MW01155225

The Oxford Handbook of
Positive Organizational Scholarship

OXFORD LIBRARY OF PSYCHOLOGY

EDITOR-IN-CHIEF

Peter E. Nathan

AREA EDITORS:

Clinical Psychology
David H. Barlow

Cognitive Neuroscience
Kevin N. Ochsner and Stephen M. Kosslyn

Cognitive Psychology
Daniel Reisberg

Counseling Psychology
Elizabeth M. Altmaier and Jo-Ida C. Hansen

Developmental Psychology
Philip David Zelazo

Health Psychology
Howard S. Friedman

History of Psychology
David B. Baker

Industrial/Organizational Psychology
Steve W. J. Kozlowski

Methods and Measurement
Todd D. Little

Neuropsychology
Kenneth M. Adams

Personality and Social Psychology
Kay Deaux and Mark Snyder

Editor-in-Chief PETER E. NATHAN

The Oxford Handbook of Positive Organizational Scholarship

Edited by

Kim S. Cameron

Gretchen M. Spreitzer

OXFORD
UNIVERSITY PRESS

OXFORD
UNIVERSITY PRESS

Oxford University Press, Inc., publishes works that further Oxford University's
objective of excellence in research, scholarship, and education.

Oxford New York
Auckland   Cape Town   Dar es Salaam   Hong Kong   Karachi
Kuala Lumpur   Madrid   Melbourne   Mexico City   Nairobi
New Delhi   Shanghai   Taipei   Toronto

With offices in
Argentina   Austria   Brazil   Chile   Czech Republic   France   Greece
Guatemala   Hungary   Italy   Japan   Poland   Portugal   Singapore
South Korea   Switzerland   Thailand   Turkey   Ukraine   Vietnam

Copyright © 2012 by Oxford University Press, Inc.

Published by Oxford University Press, Inc.
198 Madison Avenue, New York, New York 10016
www.oup.com

Oxford is a registered trademark of Oxford University Press
All rights reserved. No part of this publication may be reproduced, stored in a
retrieval system, or transmitted, in any form or by any means, electronic, mechanical,
photocopying, recording, or otherwise, without the prior permission of
Oxford University Press

Library of Congress Cataloging-in-Publication Data

The Oxford handbook of positive organizational scholarship / edited by Kim S. Cameron,
Gretchen M. Spreitzer.
    p. cm.
ISBN 978–0–19–973461–0
1. Organizational learning. 2. Organizational effectiveness. I. Cameron, Kim S. II. Spreitzer,
Gretchen M. III. Title: Handbook of positive organizational scholarship.

HD58.82.O95 2012
302.3'5—dc22   2010054131

9 8 7 6 5 4 3 2 1

Printed in the United States of America on acid-free paper

SHORT CONTENTS

OXFORD LIBRARY OF PSYCHOLOGY

The *Oxford Library of Psychology*, a landmark series of handbooks, is published by Oxford University Press, one of the world's oldest and most highly respected publishers, with a tradition of publishing significant books in psychology. The ambitious goal of the *Oxford Library of Psychology* is nothing less than to span a vibrant, wide-ranging field and, in so doing, to fill a clear market need.

Encompassing a comprehensive set of handbooks, organized hierarchically, the *Library* incorporates volumes at different levels, each designed to meet a distinct need. At one level are a set of handbooks designed broadly to survey the major subfields of psychology; at another are numerous handbooks that cover important current focal research and scholarly areas of psychology in depth and detail. Planned as a reflection of the dynamism of psychology, the *Library* will grow and expand as psychology itself develops, thereby highlighting significant new research that will impact on the field. Adding to its accessibility and ease of use, the *Library* will be published in print and, later on, electronically.

The *Library* surveys psychology's principal subfields with a set of handbooks that capture the current status and future prospects of those major subdisciplines. This initial set includes handbooks of social and personality psychology, clinical psychology, counseling psychology, school psychology, educational psychology, industrial and organizational psychology, cognitive psychology, cognitive neuroscience, methods and measurements, history, neuropsychology, personality assessment, developmental psychology, and more. Each handbook undertakes to review one of psychology's major subdisciplines with breadth, comprehensiveness, and exemplary scholarship. In addition to these broadly conceived volumes, the *Library* also includes a large number of handbooks designed to explore in depth more specialized areas of scholarship and research, such as stress, health and coping, anxiety and related disorders, cognitive development, or child and adolescent assessment. In contrast to the broad coverage of the subfield handbooks, each of these latter volumes focuses on an especially productive, more highly focused line of scholarship and research. Whether at the broadest or most specific level, however, all of the *Library* handbooks offer synthetic coverage that reviews and evaluates the relevant past and present research and anticipates research in the future. Each handbook in the *Library* includes introductory and concluding chapters written by its editor to provide a roadmap to the handbook's table of contents and to offer informed anticipations of significant future developments in that field.

An undertaking of this scope calls for handbook editors and chapter authors who are established scholars in the areas about which they write. Many of the nation's and world's most productive and best-respected psychologists have agreed to edit *Library* handbooks or write authoritative chapters in their areas of expertise.

For whom has the *Oxford Library of Psychology* been written? Because of its breadth, depth, and accessibility, the *Library* serves a diverse audience, including graduate students in psychology and their faculty mentors, scholars, researchers, and practitioners in psychology and related fields. Each will find in the *Library* the information they seek on the subfield or focal area of psychology in which they work or are interested.

Befitting its commitment to accessibility, each handbook includes a comprehensive index, as well as extensive references to help guide research. And because the *Library* was designed from its inception as an online as well as a print resource, its structure and contents will be readily and rationally searchable online. Further, once the *Library* is released online, the handbooks will be regularly and thoroughly updated.

In summary, the *Oxford Library of Psychology* will grow organically to provide a thoroughly informed perspective on the field of psychology, one that reflects both psychology's dynamism and its increasing interdisciplinarity. Once published electronically, the *Library* is also destined to become a uniquely valuable interactive tool, with extended search and browsing capabilities. As you begin to consult this handbook, we sincerely hope you will share our enthusiasm for the more than 500-year tradition of Oxford University Press for excellence, innovation, and quality, as exemplified by the *Oxford Library of Psychology.*

Peter E. Nathan
Editor-in-Chief
Oxford Library of Psychology

ABOUT THE EDITORS

Kim S. Cameron

Kim S. Cameron is William Russell Kelly Professor of Management and Organization at the Ross School of Business and Professor of Higher Education in the School of Education at the University of Michigan. His past research on organizational effectiveness, downsizing, culture, and the development of leadership competencies has been published in more than 120 academic articles and 14 scholarly books. His current research focuses on the virtuousness of and in organizations and their relationships to organizational performance. He is one of the co-founders of the Center for Positive Organizational Scholarship at the University of Michigan, and consults with organizations throughout the United States, Europe, Asia, South America, and Africa.

Gretchen M. Spreitzer

Gretchen M. Spreitzer is Area Chair and Professor of Management and Organizations at the Ross School of Business at the University of Michigan, where she also received her Ph.D. Gretchen's research focuses on employee empowerment and leadership development, particularly within a context of organizational change and decline. Her most recent work is looking at positive deviance and how organizations enable employees to flourish. This work fits within a larger effort at Michigan's Business School to develop a Scholarship of Positive Organizing that is dedicated to understanding how work organizations contribute to the development of human strengths and virtues.

ACKNOWLEDGMENTS

We wish to acknowledge the financial and instrumental support of the Stephen M. Ross School of Business, the Center for Positive Organizational Scholarship, the Office of the Vice President for Research, and the Interdisciplinary Committee on Organizational Studies at the University of Michigan. These units provided funding for the inaugural POS conference in 2001, and this event created the stimulus for the formation of a community of positive organizational scholars. They have continued their loyal support of positive organizational scholarship (POS) throughout the entire decade.

We owe a special debt of appreciation to our colleagues in the Center for Positive Organizational Scholarship at the University of Michigan: Wayne Baker, Jane Dutton, David Mayer, Bob Quinn, and Lynn Wooten. Their encouragement for this Handbook endeavor and their feedback on its content has been invaluable. We are also indebted to the larger community of POS scholars throughout the world, who have been the producers of so much of the knowledge included in this Handbook. Although many are authors of chapters, we were limited in how many contributors could be included. The work of many stellar scholars does not appear merely because of page constraints. We also thank our colleagues—including an incredible cohort of doctoral students—in the management and organizations department at the Stephen M. Ross School of Business. Their insights, feedback, energy, and support have been incalculable.

We are especially indebted to Janet Max, the superb administrator of our Center for Positive Organizational Scholarship and to Meredith Mecham Smith, the administrator of the Handbook project at the Stephen M. Ross School of Business, for their excellent administrative support in the preparation of this book. It could not have happened without them. We also thank Abby Gross and Chad Zimmerman at Oxford University Press for their trust in us and for their helpful support in the process.

Finally, we owe a special debt of gratitude to our families (especially Melinda and Bob, our spouses) for the support and encouragement of our work. You are what makes life worth living.

Kim S. Cameron
Gretchen M. Spreitzer
Ann Arbor, Michigan
2010

CONTRIBUTORS

Blake E. Ashforth
Department of Management
W.P. Carey School of Business
Arizona State University
Tempe, Arizona

Jim Asplund
Gallup, Inc.
Washington, D.C.

Orli Avi-Yonah
Department of Psychiatry &
School of Social Work
University of Michigan
Ann Arbor, Michigan

Bruce J. Avolio
Foster School of Business
Center for Leadership & Strategic
Thinking
University of Washington
Seattle, Washington

Richard P. Bagozzi
Stephen M. Ross School of Business
University of Michigan
Ann Arbor, Michigan

Wayne Baker
Stephen M. Ross School of Business
University of Michigan
Ann Arbor, Michigan

Arnold B. Bakker
Department of Work and Organizational
Psychology
Erasmus University Rotterdam
Rotterdam, The Netherlands

Jean M. Bartunek
Organization Studies Department
Carroll School of Management
Boston College
Chestnut Hill, Massachusetts

Justin M. Berg
Management Department
The Wharton School
University of Pennsylvania
Philadelphia, Pennsylvania

Caroline Biron
Faculty of Administrative Sciences
Laval University
Quebec Canada

Nikki Blacksmith
Gallup, Inc.
Washington, D.C.

Joyce E. Bono
Department of Human Resources and
Industrial Relations
Carlson School of Management
University of Minnesota
Minneapolis, Minnesota

Shelley L. Brickson
Department of Managerial Studies
University of Illinois, Chicago
Chicago, Illinois

David S. Bright
Raj Soin College of Business
Wright State University
Dayton, Ohio

Ashley D. Brown
Sloan School of Management
Massachusetts Institute of Technology
Cambridge, Massachusetts

Larry Browning
Adjunct Professor of Management,
Bodø Graduate School of Business at
The University of Nordland, Norway
Department of Communication Studies
University of Texas at Austin
Austin, Texas

Heike Bruch
Institute for Leadership and Human
  Resource Management
University of St. Gallen
Zurich, Switzerland

Kim S. Cameron
Stephen M. Ross School of Business
University of Michigan
Ann Arbor, Michigan

Melissa S. Cardon
Lubin School of Business
Pace University
New York, New York

Arne Carlsen
SINTEF Technology and Society
Oslo, Norway

Brigid Carroll
School of Business
University of Auckland
Auckland, New Zealand

Arran Caza
Schools of Business
Wake Forest University
Winston-Salem, North Carolina

Brianna Barker Caza
Schools of Business
Wake Forest University
Winston-Salem, North Carolina

Marlys K. Christianson
Rotman School of Management
University of Toronto
Toronto, Ontario, Canada

Stewart Clegg
Centre for Management and Organization
  Studies Research
University of Technology, Sydney
Sydney, Australia

Cary L. Cooper
Lancaster University Management
SchoolLancaster University
Lancaster, England

Cecily D. Cooper
Department of Management
University of Miami
Coral Gables, Florida

David L. Cooperrider
Department of Organizational
  Behavior
Weatherhead School of Management
Case Western Reserve University
Cleveland, Ohio

Stephanie J. Creary
Organization Studies Department
Carroll School of Management
Boston College
Chestnut Hill, Massachusetts

Miguel Pina e Cunha
Nova School of Business and Economics,
Lisbon, Portugal

Jared R. Curhan
Sloan School of Management
Massachusetts Institute of Technology
Cambridge, Massachusetts

Stacy E. Davies
Department of Psychology
University of Minnesota
Minneapolis, Minnesota

Jeff DeGraff
Stephen M. Ross School of Business
University of Michigan
Ann Arbor, Michigan

D. Scott DeRue
Stephen M. Ross School of Business
University of Michigan
Ann Arbor, Michigan

Rebekah Dibble
Thunderbird School of Global
Management
Glendale, Arizona

Jane E. Dutton
Stephen M. Ross School of Business
University of Michigan
Ann Arbor, Michigan

Amy C. Edmondson
Harvard Business School
Boston, Massachusetts

Julie J. Exline
Department of Psychology
Case Western Reserve University
Cleveland, Ohio

Martha S. Feldman
School of Social Ecology
University of California, Irvine
Irvine, California

Barbara L. Fredrickson
Department of Psychology
University of North Carolina
Chapel Hill, North Carolina

Philip Gibbs
School of Management
Lancaster University
Lancaster, United Kingdom

Cristina B. Gibson
School of Business
University of Western Australia
Crawley, Western Australia

Jody Hoffer Gittell
The Heller School for Social Policy and
Management
Brandeis University
Waltham, Massachusetts

Mary Ann Glynn
Organization Studies Department
Carroll School of Management
Boston College
Chestnut Hill, Massachusetts

Roger D. Goddard
College of Education and
Human Development
Texas A&M University
College Station, Texas

Paul C. Godfrey
Marriott School of Management
Brigham Young University
Provo, Utah

Lindsey N. Godwin
Division of Business
Champlain College
Burlington, Vermont

Karen Golden-Biddle
School of Management
Boston University
Boston, Massachusetts

Adam M. Grant
Management Department
The Wharton School
University of Pennsylvania
Philadelphia, Pennsylvania

Debra Guckenheimer
Department of Sociology and
Anthropology
Bowdoin College
Brunswick, Maine

Aina Landsverk Hagen
SINTEF Technology and Society
Oslo, Norway

Nardia Haigh
College of Management
Department of Management and Marketing
University of Massachusetts Boston
Boston, Massachusetts

Douglas T. Hall
School of Management
Boston University
Boston, Massachusetts

Scott C. Hammond
Woodbury School of Business
Utah Valley University
Orem, Utah

Celia V. Harquail
Authentic Organizations
Montclair, New Jersey

Spencer Harrison
Organization Studies Department
Carroll School of Management
Boston College
Chestnut Hill, Massachusetts

Emily Heaphy
Department of Organizational Behavior
School of Management
Boston University
Boston, Massachusetts

Andrew J. Hoffman
Stephen M. Ross School of Business
School of Natural Resources &
Environment
University of Michigan
Ann Arbor, Michigan

Quy Nguyen Huy
Department of Strategic Management
INSEAD
Fontainebleau, France

Remus Ilies
Broad College of Business
Michigan State University
East Lansing, Michigan

Erika Hayes James
Darden Business School
University of Virginia
Charlottesville, Virginia

Jason Kanov
Western Washington University
College of Business and Economics
Bellingham, Washington

Ronit Kark
Department of Psychology
Bar-Ilan University
Ramat Gan, Israel

Kerk F. Kee
Department of Communication Studies
Chapman University
Orange, California

Jessica Keeney
Department of Psychology
Michigan State University
East Lansing, Michigan

Shirli Kopelman
Stephen M. Ross School of Business
University of Michigan
Ann Arbor, Michigan

Ethan Kross
Department of Psychology
University of Michigan
Ann Arbor, Michigan

Chak Fu Lam
Stephen M. Ross School of Business
University of Michigan
Ann Arbor, Michigan

Mireia Las Heras
IESE Business School
University of Navarra
Barcelona, Spain

Marc Lavine
Department of Management and Marketing
University of Massachusetts Boston
Boston, Massachusetts

Hannes Leroy
Research Centre for Organisation Studies
Catholic University of Leuven
Leuven, Belgium

Marianne W. Lewis
College of Business
University of Cincinnati
Cincinnati, Ohio

Jacoba M. Lilius
School of Policy Studies
Queen's University
Kingston, Ontario, Canada

Fred Luthans
College of Business Administration
University of Nebraska
Lincoln, Nebraska

Sally Maitlis
Sauder School of Business
University of British Columbia
Vancouver, British Columbia, Canada

Jina Mao
School of Management
Boston University
Boston, Massachusetts

David M. Mayer
Stephen M. Ross School of Business
University of Michigan
Ann Arbor, Michigan

Ketan H. Mhatre
Kravis Leadership Institute
Claremont McKenna College
Claremont, California

Laurie P. Milton
Haskayne School of Business
University of Calgary
Calgary, Alberta, Canada

Aneil Mishra
2tor, Incorporated
New York, New York

Karen Mishra
School of Business
Meredith College
Raleigh, North Carolina

G. H. Morris
Department of Communication
California State University,
    San Marcos
San Marcos, California

Tord F. Mortensen
SINTEF Technology and Society
Oslo, Norway

Karen K. Myers
Department of Communication
University of California,
    Santa Barbara
Santa Barbara, California

Dan Nathan-Roberts
Department of Industrial and Operations
   Engineering
College of Engineering
University of Michigan
Ann Arbor, Michigan

Angela Neff
Department of Psychology
University of Konstanz
Konstanz, Germany

Ingrid M. Nembhard
Schools of Medicine and Public Health
School of Management
Yale University
New Haven, Connecticut

Cornelia Niessen
Department of Psychology
University of Erlangen-Nuremberg
Erlangen, Germany

Wido G. M. Oerlemans
RISBO Contract Research
Erasmus University Rotterdam
Rotterdam, The Netherlands

Greg R. Oldham
A. B. Freeman School of Business
Tulane University
New Orleans, Louisiana

Bradley P. Owens
Stephen M. Ross School of Business
University of Michigan
Ann Arbor, Michigan

Sharon K. Parker
UWA Business School
University of Western Australia
Crawley, Australia

Shefali V. Patil
The Wharton School
University of Pennsylvania
Philadelphia, Pennsylvania

Kimberly H. Perttula
The Paul Merage
   School of Business
University of California, Irvine
Irvine, California

Christine L. Porath
McDonough School of Business
Georgetown University
Washington, D.C.

Edward H. Powley
Graduate School of Business and
   Public Policy
Naval Postgraduate School
Monterey, California

Camille Pradies
Organization Studies Department
Boston College
Chestnut Hill, Massachusetts

Michael G. Pratt
Organization Studies Department
Carroll School of Management
Boston College
Chestnut Hill, Massachusetts

Robert E. Quinn
Stephen M. Ross School of Business
University of Michigan
Ann Arbor, Michigan

Ryan W. Quinn
Darden School of Business
University of Virginia
Charlottesville, Virginia

Belle Rose Ragins
Department of Management
University of Wisconsin, Milwaukee
Milwaukee, Wisconsin

Lakshmi Ramarajan
Harvard Business School
Boston, Massachusetts

Rena L. Rasch
Department of Psychology
University of Minnesota
Minneapolis, Minnesota

Laura Rees
Stephen M. Ross School of Business
University of Michigan
Ann Arbor, Michigan

Arménio Rego
Department of Economics, Management
   and Industrial Engineering
Universidade de Aveiro
Aveiro, Portugal

Run Ren
Guanghua School of Management
Peking University
Beijing, China

Seung-Yoon Rhee
KAIST Business School
Seoul, Korea

J.B. Ritchie
Woodbury School of Business
Utah Valley University
Orem, Utah

Laura Morgan Roberts
Leadership and Change PhD Program
Antioch University
Yellow Springs, Ohio

Nancy P. Rothbard
The Wharton School
University of Pennsylvania
Philadelphia, Pennsylvania

Wade C. Rowatt
Department of Psychology and
    Neuroscience
Baylor University
Waco, Texas

Jeffrey Sanchez-Burks
Stephen M. Ross School of Business
University of Michigan
Ann Arbor, Michigan

Lloyd E. Sandelands
Stephen M. Ross School of Business
University of Michigan
Ann Arbor, Michigan

Serena J. Salloum
School of Education
University of Michigan
Ann Arbor, Michigan

Leslie E. Sekerka
Ethics in Action Research and
    Education Center
Departments of Management and
Psychology
Menlo College
Atherton, California

Tony Simons
Department of Management and
Organizational Behavior
Cornell University
Ithaca, New York

David M. Sluss
College of Management
Georgia Institute of Technology
Atlanta, Georgia

Wendy K. Smith
Lerner School of Business and Economics
University of Delaware
Newark, Delaware

Scott Sonenshein
Jesse H. Jones Graduate
    School of Business
Rice University
Houston, Texas

Sabine Sonnentag
Department of Psychology
University of Mannheim
Mannheim, Germany

John J. Sosik
Department of Management
The Pennsylvania State University
Malvern, Pennsylvania

Gretchen M. Spreitzer
Stephen M. Ross School of Business
University of Michigan
Ann Arbor, Michigan

Jason M. Stansbury
Department of Business
Calvin College
Grand Rapids, Michigan

Jacqueline M. Stavros
College of Management
Lawrence Technological University
Southfield, Michigan

John Paul Stephens
Department of Organizational Behavior
Weatherhead School of Management
Case Western Reserve University
Cleveland, Ohio

Kathleen M. Sutcliffe
Stephen M. Ross School of Business
University of Michigan
Ann Arbor, Michigan

David Thomas
Harvard Business School
Boston, Massachusetts

Edward C. Tomlinson
Department of Management, Marketing,
    and Logistics
John Carroll University
University Heights, Ohio

Michael L. Tushman
Harvard Business School
Boston, Massachusetts

Tanya Vacharkulksemsuk
Department of Psychology
University of North Carolina
Chapel Hill, North Carolina

Akshaya K. Varghese
Deloitte Consulting
Hyderabad, India

Willem J. M. I. Verbeke
Department of Marketing
Erasmus University Rotterdam
Rotterdam, The Netherlands

Bernd Vogel
Henley Business School
University of Reading
Greenlands
Henley-on-Thames, United Kingdom

Timothy J. Vogus
Owen Graduate School of Management
Vanderbilt University
Nashville, Tennessee

Lee Watkiss
Organization Studies Department
Carroll School of Management
Boston College
Chestnut Hill, Massachusetts

Ned Wellman
Stephen M. Ross School of Business
University of Michigan
Ann Arbor, Michigan

Alan L. Wilkins
Brigham Young University
Provo, Utah

Michele Williams
Department of Organizational Behavior
Cornell University
Ithaca, New York

Bradley Winn
Jon M. Huntsman School of Business
Utah State University
Logan, Utah

Richard W. Woodman
Department of Management
Mays Business School
Texas A & M University
College Station, Texas

Lynn Perry Wooten
Stephen M. Ross School of Business
University of Michigan
Ann Arbor, Michigan

Kristina M. Workman
Stephen M. Ross School of Business
University of Michigan
Ann Arbor, Michigan

Monica C. Worline
The Paul Merage School of Business
University of California, Irvine
Irvine, California

Amy Wrzesniewski
Yale School of Management
Yale University
New Haven, Connecticut

Chiahuei Wu
UWA Business School
University of Western Australia
Crawley, Australia

Oscar Ybarra
Department of Psychology
University of Michigan
Ann Arbor, Michigan

Hye Jung Yoon
School of Business
Seoul National University
Seoul, Korea

Carolyn M. Youssef
College of Business
Bellevue University
Bellevue, Nebraska

Jing Zhou
Jessie H. Jones Graduate School of Business
Rice University
Houston, Texas

CONTENTS

Introduction

What Is Positive About Positive Organizational Scholarship?

Kim S. Cameron *and* Gretchen M. Spreitzer

Abstract

The *Oxford Handbook of Positive Organizational Scholarship* synthesizes much of the knowledge that has been generated after approximately ten years of research in the area of study called Positive Organizational Scholarship (POS). The Handbook identifies what is known, what is not known, and what is in need of further investigation going forward. The Handbook clarifies the definition and domain of POS, takes special care to define what is and is not meant by the term "positive," describes the history and development of this area of scientific inquiry, and explains why research in POS is so important as a scientific endeavor.

Positive organizational scholarship rigorously seeks to understand what represents the best of the human condition based on scholarly research and theory. Just as positive psychology focuses on exploring optimal individual psychological states rather than pathological ones, organizational scholarship focuses attention on the generative dynamics in organizations that lead to the development of human strength, foster resiliency in employees, enable healing and restoration, and cultivate extraordinary individual and organizational performance. POS emphasizes what elevates individuals and organizations (in addition to what challenges them), what goes right in organizations (in addition to what goes wrong), what is life-giving (in addition to what is problematic or life-depleting), what is experienced as good (in addition to what is objectionable), and what is inspiring (in addition to what is difficult or arduous). While note ignoring dysfunctional or typical patterns of behavior, examines the enablers, motivations, and effects associated with remarkably positive phenomena—how they are facilitated, why they work, how they can be identified, and how organizations can capitalize on them. The Handbook is intended to be the "go-to" place for scholars and others interested in learning about POS.

key words: Positive Organizational Scholarship, positive, POS, POS history, POS domain, positive organizational psychology

In 2003, positive organizational scholarship was first introduced as a new field of study in the organizational sciences. The primary objective of the *Oxford Handbook of Positive Organizational Scholarship* is to compile and synthesize much of the knowledge that has been generated regarding this distinctive focus of inquiry in the past 10 years. This Handbook identifies what is known, what is not known, and what needs further investigation in positive organizational scholarship (POS). The 79 chapters in this Handbook are not intended to be a comprehensive summary of all related POS topics, but they represent a good sampling of work that has adopted a POS perspective. This introductory chapter clarifies the definition and domain of POS, why it is an important field of study, and why POS emerged as a discipline in the first place. This volume is divided into nine parts to organize the chapters' themes. The concluding chapter summarizes major contributions, key findings, and explanations for the results discussed in the volume's chapters.

What Is POS?

Positive organizational scholarship is an umbrella concept used to unify a variety of approaches in organizational studies, each of which incorporates the notion of "the positive." In previously published work, several descriptions have been used to define the domain of POS, including, "the states and processes that arise from and result in life-giving dynamics, optimal functioning, and enhanced capabilities and strengths" (Dutton & Glynn, 2007, p. 693); "an emphasis on identifying individual and collective strengths (attributes and processes) and discovering how such strengths enable human flourishing (goodness, generativity, growth, and resilience)" (Roberts, 2006, p. 292); "the study of especially positive outcomes, processes, and attributes of organizations and their members," and a "focus on dynamics that are typically described by words such as excellence, thriving, flourishing, abundance, resilience, or virtuousness" (Cameron, Dutton, & Quinn, 2003, p. 4); and "organizational research occurring at the micro, meso, and macro levels which points to unanswered questions about what processes, states, and conditions are important in explaining individual and collective flourishing. Flourishing refers to being in an optimal range of human functioning" (Dutton, 2010, OMT website). These descriptions all emphasize similar terms that describe processes, dynamics, perspectives, and outcomes considered to be positive.

In brief, the "O" (organizational) in POS focuses on investigating positive processes and states that occur in association with organizational contexts. It examines positive phenomena within organizations and among organizations, as well as positive organizational contexts themselves. The "S" (scholarship) in POS focuses on pursuing rigorous, systematic, and theory-based foundations for positive phenomena. Positive organization scholarship requires a careful definitions of terms, a rationale for prescriptions and recommendations, consistency with scientific procedures in drawing conclusions, a theoretical rationale, and grounding in previous scholarly work.

The most controversial concept associated with POS is the "P"—positive. Most of the misunderstandings and criticisms of POS have centered on this concept, creating controversy in organizational studies and spawning both skeptics and advocates. The term "positive" is accused of having a potentially restrictive connotation and values bias (Fineman, 2006; George, 2004) and as being a naïve and dangerous term producing more harm than good (Ehrenreich, 2009). It is criticized as implying that most organizational science is negative, that an ethnocentric bias is being represented, or that a narrow moral agenda is being pursued. The term has been credited, on the other hand, with expanding and enriching the domain that explains performance in organizations and with

opening up, rather than restricting, organizational studies (Dutton & Glynn, 2007; Caza & Cameron, 2008). These contradictions have arisen at least partly because of the definitional ambiguity surrounding this term.

A review of dictionary definitions of "positive" reveals that the concept has such a wide range of connotations and so many applications that it defies establishing precise conceptual boundaries (e.g., Webster's, Oxford, American Heritage). Literally scores of meanings are offered. Precise conceptual definition, however, does not necessarily provide scientific clarity: Consider, for example, definitions of terms such as "love" or "effectiveness." People know what love is through experience rather than through an explanation of its conceptual boundaries or nomological network.

On the other hand, some convergence on the meaning of "positive" has begun to occur as the term has been employed in scholarly work over the past decade. The convergence can be summarized in four approaches to help specify the domain of POS. Identifying these themes helps provide a conceptual explanation of what "positive" means in the context of POS.

One approach to "positive" is adopting *a unique lens or an alternative perspective*. Adopting a POS lens means that the interpretation of phenomena is altered. For example, challenges and obstacles are reinterpreted as opportunities and strength-building experiences rather than as tragedies or problems (Gittell, Cameron, Lim, & Rivas, 2006; Lee, Caza, Edmondson, & Thomke, 2003; Sutcliffe & Vogus, 2003). Variables not previously recognized or seriously considered become central, such as positive energy (Baker, Cross, & Wooten, 2003); moral capital (Godfrey, 2003); flow (Quinn, 2002); inspiration (Thrash & Elliot, 2003); compassion (Dutton et al., 2006); elevation (Vianello, Galliani, & Haidt, 2010); and callings (Wrzesniewski, 2003) in organizations. Adopting a POS lens means that adversities and difficulties reside as much in the domain of POS as do celebrations and successes, but a positive lens focuses attention on the life-giving elements or generative processes associated with these phenomena. It is the positive perspective—not the nature of the phenomena—that draws an issue into the POS domain.

A second consensual approach to the concept of "positive" is *a focus on extraordinarily positive outcomes or positively deviant performance* (Spreitzer & Sonenshein, 2003). This means that outcomes are investigated that dramatically exceed common or expected performance.

Investigating spectacular results, surprising outcomes, and extraordinary achievements have been the focus of several investigations (e.g., Gittell, et al., 2006; Hess & Cameron, 2006; Tutu, 1999; Worthington, 2001), with each treating "positive" as synonymous with exceptional performance. Reaching a level of positive deviance, in other words, extends beyond achieving effectiveness or ordinary success. Instead, it represents "intentional behaviors that depart from the norm of a reference group in honorable ways" (Spreitzer & Sonenshein, 2003, p. 209). For example, the closure and clean-up of the Rocky Flats Nuclear arsenal exceeded federal standards by a factor of 13–60 years ahead of schedule and $30 billion under budget (Cameron & Lavine, 2006). Examining how the number-one rated delicatessen in America—located in Ann Arbor, Michigan—achieved that distinction (Baker & Gunderson, 2005); the cultural and organizational transformations that occurred in South Africa with the release of Nelson Mandela from prison (Tutu, 1999); and the extraordinary success of a financial services organization that adopted POS as a corporate strategy (Vanette, Cameron, & Powley, 2008) illustrate these types of studies. Investigating the indicators of and explanatory processes accounting for such positively deviant performance is one area in which "positive" has taken on a consensual connotation.

A third area of convergence regarding the term "positive" is that it represents *an affirmative bias that fosters resourcefulness.* Positive organizational scholarship accepts the premise that positivity unlocks and elevates resources in individuals, groups, and organizations, so that capabilities are broadened and capacity is built and strengthened (Fredrickson, 2002, 2009). "Resourcefulness" means that individuals and organizations experience an amplifying effect when exposed to positivity, such that resources and capacity expand (Dutton & Sonenshein, 2009; Fredrickson, 2003). All living systems have a heliotropic inclination (Erhard-Seibold, 1937) toward positive energy (Cameron, 2008a), so that, indeed, positivity is life-giving (Cooperrider & Srivastra, 1987; Diener, 2009b). Adopting an affirmative bias, therefore, prioritizes positive energy, positive climate, positive relationships, positive communication, and positive meaning in organizations (Cameron, 2008b), as well as the value embedded in difficult challenges or negative events (Harter & Clifton, 2003; Losada & Heaphy, 2004; Worline & Quinn, 2003). Positive organizational scholarship is unapologetic in emphasizing affirmative attributes, capabilities, and possi-

bilities more than problems, threats, and weakness, so that strengths-based activities and outcomes are highlighted (Clifton & Harter, 2003). Again, an affirmative approach does not exclude considering negative events. Rather, these are incorporated in accounting for life-giving dynamics, generating resources, and flourishing outcomes (e.g., Dutton, et al., 2006; Dutton & Glynn, 2008; Weick, 2003).

A fourth area of convergence regarding the concept of the positive is *the examination of virtuousness or the best of the human condition.* Positive organization scholarship is based on a eudaemonic assumption— that is, the postulation that an inclination exists in all human systems toward achieving the highest aspirations of humankind (Aristotle, *Metaphysics XII*; Dutton & Sonenshein, 2009). Studying virtuousness means examining excellence and goodness for its own sake—captured by the Latin *virtus* and the Greek *arête*. Although debate has arisen regarding what constitutes goodness and whether universal human virtues can be identified, all societies and cultures possess catalogues of traits that they deem virtuous, that represent what is morally good, and that define the highest aspirations of human beings (Comte-Sponville, 2001; Peterson & Seligman, 2004).

Positive organizational scholarship examines the development of and the effects associated with virtuousness and eudaemonism (Bright, Cameron, & Caza, 2006; Cameron, 2003; Ilies, Nahrgang, & Morgeson, 2007), or "that which is good in itself and is to be chosen for its own sake" (Aristotle, *Metaphysics XII*, p. 3). Studies of virtuousness *in* organizations focus on individuals' behaviors in organizational settings that help others flourish (Fowers & Tjeltveit, 2003), including investigating character strengths, gratitude, wisdom, forgiveness, hope, and courage (Grant & Schwartz, 2011; Luthans, Norman, Avolio, & Avey, 2008). Studies of virtuousness *through* organizations focus on practices and processes in organizations that represent and perpetuate what is good, right, and worthy of cultivation (McCullough & Snyder, 2001; Park & Peterson, 2003). This includes, for example, investigating profound purpose and transcendent objectives (Emmons, 1999); healing routines (Powley & Piderit, 2008); institutionalized forgiveness (Cameron & Caza, 2002); and human sustainability (Pfeffer, 2010).

These four convergent uses of the concept of "positive"—adopting a positive lens, investigating extraordinarily positive performance, espousing an affirmative bias, and exploring virtuousness or eudaemonism—do not precisely *define* the term "positive" per se, but they do identify the scholarly domain that POS scholars are attempting to map. Similar to other concepts in organizational science that do not have precisely bounded definitions (e.g., culture, innovation, core competence), this mapping provides the conceptual boundaries required to locate POS as an area of inquiry.

It is important to underscore that POS is not value-neutral. It advocates the position that the desire to improve the human condition is universal and that the capacity to do so is latent in almost all human systems. Thus, whereas traditionally positive outcomes such as improving the organization, and achieving goals or profitability are not excluded from consideration, POS has a bias toward life-giving, generative, and ennobling human conditions regardless of whether they are attached to traditional economic or political benefits.

How Did POS Emerge?

Unlike positive psychology, POS did not emerge as an attempt to rebalance the prodigious emphasis on illness and languishing in organizations. Organizational research has not been focused overwhelmingly on failure, damage, and demise. In fact, studying organizational decline was first introduced in organizational studies in 1980 (Whetten, 1980) because most organizational theories focused almost exclusively on growth. Big was assumed to be better than small; getting more was preferable to getting less. Negative phenomena did not dominate organizational studies literature as it did in psychology, even though plenty of attention had been paid to alienation, stress, injustice, and the evils of bureaucracy in traditional organizational studies (e.g., Weber, 1997).

Rather, POS arose because an array of organizational phenomena was being ignored; consequently, such phenomena were neither systematically studied nor valued. It was usually not considered legitimate in scientific circles, for example, to discuss the effects of virtues in organizations or to use terms such as "flourishing" or "positive deviance" to describe outcomes. Studies of compassion and forgiveness—two of the early studies in the POS literature (Cameron & Caza, 2002; Dutton et al., 2002)—certainly diverged from the mainstream of organizational science. Similarly, certain kinds of organizational processes—for example, generative dynamics—remained largely uninvestigated, including high-quality connections (Dutton & Ragins, 2007); thriving (Spreitzer, Sutcliffe, Dutton, Sonenshein, & Grant, 2005); connectivity (Losada & Heaphy, 2004); and positive energy networks (Baker et al., 2003).

Positive organizational scholarship also arose because the outcome variables that dominated the organization literature focused mainly on profitability, competitive advantage, problem solving, and economic efficiency (Davis & Marquis, 2005; Goshal, 2005; Jensen, 2002). Granted, outcomes such as job satisfaction, justice, and teamwork have appeared frequently in the organizational studies literature (Guzzo & Dickson, 1996; Kramer, 1999; Smith, Kendall, & Hulin, 1969), but alternative outcomes such as psychological, social, and eudaemonic well-being (Gallagher, Lopez, & Preacher, 2009; Keyes, 2005)—including social integration, social contribution, social coherence, social actualization, and social acceptance—as well as human sustainability (Pfeffer, 2010), were largely outside the purview of mainline organizational science. The best of the human condition—what people care about deeply and profoundly—was much less visible in organizational scholarship. The famous statement by Robert Kennedy in a March 18, 1968 speech at the University of Kansas is illustrative:

> The gross national product does not allow for the health of our children, the quality of their education, or the joy of their play. It does not include the beauty of our poetry or the strength of our marriages, the intelligence of our public debate, or the integrity of our public officials. It measures neither our wit nor our courage, neither our wisdom nor our learning, neither our compassion nor our devotion to our country. It measures everything, in short, except that which makes life worthwhile.

Positive organizational scholarship might be argued to have a long history, dating back to William James' (1902) writings on what he termed "healthy mindedness,"

Allport's (1960) interest in positive human characteristics; Jahoda's (1959) emphasis on prevention-based community psychology; Maslow's (1968) advocacy for studying healthy people in lieu of sick people; Diener's (1984) investigations of happiness and subjective well-being; and Organ (1988) and Batson's (1994) consideration of "citizenship behaviors" and "prosocial" activities.

Similarly, the early foundations of the organizational development field advocated a "new attitude of optimism and hope" (Bennis, 1969, p. 3) and emphasized *The Human Side of Enterprise* (McGregor, 1960) as a reaction to the dehumanizing and economically directed emphases in work organizations. Cooperrider and Srivastva's (1987) introduction of *appreciative inquiry* spotlighted the positive dynamics associated with planned change and organizational development efforts. Positive organizational scholarship, therefore, is not as much a new field of investigation as it is a coalescing force that brings together themes, perspectives, and variables that have been dispersed in the literature and underdeveloped or ignored in scientific investigation.

Most importantly, much of this earlier positively themed work was not based on scientific research and empirical investigations. It focused instead largely on advocacy and promoting an approach to addressing problems, overcoming ills, and resolving difficulties (e.g., Bennis, 1963; Maslow, 1965). Moreover, little of this work explicitly addressed organizations as the entities of interest. Positive organizational scholarship emerging, therefore, does more than merely construct a repository for earlier work. It highlights the organization as a context for study and at the same time emphasizes the importance of multiple levels of analyses including individuals, groups, and societies. Positive organizational scholarship highlights processes and practices that occur in organizations and are associated with positive outcomes, the empirical rationale for claims about positivity, and the theoretical rationale for the life-giving dynamics and outcomes associated with organizations.

Positive organizational scholarship as an identifiable field of study essentially began in earnest approximately a decade ago at the University of Michigan. As with all historical accounts of how movements and initiatives begin, various scenarios describe the beginnings of scholarly interest in POS, with no single description capturing all the motivations and significant events that produced this field of scholarly endeavor. This said, POS emerged when Jane Dutton, studying individual and organizational compassion, and Kim Cameron, studying organizational forgiveness, joined with colleague Robert Quinn, investigating positive personal change, to sponsor a conference on topics that did not seem to have a home among mainstream organizational studies. The objective was to bring together researchers in psychology and organizational behavior to examine what could be learned collaboratively about positive phenomena in organizations.

During the planning stages of this event, the terrorist attacks on September 11, 2001 occurred in New York, Washington, D.C., and Pennsylvania. Like most other citizens, the conference organizers actualized their strong desire to contribute resources that might benefit those suffering from the pain and tragedies associated with these horrific events. The decision was made to launch a website—*Leading in Trying Times* (http://www.bus.umich.edu/Positive/CPOS/Publications/tryingtimes.html)—which shared what had been learned from research relating to positive approaches to difficult situations. Scholars contributed brief articles on topics such as compassion, transcendence, hope, resilience, healing, forgiveness, helping, courage, character, and finding strength. Responses to this website from scholars and practitioners highlighted the need for more attention directed at understanding how to cultivate flourishing in organizational settings amidst the context of challenge and pain.

The subsequent conference brought together scholars working in a variety of academic domains to discuss not only how to address difficult circumstances and problems but also how to foster flourishing and capability-building at the individual, group, and organizational levels. To advance this work, the Center for Positive Organizational Scholarship was subsequently formed at the University of Michigan (www.bus.umich.edu/positive), with colleagues Wayne Baker, David Mayer, Gretchen Spreitzer, and Lynn Wooten. The title, Positive Organizational Scholarship, was selected to describe the common themes being pursued.

Why Is Research on POS Important?

In addition to revealing and highlighting phenomena that have been largely ignored in organizational studies, scholarly attention focusing on the positive is important because positive conditions produce a "heliotropic effect" (Cooperrider & Srivastva, 1987; Drexelius, 1627, 1862). Heliotropism is defined as the tendency in all living systems toward positive energy and away from negative energy—or toward that which is life-giving and away from that which is life-depleting (e.g., D'Amato & Jagoda, 1962; Mrosovsky & Kingsmill, 1985; Smith & Baker, 1960). In nature, positive energy is most often experienced in the form of sunlight, but it may occur in other forms as well such as interpersonal kindness (Dutton & Heaphy, 2003; Erhardt-Siebold, 1937). Based on the heliotropic argument, a positive environment is the preferred condition because it engenders positive energy and life-giving resourcefulness. Following this logic, human systems, like other biological systems in nature, possess inherent inclinations toward the positive. Understanding this tendency and its implications is an important need in social and organizational sciences (Cameron, 2008a).

For example, people are more accurate in processing positive information—whether the task involves verbal discrimination, organizational behavior, or judging emotion—than negative information (Matlin & Stang, 1978). People think about a greater number of positive things than negative things, and each positive thing is thought about for a longer period of time. People are more accurate in learning and remembering positive terms than neutral or negative terms (Kunz, 1974; Matlin, 1970; Taylor, 1991). When presented with lists of positive, neutral, and negative words, for example, people are more accurate over time in recalling the positive (Akhtar, 1968; Rychlak, 1977; Thompson, 1930), and the longer the delay between learning and recalling, the more positive bias is displayed (Gilbert, 1938).

People reported thinking about positive statements 20% longer than negative statements and almost 50% longer than neutral statements, so that mental rehearsal is biased toward positivity, and positive information can be recalled more easily and more accurately (Matlin & Stang, 1978). Positive phenomena are learned more quickly than are negative phenomena (Bunch & Wientge, 1933; Rychlak, 1966), and people judge positive phenomena more accurately than negative phenomena. Managers, for example, are much more accurate in rating subordinates' competencies and proficiencies when they perform correctly than when they perform incorrectly (Gordon, 1970).

People tend to seek out positive stimuli and avoid negative stimuli (Day, 1966; Luborsky, Blinder, & Mackworth, 1963), such that people judge from two-thirds to three-quarters of the events in their lives as positive (Bradburn & Noll, 1969; Havighurst & Glasser, 1972; Meltzer & Ludwig, 1967). Further, most people judge themselves to be positive, optimistic, and happy most of the time (Goldings, 1954; Johnson, 1937; Wessman & Ricks, 1966; Young, 1937). Positive words have higher frequencies in all the languages studied, and positive words typically entered English usage more than 150 years before their negative opposites (for example, "better" entered before "worse") (Boucher & Osgood, 1968; Mann, 1968; Zajonc, 1968). Central nervous system functioning (i.e., vagus nerve health) is most effective when positive emotions are fostered (Kok & Fredrickson, 2010), and bodily rhythm "coherence" is at its peak when in a positive or virtuous state (McCraty & Childre, 2004).

A bias toward the positive, in other words, appears to characterize human beings in their thoughts, judgments, emotions, language, interactions, and physiological functioning. A tendency toward the positive appears to be a natural human inclination, and empirical evidence suggests that positivity is the preferred and natural state of human beings, just as it is among other biological systems.

Emerging empirical evidence also shows that organizations respond in a way similar to individuals in the presence of positive influences (see Cameron, 2008a, for references). The irony in these findings is that, by definition, positive influences do not need to produce traditionally pursued organizational outcomes in order to be of worth. An increase in profitability, for example, is not the criterion for determining the value of positivity in organizations. Positivity is inherently valued because it is eudaemonic.

Nevertheless, studies have shown that organizations in several industries (including financial services, health care, manufacturing, and government) that implemented and improved their positive practices over time also increased their performance in desired outcomes such as profitability, productivity, quality, customer satisfaction, and employee retention. That is, positive practices that were institutionalized in organizations, including providing compassionate support for employees, forgiving mistakes and avoiding blame, fostering the meaningfulness of work, expressing frequent gratitude, showing kindness, and caring for colleagues, led organizations to perform at significantly higher levels on desired outcomes (Cameron, Bright, & Caza, 2004; Cameron, Mora, & Leutscher, 2010; Gittell, et al., 2006).

Several explanations have been proposed for why heliotropic tendencies exist and why individuals and organizations are inclined toward the positive. For example, Erdelyi (1974) explained that mental processes develop in a way that favors the positive over the negative. Most information available to human beings is disregarded, so what is retained tends to life-giving rather than life-depleting. Becker (1973) explained natural positive biases result from the fear of death, meaning that the negative is repressed and the positive—or the life-preserving—is reinforced; consequently, people develop a bias toward the positive. Learning theorists (e.g., Skinner, 1965) explained positive biases as being associated with reinforcement; that is, positive reinforcement leads to repetitiveness. Further, Sharot, Riccardi, Raio, and Phelps (2007) found that the human brain has a tendency to produce optimistic and positive orientations in its natural state. More mental acuity and mental activation occurs in a positive compared to a negative condition.

Social process theorists have explained positive biases on the basis of the functions they perform in perpetuating social organization (Merton, 1968). Simply stated, organizing depends on positive social processes that reinforce mutual benefit. Observing and experiencing positivity unlocks predispositions to act for the benefit of others, leading to increased social connections in an organization (Feldman & Khademian, 2003; Fredrickson, 2008). Similarly, Gouldner (1960) proposed that positive role modeling and forming positive social norms create a tendency toward organizational sustainability. These positive social processes are more likely to survive and flourish over the long run than are negative social processes because they are functional for the organization's survival. Weigl, Muller, Zupanc, Glaser, & Angerer (2010) explained that "positive gain spirals" are associated with positivity because they lead individuals to protect, retain, accumulate, and conserve resources more effectively, which are then instrumental in helping organizations perform successfully.

Of course, abundant evidence also exists that human beings cognitively react more strongly to negative phenomena than to positive phenomena (Baumeister, Bratslavsky, Finkenauer, & Vohs 2001; Wang, Galinsky, & Mirnighan, 2009), and evolutionary theory reminds us that living systems respond strongly and quickly to stimuli that threaten their existence or that signal maladaptation (Darwin, 1859/2003). Negatively valenced phenomena have a greater impact on human beings than do positively valenced phenomena of the same type, so that the positive achieves precedence over the effects of the negative only by sheer force of numbers (Baumeister et al., 2001; Fredrickson & Losada, 2006).

This dynamic helps explain why a bias has existed in organizational sciences toward studying the negative much more than the positive (Czapinski, 1985; Seligman, 1999). A larger effect (R^2) can usually be detected by accounting for negative phenomena compared to positive phenomena—that is, the bad has stronger effects than the good (Baumeister, et al., 2001)—so it is understandable that researchers have focused on the strongest factors accounting for the most variance. Negative effects often dominate heliotropic inclinations; indeed, they account for a larger amount of variance in behavior change, and they capture more attention in scholarly analyses. More importantly, over time, organizations also tend to emphasize negative phenomena for the same reasons—survival and adaptation are associated with addressing obstacles, competitive pressures, or threats (Davis, 2009; Nadler & Tushman, 1997; Porter, 1998; Williamson, 1998). If greater organizational effects can be created by addressing the negative, it

is logical that organizational policies, practices, and processes will, over time, also tend toward focusing on and organizing around negative factors more than positive factors. Evidence of this tendency is confirmed by Margolis and Walsh's (2003) findings that negative phenomena dominate positive phenomena in the business press and organizational studies literature by a factor of four.

An important function of POS, therefore, is to provide more attention to the processes and practices that can unleash heliotropic effects and elevate resourcefulness. Empirical evidence has suggested that when positive factors are given greater emphases than negative factors, individuals and organizations tend to flourish. The positive then overcomes the negative primarily by sheer force of numbers (Baumeister et al., 2001). Research on POS is important, in other words, because positive phenomena in and through organizations explain variance that has largely been ignored in previous empirical investigations. Processes and attributes are highlighted that have received little attention in previous organizational research. Adopting a positive lens illuminates research questions and relationships that have been underinvestigated and are otherwise ignored. Thus, studying positivity in individuals and in organizations provides fertile territory for understanding the mechanisms and outcomes associated with the naturally occurring, but underinvestigated, inclination toward the positive.

Criticisms of POS

On the other hand, the desirability of POS as a legitimate field of scientific study is by no means universally accepted, and three primary criticisms of POS have been promoted: (a) POS ignores negative phenomena, (b) POS adopts an elitist (managerial) viewpoint, (c) POS is not defined precisely. This third criticism notes that POS does not acknowledge that "positive" may not be the same for everyone, and the concepts and phenomena associated with POS are fuzzy terms that lack construct and discriminant validity and careful measurement.

The first criticism is that POS ignores issues such as conflict, poverty, exploitation, unemployment, war, and other negative circumstances that are typical of the human condition and are commonplace in organizational functioning. Positivity is equated with Pollyannaishness and simply "putting on a happy face" in the midst or serious problems and challenges. Some authors, such as Ehrenreich (2009), for example, find little that is positive in POS, claiming that positivity unrealistically assumes unremitting growth and guaranteed success in organizations, excuses excess and folly, denies reality, mitigates against hard work, implies pride and boastfulness, avoids difficult questions, invites unpreparedness, assumes that all success is deserved, and leads to "reckless optimism" and "delusional thinking." Little evidence exists, according to these critics, that positivity fosters success (Ehrenreich, 2009; Hackman, 2008).

To be sure, empirical evidence exists that bad is stronger than good (Baumeister, et al., 2001). That is, human beings react more strongly and more quickly to negative phenomena than to positive phenomena because existence is threatened. When equal measures of good and bad are present, the psychological effects of the bad outweigh those of the good. For example, negative feedback has more emotional impact on people than does positive feedback (Coleman, Jussim, & Abraham, 1987), and the effects of negative information and negative events take longer to wear off than do the effects of positive information or pleasant events (Brickman, Coates, & Jason-Bulman, 1978). The negative tends to disrupt normal functioning longer than does the positive, such that a single traumatic event usually has longer lasting effects on behavior than does a single positive event. When negative things happen (for example, people lose a wager, endure abuse, or become a victim of a crime), they spent more time trying to explain the outcome or to make sense of it than when a positive outcome occurs (Gilovich, 1983; Pratto & John, 1991). Moreover, undesirable human traits receive more weight in forming impressions than do desirable traits (Hamilton & Huffman, 1971).

It is inaccurate, however, to argue that POS ignores negative phenomena inasmuch as some of the greatest triumphs, most noble virtues, and highest achievements have resulted from the presence of the negative (e.g., Cameron & Lavine, 2006). Common human experience and abundant scientific evidence supports the idea that negativity has an important place in investigating positive processes and outcomes. Developing positive identities in negative environments, organizational healing after trauma, and achieving virtuous outcomes in the face of trials exemplify cases in which negative conditions have been investigated with a POS lens (Kanov, Maitlis, Worline, Dutton, Frost, & Lilius, 2004; Powley & Cameron, 2006; Powley & Taylor, 2006; Weick, 2003, 2006). Positive organizational scholarship does not ignore the negative; instead, it seeks to investigate the positive processes, outcomes, and interpretations embedded in negative phenomena.

A second criticism of POS is that it adopts an elitist perspective. Critics claim that POS is oriented toward exploiting human beings in favor of corporate profits and productivity, and maintaining power for the advantaged over the disadvantaged. Perpetuating the positive for the sake of organizational success, to make managers look good, to manipulate the workforce, or to reinforce unequal employment status are common criticisms (e.g., Ehrenreich, 2009; Fineman, 2006; George, 2004). These critiques fundamentally center on the claim that POS narrowly focuses on managers rather than on the exploited underclass. Detractors accuse POS of not asking the question, "Positive for whom?" and suggest that unexamined assumptions are biased toward Western philosophies and toward power elites.

On the other hand, this criticism seems to miss the unequivocally stated focus of POS on life-giving dynamics, generating resources, and flourishing outcomes whether for workers or managers, the underclass or the upper class, the individual or the organization (e.g., Cameron, et al., 2003; Dutton & Sonenshein, 2009; Roberts, 2006). The fundamental assumption of POS is a eudaemonic one: all human systems are biased toward achieving the highest aspirations of humankind or excellence and goodness for its own sake. Adopting an affirmative bias prioritizes positive energy, positive climate, positive relationships, positive communication, and positive meaning for individuals and organizations. Indeed, exploitation that allows one party to achieve advantage over another is inconsistent with the fundamental assumptions of POS. Thus, the answer to "Positivity for whom?" is not exclusive.

Fletcher (1998), for example, documented how positive practices actually reverse the disadvantaged status of underprivileged employees. Positive energy (Baker, et al., 2003), flourishing relationships (Dutton & Heaphy, 2003), empowerment (Spreitzer, 1992), and virtuousness (Cameron, 2003) all represent non-zero-sum dynamics that benefit all parties. Moreover, abundant research has examined cultural differences regarding positive phenomena, including employee well-being in more than 50 countries (Diener, 2009a; Diener & Suh, 1997; Veenhoven, 1996, 2010) and has identified universal attributes and predictors, as well as unique cultural differences across a wide variety of cultures. Non-Western cultures are well-represented in positive research (including in some chapters of this Handbook).

A third criticism of POS, related to the first two, is that a precise definition of the term "positive" is lacking. Positive is experienced subjectively, such that what may be positive for one person is not necessarily positive for another. What is defined as "good" or "ennobling" may be individualistic. Imposing a definition of positive on others is an act of power and, therefore, is, by definition, nonpositive (Caza & Carroll, 2011). Moreover, other related terms used in POS research lack precise definition and scientific validity.

Of course, many core scientific terms are the subjects of investigation, measurement, and theory-building without precise definitions. Well-used and frequently discussed terms such as "life," "leadership," and "quality" are examples, none of which has been precisely and consensually defined. These terms are considered to be "constructs," meaning they are terms constructed to capture the meaning of something that is ambiguous and difficult to circumscribe precisely. In such circumstances, investigators artificially constrain the meaning or dimensions of the construct in order to examine certain aspects of it. The key is to be precise about what is and is not included in measuring the construct. Individualistic definitions are addressed, therefore, by defining the concept scientifically and precisely in scholarly investigations.

As in many domains within the organizational sciences, this requirement is important in research on positive phenomena, and constant attention to this requirement is crucial. Improvement can certainly be made on this score in POS. On the other hand, a variety of positively oriented constructs such as "thriving" (Spreitzer et al., 2005), "virtuousness" (Cameron et al., 2004), "positive emotions" (Fredrickson, 1998), "meaningfulness" (Pratt & Ashforth, 2003), "energy" (Fritz, Lam, & Spreitzer, 2011), "best-self" (Roberts Dutton, Spreitzer, Heaphy, & Quinn, 2005), "resilience" (Sutcliffe & Vogus, 2003), "positive deviance" (Spreitzer & Sonenshein, 2003), and many others have been defined quite carefully in POS investigations. Scientific standards and rigor within POS research studies have not been ignored.

Nevertheless, vigilance must be maintained to be as precise as possible regarding what is and is not defined as positive. By identifying the four domains of the term "positive" (as discussed), the conceptual boundaries of POS become clearer, and the same requirement applies to all POS-related constructs. In other words, mapping the conceptual terrain of "positive" is not so much an act of power as a scientific necessity in

order for cumulative work to be conducted and for the nomological network surrounding the constructs to expand. Some progress has been made in this regard, although much is left to be done.

The Organization of the Handbook

To these ends, the domains of "positive" in the *Oxford Handbook of Positive Organizational Scholarship* have been organized into nine categories. This Handbook does not claim to contain a comprehensive list of relevant or important topics, nor does it claim to cover the entire conceptual landscape of POS. Nevertheless, the chapters represent a good sample of significant subjects in this field of study, and they help map the discipline's terrain.

Each chapter contains a relevant literature review—essentially addressing the question, "What do we now know about this topic?"—and the findings of current scholarship. Chapters also suggest and recommend needed future research—essentially addressing the question, "What else do we need to know about this topic?" Hence, chapters serve as a useful summary of up-to-date knowledge and a guide to future scholarship in POS for the decades ahead.

The chapter groupings represent a somewhat arbitrary categorization of major themes. They exemplify different levels of analysis, from individual-level topics to organization- and societal-level topics. They also include topics that are traditionally considered to be negative or problem-centered—such as trauma, stress, crises, and conflict—and topics not usually considered within the domain of POS—such as economic theory, sustainability, and social movements. Each chapter adopts a positive lens and emphasizes the relevance of these topics to the broad area of inquiry called POS.

Certain sections in the Handbook address issues of practice, such as the section on human resource practices and the section on leadership and change, while other sections address key theoretical issues embedded in organization studies, including organizational processes and positive relationships. The placement of chapters in a particular section does not imply that other sections may not also be appropriate, but the nine categories provide a reasonably clear schema to highlight the domains of POS. The chapter placements serve to illustrate and highlight these themes. The nine categories are described below.

Positive Individual Attributes
This first section contains chapters focusing on the positive attributes of individuals in organizations.

These chapters treat the individual as the relevant level of analysis but position individuals in the context of work organizations. Chapters address these themes:

- Psychological capital
- Prosocial motivation
- Callings in work
- Work engagement
- Positive identity
- Proactivity
- Creativity
- Curiosity
- Positive traits
- The neuroscience underpinnings of POS

Positive Emotions
The second section focuses on aspects of positive feelings, sentiments, and affect among individuals and groups in organizations. Examining emotions and subjective experience are the themes these chapters have in common. Topics addressed include:

- Positive energy
- Positive emotions
- Subjective well-being
- Passion
- Socioemotional intelligence
- Group emotions

Strengths and Virtues
The third section addresses the concepts of virtuousness in organizations and virtues in the individuals who work in organizations. Prior research has proposed that various virtues are universal; this section therefore contains just a limited sampling of topics, including:

- Virtuousness
- Forgiveness
- Humility
- Compassion
- Hope
- Courage
- Justice
- Integrity
- Positive ethics
- Leveraging strengths
- Character strengths in global managers

Positive Relationships
This section focuses on temporary encounters, and long-term relationships among organization members. It analyses the dynamics that emerge in interpersonal interactions, temporary connections, and

organizational processes that relate to relationships. The chapters examine these topics:

- High-quality connections
- Relational coordination
- Reciprocity
- Intimacy
- Civility
- Trust
- Trustworthiness
- Humor
- Psychological safety

Positive Human Resource Practices
The chapters in this section provide perspective on practices within organizations that relate to managing human capital and human resource systems. Topics of potential interest to human resource professionals, and that are addressed in human resource management functions, include:

- Career development
- Mentoring
- Socialization
- Diversity
- Communication
- Conflict resolution
- Negotiating
- Work–family dynamics

Positive Organizational Processes
This section contains chapters that examine the dynamics in organizations that are not usually considered to fall into the positive domain. The chapters address organization-level topics, and by adopting a positive lens, the chapters highlight how POS is relevant to a broad variety of phenomena. They include:
Symbolism in organizations

- Resourcefulness
- Collective efficacy
- The design of work
- Mindful organizing
- Goal attainment
- Organizational identity
- Organizational energy
- Innovation
- Organizational boundaries

Positive Leadership and Change
Chapters in this section address the process of positive organizational change and the leadership associated with achieving positive change. These chapters examine the strategies and approaches that enable

organizational change and the leadership qualities associated with successful organizations. The topics addressed are:

Organizational development

- Appreciative inquiry
- Positive change attributes
- Implementing positive change
- Authentic leadership
- Leadership development
- Peak performance
- Strategic change
- Strengths-based strategy

A Positive Lens on Problems and Challenges

Because POS is often accused of ignoring nonpositive phenomena, chapters in this section address challenges, issues, and problems from a positive perspective. They illustrate the importance of the negative in better understanding the positive. Chapters include:

- Managing the unexpected
- Healing after trauma
- Organizational recovery
- Responding to crisis
- Resilience under adversity
- Post-traumatic growth
- Ambivalence
- Responding to stress

Expanding Positive Organizational Scholarship

The final section features chapters that explore the relationships between POS and areas of scholarly interest other than traditional organizational behavior and organizational theory. Disciplines such as economics, sociology, religion, and political science are included in these chapters, which focus on:

- Sustainability
- Critical theory
- Economic models
- Social movements
- Spirituality
- Positive deviance
- International peacemaking

Conclusion

The *Oxford Handbook of Positive Organizational Scholarship* seeks to provide a foundation upon which POS research can continue. It summarizes the current state of the field by explaining relevant research and conceptual grounding for key concepts within the general domain of POS. Any scholarly field of

endeavor will have a short lifespan unless founded on valid evidence, theoretical explanation, and practical utility, so the chapters in this Handbook seek to provide that foundation. Equally important, however, is the guidance each chapter provides regarding unanswered questions, puzzles, and needed investigations. Our hope is that the suggested directions for future research each chapter provides will not be dismissed as perfunctory supplements to the chapters' content, but as a roadmap to make significant progress in understanding POS in the years ahead.

References

Akhtar, M. (1968). Affect and memory: An experimental note. *Pakistan Journal of Psychology, 1*(111), 25–27.

Allport, G.W. (1960). *Becoming: Basic considerations for a psychology of personality.* New Haven, CT: Yale University Press.

Aristotle, *Metaphysics XII, 7,* 3–4.

Baker, W., Cross, R., & Wooten, L. (2003). Positive organizational network analysis and energizing relationships. In K.S. Cameron, J.E. Dutton, & R.E. Quinn (Eds.) *Positive organizational scholarship: Foundations of a new discipline* (pp. 328–342). San Francisco: Berrett-Koehler.

Baker, W.B., & Gunderson, R. (2005). Zingermans community of businesses. Case Center for Positive Organizational Scholarship, University of Michigan.

Batson, C.D. (1994). Why act for the public good? Four answers. *Personality and Social Psychology Bulletin, 20,* 603–610.

Baumeister, R.F., Bratslavsky, E., Finkenauer, C., & Vohs, K.D. (2001). Bad is stronger than good. *Review of General Psychology, 5*(4), 323–370.

Becker, E. (1973). *The denial of death.* New York: Free Press.

Bennis, W. (1963). New role for the behavioral sciences: Effecting organizational change. *Administrative Science Quarterly*, 8(2), 125–165.

Bennis, W. (1969). *Organizational development: Its nature, origins, and prospects.* Reading, MA: Addison Wesley.

Boucher, J., & Osgood, C.E. (1969). Pollyanna hypothesis. *Journal of Verbal Learning and Verbal Behavior, 8*(1), 1–8.

Bradburn, N.M., & Noll, C.E. (1969). *The structure of psychological well-being.* Chicago: Aldine.

Brickman, P., Coates, D., & Janoff-Bulman, R. (1978). Lottery winners and accident victims: Is happiness relative? *Journal of Personality and Social Psychology, 36,* 917–927.

Bright, D.S., Cameron, K.S., & Caza, A. (2006). The amplifying and buffering effects of virtuousness in downsized organizations. *Journal of Business Ethics, 64,* 249–269.

Bunch, M.E., & Wientge, K. (1933). The relative susceptibility of pleasant, unpleasant, and indifferent material to retroactive inhibition. *Journal of General Psychology, 9*(114), 157–178.

Cameron, K.S. (2003). Organizational virtuousness and performance. In K.S. Cameron, J. Dutton & R.E. Quinn (Eds.), *Positive organizational scholarship* (pp. 48–65). San Francisco: Berrett-Koehler.

Cameron, K.S. (2008a). Paradox in positive organizational change. *Journal of Applied Behavioral Science, 44,* 7–24.

Cameron, K.S. (2008b). *Positive leadership.* San Francisco: Berrett Koehler.

Cameron, K.S., Bright, D., & Caza, A. (2004). Exploring the relationships between organizational virtuousness and performance. *American Behavioral Scientist, 4,* 766–790.

Cameron, K.S., & Caza, A. (2002). Organizational and leadership virtues and the role of forgiveness. *Journal of Leadership and Organizational Studies, 9,* 33–48.

Cameron, K.S., Dutton, J.E., & Quinn, R.E. (2003). *Positive organizational scholarship: foundations of a new discipline.* San Francisco: Berrett-Koehler.

Cameron, K.S., & Lavine, M. (2006). *Making the impossible possible: Leading extraordinary performance—the Rocky Flats story.* San Francisco: Berrett-Koehler.

Cameron, K.S., Mora, C.E., & Leutscher, T. (2010). Effects of positive practices on organizational effectiveness. *Journal of Applied Behavioral Science* (in press).

Caza, A., & Carroll, B. (2011). "Critical theory and POS." In K.S. Cameron, & G. Spreitzer, (Eds.), *Oxford handbook of positive organizational scholarship.* London: Oxford University Press.

Caza, A., & Cameron, K.S. (2008). Positive organizational scholarship: What does it achieve? In C.L. Cooper, & S. Clegg (Eds.), *Handbook of macro-organizational behavior.* New York: Sage.

Clifton, D.O., & Harter, J.K. (2003). Investing in strengths. In K.S. Cameron, J.E. Dutton, and R.E. Quinn (Eds.), *Positive organizational scholarship: Foundations of a new discipline* (pp. 111–121). San Francisco: Berrett-Koehler.

Coleman, L.M., Jussim, L., & Abraham, J. (1987). Students' reactions to teacher evaluations: The unique impact of negative feedback. *Journal of Applied Social Psychology, 17,* 1051–1070.

Comte-Sponville, A. (2001). *A small treatise of the great virtues.* (C. Temerson, Translator). New York: Metropolitan Books.

Cooperrider, D.L., & Sekerka, L.E. (2003). "Toward a theory of positive organizational change." In K.S. Cameron, J.E. Dutton, & R.E. Quinn, (Eds.) *Positive organizational scholarship: Foundations of a new discipline.* (pp. ages 225–240) San Francisco, CA: Berrett-Koehler.

Cooperrider, D.L., & Srivastva, S. (1987). Appreciative inquiry in organizational life. In W. Pasmore & E. Woodman (Eds.), *Research in organization change and development,* Vol. 1. Greenwich, CT: JAI Press.

Czapinksi, J. (1985). Negativity bias in psychology: An evaluation of Polish publications. *Polish Psychological Bulletin, 16,* 27–44.

D'Amato, M.R., & Jagoda, H. (1962). Effect of early exposure to photic stimulation on brightness discrimination and exploratory behavior. *Journal of Genetic Psychology, 101*(Dec), 267–271.

Darwin, C. (1859/2003). *The origin of species.* New York: Signet Classics.

Davis, G.F. (2009). *Managed by the markets.* New York: Oxford University Press.

Davis, G.F., & Marquis, C. (2005). Prospects for organizational theory in the early twenty-first century: Institutional fields and mechanisms. *Organization Science, 16,* 332–343.

Day, H. (1966). Looking time as a function of stimulus variables and individual differences. *Perceptual and Motor Skills, 22*(2), 423–428.

Diener, E. (1984). Subjective well-being. *Psychological Bulletin, 95,* 542–575.

Diener, E. (2009a) *Culture and subjective well-being.* Champaign, IL: Springer.

Diener, E. (2009b). *The science of well-being.* New York: Springer.

Diener, E., & Suh, E. (1997). Measuring quality of life: Economic, social, and subjective indicators. *Social Indicators Research, 40,* 189–216.

Diener, E., & Suh, E.M. (2000). *Culture and subjective well-being.* Cambridge, MA: MIT Press.

Drexelius, J. (1627). *The heliotropium, or conformity of the human will to the divine* (R.N. i. Translated by Shutte, Trans.). New York: The Devin-Adair Company.

Dutton, J.E. (2010). Interview on positive organizational scholarship by Mia Yan and Evelyn Micelotta. Academy of Management, Organization, Management, and Theory Division website: http://omtweb.org.

Dutton, J.E., & Glynn, M. (2007). Positive organizational scholarship. In C. Cooper & J. Barling (Eds.), *Handbook of organizational behavior.* Thousand Oaks, CA: Sage.

Dutton, J.E., & Heaphy, E. (2003). The power of high quality connections. In K.S. Cameron, J.E. Dutton, & R.E. Quinn. (Eds.), *Positive organizational scholarship: Foundations of a new discipline* (pp. 263–278). San Francisco: Berrett-Koehler.

Dutton, J.E., & Ragins, B.R. (2007). *Exploring positive relationships at work: Building a theoretical and research foundation.* Mahwah, NJ: Lawrence Erlbaum.

Dutton, J.E., & Sonenshein, S. (2009). Positive organizational scholarship. In S. Lopez (Ed.), *Encyclopedia of positive psychology* (pp. 737–742). Oxford: Wiley-Blackwell.

Dutton, J.E., M.C. Worline, P.J. Frost, & J.M. Lilius (2006). Explaining compassion organizing. *Administrative Science Quarterly, 51,* 59–96.

Ehrenreich, B. (2009). *Bright-sided: How positive thinking is undermining America.* New York: Henry Holt.

Emmons, R.A. (1999). *The psychology of ultimate concerns: Motivation and spirituality in personality.* New York: Guilford Press.

Erdelyi, E.H. (1974). A new look at a New Look: Perceptual defense and vigilance. *Psychological Review, 81,* 1–25.

Erhard-Seibold, E.V. (1937). The heliotrope tradition. *Orisis, 3*: 22–46.

Feldman, M.S., & Khademian, A.M. (2003). Empowerment and cascading vitality. In K.S. Cameron, J.E. Dutton, & R.E. Quinn (Eds.), *Positive organizational scholarship: Foundations of a New Discipline* (pp. 343–358). San Francisco: Berrett-Koehler.

Fineman, S. (2006). On being positive: Concerns and counterpoints. *Academy of Management Review, 31*(2), 270–291.

Fletcher (1998). Relational Practice: A Feminist Reconstruction of Work *Journal of Management Inquiry, 7*: 163–186.

Fowers, B.J., & Tjeltveit, A.C. (2003). Virtue obscured and retrieved: Character, community, and practices in behavioral science. *American Behavioral Scientist, 47*(4), 387–394.

Fredrickson, B.L. (1998). What good are positive emotions? *Review of General Psychology, 2,* 300–319.

Fredrickson, B.L., & Joiner, T. (2002). Positive emotions trigger upward spirals toward emotional well-being. *American Psychologist, 13,* 172–175.

Fredrickson, B.L., & Losada, M.F. (2005). Positive affect and the complex dynamics of human flourishing. *American Psychologist, 60*(7), 678–686.

Fredrickson, B.M. (2009). *Positivity.* New York: Crown.

Fritz, C., Lam, C.F., & Spreitzer, G. (2011). It's the little things that matter: An examination of knowledge workers' energy management. *Academy of Management Perspectives* (in press).

Gallagher, M.W., Lopez, S.J., & Preacher, K.J. (2009). The hierarchical structure of well-being. *Journal of Personality, 77,* 1025–1049.

George, J.M. (2004). Book review of positive organizational scholarship: Foundations of a new discipline. *Administrative Science Quarterly, 49,* 325–330.

Ghoshal, S. (2005). Bad management theories are destroying good management practice. *Academy of Management Learning and Education, 4,* 75–91.

Gilbert, G.M. (1938). The new status of experimental studies on the relationship between feeling and memory. *Psychological Bulletin, 35*, 433–441.

Gilovich, T. (1983). Biased evaluation and persistence in gambling. *Journal of Social and Personal Psychology, 44*, 110–1126.

Gittell, J.H., Cameron, K., Lim, S., & Rivas, V. (2006). Relationships, layoffs, and organizational resilience: airline industry responses to September 11. *The Journal of Applied Behavioral Science, 42*(3), 300–328.

Godfrey, P.C. (2003). The relationship between corporate philanthropy and shareholder wealth: A risk management perspective. *Academy of Management Review, 30*(4), 777–796.

Goldings, H.J. (1954). On the avowal and projection of happiness. *Journal of Personality, 23*(1), 30–47.

Gordon, M.E. (1970). Effect of correctness of behavior observed on accuracy of ratings. *Organizational Behavior and Human Performance, 5*(4), 366–377.

Gouldner, A. (1960). The norm of reciprocity: A preliminary statement. *American Sociological Review, 25*, 161–179.

Guzzo, R.A., & Dickson, M.W. (1996). Teams in organizations: Recent research on performance and effectiveness. *Annual Review of Psychology, 47*, 307–338.

Hackman, J.R. (2008). The perils of positivity. *Journal of Organizational Behavior, 30*, 309–319.

Hamilton, D.L., & Huffman, L.J. (1971). Generality of impression formation processes for evaluative and non-evaluative judgments. *Journal of Personality and Social Psychology, 20*, 200–207.

Havighurst, R.J., & Glasser, R. (1972). Exploratory study of reminiscence. *Journals of Gerontology, 27*(2), 245–253.

Hess, E.D., & Cameron, K.S. (2006). *Leading with values: Positivity, virtue, and high performance.* Cambridge: Cambridge University Press.

Ilies, R., Nahrgang, J.D., & Morgeson, F.O. (2007). Leader-member exchange and citizenship behaviors: A meta-analysis. *Journal of Applied Psychology, 92*, 269–277.

Jahoda, M. (1959). *Current concepts of positive mental health.* New York: Basic Books.

James, W. (1902). *The varieties of religious experience: A study in human nature.* London & Bombay: Longmans, Green, and Co./London: Collier-Macmillan.

Jensen, M.C. (2002). Value maximization, stakeholder theory, and the corporate objective function. *Business Ethics Quarterly, 12*, 235–256.

Johnson, W.B. (1937). Euphoric and depressed moods in normal subjects. *Character and Personality, 6*, 79–98.

Kanov, J.M., Maitlis, S., Worline, M.C., Dutton, J.E., Frost, P.J., & Lilius, J.M. (2004). Compassion in organizational life, *American Behavioral Scientist, 47*, 808–827.

Keyes, C.L.M. (2005). Mental illness and/or mental health? Investigating axioms of the complete state model of health. *Journal of Consulting and Clinical Psychology, 73*, 539–548.

Kok, B.E., & Fredrickson, B.L. (2010). Upward spirals of the heart: Autonomic flexibility, as indexed by vagal tone, reciprocally and prospectively predicts positive emotions and social connectedness. *Biological Psychology, 85*(3), 432–436.

Kramer, R.M. (1999). Trust and distrust in organizations: Emerging perspectives, enduring questions. *Annual Review of Psychology, 50*, 569–598.

Kuntz, D. (1974). Response faults on word-association as a function of associative difficulty and of affective connotation of words. *Journal of Consulting and Clinical Psychology, 42*(2), 231–235.

Lee, F., Caza, A., Edmondson, A., & Thomke, St. (2003). New knowledge creation in organizations. In K.S. Cameron, J.E. Dutton, & R.E. Quinn (Eds.), *Positive organizational scholarship: Foundations of a new discipline* (pp. 194–206). San Francisco: Berrett-Koehler.

Losada, M., & Heaphy, E. (2004). The role of positivity and connectivity in the performance of business teams: A nonlinear dynamics model. *American Behavioral Scientist, 47*(6), 740–765.

Luborsky, L., Blinder, B., & Mackworth, N. (1963). Eye fixation and recall of pictures as a function of GSR responsivity. *Perceptual and Motor Skills, 16*(2), 469–483.

Luthans, F., Norman, S.M., Avolio, B.J., & Avey, J.B. (2008). The mediating role of psychological capital in the supportive organizational climate–employee performance relationship. *Journal of Organizational Behavior, 29*, 219–238.

Mann, J.W. (1968). Defining unfavorable by denial. *Journal of Verbal Learning and Verbal Behavior, 7*(4), 760–766.

Margolis, J.D., & Walsh, J.P. (2003). Misery loves companies: Rethinking social initiatives by business. *Administrative Science Quarterly, 48*(2), 268–305.

Maslow, A. (1965). *Eupsychian management: A journal.* Homewood, IL: Irwin-Dorsey.

Maslow, A.H. (1968). *Toward a psychology of being.* New York: Van Nostrand.

Matlin, M.W. (1970). Response competition as a mediating factor in frequency-affect relationship. *Journal of Personality and Social Psychology, 16*(3), 536–552.

Matlin, M., & Stang, D. (1978). *The pollyanna principle.* Cambridge, MA: Schenkman Publishing Company.

McCullough, M.E., & Snyder, C.R. (2001). Classical sources of human strength: Revisiting an old home and building a new one. *Journal of Social and Clinical Psychology, 19*, 1–10.

McGregor, D. (1960). *The human side of enterprise.* New York: McGraw-Hill.

Meltzer, H., & Ludwig, D. (1967). Age differences in memory optimism and pessimism in workers. *Journal of Genetic Psychology, 110*(1), 17–30.

Merton, R.K. (1968). *Social organization and social structure.* New York: Free Press.

Mrosovsky, N., & Kingsmill, S.F. (1985). How turtles find the sea. *Zeitschrift Fur Tierpsychologie-Journal of Comparative Ethology, 67*(1–4), 237–256.

Nadler, D., & Tushman, M. (1997). *Competing by design.* New York: Oxford University Press.

Organ, D.W. (1988). *Organizational citizenship behavior: The good soldier syndrome.* Lexington, MA: Lexington Books.

Park, N., & Peterson, C.M. (2003). Virtues and organizations. In K.S. Cameron, J.E. Dutton, & R.E. Quinn (Eds.), *Positive organizational scholarship: Foundations of a new discipline* (pp. 33–47). San Francisco: Berrett Koehler.

Peterson, C., & Seligman, M.E.P. (2004). *Character strengths and virtues.* New York: Oxford University Press.

Pfeffer, J. (2010). Building sustainable organizations: The human factor. *Academy of Management Perspectives, 8*, 34–45.

Porter, M. (1998). *Competitive strategy: Techniques for analyzing industries and competitors.* New York: Free Press.

Powley, E.H., & Cameron, K.S. (2006). Organizational healing: Lived virtuousness amidst organizational crisis. *Journal of Management, Spirituality, and Religion, 3*, 13–33.

Powley, E.H., & Smith, S.N. (2006). Values and leadership in organizational crisis. In E.D. Hess & K.S. Cameron (Eds.), *Leading with values: Positivity, virtue, and high performance* (pp. 194–212). New York: Cambridge University Press.

Powley, E.H., & Piderit, K. (2008). Tending wounds: Elements of the organizational healing process. *Journal of Applied Behavioral Science, 44*(1), 134–149.

Pratt, M.G., & Ashforth, B.E. (2003). Fostering meaningfulness in work and at work. In K.S. Cameron, J.E. Dutton, & R.E. Quinn (Eds.), *Positive organizational scholarship: Foundations of a new discipline* (pp. 309–327). San Francisco: Berrett-Koehler.

Pratto, F., & John, O.P. (1991). Automatic vigilance: The attention-grabbing power of negative social information. *Journal of Personality and Social Psychology, 61*, 380–391.

Quinn, R.W. (2002). Flow in knowledge work: High performance experience in the design of national security technology. *Administrative Science Quarterly, 50*, 610–642.

Roberts, L.M. (2006). Shifting the lens on organizational life: The added value of positive scholarship. *Academy of Management Review, 31*, 292–305.

Roberts, L.M., Dutton, J.E., Spreitzer, G.M., Heaphy, E.D., & Quinn, R.E. (2005). Composing the reflected best-self-portrait: Building pathways for becoming extraordinary in work organizations. *Academy of Management Review, 30*, 712–736.

Rychlak, J.F. (1966). Reinforcement value: A suggested idiographic intensity dimension of meaningfulness for personality theorist. *Journal of Personality, 34*(3), 311–335.

Rychlak, J.F. (1977). *The psychology of rigorous humanism.* New York: Wiley-Interscience.

Seligman, M.E.P. (1999). The president's address. *American Psychologist, 54*, 559–562.

Sharot, T., Riccardi, A.M., Raio, C.M., & Phelps, E.A. (2007). Neural mechanisms mediating optimism bias. *Nature, 450*, 102–106.

Skinner, B.F. (1965). *Science and human behavior.* New York: Free Press.

Smith, J.C., & Baker, H.D. (1960). Conditioning in the horseshoe crab. *Journal of Comparative and Physiological Psychology, 53*(3), 279–281.

Smith, P.C., Kendall, L.M., & Hulin, C.L. (1969). *The measurement of satisfaction in work and retirement.* Chicago: Rand McNally.

Spreitzer, G.M. (1995). Psychological empowerment in the workplace: Dimensions, measurement, and validation. *Academy of Management Journal, 38*(5): 1442–1465.

Spreitzer, G., Sutcliffe, K., Dutton, J., Sonenshein, S., & Grant, A. (2005). A socially embedded model of thriving at work. *Organization Science, 16*(5), 537–549.

Spreitzer, G.M., & Sonenshein, S. (2003). Positive deviance and extraordinary performance. In K.S. Cameron, J.E. Dutton, & R.E. Quinn (Eds.), *Positive organizational scholarship: Foundations of a new discipline* (pp. 207–224). San Francisco: Berrett-Koehler.

Sutcliffe, K.M., & Vogus, T.J. (2003). Organizing for resilience. In K.S. Cameron, J.E. Dutton, & R.E. Quinn (Eds.), *Positive organizational scholarship: Foundations of a new discipline* (pp. 94–110). San Francisco: Berrett-Koehler.

Taylor, S.E. (1991). Asymmetrical effects of positive and negative events: The mobilization-minimization hypothesis. *Psychological Bulletin, 110*(1), 67.

Thomson, R.H. (1930). An experimental study of memory as influenced by feeling tone. *Journal of Experimental Psychology, 13*, 462–468.

Thrash, T.M., & Elliott, A.J. (2003). Inspiration as a psychological construct. *Journal of Personality and Social Psychology.* 2003; *84*(4), 871–889.

Tutu, D. (1999). *No future without forgiveness.* New York: Doubleday.

Vanette, D., Cameron, K.S., & Powley, E. (2006). Implementing positive organizational scholarship at Prudential. Center for Positive Organizational Scholarship, University of Michigan.

Veenhoven, R. (2010). *World databook on happiness (since 1984).* Boston: Dordrecht.

Veenhoven, R. (1996). Happy life-expectancy. A comprehensive measure of quality-of-life in nations. *Social Indicators Research, 39*, 1–58.

Vianello, M., Galliani, E.M., & Haidt, J. (2010). Elevation at work: The effects of leaders' moral excellence. *Journal of Positive Psychology, 4*, 105–127.

Vinokur, A.D., & van Ryn, M. (1993). Social support and undermining in close relationships: Their independent effects on the mental health of unemployed persons. *Journal of Personality and Social Psychology, 65*, 350–359.

Wang, C.S., Galinsky, A.D., & Murnighan, J.K. (2009). Bad drives psychological reactions, but good propels behavior. *Psychological Science, 20*, 634–644.

Weber, M. (1997). *The theory of social and economic organization.* New York: Free Press.

Weick, K.E. (2003). Positive organizing and organizational tragedy. In K.S. Cameron, J.E. Dutton, & R.E. Quinn (Eds.), *Positive organizational scholarship: Foundations of a new discipline* (pp. 66–80) San Francisco: Berrett-Koehler.

Weick, K.E. (2006). The role of values in high-risk organizations. In E.D. Hess & K.S. Cameron. *Leading with values: Positivity, virtue, and high performance* (pp. 55–67), New York: Cambridge University Press.

Wessman, A.E., & Ricks, D.F. (1966). *Mood and personality.* New York: Holt, Rinehart, & Winston.

Whetten, D.A. (1980). Organizational decline. *Academy of Management Review, 5,* 577–588.

Williamson, O. (1998). *The economic institutions of capitalism.* New York: Free Press.

Worline, M.C., & Quinn, R.W. (2003). Courageous principled action. In K.S. Cameron, J.E. Dutton, & R.E. Quinn (Eds.), *Positive organizational scholarship: Foundations of a new discipline* (pp. 138–158) San Francisco: Berrett-Koehler.

Worthington, E.L. (2001). Unforgiveness, forgiveness, and reconciliation and their implications for societal interventions. In R.G. Helmick & R.L. Petersen (Eds.), *Forgiveness and reconciliation: Religion, public policy, and conflict transformation* (pp. 161–182) Philadelphia: Templeton Foundation Press.

Wrzesniewski, A. (2003). Finding positive meaning in work. In K.S. Cameron, J.E. Dutton, & R.E. Quinn (Eds.), *Positive organizational scholarship: Foundations of a new discipline* (pp. 296–308) San Francisco: Berrett-Koehler.

Wrzesniewski, A., & Dutton, J.E. (2001). Crafting a job: Employees as active crafters of their work. *Academy of Management Review, 26*, 179–201.

Young, P.T. (1937). Laughing and weeping, cheerfulness and depression: A study of moods among college students. *Journal of Social Psychology, 8*, 311–334.

Zajonc, R.B. (1968). Attitudinal effects of mere exposure. *Journal of Personality and Social Psychology, 9*, 1–27.

PART 1

Positive Individual Attributes

Psychological Capital

Meaning, Findings and Future Directions

Carolyn M. Youssef *and* Fred Luthans

Abstract

Although the value of positivity has always been recognized, only in the past decade has there been renewed interest and a refocus in both psychology as a whole and in organizational studies. This chapter summarizes the theory-building and research findings to date on positive organizational behavior (POB) and psychological capital (PsyCap). The chapter then concludes by featuring a number of future directions for needed research and extensions of the domain of psychological capital.

Keywords: Positivity, positive organizational behavior, psychological capital, self-efficacy, hope, optimism, resilience

Over the last decade, led by the field of psychology and soon followed by organizational studies, there has been a surge of interest and refocus on positive-oriented research. Although positivity is certainly not new to either of these disciplines, the positive psychology movement (Seligman & Csikszentmihalyi, 2000; Snyder & Lopez, 2002) has rekindled a passion for further understanding the unique contributions of positive constructs in various life domains, including the workplace. The first part of the chapter defines what is meant by positive organizational behavior (POB) and psychological capital (PsyCap). Then, we give an overview of the theory-building and research findings to date on PsyCap and conclude by featuring future needed directions for research and suggested extensions of the domain of PsyCap.

Meaning of Positive Organizational Behavior

Positive organizational behavior is defined as "the study and application of positively oriented human resource strengths and psychological capacities that can be measured, developed, and effectively managed for performance improvement" (Luthans, 2002b, p. 59).

As inferred in this definition, the motivation behind initiating POB was to address the underrepresented positive perspective, approach, and constructs in the organizational literature (Luthans, 2002a, b). We briefly describe these perceived needs here, and revisit them throughout the chapter.

- *The need for more positivity*: Although positivity is recognized to be foundational to the field of organizational behavior since its inception (e.g., the Hawthorne studies and seminal motivation and leadership theories), a preoccupation with negativity appears to have been incessantly creeping and threatening to dominate the field, at least in the academic literature. This trend of seemingly moving away from the positive has been referred to in psychology as the "forgotten mission." Although dealing with dysfunctional employees, ineffective leaders, abusive supervision, unethical behaviors, stress and burnout in the workplace are invaluable topics to address, the relatively less attention given to positive organizational research signaled the need for a more balanced research agenda.

- *The need for evidence-based positivity*: It did not take long for the gap in the positivity academic literature, both in psychology and in organizational research, to be filled by the popular self-help literature, which almost universally lacked scientific rigor. On the other hand, POB made the case for evidence-based positivity, placing theory, research, and valid and reliable measurement as key selection criteria for the psychological resources to be included in its domain of study and application.

- *The need for uniqueness*: Related to the previous two points, it appeared that organizational research was ripe for introducing and integrating new or unique perspectives, approaches, and constructs to meet challenges associated with the newly emerging 21st century environment. This is what Luthans and Avolio (2009) referred to as "old wine, old bottles, but perhaps a new restaurant."

- *The need for a developmental approach*: Although positivity is not new to organizational sciences (including human resource management and organizational development), for a long time the relative emphasis has been on stable traits and selection-based approaches. On the other hand, POB seeks to build, develop, and nurture positivity in the workplace.

- *The need for a performance orientation*: Although positivity may be important and valuable in its own right, the realities of today's competitive environment make it necessary to link it to performance outcomes with measurable impact on the bottom line. Positive organizational behavior recognizes and addresses this need by focusing on psychological resources that can have a quantifiable performance impact and that can yield an attractive return on investment.

Four specific positive psychological resources have been determined to best fit the inclusion criteria of being theory and research-driven, measurable, developmental, and related to performance and other desirable work-related outcomes. These psychological resources are:

- *Hope*: Based on Snyder's (2000) theory-building and research, hope is defined as "a positive motivational state that is based on an interactively derived sense of successful

(1) agency (goal-directed energy) and (2) pathways (planning to meet goals)" (Snyder, Irving, & Anderson, 1991, p. 287).

- *Efficacy*: Drawing from Bandura's (1997) social cognitive theory, efficacy or confidence applied to the workplace can be defined as: "one's belief about his or her ability to mobilize the motivation, cognitive resources, and courses of action necessary to execute a specific action within a given context" (Stajkovic & Luthans, 1998b, p. 66).

- *Resilience*: Drawing from developmental psychology (Masten, 2001; Masten & Reed, 2002), we define resiliency as "the developable capacity to rebound or bounce back from adversity, conflict, and failure, or even positive events, progress, and increased responsibility" (Luthans, 2002a, p. 702).

- *Optimism*: We integrate two prevailing views of optimism, as a generalized positive expectancy (Carver & Scheier, 2002), and as an optimistic explanatory (attributional) style (Seligman, 1998).

These four widely recognized resources in positive psychology (Snyder & Lopez, 2002), when combined, form what we have termed psychological capital or simply PsyCap (Luthans, Luthans, & Luthans, 2004; Luthans & Youssef, 2004; Luthans, Youssef, & Avolio, 2007).

Meaning and Conceptual Development of Psychological Capital

Using POB and its inclusion criteria as a framework and point of departure, PsyCap expands and applies the POB theory and research. In terms of theory and construct validity, the four psychological resources of hope, efficacy, resiliency, and optimism have been found to constitute the measurably reliable and valid higher-order, latent multidimensional construct of PsyCap (see Luthans, Avolio, Avey, & Norman, 2007 for this research). We have defined this core construct of PsyCap as "an individual's positive psychological state of development that is characterized by: (1) having confidence (self-efficacy) to take on and put in the necessary effort to succeed at challenging tasks; (2) making a positive attribution (optimism) about succeeding now and in the future; (3) persevering toward goals and, when necessary, redirecting paths to goals (hope) in order to succeed; and (4) when beset by problems and adversity, sustaining and bouncing back and even beyond (resiliency) to attain success" (Luthans, Youssef, et al., 2007, p. 3).

The underlying theoretical mechanism shared among PsyCap's four constituent psychological resources is a cognitive, agentic, developmental capacity representing "one's positive appraisal of circumstances and probability for success based on motivated effort and perseverance" (Luthans, Avolio, et al., 2007, p. 550).

In terms of fit with other intangible forms of "capital," we position PsyCap as a resource that goes beyond human capital, or "what you know" (i.e., experience, knowledge, skills and abilities), and social capital, or "who you know" (i.e., relationships, networks). It deals with "who you are" here and now, and "who you can become" in the proximal future if your psychological resources are developed and nurtured in the workplace (Luthans, Luthans et al., 2004; Luthans & Youssef, 2004). In PsyCap's conceptualization as a higher-order construct, and as a construct that builds upon and goes beyond human and social capital, it also resembles the notion of "resource caravans" from psychological resource theories (Hobfoll, 2002). This theoretical lens is also consistent with Fredrickson's (2009) broaden-and-build theory, in which positivity can help build psychological resource repertoires that can be later drawn upon.

In terms of measurement, a valid and reliable PsyCap Questionnaire (PCQ) has been developed (Luthans, Youssef, et al., 2007), empirically validated (Luthans, Avolio, et al., 2007), and now recognized and used in the POB literature. In terms of malleability and developmental potential, PsyCap has been conceptualized and empirically supported as a "state-like" core construct that is open to development and management (Luthans & Youssef, 2007; Luthans, Avolio, et al., 2007; Luthans, Avey, Avolio, & Peterson, 2010; Luthans, Avey, & Patera, 2008). We conceptually place PsyCap close to (but not at) the "state" end on a continuum that ranges from "pure" traits to "pure" states. Compared to very stable talents (e.g., intelligence, Schmidt & Hunter, 2000) and relatively stable personality traits and characteristics (e.g., the Big Five personality traits, Barrick & Mount, 1991; core self-evaluations, Judge & Bono, 2001), PsyCap is significantly more dynamic (Luthans, Avolio et al., 2007) and thus open to change and development (Luthans, Avey et al., 2010; Luthans, Avey, & Patera, 2008). Also compared to character strengths and virtues from positive psychology (Peterson & Seligman, 2004), PsyCap development can more readily take place in work settings through brief training interventions, rather than over one's lifespan. In these training interventions, participants develop their PsyCap through mastery of job-related tasks, setting approach goals, future-oriented thinking, and anticipation of and pathway planning for potential obstacles and setbacks (see Luthans, Youssef et al., 2007).

On the other hand, compared to "pure" states, such as very temporary positive pleasures/moods or fleeting positive emotions, PsyCap shows relatively greater stability over time (see Luthans & Youssef, 2007 for a comprehensive discussion of the trait-state continuum and Luthans, Avolio et al., 2007 for empirical evidence). This relative stability or state-like nature of PsyCap makes the return on investment in its development more sustainable in the workplace. Similarly, in positive psychology, happiness or subjective well-being, which, although previously conceptualized as a trait-like individual difference (e.g., see Wright, 2005), has been shown to lend itself to enduring sustainable changes over time through intentional activities targeted at increasing happiness (Lyubomirsky, King, & Diener, 2005). This is also in line with the accumulated findings in positive psychology that about 50% of happiness and positivity can be accounted for by a "set point" (i.e., inherited and trait-like characteristics), whereas only 10% can be accounted for by circumstances (i.e., income, location), leaving 40% open to development through intentional activities (Lucas & Donnellan, 2007; Lyubomirsky, 2007; Lyubomirsky, Sheldon, & Schkade, 2005).

In terms of level of analysis, POB and PsyCap would tend to be characterized by what Whetten and colleagues (2009) would call "theories in organizations." Positive organizational behavior emphasizes constructs and models that can facilitate the prediction, explanation, and development of positive attitudes, behaviors, and performance outcomes primarily at the individual level. For example, each of the components (i.e., hope, efficacy, resilience, and optimism) and the overall PsyCap core construct has been clearly demonstrated to be positively related to a wide variety of desired outcomes (and negatively to undesired) (see Avey, Reichard, Luthans, & Mhatre, 2011; Avey, Luthans, & Youssef, 2010; Avey, Patera, & West, 2006; Avey, Wernsing, & Luthans, 2008; Luthans, Avolio et al., 2007; Luthans, Norman, Avolio, & Avey, 2008; Peterson & Byron, 2008; Peterson, Luthans, Avolio, Walumbwa, & Zhang, in press; Stajkovic & Luthans, 1998; Youssef & Luthans, 2007).

Finally, besides Whetten's theory in organizations perspective, to further understand PsyCap, we can draw from Pfeffer's (1997) five models of behavior and the classic Burrell and Morgan (1979) sociological paradigms. Pfeffer (1997) posits that models attempting to understand the nature of behavior in organizations, as well as their underlying assumptions and premises for their development and testing, can be based on economic, social, moral, interpretive cognitive, or retrospectively rational, theoretical lenses. Burrell and Morgan (1979), on the other hand, offer four paradigms for the analysis of social theories in organizations: functionalist, interpretive, radical structuralist, and radical humanist. These two classic typologies can be used to further elaborate and understand the philosophical foundations underlying POB and PsyCap.

The emphasis on demonstrating the objective work-related outcomes of PsyCap best fits Pfeffer's (1997) economic model of behavior. Furthermore, in PsyCap, work-related positivity is viewed as antecedent not only for proximal work outcomes, but also for overall well-being over time (Avey, Luthans, Smith, & Palmer, 2010). Our recent POB theory-building is also exploring reciprocal relationships between various life domains, such as work, relationships, and health, with higher levels of positivity, thriving, and well-being evolving over time from various psychological resources and mechanisms, such as human agency and malleability (Youssef & Luthans, 2010). Empirical research is also indicating that positive appraisals of life domains besides work (i.e., Relationship PsyCap and Health PsyCap) impact on employee's overall well-being (Luthans, Youssef, Sweetman, & Harms, 2011). This approach to positivity in PsyCap theory-building and empirical research can be best aligned with Burrell and Morgan's (1979) functionalist paradigm.

Summary of Research Findings on Psychological Capital

As indicated, a PsyCap measure has been developed and validated (Luthans, Avolio, et al., 2007; Luthans, Youssef, et al., 2007). Furthermore, PsyCap development interventions have been supported by experimental studies in a variety of work and training settings (Luthans, Avey et al., 2010), including delivery online (Luthans, Avey, & Patera, 2008). Besides meeting the criteria of valid measurement and being open to development, a growing number of studies have clearly demonstrated that PsyCap has impact on desired outcomes in the workplace. For example, in one major study, PsyCap, measured using the PCQ, was shown to be positively related to employee performance and satisfaction (Luthans, Avolio, et al., 2007). Two samples were utilized, including one with 144 employees in various functions and levels of a midsized insurance services firm. The analysis supported PsyCap as a higher-order construct, manifested in its four constituent psychological resources of efficacy, hope, optimism, and resilience. The composite PsyCap factor was also shown to be a better predictor of performance and satisfaction than its four individual facets.

Broadly defined, outcomes in most of the PsyCap studies refer to immediate in-role productivity, as well as various desired (e.g., satisfaction and commitment) and undesired (e.g., cynicism) attitudes, intentions (e.g., intent to quit) and behaviors (e.g., desired organizational citizenship behaviors, undesired counterproductive behaviors) that are closely associated and have empirically supported relationships with organizational performance. This broader, holistic approach to positivity has been conceptually (Youssef & Luthans, 2009) and, as discussed earlier, empirically supported (e.g., Luthans, Youssef et al., 2011). For example, in a study of 336 employees from a broad cross-section of organizations and jobs, Avey, Luthans, and Youssef (2010) found PsyCap to be positively related to extra-role organizational citizenship behaviors (OCBs) and negatively related to organizational cynicism, intentions to quit, and counterproductive workplace behaviors beyond what can be accounted for by demographics, personality traits, and person–organization fit and person–job fit. Another study found that PsyCap is negatively related to occupational stress symptoms, intentions to quit, and job search behaviors (Avey, Luthans, & Jensen, 2009).

Initial experimental (Luthans, Avey, et al., 2010) and longitudinal (Peterson, Luthans et al., in press) research also supports the causality between PsyCap and performance. Although positivity may have a terminal value for individuals at and beyond the workplace, the economic lens (Pfeffer, 1997) of POB and alignment with a functionalist paradigm (Burrell & Morgan, 1979) are necessary for resource allocation in bottom-line–oriented organizational settings. Return on investment (ROI) in PsyCap development has been determined, through utility analysis using real data, to be over 200% (Luthans, Youssef, et al., 2007). This impressive ROI on PsyCap, of course, would be substantially higher than other investments, and is likely to powerfully resonate with financially minded, pragmatic practitioners in organizational settings.

Although PsyCap primarily focuses on positivity at the individual level, it has also been supported as a mediator of the relationship between a supportive organizational climate and employee performance (Luthans, Norman, et al., 2008) and between authentic leadership and intact work groups' performance and citizenship behavior (Walumbwa, Luthans, Avey, & Oke, 2011). It has also been shown to moderate the relationship between organizational identity and employee citizenship and deviance behaviors (Norman, Avey, Nimnicht, & Graber Pigeon, 2010). Furthermore, research has found employees with higher PsyCap may proactively facilitate positive changes in organizations (Avey, Wensing, & Luthans, 2008). In other words, PsyCap has been shown to be instrumental in facilitating the impact of a positive organizational context on various desirable outcomes.

In addition to the above developments and findings along PsyCap's inclusion criteria, evidence for the external validity of PsyCap is also emerging. For example, studies in other cultures support the relationship between PsyCap and performance outcomes (Luthans, Avey, Clapp-Smith, & Li, 2008; Luthans, Avolio, Walumbwa, & Li, 2005; Tantiukoskula, Luthans, & Luthans, 2010), and very recent meta-analytical research revealed some differentials across countries and industries (Avey, Reichard, et al., 2011). In positive psychology, a strong emphasis has been placed on cultural differences and a clear awareness of the potential for positivity and its underlying assumptions to be culturally based (Snyder & Lopez, 2002). However, recent empirical findings show that these cultural differences may be smaller than had been assumed (Diener & Biswas-Diener, 2008).

Current Developments in Practice

On the practice side, positivity in general has always received widespread acceptance from practicing managers. However, the primary mode of application of positivity has almost solely been driven by the popular self-help literature, rather than scientifically based positive psychology, positive organizational scholarship (POS) or POB. One exception would be Gallup's strengths-based approach (Rath, 2007), although, unlike POB, it has been focused on hard-wired talents and trait-like strengths. Unfortunately, the flood of positively oriented management fads and unsubstantiated feel-good approaches over the years may have created hesitation or disbelief, with resulting resistance in many practicing managers and organizational decision makers. The failures of the fads carry over to the allocation of substantial resources toward the

positive applications advocated by positive psychology, POS, and POB. Fortunately, the emerging academically based consulting groups and their practitioner-oriented evidence-based programs and interventions seem to lately be gaining ground in appealing to positively oriented managers and organizations seeking rigorous, evidence-based positive approaches (e.g., see Linley, Harrington, & Garcea, 2010).

PsyCap is positioned to be closely aligned with the currently recognized needs in today's workplace due to its demonstrable positive impact and its specific emphasis on development, performance management, and ROI. However, today's turbulent economic, political, social, and ethical landscape also seems to be in dire need for positivity at the organizational (and community, country, and global) levels, to which the organizational sciences in general seem well positioned to contribute. Moreover, the prevailing overall negativity due to terrorism, unemployment, loss of material and social wealth, and, many would argue, deteriorating cultural values, calls for a positive psychology that emphasizes human strengths and values, both at and beyond the workplace. The sales volume of self-help bestsellers indicates the tremendous need people have for positivity. Overall, the general public, organizations, and individual leaders/employees are demanding more positivity. Although the academic debate surrounding positive psychology, POS, and POB is certainly healthy and insightful (e.g., see Fineman, 2006; Hackman, 2009; Lazarus, 2003; Luthans & Avolio, 2009; Roberts, 2006), the popular book market and the many "how-to" websites will continue to provide less rigorous, and, too often, unsustainable (at best) and misleading (at worst) alternatives. On this matter, the need for evidence-based management practices and the development of scientist–practitioners from the academic side and practitioner–scientists from consultants and professional managers seems more needed than ever (Pfeffer & Sutton, 2006; Rousseau, 2006).

Future Directions

In its current nascent, emergent state, there are numerous directions for future research and application in POB and PsyCap. We propose the following as some of the most needed future directions for both the research and extended application of POB in general, and PsyCap, in particular.

- *Expanding the breadth of POB and the PsyCap construct*: To date, the four positive psychological resources of hope, efficacy, resilience, and optimism have been identified (and empirically verified) as the best-fit positive psychological resources to be included in the core construct of PsyCap. Other positive constructs have also been evaluated, and the potential for their inclusion has been assessed (see Chapters 6 and 7 of Luthans, Youssef, et al., 2007, which feature the cognitive resources of creativity and wisdom; the affective resources of well-being, flow, and humor; the social resources of gratitude, forgiveness, and emotional intelligence; and the higher-order resources of spirituality, authenticity, and courage). Research should continue to further investigate these and other psychological resources for potential integration into PsyCap, both conceptually, and in terms of meeting the inclusion criteria of valid measurement, development, and performance impact.

- *Expanding the scope of the PsyCap construct to other domains*: Although the workplace is certainly one of the most important domains of life, PsyCap is applicable to other domains as well. For example, very recent theory (Youssef & Luthans, 2010) and research (Luthans, Youssef et al., 2011) have included relationships, health, and overall well-being. Some of PsyCap's constituent resources also need to be explored in relation to academic and athletic performance. Future research should assess the validity of PsyCap in these other life domains that are beyond the workplace. Furthermore, the relative contribution of PsyCap in these life domains to overall positivity, as well as the spillover effects of PsyCap across these domains, would seem to be interesting extensions to be tested by future research.

- *Expanding the boundaries of PsyCap to other contexts*: The empirical studies conducted to date mainly utilized samples from for-profit organizations in the United States. The exceptions were a couple of published studies conducted in China (Luthans, Avey, Clapp-Smith, & Li, 2008; Luthans, Avolio, et al., 2005) and preliminary research in Southeast Asia (Tantiukoskula et al., 2010), and some conceptual developments in relation to South Africa (Luthans, Van Wyk, & Walumbwa, 2004) and the Middle East (Youssef & Luthans, 2006). The external

validity and applicability of PsyCap can be significantly enhanced by replicating these studies in new organizational contexts, such as nonprofits, hospitals, governmental and regulatory agencies, and educational institutions. Furthermore, since positivity may be culturally sensitive, if not determined, examining the underlying assumptions of U.S.-based positive models in other cultures is necessary for better understanding and extensions of positive constructs and models.

- *Expanding the boundaries of PsyCap to other levels of analysis*: Individual-level PsyCap is influenced by a wide range of contextual factors at the group and organizational levels, and is affected by and can affect positivity at these levels as well. Theories and empirical studies of positivity should account for such linkages through multilevel conceptual frameworks and empirical analyses. Moreover, although collective PsyCap has very recently been found to be related to group citizenship behavior and group performance (Walumbwa, Luthans et al., 2011), the construct validity of PsyCap and its measurement scales should be tested further at the group and, especially, organizational levels, and in the future, at community and even country levels.

- *Examining new theoretical lenses and paradigms for POB and PsyCap*: Integration of other theoretical lenses and paradigms (as we touched on in this chapter with Burrell & Morgan, 1979 and Pfeffer, 1997) into POB and PsyCap beyond the economic, functionalist approach can help expand its understanding as a multifaceted approach. Future theory-building can facilitate its development into a multidisciplinary approach with other related fields such as sociology, anthropology, political science, economics, and others. For example, a social lens can produce more contextualized conceptual frameworks. An interpretive lens with a humanistic paradigm may promote a wider range of research methods.

- *Examining new approaches and methodologies for POB and PsyCap*: Related to the point above, limiting PsyCap to deductive hypothesis testing may not be the most effective approach in the development of a relatively new area of inquiry. Instead, inductive theory-building strategies (Ketokivi & Mantere, 2010; Locke, 2007), paradigmatic theories, and metaphorical theory borrowing (Whetten et al., 2009) may be better suited to the current level of theory development in the POB literature. In a related manner, quantitative research methods need to be balanced with qualitative and mixed methods in order to add more depth, richness, and flexibility to the development process and avoid the premature creation of rigid boundaries around a still emerging area of study, such as POB and PsyCap.

- *Examining causal directions, curvilinear relationships, mediators, and moderators*: As indicated in the earlier summary of research on PsyCap relating to a wide variety of attitudes, behaviors, and performances, it is still possible that these outcomes may cause increased PsyCap in employees. For example, although employees' high PsyCap may increase their performance through their efficacious, agentic beliefs, the reverse may also be the case. That is, it is also possible that high performance enhances their PsyCap efficacy. Causal models need to be tested through experimental designs, such as the very recent Luthans, Avey, et al. (2010) study and also longitudinal studies (Avey, Luthans, & Mhatre, 2008; Peterson, Luthans et al., in press). Furthermore, although extreme positivity has been found optimal in some life domains (e.g., intimate relationships), more moderate levels of happiness have been found optimal in achievement-oriented domains such as work and education (Oishi, Diener, & Lucas, 2007). This may be because extreme positivity (e.g., very high PsyCap) may promote undesirable work behaviors leading to, for example, accidents and/or turnover. Specific examination of discontinuities at very high (and very low) PsyCap levels is necessary. For example, optimal positivity-to-negativity ratios of 3:1 for effective performance in work settings have been found (Fredrickson, 2009), but the best ratio for positive appraisals of personal relationships has been determined to be 6:1 (Gottman, 1994). These findings call for the examination of nonlinear models in positivity research. Various mediators and moderators should also be examined, including organizational, group, and leader characteristics, as well as individual differences and emotional states and, of course, different contexts.

- *Alternative interventions*: To date, the development of PsyCap has primarily focused on training interventions ranging from 1 to 4 hours. Both face-to-face (Luthans, Avey et al., 2010) and online (Luthans, Avey & Patera, 2008) training interventions have been successfully implemented. Future research and practice should examine the efficacy of other types of interventions, both to increase PsyCap and to enhance the sustainability of PsyCap increases over time after an initial intervention has been implemented. For example, employees can be provided with alternative PsyCap-enhancing activities to choose from and implement, and a forum can be created for communication and follow-up on those activities. Successful positivity-enhancing activities from positive psychology that can be adapted into workplace interventions include using gratitude journals, pursuing self-concordant goals, positive reframing of negative events, savoring, mindfulness, meditation, forgiveness, and engaging in activities that can promote the experience of flow (Fredrickson, 2009; Lyubomirsky, 2007). These activities are also likely to address the positivity needs of the whole person beyond immediate work responsibility, which initial research has indicated can promote overall well-being (Luthans, Youssef, et al., 2011). Positivity and PsyCap can also be mentored and coached by high-PsyCap leaders modeling the right attitudes and behaviors (e.g., authenticity, trust), which in turn can build their followers' PsyCap (Avey, Avolio, & Luthans, in press), and by creating the right environment for them to flourish (Walumbwa, Peterson, Avolio, & Hartnell, 2010).

In addition to these needed future directions for POB and PsyCap, the integration and collaboration between all positively oriented research initiatives, as well as between positivity scholars and practitioners, can add significant value to the validity and applicability of positivity in general. Here are some examples that raise a number of research questions for future testing:

- *Cross-level facilitators and blockages*: Although it is generally recognized that positive individuals do not automatically create positive organizations, and that positive organizational initiatives do not automatically translate into increased positivity in individual employees, the underlying mechanisms that facilitate or hinder such cross-level transfer of positivity remain largely unexplored. This goes beyond the integration of organizational- and individual-level constructs into more comprehensive models (e.g., see Youssef & Luthans, 2009). Mechanisms that may accelerate or block cross-level linkages would be dynamic in nature, requiring unique research methodologies (e.g., growth models), rather than traditional multilevel research. This is not to deny the importance of exploring contextual factors, antecedents, and outcomes at various levels of analysis, but rather to promote exploring the interrelationships of these constructs within dynamic frameworks. For example, how does time as a variable affect the interrelationship between a positive organizational culture and individual employees' level of positivity? Is there a tenure effect, in which employees become more in tune with their organization's positivity over time? Is there a "honeymoon effect," in which employees' positivity receives an initial boost upon joining a positive organization? Is there a self-selection, congruence, or "fit" effect, in which positive employees "click" with positive organizations, and thus both the employee and the organization become more positive, whereas negative employees are alienated or self-select out of the organization? These types of questions could provide a starting point for researchers and practitioners interested in exploring such cross-level linkages.
- *Cross-domain facilitators, blockages, and the overall impact on positivity*: Positive and negative spillover and/or interactive effects between work and other life domains have been recognized and supported (Judge & Ilies, 2004; Luthans, Youssef, et al., 2011). Also emerging is the recognition of cross-over

effects (Bakker, Westman, & Van Emmerik, 2009). For example, there may be a cross-over from an employee's work affect to a spouse's work outcomes. Similar to the cross-level linkages discussed in the point above, the dynamic mechanisms that may either accelerate or block cross-domain linkages need to be explored. Moreover, research should investigate the causal directions and thresholds for such cross-domain linkages to occur, as well as their overall impact on positivity. For example, how many positive interactions at work can compensate for one negative social interaction with family members or friends? How positive does one's relationship with a spouse or child need to be before it can render positivity at work redundant or unnecessary for increasing productivity or enhancing desired work attitudes? Does positivity across life domains qualitatively differ from "concentrated" positivity in one domain (e.g., work, personal relationships) in terms of impact on employee productivity and/or well-being? Is there a point at which an employee's level of negativity, due to personality dispositions, mental or physical illness, broken social relationships, or other reasons, renders any positive initiatives in the workplace ineffective for that employee? How can organizations mitigate the potentially toxic impact of jobs that require negativity (e.g., safety and security, auditing, quality control) on employees' other life domains or overall positivity and well-being?
- *Bridging the academic–practitioner divide*: The need for scientist–practitioners and practitioner–scientists has been recognized over the years. However, recently, an added emphasis has been placed on linking academic research with practice, particularly in the area of positivity, as evidenced by the themes selected over the last few years for predominantly academic forums such as the Academy of Management, the Positive Psychology Summit, and handbooks such as this and others (e.g., Linley et al., 2010). Even with this emphasis on the need to close the theory–practice gap, positive psychology, POS, and POB still need to engage in continuous dialogue with professionals and thought leaders in practice, in order to foster the relevance of positivity to their everyday

decisions and applications. As discussed earlier, PsyCap's economic perspective represents a good fit with the bottom-line orientation of management practices. However, a broader impact can be achieved if positivity can penetrate decisions related to organizational strategy, structure, and culture, with a demonstrable, quantifiable ROI. As indicated, PsyCap has made some inroads in this regard with utility analysis calculating the actual dollar ROI (Luthans, Youssef, et al., 2007). Positive organizational sciences in general need to give more emphasis to such specific approaches (rather than just "lip service") in order to complement and expand the reach and practical relevance of their findings. Furthermore, in the same way that positive organizational approaches were informed by the positive psychology movement, positive psychology can also use POB and POS as applied forms of its theories to further inform applications that can enhance counseling, therapy, mental rehabilitation, and other areas such as in education, sports, and health care.

Even though the positive movement in general and POB/PsyCap as summarized in this chapter are off to a good start, as these future directions indicate, a long, but exciting, journey still lies ahead.

Conclusion

This review indicates that PsyCap provides organizational researchers and practitioners with a largely untapped resource that is theoretically and empirically supported, validly measurable, developmental and significantly predictive of a wide range of highly desirable attitudinal, behavioral, and performance outcomes in the workplace. Positive organizational scholarship, positive psychology, and POB/PsyCap are linked by a passion for positivity and an open-ended inquiry mode (Luthans & Avolio, 2009). These positively oriented approaches represent a paradigm shift from mainstream psychology and organizational sciences, rather than merely extrapolation from existing negatively oriented constructs or neutral, deterministic views of employee attitudes, behaviors, and performance in today's workplace. This is not to say that these positive approaches should abandon their obviously rich historical roots or scientific traditions. On the contrary, from its very beginning, POB called for a theory- and research-based approach to positivity that would be founded on established scientific knowledge (Luthans, 2002a, b). The paradigm shift called for by positivity researchers is in recognizing the new environment in which the established positively oriented theories and processes, such as self-efficacy, agency, goal setting, expectancy, attribution, coping, and conservation of resources, to name but a few, can now be revived, refocused, and synergistically integrated to achieve higher levels of productivity and organizational effectiveness, as well as personal fulfillment and well-being.

References

Avey, J.B., Avolio, B.J., & Luthans, F. (in press). Experimentally analyzing the impact of leader positivity on follower positivity and performance. *The Leadership Quarterly.*

Avey, J.B., Luthans, F., & Jensen, S. (2009). Psychological capital: A positive resource for combating employee stress and turnover. *Human Resource Management, 48,* 677–693.

Avey, J.B., Luthans, F., & Mhatre, K. (2008). A call for longitudinal research in positive organizational behavior. *Journal of Organizational Behavior, 29,* 705–711.

Avey, J.B., Luthans, F., Smith, R., & Palmer, N. (2010). Impact of positive psychological capital on employee well-being over time. *Journal of Occupational Health Psychology, 12,* 17–28.

Avey, J.B., Luthans, F., & Youssef, C.M. (2010). The additive value of psychological capital: Predicting positive and negative work attitudes and behaviors. *Journal of Management, 36,* 430–452.

Avey, J.B., Patera, J.L., & West, B.J. (2006). The implications of positive psychological capital on employee absenteeism. *Journal of Leadership and Organizational Studies, 13,* 42–60.

Avey, J.B., Reichard, R., Luthans, F., & Mhatre, K. (2011). Meta-analysis of the impact of positive psychological capital on employee attitudes, behaviors and performance. *Human Resource Development Quarterly,* still in press.

Avey, J.B., Wernsing, T.S., & Luthans, F. (2008). Can positive employees help positive organizational change? *Journal of Applied Behavioral Science, 44,* 48–70.

Bakker, A.B., Westman, M., & Van Emmerik, I.J.H. (2009). Advances in crossover theory. *Journal of Managerial Psychology, 24,* 206–219.

Bandura, A. (1997). *Self-efficacy: The exercise of control.* New York: Freeman.

Barrick, M.R., & Mount, M.K. (1991). The big five personality dimensions and job performance: A meta-analysis. *Personnel Psychology, 44,* 1–26

Burrell, G., & Morgan, G. (1979). *Sociological paradigms and organizational analysis.* Farnham, UK: Ashgate.

Carver, C., & Scheier, M. (2002). Optimism. In C.R. Snyder, & S. Lopez (Eds.), *Handbook of positive psychology* (pp. 231–243). Oxford, UK: Oxford University Press.

Diener, E., & Biswas-Diener, R. (2008). *Happiness: Unlocking the mysteries of psychological wealth.* Malden, MA: Blackwell.

Fineman, S. (2006). On being positive: Concerns and counterpoints. *Academy of Management Review, 31,* 270–291.

Fredrickson, B.L. (2009). *Positivity.* New York: Crown/Random House.

Gottman, J.M. (1994). *What predicts divorce? The relationship between marital processes and marital outcomes.* Hillsdale, NJ: Lawrence Erlbaum Associates.

Hackman, J.R. (2009). The perils of positivity. *Journal of Organizational Behavior, 30,* 309–319.

Hobfoll, S. (2002). Social and psychological resources and adaptation. *Review of General Psychology, 6,* 307–324.

Judge, T.A., & Bono, J.E. (2001). Relationship of core self-evaluations traits—self-esteem, generalized self-efficacy, locus of control, and emotional stability—with job satisfaction and job performance: A meta-analysis. *Journal of Applied Psychology, 86,* 80–92.

Judge, T.A., & Ilies, R. (2004). Affect and job satisfaction: A study of their relationship at work and at home. *Journal of Applied Psychology, 89,* 661–673.

Ketokivi, K., & Mantere, S. (2010). Two strategies for inductive reasoning in organizational research. *Academy of Management Review, 35,* 315–333.

Lazarus, R.S. (2003). Does the positive psychology movement have legs? *Psychological Inquiry, 14,* 93–109.

Linley, P.A., Harrington, S., & Garcea, N. (Eds.). (2010). *Oxford handbook of positive psychology and work.* Oxford, UK: Oxford University Press.

Locke, E. (2007). The case for inductive theory building. *Journal of Management, 33,* 867–890.

Lucas, R.E., & Donnellan, M.B. (2007). How stable is happiness: Using the STARTS model to estimate the stability of life satisfaction. *Journal of Research in Personality, 41,* 1091–1098.

Luthans, F. (2002a). The need for and meaning of positive organizational behavior. *Journal of Organizational Behavior, 23,* 695–706.

Luthans, F. (2002b). Positive organizational behavior: Developing and managing psychological strengths. *Academy of Management Executive, 16,* 57–72.

Luthans, F., Avey, J.B., Avolio, B.J., & Peterson, S.J. (2010). The development and resulting performance impact of positive psychological capital. *Human Resource Development Quarterly, 21,* 41–67.

Luthans, F., Avey, J.B., Clapp-Smith, R., & Li, W. (2008). More evidence on the value of Chinese workers' psychological capital: A potentially unlimited competitive resource? *International Journal of Human Resource Management, 19,* 818–827.

Luthans, F., Avey, J.B., & Patera, J.L. (2008). Experimental analysis of a web-based training intervention to develop positive psychological capital. *Academy of Management Learning and Education, 7,* 209–221.

Luthans, F., & Avolio, B.J. (2009). The "point" of positive organizational behavior. *Journal of Organizational Behavior, 30,* 291–307.

Luthans, F., Avolio, B.J., Avey, J.B, & Norman, S.M. (2007). Psychological capital: Measurement and relationship with performance and satisfaction. *Personnel Psychology, 60,* 541–572.

Luthans, F., Avolio, B., Walumbwa, F., & Li, W. (2005). The psychological capital of Chinese workers: Exploring the relationship with performance. *Management and Organization Review, 1,* 247–269.

Luthans, F., Luthans, K., & Luthans, B. (2004). Positive psychological capital: Going beyond human and social capital. *Business Horizons, 47*(1), 45–50.

Luthans, F., Norman, S.M., Avolio, B.J., & Avey, J.B. (2008). The mediating role of psychological capital in the supportive organizational climate-employee performance relationship. *Journal of Organizational Behavior, 29,* 219–238.

Luthans, F., Van Wyk, R., & Walumbwa, F.O. (2004). Recognition and development of hope for South African organizational leaders. *Leadership & Organization Development Journal, 25,* 512–527.

Luthans, F., & Youssef, C.M. (2004). Human, social, and now positive psychological capital management: Investing in people for competitive advantage. *Organizational Dynamics, 33*(2), 143–160.

Luthans, F., & Youssef, C.M. (2007). Emerging positive organizational behavior. *Journal of Management, 33,* 321–349.

Luthans, F., Youssef, C.M., & Avolio, B.J. (2007). *Psychological capital: Developing the human competitive edge.* Oxford, UK: Oxford University Press.

Luthans, F., Youssef, C.M., Sweetman, D., & Harms, P.D. (2011). Impact of positive appraisals of relationships and health on employees' overall well-being. *Under journal review.*

Lyubomirsky, S. (2007). *The how of happiness: A new approach to getting the life you want.* New York: Penguin.

Lyubomirsky, S., King, L., & Diener, E. (2005). The benefits of frequent positive affect: Does happiness lead to success? *Psychological Bulletin, 131,* 803–855.

Lyubomirsky, S., Sheldon, K.M., & Schkade, D. (2005). Pursuing happiness: The architecture of sustainable change. *Review of General Psychology, 9,* 111–131.

Masten, A.S. (2001). Ordinary magic: Resilience process in development. *American Psychologist, 56,* 227–239.

Masten, A.S., & Reed, M.G. J. (2002). Resilience in development. In C.R. Snyder, & S. Lopez (Eds.), *Handbook of positive psychology* (pp. 74–88). Oxford, UK: Oxford University Press.

Norman, S.M., Avey, J.B., Nimnicht, J.L., & Graber Pigeon, N. (2010). The interactive effects of psychological capital and organizational identity on employee citizenship and deviance behaviors. *Journal of Leadership and Organizational Studies, 17,* 380–391.

Oishi, S., Diener, E., & Lucas, R. (2007). The optimum level of well-being: Can people be too happy? *Perspectives on Psychological Science, 2,* 346–360.

Peterson, S.J., & Byron, K. (2008). Exploring the role of hope in job performance: Results from four studies. *Journal of Organizational Behavior, 29,* 785–803.

Peterson, S.J., Luthans, F., Avolio, B.J., Walumbwa, F.O., & Zhang, Z. (in press). Psychological capital and employee performance: A latent growth modeling approach, *Personnel Psychology.*

Peterson, C., & Seligman, M. (2004). *Character strengths and virtues: A handbook and classification.* New York: Oxford University Press.

Pfeffer, J. (1997). *New directions for organizational theory.* New York: Oxford University Press.

Pfeffer, J., & Sutton R.I. (2006). Evidenced-based management. *Harvard Business Review, 84*(1), 63–74.

Rath, T. (2007). *Strengths finder 2.0.* New York: Gallup.

Roberts, L.M. (2006). Shifting the lens on organizational life: The added value of positive scholarship. *Academy of Management Review, 31,* 292–305.

Rousseau, D. (2006). Is there such a thing as evidence-based management? *Academy of Management Review, 31,* 256–269.

Schmidt, F., & Hunter, J. (2000). Select on intelligence. In E. Locke (Ed.), *The Blackwell handbook of principles of organizational behavior* (pp. 3–14). Oxford, UK: Blackwell.

Seligman, M.E.P. (1998). *Learned optimism.* New York: Pocket Books.

Seligman, M.E.P., & Csikszentmihalyi, M. (2000). Positive psychology. *American Psychologist, 55,* 5–14.

Snyder, C.R. (2000). *Handbook of hope.* San Diego: Academic Press.

Snyder, C.R., Irving, L., & Anderson, J. (1991). Hope and health. In C.R. Snyder & D.R. Forsyth (Eds.). *Handbook of social and clinical psychology* (pp. 285–305). Elmsford, NY: Pergamon.

Snyder, C.R., & Lopez, S. (Eds.). (2002). *Handbook of positive psychology*. Oxford, UK: Oxford University Press.

Stajkovic, A.D., & Luthans, F. (1998). Self-efficacy and work-related performance: A meta-analysis. *Psychological Bulletin, 124*, 240–261.

Tatiukoskula, S., Luthans, B.C., & Luthans, F. (2010). Empirical evidence of the value of an unrecognized resource for economic development in Southeast Asia: The psychological capital of Thai entrepreneurs. Paper presented at Pan Pacific Conference, Bali, Indonesia.

Walumbwa, F.O., Luthans, F., Avey, J.B., & Oke, A. (2011). Authentically leading groups: The mediating role of collective psychological capital and trust. *Journal of Organizational Behavior, 32*, 4–24.

Walumbwa, F.O., Peterson, S.J., Avolio, B.J., & Hartnell, C.A. (2010). An investigation of the relationships among leader and follower psychological capital, service climate and job performance. *Personnel Psychology, 63*, 937–963.

Whetten, D., Felin, T., & King, B. (2009). The practice of theory borrowing in organizational studies: Current issues and future directions. *Journal of Management, 35*, 537–563.

Wright, T.A. (2005). The role of "happiness" in organizational research: Past, present and future directions. In P.L. Perrewe, & D.C. Ganster (Eds.), *Research in occupational stress and well-being* Vol. 4 (pp. 221–264). Amsterdam: JAI Press.

Youssef, C.M., & Luthans, F. (2006). Time for positivity in the Middle East. In W. Mobley, & E. Weldon (Eds.), *Advances in global leadership*, Vol. 4 (pp. 283–297). Oxford, UK: Elsevier Science/JAI.

Youssef, C.M., & Luthans, F. (2007). Positive organizational behavior in the workplace: The impact of hope, optimism, and resilience. *Journal of Management, 33*, 774–800.

Youssef, C.M., & Luthans, F. (2009). An integrated model of psychological capital in the workplace. In A. Linley, S. Harrington, & N. Garcea (Eds.), *Oxford handbook of positive psychology and work* (pp. 277–288). New York: Oxford University Press.

Youssef, C., & Luthans, F. (2010). Toward an inductive theory of positivity in the workplace: The role of agency, malleability and sociability. Conference presentation at the National Academy of Management, Montreal, Quebec, Canada.

Prosocial Motivation at Work

When, Why, and How Making a Difference Makes a Difference

Adam M. Grant *and* Justin M. Berg

Abstract

This chapter examines the nature, contextual and dispositional antecedents, contingent behavioral consequences, and moderating effects of prosocial motivation at work. Prosocial motivation—the desire to protect and promote the well-being of others—is distinct from altruism and independent of self-interested motivations. Key antecedents include relational job design, collectivistic norms and rewards, transformational leadership, and individual differences in other-oriented values, agreeableness, and conscientiousness. Prosocial motivation more strongly predicts persistence, performance, and productivity when it is intrinsic rather than extrinsic; citizenship behaviors when it is accompanied by impression management motivation; and performance when manager trustworthiness is high. Prosocial motivation strengthens the relationships of intrinsic motivation with creativity, core self-evaluations with performance, and proactive behaviors with performance evaluations. Future directions include studying the conditions under which prosocial motivation fuels unethical behavior and harm-doing, collective prosocial motivation, behavior as a cause rather than consequence of prosocial motivation, new organizational antecedents of prosocial motivation, and implications for social entrepreneurship, corporate social responsibility, and the natural environment.

Keywords: Work motivation, prosocial behavior, job design, organizational citizenship, other-orientation

It really makes a difference if you have a good anesthesiologist in the operating room. . . . I've had so many important moments, incidents where I helped someone. . . . And many of these trauma cases have happened where I've thought, 'I'm glad I was there to make a difference,' you know? I really, really enjoy taking pain away from people . . . my favorite operation is childbirth. Because you give something to the patient. You take away pain and help give them a baby.

—*Anesthesiologist (Bowe, Bowe, & Streeter*, 2000, pp. 620–621)

This is a dream job for me. It's the best job in the world. It doesn't change the world for the better, but it's at least giving people some enjoyment for a couple of hours a day. . . . I'm all for education, but I'm also for entertainment. I'm for a balanced life, you know? And these things are really entertaining. People love them, and it's such a great feeling to make something that people love."

—*Video game designer (Bowe et al.,* 2000, pp. 377–378)

What motivates employees to care about making a positive difference in the lives of others, and what actions and experiences does this motivation fuel? Our chapter focuses on prosocial motivation, the desire to have a positive impact on other people or social collectives (Batson, 1987; Grant, 2007). Theoretically, research on prosocial motivation begins to illuminate when, why, and how employees' thoughts, feelings, and actions are often driven by a concern for benefiting others, answering calls to explain the motivations underlying individual and organizational behavior through perspectives other than rational self-interest (Kahn, 1990; Meglino & Korsgaard, 2004; Shamir, 1990, 1991). Practically, prosocial motivation is a timely topic, given the international growth of the service sector and the rise of teamwork; both of these trends have increased employees' interpersonal interactions and provided new work relationships in which employees can experience and express prosocial motivation (Grant, 2007; Kanfer, 2009).

Furthermore, prosocial motivation is a theoretically and practically significant phenomenon because it has a substantial influence on employees' work behaviors and job performance. Recent research suggests that prosocial motivation can drive employees to take initiative (De Dreu & Nauta, 2009), help others (Rioux & Penner, 2001), persist in meaningful tasks (Grant et al., 2007), and accept negative feedback (Korsgaard, Meglino, & Lester, 1997). Evidence also indicates that prosocial motivation can enable employees to receive more credit for proactive behaviors, such as helping, voice, issue-selling, and taking charge (Grant, Parker, & Collins, 2009); prevent employees with positive self-concepts from becoming complacent (Grant & Wrzesniewski, 2010); channel the efforts of employees who care about managing impressions toward becoming better citizens (Grant & Mayer, 2009); direct intrinsically motivated employees toward greater task persistence, performance, and productivity (Grant, 2008a); and focus intrinsically motivated employees on developing ideas that are not only novel, but also useful, thus fostering greater creativity (Grant & Berry, 2011).

Our chapter unfolds in the following steps. We begin by discussing definitional and dimensional issues: What are the key features of prosocial motivation? Second, we turn our attention to the contextual and dispositional antecedents of prosocial motivation at work. Third, we consider the behavioral consequences of prosocial motivation at work, with particular reference to the contingencies that moderate

whether prosocial motivation leads to higher levels of persistence, performance, productivity, citizenship, and initiative. Fourth, we discuss research on prosocial motivation as a moderator of the effects of other traits, states, and behaviors on performance and creativity. Finally, we identify unanswered questions and new directions to be explored in future research. We hope that our chapter will motivate other scholars to pursue new lines of inquiry that advance knowledge about—and provide practical implications for managing—prosocial motivation at work.

Definition and Dimensions

Motivation denotes a desire or reason to act, and "prosocial" literally means for the benefit of others or with the intention of helping others (Oxford English Dictionary, 2009). As such, prosocial motivation is the desire to benefit other people or groups (Batson, 1987; Grant, 2007). To gain a deeper understanding of the construct, it is useful to situate our view of prosocial motivation in basic frameworks of motivation. Psychologists have argued that motivation operates at three hierarchical levels of generality: global, contextual, and situational (Vallerand, 1997). *Global motivation* focuses on an employee's relatively stable dispositional orientation toward particular goals and actions across time and situations. *Contextual motivation* focuses on an employee's motivation toward a specific domain or class of behavior, and is moderately variable across time and situations. *Situational motivation* focuses on an employee's motivation toward a particular behavior in a particular moment in time, and is highly variable. Thus, at the extremes, global motivation can be viewed as a trait-like concept, whereas situational motivation matches prototypes of psychological states (Chaplin, John, & Goldberg, 1988).

Prosocial motivation can be conceptualized and studied at all three levels of generality. Global prosocial motivation refers to an employee's tendency to care about benefiting others and is thus perhaps best conceptualized in terms of prosocial values, or placing importance on protecting and promoting the well-being of others in general (Schwartz & Bardi, 2001). Contextual prosocial motivation refers to an employee's desire to benefit a particular category of other people through a particular occupation, job, or role. For example, contextual prosocial motivation would capture a nurse or doctor's concern for helping patients, a musician's quest to entertain and move audiences, a banker's goal of helping clients finance the purchase of a home, or a teacher's passion for educating students. Situational prosocial motivation refers to an employee's desire to benefit a specific group of other people in a specific situation. For example, returning to the previous examples, situational prosocial motivation would capture the nurse or doctor's desire to cure the patient in room 231, the musician's desire to entertain the audience at an 8 o'clock show, the banker's desire to help Lois and Clark afford a home, and the teacher's desire to help her classroom of 25 kindergartners learn to read today.[1]

Relationship with Self-interest

These distinctions help to resolve a debate about whether prosocial motivation is the opposite of, or independent of, self-interested motivations. A number of scholars have assumed that high prosocial motivation involves low self-interested motivation, and vice versa (e.g., Cialdini et al., 1997; Meglino & Korsgaard, 2004; Schwartz & Bardi, 2001). However, other scholars have argued that these motivations are independent or even orthogonal (Bolino, 1999; Crocker, 2008; De Dreu, 2006; Deutsch, 1973; Grant, 2007, 2008a, 2009; McAdams & de St. Aubin, 1992). For example, Shamir (1990, p. 314) explained:

> . . . between totally selfish work behaviors and pure altruistic behaviors that are specifically performed for the benefit of others, many organizationally relevant actions are probably performed both for a person's own sake and for the sake of a collectivity such as a team, department, or organization . . . with a wide range of motivational orientations that are neither purely individualistic (concerned only with one's satisfaction) nor purely altruistic (concerned only with maximizing the other's satisfaction).

We propose that the relationship between prosocial and self-interested motivations is likely to vary as a function of the hierarchical level of motivation under consideration. The negative, bipolar relationship between the two motivations is most likely to occur at situational levels, where there are moments and circumstances in which prosocial motivation and self-interested motivation guide employees toward conflicting courses of action. For example, social dilemma situations are explicitly defined as those in which employees are required to choose between personal and collective welfare (e.g., Weber, Kopelman, & Messick, 2004). It is worth noting that even in these situations, prosocially motivated employees are sometimes able to identify integrative solutions that "expand the pie," aligning their goals with others' (e.g., De Dreu, Weingart, & Kwon, 2000). However, we recognize that, inevitably, situations arise in which employees face conflicts between expressing prosocial and self-interested motivations.

At the contextual and global levels, these conflicts appear to disappear—or at least become resolved. Over time and across situations, employees can make choices to pursue actions that benefit others independent of—and often in conjunction with—their choices about actions that benefit themselves. For example, Sheldon, Arndt, and Houser-Marko (2003) found that over time, individuals gravitate toward, and self-select into, situations that allow them to simultaneously benefit others and themselves. Similarly, McAdams and de St. Aubin (1992) presented evidence that individuals with strong communal (prosocial) and agentic (self-interested) motivations achieve generativity by selecting activities that allow them to express both sets of motivations. In addition, studies have shown that contextual prosocial motivation in work settings is independent of—and even positively correlated with—self-interested motivations such as self-concern (De Dreu & Nauta, 2009) and impression management motivation (Grant & Mayer, 2009). Finally, studying dispositional values, Schwartz et al. (2001) found a manifold of weak correlations between prosocial and self-interested values. Thus, although prosocial motivation is often confused with altruism, Grant and Berry (2011) summarized that "prosocial motivation can involve, but should not necessarily be equated with, altruism; it refers to a concern for others, not a concern for others at the expense of self-interest."

Building on these arguments, Batson and colleagues have proposed that prosocial motivation can be based on one or more of four different ultimate goals (Batson, 1994; Batson, Ahmad, Powell, & Stocks, 2008): altruism, egoism, principlism, and collectivism. Prosocial motivation serves altruistic goals when it protects or promotes the well-being of other individuals without the intention of personal benefit. It serves egoistic goals when it increases positive affect, reduces negative affect, boosts self-esteem, provides material rewards, or prevents material punishments. It serves principlistic goals when it advances a moral value or ethical cause. And it serves collectivistic goals when it defends or strengthens one's bond with a group. In short, Batson and colleagues (2008) suggest that employees can be prosocially motivated for any combination of these four reasons: to genuinely help another in need, to protect and enhance their egos, to uphold moral principles, and to defend or advance their relationships with a group.

Now that we have clarified the nature of prosocial motivation, what are the dimensions along which it varies? Motivation is typically viewed as encapsulating three core psychological processes: the direction, intensity, and persistence of effort (Kanfer, 1990; Mitchell & Daniels, 2003). From a directional standpoint, prosocial motivation can be experienced and expressed toward different domains and beneficiaries of impact (Grant, 2007). In terms of domains, employees can be prosocially motivated to protect and promote others' physical well-being (health and safety), developmental well-being (learning and growth), psychological well-being (happiness and enjoyment), or material well-being (economic and financial status). In terms of beneficiaries, prosocial motivation can vary in whether it is directed toward other individuals, groups, or larger social collectives, such as organizations, nations, or societies. It can also vary in whether it is directed toward in-group or out-group members, and toward others inside the organization (coworkers, supervisors) or outside the organization (clients, customers, suppliers).

Prosocial motivation can also vary in terms of its intensity and persistence. From the standpoint of intensity, the more extreme the prosocial motivation, the more likely it is to be governed by the "hot" experiential system rather than the "cool" cognitive system (Loewenstein & Small, 2007; Metcalfe & Mischel, 1999; see also Grant & Wade-Benzoni, 2009). From the standpoint of persistence, prosocial motivation can be very short in duration, lasting only a few moments or hours when a particular beneficiary is in need (Batson 1998), or much longer in duration, such as in the case of an engineer's enduring lifetime commitment to helping mankind (e.g., Sieden, 1989). Finally, prosocial motivation is distinct from intrinsic motivation in terms of being outcome-focused rather than process-focused, future-focused rather than present-focused, and requiring greater conscious self-regulation and self-control (Grant, 2008a). As will be discussed in more detail later, prosocial motivation can vary in the degree to which it is intrinsic (autonomous) and extrinsic (controlled) in origin. Employees can autonomously choose to be prosocially motivated based on its identification or integration with their values, or feel pressured into prosocial motivation by feelings of guilt, obligation, and external control (e.g., Gebauer, Riketta, Broemer, & Maio, 2008).

The construct of prosocial motivation is important to positive organizational scholarship (POS) (Cameron, Dutton, & Quinn, 2003) for three core reasons. First, research on prosocial motivation challenges the often-cynical assumption that employees' goals are exclusively self-interested and egoistic, opening up a more balanced, pluralistic, and comprehensive approach to exploring and explaining the forces that guide and constrain individual and organizational action. Second, prosocial motivation can serve as a lens for understanding employees' quests to create "positive" outcomes for others, providing insight into how employees experience and pursue the desire to protect and promote the well-being of coworkers, customers, and communities. Third, prosocial motivation can operate as an enabling condition for outcomes that are often viewed as "positive" for employees, such as meaningful work and strengthened social bonds, and for organizations, such as effort, persistence, performance, creativity, citizenship and proactive behaviors.

Antecedents of Prosocial Motivation: When Employees Want to Make a Difference

Having defined the dimensions along which prosocial motivation can vary, we turn our attention to its antecedents: What causes it? Existing research on the antecedents of prosocial motivation can be organized into four categories: relational job design, collectivistic rewards, leadership, and individual differences. In the following sections, we discuss representative findings from key studies and summary themes from relevant literatures.

Relational Job Design

Job design has received the most explicit attention as a driver of prosocial motivation. Recent theory and research suggest that job design plays an important role in shaping employees' prosocial motivation. Grant (2007) developed a conceptual framework to explain how the relational architectures of jobs—the structural characteristics of work that affect employees' relationships with other people—influences prosocial motivation. He proposed that when jobs are designed to connect employees to the impact they have on the beneficiaries of their work (such as clients, customers, and patients), they experience higher levels of prosocial motivation, which encourages them to invest more time and energy in their assigned tasks and in helping these beneficiaries. Grant (2007) identified two relational job characteristics that connect employees to their impact on beneficiaries: task significance and contact with beneficiaries. Task significance is the extent to which a job provides opportunities to have an impact on other people (Hackman & Oldham, 1976), and contact with beneficiaries is the extent to which a job provides opportunities to communicate with these people (Gutek, Bhappu, Liao-Troth, & Cherry, 1999).

Grant (2007) proposed that task significance provides employees with knowledge about how their work affects beneficiaries, strengthening *perceived impact on beneficiaries*, and contact with beneficiaries enables employees to identify and empathize with beneficiaries, strengthening *affective commitment to beneficiaries*. These two psychological states fuel prosocial motivation, thereby increasing effort, persistence, and helping behavior. In the language of expectancy theory (Van Eerde & Thierry, 1996; Vroom, 1964), perceived impact constitutes instrumentality beliefs ("My performance has consequences for beneficiaries"), and affective commitment constitutes valence beliefs ("I care about beneficiaries"). As such, prosocial motivation—and thus effort, persistence, and helping behaviors directed toward having a positive impact on beneficiaries—should be highest when jobs are relationally designed to provide both task significance and contact with beneficiaries. For example, an automotive engineer should experience the strongest prosocial motivation when she is responsible for designing safety mechanisms that have the potential to prevent deaths and serious injuries *and* has the opportunity to meet actual drivers of her company's cars.

To test these hypotheses, Grant et al. (2007) conducted a field experiment and two laboratory experiments. The field experiment focused on fundraising callers responsible for soliciting alumni donations to a university. The callers had no contact with student scholarship recipients, the primary beneficiaries of the funds they raised. In the contact condition, callers spent 5 minutes interacting with a scholarship recipient, learning about how he received his scholarship and how it had improved his life. In the control condition, callers had no contact with the scholarship recipient. The callers in the contact condition showed substantial increases in task persistence and performance over the following month: Meeting a single scholarship student motivated the average caller to spend 142% more weekly time on the phone, resulting in average increases of 171% in weekly revenue raised. More specifically, the average caller increased in weekly phone time from 1 hour and 47 minutes to 4 hours and 20 minutes, and in weekly donation money raised from $185.94 to $503.22 (Grant et al., 2007). Notably, in this experiment, the callers were contacting nondonors who rarely gave money to the university. The effects were even more dramatic in a subsequent experiment in which callers were contacting repeat donors who gave in higher frequencies and amounts. When callers contacting repeat donors met a single scholarship recipient, their average weekly revenue increased more than fivefold from $411.74 to $2,083.52 (Grant, 2008c). In both field experiments, callers in the control condition showed no statistically significant changes in either persistence or performance.

To rule out Hawthorne effects by demonstrating that these effects were caused by the human connection with the scholarship recipient, and not by extraneous factors such as increased managerial attention, Grant et al. (2007) included a third condition in which the callers read a letter by the scholarship recipient but did not meet him in person. Thus, the callers received equivalent information content across the two conditions; the only difference was the physical presence of the scholarship recipient. The callers' persistence and performance increased only in the interpersonal contact condition. However, subsequent experiments showed that the letter, if it contained adequately vivid and emotionally evocative cues, was sufficient to increase perceived impact and thus motivate higher performance (Grant, 2008b). Finally, the Grant et al. (2007) experiment involved callers who knew each other, which raises the possibility of implementation threats related to callers in one condition changing their behavior as a result of learning about the treatment given to those in another condition (see Cook & Campbell, 1979). To prevent these threats, the Grant (2008c) experiment took place in different shifts, so the callers did not interact with each other and thus could not learn about alternative treatments. Such a balance of randomization within a single organization and stratified randomization at the site level strengthened conclusions about internal validity.

Another limitation of a randomized, controlled field experiment is that the involvement of researchers (Argyris, 1975), or even their mere presence (Rosenthal, 1994) can change participants' experiences, threatening the external validity of the results by calling into question whether the effects will generalize to organizations in which researchers are not involved. Thus, whereas the original field experiment was a randomized, controlled experiment designed by researchers (Grant et al., 2007), the next field experiment was a naturally occurring quasi-experiment (Grant, 2008c). While planning the original experiment, the research team learned that the manager at the university's call center had spontaneously invited a fellowship recipient to address callers during a shift. This was not a perfect experiment, as the callers were not randomly assigned to this treatment condition, but the manager did not make an announcement about the fellowship recipient's arrival, which prevented callers from self-selecting into the treatment condition. The results replicated the effects from previous experiments, demonstrating performance increases in the experimental group but not the control group.

In two laboratory experiments, Grant et al. (2007) found that perceptions of impact on and affective commitment to beneficiaries—the two psychological states that undergird prosocial motivation—mediated the effects of contact with beneficiaries on persistence in a letter-editing task. Participants spent more time editing a student's job application cover letter when they had a brief conversation with him or even only saw him, which increased their beliefs that additional effort would benefit the student (perceived impact) and that they cared about benefiting the student (affective commitment). In one of the experiments, the effects of contact with beneficiaries on persistence were moderated by task significance, such that contact with beneficiaries only motivated higher persistence when participants learned that the student was in dire need of a job.

In summary, this research demonstrates how jobs can be relationally structured to enhance prosocial motivation (for reviews, see Fried, Levi, & Laurence, 2008; Grant & Parker, 2009; Morgeson & Humphrey, 2008; Parker & Ohly, 2008; Vough & Parker, 2008). Rather than focusing on enriching task characteristics such as autonomy, variety, and feedback, as traditionally done in job design research (Hackman & Oldham, 1976), this research highlights the important role that relational characteristics of employees' jobs play in shaping their prosocial motivation. As Kanfer (2009) summarizes, these findings "suggest that organizations may strengthen work motivation by elaborating the employee–client relationship in particular ways" (p. 120) and "The notion of a relational contract between the employee and the customer or client who is affected by the employee's work is particularly germane to work motivation in the service sector and represents an important new direction in the field" (p. 122).

Further reinforcing the relational nature of task significance, Grant (2008b) has shown how, in jobs that are high in potential task significance, but in which employees rarely have the opportunity to

experience this potential, stories can serve as "corrective lenses" that reinforce and sharpen employees' perceptions of impact. In a field experiment with lifeguards who had never performed a rescue, those who read stories about other lifeguards performing rescues increased in perceived impact, which motivated them to spend more time working in the subsequent month. The lifeguards also increased in perceived social worth (feeling valued by guests), which motivated them to spend more time engaging in helping and safety behaviors to benefit guests, as rated by supervisors blind to the experimental design and conditions. Lifeguards in a control condition read stories about how other lifeguards had benefited personally from the job, and did not show any changes in job perceptions or behaviors.

Thus, prosocial motivation can be enhanced not only by designing jobs to be high in significance, but also by connecting employees directly to the beneficiaries of these jobs and providing vivid information about potential impact on beneficiaries. Across these studies, it is interesting to observe that Grant and colleagues have connected employees to their impact on future beneficiaries (lifeguards), past beneficiaries (fundraisers), and current beneficiaries (editors). These different enactments of relational job design may serve different functions of inspiration, gratitude, and empathy.

Connecting employees to future beneficiaries may serve the function of *inspiring* employees to focus on higher goals and standards by highlighting that their work has the potential to advance a more significant purpose (e.g., Shamir, Zakay, Breinin, & Popper, 1998; Thompson & Bunderson, 2003). A sports agent described how exposure to the potential financial disasters that befall professional athletes after retirement inspires him to care about making a difference in their lives: "to help guys like that . . . really motivates me . . . The young players, when they choose representation, are making one of the most important decisions of their young lives. It can mean the difference between leading a life of financial security and being a twenty-eight-year-old guy with no money in the bank and no real way of getting any" (Bowe et al., 2000, pp. 416–417).

Connecting employees to past beneficiaries may serve the function of communicating *gratitude* to employees by highlighting how their efforts have been appreciated and valued (Grant & Gino, 2010). As a construction foreman explained, "A lot of times you'll build a house for a family, and you see them move in, that's pretty gratifying. There's one particular family I've had dinner numerous times with after we did their project . . . I'm proud of that" (Bowe et al., 2000, p. 36). Similarly, an assistant director of a boys and girls club expressed, "What I get out of it is the personal satisfaction of watching them grow up into mature young adults . . . you end up over a period of time developing relationships with certain kids. There's an impact on their life, and they'll come down to me when they're adults to talk to me about it. The reward is teaching a kid a new skill" (Colby, Sippola, & Phelps, 2001, p. 476). These examples convey how meeting past beneficiaries can cultivate prosocial motivation by reminding employees of how their work is appreciated.

Connecting employees to present beneficiaries may serve the function of cultivating feelings of *empathy* by highlighting how beneficiaries are currently in need or distress (Batson, 1998). As a police officer in a Chicago housing project articulated, "I extend myself quite a bit for people through my job. I spent three years trying to help this one girl and her kids . . . She was a witness in a murder case; I was there for her, took her shopping every week . . . People are hungry" (Colby et al., 2001, p. 477). This example illustrates how meeting present beneficiaries can cultivate prosocial motivation by fostering feelings of empathy. Indeed, a recent experiment with radiologists showed that when patient photos were included with x-rays, radiologists reported more empathy and achieved greater diagnostic accuracy (Turner, Hadas-Halperin, & Raveh, 2008).

Collectivistic Norms and Rewards

Research also suggests that employees are more likely to experience prosocial motivation when organizations maintain collectivistic rather than individualistic norms and rewards. Norms influence motivation by specifying shared standards and expectations for appropriate behavior (Ajzen, 1991; Hackman, 1992). Collectivistic norms emphasize the importance of contributing to group goals, whereas individualistic norms emphasize the importance of prioritizing self-interest (Chatman & Barsade, 1995). When collectivistic norms are prevalent, employees are more likely to experience and express prosocial motivation (Batson, 1994; Miller, 1999) because they feel it is appropriate and legitimate to feel concerned about the well-being of others. For example, when engineering companies emphasize collectivistic norms, it appears that employees are more likely to experience prosocial motivation toward helping colleagues (e.g., Perlow & Weeks, 2002).

On the other hand, when individualistic norms are prevalent, self-interest is descriptively and prescriptively dominant—there is a shared belief that employees do and should pursue their own independent interests (Miller, 1999). Individualistic norms can signal to employees that expressing prosocial motivation is inappropriate, which may lead them to suppress their desires to benefit others and the organization, and focus on taking actions that advance their personal utility (Ferraro, Pfeffer, & Sutton, 2005; Miller, 1999). For example, when an accountant notices a marketing manager appearing dejected during a discussion of a new product launch, if the company maintains individualistic norms, she may withhold inquiring about the problem because she wishes to avoid appearing overly concerned about an issue in which she has no vested interest (Ratner & Miller, 2001). As an illustration of the power of norms, Kay and Ross (2003) demonstrated in laboratory experiments that the mere title of a "prisoner's dilemma" task was sufficient to influence participants' construals of appropriate responses and their actual behaviors. When the prisoner's dilemma task was introduced using prosocial labels (e.g., the "Community Game" or the "Team Game"), participants construed the labels as more appropriate and acted more cooperatively as compared to when the game was called the "Wall Street Game," "Battle of Wits," or "Numbers Game."

Parallel evidence suggests that collectivistic rewards can increase prosocial motivation. In a series of laboratory experiments, primarily using negotiation role-plays, psychologists have shown that providing collective incentives increases participants' prosocial motivation (De Dreu et al., 2000). For instance, De Dreu, Giebels, and Van de Vliert (1998) found that when negotiators were rewarded as pairs rather than as individuals, they experienced more concern for each other's outcomes and exchanged more information. Similarly, Weingart, Bennett, and Brett (1993) found that when negotiators were told that their success—and thus their payoffs—depended on maximizing group rather than individual outcomes, they reported more concern for group outcomes and thus engaged in more cooperative behaviors, experienced greater trust, and enacted more perspective-taking. These experiments highlight how rewarding employees in groups, rather than as individuals, can increase their prosocial motivation to benefit each other.

Transformational Leadership

Although this link has rarely been made explicitly, theory and research suggests that transformational leadership may also play an important role in shaping prosocial motivation. Broadly speaking, transformational leadership refers to a behavioral style of inspirational motivation, idealized influence, intellectual stimulation, and individualized consideration (Avolio, Bass, & Jung, 1999). Scholars have proposed that transformational leaders motivate employees by linking their work to their core values (Bono & Judge, 2003; Piccolo & Colquitt, 2006; Shamir, House, & Arthur, 1993). Insofar as this leads employees to prioritize the interests of the organization over and above their own self-interests (Bass, 1999), we can infer that transformational leadership has the potential to increase employees' prosocial motivations to benefit the organization and the causes valued by its members. Transformational leaders act as role models by exhibiting commitment to the greater organizational good, using symbolic and emotional appeals to foster a stronger sense of collective identity and impact among followers (Conger, Kanungo, & Menon, 2000), which may enhance their prosocial motivation to help one another and the organization. In addition, through individualized consideration, they provide support to their followers, who reciprocate by committing to the goals of the organization and engaging in behaviors that help the organization attain these goals. Furthermore, research suggests that transformational leadership often involves self-sacrificing behaviors, which can stimulate giving and helping behaviors among followers (e.g., Choi & Mai-Dalton, 1999; Singh & Krishnan, 2008; Van Knippenberg & Hogg, 2003). Prosocial motivation is likely to be a key psychological mechanism through which the self-sacrificing behaviors of transformational leaders operate to influence followers. Indeed, Grant (in press a) found that perceived impact mediated the relationship between transformational leadership and job performance, even after accounting for psychological empowerment.

However, the effects of transformational leadership may vary as a function of the type of charismatic relationship that employees have with their leaders. Scholars have distinguished between two forms of charismatic relationships: socialized and personalized (Howell & Shamir, 2005). Socialized charismatic relationships are based on a strong sense of identification with leaders' goals and strategies, which provides a pathway for expressing shared values. Personalized charismatic relationships are based on a strong sense of identification with leaders themselves, which may provide self-esteem but leave employees dependent on and vulnerable to leaders. As such, socialized charismatic relationships may inspire prosocial motivation directed toward benefiting the organization, whereas personalized charismatic relationships may inspire prosocial motivation directed toward benefiting the leader, even at the expense of others.

Individual Differences: Which Employees Are Prosocially Motivated?

Employees also differ in their dispositional tendencies to experience prosocial motivation. Meglino and Korsgaard (2004, 2006) have developed an interesting theory focusing on individual differences in other-orientation—akin to the notion of global, value-based prosocial motivation discussed earlier. One of the broad implications of their theory is that employees react differently to contextual influences as a function of the strength of their other-oriented values. For example, Korsgaard et al. (1997) found in laboratory experiments that participants with stronger other-oriented values were more receptive to negative feedback, whereas participants with weaker other-oriented values found negative feedback ego-threatening and were thus less able to benefit from it. As another example, Grant (2008b) conducted a field experiment with fundraising callers showing that the performance of those with strong other-oriented values was more dependent on task significance cues than of those with weak other-oriented values, as the former were more concerned about doing work that benefits others. Schwartz and colleagues have distinguished between two types of other-oriented values. *Benevolence values* refer to placing importance on protecting and promoting the well-being of others with whom one is in personal contact, and *universalism values* refer to placing importance on broader concerns, such as social justice and equality and protecting the environment (Schwartz & Bardi, 2001). This distinction suggests that employees with strong benevolence values will primarily experience prosocial motivation directed toward familiar beneficiaries, and their levels of prosocial motivation will be especially sensitive to contact and relationships with beneficiaries. Employees with strong universalism values may have a broader circle of concern that is less dependent on personal contact and more sustainable in the face of abstract information about task significance.

Beyond values, researchers have identified two broad personality traits that have implications for employees' proclivities toward prosocial motivation: agreeableness and conscientiousness. Agreeableness refers to a positive orientation toward others, and is manifested in higher tendencies toward altruism, cooperation, sympathy, trust, morality, and modesty

(Barrick & Mount, 1991; Costa, McCrae, & Dye, 1991). Conscientiousness refers to dependability, and is manifested in higher tendencies toward dutifulness, competence, self-discipline, achievement striving, orderliness, and cautiousness (Barrick & Mount, 1991; Costa et al., 1991). We expect that these two traits tend to foster prosocial motivation toward different targets. Agreeable employees typically focus on relationships with other people, and thus tend to direct their prosocial motivation toward individuals (Graziano, Habashi, Sheese, & Tobin, 2007; LePine & Van Dyne, 2001). Conscientious employees typically focus on being responsible and complying with rules, and thus tend to direct their prosocial motivation toward contributions that "are more impersonal, i.e. not directed to specific persons but constitute commendable, constructive forms of supporting the larger context of organized efforts" (Konovsky & Organ, 1996, p. 255). Indeed, conscientiousness is a better predictor of citizenship behaviors directed toward benefiting the organization than other people (Podsakoff et al., 2000).

Contingent Consequences of Prosocial Motivation: When Making a Difference Makes a Difference

Researchers have often assumed that prosocial motivation directly increases task effort, persistence, and helping and citizenship behaviors (e.g., Grant, 2007; Rioux & Penner, 2001). More recently, however, researchers have begun to challenge this assumption by examining contingencies that moderate the effects of prosocial motivation on behavior and performance outcomes. Here, we review evidence about intrinsic versus extrinsic forms of prosocial motivation, impression management motivation, and manager trustworthiness as important contingencies.

The Moderating Role of Intrinsic Motivation

Researchers have begun to examine whether the relationship between prosocial motivation and persistence, performance, and productivity varies as a function of whether the source of prosocial motivation is intrinsic or extrinsic. Building on self-determination theory (Gagné & Deci, 2005; Ryan & Deci, 2000), Grant (2008a) distinguished between intrinsic and extrinsic forms of prosocial motivation. Intrinsic prosocial motivation is autonomous and self-determined, and is associated with the pleasure-based feeling (Gebauer et al., 2008) of "wanting to help" (Cunningham, Steinberg, & Grey, 1980). Extrinsic prosocial motivation, on the other hand, is more externally controlled, and is

associated with the pressure-based feeling (Gebauer et al., 2008) of "having to help" (Cunningham et al., 1980). Grant (2008a) proposed that intrinsic motivation is more sustainable than extrinsic motivation, as the pressure associated with the latter causes stress and depletes energy. He thus hypothesized that prosocial motivation would be more positively associated with persistence, performance, and productivity when it was accompanied by intrinsic rather than extrinsic motivation, and studies of both firefighters and fundraisers supported this hypothesis (Grant, 2008a). This research identifies the source of prosocial motivation—intrinsic or extrinsic—as an important moderator of its effects.

The Moderating Role of Impression Management Motivation

Research has also investigated whether another type of motivation—impression management motivation, the desire to protect and enhance one's image—moderates the relationship between prosocial motivation and organizational citizenship behaviors. Grant and Mayer (2009) reconciled conflicting findings about whether prosocially motivated employees engage in more citizenship by arguing that impression management motivation encourages employees to express their prosocial motivation toward affiliative citizenship behaviors such as helping, courtesy, and initiative. They proposed that in the absence of impression management motivation, prosocially motivated employees may be more inclined to undertake self-sacrificing citizenship behaviors—engaging in challenging forms of citizenship such as voice—that run the risk of threatening their reputations. When impression management motivation is also present, employees may express their prosocial motivations in the form of affiliative citizenship behaviors that both do good and look good. In two field studies, they found support for this hypothesis: Impression management motivation strengthened the relationship between prosocial motivation and the affiliative citizenship behaviors of helping, courtesy, and initiative (Grant & Mayer, 2009). Whereas previous research (Bolino, 1999; Rioux & Penner, 2001) suggested that some employees engaged in citizenship based on prosocial motivation (good soldiers) and other employees did so based on impression management motivation (good actors), this research shows that these two motivations can coexist in the same employee, interacting to increase the likelihood of affiliative citizenship. More generally, this research reinforces our earlier point that prosocial motivation should not be equated with altruism and is independent of self-interested motivations. Grant and

Mayer found that the relationship between prosocial motivation and citizenship can be strengthened by a form of self-interested motivation: the desire to protect and promote one's image.

The Moderating Role of Manager Trustworthiness

Moving beyond other motivations as moderators, research has also addressed manager trustworthiness as a contingency. Grant and Sumanth (2009) proposed that trustworthy managers, whose values emphasize benevolence and integrity, are more likely to share information with employees about how their work benefits others and serves an important mission. This information will increase employees' perceptions of task significance, and since prosocially motivated employees place particular importance on doing work that benefits others, such employees will display higher performance when they perceive their managers as trustworthy. In three field studies of fundraisers, they found that manager trustworthiness strengthened the relationship between prosocial motivation and performance. Two of these studies showed that this moderating relationship was mediated by stronger perceptions of task significance. Furthermore, two of these studies also showed a three-way interaction among prosocial motivation, manager trustworthiness, and employees' dispositional trust propensities in predicting performance. When employees perceived their managers as trustworthy, prosocial motivation predicted higher performance. However, when employees questioned whether their managers were trustworthy, they appeared to rely on their own trust propensities as a cue to resolve the uncertainty inherent in this weak situation, and having a strong dispositional propensity toward trust compensated or substituted for low perceptions of manager trustworthiness to strengthen the relationship between prosocial motivation and performance. This research shows how manager trustworthiness, by enhancing employees' perceptions of task significance, plays an important role in strengthening the relationship between prosocial motivation and performance. It also indicates that manager trustworthiness is a particularly important facilitator of the performance of prosocially motivated employees whose dispositional inclinations toward trusting others are low.

Prosocial Motivation As a Moderator

The previous series of studies focused on the role of intrinsic motivation, impression management motivation, and manager trustworthiness as moderators

of the effects of prosocial motivation on employees' behaviors and performance. Research has also begun to focus on the role of prosocial motivation in moderating the effects of other factors on employees' behaviors and performance. In this section, we review research indicating that prosocial motivation strengthens the relationship between intrinsic motivation and creativity, proactive behaviors and supervisor performance evaluations, and core self-evaluations and job performance.

Prosocial Motivation Strengthens the Relationship Between Intrinsic Motivation and Creativity

A rich history of field studies and laboratory experiments reveals inconsistent effects of intrinsic motivation on creativity: "Now you see it, now you don't." To resolve this conflicting evidence, Grant and Berry (2011) proposed that prosocial motivation moderates the effect of intrinsic motivation on creativity. Creativity is the production of ideas that are both novel and useful (e.g., Amabile, Barsade, Mueller, & Staw, 2005), and Grant and Berry argued that intrinsic motivation encourages a focus on ideas that are novel but not necessarily useful. In essence, intrinsic motivation cultivates a desire to explore, learn, and pursue one's curiosities by focusing on ideas that are original and personally interesting and viewing the process of producing novel ideas as an enjoyable end in and of itself. Prosocial motivation encourages employees to take the perspectives of others, which draws their attention toward how their novel ideas can also be useful to others. By fostering perspective-taking, prosocial motivation may encourage employees to develop useful applications of their novel ideas, and to filter out their least useful novel ideas and select the most useful of their novel ideas. In two field studies of U.S. military employees and water treatment employees, and a laboratory experiment with participants generating ideas to help a band create sources of revenue, prosocial motivation strengthened the relationship between intrinsic motivation and independent ratings of creativity (Grant & Berry, 2011). Moreover, in the field study with water treatment employees and the laboratory experiment, perspective-taking mediated this moderating relationship: Prosocial motivation encouraged employees to take others' perspectives, which in turn enhanced the association between intrinsic motivation and creativity. This research extends the interaction of prosocial and intrinsic motivations to the new domain of creativity, and introduces perspective-taking as a new mechanism for channeling intrinsic motivation in a useful direction.

Prosocial Motivation Enhances the Association Between Core Self-evaluations and Job Performance

Recent research has examined how prosocial motivation influences the performance of employees with high core self-evaluations. Research shows variability in whether employees with high core self-evaluations—positive self-concepts based on high self-esteem, general self-efficacy, emotional stability, and an internal locus of control—attain higher performance (Judge & Bono, 2001). Although high core self-evaluations can provide employees with the confidence necessary to be effective, they can also cause complacency. Grant and Wrzesniewski (2010) examined whether prosocial motivation prevents complacency by fostering anticipatory feelings of guilt and gratitude: Because prosocially motivated employees are more concerned about benefiting others, they are more prone to feeling guilty if they fail and recognizing that others will feel grateful if they succeed. Anticipating these feelings leads those with high core self-evaluations to invest greater effort in their tasks, thus enhancing their performance. In two field studies with professional fundraisers and public service employees, prosocial motivation strengthened the relationship between core self-evaluations and job performance. In a third field study with outbound call center employees, this moderating relationship was mediated by anticipated guilt and gratitude (Grant & Wrzesniewski, 2010). This research shows how prosocial motivation can channel confidence in productive directions, and introduces anticipatory social emotions as important mediators toward this end.

Prosocially Motivated Employees Get More Credit for Proactive Behavior

Research has also explored whether prosocial motivation enhances the degree to which supervisors give employees credit for proactive behaviors in performance evaluations. Although proactive behaviors such as voice, issue-selling, taking charge, and offering help can make important contributions to organizational effectiveness, these behaviors have the potential to threaten others. Grant, Parker, and Collins (2009) proposed that supervisors make more benevolent attributions for the proactive behaviors of prosocially motivated employees, whose actions and communications signal that their proactive behaviors are driven by good intentions. In addition, prosocially motivated employees may actually express their proactive behaviors more constructively. As such, supervisors will evaluate proactive behaviors more favorably when employees are prosocially motivated. In two field studies with managers and firefighters, employees' proactive behaviors were more positively associated with supervisors' performance evaluations when employees were prosocially motivated (Grant et al., 2009). This research shows how prosocial motivation can not only directly increase performance; it may also enhance the credit that employees receive for taking the initiative to engage in anticipatory, change-oriented behaviors.

Future Directions

Although these findings provide useful insights, many exciting questions about prosocial motivation have yet to be explored. In this section, we call attention to five key categories of future directions: studying effects on unethical behavior and harmdoing, examining collective prosocial motivation, reversing the causal arrow between prosocial motivation and behavior, considering novel organizational influences on prosocial motivation, and studying prosocial motivation in the context of social entrepreneurship, corporate social responsibility, and the natural environment.

Ties That Blind: Unethical Behavior and Harm-doing

In our view, the most important new direction for inquiry involves gaining a deeper understanding of the dark sides of prosocial motivation. Although little research has explicitly explored this idea, we believe that prosocial motivation is a double-edged sword: Many acts of harm and unethical behavior are committed under the guise of the desire to make a difference. We encourage researchers to begin studying when, why, and how prosocial motivation can lead to an unwillingness to perform tasks that do not align with the particular causes and beneficiaries that one values (Bunderson & Thompson, 2009); a form of "benevolent narcissism" that involves positive illusions about one's capabilities to make a difference and vulnerability to social control (e.g., Ashforth & Kreiner, 1999; Fineman, 2006; Lofland, 1977; O'Reilly & Chatman, 1996; Pratt, 2000), such that managers and leaders mistakenly or purposefully exploit prosocially motivated employees by overworking or underpaying them (e.g., Bunderson & Thompson, 2009); a tendency to give unwanted help that leaves beneficiaries feeling incompetent, dependent, or embarrassed (Beehr, Bowling, &

Bennett, 2010; Deelstra et al., 2003; Fisher, Nadler, & Whitcher-Alagna, 1982); and meaning–manage-ability tradeoffs (McGregor & Little, 1998) that may encourage employees to focus on small wins (Weick, 1984) and incremental changes (Meyerson & Scully, 1995) at the expense of more radical, dramatic changes. There are also risks of selective moral disengagement (Bandura, 1999), single-minded convictions (McGregor, 2007), a willingness to break rules to benefit others (Morrison, 2006), nepotism toward favored beneficiaries coupled with discrimination and prejudice toward others (Batson, Klein, Highberger, & Shaw, 1995; Gino & Pierce, 2010), excessive loyalty toward beneficiaries that interferes with recognizing and reporting violations of justice and ethics (Somers & Casal, 1994), and ends-justify-the-means thinking that gives rise to a willingness to do harm in the interest of a perceived "greater good" (Margolis & Molinsky, 2008; Molinsky & Margolis, 2005). In short, prosocial motivation has the potential to both discourage unethical behavior and provide a moral justification for this behavior, and it may lead employees to craft their jobs (Wrzesniewski & Dutton, 2001) in harmful as well as helpful ways. Gaining a deeper understanding of these mixed effects represents an important opportunity for future research.

Collective Prosocial Motivation

Existing research has primarily examined prosocial motivation at the level of the individual employee. However, it is noteworthy that interventions to increase prosocial motivation have often taken place with groups of employees. For example, each scholarship recipient thanked groups of fundraisers together (Grant et al., 2007; Grant, 2008c), and both fundraisers and lifeguards met in groups to read stories about the past and potential impact of their jobs (Grant, 2008b). As another example, the medical technology company Medtronic holds an annual party at which patients whose lives have been changed by the company's products address more than 30,000 employees together (George, 2003). This raises important questions about whether prosocial motivation is contagious and exists at the group level. Do employees who experience prosocial motivation together develop shared identities, goals, and missions that reinforce and enhance their collective prosocial motivation? Is prosocial motivation more potent when activated and experienced in groups than among isolated individual employees? Given the focus of POS on enabling group and organizational flourishing (Cameron et al., 2003), it

will be both theoretically interesting and practically important to explore the development and impact of collective prosocial motivation.

Enacting Your Way Into Prosocial Motivation

Although the vast majority of research has focused on the effects of prosocial motivation on behavior, there is good reason to believe that there are reciprocal effects of behavior on prosocial motivation. To the extent that employees engage in prosocial behaviors such as helping and giving, theories of self-perception (Bem, 1972) and sense-making (Weick, 1995) suggest that they may develop stronger prosocial motivations toward the particular beneficiaries to whom they have given. Social psychological research has shown that individuals often make sense of the act of giving help by coming to believe that they care about the recipient (Flynn & Brockner, 2003; Jecker & Landy, 1969). In addition, Grant, Dutton, and Rosso (2008) found in qualitative and quantitative studies that when employees at a Fortune 500 retail company gave time or money to coworkers in need, they developed stronger prosocial identities as caring, compassionate individuals. There is also evidence that the act of volunteering fosters prosocial role identities as a person who is committed to helping a particular group of beneficiaries, such as AIDS victims, or furthering particular causes, such as fighting cancer (Grant, in press b; Grube & Piliavin, 2000; Penner & Finkelstein, 1998; Penner, Dovidio, Piliavin, & Schroeder, 2005). A fascinating question in this area concerns how individuals cross the boundary from developing these specific role identities toward viewing themselves in more general prosocial terms as caring, compassionate people who are motivated to make a positive difference in the lives of a wide range of others and advance a broader set of causes. The distinction between benevolence values emphasizing concern for close others versus universalism values emphasizing concern for the wider world (Schwartz & Bardi, 2001; see also Reed & Aquino, 2003) is again relevant here. Are employees with strong universalism values more likely to develop broader, more generalized prosocial identities and motivations after enacting prosocial behaviors than are employees with strong benevolence values? Through what processes do behaviors foster more universalistic values?

Sparking, Supporting, Sustaining, and Stifling Prosocial Motivation

We hope to see more research on how organizations initiate, maintain, and suppress prosocial motivation.

Do organizations encourage employees to express prosocial motivation in productive ways when they provide autonomy to pursue unanswered callings through job crafting (see Berg, Grant, & Johnson, 2010)? Do organizational responses to death affect prosocial motivation? Grant and Wade-Benzoni (2009) argued that when employees are exposed to mortality cues, those who reflect on death—as opposed to experiencing existential anxiety about it—come to think about the meaningfulness of their contributions, which triggers prosocial motivation. In the face of tragedies and accidents, how do organizations walk the tightrope of encouraging employees to engage in meaningful reflection without distracting their attention away from work and interfering in their private lives?

Researchers may also wish to explore how prosocial motivation influences—and is influenced by—psychological contracts, which capture the unwritten obligations and expectations that employees use to understand what they will give and receive as organizational members (Schein, 1980). Scholars have identified three basic types of psychological contracts: transactional, relational, and principled. *Transactional contracts* are based on economic currency, as employees give time and energy in exchange for pay and benefits (Rousseau & McLean Parks, 1993). *Relational contracts* are based on socioemotional currency, as employees give loyalty in exchange for belongingness, personal growth, and security (Morrison & Robinson, 1997). *Principled contracts* are based on ideological currency, as employees give initiative and dedication in exchange for the opportunity to contribute to a valued cause or mission (Thompson & Bunderson, 2003). We expect that employees with relational contracts are more likely to experience prosocial motivation toward the organization and its members, where they define their community, whereas employees with principled contracts are more likely to view the organization as a vehicle for expressing prosocial motivation toward valued beneficiaries. For instance, many employees have principled contracts with Google. As research director Peter Norwing explained, "we're all here because we want to discover and build useful things that will change the world" (Google Research Blog, 2006). Employees with transactional contracts, on the other hand, may experience and express prosocial motivation primarily outside the domain of work, such as toward their families or causes for which they volunteer.

Prosocial Motivation, Social Entrepreneurship, CSR, and the Natural Environment

Research to date has principally focused on the impact of prosocial motivation on how employees enact their jobs. However, it is likely that prosocial motivation has broader organizational and social implications. Indeed, research in public management has shown that prosocial motivation can affect the very types of jobs, careers, and industries that individuals pursue (Perry & Hondeghem, 2008). We hope to see researchers begin to study the role of prosocial motivation in solving problems of growing social and societal importance. For example, is prosocial motivation one of the driving factors that distinguishes social entrepreneurs from business entrepreneurs? Do firms run by prosocially motivated executives engage in more corporate social responsibility and philanthropy (see Agle, Mitchell, & Sonnenfeld, 1999)? How can social movements increase or tap into employees' prosocial motivations? The recent movement to "go green" provides a ripe context for studying the intersection of social movements and prosocial motivation. As concerns about protecting the planet and preventing climate change rise, how does prosocial motivation influence individual and organizational actions toward the environment? For individuals who care about the planet primarily because it provides a home for current and future generations of people (e.g., McAdams & de St. Aubin, 1992), is prosocial motivation a catalyst behind care for and action to protect the environment? All of these questions merit wider and deeper investigation, and prosocial motivation may be a fruitful conceptual lens for pursuing them. As an environmental protection agency specialist reflected (Bowe et al., 2000, pp. 578–579):

> I've always felt a personal obligation to be doing something that is for the betterment of everyone. And the environment is like, well, what could be more important than that? So even though it's frustrating sometimes, I couldn't just stop and follow something that might be extremely interesting to me but didn't help the world . . . I have this deep-rooted need to feel that my job is of public service.

Conclusion

The research reviewed in this chapter provides insights about the antecedents, contingent consequences, moderating effects, and mediating psychological mechanisms associated with prosocial motivation. In terms of antecedents, relational job design, collectivistic norms and rewards, transformational leadership, and individual differences in other-oriented values, agreeableness, and conscientiousness are important influences on prosocial motivation. In terms of contingent consequences, prosocial motivation is a stronger predictor of persistence, performance, and productivity when it is accompanied by intrinsic motivation; a stronger predictor of affiliative citizenship behaviors when it is accompanied by impression management motivation; and a stronger predictor of job performance when managers are trustworthy. In terms of moderating effects, prosocial motivation can enhance the creativity of intrinsically motivated employees, the performance of employees with high core self-evaluations, and the performance evaluations of proactive employees. In terms of psychological mechanisms, prosocial motivation accomplishes these effects by increasing the importance placed on task significance, encouraging perspective-taking and fostering anticipatory social emotions of anticipated guilt and gratitude. Prosocial motivation is thus an important motor behind many individual and collective accomplishments at work. As Ciulla (2000, pp. 225–226) reflected, "On a day-to-day basis most jobs can't fill the tall order of making the world better, but particular incidents at work have meaning because you make a valuable contribution or you are able to genuinely help someone in need."

Note

1. As organizational psychologists, our interest is in understanding how prosocial motivation at work can change, but also in how these changes can be sustained. As such, we find it most fruitful to focus on contextual prosocial motivation, which operates at a desirable middle range (Weick, 1974; see also Little, 2005) between global and situational motivation for achieving a balance between malleability and sustainability. In this chapter, unless otherwise indicated, our use of the term "prosocial motivation" will refer primarily to contextual prosocial motivation.

References

Agle, B.R., Mitchell, R.K., & Sonnenfeld, J.A. (1999). Who matters to CEOs? An investigation of stakeholder attributes and salience, corporate performance, and CEO values. *Academy of Management Journal, 42*, 507–525.

Ajzen, I. (1991). The theory of planned behavior. *Organizational Behavior and Human Decision Processes, 50*, 179–211.

Amabile, T.M., Barsade, S.G., Mueller, J.S., & Staw, B.M. (2005). Affect and creativity at work. *Administrative Science Quarterly, 50*, 367–403.

Argyris, C. (1975). Dangers in applying results from experimental social psychology. *American Psychologist, 30*, 469–485.

Ashforth, B.E., & Kreiner, G.E. (1999). "How can you do it?": Dirty work and the challenge of constructing a positive identity. *Academy of Management Review, 24*, 413–434.

Avolio, B.J., Bass, B.M., & Jung, D.I. (1999). Re-examining the components of transformational and transactional leadership using the Multifactor Leadership Questionnaire. *Journal of Occupational and Organizational Psychology, 72*, 441–462.

Bandura, A. (1999). Moral disengagement in the perpetration of inhumanities. *Personality and Social Psychology Review, 3*, 193–209.

Barrick, M.R., & Mount, M.K. (1991). The Big Five personality dimensions and job performance: A meta-analysis. *Personnel Psychology, 44*, 1–26.

Bass, B.M. (1999). Two decades of research and development in transformational leadership. *European Journal of Work and Organizational Psychology, 8*, 9–32.

Batson, C.D. (1987). Prosocial motivation: Is it ever truly altruistic? In L. Berkowitz (Ed.), *Advances in experimental social psychology* Vol. 20 (pp. 65–122). New York: Academic Press.

Batson, C.D. (1994). Why act for the public good? Four answers. *Personality and Social Psychology Bulletin, 20*, 603–610.

Batson, C.D. (1998). Altruism and prosocial behavior. In D.T. Gilbert, S.T. Fiske, & G. Lindzey (Eds.), *The handbook of social psychology,* Vol. 2 (4th ed., pp. 282–316). New York: McGraw-Hill.

Batson, C.D., Ahmad, N., Powell, A.A., & Stocks, E.L. (2008). Prosocial motivation. In J.Y. Shah, & W.L. Gardner (Eds.), *Handbook of motivation science* (pp. 135–149). New York: Guilford Press.

Batson, C.D., Klein, T.R., Highberger, L., & Shaw, L.L. (1995). Immorality from empathy-induced altruism: When compassion and justice conflict. *Journal of Personality and Social Psychology, 68*, 1042–1054.

Beehr, T.A., Bowling, N.A., & Bennett, M.M. (2010). Occupational stress and failures of social support: When helping hurts. *Journal of Occupational Health Psychology, 15*, 45–59.

Bem, D.J. (1972). Self-perception theory. In L. Berkowitz (Ed.), *Advances in Experimental Social Psychology* Vol. 6 (pp. 1–62). New York: Academic Press.

Berg, J.M., Grant, A.M., & Johnson, V. (2010). When callings are calling: Crafting work and leisure in pursuit of unanswered occupational callings. *Organization Science, 21*, 973–994.

Bolino, M.C. (1999). Citizenship and impression management: Good soldiers or good actors? *Academy of Management Review, 24*, 82–98.

Bono, J.E., & Judge, T.A. (2003). Self-concordance at work: Toward understanding the motivational effects of transformational leaders. *Academy of Management Journal, 46*, 554–571.

Bowe, J., Bowe, M., & Streeter, S. (2000). *Gig: Americans talk about their jobs*. New York: Three Rivers Press.

Bunderson, J.S., & Thompson, J.A. (2009). The call of the wild: Zookeepers, callings, and the double-edged sword of deeply meaningful work. *Administrative Science Quarterly, 54*, 32–57.

Cameron, K., Dutton, J.E., & Quinn, R.E. (2003). *Positive organizational scholarship: Foundations of a new discipline.* San Francisco: Berrett-Koehler.

Chaplin, W.F., John, O.P., & Goldberg, L.R. (1988). Conceptions of states and traits: Dimensional attributes with ideals as prototypes. *Journal of Personality and Social Psychology, 54*, 541–557.

Chatman, J.A., & Barsade, S.G. (1995). Personality, organizational culture, and cooperation: Evidence from a business simulation. *Administrative Science Quarterly, 40*, 423–443.

Choi, Y., & Mai-Dalton, R.R. (1999). The model of followers' responses to self-sacrificial leadership: An empirical test. *Leadership Quarterly, 10,* 397–421.

Cialdini, R.B., Brown, S.L., Lewis, B.P., Luce, C., & Neuberg, S.L. (1997). Reinterpreting the empathy-altruism relationship: When one into one equals oneness. *Journal of Personality and Social Psychology, 73,* 481–494.

Ciulla, J.B. (2000). *The working life: The promise and betrayal of modern work.* New York: Three Rivers Press.

Colby, A., Sippola, L., & Phelps, E. (2001). Social responsibility and paid work in contemporary American life. In A. Rossi (Ed.), *Caring and doing for others: Social responsibility in the domains of family, work, and community* (pp. 463–501). Chicago: University of Chicago Press.

Conger, J.A., Kanungo, R.N., & Menon, S.T. (2000). Charismatic leadership and follower effects. *Journal of Organizational Behavior, 21,* 747–767.

Cook, T.D., & Campbell, D.T. (1979). *Quasi-experimentation: Design and analysis issues for field settings.* Boston: Houghton-Mifflin.

Costa, P.T., Jr., McCrae, R.R., & Dye, D.A. (1991). Facet scales for agreeableness and conscientiousness: A revision of the NEO Personality Inventory. *Personality and Individual Differences, 12,* 887–898.

Crocker, J. (2008). From egosystem to ecosystem: Implications for learning, relationships, and well-being. In H. Wayment, & J. Brauer (Eds.), *Transcending self-interest: Psychological explorations of the quiet ego* (pp. 63–72). Washington, DC: American Psychological Association.

Cunningham, M.R., Steinberg, J., & Grey, R. (1980). Wanting to and having to help: Separate motivations for positive mood and guilt-induced helping. *Journal of Personality and Social Psychology, 38,* 181–192.

De Dreu, C.K.W. (2006). Rational self-interest and other orientation in organizational behavior: A critical appraisal and extension of Meglino and Korsgaard (2004). *Journal of Applied Psychology, 91,* 1245–1252.

De Dreu, C.K.W., Giebels, E., & Van de Vliert, E. (1998). Social motives and trust in integrative negotiation: The disruptive effects of punitive capability. *Journal of Applied Psychology, 83,* 408–422.

De Dreu, C.K.W., & Nauta, A. (2009). Self-interest and other-orientation in organizational behavior: Implications for job performance, prosocial behavior, and personal initiative. *Journal of Applied Psychology, 94,* 913–926.

De Dreu, C.K.W., Weingart, L.R., & Kwon, S. (2000). Influence of social motives on integrative negotiation: A meta-analytic review and test of two theories. *Journal of Personality and Social Psychology, 78,* 889–905.

Deelstra, J.T., Peeters, M.C.W., Schaufeli, W.B., Stroebe, W., Zijlstra, F.R.H., & van Doornen, L.P. (2003). Receiving instrumental support at work: When help is not welcome. *Journal of Applied Psychology, 88,* 324–331.

Deutsch, M. (1973). *The resolution of conflict.* New Haven, CT: Yale University Press.

Ferraro, F., Pfeffer, J., & Sutton, R.I. (2005). Economics language and assumptions: How theories can become self-fulfilling. *Academy of Management Review, 30,* 8–24.

Fineman, S. (2006). On being positive: Concerns and counterpoints. *Academy of Management Review, 31,* 270–291.

Fisher, J.D., Nadler, A., & Whitcher-Alagna, S. (1982). Recipient reactions to aid. *Psychological Bulletin, 91,* 27–54.

Flynn, F.J., & Brockner, J. (2003). It's different to give than to receive: Predictors of givers' and receivers' reactions to favor exchange. *Journal of Applied Psychology, 88,* 1034–1045.

Fried, Y., Levi, A.S., & Laurence, G. (2008). Motivation and job design in the new world of work. In C. Cooper, & C. Cartwright (Eds.), *The Oxford handbook of personnel psychology* (pp. 586–611). Oxford: Oxford University Press.

Gagné, M., & Deci, E.L. (2005). Self-determination theory and work motivation. *Journal of Organizational Behavior, 26,* 331–362.

Gebauer, J.E., Riketta, M., Broemer, P., & Maio, G.R. (2008). Pleasure and pressure based prosocial motivation: Divergent relations to subjective well-being. *Journal of Research in Personality, 42,* 399–420.

George, B. (2003). *Authentic leadership: Rediscovering the secrets to creating lasting value.* San Francisco: Jossey-Bass.

Gino, F., & Pierce, L. (2010). Robin Hood under the hood: Wealth-based discrimination in illicit customer help. *Organization Science, 21*(6), 1176–1194.

Norvig, P. (2006). Making a difference. Retrieved March 4, 2010 from http://googleresearch.blogspot.com/2006/02/making-difference.html.

Grant, A.M. (2007). Relational job design and the motivation to make a prosocial difference. *Academy of Management Review, 32,* 393–417.

Grant, A.M. (2008a). Does intrinsic motivation fuel the prosocial fire? Motivational synergy in predicting persistence, performance, and productivity. *Journal of Applied Psychology, 93,* 48–58.

Grant, A.M. (2008b). The significance of task significance: Job performance effects, relational mechanisms, and boundary conditions. *Journal of Applied Psychology, 93,* 108–124.

Grant, A.M. (2008c). Employees without a cause: The motivational effects of prosocial impact in public service. *International Public Management Journal, 11,* 48–66.

Grant, A.M. (2009). Putting self-interest out of business? Contributions and unanswered questions from use-inspired research on prosocial motivation. *Industrial and Organizational Psychology, 2,* 94–98.

Grant, A.M. (in press a). Leading with meaning: Beneficiary contact, prosocial impact, and the performance effects of transformational leadership. Academy of Management Journal.

Grant, A.M. (in press b). Giving time, time after time: Work design and sustained employee participation in corporate volunteering. Academy of Management Review.

Grant, A.M., & Berry, J. (2011). The necessity of others is the mother of invention: Intrinsic and prosocial motivations, perspective-taking, and creativity. Forthcoming in the *Academy of Management Journal, 54,* 73–96.

Grant, A.M., Campbell, E.M., Chen, G., Cottone, K., Lapedis, D., & Lee, K. (2007). Impact and the art of motivation maintenance: The effects of contact with beneficiaries on persistence behavior. *Organizational Behavior and Human Decision Processes, 103,* 53–67.

Grant, A.M., Dutton, J.E., & Rosso, B. (2008). Giving commitment: Employee support programs and the prosocial sensemaking process. *Academy of Management Journal, 51,* 898–918.

Grant, A.M., & Gino, F. (2010). A little thanks goes a long way: Explaining why gratitude expressions motivate prosocial behavior. Forthcoming in the *Journal of Personality and Social Psychology, 98*(6), 946–955.

Grant, A.M., & Mayer, D.M. (2009). Good soldiers and good actors: Prosocial and impression management motives as interactive predictors of affiliative citizenship behaviors. *Journal of Applied Psychology, 94,* 900–912.

Grant, A.M., & Parker, S.K. (2009). Redesigning work design theories: The rise of relational and proactive perspectives. *Academy of Management Annals, 3*, 317–375.

Grant, A.M., Parker, S.K., & Collins, C.G. (2009). Getting credit for proactive behavior: Supervisor reactions depend on what you value and how you feel. *Personnel Psychology, 62*, 31–55.

Grant, A.M., & Sumanth, J.J. (2009). Mission possible? The performance of prosocially motivated employees depends on manager trustworthiness. *Journal of Applied Psychology, 94*, 927–944.

Grant, A.M., & Wade-Benzoni, K. (2009). The hot and cool of death awareness at work: Mortality cues, aging, and self-protective and prosocial motivations. *Academy of Management Review, 34*, 600–622.

Grant, A.M., & Wrzesniewski, A. (2010). I won't let you down . . . or will I? Core self-evaluations, other-orientation, anticipated guilt and gratitude, and job performance. *Journal of Applied Psychology, 95*, 108–121.

Graziano, W.G., Habashi, M.M., Sheese, B.E., & Tobin, R.M. (2007). Agreeableness, empathy, and helping: A person X situation perspective. *Journal of Personality and Social Psychology, 93*, 583–599.

Grube, J.A., & Piliavin, J.A. (2000). Role identity, organizational experiences, and volunteer performance. *Personality and Social Psychology Bulletin, 26*, 1108–1119.

Gutek, B.A., Bhappu, A.D., Liao-Troth, M.A., & Cherry, B. (1999). Distinguishing between service relationships and encounters. *Journal of Applied Psychology, 84*, 218–233.

Hackman, J.R. (1992). Group influences on individuals in organizations. In M.D. Dunnette, & L.M. Hough (Eds.), *Handbook of industrial and organizational psychology* Vol. 2 (pp. 199–267). Palo Alto, CA: Consulting Psychologists Press.

Hackman, J.R., & Oldham, G.R. (1976). Motivation through the design of work: Test of a theory. *Organizational Behavior and Human Performance, 16*, 250–279.

Howell, J.M., & Shamir, B. (2005). The role of followers in the charismatic leadership process: Relationships and their consequences. *Academy of Management Review, 30*, 96–112.

Jecker, J., & Landy, D. (1969). Liking a person as function of doing him a favor. *Human Relations, 22*, 371–378.

Judge, T.A., & Bono, J.E. (2001). Relationship of core self-evaluations traits—self-esteem, generalized self-efficacy, locus of control, and emotional stability—with job satisfaction and job performance: A meta-analysis. *Journal of Applied Psychology, 86*, 80–92.

Kahn, W.A. (1990). Psychological conditions of personal engagement and disengagement at work. *Academy of Management Journal, 33*, 692–724.

Kanfer, R. (1990). Motivation theory and industrial/organizational psychology. In M.D. Dunnette & L.M. Hough (Eds.), *Handbook of industrial and organizational psychology* Vol. 1 (pp. 75–170). Palo Alto, CA: Consulting Psychologists Press.

Kanfer, R. (2009). Work motivation: Advancing theory and impact. *Industrial and Organizational Psychology, 2*, 118–127.

Kay, A.C., & Ross, L. (2003). The perceptual push: The interplay of implicit cues and explicit situational construals on behavioral intentions in the Prisoner's Dilemma. *Journal of Experimental Social Psychology, 39*, 634–643.

Konovsky, M.A., & Organ, D.W. (1996). Dispositional and contextual determinants of organizational citizenship behavior. *Journal of Organizational Behavior, 17*, 253–266.

Korsgaard, M.A., Meglino, B.M., & Lester, S.W. (1997). Beyond helping: Do other-oriented values have broader implications in organizations? *Journal of Applied Psychology, 82*, 160–177.

LePine, J.A., & Van Dyne, L. (2001). Voice and cooperative behavior as contrasting forms of contextual performance: Evidence of differential relationships with big five personality characteristics and cognitive ability. *Journal of Applied Psychology, 86*, 325–336.

Little, B.R. (2005). Personality science and personal projects: Six impossible things before breakfast. *Journal of Research in Personality, 39*, 4–21.

Loewenstein, G., & Small, D.A. (2007). The scarecrow and the tin man: The vicissitudes of human sympathy and caring. *Review of General Psychology, 11*, 112–126.

Lofland, J. (1977). Becoming a world-saver revisited. *American Behavioral Scientist, 20*, 805–818.

Margolis, J.D., & Molinsky, A. (2008). Navigating the bind of necessary evils: Psychological engagement and the production of interpersonally sensitive behavior. *Academy of Management Journal, 51*, 847–872.

McAdams, D.P., & de St. Aubin, E. (1992). A theory of generativity and its assessment through self-report, behavioral acts, and narrative themes in autobiography. *Journal of Personality and Social Psychology, 62*, 1003–1015.

McGregor, I. (2007). Personal projects as compensatory convictions: Passionate pursuit and the fugitive self. In B.R. Little, K. Salmela-Aro, & S.D. Phillips (Eds.), *Personal project pursuit: Goals, action, and human flourishing* (pp. 171–195). Mahwah, NJ: Erlbaum.

McGregor, I., & Little, B.R. (1998). Personal projects, happiness, and meaning: On doing well and being yourself. *Journal of Personality and Social Psychology, 74*, 494–512.

Meglino, B.M., & Korsgaard, M.A. (2004). Considering rational self-interest as a disposition: Organizational implications of other orientation. *Journal of Applied Psychology, 89*, 946–959.

Meglino, B.M., & Korsgaard, M.A. (2006). Considering situational and dispositional approaches to rational self-interest: An extension and response to De Dreu (2006). *Journal of Applied Psychology, 91*, 1253–1259.

Metcalfe, J., & Mischel, W. (1999). A hot/cool-system analysis of delay of gratification: Dynamics of willpower. *Psychological Review, 106*, 3–19.

Meyerson, D.E., & Scully, M.A. (1995). Tempered radicalism and the politics of ambivalence and change. *Organization Science, 6*, 585–600.

Miller, D.T. (1999). The norm of self-interest. *American Psychologist, 54*, 1053–1060.

Mitchell, T.R., & Daniels, D. (2003). Motivation. In W.C. Borman, D.R. Ilgen, & R.J. Klimoski (Eds.), *Handbook of psychology*, Vol. 12: *Industrial and organizational psychology* (pp. 225–254). New York: John Wiley.

Molinsky, A., & Margolis, J. (2005). Necessary evils and interpersonal sensitivity in organizations. *Academy of Management Review, 30*, 245–268.

Morgeson, F.P., & Humphrey, S.E. (2008). Job and team design: Toward a more integrative conceptualization of work design. In J. Martocchio (Ed.), *Research in personnel and human resource management* Vol. 27 (pp. 39–92). Bingley, UK: Emerald Group Publishing Limited.

Morrison, E.W. (2006). Doing the job well: An investigation of pro-social rule breaking. *Journal of Management, 32*, 5–28.

Morrison, E.W., & Robinson, S.L. (1997). When employees feel betrayed: A model of how psychological contract violation develops. *Academy of Management Review, 22*, 226–256.

O'Reilly, C., & Chatman, J. (1996). Culture as social control: Corporations, cults, and commitment. In B.M. Staw, & L.L. Cummings (Eds.), *Research in organizational behavior*

Vol. 18 (pp. 157–200). New York: Elsevier Science/JAI Press.

Oxford English Dictionary Online. (2009). Retrieved February 20, 2010 from library.upenn.edu.

Parker, S.K., & Ohly, S. (2008). Designing motivating jobs: An expanded framework for linking work characteristics and motivation. In R. Kanfer, G. Chen, & R.D. Pritchard (Eds.), Work motivation: Past, present and future (pp. 233–284). New York: LEA/Psychology Press.

Penner, L.A., Dovidio, J.F., Piliavin, J.A., & Schroeder, D.A. (2005). Prosocial behavior: Multilevel perspectives. Annual Review of Psychology, 56, 365–392.

Penner, L.A., & Finkelstein, M.A. (1998). Dispositional and structural determinants of volunteerism. Journal of Personality & Social Psychology, 74, 525–537.

Perlow, L., & Weeks, J. (2002). Who's helping whom? Layers of culture and workplace behavior. Journal of Organizational Behavior, 23, 345–361.

Perry, J.L., & Hondeghem, A. (Eds.) (2008). Motivation in public management: The call of public service. Oxford: Oxford University Press.

Piccolo, R.F., & Colquitt, J.A. (2006). Transformational leadership and job behaviors: The mediating role of core job characteristics. Academy of Management Journal, 49, 327–340.

Podsakoff, P.M., MacKenzie, S.B., Paine, J.B., & Bachrach, D.G. (2000). Organizational citizenship behaviors: A critical review of the theoretical and empirical literature and suggestions for future research. Journal of Management, 26, 513–563.

Pratt, M.G. (2000). The good, the bad, and the ambivalent: Managing identification among Amway distributors. Administrative Science Quarterly, 45, 456–493.

Ratner, R.K., & Miller, D.T. (2001). The norm of self-interest and its effects on social action. Journal of Personality and Social Psychology, 81, 5–16.

Reed, A., II., & Aquino, K.F. (2003). Moral identity and the expanding circle of moral regard toward out-groups. Journal of Personality and Social Psychology, 84, 1270–1286.

Rioux, S.M., & Penner, L.A. (2001). The causes of organizational citizenship behavior: A motivational analysis. Journal of Applied Psychology, 86, 1306–1314.

Rosenthal, R. (1994). Interpersonal expectancy effects: A 30-year perspective. Current Directions in Psychological Science, 3, 176–179.

Rousseau, D.M., & McLean Parks, J. (1993). The contracts of individuals and organizations. Research in Organizational Behavior, 15, 1–47.

Ryan, R.M., & Deci, E.L. (2000). Self-determination theory and the facilitation of intrinsic motivation, social development, and well-being. American Psychologist, 55, 68–78.

Schein, E.H. (1980). Organizational psychology. Englewood Cliffs, NJ: Prentice-Hall.

Schwartz, S.H., & Bardi, A. (2001). Value hierarchies across cultures: Taking a similarities perspective. Journal of Cross-Cultural Psychology, 32, 268–290.

Schwartz, S.H., Melech, G., Lehmann, A., Burgess, S., Harris, M., & Owens, V. (2001). Extending the cross-cultural validity of the theory of basic human values with a different method of measurement. Journal of Cross-Cultural Psychology, 32, 519–542.

Shamir, B. (1990). Calculations, values, and identities: The sources of collectivistic work motivation. Human Relations, 43, 313–332.

Shamir, B. (1991). Meaning, self and motivation in organizations. Organization Studies, 12, 405–424.

Shamir, B., House, R.J., & Arthur, M.B. (1993). The motivational effects of charismatic leadership: A self-concept based theory. Organization Science, 4, 577–594.

Shamir, B., Zakay, E., Breinin, E., & Popper, M. (1998). Correlates of charismatic leader behavior in military units: Subordinates' attitudes, unit characteristics, and superiors' appraisals of leader performance. Academy of Management Journal, 41, 387–409.

Sheldon, K.M., Arndt, J., & Houser-Marko, L. (2003). In search of the organismic valuing process: The human tendency to move towards beneficial goal choices. Journal of Personality, 71, 835–869.

Sieden, L.S. (1989). Buckminster Fuller's universe: His life and work. Cambridge: Perseus.

Singh, N., & Krishnan, V.R. (2008). Self-sacrifice and transformational leadership: Mediating role of altruism. Leadership & Organization Development Journal, 29, 261–274.

Somers, M.J., & Casal, J.C. (1994). Organizational commitment and whistle-blowing: A test of the reformer and the organization man hypotheses. Group & Organization Management, 19, 270–284.

Thompson, J.A., & Bunderson, J.S. (2003). Violations of principle: Ideological currency in the psychological contract. Academy of Management Review, 28, 571–586.

Turner, Y.N., Hadas-Halperin, I., & Raveh, D. (2008). Patient photos spur radiologist empathy and eye for detail. Paper presented at the annual meeting of the Radiological Society of North America, November.

Vallerand, R.J. (1997). Toward a hierarchical model of intrinsic and extrinsic motivation. In M.P. Zanna (Ed.), Advances in experimental social psychology Vol. 29 (pp. 271–359). New York: Academic.

Van Eerde, W., & Thierry, H. (1996). Vroom's expectancy models and work-related criteria: A meta-analysis. Journal of Applied Psychology, 81, 575–586.

van Knippenberg, D., & Hogg, M.A. (2003), A social identity model of leadership effectiveness in organizations", In R.M. Kramer & B.M. Staw (Eds), Research in Organizational Behavior, Vol. 25 (pp. 243–95). New York: Elsevier.

Vough, H., & Parker, S.K. (2008). Work design research: Still going strong. In C.L. Cooper, & J. Barling (Eds.), Handbook of organizational behavior. London: Sage Publications.

Vroom, V.H. (1964). Work and motivation. New York: Wiley.

Weber, J.M., Kopelman, S., & Messick, D.M. (2004). A conceptual review of decision making in social dilemmas: Applying a logic of appropriateness. Personality and Social Psychology Review, 8, 281–307.

Weick, K.E. (1974). Middle range theories of social systems. Behavioral Science, 19, 357–367.

Weick, K.E. (1984). Small wins: Redefining the scale of social problems. American Psychologist, 39, 40–49.

Weick, K.E. (1995). Sensemaking in organizations. Thousand Oaks, CA: Sage.

Weingart, L.R., Bennett, R.J., & Brett, J.M. (1993). The impact of consideration of issues and motivational orientation on group negotiation process and outcome. Journal of Applied Psychology, 78, 504–517.

Wrzesniewski, A., & Dutton, J.E. (2001). Crafting a job: Revisioning employees as active crafters of their work. Academy of Management Review, 26, 179–201.

CHAPTER
4

Callings

Amy Wrzesniewski

Abstract

The concept of work as a calling has generated considerable interest among researchers, inspiring a number of new lines of research into this intriguing experience of work. This chapter describes the different approaches to defining what a calling is, where it comes from, and its effects for individuals and organizations. Rather than treating the variety of perspectives on callings as a liability, it considers the many opportunities for rich empirical work that it suggests. The chapter highlights promising areas for future inquiry while sparking new questions to help spur researchers to continue to deepen our understanding of the nature of callings.

Keywords: Calling, meaningful work, meaning of work, work orientation

> If a man loves the labour of his trade, apart from any question of success
> or fame, the gods have called him.
> —*Robert Louis Stevenson*

Few topics inspire as much idealism and positivity as the notion of work as a calling. Practitioners and popular authors strive to help seekers find (or create) their callings, academics and scholars aim to understand the nature of callings as well as their antecedents and effects, and countless individuals simply wonder about what their calling might be, how to find it, and, if they have found it, how to successfully pursue it. Other orientations toward work certainly exist; work can be experienced as an alienating grind, an opportunity for challenge and growth, or through any number of other framings. But callings have stolen center stage in our imaginations as offering some sort of special gateway to fulfillment and meaning in work. As a window onto the individual experience of work, callings are of central importance to positive organizational scholarship (POS), because they capture the most positive and generative manifestation of the connection between people and their work that scholars have studied. Yet, callings

are somewhat of a Rorschach test in organizational behavior and psychology—viewed from various angles, callings reveal different understandings, assumptions, and predictions regarding their nature and form. Although the variety of viewpoints on callings may seem confusing, I attempt to trace these viewpoints to their roots in earlier research and writing in order to reconcile different approaches to the topic.

The goal of this chapter is to elucidate the construct of callings, defining their structure and content, their antecedents and outcomes, and the debates that continue over their very essence. It is at the intersections of these different findings and viewpoints on callings that the most fruitful ground for future empirical research exists. Treating the variety of perspectives on callings as a valuable set of research opportunities, rather than a liability, I highlight promising areas for future inquiry with an eye toward bringing helpful resolution to some of the debates in this area while sparking new questions to help spur researchers to continue to deepen our understanding of the nature of callings.

What Is a Calling?

There is not, to date, a single universally accepted meaning of the term "callings," as the term has been given a broad range of definitions in the organizational literature. Many of these definitions differ because they are derivative of those offered in the social sciences or in much earlier philosophical and religious works. It is a sign of the evolving and dynamic nature of research on and inquiry into callings that the definition of callings is the subject of ongoing debate.

Beginning with the social sciences, sociologist Robert Bellah and his colleagues (Bellah, Madsen, Sullivan, Swidler, & Tipton, 1985), in the context of their influential discussion of individualism and commitment in different domains of life in the United States, argued that work can be subjectively experienced as a calling (see also Baumeister, 1991). In their view, those with callings work not primarily for financial gain or career advancement, but instead for the fulfillment that the work itself brings to the individual. In a sense, the work is an end in itself. This definition is emblematic of the largely secular and individually based view of work as a calling that has dominated the organizational literature. Later, Wrzesniewski and colleagues (1997) drew on this definition to define callings as work that people feel is usually seen as socially valuable—an end in itself—involving activities that may, but need not be, pleasurable (Wrzesniewski, McCauley, Rozin, & Schwartz, 1997). More fully, a calling is traditionally defined as a meaningful beckoning toward activities that are morally, socially, and personally significant (Baumeister, 1991; Bellah et al., 1985; Wrzesniewski, Dekas, & Rosso, 2009). A calling is assumed to be unique to the person, comprising activities people believe they must do to fulfill their unique purpose in life, and offering a path to connect with one's true self (Bunderson & Thompson, 2009; Levoy, 1997; Novak, 1996). A calling refers to the enactment of personally significant beliefs through work (Elangovan, Pinder, & McLean, 2010; Myers, 2007, 2009); an enactment that has been referred to as the highest form of subjective career success (Dobrow, 2006; Hall & Chandler, 2005). Those who view their work as a calling understand their work to be an end in itself, rather than a means to some other end (Wrzesniewski et al., 1997).

Callings As a Religious Entity

The term "calling" clearly has religious roots. Specifically, callings are a product of Christian theology. Traditionally, callings were rooted in an understanding that people were "called" by God to do morally and socially significant work (Weber, 1956, 1963). Organizational scholars note that the Protestant Reformation saw a significant shift in the meaning of work, converting it from a pursuit that lacked intrinsic value to an activity that was glorified in its own right (Ciulla, 2000). This shift occurred as Martin Luther's theology promoted the concept of a calling, defined by him as a vocational direction from God about how best to serve God and the community (Weber, 1958). Later, John Calvin defined callings as a divine ordinance to which individuals have a duty and responsibility. As a result, any activity done to serve God was considered intrinsically valuable, and failure to fulfill one's calling was seen as immoral (Nord, Brief, Atieh, & Doherty, 1990). This perspective suggests that callings are revealed by God, either directly or through one's abilities, thus suggesting that callings are religious endeavors rather than expressions of the self. Later, Weber suggested that Calvin's interpretation of callings helped to enable the development of modern capitalism by producing a "Protestant work ethic" that greatly increased a societal emphasis on the individual pursuit of success. Although the accuracy of Weber's interpretation of Calvin has been debated, the impact of his perspective on callings is hard to overstate.

In modern times, the use of callings in a religious sense has come to be defined as a beckoning from God to a vocation, the acceptance and execution of which is thought to carry out the will of God (Hardy, 1990; Weiss, Skelley, Haughey, & Hall, 2004). According to this perspective, work, if carried out for purposes other than service to God, is of little spiritual significance. However, *any* work can become holy if dedicated to God (Steger, Pickering, Shin, & Dik, 2010), as answered callings are understood to be a pathway through which individuals act as the hands of God on earth (Dik & Duffy, 2009). Even without explicit reference to God or spirituality, a sense of calling as the expression of one's duty or destiny on Earth through work is evident in modern society (Bunderson & Thompson, 2009).

More recently, organizational scholars have again revisited the traditional religious roots of callings, reaching a better understanding of the impact of experiencing a calling in a neoclassical sense—reflecting the Protestant Reformation concept of calling as a duty to society rather than as a satisfying exercise in pleasure in one's work (Bunderson & Thompson, 2009). However, callings have largely lost this religious connotation and tend to be defined in the secular sense as consisting of enjoyable or pleasurable work that the individual believes is making the world a better place. Thus, the concept of a calling has taken on other forms in the modern era, and is one of several kinds of meanings that people attach to their work (Wrzesniewski et al., 2009). These meanings may also guide individuals in how they enact the tasks and relationships that comprise their jobs (Berg, Grant, & Johnson, 2010; Wrzesniewski & Dutton, 2001).

A recent review of research on callings in organizational behavior suggests that the set of definitions of callings in use share three important elements (Elangovan et al., 2010; Myers, 2007, 2009): First, callings are action-oriented; second, callings suggest a sense of meaning and mission (Dik & Duffy, 2009); and third, callings are prosocial in their focus. As well, Dobrow (2006) has suggested a broader set of elements of a calling, moving beyond a sense of fulfillment in the work and contribution to the greater good to include a sense of urgency and self-esteem from the activity of work. In the next section, I consider the experience of work as a calling in relation to other meanings of work.

Calling As a Work Orientation

The concept of work orientation builds on theoretical assertions from sociology and psychology that work is subjectively experienced by individuals in one of three distinct ways: as a job, in which the focus of the work is on income; a career, in which the focus is on advancement in one's line of work; or a calling (Baumeister, 1991; Bellah et al., 1985; Schwartz, 1986, 1994). These three categories represent three different work orientations, which guide individuals' basic goals for working, capture beliefs about the role of work in life, and are reflected in work-related feelings and behaviors (Wrzesniewski, 2003; Wrzesniewski et al., 1997). Work orientation provides a helpful framework with which to understand how individuals make meaning of their work and how they enact their jobs to reflect these meanings (Scott Morton & Podolny, 2002; Peterson, Park, Hall, & Seligman, 2009; Wrzesniewski & Dutton, 2001).

Callings have come to be defined as work that is viewed as a duty and destiny (Bunderson & Thompson, 2009), a source of fulfillment that is important to one's identity (Berg et al., 2010;

Wrzesniewski et al., 1997), a social contribution to others or the wider world (Wrzesniewski et al., 1997; Wrzesniewski, 2003), work that is an expression of one's purpose (Hall & Chandler, 2005), or as comprising one's passion, identity, urgency, engulfing consciousness, longevity, sense of meaning, and domain-specific self-esteem (Dobrow, 2006). Thus, it is likely no surprise that many of the most popular examples of callings draw from work in which passion and meaning are often assumed, such as the arts or helping professions (e.g., medicine, advocacy work), as individuals in these occupations are thought to be compelled to do expressive work or be of service to others. Research has suggested that callings can be experienced in work that runs the gamut from lofty to lowly (e.g., Berg et al., 2010; Bunderson & Thompson, 2009; Wrzesniewski & Dutton, 2001; Wrzesniewski, 2003; Wrzesniewski et al., 1997).

In this volume, Perttula and Cardon (2011, Chapter 15) note that passion for work is a hallmark of meaningful work more generally, and consider the passion that individuals experience for their work in entrepreneurial ventures and in their jobs in general (see also Wrzesniewski, Rozin, & Bennett, 2002, for a discussion of passion and work). Thus, the connection between callings and passions are clear. Both involve a sense of meaningful connection to the work that is often the source of great pleasure. Callings and passions differ, however, in two important ways. First, callings typically involve a sense that the work contributes to the world in a meaningful way (Bunderson & Thompson, 2009; Wrzesniewski et al., 1997), whereas passions do not necessarily have a social component to them. Second, passions are marked by the experience of joy and subjective vitality (Perttula & Cardon, 2010), which may or may not also accompany the experience of work as a calling. In fact, Bunderson and Thompson (2009) suggest that some may experience a calling more through a lens of duty and destiny, without the deep pleasure that is often assumed to be a part of a calling.

The evidence of the broad types of work that can be experienced as a calling is consistent with research that suggests that *any* kind of work can be a calling. Work orientations are essentially frames of meaning applied to the work one does; thus, it is possible for different people to do the same work and view it quite differently, based on which orientation each has toward the work. For example, a bank president can view the work as a way to enjoy a large income (job orientation), as a way to move into leadership positions in national banking organizations that set banking policy (career orientation), or as a way to carry out the enjoyable, fulfilling work of contributing to the financial security and well-being of a lifetime of clients (calling orientation). Likewise, a laborer can view the work as a way to cover the mortgage (job orientation), an opportunity to become crew foreperson and someday, a supervisor (career orientation), or as a way to build the infrastructure of a city, thus ensuring the safety and futures of millions of people who will live and work there (calling orientation). Regardless of the kind of work, those with calling orientations are likely to experience their work as deeply meaningful.

Callings As a Secular Entity

Although religious connotations of callings survive, the concept of a calling has taken on stronger secular tones over time. This shift is reminiscent of much older conceptions of the meaning of work which, reaching back to the Greek philosophers, including Aristotle, held that authentic fulfillment would be found through personally meaningful and intrinsically motivating pursuits (Aristotle, 1912). Indeed, much as the Greek philosophers put the individual at the center of meaningful work, modern conceptions of callings emphasize the individual as the primary entity that defines and is served by callings as well.

There seems to be little disagreement in the emerging organizational literature on callings that the sense of calling is defined by the individual doing the work. Thus, a humanitarian aid worker who primarily views the work as a way to advance into a job at the United Nations, for example, does not have a calling, whereas a groundskeeper at a professional baseball stadium who sees the work as deeply enjoyable and essential to the pursuit of the country's favorite pastime could have a calling. Both religious and secular traditions emphasize that callings include a sense that the work has a positive impact on the world and is intrinsically motivating as an end in itself. Individuals pursuing their calling often feel a great sense of urgency for following the path to which they feel intended (Bunderson & Thompson, 2009).

Callings both in the modern secular sense and the religious sense have enjoyed a surge of interest in research and the popular press. This is likely due to the pressures that stem from the increasing tendency for people to define themselves, and be defined by others, through their work (Casey, 1995). The sense that work ought to represent a meaningful, important

contribution is evident in the burgeoning career counseling and coaching industry, to which individuals flock in the hopes of identifying or creating a calling, or turning their current job into a calling. This interest in work as a calling is likely to continue as long as work is emphasized as a source of fulfillment, meaning, and purpose in life, and as individuals work more hours than ever (Schor, 1992) and change jobs more often than in the past (Sennett, 2005), potentially creating a need to understand one's own path through the lens of the work in addition to the lens of the organization (Pratt & Ashforth, 2003).

Although religious callings involve a beckoning from outside of the self that is heeded (or not), secular callings differ in that the pursuit of the calling tends to be oriented within the self (e.g., Rosso, Dekas, & Wrzesniewski, 2010). In research on secular callings, self-fulfillment is the primary focus. Individuals are depicted as following paths chosen by the self, rather than by God or some other higher power (Berg et al., 2010; Rosso et al., 2010). Although the self is most salient in secular callings, scholars still define callings both as a source of intrinsic fulfillment and as a way of making a contribution to the wider world. However, the connection between internally directed fulfillment and work done in service of others is still unclear in the literature on callings. Future work that delineates the nature and forms of calling (e.g., Bunderson & Thompson, 2009) would mark an important research contribution. In the next section, I consider related concepts that are different from, but likely are related to, the experience of work as a calling.

What Callings Are Not

Several constructs from the organizational psychology and organizational behavior literatures are likely related to callings. Although these relationships are instructive for understanding markers of callings among existing constructs, these constructs do not, in part or whole, capture what a calling is. Rather, they reflect elements of work attitudes and experience that individuals with callings might be expected to endorse. In most cases, the difference between each of these constructs and a calling is the fact that each of the former is a reflection of how deeply one is engaged in or committed to work, rather than the nature of or reasons for these attachments—which a calling more clearly captures.

Work centrality, defined as how work compares with other life spheres in its importance, and work commitment, defined as the importance of work to people's sense of self (Dubin, 1956; MOW, 1987; Loscocco, 1989), are likely related to callings. Individuals who view their work as a calling would, by definition, have high work centrality and high work commitment. However, one could have high work centrality and commitment for reasons other than having a calling; for example, a mid-level manager with a strong career orientation (Wrzesniewski et al., 1997) who is primarily focused in advancement in her work life would likely report high work centrality and commitment, but toward quite different ends than would a manager who views the work as a calling.

Similarly, work and job involvement (Kanungo, 1982; Lodahl & Kejner, 1965), defined as one's attachment to work and beliefs about the importance of work in life, respectively, are also likely to be related to callings. However, like work centrality and work commitment, they are unlikely to differentiate between those with callings and those who are deeply involved in their work and jobs for other reasons. In a basic sense, a broad swath of constructs that represent a unidimensional focus on the strength of attachment to a job or to work more generally cannot capture the *nature* of that attachment. Callings are a special case of a unique kind of relationship with and experience of work, with implications for the strength of one's attachment to work. However, callings are not solely defined by the strength of this attachment.

Finally, callings are not simply a function of intrinsic motivation toward one's work. Although those who view work as a calling are likely to be highly motivated by the content of the work itself, it is the direction toward which this motivation is oriented that defines a calling. One can be motivated to engage in an activity for its own sake because it is engaging or fun, but the personal fulfillment and social contribution inherent in callings denote a more complex relationship to the activity of work. An employee in the emergency lending arm of an institution who enjoys fielding calls from clients because it is interesting and absorbing is intrinsically motivated; an employee who enjoys fielding calls from clients because it is engaging and means that those clients can make the financial arrangements necessary to live their lives, thus impacting society in positive and potentially profound ways, may have a calling.

In the next section, I consider the antecedents of a calling orientation. Regardless of whether callings issue forth from a religious entity or well up from within, considering the sources from which they may emerge can shed helpful light on the nature of callings more generally. As well, the sources of callings raise important questions about whether callings are answered, found, or made.

The Path to Callings: Antecedents and Sources

A review of the literature quickly reveals an interesting distinction between two basic but competing assumptions that are made about the very nature of a calling. An interesting tension exists regarding whether callings are found, or discovered, and whether they are created, or made. Callings that are religious in origin are positioned as calls to be answered that issue forth from a sacred source or an entity beyond the self (Bunderson & Thompson, 2009; Rosso et al., 2010). Callings that are secular in focus have also been treated as preexisting entities to be discovered by or about the individual (Chandler & Hall, 2005), rather than as understandings of the meaning of work to be created or enacted by the individual (Wrzesniewski, 2003; Wrzesniewski & Dutton, 2001). For example, consider the difference between someone who becomes a claims administrator because he believes God has called him to do so, someone who takes the same job because a series of occupational and career tests point him to that work as his calling, and someone who takes the job because it is the best opportunity available, but soon changes elements of the job to align the work with a passion for helping others in need (Berg et al., 2010). In a basic sense, all three are pursuing callings, but whether that calling was issued, discovered, or created in the work differs.

The differences among these assumptions on the sources of callings matter, and the practical implications are clear. In the first case, one should engage in introspection and reflection so as to better "hear" the call that is issuing forth from a sacred source. In the second case, one should look deeply within the self and search high and low for feedback and data that will point one in the correct direction, toward work that will be experienced as deeply meaningful. In the third case, neither of these requirements applies; instead, one is challenged to craft the elements of a job—ostensibly any job—to align it with one's sense of a calling.

Of course, callings may evolve over the course of one's working life. Dobrow (2010a) suggests in her research on young musicians that a sense of calling changes over time, becoming reinforced or undermined as a result of one's behavioral investments in and social support of the calling. As well,

Wrzesniewski (2002, 2003) suggests that a sense of calling can grow or diminish in one's work as a result of contextual factors ranging from features of the work context to shocks in the external environment. Whether callings are found or made, and whether they evolve over time as circumstances change, are important questions requiring further study (Rosso et al., 2010).

Thus, the origins of callings are represented differently depending upon researchers' understanding of what a calling is. In a sense, the debate over the sources and nature of callings has limited exploration of the role of other forces in shaping the experience of a calling. This oversight is important, for it concerns our ability to comprehend the origins of callings and the relationships people will have with their work throughout the course of their lives. Understanding how it is that one develops an understanding of what it means to work and how one's work relates to the rest of life is a rather lofty goal, and several models can be used to elaborate a set of arguments about the development of work orientation. For example, object relations theory (Masling & Bornstein, 1994) and theories of social representations of reality (Mannetti & Tanucci, 1993) both offer explanations of how people are likely to develop a particular kind of relationship to or representation of their work.

Other possible paths of development are suggested by Bandura's social learning theory (1977). Social learning theory, unlike object relations theory, offers a clear argument for the paths of transmission that work values are likely to take. In contrast, object relations theory focuses on the complex personal configurations of one's inner and outer worlds, without making a statement about how these configurations are created (Bocknek & Perna, 1994).

The development of a calling may begin long before one enters the workforce. Social learning theory (Bandura, 1977) maintains that learning takes place via the imitation of observed behavior, which would predict that parental influences and early models of what it means to work would act together to shape a sense of work as a calling. Powerful influences, such as parental socialization with reference to the world of work, can shape one's expectations and understanding of what the experience of work will be like (Mannetti & Tanucci, 1993). Indeed, Baker and Dekas (2009) find evidence that individuals primarily "inherit" their orientations toward their work from their parents. Specifically, callings seem to be influenced by the interaction of both parents' own calling orientations toward work. In a most obvious example of social learning about work, most children see their parents go to and return from work every day over the course of many years. What their parents do, say, and teach (or, conversely, do not do, say, or teach) to their children about their work communicates a powerful message about what work is and what it is not. Children observe these behaviors of parents and other role models (Grusec & Kuczynski, 1997; Higgins, Fazio, Rohan, Zanna, & Gergen, 1998), and learn how people are rewarded or not rewarded for the general orientation they bring to their work.

Just as orientations toward work may be forming as the life course unfolds, so do individual identities. As Roberts and Creary (2010) suggest in their chapter on identity in this volume, individuals are motivated to construct and validate positive identities in their own eyes and the eyes of others. Identity theorists suggest that the pathway to a positive identity is guided by the sense that one's group memberships create endowments of favorable comparisons with others (Tajfel & Turner, 1979). Another pathway suggested by identity theory hinges on one's prototypicality as a member of the group—to the extent that one represents the group prototype, one is evaluated positively by others (Turner, 1987). The implications for work as a calling are interesting when viewed through this lens. Having a calling orientation may endow people with a sense that they represent the best of their category—the zookeepers with callings studied by Bunderson and Thompson (2009) come to mind as reaping strong benefits from their sense of themselves (and, likely, others' sense of them) as exemplars of their occupational group.

In addition, social class extends its influence into important areas, including educational opportunities, social networks, and opportunity structures more generally. It is widely assumed in theories of social and educational reproduction that parents use their socioeconomic and cultural standing to confer upon their children the necessary educational and cultural experiences to secure their places in occupational and class levels close to their own. It is therefore not surprising that most children follow their parents into the same levels and types of work to which they were exposed as children (Sennett & Cobb, 1972; Willis, 1977). Social reproduction theory (Bourdieu & Passeron, 1977) is built around this set of assertions, and predicts rather successfully the occupational levels reached by children based on their fathers' occupational position (Robinson & Garnier, 1985). The cycle in which this process occurs begins in childhood, but continues throughout the lives of children as they age and enter the workforce.

After one's sense of work has started to form in childhood, adolescents and young adults experience their first few jobs and may find a sense of calling to be reinforced, invalidated, or simply made more ambiguous by this set of experiences (see Roberson, 1990, for a discussion of how stable individual differences in work meanings develop through early socialization and work experiences). For example, a new entrant into the workforce may believe that work is meant to be a meaningful and fulfilling experience, only to find that the work is tedious and void of positive meaning. In contrast, another new entrant might expect that work is meant to yield a paycheck and nothing more, but find that the work is interesting, enjoyable, contributes to the common good, and is deeply meaningful. Whether one learns that expecting nothing of work but a paycheck is an undesirable approach to work, or that attempting to scale the hierarchical set of positions in an occupation is exciting and personally meaningful, one's expectations are challenged by the experiences encountered in the workplace, which act to further develop one's sense of work as a calling. Eventually, based on what one has learned about work through learning from role models and from actual work experience, a work orientation develops and becomes a guiding principle for making sense of how work fits in relation to the rest of life.

Dobrow (2010a) also challenges the assumption that callings are discovered rather than developed. In a longitudinal study of young musicians, she explores the antecedents of callings, suggesting that one's early experiences shape the degree to which one views music as a calling over time. Berg and colleagues (2010) note in their study of unanswered callings that individuals may have multiple callings for different occupations and activities, thus suggesting that the roots of a calling may be more complex than a single detected signal or discovery of one particular path. Their study reveals the strategies used by individuals in pursuit of unanswered callings to craft their work and leisure activities in order to realize their callings (Berg et al., 2010), thus reinforcing the importance of understanding how different understandings of the meaning of work are shaped over the life course.

Whether callings issue forth from spiritual sources, the self, one's upbringing and circumstances, or some combination of these, one point of agreement in the literature on callings is that they have largely positive effects in work and life. However, researchers have recently begun to theorize about the potential drawbacks of callings as well. In the next section, I consider the evidence that callings influence positive and negative outcomes for individuals and organizations.

Outcomes of Callings

To date, much of the empirical research on callings has been correlational in design. Several positive outcomes have been associated with having a calling, including higher levels of work, life, and health satisfaction (Dobrow, 2006; Wrzesniewski et al., 1997) and lower absenteeism from work (Wrzesniewski et al., 1997)—effects that remain even when controlling for one's income, education, and type of occupation. Callings are also associated with higher levels of intrinsic motivation at work (Wrzesniewski, Tosti, & Landman, 2011) and the derivation of more satisfaction from the work domain than from other major life domains (Wrzesniewski et al., 1997). Individuals with callings tend to put more time in at work, whether or not this time is compensated, which is perhaps not surprising in light of the finding that those with callings are more likely to report intentions to keep working even if they did not need the money (Wrzesniewski et al., 1997). Individuals with callings report higher levels of passion for and enjoyment of their work (Novak, 2006; Vallerand et al., 2003), have stronger identification and engagement with their work (Bunderson & Thompson, 2009; Dobrow, 2006), and perform at higher levels than do their peers (Hall & Chandler, 2005). As Bunderson and Thompson (2009) note, those with callings are less likely to suffer from stress, depression, and conflict between the work and nonwork spheres of their lives (Oates, Hall, & Anderson, 2005; Treadgold, 1999).

Although most of the research findings on the outcomes associated with callings are quite positive, more recent studies are beginning to consider the potential drawbacks associated with seeing work as a calling (Bunderson & Thompson, 2009; Dobrow, 2006). This research marks an important development, as it deepens scholars' understanding of the nature and impact of callings and challenges an implicit assumption that callings are universally positive experiences. For example, although Bunderson and Thompson (2009) found that a sense of calling among the zookeepers they studied was associated with a sense of transcendent meaning, identity, and significance, the basis of a sense of calling in their sample was rooted in a feeling of duty and destiny to do zookeeping work. This sense of duty and destiny may explain the sometimes profound experience of sacrifice and vigilance that the zookeepers also reported; an experience the authors described as a double-edged sword, to reflect the simultaneously positive and difficult experience of having a neo-classical calling (Bunderson & Thompson, 2009). Although Wrzesniewski and colleagues (1997) defined callings as an experience of the work as an end in itself, in which the activities of the job may or may not be pleasurable, most subsequent research on callings has primarily highlighted the enjoyment of work as the marker of a calling. Bunderson and Thompson's (2009) study marks an important step forward in building a more complete and nuanced understanding of the nature of callings in modern work.

Recent research also suggests that callings may limit individuals' ability to correctly calibrate their abilities in the domain of their calling. Dobrow (2010b) finds that, among young musicians, a sense of calling is associated with overestimation of one's own musical ability relative to ability as rated by outside experts. This discrepancy may be costly, as a sense of calling is also associated with intentions to pursue and actual pursuit of a professional music career. Given the sense of passion experienced by those with callings, it is perhaps not surprising that they are more likely to pursue the calling in their occupational path (Berg et al., 2010). But Dobrow (2010b) suggests that a sense of calling may be setting individuals up for a fall if they do not have the requisite talent to succeed. It is possible, however, that those with callings may, even in spite of less objective ability, work harder to develop their abilities and ultimately be more likely to succeed. Resolving this question represents a fascinating opportunity to better understand the link between callings and activities in the work domain, and would be relevant to the growing literature about people's ability to build on their talents through their efforts to develop them (e.g., Dweck, 1986).

Finally, emerging theoretical work has taken on the question of whether callings have the potential to be unhealthy for individuals and organizations if they are taken to an extreme that makes them unsustainable (Caza & Cardador, 2009). Clearly, callings have all the markings of an orientation toward work that could lead to exhaustion and burnout if approached as an all-consuming activity in life (Maslach, Schaufeli, & Leiter, 2001). Although most research on callings suggests positive outcomes, the field may be suffering from a sampling issue, in which individuals who experience their work as a calling and are still working in their occupations, and thus available for research, are the individuals researchers have studied. Future research should assess the extent to which individuals may have experienced their work as a calling in the past and should also include individuals who have exited a calling due to their inability to sustain it. These exits may be due to lack of ability (Dobrow, 2010b), an unhealthy experience of the calling (Caza & Cardador, 2009), or other dynamics. Only through studying those who have experienced the drawbacks of callings can researchers gain a deeper understanding of the full scope of the construct.

Conclusion
Future Directions: Unresolved Questions and Promising Threads
As noted above, areas of great promise abound in the future of callings research. Callings represent an ancient notion, but research on callings is still relatively young. The multiple emerging threads of inquiry are a testament to this, as are the conflicting assumptions and approaches taken to understanding what a calling is and why it matters. Although callings have captured the imagination of organizational researchers, the current body of work is still developing and in need of deeper study. Below, I outline several threads for future research that could help to increase our understanding of the experience of work as a calling.

First and foremost, more rigorous empirical research on callings is needed. The concept of callings entered the organizational literature from theoretical work in the social sciences (e.g., Bellah et al., 1985) and has been the subject of many empirical investigations, as noted here. However, there remains a relative dearth of studies that are empirical and longitudinal in nature to allow for a deeper understanding of the nature of callings. Qualitative studies have shed helpful light on the nature of callings in different occupations. Combined with careful measurement of the antecedents and effects of callings, this type of inquiry can help build a strong body of research in this area of inquiry. Regardless of the nature of the questions outlined below, careful empirical study marks our best opportunity as a field to move this area of research forward in a meaningful way.

Second, as might be expected in a relatively young area of research, there is work to be done on the measurement of callings. Although various measurement instruments have been developed (e.g., Bunderson & Thompson, 2009; Dobrow, 2006; Wrzesniewski et al., 1997), each emphasizes different aspects of having a calling. The focus of recent research on defining, measuring, and validating the calling construct (Berg et al., 2010; Dik & Duffy, 2009; Dobrow, 2004) and analyzing how callings are experienced (Berg, et al., 2010; Bunderson & Thompson, 2009; Dobrow, 2006) is likely to usher in a period in which additional perspectives and elements of callings are advanced before the construct is reduced to its core. This period represents an opportunity to carefully examine whether we are fully capturing what a calling is in our measurement of it. Specifically, the field needs to eventually converge on an understanding of whether callings are a loose amalgamation of different experiences of work, or whether they have particular hallmarks that define them—for example, a sense of the work as being a critically important end in itself for the individual, as well as a belief that the work contributes to the greater good in a meaningful way. Likewise, measurement advances that help differentiate a sense of calling in general from the extent to which individuals experience a calling in their current job would be helpful. To date, both treatments of callings have coexisted, but clearly mean different things (Rosso et al., 2010).

Third, research in organizational behavior continually emphasizes the impact of changing structures of careers and work in organizations on any number of variables of interest. In this sense, callings are no different, and they represent an opportunity to explore whether those with callings enjoy an additional advantage over others beyond those reported in this chapter. Specifically, it is possible that those who experience their work as a calling may be more protected from negative effects of the episodic and uncertain nature of career progression in organizations. Because those with callings primarily define their attachment to the work domain through the work itself, rather than through membership in the organization or the status of their occupation, they may find that over the various employment shifts that are likely in a career, they are relatively protected from the stresses that others experience during such transitions. To the extent that one is able to engage in work that represents one's calling, changes in the kind of position one holds, and the organization in which one holds that position, are less important than they would be for those who are more likely to define themselves on these bases. Understanding callings in the broader context of organizational life also yields opportunities to study what happens to callings in lean economic times. In economic environments that give rise to layoffs, it is possible that those with callings are both less likely to lose their jobs (if the positive performance effects of having a calling are predictive) and more likely to experience unemployment as a particularly hard time if they do lose their jobs.

Fourth, although this chapter has highlighted the role of callings in work, it would be unfortunate if research on callings advanced without an accompanying focus on other meanings of work. Research on the positive side of work and organizational life is incomplete without an anchoring in the full sweep of experience of these domains. Although callings represent one kind of relationship people can have with their work, just as worthy of study are relationships to work as a job, a career, or something else entirely. Callings help us to understand the nature of deep fulfillment and service to others in work. But many, even most, people who work do not have the luxury of finding, pursuing, enacting, or creating their callings (Berg et al., 2010; Wrzesniewski et al., 1997). Yet, each has a relationship to work that has meaning and is deserving of understanding. Indeed, any efforts to create conditions in which individuals may more likely to experience their work as a calling likely depend on understanding the kind of orientation toward work they currently have.

Fifth, recent research on moral psychology (e.g., Haidt, 2007) presents an interesting opportunity to understand the possible moral underpinnings of callings. Bunderson and Thompson (2009) suggest that callings may be experienced as a kind of moral imperative, in which individuals have a strong sense of duty, together with expectations that others should uphold the standards implied by a calling orientation. Haidt's emerging work on moral foundations of human cognition suggests that concerns regarding purity and sanctity underlie motivation to live life in a noble and elevated way (Haidt & Joseph, 2007). Future research should consider whether callings that represent either deep expressions of the self or the enactment of a life of service to others or to God may tap a fundamental moral foundation upon which people build their understanding of their actions.

To summarize, callings represent a unique and potentially multifaceted relationship between individuals and their work. Although promising progress is being made in understanding the antecedents of callings and especially the outcomes of callings, basic questions remain regarding their structure and function in social life. Their power in shaping the human experience of work has been established. What remains is the drive for explaining why, and how, callings exert the influence they do over our experience of work.

References

Aristotle. (1912). *Politics*. London: J.M.Dent and Sons.

Baker, W.E., & Dekas, K. (2009). *Examining the origins of work orientations*. Working paper.

Bandura, A. (1977). *Social learning theory*. Englewood Cliffs, NJ: Prentice-Hall.

Baumeister, R.F. (1991). *Meanings of life*. New York: The Guilford Press.

Bellah, R.N., Madsen, R., Sullivan, W.M., Swidler, A., & Tipton, S.M. (1985). *Habits of the heart: Individualism and commitment in American life*. New York: Harper and Row.

Berg, J.M., Grant, A.M., & Johnson, V. (2010). When callings are calling: Crafting work and leisure in pursuit of unanswered occupational callings. *Organization Science, 21*, 973–994.

Bocknek, G., & Perna, F. (1994). Studies in self-representation beyond childhood. In J.M. Masling, & R.F. Bornstein (Eds.), *Empirical perspectives on object relations theory* (pp. 29–58). Washington, DC: American Psychological Association.

Bourdieu, P., & Passeron, J.C. (1977). *Reproduction in education, society and culture*. London: Sage.

Bunderson, J.S., & Thompson, J.A. (2009). The call of the wild: Zookeepers, callings, and the dual edges of deeply meaningful work. *Administrative Science Quarterly, 54*, 32–57.

Casey, C. (1995). *Work, self, and society: After industrialism*. New York: Routledge.

Caza, B., & Cardador, T. (2009). *Sustaining a calling orientation toward work: The case for healthy vs. unhealthy callings*. Paper presented at Academy of Management Meetings, Chicago, IL.

Ciulla, J.B. (2000). *The working life: The promise and betrayal of modern work*. New York: Three Rivers Press.

Dik, B.J., & Duffy, R.D. (2009). Calling and vocation at work. *The Counseling Psychologist, 37*(3), 424–450.

Dobrow, S.R. (2004). *Extreme subjective career success: A new integrated view of having a calling*. Paper presented at the Academy of Management Conference, New Orleans.

Dobrow, S.R. (2006). *Having a calling: A longitudinal study of young musicians*. Doctoral dissertation, Harvard University, Cambridge, MA.

Dobrow, S.R. (2010a). *The dynamics of calling: A longitudinal study of musicians*. Working paper.

Dobrow, S.R. (2010b). *A siren song?: A longitudinal study of calling and ability (mis)perception in musicians' careers*. Working paper.

Dubin, R. (1956). Industrial workers' worlds: A study of the "central life interests" of industrial workers. *Social Problems, 3*, 131–142.

Dweck, C.S. (1986). Motivational processes affecting learning. *American Psychologist, 41*, 1040–1048.

Elangovan, A.R., Pinder, C.C., & McLean, M. (2010). Callings and organizational behavior. *Journal of Vocational Behavior, 76*(3), 428–440.

Grusec, J.E., & Kuczynski, L. (1997). *Parenting and children's internalization of values: A handbook of contemporary theory*. New York: John Wiley & Sons, Inc.

Haidt, J. (2007). The new synthesis in moral psychology. *Science, 316*, 998–1002.

Haidt, J., & Joseph, C. (2007). The moral mind: How 5 sets of innate moral intuitions guide the development of many culture-specific virtues, and perhaps even modules. In P. Carruthers, S. Laurence, & S. Stich (Eds.), *The innate mind*, Vol. 3 (pp. 367–391). New York: Oxford University Press.

Hall, D.T., & Chandler, D.E. (2005). Psychological success: When the career is a calling. *Journal of Organizational Behavior, 26*, 155–176.

Hardy, L. (1990). *The fabric of this world: Inquiries into calling, career choice, and the design of human work*. Grand Rapids, MI: W.B. Eerdmans Publishing Co.

Higgins, E.T., Fazio, R.H., Rohan, M.J., Zanna, M.P., & Gergen, K.J. (1998). From expectancies to worldviews: Regulatory focus in socialization and cognition. In J. Darley, & J. Cooper (Eds.), *Attribution and social interaction: The legacy of Edward E. Jones* (pp. 243–309). Washington, DC: American Psychological Association.

Kanungo, R.N. (1982). Measurement of job and work involvement. *Journal of Applied Psychology, 67*(3), 341–349.

Levoy, G. (1997). *Callings: Finding and following an authentic life*. New York: Three Rivers Press.

Lodahl, T.M., & Kejner, M. (1965). The definition and measurement of job involvement. *Journal of Applied Psychology, 49*(1), 24–33.

Loscocco, K.A. (1989). The interplay of personal and job characteristics in determining work commitment. *Social Science Research, 18*, 370–394.

Mannetti, L., & Tanucci, G. (1993). The meaning of work for young people: The role of parents in the transmission of a social representation. In G.M. Breakwell, & D.V. Canter (Eds.), *Empirical approaches to social representations* (pp. 298–314). Oxford: Clarendon Press/Oxford University Press.

Maslach, C., Schaufeli, W.B., & Leiter, M.P. (2001). Job burnout. *Annual Review of Psychology, 52*, 397–422.

Masling, J.M., & Bornstein, R.F. (1994). *Empirical perspectives on object relations theory*. Washington, DC: American Psychological Association.

Myers, V.L. (2007). An ontology of calling: Examining mechanisms and the transcendent possibilities of work orientation theory. *Critical Management Studies Conference Proceedings*. Manchester Business School. Manchester England.

Myers, V.L. (2009) What did Weber say? A comprehensive materialization of his implicit ontology and theory of calling. Research paper presented at *Academy of Management Annual Meetings*.

MOW International Research Team. (1987). *The meaning of working*. New York: Academic Press.

Nord, W.R., Brief, A.P., Atieh, J.M., & Doherty, E.M. (1990). Studying meanings of work: The case of work values. In A.P. Brief, & W.R. Nord (Eds.), *Meanings of occupational work* (pp. 21–64). Lexington, MA: Lexington Books.

Novak, M. (1996). *Business as a calling: Work and the examined life*. New York: The Free Press.

Oates, K.L.M., Hall, M.E.L., & Anderson, T.L. (2005). Calling and conflict: A qualitative exploration of interrole conflict and the sanctification of work in Christian mothers in academia. *Journal of Psychology and Theology, 33*, 210–223.

Perttula, K.H., & Cardon, M.S. (2011). Passion. In K.S. Cameron, & G. Spreitzer (Eds.), *Handbook of positive organizational scholarship*. Oxford: Oxford University Press.

Peterson, C., Park, N., Hall, N., & Seligman, M.E.P. (2009). Zest and work. *Journal of Organizational Behavior, 30*, 161–172.

Pratt, M.G., & Ashforth, B.E. (2003). Fostering meaningfulness in working and at work. In K.S. Cameron, J.E. Dutton, & R.E. Quinn (Eds.), *Positive organizational scholarship* (pp. 309–327). San Francisco: Berrett-Koehler Publishers, Inc.

Roberson, L. (1990). Functions of work meanings in organizations: Work meanings and work motivation. In A.P. Brief, & W.R. Nord (Eds.), *Meanings of occupational work* (pp. 107–134). Lexington, MA: Lexington Books.

Roberts, L.M., & Creary, S.J. (2010). Positive individual identities: Insights from classical and contemporary theoretical perspectives. In K.S., & G. Spreitzer (Eds.), *Handbook of positive organizational scholarship*. Oxford: Oxford University Press.

Robinson, R.V., & Garnier, M.A. (1985). Class reproduction among men and women in France: Reproduction theory on its home ground. *American Journal of Sociology, 91*, 250–280.

Rosso, B., Dekas, K., & Wrzesniewski, A. (2010). On the meaning of work: A theoretical integration and review. *Research in Organizational Behavior, 30*, 91–127.

Schor, J. (1992). *The overworked American: The unexpected decline in leisure*. New York: Basic Books.

Schwartz, B. (1986). *The battle for human nature: Science, morality, and modern life*. New York: Norton.

Schwartz, B. (1994). *The costs of living: How market freedom erodes the best things in life*. New York: Norton.

Scott Morton, F.M., & Podolny, J.M. (2002). Love or money? The effects of owner motivation in the California wine industry. *Journal of Industrial Economics, 50*(4), 431–456.

Sennett, R. (2005). *The culture of the new capitalism*. New Haven, CT: Yale University Press.

Sennett, R., & Cobb, R. (1972). *The hidden injuries of class*. New York: Random House.

Steger, M.F., Pickering, N.K., Shin, J.Y., & Dik, B.J. (2010). Calling in work: Secular or sacred? *Journal of Career Assessment, 18*(1), 82–96.

Tajfel, H., & Turner, J.C. (1979). An integrative theory of intergroup conflict. In W.G. Austin, & S. Worchel (Eds.), *The social psychology of intergroup relations* (pp. 33–47). Monterey, CA: Brooks-Cole.

Turner, J.C. (1987). *Rediscovering the social group: A self-categorization theory*. New York: Blackwell.

Treadgold, R. (1999). Transcendent vocations: Their relationship to stress, depression, and clarity of self-concept. *Journal of Humanistic Psychology, 39*, 81–105.

Vallerand, R.J., Blanchard, C., Mageau, G.A., Koestner, R., Ratelle, C., Leonard, M., et al. (2003). Les passions de l'ame: On obsessive and harmonious passion. *Journal of Personality and Social Psychology, 85*, 756–767.

Weber, M. (1958). *The Protestant ethic and the spirit of capitalism*. New York: Scribner.

Weber, M. (1963). *The sociology of religion*. Boston: Beacon.

Weiss, J.W., Skelley, M.F., Haughey, J.C., & Hall, D.T. (2004). Calling, new careers and spirituality: A reflective perspective for organizational leaders and professionals. In M.L. Pava & P. Primeaux (Eds.), *Spiritual intelligence at work: Meaning, metaphor and morals* (pp. 175–201). Amsterdam: Elsevier, Ltd.

Willis, P.E. (1977). *Learning to labor: How working class kids get working class jobs*. New York: Columbia University Press.

Wrzesniewski, A. (2002). "It's not just a job": Shifting meanings of work in the wake of 9/11. *Journal of Management Inquiry, 11*(2), 230–234.

Wrzesniewski, A. (2003). Finding positive meaning in work. In K.S. Cameron, J.E. Dutton, & R.E. Quinn (Eds.), *Positive organizational scholarship* (pp. 296–308). San Francisco: Berrett-Koehler Publishers, Inc.

Wrzesniewski, A., Dekas, K., & Rosso, B. (2009). Calling. In S.J. Lopez & A. Beauchamp (Eds.), *The encyclopedia of positive psychology* (pp. 115–118). Oxford: Blackwell Publishing.

Wrzesniewski, A., & Dutton, J.E. (2001). Crafting a job: Revisioning employees as active crafters of their work. *Academy of Management Review, 26*, 179–201.

Wrzesniewski, A., McCauley, C.R., Rozin, P., & Schwartz, B. (1997). Jobs, careers, and callings: People's relations to their work. *Journal of Research in Personality, 31*, 21–33.

Wrzesniewski, A., Rozin, P., & Bennett, G. (2002). Working, playing, and eating: Making the most of most moments. In C.L. M. Keyes, & J. Haidt (Eds.), *Flourishing: The positive person and the good life*. Washington, DC: American Psychological Association.

Wrzesniewski, A., Tosti, J., & Landman, J. (2011). *If I could turn back time: Occupational regret and its consequences for work and life*. Working paper.

Being There

Work Engagement and Positive Organizational Scholarship

Nancy P. Rothbard *and* Shefali V. Patil

Abstract

In this chapter, we examine the psychological state of employee work engagement. Our objective is to provide an overview of the engagement construct, clarify its definition, and discuss its behavioral outcomes. We discuss the development of the work engagement construct, which has led to many inconsistencies among scholars about its definition. We clarify that engagement captures employees' strong focus of attention, intense absorption, and high energy toward their work-related tasks. Work engagement is important to the positive organizational scholarship (POS) field because engagement can lead to a number of positive outcomes, such as in-role and extra-role performance, client satisfaction, proactivity, adaptivity, and creativity. Managers, however, must ensure that employees have adequate resources and sufficient breaks, so that engagement does not lead to burnout or depletion. We encourage scholars interested in studying engagement in the future to investigate the contextual moderators that affect the relationship between engagement and employee behavior and examine the differential effects of the components of engagement—attention, absorption, and energy.

Keywords: Engagement, energy, attention, absorption, internal resources

Today's dynamic and high-pressure workplace raises interesting questions about employee work engagement—the degree to which employees are focused on and present in their roles. Indeed, as the pace of work increases and the phenomenon of being available around the clock become more prevalent with the rise of smart phones and other technologies, the importance and the limitations of work engagement become even more central. On the one hand, being available 24/7 can facilitate work and create flexibility in one's life; but on the other hand, it can also threaten to strain employees' attentiveness and engagement with their work tasks as they reach their cognitive and motivational limits. The scholarly study of engagement in organizations has risen in popularity over the past several years (Rich, LePine, & Crawford, 2010). For example, engagement took center stage in Issue 1, Volume 1 of the newly

established journal, *Industrial and Organizational Psychology*, in which the opening article was devoted to an examination of the meaning of employee engagement (Macey & Schneider, 2008), followed by 13 commentaries on the topic.

Although generating a great deal of intellectual inquiry, research on engagement is still nascent and encompasses a broad array of constructs from traits, to psychological states, to behaviors (Macey & Schneider, 2008). In this chapter, we focus on engagement as a psychological state, and more specifically, engagement as psychological presence in a role. Engagement is important to organizational scholarship in particular because it is a psychological process that helps to explain the quality of participation in role activities (Rothbard, 2001). Especially in the context of studying positive organizational scholarship (POS), engagement may be a key ingredient for employee and organizational success.

Yet, even within research that examines engagement as a psychological state, inconsistencies in construct definition and measurement have arisen. Thus, in this chapter, we aim to outline the various ways psychological engagement has been defined and measured, consolidate and clarify these measurements and related constructs, and present a unified definition of the engagement construct as psychological presence in a role. We then describe the contributions of engagement to POS, with respect to behavioral outcomes of psychological engagement and what managers can do to foster engagement.

Development of the Work Engagement Construct

Recent interest in the study of work engagement has led to a proliferation of construct dimensions and operationalizations for measurement. Although scholars agree that engagement is a multidimensional construct, there is little consensus as to its dimensions and valid measurement (Macey & Schneider, 2008; Newman & Harrison, 2008). In an effort to provide construct clarity, we begin by reviewing the development of the psychological engagement construct and discuss the strengths and weaknesses of its current conceptualizations.

Kahn's (1990, 1992) examination of work engagement laid the groundwork for recent research on work engagement as a psychological state. Kahn (1990, p. 694) defined engagement as "the harnessing of organization members' selves to their work roles." Kahn (1992) suggests that engagement captures an employee's psychological presence, or "being there." Psychological presence is defined as the extent to which people are attentive, connected, integrated, and focused in their role performances. Engagement has important implications for an individual's own success and that of the organization. Indeed, Kahn (1992) states that engagement is a measure of "what enables the depths of workers' personal selves to come forth in the service of their own growth and development and that of their organizations" (Kahn, 1992, p. 322). It can also be seen as a negotiable relationship in which a person both drives personal energies into role behaviors (self-employment) and displays the self within the role (self-expression). As such, it explains the holistic investment of the self into one's work role (Ashforth & Humphrey, 1995; Goffman, 1961; Kahn, 1990). Seen in this way, engagement can be

differentiated from alienation at work (Blauner, 1964) or psychological absence. In such states of alienation, employees appear mechanical, robotic, and inauthentic (Hochschild, 1983), and estrange themselves from others (Seeman, 1975). In contrast, engaged employees are able to access their considerable energies and talents in the fulfillment of work-related tasks and goals.

Building on Kahn's (1990, 1992) work on psychological engagement and presence, Rothbard (2001, p. 656) defines engagement as "one's psychological presence in or focus on role activities." Rothbard (2001) draws on Kahn's notion that engagement and psychological presence involve being attentive and focused on a role and elaborates on this concept by suggesting that there are two critical components of role engagement: attention and absorption. Attention is defined by a person's cognitive availability and the amount of time one spends focused on a role. Absorption is defined by the intensity of the person's focus and the degree to which a person is engrossed in a role.

Approaching the construct of engagement from a different theoretical tradition, Maslach, Schaufeli, and colleagues conceptualized engagement as the opposite of job burnout. In their Maslach Burnout Inventory (MBI), Maslach and Leiter (1997) and Maslach, Schaufeli, and Leiter (2001) define job engagement as the opposite end of a continuum between engagement and burnout. They also define the engagement construct as an indicator of work-related well-being. Accordingly, they operationalize engagement in the following way: *Energy* is the opposite of exhaustion, *involvement* is the opposite of cynicism and depersonalization, and *efficacy* is the opposite of reduced professional efficacy. Initially using the same scale to measure burnout and engagement, they assumed that low scores on exhaustion, cynicism, and reduced professional efficacy would automatically imply engagement. In an important development, Schaufeli and colleagues proposed a new construct, based on the belief that the opposite of burnout did not necessarily capture the construct of engagement. In a measurement study in which they treated engagement and burnout as distinct factors, Schaufeli and Bakker (2004) recharacterized engagement as consisting of three dimensions: vigor, dedication, and absorption. *Vigor* refers to having high levels of energy and mental resilience; *dedication* refers to being challenged, inspired, and enthusiastic about one's work; and *absorption* is defined as fully concentrating and being engrossed in one's work. Schaufeli and Bakker (2003) conceptualize work engagement as the antipode of burnout and as a "positive, fulfilling, work-related state of mind characterized by . . . a more persistent and pervasive affective-cognitive state that is not focused on any particular object, event, individual, or behavior" (Schaufeli & Bakker, 2003, pp. 4–5).

Although several empirical studies have utilized the Schaufeli and Bakker (2004, 2003) measure, and the theoretical distinction between burnout and engagement is an important one, several problems have been identified with this approach and scale (Newman & Harrison, 2008; Rich, LePine, & Crawford, 2010; Zhang, Rich, & LePine, 2009). In particular, Zhang, Rich, and LePine (2009) argue that despite Schaufeli and colleagues' attempt to operationalize engagement as the positive antipode of burnout, the continued theoretical dependence on burnout constrains the incremental contributions to the literature. For example, in their handbook of the Utrecht Work Engagement Scale (UWES), Schaufeli and Bakker (2003) claim vigor and dedication are direct opposites of exhaustion and cynicism, two dimensions from Maslach's scale of burnout. Moreover, Zhang, Rich, and LePine (2009) argue that the highly correlated subdimensions of this measure prevent the concept from providing comprehensive analyses. In addition, the measurement of the Schaufeli and Bakker (2004, 2003) engagement subscales is problematic, in that the items that comprise the subdimensions of vigor, dedication, and absorption have conceptual overlap with other well-established constructs (Newman & Harrison, 2008). For example, the dedication scale has items such as "I am enthusiastic about my work" and "I am proud of the work that I do." Both of these items conceptually overlap with the notion of positive affect. Indeed, enthusiasm and pride are two of the items on the Positive Affect Negative Affect Scale (PANAS; Watson, Clark, & Tellegen, 1988). The conceptual overlap between these items in particular is problematic because confounding positive affect with engagement makes it very difficult to know what is driving the findings—positive affect or engagement. The other items on the dedication subdimension refer to the meaningfulness of and perceived challenge of work, both of which have been conceptualized as antecedents of engagement (Kahn, 1990). The vigor dimension also represents a mixing of constructs within the subscale by simultaneously referring to energy, perseverance, and resilience. The absorption subscale is the cleanest one, with the exception of one item "I feel happy when I am working intensely," which confounds

affect and engagement. Thus, the conceptual overlap with other constructs in the literature and the mixing of these constructs within the subscales makes interpretation of these dimensions problematic.

As a result, recent work by Rich and colleagues has gone back to the earlier theorizing of Kahn (1990, 1992) and Rothbard (2001) to develop a measure of engagement that includes three components: physical, emotional, and cognitive engagement (Rich, LePine, & Crawford, 2010). In their conceptualization, *physical* engagement involves the purposeful exertion of physical energy in one's role–it draws from Brown and Leigh's (1996) measure of work intensity. *Emotional* engagement involves high pleasantness and activation of positive affect in the work role. It is derived from Russell and Barrett's (1999) research on core affect and the generalized emotional state of pleasantness. Finally, *cognitive* engagement builds on Rothbard's (2001) scales of absorption and attention. Rich and colleagues have taken a meaningful step in measuring engagement as a construct that is broad and distinct from burnout. Moreover, going beyond Rothbard's (2001) more narrow conceptualization of engagement as a cognitive state to include physical energy is an additional strength of this paper. Moreover, as Spreitzer, Lam, and Quinn (2011; Chapter 12) discuss in this Handbook, energy is likely to be a subdimension of being engaged in one's work.

Two issues with this approach should be addressed. First, the emotional engagement subcomponent is difficult to disentangle from the construct of positive affect, as we have indicated in the discussion of the Schaufeli and Bakker measure. Indeed, affect may be a critical construct that relates to engagement in important ways (e.g., Rothbard, 2001). However, to build good theory about engagement, it is important to understand that positive and negative affect can both relate to engagement in important ways and that the combination of positive affect and engagement may result in very different outcomes than the combination of negative affect and engagement. In Rothbard's (2001) work on engagement in work and family roles, positive and negative affect from one role were both related to attention and absorption in that role, but had differential effects on attention and absorption in other roles. In other words, absorption and attention did not necessarily evoke a positive emotional state. It is possible that an employee could be very absorbed and attentive to a task but still feel frustrated and annoyed due to the difficulty of the task.

Second, although Rich et al. (2010) make distinctions among the physical, emotional, and cognitive components of engagement, they collapse the notions of attention and absorption into one construct within cognitive engagement, and on this six-item scale, only include one of the absorption items from Rothbard's (2001) scale. Thus, it is not surprising that they do not find a distinct factoring of attention and absorption within the cognitive engagement subscale. However, the evidence suggests that these two subdimensions of engagement are distinct and, although highly related to one another, can have different antecedents and outcomes (Perry-Smith & Dumas, 2010; Rothbard, 2001; Rothbard & Wilk, working paper).

In sum, we believe the Rich et al. (2010) approach is a step in the right direction. Based on the two issues discussed above, however, we propose that work engagement be conceptualized and measured such that there are three subcomponents: attention, absorption, and energy. Appendix 5.1 shows the items for each of these subscales. Moreover, we advocate careful attention to the way in which affect is used in modeling and theorizing about engagement.

Work Engagement and Related Constructs

Engagement is related to but distinct from other constructs in the literature. Macey and Schneider (2008) refer to several attitudes, such as organizational commitment, job satisfaction, and job involvement, that they include under a broad umbrella of state engagement. We take a different approach and contend that the distinctions between engagement and these related constructs are important particularly because these related constructs might be antecedents or outcomes of engagement.

First, engagement is distinct from organizational commitment and job satisfaction, both of which are attitudes toward the organization and job, respectively. These constructs differ from engagement in that engagement, defined as one's psychological presence in a role, is not an attitude (Saks, 2006). Moreover, engagement may result from greater organizational commitment and job satisfaction, as individuals may be willing to bring more of themselves to their work when they have a positive attitude toward their organization and the job.

Second, engagement also differs from the construct of job involvement. Lodahl and Kejner (1965) define job involvement as the importance of work to an employee and the effect his or her performance has on the individual's self-esteem.

Likewise, Kanungo (1982) defines job involvement as a cognition regarding one's psychological identification with his or her job, which is dependent on the individual's needs and the potential of the job to satisfy those needs. Fulfillment of these needs is consequently tied to one's self-image. In contrast, psychological engagement refers to the way in which individuals actually employ themselves during the performance of their work (Saks, 2006). It does not measure the reflection of needs fulfillment on the self. Moreover, May, Gilson, and Harter (2004) indicate that engagement may be an antecedent of job involvement—that is, increased cognitive availability and intensity of work performance can lead to the satisfaction of needs generated from job fulfillment. Alternatively, job involvement, defined as identification with a role, may be an antecedent to engagement in that those with greater psychological identification with a role and attachment to it may be more likely to be attentive and absorbed in the performance of that role (Rothbard, 2001).

Defining the Work Engagement Construct

As can be seen from the above discussion of engagement and related constructs, even within the perspective of engagement as a psychological state, the construct of engagement has been through considerable development and change. As such, we would like to be clear about our definition of work engagement. Consistent with the initial theorizing of Kahn (1990), the subsequent adaptation by Rothbard (2001), and work by Rich et al. (2010), we define individual work engagement as an employee's psychological presence in a role—or "being there." It is the person's focus of attention, their absorption, and their available energy directed toward work-related tasks.

In the process of defining engagement, we draw on work from various traditions. Of importance for POS, the construct of work engagement has roots in the notion of authenticity and the idea that there can be value in bringing one's whole self to work in terms of the types of resources (i.e., energy, perseverance, information) that can be harnessed to benefit the work. Kahn's (1990, 1992) definition of engagement captured the value of employing the whole self as "what enables the depths of workers' personal selves to come forth in the service of their own growth and development and that of their organizations" (Kahn, 1992, p. 322). In this way, engagement can be seen as a dynamic process in which a person both pours personal energies into role behaviors (self-employment) and displays the self within the role (self-expression), exhibiting a type of authenticity, or a true expression of their thoughts, feelings, and beliefs (Argyris, 1982).

In clarifying the definition of engagement, it is also important to note that engagement does not inherently mean the expression of "positive" affect. This stands in contrast to perspectives on engagement that equate engagement with high positive affect (e.g., Bakker & Oerlemans, 2011; Chapter 14). We propose that psychological presence conceived as focus of attention, absorption, and energy, and the notion of authentic self-expression can be associated with either positive or negative affect. In particular, one can be engaged in something because it is a problem that needs to be solved, and this can be associated with negative affect; or, one can be engaged in an activity that is joyful (Rothbard, 2001). Likewise, authenticity implies that the employee will express his or her true self at any point in time, as shown in Kahn's (1990, 1992) ethnographic studies of architecture workers and camp counselors. For example, Kahn found that an engaged senior designer at an architecture firm empathized with other people's positive or negative feelings, whereas a disengaged camp counselor became bland and superficial in addressing her campers (i.e., exhibiting affective neutrality). In these examples, engagement as represented in the senior designer example was expressed both as positive and negative affectivity, whereas disengagement was expressed as affective neutrality. The notion that engagement is conceptually distinct from positive and negative affectivity is an important one that should be taken seriously in future work on engagement as it has powerful implications for the outcomes of engagement. As we briefly discussed in the previous section, engagement that is associated with positive affect can lead to quite different outcomes from engagement associated with negative outcomes (Rothbard, 2001).

Additionally, in defining engagement, we want to reiterate that engagement is conceptually distinct from burnout and not simply the opposite of burnout. Although burnout is characterized by exhaustion, cynicism, and a decline in efficacy for a prolonged period of time (Schaufeli & Bakker, 2004), engagement represents a different motivational construct that involves a proactive garnering and application of resources to fully concentrate and dedicate oneself to a certain task. This conceptual distinction is especially important as too much engagement could potentially lead to burnout. We will continue this discussion of excessive, continuous engagement and burnout in our section on POS.

In sum, as we have defined it, the engagement construct consists of both cognitive and physical subcomponents. We suggest that scholars continue to examine two cognitive subcomponents—absorption and attention—as these have shown differential effects on outcomes (Rothbard, 2001). *Attention* refers to material resources within a person that can be applied to a given task. It is a resource-based motivational construct because it relies on the exertion of resources as a source of motivation. *Absorption*, on the other hand, refers to one's capacity and ability to apply those resources with intensity. Last, engagement consists of a physical component in the form of *energy* that can be directed toward a task.

Sustaining Engagement

Although up to this point we have concentrated solely on engagement as a static construct, there is a dynamic and temporal aspect of work engagement that should be examined as well. Questions of whether individuals can sustain high levels of engagement over time are critical to explore. Indeed, in one recent study of state engagement, being too engaged in work led to greater work–family interference (Halbesleben, Harvey, & Bolino, 2009), suggesting that there can be negative consequences of excessive focus on work. How, then, can engagement be effectively harnessed over time? Drazin, Glynn, and Kazanjian (1999) developed a theoretical argument about creative engagement at the group level and suggested that it is the *shifts* in (as opposed to sustained) engagement that are most beneficial for creativity. In contrast to being the opposite of burnout, sustained engagement could possibly lead to negative effects such as burnout (Kunda, 1992). Particularly with respect to groups with high collective engagement, individuals may alternate between episodes of intense individual work/concentration and downtime. In a recent study of software development teams, Metiu and Rothbard (working paper) found that individuals were highly engaged, but took "time-outs," breaks to replenish their energy and refocus. Such time-outs led to increased engagement and thus increased performance on the project team.

This notion that periods of disengagement or breaks can sustain engagement over time is consistent with research on recovery experiences (i.e., respite) and work engagement. For example, in a study of 527 Finnish employees, Sonnentag and

Fritz (2007) found that employees who tend to disconnect from their jobs when not at work are more likely to exhibit work engagement (Sonnentag, Niessen, & Neff, 2010). In Chapter 66 of this Handbook, Sonnentag, Niessen, and Neff discuss additional studies (e.g., Kuhnel & Sonnentag, in press; Sonnentag, 2003; Sonnentag & Bayer, 2005; Sonnentag, Binnewies, & Mojza, in press; Westman, 1999) that consistently demonstrate that psychological detachment from work can foster increased engagement with work over time.

The concept of breaks is also consistent with other research on the effects of scheduled downtime, social interactions with colleagues (Hollander, 1958), and informal joking (Bechky, 2006). Of course, in some groups, downtime is informally and naturally induced by group members to prevent boredom (Roy, 1959), whereas in other groups, downtime needs to be mandated or encouraged by management. Recent research on redesigning the workday advocates forced intermittent downtime (Elsbach & Hargadon, 2006), which challenges the general notion that job complexity at all times is a requirement for creativity (Oldham & Cummings, 1996). Levinthal and Rerup (2006) also discuss an analogous process of *mindlessness* (synonymous with disengagement) and *mindfulness* (synonymous with engagement) that follows a temporal approach. Interruptions in mindlessness lead to consciousness and then the subsequent adoption of new routines, a form of creativity (Cyert & March, 1963).

In addition to the importance of recovery and respite for energy replenishment at the general work and personal-being levels (Fritz & Sonnentag; 2005; Halbesleben, Harvey, & Bolino, 2009), scholars have also demonstrated the importance of respite at the task level. For example, experimental research has shown that disengaging from a core work problem and engaging in a distracting task is associated with better decision making on the initial set of complex problems (Dijksterhuis, Bos, Nordgren, & Van Baaren, 2006). Moreover, research finds that creative breakthroughs often occur after a break that follows an intense period of concentration because the break provides time for subconscious processing of the problem (Csikszentmihalyi & Sawyer, 1995). Thus, it is important for future research to conceptualize engagement, not as a continuous process filled with constant intensity, but rather as a noncontinuous process with intermittent exhibitions of disengagement followed by renewed focus.

Engagement and Positive Organizational Scholarship

Having defined what we mean by engagement—one's psychological presence in a role—we next consider why engagement has the potential to contribute to POS. Engagement in a role is thought to lead individuals to do their work in a way that better supports organizational effectiveness (Kahn, 1992; Saks, 2008). In some research, this has been taken to mean that engagement leads people to do what they are supposed to do in their roles better (Kahn, 1992; Saks, 2008), whereas in other research, engagement has been thought to lead employees to engage in discretionary behaviors beyond what they are supposed to do in their roles (e.g., Bakker, Demerouti, & Verbeke, 2004; Macey & Schneider, 2008). Both of these outcomes are central to further developing POS.

We illustrate how engagement, as a construct, fits into a positive view of organizational behavior by discussing the link between the psychological state of engagement and several behavioral outcomes, especially those highly relevant to POS scholars. Additionally, we discuss what managers can do to promote employee engagement in their workplaces, and therefore increase the likelihood that several positive behaviors will be exhibited by employees.

Engagement's Link to Positive Behavioral Outcomes

In the preceding discussion, we have discussed engagement as a psychological state—conceptualizing engagement as the *manner* or process in which work is conducted, not as a behavioral outcome (Saks, 2008; cf. Macey & Schneider, 2008). Investigating the behavioral outcomes of engagement is critically important to further understand the benefits of the engagement construct for scholarly research and the broader practical implications of engagement in today's workplace. In other words, what are the behavioral benefits of highly engaged employees? In the following section, we discuss several possible behaviors that may result from greater psychological engagement in work.

One key reason why engagement has captured the interests of scholars and managers is that across a wide array of studies using different operationalizations of engagement, many studies have demonstrated a positive relationship between engagement and performance. Specifically, engagement has been linked to increased in-role (Schaufeli, Taris, & Bakker, 2006) and extra-role behaviors (Macey &

Schneider, 2008; Bakker, Demerouti, & Verbeke, 2004). This translates into increased productivity and efficiency in increasingly competitive global work environments (Masson, Royal, Agnew, & Fine, 2008). Along these lines, engagement has been shown to lead to a variety of positive behaviors—increased task performance and exhibition of organizational citizenship behaviors (Rich et al., 2010), enhanced overall performance (Bakker & Demerouti, 2008; Schaufeli & Salanova, 2007), specific business-unit (Harter, Schmidt, & Hayes, 2002) and client-related performance (Salanova, Agut, & Peiro, 2005), and client satisfaction (Bakker & Demerouti, 2008). Last, Metiu and Rothbard (working paper) show that individual engagement can lead to group-level collective energy, in the form of mutual focus of attention, intensity of interactions among team members, increased coworker motivation, and positive interaction rituals.

The context or situation, such as the team or organization in which an individual works, can also moderate the effects of engagement on various behaviors. In other words, engagement may lead to different behavioral outcomes depending on the context. For example, Griffin, Parker, and Neal (2008) identify two key contextual moderators: uncertainty and interdependence. Under conditions of uncertainty, inputs, processes, and outputs of work systems lack predictability. In such situations, engagement may lead individuals to be more responsive and adaptive to change (Griffin et al., 2008; Saks, 2006) because they are vigilant and attentive to their work. Moreover, the focus of attention and cognitive availability of engaged employees may lead them to enact more proactive or anticipatory behaviors (Grant & Ashford, 2008) that can assist in dynamically creating emergent roles that are necessary for dealing with change and uncertainty (Saks, 2008). Thus, under conditions of uncertainty, engagement may lead to more proactive and adaptive behaviors. In contrast, under conditions of certainty, expectations are clear and predictable, and thus, engagement is likely to lead to better team and individual task performance because an individual's focus of attention can be directed toward the core tasks that comprise the job.

A second contextual moderator of the effects of engagement on behavioral outcomes is interdependence, in which individuals need to cooperate and coordinate in order to achieve shared goals (Bond & Smith, 1996). When interdependence is low, similar to situations of certainty and stability, engagement can lead to better individual task performance.

However, when interdependence is high, individual work engagement alone may not be enough to sustain group outcomes such as better team coordination, cooperation, and unification. Indeed, individual engagement may be a necessary but insufficient condition that needs to be coupled with shared and inspiring goals, identification with the group, and patterns of relational interaction that support such group-level outcomes (Metiu & Rothbard, working paper).

In addition to contextual moderators, the relationship between engagement and behaviors can be affected by which subcomponent of engagement is primarily activated. Engagement is defined as people's focus of attention, their absorption, and their available energy directed toward work-related tasks. Attention captures both an inward and outward focus and is likely to lead to better task performance and impression management. In particular, Rothbard and Wilk (working paper) find that employee attention, but not absorption, is significantly related to supervisors' perceptions of the employee's engagement. This is perhaps because attentive employees are vigilant about their task, but also about the workplace around them and may be more likely to engage in impression management techniques to control other's perceptions of them than those who are less attentive or than those who are highly absorbed in their work. Indeed, the items often used to measure absorption refer to being engrossed and losing track of time. Absorption, the second component of engagement, has an inward focus, and while it may not lead to better impression management and perceived performance (Rothbard & Wilk, working paper), it may very well lead to greater creativity, which can benefit from more solitary and intense idea generation (Griffin et al., 2008). The proposed relationship between absorption and creativity is similar to the studies on independent brainstorming and idea generation, in which production of ideas is greater when individuals work alone to brainstorm (Diehl & Stroebe, 1987). Individuals who are absorbed in their work and working alone may be less likely to engage in negative social behaviors such as social loafing (Diehl & Stroebe, 1987) and groupthink (Aldag & Fuller, 1993), thus increasing their concentration and subsequent creativity.

Last, engagement is characterized by high energy. This high energy may fuel extra-role, proactive behaviors (Grant & Ashford, 2008), such as organizational citizenship behaviors (Organ, 1988), seeking feedback (Ashford, Blatt, & VandeWalle, 2003), taking initiative in pursuing personal and organizational goals (Frese & Fay, 2001), expressing voice (LePine & Van Dyne, 2001), taking charge (Morrison & Phelps, 1999), and crafting jobs (Wrzesniewski & Dutton, 2001). Such proactive behaviors may require "extra" energy outside of that which is required for the completion of specified tasks, and highly engaged employees who have greater amounts of energy may be more capable of meeting those "extra" energy requirements.

The Downside to Engagement: Burnout and Workaholism

Although engagement can lead to many positive behavioral outcomes, as we have discussed above, it is important to acknowledge that there may be downsides to engagement. In particular, there may be detrimental effects of too much engagement, without the opportunity for recovery and respite. Indeed, too much work engagement may result in both burnout and workaholism, an extreme, negative form of engagement.

First, there may be an upper limit for how engaged individuals can be without having effects on strain, time allocation, and functioning in other roles. Recent research, drawing on conservation of resources theory, shows that, for some employees, being highly engaged at work is associated with greater work–family and strain-based conflict (Halbesleben, Harvey, & Bolino, 2009). Moreover, if engagement leads to negative affect in a particular situation, even a moderate level of engagement may be depleting, leading to lower levels of attention, absorption, and energy overall (Rothbard, 2001).

Second, too much engagement at work may be evidenced by workaholics, who tend to be very absorbed and attentive employees who are devoted to their jobs, often working long hours without breaks. When engagement is associated with the pressing, almost addicting need to work (Bonebright, Clay, & Ankenmann, 2000) and the sacrifice of family and social lives for the sake of work, it may lead to negative outcomes for the individual. However, it is important to note that there is an important distinction between engagement and workaholism. Although engagement is an intermittent motivational state, workaholism is a stable, steady, and sustained outlook on work. This is why workaholism has been shown to lead to poor mental health; extreme perfectionism (and decreased self-esteem for not reaching high goals); social and relationship problems, particularly with respect to work–family conflict (Bakker, Demerouti, & Burke,

2009); and overall poor psychological and physical well-being (Burke & Matthiesen, 2004). Moreover, workaholics have been shown to have long-term health problems and suffer from eventual burnout (Piotrowski & Vodanovich, 2008). Importantly, we view the relationship between work engagement and workaholism as correlational and not causal. The antecedents of workaholism are distinct from engagement, but if engagement is associated with workaholic behaviors, then deleterious outcomes may result.

What Managers Can Do to Increase Engagement

If engagement is likely to lead to several positive behaviors, it is important for us to understand what managers can do to encourage greater engagement while recognizing the importance of respite and recovery. First, a key factor for increasing work engagement is psychological safety (Kahn, 1990). *Psychological safety* refers to being able to employ one's self without fear of negative consequences to self-image, status, or career—it allows an employee or team member to engage in interpersonal risk-taking (Edmondson, 1999). When employees perceive psychological safety, they are less likely to be distracted by negative emotions such as fear, which stem from worrying about controlling perceptions of managers and colleagues. In addition to being a significant distraction, dealing with fear requires intense emotional regulation (Barsade, Brief, & Spataro, 2003), which takes away from the ability of an individual to fully immerse him or herself in his or her work tasks. Psychological safety, on the other hand, decreases such distracters and allows an employee to expend his or her energy toward being absorbed and attentive to work tasks. Managers can initiate psychological safety in the workplace by introducing effective structural features, such as coaching leadership and context support (Hackman, 1987). Team leader behavior can greatly influence the behavior of members, leading to greater trust (Tyler & Lind, 1992). Supportive, coaching-oriented, and nondefensive responses to employee concerns and questions can lead to heightened feelings of security, as opposed to authoritarian and punitive leadership (Edmondson,1996). Autonomy, especially in decision-making (Salanova, Agut, & Peiro, 2005), and feedback from coaches (in the form of information and rewards) also leads to such safety (Bakker & Demerouti, 2008; Edmondson, 1999; May, Gilson, & Harter, 2004) and consequently increased work engagement.

A second factor for increasing work engagement is the *balance* between the demands and resources that an employee has. Job demands often stem from time pressures, high-priority work, shift work, and physical demands. Both demands and resources can increase engagement, but it is important that employees perceive that they have sufficient resources to deal with their work demands (Rich et al., 2010). Challenging demands require that employees be more attentive and absorbed, and direct more energy toward their work. These high demands can often be an energizing force themselves, by helping employees achieve their goals and by stimulating their personal growth (Bakker & Demerouti, 2008). But, such energy will be depleting, if employees perceive that they do not have enough control to tackle these challenging demands (Karasek, 1979). Perceived control is increased with the granting of sufficient resources, such as managerial and collegial support. Similar to the effects of psychological safety, adequate resources ensure that employees are not hindered by distracters that can limit the attention, absorption, and energy that they put toward their work. Sufficient resources are thus especially crucial to sustaining a positive level of engagement that does not eventually lead to discouragement or burnout. The relationship between adequate resources and engagement has been discussed by Demerouti, Bakker, Nachreiner, and Schaufeli's (2001) Job Demand–Resources (JD-R) occupational stress model, which suggests that job demands that force employees to be attentive and absorbed can be depleting, if not coupled with adequate resources. The relationship has also been evidenced in a 2-year longitudinal study of Finnish health care workers: Having adequate job resources was a strong predictor of work engagement (Mauno, Kinnunen, & Ruokolainen, 2007; also see Hakanen, Bakker, & Schaufeli, 2006 and Salanova & Schaufeli, 2008). Therefore, managers should ensure that the resources they provide for their employees are commensurate with the demands placed on them.

Another set of factors that are critical for increasing work engagement involve core self-evaluations and self-concept (Judge & Bono, 2001). Self-esteem, efficacy, locus of control, identity, and perceived social impact may be critical drivers of an individual's psychological availability as evident in the attention, absorption, and energy directed toward their work. Self-esteem and efficacy are enhanced by increasing employees' general confidence in their abilities (Rich et al., 2010), which in turn assists in making them feel secure about themselves and less

self-conscious about how other people are perceiving or judging them (Kahn, 1990). Employees also gain increased control and efficacy when they perceive that they are receiving important returns on their physical, cognitive, and emotional investments (Kahn, 1990). Managers can attain this by increasing the significance of their task (i.e., the extent to which the job improves the welfare of others (Hackman & Oldham, 1976)). When employees see their tasks as significant, they feel that their own actions are improving the welfare of others (Grant, 2007, 2008; Small & Loewenstein, 2003). Finally, core self-evaluations can be enhanced by increasing an employee's identity with his or her role (May et al., 2004). This can be done by increasing employee opportunities for job enrichment and increasing the internalization of organizational goals, so that employees perceive deep meaning in their work. By increasing employee core self-evaluations, managers are ensuring that employees will want to *intrinsically* feel motivated to engage in their work, and will feel they are capable of exerting such high energy in their jobs.

Future Directions

Throughout this chapter, we have mentioned numerous directions for future research on work engagement. Because engagement is a psychological state that focuses on attention, absorption, and energy directed toward work, we see this construct as an important and central one for research in organizational behavior and positive organizational behavior, in particular. To push forward research in this area, we focus on six issues that warrant more attention.

Measuring Engagement

We have discussed several approaches that scholars have used to measure engagement and the benefits and drawbacks of each. We suggest that researchers continue to explore multiple dimensions of engagement, but focus on the three subcomponents shown in Appendix 5.1 (attention, absorption, and energy).

Subcomponents of Engagement

Similarly, given that some empirical evidence also suggests that the specific subcomponents of engagement have different effects on behavioral outcomes, we propose that future research look more closely at these relationships. For example, it is possible that intense absorption is coupled with decreased impression management behaviors, such as boasting about one's accomplishments (Ferris, Judge, Rowland, &

Fitzgibbons, 1994), which causes managers to perceive absorbed employees less positively (Rothbard & Wilk, working paper). On the other hand, attentive employees are perhaps more vigilant about their task and the workplace around them, making them more likely to engage in impression management techniques to control other's perceptions of them. High energy, the third component of engagement, may be related to other behaviors, such as proactive behaviors that require "extra energy." Thus, we encourage future scholars to examine the outcomes that result from each of the subcomponents of engagement, rather than simply aggregating them into an overarching construct, unless they do indeed operate similarly.

Contextual Moderators

We have discussed a few contextual moderators of the relationship between engagement and behaviors; namely, uncertainty and interdependence (Griffin et al., 2008). We encourage scholars to continue to search for additional contextual moderators of the relationship between engagement and behavioral outcomes. Some potential moderators include task-related moderators, such as routine versus creative or complex work assignments; group-related moderators, such as temporary versus permanent work groups; and organization-related moderators, such as security and psychological safety that might result from downsizing versus job-secure organizations.

Longitudinal Designs

In discussing several potential antecedents and consequences of engagement, such as organizational commitment, job satisfaction, and role performance, we noted that it is highly likely that these constructs relate to one another in a dynamic fashion, such that they are reciprocally related to engagement. Figure 5.1 provides a diagram of these proposed relationships. However, future research should examine these dynamic relationships empirically to help us better understand the role that engagement plays as a process linking important organizational antecedents and outcomes. An important way to do so is to examine the relationships between engagement and related constructs over time. We encourage scholars to utilize longitudinal designs to examine the ebb and flow of engagement in future research. It would also be interesting to explore if and how each of the subcomponents of engagement—attention, absorption, and energy—are affected over time and in similar or different ways.

Levels of Analysis

Most research on engagement to date has examined it as an individual-level construct; however, engagement can also be exhibited at the group and organizational levels of analysis. At the group-level of analysis, very recent empirical work (Metiu & Rothbard, working paper) demonstrates the nonadditive effects (Hertel, Kerr, & Messe, 2000;

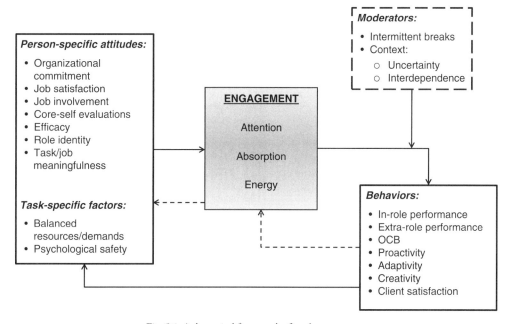

Fig. 5.1 A theoretical framework of work engagement.

Kohler, 1926) of individual engagement on group engagement for a team working on a complex task. However, more work needs to be done to understand what the antecedents and consequences of engagement at the individual, group, and organizational levels are.

Conclusion

Work engagement is an important construct that can lead to a number of positive outcomes, such as in-role and extra-role performance, client satisfaction, proactivity, adaptivity, and creativity. Managers, however, must ensure that employees have adequate resources and sufficient breaks, as well as psychological safety, so that engagement does not lead to burnout, depletion, or distraction. We encourage scholars interested in studying engagement in the future to investigate the contextual moderators that affect the relationship between engagement and employee behavior and to examine the differential effects of the components of engagement: attention, absorption, and energy. It is an exciting time to be engaged in research on engagement.

References

Aldag, R.J., & Fuller, S.R. (1993). Beyond fiasco: A reappraisal of the groupthink phenomenon and a new model of group decision processes. *Psychological Bulletin, 113*, 553–552.

Argyris, C. (1982). *Reasoning, learning, and action: Individual and organizational,* San Francisco: Jossey-Bass.

Ashford, S.J., Blatt, R., & VandeWalle, D. (2003). Reflections on the looking glass: A review of research on feedback-seeking behavior in organizations. *Journal of Management, 29*, 773–799.

Ashforth, B., & Humphrey, R. (1995). Emotion in the workplace: A reappraisal. *Human Relations, 48*(2), 97–125.

Bakker, A.B., & Demerouti, E. (2008). Towards a model of work engagement. *Career Development International, 13*, 209–223.

Bakker, A.B., Demerouti, E., & Burke, R. (2009). Workaholism and relationship quality: A spillover-crossover perspective. *Journal of Occupational Health Psychology, 14*(1), 23–33.

Bakker, A.B., Demerouti, E., & Verbeke, W. (2004). Using the job demands–resources model to predict burnout and performance. *Human Resource Management, 43*(1), 83–104.

Bakker, A.B., & Demerouti, E. (2008). Towards a model of work engagement. *Career Development International, 13*, 209–223.

Bakker, A.B., & Oerlemans, W.G.M. (2011). Subjective well-being in organizations. In K. Cameron & G. Spreitzer (Eds.), *Handbook of Positive Organizational Scholarship.* Oxford University Press.

Barsade, S.G., Brief, A.P., & Spataro, S.E. (2003). The affective revolution in organizational behavior: The emergence of a paradigm. In J. Greenberg (Ed.), *OB: The state of the science* (2nd ed., pp. 3–52). Hillsdale, NJ: L. Erlbaum Associates.

Blauner, B. (1964). *Alienation and freedom: The factory worker and his industry.* Chicago: University of Chicago Press.

Bond, R.A., & Smith, P.B. (1996). Culture and conformity: A meta-analysis of studies using Asch's (1952, 1956) line judgment task. *Psychological Bulletin, 119*, 111–137.

Bonebright, C.A., Clay, D.L., & Ankenmann, R.D. (2000). The relationship of workaholism with work-life conflict, life satisfaction, and purpose in life. *Journal of Counseling Psychology, 47*(4), 469–477.

Brown, S.P., & Leigh, T.W. (1996). A new look at psychological climate and its relationship to job involvement, effort, and performance. *Journal of Applied Psychology, 81*, 358–368.

Burke, R.J., & Matthiesen, S.B. (2004). Workaholism among Norwegian journalists: Antecedents and consequences. *Stress and Health, 20*, 301–308.

Csikszentmihalyi, M., & Sawyer, K. (1995). Creative insight: The social dimension of a solitary moment. In R. Steinberg, & J. Davidson (Eds.), *The nature of insight* (pp. 329–361). Cambridge, MA: MIT Press.

Cyert, R.M., & March, J.G. (1963). *A behavioral theory of the firm.* Englewood Cliffs, NJ: Prentice-Hall.

Demerouti, E., Bakker, A.B., Nachreiner, F., & Schaufeli, W.B. (2001). The job demands-resources model of burnout. *Journal of Applied Psychology, 86*(3), 499–512.

Diehl, M., & Stroebe, W. (1987). Productivity loss in brainstorming groups: Toward the solution of a riddle. *Journal of Personality and Social Psychology, 53*(3), 497–509.

Dijksterhuis, A., Bos, M.W., Nordgren, L.F., & van Baaren, R.B. (2006). On making the right choice: The deliberation-without-attention effect. *Science, 311*, 1005–1007.

Drazin, R., Glynn, M.A., & Kazanjian, R.K. (1999). Multilevel theorizing about creativity in organizations: A sensemaking perspective. *Academy of Management Review, 24*, 286–307.

Edmondson, A.C. (1996). *Group and organizational influences on team learning.* Unpublished doctoral dissertation, Harvard University, Boston.

Edmondson, A. (1999). Psychological safety and learning behavior in work teams. *Administrative Science Quarterly, 44*, 350–383.

Elsbach, K.D., & Hargadon, A.B. (2006). Enhancing creativity through "mind-less" work: A framework of workday design. *Organization Science, 17*, 470–483.

Ferris, G.R., Judge, T.A., Rowland, K.M., & Fitzgibbons, D.E. (1994). Subordinate influence and the performance evaluation process: Test of a model. *Organizational Behavior and Human Decision Processes, 58*, 101–135.

Frese, M., & Fay, D. (2001). Personal initiative (PI): A concept for work in the 21st century. *Research in Organizational Behavior, 23*, 133–188.

Fritz, C., & Sonnentag, S. (2005). Recovery, well-being and job performance: Effects of weekend experiences. *Journal of Occupational Health Psychology, 10*, 187–199.

Goffman, E. (1961). *Asylums.* Harmondsworth, UK: Penguin Press.

Grant, A.M. (2007). Relational job design and the motivation to make a prosocial difference. *Academy of Management Review, 32*, 393–417.

Grant, A.M. (2008). The significance of task significance: Job performance effects, relational mechanisms, and boundary conditions. *Journal of Applied Psychology, 93*, 108–124.

Grant, A.M., & Ashford, S.J. (2008). The dynamics of proactivity at work. *Research in Organizational Behavior, 28*, 3–34.

Griffin, M.A., Parker, S.K., & Neal, A. (2008). Is behavioral engagement a distinct and useful construct? *Industrial and Organizational Psychology, 1*, 48–51.

Hackman, J.R. (1987). The design of work teams. In J.W.E. Lorsch (Ed.), *Handbook of Organizational Behavior*. Englewood Cliffs, NJ: Prentice-Hall.

Hackman, J.R., & Oldham, G.R. (1976). Motivation through the design of work: Test of a theory. *Organizational Behavior and Human Performance, 16*, 250–279.

Hakanen, J.J., Bakker, A.B., & Schaufeli, W.B. (2006). Burnout and work engagement among teachers. *Journal of School Psychology, 43*, 495–513.

Halbesleben, J.R., Harvey, J., & Bolino, M.C. (2009). Too engaged? A conservation of resources view of the relationship between work engagement and work interference with family. *Journal of Applied Psychology, 94*(6), 1452–1465.

Harter, J.K., Schmidt, F.L., & Hayes, T.L. (2002). Business-unit-level relationship between employee satisfaction, employee engagement, and business outcomes: A metaanalysis. *Journal of Applied Psychology, 87*, 268–279.

Hertel, G., Kerr, N.L., & Messe, L.A. (2000). Motivation gains in performance groups: Paradigmatic and theoretical developments on the Kohler effect. *Journal of Personality and Social Psychology 79*(4), 580–601.

Hollander, E.P. (1958). Conformity, status, and idiosyncrasy credit. *Psychological Review, 65*, 117–127.

Hochschild, A.R. (1983). *The managed heart: Commercialization of human feeling*. Berkeley: University of California Press.

Judge, T.A., & Bono, J.E. (2001). Relationship of core self-evaluations traits–self-esteem, generalized self-efficacy, locus of control, and emotional stability–with job satisfaction and job performance: A meta-analysis. *Journal of Applied Psychology, 86*, 80–92.

Kahn, W.A. (1990). Psychological conditions of personal engagement and disengagement at work. *Academy of Management Journal, 33*, 692–724.

Kahn, W.A. (1992). To be fully there: Psychological presence at work. *Human Relations, 45*(4), 321–349.

Kanungo, R.N. (1982). *Work alienation: An integrative approach*. New York: Praeger Publishers.

Karasek, R. (1979). Job demands, job decision latitude and mental strain: Implications for job redesign. *Administrative Science Quarterly, 24*, 285–306.

Kohler, O. (1926). Kraftleistungen bei Einzel- und gruppenarbeit [Physical performance in individual and group situations]. *Industrielle Psychotechnik 3*, 274–282.

Kuhnel, J., & Sonnentag, S. (in press). How long do you benefit from vacation? A closer look at the fade-out of vacation effects. *Journal of Organizational Behavior*.

Kunda, G. (1992). *Engineering culture: Control and commitment in a high tech corporation*. Philadelphia: Temple University Press.

LePine, J.A., & Van Dyne, L. (2001). Voice and cooperative behavior as contrasting forms of contextual performance: Evidence of differential relationships with big five personality characteristics and cognitive ability. *Journal of Applied Psychology, 86*(2), 326–336.

Levinthal, D.A., & Rerup, C. (2006). Crossing an apparent chasm: Bridging mindful and less-mindful perspectives on organizational learning, *Organization Science, 17*(4), 502–513.

Lodahl, T.M., & Kejner, M. (1965). The definition and measurement of job involvement. *Journal of Applied Psychology, 49*, 24–33.

Macey, W.H., & Schneider, B. (2008). The meaning of employee engagement. *Industrial and Organizational Psychology, 1*, 3–30.

Maslach, C., Schaufeli, W.B., & Leiter, M.P. (2001). Job burnout. In S.T. Fiske, D.L. Schacter, & C. Zahn-Waxler (Eds.), *Annual Review of Psychology, 52*, 397–422.

Masson, R.C., Royal, M.A., Agnew, T.G., & Fine, S. (2008). Leveraging employee engagement: The practical implications. *Industrial and Organizational Psychology, 1*, 56–59.

Mauno, A., Kinnunen, U., & Ruokolainen, M. (2007). Job demands and resources as antecedents of work engagement: A longitudinal study. *Journal of Vocational Behavior, 70*, 149–171.

May, D.R., Gilson, R.L., & Harter, L.M. (2004). The psychological conditions of meaningfulness, safety and availability and the engagement of the human spirit at work. *Journal of Occupational and Organizational Psychology, 77*, 11–37.

Metiu, A., & Rothbard, N.P. (working paper). More than just the sum of the parts: How individual engagement and disengagement give rise to group engagement.

Morrison, E.W., & Phelps, C. (1999). Taking charge: Extra-role efforts to initiate workplace change. *Academy of Management Journal, 42*, 403–419.

Newman, D.A., & Harrison, D.A. (2008). Been there, bottled that: Are state and behavioral work engagement new and useful construct "wines"? *Industrial and Organizational Psychology, 1*, 31–35.

Oldham, G.R., & Cummings, A. (1996). Employee creativity: Personal and contextual factors at work. *Academy of Management Journal, 39*, 607–634.

Organ, D.W. (1988). *Organizational citizenship behavior—The good soldier syndrome*. (1st ed.). Lexington, MA/Toronto: D.C. Heath and Company.

Perry-Smith, J., & Dumas, T.L. (working paper). Debunking the ideal worker myth: The effects of family configuration and temporal flexibility on work engagement.

Piotrowski, C., & Vodanovich, S.J. (2008). The workaholism syndrome: An emerging issue in the psychological literature. *Journal of Instructional Psychology, 35*(1), 103–105.

Rich, B.L., LePine, J.A., & Crawford, E.R. (2010). Job engagement: Antecedents and effectson job performance. *Academy of Management Journal, 53*(3), 617–635.

Rothbard, N.P. (2001). Enriching or depleting? The dynamics of engagement in work and family roles. *Administrative Science Quarterly, 46*, 655–684.

Rothbard, N.P., & Wilk, S.L. (working paper). In the eye of the beholder: The relationship between employee and supervisor perceptions of engagement and their effect on performance.

Roy, D.F. (1959). Banana time: Job satisfaction and informal interaction. *Human Organization, 18*(4), 158–168.

Russell, J.A., & Barrett, L.F. (1999). Core affect, prototypical emotional episodes, and other things called emotion: Dissecting the elephant. *Journal of Personality and Social Psychology, 76*(5), 805–819.

Saks, A.M. (2006). Multiple predictors and criteria of job search success. *Journal of Vocational Behavior, 68*, 400–415.

Saks, A.M. (2008). The meaning and bleeding of employee engagement: How muddy is the water? *Industrial and Organizational Psychology, 1*, 40–43.

Salanova, M., Agut, S., & Perió, J.M. (2005). Linking organizational resources and work engagement to employee performance and customer loyalty: The mediation of service climate. *Journal of Applied Psychology, 90*, 1217–1227.

Salanova, M., & Schaufeli, W.B. (2008). A cross-national study of work engagement as a mediator between job resources and proactive behavior: A cross-national study. *International Journal of Human Resources Management, 19*, 226–231.

Schaufeli, W., & Bakker, A. (2003). *Utrecht work engagement scale*. Preliminary manual. Occupational Health Psychology Unit: Utrecht University, Holland.

Schaufeli, W., & Bakker, A. (2004). Job demands, job resources, and their relationship with burnout and engagement: A multi-sample study. *Journal of Organizational Behavior, 25*, 293–315.

Schaufeli, W.B., & Salanova, M. (2007). Efficacy or inefficacy, that's the question: Burnout and work engagement, and their relationships with efficacy beliefs. *Anxiety, Stress, and Coping, 20*(2), 177–196.

Schaufeli, W.B., Taris, T.W., & Bakker, A. (2006). Dr. Jekyll and Mr. Hide: On the differences between work engagement and workaholism. In R. Burke (Ed.), *Work hours and work addiction* (pp. 193–252). Northhampton, UK: Edward Elgar.

Seeman, M. (1975). Alienation Studies. *Annual Review of Sociology, 1*, 91–123.

Small, D.A., & Loewenstein, G. (2003). Helping a victim or helping the victim: Altruism and identifiability. *Journal of Risk and Uncertainty, 26*(1), 5–16.

Sonnentag, S. (2003). Recovery, work engagement, and proactive behavior: A new look at the interface between non-work and work. *Journal of Applied Psychology, 88*, 518–528.

Sonnentag, S., & Bayer, U. (2005). Switching off mentally: Predictors and consequences of psychological detachment from work during off-job time. *Journal of Occupational Health Psychology, 10*(4), 393–414.

Sonnentag, S., Binnewies, C., & Mojza, E.J. (in press). Staying well and engaged when demands are high: The role of psychological detachment. *Journal of Applied Psychology.*

Sonnentag, S., & Fritz, C. (2007). The recovery experience questionnaire: Development and validation of a measure for assessing recuperation and unwinding from work. *Journal of Occupational Health Psychology, 12*(3), 204–221.

Sonnentag, S., Niessen, C., & Neff, A. (2010). Recovery: Non-work experiences that promote positive states. In K. Cameron, & G. Spreitzer (Eds.), *Handbook of positive organizational scholarship*. Oxford University Press.

Spreitzer, G.M., Lam, C.F., & Quinn, R. (2010). Human energy in organizations: Implications for POS from six interdisciplinary streams. In K. Cameron, & G. Spreitzer (Eds.), *Handbook of positive organizational scholarship*. Oxford University Press.

Tyler, T.R., & Lind, E.A. (1992). A relational model of authority in groups. *Advances in Experimental Social Psychology, 25*, 115–191.

Watson, D., Clark, L.A., & Tellegen, A. (1988). Development and validation of brief measures of positive and negative affect: The PANAS scales. *Journal of Personality and Social Psychology, 54*, 1063–1070.

Westman, J.A. (1999). A test for the future. *Gynecologic Oncology, 74*(3), 329–330.

Wrzesniewski, A., & Dutton, J.E. (2001). Crafting a job: Revisioning employees as active crafters of their work. *Academy of Management Review, 26*(2), 179–201.

Zhang, Y., Rich, B.L., & LePine, J.A. (2009). Transformational leadership and job performance: The mediating role of job engagement. Presented in an interactive paper session at the annual meeting of the Academy of Management, Chicago, August 8–11.

Appendix 5.1

Work Engagement Scale
Attention
(*from Rothbard, 2001*)
I spend a lot of time thinking about my work.
I focus a great deal of attention on my work.
I concentrate a lot on my work.
I pay a lot of attention to my work.

Absorption
(*from Rothbard, 2001*)
When I am working, I often lose track of time.
I often get carried away by what I am working on.
When I am working, I am completely engrossed by my work.
When I am working, I am totally absorbed by it.
Nothing can distract me when I am working.

Energy
(*from Rich, LePine, & Crawford, 2010*)
I work with intensity on my job.
I exert my full effort to my job.
I devote a lot of energy to my job.
I try my hardest to perform well on my job.
I strive as hard as I can to complete my job.
I exert a lot of energy on my job.

Positive Identity Construction

Insights from Classical and Contemporary Theoretical Perspectives

Laura Morgan Roberts *and* Stephanie J. Creary

Abstract

This chapter develops a more comprehensive theory of positive identity construction by explicating proposed mechanisms for constructing and sustaining positive individual identities. The chapter offers a broad, illustrative sampling of mechanisms for positive identity construction that are grounded in various theoretical traditions within identity scholarship. Four classical theories of identity—social identity theory, identity theory, narrative-as-identity, and identity work—offer perspectives on the impetus and mechanisms for positive identity construction. The Dutton et al. (2010) typology of positive identity is revisited to highlight those sources of positivity that each classical theory explains how to enhance. As a next step in research, positive organizational scholarship (POS) scholars and identity scholars are encouraged to examine the conditions under which increasing the positivity of an identity is associated with generative social outcomes (e.g., engaging in prosocial practices, being invested in others' positive identity development, and deepening mutual understanding of the complex, multifaceted nature of identity).

Keywords: Identity, positive identity, identity construction, positive organizational scholarship, generative outcomes

Identities situate an entity within a social world through the construction of defining characteristics and relationships with other entities; they also evoke a set of cognitions, feelings, and behaviors that are associated with such characteristics and relationships. The study of identity reveals the meaning and significance of such self-relevant constructions for both individuals and organizations. In this chapter, we explore the intersection between positive organizational scholarship (POS) and individual identities.

Within the vast domain of identity research, general agreement exists that most individuals seek to hold positive self-views (Gecas, 1982), desire to be viewed positively by others (Swann, Pelham, & Krull, 1989), and, as a result, seek to construct positive identities—those that consist of a self-definition that is favorable or valuable in some way (Dutton & Roberts, 2009). Yet, the vast amount of research in the identity domain has also made it difficult to

discern what might be "positive" about identity. The POS lens on "positive identity" reflects an intentional inquiry into the sources of positivity for identity and the mechanisms for positive identity construction. Building upon the body of work on positive identities and organizations (see Dutton, Roberts, & Bednar, 2010; Roberts & Dutton, 2009), we first describe the various ways in which an individual might derive a positive sense of self at work. We then examine the proposed mechanisms for constructing and sustaining positive individual identities that are embedded in theoretical approaches toward the study of identity in organizations. Each of the classical theories of identity that we review—social identity theory, identity theory, narrative-as-identity, and identity work—offers a perspective on the ways in which positive identities are shaped, formed, organized, constructed, evaluated, and/or maintained. Following this review, we offer guiding principles and driving questions from the POS approach to inquiry that might illuminate generative mechanisms for positive identity construction, whereby mutual growth, enhancement, and shared empowerment co-occur as a person views herself as more virtuous, worthy, evolving, adapting, balanced, and coherent.

What Is a Positive Identity?

Dutton et al. (2010) synthesized literature on identity in organizations into a four-part typology that answers the question, "What makes a work-related identity positive?" We briefly summarize this typology below, as it provides an important review and synthesis of potential sources of positivity in work-related identities. We point readers to the full elaboration of each perspective in the Dutton et al. (2010) review article.

The four-part typology includes the virtue perspective, the evaluative perspective, the developmental perspective, and the structural perspective, each of which highlights a different source of positivity. According to the virtue perspective, an identity is positive when it is infused with the qualities associated with people of good character, such as "master virtues" (Park & Peterson, 2003) like wisdom, integrity, courage, justice, transcendence, redemption, and resilience. The evaluative perspective focuses on the regard in which individuals hold their personal identity (i.e., as an individual), relational identity (i.e., as a member of a relationship), and social identities (i.e., as members of social groups). According to this perspective, an identity is positive when it is regarded favorably by the individual who holds it and/or by referent others who regard the identity favorably. The developmental perspective focuses on changes in identity over time and assumes that identity is capable of progress and adaptation. The developmental perspective asserts that an identity is positive when it progresses toward a higher-order stage of development (for an example, see Hall's [2002] description of progress through distinct career stages). The developmental perspective also asserts that an identity is positive when the individual defines him- or herself in a way that generates fit between the content of the identity and internal or external standards (e.g., adapting to new roles at work, see Ibarra [1999]; resisting stigmatization and oppression, see Creed, DeJordy & Lok [2010] and Meyerson & Scully [1995]). The structural perspective focuses on the ways in which the self-concept is organized. Research fitting this perspective asserts that an individual's identity structure is more positive

when the multiple facets of the identity are in balanced and/or complementary relationship with one another, rather than in tension or conflict with one another (see Cheng, Sanchez-Burks, & Lee, 2008; Kreiner, Hollensbe, & Sheep, 2006; Powell & Greenhaus, 2010).

In the next section, we turn to four prominent theoretical approaches to identity in organizational studies that unearth potential mechanisms for enhancing one's sense of self as virtuous, favorably regarded, progressive, adaptive, balanced, and "whole." We refer to these theoretical approaches as "classical theories of identity," due to their well-established trajectories of conceptual and empirical scholarship.

Classical Theories of Identity

Classical theories of identity—social identity theory, identity theory, narrative-as-identity, and identity work—suggest several different mechanisms through which individuals construct positive identities. By "mechanism" we refer to "a process that explains an observed relationship . . . how and/or why one thing leads to another" (Anderson et al., 2006; see also Hedstrom & Swedberg, 1998). In this section, we discuss each of the classical theories, identifying the different mechanisms for positive identity construction that theory proposes. We do not attempt to provide an exhaustive list of possible mechanisms for positive identity construction, but rather aim to offer a broad, illustrative sampling of mechanisms that are grounded in various theoretical traditions within identity scholarship. Throughout this section, we also revisit the typology proposed by Dutton et al. (2010) in order to establish clearer linkages among past and current perspectives on positive identity, in hopes of developing a more comprehensive theory of positive identity that highlights the sources of positivity each theory explains how to enhance.

We chose to focus on these four theoretical perspectives because they offer varied accounts of the nature, origin, and influences of identity, yet they hold in common the core assumption that individuals possess a certain degree of agency in defining themselves in "positive" ways. Given our primary interest in how individuals co-construct positive identities at work, our review does not feature theoretical perspectives that view identity as essentially rigid, structurally bound, narrowly defined, and/or exploitative. However, our account of positive identity construction does feature explanatory mechanisms for coping with devaluation, stigmatization, and oppression, as well as those mechanisms for cultivating more positive identities that are not catalyzed by identity threat.

Table 6.1 Positive identity construction

	Impetus for Construction	Mechanism of Construction	Effect on Self-views
Social Identity Theory	1. Group identification	→ Pursue optimal distinctiveness	→ More Positive identity structure and identity evaluation
	2. Categorizing into social groups	→ Make favorable self-enhancing comparisons	→ More Positive identity evaluation
	3. Identity devaluation	→ Enhance social valuation of identity	→ More Positive identity evaluation
Identity Theory	1. Role–identity mismatch	→ Align actions with expectations	→ More Positive sense of adaptation and identity structure
	2. Identity activation/salience	→ Prioritize identities	→ More Positive identity structure
	3. Identity conflict	→ Segment or integrate identities	→ More Positive identity structure
Narrative-as-Identity	1. Identity transition	→ Integrate life experiences across time	→ More Positive identity structure
	2. Unexpected, untimely, involuntary, or uncertain circumstances	→ Craft narratives of growth	→ More Positive sense of development
Identity Work	1. Stereotyping	→ Engage in agentic identity performance	→ More Positive identity evaluation and identity structure
	2. Desire for authenticity	→ Engage in agentic identity performance	→ More Positive identity evaluation and identity structure
	3. Desire for social validation	→ Negotiate identity through claiming and granting	→ More Positive identity evaluation, identity structure, and sense of self as virtuous

Table 6.1 gives an overview of each of the classical theories of identity according to the impetus for positive identity construction, proposed mechanisms for positive identity construction, and the effect these behaviors have on self-views.

Social Identity Theory
CORE ASSUMPTIONS ABOUT IDENTITY
Social identity theorists purport that individuals belong to multiple social categories, including those inclusive of organizational membership, race/ethnicity, gender, and age cohort (Ashforth & Mael, 1989). Through self-categorization, individuals segment, classify, and order the social environment and their place in it (Turner, 1987). According to researchers, the existence of a social identity constitutes both a person's knowledge that he or she belongs to a social group or category (Tajfel & Turner, 1979) and the feelings associated with that membership. A social category is represented in the self-concept as a social identity that both describes and prescribes how one should think, feel, and behave as a member of that social group (Hogg, Terry, & White, 1995; Tajfel & Turner, 1979). As a member of a social group, an individual shares some degree of emotional involvement in and degree of

social consensus about the evaluation of his group and of his membership in it with other group members (Tajfel & Turner, 1979).

PROPOSED MECHANISMS FOR POSITIVE IDENTITY CONSTRUCTION
Pursue Optimal Distinctiveness
Group memberships provide opportunities for optimal distinctiveness (Brewer, 1991); people experience belonging and differentiation simultaneously, as they define themselves as similar to their in-group, yet distinct in positive ways from members of other groups. Optimal distinctiveness elevates self-esteem and thus fosters more positive identity evaluations (Brewer, 1991). Kreiner, Hollensbe, and Sheep's (2006) study of Episcopal priests suggests a link between optimal distinctiveness and positive identity structures. They detail several boundary work tactics that priests employ to identify strongly with their vocation, but protect their personal identity from being overpowered by their professional demands. The priests' continued pursuit of optimal distinctiveness helps to increase the positivity of their identity structures by balancing their needs for belonging and differentiation. Thus, optimal distinctiveness research helps to explain how group

identification cultivates more positive identity evaluations and structures.

Make Favorable, Self-enhancing Comparisons Between In-groups and Out-groups

The favorable comparison mechanism explains how categorization into social groups might increase positive self-regard. According to social identity theory, members make favorable comparisons between their in-group and a relevant out-group in order to sustain their perception that the in-group is positively distinct from the out-group (Tajfel & Turner, 1979). According to Tajfel and Turner (1979), group identifications are "relational and comparative: they define the individual as similar to or different from, as 'better' or 'worse' than members of other groups" (p. 101). Tajfel and Turner's (1979) proposition that "positive social identity is based to a large extent on favorable comparisons that can be made between the in-group and some relevant out-groups" (p. 41) suggests that the favorable comparison mechanism explains the linkage between social group categorization and positive identity from the evaluative perspective.

Enhance social valuation of identity. Tajfel and Turner's (1979) early propositions of social identity theory also indicate how people enhance the social valuation of their identity when facing identity threats. Specifically, their proposed mechanisms for coping with identity threat and devaluation help to explain how individuals increase the positivity of their identity evaluation. These mechanisms are particularly relevant for members of socially devalued groups (i.e., groups that are generally characterized within society as possessing unfavorable defining characteristics, and that are often stigmatized by negative stereotypes and low relative status in social hierarchies). Members of socially devalued groups face an unusual predicament in constructing positive identities; rather than belong to a positively distinct group, instead, they belong to group that likely distinguishes them on the basis of negative attributes.

To cope with the social identity threats that result from a lack of positive distinctiveness, some members of devalued groups may attempt to symbolically or physically exit their devalued group in order to join a more positively regarded group. They might attempt to affiliate with a highly regarded group by portraying themselves as prototypical members of that group—demonstrating that they possess the defining characteristics of the valued group (rather than the devalued group), so that they will be viewed as legitimate members. For example, certain people attempt to suppress their invisible devalued identities while in the workplace, so they will be perceived as members of their higher-status work groups (Clair, Beatty, & MacLean, 2005; Ragins, 2008).

Other members may use cognitive tactics to reevaluate their in-group using a set of criteria that will reestablish positive distinctiveness. For example, individuals whose occupations involve dirty work (Hughes, 1951) seek to negotiate and secure social affirmation for their identities (Ashforth & Kreiner, 1999). Specifically, these individuals may transform the meaning of their marginalized work and tainted identities by devaluing negative attributions and revaluing positive ones to make the occupation more attractive to insiders and outsiders (Ashforth & Kreiner, 1999). Positive self-regard is maintained by dis-identifying with a negatively regarded group or by reweighting evaluative criteria to maintain the in-group's relative worth. In sum, these social identity enhancement tactics are examples of the mechanism through which people sustain positive identity evaluations in the face of identity devaluation.

Identity Theory

CORE ASSUMPTIONS ABOUT IDENTITY

Like social identity theory, identity theory offers perspectives on the social nature of the self-concept and the socially constructed nature of the self (Hogg et al., 1995). Yet, identity theory also emphasizes a multifaceted self that mediates the relationship between social structure and individual behavior (Hogg et al., 1995). Identity theory differs from social identity theory in its primary focus on the identities attached to the multiple roles that individuals occupy in society, rather than on the wider range of master statuses (i.e., gender, race, ethnicity) that can be ascribed to individuals (Hogg et al., 1995).

Identity theory refers to two different yet strongly related strands of identity research (Stryker & Burke, 2000). The first strand, rooted in traditional symbolic interactionism, claims that social structures affect the self, and the structure of the self influences social behavior (Stryker & Burke, 2000; see also Stryker 1980; Stryker & Serpe, 1982). In this regard, identity theory reflects Mead's (1934) assertion that "society shapes self shapes social behavior" (quoted by Stryker & Burke, 2000, p. 285). Sluss and Ashforth (2007) expound upon this core premise in their work on relational identities in the workplace; they describe how individuals derive a sense of self from their various role-based interpersonal relationships and how relational identities shape patterns of interaction.

The second strand of identity theory focuses on the internal dynamics of self-processes that impact social behavior (Stryker & Burke, 2000; see also Burke, 1991; Burke & Reitzes, 1991; Burke & Stets, 1999). Identities are thought of as "self-meanings" that are attached to the multiple roles an individual performs and the meanings of an individuals' behavior (Stryker & Burke, 2000). For example, Burke and Reitzes (1981) found that college students' self-views of academic responsibility (a dimension of the student identity) were a strong predictor of college plans, suggesting that individuals will align their behaviors with their sense of self when both factors share meaning. Both strands of identity theory hold in common the belief that external social structures and the structure of the self are inextricably linked (Stryker & Burke, 2000).

PROPOSED MECHANISMS FOR POSITIVE IDENTITY CONSTRUCTION

Align Actions with Role Expectations

This mechanism explains how behavioral congruence with role expectations cultivates more positive identities according to the developmental and structural perspectives. Given that the self is multifaceted and that individuals have as many identities as they have social roles (Stryker & Burke, 2000), it is important for individuals to align their actions and sense of self with the expectations of a given role. At times, people may experience a mismatch between role expectations and their sense of self. In response, they may modify their behavior or expectations to increase alignment. For example, professionals who experience a mismatch between their roles and their identities may customize or alter their identities to fit work demands (Pratt, Rockmann, & Kaufmann, 2006). Pratt et al. (2006) uncovered three types of identity customization processes that are used among medical residents—identity enriching, identity patching, and identity splinting. *Identity enriching* occurs when professionals deepen their understanding of their professional identity without changing an identity structure (e.g., evolving definitions of what it means to be a physician). *Identity patching* occurs when professionals draw upon one identity to make sense of another identity, and when professionals make sense of workplace situations by changing their identities to fit how they do their jobs. *Identity splinting* occurs when professionals

adopt a prior identity to support the development of a new identity that is less secure (e.g., a new resident adopting the identity of a medical student). These examples of alignment help to show how meeting role expectations fosters a sense of self as capable of adapting to internal and external demands without subjugating self-interest to role expectations. In addition, aligning actions with role expectations helps to negotiate potential conflicts within one's multifaceted self-concept, thus promoting the construction of positive identity structures.

Prioritize Roles in the Salience Hierarchy

The prioritization mechanism is a pathway to constructing more positive identity structures by negotiating and balancing multiple role demands. According to identity theory, identities are organized in a salience hierarchy, such that an identity that is higher in the salience hierarchy is more likely to be invoked across a variety of situations (Stryker & Burke, 2000). The salience of an identity reflects commitment to the role relationships associated with that identity because an individual is more likely to behave in accordance with an identity that is higher in the salience hierarchy than one that is lower (Stryker & Burke, 2000). For example, Ragins (2008) describes how social experiences can shape the extent to which a person identifies him- or herself as a mentor (i.e., prioritizing the identity higher in the salience hierarchy) and, consequently, can increase commitment to performing acts consistent with the positively regarded mentor identity. Given the multitude of role expectations, identity theorists purport that role prioritization may be important for increasing the clarity of relational identities and commitment to varied role expectations (Ashforth, Harrison, & Corley, 2008). Thus, prioritization helps people cultivate more positive identity structures by shaping commitment to particular actions.

Segment or Integrate Multiple Identities

According to identity theory, a third mechanism for positive identity construction is to cognitively structure the multiple facets of one's own identities in ways that promote complementarity. Like the prioritization mechanism, this mechanism is important for reducing or preventing the internal identity conflicts that may arise when multiple identities are not mutually reinforcing (Stryker, 2000). If the conflicting identities differ greatly in salience, then the identity higher in salience will be invoked. However, if the conflicting identities reflect similar positions in the salience hierarchy, stress is likely to ensue (Burke, 1991), and individuals will be motivated to employ coping strategies to construct positive structural identities.

Segmentation and integration are both viable strategies for mitigating identity conflict (see Ashforth et al., 2008 for a review). Individuals who use segmentation tactics tend to compartmentalize multiple identities, whereas those who integrate their identities may experience their multiple identities as compatible and mutually enhancing, rather than in conflict or in opposition with one another (Caza & Wilson, 2009; Rothbard & Ramarajan, 2009). Although compartmentalization may reduce the impact of stress in various life domains, it may also inhibit a person's ability to draw upon the psychological, social, and cognitive resources that accompany various role identities across domains. Therefore, both segmentation and integration are mechanisms that help cultivate more positive identity structures. However, Dutton et al. (2010) conclude that in low-stress situations, integration tactics may be most potent for enhancing the degree of complementarity that an individual experiences between his or her multiple identities.

Narrative-as-Identity

CORE ASSUMPTIONS ABOUT IDENTITY

The narrative-as-identity approach views identity as an emergent, interpretive process rather than as a static structure. Specifically, narrative-as-identity scholarship refers to "the stories people construct and tell about themselves to define who they are for themselves and for others" (McAdams, Josselson, & Lieblich, 2006, p. 4). According to this perspective, an identity is comprised of an individual's narratives or stories of interaction with his or her social world. Identity narratives contain key themes that situate one's existence within a plot of unfolding events. These narratives provide people with a sense of order and continuity, in the midst of potentially disconnected or even conflicting life episodes.

PROPOSED MECHANISMS FOR POSITIVE IDENTITY CONSTRUCTION

Integrate Life Experiences Across Time

The integration mechanism is particularly important for making sense of identity transitions over time. Narrative identity scholars explain how to construct more positive identity structures through integrating experiences to provide a sense of unity and purpose (Erikson, 1959) and to bring coherence to life (McAdams, 1985, 1997). Some theorists emphasize that integrative narratives are not simplistic; they contain many voices in dialogue with each other (Gergen, 1991). This "conversation among narrators" or "war of historians" (Raggat, 2006) accounts for the opposition that is inherent within selfhood (Gregg, 2006). Regardless of the degree of contradiction within one's life story, self-narration represents the construction of a coherent sense of self across time and circumstance, by enabling individuals to simultaneously accommodate change and consistency (Ashforth et al., 2008). For example, according to Ibarra and Barbulescu's (2010) discussion of career transitions, self-narratives enable a person to bridge gaps between old and new roles and identities. A coherent self-narrative allows an individual to explain career and identity transitions through stories that depict one's career trajectory as a series of purposive events. To appeal to different audiences, an individual may create multiple self-narratives, such that each individual self-narrative becomes part of a larger and more varied narrative repertoire (Ibarra & Barbulescu, 2010). Thus, the mechanism of integrating life experiences helps to explain how individuals construct positive identities from a structural perspective by increasing the sense of coherence and continuity between various aspects of one's identity and related experiences.

Craft Narratives of Growth

Narrative-as-identity scholarship also unearths the process by which individuals craft stories of growth, which fosters the creation of positive identities from a developmental perspective. Narrative construction involves sense-making activities (inquiring and interpreting one's embeddedness within a social context), which help people to derive meaning from challenging situations and to (re)construct a positive sense of self even through disappointment and unexpected changes (Ashforth et al., 2008). Growth narratives are particularly potent when individuals seek to construct positive identities in the face of unexpected, untimely, involuntary, or uncertain circumstances. For example, growth is a central theme in the derivation of redemptive meaning from negative life stories (McAdams, 2006), in reflection and sense-making about traumatic events (Maitlis, 2009), as well as in narratives of hope that reflect anticipation of future growth (Carlsen & Pitsis, 2009). Maitlis' (2009) research on positive identity construction reveals how musicians who have suffered career-altering injuries compose self-narratives that enable them to make sense of who they are as professionals and humans post-injury. Some musicians in her study developed narratives of growth that signaled a greater sense of empowerment and agency in crafting a fulfilling professional and personal life, even though the shift was brought on by an unexpected, untimely, or involuntary circumstance. Thus, this mechanism suggests that, as people craft narratives of growth, they come to see themselves as evolving in positive ways, which forms a basis of positive identity from the developmental point of view.

Identity Work
CORE ASSUMPTIONS ABOUT IDENTITY
Although social identity, identity theory, and narrative-as-identity approaches each offer perspectives on the socially constructed nature of the self, the identity work approach develops this notion further to posit that the self emerges from the dynamism of interaction with one's social world. In the tradition of symbolic interactionism, the identity work perspective includes a broad body of research on the interpersonal nature of identity construction (Stryker, 1980). The phrase "identity work" is often attributed to Snow and Anderson (1987), who defined identity work as "the range of activities individuals engage in to create, present, and sustain personal identities that are congruent with and supportive of the self-concept" (p. 1348). In other words, individuals do not simply respond to external stimuli in developing positive identities, but are proactive agents in constructing socially validated identities that reflect aspects they deem most central to their sense of self.

Identity work encompasses a range of agentic tactics that people employ to proactively shape the meaning or significance of their identity in a given context. The identity work perspective typically illustrates the ways in which people respond to discrepancies or threats to their identities, such as those prompted by stereotyping, stigmatization, or legitimacy challenges (Ashforth & Kreiner, 1999; Branscombe, Ellemers, Spears, & Doosje, 1998; Ibarra, 1999). However, recent scholarship on positive identity also raises the possibility that "identity work . . . is inspired by an entity's desire to grow and evolve rather than a need to maintain social status or self-worth in the face of threat" (Roberts, Dutton, & Bednar, 2009, p. 510; see also Kreiner & Sheep, 2009). Below, we highlight two identity work mechanisms that have garnered considerable attention within the organizational psychology and organizational behavior literatures. We focus here on distinct *behavioral* identity work mechanisms that are not explicitly addressed by the

other three classical identity theories. Unlike cognitive approaches to identity work (e.g., shifting dimensions of comparison to evaluate one's own social identity more favorably, sense-making of past experiences to story oneself in more positive ways), behavioral techniques focus on active and relational sense-making processes that help individuals construct more positive identities.

PROPOSED MECHANISMS FOR POSITIVE IDENTITY CONSTRUCTION
Engage in Agentic Identity Performance
Identity performance involves proactively shaping others' perceptions of one's social group memberships and identification (Roberts & Roberts, 2007), which helps to increase the positivity of identity evaluations and structures. Agentic identity performance may be a mechanism for positive identity construction in two circumstances: when an individual desires to increase his or her experience of authentic engagement (see Roberts & Roberts, 2007, for a review); and when an individual seeks to counter negative stereotypes (see Roberts, 2005, for a review). For example, individuals often disclose their feelings about group membership and involvement in social-identity group activities in order to communicate how important those identities are to their self-concept and daily living (Bell & Nkomo, 2001; Meyerson & Scully; 1995; Roberts, Cha, Hewlin, & Settles, 2009). They may also educate others about the inaccuracies of group stereotypes, hold themselves up as a positive exemplar who does not embody the stereotypes, play into group stereotypes to accrue social benefits, or avoid discussions of difference altogether (Creed & Scully, 2000; Ely, 1994; Roberts, Settles, & Jellison, 2008). These attempts to claim or suppress identities occur via strategic self-presentation—visible displays of physical appearance (hair, makeup, clothing, jewelry); use of symbolic gestures to emphasize certain cultural orientations (displaying photos or cultural artifacts, engaging in cultural rituals); the use of strategic verbal disclosures to shape perceptions of competence or fit; or the enactment of certain public affiliations (i.e., strategic socialization) (Bell, 1990; Clair et al., 2005; Roberts & Roberts, 2007). The central insight from this body of work is that individuals take on an agentic role in constructing positive identities. Specifically, as individuals make strategic choices about identity displays and disclosures (even in the case of coping with identity threat), they increase the positivity of identity from the evaluative perspective by publicly claiming the identities they

hold in high regard (Roberts et al., 2009) and showing themselves as prototypical members who possess the favorable, defining qualities of a social identity group (Branscombe et al., 1998; Turner, 1987). The identity performance mechanism can also help to increase the complementarity of identity structures by integrating the most valued and valuable aspects of one's nonwork identities into one's work identity (Cha & Roberts, 2010).

Identity Negotiation Through Claiming and Granting
Although identity performance research tends to focus on an actor's deliberate attempts to navigate his or her social context via self-expression and impression management, research on identity negotiation illuminates the iterative, interactive nature of positive identity construction. Specifically, identity negotiation research suggests that individuals will negotiate with themselves and with others to enhance their identities and to ultimately achieve social validation of their authentic selves (Swann, 1987). As such, this mechanism helps to explain how individuals form more positive identities from the evaluative, virtue, and structural perspectives. Bartel and Dutton (2001) provide a useful framing of these identity negotiation techniques in their discussion of the claiming–granting processes by which identities are socially constructed. The claiming–granting perspective offers a dynamic account of the identity work that unfolds during interpersonal encounters and thus emphasizes the interdependence of an actor and audience when constructing positive identities within a social context. Claiming occurs when individuals perform acts that they believe embody their self-view. Granting occurs when others within the social environment engage in comparison processes that allow them to affirm or disaffirm the identity an individual desires. We offer a few illustrations of this mechanism in organizational studies: DeRue, Ashford, and Cotton (2009) describe claiming and granting of the leader identity; MacPhail, Roloff, and Edmondson (2009) describe shared recognition of and appreciation for team members' expert identities; and Milton (2009) and Polzer, Milton, and Swann (2002) describe identity confirmation processes in work groups. Each study illuminates how identity claims are validated by others in order to legitimate the credibility of an identity and attain interpersonal goals. To the extent that discrepancies exist between identities claimed and granted in social interactions, individuals may also engage in narrative identity work (cognitive and interpersonal tactics) to bridge these gaps

(Ibarra & Barbalescu, 2010). In sum, the identity negotiation research helps to show how the dynamic process of claiming and granting positive identities helps to enhance a person's sense of self as favorably regarded (i.e., validated by others) and authentic or "whole" from a structural perspective (i.e., reducing discrepancies between self-and-other views). This mechanism also reveals how virtuous identity claims are validated, as an individual is viewed as the possessor of qualities that distinguish people of good character and that are defined as inherently good.

Summary of Explanatory Mechanisms for Positive Identity Construction
To summarize, each of the four classical approaches to identity research imply different mechanisms for how individuals might strengthen the positivity of their identities at work. The implied mechanisms specify several potential links between Dutton et al.'s (2010) four-part typology and these classical identity perspectives; namely, in how they function to increase the positivity of one's feelings, sense of growth, development, adaptation, and coherence or balance.

Social identity theory and identity work theories help explain how individuals construct identities that are evaluated more favorably. Social identity theory's emphasis on one's sense of self-regard enables the construction of identities that are more positive from an evaluative perspective. The identity work research, although broad and varied, points to the means through which individuals seek and attain self-verification or identity-granting through proactive, agentic identity claims. This work also aligns with the evaluative perspective on positive identity, in that it explicates the process of constructing identities that are personally and socially valued.

Social identity theory, identity theory, and narrative-as-identity scholarship reveals mechanisms for creating more positive identity structures. The emphasis on optimal distinctiveness in social identity theory is related to the structural perspective's characterization of positive, multifaceted identities that are balanced. Identity theory's focus on boundary management and prioritization within one's identity also illuminates how individuals construct positive identity structures that are complementary. Narrative-as-identity scholarship features sense-making and story-telling as critical processes for building a sense of coherence between one's past, present, and future selves—another indicator of a positive structural identity.

Each of the four classical theories suggests how to construct identities that are more positive from a developmental perspective. Narratives of growth capture an individual's sense of evolving and becoming stronger, wiser, more capable, or better in some way. Narratives of hope incorporate expectations of oneself and one's circumstances becoming more positive in the future. The emphasis on adaptive identity development is prevalent in role identity research. Identity customization tactics promote adaptation through altering one's thoughts and behaviors, so that they align with internal values and situational expectations.

The virtue perspective is least obvious in each of the proposed mechanisms for increasing the positivity of one's identity. Although researchers do not explicitly document the impact of such mechanisms on defining oneself as virtuous in some way, certain mechanisms might be useful in constructing more virtuous identities. For instance, identity work could increase the likelihood that others will perceive a person as virtuous (e.g., moral, authentic, compassionate, courageous, generous), which could increase both positive evaluations and the positivity of virtuous identity content. Likewise, if one's growth narrative includes the self-characterization of becoming more virtuous over time, narrative-as-identity theories will align with developmental views of positive identity. If an individual identifies with a group or role that is viewed as noble, righteous, courageous, or moral in some way, social identity theory and identity theory can inform our understanding of the construction of more virtuous identities.

Future Directions

In this section, we offer two avenues for future research in this domain that would help to further examine the mechanisms through which individuals cultivate more positive identities at work: constructing positive complex identities, and evaluating the generative potential of mechanisms for positive identity construction.

Constructing Positive Complex Identities

Workplace and social trends suggest that identity complexity is becoming a more salient and central issue for organizations and their members, since the workplace is becoming increasingly diverse (Johnston & Packer, 1987), boundaries between work and nonwork roles are blurring (Ashforth, 2001), and personal and professional networks are intersecting through online social networking sites. To add another layer to positive identity research,

we encourage scholars to develop theories of positive identity that more fully explicate how individuals develop and sustain socially validated, positive complex identities. We suggest that this underexplored mechanism is central to discovering how positive identities can enable people to build positive relationships at work.

The structural perspective on positive identity offers preliminary insight on this topic, as it expounds upon the multifaceted nature of identity construction and the importance of viewing one's various roles and identities as balanced and complementary. Yet, research to date does not focus on how individuals develop a shared understanding of one another as people who possess multiple identities. Instead, identity theories typically focus on cognitive processes for simplifying one's own identity structures (e.g., hierarchical ranking) and for simplifying others' identity structures (e.g., categorization). Much of the popular identity research purports that identities are arranged according to a presumed hierarchy of identity and then viewed in terms of the most situationally salient identities, for example, master statuses (Hughes, 1945) or distinctive (token) identities (Kanter, 2003). Individuals are said to be motivated to identify with *one* group in order to resolve the tensions of belonging and distinctiveness (as with optimal distinctiveness; Brewer, 1991). Classical perspectives also suggest that individuals will use segmentation tactics, such as dis-identification (Steele, 1997) and compartmentalization (Roccas & Brewer, 2002), to create boundaries between identities (Ashforth & Mael, 1989), or use integration tactics, such as dual identification (Hornsey & Hogg, 2000), superordinate categorization (Chatman, Polzer, Barsade, & Neale, 1998), and hyphenation (Roccas & Brewer, 2002) to combine two or more identities so that they are no longer viewed as separate (Ashforth et al., 2009; Caza & Wilson, 2009; Johnson et al., 2006; Russo, Mattarelli, & Tagliaventi, 2008). The aforementioned studies focus primarily on how individuals structure their own identities into more positive ones, according to social identity theory and identity theory. Identity work's emphasis on claiming–granting processes and self-verification offers little explanation of how individuals construct socially validated positive, complex identities. We believe this gap presents an opportunity for future research on positive identity construction.

Regardless of the cognitive structure of one's identity, we learn from identity work research that individuals seek social validation for their own sense of self. Self-verification theory suggests that people want self-confirmatory feedback and assumes that an individual's ability to recognize how others perceive them is the key to successful interpersonal relationships (Swann, Stein-Seroussi, & Geisler, 1992). To the extent that a person defines oneself in complex (and perhaps even paradoxical) terms, we propose that he or she will also seek to gain interpersonal understanding of her complex existence. Research has not explicitly examined this process of claiming and granting complex identities. Thus, we invite scholars to consider how an individual may employ "identity expansion" tactics to foster a shared understanding as one who belongs to multiple groups and possesses multiple roles, all of which are significant and related to one another. Identity expansion occurs when an individual socially constructs a more complex identity by communicating to others that they are "both A and B" where "and" means either that identities are embedded or that A and B are perceived as two distinct in-group identities (Roccas & Brewer, 2002). Identity expansion can lead to shared understanding, especially in situations where mistaken assumptions regarding the membership, significance, or valence of another person's multiple identities surface. For example, during the 2008 U.S. Democratic primaries, then Senator Barack Obama repeatedly introduced himself in large and small gatherings as both the son of a Kenyan immigrant and a white woman with Midwestern roots. In so doing, he countered public pressures to identify himself in either-or terms (Thomas, Roberts, & Creary, 2009):

> I am the son of a black man from Kenya and a white woman from Kansas. I was raised with the help of a white grandfather who survived a Depression to serve in Patton's Army during World War II and a white grandmother who worked on a bomber assembly line at Fort Leavenworth while he was overseas. I've gone to some of the best schools in America and lived in one of the world's poorest nations. I am married to a black American who carries within her the blood of slaves and slaveowners—an inheritance we pass on to our two precious daughters. I have brothers, sisters, nieces, nephews, uncles, and cousins, of every race and every hue, scattered across three continents, and for as long as I live, I will never forget that in no other country on Earth is my story even possible. It's a story that hasn't made me the most conventional candidate. But it is a story that has seared into my genetic makeup the idea that this nation is more than the sum of its parts—that out of many, we are

truly one. (Barack Obama "A More Perfect Union" March 18, 2008)

This example reveals how Barack Obama directly communicated the complexity of his social and professional identities, ultimately increasing the salience of multiple facets of identity and shared understanding and acceptance of such complexity. To this end, we invite scholars to consider two questions related to the claiming and granting of complex identities: Under what circumstances might an individual pursue self-verification of positive complex identities? And, how might "identity expansion" impact the nature of interpersonal relationships?

Evaluating the Generative Potential of Mechanisms for Positive Identity Construction

The second avenue for future research in this domain involves examining the social consequences of positive identity construction mechanisms. Concerns about the potentially problematic nature of positive identity construction often point to the potentially destructive nature of inflated self-views that are not grounded in reality (e.g., egotism, narcissism—as embodied in the sarcastic phrase, "a legend in one's own mind") and therefore may promote behaviors that compromise individual and group well-being (even if they garner material success) (Ashforth, 2009; Brookings & Serratelli, 2006; Colvin, Funder, & Block, 1995; Fineman, 2006; Lee & Klein, 2002). Although Dutton, Roberts, and Bednar (2010; see also forthcoming) address some of these concerns, our synopsis of mechanisms presents additional research questions.

Some mechanisms feature the social construction of positive identity through cognition and behavior, whereas other mechanisms place a primacy on cognition over behavior. This distinction may be indicative of epistemological and philosophical debates on the nature of human existence. Although Descartes concluded that cognitions alone define human existence ("I think, therefore I am"), Carl Jung stated that "You are what you do, not what you say you'll do." According to Jung, espoused self-views may be inconsistent with actual behaviors, and Jung considers the latter to be more revealing of the true essence of one's identity than who one might think that he or she is. We encourage scholars to articulate their core assumptions about defining characteristics of positive identity— behavior, cognition, or both—as they evaluate the potency of these mechanisms for cultivating more positive identities. This distinction is particularly important because some of the proposed mechanisms may be quite effective in increasing the positivity of one's identity through cognitions and emotions, but may be disconnected from actual practices that one would deem to be generative (i.e., growth-enhancing and beneficial in some way, generally producing a favorable impact on people or situations beyond one's own self-interest). For example, one might successfully claim an identity as a "powerful leader" among her peers by manipulating and disempowering others, even while those who are oppressed attempt to contest her leadership position. As another example, a religious leader might consider himself exempt from the moral consequences of his continued ethical violations due to his ingrained growth narrative of forgiveness and redemption. The impact of these identity mechanisms for reinforcing toxic behaviors must be examined within a social context.

An area of particular concern emerges from social identity theory, in which categorization processes prompt the elevation of one's own reference group in comparison to others. This zero-sum equation for positive identity enhancement dictates that a person diminishes her regard for another individual or group in order to elevate her own sense of relative worth. In order for one person's identity becomes more positive, another's must become less positive. This "zero-sum/better-than" view of positive identity construction directly counters Rev. Dr. Martin Luther King's observation about the importance of mutuality in building relationships across difference. The famous civil rights leader stated that "all [humans] are caught in an inescapable network of mutuality, tied with a single garment of destiny, [such that] I can never be what I ought to be until you are what you ought to be." The West African proverb "I am, because we are" implies the same equation of mutual interdependence in cultivating positive identities. Positive organizational scholarship research on relationships points to the importance of mutual regard in developing high-quality connections, even across dimensions of difference (James & Davidson, 2007; Roberts, 2007; Stephens, Heaphy, & Dutton, 2011, Chapter 29). Ironically, the pursuit of positive identity cultivation through relative comparisons can obstruct mutual regard, particularly during intergroup interactions. Social identity research often points to the self-enhancement motive as a root cause for in-group bias, out-group discrimination, and intergroup conflict (Tajfel & Turner, 1979).

Given that POS emphasizes a focus on individual and collective strengths, generative mechanisms, and positive outcomes, we suggest that it also introduces a higher standard for the conception of a positive identity. Whereas psychologists might emphasize how individual cognitions and emotions can meet self-focused needs (e.g., ego preservation, self-actualization), a POS perspective on positive identity invites scholars to consider also the externalities of these mechanisms for the self and others through the embodiment of generative practices at work. For example, experimental research might trigger various mechanisms of positive identity construction and then assess their impact on actors' and observers' identities. Archival data might also provide rich illustrations of the varied mechanisms for positive identity construction and their impact on social approval, performance, and social outcomes (e.g., among political candidates, elected officials, and religious leaders).

Finally, we encourage scholars to extend beyond these four identity research traditions to discover alternate mechanisms through which individuals might cultivate a positive sense of self in organizational contexts other than those we have presented. For example, Wrzesniewski's (2011; Chapter 4) chapter in this Handbook of POS on "callings" reviews how responding to "a meaningful beckoning toward activities that are morally, socially, and personally significant" (pp. 46) can increase one's sense of self as a social contribution (i.e., virtuous identity) and elevate self-esteem (i.e., positive identity evaluation). Composing a *reflected best self-portrait* (Roberts, Dutton, Spreitzer, Heaphy, & Quinn, 2005) is another mechanism for positive identity construction that helps people understand how to associate their own strengths (virtues and core competencies) with large- and small-scale generative contributions to society. Studies of prosocial behavior in work organizations also suggest that engaging in helping behavior (e.g., community service, coming into contact with fundraising beneficiaries) can reinforce the construction of virtuous and favorably regarded identities (Dutton, Roberts, & Bednar, in press).

In conclusion, our broad, illustrative sampling of mechanisms for positive identity construction that are grounded in various classical and contemporary theoretical traditions within identity scholarship offers a set of perspectives whereby mutual growth, enhancement, and shared empowerment co-occur as a person views herself as more virtuous, worthy, evolving, adapting, balanced, and coherent.

We invite POS and identity scholars to continue to examine sources of positivity and generative mechanisms for identity construction that promote truly extraordinary social outcomes.

Acknowledgments

We wish to thank Jane Dutton, Brad Owens, Gretchen Spreitzer, and the Center for POS Research Incubator participants for their feedback and contributions to this chapter.

References

Anderson, P.J.J, Blatt, R., Christianson, M.K., Grant, A.M., Marquis, C., Neuman, E. et al. (2006). Understanding mechanisms in organizational research: Reflections from a collective journey. *Journal of Management Inquiry, 15*, 102–113.

Ashforth, B.E. (2009). Commentary: Positive identities and the individual. In L.M. Roberts, & J.E. Dutton (Eds.), *Exploring positive identities and organizations: Building a theoretical and research foundation* (pp. 171–187). New York: Routledge.

Ashforth, B.E. (2001). *Role transitions in organizational life.* LEA's Organization and Management Series. Mahwah, NJ: Lawrence Erlbaum Associates, Inc.

Ashforth, B.E., Harrison, S.H., & Corley, K.G. (2008). Identification in organizations: An examination of four fundamental questions. *Journal of Management, 34*, 325–374.

Ashforth, B.E., & Kreiner, G. (1999). How can you do it? Dirty work and the challenge of constructing a positive identity. *Academy of Management Review, 24*, 413–434.

Ashforth, B.E., & Mael, F. (1989). Social identity theory and the organization. *Academy of Management Review, 14*, 20–39.

Bartel, C., & Dutton, J.E. (2001). Ambiguous organizational memberships: Constructing organizational identities in interactions with others. In M.A. Hogg, & D.J. Terry (Eds.), *Social identity processes in organizational contexts* (pp. 115–130). Philadelphia: Psychology Press.

Bell, E. (1990). The bicultural life experience of career oriented black women. *Journal of Organizational Behavior, 11*, 459–477.

Bell, E., & Nkomo, S. (2001). *Our separate ways: Black and white women and the struggle for professional identity.* Boston: Harvard Business School Press.

Branscombe, N.R., Ellemers, N., Spears, R., & Doosje, B. (1999). The context and content of social identity threat. In N. Ellemers, R. Spears, & B. Doosje (Eds.), *Social identity context, commitment, content* (pp. 35–58). Blackwell: London.

Brewer, M.B. (1991). The social self: On being the same and different at the same time. *Personality and Social Psychology Bulletin, 17*, 475–482.

Brookings, J.B., & Serratelli, A.J. (2006). Positive illusions: Positively correlated with subjective well-being, negatively correlated with a measure of personal growth. *Psychological Reports, 98*, 407–413.

Burke, P.J. (1991). Identities and social structure: The 2003 Cooley-Mead Award address. *Social Psychology Quarterly, 67*, 5–15.

Burke, P.J., & Reitzes, D.C. (1981). The link between identity and role performance. *Social Psychology Quarterly, 44*, 83–92.

Burke, P.J., & Stets, J.E. (1999). Trust and commitment through self-verification. *Social Psychology Quarterly, 62*, 347–366.

Carlsen, A., & Pitsis, T. (2009). Experiencing hope in organization lives. In L.M. Roberts, & J.E. Dutton (Eds.), *Exploring positive identities and organizations: Building a theoretical and research foundation* (pp. 77–98). New York: Routledge.

Caza, B.B., & Wilson, M.G. (2009). Me, myself, and I: The benefits of work-identity complexity. In L.M. Roberts, & J.E. Dutton (Eds.), *Exploring positive identities and organizations: Building a theoretical and research foundation* (pp. 99–123). New York: Routledge.

Cha, S., & Roberts, L.M. (2010). Navigating Race: Asian American Journalists' Engagement of Identity-related Resources at Work. Unpublished manuscript. McGill University: Toronto.

Cheng, C., Sanchez-Burks, J., & Lee, F. (2008). Connecting the dots within: Creative performance and identity integration. *Psychological Science, 19*, 1178–1184.

Clair, J., Beatty, J., & Maclean, T. (2005). Out of sight but not out of mind: Managing invisible social identities in the workplace. *Academy of Management Review, 30*, 78–95.

Chatman, J.A., Polzer, J.T., Barsade, S.G., & Neale, M.A. (1998). Being different yet feeling similar: The influence of demographic composition and organizational culture on work processes and outcomes. *Administrative Science Quarterly, 43*, 749–780.

Colvin, C.R., Funder, D.C., & Block, J. (1995). Overly positive self-evaluations and personality: Negative implications for mental health. *Journal of Personality and Social Psychology, 68*, 1152–1162.

Creed, W.E., DeJordy, R., & Lok, J. (2010). Being the change: Resolving institutional contradiction through identity work. *Academy of Management Journal*, forthcoming.

Creed, D., & Scully, M. (2000). Songs of ourselves: Employees' deployment of social identity in workplace encounters. *Journal of Management Inquiry, 9*, 391–412.

Davidson, M., & James, E.H. (2007). The engines of positive relationships across difference: Conflict and learning. In J. Dutton, & B. Rose Ragins (Eds.), *Exploring positive relationships at work: Building a theoretical and research foundation* (pp. 137–158). Mahwah, NJ: Lawrence Erlbaum Associates.

DeRue, D.S., Ashford, S.J., & Cotton, N.C. (2009). Assuming the mantle: Unpacking the process by which individuals internalize a leader identity. In L.M. Roberts & J.E. Dutton (Eds.), *Exploring positive identities and organizations: Building a theoretical and research foundation* (pp. 217–236). New York: Routledge.

Dutton, J.E., & Roberts, L.M. (2009). *Exploring positive identities and organizations: Building a theoretical and research foundation.* New York: Routledge.

Dutton, J.E., Roberts, L.M., & Bednar, J.S. (in press). Positive Identity Rejoinder. In press. *Academy of Management Review.*

Dutton, J.E., Roberts, L.M., & Bednar, J.S. (2010). Pathways for positive identity construction at work: Four types of positive identity and the building of social resources. *Academy of Management Review, 35*, 265–293.

Dutton, J., Roberts, L., & Bednar, J. (in press). Prosocial practices, positive identity, and flourishing at work. In S. Donaldson, M. Csikszentmihalyi, & J. Nakamura (Eds.), *Applied positive psychology: Improving everyday life, schools, work, health, and society.* New York: Routledge.

Ely, R.J. (1994). The effects of organizational demographics and social identity on relationships among professional women. *Administrative Science Quarterly, 39,* 203–238.

Erikson, E.H. (1959). Identity and the life cycle: Selected papers. *Psychological Issues, 1,* 1–171.

Fineman, S. (2006). On being positive: Concerns and counterpoints. *Academy of Management Review, 31,* 270–291.

Gecas, V. (1982). The self-concept. *Annual Review of Sociology, 8,* 1–33.

Gergen, K.J. (1991). *The saturated self: Dilemmas of identity in contemporary life.* New York: Basic Books.

Gregg, G.S. (2006). The raw and the bland: A structural model of narrative identity. In D.P. McAdams, R. Josselson, & A. Lieblich (Eds.), *Identity and story: Creating self in narrative. Narrative study of lives* Vol. 4 (pp. 63–88). Washington, DC: American Psychological Association.

Hall, D.T. (2002). *Careers in and out of organizations.* Thousand Oaks, CA: Sage.

Hedstrom, P., & Swedborg, R. (1998). Social mechanisms: An introductory essay. In P. Hedstrom, & R. Swedborg (Eds.), *Social mechanisms: An analytical approach to social theory* (pp. 1–31). Cambridge: Cambridge University Press.

Hogg, M.A., Terry, D.J., & White, K.M. (1995). A tale of two theories: A critical comparison of identity theory with social identity theory. *Social Psychology Quarterly, 58,* 255–269.

Hornsey, M.J., & Hogg, M.A. (2000). Assimilation and diversity: An integrative model of subgroup relations. *Personality and Social Psychology Review, 4,* 143–156.

Hughes, E.C. (1945). Dilemmas and contradictions of status. *American Journal of Sociology, 50,* 353–359.

Hughes, E.C. (1951). *Group psychology and the analysis of the ego.* New York: Liveright.

Ibarra, H. (1999). Provisional selves: Experimenting with image and identity in professional adaptation. *Administrative Science Quarterly, 44,* 764–791.

Ibarra, H., & Barbulescu, R. (2010). Identity as narrative: Prevalence, effectiveness, and consequences of narrative identity work in macro work role transitions. *Academy of Management Review, 35,* 135–154.

Johnston, W.B., & Packer, A.H. (1987). *Work force 2000.* Indianapolis: Hudson Institute.

Johnson, M.D., Morgeson, F.P., Ilgen, D.R., Meyer, C.J., & Lloyd, J.W. (2006). Multiple professional identities: Examining differences in identification across work-related targets. *Journal of Applied Psychology, 91,* 498–506.

Kanter, R.M. (2003). Men and women of the corporation. In R.J. Ely, E.G. Foldy, & M.A. Scully (Eds.), *Reader in gender, work, and organization* (pp. 34–48). Malden, MA: Blackwell Publishing.

Kreiner, G.E., Hollensbe, E.C., & Sheep, M.L. (2006). Where is the "me" among the "we"? Identity work and the search for optimal balance. *Academy of Management Journal, 49,* 1031–1057.

Kreiner, G., & Sheep, M. (2009). Growing pains and gains: Framing identity dynamics as opportunities for identity growth. In L.M. Roberts, & J.E. Dutton (Eds.), *Exploring positive identities and organizations: Building a theoretical and research foundation* (pp. 23–46). New York: Routledge.

Lee, S., & Klein, H.J. (2002). Relationships between conscientiousness, self-efficacy, self-deception, and learning over time. *Journal of Applied Psychology, 87,* 1175–1182.

MacPhail, L., Roloff, K., & Edmondson, A. (2009). Collaboration across knowledge boundaries within diverse teams: Reciprocal expertise affirmation as an enabling condition. In L.M. Roberts & J.E. (Eds.), *Exploring positive identities and organizations: Building a theoretical and research foundation* (pp. 319–340). New York: Routledge.

Maitlis, S. (2009). Who am I now? Sensemaking and identity in posttraumatic growth. In L.M. Roberts, & J.E. Dutton (Eds.), *Exploring positive identities and organizations: Building a theoretical and research foundation* (pp. 47–76). New York: Routledge.

McAdams, D.P. (1985). *Power, intimacy, and the life story: Personological inquiries into identity.* New York: Guilford.

McAdams, D.P. (1997). The case for unity in the (post)modern self: A modest proposal. In R.D. Ashmore, & L. Jussim (Eds.), *Self and identity. Fundamental issues* (pp. 46–78). New York: Oxford University Press.

McAdams, D.P. (2006). *The redemptive self: Stories Americans live by.* New York: Oxford University Press.

McAdams, D.P. Josselson, R., & Lieblich, A. (2006). *Identity and story: Creating self in narrative. Narrative study of lives* Vol. 4. Washington, D.C.: American Psychological Association.

Mead, G.H. (1934). *Mind, Self and Society.* Chicago: University of Chicago Press.

Meyerson, D., & Scully, M. (1995). Tempered radicalism and the politics of ambivalence and change. *Organization Science, 6*(5), 585–600.

Milton, L. (2009). Creating and sustaining cooperation in interdependent groups: Positive relational identities, identity confirmation, and cooperative capacity. In L.M. Roberts & J.E. Dutton (Eds.), *Exploring Positive Identities and Organizations: Building a Theoretical and Research Foundation.* (pp. 289–317). New York: Routledge Press.

Park, N., & Peterson, C. (2003). Virtues and organizations. In K.S. Cameron, J.E. Dutton, & R.E. Quinn (Eds.), *Positive organizational scholarship: Foundations of a new discipline* (pp. 33–47). San Francisco: Berrett-Koehler.

Polzer, J., Milton, L., & Swann, W. (2002). Capitalizing on diversity: Interpersonal congruence in small work groups. *Administrative Science Quarterly, 47,* 296–324.

Powell, G., & Greenhaus, J. (2010). Sex, gender and the work–to–family interface: Exploring negative and positive interdependencies. *Academy of Management Journal, 53,* 513–534.

Pratt, M.G., Rockmann, K.W., & Kaufmann, J.B. (2006). Constructing professional identity: The role of work and identity learning cycles in the customization of identity among medical residents. *Academy of Management Journal, 49,* 235–262.

Raggat, P.T.F. (2006). Multiplicity and conflict in the dialogical self: A life-narrative approach. In. D.P. McAdams, R. Josselson, & A. Lieblich, *Identity and story: Creating self in narrative. Narrative study of lives* Vol. 4 (pp. 15–35). Washington, D.C.: American Psychological Association.

Ragins, B.R. (2008). Disclosure disconnects: Antecedents and consequences of disclosing invisible stigmas across life domains. *Academy of Management Review, 33,* 194–215.

Roberts, L.M. (2005). Changing faces: Professional image construction in diverse organizational settings. *Academy of Management Review, 30,* 685–711.

Roberts, L.M. (2007). From proving to becoming: How positive relationships create a context for self-discovery and self-actualization. In Dutton, J.E., & Ragins, B.R. (Eds.), *Exploring positive relationships at work: Building a theoretical and research foundation.* (pp. 29–46). New York: Lawrence Erlbaum Associates.

Roberts, L.M., Cha, S.E., Hewlin, P.F., & Settles, I.H. (2009). Bringing the inside out: Enhancing authenticity and positive identity in organizations. In L.M. Roberts, & J.E. Dutton (Eds.), *Exploring positive identities and organizations: Building a theoretical and research foundation* (pp. 149–169). New York: Routledge.

Roberts, L.M., Dutton, J.E., Spreitzer, G.M., Heaphy, E.D., & Quinn, R.E. (2005). Composing the Reflected Best-Self Portrait: Building pathways for becoming extraordinary in work organizations. *Academy of Management Review, 30*, 712–736.

Roberts, L.M., Settles, I., & Jellison, W. (2008). Predicting the strategic identity management of gender and race. *Identity, 8*(4), 269–306.

Roberts, L.M., & Roberts, D.D. (2007). Testing the limits of antidiscrimination law: The business, legal, and ethical ramifications of cultural profiling at work. *Duke Journal of Gender Law & Policy, 14*, 369–405.

Roccas, S., & Brewer, M.B. (2002). Social identity complexity. *Personality and Social Psychology Review, 6*, 88–106.

Rothbard, N.P., & Ramarajan, L. (2009). Checking your identities at the door: Positive relationships between non-work and work identities. In L.M. Roberts, & J.E. Dutton (Eds.), *Exploring positive identities and organizations: Building a theoretical and research foundation* (pp. 125–148). New York: Routledge.

Russo, D., Mattarelli, E., & Tagliaventi, M.R. (2008). Multiple professional identities: One big happy family? Unpublished manuscript, presented at the Academy of Management Meeting, Anaheim, CA.

Sluss, D., & Ashforth, B. (2007). Relational identities and identification: Defining ourselves through work relationships. *Academy of Management Review, 32*, 9–32.

Snow, D.A., & Anderson, L. (1987). Identity work among the homeless: The verbal construction and avowal of personal identities. *American Journal of Sociology, 92*, 1336–1371.

Steele, C.M. (1997). A threat in the air: How stereotypes shape intellectual identity and performance. *American Psychologist, 52*, 613–629.

Stephens, J.P., Heaphy, E., & Dutton, J.E. (2011). High quality connections. In K.S. Cameron & G.M. Spreitzer (Eds.), *The Oxford handbook of positive organizational scholarship*. New York: Oxford University Press.

Stryker, S. (1980). *Symbolic interactionism: A social structural version*. Menlo Park, CA: Benjamin Cummings.

Stryker, S. (2000). Identity competition: Key to differential social movement involvement. In S. Stryker, T. Owens, & R. White (Eds.), *Identity, self, and social movements* (pp. 21–40). Minneapolis: University of Minnesota Press.

Stryker, S., & Burke, P.J. (2000). The past, present, and future of an identity theory. *Social Psychology Quarterly, 63*, 284–297.

Stryker, S., & Serpe, R.T. (1982). Commitment, identity salience, and role behavior: A theory and research example. In W. Ickes, & E.S. Knowles (Eds.) *Personality, roles, and social behavior* (pp. 199–218). New York: Springer-Verlag.

Swann, W.B., Jr. (1987). Identity negotiation: Where two roads meet. *Journal of Personality and Social Psychology, 53*, 1038–1051.

Swann, W.B., Pelham, B., & Krull, D. (1989). Agreeable fancy or disagreeable truth? Reconciling self-enhancement and self-verification. *Journal of Personality and Social Psychology, 57*, 782–791.

Swann, W.B., Jr., Stein-Seroussi, A., & Geisler, B. (1992). Why people self-verify. *Journal of Personality and Social Psychology, 62*, 392–401.

Tajfel, H., & Turner, J.C. (1979). An integrative theory of intergroup conflict. In W.G. Austin, & S. Worchel (Eds.), *The social psychology of intergroup relations* (pp. 33–47). Monterey, CA: Brooks-Cole.

Thomas, D.A, Roberts, L.M., & Creary, S.J. (2009). The rise of President Barack Hussein Obama. *Harvard Business School Case No. 409115.*

Turner, J.C. (1987). *Rediscovering the social group: A self-categorization theory*. New York: Blackwell.

Wrzesniewski, A. (2011). Callings. In K.S. Cameron & G.M. Spreitzer (Eds.), *The Oxford handbook of positive organizational scholarship*. New York: Oxford University Press.

Proactivity in the Workplace

Looking Back and Looking Forward

Chiahuei Wu *and* Sharon K. Parker

Abstract

Being proactive involves self-initiated efforts to bring about a change in the work environment and/or oneself in order to achieve a different future. Proactivity is future-focused, self-starting, and change-oriented in its emphasis. There is clear evidence that proactivity makes a difference—studies show its value for outcomes like job performance, innovation, and career success. It is thus important to understand the drivers of proactivity, which is our focus here. We review how the concept of proactivity has evolved, most recently being considered as a goal-driven process. Next, we summarize motivational mechanisms that underpin proactivity. We then identify distal antecedents, reviewing individual differences and contextual influences on proactivity. Finally, we identify promising areas for future research. In particular, we advocate the need to explore the dynamic spirals of primary and secondary control processes inherent in proactive goal pursuit. For example, after an initial period of adapting to an environment, individuals might proactively introduce change into that environment, and then face a new environment, created in part by them, that requires further adaptivity.

Keywords: Proactivity, work behavior, proactive behavior, future-orientation, change, personal initiative, self-starting, proactive feedback seeking, taking charge

Work behaviors that increase the flexibility and effectiveness with which individuals meet unpredictable task demands are more important than ever in today's dynamic work environments (Griffin, Neal, & Parker, 2007). Being proactive is one such type of behavior. Being proactive involves self-initiated efforts to bring about change in the work environment and/or oneself to achieve a different future (Grant & Ashford, 2008; Parker, Bindl, & Strauss, 2010; Parker, Williams, & Turner, 2006). This future-focused, change-oriented way of behaving can prevent potential problems and enable the exploitation of opportunities for future development, thereby resulting in greater individual or organizational effectiveness.

The benefits of proactive behavior have been widely demonstrated. Fuller and Marler (2009) reported a meta-analysis that showed individuals with

a proactive personality reported higher career success and job performance. Other reviews (e.g., Bindl & Parker, 2010) have similarly identified positive consequences of proactivity for multiple outcomes, albeit with some evidence that these positive outcomes depend on attributes such as situational judgment (Chan, 2006) or negative affect and prosocial motivation (Grant, Parker, & Collins, 2009). It is therefore clear that proactive action can make a positive difference, both for individuals and organizations (see Bindl & Parker, 2010; Fuller & Marler, 2009, for fuller discussions of outcomes of proactivity).

What is less clear is how to motivate proactive action at work. Given its positive value, it is important to consider the drivers of proactivity in the workplace. This is our focus here. In the first part of the chapter, we review concepts of proactivity and make clear our focus on proactivity as a malleable goal process rather than a stable trait. In the second part of the chapter, we review motivational mechanisms underpinning proactivity. Drawing on this motivational perspective, in the third part of the chapter, we identify key antecedents of proactivity in the workplace. In the fourth and final part of the chapter, we identify issues for future research and make a general conclusion based on the current review. To facilitate understanding, Figure 7.1 presents a summary model of the variables and relationships we review in this chapter.

Conceptualizations of Proactivity

Although the concept of proactivity has been widely discussed in several domains (Crant, 2000), early research on proactive personality (Bateman & Crant, 1993) and personal initiative highlights its main characteristics (Frees & Fay 2001). In regard to the former, Bateman and Crant (1993) indicated that individuals with a proactive personality do not merely react to their environments but rather seek to actively master their environments through selecting situations, reconstructing their perceptions and appraisals, and intentionally manipulating the situation. Proactive people thus "scan for opportunities, show initiative, take action, and persevere until they reach closure by bringing about change" (p. 105). Proactive personality was shown to be distinct from the Big Five personality characteristics, both structurally and in terms of outcomes.

Rather than proactive personality's focus on the general tendency to effect change, the concept of personal initiative (Frese, Kring, Soose, & Zempel, 1996, p. 38) is defined as "a behavior syndrome" defined by three key elements: self-starting, future-focused (referred to as "proactive"), and persistent. *Self-starting* means that people do things with their own will, without requiring an external force, such as the assigning of a task. A *future focus* refers to having a long-term focus, in which people anticipate future opportunities or challenges rather than only focusing on problems or demands at hand. Because enacting change potentially entails difficulties, such as lack of resources or resistance from others, *persistence* is needed to overcome barriers to bring about change. The three features are proposed to reinforce each other in a sequence of actions to bring about change (Frese & Fay, 2001).

As well as these influential developments, the notion of proactivity was identified in a range of different topic domains, such as careers (e.g., career initiative), work design (e.g., role breadth self-efficacy), and occupational socialization (e.g., proactive feedback seeking). Crant (2000) identified commonalities across these concepts, labeling them as examples of a more generic concept, "proactive behavior." Parker, Williams, and Turner (2006) similarly argued that "despite different labels and theoretical underpinnings, concepts that relate to individual-level proactive behavior typically focus on self-initiated and future-oriented action that aims to change and improve the situation or oneself" (p. 636). Grant and Ashford (2008) reiterated this perspective, making it clear that proactivity is not "extra-role" as some have claimed, but rather is best thought of as an active way of behaving that involves anticipating and creating a new future. These developments recognize there is no need to confine proactivity to being a stable personality trait; instead, proactivity can be considered as a way of behaving, with proactive personality as an individual tendency in this behavior.[1]

In an extension of the idea that proactivity is a way of behaving that can apply across multiple

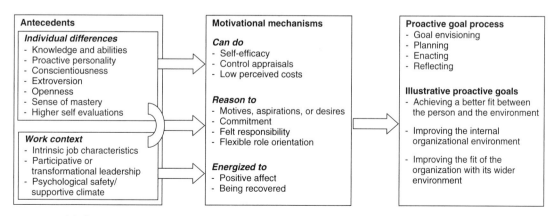

Fig. 7.1 Model of antecedents and motivational determinants of proactivity. Adapted from Parker, S. K., Bindl, U., & Strauss, K. (2010). Proactivity in the workplace: Advances, synthesis and future directions. *Journal of Management, 36*, 827–856.

domains, scholars have recently conceptualized pro-activity as a goal process (Bindl & Parker, 2009; Frese & Fay, 2001; Grant & Ashford, 2008; Parker, Bindl, & Strauss, 2010). In other words, when an individual tries to bring about a different future via change, they engage in conscious goal-directed processes, including both goal generation and goal striving (e.g., Chen & Kanfer, 2006). Goal generation involves, for example, envisioning a different future and planning to bring about a change, whereas goal striving involves concrete steps to bring about the change, as well as reflections on these actions and their consequences. Considering proactivity as involving a goal process recognizes that both goal generation and striving are necessary for bringing about change and also acknowledges that these processes are likely to be influenced by different antecedents (Bindl & Parker, 2009). From this perspective, proactivity is more than observable behavior but a broader process that also involves unobservable elements like envisioning, planning, and reflecting.

In sum, from an initial emphasis on proactive personality as a stable dispositional tendency, proactivity is now often considered as a future-focused, change-oriented way of behaving. To understand this behavior, scholars suggest that effective proactivity likely involves both the generation of a proactive goal to bring about a different future through changing one's self or the situation, and then striving to achieve this goal. There are many different futures an individual might aspire to bring about. Parker and Collins (2010) identified three: achieving a better fit between the person and the environment ("proactive person–environment fit behavior"), improving the internal organizational environment ("proactive work behavior"), and improving the fit of the organization with its wider environment ("proactive strategic behavior"). We turn now to consider what motivates the setting of, and striving for, these various proactive goals.

Motivational Mechanisms Underpinning Proactivity

Drawing on various existing motivational theories, Parker, Bindl, and Strauss (2010) proposed that proactive goal generation and striving will depend on whether individuals feel capable of being proactive (a "can do" pathway), whether they have some sense that they want to bring about a different future (a "reason to" pathway), and whether they have positive affect to foster their proactive actions (an "energized to" pathway). We describe each mechanism in turn.

Within the "can-do" pathway, self-efficacy is a key construct. Self-efficacy refers to "people's beliefs

about their capabilities to produce designated levels of performance that exercise influence over events that affect their lives" (Bandura, 1994, p. 71). Drawing on expectancy theory (Vroom, 1964), Morrison and Phelps (1999) suggested that behaving proactively can be risky—it can damage one's reputation if the action fails or incurs disapproval from others. Individuals with high self-efficacy will be more likely to positively weigh the costs of such risky action against the benefits, to believe they can cope with any potential setbacks, and will perceive a higher likelihood of success. Therefore, self-efficacy has been proposed as a key cognitive-motivational process that drives proactive action (Parker et al., 2006). Empirically, studies have shown that self-efficacy predicts personal initiative (e.g., Bledow & Frese, 2009; Frese, Garst, & Fay, 2007; Speier & Frese, 1997), job search behavior (Brown, Cober, Kane, & Shalhoop, 2006; Kanfer, Wanberg, & Kantrowitz, 2001; Saks & Ashforth, 1999), and other proactive behaviors (e.g., Axtell, Holman, Unsworth, Wall, & Waterson, 2000; Gruman, Saks, & Zweig, 2006; Morrison & Phelps, 1999; Ohly & Fritz, 2007). Other can-do elements for proactive goals proposed by Parker et al. (2010) include beliefs that action is feasible (e.g., control appraisals) and low perceived costs of action.

As stated by Eccles and Wigfield (2002), "even if people are certain they can do a task, they may have no compelling reason to do it" (p. 112). Thus, it is important to also consider an individual's reasons for behaving proactively. Drawing on self-determination theory, Parker et al. (2010) argued for the importance of internalized or autonomous, rather than controlled, forms of motivation for prompting proactivity. Thus, generating and striving for proactive goals can be a means for fulfilling motives, aspirations, or desires. For example, proactive socialization tactics (e.g., information seeking, networking, job change negotiation) are partly led by a desire for control (Ashford & Black, 1996); personal initiative is associated with aspiration for control (Fay & Frese, 2001); feedback seeking is led by the desire for useful information (Tuckey, Brewer, & Williamson, 2002); and initiative at work and voice are influenced by prosocial motives (Grant & Mayer, 2009). One's commitment toward career, teams, and organizations also provide reasons to enact proactive behavior. For example, Den Hartog and Belschak (2007; Belschak & Den Hartog, 2010) reported that different foci of commitment (career, supervisor, team, and organization) were positively related to personal initiative and proactive behavior at personal, interpersonal, and organizational level. Similar findings have been obtained in other studies focusing on organizational commitment (e.g., Burris, Detert, & Chiaburu, 2008; Chiaburu, Marinova, & Lim, 2007; Griffin et al., 2007; Rank, Carsten, Unger, & Spector, 2007).

Felt responsibility is another reason for enacting proactive behavior. An individual's belief that he or she is personally obligated to bring about environmental change has been repeatedly positively linked with personal initiative (Bledow & Frese, 2009) and proactive behaviors, such as taking charge (Morrison & Phelps, 1999; Parker & Collins, 2010), voice (Fuller, Marler, & Hester, 2006; Grant & Mayer, 2009; Parker & Collins, 2010; Tangirala & Ramanujam, 2008), individual innovation and problem prevention (Parker & Collins, 2010), continuous improvement (Fuller et al., 2006), change-oriented behavior (Choi, 2007), and initiative (Grant & Mayer, 2009). A related construct is flexible role orientation, which emphasizes employees' perceived breadth of experienced responsibility within the work environment (Parker, Wall, & Jackson, 1997). Several studies have found that flexible role orientation predicts proactive behaviors, including idea suggestion (Axtell et al., 2000; Dorenbosch, Van Engen, & Verhagen, 2005) and idea implementation and problem solving (Dorenbosch et al., 2005; Parker et al., 2006).

Over and above the mechanisms denoted by "can do" and "reason to" pathways, proactive behavior is also potentially fostered through an affective pathway. Drawing on Fredrickson's (1998) broaden-and-build theory of positive emotion, Parker (2007) proposed that positive affect is likely to influence the selection of proactive goals because it expands thinking and result in more flexible cognitive processes (Fredrickson, 1998, 2001; Isen, 1999), which in turn help individuals to think ahead and rise to the challenge in pursuing proactive goals. Consistent with these ideas, positive affect has been linked with the setting of more challenging goals (Ilies & Judge, 2005). Studies support the idea that positive affect can influence proactive behavior (e.g., Parker, Collins, & Grant, 2008). For example, Ashforth, Sluss, and Saks (2007) reported a positive correlation between positive affectivity and proactive socialization behaviors, and Bindl and Parker (2009) showed that positive affect had its strongest relationship with envisioning (an aspect of proactive goal generation) rather than three other phases of proactive goal pursuit (planning, enacting, reflecting). Within-person studies also suggest the benefits of positive affect for

proactive behavior. For example, Fritz and Sonnentag (2009) found positive affect related to taking charge behaviors both on the same and the following day, and Sonnentag (2003) found that the feeling of being recovered from work in the morning predicted personal initiative and pursuit of learning on the same day (see also Binnewies, Sonnentag, & Mojza, 2009a, 2010).

Individual Differences and Work Context Antecedents of Proactive Behavior
In this section, we review how individual differences and work context factors can influence individuals' proactive action, in part at least through influencing their can do, reason to, and energized to motivational states. Drawing on contingent perspectives, we also review research on the interaction between individual differences and contextual factors in shaping individuals' proactivity at work.

Individual Differences
The importance of knowledge and abilities for being proactive was suggested by Fay and Frese (2001): "To be able to take initiative, one needs a good and thorough understanding of what one's work is, that is, one needs job-relevant knowledge, skills, and cognitive ability" (p. 104). Research supports this argument showing, for example, a link between job qualifications and personal initiative (Fay & Frese, 2001), cognitive ability and personal initiative (Fay & Frese, 2001), educational background and job search behavior (Kanfer et al., 2001), educational background and voice (LePine & Van Dyne, 1998), knowledge (relational, normative, and strategic) and issue selling (Dutton, Ashford, O'Neill, & Lawrence, 1997), and contextual knowledge and packaging ideas for promotion (Howell & Boies, 2004). The mechanisms by which knowledge and ability affect proactivity have not be examined, but it is plausible to expect at least a partial pathway via motivation. For example, individuals with expertise will likely have experience confidence in the quality of their ideas for change ("can do" pathway).

Personality attributes have also been shown to predict proactive behavior. As discussed above, the most relevant construct is proactive personality (Bateman & Crant, 1993). Rather unsurprisingly, proactive personality predicts multiple proactive behaviors, such as network building (Lambert, Eby, & Reeves, 2006; Thompson, 2005), proactive socialization (Kammeyer-Mueller & Wanberg, 2003), career initiative (Seibert, Kraimer, & Crant, 2001), and proactive work behaviors such as taking charge, individual innovation, problem prevention, and voice (Parker & Collins, 2010).

Big Five personality factors also play a potential role. Conscientiousness and extroversion were positively related to proactive personality (e.g., Bateman & Crant, 1993; Crant & Bateman, 2000; Major, Turner, & Fletcher, 2006), and have been found to predict proactive behavior (e.g., Fay & Frese, 2001; Lepine & VanDyne, 2001; Tidwell & Sias, 2005). Openness to experiences might be expected to contribute to proactive behavior because it implies exploration of the unfamiliar, a feature embedded in proactive behavior. Supporting this view, facets of actions, ideas, and values in openness personality positively predicted proactive personality (Major et al., 2006) or voice (Lepine & VanDyne, 2001). Agreeableness, however, is generally unrelated to proactivity (Bateman & Crant, 1993; Crant & Bateman, 2000; Fay & Frese, 2001), although some studies found it is positively related to information seeking (Tidwell & Sias, 2005) and negatively related to voice (Lepine & VanDyne, 2001). Neuroticism generally has a negative (e.g., Crant & Bateman, 2000; Lepine & VanDyne, 2001; Major et al., 2006; Tidwell & Sias, 2005) or nonsignificant (e.g., Bateman & Crant, 1993; Fay & Frese, 2001; Griffin et al., 2007) relationship with proactive personality or proactive behavior. The negative impact of neuroticism mainly reflects the facet of vulnerability, which is represented by an inability to cope with stress, and being hopeless or panicked in difficult situations (Lepine & VanDyne, 2001; Major et al., 2006), aspects that are likely to impair proactive goal striving.

Consistent with the importance of perceived capability for engaging in proactive behaviors ("can do" pathways), dispositional constructs related to individuals' perception of control and self-worth have also been positively linked to proactive behavior (e.g., self-esteem, Kanfer et al., 2001; see e.g. Wrzesniewski & Dutton, 2001, for a theoretical elaboration on the relationship between control-related needs and job crafting). Parker and Sprigg (1999) also reported that proactive employees have a higher sense of mastery, showing they believe they can control or act on job demands that occur. Fay and Frese (2001) found that constructs related to actively managing undesirable situations, such as problem-focused coping and error handling, were positively related to personal initiative. Behaviorally, Johnson, Kristof-Brown, Van Vianen, De Pater, and Klein (2003) reported that people with positive core self-evaluations tend to pursue more social network-building activities, a form of proactive behaviors in social domains.

Work Context Antecedents

Situational factors are also crucial for proactive behavior because they represent conditions that allow or encourage (or constrain/inhibit) an individual to enact proactive behavior. Here, we summarize findings concerning job design, leadership, and organizational climate; factors for which the clearest evidence exists. We identify antecedents of proactive behaviors, rather than other aspects of a proactive goal process (e.g., envisioning a proactive goal), because this has been the focus of research to date.

Job characteristics play an important role in motivation, behavior, and well-being more generally (e.g. Latham & Pinder, 2005; Morgeson & Campion, 2003; Parker & Ohly, 2008), and also are important for proactivity. Because being proactive is rooted in the sense of mastery (Batement & Crant, 1993) or "can do" motivation, job characteristics that can foster this perception have been found to be positively linked to proactive behavior. For example, job autonomy, complexity, and control, positively relate to proactive behaviors (e.g., Axtell et al., 2000; Axtell, Holman, & Wall, 2006; Fay & Frese, 2001; Fay & Sonnentag, 2002; Frese et al., 1996, 2007; Hornung & Rousseau, 2007; Morrison, 2006; Ohly & Fritz, 2010; Ohly, Sonnentag, &, Pluntke, 2006; Parker et al., 2006; Rank et al., 2007; Speier & Frese, 1997). Interestingly, negative job characteristics might also play a positive role in activating proactivity. Drawing on control theory (Carver & Scheier, 1982), Fay and Sonnentag (2002) proposed that job stressors denote a deviation between a desired and an actual situation, thereby motivating employees to take an active approach to decrease the difference between the desired and actual states. In support of this view, Ashford and Cummins (1985) reported that employees having jobs with higher role ambiguity and uncertainty tend to seek feedback in order to reduce this uncertainty, especially among employees low in tolerance for ambiguity. Similarly, job stressors, such as time pressure or situational constraints, have been positively related to various proactive behaviors (Binnewies et al.; 2009a; Fay & Sonnentag, 2002; Fritz & Sonnentag, 2009; Ohly & Fritz, 2010). Suggesting a more contingent relationship, Ohly et al. (2006) found an inverted U-shaped curve that suggests that moderate time pressure is best for creativity and innovation, with low or very high levels of time pressure being problematic.

Leadership is a further important antecedent, likely influencing proactivity through each of the can do, reason to, and energized to paths. First, participative leadership, which emphasizes the value of subordinates' contributions and involvement in decision making, predicted higher levels of proactive service performance (Rank et al., 2007). Contingent reward leadership, which emphasizes the recognition and approval for subordinate effort or performance, and transformational leadership, which emphasizes motivating employees to go beyond standard expectations, were also found to have positive relationships with change-oriented citizenship behaviors via leader–member exchange (LMX) quality (Bettencourt, 2004). Transformational leadership also positively predicts proactive behavior (Belschak & Den Hartog, 2010; Rank, Nelson, Allen, & Xu, 2009), albeit potentially in a level-consistent way (Strauss et al., 2009). Strauss et al. found that team leaders' transformational leadership predicted role breadth self-efficacy (can do motivation) and in turn team member proactivity, whereas organizational leaders' transformational leadership predicted affective commitment (reason to motivation), which in turn predicted organization member proactivity. Not only leadership style, but the quality of exchange relationship between leader and employee can also affect proactive behavior. For example, higher LMX has been positively related to individual innovation (Janssen & Van Yperen, 2004; Scott & Bruce, 1994), voice (Burris et al., 2008), and change-oriented organizational citizenship behaviors (Bettencourt, 2004). Leader consideration also enhanced an employee's feedback-seeking behavior (VandeWalle, Ganesan, Challagalla, & Brown, 2000).

In contrast to the positive effect of particular leadership styles (participative leadership, transformational leadership, vision) and the quality of exchange between a leader and employee, some kinds of leadership have negative effects on proactive behavior, such as active-corrective transactional leadership, represented by monitoring subordinates to detect errors and deviations from standards and taking corrective action (Rank et al., 2009). In addition, findings regarding the relationship between supportive leadership with proactive behaviors are inconsistent. Some research has found that supervisor support predicts proactive behaviors (Axtell et al., 2000; Ohly et al., 2006; Ramus & Steger, 2000), but other research has found nonsignificant relationships between supportive leadership and proactivity (Frese, Teng, & Wijnen, 1999; Parker et al., 2006). Parker et al. (2006) suggested that supervisors might experience an "initiative paradox" (Campbell, 2000) in which they feel threatened by their employees' proactive behavior, which might explain why supportive leadership is not always beneficial.

Finally, organizational or work unit climate that can provide a supportive and safe environment is helpful for fostering proactive behavior. Proactive behavior often implies changing how others work, or altering the broader rules and procedures in an organization, which can induce feelings of discomfort in coworkers or managers. Proactivity can therefore be risky. The stronger the feeling of risk, the less likely the behavior. For example, Tidwell and Sias (2005) found that the perceived social cost in information seeking in organizations has a negative impact on overt information-seeking behavior among newcomers. A supportive climate can help to reduce the perceived cost of proactivity, or the perceived risks. The importance of a positive climate and supportive relationships in relation to proactivity has been suggested in various studies (Axtell et al., 2000; Griffin et al., 2007; Kanfer et al., 2001; LePine & Van Dyne, 1998).

In a longitudinal analysis, Axtell et al. (2006) further reported that change in management support was positively related to change in suggestions, and change in team support for innovation was positively related to change in implementations. Similarly, Scott and Bruce (1994) also found that employees who perceived higher levels of support for innovation in organizations are more likely to exhibit innovative behavior. Regarding issue selling, Ashford, Rothbard, Piderit, and Dutton (1998) found that perceived organizational support, norms favoring issue selling, and higher quality of relationships with the individuals who would be sold the issues, are three favorable contextual factors that foster a willingness to sell issues via "can do" mechanism (perceived higher probability of success and lower image risk). In a qualitative study, Dutton, Ashford, O'Neill, Hayes, and Wierba (1997) not only found organizational support is favorable in issue selling, but also further indicated that context factors related to fear of negative consequences, uncertainty, downsizing conditions, and conservativeness of the culture can impede the willingness for issue selling. Together, these findings confirm the importance of a supportive climate, either at the work unit or organizational level, in cultivating proactive behavior.

Interaction Between Individual Differences and Work Context Antecedents

Individual and situational forces are not independent; they work together to influence an individual's proactivity. First, favorable conditions for proactivity, such as autonomy, can strengthen the positive effect of dispositional forces on proactive behavior. For example, Binnewies et al. (2009a) showed that the positive relationship between recovery in the morning and personal initiative on the same day was stronger among employees with higher job control. Parker and Sprigg (1999) similarly showed that job control mitigated the stressful effects of high job demands for employees high in proactive personality, whereas control made little difference for more passive individuals. They argued that employees who have highly proactive personalities take advantage of job control to manage their job demands more effectively, compared to employees who have low proactive personalities. These findings are in line with the hypothesis that personality has a strong effect in relatively weak situations (e.g., high autonomy contexts) and has less effect in stronger situations (Davis-Blake & Pfeffer, 1989; Mischel & Shoda, 1995).

Second, situational characteristics can enable an individual to exhibit his or her dispositional tendency to be proactive. For example, Kim and Wang (2008) showed that individuals who are high in proactive personality tend to seek feedback from their supervisors when organizational fairness is high, and their supervisor usually provides positive feedback. McAllister, Kamdar, Morrison, and Turban (2007) found that employees who perceive their organizations as high in procedural justice and who define their job roles more broadly had higher ratings of taking charge at work by their supervisors. Griffin, Parker, and Mason (2010) found that leader vision enhanced employees' proactivity 1 year later for employees with high role breadth self-efficacy. The authors suggested that a clear and compelling vision establishes a discrepancy between the present and the future, and thereby provides a "reason to" be proactive and help achieve the different future.

Third, situations can potentially suppress an individual's tendency to be proactive. Gupta and Bhawe (2007) proposed that a gender-based stereotype threat has a negative impact on women's entrepreneurship intention because entrepreneurship is related to a masculine stereotype. Gupta and Bhawe (2007) also proposed that the impact of stereotype threat on women's entrepreneurship intention is greater among women with more highly proactive personalities, because the effect of stereotype threat is stronger among those who care most about the stereotyped task (Steele, 1998), and people high in proactivity have a tendency to become entrepreneurs (Frese, Fay, Hilburger, Leng, & Tag, 1997). Their hypotheses were supported in an experiment, in which the negative impact of stereotype threat on entrepreneurship intention was stronger among women with more highly proactive personality,

showing that an individual's tendency to be proactive can also be constrained in certain situations.

Fourth, studies suggest that situational characteristics can lead an individual to enact proactive behavior if he or she lacks the relevant tendency. For example, LePine and Van Dyne (1998) showed that individuals with low self-esteem were more receptive to situational characteristics promoting voice behaviors in a group with high autonomy than were individuals with high levels of self-esteem. Similarly, Rank et al. (2009) found that transformational leadership was more strongly positively related to individual innovation for individuals with lower organization-based self-esteem than for those with higher self-esteem. In the same vein, Bettencourt (2004) found that contingent reward leadership had a negative relationship with change-oriented citizenship among people high in performance goal orientation. Because contingent reward leadership focuses on in-role task responsibilities, people high in performance goal orientation tend to focus on core tasks to achieve their competence at work, rather than change-oriented citizenship. However, when people high in performance goal orientation encounter transformational leaders, they are likely to engage in change-oriented citizenship because these individuals tune into the values and goals highlighted by transformational leaders, and then enact proactive behaviors to achieve their competence. These findings suggest a compensatory effect of situations on individual differences.

It is also possible that dispositional forces can compensate for situational factors. For example, Grant and Sumanth (2009) found that those individuals who were high in dispositional trust and who were prosocially motivated showed high job-related initiative, even if they indicated their managers were not trustworthy. Thus, trust propensity compensated for manager trustworthiness. As another example, VandeWalle et al. (2000) reported that individuals' learning goal orientation was more important for perceiving higher value and lower cost in feedback seeking when they worked with inconsiderate supervisors. Taken together, the interaction effects between individual and situational antecedents are complex. We recommend further theoretical development to synthesize the potential interaction effects into a coherent framework.

Future Research

Although this chapter suggests a good understanding of key aspects of proactivity, unanswered questions remain. Some questions relate to our review—regarding measures, goal processes, mechanisms, and antecedents. In addition, we highlight how proactivity might be considered at the team or organizational level. To extend its theoretical depth, we advocate linking proactivity into a dynamic view on the relationship between self and environment. We elaborate these ways forward next.

Measures, Mechanism, and Antecedents of Proactivity

Well-established measures of proactive dispositions (e.g., Bateman & Crant's 1993 measure of proactive personality) and of domain-specific proactive behaviors (see Parker & Collins, 2010) currently exist. Nevertheless, there is room for further development.

First, proactive personality is currently treated as a unidimensional construct, yet a recent study (Wu, Wang, & Mobley, 2010) showed that proactive personality has two dimensions: *initiative,* or the tendency to actively generate ideas and take unrequested action; and *persistence,* the tendency to continuously invest efforts to accomplish goals. Their study provided preliminary evidence that initiative and persistence interact to predict proactive outcomes, suggesting the value of a multidimensional perspective on proactive personality. Second, regarding the measure of specific proactive behaviors, Parker and Collins (2010) summarized and classified 11 specific proactive behaviors into three broad factors: proactive person–environment fit behavior (feedback inquiry, feedback monitoring, job change negotiation, career initiative), proactive work behavior (taking charge, voice, problem prevention, and individual innovation), and proactive strategic behavior (strategic scanning, issue selling). However, not all proactive behaviors in the literature were included in their framework, such as network building and proactive coping. As such, it is possible that further higher-order factors of proactivity exist. Finally, although a process measure of proactivity has been recently developed that assesses not only observable behaviors but also unobservable elements such as envisioning, planning, and reflecting (see Bindl & Parker, 2009), this approach is relatively untested.

Beyond measurement, there are substantive issues to consider. As discussed, scholars have proposed that proactivity should be considered as a goal process. Yet, with one unpublished exception (Bindl & Parker, 2009), studies continue to measure only observable proactive behaviors. We advocate that scholars adopt a process perspective, especially since motivation research suggests that different elements of a proactive process are likely to be driven by different antecedents.

In addition, the motivational pathways proposed by Parker et al. (2010) have yet to be tested simultaneously: We know little about how can do, reason to, and energized to mechanisms work together. Moreover, as these authors themselves identified, unanswered questions remain about each pathway. For example, in relation to the "reason to" process, they "recommend a focus on how external goals are internalized, on the role of identity, and on how multiple motivations might play out" (p. 848). The "energized to" pathway also has had less attention, such as the role of negative affect. Some studies have found that negative affect is associated with less proactivity (Ashforth et al., 2007; Grant et al., 2009), or that a null association exists (Binnewies et al., 2009b; Binnewies et al., 2010; Fritz & Sonnentag, 2009; Griffin et al., 2007). However, in some situations, negative affect might signal a discrepancy between an actual situation and a desired situation, thereby stimulating individuals to engage in change to reduce the perceived discrepancy (Carver & Scheier, 1982). In support of this view, Den Hartog and Belschak (2007) reported one study in which negative affect was positively related to personal initiative. These findings suggest that negative affect is not the opposite construct of positive affect. It might also be that the type of negative affect is relevant. Most focus has thus far been on anxiety or depression, but activated negative affect in the form of frustration and anger might energize proactivity under some circumstances.

Regarding the individual antecedents of proactivity, as noted above, proactive personality is a powerful dispositional antecedent in predicting proactive behaviors. However, in their seminal work, Bateman and Crant (1993) did not elaborate on why there are individual differences in proactive tendency, or how this personal tendency is developed. Wu and Parker (2010) drew on attachment theory (Bowlby, 1969) to propose that proactive personality can be regarded as an exploration tendency in mastering environments, and this kind of exploration tendency is related to individuals' attachment styles developed from earlier social interactions with their caregivers. Their study provides preliminary evidence to support this proposition. A further intriguing possibility to explore is that proactive personality might change over time. Current arguments suggest that "personality traits continue to change in adulthood and often into old age, and that these changes may be quite substantial and consequential" (Roberts & Mroczek, 2008, p. 31), and several studies link personality change to life experiences (Agronick & Duncan, 1998).

Research has focused on how proactive personality influences the environment via proactive actions, but neglects the possibility that proactive personality can be influenced by environment and experiences, albeit likely over the longer term.

Beyond proactive personality, several dispositions have had short shrift thus far in the proactivity literature, especially attributes relating to the "striving" element of proactive goal regulation (Parker et al., 2010). For example, these authors proposed the importance of dispositions relating to hardiness and resilience in promoting persistence and the overcoming of setbacks.

A further important area for enquiry concerns "how" situational antecedents influence proactivity, or the underpinning mechanisms. For example, a supportive climate has usually been assumed to influence proactivity because it enhances the psychological safety to enact proactive behavior. However, support might also contribute to higher perceived efficacy to behave proactively because it ensures more resources to take proactive action. Moreover, the positive affect induced from receiving support can fuel proactivity via the affect (energized to) mechanism. From a social exchange perspective, receiving contextual support could provide a "reason to" take proactive action because support is interpreted as a favor provided by others, with taking charge being seen as a way to reciprocate the favor. Thus, situational antecedents might trigger proactive behavior through multiple pathways, but such processes have had little attention thus far.

We also suggest that antecedents vary in the extent to which they create a strong situation. We propose that situational forces can be considered as "enabling" factors or "expected to" factors. Situational factors such as job autonomy are enabling factors because they enable or allow proactivity. As suggested by Meyer, Dalal, and Hermida (2010), job autonomy results in a weak situation because it is associated with lower constraints in making decision and doing tasks. However, factors such as situational accountability or leader vision are classified as "expected to" factors because they involve stronger situational guidance to enact proactive behavior. From Meyer et al.'s perspective, accountability renders a stronger situation because it is associated with higher clarity as to individuals' work-related responsibilities.

This way of thinking about situational forces provides a hint as to theorizing about their mechanisms. For example, enabling factors might be more important for promoting proactivity among individuals who already have conducive abilities or personality tendencies, and who already possess strong "reason to" motivation. For such individuals, "enabling" factors likely enhance "can do" motivation. However, "expected to" factors might be more effective for people who lack strong reasons to act proactively: Such factors might promote greater internalization of proactive expectations and external change goals, enhancing the extent to which individuals see it as important and "their job" to be proactive. Parker et al. (2010) proposed that proactive goals need to be internalized if individuals are to sustain their proactive action through setbacks and over time.

Proactivity Beyond the Individual Level

So far, we have discussed proactivity only at the individual level. Proactivity and its benefits have also been observed at higher levels. For example, team proactive behavior positively relates to team outcomes like customer service (Kirkman & Rosen, 1999), team effectiveness (Hyatt & Ruddy, 1997), and team learning (Druskat & Kayes, 2000). Studies also indicate benefits of proactivity at an organizational level (Baer & Frese, 2003; Fay, Lührmann, & Kohl, 2004). For example, Aragón-Correa, Hurtado-Torres, Sharma, and García-Morales (2008) found that organizations with higher strategic proactivity adopted more innovative preventive practices and eco-efficient practices in their environmental strategy, which then linked to higher financial performance. Nevertheless, the mechanisms driving proactivity at higher levels are unclear. In one of the few studies considering this issue, Williams, Parker, and Turner (2010) found that, consistent with individual-level studies, a supportive team climate and high levels of self-management were associated with team proactivity. However, composition of the team was also important. The most proactive teams had members with higher-than-average proactive personality, but also low heterogeneity in proactive personality. Having team members who vary a great deal in their tendency to be proactive appeared to result in a less positive climate, thereby lowering team proactive performance.

The Role of Proactivity in Relations Between Self and Environment

According to triadic reciprocal causation (Bandura, 1999), self, environment, and behavior influence each other in dynamic ways. Many proactive behaviors, such as taking charge and innovation, describe the self as exerting its influence on the environment via proactive goal setting and striving. This relationship from self to environment is in line with the concept of primary control, or "attempts to change the world so that it fits the self's needs" (Rothbaum, Weisz, & Snyder, 1982, p. 8). However, the environment can also exert an influence on the self. The relationship from environment to self is in line with the concept of secondary control, or "attempts to fit in with the world and to flow with the current" (Rothbaum et al., 1982, p. 8).

At first glance, the concept of secondary control seems to be inconsistent with the idea of proactivity, instead being relatively more important for adaptivity (Griffin et al., 2007). However, as noted by Parker et al. (2010), proactive goals can involve changing the situation (akin to primary control) or changing the self (potentially involving secondary control). As an example, proactive feedback seeking and career initiative are two kinds of proactivity that mainly focus on changing the self, such as via seeking out feedback to improve one's own performance. We recommend considering primary and secondary control as two dynamic processes involved in proactivity. For example, newcomers can engage in proactive socialization behaviors, such as feedback seeking and relationship building, to achieve social integration and role clarity (Wanberg & Kammeyer-Mueller, 2000), a type of secondary control process in which people try to fit in the environment. After newcomers are familiar with the work environment, they may try to change their work environment through various proactive behaviors such as innovation, voice, and taking charge. At this stage, people try to master their environment according to their needs, interests, or ideas, which is in line with a primary control process. An example of this type of interplay between primary and secondary control processes in sustaining proactivity was provided by Berg, Wrzesniewski, and Dutton (2010), who reported that employees tend to use adaptive behaviors to create and seize the opportunities for proactive job crafting.

We recommend longitudinal studies to investigate the chain of dynamics between self and environment via primary and secondary control processes. People might first adapt to the environment in order to create opportunities to master and change that environment. After people bring about changes to the environment via their proactive actions, they face a new environment again, created in part by them. For example, if an individual who works independently implements an innovative procedure at work that requires consultation with colleagues in different divisions, her or his work environment as a whole will be different because of that innovation. She or he now faces a new environment that will potentially require adaptation. Proactivity research will likely be enriched by exploring and testing the dynamic linkages between self and the environment.

Conclusion

Actively trying to take charge of one's self or the environment to bring about a different future—in other words, being proactive—is an increasingly vital way of behaving in today's workplaces. In this chapter, we reviewed the concept of proactivity in terms of dispositional, behavioral, and goal process perspectives. We summarized evidence that an individual's motivation to behave in a proactive way derives from three states: the belief that one is able to be proactive (can do), that one wants to be proactive (reason to), and the experience of activated positive affect (energized to). These motivational pathways are in turn shaped and influenced by an individual's personality, the work context they are in, and the interaction between person and context. Job design, leadership, and work climate appear to be three especially important aspects of the work context for promoting proactivity. Nevertheless, although there is already a good evidence base to guide practitioners and scholars in this area, we recommended several ways that proactivity research can be enriched and extended, including a fuller consideration of the dynamics underpinning the reciprocal link between self and environment.

Note

1. From here on, we describe references to the stable, dispositional concept of proactivity as "proactive personality," to distinguish it from the more malleable concept of proactive behavior.

References

Agronick, G.S., & Duncan, L.E. (1998). Personality and social change: Individual differences, life path, and importance attributed to the women's movement. *Journal of Personality and Social Psychology, 74,* 1545–1555.

Aragón-Correa, J.A., Hurtado-Torres, N., Sharma, S., & García-Morales, V.J. (2008). Environmental strategy and performance in small firms: A resource-based perspective. *Journal of Environmental Management, 86,* 88–103.

Ashford, S.J., & Black, J.S. (1996). Proactivity during organizational entry: The role of desire for control. *Journal of Applied Psychology, 81,* 199–214.

Ashford, S.J., & Cummings L.L. (1985). Proactive feedback seeking: The instrumental use of the information environment. *Journal of Occupational Psychology, 58,* 67–79.

Ashford, S.J., Rothbard, N.P., Piderit, S.K., & Dutton, J.E. (1998). Out on a limb: The role of context and impression management in selling gender-equity issues. *Administrative Science Quarterly, 43,* 23–57.

Ashforth, B.E., Sluss, D.M., & Saks, A.M. (2007). Socialization tactics, proactive behavior, and newcomer learning: Integrating socialization models. *Journal of Vocational Behavior, 70,* 447–462.

Axtell, C.M., Holman, D.J., Unsworth, K.L., Wall, T.D., & Waterson, P.E. (2000). Shopfloor innovation: Facilitating the suggestion and implementation of ideas. *Journal of Occupational and Organizational Psychology, 73,* 265–285.

Axtell, C.M., Holman, D., & Wall, T.D. (2006). Promoting innovation: A change study. *Journal of Occupational and Organizational Psychology, 79,* 509–516.

Baer, M., & Frese, M. (2003). Innovation is not enough: climates for initiative and psychological safety, process innovations, and firm performance. *Journal of Organizational Behavior, 24,* 45–68.

Bandura, A. (1994). Self-efficacy. In V.S. Ramachaudran (Ed.), *Encyclopedia of human behaviour* (Vol. 4, pp. 71–81). New York: Academic Press.

Bandura, A. (1999). A social cognitive theory of personality. In L. Pervin & O. John (Ed.), *Handbook of personality* (2nd ed., pp. 154–196). New York: Guilford Publications.

Bateman, T.S., & Crant, J.M. (1993). The proactive component of organizational behavior: A measure and correlates. *Journal of Organizational Behavior, 14,* 103–118.

Belschak, F.D., & Den Hartog, D.N. (2010). Pro-self, pro-social, and pro-organizational foci of proactive behavior: Differential antecedents and consequences. *Journal of Occupational and Organizational Psychology, 83,* 475–498.

Berg, J.M., Wrzesniewski, A., & Dutton, J.E. (2010). Perceiving and responding to challenges in job crafting at different ranks: When proactivity requires adaptivity. *Journal of Organizational Behavior, 31,* 158–186.

Bettencourt, L.A. (2004). Change-oriented organizational citizenship behaviors: The direct and moderating influence of goal orientation. *Journal of Retailing, 80,* 165–180.

Bindl, U.K., & Parker, S.K. (2010). Proactive work behavior: Forward-thinking and change-oriented action in organizations. In S. Zedeck (Ed.), *APA handbook of industrial and organizational psychology.* Washington, DC: American Psychological Association.

Bindl, U.K., & Parker, S.K. (2009). Phases of Proactivity: How do we actually go the extra mile? In M. Frese, & S.K. Parker. Proactivity/Personal Initiative: Untangling the concept. (Invited symposium). Paper presented at the European Congress of Work and Organizational Psychology, Santiago de Compostela, Spain.

Binnewies, C., Sonnentag, S., & Mojza, E.J. (2009a). Daily performance at work: Feeling recovered in the morning as a predictor of day-level job performance. *Journal of Organizational Behavior, 30,* 67–93.

Binnewies, C., Sonnentag, S., & Mojza, E.J. (2009b). Feeling recovered and thinking about them good sides of one's work. A longitudinal study on the benefits of non-work experiences for job performance. *Journal of Occupational Health Psychology, 14,* 243–256.

Binnewies, C., Sonnentag, S., & Mojza, E.J. (2010). Recovery during the weekend and fluctuations in weekly job performance: A week-level study examining intra-individual relations. *Journal of Occupational and Organizational Psychology, 83,* 419–441.

Bledow, R., & Frese, M. (2009). A situational judgment test of personal initiative and its relationship to performance. *Personnel Psychology, 62,* 229–258.

Bowlby, J. (1969). *Attachment and Loss: Vol. 1. Attachment.* New York: Basic Books.

Brown, D.J., Cober, R.T., Kane, K., & Shalhoop, J. (2006). Proactive personality and the successful job search: A field investigation with college graduates. *Journal of Applied Psychology, 91,* 717–726.

Burris, E.R., Detert, J.R., & Chiaburu, D.S. (2008). Quitting before leaving: The mediating effects of psychological attachment and detachment on voice. *Journal of Applied Psychology, 93,* 912–922.

Campbell, D.J. (2000). The proactive employee: Managing workplace initiative. *Academy of Management Executive, 14,* 52–66.

Carver, C.S., & Scheier, M.F. (1982). Control theory: A useful conceptual framework for personality-social, clinical, and health psychology. *Psychological Bulletin, 92*(1), 111–135.

Chan, D. (2006). Interactive effects of situational judgment effectiveness and proactive personality on work perceptions and work outcomes. *Journal of Applied Psychology, 91,* 475–481.

Chen, G., & Kanfer, R. (2006). Toward a system theory of motivated behavior in work teams. In B.M. Staw (Ed.), *Research in organizational behavior* (Vol. 27), 223–267. Greenwich, CT: JAI.

Chiaburu, D.S., Marinova, S.V., & Lim, A.S. (2007). Helping and proactive extra-role behaviors: The influence of motives, goal orientation and social context. *Personality and Individual Differences, 43,* 2282–2293.

Choi, J.N. (2007). Change-oriented organizational citizenship behavior: Effects of work environment characteristics and intervening psychological processes. *Journal of Organizational Behavior, 28,* 467–484.

Crant, J.M. (2000). Proactive behavior in organizations. *Journal of Management, 26,* 435–462.

Crant, J.M., & Bateman, T.S. (2000). Charismatic leadership viewed from above: The impact of proactive personality. *Journal of Organizational Behavior, 21,* 63–75.

Davis-Blake, A., & Pfeffer, J. (1989). Just a mirage: The search for dispositional effects in organizational research. *Academy of Management Review, 14,* 385–400.

Den Hartog, D.N., & Belschak F.D. (2007). Personal initiative, commitment and affect at work. *Journal of Occupational and Organizational Psychology, 80,* 601–622.

Dorenbosch, L., Van Engen, M.L., & Verhagen, M. (2005). On-the-job innovation: The impact of job design and human resource management through production ownership. *Creativity and Innovation Management, 14,* 129–141.

Druskat, V.U., & Kayes, D.C. (2000). Learning versus performance in short-term project teams. *Small Group Research, 31,* 328–353.

Dutton, J.E., Ashford, S.J., O'Neill, R.M., Hayes, E., & Wierba, E.E. (1997). Reading the wind: How middle managers assess the context for selling issues to top managers. *Strategic Management Journal, 18,* 407–425.

Eccles, J.S., & Wigfield, A. (2002). Motivational beliefs, values, and goals. *Annual Review of Psychology, 53,* 109–132.

Fay, D., & Frese, M. (2001). The concept of personal initiative: An overview of validity studies. *Human Performance, 14,* 97–124.

Fay, D., Lührmann, H., & Kohl, C. (2004). Proactive climate in a post-reorganization setting: When staff compensates managers' weakness. *European Journal of Work and Organizational Psychology, 13,* 241–267.

Fay, D., & Sonnentag, S. (2002). Rethinking the effects of stressors: A longitudinal study on personal initiative. *Journal of Occupational Health Psychology, 7,* 221–234.

Fredrickson, B.L. (1998). What good are positive emotions? *Review of General Psychology, 2*, 300–319.

Fredrickson, B.L. (2001). The role of positive emotions in positive psychology: The broaden-and-build theory of positive emotions. *American Psychologist, 56*(3), 218–226.

Frese, M., & Fay, D. (2001). Personal initiative: An active performance concept for work in the 21st century. *Research in Organizational Behavior, 23*, 133–187.

Frese, M., Fay, D., Hilburger, T., Leng, K., & Tag, A. (1997). The concept of personal initiative: Operationalization, reliability and validity in two German samples. *Journal of Occupational and Organizational Psychology, 70*, 139–161.

Frese, M., Garst, H., & Fay, D. (2007). Making things happen: Reciprocal relationships between work characteristics and personal initiative in a four-wave longitudinal structural equation model. *Journal of Applied Psychology, 92*, 1084–1102.

Frese, M., Kring, W., Soose, A., & Zempel, J. (1996). Personal initiative at work: Differences between East and West Germany. *Academy of Management Journal, 39*, 37–63.

Frese, M., Teng, E., & Wijnen, C.J.D. (1999). Helping to improve suggestion systems: Predictors of making suggestions in companies. *Journal of Organizational Behavior, 20*, 1139–1155.

Fritz, C., & Sonnentag, S. (2009). Antecedents of day-level proactive behavior: A look at job stressors and positive affect during the workday. *Journal of Management, 35*, 94–111.

Fuller, J.B., Marler, L.E., & Hester, K. (2006). Promoting felt responsibility for constructive change and proactive behavior: Exploring aspects of an elaborated model of work design. *Journal of Organizational Behavior, 27*, 1089–1120.

Fuller, J.B., & Marler, L.E. (2009). Change driven by nature: A meta-analytic review of the proactive personality literature. *Journal of Vocational Behavior, 75*, 329–345.

Grant, A.M., & Ashford, S.J. (2008). The dynamics of proactivity at work. *Research in Organizational Behavior, 28*, 3–34.

Grant, A.M., & Mayer, D.M. (2009). Good soldiers *and* good actors: Prosocial and impression management motives as interactive predictors of affiliative citizenship behaviors. *Journal of Applied Psychology, 94*, 900–912.

Grant, A.M., Parker, S.K., & Collins, C.G. (2009). Getting credit for proactive behavior: supervisor reactions depend on what you value and how you feel. *Personnel Psychology, 62*, 31–55.

Grant, A.M., & Sumanth, J.J. (2009). Mission possible: The performance of prosocially motivated employees depends on manager trustworthiness. *Journal of Applied Psychology, 94*, 927–944.

Griffin, M.A., Neal, A., & Parker, S.K. (2007). A new model of work role performance: Positive behavior in uncertain and interdependent contexts. *Academy of Management Journal, 50*, 327–347.

Griffin, M.A., Parker, S.K., & Mason, C.M. (2010). Leader vision and the development of adaptive and proactive performance: A longitudinal study. *Journal of Applied Psychology, 95*, 174–182.

Gruman, J.A., Saks, A.M., & Zweig, D.I. (2006). Organizational socialization tactics and newcomer proactive behaviors: An integrative study. *Journal of Vocational Behavior, 69*, 90–118.

Gupta, V.K., & Bhawe, N.M. (2007). The influence of proactive personality and stereotype threat on women's entrepreneurial intentions. *Journal of Leadership & Organizational Studies, 13*, 73–85.

Hornung, S., & Rousseau, D.M. (2007). Active on the job-proactive in change: How autonomy at work contributes to employee support for organizational change. *Journal of Applied Behavioral Science, 43*, 401–426.

Howell, J.M., & Boies, K. (2004). Champions of technological innovation: The influence of contextual knowledge, role orientation, idea generation, and idea promotion on champion emergence. *Leadership Quarterly, 15*, 123–143.

Hyatt, D.E., & Ruddy, T.M. (1997). An examination of the relationship between work group characteristics and performance: Once more into the breech. *Personnel Psychology, 50*, 553–585.

Ilies, R., & Judge, T.A. (2005). Goal regulation across time: The effects of feedback and affect. *Journal of Applied Psychology, 90*, 453–467.

Isen, A.M. (1999). On the relationship between affect and creative problem solving. In S.W. Russ (Ed.), *Affect, creative experience, and psychological adjustment* (pp. 3–17). Philadelphia: Taylor & Francis.

Janssen, O., & Van Yperen, N.W. (2004). Employees' goal orientations, the quality of leader–member exchange, and the outcomes of job performance and job satisfaction. *Academy of Management Journal, 47*, 368–384.

Johnson, E.C., Kristof-Brown, A.J., Van Vianen, A.E.M., De Pater, I.E., & Klein, M.R. (2003). Expatriate social ties: Personality antecedents and consequences for adjustment. *International Journal of Selection and Assessment, 11*, 277–288.

Kammeyer-Mueller, J.D., & Wanberg, C.R. (2003). Unwrapping the organizational entry process: Disentangling multiple antecedents and their pathways to adjustment. *Journal of Applied Psychology, 88*, 779–794.

Kanfer, R., Wanberg, C.R., & Kantrowitz, T.M. (2001). Job search and employment: A personality-motivational analysis and meta-analytic review. *Journal of Applied Psychology, 86*, 837–855.

Kim, T.Y., & Wang, J. (2008). Proactive personality and newcomer feedback seeking: The moderating roles of supervisor feedback and organizational justice. In M.A. Rahim (Ed.), *Current Topics in Management* (Vol. 13, pp. 91–108). London: Transaction Publishers.

Kirkman, B.L., & Rosen, B. (1999). Beyond self-management: Antecedents and consequences of team empowerment. *Academy of Management Journal, 42*, 58–74.

Lambert, T.A., Eby, L.T., & Reeves, M.P. (2006). Predictors of networking intensity and network quality among white-collar job seekers. *Journal of Career Development, 32*(4), 351–365.

Latham, G.P., & Pinder, C.C. (2005). Work motivation theory and research at the dawn of the twenty-first century. *Annual Review of Psychology, 56*, 485–516.

LePine, J.A., & Van Dyne, L. (1998). Predicting voice behavior in work groups. *Journal of Applied Psychology, 83*, 853–868.

Lepine, J.A., & VanDyne, L. (2001). Voice and cooperative behavior as contrasting forms of contextual performance: Evidence of differential relationships with big five personality characteristics and cognitive ability. *Journal of Applied Psychology, 86*, 326–336.

Major, D.A., Turner, J.E., & Fletcher, T.D. (2006). Linking proactive personality and the big five to motivation to learn and development activity. *Journal of Applied Psychology, 91*, 927–935.

McAllister, D.J., Kamdar, D., Morrison, E.W., & Turban, D.B. (2007). Disentangling role perceptions: How perceived role breadth, discretion, instrumentality, and efficacy relate to helping and taking charge. *Journal of Applied Psychology, 92*, 1200–1211.

Meyer, R.D., Dalal, R.S., & Hermida, R. (2010). A review and synthesis of situational strength in the organizational sciences. *Journal of Management, 36*, 121–140.

Mischel, W., & Shoda, Y. (1995). A cognitive-affective system theory of personality: Reconceptualizing situations, dispositions, dynamics, and invariance in personality structure. *Psychological Review, 102*, 246–268.

Morgeson, F.P., & Campion, M.A. (2003). Work Design. In W.C. Borman, D.R. Ilgen & R.J. Klimoski (Eds.), *Handbook of psychology: Industrial and organizational psychology* (Vol. 12, pp. 423–452). Hoboken, NJ: John Wiley.

Morrison, E.W. (2006). Doing the job well: An investigation of pro-social rule breaking. *Journal of Management, 32*, 5–28.

Morrison, E.W., & Phelps, C.C. (1999). Taking charge at work: Extra-role efforts to initiate workplace change. *Academy of Management Journal, 42,* 403–419.

Ohly, S., & Fritz, C. (2007). Challenging the status quo: What motivates proactive behavior? *Journal of Occupational and Organizational Psychology, 80*, 623–629.

Ohly, S., & Fritz, C. (2010). Work characteristics, challenge appraisal, creativity and proactive behavior: A multi-level study. *Journal of Organizational Behavior, 31,* 543–565.

Ohly, S., Sonnentag, S., & Pluntke, F. (2006). Routinization, work characteristics and their relationships with creative and proactive behaviors. *Journal of Organizational Behavior, 27*, 257–279.

Parker, S.K. (2007). *How positive affect can facilitate proactive behavior in the work place.* Paper presented at the Academy of Management Conference, Philadelphia, USA.

Parker, S.K., Bindl, U., & Strauss, K. (2010). Proactivity in the workplace: Advances, synthesis and future directions. *Journal of Management, 36*, 827–856.

Parker, S.K., & Collins, C.G. (2010). Taking stock: Integrating and differentiating multiple proactive behaviors. *Journal of Management, 36*, 633–662.

Parker, S.K., Collins, C.G., & Grant, A. (2008). *The role of positive affect in making things happen.* Paper presented at the Annual SIOP Conference, San Francisco, USA.

Parker, S.K., & Ohly, S. (2008). Designing motivating work. In R. Kanfer, G. Chen & R.D. Pritchard (Eds.), *Work motivation: Past, present, and future* (pp. 233–384). New York: Routledge.

Parker, S.K., & Sprigg, C.A. (1999). Minimizing strain and maximizing learning: The role of job demands, job control, and proactive personality. *Journal of Applied Psychology, 84*, 925–939.

Parker, S.K., Wall, T.D., & Jackson, P.R. (1997). "That's not my job": Developing flexible employee work orientations. *Academy of Management Journal, 40,* 899–929.

Parker, S.K., Williams, H., & Turner, N. (2006). Modeling the antecedents of proactive behavior at work. *Journal of Applied Psychology, 91*, 636–652.

Ramus, C.A., & Steger, U. (2000). The roles of supervisory support behaviors and environmental policy in employee "ecoinitiatives" at leading-edge European companies. *Academy of Management Journal, 43*, 605–626.

Rank, J., Carsten, J.M., Unger, J.M., & Spector, P.E. (2007). Proactive customer service performance: Relationships with individual, task, and leadership variables. *Human Performance, 20*, 363–390.

Rank, J., Nelson, N.E., Allen, T.D., & Xu, X. (2009). Leadership predictors of innovation and task performance: Subordinates' self-esteem and self-presentation as moderators. *Journal of Occupational and Organizational Psychology, 82,* 465–489.

Roberts, B.W., & Mroczek, D.K. (2008). Personality trait stability and change. *Current Directions in Psychological Science, 17*, 31–35.

Rothbaum, F., Weisz, J.R., & Snyder, S.S. (1982). Changing the world and changing the self: A two process model of perceived control. *Journal of Personality and Social Psychology Bulletin, 42*, 5–37.

Saks, A.M., & Ashforth, B.E. (1999). Effects of individual differences and job search behaviors on the employment status of recent university graduates. *Journal of Vocational Behavior, 54*, 335–349.

Scott, S.G., & Bruce, R.A. (1994). Determinants of innovative behavior: A path model of individual innovation in workplace. *Academy of Management Journal, 37*, 580–607.

Seibert, S.E., Kraimer, M.L., & Crant, J.M. (2001). What do proactive people do? A longitudinal model linking proactive personality and career success. *Personnel Psychology, 54*, 845–874.

Sonnentag, S. (2003). Recovery, work engagement, and proactive behavior: A new look at the interface between nonwork and work. *Journal of Applied Psychology, 88*, 518–528.

Speier, C., & Frese, M. (1997). Generalized self-efficacy as a mediator and moderator between control and complexity at work and personal initiative: A longitudinal field study in East Germany. *Human Performance, 10*, 171–192.

Strauss, K., Griffin, M.A., & Rafferty, A.E. (2009). Proactivity directed toward the team and organization: The role of leadership, commitment and role-breadth self-efficacy. *British Journal of Management, 20*, 279–291.

Steele, C. (1998). Stereotyping and its threats are real. *American Psychologist, 53*, 680–681.

Tangirala, S., & Ramanujam, R. (2008) Exploring Non-Linearity in Employee Voice: The Effects of Personal Control and Organizational Identification, *Academy of Management Journal, 51*, 1189–1203.

Tidwell, M., & Sias, P. (2005). Personality and information seeking: Understanding how traits influence information-seeking behaviors. *Journal of Business Communication, 42*, 51–77.

Thompson, J.A. (2005). Proactive personality and job performance: A social capital perspective. *Journal of Applied Psychology, 90*(5), 1011–1017.

Tuckey, M., Brewer, N., & Williamson, P. (2002). The influence of motives and goal orientation on feedback seeking. *Journal of Occupational and Organizational Psychology, 75*, 195–216.

VandeWalle, D., Ganesan, S., Challagalla, G.N., & Brown, S.P. (2000). An integrated model of feedback-seeking behavior: Disposition, context, and cognition. *Journal of Applied Psychology, 85*, 996–1003.

Vroom, V.H. (1964). *Work and motivation.* New York: Wiley.

Wanberg, C.R., & Kammeyer-Mueller, J.D. (2000). Predictors and outcomes of proactivity in the socialization process. *Journal of Applied Psychology, 85*, 373–385.

Williams, H.M., Parker, S.K., & Turner, N. (2010). Proactively performing teams: The role of work design, transformational leadership, and team composition *Journal of Occupational and Organizational Psychology, 83*, 301–324.

Wrzesniewski, A., & Dutton, J.E. (2001). Crafting a job: Revisioning employees as active crafters of their work. *Academy of Management Review, 26*, 179–201.

Wu, C.H., & Parker, S.K. (2010). Effects of attachment styles in predicting individual differences in proactivity. Manuscript submitted to publish.

Wu, C.H., Wang, Y., & Mobley, W.H. (2010). The role of initiative and persistence in proactivity: A process view. Manuscript submitted to publish.

Striving for Creativity

Building Positive Contexts in the Workplace

Jing Zhou *and* Run Ren

Abstract

This chapter reviews the organizational creativity literature. The literature review demonstrates that social context (leadership and supervision, coworker influences, social networks, and cultural influences) and task context (job complexity, feedback and evaluation, goals, creativity expectations, and job requirements, feedback and evaluation, autonomy and discretion, time and stress, and rewards) substantially influence employees' creativity. Further, extant theories suggest that contextual factors affect creativity by influencing individuals' motivation, creative cognition, or affect. Implications for future research, especially research that is related to positive organizational scholarship (POS), are discussed. Among future research directions, the need to investigate how adversity triggers creativity is underscored.

Keywords: Creativity, innovation, entrepreneurship, motivation, creative cognition, affect and creativity, leadership, coworker influences, social networks, creativity and positive organizational scholarship

Being one of the most intriguing human capacities, creativity is essential for organizational change, adaptation, and effectiveness (Amabile, 1988; Oldham & Cummings, 1996; Woodman, Sawyer, & Griffin, 1993; Zhou & Shalley, 2003). The literature on creativity in the workplace has documented numerous studies that demonstrated that social and task contexts in organizations have profound impact on individual employees' creativity: whereas some contextual factors unleash, develop, or enhance employees' creativity, other contextual factors kill creativity everyday (Shalley, Zhou, & Oldham, 2004). This literature is usually referred to as the *organizational creativity literature*, and the term "organizational context" is often used as an umbrella term that encompass social and task contexts in organizations (Woodman et al., 1993; Zhou & Shalley, 2008a).

Organizational creativity is related to positive organizational scholarship (POS). According to the POS research community, "At its core, positive organizational scholarship investigates 'positive deviance,' or the ways in which organizations and their members flourish and prosper in extraordinary ways" (Cameron, Dutton, & Quinn, 2003). By definition, creativity is positive deviance. It represents deviance because by generating ways of doing things better, and doing things differently, creativity deviates from the status quo. It is also positive—if used appropriately, creativity may also be the key driver for positive progress, ultimately leading to successful companies, fulfilled employees, economic prosperity, and social development. Creativity is also extraordinary, because it represents unusual and unique contributions.

In this chapter, we review the organizational creativity literature, with a focus on studies that examined effects of organizational context on employee creativity. As mentioned above, examining effects of organizational context on creativity represents the bulk of work in the contemporary organizational creativity literature. After the review, we conclude this chapter by briefly discussing the implications of this body of work for POS.

What Is Organizational Creativity?

Organizational creativity refers to the generation of novel and useful ideas concerning products, services, processes, management practices, business models, and competitive strategies (Amabile, 1996; Oldham & Cummings, 1996; Shalley, 1991; Zhou, 1998). This definition suggests that to be judged as creative is to have produced tangible outcomes (e.g., an idea), instead of simply stating a mental process is creative or not, which at the present time there is no scientific way of measuring. Both novelty and usefulness are necessary elements in the definition of creativity. A novel idea needs to be new to a particular job or a particular organization, and yet it does not have to be the very first anywhere in the world; a useful idea means that it is potentially implementable and valuable.

As this definition implies, organizational members holding different positions in the organizational hierarchy, from top executives to rank-and-file employees, and working in different functional areas, from research labs to the manufacturing floor, all have the potential to be creative. Their creativity, whether generating ideas on how to do what they do currently more effectively or more efficiently, or generating ideas on completely new ways of doing things, could ultimately drive organizations' change and sustainable growth.

This definition also differentiates creativity from innovation. Whereas creativity emphasizes the generation of new ideas, *innovation* typically includes both the generation and implementation of new ideas, but with an emphasis on the implementation of new ideas. Hence, whereas creativity requires that the new and useful ideas are generated by employees and managers in a focal organization, innovation may involve the implementation of new and useful ideas generated by individuals outside of the focal organization (Zhou & Shalley, 2010). In this sense, other things being equal, organizations in which members exhibit higher levels of creativity are those organizations that do a better job at utilizing their members' human potential than do organizations in which members show relatively low levels of creativity.

The aforementioned definition of creativity is the commonly accepted and used definition of creativity in the contemporary creativity literature. It emphasizes creativity as an outcome, and makes no distinction between types of creativity.

However, Unsworth (2001) argues that creativity research may make even greater strides if, on the basis of how a creative activity gets started, creativity is conceptually divided into four categories. These four categories result from crossing two dimensions, each of which has two types: the driver for creative engagement (externally driven vs. internally driven), and the problem type (open vs. closed). *Open ideas* are those ideas that are discovered by the individual, whereas *closed ideas* are presented to the individual. The four creativity types are: responsive (external and closed), expected (external and open), contributory (internal and closed), and proactive (internal and open).

Whereas Unsworth (2001) categorizes creativity into different types based on the drivers that start the creative engagement, creativity may also be categorized into different types based on the nature of an idea or solution. For example, Mumford and Gustafson (1988) suggest that there are two different types of creativity: minor versus major contributions. *Minor contributions* refer to adjustments, recombinations, and extensions of existing ideas, whereas *major contributions* refer to groundbreaking ideas or solutions. Although these conceptual distinctions are interesting, empirical research that has clearly demonstrated the existence of these different types of creativity has been rare. For practicing managers, it is important to know that, although major creativity sounds exciting, relatively minor forms of creativity produced by hundreds if not thousands of employees in a focal organization may also add tremendous value to the organization.

Why Are Contexts Important Determinants of Creativity in the Workplace?

Organizational contexts affect creativity in two ways. First, contexts may directly influence the motivational, cognitive, and affective processes that are related to creativity (Zhou & Shalley, 2010). Second, contexts may interact with individual differences to affect creativity (Shalley et al., 2004).

Zhou and Shalley (2010) categorize previous theorizing and research on organizational creativity into three broad approaches: motivational, cognitive, and affective. These broad categories reflect researchers' focuses on different aspects of an individual's psychological processes that influence that individual's creative idea generation. Among the three approaches, the motivational approach to creativity has received the most research attention in the field of organizational creativity.

Contexts and Creativity-related Motivation

In essence, the motivational approach posits that employees will exhibit high levels of creativity when they are highly motivated, especially by intrinsic motivation (Amabile, 1988, 1996). One of the earliest theories concerning the motivational approach to creativity was formulated by Amabile (1988, 1996). According to Amabile's componential theory of creativity, three components are necessary for creativity to occur: domain-relevant knowledge (knowledge and expertise in a given domain), creativity-relevant processes (skills and strategies concerning proper ways to generate creative ideas), and task motivation (intrinsic motivation or interests in the task itself). High levels of intrinsic motivation lead to high levels of creativity. Because of its emphasis on the role of intrinsic motivation in the creative process, the componential theory of creativity is sometimes known as the *intrinsic motivation perspective of creativity*.

Many prior studies that used a motivational approach to examining creativity identified study variables and hypothesized relations among these variables by relying on the intrinsic motivation perspective of creativity and the cognitive evaluation theory (Deci & Ryan, 1980, 1985) concerning how contextual factors influence intrinsic motivation. According to the intrinsic motivation perspective of creativity, contextual factors lead to high levels of creativity when they enhance or maintain employees' intrinsic motivation; contextual factors lead to low levels of creativity when they undermine or reduce intrinsic motivation.

How do contextual factors enhance or undermine intrinsic motivation? According to the cognitive evaluation theory, employees experience high levels of intrinsic motivation when they feel competent and self-determining. Contextual factors may be either informational or controlling. The relative salience of the informational or controlling aspect of the contextual factor determines whether contextual factors enhance or undermine intrinsic motivation. When the informational aspect is salient, intrinsic motivation is enhanced or maintained. On the other hand, when the controlling aspect is salient, intrinsic motivation is undermined or reduced.

Contexts and Creativity-related Cognition

The cognitive approach rests on the assumption that, to generate creative ideas, one needs to have access to diverse raw materials (e.g., information, knowledge, experiences), and one also needs to translate these raw materials into new and useful ideas via creative cognition (Zhou & Shalley, 2010). Although in cognitive psychology, models have been developed to guide experimental studies on creative cognition (Smith, Ward, & Finke, 1995), in the field of organizational creativity, no unifying theoretical framework has been developed to comprehensively depict the precise structure, function, and processes of creative cognition, and the full-range of organizational contextual factors that lead to employees' creative cognition.

Instead, researchers have relied on theoretical arguments advanced in sociology or psychology to investigate different aspects of cognitive processes that are relevant to creativity in the workplace. For example, social network analysis has been used to examine how networks are related to employees' creativity, presumably via influence on the employees' access to diverse information and knowledge (e.g., Perry-Smith & Shalley, 2003). As another example, contextual factors have been shown to influence employees' creative self-efficacy (employees' beliefs concerning the extents to which they are capable of being creative in their work organizations), which leads to creativity (Tierney & Farmer, 2002).

A theoretical perspective that is related to the cognitive process of creativity is the sense-making perspective (Ford, 1996; Drazin, Glynn, & Kazanjian, 1999). An idea belonging to this perspective includes that employees' sense-making determines their engagement in the creative process. They make sense on the basis of contextual cues. The employees will engage in the creative process if they believe that their creative endeavor will be meaningful and influential. Few empirical studies have been conducted to test this perspective. Additional theoretical work is also needed to more comprehensively map out which contextual factors influence sense-making, and how these factors influence employees' creativity via sense-making.

Contexts and Creativity-related Affect

Compared with the motivational and cognitive approaches to creativity, the affective approach perhaps is the least well-developed and agreed upon in the field of organizational creativity. The number of published studies specifically devoted to reveal effects of affect on creativity in the workplace is relatively small. In fact, no overarching theoretical framework has been specifically developed for the purpose of delineating the relation between affect and creativity in a comprehensive fashion. Instead, in the small number of published empirical studies on affect and employee creativity, researchers have relied on psychological research and theories on the structure, nature, and functions of affective experiences to deduce effects of positive and negative affect on creativity in the workplace.

Among the relatively small number of studies concerning affect and organizational creativity, more studies examined effects of positive affect than negative affect (Shalley et al., 2004). Moreover, the results have been quite diverse, revealing complex relations among positive affect, negative affect, and creativity. Taken together, extant work concerning affect and creativity in the workplace suggests that affect serves at least four functions in the unfolding processes of generating creative ideas in organizational settings: (a) negative affect may prompt individuals to start engaging in the process of generating creative ideas or solutions (George & Zhou, 2007; Zhou & George, 2001); (b) once individuals have started the creativity process, positive affect may help them to gain access to information from their memory that would have been difficult to access when they were not in certain affective states, or it may facilitate cognitive variation (Amabile, Barsade, Mueller, & Staw, 2005); (c) during the creative idea generation process, negative affect may cue individuals that they need to exert effort and persist until they produce ideas and solutions that are truly creative (George & Zhou, 2002); and (d) the link between affect and creativity is dynamic in that positive affect may be both an antecedent and consequence of creativity, hence, a creative activity "can be an emotional experience in and of itself"(Amabile et al., 2005, p. 393).

As mentioned earlier, organizational contexts are expected to affect employees' creativity by influencing motivational, cognitive, or affective processes related to creative idea generation. In addition, organizational contexts are said to interact with individual differences to affect creativity. We now turn to a review of empirical studies that investigated effects of organizational contexts on employees' creativity. We organize this review into two parts: the first part is concerned with the impact of social or interpersonal contexts, and the second part is concerned with the impact of task contexts. As with many similar attempts at classifying studies and variables in organizational sciences, we recognize that classifying contextual factors into social versus task contexts is only relative instead of being absolute; in some instances, these two types of contexts are related. For example, although we classify goals and feedback as part of the employees' task context,

we recognize that goals may be set by supervisors, and feedback is often provided by supervisors and coworkers. As such, social and task contexts can be related to each other.

How Do Social Contexts Influence Employee Creativity?

In organizations, social contexts that have been linked to creativity include leadership and supervisory behaviors, coworker influences, social networks, and cultural influences. We will review representative studies in each of these four categories. Overall, this body of work showed that social contexts have significant impact on creativity in the workplace, suggesting that creativity represents "positive deviance" that is essential for organizations' survival, growth, and progress. It benefits from conducive social relationships in the workplace. Therefore, organizations and managers need to build positive social contexts for creativity to flourish.

Leadership and Supervision

How leadership and supervisory behaviors influence employees' creativity has attracted a great deal of research attention. A number of studies relied on leadership theories to formulate hypotheses concerning how various leadership behaviors affect creativity in the workplace. Theories presented in most of these studies resembled the motivational approach to creativity.

Several studies have examined the impact of transformational leadership on creativity (e.g., Gong, Huang, & Farh, 2009; Shin & Zhou, 2003). For example, integrating transformational leadership theory (Bass, 1985) and the intrinsic motivation perspective (Amabile, 1996), Shin and Zhou (2003) found that transformational leadership was positively related to employees' creativity, and this relation was partially mediated by intrinsic motivation.

Researchers (e.g., Jassen & van Yperren, 2004; Scott & Bruce, 1994; Tierney, Farmer, & Graen, 1999) have also used LMX theory (Dansereau, Graen, & Haga, 1975) to investigate creativity. For example, Tierney and coauthors (1999) found that LMX was positively related to creativity. As another example, Atwater and Carmeli (2009) found that LMX had a positive influence on employees' felt energy, which consequently resulted in creativity involvement at work.

A large number of studies have investigated how supervisory behaviors affect employees' creativity (e.g., Amabile & Conti, 1999; Amabile, Conti, Coon, Lazenby, & Herron, 1996; Amabile, Schatzel,

Moneta, & Kramer, 2004; Andrews & Farris, 1967; Chen & Aryee, 2007; Frese, Teng, & Wijnen, 1999; George & Zhou, 2001; Krause 2004; Oldham & Cummings, 1996; Shalley & Gilson, 2004; Yuan & Woodman, 2010; Zhou, 2003). Most of these studies took a motivational approach to theorize how and why the supervisory behaviors being investigated influence employees' creativity.

Jaussi and Dionne (2003) explored the effects of a leader's unconventional behaviors, such as standing on furniture and hanging ideas on clotheslines, on individual creativity. They found that after controlling for transformational leadership, leader's role modeling had a positive effect on followers' creativity, and this relation was also moderated by leaders' unconventional behaviors in such a way that the positive effect of role modeling on creativity was stronger when leaders' unconventional behaviors were high rather than low.

Empowering leadership involves emphasizing the job significance of the employee, allowing autonomy in decision-making, showing confidence in the employee's capabilities, and getting rid of constraints of employee performance (Ahearne, Mathieu, & Rapp, 2005; Arnold, Arad, Rhoades, & Drasgow, 2000). Zhang and Bartol (2010) found that empowerment leadership led to increased employee creativity through psychological empowerment, which in turn was related to creative process engagement and intrinsic motivation.

On the other hand, researchers also identified supervisory behaviors that negatively affect their employees' creativity. For example, Oldham and Cummings (1996) found that controlling supervision negatively related to creativity. Zhou (2003) showed that supervisors' close monitoring behavior was negatively related to employees' creativity. Porath and Erez (2007) found that rudeness from a direct authority reduced the target individual's creativity.

Taken together, prior research on effects of leadership and supervision suggest that managers should exhibit transformational leadership behavior, develop high-quality LMX relationships, and exhibit various supportive supervisory behaviors that have been found to lead to employee's creativity, and they should avoid engaging in behaviors such as close monitoring, which has been shown to lead to low levels of employee creativity.

Coworkers' Influences

Coworkers may also influence employee creativity. A large number of studies have investigated how and why such influences occur (e.g., Farmer, Tierney, & Kung-McIntyre, 2003; George & Zhou, 2001; Madjar, Oldham, & Pratt, 2002; Pearsall, Ellis, & Evans, 2008; Shalley & Oldham, 1997; Van Dyne, Jehn, & Cummings, 2002; Zhou & George, 2001; Zhou, 2003). For example, prior research suggests that coworkers may influence creativity by serving as creative role models (Zhou, 2003), by engaging in helping and supportive behaviors (e.g., Zhou & George, 2001), by setting creativity expectations (e.g., Farmer et al., 2003), and by posing as competition (Shalley & Oldham, 1997).

Prior research showed that creative role models have positive influences on eminent individuals' creativity (Bloom & Sosniak, 1981; Simonton 1975, 1984; Zuckerman, 1977). In the organizational creativity literature, research has demonstrated that the presence of creative models is beneficial to employees' creativity, although the relationship is complex.

In particular, Zhou (2003) examined conditions under which the presence of creative coworkers is beneficial for employees' creativity. She theorized that, when creative coworkers were present, employees could learn and acquire creativity-relevant skills and strategies. However, intrinsic motivation would be needed to propel the employees to learn and acquire these skills and strategies. Supervisors could enhance employees' intrinsic motivation by either providing developmental feedback or avoid engaging in close monitoring behaviors (i.e., the extent to which supervisors keep close tabs on their employees to ensure that the employees do exactly what they are told, perform tasks in expected ways, and do not do things that supervisors might disapprove of). Converging results from two field studies demonstrated that, as hypothesized, when creative coworkers were present and the less supervisors engaged in close monitoring, the greater the employees' creativity. Study 2 showed that the contribution of this joint condition was stronger for employees with less creative personalities. In addition, Study 2 found that, when creative coworkers were present, the more supervisors provided developmental feedback, the greater the employees' creativity.

Shalley and Oldham (1997) examined the impact of competition on creativity. Using the intrinsic motivation perspective, they argued it was necessary to distinguish two aspects of competition: informational and controlling. Results showed participants exhibited higher levels of creativity in two informational conditions (i.e., when participants were in competition with others present but not visible, and when they were in competition with absent others and were visible to noncompetitive others) than in a controlling condition (i.e., when participants were in competition with present others and visible to them), thereby supporting the informational versus controlling competition hypothesis. However, other results failed to support the hypothesis. Taken together, results of this study provided mixed support to the hypotheses concerning effects of informational versus controlling competition. More research is needed to shed light on the complex relation between the presence of competitive coworkers and employees' creativity.

Hirst, Van Knippenberg, and Zhou (2009) investigated the cross-level interaction between goal orientation and team learning behavior. They found that a nonlinear interaction existed between team members' learning orientation and team learning behavior on individual creativity. When team learning behavior was high, learning orientation had the strongest positive effect on employee creativity when learning orientation was at a moderate level rather than at lower or higher levels. They also found that approach orientation interacted with team learning behavior in that approach orientation was positively associated with employee creativity only when team learning behavior was high.

Social Networks

Shalley, Zhou, and Oldham (2004) argue that social networks should be one of the new directions in creativity research. Fortunately, how social networks influence creativity or the idea generation component in the entire innovation process has attracted increasing research attention in recent years. As mentioned earlier, studies on effects of social networks on creativity have taken a largely cognitive approach to creativity, theorizing that certain network positions or configurations facilitate access to diverse information or different perspectives, and their effectiveness in using such information in creative idea production (e.g., Cattani & Ferriani, 2008; Fleming, Mingo, & Chen, 2007; Lingo & O'Mahony, 2010; Perry-Smith, 2006; Perry-Smith & Shalley, 2003; Zhou, Shin, Brass, Choi, & Zhang, 2009).

According to the concept of *Simmelian tie* (e.g., Simmel, 1950), the context could significantly change the character and quality of dynamic relationships embedded in the context. "A tie becomes Simmelian when the parties involved in it are reciprocally connected to one another and each is reciprocally connected to another, third party"

(Krackhardt, 1998). Based on the Simmelian tie concept, Tortoriello and Krackhardt (2010) argued that the benefits usually associated with bridging ties depended on the nature of such ties. More specifically, individuals could produce more innovations when they share common third-party ties in boundary-spanning relationships than when they lack such common third-party ties. This is because, in a Simmelian structure, the common third party enhances the stability of the bridging relationship, with reduced dissension and better conflict resolution (Burt, 2002; Krackhardt, 1998), and the cooperation is of a higher level among people with common third parties (Reagans & McEvily, 2003).

Perry-Smith (2006) examined the impact of social network characteristics (i.e., relationship strength, network position, and external ties) on creativity. She found that weaker ties enhanced creativity, but not strong ties. The reason is that weak ties may be related to nonredundant information, which may enhance domain-relevant knowledge (Glynn, 1996; Simonton, 1999), and may provide access to diverse perspectives that facilitates divergent and flexible thinking (Coser, 1975; Granovetter, 1982). Furthermore, the relationship between weak ties and creativity was mediated by access to a more heterogeneous set of direct contacts. In addition, the effect of network centrality on creativity depended on the number of external ties. Centrality was more positively related to creativity when employees had few rather than many external ties.

Fleming, Mingo, and Chen (2007) studied the effect of brokered and cohesive collaboration on an individual's creativity. In a *cohesive network*, most people have direct ties to each other, but in *brokered network*, one person links two or more others who do not have direct ties to each other. Fleming et al. (2007) found that cohesion resulted in marginal benefits for generative creativity when inventors or their collaborators had broader experience, or inventors had worked in many organizations, or inventors' collaborators also worked with external collaborators. In addition, results showed that ideas coming out of a brokered collaboration were less likely to be used in the future. Thus, the collaborative brokerage helped in the idea generation, but hindered idea diffusion and use by others.

Zhou and colleagues (Zhou et al., 2009) examined the effect of weak ties on employee creativity. They argued that more weak ties should provide more sources of novel ideas and therefore increase the probability of creativity (Campbell, 1960; Simonton, 1999). But too many weak ties would be demanding regarding the time and effort to maintain them, thus distracting from one's creative endeavors; could not guarantee productive discussion with each contact; and might bring information overload to the individual. Consistent with their predictions, a curvilinear relationship was seen between the number of weak ties and employee creativity. Specifically, employees showed more creativity when their number of weak ties was at moderate rather than lower or higher levels. Furthermore, employees' conformity value, which refers to the extent that individuals prefer "restraint of actions, inclinations, and impulses that may upset or harm others, and violate social expectations or norms" (Schwartz, 1994, p. 22), moderated the curvilinear relationship in such a way that employees had higher level of creativity at a moderate number of weak ties when conformity was low rather than high.

Baer (2010) extended the strength-of-weak-ties perspective on creativity. He found that network size, strength, and diversity interacted to influence employee creativity. In particular, people exhibited the highest level of creativity when they developed and maintained idea networks of moderate size and weak strength, and when networks diversity was high. The diverse network provided the person access to a variety of different networks that offered a wide range of information. Furthermore, Baer (2010) also tested and found that openness to experience facilitated the absorption and integration of the diverse range of information. Specifically, employees showed the highest level of creativity when they maintained a network of moderate size, weak strength, and high diversity, and were open to experiences.

Cultural Influences

Shalley, Zhou, and Oldham (2004) call for more research on cultural influences on creativity, or creativity in the international context. Although the number of studies devoted to an understanding of how culture influences creativity in the workplace continues to be small, there are two noteworthy developments in this aspect of the literature. First, more studies used data collected from countries other than those where most organizational creativity research has been conducted (i.e., the United States and European countries) (e.g., Farmer et al., 2003; Gong et al., 2009; Zhang & Bartol, 2010; Zhou et al., 2009). Even though these studies were not designed to specifically focus on effects of culture on creativity, the increased number of studies that used international samples suggests data access is becoming less of a concern.

Second, there is increased interest in this topic. For example, a special issue on culture and creativity is forthcoming in the journal *Management and Organization Review*, and researchers have proposed ideas for new research directions in this regard (e.g., Leung & Morris, 2010; Zhou & Su, 2010).

Third, several recent papers have been published on cultural influences. For example, premised on the notion that individuals may belong to different social groups or have different cultural backgrounds, and some individuals have developed multiple social identities, a recent study showed the beneficial effects of individuals' identity integration (Cheng, Sanchez-Burks, & Lee, 2008) on creativity. Identify integration refers to the degree to which the individuals perceive the two identities as compatible or conflicting with each other (Benet-Martínez & Haritatos, 2005). Cheng et al. (2008) found that Asian Americans with higher identity integration exhibited greater creativity. They also showed that female engineers with higher identity integration were more creative in designing a product. The researchers theorized that psychologically managing multiple social identities may facilitate access to multiple knowledge domains, resulting in greater creativity.

How Do Task Contexts Influence Employee Creativity?

Previous studies have found that the task contexts surrounding employees may have profound impact on the employees' creativity (e.g., Hatcher, Ross, & Collins, 1989; Oldham & Cummings, 1996; Shalley, 1991, 1995; Tierney & Farmer, 2002, 2004; Yuan & Zhou, 2008; Zhou, 1998). By task contexts, we refer to job complexity, goals, creativity expectations, and job requirements, feedback and evaluation, autonomy and discretion, time and resources, and rewards. Much of this body of research followed the motivational approach to creativity, mentioned earlier in this chapter. We will review a few representative studies under each of these categories of variables. Overall, the implication from this body of work for POS is that, to encourage employee creativity and "positive deviance," organizations and managers need to ensure that the task contexts boost the employees' motivation, especially intrinsic motivation.

Job Complexity

A number of studies examined effects of a job's overall complexity on creativity (Hatcher et al., 1989; Oldham & Cummings, 1996; Tierney &

Farmer, 2002, 2004). In general, results showed that high levels of job complexity (Hackman & Oldham, 1980) led to high levels of creativity.

Goals, Creativity Expectations, and Job Requirements

Several studies examined goals, creativity expectations, and job requirements on employees' creativity (Carson & Carson, 1993; Madjar & Shalley, 2008; Shalley, 1991, 1995; Shalley, Gilson, & Blum, 2000; Tierney & Farmer, 2004; Unsworth, Wall, & Carter, 2005). For example, Shalley (1991) investigated effects of a creativity goal versus a productivity goal on creativity, and found an interactive effect for goal type on creativity: Individuals exhibited high levels of both creativity and productivity if they were assigned a do-your-best or difficult creativity goal and a difficult productivity goal, and creativity was low if individuals were given a do-your-best or difficult productivity goal without also assigning a creativity goal.

Feedback and Evaluation

Employees routinely receive feedback and evaluation in the workplace. Partially because of the widespread use of feedback and evaluations in individuals' daily lives and in work settings, researchers have investigated whether and how feedback and evaluations can be structured in such a way that they facilitate, rather than inhibit, employees' creativity (e.g., Amabile, 1979; Amabile, Goldfarb, & Brackfield, 1990; Bartis, Szymanski, & Harkins, 1988; Shalley, 1995; Shalley & Oldham, 1985; Shalley & Perry-Smith, 2001; Zhou, 1998, 2003; Zhou & Oldham, 2001). In general, research has shown that feedback and evaluation significantly affect employees' creativity, suggesting that to promote creativity, organizations and managers need to provide the employees with feedback and evaluations in an informational, instead of controlling, manner (cf. Zhou, 1998).

Different from most studies on this topic, which took the motivational approach to an understanding of how and why feedback and evaluations affect creativity, Yuan and Zhou (2008) used a cognitive approach. They suggested that the mixed results in the literature about the effect of external evaluation expectation on creativity may be due to the fact that there are different phases in the production process of creative ideas (i.e., variation and selective retention; Campbell, 1960). Indeed, they found that at the variation phase, participants expecting external evaluation came up with fewer creative ideas.

But, during the selective retention phase, participants expecting external evaluation were more effective in improving idea appropriateness. In addition, participants with the most creative ideas were those expecting external evaluation only during selective retention phase.

Autonomy and Discretion

A few studies relied on the intrinsic motivation perspective to examine effects of autonomy or job discretion on employee creativity. These studies consistently found that high levels of autonomy or discretion led to high levels of creativity (e.g., Shalley, 1991; Zhou, 1998).

Time and Stress

Baer and Oldham (2006) argued that creative time pressure experienced by employees might have an inverted U-shape influence on employee creativity. Although they failed to find support for the simple curvilinear relationship, they found that support for creativity moderated this relationship in that employees exhibited the highest level of creativity when they experienced moderate levels of creativity time pressure and received support for creativity. In addition, support for creativity and openness for experience also jointly moderated the curvilinear relationship between creative time pressure and employee creativity. That is, employees had the highest level of creativity when creative time pressure was intermediate, employees received support for creativity, and they had high levels of openness to experience.

Time pressure is a challenge-related stressor and can result in desirable outcomes. Ohly and Fritz (2010) studied the effects of time pressure and job control on creativity and proactive behaviors on a daily basis. Using multilevel analyses, they found that time pressure and job control were positively related to challenge appraisal, which in turn was positively related to creativity and proactive behaviors. In addition, cross-level analyses showed that daily time pressure and job control partially mediated the relationship between chronic time pressure and job control and challenge appraisal, respectively.

Byron, Khazanchi, and Nazarian (2010) conducted a meta-analysis on the effect of stressors on creativity. Based on 76 experimental studies (including 82 independent samples), they found that the effect of stressors on creativity was contingent on how stress-inducing the stressor was and the type of stress induced. Results showed that evaluative stress had a curvilinear relationship with creativity.

Individuals were more creative in low evaluative contexts than were those in control conditions; but those in highly evaluative contexts had lower creativity than did individuals in control conditions. The meta-analysis also showed that uncontrollability had a negative effect on creativity.

Rewards

One of the most intriguing, heated debates about organizational creativity is concerned with the effects of rewards on creativity in the workplace, with some researchers arguing that rewards undermine creativity, and others maintaining that rewards enhance creativity (e.g., Abbey & Dickson, 1983; Amabile, 1996; Amabile, Hennessey, & Grossman, 1986; Baer, Oldham, & Cummings, 2003; Eisenberger & Armeli, 1997; Eisenberger & Aselage, 2009; Eisenberger & Selbst, 1994; Friedman, 2009; George & Zhou, 2002; Kahai, Sosik, & Avolio, 2003). One might argue that if creativity is so important for organizations' survival and growth, employees who come up with creative ideas should be rewarded. However, results obtained from prior research suggest that the relation between rewards and creativity is more complex than most would have expected. To illustrate, we review a few prior studies.

Eisenberger and Armeli (1997) argue that rewards are given in recognition of individuals' competence, their effort at engaging in creativity, and their actual creative achievements. Using terms from cognitive evaluation theory and the intrinsic motivation perspective of creativity, if rewards are perceived as informational, they are likely to promote employees' creativity. Indeed, Eisenberger and Rhoades (2001) found that promised reward improved creativity when the reward was contingent upon creativity. They also found that rewards increased creativity via two underlying mechanisms. First, rewards contingent on creativity increased participants' extrinsic motivation. Second, such rewards also enhanced participants' perceived self-determination, and consequently intrinsic motivation, which in turn led to creativity.

George and Zhou (2002) did not find any main effect of rewards and recognition on creativity. However, their results demonstrated that rewards and recognition interacted with negative moods and clarity of feelings in such a way that negative moods were positively related to creativity when clarity of feelings and rewards and recognition were both at high levels.

Baer, Oldham, and Cummings (2003) showed that extrinsic rewards were positively related to employee creativity when employees are given simpler rather than complex and difficult jobs. In addition, this relation was true only for employees with an adaptive cognitive style. Furthermore, employees' creativity was not affected by extrinsic rewards when they had an innovative style and worked on complex jobs, and extrinsic rewards decreased employee creativity for those in the adaptive style/complex job or innovative style/simple job conditions.

Future Directions

In sum, prior research on organizational creativity has shown that social and task contexts may promote or restrict employees' creativity. These contextual effects are theorized to influence creativity via motivational, cognitive, and affective mechanisms. Thus, to enhance employee creativity, organizations, managers, and coworkers need to engage in behaviors that enhance creativity, and to set up task contexts that are conducive to creativity.

There are many possibilities for future creativity research. For example, Shalley, Zhou, and Oldham (2004) call for more research on directly testing intrinsic motivation as a mediator, differential functions of positive versus negative mood states, individuals' self-concepts such as creative self-efficacy and creative role identity, creative role models, creative process, creativity in the international contexts, social networks, different types of creativity, measurements of creativity, and team creativity. Since Shalley and coauthors issued their call, much progress has made on some of the directions that they encouraged researchers to pay more attention to. Nonetheless, as our literature review suggests, among the research directions identified by Shalley and coauthors, we still know little about whether contextual factors differentially influence different stages of the creative process, similarities and differences in how contextual factors influence creativity in different cultures, and whether different contextual factors lead to different types of creativity. More research is needed along these lines of inquiry.

In addition, there are exciting avenues for research that would explicitly link the organizational creativity and POS literatures together. These include: What is the relationship between creativity and organizational flourishing? When do the positive and negative consequences of creativity occur (Zhou & Shalley, 2008b)? What are the relationships between organizational vitality, virtuousness, or positive energy and creativity?

Conclusion

What Is Missing from Organizational Creativity Literature: Adversity and Creativity

Although our review of the organizational creativity literature suggests that, to enhance employees' creativity, it is advisable that managers and organizations build positive contexts in the workplace, we do not mean to suggest that creativity can only occur under conditions that are favorable, positive, and pleasant. In fact, Anderson, De Dreu, and Nijstad (2004) note that "Organizational life is full of negatively connotated phenomena" (p. 166). Such negative phenomena may range from individual-level adversities, such as obstacles encountered by individual employees while they perform their work, employees' job dissatisfaction and negative mood, to organizational-level adversities, such as crises or budget constraints.

Intuitively, one might argue that adversity promotes creativity because it is under challenging or adverse conditions that ordinary employees, whose jobs do not revolve around creativity, will awaken and engage in the search for new and better ways of doing things. However, the organizational creativity literature is surprisingly lacking in what factors propel employees to engage in creativity, when these employees are faced with adverse conditions.

A few extant studies suggest that this line of inquiry will be interesting and fruitful. For example, Zhou and George (2001) demonstrated that when employees experience dissatisfaction with their jobs, and yet have high continuance commitment (they cannot quit their job for a variety of reasons, Allen & Meyer, 1996), their job dissatisfaction was *positively* related to their creativity when one of three conditions existed: useful feedback from coworkers, coworker helping and support, and organizational support for creativity.

In addition, previous studies suggest that, under certain conditions, negative moods may be positively related to creativity in the workplace (George & Zhou, 2002, 2007). For example, George and Zhou (2007) found that positive and negative mood interacted to influence employee creativity in a supportive context. More specifically, based on the mood-as-information theory (Schwarz & Clore, 2003), they theorized that both positive and negative moods were functional for creativity, in that the employees' cognitive processes and behaviors would be tuned on the basis of the signal sent from their moods (Schwarz, 2002). Whereas negative moods alert the employees that the status quo might be problematic, thereby propelling them to engage in the search for new and better ways of doing things, positive moods might facilitate divergent thinking once the employees have engaged in the creative process. Moreover, negative moods may cue employees to exert continued effort until truly creative ideas or solutions have been formed. Results showed that when supervisors were supportive (i.e., providing developmental feedback, showing interactional justice, and being trustworthy), and when employee positive mood was high, negative mood had a positive effect on employee creativity.

Adverse conditions in organizations are bound to happen. Organizations that are able to seize the opportunity to promote creativity may be able to turn things around and become stronger, and those that are not able to do this may decline and even fail. Therefore, we believe it is time for researchers to pursue this important phenomenon. We join Anderson and colleagues (2004) in calling for more research that identifies the full range of conditions under which adversity promotes creativity in the workplace.

Acknowledgments

We greatly appreciate the helpful feedback provided by Professor Kim Cameron on an earlier version of this chapter. The section on future research directions that would connect organizational creativity and POS literatures especially benefited from his ideas and insights.

References

Abbey, A., & Dickson, J.W. (1983). R&D work climate and innovation in semiconductors. *Academy of Management Journal, 26*, 362–368.

Ahearne, M., Mathieu, J., & Rapp, A. (2005). To empower or not to empower your sales force? An empirical examination of the influence of leadership empowerment behavior on customer satisfaction and performance. *Journal of Applied Psychology, 90*, 945–955.

Allen, N.J., & Meyer, J.P. (1996). Affective, continuance, and normative commitment To the organization: An examination of construct validity. *Journal of Vocational Behavior, 49*, 252–276.

Amabile, T.M. (1979). Effects of external evaluation on artistic creativity. *Journal of Personality and Social Psychology, 37*, 221–233.

Amabile, T.M. (1988). A model of creativity and innovation in organizations. In B.M. Staw, & L.L. Cummings (Eds.), *Research in organizational behavior* Vol. 10 (pp. 123–167). Greenwich, CT: JAI Press.

Amabile, T.M. (1996). *Creativity in context*. Boulder, CO: Westview Press.

Amabile, T.M., Barsade, S.G., Mueller, J.S., & Staw, B.M. (2005). Affect and creativity at work. *Administrative Science Quarterly, 50*, 367–403.

Amabile, T.M., & Conti, R. (1999). Changes in the work environment for creativity during downsizing. *Academy of Management Journal, 42*, 630–640.

Amabile, T.M., Conti, R., Coon, H., Lazenby, J., & Herron, M. (1996). Assessing the work environment for creativity. *Academy of Management Journal, 39*, 1154–1184.

Amabile, T.M., Goldfarb, P., & Brackfield, S.C. (1990). Social influences on creativity: Evaluation, coaction, and surveillance. *Creativity Research Journal, 3*, 6–21.

Amabile, T.M., Hennessey, B.A., & Grossman, B.S. (1986). Social influences on creativity: The effects of contracted-for reward. *Journal of Personality and Social Psychology, 50*, 14–23.

Amabile, T., Schatzel, E., Moneta, G., & Kramer, S. (2004). Leader behaviors and the work environment for creativity: Perceived leader support. *Leadership Quarterly, 15*(1), 5–32.

Anderson, N., De Dreu, C.K.W., & Nijstad, B.A. (2004). The routinization of innovation research: A constructively critical review of the state-of-the-science. *Journal of Organizational Behavior, 25*, 147–173.

Andrews, F.M., & Farris, G. F. (1967). Supervisory practices and innovation in scientific teams. *Personnel Psychology, 20*, 497–575.

Arnold, J.J., Arad, S., Rhoades, J.A., & Drasgow, F. (2000). The Empowering Leadership Questionnaire: The construction and validation of a new scale for measuring leader behaviors. *Journal of Organizational Behavior, 21*, 249–269.

Atwater, L., & Carmeli, A. (2009). Leader–member exchange, feelings of energy, and involvement in creative work. *Leadership Quarterly, 20*(3), 264–275.

Baer, M. (2010). The strength-of-weak-ties perspective on creativity: A comprehensive examination and extension. *Journal of Applied Psychology, 95*, 592–601.

Baer, M., & Oldham, G. (2006). The curvilinear relation between experienced creative time pressure and creativity: Moderating effects of openness to experience and support for creativity. *Journal of Applied Psychology, 91*, 963–970.

Baer, M., Oldham, G.R., & Cummings, A. (2003). Rewarding creativity: When does it really matter? *Leadership Quarterly, 14*, 569–586

Bartis, S., Szymanski, K., & Harkins, S.G. (1988). Evaluation and performance: A two edged knife. *Personality and Social Psychology Bulletin, 14*, 242–251.

Bass, B.M. (1985). *Leadership and performance beyond expectation.* New York: Free Press.

Benet-Martínez, V., Leu, J., Lee, F., & Morris, M. (2005). Negotiating biculturalism: Cultural frame switching in biculturals with oppositional versus compatible cultural identities. *Journal of Cross-Cultural Psychology, 33*, 492–516.

Bloom, B.S., & Sosniak, L.A. (1981). Talent development vs. schooling. *Educational Leadership, 39*(2), 86–94.

Byron, K., Khazanchi, S., & Nazarian, D. (2010). The relationship between stressors and creativity: A meta-analysis examining competing theoretical models. *Journal of Applied Psychology, 95*, 201–212.

Burt, R.S. (2002). Bridge decay. *Social Networks, 24*, 333–363.

Cameron, K.S., Dutton, J.E., & Quinn, R. E. (2003). *Positive Organizational Scholarship.* San Francisco: Barrett-Koehler.

Campbell, D.T. (1960). Blind variation and selective retention in creative thought as to other knowledge processes. *Psychological Review, 67*, 380–400.

Carson, P.P., & Carson, K.D. (1993). Managing creativity enhancement through goal setting and feedback. *Journal of Creative Behavior, 27*, 36–45.

Cattani, G., & Ferriani, S. (2008). A core/periphery perspective on individual creative performance: Social networks and cinematic achievements in the Hollywood film industry. *Organization Science, 19*, 824–844.

Chen, Z.X., & Aryee, S. (2007). Delegation and employee work outcomes: An examination of the cultural context of mediating processes in China. *Academy of Management Journal, 50*(1), 226–238.

Cheng, C., Sanchez-Burks, J., & Lee, F. (2008). Connecting the dots within: Creative performance and identity integration. *Psychological Science, 19*, 1178–1184.

Coser, R. (1975). The complexity of roles as a seedbed of individual autonomy. In L. Coser (Ed.), *The idea of social structure: Papers in honor of Robert K. Merton* (pp. 237–263). New York: Harcourt Brace.

Deci, E.L., & Ryan, R.M. (1980). The empirical exploration of intrinsic motivational processes. In L. Berkowitz (Ed.), *Advances in experimental social psychology* (pp. 39–80). New York: Academic Press.

Deci, E.L., & Ryan, R.M. (1985). *Intrinsic motivation and self-determination in human behavior.* New York: Plenum.

Drazin, R., Glynn, M.A., & Kazanjian, R.K. (1999). Multilevel theorizing about creativity in organizations: A sensemaking perspective. *Academy of Management Review, 24*, 286–307.

Eisenberger, R., & Armeli, S. (1997). Can salient reward increase creative performance without reducing intrinsic creative interest? *Journal of Personality and Social Psychology, 72*, 652–663.

Eisenberger, R., & Aselage, J. (2009). Incremental effects of reward on experienced performance pressure: positive outcomes for intrinsic interest and creativity. *Journal of Organizational Behavior, 30*, 95–117.

Eisenberger, R., & Rhoades, L. (2001). Incremental effects of reward on creativity. *Journal of Personality and Social Psychology, 81*, 728–741.

Eisenberger, R., & Selbst, M. (1994). Does reward increase or decrease creativity? *Journal of Personality and Social Psychology, 66*, 1116–1127.

Farmer, S.M., Tierney, P., & Kung-McIntyre, K. (2003). Employee creativity in Taiwan: An application of role identity theory. *Academy of Management Journal, 46*, 618–630.

Fleming, L., Mingo, S., & Chen, D. (2007). Collaborative brokerage, generative creativity, and creative success. *Administrative Science Quarterly, 52*, 443–475.

Ford, C. (1996). A theory of individual creative action in multiple social domains. *Academy of Management Review, 21*, 1112–1142.

Frese, M., Teng, E., & Wijnen, C.J. (1999). Helping to improve suggestion systems: Predictors of making suggestions in companies. *Journal of Organizational Behavior, 20*, 1139–1155.

Friedman, R. S. (2009). Reinvestigating the effects of promised reward on creativity. *Creativity Research Journal, 21*, 258–264.

George, J.M., & Zhou, J. (2001). When openness to experience and conscientiousness are related to creative behavior: An interactional approach. *Journal of Applied Psychology, 86*, 513–524.

George, J.M., & Zhou, J. (2002). Understanding when bad moods foster creativity and good ones don't: The role of context and clarity of feelings. *Journal of Applied Psychology, 87*, 687–697.

George, J.M., & Zhou, J. (2007). Dual tuning in a supportive context: Joint contributions of positive mood, negative mood, and supervisory behaviors to employee creativity. *Academy of Management Journal, 50*, 605–622.

Glynn, M.A. (1996). Innovative genius: A framework for relating individual and organizational intelligences to innovation. *Academy of Management Review, 21*, 1081–1111.

Gong, Y., Huang, J. C., & Farh, J. L. (2009). Employee learning orientation, transformational leadership, and employee creativity: The mediating role of employee creative self-efficacy. *Academy of Management Journal, 52*, 765–778.

Granovetter, M.S. (1982). The strength of weak ties: A network theory revisited. In P.V. Marsden, & N. Lin (Eds.), *Social structure and network analysis* (pp. 105–130). Beverly Hills, CA: Sage.

Hackman, J.R., & Oldham, G.R. (1980). *Work redesign.* Reading, MA: Addison-Wesley.

Hatcher, L., Ross, T.L., & Collins, D. (1989). Prosocial behavior, job complexity, and suggestion contribution under gainsharing plans. *Journal of Applied Behavioral Science, 25*, 231–248.

Hirst, G., van Knippenberg D., & Zhou, J. (2009). A cross-level perspective on employee creativity: Goal orientation, team learning behavior, and individual creativity. *Academy of Management Journal, 52*, 280–293.

Janssen, O., & Van Yperen, N. W. (2004). Employees' goal orientations, the quality of leader-member exchange, and the outcomes of job performance and job satisfaction. *Academy of Management Journal, 47*, 368–384.

Jaussi, K., & Dionne, S. (2003). Leading for creativity: The role of unconventional leader behavior. *Leadership Quarterly, 14*, 475–498.

Kahai, S.S., Sosik, J.J., & Avolio, B.J. (2003). Effects of leadership style, anonymity, and rewards on creativity-relevant processes and outcomes in an electronic meeting system context. *Leadership Quarterly, 14*, 499–524.

Krackhardt, D. (1998). Simmelian tie: Super strong and sticky. In R.M. Kramer, & M.A. Neale (Eds.), *Power and influence in organizations* (pp. 21–38). Thousand Oaks, CA: Sage.

Krause, D.E. (2004). Influence-based leadership as a determinant of the inclination to innovate and of innovation-related behaviors: An empirical investigation. *Leadership Quarterly, 15*(1), 79–102.

Leung, K., & Morris, M.W. (2010). Culture and creativity: A social psychological analysis. In D. de Cremer, J.K. Murnighan, & R. van Dick (Eds.), *Social psychology and organizations.* New York: Routledge.

Lingo, E.L., O'Mahony, S. (2010). Nexus work: Brokerage on creative projects. *Administrative Science Quarterly, 55*, 47–81.

Madjar, N., Oldham, G.R., & Pratt, M.G. (2002). There's no place like home? The contributions of work and non-work creativity support to employees' creative performance. *Academy of Management Journal, 45*, 757–767.

Madjar, N., & Shalley, C.E. (2008). Multiple tasks' and multiple goals' effect on creativity: forced incubation or just a distraction? *Journal of Management, 34*, 786–805.

Mumford, M.D., & Gustafson, S.B. (1988). Creativity syndrome: Integration, application, and innovation. *Psychological Bulletin, 103*, 27–43.

Ohly, S., & Fritz, C. (2010). Work characteristics, challenge appraisal, creativity, and proactive behavior: A multi-level study. *Journal of Organizational Behavior, 31*, 543–565.

Oldham, G.R., & Cummings, A. (1996). Employee creativity: Personal and contextual factors at work. *Academy of Management Journal, 39*, 607–634.

Pearsall, M., Ellis, A., & Evans, J. (2008). Unlocking the effects of gender faultlines on team creativity: Is activation the key? *Journal of Applied Psychology, 93*, 225–234.

Perry-Smith, J.E. (2006). Social yet creative: The role of social relationships in facilitating individual creativity. *Academy of Management Journal, 49*, 85–101.

Perry-Smith, J.E., & Shalley, C.E. (2003). The social side of creativity: A static and dynamic social network perspective. *Academy of Management Review, 28*, 89–106.

Porath, C.L., & Erez, A. (2007). Does rudeness really matter? The effects of rudeness on task performance and helpfulness. *Academy of Management Journal, 50*, 1181–1197.

Reagans, R., & McEvily, B. (2003). Network structure and knowledge transfer: The effects of cohesion and range. *Administrative Science Quarterly, 48*, 240–267.

Schwarz, N. (2002). Situated cognition and the wisdom of feelings: Cognitive tuning. In L. Feldman Barrett, & P. Salovey (Eds.), *The wisdom in feelings* (pp. 144–166). New York: Guilford.

Schwarz, N., & Clore, G.L. (2003). Mood as information. *Psychological Inquiry, 14*, 296–303.

Schwartz, S.J. (1994). Are there universal aspects in the structure and content of human values? *Journal of Social Issues, 50*, 19–45.

Scott, S.G., & Bruce, R.A. (1994). Determinants of innovative behavior: A path model of individual innovation in the workplace. *Academy of Management Journal, 37*, 580–607.

Shalley, C.E. (1991). Effects of productivity goals, creativity goals, and personal discretion on individual creativity. *Journal of Applied Psychology, 76*, 179–185.

Shalley, C.E. (1995). Effects of coaction, expected evaluation, and goal setting on creativity and productivity. *Academy of Management Journal, 38*, 483–503.

Shalley, C.E., & Gilson, L.L. (2004). What leaders need to know: A review of social and contextual factors that can foster or hinder creativity. *Leadership Quarterly, 15*, 33–53.

Shalley, C.E., Gilson, L.L., & Blum, T.C. (2000). Matching creativity requirements and the work environment: Effects on satisfaction and intention to leave. *Academy of Management Journal, 43*, 215–223.

Shalley, C.E., & Oldham, G.R. (1985). Effects of goal difficulty and expected evaluation on intrinsic motivation: A laboratory study. *Academy of Management Journal, 28*, 628–640.

Shalley, C.E., & Oldham, G.R. (1997). Competition and creative performance: Effects of competitor presence and visibility. *Creativity Research Journal, 10*, 337–345.

Shalley, C.E., & Perry-Smith, J.E. (2001). Effects of social-psychological factors on creative performance: The role of informational and controlling expected evaluation and modeling experience. *Organizational Behavior and Human Decision Processes, 84*, 1–22.

Shalley, C.E., Zhou, J., & Oldham, G.R. (2004). The effects of personal and contextual characteristics on creativity: Where should we go from here? *Journal of Management, 30*, 933–958.

Shin, S., & Zhou, J. (2003). Transformational leadership, conservation, and creativity: Evidence from Korea. *Academy of Management Journal, 46*, 703–714.

Simmel, G. (1950). *The sociology of Georg Simmel.* K.H. Wolff (Ed.). Glencoe, IL: Free Press.

Simonton, D.K. (1975). Sociocultural context of individual creativity: A transhistorical time-series analysis. *Journal of Personality and Social Psychology, 32*, 1119–1133.

Simonton, D.K. (1984). Artistic creativity and interpersonal relationships across and within generations. *Journal of Personality and Social Psychology, 46*, 1273–1286.

Simonton, D.K. (1999). *Origins of genius.* New York: Oxford University Press.

Smith, S.M., Ward, T.B., & Finke, R.A. (Eds.). (1995). *The creative cognition approach.* Cambridge, MA: MIT Press.

Tierney, P., & Farmer, S.M. (2002). Creative self-efficacy: Potential antecedents and relationship to creative performance. *Academy of Management Journal, 45*, 1137–1148.

Tierney, P., & Farmer, S. (2004). The Pygmalion Process and Employee Creativity. *Journal of Management, 30*, 413–432.

Tierney, P., Farmer, S.M., & Graen, G.B. (1999). An examination of leadership and employee creativity: The relevance of traits and relationships. *Personnel Psychology, 52*, 591–620.

Tortoriello, M., & Krackhardt, D. (2010). Activating cross-boundary knowledge: The role of Simmelian ties in the generation of innovations. *Academy of Management Journal, 53*, 167–181.

Unsworth, K. (2001). Unpacking creativity. *Academy of Management Review, 26*, 289–297.

Unsworth, K.L., Wall, T.B., & Carter, A. (2005). Creative requirement: A neglected construct in the study of employee creativity? *Group and Organization Management, 30*, 541–560.

Van Dyne, L., Jehn, K.A., & Cummings, A. (2002). Differential effects of strain on two forms of work performance: Individual employee sales and creativity. *Journal of Organizational Behavior, 23*, 57–74.

Woodman, R.W., Sawyer, J.E., & Griffin, R.W. (1993). Toward a theory of organizational creativity. *Academy of Management Review, 18*, 293–321.

Yuan, F., & Woodman, R.W. (2010). Innovative behavior in the workplace: the role of performance and image outcome expectations. *Academy of Management Journal, 53*, 323–342.

Yuan, F., & Zhou, J. (2008). Differential effects of expected external evaluation on different parts of the creative idea production process and on final product creativity. *Creativity Research Journal, 20*, 391–403.

Zhang, X., & Bartol, K. M. (2010). Linking empowering leadership and employee creativity: The influence of psychological empowerment, intrinsic motivation, and creative process engagement. *Academy of Management Journal, 53*, 107–128.

Zhou, J. (2003). When the presence of creative coworkers is related to creativity: Role of supervisor close monitoring, developmental feedback, and creative personality. *Journal of Applied Psychology, 88*, 413–422.

Zhou, J. (1998). Feedback valence, feedback style, task autonomy, and achievement orientation: Interactive effects on creative performance. *Journal of Applied Psychology, 83*, 261–276.

Zhou, J., & George, J.M. (2001). When job dissatisfaction leads to creativity: Encouraging the expression of voice. *Academy of Management Journal, 44*, 682–696.

Zhou, J., & Oldham, G.R. (2001). Enhancing creative performance: Effects of expected developmental assessment strategies and creative personality. *Journal of Creative Behavior, 35*, 151–167.

Zhou, J., & Shalley, C.E. (2003). Research on employee creativity: A critical review and directions for future research. In J.J. Martocchio, & G.R. Ferris (Eds.), *Research in personnel and human resource management* Vol. 22 (pp. 165–217). Oxford: Elsevier Science.

Zhou, J., & Shalley, C.E. (Eds.). (2008a). *Handbook of organizational creativity.* New York: Lawrence Erlbaum.

Zhou, J., & Shalley, C.E. (2008b). Expanding the scope and impact of organizational creativity research. In J. Zhou, & C.E. Shalley (Eds.), *Handbook of organizational creativity* (pp. 347–368). Hillsdale, NJ: Lawrence Erlbaum.

Zhou, J., & Shalley, C.E. (2010). Deepening our understanding of creativity in the workplace. In S. Zedeck, et al. (Eds.), *APA handbook of industrial–organizational psychology* Vol. 1 (pp. 275–302). Washington, DC: American Psychological Association.

Zhou, J., Shin, S. J., Brass, D.J., Choi, J., & Zhang, Z. (2009). Social networks, personal values, and creativity: Evidence for curvilinear and interaction effects. *Journal of Applied Psychology, 94*, 1544–1552.

Zhou, J., & Su, Y. (2010). A missing piece of the puzzle: The organizational context in cultural patterns of creativity. *Management and Organization Review, 6*(3), 391–413.

Zuckerman, H. (1977). *Scientific elite: Nobel laureates in the U.S.* New York: The Free Press.

Organizing the Cat? Generative Aspects of Curiosity in Organizational Life

Spencer Harrison

Abstract

Research on curiosity in organizations is still in a relatively nascent state. In this chapter, I attempt to provide a foundation for research on curiosity in organizational life, with particular attention to the generative properties of curiosity. I review research on the psychology of curiosity, focusing on the distinction between specific and diversive curiosity. I use this foundation as a springboard for understanding the role of individual curiosity in organizations and exploring curiosity at collective levels of analysis. I also consider existing constructs and discuss their similarities and differences with curiosity and conclude with opportunities for future research.

Keywords: Curiosity, specific curiosity, diversive curiosity, curiosity organizing, cue labeling, learning, creativity, puzzles, problems

It may be that it was curiosity that killed the cat, but for human beings it is a very desirable quality. Without it, material progress would slow up and finally stop.
Merritt, 1925, p. 455

Curiosity is a "desire to know, to see, or to experience that motivates exploratory behavior" (Litman, 2005, p. 793). Throughout history, thinkers from a variety of disciplines and backgrounds have recognized the importance of curiosity as a catalyst for human behavior. Philosophers, including Aristotle, Plato, Augustine, Hume, Bentham, and Kant, among others, noted the power of curiosity, calling it a "passion," an "appetite," or even "an innate love of learning" (Loewenstein, 1994, p. 76). Educators have routinely emphasized the significance of curiosity as a motivation that encourages students to inquire, explore, and ultimately, to learn (Dewey, 1910). Artists seem to rely on curiosity for impulses to generate new ideas and to experiment with new artistic techniques (Leuba, 1958). Likewise, writers often rely on generating curiosity within their reader

to impel a plot along (Knobloch, Patzig, Mende, & Hastall, 2004). In a similar vein, scientists have consistently described curiosity as a wellspring of motivation for discovery (Simon, 2001). In sum, a variety of disciplines have consistently recognized curiosity as a generative force.

What do organizational scholars have to say about curiosity? To answer this question, it is instructive to examine to an example of the role of curiosity in science. Scientists have recently begun operating the Large Hadron Collider (LHC). The LHC is the largest particle accelerator ever built. It has cost an estimated $10 billion and requires the coordination of over 10,000 scientists from over 100 countries and hundreds of universities. If the LHC's budget were used as an estimate of its market value, it would rank in the 25th percentile on Forbes' list of

The Biggest Companies. Put simply, it's a large organization. So, what motivates the scientists? What catalyzes all of this organizing? And, what is the mission or the underlying purpose of this organization? When asked this sort of question during an interview for the TV show *60 Minutes*, James Gillies, the spokesman for the project explained:

> Gillies: I would say it's all being done to satisfy human curiosity.
>
> Interviewer: But are there practical things that are likely to come out of it?
>
> Gillies: I'm pretty sure there will be in the long-term. I mean, the history of science shows us that the big advances in human technology come about through curiosity-driven research. (Kroft, 2008)

By its very scale and complexity, this example demonstrates that curiosity does not simply motivate the exploration of individual scientists; it also seems to catalyze organizing activity, in this case creating a rich nexus of resources, individuals, and knowledge. Organizational scholars should have a lot to say about examples like the LHC specifically and the role of curiosity in organizational life generally. But, as of yet, organizational scholarship is relatively silent about the role of curiosity in organizations. With few exceptions, curiosity has rarely been the focal point of study in organizational scholarship (cf. Harrison, 2009; Harvey, Novicevic, Leonard, & Payne, 2007). This dearth of scholarship is surprising, given the fact that curiosity has consistently been shown to be associated with learning, a prime goal of modern organizations (Argyris & Schön, 1978; Gherardi, 1999; Hedberg, 1981; Huber, 1991; Levitt & March, 1988; Weick & Ashford, 2001) and other generative outcomes like increased well-being (Gallagher & Lopez, 2007), longevity (Swan & Carmelli, 1996), the development of emotional intelligence (Leonard & Harvey, 2007), and daily experiences of growth and life satisfaction (Kashdan & Steger, 2007).

The goal of this chapter is to preview the possibilities of curiosity in organizational life, with an emphasis on the generative properties of curiosity. To do so, I begin by defining curiosity and providing a brief review of the psychological literature on curiosity. I use this literature as a backdrop for the final sections, which represent the main thrust of the chapter. In these sections, I review examples of curiosity in organizational life. Most of these examples are fairly minimalistic, some are almost "throw away" quotes in qualitative studies focused on topics of seemingly little relation to curiosity. Others are written by scholars outside of the field of organizational

scholarship that "happened" to be studying work life. Separately, these examples might amount to very little, but I hope, by fitting them together, I can suggest fertile directions for new research. To accomplish this "fitting together," I structure the chapter by focusing on two levels of analysis: examining the potential role of individual curiosity in organizations, and exploring curiosity at collective levels of analysis. In each of these sections, I temper my discussion by considering existing paradigms and research agendas that likely represent complementary or alternative explanations for the role of curiosity in organizations. The underlying thesis is that curiosity is a worthy topic for organizational scholarship and should be a particularly fertile topic of inquiry for scholars concerned with positive organizational processes and outcomes.

Defining Curiosity

Most researchers define curiosity as a desire for knowledge and experience that motivates exploration (Berlyne, 1954, 1966; Fowler, 1965; T. B. Kashdan, Rose, & Fincham, 2004; Keller, 1987; Litman, Hutchins, & Russon, 2005; Loewenstein, 1994; Spielberger & Starr, 1994; Voss & Keller, 1983). Curiosity is often considered a "fundamental" human motivation (Maner & Gerend, 2007), playing a central role in foundational stories—like those of Pandora and Eve (Harrison, 2001).[1]— stories that attempt to address the very essence of the human experience. Perhaps it is appropriate then that studies indicate that curiosity plays a role throughout the life course, manifesting itself during infancy (Piaget, 1936) and continuing to influence behavior well into the twilight of life (Giambra, Camp, & Grodsky, 1992). Because of the relative durability of curiosity throughout life, curiosity seems best described by trait theory (Matthews, Deary, & Whiteman, 2003). In other words, curiosity is a durable individual difference or personality trait that prescribes individuals' typical exploratory responses, and these responses are experienced as dynamic states. What this means is that individuals with higher baseline levels of curiosity are likely to experience states of curiosity more frequently and more intensely. For example, when asked in a recent interview "What is your most marked characteristic?" Charlie Rose, a successful talk show host and journalist, responded, "Curiosity" (Proust Questionnaire, 2010). In other words, he is acknowledging the importance of curiosity as a trait in his life. However, in an earlier interview, he alluded to state-like mechanics of how curiosity functions during his work, referring to a specific set of interviews he had conducted:

> Interviewer: Tell me, you also said you're curious about what makes people tick, what they dream about. Mr. Rose–What is your dream?
>
> Charlie Rose: My dream most of all is to engage life and to have the experience of discovery . . . But I also want to create, in a very specific way, a true global conversation.
>
> Interviewer: And how do you intend to do that? Or, are you doing that already?
>
> Charlie Rose: I am doing that already, but I can do that in a much more, sort of, ordered way.
>
> Interviewer: Are you planning to use the web?
>
> Charlie Rose: I am using the web—that's a given right now.
>
> Interviewer: But . . . further, into China, etc.?
>
> Charlie Rose: Sure, sure. Not only that but over the air and on cable broadcast. It is my curiosity about those things that drives me forward. I mean, this has been a great day—I learned more about Twitter today because I had the CEO of Twitter on the show today; I learned more about LinkedIn because I had the CEO and cofounder of LinkedIn on. I have a greater sense of where Stanford stands today because of my experience with John Hennessy, the President of Stanford. I mean, all of that feeds my curiosity, and it takes me to another place. (van Diggelen, 2009)

What becomes evident is that Rose's curiosity is experienced as a series of states—in his case, due to his profession, a series of conversations that generate new knowledge and lead to new questions. As this example illustrates, and, as with other dispositions (Chen, Gully, & Eden, 2001), the influence of trait curiosity is likely mediated by the experience of states of curiosity. In sum, the trait-state nature of curiosity (and other traits) necessitates attention to individual differences but also to contexts that can trigger curious states.

Types of Curiosity

How curiosity is experienced and the form of exploration that emerges as a result has generated considerable debate. For example, Loewenstein (1994) argues that curiosity has a negative emotional valence; that it is experienced as a state of deprivation that surfaces when individuals become aware of the potential for new knowledge. In contrast, Kashdan, Rose, and Fincham (2004) assert that curiosity arises from the challenge of finding new knowledge, precipitating a flow-like state associated with positive emotions. However, most scholars have noted that episodes of curiosity are more emotionally complex, rife at the moment of inception with conflicting emotions (Berlyne, 1966; Litman, 2005; Spielberger & Starr, 1994) that give way to distinct forms of exploration.

Berlyne (1966) concluded that curiosity tends to emerge as one of two types that he labeled *specific* and *diversive curiosity*. Berlyne's labels are suggestive of the scope each form of curiosity entails. Specific curiosity tends to be narrow in scope, as when a plumber is trying to find a leak (Rose, 2004), an investigator is trying to figure out how to find enough evidence to stop a particular criminal (Collison, 1995), or a potential customer is trying to decode a mystery ad (Fazio, Herr, & Powell, 1992). In each case, the person is looking for a detail or a relatively concrete piece of information that he is fairly certain exists and that, if found, will solve his problem. In contrast, diversive curiosity tends to be very broad in scope, as when industrial designers play with potential features for prototypes (Sutton & Hargadon, 1996) or doctors try to discover the interesting backstories of their patients (Fitzgerald, 1999). In these examples, the person feeling curious is simply looking for new information and seeking novel ways to combine this information with what she already knows. Berlyne (1966) theorized that these differences in scope were born out of differences in emotion, hypothesizing that specific curiosity should be associated with negative emotions, whereas diversive curiosity should be associated with positive emotions. Studies by Litman and coauthors (Litman & Jimerson, 2004; Litman & Silvia, 2006) and Harrison (2009) provide empirical evidence for this claim. However, even given the emotional and exploratory distinctions between the two forms of curiosity, they generally correlate with one another (Harrison, 2009; Litman & Jimerson, 2004; Litman & Silvia, 2006) and likely work together.

Support for Berlyne's Typology

Research on information theories of emotion helps to explain why the emotional valence of curiosity may influence differences in the scope of exploration. Negative affect causes a narrowing of attention, an emphasis on data-driven or controlled processing (Forgas, 2000; Schwarz, 2002), and, in this frame of mind, novelty is more likely to be experienced as a problem to be solved or a mistake to be corrected (Crowe & Higgins, 1997). In contrast, positive feelings like excitement and pleasure tend to communicate a context that is safe for exploring and thereby drive playful behaviors that help individuals reorganize their understanding of the world (Fredrickson, 2001). These findings buttress Berlyne's intuition about the differences between specific and diversive curiosity, outlining the relationships between emotion and cognition during exploration.

Litman's work (2005) has furthered Berlyne's typology. Litman notes that the negative emotion that accompanies specific curiosity is often a sense of deprivation,

> [A]ctivated when individuals feel they are lacking needed information . . . [the] information sought during [this sense of deprivation] is theorized to be substantive, meaningful, and capable of increasing subjective feelings of competence, such as the answer to a complex question, a valuable fact, or solution to a difficult problem. (2005, p. 799)

In contrast, the positive emotions that accompany diversive curiosity emerge as feelings of interest, when individuals sense

> [T]hat it would be enjoyable to discover something new. Thus [curiosity as a feeling of interest] is related to the anticipated pleasure from finding out information of a more casual, unessential, entertaining, or aesthetically pleasing nature, such as juicy gossip, an amusing anecdote, or an entertaining story. (2005, p. 799–800)

Litman traces these differences between deprivation and interest to the interaction of the mesolimbic dopamine activation system and the opioid activation system in the nucleus accumbens. Litman's work provides a physiological explanation that helps integrate the competing ideas of Loewenstein (1994) and Kashdan (2009) within Berlyne's earlier work. Hence, work on information theories of emotion and recent work in neuroscience help to validate the notion that curiosity can be either specific or diversive in nature, generating distinct forms of exploration that lead to different types of information and different types of learning. Put more simply, why we explore influences how we explore, and how we explore influences what we might learn. Hence, the emotional duality of curiosity is important because curiosity helps to explain exploration and ultimately learning motivated by the frustration of attempting to solve a difficult problem or the excitement of trying to combine disparate ideas in new ways.

These distinct forms of curiosity become more intelligible when considering contexts that activate states of curiosity. Berlyne (1960) proposes that novel, discrepant, or anomalous cues, when noticed, evoke curiosity. Loewenstein (1994) argues that when these cues signal a deficit or gap in existing knowledge, then individuals are likely to experience a state of specific curiosity and concomitant feelings of anxiety. Litman (2005) agrees with Loewenstein's prescription for specific curiosity, but he also argues that some novel cues may evoke excitement and signal an opportunity for playing with ideas. The point seems to be that, although some cues might unequivocally contain strong signals for one type of curiosity or another, most novel cues are inherently ambiguous stimuli, and hence the nature of the social context at the moment when the cue emerges can have a huge influence on how the cue is labelled and what form of curiosity it evokes (a point I explore further below).

Using Berlyne's typology, my work (Harrison, 2009) suggests a mediated model (see Figure 9.1) as a baseline for understanding curiosity in organizations. The model metaphorically represents each step of this process as a series of ripples. The implication is that a state of curiosity tends to lead to exploratory behaviors that, in turn, tend to lead to certain outcomes—each element produces ripples that influence the next. For example, states of specific curiosity engender feelings of deprivation and anxiety that help to cognitively narrow exploratory behavior to search for concrete or detailed pieces of information. If the exploration generates new knowledge, the result is a deepening of existing schema that enables greater efficiency in performing existing tasks. In contrast, states of diversive curiosity engender feelings of excitement and anticipation, stimulating a cognitively broader search pattern and leading to the acquisition of often unexpected information. The result is an uptick in cognitive flexibility, enabling creativity and innovation. In the latter part of this chapter, I will revisit this model to show how these ripples are not strictly intrapersonal, but can have interpersonal and ultimately organizational implications.

Examining Individual Curiosity in Organizations

In his paper on longitudinal ethnographic research, Barley comments on the unique role researchers play in organizations. He notes, "by becoming a participant observer, one creates for the ecology of an organization a role that did not exist before: namely,

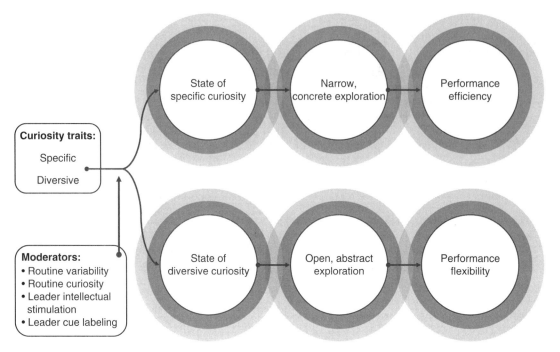

Fig. 9.1 A mediated model of individual curiosity.

the role of the ever-present and ever-curious observer" (1990, p. 240). Perhaps it is ironic then that the organizational research that provides the best evidence of the importance of individual curiosity in organizations tends to be found in qualitative studies. It is clear from this body of research that organizations often have many "ever-curious observers" within their ranks (without relying on researchers). I begin by considering evidence about the role of trait curiosity in organizations and then move on to consider the role of states of curiosity.

Trait Curiosity in Organizations

The empirical evidence suggests that curiosity is an important trait for individuals at any organizational level. The importance of trait curiosity has been mentioned in a variety of work. Studies suggest that trait curiosity is important in a wide variety of fields like therapy (Goldberg, 2002), dentistry, social work, and law (Nachmann, 1960), psychology and physics (Bordin, 1966; Galinsky, 1962), medicine (Fitzgerald, 1999), and call centers (Harrison, Sluss, & Ashforth, 2010) among others. One particularly intriguing example of the significance of curiosity in work is described in Sutton and Hargadon's (1996) ethnographic study of IDEO, the industrial design firm. They observed that IDEO specifically looks for curiosity when hiring employees. As one of their designers explains, "the kinds of people who work

here are intellectually curious, inquisitive; they like the design process. They are here because they love designing stuff, and you get to stick your fingers into more things to design" (1996, p. 702). They go on to explain that, beyond improving design, trait curiosity seems to enable being "adaptive in the face of uncertainty" (see also K. E. Weick, 1993). It's likely this overall adaptability that makes curiosity so invaluable to the doing of work in such a wide range of fields.

Curiosity seems to not only be important as part of the primary skills that enable individuals to do their work, it is also implicated in how people manage work and lead within organizations. For example, Cummings (1967) found that curiosity was an important factor in determining the effectiveness of middle managers. A study by Browning, Beyer, and Shetler (1995) might shed some light on how trait curiosity enables certain mechanisms that make managers effective. They studied cooperation across organizations in the hypercompetitive semiconductor industry. One of their informants stood out as being particularly influential in creating cooperative bridges because of his curiosity. They observed:

[Bob] Noyce was a curious genius who liked to hear about almost any topic. This curiosity and his general interpersonal style made him very approachable. . . . These qualities empowered people to act on the clarity they gained from conversations with Noyce. . . . In this way, Noyce's curiosity indirectly increased individual commitment and cooperation. (1995, p. 128)

In this example, curiosity made the leader more approachable (in contrast, Fowlie and Wood [2009] found that being unapproachable was one of the most mentioned attributes of bad leaders). Because curiosity intimates a willingness to learn about "almost any topic," curiosity generates a psychologically safe space (Edmondson, 1999) between leaders and followers, wherein followers can explore and refine new ideas. The result is that the followers ultimately feel energized to pursue new objectives with increased commitment.

Although all of these studies make a case for curiosity as a desirable trait for employees and leaders alike, they offer very few levers for managing curiosity. For instance, the IDEO example indicates that selecting individuals based on their disposition for curiosity is important. But is selection the only way to engender curiosity in organizations? Moreover, by simply considering traits, we are left with a fairly coarse understanding of the behaviors curiosity promotes and how they link to organizational outcomes. Considering the dynamics of curiosity states has the potential to offer more levers for stimulating curiosity and for understanding how curiosity motivates behavior and organizationally relevant outcomes.

State Curiosity

Individuals with higher traits for curiosity tend to experience states of curiosity more frequently and more intensely (Spielberger & Starr, 1994). Organizations often serve as strong situations (Mischel, 1968) or provide strong triggers (Louis & Sutton, 1991) that might catalyze curiosity. A delightfully simple experiment conducted by Heckel (1969) illustrates how easy it is to trigger states of curiosity at work. He mailed envelopes to psychologists: Half of his sample received an empty envelope, and the other half received one that appeared to only include the second page of a message. This second page read: "In light of the foregoing information you can understand why I contacted you" (1969, p. 754). Forty-two of the 50 psychologists receiving this half-letter responded (five even went so far as to call Heckel's office). In a follow-up survey, participants noted that the half-letters generated quite a bit of curiosity, apparently both

specific (some reported feeling frustrated and annoyed) and diverse (others reported feeling playful and humorous). Heckel concluded that "the implications for further research on curiosity in a life situation are extensive" (1969, p. 756).

Much like Heckel's letters, cues that trigger states of curiosity likely abound in organizations. This might seem paradoxical, given the fact that organizations, almost by definition, are often viewed as centers of stability. For example, at the organizational level, culture, norms, routines, and structure have a propensity to disseminate and sustain the status quo. Shared schema, roles, and socialization serve a similar function at the individual level. As a result, organizational life often seems mindless (Ashforth & Fried, 1988), mechanistic (Morgan, 2006), and simplified (Miller, 1993)—indeed, organizational life often seems "routine" in the colloquial sense. But it is the apparent *routineness* of organizational behavior that creates a context that emphasizes its foils—surprises and shocks, unexpected outcomes, new ideas, novel products. Novelty arrests attention (Wegner, 1989), and explanations of novelty dominate our interpretations of the world (Taleb, 2007). Hence, organizations often provide a stable backdrop that makes mysterious pieces of information, problems, and puzzles stick out as triggers for states of curiosity. Two organizational mechanisms seem paramount in triggering states of curiosity: routines and leaders (see Figure 9.2).

ROUTINE VARIABILITY AND ROUTINE CURIOSITY

Research by Feldman (2000) indicates that routines are not simply "genealogical entities" that cyclically reproduce the same information and the same outcomes (2000, p. 612). Instead, routines "are flows of connected ideas, actions, and outcomes" and because "the fit between ideas, actions, and outcomes is not always tight" (2000, p. 613) enacting routines can easily produce novel triggers that spur curiosity. Put differently, the lack of fit in a routine feels similar to getting one of Heckel's incomplete letters—lack of fit, loose connections, incompleteness all denote a space that seems like it should be filled, and this engenders a sense of curiosity that spurs the need for investigation.

Illustrations of the propensity for routines to catalyze states of curiosity abound. For example, Comer (1994) relates how an organization had implemented routine skill testing to ensure employees were not under the influence of drugs or alcohol during work. The general manager seems to have

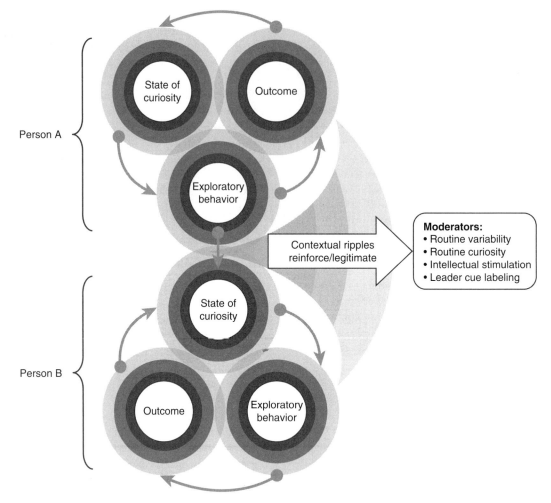

Fig. 9.2 The emergence of curiosity organizing.

sensed some slippage between differing levels of difficulty in the tests indicative of a lack of fit in the routine. As a result:

> One evening when this manager thought he had drunk too much alcohol to risk driving home from a restaurant, he decided to satisfy his curiosity about the effectiveness of the critical tracking test. He asked his dinner companion to drive him to his office, where he sat in front of the video monitor and passed the test on his first attempt. (1994, p. 264)

When the lack of fit in the routine becomes high, it might even lead to chronic states of curiosity. Given enough slippage in routine fit, rules might often be "abandoned simply because someone on the team had the time and the curiosity to work at finding a better rule" (Cangelosi & Dill, 1965, p. 197).

Variability in routines is not the only way in which routines can trigger curiosity; routines might often evoke curiosity because the routine itself was designed to do so. Returning to the IDEO example described earlier, one of the reasons for hiring curious employees is that the brainstorming routines that serves as the backbone of IDEO's work process seems to stimulate states of curiosity, so much so that designers not explicitly assigned to a particular brainstorm session may show up anyway (Sutton & Hargadon, 1996). Similarly, in recounting the routines used for clinical studies at the Centre de Reherche en Gestion (CRG), Berry notes that researchers and practitioners engage in a routine of "problem-sharing" discussions wherein "curiosity is the basic catalyst for analytical thought" (1995, p. 112). It is probable that routines like those at IDEO and the CRG might be common in organizations that place a premium on "expected creativity" (Unsworth, 2001, p. 292). In sum, routines, through inherent variability in successive performance or by design, serve as an important source of novel cues that can trigger states of curiosity.

LEADER INTELLECTUAL STIMULATION AND LEADER CUE LABELING

Leaders also play an important role in stimulating states of curiosity among their followers. As implied by the Bob Noyce example above, part of this dynamic might simply emerge from a leader being innately curious. However, the leadership role imparts special responsibility that may contribute to leaders catalyzing curiosity without necessarily being curious themselves. As Mintzberg (1971) notes, leaders often serve as the informational nerve centers of organizations, and therefore how they disseminate information can have a huge influence on the curiosity of their followers.

One mechanism through which leaders cultivate states of curiosity is intellectual stimulation (Bass, 1985). As Shin and Zhou observed, when leaders intellectually stimulate followers, followers "are encouraged to reformulate issues and problems, to pursue and satisfy their intellectual curiosity, to use their imaginations, and to be playful with ideas and solutions" (2003, p. 704). That is, leaders might deliberately try to problematize a follower's way of seeing the world, catalyzing curiosity, and thereby generating the exploration necessary to dislodge existing assumptions about the way things work. Or, perhaps more simply, a leader can provide intellectual stimulation simply by legitimizing a curiosity. For example, Orit Gadiesh, the chairman of Bain and Company, recalls an early experience in which a teacher legitimated her curiosity:

> Our homeroom teacher, whom we all adored, wrote in [my notebook], "Orit, always ask those two questions, and then the third, and the fourth. Don't ever stop being curious—and never let go until you find the answers." Though I was inquisitive before then, that advice cemented it. (Gadiesh & Dowling, 2009, p. 1)

A complementary mechanism for triggering states of curiosity is by managing information and the social cues or labels that help shape the way information is perceived. For instance, Griffin hypothesized that leaders can manipulate social cues to influence follower behavior:

> The potential power of the leader as a provider of information stems from the fact that the leader is uniquely a part of both the objective work environment and the social work environment. As an individual, and therefore a part of the social environment, the leader can make comments, display facial expressions, and otherwise provide task-related cues to subordinates. At the same time, however, the leader also has the potential to manipulate the objective work environment by redefining tasks. (1983, p. 186)

Redefining task-related cues or *cue labeling* might be considered the downward analog of issue selling (Dutton & Ashford, 1993)—instead of labeling strategic issues to capture attention up the chain of command, leaders can provide task cues that transforms information into a salient "signal" (Feldman & March, 1981) sent down the chain of command. One of the most well researched examples of this is problem solving. Problem solving is a key managerial activity (Lang, Dittrich, & White, 1978); however, the word "problem" serves as one of many labels that may be applied to situations in which problem solving classically occurs. Smith proposes that a problem is really just a sense of "the existence of a gap, difference, or disparity . . . This problematic gap can involve anything" (1988, p. 1491). Later, Smith notes that problems are "constructs, largely undetermined by existing information" (1989, p. 965).

Similar to the dichotomy between opportunities and threats common in issue selling, cue labeling might fall into one of two categories. The most common category that leaders use in cue labeling would be defining novel cues as problems. A less common but equally justifiable approach would be to label the cues as puzzles (mysteries, conundrums, riddles). Although the denotations of problems and puzzles are synonymous, the connotative contrasts are critical. Note that each label provides a different curiosity trajectory: Problems readily map onto states of specific curiosity, in which individuals explore in a relatively linear pattern, whereas puzzles suggest that the issue is fairly hazy and that exploration should likely be broad and expansive. Each label also connotes a different set of emotions— problems hint at negative affect, indicating that something is wrong whereas puzzles hint at more positive affective responses, indicating that there is an opportunity for play and discovery. Because the notion of "problems" has received more attention from scholars, I will pay more attention to the notion of labeling discrepant cues as puzzles. For example, reflective research by Locke, Golden-Biddle, and Feldman (2008) suggests that the discrepant cues labeled as doubts give rise to deductive thinking, but those labeled as generative doubts promote abductive thinking, a more open-ended questioning and exploration. More forcefully,

Cooperrider suggests that "instead of negation, criticism, and spiraling diagnosis" associated with problem solving, we need new labels like "discovery, dream, and design" to create room for inquiry (1996, p. 6). These labels are important because they do not connote that something is wrong, they imply that anything is possible. The point is not that all problems need not be labeled as "problems," but that managers be more willing to consider different ways of labeling cues. As Astely and Zammuto conclude: "Paradoxically, the best way to cope with ambiguous and changing events is to preserve a high level of ambiguity in the language that is used in dealing with them" (1992, p. 451).

To summarize, leaders, because they often serve as a nexus of information, likely play a big role in catalyzing states of curiosity. They might do so by directly attempting to trigger curiosity by purposefully engaging in intellectually stimulating conversations, activities, or challenges. Similarly, leaders might catalyze curiosity more indirectly, simply by how they label cues. It is likely that these two mechanisms often work in tandem and are perhaps more likely to trigger strong feelings of curiosity when they are aligned.

Alternative Individual-level Explanations

When considering individual curiosity, whether trait or state, it is often difficult to see the difference between curiosity and other constructs that concern motivations to learn and adapt. One common point of confusion is the difference between curiosity and creativity. Curiosity, especially diversive curiosity, is likely an upstream contributor to creativity (Kashdan & Fincham, 2002; Loewenstein, 1994), providing the novel raw material needed to recombine ideas and generate creative solutions. Perhaps the most difficult construct to differentiate from curiosity is openness to experience. However, there are compelling theoretical and empirical reasons for dissociating the two. Theoretically, openness to experience, as much as it seems to be widely accepted, is still a fairly nebulously defined personality trait. Of the Big Five personality dimensions, openness to experience is the dimensions that tends to be defined most differently across the different measures, also being called Intellectance (intelligence and mental agility with ideas) and Culture (an interest in aesthetics and art). As McCrae observes, "openness to experience is actually the most controversial, least understood, and least researched of the five factors" (as quoted in Griffin & Hesketh, 2004, p. 243). Although all of these definitions seem to share

curiosity's connection with novelty and/or learning, most of them posit individuals as passive observers, willing to be "open" to new ideas that pass in front of them, rather than agents actively seeking new puzzles and problems to solve.

The lack of conceptual clarity regarding openness to experience bleeds into the empirical utility of the construct. A recent meta-analysis (Barrick, Mount, & Judge, 2001) found that openness to experience had the lowest true score correlations with job performance. Griffin and Hesketh (2004) argue that this might be due to the fact that openness to experience is actually at least two distinct factors, and they found evidence to support that view. In contrast, the few studies of curiosity in organizations have shown relatively strong criterion-validity with job performance (Harrison, 2009; Reio & Callahan, 2004), or with other relevant outcomes like well-being (Gallagher & Lopez, 2007). Finally, and perhaps most tellingly, one of the foundational studies of the Big Five (McCrae & Costa, 1985) included measures of curiosity that did not load on the openness to experience measure (they loaded on conscientiousness). The upshot is that, although curiosity and openness to experience are conceptual relatives, they are not duplicate constructs (similar to the relationship between proactivity and extraversion or conscientiousness). Indeed, curiosity seems to be either a more specific trait or perhaps a lower-order trait of openness to experience that gets obscured when factored with other the other dimensions of the construct. However, given the variety of measures of openness to experience in existence and the variability of subdimensions included in each, it would be theoretically naïve to assume that a measure of openness to experience adequately captures curiosity, and certainly none of them captures the more fine-grained dynamics of specific and diversive curiosity.

Collective Curiosity

Although curiosity is most commonly described as a trait or state of an individual, many (if not most) of the examples of curiosity in organizations ascribe curiosity to a group or to some aspect of the organization as a whole. Indeed, evidence seems to suggest that curiosity can be a quality of the organization (e.g., a central value in organizational culture, an enduring feature of an organization's identity, a fundamental feature of routines), or it can be a catalyzing factor in organizing (e.g., a collective, contagious experience, or an impetus for collective action).

Curiosity as a Quality of Organizations

Saunders and Gero's (2004) computer simulation of visitor behavior in a museum provides an example of what collective curiosity might look like. They contrasted painting arrangements that enhanced curiosity—each painting was slightly more novel than the next, with clean sight lines to the next room highlighting even more novel paintings—with those that effectively impeded curiosity by dampening the experience of novelty and not creating mystery about what might be in the next room. They concluded:

> The consequences of a more appropriate arrangement of paintings is that the agents explore effectively and comfortably, they report a higher level of interest in the artworks throughout their exploration, and as a result, they learn a better representation of the conceptual space. (2004, p. 160)

In contrast, in the noncurious setting, the simulation produced crowding around paintings that were most familiar, which blocked access to additional rooms and ruined the overall flow of the experience. Saunders and Gero's simulation might feel esoteric, but several organizations have literally used museums as a way to incite collective curiosity within their ranks. For example, Olivetti, an Italian computer manufacturer, funds purposely bizarre art exhibits at museums close their headquarters. When asked to explain why the company would invest in something so seemingly tangential, one executive responded, because "intellectual curiosity is the raw material of our business" (Pitt, 1992). A similar story recounts how executives from Rubber Maid went to an Egyptian exhibit at the British Museum in London. This visit spawned 11 new product ideas (Higgins, 1995). But organizations need not go outside of their physical boundaries to have this experience. For example, Merkle, a mid-sized organization has within its customer relations marketing a corporate university that offers a variety of courses, many of which are "eclectic," nonbusiness focused. The CEO explains that the point is to allow "employees to investigate whatever strikes their curiosity" (Gull, 2003). The upshot of these examples is that organizations can literally craft their environments in ways that continually stimulate curiosity. As such, curiosity becomes woven into the normative ideology of the organization, making the organization itself a sort of sanctuary for exploration.

Curiosity As a Catalyst for Organizing

Up to this point, most of the discussion of curiosity in organizations has focused on relatively overt triggers of curiosity, but perhaps the most powerful influence of curiosity emerges from more subtle micro-interactions, often during the genesis of a project or organization. For example, consider the following footnote that explains the initiation of a research project on information sharing during engineering and design in the automotive industry: "We received no pay or financial support from our host company. We were permitted access to the company based on prior relations between ourselves and the host company, and because of the *joint curiosity* that was created during our initial meeting" (Terwiesch, Loch, & Meyer, 2002, p. 418, emphasis added).[2] In their methods section they explained,

> Our effort to extend previous research on preliminary information started with a visit to our host company, where we presented results from our own modeling (Loch and Terwiesch 1998) and survey-based (Terwiesch and Loch 1999) research. While the audience did not disagree with any of the arguments presented, including the need for greater concurrency and for frequent information exchange between parties working concurrently, they cited other problems. . . . At a follow-up meeting, we agreed to explore preliminary information further and defined specific research objectives. (Terwiesch, et al., 2002, p. 405)

In this example, the conversation about an initial problem unearthed new problems, and it was the mutual discovery of these new problems that generated enough collective curiosity to initiate the research effort with both parties. Research by Elsbach and Kramer (2003) on Hollywood pitch meetings provides a similar narrative. One of their informants, a writer pitching a show, observed that:

> You wanna get them in a mode of them [the person "catching" the idea] asking you questions as quickly as possible. Because then you're controlling the meeting. Now you did the pitch, now they're asking the questions, and you're filling in the gaps with more good stuff. . . . You want to stimulate them, you want to get their curiosity going. And then you want them to be a team player with you. . . . That's what you want to happen. (p. 296)

In other words, one person's curiosity can trigger another's, making curiosity a shared experience. In concrete terms: Curiosity can be contagious. Or, more precisely, when one person (or group) is curious, the curiosity drives exploratory behavior. In the case of an automotive research project, the researchers were curious about a problem and this led them to explore that problem with executives at a company. Their exploratory behavior seems to have catalyzed the curiosity of the executives, thus leading to new exploratory behavior (see Figure 9.2). As a sort of reversal in the case of pitch meetings, once the catchers became curious, they began inserting new ideas that likely catalyze the curiosity of the pitchers, leading to an upward spiral of curiosity (Fredrickson, 2001). This sort of interaction is pretty common in organizations—people are always pitching and catching ideas, proactively challenging ideas (Crant, 2000), and engaging in information seeking (Ashford & Black, 1996; Morrison, 2002). And, it is likely that the cross-fire of this behavior produces the novelty necessary to evoke curiosity. As this happens, curiosity becomes the driving force that coordinates collective action (Heath & Sitkin, 2001) as exploration generates new curiosity, which generates new exploration.

The effects of curiosity organizing over time are understudied at this point, but there is some evidence that can be used for healthy speculation. Some of this evidence comes from sociological research on hackers. Research suggest that hackers, as individuals, are "curiosity-driven [in the] relentless pursuit of the answer to a technological problem" (Taylor, 1999, p. 51), but this curiosity is often ignited by descriptions of others' explorations within the media or in popular culture (Thomas, 2002). Hence, hackers are drawn to one another and feed off one another's curiosity. As they share information, the information itself becomes more than data, it becomes a relational, "social fabric" (Thomas, 2002, p. 21) infused with values based on the motivations that engendered hacking in the first place. In other words, as individuals express and interpret their own curiosity they "develop a sense of community. It is this double movement in which individual motivations express the nature of a community, that makes motivations important for hackers" (Jordan & Taylor, 1998, p. 769).

Curiosity organizing seems to embed curiosity as both a driver of work (e.g., gathering new information, exploring new opportunities, etc.) but also as a sort of relational gravity that pulls people together. This increased interaction tends to change the nature of the perceptions of the work the people jointly perform (Griffin, 1983; Meyer, 1982). Over time, the curiosity that brings people together becomes embedded as one of the central values in the relational and cultural fabric of the collective pursuit. Collectives then begin to own the curiosity, whether

identified as a set of values like those observed in Meyers' (1982) study of hospitals or as a "plural form" of collective competence (Bradach, 1997, p. 297). Sustained curiosity organizing likely feeds back into qualities of the organization mentioned earlier. In other words, it is likely that the fairly static descriptor of "curiosity as a quality of an organization" emerges from the dynamic churning of "curiosity as a catalyst for organizing." For example, Dorkbot began as a small group of technology enthusiasts and has grown into a self-organizing collective of "people doing strange things with electricity" (dorkbot.org, 2010). There are now well over 100 Dorkbot groups all over the world. One of the members describes the meetings as "a group critique. The questions asked were informal and curious (Braiker, 2006). Founder Douglas Repetto's thoughts on the future of Dorkbot help illustrate some of the organizing features:

> I try to stay kind of neutral about the future of dorkbot. As organizations grow they often develop self-protection mechanisms, and sometimes maintaining the organization becomes more important than the actual activities of the organization. If dorkbot is no longer useful or interesting in a particular city, then we just let it die. (Repetto, 2008)

In other words, if the curiosity, the basic energy for Dorkbot organizing evaporates, so too does the organization.

To this point, in discussing the potential for collective curiosity, I have largely ignored Berlyne's distinction between specific and diversive curiosity. Part of the reason for this omission is that the studies and examples provided do not specify a type of curiosity per se. However, it is likely that some organizations take on a collective character of one type of curiosity versus the other. For example, consider the amount of curiosity organizing that occurs for an organization during a crisis, such as occurred in NASA following the disintegration of the Space Shuttle Columbia. Following the disaster, investigators collected over 2,000 pieces of debris in what was labeled the "largest land search ever conducted" (NASA, 2003). Certainly, these sorts of investigations are most likely examples of collective specific curiosity because of the suffusion of negative emotion and the overriding sense that there is a concrete answer to the problem. In contrast, the opening description of the LHC or the work described at IDEO are most likely examples of collective diversive curiosity since they seem rife with positive emotion and tend to have fairly open-ended objectives about the purpose of their collective exploration.

Alternative Collective-level Explanations

To some, the discussion of curiosity as a collective phenomenon may sound too similar to literature on organizational ambidexterity or research on organizational modes of exploration and exploitation. However, adding curiosity to these research streams holds some promising possibilities. In the opening essay of a special issue on organizational ambidexterity, the editors noted that research on ambidexterity has yet to ask: "What is the individual- and/or team-level origin of organizational capabilities for exploration and exploitation?" (Gupta, Smith, & Shalley, 2006, p. 704). In a related vein, but focusing specifically on senior-level leaders, Benner and Tushman note: "If dynamic capabilities require exploitation as well as exploration, more complex organizational forms are required, which, in turn, demand more complex senior team capabilities" (2003, p. 252). The study of curiosity, with particular attention to the differential properties and outcomes of the specific and diverse subtypes, provides a low-hanging fruit for exploring these shortcomings. Moreover, the study of how curiosity changes as it moves up levels of analysis, from individual states of curiosity to curiosity organizing to curiosity as a quality of the organization itself might provide the phenomenological leverage to better examine how ambidexterity plays out over time or how organizations might develop ambidexterity.

Future Directions

At the opening of this chapter, I noted that the majority of organizational research that mentions curiosity does so in a very tangential fashion. The relative scarcity of organizational research that focuses on curiosity serves as a boon to future researchers since a host of potential research questions abound at both the individual and collective level. For example, researchers still need to examine individuals' experiences of specific and diverse curiosity in tandem to better understand how they function within organizations and the specific and perhaps momentary interactions that might precipitate them. Similarly, in addition to testing the moderating mechanisms suggested here or elaborating others, researchers might be keen to assess the role of curiosity in contexts that necessitate rapid adaptation, like those of recently hired newcomers, expatriates adjusting to international assignments, or individuals coping with

organizational change. At the collective level, the notion of curiosity organizing provides a unique lens for understanding the emergence of social energy that can catalyze new organizations and might provide leverage for understanding temporary organizations, entrepreneurship, or organizational responses to crisis and more positive changes. Attention to collective curiosity can also provide a lens for understanding organizational communication during these events: Is the organization communicating in a way to generate more curiosity, mystery, and interest in what is going on? Do organizations attempt to diffuse curiosity in a way that actually engenders it? Moreover, the model of curiosity organizing presented here only accounts for curiosity generally, but I suggest that differences likely exist in curiosity organizing born out of specific or diverse curiosity: Are they sustained differently? Do they develop along unique trajectories? Answers to these questions promise to reveal interesting cross-level interactions and better inform our understanding of organizational becoming.

A common theme across all of the future research directions just suggested is the issue of time and attention to momentary interactions. Curiosity can be ephemeral, but when it is activated, it serves as a potent force (Loewenstein, 1994). To study curiosity, researchers need to adopt flexible methodologies that enable attention to ebbs and flows over time, exploring how moments of curiosity might catalyze future interactions or lay dormant or simply play themselves out. Experience sampling methods (ESM) seem particularly apropos for studying curiosity at the individual level because experience sampling elegantly controls for the influence of traits, attends to state dynamics, and can be used to capture contextual dynamics as well (Barrett & Barrett, 2001; Csikzentmihalyi & Larson, 1987; Scollon, Kim-Prieto, & Diener, 2003). Existing measures used by Litman (Litman, 2008; Litman & Silvia, 2006) capture Berlyne's dimensions, although there is also a case to be made for using or developing other measures that are more affect-independent (Kashdan et al., 2004). Although ESM studies are possible at the collective level, it would also be beneficial for researchers to also adopt a quiver of qualitative strategies to build theory about how organizational curiosity or curiosity organizing might emerge, function, evolve into new dynamics, or fade away.

Conclusion

The purpose of this chapter has been to highlight the role of curiosity in organizational life, emphasizing the potential for curiosity at both the individual and collective levels. The chapter has highlighted the link between curiosity and exploratory learning behaviors and hinted at the generally positive outcomes of curiosity. However, curiosity, like any motivation, is only as generative as its target. For example, although hackers see themselves as a democratizing force on the flow of information, organizations that are the victims of hacks would likely see their curiosity as destructive. Indeed, throughout history, scholars have contended that "idle curiosity" has a negative effect on society. In modern organizations, it is possible that curiosity is linked to gossip, time spent surfing on the Internet, or just time spent not focusing on a particular job task. Future research should assess the full range of behaviors curiosity might catalyze to provide a clearer picture of the benefits and costs of curiosity in organizations. However, to date, the balance of the literature seems to support the idea that the net result of curiosity in organizations is generative and that organizations should do more to cultivate curiosity (Weick, 1993), particularly to enable adaptation and innovation in dynamic environments.

Notes

1. According to Mulvey, in Greek mythology, Pandora "was sent to earth with a box that secretly contained all the evils of the worlds. The box and the forbidden nature of its contents excited her curiosity and she opened it . . . Pandora's story is a warning of the dangers of curiosity. And this theme also links her story to Eve, the first woman of Christian mythology, who persuaded Adam to eat the apple of knowledge" (1995, pp. 3–8).
2. It is worth noting that an informal count of how the words "curious" and "curiosity" are used in organizational journals reveals that authors are usually explaining their own curiosity as a motivation for the study as a way of energizing the reader, perhaps in part because curious narratives are often more interesting (Knobloch, Patzig, & Mende, 2004).

References

Argyris, C.A., & Schön, D.A. (1978). *Organizational learning*. Reading, MA: Addison-Wesley.

Ashford, S.J., & Black, J.S. (1996). Proactivity during organizational entry: The role of desire for control. *Journal of Applied Psychology, 81*(2), 199–214.

Ashforth, B.E., & Fried, Y. (1988). The mindlessness of organizational behaviors. *Human Relations, 41*(4), 305–329.

Barley, S.R. (1990). Images of imaging: Notes on doing longitudinal field work. *Organization Science, 1*, 220–247.

Barrett, L.F., & Barrett, D.J. (2001). An introduction to computerized experience sampling in psychology. *Social Science Computer Review, 19*(2), 175–185.

Barrick, M.R., Mount, M.K., & Judge, T.A. (2001). Personality and performance at the beginning of the new millennium: What do

we know and where do we go next? *International Journal of Selection and Assessment, 9*, 9–30.

Bass, B. (1985). *Leadership and Performance Beyond Expectations*. New York: Free Press.

Benner, M.J., & Tushman, M.L. (2003). Exploitation, exploration, and process management: The productivity dilemma revisited. *Academy of Management Review, 28*, 238–256.

Berlyne, D.E. (1954). A theory of human curiosity. *British Journal of Psychology, 45*, 180–191.

Berlyne, D.E. (1960). *Conflict, arousal, and curiosity*. New York: McGraw-Hill.

Berlyne, D.E. (1966). Curiosity and exploration. *Science, 153*, 25–33.

Berry, M. (1995). Research and the practice of management: A French view. *Organization Science, 6*, 104–116.

Bordin, E.S. (1966). Curiosity, compassion, and doubt: The dilemma of the psychologist. *American Psychologist, 21*, 117–121.

Bradach, J.L. (1997). Using the plural form in the management of restaurant chains. *Administrative Science Quarterly, 42*, 276–303.

Braiker, B. (2006, January 17). When art and science collide, a Dorkbot meeting begins. *The New York Times*. Retrieved from http://www.nytimes.com/.

Browning, L.D., Beyer, J.M., & Shetler, J.C. (1995). Building cooperation in a competitive industry: Sematech and the semiconductor industry. *Academy of Management Journal, 38*(1), 113–151.

Cangelosi, V.E., & Dill, W.R. (1965). Organizational learning: Observations toward a theory. *Administrative Science Quarterly, 10*, 175–203.

Chen, G., Gully, S.M., & Eden, D. (2001). Validation of a new general self-efficacy scale. *Organizational Research Methods, 4*(1), 62–83.

Collison, M. (1995). *Police, drugs and community*. London: Free Association Books.

Comer, D.R. (1994). A case against workplace drug testing. *Organization Science, 5*, 259–267.

Crant, J.M. (2000). Proactive behavior in organizations. *Journal of Management, 26*, 435–462.

Crowe, E., & Higgins, E.T. (1997). Regulatory focus and strategic inclinations: Promotion and prevention in decision-making. *Organizational Behavior and Human Decision Processes, 69*(2), 117–132.

Csikzentmihalyi, M., & Larson, R. (1987). Validity and reliability of the experience-sampling method. *Journal of Nervous and Mental Disease, 175*, 526–536.

Cummings, L.L. (1967). Managerial effectiveness II: Performance at the graduate student level. *Academy of Management Journal, 10*, 145–160.

Dewey, J.D. (1910). *How we think*. Boston: D.C. Heath.

dorkbot.org (2010). *Start a Dorkbot in your city*. Retrieved Aug. 25, 2010, from http://www.dorkbot.org/startadorkbot/.

Dutton, J.E., & Ashford, S.J. (1993). Selling issues to top management. *Academy of Management Review, 18*(3), 397–428.

Edmondson, A. (1999). Psychological safety and learning behavior in work teams. *Administrative Science Quarterly, 44*, 350–383.

Elsbach, K.D., & Kramer, R.M. (2003). Assessing creativity in Hollywood pitch meetings: Evidence for a dual-process model of creativity judgments. *Academy of Management Journal, 46*(3), 283–301.

Fazio, R.H., Herr, P.M., & Powell, M.C. (1992). On the development and strength of category and associations in memory: The case of mystery ads. *Journal of Consumer Psychology, 1*(1), 1–13.

Feldman, M.S. (2000). Organizational routines as a source of continuous change. *Organization Science, 11*(6), 611–629.

Feldman, M.S., & March, J.G. (1981). Information in organizations as signal and symbol. *Administrative Science Quarterly, 26*(2), 171–186.

Fitzgerald, F.T. (1999). On being a doctor: Curiosity. *Annals of Internal Medicine, 130,* 70–72.

Forgas, J.P. (2000). *Feeling and thinking: The role of affect in social cognition.* Cambridge: Cambridge University Press.

Fowler, H. (1965). *Curiosity and exploratory behavior.* New York: Macmillan.

Fowlie, J., & Wood, M. (2009). The emotional impact of leaders' behaviours. *Journal of European Industrial Training, 33,* 559–572.

Fredrickson, B.L. (2001). The role of positive emotions in positive psychology: The broaden-and-build theory of positive emotions. *American Psychologist, 56*(3), 218–226.

Gadiesh, O., & Dowling, D.W. (2009, September). Bain & Company chairman Orit Gadiesh on the importance of curiosity. *Harvard Business Review.*

Galinsky, M.D. (1962). Personality development and vocational choice of clinical psychologists and physicists. *Journal of Counseling Psychology, 9,* 299–305.

Gallagher, M.W., & Lopez, S.J. (2007). Curiosity and well-being. *The Journal of Positive Psychology, 2,* 236–248.

Gherardi, S. (1999). Learning as problem-driven or in the face of mystery? *Organization Studies, 20*(1), 101–124.

Giambra, L.M., Camp, C.J., & Grodsky, A. (1992). Curiosity and stimulation seeking across the adult life span: Cross-sectional and 6- to 8-year longitudinal findings. *Psychology & Aging, 7*(1), 150–157.

Goldberg, C. (2002). Escaping the dark side of curiosity. *American Journal of Psychoanalysis, 62,* 185–199.

Griffin, B., & Hesketh, B. (2004). Why openness to experience is not a good predictor of job performance. *International Journal of Selection and Assessment, 12,* 243–251.

Griffin, R. (1983). Objective and social sources of information task redesign: a field experiment. *Administrative Science Quarterly, 28,* 184–200.

Gull, N. (2003). Back to school: At Merkle Direct Marketing, education is not an option—it's a job requirement. *Inc.* Retrieved from http://www.inc.com/magazine/20030901/managing.html.

Gupta, A.K., Smith, K.G., & Shalley, C.E. (2006). The interplay between exploration and exploitation. *Academy of Management Journal, 49,* 693–706.

Harrison, P. (2001). Curiosity, forbidden knowledge, and the reformation of natural philosophy in early modern England. *Isis, 92*(2), 265–290.

Harrison, S.H. (2009). *Curiosity in organizations.* Unpublished dissertation: Arizona State University.

Harrison, S.H., Sluss, D.M., & Ashforth, B.E. (2010). *Curiosity adapted the cat: The role of trait curiosity in newcomer adaptation.* Manuscript submitted for publication.

Harvey, M., Novicevic, M., Leonard, N., & Payne, D. (2007). The role of curiosity in global managers' decision-making. *Journal of Leadership and Organizational Studies, 13*(3), 45–61.

Heath, C., & Sitkin, S.B. (2001). Big-B versus Big-O: What is organizational about organizational behavior. *Journal of Organizational Behavior, 22,* 43–58.

Heckel, R.V. (1969). Curiosity in young psychologists. *American Psychologist, 24,* 754–756.

Hedberg, B. (1981). How organizations learn and unlearn. In C.P. Nystrom & W.H. Starbuck (Eds.), *Handbook of organizational design* Vol. 1. New York: Oxford University Press.

Higgins, J.M. (1995). *Innovate or evaporate: Test & improve your organization's IQ: Its innovation quotient.* Winter Park, FL: New Management Publishing.

Huber, G.P. (1991). Organizational learning: The contributing processes and the literatures. *Organization Science, 2*(1), 88–115.

Jordan, T., & Taylor, P. (1998). A sociology of hackers. *Sociological Review, 46,* 757–780.

Kashdan, T. (2009). *Curious? Discover the missing ingredient to a fulfilling life.* New York: Willam Morrow.

Kashdan, T.B., & Fincham, F.D. (2002). Facilitating creativity by regulating curiosity. *American Psychologist, 57*(5), 373–374.

Kashdan, T.B., Rose, P., & Fincham, F.D. (2004). Curiosity and exploration: Facilitating positive subjective experiences and personal growth opportunities. *Journal of Personality Assessment, 82*(3), 291–305.

Kashdan, T.B., & Steger, M.F. (2007). Curiosity and pathways to well-being and meaning in life: Traits, states, and everyday behaviors. *Motivation and Emotion, 31,* 159–173.

Keller, J.A. (1987). Motivational aspects of exploratory behavior. In D. Görlitz & J.F. Wohlwill (Eds.), *Curiosity, imagination, and play: On the development of spontaneous cognitive and motivational processes* (pp. 25–42). Hillsdale, NJ: Lawrence Erlbaum Associates.

Knobloch, S., Patzig, G., Mende, A.-M., & Hastall, M. (2004). Affective news: Effects of discourse structure in narratives on suspense, curiosity, and enjoyment while reading news and novels. *Communication Research, 31,* 259–287.

Kroft, S. (2008, September 28). A trip inside the "Big Bang machine." [Television Broadcast]. In *60 Minutes.* New York: CBS News.

Lang, J.R., Dittrich, J.E., & White, S.E. (1978). Managerial problem solving models: A review and proposal. *Academy of Management Review, 3,* 854–866.

Leonard, N.H., & Harvey, M. (2007). The trait of curiosity as a predictor of emotional intelligence. *Journal of Applied Social Psychology, 37,* 1545–1561.

Leuba, C. (1958). A new look at curiosity and creativity. *Journal of Higher Education, 29,* 132–140.

Levitt, B., & March, J.G. (1988). Organizational learning. *Annual Review of Sociology, 14,* 319–340.

Litman, J.A. (2005). Curiosity and the pleasures of learning: Wanting and liking new information. *Cognition and Emotion, 19*(1), 793–814.

Litman, J.A. (2008). Interest and deprivation factors of epistemic curiosity. *Personality and Individual Differences, 44,* 1585–1595.

Litman, J.A., Hutchins, T.L., & Russon, R.K. (2005). Epistemic curiosity, feeling-of-knowing, and exploratory behaviour. *Cognition and Emotion, 19*(4), 559–582.

Litman, J.A., & Jimerson, T.L. (2004). The measurement of curiosity as a feeling of deprivation. *Journal of Personality Assessment, 82*(2), 147–157.

Litman, J.A., & Silvia, P.J. (2006). The latent structure of trait curiosity: Evidence for interest and deprivation curiosity dimensions. *Journal of Personality Assessment, 86*(3), 318–328.

Locke, K., Golden-Biddle, K., & Feldman, M.S. (2008). Making doubt generative: Rethinking the role of doubt in the research process. *Organization Science, 19*, 907–918.

Loewenstein, G. (1994). The psychology of curiosity: A review and reinterpretation. *Psychological Bulletin, 116*(1), 75–98.

Louis, M.R., & Sutton, R.I. (1991). Switching cognitive gears: From habits of mind to active thinking. *Human Relations, 44*(1), 55–76.

Maner, J.K., & Gerend, M.A. (2007). Motivationally selective risk judgments: Do fear and curiosity boost the boons or the banes? *Organizational Behavior and Human Decision Processes, 103*, 256–267.

Matthews, G., Deary, I.J., & Whiteman, M.C. (2003). *Personality traits* (2nd ed.). Cambridge: Cambridge University Press.

McCrae, R.R., & Costa, P.T. (1985). Updating Norman's "adequate taxonomy": Intelligence and personality dimensions in natural language and in questionnaires. *Journal of Personality and Social Psychology, 49*, 710–721.

Merritt, E. (1925). Carving the scientific possum. *Scientific Monthly, 21*, 452–456.

Meyer, A.D. (1982). Adapting to environmental jolts. *Administrative Science Quarterly, 27*, 515–537.

Miller, D. (1993). The architecture of simplicity. *Academy of Management Review, 18*(1), 116–138.

Mintzberg, H. (1971). Managerial work: Analysis from observation. *Management Science, 18*(2), B97–B110.

Mischel, W. (1968). Personality and prediction. In W. Mischel (Ed.), *Personality and assessment*. New York: Wiley and Sons, Inc.

Morgan, G. (2006). *Images of organization* (3rd ed.). Thousand Oaks, CA: Sage Publications.

Morrison, E.W. (2002). Information seeking within organizations. *Human Communication Research, 28*(2), 229–242.

Mulvey, L. (1995). The myth of Pandora: A psychoanalytical approach. In L. Pietropaolo, & A. Testaferri (Eds.), *Feminisms in the cinema*. Bloomington, IN: Indiana University Press.

Nachmann, B. (1960). Childhood experience and vocational choice in law, dentistry, and social work. *Journal of Counseling Psychology, 7*, 243–250.

Roberts, J. (2003). In search of. *NASA Researcher News*. Retrieved March 5, 2010 from http://researchernews.larc.nasa.gov/archives/2003/050903/.

Piaget, J. (1936). *Origins of intelligence in children*. New York: International Universities Press.

Pitt, W. (1992, August 4). An Italian computer maker as art patron. *Wall Street Journal*, p. A12.

Proust Questionnaire: Charlie Rose. (2010, July). *Vanity Fair*, p. 150.

Reio, T.G., & Callahan, J.L. (2004). Affect, curiosity, and socialization-related learning: A path, analysis of antecedents to job performance. *Journal of Business and Psychology, 19*(1), 3–22.

Pixelache University, Helsinki. (2008). *Interview of Douglas Repetto: Questions about self-organisation*. Retrieved from http://university.pixelache.ac/.

Rose, M. (2004). *The mind at work: Valuing the intelligence of the American worker*. New York: Penguin.

Saunders, R., & Gero, J.S. (2004). Curious agents and situated design evaluations. *Artificial Intelligence for Engineering Design Analysis and Manufacturing, 18*(2), 153–161.

Schwarz, N. (2002). Situated cognition and the wisdom of feelings: Cognitive tuning. In L.F. Barrett, & P. Salovey (Eds.), *The wisdom in feeling* (pp. 144–166). New York: Guilford Press.

Scollon, C.N., Kim-Prieto, C., & Diener, E. (2003). Experience sampling: Promises and pitfalls, strengths and weaknesses. *Journal of Happiness Studies, 4*, 5–34.

Shin, S.J., & Zhou, J. (2003). Transformational leadership, conservation, and creativity: Evidence from Korea. *Academy of Management Journal, 46*(6), 685–702.

Simon, H.A. (2001). "Seek and ye shall find". How curiosity engenders discovery. In K.D. Crowley, C.D. Schunn, & T. Okada (Eds.), *Designing for science: Implications from everyday, classroom, and professional settings* (pp. 5–18). Mahwah, NJ: Lawrence Erlbaum.

Smith, G.F. (1988). Towards a heuristic theory of problem structuring. *Management Science, 34*, 1489–1506.

Smith, G.F. (1989). Defining Managerial Problems—a framework for prescriptive theorizing. *Management Science, 35*(8), 963–981.

Spielberger, C.D., & Starr, L.M. (1994). Curiosity and exploratory behavior. In H.F. O'Neil, Jr., & M. Drillings (Eds.), *Motivation: Theory and research* (pp. 221–243). Hillsdale, NJ: Erlbaum.

Sutton, R.I., & Hargadon, A. (1996). Brainstorming in groups context: Effectiveness in a product design firm. *Administrative Science Quarterly, 41*(4), 685–718.

Swan, G.E., & Carmelli, D. (1996). Curiosity and mortality in aging adults: A 5-year follow-up of the Western Collaborative Group study. *Psychology and Aging, 11*(3), 449–453.

Taleb, N. (2007). *The black swan: The impact of the highly improbable* (1st ed.). New York: Random House.

Taylor, P.A. (1999). *Hackers*. London: Routledge.

Terwiesch, C., Loch, C.H., & Meyer, A. (2002). Exchanging preliminary information in concurrent engineering: Alternative coordination strategies. *Organization Science, 13*, 402–419.

Thomas, D. (2002). *Hacker culture*. Minneapolis: University of Minnesota Press.

Unsworth, K. (2001). Unpacking creativity. *Academy of Management Review, 26*(2), 289–297.

van Diggelen, A. (2009, March 3). Charlie Rose talks about his great and glorious life. *Fresh Dialogues*. Retrieved from http://www.freshdialogues.com/2009/03/03/charlie-rose-talks-about-his-great-and-glorious-life/.

Voss, H.G., & Keller, H. (1983). *Curiosity and exploration: Theory and results*. San Diego: Academic Press.

Wegner, D.M. (1989). *White bears and other unwanted thoughts: Suppression, obsession, and the psychology of mental control*. New York: Viking.

Weick, K.E. (1993). The collapse of sensemaking in organizations: The Mann Gulch disaster. *Administrative Science Quarterly, 38*(4), 628–652.

Weick, K.E., & Ashford, S.J. (2001). Learning in organizations. In F.M. Jablin, & L.L. Putnam (Eds.), *The new handbook of organizational communication: Advances in theory, research, and methods* (pp. 704–731). Thousand Oaks, CA: Sage.

Some Traits Associated with Flourishing at Work

Joyce E. Bono, Stacy E. Davies, *and* Rena L. Rasch

Abstract

This chapter focuses on personality traits associated with flourishing at work. Flourishing is defined broadly to include employee thriving (e.g., vitality and learning), happiness (e.g., positive moods and emotions), and engagement (e.g., job satisfaction and self-determined motivation). Two broad traits (extraversion and core self-evaluations) were identified as being central to employee flourishing. Examination of the behaviors, attitudes, emotions, and outcomes experienced by people high in these traits leads to the conclusion that people who naturally flourish at work (because of their personality) tend to have a positive approach to the self, others, and work situations, and also tend to take an active, engaged, and forward-looking approach to work, especially in novel or challenging situations.

Keywords: Self-determination, core-self evaluations, positive emotions, extraversion, flourishing

The focus of positive organizational scholarship has been on understanding and supporting aspects of the work environment that foster, develop, and support employee thriving (Cameron, Dutton, & Quinn, 2003). In this context, it may seem odd that we are writing about personality traits, which are associated with consistency in behavior across work environments. Our focus on personality is in recognition of the fact that—no matter what conditions exist in a work environment or culture—some individuals are more likely than others to experience and express positive emotions, some individuals are more likely than others to be autonomously motivated, and some individuals are more likely than others to seek out opportunities to learn and grow. Some employees are simply more likely than others to flourish, even when they share the same working conditions, because their personality traits lead them to engage in certain behaviors, to pursue specific goals or strategies, and to interpret and make meaning of their experiences in systematic ways (McAdams, 1995).

Our goal is to examine traits—and associated behaviors, attitudes, and goals—of individuals who seem to naturally flourish at work. We write from the perspective of personality traits as sets of stable, enduring characteristics of individuals associated with some degree of behavioral consistency across situations. Despite mean level changes that may occur with life experiences (e.g., people become more conscientious when they marry and have children; Roberts, Walton, & Viechtbauer, 2006), there is considerable evidence that rank ordering of personality traits across individuals remains somewhat stable over the lifetime, especially in adulthood (see Roberts & Delvecchio, 2000, for a review).

In this chapter, we use the word *flourishing* in reference to individuals who prosper at work, to those who are happy, engaged, self-motivated, successful, and learning. This definition is congruent with Spreitzer, Sutcliffe, Dutton, Sonenshein, and Grant's (2005) definition of employee thriving, as it includes the experience of vitality and learning, but it is a bit broader in that we also include happiness, positive moods and emotions, and work engagement. Our view of flourishing at work includes both a hedonic aspect, wherein it involves positive emotions and satisfaction at work, and a eudemonic aspect, wherein flourishing involves being fully engaged, and work is viewed as an expression of the true self (see Peterson, Park, & Seligman, 2005, for a comprehensive but concise description of the foundations of hedonic and eudemonic approaches to flourishing). We do not explicitly include job performance as a measure of flourishing because there may be cases in which high task performance diminishes flourishing. Yet, it is plausible that flourishing at work leads to strong performance (see Spreitzer, Porath, Gibson, & Stevens, 2010), and it is equally plausible that performing well at work might be a source of feelings of vitality, satisfaction, and meaningfulness. Thus, job performance probably plays an important role in employee flourishing, but it is not a defining element.

Historically, the literature on flourishing at work (e.g., happiness, job satisfaction, autonomy, self-determination) has been primarily focused on the work itself as a determinant (e.g., the job characteristics model; Hackman & Oldham, 1980). Some attention has also been paid to the context of work relative to employee flourishing, including examination of leader behavior (Bono & Judge, 2003). Other research examines the worker herself as a source of flourishing. Staw and Ross (1985) demonstrated a surprising level of consistency in job satisfaction over time for people who had changed both occupations and employers. Moreover, Arvey, Bouchard, Segal, and Abraham (1989) showed that about 30% of the variability in job satisfaction could be attributed to genetic factors; Ilies and Judge (2003) confirmed that 13%–45% of these genetic effects were due to personality. The general conclusion of this research is that some people have more of a natural tendency to flourish than others.

Our goal in this chapter is to examine specific personality traits associated with flourishing. As a point of departure, we review the literature linking personality with job satisfaction (reflecting hedonic aspects of flourishing) and self-determination (reflecting eudemonic aspect of flourishing), both of which have been linked to employee well-being, at work and in life. Our aim is to identify a small set of traits that are broadly associated with these core aspects of flourishing.

Traits Linked to Aspects of Flourishing
Personality and Job Satisfaction
Early research on job satisfaction focused on traits that were associated with poor emotional adjustment (e.g., Hoppock, 1935). Indeed, much research historically focused on work stress, work dissatisfaction, or coping with work demands. Taking a positive organizational scholarship (POS) approach to flourishing at work, we explicitly focused on the traits associated with the experience and expression of positive emotions and with high levels of job satisfaction. Given the topic of our chapter—positive traits—we explicitly ignored traits associated with failure to thrive at work (e.g., neuroticism), about which much has already been written.

Judge, Heller, and Mount (2002) used the Big Five framework (a taxonomy of five broad traits shown to capture most of the variance among individuals; see Goldberg, 1990) to aggregate the results of over 100 studies linking personality to job satisfaction. Extraversion was the only trait that consistently (90% of the correlations were positive) showed a positive association with job satisfaction ($\rho = 0.25$). When the Big Five traits were considered together in a regression, the two traits with the strongest positive association with job satisfaction were extraversion and conscientiousness. Using an alternative model of personality—positive and negative affectivity—Connolly and Viswesvaran (2000) also conducted a meta-analysis linking job satisfaction to personality, reporting an estimated true correlation between positive affect and job satisfaction of 0.49. Subsequently, Thoresen, Kaplan, Barsky, Warren, and de Chermont (2003) examined a larger pool of studies and also found a moderate positive association between trait positive affect and job satisfaction ($\rho = 0.34$). Using yet a third personality framework, Judge and Bono's (2001) meta-analysis examined the link between several related traits and job satisfaction. Traits associated with high levels of satisfaction in their study were self-esteem ($\rho = 0.26$), generalized self-efficacy ($\rho = 0.45$), and internal locus of control (LOC) ($\rho = 0.32$). When Judge and Bono combined these traits, along with emotional stability (reversed neuroticism) into a single construct labeled *core self-evaluations* (CSE), the correlation between CSE and job satisfaction was 0.41.

Personality and Self-determination
Although there is a long history of studying personality and job satisfaction, there is a smaller literature on traits associated with eudemonic aspects of flourishing. According to Ryan and Deci's (2000) self-determination theory, intentional behavior can be freely chosen (intrinsically or autonomously motivated), or it can be influenced by external constraints or pressures (controlled motivation), but only autonomous and intrinsic motivation are associated

with flourishing. Building on self-determination theory, Sheldon and Elliot (1998, 1999) showed that when individuals' goals are congruent with their personal values and beliefs (autonomous motivation; self-concordant goals), they are more likely to attain their goals and to experience general well-being. Typically, intrinsic motivation, autonomy, and self-determination tend to be linked more to elements of the work context (e.g., Spreitzer, 1996) rather than to stable individual dispositions. However, some studies have linked personality to self-determination (Ryan & Deci, 2000). Our goal was to identify traits associated with self-determination, autonomous motivation, goal self-concordance, or related self-regulation processes.

Judge, Bono, Erez, and Locke (2005) used the Sheldon and Elliot (1998, 1999) self-concordance framework in a work context, examining personality antecedents to self-concordance. Their results showed that CSE was positively associated with autonomous motivation and a self-concordance composite (r's from 0.18 to 0.33). A study by Heimpel, Elliot, and Wood (2006) also examined the link between autonomous motivation and one of the CSE personality traits, reporting a positive association with self-esteem (r =.35). Ng, Sorensen, and Eby (2006) linked intrinsic motivation to another CSE trait, internal LOC (ρ = .18). Focusing on motivation for healthy behaviors, but using a self-determination framework, Ingledew, Markland, and Sheppard (2004) linked extraversion to autonomous motivation (r = 0.28) and conscientiousness to intrinsic motivation (r = 0.42). Recognizing that individuals varied in the extent to which they were autonomously motivated, Deci and Ryan (1985) developed a personality measure to capture individual differences in self-determination (i.e., general causality orientation scale). This scale was moderately correlated (r = 0.35) with self-esteem, a CSE trait.

Summary

Our understanding of the literature suggests that two broad traits (or facets of those traits) tend to emerge consistently as correlates of those eudemonic and hedonic aspects of flourishing we examined (e.g., job satisfaction and self-determination). These traits were *extraversion*, which includes positive affectivity as a dimension (see Watson & Clark, 1997), and *core self-evaluations*, which includes self-esteem and LOC. In the following sections, we take a closer look at these two traits, with an explicit focus on the mechanisms by which they are associated with flourishing. Although other traits occasionally emerged in our review (e.g., conscientiousness), we excluded them from detailed analysis in this chapter because they did not emerge consistently across studies or aspects of flourishing.

Extraversion

Extraversion is a central personality trait that can be found in most personality taxonomies. People who score high on extraversion have been described as assertive, dominant, ambitious, sociable, active, energetic, talkative, enthusiastic, people-oriented, and fun-loving (e.g., Costa & McCrae, 1992). Given extraversion is such a central trait in the personality domain, one might expect consensus on what the trait and its dimensions are; that is not the case (Lucas, Diener, Grob, Suh, & Shao, 2000). The term *extraversion* was first used by Jung (1921) to differentiate between people with an inward (oriented toward the self) or outward (oriented toward the world) orientation; Guilford (e.g., Guilford, Zimmerman, & Guilford, 1976) said the core of extraversion was impulsivity; Eysenck's (e.g, Eysenck & Eysenck, 1968; Eysenck & Eysenck, 1975) view of extraversion originally included both impulsivity and sociability, but impulsivity was later moved to another dimension of personality; Cattell (e.g., Cattell, Eber, & Tatsuoka, 1980) described extraverts as warm, dominant, enthusiastic, bold, and socially enmeshed. More recent conceptualizations include McCrae and Costa's (1987) version of extraversion with sociability at the core and facets of warmth, assertiveness, excitement-seeking, activity, and positive emotions. Tellegen (e.g., Tellegen, Lykken, Bouchard, Wilcox, Segal, & Rich, 1988) views positive emotionality as the core of extraversion, but also includes well-being, social potency, social closeness, and achievement. In a comprehensive review of the trait, Watson and Clark (1997) concluded that the core of extraversion is positive emotionality, because extraversion and positive affectivity are similarly correlated with attitudes and behavior, and they are highly correlated with each other as well (r = 0.51; Watson, Wiese, Vaidya, & Tellegen, 1999). Meta-analytic work also indicates positive emotionality is the core of extraversion, since the positive emotionality facet loads most highly on the general extraversion trait (Davies, Connelly, & Ones, 2009). Over time, conceptualizations have evolved from thinking of extraverts as impulsive, poorly socialized people, to thinking of them as well-socialized people who are happy, enthusiastic, dominant, socially adept, and who "view themselves as more effectively and pleasurably engaged in various aspects of their lives" (Watson &

Clark, 1997, p. 788). Given this view of extraversion, it is no surprise our review identified extraversion as a trait associated with flourishing at work. Because positive emotions are at the core of extraversion, we include positive affectivity as a dimension of extraversion and do not discuss it as a separate trait.

Why Do Extraverts Flourish at Work?
Theory

H. J. Eysenck (1967) developed the first major theory involving extraversion. He posited that the activity of the cerebral cortex is regulated by the ascending reticular activating system (ARAS). In his view, extraverts are chronically underaroused and are more likely to partake in, or approach, exciting and arousing activities in attempts to raise their arousal to an "optimal level." Gray (1970) proposed an alternative model involving two motivational systems, called the behavioral approach or activation system (BAS) and the behavioral inhibition system (BIS). The core of this model revolves around reward sensitivity, with extraverts being more sensitive (or reactive) to reward cues, because the BAS is more activated in extraverts. Depue and Collins (1999) built on Gray's model and posit that differences between people in extraversion reflect variation in how sensitive (i.e., neurologically reactive) they are to reward cues in the environment.

Although not a theory of the biological basis of extraversion, Frederickson's broaden-and-build theory (e.g., Fredrickson & Losada, 2005) is also relevant to how extraversion and its core of positive emotions can lead to happiness and thriving at work. Fredrickson argued that positive emotions may have evolved to aid human survival by causing people to broaden their repertoire of behaviors to include activities such as exploration and play.

Fredrickson's theory states that positive emotions and the broad thinking they inspire may be useful in the long run because they allow people to gain resources such as "social connections, coping strategies, and environmental knowledge" (p. 679).

Considering these theories as a whole, extraverts are likely to flourish at work because they are approach-oriented with goals, people, and information; they are sensitive to rewards; and they experience and express positive emotions, leading them to be happy with their accomplishments and making them likely to keep an eye out for opportunities for success in the future. These tendencies lead extraverts to make positive evaluations of themselves and others, develop wide-ranging social relationships, attain positions of leadership and succeed in them, acquire broad-ranging knowledge and skills, and be more creative and innovative (see Figure 10.1).

Positive Evaluations

One of the mechanisms by which extraverts flourish at work is that they tend to interpret situations positively. Empirical evidence supports the notion that extraverts and introverts assign different meanings to the same life events. Uziel (2006) presented participants with a list of situations (e.g., getting promoted, a meeting with a supervisor, going out with friends, getting laid off, etc.) and asked them to rate each situation on its positivity and negativity. They found extraversion scores were positively correlated with positive situational evaluations ($r = 0.28$), but not negativity ratings. Thus, an extraverted person will tend to interpret work events such as a meeting with a supervisor positively (e.g., thinking of possible rewards, such as the opportunity for mentoring, or an opportunity to enact positive job change). Extraverts' positive interpretations make them more likely to

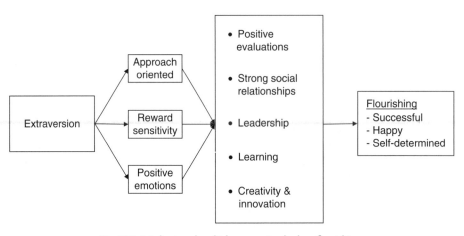

Fig. 10.1 Mechanisms by which extraversion leads to flourishing.

approach novel situations and gain access to greater opportunity.

Social Relationships

A second mechanism by which extraversion may be linked to flourishing is via strong social relationships. According to self-determination theory (Ryan & Deci, 2000), one of three core human needs is the need for relatedness. Thus, extraverts' tendencies to develop and maintain social relationships will meet a fundamental need, causing them to prosper and flourish at work. In support of the notion that extraverts have increased social relations, Watson and Clark (1997) report extraverts have more friends ($r = 0.30$), dating partners ($r = 0.19$), and attend more parties ($r = 0.33$). They are also more active in developing social networks ($r = 0.34$; Wanberg, Kanfer, & Banas, 2000). In a study of community leadership programs, Bono, Snyder, and Davies (2007) found participants high on extraversion were more central in friendship networks during the program, and more engaged in their communities following program completion, suggesting the social relationships formed by extraverts provide them with opportunities for future success.

Extraverts are also more likely to receive social support from others, which is not surprising given that they simply know more people than introverts (i.e., have larger social networks). An interesting finding was that the association between extraversion and receiving social support was mediated by the social support extraverts gave to others (Bowling, Beehr, & Swader, 2005). In other words, extraverts are more likely (than introverts) to provide others with social support, which makes them more likely to receive support during their own time of need. This may be why they tend to be more satisfied with their social relationships than less extraverted people (Lopes, Salovey, & Straus, 2003).

Leadership

Another mechanism by which extraverts flourish at work is by obtaining power and influence. Although formal power alone is not sufficient (or necessary) for flourishing, management positions tend to provide workers more discretion over their time, more decision making authority, and more autonomy and self-determination. Extraverts are more likely to emerge as leaders ($\rho = 0.33$) and to be more effective in leadership positions ($\rho = 0.24$; Judge, Bono, Ilies, & Gerhardt, 2002). They also tend to perform better when in management positions ($r = 0.10$, $\rho = 0.17$; Barrick, Mount, & Judge, 2001).

There are several reasons why extraverts are more successful in leadership positions. First, they experience and express positive emotions (Bono & Ilies, 2006), and transfer those positive emotions to those they supervise (Bono, Jackson Foldes, Vinson, & Muros, 2007). Second, extraverts are more likely than introverts to engage in the types of behaviors (i.e., transformational leadership, $\rho = 0.24$; Bono & Judge, 2004) associated with leadership success (Judge & Piccolo, 2004). Extraverted leaders may also be more effective because their approach motivation leads them to assertively approach problems and goals, they are less likely to procrastinate ($\rho = -.14$; Steel, 2007), and they build extensive social networks that provide them with increased access to resources. The trait of extraversion may also be associated with flourishing at work because extraverts tend to attain the types of positions that provide them with rewards, such as status, salary, or power, to which they are especially sensitive.

Learning

Learning plays a key role in the Spreitzer et al. (2005) definition of thriving, and extraverts' eagerness to learn may be an important mechanism by which they flourish at work. Extraverts are more likely than introverts to focus their goals on learning $\rho = 0.29$ (Payne, Youngcourt, & Beaubien, 2007); choosing "to understand or master something new" rather than to gain "favorable judgments of their competence" (Dweck, 1986, p. 1040). This makes extraverts particularly successful in training situations. In a second-order meta-analysis, Barrick, Mount, and Judge (2001) found extraversion was positively related to training performance ($\rho = 0.28$), which included performance ratings, grades, and field test scores (Barrick & Mount, 1991). Another reason extraverts excel at learning may be their approach motivation, which leads them to be more engaged during training by asking questions and interacting with the trainer and fellow trainees. Extraverts are also high in self-efficacy ($\rho = 0.33$; Judge & Ilies, 2002), which aids in learning. In sum, extraverts focus on learning for its own sake and mastering new information or skills, and therefore tend to flourish at work in part because they excel in situations in which new information is required, and in part because—over time—they acquire a stronger base of job-relevant knowledge and skills.

Creativity

Extraverts' positive emotions and eagerness to learn may lead them to be more creative, providing another mechanism by which they flourish at work.

Fredrickson's (2005) broaden-and-build theory, and a body of research by Isen and her colleagues (see Isen, Daubman, & Nowicki, 1987, for an example), clearly establish a connection between positive mood and creativity. Given the positive emotions experienced by extraverts, it is not surprising they have been found to use more divergent thinking (e.g., listing as many unusual uses for a common object as possible) and creative behaviors (e.g., creative accomplishments in the arts). Extraverts may also flourish because they are more likely to have an adaption-innovation style and tend to be more original ($r = 0.25$ and $r = 0.32$, respectively; Jacobson, 1993). There may be a biological basis to extraverts' creativity and divergent thinking, as Peterson, Smith, and Carson (2002) found extraverts have reduced latent inhibition, a neurological mechanism that allows people to ignore irrelevant stimuli. Although sometimes viewed as a limitation, this inability to block out distraction has been positively associated with creativity. Extraverts' tendencies to attend broadly to stimuli in their environment and to be creative problem solvers may also explain why they are effective leaders.

Core Self-Evaluations

Core self-evaluations is a constellation of global, evaluative personality traits reflecting a person's perceptions of self-worth, capabilities, and control. Initially, CSE was developed to explain why some individuals are happier with their jobs than others (Judge, Locke, & Durham, 1997), although CSE research quickly expanded to include other criteria, such as motivation and job performance (Judge, Erez, & Bono, 1998). In their development of the CSE construct, Judge and colleagues (1997) defined core evaluations as "basic conclusions, bottom-line evaluations, that we all hold subconsciously pertaining to self, reality, and other people". Thus, core evaluations of the *self* included individual characteristics such as self-esteem, generalized self-efficacy, and LOC. According to Judge and colleagues, people with positive core self-evaluations consider themselves capable, worthy, and in control of their lives (Judge, Van Vianen, & De Pater, 2004). From its inception, CSE was thought of as a general evaluative tendency that influenced more situation-specific evaluations, such as job satisfaction (Judge, Locke, & Durham, 1997).

Of the traits initially suggested by Judge and colleagues (1997), empirical research has consistently examined four core traits: self-esteem, generalized self-efficacy, neuroticism (reverse emotional stability),

and LOC. Self-esteem is the evaluative component of self-concept, and has been dubbed the most central of the CSE core traits, because it is the overall value a person attributes to him- or herself (Judge & Bono, 2001; Judge, Locke, Durham, & Kluger, 1998). Bandura (1982) defines self-efficacy as "judgments of how well one can execute courses of action required to deal with prospective situations" (p. 122). Judge and colleagues (1997) argued generalized self-efficacy is the subconscious evaluation of a person's capability across situations. Judge and colleagues' (1997) conceptualization of CSE also included emotional stability (i.e., reverse neuroticism) as an analog of self-esteem and LOC. The final core trait included in the CSE construct is LOC (see Rotter, 1966). People with an internal LOC believe they are masters of their own fate, having some control over events and outcomes achieved; this is in contrast to people with an external LOC, who tend to view themselves as victims of their circumstances.

Core self-evaluation was initially conceptualized as a general latent factor representing the shared variance among the four core traits (self-esteem, generalized self-efficacy, emotional stability, and internal LOC; Judge, Locke, & Durham, 1997), although it has since been acknowledged that CSE could be a compound trait (Judge & Larsen, 2001). Empirical research demonstrates clear overlap between the four CSE traits; the mean corrected meta-analytic correlation between them is 0.60 (Judge, Erez, Bono, & Thoresen, 2002). Furthermore, multiple studies have examined the factor structure of CSE and both principal components analysis (Judge, Erez, & Bono, 1998) and confirmatory factor analyses (e.g., Judge, Erez, Bono, & Thoresen, 2002, 2003) support the notion of a broad CSE trait.

Why Do People With High Core Self-evaluations Flourish At Work?
Theory

An important concept, relevant to CSE, is that CSEs are not simply the aggregation of a series of positive evaluations (e.g., of one's job, boss, or company). Rather, Judge, Locke, and Durham (1997) argued that CSE represents the tendency to view the self in a generally positive way. It is this generally positive view of the self (and the world) that is the cause of more specific evaluations. Thus, one reason CSE may be related to flourishing at work is that people who score high in the trait tend to view their work more positively than do low scorers. Judge and Larsen (2001) flesh out this idea by noting that CSE influences how people perceive stimuli, such that a person high on CSE will perceive the same stimulus (e.g., work event) in a different way (e.g., more positively) than will a person low on CSE. Judge et al. (1998) posit a more positive explanatory style for those high in CSE, such that those high on the trait tend to appraise events as challenges rather than threats.

A second theoretical reason that CSE may be related to flourishing at work is how it affects motivation and behavioral regulation. An underlying assumption of many work motivation theories (e.g., expectancy theory, self-efficacy theory, goal setting) is that employees, at some point in the process of deciding how much effort to expend, ask themselves, "Am I capable of accomplishing this task?" (Judge et al., 1998). According to Bandura (1982), people will select tasks that are within their self-efficacy range, and avoid tasks outside that range. According to Judge et al. (1998), individuals with high CSE are more likely to believe they are capable of managing the task. Thus, individuals high on CSE—because of their positive self-evaluations and high self-efficacy—are likely to be approach-orientated, especially in novel situations, and to set higher goals, because they believe they can attain them. Furthermore, Bandura's (1982) assertion that self-efficacy has a spiral effect (i.e., those with high self-efficacy develop even higher self-efficacy in the face of success) suggests high CSE will put people in a position for steadily increasing efficacy, further supporting an approach-oriented motivation.

A third theoretical reason why CSE may be related to flourishing at work is that people high in the trait may persist longer in the face of obstacles. There are two reasons to expect that high-CSE individuals will do this. The first is noted above; high CSEs are likely to evaluate their failures positively. Thus, rather than interpreting a stumbling block as a failure, they may interpret it as an opportunity to grow and learn. Secondly, Korman's (1970) self-consistency theory suggests that individuals will behave in ways that maintain their self-image. Since individuals with high CSE have positive self-views, they will be motivated to perform successfully. Research by Bono and Colbert (2005) generally supports this notion, finding that when individuals with high CSE received negatively discrepant feedback (i.e., others' ratings on a leadership 360 were lower than self-ratings), they were more committed to their development goals over time than were low CSEs.

In summary, individuals high in CSE tend to flourish at work because they evaluate themselves and their work environments positively, they persevere in the face of obstacles and change, and they have an approach-oriented motivational style. These three tendencies lead them to obtain and create better jobs; set self-concordant, difficult goals and commit to them; cope well with stress; and make good use of the resources available to them (see Figure 10.2).

Job Characteristics

One of the primary mechanisms by which individuals with high CSE flourish is the work itself. Those with high CSE both attain more complex jobs and subjectively perceive their jobs as more complex (Judge, Locke, Durham, & Kluger, 1998). Using the *Dictionary of Occupational Titles* (DOT) to code participant job titles for objective complexity, Judge, Bono, and Locke (2000) found high-CSE individuals held more complex jobs than did their low-CSE counterparts. Moreover, even after controlling for objective characteristics of the job, high CSEs perceived their jobs to have more autonomy, variety, and feedback than did people low on CSE. Adding support to the notion that CSE is linked to perceptions

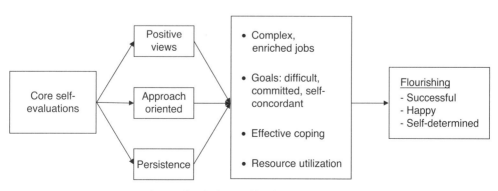

Fig. 10.2 Mechanisms by which core self-evaluation (CSE) leads to flourishing.

of job characteristics, Brown, Ferris, Heller, and Keeping (2007) found that people high in CSE viewed their jobs as less ambiguous than did low CSEs. A clear finding of the job design literature (Hackman & Oldham, 1976; Loher, Noe, Moeller, & Fitzgerald, 1985) is that job characteristics, such as autonomy, feedback, and complexity, are associated with job satisfaction. Mediation analysis (Judge, Bono, & Locke 2000; Judge, Locke, Durham, & Kluger, 1998) shows that the reason those high in CSE are happier at work is because they have more complex, enriched jobs.

Goals

Another mechanism linking CSE to flourishing is related to goals. Because they have high self-efficacy, high CSEs approach goals with confidence, leading them to set more difficult goals (Erez & Judge, 2001). In addition to setting higher goals, high CSEs also reported greater task motivation and persisted longer in the face of a difficult task. Furthermore, in a sample of sales representatives, Erez and Judge (2001) found high CSEs were more committed to their goals (an effect replicated by Bono & Colbert, 2005), engaged in more task-related activity (per company records), and thus had higher sales volume and better performance ratings. One of the mechanisms by which difficult goals lead to performance is that they encourage people with high goals to seek out new information or develop new skills (Locke & Latham, 2002). Thus, in addition to the satisfaction of performing well and the general well-being effects of goal attainment (Latham & Budworth, 2007), their tendency to set and commit to difficult goals is likely to result in increased learning for high CSEs.

Core self-evaluations may also be related to flourishing because of the types of goals people high on the trait tend to pursue. Sheldon and Eillot (1999) showed that if goals are aligned with a person's values (self-concordant goals), there is increased motivation, high levels of achievement, and greater satisfaction with goal attainment. Judge, Erez, Bono, and Locke (2005) found that individuals with high CSE were more likely to select self-concordant goals, and to put more effort into those goals, which resulted in enhanced job and life satisfaction.

Stress and Coping

More positive interpretations of stressful events, greater cognitive resources, and better coping skills may also be mechanisms through which those high in CSE flourish at work. Those with high CSE perceive stressors differently than do those low on the trait,

and they tend to use more adaptive coping strategies. The coping process begins with a primary appraisal (Lazarus & Folkman, 1984); when an event occurs, high CSEs are more likely to see the event as a challenge than as a threat. Self-esteem, a CSE trait, is positively associated both with appraising work events as challenges and to lessened fear of failure (Locke, McClear, & Knight, 1996). Kammeyer-Mueller, Judge, and Scott (2009) recently proposed a model of coping in which they hypothesized that individuals high in CSE would perceive fewer stressors in their work environment, would be less reactive to them, and would choose better coping strategies (e.g., problem-focused coping). Although results were not perfectly consistent across the four CSE traits, they generally supported a model in which CSE is related to perceiving fewer stressors, experiencing less strain, and using more effective coping techniques.

Using conservation of resources theory (Hobfoll, 1989), Harris, Harvey, and Kacmar (2009) argued that CSE represents a set of cognitive resources. Those high in CSE have a greater capacity to absorb the resource losses associated with stressors. Accordingly, they hypothesized that social stressors at work would be less related to job satisfaction for those high in CSE than for low scorers, because high CSEs had more cognitive resources available to them. Results supported this notion, as the negative effects of work stressors on job satisfaction were lower for high CSEs than for low. High CSEs ability to cope well with stress may also help them flourish in an environment of organizational change (e.g., major reorganization efforts or downsizing, mergers and acquisitions). In a study of managers in six companies on four continents, Judge, Thoresen, Pucik, and Welbourne (1999) found CSE was associated with career success, in part because of effective coping with change.

Use of Resources

Another mechanism through which people high on CSE flourish is their better use of resources. Judge and Hurst (2007) linked childhood CSE and socio-economic status to career success (i.e., income) in adulthood. They found CSE moderated the relationship between resources in childhood and young adulthood (e.g., higher socioeconomic status, good academic performance) and income later in life, such that those with higher CSE benefited more from their resources. Whereas we do not include income as an indicator of flourishing at work, this study is a nice example of how those high in CSE are able to make full use of resources available to them, over the course of their lives.

Another work-related resource is mentoring. Meta-analytic findings show those with high CSE are slightly more likely than those low on the trait to be mentored at work (ρ = 0.10). Furthermore, employees high on CSE tend to be more satisfied with their mentoring, in part because they perceive it to be more effective (Kammeyer-Mueller & Judge, 2008). It may be that high CSEs receive more effective mentoring because they are confident and autonomously motivated, leading them to be good mentees. More and better mentoring may lead to flourishing directly through increasing job satisfaction, but also indirectly through facilitating engagement and learning at work (Allen, Eby, Poteet, Lentz, & Lima, 2004). Another important resource for employees is their social connections to others. In a study of expatriates, those with high CSE formed a greater number of social relationships (Johnson, Kristof-Brown, Van Vianen, De Pater, & Klein, 2003). Thus, individuals high in CSE appear to form more and better social relationships, which they fully utilize for career advancement, learning, and support.

Future Directions

Although we focused on flourishing specifically in the work domain, there is research in the domain of positive psychology and positive organizational scholarship focused on the characteristics of individuals who experience optimal functioning in life (e.g., happiness and self-determination). On the one hand, the story looks similar to that which we tell here, specifically that positive emotions (e.g., optimism, positive affectivity) and positive self regard (i.e., self-esteem), along with autonomy and self-determination, are associated with successful pursuit of personal goals and life satisfaction. On the other hand, recent research on the character strengths and virtues associated with human flourishing (see Peterson & Seligman, 2004) has not, to our knowledge, been directly applied to flourishing at work. Researchers are currently defining and studying the concept of character and how it affects human flourishing. As this research develops, it has the potential to also shed light on our understanding of flourishing at work. Indeed, an important area for future research is whether character strengths and virtues can be developed, fostered, or elicited at work, and if so, whether doing so would increase the extent to which employees flourish on the job.

One clear question raised by this chapter is whether organizations would benefit if all their workers flourished. We have taken an employee-centric approach here, focusing on individual employee flourishing. It does not necessarily follow that staffing an organization (or work group) composed of all individuals who are high in CSEs or extraversion, or even all workers who are flourishing, would help organizations meet their objectives for growth, sustainability, or financial success. On the one hand, it is difficult to imagine not wanting an organization or workgroup composed of individuals with the traits we examined; individuals who are interested in learning; who approach challenges with confidence and enthusiasm; who evaluate themselves positively; and who are creative, cope well, make good use of resources, and are responsive to rewards. Indeed, the existing literature provides many points of evidence that when employees flourish, specifically when they are autonomously motivated, happy with their jobs, and engaged with their work, they also perform better and are less likely to leave the organization. On the other hand, existing research suggests homogeneity in the traits we examined may not always lead to desired group or organizational outcomes. It is very clear from the existing literature that negative emotions can sometimes be good for creativity (George & Zhou, 2007), but also that positive affect in a group has beneficial effects on decision quality (Staw & Barsade, 1993). Research on team extraversion shows that having a high mean in the team is associated with social cohesion and reduced conflict (Barrick, Stewart, Neubert, & Mount, 1998), but diversity on extraversion has been positively associated with team performance (Neuman, Wagner, & Christiansen, 1999), suggesting that a group with all members high on extraversion may not lead to high performance. It is beyond the scope of this chapter to develop a comprehensive theory about what configuration of the positive traits we identified would be good for work groups and organizations, but this is an important issue for future research. We should not blindly assume that because these traits are associated with employee flourishing that groups of individuals with these traits are well suited to work together in pursuit of organizational objectives.

Another important topic for future research is how to create the types of environments in which all employees can flourish. The environments in which extraverts and those high on CSE succeed are full of challenges, learning, difficult goals, strong relationships, and sensitivity to rewards. But, building these dimensions into a work environment is unlikely to lead to flourishing for employees who lack confidence, who tend to experience and express negative emotions, who expect the worst, and who are afraid to take chances. Perhaps what we have really identified in this chapter are the traits of workers who will flourish if left on their own with minimal intervention from the organization. If this is true, then the challenge of organizational leaders is how to create the freedom so that these individuals can flourish on their own, while at the same time using organizational interventions or leadership practices to bring out the best in employees who need more support and nurturing. An important practical and theoretical question for future research is how best to manage, support, and nourish individuals who do not score high on these traits.

Another issue that is not clear from the existing research literature is whether the attitudes, behaviors, and activities of employees who flourish are contagious. There is research on how organizations can support various aspects of flourishing—indeed, many of these ideas are addressed in other chapters of this volume. But one thing is not clear: whether seeding a team, workgroup, or organization with individuals who are naturally positive and approach oriented can help support the efforts of managers and organizations who wish to foster learning- and autonomy-supportive environments. Does the notion of a tipping point make sense in this context? Is there some proportion of positive approach-oriented employees necessary to change the tone of the group? Is it critical that these individuals be in leadership positions?

More research is also needed to understand the mechanisms by which positive views of the self or work events, positive expectations for the future, or positive emotions lead to positive outcomes for individuals and organizations. It is clear from the research literature that the beneficial effects of positive emotions are deep and complex, and represent far more than a Pollyanna view of the world. Fredrickson's (2005) broaden-and-build theory provides a framework for future research in this area, as she argues that positive emotions may be the means by which people gain resources. In the context of work, these might be social resources in terms of positive relationships and support from others, cognitive resources (positive emotions → exploration and play → learning → knowledge), skills (approach motivation → take on challenges → develop new skills), or psychological and emotional resources. We can learn about these mechanisms by manipulating emotions, an approach taken by Isen and colleagues, although most of their research focused on short-term mood changes. We can also learn about these

mechanisms by conducting research that assesses long-term change in emotions and resources following deeper interventions, such as mindfulness meditation (see Davidson, Kabat-Zinn, Schumacher, Rosenkranz, Muller, et al., 2003), which affect the brain and immune functioning.

Conclusion

Our review identified two broad positive traits associated with employee flourishing—extraversion and core self-evaluations—and there was a surprising degree of overlap in the mechanisms by which people high in those two traits flourished. We identified two strong underlying themes. People who flourish at work have a positive approach to the self, others, and work situations; and they have an active, engaged, and forward-looking approach to work, including novel or challenging situations.

Our focus on positive traits can be applied in work organizations in at least two ways. First, if extraversion and CSEs are associated with employee flourishing (prospering, thriving, succeeding, and being happy and self-determined at work) and are stable characteristics of individuals (even genetically determined, in part), organizations could consider these traits in hiring and staffing decisions, at least for certain jobs and with appropriate evidence that doing so would not have adverse impact on protected classes of employees. Second, our examination of these two traits sheds light on the mechanisms by which employees flourish. This information can be used by organizations to help them create the conditions that would foster flourishing among all employees, irrespective of their personality. For example, our review makes it clear that some employees (extraverts) come to work with a natural tendency to experience and express positive emotions, and others (CSEs) with a natural tendency to see themselves as authors of their own actions. But, we also know managers can engage in leadership behaviors that will increase both the positive emotions felt by employees (Bono et al., 2007, Bono & Ilies, 2006) and the extent to which they perceive their work to be self-determined (Bono & Judge, 2003), regardless of their standing on extraversion and CSE.

Given that our goal was to identify a set of traits associated with employee flourishing, we were a bit surprised to identify only two key traits. Perhaps our general approach of looking for traits that showed up consistently across studies and across our two key indicators of employee flourishing (self-determination and job satisfaction) necessarily produced a short list. In taking this broad-brush approach to the existing literature, it is likely that we overlooked some traits, especially narrow traits or facets of personality that might be associated with some aspects of flourishing at work. For example, Macey and Schneider (2008) linked employee engagement (which includes both aspects of flourishing that we focused on: job satisfaction and self-determination) to traits such as proactive personality and autotelic personality, traits we did not explicitly include in our review. Yet, upon examination, the mechanisms by which these traits are associated with employee engagement look very similar to our two underlying themes; individuals with these traits take a positive and/or proactive approach to work.

We also did not focus on conscientiousness, which has been consistently linked to job performance (see Hurtz & Donovan, 2000), but less so with job satisfaction (Judge et al., 2002). Clearly, conscientiousness has some association with employee flourishing, especially to the extent that performing well on the job may be a cause of flourishing. Yet, it was not clear to us in our review of the literature whether the achievement motivation of individuals high in conscientiousness stems from their tendency to follow rules (externally motivated), or whether it is self-determined (autonomously motivated). For this reason, we did not include conscientiousness as a central trait, although we believe it bears further investigation relative to employee flourishing. There are many ways to organize and categorize personality traits (e.g., Big Five), and it is likely that our own biases influenced the way we organized the literature. Another set of authors might have—for example—chosen positive affectivity and self-esteem as the two core traits associated with flourishing at work (although it is worth noting that those authors would likely have found the same central themes and mechanisms we did).

Finally, we can learn more by taking a fine-grained look at how individuals, such as those high in CSE, are able to better capitalize on their resources, and on how positive psychology interventions (see Seligman, Steen, Park, & Peterson, 2005) differentially affect those high and low in positive traits, such as CSEs. Are interventions—such as positive reflections or gratitude journals—only (or most) effective for individuals who score low on extraversion and CSE, or can they improve flourishing, in life and at work, for all individuals?

References

Allen, T. A., Eby, L.T., Poteet, M.L., Lentz, E., & Lima, L. (2004). Career benefits associated with mentoring for protégés: A meta-analysis. *Journal of Applied Psychology, 89,* 127–136.

Arvey, R.D., Bouchard, T.J., Segal, N.L., & Abraham, L.M. (1989). Job satisfaction: Environmental and genetic components. *Journal of Applied Psychology, 74,* 187–192.

Bandura, A. (1982). Self-efficacy mechanism in human agency. *American Psychologist, 37,* 122–147.

Barrick, M.J., & Mount, M.K. (1991). The Big Five personality dimensions and job performance: A meta-analysis. *Personnel Psychology, 44,* 1–26.

Barrick, M.R., Mount, M.K., & Judge, T.A. (2001). Personality and performance at the beginning of the new millennium: What do we know and where do we go next? *International Journal of Selection and Assessment, 9,* 9–30.

Barrick, M.R., Stewart, G.L., Neubert, M.J., & Mount, M.K. (1998). Relating member ability and personality to work-team processes and team effectiveness. *Journal of Applied Psychology, 83,* 377–391.

Bono, J.E., & Colbert, A.E. (2005). Understanding responses to multi-source feedback: The role of core self-evaluations. *Personnel Psychology, 58,* 171–203.

Bono, J.E., & Ilies, R. (2006). Charisma, positive emotions, and mood contagion. *The Leadership Quarterly, 17,* 317–334.

Bono, J.E., & Judge, T.A. (2003). Core self-evaluations: a review of the trait and its role in job satisfaction and job performance. *European Journal of Personality, 17,* S5–S18.

Bono, J.E., Jackson Foldes, H., Vinson, G., & Muros, J.P. (2007). Workplace emotions: The role of supervision and leadership. *Journal of Applied Psychology, 92,* 1357–1367.

Bono, J., Snyder, M., & Davies, S.E. (2007). *Individual characteristics, performance, and network centrality: Does performance lead to network centrality or does network centrality lead to performance?* Symposium presentation at the Academy of Management annual meeting, Philadelphia, PA.

Bowling, N.A., Beehr, T.A., & Swader, W.M. (2005). Giving and receiving social support at work: The roles of personality and reciprocity. *Journal of Vocational Behavior, 67,* 476–489.

Brown, D.J., Ferris, D.L., Heller, D., & Keeping, L.M. (2007). Antecedents and consequences of the frequency of upward and downward social comparisons at work. *Organizational Behavior and Human Decision Processes, 102,* 59–75.

Cameron, K.S., Dutton, J.E., & Quinn, R.E. (2003). *Positive organizational scholarship: Foundations of a new discipline.* San Francisco: Berrett-Koehler.

Cattell, R.B., Eber, H.W., & Tatsuoka, M.M. (1980). *Handbook for the sixteen personality questionnaire (16PF).* Champaign, IL: Institute for Personality and Ability Testing.

Connolly, J.J., & Viswesvaran, C. (2000). The role of affectivity in job satisfaction: A meta-analysis. *Personality and Individual Differences, 29,* 265–281.

Costa, P.T., Jr., & McCrae, R.R. (1992). *Revised NEO Personality Inventory (NEO-PI-R) and NEO Five-Factor Inventory (NEO-FFI) professional manual.* Odessa, FL: Psychological Assessment Resources.

Davidson, R.J., Kabat-Zinn, J., Schumacher, J, Rosenkranz, M., Muller, D., Santorelli, S., et al. (2003). Alterations in brain and immune function produced by Mindfulness Meditation. *Psychosomatic Medicine, 65,* 564–570.

Davies, S.E., Connelly, B.S., & Ones, D.S. (2009). *Exploring the dimensionality of extraversion: Factors and facets.* Poster presented at the 24th annual convention of the Society for Industrial and Organizational Society, New Orleans, LA, April, 2009.

Deci, E.L., & Ryan, R.M. (1985). *Intrinsic motivation and self-determination in human behavior.* New York: Plenum.

Depue, R.A., & Collins, P.F. (1999). Neurobiology of the structure of personality: Dopamine, facilitation of incentive motivation, and extraversion. *Behavioral and Brain Sciences, 22*, 491–569.

Dweck, C.S. (1986). Motivational processes affecting learning. *American Psychologist, 41*, 1040–1048.

Erez, A., & Judge, T.A. (2001). Relationship of core-self-evaluations to goal-setting, motivation, and performance. *Journal of Applied Psychology, 86*, 1270–1279.

Eysenck, H.J. (1967). *The biological basis of personality.* Springfield, IL: C.C. Thomas.

Eysenck, H.J., & Eysenck, S.B.G. (1968). *Manual of the Eysenck personality inventory.* San Diego: Educational and Industrial Testing Service.

Eysenck, H.J., & Eysenck, S.B.G. (1975). *Manual of the Eysenck Personality Questionnaire.* San Diego: Educational and Industrial Testing Service.

Fredrickson, B.L., & Losada, M.F. (2005). Positive affect and the complex dynamics of human flourishing. *American Psychologist, 60*, 678–686.

George, J.M., & Zhou, J. (2007). Dual tuning in a supportive context: Joint contributions of positive mood, negative mood, and supervisory behaviors to employee creativity. *Journal of Applied Psychology, 50*, 605–622.

Gray, J.A. (1970). The psychophysiological basis of introversion-extraversion. *Behaviour Research and Therapy, 8*, 249–266.

Goldberg, L.R. (1990). An alternative "description of personality": The big-five factor structure. *Journal of Personality and Social Psychology, 59*, 1216–1229.

Guilford, J.S., Zimmerman, W.S., & Guilford, J.P. (1976). *The Guilford-Zimmerman temperament survey handbook.* San Diego: Educational and Industrial Testing Service.

Hackman, J.R., & Oldham, G.R. (1976). Motivation through the design of work: Test of a theory. *Organizational Behavior and Human Performance, 16*, 250–279.

Hackman, J., & Oldham, G. (1980). *Work redesign.* Reading, MA: Addison-Wesley.

Harris, K.J., Harvey, P., & Kacmar, K.M. (2009). Do social stressors impact everyone equally? An examination of the moderating impact of core self-evaluations. *Journal of Business and Psychology, 24*, 153–164.

Heimpel, S.A., Elliot, A.J., & Wood, J.V. (2006). Basic personality dispositions, self-esteem, and personal goals: An approach-avoidance analysis. *Journal of Personality, 74*, 1293–1319.

Hobfoll, S.E. (1989). Conservation of resources: A new attempt at conceptualizing stress. *American Psychologist, 44*, 513–524.

Hoppock, R. (1935). *Job satisfaction.* New York: Harper.

Hurtz, G.M., & Donovan, J.J. (2000). Personality and job performance: The big five revisited. *Journal of Applied Psychology, 85*, 869–879.

Ilies, R., & Judge, T.A. (2003). On the heritability of job satisfaction: The mediating role of personality. *Journal of Applied Psychology, 88*, 750–759.

Ingledew, D.K., Markland, D., & Sheppard, K.E. (2004). Personality and self-determination of exercise behaviour. *Personality and Individual Differences, 36*, 1921–1932.

Isen, A.M., Daubman, K.A., & Nowicki, G.P. (1987). Positive affect facilitates creative problem solving. *Journal of Personality and Social Psychology, 52*, 122–1131.

Jacobson, C.K. (1993). Cognitive styles of creativity: Relations of scores on the Kirton adaption-innovation inventory and the Myers-Briggs type indicator among managers in the USA. *Psychological Reports, 72*, 1131–1138.

Johnson, E.C., Kristof-Brown, A.L., Van Vianen, A.E.M., De Pater, I.E., & Klein, M.R. (2003). Expatriate social ties: Personality antecedents and consequences for adjustment. *International Journal of Selection and Assessment, 11*, 277–288.

Judge, T.A., & Bono, J.E. (2001). A rose by any other name. . . . Are self-esteem, generalized self-efficacy, neuroticism, and locus of control indicators of a common construct? In B.W. Roberts, & R. Hogan (Eds.), *Personality psychology in the workplace.* Washington, DC: American Psychological Association.

Judge, T.A., & Ilies, R. (2002). Relationship of personality to performance motivation: A meta-analysis review. *Journal of Applied Psychology, 87*, 797–807.

Judge, T.A., & Larsen, R.J. (2001). Dispositional affect and job satisfaction: A review and theoretical extension. *Organizational Behavior and Human Decision Processes, 86*, 67–98.

Judge, T.A., & Piccolo, R.F. (2004). Transformational and trans-actional leadership: A meta-analytic test of their relative validity. *Journal of Applied Psychology, 89*, 755–768.

Judge, T.A., Bono, J.E., & Locke, E.A. (2000). Personality and job satisfaction: The mediating role of job characteristics. *Journal of Applied Psychology, 85*, 237–249.

Judge, T.A., Bono, J.E., Erez, A., & Locke, E.A. (2005). Core self-evaluations and job and life satisfaction: The role of self-concordance and goal attainment. *Journal of Applied Psychology, 90*, 257–268.

Judge, T.A., Bono, J.E., Ilies, R., & Gerhardt, M.W. (2002). Personality and leadership: A qualitative and quantitative review. *Journal of Applied Psychology, 87*, 765–780.

Judge, T.A., Erez, A., & Bono, J.E. (1998). The power of being positive: The relation between positive self-concept and job performance. *Human Performance, 11*, 167.

Judge, T.A., Bono, J.E., Erez, A., & Locke, E.A. (2005). Core self-evaluations and job and life satisfaction: The role of self-concordance and goal attainment. *Journal of Applied Psychology, 90*, 257–268.

Judge, T.A., Erez, A., Bono, J.E., & Thoresen, C.J. (2002). Are measures of self-esteem, neuroticism, locus of control, and generalized self-efficacy indicators of a common core construct? *Journal of Personality and Social Psychology, 83*, 693–710.

Judge, T.A., Erez, A., Bono, J.E., & Thoresen, C.J. (2003). The core self-evaluations scale: Development of a measure. *Personnel Psychology, 56*, 303–331.

Judge, T.A., Heller, D., & Mount, M.K. (2002). Five-factor model of personality and job satisfaction: A meta-analysis. *Journal of Applied Psychology, 87*, 530–541.

Judge, T.A., & Hurst, C. (2007). Capitalizing on one's advantages: Role of core self-evaluations. *Journal of Applied Psychology, 92*, 1212–1227.

Judge, T.A., Locke, E.A., & Durham, C.C. (1997). The dispositional causes of job satisfaction: A core evaluations approach. *Research in Organizational Behavior, 19*, 151–188.

Judge, T.A., Locke, E.A., Durham, C.C., & Kluger, A.N. (1998). Dispositional effects on job and life satisfaction: The role of core evaluations. *Journal of Applied Psychology, 83*, 17–34.

Judge, T.A., Thoresen, C.J., Pucik, V., & Welbourne, T.M. (1999). Managerial coping with organizational change: A dispositional perspective. *Journal of Applied Psychology, 84*, 107–122.

Judge, T.A., Van Vianen, A.E.M., & De Pater, I.E. (2004). Emotional stability, core self-evaluations, and job outcomes: A review of the evidence and an agenda for future research. *Human Performance, 17*, 325–346.

Jung, C.G. (1921). *Psychological types*. New York: Harcourt, Brace, & Co.

Kammeyer-Mueller, J.D., & Judge, T.A. (2008). A quantitative review of mentoring research: Test of a model. *Journal of Vocational Behavior, 72*, 269–283.

Kammeyer-Mueller, J.D., Judge, T.A., & Scott, B.A. (2009). The role of core self-evaluations in the coping process. *Journal of Applied Psychology, 94*, 177–195.

Korman, A.K. (1970). Toward a hypothesis of work behavior. *Journal of Applied Psychology, 54*, 31–41.

Latham, G.P., & Budworth, M.H. (2007). The study of work motivation in the 20th century. In L.L. Koppes (Ed.), *Historical perspectives in industrial and organizational psychology* (pp. 353–382). Mahwah, NJ: Erlbaum.

Lazarus, R.S., & Folkman, S. (1984). Coping and adaptation. In W.D. Gentry (Ed.), *The handbook of behavioral medicine* (pp. 282–325). New York: Guilford.

Locke, E.A., & Latham, G.P. (2002). Building a practically useful theory of goal setting and task motivation: A 35-year odyssey. *American Psychologist, 57*, 705–717.

Locke, E.A., McClear, K., & Knight, D. (1996). Self-esteem and work. *International Review of Industrial/Organizational Psychology, 11*, 1–32.

Loher, B.T., Noe, R.A., Moeller, N.L., & Fitzgerald, M.P. (1985). A meta-analysis of the relation of job characteristics to job satisfaction. *Journal of Applied Psychology, 70*, 280–289.

Lopes, P.N., Salovey, P., & Straus, R. (2003). Emotional intelligence, personality, and the perceived quality of social relationships. *Personality and Individual Differences, 35*, 641–658.

Lucas, R.E., Diener, E., Grob, A., Suh, E.M., & Shao, L. (2000). Cross-cultural evidence for the fundamental features of extraversion. *Journal of Personality and Social Psychology, 79*, 452–468.

Macey, W.H., & Schneider, B. (2008). The meaning of employee engagement. *Industrial and Organizational Psychology, 1*, 3–30.

McAdams, D.P. (1995). What do we know when we know a person? *Journal of Personality, 63*, 365–396.

McCrae, R.R., & Costa, P.T., Jr. (1987). Validation of a five-factor model of personality across instruments and observers. *Journal of Personality and Social Psychology, 52*, 81–90.

Neuman, G.A., Wagner, S.H., & Christiansen, N.D. (1999). The relationship between work-team personality composition and the job performance of teams. *Group and Organization Management, 24*, 28–45.

Ng, T.W.H., Sorensen, K.L., & Eby, L.T. (2006). Locus of control at work: A meta-analysis. *Journal of Organizational Behavior, 27*, 1057–1087.

Payne, S.C., Youngcourt, S.S., & Beaubien, J. (2007). A meta-analytic examination of the goal orientation nomological net. *Journal of Applied Psychology, 92*, 128–150.

Peterson, C., Park, N., & Seligman, M.E.P. (2005). Orientations to happiness and life satisfaction: The full life versus the empty life. *Journal of Happiness Studies, 6*, 25–41.

Peterson, J.B., Smith, K.W., & Carson, S. (2002). Openness and extraversion are associated with reduced latent inhibition: replication and commentary. *Personality and Individual Differences, 33*, 1137–1147.

Peterson, C., & Seligman, M.E.P. (2004). *Character strengths and virtues: A handbook and classification*. Washington, DC: American Psychological Association and New York: Oxford University Press.

Roberts, B.W., & DelVecchio, W.F. (2000). The rank-order consistency of personality traits from childhood to old age: A quantitative review of longitudinal studies. *Psychological Bulletin, 126*, 3–25.

Roberts, B.W., Walton, K., & Viechtbauer, W. (2006). Patterns of mean-level change in personality traits across the life course: A meta-analysis of longitudinal studies. *Psychological Bulletin, 132*, 1–25.

Rotter, J.B. (1966). Generalized expectancies for internal versus external control of reinforcement. *Psychological Monographs, 80*, 1–28.

Ryan, R.M., & Deci, E.L. (2000). Self-determination theory and the facilitation of intrinsic motivation, social development, and well-being. *American Psychologist, 55*, 68–78.

Seligman, M.E.P., Steen., T.A., Park, N., & Peterson, C. (2005). Positive psychology progress: Empirical validation of interventions. *American Psychologist, 60*, 410–421.

Sheldon, K.M., & Elliot, A.J. (1998). Not all personal goals are personal: Comparing autonomous and controlled reasons for goals as predictors of effort and attainment. *Personality and Social Psychology Bulletin, 24*, 546–557.

Sheldon, K.M., & Elliot, A.J. (1999). Goal striving, need satisfaction, and longitudinal well-being: The self-concordance model. *Journal of Personality and Social Psychology, 76*, 482–497.

Spreitzer, G. (1996). Social structural characteristics of psychological empowerment. *Academy of Management Journal, 39*, 483–504.

Spreitzer, G., Porath, C., Gibson, C., & Stevens, F. (2010). *Thriving at work: Toward its measurement, construct validation, and theoretical refinement*. Working paper, University of Michigan, Ann Arbor, MI.

Spreitzer, G., Sutcliffe, K., Dutton, J., Sonenshein, S., & Grant, A.M. (2005). A socially embedded model of thriving at work. *Organization Science, 16*, 537–549.

Staw, B.M., & Barsade, S.G. (1993). Affect and managerial performance: A test of the sadder but wiser vs. happier and smarter hypotheses. *Administrative Science Quarterly, 38*, 304–331

Staw, B.M., & Ross, J. (1985). Stability in the midst of change: a dispositional approach to job attitudes. *Journal of Applied Psychology, 70*, 469–480.

Steel, P. (2007). The nature of procrastination: A meta-analytic and theoretical review of quintessential self-regulatory failure. *Psychological Bulletin, 133*, 65–94.

Tellegen, A., Lykken, D.T., Bouchard, T.J., Jr., Wilcox, K.J., Segal, N.L., & Rich, S. (1988). Personality similarity in twins reared apart and together. *Journal of Personality and Social Psychology, 54*, 1031–1039.

Thoresen, C.J., Kaplan, S.A., Barsky, A.P., Warren, C.R., & de Chermont, K. (2003). The affective underpinnings of job perceptions and attitudes: A meta-analytic review and integration. *Psychological Bulletin, 129*, 914–945.

Uziel, L. (2006). The extraverted and the neurotic glasses are of a different color. *Personality and Individual Differences, 41*, 745–754.

Wanberg, C.R., Kanfer, R., & Banas, J.T. (2000). Predictors and outcomes of networking intensity among unemployed job seekers. *Journal of Applied Psychology, 85*, 491–503.

Watson, D., & Clark, L.A. (1997). Extraversion and its positive emotional core. In R.Hogan, J.A. Johnson, & S.R. Briggs (Eds.), *Handbook of personality psychology* (pp. 767–793). San Diego: Academic Press.

Watson, D., Wiese, D., Vaidya, J., & Tellegen, A. (1999). The two general activation systems of affect: Structural findings, evolutionary considerations, and psychobiological evidence. *Journal of Personality and Social Psychology, 76*, 820–838.

Exploring the Minds of Managers

Insights from Three Neuroscience Studies

Richard P. Bagozzi *and* Willem J.M.I. Verbeke

Abstract

Neuroscience provides new ways to think about and conduct research in organizations. We summarize findings from three of our studies that explore how theory of mind (ToM), empathy, and Machiavellianism function in organizations, particularly for sales managers. Study 1 derives a 13-item theory of mind scale and validates it; Study 2 shows how empathy and ToM undergrid customer orientation, and Study 3 reveals that Machiavellians versus non-Machiavellians are better at resonating to the feelings of others in automatic ways but at the same time are less able to take the perspective of others (put themselves in the shoes of others) and feel more anxiety in interactions, among other differences.

Keywords: Theory of mind, empathy, customer orientation, neuroscience, interpersonal mentalizing, sales managers, Machiavellianism

In this chapter, we present the results of three studies examining the mental processes of managers. The studies each consist of neuroscience experiments and complementary field studies and aim to provide insights into how and why managers behave and act the ways they do.

Although our research was not intended to explore positive organizational scholarship (POS) topics, per se, and applies to areas outside of POS as well, our three investigations have implications for POS. Our first study investigates theory of mind (ToM) processes and their implications. Theory of mind processes refer to capacities for inferring and understanding the mental states of oneself and others. These processes are obviously important for mutual understanding and in the initiation and resolution of interpersonal behavior in organizations. They thus provide a basis or means for positive organizing and leadership.

Our second study examines the functioning of customer versus sales orientations by managers. Under a customer orientation, a manager asks (speaking figuratively): What is in the best interests of the customer, and how can I best respond to those interests? Under a sales orientation, the manager asks: How can I convince the customer to buy our product or service? The former entails a perspective of attempting to satisfy mutual needs, the latter a perspective on self gain, even at the expense of the other. In this study, we scrutinize ToM processes and empathy in a functional magnetic resonance imaging (fMRI) experiment and relate these to customer alliance building in a field study. Decidedly, a customer orientation focuses on POS principles—in this case, as much on interorganizational as on intraorganizational capabilities.

Our third study also explores empathy in managers to see how those failing to exhibit POS values (i.e., Machiavellians) compare to those who do. Relationships with colleagues and customers are examined, as well as associations of positive and negative orientations with various personality traits. Destructive and constructive aspects of high and low Machiavellianism are scrutinized for customers and the organization.

Study 1: Theory of Mind

The study of the human mind and its relationship to behavior and action in business has been investigated to date primarily with qualitative research, survey methods, and psychological experiments. Only recently have researchers begun to use methods from neuroscience to study the minds of consumers and managers (e.g., Dietvorst et al., 2009; Yoon et al., 2006). Neuroscience methods are particularly suited to the investigation of memory, decision processes, and emotional processes, as well as to social and cultural behavior.

Theory of mind processes, or *interpersonal mentalizing* as it is also termed, refer to the ability to infer the beliefs, feelings, desires, intentions, and other mental states or events of other people one observes or with whom one interacts (e.g., Frith & Frith, 2003, p. 80; Singer & Fehr, 2005). The processes involved in ToM are automatic or reflexive and encompass specialized regions of the brain (e.g., Saxe, Carey, & Kanwisher, 2004).

During typical ToM processing, people are thought to make inferences about the states of mind or mental events of other people and use this information to make predictions about other people's future behavior. Although such processes can entail any mental state or event, they are especially believed to encompass inferring or attributing the direction of attention of another person, as well as their intentions. Theory of mind also can includes imitative behavior and taking the perspective of another in empathy-like processes. People with autism have difficulty engaging in ToM processes as a result of underdevelopment of the areas of the brain associated with ToM processes. Such areas of the brain as the medial prefrontal cortex (mPFC), precuneus, and temporoparietal junction (TPJ) (e.g., Saxe & Kanwisher, 2003; Saxe & Powell, 2006), temporal poles (TP) (Frith & Frith, 2003), posterior superior temporal sulcus (pSTS; Allison, Puce, & McCarthy, 2000), and possibly mirror neuron regions (e.g., the premotor cortex; Iacoboni et al., 2005) are involved in ToM processes.

To develop a sales theory of mind (SToM) scale, we conducted a literature search and performed a content analysis of research in neuroscience, sales force behavior, and communication to find items that could be used in the scale. This was done to isolate different social situations and interactions in which people low in interpersonal mentalizing ability would presumably encounter difficulties (Frith & Frith, 2003). The literature suggests that people low in interpersonal mentalizing skills exhibit several characteristics. First, they have difficulty strategically taking the initiative in conversations, which is needed to address needs, cajole, and gauge responses from customers. Second, they lack the ability to process indirect information and hints because they tend to focus on bare utterances or literal meaning and are less able to grasp and act on the ostensive meanings in communications or take a bird's-eye view or ironic perspective on interactions and their own behavior in these interactions (Soldow & Thomas, 1984). A third variable differentiating high from low mentalizers is the ability to engage in mutually rewarding interactions. People with low mentalizing skills have difficulties engaging in tasks that require joint attention and reciprocity; from a salesperson's perspective, the establishment of joint attention implies that a conversational context has been created, such that the salesperson and the customer cognitively elaborate on the same conversational topics to each other's advantage (see Grice's [1975] cooperative principle). Finally, people with low mentalizing skills have difficulties shaping or providing direction in conversations (Sujan, Weitz, & Kumar, 1994).

We generated a total of 33 items and administered them to 132 salespersons; on the basis of an exploratory factor analysis four factors comprised of 13 items were selected for the SToM scale. The reliabilities of the four subscales were .69, .76, .66, and .79, respectively, and address rapport building, detecting nonverbal cues, taking a bird's-eye view, and shaping the interaction (see Table 11.1).

Next, we applied a confirmatory factor analysis (CFA) to the data to establish the convergent and discriminant validity of items for the four subscales. We combined items according to the partial disaggregation model to yield two indicators per factor (Bagozzi & Heatherton, 1994; Bagozzi & Edwards, 1998). Using criteria from the structural equation modeling literature (e.g., Hu and Bentler, 1999), we found that this model fit very well: $\chi^2(14) = 17.51$, $p = .23$, root mean square error of approximation (RMSEA) = .05, non-normed fit index (NNFI) = .99, comparative fit index CFI = .99, and standardized root mean square residual (SRMR) = .04. As factor loadings were relatively high (.54–.97), and given the good model fit, convergent validity was established. Discriminant validity was also achieved (correlations among factors were .43–.71, all significantly less than 1.00).

We examined criterion-related validity with a seven-factor CFA where the four SToM factors and three ToM factors corresponding to the first three SToM factors were modeled (the fourth SToM

Table 11.1   The SToM Scale

Factor 1: Rapport building

---

1. When I am with a customer (e.g., in the elevator before a sales meeting) I can easily kindle a small conversation

2. I find it difficult to talk to a customer about topics that are not business-related. (R)

3. When at a business meeting or a reception, I can easily start off a conversation on a general topic such as the weather.

Factor 2: Detecting nonverbal cues

---

4. I find it difficult to discern the nonverbal cues of customers during a conversation. (R)

5. At times I realize that I do not pick up the hints in sales conversations; after the meeting colleagues explain to me what happened during the conversations. Only then do I realize what happened during the conversation. (R)

6. During a sales conversation, if customers hint of something, I do take that into consideration as we are speaking together.

Factor 3: Supplying missing information

---

7. When I realize that someone does not possess the right amount of knowledge in or during a sales conversation, I can easily add some information to bring focus to the conversation, thus making it easier for people to understand what I want to say.

8. When I realize that people do not understand what I'm saying, I put what I want to say in a broader perspective in order to explain what I mean.

9. I always try to understand the industry context in which a customer operates; and by using examples from that context, I add any missing information.

10. Sometimes I summarize for customers what has been said up to that point in the meeting, this make for a smoother conversation!

Factor 4: shaping the interaction

---

11. I make sure that I positively influence the atmosphere in a sales conversation.

12. I can easily act in ways that gives a sales conversation a positive twist.

13. I can easily make people feel more comfortable during a sales conversation.

R = reverse coded.

factor was expected to correlate with the three ToM factors). This model fit very well: $\chi^2(56) = 60.91$, $p = .30$, RMSEA $= .02$, NNFI $= .99$, CFI $= 1.00$, and SRMR $= .05$. As hypothesized, ToM$_1$ and SToM$_1$ were highly correlated (.90), ToM$_2$ and SToM$_2$ were highly correlated (.90), and ToM$_3$ and SToM$_3$ were moderately highly correlated (.45). Positive correlations between SToM$_4$ and ToM$_1$ – ToM$_3$ also occurred (.39, .63, and .18).

Finally, we investigated discriminant validity of the measures of the SToM subscales with measures of a social anxiety scale (Watson & Friend, 1969), a perspective taking scale (Davis, 1994), and the adaptive selling scale (Spiro & Weitz, 1990). The CFA model fit very well: $\chi^2(76) = 95.26$, $p = .07$, RMSEA $= .04$, NNFI $= .98$, CFI $= .99$, and SRMR $= .05$. The four dimensions of SToM correlate negatively with social anxiety ($-.22 - -.53$), and positively with

perspective taking (.27–.40) and adaptiveness (.46–.61), as hypothesized. Yet, also as hypothesized, the four SToM subscales were correlated with the other factors significantly less than 1.00, showing discriminant validity.

On a new sample of 126 salespersons, we examined construct and predictive validity. The same measures were administered as in the analyses described above, plus items from Behrman and Perrault's (1982) performance scale.

Based on high factor loadings (.70–.89) and a very good fitting model ($\chi^2(14) = 17.66$, $p = .22$, RMSEA $= .04$, NNFI $= .99$, CFI $= .99$, and SRMR $= .02$), convergent validity of the measures of SToM was again established. Likewise the correlations among the factors (.33–.77) demonstrated discriminant validity between measures of the different SToM subscales.

We also investigated criterion-related validity of the measures of the SToM scale. The overall model fit well: $\chi^2(56) = 99.54$, $p = .00$, RMSEA = .066, NNFI = .96, CFI = .98, and SRMR = .05. As hypothesized, ToM_1 and $SToM_1$ were highly correlated (.97), ToM_2 and $SToM_2$ were highly correlated (.87), and ToM_3 and $SToM_3$ were moderately highly correlated (.48). Positive correlations between $SToM_4$ and ToM_1 – ToM_3 also occurred, as predicted (.61, .61, and .42).

We assessed discriminant validity of measures of the dimensions of SToM against measures of three constructs. The overall model fit very well: $\chi^2(56) = 75.18$, $p = .05$, RMSEA = .04, NNFI = .98, CFI = .99, and SRMR = .04. The four dimensions of SToM correlated negatively with social anxiety (−.23−−.38) and positively with perspective taking (.28−.33) and adaptiveness (.46−.78), as forecasted. Yet the correlations were significantly less than 1.00 in all cases, demonstrating discriminant validity.

We also ascertained the predictive validity of performance. Performance correlated .31, .56, .31, and .48 with the four respective dimensions of SToM and −.35, .25, and .49 with anxiety, perspective taking, and adaptiveness, respectively. The performance measures were further validated by testing the mean differences of scores on the measures on a new sample of salespeople (N = 102) wherein 57 top performers were compared to bottom performers (as identified by managers). Means of high performers (M_h = 7.70) were significantly (t = 4.19) higher than the means of low performers (M_l = 6.95).

The above investigations used only a single method to scrutinize construct validity. We performed a true construct validity assessment in Study 3 by use of CFA applied to a third data item gathered by two methods (a "Does not describe me/ describes me completely" scale and a "Disagree/ Agree" scale). This allowed us to ascertain and rule out common method biases (Bagozzi, 2011). A total of 132 salespeople filled out both scales in this multitrait-multimethod study. The model fit well (where the two methods were collapsed into one method factor based on a correlation of .96, s.e. = .04, between the two): $\chi^2(82) = 169.55$, $p = .00$, RMSEA = .08, NNFI = .97, CFI = .98, and SRMR = .04. Trait variance ranged from .46 to .85 (average = .66), and of the 16 measures, only one ($StoM_{3a}$) yielded less than 50% trait variance, and even then only slightly below the .50 standard. Random error variance ranged from .00 to .49 (average = .25), which is desirably low. Method variance

ranged from .00 to .44 (average = .09), which is also desirably low; indeed, only one of 16 method factor loadings was significant.

We also examined nomological validity of the SToM scale, where the four subfactors predicted adaptiveness, perspective taking, social anxiety, and performance. The major findings were that rapport building ($SToM_1$) influenced performance but only through social anxiety. That is, the stronger the skill in building rapport, the less the felt social anxiety, and the less social anxiety, the greater the performance. The other three SToM subfactors loaded on a second-order factor, and this factor directly influenced performance. Neither adaptiveness nor perspective taking influenced performance, while taking into account SToM. The second-order SToM factor significantly influenced adaptiveness and perspective taking.

The interpretation of the nomological validity model is as follows. The rapport building dimension of SToM captures a quality of the relationship between salesperson and customer such that enhanced rapport reduces social anxiety and, through this reduction, increases performance. The other three dimensions of SToM (detecting nonverbal cues, taking a bird's-eye view, and shaping the interaction) reflect particular practices or things salespeople do to influence the sales outcome. Their influence on performance is thus direct and not mediated by adaptiveness, perspective taking, or social anxiety.

Summary of SToM Validity Analyses

The above analyses show that the measures of the four dimensions of SToM achieve convergent and discriminant validity within and across the dimensions of the scale, respectively. The findings also demonstrate that the four dimensions achieve criterion-related, predictive, discriminant, and nomological validity with such conceptually related variables as adaptive resource utilization, perspective taking, and performance, according to theory (for details on the theoretical arguments, see Dietvorst et al., 2009).

As adaptive resource utilization is a leading scale (Spiro & Weitz, 1990) and on the surface at least seems similar in meaning to ToM processes, it is useful to consider differences between the concepts. Spiro and Weitz (1990) consider the adaptive resource utilization concept and scale as unidimensional. That is, the concept and measures are claimed to capture a general or overall tendency to practice adaptive selling. The processes are presumed to be deliberative. But SToM and its measures refer to largely automatic processes in which salespeople "read the minds" of customers, so to speak, and, in turn, co-create the nature and course of the interaction with customers. Adaptive resource utilization is a conscious process in which salespeople identify customers and selling situations so as to respond according to coarse-grained a priori learned categories. Thus, adaptive selling is more of a one-way pattern of communication, albeit informed by learning in an adaptive sense in the long run. Furthermore, the measures of adaptive resource utilization do not identify the specific reasons for or mechanisms behind their effects, whereas the SToM scale measures things that might be considered the bases for general adaptiveness and thus constitute managerial policy variables for which salespeople can be selected, trained, and coached to improve adaptiveness (and as found in the study by Dietvorst et al. 2009, influence perspective taking, social anxiety coping, and performance). Hence, SToM might not only be considered more psychologically fundamental and managerially useful than measures of adaptive resource utilization, but it also might supersede measures of adaptive resource utilization in its effects on performance especially, as found by Dietvorst et al. (2009). The sub-study described hereafter explores the neuroscience foundation of the SToM scale.

We next asked the question, "Do different patterns of brain activity occur between high- and low-interpersonal mentalizing tasks?" Building on basic research in neuroscience, we hypothesized that salespersons scoring high (vs. low) in interpersonal mentalizing (i.e., high vs. low on the SToM scale) would experience greater activation of the MPFC, TPJ, TP, and precuneus regions of the brain (e.g., Amodio & Frith, 2006; Castelli et al., 2002). For more information, diagrams, and related information on neuroscience, see Bear, Connors, and Paradiso (2007). See also Dietvorst et al. (2009) and http://www.marketingpower.com/jmroct09.

From a sample of 132 salespeople who filled out the SToM scale, we selected the top ten and bottom ten right-handed male scorers for participation in the experimental tasks. The fMRI protocol consisted of three experimental conditions: interpersonal mentalizing, process, and unlinked sentences. Participants listened to five stories of each type presented in one of two different counterbalanced orders. Interpersonal mentalizing is the critical condition in which the cognitive task involves the use of ToM in order to understand why and how the characters in the story interact. The process condition serves as a closely matching control condition, in which the cognitive task involves nearly the same cognitive processes as in the interpersonal mentalizing condition, with the exception that the stories do not explicitly require the use of ToM in order to understand why and how the characters operate or interact. Finally, in the unlinked sentences condition, participants listened to a series of sentences that did not form a coherent story. The unlinked sentences condition serves as a baseline control condition, in which the cognitive task involves the use of language and memory. Under each experimental condition, every story was followed by a question that the respondent was asked to answer silently to himself. The number of words and types of words in the stories were distributed as evenly as possible over the different conditions. The stimuli were presented in the participant's mother tongue; an English translation is presented in http://marketingpower.com/jmroct09. Durations of the stories, including the questions, were between 33 and 36 seconds long, and were on average equivalent in terms of time length across the three experimental conditions. Each participant was then given about 6 seconds to think about an answer for each question following the presentation of a story.

Imaging was conducted by a General Electric fMRI scanner (see Dietvorst et al., 2009). The following website provides a brief primer on fMRI methodology and technical details on the experiment: http:\\marketingpower.com/jmroct09.

The results showed the following. First, with regard to the activation of specific anatomical areas, a region of interest (ROI) approach was used. We tested hypotheses conservatively with a random-effects group analysis at coordinates defined by previous studies and then in an exploratory way by searching for groups of voxels in which the activity across participants correlates with the individual SToM measures. Small volume corrections were applied to the four a priori ROI, according to common practice (Worsley et al., 1996). For definitions of predefined areas of focus, see Dietvorst et al. (2009, p. 663). The findings revealed that two areas of the right MPFC, the left MPFC, the right TPJ, and the precuneus were activated greater for high (vs. low) interpersonal mentalizers, when the process task was used as a control. Similarly, when the unlinked sentences condition was used as a control, greater activation for high (vs. low) interpersonal mentalizers was found for the left MPFC and the right TPJ. Thus, support of hypotheses was found for three of four brain areas. For the TP regions, differential brain activation was not found for high (vs. low) interpersonal mentalizers. Indeed, both groups experienced equal activation. See Dietvorst et al. (2009) for specific results of all activations.

For the correlational analysis, the mean percentage signal changes associated with interpersonal mentalizing compared with the process condition and compared with the unlinked-sentences condition were extracted, and then their correlations with participants' SToM scores were examined. The sizes of the ROIs are larger for the correlational analysis and were created with SFU Pickatlas software toolbox by selecting the left and right temporal lobes and the MPFC. As further tests of our hypotheses, a correlational analysis was performed between the individual SToM scores and the activity during the interpersonal mentalizing versus process task, and the interpersonal mentalizing versus unlinked sentences task. Results revealed three areas in which the activity showed significant positive correlations with SToM scores for the interpersonal mentalizing versus process task (where the numbers in brackets give the x, y, z conventual coordinate locations): right MPFC ([8 58 20], $r = .69$, $p < .005$), right TPJ ([54 −68 −2], $r = .69$, $p < .005$), and left TPJ ([−66 −28 −4], $r = .61$, $p < .005$). Two clusters in the left and right TP showed a similar but nonsignificant trend in terms of correlations with SToM scores for the interpersonal mentalizing versus process task; left TP ([−38, 10, −30], $r = .52$, $p < .05$), right TP ([48, 2, −8], $r = .45$, $p < .05$). Significant positive correlations were also found with SToM scores for the interpersonal mentalizing versus unlinked sentences task in the following regions: left TPJ ([−64 −28 −4], $r = .67$, $p < .005$), left TPJ/STS ([−60 −12 4], $r = .63$, $p < .005$), and right TPJ ([64 −42 6], $r = .60$, $p < .01$). Two small clusters in the MPFC showed a similar trend in terms of correlations with SToM scores for the interpersonal mentalizing versus unlinked sentences task, but the cluster sizes were smaller than ten voxels. Furthermore, for both contrasts, interpersonal mentalizing versus process, and interpersonal mentalizing versus unlinked sentences, none of the regions showed a negative correlation with SToM measures. In sum, we generally find support for our hypotheses: that is, when the neural responses in the interpersonal mentalizing condition were compared with those in the process and unlinked sentences conditions, the MPFC and right TPJ regions were differentially activated in the high as opposed to the low interpersonal mentalizing

group. In addition to the MPFC and right TPJ, a correlational analysis revealed that the left TPJ was also significantly correlated with SToM measures. This effect was, however, weaker in the TP region for the contrast of interpersonal mentalizing versus process, and the TP was equally activated in high and low mentalizers for the contrast of interpersonal mentalizing versus unlinked sentences.

Finally, the tests for the contrasts between interpersonal mentalizing versus process and interpersonal mentalizing versus unlinked sentences conditions yielded somewhat different results. This was mainly due to the noisy nature of the experiment, and because of the different cognitive tasks involved in the process task and unlinked sentences task.

Thus, across the four substudies investigating ToM, interpersonal mentalizing for high (vs. low) scorers on the SToM scale was consistent with research on ToM, which has been conducted largely in the context of the study of autism, in which autistic persons are compared to mentally retarded persons or, on occasion, to normal persons. Therefore, similar mental processes appear to be activated in the regions of the brain implicated in nonautistic versus autistic persons, when comparing high (vs. low) interpersonal mentalizing salespersons. Of course, most if not all participants in the Dietvorst study were not autistic; hence, the SToM scale seems to be very sensitive in detecting the four skills implicated in the scale. Moreover, the scale was found to predict performance, as well as social anxiety, adaptiveness, and perspective taking. As the adaptiveness and perspective taking scales failed to predict performance once the SToM dimensions were included as predictors, it seems that interpersonal mentalizing processes are more fundamental. Indeed, adaptiveness and perspective taking were dependent on interpersonal mentalizing, which also points to the importance of the latter.

Study 2: Theory of Mind and Emotional Bases of Customer Orientation

We studied the roles of ToM and empathy in customer orientation (Bagozzi, Verbeke, Dietvorst, & Shraa-Tam, 2011a). Customer orientation is guided by such questions as "How can I help a customer meet his or her needs by matching our product/service offerings to those needs?" and is contrasted to a sales orientation that focuses instead on such questions as "How can I convince the customer to buy our product?" The former involves mutual problem solving and is primarily two-sided, with the goal of building long-term relationships; the latter involves primarily persuasion, is mainly one-sided, and frequently leads to or is found in short-run relationships.

The main hypotheses are that salespeople scoring high (vs. low) on customer orientation should exhibit brain activation suggesting greater activation of ToM processes, perspective taking, and empathetic concern. Second, we hypothesized that customer orientation will lead to greater alliance building with customers in three senses: seeking to uncover competencies and practices in the buying center, learning from customers, and acquiring contextual knowledge about the industry and environment.

An initial set of hypotheses concerns the role of mirror neurons in salesperson interactions. Mirror neurons are particular kinds of brain neurons that function in imitative or mimicry ways. Empathetic concern, emotional sharing during the experience of empathy, occurs automatically (subject to limited inhibition under some conditions) in the mirror neuron system (MNS). The MNS is located in the premotor and parietal areas of the brain, more specifically in the posterior part of the inferior frontal cortex and the anterior part of the inferior parietal lobule (Iacoboni & Dapretto, 2006). Mirror neurons play important roles in understanding and reacting to (mimicking) the emotions of others, as well as their intentions. People with dysfunctional MNSs are unable to attune well to others in interactions (e.g., Oberman & Ramachandran, 2007).

The way mirror neurons function may be described as follows (Gallese, 2003). When we observe or hear another person performing an action, premotor sectors of the brain become active that are identical to those that would become activated had we performed the action ourself. These premotor activations are in addition to visual system activations and show that motor circuits in common to observer and observed are simultaneously shared, so to speak. Such processes are characteristic of nonconscious mimicry of facial expressions, posture, gestures, and mannerisms observed in self and others when we interact with them. At the same time, in addition to action recognition, mirror neurons code and interpret the intentions of others under observation (hence people come to remember a common representation or ideomotor program; Iacoboni, 2009); this occurs in the posterior part of the inferior frontal gyrus and the adjacent sector of the ventral

premotor cortex (Iacoboni et al., 2005). The actual emotional reactions happen in the limbic system, which is linked to the mirror neuron system through the pars opercularis (Iacoboni & Dapretto, 2006) and insula (Carr et al., 2003; Lamm, Batson, & Decety, 2007) regions of the brain. Within the limbic system, the amygdala plays a key role in emotional responding (Lamm et al., 2007).

Empathy arises from the apprehension or comprehension of another person's emotional state (e.g., Eisenberg, 2000). From a psychological perspective, empathy consists of three components: (a) an emotional reaction that might include a sharing of the other's feelings, (b) a cognitive capacity to take the perspective of the other, and (c) a monitoring mechanism that registers the source of the experienced affect in a way differentiating self from other (Lamm, Batson, & Decety, 2007, p. 42). These psychological components of empathy can be linked to neural mechanisms as follows:

a. The emotional response associated with empathy can be one of two kinds. Empathic concern consists of focus on the plight of another person and feeling compassion-like or sympathetic-like emotions. Personal distress consists of a projection of the self into an adverse situation and feeling fear-like emotions. The insula, anterior medial cingulated cortex (aMCC), and the amygdala are three key brain regions that are activated in emotional aspects of empathy (Decety & Lamm, 2006, p. 1152).

b. Decety and Lamm (2006, p. 1151) point out that taking the perspective of another person "allows us to overcome our usual egocentrism, tailor our behaviors to others' expectations, and thus make satisfying interpersonal relations possible" (see also Davis, 1994). When people take the perspective of others, similar neural circuits are activated in the self, as in the other person undergoing an experience or action under observation. The common neural processes will be discussed in the next paragraph. For now, it is sufficient to point out that perspective taking entails top-down information processing (also termed *executive functioning*) that regulates cognition and emotion through such processes as selective attention and self-regulation. The executive functions occur in such parts of the prefrontal cortex as the medial region and in the inferior parietal lobule (e.g., Decety & Lamm, 2006, p. 1151; Decety & Jackson, 2004). In addition, the precuneus region has been implicated in perspective taking (e.g., Cavanna & Trimble, 2006; Ruby & Decety, 2004; Vogeley et al., 2001, 2004).

c. A third aspect of empathy, the monitoring mechanism, which registers the source of experienced affect in terms of self–other, is important for differentiating empathic concern from emotional distress. Whereas the former is part of the meaning of empathy, the latter is a personal reaction not constitutive of empathy. In other words, empathy is an other-oriented emotional reaction, but personal distress is a self-oriented emotional reaction. As Decety and Lamm (2006, p. 1154) note:

> [I]n the experience of empathy, individuals must be able to disentangle their own feelings from the feelings shared with others to attribute mental states to the target. Self-awareness is a necessary condition for making inference about the mental states in others . . . Therefore, "agency" is a crucial aspect for successfully navigating shared representations between self and other . . . the ability to recognize oneself as the agent of a behavior is the way one builds as an entity independent from the external world . . . affective sharing must be modulated and monitored by the sense of whose feelings belong to whom . . ., and thus, agency is a crucial aspect that enables a selfless regard for the other rather than a selfish desire. . . .

The balance between self and other perceptions and the experience of agency have been observed in the inferior parietal lobule (e.g., Decety & Lamm, 2007).

With this as background, we propose the following hypotheses constitute important aspects of mirror neuron coordination:

As the MNS functions in an automatic, bottom-up manner to produce emotional sharing and the interpretation of the intentions of others with whom one interacts, it was hypothesized:

- *Hypothesis 1* (the mirror neuron system): Salespersons scoring high versus low in customer orientation will display greater coordinated activation of the posterior inferior frontal cortex, Broca's area, and the anterior inferior parietal lobule.

For empathic concern, a bottom-up emotional response, a number of regions of the brain have been implicated (e.g., Carr et al., 2003; Decety & Lamm, 2006). Hence we hypothesize:

- *Hypothesis 2* (empathetic concern): Salespeople scoring high versus low in customer orientation will display greater

coordinated activation of the insula and amygdala regions of the brain.

For taking the perspective of another person, which is largely a top-down executive function, we draw upon the following studies from the basic neuroscience literature to identify the appropriate regions of the brain: Decety and Lamm (2006), Cavanna and Trimble (2006), and Vogeley et al. (2004). Thus we propose:

- *Hypothesis 3* (perspective taking): Salespeople scoring high versus low in customer orientation will display greater coordinated activation of the MPFC, the precuneus, and the right inferior parietal cortex regions of the brain.

For the self–other monitoring mechanism, which regulates the proper other-oriented emotional reaction constitutive of empathy, a number of brain regions have been identified (e.g., Decety & Lamm, 2007). As a consequence, we forecast:

- *Hypothesis 4* (self–other monitoring): Salespersons scoring high versus low in customer orientation will display greater coordinated activation of the inferior parietal lobule.

A second set of hypotheses deals with ToM processes in customer orientation. According to the simulation account of human understanding, ToM is conceived to be an outgrowth of the ability to interpret others' actions through mental simulation (Oberman & Ramachandran, 2007, p. 316). The brain processes involved are automatic and reflexive, even prereflexive (e.g., Gallese, 2003). Research implicates the MPFC, the TP, and the TPJ as underpinning ToM. Although Dietvorst et al. (2009) studied ToM processes in salespeople, they did not explicitly address other-oriented processes that are definitive and constitutive of customer orientation skills. They also did not study empathetic processes, as was done in this study.

We expect that customer orientation will be associated with greater interpersonal mentalizing skills as reflected in the ability to infer another person's thoughts, feelings, and intentions (e.g., Dietvorst et al., 2009; Frith & Frith, 2003; Singer & Feln, 2005). Therefore, we hypothesize:

- *Hypothesis 5* (theory of mind processing): Salespeople scoring high versus low in customer orientation will display greater coordinated activation of the MPFC, TP, precuneus, and TPJ regions of the brain.

Based on previous research and a factor analysis of the sales orientation–customer orientation scale (Saxe & Weitz, 1982), we used a five-item customer orientation scale to represent degree of customer orientation, and a five-item sales orientation scale to represent degree of sales orientation. The experimental stimuli consisted of full-face, full-color video clips of five males and five females displaying various emotional states (anger, disgust, happiness, surprise, and neutrality). The control stimuli were clips of moving geometrical shapes. Thus, the four experimental conditions included: (1) positive emotional faces: happy and surprised, (2) negative emotional faces: angry and disgusted, (3) neutral faces, and (4) moving geometrical shapes. Each clip was played for 3 seconds in 12-second blocks of three clips plus interstimulus intervals of 1 second. Each block consisted of either only positive, negative, or neutral emotions or moving geometrical shapes. We employed counterbalanced versions of the stimuli. The blocks allowed us to test two hypotheses while controlling for baseline effects: (a) positive and negative faces minus moving geometrical shapes, and (b) positive and negative faces minus neutral faces. This design is similar to that employed frequently in the neuroscience literature (e.g., Wicker et al., 2003). We used fMRI acquisition and functional image analysis similar to that done in Study 4 of Dietvorst et al. (2009) to test hypotheses.

The findings for MNS hypotheses show that scores on customer orientation correlate with the right supplemental motor area (.55), right precentral gyrus (.72), right postcentral gyrus (.67), and right pars opercularis/pars triangularis (Broca's area, .72). Further, positive correlations were found between the customer orientation scale and the left amygdala (.49) and left insula (.50).

The results for the tests of ToM reveal that scores on customer orientation correlate with the left superior TP (.58), right TP (.57), left middle TP (.54), left superior temporal gyrus (STG, .49), left middle temporal gyrus (MTG, .75), left inferior temporal gyrus (.66), right STG (.62), and right middle frontal gyrus (.56). Also scores on customer orientation correlate with the right inferior parietal lobule (.54) and the right superior parietal lobule (.68).

The precuneus, which relates to both ToM and perspective taking, was found to be correlated with the customer orientation scale. Specifically, the customer orientation scale correlated with the right precuneus (.57) and left precuneus (.57).

In sum, a number of conclusions can be made from the research reported in Bagozzi, Verbeke, Dietvorst, and Schraa-Tam, (2011a). The first and perhaps most important skill found, associated with high versus low scores on customer orientation, was empathetic concern, which emerges from embodied simulation processes in the MNS: the fundamental interpersonal mental driver that occurs as bottom-up, automatic, prereflexive emotional responses in the brain. This embodied aspect of empathy entails a sharing of emotional concern and experiences with another person with whom one interacts. It functions to build a shared identity, to facilitate the ascription of intentions to others, to forge emotional bonds, and in general to foster intersubjective understanding and communication. Other evidence for empathetic concern can be seen in nonconscious imitation or mimicry of gestures, facial expressions, mannerisms, and posture. The brain regions found, associated with high versus low customer orientation scores, included the right temporoparietal junction, the supplemental motor area, the precentral and postcentral gyrus, and Broca's region. The experience of empathy as manifest in the MNS is linked to emotions through the insula.

Emotional responses in the limbic system, particularly the amygdala, are a second outcome evident in salespersons scoring high versus low in customer orientation. Such heightened emotionality goes hand in hand with relationship building and effective communication, and tends to cement the social identity of persons who interact and share empathetic moments together.

Third, largely top-down cognitive processes in the form of perspective taking and self–other differentiation also constitute important brain activities defining empathy and the grasping of an interaction partner's intentions. Brain activation in the precuneus and temporoparietal junction were found to be associated, too, with salespersons scoring high versus low in customer orientation. Such activity functions to regulate the experience and consequences of empathy and accompanying emotions. Too little empathy and emotional concern risks preventing the establishment of a shared identity and rapport; too much empathy and personal distress risks disrupting relationships and interfering with communication.

Fourth, evidence was found for ToM processing in customer orientation. Theory of mind refers to the ability to infer the beliefs, feelings, and intentions of other persons with whom one interacts or with persons one observes in an interaction. Such skills seem essential to promoting fruitful communication and effective interactions. Salespersons scoring high versus low on customer orientation had significantly greater activation of brain regions identified recently with interpersonal mentalizing: namely, the temporal pole and temporoparietal regions (Dietvorst et al., 2009, found evidence for the latter, not the former). Although no evidence was found for changes in activation in the mPFC, salespersons scoring high versus low on customer orientation had greater activation of the middle frontal gyrus, which is adjacent to the mPFV (cf., Dietvorst et al., 2009). Theory of mind processes are top-down, yet largely automatic, cognitive or executive processes.

In a field investigation, we next scrutinized whether interpersonal and interorganizational knowledge coupling is initiated through three actions taken by salespeople: discerning capabilities and practices in the buying center, acquiring knowledge from customers about their needs, and forming contextual knowledge about the industry and competition in which customer–salesperson interactions occur. We administered the customer and sales orientations subscales and three alliance building scales to 132 salespersons in a field study. See Bagozzi, Verbeke, Dietvorst, and Schraa-Tam, (2011a) for details on the hypotheses, their rationale, and measures. The findings showed that customer orientation correlated .56, .66, and .44, respectively, with discernment of capabilities and practices in the buying center, acquiring knowledge from customers, and forming contextual knowledge. By contrast, the respective correlations between scores on the sales orientation scale and the three dimensions were .25, .41, and .21. In sum, alliance building between salespeople and customers is enhanced when the mental structures and processes of seller attune to those of the buyer. That is, a customer as opposed to a seller orientation is more strongly related to alliance building between customers and salespersons. This corroborates our MNS and ToM findings described earlier.

Study 3: Theory of Mind and Empathy Underlying Machiavellianism in the Sales Force: Good or Bad?

Machiavellianism, the personality style that involves manipulation of other persons for personal gain, has not been studied much in the sales force. But given the suggestion that it or its close cousin, psychopathy, occurs frequently in the business world (Babiak & Hare, 2006), its role in personal selling deserves scrutiny. This is all the more timely in that it has been recently suggested that Machiavellians might be genuinely cooperative and trustworthy when doing so suits their interests (Wilson et al., 1996, 1998). Other researchers propose that Machiavellians in fact administer influence in both coercive and prosocial ways (Hawley, 2003). Still other researchers assert that Machiavellianism might be associated with perspective taking and empathetic concern (Nichols, 2001). An unstudied theme suggested in the anecdotal world is that Machiavellians perform better than non-Machiavellians. All the above mentioned studies were done in survey or experimental contexts or entailed speculations based on this research. In this third major part of the chapter, we examine aspects of these questions by use of fMRI techniques and also investigate correlates of Machiavellianism in field studies by survey methods to complement the fMRI findings (see Bagozzi, Verbeke, Dietvorst, Belschak, & Schraa-Tam, 2011b).

We hypothesized that Machiavellians actually perform worse than non-Machiavellians in ToM skills as measured by neuroscience markers. The rationale is that Machiavellians appear to enter social interactions with rigid mindsets, in which they mistrust others and experience action tendencies and predispositions to respond automatically with manipulative intentions (e.g., Wilson et al., 1998). Compared to non-Machiavellians, they fail to engage interaction partners in open, egalitarian, and cooperative ways but rather are selfish, short-run oriented, socially anxious, and lacking in the ability to build rapport and deeper social relations based on mutuality and give and take (e.g., Repacholi et al., 2003). If Machiavellians indeed exhibit weaker ToM skills than non-Machiavellians, then they should experience less activation of the MPFC, TP, TPJ, and precuneus regions in appropriate experimental conditions.

To study Machiavellianism and ToM processes, we used the same methods as described in Dietvorst et al. (2009) and Bagozzi, Verbeke, Dietvorst, and Schraa-Tam, (2011a), in which participants heard five ToM, five process, and five unlined sentence scenarios. We examined 43 salespeople and used Machiavellianism scores on the scale developed by Christie and Geis (1970) as covariates.

The findings showed that low scores on Machiavellianism were associated with greater activation of the right MPFC (−.41), right TPJ (−.49), left TPJ (−.33), and right precuneus (−.32), with the unlinked sentences condition as the control. With the process condition as the control, Machiavellianism was again negatively associated with the right MPFC (–.40) and the left precuneus (–.37). In sum, Machiavellians show less activation of brain areas associated with ToM than non-Machiavellians. See Bagozzi, Verbeke, Dietvorst, Belschak, and Schraa-Tam, (2011b).

Next we hypothesized that Machiavellians will score higher on emotional aspects of empathy than non-Machiavellians. Imitative aspects of empathy occur automatically in bottom-up ways (e.g., Decety & Lamm, 2006). Based on research on empathy (e.g., Decety & Lamm, 2006; Lamm, Batson, & Decety, 2007) and mirror neurons (e.g., Carr et al., 2003; Gallese, 2003; Iacoboni & Dapretto, 2006), we hypothesized that Machiavellians (versus non-Machiavellians) will show greater activation of the pars opercularis and insula regions. These brain regions reflect the automatic responses of mirror neurons to the facial and related gestural reactions of interaction partners. On the other hand, we expect no difference in activation of the amygdala based on correlation research showing that Machiavellians take a manipulative stance vis-à-vis others and tend not to be affected much by the suffering of others or moral imperatives to help others (e.g., Christie & Geis, 1970; Rushton et al., 1981; Wilson et al. 1996). We speculate that it is the greater ability of Machiavellians versus non-Machiavellians to resonate or attune emotionally to others, without feeling empathetic concern, that accounts for their ability to often outperform non-Machiavellians.

We used the same methodology with the presentation of positive emotional, negative emotional, and neutral faces, plus geometric figures, as described above in the second major part of the chapter (see Bagozzi, Verbeke, Dietvorst, Belschak, & Schraa-Tam, 2011a). The findings support these conjectures. Machiavellianism is positively associated with greater activation of right insula (.64), left insula (.56), right pars opercularis (.48), and left pars opercularis (.51) for the negative emotional condition versus rotating geometrical shapes control. Likewise for the positive emotional expressions versus rotating geometric shapes conditions, greater activation for Machiavellians was shown for the left insula (.40) and the right insula (.36). Again less activity occurred in the precuneus region (–.52), which is associated with perspective taking.

The picture emerging from the two investigations just described is that Machiavellians are less facile than non-Machiavellians in top-down, executive processes associated with both ToM and empathy (perspective taking) but more skilled in bottom-up, automatic processes associated with emotional attunement with others (the emotional concern component of empathy). This suggests that the classic psychological dimensions of empathy (perspective taking and emotional concern) might be dissociated in Machiavellians (cf., Eisenberg, 2000).

We then conducted three field studies. In the first, we surveyed 171 salespeople. The findings showed that, although Machiavellianism is not related to general intelligence, it is associated with less social intelligence (–.36) and less emotional intelligence (–.36).

In the second field study, we surveyed 101 salespeople. The results showed that Machiavellianism is negatively associated with perspective taking (–.29), customer orientation (–.32), adaptive selling (–.26), social networking (–.23), and empathy (–.25). Machiavellianism was positively correlated with social anxiety (.22) and sales orientation (.48),

For the final field study, we addressed the question: What conditions might facilitate or hamper the actions of Machiavellian salespersons in the organization? We hypothesized and found that Machiavellians thrive in situations in which explorative, opportunistic, and manipulative tactics can be employed in unhindered ways: namely, when managerial control is weak, but not when managerial control is strong. We used multiple regression to test the effects of the interaction between Machiavellianism and degree of managerial control on performance and organizational citizenship behaviors. The findings in a study of 198 salespersons showed that performance is highest when managerial control is strong and Machiavellianism low; all other combinations of control and Machiavellianism resulted in lower performance. By contrast, we found that when managerial control is low, Machiavellians perform the least amount of organizationally directed altruistic actions toward the firm (e.g., attending organizational functions that are not required but help the company image); for all other combinations of managerial control and Machiavellianism, high levels of organizationally directed altruistic actions toward the firm were taken. Last, we found that individually directed altruistic actions directed to colleagues (e.g., touching bases with colleagues before initiating actions that might affect them; helping orient new colleagues) are inhibited for those scoring low in Machiavellianism and working in an environment with low managerial control. However, compared to the performance of organizationally directed altruistic action, all salespersons performed fewer individually directed altruistic actions on average. This is probably because the latter are less visible and require intrinsic motivation, whereas the former are likely observed by management and are driven by external or extrinsic rewards.

Future Directions

Neuroscience as applied to organizational research is very new, but many opportunities exist for future research. Some questions that might be addressed in this regard include:

- Does a customer orientation relate to networks within one's organization and social capital, and if so, what neural correlates are implicated?
- How do genetic and hormonal variables relate to neural correlates of theory of mind, empathy, and Machiavellianism?
- What is the relationship between interorganizational and intraorganizational skills and processes, and how can neuroscience principles inform our understanding thereof?
- What are the neuro correlates of organizational citizenship behaviors, and how do they relate to ToM, empathy, and Machiavellianism?
- Are there neural correlates of psychological safety and knowledge sharing in organizations that provide new insights into what they are and how they function?
- Does empathy relate to organizational hostility and kindness in terms of the distinct aspects of empathy and its unique neural correlates?

Conclusion

Our use of neuroscience in the three studies summarized in this chapter was a specific one. We studied functional specialization of regions of the brain by use of fMRI procedures and also investigated what was learned in this regard by coupling each study with field surveys. In all cases, we studied mental processes in real sales managers.

Our neuroscience experiments were conducted to validate the engagement of regions of the brain suggested by basic research with autistic subjects and with activation of mirror neurons in normal subjects. The basic research upon which we drew had purposes different from our studies in that it studied developmental disorders or controlled investigations of empathetic responses to emotional invoking stimuli in normal subjects for samples not specific to people in organizations.

In our ToM investigations, we aimed to verify abilities that sales managers have in inferring the thoughts, feelings, and intentions of other people and how these relate to four specific interpersonal skills: building rapport, detecting nonverbal cues, taking a bird's-eye view and ironic perspective, and shaping the course of interaction. The 13-item scale we developed was validated in multiple samples by traditional psychometric procedures, including reliability, construct validity (i.e., convergent and discriminant validity), criterion-related validity, and predictive and nomological validity. We went further than traditional methods and verified the functioning of regions of the brain associated with our SToM scale: namely, the MPFC, right and left TPJ, and precuneus regions. The TP regions, although activated for both those scoring high versus low on the SToM scale, did not differ.

Study 1 illustrates the use of fMRI procedures in the assessment of the validity of a psychological scale, which has rarely been done in research to date. Our scale might be used to select and train employees, as well as to provide input for coaching and evaluation of existing employees. Along with the SToM scale, we believe that management can develop the capabilities of employees to "read the minds" of people with whom they interact, so to speak. For example, by having employees observe good and bad interactions, role play, and receive thoughtful feedback concerning ToM processes, skills might be fostered in mind reading to a certain extent. The four areas of the SToM scale should receive specific emphasis in this regard as training and coaching targets.

Theory of mind skills were also observed in our Study 2, in which we investigated customer orientation of sales managers. The findings showed that the greater the customer orientation, the higher the activation of the left and right TPs, STG, MTG left and right precuneus, left middle, left inferior, and right superior TG, right middle frontal gyrus, and right inferior and right superior parietal lobules. Thus, the TP, TPJ, and precuneus regions, three important areas in ToM processing, were related to customer orientation. Activation of the MPFC cortex did not differentiate high from low customer-oriented sales people, however. Overall, customer-oriented sales managers appear to be particular facile in interpersonal mentalizing.

Study 3 also revealed the role of ToM processing in differentiating people scoring high versus low in Machiavellianism. Here, the MPFC, precuneus, and right and left TPJ regions were instrumental in this regard, but as in Study 1, the TP failed to show differences. In Study 3, people scoring high in Machiavellianism actually were less able in ToM processing than those scoring low. We interpret this as being a consequence, at least in part, of the world view of Machiavellians, which is cynical and distrustful of people, their higher felt social anxiety in interpersonal encounters, and their lack of concern for and commitment to people.

Studies 2 and 3 provide evidence for the role of MNS in interpersonal transactions. In Study 2, we discovered that the MNS is indeed important in assuming a customer orientation. Specifically, the right supplemental motor area, right precentral gyrus, right post central gyrus, Broca's area, left amygdala, and left insula were implicated. People high versus low in customer orientation showed greater coordination of the insula and amygdala with respect to empathetic concern. Customer orientation appears to be fostered by greater emotional attunement toward customers.

Study 3 examined the mental correlates of Machiavellianism and found that those sales managers scoring high in Machiavellianism resonate empathically with customers to a greater extent than those scoring low. The former showed greater activation of left and right insulae and the left and right pars opercularis. The suggestion is that Machiavellians versus non-Machiavellians have the ability to detect or share in the feelings of others with whom they interact. As this is an automatic, bottom-up process, such abilities are not likely to be subject to self-regulation, at least not to a great extent. Coupled with our findings that Machiavellians versus non-Machiavellians are actually less facile in ToM and perspective processes, which are more executive-like and top-down, we see that Machiavellians appear to exhibit a decoupling of the two main aspects of empathy that psychologists have traditionally characterized as defining qualities of empathy: namely, empathetic concern and perspective taking. We note in this regard that empathetic concern in Machiavellians seems to be limited to an automatic, nonconscious emotional response and not entailing conscious concern. Indeed, research in psychology not based on brain investigation suggests that Machiavellians are uncaring and indifferent to the suffering of others and moral concerns.

Neuroscience is a promising area for future research in management and organizations in general and in POS in particular. It would seem to be particularly useful in the study of the bases for interpersonal communication and joint welfare, and to provide insight into the social or self-conscious (e.g., pride, shame, guilt, embarrassment, envy, jealousy) and moral emotions (e.g., anger, disgust, contempt, awe, gratitude, and elevation), as well as ToM and empathy.

References

Allison, T., Puce, A., & McCarthy, G. (2000). Social perception from visual cues: Role of the STS region. *Trends in Cognitive Sciences, 4*(7), 251–291.

Amodio, D., & Frith, C.D. (2006). Meeting of minds: The medial frontal cortex and social cognition. *Nature Reviews, 7,* 268–277.

Babiak, P., & Hare, R.D. (2006). *Snakes in suits: When psychopaths go to work.* New York: Regan Books

Bagozzi, R.P. (2011). Measurement and meaning in information systems and organizational research: Methodological and philosophical foundations. *MIS Quarterly,* 35, 261–292.

Bagozzi, R.P., & Edwards, J.R. (1998). A general approach for representing constructs in organizational research. *Organizational Research Methods, 1,* 45–87.

Bagozzi, R.P., & Heatherton, T.F. (1994). A general approach for representing multifaceted personality constructs: Application to state self-esteem. *Structural Equation Modeling, 1,* 35–67.

Bagozzi, R.P., Verbeke, W.J.M.I., Dietvorst, R., & Schraa-Tam, C. (2011a). *Leveraging salespeople's ability to simulate emotions and enhance customer orientation: How mirror neurons function in sales encounters.* Unpublished working paper, University of Michigan, Ann Arbor, MI.

Bagozzi, R.P., Verbeke, W.J.M.I., Dietvorst, R., Belschak, F.D., & Schraa-Tam, C. (2011b). Looking into the minds of Machiavellian salespeople: Neural mechanisms underlying instrumental action. Unpublished working paper, University of Michigan, Ann Arbor, MI.

Bear, M.F., Connors, B.W., & Paradiso, M.A. (2007). *Exploring the brain.* Philadelphia: Lippincott, Williams, & Wilkins.

Behrman, D.N., & Perreault, W.D., Jr. (1982). Measuring the performance of industrial salespersons. *Journal of Business Research, 10*(September), 355–370.

Carr, L.M., Iacoboni, M.C., Dubeau, M.C., Mazziotta, J.C., & Lenzi, G.L. (2003). Neural mechanisms of empathy in humans: A relay from neural systems for imitation to limbic areas. *Proceedings of the National Academy of Science USA, 100,* 5497–5502.

Castelli, F., Frith, C.D., Happé, F., & Frith, U. (2002). Autism, Asperger Syndrome, and brain mechanisms for the attribution of mental states to animated shapes. *Brain, 125*(August), 1839–1849.

Cavanna, A.E., & Trimble, M.R. (2006). The precuneus: A review of its functional anatomy and behavioural correlates. *Brain, 129,* 564–583.

Christie, R., & Geis, F. (1970). *Studies in Machiavellianism.* New York: Academic Press.

Davis, M.H. (1994). *Empathy: A social psychological approach.* Dubuque, IA: Brown and Benchmark.

Decety, J., & Jackson, P.L. (2004). The functional architecture of human empathy. *Behavioral and Cognitive Neuroscience Reviews, 3*(2), 71–100.

Decety, J., & Lamm, C. (2006). Human empathy through the lens of social neuroscience. *The Scientific World Journal, 6,* 1146–1163.

Decety, J., & Lamm, C. (2007). The role of the right temporoparietal junction in social interaction: How low-level computational processes contribute to meta-cognition. *The Neuroscientist, 13,* 580–593.

Dietvorst, R.C., Verbeke, W.J.M.I., Bagozzi, R.P., Yoon, C., Smits, M., & van der Lugt, A. (2009). A salesforce-specific theory of mind scale: Tests of its validity by multitrait-multimethod matrix, confirmatory factor analysis, structural equation models, and functional magnetic resonance imaging. *Journal of Marketing Research, 46,* 653–668.

Eisenberg, N. (2000). Empathy and sympathy. In M. Lewis, & J.M. Haviland-Jones (Eds.), *Handbook of emotion* (2nd ed., 677–691). New York: Guilford.

Frith, U., & Frith, C.D. (2003). Development and neurophysiology of mentalizing. *Philosophical Transactions of the Royal Society, 358,* 59–473.

Gallese, V. (2003). The manifold nature of interpersonal relations: The quest of a common mechanism. *Philosophical Transactions of the Royal Society London Biological Sciences, 358,* 517–528.

Grice, H.P. (1975). Logic and conversation. In P. Cole & J. Morgan (Eds.), *Syntax and semantics* Vol. 3 (pp. 41–58). New York: Academic Press.

Hawley, P.H. (2003). Prosocial and coercive configurations of resource control in early adolescence: A case for the well-adapted Machiavellian. *Merrill-Palmer Quarterly, 49,* 279–309.

Hu, L.-T., & Bentler, P.M. (1999). Cutoff criteria for fit indexes in covariance structure analysis: Conventional criteria versus new alternatives. *Structural Equation Modeling, 6,* 1–55.

Iacoboni, M. (2009). Imitation, empathy, and mirror neurons. *Annual Review of Psychology, 60,* 653–670.

Iacoboni, M., & Dapretto, M. (2006). The mirror neuron system and the consequences of its dysfunction. *Nature Reviews Neuroscience, 7,* 942–951.

Iacoboni, M., Molnar-Szakacs, I., Gallese, V., Buccino, G., Maxxiotta, J.C., & Rizzolatti, G. (2005). Grasping the intentions of others with one's own mirror neuron system. *PLoS Biology, 3,* 0529–0535.

Lamm, C.C., Batson, C.D., & Decety, J. (2007). The neural substrate of human empathy: Effects of perspective-taking and cognitive appraisal. *Journal of Cognitive Neuroscience, 19,* 42–58.

Nichols, S. (2001). Mindreading and the cognitive architecture underlying altruistic motivation. *Mind and Language, 16,* 425–455.

Oberman, L.M., & Ramachandran, V.S. (2007). The stimulating social mind: The role of the mirror neuron system and simulation in the social and communicative deficits of autism spectrum disorders. *Psychological Bulletin, 133,* 310–327.

Rapacholi, B., Slaughter, V., Pritchard, M., & Gibbs, V. (2003). Theory of mind, Machiavellism, and social functioning in childhood. In B. Rapacholi, & V. Slaughter (Eds.), *Individual differences in theory of mind. Macquarie monographs in cognitive science* (pp. 99–120). New York: Psychology Press.

Ruby, P., & Decety, J. (2004). How would you feel versus how do you think she would feel? A neuroimagining study of perspective taking with social emotion. *Journal of Cognitive Neuroscience, 16,* 988–999.

Rushton, J.P., Chrisjohn, R.D., & Fekken, G.C. (1981). The altruistic personality and the self-report altruism scale. *Personality and Individual Differences, 2,* 293–302.

Saxe, R., & Kanwisher, N. (2003). People thinking about thinking people: The role of the temporo-parietal junction in "theory of mind". *NueroImage, 19,* 1835–1842.

Saxe, R., & Powell, L.J. (2006). It's the thought that counts: Specific brain regions for one component of theory of mind. *Psychological Science, 17*(8), 692–699.

Saxe, R., & Weitz, B.A. (1982). The SOCO scale: A measure of the customer orientation of salespeople. *Journal of Marketing Research, 19,* 343–351.

Saxe, R., Carey, S., & Kanwisher, N. (2004). Understanding other minds: Linking developmental psychology in functional neuroimaging. *Annual Review of Psychology, 55,* 87–124.

Singer, T., & Fehr, E. (2005). The neuroeconomics of mind reading and empathy. *Neuroscientific Foundations of Economic Decision-Making, 95*(2), 340–345.

Soldow, G.F., & Thomas, G.P. (1984). Relational communication: Form versus content in the sales interaction. *Journal of Marketing, 48*(October), 84–93.

Spiro, R., & Weitz, B. (1990). Adaptive selling: Conceptualization, measurement, and nomological validity. *Journal of Marketing Research, 27,* 61–69.

Sujan, H., Weitz, B.A., & Kumar, N. (1994). Learning orientation, working smart, and effective selling. *Journal of Marketing, 58*(July), 39–52.

Vogeley, K., Bussfeld, P., Newen, A., Herrmann, S., Happe, F., Falkai, P., et al. (2001). Mind reading: Neural mechanisms of theory of mind and self-perspective. *NeuroImage, 14,* 170–181.

Vogeley, K., May, M., Ritzl, A., Falkai, P., Zilles, K., & Fink, G.R. (2004). Neural correlates of first-person perspective as one constituent of human self-consciousness. *Journal of Cognitive Neuroscience, 16,* 817–827.

Watson, D., & Friend, R. (1969). Measurement of social-evaluative anxiety. *Journal of Consulting and Clinical Psychology, 3*(August), 448–457.

Wicker, B., Keysers, C., Plailly, J., Royet, J.-P., Gallese, V., & Rizzolatti, G. (2003). Both of us disgusted in my insula: The common neural basis of seeing and feeling disgust. *Neuron, 40*(October 30), 655–664.

Wilson, D.S., Near, D., & Miller, R.R. (1996). Machiavellianism: A synthesis of the evolutionary and psychological literatures. *Psychological Bulletin, 119,* 285–299.

Wilson, D.S., Near, D., & Miller, R.R. (1998). Individual differences in Machiavellianism as a mix of cooperative and exploitative strategies. *Evolution and Human Behavior, 19,* 203–212.

Worsley, K.J., Marrett, S., Neelin, P., Vandal, A.C., Friston, K.J., & Evans, A.C. (1996). A unified statistical approach for determining significant signals in images of cerebral activation. *Human Brain Mapping, 4*(1), 58–73.

Yoon, C., Gutchess, A.H., Feinberg, F., & Polk, T.A. (2006). A functional magnetic resonance imaging study of neural dissociations between brand and person judgments. *Journal of Consumer Research, 33,* 31–40.

PART 2

Positive Emotions

Human Energy in Organizations

Implications for POS from Six Interdisciplinary Streams

Gretchen M. Spreitzer, Chak Fu Lam, *and* Ryan W. Quinn

Abstract

Energy is often viewed as the basic fuel for individual action and cognition, yet what exactly is energy? How can it be defined? How should it be measured? And, most importantly, why should organizational scholars, especially positive organization scholarship (POS) scholars, care about it? This chapter reviews the burgeoning interdisciplinary literature on energy-related constructs. We identify six distinct streams of energy-related literature. We then highlight how human energy at work can contribute to our understanding of POS.

Keywords: Energy, fuel, resources, thriving, self-regulation

Today, more than ever before, people juggle multiple roles (Perlow, 1998), work long hours, and are tethered to work through technology. Fatigue has been a culprit in occupational and mechanical safety hazards and errors (Landrigan et al., 2004; Rogers, Hwang, Scott, Aiken, & Dinges, 2004), and poor performance (Barnes & Hollenbeck, 2009; Dawson & Reid, 1997). Often, workers feel depleted, with little energy for family or community activities (Putnam, 2000). Clearly, energy matters.

The notion of energy has been implicit in many theories of motivation and self-regulation as the force or effort that drives our behavior (Gardner & Cummings, 1988; Mitchell, 1982). Notions of human energy are captured in research on job engagement (Kahn, 1990; Loehr & Schwartz, 2003; Rothbard, 2001; Schlaufeli & Bakker, 2004; Shirom, 2003), subjective vitality (Ryan & Fredrick, 1997), flow (Csikszentmihalyi, 1990), zest (Peterson, Park, Hall, & Seligman, 2009), and thriving (Spreitzer, Sutcliffe, Dutton, Sonenshein, & Grant, 2005). In terms of energy between and among individuals, researchers have examined energy networks (Cross, Baker, & Parker, 2003) and energy-in-conversation

(Quinn & Dutton, 2005). Finally, researchers have started to explore energy at the organizational level, such as momentum (Jansen, 2004), in describing organizational change initiatives (Huy, 2002).

To date, energy research has been concentrated within disparate streams. Consequently, we lack consensus on a definition of energy. Without a clear definition, no conceptualization or measure of energy can be validated. Lacking synthesis, we have disparate views of how work impacts energy and of why energy matters. Thus, through our literature review, we hope to synthesize and extend our current understanding of human energy at work. The goal of this chapter is to provide a comprehensive review of the interdisciplinary literature, including sociology and psychology, as well as recent work by organizational scholars. We focus exclusively on human energy, given that another chapter in the Handbook by Vogel and Bruch (2011) addresses organizational energy. We make sense of the divergent perspectives on human energy by organizing the literature in six distinct streams. We then distill and extend the streams of energy research to discuss implications for positive organizational scholarship (POS). We conclude the paper with some practical implications for how individuals and their organizations can cultivate and self-regulate their energy at and off work. Our hope is that our review will spur more conceptual and empirical research to address important conceptual puzzles and gaps in our understanding.

Energy-related Literature: A Review

In our review of the energy literature (Quinn, Spreitzer, & Lam, 2011), we searched for research related to the notion of energy at work. We looked not only in organizational studies, but also in the fields of psychology and sociology. We searched on the word "energy" and variants including vitality and vigor in ABI-Inform, PsycInfo, and EBSCO. We also traced papers cited in major articles. Finally, we spoke to a variety of researchers who have examined the topic of human energy. As we examined the literature, we identified six research streams. For our purposes, to qualify as a stream, the literature must include: (a) a distinctive theoretical logic for energy, (b) empirical research that tests the theoretical logic, and (c) boundaries manifest as identifiable labels for energy-related constructs and citations to common foundational studies.

Our descriptions of each stream are organized as follows: First, we provide a brief overview of its definition of energy. Second, we review empirical work that tests the stream's conceptualization of energy, its antecedents, and its outcomes, highlighting the methodology employed to measure energy. Third, we identify extensions of the stream to organizational- and work-related settings. Finally, we conclude our summary of each stream by articulating key insights derived from that stream, as well as possible ways in which the stream can contribute to other streams.

Stream 1: Ego-depletion Theory

The first stream is research on ego-depletion theory, first proposed by social psychologist Roy Baumeister and his colleagues (Baumeister, Bratslavsky, Muraven, & Tice, 1998). For ego-depletion theorists, energy is a physical, biological construct: The capacity to act or exert effort, actualized in creating and breaking down chemical bonds (particularly glucose and adenosine triphosphate [ATP]) in the human body. As a result, ego-depletion theorists assume that energy is a finite, limited resource, depleted through activities that require the "exertion of control over the self by the self" (Muraven & Baumeister, 2000, p. 247).

EMPIRICAL RESEARCH

Mostly conducted in laboratory studies, research on self-regulation demonstrates that individuals consume a high level of energy when they engage in self-control activities, such as maintaining physical stamina (Muraven, Tice, & Baumeister, 1998), regulating emotions (Baumeister et al., 1998), suppressing thoughts (Muraven et al., 1998), coping with stress (Muraven & Baumeister, 2000), persisting on unsolvable puzzles (Webb & Sheeran, 2002), and resisting impulse (Vohs & Heatherton, 2000). If such energy is not replenished, or if there is no opportunity for rest, subjects perform worse on subsequent self-control tasks (Muraven & Baumeister, 2000) and provide fewer helping behaviors to others (DeWall, Baumeister, Gailliot, & Maner, 2008).

Despite the overwhelming evidence of the importance of energy for self-control activities, only a few studies have examined the effect of self-control on energy in an organizational context. Trougakos, Beal, Green, and Weiss (2008) found that respite breaks that do not require self-regulation are more likely to result in positive affective displays with customers following the break. Sonnentag and Jelden (in press) found that after a stressful day of work, police officers reported being too drained to engage in sports activities—even though exercise has been shown to be an important recovery experience.

KEY INSIGHTS

Ego-depletion research has shown us that energy, in the form of glucose and ATP, is depleted for activities that require a high level of self-control and choice decisions. Other research has examined changes in energy measured as active blood glucose (Gailliot & Baumeister, 2007; Gailliot et al., 2007). In a series of nine laboratory experiments, Gailliot et al. (2007) demonstrated that self-control activities reduced bloodstream glucose, with this reduction associated with the subsequent impairment on self-control activities. The negative effect of reduced blood glucose on subsequent self-control activities, however, is counteracted when subjects consume a drink containing glucose. These studies confirm that physiological energy is an important fuel for self-control.

Another insight from ego-depletion theory is that self-regulation works like a muscle. Like using a muscle, energy must be expended to regulate oneself. However, the amount of energy that is required to regulate oneself decreases when a person engages in the regular practice of self-control activities (Baumeister, Gailliot, DeWall, & Oaten, 2006).

Several longitudinal studies have demonstrated that exercising self-control can improve one's ability to self-regulate in a subsequent activity (Gailliot et al., 2007; Muraven, Baumeister, & Tice, 1999; Oaten & Cheng, 2006, 2007). Overall, the empirical evidence suggests that using energy to engage in self-control activities, though draining in the short-run, can actually increase one's energy level for (related and unrelated) self-control activities over the long run.

Ego-depletion research, then, establishes the relationship between self-regulation activities, which are common in work experience and the use of human energy. The next stream—attention restoration theory—uses a similar approach, but raises questions about where and how these concepts of energy should be applied.

Stream 2: Attention Restoration Theory

The second stream of energy research is attention restoration theory (ART), first proposed by environmental psychologists Steven and Rachel Kaplan (1989). Like ego-depletion theory, ART posits that energy is finite and depletable. Unlike ego-depletion theory, however, Kaplan and Kaplan examine energy as *directed attention*. Directed attention refers to an individual's capacity to focus his or her attention (Kaplan, 1993). To measure directed attention, Cimprich (1992, 1993) introduced a validated measure of attentional function to measure one's state of focus and concentration. Sample items include "Keeping your mind on what you are doing" and "Doing things that take time and effort." Attention restoration theory researchers, then, focus on how people regulate their attention—a kind of mental effort focused on cognitive tasks—while ego-depletion researchers focus on regulation more broadly.

According to ART, energy can be drained in two ways. First, similar to ego-depletion, inhibiting distractions such as worry, stress, and unrelated thoughts contribute to a greater clarity of mind, but deplete energy and lead to mental fatigue (Kaplan, 1995). Second, information processing also depletes energy over time (Kaplan, 2001). When problem-solving, individuals have access to a vast array of stored knowledge, much of which is irrelevant to a solution. Solving the problem requires individuals to search for and focus on a small portion of their existing knowledge base.

Attention restoration theory also explains how energy in the form of directed attention can be restored. Whereas ego-depletion theory suggests that one way to restore energy is by ingesting glucose, Kaplan (2001) offered four additional ways to restore energy depleted through directed attention: *find fascination* (a type of attention that is assumed to be effortless and without capacity limitations); *being away* (being in a different place physically and mentally from an environment demanding directed attention—similar to detachment in the recovery literature); *levels of extent and coherence* (locating in a holistically rich ambience); and *compatibility* (engaging in activities that are consistent with one's preferences).

We should note here that the language of depleting and restoring energy used in these two literatures is not consistent with the laws of physics surrounding energy. Energy is never depleted or restored; instead, it is conserved and transformed. Glucose and ATP in the human body contain what physicists would call "potential energy," which exists because of a complex configuration of atoms in these molecules. When human bodies act, whether through regulated (effortful) activities or unregulated (effortless or unintentional) activities, these activities occur by transforming potential energy into kinetic energy as molecules break down into simpler structures. This observation is important for understanding ART findings and how they relate to findings from other streams.

EMPIRICAL RESEARCH

Empirical research in this stream demonstrates the beneficial effects of the four restorative mechanisms as manifest in exposure to the natural environment (e.g., Korpela & Hartig, 1996; Korpela, Hartig, Kaiser, & Fuhrer, 2001; Kaplan, Bardwell, & Slakter, 1993). Kaplan (2001) found that individuals who spend time outdoors, take walks or hikes, go to a park, or bike or jog in the neighborhood were more likely to indicate that they felt positive, focused, effective, and alert. In an experimental design, Kuo and Sullivan (2001) found that directed attention, not positive moods, stress, or social integration, fully mediated the relationship between the exposure to the natural environment and aggression. Other studies have demonstrated the beneficial effect of the natural environment in restoring energy and directed attention (Berto, 2005; Kweon, Ulrich, Walker, & Tassinary, 2008).

Empirical research on ART in the workplace has focused on the psychological benefits of a windowed work setting (Biner, Butler, Lovegrove, & Burns, 1993). Individuals who have a view of nature reported fewer ailments than did those who had more of an urban view (Kaplan, 1993). Those with a view of nature also had more positive feelings about their workplace setting, including their work and life satisfaction. Finally, Leather, Pyrgas, Beale, and Lawrence (1998) reported that a view of greenery buffered the effects of job stress on intention to quit and well-being. This work suggests parallels to the recovery literature discussed above, which indicates that being psychologically away from work predicts positive job outcomes such as job performance and proactive behaviors (Sonnentag, 2003).

KEY INSIGHTS

Attention restoration theory research corroborates the finding of ego-depletion theory that directed attention, as a regulated activity, converts potential energy into kinetic energy. Its second finding, however—that there are numerous pathways other than consuming glucose to restore energy—is more puzzling. Clearly, going for a walk is a physical activity that requires the body to transform potential energy into kinetic energy; therefore, how can energy be "restored" by such an activity? And, having a view of nature in one's workplace environment does not cause simple chemicals in the body to reform into more complex ones; therefore, how can an activity like this be "restorative"? The next stream, self-determination theory (SDT), provides us with some answers.

Stream 3: Self-determination Theory

The third stream is derived from SDT. Self-determination theory provides us with yet another definition of energy: *subjective vitality*; that is, a feeling of enthusiasm, aliveness, and positive energy (Ryan & Frederick, 1997). Subjective vitality as a psychological state is typically measured with seven items, including "I feel alive and vital," "I have energy and spirit," and "I feel energized."

Subjective vitality is embedded in a larger body of research on SDT developed by Ryan and Deci (2000). At its core, SDT proposes that when we are intrinsically motivated (i.e., doing something for its own enjoyment or interest rather than being compelled for instrumental reasons), we feel more vitality and our behaviors require less regulation. Self-determination theory posits that the social context can contribute to feelings of vitality by satisfying psychological needs for relatedness, competence, and autonomy.

EMPIRICAL RESEARCH

Self-determination theory research confirms that people feel more vitality in self-directed activities than other-directed, or controlled, activities (Nix, Ryan, Manly, & Deci, 1999), even though participants doing both kinds of activities were equally happy (which suggests that happiness is different from vitality). Relative to our puzzle about how activities such as going for a walk can have "restorative" effects, SDT research (e.g., Moller, Deci, & Ryan, 2006) has also shown that experimental participants only experienced feelings of fatigue (ego-depletion) when the activity was other-directed rather than autonomously chosen. This suggests that even though human action transforms potential energy (ATP) into kinetic energy (activity), people can still feel energized in spite of the fact that their stores of glucose or ATP may be diminishing. Marks (1977) explained this phenomenon more than three decades ago: In countries or communities in which people have sufficient nutrition on a daily basis, their stores of ATP are more than sufficient to fuel their activities for hours or even days. Ego-depletion may have more to do with the interest people have in, or the feelings of energy they have for, their activities than with their ATP or glucose levels per se.

Other SDT research has used an experience sampling method with college students to show that autonomy, competence, and relatedness were associated with greater vitality (Sheldon, Ryan, & Reis, 1996; Reis, Sheldon, Gable, Roscoe, & Ryan, 2000). And, in longitudinal research of elite female gymnasts, support was again found for the vitality-increasing effects of autonomy, competence, and relatedness even when the gymnasts had engaged in physically demanding and calorie-draining activities. Finally, autonomous individuals performed better on subsequent self-control activities than did individuals whose behavior was controlled by external forces, even when controlling for anxiety, stress, unpleasantness, or reduced motivation (Muraven, Gagne, & Rosman, 2008).

Vitality has been linked to organismic well-being, including better mental health and fewer reports of physical symptoms (Ryan & Frederick, 1997). In a study of nursing home residents, those that reported more vitality engaged in more autonomously regulating their daily activities (Sheldon, Ryan, & Reis, 1996). In a study explaining health outcomes following a natural disaster, individuals who reported vitality before the disaster were less depressed afterward (Tremblay, Blanchard, Pelletier, & Vallerand, 2006). And, in three experiments Muraven et al. (2008) conducted, the feeling of vitality resulting from autonomous behavior related to reduced physical symptoms, faster recovery from fatigue, and increased performance.

Researchers have also started to study vitality in organizational settings. A diary study found that people felt more vitality when they experienced self-determination in their daily experiences (Ryan, Bernstein, & Brown, 2010). Vitality was higher on weekends, when the participants experienced more opportunities for autonomy and relatedness activities in weekend social and leisure activities. Spreitzer et al. (2005) theorized about the effect of vitality in conjunction with learning when developing a model of human "thriving" at work. They suggested that when people are thriving at work (i.e., experience both vitality and a sense of learning), they experience personal growth and a sense of forward progress. Consequently, when thriving, individuals are more adaptive (less burnout and more career initiative) and have better in-role and extra-role job performance as reported by their bosses (Porath, Spreitzer, Gibson, & Stevens, 2008). Others have found subjective vitality to be related to creative work (Atwater & Carmeli, 2009; Kark & Carmeli, 2008).

KEY INSIGHTS

Self-determination theory, then, helps us to see how activity—even self-regulated activity—can be vitality-enhancing rather than ego-depleting if it satisfies a person's needs for autonomy, competence, and relatedness. All human activity requires transforming potential energy in the form of glucose and ATP into kinetic energy in the form of action, but some of these activities are more emotionally depleting than others. We gain insight into how this might work physiologically by reviewing the literature on energetic and tense arousal.

Stream 4: Energetic Arousal

Energetic arousal (Thayer, 1989) is the subjective experience that accompanies the activation of the body's subsystem in a way that creates feelings of enthusiasm, excitement, and vitality. In fact, Nix and his colleagues (1999) used energetic arousal survey scales in an SDT experiment in which they measured vitality. Energetic arousal is also the same construct as positive activation (Watson, Clark, & Tellegen, 1988) and is orthogonal to tense arousal or negative activation—a feeling of tension or anxiety that "coils" bodily subsystems in preparation for action—on the emotional circumplex (Russell & Feldman Barrett, 1999). Thayer (1989) developed the construct of energetic activation in

his research on mood and measured it with the Activation-Deactivation Adjective Check List (Thayer, 1978) with adjectives such as "vigorous," "energetic," and "active." The PANAS scale (Watson et al., 1988) provides an alternative to measure positive activation.

Research on energetic and tense arousal (and research on positive and negative activation) contributes to our growing understanding of how potential energy, kinetic energy, and the subjective experience of energy work together by identifying the different physiological reactions involved in each type of activation. Metaphorically, tense activation treats the body like a spring, narrowing people's attention, motivating them to address interruptions to their expectations, and preparing them to act. Acting in this state can be a highly inefficient use of physiological, potential energy because energy is spent on keeping the body tense and consciously focusing attention while also acting. The constant effortfulness and intentionality is consuming and requires a physiological adjustment to feeling energetic arousal for the body to "wind down" (Fredrickson, 1998). In contrast, action tends to be a natural and automatic part of energetic arousal, and as a result, transforming potential energy into kinetic energy is much more efficient when people feel energized.

EMPIRICAL RESEARCH

More research on energetic arousal and positive activation has been conducted in both psychology and organizational scholarship than we could possibly review. Thus, we highlight only a few studies that cover a few key points. To start, it is useful to note from Thayer's (1987) research that although one might imagine that exercise depletes energy, the *feeling* of energetic arousal is enhanced through exercise. For example, Thayer found that a walk increases energetic arousal over time more than consuming a sugary snack. Individuals can also engage in mood regulating behaviors to increase their energetic arousal (Thayer, Newman, & McClain, 1994), including stress management (e.g., relaxation techniques), social interaction (e.g., chat with a friend), and, perhaps most dominantly, physical exercise (Thayer, Peters, Takahashi, & Birkhead-Flight, 1993).

In organizational scholarship, energetic arousal is associated with creative outcomes (e.g., De Dreu, Baas, & Nijstad, 2008), entrepreneurial passion (Cardon, Wincent, Singh, & Drnovsek, 2009; Chen, Yao, & Kotha, in press), and mood convergence and emotional contagion in ork groups (Bartel & Saavedra, 2000), to give a few examples. At an organizational level of analysis, Huy (2002) examined how middle managers' positive activation associated with a radical organizational change project can set the tone for followers' to immediately commit to and maintain a change project. Learning from the change processes is more likely to occur as a result of attending to recipients' emotions by continuous effort to induce emotional excitement about the change project. Jansen (2004) used the term "momentum" to describe the positive activation associated with organizational change. She found that two organizational events are likely to influence the change momentum. At the beginning of the change, the urgency and feasibility of the change are primary predictors of change momentum. As changes proceed, an important predictor is one's judgment of whether the change is progressing in the right direction. With a high level of self-efficacy as a result of change progress, momentum is increased over time, which increases one's commitment to the change.

KEY INSIGHTS

The extensive research on energetic arousal/positive activation gives us deep insight into the causes, phenomenology, and consequences of energetic activation. This research is important for many reasons, but one of the most important for our review is that identifying the antecedents of energetic arousal can help us to understand which organizational conditions are likely to lead to the efficient (and, incidentally, enjoyable and creative) use of human energy in the work that people perform. The usefulness of this construct expands when researchers take into account the work groups' contagion and emotional momentum properties of energetic arousal at a higher level of analysis. There has been more research in organizational scholarship, however, on the consequences of energetic arousal than on its organizational antecedents. This presents an important opportunity for future research. Further, it presents a reason to integrate this research with the next stream, which helps us to see social and organizational causes and consequences of energetic arousal.

Stream 5: Interactional Ritual Chain Theory

Interactional ritual chain (IRC) theory focuses us on the social functions of energetic arousal (or subjective vitality or positive activation). The most influential scholar in this stream is Randal Collins

(1981), a sociologist who treats emotional energy as a mechanism to help understand how social interactions aggregate to create society's social structures, including organizations (Collins, 1981), stratification (Collins, 1990), markets (Collins, 1993), and social trends (Collins, 2004). Emotional energy (Collins' word for energetic arousal, subjective vitality, or positive activation) is a mechanism that can be used to explain how social structures are created and re-created: People like to feel energized and seek to re-create that experience by reengaging in the activities that they think will increase their emotional energy (Collins, 2004). This is particularly true in social interactions, which often take on a ritualistic flavor, even if people are not aware of this when they participate in them. This is one reason why people seek out social interactions and, through repetition, create social structures.

Emotional energy according to Collins (1993, p. 211) is the activation that people feel in their everyday experience, ranging from "enthusiasm and confidence" to "apathy and depression." Most of the time, most people experience moderate levels of energy, enough to carry out the usual flow of everyday interactions and activities. They only notice aberrations in their experience when energy is higher or lower than normal.

The IRC stream differs from other streams in its focus on social structure and social cognition. Self-determination theorists largely take an individual focus to energy, seeing energy as an outcome that people experience when their needs are met (Ryan & Deci, 2000). Interactional ritual chain scholars (Collins, 1993), in contrast, see energy as the outcome of a successful interaction ritual. (Interestingly, however, what makes an interaction ritual successful could be that it meets people's needs for autonomy, competence, and—most especially—relatedness.) An interaction is "successful" as a ritual when the people who are interacting are co-present, have boundaries that define their participation in the interaction, share the same focus of their attention, and experience the same feelings about whatever they are focusing on. When this happens, the shared emotions and shared focus increase until the people involved become entrained in each other's bodily micro-rhythms. When people experience this entrainment, their individual energy increases, and they identify with the people with whom they are interacting. The desire to experience emotional energy again motivates people to participate in subsequent interactions. The unit of analysis in IRC theory is interactions, which may be conversations between two people, small group meetings or discussions, or large crowds in a football stadium.

EMPIRICAL RESEARCH

Researchers that study attachment theory (e.g., Field, 1985) and social neuroscience (Panskepp, 1998) have provided evidence that human beings do, in fact, entrain themselves to one another's emotional rhythms, releasing hormones that can create energy. In clinical psychology, Miller and Stiver (1997) found that their patients would grow as people when they experienced empathic connections and that these empathic connections also generated zest or energy.

In organizational scholarship, Dutton (2003) argued that energy increases when people engage in specific relational activities: respectful engagement, task enabling, and trust. When people use these activities in their interpersonal interactions, Dutton and Heaphy (2003) argued that energy increases because (a) people derive utility or receive valued goods through these interactions; (b) people generate identities that give them meaning and self-worth; (c) people feel empowered; and (d) people help people grow and develop. Supporting Dutton and Heaphy's arguments, Carmeli and Spreitzer (2009) found that connectivity increased energy.

Quinn (2007) also pointed out that the energy that people bring to their interactions can influence the quality of the relationships that develop from those interactions, and Quinn and Dutton (2005) described how changes in energy within an interaction help coordinate both that interaction and the activities that follow that interaction. These theories lay the groundwork for research on energy networks because energy-based network relationships assume that energy is both an input and an output of interaction. As Baker and Quinn (2009) suggested in their computational model of energy networks, energy-based network relationships consisted of the attributions people make about how energizing they think others are and the expectations they have of feeling energized in their subsequent interactions with those people. Baker and Quinn's model suggests that the energy that people feel in their interactions with others affects the form and density of the relationships that evolve and the performance of the organizational network. A simple strategy of avoiding interactions with people that were perceived to be deenergizing, for example, led to relatively high levels of information use and performance. Empirical data suggest that similar principles hold true with individual performance. For example,

Baker, Cross, and Wooten (2003) found that the degree to which a person in an organizational network was considered by his or her peers to be an energizing person with whom to interact predicted that person's performance better on multiple measures of performance than that person's centrality in the organization's information network.

At least one other domain within organizational scholarship has drawn heavily from Collins' work: Research on strategic conversations and the dynamics of inclusion. Westley (1990) began examining this question using Collins' theory to show how organizational participants could be more or less energized about developing and implementing a firm's strategy depending on the degree to which they were included, dominated, and ideologically involved in conversations about strategy. In a similar vein, Brundin and Nordqvist (2008) found that the energy experienced in the board room influenced power and status dynamics.

KEY INSIGHTS

The IRC stream is particularly important for understanding energy in organizations. More than any other stream, this stream examines the relationship between energy and specific forms of social organization. It does this by introducing mechanisms such as energy tropism, interaction rituals, practices, attributions, expectations, inclusion, dominance, and ideologies to tie personal and interpersonal experiences to social structures. As people try to maximize their energetic arousal, they treat their social world like a marketplace, seeking interactions that increase energetic arousal and avoiding interactions that decrease it (Collins, 1993).

Stream 6: Conservation of Resources

The final stream of energy research—conservation of resources (CoR) theory (Hobfoll, 1989)—provides one more way to think about the organizational role of energy. Although its roots are psychological rather than organizational, it positions energy within a construct—resources—that is central to many theories of organization. Resources refer to any "objects, personal characteristics, conditions, or energies that are valued by the individual" (Hobfoll, 1989, p. 516). Of particular relevance to this review is the specific "intrinsic energetic resource" of vigor, defined as an individual possessing physical presence, cognitive alertness, and emotional energy (Hobfoll & Shirom, 2001). Stress results from depleting resources. As a result, resources must be conserved or replenished to maintain psychological well-being (Hobfoll, 1989). The CoR theory's manifestation of energy is measured with a 12-item scale that includes items such as "I feel I have physical strength" (physical energy); "I feel I can think rapidly" (cognitive energy); and "I feel capable of being sympathetic to coworkers and customers" (emotional energy). Given the types of energy we have identified in reviewing the other energy research streams, we can now articulate more clearly that when researchers use terms such as "physical energy," "cognitive energy," or "emotional energy," what they mean is the energetic arousal a person feels about investing effort (kinetic energy) into particular activities (physical, cognitive, or emotional).

EMPIRICAL RESEARCH

Conservation of resources theory has spawned empirical research on both work engagement and recovery. Schaufeli, Salanova, Gonzalez-Roma, and Bakker (2002) see the notion of vigor as one key element of the broader construct of the work engagement construct. Vigor is conceptualized as the direct opposite of emotional exhaustion (Maslach & Leiter, 2008). Schaufeli et al. (2002) broadened the definition of vigor beyond energy to include mental resilience, willingness to invest effort in one's work, and persistence in the face of difficulties. Although the engagement researchers have broadened Hobfoll's (1989) definition of vigor, it is safe to say that feeling energetic is a subdimension of being engaged in one's work. Energy is thus a key resource to conserve in order to minimize stress.

Job demands and job resources have been examined empirically as key antecedents of vigor at work. Job demands such as workload have been found to deplete vigor, whereas job resources such as supervisory and coworker support (Demerouti, Bakker, Nachreiner, & Schaufeli, 2001), social capital (Carmeli, Ben-Hador, Waldman, & Rupp, 2009), and performance feedback (Schaufeli & Bakker, 2004) have been found to enhance vigor. Salanova, Agut, and Peiro (2005) also found that more organizational resources (i.e., supervisory training, levels of autonomy, and presence of technology) increased unit-level vigor, which in turn predicted customer service performance and customer loyalty. Other empirical research points to the similar conclusions that job resources enhance vigor and reduce emotional exhaustion (e.g., Halbesleben, 2006).

Another domain of organizational research that draws upon CoR is the recovery literature pioneered by Sabine Sonnentag (2003). Given the presence of

daily job demands and the draining nature of our work (Sonnentag & Zijlstra, 2006), this research has examined how employees recover from work during off-work periods such as vacations (Eden, 1990; Fritz & Sonnentag, 2006; Westman & Eden, 1997), weekends (Fritz & Sonnentag, 2005), and evenings (Sonnentag, Binnewies, & Mojza, 2008). Sonnentag and Fritz (2007) identified four dimensions of recovery experiences that help recover vigor: detachment from work, such as not thinking about work during off-work period (Etzion, Eden, & Lapidot, 1998), relaxation, mastery experiences, and experiences of control during leisure time. Overall, findings from the recovery literature are consistent with the CoR framework in that recovery experiences that allow individuals to replenish depleted energetic resources will have a beneficial impact on subsequent well-being and job performance.

KEY INSIGHTS

In summary, an important insight of CoR theory is that job resources/demands serve as a strong predictor of vigor. Vigor can be depleted when job demands are high and depleting vigor over the long run is likely to lead to emotional exhaustion (Sonnentag & Niessen, 2008). To restore vigor, one must either engage in recovery processes or obtain job resources.

Now that we have reviewed the six streams of research on human energy the next section of this chapter synthesizes and applies these streams to POS.

Synthesizing the Six Streams: Implications for Positive Organizational Scholarship

Positive organizational scholarship, drawing on the fields of organizational studies, psychology, and sociology, focuses on the "generative dynamics in organizations that promote human strength, resiliency, healing, and restoration" (Cameron, Dutton, & Quinn, 2003). Indeed, its name embodies the core values of the movement: "Positive" addresses the discipline's elevating and affirmative focus; "organizational" focuses on the processes and conditions that occur in organizational contexts; and "scholarship" reflects the rigor, theory, scientific procedures, precise definition, and empirical validation in which the approach is grounded (Bernstein, 2003). A POS perspective assumes that understanding how to enable human excellence in organizations will unlock potential, reveal possibilities, and move us along a more positive course of human and organizational functioning. At its core, POS investigates "positive deviance," or the ways in which organizations and their members flourish and prosper in extraordinary ways (Spreitzer & Sonenshein, 2004). In this section of the chapter, we offer insights into how energy at work can contribute to a deeper understanding of POS.

What Is Energy and How Does It Matter for POS Research?

Looking across the six streams, Quinn, et al. (2011) identified three key facets of human energy: subjective, physiological/potential, and kinetic. By comparing different streams of energy research, we begin to see how these three types of energy interact. We see how organizational scholars have started to incorporate each of these ideas into their research. And, we see how much more can be learned by incorporating the interactions among these ideas into organizational research by asking questions about which resources and constraints influence the experience and transformation of energy the most; how energy is used as a resource; and how each type of energy aggregates (or fails to aggregate) across levels of analysis and over time. The connection between energy and resources seems particularly intriguing. For example, Feldman (2004) and Orlikowski (2000) showed that resources are not preexisting assets to be stored, used, and lost, but are created in practice when used to enact schema. Human energy may, in fact, be the most fundamental resource created in organizational activity. This idea was intuited by Katz and Kahn (1966) who used the word "energic" to describe resources and their functions in open systems and also by Feldman (2004) who used the word "energize" to describe how resources effect organizational schema.

Additional Implications of Human Energy for POS Research

In this section, we offer some additional implications for POS research. First, POS scholars working in the area of thriving and recovery are interested in how energy can be generated or sustained in the doing of one's work, not just depleted or drained. Although we have some understanding of how breaks and time away from work can restore human energy, we know less about how the content of work itself and the way it is accomplished can also be restorative. Spreitzer et al. (2005) suggested that resources including positive meaning, positive agency, positive emotions, and knowledge are likely to create feelings of vitality. Fritz, Lam, and Spreitzer

(2010) provided support for this assertion in an empirical study of energy management strategies used by knowledge workers. They found that strategies that are learning-oriented (e.g., set a new goal), relational (do something to make a colleague happy), and meaning-creating (reflect on the meaning of your work) are more related to having more energy than commonly reported energy management strategies such as switching tasks or taking a break. Further, research on job crafting has demonstrated that individuals can find ways to create more meaning in their work (Wrzesniewski & Dutton, 2001). Clearly, an important direction for future research within the domain of thriving and recovery will be how different aspects of work generate, not merely deplete, human energy.

Second, POS scholars are interested in the contagion of positive energy across individuals and organizations. Prior network research has shown that some people are energizers who attract others, while others are deenergizing and repel others (Baker & Quinn, 2009). While we can document the existence of energizers and deenergizers, future research can extend this area of inquiry to understand the features and qualities of energizing and deenergizing individuals better. Such knowledge is crucial to understanding how to transform deenergizers into energizers or at least neutralize them. Scholars should pay particular attention to these processes in organizational change, given the role that energy plays (Huy, 2002; Jansen, 2004).

Third, POS scholars are interested in what enables people to be resilient in difficult times (Sutcliffe & Vogus, 2003). Energy may be a critical ingredient for fortifying individuals to see opportunities and not just the inherent threat in crises and difficult times. If we want people and organizations to learn and grow through crises (Christianson, Farkas, Sutcliffe, & Weick, 2009), scholars and managers should think about ways to energize people to broaden their perspectives; indeed, so that they can see possibilities for something new. Prior research on energy amid the change process gives us some early clues (Jensen, 2004; Huy, 2002), but we have limited knowledge of the role of energy in the change process, particularly transformational or radical changes, in which burnout and exhaustion are common.

Finally, POS scholars are interested in how positive organizational practices contribute to important work outcomes. Research related to ego-depletion theory has suggested that self-control activities demand a large amount of energy. If not replenished, individuals are at risk of failing to self-control their behaviors at work. Research related to work engagement further illustrates that engagement more strongly predicts work and citizenship behaviors than job involvement or intrinsic motivation (Rich, LePine, & Crawford, 2009). This raises other questions of interest to POS scholars. For example, what role does self-regulation play in employee and organizational virtuousness? What factors determine whether work activities will require self-regulation? What management designs facilitate self-regulation or make it unnecessary?

Conclusion

Although much work has been done on the notion of energy, little integration has occurred across approaches. In this chapter, we have looked across the six streams of energy-related research to offer implications for POS. We hope that by synthesizing to three key energy constructs and identifying areas of intersection—and critical gaps—we can advance an agenda for future research on energy at work. We hope that you will join us by devoting your energy to this important endeavor.

References

Atwater, L., & Carmeli, A. (2009). Leader-member exchange, feelings of energy and involvement in creative work. *The Leadership Quarterly, 20*(3), 264–275.

Baker, W.E., Cross, R., & Wooten, M. (2003). Positive organizational network analysis and energizing relationships. In K.S. Cameron, J.E. Dutton, & R. Quinn (Eds.), *Positive organizational scholarship*. San Francisco: Berrett-Koehler Publishers.

Baker, W.E., & Quinn, R. (2009). *Energy networks and information use*. Working paper, Ross School of Business, Ann Arbor, MI.

Bartel, C.A., & Saavedra, R. (2000). The collective construction of work group moods. *Administrative Science Quarterly, 45*, 197–231.

Baumeister, R.F., Bratslavsky, E., Muraven, M., & Tice, D.M. (1998). Ego depletion: Is the active self a limited resource? *Personality processes and individual differences, 74*, 1252–1265.

Baumeister, R.F., Gailliot, M., DeWall, C.N., & Oaten, M. (2006). Self-regulation and personality: How interventions increase regulatory success, and how depletion moderates the effects of traits on behavior. *Journal of Personality, 74*, 1773–1801.

Bernstein, S.D. (2003). Positive Organizational Scholarship: Meet the Movement. *Journal of Management Inquiry, 12*(3): 266–271.

Berto, R. (2005). Exposure to restorative environments helps restore attentional capacity. *Journal of Environmental Psychology, 25*, 249–259.

Biner, P.M., Butler, D.L., Lovegrove, T.E., & Burns, R.L. (1993). Windowlessness in the workplace: A reexamination of the compensation hypothesis. *Environment and Behavior, 25*, 205–227.

Barnes, C.M., & Hollenbeck, J.R. (2009). Sleep deprivation and decision-making teams: Burning the midnight oil or playing with fire? *Academy of Management Review, 34*, 56–66.

Brundin, E., & Nordqvist, M. (2008). Beyond facts and figures: The role of emotions in boardroom dynamics. *Corporate Governance: An International Review, 16*, 326–341.

Cameron, K.S., Dutton, J.E., & Quinn, R.E. (2003). *Positive organizational scholarship: Foundations of a new discipline*. San Francisco: Berrett-Koehler.

Cardon, M.S., Wincent, J., Singh, J., & Drnovsek, M. (2009). The nature and experience of entrepreneurial passion. *Academy of Management Review, 34*, 511–532.

Carmeli, A., Ben-Hador, B., Waldman, D.A., & Rupp, D.E. (2009). How leaders cultivate social capital and nurture employee vigor: Implications for job performance. *Journal of Applied Psychology, 94*(6), 1553–1561.

Carmeli, A., & Spreitzer, G. (2009). Trust, connectivity, and thriving: Implications for innovative work behavior. *Journal of Creative Behavior, 43*(3), 169–191.

Chen, X.P., Yao, X., & Kotha, S. (in press). Passion and preparedness in entrepreneurs' business plan presentations: A persuasion analysis of venture capitalists' funding decisions. Forthcoming in *Academy of Management Journal*.

Christianson, M., Farkas, M., Sutcliffe, K.M., & Weick, K.E. (2009). Rare events as catalysts for learning: The case of the Baltimore and Ohio Railroad Museum. *Organization Science, 20*(5), 846–860.

Cimprich, B. (1992). A theoretical perspective on attention and patient education. *Advances in Nursing Science, 14*, 39–51.

Cimprich, B. (1993). Development of an intervention to restore attention in cancer patients. *Cancer Nursing, 16*, 83–92.

Collins, R. (1981). On the microfoundations of macrosociology. *American Journal of Sociology, 86*, 984–1014.

Collins, R. (1990). Stratification, emotional energy, and the transient emotions. In D. Kemper (Ed.), *Research agendas in the sociology of emotions* (pp. 27–57). Albany, NY: State University of New York Press.

Collins, R. (1993). Emotional energy as the common denominator of rational action. *Rationality and Society, 5*, 203–230.

Collins, R. (2004). *Interactional ritual chain*. Princeton, NJ: Princeton University Press.

Cross, R., Baker, W., & Parker, A. (2003). What creates energy in organizations? *MIT Sloan Management Review, 44*, 51–56.

Csikszentmihalyi, M. (1990). *Flow: The psychology of optimal experience*. New York: Harper Perennial.

Dawson, D., & Reid, K. (1997). Fatigue, alcohol and performance impairment. *Nature, 388*, 235.

De Dreu, C.K. W., Baas, M., & Nijstad, B.A. (2008). Hedonic tone and activation level in the mood-creativity link: Toward a dual pathway to creativity model. *Journal of Personality and Social Psychology, 94*, 739–756.

Demerouti, E., Bakker, A.B., Nachreiner, F., & Schaufeli, W.B. (2001). The job demands-resources model of burnout. *Journal of Applied Psychology, 86*, 499.

DeWall, C.N., Baumeister, R.F., Gailliot, M.T., & Maner, J.K. (2008). Depletion makes the heart grow less helpful: Helping as a function of self-regulatory energy and genetic relatedness. *Personality and Social Psychology Bulletin, 34*, 1663–1676.

Dutton, J.E. (2003). *Energize your workplace: How to build and sustain high-quality connections at work*. San Francisco: Jossey-Bass Publishers.

Dutton, J.E., & Heaphy, E.D. (2003). The power of high-quality connections. In K.S. Cameron, J.E. Dutton, & R.E. Quinn (Eds.), *Positive organizational scholarship: Foundations of a new discipline*. San Francisco: Berrett-Koehler.

Eden, D. (1990). Acute and chronic job stress, strain, and vacation relief. *Organizational Behavior and Human Decision Processes, 45*, 175–193.

Etzion, D., Eden, D., & Lapidot, Y. (1998). Relief from job stressors and burnout: Reserve service as a respite. *Journal of Applied Psychology, 83*, 577–585.

Feldman, M.S. (2004). Resources in emerging structures and processes of change. *Organization Science, 15*, 295–309.

Field, T. (1985). Attachment as psychobiological attunement: Being on the same wavelength. In M. Reite, & T. Field (Eds.), *The psychobiology of attachment and separation* (pp. 415–454). San Diego: Academic Press.

Fredrickson, B.L. (1998). Positive emotions speed recovery from the cardiovascular sequelae of negative emotions. *Cognition and Emotion, 12*(2), 191–220.

Fritz, C., Lam, C., & Spreitzer, G. (2010). *It's the little things that matter*. Working paper, Ross School of Business, Ann Arbor, MI.

Fritz, C., & Sonnentag, S. (2005). Recovery, health, and job performance: Effects of weekend experiences. *Journal of Occupational Health Psychology, 10*, 187–199.

Fritz, C., & Sonnentag, S. (2006). Recovery, well-being, and performance-related outcomes: The role of workload and vacation experiences. *Journal of Applied Psychology, 4*, 936–945.

Gailliot, M.T., & Baumeister, R.F. (2007). The physiology of willpower linking blood glucose to self-control. *Personality and Social Psychology Review, 11*, 303–327.

Gailliot, M., Baumeister, R.F., DeWall, C.N., Maner, J.K., Plant, E.A., Tice, D.M., et al. (2007). Self-control relies on glucose as a limited energy source: Willpower is more than a metaphor. *Journal of Personality and Social Psychology, 92*, 325–336.

Gardner, D.G., & Cummings, L.L. (1988). Activation theory and job design: Review and reconceptualization. *Research in Organizational Behavior, 10*, 81–122.

Halbesleben, J.R.B. (2006). Sources of social support and burnout: A meta-analytic test of the conservation of resources model. *Journal of Applied Psychology, 91*, 1134–1145.

Hobfoll, S.E. (1989). Conservation of resources: A new attempt at conceptualizing stress. *American Psychologist, 44*, 513–524.

Hobfoll, S.E., & Shirom, A. (2001). Conservation of resources theory: Applications to stress and management in the workplace. In R.T. Golembiewski (Ed.), *Handbook of organizational behavior* (2nd ed., pp. 57–80). New York: Marcel Dekker, Inc.

Huy, Q.N. (2002). Emotional balancing of organizational continuity and radical change: The contribution of middle managers. *Administrative Science Quarterly, 47*, 31–69.

Jansen, K.J. (2004). From persistence to pursuit: A longitudinal examination of momentum during the early stages of strategic change. *Organization Science, 15*, 276–294.

Kahn, W.A. (1990). Psychological conditions of personal engagement and disengagement at work. *Academy of Management Journal, 33*, 692–724.

Kaplan, R. (1993). The role of nature in the context of the workplace. *Landscape and Urban Planning, 26*, 193–201.

Kaplan, S. (1995). The restorative benefits of nature: Toward an integrative framework. *Journal of Environmental Psychology, 15*, 169–182.

Kaplan, S. (2001). Meditation, restoration, and the management of mental fatigue. *Environment and Behavior, 33*, 480–506.

Kaplan, S., Bardwell, L.V., & Slakter, D.B. (1993). The museum as a restorative environment. *Environment and Behavior, 25*, 725–742.

Kaplan, R., & Kaplan, S. (1989). *The experience of nature: A psychological perspective*. New York: Cambridge University Press.

Kark, R., & Carmeli, A. (2008). Alive and creating: The mediating role of vitality in the relationship between psychological safety and creative work involvement. *Journal of Organizational Behavior, 30*, 785–804.

Katz, D., & Kahn, R.L. (1966). *The social psychology of organizations*. New York: Wiley.

Korpela, K.M., & Hartig, T. (1996). Restorative qualities of favorite places. *Journal of Environmental Psychology, 16*, 221–233.

Korpela, K.M., Hartig, T., Kaiser, F.G., & Fuhrer, U. (2001). Restorative experience and self-regulation in favorite places. *Environment and Behavior, 33*, 572–589.

Kuo, F.E., & Sullivan, W.C. (2001). Aggression and violence in the inner city: Effects of environment via mental fatigue. *Environment and Behavior, 33*, 543–571.

Kweon, B., Ulrich, R.S., Walker, V.D., & Tassinary, L.G. (2008). Anger and stress: The role of landscape posters in an office setting. *Environment and Behavior, 40*, 355–381.

Landrigan, C.P., Rothschild, J.M., Cronin, J.W., Kaushal, R., Burdick, E., Katz, J.T., & Czeisler, C.A. (2004). Effect of reducing interns' work hours on serious medical errors in intensive care units. *The New England Journal of Medicine, 351*, 1838–1848.

Leather, P., Pyrgas, M., Beale, D., & Lawrence, C. (1998). Windows in the workplace: Sunlight, view, and occupational stress. *Environment and Behavior, 30*, 739–762

Loehr, J., & Schwartz, T. (2003). *The power of full engagement*. New York: Free Press.

Marks, S.R. (1977). Multiple Roles and Role Strain: Some notes on human energy, time, and commitment. *American Sociological Review, 42*(6), 921–936.

Maslach, C., & Leiter, M.P. (2008). Early predictors of job burnout and engagement. *Journal of Applied Psychology, 93*, 498–512.

Miller, J.B., & Stiver, I.P. (1997). *The healing connection: How women form relationships in therapy and in life*. Boston: Beacon Press.

Mitchell, T.R. (1982). Motivation: New directions for theory, research, and practice. *Academy of Management Review, 7*, 80–88.

Moller, A.C., Deci, E.L., & Ryan, R.M. (2006). Choice and ego-depletion: The moderating role of autonomy. *Personality and Social Psychology Bulletin, 32*, 1024–1036.

Muraven, M., & Baumeister, R.F. (2000). Self-regulation and depletion of limited resources: Does self-control resemble a muscle? *Psychological Bulletin, 126*, 247–259.

Muraven, M., Baumeister, R.F., & Tice, D.M. (1999). Longitudinal improvement of self-regulation through practice. *The Journal of Social Psychology, 139*, 446–457.

Muraven, M., Gagne, M., & Rosman, H. (2008). Helpful self-control: Autonomy support vitality, and depletion. *Journal of Experimental Social Psychology, 44*, 573–585.

Muraven, M., Tice, D.M., & Baumeister, R.F. (1998). Self-control as limited resource: Regulatory depletion patterns. *Journal of Personality and Social Psychology, 74*, 774–789.

Nix, G.A., Ryan, R.M., Manly, J.B., & Deci, E.L. (1999). Revitalization through self-regulation: The effects of autonomous and controlled motivation on happiness and vitality. *Journal of Experimental Social Psychology, 35,* 266–284.

Oaten, M., & Cheng, K. (2006). Improved self-control: The benefits of a regular program of academic study. *Basic and Applied Social Psychology, 28,* 1–16.

Oaten, M., & Cheng, K. (2007). Improvements in self-control from financial monitoring. *Journal of Economic Psychology, 28,* 487–501.

Orlikowski, W.J. (2000). Using Technology and constituting structures: A practice lens for studying technology in organizations. *Organization Science, 11,* 404–428.

Panskepp, J. (1998). *Affective neuroscience: The foundations of human and animal emotions.* Oxford: Oxford University Press.

Perlow, L.A. (1998). Boundary control: The social ordering of work and family time in a high-tech corporation. *Administrative Science Quarterly, 43,* 326–357.

Peterson, C., Park, N., Hall, N., & Seligman, M.E.P. (2009). Zest and work. *Journal of Organizational Behavior, 30,* 161–172.

Porath, C., Spreitzer, G., Gibson, C., & Stevens, F. (2008). *Human thriving at work: Antecedents and outcomes.* Working paper, Ross School of Business, Ann Arbor, MI.

Putnam, R.D. (2000). *Bowling alone: The collapse and revival of American community.* New York: Simon & Schuster.

Quinn, R.W. (2007). Energizing others in work relationships. In J.E. Dutton, & B.R. Ragins (Eds.), *Exploring positive relationships at work: Building a theoretical and research foundation* (pp. 73–90). New York: Routledge.

Quinn, R., & Dutton, J.E. (2005). Coordination as Energy-in-Conversation: A process theory of organizing. *Academy of Management Review, 30,* 36–57.

Quinn, R., Spreitzer, G., & Lam, C.F. (2011). An integrative model of human energy at work. Working paper, Ross School of Business, Ann Arbor, MI.

Reis, H.T., Sheldon, K.M., Gable, S.L., Roscoe, J., & Ryan, R.M. (2000). Daily well-being: The role of autonomy, competence, and relatedness. *Personality and Social Psychology Bulletin, 26,* 419–435.

Rich, B.L., LePine, J.A., & Crawford, E.R. (2009). Job engagement: Antecedents and effects on job performance. *Academy of Management Journal, 53,* 617–635.

Rogers, A.E., Hwang, W., Scott, L.D., Aiken, L.H., & Dinges, D.F. (2004). The working hours of hospital staff nurses and patient safety. *Health Affairs, 23,* 202–212.

Rothbard, N.P. (2001). Enriching or depleting? The dynamics of engagement in work and family roles. *Administrative Science Quarterly, 46,* 655.

Russell, J.A., & Feldman Barrett, L. (1999). Core affect, prototypical emotional episodes, and other things called *emotion*: Dissecting the elephant. *Journal of Personality and Social Psychology, 76,* 805–819.

Ryan, R.M., Bernstein, J.H., & Brown, K.W. (2010). Weekends, work, and wellbeing: Psychological need satisfactions and day of the week effects on mood, vitality, and physical symptoms. *Journal of Social and Clinical Psychology, 29,* 95–122.

Ryan, R.M., & Deci, E.L. (2000). Self-determination theory and the facilitation of intrinsic motivation, social development, and well-being. *American Psychologist, 55,* 58–68.

Ryan, R.M., & Frederick, C.M. (1997). On energy, personality and health: Subjective vitality as a dynamic reflection of well-being. *Journal of Personality, 65,* 529–565.

Salanova, M., Agut, S., & Peiro, J.M. (2005). Linking organizational resources and work engagement to employee performance and customer loyalty: The mediation of service climate. *Journal of Applied Psychology, 90,* 1217–1227.

Schaufeli, W.B., & Bakker, A.B. (2004). Job demands, job resources, and their relationship with burnout and engagement: A multi-sample study. *Journal of Organizational Behavior, 25,* 293.

Schaufeli, W.B., Salanova, M., Gonzalez-Roma, V., & Bakker, A.B. (2002). The measurement of engagement and burnout: A two sample confirmatory factor analytic approach. *Journal of Happiness Studies, 3,* 71–92.

Sheldon, K.M., Ryan, R., & Reis, H.T. (1996). What makes for a good day? Competence and autonomy in the day and in the person. *Personality and Social Psychology Bulletin, 22,* 1270–1279.

Shirom, A. (2003). Feeling vigorous at work? The construct of vigor and the study of positive affect in organizations. In D.G.P.L. Perrewe (Ed.), *Research in organizational stress and well-being* Vol. 3 (pp. 135–165). Greenwich, CT: JAI Press.

Sonnentag, S. (2003). Recovery, work engagement, and proactive behavior: A new look at the interface between nonwork and work. *Journal of Applied Psychology, 88,* 518–528.

Sonnentag, S., Binnewies, C., & Mojza, E.J. (2008). "Did you have a nice evening?" A day-level study on recovery experiences, sleep, and affect. *Journal of Applied Psychology, 93,* 674–684.

Sonnentag, S., & Fritz, C. (2007). The recovery experience questionnaire: Development and validation of a measure for assessing recuperation and unwinding from work. *Journal of Occupational Health Psychology, 12,* 204–221.

Sonnentag, S., & Jelden, S. (in press). Job stressors and the pursuit of sport activities: A day-level perspective. *Journal of Occupational Health Psychology.*

Sonnentag, S., & Niessen, C. (2008). Staying vigorous until work is over: The role of trait vigour, day-specific work experiences, and recovery. *Journal of Occupational and Organizational Psychology, 81,* 435–458.

Sonnentag, S., & Zijlstra, F.R.H. (2006). Job characteristics and off-job activities as predictors of need for recovery, well-being, and fatigue. *Journal of Applied Psychology, 91,* 330–350.

Spreitzer, G., & Sonenshein, S. (2004). Toward the construct definition of positive deviance. *American Behavioral Scientist, 77,* 828–847.

Spreitzer, G., Sutcliffe, K., Dutton, J., Sonenshein, S., & Grant, A.M. (2005). A socially embedded model of thriving at work. *Organization Science, 16,* 537–549.

Sutcliffe, K.M., & Vogus, T.J. (2003). Organizing for resilience. In K.S. Cameron, J.E. Dutton, & R. Quinn (Eds.), *Positive organizational scholarship: Foundations of a new discipline* (pp. 94–110). San Francisco: Berrett-Koehler.

Thayer, R.E. (1978). Toward a psychological theory of multidimensional activation (arousal). *Motivation and Emotion, 2,* 1–34.

Thayer, R.E. (1987). Energy, tiredness, and tension effects as a function of a sugar snack versus moderate exercise. *Journal of Personality and Social Psychology, 52,* 119–125.

Thayer, R.E. (1989). *The biopsychology of mood and arousal.* New York: Oxford University Press.

Thayer, R.E., Newman, R., & McClain, T.M. (1994). Self-regulation of mood: Strategies for changing a bad mood, raising energy, and reducing tension. *Journal of Personality and Social Psychology, 67,* 910–925.

Thayer, R.E., Peters, D.P., Takahashi, P.J., & Birkhead-Flight, A.M. (1993). Mood and behavior (smoking and sugar snacking) following moderate exercise: A partial test of self-regulation theory. *Personality and individual differences, 14,* 97–104.

Tremblay, M.A., Blanchard, C.M., Pelletier, L.G., & Vallerand, R.J. (2006). A dual route in explaining health outcomes in natural disaster. *Journal of Applied Social Psychology, 36,* 1502–1522.

Trougakos, J.P., Beal, D.J., Green, S.G., & Weiss, H.M. (2008). Making the break count: An episodic examination of recovery activities, emotional experiences, and positive affective displays. *Academy of Management Journal, 51,* 131–146.

Vogel, B., & Bruch, H. (2011). Organizational energy. In K. Cameron, & G. Spreitzer (Eds.), *Oxford handbook of positive organizational scholarship.* New York: Oxford University Press.

Vohs, K.D., & Heatherton, T.F. (2000). Self-regulatory failure: A resource-depletion approach. *Psychological Science, 121,* 249–254.

Watson, D., Clark, L.A., & Tellegen, A. (1988). Development and validation of brief measures of Positive and Negative Affect: The PANAS scales. *Journal of Personality and Social Psychology, 54,* 1063–1070.

Webb, T.L., & Sheeran, P. (2002). Can implementation intentions help to overcome ego-depletion? *Journal of Experimental Social Psychology, 39,* 279–286.

Westley, F.R. (1990). Middle managers and strategy: Microdynamics of inclusion. *Strategic Management Journal, 11,* 337–351.

Westman, M., & Eden, D. (1997). Effects of a respite from work on burnout: Vacation relief and fade-out. *Journal of Applied Psychology, 82,* 516–527.

Wrzesniewski, A., & Dutton, J.E. (2001). Crafting a Job: Employees as active crafters of their work. *Academy of Management Review, 26*(2), 179–201.

Positive Emotions

Broadening and Building Upward Spirals of Sustainable Enterprise

Leslie E. Sekerka, Tanya Vacharkulksemsuk, *and* Barbara L. Fredrickson

Abstract

Research to better understand the broaden-and-build theory of positive emotions has provided new vistas for how emotions impact people in their daily organizational life. In this chapter, we draw from a decade of research to show how positive emotions, fueled by strength-based inquiry, can help create upward spirals of positive development through transformative cooperation. We show how the benefits of these emotions can transcend the individual experience and expand through the organization and into the broader community, thus contributing to sustainable enterprise.

Keywords: Positive emotions, broaden-and-build theory, sustainable enterprise, strength-based inquiry, transformative cooperation

It has been more than a decade since Fredrickson (1998) first asked: *What good are positive emotions?* Since then, applications of the broaden-and-build theory have provided new vistas for how emotions impact people in their organizational life. Researchers have moved to validate how employee decisions are inextricably linked to emotions at every level of analysis, from the individual up to the organizational (e.g., Elfenbein, 2007). Research reflects how positive emotions shape favorable attitudes and outlooks known to stimulate learning and task accomplishment and are associated with successful actions, such as prosocial behaviors, group development, and establishing ethical cultures and ongoing learning (Arnaud & Sekerka, 2010; Akrivou, Boyatzis, & McLeod, 2006; Luthans, Vogelgesang, & Lester, 2006; Triliva & Dafermos, 2008). Thus, the exploration of positive emotions has demonstrated how to cultivate workplace climates that foster new ways of thinking that may help generate more sustainable and healthier business practices. Although today's managers are now aware that they need to spend time dealing with the emotional aspects of work, the desire to achieve efficiency and effectiveness through a more strategic cognitive-based approach remains dominant in many organizations.

In this chapter, we examine how the benefits of positive emotions serve as a mechanism to achieve transformation, contributing to an organization's dynamic evolution through upward spirals of development. Establishing cooperation toward change and innovation is especially important in today's global workplace, where positive emotions may be useful to cultivate responsibility toward broadening and building organizational development. The long-term existence and development of humans and organizations depend, largely, on application of the concept of sustainable enterprise. As described by Potocan and Mulej (2007) and Pfeffer (2010), this means evidence of moving toward the achievement of economic, ecological, ethical, and social aims. Our review of the research on positive emotions demonstrates how they are an important feature of organizations that hope to foster this type of healthy growth and ongoing development.

Broaden-and-Build Theory of Positive Emotions

The basis of our discussion stems from Fredrickson's (1998, 2001, 2009) *broaden-and-build theory* of positive emotions. Unlike negative emotions (e.g., anger, fear, worry), which narrow people's attention and mobilize cardiovascular and other bodily systems to support quick, survival-promoting action, positive emotions (e.g., joy, interest, appreciation) function in the short term to *broaden* one's attention and quell heightened bodily reactivity to *build* one's cognitive, social, psychological, and physical resources over the long term.

Overview of the Broaden Effects

Decades of experimental research pioneered by Isen and her colleagues provide evidence suggesting the causal effects of emotions such as joy. We know that positive emotions can influence a wide range of cognitive outcomes, including patterns of unusual thought (Isen, Johnson, Mertz, & Robinson, 1985), flexibility and inclusion (Isen & Daubman, 1984), creativity (Isen, Daubman, & Nowicki, 1987), and receptivity to new information (Estrada, Isen, & Young, 1997). Further social psychological inquiry into positive emotions reflects their ability to favorably alter thoughts and attention. In behavioral lab studies, for example, Fredrickson and Branigan (2005) induced different emotions in people, followed by a task asking participants to list the things that they felt like doing at that time, given their current emotional state. Those prompted to feel positive emotions listed more varied potential actions as compared to those feeling negative or no emotions. More recently, laboratory evidence for the broaden effects of positive emotions appear in studies using neuroimaging (Schmitz, De Rosa, & Anderson, 2009), eyetracking (Wadlinger & Isaacowitz, 2006), and autobiographical memory recall tasks (Talarico, Berntsen, & Rubin, 2009), showing that positive emotions shift participants' attention to perceive a wider scope.

At the interpersonal level, positive emotions have been associated with enhanced attention to others and reduced distinctions between the self and others. For example, researchers found that students who experienced more positive emotions during their first weeks at their university reported a greater sense of "oneness" between themselves and their newly assigned roommates, and then moved to develop a more complex understanding of that person (Waugh & Fredrickson, 2006). Furthermore, induced positive emotions increase trust between acquaintances (Dunn & Schweitzer, 2005), strengthen existing interpersonal relationships (Algoe, Fredrickson, Gable, & Strachman,

under review), and are foundational in creating bonds and opportunities for interdependence (Cohn & Fredrickson, 2006; Gable, Reis, Impett, & Asher, 2004). In sum, empirical evidence demonstrates the many ways in which positive emotions broaden people's mindsets, expand how they view the self in relation to others, and influence the inner workings of one's social world.

Overview of the Build Effects

The notion that positive emotions help to build capacity reflects the fact that the benefits of these emotions extend beyond simply feeling good at any moment. The terms, as suggested by the theory's name, are corollary: *broadened* awareness actually *builds* enduring personal resources. These resources can emerge in several different forms, including cognitive (e.g., mindfulness skills or intellectual complexity); social (e.g., high-quality friendships and strong social support networks); psychological (exercising resilience or optimism in challenging life situations); or physical (e.g., the ability to rebound from stress-induced peaks in blood pressure). Hence, rather than merely signaling optimal functioning, positive emotions actually help to generate personal, interpersonal, and organizational growth. To examine the build effect, Fredrickson and her colleagues (Fredrickson, Cohn, Coffey, Pek, & Finkel, 2008) followed research participants who were randomly assigned to a group that learned skills to self-generate positive emotions (via loving-kindness meditation workshops) or a monitoring, waitlist control condition. After the meditation workshops ended, those in the loving-kindness meditation group reported greater levels of mindfulness, self-acceptance, positive relations with others, better physical health, and fewer symptoms of depression, effects fully mediated by increases in daily positive emotions.

Positive Emotions in the Workplace

Correlational studies in organizational behavior also suggest an association between positive emotions and built resources. Positive emotions are linked with work achievement and high-quality social environments (Staw, Sutton, & Pelled, 1994), and creativity (Amabile, Barsade, Mueller, & Staw, 2005). Scholars continue to investigate how positive approaches are associated with enhanced satisfaction, motivation, and productivity (Martin, 2005). For example, George (1998) found that those with a "can-do" attitude can help create positive emotional climates that contribute to increases in company sales and customers. Given that positive emotions are drivers of positive attitudes, high-quality social milieus, and generative environments, the broaden-and-build capabilities produced by them are particularly relevant when leaders want to cultivate organizational change and development. We now take a closer look at how positive emotions are recognized as valuable assets in the workplace.

Since the introduction of the broaden-and-build theory, a host of revelations have emerged, showing that individual decisions, actions, and competencies are associated with positive emotions. For example, leaders with tendencies toward feeling pride and gratitude are likely to demonstrate prosocial behaviors, namely, engagement in activities displaying social justice and altruism (Michie, 2009). Positive emotions are also more closely associated with transformational leadership, rather than transactional leadership (Rowold & Rohmann, 2009). In fact, Bono and Ilies (2006) found that leaders' expression of positive emotions in the workplace creates perceptions among employees of leaders' effectiveness and elevates their desire to work for them. Because leaders often drive how employees feel, emotions expressed from the "top" can truly make a difference in the organization's climate, which can contribute to higher revenue and growth (Ozcelik, Langton, & Aldrich, 2008). Evidence continues to emerge reflecting how employee performance is associated with positive emotional experiences. For example, the display of positive social self-conscious emotions, such as pride and empathy, have beneficial effects on personal accomplishment (Zapf & Holz, 2006) and can favorably impact customer relations (Bagozzi, 2006).

Research on compassion in the workplace, concern for those suffering or facing difficulty, has been associated with positive emotions and affective commitment (Lilius et al., 2008). Here, we see that having an ability to cope and provide support to others in organizational settings is essential, but especially during recessionary periods when downsizing and layoffs persist, leading to extended periods of stress. We also know that proactive engagement in issues that produce worry and concern, such as environmental and global justice, employ cognitive strategies that activate positive emotions and constructive action (Ojala, 2007). Research shows how organizational citizenship behavior associated with pride can help people deal with difficult and even oppressive circumstances (Hareli & Tzafrir, 2006).

We know that helping individuals establish positive meaning in their job and organizational role contributes to competence, achievement, involvement, and social connection (Folkman, 1997; Ryff & Singer, 1998; Wrzesniewski & Dutton, 2001). When individuals support others to seek positive meaning in their work—bringing forward what they value most—gratitude and enthusiasm freely emerge. Positive emotions bolster cooperation as employees prepare for organizational change (Sekerka, Zolin, & Goosby Smith, 2009). We also know that character strengths closely associated with positive emotions, such as optimism, hope, efficacy, and resilience, favorably impact employees' attitudes and behaviors that support transformation. In fact, psychologists studying success in business point to such character strengths as playing a more important role in success—more so than skill, education, and to some degree, even talent (Siegel, 2006).

In terms of groups, positive emotions are associated with high-quality team member exchange linked with productivity (Tse & Dasborough, 2008). When groups share relational outcomes, positive emotions and learning contribute to a sense of empowerment and community. And, there is theoretical work that describes how intentional group change can benefit from positive emotions (Howard, 2006). At the organizational level, research has found correlations with positive emotional climates and fostering development, connections, and social and psychological capital (e.g., Bushell, 1998; Avey, Wernsing, & Luthans, 2008). Positive emotions can also favorably impact employee development and retention rates (Dries & Pepermans, 2007). Finally, a theoretical explication has described how positive emotions contribute to the development of psychological capital, which helps employees build resiliency through self-enhancement, external attribution, and hardiness (Luthans, Vgelgesang, & Lester, 2006).

Losada and Heaphy (2004) used nonlinear dynamical modeling to show that a high degree of connectivity and positive-to-negative ratios within an organization correlated with higher team performance. Not only did the mathematical models show that high-performance teams utilized a broader range of behavioral repertoires in the short term, but they also built durable psychological and social resources through strong connections with fellow team members. In contrast, lower-performing teams appeared to have low levels of connectivity and lower positive-to-negative ratios, which made them more likely to get "stuck" in situations because of a limited behavioral repertoire and decreased likelihood of building strong team member connections. With this information, research suggests that people simply perform better when their workday experiences include more positive emotions, adding to intrinsic motivation and more favorable perceptions of their work, team, leaders, and organizations (Amabile & Kramer, 2007). Indeed, later work by Fredrickson and Losada (2005) suggests that an optimal positivity ratio is above 2.9:1.

That said, we recognize that negativity inevitably arises in the workplace, and when it does, the negativity bias (Baumeister, Bratslavsky, Finkenauer, & Vohs, 2001) tends to take over. It would thus be advantageous for organizations to be equipped with positive emotions when faced with such situations in order to achieve, or maintain, an optimal positivity ratio. Given the attractive outcomes associated with an effective positive emotional ratio, leaders may be interested in cultivating them, especially if they want to extend their organization's capacity. We now turn to a particular form of change resourced by positive emotions: *transformative cooperation*. In describing this process, we discuss how the effects that stem from positive emotional climates both create and fuel this process. Then, we consider how these benefits can extend into the stakeholder community through upward spirals of growth and development.

Positive Emotions Fuel Transformative Cooperation

Transformation is a fundamental shift in how people view, understand, interpret, or make use of their organization and their role within it. Aspects of the phenomenon are described by change management scholars, who refer to second-order, radical, or gamma change (e.g., Golembiewski, Billingsely, & Yeager, 1979). This type of change goes to the root of how people frame and define their organization and work, in contrast to first-order or alpha change, which incrementally focuses on resolving specific problems (Bartunek & Moch, 1987). *Cooperation* is when people come together to produce output that provides those involved with something of value, a collaborative endeavor in which mutual benefits are achieved as a result of shared actions (Agnes & Laird, 1996).

Thus, the term *transformative cooperation* is described as a specific type of change initiated by people who pool their knowledge, skills, and passion to collectively conceptualize and construct a novel and dynamic future (Sekerka & Fredrickson, 2008). This form of change is not about fixing the current system; rather, it is a deliberate and continuous effort toward creating new forms of organizing. Transformative cooperation is a platform to marshal shared values and mutual benefits for all involved. But, because it is a generative process, it cannot be declared, ordered, or implemented via mandate. Rather, it is through strength-based discovery into what people collectively value that employees co-create the purpose and meaning of their work—from this point of mutual understanding where strengths can be elevated and where assumptions can be altered.

So, how do positive emotions fuel such an effort, contributing to individual and organizational development? We argue that positive emotions that stem from strength-based inquiry initiate transformative cooperation. This helps to establish a positive emotional climate that broadens and builds relational strength, thereby expanding individual, as well as collective capacity toward innovation. As depicted in Figure 13.1, inquiry into the strengths within the organization helps to create upward spirals of growth and development, starting with individuals and extending outward toward the community.

Creating Upward Spirals of Organizational Development
STRENGTH-BASED INQUIRY
Discovery based upon targeting individual and collective strengths is a portal to transformative cooperation. Through a variety of collaborative exercises, strength-based organizational development techniques encourage people to share positive memories through stories, testimonials, and discussions that outline what they appreciate and value about their work. This process helps people discover the best of their organization and themselves as the focal point for change, rather than looking at problems and symptoms of dysfunction. An *appreciative inquiry* (AI) summit, for example, is a platform for creating a positive, emotionally charged event that, when followed by the implementation of practices, supports the cultivation of whole-scale transformation (Cooperrider & Srivastva, 1999).

As people work together to highlight, observe, and define their organization's positive core, they are better able to identify what they deeply value. From these shared values, an ideal vision is imagined; here, participants ascertain what needs to be done and how they can work together to achieve it. Building from existing assets, the positive core of

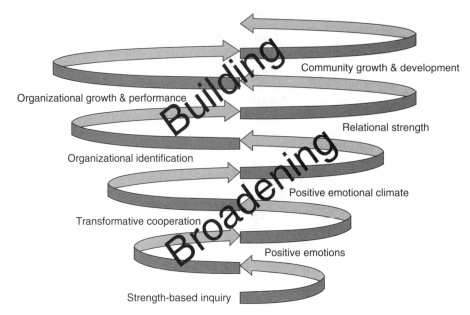

Fig. 13.1 Broadening and building in organizational settings. Strength-based inquiry fuels the beneficial effects of positive emotions at multiple levels, broadening and building sustainable enterprise.

their personal and collective strengths, employees begin a process of self-directed organizing (Cooperrider & Whitney, 2001). Employees then align themselves in unique ways by forming groups and taking on new roles and functions. They rally around shared strengths, generating positive energy via interests that help them produce new organizational relationships. This creates fresh ways to accomplish their work, shaping different constellations of organizational forms for task accomplishment. As described by Bartunek and Woodman (2011; Chapter 55, this volume), focusing on the positive in organizational settings contributes to positive psychological capital (hope, optimism, resilience), an important factor in reducing dysfunctional attitudes and behaviors during organizational change. Positive relationships and relational coordination have also been shown to contribute to resiliency in the face of work stressors that stem from external pressures (Gittell, 2008).

The act of working on a collective effort, using positive experiences as levers for development, prompts the creative thinking necessary to envision an innovative future. This process is explicit, establishes joint ownership and buy-in, and fosters transformative cooperation. Given the distinct social origins of positive emotions that people experience when interacting with others (e.g., Vittengl & Holt, 2000; Watson, Clark, McIntyre, & Hamaker, 1992), it is no surprise that people feel good when working together in this fashion. As positively

charged discovery continues, a cascade of ideas stimulates more activity and innovation. The process is described in the theory of positive change (Cooperrider & Sekerka, 2006), with positive emotions serving as the initiators (for examples see http://appreciativeinquiry.case.edu/).

POSITIVE EMOTIONS: BROADENING RELATIONSHIPS

Once initiated, the broadening effects of transformative cooperation continue to build capacity through inclusion and empowerment. When positive emotional experiences influence how we see ourselves, broadening the scope of self-perception to include others, the distinction between self and others becomes blurred. As a result, people become more likely to adopt the characteristics of others, escalating inclusivity. Responsibility toward others and shared resources can be nurtured in opposition to fueling competition over scarcity or a sense of entitlement, often the by-products of analyzing dysfunction (Sekerka, Zolin, & Goosby Smith, 2009). As employees engender appreciation and target their common values, it becomes easier to build and extend relationships and trust. Conversely, a focus on differences and problems cultivates an "us-versus-them" mindset, which fosters resentments (Gilmore, Shea, & Useem, 1997). As people reframe and expand their identity, they can begin to alter their assumptions and create new perspectives. This can be a turning point, moving organizations from a self-interest orientation, in which reactionary problem solving is directed toward survival, to a more generative other-orientation, in which interdependencies support the concept of collaborative thriving.

Given that positive emotions contribute to an expansion of the self, experiences associated with gratitude, appreciation, and other positive emotions are expected to increase employees' personal identification with others in the organization (Dutton & Dukerich, 1991; Dutton, Dukerich, & Harquail, 1994). Positive experiences that call for participation in co-creating what it means to be at work help people see themselves aligned with others. Furthermore, people experiencing positive emotions become more helpful to others, which is attributable to people becoming more flexible, creative, empathic, compassionate, and respectful.

But being helpful not only springs from positive emotional states—it can also produce them. For example, those who give help may feel proud of their actions. This experience not only creates a momentary boost in self-esteem, but can also prompt people to envisage future achievements in similar domains, motivating them to help again (Fredrickson, 2000). Social psychologists have also found a robust reciprocal association between gratitude and social support, edifying relational strength. Just as the person who gives help experiences positive emotions, the one who receives it is likely to feel grateful. Gratitude not only creates good feelings but also produces a myriad of beneficial social outcomes (e.g., Algoe, Haidt, & Gable, 2008; Algoe & Haidt, 2009; McCullough, Kilpatrick, Emmons, & Larson, 2001). For example, recall the last time someone engaged in an act of kindness toward you. Did you feel the desire to do something nice for them in return? Research shows that grateful people often feel the urge to "give back." This reciprocal nature of gratitude reinforces positive action and endorses its continuance.

POSITIVE EMOTIONS: BUILDING OUTWARD EXPANSION

Moving beyond the broadening effects of positive emotions, we see how they also build capacity, strengthening social relationships over time. People who experience positive emotions continually grow toward further optimal functioning (Fredrickson, 2003; Fredrickson & Joiner, 2002; Fredrickson et al., 2008). When genuine feelings of appreciation are cultivated, employees are more interested in working together to forge teams and coalitions in which

they stimulate ideas, achieve shared goals, and foster ongoing learning and development (Neville, 2008). As organizations continue to cultivate a positive emotional climate, they will likely benefit from the increased strength of their relationships. Such experiences can accumulate, compound, and ultimately, serve to strengthen the collective. Positive emotions promote constructive interpersonal engagement and encourage trust, which predicts effective and integrative negotiations (Anderson & Thompson, 2004), as well as the desire to contribute to the effectiveness of the organization (Fredrickson, 2000). This gives us a sense of the build effects, reflecting the macro outcomes associated with positive emotional experiences.

Again, looking to Figure 13.1, we see that as positive emotions contribute to the relational strength of organizations, this builds capacity by increasing relational expansion. In turn, this helps increase social capital, a resource that can contribute to growth and favorable performance outcomes, antecedents for work-related effectiveness. As positive emotional climates foster relational strength and growth, more people want to engage and become part of the whole, one that is working to serve a greater good (Barros & Cooperrider, 2000). Positive emotions are also associated with cultivating an ethical climate, one that supports sustainable enterprise (Arnaud & Sekerka, 2010). The strengthening of relationships through trust and cooperation creates an upward spiral of positive development through a sustained openness to expansion, energizing a holistic stance through acts of social support. As this cycle is established—one of continuous value creation—whole communities can be transformed into a more integrated complementary atmosphere. This relates nicely to what Hoffman and Haigh describe as a shift to a focus on abundance, rather than traditional deficit-based thinking. Such a perspective can provide people and their organizations with an opportunity to flourish more broadly, extending awareness and appreciation for economic growth pursued in a manner that assures protection of both social and natural environmental systems.

The benefits of positive emotions and their association with an expansion of relational capacities are boundary-free. That is, positive emotions provide the foundation for optimal functioning, which has unlimited potential to extend outward to society. The implication is that the positive emotions of employees' momentary experiences can be both generators and long-range indicators of performance and sustained well-being. Once initiated, transformative cooperation can help generate outcomes that contribute to upward growth spirals that reverberate outward to help build stronger communities.

Given the negativity bias noted earlier, especially in today's economically distressed workplace environments, the notion of too much positivity has not been an overt concern as of late. However, evidence suggests that some people value change processes that stem from a problem-based focus, which can effectively drive change (Sekerka, Zolin, & Goosby Smith, 2009). But the negative sentiments that typically accompany this process, emotions used to rally energy for transformation, are not sustainable. When fear or anger are used as levers for creating deep change, they will be unlikely contributors to individual or collective well-being. To address this concern, new process forms, such as *balanced experience inquiry*, have emerged. This particular process moves to cultivate positive emotions, while still honoring the relevance and value of issues underlying the need for change (Sekerka & Godwin, 2010). Such techniques accentuate strengths, but do not ignore the negative issues typically associated with the desire for change. Clearly, there is much work to be done to understand how to cultivate balance in an effort to create and support transformative cooperation. But, establishing this balance will unlikely emerge from a focus on achieving one particular goal or ideal. Rather, it will be an effort in flexibility and resilience, bending and integrating process components that address differences in people and their situational contexts. A robust form of positive adaptation will access the broadening and building benefits that stem from cultivating positive emotions, while also attending to systemic realities that generate negativity.

One thing is sure, regardless of the process selected, as employees work to develop new methods and technologies to support sustainable development in practice, obstacles will occur. Positive emotions, with their durable benefits, will likely support resiliency in times of difficulty to help people rebound from these challenges. The link between positive emotions and their role in helping people transform assumptions also helps them build resiliency and social integration. Such benefits are ideally suited toward creating organizations that want to become more responsible in their everyday business practices. Fostering a shared commitment to sustainable development means that relational strength will contribute to the organization's growth and performance, regardless of setbacks that may temporarily hinder progress. When people recognize that they are part of something that adds to the greater good, motivation and commitment can become protracted over time. Key to such efforts is maintaining a shared respect for ecological values that go beyond the self, actualized through cooperation and empathy. Partnerships and cooperatives help bolster this commitment within organizations, then outwardly toward stakeholders and among different institutions. As this cycle of value creation is established, industries can be transformed into more responsible and mindful entities.

Future Directions

We opened the chapter by referring to Fredrickson's original question: *What good are positive emotions?* A case has been made that positive emotions are indeed useful; yet, some scholars remain dubious (cf. Linley, Joseph, Harrington, & Wood, 2006). For scholars to remain productive in this area of study, they will need to integrate disorder and dysfunction with achievement, aspirations, and performance. To achieve robust outcomes, organizations must not only support the cultivation and extension of positive emotions, but also work at understanding how to effectively address and draw strength from negative emotions as well. Researchers must continue to explore how people can better manage and work through both positive and negative affective events (rather than simply reducing the negative) to maintain a more balanced approach toward task accomplishment and overall performance. In pursuing this focus on integration and balance, questions for future research include:

- Given individual and situational differences, how can people learn to achieve a productive ratio of emotional states to obtain performance goals while also maintaining their mental and physical health?
- How do emotions operate at the dyadic and small-group level to influence an organization's performance outcomes?
- What training and development processes can be used to cultivate change from a balanced perspective leveraging strengths, while also honoring areas of dysfunction?
- What drives the build effects of positive emotions in workplace settings? To what extent are the long-term effects sustained in organizations by bottom-up versus top-down forces?
- What role does resiliency play in how emotions marshal commitment within and among organizations?

- How can the broaden-and-build theory of positive emotions be used on a larger scale, to help explain protracted efforts toward sustainable enterprise?
- What insights can be drawn from research on the positivity ratio? Specifically, how does this work inform the development of change processes to achieve a more balanced effort, finding a sustainable weave to generate benefits from positive emotions, while also moving to address problems typically associated with negative emotions?

Although our discussion has highlighted the broaden-and-build effects of positive emotions, research has just scratched the surface of how the theory can be applied to better understand individual, organizational, and community development. We have come a long way in showing how individual feelings of gratitude, pride, appreciation, interest, and enthusiasm can instill upward spirals of development. It is up to the next generation of scholars to use these insights to help create healthier more sustainable organizations, and, in doing so, widen the interdisciplinary bridge between social psychology and organizational sciences.

Conclusion

Understanding what creates an effective and sustainable workplace is nearly impossible without considering the influence of emotions. In this chapter, we explained how positive emotions can be a powerful mechanism for organizational development. Given the research prompted by scholars to date, we know that a focus on the mechanistic operations and one-time fixes to drive production are not enough to promote the systemic and dynamic processes needed for organizations in the 21st century. As our chapter suggests, the broaden-and-build effects of positive emotions can be used as drivers for ongoing change dynamics, such as the creation of organizations that genuinely reflect the meaning of sustainable enterprise. Evidence from both social psychological and organizational studies suggests that positive emotions hold adaptive value that transcends "feeling good" at the individual level in a way to influence grander reverberating effects on larger contexts. Positive emotions have been shown to have the power to transform individuals, small groups, and whole organizations, in both the short and long term, giving us reason to be optimistic about successful sustainable enterprise in organizations.

References

Agnes, M., & Laird, C. (1996). *Webster's new world dictionary and thesaurus.* New York: Macmillan.

Akrivou, K., Boyatzis, R.E., & McLeod, P.L. (2006). The evolving group: Towards a prescriptive theory of intentional group development. *The Journal of Management Development, 25,* 689–706.

Algoe, S.B., Fredrickson, B.L., Gable, S.L., & Strachman, A. (under review). Beyond "thanks!": High-quality expressions of appreciation strengthen relationships. Manuscript submitted for publication.

Algoe, S.B., & Haidt, J. (2009). Witnessing excellence in action: The "other-praising" emotions of elevation, gratitude, and admiration. *Journal of Positive Psychology, 4,* 105–127.

Algoe, S.B., Haidt, J., & Gable, S.L. (2008). Beyond reciprocity: Gratitude and relationships in everyday life. *Emotion, 8,* 425–429.

Amabile, T.M., Barsade, S.G., Mueller, J.S., & Staw, B.M. (2005). Affect and creativity at work. *Administrative Science Quarterly, 50,* 367–403.

Amabile, T.M., & Kramer, S.J. (2007). Inner work life: Understanding the subtext of business performance. *Harvard Business Review, 85,* 72–86.

Anderson, C., & Thompson, L. (2004). Affect from the top down: How powerful individuals' positive affect shapes negotiations. *Organizational Behavior and Human Decision Processes, 95,* 125–139.

Arnaud, A., & Sekerka, L.E. (2010). Positively ethical: The establishment of innovation in support of sustainability. *International Journal of Sustainable Strategic Management. 2,* 121–137.

Avey, J., Wernsing, T., & Luthans, F. (2008). Can positive employees help positive organizational change? Impact of psychological capital and emotions on relevant attitudes and behaviors. *Journal of Applied Behavioral Science, 44,* 48–70.

Bagozzi, R.E. (2006). The role of social and self-conscious emotions in the regulation of business-to-business relationships in salesperson-customer interactions. *The Journal of Business & Industrial Marketing, 21,* 453–457.

Barros, I.O., & Cooperrider, D.L. (2000). A story of Nutrimental in Brazil: How wholeness, appreciation, and inquiry bring out the best in human organization. *Organizational Development Journal, 18,* 22–29.

Bartunek, J.M., & Moch, M. (1987). First order, second order and third order change and OD interventions. *Journal of Applied Behavioral Science, 23,* 483–500.

Bartunek, J.M., & Woodman, R.W. (2011). Organizational development. In K.S. Cameron & G.M. Spreitzer (Eds.), *The Oxford handbook of positive organizational scholarship.* New York: Oxford University Press.

Baumeister, R., Bratslavsky, E., Finkenauer, C., & Vohs, K. (2001). Bad is stronger than good. *Review of General Psychology, 5,* 323–370.

Bono, J.E., & Ilies, R. (2006). Charisma, positive emotions and mood contagion. *Leadership Quarterly, 17*(4), 317–344.

Bushell, S. (1998). Putting your emotions to work. *The Journal for Quality and Participation, 21,* 49–54.

Cohn, M.A., & Fredrickson, B.L. (2006). Beyond the moment, beyond the self: Shared ground between selective investment theory and the broaden-and-build theory of positive emotions. *Psychological Inquiry, 17,* 39–44.

Cooperrider, D.L., & Sekerka, L.E. (2006). Toward a theory of positive organizational change. In J.V. Gallos (Ed.),

Organization development: A Jossey-Bass reader (pp. 223–238). San Francisco: John Wiley & Sons.

Cooperrider, D.L., & Srivastva, S. (1999). Appreciative inquiry in organizational life. In S. Srivastva, & D.L. Cooperrider (Eds.), *Appreciative management and leadership: The power of positive thought and action in organization* (rev. ed., pp. 401–441). Cleveland, OH: Lakeshore Communications.

Cooperrider, D.L., & Whitney, D. (2001). A positive revolution in change. In D.L. Cooperrider, P. Sorenson, D. Whitney, & T. Yeager (Eds.), *Appreciative inquiry: An emerging direction for organization development* (pp. 9–29). Champaign, IL: Stipes.

Dries, N., & Pepermans, R. (2007). Using emotional intelligence to identify high potential: A metacompetency perspective. *Leadership & Organization Development Journal, 28*, 749–770.

Dunn, J., & Schweitzer, M. (2005). Feeling and believing: The influence of emotion on trust. *Journal of Personality and Social Psychology, 88*, 736–748.

Dutton, J.E., & Dukerich, J.M. (1991). Keeping an eye on the mirror: Image and identity in organizational adaptation. *Academy of Management Journal, 34*, 517–554.

Dutton, J.E., Dukerich, J.M., & Harquail, C.V. (1994). Organizational images and member identification. *Administrative Science Quarterly, 39*, 239–263.

Elfenbein, H.A. (2007). Chapter 7: Emotion in organizations. *The Academy of Management Annals, 1*, 315–386.

Estrada, C.A., Isen, A.M., & Young, M.J. (1997). Positive affect facilitates integration of information and decreases anchoring in reasoning among physicians. *Organizational Behavior and Human Decision Processes, 72*, 117–135.

Folkman, S. (1997). Positive psychological states and coping with severe stress. *Social Science Medicine, 45*, 1207–1221.

Fredrickson, B.L. (1998). What good are positive emotions? *Review of General Psychology, 2*, 300–319.

Fredrickson, B.L. (2000). Why positive emotions matter in organizations: Lessons from the broaden-and-build model. *Psychologist-Manager's Journal, Special Issue: Positive Psychology and Its Implications for the Psychologist-Manager, 4*, 131–142.

Fredrickson, B.L. (2001). The role of positive emotions in positive psychology: The broaden-and-build theory of positive emotions. *American Psychologist, 56*, 218–226.

Fredrickson, B.L. (2003). The value of positive emotions. *American Scientist, 91*, 330–335.

Fredrickson, B.L. (2009). *Positivity: Groundbreaking research reveals how to embrace the hidden strength of positive emotions, overcome negativity, and thrive.* New York: Crown.

Fredrickson, B.L., & Branigan, C. (2005). Positive emotions broaden the scope of attention and thought-action repertoires. *Cognition and Emotion, 19*, 313–332.

Fredrickson, B.L., Cohn, M.A., Coffey, K.A., Pek, J., & Finkel, S.M. (2008). Open hearts build lives: Positive emotions, induced through loving-kindness meditation, build consequential personal resources. *Journal of Personality and Social Psychology, 95*, 1045–1062.

Fredrickson, B.L., & Joiner, J. (2002). Positive emotions trigger upward spirals toward emotional well-being. *Psychological Science, 13*, 172–175.

Fredrickson, B.L., & Losada, M. (2005). Positive affect and the complex dynamics of human flourishing. *American Psychologist, 60*, 678–686.

Gable, S.L., Reis, H.T., Impett, E.A., & Asher, E.R. (2004). What do you do when things go right? The intrapersonal and interpersonal benefits of sharing positive events. *Journal of Personality and Social Psychology, 87*, 228–245.

George, J.M. (1998). Salesperson and mood at work: Implications for helping customers. *Journal of Personal Selling and Sales Management, 17*, 23–30.

Gilmore, T.N., Shea, G.P., & Useem, M. (1997). Side effects of corporate cultural transformations. *Journal of Applied Behavioral Science, 33*, 174–190.

Gittell, J.H. (2008). Relationships and resilience: Care provider responses to pressures from managed care. *Journal of Applied Behavioral Science, 44*, 25–47.

Golembiewski, R.T., Billingsely, K., & Yeager, S. (1979). Measuring change and persistence in human affairs: Types of change generated by OD designs. *Journal of Applied Behavioral Science, 1*, 143–155.

Hareli, S., & Tzafrir, S.S. (2006). The role of causal attributions in survivors' emotional reactions to downsizing. *Human Resource Development Review, 5*, 400–422.

Howard, A. (2006). Positive and negative emotional attractors and intentional change. *The Journal of Management Development, 25*, 657–670.

Isen, A.M., & Daubman, K.A. (1984). The influence of affect on categorization. *Journal of Personality and Social Psychology, 47*, 1206–1217.

Isen, A.M., Daubman, K.A., & Nowicki, G.P. (1987). Positive affect facilitates creative problem solving. *Journal of Personality and Social Psychology, 52*, 1122–1131.

Isen, A.M., Johnson, M.M.S., Mertz, E., & Robinson, G.F. (1985). The influence of positive affect on the unusualness of word associations. *Journal of Personality and Social Psychology, 48*, 1413–1426.

Lilius, J.M., Worline, M.C., Maitlis, S., Kanov, J., Dutton, J.E., & Frost, P. (2008). The contours and consequences of compassion at work. *Journal of Organizational Behavior, 29*, 193–218.

Linley, P.A., Joseph, S., Harrington, S., & Wood, A.M. (2006). Positive psychology: Past, present, and (possible) future. *Journal of Positive Psychology, 1*, 3–16.

Losada, M., & Heaphy, E. (2004). The role of positivity and connectivity in the performance of business teams: A nonlinear dynamics model. *American Behavioral Scientist, 47*, 740–765.

Luthans, F., Vogelgesang, G.R., & Lester, P.B. (2006). Developing the psychological capital of resiliency. *Human Resource Development Review, 5*, 25–45.

Martin, A.J. (2005). The role of positive psychology in enhancing satisfaction, motivation, and productivity in the workplace. *Journal of Organizational Behavior Management, 24*, 111–131.

McCullough, M.E., Kilpatrick, S.D., Emmons, R.A., & Larson, D.B. (2001). Is gratitude a moral affect? *Psychological Bulletin, 127*, 249–266.

Michie, S. (2009). Pride and gratitude: How *positive emotions* influence the prosocial behaviors of organizational leaders. *Journal of Leadership & Organizational Studies, 15*, 393–403.

Neville, M. (2008). Positive deviance on the ethical continuum: Green Mountain coffee as a case study in conscientious capitalism, *Business and Society Review, 113*, 555–576.

Ojala, M. (2007). Confronting macrosocial worries: Worry about environmental problems and proactive coping among a group of young volunteers. *Futures, 39*, 729–745.

Ozcelik, H., Langton, N., & Aldrich, H. (2008). Doing well and doing good: The relationship between leadership practices that facilitate a positive emotional climate and organizational performance. *Journal of Managerial Psychology, 23*, 186–203.

Pfeffer, J. (2010). Building sustainable organizations: The human factor. *Academy of Management Perspectives, 24*, 34–45.

Potocan, P., & Mulej, M. (2007). Ethics of a sustainable enterprise and the need for it. *Systemic Practice and Action Research, 20*, 127–140.

Rowold, J., & Rohmann, A. (2009). Transformational and transactional leadership styles, followers' positive and negative emotions, and performance in German nonprofit orchestras. *Nonprofit Management and Leadership, 20*, 41–59.

Ryff, C.D., & Singer, B. (1998). The contours of positive human health. *Psychological Inquiry, 9*, 1–28.

Schmitz, T.W., De Rosa, E., & Anderson, A.K. (2009). Opposing influences of affective state valence on visual cortical encoding. *Journal of Neuroscience, 3*, 7199–7207.

Siegel, L. (2006). *Suite success*. West Babylon, NY: AMACOM.

Sekerka, L.E., & Fredrickson, B.L. (2008). Establishing positive emotional climates to advance organizational transformation. In N.M. Ashkanasy, & C.L. Cooper (Eds.), *Research companion to emotion in organizations* (pp. 531–545). Cheltenham, UK: Edward Elgar Publishing.

Sekerka, L.E., & Godwin, L. (2010). Strengthening professional moral courage: A balanced approach to ethics training. *Training & Management Development Methods, 24*(4), 63–74.

Sekerka, L.E., Zolin, R., & Goosby Smith, J. (2009). Careful what you ask for: How inquiry strategy influences readiness mode. *Organizational Management Journal, 6*, 106–122.

Talarico, J.M., Berntsen, D., & Rubin, D.C. (2009). Positive emotions enhance recall of peripheral details. *Cognition & Emotion, 23*, 380–398.

Triliva, S., & Dafermos, M. (2008). Philosophical dialogues as paths to a more positive psychology. *Journal of Community & Applied Social Psychology, 18*, 17–38.

Tse, H., & Dasborough, M. (2008). A study of exchange and emotions in team member relationships. *Group & Organization Management, 33*, 194–215.

Vittengl, J.R., & Holt, C.S. (2000). Getting acquainted: The relationship of self-disclosure and social attraction to positive affect. *Journal of Social and Personal Relationships, 17*, 53–66.

Wadlinger, H.A., & Isaacowitz, D.M. (2006). Positive mood broadens visual attention to positive stimuli. *Motivation and Emotion, 30*, 89–101.

Watson, D., Clark, L.A., McIntyre, C.W., & Hamaker, S. (1992). Affect, personality, and social activity. *Journal of Personality and Social Psychology, 63*, 1011–1025.

Waugh, C.E., & Fredrickson, B.L. (2006). Nice to know you: Positive emotions, self-other overlap, and complex understanding in the formation of a new relationship. *The Journal of Positive Psychology, 1*, 93–106.

Wrzesniewski, A., & Dutton, J.E. (2001). Crafting a job: Revisioning employees as active crafters of their work. *Academy of Management Review, 26*, 179–201.

Zapf, D., & Holz, M. (2006). On the positive and negative effects of emotion work in organizations. *European Journal of Work and Organizational Psychology, 15*, 1–28.

Subjective Well-being in Organizations

Arnold B. Bakker *and* Wido G.M. Oerlemans

Abstract

This chapter focuses on the concept of subjective well-being (SWB) in organizations. We use the circumplex model of affect as a theoretical framework to distinguish between specific types of work-related subjective well-being, including work engagement, job satisfaction, happiness at work, workaholism, and burnout. In addition, we will link positive types of work-related SWB to job performance. Specific attention is paid to capturing the dynamics of SWB in work settings on a daily basis.

Keywords: Burnout, employee engagement, happiness, job satisfaction, subjective well-being, workaholism

Modern organizations expect their employees to be proactive and show initiative, take responsibility for their own professional development, and to be committed to high-quality performance standards. Thus, employees are needed who feel energetic and dedicated—organizations need engaged workers (Bakker & Schaufeli, 2008). This is illustrated by Ulrich (1997), who writes in his seminal book *Human Resources Champions*: "Employee contribution becomes a critical business issue because in trying to produce more output with less employee input, companies have no choice but to try to engage not only the body but the mind and soul of every employee" (p. 125).

Research has shown that about 85% of all employees in the European Union (Parent-Thirion, Fernández-Macías, Hurley, & Vermeylen, 2007) and 86% of all employees in the United States (Handel, 2005) are (very) satisfied with their jobs. Do these high levels of job satisfaction coincide with high levels of job performance, or is more needed than job satisfaction alone? In recent years, a growing number of researchers have focused on positive indicators of Subjective Well-Being (SWB), including job satisfaction (Judge, Thorensen, Bono, & Patton, 2001), work

engagement (Bakker & Leiter, 2010; Bakker, Schaufeli, Leiter, & Taris, 2008), and happiness at work (e.g., Diener & Biswas-Diener, 2008; Warr, 2007).

This chapter focuses on the concept of positive subjective well-being (SWB) in organizations. In particular, we will use the circumplex model (Russell, 1980, 2003) as a broad theoretical framework to distinguish between positive and negative types of work-related well-being. Positive indicators of SWB include work engagement, happiness at work, and job satisfaction. Negative indicators include workaholism and burnout. In addition, we will discuss the impact of positive work-related SWB on job performance. We will argue that a combination of high pleasure and high activation is needed for optimal job performance. We will close this chapter with a description of exciting new ways to capture the link between positive forms of SWB at work and job performance on an intraindividual and daily basis by using diary study designs and the day reconstruction method.

Defining Subjective Well-being

Subjective well-being refers to how people evaluate their lives. This evaluation may take the form of cognitions when a person makes a conscious evaluative judgment about his or her satisfaction with life as a whole. However, the evaluation of one's life may also be in the form of affect (i.e., as the experience of unpleasant or pleasant emotions in reaction to life). Thus, a person is said to have high SWB if he or she is (a) satisfied with his or her life, and (b) experiences frequent positive emotions such as joy and happiness, and infrequent negative emotions such as sadness and anger (Diener, Sandvik, & Pavot, 1991).

Circumplex Model of Affect

How can experiences of positive emotions be further defined? Russell's (1980, 2003) circumplex model proposes that affective states arise from two fundamental neurophysiological systems, one related to a pleasure–displeasure continuum and the other to arousal, activation, or alertness. Each emotion can be understood as a linear combination of these two dimensions as varying degrees of both pleasure and activation (see Figure 14.1). Specific emotions arise out of patterns of activation within these two neurophysiological systems, together with interpretations and labeling of these emotional experiences.

For instance, the degree of activation while experiencing positive (pleasurable) emotions varies considerably (Freedmann, 1978; Warr, 2007). "Feeling calm and content" implies a lower level of activation compared to "feeling happy, engaged, excited, or enthusiastic". Similarly, unpleasant emotions may range from "feeling bored or depressed" to "feeling upset, anxious, or tense." The circumplex model emphasizes that emotions are not discrete and isolated entities but instead are interrelated based on the two neurophysiological systems of pleasure and activation. Corroborating this, researchers have long noted the difficulty that people have in assessing, discerning, and describing their own emotions (Saarni, 1999). This difficulty suggests that individuals recognize emotions as ambiguous and overlapping experiences. Similar to the spectrum of color, emotions seem to lack the discrete borders that would clearly differentiate one from another (Russell & Fehr, 1994). Indeed, researchers exploring the subjective experience of emotion have noted that emotions are highly intercorrelated both within and between the persons reporting them (Russell & Carroll, 1999). Using statistical techniques such as multidimensional scaling and factor analysis of subjective reports of emotional words, faces, and experiences, research has repeatedly yielded two-dimensional (2-D) models of affective experience (Lang, Bradley, & Cuthbert, 1998; Larsen & Diener, 1992; Russell, 1980; Thayer, 1989).

Work-related Subjective Well-being

Applying Diener et al.'s (1991) definition of SWB to the workplace, an employee has high work-related

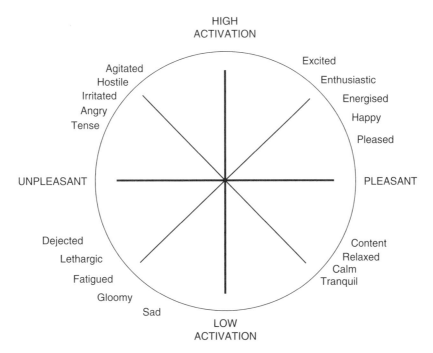

Fig. 14.1 A two-dimensional view of subjective well-being. Adapted from Russell, J.A. (1980). A circumplex model of affect. *Journal of Personality and Social Psychology, 39*, 1161–1178; and Russell, J.A. (2003). Core affect and the psychological construction of emotion. *Psychological Review, 110*, 145–172, with permission of American Psychological Association.

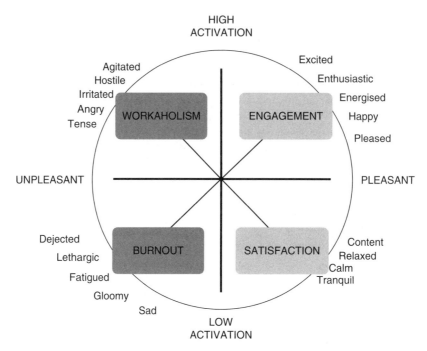

Fig. 14.2 A two-dimensional view of work-related subjective well-being. Adapted from Russell, J.A. (1980). A circumplex model of affect. *Journal of Personality and Social Psychology, 39,* 1161–1178; and Russell, J.A. (2003). Core affect and the psychological construction of emotion. *Psychological Review, 110,* 145–172, with permission of American Psychological Association.

SWB if he or she is (a) satisfied with his or her job and (b) experiences frequent positive emotions and infrequent negative emotions. The former refers to job satisfaction as a cognitive evaluation of one's job. The latter refers to positive emotions employees experience at work indicative of engagement, happiness, or satisfaction (as an affective experience). In contrast, employees who experience mainly negative emotions at work may suffer from burnout or workaholism. Further on, employees may either experience high activation levels (workaholism, engagement, happiness) or low activation (satisfaction, burnout) at work. In this section, we discuss positive and negative forms of work-related SWB in more detail, and we place them within the circumplex model of affect as demonstrated in Figure 14.2.

Positive Forms of Work-related Subjective Well-being

WORK ENGAGEMENT

Work engagement is positioned in the upper right quadrant of the circumplex model as it resemblances high levels of pleasure and activation (see Figure 14.2). Work engagement is most often defined as "a positive, fulfilling, work-related state of mind that is characterized by vigor, dedication, and absorption" (Schaufeli & Bakker, 2010; Schaufeli, Salanova, González-Romá, & Bakker, 2002, p. 74). In engagement, fulfillment

exists in contrast to the voids of life that leave people feeling empty, as in burnout. Vigor is characterized by high levels of energy and mental resilience while working, and persistence even in the face of difficulties. Dedication refers to being strongly involved in one's work, and experiencing a sense of significance and enthusiasm. Absorption is characterized by being fully concentrated and happily engrossed in one's work. Note that there are other perspectives on work engagement in the literature as well (e.g., Kahn, 1990; Rich, Lepine, & Crawford, 2010; Rothbard & Patil, 2011, Chapter 5, this volume).

In essence, work engagement captures how workers experience their work: as stimulating and energetic and something to which they really want to devote time and effort (the *vigor* component); as a significant and meaningful pursuit (*dedication*); and as engrossing and interesting (*absorption*; Bakker et al., 2008). Research has revealed that engaged employees are highly energetic, self-efficacious individuals who exercise influence over events that affect their lives (Schaufeli et al., 2001). Because of their positive attitude and high activity level, engaged employees create their own positive feedback, in terms of appreciation, recognition, and success (Bakker, 2009; Rothbard & Patil, 2011, Chapter 5, this volume). Engaged employees often indicate that their enthusiasm and energy also appear outside work, for example in sports, creative hobbies, and volunteer work. Engaged employees are no supermen—they do feel tired after a long day of hard work. However, they describe their tiredness as a rather pleasant state because it is associated with positive accomplishments. Finally, engaged employees are not addicted to their work. They enjoy other things outside work and, unlike workaholics, they do not work hard because of a strong and irresistible inner drive, but because for them working is fun (Schaufeli, Taris & Bakker, 2006).

The most often used instrument to measure engagement is the Utrecht Work Engagement Scale (UWES; Schaufeli & Bakker, 2010; Schaufeli et al., 2002) that includes a subscale for each of the three engagement dimensions: vigor, dedication, and absorption. The UWES has been validated in several countries in Europe, but also in North America, Africa, Asia, and Australia (Bakker, 2009).

HAPPINESS AT WORK

Several researchers (e.g., Cropanzano & Wright, 1999; Easterlin, 2001; Lyubomirski, 2001; Seligman, 2002) have equated the term *subjective well-being* with the term *happiness*. In this chapter, however, we will treat happiness as a positive form of SWB, equating high pleasure and moderate levels of activation. Being happy refers to somewhat higher levels of activation as being satisfied or content and somewhat lower compared to being enthusiastic or excited (see Figure 14.2).

More than 90% of all people agree with the statement "a happy worker is a productive worker" (Fisher, 2003). Why? One explanation could be that happy individuals are more active, approach-oriented, energetic, interested in their work, sympathetic to their colleagues, and persistent in the face of difficulties compared to unhappy employees. Another explanation is that employees' happiness may generate more job-related resources. For instance, happy employees may act in a pleasant way, so that colleagues are more inclined to provide instrumental, social, or emotional support.

Happiness is often operationalized by a single question (e.g., "How happy are you?"; Veenhoven, 1984). It is important to distinguish happiness as a specific emotion from other measures that cover a whole range of positive and negative emotions. One example is the Job Affect Scale (JAS), which includes various emotional states at work (e.g., excited, happy, relaxed, nervous) that are felt by employees during the preceding week (Brief, Burke, George, Robinson, & Webster, 1988; Burke, Brief, George, Robertson,

& Webster, 1989). Another popular measure is the Positive Affect and Negative Affect Scale (PANAS), consisting of ten positive affect and ten negative affect items (Watson & Clark, 1992). In line with other researchers (e.g. Fredrickson, 2001), however, we argue that it is important to differentiate between various types of positive emotions (e.g., based on both pleasure and activation levels) to better understand consequences of SWB in the workplace.

JOB SATISFACTION

Job satisfaction is probably the most studied form of work-related SWB at this point in time. Satisfaction—as a form of affect—can be positioned in the right lower quadrant of Figure 14.2, as it reflects a high level of pleasure and a low level of activation. Locke (1969) defined job satisfaction as a "pleasurable emotional state resulting from the appraisal of one's job" (p. 317). Employees who are satisfied with their jobs experience high pleasure, but may have limited energy or aspirations (Grebner, Semmer, & Elfering, 2005). For instance, employees in this low activation–high pleasure quadrant may recognize that their job is not ideal, but realize that it could be worse. According to Büssing, Bissels, Fuchs, and Perrar (1999), a decrease in level of aspiration could result in a positive state of satisfaction. This may explain the high percentage of satisfied workers often found in attitudinal studies.

It is important to distinguish between *overall* measures of job satisfaction that reflect an affective evaluation of the job, and *facet-specific* measures of job satisfaction that reflect a more cognitive evaluation of being satisfied with individual facets of the job. *Overall* job satisfaction is often assessed with a single item. For instance, Kunin (1955) developed an outline of faces that range from unhappy to happy. Later versions have varied the number of faces, as well as gender (Dunham & Herman, 1975). More recently, asexual smiley faces are used (Warr, 2007). Single-item assessments often boil down to questions like "All things considered, how satisfied are you with your job in general?" As such, *overall* job satisfaction is closely related to the experience of satisfaction as a positive emotion in the workplace.

Alternatively, separate satisfaction items may cover specific features of the job. For instance, twenty specific job features are covered in the Minnesota Satisfaction Questionnaire (Weiss, Dawis, England, & Lofquist, 1967). In such questionnaires, "intrinsic" job features are often distinguished from "extrinsic" features. For instance, satisfaction may be focused on job content (e.g., the amount of cognitive and physical workload, or autonomy in the job) or extrinsic features (e.g., one's salary). Another facet-specific measure of job satisfaction is the Job Descriptive Index (JDI; Kinicki, McKee-Ryan, Schriesheim, & Carlson, 2002) that covers five different aspects of the job: satisfaction with work itself, pay, promotion opportunities, supervision, and coworkers. As such, facet-specific measures of job satisfaction represent a rather cognitive evaluation of one's job.

Negative Forms of Work-related Subjective Well-being

WORKAHOLISM

In the circumplex model, workaholism is positioned in the upper left quadrant, as it reflects low(er) levels of pleasure and a high level of activation regarding work. Workaholism is defined as a strong inner drive to work excessively hard (Oates, 1971; Schaufeli et al., 2008). Workaholics have the compulsion to work incessantly, and tend to allocate an exceptional amount of time to work. They work beyond what is reasonably expected to meet organizational or economic requirements (Taris, Schaufeli, & Shimazu, 2010). Their compulsive tendencies make workaholics devote more resources (e.g., time, effort) to work, leaving them with fewer resources to devote to their family and other facets of their nonwork life. As a consequence, workaholics often neglect their life outside their job.

Indeed, survey studies have shown that workaholism is positively related to working overtime and work–family conflict (Bonebright, Clay, & Ankenmann, 2000). Because workaholics are willing to sacrifice personal relationships to derive satisfaction from work (Porter, 2001), it is not surprising that research shows a negative relationship between workaholism and relationship quality (Bakker, Demerouti, & Burke, 2009). There is also accumulating evidence that workaholism is related to poorer psychological and physical well-being (e.g., Andreassen, Ursin, & Eriksen, 2007; Burke & Matthiesen, 2004). Workaholics love to work, but the repetitive and addictive character of their behaviors seems to drain their energy resources.

BURNOUT

Burnout is positioned on the lower left quadrant of the circumplex model as it reflects low levels of pleasure and activation. Burnout was originally conceived as a work-related syndrome that most often occurs among individuals who work with other people (Maslach & Jackson, 1986; Maslach, Schaufeli & Leiter, 2001). However, research of the past decade has shown that the two core burnout dimensions—emotional exhaustion and cynicism—can be observed in virtually any occupational group (Bakker, Demerouti, & Schaufeli, 2002). *Emotional exhaustion* refers to a general feeling of extreme chronic fatigue, caused by continuous exposure to demanding working conditions. *Cynicism* is defined as a callous, distanced, and cynical attitude toward the work itself or the people with whom one works.

Of these two burnout dimensions, emotional exhaustion appears to be the central variable in the burnout process (Shirom, 2005). A number of studies have indeed shown that exhaustion is more strongly related to important outcome variables (such as absenteeism) than the other burnout dimensions (Lee & Ashforth, 1996). Leiter's (1993) process model of burnout proposes that cynicism should be seen as a consequence of emotional exhaustion. Accordingly, feelings of exhaustion arise from stressful working conditions, whereby employees are repeatedly confronted with high job demands (such as work pressure or high emotional demands) and, as a consequence, they can develop a cynical attitude as a coping strategy to distance themselves emotionally and mentally from work (e.g., Bakker, Schaufeli, Sixma, Bosveld, & Van Dierendonck, 2000). Consistent with our categorization of SWB using the circumplex model (see Figure 14.2), some studies have suggested that burnout is the opposite of work engagement (González-Romá, Schaufeli, Bakker, & Lloret, 2006).

Positive Work-related Subjective Well-being and Job Performance

How do different forms of work-related SWB relate to job performance? Traditionally, organizational psychologists have examined the link between employees' job satisfaction and performance (e.g., Judge, Thorensen, Bono, & Patton, 2001). More recently, however, scholars have started to examine other indicators of positive work-related SWB (e.g., work engagement; Bakker & Leiter, 2010; Warr, 2007) to better understand how SWB relates to job performance. Here, we discuss how three different forms of positive work-related SWB (work engagement, happiness at work, and job satisfaction) are associated with job performance.

Work Engagement

There are at least four reasons why engaged workers perform better than nonengaged workers (Bakker, 2009). First, engaged employees often experience active, positive emotions, including joy and enthusiasm. These positive emotions seem to broaden people's thought–action repertoire (Fredrickson, 2001; Sekerka, Vacharkulksemsuk, & Fredrickson, 2011, Chapter 13, this volume), implying that they constantly work on their personal resources. Second, engaged workers experience better health. Thus, they can focus and dedicate all their energy resources to their work. Third, engaged employees create their own job and personal resources. If needed, they ask for performance feedback, or they ask colleagues for help. Finally, engaged workers transfer their engagement to others in their immediate environment (Bakker & Demerouti, 2009; Bakker & Xanthopoulou, 2009). Since, in most organizations, performance is the result of collaborative effort, the engagement of one person may transfer to others and indirectly improve team performance.

The number of studies showing a positive relationship between employee engagement and job performance is increasing (Demerouti & Cropanzano, 2010). For example, Bakker, Demerouti, and Verbeke (2004) showed that engaged Dutch employees received higher ratings from their colleagues on in-role and extra-role performance, indicating that engaged employees perform well and are willing to go the extra mile. In addition, Halbesleben and Wheeler (2008), in their study among American employees, their supervisors, and their closest coworkers from a wide variety of industries and occupations, showed that work engagement made a unique contribution (after controlling for job embeddedness) to explaining variance in job performance.

Salanova, Agut, and Peiró (2005) conducted an important study among personnel working in Spanish restaurants and hotels. Contact employees (N = 342) from 58 hotel front desks and 56 restaurants provided information about organizational resources, engagement, and service climate. Furthermore, customers (N = 1,140) from these units provided information on employee performance and customer loyalty. Structural equation modeling analyses were consistent with a full mediation model in which organizational resources and work engagement predicted service climate, which in turn predicted employee performance and then customer loyalty.

As a final example, in their recent study among Greek employees working in fast-food restaurants, Xanthopoulou, Bakker, Demerouti, and Schaufeli (2009) made a compelling case for the predictive value of work engagement for job performance on a daily basis. Consistent with hypotheses, results

showed that employees were more engaged on days that were characterized by many job resources. Daily job resources, such as supervisor coaching and team atmosphere, contributed to employees' day levels of optimism, self-efficacy, and self-esteem, which, in turn, explained daily work engagement. Importantly, employees with higher levels of daily engagement produced higher objective daily financial returns.

Happiness and Job Satisfaction

Does scientific research confirm the positive link between happiness and performance? There are various challenges in answering this question. First, the terms *happiness* and *job satisfaction* are often used interchangeably in organizational research (Hosie et al., 2006). However, as discussed, happiness can be distinguished from satisfaction as an emotion that reflects higher levels of activation. Furthermore, facet-specific job satisfaction reflects a more cognitive evaluation toward various features of the job, whereas overall measures of job satisfaction seem to tap the affective experiences of employees. Each type may have a different effect on job performance (e.g., Schleicher, Watt, & Greguras, 2004).

A review that incorporated 254 studies showed an average correlation between overall job satisfaction and performance of 0.30 after correction for measurement errors, with a stronger correlation for employees who performed tasks of higher complexity (Judge et al., 2001). Interestingly, the authors compared this result with a previous meta-analysis of Iaffaldano and Muchinsky (1985), who reported a correlation of 0.17 between *facet-specific* measures of job satisfaction and job performance across 74 studies. Thus, it appears that overall job satisfaction relates more strongly to job performance compared to facet-specific measures of job satisfaction. Likewise, an influential meta-analyses of Lyubomirsky, King, and Diener (2005) reported studies that link happiness—defined as the experience of positive emotions (both context-free and at work)—and job performance. The authors reported an average correlation of 0.27.

Taking a more detailed approach, Fisher and Noble (2004) related employees' current mood to the way they evaluated their task performance while executing the task and afterward. Not surprisingly, correlations between current mood and performance ratings while performing the task (r = 0.41) and afterward (r = 0.57) were strong. As self-ratings of performance are biased by an individual's feelings, it is important to have information about employee performance that is independent from the target person. Lee and Allen (2002) showed that work-related positive affect (e.g., enthusiasm, excitation) was positively correlated with colleagues' ratings of help provided to other individuals ($r = 0.18$), and with ratings of citizenship behavior directed at the organization more broadly ($r = 0.24$). Other studies have operationalized organizational performance as financial turnover. For instance, Koys (2001) showed that overall employee satisfaction correlated 0.35 with store profitability in the subsequent year.

It should be noted that many of the studies reported above are cross-sectional in nature. Such studies cannot determine causality. Job satisfaction or happiness may either *cause* good performance, *follow from* good performance, or both. Looking into this issue, Lyubomirsky et al. (2005) analyzed ten studies with longitudinal research designs that included a diverse set of SWB measures that were affective in nature (e.g., PANAS, one-item happiness, positive emotions on the job), as well as job performance (e.g., supervisory evaluations, salary, absenteeism, second interviews), across different time frames (ranging from 3 months to 19 years). On the whole, the authors reported an average longitudinal correlation of 0.24, suggesting that happiness *precedes* job performance.

Preliminary Conclusions

We addressed the question whether high levels of job satisfaction would coincide with high levels of job performance or whether more is needed than job satisfaction alone. Results show that, in addition to job satisfaction, positive affective states of SWB that are characterized by high levels of pleasure and higher levels of activation—such as work engagement and happiness at work—are positively related to high levels of job performance. Further on, results show that *overall* job satisfaction—reflecting high pleasure, but low activation—is also associated with job performance. However *facet-specific* job satisfaction—reflecting a more cognitive evaluation of various job features—appears to be only weakly or not associated to job performance. In conclusion, other types of work-related SWB besides job satisfaction do relate to high levels of job performance. Also, it appears that emotional, rather than cognitive, forms of job satisfaction are positively related to job performance.

Daily Subjective Well-being

As affective forms of work-related SWB relate to job performance, it becomes critical to accurately capture emotional experiences of employees in real-time or on a daily basis. It is challenging to capture emotional experiences in the workplace, because emotions are usually short-lived (Fredrickson, 2001; Sekerka et al., 2011, Chapter 13, this volume). General survey methods are therefore not able to capture such within-person fluctuations in emotional experiences. In this section, we discuss two exciting new ways to capture the link between positive forms of SWB at work and job performance on an intraindividual and daily basis: the diary study and the day reconstruction method.

Diary Research

In diary studies, employees are kindly requested to fill in short questionnaires including state measures once or several times a day, for several days in a row (e.g., 5 or 10 successive days). An important advantage of diary research is that it relies less on retrospective recall than regular surveys, since the questions relate to individuals' perceptions and feelings on a certain day. In addition, when daily changes in, for example, work engagement are temporarily separated from daily changes in outcomes like performance and personal initiative, state work engagement can be causally related to such outcomes.

Moreover, diary research may also reveal what the day-to-day triggers are of state engagement. For example, Xanthopoulou et al. (2009) investigated how daily fluctuations in job resources (i.e., autonomy, coaching, and team climate) were related to employee's personal resources (i.e., self-efficacy, self-esteem, and optimism), work engagement, and company's financial returns. Forty-two employees working in three branches of a fast-food company completed a questionnaire and a diary booklet over 5 consecutive workdays. One of the most significant findings of this study was that previous days' coaching had a positive, lagged effect on next days' work engagement (through next days' optimism), and on next days' financial returns.

As another example, Xanthopoulou, Bakker, Heuven, Demerouti, and Schaufeli (2008) examined whether daily fluctuations in colleague support predicted day levels of job performance through first self-efficacy and then work engagement. Forty-four flight attendants filled in a questionnaire and a diary booklet before and after consecutive flights to three intercontinental destinations. As in the previous study, the dynamic nature of the relationships among the study variables were investigated using a within-subjects design, in which employees were followed on multiple occasions over a number of days. Results of multilevel analyses revealed that colleague support had unique positive lagged effects on work engagement and self-efficacy, and indirectly influenced job performance.

Sonnentag, Dormann, and Demerouti (2010) suggest intensifying conceptual development on day-specific (or even momentary) work engagement in order to arrive at a better understanding of how day-specific engagement corresponds to enduring engagement in experienced quality and configuration. In addition, they argue that it is an open question whether the scales used to assess enduring work engagement (see Schaufeli & Bakker, 2010) are valid for the measurement of state work engagement. Clearly, the time anchors on the UWES (e.g., "a few times a month") do not fit with a daily reporting schedule. The appropriateness of item wording to capture the day-to-day variations in energy and dedication remains an open question. Expanding existing measures with new items or alternative response formats would help to refine critical instruments.

Until now, individual difference variables have made a minor contribution in research on state work engagement. According to Sonnentag et al. (2010), personality may influence the variability of work engagement within a person, interacting between predictors and state work engagement, or between engagement and outcomes. As an example of this kind of research, Bledow and Schmitt (2008) argued that positive affectivity would make employees less dependent on positive events occurring during a work day. Consistent with this hypothesis, their diary study among German software engineers showed that positive affectivity moderated the relationship between positive events and work engagement. The positive relationship was stronger for engineers low in positive affectivity. In another diary study, Bakker and Xanthopoulou (2009) hypothesized that daily engagement would cross over from one colleague to another. In addition, since extraversion is the disposition to be sociable and cheerful, they predicted that extraverts (vs. introverts) would interact more often with their colleagues. The frequency of daily communication was expected to moderate the cross-over of daily work engagement, which in turn would determine colleagues' daily performance. Results confirmed the cross-over of daily work engagement, but only on days that employees within a dyad interacted frequently. Moreover, as predicted, members of the dyad influenced each other's daily performance through a process of engagement cross-over.

Day Reconstruction Method

The day reconstruction method (DRM; Kahneman, Schkade, Schwartz, & Stone, 2004) is a useful and innovative way to capture how employees experience their job from moment to moment as reflected in the positive and negative feelings that accompany their daily activities. The DRM combines elements of experience sampling and time diaries, and is designed specifically to facilitate accurate emotional recall. Respondents are first asked to fill out a time diary summarizing episodes that occurred in the preceding day. In particular, respondents describe each episode of the day by indicating when the episode began and ended, what they were doing (by selecting activities from a provided list), where they were, and with whom they were interacting. To ascertain how employees feel, respondents are asked to report the pleasure and intensity of their feelings in accordance with the circumplex model of affect (Russell, 1980, 2003). For instance, affective response categories can be based on adjectives such as feeling happy, engaged, bored, or stressed.

Importantly, when people report on their current feelings, the feelings themselves are accessible to introspection, allowing for more accurate reports on the basis of experiential information. Affective experiences are fleeting and thus not available to introspection once the feeling dissipated. Accordingly, the opportunity to assess emotion reports based on experiential information is limited to methods of momentary data capture (Stone, Shiffman, Atienza, & Nebeling, 2007). Once the feeling has dissipated, the affective experiences need to be reconstructed on the basis of other information. The DRM pertains to a specific *recent episode*, so that people can draw on episodic memory, retrieving specific moments and details of the recent past. Such reports can often recover the actual experience with some accuracy, as indicated by their convergence with concurrent mood reports used in experience sampling methods (e.g., Kahneman et al., 2004; Stone et al., 2007).

It is important to emphasize that *global* reports of past feelings are based on semantic knowledge. When asked how people "usually" feel during a particular activity (e.g., at work), people draw on their general beliefs about the activity and its attributes to arrive at a report. The actual experience does not figure prominently in these global reports because the experience itself is no longer accessible to introspection, and episodic reconstruction is not used to answer a global question. Importantly, a person's "global memory" often fails to reflect what he or she actually experienced from moment to moment (Schwarz, Kahneman, & Xu, 2009).

In sum, the DRM method can be used for assessing (a) within-person fluctuations in daily emotions and (b) relate these emotions to actual behavior (activity), circumstances (time, place, social interaction), and—if desired—daily performance. For example, research has demonstrated that work engagement is associated with in-role performance, whereas workaholism is not (Schaufeli, Taris, & Bakker, 2006). Looking into this issue, Bakker, Oerlemans, Demerouti, and Sonnentag (2010) followed 85 employees during nonwork hours by using a day reconstruction approach. Results show that daily work-related activities during nonwork hours at night have a stronger negative relationship with daily SWB (feeling happy, vigorous, and recovered) for employees who score high (vs. low) on trait workaholism *and* that physical activities have a stronger positive relationship with SWB for employees high (vs. low) on trait workaholism. These results imply that organizations should actively restrain employees and particularly workaholics from working during nonwork time and instead promote physical exercise.

Future Directions

This chapter clearly shows that positive SWB is very important in organizations, since it contributes to bottom-line outcomes such as job performance. Despite these promising results, further research is needed. First of all, most previous studies on SWB in organizations are cross-sectional in nature. Longitudinal studies are needed to examine the possibility that positive forms of work-related SWB either precede job performance, follow from job performance, or are reciprocally related to performance. In addition, we need a better understanding of how organizations can enable SWB. Previous research has suggested that increasing job resources would facilitate work engagement and thriving (Bakker & Leiter, 2010; Spreitzer, Lam, & Fritz, 2010), but we need more research on the specific SWB interventions that are effective.

Furthermore, it would be very interesting and relevant to find out what the prevalence is of job satisfaction. What percentage of the workforce has decreased its level of aspiration (i.e., activation) in order to adapt to negative aspects of the work environment? What type of interventions do we need to turn job satisfaction into more positive forms of SWB, such as work engagement and happiness at work?

It is also important to better understand the underlying psychological and behavioral processes that explain why positive forms of work-related SWB relate to job performance. Are engaged workers more proactive than those characterized by job satisfaction? Do energetic and dedicated employees engage in job crafting behaviors (Wrzesniewski & Dutton, 2001), through which they optimize their work environment and thrive? There is indeed some preliminary evidence for the idea that engaged employees are more inclined to mobilize their job resources and look for challenges (Tims & Bakker, 2010).

Future research should also aim to answer the question whether there is a dark side to positive SWB. Halbesleben, Harvey, and Bolino (2009) hypothesized and found that engagement was associated with higher work interference with family due to the resources that engaged employees expended when they engaged in extra-role work behavior, such as organizational citizenship behaviors. These findings illustrate that employees may become too engaged or even addicted to their work, which eventually may interfere with opportunities to recover from work-related efforts during off-job time.

Finally, we believe that there is a great future for diary and DRM research on SWB in organizations. Such research designs enable an examination of the most proximal processes at work leading to state SWB. Daily recordings of positive SWB, if combined with daily measures of job demands and resources, may reveal which aspects of the work environment facilitate flow and engagement at work. In addition, daily changes in flow and engagement may be related to daily learning behavior and job performance.

Conclusion

We started this chapter asking whether high levels of job satisfaction coincide with high levels of job performance, or whether more is needed than job satisfaction alone. Our review of research on SWB in organizations suggests that optimal job performance is most likely when SWB is a combination of high activation and high pleasure. Job satisfaction reflects only low to average levels of activation (and high pleasure) and refers to a more cognitive evaluation of one's job, which may not be enough to enhance performance. Work engagement and happiness at work are more likely predictors of job performance— organizations need engaged workers (Bakker & Leiter, 2010; Bakker & Schaufeli, 2008). In addition, we conclude that the best methods to assess these states may be daily diaries and DRM, since emotions are fleeting and require a real-time approach.

References

Andreassen, C.S., Ursin, H., & Eriksen, H.R. (2007). The relationship between strong motivation to work ("workaholism") and health. *Psychology and Health, 22*, 615–629.

Bakker, A.B. (2009). Building engagement in the workplace. In R.J. Burke, & C.L. Cooper (Eds.), *The peak performing organization* (pp. 50–72). Oxon, UK: Routledge.

Bakker, A.B., & Demerouti, E. (2009). The crossover of work engagement between working couples: A closer look at the role of empathy. *Journal of Managerial Psychology, 24,* 220–236.

Bakker, A.B., Demerouti, E., & Burke, R. (2009). Workaholism and relationship quality: A spillover-crossover perspective. *Journal of Occupational Health Psychology, 14,* 23–33.

Bakker, A.B., Demerouti, E., & Schaufeli, W.B. (2002). Validation of the Maslach burnout inventory–general survey: An internet study. *Anxiety, Stress, and Coping, 15,* 245–260.

Bakker, A.B., Demerouti, E., & Verbeke, W. (2004). Using the job demands–resources model to predict burnout and performance. *Human Resource Management, 43,* 83–104.

Bakker, A.B., & Leiter, M.P. (Eds.) (2010). *Work engagement: A handbook of essential theory and research.* New York: Psychology Press.

Bakker, A.B., Oerlemans, W., Demerouti, E., & Sonnentag, S. (2010). Daily recovery among workaholics: A day reconstruction study of leisure activities. Manuscript submitted for publication.

Bakker, A.B., & Schaufeli, W.B. (2008). Positive organizational behavior: Engaged employees in flourishing organizations. *Journal of Organizational Behavior, 29,* 147–154.

Bakker, A.B., Schaufeli, W.B., Leiter, M.P., & Taris, T.W. (2008). Work engagement: An emerging concept in occupational health psychology. *Work & Stress, 22,* 187–200.

Bakker, A.B., Schaufeli, W.B., Sixma, H., Bosveld, W., & Van Dierendonck, D. (2000). Patient demands, lack of reciprocity, and burnout: A five-year longitudinal study among general practitioners. *Journal of Organizational Behavior, 21,* 425–441.

Bakker, A.B., & Xanthopoulou, D. (2009). The crossover of daily work engagement: Test of an actor-partner interdependence model. *Journal of Applied Psychology, 94,* 1562–1571.

Bledow, R., & Schmitt, A. (2008). *Work engagement as a dynamic process: The interplay between events, emotions, and resources.* Poster presented at the 2008 conference of the Society of Industrial and Organizational Psychology, San Francisco, CA.

Bonebright, C.A., Clay, D.L., & Ankenmann, R.D. (2000). The relationship of workaholism with work-life conflict, life satisfaction, and purpose in life. *Journal of Counseling Psychology, 47,* 469–477.

Brief, A.P., Burke, M.J., George, J.M., Robinson, B.S., & Webster, J. (1988). Should negative affectivity remain an unmeasured variable in the study of job stress? *Journal of Applied Psychology, 73,* 193–198.

Burke, M.J., Brief, A.P., George, J.M., Robertson, L., & Webster, J. (1989). Measuring affect at work: Confirmatory factor analyses of competing mood structures with conceptual linkage to cortical regulatory systems. *Journal of Personality and Social Psychology, 57,* 1091–1102.

Burke, R.J., & Matthiesen, S.B. (2004). Workaholism among Norwegian journalists: Antecedents and consequences. *Stress and Health, 20,* 301–308.

Büssing, A., Bissels, T., Fuchs, V., Perrar, K.M. (1999). A dynamic model of work satisfaction: Qualitative approaches. Human Relations, 52, 999–1028.

Cropanzano, R., & Wright, T.A. (1999). A 5-year study of change in the relationship between well-being and job performance. *Consulting Psychology Journal, 51,* 252–265.

Demerouti, E., & Cropanzano, R. (2010). From thought to action: Employee work engagement and job performance.

In A.B. Bakker, & M.P. Leiter (Eds.), *Work engagement: A handbook of essential theory and research* (pp. 147–163). New York: Psychology Press.

Diener, E., & Biswas-Diener, R. (2008). *Happiness: Unlocking the mysteries of psychological wealth.* Malden, MA: Blackwell.

Diener, E., Sandvik, E., & Pavot, W. (1991). Happiness is the frequency, not the intensity, of positive versus negative affect. In F. Strack, M. Argyle, & N. Schwarz (Eds.), Subjective well-being: An interdisciplinary perspective. New York: Pergamon.

Dunham, R.B., & J.B. Herman. (1975). Development of a female faces scale for measuring job satisfaction. *Journal of Applied Psychology, 60,* 629–631.

Easterlin, R.A. (2001). Income and happiness: Towards a unified theory. *The Economic Journal, 111,* 465–484.

Fisher, C.D. (2003). Why do lay people believe that satisfaction and performance are correlated? Possible sources of a commonsense theory. *Journal of Organizational Behavior, 24,* 753–777.

Fisher, C.D, & Noble, C.S. (2004). A within-person examination of correlates of performance and emotions while working. *Human Performance, 17,* 145–168.

Fredrickson, B.L. (2001). The role of positive emotions in positive psychology: The broaden-and-build theory of positive emotions. *American Psychologist, 56,* 218–226.

Freedmann, J.L. (1978). *What happiness is, who has it, and why.* New York: Harcourt Brace Jovanovich.

González-Romá, V., Schaufeli, W.B., Bakker, A.B., & Lloret, S. (2006). Burnout and work engagement: Independent factors or opposite poles? *Journal of Vocational Behavior, 62,* 165–174.

Grebner, S., Semmer, N.K., & Elfering, A. (2005). Working conditions and three types of well-being: A longitudinal study with self-report and rating data. *Journal of Occupational Health Psychology, 10,* 31–43.

Halbesleben, J.R., Harvey, J., & Bolino, M.C. (2009). Too engaged? A conservation of resources view of the relationship between work engagement and work interference with family. *Journal of Applied Psychology, 94,* 1452–1465.

Halbesleben, J.R. B., & Wheeler, A.R. (2008). The relative roles of engagement and embeddedness in predicting job performance and intention to leave. *Work & Stress, 22,* 242–256.

Handel, M.J. (2005). Trends in perceived job quality, 1989 to 1998. *Work and Occupations, 32*(1), 66–94.

Hosie, P.J., Sevastos, P.P., & Cooper, C.L. (2006). Happy performing managers: The impact of affective wellbeing and intrinsic job satisfaction in the workplace. Northampton, MA: Edward Elgar Publishing Ltd.

Iaffaldano, M.T., & Muchinsky, P.M. (1985). Job satisfaction and job performance: A meta-analysis. *Psychological Bulletin, 97*(2), 251–273.

Judge, T.A., Thorensen, C.J., Bono, J.E., & Patton, G.K. (2001). The job satisfaction-job performance relationship: A qualitative and quantitative review. *Psychological Bulletin, 127,* 376–407.

Kahn, W.A. (1990). Psychological conditions of personal engagement and disengagement at work. *Academy of Management Journal, 33,* 692–724.

Kahneman, D., Krueger, A., Schkade, D., Schwarz N., & Stone, A. (2004). A survey method for characterizing daily life experience: The Day Reconstruction Method. *Science, 306,* 1776–1780.

Kinicki, A.J., McKee-Ryan, F.M., Schriesheim, C.A., & Carlson, K.P. (2002). Assessing the construct validity of the Job Descriptive Index: A review and meta-analysis. *Journal of Applied Psychology, 87,* 14–32.

Koys, D.J. (2001). The effects of employee satisfaction, organizational citizenship behavior, and turnover on organizational effectiveness: A unit-level, longitudinal study. *Personnel Psychology, 54*, 101–114.

Kunin, T. (1955). The construction of a new type of attitude measure. *Personnel Psychology, 58*, 281–342.

Lang P.J., Bradley, M.M., & Cuthbert, B.N. (1998). Emotion, motivation, and anxiety: Brain mechanisms and psychophysiology. *Biological Psychiatry, 44*, 1248–1263.

Larsen, R.J., & Diener, E. (1992). Promises and problems with the circumplex model of emotion. In M.S. Clark (Ed.), *Review of personality and social psychology* Vol. 13 (pp. 25–59). Newbury Park, CA: Sage.

Lee, R., & Allen, N.J. (2002).Organizational citizenship behavior and workplace deviance: The role of affect and cognitions. *Journal of Applied Psychology, 87*, 131–142.

Lee, R.T., & Ashforth, B.E. (1996). A meta-analytic examination of the correlates of the three dimensions of job burnout. *Journal of Applied Psychology, 81*, 123–133.

Leiter, M.P. (1993). Burnout as a developmental process: Consideration of models. In W.B. Schaufeli, C. Maslach, & T. Marek (Eds.), *Professional burnout: Recent developments in theory and research* (pp. 237–250). Washington, DC: Taylor & Francis.

Locke, E.A. (1969). What is job satisfaction? *Organizational Behavior and Human Performance, 4*, 309–336.

Lyubomirski, S. (2001). Why are some people happier than others? The role of cognitive and motivational processes in well-being. *American Psychologist, 56*, 239–249.

Lyubomirsky, S., King, L., & Diener, E. (2005). The benefits of frequent positive affect: Does happiness lead to success? *Psychological Bulletin, 131*, 803–855.

Maslach, C., & Jackson, S. (1986). Patterns of burnout among a national sample of public contact workers. *Journal of Health and Human Resources Administration, 7*, 189–212.

Maslach, C., Schaufeli, W.B., & Leiter, M.P. (2001). Job burnout. *Annual Review of Psychology, 52*, 397–422.

Oates, W. (1971). *Confessions of a workaholic: The facts about work addiction*. New York: World.

Parent-Thirion, A., Fernández-Macías, E., Hurley, J., & Vermeylen, G. (2007). *Fourth European working conditions survey*. Luxembourg: Office for Official Publications of the European Communities.

Porter, G. (2001). Workaholic tendencies and the high potential for stress among co-workers. *International Journal of Stress Management, 8*, 147–164.

Rich, B.R., LePine, J.A., & Crawford, E.R. (2010). Job engagement: Antecedents and effects on job performance. *Academy of Management Journal, 53*(3), 617–635.

Rothbard, N.P., & Patil, S.V. (2011). Being there: Work engagement and positive organizational scholarship. In K.S. Cameron & G.M. Spreitzer (Eds.), *The Oxford handbook of positive organizational scholarship*. New York: Oxford University Press.

Russell, J.A. (1980). A circumplex model of affect. *Journal of Personality and Social Psychology, 39*, 1161–1178.

Russell, J.A. (2003). Core affect and the psychological construction of emotion. *Psychological Review, 110*, 145–172.

Russell J.A., & Carroll, J.M. (1999). On the bipolarity of positive and negative affect. *Psychology Bulletin, 125*, 3–30.

Russell, J.A., & Fehr, B. (1994). Fuzzy concepts in a fuzzy hierarchy: Varieties of anger. *Journal of Personality and Social Psychology, 67*(2), 186–205.

Saarni, C. (1999). *Development of emotional competence*. New York: Guilford Press.

Salanova, M., Agut, S., & Peiró, J.M. (2005). Linking organizational resources and work engagement to employee performance and customer loyalty: The mediation of service climate. *Journal of Applied Psychology, 90*, 1217–1227.

Schaufeli, W.B., & Bakker, A.B. (2010). Defining and measuring work engagement: Bringing clarity to the concept. In A.B. Bakker, & M.P. Leiter (Eds.), *Work engagement: A handbook of essential theory and research* (pp. 10–24). New York: Psychology Press.

Schaufeli, W.B., Salanova, M., González-Romá, V., & Bakker, A.B. (2002). The measurement of engagement and burnout: A two sample confirmatory factor analytic approach. *Journal of Happiness Studies, 3*, 71–92.

Schaufeli, W.B., Taris, T.W., Le Blanc, P., Peeters, M., Bakker, A.B., & De Jonge, J. (2001). Maakt arbeid gezond? Op zoek naar de bevlogen werknemer [Does work make happy? In search of the engaged worker]. *De Psycholoog, 36*, 422–428.

Schaufeli, W.B., Taris, T.W., & Bakker, A.B. (2006). Dr. Jekyll and Mr. Hide: On the differences between work engagement and workaholism. In: R. Burke (Ed.), *Work hours and work addiction* (pp. 193–252). Edward Elgar: Northhampton, UK.

Schaufeli, W.B., Taris, T.W., & Van Rhenen, W. (2008). Workaholism, burnout, and work engagement: Three of a kind or three different kinds of employee well-being? *Applied Psychology: An International Review, 57*, 173–203.

Schleicher, D.J., Watt, J.D., & Greguras, G.J. (2004). Reexamining the job satisfaction-performance relationship: The complexity of attitudes. *Journal of Applied Psychology, 89*(1), 165–177.

Schwarz, N., Kahneman, D., & Xu, J. (2009). Global and episodic reports of hedonic experience. In R. Belli, F.P. Stafford, & D.F. Alwin (Eds.), *Calendar and time diary methods in life course research* (pp. 157–174). Newbury Park, CA: Sage.

Sekerka, L.E., Vacharkulksemsuk, T., & Fredrickson, B.L. (2011). Positive emotions: Broadening and building upward spirals of sustainable enterprises. In K.S. Cameron & G.M. Spreitzer (Eds.), *The Oxford handbook of positive organizational scholarship*. New York: Oxford University Press.

Seligman, M.E.P. (2002). *Authentic happiness*. New York: Free Press.

Shirom, A. (2005). Reflections on the study of burnout. *Work & Stress, 19*, 263–270.

Sonnentag, S., Dormann, C., & Demerouti, E. (2010). Not all days are created equal: The concept of state work engagement. In A.B. Bakker, & M.P. Leiter (Eds.), *Work engagement: A handbook of essential theory and research* (pp. 25–38). New York: Psychology Press.

Spreitzer, G.M., Lam, C.F., & Fritz, C. (2010). Engagement and human thriving: Complementary perspectives on energy and connections to work. In A.B. Bakker, & M.P. Leiter (Eds.), *Work engagement: A handbook of essential theory and research* (pp. 132–146). New York: Psychology Press.

Stone, A., Shiffman, S., Atienza, A., & Nebeling, L. (2007). *The science of real-time data capture: Self-reports in health research*. Oxford: Oxford University Press.

Taris, T.W., Schaufeli, W.B., & Shimazu, A. (2010). The push and pull of work: The differences between workaholism and work engagement. In A.B. Bakker, & M.P. Leiter (Eds.), *Work engagement: A handbook of essential theory and research* (39–53). New York: Psychology Press.

Thayer, R.E. (1989). *The origin of everyday moods: Managing energy, tension and stress*. New York: Oxford University Press.

Tims, M., & Bakker, A.B. (2010). Job crafting: Towards a new model of individual job redesign. *South African Journal of Industrial Psychology, 36*, 1–9.

Ulrich, D. (1997). *Human resource champions*. Boston: Harvard Business School.

Veenhoven, (1984). *Conditions of happiness*. Dordrecht: Reidel.

Warr, P. (2007). *Work, happiness, and unhappiness*. Mahwah, NJ: Lawrence Erlbaum.

Watson, D., & Clark, L.A. (1992). On traits and temperament: General and specific factors of emotional experience and their relation to the five-factor model. *Journal of Personality, 60*, 441–476.

Weiss, H.M., Dawis, R.V., England, G.W., & Lofquist, L.H. (1967). *Manual of the Minnesota satisfaction questionnaire*. Minneapolis, MN: University of Minnesota.

Wrzesniewski, A., & Dutton, J.E. (2001). Crafting a job: Revisioning employees as active crafters of their work. *Academy of Management Review, 26*, 179–201.

Xanthopoulou, D., Bakker, A.B., Demerouti, E., & Schaufeli, W.B. (2009). Work engagement and financial returns: A diary study on the role of job and personal resources. *Journal of Occupational and Organizational Psychology, 82*, 183–200.

Xanthopoulou, D., Bakker, A.B., Heuven, E., Demerouti, E., & Schaufeli, W.B. (2008). Working in the sky: A diary study on work engagement among flight attendants. *Journal of Occupational Health Psychology, 13*, 345–356.

CHAPTER

15 | Passion

Kimberly H. Perttula *and* Melissa S. Cardon

Abstract

The purpose of this chapter is to present an overview of research on passion and show its relevance to the realm of work and organizations. We first provide a brief review of how passion has been used in research from a historical perspective. We then explain in detail three different conceptualizations of passion, each at a different level of abstraction or specificity: generalized harmonious and obsessive passion (Vallerand and colleagues), passion for work (Perttula), and passion in an entrepreneurial work context (Cardon and colleagues). Finally, directions for future research are suggested.

Keywords: Passion, love, conceptualization

Passion is what we are most deeply curious about, most hungry for, will most hate to lose in life. It is the most desperate wish we need to yell down the well of our lives. It is whatever we pursue merely for its own sake, what we study when there are no tests to take, what we create though no one may ever see it. It makes us forget that the sun rose and set, that we have bodily functions, and personal relations that could use a little tending. It is what we'd do if we weren't worried about consequences, money, about making anybody happy except ourselves . . . it is what matters most, whether we're doing it or not.
—*Levoy*, 1997, p. 69

Both organizational researchers and practitioners have noted the importance of passion in the workplace (Boyatzis, McKee, & Goleman, 2002; Baum & Locke, 2004; Cardon et al., 2009; Chang, 2000; Perttula, 2010; Vallerand & Houlfort, 2003). Increasing interest in passion for work comes at a time when global competition and environmental turbulence demand that employers focus more and more attention on cultivating passion within their people in order to boost employee recruitment, retention, and commitment. This interest also arises at a time when corporate scandals, layoffs, and post 9/11 reflection prompt scores of employees to question what they really want out of life and work (Caudron, 1997; Wrzesniewski, 2002), and what they truly feel passionate about.

Scholars consider passion for work to be vital because without it, employees can't sustain the energy essential to organizational excellence and managers can't motivate or inspire others (Boyatzis, McKee, & Goleman, 2002). In fact, passion for work has been hailed as one of the most important factors in the success of a manager and leader (Bass, 1990; House & Howell, 1992; Locke, 1997). Furthermore, we have learned from recent research regarding the positive psychology of subjective experience that making more money does not necessarily bring an increase in life satisfaction (Seligman, 2004). Finding passion in your work may be an alternative means to do so.

The purpose of this chapter is to present an overview of passion and show its relevance to the realm of work and organizations. We first provide a brief review of how passion has been used in research from a historical perspective. We then explain in detail three different conceptualizations of passion, from the general to the context specific, for clarity of presentation. Each conceptualization of passion represents a different level of abstraction or specificity: generalized harmonious and obsessive passion (Vallerand and colleagues), passion for work (Perttula), and passion for specific roles and activities in an entrepreneurial work context (Cardon and colleagues). We include these particular models because of their detailed conceptualizations and grounding in empirical research. Finally, we share our observations concerning areas ripe for future research on passion and work.

History of Passion

Passion has been studied for a long time in various contexts including philosophy, theology, political science, social psychology, and psychology (Cardon et al., 2009). Most of these writings argue that passion is an intense emotion that interacts with cognition (some say it impairs, whereas others argue it empowers reason) and has a motivating impact on individual behaviors. Many authors suggest that passion gives individuals a sense of purpose (Rockwell, 2002), that it guides the creation and adherence to goals (Frijda, 2005), and that it leads individuals to become heavily involved and invested in their activities (Csikszentmihalyi, 1990). Interestingly, though, while these generalizations about passion are relevant to the workplace, the majority of research involving passion has been done outside of a work context. In particular, research in psychology and social psychology has historically looked at passion as unique to interpersonal relationships and in particular intimate relationships (e.g., Fletcher, Rosanowski, & Fitness, 1994). Only more recently has passion been incorporated in a work environment with concepts such as "passion for work" emerging (e.g., Martin, 2005; Baum et al. 2001). Even in the popular press, several books have appeared encouraging people to "work with passion" and "find work you love" (e.g., Chang, 2000; Anderson, 2004; Kang & Albion, 2009). However, these writings are not based on empirical findings nor are they grounded in the rich academic literature that underpins the conceptualizations we focus on here. In this chapter, we focus on passion in organizations from a research standpoint.

Models of Passion: Variations in Conception and Measurement

Although some claim that passion is one of the most important factors in the success of a manager and leader (Bass, 1990; House & Howell, 1992; Locke, 2000), systematic attempts to conceptualize passion are rare. In fact, a review of all related literature suggests that the literature is disjointed, with few definitive conclusions to be drawn and no integration existing across these studies in terms of approaches, definitions, or measures. In attempting to reconcile the considerable variation in conceptualizations, we note that one key variation is the level of abstraction or specificity the conceptualizations of passion provide. For example, there is considerable research in the field of psychology on generalized passion as it applies to a host of activities and settings (e.g., sports, gambling, music, etc.). Second, there is a body of work on passion in terms of passion experienced in a work context, rather than for hobbies or lifestyle activities such as gambling or bike riding. Finally, some research has conceptualized passion in terms of specific work contexts, such as entrepreneurship. Each perspective has value and provides different insights into the concept of passion. In the following section, we provide an overview of research on passion at each level of abstraction, including the current state of our knowledge concerning the definition, measurement, and association of passion with antecedents, as well as different affective, cognitive, and behavioral outcomes. A summary is provided in Table 15.1.

Passion Defined

At a very general level, Vallerand and his colleagues (2003; Vallerand & Houlfort, 2003; Vallerand & Miquelon, 2007) define passion as a strong inclination or desire toward a self-defining activity that one likes (or loves), finds important, and in which one invests time and energy. They proposed a dualistic model of passion that include two types of passion: harmonious and obsessive. *Harmonious passion* concerns a strong desire to engage in a passionate activity that remains under the individual's control. It is proposed, in line with self-determination theory (Deci & Ryan, 2000), that this type of passion comes from an autonomous internalization of the activity into the person's identity (Vallerand et al., 2003). Such an autonomous internalization occurs when an individual has voluntarily accepted the activity as important without any contingencies associated with it (Sheldon, 2002; Vallerand, 1997). Behavioral engagement in the passionate activity is flexible.

Obsessive passion, however, concerns a controlled internalization of the activity into one's identity (Vallerand et al., 2003). In this type of passion, the

Table 15.1 Comparisons of passion across conceptualizations and measurements

	Passion (Vallerand & Colleagues)	Passion for Work (Perttula & Colleagues)	Entrepreneurial Passion (Cardon & Colleagues)
Level of abstraction/ specificity	Very general; focused on any activity	Focused on work	Very specific; focused on three specific sets of activities/roles in entrepreneurship
Definition– dimensions	Like/love for an activity Activity is important Time and energy spent	Intense positive emotions (joy, subjective vitality) Meaningful connection toward one's work (tasks, responsibilities, activities) Internal drive	Positive and intense feelings for activities associated with roles that are identity meaningful
Types	Harmonious Obsessive		Passion for inventing Passion for founding Passion for developing
Outcomes	Flow, positive affect, life satisfaction, physical and mental health, affective commitment, performance (harmonious) Shame, interference with social relationships (obsessive)	Lower job burnout, effectiveness, creativity in some work contexts	Persistence, creativity, venture growth
Antecedents	Identification with an activity Activity specialization Parental activity valuation Autonomy	Autonomy (related) Self-esteem (related) Positive organizational support (related)	Self-efficacy (related)
Measurement	Two scales—harmonious and obsessive passion—focused on how passion fits with rest of life	PWS with four dimensions—joy, subjective vitality, meaningful connection, internal drive—focused on components of passion experience	EPS with three dimensions— passion for inventing, founding, developing—focused on different sets of activities/roles entrepreneurs could be passionate about

strong desire to engage in an activity is not under an individual's control, and certain contingencies are attached to the activity. Specifically, internalization results from intra- and/or interpersonal pressure, such as feelings of social acceptance, self-esteem, or performance. Behavioral engagement in the passionate activity is rigid.

Research has provided support for the dualistic model of passion and the validity of the Passion Scale (Vallerand et. al., 2003). The Passion Scale consists of two components. The first component includes a three-item scale that differentiates between passionate and nonpassionate individuals. Specifically, these items measure the three components of the proposed definition of passion: activity valuation, love for the activity, and time spent on the activity. The second component includes two seven-item subscales[1] that measure the relative

importance of harmonious (e.g., "This activity is in harmony with other activities in my life") and obsessive passion (e.g., "I almost have an obsessive feeling toward this activity").

Research by Vallerand and colleagues suggests that, not surprisingly, harmonious passion is generally associated with positive outcomes (e.g., positive affect, life satisfaction, good physical health, and good performance), and obsessive passion is usually associated with negative outcomes (e.g., shame, interference with social relationships).[2] In addition, in a series of studies, harmonious passion has been found to be positively correlated with flow and positive emotions (Mageau, Vallerand, Rousseau, Ratelle, & Provencher, 2005; Vallerand et al., 2003, Study 1; Vallerand et al., 2006, Studies 2 and 3), mental health, vitality, and affective commitment (Forest, Mageau, Sarrazin, & Morin, 2010), general subjective well-being (Vallerand et al., 2003, Study 2; Vallerand et al., 2007), limited negative emotions (Mageau et al., 2005; Vallerand et al., 2003, Study 1), higher levels of concentration during task engagement (Mageau et al., 2005; Vallerand et al., 2003, Study 1), and indices of psychological adjustment (Rousseau & Vallerand, 2003; Vallerand et al., 2008, Study 2; Vallerand et al., 2007, Studies 1 and 2). In contrast, obsessive passion has been found to be positively related to negative emotions during task engagement (Vallerand et al., 2003, Study 1), lower levels of positive affect (Mageau & Vallerand, 2007), rumination when the person is not allowed to engage in his or her passionate activity (Ratelle, Vallerand, Mageau, Rousseau, & Provencher, 2004; Vallerand et al., 2003, Study 1) and with ill-advised persistent behavior in conditions in which engagement in the activity should be stopped (Rip, Fortin, & Vallerand, 2006; Vallerand et al., 2003, Studies 3 and 4).

Although an increasing amount of research has looked at the two types of passion and their association with a variety of outcomes, very little research has studied the variables (i.e., antecedents) involved in the development of passion. However, a recent three-part study by Mageau, Vallerand, Charest, Salvy, Lacaille, Bouffard, and Koestner (2009) involving novice, intermediate, and expert participants revealed that identification with the activity, activity specialization, parental activity valuation, and autonomy support predict the development of passion.

In terms of direct applicability to positive organizational scholarship (POS) concepts, it should be noted that Vallerand and colleagues conducted a limited number of studies regarding passion in an organizational context. Results from these series of experiments (Houlfort, Koestner, Vallerand, & Blanchard, 2003a; Houlfort, Koestner, & Vallerand, 2003b) demonstrated the applicability of the passion concept in the workplace.[3] Specifically, it appears that having harmonious passion toward work is related to feelings of autonomy, competence, and relatedness in organizations, whereas obsessive passion is not. In addition, psychological need satisfaction and psychological adjustment in the workplace successfully mediated the relationship between harmonious passion and global psychological adjustment. Such effects may even predict how healthy and adaptive one's retirement may be. Liu, Chen, and Yao (2011) recently found a mediating role of harmonious passion between autonomy and creativity in two organizational

contexts, suggesting that passion may play a mediating role in the workplace as well. In sum, harmonious and obsessive passion have varied and somewhat opposite effects on workers' psychological adjustment.

Passion for Work

Although Vallerand and colleagues focus on individual passion for a wide variety of activities, Perttula's research on passion (Lam & Perttula, 2008; McDaniel et al., 2009; Perttula, 2003, 2004, 2010) is focused entirely on the domain of work. In this model, passion for work is defined as a psychological state characterized by the experience of intense positive emotions, an internal drive to do the work, and a sense of meaningful connection toward one's work. Specifically, passion for work contains a cognitive aspect that includes two dimensions—meaningful connection and internal drive—and an emotional aspect that include two dimensions—joy and subjective vitality. The meaningful connection dimension refers to how an individual's identity is intertwined with his or her work. An intense inner drive that propels individuals in their work reflects the second dimension of passion for work. Feelings of enjoyment, happiness, and love toward work describe the joy dimension of passion for work. The subjective vitality dimension refers to a feeling of energy and aliveness at work (Ryan & Frederick, 1997). In this model, passion is not assumed to be a stable trait or personality attribute, but is seen as a dynamic phenomenon that can be influenced by the context in which one is embedded. Although it is possible that passion could be viewed as being dispositional in nature (e.g., optimism), all three models discussed in this chapter suggest that passion is state-like and pertains to specific aspects of the work itself and/or the work role. This view argues that an individual is passionate about a particular set of work activities—ones that evoke identification and meaning—not just any or all work.

A distinction is also made between passion for one's *job* and passion for work. This line of research has focused on the passion an employee experiences due to the content of the actual work (i.e., what employees actually do) instead of their job (i.e., a formal set of responsibilities). For example, if the employee is a management professor (the job), the passion he or she has for research, teaching, and service (the work) would be the focus of the research. When discussing one's job, one is likely to turn to a myriad of aspects, such as compensation, supervision, number of hours spent working, etc. However, when discussing one's work, the focus is more specific and includes work tasks, responsibilities, and activities.

Research has provided empirical support for the concept of passion for work. Results from exploratory and confirmatory factor analyses supported the four-dimensional second-order factor structure of the Passion for Work Scale (PWS; Perttula, 2010). The PWS has shown high levels of internal consistency, as well as initial convergent, discriminant, and criterion-related validity. The measure also offers a unique contribution to our current view of employees' experiences at work by capturing both affective and cognitive components of the work experience. For example, the 13-item scale includes items such as, "I feel a strong connection between my inner self and my work," "A sense of inner urgency drives me in my work," "I have energy and spirit when working," and "I really love my work." This measure of passion for work specifically captures the *personally meaningful* aspect of experiencing passion, which has been implied but not adequately measured in prior conceptualizations of this construct.

Passion for work has been found to be associated with a variety of outcomes. Perttula (2010) found that passion for work resulted in lower levels of job burnout. However, additional results indicated that how passion is viewed and understood varies across organizational contexts. In some environments, such as a retail outdoor company, greater passion led to greater employee creativity and effectiveness. Supervisors viewed those employees who are passionate to be exhibiting innovative behaviors and to be performing at high levels. However, in other environments, such as a not-for-profit health care clinic, in which the nature of the work is more bureaucratic and technical, higher levels of employee passion did not lead to greater creativity. When passion was high in this context, supervisors viewed employees as less creative.

Despite the increasing amount of interest in passion for work, surprisingly very few studies have empirically investigated what leads to passion. However, a study by Perttula (2004) revealed that autonomy, self-esteem, and perceived organizational support were found to be positively related to passion for work.

Entrepreneurial Passion

Cardon et al. (2009) and other scholars have explored the concept of passion in a particular work setting, the entrepreneurial context. Entrepreneurship is in some ways a unique work context, given the great uncertainty (Baron, 2008), huge personal responsibility for the success of the organization (Thompson, Kopelman, & Schriesheim, 1992), and overwhelming stress levels that entrepreneurs typically experience (Baron, 2008; Rahim, 1996) compared to a general population (Brockhaus, 1980) and to managers (Busenitz et al., 1997). Given the distinctions made in the literature about this particular work context, Cardon et al. (2009) focus their conceptualization of passion on the unique types of activities involved in an entrepreneurial work role. In this context, passion is defined as "consciously accessible intense positive feelings experienced by engagement in entrepreneurial activities associated with roles that are meaningful and salient to the self-identity of the entrepreneur" (Cardon et al., 2009, p. 517).

Two primary dimensions are evident in this definition: (a) passion involves positive and intense feelings (b) that are directed toward activities and roles that are meaningful to the self-identity of the entrepreneur. Both dimensions are consistent with the conceptualizations above. For example, positive and intense feelings noted here are consistent with Vallerand's definition of passion as involving like or love for an activity and with Perttula's conceptualization of passion including intense positive feelings of joy and subjective vitality. The second dimension noted by Cardon and colleagues, the identity meaningfulness of whatever the entrepreneur is passionate for, is also consistent with the earlier conceptualizations. Vallerand notes that passion is experienced for activities that are important, and Mageau and colleagues (2009) noted that identification with an activity is an antecedent of passion. Similarly, Perttula's conceptualization has a dimension of meaningful connection toward one's work, consistent with the identity meaningfulness noted by Cardon and colleagues. In addition, Cardon's conceptualization is similar to Perttula's in that it focuses on passion for specific tasks, responsibilities, and activities experienced at work, here focusing on activities and roles that are key aspects of entrepreneurship.

The primary distinction in conceptualization is the specificity of this definition of passion for the specific types of activities and roles in this particular work context. In particular, Cardon notes that entrepreneurial passion may be experienced for activities associated with inventing new products and services (passion for inventing), activities associated with founding and establishing ventures (passion for founding), or activities associated with growing fledgling firms and developing their capabilities (passion for developing). Application of Cardon's model of passion to nonentrepreneurial contexts would require determination of the key roles associated with the context, and measurement of passion (including feelings and identity connection) for each role embedded within the work context. For example, if one wanted to better understand passion for professors of management, you might look at passion for the three common roles within a professorial job—teaching, research, and service—separately. The focus of this model is varying levels of passion for specific sets of activities associated with key roles that are all contained in one job or work context.

A key contribution of Cardon and colleagues' conceptualization of passion goes beyond the definition of what passion is to developing a model of what passion does in entrepreneurship. Specifically, they argue that passion plays a role in coordinating cognitions, emotions, and behaviors directed towards pursuit of goals. This is consistent with the contribution of Perttula, in which she incorporates both affective and cognitive components into her conceptualization of passion.

A three-dimensional model of entrepreneurial passion has been supported by several studies (Cardon, 2010; Cardon & Kirk, 2010; Drnovsek, Cardon, & Patel, 2010). In particular, Cardon, Gregoire, and Stevens (2010) conducted a series of validation studies to assess and demonstrate the convergent, discriminant, content, criterion, and test–retest validity of the Entrepreneurial Passion Scale (EPS) across a number of different samples.

Although empirical support for the importance of passion in entrepreneurship is still in its infancy, as is empirical work on passion for work more broadly defined (Perttula, 2010), this empirical evidence is steadily growing. In particular, passion for inventing and passion for founding appear to lead to greater persistence (Cardon & Kirk, 2010), whereas passion for inventing and developing lead to more creativity in goal pursuit (Cardon, 2010), and all three types of passion are correlated highly with self-efficacy (Cardon & Kirk, 2010). In addition, passion for founding and passion for developing lead directly to venture growth (Drnovsek et al., 2010). This stream of research has also found evidence that entrepreneurial passion interacts with the experience of positive and negative affect, an idea first suggested by Wincent and colleagues (2008).

In particular, passion enhances the impact of positive affect on venture growth, whereas it mitigates the negative impact of negative affect on venture growth (Drnovsek et al., 2010). As such, entrepreneurs who experience both positive affect and passion have the highest levels of venture growth, whereas entrepreneurs who experience negative affect and low passion have the lowest levels of venture growth (often decline in sales rather than growth) (Drnovsek et al., 2010). Interestingly, there is no work to date on the antecedents of entrepreneurial passion.

Comparisons Across Conceptualizations and Measurements

Many similarities exist in the conceptualizations of passion across these three levels of abstraction (see Table 15.1). First, it is clear that passion is experienced as something intense and overwhelmingly positive, even though it may have negative consequences (such as by becoming obsessive and taking over one's life). Second, all three conceptualizations argue that passion is experienced for things that are personally important and meaningful to the individual. Third, passion appears to have motivating potential, since it involves time and energy spent on a task or activity (Vallerand et al., 2003), an internal drive to do work (Perttula, 2008), and may lead to behaviors such as persistence toward one's goals (Cardon & Kirk, 2010).

The conceptual distinctions between these three models are not as much about the content or even definition of passion as they are about the focus of each set of scholars' work. At the most obvious level, Vallerand and colleagues provide a very general model of passion for any activity in one's life, Perttula provides a focus on passion experienced at work, and Cardon looks at passion for specific roles in a very specific work context, that of entrepreneurs. At a more nuanced level, though, Vallerand's focus is on how the experience of passion relates to other elements in one's life, whether it exists in harmony or takes over those other elements. Perttula, in contrast, focuses on the experience itself of passion—what is it like and how is it experienced, what are the components of that experience of passion—within the broad context of work. Her specificity concerns what passion is, whereas Cardon's specificity concerns what passion is for. Cardon and colleagues focus on the specific types of activities or roles that a specific type of worker (entrepreneurs) may be passionate about, noting that, within the broad work context, employees may be more passionate about some aspects of their work than others.

It is interesting to note that these distinctions carry through in how passion is measured among the three levels of abstraction noted above. First, identity meaningfulness is implied but not explicitly measured by Vallerand and colleagues as part of passion in their dualistic measures of harmonious and obsessive passion. In contrast, identity meaningfulness of the work is captured explicitly in the Perttula PWS and in the Cardon EPS. Second, all three scales have subdimensions that capture very different things. In the Vallerand scales, the two dimensions reflect the type of passion experienced and whether passion (and the activity for which one is passionate) is in harmony with other aspects of your life, or whether that passion has consumed your life in an obsessive manner. In this way, harmonious and obsessive passion are somewhat contradictory to one another.

In the Perttula scale, the four dimensions of passion are focused on the subjective experience of passion, the components that make up the overall experience of passion: joy, subjective vitality, meaningful connection, and internal drive. The focus here is not on whether passion is experienced in balance with other aspects of one's life, but rather on the different factors that together make one more or less passionate. As such, this is a reflective scale in that all four factors should be present for an individual to experience passion.

Finally, in the Cardon scale the three dimensions of passion distinguish between the target activities of passion—what one is passionate about (inventing, founding, or developing activities related to one's business)—rather than the components of the sensation of passion. Cardon, Gregoire, and Stevens (2010) clarify that an entrepreneur may be passionate about one or more of these activities without being passionate about the others. This indicates that the EPS is a formative construct, and the subdimensions can be experienced separately from one another. The implication of these distinctions is that these three conceptualizations are not necessarily contradictory to one another, but instead provide different perspectives on the experience of passion. Each perspective provides the researcher with a unique model and scale to use depending upon the nature of the research question. For example, if one is studying general passion for work in any work setting, the Perttula model may be best. However, if one is studying passion in an entrepreneurial context, or another context in which a specific set of

work-related activities is particularly relevant, the Cardon model would be most appropriate. Similarly, if a researcher wants to understand which specific aspects of one's job or work environment engender passion, then a focus like Cardon's on the particular roles or sets of activities embedded within a context would be most appropriate. However, this would require development or adaptation of scales, so that one can measure passionate feelings and identity connections specific to each work role.

Future Directions

Results from research in organizations presented in this chapter have provided support for the concept of passion on a number of levels. We know that passion is an important part of work, and there is an increasing interest in researching the topic of passion. In fact, it would appear that the term *passion* has become part of the general vernacular in the business world (Welch, 2005). Although an increased interest in and noted relevance of "passion" is an exciting development, it also comes at a price. Like the term *leadership*, passion runs the risk of becoming an elusive term with no clear definition or boundaries. To establish a solid foundation in this area of research, we suggest that scholars should identify the level of abstraction or specificity they wish to study. Will the research focus on generalized passion as it applies to various activities or settings? Or, will the focus be the experience of passion in a general work context? Or, will it focus on a specific work context such as entrepreneurship or passion for particular sets of activities within the work context? Scholars must first determine the level of specificity and focus of the research, then develop the subsequent model and choose the appropriate measure based on that specificity. Carefully selecting the appropriate model and measure will help facilitate the development of a systematic body of work regarding passion. Given the scarcity of theoretical and empirical research on passion, numerous directions for future research exist. We discuss some specific research questions below.

The Importance of Passion for Work

First, although it appears as if having a workforce with passion is a desirable characteristic in an organization, exactly how does passion contribute to positive outcomes? In other words, why does passion for work matter? Research should look further than creativity, flow, venture growth, and performance, and explore potential relationships among passion and other organizationally relevant variables, such as resilience, turnover, organizational citizenship behaviors, career progress, and promotions, to name just a few. For example, employees who are not passionate at work may be more likely to voluntarily leave an organization in pursuit of work that is more meaningful to them. Or, employees who experience passion for work may be more likely to perform organizational citizenship behaviors (OCB). It is likely that if employees have a meaningful connection to their work and are happy, they may want to invest the extra time and effort associated with OCBs. And finally, individuals who exhibit high levels of passion at work may be recognized to a greater degree for their contribution and thus may rise through the corporate ranks more quickly. Alternatively, employees who experience passion for work may prefer the intangible rewards such meaningfulness provides them and shy away from external recognition or promotions that could shift them into roles and duties (e.g., managerial) that are less meaningful to them. Research is needed to look at the implications of passion for relevant outcomes in the workplace.

Second, if passion is an important outcome in an organization, what fosters passion? If passionate workers lead to happier workers and more productive outcomes, then a key question is how an organization can either foster passion in its employees or harness passion that does exist in order to maximize passion's productive potential and minimize its potentially harmful effects (e.g., from obsessive passion). Autonomy, organizational support, self-efficacy, and self-esteem appear to be related to greater passion, as does finding or creating work that is personally meaningful to the individual. But how does one do that? What are the mechanisms by which passion is realized, unleashed, or sustained? Longitudinal research may be needed to tease out the sources and mechanisms through which passion is discovered, developed, and sustained (or not).

Discovery of the mechanisms through which passion works may enable us to develop guidelines for managers on how to harness the productive potential of passion in their workers. For example, does empowerment of employees or jobs designed with greater autonomy and self-management opportunity lead to greater passion? Does organizational or leader support enable employees to be less concerned for job security or performance, and thus freer to experience or express their passion? Would helping employees discover for themselves which work activities are meaningful be an important step in igniting passion within a workforce (or college students, for that matter)? Special training sessions or coaches to help employees identify their talents and skills, uncover their work and life values, and assess their current environments could be helpful in this endeavor. Managers should initiate conversations about employee work goals and personal goals in order to help shape meaningful work activities, if such relationships are found through our research.

We also need to explore ways in which employees can learn to cultivate their own passion. Boyatzis and colleagues (2002) suggest taking time out to periodically evaluate quality of life, personal values, and goals. Bennis (1989) has also touted the importance of building time into one's life for reflection and self-examination, whether it be a few hours a week or one day a month or year. Such activities may increase the likelihood that one recognizes signals and signs of discontent or unhappiness at work, which can then lead to attempts to make appropriate changes. Finally, the use of job crafting exercises (Wrzesniewski & Dutton, 2001) or tools that help one identify one's "calling" (see Wrzesniewski, 2011, Chapter 4, this volume) could be a source of creating passion.

A third area of future research opportunity involves the negative or dark side of passion for work. Perhaps having too much passion could be detrimental, as with obsessive passion, and it would be interesting to investigate whether passion exhibits a negative or curvilinear relationship with outcomes such as work–family balance or performance. This may be especially problematic in some contexts or for some jobs, where getting input from other people is a key aspect of the job (such as for CEOs or entrepreneurs), and excessive passion may lead to individuals discounting the ideas of others, especially when such ideas are contrary to their own. Furthermore, as noted by Perttula (2010), across various organizational contexts, supervisors appeared to perceive the outcomes of passion quite differently. Perhaps passion for work is viewed as attractive in theory, but problematic in practice in some organizational contexts. Supervisors may preach the value of creating passion within their employees, but they may not truly value the consequences of such a passionate workforce. Specifically, supervisors may view employees with high levels of passion as difficult to manage and control, or as unreliable and too impulsive. Additional data might be collected to examine determinants of effective versus ineffective passion for work, which may involve not only the experience of passion itself, but also the specific types of work one is passionate for, or how one chooses to express that passion.

Although we have focused on the experience of passion, the display of passion at work is a distinct but related fourth area of future inquiry. Although it may be desirable to have employees feel passion, in some work contexts, it may not be desirable for them to display such passion. Wincent and colleagues (2008) suggested that self-regulation is an important aspect of the experience of passion, as passion without self-reflection and self-control could be detrimental or dangerous in the workplace. In contrast, the effective display of passion can lead to contagion of that passion to others in the workplace (Cardon, 2008), and can lead to financial and social support from outsiders, such as investors (Sudek, Mitteness, & Cardon, 2009). Further research on the distinctions between the experience and display of passion and the implications of each is needed.

Finally, while research to date has primarily considered passion of a focal individual (person, employee, or entrepreneur), there is virtually no work on collective passion. Most work contexts involve groups of people, whether as employees, managers, or an entrepreneurial founding team, and we have very little understanding of how such collective passion might operate. When would collective passion be synergistic, and when would it be restrictive or debilitating to an organization? For example, if individuals are equally passionate about the same work tasks, yet have different ideas for how to complete those tasks, there is great potential for conflict, more so than if those same employees disagreed concerning tasks they were not passionate about (e.g., Drnovsek, Cardon, & Murnieks, 2009). Similar to concepts of shared or collective sensemaking (Weick, 1995), we need research to explore how the passion of different employees working together operates.

Conclusion

The purpose of this chapter was to present an overview of passion and show its relevance to the realm of work and organizations. Although there has been growing interest and research regarding passion among both academics and business practitioners, at present there exists little systematic conceptual or empirical knowledge about passion for work in general or across various work contexts. To better understand passion as applied to work, we presented three conceptualizations of passion across three different levels of abstraction. Work represents a significant part of our lives, and further pursuit of the ideas and future research questions presented here

will increase our understanding of why people are passionate about their work, why they are able to maintain or lose their passion, and how those actions can be influenced.

Three very different research streams exist in this area each with a different level of specificity of focus on passion. However, clear similarities exist across the streams. Taken together, it is important to realize that passion is not independent across different levels of analysis or individuals experiencing it. Passion involves an interaction between individuals, organizations, and most clearly, environments, and is an area ripe for additional research.

Notes

1. A revised scale consisting of two 6-item scales is now often used and yields similar findings (Vallerand, 2008).
2. See Vallerand (2008) for a comprehensive review of the results of these studies.
3. See Vallerand and Houlfort (2003) for the Passion Toward Work Scale, a modified version of the Passion Scale.

References

Anderson, N. (2004). *Work with passion: How to do what you love for a living*. Novato: New World Library.

Baron, R.A. (2008). The role of affect in the entrepreneurial process. *Academy of Management Review, 33*(2), 328–340.

Bass, B.M. (1990). *Handbook of leadership*. New York: Free Press.

Baum, J.R., & Locke, E.A. (2004). The relationship of entrepreneurial traits, skills, and motivation to subsequent venture growth. *Journal of Applied Psychology, 89*, 587–598.

Baum, J.R., Locke, E.A., & Smith, K.G. (2001). A multidimensional model of venture growth. *Academy of Management Journal, 44*(2), 292–303.

Bennis, W. (1989). *On becoming a leader*. Reading, MA: Addison-Wesley Publishing.

Boyatzis, R., McKee, A., & Goleman, D. (2002). Reawakening your passion for work. *HBR OnPoint, April*, 5–11.

Brockhaus, R.H. (1980). Risk taking propensity of entrepreneurs. *Academy of Management Journal, 23*, 509–520.

Busenitz, L.W., & Barney, J.B. (1997). Differences between entrepreneurs and managers in large organizations: Biases and heuristics in strategic decision-making. *Journal of Business Venturing, 12*(1), 9–30.

Cardon, M.S., & Kirk, C. (2010). Passion, self-efficacy, and persistence in entrepreneurship. Presented at the Academy of Management conference, Montreal, Canada.

Cardon, M.S. (2008). Is passion contagious? The transference of entrepreneurial emotion to employees. *Human Resource Management Review, 18*(2), 77–86.

Cardon, M.S. (2010). Hot flashes versus global warming: Which type of affect drives entrepreneurial creativity? Presented at the Babson College Entrepreneurship Research conference, Lausanne, Switzerland.

Cardon, M.S., Gregoire, D., & Stevens, C. (2010). Measuring entrepreneurial passion: Conceptual development and scale validation. Manuscript in preparation.

Cardon, M., Wincent, J., Singh, J., & Drnovsek, M. (2009). The nature and experience of entrepreneurial passion. *Academy of Management Review, 34*(3), 511–532.

Caudron, S. (1997). The search for meaning at work. *Training and Development, 51*(9), 24–27.

Chang, R. (2000). *The passion plan: A step-by-step guide to discovering, developing, and living your passion.* San Francisco: Jossey-Bass.

Csikszentmihalyi, M. (1990). *Flow: The psychology of optimal experience.* New York: Harper Perennial.

Deci, E.L., & Ryan, R.M. (2000). The "what" and "why" of goal pursuits: Human needs and the self-determination of behavior. *Psychological Inquiry, 11*, 227–268.

Drnovsek, M., Cardon, M.S., & Murnieks, C.Y. (2009). Collective passion in entrepreneurial teams. In A. Carsrud, & M. Brannback (Eds.), *Understanding the entrepreneurial mind: Opening the black box.* New York: Springer Publishing.

Drnovsek, M., Cardon, M.S., & Patel, P. (2010). *Passion, affect, and venture growth.* Manuscript in preparation.

Fletcher, G.J.O., Rosanowski, J., & Fitness, J. (1994). Automatic processing in intimate contexts: The role of close-relationship beliefs. *Journal of Personality and Social Psychology, 67*(5), 888–897.

Forest, J., Mageau, G., Sarrazin, C., & Morin, E. (2010). "Work is my passion": The different affective, behavioural and cognitive consequences of harmonious and obsessive passion. *Canadian Journal of Administrative Sciences.* DOI: 10.1002/CJAS.170

Frijda, N. (2005). Emotion experience. *Cognition and Emotion, 19*(4), 473-497.

House, R.J., & Howell, J.M. (1992). Personality and charismatic leadership. *Leadership Quarterly, 3*, 81–108.

Houlfort, N., Koestner, R., Vallerand, R.J., & Blanchard, C.B. (2003a). *Passion at work: A look at psychological adjustment.* Manuscript in preparation, McGill University.

Houlfort, N., Koestner, R., & Vallerand, R.J. (2003b). *On the development of passion at work: The role of organizational support.* Manuscript in preparation, McGill University, Montreal, Quebec.

Kang, L., & Albion, M. (2009). *Passion at work: How to find work you love and live the time of your life.* Upper Saddle River, NJ: Prentice Hall.

Lam, C., & Perttula, K. (2008). *Work is my passion.* Presented at the Academy of Management, Anaheim, CA.

Levoy, G. (1997). *Callings: Finding and following an authentic life.* New York: Three Rivers Press.

Liu, D, Chen, X., & Yao, X. (2011). From autonomy to creativity: A multilevel investigation of the mediating role of harmonious passion. *Journal of Applied Psychology, 96*(2), 294–309.

Locke, E.A. (1997). Prime movers: The traits of great business leaders. In G. Cooper, & S. Jackson (Eds.), *Creating tomorrow's organizations* (pp. 75–96). Chichester, England: Wiley.

Locke, E.A. (2000). *The prime movers.* New York: AMACOM.

Mageau, G.A., & Vallerand, R.J. (2007). The moderating effect of passion on the relation between activity engagement and positive affect. *Motivation and Emotion, 31*, 312–321.

Mageau, G.A., Vallerand, R.J., Charest, J., Salvy, S., Lacaille, N., Bouffard, T., & Koestner, R. (2009). On the development of harmonious and obsessive passion: The role of autonomy support, activity specialization, and identification with the activity. *Journal of Personality, 77*(3), 601–646.

Mageau, G.A., Vallerand, R.J., Rousseau, F.L., Ratelle, C.F., & Provencher, P.J. (2005). Passion and gambling: Investigating the divergent affective and cognitive consequences of gambling. *Journal of Applied Social Psychology, 35*, 100–118.

Martin, A. (2005). Perplexity and passion: Further consideration of the role of positive psychology in the workplace. *Journal of Organizational Behavior, 24*, 197–199.

McDaniel, D., Harrison, S., Perttula, K., Corley, K., Lam, C.F., Spreitzer, G., & Quinn, R. (2009). *Snap, Crackle, Pop! Energy and passion in organizations.* Presented at the Academy of Management, Chicago, IL.

Perttula, K. (2003). *The POW factor: Understanding passion for one's work,* Presented at the Academy of Management, Seattle, WA.

Perttula, K. (2004). *The POW factor: Understanding and igniting passion for one's work.* Unpublished doctoral dissertation, University of Southern California, Los Angeles, California.

Perttula, K. (2010). *Passion for work: Initial measurement and construct validation.* Manuscript in preparation.

Ratelle, C.F., Vallerand, R.J., Mageau, G.A., Rousseau, F.L., & Provencher, P.J. (2004). When passion leads to pathology: A look at gambling. *Journal of Gambling Studies, 20*, 105–119.

Rahim, A. (1996). Stress, strain, and their moderators: An empirical comparison of entrepreneurs and managers. *Journal of Small Business Management, 34*(1), 46–58.

Rip, B., Fortin, S., & Vallerand, R.J. (2006). The relationship between passion and injury in dance students. *Journal of Dance Medicine & Science, 10*, 14–20.

Rousseau, F.L., Vallerand, R.J. (2003). *The role of passion in the psychological adjustment of elderly individuals.* Manuscript in preparation, Universite du Quebec a Montreal.

Rockwell, I. (2002). *The five wisdom energies: A Buddhist way of understanding personalities, emotions, and relationships.* Boston: Shambhala.

Ryan, R.M., & Frederick, C.M. (1997). On energy, personality, and health: Subjective vitality as dynamic reflection of well-being. *Journal of Personality, 65*, 529–565.

Seligman, M. (2004). Work and personal satisfaction. In *Authentic happiness: Using the new positive psychology to realize your potential for lasting fulfillment* (pp. 165–187). New York: The Free Press.

Sheldon, K.M. (2002). The self-concordance model of healthy goal striving: When personal goals correctly represent the person. In E.L. Deci, & R.M. Ryan (Eds.), *Handbook of self-determination research* (pp. 65–88). Rochester, NY: The University of Rochester Press.

Sudek, R., Mitteness, C., & Cardon, M. (2009). *The impact of displayed and perceived entrepreneurial passion on angel investing.* Paper presented at the Babson College Entrepreneurship Research conference, Wellesley, MA.

Thompson, C.A., Kopelman, R., & Schriesheim, C. (1992). Putting all one's eggs in the same basket: A comparison of commitment and satisfaction among self- and organizationally employed men. *Journal of Applied Psychology, 77*(5), 738–743.

Vallerand, R.J. (1997). Toward a hierarchical model of intrinsic and extrinsic motivation. *Advances in Experimental and Social Psychology, 29*, 271–360.

Vallerand, R.J., Blanchard, C., Mageau, G.A., Koestner, R., Ratelle, C., Leonard, M., et al. (2003). Les passions de l'ame: On obsessive and harmonious passion. *Journal of Personality and Social Psychology, 85*, 756–767.

Vallerand, R.J., & Houlfort, N. (2003). Passion at work: Toward a new conceptualization. In S.W. Gilliland, D.D. Steiner, & D.P. Skarlicki (Eds.), *Emerging perspectives on values in organizations* (pp. 175–204). Greenwich, CT: Information Age Publishing.

Vallerand, R.J., Mageau, G.A., Elliot, A.J., Dumais, A., Demers, M. -A., & Rousseau, F. (2008). Passion and performance attainment in sport. *Psychology of Sport and Exercise, 9*, 373–392.

Vallerand, R.J., & Miquelon, P. (2007). Passion for sport in athletes. In D. Lavallée, & S. Jowett (Eds.), *Social psychology in sport* (pp. 249–263). Champaign, IL: Human Kinetics.

Vallerand, R.J., Rousseau, F.L., Grouzet, F.M.E., Dumais, A., Grenier, S., & Blanchard, C.B. (2006). Passion in sport: A look at determinants and affective experiences. *Journal of Sport & Exercise Psychology, 28*, 454–478.

Vallerand, R.J., Salvy, S.J., Mageau, G.A., Elliot, A.J., Denis, P., Grouzet, F.M.E., et al. (2007). On the role of passion in performance. *Journal of Personality, 75*, 505–533.

Weick, K. (1995). *Sensemaking in organizations.* Thousand Oaks, CA: Sage.

Welch, J. (2005). *Winning.* New York: HarperCollins.

Wincent, J., Cardon, M.S., Singh, J., & Drnovsek, M. (2008). Entrepreneurial affect: The distinction between emotion and passion. Presented at the Academy of Management conference, Anaheim, CA.

Wrzesniewski, A. (2002). It's not just a job: Shifting meanings of work in the wake of 9/11. *Journal of Management Inquiry, 11*(3), 230–234.

Wrzesniewski, A. (2011). Callings. In K.S. Cameron & G.M. Spreitzer (Eds.), *The Oxford handbook of positive organizational scholarship.* New York: Oxford University Press.

Wrzesniewski, A., & Dutton, J.E. (2001). Crafting a job: Revisioning employees as active crafters of their work. *Academy of Management Review, 26*(2), 179–201.

Social Context and the Psychology of Emotional Intelligence

A Key to Creating Positive Organizations

Oscar Ybarra, Laura Rees, Ethan Kross, *and* Jeffrey Sanchez-Burks

Abstract

In this chapter, we bridge work on positive organizational scholarship (POS) and emotional intelligence by focusing on their common element—an emphasis on how people navigate social interactions and relationships. We put forth a synthesis—*social-emotional intelligence*—based on two assumptions: (a) a useful integration of POS and emotional intelligence needs to describe the social context in order to understand *when* and *why* people apply their emotional intelligence skills; and (b) a useful model of emotional intelligence needs to be based on agreed upon conceptions of *how* the mind works—namely, by defining the interaction between intuitive (automatic) and deliberative (controlled) processes that underlie emotional intelligence abilities (e.g., emotional recognition and control). Our synthesis adds flexibility and adaptability to the emotional intelligence process and takes into account how it interacts with the presence or absence of positive organizational environments.

Keywords: Social context, emotional intelligence, dual psychological processes, dynamic social intelligence

Positive organizational scholarship (POS) provides a perspective for creating exceptional performance through a focus on the internal, social environment of organizations (e.g., Cameron, 2008). This perspective is essential to developing successful organizations that foster "positive deviance," or performance above the norm (e.g., Spreitzer & Sonenshein, 2003). Emotional intelligence, as currently understood however, is a diffuse construct. As O'Sullivan (2007, p. 260) notes, "Clinical practitioners, business consultants, popular writers, serious researchers, and scores of other groups use the term *emotional intelligence* (EI) to refer to anything related to understanding oneself and other people, even if the 'emotional' connection is rather tenuous." This critique notwithstanding, the construct of EI is germane to the issue of creating positive organizational environments. However, clarity, precision, and elaboration are needed in order to refine this construct, increase its explanatory value, and link it directly to POS. This chapter aims to provide such a

bridge by creating a synthesis—*social-emotional intelligence*—based on two assumptions:

- *Assumption 1*: A useful model of POS and emotional intelligence in relation to each other needs to delineate the nature of the social context in order to understand *when* and *why* people apply their EI skills.
- *Assumption 2*: A useful model of EI needs to integrate fundamental conceptions of *how* the mind works—namely, by defining the interaction between intuitive (automatic) and deliberative (controlled) mental processes—to fully capture the flexibility with which people make sense of their social worlds and are influenced by it.

We begin by reviewing the predictive ability of EI measures. Then, we turn to the diverse approaches to conceptualizing EI. Finally, we elaborate the two assumptions of social-emotional intelligence, discuss their implications for research and theory on

POS and EI, and highlight important future research directions.

What Emotional Intelligence Assessments Predict

Over the past two decades, a great deal of research has examined the relationship between EI and various outcomes for individuals, such as job satisfaction, quality of relationships, and well-being. Here, we review findings on what EI measures predict. The review is by necessity selective, given the numerous studies conducted on EI (for more extensive reviews, see Mayer, Roberts, & Barsade, 2008; Zeidner, Matthews, & Roberts, 2004).

Some research findings indicate that low levels of EI are associated with negative emotional reactions and negative coping strategies in response to stress (Jordan, Ashkanasy, & Hartel, 2002). Low EI has also been related to worry and avoidance coping (Matthews et al., 2006). On the other hand, high EI has been associated with greater well-being (positive mood and high self-esteem), higher economic self-efficacy (Engelberg & Sjoberg, 2006), and adaptive coping following negative events (Schutte, Malouff, Simunek, McKenley, & Hollander, 2002). Importantly, recent work demonstrates that trait EI is associated with such positive outcomes (e.g., job satisfaction; well-being) over and above that predicted by personality (Singh & Woods, 2008).

Emotional Intelligence Assessments and Organizational Outcomes

In organizational research, emotions and their effective management have significant implications for employees, managers, and organizations (Barsade & Gibson, 2007). Although cognitive intelligence is often prized as an ideal quality in employees, EI has also been found to have significant positive relationships with in-role, task performance, and citizenship behaviors (i.e., out-of-role performance that goes "above and beyond" one's job; Côté & Miners, 2006). These effects persist after controlling for cognitive intelligence, suggesting that EI facilitates worker's performance.

More recent work has linked EI with higher merit increases in salary and increases in company rank among members of the finance department of a Fortune 400 insurance company (Lopes et al., 2006). Supervisors and peers also rated individuals who scored higher on EI as possessing better social skills (e.g., stress tolerance). Some recent work has also shown positive relationships between EI and objective performance measures. For example, a recent study of Singaporean sellers in a buyer–seller negotiation exercise found that better emotion recognition was associated with better individual negotiation outcomes based on objective performance measures, including value created and share captured (Elfenbein et al., 2007).

Although many studies focus on individual-level implications of EI, some studies have begun to study the broader social ramifications of EI. On a dyadic relationship level, for example, studies have illustrated the intrinsically social nature of EI by finding positive relationships between EI—particularly the ability to manage emotions—and the quality of social interactions (Lopes, Brackett, Nezlek, Schutz, Sellin, & Salovey, 2004). In teams, EI—specifically, the awareness and management of one's own and others' emotions—has been linked to performance (based on a self-report workgroup-level scale, Jordan & Lawrence, 2009). Emotional intelligence has also been studied in relation to transformational leadership (Brown & Moshavi, 2005), which has been shown to have significant effects on followers' performance, motivation, and other work outcomes (Bono & Judge, 2003; Divr, Eden, Avolio, & Shamir, 2002). One study has even proposed a multilevel theory of individual-level EI and organizational-level emotional capability (including receptivity, mobilization, and learning) as significant influences on an organization's ability to change (Huy, 1999).

Despite the seemingly high level of consensus among researchers regarding EI and its predictive value, it remains a multifaceted concept, which means different things to different people—conceptually, operationally, and empirically. In the next section, we provide a brief overview of the different ways in which EI is conceptualized to illustrate this point.

Conceptualizing and Assessing Emotional Intelligence

There exists a diversity of approaches to conceptualizing and assessing EI. Some researchers think of it more in terms of personality tendencies or traits, akin to extraversion, whereas other researchers regard EI more as an ability or set of abilities. Regardless of the definitional approach to EI, researchers have created various measures that fit with their definitions. Some researchers have developed ability measures of EI, whether as trait tendencies people can self-report (Tett, Fox, & Wang, 2005) or as assessments developed to measure specific components of EI (e.g., Nowicki & Duke, 1994).

Other approaches combine self-reported EI tendencies with broader personality constructs. The diversity of treatments of EI has, in the estimates of some authors, given rise to a conceptual morass (Conte, 2005). Nevertheless, by briefly surveying the literature, we can arrive at a working understanding of what EI is.

Mixed Models

Mixed models start with self-reported qualities that appear related to EI abilities, but they also consider more molar qualities, such as one's motives, mood, self assessments, self-esteem, and coping tendencies. Some of these measures include the Emotional Quotient Inventory (EQ-i; Bar-On, 1997), the Self-Report Emotional Intelligence Test (SREIT; Schutte et al., 1998), and the Multidimensional Emotional Intelligence Assessment (MEIA; Tett, Fox, & Wang, 2005). Such mixed approaches are considered by some not to provide real assessments of EI, as they tend to heavily overlap with other personality traits, assess self-judgments rather than abilities related to EI, and measure tendencies such as assertiveness and flexibility (Mayer et. al., 2008). Indeed, studies have reported correlations above 0.70 between the EQ-i and the Big Five personality scales (e.g., Brackett & Mayer, 2003). Thus, although popular and easy to administer, it is not clear what such assessments offer beyond available personality measures, in addition to the problem that they can be faked in a socially desirable direction (Day & Carroll, 2008; Grubb & McDaniel, 2007).

Ability Models

In addition to mixed-model assessments of EI, there are a variety of ability-related models. In ability models researchers focus on single abilities, such as how people reason about emotions (e.g., Clore, Ortony, & Foss, 1987; Roseman, 1984) or how emotions influence thought (e.g., Damasio, 1994; Frigda, 1988; George & Brief, 1996; Isen, Johnson, Mertz, & Robinson, 1985; Salovey, Hsee, & Mayer, 1993; for a review, see George, 2000). Other researchers have studied different abilities such as accuracy in facial recognition and emotion perception (Ekman & Friesen, 1975; Matsumoto et al., 2000; Nowicki & Duke, 1994; O'Sullivan, 1982; Sanchez-Burks & Huy, 2009) and emotion management (e.g., Gross, 1998; Kross, Ayduk, & Mischel, 2005; Lazarus, 1994). That these abilities are considered distinct stems in part from their separate historical and intellectual traditions. For example, whereas emotional perception has its roots in non-verbal perception and facial recognition (e.g., Buck, 1984; Nowicki & Duke, 1994; Rosenthal, Hall, DiMatteo, Rogers, & Archer, 1979), an interest in emotion management seems to be rooted in part in the clinical tradition (e.g., Beck, 1979; Ellis, 2001) and social cognitive research on impulse control (e.g., Mischel, Shoda, & Rodriguez, 1989).

Integrative Models

On the other hand, integrative models, such as the four-branch model of EI (Mayer & Salovey, 1997; Mayer et al., 1997), integrate four separate-but-related abilities under one overarching concept. The four-branch model deals with people's ability to *recognize* emotions (in self and others), the ability to *use* emotion to influence thought, the ability to *understand* emotions, and the ability to *manage* emotions (Mayer & Salovey, 1997; Mayer et al., 1997). Although sometimes studied individually, together, this group of abilities gives rise to an individual's overall EI under the four-branch model (Mayer et al., 2008). Integrating different abilities into an overarching EI framework in this way acknowledges that the person has a variety of EI tools at his or her disposal to make sense of his or her environments and to adapt.

Critical Synthesis: Seeking Common Ground by Explicating the Social Context and Psychology of Emotional Intelligence

Given the diversity in theoretical and empirical approaches to the study of EI, and the varied research findings in which these different conceptions have been studied, it is challenging for even a trained researcher to understand what EI is. Such a lack of conceptual coherence promotes confusion as researchers do not have a lingua franca to use in integrating and growing their research field. This problem is compounded as practitioners propagate well-intentioned but simplified views and findings from the EI field.

However, our goal is not to throw out the proverbial EI baby with the bath water. The research and conceptions described thus far provide important early steps in the study of EI, but these approaches lack two things. First, they do not fully explicate the importance of the social context in which people apply their EI toolkit. How do we answer questions such as: How is EI influenced by the social context? What perils lurk in the social world that can make the most emotionally intelligent person ineffective at times? Once the social context is considered more explicitly, it will become clearer that the social world people navigate can shape, direct, and place constraints on a person's EI, regardless of the EI level they think they have (for similar argument in the domain of personality see Mischel & Shoda, 1995).

Second, the research described thus far assumes a very "conscious" or deliberate view of EI. For example, participants in laboratory settings are often asked to judge faces or scenes for emotional content and describe what they see. At other times, participants are presented with hypothetical, verbal descriptions of social situations and asked to report how they and the other person in the situation would feel. Communicating and reporting on one's opinions and feelings are very conscious activities (e.g., Smith & DeCoster, 2000), and they can also be cognitively demanding. In popular writing on EI, one feature that made EI promising, in addition to its potential predictive power compared to cognitive intelligence (which is quite modest for current EI assessments), was the possibility that some EI processes might be carried out automatically. Terrific links were made to the neuropsychological literature that suggest, for example, the efficiency with which the amygdala and related neural circuits can process emotional information even with little involvement of higher-level thought (e.g., Goleman, 1995; based on work by LeDoux). Although it was insightful to relate the idea of automatic and efficient mental processes to EI, in actuality, little research on automatic processes has been carried out by EI researchers. This limits most current EI conceptions.

Given these concerns, our aim in the remaining part of this chapter is to provide a framework to guide research on EI, especially in the context of POS. One aspect of our approach is to consider the social context in which EI-related tools are applied (Assumption 1). It is in this sense that POS, with its explicit focus on social interaction and relationships, can ground the concept and study of EI. The second element of our approach is to take seriously the notion that EI involves a set of mental processes, not just a score a person is given on an EI test. By delving deeper into the psychology of EI and relating it to widely accepted dual-process models (Assumption 2), we delineate a conception of EI that is more realistic psychologically, dynamic, and open to inefficiencies, but also more amenable to the goals of creating positive organizational environments. We turn to the two assumptions of our framework next.

Two Assumptions
Social-Emotional Intelligence Assumption 1: Unpacking Challenges in Social Contexts to Understand the "When" and "Why" of Emotional Intelligence

Implied in many discussions of EI is that what also matters in performance such as in one's job, in addition to cognitive intelligence (e.g., crystallized and fluid), is how people respond to and manage aspects of the social environment. This proposal may stem from findings that suggest traditional IQ types of assessments account for only 20%–25% of the variance in academic and job-related outcomes (for a review, see Neisser et al., 1996). Such a conclusion, though, rests on the assumption that measures of intelligence are based on an agreed-upon definition of intelligence and how best to measure it. Nevertheless, the remaining variance to be explained invites conjectures about what other skills and domains of life influence a person's success. One domain that has historically attracted such attention is that of social interaction and relationships.

Although it appears that putting the focus on the social domain was a coup for the field of EI, it is important to appreciate that a long history of research has dealt directly with how people make sense of their social environments, such as work on social intelligence and social cognition, as we will discuss (for reviews see Kilhstrom & Cantor, 1989, 2000). At times, EI researchers have attempted to distinguish EI from social intelligence (Mayer, Caruso, & Salovey, 1999). However, conceptually and operationally, many EI approaches emphasize the social domain. For example, some of the sub-scales of the EQ-i (Bar-On, 1997) converge onto an interpersonal factor, and many of the ability models deal with emotion recognition in others (e.g., the DANVA, Nowicki & Duke, 1994; the Japanese and Caucasian Brief Affect Recognition Test, or JACBART, Matsumoto et al., 2000) and the ability to manage emotions in others (e.g., the portion of the Mayer-Salovey-Caruso Emotional Intelligence Test, or MSCEIT, Four-Branch Model dealing with emotion management, Mayer, Salovey, & Caruso, 2002). Popular treatments have also moved beyond the term *emotional intelligence* and refer to *social intelligence* (Goleman, 2006) to make explicit the connection between EI and interpersonal processes.

Empirically, some studies of EI have been related to social outcomes, such as the quality of a person's interactions with others (Lopes et al., 2004), negotiation results (Elfenbein et al., 2007), leaders' interaction with followers (Bono & Judge, 2003; Divr et al., 2002), and the extent to which workers pursue organizational citizenship behaviors (Côté & Miners, 2006), as reviewed above. However, although navigating the social world is implied to be part of the purview of EI, it is rarely discussed in depth in terms of how EI is influenced by the social context. For example, why is it that otherwise emotionally intelligent and savvy individuals crumble when faced with temptation, such as President Clinton with Monica Lewinsky, and more recent occurrences involving other prominent individuals, such as Eliot Spitzer and John Edwards. President Clinton, for example, won two elections—achievements based on the precise navigation of the social and perilous world of U.S. politics. Yet, his downfall with regard to the Lewinsky debacle also resulted from a failure to read the social landscape and control his emotions. The inability to deal with such judgmental and behavioral outcomes performed by people considered emotionally intelligent is a serious limitation of most models of EI, and it is why we make the social context an explicit element in our analysis.

At one level, it is perplexing that, despite some allusion to the social aspect of EI, most available treatments of EI pay scant direct attention to the nature of the social world. It is also perplexing that little of the research on what was previously referred to as "social intelligence" is rarely reviewed or referred to by EI researchers. This is despite the fact that considerable research has been carried out in this area, for example, on the psychometrics of social intelligence and related social intelligence skills, which predates work on EI (e.g., Hendricks, Guilford, & Hoepfner, 1969; Hunt, 1928; Gardner, 1983; Guilford, 1967; Moss, Hunt, Omwake, & Ronning, 1927; O'Sullivan, Guilford, & deMille, 1965; also for a review see Kilhstrom & Cantor, 2000). Decades before the term "emotional intelligence" gained popularity, researchers were investigating how social intelligence differs from nonsocial intelligence and whether they can be distinguished from each other (Ford & Tisak, 1983; Riggio, Messamer, & Throckmorton, 1991; Shanley, Walker, & Foley, 1971; Thorndike & Stein, 1937; Wechsler, 1958; Woodrow, 1939), in addition to examining the role of personality factors in social intelligence (e.g., Ford & Tisak, 1983; Gough, 1966; Marlowe, 1986). Much of the work on social intelligence serves as the basis for the social cognition frameworks that have had much success in psychology in the last four decades.

Emotional intelligence is germane to navigating social interactions and relationships, but any such treatment can be greatly enhanced by considering social context and being open to available research and concepts on social intelligence and social cognition.

Thus, we take as our starting point the proposal that a useful model of EI needs to carefully, deliberately, and explicitly consider the social world that people navigate, in particular from the perspective that the social world is "fuzzy"—it is comprised of negotiable facts whose perception is driven by people's subjective construals and the meaning they ascribe to social events. It is in this regard that most models of EI are limited, in that they assume that a high score on a measure of EI represents a skill that will yield high performance across all contexts, and that the efficacy with which a person applies that skill can be determined. But truth and accuracy are difficult to establish when dealing with social events whose meanings are pliable and interpretable (for a similar discussion, see Kilhstrom & Cantor, 2000). Most EI models also neglect to consider that people's goals, unfulfilled needs, time pressures, or lack of cognitive resources can shape their construals. It is in the fuzzy zone of the social world, with its labile nature, that the promise of creating positive organizations becomes clear, as such an emphasis challenges researchers and practitioners to help shape how people construe their social surroundings and the goals they seek. Before pursuing these implications, though, it is important to address one of the assumptions of POS, which is that people value and strive for positive social connections with others. This desire for positive social connections will help put into even sharper relief the need to incorporate the social into any model of EI.

The Value of the Social

That people should strive to form supportive social connections with others is in line with the proposal of Trivers' (1971) classic paper. In an extensive review of varied psychological and related literatures, the renowned biologist convincingly concludes that people are driven to establish relationships with others, at times even at great cost to the self (Baumeister & Leary, 1995). Supportive research has shown, for instance, that people are faster to notice information with social versus nonsocial implications (Ybarra, Chan, & Park, 2001), and when getting to know someone, people prefer receiving information that tells them about the person's social versus work-related qualities (Wojciske, Bazinska,

& Jawoski, 1998). People also constantly talk about others (Dunbar, Marriott, & Duncan, 1997), and they also think about others even while sleeping (McNamara, McLaren, Smith, Brown, & Stickgold, 2005). Relationships and connections with others are fundamental drivers of individuals' judgment and behavior.

This drive to create social and emotional bonds emerges and asserts itself even in work- and task-related contexts. Classic examples of this can be found in the organizational literature dealing with groups. This research showed that, when formal groups were put in place to perform tasks relevant to organizational goals, informal groups—such as employees from different units gathering to eat lunch—were spontaneously created as a response to people's need for social contact (e.g., Hamner & Organ, 1982; Sayles, 1957). As many of the contributors to this volume discuss, such positive connections at work can lead to benefits for the organization, and their absence can lead to detrimental outcomes.

The above discussion suggests that a more complete model of EI needs to incorporate information about people's social goals and whether such goals are being met. For example, research has shown that when people do not feel socially accepted, they become emotionally negative and their ability to reason is reduced (e.g., Baumeister, Twenge, & Nuss, 2002). They also tend to focus on information related to fulfilling the need to connect (Gardner, Pickett, & Brewer, 2000), which can limit their ability to take in information relevant to the task at hand—goals have a way of blinding people to other aspects of their environments (Ordóñez, Schweitzer, Galinsky, & Bazerman, 2009).

This aspect of the social context—in terms of people's need to form and maintain social connections with others—suggests that the EI process is fluid and at times open to inefficiencies. It suggests that when people are lacking in positive social connections or have been rejected, they may be subject to experience some emotions over others and may be apt to misread or focus more on goal-relevant information, even seeing social cues where there are none (Epley, Akalis, Waytz, & Cacioppo, 2008; Humphrey, 1976). Further, given that some social inferential processes depend on limited cognitive capacity, as we will discuss in Assumption 2 of our analysis, a strong social goal that is not being met may short-circuit higher-level reasoning processes when such processes are most needed.

Available models of EI have little to say about people's need to connect and the implications such unmet needs have for social thinking and social navigation. It is usually assumed that people apply their EI skills—whatever level they happen to have—consistently across time, but we have known for some time that traits and abilities are not expressed consistently across situations (Mischel & Shoda, 1995).

The Veridicality of Emotional Displays and Chronic Perceptual Biases

In addition to not explicitly considering issues of social motivation and how this can influence social thinking, EI models assume that assessments of the social world—assuming a person has scored high on some measure of EI—are static and valid. It is comforting to assume so, but just as smart people can be foolish for a host of reasons (Sternberg, 2002), people who score high on EI may also exhibit socially inefficient behavior for a host of reasons. One way this can happen is by assuming that the emotions of others can actually be recognized (as most EI models assume), for example. In complex and mixed-motive environments in which people deal with strangers or competitors (e.g., large organizations), those being perceived many times can enact unpredictable behaviors or limit the degree to which they are "readable" (Ybarra et al., 2010). At best, it could be argued that a person high on EI would not render a judgment of another person in such cases, but no conception or assessment of EI has been created to capture this "skeptical" approach to information presented by others. At worst, the person will inaccurately read the target's emotions, triggering a cascade of inferences and assumptions that could potentially lead to a suboptimal way of interacting. Ecologically valid models of EI need to incorporate such knowledge of others and the social conditions that are more or less likely to trigger attempts not to be figured out and predicted (e.g., Ybarra et al., 2010).

Certain social environments can also chronically shape the construals people make and inferences that they draw. Although various psychological and behavioral processes are in place that prompt people to form social connections with others, people are also attuned to potential interpersonal costs, such as being betrayed by a coworker, overlooked by a boss, or treated with disrespect in front of other employees. This sensitivity to potential costs can create barriers to positive organizing as people have lower thresholds for noticing the bad and drawing negative inferences about others, and higher thresholds for accepting at face value others' positive acts. Evidence that this is the case is well documented in several domains (Ybarra, 2001, 2002; Ybarra, Schaberg, & Keiper, 1999; Ybarra & Stephan, 1996, 1999). One implication of this is that organizational values that facilitate competitiveness, distrust, and behavioral practices harmful to an organization's "social glue" could trigger less-than-generous and erroneous inferences and thus ineffective EI, due in part to supporting some beliefs over others (e.g., "My colleagues only care about themselves"), but also due to social stress and diminished cognitive resources, as we discuss under Assumption 2.

SUMMARY

Thus, with regard to Assumption 1 of our analysis, we propose that what is needed to enhance current conceptions of EI is an explicit exposition of the social context in which people apply their EI skills as they attempt to navigate their interactions and relationships with others and how the pursuit of positive organizational goals (or lack thereof) impacts the EI process. Such considerations help inform the *when* and *why* of EI. All people have a need to connect, but *when* such a need is unfulfilled, they may exhibit low EI despite having scored high on an EI assessment. A better understanding of the social context thus can also help us explain *why* people considered emotionally intelligent can be socially inefficient as a function of context—a scenario no current model of EI addresses.

We next turn to Assumption 2 of our analysis, which provides a fuller and more nuanced analysis of *how* people think, which should also help us to better predict when people will be effective in deploying their EI.

Social-Emotional Intelligence Assumption 2: Specifying the Mental Processes Involved in Emotional Intelligence and How They Interact (the "How" of Emotional Intelligence)

Most EI research assumes a very "conscious" or deliberate view of EI. For example, many times, participants in studies are asked to judge scenarios or facial stimuli and then describe what they have seen or complete self-report personality-type inventories. Thus, although EI researchers acknowledge the possibility that some mental and brain processes can operate efficiently, few if any researchers have taken seriously the distinction between intuitive

and deliberate processes, or their potential interactions (for an exception, see Fiori, 2009).

In contrast, cognitive and social psychologists (and also philosophers, political scientists, economists, and developmentalists) have described in many theoretical treatments automatic or intuitive mental processes and how they differ from more conscious and deliberate ones (e.g., Chaiken & Trope, 1999; Epstein, 1994; Evans, 2008; Hofman, Friese, & Strack, 2009; Kross & Mischel, 2010; McClure, Laibson, Loewenstein, & Cohen, 2004; Milkman, Rogers, & Bazerman, 2008; Posner & Snyder, 1975; Shiffrin & Schneider, 1977; Sloman, 1996; Smith & DeCoster, 2000; Stanovich & West, 2000). In our analysis, we integrate deliberate and intuitive components in a model of social-EI.

The abilities to communicate and report on one's opinions and feelings are very conscious activities (e.g., Smith & DeCoster, 2000)—activities that many times depend on limited cognitive resources. We refer to this aspect of EI as *deliberate*—individuals consciously use their EI to judge and analyze social and emotional situations. On the other hand, research from other areas has begun to show that processes related to EI can actually be carried out automatically and with little awareness. We refer to this as the *intuitive* aspect of EI, and discuss the deliberate–intuitive distinction presently. As we elaborate in the next section, taking seriously the distinction between intuitive and deliberate processes not only adds dynamism and context sensitivity to our framework, it also suggests novel hypotheses and implications, in addition to laying the groundwork for applying social-EI to enabling positive organizations.

Two General Abilities and Two Types of Processing for Social-Emotional Intelligence

Although a variety of abilities relevant to EI are assessed by EI instruments, here we focus on two abilities that are common to many EI models. These are the meta-capabilities of *emotional recognition* and *emotional control*. Emotional recognition and control are the workhorses of social navigation and provide the most common ground across different theoretical perspectives. Beyond this, however, our framework also incorporates the two types of information processing we discussed above—*intuitive* and *deliberate* processing. This also helps place our framework in the context of similarly distinctive dual-process models used in various disciplines, including social cognition, cognitive science, reasoning and rationality, personality, behavioral economics, and emotion regulation, for example (e.g., Chaiken & Trope, 1999; Epstein, 1994; Evans, 2008; Kross & Mischel, 2010; Posner & Snyder, 1975; Shiffrin & Schneider, 1977; Sloman, 1996; Smith & DeCoster, 2000; Stanovich & West, 2000). Going forward, we refer to these four concepts—recognition, control, intuitive, and deliberate—in terms of the *social* aspect of EI to help emphasize Assumption 1 of our analysis.

Social-emotional recognition traditionally deals with people's ability to determine in the self and others which emotions are being felt or expressed verbally and nonverbally and is rooted in earlier work on nonverbal sensitivity (e.g., Buck, 1984; Rosenthal et al., 1979). Social-emotional control refers to a person's ability to manage moods and emotions in the self and others, and research has shown this is usually in the service of maintaining or creating positive affective states and eliminating or minimizing negative ones (e.g., Clark & Isen, 1982; Erber & Erber, 2001; Larsen, 2000; Mischel, Ebbesen, & Zeiss, 1973).

Both social-emotional recognition and control can operate through a deliberate process (see Table 16.1). For example, an employee can consciously focus on what his boss is saying and attend to the boss' facial expression and gestures to infer not only what the boss wants done, but when and by whom. In terms of social-emotional control, a leader could guide her attention to think differently about the impending downsizing of her unit, a conscious frame switching that might not only help quell personal distress and anxiety, but might suggest different ways of helping the affected employees (instead of focusing on the self, for instance, the leader could focus on employee needs).

As already mentioned, in the majority of EI models, social-emotional recognition and control are considered to operate through a deliberate process (Mayer & Salovey, 1997; for an exception, see Fiori, 2009),

and research indicates that there are deliberate components to the operation of both of these skills. For example, the use of pattern matching procedures to recognize faces by certain people—those who suffer from autism spectrum disorder—necessitates deliberate attempts at recognition through the application of rules and knowledge to make inferences about what another person is feeling (Winkielman, McIntosh, & Oberman, 2009). In terms of social-emotional control, researchers have been able to manipulate the particular deliberate manner in which people approach a negative emotional experience—for instance, whether they immerse themselves or take a step back from the experience. Their findings indicate that people's cognitive approach to the situation matters, with the ability to take in more information about the social situation and not remain immersed in one's feelings helping to buffer against reexperiencing intense negative emotions associated with the event (Kross, Ayduk, & Mischel, 2005). This type of conscious, controlled approach—at least when people are first developing such skills—is at the heart of many cognitive-behavioral therapy techniques (e.g., Ellis, 2001). Deliberate steps taken by a unit leader to distance herself from the distress of impending layoffs, for example, may be effective for managing emotions (for discussion see Mischel, DeSmet, & Kross, 2006).

Although these deliberately implemented skills are critical to helping people interact effectively in social contexts, they require cognitive effort. Thus, their use is restricted by a person's level of cognitive resources. Fortunately, these skills can also operate *intuitively* through a process that is more immune to cognitive resource level (e.g., Smith & DeCoster, 2000). For example, a service provider might readily notice among a group of jockeying customers one who is smiling and who seems friendly, even if the provider is not aware of why that person captured his attention. With regard to emotion control, an employee, without deliberating but almost

Table 16.1 2 × 2 Model of social-emotional intelligence

Type of Processing

	Social-emotional recognition	Social-emotional control
Deliberate	Consciously focusing on the new boss' communications and expressions to infer intentions and what the boss wants done.	Exerting cognitive resources (attention, working memory) to switch mindsets and reappraise the meaning or consequences of impending layoffs.
Intuitive	Quickly recognizing a smile or friendliness in a customer's face, even when the customer is at a distance.	With the help of internalized organizational values, automatically speaking up against a coworker who makes a discriminatory comment.

impulsively, could speak up when a coworker says something discriminatory that goes against the company's egalitarian mantra.

Recent research has delved deeper into the intuitive operation of social-emotional abilities. For example, in terms of emotion recognition, research indicates that people can recognize the valence of faces (positive, negative) even when the faces are presented too fast to engage higher-level cognitive skills (e.g., Clark, Winkielman, & McIntosh, 2008). Recent findings also suggest that some elements of emotion control can occur quite efficiently with little deliberation (for reviews see Bargh & Williams, 2007; Mauss, Bunge, & Gross, 2007). In one study, Mauss, Cook, and Gross (2007, Experiment 1) primed participants either with words related to the concept of "control" or to the concept of "express" to activate these goal-related concepts outside of people's awareness. Following the priming task, the participants completed a mood questionnaire, which was followed by an anger-inducing situation and then a second mood questionnaire. The results indicated that participants with the "control" goal expressed less anger at Time 2 than did participants for whom the goal of "express" had been activated. This use of activated goal concepts without any awareness is taken as evidence of an efficient, intuitive type of process. These results also support prior findings that preference judgments can occur without conscious cognitive processing. In this sense, immediate feeling may not depend directly on thinking but can occur automatically (Zajonc, 1980).

Although the operation of social-EI can occur quite efficiently through intuitive processing, it does not mean this type of processing will always be effective. People create bad habits out of thoughts and behaviors all the time, and on occasion, intuitive skills can be misapplied. For example, the service provider may see a smiling customer, and only later realize the customer's smile was really an anxious grin. In cases such as these, conscious and deliberate processes are useful in conjunction with intuitive skills in order to unlearn potentially ineffective ways of relating to others, and for controlling and modulating initial assessments of others to correct for inaccurate inferences.

For example, although some aspects of emotion recognition can operate intuitively (Elfenbein & Ambady, 2002), some cultural contexts may make recognition challenging because the culture may reinforce display rules in its citizens that foster the reduction of emotion expression when dealing with strangers (e.g., Matsumoto, HeeYoo, Fontaine, Anguas-Wong, Arriola, & Ataca, 2008), making it harder for those unfamiliar with the context to judge emotions accurately. This issue is akin to that raised earlier in the context of the social context and how at times people will be less readable and predictable to others, regardless of the perceiver's EI ability. With regard to the culture example, in this case, the integration of deliberate social-emotional capabilities allows for emotion recognition to include controlled elements, in that, in addition to intuitive recognition processes, people may also have explicit knowledge about display rules for a specific culture, which can then be used to inform emotion recognition.

However, because deliberate processing tends to be more controlled and linked to limited cognitive resources, such processing should influence emotion recognition only to the extent that people are not cognitively overloaded. This assumption may not hold if people are dealing with cognitive fatigue (e.g., Winkelman, 1994). Similarly, if people are under time pressure, or if they are not motivated to undertake such deliberate processing (cf. Smith & DeCoster, 2000), social-emotional recognition (or control) could be compromised—instead of reserving judgment about the emotion being perceived, for instance, an individual might jump to conclusions and judge inaccurately. In another example, the employee lacking sleep and overwhelmed by the tasks piling up on his desk may not have the cognitive resources to discern the boss' intent (assuming they have little experience with the boss), which could compromise subsequent performance on the job. Similarly, the boss who has been traveling nonstop and putting in 14-hour days is not likely to have the cognitive wherewithal to step back from their distress and take somebody else's perspective, as doing so requires cognitive resources (e.g., Carlson, Moses, & Breton, 2002; Ruby & Decety, 2003).

Overall, the above discussion suggests that people can be flexible and even strategic in how they integrate their social-emotional abilities, playing them off each other to arrive at effective assessments of their social surroundings, but this use of deliberate processing to restrain or inform intuitive processes is restricted by the availability of limited cognitive resources. However, social-emotional abilities can become efficient and automatized through practice, much like other skills. This bodes well for organizations and employees who want to develop their social-EI potential. It suggests that, although work can be stressful and employees can be fatigued, factors that impact the availability of cognitive resources can be less of a concern because well-practiced skills and abilities can be executed with little need for cognitive resources (Bargh & Chartrand, 1999; Smith & DeCoster, 2000). In order for this to happen, however, an organization has to explicitly provide its employees regular opportunities for developing and practicing these social-emotional abilities. The only way that skills can become intuitive and automatically implemented is through repeated practice and application. As the lower right-hand quadrant in Table 16.1 indicates, the automatic, egalitarian response of the employee is likely made possible by organizational practices that lead to internalizing those values (i.e., a focus on developing positive organizations). A person could want to be egalitarian and ethical, but if the organizational environment does not support that implicitly or explicitly, those behaviors and skills will not be practiced.[1]

Overall then, factors in Assumption 2 that will impact a person's social-EI fall into two related categories: (a) the availability of cognitive resources and (b) the determination of appropriate individual reactions. Recall that, even though a skill can be executed efficiently does not imply appropriateness, as skills at times can be misapplied. In some contexts, automatically triggered reactions might need to be considered more carefully or "shelved" temporarily before acting on them. Many times, the outcomes of intuitive processes represent proposed solutions that must be monitored for their appropriateness, which requires cognitive resources. The level of individual cognitive resources—which different organizational practices can impinge upon—thus allows for various idiosyncrasies in how people manifest their social-EI, but so does the degree to which people practice and make more intuitive some EI reactions over others.

Future Directions

Many questions remain regarding the definition, measurement, and application of social-EI, so we concur with many of our colleagues' previous calls for further study of EI to help address these issues. But to this we would add that what is also needed is more conceptual work that takes the social context seriously, with all its implications, and that provides a model of mental processes, given what is known in the psychological literature. In this vein, we have proposed one approach for doing this. With regard to Assumption 1 of our analysis, we have argued

that social context has the capacity to create inefficiencies in people's EI. Most models of EI are person-centered and assume that the person or perceiver can make sense of situations as a function of their level of EI, but these models rarely consider the possibility that social and relational factors are at work to influence, bias, if not preclude a person's attempts to use their EI. Models of EI need to be more explicit about the interaction of the individuals with their social worlds, and we have argued that one of the most positive implications of positive organizational environments is its potential to constrain, simplify, and make more generous how people make sense of social and emotionally tinged situations.

Our approach also delineates the mental processes that underlie how people exercise EI and the conditions that may impact it. We regard EI to be based generally on two meta-capabilities, social-emotional recognition and control. These, of course, can be broken down further, but in the interest of simplification, these two meta-capabilities provide the most common ground across conceptions of EI. In addition, we regard both social-emotional recognition and control as being implemented through either an intuitive or deliberative process. The former processes are well practiced and can give rise to social-emotional understanding even under conditions that involve time pressure and limited cognitive resources. The latter processes are more reliant on limited cognitive resources, but they can be deployed to monitor and inform the products of intuitive EI. Such a conception adds dynamism, flexibility, and a sense of process (vs. a static EI "score" or assessment) to EI and suggests how context, especially the social context, can interact with these mental processes. We conclude by highlighting directions for future research and questions that should be answered to flesh out the present analysis:

- For us, the person matters but so does the social context. Thus, with regard to the social context, how do organizations that differ in their values, in particular the pursuit of positive organizational values and practices, influence employee EI, independent of what these individuals score on EI assessments? Moreover, how do these features of organizations interact directly with people's EI scores/abilities?
- Related to the above point, how do organizations dominated by a competitive

ethos or low levels of trust influence people's willingness to be "figured out" and predicted, and how does this affect social-emotional recognition and control?

- What organizational practices influence employee cognitive resource levels (e.g., time pressure, fatigue), and how does this state of affairs influence employee flexibility in applying the EI toolkit, especially when the context of social-emotional recognition or control calls for deliberate or conscious approaches?

- In terms of Assumption 2 of the present analysis, what are methods by which to measure intuitive versus deliberate forms of EI abilities? In terms of current EI assessments, how do such measures respond to manipulations that impact cognitive resources, and how do people who score at a certain level of EI on some measurement respond to time pressure or cognitive fatigue?

- What are the most effective ways by which individuals can transfer deliberate EI skills into intuitive ones, and how can organizations support employees in doing this (e.g., "practice" of social-emotional abilities in the workplace; organizational policies that limit threats posed by unmet social needs)?

- Are some intuitive and deliberative processes, or some interactions between the two (e.g., judgment being overwhelmed by intuitive processes), more likely in some contexts than others? Also, when is it better for a person to consider different explanations for individually perceived emotional expressions before rushing to conclusions, and how do positive organizational environments influence this process?

- Finally, when are people who score high on EI apt to act inefficiently in the social realm, and is it possible for a person who is low on some measure of EI to display socially intelligent behavior given environmental supports (e.g., internalization of organization's values)?

Conclusion

The interplay of Assumption 1 and Assumption 2 of our synthesis, along with the interactions possible in our 2 × 2 framework (Assumption 2), are ripe areas for future research. We have mentioned some

possibilities, but there are likely to be many others. It is our hope that, by delving deeper into both the social context and psychology of EI, researchers will have more knowledge at their disposal and guidance to pursue research questions that can ultimately help bridge the promise of EI with POS. Such a bridge can show us how the interplay of individual mental processes applied to interactions and relationships with others can be fostered to support positive social connections to influence organizational and individual performance.

Note

1. Most skills follow the path of explicit practice to automaticity, from being deliberate to becoming more automatic and intuitive. This is not to say that skill acquisition cannot occur implicitly and with little awareness (Bargh & Chartrand, 1999; Lewicki et al., 1992).

References

Bargh, J.A., & Chartrand, T.L. (1999). The unbearable automaticity of being. *American Psychologist, 54*, 462–479.

Bargh, J.A., & Williams, L.E. (2007). The nonconscious regulation of emotion. In J. Gross (Ed.), *Handbook of emotion regulation* (pp. 429–225). New York: Guilford.

Bar-On, R. (1997). BarOn emotional quotient inventory: Technical manual. Toronto: Multi-Health Systems.

Barsade, S., & Gibson, D. (2007). Why does affect matter in organizations? *Academy of Management Perspectives, 21*, 36–59.

Baumeister, R., Leary, M. (1995). The need to belong: Desire for interpersonal attachments as a fundamental human motivation. *Psychological Bulletin, 117*, 497–529.

Baumeister, R.F., Twenge, J.M., & Nuss, C. (2002). Effects of social exclusion on cognitive processes: Anticipated aloneness reduces intelligent thought. *Journal of Personality and Social Psychology, 83*, 817–827.

Beck. A.T. (1979). *Cognitive therapy and the emotional disorders.* New York: Penguin.

Bono, J.E., & Judge, T.A. (2003). Self-concordance at work: Toward understanding the motivational effects of transformational leaders. *Academy of Management Journal, 46*, 554–571.

Brackett, M., & Mayer, J. (2003). Convergent, discriminant, and incremental validity of competing measures of emotional intelligence. *Personality and Social Psychology Bulletin, 29*(9), 1147–1158.

Brown, F., & Moshavi, D. (2005). Transformational leadership and emotional intelligence: A potential pathway for an increased understanding of interpersonal influence. *Journal of Organizational Behavior, 26*(7), 867–871.

Buck, R. (1984). *The communication of emotion.* New York: Guilford Press.

Cameron, K.S. (2008). *Positive leadership: Strategies for extraordinary performance.* San Francisco: Berrett-Koehler Publishers, Inc.

Carlson, S.M., Moses, L.J., & Breton, C. (2002). How specific is the relation between executive function and theory of mind? Contributions of inhibitory control and working memory. *Infant and Child Development, 11*, 73–92.

Chaiken, S., & Trope, Y. (Eds.). (1999). *Dual process theories in social psychology.* New York: Guilford Press.

Clark, M.S., & Isen, A.M. (1982). Toward understanding the relationship between feeling states and social behavior. In A. Hastorf, & A.M. Isen (Eds.), *Cognitive social psychology*. New York: Elsevier

Clark, T.F., Winkielman, P., & McIntosh, D.N. (2008). Autism and the extraction of emotion from briefly presented facial expressions: Stumbling at the first step of empathy. *Emotion, 8*, 803–809.

Clore, G.L., Ortony, A., & Foss, M.A. (1987). The psychological foundations of the affective lexicon. *Journal of Personality and Social Psychology, 53*, 751–766.

Conte, J. (2005). A review and critique of emotional intelligence measures. *Journal of Organizational Behavior, 26*, 433–440.

Côté, S., & Miners, C. (2006). Emotional intelligence, cognitive intelligence, and job performance. *Administrative Science Quarterly, 51*, 1–28.

Damasio, A.R. (1994). *Descartes error: Emotion, reason, and the human brain*. New York: Grossett/Putnam & Sons.

Day, A., & Carroll, S. (2008). Faking emotional intelligence (EI): Comparing response distortion on ability and trait-based EI measures. *Journal of Organizational Behavior, 29*(6), 761–784.

Dvir, T., Eden, D., Avolio, B.J., & Shamir, B. (2002). Impact of transformational leadership on follower development and performance: A field experiment. *Academy of Management Journal, 45*, 735–744.

Dunbar, R.I.M., Marriott, A., & Duncan, N.D.C. (1997). Human conversational behavior. *Human Nature, 8*, 231–246.

Ekman, P., & Friesen, W.V. (1975). *Unmasking the Face: A guide to recognizing emotions from facial clues*. Englewood Cliffs, NJ: Prentice-Hall.

Elfenbein, H.A., & Ambady, N. (2002). On the universality and cultural specificity of emotion recognition: A meta-analysis. *Psychological Bulletin, 128*, 203–235.

Elfenbein, H.A., Foo, M.D., White, J.B., Tan, H.H, & Aik, V.C. (2007). Reading your counterpart: The benefit of emotion recognition ability for effectiveness in negotiation. *Journal of Nonverbal Behavior, 31*, 205–223.

Ellis, A. (2001). *Overcoming destructive beliefs, feelings and behaviors*. New York: Prometheus Books.

Engelberg, E., & Sjoberg, L. (2006). Money attitudes and emotional intelligence. *Journal of Applied Social Psychology, 36*(8), 2027–2047.

Epley, N., Akalis, S., Waytz, A., & Cacioppo, J.T. (2008). Creating social connection through inferential reproduction—Loneliness and perceived agency in gadgets, gods, and greyhounds. *Psychological Science, 19*, 114–120.

Epstein, S. (1994). Integration of the cognitive and the psychodynamic unconscious. *American Psychologist, 49*, 709–724.

Erber, R., & Erber, M.W. (2001). Mood and processing: A view from a self-regulation perspective. In L.L. Martin, & G.L. Clore (Eds.), *Theories of mood and cognition: A user's guidebook*. Mahwah, NJ: Erlbaum.

Evans, J.S.B.T. (2008). Dual process accounts of reasoning. *Annual Review of Psychology, 59*, 255–278.

Fiori, M. (2009). A new look at emotional intelligence: A dual process framework. *Personality and Social Psychology Review, 13*, 21–44.

Ford, M.E., & Tisak, M.S. (1983). A further search for social intelligence. *Journal of Educational Psychology, 75*, 196–206.

Frijda, N.H. (1988). *The laws of emotions*. Mahwah, NJ: Erlbaum.

Gardner, H. (1983). *Frames of mind: The theory of multiple intelligences*. New York: Basic Books.

Gardner, W.L., Pickett, C.L., & Brewer, M.B. (2000). Social exclusion and selective memory: How the need to belong influences memory for social events. *Personality and Social Psychology Bulletin, 26*, 286–296.

George, J.M. (2000). Emotions and leadership: The role of emotional intelligence. *Human Relations, 53*, 1027–1055.

George, J.M., & Brief, A.P. (1996). Motivational agendas in the workplace: The effects of feelings on focus of attention and work motivation. In B.M. Staw, & L.L. Cummings (Eds.), *Research in organizational behavior* Vol.18 (pp. 75–109). Greenwich, CT: JAI Press.

Goleman, D. (2006). *Social intelligence: The new science of human relationships*. New York: Bantam.

Goleman, D. (1995). *Emotional intelligence*. New York: Bantam.

Gough, H.G. (1966). Appraisal of social maturity by means of the CPI. *Journal of Abnormal Psychology, 71*, 189–195.

Gross, J.J. (1998). The emerging field of emotion regulation: An integrative review. *Review of General Psychology, 2*, 271–299.

Grubb, W., & McDaniel, M. (2007). The fakability of Bar-On's emotional quotient inventory short form: Catch me if you can. *Human Performance, 20*(1), 43–59.

Guilford, J.P. (1967). *The nature of intelligence*. New York: McGraw-Hill.

Hamner, W.C., & Organ, D.W. (1982). *Organizational behaviour: An applied psychological approach*. Dallas: Business Publications Inc.

Hendricks, M., Guilford, J.P., & Hoepfner, R. (1969). Measuring creative social intelligence. *Reports from the Psychological Laboratory, University of Southern California*, No. 42.

Hofman, W., Friese, M., & Strack, F. (2009). Impulse and self-control from a dual systems perspective. *Perspectives on Psychological Science, 4*, 162–176.

Humphrey, N.K. (1976). The social function of intellect. In P.P.G. Bateson, & R.A. Hinde (Eds.), *Growing points in ethology* (pp. 303–317). Cambridge: Cambridge University Press.

Hunt, T. (1928). The measurement of social intelligence. *Journal of Applied Psychology, 12*, 317–334.

Huy, Q. (1999). Emotional capability, emotional intelligence, and radical change. *Academy of Management Review, 24*(2), 325–345.

Isen, A.M., Johnson, M.M.S., Mertz, E., & Robinson, G.F. (1985). The influence of positive affect on the unusualness of word associations. *Journal of Personality and Social Psychology, 48*, 1413–1426.

Jordan, P., Ashkanasy, N., & Hartel, C. (2002). Emotional intelligence as a moderator of emotional and behavioral reactions to job insecurity. *Academy of Management Review, 27*(3), 361–372.

Jordan, P., & Lawrence, S. (2009). Emotional intelligence in teams: Development and initial validation of the short version of the Workgroup Emotional Intelligence Profile (WEIP-S). *Journal of Management and Organization, 15*(4), 452–469.

Kihlstrom, J.F., & Cantor, N. (2000). Social intelligence. In R.J. Sternberg (Ed.), *Handbook of intelligence* (2nd ed., pp. 359–379). Cambridge, U.K.: Cambridge University Press.

Kihlstrom, J.F., & Cantor, N. (1989). Social intelligence and personality: There's room for growth. In R.S. Wyer, & T.K. Srull (Eds.), *Advances in social cognition* Vol. 2 (pp. 197–214). Hillsdale, NJ: Erlbaum.

Kross, E., Ayduk, O., & Mischel, W. (2005). When asking "'why'" does not hurt: Distinguishing rumination from reflective processing of negative emotions. *Psychological Science, 16*, 709–715.

Kross, E., & Mischel, W. (2010). From stimulus control to self-control. Towards an integrative understanding of the processes underlying willpower. In R. Hassin, K. Ochsner, & Y. Trope (Eds.), *From society to brain: The new sciences of self-control* (pp. 428–446). New York: Oxford University Press.

Larsen, R.J. (2000). Toward a science of mood regulation. *Psychological Inquiry, 11*, 129–141.

Lazarus, R.S. (1994). *Emotion and adaptation.* Oxford, UK: Oxford University Press.

Lewicki, P., Hill, T., & Czyzewska, M. (1992). Nonconscious acquisition of information. *American Psychologist, 47*, 796–801.

Lopes, P., Brackett, M., Nezlek, J., Schutz, A., Sellin, I., & Salovey, P. (2004). Emotional intelligence and social interaction. *Personality and Social Psychology Bulletin, 30*(8), 1018–1034.

Lopes, P., Grewa, D., Kadis, J., Gall, M., & Salovey, P. (2006). Evidence that emotional intelligence is related to job performance and affect and attitudes at work. *Psicothema, 18*, 132–138.

Marlowe, H.A. (1986). Social intelligence: Evidence for multidimensionality and construct independence. *Journal of Educational Psychology, 78*, 52–58.

Matthews, G., Emo, A., Funke, G., Zeidner, M., Roberts, R., Costa, P., & Schulze, R. (2006). Emotional intelligence, personality, and task-induced stress. *Journal of Experimental Psychology-Applied, 12*(2), 96–107.

Matsumoto, D., LeRoux, J., Wilson-Cohn, C., Raroque, J., Kooken, K., Ekman, P., et al. (2000). A new test to measure emotion recognition ability: Matsumoto and Ekman's Japanese and Caucasian brief affect recognition test (JACBART). *Journal of Nonverbal Behavior, 24*, 179–209.

Matsumoto, D., HeeYoo, S., Fontaine, J., Anguas-Wong, A.M., Arriola, M., & Ataca, B. (2008). Mapping expressive differences around the world: The relationship between emotional display rules and individualism versus collectivism. *Journal of Cross-Cultural Psychology, 39*, 55–74.

Mauss, I.B., Bunge, S.A., & Gross, J.J. (2007). Automatic emotion regulation. *Social and Personality Psychology Compass, 1*, 146–167.

Mauss, I.B., Cook, C., &, Gross, J.J. (2007). Automatic emotion regulation during anger provocation. *Journal of Experimental Social Psychology, 43*, 698–711.

Mayer, J.D., Caruso, D., & Salovey, P. (1999). Emotional intelligence meets traditional standards for an intelligence. *Intelligence, 27*(4), 267–298.

Mayer, J.D., Roberts, R.D., Barsade, S.G. (2008). Human abilities: Emotional intelligence. *Annual Review of Psychology, 59*, 507–536.

Mayer, J.D., & Salovey, P. (1997). What is emotional intelligence? In P. Salovey, & D. Sluyter (Eds.), *Emotional development and emotional intelligence: Educational implications* (pp. 3–31). New York: Basic.

Mayer, J.D., Salovey, P., & Caruso, D.R. (2002). *Mayer-Salovey-Caruso emotional intelligence test (MSCEIT) user's manual.* Toronto: MHS Publ.

Mayer, J.D., Salovey, P., & Caruso, D. (1997). *Emotional IQ test.* Needham, MA: Virtual Knowledge.

McClure, S.M., Laibson, D.I., Loewenstein, G., & Cohen, J.D. (2004). Separate neural systems value immediate and delayed monetary rewards. *Science, 306*, 503–507.

McNamara, P., McLaren, D., Smith, D., Brown, A., & Stickgold, R. (2005). A "Jekyll and Hyde" within: Aggressive versus friendly interactions in REM and non-REM dreams. *Psychological Science, 16*, 130–136.

Milkman, K.L., Rogers, T., & Bazerman, M. (2008). Harnessing our inner angels and demons. *Psychological Science, 3*, 324–338.

Mischel, W., DeSmet, A., & Kross, E. (2006). Self-regulation in the service of conflict resolution. In M. Deutsch, P.T. Coleman, & E.C. Marcus (Eds.), *Handbook of conflict resolution* (pp. 294–313). San Francisco: Jossey-Bass.

Mischel, W., & Shoda, Y. (1995). A cognitive-affective system theory of personality: Reconceptualizing situations, dispositions, dynamics, and invariance in personality structure. *Psychological Review, 102*, 246–268. [Article also reprinted as a chapter in Higgins, E.T., & Kruglanski, A.W. (Eds). 2000. *Motivational science: Social and personality perspectives. Key reading in social psychology.* (pp. 150–176). Philadelphia: Psychology Press/Taylor & Francis.]

Mischel, W., Shoda, Y., & Rodriguez, M.L. (1989). Delay of gratification in children. *Science, 244*, 933–938.

Mischel, W., Ebbesen, E.B., & Zeiss, A.R. (1973). Selective attention to the self: Situational and dispositional determinants. *Journal of Personality and Social Psychology, 27*, 129–142.

Moss, F.A., Hunt, T., Omwake, K.T., & Ronning, M.M. (1927). *Social intelligence test.* Washington, DC: Center for Psychological Service.

Neisser, U., Boodoo, G., Bouchard, T.J., Boykin, A.W., Brody, N., Ceci, S.J., et al. (1996). Intelligence: Knowns and unknowns. *American Psychologist, 51*, 77–101.

Nowicki, S., Jr., & Duke, M. (1994). Individual differences in the nonverbal communication of affect: The diagnostic analysis of nonverbal accuracy scale. *Journal of Nonverbal Behavior, 18*, 9–35.

O'Sullivan, M. (2007). Trolling for trout, trawling for tuna: The methodological morass in measuring emotional intelligence. In G. Mattthews, M. Zeidner, & R.D. Roberts (Eds.), *The science of emotional intelligence: Knowns and unknowns* (pp. 258–287). New York: Oxford University Press.

O'Sullivan, M. (1982). Measuring the ability to recognize facial expressions of emotion. In P. Ekman (Ed.), *Emotion in the human face* (pp. 281–317). Cambridge, UK: Cambridge University Press.

O'Sullivan, M., Guilford, J.P., & deMille, R. (1965). *The measurement of social intelligence. Reports from the psychological laboratory, University of Southern California*, No. 34.

Ordoñez, L.D., Schweitzer, M.E., Galinsky, A.D., & Bazerman, M.H. (2009). Goals gone wild: The systemic side effects of overprescribing goal setting. *Academy of Management Perspectives, 23*, 6–16.

Posner, M.I., & Snyder, C.R.R. (1975). Attention and cognitive control. In R.L. Solso (Ed.), *Information processing and cognition: The Loyola symposium.* Hillsdale, NJ: Erlbaum.

Riggio, R.E., Messamer, J., & Throckmorton, B. (1991). Social and academic intelligence: Conceptually distinct but overlapping constructs. *Personality & Individual Differences, 12*, 695–702.

Roseman, I.J. (1984). Cognitive determinants of emotion. *Review of Personality and Social Psychology, 5*, 11–36.

Rosenthal, R., Hall, J.A., DiMatteo, M.R., Rogers, P.L., & Archer, D. (1979). *Sensitivity to Nonverbal Communication.* Baltimore, MD: Johns Hopkins University Press.

Ruby, P., & Decety, J. (2003). What you believe versus what you think they believe: A neuroimaging study of conceptual perspective taking. *European Journal of Neuroscience, 17,* 2475–2480.

Salovey, P., Hsee, C., & Mayer, J.D. (1993). Emotional intelligence and the self-regulation of affect. In D.M. Wegner, & J.W. Pennebaker (Eds.), *Handbook of Mental Control* (pp. 258–277). Englewood Cliffs, NJ: Prentice-Hall.

Sanchez-Burks, J., & Huy, Q. (2009). Emotional aperture: The accurate recognition of collective emotions. *Organization Science, 20,* 22–34.

Sayles, L.R. (1957). Work group behavior and the larger organization. In C. Arensburg, et al. (Eds.), *Research in industrial relations* (pp. 131–145). New York: Harper & Row.

Schutte, N., Malouff, J., Hall, L., Haggerty, D., Cooper, J., Golden, C., & Dornheim, L. (1998). Development and validation of a measure of emotional intelligence. *Personality and Individual Differences, 25,* 167–177.

Schutte, N., Malouff, J., Simunek, M., McKenley, J., & Hollander, S. (2002). Characteristic emotional intelligence and emotional well-being. *Cognition and Emotion, 16*(6), 769–785.

Shanley, L.A., Walker, R.E., & Foley, J.M. (1971). Social intelligence: A concept in search of data. *Psychological Reports, 29,* 1123–1132.

Shiffrin, R.M., & Schneider, W. (1977). Controlled and automatic human information processing: Perceptual learning, automatic attending and a general theory. *Psychological Review, 84,* 127–190.

Singh, M., & Woods, S. (2008). Predicting general well-being from emotional intelligence and three broad personality traits. *Journal of Applied Social Psychology, 38*(3), 635–646.

Sloman, S.A. (1996). The empirical case for two systems of reasoning. *Psychological Bulletin, 199,* 3–22.

Smith, E.R., & DeCoster, J. (2000). Dual process models in social and cognitive psychology: Conceptual integration and links to underlying memory systems. *Personality and Social Psychology Review, 4,* 108–131.

Spreitzer, G.M., & Sonenshein, S. (2003). Positive deviance and extraordinary organizing. In K.S. Cameron, J.E. Dutton, & R.E. Quinn (Eds.), *Positive organizational scholarship* (pp. 207–224). San Francisco: Berrett-Koehler.

Stanovich, K.E., & West, R.F. (2000). Individual differences in reasoning. Implications for the rationality debate. *Behavioral and Brain Sciences, 23,* 645–726.

Sternberg, R.J. (2002). Smart people are not stupid, but they sure can be foolish: The imbalance theory of foolishness. In R.J. Sternberg (Ed.), *Why smart people can be so stupid* (pp. 232–242). New Haven: Yale University Press.

Tett, R.P., Fox, K.E., & Wang, A. (2005). Development and validation of a self-report measure of emotional intelligence as a multidimensional trait domain. *Personality and Social Psychology Bulletin, 31,* 859–888.

Thorndike, R.L., & Stein, S. (1937). An evaluation of the attempts to measure social intelligence. *Psychological Bulletin, 34,* 275–285.

Trivers, R.L. (1971). The Evolution of Reciprocal Altruism. *The Quarterly Review of Biology, 46,* 35–57.

Wechsler, D. (1958). *The measurement and appraisal of adult intelligence* (4th ed.). Baltimore: Williams & Wilkins.

Winkelman, M. (1994). Cultural shock and adaptation. *Journal of Counseling & Development, 73*(6), 121–126.

Winkielman, P., McIntosh, D.N., & Oberman, L. (2009). Embodied and disembodied emotion processing: Learning from and about typical and autistic individuals. *Emotion Review, 1,* 178–190.

Wojciszke, B., Bazinska, R., & Jaworski, M. (1998). On the dominance of moral categories in impression formation. *Personality and Social Psychology Bulletin, 24,* 1251–1263.

Woodrow, H. (1939). The common factors in 52 mental tests. *Psychometrika, 4,* 99–108.

Ybarra, O. (2001). When first impressions don't last: The role of isolation and adaptation processes in impression revision. *Social Cognition, 19,* 491–520.

Ybarra, O. (2002). Naive causal understanding of valenced behaviors and its implications for social information processing. *Psychological Bulletin, 128,* 421–441.

Ybarra, O., Chan, E., & Park. D.C. (2001). Young and old adults' concerns with morality and competence. *Motivation and Emotion, 25,* 85–100.

Ybarra, O., Keller, M., Chan, E., Garcia, S., Sanchez-Burks, J., Rios Morrison, K., & Baron, A. (2010). Being unpredictable: Friend or foe matters. *Social Psychological and Personality Science, 1*(3), 259–267.

Ybarra, O., Schaberg, L.A., & Keiper, S.N. (1999). Favorable and unfavorable target expectancies and social information processing. *Journal of Personality and Social Psychology, 77,* 698–709.

Ybarra, O., & Stephan, W.G. (1999). Attributional orientations and the prediction of behavior: The attribution-prediction bias. *Journal of Personality and Social Psychology, 76,* 718–727.

Ybarra, O., & Stephan, W.G. (1996). Misanthropic person memory. *Journal of Personality and Social Psychology, 70,* 691–700.

Zajonc, R. (1980). Feeling and thinking: Preferences need no inferences. *American Psychologist, 35*(2), 151–175.

Zeidner, M., Matthews, G., & Roberts, R. (2004). Emotional intelligence in the workplace: A critical review. *Applied Psychology: An International Review, 53*(3), 371–399.

Shared Positive Affect in Workgroups

Seung-Yoon Rhee *and* Hye Jung Yoon

Abstract

In this chapter, we present a theoretical framework that integrates recent theorizing and empirical research on shared positive affect in workgroups. Within this framework, we outline both subconscious and conscious mechanisms for sharing of positive affect. In addition, we describe key intra- and interpersonal and social structural/contextual enablers that facilitate positive affect sharing among workgroup members and the consequences of shared positive affect for group social processes and performance outcomes. We further discuss how shared positive affect can undo the negative influences of shared negative affect and turn the negative state into a positive one. A deeper exploration of the phenomenon of shared positive affect has important ramifications for workgroups and organizations, as overall positivity can be fostered through such fundamental mechanisms as emotions and feelings. We conclude by highlighting several important yet unresolved issues for future research.

Keywords: Shared positive affect, emotion, mood, group social process, group performance, group creativity, group decision, emotional contagion, group affective tone

The rising importance of workgroups as a work unit in organizations has spurred organizational research aimed at understanding the internal and external dynamics of workgroups. One topic of interest is shared cognition and affect within workgroups. Previous research on shared cognition has revealed how ideas and knowledge are shared and stored within workgroups, and has suggested that shared knowledge structures among group members facilitate coordination and effectiveness (e.g., Hollingshead, 1998; Klimoski & Mohammed, 1994).

On the other hand, shared affect[1] within workgroups has only recently attracted the interest of organization researchers. This is quite surprising, as emotions and moods are an essential part of group experience. For example, a group member talks buoyantly to other members about how happy she felt teaching orphans at a local orphanage as a community service activity. While listening to her story, other group members may also feel happy about what she has done and about the potential positive consequences of her action, thus resulting in shared happiness in the group. Through social interactions such as this, workgroup members can influence each other's emotions and feelings. This experience of shared affect may occur more frequently in workgroups in which members actively interact with each other to accomplish task goals. Exposure to common events and a sense of shared fate among workgroup members also facilitate the experience of shared affect within workgroups (Parkinson, Fischer, & Manstead, 2005).

An emerging research domain focuses on the antecedents, processes, and outcomes of shared affect in groups. Psychologists and organizational researchers have explored the conditions that facilitate affective sharing, the mechanisms and processes of affective sharing, and the outcomes of shared affect at the interpersonal, group, and organizational levels (e.g., Barsade, 2002; Barsade & O'Neill, 2009; Bartel & Saavedra, 2000; George, 1990; Totterdell, 2000). This is the focus of our chapter. In particular, we focus on shared *positive*[2] affect in workgroups, and develop a conceptual framework for understanding the antecedents and processes of sharing of positive affect, and the consequences of shared positive affect in workgroups.

Our focus on shared positive affect is aligned with the growing interest in exploring the positive aspects of workgroup and organizational life (e.g., Cameron, Dutton, & Quinn, 2003). Previous studies on groups have included variables of positive nature, such as cooperation, group cohesiveness, and members' satisfaction with the group. However, most research on groups has focused on how to remedy negative group phenomena, including conflict among group members (Jehn, 1995), biases in group decision-making (Janis & Mann, 1977), and problematic group processes, such as the free-rider problem and conformity pressure (McGrath, 1984). Although an awareness of such group-level shortcomings and their solutions may help workgroups function normally, just remedying the negative group phenomena may not lead to extraordinarily positive outcomes (e.g., Cameron et al., 2003). By exclusively focusing on the positive side of group life, with an emphasis on shared positive affect in work groups, we attempt to increase the understanding of how both workgroup members and their groups can thrive in organizations.

Mostly through psychological research, much has been learned about positive affect at an individual level. For instance, experience of positive affect increases cognitive flexibility and creativity (Isen & Daubman, 1984), and prosocial behaviors including helping (George, 1991; Isen, Clark & Schwartz, 1976) and cooperativeness (Carnevale & Isen, 1986). Furthermore, positive emotions broaden individuals' cognitive repertoire and attention span and build long-term physical, intellectual, and social resources (Fredrickson, 1988). On the other hand, positive affect tends to inhibit analytical and critical thinking, instead increasing the use of intuitive or heuristic processes in decision making (Bless, Bohner, Schwarz, & Strack, 1990; Isen, 2000).

What, then, is the effect of shared positive affect at the group level? When workgroup members share positive affect, will the group exhibit more creativity and prosocial behavior and less analytical decision making, as in the individual-level case? What situations will facilitate or hamper the sharing of positive affect in workgroups? In this chapter, we develop a conceptual framework that integrates recent research on shared positive affect. Figure 17.1 depicts this framework. We hope to increase the understanding of why and how shared positive affect among workgroup members can contribute to the creation of a healthier workplace, wherein individual members and their groups can flourish and excel.

In the following sections, we first provide an overview of the literature on shared affect in groups. Next, we describe some of the mechanisms for affect

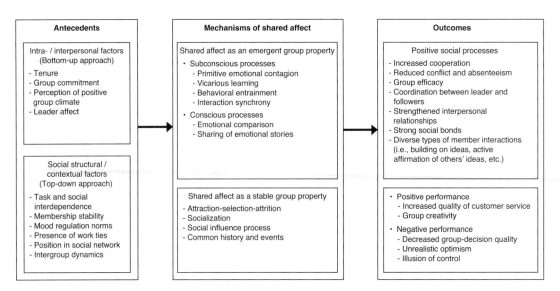

Fig. 17.1 Conceptual framework of shared positive affect in workgroups.

sharing, the conditions that enhance the sharing of positive affect among group members, and the outcomes of shared positive affect in workgroups. Then, we discuss how shared positive affect can undo the negative impact of shared negative affect. We conclude by highlighting several important yet unresolved issues for future research.

Some Background on Shared Affect in Workgroups

Two major research streams have emerged in the field of inquiry on shared affect. One stream of research focuses on shared affect as a temporary property of groups; an emergent property that arises during member interactions (Barsade, 2002; Bartel & Saavedra, 2000; Totterdell, 2000; Totterdell, Kellett, Teuchmann, & Briner, 1998). Shared affect has been found between leaders and followers (Sy, Cote, & Saavedra, 2005), within teams of community nurses and accountants (Totterdell et al., 1998), within professional cricket teams (Totterdell, 2000), and among employees tied together through a work interaction network (Totterdell, Wall, Holman, Diamond, & Epitropaki, 2004).

The other stream of research deals with shared affect as a stable property of groups, and includes studies of group affective tone (George, 1990; for review see George & Brief, 1992) and homogeneity in members' trait affectivity (Barsade, Ward, Turner, & Sonnenfeld, 2000). Group affective tone refers to "consistent or homogeneous affective reactions within a group" (George, 1990, p. 108) whereby group members develop similar affective tendencies and responses over time. George (1990) empirically showed the existence of group affective tone in workgroups at a large retail store, and found positive group affective tone associated with less absenteeism. Barsade and colleagues discovered that similarities in trait positive affect in top management teams increased the level of satisfaction, cooperation, and performance (Barsade et al., 2000).

In this chapter, we assume that repeated experience of emergent shared affect in groups will, over time, result in more stable affective characteristics such as group affective tone. Accordingly, we do not make explicit distinction between the antecedents and outcomes of the two types of processes for affective sharing. However, the affect sharing mechanisms of the two research streams will differ, as shared effect as an emergent property assumes a relatively shorter time frame whereas group affective tone as a stable property assumes a longer one.

Mechanisms for Sharing of Affect in Workgroups
Shared Affect As an Emergent Group Property

Research that treats shared affect as an emergent property of groups has focused on both the subconscious and conscious processes through which individual group members share affect. Subconscious processes are implicit, automatic processes whereby individuals unconsciously mimic others' affective experience (Barsade, Ramarajan, & Westen, 2009). The predominant mechanism in explaining collective affect by subconscious processes is primitive emotional contagion: "the tendency to automatically mimic and synchronize facial expressions, vocalizations, postures, and movements with those of another persona and consequently to converge emotionally" (Hatfield, Cacioppo, & Rapson, 1994, pp. 153–154). Individuals acquire affective cues by observing others' facial, postural, and behavioral expressions, and this facilitates the subconscious process of affect sharing (Neumann & Strack, 2000). A shared affective event can also cause the subconscious process. For example, upon hearing their company's downsizing announcement, employees may experience shared emotions of anxiety and anger (e.g., Huy, 2002). In this case, individuals do not need to observe others' affective expressions, nor even be colocated for the affective experiences to be shared. Group or organizational membership by itself can induce the subconscious process of affect sharing by binding individuals to a common interest or shared fate.

Other subconscious processes of affect sharing include vicarious learning, behavioral entrainment, and interaction synchrony (for a review, see Barsade, Brief, & Spataro, 2003; Kelly & Barsade, 2001). Vicarious affective learning occurs when individuals experience affect while observing others' affective expressions. Behavioral entrainment and interaction synchrony involve subconscious modification and adjustment of individual behaviors and affective experience for the purpose of maintaining coordinated and synchronized interactions with other people (Totterdell et al., 1998).

A more conscious, deliberate process of affect sharing occurs through emotional comparison. Through this process, individuals consciously seek and acquire affective cues from others' expressions, and judge whether their current affective experience is appropriate or not in a given situation (Schachter, 1959). Explicit sharing of affective stories also facilitates social sharing of affect (Rimé, 1995), which "occurs in discourse, when individuals communicate openly with one or more persons about the circumstances of the emotion-eliciting event and about their own feelings and emotional reactions" (Rimé, 2009, p. 65). Being exposed to a sender's emotional stories can trigger the receiver's experience of similar emotions, which often results in empathy and a feeling of emotional communion (Christophe & Rimé, 1997; Rimé, 2009).

Although the implicit, subconscious process of primitive emotional contagion does not involve individuals' intention to share affect, the more explicit, conscious process is clearly associated with motives. By ruminating or talking about past episodes and stories of a positive nature, individuals can savor the past and experience positive emotions once again. Furthermore, the strength of individuals' positive emotions is augmented when they share these positive stories with other people (Langston, 1994, as cited in Rimé, 2009). Thus, sharing positive stories with other people clearly has benefits for the narrator of the stories.

Shared Affect As a Stable Group Property

Research that focuses on shared affect as a stable property of groups introduces mechanisms of affect sharing with a longer time frame. George (1990) proposes several mechanisms that lead to the development of group affective tone. Through an attraction-selection-attrition mechanism (Schneider, 1987), individuals with similar affective tendencies tend to be attracted to and selected for group membership, whereas those with dissimilar affective tendencies are likely to leave, thus resulting in a group composed of members with similar affective tendencies. Socialization and social influence processes also contribute to the homogenization of members' affective tendencies. In addition, being exposed to a common history such as common tasks, events, and shared outcomes can lead to homogeneous affective reactions of group members.

Overall, the conceptual explanations and empirical findings on the mechanisms of affect sharing suggest that workgroup members do share positive affect. Although researchers focusing on temporary affect sharing suggest subconscious and conscious processes of affect sharing, those interested in stable affective reactions of workgroups propose social-structural mechanisms with a longer time frame. In the next section, we discuss some of the antecedents that have been found to facilitate sharing of positive affect in workgroups.

Antecedents of Shared Positive Affect in Workgroups

Researchers have examined antecedents of sharing of positive affect in both laboratory (Barsade, 2002; Sy et al., 2005) and field settings (Bartel & Saavedra, 2000; Totterdell, 2000; Totterdell et al., 1998, 2004). They have adopted two major approaches for understanding the antecedents or conditions that foster the sharing of positive affect in workgroups (Barsade & Gibson, 1998; Kelly & Barsade, 2001). A bottom-up approach focuses on how intra- and interpersonal factors, such as individual emotions, affective dispositions and interpersonal relationship strengths, contribute to affective homogeneity in workgroups. On the other hand, a top-down approach emphasizes the role that social structures, contextual factors, and organizations' emotional norms and history play in shaping the sharing of affect in groups.

The bottom-up approach describes intra- or interpersonal characteristics as preconditions for sharing of positive affect in workgroups. Totterdell and colleagues (1998) conducted two longitudinal field studies with 13 groups of community nurses who reported their daily mood for 3 weeks, and nine members of an accounting group who reported their mood three times per day for a period of 4 weeks. They argued that moods tended to be reciprocated among workgroup members through interpersonal processes over time, which led to a sense of shared affect. The correlation between individual and collective affect was greater if nurses were older, more committed to the group, perceived a positive group climate, and had fewer problems with coworkers. Leaders and their followers are likely to experience emotional contagion as well. Sy, Côté, and Saavedra (2005) discovered that leader affect influenced followers' affect. In a study of 20 different groups including jazz music groups and collegiate rowing crews, Pescosolido (2002) observed that emergent leaders tended to display a particular emotional response to uncertain situations, which was adopted by the rest of the group.

The top-down approach takes a more social structural perspective. Bartel and Saavedra (2000) examined the effects of workgroup structure on the degree of affective convergence among the members. Their focus on the impact of workgroup structure is based on the idea that the group's social system can influence the extent to which members can disseminate and acquire emotional information through social interaction. With a sample of 70 workgroups from diverse organizations, they found that task and social interdependence, membership stability, and the existence of mood regulation norms enhanced affective convergence within workgroups. Totterdell, Wall, Holman, Diamond, and Epitropaki (2004) showed that similarity of affect depended on the presence of work ties, and that similarity in affective response was more pronounced among employees who occupied similar positions in the social network structure.

Intergroup dynamics can also influence the extent to which affect is shared among group members. When a certain social identity or category becomes salient for individuals (e.g., Asian, female, etc.), they experience affect pertinent to the salient identity and, within the identity group, members are likely to experience similar feelings (Mackie, Devos, & Smith, 2000; Smith, 1993). For example, a big win by the school football team may activate students' sense of belonging to the school as an in-group member, which encourages them to bask in the reflected glory of the football team (e.g., Cialdini, Borden, Thorne, Walker, Freeman, & Sloan, 1976). The stronger in-group members' identification is with the group, the more intense the positive ingroup-directed affect is (Mackie, Silver, & Smith, 2004), and the more likely that the positive affect will be shared among the in-group members.

At a more macro level, affective culture in organizations has been shown to have the potential to exert great influence on individual members' affective experience (Barsade & O'Neill, 2009; Martin, Knopoff, & Beckman, 1998). Barsade and O'Neill (2009) define affective culture as "the manifestation of specific emotions (or moods) that help members understand and communicate the affective meaning of their group or organizational environment and the shared norms for the appropriate enactment of these emotions (or moods)" (cited in Barsade et al., 2009, p. 152). In their qualitative study of The Body Shop's affective culture, Martin, Knopoff and Beckman (1998) found norms of emotional display that encouraged expression of a wide range of emotions while simultaneously maintaining interpersonally sensitive boundaries between what was felt and what was expressed.

A growing body of research confirms the effects of both intra- and interpersonal factors and social-structural and contextual factors on the emergence of shared positive affect in workgroups. Given the positive nature of outcomes of shared positive affect

in general, which will be discussed in the following section, research on the antecedents of shared positive affect has important practical implications for developing interventions in workgroups.

Outcomes of Shared Positive Affect in Workgroups

Positive affect shared among group members can influence various aspects of group life, including the behaviors or attitudes of individual members and the group's performance. We discuss the outcomes of shared positive affect along the group effectiveness criteria suggested by Hackman and Oldham (1980), with a specific focus on satisfactory group social processes and task performance.

Shared positive affect among group members has been found to foster positive group processes in workgroups. Barsade (2002) demonstrated mood contagion between a confederate and other group members in a laboratory study with 29 groups of undergraduate students performing a managerial decision making task. Shared positive affect in groups led to more cooperation and less conflict among members. In addition, group members with shared positive affect evaluated the group's performance in a more positive light, demonstrating a link between members' sense of group efficacy and shared positive affect (e.g., Totterdell, 2000). Gibson (2003) corroborated this link through a field study of nurses and a laboratory simulation. Mason and Griffin (2003) found that a positive affective tone in groups also reduced group absenteeism.

Social sharing of affect, in which people explicitly share emotion-laden stories with others, has been found to strengthen interpersonal relationships (Peters & Kashima, 2007; Rimé, 2009), more so than did sharing of facts and information (Laurenceau, Feldman-Barrett, & Pietromonaco, 1998). Furthermore, the narrator of emotional stories and her audience tend to develop a stronger social bond when the audiences respond with enthusiasm (Gable, Reis, Impett, & Asher, 2004, as cited in Rimé, 2009). Sharing of emotional stories and episodes has also been found to increase narrators' health and subjective well-being (Finkenauer & Rimé, 1998).

Although these studies examined the impact of shared positive affect on groups' social processes and dynamics, Rhee (2006; 2007) proposed the importance of understanding how shared positive affect can trigger specific types of interactions among group members, based on Frijda's (1986) notion that each emotion is associated with specific action tendencies. For instance, individuals experiencing the emotions of joy and happiness tend to approach others and share positive outcomes, whereas individuals feeling anxious or fearful tend to avoid or escape from uncertainties (Lazarus, 1991). Rhee (2006) found in her study of 72 existing groups that shared positive affect encouraged specific types of interactions among members, analogous to the results at the individual level. Groups that shared joy and happiness engaged in building on and actively affirming each other's ideas. Building on each other's ideas contributes to a broadened scope of cognition and attention, and active affirmation of ideas contributes to building relational bonds among the members. These types of interactions have the core characteristics of playful interactions—cognitive and social spontaneity—that follow shared positive affect in groups (Rhee, 2007).

Group performance, another indicator of group effectiveness, is also enhanced by shared positive affect in workgroups. In her study of 51 sales groups in a large department store, George (1995) showed that groups that developed a positive affective tone increased their quality of customer service. Teammates' happy moods also increased individual member performance (Totterdell, 2000). At a dyadic level, several researchers have explored sharing of affect between client and service provider. Pugh (2001) showed that service providers' display of positive affect, such as smiling and making eye contact, facilitated customers' experience of positive affect, which increased the customers' ratings of service quality. Customers' trait positive affect, in turn, was associated with positive emotional display of cashiers in a fast-food restaurant observed by external raters, which resulted in increased customer satisfaction (Tan, Foo, & Kwek, 2004).

As individuals' experience of positive affect facilitates creative thinking (Isen & Daubman, 1984; Isen et al., 1992), so does shared positive affect in groups. Rhee's (2006) aforementioned laboratory study showed that shared affect of joy and happiness encouraged two types of interactions—building on and actively affirming each other's ideas—which increased group creativity. Building on each other's ideas stimulates individual members' cognition (Paulus & Yang, 2000) and enables them to combine original ideas and new ideas together in new ways, thus enhancing group creativity. Also, active affirmation of each other's ideas can create a supportive, noncritical group climate that can facilitate brainstorming and creativity in groups (Amabile, 1988; Connolly, Jessup, & Valacich, 1990). Grawitch and colleagues also found that shared positive affect in temporary groups enhanced group creativity through the generation of more original and important ideas on a brainstorming task (Grawitch, Munz, Elliott, & Mathis, 2003; Grawitch, Munz, & Kramer, 2003).

Although a general conclusion is that shared positive affect is associated with group creativity, certain types of tasks that require critical, logical cognitive processes, such as group decision making tasks, may benefit from shared affect with more negative valence. Rhee (2006) revealed that the types of interactions that enhanced group creativity actually hampered the quality of group decisions. Building on to and actively affirming each other's ideas tend to reinforce group members' positive affective state, which can motivate the members to avoid effortful, unpleasant analytical processes (Bless et al., 1990; Isen, 2000). Groups experiencing shared positive affect may engage in heuristic information processing, such as relying on simple decision rules, rather than using systematic, logical information processing in making decisions, which is likely to reduce the group's decision quality (Forgas, 1990; Kelly & Spoor, 2006). Furthermore, a group's positive emotional state can foster unrealistic optimism (Barsade, 2002) and an illusion of control (Langer, 1975), which has been found to negatively impact group performance. In addition to the reduced quality of group decisions, shared positive affect has potential to bring about negative group processes in certain situations. For example, although strong in-group identification enhances members' attachment to the group, such shared positive affect based on positive in-group identity can trigger the emotion of anger toward out-groups (Smith, Seger, & Mackie, 2006). Also, social cohesion developed through positive interactions can instigate "groupthink" by suppressing disagreements and minority opinions (Janis & Mann, 1977).

In sum, existing research confirms the important social consequences of shared positive affect in a workgroup context. Shared positive affect fosters positive social processes including cooperation, coordination, and the formation of strong social bonds. Shared positive affect also enhances group creativity, service quality during encounters with customers, and groups' task performance in general, although tasks that require logical, critical thinking and systematic information processing may not benefit as much from the shared positive affect.

Shared Positive Affect Versus Shared Negative Affect in Workgroups

Another important role that shared positive affect may play in group life is undoing the negative effects of shared negative affect. Past research on the physiological effects of positive emotions has shown that experience of positive emotions can quell or undo the cardiovascular effects of negative emotions such as anger, fear, and anxiety (Fredrickson, Mancuso, Branigan, & Tugade, 2000). Fredrickson and colleagues provided additional corroborating evidence in the context of the September 11, 2001 terrorist attacks, finding that individuals scoring high on trait resilience showed low depressive symptoms and higher life satisfaction and optimism through their experience of positive emotions such as gratitude and love (Fredrickson, Tugade, Waugh, & Larkin, 2003).

We propose that such an undoing effect may occur through shared positive affect at the group level as well. Consider the social sharing of affect, in which individuals share emotional stories and episodes with others. When exposed to negative emotional situations, individuals are motivated to seek social contact and engage in emotional conversations (Gump & Kulik, 1997; Rimé, 2009) and to share emotional stories with others (Rimé, 2009). Negative emotion occurs when expectations are violated or when unfamiliar objects or events destabilize our basis of knowledge and belief. By story-telling, narration, and conversation about emotional events and episodes, individuals acquire emotional support and reduce their anxiety, thus alleviating the initial negative emotions and feelings.

What is interesting is that narrators of negative emotional stories recovered from the negative emotional state to a greater extent when the sharing partner stimulated the narrators' cognitive work, which involved "recreat[ion] of meaning and reframe[ing] or re-apprais[al of] the episode" (Rimé, 2009, p. 77). Rimé (2009) concludes that, although empathetic sharing that involves emotional support and consolation can relieve narrators' emotional distress only temporarily, cognitive stimulation and reframing of negative events may result in a fuller recovery effect for the narrators. Here, the role of listeners of negative emotional stories becomes important, and we assume that listeners experiencing positive affect may be better equipped for cognitive reframing or reappraisal of the negative episode. Psychological literature on positive emotion has consistently found that individuals experiencing positive emotions tend to exhibit a broadened scope of cognition, attention, and action (Fredrickson, 1998).

Therefore, we predict that workgroup members experiencing positive affect will exercise cognitive flexibility to reframe negative events into positive ones, thus helping other members recover from the negative state.

The undoing effect of shared positive affect can also be observed in dynamic intergroup contexts. In the previous section, we explained how intergroup dynamics can cause members to feel positive about the in-group and to experience an emotion of anger toward out-groups (Smith et al., 2006). However, several researchers have shown that when individuals feel positive emotions, they tend to perceive out-group members similarly to the way they perceive in-group members (Dovidio, Gaertner, Isen, & Lowrance, 1995; Johnson & Fredrickson, 2005). Dovidio and colleagues (1995) found that individuals with positive emotions tended to give resources to out-group members and to see both in-group and out-group as one superordinate group. In a study examining the effect of positive emotions on the own-race bias in face perception, Johnson and Fredrickson (2005) found that white participants' experience of positive emotions enabled them to recognize black faces as well as they recognized white faces. Positive emotion thus broadens peoples' sense of self to include others and engenders feelings of oneness (Waugh & Fredrickson, 2006). Perhaps we may also observe such broadening effects of positive emotion in workgroups in which members experience shared positive affect.

The empirical studies mentioned above suggest that shared positive affect can influence group outcomes in both direct and indirect ways: directly, by impacting group social processes and performance outcomes, and indirectly, by undoing the negative effects of shared negative affect. We acknowledge that shared negative affect sometimes can result in positive outcomes. For example, shared negative affect between leader and followers encouraged the followers to exert more effort in order to overcome the current negative affective state (Sy et al., 2005). However, the majority of research exhibits negative outcomes associated with shared negative affect, including low group performance and satisfaction, high absenteeism (Duffy & Shaw, 2000), and rigid and narrow information processing (Staw, Sandelands, & Dutton, 1981). Therefore, through the undoing of negative effects of shared negative outcomes, shared positive affect has potential to break the negative spiral (e.g., more conflict, less cooperation, more absenteeism, rigid group processes) and turn it into a positive one.

Discussion

In this chapter, we developed a conceptual framework to enhance our understanding of shared positive affect as a group-level phenomenon. Using the framework, we reviewed the current literature on shared positive affect in workgroups, with a focus on shared positive affect's antecedents and outcomes and the mechanism of affect sharing.

The literature on shared positive affect demonstrates the breadth of its social consequences. Past research confirms that shared positive affect has great potential to foster positivity in workgroups, not only through building healthier, stronger social relationships but also through achievement of excellent performance, which may in turn reinforce the strength of shared positive affect. We also discussed ways in which shared positive affect can minimize the negative effects of shared negative affect or further energize workgroups to bounce back from the negative affective state. In this manner, shared positive affect may eventually create a social environment in which members can flourish, thrive, and excel in groups and organizations.

Future Directions

There is much left to be understood about the phenomenon of shared affect in workgroups and organizations and about shared positive affect in particular. First, an intriguing aspect of shared affect in workgroups is consideration of the degree of affective sharing or affective convergence and its effect on group processes and outcomes. The notion of convergent and divergent affective composition of workgroups builds on the research on homogeneity and heterogeneity of groups in terms of personality, ethnicity, and cultural or functional backgrounds. George and King (2007) emphasized the limitations of affective homogeneity. They argued that, for real teams in complex, dynamic environments, affective homogeneity might lead to a single shared reality, and the group may be equipped poorly to deal with the uncertain, ever-changing environment. Rather than acknowledging multiple, alternative views, shared positive affect can provide members with a false sense of security—leading to an erroneous belief that everything is fine and on track.

Tiedens, Sutton, and Fong (2004) proposed that affective heterogeneity, instead of homogeneity, may have positive impact on group creativity, decision quality, and ability to persuade others. In a study of 60 business teams, Losada and Heaphy (2004) discovered that the ratio of positive to negative utterances

in team communication impacted team performance. More specifically, the highest performing teams exhibited the positivity ratio of 2.9 in team communication, and individuals experiencing daily positive and negative emotions with the ratio of 2.9 showed a higher level of mental flourishing (Fredrickson & Losada, 2005). Taken together, these findings suggest the potential positive effects of affective heterogeneity in workgroups.

Several social structural characteristics of groups have the potential to influence the extent to which affect can be shared among the members. First, power and status differences among group members are likely to result in affective heterogeneity. According to Tiedens, Ellsworth, and Mesquita (2000), powerful individuals tend to show high-arousal positive or negative emotions (e.g., excitement or anger), whereas individuals possessing less power mostly respond with low-arousal emotions (e.g., contentment or guilt). Second, a strong group identity and strong identification with the group enhance the possibility that members will experience feelings similar to each other. In contrast, if members have multiple identities, or if they do not strongly identify with the group, it is likely that the members will experience divergent affect in reaction to group events (Garcia-Prieto, Mackie, Tran, & Smith, 2007).

In addition, cross-cultural differences may influence the extent to which affect is shared among group members. For instance, Asian culture is often reported to score high on the power distance index (Hofstede, 2001). In this circumstance, leaders or more powerful people may enjoy more freedom to express their emotions (e.g., Tiedens et al., 2000), and their emotions may be more likely to cascade down and be transferred to their followers, rather than the other way round. Rimé (2009) argues that Asians tend to share emotional episodes particularly with peers including siblings, cousins, and close friends. Thus, perhaps, the difference between Asians and Westerners could be with whom they share affect most actively. More specifically, Asians tend to exhibit larger overlap between task and social relationships, whereas Westerners show little overlap (Sanchez-Burks, Lee, Choi, Nisbett, Zhao, & Koo, 2003). This suggests that Asians may feel comfortable sharing emotional stories in workgroups when their task relationships are social relationships as well. We believe that it is meaningful to look deeper into the affective side of group composition, in the fashion of previous research on group composition effects (e.g., homogeneity or heterogeneity of member personality, cultural, or functional backgrounds).

The second topic for future research involves a deeper exploration of the role that group-level constructs play in the process or outcome of shared positive affect. Psychological findings of individual-level positive affect have provided important insights for studies on shared positive affect at the group level (Kelly & Spoor, 2006). However, given the nature of shared positive affect as a group-level phenomenon, group-level constructs (e.g., member interactions, groupthink, majority and minority status, core and periphery group members, boundary spanners, and homogeneous and heterogeneous member compositions) may have important theoretical and empirical implications as well.

For instance, Duffy and Shaw (2000) empirically found that a shared negative emotion of envy (envy toward other in-group members) indirectly influenced group performance, absenteeism, and group satisfaction through increased social loafing and decreased cohesion and group self-efficacy. Rhee (2006) also showed that certain types of social interactions mediated the link between shared positive affect of joy and happiness and group outcomes. By explaining the underlying mechanism for how shared affect impacted group outcomes, these studies demonstrated that group-level constructs can provide for a fuller, richer understanding of the phenomenon of shared affect in workgroups.

A third clear avenue for future research is to examine how outside observers perceive a group's affective state, and how such perceptions impact observers' evaluations of and attitudes toward the group. This approach focuses on the observers' evaluation of the group on the basis of valence of members' affective expressions (Magee & Tiedens, 2006) or on how accurately outside observers can capture members' affective state as a whole (Sanchez-Burks & Huy, 2009). Through a series of laboratory experiments in which participants saw pictures of or read stories about group members, Magee and Tiedens (2006) found that the observers evaluated groups as cohesive when members looked happy. Also, homogeneity of emotional expression across group members functioned as an indicator that they had experienced similar events and outcomes. Furthermore, observers are likely to use group's affective information in predicting group outcomes. Kelly and Spoor (2007) discovered that individuals used naïve theories, that is "organized knowledge and beliefs that people have regarding a particular target or situation" (p. 204), in predicting

consequences of shared positive or negative affect in workgroups. A compelling example they mention is that of a supervisor not taking recommendations from a group with shared negative affect, as she believed that the negative affect reduced the group's decision quality. We see that taking an outside observer's perspective can have important implications for a group's external relationships and boundary management.

Fourth, a longitudinal perspective in exploring complex and dynamic processes of shared positive affect is warranted. Fredrickson (1998) proposes that positive emotions build long-term social, intellectual, and physical resources for individuals. Similarly, shared positive affect has potential to build sustainable resources within workgroups, such as strong emotional bond and accumulated shared knowledge among the members, for instance. In their dynamic model, Walter and Bruch (2008) suggest a term, "positive group affect spiral," which contends that shared positive affect enhances quality of member relationships because the group members are likely to be attracted to each other due to similar emotional experiences. High-quality member relationships, in turn, will promote sharing of positive affect through open expressions of positive feelings. In addition, an empirical finding links changes in shared positive affect and group outcomes over time. Mason and Griffin (2003) found in their longitudinal study that groups with the greatest improvement in their level of absenteeism were those with an increased level of positive affective tone over time. These studies suggest the importance of monitoring and maintaining the positive affective spiral in workgroups to build long-term high-quality relationships and group attachment.

Several contextual factors, such as charismatic leadership, an attractive organizational identity, and emotion norms that encourage positive affective expressions, have been suggested to reinforce the positive group affect spiral (Walter & Bruch, 2008). Emotionally intelligent workgroups also have potential to enhance the spiral not only because of individual emotional resources that members have available for teamwork but also because of "emotionally competent group norms" developed throughout the group life (i.e., Druskat & Wolff, 2001; Elfenbein, 2006). Workgroup members with emotional intelligence are capable of detecting and managing others' emotions. Emotionally competent group norms include acceptance of emotions as part of the group work, expression and examination of member feelings, and promotion of group self-efficacy.

These individual emotional resources and emotionally healthy norms enhance the likelihood that members will share positive affect and develop high-quality relationships, thus strengthening the positive affect spiral in workgroups.

Finally, there is a growing interest in understanding how individuals share affect with others in non–face-to-face contexts, such as occur in virtual teams or telecommuting contexts (Friedman, Anderson, Brett, Olekalns, Goates, & Lisco, 2004; McGinn & Keros, 2002; Moore, Kurtzberg, Thompson, & Morris, 1999; Van Kleef et al., 2004ab,). During electronic negotiations, individuals tend to "nonconsciously imitate not only the linguistic structure of each other's messages (e.g., message length, informational context, grammar), but also the social-emotional connotations of the other's message (e.g., tone, directness)" (Thompson & Nadler, 2002, p. 113). Although individuals do mimic each other's affective expressions online, it may be more difficult to transfer affect through electronic media than through face-to-face interaction because electronic communication involves ambiguity and the absence of nonverbal cues (Belkin, 2009). Negative affect may be more easily transmitted electronically than positive affect, because negative expressions violate societal norms and thus may be more noticeable and contagious. By uncovering how workgroup members in non–face-to-face work settings share affect and examining the impact of such shared positive affect is, we may deepen our understanding of the affective dynamics in workgroups interacting in this relatively new way of working.

Conclusion

Despite an enduring interest in emotions, moods, and feelings as an essential part of our everyday lives, only recently have researchers begun to explore the role shared affect plays in group life. Our focus on shared positive affect opens up the possibility of fostering positivity in workgroups through such fundamental mechanisms as positive emotions and feelings shared within groups. According to Fredrickson and Losada (2005), "to flourish means to live within an optimal range of human functioning, one that connotes goodness, generativity, growth, and resilience" (p. 678). We believe that shared positive affect can help achieve this end in workgroups by building strong social bonds, motivating excellent performance, and enabling groups to resiliently bounce back from negative affective states. We hope that the theoretical framework outlined in this chapter will facilitate research in the fertile field of inquiry of shared positive affect in workgroups.

Notes

1. Following Barsade (2002) and Hatfield, Cacioppo, and Rapson (1994), we use the term *affect* in this study as a broad label. Affect is often used as an umbrella term for emotions and moods. Researchers distinguish emotion from mood in terms of whether an object or stimuli caused the feelings or in terms of the duration and intensity of the feelings (Weiss & Cropanzano, 1996). Emotions are relatively intense and short-lived, with specific targets, and can interrupt ongoing cognitive and behavioral processes. On the other hand, moods are weaker or diffuse, last longer, and lack causal object. They do not interrupt, but have a subtler impact (Clark & Isen, 1982). Moods tend to elicit a wider range of cognitive and behavioral responses than do emotions because they are not targeted toward specific causes. However, the distinction between moods and emotions is subtle, and researchers often use the terms interchangeably for semantic ease and to reflect the ambiguity in distinguishing moods and emotions (Barsade, 2002). Therefore, we use the term *affect* to capture both emotions and moods.

2. Our definition of shared positive affect includes both high-arousal positive affect (e.g., enthusiasm, joy) and low-arousal positive affect (e.g., contentment, calmness). Individual-level research finds that high-arousal positive affect (e.g., joy, excitement) activates individuals' motivation to approach others and share the positive story, whereas individuals experiencing low-arousal positive affect (e.g., contentment, relaxedness) tend to savor the moment and do nothing (Fredrickson, 1998). Therefore, it is likely that group processes and outcomes are influenced differently by high-arousal and low-arousal shared positive affect. However, current literature on shared affect mostly focuses on the valence dimension (pleasant–unpleasant affect) rather than on the arousal dimension (high arousal–low arousal affect). Thus, in this chapter, our definition of shared positive affect includes both high- and low-arousal positive affect.

References

Amabile, T.M. (1988). A model of creativity and innovation in organizations. In B.M. Staw, & L.L. Cummings (Eds.), *Research in organizational behavior* (pp. 123–167). Greenwich, CT: JAI Press.

Barsade, S.G. (2002). The ripple effect: Emotional contagion and its influence on group behavior. *Administrative Science Quarterly, 47,* 644–675.

Barsade, S.G., Brief, A.P., & Spataro, S.E. (2003). The affective revolution in organizational behavior: The emergence of a paradigm. In J. Greenberg (Ed.), *Organizational behavior: The state of the science* (2nd ed., pp. 3–52). Hillsdale, NJ: L.Erlbaum & Associates.

Barsade, S.G., & Gibson, D.E. (1998). Group emotion: A view from top and bottom. In M.A. Neale, & E.A. Mannix (Eds.), *Research on managing groups and teams* (pp. 81–102). Stamford, CT: JAI Press.

Barsade, S.G., & O'Neill, O.A. (2009). Affective organizational culture: Its influence in the long-term care setting. Working paper.

Barsade, S.G., Lamarajan, L., & Western, D. (2009). Implicit affect in organizations. *Research in Organizational Behavior, 29*, 135–162.

Barsade, S.G., Ward, A.J., Turner, J.D., & Sonnenfeld, J.A. (2000). To your heart's content: A model of affective diversity in top management teams. *Administrative Science Quarterly, 45*, 802–836.

Bartel, C.A., & Saavedra, R. (2000). The collective construction of work group moods. *Administrative Science Quarterly, 45*, 197–231.

Belkin, L.Y. (2009). Emotional contagion in the electronic communication context: Conceptualizing the dynamics and implications of electronic emotional encounters in organizations. *Journal of Organizational Culture, Communications and Conflict, 13*, 105–122.

Bless, H., Bohner, G., Schwarz, N., & Strack, F. (1990). Mood and persuasion: A cognitive response analysis. *Personality and Social Psychology Bulletin, 16*, 331–345.

Cameron, K.S., Dutton, J.E., & Quinn, R. (Eds.). (2003). *Positive organizational scholarship*. San Francisco: Berrett-Koehler.

Carnevale, P.J.D., & Isen, A.M. (1986). The influence of positive affect and visual access on the discovery of integrative solutions in bilateral negotiation. *Organizational Behavior and Human Decision Processes, 37*, 1–13.

Christophe, V., & Rimé, B. (1997). Exposure to the social sharing of emotion: Emotional impact, listener responses and the secondary social sharing. *European Journal of Social Psychology, 27*, 37–54.

Cialdini, R.B., Borden, R.J., Thorne, A., Walker, M.R., Freeman, S., & Sloan, L.R. (1976). Basking in reflected glory: Three (football) field studies. *Journal of Personality and Social Psychology, 34*, 366–375.

Clark, M.S., & Isen, A.M. (1982). Toward understanding the relationship between feeling states and social behavior. In A.H. Hastorf, & A.M. Isen (Eds.), *Cognitive social psychology* (pp. 73–108). New York: Elsevier Science.

Connolly, T., Jessup, L.M., & Valacich, J.S. (1990). Effects of anonymity and evaluative tone on idea generation in computer-mediated groups. *Management Science, 36*, 689–703.

Dovidio, J.F., Gaertner, S.L., Isen, A.M., & Lowrance, R. (1995). Group representations and intergroup bias: Positive affect, similarity, and group size. *Personality and Social Psychology Bulletin, 21*, 856–865.

Druskat, V.U., & Wolff, S.B. (2001). Building the emotional intelligence of groups. *Harvard Business Review, 79*, 81–90.

Duffy, M.K., & Shaw, J.D. (2000). The Salieri syndrome: Consequences of envy in groups. *Small Group Research, 31*, 3–23.

Elfenbein, H.A. (2006). Team emotional intelligence: What it can mean and how it can impact performance. In V. Druskat, F. Sala, & G. Mount (Eds.), *The link between emotional intelligence and effective performance* (pp. 165–184). Mahwah, NJ: Lawrence Erlbaum.

Finkenauer, C., & Rimé, B. (1998). Keeping emotional memories secret: Health and subjective well-being when emotions are not shared. *Journal of Health Psychology, 3*, 47–58.

Forgas, J.P. (1990). Affective influences on individual and group judgments. *European Journal of Social Psychology, 20*, 441–453.

Fredrickson, B.L. (1998). What good are positive emotions? *Review of General Psychology, 2*, 300–319.

Fredrickson, B.L., & Losada, M.F. (2005). Positive affect and the complex dynamics of human flourishing. *American Psychologist, 60*, 678–686.

Fredrickson, B.L., Mancuso, R.A., Branigan, C., & Tugade, M.M. (2000). The undoing effect of positive emotions. *Motivation and Emotion, 24*, 237–258.

Fredrickson, B.L., Tugade, M.M., Waugh, C.E., & Larkin, G. (2003). What good are positive emotions in crises? A prospective study of resilience and emotions following the terrorist attacks on the United States on September 11th, 2001. *Journal of Personality and Social Psychology, 84*, 365–376.

Friedman, R., Anderson, C., Brett, J., Olekalns, M., Goates, N., & Lisco, C.C. (2004). The positive and negative effects of anger on dispute resolution: Evidence from electronically mediated disputes. *Journal of Applied Psychology, 89*, 369–376.

Frijda, N.H. (1986). *The emotions*. New York: Cambridge University Press.

Gable, S.L., Reis, H.T., Impett, E.A., & Asher, E.R. (2004). What do you do when things go right? The intrapersonal and interpersonal benefits of sharing positive events. *Journal of Personality and Social Psychology, 87*, 228–245.

Garcia-Prieto, P., Mackie, D.M., Tran, V., & Smith, E.R. (2007). Intergroup emotions in workgroups: Some emotional antecedents and consequences of belonging. In E.A. Mannix, M.A. Neal, & C.P. Anderson (Eds.), *Research on managing groups and teams* Vol. 10 (pp. 145–184). Oxford, UK: Elsevier Science Press.

George, J.M. (1990). Personality, affect, and behavior in groups. *Journal of Applied Psychology, 75*, 107–116.

George, J.M. (1991). State or trait: Effects of positive mood on prosocial behaviors at work. *Journal of Applied Psychology, 76*, 299–307.

George, J.M. (1995). Leader positive mood and group performance: The case of customer service. *Journal of Applied Social Psychology, 25*, 778–794.

George, J.M., & Brief, A.P. (1992). Feeling good, doing good: A conceptual analysis of the mood at work - organizational spontaneity relationship. *Psychological Bulletin, 112*, 310–329.

George, J.M., & King, E.B. (2007). Potential pitfalls of affect convergence in teams: Functions and dysfunctions of group affective tone. In E.A. Mannix, M.A. Neal, & C.P. Anderson (Eds.), *Research on managing groups and teams* Vol. 10 (pp. 97–124). Oxford, UK: Elsevier Science Press.

Gibson, C.B. (2003). The efficacy advantage: Factors related to the formation of group efficacy. *Journal of Applied Social Psychology, 33*, 2153–2186.

Grawitch, M.J., Munz, D.C., Elliott, E.K., & Mathis, A. (2003). Promoting creativity in temporary problem-solving groups: The effects of positive mood and autonomy in problem definition on idea-generating performance. *Group Dynamics: Theory, Research and Practice, 7*, 200–213.

Grawitch, M.J., Munz, D.C., & Kramer, T.J. (2003). Effects of member mood states on creative performance in temporary workgroups. *Group Dynamics-Theory Research and Practice, 7*, 41–54.

Gump, B.B., & Kulik, J.A. (1997). Stress, affiliation, and emotional contagion. *Journal of Personality and Social Psychology, 72*, 305–319.

Hackman, J.R., & Oldham, G.R. (1980). *Work redesign*. Reading, MA: Addison-Wesley Publishing.

Hatfield, E., Cacioppo, J., & Rapson, R.L. (1994). Primitive emotional contagion. In M.S. Clark (Ed.), *Review of personality and social psychology: Emotion and social behavior* Vol. 14 (pp. 151–177). Newbury Park, CA: Sage.

Hofstede, G. (2001). *Culture's consequences: Comparing values, behaviors, institutions, and organizations across nations.* Thousand Oaks, CA: Sage.

Hollingshead, A.B. (1998). Retrieval processes in transactive memory systems. *Journal of Personality and Social Psychology, 74,* 659–671.

Huy, Q.N. (2002). Emotional balancing of organizational continuity and radical change: The contribution of middle managers. *Administrative Science Quarterly, 47,* 31–69.

Isen, A.M. (2000). Positive affect and decision making. In M.Lewis, & J.M. Haviland-Jones (Eds.), *Handbook of emotions (*2nd ed., pp. 417–435). New York: Guilford Press.

Isen, A.M., Clark, M., & Schwartz, M.F. (1976). Duration of the effect of good mood on helping: "Footprints on the sands of time". *Journal of Personality and Social Psychology, 34,* 385–393.

Isen, A.M., & Daubman, K.A. (1984). The influence of affect on categorization. *Journal of Personality and Social Psychology, 47,* 1206–1217.

Isen, A.M., Niedenthal, P., & Cantor, N. (1992). An influence of positive affect on social categorization. *Motivation and Emotion, 16,* 65–78.

Janis, I., & Mann, L. (1977). *Decision making: A psychological analysis of conflict, choice, and commitment.* New York: Free Press.

Jehn, K.A. (1995). A multimethod examination of the benefits and detriments of intragroup conflict. *Administrative Science Quarterly, 40,* 256–282.

Johnson, K.J., & Fredrickson, B.L. (2005). We all look the same to me: Positive emotions eliminate the own-race bias in face recognition. *Psychological Science, 16,* 875–881.

Kelly, J.R., & Barsade, S.G. (2001). Mood and emotions in small groups and work teams. *Organizational Behavior and Human Decision Processes, 86,* 99–130.

Kelly, J.R., & Spoor, J.R. (2006). Affective influences in groups. In J. Forgas (Ed.), *Affect in social thinking and behavior* (pp. 311–325). New York: Psychology Press.

Kelly, J.R., & Spoor J.R. (2007). Naive theories about the effects of mood in groups: A preliminary investigation. *Group Processes & Intergroup Relations, 10,* 203–222.

Klimoski, R., & Mohammed, S. (1994). Team mental model: Construct or metaphor? *Journal of Management, 20,* 403–437.

Langer, E.J. (1975). The illusion of control. *Journal of Personality and Social Psychology, 32,* 311–328.

Langston, C.A. (1994). Capitalizing on and coping with daily-life events: Expressive responses to positive events. *Journal of Personality and Social Psychology, 67,* 1112–1125.

Laurenceau, J.P., Feldman-Barrett, L., & Pietromonaco, P.R. (1998). Intimacy as an interpersonal process: The importance of self-disclosure, partner disclosure, and perceived partner responsiveness in interpersonal exchanges. *Journal of Personality and Social Psychology, 74,* 1238–1251.

Lazarus, R.S. (1991). *Emotion and adaptation.* New York: Oxford University Press.

Losada, M., & Heaphy, E. (2004). The role of positivity and connectivity in the performance of business teams: A nonlinear dynamics model. *American Behavioral Scientist, 47,* 740–765.

Mackie, D.M., Devos, T., & Smith, E.R. (2000). Intergroup emotions: Explaining offensive action tendencies in an intergroup context. *Journal of Personality and Social Psychology, 79,* 602–616.

Mackie, D.M., Silver, L.A., & Smith, E.R. (2004). Intergroup emotions: Emotion as intergroup phenomena. In L.Z. Tiedens, & C.W. Leach (Eds.), *The social life of emotions* (pp. 227–245). Cambridge: Cambridge University Press.

Magee, J.C., & Tiedens, L.Z. (2006). Emotional ties that bind: The roles of valence and consistency of group emotion in inferences of cohesiveness and common fate. *Personality and Social Psychology Bulletin, 32,* 1703–1715.

Martin, J., Knopoff, K., & Beckman, C. (1998). An alternative to bureaucratic impersonality and emotional labor: Bounded emotionality at the Body Shop. *Administrative Science Quarterly, 43,* 429–469.

Mason, C.M., & Griffin, M.A. (2003). Group absenteeism and positive affective tone: A longitudinal study. *Journal of Organizational Behavior, 24,* 667–687.

McGinn, K.L., & Keros, A.T. (2002). Improvisation and the logic of exchange in socially embedded transactions. *Administrative Science Quarterly, 47,* 442–473.

McGrath, J.E. (1984). *Groups: Interaction and performance.* Englewood Cliffs, NJ: Prentice Hall.

Moore, D., Kurtzberg, T.R., Thompson, L.L., & Morris, M.W. (1999). Long and short routes to success in electronically mediated negotiations: Group affiliations and good vibrations. *Organizational Behavior and Human Decision Processes, 77,* 22–43.

Neumann, R., & Strack, F. (2000). Mood contagion: The automatic transfer of mood between persons. *Journal of Personality and Social Psychology, 79,* 211–223.

Parkinson, B., Fischer, A.H., & Manstead, A.S.R. (2005). *Emotion in social relations.* New York: Psychology Press.

Paulus, P.B., & Yang, H.C. (2000). Idea generation in groups: A basis for creativity in groups. *Organizational Behavior and Human Decision Processes, 82,* 76–87.

Pescosolido, A.T. (2002). Emergent leaders as managers of group emotion. *Leadership Quarterly, 13,* 583–599.

Peters, K., & Kashima, Y. (2007). From social talk to social action: Shaping the social triad with emotion sharing. *Journal of Personality and Social Psychology, 93,* 780–797.

Pugh, S.D. (2001). Service with a smile: Emotional contagion in the service encounter. *Academy of Management Journal, 44,* 1018–1027.

Rhee, S.Y. (2007). Shared emotions and group outcomes: The role of group member interactions. In E.A. Mannix, M.A. Neal, & C.P. Anderson (Eds.), *Research on managing groups and teams* Vol. 10 (pp. 65–95). Oxford, UK: Elsevier Science Press.

Rhee, S.Y. (2006). Shared emotions and group effectiveness: The role of broadening-and-building interactions. In K. Mark Weaver (Ed.), *Proceedings of the sixty-fifth annual meeting of the Academy of Management (CD),* ISSN 1543–8643.

Rimé, B. (1995). The social sharing of emotional experience as a source for the social knowledge of emotion. In J.A. Russell, J.M. Fernandez-Dols, A.S.R. Manstead, & J.C. Wellenkamp (Eds.), *Everyday conceptions of emotions: An introduction to the psychology, anthropology and linguistics of emotion* (pp.475–489). Doordrecht, NL: Kluwer.

Rimé, B. (2009). Emotion elicits the social sharing of emotion: Theory and empirical review. *Emotion Review, 1,* 60–85.

Sanchez-Burks, J., & Huy, Q.N. (2009). Emotional aperture and strategic change: The accurate recognition of collective emotions. *Organization Science, 20,* 22–34.

Sanchez-Burks, J., Lee, F., Choi, I., Nisbett, R., Zhao, S., & Koo, J. (2003). Conversing across cultures: East-West communication styles in work and nonwork contexts. *Journal of Personality and Social Psychology, 85,* 363–372.

Schachter, S. (1959). *The psychology of affiliation.* Stanford, CA: Stanford University Press.

Schneider, B. (1987). The people make the place. *Personnel Psychology, 40,* 437–453.

Smith, E.R. (1993). Social identity and social emotions: Toward new conceptualizations of prejudice. In D.M. Mackie, & D.L. Hamilton (Eds.), *Affect, cognition and stereotyping: Interaction processes in group perception* (pp. 297–315). New York: Academic Press.

Smith, E.R., Seger, C.R., & Mackie, D.M. (2006). Can emotions be truly group-level? Evidence regarding four conceptual criteria. Unpublished manuscript, Indiana University, Bloomington, IN.

Staw, B.M., Sandelands, L.E., & Dutton, J.E. (1981). Threat rigidity effects in organizational behavior: A multilevel analysis. *Administrative Science Quarterly, 26,* 501–524.

Sy, T., Côté, S., & Saavedra, R. (2005). The contagious leader: Impact of the leader's mood on the mood of group members, group affective tone, and group processes. *Journal of Applied Psychology, 90,* 295–305.

Tan, H.H., Foo, M.D., & Kwek, M.H. (2004). The effects of customer personality traits on the display of positive emotions. *Academy of Management Journal, 47,* 287–296.

Thompson, L., & Nadler, J. (2002). Negotiating via information technology: Theory and application. *Journal of Social Issues, 58,* 109–124.

Tiedens, L.Z., Ellsworth, P.C., & Mesquita, B. (2000). Stereotypes about sentiments and status: Emotional expectations for high- and low-status group members. *Personality and Social Psychology Bulletin, 26,* 560–574.

Tiedens, L.Z., Sutton, R.I., & Fong, C.T. (2004). Emotional variation within work groups: Causes and performance consequences. In C.W. Leach, & L.Z. Tiedens (Eds.), *The social life of emotions.* Cambridge, UK: Cambridge University Press.

Totterdell, P. (2000). Catching moods and hitting runs: Mood linkage and subjective performance in professional sport teams. *Journal of Applied Psychology, 85,* 848–859.

Totterdell, P., Kellett, S., Teuchmann, K., & Briner, R.B. (1998). Evidence of mood linkage in work groups. *Journal of Personality and Social Psychology, 74,* 1504–1515.

Totterdell, P., Wall, T., Holman, D., Diamond, H., & Epitropaki, O. (2004). Affect networks: A structural analysis of the relationship between work ties and job-related affect. *Journal of Applied Psychology, 89,* 854–867.

Van Kleef, G.A., De Dreu, C.K.W., & Manstead, A.S.R. (2004a). The interpersonal effects of anger and happiness in negotiation. *Journal of Personality and Social Psychology, 86,* 57–76.

Van Kleef, G.A., De Dreu, C.K.W., & Manstead, A.S.R. (2004b). The interpersonal effects of emotions in negotiations: A motivated information processing approach. *Journal of Personality and Social Psychology, 87,* 510–528.

Walter, F., & Bruch, H. (2008). The positive group affect spiral: A dynamic model of the emergence of positive affective similarity in work groups. *Journal of Organizational Behavior, 29,* 239–261.

Waugh, C.E., & Fredrickson, B.L. (2006). Nice to know you: Positive emotions, self-other overlap, and complex understanding in the formation of a new relationship. *Journal of Positive Psychology, 1,* 93–106.

Weiss, H.M., & Cropanzano, R. (1996). Affective events theory: A theoretical discussion of the structure, causes and consequences of affective experiences at work. In B.M. Staw, & L.L. Cummings (Eds.), *Research in organizational behavior* (pp. 1–74). Greenwich, CT: JAI Press.

PART 3

Strengths and Virtues

Virtuousness in Organizations

Kim Cameron *and* Bradley Winn

Abstract

Virtuousness represents the best of the human condition or the highest aspirations human beings hold for themselves. In organizations, virtuousness is often manifest in collective displays of moral excellence. It signifies a core concept within positive organizational scholarship (POS), and the legitimacy and credibility of POS is at least partly dependent on whether virtuousness exists in organizations and whether it has pragmatic value. Yet, little agreement characterizes the current literature regarding the definition and relevance of virtuousness, and almost no empirical investigations have been published on virtuousness in organizations. This chapter carefully defines and explains the key attributes of virtuousness in organizations, summarizes the main findings from the few empirical studies that have been conducted, and offers a research agenda to guide future research on virtuousness in the coming years.

Keywords: Virtuousness, virtues, organizational performance, organizational virtuousness, strengths, virtue ethics, moral virtues

On June 2, 2010, Amando Galarraga, a pitcher for the Detroit Tigers major league baseball team, was on the verge of achieving something that no one in the history of Detroit Tigers baseball had achieved. Only 20 other pitchers since baseball's beginning in 1894 had ever pitched a perfect game. With two outs in the last inning, 40,000 fans watched the batter, the Cleveland Indians' shortstop, hit a ground ball to the Tigers' first baseman who fielded the ball and threw to Galarraga covering first base. The 40,000 fans erupted as the runner was clearly out and Galarraga had accomplished this near-impossible feat—that is, until the first base umpire, Jim Joyce, signaled the runner safe. Fans and players screamed their displeasure at what seemed clearly to be a blown call. Radio and television announcers in the broadcast booth opined that the entire sport of baseball had been cheated by the umpire. Yet, incredibly, Galarraga's reaction to the call was a smile, a shrug of the shoulders, and a return to the pitcher's mound to retire the 28th batter.

After the game, Jim Joyce watched the replay in the umpire's dressing room. As soon as he saw the play, he admitted, "I just cost that kid a perfect game." He had clearly missed the call. Joyce immediately went to the Tigers' dressing room, found Galarraga, and admitted his mistake. He was reportedly near tears as he hugged the pitcher and apologized for costing him a place in history.

The next night, Jim Joyce was scheduled to umpire again in the same baseball stadium with the same two teams. He expected to be criticized, booed, and abused by the fans. Instead, as he entered the field of play, most of the fans clapped. Galarraga met him at home plate at the beginning of the game to shake his hand and present him with the game's stating line-up of players. Despite the famous line by Tom Hanks, "There's no crying in baseball," Joyce was brought to tears as he experienced a completely unexpected, magnanimous response to his admitted mistake. Not only had Galarraga demonstrated forgiveness, but so had 40,000 Tigers fans—an incredible display of collective virtuousness.

Although displays of virtuousness are recognized as admirable and desirable, systematic, empirical investigations of virtuousness are rare, especially in organizations. Virtuousness has remained largely beyond the purview of organizational science. The prevailing tradition has been that examinations of virtues and virtuousness are associated with social conservatism, religious dogmatism, and scientific irrelevance (Chapman & Galston, 1992; MacIntyre, 1984; Schimmel, 1997). They are often relegated to theology, philosophy, or mere naïveté. Fineman (2006) argued, for example, that virtuousness is culturally restrictive and narrow-minded. Its relevance in the world of work or in organizations receives little credence in the face of economic pressures and stakeholder demands. Walsh (1999) analyzed word usage in the *Wall Street Journal* from 1984 through 2000 and reported that the appearance of terms such as "win," "advantage," and "beat" had risen more than four-fold over that 17 year period in reference to business organizations. On the other hand, terms such as "virtue," "caring," and "compassion" seldom appeared at all in reference to business. The use of these terms remained negligible across the same 17-year period.

On the other hand, economist Adam Smith (1976/1790) and sociologist Georg Simmel (1950), argued that virtuousness is the basis upon which all societies and economies flourish, since virtuousness is synonymous with the internalization of moral rules that produce social harmony (Baumeister & Exline, 1999). Virtuousness in societies provides the integral elements of good citizenship (White, 1996), reciprocity (Simmel, 1950), and stability (Smith, 1976/1790) needed to ensure societal longevity.

For the most part, virtuousness has been replaced in organizational studies by more morally neutral terms such as corporate social responsibility, business ethics, prosocial behavior, and employee well-being (George, 1991; McNeeley & Meglino, 1994; Piliavin & Charng, 1990). One result of this neutralized language is that systematic investigations of virtuousness in organizations have been rare, and virtuousness has been considered too saccharine to be taken seriously by most organizational scholars.

A review of scholarly literature relating to the concept of virtuousness (including the terms "virtues," "civic virtues," "moral virtues," and "virtue ethics") reveals that little agreement exists regarding its definition and attributes. Most articles in the academic literature focus on the debate about whether virtuousness actually exists (Alzola, 2008; Weaver, 2006; Whetstone, 2003; Wright &

Goodstein, 2007), on the definition of virtues and virtuousness (Fowers, 2009; Moberg, 1999; Rachels, 1999), or on the development of virtue in societies (Moore & Beadle, 2006; Nielsen, 2006). A few articles have attempted to identify universalistic virtues and to develop instruments for measuring them (Chun, 2005; Peterson & Seligman, 2004; Shanahan & Hyman, 2003), but the most striking feature of this literature is that very few empirical studies have been conducted in which virtue or virtuousness is investigated empirically (Bright, Cameron, & Caza, 2006; Caza, Barker, & Cameron, 2004; Cameron, Bright, & Caza, 2004; Den Hartog & De Hoogh, 2009; Rego, Ribeiro, & Cunha, 2010).

This chapter, therefore, puts a great deal of emphasis on clarifying the definition of virtuousness and specifying its primary attributes. A clear understanding of virtuousness and its role in organizations will not occur without a lucid definition. The second section of the chapter reviews empirical literature relating to virtuousness in organizations. Whereas an extensive literature exists on virtuousness in individuals (Peterson & Seligman, 2004; Weaver, 2006), very little has documented the investigation of virtuousness in organizations. A few studies have examined the relationship between virtuousness and organizational performance, and those key findings are summarized. Because this literature is so limited, expanding and enriching an understanding of virtuousness and its role in organizations is fertile territory. Therefore, potential research questions and an agenda for future investigations are discussed in the third and concluding section.

The Definition and Attributes of Virtuousness

To begin, it is important to differentiate the concepts of virtues and virtuousness. The term *virtues* refers to individual attributes that represent moral excellence, inherent goodness, and what represents humanity's very best qualities. Aristotle (1999) equated it with "excellence in the human soul." Examples include displays of forgiveness, humility, wisdom, and compassion. Virtues are sometimes equated with personal strengths, but as is discussed later, virtues and personal strengths are not synonymous.

Virtuousness, on the other hand, refers to a constellation of virtues in the aggregate. Virtuousness is manifest by collectives of people, and it can be fostered by organizational policies, processes, and practices. Just as individuals possess more than one virtue (and strength), organizations also display and enable more than one virtue.[1] It is also the case, as explained later, that virtuousness (a combination of virtues) is more likely to be associated with organization-level outcomes than a single virtue in isolation.

This does not mean, of course, that single virtues are not important in positive organizational scholarship (POS) research. As illustrated by several chapters in this Handbook, individual virtues have received a considerable attention in empirical investigations. The concept of virtuousness, on the other hand, has been largely ignored in POS research and is in need of conceptual and empirical development. Virtuousness in this chapter, therefore, refers to aggregates of virtues, acting in combination, which manifests itself as behaviors, processes, and routines in organizational settings. Virtuousness and its consequences remain under-developed theoretically and empirically.

One reason for the dearth of empirical research on virtuousness is the confusion that exists regarding its meaning. Virtuousness has been used interchangeably in the literature with corporate social responsibility (CSR), citizenship behavior, business ethics, justice, and strengths. Illustrations of the variety of definitions include Moberg's (1999) equating virtuousness with some of the Big Five personality attributes—namely, agreeableness and conscientiousness of managers in organizations—or Ewin's (1995) proposal that a virtue is exemplified by the persuasive ability and influence techniques of a salesperson. Fowers (2005) equated virtuousness with ethics and with personal strengths, and he defined virtuousness as the pursuit of that which leads to instrumental outcomes beneficial for human beings. Virtuousness "does not involve self-sacrifice or self-denial," so by implication, it is similar to a hedonistic pursuit of fulfillment. "Virtue is the form of excellence that allows an individual to pursue worthwhile ends in everyday activities . . . so virtue is not its own reward" (Fowers, 2009, p. 1013). A key objective of this chapter is to clarify what is and is not a virtue or virtuousness, especially in light of these multiple and conflicting perspectives and definitions.

Rooted in the Latin word *virtus,* or the Greek *arête,* meaning excellence, Plato and Aristotle described virtuousness as the desires and actions that produce personal and social good (or instrumental outcomes). More recently, virtuousness has been described as the best of the human condition, the most ennobling behaviors and outcomes of people, the excellence and essence of humankind, and the highest aspirations of human beings (Chapman, & Galston, 1992; Comte-Sponville, 2001; Dent, 1984; MacIntyre, 1984; Weiner, 1993). That is, the meaning of virtuousness has shifted from being a means to another more desirable outcome to representing an ultimate good itself.

The definition of virtuousness adopted thus far in POS equates it to an end, not a means to an end. Virtuousness is not subservient to the desire for profitability, for example, nor to any instrumental outcome. Virtuousness is characterized by at least three core attributes.

The Eudaemonic Assumption

First, virtuousness is synonymous with the *eudaemonic assumption*—this is the assumption that an inclination exists in all human beings toward goodness for its intrinsic value (Aristotle, *Metaphysics;* Dutton & Sonenshein, 2007). Several authors have provided evidence that the human inclination toward virtuousness is inherent and evolutionarily developed (Miller, 2007; Tangley, Stuewig, & Mashek, 2007). Inherent virtuousness, or an inclination toward the best of the human condition, develops in the brain before the development of language. Studies of the human brain indicate that individuals appear to have a basic instinct toward morality and are organically inclined to be virtuous (Haight, 2006; Hauser, 2006; Pinker, 1997). Krebs (1987, p. 113) asserted that human beings are "genetically disposed" to acts of virtuousness, and observing and experiencing virtuousness helps unlock the human predisposition toward behaving in ways that benefit others.

In functional terms, virtuousness is evolutionarily developed because it allows people to live together, pursue collective ends, and protect against those who endanger the social order. From a genetic or biological perspective, virtuousness plays a role in the development and perpetuation of humanity. This also explains why virtuousness is highly prized and admired, and why virtuous individuals are almost universally revered, emulated, and even sainted. They help perpetuate the human species. Miller (2007) pointed out, for example, that a selective genetic bias for human moral virtues exists. He argued that mate selection evolved at least partly on the basis of displays of virtue.

This also explains why virtuousness is associated exclusively with human beings, with flourishing and moral character (Doherty, 1995; Ryff & Singer, 1998), with human strength, self-control, and resilience

(Baumeister & Exline, 1999, 2000), and with meaningful human purpose and transcendent principles (Dent, 1984; Emmons, 1999; Roberts, 1988). Inanimate objects or ideas cannot be virtuous. The structure of an organization can facilitate or perpetuate virtuousness, but there is nothing inherently virtuous or nonvirtuous about the arrangements of functions, offices, or structures.

The concept of virtuousness also differs from the concept of ethics in that the dominant (although not exclusive) emphasis in the ethics literature is on avoiding harm, fulfilling contracts, and obeying rules and laws (Handselsman, Knapp, & Gottlieb, 2002; Paine, 2003). In practice, ethics are understood and implemented as duties (Rawls, 1971). They are usually specifications designed to prevent damage or avoid injury (Orlikowski, 2000). Unethical action is harmful, detrimental, or destructive, so to behave ethically is to avoid doing harm, damaging another individual, or destroying something valuable. Virtuousness, on the other hand, possesses an affirmative bias and focuses on elevating, flourishing, and enriching actions. Virtuousness pursues the ultimate best—eudaemonism—rather than merely avoiding the negative.

Inherent Value

A second core attribute of virtuousness is that it represents "goods of first intent" (Aristotle, *Metaphysics XII*, p. 3), meaning that it represents inherent value. Virtuousness is not a means to obtain another end, but it is considered to be an end in itself. In fact, virtuousness in pursuit of another more attractive outcome ceases by definition to be virtuousness. Forgiveness, compassion, and courage in search of recompense are not virtuous. If kindness toward employees is fostered in an organization, for example, solely to obtain a payback or an advantage, it ceases to be kindness and is, instead, manipulation. Virtuousness is associated with social betterment, but this betterment extends beyond mere self-interested benefit. Virtuousness creates social value that transcends the instrumental desires of the actor (Aristotle, 1999: 1106a22–23). Virtuous actions produce advantage to others in addition to, or even exclusive of, recognition, benefit, or advantage to the actor (Cawley, Martin, & Johnson, 2000).

This also explains why virtuousness in organizations is different from participation in normatively prescribed corporate social responsibility, such as sponsoring environmentally friendly programs or utilizing renewable resources (Bollier, 1996). Whereas some activities included in the corporate social responsibility and corporate citizenship domains may represent organizational virtuousness, these activities are typically explained as motivated by instrumental benefit or exchange relationships. That is, engagement in these actions is initiated in order to acquire benefit to the firm or result from a reciprocal arrangement (Batson, Klein, Highberger, & Shaw, 1995; Fry, Keim, & Meiners, 1982; Moore & Richardson, 1988; Piliavin & Charng, 1990; Sanchez, 2000). Exchange, reciprocity, and self-serving motives, however, are not indicative of virtuousness. Barge and Oliver (2003) and Gergen (1999) argued that associating an instrumental motive with organizational virtuousness changes the nature of the relationships among organization members and causes the behavior to evolve into "another technique of manipulation and discipline" (Barge & Oliver, 2003, p. 11). Of course, virtuousness does not stand in opposition to concepts such as citizenship, social responsibility, or ethics, but it extends beyond them.

Amplifying Effect

A third attribute of virtuousness is that it creates and fosters sustainable positive energy. It is elevating and self-perpetuating, and it requires no external motivator for its pursuit. As an ultimate end, and as an inherent attribute of human beings, virtuousness has an elevating effect. This is to say that virtuousness is amplifying when it is experienced (George, 1995). Observing virtuousness creates a self-reinforcing inclination toward more of the same. One difference between Aristotle's "goods of first intent" and "goods of second intent" is that people never tire of or become satiated with goods of first intent. There is never too much virtuousness.

Fredrickson and Joiner (2002) found evidence that observing virtuousness in organizations creates upward spirals of positive dynamics. Compassion begets gratitude, witnessing good deeds leads to elevation, and observing virtuousness fosters even more virtuousness (also see Hatch, 1999; Maslow, 1971; Sethi & Nicholson, 2001). Studies reported by Cialdini (2000) and Ashe (1952) also support the idea that when people observe exemplary or virtuous behavior, their inclination is to follow suit. Fredrickson (2003) applied her *broaden-and-build* theory—explaining the effects of experiencing positive emotions—to virtuousness in organizations. Employees' and organizations' social, intellectual, and emotional capacities are expanded and increased as a result of experiencing and observing virtuousness (Fredrickson, 2009).

This amplifying quality of virtuousness can be explained by its association with the *heliotropic effect*. The heliotropic effect is the attraction of all living systems toward positive energy and away from negative energy, or toward that which is life-giving and away from that which is life-depleting (D'Amato & Jagoda, 1962; Mrosovsky & Kingsmill, 1985; Smith & Baker, 1960). In nature, this is usually light from the sun. Several researchers have described the dynamics of individuals and groups that experience virtuousness (e.g., Eisenberg, 1990; Hatch, 1999; Leavitt, 1996; Sethi & Nicholson, 2001) proposing that, under such conditions, individuals experience a compelling urge to build upon the contributions of others and to perpetuate a virtuous spiral (Dutton & Heaphy, 2003; Erhardt-Siebold, 1937; Fredrickson, 2003, 2009). Observing virtuousness creates a self-reinforcing cycle toward more virtuousness. As Nobel laureate Desmond Tutu (1999, p. 263) asserted: "The world is hungry for goodness and it recognizes it when it sees it—and has incredible responses to the good. There is something in all of us that hungers after the good and true, and when we glimpse it in people, we applaud them for it. We long to be just like them. Their inspiration reminds us of the tenderness for life that we all can feel."

In sum, virtuousness in organizations refers to the processes and practices that support and manifest the display of virtuous behavior. In virtuous organizations, employees collectively behave in ways that are consistent with the best of the human condition and the highest aspirations of human kind. Virtuousness is heliotropic and a natural inclination of human beings. It is self-perpetuating and results in amplifying and elevating effects. Virtuousness is its own reward and its own source of positive energy.[2]

An Alternative Viewpoint: Strengths and Virtuousness

To be fair, Grant and Schwartz (2011) have presented an alternative view of virtuousness that is worth discussing because it helps clarify differences between *virtuousness* and *character strengths*—two concepts that are frequently used synonymously. These authors suggest that virtuousness is characterized by a nonmonotonic inverted-U effect. Relying on Aristotle's (1999) notion of the "grand mean," they argued that virtuousness can be taken too far. Too much virtuousness leads to negative effects. The ideal is (1999, p. 32) "a mean between two vices, the one involving excess, the other deficiency . . . its

character is to aim at what is intermediate in passions and in actions." Schwartz and Sharpe (2006, p. 383) argued that "too much of a virtue can be as big an enemy of eudemonia as too little." Virtuousness, in other words, can be excessive or can be deficient. The midpoint between recklessness and cowardice, for example, is courage. The midpoint between miserliness and overindulgence is prudence.

To provide empirical evidence for the inverted-U continuum, Grant and Schwartz relied on Peterson and Seligman's (2004) classification system for organizing 24 character strengths. Peterson and Seligman proposed that the six clusters of character strengths can be labeled as universal "virtues," so that each virtue is indicated by a set of character strengths. Grant and Schwartz summarized evidence that too much of a strength leads to negative effects, or too much virtuousness is a vice.

As examples, too much *learning orientation* (an indicator of the virtue of wisdom and knowledge) can lead to overlearning, rigidity, and to lower levels of goal accomplishment and profitability (Bunderson & Sutcliffe, 2003). Too much *persistence* (an indicator of the virtue of courage) in the form of *task practice*, as well as too much *optimism* and *self-confidence* (other indicators of the virtue of courage) and *cheerfulness* (another indicator of courage) can lead to complacency (Berman, Down, & Hill, 2002; Brown & Marshall, 2001; Haaga & Stewart, 1992; Langer & Imber, 1979), to escalating commitment to ineffective courses of action (Moon, 2001; Whyte & Saks, 2007), and to engaging in risky behaviors (Martin, Friedman, Tucker, Tomlinson-Keasey, Criqui, & Schwartz, 2002; Milam, Richardson, Marks, Kemper, & McCutchan, 2004). Too much *generosity* (an indicator of the virtue of humanity and love) can lead to diminished time, energy, and needed resources (Flynn, 2003), and too much *volunteering* (another indicator of the virtue of humanity and love) can produce role overload and stress (Windsor, Anstey, & Rogers, 2008). Too much *commitment* and too much *teamwork* (indicators of the virtue of justice) can lead people to avoid conflict, overlook illegal practices, and to groupthink in organizations (Barrick, Stewart, Neubert, & Mount, 1998; Somers & Casal, 1994).

In other words, a variety of empirical studies suggest that an overemphasis on certain behaviors or orientations does not lead to positive outcomes. A "mean" state is needed in order to have true virtuousness.

Several differences exist between Grant and Schwartz's cited evidence, however, and the definition of virtuousness. First, the practices listed as character strengths are not the same as virtues or virtuousness. They are defined by Peterson and Seligman (2004) as mechanisms by which virtues are frequently manifested, but they are not virtues themselves. They do not meet the criteria of virtuousness in either ancient or modern definitions (i.e., eudaemonic, heliotropic, inherently valuable).

Specifically, learning orientation is not necessarily virtuous, nor is persistently practicing a task. Self-efficacy has never been considered a virtue (Bandura, 1997), nor has the possession of self-confidence and self-esteem. Commitment to an organization and a sense of teamwork also are not consistent with the concept of virtue but, rather, are often outcomes, end states, or means to another end. Admittedly, optimism and generosity are sometimes included in lists of virtues, but as used in the cited research, they are not consistent with virtuousness since they can be demonstrated in excess. If optimism is replaced by the concept of *faith*, for example, and if generosity is replaced by the concept of *charity*, then both concepts are conceptually consistent but become virtuous in their definition. They produce a monotonic elevating spiral rather than an inverted-U shaped continuum.

Second, virtuousness itself represents Aristotle's grand mean. Excessive or deficient forms of behavior or orientation are qualitatively different from virtuousness. They are not merely variations in the quantity of virtuousness. In the presence of fear, for example, Grant and Schwartz suggested that cowardice is a deficient form of courage and recklessness is an excessive form of courage. Yet, no one would argue that cowardice or recklessness is virtuous. These concepts do not represent a quantitative variation on courage but rather qualitatively different concepts. The implication is that virtuousness implies inherent excellence, not excess, and virtuousness perpetuates an elevating, amplifying cycle, not a recursive cycle. In fact, an inherent attribute of virtuousness is the quality of *phronesis*, often translated as practical wisdom or judgment, or "to decide what actions are appropriate both to the situation and to producing what is good" (Fowers, 2009, p. 1018). An important difference between strengths and virtuousness, therefore, is that strengths are nonmonotonic in an inverted-U shape, whereas virtuousness is monotonic and self-reinforcing.

Research on Virtuousness in Organizations

An extensive amount of evidence has been produced showing that virtues in individuals are associated with desirable outcomes. For example, honesty, transcendent meaning, caring and giving behavior, gratitude, hope, empathy, love, and forgiveness, among other virtues, have been found to predict desired outcomes, such as an individual's commitment, satisfaction, motivation, positive emotions, effort, physical health, and psychological health (Andersson, et al., 2007; Cameron & Caza, 2004; Dutton et al., 2006; Emmons, 1999; Fry et al., 2005; Giacalone et al., 2005; Gittell et al., 2006; Grant et al, 2007; Harker & Keltner, 2001; Kellett et al., 2006; Luthans et al., 2007; McCullough, Pargament, & Thoreson, 2000; Peterson & Bossio, 1991; Seligman, 2002; Snyder, 1994; Sternberg, 1998). The organization level of analysis, however, has received very little attention in these empirical investigations.

Despite the fact that virtuousness is its own reward and does not require an instrumental outcome to be of worth, a few studies have explored the effects of virtuousness on organizational performance. The irony in this research is that, whereas virtuousness does not require a visible, instrumental pay-off to be of worth, if observable, bottom-line impacts are not detected, attention to virtuousness usually becomes subservient to the very real pressures related to enhancing financial return and organizational value (Davis, 2008; Jensen, 2002). Few leaders invest in practices or processes that do not produce higher returns to shareholders, profitability, productivity, and customer satisfaction. Without visible payoff, in other words, those with stewardship for organizational resources ignore virtuousness and consider it of little relevance to important stakeholders. Hence, if associations between virtuousness and desired outcomes were to be observed in organizations, evidence of pragmatic utility would be of value. This has been the motive for investigating the relationships between virtuousness and performance in organizations. A few studies have explored these relationships, and the key results of those investigations are summarized in this section.

Virtuousness After Downsizing

Cameron and Caza (2002) and Cameron, Bright, and Caza (2004) conducted a series of studies in which indicators of virtuousness and of performance outcomes were assessed in organizations. One study investigated eight independent business units randomly selected within a large corporation in the transportation industry. All eight units had recently downsized, so that the well-documented negative effects associated with downsizing were likely to ensure deteriorating performance (Cameron, 1994, 1998; Cascio, Young, & Morris, 1997). Organizational virtuousness scores for each business unit were measured by survey items measuring compassion, integrity, forgiveness, trust, and optimism (concepts included on lists of universally valued virtues such as those compiled by Chun, 2005; Peterson & Seligman, 2004). Organizational performance outcomes consisted of objective measures of productivity (efficiency ratios), quality (customer claims), and employee commitment (voluntary turnover) from company records, as well as employee ratings of productivity, quality, profitability, customer retention, and compensation. Despite a small sample size limiting the probability of statistical significance in the results, statistically significant relationships were found between organizational virtuousness scores and the performance outcomes. Organizations with higher virtuousness scores had significantly higher productivity, quality outputs, profitability, productivity, quality, and customer retention, and lower employee turnover.

Another investigation of a larger sample of organizations was conducted across 16 industries (e.g., retail, automotive, consulting, health care, manufacturing, financial services, not-for-profit), and all these organizations had also recently engaged in downsizing. The same measures of organizational virtuousness were obtained as in the smaller study from a representative sample of employees in each organization. Profitability (net income relative to total sales), quality, innovation, employee turnover, and customer retention were all measured as outcomes.

Findings from the smaller study were replicated in this larger sample of organizations. When controlling for factors such as size, industry, and amount of downsizing, organizations scoring higher in virtuousness were significantly more profitable, and, when compared to competitors, industry averages, stated goals, and past performance, they also achieved significantly higher performance on the other outcome measures.

In another investigation, Bright, Cameron, and Caza (2006) reported that *tonic* virtuousness (virtuousness that occurs irrespective of conditions) and *phasic* virtuousness (virtuousness that is dependent on certain circumstances, such as forgiveness when harm is done, or courage when danger is present) both perform a buffering function after organizational downsizing. Buffering is manifest in organizations as a capacity to absorb systems shocks,

bounce back, heal relationships, and collaborate. It provides a form of resilience in organizations (Sutcliffe & Vogus, 2003). When organizations scored high in virtuousness, they were also more proficient at carrying on effectively in spite of the setbacks associated with downsizing.

A different kind of study was conducted in the U.S. airline industry after the tragedy of September 11, 2001 (9/11), in which several commercial jets were used in a terroristic attack on New York City, Washington D.C., and rural Pennsylvania. More than 3000 innocent people lost their lives, and the event led to the United States declaring a formal "war on terrorism." This study investigated the relationships between virtuous downsizing strategies and financial return (Gittell, Cameron, Lim, & Rivas, 2006). The tragedy of 9/11 led to enormous financial losses for U.S. airline companies as a result of plummeting ridership after loaded planes were used as bombs. The study examined the extent to which different firms approached financial setbacks in virtuous ways. Virtuousness in this study was defined as preserving human dignity, investing in human capital, and providing an environment in which employee well-being was a priority. The two most dramatic examples of differences in approach to financial losses were the two short-haul carriers— US Airways and Southwest Airlines. One firm downsized more than was needed and, by declaring financial exigency, voided contracts and laid off employees without severance or benefits. The other company laid off no employees, stating publicly that the company adopted this strategy to demonstrate its espoused culture of virtuousness. Eight of ten U.S. airline companies downsized after this period, but some did so in ways that were more virtuous than others. Controlling for unionization, fuel price hedging, and financial reserves, the study found that the correlation between the virtuousness of the downsizing strategy and financial return (as measured by stock price gains) was $p = 0.86$ in the first 12 months and $p = 0.79$ over the next 5 years. The company that refused to engage in lay-offs because of its commitment to virtuousness earned the highest level of financial return in the industry. Virtuousness and financial return were again found to be positively and significantly related.

Virtuousness and Causality
None of the studies mentioned above provides evidence that a temporal or causal relationship exists between virtuousness and performance in organizations. Other studies were conducted,

however, in which the impact of implementing virtuous practices in organizations over time was the focus of investigation. Virtuous practices in these studies were defined as those collective behaviors or activities sponsored by and characteristic of an organization that were consistent with virtuousness. They were measured by another survey initially consisting of 114 items that revealed six stable dimensions: *caring* (people care for, are interested in, and maintain responsibility for one another as friends), *compassionate support* (people provide support for one another including kindness and compassion when others are struggling), *forgiveness* (people avoid blaming and forgive mistakes), *inspiration* (people inspire one another at work), *meaning* (the meaningfulness of the work is emphasized, and people are elevated and renewed by their work), and *respect, integrity, and gratitude* (people treat one another with respect and express appreciation for one another, as well as trusting one another and maintaining integrity).[3]

One study was conducted in the financial services industry because, stereotypically, it is among the least likely industries to be interested in virtuousness. A focus on short-term monetary returns, high-pressured environments, financial trading, and a win-at-all-costs climate is typically characteristic of this sector (Burrough & Helyar, 1990; Jensen, 2002; Korten, 2001; McLean & Elkind, 2003). Forty business units within a large northeast financial services company were investigated. The firm had embarked on a systematic effort to incorporate virtuous practices into its corporate culture in early 2005 when the CEO declared that a virtuous culture would guide the strategic direction of the firm (Vanette & Cameron, 2008). Data on employee turnover, organizational climate, and six financial performance indicators were obtained from company records.

The correlation between the aggregated virtuousness score for each business unit and the aggregation of the six measures of financial performance was $r = 0.54$, significant at the $p < 0.05$ level with only six degrees of freedom. A 1-year lag in virtuousness scores and financial outcome measures provided evidence that organizational virtuousness was predicting financial results rather than the reverse. Similarly, significant associations were found between virtuousness scores and employee turnover and organizational climate scores the following year (Cameron, Mora, Leutscher, & Calarco, 2011).

Another study exploring potential causal associations between virtuousness and performance was carried out in 29 nursing units in a large, comprehensive health care system. A multiyear study was conducted to investigate the effects of organizational virtuousness on indicators of performance. Multiday sessions were held with the nursing leaders and directors in this health system which exposed them to virtuous practices, and day-long implementation sessions were conducted by an external consultant with the 29 nursing units as a follow-up.

Two findings of interest were produced by this study (Cameron, Mora, Leutscher, & Calarco, 2011). One is that units exposed to virtuousness training improved their virtuous practice scores significantly over the 2005–2007 period. Units not exposed to virtuousness training did not improve. This implies that virtuousness in organizations can be enhanced and improved through systematic intervention. A second important finding was that the units improving the most in virtuousness also produced the most improvement in the outcome measures in subsequent years. Figure 18.1 summarizes the results. Double-digit improvement was detected over the 2-year period on most outcome measures included in the study. On each performance indicator, units that improved in overall virtuousness outperformed units that did not in subsequent years. No one virtue stood out as the single most important determinant of improvement in outcomes, but virtuousness in combination accounted for the higher performance.

These studies provide evidence that virtuousness in organizations is associated with, and may even produce, desired performance in areas such as profitability, productivity, quality, customer satisfaction, climate, and employee retention. Although the value of virtuousness in organizations does not require that it be associated with other outcomes, when faced with stockholder demands for measurable results, when helping organizations find ways to improve mandated performance measures, or when trying to lead an organization through trying times, leaders may find pragmatic utility in previously ignored virtuous practices.

Future Directions

Because the amount and scope of research on virtuousness in organizations has been limited to date, a variety of research questions remain to be investigated. Among the key areas of needed research are the measurement of virtuousness, the predictive power of virtuousness, and the moderators and mediators of the effects of virtuousness on performance outcomes.

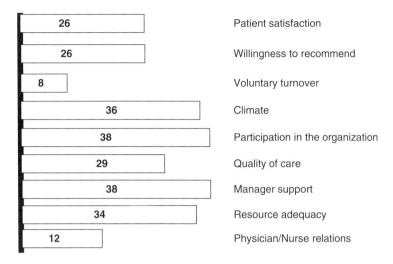

26	Patient satisfaction
26	Willingness to recommend
8	Voluntary turnover
36	Climate
38	Participation in the organization
29	Quality of care
38	Manager support
34	Resource adequacy
12	Physician/Nurse relations

Fig. 18.1 Percent improvement in performance as a result of improvement in virtuousness scores over 2 years.

Measurement

To date, no standardized measures have been developed for assessing the concept of virtuousness or its component elements. Two different instruments have been used in the studies mentioned above, but the specific virtues to be incorporated into the concept of virtuousness have not been specified. The psychometric analyses that have been conducted to date (e.g., Cameron, Bright, & Caza, 2004; Cameron, Mora, & Leutscher, 2010) have not provided a rationale for why some virtues are assessed and some are not. The conceptual boundaries and nomological network have yet to be precisely established for the concept of virtuousness, and, therefore, the groundwork for theories of virtuousness has not yet been established. The surveys used to assess virtuousness to date might be referred to as "blunt" instruments in that they provide aggregated ratings of virtuous practices in organizations, but experimental manipulations and carefully designed organizational interventions will help clarify the meaning and practice of virtuousness. Investigating which individual virtues are most important in creating high levels of virtuousness is an important challenge for future researchers.

Prediction

The challenge is the same in predicting the relationships between virtuousness and performance outcomes. Thus far, aggregated virtuousness scores in organizations have been found to be the major predictors of outcomes, and no single virtue appears to account for any more variance than others. This may be a product of imprecise measurement, or it may be a product of virtues not being displayed in

isolation from one another. If the latter is true, then investigations of which clusters of virtues occur naturally together in organizations would be most useful. Moreover, identifying which virtue clusters are most closely associated with which outcomes is also an important area for study. Are the same virtues, for example, predictive of financial performance as of employee engagement or of customer satisfaction? Are tonic virtues (such as love and integrity) more or less predictive of particular positive outcomes than phasic virtues (such as forgiveness and compassion)?

Further, in the studies reviewed that described investigations of causal associations, interventions occurred that exposed organizations to virtuous practices, and some organizations subsequently improved their scores. It is not clear, however, which specific interventions were most helpful in raising organizational virtuousness scores. Determining explicitly how to assist organizations to become more virtuous is an area of needed investigation. Moreover, consistent with Gladwell's (2002) concept of "tipping point," it is important to understand how much virtuousness is enough. Is there a ratio—such as the now-famous 3:1 ratio of positive to negative emotions that predicts flourishing outcomes (Fredrickson, 2009)—which also predicts organizational outcomes? How much virtuousness is enough?

Moderators and Mediators

Another set of issues has to do with the extent to which virtuousness has direct or moderated effects on desired outcomes. What moderators exist in determining how virtuousness acts upon the organization to produce performance outcomes? Cameron (2003) summarized literature suggesting that virtuousness elevates positive emotions which, in turn, fosters higher performance. Virtuousness also enhances social capital, which reduces transaction costs, facilitates communication and cooperation, enhances employee commitment, fosters individual learning, and strengthens relationships and involvement. All of these factors have a positive relationship with performance. Virtuousness also fosters prosocial behavior, which provides benefit to others and, ostensibly, would likely lead to higher performance. Investigating which factors, if any, serve as moderators between virtuousness and performance will certainly be a fruitful area for future investigations.

Other factors may mediate the effects of virtuousness in organizations, but to date, almost no attention has been paid to what these factors might be. For example, demographic differences such as the size of an organization, its culture, the demographic make-up of the top management team, the explicit goals and strategy of the organization, certain industry dynamics, and so forth, may be important mediators of the relationships between virtuousness and performance. Limited examination of moderators and mediators has occurred to date.

Conclusion

The credibility and legitimacy of positive organizational scholarship is at least partly dependent on its connection to organizational performance. Positive organizational scholarship researchers have advocated that positive factors should be included in organizational science because, ostensibly, they account for variance in performance that may have been otherwise overlooked (Cameron, Dutton, & Quinn, 2003; Dutton & Sonenshein, 2007; Roberts, 2006). Some have challenged this claim as being overly optimistic and more typical of aspiration than realism (Fineman, 2006; Hackman, 2008). Although investigations of positive phenomena in organizational science are still relatively sparse and underdeveloped, and only a few studies have examined systematically the effects of positive factors on organizational performance, some evidence is beginning to emerge that positive factors—virtuousness in particular—may provide an important arena for leaders of organizations to enhance their organizations' performance. Much is left to be done to make the causal case unequivocally, but enough evidence exists to be very optimistic that virtuous organizations significantly outshine normal organizations in performance.

Notes

1. Individual virtues seldom occur singly, and they cannot be demonstrated fully in isolation. For example, to demonstrate genuine forgiveness implies love, empathy, and wisdom. To demonstrate genuine kindness implies compassion, charity, and gratitude. Virtuousness—the possession of multiple virtues—is a more relevant concept in the study of organizations than single virtues in isolation.

2. In combination, these attributes of virtuousness have substantial overlap with the characteristics Peterson and Seligman (2004) identify for their character strengths. Strengths and virtues are closely related, even if not synonymous. Peterson and Seligman described a character strength as something that: (a) Helps fulfill an individual and foster the good life for oneself and others; (b) is morally valued in its own right, even in the absence of obvious benefits; (c) demonstrating the strength does not diminish others, because observers are elevated; (d) has no meaningful (virtuous) opposite; (e) is manifest across thoughts, feelings, and actions—and across situations and time; (f) is distinct from other character strengths; (g) is demonstrated by role models; (h) is demonstrated by prodigies; (i) some people can have a total lack of the strength; (j) society cultivates the strength.

3. These six dimensions of virtuousness, as it turns out, are very similar to a proposed comprehensive list of virtues reported in prior published literature. Specifically, in one of the few published listings of proposed virtuous practices in organizations, Chun (2005) reviewed several previous inventories of virtues and analyzed the corporate ethical value statements of 158 *Fortune Global* firms. Her analyses produced six dimensions of virtuous practices. Her six dimensions incorporated lists of individual virtues proposed by Aristotle, Solomon (1999), Murphy (1999), Moberg (1999), and Shanahan and Hyman (2003). Each of Chun's six dimensions is incorporated within the six positive practice dimensions that emerged in these studies. Specifically, Chun's "integrity" is assessed as "respect, integrity, and gratitude" in this study. Chun's "empathy" is assessed as "compassionate support" in this study. Chun's "warmth" is assessed as "caring" in this study. Chun's "courage" has similar items as "meaning" in this study. Chun's "conscientiousness" has similar items as "forgiveness" in this study. And Chun's "zeal" is assessed at "inspiration" in this study.

References

Alzola, M. (2008). Character and environment: The status of virtues in organizations. *Journal of Business Ethics, 78*, 343–357.

Andersson, L.M., Giacalone, R.A., & Jurkiewicz, C.L. (2007). On the relationship of hope and gratitude to corporate social responsibility. *Journal of Business Ethics, 70*, 401–409.

Aristotle. (1999). *Nicomachean Ethics*. (M. Oswald, Trans.). Upper Saddler River, NJ: Prentice Hall.

Aristotle. *Metaphysics XII*, 7, 3–4.

Asche, S.E. (1952). *Social psychology*. Englewood Cliffs, NJ: Prentice Hall.

Bandura, A. (1997). *Self-efficacy: The exercise of control*. New York: W.H. Freeman.

Barge, J.K., & Oliver, C. (2003). Working with appreciation in managerial practice. *Academy of Management Review, 28*(1), 124–142.

Barrick, M.R., Stewart, G.L., Neubert, M.J., & Mount, M.K. (1998). Relating member ability and personality to work-team processes and team effectiveness. *Journal of Applied Psychology, 83*, 377–391.

Batson, C.D., Klein, T.R., Highberger, L., & Shaw, L.L. (1995). Immorality from empathy-induced altruism: When compassion and justice conflict. *Journal of Personality and Social Psychology, 68*, 1042–1054.

Baumeister, R.F., & Exline, J.J. (1999). Virtue, personality, and social relations: Self-control as the moral muscle. *Journal of Personality, 67*, 1165–1194.

Baumeister, R.F., & Exline, J.J. (2000). Self-control, morality, and human strength. *Journal of Social and Clinical Psychology, 19*, 29–42.

Berman, S.L., Down, J., & Hill, C.W.L. (2002). Tacit knowledge as a source of competitive advantage in the National Basketball Association. *Academy of Management Journal, 45*, 13–31.

Bollier, D. (1996). *Aiming higher: 25 stories of how companies prosper by combining sound management and social vision.* New York: Amacom.

Bright, D.S., Cameron, K.S., & Caza, A. (2006). The amplifying and buffering effects of virtuousness in downsized organizations. *Journal of Business Ethics, 64*, 249–269.

Brown, J.D., & Marshall, M.A. (2001). Great expectations: Optimism and pessimism in achievement settings. In E.C. Chang (Ed.), *Optimism and pessimism: Implications for theory, research, and practice* (pp. 239–255). Washington, DC: American Psychological Association.

Bunderson, J.S., & Sutcliffe, K.M. (2003). Management team learning orientation and business unit performance. *Journal of Applied Psychology, 88*, 552–560.

Burrough, B., & Helyar, J. (1990). *Barbarians at the gate.* New York: Harper & Row.

Cameron, K.S. (1994). Strategies for successful organizational downsizing. *Human Resource Management, 33*(2), 189–211.

Cameron, K.S. (2003). Organizational virtuousness and performance. In K.S. Cameron, J. Dutton, & R.E. Quinn (Eds.), *Positive organizational scholarship* (pp. 48–65). San Francisco: Berrett-Koehler.

Cameron, K.S., & Caza, A. (2002). Organizational and leadership virtues and the role of forgiveness. *Journal of Leadership and Organizational Studies, 9*, 33–48.

Cameron, K.S., Bright, D., & Caza, A. (2004). Exploring the relationships between organizational virtuousness and performance. *American Behavioral Scientist, 4*, 766–790.

Cameron, K.S., Dutton, J.E., & Quinn, R.E. (2003). *Positive organizational scholarship.* San Francisco: Berrett-Koehler.

Cameron, K.S., Mora, C.E., Leutscher, T., & Calarco, M. (2011). Effects of positive practices on organizational effectiveness. *Journal of Applied Behavioral Science, 47*, 1–43.

Cascio, W.F., Young, C.E., & Morris, J.R. (1997). Financial consequences of employment change decisions in major U.S. corporations. *Academy of Management Journal, 40*, 1175–1189.

Cawley, M.J., Martin, J.E., & Johnson, J.A. (2000). A virtues approach to personality. *Personality and Individual Differences, 28*, 997–1013.

Caza, A., Barker, B.A., & Cameron, K.S. (2004). Ethics and ethos: The buffering and amplifying effects of ethical behavior and virtuousness. *Journal of Business Ethics, 52*, 169–178.

Chapman, J.W., & Galston, W.A. (1992). *Virtue.* New York: New York University Press.

Chun, R. (2005). Ethical character and virtue of organizations: An empirical assessment and strategic implications. *Journal of Business Ethics, 57*, 269–284.

Cialdini, R.B. (2000). *Influence: The science of persuasion.* New York: Allyn Bacon.

Comte-Sponville, A. (2001). *A small treatise of the great virtues* (C. Temerson, Trans.). New York: Metropolitan Books.

D'Amato, M.R., & Jagoda, H. (1962). Effect of early exposure to photic stimulation on brightness discrimination and exploratory behavior. *Journal of Genetic Psychology, 101*(Dec), 267–271.

Davis, G.F. (2008). The rise and fall of finance and the end of the society of organizations. *Academy of Management Perspectives, 23*, 27–44.

Den Hartog, D.N., & De Hoogh, A.H.B. (2009). Empowering behavior and leader effectiveness and integrity: Studying perceptions of ethical leader behavior from a levels-of-analysis perspective. *European Journal of Work and Organizational Psychology, 18*, 199–230.

Dent, N. (1984). *The moral psychology of the virtues.* New York: Cambridge University Press.

Doherty, W.J. (1995). *Soul searching: Why psychotherapy must promote moral responsibility.* New York: Basic Books.

Dutton, J., & Heaphy, E. (2003). The power of high-quality connections. In K.S. Cameron, J.E. Dutton, & R.E. Quinn (Eds.), *Positive organizational scholarship.* San Francisco: Berrett Koehler.

Dutton, J.E., Worline, M.C., Frost, P.J., & Lilius, J. (2006). Explaining compassion organizing. *Administrative Science Quarterly, 51*(1), 59–96.

Dutton, J.E., & Sonenshein, S. (2007). Positive organizational scholarship. In S. Lopez & A. Beauchamps (Eds.), *Encyclopedia of positive psychology.* Malden, MA: Blackwell Publishing.

Eisenberg, N. (1986). *Altruistic emotion, cognition, and behavior.* Hillsdale, NJ: Erlbaum.

Eisenberg, E.M. (1990). Jamming: Transcendence through organizing. *Communication Research, 17*, 139–164.

Emmons, R.A. (1999). *The psychology of ultimate concerns: Motivation and spirituality in personality.* New York: Guilford Press.

Erhard-Seibold, E.V. (1937). The heliotrope tradition. *Orisis, 3*, 22–46.

Fineman, S. (2006). On being positive: Concerns and counterpoints. *Academy of Management Review, 31*(2), 270–291.

Flynn, F.J. (2003). How much should I give and how often? The effects of generosity and frequency of favor exchange on social status and productivity. *Academy of Management Journal, 46*, 539–553.

Fowers, B.J. (2005). *Virtue and psychology: Pursuing excellence in ordinary practices.* Washington, DC: APA Press.

Fowers, B.J. (2009). Virtue. In S.J. Lopez (Ed.), *The Encyclopedia of positive psychology.* West Sussex, UK: Blackwell.

Fredrickson, B.L. (2003). Positive emotions and upward spirals in organizations. In K.S. Cameron, J.E. Dutton, & R.E. Quinn (Eds.), *Positive organizational scholarship: Foundations of a new discipline* (pp. 163–175). San Francisco: Berrett-Koehler.

Fredrickson, B.L. (2009). *Positivity.* New York: Crown.

Fredrickson, B.L., & Joiner, T. (2002). Positive emotions trigger upward spirals toward emotional well-being. *American Psychologist, 13*, 172–175.

Fry, L.W., Keim, G.D., & Meiners, R.E. (1982). Corporate contributions: Altruistic of for-profit? *Academy of Management Journal, 25*, 94–106.

Fry, L.W., Vitucci, S., & Cedillo, M. (2005). Spiritual leadership and army transformation: Theory, measurement, and establishing a baseline. *Leadership Quarterly, 16,* 835–862.

George, J.M. (1991). State or trait: Effects of positive mood on prosocial behaviors at work. *Journal of Applied Psychology, 76,* 229–307.

George, J.M. (1995). Leader positive mood and group performance: The case of customer service. *Journal of Applied Social Psychology, 25,* 778–794.

Gergen, K.J. (1999). *An invitation to social constructionism.* London: Sage.

Giacalone, R.A., Paul, K., & Jurkiewicz, C.L. (2005). A preliminary investigation into the role of positive psychology in consumer sensitivity to corporate social performance. *Journal of Business Ethics, 58,* 295–305.

Gittell, J.H., Cameron, K.S., Lim, S., & Rivas, V. (2006). Relationships, layoffs, and organizational resilience. *Journal of Applied Behavioral Science, 42,* 300–328.

Gladwell, M. (2002). *The tipping point: How little things make a big difference.* Boston: Back Bay Publishers.

Grant, A.M. (2007). Relational job design and the motivation to make a prosocial difference. *Academy of Management Journal, 32*(2), 393–417.

Grant, A.M., & Schwartz, B. (2011). Too much of a good thing: The challenges and opportunity of the Inverted-U. *Perspectives in Psychological Science* (in press).

Haaga, D.A.F., & Stewart, B.L. (1992). Self-efficacy for recovery from a lapse after smoking cessation. *Journal of Consulting and Clinical Psychology, 60,* 24–28.

Hackman, J.R. (2008). The perils of positivity. *Journal of Organizational Behavior, 30,* 309–319.

Haight, J. (2006). *The happiness hypothesis: Finding modern truth in ancient wisdom.* New York: Basic Books.

Handelsman, M.M., Knapp, S., & Gottlieb, M.C. (2002). Positive ethics. In C.R. Snyder, & S.J. Lopez (Eds.), *Handbook of positive psychology* (pp. 731–744). New York: Oxford University Press.

Harker, L.A., & Keltner, D. (2001). Expressions of positive emotion in women's college yearbook pictures and their relationship to personality and life outcomes across adulthood. *Journal of Personality and Social Psychology, 80,* 112–124.

Hatch, M.J. (1999). Exploring the empty spaces of organizing: How improvisational jazz helps redescribe organizational structure. *Organizational Studies, 20,* 75–100.

Hauser, M. (2006). *Moral minds: How nature designed our universal sense of right and wrong.* New York: ECCO.

Jenson, M.C. (2002). Value maximization, stakeholder theory and the corporate objective function. *Business Ethics Quarterly, 12,* 235–256.

Kellett, J.B., Humphrey, R.H., & Sleeth, R.G. (2006). Empathy and the emergence of task and relations leaders. *Leadership Quarterly, 17,* 146–162.

Korten, D.C. (2001). *When corporations rule the world.* San Francisco: Berrett Koehler.

Krebs, D. (1987). The challenge of altruism in biology and psychology. In C. Crawford, M. Smith, & D. Krebs (Eds.), *Sociobiology and psychology.* Hillsdale, NJ: Lawrence Erlbaum.

Langer, E.J., & Imber, L.G. (1979). When practice makes imperfect: Debilitating effects of overlearning. *Journal of Personality and Social Psychology, 37,* 2014–2024.

Leavitt, H.J. (1996). The old days, hot groups, and managers' lib. *Administrative Science Quarterly, 41,* 288–300.

MacIntyre, A. (1984). *After virtue: A study in moral theory* (2nd ed.). Notre Dame, IN: University of Notre Dame Press.

Martin, L.R., Friedman, H.S., Tucker, J.S., Tomlinson-Keasey, C., Criqui, M.H., & Schwartz, J.E. (2002). A life course perspective on childhood cheerfulness and its relation to mortality risk. *Personality and Social Psychology Bulletin, 28,* 1155–1165.

Maslow, A. (1971). *The farthest reaches of human nature.* New York: Viking.

McCullough, M.E., Pargament, K.I., & Thoreson, C. (2000). *Forgiveness: Theory, research, and practice.* New York: Guilford.

McLean, B., & Elkind, P. (2003). *The smartest guys in the room.* New York: Penguin.

Milam, J.E., Richardson, J.L., Marks, G., Kemper, C.A., & McCutchan, A.J. (2004). The roles of disposition optimism and pessimism in HIV disease progression. *Psychology and Heath, 19,* 167–181.

Miller, G.F. (2007). Sexual selection for moral virtues. *The Quarterly Review of Biology, 82*(2), 97–125.

McNeely, B.L., & Meglino, B.M. (1994). The role of dispositional and situational antecedents in prosocial organizational behavior: An examination of the intended beneficiaries of prosocial behavior. *Journal of Applied Psychology, 79,* 836–844.

Moberg, D.J. (1999). The big five and organizational virtue. *Business Ethics Quarterly, 9,* 245–272.

Moon, H. (2001). The two faces of conscientiousness: Duty and achievement striving in escalation of commitment dilemmas. *Journal of Applied Psychology, 86,* 533–540.

Moore, C., & Richardson, J.J. (1988). The politics and practice of corporate responsibility is Great Britain. *Research in Corporate Social Performance and Policy, 10,* 267–290.

Moore, G., & Beadle, R. (2006). In search of organizational virtue in business: Agents, goods, practices, institutions, and environments. *Organization Studies, 27,* 369–389.

Mrosovsky, N., & Kingsmill, S.F. (1985). How turtles find the sea. *Zeitschrift Für Tierpsychologie-Journal of Comparative Ethology, 67,* 237–256.

Nielsen, R. (2006). Introduction to the special issue–In search of organizational virtue: Moral agency in organizations. *Organization Studies, 27,* 318–321.

Orlikowski, W.J. 2000. Using technology and constituting structures: A practice lens for studying technology in organizations. *Organization Science, 11*(4), 404–428.

Peterson, C., & Bossio, L.M. (1991). *Health and optimism.* New York: Free Press.

Peterson, C., & Seligman, M.E.P. (2004). *Character strengths and virtues.* New York: Oxford University Press.

Piliavin, J.A., & Charng, H. (1990). Altruism: A review of recent theory and research. *Annual Review of Sociology, 16,* 27–65.

Pinker, S. (1997). *How the mind works.* New York: W.W. Norton.

Rachels, J. (1999). *The elements of moral philosophy* (3rd ed.). New York: McGraw-Hill.

Rawls, J. (1971). *A theory of justice.* Cambridge, MA: Harvard University Press.

Rego, A., Ribeiro, N., & Cunha, M. (2010). Perceptions of organizational virtuousness and happiness as predictors of organizational citizenship behaviors. *Journal of Business Ethics, 93,* 215–235.

Roberts, L.M. (2006). Shifting the lens on organizational life: The added value of positive scholarship. *Academy of Management Review, 31,* 292–305.

Roberts, R.C. (1988). Therapies and the grammar of virtue. In R.H. Bell (Ed.), *The grammar of the heart: New essays in moral philosophy and theology* (pp. 149–170). San Francisco: Harper & Row.

Ryff, C.D., & Singer, B. (1998). The contours of positive human health. *Psychological Inquiry, 9*, 1–28.

Sánchez, C.M. (2000). Motives for corporate philanthropy in El Salvador: Altruism and political legitimacy. *Journal of Business Ethics, 27*, 363–375.

Schimmel, S. (1997). *The seven deadly sins: Jewish, Christian, and classical reflections on human nature.* New York: The Free Press.

Sethi, R., & Nicholson, C.Y. (2001). Structural and contextual correlates of charged behavior in product development teams. *Journal of Product Innovation Management, 18*, 154–168.

Schwartz, B., & Sharpe, K. (2006). Practical wisdom: Aristotle meets positive psychology. *Journal of Happiness Studies, 7*, 377–395.

Seligman, M.E.P. (2002). *Authentic happiness.* New York: Free Press.

Shanahan, K.J., & Hyman, M.R. (2003). The development of a virtue ethics scale. *Journal of Business Ethics, 42*, 197–208.

Simmel, G. (1950). *The sociology of Georg Simmel.* New York: Free Press.

Smith, A. (1976/1790). *The theory of moral sentiments* (6th ed.). Oxford: Clarendon Press.

Smith, J.C., & Baker, H.D. (1960). Conditioning in the horseshoe crab. *Journal of Comparative and Physiological Psychology, 53*, 279–281.

Snyder C.R. (1994). *The psychology of hope.* New York: Free Press.

Somers, M.J., & Casal, J.C. (1994). Organizational commitment and whistle-blowing: A test of the reformer and the organization man hypothesis. *Group and Organization Management, 19*, 270–284.

Sternberg, J.J. (1998). A balanced theory of wisdom. *Review of General Psychology, 2*, 347–365.

Tangley, J., Stuewig, J., & Mashek, D. (2007). Moral emotions and moral behavior. *Annual Review of Psychology, 58*, 345–372.

Tutu, D. (1999). *No future without forgiveness.* New York: Doubleday.

Vannette, D., & Cameron, K.S. (2008). *Implementing Positive Organizational Scholarship at Prudential* (Case study 1-428-869). Ross School of Business, University of Michigan. Ann Arbor, MI: William Davidson Institute.

Vogel, D.J. (2005). Is there a market for virtue? The business case for corporate social responsibility. *California Management Review, 47*, 19–45.

Walsh, J.P. (1999). Business must talk about its social role. In T. Dickson (Ed.), *Mastering strategy* (pp. 289–294). London: Financial Times/Prentice Hall.

Weaver, G.R. (2006). Virtue in organizations: Moral identity as a foundation for moral agency. *Organization Studies, 27*, 341–368.

Weiner, N.O. (1993). *The harmony of the soul: mental health and moral virtue reconsidered.* Albany, NY: State University of New York Press.

Whetstone, T.J. (2003). The language of managerial excellence: Virtues as understood and applied. *Journal of Business Ethics, 44*, 343–357.

Whyte, G., & Saks, A.M. (2007). The effects of self-efficacy on behavior in escalation situations. *Human Performance, 20*, 23–42.

Windsor, T.D., Anstey, K.J., & Rodgers, B. (2008). Volunteering and psychological well-being among young-old adults: How much is too much? *The Gerontologist, 48*, 59–70.

Wright, T.A., & Goodstein, J. (2007). Character is not dead in management research: A review of individual character and organization-level virtue. *Journal of Management, 33*, 928–948.

Forgiveness at Four Levels

Intrapersonal, Relational, Organizational, and Collective-Group

David S. Bright *and* Julie J. Exline

Abstract

Forgiveness describes a family of actions intended to break or prevent destructive cycles of human interaction. This chapter describes how forgiveness might be conceptualized at four levels: intrapersonal, relational, organizational, and collective-group. The chapter provides an overview of these four different conceptualizations on forgiveness, the work that has been accomplished relative to each conceptualization, and potential avenues for new research. Although research on forgiveness has exploded, most work has focused on forgiveness at the individual level. It is rare to find studies that examine forgiveness in organizational contexts; yet, forgiveness concepts have substantial potential and relevance in organization studies.

Keywords: Forgiveness, intrapersonal forgiveness, relational forgiveness, interpersonal forgiveness, intergroup forgiveness, organizational forgiveness, collective-group forgiveness

Research on forgiveness has increased dramatically during the last two decades. Most of this work has been done in the discipline of psychology. As a result, only a few studies have explored forgiveness in organizational settings; yet, there is substantial reason to believe that forgiveness may be of particular relevance in an organizational context (Aquino, Grover, Goldman, & Folger, 2003). Thus, this chapter reviews writing and proposes a research framework on forgiveness from the perspective of positive organizational scholarship (POS).

In general terms, forgiveness can be understood as a family of related concepts. After providing an overview of the common characteristics of all forgiveness constructs, this chapter will introduce a multilevel framework to highlight distinctive features of forgiveness at various levels of human experience and organization. Each level of forgiveness is then described in more detail, noting how existing definitions and research findings are located within the framework. Using this framework, several questions are proposed to highlight potential areas of

research. The reader may also note that forgiveness is treated extensively in religious and theological writings; however, for purposes of this chapter, forgiveness will be discussed from a secular perspective as a universal human practice (Arendt, 1958).

General Properties of Forgiveness

Philosophically, forgiveness can be considered as a human virtue or strength (Bright, 2005; Bright, Cameron, & Caza, 2006; Peterson & Seligman, 2004), one that becomes relevant when people are harmed or offended by human-initiated action. From an interdisciplinary perspective, the term "forgiveness" is a word with many layers and dimensions. Several authors, debating the precise meaning of forgiveness, note a lack of consensus about its definition in scientific studies (see Exline et al., 2003, for a review). Because research on forgiveness has arisen primarily from the discipline of psychology, existing definitions focus on its meaning and practice at an individual level. From the perspective of POS, this is problematic because forgiveness often involves actions at multiple levels of human experience (e.g., individual, relational, organizational, or collective-group). A general understanding of forgiveness is needed that captures the essence of forgiveness while allowing for variations in definition among levels of the human experience. We suggest three characteristics of forgiveness, irrespective of its level of manifestation.

First, forgiveness is an intentional response to offense that breaks or prevents a destructive cycle of action and reaction. When people believe that they have been victimized, the typical reaction includes a negative response wherein people experience negative emotions (e.g., anger, bitterness) and cognitions (e.g., thoughts of vengeance) toward perceived offenders (McCullough & Witvliet, 2002). If these reactions are acted on, they may transfer to behaviors, usually seen as the act of seeking vengeance or retribution. Many authors note that, unless otherwise broken through forgiveness, these reactive tendencies can produce cycles of offensive action and offense-taking reaction. Arendt (1958) provides a cogent summary:

> Trespassing is an everyday occurrence which is in the very nature of action's constant establishment of new relationships within a web of relations, and it needs forgiving, dismissing, in order to make it possible for life to go on by constantly releasing men from what they have done. Only through this constant mutual release from what they do can men remain free agents, only by constant willingness to change their minds and start again can they be trusted with so great a power as to begin something new. (p. 240)

The forgiver reacts in a manner that is contrary to the seeking of revenge, such that this action breaks or prevents a cycle of offense and retaliation. The forgiver does not merely react to a harmful act, the forgiver "acts anew and unexpectedly, unconditioned by the act which provoked it" (p. 241). In the absence of forgiveness, "everybody remains bound to the process [of offense and retaliation], permitting [a] chain reaction . . . to take its unhindered course" (p. 241). In sum, forgiveness can be understood as a choice (Enright, 2001), one in which the offended party foregoes retaliation or retribution, thereby establishing the possibility for a healthy, functional way of being within oneself or of relating to others who have committed offenses.

Second, scholars maintain that forgiveness is distinct from other related concepts. Although forgiveness may offer a break from a dysfunctional cycle of harm and retaliation, it does not require

that offenders and victims reconcile or develop a trusting relationship (Enright & Fitzgibbons, 2000; Exline et al., 2003). Reconciliation may occur independently of forgiveness and vice versa (Freedman, 1998). In addition, forgiveness does not equate to forgetting, condoning, or excusing offenses (Exline et al., 2003). Those who are forgiven may still be held accountable for their actions.

Finally, forgiveness is a multilevel concept. Consider the perspectives illustrated in Table 19.1, which juxtaposes potential configurations of forgivers and offenders. Different levels of offenders are shown horizontally, indicating different sources of human-initiated offense. At the individual level, the offense can be traced to specific actors. Group-initiated offenses originate from collections of people with a common identity (e.g., religious or ideological). Organization-initiated offenses are created through formal institutional action (e.g., a company or branch of government). These forms of human-initiated action often involve multiple levels. For example, an organization-initiated action is usually carried out by individuals acting for the organization.

The vertical dimension of Table 19.1 outlines the different levels or forms of forgiveness as related to the forgiving party. At the intrapersonal level, forgiveness involves a cognitive and emotional process that functions almost entirely within a person as he or she confronts the negativity that arises when dealing with the experience of being victimized. Negative intrapsychic impacts may arise from the harmful actions of other individual, group, or organization actors. Regardless of the perpetrator, intrapsychic forgiveness allows the person to displace or dissolve the negativity (Bright, Fry, & Cooperrider, 2008) and thereby return to or maintain a healthy intrapersonal state. This is, by far, the most researched aspect of forgiveness.

The other three levels of forgiveness all deal with behavioral aspects of forgiveness. Typically, the behavioral forms of forgiveness focus on three aims: ensuring that the offensive activity stops, acknowledging that the perpetrators have ceased their harmful action, and foregoing retributive actions that might be justified from a retaliatory perspective.

At the relational level in the individual-to-individual configuration, forgiveness occurs between individually identifiable forgivers and the offender; a spouse might be forgiven by his or her partner for past abusive behavior or an employee might forgive an abusive boss. In the individual-to-group configuration, a person might express forgiveness toward a

Table 19.1 Comparison of forms of forgiveness: Configurations of forgivers and offenders

Forgiver: Form of Forgiveness	Offender: Origin of Human-initiated Action		
	Individual	Organization	Collective-Group
Intrapersonal			
Context	An individual offends or harms another individual.	An organization generates activity that causes harm to an individual.	A group perpetuates activity that harms an individual.
Forgiving Action	The forgiver frames a response that allows for intrapersonal healing.		
Examples	A supervisor berates a subordinate employee using harsh language. The berated employee displaces or dissolves his internal negative feelings and thoughts toward the supervisor.	An employee forgives her employer for the negative impacts of a policy decision. She refuses to harbor negativity toward the company.	A group of union employees does something that offends one member. That member, although offended, displaces or dissolves the internal negativity toward the group.
Interpersonal/ Relational			
Context	An individual offends or harms another individual.	An organization generates activity that causes harm to an individual.	A group generates activity that causes harm to an individual.
Forgiving Action	After sharing how the offender's actions have affected him or her, the offended employee expresses forgiveness toward the offender.	After demonstrating how the organization's action has affected him or her, the harmed person expresses forgiveness.	After sharing how the offenders' actions have affected him or her, the offended member expresses forgiveness toward the group.
Examples	A supervisor berates a subordinate employee using harsh language. The employee explains that this language is offensive to her. When the supervisor apologizes, the employee expresses forgiveness toward him.	A company fires an employee in inappropriately, then offers to rehire her. When satisfied with the company's attempts at restitution, the employee expresses forgiveness toward the company.	A group of union employees does something that offends one member. The employee makes known how the action has harmed him. When members of the group apologize, he expresses forgiveness of the group.

Organization

Context	An individual does something that threatens an organization or breaks one of its rules.	One organization threatens another organization.	A group creates activity that threatens an organization.
Forgiving Action	The forgiving organization frames a response, usually in judicial terms, that ensures that the individual has changed and will not repeat the offensive activity.		The organization frames a response, often including a judicial process, to ensure that the offensive activity will not continue. The forgiver foregoes retributive justice against the offender.
Examples	A religious leader breaks a vow and harms a member of a church. He is excommunicated. When he demonstrates that he has changed and will no longer engage in harmful activity, he is allowed to become a member again.	One company sues another company for trade infractions. When the harmful activity ceases, the suing company foregoes retributive measures.	A citizen's group uses defamatory tactics against a company. The company engages in dialogue with the group to understand the issues, and the group ceases its defamatory activity. The company foregoes retributive measures.

Collective-group

Context	Individual offenders have perpetuated an offense against a collective-group.	Institutionally sponsored harms are perpetuated against a group.	One group creates activity that causes harm to another group.
Forgiving Action	After ensuring the offender has made efforts at restitution and will not repeat the offense, the offended group expresses forgiveness toward the offender.		The offended group actively works toward the cessation of harmful activity. After gaining reasonable assurance that the offense will not continue, the offended group expresses forgiveness. The group also provides narrative support for intrapersonal and/or interpersonal forgiveness by its individual members toward the offending group.
Examples	South Africa's Truth-and-Reconciliation process allows for perpetrators to confess and for members of the offended group to understand the offense. A collective expression of forgiveness may occur (Tutu, 1999).		In Ireland, Catholics and Protestants were in perpetual conflict. After reaching a political solution, education initiatives were initiated to help members of each group forgive the other group.

group of people who have harmed him or her. In the individual-to-organization configuration, an individual consumer might forgive a company for generating a faulty, harmful product.

At the organizational level, an offender violates an institutional standard or threatens an organization's well-being. The organization-to-individual configuration is relevant when members of an organization make mistakes or commit serious errors (e.g., a physician commits an error). The organization-to-group scenario applies when an organization is harmed by collective-groups. The organization-to-organization configuration occurs when two organizations are at odds.

At the collective-group level, forgiveness is relevant in situations that arise from conflicts that affect an identity group, in which people are harmed because of their affiliation with a particular class or label. In the group-to-individual configuration, an identifiable offender may have harmed a group. The group-to-group configuration calls for *intergroup forgiveness* (Wohl & Branscombe, 2005), which is relevant to situations in which groups are locked in conflict because of identity differences. The group-to-organization configuration occurs when an identity group has been harmed by a formal institutional organization.

It has been rare for researchers to specify the configuration of forgiveness to be studied. However, the meaning, potential, and aim of forgiveness may differ in dramatic ways depending on the configuration of activity involved. Indeed, some of the conceptual difficulty associated with forgiveness may relate to confusion over the level of forgiveness activity. Forgiveness may operate somewhat independently across different levels and configurations of forgivers and offenders. For example, a person who is harmed by another individual in an organizational environment may invoke the need for three levels of forgiveness activity: the harmed person may work toward intrapsychic forgiveness, the injured person may choose to express forgiveness as way of addressing his or her interpersonal relationship with the offender, and the organization may choose to forgive the offender by resolving the question of continued organizational membership.

Forgiveness at the Intrapersonal Level

At the intrapersonal level, forgiveness is a process that focuses on a person's internal responses to an offense, including emotions and associated thoughts. When people are hurt or offended by others, they may experience many negative emotions including

anger, fear, shame, disappointment, and sorrow. When framed as an internal process of emotion regulation, forgiveness focuses on reducing or eliminating these negative emotional responses and desires for revenge (e.g., Enright, Freedman, & Rique, 1998; McCullough, Fincham, & Tsang, 2003). Negative emotions may be neutralized or replaced with positive emotions (e.g., Worthington & Wade, 1999; Yamhure-Thompson, & Shahen, 2003). Intrapsychic forgiveness has been linked with better mental and physical health (e.g., Coyle & Enright, 1997; Reed & Enright, 2006; Lawler et al., 2003; Witvliet & McCullough, 2007). Among psychologists there is some agreement that intrapersonal forgiveness may be unconditional; it may occur irrespective of contextual factors, such as lack of reformation on the part of the offender (e.g., Enright & Fitzgibbons, 2000; Worthington, 1998, 2003), or a climate that fails to encourage forgiveness.

Intrapersonal forgiveness is the most researched of all forms of forgiveness, with no less than 200 empirical articles examining its many facets. Because intrapersonal forgiveness occurs irrespective of context, the process may be quite similar, regardless of the level of the offending party. Examples of research include the areas described below.

Emotion

Forgiveness has been explored as an emotion-focused coping strategy (Worthington & Scherer, 2004). Most forgiveness interventions (e.g., Enright & Fitzgibbons, 2000; Worthington, 1998, 2003) clarify that recognizing one's right to be angry is a vital part of the process of forgiveness—and one that can protect people from the dangers of minimizing, excusing, or ignoring serious offenses. Anger is a natural response to injustice, one that can energize people and make them feel strong. In fact, because anger tends to be an empowering emotion, some people might hold on to anger because it helps them to feel powerful, dominant, and "in the right" rather than feeling the other, more vulnerable emotions associated with being victimized, such as shame, fear, or sadness. When people are in the self-protective mode that anger brings, they may be motivated to take actions that will protect themselves (or others) in the future. For example, anger may encourage people to confront their offenders, seek retributive justice, set limits, or end a relationship.

Prolonged angry feelings carry serious costs for an individual. Rumination about offenses may become a source of torment if it does not lead to a sense of meaning or resolution. Because negative emotions tend to cluster together (e.g., Watson, Clark, & Tellegen, 1988), the prolonged anger of grudge-holding increases a person's vulnerability to negative emotional states such as depression and anxiety. Chronic anger and hostility also carry serious health costs, from impaired immunity (e.g., Gouin, Kiecolt-Glaser, Malarkey, & Glaser, 2008) to cardiovascular disease (e.g., Boyle et al., 2004). Also, because most world religions promote forgiveness (e.g., Rye et al., 2000), people may see nonforgiveness as a sin that causes strain in their religious or spiritual lives. Through intrapersonal forgiveness, people reduce chronic feelings of anger, and often replace negative emotion with positive emotion (Worthington & Scherer, 2004).

Cognition

Numerous studies explore the specific thoughts and cognitive processes associated with forgiveness. Victims often begin to demonize their offenders (Ellard, Miller, Baumle, & Olson, 2002), seeing them as evil or monstrous objects rather than as people whose motives and actions might have more benevolent explanations. Rumination can worsen this effect (McCullough, Bono, & Root, 2007). Empathic perspective-taking, in contrast, facilitates forgiveness (e.g., McCullough, Worthington, & Rachal., 1997; Takaku, 2001). When people try to imagine the situation from the offender's perspective, they often find reasonable, nondemonizing explanations for why the offense occurred. Also, to the extent that people can recall or envision themselves committing a similar type of offense, they find forgiveness easier (e.g., Exline, Baumeister, Zell, Kraft, & Witvliet, 2008). Seeing oneself as capable of a similar offense makes the offense seem smaller and easier to understand. It also increases one's sense of connection with the offender. All of these factors, in turn, predict more forgiving attitudes.

Any strategy that helps to shrink perceptions of the offense or warm attitudes toward the offender could help reduce anger. In some cases, forgiveness-related thought processes unfold at a relatively unconscious, implicit level (e.g., Karremans & Aarts, 2007). In other cases, people benefit from making a decision to release negative feelings (Worthington & Scherer, 2004). These benefits may be possible even when the offense is one that a person simply cannot relate to, an action that he or she sees as completely heinous or unfathomable (Govier, 2002; Janover, 2005). One set of studies

(Wohl & Branscombe, 2005) demonstrated that forgiveness was facilitated when people were prompted to focus on their common humanity with their offenders—the notion that, universally, human beings do terrible things to each other. We, as part of that common humanity, are also flawed and in need of forgiveness (Worthington, 1998). Nonetheless, if people find themselves unable or unwilling to see their offenders in a positive light, they may be motivated by the idea of reducing their anger levels to provide emotional relief, and perhaps associated health benefits.

Personality

Some people, at a personality level, are more likely than others to use forgiveness in daily life, as captured in dispositional measures of forgiveness (e.g., Berry, Worthington, O'Connor, Parrott, & Wade, 2005; Berry, Worthington, Parrott, O'Connor, & Wade, N. G., 2001; Thompson et al., 2005), also referred to as *forgivingness* (Roberts, 1995). Broadly speaking, people who forgive readily tend to be agreeable and emotionally stable (e.g., Berry et al., 2001; Brown, 2003). In contrast, people have more difficulty forgiving if they are high in *narcissistic entitlement*—that is, if they hold inflated views of themselves and are preoccupied with obtaining special treatment and defending their rights (Exline, Baumeister, Bushman, Campbell, & Finkel, 2004).

Process, Counseling, and Intervention Models

Because forgiveness is now seen as a beneficial process in the recovery of psychologically damaged individuals, many intervention models have been generated for use in counseling and therapy (Day, Gerace, Wilson, & Howells, 2008; Kaminer, Stein, Mbanga, & Zungu-Dirwayi, 2000; Legaree, Turner, & Lollis, 2007). In this regard, several authors have explored the steps or "pathway" of a process that leads to forgiveness (e.g., Enright, 2001; Luskin, 2003; Worthington, 1998, 2001). These models have found support in the literature (Knutson, Enright, & Garbers, 2008; Lundahl, Taylor, Stevenson, & Roberts, 2008) but need further refinement. Related studies have also found that the development of an ability to forgive has been associated with a person's level of moral reasoning (Kaminer et. al., 2000; Romig & Veestra, 1998).

Forgiveness at the Relational Level

When viewed at the relational level, forgiveness once again focuses on the response of an offended individual. In this case, however, the emphasis is on behavioral responses toward the offender rather than on cognitive and emotional responses. Research on relational forgiveness focuses primarily on interpersonal relations, termed *interpersonal forgiveness*, as shown in the individual-to-individual configuration of Table 19.1.

Several psychological theories help to frame the process of offense and forgiveness in interpersonal terms. According to social exchange theory (Blau, 1964), people who harm others create interpersonal debts, debts that must be repaid in order to restore justice. In addition, equity theory (Adams, 1965; Walster, Berscheid, & Walster, 1973) predicts that interpersonal harm creates a sense of inequity or imbalance: The offender has received better-than-deserved outcomes, whereas the victim has received worse-than-deserved outcomes. These outcomes must be balanced for a sense of fairness to be restored.

Some offended parties will use retributive means to pursue justice, seeking retribution (to balance the scales) or revenge (to go a step further, attaining a dominant position). However, a risk of such strategies is that they often lead to continuation or escalation of conflict. All parties to conflict tend to downplay their own wrongdoing and to exaggerate the other's blame (e.g., Baumeister, Stillwell, & Wotman, 1990). Feeling victimized, the parties may counterattack, creating a cycle of aggression that may continue indefinitely.

Interpersonal forgiveness is one type of behavior that can prevent or interrupt this destructive cycle. Offenders might apologize or offer amends. In symbolic terms, offenders who freely apologize or offer restitution are willingly lowering their own status and improving the outcomes of the offended person. Such actions may be interpreted as attempts to repay the interpersonal debt, thereby helping to restore a sense of fairness. Offended parties, in turn, may express interpersonal forgiveness, which may help to deescalate conflicts. There are several themes of research on relational forgiveness, as indicated below:

Relational Context
One finding that emerges clearly from existing research is that the closer and more committed the relationship, the more likely that offended persons will forgive (e.g., Fincham, Paleari, & Regalia, 2002; Finkel, Rusbult, Kumashiro, & Hannon, 2002). In addition, the notion that apologies increase the odds of forgiveness has received

solid support (e.g., Darby & Schlenker, 1982; McCullough et al., 1998; Witvliet et al., 2008). Granted, there are some caveats. Apologies can backfire if they are seen as insincere (Skarlicki, Folger, & Gee, 2004). Effective apologies include clear acknowledgment of wrongdoing (Eaton, Struthers, & Santelli, 2006), expressions of remorse (e.g., Darby & Schlenker, 1989), and offers of restitution (e.g., Bottom, Gibson, Daniels, & Murnighan, 2002; Witvliet et al., 2008). Strong evidence indicates that apologies (and related actions such as restitution) facilitate forgiveness.

Restorative Justice
All of these strategies—apologies, restitution, and forgiveness—have received attention in the context of the restorative justice movement (e.g., Bazemore, 1998; Umbreit, 2001). In fact, simply being primed with the idea of restorative justice may facilitate forgiveness (e.g., Karremans & van Lange, 2005; Strelan, Feather, & McKee, 2008). Yet, framing the concept of forgiveness in the context of the legal system raises some other thorny issues surrounding interpersonal forgiveness. For example, when an offender receives a message of being forgiven, will this person be more or less likely to repeat a similar offense in the future?

The Effect of Forgiveness on Offenders
On the one hand, when perpetrators believe that they have been forgiven, there is evidence that their behavior changes. Three studies by Wallace, Exline, and Baumeister (2008) showed that offenders who felt forgiven were less likely to harm their forgivers in the future. Perhaps people who feel forgiven avoid causing additional hurt. Such logic might especially hold for offenders who clearly felt responsible for the harm.

On the other hand, some offenders may want to harm or exploit their forgivers. In relationships that are abusive or otherwise dangerous, victims who readily express forgiveness behaviors without setting limits to protect themselves may remain at risk. Readiness to forgive might be linked with a decision to stay in an abusive relationship (Katz, Street, & Arias, 1997). Recent studies also suggest that when people forgive partners who are not repentant or kind to them, they decrease in self-respect (Luchies, Finkel, McNulty, & Kumashiro, in press). Thus, although intrapersonal forgiveness may bring mental health benefits, especially after a damaging relationship has ended (e.g., Reed & Enright, 2006), quick interpersonal forgiveness while in a harmful relationship may increase victimization. For this reason, interpersonal forgiveness can be conditional. The forgiver seeks evidence that the harmful behavior has ceased, acknowledges when it has stopped, and foregoes behavioral retribution.

Communication of Forgiveness

To determine whether an expression of forgiveness will increase or decrease the risk of harm to the offended party, it may be important to consider how forgiveness is expressed. Explicit communications of forgiveness, such as saying "I forgive you," have an "illocutionary force" (Pettigrove, 2008, p. 371) that changes the context of a relationship. Explicit communications of forgiveness have the advantage of being clear; however, they also imply accusation of wrong-doing and may thus not be welcomed by offenders (Kelln & Ellard, 1999; Struthers, Eaton, Shirvani, Georghiou, & Edell, 2008). In daily life, expressions of forgiveness are often implicit. For example, forgivers might say, "Forget it," or "It's nothing." Or, they might simply forego revenge, fail to press charges, or quietly continue a relationship as though no offense had occurred. Of course, such behaviors might not indicate intrapsychic forgiveness; instead, they could reflect unassertive behavior, attempts to follow social norms, or even calculated plans to win trust in the hopes of getting later revenge. But in terms of overt behavior, such actions may be seen as forgiving.

Forgiveness at the Organizational Level

Next, we consider forgiveness at the organization level, or *organizational forgiveness*, which entails the "capacity to foster collective abandonment of justified resentment, bitterness, and blame, and, instead, it is the adoption of positive, forward-looking approaches in response to harm or damage" (Cameron & Caza, 2002, p. 39). The organization becomes involved when a person or a few individuals are found to be in violation of the organization's code of conduct or rules of membership, or when an individual's actions may be placing the organization or others at risk. Forgiveness can be practiced both *in* and also *through* organizations (Bright, Cameron, & Caza, 2006). Existing research on organizational forgiveness focuses mostly on the organization-to-individual relationship shown in Table 19.1.

Employee Error

The most common research focuses on organizational response to employee error. An organization ensures that the offender discontinues the harmful behavior, acknowledges that the offender has done so, and sets the stage for a continued relationship between an offender and an organization. For example, an offending leader or employee may regain or retain his or her membership in the organization after issues of concern to both parties have been addressed, lessons learned, and changes incorporated (Sutton & Thomas, 2005).

In one of the first studies on this topic, Bosk (1979) conducted an ethnographic study in an elite hospital on the west coast of the United States. The study specifically examined the responsiveness of a hospital establishment when a surgical resident in training committed an error in treatment. Bosk documented the forms of social control that a resident encounters when learning professional standards of conduct. From the perspective of organizational forgiveness, his depiction portrays the hospital medical hierarchy as a self-policing entity. As an establishment, the organization's leaders made career-shaping decisions about the residents' performance whenever they committed errors. Bosk documented how, because of frequent, harsh punishments, the perception of nonforgiveness suppressed a discussion of error (Condon, 2007).

In a later reflection, Bosk (2003) described the seriousness with which errors were considered (p. xvi). Some offenses were deemed more forgivable than others, and one question above all seemed important when making these judgments: To what extent was the offender blameworthy? Forgiveness was more forthcoming if the offender was seen as blameless, while otherwise the organization was less forgiving. Forgiveness was clearly dependent on the capacity of residents to reform and learn from their mistakes. Recent work encourages a "culture of forgiveness" and a systems approach to self-examination in medical organizations, such that the occurrence of error can serve as a mechanism of organizational change (Berlinger, 2003). Such processes may include a dialogue with those who are injured (Berlinger, 2003). The effects of these developments are apparently creating some shift in medical practice (Purtilo, 2005). A perspective that encourages organizational forgiveness may promote examinations of the sources of error, both personal and systemic, in the aftermath of medical tragedies (e.g., Sachs, 2005).

Culture or Climate of Forgiveness

In literature outside of medicine, researchers have conducted studies to explore forgiveness as a dimension of organizational culture or climate

(Bright, 2005; Cox, 2008). Typically, these studies examine perceptions of environmental conditions that may encourage forgiveness in the workplace. The basic proposition is that forgiving behaviors, as expressed in organizations, are a function of the dispositions of individuals to forgive and environmental factors such as organizational decisions, policies, system-wide events, and interventions. Cox (2008) has created and validated an early measure of forgiveness climate, showing its relation to a willingness to forgive among individual employees.

The benefits to organizations of a forgiving climate may be significant. For example, it has been found that perceptions of forgiveness are associated with the absence of long-term organizational decline in the aftermath of downsizing (Bright, Cameron, & Caza, 2006; Cameron, Bright, & Caza, 2004). Employees may be forgiving of an organization and its leaders to the extent that they receive forgiveness in their organizational experience (Bright, Cameron, & Caza, 2006; Cameron & Caza, 2002). A culture of forgiveness may provide leaders with more latitude during moments when they need to make tough decisions that may result in harm to some employees (Bright, 2005; Bright, Cameron, & Caza, 2006).

Bright (2005), in a qualitative study of forgiveness in a trucking company, found two forms or modes of narrative that promote forgiveness. In the most common, *pragmatic* mode, forgiveness was seen as necessary practice that was needed to support ongoing relationships: The benefits of forgiving outweighed the costs of not forgiving. In the less common, *transcendent* mode, forgiveness was viewed as a transformational practice, a means to learn from and encourage positive transformations after difficult interpersonal moments. Evidence also suggested that an organization-wide intervention could shift the common narrative from the pragmatic to the transcendent mode, indicating a change in climate. Policies and practices that encourage dialogue, an appreciation for the others' perspectives, and systems-thinking may give employees a perspective that facilitates forgiveness, even when forgiveness is not an overt objective. Many organizational development practices may create such effects, including those shaped by appreciative inquiry (Cooperrider, 1990; Whitney & Trosten-Bloom, 2003), open-systems (Owen, 2008), or complex systems (Olson & Eoyang, 2001).

In other developments, Kurzynski (1998) was among the first to suggest that forgiveness should be considered as part of an organization's human resource management strategy, noting that forgiveness provides an essential, long-term benefit to organizations by allowing employees to recuperate after missteps. Nussbaum (2007) takes this idea further, arguing that a forgiving culture can be shaped through a policy and practice of counseling with employees who may have performance problems. He outlines five questions to consider when outlining a path to forgiveness for an employee, including an analysis of behaviors, consequences, and extenuating circumstances, then focusing on how and when reforms in behavior will be achieved in the future. The implicit message for employees is that they should have the benefit of learning from the experience, as well as a clear understanding of organizational expectations. Pignatelli (2006) explored a similar idea in the context of teacher development in educational institutions. Salvador and Folger (2009) found that the intention among managers to punish misconduct was inversely associated with perceptions of organizational forgiveness. Such studies suggest the potential for strong interactions between levels of forgiveness.

Forgiveness at the Collective-group Level

Next, we consider forgiveness at the collective-group level, in which victims are harmed because of an affiliation with a social category or identity (Cehajic, Brown, & Castano, 2008; Hewstone, Cairns, Voci, Hamberger, & Niens, 2006). When people are targeted because of their membership in a collective group, "a victim can feel his or her right to live in this world has been challenged and his or her very identity is unacceptable" (Lamb, 2006, p. 45). Victims often recognize that their response (e.g., forgiving or unforgiving) will represent the group members "who were not themselves harmed [but who] can feel the pain and experience the trauma in solidarity with the wounded" (p. 45). People may endure the experience of suffering when others within their identity group are harmed (Brown, Wohl, & Exline, 2008; Govier, 2002).

There is some debate in the literature about the degree to which a collective-group can be considered as a forgiving entity (Bernstein, 2006; Shriver, 1995). Govier (2002) offers an excellent summary and rebuttal of the critiques, noting that "to accept the view that forgiveness is not humanly realistic for groups is to accept that no efforts should be made to overcome or transform feelings of grievance, bitterness or resentment . . . There is no logical or metaphysical mistake involved in believing that groups can forgive" (p. 99).

A point of contention arises from the fact that collective-groups often lack a formal structure through which they mobilize or communicate forgiveness (Blumenthal, 2005; Govier, 2002). Thus, collective-group forgiveness can be understood as a narrative response from a group toward a perceived offender (Malcolm & Ramsey, 2006), one that represents the general group sentiment, and it may not include any formal group action (Blumenthal, 2005). The forgiving group, over time, generates and perpetuates a narrative understanding of the offender that acknowledges that the offender has ceased to engage in harmful behavior and that collective-group members no longer seek retributive justice (Digeser, 1998; Griswold, 2007).

From this perspective, collective-group forgiveness is an emergent phenomenon that unfolds through an evolution in a group's "collective memory" (Kaiser, 2005). The appearance of collective-group forgiveness may require a substantial amount of time, even many generations (Kampf, 2008). Like other forms of behavioral forgiveness, collective-group forgiveness may be communicated directly but is more likely to be indirect and informal (Merolla, 2008).

Collective-group forgiveness is considered most frequently in the group-to-group configuration illustrated in Table 19.1, and it is referred to in the literature as *sociopolitical forgiveness* (Montiel, 2000) or *intergroup forgiveness* (Wohl & Branscombe, 2006; Hewstone, et al., 2006). Empirical research on the topic is rare, although intergroup forgiveness has been studied in ongoing conflicts around the world: Protestant–Catholic relations in Northern Ireland (Hewstone, et al., 2006), the ethnic relations of the Balkans (Cehajic, 2008), and the relationship between Germans and Jews in the aftermath of the Holocaust (Wohl & Branscombe, 2006).

Collective-group forgiveness is also considered in numerous conceptual papers that focus on its potential to break cycles of violence. For instance, Tutu (1999) notes that, when members of an identity group forgive, they recognize that "there is no point in exacting vengeance, knowing that it will be the cause of future vengeance by the offspring of those we punish" (p. 155). That is, in keeping with the general characteristics of forgiveness, collective-group forgiveness holds potential as a practice that can break the cycle of vengeance in the

context of intergroup violence. At least four streams of research are promising.

The Truth-and-Reconciliation Process

Probably the best known of approaches used to foster the potential for collective-group forgiveness is the truth-and-reconciliation process pioneered in the aftermath of apartheid in South Africa (Gobodo-Madikizela, 2003; Tutu, 1999). Montiel (2000, p. 100) suggests that, in a sociopolitical context, there are "constructive" and "destructive" forms of forgiveness, in which constructive forgiveness occurs in a "pragmatic combination of forgiveness and justice." For this reason, it is essential to address both the "subjective-psychological" and "objective-systemic" consequences of conflict, thus averting the possibility of future conflict. The truth-and-reconciliation movement aims to achieve this pragmatic combination through the creation of a formal, government-sanctioned organization that has the prerogative to investigate harmful past actions. In the context of socio-political conflict, in which offending actors were usually agents of the system, this process allows for the victims to have a voice and for the full documentation of harms suffered. Hypothetically, the process provides a public forum in which people can develop an empathetic understanding of the traumas that have been experienced by those who have been victimized. "Empathy is essential for the development of remorse on the part of perpetrators, and of forgiveness on the part of victims" (Gobodo-Madikizela, 2008, p. 169). When this occurs, "forgiving is not necessarily about forgetting, but forgiving is a prelude to moving on and focusing on the future, rather than the past" (Boettke & Coyne, 2007, p. 55).

The Contact Hypothesis

The next area focuses on the degree to which contact between members of opposing groups fosters an improvement in intergroup relations. The contact hypothesis was first articulated by Allport (1954) and has spawned work throughout the world (Hewstone & Brown, 1986). Allport (1954) proposed four conditions for contact that should lead to improved intergroup relations: the participants should have equal status, they seek "common goals," they are supported by the institutions they represent, and the interaction broadens the "perception of common interests and humanity between members of the two groups" (Hewstone,

Cairns, Voci, Manberger, & Niens, 2006, p. 102). Cehajic (2008) explains that the contact hypothesis predicts the emergence of several mediating mechanisms that should lead to greater intergroup forgivingness among participants, including trust, empathy for the other, and a decrease in the "outgroup homogeneity effect" (p. 354). For example, in the Jewish–German identity relationship, Wohl and Branscombe (2005) demonstrated that people are more forgiving of other in-group members than they are of out-group members, and that they become more forgiving of others when they move from out-group to in-group status. In Northern Ireland and the former Yugoslavia, respectively, both Hewstone et al. (2006) and Cehajic (2008) demonstrated that intergroup contact helps participants to view one another as part of a larger in-group and that these perceptions correlated with intergroup forgiveness.

In applied work, McGlynn, Niens, Cairns, and Hewstone (2004) found that the integration of students in school is associated with forgiveness between students of opposing groups. The contact hypothesis is also the basis of several social entrepreneurial ventures in the business community, in which business models are purposely framed to create opportunities for members of conflicting groups to come in contact one with another. In this work, it is assumed that local business provides a setting for relationship building and, furthermore, that such relationships will serve as a catalyst for peace. Numerous examples of such work can be found throughout the world (International Alert, 2006; Sweetman, 2009).

The Education Hypothesis

A third approach to fostering intergroup forgiveness might be termed the *education hypothesis*. This approach proposes that individuals who learn about the meaning and practice of forgiveness when they are young will practice forgiveness when they are older (Klatt & Enright, 2009; Rodden, 2003). This supposition is potentially important in the context of intergroup conflict, in which a cycle of dysfunctional conflict may carry on for generations. Interventions have been implemented and measured in several locations throughout the world, perhaps most notably in Northern Ireland (Hill, 2007). Studies show that students in Hong Kong (Hui & Ho, 2004) and in inner-city Milwaukee (Gassin, Enright, & Knutsen, 2005) were positively influenced by educational programs to understand and be willing to apply forgiveness.

Collective-group Forgiveness of Institutions

A final, emerging area of collective-group forgiveness pertains to the group-to-organization cell of Table 19.1. Specifically, organizational institutions sometimes create harmful impacts on collective-groups of people through their corporate activities. Usually, such discussions are considered in light of an organization's reputation and moral capital (Godfrey, 2005); however, a potentially interesting direction for research focuses on *consumer forgiveness* (Chung & Beverland, 2006). When consumers are harmed by an organization, they may forgive that organization by releasing negative emotions at the intrapersonal level and by "acting constructively toward the relationship" (p. 98) at the collective-group level. Research on forgiveness in this domain is rare, and could generate important insight, especially given the examples of corporate offense in recent decades.

Potential Questions for Future Research

Despite the surge of work on the topic, research on forgiveness is still in its infancy. The following six areas present high potential for a deepened understanding of forgiveness.

First, many authors have noted a lack of consensus about the meaning of forgiveness. The model in this chapter demonstrates that one reason for this is that forgiveness as a general concept is best understood as a family of qualitatively different concepts. The meaning and practice of forgiveness may differ in significant ways depending on the level of forgiveness (e.g., intrapersonal, relational) and dimension (e.g., emotional, cognitive, behavioral) under consideration. Each form of forgiveness represents a distinct phenomenon that may operate somewhat independently of the others. We suggest that it will be beneficial to the field if future forgiveness researchers were to specify which area of the conceptual family their research emphasizes. This practice would help to develop greater conceptual clarity.

Second, there is abundant opportunity to explore forgiveness within the various configurations of relationships outlined in Table 19.1. At the intrapersonal level, for example, research could focus on how to discriminate between forgiveness and related (but troublesome) processes like minimizing and excusing. In addition, it would be interesting to examine how often people really go through a full process of forgiveness, as described in the intrapersonal process models. Such work might help to identify the key ingredients in forgiveness interventions that make them effective at the intrapersonal level. Also, the relationship between forgiveness and personality needs to be deepened.

Third, at the relational level, there is a need to understand and better discriminate between interpersonal and intrapersonal forgiveness and to understand the multilevel relationship between the two. It would be useful to look at situations in which people express forgiveness but do not feel it inside (intrapersonal) and vice versa: What are the predictors? What are the consequences? In addition, it is possible that forgiveness behaviors may be taken as de facto condoning of harmful relational behaviors. Even if a person forgives at the intrapersonal level, it may be important to understand the potential risks and dangers of expressing forgiveness—perhaps especially implicit forgiveness—in volatile situations. Finally, most relational research focuses on interpersonal relations. It could be interesting to examine how individuals forgive institutions (e.g., Chung, 2006) or collective-groups.

Fourth, the field is wide open with respect to the work that may be accomplished at the organization and collective-group levels of forgiveness. As documented in this chapter, work on forgiveness in relation to employee error might help the development of perspectives on how to manage internal errors in ways that allow for multilevel learning and long-term systemic change. For example, how do organizations determine when it is appropriate to forgive in an organizational environment? What policies exist that encourage or discourage cultures of forgiveness? Is there a relationship between a climate of forgiveness and organizational adaptive capacity or organization innovation capacity? The answers to these types of questions may have implications not just for the individuals involved but for the health of organizations.

At the collective-level, the work on the contact hypothesis and the education hypothesis is completely new. What are the conditions under which the contact hypothesis works to generate more forgiveness between opposing groups? How do the narratives about "the other" differ with respect to forgiveness between those of one group who have had more contact with members of an opposing group? Given the myriad of business-oriented peace-building experiments around the world, are these actually increasing intergroup forgiveness?

Fifth, forgiveness research has focused almost exclusively on the forgiver. Yet, as illustrated in Table 19.1, there are many potential offenders as well, each of whom creates human-initiated activity.

How might forgiveness potentially benefit these offenders? For instance, how might the possibility of forgiveness (at all levels) help a physician who makes a life-critical mistake or a soldier who puts his unit at risk because of an error of judgment? How might interpersonal forgiveness be a part of the healing and personal change in an abusive spouse or an unruly supervisor? The nearly exclusive focus on forgivers in research may be overlooking an essential, important set of benefits and impacts on the other parties involved.

Sixth, a multilevel view of forgiveness suggests the need to understand the relationships between qualitatively different forgiveness practices across levels. The fact that forgiveness occurs at one level does not necessarily mean that it occurs at other levels. Does intrapersonal forgiveness on a large scale facilitate a shift in the narrative of a collective-group that would indicate that it has forgiven? Does a narrative of forgiveness at the collective-group level facilitate intrapersonal or interpersonal forgiveness toward perpetrators of past harms? Forgiveness may invoke a complex array of considerations that should be clarified and explored.

Conclusion

This chapter demonstrates that forgiveness is an important multilevel family of concepts that describes how people deal with human-initiated difficulties. It is a central virtue, or human strength, because it acts as a key mechanism for escaping or preventing dysfunctional cycles of interaction in the human experience. We have suggested that research on forgiveness is at an early stage, and we have highlighted many promising areas for future work. The framework described in this chapter will hopefully provide conceptual clarity as this work progresses and an understanding of the forms of forgiveness is developed.

Acknowledgment

We thank Anindita Sengupta at Wright State University for her invaluable support. Her effort to track down an innumerable number of references made this chapter possible.

References

Adams, J.S. (1965). Inequity in social exchange. In L. Berkowitz (Ed.), *Advances in experimental social psychology* Vol. 2 (pp. 267–299). New York: Academic Press.

Allport, G.W. (1954). *The nature of prejudice*. Cambridge, MA: Addison-Wesley.

Aquino, K., Grover, S.L., Goldman, B., & Folger, R. (2003). When push doesn't come to shove: Interpersonal forgiveness in workplace relationships. *Journal of Management Inquiry, 12*(3), 209–216. doi:10.1177/1056492603256337.

Arendt, H. (1958). Irreversibility and the power to forgive. In H. Arendt (Ed.), *The human condition* (pp. 233–247). Chicago: University of Chicago Press.

Baumeister, R.F., Stillwell, A., & Wotman, S.R. (1990). Victim and perpetrator accounts of interpersonal conflict: Autobiographical narratives about anger. *Journal of Personality and Social Psychology, 59*, 994–1005.

Bazemore, G. (1998). Restorative justice and earned redemption: Communities, victims, and offender reintegration. *American Behavioral Scientist, 41*, 768–813.

Berlinger, N. (2003). Avoiding cheap grace: Medical harm, patient safety, and the culture(s) of forgiveness. *The Hastings Center Report, 33*(6), 28–38.

Bernstein, R.J. (2006). Derrida: The aporia of forgiveness? *Constellations, 13*(3), 394–406. doi:10.1111/j.1467–8675.2006.00400.x.

Berry, J.W., Worthington, E.L., Jr., Parrott, L., III, O'Connor, L.E., & Wade, N.G. (2001). Dispositional forgivingness: Development and construct validity of the Transgression Narrative Test of Forgivingness (TNTF). *Personality and Social Psychology Bulletin, 27*, 1277–1290.

Berry, J.W., Worthington, E.L., O'Connor, L.E., Parrott, L. III, & Wade, N.G. (2005). Forgivingness, vengeful rumination, and affective traits. *Journal of Personality, 73*, 183–225.

Blau, P.M. (1964). *Exchange and power in social life*. New York: Wiley.

Blumenthal, D. (2005). Repentance and forgiveness. *Journal of Religion & Abuse, 7*(2), 69. doi:10.1300/J154v07n02_05.

Boettke, P.J., & Coyne, C.J. (2007). Political economy of forgiveness. *Society, 44*(2), 53–59.

Bosk, C.L. (2003). *Forgive and remember: Managing medical failure* (2nd ed.). Chicago: University of Chicago Press.

Bosk, C.L. (1979). *Forgive and remember: Managing medical failure*. Chicago: University of Chicago Press.

Bottom, W.P., Gibson, K., Daniels, S.E., & Murnighan, J.K. (2002). When talk is not cheap: Substantive penance and expressions of intent in rebuilding cooperation. *Organization Science, 13*, 497–513.

Boyle, S.H., Williams, R.B., Mark, D.B., Brummett, B.H., Siegler, I.C., Helms, M.J., et al. (2004). Hostility as a predictor of survival in patients with coronary artery disease. *Psychosomatic Medicine, 66*, 629–632.

Bright, D.S. (2005). *Forgiveness and change: Begrudging, pragmatic, and transcendent responses to discomfiture in a unionized trucking company*. Unpublished dissertation, Case Western Reserve University, Cleveland, OH.

Bright, D.S., Cameron, K., & Caza, A. (2006). The amplifying and buffering effects of virtuousness in downsized organizations. *Journal of Business Ethics, 64*(3), 249–269.

Bright, D.S., Fry, R.E., & Cooperrider, D.L. (2008). Forgiveness from the perspectives of three response modes: Begrudgment, pragmatism, and transcendence. In C.C. Manz, K.S. Cameron, K. Manz & R.D. Marx (Eds.), *The virtuous organization* (pp. 67–95). New Jersey: World Scientific Publishing.

Brown, R.P. (2003). Measuring individual differences in the tendency to forgive: Construct validity and links with depression. *Personality and Social Psychology Bulletin, 29*, 759–771.

Brown, R.P., Wohl, M.J.A., & Exline, J.J. (2008). Taking up offenses: Secondhand forgiveness and group identification.

Personality and Social Psychology Bulletin, 34(10), 1406–1419. doi:10.1177/0146167208321538.

Cameron, K.S., Bright, D.S., & Caza, A. (2004). Exploring the relationships between organizational virtuousness and performance. *American Behavioral Scientist, 47*(6), 766–790.

Cameron, K., & Caza, A. (2002). Organizational and leadership virtues and the role of forgiveness. *Journal of Leadership & Organizational Studies, 9*(1), 33.

Cehajic, S., Brown, R., & Castano, E. (2008). Forgive and forget? Antecedents and consequences of intergroup forgiveness in Bosnia and Herzegovina. *Political Psychology, 29*(3), 351–367.

Chung, E., & Beverland, M. (2006). An exploration of consumer forgiveness following marketer transgressions. *Advances in Consumer Research, 33*, 98.

Condon, R.E. (2007). Forgive and remember revisited. *The American Journal of Surgery, 194*(1), 1–2.

Cooperrider, D.L. (1990). Positive image, positive action: The affirmative basis of organizing. In S. Srivastva, & D.L. Cooperrider (Eds.), *Appreciative management and leadership: The power of positive thought and action in organizations* (pp. 91–125). San Francisco: Jossey-Bass Inc.

Cox, S. (2008). *A forgiving workplace: An investigation of forgiveness climate, individual differences and workplace outcomes*. Dissertation, Louisiana Tech University, Ruston, LA.

Coyle, C.T., & Enright, R.D. (1997). Forgiveness intervention with post-abortion men. *Journal of Consulting and Clinical Psychology, 65*, 1042–1046.

Darby, B.W., & Schlenker, B.R. (1982). Children's reactions to apologies. *Journal of Personality and Social Psychology, 43*, 742–753.

Day, A., Gerace, A., Wilson, C., & Howells, K. (2008). Promoting forgiveness in violent offenders: A more positive approach to offender rehabilitation? *Aggression and Violent Behavior, 13*(3), 195–200.

Digeser, P. (1998). Forgiveness and politics: Dirty hands and imperfect procedures. *Political Theory, 26*(5), 700–724.

Eaton, J., Struthers, C.W., & Santelli, A.G. (2006). The mediating role of the perceptual validation in the repentance-forgiveness process. *Personality and Social Psychology Bulletin, 32*, 1389–1401.

Ellard, J.H., Miller, C.D., Baumle, T., & Olson, J.M. (2002). Just world processes in demonizing. In M. Ross, & D.T. Miller (Eds.), *The justice motive in everyday life* (pp. 350–362). Cambridge: Cambridge University Press.

Enright, R.D. (2001). *Forgiveness is a choice: A step-by-step process for resolving anger and restoring hope*. Washington, DC: APA Life Tools.

Enright, R.D., & Fitzgibbons, R.P. (2000). *Helping clients forgive: An empirical guide for resolving anger and restoring hope*. Washington, DC: American Psychological Association Books.

Enright, R.D., Freedman, S., & Rique, J. (1998). The psychology of interpersonal forgiveness. In R.D. Enright, & J. North (Eds.), *Exploring forgiveness* (pp. 46–63). Madison: University of Wisconsin Press.

Enright, R.D., & Fitzgibbons, R.P. (2000). *Helping clients forgive: An empirical guide for resolving anger and restoring hope*. Washington, DC: American Psychological Association.

Exline, J.J., Baumeister, R.F., Bushman, B.J., Campbell, W.K., & Finkel, E.J. (2004). Too proud to let go: Narcissistic entitlement as a barrier to forgiveness. *Journal of Personality and Social Psychology, 87*, 894–912.

Exline, J.J., Baumeister, R.F., Zell, A.L., Kraft, A., & Witvliet, C.V.O. (2008). Not so innocent: Does seeing one's own capability for wrongdoing predict forgiveness? *Journal of Personality and Social Psychology, 94*, 495–515.

Exline, J.J., Worthington, E.L., Jr., Hill, P., & McCullough, M.E. (2003). Forgiveness and justice: A research agenda for social and personality psychology. *Personality and Social Psychology Review, 7*(4), 337.

Fincham, F.D., Paleari, F.G., & Regalia, C. (2002). Forgiveness in marriage: The role of relationship quality, attributions and empathy. *Personal Relationships, 9*, 27–37.

Finkel, E.J., Rusbult, C.E., Kumashiro, M., & Hannon, P. (2002). Dealing with betrayal in close relationships: Does commitment promote forgiveness? *Journal of Personality & Social Psychology, 82*, 956–974.

Freedman, S. (1998). Forgiveness and reconciliation: The importance of understanding how they differ. *Counseling and Values, 42*(3), 200–216.

Gassin, E.A., Enright, R.D., & Knutson, J.A. (2005). Bringing peace to the central city: Forgiveness education in Milwaukee. *Theory Into Practice, 44*(4), 319–328.

Godfrey, P.C. (2005). The relationship between corporate philanthropy and shareholder wealth: A risk management perspective. *Academy of Management Review, 30*(4), 777–798.

Gobodo-Madikizela, P. (2008). Trauma, forgiveness and the witnessing dance: Making public spaces intimate. *Journal of Analytical Psychology, 53*(2), 169–188.

Gobodo-Madikizela, P. (2003). *A human being died that night: A South African story of forgiveness.* Boston: Houghton Mifflin Harcourt.

Govier, T. (2002). *Forgiveness and Revenge* (1st ed.). New York: Routledge.

Gouin, J.-P., Kiecolt-Glaser, J.K., Malarkey, W.B., & Glaser, R. (2008). The influence of anger expression on wound healing. *Brain, Behavior, and Immunity, 22*, 699–708.

Griswold, C.L. (2007). *Forgiveness.* New York: Cambridge University Press.

Hewstone, M., & Brown, R. (1986). Contact is not enough: An intergroup perspective on the "contact hypothesis." In M. Hewstone, & R.J. Brown (Eds.), *Contact and conflict in intergroup encounters* (pp. 1–44). Oxford: Blackwell.

Hewstone, M., Cairns, E., Voci, A., Hamberger, J., & Niens, U. (2006). Intergroup contact, forgiveness, and experience of "The Troubles" in Northern Ireland. *Journal of Social Issues, 62*(1), 99–120. doi:10.1111/j.1540–4560.2006.00441.x.

Hill, E.W. (2001). Understanding forgiveness as discovery: Implications for marital and family therapy. *Contemporary Family Therapy, 23*(4), 369–384.

Hui, E.K.P., & Ho, D.K.Y. (2004). Forgiveness in the context of developmental guidance: Implementation and evaluation. *British Journal of Guidance and Counseling, 32*(4), 477–492. doi:10.1080/03069880412331303286.

International Alert. (2006). *Local business, local peace.* London: International Alert.

Janover, M. (2005). The limits of forgiveness and the ends of politics. *Journal of Intercultural Studies, 26*(3), 221. doi:10.1080/07256860500153500.

Kaiser, S. (2005). To punish or to forgive? Young citizens' attitudes on impunity and accountability in contemporary Argentina. *Journal of Human Rights, 4*(2), 171. doi:10.1080/14754830590952116.

Kaminer, D., Stein, D.J., Mbanga, I., & Zungu-Dirwayi, N. (2000). Forgiveness: Toward an integration of theoretical models. *Psychiatry, 63*, 344–357.

Kampf, Z. (2008). The pragmatics of forgiveness: Judgments of apologies in the Israeli political arena. *Discourse Society, 19*(5), 577–598. doi:10.1177/0957926508092244.

Karremans, J.C., & Aarts, H. (2007). The role of automaticity in determining the inclination to forgive close others. *Journal of Experimental Social Psychology, 43*, 902–917.

Karremans, J.C., & van Lange, P.A.M. (2005). Does activating justice help or hurt in promoting forgiveness? *Journal of Experimental Social Psychology, 41*, 290–297.

Katz, J., Street, A., & Arias, I. (1997). Individual differences in self-appraisals and responses to dating violence scenarios. *Violence and Victims, 12*, 265–276.

Kelln, B.R.C., & Ellard, J.H. (1999). An equity theory analysis of the impact of forgiveness and retribution on transgressor compliance. *Personality and Social Psychology Bulletin, 25*, 864–872.

Klatt, J., & Enright, R. (2009). Investigating the place of forgiveness within the positive youth development paradigm. *Journal of Moral Education, 38*(1), 35–52.

Knutson, J., Enright, R., & Garbers, B. (2008). Validating the developmental pathway of forgiveness. *Journal of Counseling & Development, 86*(2), 193–199.

Kurzynski, M.J. (1998). The virtue of forgiveness as a human resource management strategy. *Journal of Business Ethics, 17*(1), 77–85.

Lamb, S. (2006). Forgiveness, women, and responsibility to the group. *Journal of Human Rights, 5*(1), 45–60. doi:10.1080/14754830500485874.

Lawler, K.A., Younger, J.W., Piferi, R.L., Billington, E., Jobe, R., Edmonson, K., et al. (2003). A change of heart: Cardiovascular correlates of forgiveness in response to interpersonal conflict. *Journal of Behavioral Medicine, 26*, 373–393.

Legaree, T.A., Turner, J., & Lollis, S. (2007). Forgiveness and therapy: A critical review of conceptualizations, practices, and values found in the literature. *Journal of Marital and Family Therapy, 33*(2), 192.

Luchies, L.B., Finkel, E.J., McNulty, J.K., & Kumashiro, M. (in press). The doormat effect: When forgiving erodes self-respect and self-concept clarity. *Journal of Personality and Social Psychology.*

Lundahl, B.W., Taylor, M.J., Stevenson, R., & Roberts, K.D. (2008). Process-based forgiveness interventions: A Meta-analytic review. *Research on Social Work Practice, 18*(5), 465–478. doi:10.1177/1049731507313979.

Luskin, F. (2003). *Forgive for good.* San Francisco: Harper.

Malcolm, L., & Ramsey, J. (2006). Teaching and learning forgiveness: A multidimensional approach. *Teaching Theology and Religion, 9*(3), 175–185. doi:10.1111/j.1467–9647.2006.00281.x.

McCullough, M.E., Bono, G., & Root, L.M. (2007). Rumination, emotion, and forgiveness: Three longitudinal studies. *Journal of Personality and Social Psychology, 92*(3), 490–505.

McCullough, M.E., Fincham, F.D., & Tsang, J.A. (2003). Forgiveness, forbearance, and time: The temporal unfolding of transgression-related interpersonal motivations. *Journal of Personality and Social Psychology, 84*(3), 540–557.

McCullough, M.E., Rachal, K.C., Sandage, S.J., Worthington, E.L., Jr., Brown, S.W., & Hight, T.L. (1998). Interpersonal forgiving in close relationships II: Theoretical elaboration and measurement. *Journal of Personality and Social Psychology, 75*, 1586–1603.

McCullough, M.E., & Witvliet, C.V. (2002). The psychology of forgiveness. In C.R. Snyder, & S.J. Lopez (Eds.), *Handbook* of positive psychology (pp. 446–458). London: Oxford University Press.

McCullough, M.E., Worthington, E.L., Jr., & Rachal, K.C. (1997). Interpersonal forgiving in close relationships. *Journal of Personality and Social Psychology, 73*, 321–336.

McGlynn, C., Niens, U., Cairns, E., & Hewstone, M. (2004). Moving out of conflict: The contribution of integrated schools in Northern Ireland to identity, attitudes, forgiveness and reconciliation. *Journal of Peace Education, 1*(2), 147–163. doi:10.1080/1740020042000253712.

Merolla, A. (2008). Communicating forgiveness in friendships and dating relationships. *Communication Studies, 59*(2), 114–131. doi:10.1080/10510970802062428.

Montiel, C.J. (2002). Sociopolitical forgiveness. *Peace Review, 14*(3), 271–277.

Montiel, C.J. (2000). Constructive and destructive post-conflict forgiveness. *Peace Review, 12*(1), 95–101.

Nussbaum, G.F. (2007). Counseling: Establishing a culture of forgiveness. *AORN Journal, 86*(3), 415–422.

Olson, E.E., & Eoyang, G.H. (2001). *Facilitating organization change: Lessons from complexity science* (1st ed.). San Francisco: Pfeiffer.

Owen, H. (2008). *Open space technology: A user's guide* (3rd ed.). San Francisco: Berrett-Koehler Publishers.

Peterson, C., & Seligman, M.E.P. (2004). *Character strengths and virtues: A handbook and classification*. New York: Oxford University Press.

Pettigrove, G. (2004). The Forgiveness We Speak: The Illocutionary Force of Forgiving. *The Southern Journal of Philosophy, 42*(3), 371–392. doi:10.1111/j.2041-6962.2004.tb01938.x.

Pignatelli, F. (2006). Forgiveness in progressive education. *Encounter, 19*(3), 6–13.

Purtilo, R.B. (2005). Beyond disclosure: Seeking forgiveness. *Physical Therapy, 85*(11), 1124–1126.

Reed, G.L., & Enright, R.D. (2006). The effects of forgiveness therapy on depression, anxiety, and posttraumatic stress for women after spousal emotional abuse. *Journal of Consulting and Clinical Psychology, 74*, 920–929.

Roberts, R.C. (1995). Forgivingness. *American Philosophical Quarterly, 32*(4), 289–306.

Rodden, J. (2003). Forgiveness, education, public policy: The road not yet taken. *Modern Age, 46*(4), 333–341.

Romig, C.A., & Veenstra, G. (1998). Forgiveness and psychosocial development: Implications for clinical practice. *Counseling and Values, 42*(3), 185–199.

Rye, M.S., Pargament, K.I., Ali, M.A., Beck, G.L., Dorff, E.N., Hallisey, C., et al. (2000). Religious perspectives on forgiveness. In M.E. McCullough, K.I. Pargament, & C.E. Thoresen (Eds.), *Forgiveness: Theory, research, and practice* (pp. 17–40). New York: Guilford.

Sachs, B.P. (2005). A 38-year-old woman with fetal loss and hysterectomy. *Journal of the American Medical Association, 294*(7), 833–840. doi:10.1001/jama.294.7.833.

Salvador, R., & Folger, R.G. (2009). *Organizational forgiveness and punishing ethical misconduct*. Presented at the Society for Industrial/Organizational Psychology, New Orleans, LA.

Shriver, D.W. (1995). *An ethic for enemies*. New York: Oxford University Press.

Skarlicki, D.P., Folger, R., & Gee, J. (2004). When social accounts backfire: The exacerbating effects of a polite message or an apology on reactions to an unfair outcome. *Journal of Applied Social Psychology, 34*, 322–341.

Strelan, P., Feather, N.T., & McKee, I. (2008). Justice and forgiveness: Experimental evidence for compatibility. *Journal of Experimental Social Psychology, 44*, 1538–1544.

Struthers, C.W., Eaton, J., Shirvani, N., Georghiou, M., & Edell, E. (2008). The effect of preemptive forgiveness and a transgressor's responsibility on shame, motivation to reconcile, and repentance. *Basic and Applied Social Psychology, 30*, 130–141.

Sutton, G.W., & Thomas, E.K. (2005). Restoring Christian leaders. *American Journal of Pastoral Counseling, 8*(2), 27–42.

Sweetman, D. (2009). *Business, conflict resolution and peacebuilding: Contributions from the private sector to address violent conflict*. London: Routledge.

Takaku, S. (2001). The effects of apology and perspective taking on interpersonal forgiveness: A dissonance-attribution model of interpersonal forgiveness. *Journal of Social Psychology, 141*, 494–508.

Thompson, L.Y., Snyder, C.R., Hoffman, L., Michael, S.T., Rasmussen, H.N., Billings, L.S., et al. (2005). Dispositional forgiveness of self, others, and situations. *Journal of Personality, 73*, 313–359.

Tutu, D. (1999). *No future without forgiveness*. New York: Doubleday.

Umbreit, M.S. (2001). *The handbook of victim offender mediation*. San Francisco: Jossey-Bass.

Wallace, H.M., Exline, J.J., & Baumeister, R.F. (2008). Interpersonal consequences of forgiveness: Does forgiveness deter or encourage repeat offenses? *Journal of Experimental Social Psychology, 44*, 453–460.

Walster, E., Berscheid, E., & Walster, G.W. (1973). New directions in equity research. *Journal of Personality and Social Psychology, 25*, 151–176.

Watson, D., Clark, L., & Tellegen, A. (1988). Development and validation of brief measures of positive and negative affect: The PANAS scales. *Journal of Personality and Social Psychology, 54*, 1063–1070.

Whitney, D.K., & Trosten-Bloom, A. (2003). *The power of appreciative inquiry*. San Francisco: Berrett-Koehler Publishers.

Witvliet, C.V.O., & McCullough, M.E. (2007). Forgiveness and health: A review and theoretical exploration of emotion pathways. In S.G. Post (Ed.), *Altruism and health: Perspectives from empirical research*. Oxford: Oxford University Press.

Witvliet, C.V.O., Worthington, E.L., Jr., Root, L.M., Sato, A.F., Ludwig, T.E., & Exline, J.J. (2008). Retributive justice, restorative justice, and forgiveness: A psychophysiological analysis. *Journal of Experimental Social Psychology, 44*, 10–25.

Wohl, M.J.A., & Branscombe, N.R. (2005). Forgiveness and collective guilt assignment to historical perpetrator groups depend on level of social category inclusiveness. *Journal of Personality and Social Psychology, 88*, 288–303.

Worthington, E.L., Jr. (2003). *Forgiving and reconciling*. Downers Grove, IL: Intervarsity.

Worthington, E.L. (2001). *Five steps to forgiveness*. New York: Crown.

Worthington, E.L., Jr. (Ed.). (1998). *Dimensions of forgiveness: Psychological research and theological perspectives*. Randor, PA: Templeton Foundation Press.

Worthington, E.L., Jr., & Scherer, M. (2004). Forgiveness is an emotion-focused coping strategy that can reduce health risks and promote health resilience: Theory, review, and hypotheses. *Psychology and Health, 19*, 385–405.

Worthington, E.L., Jr., & Wade, N.G. (1999). The social psychology of unforgiveness and forgiveness and implications for clinical practice. *Journal of Social and Clinical Psychology, 18*, 385–418.

Yamhure Thompson, L., & Shahen, P.E. (2003). Forgiveness in the workplace. In R.C. Giacalone, & C.L. Jurkiewicz (Eds.), *Handbook of spirituality and organizational performance* (pp. 405–420). New York: M.E.Sharpe.

Exploring the Relevance and Implications of Humility in Organizations

Bradley P. Owens, Wade C. Rowatt, *and* Alan L. Wilkins

Abstract

In this chapter, we explore the meaning and relevance of humility within the context of organizations. After briefly reviewing the history of the construct of humility and synthesizing past definitions of humility, we discuss extant research exploring the impact of humility on individual performance, prosocial behavior, team processes, and leadership. We conclude by discussing the potential boundary conditions for the usefulness of humility in organizations and offering ideas for future research.

Keywords: Humility, virtues, leadership, teams, learning, adaptation

Sense shines with a double luster when it is set in humility. An able yet humble man is a jewel worth a kingdom.
—*William Penn*

Humility is the foundation of all the other virtues: hence, in the soul in which this virtue does not exist there cannot be any other virtue except in mere appearance.
—*St. Augustine*

Why Should We Care About Humility?

One misunderstanding of positive organizational scholarship (POS) is that it is a rosy lens that attends exclusively to strengths, abundance, and *the positive*, and largely ignores real limits, set backs, and problems (Fineman, 2006). Contrary to this view, POS entails viewing negative events, limits, and failures as important catalysts that can facilitate adaptation, reawakening, resilience, and growth (Cameron, Dutton, & Quinn, 2003).

Similarly, humility is a virtue that concerns human limits—how to view and handle human limits productively, adaptively, and constructively. Given its focus on limits, no wonder humility makes some uncomfortable (Hume, 1994, 219/270; see also Grenberg, 2005, pp. 1–5) and has been identified as a much neglected topic in social science (Tangney, 2000). Despite past neglect, we propose that general

workplace trends such as global competition, technological innovation, team-based structures, information-based economies—all of which make the workplace increasingly dynamic, turbulent, interdependent, and uncertain (Crossan et al., 2008; Ireland & Hitt, 1999)—make humility in organizations an "idea whose time has come" (Hugo, 1877/2005). In light of anticipated challenges and changes that continue to unfold in the 21st century, scholars have suggested a greater need for organizational members to have the humility to acknowledge areas of ignorance and inexperience and to foster the learning and adaptation that will be required to succeed in an increasingly unpredictable workplace (see Kotter, 1995; Senge, 2006; Weick, 2001). Theorists have proposed further that humility is the "cornerstone of organizational learning, high-quality service to customers and employees, and organizational resilience" (Vera &

Rodriguez-Lopez, 2004, p. 393; see also Hamel, 2007, p. 96) since it fosters an openness to new paradigms, an eagerness to learn from others, an acknowledgment of limitations and mistakes, and a more realistic picture of both the firm and the firm's external environment.

Our Focus

Outside of the organizational literature, this last decade has seen a resurgence of interest in the construct of humility. For instance, philosophers have recently reopened discussion about the meaning, merits, and implications of humility in leading a moral and happy life (Grenberg, 2005; Roberts & Wood, 2003). Psychologists also have begun discussing and theorizing about humility (i.e., Exline et al. 2004; Morris, Brotheridge, & Urbanski, 2005; Tangney, 2000), undoubtedly sparked by the general movement of positive psychology (Seligman & Csikszentmihaly, 2000). We acknowledge our debt to philosophers and psychologists for providing a theoretical foundation for our understanding of humility. However, in this chapter, our primary purpose is not to offer an extensive review of all that past philosophers and psychologists have said about humility (for such reviews see Exline et al., 2004; Grenberg, 2005; Tangney, 2000) or to discuss the nuanced conceptual distinctions between humility and related constructs (for such discussions see Exline et al., 2004; Owens, 2009a; Peterson & Seligman, 2004). Rather, our main goal is to sketch a potential research stream exploring humility in the context of organizations. To accomplish this goal, we will briefly discuss the historical roots, meaning, and past operationalizations of humility; discuss the increasing relevance of humility in today's organizations; highlight extant research on humility; consider possible disadvantages to humility in organizations; and offer recommendations for future research.

The History and Meaning of Humility

The topic of humility has a rich background in theology and philosophy. Because humility often entails the appreciation of knowledge and worth beyond the self, it is a foundational principle in most world religions. Humility is also central to many philosophical discussions of morality. Immanuel Kant, for example, viewed humility as a "meta-attitude which constitutes the moral agent's proper perspective on himself" and a virtue foundational to most other virtues (Grenberg, 2005, p. 133) because humility tempers other virtues, opens one to the influence and needs of others, and insists on reality rather than pretense. Psychologists categorize humility as a "temperance virtue" that guards against excess (i.e., excessive self-focus or inflated estimation of one's own knowledge and abilities; see Park & Peterson, 2003) and have held up humility as a historically revered characteristic and a multifaceted strength (Tangney, 2000).

The word *humility* is rooted in the Latin word *humus* meaning "earth" or "ground," and from the Latin word *humilis* meaning "on the ground" (Online Etymology Dictionary, 2010). Colloquialisms such as "down-to-earth" and "having a grounded view" reflect humility's lexical origin. Thus, in general terms, humility means to have a grounded view or perspective of oneself and others. One scholar suggests that humility entails a deeply held "belief in the equal dignity and shared limits of all persons" (Grenberg, 2005, p. 164). From this perspective, humility may entail seeing the self and others as sharing general human limitations, as well as worth and dignity (see humanity self-construal, Harb & Smith, 2008). This grounded view of self and others enables a humble person to acknowledge his or her own personal qualities and limitations (as well as those of others) without producing feelings of superiority or inferiority. Associating humility with inferiority has been, we believe, an unfortunate (and incorrect) conceptualization which has led some thinkers and scholars to question its worthiness as a virtue.[1]

The main distinction between nonvirtuous and virtuous conceptualizations of humility depends upon whether self-respect and a stable sense of self-worth are proposed to accompany humility. In other words, a stable sense of self-worth is fundamental to virtuous humility.[2] From an Aristotelian ethics standpoint, in which virtues represent the "golden mean" or middle ground between two extremes, humility represents "the mid-point between the two negative extremes of arrogance and lack of self-esteem" (Vera & Rodriguez-Lopez, 2004, p. 395) or "that crest of human excellence between arrogance and lowliness" (Morris et al., 2005, p. 1331). As Grenberg (2005) aptly states: "The humble person is one who has achieved a balance of appreciation of [personal] worth and limit, and thereby avoids despair. Humility . . . would not be a virtuous state unless it maintained just this balance. The humble person takes her awareness of limit as an impetus to action instead of as a warrant for despairing inaction" (p. 181).

Aside from the general, philosophical roots of humility, psychologists have conceptualized humility as a "multifaceted strength" (Morris et al., 2005;

Tangney, 2000), having multiple dimensions. As a newly considered construct in the field of psychology, the proposed dimensions of humility vary widely and have yet to reach consensus. However, in one systematic review of the humility literature, Owens (2009a)[3] identified the most commonly attributed or core facets of humility. Given space restrictions, we will highlight the three most prevalent dimensions that appear in past definitions of humility.

The most commonly cited dimension of humility involves the capacity or willingness to evaluate oneself without positive or negative exaggeration, leading to a more accurate, nondefensive, objective self-view. For instance, psychologists propose that humility entails an "accurate assessment of one's abilities and achievements" and the "ability to acknowledge one's mistakes, imperfections, gaps in knowledge, and limitations" (Tangney, 2002, p. 73), a nondefensive acknowledgment of strengths and limitations (Exline et al., 2004), and a willingness to see the self accurately (Morris, Brotheridge, & Urbanski, 2005; Owens, 2009a). In organizational parlance, humility appears to enable a person to conduct a more accurate S.W.O.T. analysis (i.e., Strengths, Weakness, Opportunities, and Threats) of intrapersonal resources.

Another common element of past definitions entails viewing others in an appreciative, nonthreatened way. For example, humility involves appreciating the value and contributions of others (Tangney, 2002, p. 74), acknowledging the strengths of others without feeling threatened by them (Exline et al., 2004), and having "an exalted view of the capacities of others rather than a negative view of oneself" (King & Hicks, 2007). In other words, humility allows a person to see and acknowledge the strengths of others without eliciting feelings of inferiority. If humility, derived from "humus," entails beliefs in shared human limit and dignity, this perspective makes the specialized knowledge, skills, and unique strengths of others more interesting and more admirable. Those who possess unique strengths may be seen as exemplars who have excelled despite ubiquitous human limits. Thus, humility may enable a person to transcend the comparative-competitive model of self-evaluation, allowing the humble person to view others as exemplars from whom she might learn.[4]

Last, previous definitions of humility often entail "teachability" or openness to new ideas, feedback, and advice. Tangney (2000, p. 72), for example, argued that "humility carries with it an open-mindedness, a willingness to . . . seek advice, and a desire to learn." Humility is said to connote being "open to new

paradigms . . . eager to learn from others" (Vera & Rodriguez-Lopez, 2004, p. 395). Templeton (1997) said, "Inherent in humility resides an open and receptive mind . . . it leaves us more open to learn from others" (p. 162). In other words, humility reflects openness to new ideas, advice, and information. In summary, by linking philosophical roots with psychological conceptualizations, we propose that humility entails a deeply held belief of shared human limits and worth that shapes how individuals view themselves (objectively), others (appreciatively), and new information (openly).[5]

Humility has been considered to be a trait (Ashton & Lee, 2008), an orientation (Morris, Brotheridge, & Urbanski, 2005; Owens, 2009b), and a "meta-attitude" (Grenberg, 2005). Despite differences in labeling the core nature of humility, there seems to be some agreement in the psychological literature that humility is something that can be developed[6] and that its expression may vary according to situational cues (Owens, Rubenstein, & Hekman, 2010; Tangney, 2002).

Past Operationalizations of Humility

One of the major obstacles to launching a rigorous study of humility is the challenge of measurement. One group of researchers asserts that trying to conduct research on humility is "humbling" because of difficulties in measuring this elusive construct (Halling et al., 1994). To date, researchers have developed self-report, implicit, other-report, and indirect measures of humility (or closely related constructs). Oddly, there does not appear to be a published self-report measure of trait humility independent from other constructs. Existing self-report measures of humility that do exist, blend it with *modesty*[7] (Peterson & Seligman, 2004), *honesty*[8] (Lee & Ashton, 2004), and *arrogance*[9] (Rowatt et al., 2006). An independent self-report measure of humility could be very useful.

However, self-reported measures should be interpreted with caution. Genuinely humble persons may not self-report being humble; whereas, narcissists sometimes create the appearance of humility to mask their arrogance or grandiose sense of self (American Psychiatric Association, 2004). According to some scholars, it takes cognitive effort to resist the temptation to present oneself in an overly positive fashion. When cognitive resources are depleted, people described the self as more narcissistic (i.e., arrogant, egotistical; see Vohs, Baumeister, & Ciarocco, 2005). Furthermore, since self-report measures of humility can easily be exaggerated (positively or negatively), researchers would be wise to assess and control for desirable responding as well.

Because self-report measures have proven less reliable (Exline et al., 2004; Owens, 2009a; Tangney, 2002) and somewhat paradoxical (i.e., what do we make of someone who reports themselves to be exceptionally humble?), scholars have attempted to tap humility indirectly. For example, humility has been operationalized as low self-esteem (Knight & Nadel, 1986; Weiss & Knight, 1980) and the negative difference between self and other evaluations (i.e., evaluating self lower than others, Furnham, Hosoe, & Tang, 2001). But these two operationalizations fail to capture the virtuous view of humility mentioned above.

In an attempt to circumvent limits of self-report, Rowatt et al. (2006) developed a Humility-Arrogance Implicit Association Test (IAT; Greenwald, McGhee, & Schwartz, 1998) that relies on reaction times to associate humility or arrogant trait terms with the self. The implicit measure of humility was internally and temporally consistent. Implicit humility correlated with implicit self-esteem, self-reported humility relative to arrogance, and self-reported narcissism (inversely) among college students (Rowatt et al., 2006). In general, implicit measures hold promise for accurately capturing personal humility because they are more difficult to manipulate or exaggerate than are explicit, self-report measures (Fiedler & Bluemke, 2005). However, the Humility-Arrogance IAT may not be widely used because it requires a personal computer and reaction-time software to administer and score. Low-tech, paper-pencil IATs exist to measure prejudice (Lemm et al., 2008), but have not yet been adapted to assess humility.

Other-report is a viable alternative to self-report or implicit measurement of humility, and several scholars have suggested using the consensus of "close observers" as the best approach (Exline et al., 2004; see also Davis, Worthington, & Hook, 2010). For instance, Richards (1992) argued that, although those who actually possess humility are not likely to attribute this virtue to themselves, close others may be able to observe this virtue more accurately. Testing this idea, Owens (2009a) developed and administered a self-report and other-report humility scale to multiple samples and found that, compared to self-report humility, measuring other-report humility is more reliable (i.e., has internal consistency and test–retest reliability) and has higher nomological validity (i.e., associated with other theoretically related constructs as expected).[10] In another study, other-report humility predicted performance and performance improvement, whereas self-reported humility did not (Owens, 2009a). This finding provides support for the claim that, compared to explicit self-report measures, other-report methodologies are the more effective method for capturing the seemingly elusive humility construct.

The Growing Importance of Humility in Organizations

At the beginning of this chapter, we claimed that humility in organizations was an idea whose time has come. As a virtue thought to foster learning, we suggest that the importance of humility is growing because work trends make learning within organizational contexts a key to maintaining competitive advantage. Trends such as increasingly fast-paced technological innovation, a global marketplace that requires understanding of and competition with local and international competitors, teams-based structures that entail increased collaboration and interdependence, and in general, an increasing amount of work centered on information and knowledge (i.e., inherent in this "information age") all suggest a premium to be placed on factors such as humility that foster individual and organizational learning capability (Bassi, Cheney, & Lewis, 1998; Senge, 2006). Indeed, it has been clear to organizational researchers since at least the classic work by Lawrence and Lorsch (1967) that the most successful organizations were more adaptive (learn more quickly) as their competitive environment became more turbulent. More recently, other researchers have demonstrated that with even more turbulent "high-velocity" environments like those facing the computer industry, successful organizations would have to learn how to change continuously (see Brown & Eisenhardt, 1997).

Acknowledging similar conditions of rapid change and uncertainty, Weick (2001) argued that leaders in the 21st century will need to allow "more migration of decisions to those with the expertise to handle them, and less convergence of decisions on people entitled by rank to make them" (p. 106). However, the leadership literature suggests that many organizational actors have an implicit theory that leaders do not admit mistakes, do not seek subordinate advice or approval on issues or decisions, and want their own way (Ensari & Murphy, 2003; Frasier & Lord, 1988). Certainly, leaders with such an orientation are a poor fit for organizations in dynamic, fast-paced industries that tend to be extremely reliant on specialists.

Of course, leaders are not the only participants in organizations who might fail to listen to and learn from others. Experts of differing specialties, participants from different functions or divisions, and those who represent yet other perspectives (e.g., different national cultures, labor vs. management) may resist understanding and learning from one another. Pfeffer and Sutton (2000) document a ubiquitous tendency for organizational participants to know intellectually (and generally) what to do, much more than what they actually try to implement. They discovered that this "knowing–doing gap" often related to the tendency for participants to value talking more than taking action and looking smart more than learning from mistakes. Trial-and-error learning is often rejected for fear of critique and rejection by others. Participants also often perceived themselves as competitors with others inside the organization more than with external competitors, leading to less knowledge sharing and collaboration. These individual and organizational tendencies described by the knowing–doing gap seem particularly counterproductive in a marketplace that is expected to increasingly reward learning and adaptation (Senge, 2006).

What does all of this have to do with humility? Given the elements of humility reviewed above, we propose that humility may mitigate the conflicts and organizational problems just described. Specifically, given its roots in grounded perceptions of shared limits and dignity (Grenberg, 2005) and the way humility entails acknowledging the strengths of others, we suggest that humility will enable greater acknowledgment and utilization of specialized expertise and foster less of an emphasis on hierarchy. Furthermore, organizational participants possessing humility are a better fit for firms in dynamic environments since they are more likely to admit their own knowledge gaps, admit past mistakes, genuinely value the expertise of others, and embrace trial-and-error learning.

Review of Extant Humility Research

One of the major purposes of this chapter is to outline a research stream for humility in organizations. In this section, we discuss current and developing theory and research on humility. Because humility in psychological and organizational studies is still in its early stages, we will report both published research and preliminary evidence from research in progress.[11] Although much has been said and theorized about the importance of humility in organizations, most of these propositions have not been tested. However, a few examples of recent research hypothesize and test the relationship between humility and individual performance, prosocial behavior, positive team environments (psychological safety, cohesion), team performance, and effective leadership.

Humility and Performance

The usefulness or relevance of any construct within organizational research is often judged by whether it has a significant impact on performance, which some consider the core criterion of organizational research (Wall et al., 2004). Although humility has been theoretically and qualitatively connected with high performance (Collins, 2005; Vera & Rodriguez-Lopez, 2004), until recently, this connection has not been rigorously tested through empirical study.

Some have hypothesized that humble persons perform at a higher level than less humble persons. For instance, among college students, implicit humility correlated positively with academic performance even after narcissism and conscientiousness were statistically controlled (see Rowatt et al., 2006, Study 2). In related research, Owens (2009b) suggested that humility would influence performance through the mechanisms of (a) better awareness of strengths and weaknesses informing decisions about the time and effort one would need to allocate to accomplish performance related tasks, (b) more attention to and benefitting from the positive social modeling of others (i.e., enhanced social learning from strong performers), and (c) more receptivity to feedback leading to adaptability (e.g., taking remedial action) after showings of poor or mediocre performance. In this study, at the end of the quarter, business students who had worked together on project teams for over 2 months rated each of their team members on humility (using an other-report humility scale developed by Owens, 2009a).[12] Individual grades on tests and assignments throughout the quarter represented individual performance. Overall, humility predicted individual performance beyond the common performance predictors of conscientiousness (Barrick & Mount, 2001), general mental ability (Dodrill, 1983; Wonderlic, 1973), and generalized self-efficacy (Schwarzer & Jerusalem, 1995). Furthermore, humility was the strongest predictor of performance improvement over the course of the term and showed a compensatory effect on performance for those with lower general mental ability. In other words, students with lower general mental ability performed poorly without humility but well with humility.

In a work context, the self-reported honesty-humility of employees predicted job performance ratings by their supervisors (Johnson, Rowatt, & Petrini, 2010). The significant relationship between honesty-humility and job performance persisted when conscientiousness and other personality dimensions were statistically controlled. It should be noted that honesty-humility predicted job performance among employees providing health care service to challenging clients. Thus, humility might be especially predictive of job performance in service-oriented industries.

Humility and Prosocial Behavior

With few exceptions, characteristics such as narcissism, with its attendant patterns of "self-aggrandizing arrogant behavior, hostility, entitlement, and lack of empathy toward others" (Morf & Rhodewalt, 2001, p. 178) consistently have been found to be associated with poor interpersonal relating (Vazire & Funder, 2006), conflict, and lower social acceptance (Paulus, 1998). In contrast, several scholars suggest that humility, which is considered the conceptual opposite of narcissism and arrogance (Tangney, 2000), will foster more positive, satisfying interpersonal relating (i.e., Exline et al., 2004). Specifically, where humility exists, more satisfying interrelating may occur since humility has been associated with taking the focus off the self and focusing more on others, and acknowledging others' strengths (Tangney, 2000). In support of this idea, clinical psychologists have employed "humility training" to help patients with overcompensating personality disorders (i.e., overly aggressive, lacking empathy) to learn to develop more satisfying and lasting interpersonal relationships (Means et al., 1990). In this training, humility is explained and offered as an alternative to assertiveness and is coupled with aggression/anger control interventions (p. 211).

Humility also appears to be a prosocial quality linked with good citizenship behaviors like cooperation and helping. Honesty-humility, for example, was found to correlate positively with cooperation in an economic game (Hilbig & Zettler, 2009). Among college students, self-reported humility and helping correlated positively, and implicit humility correlated positively with the amount of time volunteered to help a peer in need (LaBouff et al., 2010). Also, Exline and Geyer (2004) found that students who were primed with humility (i.e., they were asked to write about "an experience when you felt humble") took longer to defect in a prisoner's dilemma game. This evidence for the connection between humility and the prosocial behaviors of helping and cooperation has important implications for teams.

Humility in Teams

Given its characteristics, we propose that humility has significant relevance in the context of teams. In past research, team members who display characteristics that are considered the opposite of humility, such as self-enhancement and arrogance, are punished by team members because of their disruptiveness to team functioning (Anderson et al., 2006; Horowitz et al., 2006). A review of the teams literature yields ample evidence to support the claim that narcissism, arrogance, self-enhancement, and egocentrism are generally found to be counterproductive characteristics in teams because of their tendency to inhibit team functioning and to foster team member incompatibility (see Foushee, et al., 1986; Steiner, 1986).

One of the benefits of teams is the synergy that can occur as individual team member strengths are combined and as individual limitations are made up for by these strengths (Cannon-Bowers, Salas, & Converse, 1993). However, if team members do not acknowledge personal limits, or acknowledge the strengths of other team members, the intended benefits of teams may go unrealized.

To date, we are not aware of published research that examines the impact of humility in teams. However, an example of unpublished research using 85 student project teams showed a positive relationship between team member humble behaviors and the emergence of shared team processes such as task allocation effectiveness, cohesion, efficacy, citizenship behavior, and psychological safety (Owens & McCornack, 2010). This study also showed a strong, positive relationship between humility and team performance (the assessed quality of team projects by judges who were blind to the study's purpose), which was fully mediated by team cohesion.

Humility in Leadership

Much of the recent attention directed toward humility in management literature relates to its importance in leadership. Theorists have suggested that humility is becoming more critical for leaders who direct their organizations in increasingly dynamic and turbulent environments. For instance, Weick (2001) suggested that the increasing "unpredictability and unknowability" organizations face will require leaders of the 21st century to have "more humility and less hubris" (p. 106).

Humility may be viewed as a characteristic more typical and expected of followers rather than leaders. Indeed, some may view humility and leadership as oxymoronic since the prototypical leader often is perceived as being a strong-willed individual who exerts great influence on his or her subordinates (Ensari & Murphy, 2003). Leadership has long been associated with the personality characteristics of dominance, aggressiveness, and ascendancy; not the characteristics one usually associates with a humble leader. However, scholars who have carefully examined this construct insist that humility does not equate to weakness but rather requires a "unique sort of courage" (Exline et al. 2004, p. 64) to be willing to be vulnerable in order to improve oneself and help others.

One group of theorists argued that humility "is a critical strength for leaders and organizations possessing it, and a dangerous weakness for those lacking it" (Vera & Rodriguez-Lopez, 2004, p. 393). Past images of leaders who put on a front, who "fake it 'til they make it" and appear to know all the answers, seem especially outmoded in this new, dynamic "knowledge economy" (Dane & Pratt, 2007, p. 49) where it is becoming increasingly difficult to "figure it all out at the top" (Senge, 1990, p. 7). A growing number of scholars insist that humility is not incompatible with strong and effective leadership (Dhiman, 2002; Kerfoot, 1998; Lu, Gilmour, & Kao, 2001, 2004; Reimann, 1995). For example, Weick (2001) insists that, for a leader to humbly admit, "I don't know" is a sign of strong rather than weak leadership because such an action will foster learning, trust, and better direction-taking (p. 105). Admitting areas of ignorance as a leader and asking for the input of others, Weick argued, "establishes leader credibility in an unknowable world . . . strengthens rather than weakens relationship[s]" and activates follower sense-making (Weick, 2001, p. 112). Indeed, one of the main benefits of leader humility may be that such leaders act as exemplars to others of how to make sense of an increasingly uncertain and unpredictable workplace (p. 107). Further, Morris, Brotheridge, and Urbanski (2005) propose a theoretical model in which leader humility is viewed as an important characteristic for leadership effectiveness fostering supportiveness, socialized power, and participation. Kerfoot (1998) also argues the necessity of humility when speaking of leadership in a dynamic health care context.

Work on humility in leadership remains mostly theoretical at this point. However, we have discovered a few examples of research on humility in leadership. For instance, in a qualitative study, Reimann (1995) reports humility to be an important characteristic of strategic leaders who were best able to cope with rapid change. In addition, the results of Collin's (2001) inductive work examining why some companies reach and sustain exceptional performance showed that humility was one of the most important and pervasive traits possessed by leaders of these "Good to Great" firms. More specifically, Collins proposes

that realizing the highest, most effective level of leadership (i.e., Level 5 Leadership) entails achieving a "paradoxical blend of humility and intense professional will" (Collins, 2001, 2005).[13]

In a study of 111 CEO's in 105 computer and software firms between 1992 and 2004, Chatterjee and Hambrick (2007) found that those who were more "narcissistic" were associated with different firm outcomes than their more humble competitor CEOs. The more narcissistic a CEO, the more he or she tends to "swing for the fences," to change strategy more often and to pursue larger and more frequent acquisitions. The performance of the narcissistic CEOs was either much higher or much lower than less narcissistic CEOs, but their average performance was not worse. Humbler CEOs, as measured in this study, were more likely to pursue incremental improvements and to have less variable performance. These researchers measured narcissism (which they conceived of as the opposite of humility) using five measures: the size of the CEO's picture in the company's annual report; the number of times a CEO's name appeared in company news releases; the number of times a CEO referred to singular personal pronouns such as "I" or "me" in interviews; and two measures of the CEO's pay compared with the next highest-paid executive. Such measures emphasize self-focus, imply but do not measure an orientation to others, and fail to capture openness to learning, the principal humility dimensions measured in many other studies.

More recently, Owens, Rubenstein, and Hekman (2010) developed a theoretical model outlining the situational triggers, drivers, consequences, and contingencies of humility in organizational leadership based on 64 semistructured interviews with leaders from business, health care, military, government, nonprofit, and educational settings. The model assimilates insights[14] from these interviews into propositions about the enablers of developing and expressing humility in a leadership role, the contingencies that determine the efficacy of humility in leadership, and the individual- and team-/unit-level consequences of humility in leadership. Overall, there was a high level of consensus that humility in leadership could be developed (it is not a static trait) and that leader humility would positively influence performance through enhanced learning, more comprehensive decision-making, follower empowerment, and employee retention.

One critical question about the usefulness of studying humility in leadership is whether it is distinct from other established leadership approaches or styles. To address this question, preliminary evidence from roughly 1,500 employee ratings of their leaders indicates that leader humility is conceptually distinct[15] from transformational leadership (MLQ-5X, Bass & Avolio, 1994), charismatic leadership (Conger & Kanungo, 1994), authentic leadership (ALQ; Walumbwa, et al., 2008), and servant leadership (Greenleaf & Spears, 2002; Liden, Wayne, Zhao, & Henderson, 2008). The same study showed that leader humility is positively associated with unit cohesion, experimentation, and learning goal orientation (Owens, 2010, working paper).

Possible Disadvantages of Humility

Does humility fit in a volume devoted to extraordinary performance, outcomes, and processes in organizations? That is, will those who are humble put themselves and their groups forward enough to excel? Or, will they be so realistic in their views of self and others that they will fail to take risks and "shoot for the stars," as the study by Chatterjee and Hambrick (2007) suggests? Although we have made the opposite argument, in the business world, some may view "softer" traits like humility as irrelevant or even counterproductive in an economically driven, often cut-throat, competitive marketplace. In this section, we acknowledge some possible disadvantages of humility and discuss the potential boundary conditions for the usefulness of humility in organizations.

In the context of leadership, humble leaders are more likely to admit their mistakes or present themselves as less than perfect. We can imagine conditions in which such humility or honesty could be problematic. Goffee and Jones (2000) suggest that charismatic leaders should admit weakness, but only "selective" ones (not fatal flaws) and perhaps ones that might be considered a strength from another point of view (e.g., "workaholic"). However, these seem to be strategies that humble leaders would dismiss.

In addition, although we believe humility is a very positive trait in organizations, it is unclear to us whether humility will predict upward movement in an organization. Humble people might be perceived as unassertive or lacking in initiative. Or, they might not be noticed by their superiors, even though their work is good, because they attribute credit to others and honestly see themselves as being only partly responsible for successes. This effect may be magnified further if the peers of humble individuals are engaging in strategic self-enhancement in order to gain promotions and influence (see Pfeffer & Fong, 2005).

Finally, we also note a potential irony in the way we might study and write about humility in organizational contexts where this characteristic is likely to be treated instrumentally and with self-interest. From the Aristotelian point of view, virtues become self-reinforcing as they are internalized and as their practice creates a sense of self-actualization (personal fulfillment through acting with excellence, employing one's best strengths). Further they would not be individual character virtues if they were under strong situational control. Rather, they would merely be the demonstration of a skill of "situational virtue."[16] In summary, humility is most virtuous if it is practiced to a significant extent in the face of situational opposition (temptations to be arrogant, self-defensive, etc.), and practiced excellently, such that it becomes a "signature strength" that is able to give one a sense of self-mastery and joy in its use.

In this context, we note some important issues in approaches that could be taken in studying humility and acting on the findings we have reviewed thus far. For example, will an emphasis on the instrumental benefits of humility lead to organizational training and personal improvement efforts to "act humbly" that yield neither the sought-for performance benefits nor the personal character excellence and self-actualization? To what extent will participants in such training and organizations discount apparently humble behavior? To what extent will participants who act humbly but with self-interested motives fail to achieve the *eudaimonia* (sense of mastery and joy) described by Aristotle? That is, the way we study and talk about humility could tend to "commoditize" it and create a sense that it is a variable to be manipulated more than a virtue to be developed and internalized for proper motives and across challenging situations.

What Should Future Research Examine?

Since examining humility within the context of organizations is a relatively new effort, there are many potentially fruitful areas for future research. We will highlight a few areas that we feel are most important for the immediate progression of this research stream.

First, future research should examine and compare the agreement of other-report with implicit self-report measures of humility. It may be that implicit measures of humility might capture more cognitive aspects of humility, whereas other-report measures might tap more social aspects of humility. From a predictive validity standpoint, future research should consider selecting the method of measuring humility based on the nature of the outcome being predicted. For example, to test whether humility influences cognitive decision-making biases, such as overconfidence and hindsight bias, measuring humility implicitly may be the best approach. For predicting outcomes like prosocial behavior, leadership dynamics, or team relational processes, measuring humility via other-report may be the best approach.

Second, future research should examine the origins or antecedents of humility. As previously suggested, humility might stem from innate motivations or experiences or both. For instance, humility has been proposed to be driven by a deeply held belief in personal malleability (i.e., an incremental implicit theory of the self, Owens, 2009a; see also Dweck 1999). Humility may also be motivated by the "drive to learn," which has been identified as one of the "four innate drives," along with the drive to acquire, the drive to bond, and the drive to defend (Lawrence & Nohria, 2002, p. 5). Aside from innate needs or implicit theories, scholars have also suggested that humility may stem from past experiences of secure relational attachments, reality-based feedback about one's strengths and weaknesses, and not to have extreme emphasis placed on performance in one's past school (and perhaps work) experience (Exline et al., 2004). Other suggested antecedents include significant life reversals, having humble mentors (Collins, 2001), and religiosity (Tangney, 2000).

The innate motivations and experiential antecedents of humility, if understood, would enable organizations to better promote this characteristic and/or create a work environment in which humility can thrive. More fully understanding the antecedents of humility will also help to better inform organizations how to select for or develop this attribute in employees and leaders.

Third, given increased interest in organizational virtues in general (Cameron, Dutton, & Quinn, 2003), future research should examine the interaction between humility and other virtues. Aristotle's Golden Mean perspective suggests that virtues taken to an extreme can become vices. As a "temperance virtue" that helps to guard against excess (Park & Peterson, 2003), some have suggested that humility may be an important "balancer" of other positive characteristics or virtues. For example, Vera and Rodriguez-Lopez suggest that "courage without humility might become rashness" (2003 p. 397). In addition, since it has been suggested that humility is foundational to most other virtues (Grenberg, 2005), future research should also address the potential connections between humility and virtues such as forgiveness, gratitude, integrity, honesty, and empathy.

Fourth, it may also be meaningful to understand humility in teams within the framework of existing team development models. For instance, with reference to the punctuated equilibrium model (Gersick, 1988), future research might test whether teams with more humility may be quicker to recognize and break out of the initial inertia phase and transition to more effective team patterns (i.e., would "punctuate" more quickly). As companies continue to organize around teams, understanding the factors that contribute to quicker and more effective team adaptability and learning seems especially important in an increasingly dynamic, unpredictable, and information-rich workplace (see Kim & Mauborgne, 1998).

Fifth, in the domain of leadership, humility may also be "credited" differently depending on the role relationship. For example, what peers may view as humility, bosses may view as weakness, and subordinates may view as pandering. Future research should empirically address whether humility perceptions systematically differ across role relationships and whether the proposed relational outcomes associated with humility also differ by roles (i.e., whether humility is more strongly related to trust and loyalty for peers than for subordinates).

Understanding the relationship between leader humility and other established leadership approaches may be important to identifying where leader humility might supplement or provide elaborative insight to existing leadership models and thought. For instance, Morris et al. (2005) suggested that humility may be the differentiator between perceptions of genuine and pseudo-transformational leadership. Such propositions still need to be tested. Also, the degree and direction to which humility is related to and interacts with other positive leadership approaches, such as servant, authentic, and charismatic leadership, might also be important areas to explore in the future.

Sixth, future research should examine humility as an organizational characteristic. Vera and Rodriguez-Lopez (2004) write about organizational humility and share qualitative insights from a "humble organization." However, more needs to be understood about how to instill humility in organizational processes and culture, and how these organizational characteristics might enable the development of individual humility. Alisdair MacIntyre (1984) presents a neo-Aristotelian perspective on the development and practice of virtues that suggests some of the organizational elements that might be important to the development of organizational support for virtues. He argues that the Greek conception of virtues was that they were learned and practiced in community and that, without such community support and practice, excellence in virtues cannot be achieved. He posits that such communities make it clear "of what narrative we are a part." That master narrative identifies and illustrates the community's virtues and helps community members define and practice excellence in those virtues. Moore's (2002) analysis of MacIntyre suggests that this perspective has relevance for modern work organizations if they can establish communities of practice around particular virtues to become excellent in their practice and if they can orient the particular virtues to addressing the demands of external stakeholders (who are not likely to understand or value such virtues per se). Collins' (2001) qualitative and inductive work may also point to organization-level approaches that foster the development of humility along with other virtues and are thus more likely to facilitate extraordinary organizational and personal outcomes.

Such contributions raise a number of possibilities and questions. First, we could consider the organization as a context for the development of humility in participants and ask: What organizational contexts are most and least conducive to the development of humility in participants? Next, we might consider how such organizational contexts are developed. Further, we could consider the extent to which organizational contexts that are composed of high proportions of humble participants and that provide a refining host for learning and practicing the virtue of humility facilitate accomplishing extraordinary outcomes. In the spirit of the psychological and philosophical interests in character virtues and strengths (see Peterson & Seligman, 2004), we could ask whether the adoption and practice of classic virtues (including humility) is conducive to "the good life" of individuals, as well as to overall organizational performance, or whether these pursuits are potentially in conflict with one another (see Moore & Beadle, 2006).

Conclusion

In this chapter, we made a case for the growing importance of humility within organizational contexts. Increasingly uncertain and dynamic work environments make humility not only relevant but requisite for success in today's work world, offering "strategic value for firms by furnishing organizational members with a realistic perspective on themselves, the firm, and the environment" (Vera & Rodriguez-Lopez, 2004, p. 393). We hope the points discussed in this chapter spur further interest in humility and enable further examination of this "classical source of strength" (Tangney, 2000, p. 70) within an organizational context.

Acknowledgments
We would like to thank Julia Exline and Kim Cameron for their helpful comments on an earlier draft of this chapter.

Notes

1. For instance, David Hume (1994, p. 219/270) said: "Humility . . . and the whole train of the monkish virtues; for what reason are they everywhere rejected by men of sense, but because they serve to no purpose? We justly, therefore, transfer them to the opposite column, and place them in the catalogue of vices."

2. According to Grenberg (2005), for the humble person "The urgency of the questions of self-worth recedes because they have been adequately answered. The judgments and feelings which constitute her meta-attitude [about herself] are not being made constantly but rather, for the successfully humble person, are completed and receded into the background" (p. 159). Tendencies to self-enhance and to maintain an inflated view of oneself (Kruger & Dunning, 1999; Taylor & Brown, 1994) may stem from lingering or unresolved questions about one's self-worth and have been associated with maladjustment, brittle ego-defense systems, deceitfulness, and lower productivity (see Colvin, Block, & Funder, 1995).

3. This literature analysis of the definitional dimensions of humility was conducted independently by Owens and a research assistant, then compared for agreement.

4. The concept of appreciative inquiry (Cooperrider & Srivastva, 1987) seems relevant to this facet of humility, especially if considered at the dyadic or interpersonal level.

5. Past definitions of humility have also mentioned, although less often, the dimensions of self-transcendence (Morris et. al, 2005), low self-focus (Tangney, 2002), an orientation toward service, and self-complacency avoidance (Vera & Rodriguez-Lopez, 2004).

6. Humility, as a virtue, is "dynamic in nature and capable of improvement or deterioration" (Vera & Rodriguez-Lopez, 2004, p. 394).

7. Modesty connotes a *restrained* or 'played down' estimation of one's accomplishments and having the social savvy not to boast or talk too much about oneself. (Exline, et al., 2004; Owens, Johnson, & Mitchell, 2010)

8. In this study, honesty seems to capture sincerity when interacting with others.

9. In this study, arrogance is operationalized simply as the conceptual opposite of humility.

10. These scales were empirically tested with student and field samples and found to be related to, but distinct from the constructs of openness to experience (McCrae & Costa, 1987), modesty (Peterson & Seligman, 2004), learning goal orientation (VandeWalle, 1997), honesty-humility (Ashton & Lee, 2008), narcissism (Margolis & Thomas, 1980), and core self-evaluations (Judge, Erez, Bono, & Thoresen, 2003; Owens, 2009).

11. I.e., from doctoral dissertations and peer-reviewed conference proceedings.

12. In this study, team member ratings of team participation and contribution were also assessed and controlled for to help rule out explanations that the results were driven by general classroom engagement or interpersonal liking.

13. Examples of successful executives recognized for their humility include Sam Walton (WalMart), Mary Kay Ash (Mary Kay),

Herb Keller (Southwest), Craig Weatherup (Pepsi Cola Company), Darwin Smith (Kimberly-Clark), Ingvar Kamprad (IKEA), David Neeleman (JetBlue), and Joe Lee (Darden Restaurants).

14. Using conventional guidelines for analyzing qualitative data (i.e., from Miles & Huberman, 1994; Lee, 1999), transcribed interview responses were content analyzed and coded by independent researchers. The Cohen's κ agreement score across independent codings was 0.82.

15. Principal components analyses were conducted for each leadership scale and humility. Factors were set so that they were free to vary. No cross-loadings were observed between the humility items and all other leadership measures. Two items from established leadership scales loaded above 0.40 onto the humility factor.

16. We agree with Peterson and Seligman (2004) that humility and other virtues may find varied expression across situations and that they may also be developed by particular enabling conditions (family, school, mentors, etc.). However, we are also seeking to discover individual differences that serve as character strengths and that are relatively consistent across situations. If we are only considering behavior that is to a large extent situationally determined, we miss the element of choice and will that are essential to virtue.

References

American Psychiatric Association. (2004). *Diagnostic and statistical manual of mental disorders*. (4th ed., text rev.). Washington, DC: Author.

Anderson, C., Srivastava, S., Beer, J.S., Spataro, S., & Chatman, J.A. (2006). Knowing your place: Self-perceptions of status in face-to-face groups. *Journal of Personality and Social Psychology, 91*(6), 1094–1110.

Ashton, M.C., & Lee, K. (2008). The HEXACO model of personality structure and the importance of the H factor. *Social and Personality Psychology Compass, 2*, 1952–1962.

Barrick, M.R., Mount, M.K., & Judge, T.A. (2001). Personality and performance at the beginning of the new millennium: What do we know and where do we go next? *International Journal of Selection and Assessment, 9*, 2–29.

Bass, B.M., & Avolio, B.J. (1994). *Improving organizational effectiveness through transformational leadership*. Thousand Oaks, CA: Sage Publications.

Bassi, L., Cheney, S., & Lewis, E. (1998). Trends in workplace learning: Supply and demand in interesting times. *Training and Development, 52*, 51.

Brown, S.L., & Eisenhardt, K.M. (1997). The art of continuous change: Linking complexity theory and time-paced evolution in relentlessly shifting organizations. *Administrative Science Quarterly, 42*(1), 1–34.

Cameron, K.S., Dutton, J.E., & Quinn, R.E. (2003). *Positive organizational scholarship: Foundations of a new discipline*. San Francisco: Berrett-Koehler.

Cannon-Bowers, J.A., Salas, E., & Converse, S.A. (1993). Shared mental models in expert team decision making. In N.J. Castellan, Jr. (Ed.), *Individual and group decision making: Current issues* (pp. 221–246). Hillsdale, NJ: Erlbaum.

Chatterjee, A., & Hambrick, D.C. (2007). It's all about me: Narcissistic chief executive officers and their effects on company strategy and performance. *Administrative Science Quarterly, 52*, 351–386.

Collins, J. (2001). *Good to great*. New York: Harper, Collins.

Collins, J. (2005). Level 5 leadership: The triumph of humility and fierce resolve. *Harvard Business Review, 7*, 136–146.

Colvin, C.R., Block, J., & Funder, D.C. (1995). Overly positive self-evaluations and personality: Negative implications for mental health. *Journal of Personality and Social Psychology, 68*, 1152–1162.

Conger, J.A., & Kanungo, R.N. (1994). Charismatic leadership in organizations: Perceived behavioral attributes and their measurement. *Journal of Organizational Behavior, 15*, 439–452.

Cooperrider, D.L., & Srivastva, S. (1987). Appreciative inquiry in organizational life. *Research in Organizational Change and Development, 1*, 129–169.

Crossan, M., Vera, D., & Nanjad, L. (2008). Transcendent leadership: Strategic leadership in dynamic environments. *Leadership Quarterly, 19*, 569–581.

Dane, E., & Pratt, M.G. (2007). Exploring intuition and its role in managerial decision making. *Academy of Management Journal, 32*, 33–54.

Davis, D.E., Worthington, E.L., Jr., & Hook, J.N. (2010). Humility: Review of measurement strategies and conceptualization as personality judgment. *The Journal of Positive Psychology, 5*, 243–252.

Dhiman, S. (2002). Zen of Learning: Folkways through wisdom traditions. *The Journal of American Academy of Business, Cambridge, 2*, 1.

Dodrill, C.B. (1983). Long-term reliability of the Wonderlic Personnel Test. *Journal of Consulting and Clinical Psychology, 51*, 316–317.

Dweck, C.S. (1999). *Self-theories: Their role in motivation, personality and development*. Philadelphia: Taylor and Francis/Psychology Press.

Ensari, N., & Murphy, E.S. (2003). Cross-cultural variations in leadership perceptions and attribution of charisma to the leader. *Organizational Behavior & Human Decision Processes, 92*, 52–66.

Exline, J.J., Campbell, W.K., Baumeister, R.F., Joiner, T.E., & Krueger, J.I. (2004). Humility and modesty. In C. Peterson, & M. Seligman (Eds.), *The Values In Action (VIA) classification of strengths* (pp. 461–475). Cincinnati: Values in Action Institute.

Exline, J., & Geyer, A. (2004). Perceptions of humility: A preliminary study. *Self and Identity, 3*(2), 95–115.

Fiedler, L., & Bluemke, M. (2005). Faking the IAT: Aided and unaided response control on the Implicit Association Tests. *Basic and Applied Social Psychology, 27*, 307–316.

Fineman, S. (2006). On being positive: Concerns and counterpoints. *Academy of Management Review, 31*, 270–291.

Foushee, H.C., Lauber, J.K., Baetge, M.M., & Acomb, D.B. (1986). *Crew factors in flight operations III: The operational significance of exposure to short-haul air transport operations*. (NASA Technical Memorandum 88322). Washington, DC: National Aeronautics and Space Administration.

Fraser, S.L., & Lord, R.G. (1988). Stimulus prototypicality and general leadership impressions: Their role in leadership and behavioral ratings. *Journal of Psychology, 122*, 291–303.

Furnham, A., Hosoe, T., & Tang, T. (2001). Male hubris and female humility? A cross-cultural study of ratings of self, parental and sibling multiple intelligence in America, Britain and Japan. *Intelligence, 30*, 101–115.

Gersick, C. (1988). Time and transition in work teams: Toward a new model of group development. *Academy of Management Journal, 31*, 9–41.

Goffee, R., & Jones, G. (2000). Why should anyone be led by you? *Harvard Business Review, September-October*, 63–70.

Greenleaf, R.K., & Spears, L.C. (2002). *Servant leadership: A journey into the nature of legitimate power and greatness* (25th anniversary edition). Mahwah, NJ: Paulist Press.

Greenwald, A.G., McGhee, D.E., & Schwartz, J.L.K. (1998). Measuring individual differences in implicit cognition: The implicit association test. *Journal of Personality and Social Psychology, 74*, 1464–1480.

Grenberg, J.M. (2005). *Kant and the ethics of humility: A story of dependence, corruption and virtue.* Cambridge, MA: Cambridge University Press.

Harb, C., & Smith, P.B. (2008). Self-construals across cultures: Beyond independence-interdependence. *Journal of Cross-Cultural Psychology, 39*, 178–197.

Halling, S., Kunz, G., & Rowe, J.O. (1994). The contributions of dialogal psychology to phenomenological research. *Journal of Humanistic Psychology, 34*, 109–131.

Hamel, G. (2007). Competition for competence and interpartner learning within international strategic alliances. *Strategic Management Journal, 12*, 83–103.

Hilbig, B.E., & Zettler, I. (2009). Pillars of cooperation: Honesty-humility, social value orientations, and economic behavior. *Journal of Research in Personality, 43*, 516–519.

Horowitz, L.M., Wilson, K.R., Turan, B., Zolotsev, P., Constantino, M.J., & Henderson, L. (2006). How interpersonal motives clarify the meaning of interpersonal behavior: A revised circumplex model. *Personality and Social Psychology Review, 10*(1), 67–86.

Hugo, V. (1877/2005). *The history of a crime.* (T. H. Joyce, & A. Locker, Trans.). New York: Mondial. (Original work published 1877).

Humble. (2010). In *Online Etymology Dictionary.* Retrieved March 09, 2010, from http://dictionary.reference.com/browse/humble.

Hume, D. (1994). *Hume: Political essays (Cambridge texts in the history of political thought)* K. Haakonssen (Ed.). New York: Cambridge University Press.

Ireland, R.D., & Hitt, M.A. (1999). Achieving and maintaining strategic competitiveness in the 21st century: The role of strategic leadership. *Academy of Management Executive, 13*(1), 43–57.

Johnson, M., Rowatt, W.C., & Petrini, L. (2010). Humility predicts job performance. Manuscript in preparation.

Judge, T.A., Erez, A., Bono, J., & Thoresen, C.J. (2003). The core self-evaluations scale: Development of a measure. *Personnel Psychology, 56*, 303–331.

Kerfoot, K. (1998). The strategic use of humility. *Nursing Economics, 16*, 238–239.

Kim, W.C., & Mauborgne, R. (1998). Procedural justice, strategic decision making, and the knowledge economy. *Strategic Management Journal, 19*, 323–338.

King, L.A., & Hicks, J.A. (2007). What ever happened to "What might have been"? *American Psychologist, 62*, 625–636.

Knight, P., & Nadel, J. (1986). Humility revisited: Self-esteem, information search, and policy consistency. *Organizational Behavior and Human Decision Processes, 38*, 196–207.

Kotter, J.P. (1995). Leading change: Why transformation efforts fail. *Harvard Business Review, 73*(2), 59–67.

Kruger, J., & Dunning, D. (1999). Unskilled and unaware of it: How difficulties in recognizing one's own incompetence lead to inflated self-assessments. *Journal of Personality and Social Psychology, 77*, 1121–1134.

LaBouff, J., Rowatt, W.C., Johnson, M., & McCullough, G. (2010). Humble people are more helpful than less humble people: Evidence from three studies. Manuscript under review.

Lawrence, P.R., Lorsch, J.W. (1967). Differentiation and integration in complex organizations. *Administrative Science Quarterly, 12*(1), 1–47.

Lawrence, P.R., Nohria, N. (2002). *Driven: How human nature shapes our choices.* San Francisco: Jossey-Bass.

Lee, T.W. (1999). *Using qualitative methods in organizational research.* Thousand Oaks, CA: Sage Publications.

Lee, K., & Ashton, M.C. (2004). Psychometric properties of the HEXACO Personality Inventory. *Multivariate Behavioral Research, 39*, 329–358.

Lemm, K.M., Lane, K.A., Sattler, D.N., Khan, S.R., & Nosek, B.A (2008). Assessing implicit cognitions with a paper-format Implicit Association Test. In M.A. Morrison, & T.G. Morrison (Eds.), *The psychology of modern prejudice* (pp. 123–146). Hauppauge, NY: Nova Science Publishers.

Liden, R.C., Wayne, S.J., Zhao, H., & Henderson, D. (2008). Servant leadership: Development of a multidimensional measure and multi-level assessment. *The Leadership Quarterly, 19*, 161–177.

Lu, L., Gilmour, R., & Kao, S.F. (2001). Cultural values and happiness: An East-West dialogue. *Journal of Social Psychology, 141*, 477–493.

MacIntyre, A. (1984). *After virtue* (2nd ed.). Notre Dame, IN: University of Notre Dame Press.

Margolis, H.D., & Thomas, V. (1980). The measurement of narcissism in adolescents with and without behavioral and emotional disabilities. Unpublished master's thesis, United States International University, San Diego, CA.

McCrae, R.R., & Costa, P.T. (1987). Validation of the 5-factor model of personality across instruments and observers. *Journal of Personality and Social Psychology, 52*, 81–90.

Means, J.R., Wilson, G.L., Sturm, C., Biron, J.E., & Bach, P.J. (1990). Theory and practice: Humility as a psychotherapeutic formulation. *Counseling Quarterly, 3*, 211–215.

Miles, M.B., & Huberman, A.M. (1994). *Qualitative data analysis: An expanded sourcebook.* Thousand Oaks, CA: Sage Publications.

Moore, G. (2002). On the implications of the practice-institution distinction: MacIntyre and the application of modern virtue ethics to business. *Business Ethics Quarterly, 12*(1), 19–32.

Moore, G., & Beadle, R. (2006). In search of organizational virtue in business: Agents, goods, practices, institutions, and environments. *Organization Studies, 27*, 369–389.

Morf, C.C., & Rhodewalt, F. (2001). Unraveling the paradoxes of narcissism: A dynamic self-regulatory processing model. *Psychological Inquiry, 12*(4), 177–196. http://www.informaworld.com/smpp/title~db=all~content=t775648164~tab=issueslist~branches=12-v12.

Morris, J.A., Brotheridge, C.M., & Urbanski, J.C. (2005). Bringing humility to leadership: Antecedents and consequences of leader humility. *Human Relations, 58*, 1323–1350.

Owens, B.P. (2009a). Humility in organizational leadership. *Dissertation Abstract International, 70*(8) (UMI No. AAT 3370531) Retrieved March 20, 2010.

Owens, B.P. (2009b). Humility in organizations: Establishing construct, nomological, and predictive validity. *Academy of Management Best Paper Proceedings*, 1–6.

Owens, B.P. (2010). *Is it distinct? Establishing conceptual and empirical validity for leader humility.* Working paper.

Owens, B.P., & McCornack, D. (2010, August). *The influence of humility on team psychological safety, cohesion, task allocation effectiveness, efficacy, and performance.* Paper presented at the Academy of Management meetings, Montreal, Canada.

Owens, B.P., Rubenstein, A., & Hekman, D.R. (2010, August). *The antecedents, consequences, and contingencies of humility in leadership: A qualitative approach*. Paper presented at the Academy of Management meetings, Montreal, Canada.

Park, N., & Peterson, C.M. (2003). Virtues and organizations. In K. Cameron, J. Dutton, & R. Quinn (Eds.), *Positive organizational scholarship: Foundations of a new discipline*. San Francisco: Berrett-Koehler Publishers.

Paulhus, D.L. (1998). Interpersonal and intrapsychic adaptiveness of trait self-enhancement: A mixed blessing? *Journal of Personality and Social Psychology, 74*, 1197–1208.

Peterson, C., & Seligman, M.E.P. (2004). *Character strengths and virtues: A handbook and classification*. Washington, DC: American Psychological Association; New York: Oxford University Press.

Pfeffer, J., & Fong, C.T. (2005). Building organization theory from first principles: The self-enhancement motive and understanding power and influence. *Organization Science, 16*(4), 372–388.

Pfeffer, J., & Sutton R.I. (2000). *The knowing-doing gap: How smart companies turn knowledge into action*. Boston: Harvard Business School Press.

Reimann, B.C. (1995). Leading strategic change. *Planning Review, 23*, 6–10.

Richards, N. (1992). *Humility*. Philadelphia: Temple University Press.

Roberts, C.R., & Wood, W.J. (2003). Humility and epistemic goods. In M. DePaul, & L. Zagzebski (Eds.), *Intellectual virtue: Perspectives from ethics and epistemology*. Oxford: Oxford University Press.

Rowatt, W.C., Powers, C., Targhetta, V., Comer, J., Kennedy, S., & LaBouff, J. (2006). Development and initial validation of an implicit measure of humility relative to arrogance. *Journal of Positive Psychology, 1*, 198–211.

Seligman, M.E. P., & Csikszentmihaly, M. (2000). Positive psychology: An introduction. *American Psychologist, 55*, 5–14.

Senge, P.M. (1990). *The fifth discipline: The art and practice of the learning organization*. New York: Currency/Doubleday.

Senge, P.M. (2006). *The fifth discipline: The art and practice of the learning organization* (Rev. ed.). New York: Currency/Doubleday.

Schwarzer, R., & Jerusalem, M. (1995). Generalized Self-Efficacy scale. In J. Weinman, S. Wright, & M. Johnston (Eds.), *Measures in health psychology: A user's portfolio. Causal and control beliefs* (pp. 35–37). Windsor, UK: Nfer-Nelson.

Steiner, I.D. (1986). Paradigms and groups. In L. Berkowitz (Ed.), *Advances in experimental social psychology* Vol. 19 (pp. 251–289). Orlando: Academic Press.

Tangney, J.P. (2000). Humility: Theoretical perspectives, empirical findings and directions for future research. *Journal of Social and Clinical Psychology, 19*, 70–82.

Tangney, J.P. (2002). Humility. In C.R. Snyder, & S.J. Lopez (Eds.), *Handbook of positive psychology*. New York: Oxford University Press.

Taylor, S.E., & Brown, J.D. (1994). Positive illusions and well-being revisited: Separating fact from fiction. *Psychological Bulletin, 116*, 21–27.

Templeton, J. (1997). *Worldwide laws of life*. Philadelphia: Templeton Foundation Press.

VandeWalle, D. (1997). Development and validation of a work domain goal orientation instrument. *Educational and Psychological Measurement, 57*(6), 995–1015.

Vazire, S., & Funder, D.C. (2006). Impulsivity and the self-defeating behavior of narcissists. *Personality and Social Psychology Review, 10*, 154–165.

Vera, D., & Rodriguez-Lopez, A. (2004). Humility as a source of competitive advantage. *Organizational Dynamics, 33*(4), 393–408.

Vohs, K.D., Baumeister, R.F., & Ciarocco, N.J. (2005). Self-regulation and self-presentation: Regulatory resource depletion impairs impression management and effortful self-presentation depletes regulatory resources. *Journal of Personality and Social Psychology, 88*, 632–657.

Wall, T.D., Michie, J., Patterson, M., Wood. S.J., Sheehan, M., Clegg. C.W., & West, M. (2004). On the validity of subjective measures of company performance. *Personnel Psychology, 57*, 95–118.

Walumbwa, F.O., Avolio, B.J., Gardner, W.L., Wernsing, T.S., & Peterson, S.J. (2008). Authentic leadership: Development and validation of a theory-based measure. *Journal of Management, 34*, 89–126.

Weick, K.E. (2001). Leadership as the legitimation of doubt. In W. Bennis, G.M. Spreitzer, & T.G. Cummings (Eds.), *The future of leadership: Today's top leadership thinkers speak to tomorrow's leaders*. San Francisco: Jossey—Bass.

Weiss, H., & Knight, P. (1980). The utility of humility: Self-esteem, information search, and problem-solving efficiency. *Organizational Behavior and Human Performance, 25*, 216–223.

Wonderlic, E.F. (1973). *Wonderlic personnel test: Manual*. Los Angeles: Western Psychological Services.

Compassion Revealed

What We Know About Compassion at Work (and Where We Need to Know More)

Jacoba M. Lilius, Jason Kanov, Jane E. Dutton, Monica C. Worline, *and* Sally Maitlis

Abstract

In this chapter, we examine work by those who have responded to Frost's (1999) call for research that accounts for suffering and compassion in work organizations. We add to this line of inquiry by reviewing the organizational research on compassion published over the past decade and illuminating connections with extant research on related phenomena. In particular, we explore current understandings of the nature and impact of compassion at work, the conditions that facilitate compassion in work organizations, and efforts to institutionalize compassion. In pointing to what we see as fruitful directions for future research, we invite more scholars to see suffering and compassion as critical and pervasive aspects of organizational life.

Keywords: Compassion, suffering, care, empathy, emotion

As organizational researchers, we tend to see organizations and their members with little other than a dispassionate eye and a training that inclines us toward abstractions that do not include consideration of the dignity and humanity of those in our lens. Our hearts, our compassion, are not engaged and we end up being outside of and missing the humanity, the "aliveness" of organizational life. . . . As a result, we miss some pretty fundamental and important aspects of organizational life and functioning, and our theories and practices probably distort more than they illuminate what they purport to explain. If, as the Buddha is reported to have said, "suffering is optional but an inevitable part of the human condition," then we ought to find suffering as a significant aspect of organizational life . . . our theories ought to reflect this somehow.

—*Frost*, 1999, p. 128

It has been over a decade since Frost issued this resounding call for organizational scholars to rethink our theories and practices in ways that more fully see, appreciate, and account for suffering and compassion as essential in organizational life. At the heart of Frost's call is the intuitive understanding that suffering is a fundamental and inevitable aspect of the human condition (Barasch, 2005; Dalai Lama, 1995; Nussbaum, 1996; Wuthnow, 1991)

and that compassion is both needed and more likely to occur when it is present.

Suffering is a broad term that encompasses a wide range of unpleasant subjective experiences including physical and emotional pain, trauma, psychological distress, and existential anguish, and feelings of disconnection (Baumeister & Leary, 1995; Blauner, 1964; Driver, 2007; Durkheim, 1897; Kanov, 2005; Leary & Kowalski, 1995; Leary,

Springer, Negel, Ansell, & Evans, 1998; Miller & Stiver, 1997; Pollock & Sands, 1997; Reich, 1989; Scarry, 1985; Schulz et al., 2007; Tangney & Fischer, 1995; Weiss, Bowlby, & Riesman, 1973) that may be triggered by the occurrence of certain events or circumstances (Cassell, 1999; Schulz et al., 2007). For example, suffering may stem from events in an employee's personal life, such as the loss or illness of a loved one (Hazen, 2003; Lilius et al., 2008), the breakup of a romantic relationship (Manns & Little, 2010), physical illness and chronic pain (Dewa & Lin, 2000), or mental illnesses (World Health Organization, 1996, cited in Dewa & Lin, 2000). Suffering can also be triggered by events within the workplace, such as incivility from colleagues (e.g., Cortina, Magley, Williams, & Langhout, 2001) or simply the toll of caring for others as part of the work role (e.g., Figley, 1995; Jacobson, 2006; Maslach, 1982) (see Driver, 2007 for a review of various causes of suffering at work; see also Bhagat, McQuaid, Lindholm, & Segovis, 1985).

Regardless of whether these events occur within or outside of the organization, suffering knows no such boundaries (Burke & Greenglass, 1987; Fox & Dwyer, 1999; Frone, Russell, & Cooper, 1992; Hazen, 2008; Lilius et al., 2010; Zedeck & Mosier, 1990); thus, as part of the human condition, it is a ubiquitous feature of all workplaces. This is not only a moral concern, but also a financial one. It is estimated that employee grief, for example, costs U.S. businesses upward of $75 billion annually (Zaslow, 2002), whereas job stress and burnout have been estimated to cost industry hundreds of billions of dollars annually (Butts, 1997). These estimates are staggering, and even more so considering that they are relatively dated and capture only two forms of suffering.

This brief overview of the triggers and kinds of suffering found in organizations clearly conveys the multiple opportunities for and importance of compassion at work. Frost's call for scholars to acknowledge the presence of suffering and compassion in organizations inspired research that has contributed to our understanding of the nature of compassion and suffering in work organizations and of the powerful effects of compassion on those who receive it, witness its accomplishment, and are involved in its delivery. In addition, scholars are now exploring the organizational conditions that foster compassion. This chapter adds to this line of inquiry by reviewing the organizational research on compassion published over the past decade,

illuminating connections to extant research on related phenomena, and inviting scholars to see suffering and compassion as critical and pervasive aspects of organizational life.

Below, we introduce our conceptualization of compassion and discuss its relationship to pain and suffering. We then review the impact of compassion, its facilitating conditions in work organizations, and efforts to institutionalize compassion. We end the chapter with a discussion of what we see as fruitful directions for future research.

Conceptual Foundations of the Study of Compassion

Compassion comes into the English language by way of the Latin root *passio*, which means to suffer, paired with the Latin prefix *com*, meaning together—to suffer together. The concept of compassion and its link to suffering has deep philosophical and religious roots. For instance, Christian theologian Thomas Aquinas noted the interdependence of suffering and compassion when he wrote: "No one becomes compassionate unless he suffers" (cited in Barasch, 2005, p. 13). Ancient Chinese traditions acknowledge the interrelationship of suffering and human concern in the figure of Kwan Yin, often referred to as the goddess of compassion. Hindu imagery depicts compassion through a half-ape half-human deity, Hanuman, whose chest is cleaved open to reveal his heart to others undefended. Some Buddhist traditions induct individuals seeking to cultivate their compassion into the vow of the Boddhisattva, whose life is dedicated to being present with and relieving the suffering of all beings (Barasch, 2005; Chodron, 1997). A recurring theme is thus the relationship between one's own suffering and self-oriented compassion, and compassion for others (Neff, 2003, 2009).

Another important thread is the fundamental nature of compassion and suffering to our basic humanity. Modern philosophers, spiritual thinkers, and social scientists note the importance of compassion in social life (e.g., Blum, 1980; Frost, 1999; Keltner, 2008; Nussbaum, 1996, 2001; Post, 2003; Solomon, 1998; Wuthnow, 1991) and the Dalai Lama (1995) equates compassion with humanity. Keltner (2008) goes a step further, arguing that humans have evolved to be compassionate. Compassion, as inextricably linked with suffering and as core to our humanity, is thus an age-old concept that pervades writing and thinking across diverse cultures and traditions.

How Is Compassion Manifest in Work Organizations?

Writing for organizational scholarship, Kanov et al. (2004) represent compassion as a three-part process hinging on the interrelationship of self and other in the midst of suffering. More specifically, compassion consists of attention to or noticing of suffering; empathic concern, a felt relation with the other; and action to lessen or relieve suffering (see also Clark, 1997). This conceptualization defines compassion from the perspective of the compassion provider and differentiates compassion from empathy (Davis, 1996). It also stands apart from conceptualizations of compassion as a trait (e.g., Cosley, McCoy, Saslow, & Epel, 2010) and moves beyond a view of compassion as an emotion (Goetz, Keltner, & Simon-Thomas, 2010; Lazarus, 1991; Nussbaum, 1996).

The noticing of suffering involves awareness of the presence or possible presence of suffering. That is, one may notice that someone else is suffering or that an individual is under some kind of duress without being certain that that person is suffering. Because noticing brings awareness, it is therefore a necessary (but not sufficient) precondition for the subsequent steps of the compassion process (Frost, 2003). Felt empathic concern, the second part of the compassion process, is the feeling of compassion (for a review, see Goetz et al., 2010)—the "suffering with" that emotionally connects one person to another who is struggling or suffering (Kanov et al., 2004). Research reveals the role of perspective-taking for a host of organizational processes, including the production and transfer of knowledge (Boland & Tenkasi, 1995), negotiation (e.g., Galinsky & Moskowitz, 2000), and contextual performance (Parker & Axtell, 2001). Our framework builds on this research to suggest that empathic concern, which involves perspective-taking, plays an important role in organizations by connecting the awareness of suffering to compassionate responding (Kanov et al., 2004; see also Oveis, Horberg, & Keltner, 2010).

Compassionate responding is the third part of the compassion process and refers to actions or displays that occur in response to others' suffering with the aim of lessening, alleviating, or making it more bearable (Kanov et al., 2004; see also Reich, 1989). Research suggests that compassionate responding in work organizations can take at least three forms: emotional support, material goods, and the granting of time and flexibility (Dutton, Worline, Frost, & Lilius, 2006; Frost, Dutton, Worline, &

Wilson, 2000; Lilius et al., 2008), which can be either work-related or home-related (Dutton, Spreitzer, Heaphy, & Stephens, 2010). In this way, the responding component of the compassion process is closely linked to the family of prosocial behaviors (Brief & Motowidlo, 1986; Penner, Dovidio, Piliavin, & Schroeder, 2004) or interpersonal citizenship (for a review, see Podsakoff, MacKenzie, Paine, & Bachrach, 2000), which focuses on helping behaviors or intentional actions that benefit another (Dovidio & Penner, 2004).

FORMS OF COMPASSION

With the above three-part definition as a foundation, research has demonstrated that compassion varies in two key ways. First, compassion can range in form from a more dyadic process to a more collective and organized one. Dyadic compassion is present when one person (e.g., an employee or customer) notices the suffering of another person, feels empathic concern, and responds (e.g., Kahn, 1993; Lilius et al., 2008; Margolis & Molinsky, 2008; Miller, 2007). This form of compassion is illustrated in the following story:

> A coworker, Katrice, had an adverse outcome to her abdominal surgery, which resulted in several weeks of prolonged absence from work beyond her expected surgical leave. She has three young children for whom she was the primary caregiver. . . . Cara, another coworker who shares our office, called her daily to offer emotional support, ran errands, and helped with the children during her off-duty hours until the wounds healed and she was able to resume her normal physical activities. Cara even rearranged her work schedule to help drive Katrice to the doctor's visits so Katrice's husband wouldn't have to miss more work time (provided by a participant in Lilius et al., 2008)

In work organizations, compassion is often not limited to an interaction between two individuals, but rather may take the form of a more collective accomplishment. Recognizing this, Kanov et al. (2004) proposed a framework in which "organizational compassion" begins with individual noticing of a colleague's suffering, but becomes a fundamentally social process in which members of an organization come to exhibit a collective acknowledgment that pain is present, share and express their felt empathic concern, and respond to suffering in a collective, often coordinated way. An instance of collective compassion is illustrated in the following story (Lilius et al., 2008):

> A coworker was diagnosed with breast cancer. Our entire department knew about this with our coworker's permission through the Director. We all decided how to best handle the absences of the coworker. She happened to be a single mother so it was important to help her at home during her chemo. Our department set up a rotating schedule to bring the family dinner each night for a 6-week period, and her work activities were covered.

Researchers have found empirical support for the Kanov et al. (2004) model of organizational compassion. Through an in-depth focus on what they refer to as the process of compassion organizing, Dutton et al. (2006) focus on how individual compassion in response to a painful episode becomes a shared effort in which resources are collectively and competently generated and directed to alleviate suffering. O'Donohoe and Turley (2006) found evidence for collective compassion in how newspaper staff develop a communal sense of felt empathic concern and engage in coordinated compassionate responding when dealing with bereaved customers calling to place In Memoriam notices. Powley (2009) identified how collective compassion in the wake of a shooting helps to activate an organization's latent capacity for resilience, which promotes organizational healing (Powley & Cameron, 2008). Finally, building on the idea of systems of caregiving and supportive attachments among colleagues as a collective property (Kahn, 1993, 1998), compassion as a collective process has been theorized as a type of emotion-based organizational capability (e.g., Huy, 1999; Coté & Huy, 2010) that is sustainable over time (Lilius et al., 2010), reflecting a central form of what Cameron and colleagues refer to as organizational virtuousness (e.g., Cameron, 2003; Cameron, Bright, & Caza, 2004).

Compassion also may vary in the competence with which it is delivered, as reflected in the ability to respond to the unique needs and circumstances of others (Boykin & Schoenhofer, 2001; Candib, 1995). Writing about compassion in work organizations, Dutton, Frost, Worline, Lilius, and Kanov (2002) and Dutton et al. (2006) specify that compassion competence can be evaluated along four dimensions: scope, scale, speed, and specialization or customization of response. Scope refers to the breadth of resources provided to a person or group who is suffering, whereas scale refers to the volume of these resources. The speed of compassion captures the timeliness with which the resources are provided, and specialization refers to the degree to which resources are customized to the needs and circumstances of the sufferer. Competent compassion exhibited by an organizational member is a critical relational skill or practice (Fletcher, 1999; Frost et al., 2006) that could be thought of as an important form of social intelligence (e.g., Goleman, 2006). Recent research has suggested that another form of competence may be reflected when people and collectives are aware of and respect their own limits in providing compassion (Lilius et al., 2010).

MEASUREMENT OF COMPASSION

The diversity of forms of compassion described above is also reflected in research that approaches the issue of measurement in a range of ways. One approach involves coding qualitative data for evidence of noticing, feeling, and responding to suffering, as in Dutton et al. (2006) and Miller (2007). Other research has asked respondents to indicate how frequently they experience compassion in their workplace (Lilius et al., 2008). Researchers who hold a trait-based view of compassion have several measures available to them, including the Compassion subscale of the Dispositional Positive Emotion Scales (Shiota, Keltner, & John, 2006) or Davis' (1980) Interpersonal Reactivity Index. Neff (2003) also conceptualizes compassion as an individual difference, but focus on the degree to which people are self-compassionate.

In the same way that compassion can be measured as a personal trait, compassion can be conceptualized (Kanov et al., 2004) and measured as an organizational characteristic. For example, McLelland (2010) measured the compassion of an organization as the degree to which its routines are likely to facilitate noticing, feeling, and responding to suffering, whereas Muller (2010) suggested that an institution's level of corporate philanthropy is a reflection of its organizational compassion.

Finally, research also reflects efforts to capture variation in the competence with which compassion is expressed. As noted above and in Dutton et al. (2006), the competence of a compassionate response can be evaluated in terms of its speed, scope, scale, and customization to reflect a degree of competence. Dutton et al. (2010) further suggest that extensiveness is another important way that compassionate responses can vary, falling along a spectrum from more simple inquiries and expressions of concern, to work-based help, to efforts that transcend the work–personal boundary.

What Difference Does Compassion Make in Organizations?

Frost (1999) suggested that, although missing from mainstream theories, compassion is central to organizational functioning. Existing research shows that it is associated with a host of important outcomes for employees, organizations, and customers alike. Although the effects of compassion depend on whether one is on the receiving end of, bearing witness to, or participating in the delivery of compassion, research suggests that compassion has many beneficial consequences. Most intuitively, compassion makes a difference to those on its receiving end. Individuals who experience compassion in times of suffering are better able to manage and move forward from their difficult circumstances. This effect is directly visible in health care settings, where research shows the impact of compassion on reducing patient anxiety (Fogarty, Curbow, Wingard, McDonnell, & Somerfield, 1999) and fostering positive patient health outcomes (Taylor, 1997).

If compassion has positive outcomes in the context of health care, it is not hard to imagine its effects would be salutary in work organizations—for employees, customers, and others. Indeed, in the face of traumatic personal losses, evidence continues to build that compassion from one's work colleagues plays a critical role in an individual's ability to recover. This may be in part simply a function of having one's pain acknowledged, such that grief does not become disenfranchised (Bento, 1994; Doka, 1989; Manns & Little, 2010). As Hazen (2008) noted, it is extremely difficult for an employee to heal from a trauma in his or her life if one feels that they cannot openly express the loss. As such, compassion from other organizational members legitimates the painful experience and allows the grieving process to unfold for the suffering employee. In addition to legitimation of pain, the emotional support, time and flexibility, material goods, or whatever else may be part of a compassionate response (Dutton et al., 2006; Lilius et al., 2008) provide key resources that allow individuals to get back on their feet and recover from painful circumstances. For instance, some scholars have shown how the temporary suspension of work-related demands may allow employees to manage debilitating anxiety (Kahn, 2001) and readjust psychologically and emotionally following a traumatic experience (Powley, 2009). Although we are not advocating the instrumental provision of compassion to boost productivity, it is important to note that the experience of compassion may play a role in

helping suffering individuals resume or reengage with their work.

Importantly, research suggests that compassion impacts members' (e.g., employees, customers) attitudes and relational perceptions beyond alleviating suffering. Experiencing compassion shapes individuals' sense-making about the kind of organization of which they are a part and the kinds of colleagues with whom they work (Lilius et al., 2008). Organizational scholars document the importance of the belief that one's work organization values and cares about their well-being (i.e., perceived organizational support) for key outcomes favorable to the employee (e.g., job satisfaction) and the organization (e.g., affective organizational commitment) (for a review, see Rhoades & Eisenberger, 2002). In a similar vein, Lilius et al. (2008) found that employees who report experiencing compassion at work are more likely to report being affectively committed to their organization, and describe their coworkers and organizations in positive terms. Similarly, Powley (2009) found that work colleagues emerge from a shared trauma and subsequent compassionate treatment with a strengthened quality of relationship with their colleagues and a heightened sense of community and belonging. In a study of how organizational members interpreted compassionate organizational actions after the terrorist attacks of September 11, 2001 (9/11) in the United States, researchers found it changed how members felt, how they saw themselves, and how they saw the organizations (Rhee, Dutton, & Bagozzi, 2008).

Lilius et al. (2008) also found that employees who experienced compassion are more likely to report positive emotions while at work, which has been connected to a host of important organizational outcomes (for a review, see Fredrickson, 2003; Staw, Sutton, & Pelled, 1994). Organizational members who see others in relative distress arising from an inability to move toward desired goals may act to help them through "coaching with compassion" (Boyatzis, Smith, & Blaize, 2006), allowing a person to move closer to his or her aspirations and ideal self. Similarly, in the face of bad news (e.g., that one has been laid off), compassion in the form of interpersonally sensitive treatment in its delivery can "cushion the blow" (Margolis & Molinsky, 2008, p. 847) by protecting the dignity and well-being of the recipient (Tyler & Bies, 1990). Recent experimental research reveals that the inducement of compassion through loving-kindness meditation builds resources that result in higher levels of life satisfaction and lower levels of depressive symptoms (Fredrickson, Cohn, Coffey, Pek, & Finkel, 2008).

Beyond the impact of compassion on suffering individuals, research reveals patterns of compassion spirals, in which those on the receiving end of compassion are subsequently better able or more likely to direct caring and supportive behaviors toward others (Goetz et al., 2010). This is particularly important in caregiving organizational contexts, where the work itself brings about stress, burnout, and compassion fatigue (Figley, 1995). Effective organizational and individual functioning is enhanced to the extent that caregiving behaviors are exhibited among work colleagues (i.e., "caring for the caregivers"; Kahn, 1993). Not only are caregivers themselves positively impacted (e.g., through reduced stress and burnout), but such compassion also helps to replenish the emotional resources caregivers need to care for their clients. This extends to employees not typically thought of as "caregivers," such as newspaper employees whose interactions with grieving customers are enhanced as a function of support from and emotion processing with their coworkers (O'Donohoe & Turley, 2006). Indeed, evidence from research on perceived organizational support suggests that supervisors who feel that their organization values them and cares about their well-being are more likely to direct supportive behaviors toward their subordinates (Rhoades & Eisenberger, 2006).

The impact of compassion at work extends beyond those who receive it to those who witness it or participate in its delivery. First, employee sensemaking about the kind of organization for which one works is shaped not only by one's own experiences of compassion, but also by witnessed interpersonal treatment of colleagues (Grant, Dutton, & Rosso, 2008; Lilius et al., 2008). This finding is in line with research on interpersonal justice, which shows that compassion in the delivery of bad news can have a positive impact on the attitudes and perceptions of layoff survivors (Brockner et al., 1994). Similarly, perceptions of organizational support— that one's work organization values and cares about one's own well-being—may be shaped by impressions of the degree to which employees in general are supported (Rhoades & Eisenberger, 2002). Second, witnessing others engaging in virtuous action leads people to feel elevation (Haidt, 2003), a positive emotion that causes others to want to engage in similar behavior. This adds to Fredrickson's (2003) work on upward emotion spirals to show another important way that compassion may beget compassion.

Finally, existing empirical research points to the positive impact of participating in the delivery of compassion. Although there has long been an assumption that the provision of compassion is a fatiguing endeavor (Figley, 1995), recent research suggests that it may also engender compassion satisfaction, which has been defined as "the satisfaction derived from the work of helping others" (Stamm, 2002, p. 107). This notion aligns with work on the positive implications of social support provision (Brown, Nesse, Vinokur, & Smith, 2003). Recent experimental research further suggests that those who see themselves as compassionate are more receptive of others' social support, which in turn helps to mitigate their own physiological stress reactions (Cosley et al., 2010).

Acting with compassion is key for individuals who, as part of their job, must sometimes engage in behaviors that cause others pain (e.g., downsizing agents; Mishra, Mishra, & Spreitzer, 2009), in which the performance of so-called "necessary evils" is inescapable in many cases, and is often quite painful for the agents themselves (see Clair, Ladge, & Cotton, 2010; Margolis & Molinsky, 2008; Molinsky & Margolis, 2005). Engaging with and responding to the suffering inflicted on another not only helps the person in pain, but also allows the harm-doer to navigate the difficult situation (Margolis & Molinsky, 2008) and to maintain his or her moral identity (Aquino & Reed, 2002) or a type of virtuous identity (Dutton, Roberts, & Bednar, 2010). Similarly, opportunities to provide compassion to others are associated with an enhanced positive prosocial identity (Grant et al., 2008). Further, it has been shown that the provision of compassion in the delivery of bad news can have positive effects on an organization's reputation, and on stakeholders' intentions to engage in organizationally supportive behavior (Coombs, 1999).

Engaging in compassion at work also has implications for how connected individuals feel to their organization and, work colleagues, and ultimately to key organizational outcomes. At a basic level, research suggests that compassion is associated with a heightened degree of self–other similarity (Oveis et al., 2010). This heightened connection to others, in combination with the positive prosocial organizational perceptions that flow from involvement in the provision of compassion (Grant et al., 2008), culminates in a greater affective commitment to one's organization, with well-established implications for positive organizational outcomes, such as lower levels of turnover and increased organizational citizenship (for a review, see Meyer, Stanley, Herscovitch, & Topolnytzky, 2002). Finally, Dutton, Lilius, and Kanov (2007) have theorized that compassion among work colleagues contributes to an organizational capability for cooperation by generating relational resources, strengthening shared values, and cultivating critical relational skills.

In summary, research suggests that the experience of compassion—be it as a recipient, a witness, or a participant—can make an important difference for organizational members, customers, and whole organizations. In light of these findings, understanding the organizational conditions that facilitate the process of compassion becomes paramount. These are reviewed below.

How the Organizational Context Shapes Compassion

A focus on compassion directs research attention to the interweaving of attention, feeling, and action in context. To look at compassion in organizations is really to look at compassion-in-practice—how organizational contexts shape people's ability and willingness to notice, feel, and act in relation to suffering, both as individuals and as coordinated collectives (Dutton et al., 2006; Kanov et al., 2004). Although our starting assumption is that compassion is fundamental to being human, as we have discussed elsewhere (Frost et al., 2006; Lilius et al., 2010), everyday realities of organizational life and pressures for productivity and efficiency often obscure or drive out human moments at work (Frost, 2003; Hallowell, 1999) and reduce the likelihood that employees will have the capacity to notice suffering, much less have the time or resources to respond. Given the potential barriers to compassion, it is important to understand what conditions foster compassion. Existing research suggests that organizations facilitate compassion in two broad ways: indirectly, by fostering conditions under which the spontaneous process of compassion is more likely to unfold; and through explicit attempts to routinize compassion through the institutionalization of compassion processes.

Conditions That Foster Spontaneous Compassion

Here, we build on Kanov et al. (2004) to consider several conditions that foster the spontaneous expression of compassion in work organizations. We focus in particular on conditions that can be broadly categorized as relational-, cultural-, and leadership-based, under which compassion processes—noticing suffering, feeling empathic concern, and compassionate responding by both individuals and coordinated collectives—are likely to spontaneously unfold.

CONDITIONS THAT FOSTER NOTICING OF SUFFERING

Conditions that make it more likely that organizational members will become aware of the actual or possible suffering of a colleague are critical for the activation of compassion (Cassell, 1999; Dutton et al., 2006). Individual awareness can arise through at least two channels: through attunement to changes in the condition (Benner, Tanner, & Chesla, 1992) or emotional states (Coté & Huy, 2010) of another, or through an organizational member choosing to discuss his or her difficult circumstances with others at work.

At a very basic level, the noticing of suffering hinges on conditions that may be in short supply in modern organizations: time and rich forms of interaction. Pressures for productivity and efficiency reduce the likelihood that employees will notice the suffering of colleagues and diminish the capacity to connect and be present with them to inquire further (Frost, 2003; Hallowell, 1999). Similarly, the often subtle signals that someone is struggling can also be easily lost through the increasing use of less rich forms of communication and interaction, such as e-mail versus face-to-face interaction (Hallowell, 1999). As such, physical spaces, structures, and communication routines that bring colleagues into regular and close contact (e.g., face-to-face via daily or weekly department meetings, architecturally open workspaces) provide opportunities for establishing baseline understandings of what one's colleagues are typically like (e.g., their usual demeanor, attitude, etc.) and also create opportunities to notice when individuals seem to deviate from their typical selves, which may be an indication that they are suffering in some way (Kanov et al., 2004; Lilius et al., 2010).

Awareness of suffering is further facilitated by the quality of the relationships between work colleagues. Higher-quality connections between people are distinguished by how they feel (mutual, positive regard, and vitality) and how they function (process more emotional information, more flexible, and more open) (Dutton & Heaphy, 2003; Stephens, Heaphy, & Dutton, 2011; Chapter 29, this volume). As Kahn (1998) describes, work relationships vary in the strength of their emotional attachments, with strong attachments leaving people feeling "joined, seen, felt, known, and not alone" (p. 39). Knowing one's colleagues in this way provides the necessary familiarity about what their usual state and behaviors look like, which enables one to know when colleagues do not seem quite themselves. In addition, connection quality may affect whether someone who notices a change in the condition of a colleague feels comfortable to inquire further. As Miller (2007, p. 231) finds, "the process of noticing in compassionate communication involves not just noticing a need for help, but also active information-gathering about the individual in need and the context surrounding that need." The quality of relations between work colleagues also shapes the degree to which employees have enough trust in their colleagues to share their painful circumstances (Dutton et al., 2010) and the sense that it is psychologically safe to do so (Edmondson, 1999). Further, strong ties between organizational members facilitate the spread of awareness by making shared information about suffering more credible and legitimate, and multiple and diverse subnetworks within an organization increase the spread of information about suffering (Dutton et al., 2006).

Conditions that foster noticing of suffering may be cultural as well. Variation in organizational and work group norms around the nature of the boundary between work and nonwork (Ashforth, Kreiner, & Fugate, 2000; Clark, 2000) can shape how appropriate and typical it is for work colleagues to share personal details and struggles. Similarly, existing routines related to customer and community service, although not designed for collective compassion per se (as opposed to what we discuss regarding institutionalization below), may help spread information about and attention to suffering. One such example was seen in the business school studied by Dutton et al. (2006), in which a preexisting civic engagement education program enabled the rapid spread of attention to suffering students.

Organizational leaders can set an important tone for the value and legitimacy of noticing suffering (Dutton et al., 2002, 2006). For example, after 9/11, there was vivid evidence of the difference leaders made in noticing suffering (Dutton et al., 2002). Leaders' actions can be dramatic and visible, as in Dutton et al. (2006), in which a top leader (Dean of the Business School) modeled and legitimated attention to the suffering of students, unleashing a torrent of student, faculty, and staff responding. Leaders also play a key role by shaping organizational norms around caring and compassion. Symbolic and instrumental behaviors from the leader can establish and reinforce values that let others know it is appropriate and necessary to know about each other's lives and pay attention to the pain and suffering of organizational members (Delbecq, 2010; Dutton et al., 2006). Such actions can also be reflected in the more everyday model provided in managerial caring (Kroth & Keeler, 2009).

CONDITIONS THAT ENABLE EMPATHIC CONCERN

Once aware of the suffering of a work colleague, employees are more likely to feel empathic concern under particular conditions. High-quality relationships again play a key role, in that they shape the ease with which one can take the perspective of another, heightening the likelihood of empathic concern (Eisenberg, 2000; Parker & Axtell, 2001). Cultural conditions make it more likely that these emotions will be both felt and shared with others, and that the processing of difficult emotions will be normalized (Kanov et al., 2004). Normalized ways of processing difficult emotions were identified by O'Donohoe and Turley (2006) as key for managing customer grief and ones' own difficulties in doing so. Organizational values around holistic personhood and the importance of putting humanity on display foster open expressions of emotional pain that can also facilitate the propagation of empathic concern (Dutton et al., 2006).

Organizational leaders can also play an important role in enabling felt empathic concern by modeling expressions of emotion more generally (e.g., Frost, 2003), and care and concern more specifically (Kroth & Keeler, 2009; Mumby & Putnam, 1992). These findings are in line with a recent shift toward more relational models of leadership that emphasize the importance of being in tune with and responsive to the emotional states of others (Boyatzis & McKee, 2005; Goleman, Boyatzis, & McKee, 2002; Fletcher, 2007).

CONDITIONS THAT ENABLE RESPONDING

Awareness of the suffering of a work colleague and felt empathic concern are necessary but not sufficient conditions for a compassionate response. Often, the suffering is such that the nature and form of an appropriate response is not clear, which leaves the offering of help as an interpersonally risky endeavor. The risk involved means that the quality of relationships between work colleagues is again paramount. Trust is a key condition for accepting the associated vulnerability (Rousseau, Sitkin, Burt, & Camerer, 1998) that affects whether one will respond to suffering (Dutton et al., 2010; Lilius et al., 2010).

Relationship quality not only affects the likelihood that compassionate responding will occur, but it also affects the competence of the response—its speed, scope, scale, and customization (Dutton et al., 2002, 2006). "Knowing the other" (Tanner, Benner, Chesla, & Gordon, 1996) provides a foundation for understanding how to best meet the unique needs of the sufferer, thus lowering the interpersonal risk involved in responding and enhancing the competence of the response (Cassell, 1999; Clark et al., 1998; Dutton et al., 2002, 2006; Lilius et al., 2010). Diverse and strong relational networks also heighten the competence of the response (Dutton et al., 2006).

The actions of leaders again serve as a key enabler of compassionate responding. When leaders themselves demonstrate compassionate responding, they legitimate it as a valued and worthwhile endeavor toward which to devote valuable time and organizational resources, thus encouraging and empowering others to also respond to suffering (Worline & Boik, 2006). Leaders' compassionate responding also models appropriate responding (Dutton et al., 2006), thus reducing the uncertainty and vulnerability that may otherwise inhibit responding. This may be particularly important in situations in which employees want to help a suffering colleague, but do not share a close enough relationship to be comfortable doing so without this model.

The Institutionalization of Compassion

As reviewed above, compassion can be a spontaneous process that is informal and emergent, shaped by the unique conditions of compassion providers, receivers, and the broader organizational context. At the same time, organizations may take steps to institutionalize compassion by implementing different structures and programs that try to more efficiently and effectively trigger compassion to reduce suffering (Delbecq, 2010; Kanov et al., 2004). By the institutionalization of compassion, we are referring to the means by which compassion as a process becomes a type of taken-for-granted social fact and thus persists in a particular form over time within an organization (e.g., Zucker, 1977). Here, we focus on deliberate organizational attempts to institutionalize compassion.

Compassion as an organizational process can become institutionalized for both rational and symbolic reasons. On the rational side, organizations can routinize emotion-wrought processes to help minimize the uncertainty and unpredictability associated with having to notice, feel, and respond uniquely to each case of suffering that unfolds in an organization. This argument fits with the idea that organizations can use bureaucratic control to rein in and manage disruptive emotions like suffering (Martin, Knopoff, & Beckman, 1998). On the symbolic side, the institutionalization of compassion occurs to create and preserve legitimacy for actions and actors associated with noticing, feeling, and responding to suffering (Frost et al., 2006). In line with these arguments, institutionalizing compassion infuses these structures with meaning and legitimacy beyond their instrumental or rational intent (Feldman & Pentland, 2003). Accordingly, organizations deploy a variety of mechanisms that facilitate the noticing, feeling, and responding to employee's suffering as a type of collective achievement. These mechanisms come in two major forms: designated roles and formal programs.

DESIGNATED ROLES

An important and enduring means of institutionalizing compassion has been through the formal designation of roles that include the detection of and response to human suffering. For example, in universities, the role of ombudsperson includes responsibility for discerning and facilitating effective organizational responding to members' sufferings brought on by a variety of circumstances (e.g., unfair or uncivil treatment at work, Stewart, 1987). Other roles in different institutional settings, for example, patient advocates in hospital settings (Heaphy, 2010) or customer service representatives in call centers (Totterdell & Holman, 2003), are designed to systematically detect and respond to suffering (and other complaints) from organizational customers. The designation of formal roles for handling problematic interactions for the organization (Strauss, 1993) buffers organizations from interruptions and disturbances that could detract from their effectiveness. At the same time, in theory, they allow deployment of more skilled practitioners to deal with human suffering than might be otherwise available.

FORMAL PROGRAMS

Formal organizational programs that ease and systematize the process of compassion come in several forms. Some programs facilitate peer-to-peer support as a means for facilitating and delivering compassion. For example, Bacharach, Bamberger, and McKinney (2000) studied a union's member-assistance program (MAP), which, like employee assistance programs (EAPs), are formal means designed to provide services and support for individual employees who are suffering. Although EAPs offer services through professional support providers, union-based programs tend to be staffed by unpaid volunteers (Bacharach et al., 2000). Grant et al. (2008) studied an employee support program (ESP) in which employees could choose to regularly contribute to a fund that provided financial support for employees if they faced emergency conditions. Some organizations allow employees to donate vacation time that other employees in need can draw on if they face a family emergency requiring absences from work (Lilius et al., 2008). Finally, both CISCO Systems (see Dutton et al., 2002) and a university setting that we studied (Dutton et al., 2006) have harm notification networks in place to systematize awareness of any organizational members who are in painful situations. In all of these cases, the organizationally endowed and legitimated programs facilitate and routinize detecting and responding to employee pain in ways that are intended to minimize employee impairment on the job. At the same time, these programs often endow the organization (and by implications its employees) with the reputation and identity of being a caring and compassionate organization (Grant et al., 2008).

In programs like these, compassion is organized and routinized through the implementation of various practices intended to maintain standards in the ways that compassion is delivered. For example, MAPs have routines for screening and selecting peer volunteers who can participate in the program based on their ability to demonstrate skills in listening, giving support, and maintaining confidentiality (Bacharach et al., 2000). They also use training programs to equip help-providers with general crisis management preparation and to foster mutual socialization of peer helpers. Similarly, in the ESP studied by Grant et al. (2008), there were strict rules around the circumstances under which employees could apply for financial aid from the ESP foundation. Taken together, these practices may help increase the effectiveness of the program by heightening clarity for those administering it, as well as engendering a sense that it is run in a procedurally fair way and that the compassion delivery system was not exploited by those who did not really need help.

The effectiveness of these kinds of programs and roles is variable, and depends not only on how well the programs are run or how well executed the roles are, but also the degree to which the programs are utilized. For example, one study of EAPs in seven organizations found that most employees were unaware of the program's existence (Steele & Hubbard, 1985). Beyond utilization, the effectiveness of these programs could be gauged in terms of the speed, scale, scope, and customization of compassion vs. compassionate in responding to the needs of suffering employees (see Dutton et al., 2002, 2006), although we are not aware of any such published studies.

Future Research

Our foray into the domain of compassion research in organizations identifies four, among many, possible avenues for future research. First, in keeping with this volume, our focus has been on understanding the nature and positive impact of the presence of compassion. There have been hints in our research, however, that the absence of compassion may be an equally powerful force in organizations. For example, in a study by Lilius et al. (2008), almost 10% of respondents asked to provide a story of compassion at work actually provided a story of when compassion was lacking. Some of these stories were highly elaborate and emotionally charged. As such, we suspect that, although compassion may feel "above and beyond" for those who receive it, those who fail to receive compassion during times of suffering and need can feel overlooked and shortchanged. A more systematic examination of the experience and perceptions of employees when compassion might have been expected but was not forthcoming could contribute to our understanding of compassion and of respectful interpersonal treatment more generally (Miller, 2001).

Second, we need to explore when and how the presence of compassion can have negative repercussions. Compassion can be costly to receivers, givers, observers, and the organizations of which they are a part (Frost et al., 2006). For example, some individuals prefer to keep their suffering to themselves, and especially to keep it separate from their working life. These people could experience great shame at receiving the compassionate attention of colleagues who want to support them (Frost et al., 2000). Equally, others in the organization may be aware of cultural norms of compassion but feel discomfort about how to behave around a suffering colleague, or feel pressure to show compassion when they do not feel it. Such pressure may be especially intense in settings in which compassion has been institutionalized, where it may become another form of emotional labor, leading to resentment, alienation, or burnout (Figley, 1995; Hochschild, 1983; Maslach, 1982). The study of compassion would greatly benefit from further exploration of such issues.

Third, we need to study the limitations of the institutionalization of compassion. Although institutionalized roles and programs may enhance the breadth and competence of compassionate responding through legitimated means, these kinds of structures and processes can be poor substitutes for the individualized, highly situation-specific response to an individual sufferer's circumstance that may be necessary for experiencing compassion's healing effects. In addition, "forced" compassion may have negative implications (Grant et al., 2008). These limits have led some researchers to argue that compassion needs to operate in a more "organic, informal fashion that is antithetical and nonamenable to managerial systematization and control" (O'Donohoe & Turley, 2006 p. 1446).

Fourth, researchers could broaden the domain of compassion work by building on at least three new pathways. First, there is the critical new frontier of neuroscience and emotions that invites deeper inquiry into the links between compassion and the functioning of the human brain (e.g., Davidson, 2002; Goleman, 2003). Second, there is important work on self-compassion (e.g., Neff & Vonk, 2009; Neff, Kirkpatrick, & Rude, 2007) that would enlarge how organizational researchers imagine the applicability of compassion to individuals and their functioning and well-being in the workplace. Third, there is a possible pathway to study compassion at a more global or macro level than we have implied here. The call to be answered, which is as pragmatic as it is theoretical, is how to cultivate a more compassionate society. What does organization theory have to add to our understanding of compassion and compassion organizing as a societal accomplishment? We have watched with appreciation the spread of the Charter for Compassion as a type of global movement via technology to create foundation conditions for compassion globally (www.charterforcompassion.org). Could this type of effort be studied as a vehicle for illuminating new possibilities for unleashing and supporting compassion at a more global scale? We have also been encouraged by the 2010 Academy of Management theme called "Dare to Care: Passion & Compassion in Management Practice and Research." This type of invitation to consider compassion and management practice and research is sure to unlock new possibilities that hopefully will impact society in positive ways.

Conclusion

It is an exciting time to be a student of compassion in organizations. Although Adam Smith argued that empathy and compassion were at least as important and interesting as self-interest (Smith, 1976), this point has been obscured through organizational models that assume human nature to consist only of individual self-interest (see de Waal, 2009; Walsh, Weber, & Margolis, 2003). But the tide is turning. New research points to the fundamental role of empathic concern and compassion in both human biology and human social life, drawing out questions about the limitations of economic and organizational theories that rely solely on assumptions of individual self-interest (Barasch, 2005; Davidson, 2002; de Waal, 2009; Keltner, 2008; Sober & Wilson, 1999). In the preface of a book which draws from many studies of chimpanzee social interaction, primatologist de Waal (2009, p. x) makes the case that empathetic concern is central to human social life: "Being in tune with others, coordinating activities, and caring for those in need isn't restricted to our species. Human empathy has the backing of a long evolutionary history."

This chapter has offered a review of the work that demonstrates the implications of compassion for organizations and their members. This decade of work moves us beyond Frost's (1999) lamentations that we are missing fundamental and important aspects of organizational life by being blind to compassion. We hope this chapter illustrates that, with fresh eyes, there is much to see and learn about organizations and organizing using the lens of compassion.

References

Aquino, K., & Reed, A., II. (2002). The self-importance of moral identity. *Journal of Personality and Social Psychology, 83,* 1423–1440.

Ashforth, B.E., Kreiner, G.E., & Fugate, M. (2000). All in a day's work: Boundaries and micro role transitions. *Academy of Management Review, 25,* 472–491.

Bacharach, S.B., Bamberger, P., & McKinney, V. (2000). Boundary management tactics and logics of action: The case of peer support providers. *Administrative Science Quarterly, 45,* 704–736.

Barasch, M.I. (2005). *Field notes on the compassionate life: A search for the soul of kindness.* New York: Rodale Press.

Baumeister, R.F., & Leary, M.R. (1995). The need to belong: Desire for interpersonal attachments as a fundamental human motivation. *Psychological Bulletin, 117,* 497–529.

Benner, P., Tanner, C.A., & Chesla, C.A. (1992). From beginner to expert: Gaining a differentiated clinical world in critical care nursing. *Advances in Nursing Science, 14*(3), 13–28.

Bento, A. (1994). When the show must go on: Disenfranchised grief in organizations. *Journal of Managerial Psychology, 9,* 35–44.

Bhagat, R.S., McQuaid, S.J., Lindholm, H., & Segovis, J. (1985). Total life stress: A multimethod validation of the construct and its effect on organizationally valued outcomes and withdrawal behaviors. *Journal of Applied Psychology, 70,* 202–214.

Blauner, R. (1964). *Alienation and freedom.* Chicago: University of Chicago Press.

Blum, L. (1980). Compassion. In A.O. Rorty (Ed.), *Explaining emotions* (pp. 507–517). Berkley: University of California Press.

Boland, R., & Tenkasi, R. (1995). Perspective making and perspective taking in communities of knowing. *Organization Science, 6,* 350–372.

Boyatzis, R., & McKee, A. (2005). *Resonant leadership: Renewing yourself and connecting with others through mindfulness, hope, and compassion.* Boston: Harvard Business School Press.

Boyatzis, R.E., Smith, M., & Blaize, N. (2006). Developing sustainable leaders through coaching and compassion. *Academy of Management Learning and Education, 5,* 8–24.

Boykin, A., & Schoenhofer, S.O. (2001). *Nursing as caring: A model for transforming practice.* Mississauga, Ontario: Jones & Bartlett.

Brief, A.P., & Motowidlo, S.J. (1986). Prosocial organizational behaviors. *Academy of Management Review, 11,* 710–725.

Brockner, J., Konovsky, M., Cooper-Schneider, R., Folger, R., Martin, C.L., & Bies, R.J. (1994). The interactive effects of procedural justice and outcome negativity on the victims and survivors of job loss. *Academy of Management Journal, 37,* 397–409.

Brown, S.L., Nesse, R.M., Vinokur, A.D., & Smith, D.M. (2003). Providing social support may be more beneficial than receiving it: Results from a prospective study of mortality. *Psychological Science, 14,* 320–327.

Burke, R.J., & Greenglass, E.R. (1987). Work and family. In C.L. Cooper, & I.T. Robertson (Eds.), *International review of industrial and organizational psychology* (pp. 273–320). New York: John Wiley.

Butts, D. (1997). Joblessness, pain, power, pathology and promise. *Journal of Organizational Change Management, 10,* 111–129.

Cameron, K.S. (2003). Organizational virtuousness and performance. In K. Cameron, J. Dutton, & R. Quinn (Eds.), *Positive organizational scholarship* (pp. 48–65). San Francisco: Berrett-Koehler.

Cameron, K.S., Bright, D., & Caza, A. (2004). Exploring the relationships between organizational virtuousness and performance. *American Behavioral Scientist, 47,* 766–790.

Candib, L. (1995). *Medicine and the Family.* New York: Basic Books.

Cassell, E.J. (1999). Diagnosing suffering: A perspective. *Annals of Internal Medicine, 131,* 531–534.

Chodron, P. (1997). *When things fall apart: Heart advice for difficult times.* Boston, MA: Shambhala.

Clair, J., Ladge, J., & Cotton, R. (2010). In search of silver linings: How chronic downsizing agents generate positive self-states in the context of repeatedly harming others. In J. Kanov, & J. Lilius (Chairs), *Compassion research incubator: Emerging perspectives on the scholarship and practice of compassion.* Symposium conducted at the annual meeting of the Academy of Management, Montreal, Canada.

Clark, C. (1997). *Misery and company: Sympathy in everyday life.* Chicago: The University of Chicago Press.

Clark, R.A., Pierce, A.J., Finn, K., Hsu, K., Toosley, A., & Williams, L. (1998). The impact of alternative approaches to comforting, closeness of relationship, and gender on multiple measures of effectiveness. *Communication Studies, 49,* 224–239.

Clark, S.C. (2000). Work/family border theory: A new theory of work/family balance. *Human Relations, 53,* 747–770.

Coombs, W.T. (1999). Information and compassion in crisis responses: A test of their effects. *Journal of Public Relations Research, 11,* 125–142.

Cortina, L.M., Magley, V.J., Williams, J.H., & Langhout, R.D. (2001). Incivility in the workplace: Incidence and impact. *Journal of Occupational Health Psychology, 6,* 64–80.

Cosley, B.J., McCoy, S.K., Saslow, L.R., & Epel, E.S. (2010). Is compassion for others stress buffering? Consequences of compassion and social support for physiological reactivity to stress. *Journal of Experimental Social Psychology,* forthcoming.

Coté, S., & Huy, Q.N. (2010). *The nature and function of collective emotional abilities in organizations.* Working paper, INSEAD, Fontainebleau, France.

Dalai Lama (1995). *The power of compassion.* London: Thorsons.

Davidson, R. (2002). Toward a biology of positive affect and compassion. In R.J. Davidson, & A. Harrington (Eds.), *Visions of compassion: Western scientists and Tibetan Buddhists examine human nature* (pp. 107–130). Oxford, NY: Oxford University Press.

Davis, M.H. (1980). A multidimensional approach to individual differences in empathy. *Catalog of Selected Documents in Psychology, 10,* 85.

Davis, M.H. (1996). *Empathy: A social psychological approach.* Boulder, CO: Westview Press.

Delbecq, A. (2010). Organizational compassion: A litmus test for a spiritually centered organizational culture. *Journal of Spirituality, Management, and Religion,* forthcoming.

Dewa, C.S., & Lin, E. (2000). Chronic physical illness, psychiatric disorder and disability in the workplace. *Social Science & Medicine, 51,* 41–50.

De Waal, F. (2009). *The age of empathy: Nature's lessons for a kinder society.* Chatsworth, CA: Harmony.

Doka, K.J. (1989). *Disenfranchised grief: Recognizing hidden sorrow.* Lexington, MA: Lexington.

Dovidio, J.F., & Penner, L.A. (2004). Helping and altruism. In M.B. Brewer, & M. Hewstone (Eds *Emotion and motivation* (pp. 247–280). Malden, MA: Blackwell Publishing.

Driver, M. (2007). Meaning and suffering in organizations. *Journal of Organizational Change Management, 20,* 611–632.

Durkheim, E. (1997). *Suicide.* New York: The Free Press. (Original work published in 1897)

Dutton, J.E., Frost, P.J., Worline, M.C., Lilius, J.M., & Kanov, J.M. (2002). Leading in times of trauma. *Harvard Business Review, 80,* 54–61.

Dutton, J.E., & Heaphy, E. (2003). The power of high quality connections. In K. Cameron, J.E. Dutton, & R.E. Quinn (Eds.), *Positive organizational scholarship* (pp. 263–278). San Francisco: Berrett-Koehler.

Dutton, J., Lilius, J.M., & Kanov, J.M. (2007). The transformative potential of compassion at work. In D. Cooperrider, R. Fry, & S. Piderit (Eds.), *Handbook of transformative cooperation: New designs and dynamics* (pp. 107–126). Palo Alto, CA: Stanford University Press.

Dutton, J.E., Roberts, L.M., & Bednar, J. (2010). Pathways to positive identity construction at work: Four types of positive identity and the building of social resources. *Academy of Management Review, 35,* 265–293.

Dutton, J.E., Spreitzer, G.M., Heaphy, E., & Stephens, J.P. (2010). When and how employees lend a hand: Facilitators of compassion outside of work. In J. Kanov, & J. Lilius (Chairs), *Compassion research incubator: Emerging perspectives on the scholarship and practice of compassion.* Symposium conducted at the annual meeting of the Academy of Management, Montreal, Canada.

Dutton, J.E., Worline, M.C., Frost, P.J., & Lilius, J.M. (2006). Explaining compassion organizing. *Administrative Science Quarterly, 51*, 59–96.

Edmondson, A.C. (1999). Psychological safety and learning behavior in teams. *Administrative Science Quarterly, 44*, 350–383.

Eisenberg, N. (2000). Emotion, regulation, and moral development. *Annual Review of Psychology, 51*, 665–697.

Feldman, M., & Pentland, B. (2003). Reconceptualizing organizational routines as a source of flexibility and change. *Administrative Science Quarterly, 48*, 94–118.

Figley, C.R. (1995). Compassion fatigue: Toward a new understanding of the costs of caring. In B.H. Stamm (Ed.), *Secondary traumatic stress: Self-care issues for clinicians, researchers, and educators* (pp. 3–28). Baltimore, MD: Sidran Press.

Fletcher, J.K. (1999). *Disappearing acts: Gender, power and relational practice at work.* Cambridge, MA: MIT Press.

Fletcher, J.K. (2007). Leadership, power and positive relationships. In J.E. Dutton, & B.R. Ragins (Eds.), *Exploring positive relationships at work: Building a theoretical and research foundation* (pp. 347–372). Mahwah, NJ: Lawrence Erlbaum Publishers.

Fogarty, L.A., Curbow, B.A., Wingard, J.R., McDonnell, K., & Somerfield, M.R. (1999). Can 40 seconds of compassion reduce patient anxiety? *Journal of Clinical Oncology, 17*, 371–379.

Fox, M.L., & Dwyer, D.J. (1999). An investigation of the effects of time and involvement in the relationship between stressors and work–family conflict. *Journal of Occupational Health Psychology, 4*, 164–174.

Fredrickson, B.L. (2003). Positive emotions and upward spirals in organizsations. In K. Cameron, J. Dutton, & R. Quinn (Eds.), *Positive organizational scholarship: Foundations of a new discipline* (pp. 163–175). San Francisco: Berrett-Koehler.

Fredrickson, B.L., Cohn, M.A., Coffey, K.A., Pek, J., & Finkel, S.M. (2008). Open hearts build lives: Positive emotions, induced through loving-kindness meditation, build consequential personal resources. *Journal of Personality and Social Psychology, 95*, 1045–1062.

Frone, M.R., Russell, M., & Cooper, M.L. (1992). Antecedents and outcomes of work-family conflict: Testing a model of the work-family interface. *Journal of Applied Psychology, 77*, 65–78.

Frost, P.J. (1999). Why compassion counts! *Journal of Management Inquiry, 8*, 127–133.

Frost, P.J. (2003). *Toxic emotions at work: How compassionate managers handle pain and conflict.* Boston: Harvard Business School Press.

Frost, P.J., Dutton, J.E., Maitlis, S., Lilius, J.M., Kanov, J.M., & Worline, M.C. (2006). Seeing organizations differently: Three lenses on compassion. In S.R. Clegg, C. Hardy, T.B. Lawrence, & W.R. Nord. (Eds.), *The sage handbook of organization studies* (2nd ed., pp. 843–866). London: Sage Publications.

Frost, P.J., Dutton, J.E., Worline, M.C., & Wilson, A. (2000). Narratives of compassion in organizations. In S. Fineman (Ed.), *Emotion in organizations* (pp. 25–45). Thousand Oaks, CA: Sage Publications.

Galinsky, A.D., & Moskowitz, G.B. (2000). Perspective-taking: Decreasing stereotype expression, stereotype accessibility, and in-group favoritism. *Journal of Personality and Social Psychology, 78*, 708–724.

Goetz, J.L., Keltner, D., & Simon-Thomas, E. (2010). Compassion: An evolutionary analysis and empirical review. *Psychological Bulletin, 136*, 351–374.

Goleman. D. (2003). *Destructive emotions: How can we overcome them?* New York: Bantam Books.

Goleman, D. (2006). *Social intelligence: The new science of human relationships.* New York: Bantam Books.

Goleman, D., Boyatzis, R., & McKee, A. (2002). *Primal leadership: Realizing the power of emotional intelligence.* Boston: Harvard Business School Press.

Grant, A.M., Dutton, J.E., & Rosso, B. (2008). Giving commitment: Employee support programs and the prosocial sensemaking process. *Academy of Management Journal, 51*, 898–918.

Haidt, J. (2003). Elevation and the positive psychology of morality. In C.L.M. Keyes, & J. Haidt (Eds.), *Flourishing: Positive psychology and the life well-lived* (pp. 275–289). Washington, DC: American Psychological Association.

Hallowell, E.M. (1999). The human moment at work. *Harvard Business Review, 77*, 58–66.

Hazen, M.A. (2003). Societal and workplace response to perinatal loss: Disenfranchised grief or healing connection? *Human Relations, 56*, 147–156.

Hazen, M.A. (2008). Grief and the workplace. *Academy of Management Perspectives, 22*, 78–86.

Heaphy, E.D. (2010). *Storytelling as a means of organizational problem handling: The work of patient advocates.* Working paper, Boston University, Boston, MA.

Hochschild, A.R. (1983). *The managed heart: Commercialization of human feeling.* Berkeley: University of California Press.

Huy, Q.N. (1999). Emotional capability, emotional intelligence, and radical change. *Academy of Management Review, 47*, 31–69.

Jacobson, J.M. (2006). Compassion fatigue, compassion satisfaction, and burnout: Reactions among employee assistance professionals providing workplace crisis intervention and disaster management services. *Journal of Workplace Behavioral Health, 21*, 133–152.

Kahn, W.A. (1993). Caring for the caregivers: Patterns of organizational caregiving. *Administrative Science Quarterly, 38*, 539–563.

Kahn, W.A. (1998). Relational systems at work. In B.M. Staw, & L.L. Cummings (Eds.), *Research in organizational behavior* Vol. 20 (pp. 39–76). Greenwich, CT: JAI Press.

Kahn, W.A. (2001). Holding environments at work. *Journal of Applied Behavioral Science, 37*, 260–279.

Kanov, J. (2005). *Re-envisioning feeling and relating at work: An inductive study of interpersonal disconnection in organizational life.* Unpublished doctoral dissertation, University of Michigan, Ann Arbor, MI.

Kanov, J., Maitlis, S., Worline, M.C., Dutton, J.E., Frost, P.J., & Lilius, J. (2004). Compassion in organizational life. *American Behavioral Scientist, 47*, 808–827.

Keltner, D. (2008). *Born to be good: The science of meaningful life.* New York: W.W. Norton.

Kroth, M., & Keeler, C. (2009). Caring as a managerial strategy. *Human Resource Development Review, 8*, 506–531.

Lazarus, R.S. (1991). *Emotion and adaptation.* New York: Oxford University Press.

Leary, M.R., & Kowalski, R.M. (1995). *Social anxiety.* New York: Guildford Press.

Leary, M.R., Springer, C., Negel, L., Ansell, E., & Evans, K. (1998). The causes, phenomenology, and consequences of hurt feelings. *Journal of Personality and Social Psychology, 74,* 1225–1237.

Lilius, J.M., Worline, M.C., Maitlis, S., Kanov, J.M., Dutton, J.E., & Frost, P. (2008). The contours and consequences of compassion at work. *Journal of Organizational Behavior, 29,* 193–218.

Lilius, J.M., Worline, M.C., Dutton, J.E., Kanov, J.M., Maitlis, S., & Frost, P.J. (2011). Understanding compassion capability. *Human Relations,* in press. Manns, M., & Little, S. (2010). *Grief and compassion at work following the loss of a romantic relationship.* Paper presented at the annual meeting of the Academy of Management, Montreal, Canada.

Margolis, J.D., & Molinsky, A. (2008). Navigating the bind of necessary evils: Psychological engagement and the production of interpersonally sensitive behavior, *Academy of Management Journal, 51,* 847–872.

Martin, J., Knopoff, K., & Beckman, C. (1998). An alternative to bureaucratic impersonality and emotional labor: Bounded emotionality at the Body Shop. *Administrative Science Quarterly, 43,* 429–469.

Maslach, C. (1982). *Burnout: The cost of caring.* Englewood Cliffs, NJ: Prentice Hall.

McLelland, L. (2010). *From compassion to client satisfaction: Examining the relationship between routines that facilitate compassion and quality of service.* Working paper, Emory University, Atlanta, GA.

Meyer, J.P, Stanley, D.S., Herscovitch, L., & Topolnytzky, L. (2002). Affective, continuance, and normative commitment to the organization: A meta-analysis of antecedents, correlates, and consequences. *Journal of Vocational Behavior, 61,* 20–52.

Miller, D.T. (2001). Disrespect and the experience of injustice. *Annual Review of Psychology, 52,* 527–553.

Miller, J.P., & Stiver, I.P. (1997). *The healing connection.* Boston: Beacon Press.

Miller, K.I. (2007). Compassionate communication in the workplace: Exploring processes of noticing, connecting, and responding. *Journal of Applied Communication Research, 35,* 223–245.

Mishra, A., Mishra, K., & Spreitzer G. (2009). How to downsize your company without downsizing morale. *Sloan Management Review, 50,* 39–44.

Molinsky, A., & Margolis, J. (2005). Necessary evils and interpersonal sensitivity in organizations. *Academy of Management Review, 30,* 245–268.

Muller, A., & Whiteman, G. (2010). *The human focus of organizations: Corporate disaster response as organizational compassion.* Working paper, University of Washington, Seattle, WA.

Mumby, D.K., & Putnam, L.L. (1992). The politics of emotion: A feminist reading of bounded rationality. *Academy of Management Review, 17,* 465–486.

Neff, K.D. (2003). Self-compassion: An alternative conceptualization of a healthy attitude toward oneself. *Self and Identity, 2,* 85–102.

Neff, K.D. (2009). Self-Compassion. In M.R. Leary, & R.H. Hoyle (Eds.), *Handbook of individual differences in social behavior* (pp.561–573). New York: Guilford Press.

Neff, K.D., Kirkpatrick, K., & Rude, S.S. (2007). Self-compassion and its link to adaptive psychological functioning. *Journal of Research in Personality, 41,* 139–154.

Neff, K.D., & Vonk, R. (2009). Self-compassion versus global self-esteem: Two different ways of relating to oneself. *Journal of Personality, 77,* 23–50.

Nussbaum, M.C. (1996). Compassion: The basic social emotion. *Social Philosophy and Policy, 13,* 27–58.

Nussbaum, M.C. (2001). *Upheavals of thought: The intelligence of emotions.* Cambridge: Cambridge University Press.

O'Donohoe, S., & Turley, D. (2006). Compassion at the counter: Service providers and bereaved customers. *Human Relations, 59,* 1429–1448.

Oveis, C., Horberg, E.J., & Keltner, D. (2010). Compassion, pride, and social intuitions of self-other similarity. *Journal of Personality and Social Psychology, 98,* 618–630.

Parker, S.K., & Axtell, C.M. (2001). Seeing another viewpoint: Antecedents and outcomes of employee perspective taking. *Academy of Management Journal, 44,* 1085–1100.

Penner, L.A., Dovidio, J.F., Piliavin, J.A., & Schroeder, D.A. (2004). Prosocial behavior: Mulitilevel perspectives. *Annual Review of Psychology, 56,* 365–392.

Podsakoff, P.M., MacKenzie, S.B., Paine, J.B., & Bachrach, D.G. (2000). Organizational citizenship behaviors: A critical review of the theoretical and empirical literature and suggestions for future research. *Journal of Management, 26,* 513–563.

Pollock, S.E., & Sands, D. (1997). Adaptation to suffering: Meaning and implications for nursing. *Clinical Nursing Research, 6,* 171–185.

Post, S.G. (2003). *Unlimited love, altruism, compassion and service.* Philadelphia: Templeton Foundation Press.

Powley, E.H. (2009). Reclaiming resilience and safety: Resilience activation in the critical period of crisis. *Human Relations, 62,* 1289–1326.

Powley, E.H., & Cameron, K.S. (2008). Organizational healing: Lived virtuousness amidst organizational crisis. In C.C. Manz, K. Cameron, K. Manz, & R.D. Marx (Eds.), *The virtuous organization* (pp. 21–44). Hackensack, NJ: World Scientific.

Rhee, S., Dutton, J.E., & Bagozzi, R. (2008). Making sense of organizational actions with virtue frames and its links to organizational attachment." In C.C. Manz, K. Cameron, K. Manz, & R.D. Marx (Eds.), *The virtuous organization* (pp. 45–65). Hackensack, NJ: World Scientific.

Rhoades, L., & Eisenberger, R. (2002). Perceived organizational support: A review of the literature. *Journal of Applied Psychology, 87,* 698–714.

Rhoades, L., & Eisenberger, R. (2006). When supervisors feel supported: Relationships with subordinates' perceived supervisor support, perceived organizational support, and performance. *Journal of Applied Psychology, 91,* 689–695.

Reich, W.T. (1989). Speaking of suffering: A moral account of compassion. *Soundings, 72,* 83–108.

Rousseau, D., Sitkin, S., Burt, R., & Camerer, C. (1998). Not so different at all: A cross-discipline view of trust. *Academy of Management Review, 23,* 387–392.

Scarry, E. (1985). *The body in pain: The making and unmaking of the world.* New York: Oxford University Press.

Schulz, R., Hebert, R.S., Dew, M.A., Brown, S.L., Scheier, M.F., Beach, S.R., et al. (2007). Patient suffering and caregiver compassion: New opportunities for research, practice, and policy. *The Gerontologist, 47,* 4–13.

Shiota, M.N., Keltner, D., & John, O.P. (2006). Positive emotion dispositions differentially associated with Big Five personality and attachment style. *The Journal of Positive Psychology, 1,* 61–71.

Smith, A. (1976). *The theory of moral sentiments.* D.D. Raphael, & A.L. Macfie (Eds.). Oxford: Clarendon Press.

Sober, E., & Wilson, D.S. (1999). *The evolution and psychology of unselfish behavior.* Cambridge, MA: Harvard University Press.

Solomon, R.C. (1998). The moral psychology of business: Care and compassion in the corporation. *Business Ethics Quarterly, 8,* 515–533.

Stamm, B.H. (2002). Measuring compassion satisfaction as well as fatigue: Developmental history of the compassion satisfaction and fatigue test. In C.R. Figley (Ed.), *Treating compassion fatigue* (pp. 107–119). New York: Brunner-Routledge.

Staw, B.M., Sutton, R.I., & Pelled, L.H. (1994). Employee positive emotion and favorable outcomes at the workplace. *Organization Science, 5,* 51–71.

Steele, P.D., & Hubbard, R.L. (1985). Management styles, perceptions of substance abuse, and employee assistance programs in organizations. *The Journal of Applied Behavioral Science, 21,* 271–286.

Stephens, J.P., Heaphy, E., & Dutton, J.E. (2011). High-quality connections. In K.S. Cameron & G.M. Spreitzer (Eds.), *The Oxford handbook of positive organizational scholarship.* New York: Oxford University Press.

Stewart, K.L. (1987). What a university ombudsperson does: A sociological study of everyday conduct. *Journal of Higher Education, 49,* 1–22.

Strauss, A.(1993). *Continual permutations of action.* New York: de Gruyter.

Tangney, J.P., & Fischer, K.W. (1995). *Self-conscious emotions: The psychology of shame and guilt.* New York: Guilford Press.

Tanner, C.A., Benner, P. Chesla, C., & Gordon, S. (1996). The phenomenology of knowing the patient. In S. Gordon, P. Benner, & N. Noddings (Eds.), *Caregiving: Readings in knowledge, practice, ethics, and politics* (pp. 203–220). Philadelphia: University of Pennsylvania Press.

Taylor, M.B. (1997). Compassion: It's neglect and importance. *British Journal of General Practice, 47,* 521–523.

Totterdell, P., & Holman, D. (2003). Emotion regulation in customer service roles: Testing a model of emotional labor. *Journal of Occupational Health Psychology, 8,* 57–73.

Tyler, T.R., & Bies, R. (1990). Interpersonal aspects of procedural justice. In J.S. Carroll (Ed.), *Applied social psychology in business settings* (pp. 77–98). Hillsdale, NJ: Lawrence Erlbaum Associates, Inc.

Walsh, J.P., Weber, K., & Margolis, J.D. (2003). Social issues and management: Our lost cause found. *Journal of Management, 29,* 859–881.

Weiss, R.S., Bowlby, J., & Riesman, D. (1973). *Loneliness: The experience of emotional and social isolation.* Cambridge, MA: MIT Press.

Worline, M.C., & Boik, S. (2006). Leadership lessons from Sarah: Values based leadership as everyday practice. In K. Cameron, & E. Hess (Eds.), *Leading with values: Positivity, virtue, and high performance* (pp. 108–131). Cambridge: Cambridge University Press.

Wuthnow, R. (1991). *Acts of compassion: Caring for others and helping ourselves.* Princeton: Princeton University Press.

Zaslow, J. (2002). Putting a price tag on grief. *Wall Street Journal, November 20,* D1.

Zedeck, S., & Mosier, K.L. (1990). Work in the family and employing organization. *American Psychologist, 45,* 240–251.

Zucker, L. (1977). The role of institutionalization in cultural persistence. *American Sociological Review, 42,* 726–743.

Imagining Hope in Organizations

From Individual Goal-Attainment to Horizons of Relational Possibility

Arne Carlsen, Aina Landsverk Hagen, *and* Tord F. Mortensen*

Abstract

Research on hope in organizations is still at an embryonic stage. Few scholars have taken up the challenge put forth by Ludema, Wilmot, and Srivastava (1997) in terms of making use of or furthering their evocative exposition of a vocabulary of hope for organization studies. Instead, there has been a tendency in much hope research to reduce hope to notions of individual goal-attainment. This treatment of hope threatens to confound the phenomenon with self-efficacy and optimism, downplays its relational dimension, neglects the open-ended qualities of experiencing in hope, and fails to see that hope is intimately related to imagination. Resurrecting hope as a key construct in organizational research demands a broadening of its conceptual underpinnings and methodological approaches. We review and contrast traditions of hope research and point to implications for more process-oriented approaches. The interplay between imagination and hope in hydrocarbon exploration is provided as an illustrative case.

Keywords: Hope, relational possibility, imagination, agency, phenomenology, pragmatism, narrative

It is the dream we carry
that something wondrous will happen
that it must happen
time will open
hearts will open
doors will open
springs will flow—
that the dream itself will open
that one morning we'll quietly drift
into a harbor we didn't know was there.
—*Olav H. Hauge, It Is the Dream* (1966)[1]

That's what hope is. Imagining and then fighting for and struggling for and sometimes dying for what didn't seem possible before.
—*Barack Obama, The Ebenezer Baptist Church Address*, 20 January 2008, Atlanta

---

* Aina Landsverk Hagen and Tord F. Mortensen contributed equally as second authors to this chapter.

The dreams we carry in organizations are many. Sometimes, dreams take the form of goal-driven pursuits: to improve performance, to create a healthy workplace were people thrive, to conquer markets, to win against competitors, or to do good for outside beneficiaries. At other times, dreams are built on more complex longings, where it is not the prospects of a specific achievement that call upon us but the naked terrains of possibility and its unpredictable openness: to shape a new role, to form new connections with people, to embark upon a new project adventure, to enter a new industry, to marvel at the beauty and indeterminacy of a single powerful idea, to aspire to ideals of human betterment (Rorty, 2000), or simply, to believe that what we do today will somehow prove beneficial and matter tomorrow in ways we yet cannot foresee (James, 1880, 1896/2000). All of these dreams, whether goal driven or possibility expanding, pleasant or desperate, are fuelled by some shade of hope. Yet, hope in organizations is something we know little about.

What is hope, and how is hope experienced and enabled in organizations? Hope is a complex and fundamental category of human experiencing that has been approached from many parts of social science. Our nodding to pragmatism above indicates just one example, as we will show. A quest to understand hope should be a humble quest. The experiencing of hope in organizations cannot be fully appreciated if we connect it to organizational ends alone. Organizations are targets of hope, but also sites for hope that proceeds inward to individual lives and outward to broader causes and purposes.

Our aim with this chapter is paradoxical. Although being humbled by the daunting possibilities and potential reach of inquiring into hope, we also believe hope research needs a change of tracks to meet its potential in positive organizational scholarship (POS) and organization studies more broadly. In the latter sense, our purpose is that of opening up. It is probably fair to say that only *one* journal article about the construct of hope in organization theory does justice to the historical roots of the concept—a paper by Ludema, Wilmott, and Srivastava (1997) in *Human Relations*. The paper is remarkable for the breath of theory it uses and because its ambitions proceeded later efforts in terms of offering a contrast to a *vocabulary of deficit thinking* by proposing the building blocks for a *vocabulary of hope*. Since it was published in 1997, the paper has been referenced in eight articles within organization theory,[2] none of which can be said to fully adopt the authors' mission of developing a vocabulary of hope. Research on hope has so far

not been a major driving force in the development of the tradition of POS or organization theory at large.

We have organized our review of the literature on hope along three pathways that each may contribute to future work, see Table 22.1 for a summary. The first path is research on hope within positive psychology and the related emergent literature on positive psychological capital, both having a dominant focus on measuring states of hope as individual goal-attainment. This contrasts with the key notion of hope as *relational possibility* in Ludema et al. (1997), representative for a second path of research within other vistas of social science. Characteristic of this path—and we shall pay particular attention to pragmatism and narrative theory—are notions of hope as future-oriented quests for utopia, human betterment, or progression in life stories. Such approaches tend to be broad, descriptive, and conceptual in their orientations and can be hard to make operational in empirical organizational research. We thus go on to sketch a third path, in which we argue for a phenomenological approach to understand how hope is experienced and enabled at work. Here, we point to examples of process approaches within streams of health research and within POS.

We illustrate this path with a description of the dynamics between hope and imagination in hydrocarbon exploration. Throughout, we also pay brief visits to the enabling of hope in some of President Obama's speeches, reflecting the centrality of hope in his political project.[3]

The First Path: Hope As Individual Goal Attainment

A dominant pathway of hope-related research is what has come to be known as *hope theory* within positive psychology. C. Rick Snyder (2000a, 2002) has been a leading figure in this tradition, building on psychiatry (e.g., Frankl, 1963/2004) as well as clinical psychology (e.g., Stotland, 1969). Snyder took initial inspiration from interviews when doing *excuse research*. He saw that, as much as people make excuses to distance themselves from unfavorable outcomes, a more striking pattern was their striving toward meeting positive goals (Snyder, 1989, 2000b). Snyder and his colleagues have since laid the groundwork for understanding hope as a form of positive expectation for goal attainment that includes agency, pathway thinking, and affective resources. Goal-directed thinking is the heart of this set of conceptions, as Snyder sees goals as providing anchors or endpoints of mental action sequences (Snyder, 2000b). Goals include both *repair goals* of filling a profound void, everyday *maintenance goals* and *enhancement goals*

Table 22.1 Paths of hope research in comparison

	First Path: Hope As Individual Goal Attainment	Second Path: Hope As Relational Possibility	Third Path: Hope As Organizational Processes
Key conceptions	Hope as positive expectancy of goal attainment resulting from an interaction of *ways* (a sense of available pathways) and *will* (a sense of agency); primarily individual, goal-oriented, and cognitive in orientation	Hope as a mode of acting that is intensely relational, thrives on the open-ended, is sustained by moral dialogue, and is a generative engine of development; acknowledges collectivity, emergence, and emotion	Hope as phenomenon; a future-oriented and emotive quality of experiencing that interacts with other organizational processes and is contextually and situationally shaped; acknowledges collectivity, emergence, and emotion
Underpinning traditions of research and philosophy	Solid tradition dominated by the hope theory of Snyder (2000a; 2000b; 2002) and colleagues in positive psychology as well as Luthans, Youseff, and Avolio (2007) and others on positive psychological capital; antecedents in psychiatry and clinical psychology; some use of narrative theory	Fragmented field of theorizing with limited uptake in organization studies, except for the paper by Ludema, Wilmot, and Srivastava (1997); broad inspiration from many parts of social science including theology, psychology, pragmatist philosophy, and narrative theory	Established tradition of process studies of hope within health-related research; emergent tradition within positive organizational scholarship; uses broad theoretical inspiration, e.g., from positive psychology, narrative theory, and the philosophy of pragmatism
Main thrust of studies	Measurements of covariance of positive states based on standardized scales	Philosophical and conceptual work with societal focus, with the exception of mixed-methods life story studies within narrative psychology	Studies of processes and functions of hope in everyday work, mainly with a qualitative, interpretive orientation

that build on what is already satisfactory. Snyder (2002) holds that, without goals, or with vague goals, hope is not nurtured, and he sees emotion as being derived from goal-directed thought—its by-product. Positive emotions flow from perceptions of successful goal pursuits, negative emotions from perceptions of unsuccessful ones.

Snyder's hope theory is bidimensional in the sense that two forms of expectancies are held to interact: *ways*, a sense of available pathways to reach goals, and *will*, a sense of agency. Hope, according to Snyder (2002), is thus a form of goal-directed thinking in which people attach value to desired goals, see themselves as capable of producing routes (ways) to reach these goals, and have the agency (will) to move along these routes and persevere in the face of obstacles.

The two components of hope in hope theory—will and ways—are each on their side related to two other forms of cognitive expectancies held to be determinants of behavior. *Will* is seen as overlapping

with *self-efficacy* (Bandura, 1997; Stajkovic & Luthans, 1997); one's expectancy that one is capable of performing specific actions to attain specific outcomes. Contributors to this hope theory recognizes the overlap with self-efficacy for situational goal-directed thoughts, but hold that the will component of hope can be based on goal thoughts that are cross-situational and enduring (Snyder, Rand, & Sigmon, 2005). *Ways* is seen as overlapping with *optimism*; the general expectancy that one will experience good outcomes in life (Scheier & Carver, 1985) and the retrospective attribution of such outcomes to self (Seligman, 1998). Ways and optimism differ in the sense that the pathways component of the hope construct pertains uniquely to actions initiated by self, whereas optimism is more linked to outcomes that result from forces and happenings external to the individual (Snyder, 2000b).

Most contributions of hope theory repeat some version of the distinctions just made, signaling that the potential overlap and confusion between these terms is a standing concern (Luthans & Jensen, 2002; Snyder, 2000b; 2002), although several studies have concluded that each component of the two-dimensional hope theory is distinct from each other and from related concepts (e.g., Carifio & Rhodes, 2002; Luthans, Avolio, Avey, & Norman, 2007; Magaletta & Oliver, 1999; Youssef & Luthans, 2007). For example, Magaletta and Oliver (1999), working from a sample of 204 university students and investigating the relationships between expectancies and general well-being, report findings that suggest unique contributions from both components of the hope construct, as well as from the overall combined measure (although weaker). Empirical overlaps between the will component of hope and self-efficacy, as well as between the ways component and optimism, were also established in this study.

The growing theory on psychological capital adds to this stream of distinctions made. Positive psychological capital, PsyCap, is suggested as a high-level construct consisting of the components of hope, optimism, self-efficacy, and resilience, as well as their potentially synergistic interaction (Luthans, Avolio et al., 2007; Luthans, Youseff, & Avolio, 2007; see also Youseffin & Luthans, 2011, Chapter 2, this volume).

Research following this set of conceptualizations has, during the last decade, established that individually measured states of high hope are favorably associated with positive outcomes in the arenas of athletics, physical health (although no claims for increased recovery rates of severe illnesses are made), psychological adjustment, and psychotherapy (Snyder, 2000a; Snyder, Rand, & Sigmon, 2005). Recently, studies have also related hope to favorable outcomes in organizations. For example, Adams et al. (2002) claim a link between high levels of employee hope and profitable companies (further characterized by high levels of autonomy, clear goals, and two-way communication). Peterson and Luthans (2003) present a study in which high-hope as compared to low-hope leaders had more profitable work units and had better satisfaction and retention rates among their subordinates. Likewise, studies of PsyCap in the workplace have reported various links between hope and job satisfaction, organizational commitment and performance (Larson & Luthans, 2006; Luthans, Avolio, Walumbwa, & Li, 2005; Luthans, Norman, Avolio, & Avey, 2008 Youseff & Luthans, 2007).

Finally, attempts have been made to sketch strategies for accentuating hope in the workplace based on the kinds of covariances that have been reported (see Lopez et al., 2004, for a more general overview). Luthans and Jensen (2002, p. 314–315) mention, for example, the importance of solution talk, as opposed to problem talk—clarifying and forming goals that are specific and challenging at all levels, breaking goals down to manageable steps, and mentally rehearsing their completion, as well as recollection of previous successes. Part of this advice parallels the typical ways of building self-efficacy in terms of undergoing mastery experiences and learning from vicarious experience through social modeling and social persuasion (Bandura, 1997).

The merits of the research just cited should not be discredited, nor should its results be overlooked. But it seems fair to suggest that the path of hope research we find in positive psychology can be characterized not only as focused but also as overly narrow. Two sets of arguments underpin that suggestion. First, this stream of hope research shows little methodological variation. The studies referred to invariably present measures of self-reported individual states and claims of covariance with some positive outcome. Following Hackman (2009a,b) in his broader critique of the positive organizational behavior tradition—of which Luthans et al. (2008) hold research on hope, self-efficacy, optimism, and resilience to be core—we also note the lack of discussion of direction of causality and dimensionality of concepts. Moreover, current hope research says very little of how hope is experienced by organizational members, how hope is shaped over time, or how processes of enabling or restricting hope interact with other organizational processes or phenomena. The methods used are highly decontextual and atemporal.

Second, most hope research, whether in positive psychology or the PsyCap tradition, operates from a fairly confined conceptual terrain. None of the studies cited above communicates with traditions of hope research outside psychiatry or clinical and positive psychology. This is probably a main reason why the many heavy assumptions that go into the notion that hope is primarily linked to individuals' goal-directed thinking are seldom or never discussed. At least three key assumptions go virtually unquestioned: Is it meaningful to study hope as a purely *individual* phenomenon? Can one assume that hope is always tied to some form of *goal-directed* pursuit? Is it fair to assume that hope primarily is a form of *thinking*? Each of these assumptions presents opportunities for broadening the concept of hope and extending hope research. Empirically, one may simply think about the experience of having a child, probably one of the most hope-inducing and hope-intensive experiences one can undergo as a human being. Children are beacons of hope for the future and miracles of new life who renew relationships and open possibilities, sometimes not only for their close family, but for a village or for entire generations of kin. Is having a child meaningfully understood as a purely individual experience? Is it about goal attainment? Is it cognitive in origin? Organizations are not sites for birthing children but have their baby parallels in highly favored projects, adventures, and ideas, carriers of dreams that both stake out pursuits and open up to the unknown.

Theoretically, as we will show, there are many reasons for saying that hope is a quality of experiencing that is intensely relational, irreducibly open-ended, and thickly emotional at its origin rather than in its consequence. Although hoping is *sometimes* primarily individually and goal-driven, we suggest it is fruitful to regard such conceptions as reporting from a specific *mode* of hoping (Webb, 2007) rather than the whole phenomenon. There is also existential hope (Meisenhelder, 1982), utopian hope (Bloch, 1959/1995), social hope (Rorty, 2000), and open-ended hope (Carlsen & Pitsis, 2009; Crites, 1986; Crapanano, 2003). Hope is not a single undifferentiated experience that one may dissect easily into its cognitive and emotive compartments. To more fully understand hope, we must consult broader research traditions.

The Second Path: Hope As Relational Possibility

The approaches to hope that we have classified under the first and second paths share territory in terms of acknowledging hope as a positively charged experience that is directed toward the future and acts as a generative force in people's lives. They differ on all three of the identified core assumptions of the path dominated by positive psychology: individuality over relationality, goal attainment over open-endedness, and cognition over emotion.

Let us begin with the heritage of Ludema, Wilmot, and Srivastava (1997; see also Ludema, 2001). This work presents an ambitious and far-reaching agenda of offering *textured vocabularies of hope*—stories, theories, illustrations, and concepts—that can provide the linguistic resources for transformative human action and organizing. In many ways, it is an ambition that forms a parallel argument to

the genesis of positive psychology (Seligman & Csickszentmihalyi, 2000) and positive organizational scholarship (Cameron, Dutton, & Quinn 2003) in terms of being pit against deficit thinking. To Ludema et al., a vocabulary of hope counteracts an arsenal of demolishing and deriding intellectual weaponry of critical and deconstructive methods that focus on incapacities and faults (Gergen, 1994). Summarizing 40 books and 100 articles taken from Greco-Roman, Judeo-Christian, enlightenment, psychoanalytic, radical humanist, and cognitive theorist traditions, the authors land on four enduring qualities of hope:

- *Hope is relational*: Experiences of hope are intensely relational, both in how they are born and sustained and in their functions. Hope is enlivened in the personal and professional relationship. Hope may prosper when one places oneself in service to others, and hope may be a binding force in a community or society at large.
- *Hope is open-ended*: Hoping assumes a conviction that the future is open-ended, becoming, fraught with generative possibilities and can be influenced. Rather than being set on specific goals alone, the experiencing of hope presupposes dynamic and improvisational imagination that precedes anticipation of a coherent image of the future.
- *Hope is sustained by moral dialogue*: The experiencing of hope is sustained by dialogue about ultimate concerns and high human ideals. Hope is a source of moral vision that may point to possibilities for human betterment and spawn moral action.
- *Hope is generative*: Hoping is a source of positive affect and action, and as such, the engine of all human creativity and cultural development. Hope is most generative when it is inclusive, invites open dialogue, and expands people's horizons.

A noteworthy overall feature of these enduring qualities is the theme of transcendence. Along with Peterson and Seligman (2004, p. 569–582), one may regard hope as a character strength of transcendence. But the transcendence in hope conveyed by Ludema et al. (1997) does not stop at self or organizational borders. Rather, it is an expansion toward increasing relational possibility, a hoping that extends from some local core to a noble larger whole. Hope is transcendent in that it stretches beyond the status quo of present circumstances toward renewing life and improving human conditions. In the traditions of hope research referred to by Ludema et al., this stretching beyond the present tends to be directed toward some moral, spiritual, or religious visions. By such thinking, hoping is an act of transcendence that has many alternative final addressees: utopia, human betterment, or divinity.

The transcendence of hope is a core theme in the famous discussion of utopia by Ernst Bloch (1959/1995), but also follows, as we shall see, strongly from pragmatism and narrative theory. To get at several forms of transcendence, we shall invoke the metaphor of *imagined horizons*. It is a concept borrowed and adapted from a contemporary philosopher within anthropology, Vincent Crapanzano (2004). Crapanzano, who also takes a broad philosophical perspective on hope (Crapanzano, 2003), explores the dynamics of opening and closure in how people imagine—implicitly or explicitly—horizons that shape what they experience and how they interpret what they experience. Horizons are demarcated within a narrated and known landscape, ranging from the highly articulate, such as specific goals hoped for, to more vaguely shaped contours and edges that fall away but still represent imaginations that allow people to distance themselves from present realities. Horizons are dynamically related to ongoing experience in the sense that, when reaching the peak that used to be our horizon, another beyond is already forming, and this beyond instantly forms the horizon of the next search (Crapanzano, 2004). Talking about horizons and their beyond allows us to consider multiple addressees of experiences of hoping and the importance of imagination in such experiences. People ultimately hope for what they imagine, and such imaginations come in many forms.

Horizons of Hope in Pragmatism

Pragmatism may be regarded a philosophy of hope (Westbrook, 2005), one that is stretching from Emerson through James and Dewey to Rorty (Koopman, 2006). A core theme of William James' work is the twin notion of existential indeterminacy and people's will to believe (James, 1880, 1896/2000). On the one hand, in his radical theory of experience, James saw existence as fundamentally open-ended, undetermined, and in a flux of continuous becoming (Carlsen, 2009). On the other, a personal experience of emerging from suicidal depression colors James' entire scholarship. When James famously decided he would have the will to

believe, it was a belief that current thoughts and actions would be fruitful in future experience and that his sense of self would not to be destroyed but enhanced by future experience (McDermott, 2000). We may say it was a hope born out of reconciling the inherent fragility and uncertainty of existence with people's will to believe that they can make a difference. In this sense, James' will to believe mirrors a view of hope as set up by the ontological insecurity of struggling with existential angst in the face of one's inevitable death (Meisenhelder, 1982).

The centrality of belief—and thus hope—in James' scholarship partly shares the element of *will* with Snyder's hope theory but is not directed at any situational or enduring goals, nor is it a cool and exclusively positive affair. Insisting on such unitary concreteness would be anathema to James' recognition of the fragility of life, the ongoing threat of despair, and the open-ended nature of existence. Also, *belief* here should not be regarded as *faith* in terms of ascribing to specific ways of seeing (Crapanzano, 2003). Rather, James' belief should be seen as a hoping that cannot be collapsed into some specific behavioral setting but stretches toward vaguely perceived horizons and their beyond. It follows in a tradition of heralding self-reliance and transcendence in American intellectual life, a tradition in which Ralph Waldo Emerson laid the first stones (Ziff, 1982). Emerson's quest for self-reliance originated within a setting of growth of the new and promised land, an elevation of creative discovery rooted in nature over the determining seal of European history. But it was also a self-reliance that, from the beginning, addressed horizons beyond independence and growth, as famously stated in Emerson's lecture on Nature: "So we shall come to look at the world with new eyes. It shall answer the endless inquiry of the intellect, - What is truth? and of the affections,- What is good? by yielding itself passive to the educated Will" (Emerson, 1836/1982, p. 80).

Emerson's call for inquiring into *truth* and *good* as the horizon of hope for the American scholar (and worker) was also picked up by Dewey, who situated it in an ongoing quest for developing democracy (Dewey, 1903/1973). Dewey saw pragmatism as part of a larger tradition of socializing and education that furthered liberty and increased hope for the future. He spoke of the importance of moral imagination, by which people conjure ideals of human betterment to guide action in the present (Alexander, 1992; 1995). By this view, acts of hoping can be acts of moral imagination where the betterment of the human condition is the final horizon. This aspect of Deweyan thought was later celebrated by Rorty (2000, p.120): "Hope—the ability to believe that the future will be unspecifiably different from and unspecifically freer than, the past—is the condition of growth. That sort of hope was all that Dewey himself offered us, and by offering it he became our century's Philosopher of Democracy."

The relevance of the pragmatism theme of hope for our present purposes is not only to show that hope may address wide and distant horizons of relational possibility. Pragmatism also attunes us to how tightly interwoven the experiencing of hope is with imagination. In pragmatism, questions of justification in science refer to the future, truth is always provisional, subject to fallibility and improved imaginations (Carlsen, 2009). In Rorty's (2000) terms, *knowledge* (as absolute truth) is replaced with *hope* (as imagined conjectures addressing specific purposes), and hope for a better human future is the final addressee of all inquiry. Rorty's conceptual move is a reminder that hope is a fundamental and necessary ingredient in everyday creative work. Each act of creation or venturing forth, whether in everyday life or in scientific work, is a step into the unknown that presupposes some amount of hoping.

One can also turn the argument around. Must not hope presuppose imagination? Pragmatism as a philosophy of hope is also a situated theory of imagination as it extends in and through daily activities (Alexander, 1990; Joas, 1996). As such, imagination can be thought of as a human capacity to transcend limitations and convert (Kearney, 1998, p. 4) "absence into presence, actuality into potentiality, what-is into something-other-than-it-is." When President Obama speaks of hope, it may be seen as having precisely such qualities of imagination. In his Cairo speech, Obama spoke of a future that is inherent in all our acts, in our "ability to re-imagine the world, to remake this world"[4] as it was in the acts of people before us. Obama can be seen as enabling hope by attempting to expand our moral imagination, not only by speaking of ideals of conduct and human betterment in a Deweyan sense, but by urging people to imagine the situation of the other through emphatic projections.[5] It is as way of talking about hope that continues and expands the pragmatist tradition.

A role for imagination in hope can be inferred from Snyder's (2000b, 2002) hope theory in terms of the importance of conjuring pathways to reach goals. It cannot, however, be taken for granted that experiencing hope follows in a distinct phase *after* portrayal of some clear goal or vision. Rather, it seems more likely that hope often emerges from that which is imagined, whether conjuring the future possibilities of an organization, the future lives of children, or the ideals of human conduct for society at large. There are hoped-for imaginations from specific circumstances, as well as more enduring imaginations. Acts of imagination and hoping may sustain each other in processes unfolding over days, weeks, or even years.

Pragmatism has also taught us that imagination is not a mere cognitive affair. Imagination will often partly take place in a prereflective domain and can be considered the mode of reasoning that is most tightly associated with feeling (Alexander, 1990; Anderson, 2005). Indeed, the logician Peirce went as far as saying that all idea generation, all abductive inference, is in its essence a form of imaginative feeling that cannot follow from step-by-step logic but needs involvement of embodied human intuition (Peirce, 1931–1958 (CP): 1.46; 2.641–644).

Lazarus (1999) has suggested a conception of hope that is more in line with pragmatist notions of felt imaginations emerging from everyday events. To Lazarus, hoping is both an emotion and a vital coping resource. Lazarus sees hope as a product of the relational meaning an individual constructs when encountering significant situations in which something is at stake, also situations that are threatening or difficult in some way.[6] This conceptualization is in line with the centrality of *doubt* as the engine of imaginations in pragmatism (Locke, Golden-Biddle, & Feldman, 2008). Contraries to prior thinking, threats to status quo and difficulties represent problems and doubt that seed imagination, and in turn, hope.

Although being a powerful window into the dynamics of imagination and hope, pragmatist theory says little about the finer details of how language is used to build collective imagination: How is the hope that carries relational possibility created? For that we turn to narrative.

Horizons of Hope in Narrative Theory

Narrative theory, and in particular its psychological branch (e.g., Bruner, 1990; McAdams, 1993; Sarbin, 1986), provides resources to understand the experience of hope in two distinct ways. The first set of contributions revolves around how narratives constitute a primary tool for human meaning making and imagination (Kearney, 2002;

Polkinghorne, 1988). Hope is rooted in the creation of meaning in ongoing experience by the weaving stories of possibilities in new experience. Such weaving may incorporate stories of individuals within stories of the organization, within stories and hopes for outside beneficiaries and larger social wholes. It is through stories that relational being can exist (Gergen, 2009), and it is through stories that we see the multiple addressivities of hoping; hope for a *me*, a *we*, or an *other*, sometimes in the same telling (Carlsen & Pitsis, 2009). An example here may be taken from the source of one of our opening quotes, the speech U.S. President Barack Obama gave at the Ebenezer Baptist Church in Atlanta, on January 20, 2008.[7] In this speech, Obama weaves together the stories of individuals (a white young girl and a black old man, Rosa Parks, King, Obama himself) with stories of larger "we" (the church audience, the Civil Rights movement, immigrants, blacks and whites, people of all religions and atheists, America, the world) and the need for unity in the "fierce urgency of the present."[8] It is a relational and a temporal weave: Through imagination, the work of hope connects people's shared past achievements, their history, with the now and the potentiality of tomorrow.

It is inherent in Snyder's hope theory and Bandura's self-efficacy theory that stories of past achievements—whether one's own or those gained from vicarious experience—provide templates of experiences that may build belief in attaining future outcomes (e.g., McDermott & Hastings, 2000). People use stories from the past to create hope for the future. Narratives also come as scenarios of hoped-for futures, sequences of potential events, and future states that make up believed-in imaginings (Rivera & Sarbin, 1998) that may or may not be assigned social weight.[9]

It follows from what has been said so far that the stories that bring hope to people's lives are not only of an overt kind. People grab plot lines that inform what they attend to, enact, and hope for when living life forward (Ricoeur, 1991); for example, the hopes framed in stories of a mission, a mystery, a battle, or a treasure hunt (Carlsen, 2008). Such grabbing of plot lines will always take place within horizons of meaning that escape full articulation (Crapanzano, 2004; Crites, 1971; Ricoeur, 1991; Sarbin, 1997). For example, McAdams and colleagues (Bauer, McAdams, & Pals, 2008; McAdams, 2006) have identified the narrative structure of *redemption* as a mythic resource drawn upon by many Americans in how they make sense of

their lives. The theme of redemption is traced back to spiritual autobiographies of New England Puritans in the 17th century and carry heavy references to the story of Jesus Christ in the New Testament. It revolves around heroic struggles to defy convention, overcome obstacles, and endure suffering on the path to personal liberation, growth, and generativity. Redemptive stories affirm belief in progress in people's lives and hope for the future.

The second set of contributions from narrative theory that can be used to understand the experience of hope in organizations is that it offers a window into understanding its motivational dimensions. A casual use of the term *hope* may refer to almost any set of action-motive in everyday life, like "hoping to see a movie tonight" or "hoping the plane is on schedule." Most such events are not likely to figure importantly in how people see their lives or the development of organizations. By contrast, an act of hoping that concerns individual and collective life stories will be more consequential and contribute more to the intensity of the experience. According to narrative identity theory, life stories, whether individual or collective, function to achieve some semblance of continuity and purpose among the variety of situationally determined self-concepts. People experience their lives though evolving life stories that they continuously construct and reconstruct to make sense of their past and anticipate their future (Bruner, 1990; Crites, 1971; McAdams, 1993, 1999; Polkinghorne, 1988). This is a temporal process that always extends from the threefold present: a present of things present, a present of things past, and a present of things future (Crites, 1971). Hope is inherent in the experience of self in the present of things future. Maintaining the experience of hope may thus be considered a meta-motive in identity construction as it is links to favorable progression in the life stories of individuals and collectives (Carlsen & Pitsis, 2009). We shall dwell briefly on two primary forms such progression may take, corresponding to two types of hope: attainment hope and opening-up hope.

ATTAINMENT HOPE

Attainment hope is directed toward desired outcomes of goal-directed pursuits (situational or more enduring) that deeply concerns a *me* or a *we* and engender lived experience with a sense of purpose. The need for forms of goal-attainment in life is a recurring theme in the social sciences, as well as in narrative identity literature. Motives for enrichment of life stories in terms of enhancing attainment-hope range from purpose (Bruner, 1990; McAdams, 1999) to challenge (Csikszentmihalyi, 1985), drama (Carlsen, 2008; Mattingly, 1998; Scheibe, 1986), and generativity (McAdams, 2006; McAdams, Diamond, de St. Aubin, & Mansfield, 1997); the motive of leaving a legacy behind that is valuable for future generations.

This set of conceptualizations bears likeness to Snyder's hope theory in terms of assigning weight to the goal-directed dimension of the hoping experience. It differs in emphasizing that hope is relational. For example, hoping to escape from severe illnesses, such as cancer, is a hope that may be central to both patients and health personnel (Good, Good, Schaffer, & Lind, 1990). In her brilliant book about healing dramas of occupational therapy, Mattingly (1998) pointed to a similar mechanism—by instilling hope in the lives of their patients and their patients' next of kin, therapists also find deep sources of hope in their own lives. Likewise, tales from Holocaust survivors (Bratteli, 1980; Sachnowitz, 1976), often emphasize hope as a generative force that was necessary to escape death *and* leave behind a legacy that would prevent similar atrocities from happening again.

Another contrast between what we here call attainment hope and the hope theory of positive psychology is that we see hope as having a shadow of despair and risk (Carlsen, 2008; Crites, 1986; Lazarus, 1999, 2003; Scheibe, 1986). As previewed in the opening quote from Obama, hope is not an undifferentiated positive experience but rather a positively charged quality of experiencing that may be heightened by the totality of what is at stake.

OPENING-UP HOPE

Opening-up hope is oriented toward new possibilities and the open-ended qualities of experience. It springs from a need to live with indeterminacy and possibility (MacIntyre, 1981; Turner, 1980): the unforeseen, the break with the past, the new day. Its function in the life story is to maintain openness (McAdams, 1993) and prevent stagnation caused by a determining past or the imposing constraints of others. Eclea Bosi (1979) (as referred to in Scheibe, 1986) has remarked on the pleasure with which old people she interviewed about their lives remembered their youths, despite having gone through periods of poverty, deprivation, and limitation of freedom. In retrospect, the old persons viewed what many would describe as miserable childhoods with "great pleasure and warm nostalgia" (Scheibe, 1986, p. 145): "Bosi remarks that the reason for this

historical foreshortening has to do with the character of youthful perceptions of the world—perceptions that are fresh and full of adventure. No matter how hard the external conditions, the playful gathering in of fresh perceptions of the world comprise essential features—the fundaments—of the life story as it is to develop."

Along with Erikson (1959/1994), one may regard openness in life story an inevitable quality of youth that is primarily located in early stages of a life cycle. We hold that it is more fruitful to regard it a mode of hoping that endures through life (McAdams, 1993). It stands in contrast to stagnation and the potential captivity of a unitary goal-pursuit (Carlsen & Pitsis, 2009; Crites, 1986). Attainment hope and opening-up hope can be in conflict. The same desires that make people passionately pursue some possibilities may close down others.

In summary, we learn from narrative theory that the intensities of hope must be seen both as stemming from a narratively shaped field of desire in the present future and as a quality of undirected open-endedness that stands against a closedness one may bring to lived experience. Consequently, hope needs to be investigated not only as a *generative force* within established or projected trajectories of action, but also as a *subversive force* that opposes closedness.

The Phenomenological Path: Experiencing and Enabling Hope At Work

The third path of hope research that we raise in this chapter follows from the previous two, not to replace them, but as a necessary extension. Continued measuring of individual states of goal-induced hope or broad sweeping theorizing around the philosophical basis of hope will not be sufficient to resurrect hope as a key concept in POS or organization studies at large. Furthermore, when using a narrative perspective on hope, it is important to keep in mind that stories meant to invoke hope are often contested and vulnerable to critique for being loosely connected to everyday practice and action. We do not know very much about the phenomenon of hope in organizations, and we need to strengthen research that studies hope as part of organizational practice.

A phenomenological approach to hope demands that one follows people in their work settings over time and tries to capture the functions of hope in everyday work and in relation to other phenomena such as organizational change, creativity, job crafting, or positive identity construction. Sensitivity to context will be one key in such efforts. All variations of the experience of hoping are manifestations of the projective capacities of human agencies, but the intensities and functions of hoping will depend on the directionality of hope (emerging from depression, getting away from hopelessness, attaining a discovery) and the particulars of the sequences of events that form contexts for acts of hoping.

Our use of the term *acts of hoping* rather than *states of hope* is intentional. It signals a focus on verbs rather than nouns, process rather than states. Such a shift has been key to recent studies of hope processes in health-related research. Eliott and Olver (2007), in doing semistructured interviews with 28 dying cancer patients, found that a shift to the use of hope as verb rather than noun enabled the patients to focus on the positive, connect to others, and actively engage in life. Weingarten (2010) argues that seeing hope as a verb helps people focus on doing and connecting in the here and now and describes clinical practices of co-creating *reasonable hope*. (See also contributions by Miller (1985), Good et al. (1990), and Parse (2007)).

We know of no studies dedicated solely to hope phenomena in organizations, although ongoing work on *hope organizing* in the Andes flight disaster (Harrison, 2010) and hopeful social change in poor countries (Branzei, 2011) seems promising. Hope does however figure indirectly in several POS-related studies. An early account can be found in research on the survivors of downsizing applying a hopeful response (Mishra & Spreitzer, 1998). Several more recent studies have investigated shades of hope related to positive identity construction. Maitlis (2009) has beautifully described how musicians making sense of traumas that threatened or undermined their sense of self tell of a deep-seated experiencing of opening up to a discovery of new roles and pathways. Ibarra (1999, 2003, p. 91–111) has shown how experiments with provisional selves, ranging from small projects to singular acts of doing something new, highlight the opening-up function in identity construction. A related strategy revolves around telling stories of one's professional experiences in ways that open up and qualify several future possible selves and development paths (Ibarra, 2003, p. 133–158). Likewise, the notions of *jolts in experience* by Roberts, Dutton, Spreitzer, Heaphy, and Quinn (2005) and *instantiating* by Carlsen (2006) can be regarded as seeding opening-up hope. In both contributions, a breach in experience is made significant, by individuals or a collective, as opening up new growth patterns, whether possible selves (Roberts et al., 2005) or identity-salient new

trajectories of practice (Carlsen, 2006). In the latter case, two relatively small and insignificant projects that demonstrated the value of in-house technologies were projected as ideal exemplars of future practice of the firm and revitalized the life story of the organization. In the eyes of organizational members the projects represented, ". . . just the kind of work we really wanted to do" (Carlsen, 2006, p. 140). Opening-up hope charges breaches in experience with expectation. Attainment hope sets people on the pathways that have been opened up.

We shall end the chapter with a case that illustrates the potential of inquiring into hope as relational possibility. It is taken from a type of work context in which *ideas* carry hopes of both goal attainment and expanded possibility: oil exploration.

From Dusters to Play Openers: Ideas of Hope in Oil Exploration

Explorers of oil and gas have to imagine processes that took place hundreds of millions of years ago and persuade their companies to bet millions of dollars on *prospects*; ideas of where oil can be found. Explorers are in many ways modern gold miners and science-based fortune seekers, and as such, make up a case particularly thick on the phenomenon of how ideas mediate hope. The ideas that carry the most weight are *play openers*. A *play* in hydrocarbon exploration is a clustering of petroleum accumulations and prospects into natural families; a type of prospect.[10] A play opener is the demonstration of a completely new form of prospect type or the validation of a prospect type in a region where it has not been seen before.

A few years ago, two of the authors (Mortensen and Carlsen) were having lunch with a small group of exploration geologists in an oil company as part of a 4-year action research project. We were preparing a workshop on creativity in exploration, and this was the third or fourth time we met. The uplifted and enthusiastic spirit of the conversation perplexed us. Between encounters, we had tried to follow the results of the drilling program of these exploration teams, and we had just learned that their most believed-in well, drilled on a prospect they had been working on for many years, came in dry. It was a duster. Why then, this enchanted atmosphere? It turned out that the duster had not only brought disconfirmations to the group, but also new data that spurred a flurry of questions, discussions, and idea generation. Combined with other geological data, a number of potential prospects were on the brink of being developed, some with consequences for large parts of the geological region that the geologists were exploring. In an interview on one of the following days—with another geologist of the same group—a second piece of the puzzle became clear. During the point in the interview at which he shows most engagement, the explorer says the following:

And then she came in to [my office] . . . she had a seismic line that went from [another larger region] where she was interpreting it, into our [territory] . . . "You've seen this?," she said. On that one seismic line there was a bright seismic amplitude on the top, so then I say "no, I haven't seen it." . . . Then I sat a few evenings with it . . . and in the course of three to four days I had mapped out four large structures in an area where we had no real prospects . . . and that could potentially mean an extension of those play models into a vast area . . . from those four we have almost 150 structures today . . . and if that works the upside potential is just enormous, which basically all came from one person with one seismic line where she spotted an anomaly.

The exact geological connections between the lunch conversation and the mapping of the structures reported in the interview are not decisive to the present purposes. The main point to be derived from this is the sense of hopeful engagement attached to imaginations—whether rays of vague ideas derived from dusters or ideas of play openers—and the decisiveness of this engagement both for collectives and individuals.

Figure 22.1 illustrates a trajectory of idea development and the associated growing and decay of hope as interpreted by us after the events. The context for the situation is the attainment-hope attached to (1) the favored prospect idea before drilling. This idea was the explorers' most trusted prospect,

one they championed to drilling. Ideas of such prospects in no small way carry the fate of individual careers, the collective fortunes for the exploration team and the organization. When the prospect turned out to be a (2) duster, this attainment-hope was shattered. As we have learned from pragmatism, disconfirmation of prior thoughts has the power to generate new ideas as new data represent (3) new seeds of wonder. Here, we are not talking of ideas of new prospects, but rather of ideas as something more embryonic; the birthing of curiosity, the vague trajectories of thought that carry opening-up hope. From the dust of the duster, (4) ideas of new prospects emerged for the explorers, at first as tentative imaginations of where there could be oil. These ideas will also mediate attainment hope, but here it seems fair to suggest that opening-up hope plays a more significant role. For the explorers, new prospect ideas are likely to be generators of hope and sources of vitality, long before work unfolds into full-fledged drilling adventures. Finally, as can be inferred from the interview, (5) ideas of a play opener are imagined. A single seismic line was expanded into four new structures, which again opened up for vast potentials for oil and possibilities for further search. This set of ideas mediates a mixture of both strong attainment hope and opening-up hope.

The example illustrates several of the points raised previously in the chapter. Hope develops in tandem with imagination—here, the conjuring of ideas of explaining past geological processes (imagined narratives of prior happenings) brought to bear on prospects for drilling (imagined sequences of outcomes). It is a peculiar quality of this dynamic that ideas, when they are tested, may erase some forms of hope (attainment hope) and simultaneously create others (opening-up hope). The hoping going on here is both tied to specific goals of finding oil and realizing identified prospects, as well as emerging from new experiences of being proved wrong, seeing an anomaly, and generating new imaginings that are believed in. Finally, this whole process of hoping unfolds across blurred boundaries of individuals and collectives: The hoping addresses outcomes for explorers, for the teams in question, for the oil company, and for the larger geological region and the socioeconomic prosperity of the geographical region where exploitation may take place. We see a sequence of horizons of relational possibility.

Conclusion

When circumscribing his topic at the start of *The Varieties of Religious Experience*, William James

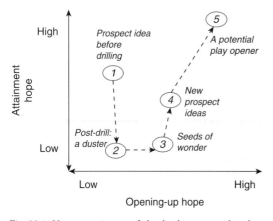

Fig. 22.1 How one trajectory of idea development mediated forms of hope.

(1902/2002) somewhat laconically expressed distaste for reducing the inquiry of so complex a field to one distinct definition. It is a sentiment we share for the phenomenon of hope. Hope should be understood in its varieties. Frustrations with a plethora of definitions (e.g., Schrank, Stanghellini, & Slade, 2008) signify the profundity of the phenomenon and its many differentiated manifestations (Webb, 2007; Weingarten, 2010) rather than intellectual confusion. It is therefore somewhat paradoxical that we shall end with a definition here. It should be understood as a summary of the argument, with each element being a vector for further inquiry rather than a demarcation of the limits of the phenomenon.

We conclude that it is fruitful to approach the phenomenon of hope in organizations as a differentiated and future-oriented quality of experiencing that may be directed toward anticipated *attainment* of specified outcomes and purposes, but can also address an expectation of *opening-up* to unknown possibilities and *unarticulated horizons* of expectations and their beyond; is *relationally* construed and sustained; presupposes and enables *believed-in imaginings* of *narrative form*; may be *inherited* from previous experience, as well as *emerge* from new events and jolts in experience; is *emotionally charged* in its origin and in mobilizing affect; and accommodates both *potentially positive outcomes* and *negative elements* of despair, doubt, conflict, and loss.

We started our chapter by questioning three sets of assumptions in psychological hope theory: individuality over relationality, goal-attainment over open-endedness, and cognition over emotion. Following the lead from Ludema et al. (1997), we have established that inquiring into the experiencing of hope in organizations should be more about imagining horizons of relational possibility than about individual goal attainment. And, as our walk through theory and empirical snippets from the worlds of oil explorers or Obama's speeches shows, experiences of hope are felt imaginings that are not singularly good or positive. The antitheses of hope do not belong to some other set of experiences or at the other end of some linear scale. They should be seen as fellow travelers that contribute to an overall charging of the experience.

Future Directions

The main research direction to come out of this chapter is a push for an increased variety of methods and conceptual underpinnings to the study of hope at work. We particularly advocate approaches in which experiences of hope and processes of enabling hope are studied in situ and in relation to other organizational processes, like organizational change and job crafting (see Carlsen & Pitsis, 2009). This is not a call to replace one monopoly (measuring individual states) with another (phenomenological work), but rather a call to expand the field. Part of such expansion should include more conceptual and empirical work on what hope stands against. What are the antitheses of hope? The research traditions encountered here have pointed to a range of answers: despair, indifference, lack of belief, doubt, closedness in experience, and fear of solitary mortality with no beyond. Investigating the basis for each of these may further contribute to our understanding of the variations of hope experiences.

Our two empirical snippets also point toward one area of investigation that seems particularly ripe for future research: the dynamics between imagination and hope. Oil exploration typifies a form of creative work in which ideas are the main input, content, and deliverable, as for example in architectural work, legal work, or research—work in which one's hopes are intensely related to microprocesses of imagination. Obama's example of leadership points to the importance of language (Holman & Thorpe, 2002) in opening up discursive space and facilitating the imagining of new possibilities. It also reminds us that hope may be ultimately about imagining the circumstances and lives of the other, whether for purposes of being creative (Grant & Berry, 2010) or as an ethical quest toward expanded moral imagination. Pursuing the dynamics of imagination and hope may allow us to drift into harbors we did not know were there. That is a dream we may carry.

Acknowledgments

We are grateful to Oana Branzei, Siv Heidi Breivik, Jane Dutton, Karoline Krauss, Tyrone Pitsis, and Lance Sandelands for useful discussions and input leading up to the final version of this paper, and to Gretchen Spreitzer for helpful editorial advice. A version of the illustrative case on hope in hydrocarbon exploration was presented at the symposium "The will and the way: New insights into the workings of hope in organizations" (OB/MOC) at the Annual Meeting of the Academy of Management, Montreal, 2010. Our work on the chapter was made possible by grant 187952/I40 of the Norwegian Research Council under the Idea Work project.

Notes

1. Translation to English by the authors, starting from a version given in Poetry Dispatch No. 199, November 1, 2007, http://www.poetrydispatch.wordpress.com/2007/11/02/olaf-h-hauge-its-the-dream/, last accessed March 26, 2010.

2. As listed at ISI web of knowledge, last accessed August 2010.

3. Obama touches upon hope in most of his major speeches, see also the book *The audacity of hope* (Obama 2006). Whether or not one shares political stance with Obama, whether or not one admires or contests his views and his public speaking of hope, his speeches are an example of leadership by trying to evoke hope within and across organizations. As such, the events of interaction that the speeches represent, in real time and retrospect, make up one of the more important current phenomena of any hope research. It is of course a much larger set of events and analytical tasks than can be reasonably gotten at here. Our purpose is merely a brief peak to point at some avenues of understanding.

4. Obama, B. June 4, 2009. *A New Beginning: Speech at Cairo University*. Cairo Egypt. www.americanrhetoric.com, last accessed August 2010.

5. Obama, 2009. Nobel Price Acceptance Speech. Transcript last accessed 2010-09-01 at http://www.cnn.com/2009/POLITICS/12/10/obama.transcript/index.html. In a follow up interview with celebrities Will Smith and Jada Pinkett Smitt, Obama qualified the term in saying that "one of the critical ingredients to peace" is "my ability to stand in your shoes, to see through your eyes, to constantly imagine, 'What's it like being a mother in Bangladesh right now?'" See http://blogs.abcnews.com/politicalpunch/2009/12/president-obama-sits-for-interviews-with-gloria-estefan-will-smith-jada-pinkett-smith.html, last accessed August 2010.

6. Snyder (2002) has attempted to counter this set of conceptualizations by claiming that the hope that can be linked to difficult situations collapses into his category of "repair goals" that are set up to fill a void. We find that argument little convincing as it neglects the possibility of emergence from both negative and positive jolts in experience and fails to consider the possibility of emotional origin of hope.

7. Obama, B. January 20, 2008. *The Ebenezer Baptist Church Address*. Ebenezer Baptist Church, Atlanta. www.americanrhetoric.com, last accessed August 2010.

8. Obama starts with a reference to the Scripture, when Joshua and the Israelites arrived at the gates of Jericho. He goes on by making a stream of references to the nearer past, tapping into a communal reservoir of shared memories,

> As I was thinking about which ones we needed to remember at this hour, my mind went back to the very beginning of the modern Civil Rights era. Because before Memphis and the mountaintop, before the bridge in Selma and the march on Washington, before Birmingham and the beatings, the fire hoses, and the loss of those four little girls, before there was King the icon and his magnificent dream, there was King the young preacher and a people who found themselves suffering under the yolk of oppression.

9. Two examples from the health sector are illustrative here: (1) HopeLab (www.hopelab.org) is a nonprofit organization that combines research with efforts to improve the health and quality of life of young people with chronic illness.

In a particularly inventive solution, HopeLab has developed a video-based game, Re-Mission™ for adolescents and young adults with cancer. In this game, players make their own stories of fighting cancer as they "pilot a nanobot named Roxxi as she travels through the bodies of fictional cancer patients destroying cancer cells, battling bacterial infections, and managing side effects associated with cancer and cancer treatment." http://www.hopelab.org/innovative-solutions/re-mission%E2%84%A2/, last accessed April 2010. HopeLab also uses digital storytelling to convey models of how young survivors of cancer have dealt with their illnesses (http://www.hopelab.org/innovative-solutions/digital-storytelling/).

(2) The psychiatric division of Stavanger Sjukehus, a major hospital in Norway, rehabilitates patients through work arrangements. A recent design of this rehabilitation, so far judged as remarkably successful by hospital staff and outside authorities, emphasizes that the patients should not just be included in any job, but one that enables them to take small steps toward their life dream. By tying everyday work, however trivial, to the narrative of the larger dream, one attempts to activate the power of hope.

10. Typically plays are defined by combination of three factors: 1) the petroleum charge system or source rock where the oil or gas was formed, 2) the reservoir rock where it migrated to and is contained, and 3) the seal formation/type of trap that prevents the hydrocarbons from leaking out of the reservoir.

References

Adams, V. H., Snyder, C.R., Rand, K.L., King, E.A., Sigman, D.R., & Pulvers, K.M. (2002). Hope in the workplace. In R.A. Giacolone, & C.L. Jurkiewicz (Eds.), *Handbook of workplace spirituality and organizational performance* (pp. 367–377). New York: Sharpe.

Alexander, T.M. (1990). Pragmatic imagination. *Transactions of the Charles S. Peirce Society, 26*, 325–348.

Alexander, T.M. (1992). Dewey and the metaphysical imagination. *Transactions of the Charles S. Peirce Society, 28*, 203–215.

Alexander, T.M. (1995.) John Dewey and the roots of democratic imagination. In L. Langsdorf & A.R. Smith (Eds.), *Recovering pragmatism's voice: The classical tradition, Rorty, and the philosophy of communication* (pp. 131–301). Albany, NY: SUNY Press.

Anderson, D.R. (2005). The esthetic attitude of abduction. *Semiotica, 153*, 9–22.

Bandura, A. (1997). *Self-efficacy: The exercise of control*. New York: W.H. Freeman and Company.

Bauer, J.J, McAdams, D., P., & Pals, J.L. (2008). Narrative identity and eudaimonic well-being. *Journal of Happiness Studies, 9*, 81–104.

Bloch, E. (1995). *The principle of hope* Vol. 2. (N. Plaice, S. Plaice & P. Knight, Trans.). Cambridge, MA: MIT Press. (Original work published in 1959)

Bosi, E. (1979). *Memoria a sociedade*. Sao Paolo, Brazil: T.A. Queiroz.

Branzei, O. (2011). Social change agentry work: Understanding the hopeful (re)production of social change. Forthcoming in K. Golden-Biddle, & J.E. Dutton (Eds.), *Exploring positive social change and organizations: Building a theoretical and research foundation*. New York: Psychology Press/Routledge.

Bratteli, T. (1980). *Fange i natt og tåke.* [Captive in night and fog] Oslo: Tiden Norsk Forlag.

Bruner, J. (1990). *Acts of meaning.* Cambridge, MA: Harvard University Press.

Cameron, K., Dutton, J.E., & Quinn, R.E. (Eds.) (2003). *Positive organizational scholarship: foundations of a new discipline.* San Francisco: Barrett Kohler.

Carifio J., & Rhodes, L. (2002). Construct validities and the empirical relationships between optimism, hope, self-efficacy, and locus of control. *Work, 19*, 125–136.

Carlsen, A. (2006). Organizational becoming as dialogic imagination of practice. The case of the indomitable Gauls. *Organization Science, 17*, 132–149.

Carlsen, A. (2008). Positive dramas. Enacting self-adventures in organizations. *Journal of Positive Psychology, 3*, 55–71.

Carlsen, A. (2009). After James on identity. In P. Adler (Ed.), *Oxford handbook of sociology and organization studies: Classical foundations* (pp. 421–443). New York: Oxford University Press.

Carlsen, A., & Pitsis, T. (2009). Experiencing hope in organizational lives. In L.M. Robert, & J. Dutton (Eds.), *Exploring positive identities and organizations: Building a theoretical and research foundation* (pp. 77–98). New York: Psychology Press.

Crapanzano, V. (2003). Reflections on hope as a category of social and psychological analysis. *Cultural Anthropology, 18*, 3–32.

Crapanzano, V. (2004). *Imaginative horizons.* Chicago: The University of Chicago Press.

Crites, S. (1971). The narrative quality of experience. *Journal of the American Academy of Religion, 39*, 291–311.

Crites, S. (1986). Storytime: Recollecting the past and projecting the future. In T.R. Sarbin (Ed.), *Narrative psychology* (pp. 152–173). Westport, CT: Praeger Publishers.

Csikszentmihalyi, M. (1985). Emergent motivation and the evolution of the self. *Advances in Motivation and Achievement, 4*, 93–119.

Dewey, J. (1973). Ralph Waldo Emerson. In J. McDermott (Ed.), *The philosophy of John Dewey* (pp. 24–31). Chicago: University of Chicago Press. (Original work published in 1903)

Eliott, J.A., & Olver, I.N. (2007). Hope and hoping in the talk of dying cancer patients. *Social Science and Medicine, 64*, 138–149.

Emerson, R.W. (1982). Nature. In L. Ziff (Ed.), *Ralph Waldo Emerson: Selected essays* (pp. 35–82). New York: Penguin Books. (Original work published in 1836)

Erikson, E.H. (1994). *Identity and the life cycle.* New York: W.W. Norton & Company. (Original work published in 1959)

Frankl, V. (1963/2004). *Man's search for meaning: The classic tribute to hope from the Holocaust.* London: Random House/ Rider.

Gergen, K.J. (1994). *Realities and relationships. Soundings in social construction.* Cambridge: Harvard University Press.

Gergen, K.J. (2009). *Relational being. Beyond belief and community.* New York: Oxford University Press.

Good, M.D.V, Good, B.J., Schaffer, C., & Lind, S.E. (1990). American oncology and the discourse on hope. *Culture, Medicine and Psychiatry, 14*, 59–79.

Grant, A.M., & Berry, J. (2010). The necessity of others is the mother of invention: Intrinsic and prosocial motivations, perspective-taking, and creativity. Manuscript submitted for publication.

Hackman, J.R. (2009a). The perils of positivity. *Journal of Organizational Behavior, 30*, 309–319.

Hackman, J.R. (2009b). The point of POB: Rejoinder. *Journal of Organizational Behavior, 30*, 321–322.

Harrison, S. (2010). Hope organizing: The case of the Andes flight disaster. In K. Krauss, & C. Wu (organizers), *The will and the way: New insights into the workings of hope in organizations.* Symposium (OB/MOC) at the annual meeting of the Academy of Management, Montreal.

Holman, D., & Thorpe, R. (2002). *Management and language.* London: Sage.

Ibarra, H. (1999). Provisional selves: Experimenting with image and identity in professional adaptation. *Administrative Science Quarterly, 44*, 764–792.

Ibarra, H. (2003). *Working identity: Unconventional strategies for reinventing your career.* Boston: Harvard Business School Press.

James, W. (1880). Great men, great thoughts and the environment. *Atlantic Monthly, 46*, 441–459.

James, W. (2000). The will to believe. In J. Stuhr (Ed.), *Pragmatism and classical American philosophy. Essential readings and interpretive essays* (2nd ed., pp. 230–241). New York: Oxford University Press. (Original work published in 1896)

James, W. (2002). *The varieties of religious experience.* Centenary Edition. London: Routledge. (Original work published in 1902)

Joas, H. (1996). *The creativity of action.* Cambridge, UK: Polity Press.

Kearney, R. (1998). *Poetics of imagining.* New York: Fordham University Press.

Kearney, R. (2002). *On stories.* London: Routledge.

Koopman C. (2006). Pragmatism as a philosophy of hope: Emerson, James, Dewey, Rorty. *Journal of Speculative Philosophy, 20*, 106–116.

Larson M., & Luthans, F. (2006). Potential added value of psychological capital in predicting work attitudes. *Journal of Leadership and Organizational Studies, 13*, 44–61.

Lazarus, R.S. (1999). Hope: An emotion and a vital coping resource against despair. *Social Research, 66*, 653–678.

Lazarus, R.S. (2003). Does the positive psychology movement have legs? *Psychological Inquiry, 14*, 93–109.

Locke, K., Golden-Biddle, K., & Feldman, M. (2008). Making doubt generative: Rethinking the role of doubt in the research process. *Organization Science, 19*, 907–918.

Lopez, S.J., Snyder, C.R., Magyar-Moe, J.L., Edwards, L., Pedrotti, J.T., Janowski, K., et al. (2004). Strategies for accentuating hope. In P.A. Linley, & S. Joseph (Eds.), *Positive psychology in practice* (pp. 388–404). New York: John Wiley & Sons.

Ludema, J.D. (2001). From deficit discourse to vocabularies of hope: The power of appreciation. In D. Cooperrider, P.F.J. Sorensen, T.F. Yaeger, & D. Whitney (Eds.), *Appreciative inquiry: An emerging direction for organizational development* (pp. 265–287). Champaign, IL: Stipes Publishing LCC.

Ludema, J.D., Wilmot, T.B., & Srivastva, S. (1997). Organizational hope: Reaffirming the constructive task of social and organizational inquiry. *Human Relations, 50*, 1015–1053.

Luthans, F., Avolio, B., Walumbwa, F., & Li, W. (2005). The psychological capital of Chinese workers: Exploring the relationship with performance. *Management and Organization Review, 1*, 247–269.

Luthans F., Norman, S.M., Avolio, B.J., & Avey, J.B. (2008). The mediating role of psychological capital in the supportive organizational climate—employee performance relationship. *Journal of Organizational Behavior, 29*, 219–238.

Luthans, F., & Jensen, S. (2002). Hope: A new positive strength for human resource development. *Human Resource Management Review, 1*, 304–322.

Luthans, F., Avolio, B., Avey, J.B., & Norman, S.M. (2007). Positive psychological capital: Measurement and relationship with performance and satisfaction. *Personnel Psychology, 60*, 541–572.

Luthans, F., Youseff, C., & Avolio, B. (2007). *Psychological capital: Developing the human competitive edge.* New York: Oxford University Press.

MacIntyre, A. (1981). *After virtue.* London: Duckworth Press.

Magaletta, P.R., & Oliver, J.M. (1999). The hope construct, will, and ways: Their relations with self-efficacy, optimism, and general well-being. *Journal of Clinical Psychology, 55*, 539–551.

Maitlis, S. (2009). Who am I now? Sensemaking and identity in posttraumatic growth. In L. Morgan Roberts, & J.E. Dutton (Eds.), *Exploring positive identities and organizations: Building a theoretical and research foundation* (pp. 47–76). Mahwah, NJ: Lawrence Erlbaum Associates.

Mattingly, C.F. (1998). *Healing dramas and clinical plots. The narrative structure of experience.* Cambridge, UK: Cambridge University Press.

McAdams, D.P. (1999). Personal narratives and the life story. In A. Pervin, & O.P. John (Eds.), *Handbook of personality. Theory and research* (2nd ed., pp. 478–500). New York: Guilford Press.

McAdams, D.P. (1993). *The stories we live by.* New York: William Morrow.

McAdams, D.P. (2006). *The redemptive self. Stories Americans live by.* New York: Oxford University Press.

McAdams, D.P., Diamond, A., de St. Aubin, E., & Mansfield, E. (1997). Stories of commitment: The psychosocial construction of generative lives. *Journal of Personality and Social Psychology, 72*, 678–694.

McDermott, D., & Hastings, S. (2000). Hope interventions for children and adolescents. In C.R. Snyder (Ed.), *Handbook of hope: Theories, measures, and applications* (pp.185–198). San Diego: Academic Press.

McDermott, J.J. (2000). William James. Introduction. In J. Stuhr. (Ed.) *Pragmatism and classical American philosophy. Essential readings and interpretive essays* (2nd ed., pp. 140–151). New York: Oxford University Press.

Meisenhelder, T. (1982). Hope: A phenomenological prelude to critical social theory. *Human Studies, 5*, 195–212.

Miller, J.F. (1985). Inspiring hope. *American Journal of Nursing, 85*, 22–25.

Mishra, A.K., & Spreitzer, G.M. (1998). Explaining how survivors respond to downsizing: The roles of trust, empowerment, justice, and work redesign. *Academy of Management Review, 23*, 567–588.

Obama, B. (2006). *The audacity of hope.* New York: Random House.

Parse, R.R. (2007). Hope in "Rita Hayworth and Shawshank Redemption": A human becoming hermeneutic study. *Nursing Science Quarterly, 20*, 148–154.

Peirce, C.S. (1931–1958). C. Hartshorne, P. Weiss, A. Burks (Eds.), *Collected papers of Charles Sanders Peirce* Vols. 1–8. Harvard, MA: Cambridge University Press.

Peterson, C., & Seligman, M.E. P. (Eds.). (2004). *Character strengths and virtues: A handbook and classification.* New York: Oxford University Press.

Peterson, S., & Luthans, F. (2003). The positive impact of development of hopeful leaders. *Leadership and Organization Development Journal, 24*, 26–31.

Polkinghorne, D.E. (1988). *Narrative knowing and the human sciences.* Albany, NY: State University of New York Press.

Ricoeur, P. (1991). Life in quest of narrative. In D. Wood (Ed.), *On Paul Ricoeur. Narrative and interpretation* (pp. 20–33). London: Routledge.

Rivera, J.D., & T.R. Sarbin. (Eds.) (1998). *Believed-in imaginings. The narrative construction of reality.* Washington, DC: American Psychological Association.

Roberts, L.M., Dutton, J.E., Spreitzer, G.M., Heaphy, E.D., & Quinn, R.E. (2005). Composing the reflected best self portrait: Building pathways for becoming extraordinary in organizations. *Academy of Management Review, 30*, 712–736.

Rorty, R. (2000). *Philosophy and social hope.* New York: Penguin.

Sachnowitz, H. (1976). *Det angår også deg.* Told to Arnold Jacoby. Oslo: Cappelen.

Sarbin, T.R. (1986). The narrative as a root metaphor for psychology. In T.R. Sarbin (Ed.), *Narrative psychology* (pp. 3–21). Westport, NY: Praeger Publishers.

Sarbin, T.R. (1997). The poetics of identity. *Theory & Psychology, 7*, 67–82.

Scheibe, K.E. (1986). Self-narratives and adventure. In T.R. Sarbin (Ed.), *Narrative psychology* (pp. 129–151). Westpost, NY: Praeger Publishers.

Scheier, M.F., & Carver, C.S. (1985). Optimism, coping, and health: Assessment and implications of generalized outcome expectancies. *Health Psychology, 4*, 219–247.

Schrank B., Stanghellini, G., & Slade, M. (2008). Hope in psychiatry: A review of the literature. *Acta Psychiatria Scandinavia, 118*, 421–433.

Seligman, M.E. P. (1998). *Learned optimism. How to change your mind and your life.* New York: Pocket Books.

Seligman, M.E. P., & Csikszentmihalyi, M. (2000). Positive psychology: An introduction. *American Psychologist, 55*(1), 5–14.

Snyder, C.R., Rand, K.L., & Sigmond, D.R. (2005). Hope theory: A member of the positive psychology family. In C.R. Snyder, & S.J. Lopez (Eds.), *Handbook of positive psychology* (pp. 257–276). New York: Oxford University Press.

Snyder, C.R. (2000b). Hypothesis: There is hope. In C.R. Snyder (Ed.). *Handbook of hope* (pp. 3–21). San Diego: Academic Press.

Snyder, C.R. (Ed.). (2000a). *Handbook of hope.* San Diego: Academic Press.

Snyder, C.R. (2002). Hope theory: Rainbows in the mind. *Psychological Inquiry, 13*, 249–279.

Stajkovic, A.D., & Luthans, F. (1997). A meta-analysis of the effects of organizational behavior modification on task performance, 1975–95. *Academy of Management Journal, 40*, 1122–1149.

Stotland, E. (1969). *The psychology of hope.* San Francisco: Jossey-Bass.

Turner, V. (1980). Social dramas and stories about them. In W.J. T. Mitchell (Ed.), *On narrative* (pp. 137–164). Chicago: The University of Chicago Press.

Webb, D. (2007). Modes of hoping. *History of the Human Sciences, 20*, 65–83.

Weingarten, K. (2010). Reasonable hope: Construct, clinical applications, and supports. *Family Process, 49*, 5–25.

Westbrook, R.B. (2005). *Democratic hope: Pragmatism and the politics of truth.* Ithaca, NY: Cornell University Press.

Youssef, C.M., & Luthans, F. (2007). Positive organizational behavior in the workplace: The impact of hope, optimism, and resilience. *Journal of Management, 33,* 774–800.

Youssef, C.M., & Luthans, F. (2011). Psychological capital: Meaning, findings, and future directions. In: K.S. Cameron & G.M. Spreitzer (Eds.), *The Oxford handbook of positive organizational scholarship.* New York: Oxford University Press.

Ziff, L. (1982). Introduction. In L. Ziff (Ed.), *Ralph Waldo Emerson: Selected essays* (pp. 7–27). New York: Penguin Books.

Courage in Organizations

An Integrative Review of the "Difficult Virtue"

Monica C. Worline

Abstract

Even everyday work has powerful consequences—a loan officer who houses a mother and her children, a teacher who moves a vulnerable student—consequences that demand courage. Courage crosses disciplinary, industrial, cultural, and historical boundaries as a cherished virtue that is necessary to social order. This chapter reviews recent research that reinforces the necessity and value of courage as a fundamental pattern of action in organizations. Necessary elements of that pattern include the simultaneous expression of individuation, an individual's ability to stand apart from the crowd; and involvement, an individual's ability to internalize the values and aims of the collective. The chapter demonstrates that understanding courage as part of organizational life involves research that taps these two important dimensions, and it offers suggestions for future research to expand our understanding of the antecedents and consequences of this pattern in organizational behavior.

Keywords: Courage, self-efficacy, leadership, emotion, prosocial behavior, conformity

Out of the night that covers me
Black as the Pit from pole to pole
I thank whatever gods may be
For my unconquerable soul.

In the fell clutch of circumstance,
I have not winced nor cried aloud.
Under the bludgeonings of chance
My head is bloody, but unbowed.

Beyond this place of wrath and tears
Looms but the Horror of the shade,
And yet the menace of the years
Finds, and shall find, me unafraid.

It matters not how strait the gate,
How charged with punishments the scroll,
I am the master of my fate,
I am the captain of my soul.
—*William Henley,* Invictus

William Henley's poem sings the indomitability of a human soul suffused with courage, a virtue that is central to social organization. The film *Invictus* (Eastwood, 2009) borrows its title from Henley's poem to portray the first days of Nelson Mandela's presidency and the challenges of radical change at the end of apartheid in South Africa. The film depicts Henley's poem as an inspiration for Mandela when he was jailed at Robin's Island—a reminder of the power of one person's courage to constructively oppose overwhelming social forces. In the film, Mandela's courage and dignity—and his gift of the poem *Invictus* to a young sports leader—inspire a group of athletes to bring the South African rugby team to international victory. We see Henley's poem providing a bridge from Victorian art to the era of South African antiapartheid civil rights activism and then on to a new era of democratic organizational leadership. It is this kind of inspirational power that makes courage such an important virtue for positive organizational scholarship (POS). *Invictus* can form a bridge across these different historical periods and social challenges because it speaks of the power of courage to sustain action in the midst of great adversity. And, for this reason, courage is a cherished virtue across almost every human culture (Peterson & Seligman, 2004) and a promising topic of study for POS.

And yet, despite its inspiring power to hold people steadfast in the face of adversity, courage has been dubbed "the difficult virtue" by philosophers, who point out that we must also come to terms with its confrontational and destructive edge (Rorty, 1988; Walton, 1986). Henley's *Invictus* proves instructive again in this regard. Although inspiring to great leaders such as Nelson Mandela and to citizens touched by his story through film, *Invictus* also has the dubious distinction of being the last words of Oklahoma City bomber Timothy McVeigh (BBC Americas, 2001). McVeigh, unbowed by a hail of criticism for his actions, stared unblinkingly into the camera during his execution, invoking Henley's poem to proclaim himself a hero to the end. Courage is the "difficult virtue" because it demands an individualistic boldness and confrontation that tends to reinforce itself over time, ultimately threatening the very foundation of the virtue itself (Rorty, 1988). Courage as a social virtue becomes susceptible to what Aquinas (2002) called "semblances" of itself—such as runaway egotism or individualism (see also Yearley, 1990). The comparison of Nelson Mandela's use of *Invictus* with Timothy McVeigh's use of the same poem highlights the problem of distinguishing

true courage from its semblances (Aquinas, 2002; Yearley, 1990), or distinguishing the true hero from the terrorist (Rorty, 1988). Distinguishing courage from its semblances in organizations is part of the work POS scholars must undertake in studying this topic. Any conversation about courage is incomplete without an understanding of the power of courage to inspire constructive confrontation (Worline, 2004b), but such a conversation must also address the virtue's relationship with war, terrorism, and martyrdom (Miller, 2000; Quinn & Worline, 2008; Rorty, 1988; Walshe, 2010).

Courage—and its status as the "difficult virtue"—provides an important focus for POS scholars working in the post-Enron era (Byrne, 2002) and living on the heels of a major 21st-century economic crisis born out of runaway risk-taking among those in the financial sector. Even a quick glance at organizations that depend on a wise relationship with risk shows us that contemporary workplaces are in need of courageous voices (Worline, 2004b), and are also susceptible to the destructive edge of runaway individualism (Sandelands, 2003; Walshe, 2010). Today's organizations depend more and more on their members' capacity to do things that may involve courage, such as persevere on difficult tasks, take initiative, and engage in innovation related to change (Badaracco, 2002; Sekerka, Bagozzi, & Charnigo, 2009). For these reasons, a deeper understanding of the "difficult virtue" is crucial for scholars interested in POS.

Understanding the Difficult Virtue

Courage is a concept with a tendency toward confrontation woven into its very fabric (Rorty, 1988), especially through its ties with conquest and military history (Aristotle, 1985; Miller, 2000; Walshe, 2010). At the same time, however, courage is praised as a cardinal virtue (Aquinas, 2002) and upheld as central to the creation of a viable society (Aristotle, 1985; Goode, 1978; Walton, 1986; Yearley, 1990). Because of its importance, and central in the creation of a good life and positive organizations, courage is important for POS scholars to grapple with despite its difficulty. Courage is an almost universal presence in the world's mythology, appearing in some form in the cultural stories told by most groups around the world (Lash, 1995; Robinson, Wilson, & Picard, 1962). Courage lies at the heart of the hero's journey (Campbell, 1949), in which one journeys out from what is familiar to encounter and conquer what is strange and return home with new understanding or enlightenment. This pattern lies at the heart of many of the world's myths

(Campbell, 1949), and many organizational scholars relate leadership, learning, and new forms of organization with a contemporary hero's journey (see, e.g., Daft & Lengel, 1998; Frost, Nord, & Krefting, 2004; Heifetz, 1994; Quinn, 1996; Whyte, 2001). In fact, courage may be distinguished from heroism simply by time and the viewpoint of history. Gibbon (2002) suggests that individual acts of courage remembered in history are what comprise heroism.

In spite of its social importance, courage has been notoriously difficult to define throughout Western history. Socrates is reputed to have failed to define the word, and henceforward its nature has been the subject of debate (Tillich, 1952; Walton, 1986). Aristotle (1985) envisioned courage embodied in the good soldier, who parceled out the "golden mean" between reason and action, knowing when and how to balance wise deliberation with bold moves. Chinese poet and philosopher Mencius also wrestled with defining courage in relation to war, looking for a meaning that gave proper weight to the social good (see Yearley, 1990). In Mencius' time, armies of soldiers were tearing apart the Chinese countryside while masquerading as heroes, and thus his writing grasped for a notion of courage that went beyond physical prowess, danger, and risk-taking. Mencius ultimately related courage to steadfastness in the face of hardship, prefiguring Henley's *Invictus* by painting a picture of courage as a moment of human indomitability that must necessarily be coupled with proper cultural values and exercised within socially set limits. Williams (1976) proposes that certain words are intrinsically bound up with the values and ideas of their time, and that, for these concepts, it is fruitless to attempt to create dictionary-style definitions because they rapidly become either useless or irrelevant. Courage seems to be such a term, where problems of meaning are inextricably bound up with the social problems of its time and place in history.

In a world that is coming to terms with the facts of terrorism and runaway risk-taking as an ongoing social reality, our current historical moment may be a particularly important one in which to revisit contemporary meanings of the word courage (Pury & Kowalski, 2007; Walshe, 2010; Worline, 2004b). Rate and colleagues (2007) conducted an extensive review of scholarly definitions of courage, showing a consensual definition as the tendency to voluntarily pursue worthy goals in the face of fear or risk. However, as noted by Schilpzand and colleagues (2008), almost all scholarly definitions of courage tend toward seeing it as an inherent quality or dispositional virtue, rather than looking at it as a quality of action embedded in

social context. For organizational scholars, who often want to understand more than dispositional factors, many of the conventional definitions of courage based in philosophy are of limited usefulness (Schilpzand et al., 2008; Quinn & Worline, 2008; Worline, 2004b). In addition, most evidence from organizational studies suggests that dispositional variables fail to predict courageous work behavior (Rothschild & Miethe, 1999; Rachman, 1990; Schilpzand, Mitchell, & Erez, 2008; Worline, 2004b).

Rachman (1990), who studied the courage of citizens in facing the bombing raids in London during World War II, found no personality-style variables that related to people's courageous response to wartime. In studies related to the work of soldiers, Rachman noted a physiological distinction between decorated and nondecorated soldiers in laboratory experiments, but found that this difference did not relate to their execution of duties (Cox, Hallam, O'Connor, & Rachman, 1983; O'Connor, Hallam, & Rachman, 1985). Nondecorated soldiers (presumably less courageous) showed a greater physiological response to pain during a painful task than did decorated soldiers; but all of the soldiers successfully completed the painful task, regardless of dispositional characteristics or physiological arousal levels. Similar results emerge from studies of whistleblowers, with dispositional factors failing to reliably predict who will report organizational corruption (Glazer & Glazer, 1989; Rothschild & Miethe, 1999). As a result of evidence like this, organizational research has moved away from a dispositional approach to the study of courage (Schilpzand, Mitchell, & Erez, 2008) and moved toward research that emphasizes courage as an emergent pattern of action in context (Quinn & Worline, 2008; Schilpzand, Mitchell, Erez, 2008; Worline, 2004b; Worline, Wrzesniewski, & Rafaeli, 2002). Working from this definition emphasizes the fact that anyone in an organization can undertake courageous action when the right combination of opportunity and resources presents itself. An accountant can draw upon his knowledge and sense of what is right to oppose fudging the numbers as an act of courage, even at the same time that a leader can draw upon her vision and sense of purpose to insist on reporting the right numbers as an act of courage. Although these are "everyday" actions in work contexts, they require individuals to stand apart from what is happening around them and engage constructively against social forces pushing them to go along. This example illuminates an emerging definition of courage in organizations that will form the foundation for the rest of this chapter: Courage is a pattern of constructive opposition, in which an individual stands against social forces in order to remedy duress in the organization.

The Difficult Virtue at Work

Organizations depend on their members to make difficult ethical choices, to accomplish ambitious tasks, to take initiative and drive performance, to persevere in the face of adversity, to engage in experimental activities related to change, and to guard what is right in the face of threats (Badaracco, 2002; Sekerka, Bagozzi, & Charnigo, 2009). Each of these activities may relate to the expression of courage in work organizations, and these actions are important for POS scholars to understand, placing courage at the heart of a POS research agenda. Because of their centrality to organizational success, these behaviors provide a focus for a good deal of research in organizational behavior, and in this way, courage has seeped into organizational studies. Behaviors such as initiative-taking (Frese et al., 1996; Morrison & Phelps, 1999), ethical decisions (Badaracco, 2002; Sekerka, Bagozzi, & Charnigo, 2009), perseverance in adversity (Heifetz, 1994; Kotter & Cohen, 2002), leadership in times of difficulty or change (Daft & Lengel, 1998; Heifetz, 1994), experimentation and innovation (Brown & Eisenhardt, 1997), whistleblowing (Glazer & Glazer, 1989), issue selling (Dutton, Ashfor, O'Neill, & Lawrence, 2001), and speaking up (Edmondson, 2003) or dissenting (Graham, 1986) may fall under the umbrella of courage at work (see Schilpzand et al., 2008).

One difficulty in establishing a research agenda related to courage is that it cannot be simplified into a list of actions that are or are not courageous. No action, in and of itself, is courageous (Aquinas, 2002; Yearley, 1990). Rather, action takes on the quality of courage when performed in constructive opposition to duress related to an ongoing social project (Worline, 2004b), rendering courage as part opportunity to remedy duress and part individual capacity to act on that opportunity. This pattern becomes important as a way to understand the unique expression of courage at work and to help scholars develop a sense of courageous behavior that is likely to be distinct from—yet overlap with— many existing constructs in organizational research. Scholars who want to understand courage in organizations will need to integrate the concept of courage with many different constructs in order to flesh out a full understanding of courage as a part of workplace behavior. Some of the most important are discussed here.

Courage As an Emergent Pattern of Activity

Building on an understanding of courage that extends beyond disposition, Worline (2004b) used narrative analysis to study courage in work contexts. Looking across hundreds of accounts of courage at work, Worline (2004b) found a recurring contextual pattern: An individual, exercising her capacity to act separately from the group, engages in constructive opposition to an important ongoing social project or endeavor in the midst of duress. Central to this understanding is the dynamic of *constructive opposition*, defined as a particular moment in social life when an individual expresses the capacity to act separately from the social forces in which he is immersed in order to protect or advance the collective good in some way (Worline, 2004b, 2009). As social psychology has made clear, individual activity is usually directed in accord with ongoing social projects, which are always unfolding in social systems (Worline, 2009). Narratives of courage at work show us that courage is manifest in moments when people draw upon their capacity for individuation and act in opposition to the flow of involvement in social life to remedy duress (Worline, 2004b, 2009). Quinn and Worline (2008) showed courage as a pattern of constructive opposition in the face of duress in their analysis of the process of a group of strangers engaging in courageous collective action.

Constructive opposition is a concept that is obviously lodged in the eye of the beholder (Worline, 2004b), and it provides room for the ongoing questions raised about the relationship between a courageous freedom fighter and a terrorist (Rorty, 1988; Walshe, 2010). As a pattern, constructive opposition that remedies duress suggests that courageous action pursues some worthy or socially valuable goal or aim, which is emphasized in most definitions of courage (Pury & Kowalski, 2007; Rate, Clarke, Lindsay, & Sternberg, 2007). This emphasis on social good may distinguish courage from the construct of bravery, which has been defined often as risky or difficult action that overcomes a fear (Walker & Hennig, 2004).

A notion of courage as an emergent pattern of activity in context suggests that understanding courage depends on a collective and historical point of view, not simply a personal one. It is a reliable fact that "heroes" often don't see themselves that way (Gibbon, 2002; Pury & Kowalski, 2007; Worline, 2004b). The identification of socially worthy or valuable aims is mostly a collective and historical endeavor, not simply an individual one (Goode, 1978; Gibbon, 2002). Sociologist Goode (1978) suggests that the celebration of heroes is a central way in which society reinforces acceptable social norms and inspires prosocial behavior. Gibbon (2002) suggests that we in contemporary society have lost sight of the fact that heroism must withstand not only tests of immediate public scrutiny but also tests of time. For Gibbon (2002), courage must be a pattern of constructive opposition that remedies duress to collective aims that can be recognized even from the distance of historical perspective. Gibbon (2002) removes from all consideration the idea that heroes must think of themselves as heroic; rather, true heroes do what is right in the difficult situations of their lives, and leave it to history to sort out the rest.

For organizational scholars, the fact that courage cannot be easily identified by the person undertaking it suggests that first-person reports of courage may be unreliable (Worline, 2004a). Both Worline (2004) and Schilpzand and colleagues (2008) have found that patterns of courageous action in context differ very little across the point of view or voice of storytellers—suggesting a pattern that goes beyond the perspective of the actor. These findings suggest that people talking about their own courageous acts describe essentially the same pattern as do people talking about the courageous acts of others in their work environment. These findings point us toward the study of behavior in context, rather than the study of individuals, in order to truly understand courage as it unfolds in organizations (Schilpzand et al., 2008; Worline, 2009).

Two Forms of Duress That Shape Courage in Organizations

Courageous behavior in organizations unfolds in response to duress—a threat to collective vitality or collective good (Quinn & Worline, 2008; Worline, 2004b). Schilpzand and colleagues (2008) studied narratives of executives and managers across industries and found that it is common for employees to be moved to undertake courageous action because they are protecting their colleagues or organization from harm—a form of felt duress in organizations. Worline (2004b) suggests that people feel duress to social life when they register things such as threat, hardship, oppression, harm, injury, or constraint. In response to these feelings, people undertake actions to remedy duress in ways that make sense, given their organizational context. Worline (2004b) identifies two forms of duress that are common antecedents of courageous action and are important in organizations.

One source of duress common in social settings arises from the threat that the individual can decide to live an entirely separate life (Worline, 2004b). The threat of runaway and/or narcissistic individualism threatens to pull groups apart (Sandelands, 2003). The idea that the individual can overreach, taking for himself or herself the vitality and power that is rightly part of social life, creates duress that Pinsky (2002) refers to as a deeply held fear of the "coming apart of civic fabrics" (p. 4). We have come, in the post-postmodern West, at least, to expect that the individual will live in conflict with social welfare (Axelrod, 1984; Putnam, 2000; Sober & Wilson, 1998). Because of this habit of mind, we see altruism as strange (Sober & Wilson, 1998), and we tend to overlook the positive social forces that spring up around us (Cameron, Dutton, & Quinn, 2003; Seligman, 2003). Social figures who draw on the notion of courage to engage in extremism, like McVeigh, show us the destructive edge of heroism taken into individual use. In response to the coming apart of civic fabric, people who feel this fear often take initiative to act in ways that remedy the threat to the common welfare. Thus, this form of duress provides a common spark for courage in organizational settings (Schilpzand et al., 2008; Worline, 2004b).

Another form of duress, no less present than the first, is an overbearing structure that stifles social life (Worline 2004). Pinsky (2002) writes of this form of duress as "the nightmare of undifferentiation" (p. 3), suggesting that one of the functions of poetry and social art is to help manage this nightmare. Indeed, we can see Henley's poem *Invictus* as a strong statement of differentiation in the face of overwhelming forces that threaten to stifle the individual. Another image that conveys the essence of this form of duress is a now-famous photograph of a lone Chinese man standing in front of a line of tanks during the 1989 protests in Tienanmann Square (see Figure 23.1). The image arrests us with the small stature of humanity standing against the machines of war. Despite his small stature, that one human being, standing against the tanks, becomes larger than any of the forces arrayed against him—as unbowed as the character of Henley's poem. His ability to stand indomitable in the face of such power calls forth the humanity in others. This kind of display of courage in the face of violence was the vision behind Gandhi's idea of nonviolent social protest, and also informed the nonviolent philosophy followed by Nelson Mandela (Hoagland, 1970). The array of military might of the Chinese government is an apt visual metaphor for an overbearing social, political, and economic structure that oppresses the capabilities and dynamism of

Fig. 23.1 Tiananmen Square, 1989. Photograph by Jeff Widener. Copyright Associated Press, reproduced with permission.

its members. Against such duress, as in the visual metaphor of this image, the individual stands out from the stifling background and acts to remedy duress by pushing back on the overbearing forces—another common spark for courage in organizational settings (Schilpzand et al., 2008; Worline, 2004b).

Integrating Future Research on the Difficult Virtue with Related Concepts

The expression of constructive opposition to remedy duress in organizations may take many forms. Sometimes constructive opposition is expressed through challenging an authority figure, sometimes it finds its form in an employee giving voice to an unpopular or undiscussible idea, and yet other times it may look like someone taking responsibility for a project that is stalled or where ownership and accountability is diffuse (Worline, 2004b). This section of the chapter offers ideas for integrating recent research on courage in organizations more broadly into organizational studies and POS. Because so few studies of courage in organizations have been published in the organization literature, this section also emphasizes many avenues for future research and integrates ideas for future research on courage with many related constructs that border on the expression of courage in organizations.

Conformity and Obedience

Worline (2009) suggests that many courageous behaviors in organizations can be mapped onto common themes established in social psychology, if we view courageous action as a form of positive deviance (Spreitzer & Sonnenshein, 2003). For instance, many themes that emerge from narratives of courage in organization reflect a positive deviant form of obedience (or disobedience) as defined in social psychology by Milgram (1974). In these forms of courage, instead of blindly going along with an authority figure's orders, people in organizations confront abusive or inappropriate use of authority as a way to remedy duress to the collective aims (Worline, 2009). How such processes unfold remains understudied. Positive organizational scholarship could pursue understudied questions about how employees and managers go about challenging authority in positively deviant ways. The results and impacts of such forms of courage in organizations is similarly understudied. Positive organizational scholarship could focus future research on the impacts of expressions of courage on both individual and organizational outcomes.

Another common theme among stories of courage as a form of positive deviance falls along the lines of conformity research established in social psychology by Asch (1956). In this form of courage in organizations, people do not simply go along with popular opinion in organizations or agree with their peers because it is the easy thing to do (Worline, 2009). Instead, they speak up to protect people and ideas, using voice as a means to remedy duress to collective aims (Edmondson, 2003; Schilpzand et al.,

2008; Worline, 2009). Sometimes this speaking up takes the form of dissent (Graham, 1986), and sometimes it takes the form of issue selling (Dutton et al., 2001). When and how people choose to speak up in organizations is a prime area for future research that links courage to broader issues in organizational studies. This offers an important counter to the pervasive silence that organizational scholars have documented (Morrison & Milliken, 2000).

Yet another point of integration with social psychological constructs comes from themes of courageous action related to responsibility and role conformity, as explored in social psychology by Darley and Latane (1968) and Zimbardo (2007). A common theme of stories of courage in organizations, especially in hierarchically flat organizations, include taking responsibility and pushing projects forward when diffusion of responsibility threatens collective aims (Schilpzand et al., 2008; Quinn & Worline, 2008; Worline, 2004b, 2009). Another common theme includes an individual standing out from a role or differentiating from others and from role definitions in order to protect someone or advance ideas in the organization (Schilpzand et al., 2008; Worline, 2004b, 2009). Although we know that organizations are subject to diffusion of responsibility, we know less about how people who want to take responsibility step up to push agendas forward in organizations. Some of the research on issue selling may be relevant here (e.g. Dutton et al., 2001), but it may be courageous in some cases to take responsibility for work issues instead of social issues. Pursuing such questions and examining the overlap of courage and issue selling in organizations is a fruitful path for future research. Using these general themes as a roadmap, POS may be able to integrate the study of courage with the study of some of the major themes of social and organizational psychology.

SILENCE, VOICE, AND DISSENT

Most people who work in organizations have ideas about how to change the status quo for the better, and yet very few give voice to those ideas (Graham, 1986; Kotter & Cohen, 2002; LePine & Van Dyne, 1998; Morrison & Milliken, 2000; Van Dyne, Ang, & Botero, 2003). Speaking up in organizations can be courageous when it involves raising concerns (Edmondson, 2003), conscientiously objecting to policies or practices (Graham, 1986), or addressing issues that are usually undiscussable (Daft & Lengel, 1998; Quinn, 1996). Worline (2004b) finds that speaking up is one of the most important themes in accounts of courageous action by knowledge workers.

Schilpzand and colleagues (2008) suggest that employees are courageous when they speak up against abusive power in organizations. This echoes findings in the domain of whistleblowing, in which courage takes the form of speaking about corruption or widespread wrongdoing (Glazer & Glazer, 1989). Despite the importance of exposing corruption, whistleblowers are still often regarded as antisocial or incompetent and are often rejected by other organizational members (Glazer & Glazer, 1989; Faunce, Bolsin, & Chan, 2004). Although speaking up is clearly important, and sometimes involves great courage on the part of an organization's members, organizational scholars still know relatively little about who speaks up and why (Edmondson, 2003; Rothschild & Miethe, 1999). Similarly understudied are processes by which organizations cultivate courageous voice among employees in the midst of duress or threat, and how organizations respond to courageous voice or principled dissent by employees (Graham, 1986). These areas of overlap between the study of courage and the concepts of voice, whistleblowing, and silence in organization offer fertile ground for future research.

PROACTIVITY, INITIATIVE, AND PROSOCIAL BEHAVIOR

Many scholars endeavor to understand why and how employees undertake self-motivated or proactive approaches to their work beyond what is required of them (Frese et al., 1996; Morrison & Phelps, 1999). Sometimes forms of initiative or proactive behavior are described as courageous by employees (Worline, 2004b), such as when initiative is directed toward organizational change that remedies duress, selling important issues (Dutton et al., 2001), taking charge of projects that need direction, or toward actively breaking rules in order to get things done (Frese et al., 1996; Morrison, 2006; Morrison & Phelps, 1999). Worline (2004b) found that, in organizational environments characterized by low levels of hierarchy and project-driven work, initiative and taking charge were commonly described themes in accounts of courage at work. Yet, few scholars who have studied initiative taking or other forms of prosocial behavior have asked about the role of courage. The overlap between these constructs provides many opportunities for scholars to explore questions about courage and organizational citizenship behavior or prosocial behavior in different types of work environments. For example, organizational scholars might usefully delve more deeply into the study of when employees choose to take initiative in the face of difficulty, why employees choose to constructively take charge of projects when responsibility is diffuse, how employees navigate the work environment when they are courageously taking initiative, and how such behaviors are received by others and rewarded or punished by the organization.

COORDINATION AND COLLECTIVE ACTION

When groups of people must unite in order to accomplish something related to the collective good—something that can involve a great deal of constructive opposition—the notion of courage may be important to forming collective identity and coordinating collective action (Quinn & Worline, 2008). Quinn and Worline (2008) analyzed data from Flight 93, which was hijacked on September 11, 2001, in order to understand how a group of strangers united to undertake courageous collective action. They found that people used conversation to create resources such as emotional calm and meaning, and these resources were part of what enabled them to act in the face of extreme adversity. Quinn and Worline also showed the process of collective narration, by which passengers on the plane arrived at a collective story that brought meaning and coherence to the extreme duress they were facing. Narrating their circumstances involved conversation with other passengers on the plane, as well as with people outside the situation. This process of narration helped the passengers make sense of the duress and also helped them form a collective identity that undergirded their trust in one another and their capacity to coordinate. The passengers were then able to draw upon their collective narrative about what was happening to enact a shared plot of counterattack against the hijackers. The evidence suggests that this collective narrative also enabled the passengers to improvise during the counterattack, fueling flexible collective action that responds to changing circumstances. This research builds a foundation for future work that explores the process of courageous collective action as it unfolds in different settings. This research also provides a link between the concept of courage and concepts such as collective identity or social movements. Future research may explore these links and show more fully how courageous collective action impacts capabilities for organizing and collective action.

EMOTION

Courage has long been linked with the emotion of fear (Rachman, 1990) and the idea of overcoming fear (Rate et al., 2007). In organization studies, Worline

(2004b) found that people named a broad range of emotions when they told stories of courage in work organizations. This finding was echoed by Schilpzand and colleagues (2008), who showed both positive and negative emotion in narrative accounts of courage from executives. Narratives of courage contain descriptions of emotions such as anger, anxiety, tension, relief, joy, and inspiration (Schilpzand et al., 2008; Worline, 2004b). A glance back at Henley's *Invictus* suggests that courage may be associated with feelings such as gratitude, faith, and confidence. Quinn and Worline (2008) suggest that the deliberate cultivation of calm may be important in the expression of courage, and that processes of collective courageous action may require ways that members maintain calm in the midst of duress. These preliminary studies open the door for further research on the range of emotion involved in the expression of courage in organizations and how particular emotions are related to processes of courage and organizing.

Beyond mapping the terrain of a range of emotion associated with the expression of courage at work, some research sheds light on the role of emotion in processes of courageous action. Worline (2004b) found that stories of courage in work organizations reliably created a feeling of inspiration in readers and shaped their intentions to act with courage in the future. Inspiration may be a lynchpin in the spread of courage in organizations. The power of inspiration becomes visible in that famous image of courage from Tiananmen Square (see Figure 23.1), where the lone figure's highly individuated action serves as a silent rallying cry to inspire others. Such ability to stand out as an individuated member of a group and act on its behalf engenders feelings of awe, inspiration, and elevation (Haidt, 2000; Worline, 2004b). Inspiration and elevation are important emotions because they predispose people to acting in a prosocial manner (Haidt, 2000; Fredrickson, 2001), and they may move others to act with the collective good in mind, engendering positive spirals (Fredrickson & Joiner, 2002). Future research questions for those interested in POS include studies to measure inspiration in organizational contexts and map its effects. Important open questions for future research focus on learning more about how inspiration functions as a both an antecedent and consequence of courage and links courage to positive spirals in organizations.

CONFIDENCE AND SELF-EFFICACY

It is surely the case that the solitary Chinese man, standing alone against the tanks, was not the only person in that time and place who felt that the collective life needed protection. And, yet, it is also the case that not everyone who registered duress to social life had the experience, the mental preparation, the training, the skill, or the confidence and fortitude that emanate from the figure in the photograph. Concepts such as confidence, experience, self-efficacy, and training could be important enablers of courage in organizations (Schilpzand et al., 2008). Some research on minority influence in groups has shown that exposure to an individual speaking up against popular opinion makes it more likely that other members will speak up in the future (Nemeth & Chiles, 1988). Rachman (1990) suggests that self-efficacy and confidence may be related to acting courageously. Schilpzand et al. (2008) report that some kinds of training and related work experience may be important antecedents to courageous action in organizations. Although this body of research hints at the importance of confidence and self-efficacy in the expression of courage, little research shows exactly how such enablers impact courage. Future research could be dedicated to understanding when and in what ways employees draw upon enablers such as confidence, self-efficacy, or prior work experience as they undertake efforts to remedy duress in organizations.

LEADERSHIP

Much of the writing on leadership in organizations invokes the idea of courage, so much so that Frost, Nord, and Krefting (2004) devote a section of their book to fostering courage and using courage to work thoughtfully with power. And, although courage is certainly part of what is necessary to stand out as a leader (Daft & Lengel, 1998), Badaracco (2002) suggests that many leaders act with a quiet courage behind the scenes, in a patient and constructive effort to remedy moral duress in organizations. Daft and Lengel (1998) suggest that leadership involves nonconformity, and thus courage is at the heart of leadership. Avolio and colleagues (2004) have begun to integrate the study of courage into the study of authentic leadership and positive organizational behavior. Future research in POS could focus on extending this promising start on integrating courage into the study of leadership by showing when and how leaders express constructive opposition to ongoing social projects in their organizations in ways that remedy duress. Future research could also examine when and how such expressions of courage by leaders impact their followers and the broader organizations they serve.

INNOVATION AND EXPERIMENTATION

Research on leadership often suggests that leaders must be able to learn from failure, which requires courage (e.g. Daft & Lengel, 1998), and that how leaders treat failure will have important consequences for followers' ability to learn (Edmondson, 1999). Research on creativity and innovation often suggests that experimentation—which necessarily involves failure—is key to creative breakthroughs and to organizational change (Edmondson, Bohmer, & Pisano, 2001). Because failure challenges people's sense of psychological safety in organizations (Edmondson, 1999), it often requires courage to engage in experimental and innovative actions (Schilpzand et al., 2008). Beyond recognizing this important link between courage and innovation, however, little research explores the deeper processes that allow people to express courage in the face of the unknown in organizational life. How employees engage in constructive opposition to duress in relation to experimentation and errors in organizations provides fertile ground for additional research integrating courage into a broader view of organizational behavior.

Extending POS Research on the Difficult Virtue

Returning to *Invictus* after a survey of courage in organizational behavior research, we now see the importance of extending our understanding of the "difficult virtue" as part of POS. Courage research will enable POS to understand what enables organizational members to remain unbowed in the "fell clutch of circumstance" and undaunted "under the bludgeonings of chance." Extending that line of research will facilitate our knowledge of what enables individuals to stand against social forces and help us understand when, how, and why people undertake difficult action in order to remedy duress in organizations.

Positive organizational scholars will want to understand more than simply individual factors related to courage. Worline (2009) showed three main themes that emerged from narrative accounts of courage at work and illuminate the social forces that prompt courageous action. Future research could replicate and extend these findings to examine the most common social factors or social forces that create conditions under which individuals are likely to engage in constructive opposition. Such research would help us understand common situations that prompt the expression of courage in organizations. Similarly, future research could examine instances of courage for common types of duress to understand if there are reliable ways in which duress prompts the expression of courage in organizations. This type of research would allow those engaged in POS to understand more clearly when the expression of courage is likely to occur.

Courage is linked with important organizational impacts such as moral and ethical outcomes in organizations (Sekerka et al., 2009). Many positive organizational scholars are likely to be interested in the relationship of courage with a variety of organizational outcomes. Are organizations with more courage also more innovative? More collaborative? More capable of learning? Such research requires large-scale, cross-level research that can measure courage reliably at the individual level and link it with organizational-level variables. Measures of courage are still in their infancy, but some measure development studies are underway (e.g. Schilpzand et al., 2008). A subscale of the Values in Action survey (Peterson & Seligman, 2004) focuses on individual valor and courage, which could provide a starting point for POS researchers interested in further survey research and measure development.

Scholars don't yet understand the extent to which courageous acts happen in organizations nor the frequency of such actions. Pointing to widespread silence and corruption, some argue that courage in organizations must be elusive and rare. Pointing to the lack of research attention to courage in organizations, however, others suggest that courage may be much quieter and everyday than we know. Are acts of courage in organizations lacking, or simply overlooked? Broader studies of courage in organizations will help address this question and bring attention to the frequency of the expression of courage as well as its impacts.

Conclusion

Writing about meaningful work and its capacity to shape our very identity, David Whyte (2001, p. 512) writes:

> It is astonishing how much of our everyday work has powerful life-or-death consequences: the firefighter on the fragile roof, the policeman on the street, the electrical engineer bringing power back to a darkened neighborhood. The teacher curses his way to school and then says exactly the right thing at the right time to the vulnerable, listening adolescent. All good work should have an edge of life and death to it, if not immediately apparent, then to be found by ardently exploring its greater context.

Courage, then, belongs right at the heart of everyday work. Recent studies of courage in organizational contexts reinforce this "everyday" quality of courageous action as something that all members of organizations can discuss as part of their work experience (Schilpzand et al., 2008; Worline, 2004b, 2009). Far from the image of the mythic hero, we find courage in every corner of every cubicle. And yet, each act of courage also contains the seeds of those myths. Whyte (2001) suggests that each act of courage at work must awaken a force of nature within us—the kind of individuation suggested by Worline (2004b) as part of the fundamental pattern of courage. When that individuation falters, our courage falters. In addition to individuation, but receiving less attention, we must also have something worth the difficulty of standing out as an individual—the kind of involvement in social projects described by Worline (2004b). That is Whyte's (2001) idea that all work has a life-or-death edge that we find by exploring its greater context—a conversation with the eternal that plays out through us and calls us to stand against the array of social forces, like the Chinese man standing for an ideal of democracy (see Figure 23.1), a social project in the service of which it becomes worthwhile to face down a line of the tanks.

That courage is not simply risk-taking or facing danger, and that it goes beyond the makeup of the actor, are lessons that are important in understanding the "difficult virtue" and its place in organization studies. That courage must be put to work in the service of social aim and becomes collectively determined is part of weaving the difficult virtue into the study of organizations. This lesson becomes vivid in the famous children's tale, *The Wizard of Oz* (Baum, 1956), in which the nature of courage becomes clear through the character of the Cowardly Lion. The Cowardly Lion is in search of courage, but he is afraid of everything, including his own shadow. As the Cowardly Lion and his friends travel the yellow brick road, we learn that to find courage is to discover participation in a vibrant social life. The Cowardly Lion ultimately discovers the essence of courage not in himself, not by meeting the wizard, and not even by acting with particular bravery; courage comes to him when he perseveres in the midst of hardship and does not give up on his friends when they need him. The Cowardly Lion's "courage" is actually only a medal of honor bestowed by the wizard after the fact; a medal that marks the kind of everyday constructive opposition to remedy duress that we see in narratives of courage at work. Whyte (2001, p. 521) says of this courage at work: "we stop looking for heroes to come and show us the path to glory, but we do not ignore the courageous example of others . . . we attempt to find the same inner correspondences in our own bodies that will allow us to take the next courageous step that we can also call our own." Whyte's words and the Cowardly Lion's example point the way toward the frontier of research on courage in POS—finding out more about the workings of that crucial intersection between the dangers to collective life and the individual's capacity for action that remedies duress.

References

Aquinas, T. (2002). *The treatise on human nature: Summa theologica* (R. Pasnau, Trans.). Indianapolis: Hackett Publishing.

Aristotle. (1985). *Nicomachean ethics* (T. Irwin, Trans.). Indianapolis: Hackett Publishing Company.

Asch, S.E. (1956). Studies of independence and conformity: A minority of one against a unanimous majority. *Psychological Monographs, 70*(9), 70–81.

Avolio, B., Gardner, W., Walumbwa, F., & Luthans, F. (2004). Unlocking the mask: A look at the process by which authentic leaders impact follower attitudes and behaviors. *Leadership Quarterly, 15*, 801–823.

Axelrod, R. (1984). *The evolution of cooperation*. New York: Basic Books.

Badaracco, J. (2002). *Leading quietly: An unorthodox guide to doing the right thing*. Boston: Harvard Business School Press.

Baum, L. (1956). *The Wizard of Oz*. Chicago: Rand McNally.

BBC Americas. (2001, June 11). McVeigh's final statement. Retrieved from *http://news.bbc.co.uk/2/hi/americas/1383206.stm*.

Brown, S., & Eisenhardt, K. (1997). The art of continuous change: Linking complexity theory and time-paced evolution in relentlessly shifting organizations. *Administrative Science Quarterly, 42*, 1–34.

Byrne, J.A. (2002, August 26). After Enron: The ideal corporation. *BusinessWeek, 68–74*.

Cameron, K., Dutton, J.E., & Quinn, R. (2003). *Positive organizational scholarship: Foundations of a new discipline*. San Francisco: Berrett-Koehler Publishers.

Campbell, J. (1949). *The Hero With a Thousand Faces*. Princeton, NJ: Princeton University Press.

Cox, D., Hallam, R., O'Connor, K., & Rachman, S. (1983). An experimental analysis of fearlessness and courage. *British Journal of Psychology, 74*, 107–117.

Daft, R.L., & Lengel, R.H. (1998). *Fusion leadership*. San Francisco: Berrett-Koehler.

Darley, J.M., & Latané, B. (1968). Bystander intervention in emergencies: Diffusion of responsibility. *Journal of Personality and Social Psychology, 8*, 377–383.

Dutton, J., Ashford, S., O'Neill, R., & Lawrence, K. (2001). Moves that matter: Issue selling and organizational change. *Academy of Management Journal, 44*, 716–736.

Eastwood, C. (Producer and Director). (2009). Invictus [Motion Picture]. United States of America: Warner Brothers.

Edmondson, A. (1999). Psychological safety and learning behavior in work teams. *Administrative Science Quarterly, 44*, 350–383.

Edmondson, A. (2003). Speaking up in the operation room: How team leaders promote learning in interdisciplinary action teams. *Journal of Management Studies, 40*, 1419–1452.

Edmondson, A., Bohmer, R., & Pisano, G. (2001). Disrupted routines: Team learning and new technology implementation in hospitals. *Administrative Science Quarterly, 46*, 685–716.

Faunce, T., Bolsin, S., & Chan, W. (2004). Supporting whistleblowers in academic medicine: Training and respecting the courage of professional conscience. *Journal of Medical Ethics, 30*, 40–43.

Fredrickson, B.L. (2001). The role of positive emotions in positive psychology - The broaden-and-build theory of positive emotions. *American Psychologist, 56*(3), 218–226.

Fredrickson, B.L., & Joiner, T. (2002). Positive emotions trigger upward spirals toward emotional well-being. *Psychological Science, 13*(2), 172–175.

Frese, M., Kring, W., Soose, A., & Zempel, J. (1996). Personal initiative at work: Differences between East and West Germany. *Academy of Management Journal, 39*, 37–63.

Frost, P., Nord, W., & Krefting, L. (2004). *Managerial and organizational reality: Stories of life and work*. New York: Pearson Prentice Hall.

Gibbon, P. (2002). *A call to heroism: Renewing America's vision of greatness*. New York: Atlantic Monthly Press.

Glazer, M.P., & Glazer, P.M. (1989). *The whistleblowers: Exposing corruption in government and industry*. New York: Basic Books.

Goode, W. (1978). *The celebration of heroes: Prestige as a social control system*. Berkeley: University of California Press.

Graham, J.W. (1986). Principled organizational dissent: A theoretical essay. In L.L. Cummings, & B.W. Staw (Eds.), *Research in organizational behavior* Vol. 8 (pp. 1–52). Greenwich, CT: JAI Press.

Haidt, J. (2000). The positive emotion of elevation. *Prevention and Treatment, 3*(3). article 3c.

Heifetz, R. (1994). *Leadership without easy answers*. Boston: Harvard University Press.

Hoagland, E. (1970). *The courage of turtles: Fifteen essays about compassion, pain, and love*. New York: Random House.

Kotter, J., & Cohen, D. (2002). *The heart of change*. Boston: Harvard Business Publishing.

Lash, J. (1995). *The hero: Manhood and power*. New York: Thames and Hudson.

LePine, J.A., & Van Dyne, L. (1998). Predicting voice behavior in work groups. *Journal of Applied Psychology, 83*, 853–868.

Milgram, S. (1974). *Obedience to authority*. New York: Harper & Row.

Miller, W.I. (2000). *The mystery of courage*. Cambridge, MA: Harvard University Press.

Morrison, E.W. (2006). Doing the job well: An investigation of pro-social rule breaking. *Journal of Management, 32*, 5–28.

Morrison, E.W., & Miliken, F. (2000). Organizational silence: A barrier to change and development in a pluralist world. *Academy of Management Review, 25*, 706–725.

Morrison, E.W., & Phelps, C. (1999). Taking charge at work: Extrarole efforts to initiate workplace change. *Academy of Management Journal, 42*, 403–419.

Nemeth, C., & Chiles, C. (1988). Modeling courage: The role of dissent in fostering independence. *European Journal of Social Psychology, 18*(3), 275–280.

O'Connor, K., Hallam, R., & Rachman, S. (1985). Fearlessness and courage: A replication experiment. *British Journal of Psychology, 76*, 187–197.

Peterson, C., & Seligman, M.E.P. (2004). *Character strengths and virtues: A handbook and classification*. Oxford: Oxford University Press.

Pinsky, R. (2002). *Democracy, culture, and the voice of poetry*. Princeton, NJ: Princeton University Press.

Pury, C., & Kowalski, R. (2007). Human strengths, courageous actions, and general and personal courage. *The Journal of Positive Psychology, 2*, 120–128.

Putnam, R. (2000). *Bowling alone: The collapse and revival of American community*. New York: Simon and Schuster.

Quinn, R.E. (1996). *Deep change: Discovering the leader within*. San Francisco: Jossey-Bass.

Quinn, R.W., & Worline, M.C. (2008). Enabling courageous collective action: Conversations from United Airlines flight 93. *Organization Science, 19*, 497–516.

Rachman, S.J. (1990). *Fear and courage* (2nd ed.). New York: W.H. Freeman and Company.

Robinson, H.S., Wilson, K., & Picard, B.L. (1962). *The Encyclopaedia of myths and legends of all nations*. London: Kaye & Ward Ltd.

Seligman, M.E. (2003). Positive psychology: Fundamental assumptions. *American Psychologist, 16*(3), 126–127.

Spreitzer, G., & Sonnenshein, S. (2003). Positive deviance and extraordinary organizing. In K. Cameron, J. Dutton, & R. Quinn (Eds.), *Positive organizational scholarship* (pp. 207–224). San Francisco: Berrett-Koehler.

Rachman, S.J. (1990). *Fear and courage* (2nd ed.). New York: W.H. Freeman and Company.

Rate, C.R., Clarke, J.A., Lindsay, D.R., & Sternberg, R.J. (2007). Implicit theories of courage. *The Journal of Positive Psychology, 2*, 80–98.

Rorty, A.O. (1988). *Mind in action: Essays in the philosophy of mind*. Boston: Beacon Press.

Rothschild, J., & Miethe, T.D. (1999). Whistle-blower disclosures and management retaliation: The battle to control information about organization corruption. *Work and Occupations, 26*(1), 107–128.

Sandelands, L. (2003). *Thinking about social life*. Lanham, MD: University Press of America.

Sekerka, L.E., Bagozzi, R.P., & Charnigo, R. (2009). Facing ethical challenges in the workplace: Conceptualizing and measuring professional moral courage. *Journal of Business Ethics, 89*(4), 565–579.

Schilpzand, P., Mitchell, T., & Erez, A. (2008). Personal courage. Working paper presented as a part of a symposium on "Courage in organizations: Asking new questions about a fundamental virtue" at the Academy of Management annual meeting, Anaheim, California.

Sober, E., & Wilson, D. (1998). *Unto others: The evolution and psychology of unselfish behavior*. Cambridge, MA: Harvard University Press.

Tillich, P. (1952). *The courage to be*. New Haven, CT: Yale University Press.

Walker, L., & Hennig, K. (2004). Differing conceptions of moral exemplarity: Just, brave, and caring. *Journal of Personality and Social Psychology, 86*, 629–647.

Walshe, N. (2010). Unpublished dissertation, Birkbeck College, University of London.

Walton, D.N. (1986). *Courage: A philosophical investigation*. Berkeley: University of California Press.

Whyte, D. (2001). *Crossing the unknown sea*. Reprinted in P. Frost, W. Nord, & L. Krefting (Eds.), Managerial and organizational reality: Stories of life and work (pp. 510–523). New York: Pearson Prentice Hall.

Williams, R. (1976). *Keywords: A vocabulary of culture and society*. New York: Oxford University Press.

Worline, M.C. (2004a). Valor. In C. Peterson, & M. Seligman (Eds.), *Character strengths and virtues: A handbook and classification* (pp. 213–228). Oxford: Oxford University Press.

Worline, M.C. (2004b). Dancing the cliff edge: The role of courage in social life. Unpublished dissertation: University of Michigan.

Worline, M.C., Wrzesniewski, A., & Rafaeli, A. (2002). Courage and work: Breaking routines to improve performance. In R.G. Lord, R.J. Klimoski, & R. Kanfer (Eds.), *Emotions in the workplace: Understanding the structure and role of emotions in organizational behavior*. San Francisco: Jossey-Bass.

Worline, M.C. (2009). Understand the role of courage in social life. Forthcoming chapter in C. Pury, & S. Lopez (Eds.), *Courage in psychology*. New York: APA Press.

Yearley, L.H. (1990). *Mencius and Aquinas: Theories of virtue and conceptions of courage*. Albany, NY: State University of New York Press.

Zimbardo, P. (2007). *The Lucifer effect*. New York: Random House.

A Positive Lens on Organizational Justice

Toward a Moral, Constructive, and Balanced Approach to Reactions to Third-party (In)justice

David M. Mayer

Abstract

Although there is a sizeable literature on one's own reactions to (in)justice, less is known about third-party reactions to other's (in)justice. The research that does exist tends to focus on self-interested explanations for caring about other's (in)justice, generally examines negative responses such as retaliation, punishment, and withdrawal, and typically does not distinguish between injustice and justice. In this chapter, I briefly review the literature on third-party reactions to (in)justice, highlight how this literature could benefit from a positive approach, present a theoretical model linking other's justice and injustice to moral emotions and ultimately to constructive and prosocial responses, and conclude with several practical and research implications.

Keywords: Organizational justice, positive organizational scholarship, third-party reactions, morality

A sizable literature examines reactions to experiences and perceptions of (in)justice in the workplace, a field that has come to be known as *organizational justice* (Greenberg & Colquitt, 2005). Empirical research on organization justice reveals that justice perceptions have important attitudinal and behavioral outcomes, such as organizational commitment, evaluations of authority, job satisfaction, trust, organizational citizenship behavior (OCB), deviance, and performance (Cohen-Charash & Spector, 2001; Colquitt, Conlon, Wesson, Porter, & Ng, 2001). A defining feature of most of the research on organizational justice is the examination of how an individual responds to his or her own experiences and/or perceptions of (in)justice. Clearly, when an individual experiences and/or perceives unjust treatment, negative outcomes ensue.

An alternative approach in the organizational justice literature is to examine third-party reactions to others' (in)justice. Beginning with the pioneering work by Brockner and colleagues (Brockner, 1990; Brockner, DeWitt, Grover, & Reed, 1990; Brockner, Greenberg, Brockner, Bortz, Davy, & Carter, 1986;

Brockner, Grover, Reed, DeWitt, & O'Mally, 1987; Brockner, Tyler, & Cooper-Schneider, 1992) in the mid-1980s and early 1990s demonstrating how "survivors" of layoffs were heavily influenced by the way those who were "let go" were treated, this area of research has gained considerable momentum in recent years (Skarlicki & Kulik, 2005). This burgeoning area of inquiry provides an interesting complement to the extant organizational justice literature by acknowledging that people care not only about their own treatment but also about how others are treated. Skarlicki and Kulik provide an excellent review of this literature and highlight how several fields (e.g., organizational behavior, social psychology, law, etc.) have contributed to understanding the conditions under which others' (in)justice is associated with third-party reactions, the underlying mechanisms responsible for these reactions, and the aftermath of third-party behavior.

Although this domain of research shows much promise, a perusal of the literature reveals a certain irony: The literature on third-party reactions, a seemingly positive notion, has taken a decidedly negative tone. Consistent with a positive organizational scholarship (POS) orientation (Cameron, 2007; Cameron, Dutton, & Quinn, 2003; Caza & Cameron, 2008; Spreitzer, 2008), I believe a positive approach to the study of third-party reactions to others' (in)justice could greatly contribute to the field of organizational justice. Specifically, I argue that there are three primary ways to study third-party (in)justice through a positive lens—and that research has typically not taken such an approach. First, many of the explanations provided for why people care about others' (in)justice are self-interested in nature (see Folger, 1994, 1998, 2001, for exceptions). Although Skarlicki and Kulik (2005) emphasize that moral explanations can be used to understand third-party reactions, the reality is that scholars have typically drawn on self-interested rationales for why an individual in the workplace may care about another's treatment (see O'Reilly & Aquino, in press for a notable exception). Second, scholars have typically studied "negative" reactions to other's mistreatment, such as blaming the victim, punishing the victim, punishing the perpetrator, and withdrawing from the organization (Skarlicki & Kulik, 2005). However, individuals can also respond with compassion to victims, with constructive conversations with perpetrators, and with prosocial behavior. Third, research on third-party reactions has tended to not differentiate between *injustice* and *just* treatment. Given that scholars are increasingly aware that positive and negative, good and bad, and just and unjust may represent different constructs, as opposed to ends of the same continuum (Baumeister, Bratslavsky, Finkenauer, & Vohs, 2001), a positive approach to third-party reactions considers not only reactions to injustice but also to justice.

In an effort to introduce a positive lens on third-party reactions to other's (in)justice, I contend that there are three defining features of this positive approach: using a *moral* explanation to explain third-party reactions; emphasizing compassionate, *constructive*, and prosocial reactions; and providing a more *balanced* approach by exploring reactions to both injustice and justice. To be clear, the focus of this chapter is not to provide a comprehensive review of the literature on reactions to third-party (in)justice (see Skarlicki & Kulik, 2005 for a review), but rather to explicate what a positive lens on third-party reactions to (in)justice might look like. In what follows, I briefly highlight the typical self-interest paradigm in third-party reaction research and then describe how a moral lens represents a more positive approach. Next,

I review the various negative outcomes associated with third-party reactions and make the case for considering constructive and prosocial reactions. Then, I suggest that justice and injustice are not separate ends of the same continuum, and assert that a positive lens is more balanced and thus focuses on reactions to justice and injustice. Finally, I present a theoretical model linking other's treatment (i.e., justice and injustice) to positive outcomes (i.e., compassion, constructive responses, prosocial behavior) through moral emotions (i.e., righteous anger, empathy, gratitude, elevation).

A Positive Lens on Third-party Reactions to (In)justice
Moral Explanations

The first hallmark of a positive lens on third-party reactions to other's (in)justice concerns the underlying motivation for the reaction. Specifically, I argue that a moral lens is a critical component of a positive approach. However, the preponderance of research on organizational justice more generally, and third-party reactions more specifically, has taken a self-interested lens.

As noted in reviews of the justice literature (see Cropanzano, Byrne, Bobocel, & Rupp, 2001; Cropanzano, Rupp, Mohler, & Schminke, M. 2001; Greenberg & Colquitt, 2005), there are several motivations for why people care about justice. These motives have traditionally focused on several self-interested explanations, such as a desire for economic gain (Thibaut & Walker, 1975), a need to feel a connection to and sense of belongingness with others (Lind & Tyler, 1988; Tyler & Lind, 1992), and a goal of reducing uncertainty (Lind, 2001; Lind & van den Bos; 2002; van den Bos & Lind, 2002). These same motives have been applied to the literature on third-party reactions to (in)justice (Skarlicki & Kulik, 2005). For example, when formulating predictions about why a third party might be affected by (in)justice, scholars have highlighted the role of these self-interested explanations (Colquitt, 2004; De Cremer, Stinglhamber, & Eisenberger, 2005; De Cremer, Van Dijke, & Mayer, 2010; De Cremer & Van Hiel, 2006, 2010; De Cremer, Wubben, & Brebels, 2008; Duffy, Ganster, Shaw, Johnson, & Pagon, 2006; Jones & Skarlicki, 2005; Lind, Kray, & Thompson, 1998; Mayer, Nishii, Schneider, & Goldstein, 2007; Tangirala & Ramanujam, 2008; van den Bos & Lind, 2001).

An alternative (and I argue more positive) way to think about third-party reactions is to take a moral lens. A moral lens suggests that people respond to third-party reactions not because the mistreatment of a third party has implications for one's own well-being, but rather because the third party believes his reaction is the right thing to do. Indeed, it is important to acknowledge that one motivation for why individuals care about other's treatment is because they believe that people deserve to be treated with respect and justice. Folger's (1994, 1998, 2001) deontic model highlights this fundamental belief about how people should be treated. In essence, the deontic model argues that people care about justice because it is simply "the right thing to do"—as opposed to a self-interested reason for wanting to see other's treated fairly.

Although scholars have typically focused on self-interested explanations for third-party reactions, some research has taken a moral lens. For example, some research in behavioral economics suggests that individuals will enforce justice rules even when it hurts their own economic self-interest (Johansson & Svedsater, 2009; Kahneman, Knetsch, & Thaler, 1986; Turillo, Folger, Lavelle, Umphress, & Gee, 2002). In addition, recent work by Rupp and colleagues (Liao & Rupp, 2005; Rupp & Bell, 2010; Skarlicki & Rupp, in press; Spencer & Rupp, 2009) draws on the deontic model and provides support for the notion that individuals care about other's treatment for moral reasons. This work, which takes a moral approach to understand third-party reactions, is a positive way to think about such behavior.

Constructive Reactions

A second characteristic of a positive lens on third-party reactions to other's (in)justice concerns the nature of the reaction. Specifically, I maintain that considering constructive reactions to others' injustice is a key aspect of a positive approach. Interestingly, the bulk of the research on third-party reactions has focused on negative reactions. For example, research has demonstrated how other's (in)justice can have negative implications for task performance, conflict, cooperation, citizenship, emotions, depression, antisocial behavior, turnover intentions, job satisfaction, commitment, and trust (Colquitt, 2004; De Cremer et al., 2005; De Cremer et al., 2010; De Cremer & Van Hiel, 2006, 2010; De Cremer et al., 2008; Duffy et al., 2006; Jones & Skarlicki, 2005; Liao & Rupp, 2005; Lind et al., 1998; Mayer et al., 2007; Rupp & Bell, 2010; Skarlicki & Rupp, in press; Spencer & Rupp, 2009; Tangirala & Ramanujam, 2008; van den Bos & Lind, 2001). In general, the only time other's treatment has a positive influence on behaviors, attitudes, and emotions is when the other person

has been treated worse than the focal employee. Consistent with social comparison theory (Festinger, 1954), research generally shows, in that situation, that the outcomes are more favorable. Even when employees act out of moral concerns as opposed to their own self-interest, individuals tend to respond to other's injustice with undesirable outcomes such as retaliation, punishment, reducing commitment and identification with the transgressor or institution, abstaining from action, or increased perceptions of emotional labor (Kahneman et al., 1986; Liao & Rupp, 2005; Skarlicki & Rupp, in press; Spencer & Rupp, 2009; Turillo et al., 2002).

Although these findings are interesting because they highlight that individuals do respond to other's justice, and the motivation appears to reside in moral rather than self-interested explanations in some cases, I would not characterize the majority of outcomes as positive. Positive, or constructive, reactions can take many forms. In terms of reactions to *injustice*, one example is to provide emotional support and compassion to an individual who was victimized by mistreatment. This behavior could take the form of listening, empathizing, helping direct the individual to a course of action, or any number of other supportive behaviors. Another positive response is to directly address the perpetrator. This behavior could entail talking to the wrongdoer, sticking up for the victim, and constructively trying to come up with a conclusion to aid the victim.

In terms of reactions to other's justice, an individual could respond by expressing gratitude to the authority figure who provided the fair treatment on the beneficiary's behalf. In addition, one could "pay it forward" by treating others in his or her social world in a similarly fair manner. Alternatively, he or she could respond by engaging in prosocial behaviors that help the authority figure and/or his or her organization. Indeed, work on virtuousness (Bright, Cameron, & Caza, 2006; Cameron, 2003a,b; Cameron Bright, & Caza, 2004; Caza, Barker, & Cameron, 2004) highlights the amplifying effects of positive emotions—and such emotions are likely to occur when others are treated fairly. Consistent with Fredrickson's (2001) broaden-and-build theory of positive emotions, the amplifying effects of positive emotions in the form of virtuousness tends to be self-perpetuating. Thus, when a third party sees another person treated in a just manner, it can lead to positive emotions that lead to prosocial and virtuous behavior. I return to these positive reactions when presenting the theoretical model later in this chapter.

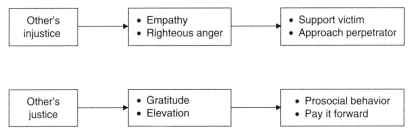

Fig. 24.1 A theoretical model of positive reactions to third-party (in)justice.

Justice and Injustice

A third component of a positive lens on third-party reactions to other's treatment concerns the inclusion of both just and unjust treatment. Specifically, I contend that exploring reactions to both other's injustice and other's just treatment is a critical way to take a positive approach. However, the majority of work on third-party reactions has not differentiated between justice and injustice but has implicitly focused on injustice. For example, Skarlicki and Kulik (2005) use the word "(mis)treatment" in the title of their review of the third-party literature and focus primarily on research in which another individual has been mistreated.

The issue of whether justice and injustice are distinct constructs or ends of the same continuum will likely become an emerging topic in the organizational justice literature. As an example, being treated with injustice could include being sexually harassed by one's boss—a clear violation of appropriate interpersonal treatment and a lack of dignity and respect. In contrast, being treated justly could involve a supervisor who goes out of his or her way to make an employee feel like a valued member of the work group and takes a genuine interest in his or her personal and professional development. I argue that justice and injustice are qualitatively different, and that many of the effects that have been found in the justice literature are a result of injustice as opposed to justice. Indeed, research on positive–negative asymmetry demonstrates that "bad is stronger than good" (Baumeister et al., 2001). However, our manipulations and measurement of (in)justice generally do not allow us to tease apart the role of injustice and justice. I argue that it is important to think about justice and injustice as distinct constructs and to explore reactions to both because reactions to each could differ.

Summary

I sought to make the case that the literature on reactions to third-party (in)justice tends to have a negative orientation. I argue for three amendments to the third-party literature in order to introduce a positive lens: a focus on the moral motivation of the action, an examination of constructive outcomes, and the presentation of a balanced approach by considering both unjust and just dynamics. In what follows, I draw on these three principles to develop a theoretical model taking a positive approach to third-party reactions to (in)justice.

Theoretical Model

This section presents a theoretical model that uses a positive lens to study third-party reactions (see Figure 24.1). As an overview, I present two separate pathways, one for justice and one for injustice, that lead to constructive reactions through the mechanisms of moral emotions. The focus on emotions is notable as most theories used to explain third-party reactions have been more cognitive in nature (Skarlicki & Kulik, 2005).

Pathway 1: Other's Injustice

The first pathway in the model begins with other's injustice. Other's injustice can take many forms. For example, consistent with the different justice dimensions (Colquitt, 2001), injustice can be about distributions, procedures, or interpersonal interactions. A distributive injustice could occur when an outcome an individual receives is unfair. For example, a person who should certainly be promoted to a higher-level position is not. A procedural injustice could occur when the procedures used to make a decision are unfair. An example might be suspending an employee for alleged wrongdoing and not allowing him to voice his side of the story first. An interactional injustice could occur when a person is not treated with dignity or respect, or provided an adequate explanation for a decision. An example would be if a coworker or supervisor belittles, makes fun of, and/or sexually harasses another employee or subordinate. These are just a few of the examples that could constitute injustice.

In response to these types of injustices, employees are likely to have emotional reactions (De Cremer, 2007). Specifically, I focus on two other-focused moral emotions: righteous anger and empathy (Tangney et al., 2007). *Righteous anger* occurs as a result of a perpetrator who violates moral standards. As Tangney et al. (p. 361) note, "In such cases, the harm need not be personally experienced. One can feel anger upon witnessing morally repulsive behavior aimed at a third party . . . Righteous anger can serve moral functions in that it can motivate 'third-party' bystanders to take action in order to remedy injustices." Indeed, when an employee witnesses the injustice of another organizational member it can lead to feelings of righteous anger as a widely held moral principle is breached.

Empathy is defined as a "shared emotional response between an observer and a stimulus person" (Feshbach, 1975, p. 25). Thus, empathy is generally conceived of as a moral emotional *process* as opposed to a discrete emotion (Eisenberg, Valiente, & Champion, 2004; Tangney et al., 2007). Other-oriented empathy involves not only taking another's perspective but also vicariously feeling the same emotions. An empathic response involves a focus on the person in need as opposed to one's own response to the situation. When someone is the victim of an injustice, it is likely that others will feel empathy toward that person because she is in a stressful and difficult situation. Empathy is closely related to compassion, which involves a consideration and concern about others' pain (Dutton, Worline, Frost, & Lilius, 2006; Kanov, Maitlis, Worline, Dutton, Frost, & Lilius, 2004; Lilius, Worline, Maitlis, Kanov, Dutton, & Frost, 2008).

The model posits that these two emotions, righteous anger and empathy, will be associated with constructive behaviors. The constructive behaviors I focus on relate to interactions with the victim (e.g., showing compassion, talking through the issue, helping develop a plan for moving forward) and interactions with the perpetrator (e.g., having a direct, honest, but nonconfrontative conversation with the perpetrator). There is reason to believe that these two emotions will lead to constructive reactions. For example, righteous anger is associated with having concern for and a desire to help distressed others (Rozin, Lowery, Imada, & Haidt, 1999). Similarly, research demonstrates that empathy promotes helping others in need (Batson, 1991) and inhibits aggressive responses that harm others (Miller & Eisenberg, 1988). Thus, righteous anger and empathy that result from another person's experienced injustice are expected to lead to constructive responses that benefit the victim.

Pathway 2: Other's Justice

The second pathway in the model begins with other's justice. In line with injustice taking multiple forms, such as distributive, procedural, and interactional, so too can justice. For example, an employee who has performed well can be appropriately rewarded for his or her work even when the boss feels pressure from higher-ups to not provide bonuses (i.e., distributive justice). Alternatively, the boss is never biased and always tries to be ethical when making tough decisions, even when others in the organization may use less transparent and more deceptive means (i.e., procedural justice). Finally, one's manager may go to great lengths to find out about each of his employees and therefore demonstrate the respect he has for his whole team, even when he is very busy (i.e., interactional justice). Clearly, there are several behaviors that one could engage in to be considered as fair.

In response to these types of just treatment, I posit that employees are likely to experience two positive other-focused moral emotions: gratitude and elevation (Tangney et al., 2007). *Gratitude* is "a feeling of thankfulness directed toward others that emerges through social exchanges between helpers and beneficiaries" (Grant & Gino, 2010, p. 946–947). Although gratitude is typically examined as a result of one's own positive experiences with another, it can also occur in a third party who witnesses another being fairly treated.

Elevation is a positive moral emotion that occurs when observing another who is virtuous or commendable (Haidt, 2000). This emotion is often accompanied by a warm, pleasant feeling in one's chest. Elevation helps to develop a "broaden-and-build" (Frederickson, 2000) approach to the world. Feeling a sense of awe by watching a manager treat others fairly even when it is not easy to do so can promote the emotion of elevation.

Consistent with the model, I predict that these two positive, other-focused moral emotions eventuate in prosocial behavior. There is considerable theoretical and empirical support for the link between these emotions and prosocial behavior. For example, research supports the notion that gratitude promotes prosocial acts (see McCullough, Kilpatrick, Emmons, & Larson, 2001 for a review). Gratitude can serve as a moral reinforcer that promotes helpful behavior. Similarly, elevation is associated with being prosocial (Algoe & Haidt, 2009; Landis,

Sherman, Piedmont, Kirkhart, Rapp, & Bike, in press; Schnall, Roper, & Fessler, 2010). Thus, I suggest that feelings of gratitude and elevation that result from observing other's justice promote prosocial behavior not only toward the person who spurred the emotion, but also can spread to others in one's social world in a "pay it forward" sense.

Summary

In this model, I posit that injustice and justice are important and drive constructive and prosocial third-party reactions. These relationships are explained by the activation of moral emotions—righteous anger and empathy for other's injustice, and gratitude and elevation for other's justice. In what follows, I highlight several practical and research implications related to this model, as well as a positive approach to third-party reactions more generally.

Practical Implications

The ideas presented in this chapter have practical implications for managers and employees working in organizations. One important implication for managers is that both other's injustice and justice can have an impact on employee reactions even if they were not directly affected. The extant third-party literature tends to warn managers that if they treat an employee unfairly it can have a negative effect on other employees. The ideas provided in this chapter suggest a positive way to view this process. Specifically, treating an employee fairly can lead to positive reactions by others in the organization, which ultimately can improve the work environment through such actions such as improved job attitudes, citizenship behavior, and ultimately, performance. Thus, managers should be aware that utilizing fair decisions, procedures, and interpersonal treatment can lead to positive outcomes not just for the person receiving the treatment but also for others in the organization.

A useful implication for employees involves how to best respond to other's injustice. Typically, scholars have examined negative responses, such as retaliation, punishment, withdrawal, and negative emotions. This approach is reasonable, given the types of responses most of us would have to witnessing a coworker being treated unfairly. However, the model presented in this chapter suggests that employees should be aware of their emotional reaction, and consider constructive ways of responding. Ultimately, harnessing one's righteous anger and/or empathy to provide compassionate responses to the victim (as opposed to blaming the victim) and interacting with the perpetrator

using a constructive approach (as opposed to retaliating or withdrawing) will likely lead to the best outcome in the future.

Research Implications

This chapter provides several avenues for future research directions. The greatest priority is empirically testing the theoretical model presented. It is important to empirically examine whether justice and injustice are associated with different third-party reactions and through different affective mechanisms. If support is found for this model, it will be important to extend the model.

One way to extend the model is to examine moderators. Are certain types of people more likely to respond to other's justice and injustice with positive emotional responses and/or constructive and prosocial reactions? For example, individuals higher in cognitive moral development (Kohlberg, 1969), dispositional empathy (Batson, 1991), moral disengagement (Bandura, 1999), and moral identity (Aquino & Reed, 2002) may have stronger reactions. Are some people more likely to respond to an injustice versus to just treatment? In addition, are there contextual variables that may serve as boundary conditions for the effects of other's justice and injustice on third-party reactions? For example, do reactions tend to be stronger when there is an ethical climate (Victor & Cullen, 1988) or the organization is virtuous (Cameron, Bright, & Caza, 2004)? Examining the model's boundary conditions is an important next step.

Another way to extend the model is to examine additional mechanisms. In the theoretical model presented in this chapter, I focused on outward-focused moral emotions. A focus on emotions is an important addition to the third-party reaction literature as the explanations have tended to be more cognitive (Skarlicki & Kulik, 2005). However, it would be interesting to examine alternative processes to better understand how other's justice and injustice are associated with positive types of reactions. For example, a third party may engage in a constructive response to another's injustice because of felt emotions, but it could also be because that individual has a strong identification with the organization and wants to ensure that she works in an ethical organization that treats people the right way. It would be fruitful to expand on the presented model by including additional mechanisms for why an individual would respond constructively to another's (in)justice.

One potential contribution of taking a positive lens to examine third-party reactions to others (in) justice is the acknowledgment that, typically, scholars have focused on negative, or at the very least less than ideal, types of reactions. I highlight several constructive, compassionate, and prosocial reactions to other's (in)justice. Although I present several types of constructive responses, it would be interesting to develop a more detailed typology of the different ways in which an individual could engage in constructive behavior. Also, more conceptual and empirical work could be dedicated toward understanding what makes a response constructive, and how such responses can be operationalized. I view this as a particularly important domain for future inquiry.

Finally, I introduce the idea that justice and injustice are qualitatively different, as opposed to being ends of the same continuum. It is important for scholars to empirically test this idea to see if measures and manipulations of justice and injustice are distinct and have different antecedents and consequences. It would be useful to follow the lead of scholars who have made similar arguments for other constructs. For example, scholars demonstrated that positive and negative affect are distinct constructs, as opposed to ends of the same continuum (Watson, Clark, & Tellegen, 1988). Organizational justice scholars could similarly develop a measure of justice and a measure of injustice and establish that they are distinct from one another empirically, with unique antecedents and consequences. If injustice and justice are distinct, this has many implications for the third-party literature, as well as for the organizational justice literature more generally.

Conclusion

In this chapter, I present a positive approach to the study of third-party reactions, highlighting the benefits of integrating the literatures on organizational justice and POS. I argue that there is a natural marriage between these fields—especially when it comes to reactions to third-party (in)justice. My hope is that this chapter will encourage additional theory and research incorporating these domains as I believe there is much to gain by taking a positive lens to the study of organizational justice.

References

Algoe, S.B., & Haidt, J. (2009). Witnessing excellence in action: The "other-praising" emotions of elevation, gratitude, and admiration. *Journal of Positive Psychology, 4*, 105–127.

Aquino, K., & Reed, A. (2002). The self-importance of moral identity. *Journal of Personality and Social Psychology, 83*, 1423–1440.

Bandura, A. (1999). Moral disengagement in the perpetration of inhumanities. *Personality and Social Psychology Review, 3*, 193–209.

Batson, C.D. (1991). *The altruism question*. Hillsdale, NJ: Erlbaum.

Baumeister, R.F., Bratslavsky, E., Finkenauer, C., & Vohs, K.D. (2001). Bad is stronger than good. *Review of General Psychology, 5*, 323–370.

Bright, D.S., Cameron, K.S., & Caza, A. (2006). The amplifying and buffering effects of virtuousness in downsized organizations. *Journal of Business Ethics, 64*, 249–269.

Brockner, J. (1990). Scope of justice in the workplace: How survivors react to co-worker layoffs. *Journal of Social Issues, 46*, 95–106.

Brockner, J., DeWitt, R., Grover, S., & Reed, T. (1990). When it is especially important to explain why: Factors affecting the relationship between managers' explanations of a layoff and survivors' reaction to the layoff. *Journal of Experimental and Social Psychology, 26*, 389–407.

Brockner, J., Greenberg, J., Brockner, A., Bortz, J., Davy, J., & Carter, C. (1986). Layoffs, equity theory and work performance: Further evidence on the impact of survivor guilt. *Academy of Management Journal, 29*, 373–384.

Brockner, J., Grover, S., Reed, T., Dewitt, R.L., & O'Malley, M. (1987). Survivors' reactions to layoffs: We get by with a little help for our friends. *Administrative Science Quarterly, 32*, 526–541.

Brockner, J., Tyler, T.R., & Cooper-Schneider, R. (1992). The influence of prior commitment to an institution on reactions to perceived unfairness: The higher they are, the harder they fall. *Administrative Science Quarterly, 37*, 241–261.

Cameron, K.S. (2007). Positive organizational scholarship. In S. Clegg, & J. Bailey (Eds.), *International encyclopedia of organizational studies*. Beverly Hills: Sage.

Cameron, K.S. (2003a). Ethics, virtuousness, and constant change. In N.M. Tichy, & A.R. McGill (Eds.), *The ethical challenge* (pp. 185–193). San Francisco: Jossey-Bass.

Cameron, K.S. (2003b). Organizational virtuousness and performance. In K.S. Cameron, J.E. Dutton, & R.E. Quinn (Eds.), *Positive organizational scholarship: Foundations of a new discipline* (pp. 48–65). San Francisco: Berrett-Koehler.

Cameron, K.S., Bright, D., & Caza, A. (2004). Exploring the relationships between organizational virtuousness and performance. *American Behavioral Scientist, 47*, 766–790.

Cameron, K.S., Dutton, J.E., & Quinn, R.E. (2003). *Positive organizational scholarship: Foundations of a new field*. San Francisco: Berrett-Koehler Publishers, Inc.

Caza, A., Barker, B.A., & Cameron, K.S. (2004). Ethics and ethos: The buffering and amplifying effects of ethical behavior and virtuousness. *Journal of Business Ethics, 52*, 169–178.

Caza, A., & Cameron, K.S. (2008). Positive organizational scholarship: What does it achieve? In S. Clegg, & C.L. Cooper (Eds.), *The sage handbook of organizational behavior: Volume 2: Macro approaches*. New York: Sage.

Cohen-Charash, Y., & Spector, P.E. (2001). The role of justice in organizations: A meta-analysis. *Organizational Behavior and Human Decision Processes, 89*, 278–321.

Colquitt, J.A. (2004). Does the justice of the one interact with the justice of the many? Reactions to procedural justice in teams. *Journal of Applied Psychology, 89*, 633–646.

Colquitt, J.A., Conlon, D.E., Wesson, M.J., Porter, C.O. L.H., & Ng, K.Y. (2001). Justice at the millennium: A meta-analytic review of 25 years of organizational justice research. *Journal of Applied Psychology, 86*, 425–445.

Cropanzano, R., Byrne, Z.S., Bobocel, D.R., & Rupp, D.E. (2001). Moral virtues, fairness heuristics, social entities, and other denizens of organizational justice. *Journal of Vocational Behavior, 58*, 164–209.

Cropanzano, R., Rupp, D.E., Mohler, C.J., & Schminke, M. (2001). Three roads to organizational justice. In J. Ferris (Ed.), *Research in personnel and human resources management* Vol. 20 (pp. 1–113). Greenwich, CT: JAI Press.

De Cremer, D. (2007). *Advances in the psychology of justice and affect.* Charlotte, NC: Information Age Publishing.

De Cremer, D., Stinglhamber, F., & Eisenberger, R. (2005). Effects of own versus other's fair treatment on positive emotions: A field study. *The Journal of Social Psychology, 145*, 741–744.

De Cremer, D., & van Hiel, A. (2006). Effects of another person's fair treatment on one's own emotions and behaviors: The moderating role of how much the other cares for you. *Organizational Behavior and Human Decision Processes, 100*, 231–249.

De Cremer, D., & van Hiel, A. (2010). Becoming angry when another is treated fairly: On understanding when own and other's fair treatment influences negative reactions. *British Journal of Management, 21*, 280–298.

De Cremer, D., Wubben, M.J.J., & Brebels, L. (2008). When unfair treatment leads to anger: The effects of other people's emotions and ambiguous unfair procedures. *Journal of Applied Social Psychology, 38*, 2518–2549.

De Cremer, D., Van Dijke, M., & Mayer, D.M. (2010). Cooperating when "You" and "I" are treated fairly: The moderating role of leader prototypicality. *Journal of Applied Psychology, 95*, 1121–1133.

Duffy, M.K., Ganster, D.C., Shaw, J.D., Johnson, J.L., & Pagon, M. (2006). The social context of undermining behavior at work. *Organizational Behavior & Human Decision Processes, 101*, 105–126.

Dutton, J., Worline, M.C., Frost, P.J., & Lilius, J. (2006). Explaining compassion organizing. *Administrative Science Quarterly, 51*, 59–96.

Eisenberg, N., Valiente, C., & Champion, C. 2004. Empathy-related responding: Moral, social, and socialization correlates. In A.G. Miller (Ed.), *The social psychology of good and evil* (pp. 386–415). New York: Guilford.

Feshbach, N.D. (1975). Empathy in children: Some theoretical and empirical considerations. *Counseling Psychology, 5*, 25–30.

Festinger, L. (1954). A theory of social comparison processes. *Human Relations, 7*, 117–140.

Folger, R. (1994). Workplace justice and employee worth. *Social Justice Research, 7*, 225–241.

Folger, R. (1998). Fairness as a moral virtue. In M. Schminke (Ed.), *Managerial ethics: Moral management of people and processes* (pp. 13–34).Mahwah, NJ: Erlbaum.

Folger, R. (2001). Fairness as deonance. In S.W. Gilliland, D.D. Steiner, & D.P. Skarlicki (Eds.), *Research in social issues in management* (pp. 3–33). New York: Information Age Publishers.

Frederickson, B.L. (2000). Cultivating positive emotions to optimize well-being and health. *Prevention Treatment, 3*, article 0001a.

Fredrickson, B.L. (2001). The role of positive emotions in positive psychology: The broaden-and-build theory of positive emotions. *American Psychologist, 56*, 218–226.

Grant, A.M., & Gino, F. (2010). A little thanks goes a long way: Explaining why gratitude expressions motivate prosocial behavior. *Journal of Personality and Social Psychology, 98*, 946–955.

Greenberg, J., & Colquitt, J.A. (2005). *The handbook of organizational justice.* Mahwah, NJ: Erlbaum.

Haidt, J. (2000). The positive emotion of elevation. *Prevention Treatment, 3*, ISSN: 1522–3736.

Johansson, L., & Svedsater, H. (2009). Piece of cake? Allocating rewards to third parties when fairness is costly. *Organizational Behavior and Human Decision Processes, 109*, 107–119.

Jones, D., & Skarlicki, D.P. (2005). The social construction of justice: The effects of overhearing peers discuss an authority's fairness reputation on reactions to subsequent treatment. *Journal of Applied Psychology, 90*, 363–372.

Kahneman, D., Knetsch, J.L., & Thaler, R.H. (1986). Fairness and the assumptions of economics. *Journal of Business, 59*, 101–116.

Kanov, J. Maitlis, S., Worline, M.C., Dutton, J.E., Frost, P.J., & Lilius, J. (2004). Compassion in organizational life. *American Behavioral Scientist, 47*, 808–827.

Kohlberg, L. (1969). *Stages in the development of moral thought and action.* New York: Holt, Rinehart & Winston.

Landis, S., Sherman, M., Piedmont, R., Kirkhart, M., Rapp, E., & Bike, D. (in press). The relation between elevation and self-reported prosocial behavior: Incremental validity over the five factor model of personality. *Journal of Positive Psychology.*

Liao, H., & Rupp, D.E. (2005). The impact of justice climate, climate strength, and justice orientation on work outcomes: A multilevel—multifoci framework. *Journal of Applied Psychology, 90*, 242–256.

Lilius, J., Worline, M., Maitlis, S., Kanov, J., Dutton, J., & Frost, P. (2008). The contours and consequences of compassion. *Journal of Organizational Behavior, 29*, 193–218.

Lind, E.A. (2001). Fairness heuristic theory: Justice judgements as pivotal cognitions in organizational relations. In J. Greenberg, & R. Cropanzano (Eds.), *Advances in organizational justice* (pp. 56–88). Stanford, CA: Stanford University Press.

Lind, E.A., Kray, L., & Thompson, L. (1998). The social construction of injustice: Fairness judgments in response to own and others' unfair treatment by authorities. *Organizational Behavior and Human Decision Processes, 75*, 1–22.

Lind, E.A., & Tyler, T.R. (1988). *The social psychology of procedural justice.* New York: Plenum.

Lind, E.A., & Van den Bos, K. (2002). When fairness works: Toward a general theory of uncertainty management. *Research in organizational behavior, 24*, 181–223.

Mayer, D.M., Nishii, L.H., Schneider, B., & Goldstein, H.W. (2007). The precursors and products of fair climates: Group leader antecedents and employee attitudinal consequences. *Personnel Psychology, 60*, 929–963.

McCullough, M.E., Kilpatrick, S., Emmons, R.A., & Larson, D. (2001). Is gratitude a moral effect? *Psychological Bulletin, 127*, 249–266.

Miller, P.A., & Eisenberg, N. (1988). The relation of empathy to aggressive and externalizing/antisocial behavior. *Psychological Bulletin, 103*, 324–344.

O'Reilly, J., & Aquino, K. (in press). A model of third parties' morally-motivated responses to mistreatment in organizations. *Academy of Management Review.*

Rozin, P., Lowery, L., Imada, S., & Haidt, J. (1999). The CAD triad hypothesis: A mapping between three moral emotions (contempt, anger, disgust) and three moral codes (community, autonomy, divinity). *Journal of Personality and Social Psychology, 76*, 574–586.

Rupp, D.E., & Bell, C.M. (2010). Extending the deontic model of justice: Moral self regulation in third-party responses to injustice. *Business Ethics Quarterly, 20*, 89–106.

Schnall, S., Roper, J., & Fessler, D.M.T. (2010). Elevation leads to altruistic behavior. *Psychological Science, 21*, 315–320.

Skarlicki, D.P., & Kulik, C. (2005). Third party reactions to employee mistreatment: A justice perspective. In B. Staw, & R. Kramer (Eds.), *Research in organizational behavior* Vol. 26 (pp. 183–230).

Skarlicki, D., & Rupp, D.E. (in press). Dual processing and organizational justice: The role of rational versus experiential processing in third party reactions to workplace mistreatment. *Journal of Applied Psychology*.

Spencer, S., & Rupp, D.E. (2009). Angry, guilty, and conflicted: Injustice toward coworkers heightens emotional labor through cognitive and emotional mechanisms. *Journal of Applied Psychology, 94*, 429–444.

Spreitzer, G.M. (2008). A note on "the future of positive organizational scholarship". In D. Barry, & H. Hansen (Eds.), *The sage handbook of new approaches in management and organization* (pp. 501–503). Thousand Oaks, CA: Sage.

Tangirala, S., & Ramanujam, R. (2008). Employee silence on critical work issues: The cross level effects of procedural justice climate. *Personnel Psychology, 61*, 37–68.

Tangney, J.P., Stuewig, J., & Mashek, D.J. (2007). Moral emotions and moral behavior. *Annual Review of Psychology, 58*, 345–372.

Thibaut, J.W., & Walker, L. (1975). *Procedural justice: A psychological perspective*. Hillsdale, NJ: Erlbaum.

Turillo, C.J., Folger, R., Lavelle, J.J., Umphress, E.E., & Gee, J.O. (2002). Is virtue its own reward? Self-sacrificial decisions for the sake of fairness. *Organizational Behavior and Human Decision Processes, 89*, 839–865.

Tyler, T.R., & Lind, E.A. (1992). A relational model of authority in groups. In M.P. Zanna (Ed.), *Advances in experimental social psychology* Vol. 25 (pp. 115–191). San Diego: Academic Press.

Van den Bos, K., & Lind, E.A. (2001). The psychology of own versus others' treatment: Self-oriented and other-oriented effects on perceptions of procedural justice. *Personality and Social Psychology Bulletin, 27*, 1324–1333.

Van den Bos, K., & Lind, E.A. (2002). Uncertainty management by means of fairness judgments. In M.P. Zanna (Ed.), *Advances in experimental social psychology* Vol. 34 (pp. 1–60). San Diego: Academic Press.

Victor, B., & Cullen, J.B. (1988). The organizational bases of ethical work climates. *Administrative Science Quarterly, 33*, 101–125.

Watson, D., Clark, L.A., & Tellegen, A. (1988). Development and validation of brief measures of positive and negative affect: The PANAS scales. *Journal of Personality and Social Psychology, 54*, 1063–1070.

Research on Behavioral Integrity

A Promising Construct for Positive Organizational Scholarship

Tony Simons, Edward C. Tomlinson, *and* Hannes Leroy

Abstract

Behavioral integrity (BI) is the perception that another person, group, or entity lives by his word –delivers on promises and enacts the same values he espouses. This construct is more basic than trust or justice, and is typically measured as the perceived pattern of alignment between words and deeds. Empirical studies have shown it to have powerful positive consequences for the attitudes and performance of followers, managers, and organizations, and also that BI moderates the impact of other leader behaviors on these outcomes. Only a few studies have examined antecedents, and fewer still have examined moderated antecedents. Although initial terrain has been sketched out by early studies, there is much yet to learn about the workings of this high-potential construct.

Keywords: Behavioral integrity, leadership, trust, values

Behavioral integrity (BI) was defined by Simons (Simons 1999, 2002) as the perceived pattern of alignment between a target's words and actions—how well that target tends to keep promises and tends to demonstrate espoused values. It is a judgment, in essence, of the strength and reliability of the other's word, and it is a trait ascribed to the target. BI or its lack can be ascribed to a person, a group (e.g., "the leadership team"), or a company. Unlike common-usage notions of integrity or trustworthiness, BI does not consider the benevolence, the moral content, or the observer's acceptance of the target's espoused values. We may dislike and mistrust someone who espouses and enacts values we consider despicable, but we will give them some credit for representing those values honestly, and thus displaying BI. This construct has attracted attention among scholars for its conceptual simplicity and apparent predictive power, and among practitioners for its intuitive appeal. The sense that another's word can be relied upon seems to be essential for effective leadership (see Mishra & Mishra [2011], Chapter 34, this volume), and for effective relationships in other settings as well.

The growing body of research on this construct has established connections spanning a wide range of organizational behavior literatures, from employee job attitudes to performance-related behaviors, and from perceptions of effective leadership to substantive measures of unit-level and organizational performance in diverse settings. The emerging BI construct is well enough grounded to sustain inquiry, has generated very promising initial research results, and is new enough to represent extremely fertile terrain for scholarship.

Here, we inventory the current state of BI research using the conceptual model presented in Figure 25.1. First, we offer a key distinction: BI is by definition an ascribed trait, in the eye of the beholder—but this perception is based in part upon the objective behavior of the target: Does this person, in fact, make promises that are not kept, and does this person, in fact, espouse values that differ from those he or she enacts? These objective facts are filtered through the observer's perceptual screens to yield a BI perception. It is useful, for both predictive and intervention purposes, to differentiate two relevant

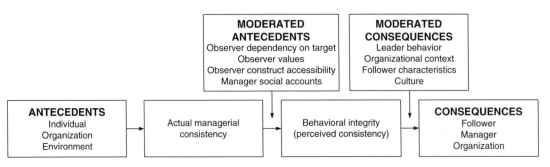

Fig. 25.1 Conceptual diagram of review.

constructs: actual word-deed alignment (an antecedent to BI) and perceived alignment (BI itself).

With this distinction in mind, we proceed by discussing the status of BI as it compares conceptually and empirically to related constructs. We review several applications of BI with different measures, different levels of analysis and aggregation, and with different referents. BI occupies a unique position in the nomological net and seems to function robustly across different applications. Next, we systematically discuss each of the components in Figure 25.1: consequences, moderated consequences, antecedents, and moderated antecedents. Table 25.1 shows all studies described in this review, sorted according to the categories in Figure 25.1, along with sample size and effect sizes.

The Behavioral Integrity Construct: Conceptualization and Measurement

Several constructs occupy a similar conceptual space to BI. Simons (2002) meaningfully differentiated BI from trust, justice, hypocrisy, psychological contracts, and credibility. Because BI is by definition a perceived attribute, and also because we expect self-assessed BI to be biased (Simons, 2002), most existing measures ask respondents to describe the BI of another—typically, their boss, supervisor, CEO, or a group such as "senior management." Aggregating responses of multiple observers' (e.g., subordinates') perceptions yields the most reliable measure of an actor's (e.g., manager's) BI, as it filters out many individual perceiver biases, but measuring individual perceptions is appropriate for some research questions.

Most empirical studies of the BI construct have used the survey measure that was developed by Simons and McLean Parks (2000) and reported in Simons, Friedman, Liu, and McLean Parks (2007). This eight-item scale has demonstrated consistently high reliabilities in English (α = 0.96), Spanish (α = 0.94), and Dutch (α = 0.90). This scale may be divided into two four-item subscales: one that focuses on

alignment between enacted and espoused values (α = 0.83) and a second that focuses on follow-through on promises (α = 0.81). These two subdimensions were intercorrelated at r = 0.94 in an initial sample of hotel employees, which rendered the subdimensions indistinguishable; but in a sample of high school teachers, the two were only intercorrelated at r = 0.72. Simons has found that a six-item version of the scale correlates with the original scale at r = 0.97 and maintains reliabilities above 0.80 for both the whole scale and for the abbreviated three-item subscales. These original BI scales and subscales can be used as general measures of a perceived attribute, or may usefully be focused on a specific value (e.g., "BI regarding safety," Leroy et al., 2010).

A second survey measure of BI was developed by Dineen, Lewicki, and Tomlinson (2006). Dineen et al. developed a four-item measure of BI that focuses on whether the manager in question enacts values *and rules* as espoused. Their measure showed reliability over α = 0.80, and it correlated with the values subcomponent of Simons and McLean Parks' (2000) scale at r = 0.72. The addition of personally adhering to and enforcing rules adds a useful element to BI that probably does not stand as a separate dimension, but is clearly appropriate for measuring the construct.

A third survey measure was developed by Palanski (2008). This measure consists of two open-ended questions that elicit the target leader's espoused values and promises, and two Likert-scaled items that ask how often those espoused values are enacted and how often the promises are kept. Palanski reported good interitem correlations and predictive power for the two closed-ended items used as a scale, and found correlations between it and the Simons and McLean Parks' (2000) scale of between r = 0.6 and r = 0.7. Open-ended questions about specific promises and values provide useful qualitative information about BI, although the statistical properties of the scale are not ideal.

Table 25.1 Overview of empirical studies linking behavioral integrity to other variables

Construct	Illustrative Study/Studies	Sample Size	Observed Correlation
CONSEQUENCES: Employee Attitudes			
Job satisfaction	Vitell & Davis, 1990[a]	61	0.40
	Robinson & Rousseau, 1994[a]	128	0.76
	Viswesvaran & Deshpande, 1996[a]	150	0.53
	Ryncarz, 1997[a]	44	0.69
	Viswesvaran et al., 1998[a]	77	0.11
	Koh & Boo, 2001[a]	237	0.38
	Johnson & O'Leary-Kelly, 2003[a]	103	0.59
	Neumann, 2005		
	• BI measures on 14 different values	3037	0.28–0.60
	Simons, Friedman, Liu, & McLean Parks, 2007	1944	0.64
	Palanski, 2008		
	• Study 1	140	0.57
	• Study 2	149	0.29
	• Study 3	83	0.68
	Prottas, 2008	2542	0.44
Negative affect toward organization	Kickul, 2001[a]	322	−0.45
Organizational commitment	Schwepker, 1999[a]	152	0.24
	Mize et al., 2000[a]	99	0.44
	Simons & McLean Parks, 2000		
	• Individual level	6800	0.55
	• Department level	597	0.44
	• Business unit level	76	0.73
	Johnson & O'Leary-Kelly, 2003[a]	103	0.52
	Narasimhan, 2007	165	
	• Supervisory BI		0.23
	• Senior management BI		0.30
	Simons, Friedman, Liu, & McLean Parks, 2007	1944	0.54
	Hinkin & Schriesheim, 2009	456	0.53
Trust	Robinson & Rousseau, 1994[a]	128	0.79
	Simons & McLean Parks, 2000		
	• Individual level	6800	0.73
	• Department level	597	0.74
	• Business unit level	76	0.82

(Continued)

Table 25.1 Overview of empirical studies linking behavioral integrity to other variables (*Continued*)

Construct	Illustrative Study/Studies	Sample Size	Observed Correlation
CONSEQUENCES: Employee Attitudes			
	Simons & Hagen, 2006	379	0.57
	Narasimhan, 2007		
	Supervisor BI		
	• Trust in senior management	165	0.26
	• Trust in supervisor	165	0.43
	Senior management BI		
	• Trust in senior management	165	0.46
	• Trust in supervisor	165	0.20
	Simons, Friedman, Liu, & McLean Parks, 2007	1944	0.74
	Palanski & Yammarino, in press		
	• Study 1	140	0.56
	• Study 2	149	0.22
	• Study 3	83	0.56
	Hinkin & Schriesheim, 2009	456	0.73
Organizational identity	Tomlinson, Ash, & Hall, 2006	51	0.40
Organizational cynicism	Johnson & O'Leary-Kelly, 2003[a]		
	• Cognitive cynicism	103	−0.62
	• Affective cynicism	103	−0.55
	Narasimhan, 2007		
	• Supervisory BI	165	−0.45
	• Senior management BI	165	−0.41
Follower Engagement	Vogelgesang & Lester, 2008		
	BI, Time 1		
	• Follower engagement, T1	418	0.16
	• Follower engagement, T2	313	0.21
	BI, Time 2		
	• Follower engagement, T1	310	0.22
	• Follower engagement, T2	344	0.28
	Leroy, 2009	210	0.39
Follower Well-being	Prottas, 2008		
	• Employee stress	2542	−0.21
	Johnson & O'Leary-Kelly, 2003[a]		
	• Emotional exhaustion	103	−0.38

Table 25.1 *(Continued)*

Construct	Illustrative Study/Studies	Sample Size	Observed Correlation
CONSEQUENCES: Employee Attitudes			
	Prottas, 2008		
	• Employee health	2542	−0.12
	Prottas, 2008		
	• Employee life satisfaction	2542	0.19
	Leroy, 2009		
	• Burnout	210	−0.36
CONSEQUENCES: Employee Judgments About Leadership			
Interpersonal justice	Simons, Friedman, Liu, & McLean Parks, 2007	1944	0.59
Interactional justice	Kickul, 2001[a]	322	0.42
	Narasimhan, 2007	165	
	• Supervisory BI		0.76
	• Senior management BI		0.45
Procedural justice	Kickul, 2001[a]	322	0.34
	Dineen, Lewicki, & Tomlinson, 2006		
	• Bank A (individual level)	838	0.44
	• Bank B (group level)	264	0.38
	Narasimhan, 2007		
	• Supervisory BI	165	0.51
	• Senior management BI	165	0.70
Leadership perceptions	Palanski & Carroll, 2006		
	• Leader emergence	213	0.50
	Palanski & Yammarino, in press		
	• Study 2: satisfaction with leader	83	0.83
	• Study 3: satisfaction with leader	113	0.35
CONSEQUENCES: Employee Behaviors			
In-role performance	Johnson & O'Leary-Kelly, 2003[a]	103	0.33
	Leroy, 2009		
	• Proactive performance	210	0.13
	• Adaptive performance	210	0.18
Job performance	Way, Simons, & Tuleja, 2010	89	0.26–0.27[b]
	Palanski & Yammarino, in press		
	• Study 2	83	0.43
	• Study 3	113	0.27

(Continued)

Table 25.1 **Overview of empirical studies linking behavioral integrity to other variables** (*Continued*)

Construct	Illustrative Study/Studies	Sample Size	Observed Correlation
CONSEQUENCES: Employee Behaviors			
Discretionary service behaviors	Simons & McLean Parks, 2000		
	• Department level	597	0.17
	• Business unit level	76	0.42
Organizational citizenship behaviors	Johnson & O'Leary-Kelly, 2003[a]		
	• Helping behaviors	103	0.07
	Dineen, Lewicki, & Tomlinson, 2006		
	• Bank A (individual level)	838	0.13
	• Bank B (group level)	264	0.17
Deviant behavior	Kickul, 2001[a]	322	−0.33
	Dineen, Lewicki, & Tomlinson, 2006		
	• Individual/Organizational deviance		
	• Bank A (individual level)	838	−0.14/−0.06
	• Bank B (group level)	264	−0.11/−0.16
Absenteeism	Johnson & O'Leary-Kelly, 2003[a]	103	−0.27
	Prottas, 2008	2542	−0.06
Intent to stay	Robinson & Rousseau, 1994[a]		
	• Time 2	128	0.42
	Simons, Friedman, Liu, & McLean Parks, 2007	1944	0.33
Intent to quit	Narasimhan, 2007		
	• Supervisory BI	165	−0.25
	• Senior management BI	165	−0.17
Turnover	Robinson & Rousseau, 1994[a]	128	0.32
	Simons & McLean Parks, 2000 Business unit level	76	−.11
CONSEQUENCES: Organizational Performance			
Profitability	Simons & McLean Parks, 2000		
	• Business unit level	76	0.36
Organizational effectiveness	Parry & Proctor-Thomson, 2002[a]	1354	0.34
Ability to achieve bottom-line	Parry & Proctor-Thomson, 2002[a]	1354	0.19
Satisfaction with purchasing executive (two studies)	Simons & Hagen, 2006		
	• With purchasing executive	384	0.79–0.80
	• With client company	384	0.53–0.67

Table 25.1 (*Continued*)

Construct	Illustrative Study/Studies	Sample Size	Observed Correlation
MODERATED CONSEQUENCES			
Supervisory guidance * BI → employee deviance/OCB	Dineen, Lewicki, & Tomlinson, 2006		
Role overload * BI → expedience	Ma, Mclean Parks, & Gallagher, 2010		
Value breach * culture strength → cynical attributions	Cha, 2009		
Volition of others * BI → trust	Simons & Hagen, 2006		
Congruence * BI → organizational identity	Tomlinson, Ash, & Hall, 2006		
Culture * BI → trust	Friedman, Simons, & Hong, 2009		
ANTECEDENTS: Personal characteristics			
Leadership behaviors	Parry & Proctor-Thomson, 2002[a]		
	• Transformational leadership	1354	0.44
	Palanski, 2008		
	• Charisma, Study 2	149	0.57
	• Charisma, Study 3	83	0.72
	Leroy, 2009		
	• Authentic leadership	210	0.49
	Basik, 2010		
	• Leader political skills	99–108	0.65–0.68
Personal characteristics	Palanski & Carroll, 2006		
	• Conscientiousness	213	0.18
	Vogelgesang & Lester, 2008		
	• BI, Time 1		
	• Interactional transparency T1	422	0.53
	• Interactional transparency T2	314	0.44
	• BI, Time 2		
	• Interactional transparency T1	315	0.36
	• Interactional transparency T2	345	0.62
Leader contingent reward or punishment	Palanski, 2008		
	• Leader contingent reward, Study 1	140	0.29
	• Leader contingent reward, Study 2	149	0.53
	• Leader contingent reward, Study 3	83	0.57
	Hinkin & Schriesheim, 2005		
	• Contingent reward	456	0.61

(Continued)

Table 25.1   Overview of empirical studies linking behavioral integrity to other variables (*Continued*)

Construct	Illustrative Study/Studies	Sample Size	Observed Correlation
ANTECEDENTS: Personal characteristics			
	Hinkin & Schresheim, 2005		
	• Contingent punishment	456	0.38
	• Reward omission	456	−0.52
	• Punishment omission	456	−0.31
ANTECEDENTS: Contextual effects			
Organizational culture	Way, Simons, & Tuleja, 2010		
	• Perceived organizational support	87	0.30[b]
	Leroy, 2009		
	• Ethical culture	210	0.42[b]
Trickle-down	Simons, Friedman, Liu, & Mclean Parks, 2007		
	• Upper management BI		
	Palanski, 2008		
	• Leader BI		
ANTECEDENTS: Historical effects			
Previous value breaches	Cha, 2009		
	Hewlin, Cha, & Hewlin, 2010		
Morality of value-content	Clemenson, 2007		
	• Leader's follower-rated value for achievement	286	0.46
	• Leader's follower-rated value for integrity	286	0.29
	• Leader's follower-rated value for fairness	286	0.29
MODERATED ANTECEDENTS			
BI violation * race (Black)	Simons, Friedman, Liu, & Mclean Parks, 2007		
BI violation * culture	Friedman, Simons, & Hong, 2009		
Morality of value content * value congruence	Clemenson, 2007		

[a] Studies were included in a meta-analysis on behavioral integrity by Davis and Rothstein (2006), and include narrow measures that are consistent with, but do not fully capture, BI (e.g., psychological contract breach).
[b] Path coefficient from a structural equation model.

A fourth approach to BI measurement focuses on particular values relevant to the context, and measures espousal and enactment separately. This approach allows targeting of a particular slice of word–action consistency that might be especially predictive of the outcomes under study. It also allows for examination of the unresolved question about the relationship between issue-specific BI and generalized perceptions of it. Finally, it allows for consideration of asymmetries between overpromising and underpromising, and the differentiation of the benefits of simple enactment as opposed to the alignment between espousal and enactment. Leroy, Halbesleben, Dierynck, Savage, and Simons (2010), in a study of safety in hospitals, developed separate scales for supervising nurses' espousal of safety protocols and their enactment and enforcement of these protocols. Cording, Simons, and Smith (2009) examined the espoused value placed on employees and customers in a sample of annual reports (using word/phrase frequencies as an indicator) and compared those with an index of the enactment of these values in their respective companies' policies. Note that this approach measured *actual* rather than *perceived* word–action consistency—BI is the latter. This approach, distinguishing value-specific espousals and enactments, shows promise. It would be especially useful to assess how the separate espousal and enactment scales combine and relate to one of the generalized BI scales.

Other measures have been used to approximate BI with varying levels of accuracy. Prottas (2008) measured BI using two items: "I can trust what my managers say in this organization," which is a reasonable BI item, and "Managers in my organization behave honestly and ethically when dealing with employees and clients or customers," which extends well beyond BI toward ethics (see Stansbury & Sonenshein [2011], Chapter 26, this volume, for treatment of the latter). BI is explicitly void of ethical or moral content, as it focuses exclusively on alignment between words and deeds. Several of the studies drawn upon in Davis and Rothstein's (2006) meta-analysis of BI and attitudinal consequences use the Perceived Leader Integrity Scale (PLIS; Craig & Gustafson, 1998), which similarly includes an ethical dimension that is explicitly distinct from the BI construct. However, measures of psychological contract breach (e.g., Robinson & Rousseau, 1994) may be considered as assessing an element of BI that is especially germane for employees in organizations (Simons, 2002). In this vein, Deery et al. (2006) examined discrepancies between espoused and enacted behavioral standards at an organization in their study of psychological contract breach. This approach may be described as an assessment of organization-level BI.

In sum, the scale developed by Simons et al. (2007) has shown very strong psychometric properties in a variety of settings, and it and its two subscales can be adapted or focused for different uses. The notion of separate measures of espousal and enactment also shows promise for further exploring how BI functions. In considering additional measures, care must be taken to avoid assessing concepts that are not part of the BI construct (e.g., moral rectitude, benevolence) and to remain cognizant of the distinction between a *perceived* pattern of word–action consistency (BI) and *actual* consistency (an antecedent to BI).

Consequences of Behavioral Integrity

Simons (2002) argued that managerial BI would drive specific follower attitudes and behaviors. Subsequent research has confirmed these relationships and demonstrated how BI relates to manager performance and organization-level operational and financial measures as well. In Figure 25.1, we argue that BI has consequences at three levels: follower, managerial, and organizational. We discuss each of these outcomes in turn.

Follower Outcomes

Empirical work on BI has confirmed its association with key employee attitudes, employee well-being, and performance-related behaviors at both individual and group levels.

Employee Attitudes

An examination of the attitudinal consequences of BI is useful for understanding how BI works to ultimately affect behavioral, operational, and financial outcomes. Attitudes likely mediate the practical impact of BI. In a meta-analysis on the relationship between BI and employee attitudes, Davis and Rothstein (2006) found strong positive relationships between perceptions of supervisor BI and employee job satisfaction, organizational commitment, satisfaction with the leader, and affect toward the organization (overall average $r = 0.48$, $p < 0.01$). Supervisory BI has also been found to predict follower engagement (Vogelgesang et al., 2010) and followers' organizational identity (Tomlinson et al., 2006).

Simons (2002) specifically posited that BI would be a significant predictor of trust as it directly pertains to the issue of reliability of one's word, a position that is consistent with several prominent theories of trust development (e.g., Lewicki & Bunker, 1996; Mayer et al., 1995). A number of studies have confirmed this relationship (Simons et al., 2007; Simons & Hagen, 2006; Simons & McLean Parks, 2000; Velez, 2000). There has also been some empirical support for the prediction that trust mediates the positive relationships between BI and employee attitudinal and behavioral outcomes (Simons, 2002). Kannan-Narasimhan and Lawrence (2010) found that trust completely mediated the relationship between senior management BI and organizational commitment; trust partially mediated the relationship between supervisory BI and organizational cynicism, and fully mediated the relationship between supervisory BI and turnover intentions. Similarly, Hinkin and Schriesheim (2009) found that trust partially mediated the impact of supervisory BI on organizational commitment and satisfaction (but not leader effectiveness). When the impact of BI is mediated by trust and when it is not is an open question.

More recently, Simons (2008) has asserted that leader BI affects employee engagement and performance through the additional mediation of communication clarity. Although BI increases trust in leadership, which has positive effects, it also means that leadership is sending congruent messages through its various verbal and nonverbal channels; as a consequence, subordinates know more precisely what is expected or desired of them. Leroy et al. (2010) found preliminary support for this dual-mechanism model.

Employee Well-being and Performance-related Behaviors

Managers' BI has been associated with employee stress- and health-related outcomes, such as burnout (Leroy, 2009; Prottas, 2008), as well as life satisfaction (Prottas, 2008). These consequences likely emerge from the mediation of uncertainty, mistrust, and possibly anger.

Simons (2002) posited that supervisory BI would predict several employee performance-related behaviors (intent to stay, organizational citizenship behaviors [OCBs], receptiveness to change efforts, and job performance). Empirical research has generally confirmed these relationships and uncovered other performance-related consequences of BI. Leroy (2009) found that BI was positively associated with employee proficiency and adaptability. Palanski and Yammarino (in press) show that leader BI indirectly affects follower job performance through trust in and satisfaction with the leader. They further found that follower job performance was predicted by the *follower's* BI. Vogelgesang et al. (2010) found that manager BI predicted military cadets' engagement, which in turn predicted their performance ratings.

In a study of a large banking organization, Dineen et al. (2006) found that individual employee perceptions of supervisory BI were positively related to employee intentions to perform OCBs. Furthermore, they found that BI was negatively related to deviance directed at the organization, and that aggregate perceptions of BI (in a separate field sample) were negatively related to individual-level deviance (cf. Tang & Liu, 2010). Way, Simons, and Tuleja (2010) demonstrated the impact of BI on employee job performance behaviors (OCBI, OCBO, and task performance). McLean Parks and Ma (2008) found that supervisory BI negatively predicted employee expedience behaviors (i.e., cutting corners). Recent work has also begun to explore how managerial BI negatively affects employee absenteeism (Prottas, 2008) and turnover (Simons et al., 2007; Simons & McLean Parks, 2000).

Examination of aggregate group-level BI perceptions allows examination of group and organization-level outcomes. Simons and McLean Parks (2000) found that, in a sample of 6,800 employees at 597 hotel departments, department-level perceptions of manager BI were positively related to discretionary service behavior. BI perceptions have further been found to have an impact on group-level phenomena such as higher group cohesion and effective group processes and outcomes (Rozell & Gunderson, 2003). In both lab and field studies, Palanski, Kahai, and Yammarino (2010) found that information sharing within teams affects team-level perceptions of BI, which in turn affects team-level trust and performance.

Managerial Outcomes
Perceptions of Leadership

Initial conceptual work on BI also posited its relationship to effective leadership (Simons, 1999, 2002). Parry and Proctor-Thomson (2002) found ratings of integrity to be significantly correlated with transformational leadership behaviors. In leaderless work groups, BI predicted leader emergence (Palanski & Carroll, 2006).

Job Performance Behaviors

Way et al. (2010) found that managerial BI, as rated by a subordinate, predicted the manager's own job performance behaviors as rated by his or her supervisor.

Organizational Outcomes

A small number of studies have examined BI in relation to various metrics of operational and/or financial success. Simons and McLean Parks (2000) found in a sample of 76 hotels that BI was correlated with customer satisfaction scores, employee turnover rates, and unit-level hotel profitability. In fact, BI accounted for 13% of the variance in profitability among this sample of hotels. A study by Cording et al. (2009) found that alignment between espousal and action, in a sample of 377 acquired companies in various industries, was associated with employee performance and ultimately with company stock performance. Given the practical implications of these effects, further study in this area is definitely warranted.

Summary

The initial examinations of BI outcomes have been impressive. To our knowledge, no studies examine employee willingness to implement espoused change, which is a proposed outcome in the Simons (2002) model. Research has also begun to explore novel outcomes that do not fit neatly within the traditional categories listed above. For example, data from a large mega-church indicated that low leader (pastor) BI was associated with follower façade creation (i.e., falsely portraying oneself as embracing organizational values) (Hewlin et al., 2010). New research is also examining the effect that nursing supervisor BI has on follower psychological safety, adherence to safety protocols, and ultimately accident rates (Leroy et al., 2010).

It would be useful to have more studies that examine job/task performance as an outcome. Davis and Rothstein (2006) called for more research on how BI affects individual behavior and organizational performance, and we agree. The bottom-line impact of BI needs to be demonstrated in more industries, manufacturing as well as service. It is possible that service industries are more sensitive to managerial BI, as problems with employee morale directly and immediately affect the customer (Simons, 1999). Further, the mechanisms by which BI affects performance need to be more fully articulated and tested. The relationship between BI and certain outcome variables might be determined by the referent of the BI perception. Kannan-Narasimhan and Lawrence (2010) found that top management BI predicted organizational commitment, whereas supervisory BI did not; conversely, supervisory BI predicted turnover intentions and organizational cynicism.

Moderated Consequences of Behavioral Integrity

Although not specified in Simons' (2002) model, an increasing number of scholars have begun to consider BI as a moderator of the effects of other leader behavior. This approach is based on the insight that just about anything a leader says will be interpreted through a lens that asks whether the leader truly means it—whether, in fact, she demonstrates BI. Leaders' exhortations, directions, standards, espousals, or coaching must depend ultimately on the leader's credibility to make them work. Simons (2008) has proposed BI as a *necessary but not sufficient* condition for effective leadership to occur. Accordingly, researchers have explored interactions between BI and a variety of moderators on key outcomes. In Figure 25.1, we include leader behaviors, organizational context, national culture, and follower characteristics.

Leader Behavior

Dineen et al. (2006) posited that BI and supervisory guidance would exert independent and interactive relationships on employee conduct. In two separate samples of banking employees, Dineen et al. found that supervisory guidance (providing instruction to employees) interacted with supervisory BI to affect both OCBs and deviance. Specifically, OCBs were highest and deviance was lowest when high guidance was accompanied by high BI. Conversely, the worst outcomes (lowest OCBs, highest deviance) were associated with high guidance, but low BI.

Contextual Factors

Ma, McLean Parks, and Gallagher (2010) found that BI perceptions moderated the impact of workers' role overload on expediency behaviors (i.e., bending or breaking rules in order to fulfill organizational objectives), with more constructive responses resulting when perceived leader BI was high. Simons and Hagen (2006) found in separate samples of supermarket buyers and suppliers that volition power moderates the impact of BI on trust, such that BI is a more powerful predictor of trust when the trustee has more relative power than the trustor.

Follower Characteristics

Recent research has focused attention on how BI may interact with value congruence (i.e., alignment between the employee's and manager's views on work-related issues). In a sample of manufacturing employees, perceptions of managers' BI interacted with value congruence to affect organizational identity, such that when congruence is high, organizational identity remains at a relatively high level regardless of BI; however, when congruence is low, organizational identity increases at a small rate as BI increases (Tomlinson et al., 2006). Thus, BI serves as a partial substitute for value congruence—if the boss does not agree with you, it lessens the negative impact if she can at least be consistent.

In terms of other potential moderators, Davis and Rothstein (2006) did not find any support for cultural effects on the relationship between BI and employee attitudes, but their meta-analysis did suggest that employee gender and number of levels separating employee and manager may moderate the BI–employee attitude relationship (although Prottas [2008] did not find support for a gender moderator). Prottas (2008) proposed the degree of interdependence and degree of employee autonomy as potential moderators of the impact of BI.

Antecedents to Behavioral Integrity

In Figure 25.1, one of most the important drivers of BI is actual managerial consistency. In turn, actual managerial consistency is a function of individual, organizational, and environmental variables. In this section, we look at these different antecedents to BI. We indicate which relationships have been supported by existing research and which need to be examined further.

Simons (1999) asserted that BI would be associated with effective transformational leadership, as the trust that it engenders is necessary for profound interpersonal influence. Subsequent empirical studies confirmed BI to be associated with transformational leadership behavior (Parry & Proctor-Thomson, 2002) and leader charisma (Palanski, 2008), authentic leadership behaviors (Leroy, 2009), and leader political skills (Basik, 2010). BI has thus been shown to be associated with a broad range of effective leadership behaviors. Future research should continue to clarify what role leader BI plays in different leadership models, as a cause or a consequence of other leader behaviors.

Simons (2002) proposed several leader personal characteristics that would affect their actual word–action alignment and so drive BI. These include ambivalence toward change, self-awareness, and personality traits of self-monitoring and conscientiousness. Palanski and Carroll (2006) confirmed BI to be related to the Big Five personality trait of conscientiousness. Simons (2008) suggested that personal discipline supports BI, and that it can be developed through developing skills and habits of delaying gratification, facing personal fears, building self-awareness, vigilance, and other self-management techniques.

A few behavioral antecedents have been examined. Hinkin and Schriesheim (2009) showed that a leader-contingent display of both rewards and punishment to followers had a positive impact on follower perceptions of leader BI (see also Palanski, 2008). Vogelgesang and Lester (2008) found in a sample of army cadets that leader interactional transparency was associated with BI.

In addition to leaders' personal characteristics and behaviors, Simons (2002) posited that alignment between a manager's words and deeds can be a function of contextual factors. For instance, actual BI may be impaired because of the job complexity and role ambiguity the manager faces. Managers need to satisfy diverse stakeholders and are sometimes confronted with opposing demands that make them renege on their promises. Another example of an impeding factor to word–deed alignment is organizational change. Whether institutionally driven through managerial fads and fashions or specific organizational change initiatives, change may impair the manager's ability to be true to his or her word. Even the best managers in some companies may face the implementation of multiple but partial change efforts over time, the poor integration of management techniques and technology, and overall poorly integrated policies and procedures. The initial studies of BI impact have examined companies in volatile industries (e.g., hospitality industry; Simons, 2000). No studies have examined BI in the dwindling pool of stable industries. Also, none has looked explicitly at the impact of managerial role ambiguity, multiple accountabilities, or change initiatives on BI.

In addition to environmental turbulence, Simons (2008) suggested that BI can be a function of the overall culture of the organization. Way et al. (2010) found that leader perceptions of positive organizational support were associated with followers' perceptions that the leader displays high BI. Friedman et al. (2007) found that leaders' perceptions of *their* leaders' BI "trickled down" to affect their *own* BI as assessed by their followers. This trickle-down effect could be a result of emulation of superiors, or of leaders simply passing along the fair treatment they receive. Palanski (2008) similarly found that the BI of leaders trickles down to influence follower BI. Leroy (2010) demonstrated that BI is associated with an ethical organizational culture that values accountability, sanctionability, and discussability. Kannan-Narasimhan (2006) proposed that alignment between corporate culture and climate would support BI.

Summary

In sum, theory on BI (Simons, 1999, 2002, 2008) has suggested several different antecedents to BI, and those that have been tested were largely supported. Research has confirmed that BI is influenced by personal characteristics (specific leadership behaviors and personality factors) and contextual characteristics (organizational and environmental factors). Yet, several theoretical propositions have been left unexplored. For instance, future research may examine the impact of managerial role ambiguity or change initiatives on perceived BI.

Moderated Antecedents to Behavioral Integrity

Simons (2002) suggested that a number of perceptual filters moderate between the manager's *actual* word–deed alignment and the *perceived* pattern of word–deed alignment that is BI, as BI is subjectively determined and ascribed. In Figure 25.1, we include several factors as moderators of the association between actual managerial consistency and BI: observer's dependence on the manager (for instance through a hierarchical relationship), observer caring about the promise or underlying value that is espoused, manager's social accounts of potential mismatches, and observer's chronic construct accessibility for related concepts (integrity, honesty, sincerity, or hypocrisy). Empirical examination of these propositions is just beginning.

Simons et al. (2007) found that black employees were more likely to notice and respond to BI violations than were nonblack employees, suggesting that BI is a more salient concept to them. Friedman et al. (2009) found in a vignette study that Indian respondents were less likely to interpret a leader's promise breach as indicative of low BI than were American respondents. Future research needs to consider these effects in sample selection, and to further articulate the role of culture and demographics in the attribution and significance of BI.

The role of values content in driving BI perceptions is relatively unexplored. Clemenson (2008) found that the impact of managers' perceived value content on BI was moderated by employees' assessment of value congruence with their managers. The relationships among BI, value congruence, and value content have not yet been conclusively unpacked.

Finally, the context and history through which the observer views the target affect BI perceptions.

When a leader breaks a promise, followers become more vigilant for future promise-breaking behavior (Simons, 2002). Cha and Edmondson (2006) studied how employees form attributions of discrepancies between values and actions. When such discrepancies were attributed to hypocrisy, employees became disenchanted. Cha (2009) found that strong organizational values can create a "buffer" that reduces negative BI attributions in response to a leader's value breaches. The role of attribution also highlights the importance of a leaders' ability to communicate in such a way as to allow followers to *perceive* consistency and recognize it as BI.

Future research should continue to consider observer and context effects that determine how a given manager's conduct will affect BI perceptions. BI perceptions appear to be strongly influenced by the demographics and sense-making processes of the perceiver(s). One unexplored area is that managers' social accounts may moderate the impact of a leader's value breach on BI.

Future Directions

Regarding the BI construct itself, open questions remain regarding the relationship between value-specific BI and broader BI ascriptions. Do people form multiple assessments of their leaders' BI, perhaps focusing on various specific values, or do they form a unitary judgment? Does perceived hypocrisy regarding a single value taint all judgments of that leader's BI? Does it depend on the value violated (e.g., presidential marital infidelity)? Does it depend on characteristics of the observer? New BI measures that focus on single values, and that separately assess enactment and espousal, can be compared to general measures to address these questions.

At this point, the most well-established outcomes of BI are individual attitudes: Trust, commitment, and satisfaction of various types have been replicated across diverse settings. Individual, group, and organizational performance and operational outcomes have been demonstrated in service industries, but need to be replicated in a manufacturing setting. Such outcomes are especially critical for attracting the attention of executives and intervention-oriented practitioners. Further, there has been little longitudinal research into this area to cement causal assertions. Especially needed are intervention studies that track the performance implications of a BI intervention over time.

An additional realm that is relatively untapped is the notion of moderated consequences. It stands to reason that a leader's BI will strongly affect the success or failure of her managerial initiatives. Is the leader—who is exhorting behavioral change, heightened standards, or a particular value—someone to be believed or not? One can imagine that the consequence of many leader initiatives depends on the leader's BI. Again, a few studies have begun to explore this area, but the potential seems huge.

Relatively unexplored are the antecedents of BI. What conditions, at the individual, organizational, and environmental levels, cause managers to behave inconsistently, and so to be seen as having low BI? Simons (1999, 2002) proposed that times of organizational change and environmental uncertainty are especially challenging for BI, but hard numbers have not yet been attached to that assertion. Is it harder to maintain BI when your job requires juggling the needs of multiple, diverse stakeholders? Does self-knowledge really help with the maintenance of BI? Are some leader personality traits beyond conscientiousness associated with subordinate perceptions of BI?

Perceptual moderators, several of which were proposed by Simons (2002), also represent a relatively untapped area for research questions. What factors on the part of observers make them especially sensitive or insensitive to leaders' behavioral inconsistencies? Studies of cultural and cross-cultural effects can fall into this category, as would considerations of observers' personalities or value structures as perceptual moderators. Are some kinds of people more harsh or forgiving when judging the BI of other groups of people? It is worth noting that a study of perceptual moderators with a single given target of observation—a sample of a company's employees asked to assess their CEOs BI, for example, or employee responses to a given vignette—will appear in that study as main effects. Conceptually, though, these phenomena represent filters through which objective reality is perceived, and thus fall into this category of perceptual moderators.

In sum, there is little one might ask about the BI construct that would *not* represent a new and promising area for research.

Conclusion

Behavioral integrity is a relatively new construct for research, but it is one with great intuitive appeal, as most businesspeople track closely whose word can be relied upon and whose cannot. The notion that an effective leader must walk her talk, lead by example, and keep her promises is hardly novel. Most treatises on leadership address the idea in some way, but the construct has not yet received the focused and sustained research attention it warrants. Initial tests of

attitudinal correlates have been solid and leave room for incremental advances as one looks at the relative importance of BI among other drivers of trust, commitment, and engagement. When one extends beyond attitudes to examine behavioral and organizational performance outcomes, the story becomes much more exciting: Initial studies suggest very substantial behavioral and bottom-line performance consequences for BI. Most of the empirical studies to date are cross-sectional survey studies, so that these results limit inferences of causality. However, some studies are longitudinal (e.g., Kannan-Narasimhan & Lawrence, 2010), employ methods that rely on covariance structure analysis that evaluates the plausibility of causality (e.g., Simons & McLean Parks, 2000), or use an experimental method (e.g., Palanski et al., 2010), and these studies generate more confidence in asserting causal direction.

References

Basik, K. (2010). Expanding the boundaries of behavioral integrity in organizations. Dissertation, The Florida State University, College of Business, Florida, US.

Cha, S.E. (2009). *Leadership and the ideological halo: How employees respond to violations of organizational values*, Paper presented at the Academy of Management Conference, Chicago.

Cha, S.E., & A.C. Edmondson (2006). When values backfire: Leadership, attribution, and disenchantment in a values-driven organization. *The Leadership Quarterly, 17,* 57–78.

Clemenson, B. (2008). Authentic leadership: Do leader's values impact their authenticity in the eyes of their followers? A quantitative study. Dissertation, Case Western Reserve University, Weatherhead School of Management.

Cording, M., Simons, T.L., et al. (2009). *Behavioral integrity and acquisition performance: Evidence of proximal and distal effects.* Paper presented at the annual meeting of the Academy of Management, Chicago, IL.

Craig, S.B., & Gustafson, S.B. (1998). Perceived leader integrity scale: An instrument for assessing employee perceptions of leader integrity. *The Leadership Quarterly, 9,* 127–145.

Davis, A.L., & Rothstein, H.R. (2006). The effects of the perceived behavioral integrity of managers on employee attitudes: A meta-analysis. *Journal of Business Ethics, 67,* 407–419.

Deery, S., Iverson, R.D., & Walsh, J.T. (2006) Toward a better understanding of psychological contract breach: A study of customer service employees, *Journal of Applied Psychology 91,* 166–175.

Dineen, B.R., Lewicki, R.J., et al. (2006). Supervisory guidance and behavioral integrity: Relationships with employee citizenship and deviant behavior. *Journal of Applied Psychology, 91,* 622–635.

Friedman, R., Simons, T., et al. (2009). *Culture's impact on behavioral integrity: When is a promise not a promise?* Paper presented at the annual meeting of the Academy of Management, Chicago, IL.

Hewlin, P., Cha, S.E., et al. (2010). *Value breaches and follower façade creation in a megachurch: The role of leader behavioral integrity versus leader charisma.* Paper to be presented at the annual meeting of the Academy of Management, Montreal, Canada.

Hinkin, T.R., & Schriesheim, C.A. (2005). A theoretical and empirical examination of Bass' transactional leadership dimensions.

Paper presented at the annual meeting of the Academy of Management, Honolulu.

Hinkin, T.R., & Schriesheim, C.A. (2009). *The psychological contract at work: Testing a model of leader reinforcement practices, behavioral integrity, trust, and subordinate outcomes.* Paper presented at the annual meeting of the Academy of Management, Chicago, IL.

Johnson, J.L., & O'Leary-Kelly, A.M. (2003). The effects of psychological contract breach and organizational cynicism: not all social exchange violations are created equal. *Journal of Organizational Behavior, 24,* 627–647.

Kannan-Narasimhan, R. (2006). *Aligning organizational climate with culture: The role of behavioral integrity.* Paper presented at the annual meeting of the Academy of Management, Atlanta, GA.

Kannan-Narasimhan, R., & Lawrence, B.S. (2010). Behavioral integrity: How referents and trust matter to workplace outcomes. Working paper.

Koh, H.C., & Boo, E.H.Y. (2001). The link between organizational ethics and job satisfaction: A study of managers in Singapore. *Journal of Business Ethics, 29,* 309–324.

Leroy, H. (2009). *Behavioral integrity and authentic leadership.* Paper presented at the annual meeting of the Academy of Management, Chicago, IL.

Leroy, H., Halbesleben, J., et al. (2010). *Living up to safety values in health care: Effects of a leader's behavioral integrity on nurse and patient safety.* Paper to be presented at the annual meeting of the Academy of Management, Montreal, Canada.

Lewicki, R.J., & Bunker, B.B. (1996). Developing and maintaining trust in work relationships. In R.M. Kramer, & T.R. Tyler (Eds.), *Trust in organizations: Frontiers of theory and research* (pp. 114–139). Thousand Oaks, CA: Sage.

Ma, L., McLean Parks, J., et al. (2010). *Breaking rules and getting things done: Organizational expedience and intrapreneurship.* Paper to be presented at the annual meeting of the Academy of Management, Montreal, Canada.

Mayer, R.C., Davis, J.H., et al. (1995). An integrative model of organizational trust. *Academy of Management Review, 20,* 709–734.

McLean Parks, J., & Ma, L. (2008). *Behavioral integrity and elasticity in the "rules" of the game.* Paper presented at the annual meeting of the Academy of Management, Anaheim, CA.

Mishra, A.K., & Mishra, K.E. (2011). POS and trust in leaders. In K.S. Cameron & G.M. Spreitzer (Eds.), The Oxford handbook of positive organizational scholarship. New York: Oxford University Press.

Palanski, M.E. (2008). *The behavioral frequency integrity scale as an alternative measure of behavioral integrity.* Paper presented at the annual meeting of the Academy of Management, Anaheim, CA.

Palanski, M.E., & Carroll, E.A. (2006). *Behavioral integrity as an antecedent to leader emergence.* Paper presented at the annual meeting of the Academy of Management, Atlanta, GA.

Palanski, M.E., Kahai, S., et al. (2010). *How transparency, behavioral integrity, and trust enhance team performance.* Working paper.

Palanski, M.E., & Yammarino, F.J. (in press). Impact of behavioral integrity on follower job performance: A three study examination. *Leadership Quarterly,* forthcoming.

Parry, K.W., & Proctor-Thomson, S.B. (2002). Perceived integrity of transformational leaders in organizational settings *Journal of Business Ethics, 35,* 75–96.

Prottas, D. (2008). Perceived behavioral integrity: Relationships with employee attitudes, well-being, and absenteeism. *Journal of Business Ethics, 81,* 313–322.

Robinson, S.L., & Rousseau, D.M. (1994). Violating the psychological contract: Not the exception but the norm. *Journal of Organizational Behavior, 15,* 245–259.

Rozell, E.J., & Gunderson, D.E. (2003). The effects of leader impression management on group perceptions of cohesion, consensus, and communication. *Small Group Research, 34,* 197–222.

Simons, T. (1999). Behavioral integrity as a critical ingredient for transformational leadership. *Journal of Organizational Change Management, 12,* 89–104.

Simons, T. (2002). Behavioral integrity: The perceived alignment between managers' words and deeds as a research focus. *Organization Science, 13,* 18–35.

Simons, T. (2008). *The integrity dividend: Leading by the power of your word.* San Francisco: Jossey Bass.

Simons, T., Friedman, R., et al. (2007). Racial differences in sensitivity to behavioral integrity: Attitudinal consequences, in-group effects, and 'trickle down' among black and non-black employees. *Journal of Applied Psychology, 92,* 650–665.

Simons, T., & Hagen, J. (2006). *The impact of behavioral integrity in supply chain management.* Paper presented at the annual meeting of the Academy of Management, Atlanta, GA.

Simons, T., & McLean Parks, J. (2000). *The sequential impact of behavioral integrity on trust, commitment, discretionary service behavior, customer satisfaction, and profitability.* Paper presented at the annual meeting of the Academy of Management, Toronto, Canada.

Stansbury, J.M., & Sonenshein, S. (2011). Positive business ethics: Grounding and elaborating a theory of good works. In K.S. Cameron & G.M. Spreitzer (Eds.), The Oxford handbook of positive organizational scholarship. New York: Oxford University Press.

Tang, T.L., & Liu, H. (2010). *Love of money and unethical behavior intention: Does an authentic supervisor's personal integrity and character (ASPIRE) make a difference?* Working paper.

Tomlinson, E.C., Ash, S.R., et al. (2006). *When we don't see eye-to-eye: The moderating effect of behavioral integrity on organizational identity.* Paper presented at the annual meeting of the Academy of Management, Atlanta, GA.

Viswesvaran, C., & Deshpande, S.P. (1996). Ethics, success, and job satisfaction: A test of dissonance theory in India, *Journal of Business Ethics, 15,* 1065–1069.

Viswesvaran, C., & Deshpande, S.P. (1998). Job satisfaction as a function of top management support for ethical behavior: A study of Indian managers, *Journal of Business Ethics, 17,* 365–371.

Vitell, S.J., & Davis, D.L. (1990). The relationship between ethics and job satisfaction: An empirical investigation, *Journal of Business Ethics, 9,* 489–494.

Velez, P. (2000). *Interpersonal trust between a supervisor and subordinate.* Unpublished doctoral dissertation, University of California, Berkeley.

Vogelgesang, G., & Lester, P.B. (2008). *Behavioral integrity and interactional transparency as drivers of engagement.* Paper presented at the annual meeting of the Academy of Management, Anaheim, CA.

Vogelgesang, G., Simons, T.L., et al. (2010). *How leader interactional transparency drives employee engagement: The complementary roles of participative decision making and behavioral integrity.* Working paper.

Way, S.A., Simons, T., et al. (2010). *Perceived organizational support, behavioral integrity, and job performance behaviors of Chinese subordinates and managers.* Working paper.

Positive Business Ethics

Grounding and Elaborating a Theory of Good Works

Jason M. Stansbury *and* Scott Sonenshein

Abstract

Although the normative business ethics literature elaborates positive visions of the "good," the behavioral ethics literature primarily focuses on unethical behaviors or decision processes that either lead to or prevent those behaviors. The former literature is valuable for rigorously defining what makes "positive" phenomena so, thereby philosophically grounding "positive"—something that has been often only implicit in positive organizational scholarship (POS). To better theorize a positive counterpart to unethical behavior, this chapter defines a construct called "good works," which are behaviors that are morally praiseworthy, discretionary, and positively deviant. Elucidation of these three criteria based on their theoretical foundations helps to distinguish good works from other related behaviors. The chapter proposes a model of the decision process that precedes good works, based in part upon moral identity, moral imagination, and the sensemaking intuition model, and concludes with directions for future research into the individual and organizational antecedents and consequences of good works.

Keywords: Positive, ethics, behavioral ethics, normative ethics, moral identity, moral imagination, sensemaking–intuition model, supererogation, positive deviance

Positive business ethics is the study of that which is morally excellent or praiseworthy in business. Although the field of business ethics has seen increasing attention by management scholars, we argue in this chapter that a majority of the research in business ethics has focused on attempting to unpack dependent variables, processes, and conceptions of the "good" that disproportionately (but certainly not exclusively) focus on negative aspects of human behavior and morality. Our ambition in this chapter is to briefly review this negative tendency that we see in the descriptive business ethics literature, followed by the presentation of a more positive view of business ethics. We offer several different ways of theorizing "positive," drawing from normative theories of the good. By grounding "positive" in a discussion of the good, we help inform descriptive research in business ethics, and more generally positive organizational scholarship (POS), which has often struggled to understand and define "positive." Our model of positive business ethics—something we call a model of "good works"—explains actions that are positively deviant (Spreitzer & Sonenshein, 2004), are perceived by the people who perform them (and their salient referents) as morally praiseworthy or excellent, and are perceived to be discretionary rather than obligatory. We differentiate our view of good works from related research that has sought to understand morally excellent or praiseworthy behaviors, and propose a model whereby decision-makers identify and determine how to perform good works. We conclude with a call to scholars to be cognizant of the negative–positive biases they bring to their study of business (un)ethics and illustrate how a view of good works expands the domain of business ethics and POS.

Business Ethics: A Brief Overview of Its Negative Tendency

Business ethics is a bit unique as compared to other possible fields to examine through a POS lens, in that it involves both a descriptive study of human behavior more familiar to social scientists, as well as a normative one that is less familiar. For descriptive studies, behavioral ethicists describe and explain organizational behaviors that are recognized by participants or affected parties as (un)ethical, as well as the rational and nonrational decision processes whereby individuals in organizational contexts (fail to) evaluate their actions in ethical terms (O'Fallon & Butterfield, 2005; Sonenshein, 2007; Tenbrunsel & Smith-Crowe, 2008; Trevino, Weaver, & Reynolds, 2006). On the other hand, normative business ethicists elaborate different philosophical visions of the good that can be used to articulate why one decision or outcome is morally better than another.

Although there have been descriptive theories and studies of praiseworthy phenomena such as organizational citizenship behaviors (OCBs; LePine, Erez, & Johnson, 2002; Organ, 1997; Van Dyne, Cummings, & Parks, 1995; Van Dyne & LePine, 1998), corporate social responsibility (CSR; Barnett, 2007; Margolis & Walsh, 2003; Scherer & Palazzo, 2007), whistle-blowing (Mesmer-Magnus & Viswesvaran, 2005; Miceli & Near, 1992), and positive deviance (Spreitzer & Sonenshein, 2003 & 2004; Warren, 2003), much of the work in behavioral ethics has been focused on ethical deficiencies and their prevention. Articles about behavioral business ethics written for audiences of management scholars broader than the community of business ethicists often seize their readers' attention by beginning with a reference to scandals and the need for a better understanding of how to prevent them (e.g., Brown, Trevino, & Harrison, 2005; Jones, 1991; Reynolds, 2006; Scherer & Palazzo, 2007; Street, Douglas, Geiger, & Martinko, 2001; Trevino, Weaver, & Reynolds, 2006). Moreover, a prevailing concern with the study of deficiencies in ethical decision-making and behavior is evident in much research. For example, Reynolds (2006), in his study of the biopsychological bases of moral awareness states, "I will use the neurocognitive model to develop research propositions around the central concern of ethics research: unethical behavior" (p. 742). When introducing moral imagination, Moberg and Seabright (2000) call it "a form of reasoning that serves as an antidote to decision environments that normally lead to morally defective choices" (p. 845). Although the modeling and prevention of legally and morally unacceptable behavior is plainly quite important, we believe that the descriptive domain of ethically excellent or praiseworthy behaviors in business appears to be relatively undertheorized and underexamined. A focus on a more positive perspective on business ethics is not meant to relegate traditional research to the side; quite the opposite, we believe that explaining unethical behavior as well as positive ethical behavior are both important research endeavors. However, we believe that current theoretical frameworks have a tendency to focus on explaining unethical behavior, and that theories needed to explain ethical behavior are not necessarily the same as those used to explain unethical behavior.

Positive Business Ethics: Summary of the Good Works Construct

In contrast to much of the literature briefly reviewed so far, we will focus this chapter on a more positive set of phenomena that we call "good works": actions that are positively deviant (Spreitzer & Sonenshein, 2004), are perceived by the people who perform them (and their salient referents) as morally praiseworthy or excellent, and are perceived to be discretionary rather than obligatory. We will also examine the positive processes and mechanisms that help explain such behaviors.

To begin our discussion of good works, consider some examples that have focused on more positive aspects of ethical behavior. Examples might include Howard Lutnick's decision to pay 10 years' worth of health insurance and profit sharing to the dependents of 658 Cantor Fitzgerald employees killed on September 11, 2001 (Gordon, 2001), John Rockwell's development of McDonald's Corporation's Green Building Strategy (Net Impact, 2009), or Ajay Badhwar's conception and development of a carbon-capture business that leverages the engineering and project management strengths of Alstom Power and the Dow Chemical Company (Net Impact, 2009). All of these examples are positively deviant in that they depart from the typical behavior of managers in these decision-makers' industries and perhaps even their own companies; they are morally praiseworthy in their contribution to individual and collective well-being; and they are discretionary, in that no blame would accrue for not doing them, nor were they coerced by others.

Good works are conceptually distinct phenomena from other constructs that emphasize descriptively positive behaviors. For example, they are different from OCBs because, although they are discretionary and praiseworthy, they are also positively deviant, that is, nontrivially outside of the norms of behavior typical to an organization or other relevant referent. Similarly, they are different from CSR for the same reason. They are a subset of positively deviant behaviors in that they are considered excellent or praiseworthy according to some moral standard, whereas other positively deviant behaviors may perhaps be honorable for their beauty (like the construction of architecturally attractive facilities or the placement of aesthetically excellent advertising) or their cleverness (like the use of industrial ecology to capture the waste streams from one production process as the inputs for another) but not morally excellent per se. Finally, good works are not simply the inverse of ethical misbehaviors or the results of not engaging in misbehavior, such that it is reasonable to suppose that they may be described using the same processes: Rather, their discretionary, praiseworthy, and positively deviant nature makes it likely that they are governed by decision processes that do not draw on the same cognitive resources as more urgent problems whose neglect may lead to negative sanctions (Baumeister, Bratslavsky, Finkenauer, & Vohs, 2001).

Although good works may exist at the individual or the organizational level, we are focusing this chapter on good works as individual actions that result from individual-level decision processes. Individual decisions often have organizational implications, especially when individual decision-makers are acting on behalf of, or directing, the organization. However, to develop the idea of good works at the organizational level would require a theoretical focus that goes beyond our largely psychological and social-psychological approach and would take us to a more sociological analysis that warrants its own treatment. As a result, we believe that a theory of good works at the organizational level remains a fertile opportunity for future research, but one that we do not take up here.

Having broadly discussed good works, we turn to better grounding the construct, first by considering its normative underpinnings and then moving to elaborate the construct for descriptively oriented views of business ethics.

Good Works: A Normative Grounding

A normative grounding of good works is important because it adds theoretical clarity to what "positive" is—that is, what makes some behaviors morally praiseworthy. Although such a grounding can add important clarity to the POS literature, it is not without controversy. The content and justification of the good life and of good actions have been subjects

of ongoing philosophical inquiry for thousands of years (e.g., Aristotle, 350 BCE/1985; Foucault, 1988; Taylor, 1989), and business ethicists continue to theorize applications of these visions of the good life to and within organizations (e.g., Crane, Knights, & Starkey, 2008; Hartman, 1996; Solomon, 1992). In fact, there is an indefinite number of visions of the good (Lyotard, 1984; Taylor, 1989) that may have an indefinite set of implications for business ethics (Rorty, 2006). Our purpose here is not to recommend one normative vision of the good over the others, but rather to sketch a few of them briefly, highlight some continuities between them, and illustrate their potential implications for grounding a view of good works. We believe that normative ethics can helpfully elaborate what it is that makes good works "good," and perhaps commend some that have not often occurred to decision-makers. This is important because one of the difficulties of the development of POS is that scholars often do not have a sound basis for what "positive" means (George, 2004).

Importantly, we are not attempting to subsume all that might be positive under the moral good. Rather, moral praiseworthiness pertains to a subset of all honorable behaviors, specifically those actions that contribute to the good life of individuals and the communities within which they live and work. Spreitzer and Sonenshein (2004) characterized the positive aspect of positive deviance as that which is honorable; positive acts do or would meet with the approval and even acclaim of a relevant referent group because those acts exceed the norms that such a group holds for the relevant behavior. But that which is honorable includes more than just that which is morally good, whether as a matter of definition or perception (Scott, 1996). Aquinas (1984) distinguished between intellectual and moral virtues, noting that the former are useful for reasoning accurately and insightfully from both principles and evidence, regardless of the moral or immoral purposes to which they are put. A skilled integrative bargainer may discern that two children fighting over an orange can both be satisfied if one is given the peel for baking and the other the flesh for eating (Fisher, Ury, & Patton, 1991); she has solved a problem through a laudable rational insight, but not through strength of her moral character or brilliance of her moral vision. Similarly, aesthetic beauty is also independent of ethics (Adorno, 2004; Rothko, 2004). A well-dressed employee may be a credit to his role or organization (Rafaeli & Pratt, 1993) and be complimented accordingly, whereas a skilled public speaker may be much appreciated by his audience, but neither one has demonstrated moral character or moral vision, at least through their aesthetic excellences. These honorable characteristics are nonexclusive; for instance, a speech may simultaneously contribute to the good life of the community by discrediting discriminatory practices, ingeniously refer to cherished identities shared by the speaker and the parties being addressed (Nielsen, 1996), and impart excitement to its message through the cadence of its delivery. But, it is the first characteristic that makes it morally praiseworthy.

One stream of theorizing about the good life in business ethics is drawn from the virtue tradition that stretches back to Aristotle, a theme that POS scholars have frequently used (Cameron, 2003). On the insistence that individual happiness is enabled by the well-functioning of the surrounding community, Solomon (1992) elaborated a set of classically grounded virtues that, when practiced by individual businesspeople, would be conducive to collective well-being in organizations. His vision was expansive, encompassing organizations characterized by "continuity and stability, clearness of vision and constancy of purpose, corporate loyalty and individual integrity" (p. 104), in which each employee has a job that "means something, one that has (more or less) tangible and clearly beneficial results, one that (despite inevitable periods of frustration) one enjoys doing" (p. 105–106). Solomon (1992) placed a high value on congenial virtues like friendliness, compassion, caring, and wit, which, along with courage, toughness, and justice, complemented by intellectual virtues like vision and creativity, are important for creating and sustaining organizations that exemplify the vision quoted above. Good works in such a framework might include acts of compassionate generosity to organization members who are victims of some misfortune (e.g., the responses to victims of an apartment fire chronicled in Dutton, Worline, Frost, & Lilius, 2006), which would enhance the solidarity of the community and the well-being of its members.

Hartman (1996) similarly emphasized the importance of theorizing business organizations as communities (and as elements of broader communities) in which the well-being of individuals may be promoted. Hartman's (1996) overriding concern is the cultivation of moral autonomy, such that individuals are able to make (and take responsibility for) their own decisions according to the demands of their own consciences. This moral autonomy requires a context that enhances its inhabitants' abilities and opportunities to exercise it—one in which there are responsibilities to be discharged, authorities to be exercised, and goods to be justly distributed. That good community, of which the business organization is a microcosm, requires careful development and maintenance: Good works there would enhance both the loyalty of its constituents and the scope of their autonomy, often through greater justice and transparency. For instance, an HR manager might promote both the availability of disability accommodations and the procedures through which their reasonability is determined. This would enhance the quality of work and life for employees who would otherwise suffer silently rather than self-identify their disability, thus increasing their loyalty and autonomy; it would also increase perceptions of procedural fairness among their coworkers (Colella, Paetzold, & Belliveau, 2004), to similar effect.

Other streams draw from even newer traditions in philosophical ethics. For instance, Crane, Knights, and Starkey (2008) have explored implications for the workplace of an even more radical ideal of moral autonomy drawn from the work of Michel Foucault. This radical autonomy recognizes that people need communities if they are to realize aspirations greater than social isolation, and that joining communities requires submitting to the authority of those communities' norms; however, individuals should choose for themselves with which communities they will affiliate themselves, and therefore to which norms and authorities they will submit themselves (Crane et al., 2008). Gardner, Stansbury, and Hart (2010) have applied just such a Foucauldian approach to the practice of "poaching" employees from other firms, arguing that norms against lateral hiring among employers are in fact simply a form of opportunistic economic collusion masquerading as ethics; instead, employees ought to decide for themselves what outside offers to entertain, on the basis of relationships of loyalty mutually forged between them and their employers. One example of a good work that might be relevant to such an approach is the formation of network groups for diverse sets of minority employees or the promulgation of policies that encourage the formation of those groups (Friedman & Holtom, 2002); such groups provide employees with a choice of affiliations and the opportunity to challenge the norms of one affiliation through the strength of another.

Aside from theorizing about the nature of the good itself, a different stream of philosophical thought analyzes the content and possibility of actions that are both praiseworthy and discretionary. Mellema (1991a) defines actions that fulfill no moral duty or obligation, that are praiseworthy, and whose omission is not blameworthy (p. 3) as supererogatory; that is, as being "above and beyond" what is necessary. Seven types of action are generally understood to be supererogatory: beneficence (i.e., giving gifts or charity), doing favors, volunteering, declining to claim one's rights, forgiveness, heroism (i.e., taking on extraordinary responsibilities), and saintliness (i.e., forbearing extraordinary hardships or temptations) (Heyd, 1982). Importantly, supererogatory actions need not be altruistic; good works need not be wholly selfless to be good, although praiseworthy actions typically benefit or at least attempt to benefit someone else as well (Mellema, 1991a; Solomon, 1992).

Some cases illustrate situations in which a praiseworthy action is actually not entirely discretionary. These actions may fall into the category of quasi-supererogation if they are the sort of action that someone is obligated to do sooner or later, but that a person may decline any instance of without qualms (Mellema, 1991a,b). Reviewing manuscripts for a journal that one submits manuscripts to would be a case of quasi-supererogation, because declining any single review request is not a failure to fulfill one's duty to review, but declining all of them is. Similarly, some actions are quasi-supererogatory because their omission signals (howsoever accurately or inaccurately) a lack of some virtue (Mellema, 1991b). Contributing to the annual United Way drive is praiseworthy, but not doing so may imply a lack of generosity, team spirit, or both; depending on one's reasons for declining, it may be blameworthy not to contribute.

The foregoing thumbnail sketch of a normative grounding of positive business ethics highlights a pair of important points. First, the analytical study of supererogatory (henceforth praiseworthy and discretionary) actions reveals a typology of those actions, points out that those actions need not be altruistic, and highlights that some such actions are not as discretionary as they may seem. Second, various conceptions of the good generally concern themselves with the well-being of the individual embedded within a social system that must also be sustained in a well-functioning state. Businesses are subsystems of larger social systems, and happen to be especially important for the well-being of the people within them, so that the individual, organizational, and social levels of analysis are interdependent. Thus, good works can entail contributions to specific individuals, such as doing favors for overwhelmed coworkers or customers, or contributions to the well-functioning of the system upon which individuals depend, such as reducing waste in the company cafeteria or appointing an ombudsperson.

Good Works: A Descriptive Grounding
In this section, we will further elaborate the good works construct as an important and understudied domain within descriptive positive business ethics. Its defining features are its moral praiseworthiness, its discretionary character, and its positive deviance, as perceived by the person performing the good work and that person's salient referents.

Moral Praiseworthiness
An action is morally praiseworthy if it exemplifies or promotes some vision of the good life, as the examples cited in the foregoing section do. For our descriptive purposes, we will define moral praiseworthiness with reference to the visions of the good held by some referent group (Warren, 2003), which may likely hold visions of the good that bear some resemblance to those outlined in the preceding section. These might not adhere strictly to some particular normative standard; for instance, businesspeople may consider some actions morally praiseworthy that normative ethicists, activists, or other observers do not. The generation of ecologically unsustainable waste streams is self-defeating in the long run if widely practiced, making such behavior potentially unethical (e.g., Kant, 1998), yet sustainability projects that reduce but do not eliminate emissions are viewed by many businesspeople as praiseworthy contributions to the world in which they and their children will live (Environmental Defense Fund, 2008). Even with reference to the same vision of the good (a world characterized by both prosperity and a stable ecosystem), the line that descriptively delineates praise from blame varies with the issue at hand and the parties who take an interest in it and offer an interpretation of it.

Some actions are positively deviant and discretionary but not morally praiseworthy per se. An example of such a behavior would be Cummins Engine Company's commitment to pay architecture fees for public buildings in its hometown of Columbus, Indiana (Cummins Engine Company, n. d.; Csikszentmihalyi, 2003); honorable though Cummins's commitment is, it does not appear to enhance moral autonomy or bolster the position of the least-advantaged in the community (for instance). Similarly, Southwest Airlines' policy of not charging passengers to check bags is clever, discretionary, and positively deviant, but not morally praiseworthy per se, since the good at issue is simply a few extra dollars in its (many) customers' pockets. Such behaviors may be honorable for nonmoral reasons, but behaviors that are positively deviant without being morally praiseworthy per se are likely to be better understood with models of innovation than with models of good works.

Discretion

Discretionary actions are those for which no moral condemnation applies upon their omission. Not all volitional actions are discretionary; writing about organizational citizenship behaviors, Organ (1988) stated that "By discretionary, we mean that the behavior is not an enforceable requirement of the role or the job description . . . the behavior is rather a matter of personal choice, such that its omission is not generally understood as punishable" (p. 4). Whereas Organ's interest was in behaviors that were not required by the employee's job role, our interest is in behaviors that are not required by moral considerations, which is to say, behaviors that are supererogatory or quasi-supererogatory according to the definition in the foregoing section. The case of quasi-supererogatory behaviors is an interesting boundary condition, because these are boundedly discretionary: They fulfill a duty that must be honored in some way, but the particular action with which to fulfill the duty is up to the decision maker. For instance, the example above of soliciting requests for accommodation from employees under the Americans with Disabilities Act is quasi-supererogatory: The action is praiseworthy, and its omission is not blameworthy, but it fulfills the employer's duty to accommodate the disabled. Since making accommodations is a duty under United States law, this proactive approach qualifies merely as an excellent way of meeting an obligation that the employer would have to fulfill anyway. Similarly, giving to the annual United Way drive may be a signal of one's generosity; not giving is not an indicator of a lack of generosity if one's generosity is alternatively expressed through gifts given directly to other charities, or even directly to people in need. That said, we believe that even quasi-supererogatory actions that fulfill some minimum duty, if performed in a way that is morally praiseworthy and positively deviant, are deserving of study—it is worth asking, "Why fulfill the duty in this way, at this time?"

Some actions may be morally praiseworthy, positively deviant, but not discretionary. Instances of whistle-blowing that expose a significant and imminent harm would fall into this category; for instance, blowing the whistle on the harmful health effects of tobacco use, asbestos exposure, or some as-yet-unexposed dangerous product is praiseworthy, but suppressing the same information is blameworthy, so that such an act of whistle-blowing is not discretionary. Consider also James Burke's decision on behalf of Johnson & Johnson to recall all Tylenol during the cyanide adulteration crisis of 1982: Burke was deservedly praised for his decisive and comprehensive response to the threat, but the blame that would have accrued if more people had died after a more measured response would have been fearsome. The Credo at Johnson & Johnson famously states in its opening lines that "We believe our first responsibility is to the doctors, nurses and patients, to mothers and fathers and all others who use our products and services. In meeting their needs everything we do must be of high quality" (Johnson, 1943). The Credo's clear focus on the firm's responsibility to provide high-quality medicines to its consumers highlighted the unacceptability of further deaths from a poisoned product. Therefore, morally praiseworthy and positively deviant though this decision was, it was not truly discretionary; this decision is better described by moral approbation (Jones & Ryan, 1997) than by our good works construct.

Positive Deviance

Positive deviance is behavior that violates existing norms (i.e., deviates) in a way that is honorable (i.e., positive) (Spreitzer & Sonenshein, 2004). For our purposes, "morally praiseworthy" is a subset of "honorable," as elaborated above. Deviance is behavior that is exceptional in some respect relative to typical or routine behaviors among a reference group; it may be statistically rare, supraconforming, or simply behavior that members of the reference group identify or would identify as deviant, but it should not have the negative connotations that are often ascribed to the term (Spreitzer & Sonenshein, 2004). Therefore, when we state that good works are positively deviant, we emphasize that they are exceptional rather than common, they are not well characterized by typical models of similar behavior, and they do not conform to typical routines.

Some actions may be morally praiseworthy and discretionary but not positively deviant. Helping a coworker move into a new home, advising a new hire about how to comply with the code of conduct, walking a disabled customer to his car, or suggesting a process change that will reduce electricity consumption might all be well within the norms and routines of many workplaces. Many such behaviors would be appropriately classified as OCBs (LePine, Erez, & Johnson, 2002; Organ, 1997) or prosocial organizational behaviors (Brief & Motowidlo, 1986), and can be modeled accordingly. However, it is important to note that, as the requirements of many jobs become more vague and expansive, what is considered in-role behavior has also expanded, to the extent that many prototypical OCBs are considered in-role by many employees and managers (Organ, 1997); moreover, meta-analysis suggests that OCBs may be most accurately understood as a "general tendency to be cooperative and helpful in organizational settings" (LePine, Erez, & Johnson, 2002). Therefore, we suggest that, although the OCB construct may incorporate some good works, the positively deviant character of the latter will tend to separate it from the mundane (although not thereby unimportant) character of most of the former (Spreizer & Sonenshein, 2004). Brief and Motowidlo's (1986) prosocial organizational behavior construct is even broader, incorporating behaviors that may or may not be directed toward the organization or its members and may or may not benefit them. Brief and Motowidlo (1986) themselves noted that the term *prosocial* is quite value-laden, but that neither researchers nor managers should presume that a prosocial behavior ought to be promoted for practical or ethical reasons. Therefore, we similarly suggest that, although some prosocial organizational behaviors may also qualify as good works, we believe that the more restricted domain of the latter is useful for research and practice.

Similarly, CSR may be discretionary and praiseworthy but not positively deviant. Barnett (2007) characterizes it as discretionary corporate activity intended to both improve social welfare and enhance stakeholder relationships. It need not be altruistic, and in fact, the intention to enhance stakeholder relationships means that genuinely altruistic acts of CSR are likely to be accidental. Barnett (2007) also characterizes CSR as nearly universal, rather than positively deviant. Moreover, Barnett (2007), Margolis and Walsh (2003), and Scherer and Palazzo (2007) define it as an organization-level phenomenon, in the domain of strategy and organization theory. We are focusing on good works as individual behaviors; those behaviors may have organization-level implications, especially if the actors are important organizational decision-makers, but theories of organization-level good works informed by the CSR literature must remain for future research.

Prototypical Good Works

Having described the attributes of good works, and the conditions that mark their absence, we will now illustrate some prototypical good works. Nike has been working to enhance its sustainability since the early 1990s, and despite a major setback during the sweatshop scandal of that same decade, it has made enormous progress (Arnold & Hartman, 2003; McDonough & Braungart, 2002; York & Larson, 2006). A small group of employees organized as the Nike Environmental Action Team (i.e., NEAT) in 1993, which promoted recycling programs including Reuse-A-Shoe (Nike, 2001), which has recycled over 24 million shoes into rubberized sports surfaces and other materials since 1990; 300 basketball courts, tracks, and other surfaces had been donated to communities by Nike by 2008 (Nike, n. d.). Then, in 1995, NEAT heard a galvanizing presentation by Paul Hawken, which convinced its members that businesses like Nike needed to "enter a new era of commerce where human and business needs don't deplete living systems" (Nike, 2001, p. 5). In 1996, Nike commissioned a new green European headquarters campus with extensive recreational facilities (McDonough & Braungart, 2002), and by 1998, Nike had an official sustainability policy, even as it was inundated by a rising tide of bad publicity over the labor and environmental practices of its contract manufacturers (York & Larson, 2006). In July 1998, CEO Phil Knight committed Nike to holding its suppliers to U.S. Occupational Safety and Health Administration (OSHA) indoor air-quality standards, to a 16-year-old lower age limit for apparel workers, and an 18-year-old limit for footwear workers, and nongovernmental organization (NGO) involvement in monitoring of its factories' labor and environmental practices (Arnold & Hartman, 2003). Moreover, Nike has led its industry by requiring after-work educational programs for workers in its contract factories; these programs have meaningfully enhanced educational attainment and promotion opportunities for personnel who otherwise would not be able to pursue formal education; in Vietnam, all contract factories offer education leading to the local equivalent of a U.S. high school level diploma (GED) (Arnold & Hartman, 2003). In the United States, Nike has been gradually eliminating its use of materials, like polyvinyl chloride, that are neither biodegradable nor indefinitely recyclable, incorporating ever-greater quantities of organic cotton into its garments, and reducing the use of nonregulated hazardous materials in its contractors' manufacturing processes (McDonough & Braungart, 2002; York & Larson, 2006). These actions qualify as good works, because they embody a morally praiseworthy commitment to social and environmental good dating back to NEAT's original epiphany in 1995; they are discretionary in the sense that they more than meet the legal requirements that Nike faces and are in many cases invisible to consumers; and they are positively deviant in that Nike has often pioneered these activities in its industry.

Toward a Model of Good Works

An indefinite number of potential good works exist, as well as a great many possible antecedents and moderators of their incidence. Accordingly, we will next focus our attention on the decision process whereby individuals identify and carry out good works. We believe that this process is important because it highlights one of the most important mechanisms for the genesis of good works, and because it provides an opportunity-oriented counterpart to problem-focused moral decision-making.

The decision process that precedes a good work is partly rational and partly intuitive. Rational processes are important for choosing to do a good work, because positively deviant actions are unlikely to result from the peripheral information processing that occurs when decision makers devote little cognitive attention to decisions that they do not view as ethically important (Street et al., 2001). However, a systematic normative analysis of the set of possible good works, followed by an optimizing (or even satisficing) choice among them, seems to be beyond the cognitive resources of business decision makers (Sonenshein, 2007). Rather, we propose that businesspeople have moral identities that are, to some greater or lesser extent, central to their senses of self (Aquino & Reed, 2002). Those identities will encompass a set of scripts for action that the individual considers moral; for positively deviant actions that depart from the set of behaviors typical in the work role, these scripts may belong to a different role, and be enacted in the work role as an act of moral imagination (Werhane, 1999). A given individual will recognize an opportunity for a good work in the workplace through reflexive pattern matching (Reynolds, 2006) of the attributes of the situation with the schemas that comprise their moral identity. That recognition will prompt an intuitive determination of whether they would or would not like to perform that good work (Sonenshein, 2007). Afterward, the individual will rationally consider the practical constraints he will face, strategies he will follow, and justifications he will offer in order to perform the good work (Sonenshein, 2007). The ensuing rational consideration may dissuade the individual from performing the good work, or encourage him to do so, depending on whether the justifications and strategies he is able to formulate are adequate to overcome the constraints he will face in enacting his deviance. We will elaborate the elements of this model below.

Moral identity (Aquino & Reed, 2002; McFerran, Aquino, & Duffy, 2010; Shao, Aquino, & Freeman, 2008) is "a self-conception organized around a set of moral traits" (Aquino & Reed, 2002, p. 1424). Individuals will consider themselves, to a greater or lesser extent, to be people that cherish and demonstrate (or internalize and symbolize) attributes like caring, compassion, fairness, friendliness, generosity, helpfulness, hard work, honesty, and kindness (Aquino & Reed, 2002). The foregoing set of attributes is not exhaustive, and in fact different individuals will incorporate different attributes that they consider moral; however, the foregoing set is usefully general in its acceptance as typically moral by a wide range of people (Aquino & Reed, 2002). Moreover, empirical studies have found that individuals who internalize these attributes are more likely to self-report volunteerism, to actually engage in charitable giving (Aquino & Reed, 2002), and to both subscribe to a principled ethical ideology and subsequently engage in OCBs (McFerran, Aquino, & Duffy, 2010). Moral identity appears to be a self-schema that prompts prosocial behavior.

Moral imagination (Moberg & Seabright, 2000; Werhane, 1999) is also important for decisions to perform good works, because the positive deviance of those good works requires a creative awareness of both the immediate situation and of other honorable possibilities: A lack of creativity leads to actions that are positively mundane, whereas a lack of awareness leads to actions that are flatly deviant. Werhane (1999) characterized moral imagination as being aware of the schemas guiding one's own ethical thinking in a given situation, considering other possibly relevant schemas from outside of that situation, and imagining new possibilities of action that draw on both sets of schemas. She elaborated on contemporary social psychological and philosophical conceptions of the self to propose that each person has different "thick selves," one for each set of different activities and matching reference groups one participates in. One also has a "thin self" that exists at the intersection of those many thick selves, which comprises one's consistent moral core, regardless of the situation. The thin self is able to mediate between different thick selves to bring to bear schemas that facilitate understanding and scripts that guide action as needed and as appropriate, and that bringing of different aspects of self to bear from outside of the situation at hand is constitutive of moral imagination (Werhane, 1999). For instance, a committed environmentalist may have a "thick self" that spends weekends knee-deep in mud doing wetlands restoration, and another "thick self" that spends workdays striving for efficiency as a facilities manager. Her "thin self" may incorporate an abhorrence of waste and a hands-on practicality; she may exercise moral imagination by proposing that a new parking lot incorporate a runoff-capture cistern to irrigate the grounds and prevent contamination of the watershed. We argue that the positive deviance that differentiates good works from more mundane prosocial behaviors can be understood as an enactment of a different but appropriate thick self, characterized by a moral identity (Aquino & Reed, 2002), in a situation in which the work self would typically apply.

The Sensemaking-Intuition Model (SIM; Sonenshein, 2007) describes how a decision maker faces a situation of moral equivocality, in which it is not clear what the right thing to do is. Incidents of positive deviance would seem to qualify as equivocal because they depart from the typical routines and practices of a workplace, and therefore would seem to require some degree of consideration. The SIM posits that a given decision begins with an issue construction, in which the decision maker or others in the social environment interpret a set of social cues as marking an ethical issue (Sonenshein, 2007). Opportunities to perform good works are similarly constructed from the schemas that identify goods and opportunities, and the scripts that guide actions, through moral imagination. A decision maker's moral identity, as an element of the thin self at the nexus of many thick selves, will organize cues according to the self-schemas drawn from those thick selves. That organization may sometimes reveal an opportunity for a good work that complements and reinforces moral identity. A given decision maker's schemas and scripts may be well-developed, whether through careful upbringing, education in moral reasoning or practical ethics, or exposure to moral exemplars (Moberg & Seabright, 2000; Weaver, 2006; Weaver, Trevino, & Agle, 2005); more numerous and well-developed schemas and scripts are useful for better matching actions to the environment (Weick, 1979), and in this case, for exercising moral imagination to construct opportunities to do good works. For instance, our wetlands-loving facilities manager likely learned about the effect of runoff from paved surfaces on local wetlands through education, hands-on exposure to those wetlands, or both; her thick self who restores wetlands on the weekends recognized the runoff from a parking lot as harmful. Her waste-loathing thin self aligned that schema with the efficiency-seeking

schema of her facilities manager thick self to highlight the value of capturing the runoff. She constructed an opportunity to do a good work through an act of moral imagination.

Once an opportunity has been constructed, according to the SIM, the decision maker will intuitively and instantaneously make a moral judgment (Sonenshein, 2007), which in this case will be whether the good work at hand is something to perform or not. That intuition will stem from the degree to which the pattern of attributes in the opportunity construction match the pattern of attributes of a moral schema that has a positive valence (Reynolds, 2006; Sonenshein, 2007). The self-importance of one's moral identity (Aquino & Reed, 2002) is likely to influence that judgment, as are the type and length of the decision maker's experiences with good works, and the social influences for or against good works to which she has been exposed (Sonenshein, 2007). Our facilities manager is likely to judge her runoff-capture opportunity as worth pursuing, in light of its strong match with a positively valued schema.

Finally, the decision maker will formulate explanations and justifications of her intuition (Sonenshein, 2007). This is the point at which formal ethical reasoning can be engaged to evaluate the normative excellence of a good work, although often a decision maker may instead formulate her explanation to others using non-normative terms (Sonenshein, 2006), and the degree of normative justification that she requires for her own satisfaction may be quite small. At this stage, the decision maker may also reassess the feasibility of performing the good work, if the explanations and justifications formulated are inadequate for overcoming the expected barriers and objections to the action. Our facilities manager may justify her runoff-capture proposal to others in terms of both rational efficiency (not consuming municipal water, and perhaps earning public goodwill in times of drought), and the ecological benefit of reducing runoff.

Conclusion

Positive business ethics offers the promise of better articulating the positive foundations of ethical versus unethical behavior, as well as for providing a model for how other research streams in POS can use normative theories to better understand what "positive" means. Although our review of normative theories was far from comprehensive, it suggests an opportunity for crisper theorizing for POS scholars. We took on this challenge of crisper theorizing through the development of the good works construct and its integration into a decision making model that, unlike many other models in the business ethics literature, explicitly focuses on explaining positive ethical behavior—not unethical transgressions. In doing so, we hope to have taken an important step in helping explain some of the extraordinary good works that organizational members undertake.

Future Directions

Positive business ethics, and especially a theory of good works, calls for the importance of understanding the normative foundation of positive behavior. Business ethics especially makes salient the need for theoretical clarity around what is positive, as in this case, positive has implications for fundamental questions of right or wrong. At the same time, the descriptive model we developed about good works is fundamentally rooted in social science, with implications for theorizing about the descriptive mechanisms and processes that lead to positive ethical behavior. Although we are certainly not the first to have noticed questions around the integration of normative and descriptive business ethics (e.g., Donaldson & Dunfee, 1994; Trevino & Weaver, 1994), we feel that the often confusing relationship between normative and descriptive aspects of business ethics is that much more important for POS. Normative theories, such as those we briefly reviewed here, help inform what is positive, whereas descriptive theories explain how we get there.

The Ends of Business Ethics—What Is "Positive"?

One of the over-arching criticisms of much of the POS literature to date has been on the murky and problematic understanding of "positive." George (2004, p. 326) put it this way: "The meaning of terms such as 'positive'. . . is implied or assumed to be universally understood and agreed upon . . . I beg to differ. Clearly, what is thought of as positive, extraordinary, or virtuous is value laden and debatable, context-dependent, and historically, ideologically, and socially constrained." Fineman, offering another critique of POS, used these words: "The revolutionary verve of positive scholars is striking yet attests ideologically to established traditions that fuse positive assumptions about human nature with moral rectitude" (Fineman, 2006, p. 272). What these criticisms rightly point out is that POS scholars have either avoided a clear definition of "positive" or made universalistic assumptions about what is positive that borders on the line of creating a "cosmology" (George, 2004, p. 326) or a "moral/ideological stand"

(Fineman, 2006, p. 271). We have tried to be both explicit and pluralistic in our use of normative theories to add more texture to the meaning of "positive." We described several possible definitions of the good that can serve as a foundation for "positive." We remain (in this chapter) agnostic about philosophical debates over which conception of the good is "right," or even if it makes sense to ask such questions in the first place (Rorty, 1982). Instead, we present a variety of conceptions of the good that can inform how we theorize which types of behaviors are viewed as positively ethical—that is, as morally praiseworthy.

No doubt our very brief review of normative theories has left out other important conceptions of the good, which may also commend otherwise-ignored opportunities for businesspeople to do and be good. If POS scholars want to overcome criticisms of being ideological (that is, affirming one conception of the good) and criticisms of not being clear on what is positive (that is, not affirming any conception of the good), we encourage a stronger dialogue with business ethicists who are better equipped to elaborate the different foundations of positivity, especially concerning moral behavior. If POS scholars ground their theorizing about the positive in philosophically articulated models of the good, then the latter criticism will be moot. Moreover, charges of ideology are troublesome mostly when the vision of the good that grounds a work of scholarship is left implicit. By making the claims to positivity explicit in a given work, positive scholars can address the weaknesses of those claims, while remaining circumspect about what they do and do not advocate.

The Means of Positive Business Ethics— How Do We Get There?

Although normative business ethicists have a vital role to play in explicating the foundations of positivity, we think that social scientists have much to learn about the mechanisms and processes that explain positive ethical behavior. Our brief review of (un)ethical behavior suggests that the field of business ethics has amassed quite a wealth of knowledge around explaining when and why individuals engage in decision making that leads to unethical behavior. But as our descriptive model of good works suggests, it is important for models of ethical decision making to also explain positive ethical behavior.

There are a number of relationships that future research into these models might explain. The internalization and symbolization of moral identity (Aquino & Reed, 2002) may be important positive antecedents of good works, as might the diversity and detail (Weick, 1979) of the schemas and scripts that comprise individuals' moral identity. Similarly, individual-level positive or negative antecedents of good works may include personality, duration, or diversity of work experiences or gender, whereas organization-level antecedents may include ethical climate (Victor & Cullen, 1988), psychological safety (Edmondson, 1999), or the presence of a values-based ethics program (Paine, 1994). Theoretically or practically important consequences of good works may also include affective or normative commitment (Meyer & Allen, 1991) at the individual level. Importantly, the foregoing adaptation of the SIM for good works implies that agents of moral change, such as tempered radicals (Meyerson & Scully, 1995), might have opportunities to appeal to other decision makers in their organizations without recrafting their presentation of the opportunity in non-normative terms (Sonenshein, 2006). Because the intuitive judgment of the attractiveness of a good work results from the similarity of the construction of the opportunity to schemas that are important to the decision maker's moral identity, tempered radicals can retain the moral character of their appeals by framing those appeals to match cherished aspects of others' moral identity. Understanding what goods or actions others hold dear may be especially helpful for formulating successful moral appeals, as might targeting those appeals to individuals for whom moral identity is self-important.

Both business ethics and POS share a common concern around positively deviant behavior that is praiseworthy, and as we argued here, both rely on some normative foundation to define what is "praiseworthy." In this chapter, we hope we have taken an important step in bridging these related disciplines in the hopes of creating more rigorous and impactful scholarship that informs both areas of research.

References

Aquino, K., & Reed, A. II. (2002). The self-importance of moral identity. *Journal of Personality and Social Psychology, 83,* 1423–1440.

Adorno, T.W. (2004). *Aesthetic theory.* London: Continuum.

Aristotle. (1985). *Nicomachean ethics.* (T. Irwin, Trans.). Indianapolis, IN: Hackett Publishing. (Original work published c350 B.C.E.)

Arnold, D.G., & Hartman, L.P. (2003). Moral imagination and the future of sweatshops. *Business and Society Review, 108,* 425–461.

Aquinas, T. (1984). *Treatise on the virtues.* (J.A. Oesterle, Trans.). Notre Dame, IN: University of Notre Dame Press.

Barnett, M.L. (2007). Stakeholder influence capacity and the variability of financial returns to corporate social responsibility. *Academy of Management Review, 32,* 794–816.

Baumeister, R.F., Bratslavsky, E., Finkenauer, C., & Vohs, K.D. (2001). Bad is stronger than good. *Review of General Psychology, 5,* 323–370.

Brief, A.P., & Motowidlo, S.J. (1986). Prosocial organizational behaviors. *Academy of Management Review, 11,* 710–725.

Brown, M.E., Trevino, L.K., & Harrison, D.A. (2005). Ethical leadership: A social learning perspective for construct development and testing. *Organizational Behavior and Human Decision Processes, 97,* 117–134.

Cameron, K. (2003). Organizational virtuousness and performance. In K. Cameron, J. Dutton, & R. Quinn (Eds.), *Positive organizational scholarship* (pp. 48–65). San Francisco: Berrett-Koehler.

Colella, A., Paetzold, R.L., & Belliveau, M.A. (2004). Factors affecting coworkers' procedural justice inferences of the workplace accommodations of employees with disabilities. *Personnel Psychology, 51,* 1–23.

Crane, A., Knights, D., & Starkey, K. (2008). The conditions of our freedom: Foucault, organization, and ethics. *Business Ethics Quarterly, 18,* 299–320.

Cummins Engine Company. (n. d.). *Milestones in the foundation's history.* Retrieved January 22, 2010, from http://www.cummins.com/cmi/content.jsp?siteId=1&langId=1033&menuId=82&overviewId=5&anchorId=374&menuIndex=none&dataId=2950&feed=1&feed=1.

Csikszentmihalyi, M. (2003). *Good business.* New York: Viking.

Donaldson, T., & Dunfee, T.W. (1994). Toward a unified conception of business ethics: Integrative social contracts theory. *Academy of Management Review, 19,* 252–284.

Dutton, J.E., Worline, M.C., Frost, P.J., & Lilius, J. (2006). Explaining compassion organizing. *Administrative Science Quarterly, 51,* 59–96.

Edmondson, A. (1999). Psychological safety and learning behavior in work teams. *Administrative Science Quarterly, 44,* 350–383.

Environmental Defense Fund. (2008). *Innovations review.* Retrieved on January 13, 2010, from http://www.edf.org/InnovationsReview.

Fineman, S. (2006). On being positive: Concerns and counterpoints. *Academy of Management Review, 31,* 270–291.

Fisher, R., Ury, W., & Patton, B. (1991). *Getting to yes: Negotiating agreement without giving in* (2nd ed.). New York: Houghton Mifflin.

Foucault, M. (1988). Technologies of the self. In L.H. Martin, H. Gutman, & P.H. Hutton (Eds.), *Technologies of the self: A seminar with Michel Foucault* (pp. 16–49). Amherst, MA: University of Massachusetts Press.

Friedman, R.A., & Holtom, B. (2002). The effects of network groups on minority employee turnover intentions. *Human Resource Management, 41,* 405–421.

Gardner, T.M., Stansbury, J., & Hart, D. (2010). The ethics of lateral hiring. *Business Ethics Quarterly. 20,* 230–269.

George, J.M. (2004). [Review of the book *Positive organizational scholarship: Foundations of a new discipline*]. *Administrative Science Quarterly, 49,* 325–330.

Gordon, M. (2001). Howard Lutnick's second life. *New York Magazine.* December 10. Retrieved November 7, 2009, from http://www.nymag.com/nymetro/news/sept11/features/5486.

Hartman, E.M. (1996). *Organizational ethics and the good life.* New York: Oxford University Press.

Heyd, D. (1982). *Supererogation.* Cambridge: Cambridge University Press.

Johnson, R.W. (1943). *Our credo.* Retrieved January 22, 2010 from http://www.jnj.com/wps/wcm/connect/c7933f004f5563d-f9e22be1bb31559c7/our-credo.pdf?MOD=AJPERES.

Jones, T.M. (1991). Ethical decision making by individuals in organizations: An issue-contingent model. *Academy of Management Review, 16,* 366–395.

Jones, T.M., & Ryan, L.V. (1997). The link between ethical judgment and action in organizations: A moral approbation approach. *Organization Science, 8,* 663–680.

Kant, I. (1998). *Groundwork of the metaphysics of morals.* (M.J. Gregor, Trans. and Ed.). Cambridge: Cambridge University Press. (Original work published 1785).

LePine, J.A., Erez, A., & Johnson, D.E. (2002). The nature and dimensionality of organizational citizenship behavior: A critical review and meta-analysis. *Journal of Applied Psychology, 87,* 52–65.

Lyotard, J.F. (1984). *The postmodern condition.* (G.Bennington, & B. Massumi, Trans.). Minneapolis: University of Minnesota Press.

Margolis, J.D., & Walsh, J.P. (2003). Misery loves companies: Rethinking social initiatives by business. *Administrative Science Quarterly, 48,* 268–305.

McDonough, W., & Braungart, M. (2002). Eco-intelligence: From inspiration to innovation. *Green@Work,* July/August. Retrieved January 23, 2010, from http://www.greenatworkmag.com/gwsubaccess/02julaug/eco.html.

McFerran, B., Aquino, K., & Duffy, M.K. (2010). Individual predictors of the commitment to integrity: The role of personality and moral identity. *Business Ethics Quarterly, 20*: 35–56.

Mellema, G. (1991). *Beyond the call of duty.* Albany, NY: State University of New York Press.

Mellema, G. (1991). Supererogation and business ethics. *Journal of Applied Philosophy, 8,* 191–199.

Mesmer-Magnus, J., & Viswesvaran, C. (2005). Whistleblowing in organizations: An examination of correlates of whistleblowing intentions, actions, and retaliation. *Journal of Business Ethics, 62,* 277–297.

Meyer, J.P., & Allen, N.J. (1991). A three-component conceptualization of organizational commitment. *Human Resource Management Review, 1,* 61–98.

Meyerson, D.E., & Scully, M.A. (1995). Tempered radicalism and the politics of ambivalence and change. *Organization Science, 6,* 585–600.

Miceli, M.P., & Near, J.P. (1992). *Blowing the whistle.* New York: Lexington Books.

Moberg, D.J., & Seabright, M.A. (2000). The development of moral imagination. *Business Ethics Quarterly, 10,* 845–884.

Net Impact. (2009). *Impact at Work.* Retrieved January 13, 2010 from http://netimpact.org/displaycommon.cfm?an=1&sub-articlenbr=399.

Nielsen, R.P. (1996). *The politics of ethics.* New York: Oxford University Press.

Nike. (2001). *Fiscal year 2001 corporate responsibility report.* Beaverton, OR: Nike.

Nike. (n.d.). *Nike reuse-a-shoe.* Retrieved January 23, 2010, from http://www.nikereuseashoe.com/.

O'Fallon, M.J., & Butterfield, K.D. (2005). A review of the empirical ethical decision-making literature: 1996–2003. *Journal of Business Ethics, 59,* 375–413.

Organ, D.W. (1988). *Organizational citizenship behavior: The good soldier syndrome.* Lexington, MA: Lexington Books.

Organ, D.W. (1997). Organizational citizenship behavior: It's construct clean-up time. *Human Performance, 10,* 85–97.

Paine, L.S. (1994). Managing for organizational integrity. *Harvard Business Review, 72,* 106–119.

Rafaeli, A., & Pratt, M.G. (1993). Tailored meanings: On the meaning and impact of organizational dress. *Academy of Management Review, 18*(1), 32–55.

Reynolds, S.J. (2006). A neurocognitive model of the ethical decision-making process: Implications for study and practice. *Journal of Applied Psychology, 91,* 737–748.

Rothko, M. (2004). *The artist's reality: Philosophies of art.* C. Rothko (Ed.). New Haven, CT: Yale University Press.

Rorty, R. (1982). *Consequences of pragmatism.* Minneapolis: University of Minnesota Press.

Rorty, R. (2006). Is philosophy relevant to applied ethics? *Business Ethics Quarterly, 16,* 369–380.

Scherer, A.G., & Palazzo, G. (2007). Toward a political conception of corporate responsibility: Business and society seen from a Habermasian perspective. *Academy of Management Review, 32,* 1096–1120.

Scott, C.E. (1996). *On the advantages and disadvantages of ethics and politics.* Bloomington, IN: Indiana University Press.

Shao, R., Aquino, K., & Freeman, D. (2008). Beyond moral reasoning: A review of moral identity research and its implications for business ethics. *Business Ethics Quarterly, 18*(4): 513–540.

Solomon, R.C. (1992). *Ethics and excellence.* New York: Oxford University Press.

Sonenshein, S. (2006). Crafting social issues at work. *Academy of Management Journal, 49,* 1158–1172.

Sonenshein, S. (2007). The role of construction, intuition and justification in responding to ethical issues at work: The sensemaking-intuition model. *Academy of Management Review, 32,* 1022–1040.

Spreitzer, G.M., & Sonenshein, S. (2003). Positive deviance and extraordinary organizing. In K. Cameron, J. Dutton, & R. Quinn (Eds.), *Positive organizational scholarship* (pp. 207–224). San Francisco: Berrett-Koehler.

Spreitzer, G.M., & Sonenshein, S. (2004). Toward the construct definition of positive deviance. *American Behavioral Scientist, 47,* 828–847.

Street, M.D., Douglas, S.C., Geiger, S.W., & Martinko, M.J. (2001). The impact of cognitive expenditure on the ethical decision-making process: The cognitive elaboration model. *Organizational Behavior and Human Decision Processes, 86,* 256–277.

Taylor, C. (1989). The diversity of goods. In S.G. Clarke, & E. Simpson (Eds.), *Anti theory in ethics and moral conservatism* (pp. 223–240). Albany, NY: State University of New York Press.

Tenbrunsel, A.E., & Smith-Crowe, K. (2008). Ethical decision making: Where we've been and where we're going. *Academy of Management Annals, 2,* 545–607.

Trevino, L.K., & Weaver, G.R. (1994). Business ETHICS/ BUSINESS ethics: one field or two? *Business Ethics Quarterly, 4,* 113–128.

Trevino, L.K., Weaver, G.R., & Reynolds, S.J. (2006). Behavioral ethics in organizations: A review. *Journal of Management, 32,* 951–990.

Van Dyne, L., Cummings, L.L., & Parks, M.J. (1995). Extra-role behaviors: In pursuit of construct and definitional clarity. In L.L. Cummings, & B.M. Staw (Eds.), *Research in organizational behavior* (pp. 215–285). Greenwich, CT: JAI Press.

Van Dyne, L., & LePine, J.A. (1998). Helping and voice extra-role behaviors: Evidence of construct and predictive validity. *Academy of Management Journal, 41,* 109–119.

Victor, B., & Cullen, J.B. (1988). The organizational bases of ethical work climates. *Administrative Science Quarterly, 33*, 101–125.

Warren, D. (2003). Constructive and destructive deviance in organizations. *Academy of Management Review, 28*, 622–633.

Weaver, G.R. (2006). Virtue in organizations: Moral identity as a foundation for moral agency. *Organization Studies, 27*, 341–368.

Weaver, G.R., Trevino, L.K., & Agle, B.R. (2005). Somebody I look up to: Ethical role modeling in organizations. *Organizational Dynamics, 34*, 313–330.

Weick, K.E. (1979). *The social psychology of organizing* (2nd ed.). New York: McGraw-Hill.

Werhane, P.H. 1999. *Moral imagination and management decision-making.* New York: Oxford University Press.

York, J., & Larson, A. (2006). *Nike: Moving down the sustainability track through chemical substitution and waste reduction* (UVA-ENT-0098). Charlottesville, VA: Darden Business Publishing.

Productivity Through Strengths

Jim Asplund *and* Nikki Blacksmith

Abstract

This chapter discusses how organizations can drive performance through strengths-based development practices. Specifically, we report the results of 40 years conducting behavioral research that has led to the development of the Clifton StrengthsFinder®, an online measure of personal talent that identifies areas in which an individual's greatest potential for building strengths exists. Through the use of this tool, managers and individuals can leverage strengths to improve employee and organization performance. This chapter reports findings, from studies of large organizations using this tool, that suggest strengths-based employee development leads to higher levels of engagement and performance within business units.

Keywords: Strengths, talent, development, engagement, productivity

Organizations are always looking for ways to improve their performance in order to maintain a competitive edge and flourish. One of the most efficient means of driving organizational performance without cutting costs is through the people of the organization. Ultimately, everything an organization does to continuously operate has some type of human component. Fleming and Asplund (2007) studied some of the world's best organizations and found that what they were doing differently was leveraging the power of their human capital. Ensuring that employees were engaged in their work was one practice that those organizations executed to drive organizational performance. Educating current employees within the organization to engage their direct reports or their coworkers can lead to better performance, especially if it's done using a strengths-based approach. One component of engagement is ensuring that employees are always learning and growing, and developing employees using strengths-based science can ensure that organizations are fully maximizing their employees' potential. Several studies have shown that strengths-based employee development in the

workplace can lead to desired behavioral change (Clifton & Harter, 2003; Hodges & Clifton, 2004). Specifically, managers who foster environments in which employees are able to leverage their talents have more productive work groups (Clifton & Harter, 2003). Strengths-based employee development has been widely applied in organizations and has been found to be linked to individual and organizational performance (e.g., Hodges & Asplund, 2009).

Employee Engagements and Organizational Performance

For decades, psychologists have been studying job attitudes and their relationship to organizational performance. A meta-analytic study of the research literature conducted by Timothy Judge and colleagues, published in *Psychological Bulletin* in 2001, found substantial correlation between job satisfaction and productivity. A similar meta-analytic study of the literature conducted by Robert Tett and John Meyer, published in *Personnel Psychology* in 1993, found substantial correlation between both job satisfaction and organizational commitment with turnover intentions and actual turnover of employees. The connections between job satisfaction and organizational commitment with productivity and turnover have potentially important practical value to most organizations. Although job satisfaction has been studied for decades, more recently, organizations have been focusing on employee engagement, as it has also been found to be linked to positive organizational performance and has components that managers and organizations can directly influence (Harter, Schmidt, & Hayes, 2002).

Employee engagement can be defined as a multidimensional construct that is comprised of positive attitudes about one's work environment that include organizational commitment, job involvement, and job satisfaction (Harter, Schmidt, & Hayes, 2002; Macy & Schneider, 2008). Recent empirical evidence shows that these constructs are highly correlated and have similar positive and negative affectivity (Le, Schmidt, Harter, & Lauver 2010). These attitudes can generally be characterized as feelings of passion, energy, enthusiasm, or activation. The conditions that lead to employee engagement are most salient in their local work teams, with significant influences from the employee's supervisor, coworkers, and their daily interactions and experiences in the workplace.

The foundation of employee engagement is in the day-to-day experiences and discretionary efforts of employees, rather than in broadly measured attitudes. Accordingly, Gallup's measure of employee engagement, the $Q^{12®}$, focuses on items reflecting the daily experiences of employees on the job. As noted by Harter et al. (2002), employee engagement also requires dimensions of both cognitive involvement and emotional enthusiasm, "Employees that are cognitively involved in their work but not enthusiastic may have a good understanding of their job requirements and enjoy their work, but [are] unwilling to turn the involvement into activity that benefits the workgroup or organization. Conversely, employees that are enthusiastic but not cognitively involved may have a great deal of undirected or unfocused energy that is similarly inefficient for the workgroup or organization."

Measuring Employee Engagement

During the 1990s, scientists at Gallup reviewed more than two decades of research on workplace conditions, across more than 1 million employees. In-depth qualitative and quantitative study of successful managers and employees revealed 12 elements that best describe the conditions of an engaging workplace, and Gallup created survey items to measure those conditions in its $Q^{12®}$ survey:

1. I know what is expected of me at work. (Q1).
2. I have the materials and equipment I need to do my work right (Q2).
3. At work, I have the opportunity to do what I do best every day (Q3).
4. In the last seven days, I have received recognition or praise for doing good work (Q4).
5. My supervisor, or someone at work, seems to care about me as a person (Q5).
6. There is someone at work who encourages my development (Q6).
7. At work, my opinions seem to count (Q7).
8. The mission or purpose of my company makes me feel my job is important (Q8).
9. My associates or fellow employees are committed to doing quality work (Q9).
10. I have a best friend at work (Q10).
11. In the last 6 months, someone at work has talked to me about my progress (Q11).
12. This last year, I have had opportunities at work to learn and grow (Q12).[1]

This survey has been validated via psychometric studies of its reliability, convergent validity, and criterion-related validity, as well as through practical validations of its contributions to positive change in the workplace. The $Q^{12®}$ instrument has a Cronbach's α of 0.91 at the business-unit level (Harter, Schmidt, Killham, & Asplund, 2006). The convergent validity of the tool, based on studies comparing the 12 items to other longer surveys of job satisfaction and engagement, is 0.91, which provides evidence that the survey is a composite measure and captures the general engagement factor.

The database on the 12 engagement items now includes responses from more than 12 million employees in 150 different countries. A 2002 Gallup meta-analysis included data from 7,939 business or organizational units and unit-level outcomes (customer ratings, profit, productivity, employee retention, and accidents), published in the *Journal of Applied Psychology* (Harter, Schmidt & Hayes, 2002). This meta-analysis has been updated a total of seven times, and the current database now includes the most recent 3 years of data from 620,000 independent business or organizational units (5.4 million independent employee responses) in 137 countries.

This survey was designed by Gallup to help organizations improve employee engagement in their teams and therefore is comprised of items that measure an actionable component of employee engagement rather than an attitudinal component (e.g., loyalty, pride, commitment). The 12 engagement items measure components of engagement that can be influenced by a manager and are therefore practical for understanding and improving engagement.

The most recent meta-analysis conducted by Gallup studied the practical implications of engaging employees in the organization (Harter, Schmidt, Killham, & Asplund, 2006). When comparing median percentages of work groups with scores in the top quartile to workgroups with scores in the bottom quartile of engagement, the top quartile groups outperformed the bottom groups. Those workgroups had lower turnover, higher customer loyalty, fewer safety incidents, less shrinkage, higher productivity, and more profitability. In addition to these empirical studies, Gallup researchers conduct ongoing investigations into the psychology of each of the key elements, and how organizations and employees may build more engaging workforces. One specific focus of Gallup research is that of employee development and the different approaches to employee development that will lead to more engaged and productive employees. Strengths-based employee development is one approach that has been shown to increase employee engagement.

Strengths-based Employee Development

Traditional employee development approaches focus on fixing the employee's areas of weakness, instead of focusing of improving on the already positive aspects of the employee. This more positive approach toward employee development purports that employees will experience greater positive outcomes when they focus efforts on their strengths more often than trying to resolve weaknesses (Hodges & Asplund, 2009). Strengths development proceeds from the "identification of positive personal and interpersonal traits (talents) in order to position and develop individuals to increase the frequency of positive subjective experience" (Clifton & Harter, p. 114). The approach suggests that people can develop most efficiently through their natural talents, by integrating knowledge and skills to natural talents, rather than attempting to fix weak or missing traits.

This approach does not signify an ignorance of weaknesses, but is rather a recognition of the greater gains to be had from focusing on strengths. These strengths are composed of:

- *Skills*: The basic abilities to perform fundamental tasks; skills do not occur naturally, but must be acquired through training and practice.

- *Knowledge*: An acquaintance with, and understanding of, facts and principles accumulated through education or experience.
- *Talents*: Natural ways of thinking, feeling, and behaving, such as a sensitivity to the needs of others, or the tendency to be outgoing at social gatherings. Talents come into existence naturally and cannot be acquired in the way one can obtain skills and knowledge.

Talents are the reliable, natural features of our personalities. For example, discipline is not a reliable or natural trait for most of us, but many of us can demonstrate it in certain situations. A person's most powerful talents represent the best of his or her natural self. They are the foundation from which a person finds the best opportunities to perform at high levels of excellence. Dominant talents naturally appear frequently and powerfully, in a variety of situations. Individuals can develop a heightened self-awareness, they can add knowledge and skills, and they can stabilize their values and beliefs as means of developing their talents into strengths. Growing evidence suggests that traits, such as talent, begin to develop at young ages and stabilize in adulthood (Hodges & Asplund, 2010; Low, Yoon, Roberts, & Rounds, 2005; Levin, 2006). Numerous studies of personality, behavior genetics, intelligence, interests, and values have documented high variability across individuals. Genetic research suggests a substantial trait component in personality and intelligence constructs, among other constructs (Arvey, Rotundo, Johnson, Zhang, & McGue, 2006; Goldsmith, 2003). The findings of high genetic composition may hint that how people most efficiently grow and develop is dynamically related to who they are to begin with. Other "attitudinal" constructs, such as job satisfaction, have a weaker genetic component (Fleming & Asplund, 2007). People can change on these more state-like factors (satisfaction, well-being, engagement, performance, etc.), but most efficiently through who they are to begin with (their inherent talents).

A strengths approach to employee development begins with identifying those talents (Clifton & Harter, 2003). Once dominant talents are identified, a person can thoughtfully appeal to them and determine how he or she will intentionally express the talent even more often in the future. The more a talent is exercised, and the more it is refined through added knowledge and skills, the more integrated and stronger it becomes, and it then can be considered a strength. Those individuals who can identify and develop a heightened self-awareness of their strengths will be more likely to leverage their positive attributes and achieve higher success than will those who do not have a self-awareness of what they do well or those who focus on improving areas of lesser aptitude (Asplund & Hodges, 2009).

Following the identification of strengths is the integration of these strengths into one's self-view. Changes in one's perceived sense of self have been found to be enduring turning points in one's life (Avolio & Luthans, 2006). Ultimately, the change in an individual's perceived sense of self helps interpret the situation and context around that person through a different lens and thus leads toward changed behaviors and improved performance at work (Clifton & Harter, 2003). Upon the identification of strengths, individuals and organizations seek to complement those strengths with additional skills and knowledge through formal and informal learning activities. This includes teaching and education, mentoring activities, individual and team coaching, and other organization learning mechanisms.

There are many benefits to strengths-based employee development interventions, including improved communication, strong workplace relationships, and effective teams (Connelly, 2002; Robison, 2003; Smith & Rutigliano, 2003). Studies using college students have also shown that strengths-based development can improve self-confidence, direction, hope, and altruism (Hodges & Clifton, 2004).

Identifying Employee Strengths

How does one discover his or her dominant talents? Dr. Donald O. Clifton, an educational psychologist and Gallup research leader, was a pioneer in the study of talent. For over 50 years at the University of Nebraska, Selection Research Incorporated, and Gallup, Clifton studied "frames of reference" (Clifton, Hollingsworth, & Hall, 1952), teacher–student rapport (Dodge & Clifton, 1956), management (Clifton, 1970, 1975, 1980), and success across a wide variety of domains. Clifton believed that individuals could learn to capitalize upon their talents; that focusing on what we do best provides the optimal route to success. In accordance with those beliefs, Clifton and other Gallup researchers worked to identify hundreds of themes of talent that predict work and academic success, and built structured interviews for measuring them.

In the course of conducting this research, Gallup researchers identified generalizable thoughts, feelings, and behaviors associated with success (Harter, Hayes, & Schmidt, 2004; Schmidt & Rader, 1999). In the mid-1990s, Clifton and colleagues systematically reviewed these interviews and the data they generated to construct an objective measure of these general talent themes. The Clifton StrengthsFinder® (CSF) is the result of those efforts. The CSF is an online assessment that presents respondents with 177 sets of paired statements. Each pair of statements is presented as if anchoring opposite poles of a continuum, and the respondent is asked to choose the statement that best describes her and the extent to which the chosen option is descriptive of her. Most of these statements are associated with one of 34 distinct talent themes, with each theme's score a function of the intensity of the respondent's self-description. Results are presented to the respondent as a ranked ordering of Signature Themes, which are the focus of the feedback provided to the respondent.

StrengthsFinder serves as a starting point in the identification of specific personal strengths. Supporting materials then help individuals through a process of discovery and development as they strategize and build upon their talents to develop strengths within their roles. StrengthsFinder has been primarily applied toward the development of individuals in the workplace and higher education domains. At the time of this writing, it has been completed by more than 4 million individuals in more than 24 languages. Several thousand individuals complete the assessment each day. (For a summary of StrengthsFinder's psychometric properties, please see Asplund, Lopez, Hodges & Harter, 2009).

In 2006, Gallup researchers conducted a comprehensive review of StrengthsFinder's psychometrics. Confirmatory studies validated the 34-theme structure in both adult and student populations. In the course of reviewing more than 1 million cases in multiple studies, some improvements were made to theme validities and reliabilities. These improvements were the result of some changes in scoring, as well as the addition of some new items. These new items were drawn from Gallup's library of thousands of talent-related questions, and from researchers' experience in building structured interviews and providing talent feedback. Finally, there were some items included in the original version of StrengthsFinder that had not previously been used in the scoring process. A thorough review of each of these items showed many to be unnecessary as either distracters or scored items. These were accordingly removed from the instrument. The result of this review was a slightly shorter assessment with improved psychometric properties, known as StrengthsFinder 2.0 (Rath, 2007).

General Usage of the Clifton StrengthsFinder

StrengthsFinder results are reported in a variety of ways, depending on the context in which individuals are introduced to the assessment. Someone who purchases an individual book receives a report listing his top five talent themes—those in which the person received his highest scores, in order of intensity. In other situations, respondents may review their full 34-theme sequence, along with developmental suggestions for each theme, in a personal feedback session with a Gallup consultant or in a supervised team performance session with colleagues. In programs designed to promote strengths-based development, feedback is often accompanied by instruction, experiential learning, and mentoring activities designed to help people develop strengths associated with occupational or educational roles.

As part of the update to StrengthsFinder 2.0, a new, more detailed type of feedback was introduced. This feedback report includes talent descriptions that go beyond the Signature Themes by looking at item-level responses. The inclusion of this item-level feedback provides a more customized version of the respondent's Signature Themes report and features a more in-depth look at the nuances of what makes one unique, using more than 5,000 new personalized strengths insights accumulated over the years by Gallup researchers.

The intended use of StrengthsFinder was to facilitate the personal development and growth of an individual, specifically self-discovery (Asplund, Lopez, Hodges, & Harter, 2007; Asplund & Hodges, 2009). The results are viewed as a preliminary hypothesis of that individual's strengths and should be verified and confirmed based on the individual's understanding of self. The CSF rank orders the top themes of talent, and each individual receives a customized report that describes her talents in detail, along with developmental suggestions that help her leverage her talents at work. Further intended use of the tool includes a foundation for discussion with managers and colleagues in order to drive behavioral change.

Gallup has created and administered development programs with hundreds of thousands of employees in hundreds of organizations all over the world. All of these programs flow out of the same theory, laid out in Clifton & Harter, 2003: Measure constructs most likely to be predisposed; identify talents and weaknesses; focus maximum learning on talents, integrate activities of one's life around talents, and manage around weaknesses; and focus

change on constructs that are changeable, rather than the missing traits.

Productivity Through Strengths

Gallup's development programs have generated substantial evidence that a strengths-based approach to employee development results in desired behavioral change (Clifton & Harter, 2003; Hodges & Asplund, 2009; Hodges & Clifton, 2004). The strengths approach has been used to overcome a specific challenge, as well as being used as part of a much larger transformation of the workplace culture (Brim, 2008). Examples of specific applications include conflict management (Brim, 2005b; Clifton & Anderson, 2002), communication (Brim, 2005c, 2007), mentoring (Clifton, 2003), time management (Brim, 2005d), and career planning (Brim, 2007; Clifton & Anderson, 2002). These are only a few examples of the many applications of strengths science across a wide range of roles and situations.

In a recent study, significant gains were observed in individuals or teams that invested in their own strengths development (Asplund, Lopez, Hodges, & Harter, 2009). Archival evidence was accumulated across multiple workplace studies to ascertain the extent to which performance increased as a result of learning or applying strengths-based management practices. Eleven companies from the retail, manufacturing, financial services, hospitality, and business services industries were included, representing an estimated 90,000 employees. Differences in performance measurement both within and across companies limited the extent to which the study data could be aggregated. Despite these limitations, adequate data existed in multiple subpopulations to indicate significant returns on these companies' investments in strengths development:

- In 896 business units, pre–post measures of employee engagement were available in the form of survey data from Gallup's Q^{12}. Those units whose managers received some strengths feedback (typically a 1-hour coaching conversation focused on understanding one's strengths) showed significantly more improvement ($d = 0.16$) on their Q^{12} Grand Mean relative to those units in which the manager received no strengths feedback. (For workgroups of this size, Gallup researchers consider growth of 0.10 to be substantial [Gallup, 2009], based on work with organizations and the amount of change in their business outcomes that can be related to change in engagement scores). This was a simple waitlist control design, in which assignment to the waitlist was unrelated to the measure of engagement. This is particularly notable because only the managers of these groups received strengths feedback during the study period—the remaining employees in both the study and control groups received nothing.

Data on individual engagement responses were also available for 12,157 employees. Among those employees receiving strengths feedback, engagement also improved significantly (d = 0.33) relative to employees without feedback. This was also largely a simple waitlist control, in which most of the "control" employees in this study eventually received strengths feedback as well.

- Turnover data were available for 65,672 employees. Among employees receiving some strengths feedback, turnover rates were 14.9% lower than for those employees receiving no feedback (controlling for job type and tenure).
- There were 530 work units with productivity data. Those whose managers received strengths feedback showed 12.5% greater productivity post-intervention relative to those units in which the manager received nothing. Similar to the engagement data discussed above, this is particularly notable because only the managers of these groups received strengths feedback during the study period, with the remainder of the employees in both the study and control groups receiving nothing in most cases. Also similar to the engagement studies, the "control" managers here were simple waitlist controls.
- Data on the productivity of 1,874 individual employees were examined for the effects of strengths feedback as well. Most of these employees were engaged in sales functions, in which the productivity data represent sales. Among those employees receiving a strengths intervention, productivity improved by 7.8% relative to employees without the intervention. This control was also largely a simple waitlist situation, in which many of the "control" employees in this study subsequently received strengths feedback and coaching as well.
- Profit data were available for 469 business units, ranging from retail stores to large manufacturing facilities. Those units whose managers received strengths feedback showed 8.9% greater profitability post-intervention

relative to units in which the manager received nothing. Again, only the managers of these groups received strengths feedback during the study period, with the remainder of the employees in both the study and control groups receiving nothing in most cases. Also similar to the engagement studies, the "control" managers here were waitlist controls for the most part.

Creating an Environment for Effective Strengths-based Development

It is important to note that strengths-based employee development is significantly affected by the social context of the workplace: Teams that encourage and support these efforts have reaped substantial rewards, whereas more laissez-faire teams have garnered much less. This observation has led us to recently begin assessing the quality of the organization's efforts.

In a recent study of college students, Bowers and Lopez (2010) identified three constructs they deemed necessary for students to successfully capitalize on their strengths: "continual social support, experiences of success, and reinforcement of personal strengths" (Bowers & Lopez, 2010, p. 6). The authors went on to note that these three constructs "represent phenomena that are interrelated, overlapping, and circular," rather than a sequential process.

Gallup researchers conducted onsite observations and follow-up interviews with employees and managers who used a strengths-based employee development approach. Gallup researchers found that there was a large amount of variability in the abilities of local workgroups to apply what they had learned. Some of this variability is unavoidable, since the underlying assumption of the strengths theory is that individuals will vary in their natural ability to learn, integrate, or apply any insights. They also found that there was a wide range of support when applying strengths science in business settings. Some of the variability is due to organizational impediments or outright obstruction—variability in the kind of social support highlighted by Bowers and Lopez (2010). In turn, the variability in social support is likely a function of the engagement of those employees receiving the strengths intervention. It therefore makes sense to assess the availability of that social support as part of any new initiative incorporating strengths science.

A strengths-based approach to management is the single best means of improving the employee–manager relationship that Gallup has observed over the years of working with organizations to improve employee engagement. Therefore, a short battery of items was developed to assess the extent to which managers and their teams leverage their strengths. The items in this Strengths Orientation (SO) index are as follows:

- Every week, I set goals and expectations based on my strengths (SO1).
- I can name the strengths of five people I work with (SO2).
- In the last 3 months, my supervisor and I have had a meaningful discussion about my strengths (SO3).
- My organization is committed to building the strengths of each associate (SO4).

These are all Likert items, rated on a scale of 1–5, with 5 labeled "strongly agree" and 1 labeled "strongly disagree."

We have tested these items with samples of the U.S. working population, and only 3% could strongly agree with all four of them. With such a low base rate of agreement in the working population, there is ample opportunity to observe improvements in this index in response to strengths development efforts.

We developed the SO index in the wake of strong evidence from a large client (Company X) with over 10 years of investment in employee engagement, in which strengths items explained incremental variance in sales and operating income among 606 business units. The four items used at Company X were different from those listed above, but results of this research encouraged us to develop a general battery of items to use with other organizations.

In a structural equation model (SEM) of employee engagement and financial performance, the path coefficient from the "employee" variable to sales increased from 0.16 to 0.25 with the addition of strengths index items, and the path coefficient from employee to operating income increased from 0.18 to 0.27. These increases in utility represent an enormous return on Company X's investments in strengths development.

The evidence at Company X informed the development of the SO index; in particular, it was clear that performance improvements hinged on specific application of strengths discoveries to the objective at hand, but that such applications could only occur after employees became aware of their strengths and their colleagues' strengths, they began to experience success through more intentional application of those strengths, and they perceived a shared commitment to the strengths philosophy among coworkers, managers, and company leadership. The reader should note the similarity of these findings to those of Bowers and Lopez cited above.

As a consequence of these discoveries, we developed the SO items to measure employees' perceptions of their work environment regarding its receptivity to, and usage of, strengths. Item candidates were tested for their reliability and validity, as well as their convergence with the Q^{12} items. Because they are intended as addenda to a longer instrument, efforts were made not only to reduce redundancy with the Q^{12} items, but also to ensure their practical usefulness in discussions with employees regarding their engagement and productivity.

Since their inception, the SO items have been administered to more than 125,000 employees in 16 different organizations. The usage of these items has been uneven, however. Only 8,362 employees in three of these organizations have been administered the entire index in its current form. As for the individual items:

- *Every week, I set goals and expectations based on my strengths (SO1)*: This item has been administered to 11,070 employees in four organizations, with a mean score of 3.81.
- *I can name the strengths of five people I work with (SO2)*: This item has been administered to 8,913 employees in three organizations, with a mean score of 3.78.
- *In the last 3 months, my supervisor and I have had a meaningful discussion about my strengths (SO3)*: This item has been administered to 19,347 employees in five organizations, and has the lowest overall mean score of 3.71.
- *My organization is committed to building the strengths of each associate (SO4)*: This item has been administered to 105,105 employees in 14 organizations, and has the highest overall mean score of 3.87.

As a group, the items provide basic coverage of the desired content area, with a modest amount of item intercorrelation, as shown in Table 27.1.

Table 27.1   Intercorrelations of items

Item	SO1	SO2	SO3	SO4
SO1	—	.41	.41	.48
SO2		—	.36	.33
SO3			—	.63
SO4				—

Cronbach's α of SO Index = 0.76.

Table 27.2 Correlations between Strengths Orientation index and Q¹² Engagement Items and Grand Mean

SO_Index			SO1	SO2	SO3	SO4
Q¹² Grand Mean	Pearson r	0.72	0.51	0.38	0.61	0.79
	N	7,776	10,095	8,110	18,157	91,272
Q01	Pearson r	0.46	0.35	0.21	0.38	0.5
	N	8,348	11,049	8,894	19,325	104,764
Q02	Pearson r	0.43	0.29	0.18	0.39	0.56
	N	8,328	11,023	8,872	19,281	104,593
Q03	Pearson r	0.55	0.43	0.31	0.48	0.63
	N	8,325	11,009	8,855	19,270	104,038
Q04	Pearson r	0.53	0.36	0.25	0.48	0.58
	N	8,268	10,920	8,783	19,155	102,621
Q05	Pearson r	0.53	0.34	0.26	0.48	0.58
	N	8,315	10,991	8,843	19,251	103,560
Q06	Pearson r	0.61	0.43	0.26	0.52	0.67
	N	8,328	11,008	8,861	19,265	103,612
Q07	Pearson r	0.59	0.4	0.34	0.52	0.66
	N	8,286	10,957	8,803	19,223	103,552
Q08	Pearson r	0.59	0.43	0.34	0.52	0.69
	N	8,313	10,991	8,849	19,241	103,759
Q09	Pearson r	0.49	0.33	0.29	0.41	0.57
	N	8,324	11,008	8,864	19,264	103,844
Q10	Pearson r	0.42	0.29	0.32	0.33	0.4
	N	8,241	10,811	8,749	19,079	100,424
Q11	Pearson r	0.57	0.38	0.21	0.49	0.57
	N	8,269	10,872	8,715	19,132	101,952
Q12	Pearson r	0.58	0.4	0.3	0.48	0.66
	N	8,213	10,838	8,666	19,037	101,718

In the interests of space, we have omitted the p-values, which are all zero. Every correlation shown is significant at the 99th confidence interval (CI). Cronbach's α of Q¹² items (Harter, Schmidt, & Hayes) = 0.91; Cronbach's α of Q¹² items (this study) = 0.94.

Table 27.2 shows the correlations between the SO index and the Q¹² Engagement Items. It also shows the correlation between the SO index and the engagement grand mean (the mean of all 12 engagement items). These correlations reveal the range in salience for the SO items with respect to the individual employee engagement items. Perceptions of organizational commitment to strengths have the highest correlations with each aspect of employee engagement. Employees who perceive an organizational commitment to building the strengths of each associate are much likelier to know what's expected of them at work, and for that to represent an opportunity to do what they do best every day. The mission or purpose of their company makes them feel their job is important, that their opinions count, and that someone at work cares about them. They also perceive greater opportunities to learn and grow, and that they have support in their developmental efforts, as well as feedback on how they are doing.

Our research shows companies achieve superior performance when they deeply involve their employees in this type of engaging culture (Fleming & Asplund, 2007). An employee who feels that someone at work cares about him, who feels a sense of progress and is encouraged to make the most of his unique personality for the benefit of the company, usually pays back that attention many times over. If he finds his employer takes an active interest in him personally, and teaches him things he never knew about himself, he is much likelier to pay back the company with the work ethic, enthusiasm, and commitment that it wants from him. And he will do so from a position of greater self-knowledge and confidence. Eisenberger, Huntington, Hutchinson, and Sowa (1986) report similar findings with regards to their social exchange view of commitment, which states that if employees perceive the organization supports them or is committed to them, then they are more likely to have feelings of obligation to the employer, which enhances organizational performance.

Getting to this point with an employee involves a significant commitment from the organization. Managers must learn to identify and develop individuals' strengths. Performance management systems must be aligned to reinforce this and provide accurate, ongoing feedback to every individual. Perhaps the largest organizational commitment of all is an extension of trust: By explicitly acknowledging the uniqueness of each employee, most organizations energize those employees' independent thinking and creativity. This in turn tends to make their activities more financially productive in many ways that were not foreseen by their executives. Engaged employees are better at knowing both the long- and short-term goals of the employee–customer interaction, and their roles in making them happen. They are also far more likely to care whether those happen, be more motivated to learn how to apply themselves, and are likelier to know how far (and when) they can stretch business rules when the situation warrants it. Strengths development can accelerate this process by helping employees learn to be more intuitive and creative within the context of who they are; this is something everyone can learn to do better, and to apply in ways that produce extraordinary financial returns.

We continue to investigate the mechanisms whereby strengths development increases performance. Having accumulated substantial evidence of the benefits of strengths development, we are confident in recommending it as a direct means of improving employee engagement, productivity,

and retention. What we would like to understand better is the degree to which the benefits are moderated by the engagement of the employees. As noted earlier, there is substantial evidence of the centrality of employee engagement to observed differences in employee performance across a wide range of measures.

At Company X, adding the SO index to our structural model of employee engagement, sales, and income growth increased effect sizes by approximately 50%. At the time, our focus was on increasing employee engagement, so we regrettably did not perform any analyses omitting employee engagement. A later qualitative review of high-performing business units within Company X strongly indicated that, in this organization at least, the engagement of employees within those business units was a key moderator of the effectiveness of the strengths program implementation and follow-through.

With the more recent development of the SO index, we have accumulated little performance data to be able to further test the findings from Company X. At this point, we have studied two organizations with SO index data and multiple waves of employee engagement data. One of these organizations also provided data on sales and productivity. We turn now to an examination of these organizations.

Incremental Validity of Strengths Orientation Index

The two organizations in this study are both retailers. We will henceforth refer to them by the unimaginative appellations "Company Y," and "Company Z," respectively. Company Y is a seller of industrial equipment with 12 locations; 410 employees participated in the two employee engagement surveys, conducted 1 year apart. This represents the entire employee population of Company Y. Company Z is a seller of automotive and trucking supplies, with 70 participating business units; 145 employees participated in the two employee engagement surveys, and 88 of these responded to the SO index items (only those employees who were exposed to the strengths stimuli were asked those items). All of these 88 employees were account managers or people managers.

We examined the influence of the strengths programs on the level of engagement of the employees who participated. To partial out the effects of their prior engagement, we conducted hierarchical regressions, following the approach described in Alf and Graf (1999).

Table 27.3 Strengths orientation increases employee engagement

	Model 1		Model 2	
	Company Y	Company Z	Company Y	Company Z
$EE_{Time 1}$	.54**	.64**	.16*	.28**
Strengths Orientation			.79**	.68**
Adjusted R^2	.29	.42	.74	.75
ΔR^2	.45		.34	
F	709.9**		146.4**	

* p <0.05, ** p <0.01.

The results in Table 27.3 show strong evidence for the SO index explaining incremental variability in employee engagement. In each company, employees' engagement at Time 1 predicted their engagement at Time 2. Adding the SO index to the regressions significantly improved those predictions. Employees who had some experiences using their strengths discoveries, and who perceived a commitment to the strengths philosophy at their organization, were much more engaged at Time 2.

Improving Financial Performance and Productivity with a Strengths-based Development Approach

Company Z provided trailing sales and productivity data for their sales teams. The productivity data consisted of pounds of units shipped. The first wave of employee engagement data was collected in October of Year 1, and the second wave in May of Year 2. The financial data were for the full calendar Year 2. With two waves of employee engagement data, the question of interest to Company Z was the extent to which improvements in employee engagement were associated with financial performance. As a result, the focus of the analysis here is on changes in employee engagement and strengths orientation.

Tables 27.4 and 27.5 show the results of hierarchical regression analyses using employee engagement and strengths orientation to predict sales performance. The SO index change scores alone predicted unit sales, whereas employee engagement alone only did so at the 90th confidence level. The model including both variables proved quite superior, with a multiple R of 0.42. The interaction term was not significant, and tests of collinearity show little cause for concern (the highest VIF = 1.4).

Tables 27.6 and 27.7 show the results of hierarchical regression analyses using employee engagement and strengths orientation to predict productivity. The SO change scores alone do not predict shipments, but employee engagement does at the 90th confidence level. Hierarchical regressions show that the model including both variables predicted shipments with a multiple R of 0.34. Again, the interaction term was not significant.

Investments in developing the strengths of Company Z's employees paid significant, measurable returns. By providing a structured way for employees and teams to observe and discuss their thoughts, feelings, and behaviors, and thereby develop greater awareness of each other, Company Z fostered greater employee engagement, financial

Table 27.4 Regressions predicting sales performance

	Model 1	Model 2
Employee Engagement	.21	.29**
Strengths Orientation		.38**
Adjusted R^2	.03	.15
ΔR^2		.12
F		9.21**

* p <0.05, ** p <0.01.

Table 27.5 Regressions predicting sales performance

	Model 1	Model 2
Strengths Orientation	.31**	.38**
Employee Engagement		.29*
Adjusted R^2	.08	.15
ΔR^2		.072
F		5.13*

* p <0.05, ** p <0.01.

Table 27.6 Regressions predicting productivity

	Model 1	Model 2
Employee Engagement	.24	.31*
Strengths Orientation		.26*
Adjusted R^2	.04	.09
ΔR^2		.05
F		3.39

* $p < 0.05$, ** $p < 0.01$.

performance, and productivity. It must be emphasized that only a small minority of employees at Company Z learned their strengths, yet the financial performance of the entire organization improved.

Future Directions

A great deal of work still needs to be done to specify how strengths development fits in to the larger nomological network of positive organizational scholarship (POS). As POS is concerned with conditions and environments that foster flourishing at all levels of the organization, strengths-based employee development has a clear connection to this body of research. Understanding how developing employees based on a strengths approach leads to organization, individual, and workgroup success is important. Future strengths-based development research should focus on understanding employee perceptions of work, and how often they claim positive experiences in the workplace and exhibit prosocial and citizenship behavior. Here, we list some areas for future research.

- Although this research focuses on the relationship between strengths-based employee development and employee morale, future research should examine how developing employees using a strengths-based

Table 27.7 Regressions predicting productivity

	Model 1	Model 2
Strengths Orientation	.31	.26*
Employee Engagement		.31*
Adjusted R^2	.01	.09
ΔR^2		.08
F		5.26*

* $p < 0.05$, ** $p < 0.01$.

approach leads to flourishing and positive states of employees, specifically perceptions and conceptualization of their work. For example, do employees perceive their work to be more meaningful and fulfilling when their managers focus on their strengths and manage around their weaknesses, instead of taking a more typical development approach and investigating levels of productivity and morale? Determining whether employees claim to experience more positive experiences such as happiness, joy, or fulfillment during the workday will add to a deeper understanding of how strengths-based development contributes to POS.

- Positive organizational scholarship should investigate how strengths-based development is related to prosocial and citizenship behavior. When managers use a positive, strengths-based approach to employee development, does that lead to or encourage positive behavior within teams and business units? Strengths-based employee development uses positive language to describe and understand one's self and one's team members, thus it may relate to better relationships on the teams and more helping behaviors on those teams.

- Research efforts should also focus on understanding how strengths-based development is related to resilience. Do those employees who participate in strengths-based developmental programs have higher resilience? Are individuals and teams who have participated in strengths programs more likely to bounce back from adversity?

- More research needs to be done on positive leadership. Do organizations that put leaders through a strengths-based employee developmental program experience more positive states of leadership? For example, are those leaders more likely to have positive deviant performance?

- Research should examine how many employees constitute a "critical mass" for the strengths science to take hold and generate downstream financial benefits. Company X and Company Z represent disparate approaches here: Company X developed tens of thousands of employees, whereas Company Z only developed a small cadre of leaders. The financial gains at Company X were much larger, but it also had a much longer track record of engaging its employees, in addition to deploying many more resources toward strengths development. The methods whereby employees received strengths feedback also differed greatly over time within each of the companies presented in this study. There is a need for research to continue to refine such workplace applications: What are the most productive and efficient means of developing an employee's strengths, and what company or employee characteristics moderate those modes? Future research needs to explore the ways in which strengths development may be employed to boost well-being. Enormous financial gains are available to companies who improve their employees' well-being (Rath & Harter, 2010). The psychobiological foundations of strengths development are little understood, and need more investigation.

We hope to address these aspects of strengths development in the coming years.

Conclusion

Strengths-based employee development approaches lead to more engaging workforces, and organizations can reap financial rewards and expect more productivity from their employees if they devote time and effort to helping each employee understand his strengths and use them in the workplace. Company Z, for example, devoted much time and effort to measuring and understanding the levels of employee engagement within the organization and took the extra effort to develop its employees using a positive, strengths-based approach. This resulted in their employees working harder and giving something more to the organization than the effort they exerted prior to being involved in a strengths-based development initiative. However, the situation at Company Z needs to be contrasted with a common view of employment, wherein employees seem to accept a purely economic view of their jobs. In this supposed purely economic transaction, employees rent their labor for financial returns. In the current economic climate, with so many people out of work or underemployed, it might seem almost intemperate to aspire to more than that. But even in times like these, the employee also experiences the workplace as a social system that significantly affects her well-being in a variety of ways.

Since 2005, Gallup has been collecting data from the first-of-its-kind poll of a representative sample of the world, comprising one of the most significant studies of human well-being ever conducted (Rath & Harter, 2010). The principal outcomes of this research have been to identify what people all over the world experience on a typical day, and to gain an understanding of the primary determinants of individual well-being. These principal factors are remarkably consistent across the world, with our careers being the most important determinants of how we evaluate our lives. Perhaps this should not be so surprising, since our careers describe what we do to occupy our time, and whether we enjoy what we do each day. Given the extreme importance of our careers, employers are exceptionally well-positioned to affect the well-being of their employees, from the obvious financial benefits to the number and types of personal relationships we have with our coworkers, and the amount of deleterious stress we experience daily on the job.

Bad workplaces create stress and damage our physical health (Stone & Harter, 2009). Employees in good workplaces enjoy their workdays almost as much as they enjoy weekends and therefore can be more productive. Many of those good workplaces, like the companies we have discussed here, got that way by focusing on employees' strengths to engage every single employee. When a manager focuses on an employee's strengths, the odds of that employee being disengaged are only 1 in 100. By comparison, if an employee's manager focuses on his weaknesses, those odds are 22 in 100. Even worse, if an employee feels his manager focuses on neither his strengths nor weaknesses—in effect, if he is ignored—his odds of being disengaged are 40 in 100 (Gallup, April 2004).

Organizations like Company X and Company Z have learned to thrive by creating conditions wherein employees can thrive; the evidence for that is compelling and substantial. In this chapter, we have presented some evidence for one of the principal pathways via which companies accrue financial benefits in this way. We submit that when such organizations improve their performance, they reinvest even more in their people, thus continuing a healthy cycle of continuous improvement. We have certainly seen evidence of that over time.

Note

1. These 12 statements cannot be reprinted or reproduced in any manner without the written consent of The Gallup Organization. Copyright © 1993–1998, The Gallup Organization, Washington, D.C. All rights reserved.

References

Alf, E., & Graf, R. (1999). Asymptotic confidence limits for the difference between two squared multiple correlations: A simplified approach. *Psychological Methods, 4,* 70–75.

Arvey, R.D., Rotundo, M., Johnson, W., Zhang, Z., & McGue, M. (2006). The determinants of leadership role occupancy: Genetic and personality factors. *The Leadership Quarterly, 17,* 1–20.

Asplund, J., Lopez, S.J., Hodges, T., & Harter, J. (2009). *The Clifton StrengthsFinder 2.0 technical report: Development and validation.* Princeton, NJ: Gallup Organization.

Avolio, B.J., & Luthans, F. (2006). *The high impact leader: Moments matter in accelerating authentic leadership development.* New York: McGraw-Hill.

Bowers, K.M., & Lopez, S.J. (2010). Capitalizing on personal strengths in college. *Journal of College and Character, 11,* 1–11.

Brim, B. (2005b). The talent to deal with conflict. *Gallup Management Journal, 5.*

Brim, B. (2005c). The talent to communicate. *Gallup Management Journal, 5.*

Brim, B. (2005d). The talent to manage your time. *Gallup Management Journal, 5.*

Brim, B. (2007). Debunking strengths myths #1. *Gallup Management Journal, 7.*

Brim, B. (2008). Debunking strengths myth #2. *Gallup Management Journal, 8.*

Clifton, D.O. (1970). *The magnificence of management.* A reprint of an address presented to the 8th Annual Life Agency Management Program. Boston.

Clifton, D.O. (1975). Interaction is: Where the action is. A reprint of a report prepared by Donald O. Clifton and presented at the 1972 Chartered Life Underwriters (CLU) Forum.

Clifton, D.O. (1980). *Varsity management: A way to increase productivity.* A reprint of an address presented to the 29th annual Consumer Credit Insurance Association (CCIA) program on June 24, 1980. Napa, California.

Clifton, D.O., & Anderson, C.E. (2002). *StrengthsQuest: Discover and develop your strengths in academics, career, and beyond.* New York: Gallup Press.

Clifton, D.O., & Harter, J.K. (2003). Investing in strengths. In K.S. Cameron, J.E., Dutton, & R.E. Quinn (Eds.), *Positive organizational scholarship* (pp. 111–121). San Francisco: Berrett-Koehler.

Clifton, D.O., Hollingsworth, F.L., & Hall, W.E. (1952). A projective technique for measuring positive and negative attitudes towards people in a real-life situation. *Journal of Educational Psychology, 43,* 273–283.

Connelly, J. (2002). All together now. *Gallup Management Journal, 2*(1), 13–18.

Dodge, G.W., & Clifton, D.O. (1956). Teacher-pupil rapport and student teacher characteristics, *Journal of Educational Psychology, 47,* 6.

Eisenberger, R., Huntington, R., Hutchinson, S., & Sowa, D. (1986). Perceived organizational support and employee diligence, commitment, and innovation. *Journal of Applied Psychology, 71,* 500–507.

Fleming, J.H., & Asplund, J. (2007). *Human sigma: Managing the employee-customer encounter.* New York: Gallup Press.

Gallup. (2004). [Gallup Workplace Poll]. Unpublished raw data.

Gallup. (2009). *Estimating meaningful differences in Q12® grand mean scores.* Unpublished manuscript.

Goldsmith, H.H. (2003). Genetics of emotional development. In R.J. Davidson, K.R. Scherer, & H.H. Goldsmith (Eds.), *Handbook of affective sciences* (pp. 300-319). New York: Oxford University Press.

Harter, J.K., Hayes, T.L., & Schmidt, F.L. (2004). *Meta-analytic predictive validity of Gallup Selection Research Instruments [technical report].* Omaha, NE: The Gallup Organization.

Harter, J.K., Schmidt, F.L., Killham, E.A., & Asplund, J.W. (2006). *Q12 Meta-analysis: The relationship between engagement at work and organizational outcomes.* Washington, DC: The Gallup Organization.

Harter, J.K., Schmidt, F.L., & Hayes, T.L. (2002). Business-unit-level relationship between employee satisfaction, employee engagement, and business outcomes: A meta-analysis. *Journal of Applied Psychology, 87,* 268–279.

Hodges, T.D., & Asplund, J. (2010). Strengths development in the workplace. In P.A. Linley, S. Harrington, & N. Garcea (Eds.), *Oxford handbook of positive psychology* (pp. 213–221). New York: Oxford University Press.

Hodges, T.D., & Clifton, D.O. (2004). Strengths-based development in practice. In A. Linley, & S. Joseph (Eds.), *Positive psychology in practice* (pp. 256–268). Hoboken, NJ: John Wiley & Sons, Inc.

Judge, T.A., Thoresen, C.J., Bono, J.E., & Patton, G.K. (2001). The job satisfaction-job performance relationship: A qualitative and quantitative review. *Psychological Bulletin, 127,* 376–407.

Le, H., Schmidt, F.L., Harter, J.K., & Lauver, K.J. (2010). The problem of empirical redundancy of constructs in organizational research: An empirical investigation. *Organizational Behavior and Human Decision Processes, 112,* 112–125.

Levin, D.J. (2006). *This is your brain on music: The science of a human obsession.* New York: Dutton.

Low, K.S.D., Yoon, M., Roberts, B.W., & Rounds, J. (2005). The stability of vocational interests from early adolescence to middle adulthood: A quantitative review of longitudinal studies. *Psychological Bulletin, 131,* 713–737.

Macey, W.H., & Schneider, B. (2008). The meaning of employee engagement. *Industrial and Organizational Psychology, 1,* 3–30.

Rath, T.C. (2007). *StrengthsFinder 2.0.* New York: Gallup Press.

Rath, T., & Harter, J. (2010). *Wellbeing: The five essential elements.* New York: Gallup Press.

Robison, J. (2003). How GlaxoSmithKline builds employee strengths. *Gallup Management Journal, 3.* Retrieved from http://gmj.gallup.com/content/1015/How-GlaxoSmith Kline-Builds-Employee-Strengths.aspx.

Schmidt, F.L., & Rader, M. (1999). Exploring the boundary conditions for interview validity: Meta-analytic validity findings for a new interview type. *Personnel Psychology, 52,* 445–464.

Smith, B., & Rutigliano, T. (2003). *Discover your sales strengths: How the world's greatest salespeople develop winning careers.* New York: Warner Books.

Stone, A., & Harter, J.K. (2009). The experience of work: A momentary perspective. Omaha, NE: Gallup.

Tett, R.P., & Meyer, J.P. (1993). Job satisfaction, organizational commitment, turnover intention, and turnover: Path analyses based on meta-analytic findings. *Personnel Psychology, 47,* 259–293.

The Positive Power of Character Strengths and Virtues for Global Leaders

Arménio Rego, Stewart Clegg, *and* Miguel Pina e Cunha

Abstract

In a globalized world, transnational companies are implicated in power relations with many other organizations, including states, and are responsible for millions of people's lives and livelihoods. Building positive organizational performance and contributing to the creation of a better planet requires having global leaders with positive qualities in senior positions in these organizations. In this chapter, using Peterson and Seligman's (2004) framework, we explore how the character strengths and virtues of global leaders can make them more effective *and* better able to develop flourishing organizations and people within and around them in the contexts in which they operate. We also explore how global leaders with such positive qualities are more motivated to accept and/or look for global leadership development opportunities, and better able to learn from such opportunities. Some research directions are also considered.

Keywords: Global leaders' effectiveness, global leaders' development, character strengths and virtues, positive organizational performance

Global firms require global leaders (Caligiuri & Tarique, 2009; Morrison, 2000). Global leaders are "high level professionals such as executives, vice presidents, directors, and managers who are in jobs with some global leadership activities such as global integration responsibilities" (Caligiuri & Tarique, 2009, p. 336). One hypothetical example of a global leader's day is provided by Nardon and Steers (2007): She is located in Bangalore, and interacts with her business partner in California, a client in Hong Kong, Australian clients, and a partner in Mexico, before preparing for a trip to Germany. Obviously, such a profile may hypothetically characterize many agendas: For instance, that of the company's CEO, one of its executive directors, one of the heads of their vertical business units, the Chief Global Delivery Officer or Chief Marketing Officer, or of an European expatriate leading a cross-cultural team working on the development of a new product. These different hypothetical leaders face different challenges, but they all operate within a complex and diverse context.

Considering the impact of transnational companies upon hundreds of thousands of organizations and millions of people worldwide, the virtuousness of these "macro agents" (Jackson, 1999) may have a significant impact in the promotion of individual, organizational, and societal well-being (Cameron, 2010; Cameron & Caza, 2004). Today, not only are they expected to develop "good businesses" (Csikszentmihalyi, 2003) but also to contribute to the creation of a better planet (George, 2003, 2009). Having despoiled the planet these past 200 years, the titans of industry now lead the shared responsibility with governments and ordinary citizens for renewing it, because it is their decisions, investments, and activities that will make the difference.

Researchers such as Beechler and Javidan (2007), Gregersen, Morrison, and Black (1998), de Vries and Mead (1992), and Moran and Riesenberger (1994) have suggested that global leader roles require specific competencies and characteristics (e.g., inquisitiveness, global mindset, ability to build and maintain organizational networks at the global level, demonstrating knowledge and respect for other countries). In some taxonomies (e.g., Brownell, 2006; Conner, 2000; Gregersen et al., 1998), character strengths and virtues are explicitly referred (e.g., integrity, character, courage, emotional intelligence). In other taxonomies, character strengths and virtues are not explicitly mentioned but are clearly viewed as implicitly necessary for developing global leadership competencies. For example: the strengths of wisdom and open-mindedness are crucial for understanding and respecting cultural differences; vitality is necessary for traveling through different time zones, dealing with massive exposure to information, and working long days in adverse conditions, and integrity is necessary for dealing with the unethical behaviors and disrespect for human rights that will be encountered in some contexts.

There is a tendency in the management literature to valorize corporate leaders as heroes—heroes who often, subsequently, turn out to have "feet of clay"; that is, they are neither as extraordinary as might be assumed, and they turn out to have character and ethical flaws, just like most of us. Leaders often do make a difference, mostly through setting parameters, tone, and examples that are adopted by those reporting to them, and they are admired or denigrated in consequence.

With this chapter, our aim is to explore the character strengths and virtues that make global leaders more effective *and* better able to develop both flourishing organizations and people within and around them in the contexts in which they operate. In a globalized world, where multinational/global companies have extensive power over a huge number of other organizations and millions of people, building positive organizational performance requires having global leaders with such positive qualities. The character strengths and virtues framework proposed by Peterson and Seligman (2004) can be used as a loose framework (Table 28.1). These authors defined virtues as "the core characteristics valued by moral philosophers and religious thinkers: wisdom, courage, humanity, justice, temperance, and transcendence" (p. 13). Character strengths are the distinguishable routes through which virtues are expressed.

The chapter is inspired by the idea that "management theories must be both right and good" (Ghoshal & Moran, 2005, p. 17). Being right, we would argue, comes from being well-grounded in coherent theory and demonstrable empirical research, while being good comes from promoting ethical rather than unethical outcomes. The chapter is organized as follows. First, we discuss the complex globalized context in which global leaders operate. Second, we explore the relevance of human strengths and virtues for global leaders' effectiveness and their fostering of positive organizational performance. Third, we explore the effects of human strengths and virtues on global leaders' development. Fourth, we integrate arguments and discuss how global leaders may combine different virtues to be both effective and a source of positive organizational performance and social betterment. Finally, some avenues for future research are suggested.

Before proceeding, three cautionary notes are necessary. First: Character strengths and virtues are relevant both for global and local leaders. However, the increased complexity, uncertainty, and diversity (Beechler & Javidan, 2007; Bird & Osland, 2004; Gregersen et al., 1998) that global leaders need to face make their character strengths and virtues more relevant for them than for normal leaders. In a "risk society," in which the dysfunctional effects of business can flow globally, far from the places where investments were made or costs incurred, global leaders have global responsibilities (Beck, 1999). Global leaders also display character strengths and virtues in a way that is different from local leaders. As Gregersen et al. (1998, p. 25) argued, all leaders must be able to manage uncertainty, but "the degree of uncertainty that global managers face is exponentially higher." Although a strong character is important for every leader, it is specially put to the test when leaders face ethical dilemmas involving social norms and beliefs that collide with those prevailing in their culture. As an example, consider the case of an American manager working in China who, because of company policy, notified the police that he had fired an employee for theft and, later, discovered that the ex-employee had been executed (Stone, 2002; Wright, Szeto, & Lee, 2003).

Second, we present examples of character strengths without, however, implying that such leaders are necessarily virtuous. For example, the fact that a leader has shown courage at a certain time or in making certain decisions does not imply that he or she may be considered a courageous/virtuous leader. A leader can show courage in certain moments/decisions *and* cowardice in others. This latter action may restrain us from calling such a leader courageous but does not destroy the courage demonstrated in the former action and its positive consequences. Likewise, the examples of leaders who failed in behaving virtuously do not mean that such leaders are devoid of virtue.

Table 28.1   Virtues and human strengths (Peterson & Seligman, 2004)

Virtues	Human Strengths
Wisdom and knowledge: Cognitive strengths that entail the acquisition and use of knowledge	• Creativity: Thinking of novel and productive/adaptive ways to conceptualize and do things • Curiosity: Taking an interest in all of ongoing experience for its own stake; exploring and discovering • Open-mindedness: Thinking things through and examining them from all sides; not jumping to conclusions; being able to change one's mind in light of evidence • Love of learning: Mastering new skills, topics, and bodies of knowledge; tendency to add *systematically* to what one knows • Perspective/wisdom: Being able to provide wise counsel to others; looking at the world in a way that make sense to oneself and to other people
Courage: Emotional strengths that involve the exercise of will to accomplish goals in the face of opposition, external or internal	• Bravery: Not shrinking from threat, challenge, difficulty, or pain; speaking up for what is right even when facing opposition; acting on convictions even if unpopular • Persistence: Finishing what one starts; persisting in a course of action in spite of obstacles; taking pleasure in completing tasks • Integrity: Speaking the truth; presenting oneself in a genuine/authentic way; acting in a sincere way; taking responsibility for one's feelings and actions • Vitality: Approaching life with excitement and energy; living life as and adventure; feeling alive and activated
Justice: Civic strengths that underlie healthy community life	• Citizenship: Working well as member of a group or team; being loyal to the group • Fairness: Treating all people the same according to notions of fairness and justice; not letting personal feelings bias decisions about others • Leadership: Organizing group activities and seeing that they happen, while promoting good relationships within the group
Humanity: Interpersonal strengths that involve "tending and befriending" others	• Love: Valuing close relations with others; being close to people • Kindness: Doing favors and good deeds for others; helping people and take care of them • Social intelligence: Being aware of the motives and feelings of self and others; knowing what to do to fit into different social situations
Temperance: Strengths that protect against excess	• Forgiveness and mercy: Forgiving those who have done wrong; giving people a second chance; nor being vengeful • Humility/modesty: Letting one's accomplishments speak for themselves; not seeking the spotlight • Prudence: Being careful about one's choices; not saying or doing things that might later be regretted • Self-regulation: Regulating what one feels and does; being disciplined; controlling one's appetites and emotions
Transcendence: Strengths that forge connections to the larger universe and provide meaning	• Appreciation of beauty and excellence: Noticing and appreciating beauty, excellence, or skilled performance in all domains of life • Gratitude: Being aware of and thankful for the good things that happen • Hope: Expecting the best and working to achieve it • Humor: Liking to laugh and tease; bringing smiles to other people; seeing the light side • Spirituality: Having coherent beliefs about the higher purpose and meaning of life; having beliefs about the meaning of life that shape conduct and provide comfort

Third, the framework suggested by Peterson and Seligman (2004) for classifying character strengths and virtues is not yet empirically validated. As the authors state (p. 31), the classification is not "a finished product" and likely to change. For example, the classifications of some strengths are debatable (e.g., humor strength within transcendence virtue, or leadership under virtue of justice). However, the framework is well-known and helpful in identifying the crucial character strengths and virtues of global leaders.

Global Leaders in a Complex and Heterogeneous World

The world, when viewed from a neo-economically liberal perspective, has been described as flat (Friedman, 2005). To see things this way is to see very little at all. As argued by Bingham, Black, and Felin (2000, p. 290), "there is no uniformity in customer preferences, competitive circumstances, economic conditions, employee relations, or governmental regulations across the various countries and cultures. We live in an increasingly borderless world that is nonetheless still filled with linguistic, cultural, political, temporal, economic, and social borders." Thus, whether a company follows the "think global and act local" or the "think local and act global" recipe, it must recognize the diversity of cultures and local markets, and see them as a source of opportunity and challenge, while at the same time pushing for strategic consistency across countries and integrated operations (Paul, 2000).

The globalized environment is full of local idiosyncrasies that can change the ways in which leaders conduct business and the competencies they need to be successful. As Black (2006, p. 185) suggested, "great *global* leaders are inquisitive about *local* conditions. This is because they know that terrain that looks flat from 30,000 feet is full of dips and bumps at ground level; and they well understand that global strategies conceived at cruise altitude mean little to nothing if they cannot gain traction where the rubber meets the road". Hitt, Javidan, and Steers (2007, p. 2) also argued that a global company, with a complex web of global interdependencies

> [N]eeds managers who can understand and are able to deal with excessive levels of ambiguity and diversity, managers who have the appropriate knowledge about diverse sociocultural and institutional systems and have the intellectual capacity to absorb but not be paralyzed by high levels of complexity, managers who have the personal attributes that enable them to work closely and effectively with those from other cultural regions of the world, managers who can build sustainable trusting relationships with individuals, groups, and organizations in different countries to ensure that they help [the company] achieve its global ambitions.

Leading globally is thus a complex endeavor, a "near-Herculean" task replete with "disorienting challenges" (Osland, Bird, Mendenhall, & Osland, 2006, pp. 197–198) proceeding from four main aspects of the global context (Lane, Maznevski, Mendenhall, 2004): multiplicity across a range of dimensions (e.g., competitors, customers, governments, nongovernmental organizations [NGOs]); interdependence among a great variety of stakeholders and of sociocultural, economic, political, and environmental systems; ambiguity (in terms of, for example, lack of information clarity, cause–effect relationships, equivocality), and flux (i.e., the whole system is always changing at a fast rate). We argue that virtues may help global leaders face such challenges in a way that makes them not only more effective but also more contributive to positive organizational performance and societal improvement.

Exploring the Role of Human Strengths and Virtues on Global Leaders' Positive Performance

Next, we explore how character strengths and virtues may help global leaders to perform activities and their strategic role in a more effective and positive way. For purposes of clarification, each core virtue (wisdom and knowledge, courage, justice, humanity, temperance, and transcendence) is discussed separately. An integrative perspective is presented in the final section, and some bridges between character strengths will be offered whenever pertinent.

Strengths of Wisdom and Knowledge

The combined virtues of wisdom and knowledge comprise five character strengths: creativity (involving originality and ingenuity), curiosity (interest, novelty-seeking, and openness to experience), open-mindedness (judgment and critical thinking), love of learning, and perspective. These strengths, frequently operating in a blended way, are crucial to global leaders' effectiveness. Black and associates (Black, 2006; Black, Morrison, & Gregersen, 1999; Gregersen et al., 1998) refer to inquisitiveness as the "fuel of the global mind" (Black, 2006, p. 183). Morrison (2000, p. 126) also noted that "true inquisitiveness produces the action associated with learning, and learning is essential for keeping savvy, character, and perspective fresh. Without inquisitiveness, an individual will never develop a solid understanding of global markets nor will s/he establish the type of vibrant internal relationships necessary to effectively access the resources of the global organization."

Wisdom can be seen as "the product of knowledge and experience" (Peterson & Seligman, 2004, p. 106), combined with an accurate view of one's own strengths and weaknesses. Using this definition, it is possible to identify some CEOs who seem to have the appropriate combinations of reflexivity, knowledge, and experience. Born in Brazil, French by nationality, raised in Lebanon, and having worked in France, Brazil, the United States, and from 1999, in Japan, Carlos Ghosn is known as a kind of "savior" of Nissan (Millikin & Fu, 2005). He embraced the cultural differences between himself and Japanese interlocutors and used differences in cultural perspective as opportunities for personal growth and to become a better leader. He approached the Nissan-Renault alliance as an opportunity for mutual learning, considering that both could learn from the strengths and perspectives of the other. Regarding Japanese culture, he said: "I did not try to learn too much about Japan before coming, because I didn't want to have too many preconceived ideas. I wanted to discover Japan by being in Japan with Japanese people" (Millikin & Fu, 2005, p. 121). Immersion is an essential trait for global leaders—it denotes a degree of anthropological curiosity essential to managing the complexities of a subtle and culturally different everyday life.

Global leaders with strengths of wisdom and knowledge are potentially more culturally sensitive; they appreciate diversity and are more open to learning about the cultural idiosyncrasies of colleagues, clients, employees, suppliers, and authorities from other cultural contexts. They express a higher capacity to build and maintain organizational networks at the global level, and they receive the respect of interlocutors around the world, thus leading, interacting, negotiating, and building partnerships in more effective ways. They are better able to identify leadership behaviors that are more appropriate in different contexts (Javidan, Dorfman, Sully de Luque, & House, 2006; Morrison, 2000), and they develop global business and global organizing expertise (Mendenhall, 2006; Osland et al., 2006) from a global perspective, integrating diverse knowledge bases (Gupta & Govindarajan, 2002) and developing strategies that take into account local and global issues. When working abroad, they develop better cross-cultural adjustment, building social and working relationships, becoming more effective, and reducing the risks of expatriation failure and premature return (Lee, 2007; Lee & Liu, 2006).

Strengths of Courage

Courage is displayed via four main human strengths: bravery, persistence (involving perseverance and industriousness), integrity (authenticity and honesty), and vitality (zest, enthusiasm, vigor, and energy). This virtue is relevant for any leader (Carey, Patsalos-Fox, & Useem, 2009), but the complexity and ambiguity involved in global business make it especially relevant for global leaders (Morrison, 2001; Spreitzer,

McCall, & Mahoney, 1997; Treasurer, 2009). Morrison (2001, p. 65) notes:

> Integrity forms the bedrock of character and is essential in sustainable global leadership. . . . While all managers inevitably confront ethical issues, global leaders confront them on a regular basis. Because of the frequency and depth of the ethical challenges they face, global leaders need a unique set of competencies in order to maintain their personal integrity and build a consistent set of values for the global organization.

The corporate scandals that have taken place in recent years, with their global consequences, could perhaps have been avoided if the companies' leaders had acted in honest, authentic, and brave ways (George, 2003, 2009). We recognize such authenticity readily when we see it; for instance, one of the most widely admired statesmen of modern times, Nelson Mandela, is recognized, above all else, for the integrity of his character despite the tribulations he had to endure and the fact that, in some assessments, he would be regarded as a terrorist. In the corporate executive field, Anne Mulcahy also gave proofs of such strength. Contradicting critics who doubted that she could be the catalyst to remake Xerox into a profitable company, she started visiting employees all over the world, "living on planes" and deciding to speak the truth directly to employees, including bad news about shutting down a business unit or making layoffs (Caminiti, 2005a; J. Collins, 2009; George, 2009). With vigor, she did not take a weekend off for 2 years and rebuffed advisors' repeated suggestions that she consider Chapter 11 (a chapter of the U.S. bankruptcy code that permits reorganization under bankruptcy laws). By 2006, the company's profits exceeded $1 billion and, in 2008, Mulcahy was selected by *Chief Executive* magazine as chief executive of the year.

Courage is relevant to several global leaders' activities and challenges. It helps them show decisiveness and integrity when making decisions (e.g., closing a plant in a poor region of a developing country) involving political, labor, and NGOs issues in other countries, thus preventing problems from escalating worldwide (Carey et al., 2009). It impels them "to walk the talk," thus creating the trust necessary for stimulating fluid and collaborative work relationships with individuals, teams, and organizations from many different economic, legal, political, social, and cultural systems (Beechler & Javidan, 2007). Courageous and honest leaders are also more able to develop trust with their subordinates and persuade them to accept challenging and difficult international assignments. Courage is also crucial for dealing with xenophobic attitudes in those countries in which the company operates (Kets de Vries, 2001).

When news disseminate swiftly at the global level, and a mistake committed in one country may damage a company's reputation worldwide, courage is necessary so that leaders can be transparent with stakeholders, assume responsibility for mistakes, and reveal uncomfortable data about the company's actions and, eventually, recall products (Bennis, Goleman, & O'Toole, 2008; George, 2009). Courage is also important when dealing with ethical dilemmas, which are magnified when a company operates across several cultures. It is especially relevant in contexts in which corruption is salient and human rights are disrespected (Morrison, 2000, 2001). As George (2003) suggested, there are cases in which a company must lose business to gain a reputation. Courage is also crucial for defining ambitious goals and strategies and for pursuing them with persistence, vitality, and bravery.

Strengths of Justice

The virtue of justice is displayed in three major human strengths: leadership, citizenship, and fairness. Arguing for leadership as an important character strength for global leaders appears tautological; however, if one considers their role complexity and the wide range and diversity of stakeholders they need to interact with, as well as the need to coordinate fluid and collaborative work relationships and to promote trust and speed of decision making throughout a global network (Beechler & Javidan, 2007), this personal quality is of great relevance. Articulating a tangible vision and strategy, clarifying values, and catalyzing cultural and strategic changes have been suggested by Mendenhall and associates (Mendenhall, 2006; Mendenhall & Osland, 2002; Osland et al., 2006) as important competencies for global leaders.

The strength of citizenship (involving social responsibility, loyalty, and teamwork) makes global leaders better able to build more sustainable and responsible organizations, more sensitive to the impacts that they have on communities and the natural environment, more receptive to social accountability norms and standards (e.g., SA8000), and more likely to follow policies and strategies that do not harm the planet or humanity. Manifestations of such character strength can be found in those leaders who infuse their actions with the Japanese concept of *kyosei* (Boardman & Kato, 2003). Ryuzaburo Kaku (1997), honorary chairman of Canon, defined *kyosei* as "'a spirit of cooperation,' in which individuals and organizations live and work together for the common good. A company that

practices *kyosei* establishes harmonious relations with its customers, its suppliers, its competitors, the governments with which it deals, and the natural environment" (p. 55).

One may presume that the strength of citizenship fuelled the Caux Round Table initiative (www. cauxroundtable.org), in which a group of Japanese, European, and United States leaders developed a set of principles for business behavior rooted in two ethical ideas: *kyosei* and human dignity (Boardman & Kato, 2003; Waddock & Smith, 2000). Improving commercial and social relationships among nations, and reducing social and economic threats to peace and world stability, were two main purposes of the initiative. Other initiatives, such as the Global Compact (http://www.unglobalcompact.org/), the Equator Principles (http://www.equator-principles.com/), the Global Business Oath (http://www.globalbusinessoath.org), and the World Business Council on Sustainable Development (http://www.wbcsd.org) also constitute the foundations of genuine citizenship initiatives. Although these citizenship purposes may be endorsed by all leaders with positive consequences for the common good, the impact of global leaders and global organizations is much more intense and extensive, not only directly (i.e., on these organizations themselves) but also indirectly on all entities with which global organizations have social, economic, or political relationships.

One may reasonably expect that, through role modeling and social learning fueled by the policies and practices they adopt, global leaders with a strong justice character will behave fairly and foster justice in their organizations, with positive consequences for employees' attitudes and behaviors (Kim & Mauborgne, 1993, 1996; Viswesvaran & Ones, 2002) across the worldwide organizational network. By practicing justice, global leaders may better bond individuals and organizations that are geographically separated and promote enhanced cooperation among the members of a global network. Practicing justice can also lead to positive consequences for customers (Clark, Adjei, & Yancey, 2009; George, 2003) and suppliers (Hornibrook, Fearne, & Lazzarin, 2009). Justice may improve corporate social responsibility compliance across the global supply chain (Boyd, Spekpman, Kamauff, & Werhane, 2007; Griffith, Harvey, & Lusch, 2006), stimulate cooperation in strategic alliances (Luo, 2008), and decrease opportunism in international joint ventures (Luo, 2007). Global leaders with justice strengths are more likely to impel their companies to stay away from countries with poor human rights records, to refrain from hiring cheap labor in the Third World, and to respect minorities in cultural contexts in which they are discriminated (Bragues, 2006). One may also consider that global leaders with commitments to higher levels of justice are better positioned to understand the justice standards (e.g., equity, need, equality) that prevail in different contexts (Greenberg, 2001; Morris & Leung, 2000; Murphy-Berman, Berman, Singh, Pachauri, & Kumar, 1984), thus adjusting decisions and policies accordingly.

Strengths of Humanity

Humanity manifests itself in caring relationships with others, including love, kindness (generosity, nurturance, care, compassion, altruistic love and "niceness"), and social intelligence (personal, emotional, and social intelligence). Both love and kindness are crucial for leaders' effectiveness (Barbuto & Wheeler, 2006; Dennis & Bocarnea, 2005; Fry, 2003; George, 2003; Liden, Wayne, Zhao, & Henderson, 2008). There are reasons to believe that they are also crucial for several global leaders' actions, including their capacity to build and develop mentoring relationships (George, 2003; Ragins & Cotton, 1999). Through mentoring, an expatriate leader may develop local country employees' competencies and strong local management teams, thus helping the company to localize their staff, decrease expatriation costs, and motivate local country employees (Law, Wong, & Wang, 2004; Mezias & Scandura, 2005; Selmer, 2003, 2004). Both strengths may also allow a global leader to mentor impatriates (Harvey & Novicevic, 2004) and/or individuals who are preparing for international assignments (Jassawalla, Asgary, & Sashittal, 2006), thus helping their cross-cultural and psychological adjustment and helping them to be more effective.

Bill George (2003), former CEO of Medtronic, argued that through "leading with heart," a leader is more able to establish closer relationships with colleagues, thus building a "closely knit team whose collective knowledge and wisdom about the business vastly exceeds" that of the leader (p. 24). Building such ties is specially challenging for leaders working within a culturally diverse team and/or with teams whose members operate in different locations. Daniel Vasella, from Novartis, gave proof of "leading with heart" when deciding to provide Gleevec for free for anyone with an income below $40,000 (George, 2003): Such action is not only important in caring for customers and making the world a better place, it also establishes the brand as compassionate.

Social intelligence has been referred as a relevant competency of global leaders (Alon, & Higgins, 2005; Brownell, 2006; McCall & Hollenbeck, 2002). A global leader with social intelligence demonstrates a sincere interest in and concern for others and a heightened ability to listen to employees, customers, suppliers, authorities, partners, and other stakeholders from different contexts, as well as a deep capacity to understand different viewpoints and to interpret emotions and verbal and nonverbal communicational cues in different cultures. As a consequence (Alon, & Higgins, 2005; Black, Morrison, & Gregersen, 1999; Goleman, 1998; Morrison, 2000; Riggio & Reichard, 2008), he or she is more able to understand local markets, customers, competitors, and governments quickly; is more effective in overcoming barriers to communication that separate people across cultures and vast geographic distances; has a higher capacity to understand the emotional tone within cross-cultural teams and thus channel such emotions in a more appropriate way; is more able to understand and manage others' emotions, thus being more effective in managing conflict and negotiating in diverse contexts; and is less likely to lose emotional control when facing unfamiliar situations in idiosyncratic cultural contexts.

Strengths of Temperance

The virtue of temperance manifests in four main character strengths: forgiveness and mercy, humility and modesty, prudence, and self-regulation. Global leaders with strong forgiveness (Bright, 2006) are potentially more able to manage conflicts constructively with employees, colleagues, customers, suppliers, and other stakeholders around the world. They are more tolerant when facing misunderstandings resulting from cross-cultural differences and conflicts, thus better able to develop positive cross-cultural interactions and global organizational networks, and to operate with cultural adaptability when carrying out international assignments. Considering its positive effects on physical, psychological, and emotional well-being (Cameron & Caza, 2002), forgiveness may also contribute to increasing global leaders' vitality and help them to deal effectively with the demands of their role. Through contagion effects, global leaders may promote forgiveness within the companies with which they interact, thus facilitating buffering and amplifying positive effects (Bright, 2006; Cameron & Caza, 2002; Cameron, Bright, & Caza, 2004; Grant, 2008) across a wide range of organizations.

Humility may also have a positive impact on global leaders' action. A humble leader is in principle more able to accept and experience comfort with the ambiguity surrounding international and cross-cultural activities than one less humble (Distefano, 1995). Vera and Rodriguez-Lopez (2004) point out several features of a humble leader with relevance for global leadership. For example, being open to new paradigms is crucial for understanding different social, economic, political, and cultural contexts, and in adopting new approaches when dealing with diverse markets, people, and entities. By acknowledging one's own limitations and mistakes, and attempting to correct them, global leaders are better able to face different contexts with interest and respect, and to learn from cultural mistakes. Asking for advice is crucial to penetrating new markets and interacting with diverse employees, customers, suppliers, and authorities. Developing others may be essential for increasing human capital in less-developed countries, thus reducing the costs of expatriation. Sharing honors and recognition with employees is crucial to being accepted and respected in unfamiliar contexts. By their example, humble leaders are also able to promote organizational humility and, indirectly, competitive advantage, because humility is a "valuable, rare, irreplaceable, and difficult to imitate" resource (Vera & Rodriguez-Lopez, 2004, p. 397).

Self-regulation is crucial to avoid being dazzled by the media spotlight; to the practice of self-restraint, rather than making megalomaniac decisions—just because one can; to making decisions that respect the interests and rights of poor communities and of partners with fragile power positions in developing countries; to avoiding "vices" when working/acting in remote cultures where human rights are disregarded; and to avoiding consumption habits that may appear extravagant/disrespectful when working/interacting with people from more deprived economic contexts. In contrast, weak self-regulation may lead global leaders to intemperate decisions with perverse consequences at the global level. Behaviors such as those of Denis Kozlowski, former CEO of Tyco, who spent $2 million in a week-long birthday party for his wife and used company resources to support a sumptuous lifestyle (Bragues, 2006; Kellerman, 2004; Vera & Lopez-Rodriguez, 2004; D. Collins, 2009), damage employees' commitment worldwide. It is difficult for employees to justify making sacrifices for the company's good when faced with a CEO who imagines himself a Bourbon monarch of the *ancien régime*, in terms if lifestyle. Intemperance may also lead to fraudulent accounting and records, hiding dishonest procedures and feeding narcissistic goals; pompous and ineffective acquisitions, and legal problems with their concurrent negative impact.

Lou Gerstner gave proof of temperance when taking the helm of IBM. In contrast to HP's Carly Fiorina, who nourished her media image as a celebrity CEO (Malone, 2007), he kept away from the media ("never allowing hype to precede results"; J. Collins, 2009, p. 165). Adopting an attitude of personal discipline (e.g., by self-regulating), engaging "in the disciplined practice of underpromising and overdelivering" (J. Collins, 2009, p. 165), and fostering a culture of discipline, he restored (at least some of) IBM's greatness. Jim Collins (2009, p. 162) referred to him this way: "Gerstner came in as a savior CEO yet clearly had the discipline to make difficult decisions (and to resist making panicky decisions). . . . In the end, Gerstner was clearly ambitious for IBM first and foremost, beyond himself." Global leaders' temperance, especially in times of crisis (Powley & Taylor, 2006), may have a strong symbolic value in bringing together the efforts and energies of the company's stakeholders operating in distant cultural contexts.

Strengths of Transcendence

Transcendence expresses itself in five character strengths: appreciation of beauty and excellence, gratitude, hope, playfulness, and spirituality. The prototype of this category is spirituality, referring to beliefs and practices grounded in the conviction that there is a transcendent (i.e., nonphysical) dimension to life. Some theoretical and empirical evidence suggests that "spirituality mobilizes the individual towards meaningful or 'transcendental' accomplishment" (Sanders III, Hopkins, & Geroy, 2003, p. 21), and that spiritual leadership has a positive impact on leaders, followers, and organizational performance, well-being, and flourishing (Fry, 2003, 2008; Fry, & Matherly, 2007; Fry & Slocum, 2008; Fry, Vitucci, & Cedillo, 2005).

Spiritual leadership refers to "motivating and inspiring workers through a transcendent vision and a corporate culture based on altruistic values to produce a highly motivated, committed and productive workforce" (Fry & Slocum, 2007, p. 90). A transcendent/meaningful vision and a virtuous organizational culture are especially fruitful for lubricating international flows of organizational learning and bringing together efforts and initiatives emerging in different locations and diverse social, political, economic, and cultural contexts. Although it is not necessary, as we shall shortly see, it helps greatly if the transcendent vision is religious in detail for it to be shared among significant communities of the citizens of the countries in question: Where it is not, then the transcendence may be strictly limited. In a context of high complexity, ambiguity, and uncertainty, as well as shared spirituality, leaders with transcendent qualities are better able to develop the bonds that allow for the integration of the efforts and energies of diverse and geographically dispersed people and units. If a virtuous vision and a positive/transcendental culture serves to clarify the general direction of change, to simplify hundreds or thousands of more detailed decisions, and to coordinate the actions of many different people quickly and efficiently (Fry, 2003), it can also serve to simplify and integrate the daily decisions and coordinate the actions of diverse people and entities operating worldwide. Virtuous visions and actions emerging within global organizations disseminate throughout a wide network of partners globally. In this way, "building enduring organizations that contribute to making this world a better place to live" (George, 2009), will be a more plausible endeavor.

A global leader who appreciates strong spirituality may also be better able to understand the diverse religiosity of employees (e.g., Joaquin, a Colombian leading a Malay branch of a Japanese company, recognized the importance of the *Haj*, the sacred journey to Mecca, and created a system allowing ten employees to go there each year without having to take vacation days; Otazo, 1999). Spirituality may also provide leaders with enough internal locus of control for dealing with strong ambiguity and stressful contingencies (Sanders, Hopkins, & Geroy, 2003).

Appreciation of beauty and excellence may also promote global leaders' effectiveness and positive performance. A leader with such strength is more likely to see beauty in what might otherwise be regarded as the idiosyncratic habits and practices of people from developing countries, when adopting an ethnocentric perspective that depreciates less sophisticated ways of life. He or she is more likely to connect deeply with other people (Peterson & Seligman, 2004) and to focus on perfecting his or her local language proficiency, instead of assuming that "English is *the* business language" and/or resorting to an interpreter. Appreciative leaders have fewer rigid views of right and wrong, and are more motivated to accept and feel good living together with diverse cultures. In this way, they develop flourishing relationships with people from different contexts, including employees, customers, suppliers, joint ventures partners, and authorities.

Humor is also important for global leaders. A global leader with a good sense of humor is better able to deal positively and with fairness when interacting with people from polychronic cultures, where "time is *not* money," and/or from countries where wealth and leisure are scarce, and communication infrastructures are poor. They may react with playfulness when making "cultural mistakes" and/or observing behaviors which, in light of their culture, appear strange. If they are also characterized by strong gratitude, it is more likely that they face diversity and adversity with positive feelings instead of with complaints about the difficulties of the job.

Finally, hope may help a global leader to maintain optimism, self-confidence, and a future orientation when facing unprecedented obstacles in problematic countries and/or when experiencing the first months of an international assignment in a completely novel culture. Certainly, the leaders of Toyota will need to draw on deep well-springs of hope if they are to emerge with any credit from the safety recall scandal of 2010, in which government officials have said that Toyota did not tell them about the problem until prompted; that Toyota decided the fault was not a safety issue when it received the first reports over a year ago; and that, initially, they treated the 26 cases across Europe in the winter of 2008/09 as "a quality issue." Only when the problem recurred 1 year later did they treat it as a safety issue. Similarly, in the United States, it was only after government pressure that Toyota admitted the extent of its liability and sought to recall over 8 million cars worldwide. Courage was in short supply in this case.

Methodologically, we would suggest that the qualities we have identified in this section should be thought of as elements or dimensions in the ideal type for a good global leader. Of course, it will be rare to find all these qualities embodied in any single person but they stand, as a condensation of many attributes, as a guide to the character of a leader conceived in ideal typical terms. We do not mean anything normative or prescriptive with this statement, but merely that such a condensation of features may guide researchers and practitioners in their identification of global leaders.

Human Strengths and Virtues as Facilitators and Enablers of Global Leader Development

With an increasing demand for global leaders to carry out global strategies, organizations need to develop global leadership competencies. However, development costs are high (Caligiuri & Tarique, 2009), and even higher are the costs of investing in individuals who later reveal themselves unable to meet the firms' needs. One way to increase the chances of

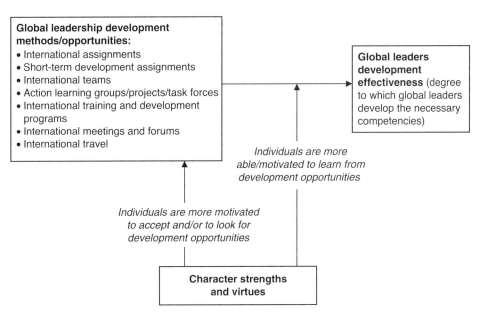

Fig. 28.1 Character strengths and virtues as moderators and antecedents of global leadership development methods.

success is to select individuals with high potential and then offer them developmental experiences (Caligiuri, 2006). We suggest that individuals with character strengths and virtues will be better motivated to accept or look for, and to take advantage (Figure 28.1) of development experiences (Suutari, 2002). Relevant international assignments, short-term development assignments, international teams, action learning projects, international training and development programs, international meetings and forums, and international travel are all arenas in which these individuals can flourish.

Human strengths and virtues make the individual more motivated to accept and/or to look for development opportunities (Osland et al., 2006). For example, individuals with high levels of curiosity, love of learning, bravery, and hope are more likely to accept and/or look for international assignments, responsibilities in international teams, and participation in international meetings and forums. Individuals with higher bravery, persistence, and vitality are more likely to accept frequent short-term assignments and frequent travelling. Individuals with higher transcendence and humanity are more likely to adhere to initiatives such as *SeitenWechsel* ("PerspectiveChange"), in which executives are assigned for a short period of time (usually 2 weeks) to social welfare projects involving less privileged members of society (e.g., homeless people, juvenile delinquents, terminally ill HIV patients, immigrants seeking asylum). According to Mendenhall et al. (2003), through such initiatives, managers may learn

how to perceive the world through the eyes of less privileged people, and, thus, develop competencies that matter for global leaders.

Human strengths and virtues also make individuals better able to learn from development experiences/opportunities (Bandura, 1997). For example, individuals with higher curiosity, open-mindedness, perspective, and love of learning are more motivated to pay attention to and to remember others' behaviors, attitudes, and values witnessed while participating in international assignments, short-term assignments, international teams, international meetings and forums, and international traveling. They are more able to learn contrasting views and values, thus forcing them to think globally (Gregersen et al., 1998). They are more motivated to translate observed behaviors into appropriate behaviors, thus satisfying their motivation for knowledge/wisdom and for mastering new skills. They tend to adopt a more inquisitive attitude when participating in action learning activities and international training and development programs, feeling attracted to the idiosyncratic behaviors of other people and asking pertinent questions to improve their cross-cultural adaptability. Bravery, vitality, and persistence make individuals more motivated to continue to learn even when facing difficulties (e.g., when working in a completely different culture from their own, or when participating in teams in which communication problems and conflicts emerge as result of cultural diversity) and after committing errors and experiencing failures.

Bridging Character Strengths and Virtues

As the foregoing discussion suggested, different groups of strengths (i.e., core virtues) tend to support different roles, activities, and competencies (Table 28.2). For example, wisdom and knowledge help global leaders to learn how to understand and interact positively with different people and stakeholders. Courage helps them to make challenging decisions and face problems honestly and energetically. Justice promotes respect, trust, cooperation, and human dignity. Humanity facilitates the promotion of trustful and cooperative relationships, caring about others, and fostering community development. Temperance helps global leaders to be cautious, to make wise decisions, to learn from mistakes, and to adopt a level-5 leadership approach (i.e., building enduring greatness through a paradoxical combination of personal humility plus professional will) (J. Collins, 2001, p.70). Transcendence facilitates the pursuit of sustainable futures.

However, different character strengths and virtues may support the same global leaders' activities and competencies. For example, open-mindedness, love of learning, social intelligence, and citizenship may be crucial for developing cultural adaptability and the ability to build positive interactions with diverse stakeholders. Moreover, some competencies, activities, or roles may require the contribution of several strengths: When they are not combined, the effects may be perverse. For example, a courageous leader without integrity may make profitable deals in corrupt contexts, putting the reputation of the company and its long-term development in serious trouble. Courage without humility makes leaders rash (Vera & Rodriguez-Lopez, 2004) and unable to develop positive and fluid interactions in the global network. A courageous leader without wisdom and temperance may accept a risky international assignment without the proper cultural preparation (Otazo, 1999), thus harming performance and jeopardizing the mission; for example, Carly Fiorina was a courageous leader, but a certain degree of intemperance led to her abrupt dismissal (Malone, 2007).

The previous argument helps us understand that "virtue is found in the middle." "Excessive" courage may lead the leader to neglect risks and difficulties that could be reasonably expected in some contexts or regarding some decisions. "Excessive" prudence and/or humanity may impede him or her from taking difficult although necessary decisions. "Excessive" transcendence (namely appreciation of excellence) may lead to the articulation of "perfect visions" that do not show much adherence to reality. These risks show one of the main features of virtues (Aristotle, 1999): They are midway between two vices—they are the golden mean between the extremes (e.g., courage is midway between cowardice and recklessness). The topic also suggests that curvilinear relationships may exist between virtues and global leader effectiveness and positive performance.

Future Directions

In contrast with cross-cultural leadership, the topic of global leadership is a nascent field in the organizational literature, having received much less attention than domestic leadership (Beechler & Javidan, 2007; Osland et al., 2006; Suutari, 2002). Naturally, studies about the character strengths and virtues of global leaders are scarce. Therefore, avenues for future research are wide and long, and countless questions are open to debate and empirical research.

One of the most important questions is how global leaders' character strengths and virtues relate effectively to organizationally positive performance. Because we do not think that the causal relations are immediate and cross-sectional but more akin to being ontogenetic, albeit socially constructed, shaping the organization's *long durée*, we suggest that the method of long-term financial performance that is used to build the "best performing CEOs in the world" ranking (Hansen, Ibarra, & Peyer, 2010) may be useful for measuring global leaders' effectiveness. For those leaders and organizations whose performance is consistent over a specified period of time, looking at the broad social media about the organizations and leaders in question, we need to ask: Are those leaders occupying the top places more virtuous than those in the lower positions? How do different global leaders' character strengths and virtues interact in predicting organizational long-term financial performance?

Measuring positive organizational performance is a complex endeavor. Although long-term financial performance may be included in the construct, other variables must be taken into account (e.g., organizational presence in rankings such as "the best places to work for"; social accountability and environment certifications; unfair downsizing practices; a diminishing carbon footprint). Are organizations led by more virtuous global leaders more frequently present in such rankings? Do they get social accountability certifications more frequently?

Future studies may also test how the relationship between global leaders' character strengths and virtues and their effectiveness is mediated or moderated by

Table 28.2 Core virtues sustaining global leaders' activities and competencies

Core Virtues	Examples of Activities/Competencies that this Virtue May Nourish, Support or Develop
Wisdom and knowledge	**Learning, understanding and interacting/networking positively** • Learning, understanding and taking advantage of the global market and the complexities of the cultural, economic and political "mosaic" • Developing global business and global organization expertise • Developing strategic plans that take local and global issues into account • Developing positive interactions with diverse stakeholders
Courage	**Taking challenging decisions and facing problems/difficulties honestly and energetically** • Keeping integrity when ethical and human rights problems need to be faced/solved in different cultural, economic, social, and political contexts • Facing the hassles of frequent travelling, working in different time zones, and working in culturally, politically, socially, and economically adverse conditions • Assuming responsibility for mistakes and preserving the company's reputation worldwide • Defining ambitious strategies and goals, and energizing stakeholders worldwide
Justice	**Leading respectfully, fostering trust and cooperation, and promoting human dignity** • Adopting a respectful leadership approach, and fostering trust and fluid cooperative work relationships between diverse stakeholders within the global network • Building "goodwill" in a wide range of stakeholders • Adopting integrative leadership efforts that allow different approaches to work in ways consistent with the global organization strategy • Adopting, implementing, and facilitating a sustainable and responsible management strategy ("people, planet, profits"), thus contributing to the common good • Promoting human dignity
Humanity	**Promoting trustful and cooperative relationships, caring about others, and fostering community development** • Building team spirit and cooperation along the global network • Fostering community development • Mentoring (e.g., expatriates, impatriates, local country nationals) • Caring about customers and making the world a better place in which to live • Empathizing, listening, and overcoming cultural communication barriers • Managing conflict and negotiating constructively
Temperance	**Being prudent, making wise decisions, learning through mistakes, and adopting a level-5 leadership approach** • Acknowledging one's own limitations, facing cultural mistakes with elevation, and learning from them • Adopting prudent decisions and preserving the company's reputation • Asking for advice, thus being more able to penetrate new markets and interact positively with diverse stakeholders • Promoting organizational humility (a valuable, rare, irreplaceable, and difficult-to-imitate resource) • Avoiding the media spotlight
Transcendence	**Pursuing excellence, sustainable management, and meaningful visions and missions** • Articulating positive and meaningful visions and missions, thus making people feel they perform meaningful work and mobilizing their energies worldwide • Maximizing the organization's triple bottom line • Promoting organizational learning within and across unities, branches, and organizations • Feeling grateful for having the opportunity to know/experience the splendid world diversity • Pursuing excellence in the company and the global network of which it is part

variables such as global mindset (Beechler & Javidan, 2007), cultural intelligence (Earley, Murnieks, & Mosakowski, 2007), and other cognitive, relational, and business competencies (Bird & Osland, 2004; Mendenhall, 2006). Mediating variables at the organizational level (e.g., trust, collective self-efficacy) may also be pertinent.

Another important research stream would be testing if the relevance of character strengths and virtues for global leaders' performance is contingent on roles and missions. For example, are integrity and bravery more relevant for global leaders who work and interact with partners from contexts where corruption is deep? Are love of learning and open-mindedness more relevant when dealing with partners from novel cultures and when leading cross-cultural teams with strong diversity?

A key variable is the extent to which global leaders' character strengths and virtues disseminate throughout the whole global organization and their subsidiaries across the world, to become embedded in routines, rituals, and rites that characterize the organization. Leadership in local sustainability and clean-up programs, in social welfare initiatives, in setting the pace for labor and management best practices, for instance, would be important. Longitudinal studies may test if the virtuousness degree of global leaders is reflected in the kind of leaders they appoint to lead subsidiaries across the world; the criteria they use in selecting expatriates, the trust bonds developed between headquarters and subsidiaries; and the levels of job performance and affective commitment developed by employees working in different branches across the world.

Do global leaders with high character strengths and virtues demonstrate better cross-cultural adjustment when working abroad? Are they more willing to join initiatives such as the Global Compact, World Business Council on Sustainable Development, or the Global Business Oath? What is the relationship between the global leaders' character strengths and virtues and the strength, breadth, and depth of the global networks they develop? How is global leader virtuousness reflected in the relationships among the organization and its customers, suppliers, authorities, and partners? Do organizations led by virtuous global leaders show less judicial problems with such stakeholders?

Future studies may also investigate to what degree the selection criteria for global leaders' comprise character strengths and virtues. Do boards, companies, and head-hunters consider such criteria when assessing the candidates' potential? Is there any relationship

between such orientation and the degree to which companies are susceptible to corporate scandals? To what extent do virtuous global leaders take into account character strengths and virtues when selecting their successors and expatriates? Is such a practice influenced by the virtuousness of their companies' culture?

Finally, future studies may empirically test the suggestion that character strengths and virtues make individuals more motivated to accept and look for development opportunities, and make them more able to learn from such opportunities. One interesting possibility is to test, with adaptations, the theoretical model proposed by Ng, Van Dyne, and Ang (2009).

Some research suggestions will not be easy endeavors on which to deliver. Collecting data about global leaders' virtues and effectiveness may be a difficult task. For example, due to both agenda constraints and desires to protect their image, the expectation that global leaders will participate in research surveys may be too optimistic. Nonetheless, global leaders leave many traces: in-depth analyses of their discourse (interviews and articles in the press, messages in company reports, letters addressed to shareholders, press releases), and the congruence between discourse and practice may allow for the collection of valuable data. Adopting the structured observation method used by Mintzberg (1971) may also be a useful way to identify global leaders' character strengths and the routes through which they are displayed (e.g., in contacts with stakeholders and other interlocutors across the world). Such a method is naturally very demanding, but one can expect that the more virtuous leaders will be motivated to contribute to improving scientific knowledge within this unexplored field.

Conclusion

This chapter explored how character strengths and virtues may help global leaders to be more effective, attain positive organizational performance, and contribute to the common good at the global level. By cultivating and developing virtuous attitudes, decisions, and actions while interacting with employees, suppliers, customers, partners, government authorities, NGOs, and local communities at the worldwide level, global leaders may build "good businesses" (Csikszentmihalyi, 2003), promote organizational virtuousness (Cameron, Bright, & Caza, 2004; Wright & Goodstein, 2007), and support human development. They may also build positive networks of self-regulation (e.g., Caux Round Table) and influence governments and transnational authorities to focus on sustainability development, improving legislation, and being better regulators of their companies' conduct. We see global leader virtuousness as a process that may drive organizations into positive spirals, rather than simply as a leader trait. The fact that global leaders are subject to intense scrutiny transforms them as role models for many aspirants to the same type of position.

Global leaders are role models both for current and future generations and, through intergenerational reciprocity (Hernandez, 2008), they may promote future leaders' and organizations' virtuousness. Hugh Grant, chairman, president, and CEO of Monsanto, noted that "I don't believe global companies can cure the world's ills, but they can be part of the cure" (Caminiti, 2005b, p. 21). Of course, it is important that the reality match the rhetoric—Monsanto, after all, is the developer of the terminator gene, which ethical.investing.com regard as "currently the greatest threat to humanity" (ethicalinvesting. com, 2010). Virtuous global leaders need to turn global companies into powerful engines of economic and human progress, rather than merely mouth rhetoric that their companies' realities belie. Of course, it is difficult, especially when they are domiciled and publically listed in countries in which rampant economic liberalism is dominant, but the difference they make and the example they present, even when flawed, offer remarkable opportunities for learning, as well as for improving the state of the world.

References

Alon, I., & Higgins, J.M. (2005). Global leadership success through emotional and cultural intelligences. *Business Horizons, 48*(6), 501–512.

Aristotle. (1999). *The Nicomachean ethics* (W.D. Ross, Trans.). New York: Batoche Books.

Bandura, A. (1997). *Self-efficacy: The exercise of control*. New York: Freeman.

Barbuto, J.E., & Wheeler, D.W. (2006). Scale development and construct clarification of servant leadership. *Group & Organization Management, 31*(3), 300–326.

Beck, U. (1999). *World risk society*. Oxford: Polity Press.

Beechler, S., & Javidan, M. (2007). Leading with a global mindset. In M. Javidan, R.M. Steers, M.A., & Hitt (Eds.), *Advances in international management* Vol. 19 (pp. 131–169). Stamford, CT: JAI Press.

Bennis, W., Goleman, D., & O'Toole, J. (Eds.). (2008). *Transparency: Creating a culture of candor* (pp. 45–92). San Francisco: Jossey Bass.

Bingham, C., Black, J.S., & Felin, T. (2000). An interview with John Pepper: What it takes to be a global leader. *Human Resource Management, 39*(2–3), 287–292.

Bird, A., & Osland, J.S. (2004). Global competencies: An introduction. In H.W. Lane, M.L. Maznevski, M.E. Mendenhall,

& J. McNett (Eds.), *The Blackwell handbook of global management* (pp. 57–80). London: Blackwell.

Black, J.S. (2006). The mindset of global leaders: Inquisitiveness and duality. In W.H. Mobley, & E. Weldon (Eds.), *Advances in global leadership* (pp. 181–200). Stamford, CT: JAI Press.

Black, J.S., Morrison, A.J., & Gregersen, H.B. (1999). *Global explorers: The next generation of leaders*. New York: Routledge.

Boardman, C.M., & Kato, H.K. (2003). The Confucian roots of business Kyosei. *Journal of Business Ethics, 48*(4), 317–333.

Boyd, D.E., Spekman, R.E., Kamauff, J.W., & Werhane, P. (2007). Corporate social responsibility in global supply chains: A procedural justice perspective. *Long Range Planning, 40*, 341–356.

Bragues, G. (2006). Seek the good life, not money: The Aristotelian approach to business ethics. *Journal of Business Ethics, 67*, 341–357.

Bright, D.S. (2006). Forgiveness as an attribute of leadership. In E.D. Hess, & K.S. Cameron (Eds.), *Leading with values* (pp. 172–193). Cambridge: Cambridge University Press.

Bronwell, J. (2006). Meeting the competency needs of global leaders: A partnership approach. *Human Resource Management, 45*(3), 309–336.

Caligiuri, P. (2006). Developing global leaders. *Human Resource Management Review, 16*, 219–228.

Caligiuri, P., & Tarique, I. (2009). Predicting effectiveness in global leadership activities. *Journal of World Business, 44*(3), 336–346.

Cameron, K. (2010). Five keys to flourishing in trying times. *Leader to Leader, 55*, 45–51.

Cameron, K.S., & Caza, A. (2004). Introduction: Contributions to the discipline of positive organizational scholarship. *American Behavioral Scientist, 47*(6), 731–739.

Cameron, K.S., Bright, D., & Caza, A. (2004). Exploring the relationships between organizational virtuousness and performance. *American Behavioral Scientist, 47*(6), 1–24.

Cameron, K.S., & Caza, A. (2002). Organizational and leadership virtues and the role of forgiveness. *Journal of Leadership & Organizational Studies, 9*(1), 33–48.

Caminiti, S. (2005a). The people company. *NYSE Magazine*. January/February, 12–16.

Caminiti, S. (2005b). The global company. *NYSE Magazine*, January/February, 17–22.

Carey, D., Patsalos-Fox, M., & Useem, M. (2009). Leadership lessons for hard times. *McKinsey Quarterly*, (4), 50.

Clark, M., Adjei, M., & Yancey, D. (2009). The impact of service fairness perceptions on relationship quality. *Services Marketing Quarterly, 30*(3), 287.

Collins, D. (2009). Kozlowski's Tyco—"I am the company." In A. Gini, & A.M. Marcoux (Eds.), *Cases studies on business ethics* (pp. 115–125). Upper Saddle River, NJ: Pearson.

Collins, J. (2001). Level 5 leadership: the triumph of humility and fierce resolve. *Harvard Business Review, 79*(1), 67–76.

Collins, J. (2009). *How the mighty fall: And why some companies never give in*. New York: Arrow.

Conner, J. (2000). Developing the global leaders of tomorrow. *Human Resource Management, 39*(2–3), 147–157.

Csikszentmihalyi, M. (2003). *Good business: Leadership, flow and the making of meaning*. New York: Viking.

Dennis, R.S., & Bocarnea, M. (2005). Development of the servant leadership assessment instrument. *Leadership & Organization Development Journal, 26*(7/8), 600–615.

Distefano, J. (1995). Tracing the vision and impact of Robert K. Greenleaf. In L. Spears (Ed.), *Reflections on leadership* (pp.61–78). New York: Wiley.

Earley, P.C., Murnieks, C., & Mosakowski, E. (2007). Cultural intelligence and the global mindset. In M. Javidan, R.M. Steers, M.A. Hitt (Eds.), *Advances in international management* Vol. 19 (pp.75–103). Stamford, CT: JAI Press.

ethicalinvesting.com. (2010). Terminator gene. Retrieved from www.ethicalinvesting.com/monsanto/terminator.shtml, accessed June 9, 2010.

Friedman, T.L. (2005). *The world is flat*. New York: Farrar, Straus and Giroux.

Fry, L.W. (2003). Toward a theory of spiritual leadership. *Leadership Quarterly, 14*, 693–727.

Fry, L.W. (2008). Spiritual leadership: State-of -the-art and future directions for theory, research, and practice. In J. Biberman, & L. Tishman (Eds.), *Spirituality in business: Theory, practice, and future directions* (pp. 106–124). New York: Palgrave.

Fry, L.W., & Matherly, L.L. (2007). Spiritual leadership and performance excellence. In S.G. Rogelberg (Ed.), *Encyclopedia of industrial/organizational psychology*. Thousand Oaks, CA: Sage.

Fry, L.W., & Slocum, J.W., Jr. (2008). Maximizing the triple bottom line through spiritual leadership. *Organizational Dynamics, 37*(1), 86–96.

Fry, L.W., Vitucci, S., & Cedillo, M. (2005). Spiritual leadership and army transformation: Theory, measurement, and establishing a baseline. *Leadership Quarterly, 16*, 835–862.

George, B. (2003). *Authentic leadership: Rediscovering the secrets to creating lasting value*. San Francisco: Jossey Bass.

George, B. (2009). *Seven lessons for leading in crisis*. San Francisco: Jossey Bass.

Ghoshal, S., & Moran, P. (2005). Towards a good theory of management. In J. Birkinshaw, & G. Piramal (Eds.), *Sumantra Ghoshal on management* (pp.1–27). London: FT/Prentice-Hall.

Goleman, D. (1998). What makes a leader? *Harvard Business Review, 76*(6), 93–102.

Grant, K. (2008). Imperfect people leading imperfect people: Creating environments of forgiveness. *Interbeing, 2*(2), 11–17.

Greenberg, J. (2001). Studying organizational justice cross-culturally: Fundamental challenges. *International Journal of Conflict Management, 12*(4), 365–375.

Gregersen, H.B., Morrison, A.J., & Black, J.S. (1998). Developing leaders for the global frontier. *Sloan Management Review, 40*(1), 21–32.

Griffith, D.A., Harvey, M.G., & Lusch, R.F. (2006). Social exchange in supply chain relationships: The resulting benefits of procedural and distributive justice. *Journal of Operations Management, 24*(2), 85–98.

Gupta, A.K., & Govindarajan, V. (2002). Cultivating a global mindset. *Academy of Management Executive, 16*(1), 116–126.

Hansen, M.T., Ibarra, H., & Peyer, U. (2010). The best-performing CEOs in the world. *Harvard Business Review, 88*(1), 104–113.

Harvey, M., & Novicevic, M.M. (2004). The development of political skill and political capital by global leaders through global assignments. *International Journal of Human Resource Management, 15*(7), 1173–1188.

Hernandez, M. (2008). Promoting stewardship behavior in organizations: A leadership model. *Journal of Business Ethics, 80*(1), 121–128.

Hitt, M.A., Javidan, M., & Steers, R.M. (2007). The global mindset: A review and proposed extensions. In M. Javidan, R.M. Steers, & M.A. Hitt (Eds.), *Advances in international management* Vol. 19 (pp.11–47). Stamford, CT: JAI Press.

Hornibrook, S., Fearne, A., & Lazzarin, M. (2009). Exploring the association between fairness and organisational outcomes in supply chain relationships. *International Journal of Retail & Distribution Management, 37*(9), 790–803.

Jackson, W.A. (1999). Dualism, duality and the complexity of economic institutions. *International Journal of Social Economics, 26*(4), 545–558.

Jassawalla, A.R., Asgary, N., & Sashittal, H.C. (2006). Managing expatriates: The role of mentors. *International Journal of Commerce and Management, 16*(2), 130–140.

Javidan, M., Dorfman, P.W., Sully de Luque, M., & House, R.J. (2006). In the eye of the beholder: Cross cultural lessons in leadership from project GLOBE. *Academy of Management Perspectives, 20*, 67–90.

Kaku, R. (1997). The path of Kyosei. *Harvard Business Review, 75*(4), 55–63.

Kellerman, B. (2004). *Bad leadership*. Boston: Harvard Business School Press.

Kets de Vries, M.F.R. (2001). The anarchist within: Clinical reflections on Russian character and leadership style. *Human Relations, 54*(5), 585–627.

Kets de Vries, M.F.R., & Mead, C. (1992). The development of the global leader within the multinational corporation. In V. Pucik, N.M. Tichy, & C. K. Bartlett (Eds.), *Globalizing management: Creating and leading the competitive organization* (pp. 187–205). New York: John Wiley & Sons.

Kim, W.C., & Mauborgne, R.A. (1993). Procedural justice, attitudes, and subsidiary top management compliance with multinationals' corporate strategic decisions. *Academy of Management Journal, 36*(3), 502–526.

Kim, W.C., & Mauborgne, R.A. (1996). Procedural justice and managers' in-role and extra-role behavior: The case of the multinational. *Management Science, 42*(4), 499–515.

Lane, H.W., Maznevski, M.L., & Mendenhall, M.E. (2004). Globalization: Hercules meets Buddha. In H.W. Lane, M.L. Maznevski, M.E. Mendenhall, & J. McNett (Eds.), *The Blackwell handbook of global management* (pp. 3–25). London: Blackwell.

Law, K., Wong, C.-S., & Wang, K.D. (2004). An empirical test of the model on managing the localization of human resources in the People's Republic of China. *International Journal of Human Resource Management, 15*(4/5), 635–648.

Lee, H.W. (2007). Factors that influence expatriate failure: An interview study. *International Journal of Management, 24*(3), 403–413.

Lee, H.W., & Liu, C.H. (2006). Determinants of the adjustment of expatriate managers to foreign countries: An empirical study. *International Journal of Management, 23*(2), 302–311.

Liden, R., Wayne, S., Zhao, H., & Henderson, D. (2008). Servant leadership: Development of a multidimensional measure and multi-level assessment. *Leadership Quarterly, 19*(2), 161–177.

Luo, Y. (2007). An integrated anti-opportunism system in international exchange. *Journal of International Business Studies, 38*(6), 855–877.

Luo, Y. (2008). Procedural fairness and interfirm cooperation in strategic alliances. *Strategic Management Journal, 29*(1), 27–46.

Malone, M.S. (2007). *Bill & Dave: How Hewlett and Packard built the worlds' greatest company*. New York: Portfolio.

McCall, M., & Hollenbeck, G. (2002). *Developing global executives: The lessons of international experience*. Boston: Harvard Business School Press.

Mendenhall, M.E. (2006). The elusive, yet critical challenge of developing global leaders. *European Management Journal, 24*(6), 422–429.

Mendenhall, M., & Osland. J.S. (2002, June). *An overview of the extant global leadership research*. Symposium presentation, Academy of International Business, Puerto Rico.

Mendenhall, M.E., Jensen, R.J., Black, J.S., & Gregersen, H.B. (2003). Seeing the elephant: Human resource management challenges in the age of globalization. *Organizational Dynamics, 32*(3), 261–274.

Mezias, J.M., & Scandura, T.A. (2005). A needs-driven approach to expatriate adjustment and career development: A multiple mentoring perspective. *Journal of International Business Studies, 36*(5), 519–538.

Millikin, J.P., & Fu, D. (2005). The global leadership of Carlos Ghosn at Nissan. *Thunderbird International Business Review, 47*(1), 121–137.

Mintzberg, H. (1971). Managerial work: Analysis from observation. *Management Science 18*(2), B97–B110.

Moran, R.T., & Riesenberger, J.R. (1994). *The global challenge: Building the new worldwide enterprise*. London: McGraw-Hill.

Morris, M., & Leung, K. (2000). Justice for all? Progress in research on cultural variation in the psychology of distributive and procedural justice. *Applied Psychology: An International Review, 49*(1), 100–132.

Morrison, A.J. (2000). Developing a global leadership model. *Human Resource Management, 39*(2–3), 117–131.

Morrison, A. (2001). Integrity and global leadership. *Journal of Business Ethics, 31*(1), 65–76.

Murphy-Berman, V., Berman, J.J., Singh, P., Pachauri, A., & Kumar, P. (1984). Factors affecting allocation to needy and meritorious recipients: A cross-cultural comparison. *Journal of Personality and Social Psychology, 46*, 1267–1272.

Nardon, L., & Steers, R.M. (2007). Learning cultures on the fly. In M. Javidan, R.M. Steers, & M.A. Hitt (Eds.), *Advances in international management* Vol. 19 (pp. 171–189). Stamford, CT: JAI Press.

Ng, K., Van Dyne, L., & Ang, S. (2009). From experience to experiential learning: Cultural intelligence as a learning capability for global leader development. *Academy of Management Learning & Education, 8*(4), 511–526.

Osland, J.S., Bird, A., Mendenhall, M., & Osland, A. (2006). Developing global leadership capabilities and global mindset: A review. In K. Stahl, & I. Bjorkman (Eds.), *Handbook of research in international human resource management* (pp. 197–222). Cheltenham: Edward Elgar.

Otazo, K.L. (1999). Global leadership: The inside story. In W.H. Mobley, M.J. Gessner, & V. Arnold (Eds.), *Advances in global leadership* Vol. 1 (pp. 317–335). Stamford, CT: JAI Press.

Paul, H. (2000). Creating a global mindset. *Thunderbird International Business Review, 42*(2), 187–200.

Peterson, C., & Seligman, M.E. P (2004). *Character strengths and virtues: A handbook and classification*. Washington: American Psychological Association and Oxford University Press.

Powley, E.H., & Taylor, S.N. (2006). Values and leadership in organizational crisis. In E.D. Hess, & K.S. Cameron (Eds.), *Leading values: Positivity, virtue, and high performance* (pp. 194–212). Cambridge: Cambridge University Press.

Ragins, B.R., & Cotton, J.L. (1999). Mentor functions and outcomes: A comparison of men and women in formal and informal mentoring relationships. *Journal of Applied Psychology, 84*(4), 529–550.

Riggio, R.E., & Reichard, R.J. (2008). The emotional and social intelligences of effective leadership: An emotional and social skill approach. *Journal of Managerial Psychology, 23*(2), 169–185.

Sanders, J.E., III, Hopkins, W.E., & Geroy, G.D. (2003). From transactional to transcendental: Toward and integrated theory of leadership. *Journal of Leadership and Organizational Studies, 9*(4), 21–31.

Selmer, J. (2003). Staff localization and organizational characteristics: Western business operations in China. *Asia Pacific Business Review, 10*(1), 43–57.

Selmer, J. (2004). Expatriates' hesitation and the localization of western business operations in China. *International Journal of Human Resource Management, 15*(6), 1094–1107.

Spreitzer, G.M., McCall, M.W., Jr., & Mahoney, J.D. (1997). The early identification of international executives. *Journal of Applied Psychology, 82*, 6–29.

Stone, R.J. (2002). *Human resource management* (4th ed.). Melbourne, Australia: John Wiley.

Suutari, V. (2002). Global leader development: An emerging research agenda. *Career Development International, 7*(4), 218–233.

Treasurer, B. (2009). Courageous leadership: Modeling the way. *Leader to Leader, 52*, 13–17.

Vera, D., & Rodriguez-Lopez, A. (2004). Strategic virtues: Humility as a source of competitive advantage. *Organizational Dynamics, 33*(4), 393–406.

Viswesvaran, C., & Ones, D.S. (2002). Examining the construct of organizational justice: A meta-analytic evaluation of relations with work attitudes and behaviors. *Journal of Business Ethics, 38*(3), 193–203.

Waddock, S., & Smith, N. (2000). Relationships: The real challenge of corporate global citizenship. *Business and Society Review, 105*(1), 47–62.

Wright, P.C., Szeto, W.F., & Lee, S.K. (2003). Ethical perceptions in China: The reality of business ethics in an international context. *Management Decision, 41*(1/2), 180–189.

Wright, T., & Goodstein, J. (2007). Character is not "dead" in management research: A review of individual character and organizational-level virtue. *Journal of Management, 33*(6), 928–958.

PART 4

Positive Relationships

High-quality Connections

John Paul Stephens, Emily Heaphy, *and* Jane E. Dutton

Abstract

High-quality connections (HQCs) are short-term, dyadic interactions that are positive in terms of the subjective experience of the connected individuals and the structural features of the connection. Although previous research has shown that HQCs are associated with individual and organizational outcomes, we advance theory by identifying cognitive, emotional, and behavioral mechanisms and aspects of the context that build and strengthen HQCs in organizations. We discuss the implications of uncovering these mechanisms for understanding processes such as relational formation and relational resilience, relational theories such as exchange theory, organizational moderators for these mechanisms, and the implications for individual agency. We close the chapter with suggestions for selecting methods and research designs that will enhance our understanding of the development and impact of HQCs at work.

Keywords: Connections, relationships, mechanisms, cognition, emotion, behavior, organizational context

Our chapter explores the theory and research behind the building of high-quality connections (HQCs) at work. *High-quality connections* is the term we use to designate short-term, dyadic, positive interactions at work. The positivity of HQCs is known by how they feel for both persons involved, what HQCs do, and the beneficial outcomes they produce. The feeling of an HQC can be experienced as the uplift felt when encountering someone who expresses genuine concern for how you are doing after a grueling meeting or work shift. The way in which HQCs function can be understood through how you think more clearly and act more competently after a particular conversation with a colleague before entering a meeting. A focus on these kinds of quality connections is part of a broader interest in understanding the foundations and impacts of positive interrelating at work (Dutton & Ragins, 2007), which include individual and collective flourishing and thriving (Dutton & Glynn, 2008; Ryff & Singer, 2000).

We begin our chapter by reviewing the definition, assumptions, and theoretical motivation behind

focusing on HQCs. We then move to laying the groundwork for a research review through a discussion of the cognitive, emotional, and behavioral mechanisms that explain how HQCs are formed, and illustrate how features of the organizational context shape how these causal mechanisms work. Considering these causal mechanisms leads to suggestions for future research and a discussion of methods that can help us better understand connections in work organizations.

Foundations of High-quality Connections Research

Building on previous research (Dutton & Heaphy, 2003), we define work connections as the dynamic, living tissue (Berscheid & Lopes, 1997) that exists between two people at work when some interaction occurs that involves mutual awareness. Connections direct researchers' attention to the experience of discrete interactions that transpire on a single occasion or within the context of an ongoing relationship between two people (e.g., a conversation, hallway interaction, or apology). Although relationships refer to an enduring association between two persons (Reis, 2001), our definition of connections does not assume that the two people have a prior history or ongoing bond. Instead, exploring connections involves a focus on the micro-bits of interrelating at work that can contribute to a relationship over time, but are important in and of themselves.

Our assertion that connections are worthy of greater theoretical attention rests on four assumptions. First, we assume that humans are intrinsically social and have a need to belong (Baumeister & Leary, 1995; Maslow, 1968), thus making connections an important aspect of people's social experience in organizations. Second, we assume that connections are dynamic and change as individuals alter how they are feeling, thinking, and behaving while interrelating with another person (Gable & La Guardia, 2007; Reis, 2007). Third, the work of organizations is performed through social processes, and connections are key elements for understanding how work is accomplished. Fourth, we assume that connections vary in quality. Differences in quality reflect variance in how healthy and well-functioning the living tissue (in this case, the dyadic connection) is at a particular point in time.

We are particularly interested in two clusters of connection-quality indicators (Dutton & Heaphy, 2003). One cluster focuses on the positivity of the subjective and emotional experience of each individual in the connection. The second taps structural features of the connection that enhance the potentiality and responsiveness of the connection.

Connection quality is marked by three subjective experiences. First, connection quality is sensed by the feelings of vitality in connection. People in an HQC are more likely to feel positive arousal and a heightened sense of positive energy (Quinn & Dutton, 2005). Second, the quality of a connection is also felt through a sense of positive regard (Rogers, 1951). Being regarded positively denotes a sense of feeling known and loved, or of being respected and cared for in the connection. Finally, the subjective experience of a connection's quality is marked by the degree of felt mutuality. Mutuality captures the feeling of potential movement in the connection, born out of mutual vulnerability and responsiveness as both people experience full participation and engagement in the connection at the moment (Miller & Stiver, 1997). These three subjective markers help to explain why HQCs are experienced as attractive and pleasant, but also as life-giving. Literally and figuratively, one senses life or being

more alive in these kinds of human-to-human connections.

High-quality connections are also defined in terms of three structural features. These three features capture the structural capacity of the connection. First, a higher connection quality implies greater emotional carrying capacity, which is evidenced by the expression of more emotion, both positive and negative, when in the connection. The tensility of the connection captures the connection's capacity to bend and withstand strain and to function in a variety of circumstances. It is the feature of the connection that indicates its resilience or its capacity to bounce back after setbacks. The third characteristic of a connection's quality is its connectivity. Connectivity describes a connection's level of openness to new ideas and influences. The three structural features help specify why connections of higher quality between two people foster beneficial outcomes.

Our conception of positive connection quality originates in relational theory, with its focus on the human growth and development that can occur while in connection with—rather than separation from—others (Miller, 1976; Miller & Stiver, 1997). On the other hand, relational concepts important to organizational research, such as trust and social support, are based in exchange theory, which emphasizes the instrumental exchange of resources between people (e.g., Blau, 1964; Homans, 1974; Thibaut & Kelley, 1959). Trust, for example, is defined in terms of how one expects another to act (Holmes & Rempel, 1989; McAllister, 1995). Similarly, social support describes the amount and content of care and aid exchanged between people at work, and how these resources buffer negativity (Uchino, 2004). Although these relational phenomena can be positive (or at least lead to positive outcomes), we believe that taking a different theoretical starting point broadens our understanding of relational phenomena in two ways. First, our theorizing about HQCs emphasizes the positive, mutually developmental experience of being in a connection, rather than the exchanges of resources and rewards. Second, by attending to the structural qualities of connection quality, we highlight how HQCs are associated with capacities that affect individual and dyadic performance, helping to explain why HQCs are associated with positive outcomes.

Why Do They Matter Theoretically? Impacts of High-quality Connections

Since HQCs are shorter-term moments within ongoing relationships or encounters between strangers, the traces of their impact have received less research attention compared to ongoing relationships. Meta-analyses of the impact of relationships at work on a variety of outcomes suggest HQCs should be impactful (e.g., Chiaburu & Harrison, 2008), and we briefly summarize other pieces of evidence that point to their value.

Evidence suggests that HQCs improve individual functioning through affecting cognitive, physiological, and behavioral processes. For example, experimental studies suggest that small amounts of interaction with others can improve both persons' cognitive performance in terms of speed of processing and working memory performance (Ybarra et al., 2008). Furthermore, in their review of medical evidence, Heaphy and Dutton (2008) show how brief interactions at work can have salutary effects on individuals through affecting the cardiovascular, neuroendocrine, and immune systems. Research also suggests that HQCs facilitate individual employees' recovery and adaptation when they are suffering from loss or illness (e.g., Lilius, Worline, Maitlis, Kanov, Dutton, & Frost, 2008), undergoing transitions in their careers or jobs (e.g., Ibarra, 2003) or need task-related help (Venkataramani & Dalal, 2007). High-quality connections are important means by which individuals develop and grow (Ragins & Verbos, 2007), enhance and enrich identities (Roberts, 2007), and form attachments to work organizations or to communities (e.g., Blatt & Camden, 2007). They can also create moments of learning and mutual inquiry in contexts as varied as negotiations (Kolb & Williams, 2003; Putnam, 2004) and organizational change (Creed & Scully, 2000; Meyerson, 2001).

At a more collective level, there is also evidence that HQCs can have beneficial effects. For example, HQCs among members of organizational units are associated with greater levels of psychological safety and trust. Higher levels of psychological safety, in turn, contribute to greater unit-level learning from failures (Carmeli, Brueller, & Dutton, 2009; Carmeli & Gittell, 2009). Higher levels of interpersonal trust can spawn spirals of increasing cooperation and trustworthiness (Ferrin, Bligh, & Kohles, 2008). Finally, HQCs are also associated with improving organizational processes such as coordination (e.g., Gittell, 2003) and error detection (e.g., Vogus, 2004).

Given the evidence for the value of HQCs to individual and organizational functioning, it is important to understand how such connections are built and strengthened. We use the terms "building" and "strengthening" to refer to the initiation of an HQC and the movement toward a connection of greater quality, respectively. We aim to further theory development by proposing mechanisms that help to build HQCs, rather than replicate research linking HQCs to positive outcomes (e.g., Carmeli, 2009; Carmeli, Brueller, & Dutton, 2009). In an effort to make our theory more flexible and precise (Elster, 1998; Stinchcombe, 1991), we explain how cognitive, emotional, behavioral, and organizational mechanisms build and strengthen HQC connections. For the most part, these are "action formation" mechanisms, in which one micro-component (e.g., cognition, emotion, or behavior) influences another (Hedstrom & Swedberg, 1998). Yet, since these connections are described within the work context, we also outline how this context shapes our action formation mechanisms.

By opening up the "black box" of how HQCs are built, we hope to provide a stronger foothold for scholars interested in developing and testing theory about how to build and strengthen the connections that aid individual (Bradbury & Lichtenstein, 2000) and collective functioning in organizations (e.g., Hargadon & Bechky, 2006; Quinn & Dutton, 2005). For example, these mechanisms can help us understand key relational processes, including relational initiation and resilience, and deepen our understanding of relational theories such as exchange theory. Our discussion of the cognitive, emotional, and behavioral mechanisms behind connection quality uncovers the myriad ways in which individuals can shape interactions more positively. Finally, describing how the connection building process is further shaped by the organizational context presents potentially significant contingencies for how we are to understand the role of these mechanisms. Substantial contributions to both scholarship and practice can thus be gained by our exploration of how cognition, emotions, behavior, and organizational context spur and strengthen HQCs.

Explaining High-quality Connections: Three Sets of Mechanisms

We focus on three major categories of contributors—cognitive, emotional, and behavioral—because they are basic social-psychological pathways through which HQCs at work are built and strengthened. Cognitive mechanisms highlight how conscious and unconscious thought processes predispose people to building HQCs. Emotional mechanisms point out how feelings open people up to connection and are shared between people in ways that build HQCs. Finally, behavioral mechanisms showcase the role of different kinds of moves (Goffman, 1959) and

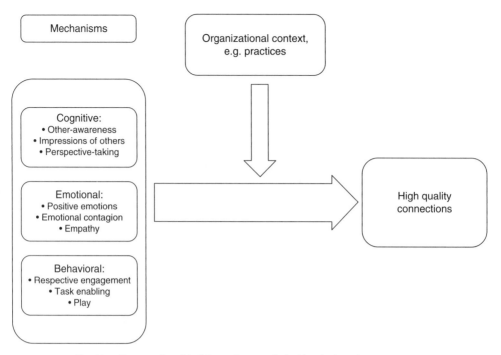

Fig. 29.1 Conceptual model of the mechanisms for building high-quality connections.

modes of interrelating that explain the quality of connection that two people form. By surveying key examples of each kind of mechanism, we aim to seed future research, rather than provide an exhaustive account of mechanisms leading to HQCs. Our overall conceptual model is summarized in Figure 29.1.

Cognitive Mechanisms

Individuals' cognitions are key building blocks for connections because the mental processing of information about others shapes people's orientation toward forming connections with others. Although cognitions ultimately inform actions (Gibson, 1979), we outline how mental processes, such as other-awareness, impression-formation, and perspective-taking, matter in the formation of HQCs.

OTHER-AWARENESS

A primary mechanism for establishing connection is being aware of another person's presence and behaviors, and recognizing that the other is a salient aspect of the environment (Davis & Holtgraves, 1984). As a basic human cognitive ability, other-awareness refers to the capacity to distinguish between the behavior, cognitions, and emotions of the self and that of others (Asendorpf & Baudonniere, 1993; Asendorpf, Warkentin, & Baudonniere, 1996). Other-awareness is necessary for accurately recalling the characteristics and behaviors that identify particular others

(Overbeck & Park, 2001). Being aware of others (viz. supervisors) at work has also been linked with intentions to stay at a particular job (Gardner, Dunham, Cummings, & Pierce, 1987), further suggesting that some sort of focus on others fosters an orientation toward connecting and a willingness to maintain current connections. Other-awareness involves being aware of what others are doing, and this is especially important for providing some context for one's own actions. For example, in a study of students in short-term, geographically distributed groups, other-awareness was displayed in requests for and the provision of information about what group members were doing or would do (Weisband, 2002). Even through e-mail, groups with members that were more aware of each other were able to better coordinate their actions, suggesting that other-awareness fostered the formation of higher-quality connections.

IMPRESSIONS OF OTHERS

Although being aware of others, who they are, and what they do fosters interrelating in a more mutual and other-regarding way, the quick impressions we form about others can also shape how connections develop. People can make rapid judgments of whether particular others are accepting, supportive, and warm, based on observing "thin slices" (less than 5 minutes) of their nonverbal behaviors, such as gestures and facial expressions (Ambady, Bernieri, & Richeson, 2000; Ambady & Rosenthal, 1993). These initial impressions of warmth and acceptance attract individuals to each other, shaping the choice of who to connect with and thereby increasing the chances of selecting someone who is able and willing to be mutually engaged.

Sensing who might be warm and accepting can aid both connection-building and strengthening. For example, for any new employee trying to get "on board" with her organization, gauging who will most likely be accepting and open to connection helps to determine who she initially approaches for information and help (Rollag, Parise, & Cross, 2005). These judgments can potentially help one select someone to connect with who will be most likely to provide positive regard, and thus be a good bet for a HQC. At the same time, these impressions can also inform how connections are undertaken within the context of longer-term relationships. Perceptions of how warm or supportive someone is based on his or her current posture and facial expression can guide the decision to interact with that person at that time (cf. Elfenbein, 2007). For example, perceiving that someone is anxious and unable to provide support could either limit requesting help from them, which might further add to their frustration, or motivate providing support to them. On the other hand, sensing that the person is accepting and able to offer support could allow for a timely request for care and support (see Baron & Boudreau, 1987).

PERSPECTIVE-TAKING

Although employees form impressions about someone's disposition based on brief glimpses of their behavior, they also imagine themselves in another person's shoes, which is called perspective-taking. Perspective-taking goes beyond other-awareness in not only recognizing another's distinct behavior and internal state, but also in mentally representing the other's experience as one's own (Epley, Keysar, Van Boven, & Gilovich, 2004; Galinsky, Ku, & Wang, 2005). Perspective-taking has been conceptualized as the cognitive component of empathy, which, in combination with empathy's affective component, motivates altruistic behavior and helping (Batson, Dyck, Brandt, Batson, Powell, McMaster, & Griffitt, 1988; Batson, Early, & Salvarani, 1997). Perspective-taking facilitates predicting another person's behavior and reactions (Davis, 1983) and the shaping of one's own behaviors in ways that demonstrate care and concern, and that can facilitate a positive response from the other. In one work example, being more adept at perspective-taking would have helped a consultant anticipate how developing changes to a project without involving his client could have threatened the client's sense of competency and made him angry (Williams, 2007). Being predisposed to imagine how the client might feel might have led the consultant to present his suggestions in ways that affirmed the client's abilities and invited further improvement, ultimately building the connection.

This description of the role of cognitive mechanisms in building HQCs reveals two key points. First, certain cognitions can predispose people to be more or less open to connect with others at work, as is the case with other-awareness and perspective-taking. Second, only small pieces of information are needed for cognition to shape organizational members' sensitivity to whether others are open to connection. In the following section, we build on these points by describing how emotions strengthen and build HQCs by altering individuals' orientations toward others and opening up and inviting in further interaction.

Emotional Mechanisms

Emotions are part of people's everyday experience in organizations (Fineman, 1993), and they help us know we are in connection with others (Sandelands & Boudens, 2000). Some psychologists argue that emotions help people navigate relationally by facilitating both their responses to problems they confront in their social worlds and the maintenance of social order (Keltner & Haidt, 1999; Morris & Keltner, 2000). We focus on three areas of emotions research useful for understanding how emotions explain the building of HQCs. Research on positive emotions, emotional contagion, and empathy provides theoretical accounts for how emotions travel between people, building and strengthening connections in the process.

POSITIVE EMOTIONS

Fredrickson's (1998, 2001) research on positive emotions has built evidence to support her hypothesis that positive emotions broaden our thinking and help build durable, social resources. This broadening and building includes the development of greater relationship closeness (self–other overlap) in new relationships (Waugh & Fredrickson, 2006) and the perception of intergroup similarity (Johnson & Fredrickson, 2005).

Positive emotions vary in their relationship consequences, and one such emotion, gratitude, may be particularly relevant for building HQCs. Gratitude, or thankfulness, occurs when an individual perceives that someone intentionally provides something valuable to another (e.g., Emmons & Shelton, 2001; Fredrickson, 2004). Feeling grateful toward others boosts attention to the positive qualities of the benefactor and the motivation to relate to the benefactor (Algoe & Haidt, 2009). There is also evidence that gratitude has both immediate and enduring effects for both members of a dyad. When one person experiences gratitude, both members of a dyad experience greater connection over time (Algoe, Gable, & Maisel, in press; Algoe, Haidt, & Gable, 2008). In an example from a product innovation firm, when design team members enthusiastically demonstrated gratitude for each other's contributions in brainstorming sessions, this thankfulness, and the connection itself, was reinforced by inviting those particular team members to future meetings (Hargadon & Bechky, 2006).

EMOTIONAL CONTAGION

Emotional contagion refers to the family of phenomena that describes the interpersonal influence of emotions (Elfenbein, 2007), or more specifically, how a person or group unwittingly or explicitly influences the emotions and attitudes of another person or group (Schoenewolf, 1990). Through emotional contagion, individuals can share similar emotional experiences as they unconsciously mimic each other's facial expressions, movements, and vocalizations (Hatfield, Cacioppo, & Rapson, 1992). This increased mimicry, in turn, has been linked to greater liking and rapport (Chartrand & Bargh, 1999; Lakin, Jefferis, Cheng, & Chartrand, 2003).

Emotional contagion can also occur through the conscious management of emotional displays through surface or deep acting, which may or may not be concordant with their underlying emotional experience (Grandey, 2000; Hochschild, 1983). These emotional displays influence how positive emotions travel between people. Researchers have studied these emotional displays in boundary spanning positions, such as customer service, and find that emotions do travel between employee and customer (Pugh, 2001). This contagion positively affects the quality of the connection, as rated by peers or customers, when the emotional display is viewed as authentic (Grandey, 2003; Grandey, Fisk, Mattila, Jansen, & Sideman, 2005; Hennig-Thurau, Groth, Paul, & Gremler, 2006).

EMPATHY

Empathy occurs when a person vicariously experiences another's emotion (Mehrabian & Epstein, 1972).

Empathy is viewed as the basis of human connection (Miller & Stiver, 1997). When people feel empathy for another, they experience warmth, compassion, and concern for the other, which, in turn, motivates altruistic (Batson, Duncan, Ackerman, Buckley, & Birch, 1981; Davis, 1983) and prosocial behavior (Brief & Motowidlo, 1986), which are markers of higher-quality relationships (Reis & Collins, 2000). In one example, McNeely and Meglino (1994) found in a study of secretaries that self-reported empathy was correlated with higher levels of prosocial behaviors toward others.

Empathy can also be skillfully enacted to facilitate quality connecting. Therapists such as Carl Rogers (1951) and Jean Baker Miller (Miller & Stiver, 1997) view empathy as an essential component in creating a relationship that can engender a feeling of interpersonal support and promote growth and change. Empathy is also considered a core part of emotional (Salovey & Mayer, 1990) as well as social intelligence (Goleman, 2006). Studies have found, for example, that when one is skilled at understanding another's emotions, the other person reports greater liking (Mueller & Curhan, 2006). In caregiving organizations, service providers are trained to provide an experience of empathy to their clients (Kahn, 1992), while managers in all types of organizations express empathy for their colleagues and employees (Frost, 2003). Through the skillful use of empathy, HQCs can be built and strengthened.

In sum, emotions powerfully influence how people at work connect with others in a range of ways, from the unconscious nonverbal communication of emotional contagion, to the felt experience of empathy. In addition, positive emotions promote more openness toward others. Emotion-based mechanisms highlight how emotions coordinate the mind, body, and feelings, orienting individuals toward others, and simultaneously inviting others to engage, build, and strengthen HQCs. We now turn to perhaps the most observable of the three mechanisms, the behaviors that bring us together.

Behavioral Mechanisms

Behaviors are observable elements of interpersonal communication and are critical means for the building of HQCs in the workplace. Research suggests that demonstrating respect, task enabling, and playing each facilitate the building of HQCs.

RESPECTFUL ENGAGEMENT

Respectful behaviors are defined by how they show esteem, dignity, and care for another person (e.g., Ramarajan, Barsade, & Burak, 2008). Research on civility (and incivility, e.g., Cortina, Magley, Williams, & Langhout, 2000; Pearson & Porath, 2009), dignity (e.g., Hodson, 2001), and respect (e.g., Lawrence-Lightfoot, 2000) suggest that everyday behaviors and small moves communicate how one person values another. Research in the traditions of symbolic interactionism (Cooley, 1902; Goffman, 1967; Mead, 1934) and ethnomethodology (Garfinkel, 1967) describes how gestures, talk, and bodily postures convey and are interpreted as respect. Since the provision and interpretation of communicative behaviors occur through interaction (Sennet, 2003), when these behaviors demonstrate the basic human entitlements of respect and dignity (Rawls, 1971), they foster peoples' chances of experiencing an HQC.

We see the link between respectful engagement with others and HQCs in several research domains. First, psychological presence or being engaged with others displays respect and encourages continued interaction (Kahn, 1992). When presence is lacking, such as when communication modes like electronic mail limit access to nontextual cues or when multitasking limits attention to the other, connection suffers (Hallowell, 1999). Second, actions that communicate affirmation and reflect respect and worth can potentially enable connections and make interactions quite meaningful. This was the case for hospital cleaners who felt respected by how they were spoken to by patients; these cleaners derived meaning and satisfaction from such interactions (e.g., Wrzesniewski & Dutton, 2001). Third, respect is important for the connections involved in recruitment and selection, in which information is exchanged between those inside and outside of an organization. In a video analysis of interview conversations, LeBaron, Glenn, and Thompson (2009) detail how micro-behaviors convey respect in interaction, which in turn shapes the possibility of the interviews' outcomes. Fourth, expressions of gratitude or thanks also affirm a recipient's worth and value. In turn, this affirmation fosters a motivation to help others, and thus increases connection quality (Grant & Gino, 2010).

TASK ENABLING

A second form of behavior important for HQCs is task enabling, or interpersonal actions that help someone complete or perform a task (Dutton, 2003b). Research on interpersonal helping (e.g., Lee, 1997), interpersonal citizenship (e.g., Podsakoff, MacKenzie, Paine, & Bachrach, 2000; Williams &

Anderson, 1991), and prosocial motivation (e.g., Penner, 2002) all suggest that the interpersonal provision of information, emotional support, and other resources can cultivate perspective-taking and gratitude, which fosters connection quality. Researchers tend to examine how the quality of a relationship enables helping (e.g., Settoon & Mossholder, 2002), and not the reverse. However, the role of reciprocity would suggest that acting generously toward another would encourage the same in return (Gouldner, 1960), engendering the mutuality, vitality, and positive regard that define an HQC. Receiving help in a way that ensures fairness, dignity, and respect elicits positive responses from recipients, such as increased commitment to the overall relationship (e.g., Flynn & Brockner, 2003). In turn, if recipients feel that help is being provided for some instrumental purpose, they are less likely to experience an HQC (Ames, Flynn, & Weber, 2004).

PLAY

A third form of interaction conducive to building HQCs is play. Play is a distinctly human capacity that develops over a person's lifetime (Huizinga, 1950), and it is seen by some as a direct expression of human community (Sandelands, 2010). Specifically, playful activities provide goods internal to the activities (e.g., skills and pleasures that are only available when participating in a playful activity; MacIntyre, 1981), are actively engaged in, contain social rules, are learned through participation, contain elements that are repeated, transcend the individual self, and involve risk (Stone, 1989). Accordingly, play enables connection at work in at least two important ways. First, play enables variation in response patterns during interaction, promoting learning about another that is less possible or likely in a work or nonplay mode. For example, in a community hospital billing department, employees developed extensive playing routines that involved squirt gun fights, elaborate play with a mascot, and routinized sunshine breaks. These instances of connection-as-play were useful for reducing stress, taking people outside their normal roles and behaviors, and thus allowing employees to see and know each other differently (Dutton, 2003a; Worline, Lilius, Dutton, Kanov, Maitlis, & Frost, 2009).

Second, as is the case with games, being fully engaged with others in the rules that set play apart from the "real world" can encourage more interpersonal risk taking, and a loss of self-consciousness (Czikszentmihalyi, 1975; Eisenberg, 1990). Through developing a concern for both self and other, and being fully present in the moment, people experience a sense of freedom and happiness. These positive feelings help open people up to connecting with others they may otherwise not know. For example, in a regional unit of the Make-A-Wish Foundation, playing is seen as an important means for cultivating connections among employees, as well as between employees and the clients they serve (Grant & Berg, 2009). Playfulness broke down hierarchy and a sense of bureaucracy, creating a different form of connection between employees used to being separated through formal roles and helping to develop rapport with donors, volunteers, and families who were being served (Make-A-Wish families).

These behavioral mechanisms all suggest that what we do and how we do it in our interactions with others at work are important for changing the possibilities for and means of connecting. The focus on respectful engagement, task enabling, and playing shows us that small moves matter for building connection and that modes of interacting can transform people's understandings of how they relate to others. Since this all occurs within the context of work, we now examine how features of the workplace would further modify these basic causal mechanisms.

The Role of the Organizational Context

The work context is likely to moderate how and to what degree these mechanisms influence connection quality (Mischel, 1977) as context alters the opportunities, forms, and meaning of connecting. Although many aspects of the organizational context are relevant for building connections, we focus on organizational practices, or the recurring bundles of behavior at work (Orlikowski, 2002) that enable or limit the opportunities or motivation to connect with others (Baker & Dutton, 2007; Feldman & Rafaeli, 2002; Fletcher, 1998). Practices can be both formal (e.g., human resource practices, such as selection and evaluation) and informal (e.g., turn-taking at meetings). We focus on practices of selection and communication in meetings that foster the HQC mechanisms outlined above. We illustrate these practices with examples from Menlo Innovations, a small software design firm in Ann Arbor, Michigan, that relies on pairs of programmers to develop computer code (DeGraff & Lawrence, 2002). By doing so we aim to demonstrate how the organizational context moderates how connection building processes are likely to work.

ORGANIZATIONAL PRACTICES AND COGNITIVE MECHANISMS

Practices have the potential to shape what people know about each other (Feldman & Rafaeli, 2002), and about the organization (Vogus & Welbourne, 2003). In the case of Menlo, the practice of "extreme interviewing" allows for the acquisition, sharing, and building of information between people. In this process for selecting new employees, 50 candidate programmers directly interact and work with the entire staff. This kind of interviewing allows potential hires to demonstrate skills like perspective-taking as they develop, correct, and share code with other interviewees and current staff. Through observing and reporting on the candidates, Menlo staff actually test out their initial perceptions and impressions of job candidates in the context of a participatory hiring process (Baker & Dutton, 2007). By selecting on demonstrated skills, Menlo increases the likelihood that employees will have perspective-taking capabilities that allow them to build HQCs, and also ensures that current staff involved in the selection process are more aware of new hires, their capabilities, and thus their potential for connection (see Prusak & Cohen, 2001).

ORGANIZATIONAL PRACTICES AND EMOTIONAL MECHANISMS

Menlo's use of daily stand-up meetings is a practice that allows employees to express needs, gratitude, and admiration for others in a public, group setting on a regular basis. Meetings matter, since they serve as arenas for situating others in their relative roles, and are where the various elements of the organization converge (Boden, 1994; Pomerantz & Denvir, 2007; Van de Ven, Delbecq, & Koenig, 1976). Every day, at approximately 10 a.m., the staff, programmers, and directors working in the Menlo office gather in a circle to each give a 20- to 60-second report on the status of their current project. Standing in a circle puts each person on an equal footing, thus decreasing status differences that can get in the way of building HQCs (Pratt & Rafaeli, 2002). These meetings give each individual the opportunity to express his or her concerns, advice, offers of assistance, and gratitude for help received. Such meetings allow people to collectively and publicly express the positive emotions of gratitude and admiration that affirm others' contributions, and foster higher-quality connections (see Dutton, 2003b).

ORGANIZATIONAL PRACTICES AND BEHAVIORAL MECHANISMS

Respectful communication is routinized through the practice of the stand-up meeting as well. The turn-taking that is enforced as part of these meetings allows for mutual and collective engagement as each individual or pair of programmers speaks out on their current needs (Schegloff, 2000). People only speak up when a Viking helmet (with two horns) is passed to them. This allows members of pairs to both signal that they "hold the floor" as a unit, delimiting who speaks when. These kinds of rituals for turn-taking can be very important for shaping interaction dynamics (Collins, 2004; Tannen, 2001). In this context, using the helmet also makes the meeting more playful; as in other contexts of play, people accept the common rules of passing around the helmet and using that to determine turn-taking. Although meetings allow for the development and dispersion of organizational knowledge (Hargadon & Sutton, 1997; Sutton & Hargadon, 1996), playful meetings help people know each other in different ways, and the fun invites a focus on the actual process of interrelating with others, and not just on the information being exchanged (Dougherty & Takacs, 2004). This play encourages people to open up even more about their struggles and successes, thus facilitating higher-quality connections.

Taken together, these intersections among the cognitive, emotional, and behavioral mechanisms and the practices of the organization provide an illustration of how social psychological mechanisms can be amplified (or diminished) through the conditions of the organizational context. Creating and sustaining HQCs at work are contingent upon the organizational context and how people engage that context—or possibly shape it in their own ways—to facilitate connection.

Future Directions

It is exciting to consider the insights revealed by the elaboration of mechanisms that help to explain how HQCs at work are built and strengthened. Using a mechanisms lens makes at least four contributions toward how we understand the role of generative micro-units of interrelating within dyads.

First, at a basic level, articulating the mechanisms underlying the building and strengthening of HQCs highlights the variety of internal and overt social psychological processes that contribute to quickly forming positive connections. The focus on connections, as opposed to relationships, emphasizes the importance of short interactions in work organizations. The elaboration of cognitive, emotional, and behavioral mechanisms further emphasizes the fast-acting causes of connecting dynamics in organizations. We live in a work world that relies increasingly on temporary collaborations (Faraj & Xiao, 2006; Lewin & Regine, 2000) and swift coordination

(Meyerson, Weick, & Kramer, 1996). Accordingly, individuals have to build HQCs quickly within and across organizational boundaries and understanding the "nuts and bolts, cogs and wheels" (Elster, 1989, p. 3) that help to explain the creation and strengthening of connection in work-based interactions is theoretically and practically useful.

Theoretically, the mechanisms-based approach to elaborating the causes of HQCs enriches theories of relational processes in organizations, such as relational formation and relational resilience. In the case of relational formation, the quality of mutual awareness in initial connections shapes how newcomers learn and are assimilated into organizations (e.g., Ashforth, Saks, & Lee, 1998; Louis, 1980; Morrison, 2002). Similarly, initial connection quality influences the development of longer-term relationships in the case of business relationships (Dwyer, Schurr, & Oh, 1987), negotiations (McGinn & Keros, 2002), and mentorship (Kram, 1988; Thomas, 1993), which are all critical relational formation domains. In the case of relational resilience, researchers studying how relationships change or adapt to setbacks can use our approach to advance theory on how the connective tissue of a relationship can be strengthened in the face of incivility (Pearson & Porath, 2009), trust violations (Pratt & Dirks, 2006), offences (Bright, Fry, & Cooperrider, 2006), or poor communication (cf. Gittell, 2002a, b). For example, perspective-taking might inform an offender in an uncivil situation that the other party feels wronged; coupled with practices set in place to address grievances, the offender can begin on the path of relational repair. In this way, our approach specifies new theoretical pathways and linkages.

Second, understanding the mechanisms of HQCs also enriches our understanding of how relationships impact people at work. For example, social exchange theory describes how people engage in relationships to exchange resources (Homans, 1974; Thibaut & Kelley, 1959). However, theories of social exchange say less about what social-psychological conditions encourage engagement in exchange relationships. Our mechanism-based approach suggests that engagement in relationships for valuable resources is facilitated by, for example, accurate other-awareness (who has what I need?), gratitude (to ensure continued exchange), and respect (demonstrating that the other is valuable). Thus, our mechanisms approach for HQCs enriches perspectives that explain how and why people in organizations engage in relationships based on exchange.

Our third contribution stems from attending to the organizational moderators arising from the organizational context in our account of the causes of HQCs. For our theory of HQC initiation and strengthening to be more flexible and precise, we have outlined how the presence of certain organizational practices is a contingency for the development of HQCs. Although we have focused on organizational practices as potential moderators of connecting mechanisms, many other important contextual features of organizations should be considered (e.g., Baker & Dutton, 2007; Rollag et al., 2005). Through a more complete articulation of contextual features, researchers are better able to see the organizational embedding of relational processes that begin with the building and strengthening of HQCs.

Fourth, and finally, a mechanisms approach exposes multiple avenues for organizational members to exercise agency in the building HQCs. Each of the mechanism clusters reveals different possible pathways for how people can proactively shape themselves and their work environment (Grant & Ashford, 2008) to foster the building of HQCs. Considering a cognitive route, for example, suggests that organizational members can shape connecting possibilities through actively judging the presence of qualities such as warmth, support, and acceptance in others. Using the emotions pathway, employees might intentionally cultivate a capacity for gratitude for the contributions of others to their success. From the behavioral pathway, individuals might experiment with different methods of playing with their work colleagues. Each option broadens the repertoire of possibilities for how individuals can actively participate in cultivating possibilities for HQCs at work for self and for others, by attending to the engines of connection-building identified in each of the mechanism discussions.

Despite these contributions, HQC research faces a number of challenges. First, although we have separated these mechanisms into discrete categories, they clearly interrelate in important ways. Future research should address how these mechanisms relate to one another. Second, as organizational researchers, it will be important to understand which mechanisms are particularly potent in specific kinds of organizational contexts, and in different forms of social relationships (e.g., those based on communal sharing, or gift exchange; Fiske, 1992). Third, more empirical work is needed to develop and validate measures of HQCs from the perspectives of both persons in a dyad, instead of from just one individual or an entire collective, although researchers have already demonstrated

the applicability of HQCs to the study of teams and units as a whole (Carmeli & Gittell, 2009; Carmeli et al., 2009). Finally, researchers of HQCs need to continue pushing the theoretical frontier on the full range of mechanisms, including further cognitive, emotional, and behavioral mechanisms, as well as additional types, such as motivational or physiological mechanisms, that explain HQC-building. This is important, as there is growing recognition of the potency and practical impact of these micro-bits of human-to-human interrelating at work.

Given these research limitations, it is important to use research methods designed to capture the core characteristics of HQCs, such as both individuals' subjective experiences and perceptions of the interaction, and their momentary as well as dynamic nature. Although Carmeli and his colleagues have developed measures of the quality of connections at the unit level, we need valid measures at the level of the dyad. This means considering a within-person approach that maps changes in each dyad member's thoughts, feeling, and behaviors over time (Gable & La Guardia, 2007). One method that might be particularly appropriate is daily diary or experience sampling (see Reis & Collins, 2000, for a review). In these approaches, dyad members synchronously complete multiple surveys over time, revealing how dyad members respond to each other, and how both intrapersonal and interpersonal associations among things like values, personality, behaviors, and the immediate context influence dyadic outcomes (e.g., Crocker & Canevello, 2008). A second approach involves the use of direct observation of interrelating (for reviews, see Gottman & Notarius, 2000; Reis & Collins, 2000). Analyzing detailed transcripts and video recordings of dyads in conversational analysis (e.g., Hopper, 1992; Schegloff & Sacks, 1973) and micro-ethnography (LeBaron, 2005) could reveal how verbal and nonverbal behavior situated in a particular context constitute a given interaction (see Goodwin, 2000; LeBaron, 2005; Streeck & Mehus, 2005). These methods reveal insights about the observable behaviors that are constructed between a pair of actors.

Conclusion

Methodological, theoretical, and practical implications are of concern to any scholar, and we hope that our framework is a useful starting point for those interested in digging deeper into how connections help individuals and organizations flourish. A complete picture of how connections are built and strengthened will be a hard-won accomplishment. However, with our initial sketch, our aim is that others will broaden and refine the picture of how people initiate and skillfully cultivate HQCs, and ultimately, positive relationships with others at work.

Authors' note: We wish to thank Gretchen Spreitzer, Avi Carmeli, Mary Ceccanese, Karen Dickinson and Kathy Kram for comments on earlier versions of the chapter.

References

Algoe, S.B., & Haidt, J.D. (2009). Witnessing excellence in action: The "other-praising" emotions of elevation, gratitude, and admiration. *Journal of Positive Psychology, 4*(2), 105–127.

Algoe, S.B., Gable, S.L., & Maisel, N. (in press). It's the little things: Everyday gratitude as a booster shot for romantic relationships. *Personal Relationships.*

Algoe, S.B., Haidt, J., & Gable, S.L. (2008). Beyond reciprocity: Gratitude and relationships in everyday life. *Emotion, 8*, 425–429.

Ambady, N., Bernieri, F.J., & Richeson, J.A. (2000). Toward a histology of social behavior: Judgmental accuracy from thin slices of the behavioral stream. In M.P. Zanna (Ed.), *Advances in experimental social psychology* Vol. 32 (pp. 201–271). San Diego: Academic Press.

Ambady N., & Rosenthal, R. (1993). Half a minute: Predicting teacher evaluations from thin slices of nonverbal behavior and physical attractiveness. *Journal of Personality and Social Psychology, 64*(3), 431–441.

Ames, D., Flynn, F.J., & Weber, E. (2004). It's the thought that counts: On perceiving how helpers decide to lend a hand. *Personality and Social Psychology Bulletin, 30*(4), 461–447.

Asendorpf, J.B., & Baudonniere, P.M. (1993). Self-awareness and other-awareness: Mirror self-recognition and synchronic imitation among unfamiliar peers. *Developmental Psychology, 29*(1), 88–95.

Asendorpf, J.B., Warkentin, V., & Baudonniere, P.M. (1996). Self-awareness and other-awareness II: Mirror self-recognition, social contingency awareness, and synchronic imitation. *Developmental Psychology, 32*(2), 313–321.

Ashforth, B.E., Saks, A.M., & Lee, R.T. (1998). Socialization and newcomer adjustment: The role of organizational context. *Human Relations, 51*, 897–926.

Baker, W.E., & Dutton, J.E. (2007). Enabling positive social capital in organizations. In J.E. Dutton, & B.R. Ragins (Eds.), *Exploring positive relationships at work* (pp. 325–246). Mahwah, NJ: Lawrence Erlbaum Associates.

Baron, R.B., & Boudreau, L.A. (1987). An ecological perspective on integrating personality and social psychology. *Journal of Personality and Social Psychology, 53*(6), 1222–1228.

Batson, C.D., Duncan, B.D., Ackerman, P., Buckley, T., & Birch, K. (1981). Is empathic emotion a source of altruistic motivation? *Journal of Personality and Social Psychology, 40*(2), 290–302.

Batson, C.D., Dyck, J.L., Brandt, J.R., Batson, J.G., Powell, A.L., McMaster, M.R., & Griffitt, C. (1988). Five studies testing two new egoistic alternatives to the empathy-altruism hypothesis. *Journal of Personality and Social Psychology, 5*(1), 52–77.

Batson, C.D., Early, S., & Salvarani, G. (1997). Perspective taking: Imagining how the other feels versus imagining how you would feel. *Personality and Social Psychology Bulletin, 23*(7), 751–758.

Baumeister, R.F., & Leary, M.R. (1995). The need to belong: Desire for interpersonal attachments as a fundamental human motivation. *Psychological Bulletin, 117*, 497–529.

Berscheid, E., & Lopes, J. (1997). A temporal model of relationship satisfaction and stability. In R.J. Sternberg, & M. Hojjat (Eds.), *Satisfaction in close relationships* (pp. 129–159). New York: Guilford Press.

Blatt, R., & Camden, C.T. (2007). Positive relationships and cultivating community. In J.E. Dutton, & B.R. Ragins (Eds.), *Exploring positive relationships at work: Building a theoretical and research foundation* (pp. 243–264). Mahwah, NJ: Lawrence Erlbaum.

Blau, P. (1964). *Exchange and power in social life.* New York: Wiley.

Boden, D. (1994). *The business of talk: Organizations in action.* Cambridge, MA: Polity.

Bradbury, H., & Lichtenstein, B.M. B. (2000). Relationality in organizational research: Exploring the space between. *Organization Science, 11*(5), 551–564.

Brief, A.P., & Motowidlo, S. (1986). Prosocial organizational behaviors. *Academy of Management Review, 11*, 710–725.

Bright, D.S., Fry, R.E., & Cooperrider, D.L. (2006). Forgiveness from the perspectives of three response modes: Begrudgement, pragmatism and transcendence. In C. Manz, K. Cameron, K. Manz, & B. Marx (Eds.), *The virtuous organization: Insights from some of the world's leading management thinkers.* Hackensack, NJ: World Scientific.

Carmeli, A. (2009). Positive work relationships, vitality, and job performance. In N. Ashkanasy, W. J. Zerbe, & C.E.J. Härtel (Eds.), *Research on emotion in organizations* Vol. 5 (pp. 45–71). Oxford: JAI Press.

Carmeli, A., Brueller, D., & Dutton, J.E. (2009). Learning behaviors in the workplace: The role of high quality interpersonal relationships and psychological safety. *Systems Research and Behavioral Science, 26*, 81–98.

Carmeli, A., & Gittell, J.H. (2009). High quality relationships, psychological safety, and learning from failures in work organizations. *Journal of Organizational Behavior, 30*, 709–729.

Chartrand, T.L., & Bargh, J.A. (1999). The chameleon effect: The perception-behavior link and social interaction. *Journal of Personality and Social Psychology, 76*, 893–910.

Chiaburu, D.S., & Harrison, D.A. (2008). Do peers make the place? Conceptual synthesis and meta-analysis of co-worker effects on perceptions, attitudes, OCBs and performance. *Journal of Applied Psychology, 93*(5), 1082–1103.

Collins, R. (2004). *Interaction ritual chains.* Princeton, NJ: Princeton University Press.

Cooley, C. (1902). *Human nature and social order.* New York: Charles Scribner's Sons.

Cortina, L.M., Magley, J.J., Williams, J.H., & Langhout, R.D. (2000). Incivility in the workplace: Incidence and impact. *Journal of Occupational Health Psychology, 6*, 64–80.

Creed, W.E.D., & Scully M. (2000). Songs of ourselves: Employees' deployment of social identity in everyday workplace encounters. *Journal of Management Inquiry, 9*(4), 391–412.

Crocker, J., & Canevello, A. (2008). Creating and undermining social support in communal relationships: The role of compassionate and self-image goals. *Journal of Personality and Social Psychology, 95*(3), 555–575.

Czikszentmihalyi, M. (1975). *Beyond boredom and anxiety.* San Francisco: Jossey-Bass.

Davis, M.H. (1983). Measuring individual differences in empathy: Evidence for a multidimensional approach. *Journal of Personality and Social Psychology, 44*(1), 113–126.

Davis, D., & Holtgraves, T. (1984). Perceptions of unresponsive others: Attributions, attraction, understandability and memory of their utterances. *Journal of Experimental Social Psychology, 20,* 383–408.

DeGraff, J., & Lawrence, K.A. (2002). *Creativity at work: Developing the right practices to make innovation happen.* San Francisco: Jossey-Bass.

Dougherty, D., & Takacs, C.H. (2004). Team play: Heedful interrelating as the boundary for innovation. *Long Range Planning, 37,* 569–590.

Dutton, J.E. (2003a). Breathing life into organizational studies. *Journal of Management Inquiry, 12,* 1–19.

Dutton, J.E. (2003b). *Energize your workplace: Building and sustaining HQC connections at work.* San Francisco: Jossey-Bass.

Dutton, J.E., & Glynn, M. (2008). Positive organizational scholarship. In C. Cooper, & J. Barling (Eds.), *Sage handbook of organizational behavior: Vol.1: Micro approaches* (pp. 693–712*).* London: Sage Publications.

Dutton, J.E., & Heaphy, E. (2003). The power of high-quality connections. In K.S. Cameron, J.E. Dutton, & R.E. Quinn (Eds.), *Positive organizational scholarship: Foundations of a new discipline* (pp. 263–278). San Francisco: Berrett-Koehler.

Dutton, J.E., & Ragins, B.R. (Eds.). (2007). *Exploring positive relationships at work: Building a theoretical and research foundation.* New York: Lawrence Erlbaum Associates.

Dwyer, F.R., Schurr, P.H., & Oh, S. (1987). Developing buyer-seller relationships. *Journal of Marketing, 51,* 11–27.

Eisenberg, E. (1990). Jamming: Transcendence through organizing. *Communication Research, 17,* 139–164.

Elfenbein, H.A. (2007). Emotion in organizations. In J.P. Walsh, & A.P. Brief (Eds.), *The Academy of Management annals* (pp 315–386). London: Routledge.

Elster, J. (1989). *Nuts and bolts for the social sciences.* Cambridge, UK: Cambridge University Press.

Elster, J. (1998). A plea for mechanisms. In P. Hedstrom, & R. Swedberg (Eds.), *Social mechanisms: An analytical approach to social theory* (pp. 45–73). Cambridge, UK: Cambridge University Press.

Emmons, R.A., & Shelton, C.S. (2001). Gratitude and the science of positive psychology. In C.R. Snyder, & S.J. Lopez (Eds.), *Oxford handbook of positive psychology* (pp. 459–471). New York: Oxford University Press.

Epley, N., Keysar, B., Van Boven, L., & Gilovich, T. (2004). Perspective taking as egocentric anchoring and adjustment. *Journal of Personality and Social Psychology, 87*(3), 327–339.

Faraj, S., & Xiao, Y. (2006). Coordination in fast-response organizations. *Management Science, 52*(8), 1155–1189.

Feldman, M., & Rafaeli, A. (2002). Organizational routines as sources of connections and understandings. *Journal of Management Studies, 39*(3), 309–331.

Ferrin, D.L., Bligh, M.C., & Kohles, J.C. (2008). It takes two to tango: An interdependence analysis of the spiraling of perceived trustworthiness and cooperation in interpersonal and intergroup relations. *Organizational Behavior and Human Decision Processes, 107,* 161–178.

Fineman, S. (1993). *Emotion in organizations.* London: Sage Publications.

Fiske, A.P. (1992). The four elementary forms of sociality: Framework for a unified theory of social relations. *Psychological Review, 99,* 689–723.

Fletcher, J.K. (1998). Relational practice: A feminist reconstruction of work. *Journal of Management Inquiry, 7*(2), 163–186.

Flynn F.J., & Brockner, J. (2003). It's different to give than to receive: Asymmetric reactions of givers and receivers to favor exchange. *Journal of Applied Psychology, 88*(6), 1–13.

Fredrickson, B.L. (1998). What good are positive emotions? *Review of General Psychology, 2,* 300–319.

Fredrickson, B.L. (2001). The role of positive emotions in positive psychology: The broaden-and-build theory of positive emotions. *American Psychologist,* 56, 218–226.

Fredrickson, B.L. (2004). Gratitude, like other positive emotions, broadens and builds. In R.A. Emmons, & M.E. McCullough (Eds.), *The psychology of gratitude* (pp. 145–166). New York: Oxford University Press.

Frost, P. (2003). *Toxic emotions at work.* Boston: Harvard Business School Press.

Gable, S., & La Guardia, J.G. (2007). Positive processes in close relationships across time, partners and context: A multi-level approach. In A.D. Ong, & M.H. M. van Dulman (Eds.), *Oxford handbook of methods in positive psychology* (pp. 576–590). New York: Oxford University Press.

Galinsky, A., Ku, G., & Wang, C.S. (2005). Perspective-taking and self-other overlap: Fostering social bonds and facilitating social coordination. *Group Processes & Intergroup Relations, 8*(2), 109–124.

Gardner, D.G., Dunham, R.B., Cummings, L.L., & Pierce, J.L. (1987). Focus of attention at work and leader-follower relationships. *Journal of Occupational Behavior, 8*(4), 277–294.

Garfinkel, H. (1967). *Studies in ethnomethodology.* Englewood Cliffs, NJ: Prentice Hall.

Gibson, J.J. (1979). *The ecological approach to visual perception.* Boston: Houghton Mifflin.

Gittell, J.H. (2002a). Coordinating mechanisms in care provider groups: Relational coordination as a mediator and input uncertainty as a moderator of performance effects. *Management Science, 48*(11), 1408–1426.

Gittell, J.H. (2002b). Relationships between service providers and their impact on customers. *Journal of Service Research, 4*(4), 299–311.

Gittell, J.H. (2003). A theory of relational coordination. In K. Cameron, J. Dutton, and R.E. Quinn (Eds.), *Positive organizational scholarship: Foundations of a new discipline* (pp. 25–27). San Francisco: Berrett-Koehler Publishers.

Goffman, E. (1959). *Presentation of self in everyday life.* New York: Anchor Books.

Goffman, E. (1967). *Interaction rituals: Essays on face-to-face behavior.* New York: Books.

Goleman, D. (2006). *Social intelligence.* New York: Random House, Inc.

Goodwin, C. (2000). Action and embodiment within situated human interaction. *Journal of Pragmatics, 32,* 1489–1522.

Gottman, J.M., & Notarius, C.I. (2000). Decade review: Observing marital interaction. *Journal of Marriage & the Family, 62*(4), 927–947.

Gouldner, A.W. (1960). The norm of reciprocity: A preliminary statement. *American Sociological Review, 25,* 161–178.

Grandey, A. (2000). Emotion regulation in the workplace: A new way to conceptualize emotional labor. *Journal of Occupational Health Psychology, 5*(1), 95–110.

Grandey, A. (2003). When "the show must go on": Surface and deep acting as determinants of emotional exhaustion and peer-rated service delivery. *Academy of Management Journal, 46*(1), 86–96.

Grandey, A., Fisk, G., Mattila, A., Jansen, K., & Sideman, L. (2005). Is service with a smile enough? Authenticity of positive displays in service encounters. *Organizational Behavior and Human Decision Processes, 96,* 38–55.

Grant, A.M., & Ashford, S.J. (2008). The dynamics of proactivity at work. *Research in Organizational Behavior, 28,* 3–34.

Grant, A., & Berg, J. (2009). *Serious play: The quest for legitimacy in resisting institutional pressures.* Working paper, Wharton Business School, Philadelphia, PA.

Grant, A.M., & Gino, F. (2010). A little thanks goes a long way: Explaining why gratitude expressions motivate prosocial behavior. *Journal of Personality and Social Psychology, 98,* 946–955.

Hallowell, E. (1999). *Connect.* New York: Pantheon Books.

Hargadon, A.B., & Bechky, B. (2006). When collections of creatives become creative collectives: A field study of problem solving at work. *Organization Science, 17*(4), 484–500.

Hargadon, A.B., & Sutton, B.I. (1997). Technology brokering and innovation in a product development firm. *Administrative Science Quarterly, 42*(4), 716–749.

Hatfield, E., Cacioppo, J., & Rapson, R.L. (1992). Primitive emotional contagion. In M.S. Clark (Ed.), *Review of personality and social psychology: Emotion and social behavior* Vol. 14 (pp. 151–177). Newbury Park, CA: Sage.

Heaphy, E., & Dutton, J. (2008). Positive social interactions and the human body at work: Linking organizations and physiology. *Academy of Management Review, 33*(1), 137–162.

Hedstrom, P., & Swedberg, R. (1998). Social mechanisms: An introductory essay. In P. Hedstrom, & R. Swedberg (Eds.), *Social mechanisms: An analytical approach to social theory* (pp. 1–31). Cambridge, UK: Cambridge University Press.

Hennig-Thurau, T., Groth, M., Paul, M., & Gremler, D.D. (2006). Are all smiles created equal? How emotional contagion and emotional labor affect service relationships. *Journal of Marketing, 7*(3), 58–73.

Hochschild, A. (1983). *The managed heart: Commercialization of human feeling.* Berkeley, CA: University of California Press.

Hodson, R. (2001). *Dignity at work.* Cambridge, UK: Cambridge University Press.

Holmes, J.G., & Rempel, J.K. (1989). Trust in close relationships. In C. Hendrick (Ed.), *Review of personality and social psychology* Vol. 10 (pp. 187–220). Beverly Hills: Sage.

Homans, G.C. (1974). *Social behaviour: Its elementary forms* (Rev. ed.). New York: Harcourt Brace Jovanovich, Inc.

Hopper, R. (1992). *Telephone conversation.* Bloomington, IN: Indiana University Press.

Huizinga, J. (1950). *Homo ludens: A study of play-element in culture.* Boston: Beacon Press.

Ibarra, H. (2003). *Working identity.* Boston: Harvard Business School Press.

Johnson, K.J., & Fredrickson, B.L. (2005). "We all look the same to me:" Positive emotions eliminate the own-race bias in face recognition. *Psychological Science, 16,* 875–881.

Kahn, W. (1992). To be fully there: Psychological presence at work. *Human Relations, 45*(5), 321–349.

Keltner, D., & Haidt, J. (1999). Social functions of emotions at multiple levels of analysis. *Cognition and Emotion, 13,* 505–522.

Kolb, D.M., & Williams, J. (2003). *Everyday negotiation.* San Francisco: Jossey-Bass.

Kram, K. (1988). *Mentoring at work: Developmental relationships in organizational life.* Lanham, MD: University Press of America.

Lakin, J.L., Jefferis, V.E., Cheng, C.M., & Chartrand, T.L. (2003). The Chameleon Effect as social glue: Evidence for the evolutionary significance of nonconscious mimicry. *Journal of Nonverbal Behavior, 27,* 145–162.

Lawrence-Lightfoot, S.L. (2000). *Respect: An exploration.* New York: Perseus Books.

LeBaron, C. (2005). Considering the social and material surround: Toward microethnographic understandings of nonverbal behavior. In V. Manusov (Ed.), *The sourcebook of nonverbal measure* (pp. 493–506). Mahwah, NJ: Erlbaum.

LeBaron, C., Glenn, P., & Thompson, M. (2009). Identity work during boundary moments: Managing positive identities through talk and embodied interaction. In L.M. Roberts, & J. Dutton (Eds.), *Exploring positive identities and organizations* (pp. 191–215). New York: Routledge.

Lee, F. (1997). When the going gets tough, the tough ask for help? Help seeking and power motivations in organizations. *Organizational Behavior and Human Decision Processes, 72,* 336–363.

Lewin, R., & Regine, B. (2000). *The soul at work.* New York: Simon & Schuster.

Lilius, J.M., Worline, M.C., Maitlis, S., Kanov, J.M., Dutton, J.E., & Frost, P. (2008). The contours and consequences of compassion at work. *Journal of Organizational Behavior, 29,* 193–218.

Louis, M.R. (1980). Surprise and sense making: What newcomers experience in entering unfamiliar organizational settings. *Administrative Science Quarterly, 25,* 226–251.

MacIntyre, A. (1981). *After virtue.* Notre Dame, IN: Notre Dame University Press.

Maslow, A. (1968). *Toward a psychology of being* (2nd ed.). Princeton, NJ: Van Nostrand.

McAllister, D.J. (1995). Affect- and cognition-based trust as foundations for interpersonal cooperation in organizations. *Academy of Management Journal, 38,* 24–59.

McGinn, K.L., & Keros, A. (2002). Improvisation and the logic of exchange in embedded negotiations. *Administrative Science Quarterly, 47*(3), 442–473.

McNeely, B.L., & Meglino, B.M. (1994). The role of dispositional and situational antecedents in prosocial behavior: An examination of the intended beneficiaries of prosocial behavior. *Journal of Applied Psychology, 79,* 836–844.

Mead, G.H. (1934). *Mind, self and society.* Chicago: Chicago University Press.

Mehrabian, A., & Epstein, N.A. (1972). A measure of emotional empathy. *Journal of Personality, 40,* 523–543.

Meyerson, D.E. (2001). *Tempered radicals.* Boston: Harvard Business School Press.

Meyerson, D., Weick, K., & Kramer, R.M. (1996). Swift trust and temporary systems. In R.M. Kramer, & T.R. Tyler (Eds.), *Trust in organizations* (pp. 166–195). Thousand Oaks, CA: Sage.

Miller, J.B. (1976). *Toward a new psychology of women.* Boston: Beacon Press.

Miller, J.B., & Stiver, I.P. (1997). *The healing connection.* Boston: Beacon Press.

Mischel, W. (1977). The interaction of person and situation. In D. Magnusson, & N.S. Endler (Eds.), *Personality at the crossroads: Current issues in interactional psychology* (pp. 333–352). Hillsdale, NJ: Erlbaum.

Morris, M.W., & Keltner, D. (2000). How emotions work: the social function of emotional expression in negotiations. *Research in Organizational Behaviour, 22,* 1–50.

Morrison, E. (2002). Newcomers' relationships: The role of social network ties during socialization. *Academy of Management Journal, 45*(6), 1149–1160.

Mueller, J.S., & Curhan, J.R. (2006). Emotional intelligence and counterpart mood induction in a negotiation. *International Journal of Conflict Management, 17*(2), 110–128.

Orlikowski, W. (2002). Knowing in practice: Enacting a collective capability in distributed organizing. *Organization Science, 13*(3), 249–273.

Overbeck, J.R., & Park, B. (2001). When power does not corrupt: Superior individuation processes among powerful perceivers. *Journal of Personality and Social Psychology, 81*(4), 549–565.

Pearson, C., & Porath, C. (2009). *The costs of bad behavior.* New York: Portfolio.

Penner, L.A. (2002). The causes of sustained volunteerism: An interactionist perspective. *Journal of Social Issues, 58,* 447–467.

Podsakoff, P.M., MacKenzie, S.B., Paine, J.B., & Bachrach, D.G. (2000). Organizational citizenship behaviors: A critical review of the theoretical and empirical literature and suggestions for future research. *Journal of Management, 26,* 513–563.

Pomerantz, A., & Denvir, P. (2007). Enacting the institutional role of chairperson in upper management meetings: The interactional realization of provisional authority. In F. Cooren (Ed.), *Interacting and organizing: Analyses of a management meeting* (pp. 31–51). Mahwah, NJ: Erlbaum.

Pratt, M., & Dirks, K.T. (2006). Rebuilding trust and restoring positive relationships: A commitment-based view of trust. In J. Dutton, & B. Ragins (Eds.), *Exploring positive relationships at work: Building a theoretical and research foundation* (pp. 117–136). Mahwah, NJ: Lawrence Earlbaum Associates.

Pratt, M.G., & Rafaeli, A. (2002). Symbols as a language of organizational relationships. In B. Staw, & R.I. Sutton (Eds.), *Research in organizational behavior* Vol. 24 (pp. 93–133). Greenwich, CT: JAI Press.

Prusak, L., & Cohen, D. (2001). How to invest in social capital. *Harvard Business Review, 79,* 86–93.

Pugh, S.D. (2001). Service with a smile: Emotional contagion in the service encounter. *Academy of Management Journal, 44,* 1018–1027.

Putnam, L.L. (2004). Transformations and critical moments in negotiations. *Negotiation Journal, 20*(2), 275–295.

Quinn, R., & Dutton, J. (2005). Coordination as energy-in-conversation: A process theory of organizing. *Academy of Management Review, 30*(1), 38–57.

Ragins, B.R., & Verbos, A.K. (2007). Positive relationships in action: Relational mentoring and mentoring schemas in the workplace. In J.E. Dutton, & B.R. Ragins (Eds.), *Exploring positive relationships at work: Building a theoretical and research foundation* (pp. 91–116). New York: Lawrence Erlbaum Associates.

Ramarajan, L., Barsade, S.G., & Burak, O. (2008). The influence of organizational respect on emotional exhaustion in the human services. *The Journal of Positive Psychology, 3*(1), 4–18.

Rawls, J. (1971). *A theory of justice.* Cambridge, MA: Belknap Press.

Reis, H. (2001). Relationship experiences and emotional well-being. In C. Ryff, & B. Singer (Eds.), *Emotion, social relationships, and health* (pp. 57–86). Oxford: Oxford University Press.

Reis, H.T. (2007). Steps toward the ripening of relationship science. *Personal Relationships 14, 1, 23*

Reis, H.T., & Collins, N.L. (2000). Measuring supportive processes and interactions. In S. Cohen, L. Underwood, & B. Gottlieb (Eds.), *Social support measurement and intervention: a guide for health and social scientists* (pp. 136–192). New York: Oxford University Press.

Roberts, L.M. (2007). From proving to becoming: How positive relationships create a context for self-discovery and self-actualization. In J.E. Dutton, & B.R. Ragins (Eds.), *Exploring positive relationships at work: Building a theoretical and research foundation* (pp. 29–46). New York: Lawrence Erlbaum Associates.

Rogers, C.R. (1951). *Client-centered therapy.* New York: Houghton Mifflin.

Rollag, K., Parise, S., & Cross, R. (2005). Getting new hires up to speed quickly. *MIT/Sloan Management Review, 46*(2), 35–44.

Ryff, C.D., & Singer, B. (2000). Interpersonal flourishing: A positive health agenda for the new millennium. *Personality Social Psychological Review, 4,* 30–44.

Salovey, P., & Mayer, J.D. (1990). Emotional intelligence. *Imagination, Cognition, and Personality, 9,* 185–211.

Sandelands, L.E. (2010). The play of change. *Journal of Organizational Change Management, 23,* 71–86.

Sandelands, L.E., & Boudens, C.J. (2000). Feeling at work. In S. Fineman (Ed.), *Emotion in organizations* (2nd ed., pp. 25–45). London: Sage.

Schegloff, E. (2000). Overlapping talk and the organization of turn-taking for conversation. *Language and Society, 29,* 1–63.

Schegloff, E., & Sacks, H. (1973). Opening up closings. *Semiotica, 8*(4), 289–327.

Schoenewolf, G. (1990). *Turning points in analytic therapy.* Northvale, NJ: Aronson.

Sennett, R. (2003). *Respect in a world of inequality.* New York: W.W.Norton & Co.

Settoon, R.P., & Mossholder, K.W. (2002). Relationship quality and relational context as antecedents of person- and task-focused interpersonal citizenship behavior. *Journal of Applied Psychology, 87,* 255–267.

Stinchcombe, A.L. (1991). The conditions of fruitfulness of theorizing about mechanisms in social science. *Philosophy of the Social Sciences, 21*(3), 367–388.

Stone, B. (1989). The self and the play-element in culture. *Play & Culture, 2,* 64–79.

Streeck, J., & Mehus, S. (2005). Microethnography: The study of practices. In K. Fitch, & R. Sanders (Eds.), *Handbook of language and social interaction* (pp. 381–404). Mahwah, NJ: Lawrence Erlbaum.

Sutton, R.I., & Hargadon, A.B. (1996). Brainstorming groups in context: Effectiveness in a product design firm. *Administrative Science Quarterly, 41*(4), 685–718.

Tannen, D. (2001). The power of talk: Who gets heard and why. In I.G Asherman, & S.V. Asherman (Eds.), *Negotiation sourcebook* (pp. 245–258). Amherst, MA: HRD Press.

Thibaut, J.W., & Kelley, H.H. (1959). *The social psychology of groups.* New York: Wiley.

Thomas, D.A. (1993). Racial dynamics in cross-race developmental relationships. *Administrative Science Quarterly, 38*(2), 169–194.

Uchino, B. (2004). *Social support and physical health: Understanding the consequences of relationships.* New Haven, CT: Yale University Press.

Van de Ven, A.H., Delbecq, A.L., & Koenig, R., Jr. (1976). Determinants of coordination modes within organizations. *American Sociological Review, 41*(2), 322–338.

Venkataramani, V., & Dalal, R.S. (2007). Who helps and harms whom? Relational antecedents of interpersonal helping and harming in organizations. *Journal of Applied Psychology, 92*(4), 952–966.

Vogus, T.J. (2004). *In search of mechanisms: How do HR practices affect organizational performance?* Unpublished doctoral dissertation, University of Michigan, Ann Arbor, MI.

Vogus, T.J., & Welbourne, T.M. (2003). Structuring for high reliability: HR practices and mindful processes in reliability-seeking organizations. *Journal of Organizational Behavior, 24*(7), 877–903.

Waugh, C.E., & Fredrickson, B.L. (2006). Nice to know you: Positive emotions, self- other overlap, and complex understanding in the formation of new relationships. *Journal of Positive Psychology, 1*, 93–106.

Weisband, S. (2002). Maintaining awareness in distributed team collaboration: Implications for leadership and performance. In P.J. Hinds, & S. Kiesler (Eds.), *Distributed work* (pp. 311–333). Cambridge, MA: MIT Press.

Williams, L.J., & Anderson, S.E. (1991). Job satisfaction and organizational commitment as predictors of organizational citizenship and in-role behaviors. *Journal of Management, 17*, 601–617.

Williams, M. (2007). Building genuine trust through interpersonal emotion management: A threat regulation model of trust and cooperation across boundaries. *Academy of Management Review, 32*(2), 595–621.

Worline, M., Lilius, J., Dutton, J., Kanov, J., Maitlis, S., & Frost, P. (2009). *Understanding compassion capability.* Working paper, University of California, Irvine.

Wrzesniewski, A., & Dutton, J. (2001). Crafting a job: Employees as active crafters of their work. *Academy of Management Review, 26*(2), 179–201.

Ybarra, O., Burnstein, E., Winkielman, P., Keller, M.C., Manis, M., Chan, E., & Rodriquez, J. (2008). Mental exercising through simple socializing: Social interaction promotes general cognitive functioning. *Personality and Social Psychology Bulletin, 34*(2), 248–259.

New Directions for Relational Coordination Theory

Jody Hoffer Gittell

Abstract

Relational coordination theory makes visible the relational process underlying the technical process of coordination, arguing that coordination encompasses not only the management of interdependence between tasks but also between the people who perform those tasks. This chapter introduces relational coordination theory, then proposes five potential directions for its further development, each of which deepens the contribution of the theory to positive organizational scholarship. The first proposed direction is to develop the social psychological foundations of relational coordination theory, placing it more firmly into the context of relational theory. The second is to extend relational coordination theory from its focus on role relationships to include personal relationships and to explore the interplay between them. Third is to broaden relational coordination networks beyond the core workers who have typically been considered, to include multiple other participants: so-called *noncore workers*, the customer herself, and participants outside the focal organization who are involved in the same value chain. Fourth is to extend the theorized outcomes of relational coordination beyond outcomes for the organization and its customers to include outcomes for workers as well. The fifth proposed direction is to go beyond the linear model of organizational change implicit in relational coordination theory toward a more dynamic and iterative model of change. These new directions will be previewed briefly in anticipation of their future development.

Keywords: Relationships, communication, coordination, relational coordination

Positive organizational scholarship (POS) is a humanistic approach to the study of organizations, emphasizing the importance of subjectivity, intersubjectivity, and meaning at work (Cameron, Dutton, & Quinn, 2003). Relational coordination theory contributes to POS by offering a theory of coordination that makes visible the relational process underlying the technical process, arguing that coordination encompasses not only the management of interdependence between tasks (Malone & Crowston, 1994) but also the management of interdependence between the people who perform those tasks. The theory reveals the intersubjectivity of the coordination process, therefore paying close attention to the quality of communication and relationships among participants, as well as to the technical requirements of the work.

This theory shares common threads with other intersubjective or relational approaches to the coordination of work (Bechky, 2006; Faraj & Sproull, 2000; Faraj & Xiao, 2006; Gittell, 2002b; Heckscher, 1994; Heckscher & Adler, 2006; Quinn & Dutton, 2005; Weick & Roberts, 1993) but differs in several important ways.

First, relational coordination theory starts by conceptualizing coordination as occurring through a network of relationship and communication ties among participants in a work process, where a work process is a set of interdependent tasks that transforms inputs into outcomes of value to the organization. Second, this theory identifies three distinctive dimensions of relationships—shared goals, shared knowledge, and mutual respect—that together are argued to underlie the effective coordination of work. Third, these dimensions are conceived as existing between work roles rather than between individual participants. Fourth, the theory explains how relational forms of coordination influence quality and efficiency outcomes, and how this influence is weaker or stronger depending upon the nature of the work. Fifth, and finally, the theory explains how formal organizational structures can be designed to support relational forms of coordination, rather than suggesting that formal structures are necessarily substitutes or impediments to relational coordination. Despite providing a unique perspective on coordination, and despite promising results of empirical testing thus far (as well as perceived usefulness to multiple practitioner communities), the theory of relational coordination remains at an early stage of development. This chapter describes these theoretical propositions at greater length, then proposes five new directions for its further development.

Relational Coordination Theory

Mary Parker Follett appears to be the first theorist to have proposed a relational theory of coordination. She accepted the then-prevalent argument that the primary function of organizations was to coordinate work. She argued uniquely, however, that coordination at its most effective was not a mechanical process but rather a process of continuous interrelating between the parts and the whole. In her words:

> It is impossible . . . to work most effectively at coordination until you have made up your mind where you stand philosophically in regard to the relation of parts to wholes. We have spoken of the relation of departments—sales and production, advertising, and financial—to each other, but the most profound truth that philosophy has ever given us concerns not only the relation of parts, but the relation of parts to the whole, not to a stationary whole, but to a whole a-making. (Follett, 1949, p. 91)

Consistent with Follett's argument, Thompson (1967) later suggested that coordination as a process of reciprocal relating, or "mutual adjustment," can indeed be beneficial. But he offered a contingency argument, suggesting that this is true only when tasks are reciprocally interdependent, or in other words, when outcomes from one task feed back and create new information for participants who are performing related tasks (Thompson, 1967). Moreover, Thompson saw mutual adjustment as playing a limited role in organizations. Because mutual adjustment is prohibitively costly, he argued,

coordination more commonly occurs through coordinating mechanisms such as supervision, routines, scheduling, preplanning, or standardization.

Since then, the nature of work has changed. Work is characterized by increasing levels of task interdependence, uncertainty, and time constraints, expanding the relevance of mutual adjustment beyond what Thompson originally foresaw and forcing the exploration of coordination as a relational process. Organizational scholars have responded by developing relational approaches to coordination that build on Follett's concept of coordination, including the concepts of sense-making (Weick & Roberts, 1993), expertise coordination (Faraj & Sproull, 2000; Faraj & Xiao, 2006), coordination as energy-in-conversation (Quinn & Dutton, 2005), role-based coordination (Bechky, 2006), and collaborative community (Heckscher, 1994; Heckscher & Adler, 2006). As part of this stream, relational coordination theory has sought to extend Follett's work by offering a unique way to conceptualize the relational dynamics of coordination, its expected outcomes, and its structural predictors.

First, the theory of relational coordination specifies the nature of relationships through which coordination occurs, proposing that these relationships include *shared goals* that transcend participants' specific functional goals, *shared knowledge* that enables participants to see how their specific tasks interrelate with the whole process, and *mutual respect* that enables participants to overcome the status barriers that prevent them from seeing and taking account of the work of others. Together, these three relational dimensions reinforce and are reinforced by communication that is frequent, timely, accurate, and problem-solving. For example, knowledge of what each participant contributes to the overall work process enables him or her to communicate in a timely way with participants in other functions, grounded in an understanding of who needs to know what, why, and with what degree of urgency. Shared knowledge also enables participants to communicate with each other with greater accuracy due to knowing not only their own specific tasks but also how their tasks relate to the tasks of participants in other functions. Shared goals increase participants' motivation to engage in high-quality communication, as well as increasing the likelihood that they will resort to problem-solving communication rather than blaming when things go wrong. Mutual respect increases the likelihood that participants will be receptive to communication from their colleagues in other functions, irrespective of their relative status, thus increasing the quality of

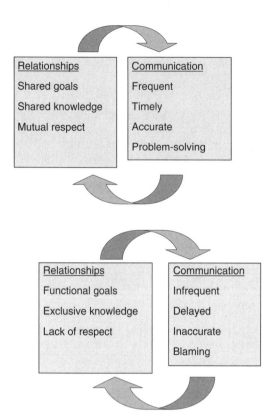

Fig. 30.1 Relational coordination as a mutually reinforcing cycle of relationships and communication.

communication, given that communication is a function of what is heard as well as what is said. Relational coordination is therefore defined as "a mutually reinforcing process of interaction between communication and relationships carried out for the purpose of task integration" (Gittell, 2002a, p. 301), as illustrated in Figure 30.1. Together, these mutually reinforcing relationship and communication ties form the basis for coordinated collective action (Gittell, 2006).

Second, consistent with Follett's thinking about the relational approach to coordination, the relational dimensions of relational coordination are not personal relationships of "liking" or "not liking" but rather are task-based relationship ties. They are conceptualized as ties between work roles, rather than personal ties between discrete individuals who inhabit those work roles. We will revisit this aspect of the theory when we propose new directions for further theoretical development.

Third, the theory of relational coordination extends Follett's work and subsequent work on relational forms of coordination by exploring *how* this approach to coordination is expected to impact performance. Follett proposed that a relational approach

to coordination is more *effective* than more mechanistic approaches, but the theory of relational coordination proposes specifically that both quality and efficiency outcomes can be improved simultaneously, moving beyond the tradeoffs between quality and efficiency that are typically found, by enabling participants to achieve better results for customers while engaging in less wasteful and more productive utilization of resources. How? In contrast to the traditional bureaucratic form of coordination that is carried out primarily by managers at the top of functional silos, relational coordination is carried out via direct contact among workers at the front line, through networks that cut across functional silos at the point of contact with the customer. Relational coordination thus improves performance of a work process by improving the work relationships (shared goals, shared knowledge, mutual respect) between people who perform different functions in that work process, leading to higher-quality communication. Task interdependencies are therefore managed more directly, in a more seamless way, with fewer redundancies, lapses, errors, and delays.

But this performance argument is not universalistic—rather, it is a contingency argument. Again going beyond Follett's conceptualization, relational coordination theory builds on information processing and contingency theories by arguing that relational forms of coordination are particularly useful for achieving desired performance outcomes under conditions of reciprocal interdependence (Thompson, 1967), task and input uncertainty (Argote, 1982; Galbraith, 1972), and time constraints (Adler, 1995). When tasks are reciprocally interdependent, feedback loops are created among them, therefore increasing the need for relational coordination to enable participants to mutually adjust their actions in response to the outcomes of each others' tasks. Furthermore, when task and/or input uncertainty is high, relational coordination becomes more important for enabling participants to adjust their activities with each other "on the fly," as new information emerges in the process of carrying out the work. Finally, as time constraints increase, as in high-velocity environments, relational coordination becomes more important for enabling participants to adjust their actions rapidly in response to each other and newly emergent information, without wasting additional time referring problems upward for resolution.

Relational coordination theory extends Follett's work and subsequent theory in one final way, by arguing that, although relational forms of coordination can and do emerge spontaneously from the

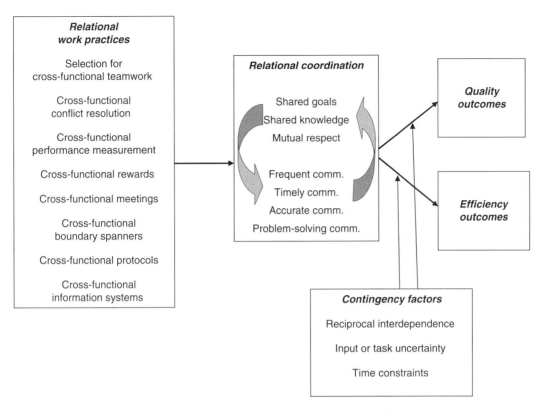

Fig. 30.2 Structure/process/outcomes model of relational coordination.

actions of individual actors, they are also fundamentally shaped by organizational structures. In organizations with traditional bureaucratic structures that tend to reinforce functional silos, relational networks are expected to exhibit strong ties within functions and weak ties between functions, resulting in fragmentation and poor handoffs among participants at the front line of production or service delivery. By contrast, in organizations with structures that cut across functional silos (structures that include, for example, selecting participants for cross-functional teamwork, measuring and rewarding participants for cross-functional teamwork, resolving conflicts proactively across functions, developing work protocols that span functional boundaries, designing jobs with flexible boundaries between areas of functional specialization, and designing boundary spanner roles to support the development of networks across functional boundaries), relationship and communication networks are expected to be more cohesive. These cross-cutting structures represent a redesign of traditional bureaucratic structures, and together they constitute a relational work system that strengthens cross-functional networks of relational coordination without sacrificing the benefits of the division of labor.

Together, these extensions of Follett's relational approach to coordination suggest a structure/process/outcomes model in which relational modes of coordination represent the process component; quality and efficiency performance represent the outcomes component moderated by task interdependence, uncertainty, and time constraints; and relational work practices represent the structure component. (See Figure 30.2 for an illustration.) This theory thus departs from information processing and organization design theories, which have tended to argue that networks *replace* formal organizational practices as information processing demands increase (Argote, 1982; Galbraith, 1972; Tushman & Nadler, 1978), and post-bureaucratic theory, which argues more universally that bureaucratic structures are *replaced* with networks in the ideal post-bureaucratic organization (Heckscher, 1994). By contrast, relational coordination theory calls for the redesign rather than the replacement of formal structures, specifically redesigning these structures to reinforce and strengthen relational processes across functional boundaries, where they tend to be weak (Gittell, Seidner, & Wimbush, 2010). In so doing, relational coordination theory contributes to high-performance work systems theories, proposing—along with Leana and Van Buren (1999), Collins and Clark (2003), Evans and Davis (2005), Vogus (2006), and others—a type of high-performance work system that strengthens employee–employee relationships, distinct from but potentially complementary to high-performance work systems that reinforce employee commitment to the organization, or that build employee knowledge and skills.

Although relational coordination theory is at a relatively early stage of development, it has received a fair amount of empirical support. Findings thus far suggest that relational coordination is an empirically coherent concept that meets standards of both internal and external validity. Furthermore, findings thus far suggest that the strength of relational coordination ties among participants in a work process predict an array of quality and efficiency outcomes that are of strategic importance to organizations (e.g., Gittell, 2001; Gittell et al., 2000; Gittell, Weinberg, Bennett, & Miller, 2008; Gittell, Weinberg, Pfefferle, & Bishop, 2008; Weinberg, Lusenhop, Gittell & Kautz, 2007). The contingency hypotheses in relational coordination theory have been explored to a more limited extent, with initial findings suggesting that the performance effects of relational coordination increase as input uncertainty increases (Gittell, 2002b). The hypothesized predictors of relational coordination have also received empirical support, with evidence suggesting that cross-cutting formal organizational structures do indeed increase the strength of relational coordination ties as reported by participants (Gittell, 2002a,b, 2002b; Gittell, Seidner, & Wimbush, 2010; Gittell, Weinberg, Bennett, & Miller, 2008).

Although further empirical testing is under way, the theory itself is also in need of further development. Accordingly, the following section proposes five directions for further development of relational coordination theory.

New Directions for Relational Coordination Theory
Building the Social Psychological Foundations of Relational Coordination Theory

Relational coordination theory is relatively unique in specifying the relational dimensions of coordination—shared goals, shared knowledge, and mutual respect—and specifying how these relational ties reinforce and are reinforced by communication ties to enable the effective coordination of work. But one promising new direction for relational coordination theory is to explore more deeply its relational underpinnings, returning to social psychological theories that posit

the self as a self-in-relation, then connecting those underpinnings in a coherent way to the organizational phenomenon of coordination.

Theorists as early as Follett (1924) have argued that relationships are the fundamental building block of human identity. "Reality is in the relating," argued Follett, "in the activity between" (p. 36). Furthermore, when we consider "the total situation," we come face to face with the "possible reciprocal influence of the subject and object" (p. 37). Through this reciprocal influence, or what she calls a circular response, "we are creating each other all the time" (p. 41). Elaborating the argument, she claims further that "I can never influence you because you have already influenced me; that is, in the very process of meeting, by the very process of meeting, we both become something different" (p. 42).

Consistent with Follett, Buber (1937) argued that the self is always by necessity constructed as a "self-in-relation," meaning that the human subject is defined through its relationships with other subjects. Based on this argument, Buber challenges the Cartesian foundations of Western ontology, in essence replacing "I think, therefore I am" with "I relate, therefore I am." Freud (1930) also gives primacy to relationships, but treats the broken relationship as the starting point for the human condition, arguing that "a primary separation [of infant from mother], arising from disappointment and fueled by rage, creates a self whose relations with others or 'objects' must then be protected by rules, a morality that contains this explosive potential" (p. 46). He points to an urge toward union with others, and calls it *altruism*, a replacement for or perhaps a return in a more limited way to the "oceanic feeling" that is left behind on the path to moral development. Connection thus appears central to civilized life.

Miller (1976) transformed the psychology of human development by questioning the Freudian conception of human development as revolving around individuation and separation. She theorized that this conception is rooted in the male experience, and is one that either ignores the female experience or interprets the female experience as an anomaly or an absence of full development. The prototypical developmental path, when considered from the standpoint of the female experience, is growth through connection, rather than growth through separation. Miller argued that the one-sided view of development ignores the reality that the human subject, and our notion of individuality, is itself socially embedded, meaning that individuation itself occurs through mutual recognition by other human subjects.

Furthermore, Miller argues, life is possible only through connection with others, starting with the mother at birth. We are, therefore, relational by nature.

Building on Miller's argument, Mitchell (2000) argued that attachment and relationality are so fundamental to the human condition that, contrary to dominant psychological theories, a concept of drive is not necessary to explain them. "To argue that we need a concept of drive to describe what the individual seeks in interactions with other people presumes that the individual qua individual is the most appropriate unit of study. It assumes that the individual, in his or her natural state, is essentially alone, and then is drawn into interaction for some purpose or need" (p. 105). "To define humans as relational is quite different from specifying object-seeking as a specific drive. . . . It is simply what we are built to do, and we do it without intentionality" (p. 106).

The common thread among these theorists is that relationships are fundamental to the life experience and identity of human beings. But what insights, if any, can we gain from these theorists regarding the role that relationships play in the coordination of work? It appears that Follett was the first to attempt to connect the relational nature of human identity to the coordination of work. Follett's writings suggest that a relational understanding of human identity is somehow connected to a relational understanding of coordination. Just as human identity and causality are characterized by reciprocal influence, so too is coordination. Coordination, Follett argued, is most effective when it occurs through mutual adjustment among the factors of a situation, starting early and continuing throughout the process. What is the rationale behind this intriguing parallel that Follett has identified between the relationality of human identity, relationality of the nature of causality itself, and relationality of the coordination of work? Are these simply analogous, or is there something more?

Other organizational theorists have drawn important insights from social psychological arguments regarding relationality, and over the past decade have begun increasingly to apply the concept of relationality to organizational life. Fletcher (1999) introduced the concept of relational practice, arguing that it tends to be "disappeared" from organizational discourse and reward structures due to our tendency to relegate it to the private sphere of women's work, despite its potential to serve as a powerful driver of organizational performance. Fletcher's work draws particularly on Miller's insights regarding the gendering of relationality, due to the tendency for males

to be socialized into the self-as-individual identity and for females to be socialized into the self-in-relation identity. Other scholars have continued the translation of relationality from the realm of social psychology into the realm of organizations, exploring relational conceptualizations of job design (e.g., Gittell, Weinberg, Bennett, & Miller, 2008; Grant, 2007; Wrzesniewski & Dutton, 2001), learning (Edmondson, 1996, 2004; Nembhard & Edmondson, 2006), professionalism (Adler, Kwon, & Heckscher, 2008; Fletcher, 1999), and coordination, as we have seen (e.g., Bechky, 2006; Faraj & Sproull, 2000; Faraj & Xiao, 2006; Gittell, 2002b; Heckscher & Adler, 2006; Quinn & Dutton, 2005; Weick & Roberts, 1993). But these scholars have not addressed the fundamental question of how the relationality of human identity informs or explains the relationality of organizational life. Furthermore, how does this dynamic play out in contexts in which the relationality of human identity is made relatively invisible through a gendered process of socialization; that is, when relationality is associated with female qualities rather than human qualities more broadly? This theoretical work remains to be done.

Extending Relational Coordination Theory to Include Personal Relationships

As noted above, relational coordination theory has been built on the concept of relationships between work roles, rather than relationships between unique individuals. The strengths of role relationships are clear from a logistical standpoint: They enable individuals to come and go without disrupting the web of relationships through which work is coordinated, thus facilitating scheduling flexibility for operational benefits, as well as for accommodating the work/life needs of employees. But are role relationships "real" relationships, in the sense of having the humanistic attributes and the potential for emotional connection that gives relationships their power to shape organizational life in a positive way? In other words, to be consistent with the humanistic strengths-based orientation of POS, must the concept of relational coordination incorporate or account for personal relationships, or can it focus solely on relationships between roles, a foundation that is arguably more flexible and sustainable over time? Much of relational theory focuses on relationships between individuals rather than roles, even in POS, where theorists have explored how relationships drive organizational performance as well as individual well-being (e.g., Dutton, 2003; Dutton & Heaphy, 2003; Dutton & Ragins, 2007).

Gilligan (1982) offers insight into this question by comparing the trajectories of male and female moral development. She summarizes the research that supported established psychological theories that women tend to have a different moral sensibility than do men. Although psychologists from Freud onward had interpreted women's differences as a failure to complete moral development, Gilligan questioned that interpretation. She listened to the ways in which girls and women spoke about moral choices relative to the ways in which boys and men spoke about moral choices. What she heard was not a deficiency in moral development, but rather a distinct voice or conception of morality. As she later summed up: "The different voice . . . is a relational voice: a voice that insists on staying in connection . . . so that the psychological separations that have long been justified in the name of autonomy, selfhood, and freedom no longer appear as the sine qua non of human development but as a human problem" (p. xiii). The notion of deficiency had come from the assumption that male moral development, predicated on achieving separation and autonomy, was the normal human development, and that other paths that deviated from it could thus be judged as lacking. She argued that "instead, the failure of women to fit existing models of human growth may point to a problem in the representation, a limitation in the conception of human condition, an omission of certain truths about life" (p. 2).

In this respect, Gilligan's argument mirrors that of Miller, and provides additional research evidence to bolster it. But, in one of her studies, Gilligan finds other aspects of these alternative male–female moral codes, in addition to the contrast between autonomous and relational models of human development. In particular, when observing patterns of play among girls and among boys, she notices that girls play in smaller groups, have a greater focus on preserving relationships than on playing the game itself, and make less use of rules to govern their play. As Mead (1934) argued earlier, girls therefore learn less to take the role of "generalized other" and learn less the abstraction of human relationships. Gilligan states the contrast in the following way: "This conception of morality as concerned with the activity of care centers moral development around the understanding of responsibility and relationships, just as the conception of morality as fairness ties moral development to the understanding of rights and rules" (p. 19).

This notion of personal connection versus generalized connection emerges again in Gilligan's analysis of Freud's (1930) "oceanic feeling," which gives rise to altruism. As Gilligan points out, this altruism is not specific to an individual person. It is a broader, more humanistic urge that does not require a personal relationship; rather, it is more a relationship among roles—e.g., between human being in a position to help and human being in need of help. One of her interviewees expresses a similar sense of collective connection, which Gilligan interprets in the following way: "In seeing individual lives as connected and embedded in a social context of relationship, she expands her moral perspective to encompass a notion of 'collective life.'" But Gilligan questions whether this is adequate, and whether indeed it qualifies as a connection at all.

Do generalized or role relationships even *count* as relationships? Can role relationships serve as a basis for effective coordination and at the same time as a source of positive connection at work? Or, must role relationships be supplemented by personal concern for individual people as specific human beings? If so, which precedes and gives rise to which?

Extending Relational Coordination Theory to Include a Broader Network of Participants

Another new direction for relational coordination theory is to extend the network of relational coordination to include a broader network of participants. These additional participants include workers who are considered to be "noncore" or peripheral to the strategic goals of the organization; customers, who are typically seen as recipients of products or services rather than participants in their production; and those who reside outside the boundaries of the focal organization and yet are participants in a work process that extends beyond the focal organization—often members of a supply chain or network.

Consider the noncore worker. Relational coordination in theory includes all workers who are engaged in interdependent tasks in a given work process. But the theory has evolved, through the studies that have been conducted, to focus on workers in the "operating core" of the organization, thereby neglecting participants who may be perceived to have "peripheral" roles but who nevertheless have tasks that are highly interdependent with those in the operating core. Thus, in practice, relational coordination theory has evolved toward a neglect of the noncore or peripheral worker, for example neglecting the skycap's role in the flight departure process, and neglecting the housekeeper's and nursing aide's roles in the patient care process, despite anecdotal evidence that these noncore functions play critical roles in achieving the desired outcomes due to their interdependence with the so-called core functions. As Wright (2010) argues, "By expanding relational coordination theory to include noncore personnel, whole organizations may benefit from improved coordination through a greater understanding of the organizations' core purpose; particularly in environments of change and uncertainty" (p. 1).

The explicit extension of relational coordination theory to include noncore workers would run counter to a more recent argument in the human resource management literature, the argument that human resource management is more "strategic" in its use of resources when it focuses attention on the core workforce—the so-called *knowledge workers* who are less replaceable and who drive those outcomes that are of strategic importance to the organization (Lepak & Snell, 1999). This argument is short-sighted from the standpoint of relational coordination theory, which implies that a work process (and its desired outcomes) is only as strong as its weakest link, thus suggesting that any participant whose tasks are included in that work process falls within the scope of strategic human resource management. Both relational coordination networks and the formal structures that are designed to support them should therefore be conceptualized explicitly as including both core and noncore workers.

Next, we can extend the relational coordination network to include the customer him- or herself as a key participant in the coordination of work. This move is already justified implicitly by the theory itself, to the extent that the customer is indeed expected to carry out tasks that are part of the work flow and are interdependent with the tasks carried out by employees. The move to include customers in the network of relational coordination is also consistent with a growing recognition of the customer as a key coproducer of outcomes in service settings. Motivations behind this trend include efficiency gains for organizations and, potentially, higher-quality outcomes, to the extent that customers can better customize services to meet their unique needs and can become empowered rather than passive recipients of services (Chappell, 1994; Marschall, 2004). This move is also consistent with the paradigm of client-centered services, and in health care with the emerging paradigm of patient-centered or relationship-centered care, both of which recognize the client and/or patient as a focal point for provider interactions, and also as an active participant in the work process, at the very least providing input regarding desired outcomes and information that will better inform providers as to the nature of the tasks that are needed to achieve those desired outcomes. In health care, for example, certain tasks are to be carried out by the patient, once labeled "compliance." These include taking the correct medications at the correct times and engaging in appropriate exercise or diet. These tasks can readily be understood as coproduction tasks that are critical to achieving desired health outcomes, when performed in cooperation with the care provider team. Engaging the customer in coproduction in such settings is increasingly understood to require a relational process of some sort (Eaton, 2000; Safran, Miller, & Beckman, 2006; Stone, 2000; Suchman, 2006), suggesting the possibility that relational coordination theory can be fruitfully extended to encompass the customer (Ple, 2009; Ryan, 2009).

Finally, we can extend relational coordination networks to include participants who are located outside the boundaries of the focal organization. Drawing upon Rousseau's (1985) guidelines for the development of multilevel theory, Gittell and Weiss (2004) developed a multilevel model of coordination networks in which relational coordination within organizations is conceptualized as extending beyond the organization to include relational coordination with other organizations in the same supply network. Network concepts are highly conducive to being conceptualized at multiple levels, from individual to organizational to cross-organizational. More recent work by Gittell, Weinberg, and Hagigi (2010) shows how relational coordination networks can be modeled across a supply chain, thus hypothesizing that these networks tend to have modular characteristics, with stronger ties within organizations than across organizations, due to the limitations posed by bounded rationality. They hypothesize further that system integrator roles are required for effective coordination of these modular networks, that system integrators require system knowledge in order to play their role effectively, and that the integrator can either bridge structural holes or serve as a connector between modules in the network. This theorizing requires further development but is promising as an avenue for expanding the relevant participants in relational coordination networks beyond the boundaries of a single organization to include the broader value chains in which organizations participate.

Extending Relational Coordination Theory to Include Outcomes for Workers

As argued above, relational coordination theory has well-developed hypotheses regarding the simultaneous effects of relational coordination on quality and efficiency outcomes, particularly under conditions of reciprocal task interdependence, task or input uncertainty, and time constraints. But the theory has largely overlooked the impact of relational coordination on outcomes for workers themselves, taking for granted that more positive and more effective working relationships would serve as a source of job satisfaction for workers. What is needed is a theoretical exploration of how and why relational coordination might affect workers, considering the potential for both positive and negative effects. On the positive side, we might anticipate that relational coordination increases job satisfaction by increasing workers' ability to accomplish their jobs (Gittell, Weinberg, Pfefferle, & Bishop, 2008). We know that having the resources necessary to accomplish one's work is a source of employee satisfaction (Hallowell Schlesinger & Zornitsky, 1996) and, similarly, that social networks enable people to more effectively accomplish their work by increasing their ability to mobilize resources (Baker, 2000; Nahapiet & Ghoshal, 1998). Moreover, we know from organizational scholars that positive relationships are a source of well-being at work (Dutton, 2003; Dutton & Heaphy, 2003; Dutton & Ragins, 2007). Dutton and Heaphy (2003) argue that high-quality connections are energizing due to creating a keen attunement and high awareness of the needs of others, as well as recognition and validation of one's self by others. In addition, recognition and validation of one's professional contribution might be expected to lead to a heightened sense of professional efficacy. These represent two compelling rationales for why relational coordination might enhance worker outcomes.

But on the negative side, it is important to explore the potential discomfort caused by transforming a siloed organization that values professional expertise and autonomy into a cross-functional organization that places increased value on relational competence and interdependence. This change may be experienced as a loss of professional status and autonomy that reduces satisfaction with work and other related outcomes, particularly for high-status workers (Adler, Kwon & Heckscher, 2008). In sum, relational coordination theory should be extended to consider the potential for both positive and negative outcomes for workers that may result when organizations seek to bridge functional boundaries to achieve a more collective or systems perspective.

Extending Relational Coordination Theory to the Process of Organizational Change

To date, relational coordination theory has not explicitly addressed the question of organizational change.

But there is an implicit theory in the existing model, as portrayed above. One tenet of relational coordination theory is that relationships and communication networks reinforce one another in a virtuous or vicious cycle, suggesting that this cycle is mutually reinforcing and thus not easily reversed. Another tenet of relational coordination theory is that the positive cycle of relational coordination is supported by a set of cross-cutting organizational practices that span functional boundaries between participants who are engaged in a work process—a process of transforming inputs into outputs of greater value. The negative cycle of relational coordination is supported instead by traditional bureaucratic organizational practices that foster strong ties within functional silos at the expense of ties between functions.

But some have questioned whether the implementation of a set of formal organizational structures—selection for cross-functional teamwork, cross-functional performance measurement, cross-functional rewards, cross-functional conflict resolution, cross-functional protocols and meetings, and so on—is even be possible in the context of a strongly negative cycle of relational coordination. Will participants adopt the newly introduced work practices and participate in them in a meaningful way, or instead follow the letter but not the spirit of the newly introduced work practices, or even reject them outright? We know from theories of organizational change that numerous conditions are needed for change efforts to succeed. These conditions include a shared vision of the change, an understanding of the behaviors that are required for the change, and a belief that the change is necessary. To successfully implement practices that foster relational coordination may require, paradoxically, the shared goals, shared knowledge, and mutual respect that are supposed to be *outcomes* of those new structures, not their antecedents. It is therefore likely that the theory of change implicit in the current theory of relational coordination is too simplistic and mechanistic, not taking sufficient account of the possibility that feedback loops exist between the newly adopted structures and the processes that they are intended to support. Indeed, a study that assessed the impact of external pressures on relational coordination found that more intense external pressures predicted higher relational coordination among participants, mediated by perceived work stressors rather than by changes in formal structures (Gittell, 2008). Changes in formal structures were the strongest predictor of relational coordination, suggesting the possibility that structural changes are important for *sustaining* changes in relational coordination, but also suggesting the possibility that changes in relational coordination may *precede* changes in formal work structures.

Conclusion

This chapter has outlined the basic contributions of relational coordination theory, and has proposed five new directions for further theoretical development: to deepen the social psychological underpinnings of the theory drawing upon relational theory; to explore and challenge the proposition that relational coordination ties are based on role relations to the exclusion of personal relations; to extend the reach of the relational coordination network to include additional participants in the work process under consideration (in particular, noncore employees, customers, and members of the organization's broader value chain); to theorize about outcomes for workers, as well as for organizations and their customers; and finally, to explore and deepen the theory of change implicit in relational coordination theory. This chapter thus outlines an ambitious agenda for theory building that deepens the potential contribution of relational coordination theory to the broader discipline of POS.

As noted at the beginning of this chapter, POS emphasizes the subjective and intersubjective experience of work, thus highlighting the need for human beings to connect and relate. To the extent that organizations create the conditions for connection and relationship to occur, they tap into this aspect of the human condition, thereby unleashing the potential for high levels of individual and collective performance. Although traditions outside of POS offer arguments about quality/efficiency trade-offs, relational coordination theory argues that organizations move beyond that trade-off by tapping into the relational nature of human beings.

At the same time, POS is the study of generative dynamics and endogenous resourcefulness. Relational coordination is the embodiment of organizational generativity and resourcefulness because, at its best, it brings together numerous parts of the organization in the pursuit of a shared and superordinate purpose. Relational coordination also captures generative dynamics because it is an inherently processual approach, as is evidenced in the interplay between shared goals, shared knowledge, and mutual respect and the ongoing communication needed to produce generativity and resourcefulness. Relational coordination theory thus provides grounded insight into the subjective and intersubjective process of coordinating and into the dynamics and experience of that process.

Positive organizational scholarship is also about finding meaning in work (e.g., Wrzesniewski & Dutton, 2001). Relational coordination theory substantially contributes to that ideal because relational coordination at its best entails more connection through one's work and with one's work, enabling front-line workers to better live out their professional ideals. Finally, relational coordination theory embodies the POS approach of viewing organizational strength as a distributed property of an organization, celebrating those on the front line and not only in the executive suite as drivers of organizational excellence.

References

Adler, P. (1995). Interdepartmental interdependence and coordination: The case of the design/manufacturing interface. *Organization Science, 6*, 147–167.

Adler, P., Kwon, S., & Heckscher, C. (2008). Professional work: The emergence of collaborative community. *Organization Science, 19*(2), 359–376.

Argote, L. (1982). Input uncertainty and organizational coordination in hospital emergency units. *Administrative Science Quarterly, 27*(3), 420–434.

Baker, W. (2000). *Achieving success through social capital.* San Francisco: Jossey-Bass.

Bechky, B.A. (2006). Gaffers, gofers and grips: Role-based coordination in temporary organizations. *Organization Science, 17*(1), 3–21.

Buber, M. (1937). *I and thou.* New York: Simon and Schuster (Original work published 1923).

Cameron, K., Dutton, J.E., & Quinn, R.E. (2003). *Positive organizational scholarship: Foundations of a new discipline.* San Francisco: Berrett-Koehler Publishers.

Chappell, R.T. (1994). Can TQM in public education survive without co-production? *Quality Progress, 27*(7), 41–45.

Collins, C.J., & Clark, K. (2003). Strategic human resource practices, top management team social networks, and firm performance. *Academy of Management Journal, 46*, 740–751.

Dutton, J.E., & Ragins, B.R. (2007). *Exploring positive relationships at work: Building a theoretical and research foundation.* Mahwah, NJ: Lawrence Ehrlbaum Associates.

Dutton, J.E., & Heaphy, E.D. (2003). The power of high-quality connections. In K.S. Cameron, J.E. Dutton, R.E. Quinn (Eds.), *Positive organizational scholarship: Foundations of a new discipline.* San Francisco: Berrett-Koehler Publishers.

Dutton, J.E. (2003). *Energize your workplace: How to create and sustain high-quality connections at work.* San Francisco: Jossey-Bass.

Eaton, S.C. (2000). Beyond "unloving care:" Linking human resource management and patient care quality in nursing homes. *International Journal of Human Resource Management, 11*(3), 591–616.

Edmondson, A.C. (1996). Learning from mistakes is easier said than done: Group and organization influences on the detection and correction of human error. *Journal of Applied Behavioral Science, 32*, 5–28.

Edmondson, A.C. (2004). Psychological safety, trust, and learning in organizations: A group-level lens. In R.M. Kramer, &

K.S. Cook (Eds.), *Trust and distrust in organizations: Dilemmas and approaches* (pp. 239–272). New York: Russell Sage.

Evans, W.R., & Davis, D. (2005). High-performance work systems and organizational performance: The mediating role of internal social structure. *Journal of Management, 31,* 758–775.

Faraj, S., & Xiao, Y. (2006). Coordination in fast response organizations. *Management Science, 52*(8), 1155–1169.

Faraj, S., & Sproull, L., 2000. Coordinating expertise in software development teams. *Management Science, 46(12):* 1554-1568.

Fletcher, J.K. (1999). *Disappearing acts: Gender, power, and relational practice at work.* Cambridge: MIT Press.

Follett, M.P. 1924. *Creative experience.* New York: Longmans, Green.

Follett, M.P. 1949. *Freedom and co-ordination: Lectures in business organization by Mary Parker Follett.* London: Management Publications Trust, Ltd.

Freud, S. (1930). Civilization and its discontents. *Standard Edition, 23:* 64–145, London: Hogarth Press, 1961.

Galbraith, J.R. (1972). Organization design: An information processing view. In J.W. Lorsch, & P.R. Lawrence (Eds.), *Organization planning: Cases and concepts* (pp. 49–74). Homewood, IL: Richard D. Irwin, Inc.

Gilligan, C. (1982). *In a different voice: Psychological theory and women's development.* Cambridge, MA: Harvard University Press.

Gittell, J.H. 2001. Supervisory span, relational coordination and flight departure performance: A reassessment of post-bureaucracy theory. *Organization Science, 12*(4): 467–482.

Gittell, J.H. (2002a). Relationships between service providers and their impact on customers. *Journal of Service Research, 4*(4), 299–311.

Gittell, J.H. (2002b). Coordinating mechanisms in care provider groups: Relational coordination as a mediator and input uncertainty as a moderator of performance effects. *Management Science, 48,* 1408–1426.

Gittell, J.H., Weinberg, D., Bennett, A., & Miller, J.A. (2008). Is the doctor in? A relational approach to job design and the coordination of work. *Human Resource Management, 47*(4), 729–755.

Gittell, J.H. (2006). Relational coordination: Coordinating work through relationships of shared goals, shared knowledge and mutual respect. In O. Kyriakidou, & M. Ozbilgin (Eds.), *Relational perspectives in organizational studies: A research companion.* London: Edward Elgar Publishers.

Gittell, J.H. (2008). Relationships and resilience: Care provider responses to pressures from managed care. *Journal of Applied Behavioral Science, 44*(1), 25–47.

Gittell, J.H., Fairfield, K., Bierbaum, B., Jackson, R., Kelly, M., Laskin, R., Lipson, S., Siliski, J., Thornhill, T., Zuckerman, J. (2000). "Impact of Relational Coordination on Quality of Care, Post-Operative Pain and Functioning, and Length of Stay: A Nine Hospital Study of Surgical Patients," *Medical Care, 38*(8): 807–819.

Gittell, J.H., Seidner, R., & Wimbush, J. (2010). A relational model of how high-performance work systems work. *Organization Science, 21*(2), 299–311.

Gittell, J.H., Weinberg, D.B., & Hagigi, F. (2010). *Modularity and the coordination of complex work: The case of post-surgical patient care.* Working Paper.

Gittell, J.H., Weinberg, D., Pfefferle, S., & Bishop, C. (2008). Impact of relational coordination on job satisfaction and quality outcomes: A study of nursing homes. *Human Resource Management Journal, 18*(2), 154–170.

Gittell, J.H., & Weiss, L. (2004). Coordination networks within and across organizations: A multi-level framework. *Journal of Management Studies, 41*(1), 127–153.

Grant, A.M. (2007). Relational job design and the motivation to make a prosocial difference. *Academy of Management Review, 32*(2), 393–417.

Hallowell, R, Schlesinger, L., & Zornitsky, J. (1996). Internal customer satisfaction, customer and job satisfaction: Linkages and implications for management. *Human Resource Planning, 192:* 20-31.

Heckscher, C. (1994). Defining the post-bureaucratic type. In C. Heckscher, & A. Donnellon (Eds.), *The post-bureaucratic organization.* Thousand Oaks, CA: Sage.

Heckscher, C., & Adler, P.S. (2006). *The firm as a collaborative community: Reconstructing trust in the knowledge economy.* Oxford: Oxford University Press.

Leana, C., & Van Buren, H.J. (1999). Organizational social capital and employment practices. *Academy of Management Review, 24,* 538–555.

Lepak, D.P., & S.A. Snell. 1999. The human resource architecture: Toward a theory of human capital allocation and development. *Academy of Management Review, 24:* 31–48.

Malone, T., & Crowston, K. (1994). The interdisciplinary study of coordination. *Computing Surveys, 26*(1), 87–119.

Marschall, M. (2004). Citizen participation and the neighborhood context: A new look at the coproduction of local public goods. *Political Research Quarterly, 57*(2), 231–245.

Mead, G.H. (1934). *Mind, self and society: From the standpoint of a social behavioralist.* Chicago: University of Chicago Press.

Miller, J.B. (1976). *Toward a new psychology of women.* Boston: Beacon Press.

Mitchell, S. (2000). *Relationality: From attachment to intersubjectivity.* Hillsdale, NJ: The Analytic Press.

Nahapiet, J., & Ghoshal, S. (1998). Social capital, intellectual capital and the organizational advantage. *Academy of Management Review, 23*(2), 242–266.

Nembhard, I.M., & Edmondson, A.C. (2006). Making it safe: The effects of leader inclusiveness and professional status on psychological safety and improvement efforts in health care teams. *Journal of Organizational Behavior, 27,* 941–966.

Ple, L. (2009). How does the customer co-construct the service organization over time? An empirical study of the impact of the customer on intra-organizational coordination. *Working paper.*

Quinn, R., & Dutton, J.E. (2005). Coordination as energy-in-conversation. *Academy of Management Review, 30*(1), 36–57.

Rousseau, D. (1985). Issues of level in organizational research: Multi-level and cross-level perspectives. *Research in Organizational Behavior, 7,* 1–37.

Ryan, M. (2009). *Care coordination for senior patients with multiple chronic diseases: Examining the association between organizational factors and patient outcomes.* Ph.D. dissertation, Heller School for Social Policy and Management, Brandeis University, Waltham, MA.

Safran, D.G., Miller, W., & Beckman, H. (2006). Organizational dimensions of relationship-centered care: Theory, evidence, and practice. *Journal of General Internal Medicine, 21,* S9–S15.

Stone, D. (2000). Caring by the book. In M.H. Meyer (Ed.), *Care work: Gender, class, and the welfare state* (pp. 89–111). New York: Routledge.

Suchman, A. (2006). A new theoretical foundation for relationship-centered care: Complex responsive processes of relating. *Journal of General Internal Medicine, 12,* S40–44.

Thompson, J.D. (1967). *Organizations in action: Social science bases of administrative theory.* New York: McGraw-Hill.

Tushman, M., & Nadler, D. (1978). Information processing as an integrating concept in organizational design. *Academy of Management Review, 3*(3), 613–124.

Vogus, T. (2006). What is it about relationships? A behavioral theory of social capital and performance. *Labor and Employment Relations Proceedings, 58,* 164–173.

Weick, K.E., & Roberts, K. (1993). Collective mind in organizations: Heedful interrelating on flight decks. *Administrative Science Quarterly, 38,* 357–381.

Weinberg, D.B., Lusenhop, W., Gittell, J.H., & Kautz, C. (2007). Coordination between formal providers and informal caregivers. *Health Care Management Review, 32*(2), 140–150.

Wright, W. (2010). *Extending relational coordination as a high performance work system.* Ph.D. dissertation proposal, Curtin University of Technology, Perth, Western Australia.

Wrzesniewski, A., & Dutton, J.E. (2001). Crafting a job: Revisioning employees as active crafters of their work. *Academy of Management Review, 26*(2), 179–120.

CHAPTER 31

A Dual Model of Reciprocity in Organizations

Moral Sentiments and Reputation

Wayne Baker

Abstract

In this chapter, I develop a dual model of reciprocity in organizations that brings together mainstream reciprocity theory and positive organizational scholarship (POS). Reciprocity theory assumes that people are self-regarding; they give only if doing so builds a reputation for generosity that pays off in the future. Positive organizational scholarship assumes that people are naturally other-regarding, giving to others without regard to self. Moral sentiments, defined as positive emotions such as gratitude, motivate prosocial behavior. I take a middle ground, arguing that most people in organizations have mixed motives, simultaneously concerned for self and for others. The dual model combines the mechanisms of reputation and moral sentiments. I describe examples of this dual model in organizations, focusing on human resource practices and everyday work practices that appeal to people with mixed motives. I conclude with a discussion of future research directions based on this dual model.

Keywords: Reciprocity, pay it forward, exchange, indirect reciprocity, moral sentiments, positive emotions, positive practices, social capital

> How selfish soever man may be supposed, there are evidently some principles in his nature, which interest him in the fortune of others, and render their happiness necessary to him, though he derives nothing from it, except the pleasure of seeing it.
> —Adam Smith, Opening sentence in *The Theory of Moral Sentiments*

Consider the expression of moral sentiments in this story: "On my way [driving] to church I slid into the ditch, buried myself [in snow] and had to rely on a couple of Good Samaritans to help me. Today I had a chance to repay that favor. A couple of ladies were stuck in Grand Rapids [Michigan] and I pulled over, fresh in my mind because I had been helped by someone else. I think a lot of the time, it's a good reminder. My faith does inform my decisions but on the other hand, there's nothing quite like being the recipient of a fleshed-out virtue to help you do what's right."

This story, told on National Public Radio's *Talk of the Nation* (February 13, 2008), contains all the elements of a common human behavior that remains a theoretical conundrum for evolutionary theory, social exchange theory, and rational choice. The behavior is a form of reciprocity known by several names: indirect reciprocity, generalized reciprocity, or generalized exchange; colloquially, it is called *paying it forward* (Hyde, 2000). Paying it forward is a chain of events that involves at least three parties and two unilateral acts of helpfulness. This three-party chain can take different forms (e.g., look ahead to Figure 31.1). For example, *A* helps *B*; *B* feels positive emotions, which motivate *B* to help *C*. In the story above, Good Samaritans (*A*) helped the storyteller (*B*) out of a ditch; the storyteller (*B*) later did the same for the ladies from Grand Rapids (*C*).

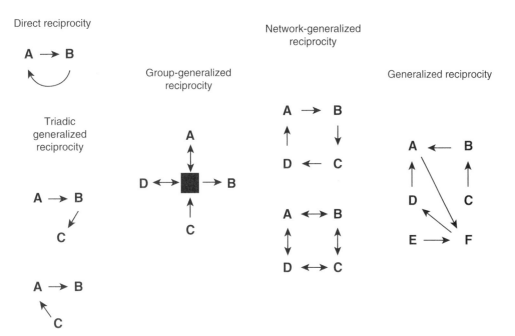

Fig. 31.1 Illustration of direct reciprocity and forms of generalized reciprocity. Sources: Reproduced or adapted from diagrams in Molm, Collett, and Schaefer (2007) Nowak and Sigmund (2005), Takahashi (2000), and Yamagishi and Cook (1993).

On indirect reciprocity, Ekeh (1974, p. 48) said, "an individual feels obliged to reciprocate another's actions, not by directly rewarding his benefactor, but by benefitting another actor implicated in a social exchange situation with his benefactor and himself."

Reciprocity is so widely observed throughout human society that Becker (1956) said our species should be renamed "*Homo reciprocus*." Reciprocity made complex social systems possible (Leakey & Lewin, 1978). Reciprocity is essential for democracy and economic growth (e.g., Putnam, 2000), as well as for the social capital of organizations (e.g., Adler & Kwon, 2002; Baker, 2000; Cohen & Prusak, 2001). Indeed, reciprocity is a key form of positive social capital in organizations when it creates and expands the generative capacity of people and groups (Baker & Dutton, 2007).

Nonetheless, the principle of reciprocity is so powerful that it can be used as a "compliance technique" to create uninvited debts and unfair exchanges, as unscrupulous salespeople, politicians, and fundraisers know quite well (Cialidini, 1993). People can strategically build a (false) reputation for generosity solely to benefit from the generosity of others. That the principle can be misused does not detract from the role reciprocity plays as a positive organizational practice. In this chapter, I develop insights into this positive practice by linking it to the mainstream literature on reciprocity and to positive organizational scholarship (POS).

These two literatures have developed separately, with opposite views of human nature. Reciprocity theory and research assume that selfish interests motivate behavior. Indirect reciprocity is a theoretical puzzle. Self-regarding people are likely to free ride, taking advantage of others and not giving their own resources (e.g., Takahashi, 2000, p. 1105). As a result, indirect reciprocity cannot get started, and if it somehow does, it would be so fragile that it would soon fall apart. Those "who think that others will not give are unlikely to give away their own resources, and generalized exchange [indirect reciprocity] may never be established" (Takahashi, 2000, p. 1107). From this perspective, other-regarding behavior appears to be irrational. Why, for example, did the Good Samaritans help the storyteller out of the snow? It was unlikely that he would repay them in kind (and certainly not with money). Why did he pay it forward? One may cite his religious convictions, but reciprocity is embedded in all moral and religious codes (Gouldner, 1960), and we would have to explain why reciprocity resides in these codes in the first place. And, in this specific case, we would have to explain why it was applied to the ladies from Grand Rapids. After all, no one would have known if the storyteller had failed to stop and help.

Positive organizational scholarship, in contrast, assumes that "unselfishness, altruism, [and] contributions without regard to self" motivate behavior (Cameron, Dutton, & Quinn, 2003, p. 4). Based on these assumptions, the helping behaviors in Grand Rapids are easily explained: People are naturally other-regarding, so indirect reciprocity (such as aiding motorists in difficulty) is commonplace. Indeed, if we assume that people are strongly other-regarding, prosocial behavior such as indirect reciprocity is no longer a puzzle to be explained. In this chapter, I take a middle position. Some people may be very selfish; some may be concerned only for others. But I assume that most people in organizations are between the poles of the selfish and the saintly, motivated both by concerns for self and concerns for others. Given that most people are in the middle, the mechanisms that facilitate indirect reciprocity in organizations must take into account mixed motives. This chapter is a step in this direction. Drawing together theory and research on reciprocity and POS, I propose a "dual model" of reciprocity in organizations that combines the mechanisms of moral sentiments and reputation.

The chapter is organized as follows. First, I provide an overview of types of reciprocity. Second, I discuss the two opposing assumptions about human nature: *Homo economicus* versus *Homo reciprocus*. Third, I propose a dual model of reciprocity in organizations, based on two key mechanisms: reputation and moral sentiments. Fourth, I describe several empirical examples of this dual model in organizations, focusing on "enablers" of positive social capital (Baker & Dutton, 2007). I conclude with a discussion of future research directions based on this dual model.

Types of Reciprocity

Reciprocity is a form of cooperation in which two or more people exchange or transfer resources at different points in time. These resources include information, ideas, advice, help, assistance, opportunities, contacts, material goods, services, financial capital, and so on (Baker, 2000). Reciprocity is an implicit understanding between two or more people; it does not involve formal agreements or legal contracts; there is no price or official exchange rate. Expectation of repayment is tacit or vague. As a result, a beneficiary of an exchange may or may not repay the benefactor, and may or may not "pay it forward" to a third party.

Direct reciprocity is an exchange or transfer of resources between two people. As illustrated in Figure 31.1, *A* provides a resource to *B* and, at some later time, *B* provides a resource to *A*. Indirect reciprocity, also known as generalized reciprocity or generalized exchange (e.g., Takahashi, 2000), occurs in larger systems and involves three or more people. The essence of indirect reciprocity is unilateral resource giving. For example, what I call *triadic generalized reciprocity* involves three people and three unilateral transfers (see Figure 31.1). Nowak and Sigmund (2005) describe two types of triads: "upstream" and "downstream." Upstream occurs when *A* provides a resource to *B*, *B* feels "positive emotions" as a result, and therefore provides resources to *C* (i.e., pays it forward). Downstream occurs when *A* provides a resource to *B*, *C* observes *A*'s generosity, feels positive emotions, and rewards by assisting *A* when *A* makes a request or expresses a need. Although Nowak and Sigmund (2005) do not mention it, downstream indirect reciprocity may include paying it forward to a fourth party: *A* provides a resource to *B*, *C* observes *A*'s generosity and feels positive emotions that motivate *C* to provide a resource to *D*.

Nowak and Sigmund (2005) are theorists who posit that "positive emotions" are the mechanisms driving indirect reciprocity, but they do not specify which positive emotions or elaborate how this mechanism might work. Research in positive psychology and POS, however, suggests that gratitude is a key positive emotion at play (and, as I argue later, a key source of moral sentiments). Gratitude promotes prosocial behavior (e.g., Emmons & McCullough, 2003, 2004). People who feel gratitude are more helpful to those in their social networks (McCullough, Emmons, & Tsang, 2002). Gratitude is a stronger motivation for prosocial behavior than feelings of indebtedness (Tsang, 2007). Indebtedness is an uncomfortable feeling of obligation that may or may not lead to reciprocity. For example, indebtedness can lead a recipient of help to avoid her benefactor (Tsang, 2007; Watkins, Scheer, Ovnicek, & Kolts, 2006), and, by implication, not participate in direct or indirect reciprocity.

Another form or reciprocity is group-generalized reciprocity (Yamagishi & Cook, 1993), which occurs when people contribute resources to a resource pool, and people receive or withdraw resources from it. Some may give and receive; others may only give; still others may only receive. Examples include voluntary donations of human blood and organs (e.g., Healy, 2006; Titmuss, 1971) and voluntary participation in rotating savings and credit associations (Biggart & Castanias, 2001). Examples also include involuntary systems of "redistribution" documented by anthropologists (e.g., Polanyi, 1957/1971) and modern taxation. Network-generalized reciprocity

(Yamagishi & Cook, 1993), also called *chain-generalized reciprocity* (Molm, Collett, & Schaefer, 2007) follows fixed patterns of exchange, such as one-way and two-way cycles (see Figure 31.1).[1] The classic example is the Kula Ring in the South Pacific Trobriand Islands, in which valuables changed hands from island to island in a fixed circular pattern (e.g., Malinowski, 1922; see, also, Strathern, 1975).

Pure generalized reciprocity does not involve fixed networks of giving or receiving (Takahashi, 2000). Putnam (2000) provides a prosaic definition that captures the emergent and unplanned nature of this form of reciprocity: "I'll do this for you now, without expecting anything immediately in return and perhaps without even knowing you, confident that down the road you or someone else will return the favor" (p. 134). Aiding a stranded motorist (as in the lead story to this chapter) is a good example. It is difficult to predict when and where one might encounter a stranded motorist; it is difficult to predict when and where one might become a stranded motorist; and direct reciprocity (see Figure 31.1) is unlikely.

Homo Economicus Versus Homo Reciprocus

Why do people engage in reciprocity? We do not have to go beyond rational self-interest to explain *direct* reciprocity, the exchange of favors between two people. But indirect reciprocity is a puzzle if we assume self-interested behavior. This assumption implies that people cooperate only if forced to do so, or if they are convinced that their seemingly generous behavior will pay off in the future. This is the well-known "*Homo economicus*" or "economic man"—the hyper-rational, coldly calculating, self-interested habitué of classical economic theory.

H. economicus is, of course, a fiction. Some people are quite self-regarding, but few real people live up to this extremely selfish view of human nature. Yet, the fiction contains an important truth: Self-interest is undeniably part of human nature. The problem comes in when theories of reciprocity make the assumption of homogenous social preferences. As Simpson and Willer (2008) note, almost all studies of indirect reciprocity assume that people are self-regarding "egoists." This assumption is at odds with research in mainstream social psychology, which demonstrates that social preferences (or social motives) are heterogeneous. Many people, for example, behave like "*Homo reciprocus*," which I define as a pronounced propensity to reciprocate directly and indirectly with others, engaging in and creating a dynamic network of interactions.[2]

This propensity to reciprocate is variable. There is a distribution of social preferences in a population, ranging from self-regarding egoists (like *H. economicus*) on one end to other-regarding altruists on the other. Surprisingly, a number of behavioral economists have come to share the view that preferences are heterogeneous, convinced by years of experimental evidence that there is a tendency for some people to behave prosocially (see, e.g., Gintis, Bowles, Boyd, & Fehr, 2005). Neuroscience shows that social preferences are part of human brain circuitry, confirming that they are genuine (e.g., Fehr & Camerer, 2007).

Nonetheless, the social science research on social preferences and reciprocity typically makes simplifying assumptions about the distribution of preferences, placing people into a few discrete categories. Simpson and Willer (2008), for example, divide the subjects in their experiments into two categories: egoists or altruists. Egoists are concerned about their own welfare; altruists balance concern for self with concern for others. Weber and Murnighan (2008) describe "consistent contributors" who "always contribute, regardless of others' choices" (pp. 1340–1341), in contrast to free riders who take advantage of the system when they can and cooperate only if it pays off. And, behavioral economists posit the existence of "strong reciprocators," people with a predisposition to cooperate and to punish those who do not, even at personal cost (e.g., Fehr, Fischbacher, & Gächter, 2002; Gintis, Bowles, Boyd, & Fehr, 2005).

Discrete categories capture important tendencies in a population, but it is more likely that the distribution of preferences is continuous. For example, Baker and Levine (2010) used a continuous measure of social preferences—values—in their study of the mechanisms of indirect reciprocity. The participants in their experiments had values that ranged between extreme self-regarding values and extreme other-regarding values. At one end, people had very strong preferences for achievement (winning in competitive situations) and power (control of people and resources; status and prestige). At the other, people had very strong preferences for universalism (concern for the welfare of people in general) and benevolence (concern for the welfare of members of one's social network).[3] Most participants, however, fell between the extremes, having values that mixed concern for self and concern for others. In other words, they combined the motivations of *H. economicus* and *H. reciprocus*. In this chapter, I assume that most organizations are populated with people who have mixed motives, consistent with Baker and Levine's (2010) finding.

A Dual Model of Reciprocity in Organizations

If people embody the spirit of *H. economicus*, then reciprocity occurs only if forced, or as a response to rewards and punishments. If humans embody the spirit of *H. reciprocus*, then reciprocity occurs freely, as long as obstacles do not stand in the way. Since social preferences vary, with most people in the middle, organizations must manage a population of people with mixed motives. Mechanisms, therefore, must elicit moral sentiments and appeal to rational choice. Although POS offers a wide range of possibilities, I focus on mechanisms that have a basis in *both* the mainstream reciprocity literature and POS. As noted above, these fields exist in parallel and separate universes. Linking these fields generates both insights into reciprocity as a key form of positive social capital (Baker & Dutton, 2007) and leads to the future directions for research, which are presented at the end of this chapter.

I propose a dual model of reciprocity in organizations.[4] The first of two mechanisms is moral sentiments driven by positive emotions. As I elaborate below, gratitude in particular promotes indirect reciprocity. Positive emotions are the domain of positive psychology and POS but have a few links to the reciprocity literature (e.g., Nowak & Sigmund, 2005). The second mechanism is reputation, which is the dominant mechanism in the mainstream reciprocity literature, but also has connections to positive psychology and POS.

Mechanism 1: Moral Sentiments

Moral sentiments encourage other-regarding behavior. This mechanism, I argue, operates through emotions. Adam Smith (1759) argued in *The Theory of Moral Sentiments* that "sympathy" motivated other-regarding behavior. This innate human ability enabled one person to understand what another person feels by imagining what one would feel in the same situation. Centuries later, neuroscience confirms the existence of "mirror neurons" (e.g., Rizzolatti & Craighero, 2004) that behave in a similar manner, enabling one person to "sympathize" with another and feel what the other person feels.

The act of giving itself generates positive emotions or what Becker (1974) called a "warm glow" in the giver. That this "warm glow" is a reason for giving has received empirical support (e.g., Andreoni 1989, 1990). Receiving help elicits the positive

emotion of *gratitude*. Gratitude is a recognition of the "unearned increments of value in one's experience" (Bertocci & Millard, 1963, p. 389). Gratitude is one of the "moral emotions." These are emotions "linked to the interests or welfare either of society as a whole or at least of persons other than the judge or agent" (Haidt, 2003, p. 276). Negative moral emotions, such as guilt, shame, or embarrassment, have received more attention in psychology (e.g., Tangney, Stuewig, & Mashek, 2007) but positive psychologists emphasize positive moral emotions—especially gratitude (e.g., Emmons, 2003; McCullough, Kilpatrick, Emmons, & Larson, 2001).

Feelings of gratitude are the specific positive emotions behind the moral sentiments driving reciprocity. For example, Simmel (1950) observed that gratitude is the "moral memory" that reminds a beneficiary of reciprocal obligations. Generally, gratitude promotes prosocial behavior (e.g., Emmons & McCullough, 2003, 2004; Tsang, 2007), such as helping others in one's social networks (McCullough, Emmons, & Tsang, 2002). Gratitude for benefits received motivates paying it forward to others, according to evidence from experiments (Baker & Levine, 2010) and field studies (Baker & Bulkley, 2009) of positive organizing and reciprocity.[5] More generally, successful exchanges generate positive emotions, which, in turn, increase cohesion and commitment to the exchange relationship (Lawler, 2001; see also, Collins, 2004) and social solidarity—feelings of belonging, relational commitment, and mutual trust (Molm, Collett, & Schaefer, 2007). Increased cohesion, commitment, and solidarity all promote future acts of reciprocity.

Mechanism 2: Reputation

Alexander (1987) argued that reputation is necessary to sustain indirect reciprocity. Those who earn a reputation for generosity are more likely to receive help from others, compared to those who have a reputation for stinginess. According to this line of argument, without reputation—that is, without knowing what others have done in the past—a system of indirect reciprocity cannot arise. Alexander's argument spurred a vigorous program of research on reciprocity, in which reputation is considered to be the dominant mechanism. Evolutionary biologists, for example, operationalize reputation as "image" and propose that "image scoring" is a strategy people use to build a positive reputation (Nowak & Sigmund, 1998). Those who operate with this strategy act generously only to improve their image. Simpson and Willer (2008) found evidence of image scoring in their experiments on indirect reciprocity. The egoists in their studies were sensitive to "reputational incentives," behaving in ways that are consistent with an image scoring strategy. For example, egoists were more likely to give when their behavior was public than when it was private. Altruists, however, were less sensitive to the presence or absence of these reputational incentives. Other experiments and computer simulations have shown similar results (e.g., Seinen & Schram, 2006; Wedekind & Milinski, 2000). Building on these studies, Baker and Levine (2010) assessed the effects of reputational incentives, using a continuous measure of social preferences rather than an egoist–altruist divide. They found that most people respond to reputational incentives. Only the small minority who had very strong other-regarding values ignored these incentives, behaving generously regardless of the past behaviors of others.

Fairness is the other side of reputation. Building an altruistic image pays off only if others use fairness criteria, rewarding those who are (or appear to be) generous and punishing others who are stingy. Using an agent-based simulation, Takahashi (2000) showed that generalized reciprocity can evolve without social norms, altruism, or central authority as long as each agent (i.e., person) has some sense of fairness and information about other agents. Fairness is an agent's evaluation of the past behavior of a potential recipient. An agent uses these evaluations to make decisions about giving. In this simulation, an agent gives resources to another agent who satisfies the giver's criterion for fairness and denies resources to agents who do not. Fairness-based selective giving evolves into a system of indirect reciprocity if each agent has information about all other agents or about those in one's neighborhood.

In the only study of the evolution of reciprocity in real groups, Baker and Bulkley (2009) found that people indeed use fairness criteria when they decide whether to help someone. In this setting, people could observe others' behavior, seeing whether they were generous or not in their responses to others' requests for help. When generous people made requests, they were more likely to get a response, and to get more responses, compared to stingy people who made requests. However, as Takahashi (2000) suggested, each person has his or her own fairness criteria. Some people in the groups studied by Baker and Bulkley (2009) reported that they always used fairness criteria; others said that they

applied fairness criteria only in extreme cases; still others said they never used fairness to determine whether or not to respond to someone.

The effects of fairness on organizational citizenship behaviors (OCBs), which include reciprocity, are well documented at the individual and group levels. For example, the more people feel they are treated fairly, the more they engage in reciprocity (e.g., Stamper & Van Dyne, 2001). Fairness is a component of the "procedural justice climate" of a group—"a distinct group-level cognition about how a work group as a whole is treated" (Naumann & Bennett, 2000, p. 882). The more the members of a group feel their group is treated fairly, the more they engage in reciprocity and other OCBs (e.g., Dekas, 2009; Mayer, Nishii, Schneider, & Goldstein, 2007; Naumann & Bennett, 2000).

Examples of the Dual Model of Reciprocity in Action

This dual model of reciprocity in organizations— moral sentiments and reputation—is a synthesis of the literatures on reciprocity and POS, highlighting some of the links between these disparate lines of work. This dual model assumes that most (but not all) people are motivated to give by a combination of selfish and unselfish reasons. Effective organizational procedures and practices may appeal to one or both of the mechanisms in this dual model.

Any number of positive organizational practices could encourage the expression of moral sentiments and create opportunities for reputation building. Given the relative lack of POS theory and research about reciprocity, however, I focus on some of the key "enablers" of positive social capital proposed by Baker and Dutton (2007) and describe how they connect to the two mechanisms in the dual model. I consider these connections to be areas of future research, as I discuss in the conclusion to the chapter.

Baker and Dutton (2007, p. 330) define "enabler" as "any practice or condition that makes a process or state more likely to occur." They present several clusters of positive organizational practices. Some are human resource practices, such as selection and socialization; others are everyday work practices, such as the conduct of meetings and collaborative technologies (Baker & Dutton, 2007, pp. 331, 334). These enablers influence motivations and opportunity structures for positive social capital. Applied here, these enablers heighten moral sentiments and create opportunities for their expression; at the same time, these enablers dampen the expression of

Table 31.1 Links between enablers of positive social capital and two mechanisms of reciprocity in organizations

Enabler	Moral Sentiments	Reputation
Selecting on relational skills	Populates an organization with members who have other-regarding social preferences.	___
Participatory selection practices	Interactions with a diverse set of current employees helps to identify candidates with other-regarding values and produces positive emotions	Creates opportunities for reputation building with a diverse social networks; increases interpersonal knowledge and more and earlier exposure to others' needs and potential contributions to them
Relational socialization practices	Cultivates conditions of high-quality connections (trusting and respectful engagement) and the positive emotions they come from them; decreases the motivation to misuse the reciprocity principle to trigger unwanted exchanges or create unfair debts	Creates more connections earlier and creates more opportunities for creating high-quality connections, including opportunities to build reputation by helping others. Greater and earlier exposure to others' needs increases opportunities to respond to them and build reputation
Using group incentives	Group incentives link and align self-interest with moral sentiments	Promotes and rewards other-regarding behavior
Relational meeting practices	Cultivates trusting and respectful engagement, which encourages the expression of moral sentiments and dampen self-interest	Provides new and more venues and occasions for reputation building
Using collaborative technologies	Uses technology as a means to express moral sentiments in exchange	Provides means (tools) for building reputation by practicing reciprocity

Source: Modification of Table 2 in Baker and Dutton (2007).

self-interest, but also provide opportunities for its expression in positive reputation building. These are summarized in Table 31.1.

Consider, for example, selecting on relational skills and participatory selection practices. These two enablers populate an organization with members who have desirable social preferences and build positive ties with current employees during the selection process. Both POS case studies and experimental evidence show that selecting on the basis of social preferences influences cooperative behavior. For example, two-part experiments show that selecting participants who demonstrated other-regarding behavior in one experiment and putting them in a second experiment will increase rates of cooperation in the second experiment (Fischbacher & Gaechter, 2008). Some companies intentionally search for and hire people with the "right attitude" and "relational competence" to build a population of members with other-regarding values. Examples include Southwest Airlines (Gittell, 2003), along with Zingerman's (Baker & Gunderson, 2005) and the other "small giants" chronicled by Burlingham (2005). (Zingerman's is a family of high-quality food-related businesses in Ann Arbor, Michigan.)

Companies noted for high levels of social capital, such as Viant, IDEO, and Russell Reynolds Associates (Cohen & Prusak, 2001, pp. 137–138), employ a long interview process to vet candidates for cooperativeness. A long interview process is a participatory process in which current employees and prospective employees build positive ties with one another; the process helps to screen out candidates who attempt to present themselves as other-regarding when they are not. In addition to a recruitment process that involves many interviews with current employees, companies use other methods to identify candidates with the right attitude. Zingerman's, for example, requires candidates to write several short essays about their good and bad experiences of service, teamwork, and cooperation (Baker & Gunderson, 2005).

Relational socialization refers to "the formal and informal processes that are used to bring new organizational members on board in an organization" (Baker & Dutton, 2007, p. 336). Relational socialization practices cultivate conditions of trust and respectful engagement, two components of high-quality connections. High-quality connections generate positive emotions, thus increasing prosocial behavior (such as reciprocity) and decreasing the motivation to misuse the reciprocity principle. Relational meeting practices also enable high-quality connections and provide opportunities for reciprocity. Both enablers are evident in the informal practices used at IDEO, the premiere new product design firm (Hargadon & Sutton, 1997). "Brainstorming meetings" and "Monday morning meetings" socialize newcomers by making visible and reinforcing strong norms of direct and indirect reciprocity.[6] These are also regular and routine relational meeting practices that build moral sentiments and provide opportunities to enhance reputations. For instance, designers call brainstorming meetings to solicit ideas, suggestions, and solutions from fellow designers. In return, they will participate in the brainstorming meetings held by other designers, whether or not they have received help from them in particular. In Monday morning meetings, designers regularly announce the problems they are working on and elicit potentially useful or helpful ideas (p. 742). "These interactions make visible the norms of asking for help, sharing knowledge, and giving help," note Hargadon and Sutton (1997, p. 742). Other-regarding designers would thrive in this cultural setting, whereas self-regarding designers would find selfish reasons to help: By helping others, they would build a reputation for generosity that would be rewarded in the future. Refusing to help others would earn a reputation for stinginess that would be punished by ostracism.

Reward and incentive systems can inhibit or facilitate positive social capital (Baker, 2000; Baker & Dutton, 2007). When people have mixed motives, reciprocity depends on the application of incentive systems that reward those who build reputations for generosity. However, organizations that hire self-regarding employees typically have incentive systems that measure and reward individual performance, making cooperation even less likely. But even in organizations that recruit and hire other-regarding employees, measuring and rewarding reciprocity elevates it to higher levels. For example, Southwest Airlines gives agent-of-the-month awards to those who enable others to succeed (Gittell, 2003). The winners are determined by fellow employees. These awards make public reputations for generosity, and, by the way they are determined, elevate moral sentiments. Similarly, Zingerman's X-tra Mile program (Baker & Gunderson, 2005) enhances moral sentiments and reputations at the same time. When one employee observes another going the extra mile (e.g., making a big contribution

by performing an unselfish act), the observer writes up the episode for publication in the company newsletter. The person who went the extra mile gets public recognition and a "very cool x-tra mile t-shirt." Practices such as these build genuine reputations for generosity, as well as make visible and reinforce strong norms of reciprocity.

Group incentives enable reciprocity because they align self-interest with moral sentiments, and promote and reward other-regarding behavior. Companies known for high social capital develop formal systems linking individual pay to group-level outcomes (see, e.g., Cohen & Prusak, 2001). Firms that utilize open book finance (OBF), such as Springfield Remanufacturing Corporation (SRC), develop hundreds of group-level incentive systems that measure and reward cooperative behavior (e.g., Stack with Burlingham, 1994). Open book finance (sometimes also called open book management) is "based on the premise that business is essentially a game"—and, to play it, people must know the rules, get enough information to know what is going on and to keep score, and have the opportunity to win or lose (Baker & Smerek, 2010, p. 1). "Mini-games" are a novel form of group-level incentive systems. These "are small-scale incentive plans designed to fix weaknesses or pursue an opportunity" (Baker & Smerek, 2010, p. 7). Each mini-game includes a common goal, a scorecard, and monetary rewards that are shared equally with members of the group playing the mini-game. For example, the catering department at Zingerman's created the 50/50 Catering Game to increase the number of on-time deliveries. Each person got $50 when 50 days had passed without a single late delivery. This mini-game forced the players to discover the root causes of late deliveries and to work together to fix problems (such as drivers not getting the right directions). With this mini-game, the catering department went from 10% late deliveries per week to a record-setting 355 days in a row without a single late delivery (Baker & Smerek, 2010, pp. 7–8).

Collaborative technologies use software or web-based tools to enable a dispersed workgroup to share information, exchange ideas, brainstorm, manage projects, and so on. These technologies "ease the difficulties of making contact with other people when physical distance or structural impediments are barriers" (Baker & Dutton, 2007, p. 340). Instant messaging, skill-profiling systems, chat rooms, team rooms, and other systems can enhance the ability of group to work together and build social capital

(Cross & Parker, 2004). Using a collaborative technology called the Reciprocity Ring™ to collect data on the evolution of reciprocity in real groups, Baker and Bulkley (2009) found strong evidence of both moral sentiments and reputation, controlling for a variety of other factors.[7] For example, participants who received help felt gratitude and were more likely to pay it forward by helping third parties. Participants were more likely to help those who were generous than to help those who were not. Over time, participants learned the value of reciprocity, especially paying it forward, as ways to get needed resources, contribute to others, and build the solidarity of the group.

Future Directions

The dual model of reciprocity in organizations is a synthesis of two separate literatures and research streams. Thus, future directions for the field include both empirical tests and theoretical refinements of the dual model.

- Positive emotions are the moral sentiments that drive reciprocity. Gratitude, in particular, motivates paying it forward. Do other positive emotions influence reciprocity? For example, what is the role of pride, hope, interest, inspiration, or even love?
- Given that positive emotions, such as gratitude, are the moral sentiments behind reciprocity, what is the role of negative emotions? Do negative emotions have the opposite effect of positive emotions? What is the role, for example, of fear, contempt, anger, or disgust?
- The dual model assumes that most people in organizations have mixed motives, a combination of self-regarding and other-regarding concerns. In other words, the model applies to the middle range of the distribution of social preferences. Does the dual model also apply at the extremes? For example, do moral sentiments play much of a role in organizations populated with extremely self-interested members? Conversely, does reputation play much of a role in organizations with extremely other-regarding members?
- Successful exchanges generate positive emotions that, in turn, facilitate additional successful exchanges (Lawler, 2001). Are there positive (or negative) spirals in the evolution of reciprocity? Are there threshold effects?
- This chapter described a number of human resource practices and everyday work practices that influence moral sentiments and reputation and enable the expression of reciprocity. An important direction of future work is to catalog additional positive practices in organizations, and to determine the relative effectiveness of various positive practices for the emergence and evolution of reciprocity.

Conclusion

This chapter brings together two disparate literatures—reciprocity theory and POS—to develop a dual model of reciprocity in organizations. Two key mechanisms of reciprocity compose this model: reputation and moral sentiments. Reciprocity theorists emphasize the role of reputation in the emergence and evolution of reciprocity. They assume that people are self-interested and will give to others only if doing so builds a reputation for generosity that will be rewarded in the future. In contrast, POS assumes that people are other-regarding and naturally inclined to give generously to others without regard to repayment. For POS, moral sentiments—defined here as positive emotions, such as gratitude—drive the evolution of reciprocity.

Based on a number of empirical studies, I assume that most people in organizations have mixed motives, simultaneously self- and other-regarding. Accordingly, effective enablers of positive social capital in organizations must be designed to motivate people with mixed motives, generating moral sentiments and providing opportunities to build reputations that pay off. I provided several empirical examples of positive practices that facilitate reciprocity, considering both human resource practices and everyday work practices. These positive practices create work environments that foster the moral sentiments at the heart of reciprocity.

Notes

1. Molm, Collett, and Schaefer (2007) would subsume my triadic generalized reciprocity in their definition of chain-generalized reciprocity, but it is useful to maintain the distinction between three-actor networks and larger networks.
2. I borrow *Homo reciprocus* from Becker (1956), although I use it in a more focused way. Becker never provides a formal definition, and uses the term *H. reciprocus* and a synonym "man in reciprocity" in many and diverse ways.
3. These values come from Schwartz's theoretical circumplex model of ten values (e.g., Schwartz, 1994, 2006; Schwartz &

Bardi, 2001). This circumplex has two higher-order dimensions, one of which is "self-enhancement" (or self-regarding values) versus "self-transcendence" (or other-regarding values). Achievement and power are self-regarding values; universalism and benevolence are other-regarding values.

4. Of course, other factors influence reciprocity. For example, cooperation tends to be high in groups that are small and/or where behavior is easily monitored, effective sanctions operate, and social relations are stable (Coleman, 1990, pp. 300–321). Ethnic rotating savings and credit associations are good examples (Biggart & Castanias, 2001). Institutional and organizational structures influence unilateral giving. For example, differences in the institutions that organize exchange explain the wide variations in rates of donating human blood and organs (Healy, 2006). In the behavioral laboratory, factors outside the specific rules of an experimental game, such as social identities, group size, time pressure, and communication influence cooperative behavior in the game (Cook & Cooper, 2003, pp. 227–231; Ostrom & Walker, 2003). Subjects from different national cultures behave differently in the same experiment (e.g., Yamagishi, 1988).

5. Baker and Bulkley (2009) observed the formation of a norm of reciprocity in real groups that used an online system of making and responding to requests. Those who benefited more from the system paid it forward more often than those who benefited less, controlling for a host of other factors. Indeed, 80% of the almost 3,000 acts of helping were unilateral, rather than direct reciprocity (Figure 31.1). This online system is called the Reciprocity Ring,™ available from Humax Corporation (www.humaxnetworks.com).

6. Generally, many attribute the practice of reciprocity to social norms (Ekeh, 1974; Lévi-Straus, 1969 [1949]; Gouldner, 1960). A norm of indirect reciprocity, for example, means that a recipient of unilateral giving feels morally motivated to continue the practice of unilateral giving and "pay it forward" to some third party. This is the form of paying it forward that Nowak and Sigmund (2005) called "upstream reciprocity" (see Figure 31.1).

7. The Reciprocity Ring™ is provided by Humax Corporation as a face-to-face activity and an online collaboration technology (www.humaxnetworks.com). Other factors included the effects of incentives, costs and risks of helping, and the passage of time.

References

Adler, P.S., & Kwon, S. (2002). Social capital: Prospects for a new concept. *Academy of Management Review, 27*(17), 40.

Andreoni, J. (1989). Giving with impure altruism: Applications to charity and Ricardian equivalence, *Journal of Political Economy, 97*, 1447–1458.

Andreoni, J. (1990). Impure altruism and donations to public goods: A theory of warm-glow giving. *Economic Journal, 100*, 464–477.

Alexander, R.D. (1987). *The biology of moral systems.* New York: Aldine de Gruyter.

Baker, W. (2000). *Achieving success through social capital.* San Francisco: Jossey-Bass.

Baker, W., & Bulkley, N. (2009). *The evolution of pure generalized reciprocity.* Paper presented at the 2009 annual meetings of the Academy of Management.

Baker, W.E., & Dutton, J.E. (2007). "Enabling Positive Social Capital in Organizations. In J.E. Dutton and B.R. Ragins (Eds.), *Exploring Positive Relationships at Work: Building a Theoretical and Research Foundation.* Mahwah, NJ: Lawrence Erlbaum Publishers.

Baker, W., & Gunderson, R. (2005). *Zingerman's Community of Businesses.* Unpublished manuscript, Center for Positive Organizational Scholarship, Stephen M. Ross School of Business, University of Michigan.

Baker, W., & Levine, S. (2010). *Mechanisms of generalized exchange: Towards an integrated model.* Working paper, University of Michigan.

Baker, W., & Smerek, R. (2010). *Open book finance.* Case 1–429–091. GlobaLens, William Davidson Institute, University of Michigan, Ann Arbor, MI.

Becker, G.S. (1974). A theory of social interactions. *Journal of Political Economy, 82*, 1063–1093.

Becker, H.P. (1956). *Man in reciprocity.* New York: Praeger.

Bearman, P. (1997). Generalized exchange. *American Journal of Sociology, 102*, 1383–1415.

Bertocci, P.A., & Millard, R.M. (1963). *Personality and the good: Psychological and ethical perspectives.* New York: David McKay.

Biggart, N.W., & Castanias, R.P. (2001). Collateralized social relations: The social in economic calculation. *American Journal of Economics and Sociology, 60*, 471–500.

Burlingham, B. (2005). *Small giants.* New York: Penguin.

Cameron, K.S., Dutton, J.E., & Quinn, R.E. (2003). Foundations of positive organizational scholarship. In K.S. Cameron, J.E. Dutton, & R.E. Quinn (Eds.), *Positive organizational scholarship* (pp. 3–13). San Francisco: Berrett-Koehler.

Coleman, J.S. (1990). *Foundations of social theory.* Cambridge, MA: Harvard University Press.

Collins, R. (2004). *Interaction ritual chains.* Princeton, NJ: Princeton University Press.

Cohen, D., & Prusak, L. (2001). *In good company: How social capital makes organizations work.* Boston: Harvard Business School Press.

Cook, K.S., & Cooper, R.M. (2003). Experimental studies of cooperation, trust & social exchange. In E. Ostrom, & J. Walker (Eds.), *Trust and reciprocity: Interdisciplinary lessons from experimental research* (pp. 209–244). New York: Russell Sage Foundation Press.

Cialdini, R.B. (1993). *Influence: The psychology of persuasion.* New York: Quill/William Morrow.

Cross, R., & Parker, A. (2004). *The hidden power of networks.* Boston: Harvard Business School Press.

Dekas, K. (2009). *Citizenship in context: Investigating the effects of work group climate on organizational citizenship perceptions, behavior & performance.* Doctoral dissertation, University of Michigan, Ann Arbor, MI.

Ekeh, P.P. (1974). *Social exchange theory: The two traditions.* Cambridge, MA: Harvard University Press.

Emmons, R.A., & McCullough, M.E. (Eds.). (2004). *The psychology of gratitude.* New York: Oxford University Press.

Emmons, R.A. (2004). Gratitude. In M.E. P. Seligman, & C. Peterson (Eds.), *Character strengths and virtues* (pp. 553–568). New York: Oxford University Press.

Emmons, R.A., & McCullough, M.E. (2003). Counting blessings versus burdens: Experimental studies of gratitude and subjective well-being. *Journal of Personality and Social Psychology, 84*, 377–389.

Emmons, R.A. (2003). Acts of gratitude in organizations. In K.S. Cameron, J.E. Dutton, & R.E. Quinn (Eds.), *Positive organizational scholarship* (pp. 81–93). San Francisco: Berrett-Koehler Publishers.

Fehr, E., & Camerer, C.F. (2007). Social neuroeconomics: The neural circuitry of social preferences. *Trends in Cognitive Sciences, 11*, 419–427.

Fehr, E., Fischbacher, U., & Simon, G. (2002). Strong reciprocity, human cooperation and the enforcement of social norms. *Human Nature, 13*, 1–25.

Fischbacher, U., & Gaechter, S. (2008). *Heterogeneous social preferences and the dynamics of free riding in public goods experiments*. Discussion papers 2008–07, The Centre for Decision Research and Experimental Economics, School of Economics, University of Nottingham, Nottingham, UK.

Hargadon, A., & Sutton, R.I. (1997). Technology brokering and innovation in a product development firm. *Administrative Science Quarterly, 42*, 746–749.

Gouldner, A.W. (1960). The norm of reciprocity. *American Journal of Sociology, 25*, 161–178.

Gintis, H., Bowles, S., Boyd, R., & Fehr, E. (Eds.). (2005). *Moral sentiments and material interests*. Cambridge, MA: MIT Press.

Gittell, J.H. (2003). *The Southwest Airlines way*. New York: McGraw-Hill.

Haidt J. (2003). Elevation and the positive psychology of morality. In C.L. Keyes, & J. Haidt (Eds.), *Flourishing: Positive psychology and the life well-lived* (pp. 275–289). Washington, DC: American Psychological Association.

Healy, K. (2006). *Last best gifts: Altruism and the market for human blood and organs*. Chicago: University of Chicago Press.

Hyde, C.R. (2000). *Pay it forward*. New York: Simon & Schuster.

Lawler, E.J. (2001). An affect theory of social exchange. *American Journal of Sociology, 107*, 321–352.

Leakey, R., & Lewin, R. (1978). *People of the lake*. New York: Anchor Press/Doubleday.

Levi-Strauss, C. ([1949] 1996). The principle of reciprocity. In A.E. Komter (Ed.), *The gift: An interdisciplinary perspective* (pp. 15–26). Amsterdam: Amsterdam University Press.

Malinowski, B. (1922). *Argonauts of the western Pacific*. London: Routledge.

Mayer, D.M., Nishii, L.H., Schneider, B., & Goldstein, H.W. (2007). The precursors and products of fair climates: Group leader antecedents and employee attitudinal consequences. *Personnel Psychology, 60*, 929–963.

McCullough, M.E., Kilpatrick, S.D., Emmons, R.A., & Larson, D.B. (2001). Is gratitude a moral affect? *Psychological Bulletin, 127*, 249–266.

McCullough, M.E., Emmons, R.A., & Tsang, J. (2002). The grateful disposition: A conceptual and empirical topography. *Journal of Personality and Social Psychology, 82*, 112–127.

Molm, L.D., Collett, J.L., & Schaefer, D.R. (2007). Building solidarity through generalized exchange: A theory of reciprocity. *American Journal of Sociology, 113*, 205–242.

Naumann, S.E., & Bennett, N. (2000). A case for procedural justice climate: Development and test of a multilevel model. *Academy of Management Journal, 43*, 81–889.

Nowak, M.A., & Sigmund, K. (1998). Evolution of indirect reciprocity by image scoring. *Nature, 393*, 573–577.

Nowak, M.A., & Sigmund, K. (2005). Evolution of indirect reciprocity. *Nature, 437*, 1291–1298.

Ostrom, E., & Walker, J. (Eds.). (2003). *Trust and reciprocity: Interdisciplinary lessons from experimental research*. New York: Russell Sage Foundation Press.

Polanyi, K. ([1957/1971]). The economy as instituted process. In K. Polanyi, C. Arensberg, & H. Pearson (Eds.), *Trade and market in the early empires: Economies in history and theory* (pp. 248–306). Chicago: Henry Regnery Company.

Putnam, R.D. (2000). *Bowling alone: The collapse and revival of American community*. New York: Simon & Schuster.

Rizzolatti, G., & Craighero, L. (2004). The mirror-neuron system. *Annual Review of Neuroscience, 27*, 169–192.

Seinen, I., & Schram, A. (2006). Social status and group norms: Indirect reciprocity in a repeated helping experiment. *European Economic Review, 50*, 581–586.

Schwartz, S. (1994). Are there universal aspects to the structure and content of human values? *Journal of Social Issues, 50*, 19–45.

Schwartz, S. (2006). A theory of cultural value orientations: Explication and applications. *Comparative Sociology, 5*, 136–182.

Schwartz, S., & Bardi, A. (2001). Values hierarchies across cultures. *Journal of Cross-Cultural Psychology, 32*, 268–290.

Simmel, G. (1950). *The sociology of Georg Simmel*. Glencoe, Illinois: Free Press.

Simpson, B., & Willer, R. (2008). Altruism and indirect reciprocity: The interaction of person and situation in prosocial behavior. *Social Psychology Quarterly, 71*, 37–52.

Stack, J., & Burlingham, B. (1994). *The great game of business*. New York: Currency/Doubleday.

Stamper, C.L., & Van Dyne, L. (2001). Work status and organizational citizenship behavior: A field study of restaurant employees. *Journal of Organizational Behavior, 22*, 517–536.

Strathern, A. (1975). *The rope of moka: Big-men and ceremonial exchange in Mount Hagen, New Guinea*. Cambridge, UK: Cambridge University Press.

Takahashi, N. (2000). The emergence of generalized exchange. *American Journal of Sociology, 105*, 1105–1134.

Tangney, J.P., Stuewig, J., & Mashek, D.J. (2007). Moral emotions and moral behavior. *Annual Review of Psychology, 58*, 345–372.

Titmuss, R. (1971). *The gift relationship: From human blood to social policy*. New York: Pantheon Books.

Tsang, J. (2007). Gratitude for small and large favors: A behavioral test. *The Journal of Positive Psychology, 2*, 157–167.

Tsang, J.A. (2006). The effects of helper intention on gratitude and indebtedness. *Motivation and Emotion, 30*, 199–205.

Watkins, P.C., Scheer, J., Ovnicek, M., & Kolts, R. (2006). The debt of gratitude: Dissociating gratitude and indebtedness. *Cognition and Emotion, 20*, 217–241.

Weber, J.M., & Murnigham, L.K. (2008). Suckers or saviors? Consistent contributors in social dilemmas. *Journal of Personality and Social Psychology, 95*, 1340–1353.

Wedekind, C., & Milinski, M. (2000). Cooperation through image scoring in humans. *Science, 288*, 850–852.

Yan, Y. (1996). *The flow of gifts: Reciprocity and social networks in a Chinese village*. Stanford, CA: Stanford University Press.

Yamagishi, T. (1988). Exit from the group as an individualistic solution to the public good. *Journal of Experimental Social Psychology, 24*, 530–542.

Yamagishi, T., & Cook, K.S. (1993). Generalized exchange and social dilemmas. *Social Psychology Quarterly, 56*(4), 235–248.

Workplace Intimacy in Leader–Follower Relationships

Ronit Kark

Abstract

Traditional leadership theories and management practices tend to distinguish between the public sphere (e.g., organizations and the workplace) characterized by control, instrumentality, and rationality, and the private sphere (the home), characterized by emotionality, spontaneity, and intimate personal relationships. Recently, new models of relational leadership have emerged. Within this stream, in this chapter, I explore the links between leadership and intimacy in the organizational context. Drawing on the psychological literature, I define the concept of workplace intimacy, present its different components, and examine how it may be enacted in the field of leadership and management. Then I present the processes of exchange (e.g., communal exchange) and identity shifts (e.g., the relational self-concept) that may underlie the development of workplace intimacy. Last, I suggest a wide array of workplace intimacy outcomes at the individual and group level and point to directions for further exploration, empirical research, and re-visioning of the leadership and management field as one that can foster meaningful, pleasurable, and valuable mutual relationships with followers.

Keywords: Relational leadership, post-heroic leadership, workplace intimacy, communal exchange, instrumental exchange, relational self-concept

At her hardest times I cried and she cried. She opened herself up to me and
I opened myself. . . . I felt her pain, so we cried. Here you spend more time with people
than with people at home. So you feel for them. (A bank employee describing how her
manager told her that her father was dying of cancer; Kark, 1999)

Organizational theories and practices have made it a point to distinguish between different frameworks by placing work outside the home sphere, and close and emotional relationships outside the workplace. According to Kanter (1977), the "myth of separate spheres" permeates our culture. The Industrial Revolution marked a fundamental change in the separation of work and family life (Perlow, 1998). Work became the public realm and was increasingly conceptualized as the political, instrumental, rational world of economic production, whereas Home was identified as private territory conceptualized as the nonpolitical, natural, irrational, emotional world focused on social and biological reproduction, economic consumption, and in terms of leisure, physical, and mental restoration for the wage laborer (Nippert-Eng, 1995). Bureaucratic models of organization proliferated across the industrial world (DiMaggio & Powell, 1983). These were designed to enhance organizational efficiency through control mechanisms such as hierarchy, the division of labor, and impersonal, unemotional, and deindividualized rules. Close relationships were discouraged so as to avoid personal favoritism and ensure uniform treatment (Martin, Knopoff, & Beckman, 1998). Although work penetrated the home environment (e.g., long working hours) to increase work productivity and profit, the tendency to infuse work with home-related elements was much less frequent (Nippert-Eng, 1995). Spontaneous feelings and close relationships were often perceived as illegitimate in the workplace and were often taxed.

The relationship between the public sphere and work shaped leadership and management theories and practices, which were increasingly dominated by an instrumental perspective geared for organizational success (Kerfoot & Knight, 1993). As Kerfoot noted (1999), "All social intercourse and interaction is subjected to a yard stick of its degree of utility to the larger goals of the organization. . . . This mode of engagement implies that all encounters and events become potential arenas for instrumental control" (p. 188).

In recent years, the theory and practice of leadership and management have undergone a noticeable change. Industrial era models of effectiveness have been superseded by newer models considered more appropriate to the knowledge-intensive realities of today's workplace, which stress relational "post-heroic" leadership (e.g., Carmeli, Ben-Hador, Waldman, & Rupp, 2009; Fletcher, 2004; Lipman Blumen, 1996; Uhl-Bien, 2006). These new models of leadership recognize that effectiveness in knowledge-based environments depends on a less individualistic, more relational concept of leadership that focuses on dynamic, interactive processes of influence and collaborative learning (Pearce & Conger, 2003). Nevertheless, Uhl Bien (2006) commented that "while relationships are at the heart of many of the new approaches emerging in the leadership literature . . . we know surprisingly little about how relationships form and develop in the workplace. Moreover, investigation into the relational dynamics of leadership as a process of organizing has been severely overlooked in leadership research" (p. 654).

In this chapter, I introduce a relational concept that has received very little attention in the field of organization studies and in the leadership field: the concept of workplace intimacy.[1] Intimacy is a form of close relatedness in which an individual shares his or her innermost emotions, experiences, and thoughts with the other and experiences empathic responsiveness, a depth of understanding and a sense of shared meaning. Researchers and psychological therapists have systematically articulated that true intimacy with others is one of the highest values of human experience. Various theoreticians

and researchers have asserted that there may be nothing more important for the well-being and optimal functioning of human beings than intimate relationships (Bowlby, 1969; Kelly, 1955; Rogers, 1951; Sullivan, 1953; for a recent review see Reis, Collins, & Berscheid, 2000). Intimacy and connections have been referred to as "the bedrock of human happiness and meaning" (Prager & Roberts, 2004, p. 44). Although intimacy has been recognized as a central concept in understanding humane existence, it has been overlooked in the study of organizations and the workplace. This is even more evident when we refer to the relationships between leaders and followers, since leadership and management have been perceived as one of the mechanisms to assure the maintenance of the logic of separation, and a means of reinforcing employees' loyalty and commitment to the organizational sphere and its aims, often at the expense of other spheres.

Thus, the purpose of this chapter is to explore the links between leadership and intimacy in the context of work. I start by defining the concept of workplace intimacy, drawing on the psychological literature, while distinguishing it from related concepts and presenting different dimensions of the concept of intimacy. Then I explore two of the major processes involved in intimate relationships (i.e., exchange schemas and the shaping of identities) and how they may inform leader–follower relationships. Next, I present different outcomes of workplace intimacy, focusing on the individual and on the group and organization level. Last, I discuss directions for future research and the possible dark sides of leader–follower workplace intimacy.

Workplace Intimacy

According to Sexton and Sexton (1982) "the word intimacy is derived from the Latin *intimus*, meaning inner or inmost. To be intimate with another is to have access to, and to comprehend, his or her inmost character" (p. 1). Intimacy is sharing what is inmost with others (Popovic, 2005), and involves "seeing" and being "seen" by having an empathic perception and a depth of understanding of the other. Intimate relating is made up of positive behavior components that are not merely ideational but have an outward manifestation, a style of communication in which both partners experience a sense of shared meaning (Firestone & Firestone, 2004).

Sullivan (1953) suggested that intimate relationships are ones in which individuals have real sensitivity to what matters to another person, supplying each other with satisfaction. In such relationships, individuals are interested in contributing and supporting the happiness and self-worth of the other as an aim in itself, rather than for specific self-interest or instrumental reasons. There is mutual validation of self-worth and collaboration. Lerner (1989) suggested that: "An intimate relationship is one in which neither party silences, sacrifices, or betrays the self" (p. 3). According to Reis and Shaver (1988), intimacy is an interpersonal process with two principal components: self-disclosure and partner responsiveness. Intimacy is initiated when one person communicates personally relevant and revealing information, thoughts, and feelings to another person. Expressions may also be nonverbal in nature, standing as communication on their own right or amplifying verbal disclosures and behaviors (Keeley & Hart, 1994).

Thus, intimacy is a personal, subjective (and often momentary) sense of connectedness that is the outcome of an interpersonal, transactional process consisting of self-disclosure and the other's responsiveness (Laurenceau, Rivera, Schaffer, & Pietromonaco, 2004). However, the definition provided by Sullivan and others that draw on his work (e.g., Sharabany, 1994), portrays intimacy as a wider concept than confident self-exposure and other-responsiveness. This definition includes other aspects of a relationship such as the readiness to ask for help, a sense of empathy and understanding, frequency of interaction, and number of mutual activities.

Drawing on the definitions provided above, workplace intimacy can be defined as a relationship or an interaction that takes place in the work context and is characterized by a sense of connectedness related to self-disclosure and the sharing of what is innermost with others, while experiencing a sense of the other as having an empathic perception, a depth of understanding, a real sensitivity to what matters, and a motivation to contribute to mutual well-being and to provide satisfaction. Workplace intimacy is a flexible process that occurs over time and is never complete or fully accomplished. It is a relationship that is pleasurable and valuable in and of itself (Aron, Mashek, & Aron, 2004; Kerfoot, 1999).

The terms *intimacy* and *closeness* are usually used interchangeably and equated with each other (e.g., Geddes & Grosset, 1999; Miller & Lefcourt, 1982). According to some researchers, intimacy is a specific form of intense closeness. It is one type of closeness, emphasizing validation and caring (Ries & Patrick, 1996). Closeness appears to be a richer, more inclusive term than intimacy, capturing a greater variety of relationships. Other types of closeness include more behaviorally based forms of independence, in which partners' influence each others' behavior (e.g., Berscheid, Snyder, & Omoto, 1989). According to Sharabany (1994), intimacy is a mature type of closeness. Thus, workplace intimacy is more specific than workplace close relationships.

The concept of workplace intimacy is also somewhat distinct from the concept of connection and high-quality connections (HQCs). Recently, the topic of positive relationships at work has become a focus of attention in the study of organizations. Dutton and Heaphy (2003) suggested the concept of HQCs, to characterize whether the connective tissue between individuals is life-giving or life-depleting (see also Stephens, Heaphy, & Dutton, 2011, Chapter 29, this volume). According to this perspective, connections with others are seen as a dynamic, living tissue that exists between two people when some contact is made between them involving mutual awareness and social interactions. Dutton and Heaphy (2003) contend that "connections do not assume intimacy or closeness" (p. 264). However, based on the definition of workplace intimacy given above, workplace intimacy is a positive connection and a specific form of close and intense HQC. This implies that not all leader–follower HQCs have the characteristics of intimate relationships; however, workplace intimacy is one specific, more discrete form of HQC and may have its distinct determinants and correlates.

Intimacy is also related to the concept of love. According to Sternberg's (1986) triangular theory, love has three components: *intimacy,* which encompasses the feelings of closeness, connectedness, and bondedness; *passion,* which encompasses the drives that lead to romance, physical attraction, and sexual consummation; and *decision/commitment,* which encompasses the decision that one loves another, and in the long term, the commitment to maintain that love (Sternberg, 1986; Sternberg & Grajek, 1984). Thus, intimacy is one specific aspect of love.

Workplace intimacy is likely to manifest itself in different types of workplace interactions (e.g., among coworkers, between employees and customers). In what follows, I explore the specific and possibly more complex dynamics of workplace intimacy between leaders and their followers, or between managers and their employees within the organizational context.

Components of Intimate Relationships

Various components of intimacy have been depicted in the psychological literature. Sharabany (1994) conceptualizes intimate relationships as comprised of eight different dimensions. According to Sharabany (1994), these dimensions may vary in terms of quantity and quality, but their sum reveals the overall assessment of intimacy in the relationship. The second conceptualization of intimacy is based on the work of Schaefer and Olson (1981), who identified seven types of intimacy that can be further applied to the workplace sphere and to leader–follower relationships. Their components deal with the "process" aspect of intimacy by distinguishing between intimate experiences and an intimate relationship. An intimate experience is a feeling of closeness or sharing with another in one or more of the seven areas suggested. It is possible to have intimate experiences with a variety of people without having or developing an intimate relationship. According to Schaefer and Olson, an intimate relationship is generally one in which an individual shares intimate experiences with the other in several areas, with the expectation that the experiences and relationship will persist over time. The different frameworks of intimacy and examples from field interviews conducted with bank-branch employees and managers[2] to demonstrate how these components may apply to the workplace and the organizational field are presented in Table 32.1.[3]

Workplace Intimacy As a Form of Communal Exchange

Work relationships and leader–follower or manager–employee relationships are often characterized as instrumental-exchange relationships, whereas intimate relationships are perceived and defined as affective-communal relationships. Based on Goffman's (1961) distinction between communal and economic exchange, Clark and colleagues compared and contrasted these two relational forms (Clark & Mills, 1979; Mills & Clark, 1982). A central distinction between communal and exchange relationships involves the rules governing the giving and receiving of benefits. In communal relationships, members are concerned about the other's welfare. They give benefits to please the other, or in response to his or her needs. In exchange relationships, members are less concerned with the other's welfare. They give benefits with the expectation of receiving comparable benefits in return in the future. Several studies support this distinction between communal and exchange relationships (e.g., Clark, 1984; Clark & Mills, 1979; Clark & Waddell, 1985). It has also been demonstrated in an empirical study that in exchange, but not in

communal relationships, people keep track of individual inputs into joint tasks. Keeping track is necessary to allocate benefits in proportion to inputs. In communal relationships, members keep track of one another's needs, because benefits are distributed to demonstrate concern or according to the other's needs (Clark, 1984). Thus, when no clear opportunity for reciprocation exists, people are more likely to attend to the needs of the other in communal rather than in exchange relationships. Exchange relationships are often exemplified by relationships between acquaintances or people who do business together. Communal relationships are often exemplified by friendships, romantic relationships, and family relationships.

Thus, when intimate leader–follower workplace relationships are formed, they are based, at least to some extent, on communal exchange relationships, in which the leader and follower have a general obligation to be concerned about the other's welfare and to give benefits in response to the other's needs. However, even within leader–follower relationships that are characterized by workplace intimacy, affective-communal feature and instrumental-exchange features are likely to coexist, since intimate relationships in an organizational context demand distinct and even conflicting strategies for relationship management (see also Ingram & Zou, 2008).

Workplace Intimacy As a Form of Identity

Workplace intimacy can be understood in terms of identity centering on the concept of the relational. For instance, the self-expansion model postulates that, in intimate relationships, each person includes in the self, to some extent, some aspects of the other (Aron & Aron, 1986; Aron, Aron, & Norman, 2001; Aron et al., 2004). This suggests that, when intimate relationships are formed, the other's resources, perspectives, and identities become part of the self. These *resources* of the other include material goods, knowledge (conceptual, informational, and procedural), and social assets that can facilitate the achievement of goals. The *perspective* aspect of inclusion refers to ways of experiencing (consciously or unconsciously) and understanding the world to some extent from the other's point of view. Perceiving oneself as including a relationship partner's resources in the self implies perceiving oneself as having access to these resources.

The resource aspect of inclusion of the other in the self is particularly crucial from a motivational point of view. This is because perceiving another's resources as one's own means that the outcomes

Table 32.1 Components of workplace intimacy

Component	Definition	Examples from interviews in an organizational context
Sharabany (1994)		
Frankness and spontaneity	Self-disclosure of negative/positive things about the self The possibility to receive and accept honest feedback	"Here we talk about every thing. Everyone knows what bothers the other. People will share small things about their kids, family. I can talk to my manager about my personal problems."
Sensitivity and knowing	A sense of empathy and understanding (not necessarily achieved through verbal self-disclosure)	"She is like a psychoanalyst's couch. She trusts me and I trust her. She can handle any problem." (A female employee talking about her manager).
Attachment to the other	Liking the other, feelings of closeness and connectedness Seeing the other as important and missing him or her when absent	Many employees and managers talked about their relationships like family relationships: "She is a great manager, she is like a mother to me." (A female employee).
Exclusiveness of the relationship	Unique qualities that are not represented in other relationships Preference for this relationship over other relationships	"She is like a sister to me. I know it is not blood relations but, like my sister, I can feel sure she will help me with any problem I might have." (A female employee describing her manager).
Giving and sharing with the other	Spending time listening to the other Sharing of material goods	"I had two pregnancies here. We chat about the pregnancy, about the process, about giving birth. We talk to each other about our children and many personal topics."
Imposition	Degree to which things can be taken from the other and imposed upon Degree of openness and readiness to request and accept the other's help	A female employee describing her relationship with her female manager, who is single at the age of 40. She suggested to her manager, who does not have children, to share her son with her: "It's like home here. I bring my kids here. Dafna (the branch manager) loves them. She spoils them, compliments them. Once I said to her: 'you can have my son for a trial.' She loves my kids. I don't let them disturb her. I bring them when I don't have an arrangement for them. On school holidays, I bring them to work because I am very concerned at what happens in the branch. Another employee would have taken the day off to stay with her children."
Common activities.	Joint activities (also outside the work context) Enjoyment of time spent together and activities done together	In the bank branches, many employees and managers talked about leisure activities they experienced with their managers after working hours. "We go together for walks after working hours." (A male employee)
Trust and loyalty	Degree to which the other can be trusted to keep secrets, be supportive, not betray, and speak up to defend when others say bad things	"I like the branch manager very much. I can tell him in the face if I am hurt or anything else. If it were another manager who would bear a grudge, and who was not trustworthy I would keep my distance and not share my feelings."

Table 32.1 Components of workplace intimacy (*continued*)

Component	Definition	Examples from interviews in an organizational context
Schaefer and Olson (1981)		
Emotional intimacy*	Experiencing a closeness of feelings	"I share joys and sorrows with her. For me, intimacy is to feel as the other person feels whether in joy or sorrow. I identify with my manager, and I feel she identifies with me. I tell her something happy, and I feel she is happy for me. It's a matter of feeling." (An employee describing her relationship with her manager)
Social intimacy	Experience of having common friends and social networks	Some of the employees talked about their family members becoming friends of other family members of the managers who worked with them and building an independent relationship.
Recreational intimacy**	Shared experience of interest in hobbies and mutual participation in recreational events	"I had a manager (male manager) whom I liked. I played with him in the workplace sports league. I knew him more than an employee–manager relationship because we played together . . . we laughed together, played together, had man to man talk . . ." (A male employee describing his manager)
Physical intimacy	Experience of sharing general affection. (e.g., a pat on the back, an affectionate handshake, a friendly hug, and looking one in the eye)	A good example of this dimension came up in an interview with a highly appreciated bank branch manager. She described situations in which she saw employees providing bank services and having a hard time with clients. In such cases, she could not interfere, but she would walk behind the employees and gently touch them on the shoulder or back, to signal to them that she was aware of the way they were managing the difficulty and understood, empathized with and supported them.
Intellectual intimacy	Experience of sharing ideas	"Sometimes when we do not agree on ideas it creates friction. Sometimes, we really squabble and raise our voices . . . I feel free with her to express my thoughts. I allow myself to raise my voice, because it's for the best. You don't have to keep everything you think inside . . . It's like at home. When you do not agree, you express your thoughts and feelings."
Spiritual intimacy	Experience of showing ultimate concern, a similar sense of meaning in life, or religious faith	An employee mentioned a situation in which the branch manager needed some help in a course in Judaism he was studying. Knowing her husband's expertise, he came with another branch manager to her small apartment to study Mishna [written compilations of Jewish oral traditions] with her husband.
Aesthetic intimacy	Closeness that results from the experience of sharing beauty	A female employee talked about the way her female manager dressed and how she liked her taste and style. She further described how this had influenced her, changing her own taste and how they went shopping for clothes together.

* Similar to Sharabany's component of "attachment to the other".
** Similar to Sharabany's component of "common activities".

(rewards and costs) the other incurs are to some extent also experienced as one's own. This suggests that, when an intimate relationship is formed between a leader and a follower, the leader may become to some extent a part of the followers' self (and vice versa). This can further influence the follower's (and leader's) identities and perceptions and enhance their resources in terms of material goods, knowledge, and social assets.

The focus on the effect of workplace intimacy on leader and follower identity is related to developing theories in the field of leadership that focus on the self-concept (e.g., Kark & Shamir, 2002; Lord, Brown, & Feiberg, 1999; van Knippenberg & Hogg, 2003). This framework promotes a view of the self-concept as dynamic and multifaceted, in which people's self-perception is composed of different aspects. Forces at various levels of analysis (e.g., personality traits, dyadic relationships, organizational culture) can influence the cognitive accessibility of a given self-concept, leading to the activation of a particular identity level at a given point in time (Brickson, 2000). Thus, different situations may bring different aspects of the self to the fore, and the self-concept may change through exposure to various external stimuli, including the influence and behavior of leaders on followers (Kark & Shamir, 2002; Lord & Brown, 2004) or that of followers on leaders (Howell & Shamir, 2005). This dynamic enables leaders and followers to interact in ways that activate various levels and aspects of the self.

Social psychological theories of the self tend to see the individual's self-identity as comprising both personal and social identities (e.g., Banaji & Prentice, 1994). Brewer and Gardner (1996) proposed an elegant theory for classification of the self, suggesting a further distinction between two levels of social selves: the relational (or interpersonal) and the collective identity. Research on leadership and the self has suggested that leaders can profoundly influence subordinates' relational and collective self-concepts by making various identity levels more salient, and thereby influence follower behavior and other social processes (e.g., Kark & Shamir, 2002; Lord et al., 1999; van Knippenberg, van Knippenberg, De Cermer, & Hogg, 2004).

The relational level of self-identity that links the individual to the leader may be central to the understanding of the effect of leader–follower workplace intimacy. The *relational self* is derived from interpersonal connections and role relationships with specific others (e.g., child–parent, subordinate–leader). At this level, individuals conceive of themselves predominantly in terms of their roles in relation to significant others, and self-worth is derived from appropriate role behavior (e.g., being a good follower), as conveyed through reflected appraisals of the other person involved in the relationship (Brewer & Gardner, 1996; Gabriel & Gardner, 1999). When a relational orientation is salient, an individual's primary motivation is to enhance the relationship partner's well-being and derive mutual benefits (Brewer & Gardner, 1996). Leader–follower workplace intimacy is a mode of relating that stresses behaviors that are in line with the construct of relational practice, as suggested by Fletcher (1999). This concept refers to a way of working that is directed toward the welfare of others. The concept of relational practice is rooted in the relational theory of human development of "growth-in-connection" (Miller, 1976; Miller & Stiver, 1997), which stresses that human growth occurs through a process of connections and relating rather than by a process of individuation and separation.

Thus, when leaders and followers enact intimate behaviors and form a close emotional bond, the relational self is likely to become salient and activated, informing their motivations and behaviors. Furthermore, in such relationships, the leader's and follower's identities and perspectives are somewhat modified by the inclusion of certain aspects of the other in the self-schema.

Workplace Intimacy in the Study of Leader–Follower Relationships

Many leadership theories acknowledge the importance of the relationship between the leader and follower. As suggested above, in recent years, the focus on relationships in leadership theories has become more central and explicit. Theorists have many different labels to describe this new form of relational leadership, including leadership forms as: distributed (Gronn, 2002), distributive (Brown & Gioia, 2002), shared (Pearce & Conger, 2003), quiet (Badaracco, 2002), connective (Lipman Blumen, 1996), inclusive (Carmeli, Reiter-Palmon, & Ziv, 2010), post-heroic (Fletcher, 2004), leader–member exchange (LMX; Graen & Uhl-Bien, 1995), and complexity leadership (Uhl-Bien, 2006). Although there are important distinctions, all share an emphasis on the egalitarian, more mutual, collaborative and fluid, less hierarchical nature of interactions and on recognition of the importance of relationships in fostering relational health and positive personal and organizational outcomes (Fletcher, 2007).

According to Fletcher (2004, 2007) relational (e.g., post-heroic) models of leadership have three characteristics that distinguish them from more traditionally individualistic models. First, leadership is shared and distributed and is not enacted by a single person. Second, leadership is a social process, in which human interactions are keys. Third, relational leadership results in outcomes of learning, growth, and well-being for the organization, as well as the people involved (Fletcher, 2007). Despite the increasing acceptance of relational leadership, works that focus on the close and intense form of leader–follower workplace intimacy are sparse.

To the best of my knowledge, only two previous works make use of the concept of intimacy to characterize leadership and management dynamics. One is a theoretical work that explored the relationship between masculinity, management, and intimacy (Kerfoot, 1999). The other is an empirical study of executive character and development with regards to a mastery-oriented approach versus an intimacy-oriented approach (Kofodimos, 1993). Although these works draw on different streams of thought, they reach somewhat similar conclusions.

Kerfoot (1999) examines the organization of intimacy with regards to management, contending that most organizational cultures are dominated by and promote management practices that are increasingly instrumental in their focus on success and utility. This form of management implies that all encounters, events, and social relationships become potential arenas for instrumental control. Kerfoot (1999) bases her analysis on the work of Bologh (1990), who suggested there were two types of intimacy: instrumental and emotional. Emotional intimacy rests on relationships with no preexisting definition of who is "in charge." The conditions for emotional intimacy are based primarily on the fact that neither party is the object or subject, but that the subjectivity of self or the other can vary as each relating to the uniqueness of the other. This strengthens the perception that the other *matters* and *makes a difference*. The precondition is that each is attuned to and, in tune with, the embodied subjectivity of the other. It involves caring for the other. Instrumental intimacy, by contrast, has the trappings of intimacy but is aimed at achieving instrumental control over the other.

According to Kerfoots' (1999) analysis, management denies the ambiguity, fluidity, and alternative possibilities of human interaction aside from that grounded in instrumental intimacy. Bologh (1990) points out that "the more that formalities predominate, the less that personal self-disclosure occurs and the more superficial the relationships remains. . . . Because intimacy breaks down the barriers that formality provides. Intimacy promotes vulnerability. Intimacy can be dangerous; one's trust can be betrayed, one's weaknesses exploited, and one's esteem or desire unreciprocated. In other words, one can be hurt and humiliated. On the other hand, intimacy can be protective and intensely pleasurable. Trust can be met with care, vulnerability, and tenderness, exposure with recognition and affirmation, esteem and desire reciprocated. In other words, one can be nurtured, affirmed, and exalted" (p. 217).

Managers are concerned about maintaining and reinforcing hierarchy and their protective barriers for fear of disclosure that might be humiliating or exploitative. They, thus further deny the possibility of removing such barriers, since to do so would be regarded as immediately giving a power advantage to the other. This managerial mode of engaging with the world and activities of management is also appealing as a way of handling the uncertain nature of many aspects of managerial work, euphemistically described as *managing change*, *downsizing*, and *restructuring* Kerfoot further contends that this type of management rationale is based on an ethos of masculinity and fits masculine subjects who are drawn into its discourse and behavioral displays.

Although Kerfoot argues that managerial and masculine practices displace and deny alternative noninstrumental expressions of intimacy, she calls for the alternative expression of emotional intimacy in leader–follower relationship at work. She offers the notion of play and playfulness as an alternative, contending that emotional intimacy presents a range of possibilities for subject/object positions, flexible exploration, and movement in a playful fashion. This allows for alternative expressions that challenge the conventional order of managerial relationships by stimulating authentic discovery, creativity, and pleasure in the workplace. Similarly, Sandeland (2003, 2010) has also recently linked love relationships and the ability to play and be playful.

Kofodimos (1993) reached somewhat similar conclusions with regards to management, masculinity, and workplace intimacy. This empirical study analyzed executive character and development. It is based on a long-term action research study of managers conducted at the Center for Creative Leadership was followed by intensive clinical studies of individual executives. The executives were interviewed, as well as their coworkers, managers, and friends; thus, the researchers obtained a range of perspectives on each executive's managerial approach, life and career history, and personal life.

Following this study, Kofodimos (1993) developed a model that distinguished between a mastery-oriented approach and an intimacy-oriented approach. Mastery, most broadly defined, is the experience of developing and exercising one's abilities and power. It involves a process or mode of functioning, and a goal or desired outcomes. Their findings show that, for executives, mastery can become the only satisfying mode of experience and the sole desired goal. Mastery is experienced and practiced by managers in terms of a constant need to control and manage others; intolerance of others' and one's own weaknesses and mistakes; task-oriented interactions with intimate others; distance in personal relationships; suppression of feelings, inner needs, and fears; striving for mastery in all activities in personal life; inability to relax; structuring of vacations; involvement in competitive leisure activities; and experiencing personal life as mundane.

An intimacy-oriented approach was defined as a mode of experience that contrasts most directly with the drive for mastery. It involves seeking connectedness with others, as well as with one's inner self. The key characteristics of the intimacy-oriented approach are an emphasis on one's own and other's feelings, concern with what people need and want, tolerance for one's own and other's weaknesses, an emphasis on a rewarding and satisfying process of accomplishing things, a desire to collaborate and be interdependent with others, an appreciation of connection, revealing emotions and one's vulnerabilities and doubts, preference for leisure and contemplation, and a playful approach to life and work.

Hence, managers in general, and in particular male managers, tend to approach the world with a mastery perspective and avoid an intimacy-oriented approach. Kofodimos also found that organizational forces support the mastery–intimacy imbalance by shaping and reinforcing the drive for mastery and avoidance of intimacy. Furthermore, she brings evidence for possible negative outcomes of managers' avoidance of workplace intimacy.

These works on leadership and intimacy suggest that intimacy is negated in leadership thinking and management practices. However, more recent relational leadership theories and studies on HQCs (e.g., Dutton & Heaphy, 2003; Fletcher, 2004) and on friendships at work (e.g., Ingram & Zou, 2008) paint a different picture. Since individuals spend most of their waking hours at work, they are likely to form intimate and close relationships at work, and these relationships are likely to characterize leader–follower relationships. Thus, there is a need rethink, re-vision, and empirically study closer forms of relating in leader–follower interactions—namely, workplace intimacy—as well as to explore the different dimensions of intimacy and the possible ways they are enacted and displayed in the workplace.

Outcomes of Leader–Follower Workplace Intimacy Relationships

Close intimate relationships can shape people by influencing the ways they think, how they think (Agnew, Van Lange, Rusbult, & Langston, 1998), and the ways in which they behave (Berscheid et al., 1989). This implies that workplace intimacy in leader–follower relationships can have perceptual, motivational, behavioral, and health consequences, and can result in a wide range of outcomes at the personal and group or organizational level.

Workplace Intimacy and Positive Individual Level Outcomes
SELF-WORTH, SELF-EFFICACY, AND ORGANIZATIONAL-BASED SELF-ESTEEM

The impact of leadership on followers' performance is often explained as stemming from followers' development and empowerment, which increase both their ability and their motivation (e.g., Bass, 1985; Dvir, Eden, Avolio, & Shamir, 2002; Kark, Shamir, & Chen, 2003). According to Brewer and Gardner (1996), at the relational level of identity, self-representations and perceptions of self-worth are dependent on the reflected self, or the self as seen through the reactions of the other person. Positive close relationships create new opportunities for enhancing one's conception of self. According to Roberts (2007), "In positive relationships, people are likely to become more self aware of strengths and limitations, to feel affirmed, and to become more open to continued growth and development. Mutual understanding, influence, benefits, and expectations create the possibility for greater self-discovery and a heightened sense of self efficacy" (p. 31). This suggests that leaders who form intimate relationships with followers are likely to increase followers' self-worth and self-efficacy, because they transmit the message that the leader believes in the follower and has high confidence in his or her integrity and ability. This process is likely to be mutual.

Furthermore, according to the self-expansion model (Aron & Aron, 1986; Aron et al., 2001), in intimate relationships, each person includes some of the other's resources and identities in the self. If the followers perceive themselves as having access to the leader's resources and as including them in the self, this is likely to enhance their sense of work self-efficacy and their organizational-based self-esteem (OBSE). Thus, workplace intimacy in leader–follower relationships is likely to lead to followers' enhanced sense of self-worth, efficacy, and OBSE. This is also likely to be mutual and affect the leaders' heightened sense of self as well.

GROWTH, VITALITY, AND ENERGY

Connections with others are vital for human development and growth. Different streams of thought link close connections with growth. Miller and Stiver (1997) argue that relational interactions are growth-fostering and result in mutually empowering connections that they refer to as the "five good things": zest, empowered action, increased knowledge, increased self-worth, and a desire for more connections. Thus, leadership practices that form close intimate relationships and prime the relational aspects of the self are likely to result in empowerment effects similar to those specified in the "five good things": followers' increased feelings of vitality, liveliness, and energy; sense of self-worth; sense of meaningfulness; and their belief in their ability to act toward achieving their personal goals (Kark & Shamir, 2002).

Researchers have linked a context of HQCs with increased vitality (Ryan & Frederick, 1997). Dutton (2003) proposes that interpersonal connections are a key mechanism to energizing people at work, giving them a "sense of being eager to act and capable of action" (p. 6). In a similar vein, Spreitzer et al. (2005) proposed that specific work environments and relational resources enhance the sense of agency experienced by individual employees, which ultimately results in individual growth, learning, and vitality. Empirical research supports this notion by showings that, in contexts in which employees feel psychological safety, they also feel vital (Kark & Carmeli, 2009). Furthermore, a recent study found that leader relational behaviors cultivate social capital among employees in community centers and that these relational ties augment feelings of vigor (Carmeli et al., 2009). Thus, workplace intimacy in leader–follower relationships is likely to enhance a sense of growth, vitality, and energy.

DEPENDENCE AND INTERDEPENDENCE

It is commonly believed that follower growth and empowerment imply greater follower independence.

However, strong emotional connections between followers and leaders may also lead to the dependency of followers on the leader (Howell, 1988). Although this has commonly been associated with a negative form of leadership (e.g., the dark side of charisma), the theoretical rationale presented above suggests that an intimate relationship, which can enhance the relational self and the inclusion of some aspects of the intimate other in the self, may increase the attachment to the leader and dependence on the leader. Relational perspectives (e.g., Miller & Stiver, 1997; Fletcher, 1999) challenge the commonly accepted opposition between dependence and empowerment, claiming that this distinction rests on traditional models of masculine development that view the development of independence and self-reliance as disengagement from significant others. In contrast, relational perspectives present a model of development within a relationship that emphasizes both independence and interdependence. Within such a model, a relationship may be characterized by both a sense of empowerment and some sense of interpersonal dependence. Thus, workplace intimacy is likely to contribute to followers' empowerment and simultaneously to followers' interdependence. In support of this thesis, recent findings from a large-scale study of bank employees and managers showed that transformational leadership was positively related simultaneously to both followers' empowerment and dependence on the leader (Kark et al., 2003). Furthermore, followers' empowerment and dependence were not negatively correlated with each other.

PHYSICAL WELL-BEING

Intimate relationships have been found to account for many health benefits. For example, some studies have shown that confiding stressful (as opposed to trivial) material in intimate relationships leads to measurable psychological benefits (Prager, 1995). Intimate behavior further buffers people from the pathogenic effects of stress. In the face of stressful life events, people who have intimate relationships have fewer stress-related symptoms, faster recovery from illness, and a lower probability for relapse or reoccurrence than do those who do not have intimate relationships. The beneficial effects of intimate relationships on health and well-being has been widely reported (Prager, 1995). Work relationships that are endowed with close supportive relationships can be construed as a set of social resources (Losada & Heaphy, 2004; Miller & Stiver, 1997) that fuel individual well-being. These social resources, which are endogenously produced through supportive interactions between an individual and others (Feldman, 2004; Lilius, Kanov, & Dutton, 2011, Chapter 21, this volume), have been found to be associated with physiological changes in the neuroendocrine, cardiovascular, and immune systems that contribute to openness to experience and to enhanced capacity to act (Reis & Gable, 2003). Heaphy and Dutton (2008) suggest that positive relationships contribute to physiological resources and lead to physical strength and health. Thus, leader–follower intimate work relations can enhance an individual's (both leader and follower) physical health and well-being.

LEARNING

Intimacy in a leader–follower relationship may lead to the followers' ability to show learning behavior and behave creatively. According to Fletcher (2004), relational leadership results in learning by enhancing the conditions under which new knowledge is co-created and implemented at the individual and team level. Strong intimate bonds can affect learning in various ways. First, knowledge is better passed from one to the other and absorbed faster (Dutton & Heaphy, 2003). Second, knowledge is generated in interactions between people (Dutton & Heaphy, 2003; Miller & Stiver, 1997; Stephens et al., 2011). Third, people in intimate interactions feel psychologically safe, and this enables them to better experience, take chances, and learn new ways of thinking and doing things. Edmondson (2004) suggested that specific aspects of leader behavior, such as accessibility, availability, and openness, are essential for promoting psychological safety and learning (e.g., Edmondson, 1996, 1999; Nembhard & Edmondson, 2006). A recent study supports this notion, showing empirically that leaders who are sensitive to relational dynamics shape a context in which people feel psychologically safe and facilitate learning from failures (Hirak, Carmeli, Peng, & Schaubroeck, 2010).

LOYALTY, COMMITMENT TO THE OTHER, AND COOPERATION

When an individual's relational self is salient, his or her primary motivation is to enhance the relationship partner's well-being and mutual benefits (Gabriel & Gardner, 1999). Batson (1994) defined this concern for the outcomes of the other as the basis of altruistic motivation to benefit the other. Following this, Kark and Shamir (2002) suggested that, when followers are focused on their relational

self this can motivate them to enhance the well-being and possible benefits of the leader, leading to followers' willingness to cooperate with the leader and their loyalty and commitment to the leader.

Workplace Intimacy and Group-focused/Group-level Outcomes

A leader who forms close intimate work relationships is likely to affect employees' attachment, motivations, and behavior toward the organization, as well as group-level behaviors. There are several ways in which the formation of intimate leader–follower relationships can have this effect. First, since a leader is often seen as a representatives figure who embodies a unit's identity and values (e.g., Kark & Van-Dijk, 2007; Shamir, Zakay, & Popper, 1998), certain intimate behaviors of leaders may increase not only the attachment of the individual to the leader, but also influence the attachment of the individual to the team. This can enhance followers' social identification and commitment to the work group and the organization.

Second, the relational leader can provide followers with an emulative role model for a close and caring relationship, and this is likely to affect the ways in which the team members interact among themselves, leading to the enhancement of the relational capital of the group (see also Mishra & Mishra, 2011, Chapter 34, this volume). The literature on leadership suggests that vicarious learning, by observing leaders' behaviors, plays a key role in shaping not only individual followers' conduct, but may be an important group process by which leader role modeling may enhance team behavior (e.g., Kozlowski & Ilgen, 2006; Trevino & Brown, 2005). Leader behavior "models the way" organizational/group goals should be pursued (Kouzes & Posner, 2003). Thus, a leader who forms close caring and intimate relationships with followers may be emulated by group members, and this behavior may become an emerging group property (Kozlowski & Klein, 2000).

Another major mechanism through which a leader can affect the relationships at the group level is through leader–follower emotional contagion processes. Various researchers have described how leaders, by creating a certain emotional environment, can affect followers (e.g., Dasborough & Ashkanasy, 2003). Fredrickson (2003) suggests that the emotions expressed by leaders may be especially contagious due to their position of power. Several recent empirical studies have examined the mood contagion process in work groups, documenting the spread of emotions from leaders to followers and among group members (e.g., Barsade, 2002; Cherulnik, Donley, Wiewel, & Miller, 2001). This may imply that leaders exhibiting emotions related to intimate relationships (caring, empathy) may affect the transfer of emotions and lead to a work culture that cultivates empathy and compassion. Last, leaders can also give rise to more intimate work relationships at the group level by shaping the work context (e.g., choice of tasks for the workgroup, task structure, allocation of rewards) (Kark & Van Dijk, 2007). For example, leaders can choose to reward followers' relational behaviors and close, caring team interactions.

Thus, leaders who enhance workplace intimacy can contribute to individuals' and the organization's relational capital (Blatt, 2009), leading to followers' sense of attachment to the group, and enhancing followers' social identification, affective commitment to the organization, and a sense of obligation between team members to meet each other's needs and act in ways that benefit the relationship. This can further affect followers' prosocial behaviors and lead to the display of organizational citizenship behavior (OCB).

Conclusion

The concept of leader–follower workplace intimacy presented here portrays intimate leader–follower relationships in the workplace as a multifaceted, complex, and dynamic form of relating. It suggests that leaders and followers can mutually affect each other by using a communal mode of exchange and by giving salience to different aspects of the other's self-concept (e.g., relational self). This is likely to enhance individual outcomes (e.g., self-efficacy, vitality, growth, and learning) and individuals' attachment to the work group and the organization (e.g., social identification, collective obligation, affective commitment, and OCB). Furthermore, this relationship can extend to the collective and influence group level outcomes, thus enhancing the organizational relational capital. It can elicit a relational work context and affect related group-level outcomes, such as an organizational culture of compassion. Thus, the theoretical framework suggested above begins to shed light on the complex ways in which leader–follower workplace intimacy can affect multiple and diverse aspects of followers' and leaders' perceptions and behaviors, resulting in positive outcomes for the individual and the organization.

The perspective developed in this chapter questions the widespread discourse of segregation between the private and public spheres that negates major aspects of the human experience at work and does not accurately capture the emotions, interactions, and relationships that may develop in the workplace. This perspective calls for rethinking leadership and management discourse and practices, and provides some directions for further research on leadership and workplace intimacy. In addition, there are some issues and questions that merit attention in future studies.

First, workplace intimacy and how it is perceived and enacted, as well as its outcomes, can be highly dependent on cultural specificities. Previous studies have demonstrated that there are cultural differences in intimacy, and that these may have important practical consequences for relational well-being (Marshall, 2008). Individualistic versus collectivistic cultures have somewhat different views of intimacy (Seki, Matsumoto, & Imahori, 2002). The effect of national culture on perceptions of leadership was also demonstrated in the Globe Study (e.g., House, Javidan, Hanges, & Dorfman, 2002). Thus, the relationship between leadership, workplace intimacy, and culture still needs to be further explored in local, as well as global, organizations.

Second, gender may play an important role in shaping workplace intimacy. Many studies have shown that women tend to be more prone to form intimate relationships in comparison to men (e.g., Hook, Gerstein, Detterich, & Gridley, 2003; Marshall, 2008). It has been demonstrated (Gabriel & Gardner, 1999) that women tend to focus more on the relational aspects of the self, whereas men tend to focus more on the collective aspects. This suggests that women might be more likely to enact relational leadership behaviors and respond to the relational aspects of leadership than are men. Furthermore, people may expect different behavior from men and women and thus may interpret and evaluate differently the enactment of a relational leadership style and the development of workplace intimacy by men versus women leaders (Fletcher, 1999; Kark & Waismel-Manor, 2005). Moreover, previous research has shown that same-sex intimate relationships are somewhat different than cross-sex intimate relationships (e.g., Monsour, 1992). This may affect the workplace intimacy dynamics of leader–follower relationships in same-sex versus cross-sex relationships, as well as reveal differences between female dyads and male dyads. Future research should therefore examine not only the relationships between various leader–follower intimate behaviors and their outcomes, but also the moderating effects of various followers' and leaders' characteristics and orientations on these relationships.

Organizational context can also impact workplace intimacy. One factor is the distance of the leader from the followers. The behaviors specified above assume direct leader–follower contact, and may therefore apply primarily to direct relationships (e.g., mid-level organizational leaders). However, there is a difference between close leadership, in which followers and leaders have daily face-to-face interactions, and leadership at a distance (Antonakis & Atwater, 2002; Shamir, 1995). This difference may be amplified when dealing with workplace intimacy. Thus, there is a need for further research to understand the role of workplace intimacy in close versus distant leadership, in particular to study whether certain components of intimacy can take place at a distance. This is pertinent in the age of globalization, in which many direct managers are physically distant from their followers, and interact with them mostly through e-mail.

Workplace intimacy is likely to be initiated and shaped by both leaders and followers. According to Howell and Shamir (2005), leaders and followers may both play an active role in forming their mutual relationships. This suggested reciprocal and possibly different dynamics in follower–leader relationships should serve as a focus of future research in the field.

Last, I have focused primarily on the positive aspects of workplace intimacy. However, it also has its dark sides. As Firestone and Firestone (2004) note: "Intimate relationship can be the ultimate source of happiness and fulfillment; at the same time, they have the potential to generate considerable pain and suffering." (p. 375). Workplace intimacy may result in tension arising from conflicting motivational concerns and different exchange patterns (communal vs. instrumental), which may clash or cause misunderstandings when both business and intimate interests are present (Ingram & Zou, 2008). For example, in a situation in which a manager has to fire an employee with whom he has an intimate relationship, this may be more painful to both of them. Second, due to the power differences in a leader–follower relationship, there is a potential danger that managers will make use of intimate relationship and followers' trust to coerce or exploit them. Employees can also exploit intimate relationships with their managers, although to a lesser extent. For example, employees can hurt their managers by making use of information that managers disclosed to them regarding their vulnerabilities and personal affairs. Third, the promise of intimate and relational leadership can be co-opted at the organizational level as a mechanism aimed merely to enhance followers' organizational conformity and to contribute to organizational utility. Intimacy can become commercialized as a contemporary instrumental management practice that seeks to capture the subtleties and nuances of social relations for organizational ends (Fletcher, 2007; Kerfoot, 1999).

It should be acknowledged, in conclusion, that I do not know the extent to which workplace intimacy is prevalent in leader–follower relationships in organizations, nor the scope and magnitude of its influence on the personal and organizational outcomes presented above. However, given the strong evidence for the effects of intimacy on individual well-being, optimal functioning, joy, and meaning, and the lack of sufficient understanding of the mechanisms by which these effects may be achieved by relational leaders within the workplace context, theoretical frameworks such as the one proposed in this chapter are needed to better characterize and conceptualize leadership theory and positive organizational scholarship.

Acknowledgement

I am thankful for the helpful suggestions of Avi Carmeli, Dana Findler, Mirav Gaziel, Amir Nehari, Gretchen Spreitzer and Liron Vinder.

Notes

1. I do not refer to sexualized forms of intimacy, which can be related to sexual harassment at work, a topic that has been well documented and researched in the organizational literature.
2. The quotations are from a large study I conducted in 70 bank branches in Israel, in which quantitative and qualitative data were collected. As a part of the study 50 in-depth semi-structured interviews were conducted among employees and managers that focused on the relationship between them.
3. Based on these typologies Sharabany (1994) and Schaefer and Olson (1981) also suggested scales for the measurement of intimacy that have been adapted to the workplace by Nehari, Kark and Findler (2010).

References

Agnew, C.R., Van Lange, P.A.M., Rusbult, C.E., & Langston, C.A. (1998). Cognitive interdependence: Commitment and the mental representation of close relationships. *Journal of Personality and Social Psychology, 74,* 939–954.

Antonakis, J., & Atwater, L. (2002). Leader distance: A review and a proposed theory. *Leadership Quarterly, 13,* 673–704.

Aron, A., & Aron, E.N. (1986*). Love as the expansion of self: Understanding attraction and satisfaction.* New York: Hemisphere.

Aron, A., Aron, E.N., & Norman, C. (2001). Self-expansion model of motivation and cognition in close relationships and beyond. In G.J.O. Fletcher, & M.S. Clark (Eds.), *Interpersonal processes* (pp. 478–501). Malden, MA: Blackwell.

Aron, A.P., Mashek, D.J., & Aron, E.N. (2004). Closeness as including other in the self. In D.J. Mashek, & A. Aron (Eds.), *The handbook of closeness and intimacy* (pp. 27–42). Mahwah, NJ: Erlbaum.

Badaracco, J. (2002). *Leading quietly.* Cambridge, MA: Harvard Business School Press.

Banaji, M.R., & Prentice, D.A. (1994). The self in social contexts. *Annual Review of Psychology, 45,* 297–332.

Barsade, S.G. (2002). The ripple effect: emotional contagion and its influence on group behavior. *Administrative Science Quarterly, 47,* 644–675.

Bass, B.M. (1985). *Leadership and performance beyond expectation.* New York: The Free Press.

Batson, C.D. (1994). Why act for the public good? Four answers. *Personality and Social Psychology Bulletin, 20,* 603–610.

Berscheid, D., Snyder, M., & Omoto, A.M. (1989). The relationship closeness inventory: Assessing the closeness of interpersonal relationships. *Journal of Personality and Social Psychology, 57,* 792–807.

Blatt, R. (2009). Tough love: How communal schemas and contracting practices build relational capital in entrepreneurial teams. *The Academy of Management Review, 34,* 533–551.

Bowlby, J. (1969). *Attachment and loss* Vol. 1. New York: Basic Books.

Brewer, M.B., & Gardner, W. (1996). Who is this "We"? Levels of collective identity and self representations. *Journal of Personality and Social Psychology, 71,* 83–93.

Brown, M.E., & Gioia, D.A. (2002). Distributive leadership in an online division of an offline organization. *The Leadership Quarterly, 13,* 397–419.

Brickson, S. (2000). The impact of identity orientation on individual and organizational outcomes in demographically diverse settings. *Academy of Management Review, 25,* 82–101.

Bologh, R.W. (1990). *Love or greatness: Max Weber and masculine thinking–a feminist inquiry.* London: Unwin Hyman.

Carmeli, A., Ben-Hador, B., Waldman, D.A., & Rupp, D.E. (2009). How leaders cultivate social capital and nurture employee vigor: Implications for job performance. *Journal of Applied Psychology, 94,* 1553–1561.

Carmeli, A., Reiter-Palmon, R., & Ziv, E. (2010). Inclusive leadership and employee involvement in creative tasks in the workplace: The mediating role of psychological safety. *Creativity Research Journal,* Forthcoming.

Cherulnik, P.D., Donley, K.A., Wiewel, T.S., & Miller, S.R. (2001). Charisma is contagious: The effects of leader's charisma on observers' affect. *Journal of Applied Social Psychology, 31,* 2149–2159.

Clark, M.S. (1984). Record keeping in two types of relationships. *Journal of Personality and Social Psychology, 47,* 549–557.

Clark, M.S., & Mills, J. (1979). Interpersonal-attraction in exchange and communal relationships. *Journal of Personality and Social Psychology, 37,* 12–24.

Clark, M.S., & Waddell, B. (1985). Perceptions of exploitation in communal and exchange relationships. *Journal of Social and Personal Relationships, 2,* 403–418.

Dasborough, M.T., & Ashkanasy, N.M. (2003). *A qualitative study of cognitive asymmetry in employee affective reactions to leadership behaviors.* Paper presented at the Academy of Management Conference, Seattle.

DiMaggio, P.J., & Powell, W.W. (1983). The iron cage revisited: Institutional isomorphism and collective rationality in organizational fields. *American Sociological Review, 48,* 147–160.

Dutton, J.E. (2003*). Energize your workplace: How to create and sustain high quality relationships at work.* San Francisco: Jossey-Bass.

Dutton, J.E., & Heaphy, E.D. (2003). The power of high-quality connections at work. In K.S. Cameron, J.E. Dutton, & R.E. Quinn (Eds.), *Positive organizational scholarship* (pp. 263–278). San Francisco: Berrett-Koehler Publishers.

Dvir, T., Eden, D., Avolio, B.J., & Shamir, B. (2002). Impact of transformational leadership on followers' development and performance: A field experiment. *Academy of Management Journal, 45,* 735–744.

Edmondson, A.C. (1996). Learning from mistakes is easier said than done: Group and organizational influences on the detection and correction of human error. *The Journal of Applied Behavioral Science, 32,* 5–28.

Edmondson, A.C. (1999). Psychological safety and learning behavior in work teams. *Administrative Science Quarterly, 44,* 350–383.

Edmondson, A.C. (2004). Psychological safety, trust, and learning in organizations: A group-level lens. In R.M. Kramer, & K.S. Cook (Eds.), *Trust and distrust in organizations: Dilemmas and approaches* (pp. 239–272). New York: Russell Sage.

Feldman, M.S. (2004). Resources in emerging structures and processes of change. *Organization Science, 15,* 295–309.

Firestone, R.W., & Firestone, L. (2004). Methods for overcoming the fear of intimacy. In D.J. Mashek, & A. Aron (Eds.), *The handbook of closeness and intimacy* (pp. 375–396). Mahwah, NJ: Erlbaum.

Fletcher, J.K. (1999). *Disappearing acts: Gender, power, and relational practice at work.* Cambridge, MA: MIT Press.

Fletcher, J.K. (2004). The paradox of postheroic leadership: An essay on gender, power, and transformational change. *The Leadership Quarterly, 15,* 647–661.

Fletcher, J.K. (2007). Leadership, power, and positive relationships. In J.E. Dutton, & B.R. Ragins (Eds.), *Exploring positive relationships at work: Building a theoretical and research foundation* (pp. 347–371). Mahwah, NJ: Lawrence Erlbaum Associates.

Fredrickson, B.L. (2003). Positive emotions and upward spirals in organizations. In K.S. Cameron, J.E. Dutton, & R.E. Quinn (Eds.), *Positive Organizational Scholarship* (pp. 163–175). San Francisco: Berrett-Koehler.

Gabriel, S., & Gardner, W.L. (1999). Are there "his" and "hers" types of interdependence? The implications of gender differences in collective versus relational interdependence for affect, behavior, and cognition. *Journal of Personality and Social Psychology, 77,* 642–655.

Geddes & Grosset (Publishers) (1999). *New English dictionary and thesaurus.* New Lanark, Scotland: Geddes & Grosset (formerly Children's Leisure Products Limited).

Goffman, E. (1961). *Encounters: Two studies in the sociology of interaction.* Indianapolis: Bobbs-Merrill.

Graen, G.B., & Uhl-Bien, M. (1995). Relationship based approach to leadership: Development of leader-member exchange (LMX) theory of leadership over 25 years: Applying a multi-level multi-domain perspective. *Leadership Quarterly, 6,* 219–247.

Gronn, P. (2002). Distributed leadership as a unit of analysis, *Leadership Quarterly, 13*, 423–451.

Heaphy, E.D., & Dutton, J.E. (2008). Positive social interactions and the human body at work: Linking organizations and physiology. *Academy of Management Review, 33*, 137–162.

Hirak, R., Carmeli, A., Peng, A.C., & Schaubroeck, J. (2010). *How leadership facilitates psychological safety and learning from failures in work teams*. Paper presented at the Academy of Management annual meeting, Montreal, Canada.

Hook, M.K., Gerstein, L.H., Detterich, L., & Gridley, B. (2003). How close are we? Measuring intimacy and examining gender differences. *Journal of Counseling & Development, 81*, 462–472.

House, R., Javidan, M., Hanges, P., & Dorfman, P. (2002). Understanding cultures and implicit leadership theories across the globe: An introduction to project GLOBE. *Journal of World Business, 37*, 3–10.

Howell, J.M. (1988). Two faces of charisma: Socialized and personalized leadership in organizations. In J.A. Conger, & R.N. Kanungo (Eds.), *Charismatic leadership* (pp. 213–236). San Francisco: Jossey-Bass.

Howell, J.M., & Shamir, B. (2005). The role of followers in the charismatic process: Relationships and their consequences. *Academy of Management Review, 30*, 96–112.

Ingram, P., & Zou, X. (2008). Business friendships. *Research in Organizational Behavior, 28*, 167–184.

Kanter, R.M. (1977). *Men and women of the corporation*. New York: Basic Books.

Kark, R. (1999). *Gendering identification processes: The deconstruction of boundaries between the private and public sphere*. Paper presented at the 7th International Interdisciplinary Congress on Women–Women's Worlds 99, Tromso, Norway.

Kark, R., & Carmeli, A. (2009). Alive and creating: The mediating role of vitality and aliveness in the relationship between interpersonal work climate and creative work involvement. *Journal of Organizational Behavior, 30*, 785–804.

Kark, R., & Shamir, B. (2002). The dual effect of transformational leadership: Priming relational and collective selves and further effects on followers. In B.J. Avolio, & F.J. Yammarino (Eds.), *Transformational and charismatic leadership: The road ahead* Vol. 2 (pp. 67–91). Amsterdam: JAI Press.

Kark, R., Shamir, B., & Chen, G. (2003). The two faces of transformational leadership: Dependence and empowerment. *Journal of Applied Psychology, 88*, 243–255.

Kark, R., & Van-Dijk, D. (2007). Motivation to lead motivation to follow: The role of the self-regulatory focus in leadership processes. *Academy of Management Review, 32*, 500–528.

Kark, R., & Waismel-Manor, R. (2005). Organizational citizenship behavior: What's gender got to do with it? *Organization, 12*, 889–917.

Keeley, M.P., & Hart, A.J. (1994). Nonverbal behavior in dyadic interactions. In S. Duck (Ed.), *Dynamics of relationships* (pp. 135–179). Thousand Oaks, CA: Sage.

Kelly, G.A. (1955). *The psychology of personal constructs*. New York: Norton.

Kerfoot, D. (1999). The organization of intimacy: Managerialism, masculinity and the masculine subject. In S. Whitehead, & R. Moodley (Eds.), *Transforming managers: Gendering change in the public sector* (pp. 184–198). London: UCL press.

Kerfoot, D., & Knights, D. (1933). Management, masculinity and manipulation: From paternalism to corporate strategy in financial services in Britain. *Journal of Management Studies, 30*, 659–679.

Kofodimos, J. (1993). *Balancing act: How managers can integrate successful careers and fulfilling personal lives*. San Francisco: Jossey-Bass.

Kouzes, J.M., & Posner, B.Z. (2003). *Credibility: How leaders gain and lose it, and why people demand it*. San Francisco: Jossey-Bass.

Kozlowski, S.W.J., & Ilgen, D.R. (2006). Enhancing the effectiveness of work groups and teams. *Psychological Science in the Public Interest, 7*, 77–124.

Kozlowski, S.W.J., & Klein, K.J. (2000). A multilevel approach to theory and research in organizations: Contextual, temporal, and emergent processes. In K.J. Klein, & S.W. J. Kozlowski (Eds.), *Multilevel theory, research, and methods in organizations: Foundations, extensions, and new directions* (pp. 3–90). San Francisco: Jossey-Bass.

Laurenceau, J.P., Rivera, L.M., Schaffer, A.R., & Pietromonaco, P.R. (2004). Intimacy as an interpersonal process: Current status and future direction. In D.J. Mashek, & A. Aron (Eds.), *Handbook of closeness and intimacy* (pp. 61–78). Mahwah, NJ: Erlbaum.

Lerner, H. (1989). *The dance of intimacy: A women's guide to courageous acts of change in key relationships*. New York: Harper Perennial.

Lilius, J.M., Kanov, J.M., & Dutton, J.E. (2011). In K. Cameron & G. Spreitzer (Eds.), *Handbook of positive organizational scholarship*. New York: Oxford University Press.

Lipman Blumen, J. (1996). *The connective edge*. San Francisco: Jossey Bass.

Lord, R.G., & Brown, D.J. (2004). *Leadership processes and follower identity*. Mahwah, NJ: Lawrence Erlbaum Associates.

Lord, R.G., Brown, D.J., & Feiberg, S.J. (1999). Understanding the dynamics of leadership: The role of follower self-concepts in the leader/follower relationship. *Organizational Behavior and Human Decision Processes, 78*, 167–203.

Losada, M., & Heaphy, E. (2004). The role of positivity and connectivity in the performance of business teams: A nonlinear dynamics model. *American Behavioral Scientist, 47*, 740–765.

Marshall, T.C. (2008). Cultural differences in intimacy: The influence of gender-role ideology and individualism–collectivism. *Journal of Social and Personal Relationships, 25*, 143–168.

Martin, J., Knopoff, K., & Beckman, C. (1998). An alternative to bureaucratic impersonality and emotional labor: Bounded emotionality at the body shop. *Administrative Science Quarterly, 43*, 429–469.

Miller, J.B. (1976). *Toward a new psychology of women*. Boston: Beacon Press.

Miller, R.S., & Lefcourt, H.M. (1982). The assessment of social intimacy. *Journal of Personality Assessment, 46*, 514–518.

Miller, J.B., & Stiver, I.P. (1997). *The healing connection: How women form relationships in therapy and in life*. Boston: Beacon Press.

Mills, J., & Clark, M.S. (1982). Communal and exchange relationships. In L. Wheeler (Ed.), *Review of personality and social psychology*. Beverly Hills: Sage.

Mishra, A.K., & Mishra, K.E. (2011). POS and trust in leaders. In K. Cameron, & G. Spreitzer (Eds.), *Handbook of positive organizational scholarship*. New York: Oxford University Press.

Monsour, M. (1992). Meaning of intimacy in cross- and same-sex friendships. *Journal of Social and Personal Relationships, 9*, 277–295.

Nehari, A., Kark, R., & Findler, D. (2010). *Developing a workplace intimacy scale*. Working paper, Department of Psychology, Bar-Ilan University, Ramat Gan, Israel.

Nembhard, I.M., & Edmondson, A.C. (2006). Making it safe: The effects of leader inclusiveness and professional status on psychological safety and improvement efforts in health care teams. *Journal of Organizational Behavior, 27*, 941–966.

Nippert-Eng, C.E. (1995). *Home and work: Negotiating boundaries through everyday life*. Chicago: University of Chicago Press.

Perlow, L.A. (1998). Boundary control: The social ordering of work and family time in a high-tech corporation. *Administrative Science Quarterly, 43*, 328–357.

Pearce, C., & Conger, J. (2003). All those years ago: The historical underpinnings of shared leadership. In C. Pearce, & J. Conger (Eds.), *Shared leadership: Reframing the hows and whys of leadership* (pp. 3–13). London: Sage.

Popovic, M. (2005). Intimacy and its relevance in human functioning. *Sexual and Relationship Therapy, 20*, 31–49.

Prager, K.J. (1995). *The psychology of intimacy*. New York: Guilford.

Prager, K.J., & Roberts, L.J. (2004). Deep intimate connections: Self and intimacy in couple relationships. In D.J. Mashek, & A. Aron (Eds.), *The handbook of closeness and intimacy* (pp. 43–60). Mahwah, NJ: Erlbaum.

Reis, H.T., Collins, W.A., & Berscheid, E. (2000). The relationship context of human behavior and development. *Psychological Bulletin, 126*, 844–872.

Reis, H.T., & Gable, S.L. (2003). Toward a positive psychology of relationships. In C.L.M. Keyes (Ed.), *Flourishing: Positive psychology and the life well-lived* (pp. 129–159). Washington, D.C: American Psychological Association.

Reis, H.T., & Patrick, B.C. (1996). Attachment and intimacy: Components processes. In A. Kruglanski, & E.T. Higgins (Eds.), *Social psychology: Handbook of basic principles* (pp. 523–563). New York: Guilford.

Reis, H.T., & Shaver, P (1988). Intimacy as interpersonal process. In S. Duck (Ed.), Handbook of close relationships: Theory, relationships and interventions. Chichester, UK: Wiley.

Roberts, L.M. (2007). From proving to becoming: How positive relationships create a context for self-discovery and self-actualization. In Dutton, J.E., & Ragins, B.R. (Eds.). Exploring positive relationships at work: Building a theoretical and research foundation. (pp. 29-46). New York: Lawrence Erlbaum Associates.

Rogers, C.R. (1951). *Client centered therapy*. Boston: Houghton Mifflin.

Ryan, R.M., & Frederick, C. (1997). On energy, personality, and health subjective vitality as a dynamic reflection of well-being. *Journal of Personality, 65*, 529–566.

Sandelands, L.E. (2003). *Thinking about social life*. Lanham, MD: University Press of America.

Sandelands, L.E. (2010). The play of change. *Journal of Organizational Change Management, 23*, 71–86.

Schaefer, M.T., & Olson, D.H. (1981). Assessing intimacy: The PAIR Inventory. *Journal of Marital and Family Therapy, 7*, 47–60.

Seki, K., Matsumoto, D., & Imahori, T.T. (2002). The conceptualization and expression of intimacy in Japan and the United States. *Journal of Cross-cultural Psychology, 33*, 303–319.

Sexton, R.E., & Sexton, V.S. (1982). Intimacy: A historical perspective. In: M. Fisher, & G. Stricker (Eds.), *Intimacy* (pp. 1–20). New York: Plenum.

Shamir, B. (1995). Social distance and charisma: Theoretical notes and an exploratory study. *The Leadership Quarterly, 6*, 19–47.

Shamir, B., Zakay, E., Breinin, E., & Popper, M. (1998). Correlates of charismatic leader behavior in military units: Subordinates' attitudes, unit characteristics, and superiors' appraisals of leader performance. *Academy of Management Journal, 41*, 387–409.

Sharabany, R. (1994). Intimate friendship scale: Conceptual underpinnings, psychometric properties and construct validity. *Journal of Social and Personal Relationships, 11*, 449–469.

Spreitzer, G., Sutcliffe, K., Dutton, J., Sonenshein, S., & Grant, A.M. (2005). A socially embedded model of thriving at work. *Organization Science, 16*, 537–549.

Stephens, J.P., Heaphy, E., & Dutton, E.J. (2011). High-quality connections. In K. Cameron, & G. Spreitzer (Eds.), *Handbook of positive organizational scholarship* (pp.). New York: Oxford University Press.

Sternberg, R.J. (1986). A triangular theory of love. *Psychological Review, 93*, 119–135.

Sternberg, R.J., & Grajek, S. (1984). The nature of love. *Journal of Personality and Social Psychology, 47*, 312–329.

Sullivan, H.S. (1953). *The interpersonal theory of psychiatry*. New York: Norton.

Trevino, L.K., & Brown, M.E. (2005). The role of leaders in influencing unethical behavior in the workplace. In R.E. Kidwell, & C.L. Martin (Eds.), *Managing organizational deviance* (pp. 69–87). Thousand Oaks, CA: Sage.

Uhl-Bien, M. (2006). Relational leadership theory: Exploring the social processes of leadership and organizing. *The Leadership Quarterly, 17*, 654–676.

van Knippenberg, D., & Hogg, M.A. (2003). A social identity model of leadership effectiveness in organizations. In R.M. Kramer, & B.M. Staw (Eds.), *Research in organizational behavior* Vol. 25 (pp.245–297). Greenwich, CT: JAI Press.

van Knippenberg, D., van Knippenberg, B., Cermer, D.D., & Hogg, M.A. (2004). Leadership, self, and identity: A review and research agenda. *Leadership Quarterly, 15*, 825–856.

Civility

Christine L. Porath

Abstract

Despite civility's natural appeal across societies historically, and recent concern over the lack of it, civility has received little attention in the management literature, and there are relatively few empirical studies. In this chapter, I review empirical findings on civility and incivility. I highlight the benefits of civility and the costs of incivility on individual outcomes, witnesses, teams, organizations, and customers. I discuss the effects of civility and incivility on health, stress, performance, creativity, helpfulness, team effectiveness, and the organization's bottom line. Then, I highlight practical applications of civility in the workplace. Finally, I close with recommendations for future research.

Keywords: Civility, incivility, courtesy, compassion, kindness, politeness, sportsmanship, rudeness, deviance, performance, stress

Civility, defined as respectful treatment of others, is continually heralded. From U.S. President Barack Obama, to former U.K. Prime Minister Tony Blair, to former Australian Prime Minister John Howard, to local civic leaders, from professional sports leagues to Little League commissioners, civility is being highlighted as necessary (e.g., Phillips & Smith, 2004; Rice-Oxley, 2006). As a society, we believe that fundamentally, civility matters. Whether it facilitates negotiations across countries or parties, promotes collegiality and teamwork, encourages the respect of diverse players and members, spreads goodwill, and helps ensure sportsmanship and safety; or decreases crime, deviance, or a host of other negative outcomes—civility seems to matter . . . a lot. Perhaps that's why people are worried about the current lack of civility in society. In a poll of U.S. adults, 79% said a lack of courtesy was a serious problem (Remington & Darden, 2002).

Despite civility's natural appeal across societies historically (cf., Pearson & Porath, 2009; Peck, 2002), and recent concern over the lack of it, civility has received little attention in the management

literature, and there are relatively few empirical studies. More recent research has focused on the lack of civility, and incivility.

One way to illustrate the concepts of civility and incivility is to place them on a continuum ranging from positive to negative deviance (see Cameron, 2003, for a review of positive organizational scholarship [POS] constructs). Civility is at the positive end of the continuum, embodying ideas such as respectful, considerate, compassionate, and caring treatment; pleasant and positive interactions or connections; and feeling valued, recognized, and appreciated. Incivility, which is defined as the exchange of seemingly inconsequential inconsiderate words and deeds that violate conventional norms of workplace conduct (Andersson & Pearson, 1999), is at the negative end of the spectrum. They aren't mere opposites. For example, by removing incivility, one doesn't necessarily feel treated civilly. Something more is required. Yet, so many civil interactions require so little effort or time. Little niceties, attention, body language, tone, responses, and gestures can make all the difference between what is perceived as civil or uncivil. It is all in the eyes of the beholder. Civility and incivility reflect people's interpretation about how actions make them feel.

In this chapter, I review empirical findings on civility and incivility. I highlight the benefits of civility and the costs of incivility on individual outcomes, witnesses, teams, organizations, and customers. Then, I highlight practical applications of civility in the workplace. Finally, I close with recommendations for future research.

Civility: Definition and Theoretical Review of the Literature

Civility can take many forms, and includes courtesy, compassion, kindness, politeness, manners, and sportsmanship (see Forni, 2002). Acting civilly entails being aware of and caring about others. It involves, "weaving restraint, respect, and consideration into the very fabric of awareness" (Forni, 2002, p. 9). Civility involves thoughtful relating to friends, family, and coworkers. However, it also extends to an active interest in the well-being of one's community, as well as a concern for the health of the planet (Forni, 2002). When we act civilly, we act in a caring and responsible way; we choose to do the right thing for others (Forni, 2002).

Although civility, courtesy, politeness, and manners are all related forms of awareness, Forni (2002) explains that etymology reveals the differences among these terms. Connected to *court*, courtesy is associated with superior character, as expected of those connected to royalty. In practice, courtesy suggests excellence in bestowing respect and attention, and it can include deference and formality (Forni, 2002 p. 10). Politeness refers to those with *polished* behavior (Forni, 2002). It is inferred that people put effort into learning polite behavior, bettering themselves along the way. Manners comes from the word *manus*, Latin for "hand, and have to do with the use of our hands and our handling of things" (Forni, 2002). Typically manner(s) is used to refer to how we behave with others (i.e., handling someone with care) (Forni, 2002). Civility is tied to *civitas*, or city or civic community (Forni, 2002). The idea is that people are shaped intellectually and socially by the city, and therefore give back to the city. Civil people are often referred to as courteous, polite, or well-mannered; however, the term invokes calls to be good citizens and neighbors (Forni, 2002). In addition to these differences based on etymology, civil is described as more much more active and positive than politeness or courtesy (Forni, 2002; p. 11).

Civility spurs positive emotions and jump-starts a process with physiological, psychological, and relational benefits. When a person perceives a civil act, it sparks emotions and prompts an appraisal process (whether conscious or unconscious) (see Porath, MacInnis, & Folkes, 2010a) that typically triggers subjective experiences, body language, cognitive processing, and physiological changes (Frederickson, 2001). Consistent with the broaden-and-build theory of positive emotions, civility broadens people's thought–action repertoires and builds enduring personal resources, ranging from physical and intellectual resources to social and psychological resources (Frederickson, 2001).

Civility engenders positive feelings of self and others. When people experience civility, they are more likely to believe that they are valued organizational members; their energy to contribute to others and engage with the organization increases (Pearson & Porath, 2009). Respectful interactions with others fuel high-quality connections (Dutton, 2003). When individuals feel respected, they feel trusted and are more likely to trust others (Edmondson, 1999). This trust can enhance feelings of efficacy and capability at work (Spreitzer 1995), and encourage individuals to engage in proactive and risk-taking behaviors (Edmondson 1999; Mayer, Davis, & Schoorman 1995). As a result, civility facilitates *thriving*, defined as the psychological state of growth in which people experience both a sense of vitality and learning, as well as performance, organizational citizenship behaviors, and health (Porath, Spreitzer, & Gibson, 2008).

Empirical Evidence: Effects of Civility and Incivility on Individual Outcomes

Empirically, little research has focused on civility. However, a related meta-analysis suggests that supportive (i.e., civil) peer relationships at work are correlated with attitudes toward work, distress, performance, and well-being (Chiaburu & Harrison, 2008). Moreover, research has shown that coworker support may buffer employees from experiencing burnout (Liang & Hsieh, 2008; Leiter & Maslach, 1988). Related work suggests that positive human connections not only reduce stress, but also promote trust, bonding, and well-being (Hallowell, 1999).

To date though, much of the empirical evidence, particularly at the individual level, has focused on the negative effects of incivility rather than the benefits of civility. One of the most costly effects of incivility is its toll on people's health. People who experience incivility report psychological distress (Cortina, Magley, Williams, & Langhout, 2001) and negative emotional effects, including fear, anger, and sadness (Pearson & Porath, 2005). Experiences of incivility reduce supervisor, coworker, and work satisfaction, which, in turn, drive intentions to quit and poor mental health (Lim, Cortina, & Magley, 2008). The more uncivil the environment, the more stressed the employees. Across a study of eight firms from diverse industries, including pharmaceuticals, health care, maritime, technology/computer services, utility, and nonprofit, I've found that more than 60% of people who work in uncivil environments experience stress (Porath, 2010). Over 80% report feeling used up at the end of the day; the majority report being emotionally exhausted, feeling burned out, and having lost enthusiasm and motivation for their work.

There are many health effects of stress, including fatigue, headaches, muscle tension, and sleep disturbances (cf. Hallowell, 1997). Stress is also associated with reduced motivation, loss of concentration, and decreased productivity and creativity. Emotional side effects of stress include anxiety, pessimism, depression, and the tendency to withdraw from others. However, the effects of stress can be even more severe if people face constant low to moderate stress, such as incivility for too long or too often. In his book, *Why Zebras Don't Get Ulcers*, Robert Sapolsky explains that average stressors over time, like incivility, can lead to severe health problems such as ulcers, cardiovascular disease, diabetes, and cancer. Research has shown that ordinary daily hassles (such as incivilities) often outstrip major life stressors, impairing social and work functioning (Lazarus & Folkman, 1984). In many cases, the more indirect, covert incivilities resulted in more extensive stress and emotional scars than outright physical abuse; and they were more debilitating to workers (Mayhew et al., 2004). People who work in a toxic environment may also experience personality changes, such as depression, hostility, and alienation (Leymann, 1996). Research has shown that, for some people more than others, stress leads to depression and other negative consequences. A person's response to threat, loss, and humiliation (all feelings associated with incivility) is significantly affected by his or her genetic makeup (Caspi et al., 2003).

Incivility-fueled stress is also costly in terms of productivity. Stress disrupts memory and hinders information processing (Sapolsky, 2004). Stress can impede problem solving and lead to more superficial and simplistic thinking. Employees under stress don't learn as well either. I've found that stressed employees tend to withdraw from their jobs psychologically and physically. Those who work in an uncivil environment report a loss of importance and meaning of work, job satisfaction, and organizational commitment (see also Cortina et al., 2001). These employees also tend to invest less time and energy in their work, are far less likely to engage in organizational citizenship behaviors, and are absent more often. Workplace incivility is associated with greater turnover (Pearson & Porath, 2005) and interpersonal and organizational deviance (Porath, Shapiro, & Duffy, 2004). Related constructs, such as supervisor undermining, are associated with retaliation (Bies & Tripp, 1996, 2005; Bies, Tripp, & Kramer, 1997; Skarlicki & Folger, 1997), counterproductive behaviors (Duffy, Ganster, & Pagon, 2002), and withdrawal of leader support (Tyler & Blader, 2000).

More recent work has emphasized the detrimental effects of incivility on performance. Pushed to study if rudeness actually affected performance, I designed experimental studies with Amir Erez to test whether, and to what extent, incivility hijacked performance (Porath & Erez, 2007). Respondents were subjected to identical treatment in either the control group (those treated civilly) or the uncivil group; the same form of incivility was delivered in the same way, in the same context. What we varied for each experiment were the occasions for incivility (or civility). Sometimes the experimenter was rude to participants for being late, sometimes a stranger treated participants uncivilly, and sometimes we asked participants to simply think about how they would react to various types of incivility. In each situation, we measured participants' performance, creativity, and helping behaviors. To measure performance, we asked participants to complete an anagram and brainstorming task.

We found that even with one-time, relatively low-intensity incidents, participants who had been treated rudely were not able to concentrate as well. Concentration also suffered for participants who were asked merely to *imagine* an uncivil event. In both cases, those treated rudely lost task focus. Their short-term memory suffered; they recalled nearly 20% less. Their performance plummeted.

In our first study, in which the experimenter had belittled a confederate for being late, *other* participants performed 33% worse on the verbal tasks and came up with 39% fewer creative ideas. In our second study, in which a stranger encountered en route to the experiment was rude to participants, their performance was 61% worse on the verbal tasks, and they produced less than half as many ideas as those who had not been treated rudely.

In both studies, participants who experienced incivility were 30% less creative. They produced 25% fewer ideas, and their ideas were less diverse. When asked what to do with a brick, they'd offer logically consistent ideas like "build a house," "build a path," and "build a school." Ideas generated by people who had not been treated uncivilly? "Sell the brick on e-bay"; "use it as a goal post for a street soccer game"; and "decorate it like a pet and then give it to a kid as a present."

We also learned a lot about how incivility affects helpfulness. When people were treated uncivilly, their inclination to help others dropped, too. In the first study, in which no incivility had occurred, 90% of participants helped pick up something that had been intentionally dropped. But when the experimenter insulted a confederate for being late, only 35% offered any assistance. In the second study, 73% of those who hadn't experienced incivility volunteered to lend a hand. But when a confederate was rude to participants who were trying to find the location where the study was taking place, only 24% of those who had been treated uncivilly offered assistance.

Civility promotes effective cognitive functioning, which leads to greater performance and helpfulness. When individuals do not feel respected, they tend to either shut down or use up valuable cognitive assets trying to make sense of the environment, determine why there is a lack of respect, and how they should respond. Thus, uncivil environments drain emotional and cognitive resources necessary for learning and performance. These negative consequences are more likely when incivility stems from unlike-minded people (see Hwang, 2009).

Effects on Witnesses

Civility, or the lack thereof, also affects witnesses who see or hear about respectful or disrespectful treatment. To better understand how just being around a civil environment affected individual performance, I collected data from employees and managers across a range of industries. I found that working in a civil atmosphere sparks energy and increases motivation and enthusiasm for the organization. People working in more civil environments more easily learn and apply knowledge and skills. When I compared employees working in the top and bottom 10% of civil and uncivil workplaces, I learned that those who worked in the most highly

civil places reported having 26% more energy. They were 30% more likely to feel motivated about learning new ideas and skills and 30% more likely to feel vital and energetic. Those working in highly civil environments were also 36% more satisfied with their jobs and 44% more committed to their organizations. These results showed: Managers rated them as performing 10%–20% better than others in the organization. Civil environments seem to enhance performance.

People who worked in civil environments were also more likely to be altruistic and courteous to other employees. They were more inclined to act in the company's best interests, whether by helping other employees with work-related problems, taking steps to prevent problems, encouraging others to do their job well, attending company functions, or participating in company meetings. Although less easily quantifiable in terms of the bottom line, these results are clearly beneficial to managers and organizations.

Just being around incivility, on the other hand, is quite detrimental. Witnesses report that incivility angers them and colors their feelings (toward the offender and the organization). To better understand the effects of incivility on witnesses, Amir Erez and I conducted more experiments (see Porath & Erez, 2009). We studied performance and creativity using the same tasks and methods that we applied to targets. The pattern of results for witnesses of incivility was extremely similar to those of targets. Those who witnessed incivility performed 20% worse on the anagrams and produced nearly 30% fewer ideas in the brainstorming task. Witnesses to incivility were also far less likely to help—even when the experimenter had no apparent connection to the uncivil participant. In both studies, only 25% of those who witnessed incivility volunteered to help, as compared to 51% who didn't witness incivility. These results are important because they illustrate that incivility has a spillover effect. It implies that the organizational functioning and climate could be affected by incivility.

Effects on Teams

Civility is a lubricant that fosters good teamwork. To learn more about how civility affects teams, I gathered information from teams in maritime, utility, pharmaceutical, technology/computer services, nonprofit and health care industries (Porath, 2010). The lesson was clear: The more civil the environment, the more employees feel connected to their teammates, and the more energy and motivation they have to do their best work. In more civil teams, trust is high, and members tend to feel appreciated and valued. As a result, members feel comfortable sharing information and ideas, collaborate more creatively, and grow.

One powerful effect of civility within teams is that it increases members' sense of psychological safety, or the feeling that the team environment is a safe place in which to take risks. Studies of cardiac surgical units at 16 hospitals revealed that psychological safety was a crucial factor in facilitating learning (Edmondson, 1999). Members of civil teams are more comfortable and more likely to seek or accept feedback. They will ask for help, talk about mistakes, and inform each other about problems.

Southwest Airlines (SWA) serves as a great example how civility facilitates teamwork. In Gittell's book *The Southwest Airlines Way*, she describes how joint problem solving and shared goals produce high efficiency, quality, and satisfaction at SWA. Southwest Airline's mission statement emphasizes how employees are internal customers, and that each employee is to be treated with respect, regardless of their job. Civil teamwork pays off for SWA in low turnaround time (20% below industry standards), increased productivity (40% above industry standards), less customer complaints (by half), fewer lost bags (by one-third), and less flight delays (by 50%) (Gittell, 2003).

Emotional contagion and the broaden-and-build model of positive emotions suggest that civility may have a number of intangible effects. Civility within or outside of the team often spreads, as teammates "catch" the positive emotions felt by their colleagues, even if they didn't share the experience or witness the civility personally (Lipps, 1903; Lakin, Jefferis, Cheng, & Chartrand, 2003). In experiments with teams from accounting, nursing, and professional sports, researchers have found that moods felt by one team member readily transfer to other members (Hatfield, Cacioppo, & Rapson, 1992, 1994; Howard & Gengler, 2001; Totterdell, 2000; Totterdell, Kellet, Teuchmann, & Briner, 1998). I have found in my research that even employees who only witness or hear about civility may display and *feel* the same emotional responses that they are mimicking. Contagion effects can also facilitate a team's thinking and behaviors (Barsade, 2002).

Effects on Organizations

At the organizational level, a climate of civility has been shown to increase individual thriving, which drives individual performance, organizational citizenship behaviors, and burnout (Porath, Spreitzer, & Gibson, 2008). In his book *Good to Great*, Jim Collins and collaborators discovered a similar relationship. Companies that went from good to great were known for civil, high-quality collegial relationships (Collins, 2001). Other case studies highlight a similar finding: Respect and civility set the stage for positive, energizing relationships and effective organizational performance (e.g., Gittell, 2003; Meyer, 2006).

Where there is incivility or destructive communication, trust and faith in the organization wane. A 4-year study of an information technology organization finds that less intense forms of incivility may have stronger negative effects on organizational trust (Gill & Sypher, 2009). Put simply: Uncivil communication prevents community building.

Effects of Customers Witnessing Civility and Incivility on Organizations

Organizations benefit from customers' witnessing employee-to-employee civility, and suffer when customers' witness incivility. Debbie MacInnis, Valerie Folkes, and I studied whether witnessing employee-to-employee civility (or incivility) would affect consumers' attitudes toward these employees, other employees of the organization, the organization itself, or the brand. Witnessing civility is powerful. In our studies, more than eight out of ten customers tell us that their attitude toward the company becomes more favorable when employees treat each other well (Porath, MacInnis, & Folkes, 2010c). Eighty-five percent say they're *more* willing to use the company's products and services in the future. Fifty-five percent are more interested in learning about new products and services offered by a company where employees are treated well. Nearly ninety percent feel more certain that they will be treated well in the future. It's tough to put a price on these benefits, but huge gains and reputational benefits are likely when customers share positive stories with others.

However, when customers witness incivility, the results are stunning: Nearly 80% of customers who had witnessed employee-to-employee incivility said that they would use the firm's products and services in the future, while only 20% of the participants who witnessed incivility agreed to do so. Nine out of ten said that their attitude toward the uncivil employee became less favorable. Nearly half were less willing to use the company's products and services. Ninety-two percent of customers who witnessed an employee acting uncivilly toward another employee spoke negatively about the firm to others based on this incident (Porath, MacInnis, & Folkes, 2010b).

It pays if your employees treat one another with respect. Customers who notice employees behaving kindly have even remarked to us that they wanted to work with them. Most of them told family members and friends about their positive feelings, too. Bain & Company research shows that when firms retain just 5% more of their best customers, corporate profits can be boosted 25%–85%, depending on the industry. If customers are witnessing employee civility, they think and respond favorably toward organizations.

Across four studies, we found that witnessing an act of incivility between employees in a firm is extremely detrimental to companies: It induces consumer anger and causes consumers to make broad and negative conclusions (generalizations) about the firm as a whole, other employees who work there, and expectations about future encounters with the firm—conclusions that go well beyond the uncivil incident. Perhaps even more surprising, consumers respond negatively to employee incivility even when the uncivil employee was trying to help the customer (by rectifying a delay in service delivery) (Porath, MacInnis, & Folkes, 2010a). In other studies, we found that customers do not tolerate an employee reprimanding another employee uncivilly, even if the reprimand is delivered offstage by a superior whose uncivil comments are related to the employee's (incompetent) job-related behaviors (Porath et al., 2010b).

Customers who witness employee incivility are not only angry at the perpetrator, but are also more likely to seek revenge against the perpetrator and the firm. What drives customer anger about witnessing employee incivility? Although witnessing employee incivility harms the customer's experience, runs counter to normative expectations, and is perceived as unjust to the victim (deontic justice), the driving mediating force responsible for the range of negative outcomes is deontic justice. Customers do not like to see others treated disrespectfully. When they see others treated unfairly, it motivates a desire to retaliate. However, this desire to retaliate is not isolated to the perpetrator of the suffering; it extends to the firm associated with the perpetrator.

Practical Applications

With growing evidence of the benefits of civility, it is no wonder that more organizations are instituting policies and initiating programs that promote civility.

Christine Pearson and I (2009) considered best practices by offering examples of some very different organizations, including Cisco, DaVita Dialysis, Microsoft, Starbucks, and O'Melveny & Myers. Although these firms vary by size, industry, locations, and business strategies, each is cultivating workplace civility, and each attributes at least some part of their success to that focus. Strategies, timing, and progression vary based on environment, norms, resources, and goals. The key seems to be that small steps are taken consistently and relentlessly.

Leaders set the tone—civility needs to start with their commitment to create a positive environment, one where bad behavior is not tolerated. There are many of excellent examples of how this can be done. Southwest Airlines' mission statement highlights respect of other employees (referring to them as "internal customers") and has outstanding hiring policies ("hire for attitude"). Microsoft now trains their employees in emotional intelligence and evaluates them on this skill every year. Cisco has designed a comprehensive Global Workplace Civility program and trains managers on how to spot and deal with bad behavior. But, there are also compelling stories of how one person can completely turn the culture and business around by focusing on civility.

When Kent Thiry came on board as CEO of DaVita (then named Total Renal Care), the organization was an absolute mess. Thiry explained that DaVita was "technically bankrupt": "It was being investigated by the SEC, sued by shareholders, had turnover at over twice the current levels, was almost out of cash, and in general, wasn't the happiest of places" (Pelosi, 2004). Thiry believed not only that a positive, respectful community would be good for employees and business, but that it was also tied to patient-well being. Among many initiatives, DaVita began socializing employees toward mutual respect through various training classes. Employees at the manager level and above receive a mission and values report card every year that includes assessments by those who report to them. Employees who live the values well at DaVita are rewarded very well. Focusing on values has paid off in remarkable ways for DaVita. Between 1999 and 2005, the company's market capitalization grew from less than $250,000 to more than $5 billion. Clinical outcomes are now the best in the industry, and there's been a 50% reduction in turnover (Pelosi, 2004). Stock has jumped more than tenfold. At DaVita, it's all about company values that focus on civility, and that has certainly paid off.

Research shows that interventions focusing on civility enhance both civility and a range of other positive outcomes. Ostatuke and colleagues (2009) developed the CREW process (Civility, Respect, and Engagement at work) to enhance civility among work colleagues. This organizational development process is designed to enhance employees' experience and well-being by improving the quality of their social environment. It includes an initial survey, a full day of community gathering, then weekly facilitated meetings (of groups of 10–15 employees) over 6 months. At the end of the 6 months, a follow-up survey occurs. Changes during this period are tracked. In this study, results from two CREW processes with a total of 23 cites with Veterans Hospitals were associated with improved participant ratings of civility, whereas the ratings of control group members remained constant.

Building on these findings, Leitner and colleagues (2009) employed the CREW process with a health care provider and studied whether this 6-month intervention process would not only improve civility, but also affect attitudes, well-being, and burnout. They found that CREW led to greater improvements in members' civility, supervisor civility, respect, cynicism, job satisfaction, and absences as compared with members of the control groups.

Positive organizational examples and CREW results suggest that interventions focused on increasing civility can improve collegiality, contribute to the well-being of employees, and positively affect the organization's bottom line.

Future Directions

Civility research is in its early stages. The development of a validated measure would be useful. Work has begun on its conceptual development and scale (four items from the 1996 General Social Survey; Ferriss, 2002), but additional work, particularly with an eye for its use in organizational research, is needed. A measure might capture the following ideas (whether in terms of experiencing or acting): treated respectfully, treated civilly, treated considerately, treated in a caring manner, treated kindly, pleasant interaction(s) or connection(s), and feeling valued, feeling recognized, and feeling appreciated. Scholars can use a validated measure to compile compelling evidence on the effects of individual, team, and organizational outcomes. Managers and organizations will be more motivated to manage for and initiate programs devoted to promoting civility with such ammunition.

Although recent research has uncovered many consequences of incivility on individuals, research that reveals the benefits of civility is lagging. Research that demonstrates shorter- and longer-term benefits of civility may answer a call for variables and research that address human sustainability (Pfeffer, 2010). If civility is associated with positive health outcomes, it may be something that organizations can and will want to nurture and develop in the future to promote human sustainability. Ideally, these benefits can also be linked to cost savings for organizations. Learning more about the health benefits of civility and their savings could have important practical implications.

Discovering more about how civility fosters positive team outcomes would also be interesting. Trust and psychological safety likely play a role, but what other mechanisms facilitate effectiveness?

Learning more about *why* civility leads to better performance and other positive outcomes is of interest. Do these effects hold for those who witness civility? What drives these effects?

Neuroscience likely holds the key to unlocking our knowledge about how civility and incivility affect our mind and shape our responses. How does civility and incivility affect our brains? Early research shows that incivility affects cognitive functioning. What processes does it impact (e.g., working memory)? Does civility enhance cognitive functioning? Although civility is likely to promote positive emotions and unlock broaden-and-build processes, additional processes such as cognitions and positive attributions may play a role. It would be interesting to learn more about these and other possibilities.

Are there times when there may be a downside to acting civilly? Does this vary by norms, industry, or followers? Stories abound about the downside to being too nice. Leaders (and women) are warned about the potential risks of appearing too nice. Yet, there are some wonderful examples of very civil leaders who are extraordinarily successful because of this style—not in spite of it.

What benefits might incivility garner for a leader or employee? Are there times when incivility is called for, such as in times of crisis? Colleagues and I have learned that civility is more effective than incivility. This is true in crises or any other circumstances (Pearson & Porath, 2009). It takes time, energy, and skill to listen through and get beyond the disrespect. That's challenging for anyone, especially in times of crises. Incivility carries an emotional sting that often knocks people off track—sometimes long term. Research shows that incivility robs concentration, hijacks task orientation, and impedes performance (Porath & Erez, 2007).

Although greater directness or assertiveness may be helpful, incivility is not.

Are there individual characteristics and personality dispositions that may make incivility more likely? Narcissism, aggressiveness, and low emotional intelligence seem likely candidates. People who suffer from social inhibitions (such as those with Asperger syndrome) might be uncivil unintentionally. Individuals from different geographic regions in the United States possess different attributes, tone, and body language and embody norms that are typically perceived as more or less civil and uncivil. Gaining a better understanding of these and their effects would be informative. People can benefit from this knowledge if they are mindful of how they are perceived, and make adjustments to interact more effectively.

Future research should study cross-cultural differences as they relate to civility and incivility. How do cultural differences explain what's perceived as civil or uncivil? Brauer and Chaurand (2009) compared responses of participants with regard to perceived normality of 46 uncivil behaviors in public settings. Substantial cultural differences existed regarding the type of behaviors that were considered uncivil. In the workplace context, it is likely that what is uncivil or civil in one cultural context might vary in another (see also Kisselburgh & Dutta, 2009). Status and power may be key variables in this context. Therefore, cultural norms and power distance might be useful to explore. As organizations become more diverse and globalization increases, it seems that gaining a better understanding of cultural norms, perceptions, and responses as they relate to civility and incivility is a fruitful endeavor with important implications. Civility may be crucial to *laterality*, defined as the ability to cut across boundaries and relate to others from different areas (Gibson & Dibble, 2008).

Finally, research has begun to document how civility initiatives benefit employees and organizations. Research focusing on how particular initiatives and contexts facilitate successful outcomes is needed. What training programs are beneficial for organizations to invest in? Much remains to be learned about how civility initiatives can be implemented best, even though it is likely to depend on a variety of circumstances.

Conclusion

Especially in these challenging times, we cannot and should not take civility lightly. It is too important to too many people. It has a direct and substantial impact on an organization's bottom line. For society, the benefits range from emotional, health (stress), and psychological benefits, to an increase of performance and well-being, to a decrease in aggressiveness and crime.

Much can be accomplished with a little civility. If managers, teammates, and employees can be examples of and find ways to foster civility in organizations, people and organizations will be all the better for it. Since civility cascades outside the organization, society benefits as well. From employee well-being to organizational performance and costs, civility appears to be a crucial behavior. Tremendous potential exists for researchers to better develop our understanding of civility, its precursors, moderators, and outcomes, and to motivate organizations to manage for it.

References

Andersson, L.M., & Pearson, C.M. (1999). Tit for tat? The spiraling effect of incivility in the workplace. *Academy of Management Review, 24*, 452–471.

Barsade, S.G. (2002). The ripple effect: Emotional contagion and its influence on group behavior. *Administrative Science Quarterly, 47*, 644–676.

Bies, R.J., & Tripp, T.M. (1996). Beyond distrust: "Getting even" and the need for revenge. In R.M. Kramer, & T.R. Tyler (Eds.), *Trust in organizations* (pp. 246–260). Thousand Oaks, CA: Sage.

Bies, R.J., & Tripp, T.M. (2005). The study of revenge in the workplace: Conceptual, ideological, and empirical issues. In S. Fox, & P.E. Spector (Eds.), *Counterproductive work behavior: Investigations of actors and targets* (pp. 65–82). Washington, DC: American Psychological Association.

Bies, R.J., Tripp, T.M., & Kramer, R.M. (1997). At the breaking point: Cognitive and social dynamics of revenge in organizations. In R.A. Giacalone, & J. Greenberg (Eds.), *Antisocial behavior in organizations* (pp. 18–36). Thousand Oaks, CA: Sage.

Brauer, M., & Chaurand, N. (2009). Descriptive norms, prescriptive norms, and social control: An intercultural comparison of people's reactions to uncivil behaviors. *European Journal of Social Psychology, 39*, 1–10.

Cameron, K.S. (2003). Organizational virtuousness and performance. In K.S. Cameron, J.E. Dutton, & R.E. Quinn (Eds.), *Positive organizational scholarship* (pp. 48–65). San Francisco: Barrett-Koehler.

Caspi, A., Sugden, K., Moffitt, T.E., Taylor, A., Craig, I.W., Harrington, H., et al. (2003). Influence of life stress on depression: Moderation by a polymorphism in the 5-HTT Gene. *Science, 301*, 386–389.

Chiaburu, D.S., & Harrison, D.A. (2008). Do peers make the place? Conceptual synthesis and meta-analysis of co-worker effects on perceptions, attitudes, OCBs, and performance. *Journal of Applied Psychology, 93*, 1082–1103.

Collins, J. (2001). *Good to great.* New York: HarperCollins.

Cortina, L.M., Magley, V.J., Williams, J.H., & Langhout, R.D. (2001). Incivility in the workplace: Incidence and impact. *Journal of Occupational Health Psychology, 6*, 64–80.

Duffy, M.K., Ganster, D.C., & Pagon, M. (2002). Social undermining in the workplace. *Academy of Management Journal, 45*, 331–351.

Dutton, J.E. (2003). *Energize your workplace: How to create and sustain high-quality connections at work.* San Francisco: Jossey-Bass.

Edmondson, A. (1999). Psychological safety and learning behavior in work teams. *Administrative Science Quarterly, 44*, 350–383.

Ferriss, A.L. (2002). Studying and measuring civility: A framework, trends, and scale. *Sociological Inquiry, 72*, 376–392.

Forni, P.M. (2002). *Choosing civility: The twenty-five rules of considerate conduct.* New York: St. Martin's Griffin.

Fredrickson, B. (2001). The role of positive emotions in positive psychology: The broaden and build theory of positive emotions. *American Psychologist, 56*, 218–226.

Gibson, C.B., & Dibble, R. (2008). Culture inside and out: Developing the collective capability to externally adjust. In S. Ang, & L. Van Dyne (Eds.), *Advances in cultural intelligence* (pp. 221–240). New York: Sharpe.

Gill, M.J., & Sypher, B.D. (2009). Workplace incivility and trust. In P. Lutgen-Sandvik, & B.D. Sypher (Eds.), *Destructive organizational communication: Processes, consequences, and constructive ways of organizing* (pp. 53–73). New York: Routledge/Taylor & Francis Group.

Gittell, J.H. (2003). *The Southwest Airlines way: Using the power of relationships to achieve high-performance.* New York: McGraw-Hill.

Hallowell, E.M. (1999). *Connect: 12 vital ties that open your heart, lengthen your life, and deepen your soul.* New York: Pocket Books.

Hallowell, E.M. (1997). *Worry.* New York: Random House.

Hatfield, E., Cacioppo, J., & Rapson, R.L. (1992). Primitive emotional contagion. In M.S. Clark (Ed.), *Emotion and social behavior: Review of personality and social psychology* Vol. 14 (pp.151–177). Newbury Park, CA: Sage.

Hatfield, E., Cacioppo, J., & Rapson, R.L. (1994). *Emotional contagion.* New York: Cambridge University Press.

Howard, D.J., & Gengler, C. (2001). Emotional contagion effects on product attitudes. *Journal of Consumer Research, 28*, 189–201.

Hwang, H. (2009). Why does incivility matter when communicating disagreement?: Examining the psychological process of antagonism in political discussion. *Dissertation Abstracts International, 69*, 9A.

Kisselburgh, L.G., & Dutta, M.J. (2009). The construction of civility in multicultural organizations. In P. Lutgen-Sandvik, & B.D. Sypher (Eds.), *Destructive organizational communication: Processes, consequences, and constructive ways of organizing* (pp. 121–142). New York: Routledge/Taylor & Francis Group.

Lakin, J.L., Jefferis, V.E., Cheng, C.M., & Chartrand, C.L. (2003). The chameleon effects as social glue: Evidence for the evolutionary significance of nonconscious mimicry. *Journal of Nonverbal Behavior, 27*, 145–162.

Lazarus, R.S., & Folkman, S. (1984). *Stress, appraisal, and coping.* New York: Springer.

Leitner, M., & Maslach, C. (1988). The impact of interpersonal environment on burnout and organizational commitment. *Journal of Organizational Behavior, 9*, 297–308.

Leitner, M.P., Laschinger, H.K.S., Day, A., & Gilin-Oore, D. (2009, November). *The role of civility and incivility in a model of burnout and engagement: An intervention study.*

Paper presented at the APA/NIOSH Conference: Work, Stress, & Health, San Juan, Puerto Rico.

Leymann, H. (1996). The content and development of mobbing at work. *European Journal of Work and Organizational Psychology, 5*, 251–276.

Liang, S.C., & Hsieh, A.T. (2008). The role of organizational socialization in burnout: A Taiwanese example. *Social Behavior and Personality, 36*, 197–216.

Lim, S., Cortina, L.M., & Magley, V.J. (2008). Personal and workgroup incivility: Impact on work and health outcomes. *Journal of Applied Psychology, 93*, 95–107.

Lipps, T. (1903). Einfühlung, innere Nachahmung und Organempfindung. *Archiv für die Gesante Psychologie, 1*, 465–519. [Original idea of emotional contagion.]

Mayer, R.C., Davis, J.H., & Schoorman, F.D. (1995). An integration model of organizational trust. *Academy of Management Review, 20*(3), 709–734.

Mayhew, C., McCarthy, P., Chappell, D., Quinlan, M., Barker, M., & Sheehan, M. (2004). Measuring the extent of impact from occupational violence and bullying on traumatized workers. *Employee Responsibilities and Rights Journal, 16*, 117–134.

Meyer, D. (2006). *Setting the table: The transforming power of hospitality in business.* New York: HarperCollins Publishers.

Ostatuke, K., Mohr, D., Ward, C., Moore, S.C., Dyrenforth, S., & Belton, L. (2009). Civility, respect, engagement in the workforce (CREW): Nationwide organizational development intervention at Veterans Health Administration. *Journal of Applied Behavioral Science, 45*, 384–410.

Pearson, C.M., & Porath, C.L. (2009). *The cost of bad behavior— how incivility damages your business and what you can do about it.* New York: Portfolio | Penguin Group (USA) Inc.

Pearson, C.M., & Porath, C.L. (2005). On the nature, consequences and remedies of workplace incivility: No time for "Nice"? Think again. *Academy of Management Executive, 19*, 7–18.

Peck, D.L. (2002). Civility: A contemporary context for a meaningful historical concept. *Sociological Inquiry, 72*, 358–375.

Pelosi, R. (2004). Corporate spotlight: DaVita. *American Health Executive Supplement,* November 1.

Pfeffer, J. (2010). Building sustainable organizations: The human factor. *Academy of Management Perspectives, 24*, 34–45.

Phillips, T., & Smith, P. (2004). Emotional and behavioral response to everyday incivility: Challenging the fear/avoidance paradigm. *Journal of Sociology, 40*, 378–399.

Porath, C.L. (2010). *The health effects of incivility.* Working paper, Georgetown University, Washington, DC.

Porath, C.L., & Erez, A. (2009). Overlooked but not untouched: How incivility reduces onlookers' performance on routine and creative tasks. *Organizational Behavior and Human Decision Processes, 109*, 29–44.

Porath, C.L., & Erez, A. (2007). Does rudeness matter? The effects of rude behavior on task performance and helpfulness. *Academy of Management Journal, 50*, 1181–1197.

Porath, C.L., MacInnis, D.J., & Folkes, V.S. (2010a). Witnessing incivility among employees: Effects on consumer anger and negative inferences about companies. *Journal of Consumer Research, 37*(2), 292–303.

Porath, C.L., MacInnis, D., & Folkes, V. (In Press). It's unfair: Why customers who merely observe an uncivil employee abandon the company. *Journal of Services Research.*

Porath, C.L., MacInnis, D., & Folkes, V. (2010c). *Witnessing uncivil interactions between employees: Effects on consumer behavior.* Working paper, Georgetown University, Washington, DC.

Porath, C.L., Shapiro, D.L., & Duffy, M.K. (2004, August). *When does perceived incivility lead to production deviance? A test of a systemwide perspective?* Paper presented at the annual Academy of Management meeting, New Orleans, LA.

Porath, C.L., Spreitzer, G., & Gibson, C. (2008, August). *Antecedents and consequences of thriving across six organizations.* Paper presented at the annual Academy of Management meeting, Anaheim, CA.

Remington, R., & Darden, M. 2002. *Aggravating circumstances: A status report on rudeness in America.* New York: Public Agenda.

Rice-Oxley, M. (2006, January 23). R-e-s-p-e-c-t, find out what it means to England. *The Christian Science Monitor.* Retrieved from http://www.csmonitor.com/2006/0123/p01s02-woeu.htm.

Sapolsky, R.M. (2004). *Why zebras don't get ulcers* (3rd ed.). New York: Owl Books, Henry Holt and Company, LLC.

Skarlicki, D.P., & Folger, R. (1997). Retaliation in the workplace: The roles of distributive, procedural, and interactional injustice. *Journal of Applied Psychology, 82,* 434–443.

Spreitzer, G.M. (1995). Psychological empowerment in the workplace: Dimensions, measurement, and validation. *Academy of Management Journal, 38*(5), 1442–1465.

Totterdell, P. (2000). Catching moods and hitting runs: Mood linkage and subjective performance in professional sports teams. *Journal of Applied Psychology, 85,* 848–859.

Totterdell, P., Kellet, S., Teuchmann, K., & Briner, R.B. (1998). Evidence of mood linkage in work groups. *Journal of Personality and Social Psychology, 74,* 1504–1515.

Tyler, T.R., & Blader, S.L. (2000). *Cooperation in groups: Procedural justice, social identity and behavioral engagement.* Philadelphia: Psychology Press.

Positive Organizational Scholarship and Trust in Leaders

Aneil K. Mishra *and* Karen E. Mishra

Abstract

In this chapter, we discuss how courage, authenticity, and humility, all key characteristics of positive organizational scholarship (POS) leaders, enable leaders to be more likely to engage in trusting behavior with others. Moreover, our research has found that a leader demonstrates his or her trustworthiness by demonstrating reliability, openness, competence, and compassion. These trustworthiness dimensions contribute to a leader's ability to create and sustain hope, thus creating a circle of trusted others that includes colleagues and subordinates whom he or she can rely on and who in turn relies on him or her. Through this trusting behavior, the leader empowers others and provides hope for the future, leading to lasting positive changes for the organization and creating a culture of trust.

Keywords: Positive organizational scholarship, trust, leadership, hope, authenticity, humility, courage

Current global economic conditions cry out for a new way for individuals to lead organizations and societies. Trust in a variety of institutions, including governmental and business, is at an all-time low. To strengthen society and its major foundations, we need to build and rebuild trust. Several of our major societal institutions have experienced major declines in how much the public trusts them. The Edelman Global Trust Barometer has been tracking trust levels in society since 1999 and includes both U.S. and international assessments. This year, Edelman found trust in business at its lowest level ever, 38%, down from 58% the year before (Edelman, 2009). This assessment is lower than when the Enron debacle occurred. The Gallup Poll of Trust in Government found that 81% of those polled trust the government to do what is right only some of the time or never, the worst percentage since the survey began in 1993 (Gallup, 2009).

Not only do we distrust those institutions that we depend on for our livelihoods and security, but we have little trust in leaders as well. A Survey by the Centre for Work-Life Policy, an American consultancy, found that between June 2007 and December 2008, the proportion of employees who professed loyalty to their employers slumped from 95% to 39%; the number voicing trust in them fell from 79% to 22% (The Economist, 2009). In 2009, the National Leadership Index found 69% of Americans believed that there is a leadership crisis in the country today—not much of an improvement from 81% in 2008 and 77% in 2007 (Harvard Kennedy School, 2009). These and other findings suggest that a leadership crisis exists in the United States just when strong leadership is most needed to address not only the current economic crisis, but also many longstanding economic and societal challenges as well.

Trust has declined for many reasons, and some of these have persisted for decades. These include societal issues, such as increasing suspicion due in part to decreased interaction among individuals, as discussed by Putnam (2000), and institutional factors, such as the recent massive failures in our financial system; significantly deficient federal disaster response, especially to Hurricane Katrina; and rampant partisanship by our elected leaders. They also include organizational malfeasance and misfeasance, as exemplified by the Lockheed bribery scandals in the 1970s, the Red Cross HIV-testing failures in the 1980s, Long Term Capital Management in the 1990s, and Enron and Tyco International in the 2000s. Finally, they include violations of trust by many business, governmental, and religious leaders, acting individually or in concert with others.

In this chapter, our focus will be on how leaders build trust between leaders and their followers in a positive organizational context. We will begin by introducing the role that trust plays in the role of a leader, including how trust has been proven to produce positive outcomes for leaders. Next, we will focus on the link between trust and positive organizational scholarship (POS), examining the links that exist between them. Then, we will delve more deeply into those positive characteristics that contribute to a leader's willingness to build trust and his ability to demonstrate trustworthiness, focusing especially on courage, authenticity, and humility. Next, we focus specifically on the four key four dimensions of trustworthiness that a leader can demonstrate to others to engender their trust, provide them with hope, and foster their empowerment. Finally, we reveal how a leader builds a culture of trust to create lasting, positive change in an organization (see Figure 34.1).

The Role of Trust in Leadership

Trust is important because it allows individuals and collectives to manage interdependence more easily by reducing the need for contracts and formal agreements. Trust reduces uncertainty and helps us to manage complexity (Luhmann, 1979, 1988). It also permits highly flexible work arrangements that promote risk-taking and innovation (Mishra, Mishra, & Spreitzer, 2009). Indeed, when trust has been established, entirely new ways of behaving are possible (Fukuyama, 1995). Based on almost two decades of research involving thousands of employees, managers, and top executives, we define interpersonal trust as one party's willingness to be vulnerable to another party, based on the belief that the latter party is Reliable, Open, Competent, and Compassionate (Mishra, 1996; Mishra & Mishra, 1994). We call these four beliefs or dimensions of trustworthiness the ROCC of Trust (Mishra & Mishra, 2008). Our definition of trust is consistent with several decades of research on trust, which incorporates the key elements of vulnerability (Deutsch, 1962; Granovetter, 1985; Zand, 1972), risk/risk-taking (Deutsch, 1973; Lewis & Weigert, 1985), and rational choice (Kramer, 1999). It also encompasses definitions that other leading trust scholars have articulated, including positive expectations regarding others' intentions or behavior (Rousseau, Sitkin, Burt, & Camerer, 1998), and in particular, their competence, integrity, and benevolence (Mayer, Davis, & Schoorman, 1995).

Previous research has shown that leaders are critical to building trust in organizations, and that trust in leadership is significantly related to a number of attitudes, behaviors, and performance outcomes. In their meta-analysis of 106 independent samples,

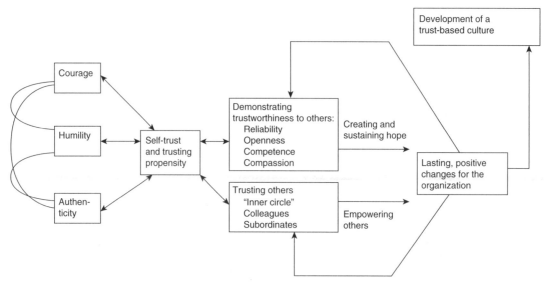

Fig. 34.1 Model of trust-based positive organizational scholarship.

Dirks and Ferrin (2002, p. 618) found that trust in leadership was positively related to a variety of outcomes, including job performance, organizational citizenship behaviors, organizational commitment, and job satisfaction, while being negatively related to intention to quit. They also found that procedural justice, distributive justice, and interactional justice were positively related to antecedents of trust in leadership, as were participative decision making and perceived organizational support (Dirks & Ferry, 2002, p. 619). In the section below, we review specific empirical studies that illustrate how trust in leadership and elements of POS have been found to be significantly related.

Trust and Positive Organizational Scholarship

Many of the assumptions and propositions underlying POS in our assessment generally depend on relationships based on trust between individuals. Positive organizational scholarship environments are typified by positive attributes, such as belief in the goodness of human contribution and human potential leading to positive performance (Cameron, 2007). Positive organizational scholarship research also advocates the belief that humans desire to make a positive contribution to the life and health of their organizations, and one key feature of positive organizations is trust (Cameron, 2007). However, just as the focus historically has been on negative organizational characteristics, there has also been a lack of emphasis on understanding how trustworthy leaders in organizations can contribute to positive organizational outcomes.

Spreitzer (2006) notes several key elements of POS that would be typical within trust-based relationships. Developmental efforts to emphasize the importance of leveraging strengths rather than focusing on performance gaps (Spreitzer, 2006) are more likely to take place if individuals trust one another based upon beliefs about each other's benevolence. Jolts that are viewed as positive and thus a stimulus for learning (Spreitzer, 2006) are more likely to be viewed as such when organizational members trust one another in terms of being competent, so that they can develop constructive solutions to the jolt, and/or they trust one another not to engage in punitive actions for any mistakes that occur in the process of responding to the jolt. Also, individuals who desire to create mutual support through the building of durable resources (Spreitzer, 2006) also are more likely to do so if they trust one another. Moreover, we believe that the

developmental processes and outcomes articulated within POS to date are likely to be enhanced by relationships based on trust between followers and their leader.

Previous Research on Trust

In his review of the research literature on trust in organizations, Kramer (1999, p. 571) identified cognitive/rational, affective, and social components, and argues that rationality is an insufficient basis for understanding why individuals choose to trust others (Kramer, 1999, p. 573). Despite a number of scholars arguing for trust as comprising affective components (Lewis & Weigert, 1985; Bromiley & Cummings, 1996), and finding empirical support for distinguishing affective from cognitive components (e.g., McAllister, 1995), affect has received relatively less attention in research on interpersonal trust. In the context of POS, with its emphasis on positive relationships, however, we would expect that affect would play an important role in individuals' decisions to trust.

More generally, Kramer (1999, p. 574) argued that context should also be considered in understanding whether, how, and why individuals choose to trust. Hardin (1993) argues that trust involves the dispositional nature of the truster, characteristics of the trustee, and the context in which the decision to trust takes place. Building on Hardin (1993), Kramer (1999, p. 574) argues that cognitive, calculative considerations would matter more in organizational contexts in which little is known about one another, "e.g., transactions involving comparative strangers," and relational considerations might be more important in contexts in which much information is known, "such as those involving members of one's own group." Relational considerations are central in trust research that utilizes a social exchange perspective (e.g., Konovsky & Pugh, 1994; Whitener, Brodt, Korsgaard, & Werner, 1998). In POS contexts, we would argue that relational considerations would matter greatly in decisions to trust. Not only would organizational members have greater knowledge of one another, but individuals also would be evaluating each other on the extent to which they adhere to the values and beliefs comprised by the positive organization.

The importance of context in shaping expectations and trust is supported by empirical research. Miller (1992, p. 197) found that Hewlett-Packard's policy of removing locks on doors and eliminating time clocks demonstrated management's trust in its employees' cooperativeness. This allowed employees to assume that their fellow colleagues would be cooperative, and thus made it more likely that they would want to trust each other. Uzzi (1997) also found evidence that contexts that assumed cooperation among organizational members made it easier for them to trust one another and help one another solve problems. When organizational contexts demonstrate that individuals are not to be trusted, contrasting behaviors can result. Hochschild (1983) found that flight attendants "came to fear and distrust their passengers because of a policy allowing passengers to write letters of complaint about in-flight service which would end up in the attendants' files, regardless of how valid the complaint" (Kramer, 1999, p. 591). More recently, Moore-Ede (1993) found that a requirement for long-distance truck drivers to keep detailed logs of their driving time led to counterproductive behavior, and encouraged some drivers to evidence distrust by keeping two sets of logs, one for company inspections and one that represented their actual behavior.

Positive Individual Characteristics Influencing Leaders' Trust-building

Cameron (2008) specifically identified positive leadership within the positive scholarship domain. Positive leaders focus on enabling "positively deviant performance, foster an affirmative orientation in organizations, and engender a focus on virtuousness" (Cameron, 2008, p. 1). He has identified four strategies that positive leaders cultivate to create a flourishing environment: create a positive climate, develop positive relationships, encourage and use positive communication, and provide positive meaning (Cameron, 2008, p. xi). Cameron (2008) submits that a leader can focus on positively deviant behaviors whether or not he or she is placed into a positive or a negative environment.

First, positive leaders create a positive climate by emphasizing the positive and growing aspects of their organizations, even in the face of a crisis (Cameron, 2008). Positive leaders develop a positive climate through demonstrating compassion, offering forgiveness, and expressing gratitude (Cameron, 2008, p. 23). Positive leadership through a positive climate leads to people in that organization acting in a more creative fashion. Positive leaders also create positive relationships when they build positive energy networks and reinforce individual's strengths (Cameron, 2008, p. 42). Other scholars have found that this positive network is more important in an individual's success in the organization than is his or her actual position in the organization

(Baker, 2004). In addition, Baker (2004) found that "high-performing organizations have three times more positive energizers than average organizations" (Cameron, 2008, p. 43). In addition, the Gallup organization has also found that a focus on strengths, rather than weaknesses, can energize an individual to better performance (Buckingham & Clifton, 2001).

Positive communication is just as important in creating a positive work environment. Cameron (2008) found that a high-performance team in a positive organization provided more positive than negative comments to team members. This factor alone predicted organizational performance. This is likely because it contributes to a sense of connectivity among team members, thus increasing levels of trust. Finally, a positive leader contributes to a positive organizational culture by providing positive meaning. Positive meaning contributes to organizational performance and trust. Positive meaning is built by work having a positive impact, work aligned with personal value, work whose impact is long lasting, and work that builds supportive relationships (Cameron, 2008, p. 72–73). All of these strategies allow a positive leader to create a positive organization.

Previous empirical studies show that trust in leaders is positively related to POS-related constructs and characteristics. In two separate studies of several hundred nurses each, structural equation models showed that empowerment, interactional justice, and recognition for work were positively related to the respect nurses felt they received from their managers and peers, which in turn was positively related to the trust they had in their managers (Laschinger, 2004; Laschinger & Finegan, 2005). In a study of two different consulting organizations, Six and Sorge (2008) found a number of factors that differentiated the organization with stronger interpersonal trust from the weaker one, including giving positive feedback or compliments, showing care and concern for others, and surfacing and settling differences in expectations. More generally, leaders who are trusted by their followers, particularly in terms of their competence, are more easily able to effect change quickly in their organization (Gabarro, 1987).

Courage, Humility, and Authenticity as Key Positive Leadership Characteristics

In our own research about many different kinds of leaders, we found that when the leader took the initiative to first demonstrate his or her trustworthiness, others within the organization (and often outside of it) came to trust the leader, and through that trust, acted in positive ways that led to lasting change and performance improvements. These positive results then helped to affirm the leaders' trustworthiness and trust-building efforts. We found that this "virtuous trust cycle" often depended on three critical leadership characteristics: courage, authenticity, and humility (Mishra & Mishra, 2008). Leaders' courage made it easier for them to be vulnerable to others, for example by sharing sensitive information or by empowering rank-and-file employees. Leaders' humility also encouraged them to be vulnerable to their followers, and even motivated these followers to build trust with one another by acknowledging their collective vulnerability. By admitting that they didn't hold all the answers and that they were just as dependent on their followers as the followers were on them, humble leaders fostered a sense of shared fate that is so often missing in organizations, especially those facing adverse circumstances. Finally, leaders' authenticity encouraged others in turn to be vulnerable to them. This authenticity in terms of transparent values and motives, coupled with behaviors that strongly corresponded to these values and motives, reassured followers and others that these leaders' motives, values, or goals did not need to be second-guessed and that trusting actions could be reciprocated without fear of being taking advantage of or receiving punishment. In contrast to organizations that often compete over resources, especially when faced with a threat or crisis, we found that organizations led by humble and trustworthy leaders instead utilized collaborative approaches to allocating resources. Building on prior POS research, we then argue that three characteristics typically ascribed to positive leaders—courage, humility, and authenticity—will contribute to their tendency to build trust with their stakeholders.

Courage

We define a leader's courage as a willingness to confront the status quo (Worline & Quinn, 2003), based on confidence in the future (Luthans & Avolio, 2003) and self-confidence about one's own ability to make a difference. Following Mishra and Mishra (2008), we argue that leaders who possess greater courage are expected to engage in greater trust-building efforts. To the extent that it requires courage to admit one's mistakes, a leader who possesses greater courage will then be more willing to build trust with others in order to overcome those mistakes. A leader who possesses a greater willingness to confront the status quo is also more likely to see the need to induce others' cooperation in overcoming this status quo, and cooperation is enhanced by trust. Courage based on greater confidence in the future will also induce leaders to build the trust that is necessary to involve others in creating such a future. It may be also be possible that leaders possessing greater self-confidence may have stronger generalized predispositions to trust others (Rotter, 1967), and therefore they would be more likely to build trust with others.

Humility

Humility is also an important characteristic possessed by leaders who are more likely to build trust with others. Nielsen, Marrone, and Slay (2010) defines humility as "a desirable personal quality reflecting the willingness to understand the self (identities, strengths, limitations), combined with perspective in the self's relationships with others (i.e., perspective that one is not the center of the universe). Humble leaders remain aware of and accept their vulnerabilities and openly discuss them with associates, so that they can be questioned to ensure that they are heading in the right direction (Luthans & Avolio, 2003). Humble leaders are also interested in how others perceive them and integrate this information with how they perceive themselves (Nielsen et al., 2010). Humility can be developed in leaders (Owens, Rowatt, & Wilkins, Chapter 20, this volume), and because humble leaders are open to receiving feedback from others, they should be more likely to build trust with others in order to receive feedback that is as complete as possible.

Authenticity

Authenticity is the third key characteristic of a leader who is likely to build trust with others. This leader lives the values that he or she preaches. Authentic leadership is defined as "a pattern of leader behavior that draws upon and promotes both positive psychological capacities and a positive ethical climate, to foster greater self-awareness, an internalized moral perspective, balanced processing of information, and relational transparency of the part of leaders working with followers, fostering positive self development" (Walumbwa, Avolio, Gardner, Wernsing, & Peterson, 2008, p. 94). Authentic leaders have no gaps between their words and actions, and thus no hypocrisy (Luthans & Avolio, 2003). An authentic leader is also self-aware, owning his personal experience and acting with the true self

(Luthans & Avolio, 2003). Authentic leaders possess a deep sense of self-awareness that informs their actions. As a result, authentic leaders "are perceived by others as being aware of their own and others' values or moral perspectives" (Helland & Winston, 2005). This allows authentic leaders to have the moral capacity to judge issues and circumstances involving "shades of grey" (Luthans & Avolio, 2003). Because their authenticity is in large part based on relationships with others, it is likely that authentic leaders will be more likely to build trust with those others, to deepen the integration between their espoused values and their own actions.

Courage, Humility, and Authenticity Often Go Together

In our previous work, we often found that courage, humility, and authenticity often coexisted within leaders who were effective at building trust and demonstrating trustworthiness (Mishra & Mishra, 2008). This is perhaps not surprising, given that "humility tempers other virtues, opens one to the influence and needs of others, and insists on reality rather than pretense" (Owens et al., 2011, Chapter 20, this volume). Luthans and Avolio (2003) argue that authentic leadership can be developed, as can other attributes such as moral reasoning, capacity, confidence, hope, optimism, resiliency, and future orientation. Authentic leaders are often courageous as well, leading from the front, and going in advance of others when there is a risk in doing so (Luthans & Avolio, 2003). They are easily motivated to work harder, more satisfied and possessing high morale, and they have high levels of motivational aspiration and set stretch goals. They persevere in the face of obstacles and difficulties; they analyze personal failures and setbacks as temporary, if not as learning experiences, and they view them as one-time, unique circumstances. Authentic leaders also tend to feel upbeat and invigorated both physically and mentally (Luthans & Avolio, 2003). Space limitations prevent further elaboration as to how courage, humility, and authentic may covary or even reinforce one another, but please see Owens et al. (2011, Chapter 20, this volume), for a rich discussion. Because of their positive relationship with such constructs as hope, optimism, and values, we believe that courage, humility, and authenticity are likely to have a strong influence upon affective components of trust, and not just trust's cognitive components.

As an example from our two decades of research, Bob Lintz, a leader who ran an automotive stamping plant in Parma, Ohio, compellingly demonstrated to us courage, humility, and authenticity. Bob took the Parma plant, which in the early 1980s was a $250 million annual revenue operation that was scheduled to be shut down in 3 years, and successfully turned the facility around over the course of several years. Today, it remains in operation, and is one of the highest-quality, most productive stamping plants in the world (Mishra & Mishra, 2008). His particular approach to building trust show how courage, humility, and authenticity all enhance a leader's ability and motivation to build trust with a wide variety of stakeholders, and build lasting positive change as well.

Bob asked the local United Auto Workers (UAW) for help in turning around the Parma stamping plant based on his own experience working at GM. This experience led him to understand that asking for help was essential in creating lasting positive changes. He shared critical business information that normally was restricted to senior management, first with Parma's UAW leaders, and ultimately with all of the hourly employees. Such sharing of information required courage from Bob, as he could have been reprimanded by his superiors for doing so. Asking for help demonstrated Bob's courage and humility because he openly acknowledged that he and the rest of the management team didn't have all the answers, when at the time, it was cultural norm for managers to in fact act as if they did have all the answers. Demonstrating courage and humility in this way also contributed to Bob's trusting the UAW leadership, because they could have interpreted a request for help as a sign of weakness (and often did based on previous instances). The approach Bob used to ask for help also evidenced his authenticity. He had learned at the very beginning of his career at GM in the 1960s just how important help was from others in creating positive change, even if that help came from people his superiors had told him not to trust (i.e., union employees).

> I had 30 people working for me from day one. Management assumed that I knew everything because I was a college graduate, but I really had no idea what I was supposed to do because I'd only received a 4-hour training program. I would try to talk to my fellow supervisors, but because I was a college graduate, and they weren't, they wouldn't talk to me. Instead of having college degrees, those supervisors got their jobs because they were the best at telling people what to do by cussing at them.
>
> On the other hand, the hourly UAW people, the ones who worked for me, went out of their way to

help me. It didn't take long before I realized that the good guys were the hourly employees. As their new supervisor, I had told them that "I'm going to have to rely on you folks to help me." My hourly employees really liked being asked for help. At the time, I was too naïve to understand how different I was from the traditional guy who came up through the ranks, and later I realized how critical it was to influence others in the organization by simply asking for help.

When asked recently what some of the turning points were in transforming the Parma plant into a trust-based culture, Bob mentioned this example:

> The regional head of the UAW had the wisdom to ask me to address all of the hourly people in a union meeting, even though that had never been done at General Motors. Management people were simply not allowed at union meetings. The regional UAW guy introduced me as having an important message: the reality of our business. I started to give my presentation and started hearing all these catcalls from throughout the plant, "Get him out of here. Get him out of here. No management people in a union meeting." It got to a point where I couldn't even speak any longer. So, the regional guy gets up and says, "give the man an opportunity, he's trying to help you." For a union leader to talk about a management guy as really sincere and trying to help was unheard of.

Bob's humble act of going to a formal UAW meeting represented an act of trust because even though he was the top manager at the Parma stamping plant, its UAW membership had ridiculed him many times during management–union meetings. So, it was very likely that when Bob went to their own meeting, where the UAW controlled the situation, they would be emboldened to act even more negatively. His willingness to expose himself in this manner led the way toward his building a more trust-based relationship with the Parma plant's UAW leadership and its rank-and-file hourly employees.

This meeting was not only an act of trust on Bob's part, but also an opportunity for him to demonstrate his trustworthiness. He did this by listening as well as articulating his future vision. Bob gave the union employees same opportunity to articulate reasons why the plant needed to change the way it operated. The local UAW, with support from their national UAW bosses, provided him with a trusted platform, the union meeting, to talk about the state of the business, and to articulate how everyone would have to work together if Parma were to win new business and avoid certain closure. The paradox then, for Bob and other leaders that we've studied like him, is that, in order for others to trust them, these leaders must often first demonstrate through their own behaviors that they trust their followers, even when those followers haven't previously justified such trust.

The Specific Ways That Leaders Demonstrate Trustworthiness

In our research, we have identified four ways in which leaders have successfully built trust with their constituents: reliability, openness, competence, and compassion (ROCC; Mishra & Mishra, 1994). The first dimension of trustworthiness is reliability. This dimension is often what people recognize first in dealing with others, including their leaders: Do they show up on time? Do they follow-up as promised? Reliability entails being consistent in words and actions, and leaders who are trusted in terms of their reliability follow through as they say they will. Individuals are more likely to trust a leader who is reliable because it reduces uncertainty regarding the leader's behavior. We argue that reliability should be a critical dimension of trustworthiness because there is a higher degree of interdependence in a POS system than in non-POS systems. Actors must be able to be counted upon to behave consistently and reliably; without reliable actions, highly interdependent coordination is impossible.

Leaders demonstrate their openness by sharing information and being honest with others. At a minimum, being open means not lying to another person. At its greatest level, it means full disclosure. Trustworthiness in terms of openness takes longer to develop than does reliability-based trustworthiness because it involves not only speaking merely the truth, but also revealing information about one's intentions and expectations, and for a leader, that can involve highly sensitive information. A leaders' openness also reduces uncertainty for followers, and thus leads them to trust the leader more. In a POS system, such openness should be especially relevant as a trustworthiness dimension because high performance depends on information that is not only timely but accurate (Gittell, 2003, p. 282).

Leaders demonstrate their competence by meeting and exceeding performance expectations and delivering results that support their organization's strategic goals and objectives. Followers want to know that they can depend on their leader to be competent to solve problems and lead them through to a solution. Because POS focuses on the development of talents and strengths instead of weaknesses, followers are more likely to respond to a leader's developmental efforts if they believe the leader has the knowledge and abilities necessary to hone their talents and strengths.

Finally, leaders can demonstrate their trustworthiness in terms of their compassion. Compassion can take a great deal of time to demonstrate because it requires first an understanding or empathy for the other party's needs and interests, and then, as Luthans and Avolio (2003) argue, a willingness to further those needs and interests. Whereas Lilius, Worline, Maitlis, Kanov, Dutton, and Frost (2008) found that most acts of compassion came from a coworker, we suggest that acts of compassion from a leader can also go a long way toward building positive connections with employees. Leaders have greater authority and access to provide the material resources that can foster followers' interests than do coworkers. Lilius et al. (2008) did find that acts of compassion generated perceptions of support and strengthened organizational commitment. Accordingly, a leader who demonstrates compassion is likely to promote those relationships that foster individual and collective growth.

How Trustworthy Leaders Create Cultures of Enduring, Positive Change and Trust
In the sections below, we will attempt to demonstrate through examples gleaned from our ongoing research program how leaders create lasting positive changes in their organizations through two key processes: creating and sustaining hope and empowering others. These positive changes not only reinforced the leaders' trustworthiness and justified their initial efforts to build trust, but they also created cultures of trust that have endured, in some cases, for decades, even years after the leader left the organization.

Creating and Sustaining Hope
One way in which leaders develop lasting positive changes and a culture of trust within their organizations is through creating and sustaining hope. Hope is defined as an activating force that enables people, even when faced with the most overwhelming obstacles, to envision a promising future and to set and pursue goals (Helland & Winston, 2005). It is not surprising to us that trust and hope often go together in the context of positive change, as both are *relational* constructs. Ludema, Wilmot, and Srivastva (1997) define four enduring qualities

of hope as being "a) born in relationships, b) inspired by the conviction that the future is open and can be influenced, c) sustained by dialogue about high human ideals, and d) generative of positive action" (p. 9). Like hope, leadership arises in relationship with others.

Peterson and Luthans (2003) describe hopeful leaders as possessing both *willpower* (agency) and *waypower* (alternate pathways). In their study of high-hope leaders, they found that these leaders (as compared to low-hope leaders) led more profitable organizations and had better retention and satisfaction rates among subordinates. Thus, hopeful leaders produce positive organizational results. Other research has found that, by demonstrating trustworthiness, leaders can engender hopeful responses among their followers in threatening contexts, such as crisis or downsizing, in which organizational members are vulnerable (Mishra & Spreitzer, 1998; Spreitzer & Mishra, 2000).

In our research, some of the most compelling examples of leaders fostering hope in others take place in health care contexts. This is not surprising, given that the hope for healing is what patients are looking for when they consult a physician or surgeon.

Kevin Lobdell, M.D., is director of Adult and Pediatric CV Critical Care, and is associate director of the Cardiothoracic Residency Program at Carolinas Heart and Vascular Institute in Charlotte, North Carolina. He has found his niche in streamlining surgical care, and has optimized a process for improving the time cardiac surgical patients are extubated after surgery by over 100%; now, as many as 80% of patients are extubated within 6 hours (Lobdell et al., 2009). He and his team have reduced mortality by nearly 50%, sepsis by 50%, and acute renal failure by 37.5%, while improving operational efficiency by reducing ICU and hospital length of stays (Lobdell et al., 2009).

These outcomes were achieved partly because Dr. Lobdell engendered optimism and confidence within his hospital unit by sharing data widely with fellow physicians, nurses, respiratory therapists, and other staff members, and by building these individuals into a cohesive team through a common goal. Dr. Lobdell argues that communicating honestly, directly, and humbly while maintaining a relentless sense of optimism have been essential to the unit's success (Mishra & Mishra, 2008). "High-hope individuals tend to be more certain of their goals and challenged by them; value progress toward goals as well as the goals themselves; enjoy interacting with others and readily adapt to new and collaborative relationships; are less anxious, especially in evaluative, stressful situations; and are more adaptive to environmental change" (Peterson & Luthans, 2003: p. 27).

A key way in which Dr. Lobdell works to resolve conflicts with his colleagues in this highly stressful work environment is through informal communication, and in particular through discussing his colleagues' children. We argue that this reinforces his authenticity, as he is indeed responsible for a number of very sick child patients in his unit. Dr. Lobdell has found this to be important in demonstrating his compassion for his team members and for them to find common ground with each other. We believe that by establishing this common ground, he has enabled them to trust each other more, and use that trust to make their patients better much more quickly.

Empowering Others

Another way in which leaders develop lasting positive changes and a culture of trust within their organizations is by empowering others. We define empowerment as a personal sense of control in the workplace, as manifested in four beliefs about the person–work relationship: meaning, competence, self-determination, and impact (Spreitzer, 1995). Meaning reflects a sense of purpose or personal connection about work, which helps individuals cope better with uncertainty. Leaders who help enhance individuals' empowerment in terms of competence, or a belief that they have the skills and abilities necessary to perform their work well, provide them with another coping resource to deal with changes at work. By enhancing their followers' empowerment in terms of self-determination, which is a sense of freedom about how individuals do their own work, leaders help feel a greater sense of control over any threatening or challenging work changes. By increasing followers' empowerment in terms of impact, leaders are able to help their followers feel that they can influence changes in the organization through their actions. We focus on empowerment because we argue that empowering others is a form of trusting them. It involves not only transferring authority from leaders to followers (Spreitzer & Mishra, 1999), but also sharing the responsibility for co-creating a meaningful, high-impact, and collaboratively designed organizational system.

By being true to themselves, authentic leaders' exhibited behavior positively transforms and develops their associates into leaders themselves (Luthans & Avolio, 2003), thus empowering them. More specifically, authentic leaders are guided by a set of end values that are oriented toward doing what's right for their constituency, in which the individual has something positive to contribute to the group, and they model these values rather than using coercion or even persuasion (Luthans & Avolio, 2003). Authentic leaders are also equally focused on developing others and task accomplishment (Luthans & Avolio, 2003). In this manner, leaders will be enhancing followers' empowerment in all four dimensions. When leaders help others to identify and nurture their strengths, they build awareness of possibilities and encourage others to take courageous action to become their hoped-for possible selves (Spreitzer, 2006).

Bob Lintz is also a great example of a leader who empowers others, especially in a context when it was not popular to do so. First, he provided others with a sense of meaning by giving them accurate and honest information about the state of the plant, and he let them know that their participation would help determine the fate of the plant's existence. In this way, he let them know that he was depending on them for their help to make sure that the plant did not fail. He was making it clear that their competence would make the difference between their plant surviving or closing. In addition, he provided them with the necessary team training to work efficiently and effectively together to generate new ideas to keep their plant open. By providing this training, he gave them a sense of competence and self-determination, knowing that their plant's future was now in their hands as much as it was in his. Finally, when the teams came up with new ideas for how to improve business practices or how to create new business from other plants, he asked them to present their findings to external customers and other GM executives, so that they could see the impact of their work. When the teams became successful in generating new business for the plant based upon their own ideas, they became co-owners of the process to keep Parma alive and thriving.

Creating Cultures of Trust

By achieving lasting, positive changes through creating hope and empowering their followers, trustworthy leaders will be able to develop cultures of trust in which organizational members not only trust their leaders, but also trust one another and identify with a common set of values incorporating the four key dimensions of trustworthiness.

Building and aligning a positive, collective identification with an organization's mission and values is one of the most important responsibilities of authentic leadership (Luthans & Avolio, 2003). To the extent that those values emphasize personal and collective competence, the organization can become what Gallup calls a strengths-based organization (Buckingham & Clifton, 2001; Luthans & Avolio, 2003). More generally, leaders intent on creating change quickly and enduringly should focus on building a culture of trust (Gabarro, 1978).

The leaders we've studied built trust not only among individuals with whom they directly interacted, but also by using broader efforts to instill the ROCC of Trust throughout their organizations and key external stakeholders. By building trust through ROCC, leaders modeled their trustworthiness, thus encouraging their followers to reciprocate. Our leaders built cultures of reliability-based trust by fostering the development of norms, processes, and systems that made high performance replicable, and by developing institutional mechanisms that reminded others of their commitments and made them more likely to keep them. Our leaders built a culture of trust based on openness by providing opportunities for their employees to talk with them without fear of reprisal, and by being transparent in their communications, often sharing sensitive information about company performance and other important issues. Leaders established competence-based trust throughout the organization by establishing high standards of excellence, with clearly defined metrics. Leaders built compassion-based trust—the form of trust that takes the longest time to build and is often the toughest piece of the ROCC of Trust—by demonstrating empathy in tangible and convincing ways, by personally making symbolic and substantive sacrifices for the betterment of the organization and demanding the same of their subordinates, and by developing innovative ways to save jobs during periods of organizational crisis or economic upheaval.

As a result of these efforts, they created lasting, positive changes in their organizations, and established a set of expectations and values that are deeply embedded in their organizations. As one compelling example, we discuss Two Men and Truck, International, Inc. (TMT), a $200 million enterprise founded by Mary Ellen Sheets in 1985 with a $350 investment in a used truck. We have been studying Two Men and a Truck, International for over a decade (Mishra & Mishra, 2008). It is the largest local moving company in the United States,

with over 200 franchisees in the United States, Canada, and Ireland.

Two Men and a Truck and its leaders established system-wide trust in terms of reliability and competence in many ways, including developing highly consistent work standards, industry-leading employee and franchisee training, and a franchise agreement that creates clear expectations for the franchisor, franchisees, and all of their customers. They also built trust in terms of competence by explicitly hiring "people brighter than they are from the firm's outset," according to the leaders of TMT, and by insisting that this "smarter than I am" approach to managing was adopted by anyone responsible for recruiting, selecting, developing, or retaining personnel. TMT fostered a culture of trust in terms of openness by sharing sensitive information about each of their 200 franchises with every franchise in the system, including operating performance, financial information, and marketing tactics. Over many years, this trusting and trust-building behavior initiated by TMT's top management has helped its franchises view one another not as competitors, but as collaborators, helping one another to improve each other's operations and grow the entire franchise system quickly and profitably. Finally, from the founder's initial act of compassion—donating the entire first year's profits to charity—TMT has evolved its compassion-based culture through its "Movers Who Care" trademark and its core values that include "Care," "Give back to the community," and the "Grandma rule." These and other TMT initiatives have resulted in a tightly knit franchise system that is encouraging of each other and is trusting of the home office. TMT has demonstrated that the actions of leaders can result in a trust-based culture that can have both cultural and financial benefits.

Future Directions

- *How long does it take to build a trusting culture in a positive organization?* In two of the examples we highlighted, Bob from Parma and the Two Men and a Truck family, both worked to build trust over a period of several years, and then spent several more years working to sustain the trust they had built. We know that trust takes time to build, and in both cases, these leaders had significant time in which to build a trusting culture. What happens when a leader is new to a culture or enters a turn-around situation? Would these characteristics of courage, authenticity, and humility facilitate the four dimensions of trust in the same way with less time?

- *What is the role of strengths in building trust?* The Gallup Organization's Strengths-based assessments have gained widespread use among practitioners. Positive organizational researchers have also begun examining a strengths-based approached to leading and manager (Roberts, Caza, Heaphy, Spreitzer, & Dutton, in progress; Spreitzer, Stephens, & Sweetman, 2009). We would like to know what the effect would be on trust within an organization if a leader managed from a viewpoint of strengths instead of weaknesses, and what would it require, in turn, from the rest of the organization.

- *Are trustworthy leaders made or born?* In light of the fact that we believe that courage, authenticity, and humility underpin trustworthy leaders, it would be interesting to discover how a leader develops these characteristics. To what extent do leaders develop these characteristics early in life, or can they acquire them in adulthood? We do believe that the leader's ability to build trust can be a foundation for lasting positive change/culture, and that the ability to demonstrate trustworthiness and build trust can be learned. The challenge is to help practitioners find the best ways in which to do so.

- *Is the process for rebuilding trust the same as building trust?* How trust can be repaired once it has been violated remains a fruitful area for research. We have found it difficult to refute the truism that trust takes time to build, but once broken is very difficult to rebuild. Citing Slovic (1993), Kramer (1999, p. 593) notes that "negative (trust-destroying) events are more visible and noticeable than positive (trust-building) events (and) trust-destroying events carry more weight in judgment than trust-building events of comparable magnitude." Although we would like to focus on the positive aspects of a trustworthy leader, we must acknowledge that there are times when a leader must enter an organization in which trust has been lost or violated, and must endeavor to rebuild trust to create a new and more positive organization if the organization is to survive. What steps must a leader take in this type of situation? How can a leader overcome broken promises and negativity to gain the confidence of an organization?

Conclusion

Despite some of the lowest levels of trust in business and government ever polled, there is hope for leaders who aspire to create positive organizations. Trusted leaders can create powerful results for their organizations by believing in the goodness of their employees and their ability to create a positive performance for the organization. By trusting their employees, leaders create a virtuous cycle of trust that permeates throughout the organization, enabling behaviors and outcomes that would not exist without such trust. Leaders' courage, authenticity, and humility allow them to both become more trusting of their subordinates, and help to demonstrate their trustworthiness to these individuals. When leaders demonstrate their reliability, openness, competence, and compassion, they are viewed as more trustworthy, and are more able to create and sustain hope among their followers, and empower them as well. Such hope and empowerment are critical to creating and sustaining lasting and positive change and a trust-based culture.

We also need to consider whether trust and trustworthiness are always something that leaders want to build. As vulnerability is at the core of trust, trusting too much can result in significant, often devastating, losses. In addition, building trust takes significant time and resources, even if it is to simply demonstrate one's trustworthiness, and leaders and organizations do not have limitless resources. Finally, leaders must always be making choices, and choosing to build trust with one set of individuals means choosing not to do so with others, at least in the short term. Leaders, then, must depend on their hard-won wisdom to be able to build trust with the right people at the right time.

References

Baker, W. (2004). *Half-baked brown bag presentation on positive energy network*. Unpublished manuscript, University of Michigan Business School, Ann Arbor, MI.

Bromiley, P., & Cummings, L.L. (1996). Transaction costs in organizations with trust. In R. Bies, R. Lewicki, & B. Sheppard (Eds.), *Research on negotiations in organizations* Vol. 5 (pp. 219–247). Greenwich, CT: JAI.

Buckingham, M., & Clifton, D.O. (2001). *Now, discover your strengths*. New York: Free Press.

Cameron, K.S. (2007). Positive organizational scholarship. In S. Clegg, & J. Bailey (Eds.), *International encyclopedia of organizational studies*. Beverly Hills: Sage.

Cameron, K.S. (2008). *Positive leadership: Strategies for extraordinary performance*. San Francisco: Berrett-Koehler Publishers.

Deutsch, M. (1962). Cooperation and trust: Some theoretical notes. In M.R. Jones (Ed.), *Nebraska symposium on motivation* (pp. 275–319). Lincoln, NE: University of Nebraska Press.

Deutsch, M. (1973). *The resolution of conflict: Constructive and destructive processes*. New Haven, CT: Yale University Press.

Dirks, K.T., & Ferrin, D.L. (2002). Trust in leadership: Meta-analytic findings and implications for research and practice, *Journal of Applied Psychology, 87*(4), 611–628.

Schumpeter, J.A. (2009, October 8). Hating what you do: Disenchantment with work is growing. *The Economist*. Retrieved from http://www.economist.com/node/14586131? story_id=14586131.

Edelman Public Relations. (2009). 2009 Trust barometer. The tenth global opinion leaders study. Retrieved April 19, 2010, from http://www.edelman.com/trust/2009/.

Fukuyama, F. (1995). *Trust: The social virtues and the creation of prosperity*. New York: Free Press.

Gabarro, J.J. (1978). The development of trust, influence and expectations. In A. Athos, & J. J. Gabarro (Eds.), *Interpersonal behavior*. Englewood Cliffs, NJ: Prentice Hall.

Gabarro, J.J. (1987). *The dynamics of taking charge*. Boston: Harvard Business School Press.

Gallup Organization. (2009). 2009 survey on trust in government. Retrieved April 19, 2010, from http://www.gallup.com/poll/5392/Trust-Government.aspx.

Gittell, J.H.(2003). A theory of relational coordination. In K.S. Cameron, J.E. Dutton, & R.E. Quinn (Eds.), *Positive organizational scholarship: Foundations of a new discipline* (pp. 279–295). San Francisco: Berrett-Koehler Publishers.

Granovetter, M. (1985). Economic action and social structure: The problem of embeddedness. *American Journal Sociology, 91*(3), 481–510.

Hardin, R. (1993). The street-level epistemology of trust. *Politics & Society, 21*(4), 505–529.

Harvard Kennedy School Center for Public Leadership in collaboration with the Merriman River Group (2009). *National leadership index 2009*. Retrieved April 19, 2010, from http://content.ksg.harvard.edu/leadership/images/CPLpdf/cpl_nli_2009.pdf.

Helland, M.R., & Winston, B.E. (2005). Towards a deeper understanding of hope and leadership. *Journal of Leadership and Organizational Studies, 12*(2), 42–54.

Hochschild, A.R. (1983). *The managed heart: Commercialization of human feeling*. Berkeley: University of California Press.

Kramer, R. (1999). Trust and distrust in organizations: Emerging perspectives, enduring questions, *Annual Review of Psychology, 50*, 569–598.

Konovsky, M., & Pugh, D. (1994). Citizenship behavior and social exchange. *Academy of Management Journal, 37*, 656–669.

Lewis, J.D., & Weigert, A. (1985). Trust as a social reality. *Social Forces, 63*, 967–985.

Lilius, J.M., Worline, M.C., Maitlis, S., Kanov, J., Dutton, J.E., & Frost, P. (2008). The contours and consequences of compassion at work. *Journal of Organizational Behavior, 29*, 192–318.

Lobdell, K., Camp, S., Stamou, S., Swanson, R., Reames, M., Madjarov, J., et al. (2009). Quality improvement in cardiac critical care. *HSR Proceedings in Intensive Care and Cardiovascular Anesthesia, 1*(1), 22–26.

Laschinger, H. (2004). Hospital nurses' perceptions of respect and organizational justice. *Journal of Nursing Administration, 34*(7/8), 354–364.

Laschinger, H., & Finegan, J. (2005). Using empowerment to build trust and respect in the workplace: A strategy for addressing the nursing shortage. *Nursing Economics, 23*(1), 6–13.

Ludema, J.D., Wilmot, J.B., & Srivastva, S. (1997). Organizational hope: Reaffirming the constructive task of social and organizational inquiry. *Human Relations, 50*(8), 1015–1053.

Luhmann, N. (1979). *Trust and power*. Hoboken, NJ: Wiley.

Luhmann, N. (1988). Familiarity, confidence, trust: Problems and alternatives. In D. Gambetta (Ed.), *Trust: Making and breaking cooperative relations* (pp. 94–107). Cambridge, MA: Basil Blackwell.

Luthans, F., & Avolio, B. (2003). Authentic leadership development. In K.S. Cameron, J.E. Dutton, & R.E. Quinn (Eds.), *Positive organizational scholarship: Foundations of a new discipline* (pp. 240–258). San Francisco: Berrett-Koehler Publishers.

Mayer, R.C., Davis, J.H., & Schoorman, F.D. (1995). An integrative model of organizational trust. *Academy of Management Review, 20*, 709–734.

McAllister, D.J. (1995). Affect- and cognition-based trust as foundations for interpersonal cooperation in organizations. *Academy of Management Journal, 38*, 24–59.

Miller, G.J. (1992). *Managerial dilemmas: The political economy of hierarchies*. New York: Cambridge University Press.

Mishra, A.K. (1996). Organizational responses to crisis: The centrality of trust. In R. Kramer, & T. Tyler (Eds.), *Trust in organizations* (pp. 261–287). Newbury Park, CA: Sage.

Mishra, A.K., & Mishra, K.E. (1994). The role of mutual trust in effective downsizing strategies, *Human Resource Management, 33*(2), 261–279.

Mishra, A.K., & Mishra, K.E. (2008). *Trust is everything: Become the leader others will follow*. Chapel Hill, NC: Author.

Mishra, A. K., Mishra, K.E., & Spreitzer, G.M. (2009). How to downsize your company without downsizing morale. *MIT Sloan Management Review*, Spring, 39–44.

Mishra, A.K., & Spreitzer, G.M. (1998). Explaining how survivors respond to downsizing: The roles of trust, empowerment, justice and work redesign. *Academy of Management Review, 23*(3), 567–588.

Moore-Ede, M. (1993). *The twenty-four hour society: Understanding human limitations in a world that never stops*. New York: Addison-Wesley.

Nielsen, R., Marrone, J.A., & Slay, H.S. (2010). A new look at humility: Exploring the humility concept and its role in socialized charismatic leadership (SCL). *Journal of Leadership & Organizational Studies, 17*(1), 33–43.

Owens, B.P., Rowatt, W.C., & Wilkins, A.L. (2011). Exploring the relevance and implications of humility in organizations. In K.S. Cameron, & G.M. Spreitzer (Eds.), *The Oxford handbook of positive organizational scholarship*. New York: Oxford University Press.

Peterson, S.J., & Luthans, F. (2003). The positive impact and development of hopeful leaders. *Leadership and Organization Development Journal, 24*(1/2), 26–31.

Putnam, R.D. (2000). *Bowling alone: The collapse and revival of American community*. New York: Simon and Schuster.

Roberts, L.M., Caza, B.B., Heaphy, E., Spreitzer, G., & Dutton, J. *Strengths in action: A build-and-broaden model of positive identity development at work*. Working paper.

Rotter, J.B. (1967). A new scale for the measurement of interpersonal trust. *Journal of Personality, 35*, 651–665.

Rousseau, D.M., Sitkin, S.B., Burt, R.S., & Camerer, C. (1998). Not so different after all: A cross-discipline view of trust. *Academy of Management Review, 23*, 393–404.

Six, F., & Sorge, A. (2008). Creating a high-trust organization: An exploration into organizational policies that stimulate interpersonal trust building. *Journal of Management Studies, 45*(5), 857–884.

Slovic, P. (1993). Perceived frisk, trust, and democracy. *Risk Analysis, 13*, 675–682.

Spreitzer, G.M. (1995). Psychological empowerment in the workplace: dimensions, measurement, and validation. *Academy of Management Journal, 38*, 1442–1465.

Spreitzer, G.M., & Mishra, A.K. (1999). Giving up control without losing control: Trust and its substitutes' effects on managers' involving employees in decision making. *Group and Organization Management, 14*(2), 155–187.

Spreitzer, G.M., & Mishra, A.K. (2000). An empirical examination of a stress-based framework of survivor responses to downsizing. In R. J. Burke, & C. L. Cooper (Eds.), *The organization in crisis: Downsizing, restructuring, and privatization* (pp. 97–118). London: Blackwell.

Spreitzer, G.M. (2006). Leading to grow and growing to lead: Leadership development lessons from positive organizational studies. *Organizational Dynamics, 35*(4), 305–331.

Spreitzer, G.M., Stephens, J.P., & Sweetman, D. (2009). The reflected best self field experiment with adolescent leaders: Exploring the psychological resources associated with feedback source and valence. *Journal of Positive Psychology, 4*(5), 331–348.

Walumbwa, F.O., Avolio, B.J., Gardner, W.L., Wernsing, T.S., & Peterson, S.J. (2008). Authentic leadership: Development and validation of a theory-based measure. *Journal of Management, 34*, 89–126.

Whitener, E., Brodt, S., Korsgaard, M.A., & Werner, J. (1998). Managers as initiators of trust: An exchange relationship for understanding managerial trustworthy behavior. *Academy of Management Journal, 23*, 513–530.

Worline, M.C., & Quinn, R. (2003). Courageous principled action. In K.S. Cameron, J.E. Dutton, & R.E. Quinn (Eds.), *Positive organizational scholarship: Foundations of a new discipline* (pp. 138–158). San Francisco: Berrett-Koehler Publishers.

Uzzi, B (1997). Social structure and competition in interfirm networks: The paradox of embeddedness. *Administrative Science Quarterly, 42*, 35–67.

Zand, D. (1972). Trust and managerial problem solving. *Administrative Science Quarterly, 17*, 229–239.

Perspective Taking

Building Positive Interpersonal Connections and Trustworthiness One Interaction at a Time

Michele Williams

Abstract

There is growing interest in the role of perspective taking in organizations. Perspective taking has been linked to enhanced interpersonal understanding and the strengthening of social bonds. In this chapter, I integrate research from sociology, communications, and psychology to provide insight into why, when, and how perspective taking facilitates the relational resources of positive connections and trustworthy actions. I introduce the importance of a three-dimensional view of perspective taking for building relational resources and present data validating this conceptualization. I conclude with directions for future research.

Keywords: Perspective taking, survey scale development, trust, trustworthiness, empathic concern, interpersonal connection

There is growing interest and debate surrounding the role of perspective taking in social interactions and organizational life. In this chapter, I examine the central role of perspective taking in building two relational resources: positive connections and trustworthy actions. Whereas some researchers focus on the ability of perspective taking to elicit empathy, concern, and cooperative behavior (Batson, Turk, Shaw & Klein, 1995; Parker & Axtell, 2001; Parker, Atkins, & Axtell, 2008), others focus on the strategic impact of perspective taking (Epley, Caruso, & Bazerman, 2006; Galinsky & Mussweiler, 2001; Galinsky, Maddux, Gilin, & White, 2008). I build on both streams by examining work that connects perspective taking to cooperative behavior and by delineating how the proactive or strategic aspects of perspective taking can also generate relational resources.

Perspective taking refers to the process of "imagining another person's thoughts or feeling from that person's point of view" (Davis, 1996; Mead, 1934). The topic of perspective taking is relevant to positive organizational scholarship (POS) because perspective taking can be considered a virtuous process.

Perspective taking not only requires discretionary cognitive and emotional effort, it paves the way for kind, understanding, compassionate actions—actions which Park and Peterson (2003) assert are related to the virtue of love (or, in the organizational context, befriending others).

Because the implications of perspective taking for interpersonal interactions have been examined by scholars in sociology, communications, and psychology (Davis, 1996; Epley et al., 2006; Galinsky et al., 2008; Krauss & Fussell, 1991; Mead, 1934), I take an interdisciplinary approach to perspective taking. Integrating the research from these disciplines provides insight into why, when, and how perspective taking facilitates the virtue of befriending others.

This chapter is organized as follows. First, I review literature that suggests that perspective taking fosters the relational resources of positive interpersonal connections and trustworthy actions. I then argue that a three-dimensional view of perspective taking, one which includes cognitive, affective, and appraisal-related perspective taking, is important for understanding the link between perspective taking and relational resources. Next, I present data validating the proposed subdimensions of perspective taking and conclude with directions for future research.

Perspective Taking and Positive Interpersonal Connections

Perspective taking builds positive connections in several ways. It facilitates interpersonal understanding, strengthens social bonds, and elicits compassionate behavior (Williams, 2008).

Perspective Taking and Interpersonal Understanding

Perspective taking is a process for gaining interpersonal understanding. It requires one to understand the meaning that a situation holds for another and to adjust to the needs of that interaction counterpart (Blumer, 1969; Goffman, 1967). Perspective taking allows people to respond to the needs and actions of others in a flexible, responsive manner (Blumer, 1969; Krauss & Fussell, 1991; Mead, 1934). It allows people to understand the values that counterparts place on various goals, possessions, achievements, and identities (Brown & Levinson, 1987). Moreover, it allows people to communicate their preferences in a way that more closely matches the underlying meaning (or symbolic level) of their interaction partner's language (Blumer, 1969; Collins, 1990; Goffman, 1967).

Scholars in the field of communications, for example, investigate perspective taking in speaker–listener dyads (Fussell & Krauss, 1992). From this standpoint, it is widely accepted that perspective taking is necessary for effective communication because speakers must take into account what a specific listener knows when deciding how to formulate a message (Fussell & Krauss, 1992). People who are asked to engage in perspective taking adjust the content of their communication to the information they believe another person possesses (Fussell & Krauss, 1992; Krauss & Fussell, 1991). This combination of perspective taking and adjustment has been linked to greater comprehension by listeners (Krauss & Fussell, 1991). Thus, perspective taking may build social bonds by fostering mutual understanding, promoting communication that makes others feel understood, and decreasing conflicts that arise because of miscommunications.

Perspective Taking and Social Bonds

In addition to good communication and mutual understanding, which are important mechanisms

for strengthening social bonds, perspective taking also strengthens social bonds by increasing perceived self–other overlap (i.e., similarity, Galinsky, Ku, & Wang, 2005; Galinsky, Wang, & Ku, 2008). Perspective taking increases positive perceptions of other individuals by increasing the overlap between the cognitive representation of the self, the representation of the other, and the representation of the group to which the other belongs. Thus, perspective taking influences the self–other overlap between people from different social groups, who may initially perceive themselves as quite different from one another. The increased self–other overlap that results from perspective taking is impactful because it decreases both stereotyping of other individuals and prejudice toward others, as well as negative perceptions of other groups, including stigmatized groups (Batson et al., 1997; Galinsky et al., 2005, 2008).

Perspective taking also helps people build social bonds by fostering emotionally positive interactions. The understanding gained through perspective taking increases individuals' ability to avoid negative interactions and foster positive interactions (i.e., interactions with energy and mutual engagement) (Blumer, 1969; Collins, 1990; Goffman, 1967).

Perspective Taking and Compassion

Finally, perspective taking increases positive interpersonal connections by eliciting tender feelings of empathic concern and compassionate actions. In contrast to the perspective taking literature in microsociology and communication, the literature in psychology has examined perspective taking primarily in the context of empathy and helping behavior (Batson, 1998; Batson, Turk, Shaw, & Klein, 1995; Eisenberg & Miller, 1987; Parker & Axtell, 2001). Although closely related to empathy and empathic concern, perspective taking refers solely to the cognitive understanding of another person's point of view (thoughts, feelings, and/or appraisals). Empathy and empathic concern, in contrast, always have an emotional or affective component that has been labeled "emotion matching," "affective attunement," and/or "emotional resonance" (Davis, 1996). Whereas symbolic interactionists highlight the strategic use of perspective taking to increase the positive emotional quality of interactions (Blumer, 1969; Collins, 1990; Goffman, 1967), social psychologists suggest that perspective taking can also evoke positive behaviors during interactions through nonstrategic, empathy-related processes (Batson et al., 1995). For example, in noncompetitive experimental studies, perspective taking consistently elicits considerate behavior (Batson, 1998; Eisenberg & Miller, 1987). In organizational contexts, the empathy-related manifestations of perspective taking have been shown to foster cooperative behavior (Parker & Axtell, 2001). Perspective taking can also lead people to value others' welfare, feel compassion for them, and engage in helpful, benevolent behavior (Batson, 1998; Batson et al., 1995; Batson, Sager, Garst, Kang, Rubchinsky, & Dawson, 1997; Lilius, Kanov, & Dutton, 2011, Chapter 20, this volume; Van Lange, 2008).

In sum, perspective taking facilitates positive interpersonal connections by promoting interpersonal understanding, strengthening social bonds, fostering emotionally positive interactions, and motivating compassionate actions.

Perspective Taking and Trustworthy Action

Perspective taking enables trustworthy action in several ways. It motivates benevolence toward others, enables positive emotional influence, and facilitates proactive trustworthiness (Williams, 2008).

Perspective Taking and Benevolence

Benevolent actions are a central component of trustworthy behavior (Mayer, Davis, & Schoorman, 1995; Mishra & Mishra, 2011, Chapter 34, this volume; Williams, 2001a). Perspective taking generates benefits that influence benevolence through motivational, affective, and cognitive mechanisms. In terms of motivation, psychologists' suggest that perspective taking can generate compassion, which "amplifies or intensifies motivation to relieve another person's need" (Batson et al., 1995, p. 300). Consequently, perspective taking may motivate individuals to prioritize the interests of others. Thereby, it can trigger benevolent behaviors, such as compassionate statements and actions (Batson et al., 1995; Davis, 1996; Eisenberg & Miller, 1987). Similarly, because perspective taking leads people to value others' welfare (Batson et al., 1995), perspective taking may motivate benevolent actions that help others. It should also decrease the likelihood that a perspective taker will ignore the concerns of others and thereby inflict harm unintentionally.

Perspective Taking and Emotional Influence

In the affective domain, perspective taking may indirectly influence trust by enabling individuals to influence the emotions of others (i.e., emotional influence). Specifically, it may help the trust builder increase positive and decrease negative affect during interactions. Williams (2007) argues that, because

perspective taking provides a mechanism for understanding when people anticipate harm and feel threatened, it provides the information that people need to actively decrease the amount of negative emotion experienced by others. Symbolic interactionists suggest that perspective taking is also likely to generate pleasant feelings in others because it enables perspective takers to maintain emotionally positive interactions (Blumer, 1969; Collins, 1990). Consistent with assertions by scholars who propose that individuals use feelings as information about trustworthiness (Dunn & Schweitzer, 2005; Jones & George, 1998; Williams, 2001a), I contend that when perspective takers generate positive feelings in others, those feelings may increase perceptions of the perspective taker's trustworthiness. Similarly, when a perspective taker prevents negative feelings, the resulting absence of negative feelings should maintain or at least not detract from the perception of his or her trustworthiness.

Perspective Taking and Proactive Trustworthiness

I define proactive trustworthiness as behavior that an individual actively engages in because she anticipates that others will view it as trustworthy (i.e., benevolent, morally appropriate, and/or competent), even if the behavior seems unnecessary from the individual's own point of view. Proactive trustworthiness is a new way of looking at trust building and trustworthiness. With few exceptions (Child & Möllering, 2003; Mishra & Mishra, 2011, Chapter 34, this volume; Whitener, Brodt, Korsgaard, & Werner, 1998; Williams, 2007), the scholarly research on trust has not focused on the intentional interpersonal processes individuals can use to build trust. Scholars most often describe trust development as a relatively passive process of gathering data about other people's trustworthiness by watching their behavior in various situations over time (Lewicki & Bunker, 1996; Ring & Van de Ven, 1994; Shapiro, Sheppard, & Cheraskin, 1992) or by using information from proxy sources (e.g., Burt & Knez, 1996; Zucker, 1986). Scant attention is given to the fact that people are evaluating the trustworthiness of individuals, who are often not passive, but engaged in proactive attempts to influence the evaluation process.

Perspective taking is a process that individuals may use proactively to avoid behavior that others will perceive as either intentionally or unintentionally harmful. Symbolic interactionists, for example, suggest that perspective taking can provide cognitive information about how others are likely to view one's actions (Blumer, 1969; Mead, 1934). This, in turn, allows one to better respond with behaviors that others will define as trustworthy and benevolent. In other words, perspective taking helps individuals negotiate the meaning of benevolence within a specific relationship.

Although organizational scholars routinely investigate a variety of proactive processes, including feedback seeking, taking charge, job crafting, and selling issues (e.g., Ashford & Tsui, 1991; Morrison & Phelps, 1999; Wrzesniewski & Dutton, 2001; see Grant & Ashford, 2008 for review), they tend to focus on behaviors rather than cognitive processes. Thus, despite the proactive implications of perspective taking for trustworthy actions, perspective taking has rarely been investigated as a proactive process (c.f., Parker & Axtell, 2001). According to Parker, Williams, and Turner (2006, p. 636), "individual-level proactive behaviors typically focus on self-initiated and future-oriented action that aims to change and improve the situation or oneself." Although perspective taking includes both the anticipatory and the impact-oriented dimensions characteristic of proactive processes (Grant & Ashford, 2008), perspective taking is atypical in that it is an intrapsychic process. Individuals *imagine* how others will experience an event and then adjust their behavior accordingly. For example, a speaker first imagines what information another individual possesses and then adjusts his or her language and level of detail accordingly (e.g., Fussell & Krauss, 1992). Because perspective taking occurs before people act, and they engage in perspective taking to obtain more positive outcomes (Blumer, 1969; Collins, 1990; Goffman, 1967), perspective taking is a quintessentially proactive process.

Thus, I argue that perspective taking is not merely a process that allows people to have a more active role in trust building, but that perspective taking allows individuals to demonstrate proactive trustworthiness.

Perspective Taking Dimensions and Context
The effect of perspective taking on relational and material resources is influenced by the type of perspective taking that one engages in and the competitiveness of the context.

Perspective Taking Dimensions: Cognitive, Affective, and Appraisal-related Perspective Taking
In contrast to the perspective taking literature in micro-sociology and communications, the psychological literature views perspective taking as a multidimensional construct. The two dimensions of perspective taking that have received the most scholarly attention are affective and cognitive perspective taking. *Affective perspective taking* refers to the intrapsychic process of imagining another's feelings from that person's point of view, whereas *cognitive perspective taking* refers to the process of imagining another's thoughts or motives from that person's point of view (Davis, 1996). Thus, although all perspective taking involves the cognitive process of imagining another's experience, its dimensions are defined by the content that one imagines (e.g., another's thoughts or feelings).

Appraisal-related perspective taking is a third underexplored component of perspective taking that is likely to have a unique impact on trustworthy behavior (Williams, 2007, 2008). Appraisal-related perspective taking refers to the process of imagining how events are relevant for others' goals, concerns, and well-being from their point of view (Williams, 2007). It requires taking perspective with respect to other people's cognitive appraisals of a situation.

Cognitive appraisals occur when people evaluate external events with respect to the implications of those events for their own goals, concerns, and general well-being (Ellsworth, 1991; Folkman, 1984; Lazarus & Folkman, 1984). These appraisals are an integral part of people's emotional experiences (Ellsworth & Scherer, 2003; Smith & Ellsworth, 1985). For example, if a decision that thwarts employees' goals is made by their supervisor, whom they then hold responsible for the negative outcomes, these employees are likely to feel anger toward their supervisor (anger involves negative goal conduciveness and attributions of responsibility to another, Smith & Ellsworth, 1985). However, if their goals are thwarted by uncontrollable circumstances, they are likely to feel sadness (sadness involves negative goal conduciveness and attributions that no one is responsible, Smith & Ellsworth, 1985).

I argue that, similar to the process of imagining how others will feel (affective perspective taking, Davis, 1996), the process of imagining how events are relevant for others goals, concerns, and well-being (appraisal-related perspective taking, Williams, 2007) will evoke concern for others and motivate compassionate behavior. However, relative to affective perspective taking, engaging in appraisal-related perspective taking attends specifically to other people's cognitive appraisals. Moreover, because people find events threatening or stressful when those events negatively impact their goals or general well-being (Folkman, 1984; Lazarus & Folkman, 1984), appraisal-related perspective taking allows the perspective taker to better understand and anticipate which situations or actions other individuals are likely to find harmful or stressful. Appraisal-related perspective taking, therefore, has the potential to provide perspective takers with an anticipatory understanding of why other people may react with negative feelings and behavior. This understanding allows perspective takers to proactively influence the elements of the situation that may be perceived as harmful and mitigate the harm that others experience.

For example, imagining that others think a project's success is important (an example of general cognitive perspective taking) may have different action implications than imagining that they view the project's success as their only chance to keep their jobs from ending (an example of appraisal-related perspective taking). In the first case, an e-mail containing data pointing to the marginal returns of the project may be surprising or unpleasant, but in the second case, the same message may be extremely threatening and anxiety provoking. Building on Williams (2007), who emphasized the importance of appraisal-related perspective taking for emotional influence, I argue here that appraisal-related perspective taking also builds trust through cognitive and motivational mechanisms. It not only motivates people to act benevolently and with compassion, but also enables them to cognitively anticipate which actions others are likely to find benevolent or harmful from their point of view.

Dimensions of Perspective Taking in Competitive and Cooperative Contexts

Recently, scholars examining perspective taking in competitive contexts have found that cognitive and affective perspective taking have different implications for acting with compassion versus acquiring material resources. They find that, in competitive contexts, cognitive perspective taking with respect to others' thoughts or strategic goals can simultaneously lead to less biased perceptions of fairness and more extreme assessments of the likelihood of competitive behavior by others (Epley et al., 2006). This more extreme assessment of others' competitive behavior increases the competitiveness of the perspective taker and his or her attainment of material resources (i.e., value claiming in negotiations). However, even in competitive contexts, affective perspective taking which occurs with respect to

people's feelings builds relational and communal resources (Galinsky et al., 2008). Affective perspective taking motivates more cooperative behavior and leads to higher joint gains (Galinsky et al., 2008).

Less is known about appraisal-related perspective taking. However, because cognitive appraisals are central to understanding people's emotional experiences (Smith & Ellsworth, 1985), appraisal-related perspective taking should enhance the perspective takers ability to anticipate and understand the emotions of others. Thereby, it may also elicit more cooperative behavior from perspective takers. Thus, although the positive impact of cognitive perspective taking on relational resources may depend upon the competitiveness of the context, the positive impact of affective perspective taking (and appraisal-related perspective taking) may be less context dependent.

Measuring Perspective Taking Dimensions

I have introduced the construct of appraisal-related perspective taking as distinct from affective and cognitive perspective taking. Moreover, I have proposed distinct informational and anticipatory advantages of appraisal-related perspective taking. A first step in testing these theoretical assertions is developing a survey measure of appraisal-related perspective taking. In this section, I present data supporting a survey measure of appraisal-related perspective taking.

Procedure

One hundred and twenty-seven undergraduates from a large northeastern university were recruited through the university's online system to participate in a narrative study. A week prior to the narrative study, they filled out an online survey about their characteristic style of social interaction. This first survey, administered at Time 1, included the three measures of perspective taking discussed below.

Measures

Three-item measures of cognitive, affective, and appraisal-related perspective taking were included in the Time 1 survey (see Appendix 35.1 for items). Responses were captured on a five-point Likert scales ranging from 1 = not at all characteristic to 5 = very characteristic. The cognitive perspective taking items were taken from Davis' (1983, 1996) measure of perspective taking. The affective perspective taking items included the one perspective taking item from Davis' scale that was purely affective and two items based on the affective perspective taking directions used by Batson et al. (1995) and Galinsky et al. (2008). The appraisal-related perspective taking scale included three items from Williams (2001b).[1]

Sample

After eliminating cases with missing data, analyses were performed on a final sample of 122 participants. Seventy-five percent were female and 25% were male. Eighty-six percent were born in the Unites States. Forty-eight percent were Caucasian, 33% were Asian, 7% were African American, and 6% were Latino or Hispanic. Six percent did not report their ethnicity or selected "other." Subjects received $15 for participating in both parts of the study (two surveys).

Analyses

Using Lisrel 8.72 (Jöreskog & Sorbom, 1997), I performed a confirmatory factor analysis using a fully-disaggregated structural equations model.

Descriptive Statistics

Descriptive statistics for the three measures of perspective taking appear in Table 35.1.

Confirmatory Factor Analysis Results

The proposed three-factor model fit well: χ^2 (24) = 22.45, p = 0.55, root mean square error of approximation (RMSEA) = 0.00, standardized root mean square residual (SRMR) = 0.03, comparative fit index (CFI) = 1.0. All factor loadings were significant and ranged from 0.77 to 0.86. To test the discriminant validity of the appraisal-related perspective taking scale, I analyzed several other models. I tested a one-factor model, in which all of the items loaded on the same general perspective taking factor (χ^2 (27) = 65.86, p = 0.00). The one-factor model fit significantly worse than the three-factor model: sequential chi-square difference test (SCDT) $\Delta\chi^2$ (3) = 43.41, p = 0.00. Next, I tested

models constraining the correlation between each two types of perspective taking to 1, where a correlation of 1 would indicate the factors were not distinct from one another. Sequential chi-square difference tests (Anderson & Gerbing, 1988; Kline, 2005) between the unconstrained three-factor model and a model constraining affective and cognitive perspective taking to a correlation of 1 (SCDT $\Delta\chi^2$ (1) = 10.53, p = 0.00); a model constraining affective and appraisal-related perspective taking to a correlation of 1 (SCDT $\Delta\chi^2$ (1) = 8.44, p = 0.00), and a model constraining appraisal-related and cognitive perspective taking to a correlation of 1 (SCDT $\Delta\chi^2$ (1) = 10.53, p = 0.00) were all highly significant. These results indicate that the different measures of perspective taking were in fact distinct.

Finally, I confirmed that all three types of perspective taking formed a higher-order construct (see Figure 35.1). A second-order factor, in which all three dimensions of perspective taking loaded onto a superordinate perspective taking factor fit well: χ^2 (24) = 22.45, p = 0.55, RMSEA = 0.00, CFI = 1.0, SRMR = 0.03. Appraisal-related perspective taking, affective perspective taking, and cognitive perspective taking all had significant relationships to the superordinate latent variable of perspective taking. The standardized parameter estimates were 0.95, 0.90, and 0.89, p <0.01, respectively.

In conclusion, these results support the contention that appraisal-related perspective taking, affective perspective taking, and cognitive perspective taking are three distinct dimensions of perspective taking.

Discussion

In this section, I presented a new three-item measure of appraisal-related perspective taking. I also used the instructions from well-validated experimental manipulations to develop a survey measure of affective perspective taking. The measure of appraisal-related perspective taking was correlated with, but

Table 35.1 Descriptive statistics and Pearson correlation table (Cronbach's α reliability coefficients along the diagonals)

	Mean	St. dev.	1	2	3
1. Appraisal-related Perspective Taking	3.6	.81	.77		
2. Affective Perspective Taking	3.7	.91	.71**	.88	
3. Cognitive perspective Taking	3.4	.88	.67**	.68**	.81

**p <0.01

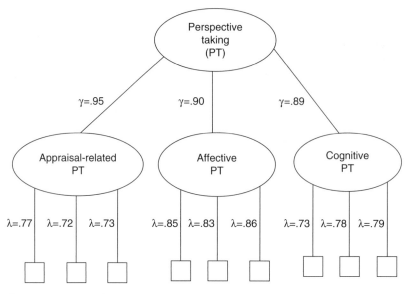

χ^2 (24)=22.45; p=.55; RMSEA=.00; CFI=1.00; RMSEA=.03

Fig. 35.1 Second-order factor of perspective taking (PT).

distinct from existing measures/manipulations of cognitive and affective perspective taking. Further, all three proposed subdimensions of perspective taking—appraisal-related, affective, and cognitive—formed a second-order factor of perspective taking. Although this is only a first step in developing and testing theoretical arguments related to appraisal-related perspective taking, it is a critical step for enabling additional research.

The measures presented here provide several opportunities for researchers. The measures of the perspective taking dimensions can be used to more distinctly capture the single dimension of perspective taking under investigation in a particular study. The individual measures of the dimensions also can be used as a manipulation check in experimental studies. These measures have also been successfully modified to investigate perspective taking with respect to a specific group (e.g., team members, doctors) and specific individuals (e.g., one's boss, assistant or team leader). Moreover, the theoretical reasons presented earlier suggest that the dimensions of perspective taking will have different influences on various outcome measures. The measures presented here may also allow researchers to amass enough empirical evidence to establish their differential relationships with outcome measures, despite the somewhat high correlations among the perspective taking dimensions (e.g., see Colquitt, Scott, & LePine, 2007, for a parallel example—a meta-analysis that

establishes the differential impact of the highly correlated dimensions of trustworthiness). Finally, the individual measures of the three dimensions of perspective taking can be aggregated to form a more comprehensive measure of perspective taking.

Additionally, recent research has begun to examine the nomological net of appraisal-related perspective taking. Appraisal-related perspective taking was found to be part of consultants' mental models of active trust building (Williams, 2001b). Knowledge workers' self-reported appraisal-related perspective taking was related to their bosses' perceptions of the workers' trustworthiness and performance (Williams, 2008). Additionally, appraisal-related perspective taking by knowledge workers was related to interpersonally sensitive and just behavior measured 1.5 years after appraisal-related perspective taking was measured (Williams, 2009).

Conclusion

This chapter used the lens of POS to address the growing interest and debate surrounding the role of perspective taking in organizational life. I asserted that perspective taking fosters kindness, understanding, and compassion—behaviors that Park and Peterson (2003) relate to the virtue of befriending others. I integrated research from the disciplines of sociology, communications, and psychology to provide insight into why, when, and how perspective taking facilitates the virtuous processes of positive interpersonal connections and trustworthy actions. Perspective taking motivates and enables positive interpersonal connections in three ways (Williams, 2008): by promoting interpersonal understanding, by strengthening social bonds, and by motivating compassionate actions. Perspective taking also influences trustworthy behavior in three ways (Williams, 2007, 2008): by motivating benevolent, trustworthy behavior; by allowing individuals to influence the emotions of others; and by facilitating proactive trustworthiness.

Finally, in this chapter, I introduced the importance of investigating different dimensions of perspective taking. I asserted that cognitive and affective perspective taking have very different outcomes in competitive contexts. I then introduced the importance of appraisal-related perspective taking. Appraisal-related perspective taking enables people to engage in proactive attempts to act with compassion and influence the emotional experiences of others. I provided support for a three-dimensional measure of perspective taking that can be used to further research the outcomes related to perspective taking.

Although the potential importance of perspective taking for a variety of interpersonal processes within organizations seems clear, there is currently a dearth of work on perspective taking in organizational contexts. In the next section, I discuss practical implications of perspective taking for organizations and then highlight three promising areas for organizational research on perspective taking.

Practical Implications

Because perspective taking requires cognitive effort (Rossnagel, 2000), cognitive constraints such as time pressure and work load are likely to inhibit perspective taking at exactly the times when it would be most helpful to understand how one's actions will impact others. Thus, reaping the benefits of perspective taking may require managerial foresight. Managers not only need to sponsor professional development seminars that enable knowledge workers to understand the benefits of perspective taking, but also encourage the use of perspective taking during slack times. Establishing perspective taking as a well-learned response to interpersonal interactions will support the effective use of perspective taking during the most critical times in an organization—when people are under pressure.

On a cautionary note, managers need to be cognizant of the type of perspective taking they encourage among their subordinates. Although cognitive perspective taking can increase understanding across functional boundaries (Boland & Tenaski, 1995) and decrease some cognitive bias (Epley et al., 2006; Galinsky & Mussweiler, 2001), it also has the potential to increase competitive behavior (Epley et al., 2006). In contrast, affective perspective taking is associated with showing concern, facilitating collaboration, and higher joint gains across contexts (e.g., Galinsky et al., 2008; Parker & Axtell, 2001). Moreover, people may be less able to use affective perspective taking to take advantage of others or behave maliciously because affective perspective taking is more likely to elicit empathic concern, and increased valuing of others' welfare. In turn, these prosocial processes would serve to undercut malevolent intentions.

Future Directions

Work on perspective taking in organizational settings is on the rise (e.g., Parker et al., 2008). Although there are many interesting directions for future research, I have selected three research areas that capture issues that are central to understanding both the role of perspective taking in organizations and the importance of perspective taking for POS. In this section, I argue that future research would benefit from investigating the implications of perspective taking for high-quality connections (HQCs), gratitude, and trust repair.

Perspective Taking and High-quality Connections

Perspective taking has a variety of positive interpersonal outcomes. It promotes interpersonal understanding (Fussell & Krauss, 1992), strengthens social bonds (Galinsky et al., 2005), fosters emotionally positive interactions (Blumer, 1969), motivates compassionate actions (Batson et al., 1995), and promotes trustworthy behavior (Williams, 2008). These positive processes are likely to contribute to HQCs. High-quality connections are important both because they contribute to personal health and well-being and because they facilitate the coordination of work (Dutton & Heaphy, 2003). Dutton and Heaphy (2003) define HQCs as relationships with three characteristics: They are high in emotional carrying capacity (i.e., the ability to weather high levels of emotional traffic), tensility (the capacity to withstand strain), and connectivity (i.e., generativity and openness to new ideas and influences, Dutton & Heaphy, 2003, p. 266). Perspective taking is likely to be particularly relevant for tensility and connectivity. In terms of tensility, perspective taking is likely to enable people to withstand the strain of interpersonal conflict. Imagining another person's perspective during a conflict situation and allowing oneself to feel empathic concern for a person who is blocking one's goals or reducing one's well-being should facilitate communication and compassionate action. Communication and compassionate action, in turn, should allow the relationship to withstand higher levels of strain than a relationship in which neither person engages in perspective taking. In terms of connectivity, the very act of perspective taking signals a degree of openness to new ideas and influences because the perspective taker wishes to understand how situations appear from a different point of view. Future research would benefit from additional exploration of how different dimensions of perspective taking can lead to and maintain HQCs.

Perspective Taking and Gratitude

In addition to compassion and trustworthiness, perspective taking is likely to foster other interpersonal virtues, such as gratitude and justice. Gratitude, for example, "is the positive recognition of benefits received" (Emmons, 2003, p. 82). It requires that a recipient recognizes that a gift or benefit was freely given. Gratitude is associated with positive relational outcomes, such as helping one's benefactor. Perspective taking facilitates gratitude because it enables individuals to understand the intentions of their benefactor and to recognize the value of the gift from the benefactor's point of view. Because of the potential for perspective taking to enhance people's ability to recognize the benefits bestowed by others, the relationship between perspective taking and gratitude represents a potentially fruitful area of research for organizational scholars.

Perspective Taking and Trust Violations

Trust repair is by nature a reactive process. Both the transgressor and the victim must respond to a violation that has already occurred. Future research, however, should explore how perspective taking can influence elements of the trust repair process in a proactive manner. I propose that perspective taking can influence the manner in which both transgressors and victims approach trust repair in three ways (Williams, forthcoming). First, perspective taking can influence the transgressor's ability to identify asymmetric trust breaks (those initially perceived by the victim only). Second, perspective taking should enhance both parties' ability to reduce negative affect and perceive factors mitigating attributions of

responsibility. Finally, because perspective taking can help victims to perceive mitigating factors, it can influence the victim's ability to approach trust repair in a more effective and socially complex manner than simply airing his or her grievances from his or her own perspective. Thus, perspective taking may play a central, but yet unexplored, role in effective trust repair.

Note

1. This chapter reports the discriminant validity of appraisal-related perspective taking from other dimensions of perspective taking. Please see Williams (2001b) for information on measure development, pretesting of the measure, and the discriminant validity of this appraisal-related perspective taking measure from other relational constructs such as trust and liking.

References

Anderson, J.C., & Gerbing, D.W. (1988). Structural equation modeling in practice: A review and recommended two-step approach. *Psychological Bulletin, 103*(3), 411–423.

Ashford, S.J., & Tsui, A.S. (1991). Self-regulation for managerial effectiveness: The role of active feedback seeking. *Academy of Management Journal, 34*(2), 251–280.

Batson, C.D. (1998). Altruism and prosocial behavior. In D.T. Gilbert, S.T. Fiske, & G. Lindzey (Eds.), *The handbook of social psychology* (pp. 282–316). New York: McGraw-Hill.

Batson, C.D., Polycarpou, M.P., Harmon-Jones, E., Imhoff, H.J., Mitchener, E.C., Bednar, L., et al. (1997). Empathy and attitudes: Can feeling for a member of a stigmatized group improve feelings toward the group? *Journal of Personality and Social Psychology, 72*(1), 105–118.

Batson, C.D., Sager, K., Garst, E., Kang, M., Rubchinsky, K., & Dawson, K. (1997). Is empathy-induced helping due to self-other merging? *Journal of Personality and Social Psychology, 73*(3), 495–509.

Batson, C.D., Turk, C.L., Shaw, L.L., & Klein, T.R. (1995). Information function of empathic emotion: Learning that we value the other's welfare. *Journal of Personality and Social Psychology, 68*(2), 300–313.

Blumer, H. (1969). *Symbolic interactionism: Perspective and method.* Englewood Cliffs, NJ: Prentice-Hall.

Boland, R.J., & Tenkasi, R.V. (1995). Perspective making and perspective-taking in communities of knowing. *Organization Science, 6*(4), 350–372.

Brown, P., & Levinson, S.C. (1987). *Politeness: Some universals in language usage.* Cambridge, UK: Cambridge University Press.

Burt, R.S., & Knez, M. (1996). Trust and third-party gossip. In R.M. Kramer, & T.R. Tyler (Eds.), *Trust in organizations: Frontiers of theory and research* (pp. 68–89). London: Sage.

Child, J., & Möllering, G. (2003). Contextual confidence and active trust development in the Chinese business environment. *Organization Science, 14,* 69–80.

Collins, R. (1990). Stratification, emotional energy, and the transient emotions. In T.D. Kemper (Ed.), *Research agendas in the sociology of emotions* (pp. 27–57). Albany, NY: State University of New York Press.

Colquitt, J.A., Scott, B.A., & Lepine, J.A. (2007). Trust, trustworthiness, and trust propensity: A meta-analytic test of their unique relationships with risk taking and job performance. *Journal of Applied Psychology, 92*(4), 909–927.

Davis, M.H. (1983). Measuring individual differences in empathy: Evidence for a multidimensional approach. *Journal of Personality and Social Psychology, 44*(1), 113–126.

Davis, M.H. (1996). *Empathy: A social psychological approach.* Madison, WI: Westview Press.

Dunn, J., & Schweitzer, M. (2005). Feeling and believing: The influence of emotion on trust. *Journal of Personality and Social Psychology, 88*(6), 736–748.

Dutton, J.E., & Heaphy, E.D. (2003). The power of high-quality connections. In K.S. Cameron, J.E. Dutton, & R.E. Quinn (Eds.), *Positive organizational scholarship: Foundations of a new discipline* Vol. 3 (pp. 263–278). San Francisco: Berrett-Koehler Publishers.

Eisenberg, N., & Miller, P.A. (1987). Empathy and prosocial behavior. *Psychological Bulletin, 101,* 91–119.

Ellsworth, P.C. (1991). Some implication of cognitive appraisal theories of emotion. In K.T. Strongman (Ed.), *International review of studies on emotion* Vol. 1 (pp. 143–161). New York: John Wiley & Sons Ltd.

Ellsworth, P.C., & Scherer, K.R. (2003). Appraisal processes in emotion. In R.J. Davidson, H.H. Goldsmith, & K.R. Scherer (Eds.), *Handbook of affective sciences* (pp. 572–595). New York and Oxford: Oxford University Press.

Emmons, R.A. (2003). Acts of gratitude in organizations. In K.S. Cameron, J.E. Dutton, & R.E. Quinn (Eds.), *Positive organizational scholarship* (pp. 81–93). San Francisco: Berrett-Koehler Publishers.

Epley, N., Caruso, E.M., & Bazerman, M.H. (2006). When perspective taking increases taking: reactive egoism in social interaction. *Journal of Personality and Social Psychology, 91*(5), 872–889.

Folkman, S. (1984). Personal control and stress and coping processes: A theoretical analysis. *Journal of Personality and Social Psychology, 46,* 839–852.

Fussell, S.R., & Krauss, R.M. (1992). Coordination of knowledge in communication: Effects of speakers' assumptions about what others know. *Journal of Personality and Social Psychology, 62*(3), 378–391.

Galinsky, A.D., Ku, G., & Wang, C.S. (2005). Perspective-taking and self-other overlap: Fostering social bonds and facilitating social coordination. *Group Processes and Intergroup Relations, 8*(2), 109–124.

Galinsky, A.D., Maddux, W., Gilin, D., & White, J.B. (2008). Why it pays to get inside the head of your opponent: The differential effects of perspective taking and empathy in strategic interactions. *Psychological Science, 19*(4), 378–384.

Galinsky, A.D., & Mussweiler, T. (2001). First offers as anchors: The role of perspective-taking and negotiator focus. *Journal of Personality and Social Psychology, 81*(4), 657–669.

Galinsky, A.D., Wang, C.S., & Ku, G. (2008). Perspective-takers behave more stereotypically. *Journal of Personality and Social Psychology, 95*(2), 404–419.

Goffman, E. (1967). *Interaction ritual: Essays in face-to-face behavior.* Garden City, NY: Anchor Books.

Grant, A.M., & Ashford, S.J. (2008). The dynamics of proactivity at work. *Research in Organizational Behavior, 28,* 3–34.

Jones, G.R., & George, J.M. (1998). The experience and evolution of trust: Implications for cooperation and teamwork. *Academy of Management Review, 23,* 531–546.

Jöreskog, K.G., & Sorbom, D. (1997). *LISREL 8: User's reference guide* (2nd ed.). Chicago: Scientific Software International, Inc.

Kline, R.B. (2005). *Principles and practices of structural equation modeling* (2nd ed.). New York: Guilford Press.

Krauss, R.M., & Fussell, S.R. (1991). Perspective taking in communication: Representations of others' knowledge in reference. *Social Cognition, 9,* 2–24.

Lazarus, R.S., & Folkman, S. (1984). *Stress, appraisal and coping.* New York: Springer.

Lewicki, R.J., & Bunker, B.B. (1996). Developing and maintaining trust in working relationships. In R.M. Kramer, & T.R. Tyler (Eds.), *Trust in organizations: Frontiers of theory and research* (pp. 114–139). London: Sage.

Lilius, J.M., Kanov, J., & Dutton, J.E. (2011). Compassion revealed: What we know about compassion at work (and where we need to know more). In K.S.Cameron & G.M.Spreitzer (Eds.), *The Oxford handbook of positive organizational scholarship.* New York: Oxford University Press.

Mayer, R.C., Davis, J.H., & Schoorman, F.D. (1995). An integrative model of organizational trust. *Academy of Management Review, 20,* 709–734.

Mead, G.H. (1934). *Mind, self, and society.* Chicago: University of Chicago Press.

Mishra, A.K., & Mishra, K.E. (2011). Positive organizational scholarship and trust in leaders. In K.S. Cameron & G.M. Spreitzer (Eds.), *The Oxford handbook of positive organizational scholarship.* New York: Oxford University Press.

Morrison, E.W., & Phelps, C.C. (1999). Taking charge at work: extra-role efforts to initiate workplace change. *Academy of Management Journal, 42*(4), 403–419.

Park, N., & Peterson, C.M. (2003). Virtues and organizations. In K.S. Cameron, J.E. Dutton, & R.E. Quinn (Eds.), *Positive organizational scholarship: Foundations of a new discipline* Vol. 1 (pp. 33–47). San Francisco: Berrett-Koehler Publishers, Inc.

Parker, S.K., Atkins, P.W., & Axtell, C.M. (2008). Building better work places through individual perspective taking: A fresh look at a fundamental human process. In G. Hodgkinson, & K. Ford (Eds.), *International review of industrial and organizational psychology* Vol. 32 (pp. 149–196). Chichester, UK: Wiley.

Parker, S.K., & Axtell, C.M. (2001). Seeing another viewpoint: Antecedents and outcomes of employee perspective taking. *Academy of Management Journal, 44,* 1085–1100.

Parker, S.K., Williams, H.M., & Turner, N. (2006). Modeling the antecedents of proactive behavior at work. *Journal of Applied Psychology, 91*(3), 636–652.

Ring, P.S., & Van de Ven, A.H. (1994). Developmental processes of cooperative interorganizational relationships. *Academy of Management Review, 19,* 90–118.

Rossnagel, C. (2000). Cognitive load and perspective-taking: Applying the automatic-controlled distinction to verbal communication. *European Journal of Social Psychology, 30*(3), 429–445.

Shapiro, D., Sheppard, B.H., & Cheraskin, L. (1992). Business on a handshake. *The Negotiation Journal, 8,* 365–377.

Smith, C.A., & Ellsworth, P.C. (1985). Patterns of cognitive appraisal in emotion. *Journal of Personality and Social Psychology, 48,* 813–838.

Van Lange, P.A. (2008). Does empathy trigger only altruistic motivation? How about selflessness or justice? *Emotion, 8*(6), 766–774.

Whitener, E.M., Brodt, S.E., Korsgaard, M.A., & Werner, J.M. (1998). Managers as initiators of trust: An exchange relationship framework for understanding managerial trustworthy behavior. *Academy of Management Review, 23*(3), 513–530.

Williams, M. (2001a). In whom we trust: Group membership as an affective context for trust development. *Academy of Management Review, 26*(3), 377–396.

Williams, M. (2001b). *Seeing through the client's eyes: Building interpersonal trust and cooperation across organizational boundaries.* Unpublished doctoral dissertation, University of Michigan, Ann Arbor.

Williams, M. (2007). Building genuine trust through interpersonal emotion management: A threat regulation model of trust and collaboration across boundaries. *Academy of Management Review, 32*(2), 595–621.

Williams, M. (2008, August). *Seeing through other's eyes: Appraisal-related perspective taking, trustworthiness, and performance.* Paper presented at the annual meeting of the American Sociological Association, Boston, MA.

Williams, M. (2009, August). *Justice is in the eye of the beholder: How does perspective taking facilitate interpersonal justice?* Paper presented at the annual meeting of the Academy of Management, Chicago, IL.

Williams, M. (in press). Building and Re-Building Trust: Why Perspective Taking Matters. In R. Kramer, & T.L. Pittinsky (Eds.), *Restoring Trust: Enduring Challenges and Emerging Answers.* New York: Oxford University Press.

Wrzesniewski, A., & Dutton, J.E. (2001). Crafting a job: Revisioning employees as active crafters of their work. *Academy of Management Review, 26*(2), 179–201.

Zucker, L.G. (1986). Production of trust: Institutional sources of economic structure, 1840–1920. In B. M. Staw & L.L. Cummings (Eds.), *Research in organization behavior* (pp. 53–111). Greenwich, CT: JAI Press.

Appendix 35.1

Perspective Taking Items by Dimension

Appraisal-related Perspective Taking Items
- When dealing with others, I try to imagine how my actions will affect things that are important to them.
- When interacting with others, I try to understand why particular issues hold emotional significance for them.
- When interacting with others, I try to look at things from their perspective.

Affective Perspective Taking
- I try to understand how other people are feeling.
- When interacting with others, I think about how I would feel if I were in their place.
- I try to think about what emotions other people may be feeling when I interact with them.

Cognitive Perspective Taking
- I try to look at everybody's side of a disagreement before I make a decision.
- I believe that there are two sides to every question, and try to look at them both.
- When I'm upset at someone, I usually try to "put myself in his shoes" for a while.

(coefficient α = 0.77; Williams, 2001b)
(coefficient α = 0.88; Davis, 1983; Batson et al., 1995; Galinsky et al., 2008)
(coefficient α = 0.81; Davis, 1983)

The Laughter Advantage

Cultivating High-quality Connections and
Workplace Outcomes Through Humor

Cecily D. Cooper *and* John J. Sosik

Abstract

Humor can be a powerful form of communication in organizations, leading to positive emotions and cognitions, high-quality interactions, and enhanced managerial and business unit performance. Humor is a valuable character strength that allows individuals to transcend mundane work, stressful situations, hardships, and the imperfections of human beings. By using humor, individuals can optimize transient encounters, as well as enhance the quality of ongoing relationships. In this chapter, we discuss how workplace humor facilitates cooperation, relationship building, creativity, and the negotiation of positive workplace identities. We conclude with practical suggestions for managers who wish to harness the potential of humor and recommendations for scholars interested in pursuing research in this fruitful area.

Keywords: Humor, joking, cooperation, creativity, leadership, ingratiation, negotiations, coping, psychological capital

I think you have got to have [humor at work], because it is such an important human emotion. I can't imagine a work environment or a living environment without humor present. (Assistant to the Superintendent of Schools for a county in Florida, Male, 51[1])

I think that when management utilizes [humor] that it can increase teamwork and comfort zone and an acceptance level. . . . I just think it's unbelievably important. And I can't imagine working in a place where [humor] couldn't be used on a regular basis. (President of a small consulting firm, Female, 46)

As these quotes illustrate, humor is an essential part of life, playing a pivotal role in the enjoyment of day-to-day life, including time spent at work. Although work is a purposeful, goal-oriented activity, people do not achieve these goals as mechanized actors. Rather, organizational members must navigate a sea of mental and emotional challenges by using various tactics that allow them to not only cope with daily stressors, but also thrive as individuals and as a collective. Humor is essential for achieving this end as it allows people to transcend mundane work, stressful situations, hardships, and the imperfections of human beings. Moreover, workplaces that foster environments in

which humor is accepted practice can expect not only more satisfied employees, but also more productive ones. Humor facilitates the attainment of various desired outcomes, including creativity (O'Quin & Derks, 1997), customer relations (Bergeron & Vachon, 2008), organizational citizenship behaviors (Cooper, 2002), and workgroup performance (Avolio, Howell, & Sosik, 1999).

Humor, as a topic of study, falls squarely within the domain of positive organizational scholarship (POS) and has been identified as a character strength reflecting the virtue of transcendence in the positive psychology literature (Peterson & Seligman, 2004).

Humor involves a positive state that can be generative, resulting in resilience, positive relationships, and modes of flourishing. Accordingly, we find it surprising that investigation of this topic is, thus far, noticeably absent from the burgeoning area of POS research (cf. Cameron, Dutton, & Quinn, 2003). Since existing research on humor implies that it is an enabler of the positive individual and organizational outcomes of interest to POS, additional theoretical and empirical research investigating this area is warranted. To illustrate the relevance of this topic for POS, as well as to stimulate thought on humor by POS scholars, this chapter will review certain areas in which we see significant overlap between the study of humor and POS. Specifically, we will discuss how humor leads to cooperation, high-quality relationships, creativity, and the creation of positive meaning at work. We begin this discussion by defining "humor" for the purpose of this review. Finally, we conclude the chapter with recommended directions for future research and practical suggestions for managers who are passionate about humor.

Humor

> I enjoy my work, because there's humor there. (Real estate agent, Female, 62)

The term *humor* can have a variety of different meanings. Some researchers conceptualize humor as a trait and study "sense of humor" as an aspect of personality, an individual difference in the propensity to create and appreciate humorous stimuli (Martin & Lefcourt, 1984; Mindess, 1971). Consistent with this perspective, positive psychologists view humor as a character strength that reflects a form of playfulness involving a predisposition to laugh and tease, bring mirth to others, and make jokes (Peterson & Seligman, 2004). Others consider it a state, a temporary condition that involves cheerfulness or mirth (Hehl & Ruch, 1985; Martin, 2007). Researchers taking this perspective are usually interested in identifying outcomes, such as liking or creativity, which may be facilitated by an induced humorous state and investigate these questions in a laboratory using cartoons or video clips to induce a humorous state (e.g., Isen & Daubman, 1984). Management scholars have most frequently taken another perspective, studying humor as a behavioral expression in a social setting, a communication shared between people. This perspective assumes that the expression of humor sometimes, but not always, results in a humorous state, depending on whether the parties involved enjoyed the humor.

However, even humor scholarship that falls within this latter perspective, similarly considering humor as a behavioral expression, includes divergent conceptualizations of humor. As Malone (1980) acknowledges, humor can have a dark side, with the ability to alienate coworkers and leave employers legally liable (Leap & Smeltzer, 1984). Cooper's discussion of humor also acknowledges this double-edged sword: "humor . . . has the power to increase liking and link parties together, or, conversely, decrease liking and push them apart" (2008, p. 1103). We believe that even some negative forms of humor can ultimately lead to positive individual and organizational outcomes. For example, if an unsatisfied customer uses crude humor that offends an employee, it might evoke self-reflection by the employee as to how the comment relates to the quality of service provided. It might also evoke compassion on the part of the employee for the customer because of the inequity, and ultimately lead to forgiveness for the wisecrack and a higher-quality employee–customer relationship in the future. However, as clarified in the next paragraph, a thorough discussion of negative humor falls outside the scope of this chapter. Other research, interested in the benefits of humor, has restricted its focus to positive aspects, such as whether an individual "uses amusing stories to defuse conflicts" and "uses wit to make friends of the opposition" (Avolio et al., 1999, p. 221). In a recent practitioner-focused review, Romero and Cruthirds also "assume that humor is funny to all participants in the humor exchange" in order to elaborate the desirable outcomes associated with humor (2006, p. 59).

Given the competing, but equally viable, treatments of this concept, how should humor be defined for inclusion within the realm of POS? Some key boundary characteristics of the POS domain are informative. First, POS is concerned with states, which can be induced and changed, rather than traits, which are not open to development (Luthans, 2002). Second, these states must be positive in nature, resulting in generative mechanisms that enable human flourishing (Roberts, 2006). Thus, studying inherently negative humor is not consistent with the positive motives typically associated with POS, and may not be informative to this area, nor is "sense of humor" of interest. For the purposes of POS, then, we define humor as *any event purposely shared by an agent (e.g., an employee or manager) with another individual (i.e., a target) that is intended to be amusing to the target and that engenders positive emotions in the target, the agent, and any other observers.* This definition is modeled after that previously offered by Cooper (2005) but differs in that the effect of the humor in the current definition is specified as being inherently positive for all parties involved. Notably, the definition encompasses any form of humor that is positively motivated and has the potential to elicit a positive reaction (e.g., sarcasm, witticisms, and puns). Research indicates that even forms of humor that may seem negative, such as putdown humor, can actually have positive benefits in certain contexts (Scogin & Pollio, 1980; Terrion & Ashforth, 2002).

Now that our use of the term humor is clarified, we will review the role of humor in facilitating four outcomes of interest to POS researchers: cooperation, high-quality relations, creativity, and finding positive meaning (see Martin, 2007, and Peterson & Seligman, 2004 for more general reviews of humor research from the field of psychology).

Cooperation

> I've been in meetings where things have gotten to an incredibly tense moment—and a well-delivered, humorous statement was like a wave that cleansed the room of the tension and delivered a fresh, tension-free space to continue discussions.
> (Susan Podziba, experienced mediator, as quoted in Forester, 2004, p. 222)

Humor's role in close relationships is well-documented within management research (refer to the next section for discussion), but less attention has been paid to the role of humor in transient encounters or with people who have an arm's-length (rather than close) relationship. However, humor can have notable consequences even for passing interactions, and these types of interactions should be of equal interest to management scholars since they reflect the context in which much business is conducted or services are rendered. Organizational members often have to make requests of administrative personnel, colleagues in other departments, and even people outside of the organization to accomplish their tasks (Brief & Motowidlo, 1986). Even if people are acquainted, they may not have the type of relationship that invites reciprocity, and their goals may not be interdependent. Thus, an organization's success often rests on the ability of employees to influence others to cooperate in the accomplishment of goals (i.e., help them out) (George & Brief, 1992).

But how does humor lead others to cooperate? A great deal of agreement exists within the management literature that "expressed positive emotions are a tool of social influence because encounters with a friendly person are positively reinforcing" (Rafaeli & Sutton, 1991, p. 750). People who express positive emotions at work, including humor, are more likely to receive assistance and support (Staw, Sutton, & Pelled, 1994). As described in Frederickson's (2001) broaden-and-build theory, sharing a positive emotion can "broaden people's momentary thought–action repertoires" and build their personal resources, including the social resources essential for cooperation (p. 219).

Positive humor can also be used to influence others to comply with requests because of humor's ability to ingratiate (Cooper, 2005). In a group setting, collectively constructed humor can facilitate collaboration (Rogerson-Revell, 2007). Humor gets people in a good mood, which then primes them to be more helpful or conciliatory. This tactic may even be used to win over others who are inclined *not* to cooperate because of previous negative interactions or negative expectations (e.g., because of competing interests). For example, Baron and Ball (1974) found that humor could reduce subjects' aggression toward people who previously offended them. As a state, humor is incompatible with feelings of anger and aggression. Thus, inducing a humorous state can promote the likelihood of positive interactions, since humor can function to build social resources, ingratiate, and/or counter feelings of aggression.

Although cooperation is important for many types of encounters (e.g., information seeking) and between various types of parties (e.g., coworkers), two streams of research specifically focus on humor's role in igniting cooperation. The first includes research on the use of humor in negotiations. Negotiators must cooperate if they want to achieve the preferred outcomes associated with integrative bargaining (Pruitt, 1981). The second deals with customer service encounters. Since customers are coproducers of the service experience, eliciting their cooperation is necessary to optimize the transaction (Crosby, Evans, & Cowles, 1990). Research demonstrates the efficacy of humor for enabling both of these outcomes.

Negotiations

Results of a number of laboratory studies suggest that humor, used appropriately and strategically during a negotiation, can influence the parties to behave more collaboratively. Humor can be used in negotiations to diffuse tension, soften the impact of offensive comments, introduce a troublesome issue, and promote one's viewpoint in a charming way (Vuorela, 2005). After being exposed to humor, negotiators in a simulated business scenario reported a greater inclination to use constructive modes of conflict resolution (rather than avoidance) and behave collaboratively with the other party in a future negotiation (Baron, 1984). In another experiment, negotiators who were exposed to humor used fewer contentious tactics when bargaining and were more likely to understand the other parties' preferences, resulting in negotiation outcomes with a greater overall benefit for both parties (Carnevale & Isen, 1986). Subsequent field studies validate and extend results reported in the aforementioned experiments.

Interviews with professional mediators imply that, in their position of formal authority, mediators can (carefully) use humor to achieve a better process and outcome for all parties (Forester, 2004). Although people are adversaries in a bargaining situation, humor can give everyone a shared experience, causing them to connect, even if that connection is only momentary. This connection can, then, lead them to reduce competitive conduct. Humor during mediations can also disarm parties from thinking only about their own idea for a solution and, instead, construct additional, more integrative solutions to the disagreement (Forester, 2004). Analysis of recorded business negotiations finds that joking is associated with both relational discourse, as well as serious, substantive issues (Adelsward & Oberg, 1998). For substantive issues, humor is most likely to occur for areas of negotiation that are important but problematic, such as the negotiation of price. The researchers observed humor and laughter could be used to save face, avoiding embarrassment while deflecting positions of the other party. An observational study of a salesman visiting a photographic shop generated similar conclusions. Specifically, the store manager (i.e., the sales prospect) initiated humor much more frequently than the salesman in order to rebuke the salesman's attempts while mitigating interactional difficulties (Mulkay, Clark, & Pinch, 1993).

Humor can even be used effectively during multicultural business negotiations (Vuorela, 2005). Granted, humor does not always transcend cultures readily. People of different nationalities may appreciate different types of humor, or humor can be difficult to understand for non-native speakers of a language. Even so, humor can be used to break down cultural barriers. For example, Vuorela observed that participants in a sales negotiation joked about their own idiosyncratic national characteristics, and this self-focused ethnic humor allowed them to acknowledge differences while building common ground in the negotiation: "the buyers and sellers used cooperative humor to work together as a team" (2005, p. 127).

Customer Relations

Humor leads to cooperation in service encounters just as it does in negotiations. Employees who experience humor in the workplace report greater job satisfaction, which can lead to higher perceptions of service quality that is reliable, responsive, and empathic. In the financial services industry, research finds that the use of humor by financial advisors is related to client satisfaction and perceived service quality (Bergeron & Vachon, 2008). Advisors who use humor during consultations leave their clients feeling "pleasantly surprised" by the service experience (Bergeron, Roy, & Fallu, 2008).

However, most research on humor in service encounters has been conducted within medical settings, studying the interactions of physicians and patients. Cooperation is particularly important in this context since patients are coparticipants in the service encounters, and their compliance affects the general quality of services generated, in terms of medical treatment or therapeutic intervention (Walsh, Leahy, & Litt, 2009). However, gaining the cooperation of patients can be challenging, because, when faced with a medical problem, the emotions of patients and their families can run high. The "customers" often enter an interaction with feelings of anxiety, fear, or even despondence (Locke, 1996). Yet, humor is uniquely suited to temporarily dispel these types of feelings, thus creating a welcome distraction.

In fact, interviews with physicians and other care providers indicate that physicians use humor as an "emotion management" tool "to build rapport, to calm and reassure, or to reduce embarrassment . . ." (Francis, Monahan, & Berger, 1999, p. 172). The case of Hunter "Patch" Adams, portrayed in a film by Robin Williams, and his Gesundheit! Institute of holistic medicine serves as an example of a physician using humor to achieve such goals (Sosik, 2006). Observing physicians in a pediatric hospital permitted Locke (1996) to uncover how this emotion management works: Humor redefines the situation, substituting positive emotions for negative emotions. Initiating this switch allows physicians to achieve their interaction goals with the patient, eliciting "client cooperation with the service delivery process"

(Locke, 1996, p. 40). Overall, many types of humor can be used in emotion management. In the aforementioned studies, physicians' humor took a variety of forms, including very spontaneous jokes, jokes of a particular type that are used repeatedly (e.g., good news–bad news jokes), teasing, and, with young patients, everything from puppeteering to peek-a-boo games (Francis et al., 1999; Locke, 1996; Walsh et al., 2009). In sum, humor served as an effective social lubricant in these transient encounters, but humor has benefits for more permanent relationships as well.

Relationship Building and Maintenance

> Humor really defines personal relationships. If you can interject appropriate humor, not only can you have fun in the workplace, but better relationships and better rapport with your coworkers. (Vice-president of a small construction company, Female, 45)

> When my boss jokes around with me, it makes me feel more comfortable around him. . . . It makes me feel like it's . . . not all business all the time [and] that we've got a relationship beyond the factual day-to-day business that we have to do. (Account manager for an entertainment management firm, Female, 33)

Humor is central to building and maintaining close workplace relationships, such as those between coworkers or manager–subordinate pairs. People are most likely to flourish when they build high-quality relationships because these connections affect how they feel about their jobs and their ability to carry out work, since most work is interdependent (Dutton & Heaphy, 2003; Gersick, Bartunek, & Dutton, 2000). High-quality leader–follower relationships that support interdependent work allow employees to develop their innate talents into character strengths as they strive toward human excellence (Sosik, 2006). Fortunately, the literature is replete with studies examining humor dynamics of workgroups and leaders (i.e., both horizontally and vertically directed interactions) that is informative to the issue of humor in workplace relations.

Coworker Relations

Humor is a common phenomenon among coworkers, who will often jointly construct humor sequences, building on one another's humorous comments (Holmes, 2006, 2007). Puns, slapstick, jokes, anecdotes, and teasing appear to be part of the socialization process that helps create bonds among employees (Vinton, 1989). Observational studies of workplace interactions are replete with accounts of employees using humor with other employees for any variety of reasons, including teasing them in order to get things done (Bradney, 1957; Collinson, 1988), dealing with stress (Parsons, Kinsman, Bosk, Sankar, & Ubel, 2001; Plester & Orams, 2008), or simply trying to alleviate boredom (Fine, 1988; Roy, 1960). The researchers often infer from these observations that the employees are able to construct and maintain "good relations with fellow workers" (Holmes, 2006, p. 26) through humor, which is a reasonable assumption but not directly tested through the research.

More conclusive evidence can be seen in a field study by Wanzer, Booth-Butterfield, and Booth-Butterfield (1996), finding that individuals who were perceived as more humorous (i.e., having a high "humor orientation") were judged to be more socially attractive by their acquaintances. A laboratory study by Fraley and Aron (2004) also tested and found a direct effect of humor on interpersonal feelings. Participants, who were same-sex strangers, worked in pairs on joint tasks that were prescreened as being particularly funny or not funny. Results indicated that sharing a humorous experience created greater feelings of closeness in initial encounters.

In sum, these studies indicate that humor can be prevalent among coworkers and facilitate positive relationships, but they do not address *why* this occurs. What is it about humor that brings people together? Recent theorizing suggests that the sharing of humor at work may affect relationship quality through any of three processes: affect-reinforcement (i.e., people are attracted to humorous others because they elicit positive affect), perceived similarity (i.e., people are attracted to others who find humor in similar things), or self-disclosure (i.e., by expressing humor, people are sharing a special type of information about themselves) (Cooper, 2008). Empirical research so far is scant but the laboratory study by Fraley and Aron (2004) offers some insight. The feelings of closeness that occurred in their study arose because humor served as a "distraction from the discomfort" (i.e., the awkwardness of an initial meeting) and "created self-expansion" (i.e., provided a new perspective to the situation). Interestingly, and contrary to speculation by Cooper (2008), humor in this experiment did not act through the process of self-disclosure, but this may have stemmed from a constraint placed on the amount of personal interaction that could occur during the experiment.

Further evidence that humor affects workplace relationships is available in studies of humor and groups. Duncan and Feisal's (1989) longitudinal study of 25 workgroups concluded that joking is a "social lubricant" that indirectly improves performance by improving group cohesiveness. Scogin and Pollio (1980) investigated the pattern and type of humor occurring in ongoing and temporary groups in various settings. Although they did not directly measure group cohesiveness, they observed that the amount and type of humor used in the groups depended on the level of familiarity among group members. Members of groups with a greater amount of history were more likely to target their humor at other group members, whereas in short-duration groups, humor would generally be undirected. Another notable observation dealt with the content of the humor: Groups used both negatively and positively toned remarks, but negatively toned humor was much more frequent in the ongoing, rather than temporary, groups. The authors speculate that "the percentage of negatively targeted remarks made by a group can be used as an unobtrusive estimate of group cohesiveness" (Scogin & Pollio, 1980, p. 849). Thus, group humor was a noticeable artifact of the amount of familiarity among group members, and the authors proposed this finding to have implications for group cohesiveness.

Recent research complements Scogin and Pollio (1980) by exploring *why* humor might impact relations among group members. Through observations and interviews of Canadian police officers in a 6-week executive development course, Terrion and Ashforth (2002) found that sharing humor (particularly putdown humor) helped the temporary group become a cohesive unit because the humor signaled growing trust and solidarity among members. To clarify, although putdowns can sometimes be used to purposefully disparage others, the officers in this study used this type of humor in a playful, positive manner, not to elevate their own status, but to "poke fun" at a target. Being the target of a putdown in this context meant that an individual was an integral part of the group and well-respected by the person expressing the humor (i.e., who knew the target could take the joke). The type of putdowns that were acceptable advanced over time from "putdowns of oneself to putdowns of shared identities, external groups, and finally, each other" (Terrion & Ashforth, 2002 p. 80). The putdowns reflected an informal rule structure that arose within the group and guided member behavior. By collectively adhering to these rules, the group furthered solidarity.

These findings are also consistent with Scogin and Pollio's (1980) contention that negatively toned humor, in this case putdown humor, often has positive effects for groups.

Leader–Subordinate Connections

Humor also enables relationships between people at different levels of an organization. This relationship building occurs because humor can inspire and challenge employees (Holmes & Marra, 2006), reduce stress in the workplace, and help employees understand management's concerns and vice versa (Davis & Kleiner, 1989). Some research has studied humor and leadership at an aggregate level, focusing on the effects that leader humor can have on groups of employees. For example, a study of principals at 50 high schools found that if teachers perceived their principal as having a good sense of humor, they expressed higher levels of loyalty to that principal (Burford, 1987).

Other research has studied humor vis-à-vis leadership style, focusing on the role of humor in transformational leadership. Transformational leaders are known for individualizing the needs of followers and attending to their development. Because of this relational focus, early research proposed that transformational leaders were likely to use humor, but did not find empirical support for this relationship (Dubinsky, Yammarino, & Jolson, 1995). However, subsequent research uncovered various relationships between leadership style, humor usage, and performance. Data collected from 115 leaders and their business units in a large Canadian financial institution indicated that transformational leadership was positively related to the use of humor, the use of humor by leaders had a positive main effect on individual and unit performance, and transformational leaders who used humor had units that performed better than leaders who did not use humor (Avolio, Howell, & Sosik, 1999). This study found that humor can be a useful tool for transformational leaders, although all leaders could not garner benefits from humor (e.g., contingent-reward leaders were worse off if they used humor).

Other research has taken a dyadic approach in studying leader humor. Survey research indicates that respondents who perceive their supervisors as using positive humor also perceive them as being higher on task and relationship behaviors and overall effectiveness (Decker & Rotondo, 2001). A slight variation of this method was used in surveying military cadets who were asked to think of someone in their past who was a particularly good or bad leader and answer a variety of questions about this leader. Results indicated that the cadets perceived good leaders as having more of a warm humorous style than they did bad leaders, even after controlling for ratings of leadership effectiveness on various dimensions (Priest & Swain, 2002). The authors then replicated these "humor and good leader" results in a second study, even after controlling for additional attributes. "In both studies, the relation between leadership effectiveness and warm humorous style was a very strong one" (Priest & Swain, 2002, p. 185).

Taken together, the prior studies indicate that leaders who use humor have higher-performing followers (Avolio et al., 1999), are perceived as exhibiting more relationship behaviors (Decker & Rotondo, 2001), and are more likely to be considered particularly good (rather than bad) leaders (Priest & Swain, 2002). These findings imply that leaders can build higher-quality relationships with their subordinates through humor, but they do not directly measure relationship quality per se. Addressing this question more directly, Cooper (2004) conducted a field study of managers and their direct reports, collecting matched survey responses to determine whether leader-reported humor usage was related to member-reported exchange quality (LMX). In fact, a significant relationship existed, even after controlling for alternative explanations, such as demographic similarity, relationship tenure, leader trait positive affect, and leader perspective taking.

Humor exchanges between leaders and subordinates do not always occur in a top-down fashion, however. Although leaders are known to set the norms for using humor (Coser, 1960), humor is a reciprocal, interactive event, and subordinates are active participants in this process (Holmes, 2006), often initiating humor. One of the most frequently cited reasons for subordinates to use humor with their managers is as a means of relaying sensitive information (Holmes, 2006; Ket De Vries, 1990). Some research on mid-level managers suggests that women are more likely to use humor for this reason than are men, to help them negotiate certain paradoxes of their identity. Instead of being direct, women managers offer feedback to their superiors through humor in order to balance the expectations associated with acting like a woman and acting like a manager (Martin, 2004). By using humor in relaying difficult information, subordinates are trying to preserve their relationship with their manager. Yet, subordinates can also use humor as a subversive tool, hiding behind the façade of humor to challenge management (Ket De Vries, 1990). Although managers could appreciate this use of humor as well, research on "jokers" indicates that subversive humor might accrue considerable risk. For example, people like the jokers they work with but do not see them as management material (Plester & Orams, 2008).

Creativity

> When things get very serious the creative juices that we need to create a good product don't exist. . . . I think, especially in my situation, sarcasm and sense of humor and fun . . . goes a long way to breaking down barriers between people . . . opening them up. And when they're opened up, then they really start getting creative, and when they really start getting creative we get more jobs, we keep our business going. Without creativity, we're pretty much dead in the water . . . and humor goes a long way to creating that situation. (Landscape architect, Male, 34)

As expressed by this landscape architect, creativity is essential across a variety of industries and can be a determinant of competitive advantage for an organization (Amabile, 1988). Accordingly, firms want to encourage the creativity of their employees. To a large extent, creativity is determined by personal characteristics, but creativity can also be influenced by contextual factors (Oldham & Cummings, 1996; Kahai, Sosik, & Avolio, 2003), and one factor of particular importance for creativity is humor. Peterson and Seligman (2004) pointed out that "the ability to create humor is correlated with . . . creativity" (p. 595). A notable body of research exists demonstrating humor's ability to facilitate creative performance (for a more general review of research on humor and creativity see O'Quin & Derks, 1997).

Exposure to humor has been shown to improve performance on a creativity test (Ziv, 1976), rating and sorting tasks (Isen & Daubman, 1984), and word association tests (Isen Johnson, Mertz, & Robinson, 1985, Study 2), all measures of creative thinking. Ziv (1976) speculated that the humor facilitated divergent thinking. Similarly, Isen and Daubman inferred that the positive affect induced through humor influences "the way in which cognitive material is categorized or grouped together" (1984, p. 1212). In a more direct test of the humor–creativity link, exposure to humor enhanced performance on a task requiring problem solving innovation (i.e., a building task) and could not be explained away as a result of arousal alone (i.e., affectless arousal) (Isen, Daubman, & Nowicki, 1987). The elated arousal resulting from humor "seems to lead to the kinds of thinking that enable people to solve problems that require ingenuity or innovation" (Isen et al., 1987, p. 1128). These results are consistent with Morreall's (1991) proposition that humor fosters creativity by enhancing mental flexibility, divergent thinking, and problem solving acuity.

However, humor is not always beneficial for performance. Belanger, Kirkpatrick, and Derks (1998) discovered that, although humor facilitated performance on creative (i.e., divergent) tasks, it actually hindered performance on noncreative (i.e., convergent) tasks for male subjects, uncovering an important boundary condition regarding humor's role in the creative process. In fact, humor may even *detract* from performance on convergent tasks.

A field study conducted by Holmes (2007) in a variety of professional organizations in New Zealand complements the aforementioned laboratory studies. Holmes (2007) noted that humor generated in meetings always seemed to provide a welcome mental break for participants, but could also help generate creative ideas for addressing the task at hand. Employees contested the status quo through humor and, in doing so, this stimulated creative thinking. Leaders often initiated the humor, but this tendency varied and "particular leaders foster different amounts and different types of humor" (Holmes, 2007, p. 533). That said, humor can also be useful even when creativity is not required. Humor benefits employees in professions that are not intrinsically interesting or challenging by infusing the work with the enjoyment or meaning that it lacks.

Finding Positive Meaning

> Even with our Committee General, when we're in a meeting—operations intelligence meeting that's top secret—and we're talking about people dying . . . we'll sometimes make a comment and all laugh. But [it is] not in a macabre way. Normally, it's just something we poke at each other to relieve the tension. I think, particularly in our profession, humor is just a way of letting off steam. (Upper level civilian employee in the U.S. Military, Male, 53)

Experiencing meaning at work is associated with better psychological and physical health. Employees create meaning through a sense-making process (Pratt & Ashforth, 2003) that is often not conducted in isolation, but socially constructed among individuals in work groups or departments (Weick, 1995), and humor plays a key role in this process (Tracy, Myers, & Scott, 2006). Humor is a vehicle through which organizational members can cope with undesirable aspects of their jobs and, in doing so, find a greater level of satisfaction in their work. Undesirable job characteristics can stem from aspects of the work itself (i.e., if the work lacks intrinsic motivators or involves "dirty" tasks) or from stigma associated with the occupation (i.e., if the public views the occupation as tainted). In fact, humor is so effective at helping employees transcend negative aspects of their jobs that newcomers are often socialized into organizations using humor to deal with the challenges of work (Parsons, Kinsman, Bosk, Sankar, & Ubel, 2001). For example, jokers help socialize newcomers by using workplace humor to help them to make sense of uncertain and stressful events. The role of the joker is to challenge management to see the folly in its initiatives, push the boundaries on what is generally accepted in the workplace, develop "fun" cultures, and provide comic relief (Plester & Orams, 2008).

Research linking humor to the creation of positive meaning at work can be classified into two related but distinct categories of outcomes. The preponderance of research in this area focuses on *collective coping*, studying how groups of employees use humor to deal with jobs (or aspects of jobs) that are not motivating as a result of boring or monotonous tasks, mundane work, unreasonable expectations, or the like (Collinson, 1988; Fine, 1988; Roy, 1960). More recent studies, however, have begun to link humor to the creation and maintenance of *positive workplace identities*. Employees required to do "dirty" tasks can use humor to negotiate preferred notions of identity, de-emphasizing the undesirable aspects of their jobs. Most identity maintenance activities occur among coworkers, focusing on the workers' feelings about their own occupation (Clair & Dufresne, 2004; Tracy et al., 2006). However, workers in tainted occupations can also use humor to manage their occupation's identity with clients and/or the general public (Ashforth, Kreiner, Clark, & Fugate, 2007).

Collective Coping

Research in psychology highlights the ability of humor to combat stress at the individual level (see Dixon, 1980, and Lefcourt, 2002 for reviews), but most research on humor and coping in organizations has focused on humor generated within a social setting and its collective advantage for all who are involved. Many of these studies take the form of participant observation in various workplace settings.

Roy (1960) worked with a small group of machine operators for 2 months, taking detailed notes of the group members' interactions and how these interactions affected the work experience. The tasks required were simple and repetitive, and the group worked in relative isolation from other employees and management. Roy (1960) observed that the workers were able to combat the monotony of meaningless work through the use of humor and play at regular times throughout each workday, interactions that he also began to anticipate eagerly. Many of the regular humor sequences were simple, involving patterns of teasing or practical jokes, but they added a source of enjoyment to the long days. Roy (1960) did not believe the humor necessarily enhanced the productivity of the group, but it enriched the job.

Fine (1988) conducted an ethnographic study of the use of humor and play among restaurant workers and, similar to Roy (1960), Fine found that restaurant employees collectively participated in play activities and humor expression to create more enjoyment in their work. The primary difference, however, stemmed from how employees fit humor into their work. Cooks have very intense pressure for a relatively short part of their shift (peak dining hours) and, during this time, the work is sufficiently challenging to require and maintain the cooks' interest. However, the remainder of the time (nonpeak hours occurring before and after the "rush"), the cooks have very little work to do, and this is when they use humor and practical jokes (e.g., asking a new employee to get a can of steam from the pantry). In sum, busyness varied for the restaurant staff, and the use of humor varied inversely to the demands imposed by work (Fine, 1988). Thus, humor did not necessarily take employees away from required tasks, as with the machine operators (Roy, 1960). Other studies conducted within factories (Collinson, 1988) and department stores (Bradney, 1957) also mention humor as a collective effort to resist boredom.

However, humor can be used to cope with things other than boredom. For example, managers in a training course used humor in the training sessions to cope with those aspects of the course that they found problematic (Grugulis, 2002). In some cases, very experienced managers felt better qualified than the tutors teaching the course and would use humor as a way to communicate frustration they had with their instructor. Alternatively, some less experienced managers found the requirements of the course to be overly challenging and used humor with each other as a way of allaying their anxiety, thus distancing themselves from the problem. Overall, many of the participants also found the reporting requirements to be excessively bureaucratic and cumbersome and would use subversive humor to communicate these thoughts. In all cases, the humor allowed managers participating in the training to collectively navigate and deal with the challenges they faced (Grugulis, 2002).

Creation of Positive Workplace Identities

In addition to coping, humor also allows employees to collaboratively make sense of identity-threatening tasks in a way that helps them affirm positive work-related identities. This tendency has been well-documented by three empirical studies conducted in various contexts. The first study, by Clair and Dufresne (2004), examined the experiences of downsizing agents from a firm in the financial services industry. Although these informants were not in a stigmatized profession per se, the task of downsizing involves social taint. Thus, these individuals had to deal with stigmatization while carrying out responsibilities in this temporary role. Interview themes indicated that downsizing agents were able to distance themselves from the stigma of the downsizing events through emotional, cognitive, or physical distancing tactics, with humor representing a common form of emotional distancing. As stated by one manager tasked with downsizing fellow workers, "we kind of joked about it to not let it directly emotionally affect us" (Clair & Dufresne, 2004, p. 1612). Overall, they consciously chose to use humor with other downsizing agents to separate themselves from the act of laying people off. Doing so helped them maintain the focus necessary to finish carrying out their job.

Tracy, Myers, and Scott (2006) also observed workers in their study using humor to collectively manage and reaffirm positive identities. The authors conducted observations, field interviews, and formal interviews of informants in three occupations, correctional officers, 911 call takers, and firefighters. Each represents a type of human service work that involves job duties that are unpredictable, dirty, and even tragic. Similar to the downsizing agents, the informants in this sample also used humor to distance themselves from identity-threatening aspects of their jobs. However, in this study, the content of the humor would often entail making fun of "clients" (i.e., people they were serving). The 911 call takers would play recordings of crazy callers, and firefighters would joke about people calling them for nonemergency situations (see Maxwell, 2003, for further review of humor in crisis situations). The correctional officers particularly resorted to humor when they had to clean up after criminals, collecting food trays and laundry, since these were the most degrading and, thus, identity-threatening tasks. Stated differently, although workers in these occupations must help (or serve) all types of people, including degenerates and criminals, they used humor as a way of expressing their distinction from and superiority over those they were serving. The workers were able to redefine interpretations of situations, clients, or tasks by joking with each other and, in doing so, preserve positive aspects of their workplace identity (Tracy et al., 2006).

Ashforth and colleagues (2007) interviewed managers who worked as correctional officers and firefighters, as did Tracy et al. (2006), but they also included informants from a broader array of "dirty work" occupations (e.g., personal injury lawyers, roofers, collection agents). As in the prior two studies, people from these occupations used humor as a means of distancing themselves from undesirable aspects of their jobs. However, the managers in this sample also addressed their occupational taint by using humor proactively with external constituents. For example, upon being teased by his clients, a personal injury lawyer made a joke about being an ambulance chaser. Injecting humor in this way allowed the dirty workers to not only cope with but challenge the stereotypes of their occupations while still positively bridging the divide between themselves and the other party. Overall, these managers felt that using humor to combat stigma in this manner enabled them to be seen more positively by the public. Thus, Ashforth and colleagues (2007) offer a contribution beyond the prior two studies by noting how organizational members can use humor to impact not only how they think about themselves, but how those outside their occupation view them.

Discussion

In order to expand our understanding of how humor can contribute to POS, we conducted a focused review of the workplace humor literature addressing the topic of humor in relation to cooperation, relationship building, creativity, and the negotiation of positive workplace identities. We see these areas of humor research as being most relevant to POS. Moving forward, knowledge of POS can accrue by furthering humor research in each of these four domains, as well as in a few others that we propose in the next section.

That said, in conducting this review, we also noted certain shortcomings in specific studies and within the field of humor research, more generally, which deserve mention. We highlight these issues, so that POS scholars do not make the same mistakes in their investigations of humor. After these critical insights, we outline additional directions for future research and conclude with practical implications for managers.

Constructive Critique

First, our literature review indicates that knowledge in this area is not accumulating in an appropriate manner. Granted, one difficulty facing humor scholarship is the lack of a clear paradigm—there is no over-arching "theory of humor." This may serve as a challenge to POS researchers since the inclusion criteria for POS constructs includes being "based on theory, research and valid measurement . . ." (Avey, Luthans, Smith & Palmer, 2010, p. 20). Even so, we still see more basic problems with the choices some researchers make when designing their studies. People doing research in this area should be careful to take prior work into consideration and scrutinize the methodological fit of their studies (Edmonson & McManus, 2007). Too often, we see humor researchers reinvent the wheel and apply qualitative (i.e., inductive) methods that then generate conclusions already drawn by prior studies, albeit perhaps in a different context. Research on organizational humor has reached a point of maturity at which published work can be used to develop specific testable hypotheses. In fact, some theoretical work in this area already presents propositions that could benefit from testing (e.g., Cooper, 2008) and can serve as a catalyst for empirical work in a positivist tradition.

Moreover, qualitative studies do not *measure* outcomes of interest, so quantitative studies can follow in various areas to test and add validity to phenomena reported by these studies (e.g., by measuring group cohesiveness rather than simply observing group members interact). That said, when conducting quantitative research we also strongly urge researchers to include appropriate control variables in their studies. Such control variables should take into account the various individual characteristics, situational influences, and moderating influences of humor as they relate to cooperation, relationship building, creativity, and the negotiation of positive workplace identities. When control variables are not included, researchers can make erroneous conclusions about the efficacy of humor when something else is actually driving the effects.

Second, our review suggests the need for POS scholars interested in the study of humor to seriously consider measurement issues and levels-of-analysis issues in their research designs. Our review indicated the use of a variety of study-specific measures of humor in the organizational literature (e.g., Avolio et al., 1999; Dubinsky et al., 1995). We believe that a need exists for the use of more established measures of humor not common in the organizational literature, with sound psychometric properties demonstrated across a stream of research. Such measures include the Situational Humor Response Survey (SHRQ; Martin & Lefcourt, 1984), the State-Trait Cheerfulness Inventory (Ruch, Kohler, & van Thriel, 1996), or the Humor Styles Questionnaire (HSQ; Martin, Puhlik-Doris, Larsen, Gray, & Weir, 2003). For example, the HSQ measures four functions of humor: self-enhancing, aggressive, affiliative, and self-defeating, which may help us better understand the motivational bases for the use of humor in the workplace.

Another issue for POS researchers to consider is how to best measure humor. The humor measures listed above are self-report survey measures, which are notorious for being laden with social desirability and self-serving bias associated with inflated ratings (Harris & Schauebroeck, 1988). Since humor has an intended audience (Martin, 2007), perhaps obtaining measures of humor from sources besides the initiator of humor is advisable, to take into account the perspectives of all parties in the humor transaction. Content analysis and case studies of humorous communication (e.g., Adelsward, & Oberg, 1998) also offer alternative forms of measurement that can triangulate the results of survey research.

Regarding levels of analysis, our review suggests another opportunity for POS scholars interested in studying humor in the workplace. Humor is a dynamic process that involves an initiator, target, and audience. This dynamic suggests a dyadic or group level of analysis, yet most research has been conducted at the individual level of analysis (cf. Martin, 2007; Peterson & Seligman, 2004). We therefore call for POS scholars to apply appropriate level-specific theorizing, measurement, and testing using multilevel data analytic tools such as within and between analysis (Dansereau, Alutto, & Yammarino, 1984).

Future Directions

In addition to the topic areas presented in this chapter, which can contribute to the POS arena, we have other general suggestions for POS researchers who desire to study humor. A novel direction for future research on humor and POS involves the concept of positive psychological capital (PsyCap; Luthans, Avolio, Avey, & Norman, 2007; Luthans & Youssef, 2007). PsyCap is a positive and developmental psychological state marked by high self-efficacy, optimism, hope, and resilience. PsyCap has been linked to different organizational outcomes, including higher levels of employee well-being, performance, and satisfaction; organizational change; a supportive work climate; reduced absenteeism; and positive organizational emotions (Avey et al., 2010; Luthans et al., 2007). To the extent that humor reflects a positive emotion or psychological state (Martin, 2007), we believe that humor may be associated with the components of PsyCap.

As noted above, the components of PsyCap include resilience, optimism, hope, and self-efficacy. Resilience describes having the ability to overcome adversity, failure, or seemingly impossible odds. We believe that resilience may be required for humor to be expressed in what Peterson and Seligman (2004) describe as "a composed and cheerful view on adversity that allows one to see its light side and thereby sustain a good mood" (p. 584). Resilience involves being adaptable by considering alternate scenarios and divergent thinking associated with humor. Optimism makes internal or dispositional attributions for positive events, and external or situational attributions for negative events. We believe that optimism may be required for humor to evolve as a defense mechanism in the presence of adversity to suppress its negative impacts (Peterson & Seligman, 2004) by focusing on those aspects of the situation that are under one's control. Humor may enable people to deflect the causes of negative outcomes toward others or external events in an optimistic manner.

Hope involves having the willpower and pathways to achieve goals. We believe that hope may be associated with humor because a cheerful or humorous psychological state (or temperament) may stimulate creative pathways for the solution to problems. Self-efficacy is one's belief of being capable of performing a specific task through the mobilization of cognitive resources (Luthans et al., 2007). Considering that self-efficacy and creativity have been linked in prior research (Amabile, 1988) and the creativity-enhancing characteristics of humor have been noted, we believe that self-efficacy and humor may be linked. Future POS research is needed to examine these potential associations.

Scholars interested in POS and humor could also benefit from conducting humor research that bolsters the business case for humor. Much of the research on workplace humor has examined subjective instead of objective outcomes. A notable exception is Avolio et al. (1999), who examined the effect of leadership styles and humor on business unit performance measures from company records. We believe that more research of this type is needed. Such research can examine positive organizational outcome measures such as actual financial performance records, balanced scorecard metrics, market share, organizational change success, quality indices, customer and employee engagement metrics, turnover, promotions, and other career development measures. Finding positive associations between humor and these measures can add credibility to discussions of humor in the workplace.

Although these avenues for future research seem most promising, other key questions regarding humor and POS are in need of answers. Although much research has examined humor (particularly in the domain of psychology), we believe that the relevance and rigor of these studies are highly variable. Moreover, the positive role of humor in organizations has not been fully examined, so that studies are needed to determine the nomological network of humor at the individual, dyadic, group, and organizational levels of analysis. In particular, we believe these areas are in need of study:

- What comprises the dark side of humor in organizations? What are the unintended negative consequences of humor in organizations? How can well-intentioned humor be misapplied, and what can be done to prevent this from happening? Under what circumstances does humor detract from employee and organizational performance?
- How does humor relate to other POS concepts, such as civility, gratitude, courageous principled action, emotional intelligence, or authentic leadership?
- How does organizational and national culture influence the antecedents, operating mechanisms, and outcomes of humor? Does culture moderate the effects that humor has on its target and audience (e.g., do the norms for humor differ in clan versus market cultures)?
- What comprises "cultures of fun" in organizations? How can a strengths-based organization or culture influence humor's mechanisms and outcomes?

- What is the role of time in the evolution of humor recognition, appreciation, and display? How do humor's styles, mechanisms, and outcomes change over an individual's, dyad's, group's, and organization's life cycle? How does organizational size, age, and industry influence the degree to which humor is appreciated and used in organizations?
- What beneficial functions can humor serve in specific jobs or organizational roles? Can humor be used to select candidates for appropriate jobs? Can humor be learned by organizational members through training, as any skill is learned? If so, does it produce meaningful change in an individual's humor abilities and styles? Can training on humor provide positive organizational outcomes and/or simply reduce the occurrence of negative organizational outcomes?

Practical Implications

As noted in this review, humor can serve many useful functions in organizations. Humor can lead to a more positive customer experience, integrative bargaining, better workplace relationships, creative performance, and a more positive view of work itself. Thus, organizations should embrace humor as an enabler of these and other positive outcomes. That said, the strategy for "embracing humor" as part of an organization's practices can be a tedious task for managers to negotiate.

Although some articles in the popular press imply that managers should try to inject humor through official workplace practices (Kilbride, 2009; Wickenheiser, 2008) or the hiring of humor consultants (O'Reilly, 2007; Walzer, 2007; Woolley, 1988), this artificial injection of humor is not without risk. For example, a recent field study observing a "culture of fun" program implemented within a call center found mixed effects in terms of employee reaction (Fleming, 2005). Management in the call center was quite well-meaning, implementing the program to help employees deal with the "exceedingly mundane and monotonous" (p. 292) nature of their jobs. Some employees appreciated these efforts to enrich their work experience and saw the program as a signal that management truly cared. However, other employees were not only skeptical but cynical about the program, viewing management's "fun" policies as inauthentic at best and condescending at worst (i.e., that they were being treated like children rather than adults). The employees were often put into contrived situations and expected to play games, have relay races, or sing songs (e.g., "The Rainbow Connection" by the Muppets). This unfortunate case is consistent with Lyttle's (2007) review of the humor literature that concluded that humor in the workplace can create many unintended consequences, such as distraction, loss of credibility, and offended individuals in diverse workplaces. Therefore, managers need to carefully evaluate how to use humor to maximize its benefits while minimizing its ill effects.

Granted, the concepts of fun and humor are not completely synonymous, but the takeaways from the Fleming (2005) study are still relevant to planned humor initiatives. As is evident in many of the studies cited in this review, employees will usually inject their own version of humor and fun at work, even without the interference of management. Thus, in many cases, managers might be able to garner the benefits of humor by simply allowing this process to occur naturally, creating a context in which these behaviors are accepted rather than reprimanded. In fact, for those managers who may not consider themselves naturally humorous, supporting the use of humor by others may be the preferred strategy for tapping into humor's benefits, since failed attempts at humor have the risk of seeming awkward, inauthentic, distracting, or even offensive. Alternatively, if management does want to take a more proactive role in encouraging humor, one of the best ways to do this may be by example. As noted earlier in this chapter, leaders often set the tone for whether humor is accepted at work, and some of the most notable examples of organizations that have embraced humor have leaders that embrace humor (e.g., Southwest Airlines, JetBlue, Sun Microsystems, Zappos) (Hof, Rebello, & Burrows, 1996; O'Reilly & Pfeffer, 1995; Gittell & O'Reilly, 2001).

Thus, we are not discouraging organizations from ever having events or initiatives with the purpose of introducing humor at work, but we are encouraging organizations to make sure that any such initiative are undertaken with the utmost consideration. Any efforts in this area will need to be received by diverse committees of employees as authentic and enjoyable in order to be effective above and beyond the informal humor that may already exist.

Conclusion

In conclusion, the aim of this chapter was to illustrate the relevance of humor research to the domain of POS scholarship. As we attempted to describe, a great deal of overlap exists between various outcomes associated with humor and outcomes of interest to POS researchers. Accordingly, furthering research on humor in organizations should also advance knowledge within this domain. In addition to the topic areas reviewed in the chapter, we also noted a number of other potentially fruitful areas for academic research on humor. That said, we introduced these ideas with certain caveats, encouraging anyone doing research in this area to think very critically about their theoretical framework and research design, in order to create scholarship that can be as impactful as possible. Addressing this topic is not without its challenges; however, a breadth of opportunities exist for contributing to knowledge in this topic area. We encourage researchers to undertake such endeavors to benefit both scholarship and practice and add to our knowledge base of POS.

Acknowledgement

The authors would like to acknowledge Michael Agard and Scott Horenziak for their research assistance.

Note

1. Unless otherwise noted, quotes are taken from interviews conducted by the first author during her dissertation research (Cooper, 2002).

References

Adelsward, V., & Oberg, B.M. (1998). The function of laughter and joking in negotiation activities. *Humor: International Journal of Humor Research, 11*(4), 411–429.

Amabile, T.M. (1988). A model of creativity and innovation in organizations. In B.M. Staw, & L.L. Cummings (Eds.), *Research in organizational behavior* Vol. 10 (pp. 123–167). Greenwich, CT: JAI Press.

Ashforth, B.E., Kreiner, G.E., Clark, M.A., & Fugate, M. (2007). Normalizing dirty work: Managerial tactics for countering occupational taint. *Academy of Management Journal, 50*(1), 149–174.

Avey, J.B., Luthans, F., Smith, R.M., & Palmer, N.F. (2010). Impact of positive psychological capital on employee well-being over time. *Journal of Occupational Health Psychology, 15*(1), 17–28.

Avolio, B.J., Howell, J.M., & Sosik, J.J. (1999). A funny thing happened on the way to the bottom line: Humor as a moderator of leadership style effects. *Academy of Management Journal, 42*(2), 219–227.

Baron, R.A. (1984). Reducing organizational conflict: An incompatible response approach. *Journal of Applied Psychology, 69*(2), 272–279.

Baron, R.A., & Ball, R.L. (1974). The aggression-inhibiting influence of nonhostile humor. *Journal of Experimental Social Psychology, 10*, 23–33.

Belanger, H.G., Kirkpatrick, L.A., & Derks, P. (1998). The effects of humor on verbal and imaginal problem solving.

Humor: International Journal of Humor Research, 11(1), 21–31.

Bergeron, J., Roy, J., & Fallu, J. (2008). Pleasantly surprising clients: A tactic in relationship marketing for building competitive advantage in the financial services sector. *Canadian Journal of Administrative Sciences, 25,* 171–184.

Bergeron, J., & Vachon, M. (2008). The effects of humor usage by financial advisors in sales encounters. *The International Journal of Bank Marketing, 26*(6), 376–398.

Bradney, P. (1957). The joking relationship in industry. *Human Relations, 10,* 179–187.

Brief, A.P., & Motowidlo, S.J. (1986). Prosocial organizational behaviors. *Academy of Management Review, 11*(4), 710–725.

Burford, C. (1987). Humour of principals and its impact on teachers and the school. *The Journal of Educational Administration, 25*(1), 29–54.

Cameron, K.S., Dutton, J.E., & Quinn, R.E. (Eds.). (2003). *Positive organizational scholarship: Foundations of a new discipline.* San Francisco: Berrett-Koehler.

Carnevale, P.J.D., & Isen, A.M. (1986). The influence of positive affect and visual access on the discovery of integrative solutions in bilateral negotiation. *Organizational Behavior and Human Decision Processes, 37,* 1–13.

Clair, J.A., & Dufresne, R.L. (2004). Playing the grim reaper: How employees experience carrying out a downsizing. *Human Relations, 57*(12), 1597–1625.

Collinson, D.L. (1988). "Engineering humor": Masculinity, joking and conflict in shop-floor relations. *Organization Studies, 9*(2), 181–199.

Cooper, C.D. (2002). *No laughing matter: The impact of supervisor humor on leader-member exchange (LMX) quality.* Doctoral dissertation, University of Southern California, Los Angeles.

Cooper, C.D. (2004). *Did you hear the one about humor and leadership? A field study of supervisor humor and leader-member exchange quality.* Paper presented at the annual meeting of the Academy of Management, New Orleans.

Cooper, C.D. (2005). Just joking around? Employee humor expression as an ingratiatory behavior. *Academy of Management Review, 30,* 765–776.

Cooper, C.D. (2008). Elucidating the bonds of workplace humor: A relational process model. *Human Relations, 61*(8), 1087–1115.

Coser, R.L. (1960). Laughter among colleagues: A study of the social functions of humor among the staff of a mental hospital. *Psychiatry, 23,* 81–95.

Crosby, L., Evans, K.R., & Cowles, D. (1990). Relationship quality in services selling: An interpersonal influence perspective. *Journal of Marketing, 54*(3), 68–81.

Dansereau, F., Alutto, J.A., & Yammarino, F.J. (1984). *Theory testing in organizational behavior: The varient approach.* Englewood Cliffs, NJ: Prentice-Hall.

Davis, A., & Kleimer, B.H. (1989). The value of humor in effective leadership. *Leadership & Organizational Journal, 10*(1), i–iii.

Decker, W.H., & Rotondo, D.M. (2001). Relationships among gender, type of humor, and perceived leader effectiveness. *Journal of Managerial Issues, 13*(4), 450–465.

Dixon, N.F. (1980). Humor: A cognitive alternative to stress? In I.G. Sarason, and C.D. Spielberger (Eds.), *Stress & anxiety* (pp. 281–289). Washington, DC: Hemisphere Publishing Corporation.

Dubinsky, A.J., Yammarino, F.J., & Jolson, M.A. (1995). An examination of linkages between personality characteristics and dimensions of transformational leadership. *Journal of Business and Psychology, 9,* 315–335.

Duncan, W.J., & Feisal, J.P. (1989). No laughing matter: Patterns of humor in the workplace. *Organizational Dynamics, 17*(4), 18–30.

Dutton, J.E., & Heaphy, E.D. (2003). The power of high-quality connections. In K.M. Cameron, J.E. Dutton, & R.E. Quinn (Eds.), *Positive organizational scholarship: Foundations of a new discipline* (pp. 263–278). San Francisco: Berrett-Koehler Publishers.

Edmondson, A.C., & McManus, S.E. (2007). Methodological fit in management field research. *Academy of Management Review, 32,* 1155–1179.

Fine, G.A. (1988). Letting off steam? Redefining a restaurant's work environment. In M.D. Moore, & R.C. Snyder (Eds.), *Inside organizations: Understanding the human dimension* (pp. 119–127). Newbury Park, CA: Sage.

Fleming, P. (2005). Workers' playtime? Boundaries and cynicism in a "culture of fun" program. *The Journal of Applied Behavioral Science, 41*(3), 285–303.

Forester, J. (2004). Responding to critical moments with humor, recognition, and hope. *Negotiation Journal, 20*(2), 221–237.

Fraley, B., & Aron, A. (2004). The effect of a shared humorous experience on closeness in initial encounters. *Personal Relationships, 11,* 61–78.

Francis, L., Monahan, K., & Berger, C. (1999). A laughing matter? The uses of humor in medical interactions. *Motivation and Emotion, 23*(2), 155–174.

Frederickson, B.L. (2001). The role of positive emotions in positive psychology: The broaden-and-build theory of positive emotions. *American Psychologist, 56*(3), 218–226.

George, J.M., & Brief, A.P. (1992). Feeling good-doing good: A conceptual analysis of the mood at work-organizational spontaneity relationship. *Psychological Bulletin, 112*(2), 310–329.

Gersick, C.J.G., Bartunek, J.M., & Dutton, J.E. (2000). Learning from academia: The importance of relationships in professional life. *Academy of Management Journal, 43,* 1026–1044.

Gittell, J.H., & O'Reilly, C. (2001). *JetBlue Airways: Starting from scratch.* Case no. 9–801-354. Boston: Harvard Business School.

Grugulis, I. (2002). Nothing serious? Candidates' use of humour in management training. *Human Relations, 55*(4), 387–406.

Harris, M., & Schauebroeck, J. (1988). A meta-analysis of self-supervisor, self-peer, and peer-supervisor ratings. *Personnel Psychology, 41,* 43–62.

Hehl, F.J., & Ruch, W. (1985). The location of sense of humor within comprehensive personality spaces: An exploratory study. *Personality and Individual Differences, 6*(6), 703–715.

Holmes, J. (2006). Sharing a laugh: Pragmatic aspects of humor and gender in the workplace. *Journal of Pragmatics, 38*(1), 26–50.

Holmes, J. (2007). Making humour work: Creativity on the job. *Applied Linguistics, 28*(4), 518–537.

Holmes, J., & Marra, M. (2006). Humor and leadership style. *Humor: International Journal of Humor Research, 19*(2), 119–138.

Hof, R.D., Rebello, K., & Burrows, P. (1996). Scott McNealy's rising sun: How he's taking the computer maker to new heights. *Business Week, January 22,* 66–73.

Isen, A.M., & Daubman, K.A. (1984). The influence of affect on categorization. *Journal of Personality and Social Psychology, 47,* 1206–1217.

Isen, A.M., Daubman, K.A., & Nowicki, G.P. (1987). Positive affect facilitates creative problem solving. *Journal of Personality and Social Psychology, 52*(6), 1122–1131.

Isen, A.M., Johnson, M.M., Mertz, E., & Robinson, G.F. (1985). The influence of positive affect on the unusualness of word associations. *Journal of Personality and Social Psychology, 48*, 1413–1426.

Kahai, S.S., Sosik, J.J., & Avolio, B.J. (2003). Effects of leadership style, anonymity, and rewards on creativity-relevant processes and outcomes in an electronic meeting system context. *The Leadership Quarterly, 14*, 499–524.

Kets de Vries, M.F.R. (1990). The organizational fool: Balancing a leader's hubris. *Human Relations, 43*(8), 751–770.

Kilbride, K. (2009). Different techniques to saying THANKS. *Tribune Business Weekly, 20*(28), 1.

Leap, T.L., & Smeltzer, L.R. (1984). Racial remarks in the workplace: Humor or harassment? *Harvard Business Review, 62*, 74–78.

Lefcourt, H.M. (2002). Humor. In C.R. Snyder, & S.J. Lopez (Eds.), *Handbook of positive psychology* (pp. 619–631). New York: Oxford University Press.

Locke, K. (1996). A funny thing happened! The management of consumer emotions in service encounters. *Organization Science, 7*(1), 40–59.

Luthans, F. (2002). The need for and meaning of positive organizational behavior. *Journal of Organizational Behavior, 23*, 695–706.

Luthans, F., Avolio, B.J., Avey, J.B., & Norman, S.M. (2007). Positive psychological capital: Measurement and relationship with performance and satisfaction. *Personnel Psychology, 60*, 541–572.

Luthans, F., & Youssef, C.M. (2007). Emerging positive organizational behavior. *Journal of Management, 33*(3), 321–349.

Lyttle, J. (2007). The judicial use and management of humor in the workplace. *Business Horizons, 50*(3), 239–245.

Malone, P.B. (1980). Humor: A double-edged tool for today's managers? *Academy of Management Review, 5*(3), 357–360.

Martin, D.M. (2004). Humor in middle management: Women negotiating the paradoxes of organizational life. *Journal of Applied Communication Research, 32*(2), 147–170.

Martin, R.A. (2007). *The psychology of humor: An integrative approach*. Burlington, MA: Elsevier Academic Press.

Martin, R.A., & Lefcourt, H.M. (1984). Situational humor response questionnaire: Quantitative measure of sense of humor. *Journal of Personality and Social Psychology, 47*(1), 145–155.

Martin, R.A., Puhlik-Doris, P., Larsen, G., Gray, J., & Weir, K. (2003). Individual differences in interpersonal and intrapersonal functions of humor: Development of the Humor Styles Questionnaire. *Journal of Research in Personality, 47*, 145–155.

Maxwell, W. (2003). The use of gallows humor and dark humor during crisis situations. *International Journal of Emergency Mental Health, 5*(2), 93–98.

Mindess, H. (1971). *Laughter and liberation*. Los Angeles: Nash Publishing.

Morreall, J. (1991). Humor and work. *Humor: International Journal of Humor Research, 4*(3–4), 359–373.

Mulkay, M., Clark, C., & Pinch, T. (1993). Laughter and the profit motive: The use of humor in a photographic shop. *Humor: International Journal of Humor Research, 6*(2), 163–193.

Oldham, G.R., & Cummings, A. (1996). Employee creativity: Personal and contextual factors at work. *Academy of Management Journal, 39*(3), 607–634.

O'Quin, K., & Derks, P. (1997). Humor and creativity: A review of the empirical literature. In M.A. Runco (Ed.), *The creativity research handbook* (pp. 227–256). Cresskill, NJ: Hampton Press.

O'Reilly, S. (2007). Laughing all the way to the bank. *Personnel Today, January 9*, 27.

O'Reilly, C.A., III, & Pfeffer, J. (1995). *Southwest Airlines: Using human resources for a competitive advantage (A)*. Case no. HR-1A. Palo Alto, CA: Stanford University.

Parsons, G., Kinsman, S.B., Bosk, C.L., Sankar, P., & Ubel, P.A. (2001). Between two worlds: Medical student perceptions of humor and slang in the hospital setting. *Journal of General Internal Medicine, 16*, 544–549.

Peterson, C., & Seligman, M.E.P. (2004). *Character strengths and virtues: A handbook and classification*. New York: Oxford/American Psychological Association.

Plester, B., & Orams, M. (2008). Send in the clowns: The role of the joker in three New Zealand IT companies. *Humor: International Journal of Humor Research, 21*(3), 253–281.

Pratt, M.G., & Ashforth, B.E. (2003). Fostering meaningfulness in working and at work. In K.M. Cameron, J.E. Dutton, & R.E. Quinn (Eds.), *Positive organizational scholarship: Foundations of a new discipline* (pp. 309–327). San Francisco: Berrett-Koehler Publishers.

Priest, R.F., & Swain, J.E. (2002). Humor and its implications for leadership effectiveness. *Humor: International Journal of Humor Research, 15*(2), 169–189.

Pruitt, D. (1981). *Negotiation behavior*. New York: Academic Press.

Rafaeli, A., & Sutton, R.I. (1991). Emotional contrast strategies as means of social influence: Lessons from criminal interrogators and bill collectors. *Academy of Management Journal, 34*(4), 749–775.

Roberts, L.M. (2006). Shifting the lens on organizational life: The added value of positive scholarship. *Academy of Management Review, 31*(2), 292–305.

Rogerson-Revell, P. (2007). Humour in business: A double-edged sword: A study of humor and style shifting in intercultural business meetings. *Journal of Pragmatics, 39*, 4–28.

Romero, E.J., & Cruthirds, K.W. (2006). The use of humor in the workplace. *Academy of Management Perspectives, 20*(2), 58–69.

Roy, D.F. (1960). "Banana time": Job satisfaction and informal interaction. *Human Organization, 18*, 158–168.

Ruch, W., Kohler, G., & van Thriel, C. (1996). Assessing the "humorous temperament": Construction of the facet and standard trait forms of the State-Trait-Cheerfulness Inventory—STCI. *Humor: International Journal of Humor Research, 9*, 303–340.

Scogin, F.R., & Pollio, H.R. (1980). Targeting and the humorous episode in group process. *Human Relations, 33*(11), 831.

Sosik, J.J. (2006). *Leading with character: Stories of valor and virtue and the principles they teach*. Greenwich, CT: Information Age Publishing.

Staw, B.M., Sutton, R.I., & Pelled, L.H. (1994). Employee positive emotion and favorable outcomes at the workplace. *Organization Science, 5*(1), 51–71.

Terrion, J.L., & Ashforth, B.E. (2002). From "I" to "we": The role of putdown humor and identity in the development of a temporary group. *Human Relations, 55*(1), 55–88.

Tracy, S.J., Myers, K.K., & Scott, C.W. (2006). Cracking jokes and crafting selves: Sensemaking and identity among human service workers. *Communication Monographs, 73*(3), 283–308.

Vinton, K.L. (1989). Humor in the workplace: Is it more than telling jokes? *Small Group Behavior, 20*(2), 151–166.

Vuorela, T. (2005). Laughing matters: A case study of humor in multicultural business negotiations. *Negotiation Journal, 21*(1), 105–129.

Walsh, I.P., Leahy, M.M., & Litt, M. (2009). "Cajoling" as a means of engagement in the dysphagia clinic. *Seminars in Speech and Language, 30*(1), 37–47.

Walzer, P. (2007, January 12). It's no joke: Laughs can be great for business. *McClatchy-Tribune News,* p. 1.

Wanzer, M.B., Booth-Butterfield, M., & Booth-Butterfield, S. (1996). Are funny people popular? An examination of humor orientation, loneliness, and social attraction. *Communication Quarterly, 44*(1), 42.

Weick, K.E. (1995). *Sensemaking in organizations.* Thousand Oaks, CA: Sage.

Wickenheiser, M. (2008, April 1). Fun, humor can provide important relief in workplace, experts say. Washington DC: *McClatchy-Tribune Business News.*

Woolley, S. (1988). Now, success is a laughing matter. *Business Week, August 8,* 81.

Ziv, A. (1976). Facilitating effects of humor on creativity. *Journal of Educational Psychology, 68*(3), 318–322.

Psychological Safety

A Foundation for Speaking Up, Collaboration, and Experimentation in Organizations

Ingrid M. Nembhard *and* Amy C. Edmondson

Abstract

In this chapter, we describe psychological safety and organizational learning, how they are related, and how they contribute to a positive work experience. We begin by defining psychological safety, then provide a theoretical and evidence-based argument that psychological safety facilitates three key determinants of organizational learning: speaking up, collaboration, and experimentation. We further propose that these activities promote both organizational performance and more satisfying work environments. We also discuss aspects of the work environment (e.g., status hierarchies and narrow performance goals) that undermine psychological safety by highlighting the interpersonal risks of engaging in learning behaviors. Finally, we address overcoming these barriers, identifying leader inclusiveness, high-quality peer relationships, and opportunities to practice offline as factors that promote psychological safety and set the stage for organizational learning and improvement. We conclude with suggestions for future research.

Keywords: Psychological safety, organizational learning, team learning, speaking up, communication, collaboration, experimentation, leadership, performance

It was a busy afternoon in the labor and delivery ward at an urban hospital in the northeastern United States. Twins were being born prematurely, and a team from the neonatal intensive care unit (NICU) was called in to assist. The babies were delivered without incident, but they were at high risk for respiratory distress syndrome (respiratory system failure) because their gestational age was only 27 weeks. It had become, relatively recently, a best practice to administer prophylactic surfactant as soon as possible after birth for such high-risk babies, to promote lung development. Yet, the neonatologist had not issued an order. The therapist, new to this NICU, noticed that the neonatologist was preparing to return to his morning rounds, during which he would be assessing the other patients in the NICU, where the twins would now reside as well. She considered reminding him about the surfactant, but then remembered how he publicly berated a nurse last week for questioning one of his orders. She rationalized—and believed—that the twins would be fine, and thus dismissed the idea of reminding the neonatologist and continued her task.

In this partly fictionalized example, derived from our field research in numerous hospitals and well-disguised for confidentiality, the therapist's choice to remain silent was not because she lacked concern for the twins; quite the contrary, she had dreamed of caring for infants in the NICU since high school. She cared passionately about those tiny patients.

In a different NICU, thousands of miles away, another respiratory therapist confronts the same situation: a neonatologist who forgets to order surfactant, this time for a baby boy of 28 weeks' gestational age. Without hesitation, without even becoming aware of it as a decision, she stops the neonatologist to remind him. He quickly agrees that the baby should receive surfactant and calls the pharmacy to request it. He ends the conversation by thanking her for "watching out for me and the patient." Shortly thereafter, as she is administering the surfactant to the boy, she thinks to herself that the NICU could ensure that all babies who need surfactant receive it by instituting a protocol. During a break, she seeks out her manager to make this suggestion.

What explains the difference in the two therapists' reactions to the same situation? Why is the therapist in the second hospital willing to remind the neonatologist about the surfactant and then take the initiative to make a corrective suggestion to her manager, whereas the therapist in the first hospital dismisses her concern about the same treatment? The therapists have made different calculations about the risks involved in voicing their concern. The therapist in the first hospital calculated—only partly consciously, with little focused attention—that the risk of suffering negative personal consequences (e.g., berating, punishment, etc.) as a result of speaking up outweighed the benefits. In contrast, the therapist at the second hospital believed that the benefits of speaking up were great and the risks were minimal. She felt it was safe to express her concern and suggestion, that no penalty would follow. In sum, she felt a sense of *psychological safety*.

In this chapter, we describe the construct of psychological safety, summarize evidence for the relationship between psychological safety and organizational learning, and discuss how both contribute to a positive work experience. We begin by defining psychological safety, then provide a theoretical and evidenced-based argument that psychological safety facilitates three key determinants of organizational learning—speaking up, collaboration, and experimentation—that ultimately result in better organizational performance and more satisfying work environments. We explain that this positive process is often thwarted by aspects of the work environment (e.g., status hierarchies and performance goals) that undermine psychological safety by highlighting the interpersonal risks of engaging in learning behaviors (e.g., appearing ignorant and incompetent). We also show that the challenges the work environment may present can be overcome. We point to leader inclusiveness, high-quality peer relationships, and opportunities to practice offline as factors that cultivate psychological safety, setting the stage for organizational learning and improvement. We conclude with suggestions for future research.

Defining Psychological Safety

Psychological safety describes individuals' perceptions related to the degree of interpersonal threat in their work environment. We define it as the general belief that one is comfortable being oneself—being open, authentic, and direct—in a particular setting or role. Psychological safety consists of taken-for-granted beliefs about how others will respond when one puts oneself on the line, such as by taking a risk, asking a question, seeking feedback, reporting a mistake, or proposing a new idea (Edmondson, 1999). At work, individuals engage in a tacit calculus at behavioral decision points, in which they assess the interpersonal risk associated with a given behavior. In this tacit process, one weighs the potential action against the particular interpersonal climate, as in, "If I do 'X' here, will I be hurt, embarrassed or criticized?" A negative answer to this tacit question constitutes a sense of psychological safety and allows the actor to proceed. In this way, an action (e.g., admitting error or asking for help) that might be unthinkable in one work setting is readily taken in another, due to different expectations about the interpersonal consequences.

Others have defined psychological safety similarly. For example, Kahn (1990, p. 708) described it as "feeling able to show and employ one's self without fear of negative consequences to self-image, status, or career." Kahn's (1990, p. 703) qualitative research found that psychological safety was one of three psychological conditions that "shaped how people inhabited their roles [in the organization]." Psychological safety does not imply a cozy environment in which people are close friends, nor does it suggest an absence of pressure or problems. Rather, it describes a climate in which the focus can be on productive discussion that enables early prevention of problems and the accomplishment of shared goals, because people are less likely to focus on self-protection. For this reason, particular attention has been paid to psychological safety in the clinical psychology literature, as an important element of the therapeutic context (Rappoport, 1997; Waks, 1988).

Prior research shows that perceptions of psychological safety tend to be similar among people who work closely together, such as members of an intact team, both because team members are subject to the same set of contextual influences and because these perceptions develop out of salient shared experiences (Edmondson, 1999). For example, members of a team will conclude that making a mistake does not lead to rejection when they have had team experiences in which appreciation and interest are expressed in response to discussions of their own and others' mistakes. The similarity of beliefs in social systems, such as workgroups, is the subject of much inquiry (see reviews by Klimoski & Mohammed, 1994; Walsh, 1995).

Researchers have also studied psychological safety at the individual and organization levels of analysis. For example, Tynan (2005) studied psychological safety at the individual level, investigating the relationship between supervisors and employees in a laboratory setting. She noted the importance of both *self* psychological safety (how safe an individual feels in relation to a specific target person) and *other* psychological safety, an individual's perception of how safe a specific other person feels. At the organizational level, Baer and Frese (2003) used surveys to assess the psychological climate of 47 mid-sized industrial and service sector firms, and found that firms with greater overall levels of psychological safety outperformed other firms.

Psychological Safety: A Foundation for Organizational Learning

During the last 20 years, the concept of psychological safety has garnered significant attention because researchers have found that it plays an important role in facilitating a positive organizational process: organizational learning. The evidence suggests that organizational learning provides a sustainable path to high performance in changing and uncertain environments, which describes many, if not most, work environments (Edmondson, 2008; Schein, 1993; Stata, 1989). Organizational learning refers to the process of improving organizational actions (e.g., customer service) by integrating new insights and knowledge (Fiol & Lyles, 1985; Garvin, 1993). In this section, we describe organizational learning, its benefits, and the risks it entails. In the next section, we then explain how psychological safety helps mitigate the risks of learning. In discussing organizational learning, we focus on deliberate learning rather than autonomous learning from accumulated experience because, although the latter is important, the former has become a core aim of organizations wishing to manage their performance (Argote, 1999).

Organizational Learning

Much like individual learning (Kolb, 1984), organizational learning encompasses iterative cycles of idea generation, planning (to execute selected ideas),

action (to trial ideas according to plans), and reflection (to critically examine the results of actions for new ideas). Each new cycle is informed by the results of the previous ones, and cycles continue until desired outcomes are achieved, or indefinitely in a more dynamic context (Edmondson, 2002). A primary difference between individual and organizational learning is that individual learning is not other-dependent, whereas organizational learning requires multiple individuals.

Through multiple individuals and teams learning while engaged in disparate tasks, organizations are able to develop new routines that allow effective performance in a changing context (Levitt & March, 1988; Schulz, 2002). Although some routines are simple and carried out by one person, most organizational routines are complex and require coordination among a group of individuals with different expertise (Parker & Wall, 1996). As these individuals engage in iterative cycles of idea generation-planning-action-reflection, they surface and integrate their differential knowledge, and learn how to effectively use their new collective knowledge to improve organizational routines. Because this process typically happens among individuals working in teams, teams and team learning are regarded as the primary vehicles of organizational learning (Edmondson, 2002; Senge, 1990). Organizations thus learn when multiple teams within them learn. Team learning describes the activities through which members acquire, share, or combine their knowledge with the goal of adapting and improving their work processes (Argote, Gruenfeld, & Naquin, 1999). Although many behaviors may serve this purpose, three behaviors are consistently associated with team learning, and hence organizational learning: speaking up, collaboration, and experimentation (Ancona & Caldwell, 1992; Edmondson, 1999; Gibson & Vermeulen, 2003). These three behaviors fuel the idea generation-planning-action-reflection cycle (Edmondson, 2002), as summarized in Table 37.1.

SPEAKING UP

The learning process in organizations depends on multiple forms of conversation between individuals in the workplace. This includes asking questions, seeking feedback, talking about errors, asking for help, offering suggestions, and discussing problems and concerns (Edmondson 1999). All of these conversations involve what is commonly referred to as speaking up—taking some degree of interpersonal risk to offer content that one believes is relevant. Speaking up is particularly crucial for raising

Table 37.1 Core learning behaviors supporting the organizational learning process

Learning Behavior	Description	Contribution to Organizational Learning
Speaking up	Open and authentic communication, including speaking up with questions, concerns and suggestions	Raises awareness of problems and opportunities for improvement, and increases knowledge transfer
Collaboration	Cooperation between individuals working toward a common goal; includes conversation and coordination	Enables the process to draw on greater expertise and facilitates action through coordination
Experimentation	Trials to develop innovations, skill with new practices, or solutions to problems	Failures motivate learning and provide lessons

awareness about problems or opportunities for improvement. It is a means of generating discussion about current practices and about ideas for improving work processes. Speaking up also fuels the decision and planning components of the learning process; the insights gained from open conversation help determine appropriate courses of action (Simons, Pelled, & Smith, 1999). In situations in which effective practices exist, and the challenge is a successful implementation of those practices, speaking up is essential to helping people learn new practices. Conversing about experiences, insights, and questions builds understanding of new practices and how to perform them.

COLLABORATION

As noted earlier, many organizational routines require individuals to work together effectively and efficiently (Parker & Wall, 1996). Collaboration refers to the degree of cooperation among individuals who seek to achieve a common goal (Gratton & Erickson, 2007). It includes conversation and coordination of actions to achieve the goal. In that sense, it mirrors relational coordination, which Gittell (2011, Chapter 30, this volume) defines as "communicating and relating for the purpose of task integration." Organizational learning depends on collaboration inside teams, and with those outside the team as well (e.g., those in other departments or organizations) (Ancona & Caldwell, 1992). Without internal and external collaboration, the learning process is hindered by ill-informed ideas and plans. It is also potentially hindered at the action stage by poor coordination. At the reflection stage, lack of collaboration may hurt learning if it portends the exclusion of expertise that would allow broader and deeper lessons to be learned from the experience. Imagine a new product development team that does not collaborate with the marketing team. It is likely not to learn as much from its product launch as it

would if it had worked with the marketing team to understand customer feedback.

EXPERIMENTATION

Learning in organizations relies on experimentation. When new practices enter an industry, individuals and teams must quickly adapt or innovate in response, if their organizations are to remain successful. They often do so through small trials to gain experience using the practices. Likewise, when organizations wish to generate ideas for new products or services, or novel solutions to existing problems, experimentation is required to find out what works and what does not. This trial-and-error process, by definition, involves failures. Failures can be invaluable learning experiences for organizations (Chuang & Baum, 2003; Miner, Kim, Holzinger, & Haunschild, 1999). Recent research suggests that failures have a higher learning value than success (Kim, Kim, & Miner, 2009; Madsen & Desai, 2010). When success occurs, celebration may follow, with little investigation of the reasons for success. In contrast, failure often motivates examination of systems to determine the causes of failure. Lessons learned allow the design of solutions that minimize such events in the future (Sitkin, 1992). Thus, despite the risk of failure that accompanies experimentation, organizations that experiment—and therefore learn—are more likely to be successful in the long term than those that do not (Thomke 2003).

Benefits of Organizational Learning

Theoretical and empirical research has identified several benefits of organizational and team learning for organizations and their staff. The benefits largely fall into two categories: better organizational or team performance, and more satisfying work environments. Most of the research showcases the positive relationship between learning behavior and performance. This relationship has been demonstrated in a variety of work settings, including for example, manufacturing (Arthur & Huntley, 2005), product development (Lynn, Mazzuca, Morone, & Paulson, 1998), and patient care delivery (Nembhard & Tucker, 2010).

The studies suggest that learning behavior affects performance by facilitating new knowledge creation and the implementation of new practices. Choo and colleagues (2007) conducted a study of 188 Six Sigma projects in a manufacturing firm and found that project performance improved because team learning behaviors (i.e., information seeking and discussion) led to performance-enhancing knowledge. However, new knowledge is not enough to improve performance. Knowledge must be implemented (March, 1991), which is also enabled by learning behaviors. A qualitative study of cardiac surgery teams at 16 hospitals showed that teams that engaged in learning behaviors were more likely to successfully implement a new technology than were those that underestimated the implementation challenge and engaged in little explicit team learning. The learning behaviors helped teams adapt to the new ways of working together required by the technology (Edmondson, Bohmer, & Pisano, 2001). Similarly, a study of hospital improvement teams found that use of learning activities aimed at adapting new practices to the setting helped teams to implement new practices (Tucker, Nembhard, & Edmondson, 2007). In both studies, learning activities were associated with better performance.

A related but distinct benefit of organizational learning is the positive effect on the experience of work for staff. In learning organizations, staff are encouraged and empowered to participate in improvement efforts. The implicit, high valuation of staff members' contributions shapes how they experience the work environment. Being involved in discussions about issues that affect their work increases staff members' feelings of empowerment, support, and value (Eby, Freeman, Rush, & Lance, 1999), which contributes to staff's favorable impression of the setting as one in which they can thrive and flourish. Further, staff involvement in organizational learning fosters the development of high-quality working relationships, which staff enjoy (Cameron, Dutton, & Quinn, 2003; Dutton, 2003). A recent study found that workgroups with greater use of learning activities not only experienced better performance, but also experienced greater interdisciplinary collaboration among staff

(Nembhard & Tucker, 2010). Moreover, the researchers found that improved collaboration explained the relationship between use of learning activities and performance. Using learning activities led to greater collaboration, and in turn, to better performance. No evidence was found to support the notion that collaboration predicted the use of deliberate learning activities, although the researchers suspected a circular relationship.

In sum, the benefits of organizational learning are significant. Engaging in the process improves the work environment for staff, making it a more enriching and satisfying environment. Thus, staff members benefit. The organization benefits as well by having satisfied, contributing staff who use their extensive knowledge about organizational processes to help the organization create and implement new knowledge that allows the organization to perform well into the future.

Interpersonal Risks Inherent in Organizational Learning

Despite the benefits of organizational learning, individuals are often hesitant to engage in this process and its associated behaviors (speaking up, collaboration, and experimentation) because they perceive the interpersonal risks to be great. In general, but particularly in the work environment, individuals are cognizant of risks to their reputation (Tedeschi, 1981). They seek to maintain a favorable reputation—being seen as smart, competent, positive, and helpful—because a favorable reputation has socioemotional and instrumental benefits (Edmondson, 2003a). Most of us like being viewed favorably, and it offers tangible benefits, especially when favorable impressions are held by those in positions of power. At work, a supervisors' favorable impression can translate into assignment to desirable projects, promotions, and special privileges (e.g., corner office), for example. Hence the saying "Reputation is everything," and the finding that individuals actively manage their reputations (Leary & Kowalski, 1990). They manage not only by performing well, but also by avoiding situations and behaviors that pose risks to their image (Tedeschi, 1981). Unfortunately, learning behaviors can entail such risks. Speaking up, collaborating with diverse others, and experimenting can be risky. Notably, individuals risk being seen as ignorant, incompetent, negative, and disruptive (Edmondson, 2003a).

When individuals speak up about concerns or ask questions, they first risk being seen as ignorant.

Others might expect that they should already know the answer or understand the situation. Similarly, speaking up about one's mistakes or seeking other's help raises concerns that others will assume that one is incompetent. If an individual speaks up about problems or errors, he or she also risks being seen as negative. Individuals in the workplace—staff and leaders alike—likely believe themselves to be working to the best of their abilities. Thus, others' negative feedback is likely to be viewed as inaccurate, and the feedback giver as a trouble-maker or a negative person. Most people do not wish to be viewed this way. Thus, they compensate for errors and withhold negative feedback, even though this information is valuable for learning and ultimately performance improvement (Tucker & Edmondson, 2003). Finally, speaking up risks giving the impression that the individual is disruptive. Work environments are filled with busy individuals trying hard to accomplish the day's tasks within work hours. Therefore, interruptions to raise concerns or ask for help can seem disruptive. However, research shows that interruptions benefit learning. In a study of 90 teams working in the pharmaceutical and medical products industry, Zellmer-Bruhn (2003) found that interruptions increased knowledge transfer effort and the acquisition of new routines. Despite such benefits of speaking up, organizational silence is prevalent due to the inherent risks and associated fear of speaking up (Milliken & Morrison, 2000; Van Dyne, Soon, & Botero, 2003). In one study, over 85% of the managers and staff interviewed admitted to remaining silent about a concern (Milliken, Morrison, & Hewlin, 2003).

The risks associated with speaking up arise with collaboration and experimentation as well. When an individual collaborates with others, thereby implicitly granting the opportunity for others' to observe his or her knowledge and performance, the individual risks others forming an unfavorable impression. Others might categorize differences in knowledge or work practices as evidence of ignorance or incompetence. By participating in experiments, individuals face similar risks. Because failure (a learning opportunity) is almost inevitable with experiments, individuals who engage in experiments risk being associated with failure and incompetence (Wolfe, Lennox, & Cutler, 1986). Additionally, they risk being seen as negative or disruptive, if their experiments challenge well-accepted practices or provide evidence that those practices are not best.

Facing these small but psychologically meaningful interpersonal risks, the easiest and most natural form of risk management is to avoid speaking up, collaboration, and experimentation. Although this approach has the advantage of minimizing individual risk, it has the disadvantage of minimizing team and organizational learning, thus limiting organizational performance and creating a less enriching work environment.

How Psychological Safety Mitigates Organizational Learning's Risks

The interpersonal risks associated with team and organizational learning are formidable but can be overcome. A growing body of research suggests that psychological safety minimizes the perceived risks of engaging in learning behaviors. In psychologically safe places, individuals feel that their actions and feedback are valued and will not result in negative consequences (e.g., censoring, ridicule, penalty, or punishment). Therefore, it is safe to take interpersonal risks, such as those required for learning (Edmondson, 1999; Jackson & Dutton, 1988; West, 1990). Studies consistently show that individuals and teams in psychologically safe places engage in core learning behaviors (i.e., speaking up, collaboration, and experimentation).

Psychological Safety and Speaking Up

Much of the research on psychological safety demonstrates its role in motivating individuals to speak up. In one of the seminal works in this area, Edmondson (1996) showed that nurses were more likely to speak up about medication errors if they described their hospital unit using terms suggestive of psychological safety, such as "nonpunitive" and "nonjudgmental." In the very different context of telecommunication, Dutton and colleagues (1997) similarly showed that middle managers decided whether to speak up about issues based on their assessment of psychological safety. When they viewed the culture as open and supportive of new ideas, managers were more likely to try to sell their issues to top management, an act that would typically be viewed as risky. In yet another distinct context, a restaurant chain, Detert and Burris (2007) showed that employees who felt psychologically safe were more likely to use improvement-oriented voice (i.e., speak up about improvements to organizational functioning to someone with perceived authority). The propensity to share one's knowledge in psychologically safe places appears repeatedly across organizational settings (Siemsen, Roth, Balasubramanian, & Anand, 2009).

Psychological Safety and Collaboration

The role of psychological safety in creating a context in which it is easier to collaborate with diverse individuals has also been documented. In the aforementioned study of 16 cardiac surgery teams implementing a new technology, the researchers found that those teams that developed psychological safety became more collaborative. Their collaboration was such a departure from their prior hierarchically driven routines that team members frequently commented on the difference in their conversations with the researchers. For example, one nurse from a team that developed psychological safety said, "We're more of a team in the operating room . . . much more interactive than I ever dreamed it could be. . . . It gave me a new lease on life" (Edmondson et al., 2001, p. 700). The positive effect of psychological safety on collaboration is also suggested by the work of Van der Vegt and Bunderson (2005) in the oil and gas industry. This work showed that expertise diversity in teams (often a barrier to collaboration) is associated with learning behavior when team identification, a concept that parallels psychological safety in its emphasis on the emotional-motivational basis for interaction, is high. This finding suggests that members overcome their differences to collaborate in learning behaviors once they identify with the team and believe it is safe.

Psychological Safety and Experimentation

Research has also found that psychological safety can motivate the experimentation needed for innovation. When support for risk-taking and tolerance for mistakes is present, teams have been found to engage in behaviors associated with innovation, such as experimentation and improvisation (Caldwell & O'Reilly III, 2003; Vera & Crossan, 2005; West, 1990). A classic example of a psychologically safe work climate fostering innovation through experimentation is 3M, where the Post-It Note was discovered. A researcher there was intrigued by a colleague's failed experiment with an adhesive, which the colleague openly shared with him and others at 3M. The researcher thought that the adhesive might be useful for keeping papers from falling out of his choir book, so he began to experiment with different versions of the adhesive. Many versions failed, yet he felt encouraged to pursue his idea because 3M encouraged intrapreneurial activity and allowed for failure. His many failed experiments, performed within the safety of the 3M organization, led to the Post-It Notes we use today (Fry, 1987).

Psychological Safety and Performance

The evidence strongly supports that psychological safety effectively mitigates the interpersonal risks of learning, such that individuals and teams in psychologically safe places readily engage in learning behavior, with consequent improved performance (e.g., Edmondson, 1999). Some studies even provide evidence of a direct relationship between psychological safety and performance (e.g., Baer & Frese, 2003; Edmondson, 1999), hence the interest in psychological safety in organizations.

Barriers to Psychological Safety and Organizational Learning

If asked whether they prefer to work in a psychologically safe place or not, we guess that most individuals would respond in the affirmative. Who would not want to work in place where the interpersonal risks are low, learning behaviors are appreciated, and individual and collective performance are high? Yet, the median rating of workplace psychological safety is 76 out of 100 across a variety of industries in numerous countries (Garvin, Edmondson, & Gino, 2008). This suggests that a significant percentage of the global workforce is employed in an organization in which psychological safety is low. Why is this the case, when most people prefer the alternative? We argue that several factors challenge the development of psychological safety in the workplace, factors related to the nature of work, workgroups, and organizations. We briefly discuss these factors, before presenting countervailing, positive influences on psychological safety in the workplace. Table 37.2 summarizes these negative and positive influences on psychological safety.

The Nature of Work and Workgroups

Organizations employ individuals with diverse expertise, experiences, and backgrounds. Often, these individuals are expected to work together to complete tasks. However, a significant body of research shows that individuals often find it difficult to work in diverse groups (Williams & O'Reilly, 1998). It can be especially challenging to work in such groups when differences translate into status and power differences. Status refers to the level of prominence, respect, and influence associated with an individual as a result of a characteristic such as age, gender, ethnicity, profession, etc. (Anderson, John, Keltner, & Kring, 2001). Power refers to the "ability to influence behavior, to change the course of events, . . . and to get people to do

Table 37.2 Positive and negative influences on psychological safety

Negative Influences	Positive Influences
Nature of work and workgroups	Nature of work and workgroups
Diverse	Leadership and leader behavior
Hierarchical based on status and power	High-quality relationships
Temporary and virtual	Nature of organizations
Nature of organizations	Opportunity for "practice"
Performance-oriented	

things that they would not otherwise do" (Pfeffer, 1994).

Individuals are well aware of where they fall in the status and power hierarchies at work (Tajfel & Turner, 1986; Webster & Foschi, 1988). Their position shapes their perceptions of how safe it is to take interpersonal risks within their workgroup. In one study of intensive care units, we found that lower-status team members reported feeling less safe than did higher-status members. The former reported feeling more uncomfortable checking with others, more fearful that mistakes would be held against them, less able to bring up tough problems and issues, and less certain that others value their unique talents and skills (Nembhard & Edmondson, 2006). Thus, simply by virtue of hierarchies in the workplace, psychological safety can be elusive for many.

Another emerging characteristic of work and workgroups that likely contributes to the elusiveness of psychological safety is their temporariness. In many organizations, work is project-based, and projects are "staffed" with individuals whose expertise is most relevant. Some individuals may have worked together before; others may not. Some may work on the project until it is complete, others may not. Some projects span a long period of time, perhaps even years, others span weeks. Although the fluctuations and variations enable project needs to be met, they can pose problems for the development of psychological safety. Although not always true, individuals are likely to feel safer with those with whom they have stable, long-term relationships. In the context of such relationships, members develop a rapport, understanding, and appreciation of each other that can cultivate psychological safety. Temporary project teams do not benefit from this familiarity, an observation that has been used to explain the unexpected death of climbers on a Mt. Everest expedition. A review of the incident concluded that lack of familiarity among members of the expedition team led to lack of psychological safety, which prevented discussion of the dire

situation the team faced and how to address it (Roberto, 2002).

Lack of familiarity, and consequently lack of psychological safety, also seems to stem from another increasingly common attribute of workgroups—their virtuality. A study by the Gartner Group found that more than 60% of professionals work in virtual teams, meaning that members are geographically dispersed and electronically dependent (Kanawattanachai & Yoo, 2002). In these teams, members' sense of belonging to a bounded group can be limited, thus lowering their psychological safety. Faraj and Yan (2009) studied 64 software development teams and found that situations that failed to reinforce and buffer team boundaries were negatively associated with psychological safety. Thus, the nature of work (virtual and temporary), as well workgroup dynamics (status and power differences), can hinder psychological safety.

The Nature of Organizational Goals

Organizational goals can also inhibit psychological safety. Goals have been classified as either performance-oriented or learning-oriented. A performance goal orientation emphasizes "demonstrating competence and avoiding failure," whereas a learning goal orientation emphasizes the "development of skill, knowledge, and competence" (Bunderson & Sutcliffe, 2003, p. 552). Individuals come to understand the goal orientation of their organizations through cues such as leadership directives, task assignments, evaluation and reward systems, and social discourse. These cues shape individuals' perceptions of what is valued in the organization. Thus, organizations whose cues indicate a performance orientation (e.g., financial bonuses for achieving a zero-failure rate or financial penalties for failing to meet sales goals) are likely to have individuals who perceive that they should focus their efforts on delivering high performance by showing successes and avoiding failures (Ames & Archer, 1988). By signaling high performance, as defined by management, they will secure their position in the organization and receive rewards. Conversely, they infer that signaling low performance will have negative consequences. Thus, there is great pressure to perform well.

Performance pressure can result in lower psychological safety and lower willingness to deviate or take risks. Experimental studies show that children with a performance goal are more risk averse, less willing to experiment, and less willing to depart from strategies to which they are accustomed than are children with a learning goal (Dweck & Leggett, 1988). Additionally, they ultimately perform worse than their learning-oriented counterparts. Research on workers in service settings similarly shows that individuals who feel pressured to perform engage in behaviors (e.g., cutting corners) that ultimately erode performance (Oliva, 2001). Lack of psychological safety prevents them from speaking up about the appropriateness of performance goals and their need for assistance to achieve those goals. Unfortunately, many organizations appear to be performance-oriented; creating learning-oriented organizations appears to take thoughtful leadership and considerable effort (Edmondson, Nembhard, & Roloff, 2007).

When It Is Safe to Learn: Positive Influences on Psychological Safety

In multiple studies, psychological safety has been shown to vary significantly across groups within the same organization (Edmondson, 1996, 1999, 2002). This implies that this important climate variable is subject to local influences—factors that vary at the group level of analysis, such as supervisory behavior, goal clarity, and task interdependence.

In particular, prior research has emphasized local leadership—the behavior of those leaders in close contact with a given workgroup or individual—as a key determinant of psychological safety (Detert & Burris, 2007; Edmondson, 1996, 2003b). In our research in hospitals, we found that leader inclusiveness—the extent to which local leaders, such as physicians or nurse managers, sought and appreciated others' input, made themselves available, and displayed fallibility—influenced others' psychological safety (Edmondson, 1996; Nembhard & Edmondson, 2006). The more inclusive the leaders were, the higher the psychological safety was in the hospital unit. Elevation in psychological safety was particularly striking for lower-status individuals. Whereas lower-status individuals (e.g., nurses) working in units with less inclusive leaders felt

significantly less safe than higher-status individuals (i.e., physicians), those working in units with higher leader inclusiveness felt a level of safety comparable to higher-status individuals. In these units, there was also greater staff engagement in quality improvement work.

Other researchers have also found this positive relationship between leader behavior and psychological safety in a variety of settings, including for example, insurance companies (May, Gilson, & Harter, 2004), technology firms (Detert & Trevino, 2010), and restaurants (Detert & Burris, 2007). In each study, researchers found that leaders' openness to new ideas was linked to staff psychological safety, and that psychological safety mediated the relationship between leaders' openness and staff's improvement-oriented behavior. In Halbesleben and Rathert's (2008) study, higher leader-associated psychological safety even predicted a reduction in staff workarounds, a prevalent behavior that undermines organizational learning because it solves problems temporarily without addressing them systematically (Tucker & Edmondson, 2003).

In addition to leaders, peers affect psychological safety. Studies show that supportive coworker relationships are significantly associated with psychological safety (e.g., May et al., 2004). Kahn's (1990) qualitative study of an architecture firm found that supportive and trusting interpersonal relationships promoted psychological safety. The informants in Kahn's study reported that they felt free to share their design ideas when they believed that criticism from their peers would be constructive rather than destructive. The belief that peers see one as competent (an aspect of respect) is salient; those who feel that their capability is in question are more likely to feel judged and thus may keep their opinions to themselves for fear of harming their reputation (Edmondson & Moingeon, 1998). In sum, if relationships within a group are characterized by trust and respect, individuals are likely to experience greater psychological safety.

Recent work on high-quality relationships in the workplace suggests why these relationships positively influence psychological safety (Carmeli, 2007; Carmeli & Gittell, 2009). This work argues that such relationships have higher capacity; they can handle the sharing of more and varied (positive and negative) emotions, withstand strain and change, and accommodate new ideas. These relationships also positively alter the subjective experience of the workplace, such that individuals in them experience vitality, positive regard for each other, and a shared sense of engagement. See Chapter 29 (this volume) by Stephens, Heaphy, and Dutton's for greater discussion of high-quality connections. Recent empirical work shows that the attributes of these relationships—their capacity and the subjective experience of individuals within them—are positively associated with psychological safety, which mediates their association with learning behavior (Carmeli, 2007; Carmeli & Gittell, 2009). Thus, there is evidence that both coworkers and leaders play key roles in the development of psychological safety.

Having the time and opportunity to practice offline also influences psychological safety. Senge (1990) observed that sports teams spend more time practicing than performing, whereas management and other organizational work teams typically do not invest in practice sessions of any kind. Senge (1990) suggested using management "practice fields," in which teams learn in management "flight simulators," dynamic models where participants can make decisions and test interrelationships without risk to their real work. In the study of cardiac surgery teams mentioned earlier, six of the eight successful teams used a form of practice field, engaging in team practice sessions (dry runs), whereas six of the eight unsuccessful teams did not do so (Edmondson et al., 2001). In these practice sessions, the teams walked through the steps of the procedure without a patient, discussing what each person would be doing if a real patient had been present. These sessions helped teams anticipate problems that might arise during surgery, and also helped them get comfortable in new interpersonal roles and relationships. Other research found that leader briefings and team training sessions promote team performance in new environments (Marks, Zaccaro, & Mathieu, 2000). Practice sessions may foster psychological safety, not only because real financial or service consequences are removed, but also because they convey to team members that learning is important and that getting it right the first time is understood to not always be possible. Figure 37.1 summarizes our discussion of the contributors and outcomes of psychological safety and organizational learning.

Future Directions

Although much is now known about psychological safety and its contribution to organizational learning, there remain numerous avenues for future research. Here, we propose just a few with the hope of providing a starting point and encouraging greater discussion and understanding of the role of psychological safety in organizations.

- *Understanding leader inclusiveness and other leadership strategies for fostering psychological safety*: Our work points to a leader attribute that fosters psychological safety: leader inclusiveness. This is a construct that we developed and measured through survey responses about three practices. Future research should develop this construct further and investigate whether there are more practices that demonstrate inclusiveness. It should also study how to help leaders become more inclusive in their approach. Additionally, future research should explore other leader behaviors that may influence psychological safety. Roussin (2008) provides a case-based argument that leaders who use dyadic discovery methods (i.e., private, individual, trust-building conversations with team members to understand their perspectives) learn more about their teams and more effectively customize their behaviors to increase psychological safety than do leaders who use a group-level discovery process. More research is needed to explore this argument, identify other effective leader behaviors, and examine the relative effectiveness of different leader behaviors for cultivating psychological safety.
- *Psychological safety as a moderator of relationships in the work environment*: In most empirical work, psychological safety has been regarded as a main effect predictor of organizational learning or performance, or as a mediator on the pathway between another antecedent (e.g., professional status) and an outcome such as learning or performance. However, some research has raised the possibility that psychological safety might also moderate relationships in the work environment. For example, Baer and Frese (2003) found that psychological safety moderated the relationship between process innovativeness and financial performance, such that a high level of psychological safety was associated with a positive relationship between process innovativeness and financial performance, whereas a low level of psychological safety was associated with a negative relationship.

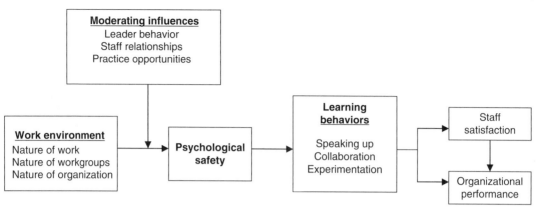

Fig. 37.1 A model of psychological safety and learning in organizations.

Other work has proposed that psychological safety moderates the relationship between learning goals and learning behavior (Edmondson, 2003a), but this hypothesis has yet to be tested. Future research may examine this hypothesis and other situations in which psychological safety may moderate as the cultivation of psychological safety may be a lever to alter other organizational processes.

- *The relationship between psychological safety and other positive phenomena*: Every chapter in this volume provides thoughtful, empirically grounded and theoretically compelling insights about a subject within the domain POS. We propose that much would be gained by considering how psychological safety might affect or be affected by other processes discussed in this volume. In particular, we think that much would be learned through consideration of possible relationships between psychological safety and mindful organizing (see Chapter 50 of this volume), managing the unexpected (see Chapter 64), and resilience at work (see Chapter 68). Our guess is that psychological safety enables each of these processes. This would suggest that positive processes beget positive processes. The question remains whether negative processes or events can also beget positive processes like psychological safety.
- *Other outcomes of psychological safety*: In our discussion, we have focused on the relationship between psychological safety, organizational learning, and performance. This focus mirrors the theoretical and

empirical research to date. Little research has considered other potential outcomes of psychological safety; yet, a range of other outcomes likely exists. Recent work shows that innovation (Gibson & Gibbs, 2006) and involvement in creative work (Kark & Carmeli, 2009) are additional outcomes of psychological safety. We encourage scholars to examine other outcomes, for example, employee well-being or health outcomes.

As scholars explore these and other avenues, it is worth remembering that organizational research on psychological safety has gone through different methodological stages. Some early work, notably by Kahn (1990) was qualitative and exploratory in nature, as needed to flesh out dimensions of the construct and how it worked in different work settings. Edmondson's (1999) study introduced a mixed-methods (qualitative and quantitative) approach that allowed tests of associations between existing team survey variables and a new measure of psychological safety developed by her, using items induced from qualitative data in two workplaces. The scale—both in full and in part—published in Edmondson (1999) has been used in several quantitative studies since (e.g., Baer & Frese, 2003; Nembhard & Edmondson, 2006; etc.). The scale turns out to be robust to small changes in wording needed to reflect different kinds of workplaces. In general, quantitative studies, often using survey scales, are appropriate for studying new relationships between existing constructs (Edmondson & McManus, 2007). Thus, future studies to investigate possible moderators of previously shown theoretical relationships between psychological safety and an outcome variable, or psychological safety's relationship to other established constructs are well suited to the use of survey approaches that modify the existing scales as needed.

We hope that scholars will work individually and together to uncover more ways in which psychological safety contributes to a positive work environment. There is still much to learn.

Conclusion

Our review of the theoretical and empirical literature suggests that psychological safety sets the stage for organizational learning, a process that enables organizations and their staff to survive and thrive in changing and uncertain environments. Many studies show that, when there is a shared belief that it is safe to take interpersonal risks (e.g., ask questions, reveal mistakes), individuals and teams are willing to speak up, collaborate, and experiment, thus facilitating organizational learning. The benefits of such learning are great. In a changing environment, organizations that learn perform better over time, while those that don't learn fall behind. Learning organizations engage employees, drawing upon their knowledge and curiosity to generate and implement new ideas, inviting and supporting their efforts to improve, experiment, and innovate. This experience can make the work environment enriching and satisfying for staff.

The link between psychological safety and organizational learning provides the foundation for a positive organizational dynamic, a positive feedback loop that promotes organizational performance. However, in practice, both psychological safety and organizational learning confront obstacles in the work environment. In this review, we highlight three factors that can inhibit the realization of psychological safety and organizational learning: status/power hierarchies, challenging job designs (e.g., temporary teams), and overly narrow goals. Our review shows that it is possible to overcome these challenges through leader inclusiveness, positive relationships among coworkers, and opportunities for offline practice, for example.

This set of findings represents POS in a number of respects. First, they demonstrate a positive phenomenon: individuals and teams overcoming the interpersonal hurdles and environmental challenges to organizational learning to the benefit of organizations and staff. Second, the findings provide reassurance for organizations: sustained performance improvement is possible, with the help of engaged, psychologically safe staff. Finally, this stream of research holds a positive message for scholars as it affirms that it is possible to identify conditions that counter negative patterns of behavior *and* that yield significant benefits for organizations and their staff.

References

Ames, C., & Archer, J. (1988). Achievement goals in the classroom: Students' learning strategies and motivation processes. *Journal of Educational Psychology, 80*, 260–267.

Ancona, D.G., & Caldwell, D.F. (1992). Bridging the boundary: External activity and performance in organizational teams. *Administrative Science Quarterly, 37*(4), 634–665.

Anderson, C., John, O.P., Keltner, D., & Kring, A.M. (2001). Who attains social status? Effects of personality and physical attractiveness in social groups. *Journal of Personality and Social Psychology, 81*, 116-132.

Argote, L. (1999). *Organizational learning: Creating, retaining and transferring knowledge.* Norwell, MA: Kluwer.Argote, L., Gruenfeld, D., & Naquin, C. (1999). Group learning in organizations. In M.E. Turner (Ed.), *Groups at work: Advances in theory and research.* New York: Erlbaum.

Arthur, J.B., & Huntley, C.L. (2005). Ramping up the organizational learning curve: Assessing the impact of deliberate learning on organizational performance under gainsharing. *Academy of Management Journal, 48*(6), 1159–1170.

Baer, M., & Frese, M. (2003). Innovation is not enough: Climates for initiative and psychological safety, process innovations, and firm performance. *Journal of Organizational Behavior, 24*(1), 45–60.

Bunderson, J.S., & Sutcliffe, K.M. (2003). Management team learning orientation and business unit performance. *Journal of Applied Psychology, 88*(3), 552.

Caldwell, D.F., & O'Reilly, C.A., III. (2003). The determinants of team-based innovation in organizations. *Small Group Research, 34*(4), 497.

Cameron, K.S., Dutton, J.E., & Quinn, R.E. (2003). *Positive organizational scholarship.* San Francisco: Berrett-Koehler.

Carmeli, A. (2007). Social capital, psychological safety and learning behaviours from failure in organisations. *Long Range Planning, 40*(1), 30–44.

Carmeli, A., & Gittell, J.H. (2009). High-quality relationships, psychological safety, and learning from failures in work organizations. *Journal of Organizational Behavior, 30*(6), 709–729.

Choo, A.S., Linderman, K.W., & Schroeder, R.G. (2007). Method and psychological effects on learning behaviors and knowledge creation in quality improvement projects. *Management Science, 53*(3), 437–450.

Chuang, Y.-T., & Baum, J.A.C. (2003). It's all in the name: Failure-induced learning by multiunit chains. *Administrative Science Quarterly, 48*(1), 33–59.

Detert, J.R., & Burris, E.R. (2007). Leadership behavior and employee voice: Is the door really open? *Academy of Management Journal, 50*(4), 869–884.

Detert, J.R., & Trevino, L.K. (2010). Speaking up to higher-ups: How supervisors and skip-level leaders influence employee voice. *Organization Science, 21*(1), 249–270.

Dutton, J.E. (2003). *Energize your workplace: How to build and sustain high-quality relationships at work.* San Francisco: Jossey-Bass.

Dutton, J.E., Ashford, S.J., O'Neill, R.M., Hayes, E., & Wierba, E.E. (1997). Reading the wind: How middle managers assess the context for selling issues to top managers. *Strategic Management Journal, 18*(5), 407–423.

Dweck, C.S., & Leggett, E.I. (1988). A social-cognitive approach to motivation and personality. *Psychological Review, 95*(2), 256–273.

Eby, L.T., Freeman, D.M., Rush, M.C., & Lance, C.E. (1999). Motivational bases of affective organizational commitment: A partial test of an integrative theoretical model. *Journal of Occupational and Organizational Psychology, 72*(4), 51–59.

Edmondson, A.C. (1996). Learning from mistakes is easier said than done: Group and organizational influences on the detection and correction of human error. *Journal of Applied Behavioral Science, 40*(1), 66–90.

Edmondson, A.C. (1999). Psychological safety and learning behavior in work teams. *Administrative Science Quarterly, 44*(2), 350–383.

Edmondson, A.C. (2002). The local and variegated nature of learning in organizations: A group-level perspective. *Organization Science, 13*(2), 128–146.

Edmondson, A.C. (2003a). Managing the risk of learning: Psychological safety in work teams. In M. West, D. Tjosvold, & K.G. Smith. (Eds.), *International handbook of organizational teamwork and cooperative working* (pp. 255–276). London: John Wiley & Sons.

Edmondson, A.C. (2003b). Speaking up in the operating room: How team leaders promote learning in interdisciplinary action teams. *The Journal of Management Studies, 40*(6), 1419–1452.

Edmondson, A.C. (2008). The competitive imperative of learning. *Harvard Business Review, 86*(7/8), 60–67.

Edmondson, A.C., Bohmer, R.M., & Pisano, G.P. (2001). Disrupted routines: Team learning and new technology implementation in hospitals. *Administrative Science Quarterly, 46*(4), 685–716.

Edmondson, A.C., & McManus, S. (2007). Methodological fit in management field research. *Academy of Management Review, 32*(4), 1155–1179.

Edmondson, A.C., & Moingeon, B. (1998). From organizational learning to learning organization. *Management Learning, 29*(1), 5–20.

Edmondson, A.C., Nembhard, I.M., & Roloff, K.S. (2007). *Children's hospital and clinics (B).* Case No. 9–608-073. Boston: Harvard Business School.

Faraj, S., & Aimin, Y. (2009). Boundary work in knowledge teams. *Journal of Applied Psychology, 94*(3), 604–617.

Fiol, C.M., & Lyles, M.A. (1985). Organizational learning. *Academy of Management Review, 10*(4), 803–813.

Fry, A. (1987). The post-it note: An intrapreneurial success. *SAM Advanced Management Journal, 52*(3), 4–9.

Garvin, D.A. (1993). Building a learning organization. *Harvard Business Review, 71*(4), 78–91.

Garvin, D.A., Edmondson, A., & Gino, F. (2008). Is yours a learning organization? *Harvard Business Review, 86*(3), 109–116.

Gibson, C., & Vermeulen, F. (2003). A healthy divide: Subgroups as a stimulus for team learning behavior. *Administrative Science Quarterly, 48*(2), 202–239.

Gibson, C.B., & Gibbs, J.L. (2006). Unpacking the concept of virtuality: The effects of geographic dispersion, electronic dependence, dynamic structure, and national diversity on team innovation. *Administrative Science Quarterly, 51*(3), 451–495.

Gittell, J.H. (2011). New directions for relational coordination theory. In K.S. Cameron & G.M. Spreitzer (Eds.), *The Oxford handbook of positive organizational scholarship.* New York: Oxford University Press.

Gratton, L., & Erickson, T.J. (2007). 8 ways to build collaborative teams. *Harvard Business Review, 85*(11), 100–109.

Halbesleben, J.R.B., & Rathert, C. (2008). The role of continuous quality improvement and psychological safety in predicting work-arounds. *Health Care Management Review, 33*(2), 134–144.

Jackson, S.J., & Dutton, J. (1988). Discerning threats and opportunities. *Administrative Science Quarterly, 33,* 370–387.

Kahn, W.A. (1990). Psychological conditions of personal engagement and disengagement at work. *Academy of Management Journal, 33*(4), 692–724.

Kanawattanachai, P., & Yoo, Y. (2002). Dynamic nature of trust in virtual teams. *The Journal of Strategic Information Systems, 11*(3–4), 187–213.

Kark, R., & Carmeli, A. (2009). Alive and creating: The mediating role of vitality and aliveness in the relationship between psychological safety and creative work involvement. *Journal of Organizational Behavior, 30*(6), 785–804.

Kim, J.-Y., Kim, J.-Y., & Miner, A.S. (2009). Organizational learning from extreme performance experience: The impact of success and recovery experience. *Organization Science, 20*(6), 958–978.

Klimoski, R., & Mohammed, S. (1994). Team mental model: Construct or metaphor? *Journal of Management, 20*(2), 403–437.

Kolb, D.A. (1984). *Experiential learning: Experience as the source of learning and development.* Englewood-Cliffs, NJ: Prentice-Hall.

Leary, M.R., & Kowalski, R.M. (1990). Impression management: A literature review and two component model. *Psychological Bulletin, 107,* 34–47.

Levitt, B., & March, J.G. (1988). Organizational learning. *Annual Review of Sociology, 14,* 319–340.

Lynn, G.S., Mazzuca, M., Morone, J.G., & Paulson, A.S. (1998). Learning is the critical success factor in developing truly new products. *Research Technology Management, 41*(3), 45–52.

Madsen, P.M., & Desai, V. (2010). Failing to learn? The effects of failure and success on organizational learning in the global orbital launch vehicle industry. *Academy of Management Journal, 53*(3), 451–476.

March, J.G. (1991). Exploration and exploitation in organizational learning. *Organization Science, 2*(1), 71–87.

Marks, M.A., Zaccaro, S., & Mathieu, J.E. (2000). Performance implications of leader briefings and team-interaction training for team adaptation to novel environments. *Journal of Applied Psychology, 85*(6), 971–986.

May, D.R., Gilson, R.L., & Harter, L.M. (2004). The psychological conditions of meaningfulness, safety and availability and the engagement of the human spirit at work. *Journal of Occupational and Organizational Psychology, 77,* 11–37.

Milliken, F.J., & Morrison, E.W. (2000). Organizational silence: A barrier to change and development in a pluralistic world. *Academy of Management Review, 25*(4), 706–725.

Milliken, F.J., Morrison, E.W., & Hewlin, P.F. (2003). An exploratory study of employee silence: Issues that employees don't communicate upward and why. *Journal of Management Studies, 40*(3), 1453–1476.

Miner, A.S., Kim, J.Y., Holzinger, I.W., & Haunschild, P.R. (1999). Fruits of failure: Organizational failure and population-level learning. In A.S. Miner, & P. Anderson (Eds.),

Advances in strategic management (pp. 187–220). Stamford, CT: JAI Press.

Nembhard, I.M., & Edmondson, A.C. (2006). Making it safe: The effects of leader inclusiveness and professional status on psychological safety and improvement efforts in health care teams. *Journal of Organizational Behavior, 27*(7), 941–966.

Nembhard, I.M., & Tucker, A.L. (2010). Deliberate learning to improve performance in dynamic service settings: Evidence from hospital intensive care units. *Organization Science.* Forthcoming.

Oliva, R. (2001). Tradeoffs in response to work pressure in the service industry. *California Management Review, 43*(4), 26–43.

Parker, S.K., & Wall, T.D. (1996). Job design and modern manufacturing. In P.B. Warr (Ed.), *Psychology at work* (pp. 333–359). London: Penguin Group.

Pfeffer, J. (1994). *Managing with power: Politics and influence in organizations.* Boston: Harvard Business School Press.

Rappoport, A. (1997). The patient's search for safety: The organizing principle in psychotherapy. *Psychotherapy, 34*(3), 250–261.

Roberto, M.A. (2002). Lessons from Everest: The interaction of cognitive bias, psychological safety, and system complexity. *California Management Review, 45*(1), 136–158.

Roussin, C.J. (2008). Increasing trust, psychological safety, and team performance through dyadic leadership discovery. *Small Group Research, 39*(2), 224–248.

Schein, E.H. (1993). How can organizations learn faster? The challenge of entering the green room. *Sloan Management Review, 34*(2), 85–92.

Schulz, M. (2002). Organizational learning. In J.A.C. Baum (Ed.), *The Blackwell companion to organizations* (pp. 415–441). Malden, MA: Blackwell Publishers Ltd.

Senge, P.M. (1990). *The fifth discipline: The art and practice of the learning organization.* New York: Currency Doubleday.

Siemsen, E., Roth, A.V., Balasubramanian, S., & Anand, G. (2009). The influence of psychological safety and confidence in knowledge on employee knowledge sharing. *Manufacturing & Service Operations Management, 11*(3), 429–447.

Simons, T., Pelled, L.H., & Smith, K.A. (1999). Making use of difference: Diversity, debate, and decision comprehensiveness in top management teams. *Academy of Management Journal, 42*(6), 662–673.

Sitkin, S.B. (1992). Learning through failure: The strategy of small losses. *Research in Organizational Behavior, 14*, 231–266.

Stata, R. (1989). Organizational learning-the key to management innovation. *Sloan Management Review, 30*(3), 63–74.

Stephens, J.P., Heaphy, E., & Dutton, J.E. (2011). High-quality connections. In K.S. Cameron & G.M. Spreitzer (Eds.), The

Oxford handbook of positive organizational scholarship. New York: Oxford University Press.

Tajfel, H., & Turner, J.C. (1986). The social identity theory of intergroup behavior. In S. Worchel, & W.G. Austin (Eds.), *Psychology of intergroup relations* (pp. 7–24). Chicago: Nelson-Hall.

Tedeschi, J.T. (1981). *Impression management theory and social psychological research.* New York: Academic Press.

Tucker, A.L., & Edmondson, A.C. (2003). Why hospitals don't learn from failures: Organizational and psychological dynamics that inhibit system change. *California Management Review, 45*(2), 55–72.

Tucker, A.L., Nembhard, I.M., & Edmondson, A.C. (2007). Implementing new practices: An empirical study of organizational learning in hospital intensive care units *Management Science, 53*(6), 894–907.

Tynan, R. (2005). The effects of threat sensitivity and face giving on dyadic psychological safety and upward communication. *Journal of Applied Social Psychology, 35*(2), 223–247.

Van der Vegt, G.S., & Bunderson, J.S. (2005). Learning and performance in multidisciplinary teams: The importance of collective team identification. *Academy of Management Journal, 48*(3), 532–547.

Van Dyne, L., Soon, A., & Botero, I.C. (2003). Conceptualizing employee silence and employee voice as multidimensional constructs. *Journal of Management Studies, 40*(6), 1359–1392.

Vera, D., & Crossan, M. (2005). Improvisation and innovative performance in teams. *Organization Science, 16*(3), 203–224.

Waks, L.J. (1988). Design principles for laboratory education in the creative process. *Person-Centered Review, 3*(4), 463–478.

Walsh, J. (1995). Managerial and organizational cognition: Notes from a trip down memory lane. *Organization Science, 6*(3), 280–321.

Webster, M., & Foschi, M. (1988). *Status generalizations.* Stanford, CA: Stanford University Press.

West, M.A. (1990). The social psychology of innovation in groups. In M.A. West, & J.L. Farr (Eds.), *Innovation and creativity at work: Psychological and organizational strategies* (pp. 309–333). Chichester, UK: Wiley.

Williams, K.Y., & O'Reilly, C.A., III. (1998). Demography and diversity in organizations: A review of the 40 years of research. *Research in Organizational Behavior, 20*, 77–140.

Wolfe, R.N., Lennox, R.D., & Cutler, B.L. (1986). Getting along and getting ahead: Empirical support for a theory of protective and acquisitive self-presentation. *Journal of Personality & Social Psychology, 50*(2), 356–361.

Zellmer-Bruhn, M.E. (2003). Interruptive events and team knowledge acquisition. *Management Science, 49*(4), 514–528.

PART 5

Positive Human Resource Practices

Personal Growth Through Career Work

A Positive Approach to Careers

Douglas T. Hall *and* Mireia Las Heras

Abstract

In this chapter we present the concept of career as one that is well suited to a POS approach, as careers involve human possibilities and lifelong work pursuits. We review different conceptual approaches to careers, including subjective vs. objective views of career experience, as well as content vs. process approaches to understanding career dynamics. We present a model of different types of careers based upon different individuals' personal definitions of success. We suggest more research on positive career concepts such as a career calling, the dream, psychological success, and the path with a heart.

Keywords: Objective career, subjective career, career success, psychological career success, developmental relationships, smart jobs, self-awareness, adaptability, career dream, reflected best self

What Is a Career? The Objective and Subjective Experience of Career

Since work is so important in many societies as a way of creating a person's sense of identity, it follows that one of the best ways to understand a person's life is to understand the person's career. Simply put, the career is the sequence of work experiences that a person has over his or her lifespan (M. B. Arthur, Hall, & Lawrence, 1989). Since work and work history or career have such an important impact on an individual's definition of oneself, a career has great potential for creating significant positive or negative personal experiences. In this chapter, we address the positive possibilities inherent in a career.

There are two ways that one can observe a career: from the inside and from the outside. The inside view, from the perspective of the individual, is called the *subjective career* and it is the individual's perception and personal experience of the events and meaning of the career. The outside view, called the *objective career*, is the events (e.g., promotions, job assignments) and career outcomes (e.g., pay and other rewards) that an outside observer can see. Much of the research on careers to date has focused on the objective career, and there is a need for more research on the subjective perspective (Arthur, Khapova, & Wilderom, 2005).

It is our intention in this chapter to give more attention to the subjective perspective of a career. In particular, we want to focus on when the career goes right for the person, providing a sense of purpose, personal growth, and fulfillment. And, as positive psychology is the "scientific study of what goes right in life, from birth to death and at all steps in between" (Peterson, 2006), this way of viewing careers is highly congruent with the perspective of positive psychology and positive organizational scholarship.

The Positive Meaning of Career in a Person's Life

How might the career contribute to positive experiences and outcomes in a person's life? To paraphrase

Elizabeth Barrett-Browning's line in her famous love poem to her husband, let us count the ways:

1. *Career work conveys identity.* In many societies, a person's occupation or work is the major component in his or her overall sense of personal identity. When people are asked who they would be if they were not doing the work they have been doing, many feel that they could not imagine who they would be. They cannot think of themselves in any other way (Hall, 2002). And, we see this identity impact of work in reverse when people retire, as many people feel lost and depressed, and it takes them a while to recover their sense of life structure and purpose (Hall, 2002).

2. *Career work reflects meaning and purpose in life.* Related to the point above, many people perceive their main contributions to society in terms of what they do in their career work. One of the important sources of stress from job loss is often the feeling that the person has no reason to get up in the morning, which in turns erodes the person's self-esteem. In fact, people approaching retirement often fantasize about dying very soon after they stop working (Sofer, 1970). And there is some evidence that mortality rates increase immediately after retirement (Haynes, McMichael, & Tyroler, 1978).

3. *Development in the career entails fulfillment of human potential.* On the other hand, when the person is learning and growing at work, this is an important method of achieving what Maslow (1954) called self-actualization or self-fulfillment. Personal growth is a process of bringing out hidden or potential strengths and other qualities, and this process often happens naturally in the course of mastering new job demands.

4. *Career, support, and challenge: growing in human development.* Two of the positive influences that promote development in the career are support and challenge. Support is necessary to help provide a "safe haven," wherein the person can experiment with new aspects of the self (Ibarra, 2003) without excessive fear of failure. Kegan (1982) referred to this as a "holding environment," a transitional space in which the person would not feel highly evaluated and in which it is seen as legitimate to try out new behaviors, perhaps to make mistakes, and to learn.

5. *The career is subject to the individual's control; it is* agentic. Another positive feature of the career is that, to a great extent, and in many contexts, it is under the control of the person. That is, it is up to the person to define what the career is and what constitutes psychological success. Through an interpretive process, the person makes sense of the career and makes choices about what kinds of career opportunities to pursue. In fact, the major behavior in the career that is studied in psychology is often called *vocational choice*. Of course, not all people have a sense of personal agency in relation to their careers, and the extent to which a person feels like a "sculptor" (agent) or the "sculpture" (product) of the career can be an important variable that warrants more attention in career research. Thus, since the person does not always feel agentic regarding the career, it is important to look at determining factors, such as self-efficacy and locus of control.

6. *Therefore, personal interpretation and framing of one's career work is critical.* This brings us back to the subjective career—what the individual sees when he or she look inside at his or her career role and identity. We need to better understand what factors are related to a person's feeling about whether his or her career has been successful. If more people had a deep sense of psychological success in their life's work, we would have healthier, happier, more hopeful children; happier marriages; healthier adults; and more vibrant, creative, and effective organizations, to name, but a few positive outcomes.

Overview of the Career Literature
Career Orientation

The career literature of the last decade distinguishes three different types of career orientations: work, career, and calling. Career orientation refers to the type of relationship that people have with their job, and what people seek to perceive as a reward from their work (Wrzesniewski, McCauley, Rozin, & Schwartz, 1997). The distinction of these three orientations was first highlighted in the best-seller *Habits of the Heart* (Bellah, Madsen, Sullivan, Swidler, & Tipton, 1985), yet the first measure of the construct comes from Wrzesniewski et al.'s study (1997). In recent work, Wrzesniewski (2010 working paper) points out that callings and jobs seem to lie at both ends of a continuum, yet she questions where career falls on such a continuum.

Following this definition, we propose (see Figure 38.1) that a career orientation is determined by the outcomes the person seeks to generate from engaging in his or her job. These outcomes can be extrinsic, that is granted by others, or intrinsic,

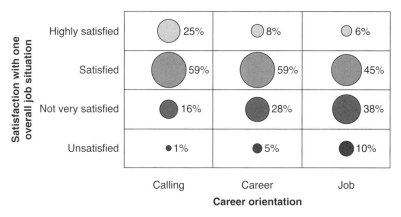

Fig. 38.1 Correlation between career orientation* and job satisfaction**.

* Career orientation was measured with Wrzesniewski et al.'s (1997) measure, forcing people to choose one of the descriptions that would fit their situation better.

** Overall job satisfaction was measured with an item measure "How satisfied do you currently feel with you job situation?"

those perceived by engaging in the work. People who have a *job orientation* are "only interested in the material benefits from work and do not seek to reap any other benefit from it. The work is not an end in itself, but instead a means that allows individuals to acquire the resources needed to enjoy their time away from the job."(. . .)"The major interests and ambitions of job holders are not expressed through their work" (Wrzesniewski, McCauley, Rozin, & Schwartz, 1997) (p. 22). People who have a *career orientation* "have a deeper personal investment in their work and mark their achievements not only through monetary gain, but through advancement within the occupational structure. This advancement often brings higher social standing, increased power within the scope of one's occupation, and higher self-esteem for the worker." Finally, people with a *calling* orientation toward their career "find that their work is inseparable from their life. A person with a calling works not for financial gain or career advancement, but instead for the fulfillment that doing the work brings to the individual."

Thus, it is not really a continuum, but a bidimensional cube, in which, on each of the axes, one can find the desire for each of these outcomes, intrinsic or extrinsic. It is interesting to note that persons may also work due to prosocial motivation-defined as an individual's motivation to have a positive effect on a person other than oneself. However, career orientation as it is defined does not refer to this kind of outcome.

It is not clear what we might call the orientation that refers to a preference for both intrinsic and extrinsic outcomes. If we use a literal definition of

the word "preference," then it would not be possible for a person to have a preference for both, and this would be an empty set. Or, if we thought of each dimension as a *value* attached to each set of outcomes, then it would be possible for a person to value highly both intrinsic and extrinsic outcomes. In that case, we might think of this quadrant as representing a desired outcome of a "privileged calling." People who have used their great wealth and public recognition to bring attention to issues such as world health or injustice (e.g., Bono, Melinda and William Gates) would be examples of successful people with this orientation.

According to this view, the person's preference for intrinsic or extrinsic outcomes would then determine the career orientation of that person. As Wrzesniewski et al. (1997) stress, the job-career-calling orientation is not necessarily dependent upon occupation; within any occupation, one could conceivably find individuals with all three kinds of relations to their work. These authors also state that people do not usually have pure orientations; that is, the distinction lies in the extremes, but individuals fall somewhere along the continuum.

The authors of this chapter call for the need to include prosocial outcomes as defining one's career orientation. Presently, orientations are exclusively defined as the preference for extrinsic or intrinsic outcomes. By including prosocial motives when defining one's orientation, we would define new categories of orientation that could solve some inconsistencies extant in the literature. First, Wrzesniewski suggests that the work that people feel called to do is usually seen as socially valuable—an end in itself—involving activities that may, but need not be, pleasurable. However, what she names a calling seems to include two different orientations. One is to serve (e.g., the poor or the immigrant, for instance). A calling to serve could be termed a socially valuable calling. The other calling orientation is that which leads to fulfilling a *passion* (does not need to be socially valuable). For instance, a person might feel a calling to be a writer, a painter, or a hiker. Those are not necessarily "socially valuable" occupations. Quite the contrary, people might tell those who feel such a calling that they should do "something useful for society," such as a career, in business or medicine. These two orientations, however, need not be exclusive (for instance, doctors may feel passionate about medicine as well as serving their clients). As a matter of fact, none of the categories need be exclusive, but a continuum may exist among them. By including prosocial outcomes and dividing the calling orientation into two (*a calling for service* and *a calling for fulfillment*), we might be solving what makes reference to when discussing the work of Wrzesniewski et al. (1997). Dobrow (2004) mentions that the calling category captures only partially what it means to have a calling. "Its weakness, in my view, is that it taps into only the basic elements of having a calling, rather than grasping its complexities" (p. B2).

Another definition of a calling is that given by Hall and Chandler (2005). They suggest that a person has a calling when he or she perceives the job as his or her purpose in life. There is a subtle difference to Wrzesniewski's (1997) definition since Hall and Chandler's definition does not refer to an orientation as the type of outcomes sought with one's work, but as the need to fully find one's purpose in life. However, Hall and Chandler's definition would also benefit from the distinction of a call to serve others and a call to fully use one's potential. The bottom line is that a person with a social call will define his or her success in terms of meeting his or her prosocial goals, whereas a person with a fulfilling call will seek to meet his or her intrinsic goals.

We would suggest that career orientation might not be stable along a person's life course because the person's preferences for outcomes might change over time, depending on experiences and circumstances (Las Heras & Hall, 2007). This is actually consistent with Wrzesniewski (and with Baumeister, 1991) since they note that a work orientation is the type of relationship that people have with their job, and it guides people's reasons for working, encompassing beliefs about the role of work in life. As such, this work orientation is reflected in work-related feelings

and behaviors. Thus, those reasons for work, feelings, and behaviors might change over time. This view is also consistent with Hall and Chandler's (2005) view that a sense of calling "can come to the person at any point in life, without having been visualized earlier (p. 161)." Thus, it seems that the career orientation need not to be stable, but that there might be triggers to "awaken" an old calling that the person never dared to investigate or pursue. It might also be that, toward the end of the person's life, he or she feels more the need of a legacy, and so, the work is viewed as "a calling" to realize that legacy.

The second author of this chapter has worked on an exploratory study of the consequences of one's career orientation on job and career outcomes (Las Heras, 2009). She found, in a sample of 1,200 employed people in Spain, that overall, people who have a calling orientation are much more satisfied with their work (Figure 38.1) than those who have either a job or a career orientation. Similarly, she's found that those with a calling orientation are more satisfied with their work–life balance (measured with Valcour's [2007] scale). Since the study is cross-sectional, it is not possible to infer causality, yet it seems plausible that a calling orientation frees the person from the constrictions of choosing the best possible paid job, and conveys a higher sense of identity, focusing on choosing a job that meets one's overall life preferences and hence, facilitating both satisfaction and a better work–life balance.

We call for more research that focuses on the antecedents, as well as on the outcomes of having one versus another career orientation. This would help us to better understand the relevance of one's career orientation and improve career counseling, as well as improve scholarship focusing on diverse positive outcomes of one's career versus concentrating on maximizing extrinsic rewards.

Different Approaches to the Study of Careers

Over the years, there have been two general approaches to the study of careers (Hall, 2002). One has been to look at the career as a *process,* that is the way that the career evolves over time. The other has looked more closely at *content*, the variables that affect a person's career experience, the factors that lead to certain career choices and behaviors, as well as the outcomes of those choices and behaviors. We will look at each of these approaches in turn.

CAREER CHOICE: CONTENT THEORIES
Early research on careers had to do with making predictions about initial career choices; that is,

about who would enter particular occupations. In psychology, where the term *vocational choice* was often used, the emphasis was on various models of the individual and various psychometric tools that measured career-related interests, values, and needs. One of the most widely tested choice models was that of John Holland (1997), who saw career choice as finding a good fit between a person's orientation and the requirements of a particular occupational environment. Holland proposed six personality types and six matching occupational environments: Realistic, Investigative, Social, Conventional, Enterprising, and Artistic. The most widely used instrument to assess a person's orientation and matching occupation is the Self-directed Search (Reardon & Lenz, 1998).

Holland proposed a hexagonal model for showing how the different personality types relate to one another. Based upon empirical analysis, personality types and occupations that are nearer to each other in the model are more similar. For example, realistic occupations (e.g., engineering, architecture) are more similar to conventional roles (e.g., accounting, finance) rather than social occupations (e.g., social work, clinical psychology).

Another content approach that involves matching of people and occupations is a stream of research and practice dealing with occupational interest. Perhaps the most widely known work on interests has been done by Frederick Kuder (Kuder Preference Record), E. K. Strong (Strong Interest Inventory), and David Campbell (Campbell Interest and Skills Inventory) (Hall, 2002). The idea here is to identify the kinds of activities that are engaged in by people who are satisfied with their career pursuits and use those as a benchmark for aspiring careerists. These interest inventories compare the test taker's profile with those of various occupations, and the occupations whose profiles best fit the test taker's are those that present a potential good fit.

One of the attractive features of looking at interests as a guide to career choices is that they are remarkably stable over a lifespan. Test–retest correlations as high as 0.70 over a 20-year period are not unusual (Hall, 2002). Thus, a career coach or counselor, in addition to using a test, can also help people by guiding them through reflections on activities that gave them pleasure in childhood and in young adulthood.

CAREER CHOICE: PROCESS THEORIES
Although the content theories help us understand *what* factors are related to career choices, they don't tell us as much about *how* or *why* people make their choices. They give us a rather static view of career matching. Therefore, if we can get a fuller view of choice, it also helps to consider the process of how people make their career decisions.

Ginzberg and his colleagues, in a classic study, identified three stages in the growing maturity of the person as a career decision-maker (Ginzberg, Ginsburg, Axelrad, & Herma, 1951). The earliest stage is a *fantasy* stage, which is when children imagine the kinds of things they would like to do when they grow up—such as a firefighter, athlete, doctor or even a superhero. This stage covers the childhood years up to about age 11.

Next, between the approximate ages of 11 to 16, the person begins to think more seriously about future work and makes some *tentative* choices. This tentative stage is initially based on interests, and then it becomes more grounded with thinking about one's capabilities and how they might rule certain occupations in or out. For example, if a child were interested in becoming an Air Force pilot, but he had poor vision, this lack of visual capability would rule out that career option. And, later in this tentative career thinking, the person's values become more crystallized, and they begin to influence career preferences.

The third stage, starting around age 17, is one of *realistic* choices. Here, the person begins to make specific career decisions, such as whether to go to college, take a job, seek further training, join the military, and so forth. There are three phases of this realistic stage. First comes an *exploratory* period, when the person examines various possible career choices. Next comes a *crystallization* phase, in which the person narrows down the choices, followed by a *specification* period, when the person makes a decision with a commitment to action.

This realistic stage continues into adulthood, as the person makes many more career choices and career changes. And each new choice involves the same substages of exploration, crystallization, and specification. Hall (2002) has described these changes in the adult years as a series of career minicycles or career learning stages.

Another way of looking at the process of career choosing is Super's (1957) description of career development as a *synthesizing process*, in which the person comes to develop a self-concept that is congruent with the career role that he or she is entering. Super's original work (Super, 1957) described career development as a life-long cycle involving early career exploration, then trial activities, leading to establishment or mastery, then a long career plateau, ending with decline or disengagement into retirement. Later, Super (1992) described the more complex world of the modern career, with multiple roles and more frequent changes, with his model of the "career rainbow," which showed how different roles could come along at different points in the life cycle.

Although they are not explicitly presented as models of career development, two theories of adult development stages by Levinson and his colleagues (1978, 1996) and Kegan (1982, 1998) have been widely used by career development scholars and practitioners. Each model posits stages of development that present certain life tasks for the person to confront, and successfully dealing with those tasks moves the person on to the next stage. Levinson's theory is generally decades-based, with the 20s being a time devoted to the task of settling down and forming an initial adult life structure. The early 30s are a time for making a transition into a revised life structure (e.g., getting married, switching career fields, going back to school, or a major geographic relocation). The 40s are a time for midlife review and transition, and the 50s should be a more stable time for the implementation of midlife changes. Levinson's model did not extend into the later career years.

Kegan's model is more complex, based on the evolution of the self in relation to the environment. As the person grows and the environment becomes more complex, the person must develop a self that is capable of comprehending that complexity. Thus, the self becomes more differentiated, but the person must be able to integrate this more complex self, as well. Maturity is therefore a process of becoming capable of taking in and mastering an increasingly complex world and seeing one's self as both part of that world and yet a separate entity from it. Thus, for example, regarding one's career, the maturing person comes to see the career as one part of the self, but not the whole self. The person is capable of observing his or her career as a distinct object, not being totally enmeshed in it or held hostage to it.

There are other content theories of careers and other process theories, to be sure, but these are some of the more widely used ones. When both approaches are understood and used together, one has richer understanding of the what and how of career development. The more fully the person invests the self in career work, the more aligned and fulfilled he or she feels, and the more effective he or she will be.

Career Success: A Confusing Term
Extrinsic and Intrinsic Dimensions of Success

Two ways of looking at career success run parallel to the objective and subjective views of careers mentioned at the beginning of this chapter. First, one can look at career success as an objective phenomenon that refers to how the focal person's extrinsic achievements compare to others', for instance in terms of money and promotions. It also relates to subjective phenomena, which explains how satisfied and content the focal person feels about the development of her or his own career. The objective–subjective distinction is not really clear cut (Arnold & Cohen, 2008) because some parameters used to measure some of those constructs have proven to have mixed meanings. Thus, instead, in this chapter, we shall refer to extrinsic and intrinsic career success. *Extrinsic career success* is that which is measured by career outcomes that are given to the focal person by an external individual. There is no interpretation, only a comparison, of levels of extrinsic achievements.

Intrinsic career success depends solely on elements that remain in the person's judgment or meaning making, even if those feelings and perceptions originate in external realities, such as pay or promotions. In the literature, two essentially different avenues exist within the intrinsic dimension of career success: one type of construct that can be clustered under the umbrella of subjective career success, and the other as a single construct coined *psychological career success* (PCS).

Thus, career success constructs can be classified in a 2 × 2 grid (see Table 38.1). On one axis, we consider the locus of the appraisal: whose perspective the appraisal is measured from, the external observer or the career pursuer. On the other axis, we have what is being measured: purely external achievements, or else overall career experiences (extrinsic and intrinsic).

The constructs under the umbrella of subjective career success are concerned with an "individuals' subjective judgments about their career attainments" (Ng, Eby, Sorensen, & Feldman, 2005, p. 369). On the other hand, the construct PCS refers to the "feeling of contentment and satisfaction and personal accomplishment" derived from career experiences (Hall & Mirvis, 1996). Thus, it seems plausible that when one says that everybody has "the desire to feel successful," one is referring to a feeling of contentment and accomplishment.

Table 38.1 Constructs that refer to career success in the literature according to the locus of appraisal (external vs. internal) and focus of what is measured (extrinsic achievements vs. overall career experiences)

	Extrinsic Achievements	Overall Career Experiences (Extrinsic and intrinsic)
External Observer's Appraisal	*Refers to*: Objective achievements and rewards *In the literature, referred to as:* Extrinsic career success/Objective career success	Not found in the careers literature Public psychological career success
Internal (Career Pursuer's) Appraisal	*Refers to*: Perceived objective career success *In the literature referred to as*: Subjective career success	*Refers to*: The feeling of satisfaction over career experiences *In the literature referred to as*: Psychological career success

Psychological Career Success

The construct of PCS responds to an internal appraisal of overall career experiences; that is, both the extrinsic and intrinsic achievements and experiences (see Figure 38.1). Psychological career success refers to the feeling of pride and fulfillment that emerges from meaningful work experiences, and not only to the perception of attaining objective success (Hall, 2002; Hall & Chandler, 2005; Hall & Mirvis, 1996).

The dissertation of the second author of this chapter (Las Heras, 2009) found that five elements characterize the career stories of those who experience different levels of PCS. Those dimensions are manifested in the person's discourse, differentiating the levels of PCS that the person feels. Las Heras' research shows that those five elements are:

- The sense of personal agency and not fate in career decisions
- The sense of being a part of the different projects one has participated in for each of one's career undertakings
- The sense of pride rather than regret about one's current career situation
- The judgment that career events, whether objectively good or not, have had positive instead of negative outcomes
- The perception that career has synergized and not interfered with goals and development in other meaningful life domains

It is critical to realize that PCS is independent from objective success. Moreover, some evidence shows that, under certain circumstances, objective career success might lead to extremely low PCS. Korman, Wittig-Berman, and Lang (1981) identified the phenomenon of "career success and personal failure."

Whereas PCS is the perception that one has done his or her best, personal failure is the perception that one has not accomplished meaningful goals. Career success and personal failure happen when there is expectancy disconfirmation, contradictory role demands, and a sense of external control. Expectancy disconfirmation is a cognitive state in which an individual realizes that he or she has been wrong in his or her orientation toward the world, expecting that salary and promotion would bring great personal satisfaction. Thus, this phenomenon points to the fact that objective success is not always conducive to the feeling of contentment and fulfillment of work experiences, which is what we call PCS.

More recent studies by Burke and Desza (1982), and Burke (1999) examine the prevalence of the career success/personal failure phenomenon. In the former, they investigate whether Type A behaviors are correlated to the feelings of personal failure. They find Type A behaviors to be significantly related to career outcomes reflecting disappointment, alienation, and personal failure. In the second study, Burke (1999) investigates whether the phenomena appears among managers in Canada, and finds that it indeed does.

In a similar vein, Bartolomé and Evans (1980) identify behaviors that lead to high objective career success and yet produce psychological failure which, again, is contrary to psychological success. They call attention to the fact that many executives accept the cliché that (objective) success always demands a price, which is usually the deterioration of private life (Bartolome & Evans, 1980). Bartolomé and Evans find that, by accepting this cliché, many executives attain high levels of objective success while experiencing low levels of satisfaction with the accumulation of their work experiences, which is equivalent to low levels of psychological success.

What about the upper right hand quadrant in Figure 38.1, external observers' appraisal of an individual's PCS? We would call this "public psychological career success," which would be the external image of the person's PCS. To our knowledge, this issue has received no attention in the literature of careers, but if we look at business and organizational life more broadly, we do see it discussed in relation to socially responsible leadership. Values-driven organizations are examples of settings in which the leader focuses on servant leadership and doing the right thing. Examples would be Malden Mills, where CEO Aaron Feurstein used his own money to continue paying workers while his burned-out factory was being rebuilt.

Other examples of leaders who were publicly known for pursuing their internal definitions of PCS are Yvon and Melinda Chouinard of Patagonia, Ben Cohen of Ben & Jerry's ice cream, and Tom Chappell of Tom's of Maine (oral and body care products). Other examples can be found in the leadership of companies such as Timberland, Wainwright Bank, The Body Shop, Starbucks, and Stonyfield Farms. Although public discussion of the leaders in these companies has focused primarily on their leadership methods and on the service-centered cultures of their organizations, little attention has been paid to the careers of the leaders and other members of the firms. By studying these phenomena—people who actually are in the upper right quadrant of Figure 38.1—we could learn more about how to create contexts that help employees have greater alignment between their personal career passions and corporate missions and, thus, to pursue their callings or paths with a heart.

Career Growth Through Early Challenge and Developmental Relationships

Development is secured when people feel challenged and supported simultaneously (Kegan, 1982; Levinson, 1978). To ensure that people are able to tackle the right challenge, strong organizational support is crucial: Trial and error should be encouraged rather than prohibited, and appropriate and prompt feedback should be given, so that individuals can clearly know where they are and what they need to do more. That support will include positive feedback, which in turn enhances one's self-efficacy (Bandura, 1997). Mentoring provides protégés with necessary psychological and career support (Kram, 1985), and a diverse developmental network (Higgins & Kram, 2001) is beneficial to one's career development and personal growth. Therefore, when

people have varied, nonredundant mentors, they benefit in terms of task and personal learning.

Just as important as support is challenge. We know that being stretched by a challenging job assignment in the person's first year out of school is related to early career success as measured by job level and salary progress (Berlew & Hall, 1966). But, relationships are critical to early challenge, as it is the boss who sets the expectations for the first job assignment; thus, unless the supervisor sets high expectations, the person will not be stretched or challenged. A "Pygmalion effect" is operating here, and if the boss sets the expectations high, the chances are that the new employee will in fact rise to the challenge and meet these expectations (Livingston, 2003).

However, we go beyond the idea of stretching early assignments, and we recommend the use of *smart jobs*. A smart job is one that facilitates the development of key career *metacompetencies* in the incumbent: self-awareness and adaptability (Hall & Las Heras, 2010). Heightened self-awareness through a job might come about through simpler, unobtrusive 360-degree feedback processes, including customer feedback, for example. Or, it could be aided by self-reflexive processes, such as periodic blogging, which we see in the film *Avatar*. Or, it could be promoted by prescribing specific training and education experiences on an annual basis for specific jobs. Self-awareness also grows through coaching processes: professional, peer and team coaching. Although there are different types that serve different goals, all of them facilitate self-awareness, and thus, help to create *smart job* situations.

Adaptability could be promoted by linking jobs to provide for periodic job rotation, which creates more variety in experience. A job could also come equipped with "term limits," so that the person cannot stay beyond the life of the job's learning curve and an additional year to reap the returns of mastering the job. Karaevli (2007) found support for the relationship between career variety and organizational adaptability and survival in her 30-year study of the U.S. airline and paint industries. The key to developing adaptability is facilitating a varied experience through the organizational and HR management systems, such as succession planning and leadership development processes (Karaevli & Hall, 2004, 2006).

This variety–adaptability link also means that succession planning systems should include selection criteria for future jobs that favor stretching and developing a high-talent manager by occasionally selecting for jobs that do not necessarily represent a perfect fit. This may mean sometimes choosing the candidate who might learn the most from a position, as opposed to the person who appears most likely to be a high performer. Also, selecting top management teams in which members possess varied career backgrounds, such as across industries, across sectors (public, private, nongovernmental organizations), and across business functions, creates greater top-level executive adaptability, which in turn leads to greater organizational long-term adaptability and survival.

What Happened to the Dream?

One of the most positive aspects of the concept of career is that it deals with the realm of *possibility*— our aspirations, hopes, and dreams. In contrast to related concepts such as jobs, work, and occupations, which are rooted in the present tense, career evokes the future and change. However, we have done little to tap the potential of these possibilities. Daniel Levinson and his colleagues (1978, 1996) found in their studies of adult development of men and women that a driving force is the *dream*. The dream is something that we all have when we are young and are imagining our futures. Then, as the expression goes, life happens. As the career gets under way, we often see choices that may be attractive in certain ways (perhaps financially, perhaps regarding quality of life), but they may not be related to the dream. Then, as we go from one step to the next in the career, the path may take us farther and farther away from the original dream.

In fact, as Levinson and his colleagues found, this growing divergence between dream and on-the-ground reality eventually reaches crisis proportions, causing a seismic shift in life structure. This is the infamous midlife transition, which often occurs in the early or mid-40s. This midlife change is perhaps one of the most familiar themes in popular writings about career (e.g., Sheehy, *Passages*), but ironically it has not received a great deal of serious scholarly attention in the organizational literature (Hall, 2002). But this is not the area where we call for more research.

Rather than focusing on the stress and crises of the midlife transition, we would argue that it would be more productive and more generative to focus on the positive—on the dream. Let our queries be: What happened to the dream? And, how can the dream be rekindled? After all, this is the person's quest during the midlife transition, and focusing

directly on how to reconnect with the dream, how to make it a practical reality in a person's life, will get us to a positive result much more quickly and efficiently than studying all of the potholes in life that impede movement toward that dream.

One suggestion for moving in this direction is to do research that builds on the reflected best self (Dutton, Spreitzer, Roberts, Heaphy, & Quinn, 2005). The reflected best self helps the person reconnect with the most inspirational aspects of his or her personal identity, and by reflecting carefully on the essence of this valued identity, the person is then in a good position to reflect back to an earlier stage in life and revisualize his or her original dream. This can be done in a guided activity, such as Shepard's (1984) career and life planning exercises. These exercises do not deal explicitly with the dream, but they do get at several valued components of the identity, and it would then be a short step to ask the person to think about his or her original aspirations and hopes for the future.

The next step, after the person has a clear sense of the original dream, would be to construct a current path to the dream. Again, we do not want to be distracted by the barriers to the dream. A realistic approach could be to think of this as an exercise in overcoming resistance to change, as proposed by Kegan and Lahey (2009). The idea here is that the dream gets sidetracked because the person has other, competing commitments that get in the way of pursuing the dream. These other commitments are often highly desirable goals and objectives in and of themselves. And, in the absence of careful analysis, we often come to the premature assumption that we cannot pursue both the competing commitments and the original dream. However, as Kegan and Lahey (2009) have found, when people go through the competing commitments "Four Column" exercise, they generally find ways to make the desired change in behavior and at the same time maintain their other valued commitments.

This would be an ideal topic for action research. In fact, we would argue that this work on reconnecting to the original dream can only be done through a process of co-inquiry. It would require the active involvement (and hard work!) of the research participant, and it would have to be a highly intentional and self-reflective process. It would require the strong application of the two major career metacompetencies, identity awareness and adaptability (Hall, 2002).

Then, as a next step, researchers could examine when the person actually engages in new behaviors to pursue the dream. Using methods similar to Ibarra's (2003), it would be possible to examine the small steps and experiments that lead to identity change. But the difference between this proposed research and Ibarra's is that we would hypothesize a correlation between the elements of the newly rediscovered dream and the person's newly emergent behaviors. Thus, the new behavior would not be so much pure trial and error, but rather dream-guided trial behavior.

Another idea for research on "good careers" was provided by the first author, in his call for more research on virtuous protean careers:

> In closing, let me appeal for your contributions to research on processes that are counter to the expedient, bottom-line-at-all-costs behaviors that have been dominating our recent headlines. We're heard enough about the "bad guys" who are being led out of their offices in handcuffs. Let us study the "good guys and good gals"—the Meg Whitmans and Herb Kellehers—who exert leadership that brings out the best in people. Let us understand better how people can grow in their awareness of themselves and of the larger community in which they live and work. Let us discover what triggers people to positive change, to generous self-determination. Let us pursue the "path with a heart," in our research and in our lives. (Hall, 2004, p. 11)

Conclusion

Since work is such a major factor affecting the quality of a person's life, and since the career represents the cumulative effects of all of a person's work experiences over the span of his or her work life, the career has great potential for creating positive experiences. However, much of the careers research literature to date has dealt with career *outcomes*, such as attainment and income, rather than experiences and process.

There is much work to be done in the study of career experiences. What factors facilitate a person's following the path with a heart? What keeps a person on track in pursuing his or her dream? What in an organizational environment or in the person's career history promotes the growth of the career metacompetencies—identity and adaptability? When do employers make choices that favor stretch and growth versus perfect fit (meaning the person has already done the job before and thus has little to learn from it)?

Another critical empirical question regarding career growth asks what factors favor movement across career learning cycles. That is, when a person is at the mastery phase of one career mini-cycle, what internal and/or external forces induce her or him to begin exploration of new possibilities that will lead to a career move and a new learning cycle?

Part of this needed research entails a focus on the *subjective career*, as opposed to the objective career, which has received most of our attention to date (Arthur, Khapova, & Wildrom, 2005). We need to attach more importance to the point of view of the individual in understanding and assessing the career. In recent years, interest has awakened in the subjective career, and it appears that we are headed in the right direction.

An important effort in seeking to understand the subjective career has been undertaken by the Collaboration for the Cross-Cultural Study of Contemporary Careers (5C) group of researchers (for more information see Briscoe et al., 2007; Chudzikowski et al., 2006, 2009). They have interviewed over 200 people in 11 countries (Austria, China, Costa Rica, Israel, Japan, Malaysia, Mexico, Serbia, South Africa, Spain, United States) that represent Schwartz's (1999) seven cultural regions. In this first qualitative phase, the 5C researchers conducted semistructured interviews with early and late career employees in three occupations: blue-collar, business, and nursing. Driving theory generation through the use of content analysis and constant comparative techniques, categories illuminating career transitions were developed at a country level. Although career transitions and career success across cultures have many features in common (e.g., achievement, job satisfaction, and the nature of the work itself), the larger cultural context and pace of change have significant impact.

For instance, in countries with a relatively stable past, the younger generation enjoys a great ability to look to the past for guidance and support. In countries where modern careers and economies co-mingle with significant political change, the younger generation must blaze its own path and often seeks success without clear guidance from traditional values or practices. Studies such as the one undertaken by the 5C group are urgently needed to understand positive career experiences, since most of our theories and models, so far, have been North America- and Europe-centric, and so might be missing relevant features of careers in other contexts.

Another important, timely question is, "What is a 'good retirement'?" This is a major issue around the world, but people who study careers have not given this question sufficient attention yet. The 5C study of cross-cultural careers has found major generational differences, such that "retirement" in rapidly changing societies like China often has little meaning, particularly for unskilled workers, who are forced to continue doing menial labor to survive (Briscoe, Hall, & Mayrhofer, 2010).

In terms of method, doing more work on the subjective career would entail more use of qualitative methods. Clinical methods, such as those employed by Levinson (1978, 1996) and Vaillant (2003) to study unfolding life course events, are not highly valued in organizational behavior and management. Yet, these methods best fit the complex interplay of intraindividual, interpersonal, network, organizational, racial, ethnic, gender, cultural, and institutional factors that shape a career. The classic works of Robert White, such as *The Study of Lives* (1972), contain straightforward clinical methods for studying individual life course development processes, and the field has virtually forgotten how to do this kind of work. It seems analogous to the field of medicine's unlearning how to reposition breech babies or even to diagnose heart or pulmonary issues with a stethoscope. Let us study more expansive, fulfilling, contributing, zestful lives, what contributes to them, and what kind of footprint they leave on the world.

References

Arnold, J., & Cohen, A. (2008). The psychology of careers in industrial and organizational settings: A critical but appreciative analysis. *International Review of Industrial and Organizational Psychology, 23*, 1–43.

Arthur, M.B., Hall, D.T., & Lawrence, B.S. (Eds.). (1989). *The handbook of career theory*. London: Cambridge University Press.

Arthur, M.B., Khapova, S.N., & Wilderom, C.P. M. (2005). Career success in a boundaryless career world. *Journal of Organizational Behavior, 26*(2), 177–202.

Bandura, A. (1997). *Self-efficacy: The exercise of control*. New York: Freeman.

Bartolome, F., & Evans, L.P. (1980). Must success cost so much? *Harvard Business Review, 58*, 137–148.

Baumeister, R.F. (1991). *Meanings of life*. New York: The Guilford Press.

Bellah, R., Madsen, R., Sullivan, W., Swidler, A., & Tipton, S. (1985). *Habits of the heart*. Berkeley: University of California Press.

Berlew, D.E., & Hall, D.T. (1966). The socialization of managers: Effects of expectations on performance. *Administrative Science Quarterly, 11*, 207–223.

Briscoe, J.P., Hall, D.T., & Mayrhofer, W. (Eds.). (2011). *Careers and cultures—A global perspective: The collaboration for the cross-cultural study of contemporary careers*. New York: Routledge.

Briscoe, J., Chudzikowski, K., Demel, B., Mayrhofer, W., Unite, J., Heras, M.L., et al. (2007). *Career success across cultures: Dancing to the beat of their own drummers*. Paper presented at the 23rd Colloquium of European Group for Organizational Studies (EGOS), Vienna, Austria.

Burke, R.J. (1999). Career success and personal failure feelings among managers. *Psychological Reports, 84*, 651–653.

Burke, R.J., & Deszca, E. (1982). Career success and personal failure experiences and Type A behaviour. *Journal of Occupational Behavior, 3*(2), 161–170.

Chudzikowski, K., Demel, B., Mayrhofer, W., Abdul-Ghani, R., Briscoe, J., Changjun, D., et al. (2006, July 6–8). *Here, there, and everywhere? Conceptualisations of career success in different cultures*. Paper presented at the 22nd Colloquium of European Group for Organizational Studies (EGOS), Bergen, Norway.

Chudzikowski, K., Demel, B., Mayrhofer, W., Briscoe, J.P., Unite, J., Milikić, B.B., et al. (2009). Career transitions and their causes: A country-comparative perspective. *Journal of Occupational & Organizational Psychology, 82*(4), 825–849.

Dobrow, S. (2004). Extreme subjective career success: A new integrated view of having a calling. *Academy of Management Proceedings,* B1–B6.

Dutton, J.E., Spreitzer, G.M., Roberts, L.M., Heaphy, E.D., & Quinn, R.E. (2005). Composing the reflected best-self portrait: Building pathways for becoming extraordinary in work organizations. *Academy of Management Review, 30*(4), 712–736.

Ginzberg, E., Ginsburg, J.W., Axelrad, S., & Herma, J.L. (1951). *Occupational choice*. New York: Columbia University Press.

Hall, D.T. (2002). *Careers in and out of organizations*. Thousand Oaks, CA: Sage.

Hall, D.T. (2004). The protean career: A quarter-century journey. *Journal of Vocational Behavior, 65*, 1–13.

Hall, D.T., & Chandler, D.E. (2005). Psychological success: When the career is a calling. *Journal of Organizational Behavior, 26*, 155–178.

Hall, D.T., & Las Heras, M. (2010). Reintegrating job design and career theory: Creating not just good jobs but smart jobs. *Journal of Organizational Behavior, 31*(2–3), 448–462.

Hall, T., & Mirvis, P. (1996). The new protean career: Psychological success and the path with a heart. In *The career is dead—long live the career* (pp. 15–46). San Francisco: Jossey-Bass.

Haynes, S.J., McMichaels, A.J., & Tyroler, H.A. (1978). Survival after early and normal retirement. *Journal of Gerontology, 33*(2), 269–278.

Higgins, M.C., & Kram, K.E. (2001). Reconceptualizing mentoring at work: A developmental network perspective. *Academy of Management Review, 26*(2), 264–288.

Holland, J. (1997). *Making vocational choice: A theory of vocational personalities and work environments* (3rd ed.). Odessa, FL: Psychological Assessment Resources.

Ibarra, H. (2003). *Working identity: Unconventional strategies for reinventing your career*. Boston: Harvard Business School Press.

Karaevli, A. (2007). Performance consequences of new CEO "outsiderness": Moderating effects of pre- and post-succession contexts. *Strategic Management Journal, 28*(7), 681–706.

Karaevli, A., & Hall, D.T. (2004). Growing leaders for turbulent times: Is succession planning up to the challenge? *Organizational Dynamics, 32*(1), 62–79.

Karaevli, A., & Hall, D.T.T. (2006). How career variety promotes the adaptability of managers: A theoretical model. *Journal of Vocational Behavior, 69*(3), 359–373.

Kegan, R. (Ed.). (1982). *The evolving self: Problem and process in human development*. Cambridge, MA: Harvard University Press.

Kegan, R., & Lahey, L.L. (2009). *Immunity to change: How to overcome it and unlock the potential in yourself and your organization*. Boston: Harvard Business School Press.

Korman, A.K., Wittig-Berman, U., & Lang, D. (1981). Career success and personal failure: Alienation in professional managers. *Academy of Management Journal, 24*, 342–360.

Kram, K.E. (1985). *Mentoring at work: Developmental relationships in organizational life*. Glenview, IL: Scott, Foresman.

Las Heras, M. (2009). *Psychological career success, preferred success set and its dynamism*. Unpublished doctoral dissertation, School of Management, Boston University, Boston.

Las Heras, M., & Hall, D.T. (2007). Integration of career and life. In D. Bilimoria & S.K. Piderit (Eds.), *Handbook of women in business and management* (pp. 178–205). Northampton, MA: Edward Elgar Publishing.

Levinson, D., Darrow, C.N., Klein, E.B., Levinson, M.H., & McKee, B. (1978). *The seasons of a man's life*. New York: Alfred A.Knopf, Inc.

Levinson, D., & Levinson, J. (1996). *The seasons of a woman's life*. New York: Knopf.

Livingston, J.S. (2003). Pygmalion in management. *Harvard Business Review, 81*(1), 97–106. (Originally published in 1969; reprinted in 2003 as an HBR Classic.)

Maslow, A.H. (1954). *Motivation and Personality*. New York: Harper.

Ng, T.W.H., Eby, L.T., Sorensen, K.L., & Feldman, D.C. (2005). Predictors of objective and subjective career success: a meta-analysis. *Personnel Psychology, 58*(2), 367–408.

Peterson, C. (2006). *A primer in positive psychology*. New York: Oxford University Press.

Reardon, R.C., & Lenz, J.G. (1998). *The self-directed search and related Holland career materials: A practitioner's guide*. New York: Psychological Assessment Resources.

Schwartz, S.H. (1999). A theory of cultural values and some implications for work. *Applied Psychology: An International Review, 48*(1): 23–47.

Shepard, H.A. (1984). On the realization of human potential: A path with a heart. In M.B. Arthur, L. Bailyn, D.J. Levinson, & H.A. Shepard (Eds.), *Working with Careers*. New York: Columbia University, Graduate School of Business, 25–46.

Super, D.E. (1957). *The psychology of careers*. New York: Harper & Row.

Super, D.E. (1992). Toward a comprehensive theory of career development. In D.H. Montross & C.J. Shinkman (Eds.), *Career development: Theory and practice*. Springfield, IL: Charles C. Thomas.

Vaillant, G.E. (2003). *Aging well: Surprising guideposts to a happier life from the landmark Harvard study of adult development*. Boston: Little, Brown & Company.

Valcour, M. (2007). Work-based resources as moderators of the relationship between work hours and satisfaction with work-family balance. *Journal of Applied Psychology, 92*(6), 1512–1523.

White, R.W. (1972). *Lives in progress: A study of the natural growth of personality*. New York: Henry Holt and Company.

Wrzesniewski, A. (2010). *Careers, and callings: How work meanings shape job transitions*. Working paper.

Wrzesniewski, A., McCauley, C., Rozin, P., & Schwartz, B. (1997). Jobs, careers, and callings: People's relations to their work. *Journal of Research in Personality, 31*, 21–33.

Relational Mentoring

A Positive Approach to Mentoring at Work

Belle Rose Ragins

Abstract

Like other relationships, the quality of mentoring relationships falls along a continuum ranging from high quality to dysfunctional. Although most mentoring research has focused on relationships that are average in quality, at its best, mentoring personifies the very essence of positive relationships at work. Using a positive lens, this chapter offers an overview of the construct of relational mentoring. Relational mentoring represents the relational state of high-quality mentoring and is defined as an interdependent and generative developmental relationship that promotes mutual growth, learning, and development within the career context. The construct of relational mentoring is presented and contrasted with traditional approaches to mentoring. The antecedents, functions, processes, and characteristics of relational mentoring are examined. Mentoring schema theory, the self-structures of mentoring framework, and the relational cache cycle are applied to relational mentoring. A preliminary measure of relational functions is presented, along with an agenda for future research on mentoring relationships and mentoring episodes.

Keywords: Mentoring relationships, positive relationships at work, relational mentoring, high-quality mentoring, developmental relationship, mentoring schema theory, self-structures of mentoring, relational cache cycle, relational functions, mentoring episodes

When asked to reflect on relationships that have made a difference in their lives, many people think about their mentoring relationships. However, like other work relationships, mentoring relationships fall along a continuum of quality (Ragins & Verbos, 2007). Mentoring researchers have focused on understanding the qualities, characteristics, and outcomes of average relationships but have not examined the high-quality end of the continuum. At its best, mentoring has the capacity to be a life-altering relationship that inspires and transforms individuals, groups, and organizations (Ragins & Kram, 2007). High-quality mentoring exemplifies positive relationships at work (Dutton & Ragins, 2007; Ragins & Verbos, 2007). By neglecting the high end of the quality continuum, we unnecessarily restrict our understanding of high-quality relationships, which in turn curtails our ability to cultivate and sustain these critical work relationships.

The field of positive organizational scholarship (POS) offers an important lens for understanding high-quality mentoring (Cameron, Dutton, & Quinn, 2003). Using a positive lens, this chapter offers an overview of the construct of relational mentoring. Relational mentoring represents the relational state of high-quality mentoring and is defined as an interdependent and generative developmental relationship that promotes mutual growth, learning, and development within the career context (Ragins, 2005). The antecedents, functions, processes, and characteristics of relational mentoring will be presented, along with an agenda for future research.

The chapter proceeds as follows. It first begins with an overview of mentoring relationships and the distinction between relational and traditional mentoring. Following this, the antecedents of relational mentoring are presented and integrated with mentoring schema theory and the self-structures of mentoring. I then examine the functions, processes, and characteristics of relational mentoring. To promote research in this area, a preliminary measure of relational mentoring is presented and an agenda for future research is provided.

Mentoring and the Relational Perspective

In this section, I first offer an overview of mentoring and define mentoring using a traditional perspective. I then describe some of the limitations of the traditional approach and present the construct of relational mentoring as an alternative frame for viewing mentoring relationships at work.

What Is a Mentor?

Traditionally, mentoring is defined as a relationship between an older, more experienced mentor and a younger less experienced protégé for the purpose of helping and developing the protégé's career (Kram, 1985; Ragins, 1989). Mentors may or may not be employed in the same organization as the protégé or be in the protégé's profession or chain of command.

Mentoring relationships may develop informally or may be assigned as part of a formal mentoring program (Baugh & Fagenson-Eland, 2007). Formal mentoring relationships are generally not as effective as informal relationships (Ragins & Cotton, 1999; Wanberg, Welsh, & Hezlett, 2003). However, the quality of the relationship has been found to matter more than whether the relationship is formally assigned or informally developed (Ragins, Cotton, & Miller, 2000); high-quality formal relationships can be more effective than low-quality informal relationships. Those with mentors, be they formal or informal, generally have more positive work and career attitudes than those lacking mentors (cf., Allen, Eby, Poteet, Lentz, & Lima 2004; Underhill, 2006).

A key feature that defines mentoring and distinguishes it from other types of work relationships is that mentoring is a relationship that is embedded within the career context (Ragins & Kram, 2007). Another distinction is that mentoring relationships evolve through stages that eventually result in the relationship either terminating or becoming redefined as a peer relationship (Kram, 1983, 1985).

Finally, it should be noted that mentoring relationships are part of a developmental network of relationships that exist within and outside the workplace (Higgins & Kram, 2001). At a given point in time, individuals may have a constellation of developmental relationships that offer career guidance and support. As discussed later, these relationships change individuals, and these changes are carried with the individual across life thresholds and the other relationships in their developmental network. As we will see, a key tenet of relational mentoring theory is that the outcomes associated with relational mentoring have the capacity to transform other relationships in the individual's developmental network.

Mentoring Episodes

Like other relationships, mentoring relationships can be viewed at the level of a single interaction, which are called *mentoring episodes* (Fletcher & Ragins, 2007). Mentoring episodes involve short-term developmental interactions that occur at a specific point in time.

Although all mentoring relationships involve mentoring episodes, individuals can engage in a mentoring episode without necessarily being in a mentoring relationship. Individuals may come to define their relationship as an informal mentoring relationship after they reach a "tipping point" in the number, length, and quality of mentoring episodes. For example, a junior faculty member may seek advice about a career-related dilemma from a more senior member of her department. Both individuals may agree that the senior faculty member engaged in mentoring behaviors during the specific episode, but neither may view it as a mentoring relationship at that point in time. However, with repeated positive interactions, they may begin to view their relationship as a mentoring relationship.

Like mentoring relationships, mentoring episodes fall along a continuum of quality. High-quality mentoring episodes are similar to high-quality connections (Dutton & Heaphy, 2003) and growth-fostering interactions (Jordan, Kaplan, Miller, Stiver, & Surrey, 1991; Miller, 1976). High-quality connections are characterized by high emotional carrying capacity (i.e., the capacity to withstand both positive and negative emotions), tensility (i.e., the capacity to withstand strain), and high connectivity (i.e., the capacity to be open to new ideas and deflect behaviors that shut down generative processes) (Dutton & Heaphy, 2003). Growth-fostering interactions are characterized by mutual empathy, authenticity, and empowerment, and lead to states of zest, empowered action, increased sense of self-worth, new knowledge, and the desire for more connection (Jordan et al., 1991; Miller, 1976). The higher the quality of the mentoring episode, the more likely individuals are to view their relationship as a mentoring relationship. Low-quality episodes are unlikely to lead to mentoring relationships. Episodes that are mixed in quality may lead to mentoring relationships, but as discussed next, these relationships are more likely to be characterized as average in quality.

The Continuum of Quality

Relational mentoring theory holds that mentoring relationships involve three relational states (dysfunctional, traditional, and relational) that reflect low, medium, and high ends of the quality continuum (Ragins, 2005). Like other relationships, no two mentoring relationships are the same or stay the same over time. Mentoring relationships provide different functions based on the needs of their members, which are continually evolving. Not only are there differences between relationships in terms of quality, but relationships also transform over time to reflect various states of quality (Ragins & Verbos, 2007). The continuum of mentoring quality therefore reflects not only differences across relationships but also within them. The field of mentoring has generally focused on mentoring relationships that reflect the midpoint of the quality continuum. There has been a significant amount of research directed toward understanding dysfunctional mentoring (e.g., Eby, 2007; Eby, Butts, Lockwood, & Simon, 2004; Eby, Evans, Durley, & Ragins, 2008; Scandura, 1998), but less is known about high-quality relationships. One reason for this is that, like other fields in organizational science, the field of mentoring focuses on phenomenon experienced by the majority of workers (e.g., average phenomenon). Although this captures the experiences of more workers, it curtails our understanding of the full range of mentoring experiences, and as discussed next, creates methodological problems and issues in our research.

The Need for a Positive Organizational Scholarship Perspective

The field of POS (Cameron et al., 2003) illuminates the problems with focusing on average phenomenon: Not only do we lose sight of the extraordinary, but the very description of our constructs suffers from conceptual and methodological inadequacy.

This problem is aptly illustrated in the field of mentoring. Traditional perspectives on mentoring describe ordinary relationships of average quality, but by focusing on average relationships, our very definition and measurement of mentoring becomes limited to these types of relationships. For example, traditional perspectives on mentoring view it as a hierarchical, one-way relationship in which the mentor serves as a "godfather" in helping the protégé's career and advancement. However, research on high-quality relationships questions this view and points to its limitations in understanding the processes and outcomes associated with high-quality relationships (Dutton & Heaphy, 2003; Dutton & Ragins, 2007; Fletcher & Ragins, 2007; Miller & Stiver, 1997). Because our theory explains average relationships, our measurement soon follows, and our empirical base of knowledge becomes limited to explaining average relationships. High-quality relationships fall off our conceptual and empirical map.

A Relational Approach to Mentoring

Relational mentoring puts high-quality mentoring back on the map. It does not reject traditional perspectives; these approaches explain average or marginally effective relationships, but do not explain high-quality relationships (Ragins & Verbos, 2007). By widening the conceptual lens of mentoring, relational mentoring allows us to assess the processes, characteristics, and outcomes of high-quality mentoring. Let us now turn to the four key principles that define relational mentoring and distinguish it from traditional approaches (Ragins, 2005; Ragins & Verbos, 2007).

USE OF A DYADIC AND RECIPROCAL PERSPECTIVE

First, relational mentoring challenges the view that all mentoring is a one-sided relationship, and instead points to the mutuality and reciprocity inherent in growth-producing relationships (cf., Fletcher & Ragins, 2007). Instead of viewing the mentor as a prevailing source of power and influence, relational mentoring recognizes that high-quality relationships involve the capacity for mutual influence, growth, and learning. Both members enter the relationship expecting to grow, learn, and be changed by the relationship, and both feel a responsibility and a desire to contribute to the growth and development of their partner.

Although the overall level of expertise between the mentor and protégé may be asymmetrical, a relational perspective recognizes that expertise shifts within a given mentoring episode, which allows for mutual learning for both members (Fletcher & Ragins, 2007). For example, a faculty mentor may help a protégé with publishing an article, but the protégé may offer expertise in new statistical analyses. Influence is shared, with the mentor using "power with" rather than "power over" influence strategies that characterize high-quality relationships (Follett, 1924; Miller, 1976). An example of mutual growth can be found in diverse mentoring relationships; diverse mentoring relationships involve individuals who differ in group memberships associated with power (e.g., race, ethnicity, gender, sexual orientation, religion, disability) (Ragins, 1997). These relationships offer an ideal platform for both mentors and protégés to learn about diversity and to grow from the unique experiences of those with different backgrounds, cultures, nationalities, and experiences.

RELIANCE ON COMMUNAL NORMS AND GENERATIVE PROCESSES

Second, relational mentoring calls to question *exchange paradigms* and the *instrumental approach* to mentoring. An instrumental approach uses a transactional frame and values the relationship for what it can *do* rather than what it can *be*. Instrumental approaches use a social exchange framework (Blau, 1964, Homans, 1958, 1974) that relies on exchange norms in the relationship. With exchange norms, partners give to each other with the expectation that they will receive a "return on their investment." For example, mentors may expect allegiance in return for the favors bestowed on their protégés. In turn, protégés may be advised to use their mentors as a career resource and to "trade them in" when a better mentor comes along. In contrast, relational mentoring is a close relationship that is governed by communal norms (Clark & Mills, 1979, 1993), in which individuals give to their partners on the basis of need rather than on the basis of expected returns.

EXTENDED RANGE OF DEPENDENT VARIABLES

Third, relational mentoring expands the range of dependent variables used to capture the effectiveness of mentoring relationships. Current approaches use traditional criteria of career success, such as advancement and compensation, which fail to capture the outcomes associated with high-quality relationships (Dutton & Heaphy, 2003; Miller & Stiver, 1997). Relational mentoring draws on the

relationship and the POS literatures to identify a broad range of dependent variables that reflect personal growth and development, as well as the acquisition of relational skills and competencies that may be transportable across work roles and organizational boundaries (Fletcher, 1996; Kram & Ragins, 2007). A POS perspective offers an array of potential outcomes that include positive psychological capital (Luthans, Youssef, & Avolio, 2007), thriving (Spreitzer, Sutcliffe, Dutton, Sonenshein, & Grant, 2005), flourishing (Diener & Biswas-Diener, 2008; Keyes & Haidt, 2003), resilience (Luthans, 2002; Luthans et al., 2007), and a host of other POS outcomes identified in this volume.

Expanding the criteria base allows for a more accurate assessment of the effectiveness of mentoring relationships. For example, a high-quality relationship may help its members develop a professional identity or balance work and family, but may not lead to a change in compensation or advancement. Researchers who use compensation or advancement as evidence of effective mentoring may conclude that the relationship is ineffective, when in fact the relationship may be exceptionally effective in meeting the unique needs of its members.

A HOLISTIC APPROACH

Finally, a relational perspective takes a holistic approach that incorporates and acknowledges the interaction between work and nonwork domains (Ragins, 2008). Although traditional perspectives view work relationships only in terms of work outcomes, a holistic perspective recognizes that high-quality relationships can influence the quality of life within and outside the workplace (Ragins & Dutton, 2007). Relationships change people, and these changes are not left at the workplace door. The reach of high-quality mentoring may extend beyond the workplace and may influence the individual's ability to cope with challenges that spill over across his or her life domains (Ragins, Lyness, & Winkel, 2010). For example, high-quality mentoring may build an individual's self-efficacy and her capacity for compassion (Boyatzis, 2007), as well as her emotional intelligence (Cherniss, 2007), her capacity to cope with stress (Kram & Hall, 1989), and her ability to balance work and family demands (Greenhaus & Singh, 2007). Although this chapter focuses on work relationships, a developmental network perspective holds that people have constellations of developmental and mentoring relationships that exist within and outside the workplace (Higgins & Kram, 2001). Using a holistic perspective, high-quality mentoring relationships outside the workplace can build an individual's relational resources, which can be carried into the workplace and influence her ability to develop high-quality relationships at work.

In sum, in contrast to traditional, one-sided approaches to mentoring that use exchange models to predict a restricted range of instrumental outcomes, a relational approach widens the lens of mentoring to include high-quality, interdependent relationships that use communal norms to facilitate mutual growth, learning, and development within a career context. Relational mentoring incorporates a holistic perspective, and views mentoring as a positive work relationship that influences the quality of life within and outside the workplace. Let us now turn to a more in-depth review of the antecedents, processes, and outcomes that may be found in high-quality mentoring relationships.

Antecedents of Relational Mentoring

In this section, I review the individual, relational, and organizational factors that may lead to high-quality mentoring relationships. A number of individual variables may predict people's ability to develop and sustain high-quality mentoring relationships (cf., Fletcher & Ragins, 2007; Ragins, 2005, 2009; Ragins & Verbos, 2007). These include their self-structures of mentoring, their relational skills and knowledge, and other individual differences variables, such as personality, attachment styles, and emotional intelligence.

The Self-structures of Mentoring

Self-structures of mentoring involve three components: mentoring identities, mentoring schemas, and mentoring as possible selves (Ragins, 2005, 2009; Ragins & Verbos, 2007).

MENTORING IDENTITIES

Individuals vary with respect to the degree to which they incorporate relationships into their identity structures (Anderson & Chen, 2002; Markus & Kitayama, 1991). Individuals who define themselves in terms of others are viewed as having interdependent self-construals (Cross, Bacon, & Morris, 2000) or relational identities (Brewer & Gardner, 1996). Since relationships are central to their sense of self, these individuals should place greater importance on relationships than others (Anderson & Chen, 2002).

Mentoring identities are a type of relational identity that involves individuals defining themselves in terms of their mentoring relationships (Ragins, 2009). Both mentors and protégés have mentoring identities, and these identities may range from positive to negative. Positive mentoring identities involve states of positive self-cognition (e.g., "Who am I? I am a good mentor."). The individual not only defines him- or herself in terms of the mentoring relationship, but this self-structure also gives the individual positive cognitive and affective associations. Individuals who have positive mentoring identities are posited to be more motivated and better able to develop high-quality mentoring relationships than are those who do not have a positive mentoring identity (Ragins, 2009).

MENTORING SCHEMAS

Mentoring schemas are the second self-structure that influences relational mentoring. Mentoring schemas are "fluid cognitive maps derived from past experiences and relationships that guide mentor's and protégé's perceptions, expectations, and behaviors in mentoring relationships." (Ragins & Verbos, 2007, p. 101) Drawing on relational schema (Baldwin, 1992; Planalp, 1985, 1987) and social cognition theory (Fiske, 1992; Markus, 1977; Markus & Zajonc, 1985), mentoring schema theory holds that individuals hold mental maps of mentoring that shape their expectations, frame their experiences, and motivate their behaviors in mentoring relationships (Ragins & Verbos, 2007). Essentially, mentoring schemas are knowledge structures of what mentoring relationships "look like." Mentoring schemas involve expectations about what mentors and protégés do in the relationship, what the relationship provides, and how it functions. As discussed later, relational mentoring involves a unique set of functions that distinguish it from average or dysfunctional relationships. Individuals who incorporate relational functions into their mental maps of mentoring should be more likely to develop high-quality mentoring relationships than are those who do not incorporate relational functions (Ragins, 2005). An example of a mentoring schema that would predict the development of a high-quality relationships is "Good mentors learn from their protégés and are able to grow in the relationship." An example of a schema that would be less likely to result in a high-quality relationship is "Protégés should always listen to their mentors as the mentor knows best."

MENTORING AS POSSIBLE SELVES

Possible selves reflect the selves we wish to become, as well as the selves we fear becoming (Markus &

Nurius, 1986). Mentoring as a possible self is defined as "a future oriented representation of oneself in a mentoring relationship" (Ragins, 2009, p. 243). The possible selves of mentoring range from positive to negative, reflecting the best and worst visions of oneself in a future mentoring relationship. Examples of different possible selves include: "I see myself as an effective, wonderful mentor," "I can't picture myself as a mentor," and "I would be an awful mentor." Those who hold positive self-visions should be more motivated to enter and sustain a high-quality mentoring relationship than are those who lack visions or hold negative visions of themselves in mentoring relationships (Ragins, 2005).

These three self-structures influence one another and are also affected by past and current experiences in mentoring relationships (Ragins, 2005). Those who have had high-quality mentoring relationships in the past, either as mentors or as protégés, may be more likely to have positive self-structures that allow them to develop and sustain high-quality relationships in the future. In contrast, those who lack these experiences may be less likely to incorporate mentoring into their identity structures; mentoring becomes tangential to who they are and who they aspire to be.

Even the experience of witnessing high-quality relationships can help individuals develop mentoring self-structures that offer a foundation for high-quality mentoring relationships. For example, high-quality mentoring relationships can be a source of role modeling for others in the organization, particularly if such relationships occur in high-ranking, visible positions. To the extent that mentoring culture is driven from the top, the presence of high-ranking relational mentoring may create mentoring cultures that both value and model high-quality relationships.

Although cognitive structures are important for guiding and framing expectations, individuals also need a certain skill set in order to develop high-quality mentoring relationships.

Relational Skills, Caches, and Differences

RELATIONAL SKILLS

Mentors and protégés should be more likely to develop and sustain high-quality relationships when they have the ability to engage in effective communication, empathic listening, personal learning, and self-reflection (Kram & Ragins, 2007). Emotional intelligence, emotional competence, and the ability to be compassionate may also help individuals develop high-quality mentoring relationships (Boyatzis, 2007; Cherniss, 2007; Fletcher,

1998; Fletcher & Ragins, 2007). Boyatzis (2007) observes that, by exhibiting compassion, mentors and protégés help each other engage in intentional change behaviors that allow them to achieve their dreams and aspirations.

Using Stone Center relational cultural theory (RCT) (Jordan et al., 1991; Miller & Stiver, 1997), Fletcher and Ragins (2007) identified a set of individual antecedents to relational mentoring. These include the ability to be authentic, adaptive, empathetic, interdependent, and vulnerable in the relationship (see also Fletcher, 1998, 1999). Another key antecedent is the ability to engage in fluid expertise; fluid expertise allows individuals to move from an expert to nonexpert role, to acknowledge help, and to give credit to others without losing self-esteem or needing to engage in "face-saving gambits" (Fletcher, 1998). Mentors in particular need to be able to put aside their hierarchical roles and formal position in order to enter the relationship from a place of mutual vulnerability, interdependence, and fluid role relationships. They must have the emotional stability and self-awareness necessary to allow for mutual influence in the relationship; influence that is based on needs and abilities, rather than on hierarchically prescribed roles and traditional power relationships.

THE RELATIONAL CACHE CYCLE

High-quality mentoring relationships are not only built on relational skills, they may also generate the relational skills needed to build other high-quality relationships. We call this *relational caches*, which are a transportable set of relational skills and competencies that transfer across time, relationships, and settings (Kram & Ragins, 2007). This reflects the idea that individuals carry their skill set with them across relationships.

Relational caches are likely to be developed in high-quality relationships, and because people share and build relational skills in growth-producing relationships (Miller & Stiver, 1997), they are also likely to be passed between members of these relationships. Moreover, since mentoring relationships exist within a broader network of other relationships (Higgins & Kram, 2001), members in high-quality mentorships may pass their relational caches to others in their social network. This becomes an iterative process in which mentors and protégés help each other broaden and build their skill caches, and in so doing develop relational caches that are passed along to members of their other relationships both within and outside the workplace.

In essence, a holistic perspective recognizes that individuals do not leave their relational skills at the workplace door, but carry them into other relationships nested within their homes, communities, and professional networks. Similarly, relational skills that are developed outside the work domain can be carried back into the workplace and can influence the quality of workplace mentoring. This suggests that the ability to develop high-quality relationships outside the workplace should spill over and influence relationships within the workplace and vice versa. An iterative cycle of positive relationships could therefore be developed that includes relationships nested in the workplace, the home, the community, and the profession.

INDIVIDUAL DIFFERENCES

A number of individual difference variables may influence an individual's ability to develop and sustain high-quality relationships. Although there has been a lack of research on personality characteristics that predict high-quality mentoring, a recent review of the literature on mentoring and personality suggests that individuals who exhibit prosocial personalities, altruism, other-oriented empathy, and openness to experience may be more likely to engage in relational mentoring than are those who lack these attributes (cf. Turban & Lee, 2007; Allen, 2003; Aryee, Chay, & Chew, 1996; Bozionelos, 2004).

Given the relational skill set identified earlier, it would be reasonable to expect that individuals who had strong self-esteem, emotional stability, and emotional intelligence would be more likely to seek and develop high-quality mentoring relationships than would those who lack these attributes. Individuals with strong learning goal orientations (Godshalk & Sosik, 2003) should be attracted to the mutual learning processes inherent in high-quality mentoring relationships. Finally, attachment styles may influence the closeness of the mentoring relationship (Noe, Greenberger, & Wang (2002) and the motivation to enter a mentoring relationship (Wang, Noe, Wang, & Greenberger, 2009). According to attachment theory (Bowlby, 1969), individuals with secure attachment styles may be better able to develop close relationships than would those who either avoid close relationships or experience anxiety in the presence of intimacy. Those with secure attachment styles are also better able to adhere to the communal norms that characterize close relationships (Bartz & Lydon, 2008). It is therefore reasonable to expect that individuals with secure attachment styles should be better able and more motivated to enter high-quality mentoring relationships than would those with insecure attachment styles.

Relationship Antecedents

At least four characteristics of the relationship should affect its ability to achieve high-quality states. First, relationships are likely to be of higher quality when the mentor and protégé share similar mentoring schemas (Ragins, 2005; Ragins & Verbos, 2007). As discussed earlier, both mentors and protégés have mentoring schemas that reflect expectations about their respective roles, as well as the behaviors, purpose, and outcomes of the relationship. Schema congruency should not only influence the satisfaction and quality of the relationship, but also its effectiveness; members may be more likely to work at cross-purposes when they do not share a common frame of reference or set of expectations about the relationship.

Second, mentoring relationships are likely to be of higher quality when both members hold communal norms. Communal norms involve members giving to their partners without the expectation or obligation of repayment (e.g., Clark & Mills, 1979) and represent a key process in relational mentoring (Ragins, 2005). Existing research indicates that commitment is a key predictor of quality of relationship (Allen & Eby, 2008), and communal norms reflect the deepest form of relational commitment (Clark & Mills, 1979, 1993); so, it is reasonable to expect that relationships will be of higher quality when *both* members hold communal rather than exchange norms. However, a state of norm incongruency, in which one member uses exchange norms while the other relies on communal, should lead to restricted levels of relational quality.

Third, the similarity of values, personality, and learning orientations should affect the quality of the mentoring relationship. Mentoring researchers have found that perceived and actual similarity in learning goal orientations and other personality and value attributes predict relationship satisfaction and liking, which are often predictors of high-quality relationships (Godshalk & Sosik, 2003; Lankau, Riordan, & Thomas, 2005; Wanberg, Kammeyer-Mueller, & Marchese, 2006). Demographic dissimilarity creates a challenge for many mentoring relationships as individuals may not be aware of "deep level" types of diversity (e.g., personality, values, interests) that can be the basis for developing a close mentoring relationship (Ragins, 1997).

However, related research indicates that, over time, individuals find deep-level similarities that form the basis of effective work relationships (Harrison, Price, & Bell, 1998). This suggests that members of diverse mentoring relationships may need to make a more concerted effort to discover similarities involving personality, values, and interests, and that diverse relationships may take more time to develop into high-quality mentoring relationships than demographically homogeneous relationships (Clutterbuck & Ragins, 2002; Ragins, 1997).

The fourth characteristic that may influence relational quality is the structure of the mentoring relationship. For example, whereas informal relationships often develop on the basis of shared interests and commonalities, formal mentoring relationships are usually assigned by a third party and are therefore less likely to have this advantage. In recognition of this limitation, some formal programs involve mentors and protégés in the matching process, and existing research indicates that this procedure may yield higher-quality relationships (Allen et al., 2006). Even so, formal relationships are usually contracted to last between 6 months and a year, which restricts the time needed to reach a high-quality state (Ragins, 2005). In contrast, informal mentoring relationships usually span between 3 and 5 years, which allows more time for members to establish trust, reciprocity, and interdependence in the mentoring relationship.

Electronic or virtual mentoring, which occurs over the Internet, also faces unique challenges to achieving high-quality states (cf. review by Ensher & Murphy, 2007; see also Ensher, Heun, & Blanchard, 2003; Hamilton & Scandura, 2003). Because of the lack of face-to-face interaction and nonverbal cues, electronic relationships are more susceptible to miscommunication, and it is more difficult and time-consuming to establish trust and rapport in these relationships than in face-to-face mentoring (Buche, 2008). Given these differences, it may not be fair to compare formal and electronic mentoring with informal mentoring. Perhaps a better approach would be to examine the predictors and the range of quality within a particular type of mentoring relationship (e.g., what does high-quality electronic mentoring look like, and what factors predict the ability of individuals to attain these relationships).

Organization Antecedents
Mentoring relationships do not exist in a vacuum but are nested within the organizational context.

Some organizations promote a mentoring culture that values shared knowledge, collaboration, and learning (Eby, Lockwood, & Butts, 2006). These cultures should be more likely to promote relational mentoring than organizations that are characterized by competitiveness, hierarchical relationships, and traditional forms of power that restrict mutual learning, reciprocity, and interdependence in work relationships (Fletcher & Ragins, 2007).

In sum, characteristics of the individual, relationship, and organization may influence the ability of individuals to develop high-quality mentoring relationships. Let us now turn to a more in-depth examination of the functions and processes of high-quality mentoring relationships.

Functions and Processes in High-quality mentoring Relationships
The Evolution of Mentoring Functions
Over 25 years ago, Kathy Kram (1985, p. 22) defined mentoring functions as "those aspects of a developmental relationship that enhance *both* individuals' growth and advancement" (italics added). Although this definition took a dyadic perspective, the functions described in her landmark book focused primarily on what the mentor provides to the protégé. Kram described two classifications of mentor functions, career development and psychosocial, and identified discrete functions or behaviors within each of these categories. *Career development* functions help protégés advance in the organization and include five subcategories: sponsoring advancement, providing job coaching, increasing positive exposure and visibility in the organization, offering protection, and giving challenging assignments. Mentors also provide *psychosocial* functions, and the four subcategories here include role modeling, acceptance and confirmation, counseling, and friendship.

Building on Kram's (1983) groundbreaking work, instruments were soon developed that allowed researchers to measure these functions from the mentor's perspective (Noe, 1988; Ragins & McFarlin, 1990; Scandura & Ragins, 1993). Twenty years later, we know that mentors do indeed provide these functions and that these functions predict protégés' career outcomes and their satisfaction with the mentor and the relationship (cf., Allen et al., 2004; Wanberg et al., 2003). *However, although high levels of these functions represent greater levels of relational quality, high-quality relationships may involve more than just these functions.*

Relational mentoring builds on this existing work in two key ways. First, hearkening back to

Kram's (1985) initial definition, relational mentoring examines the functions and processes provided by *both* members of the relationship. Second, because relational mentoring seeks to explain processes involved in high-quality relationships, the range of functions in the relationship are extended to include the qualities, behaviors, and characteristics found in close interpersonal relationships (Duck, 1994; Mashek & Aron, 2004), high-quality connections (Dutton & Heaphy, 2003), growth-fostering interactions (Jordan et al., 1991; Miller, 1976), and positive relationships at work (Dutton & Ragins, 2007).

Relational mentoring offers a third category of mentoring functions: relational functions. *Relational functions do not substitute for career development or psychosocial functions, but represent an additional category that reflects high-quality relationships.* From the negative side of the spectrum, research has presented new measures that capture the functions, behaviors, and characteristics found in dysfunctional mentoring relationships (Eby et al., 2004, 2008). Mirroring this work from a positive perspective, this section describes relational functions, and a preliminary measure of relational functions is provided in Table 39.1.

Relational Functions

Relational functions represent a third category of mentoring functions that reflects the characteristics, behaviors, and attributes that may be found in high-quality mentoring relationships. The list of such characteristics can be extensive, but here I am only identifying key functions that may be displayed by *both* mentors and protégés in high-quality relationships and episodes. This list is not meant to be exhaustive, but reflects core attributes drawn from related research and theory in the relationships, social psychology, social cognition, and mentoring literatures. Drawing on this work, relational functions may include six subcategories: personal learning and growth, inspiration, affirmation of selves, reliance on communal norms, shared influence and mutual respect, and relational trust and commitment.

PERSONAL LEARNING AND GROWTH

Learning can be both a process and an outcome of mentoring relationships (Kram & Ragins, 2007; Lankau & Scandura, 2007). In terms of process, high-quality mentorships differ from traditional relationships in the mutuality, type, and degree of learning. Traditional approaches view the mentor as the teacher or guide and the protégé as the learner.

In contrast, a relational approach recognizes that, in high-quality mentoring, both members may learn and grow from the relationship. High-quality relationships involve fluid expertise, in which expertise shifts depending on the mentoring episode or interaction (Fletcher & Ragins, 2007). For example, in a given episode, a protégé may show the mentor how to use the latest technology, or may offer insights into generational differences among new entrants into the workforce. Greater levels of mutual learning should occur in high-quality relationships because learning is based on the individual's task expertise or knowledge, rather than on their hierarchical position or role in the relationship.

The type of learning should also differ in high-quality mentoring relationships. Although there are many ways to define learning in mentoring relationships (cf., review by Lankau & Scandura, 2007), high-quality relationships are more likely to produce personal learning (Carmeli, Brueller, & Dutton, 2009; Kram & Cherniss, 2001), which involves the individual's insights into their values, strengths, and weaknesses, as well as their developmental needs, reactions, and patterns of behaviors (Kram, 1996; Higgins & Kram, 2001). Learning therefore can involve not only the sharing of information and knowledge, but also the potential for personal growth and development. By providing personal learning functions, members help each other learn more about themselves and others. For example, in high-quality relationships both mentors and protégés may provide their partner with feedback that illuminates the "blind spots" in their relationships with others, while giving them insights into their personal strengths and weaknesses.

INSPIRATION

Inspiration is an evoked psychological state derived from an episode with an object, event, or person (Thrash & Elliot, 2003, 2004). Inspiration involves seeing different and better possibilities, and can lead to a positive motivational state that involves the energization and direction of behavior (Thrash & Elliot, 2003, 2004). Inspiration scholars distinguish between being "inspired by" and being "inspired to" (e.g., one can admire a person or an object without being moved to action) (Thrash & Elliot, 2004). In a relational context that involves mutuality and reciprocity, there may be an additional process of mutual inspiration (e.g., "inspired with.").

Mentors and protégés have the capacity to inspire each other in their mentoring episodes and relationships. Traditional perspectives on mentoring hold

Table 39.1 The Relational Mentoring Index

Instructions: The following questions ask about your experience in mentoring relationships. Mentoring is a developmental relationship that pairs a more experienced and knowledgeable mentor with a less experienced protégé. The relationship supports the protégé's career, but also offers important benefits for the mentor. Both members may learn, grow, and develop from the mentoring relationship.

Some mentoring relationships develop spontaneously and informally, whereas others are part of a formal mentoring program. In formal mentoring programs, mentors and protégés are matched and assigned in some way.

(Introductory Questions)

- Do you currently have an ongoing mentoring relationship? (options: yes/no/unsure)

- When did the relationship begin?

- If you have more than one mentoring relationship, please answer the following questions in terms of your strongest relationship.

- What is your role in this relationship? (options: mentor, protégé)

- Is this relationship formally assigned as part of a formal mentoring program? (options: yes it is a formally assigned relationship/no it is not a formally assigned relationship/unsure)

Relational Mentoring Index

When thinking about this particular mentoring relationship, please indicate the degree to which you agree with the following statements using the following scale: 1 (strongly disagree) to 7 (strongly agree).

(Relational Functions and Items)

(Function: Personal Learning and Growth)

1. My partner is helping me learn and grow as a person.

2. My partner helps me learn about my personal strengths and weaknesses.

3. My partner helps me learn more about myself.

(Function: Inspiration)

4. My partner has inspired or been a source of inspiration for me.

5. My partner gives me a fresh perspective that helps me think "outside the box."

6. I am often inspired by my partner.

(Function: Self-affirmation[a]**)**

(Sub-function: Affirmation of Ideal Self)

7. My partner is helping me become the person I aspire to be.

8. My partner sees me not only for who I am now, but also for who I aspire to be.

(Sub-function: Affirmation of Best Self)

9. My partner always sees the best in me.

10. My partner seems to bring out the best in me.

(Sub-function: Affirmation of Authentic Self)

11. My partner accepts me for who I am.

12. I can be myself with my partner.

(Function: Reliance on Communal Norms)

13. In our relationship, we help each other without expecting repayment.

14. We never keep score of who gives and who gets in our relationship.

Table 39.1 *(continued)*

15. We give to each other without expecting repayment.
(Function: Shared Influence and Respect)
16. My partner and I respect and influence each other.
17. We respect each other, and we value what each person has to say.
18. There is mutual respect and influence in our relationship.
(Function: Trust and Commitment)
19. Our relationship is founded on mutual trust and commitment.
20. My partner and I trust each other, and we are committed to the relationship.
21. Trust and commitment are central to our relationship.

ᵃ Affirmation items may all load on same factor.

that mentors may serve as role models for their protégés. Role modeling approaches, but does not fully capture the possibilities for inspiration in high-quality mentoring relationships; members are not only "inspired by" others (e.g., the mentor serving as a role model), but can also be "inspired to" engage in new and creative behaviors and may also engage in a reciprocal and synergistic process of mutual inspiration (e.g., "inspired with"). Traditional perspectives on role modeling ignore the possibility of mutual inspiration in which the mentor both inspires and is inspired by his or her protégé. Another distinction is that role modeling involves emulation and admiration, whereas inspiration can involve sparks of creativity that allow both members of the relationship to think about things in fresh and new ways (Thrash, Maruskin, Cassidy, Fryer, & Ryan, 2010). Mutual inspiration can involve synergistic "thinking outside the box" behaviors that can be beneficial for both mentors and protégés (Thrash, Elliot, Maruskin, & Cassidy, 2010). High-quality relationships offer the psychological space in which inspiration can thrive (Dutton & Heaphy, 2003), and it is reasonable to expect that both mentors and protégés will report that their partner inspires them, gives them a fresh perspective, and helps them think about work and life in new ways.

AFFIRMATION OF IDEAL, BEST, AND AUTHENTIC SELVES

The self is not formed in a vacuum, but is crafted through relationships with others (Cooley, 1902; Mead, 1934). High-quality mentoring relationships may help their members develop three aspects of the self: their ideal selves (Markus & Nurius,

1986), their best selves (Roberts, Dutton, Spreitzer, Heaphy, & Quinn, 2005), and their authentic selves (Goffman, 1959; Harter, 2002).

Ideal selves represent the selves we wish to become in the future; they reflect our hopes, dreams, and aspirations, as well the skills, abilities, achievements, and accomplishments that we wish to attain (Higgins, 1987; Markus & Nurius, 1986). Research from the close relationships literature indicates that partners play a key role in helping each other reach their ideal selves. Drawing on interdependence theory (Kelley, 1983; Kelley & Thibaut, 1978; Rusbult & Van Lange, 1996) and the ideal self literature (Higgins, 1987; Markus & Nurius, 1986), Drigotas and his colleagues offer the idea of the *Michelangelo phenomenon* (Drigotas, Rusbult, Wieselquist, & Whitton, 1999). Using the metaphor of the sculptor who helps the true form emerge from the stone, the Michelangelo phenomenon describes the role that close partners play in affirming one another's pursuit of the ideal self and the means by which the self is shaped by a close partner's perceptions and behaviors (Drigotas, 2002; Drigotas et al., 1999).

The Michelangelo phenomenon has great utility for explaining the processes involved in high-quality mentoring. This phenomenon holds that an individual can help his partner reach his ideal self by offering affirmations that confirm the partner's beliefs about himself and by behaving in ways that are congruent with his partner's ideal self (Drigotas, 2002; Drigotas et al., 1999). Partner affirmations take the form of *perceptual* affirmation, in which partners view each other in terms of their ideal selves, and *behavioral* affirmations, in which individuals help their partners engage in behaviors that are aligned with their ideal selves by directly eliciting or creating opportunities to engage in desired behaviors, or by decreasing the opportunity to engage in behaviors that conflict with ideal selves. Existing research has found support for this phenomenon and has found that movement toward ideal selves predicts positive outcomes reflecting relational and personal well-being (e.g., life satisfaction, emotional well-being, self-esteem, vitality, relational stability, relational satisfaction) (Drigotas, 2002; Drigotas et al., 1999; Kumashiro, Rusbult, Finkenauer, & Stocker, 2007; Rusbult, Kumashiro, Kubacka, & Finkel, 2009).

By providing affirmation, high-quality mentoring relationships may also help their members develop their "reflected best self." Reflected best selves are defined as "an individual's cognitive representation of the qualities or characteristics an individual displays when at his or her best" (Roberts et al., 2005, p. 713). Reflected best selves share some features of the ideal self, but focus more on the qualities and characteristics the person currently has rather than on those they wish to possess (cf. Higgins, 1987). According to Roberts and colleagues, mentoring relationships are relational resources individuals can use to develop portraits or mental representations of who they are when they are at their personal best. Through behavioral and perceptual affirmation, mentors and protégés may help each other expand their collective constellation of possible selves and provide the opportunity to bring their best selves forward in their mentoring relationship.

In addition to best and ideal selves, high-quality mentoring relationships may also affirm the presentation of the authentic self. The authentic self represents one's "true or real self" (Gergen, 1991; Mitchell, 1992). Unlike ideal and best selves, authentic selves include not only our best, but also our worst traits, characteristics, and attributes. High-quality relationships allow for the affirmation of the authentic self (Mitchell, 1992; see also Roberts, 2007). Unlike other relationships in which the authentic self is repressed, hidden, or distorted (Goffman, 1959; Schlenker, 1980), high-quality relationships offer the relational space, affirmation, and acceptance needed to close the space between the presented and the actual self (Roberts, 2007; Roberts, Cha, Hewlin, & Settles, 2009). Drawing on self-verification theory, such congruence may lead to positive outcomes for the individual (Swann, 1983, 1987) and their work relationships (Swann, Polzer, Seyle, & Ko, 2004).

RELIANCE ON COMMUNAL NORMS

A key factor that distinguishes high-quality relationships from other relationships is the reliance on communal norms (Clark & Mills, 1979, 1993). In relationships governed by communal norms, the focus is on the partner's well-being, and benefits are given in response to the partner's needs without expecting repayment (Clark & Mills, 1979). In contrast, in exchange relationships benefits are given with the expectation that a comparable benefit will be provided in return. The individual receiving the benefit incurs an obligation or debt to return a comparable benefit to his or her partner. Clark and Mills point out that communal relationships vary in strength (Clark & Mills, 1993; Mills, Clark, Ford, & Johnson, 2004); in strong communal relationships individuals feel a strong responsibility for the welfare of their partner, whereas in weak communal relationships, people take on less responsibility for their partner's welfare. They observe that norms vary across relationships, with communal norms being more likely to be enacted in close relationships involving family members and friends, whereas exchange norms prevail in relationships between employers and their employees (Clark & Jordan, 2002).

Like other relationships, mentoring relationships may vary by the type and strength of relationship norms. Since mentoring relationships can range from close personal relationships to formally assigned relationships that embody a contractual relationship, it is reasonable to expect that high-quality mentoring relationships are more likely to rely on communal rather than exchange norms, and that the stronger the communal norm, the higher the quality of the relationship (Ragins, 2005). As a related construct, reciprocity can be governed by either communal or exchange norms, and it is expected that mentoring relationships that use exchange-based norms for reciprocity should be of lower quality and have more problematic outcomes than relationships that rely on communal-based norms for reciprocity. For example, mentors who expect or require that their protégés return a comparable benefit may be viewed as exploiting their protege (cf., Shore, Toyokawa, & Anderson, 2008), and protégés who give to their mentor but later expect a benefit in return may be viewed as manipulative (Eby et al., 2008). In contrast, mentors and protégés who give to each other because of concern for the well-being of their partner and their relationship not only reflect a state of relational mentoring, but also offer a foundation for other relational processes that further enhance the relationship. The use of social exchange models may therefore explain average, marginal, or even dysfunctional mentoring relationships, but do not capture the relational processes inherent in high-quality relationships.

SHARED INFLUENCE AND MUTUAL RESPECT

Relational mentoring is characterized by shared influence, which involves the process by which members influence and are influenced by each other (Ragins, 2005). Mutuality is the norm in high-quality mentoring, and influence is based on the individual's expertise in a given mentoring episode, rather than on their hierarchical position (Fletcher & Ragins, 2007). Although by definition mentors have more experience in work or career domains, protégés bring their own insights, life experiences, and talents to the table, and mentors in high-quality relationships value and are influenced by their protégés' perspectives.

Hand-in-hand with shared influence is mutual respect. Respect involves elements of admiration, appreciation, and encouragement (Ferguson, 2003), and in close personal relationships, incorporates a perception that the partner has "admirable moral qualities" that include wisdom, self-discipline, honor, patience, and self-knowledge (Frei & Shaver, 2002). Mutual respect is a prerequisite for shared influence in mentoring relationships, and these characteristics should be associated with mutual growth, learning, and development in the mentoring relationship.

Shared influence reflects interdependence in the relationship. Interdependence in close relationships involves vulnerability (Rusbult & Van Lange, 2003) and may also involve the ability of individuals to empower one another in a relational sense. Relational empowerment involves reciprocal influence, mutual empathy, concern, and vulnerability in the relationship (Surrey, 1991), and therefore differs from other forms of empowerment that focus more on control over work functions (Spreitzer, 2008). Although empowerment is often used interchangeably with shared influence, it is important to preserve this distinction when examining mentoring relationships. Mentors who are supervisors may empower their protégés by giving them more control over their work functions. This may be in addition to, or in place of, shared influence, which is a mutual process that is not limited to work functions (Jordan, 1991). Shared influence is broader in scope than empowerment, and is better able to describe processes in a range of mentoring relationships.

RELATIONAL TRUST AND COMMITMENT

Although there are many different conceptualizations of trust (Lewicki Tomlinson, & Gillespie, 2006), trust is commonly defined as "a psychological state comprising the intention to accept vulnerability based upon positive expectations of the intentions or behavior of another" (Rousseau, Sitkin, Burt, & Camerer, 1998, p. 395). Rousseau and colleagues observe that trust is not a behavior or a choice, but rather a psychological condition that reflects the willingness to be vulnerable under conditions of risk and interdependence.

Relational trust may best reflect the processes in high-quality mentoring, as this type of trust comes from the relationship itself (Lewicki, McAllister, & Bies, 1998; McAllister, 1995). *Calculus-based trust* involves the individual making a rational decision to trust using an economic transaction approach, whereas relational trust has an affective foundation based on emotional bonds and the degree to which members express genuine care and concern for their partners (Lewis & Wiegert, 1985; McAllister, 1995). Relational trust reflects communal norms (Clark & Mills, 1979), in that individuals perceive their partners as being committed to the relationship and that they give on the basis of need rather than self-interest (McAllister, 1995), and also incorporates elements of respect (Frei & Shaver, 2002). Relational trust develops through repeated interactions (Rousseau et al., 1998), or in the case of mentoring, mentoring episodes (Fletcher & Ragins, 2007). Lewicki and colleagues observe that trust is influenced not only by the length of the relationship, but also by the frequency and depth of interactions, and the diversity of challenges that are successfully faced in the relationship (Lewicki et al., 1998).

Relational trust is intricately connected to commitment in high-quality work relationships and other close relationships (Wieselquist, Rusbult, Foster, & Agnew, 1999). In their analyses of trust processes in positive relationships at work, Pratt and Dirks (2007) point out that traditional perspectives on trust use a social exchange perspective (e.g., "I'll trust you if you trust me"), which does not explain how trust can be broken and then repaired in high-quality relationships. They offer the idea that trust is a relationship-based commitment in high-quality relationships. The commitment to the relationship allows individuals to experience both the negative effects of personal vulnerability as well as the positive benefits of being in a trusting relationship.

Applying these perspectives to the mentoring arena, it is reasonable to expect that high-quality mentoring relationships involve affective forms of relational trust that are grounded not only in the commitment to the partner, but also in the commitment to the relationship. The development of this type of trust not only takes time, but the opportunity to engage in mentoring episodes that challenge the relationship and allow members to illustrate their commitment to each other and the relationship.

Future Directions

Future research could examine the antecedents, processes, and outcomes of high-quality mentoring relationships. Researchers could use the self-structure of mentoring framework (Ragins, 2009) and mentoring schema theory (Ragins & Verbos, 2007) to examine how mentoring identities, schemas, and possible selves combine to influence the development of high-quality relationships. Self-structures are shaped by past relationships and episodes, but what types of specific experiences are most important for developing relational mentoring? Can individuals develop positive self-structures from observing others, or do they need direct experience? Do these relationships differ for those in formal mentoring relationships, and how can organizations promote the development of positive self-structures in the workplace?

Future research could also empirically examine the relational cache cycle (Kram & Ragins, 2007). Do the relational competencies developed in high-quality mentoring relationships help individuals create and sustain other high-quality relationships within and outside the workplace? Are relational caches passed between partners in high-quality mentoring relationships, and can these caches be passed across relationships to social networks within and outside the workplace? Do these processes build on each other to create an iterative cycle of positive relationships across life domains?

The Relational Mentoring Index (RMI; Table 39.1) provided here offers a first step in examining the functions and processes of high-quality mentoring relationships. Future research needs to validate the instrument and assess its ability to predict outcomes of high-quality relationships. The RMI could also be tested in conjunction with traditional measures of mentoring roles and functions in order to assess the added variance in outcomes that can be accounted for by an inclusion of measures that tap the characteristics of high-quality relationships. Since the measure taps relational functions provided

by both members of the relationship, a dyadic approach can be used to assess the psychometric properties of the instrument for both mentors and protégés.

A relational approach to mentoring also opens the doors to examining an expanded array of outcomes associated with the fields of POS (Cameron et al., 2003), positive psychology (Snyder & Lopez, 2002), and positive organizational behavior (Luthans, 2002; Nelson & Cooper, 2007). Mentoring scholars have assessed the quality of mentoring relationships using traditional measures that reflect protégé's job attitudes, compensation, and advancement, but a relational approach offers an array of outcomes that reflect personal growth, learning, and development for both members of the relationship (Fletcher & Ragins, 2007; Ragins, 2005; Ragins & Verbos, 2007). Using a holistic perspective (Ragins, 2008; Ragins & Dutton, 2007) the reach of relational mentoring may extend beyond the workplace to influence quality of life in the nonwork domain, and may predict such outcomes as life satisfaction, physical and psychological health, balance, and well-being. The affirmation of identity in high-quality relationships has particular resonance among those in marginalized identity groups (Ragins, 2007; Roberts, 2007), and future research could examine the conditions under which mentoring helps workers manage marginalized and stigmatized identities (Ragins, 2008). Finally, by providing relational functions that build resilience and capacity, high-quality mentoring may be a relational resource that buffers both protégés and mentors from stressful life events and challenges that originate from within and outside the workplace.

Conclusion

In conclusion, the field of POS expands the lens used to view mentoring relationships. Relational mentoring offers mentoring and relationship scholars an unobstructed vision of the possibilities of mentoring relationships and the potential of these relationships to influence the quality of life across domains.

References

Allen, T.D. (2003). Mentoring others: A dispositional and motivational approach. *Journal of Vocational Behavior, 62*, 134–154.

Allen, T.D., & Eby, L.T. (2008). Mentor commitment in formal mentoring relationships. *Journal of Vocational Behavior, 72*, 309–316.

Allen, T.D., Eby, L.T., & Lentz, E. (2006). Mentorship behaviors and mentorship quality associated with formal mentoring programs: Closing the gap between research and practice. *Journal of Applied Psychology, 91,* 567–578.

Allen, T.D., Eby, L.T., Poteet, M.L., Lentz, E., & Lima, L. (2004). Career benefits associated with mentoring for protégés: A meta analysis. *Journal of Applied Psychology, 89,* 127–136.

Anderson, S.M., & Chen, S. (2002). The relational self: An interpersonal social-cognitive framework. *Psychological Review, 109,* 619–645.

Aryee, S., Chay, Y.W., & Chew, J. (1996). The motivation to mentor among managerial employees: An interactionist approach. *Group & Organization Management, 21,* 261–277.

Baldwin, M.W. (1992). Relational schemas and the processing of social information. *Psychological Bulletin, 112,* 461–484.

Bartz, J.A., & Lydon, J.E. (2008). Relationship-specific attachment, risk regulation, and communal norm adherence in close relationships. *Journal of Experimental Social Psychology, 44,* 655–663.

Baugh, S.G., & Fagenson-Eland, E.A. (2007). Formal mentoring programs: A "poor cousin" to informal relationships? In B.R. Ragins, & K.E. Kram (Eds.), *The handbook of mentoring at work: Theory, research and practice* (pp. 249–272). Thousand Oaks, CA: Sage.

Blau, P.M. (1964). *Exchange and power in social life.* New York: Wiley.

Bowlby, J. (1969). *Attachment and loss:* Vol. 1: *Attachment.* New York: Basic Books.

Boyatzis, R.E. (2007). Mentoring for intentional behavioral change. In B.R. Ragins, & K.E. Kram (Eds.), *The handbook of mentoring at work: Theory, research and practice* (pp. 447–470). Thousand Oaks, CA: Sage.

Bozionelos, N. (2004). Mentoring provided: Relation to mentor's career success, personality and mentoring received. *Journal of Vocational Behavior, 64,* 24–46.

Brewer, M., & Gardner, W. (1996). Who is this "we"? Levels of collective identity and self representations. *Journal of Personality and Social Psychology, 71,* 83–91.

Buche, M.W. (2008). Development of trust in electronic mentoring relationships. *International Journal of Networking and Virtual Organisations, 5,* 35–49.

Cameron, K.S., Dutton, J.E., & Quinn, R.E. (Eds.). (2003). *Positive organizational scholarship: Foundations of a new discipline.* San Francisco: Berrett-Koehler.

Carmeli, A., Brueller, D., & Dutton, J. (2009). Learning behaviours in the workplace: The role of high-quality interpersonal relationships and psychological safety. *Systems Research and Behavioral Science, 26,* 81–98.

Cherniss, C. (2007). The role of emotional intelligence in the mentoring process. In B.R. Ragins, & K.E. Kram (Eds.), *The handbook of mentoring at work: Theory, research and practice* (pp. 427–446). Thousand Oaks, CA: Sage.

Clark, M.S., & Jordan, S.D. (2002). Adherence to communal norms: What it means, when it occurs, and some thoughts on how it develops. *New Directions for Child and Adolescent Development, 95,* 3–26.

Clark, M.S., & Mills, J. (1979). Interpersonal attraction in exchange and communal relationships. *Journal of Personality and Social Psychology, 37,* 12–24.

Clark, M., & Mills, J. (1993). The difference between communal and exchange relationships. *Personality and Social Psychological Bulletin, 19,* 684–691.

Clutterbuck, D., & Ragins, B.R. (2002). *Mentoring and diversity: An international perspective.* Oxford: Butterworth-Heinemann/Elsevier.

Cooley, C.H. (1902). *Human nature and the social order.* New York: Scribner.

Cross, S.E., Bacon, P.L., & Morris, M.L. (2000). The relational-interdependent self-construal and relationships. *Journal of Personality and Social Psychology, 78,* 791–808.

Diener, E.D., & Biswas-Diener, R. (2008). *Happiness: Unlocking the mysteries of psychological wealth.* Malden, MA: Blackwell.

Drigotas, S.M. (2002). The Michelangelo phenomenon and personal well-being. *Journal of Personality, 70,* 59–77.

Drigotas, S.M., Rusbult, C.E., Wieselquist, J., & Whitton, S.W. (1999). Close partner as sculptor of the ideal self: Behavioral affirmation and the Michelangelo phenomenon. *Journal of Personality and Social Psychology, 77,* 293–323.

Duck, S. (1994). *Meaningful relationships: Talking, sense, and relating.* Thousand Oaks, CA: Sage.

Dutton, J.E., & Heaphy, E.D. (2003). The power of high-quality connections. In K.S. Cameron, J.E. Dutton, & R.E. Quinn (Eds.), *Positive organizational scholarship: Foundations of a new discipline* (pp. 263–278). San Francisco: Berrett-Koehler.

Dutton, J.E., & Ragins, B.R. (Eds.). (2007). *Exploring positive relationships at work: Building a theoretical and research foundation.* Mahwah, NJ: Erlbaum.

Eby, L.T. (2007). Understanding relational problems in mentoring. In B.R. Ragins, & K.E. Kram (Eds.), *The handbook of mentoring at work: Theory, research and practice* (pp. 323–344). Thousand Oaks, CA: Sage.

Eby, L.T., Butts, M., Lockwood, A., & Simon, S.A. (2004). Protégés' negative mentoring experiences: Construct development and nomological validation. *Personnel Psychology, 57,* 411–447.

Eby, L.T., Evans, S.C., Durley, J.R., & Ragins, B.R. (2008). Mentors' perceptions of negative mentoring experiences: Scale development and nomological validation. *Journal of Applied Psychology, 93,* 358–373.

Eby, L.T., Lockwood, A.L., & Butts, M. (2006). Perceived support for mentoring: A multiple perspectives approach. *Journal of Vocational Behavior, 68,* 267–291.

Ensher, E.A., Heun, C., & Blanchard, A. (2003). On-line mentoring and computer mediated communication: New directions in research. *Journal of Vocational Behavior, 63,* 264–288.

Ensher, E.A., & Murphy, S.E. (2007). E-mentoring: Next-generation research strategies. In B.R. Ragins, & K.E. Kram (Eds.), *The handbook of mentoring at work: Theory, research and practice* (pp. 299–322). Thousand Oaks, CA: Sage.

Ferguson, E.D. (2003). Work relationships, lifestyle and mutual respect. *Journal of Individual Psychology, 59,* 501–506.

Fiske, A.P. (1992). The four elementary forms of sociality: Framework for a unified theory of social relations. *Psychological Review, 99,* 689–723.

Fletcher, J.K. (1996). A relational approach to developing the protean worker. In D.T. Hall (Ed.), *The career is dead–Long live the career: A relational approach to careers* (pp. 105–131). San Francisco: Jossey-Bass.

Fletcher, J.K. (1998). Relational practice: A feminist reconstruction of work. *Journal of Management Inquiry, 7,* 163–187.

Fletcher, J.K. (1999). *Disappearing acts: Gender, power and relational practice at work.* Cambridge, MA: MIT Press.

Fletcher, J.K., & Ragins, B.R. (2007). Stone Center relational cultural theory: A window on relational mentoring. In B.R. Ragins, and K.E. Kram (Eds.), *The handbook of mentoring at work: Theory, research and practice* (pp. 373–399). Thousand Oaks, CA: Sage.

Follett, M.P. (1924). *Creative experience*. New York: Longmans Green.

Frei, J.R., & Shaver, P.R. (2002). Respect in close relationships: Prototype definition, self-report assessment, and initial correlates. *Personal Relationships, 9*, 121–139.

Gergen, K.J. (1991). *The saturated self*. New York: Basic Books.

Godshalk, V.M., & Sosik, J.J. (2003). Aiming for career success: The role of learning goal orientation in mentoring relationships. *Journal of Vocational Behavior, 63*, 417–437.

Goffman, E. (1959). *The presentation of self in everyday life*. Garden City, N.Y: Doubleday.

Greenhaus, J.H., & Singh, R. (2007). Mentoring and the work-family interface. In B.R. Ragins, & K.E. Kram (Eds.), *The handbook of mentoring at work: Theory, research and practice* (pp. 519–544). Thousand Oaks, CA: Sage.

Hamilton, B.A., & Scandura, T.A. (2003). E-mentoring: Implications for organizational learning and development in a wired world. *Organizational Dynamics, 31*, 388–403.

Harter, S. (2002). Authenticity. In C.R. Snyder, & S.J. Lopez (Eds.), *Handbook of positive psychology* (pp. 382–394). London: Oxford University Press.

Harrison, D.A., Price, K.H., & Bell, M.P. (1998). Beyond relational demography: Time and the effects of surface- and deep-level diversity on work group cohesion. *Academy of Management Journal, 41*, 96–107.

Higgins, E.T. (1987). Self-discrepancy: A theory relating self and affect. *Psychological Review, 94*, 319–340.

Higgins, M.C., & Kram, K.E. (2001). Reconceptualizing mentoring at work: A developmental network perspective. *Academy of Management Review, 26*, 264–288.

Homans, G.C. (1958). Social behavior as exchange. *American Journal of Sociology, 63*, 597–606.

Homans, G.C. (1974). *Social behavior: Its elementary forms*. New York: Harcourt, Brace, Jovanovich.

Jordan, J.V. (1991). *The movement of mutuality and power*. Work in progress, No. 53. Wellesley, MA: Stone Center Working Paper Series.

Jordan, J.V., Kaplan, A.G., Miller, J.B., Stiver, I.P., & Surrey, J.L. (1991). *Women's growth in connection*. New York: The Guilford Press.

Kelley, H.H. (1983). The situational origins of human tendencies: A further reason for the formal analysis of structures. *Personality and Social Psychology Bulletin, 9*, 8–30. doi:10.1177/0146167283091003.

Kelley, H.H., & Thibaut, J.W. (1978). *Interpersonal relations: A theory of interdependence*. New York: Wiley.

Keyes, C.L.M., & Haidt, J. (Eds.). (2003). *Flourishing: Positive psychology and the life well lived*. Washington, DC: American Psychological Association.

Kram, K.E. (1983). Phases of the mentor relationship. *Academy of Management Journal, 26*, 608–625.

Kram, K.E. (1985). *Mentoring at work: Developmental relationships in organizational life*. Glenview, IL: Scott, Foresman.

Kram, K.E. (1996). A relational approach to career development. In D.T. Hall (Ed.), *The career is dead–Long live the career: A relational approach to careers* (pp.132–157). San Francisco: Jossey-Bass.

Kram, K.E., & Cherniss, C. (2001). Developing emotional competence through relationships at work. In C. Cherniss, & D. Goleman (Eds.), *The emotionally intelligent workplace: How to select for, measure and improve emotional intelligence in individuals, groups and organizations* (pp. 254–285). San Francisco: Jossey Bass.

Kram, K.E., & Hall, D.T. (1989). Mentoring as an antidote to stress during corporate trauma. *Human Resource Management, 28*, 493–510.

Kram, K.E., & Ragins, B.R. (2007). The landscape of mentoring in the 21st century. In B.R. Ragins, & K.E. Kram (Eds.), *The handbook of mentoring at work: Theory, research and practice* (pp. 659–692). Thousand Oaks, CA: Sage.

Kumashiro, M., Rusbult, C.E., Finkenauer, C., & Stocker, S.L. (2007). To think or to do: The impact of assessment and locomotion orientation on the Michelangelo phenomenon. *Journal of Social and Personal Relationships, 24*, 591–611.

Lankau, M.J., Riordan, C.M., & Thomas, C.H. (2005). The effects of similarity and liking in formal relationships between mentors and protégés. *Journal of Vocational Behavior, 67*, 252–265.

Lankau, M.J., & Scandura, T.A. (2007). Mentoring as a forum for personal learning in organizations. In B.R. Ragins, and K.E. Kram (Eds.), *The handbook of mentoring at work: Theory, research and practice* (pp. 95–122). Thousand Oaks, CA: Sage.

Lewicki, R.J., McAllister, D.J., & Bies, R.J. (1998). Trust and distrust: New relationships and realities. *Academy of Management Review, 23*, 438–458.

Lewicki, R.J., Tomlinson, E.C., & Gillespie, N. (2006). Models of interpersonal trust development: Theoretical approaches, empirical evidence, and future directions. *Journal of Management, 32*, 991–1022.

Lewis, J.D., & Weigert, A. (1985). Trust as a social reality. *Social Forces, 63*, 967–985.

Luthans, F. (2002). The need for and meaning of positive organizational behavior. *Journal of Organizational Behavior, 23*, 695–706.

Luthans, F., Youssef, C.M., & Avolio, B.J. (2007). *Psychological capital: Developing the human competitive edge*. New York: Oxford University Press.

Markus, H.R. (1977). Self-schemata and processing information about the self. *Journal of Personality and Social Psychology, 35*, 63–78.

Markus, H.R., & Kitayama, S. (1991). Culture and the self: Implications for cognition, emotion, and motivation. *Psychological Review, 98*, 224–253.

Markus, H., & Nurius, P. (1986). Possible selves. *American Psychologist, 41*, 954–969.

Markus, H., & Zajonc, R.B. (1985). The cognitive perspective in social psychology. In G. Lindzey, & E. Aronson (Eds.), *Handbook of social psychology* Vol. 1 (3rd ed., pp. 137–230). New York: Random House.

Mashek, D.J., & Aron, A. (Eds.). (2004). *Handbook of closeness and intimacy*. Mahwah, NJ: Erlbaum.

McAllister, D.J. (1995). Affect- and cognition-based trust as foundations for interpersonal cooperation in organizations. *Academy of Management Journal, 38*, 24–59.

Mead, G.H. (1934). *Mind, self and society*. Chicago: University of Chicago Press.

Miller, J.B. (1976). *Toward a new psychology of women*. Boston: Beacon Press.

Miller, J.B., & Stiver, I. (1997). *The healing connection*. Boston: Beacon Press.

Mills, J., Clark, M.S., Ford, T.E., & Johnson, M. (2004). Measurement of communal strength. *Personal Relationships, 11*, 213–230.

Mitchell, S.A. (1992). True selves, false selves, and the ambiguity of authenticity. In N.J. Skolnick, & S.C. Warshaw (Eds.),

Relational perspectives in psychoanalysis (pp. 1–20). Hillsdale, NJ: Analytic Press.

Nelson, D.L., & Cooper C.L. (Eds.). (2007). *Positive organizational behavior: Accentuating the positive at work*. Thousand Oaks, CA: Sage.

Noe, R.A. (1988). An investigation of the determinants of successful assigned mentoring relationships. *Personnel Psychology, 41*, 457–479.

Noe, R.A., Greenberger, D.B., & Wang, S. (2002). Mentoring: What we know and where we might go. *Research in Personnel and Human Resources Management, 21*, 129–173.

Planalp, S. (1985). Relational schemata: A test of alternative forms of relational knowledge as guides to communication. *Human Communication Research, 12*, 3–29.

Planalp, S. (1987). Interplay between relational knowledge and events. In R. Burnett, P. McGhee, & D. Clarke (Eds.), *Accounting for relationships: Explanation, representation, & knowledge* (pp. 175–191). New York: Metheun.

Pratt, M.G., & Dirks, K.T. (2007). Rebuilding trust and restoring positive relationships: A commitment-based view of trust. In J. Dutton, & B.R. Ragins (Eds.), *Exploring positive relationships at work: Building a theoretical and research foundation* (pp. 117–136). Mahwah, NJ: Erlbaum.

Ragins, B.R. (1989). Barriers to mentoring: The female manager's dilemma. *Human Relations, 42*, 1–22.

Ragins, B.R. (1997). Diversified mentoring relationships: A power perspective. *Academy of Management Review, 22*, 482–521.

Ragins, B.R. (2005). *Towards a theory of relational mentoring*. Unpublished manuscript.

Ragins, B.R. (2007). Diversity and workplace mentoring relationships: A review and positive social capital approach. In T.D. Allen, and L.T. Eby (Eds.), *Blackwell handbook of mentoring: A multiple perspectives approach* (pp. 281–300). Oxford, UK: Blackwell.

Ragins, B.R. (2008). Disclosure disconnects: Antecedents and consequences of disclosing invisible stigmas across life domains. *Academy of Management Review, 33*, 194–215.

Ragins, B.R. (2009). Positive identities in action: A model of mentoring self-structures and the motivation to mentor. In L.M. Roberts, & J.E. Dutton (Eds.), *Exploring positive identities and organizations: Building a theoretical and research foundation* (pp. 237–263). New York: Routledge Press.

Ragins, B.R., & Cotton, J.L. (1999). Mentor functions and outcomes: A comparison of men and women in formal and informal mentoring relationships. *Journal of Applied Psychology, 84*, 529–550.

Ragins, B.R., Cotton, J.L., & Miller, J.S. (2000). Marginal mentoring: The effects of type of mentor, quality of relationship, and program design on work and career attitudes. *Academy of Management Journal, 43*, 1177–1194.

Ragins, B.R., & Dutton, J. (2007). Positive relationships at work: An introduction and invitation. In J. Dutton, & B.R. Ragins (Eds.), *Exploring positive relationships at work: Building a theoretical and research foundation* (pp. 3–25). Mahwah, NJ: Erlbaum.

Ragins, B.R., & Kram, K.E. (2007). The roots and meaning of mentoring. In B.R. Ragins, & K.E. Kram (Eds.), *The handbook of mentoring at work: Theory, research and practice* (pp. 3–15). Thousand Oaks, CA: Sage.

Ragins, B.R., Lyness, K.S., & Winkel, D. (2010, August). *Life spillovers: The impact of fear of home foreclosure on attitudes towards work, life and careers*. Paper presented at the 2010 Academy of Management meeting, Montreal, Canada.

Ragins, B.R., & McFarlin, D.B. (1990). Perceptions of mentor roles in cross-gender mentoring relationships. *Journal of Vocational Behavior, 37*, 321–339.

Ragins, B.R., & Verbos, A.K. (2007). Positive relationships in action: Relational mentoring and mentoring schemas in the workplace. In J. Dutton, & B.R. Ragins (Eds.), *Exploring positive relationships at work: Building a theoretical and research foundation* (pp. 91–116). Mahwah, NJ: Erlbaum.

Roberts, L.M. (2007). From proving to becoming: How positive relationships create a context for self-discovery and self-actualization. In J. Dutton, & B.R. Ragins (Eds.), *Exploring positive relationships at work: Building a theoretical and research foundation* (pp. 29–45). Mahwah, NJ: Erlbaum.

Roberts, L.M., Cha, S.E., Hewlin, P.F., & Settles, I.H. (2009). Bringing the inside out: Enhancing authenticity and positive identity in organizations. In L.M. Roberts, & J.E. Dutton (Eds.), *Exploring positive identities and organizations: Building a theoretical and research foundation* (pp. 149–169). New York: Routledge Press.

Roberts, L.M., Dutton, J.E., Spreitzer, G.M., Heaphy, E.D., & Quinn, R.E. (2005). Composing the reflected best-self portrait: Building pathways for becoming extraordinary in work organizations. *Academy of Management Review, 30*(4), 712–736.

Rousseau, D.M., Sitkin, S.B., Burt, R.S., & Camerer, C. (1998). Not so different after all: A cross-discipline view of trust. *Academy of Management Review, 23*, 393–404.

Rusbult, C.E., Kumashiro, M., Kubacka, K.E., & Finkel, E.J. (2009). "The part of me that you bring out": Ideal similarity and the Michelangelo phenomenon. *Journal of Personality & Social Psychology, 96*, 61–82.

Rusbult, C.E., & Van Lange, P.A.M. (1996). Interdependence processes. In E.T. Higgins, & A.W. Kruglanski (Eds.), *Social psychology: Handbook of basic principles* (pp. 564–596). New York: Guilford Press.

Rusbult, C.E., & Van Lange, P.A.M. (2003). Interdependence, interaction, and relationships. *Annual Review of Psychology, 54*, 351–375.

Scandura, T.A. (1998). Dysfunctional mentoring relationships and outcomes. *Journal of Management, 24*, 449–467.

Scandura, T.A., & Ragins, B.R. (1993). The effects of sex and gender role orientation on mentorship in male-dominated occupations. *Journal of Vocational Behavior, 43*, 251–265.

Schlenker, B.R. (1980). *Impression management: The self-concept, social identity, and interpersonal relations*. Belmont, CA: Brooks/Cole.

Shore, W.J., Toyokawa, T., & Anderson, D.D. (2008). Context-specific effects on reciprocity in mentoring relationships: Ethical implications. *Mentoring & Tutoring: Partnership in Learning, 16*, 17–29.

Snyder, C.R., & Lopez, S.J. (Eds.). (2002). *Handbook of positive psychology*. New York: Oxford University Press.

Spreitzer, G. (2008). Taking stock: A review of more than twenty years of research on empowerment at work. In J. Barling, & C.L. Cooper (Eds.), *The Sage handbook of organization behavior*: Vol. 1: *Micro approaches* (pp. 54–72). London: Sage.

Spreitzer, G., Sutcliffe, K., Dutton, J., Sonenshein, S., & Grant, A.M. (2005). A socially embedded model of thriving at work. *Organization Science, 16*, 537–549.

Surrey, J.L. (1991). Relationship and empowerment. In J.V. Jordan, A.G. Kaplan, J.B. Miller, I.P. Stiver, & J.L. Surrey (Eds.),

Women's growth and connection: Writings from the stone center (pp. 162–180). New York: Guilford Press.

Swann, W.B., Jr. (1983). Self-verification: Bringing social reality into harmony with the self. In J. Suls, & A.G. Greenwald (Eds.), *Social psychological perspectives on the self* Vol. 2 (pp. 33–66). Hillsdale, NJ: Erlbaum.

Swann, W.B., Jr. (1987). Identity negotiation: Where two roads meet. *Journal of Personality and Social Psychology, 53,* 1038–1051.

Swann, W.B., Jr., Polzer, J.T., Seyle, D.C., & Ko, S.J. (2004). Finding value in diversity: Verification of personal and social self-views in diverse groups. *Academy of Management Review, 29,* 9–27.

Thrash, T.M., & Elliot, A.J. (2003). Inspiration as a psychological construct. *Journal of Personality and Social Psychology, 84,* 871–889.

Thrash, T.M., & Elliot, A.J. (2004). Inspiration: Core characteristics, component processes, antecedents, and function. *Journal of Personality and Social Psychology, 87,* 957–973.

Thrash, T.M., Elliot, A.J., Maruskin, L.A., & Cassidy, S.E. (2010). Inspiration and the promotion of well-being: Tests of causality and mediation. *Journal of Personality and Social Psychology, 98,* 488–506.

Thrash, T.M., Maruskin, L.A., Cassidy, S.E., Fryer, J.W., & Ryan, R.M. (2010). Mediating between the muse and the masses: Inspiration and the actualization of creative ideas. *Journal of Personality & Social Psychology, 98,* 469–487.

Turban, D.B., & Lee, F.K. (2007). The role of personality in mentoring relationships: Formation, dynamics, and outcomes. In B.R. Ragins, & K.E. Kram (Eds.), *The handbook of mentoring at work: Theory, research and practice* (pp. 21–50). Thousand Oaks, CA: Sage.

Underhill, C.M. (2006). The effectiveness of mentoring programs in corporate settings: A meta-analytical review of the literature. *Journal of Vocational Behavior, 68,* 292–307.

Wanberg, C.R., Kammeyer-Mueller, J., & Marchese, M. (2006). Mentor and protégé predictors and outcomes of mentoring in a formal mentoring program. *Journal of Vocational Behavior, 69,* 410–423.

Wanberg, C.R., Welsh, E.T., & Hezlett, S.A. (2003). Mentoring research: A review and dynamic process model. *Research in Personnel and Human Resources Management, 22,* 39–124.

Wang, S., Noe, R., Wang, Z., & Greenberger, D. (2009). What affects willingness to mentor in the future? An investigation of attachment styles and mentoring experiences. *Journal of Vocational Behavior, 74,* 245–256.

Wieselquist, J., Rusbult, C.E., Foster, C.A., & Agnew, C.R. (1999). Commitment, pro-relationship behavior, and trust in close relationships. *Journal of Personality and Social Psychology, 77,* 942–966.

Socialization Perspectives and Positive Organizational Scholarship

Blake E. Ashforth, Karen K. Myers, *and* David M. Sluss[1]

Abstract

Research on socialization in organizational contexts has followed four relatively independent paths: socialization stage models, socialization tactics, newcomer proactivity, and socialization content (newcomer learning). We argue that these paths are actually intertwined, such that they jointly lead to newcomer adjustment (specifically, role clarity, task mastery, social acceptance, and role crafting). Although socialization research tends to assume that the process is somewhat negative—reducing uncertainty and anxiety—a positive organizational scholarship (POS) lens suggests that newcomers frequently view the process as a positive experience. Indeed, newcomers are apt to feel exhilarated and energized by the novelty and challenges of a new work setting. We examine how the process of socialization may foster not only the "conventional" outcomes of newcomer learning and adjustment, but greater psychological capital and a sense of thriving.

Keywords: Socialization, thriving, psychological capital, proactivity, learning, adjustment

Although organizations are usually intended by their founders to be more or less permanent institutions, they are populated with individuals who regularly come and go. How do organizations continue to function in the face of a constantly changing roster of members? The answer is through *socialization*, "the process by which individuals become part of an organization's pattern of activities" (Ashforth, Sluss, & Harrison, 2007, p. 1; see also Anderson, Riddle, & Martin, 1999). This broad definition accommodates the effect of the organization on the individual and the increasingly recognized effect of the individual on the organization, and it accommodates the fact that even organizational veterans may need socialization as they assume new responsibilities and transition into new positions. Given space limitations, we will focus on the socialization of newcomers to the organization.

Research on socialization in organizational contexts dates back many decades to various ethnographic studies of occupations, particularly those by

members of the Chicago School of Sociology (see Barley, 1989, for a review). Numerous perspectives have since been offered to explain socialization, and numerous reviews of the literature have attempted to provided some order to the resulting sprawl (e.g., Ashforth, Sluss, & Harrison, 2007; Bauer, Bodner, Erdogan, Truxillo, & Tucker, 2007; Bauer, Morrison, & Callister, 1998; Bauer & Taylor, 2002; Cooper-Thomas & Anderson, 2006; Fisher, 1986; Saks & Ashforth, 1997a; Saks, Uggerslev, & Fassina, 2007; Van Maanen, 1976; Wanous & Colella, 1989).

Our discussion will be based on the integrative socialization model by Ashforth, Sluss, and Harrison (2007), which depicts complementary relationships among the four major socialization perspectives that have emerged thus far (see Figure 40.1): socialization stage models, (institutionalized) socialization tactics, newcomer proactivity, and socialization content (or newcomer learning). *Socialization stage models* refer to the sequence of phases through which newcomers progress as they transition from inexperienced outsiders to savvy insiders. Although these models have attracted little scholarly attention during the last 25 years, they provide a useful heuristic by suggesting the challenges that newcomers may face as they settle in (Fisher, 1986). *(Institutionalized) socialization tactics* are the formalized means by which organizations structure the experiences of newcomers in order to impart certain lessons. Researchers have consistently utilized Van Maanen and Schein's (1979) typology of tactics, explained in more detail below. *Newcomer proactivity* is the means by which individuals actively engage with their work environment, largely as a means of seeking information about their role and work environment in order to reduce uncertainty. Typologies of proactivity focus primarily on behavior (e.g., observing, feedback-seeking, networking) and secondarily on cognition (i.e., positive framing; see Ashforth, Sluss, & Harrison, 2007). *Socialization content (newcomer learning)* refers to the acquisition of knowledge, skills, and abilities—the nature of what is actually learned—to transform the individual into an effective organizational member. While numerous typologies of socialization content have been proposed (see Ashforth, Sluss, & Harrison's, 2007, review), most concur that "learning spans the job and role, interpersonal and group relationships, and the nature of the organization as a whole" (p. 17).

Finally, as Figure 40.1 also depicts, *(proximal) newcomer adjustment* is the outcome of these four socialization perspectives. Although there is little consensus on what specifically constitutes proximal adjustment, Bauer et al. (2007) and D. C. Feldman (1981) provide a three-fold formulation that articulates the broad range of adjustment challenges: role clarity, task mastery, and social acceptance. We add a fourth criterion: role crafting. Building upon job crafting (Wrzesniewski & Dutton, 2001), Sluss, van Dick, and Thompson (2010) argue that role crafting is a meta-construct in which one defines, takes, makes, and "innovates" around his or her given role within the organization, ranging from minor adjustments to wholesale change to the role. Given increasing environmental complexity and dynamism, role crafting is becoming not only more common but normatively expected (Evans & Davis, 2005).

Proximal newcomer adjustment in turn predicts performance and various work-related attitudes (e.g., job satisfaction, organizational commitment, intentions to remain; Bauer et al., 2007; see also Saks et al., 2007), as well as group and organizational outcomes (e.g., cohesion, internal stability; Cooper-Thomas & Anderson, 2006; Myers &

McPhee, 2006). These more distal forms of adjustment are not depicted in Figure 40.1 as our focus is instead on the proximal forms of adjustment; again, role clarity, task mastery, social acceptance, and role crafting.

Positive Organizational Scholarship and Socialization: Thriving and Psychological Capital

How does positive organizational scholarship (POS) fit into this integrative model? Although a "metatheory" of POS relationships does not yet exist, we believe that newcomer learning and adjustment are particularly relevant to two major POS constructs: thriving and psychological capital (PsyCap) (see Figure 40.1). *Thriving* is "the psychological state in which individuals experience both a sense of vitality and a sense of learning . . . which communicates a sense of progress or forward momentum in one's development" (Spreitzer, Sutcliffe, Dutton, Sonenshein, & Grant, 2005, p. 538). Although the tie between newcomer learning and "a sense of learning" is obvious, the notion of vitality—of "aliveness" (p. 538), the "physical or mental vigor that creates the capacity to live, grow, and develop" (M. S. Feldman & Khademian, 2003, p. 344)—is quite novel to the socialization literature. This literature has tended to cast the socialization process in somewhat aversive terms, as the reduction of uncertainty and its associated anxiety (e.g., Gallagher & Sias, 2009; Kramer, 2004; Morrison, 1993). Further, although Pascale (1985) writes that Americans "are intellectually and culturally opposed to the manipulation of individuals for organizational purposes" (p. 28), he goes on to note that some individuals in his study complained about working in organizations that did *not* do a good job of socializing newcomers to the culture, and that newcomers perceived that up to three-quarters of their time was spent just trying to interpret organizational expectations. In short, newcomers often desire and expect some socialization and, as we will see, newcomers in organizations that abnegate socialization tend to be poorly adjusted.

Indeed, in terms of POS, the empirical convergence of learning and vitality onto a second-order thriving factor (Carmeli & Spreitzer, 2009)[2] suggests that newcomers may in fact view the socialization process quite positively. And, indeed, there are certainly hints in the literature, particularly in ethnographic studies, that newcomers may positively anticipate the experience of socialization, may view surprises as pleasant rather than unpleasant, may

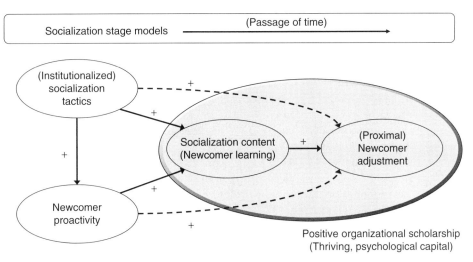

Fig. 40.1 The socialization perspectives and positive organizational scholarship. Note: The dotted lines denote that socialization content does not fully mediate the links between socialization tactics/newcomer proactivity and newcomer adjustment. Adapted from Ashforth, B. E., Sluss, D. M., & Harrison, S. H. (2007). Socialization in organizational contexts. In G. P. Hodginson, & J. K. Ford (Eds.), *International review of industrial and organizational psychology* Vol. 22 (pp. 1–70). Chichester, UK: Wiley. With permission of the publisher.

experience joy and delight at what they encounter, and may embrace novelty rather than fear its unknown qualities (e.g., Hafferty, 1991; Louis, 1980; Myers, 2005). As a result, a sense of thriving seems quite likely during the socialization experience.

The second major POS construct, PsyCap, is a state rather than a trait,

> [C]haracterized by: (1) having confidence (self efficacy) to take on and put in the necessary effort to succeed at challenging tasks; (2) making a positive attribution (optimism) about succeeding now and in the future; (3) persevering towards goals and, when necessary, redirecting paths to goals (hope) in order to succeed; and (4) when beset by problems and adversity, sustaining and bouncing back and even beyond (resilience) to attain success. (Luthans, Youssef, & Avolio, 2007, p. 3; see also Avey, Luthans, & Youssef, 2010)

Saks and Gruman (2011) argue that the emphasis on information and learning in socialization models overlooks the critical need to develop the PsyCap of newcomers. Given an increasingly dynamic and complex environment and the growing prevalence of self-directed careers and team- and project-based work, individuals need to be able to adapt to diverse and challenging roles in real time (e.g., Bridges, 1995; Hall, 2002). Saks and Gruman argue that socialization practices such as realistic orientations, mentoring, opportunities for observational learning, and developmental assignments help foster enhanced newcomer confidence,

expectations of success, motivation to realize goals, and desire to surmount problems. For example, Luthans, Avey, and Patera (2008) describe the salutary impact that a 2-hour web-based training intervention had on the PsyCap of working adults.

In the sections to follow, we will discuss the impact of the four socialization perspectives—socialization stage models, socialization tactics, newcomer proactivity, and socialization content—on one another (i.e., the arrows in Figure 40.1), as well as on (proximal) newcomer adjustment, thriving, and PsyCap. We will emphasize "best practices," although our proposed links between socialization and the POS variables will necessarily be rather speculative due to a lack of POS-focused socialization research. We will begin with socialization content, since understanding *what* newcomers are being socialized to learn will clarify *why* and *how* they are being socialized, that is, the socialization processes of socialization tactics and newcomer proactivity.

Socialization Content (Newcomer Learning)

As depicted in Figure 40.1, what newcomers learn lies "at the heart of any organizational socialization model" (Cooper-Thomas & Anderson, 2005, p. 117; Saks & Ashforth, 1997a). As noted, the various typologies of socialization content collectively suggest that learning spans the role (including job or tasks), social (including interpersonal and group), and organizational domains (Haueter, Macan, & Winter, 2003; Morrison, 1995; Ostroff & Kozlowski, 1992).

Given that the POS construct of thriving suggests that the sense of learning and of vitality are closely linked, the attainment of learning is apt to strongly predict a sense that one is also adjusting well to the new situation. Indeed, newcomer learning has been associated with a wide variety of adjustment variables (although not always consistently), including three of our four forms: role clarity, task mastery, and social acceptance (Chan & Schmitt, 2000; Hart & Miller, 2005; Kammeyer-Mueller & Wanberg, 2003; Klein, Fan, & Preacher, 2006).

Regarding the fourth form, role crafting, Chao, O'Leary-Kelly, Wolf, Klein, and Gardner (1994) found that newcomer learning was associated with "adaptability" (sample item: "I like to try new and different things in my job," Gould, 1979, p. 544). An argument could be made that the relationship between learning and role crafting is actually U-shaped. A lack of learning regarding the role and wider organization may force an individual to invent her own way of enacting the role. Indeed, she may be unaware of the assumptions and biases of veterans and try "naïve" ways that the veterans would never have considered—and possibly stumble on some more effective ways of enacting the role. Conversely, a large amount of learning provides the knowledge, PsyCap, and social credibility to try alternative ways of enacting one's role (cf. Staw & Boettger, 1990; Wrzesniewski & Dutton, 2001). On balance, we expect the impact of high learning on role crafting to be stronger than that of low learning because the impact of the latter is somewhat random and fortuitous.

Further, newcomer learning and adjustment are very likely to contribute to PsyCap. As newcomers internalize lessons about their role, interpersonal relationships, and organization and attain at least some role clarity and task mastery, it is quite likely that their confidence, expectations of success, motivation to realize goals, and desire to surmount problems will increase. Additionally, the social support and validation that typically attend social acceptance may embolden newcomers to strive harder, as may the reinforcement garnered from successful attempts at role crafting (Ashforth, 2001).[3] Finally, one's PsyCap is very likely to facilitate both learning and adjustment such that a virtuous circle ensues.

Socialization Content as the Mediator of Socialization Processes

Figure 40.1 depicts socialization content as the mediator through which the socialization processes of socialization tactics and newcomer proactivity affect

newcomer adjustment. Tests of these relationships have included various adjustment variables, but seldom one of the four focused on in this chapter. Klein et al. (2006) found that newcomer learning partially mediated the impact of socialization agent helpfulness (arguably a form of the "serial" socialization tactic, defined later) on role clarity, along with job satisfaction and organizational commitment. Ashforth, Sluss, and Saks (2007) report that newcomer learning fully mediated the impact of the socialization tactics (specifically, "institutionalized socialization," defined later) and proactive behavior on performance, job satisfaction, and organizational identification, and partially mediated the impact of tactics and proactive behavior on intentions to quit. Cooper-Thomas and Anderson (2002) found that newcomer learning fully mediated the impact of (institutionalized) socialization tactics on job satisfaction and organizational commitment. And Klein and Weaver (2000) report that learning fully mediated the influence of an orientation program ("institutionalized socialization") on organizational commitment. By inference, we strongly suspect that learning at least partially mediates the influence of both socialization tactics and newcomer proactivity on our four proximal adjustment variables.

In sum, newcomer learning is pivotal to newcomer adjustment, a sense of thriving, and the enhancement of PsyCap. The question remains, then: What socialization processes are likely to foster newcomer learning? We broach this question through discussions of socialization stage models, (institutionalized) socialization tactics, and newcomer proactivity.

Socialization Stages Models

Stage models tend to be more prescriptive than descriptive, in that each stage is predicated on resolving the challenges of the previous stage (prescription), although empirical support has been mixed (description; see Fisher's, 1986, review). As such, stage models may be seen as useful heuristics, rather than rigorously predictive models, for thinking through the challenges that newcomers may face as they progress through the socialization process. Following Ashforth, Sluss, and Harrison's (2007; see also Nicholson, 1987) review, four stages are relatively common to most models: anticipation, encounter, adjustment, and stabilization.

Stage 1: Anticipation

Anticipation includes actions through which individuals gain a sense of what to expect upon organizational entry. Individual actions range from reading organizational websites to asking questions of knowledgeable friends and family. Perhaps the most well-researched topic in this vein is the job search process, which indicates that job seekers who employ diverse sources of information and job search strategies, and invest more effort in the process, are likely to have more job offers and better person–job (P–J) and person–organization (P–O) fit (Kanfer, Wanberg, & Kantrowitz, 2001; Saks, 2005).[4]

Organizational actions range from the recruitment and selection process to internships and press releases. Organizations differ widely on two key dimensions. The first is realism–idealism. Although many organizations prefer to offer fairly idealized pronouncements about themselves, when it comes to potential organizational newcomers, research indicates the benefits of setting realistic expectations. Recruitment practices that emphasize the realities of entering a new job and organization in general, and of entering a specific job and organization—in contrast to traditional (overly positive) previews—tend to ultimately enhance distal adjustment, although our four criteria for proximal adjustment have seldom been examined (e.g., Morse & Popovich, 2009; Phillips, 1998).

The second dimension is whether individuals are hired for P–J fit and/or P–O fit. Given that contemporary organizations are less inclined to promise long-term employment, most likely hire individuals to fulfill a particular job vacancy (P–J fit), or, increasingly, a more or less organic role (Bridges, 1995). However, the less specialized the knowledge, skills, and abilities required to fulfill a particular job, and the stronger and more distinctive the culture of the organization, the more likely the organization will hire for P–O fit. Strong-culture organizations tend to believe that promising newcomers who "get it"—who understand and resonate with the culture—can be trained to fulfill particular jobs, but that individuals who don't "get it" are unlikely to ever do so. In short, strong-culture organizations often select on P–O fit and then train for P–J fit. At Microsoft, for example, in addition to the normal round of interviews, applicants are interviewed by a person who is typically not associated with the department making the hire in order to assess whether the applicant fits the wider culture (Bartlett, 2001).

Stage 2: Encounter

The second stage, *encounter*, focuses on the actual entry of new members and how they cope with what they find and with the inevitable slippage between their expectations and reality. Given the marked uncertainty and need for learning that characterizes the encounter stage, this stage clearly resonates with the topics of socialization tactics (regarding the organization's role) and newcomer proactivity (regarding the individual's role), each discussed below. For example, Ashford, Blatt, and VandeWalle's (2003) literature review indicates that feedback-seeking, a form of newcomer proactivity, tends to decline as newcomers gain experience (and exit the encounter stage). Further, as noted, the emphasis of socialization models on uncertainty and anxiety—including the encounter stage of stage models—has cast a negative pall on the socialization process. The POS notion of vitality (as a component of thriving), however, suggests that newcomers may experience this stage (at least at times) as exhilarating. The novelty of the new job, work-based relationships, and organization are very likely to make individuals more aware of their surroundings, more sensitive to the expressed views and nonverbal cues of their coworkers and manager (Korte, 2009), more receptive to sampling new experiences, and more inclined to actively process and internalize those experiences. Newcomers, in short, are likely to be highly engaged, experiencing both the highs as well as the well-researched lows of their new world.

Stage 3: Adjustment

This stage involves resolving the challenges of the new situation, such as becoming task proficient and integrated into work-based relationships, and adhering to the organization's norms and values, leading to a sense of actually fitting in. In terms of Figure 40.1, this stage is reflected in newcomer adjustment, along with concomitant increases in PsyCap; that is, this stage is an outcome of the other socialization perspectives. It should be noted that most newcomers experience a significant decline in their attitude toward the organization after an initial "honeymoon period" (e.g., Boswell, Shipp, Payne, & Culbertson, 2009). The honeymoon itself is likely attributable to most organizations overselling themselves and to newcomers romanticizing their new employer (as the saying goes, the grass is always greener on the other side of the fence). The subsequent drop in attitudes is likely attributable to the honeymoon ending and to inadequacies of the socialization process. Appropriate job search practices and realistic previews, discussed above, along with appropriate socialization tactics and newcomer proactivity, discussed below, can substantially mitigate the drop in attitudes—although the honeymoon may well remain the high-water mark for attitudes.

Stage 4: Stabilization

The final stage, *stabilization*, includes actions that signal that individuals are bona fide organizational members, such as terminating formal mentoring and learning organizational secrets (e.g., C. M. Anderson et al., 1999). As such, stabilization typically demarks the conclusion of the organization's formal socialization efforts. The encounter and adjustment stages can be regarded as a liminal period (Turner, 1969) during which newcomers are seen as (and perceive themselves to be) neither outsiders nor true insiders, not yet "real" organizational members. Liminality can be disquieting, and newcomers typically look eagerly to its resolution. Thus, research on role transitions indicates that rituals and markers that clearly signal, to the newcomers and veterans alike, that the newcomers are accepted as bona fide members help facilitate their sense of inclusion and worth (Ashforth, 2001). For instance, novice firefighters are transformed into "real" firefighters when they graduate from the training academy and can trade their red shirts for blue shirts (Myers, 2005). Nearly as important is the day when they are no longer probationary firefighters, signifying the completion of their first year, and can shed the derogatory label of "booters" and stop performing "grunt" chores.

In sum, socialization stage models regard the socialization process as a sequential series of challenges in which the resolution of each set leads to the next stage. As noted, these models are better viewed as a heuristic than as an empirically valid description of a lock-step progression. Specific elements may not occur (e.g., unmet expectations), and the stages are likely very fluid as elements of one may bleed into the next and events may induce one to recycle through the stages (e.g., Hess, 1993). The remaining process models—socialization tactics and newcomer proactivity—focus on the roles of the organization and newcomer.

Socialization Tactics

Van Maanen and Schein (1979) wrote what is arguably the most influential socialization article to date. They organized otherwise disparate socialization practices into an overarching framework that has clear implications for the effects on newcomers. The framework consists of six bipolar tactics: the *collective (vs. individualized)* tactic entails putting newcomers together and having them share the same developmental experiences, *formal (vs. informal)* involves separating newcomers from veterans, *sequential (vs. random)* includes a lock-step series of developmental experiences, *fixed (vs. variable)* entails a preset timetable for progressing through developmental experiences, *serial (vs. disjunctive)* involves learning from more experienced individuals, and *investiture (vs. divestiture)* entails affirming the newcomer's incoming self and capabilities, rather than tearing them down so that the newcomer can be reconstructed in the organization's image.

Jones (1986) argues that the collective, formal, sequential, fixed, serial, and investiture tactics comprise a gestalt of practices that encourage newcomers to accept and replicate the status quo.[5] Accordingly, Jones dubbed this set of tactics, *institutionalized socialization*. A meta-analysis by Saks et al. (2007) indicates that institutionalized socialization is indeed negatively associated with role crafting ("role innovation"). Conversely, the opposite set of tactics—*individualized socialization*—leaves newcomers to their own devices and thereby may implicitly encourage more idiosyncratic views and behavior. That said, socialization tactics describe only the *process* of socialization, not the actual *content* that is imparted via that process. Although organizations typically use institutionalized socialization to impart the message that role conformity is preferred, there is no reason why these same tactics cannot be used instead to extol role crafting (Ashforth & Saks, 1996).

A paradigmatic example of institutionalized socialization is formal training (Kozlowski & Salas, 2009). Newcomers are grouped together in a training room (collective); separated from regular employees (formal); put through a series of instructive experiences that shape knowledge, skills, and abilities (sequential) according to a preset schedule (fixed) involving experts as trainers (serial), and in a manner that builds on the incoming competencies of the newcomers (investiture). Precisely because such training is off-the-job, the effectiveness of the "transfer of training" depends on the relevance and reinforcement of what is learned in the actual work context (Holton, Bates, & Ruona, 2000). Indeed, formal training is typically supplemented with on-the-job training to crystallize how the lessons apply to the local context. In fact, most training is *on* the job as individuals learn informally as issues arise (Chao, 1997). The point, then, is that the formality of institutionalized socialization is often supplemented by informal means that are more sensitive to the actual tasks that the newcomer will perform.

Impact of Institutionalized Versus Individualized Socialization

Because institutionalized socialization represents a relatively structured set of practices intended to carefully shape the nature and sequence of developmental experiences and the lessons drawn from those experiences, it is likely to predict newcomer learning, a facet of the POS construct of thriving. The few studies that have assessed this prediction have generally been supportive (Ashforth, Sluss, & Saks, 2007; Cooper-Thomas & Anderson, 2002; Takeuchi & Takeuchi, 2009). Also, studies of specific tactics, such as the use of formal training, an orientation program (formal), and mentors (serial), have also been supportive (e.g., Hart & Miller, 2005; Klein & Weaver, 2000; Sluss & Thompson, 2009; Sonnentag, Niessen, & Ohly, 2004). (The impact of institutionalized socialization on the other facet of thriving, vitality, may depend largely on the motivating potential of the practices. Structured practices can ignite a sense of aliveness by exposing the individual to intrinsically interesting activities that foster a sense of possibility, whereas practices that involve uninteresting, tangential activities can prove psychologically deadening.)

As noted, newcomer learning is likely to substantially mediate the impact of socialization tactics (and newcomer proactivity) on newcomer adjustment. The dotted lines between socialization tactics and newcomer adjustment (and between newcomer proactivity and adjustment) denote that the process of socialization has direct, *substantive* effects (e.g., the collective tactic provides a cohort of peers, facilitating social acceptance), and direct, *symbolic* effects, whether intended or unintended (e.g., although orientation programs appear to be only moderately helpful ([Nelson & Quick, 1991], newcomers may view the *absence* of such programs as a signal that the organization does not care about them [Salzinger, 1991]). Thus, Ashforth, Sluss, and Saks (2007) found that institutionalized socialization and proactive behavior directly affected facets of newcomer adjustment (although the four criteria listed earlier were not included), while controlling for the indirect effects via newcomer learning (see also Takeuchi & Takeuchi, 2009).

Indeed, far more research has been conducted on the links between the tactics and newcomer adjustment than between the tactics and learning. A meta-analysis by Bauer et al. (2007; see also Saks et al., 2007) found that institutionalized socialization is positively related to three of our forms of newcomer adjustment: role clarity, task mastery (self-efficacy), and social acceptance (as noted earlier, institutionalized socialization has also been found to be negatively related to role crafting). Just as institutionalized socialization shapes learning, so it reduces uncertainty, builds task competencies, and provides opportunities for newcomers to bond with those "in the same boat" as well as with their socialization agents (Bauer et al., 2007; Gruman, Saks, & Zweig, 2006). This form of socialization, in short, grounds one in a well-defined role, among personalized and valued colleagues, and provides the wherewithal for negotiating one's way within the organization. Thus, institutionalized socialization is likely to foster each of the elements of PsyCap: confidence in one's capabilities, optimism about one's future as a contributing organizational member, motivation to persevere toward one's goals, and a certain resilience in the face of inevitable setbacks. Further, returning to our point about indirect symbolic effects, the very fact that socialization is structured by the organization conveys the message that the organization is concerned about and attentive to newcomers' development. This message reinforces newcomers' growing sense of psychological safety.

In contrast, individualized socialization, as the absence of structure, forces newcomers to "sink or swim" when used without the benefit of prior institutionalized socialization. The less incoming work experience a newcomer has, the more problematic this absence becomes. Although individualized socialization may implicitly foster self-reliance and almost mandates role crafting, it tends to render learning quite haphazard and it undermines adjustment. A newcomer's initial months can be described as a succession of critical incidents that he or she must "decode" to make sense of the organization and his or her role within it (Gundry & Rousseau, 1994). *Institutionalized* socialization helps order the sequence of such incidents and cues the meaning to be derived, so that newcomers' knowledge, skills, and abilities gradually accumulate; conversely, the haphazardness of individualized socialization means that a newcomer may be confronted with an almost random array of incidents, inhibiting sequential learning, and the lack of experienced guides may make decoding the incidents very problematic (Ashforth, 2001). For example, a realtor left to her own devices may be very unsure how to interpret gruff comments from her manager or whether to take the pleasant overtures of another realtor (and potential competitor) at face value. Further, although the "survival mode" that typifies individualized socialization may certainly foster a sense of aliveness—akin to that of a soldier at the front—this is not the psychologically safe and positively valenced aliveness discussed in the POS literature (e.g., Kark & Carmeli, 2009). Thus, individualized socialization may thwart both facets of thriving: learning and vitality.

Finally, individualized socialization provides a very rocky path toward PsyCap. To be sure, if one surmounts the haphazardness of the process, one may reap enhanced confidence, optimism, intrinsic motivation, and resilience; as the aphorism puts it, what doesn't kill you makes you stronger. However, the risk of floundering and failure are very high indeed. In short, if a newcomer succeeds in learning and becoming adjusted, with a concomitant sense of thriving and enhanced PsyCap, it is probably in spite of individualized socialization, not because of it.

We have thus far discussed the socialization tactics as a monolithic set. Two tactics in particular, however, shed some unique light on the dynamics of socialization.

Investiture Versus Divestiture

Following Van Maanen and Schein (1979), investiture was defined as affirming a newcomer's incoming self and capabilities. When investiture is measured according to this definition (rather than simply as social support, following Jones, 1986), it tends to correlate weakly with the other tactics (Ashforth, Saks, & Lee, 1997). Bourassa and Ashforth (1998) suggest that, although investiture is positively correlated with the other institutionalized socialization tactics in most organizations, it is negatively correlated in organizations that actively use divestiture as part of a structured socialization effort. The classic example is military boot camp, where new recruits have their heads shaved and civilian clothes replaced by a uniform, are instructed to march in unison, are subjected to a grueling physical regimen and relentless barrage of verbal harassment from drill sergeants, and must refer to themselves in the third person (i.e., "This recruit"; e.g., Ricks, 1997). The stronger and more distinctive the culture of the organization, the more likely it is to practice some degree of divestiture alongside institutionalized socialization. Other examples include medical schools, athletic teams, police academies, religious groups, firestations, coal mines, and trawlers (e.g., Bourassa & Ashforth, 1998; Conti, 2009; Hafferty, 1991; Myers, 2005; Vaught & Smith, 1980).

The links between investiture and positive newcomer adjustment, thriving, and PsyCap are readily apparent: Investiture builds on the very strengths for which the individual was hired (e.g., the creativity of the graphic artist). What, then, is the impact of its antithesis, divestiture? Paradoxically, we speculate that divestiture also tends to be associated with each of these outcomes, at least after the actual divestment practices have ceased (as in the earlier example of graduate firefighters eagerly trading in their red shirts for blue ones; Myers, 2005). This is because pronounced divestiture—like pronounced investiture—tends to be *normative* for its particular context and therefore expected and even desired by organizational applicants. Applicants to the army usually know roughly what to expect in boot camp and often look forward to being remade into a soldier. This is not to say that the grueling exercises, constant harassment, and so on are experienced as pleasurable; rather, it's the anticipation of successfully completing boot camp and being sanctified as a true soldier that gives meaning to the ordeal. The implication for POS is significant: Whereas POS focuses largely on the virtuous circle of positive inputs–positive outputs, the notion of normative divestiture suggests that thriving and PsyCap can also stem from marked adversity, depending on the personal development that is fostered and the meaning one imputes to the ordeal.

Serial Versus Disjunctive

A meta-analysis by Saks et al. (2007) found that the serial and investiture tactics, jointly, were the most strongly associated with all the adjustment variables included in their analysis: role clarity (reverse of role ambiguity and role conflict), performance (arguably a proxy for task mastery), role crafting (reverse of custodial role orientation), intentions to quit, job satisfaction, organizational commitment, and perceived fit.

Why might these so-called "social" tactics (Jones, 1986) be so important? Ashforth, Sluss, and Harrison (2007; see also N. Anderson & Thomas, 1996; Moreland & Levine, 2001) argue that "socialization is not so much 'organizational' as 'tribal'" (p. 35). Ostroff and Kozlowski (1992) found that newcomers are more interested in acquiring information about their role and local dynamics than about the wider organization. The distal and abstract organization is relevant insofar as it provides the context for the "tribe"; indeed, the organization is rendered concrete through localized enactments. Although orientation programs and formal training provide a generalized sense of the organization and a somewhat context-free sense of the work, much of the everyday tacit knowledge needed to enact a specific role is learned by ongoing social learning processes—observation, imitation and trial, and feedback (Bandura, 1977)—in the relevant context. Peers and supervisors are particularly likely to be viewed as credible social referents because they are knowledgeable about the work and localized context, share a social identity as members of the same group, are interdependent with the newcomer, and physically proximal (Ashforth, Sluss, & Harrison, 2007; Sluss & Ashforth, 2008). And, because much learning occurs from spontaneous interaction around emergent events, the ongoing accessibility of these social referents is very important.

Further, social referents play a central role in providing instrumental and expressive social support for the tensions and frustrations that inevitably accompany "breaking in" (Katz, 1985), and in validating the newcomer's adoption of identity markers (e.g., dress, jargon), behaviors (e.g., role enactment), and performance (Ashforth, 2001; Ibarra, 1999). As noted, social support and social validation reinforce the newcomer's PsyCap, emboldening future role enactment. Indeed, Saks and Gruman (2011) go so far as to state that "social support is probably the most important socialization resource for the development of PsyCap" (p. 21). Finally, the social bonds that may be facilitated by serial socialization help address the fundamental need for belonging, contributing to a sense of human connection and vitality (Baumeister & Leary, 1995; Dutton & Heaphy, 2003). It is not surprising, then, that Nelson and Quick (1991) report that newcomers ranked their interactions with peers as the most helpful of various socialization practices. And, regarding our adjustment facets, Morrison (2002) found that newcomers with stronger and denser informational networks had higher role clarity and task mastery. Indeed, Korte (2009) found that new engineers were surprised by the necessity of building relationships with coworkers and supervisors in order to attain task mastery.

MENTORS

The use of mentors is a particularly important and well-researched form of serial socialization (Kammeyer-Mueller & Judge, 2008; Underhill, 2006). Mentors are usually senior colleagues (peers, supervisors, and/or individuals outside the chain of command) who, whether formally appointed or informally emergent, facilitate a newcomer's adjustment through coaching, counseling, and role modeling, and by providing opportunities, social support, and protection (Kram, 1988; Wanberg, Welsh, & Hezlett, 2003). For example, among a sample of hospital employees, mentoring predicted learning, which in turn predicted role clarity (Lankau & Scandura, 2002). Indeed, given the intricacies of communicating tacit knowledge and sensitive information (e.g., about self, feedback, organizational politics), and the gradual nature by which some skills and abilities are shaped, mentoring relationships often add distinct value beyond traditional training programs (Hale, 2000; Swap, Leonard, Shields, & Abrams, 2001). Further, we suspect that the strong interpersonal bond that often forms between a mentor and protégé can put a "human face" on the organization for the protégé, thereby personalizing and invigorating her relationship with an otherwise abstract organization (Sluss & Ashforth, 2008). Thus, mentoring may contribute to a sense of vitality. As Quinn (2007, in Kark & Carmeli, 2009, p. 786) put it: "The higher quality of the connection between two people . . . the more energy those people will feel." Given the importance of this personal connection to the efficacy of mentoring, it is not surprising that informal mentoring relationships tend to be more effective than formal ones since participants self-select into the former (Underhill, 2006; Wanberg et al., 2003).

In sum, newcomers are largely socialized via interactions with peers, supervisors, and mentors, which are grounded in a particular context and focus largely on that context and the newcomers' roles within it. More generally, the socialization tactics provide a parsimonious framework for analyzing the impact of a variety of specific practices, from orientation programs to the use of mentors. It is equally clear that the tactics have a large impact on newcomer learning and adjustment, and thus, newcomer thriving and PsyCap.

Newcomer Proactivity

If socialization tactics pertain to what the organization does for and to the individual, newcomer proactivity pertains to what the individual does for him- or herself. As noted, newcomers seek to reduce the uncertainty they encounter upon entering a new role and organization. Unfortunately, newcomers often conclude that they need more information than the organization actually provides through its socialization tactics (Jablin, 1984) and that the information that *is* provided is relatively generic, prompting questions about how it might translate into newcomers' particular situation. Thus, newcomers tend to obtain more useful information from relatively proactive, self-directed means (Morrison, 1995; Teboul, 1994).

Research on *newcomer proactivity* explores how neophytes actively seek information about their role and organization (Ashford & Black, 1996; Crant, 2000). Miller and Jablin (1991; see also Miller, 1996) proposed essentially social means, including observing, asking questions, eavesdropping ("surveillance"), testing limits (e.g., breaking rules), disguising conversations (e.g., joking to subtly raise an issue), and using secondary sources (e.g., company website). Ashford and Black (1996) focused on means of securing a sense of control, including information-seeking, feedback-seeking, positive framing (seeing things optimistically), relationship-building, general socializing (participating in social events), networking (socializing with people outside one's unit), and role crafting ("job-change negotiating"; although Crant, 2000, also includes role crafting in his definition of proactive behavior, he notes that other scholars exclude role crafting from proactivity and that it remains an "unresolved issue," p. 457). Information- and feedback-seeking essentially collapse Miller and Jablin's (1991) social means. Jablin (2001) concluded from a literature review that newcomers use observing and direct means most frequently, but use more indirect means as the social costs increase (e.g., looking uninformed, burning goodwill). However, Finkelstein, Kulas, and Dages (2003) found that indirect means are *negatively* related with role clarity, suggesting they may generate unreliable information.

With the exception of positive framing, all the means are behavioral, raising the question of whether cognitive means have been largely overlooked (Ashford & Black, 1996). Ashforth, Sluss, and Harrison (2007) suggest several promising possibilities. One is self-regulation, the "modulation of thought, affect, and behavior" in the service of "goal-directed activities" (Porath & Bateman, 2006, p. 185). Manz (1983; Saks & Ashforth, 1996), for example, discusses self–goal setting, self-observation (monitoring one's own behavior and its causes), rehearsal of desired behaviors, and so on. Another possibility is proactive coping, including preemptive cognitive appraisals and preliminary coping, in which potentially stressful incidents are recast as challenges that spur personal growth (Folkman & Moskowitz, 2004). The upshot is that newcomer proactivity is as much a mind-set—a cognitive orientation—as a set of specific behaviors. Indeed, this cognitive orientation may be an integral newcomer resource, given the usual constraints on behavior during the newcomer adjustment process.

Socialization Tactics and Newcomer Proactivity

Figure 40.1 depicts that institutionalized socialization positively influences newcomer proactivity. Although it could be argued that the provision of institutionalized socialization encourages individuals to learn passively, Ashforth, Sluss, and Harrison (2007) speculate that just the opposite tends to occur. By providing structured opportunities for learning, institutionalized socialization underscores the importance of learning and affords opportunities to ask questions of experienced colleagues, to observe, and so forth. For example, Teboul (1995) found that institutionalized socialization reduced the perceived social costs of information-seeking, which encouraged proactivity. Thus, institutionalized socialization has been found to be positively associated with newcomers' proactive behaviors (e.g., Gruman et al., 2006; Mignerey, Rubin, & Gorden, 1995; Saks & Ashforth, 1997b). Further, by fostering a solid basis of learning, formal socialization programs, such as training centers, likely equip newcomers with the tools they need to subsequently engage their work environments in a proactive manner (e.g., Scott & Myers, 2010).

At the same time, precisely because institutionalized socialization represents structured learning, it appears to reduce the need for newcomer proactivity, suggesting that institutionalized socialization may serve as a substitute for proactivity (Gruman et al., 2006; Kim, Cable, & Kim, 2005). However, Ashforth, Sluss, and Harrison (2007) argue that "synergies" between the two socialization processes are common, such that "organizations have little to lose from encouraging proactivity in the context of institutionalized socialization" (p. 30). For instance, Kim et al. (2005) found that positive framing strengthened the relationship between institutionalized socialization and newcomer adjustment, presumably because positive framing led newcomers to interpret institutionalized socialization as helpful rather than intrusive.

Impact of Newcomer Proactivity

Given that newcomer proactivity involves actively seeking information, often to fill in the gaps left by socialization tactics and to address issues that arise spontaneously in the enactment of one's role, it is not surprising that proactive behaviors are associated with newcomer learning (Kraimer, 1997; cf. Chan & Schmidt, 2000). For example, Ashforth, Sluss, and Saks (2007) found that newcomer proactive behavior measured at 4 months predicted newcomer learning measured at 7 months. Indeed, proactivity was more strongly related to learning than was institutionalized socialization, consistent with Morrison's (1995) research suggesting that active means of socialization affect learning more strongly than passive means.

Regarding adjustment, newcomer proactivity has been linked to role clarity (Holder, 1996; Menguc, Han, & Auh, 2007; Morrison, 1993), task mastery (Morrison, 1993), and social acceptance (Chan & Schmitt, 2000; Gruman et al., 2006; Menguc et al., 2007; Morrison, 1993; Wanberg & Kammeyer-Mueller, 2000). What about role crafting? Although newcomer proactivity connotes activism, scholars have tended to treat the status quo as a given that newcomers endeavor to learn about and adapt to (the exception, of course, is the actual inclusion of role crafting in Ashford and Black's, 1996, typology, noted above). However, the activist stance of the construct suggests that proactivity may influence the nature—or at least one's enactment—of the role (Mignerey et al., 1995). For example, Ashforth, Sluss, and Saks (2007) also found that newcomer proactive behavior predicted role crafting ("role innovation").

Given the strong ties between newcomer proactive behavior and learning and adjustment, it seems likely that proactivity is also strongly related to PsyCap and newcomer thriving. Often, the absence of PsyCap (especially optimism and hope) is a product of one's ignorance of an otherwise munificent situation rather than an actual thwarting of one's efforts. Because organizations increasingly expect newcomer socialization to be at least somewhat self-directed (Frese, Garst, & Fay, 2007), self-efficacy, optimism, hope, and resilience are likely to build as one actively engages the work environment and learns more about how it operates and one's particular role within it. Regarding thriving, Spreitzer et al. (2005) argue that "agentic behaviors constitute the engine of the thriving process" (p. 538). At first blush, it might appear that activism would deplete one's energy, much as spending money depletes one's capital. However, we speculate that such engagement actually *renews* energy as individuals come to feel more engaged in their role and work setting, and through their activism acquire learning, credibility, and resources. Indeed, some conceptions of employee or work engagement (as a state) include such terms as enthusiasm, passion, and energy (Macey & Schneider, 2008). Just as exercise ultimately develops physical prowess, newcomer proactivity may contribute to the sense of vitality (and, in turn, may be galvanized by vitality) that is the hallmark of thriving. That said, if proactivity is not encouraged by the organization—or worse, is actually discouraged—individuals may well burn out from having their exertions go unrewarded.[6]

Conclusion

Although research on socialization in organizational contexts has proceeded along four relatively independent paths—socialization stage models, socialization tactics, newcomer proactivity, and socialization content—our review suggests that these paths are intertwined and lead to a common destination: an abiding sense of adjustment to the workplace. Viewed through a POS lens, it becomes clear that socialization is not simply about allaying anxiety and providing a mechanical "adjustment" to one's role and organization, but also about positively galvanizing one and providing the PsyCap for crafting and embracing one's future in the organization.

Our review suggests several overarching directions for research. First, we argued that structured socialization, in the form of institutionalized socialization, is far more likely to foster newcomer learning, adjustment, thriving, and PsyCap than is unstructured (individualized) socialization. This raises questions regarding how best to sequence developmental practices (e.g., when should novice consultants be exposed to demanding clients?), how best to realize the potential synergies of institutionalized socialization and newcomer proactivity when a structured program seemingly obviates the need for proactivity, and when best to relax or phase out the structure so that newcomers can become fully contributing members. Second, in terms of ties between socialization and POS, we characterized vitality (a facet of thriving) as a concomitant of the process of socialization, and learning (the other facet of thriving) and PsyCap gains as outcomes of that process. Important research questions here include how best to foster a sense of vitality within the context of a structured and therefore potentially stultifying program, and the impact this sense may have on both newcomer learning and adjustment, as well as on PsyCap. Given Fredrickson's (2003) broaden-and-build model (see Note 2), we suspect that a sense of vitality greatly facilitates effective socialization and may lubricate the virtuous circle noted earlier, where enhanced PsyCap in turn facilitates learning and adjustment (both proximal and distal). Third, we argued that the grueling nature of divestiture actually facilitates positive outcomes (at least when that divestiture is expected), suggesting that

POS outcomes (in this case, thriving and PsyCap) can flow from seemingly adverse experiences. This raises questions concerning when "negative" socialization experiences such as "tough love" may be more effective for the newcomer and organization than "positive" ones, whether (and if so, how) negative and positive experiences may be blended (e.g., is there a socialization analogy to "good cop/bad cop"?; cf. Bourassa & Ashforth, 1998), and what other POS constructs might follow similar dynamics.

In closing, research connecting socialization and POS may be in its infancy, but it is readily apparent that there is tremendous scholarly and practical potential to be realized from actively considering how the process of socialization facilitates—and is facilitated by—an orientation to positivity.

Notes

1. The authors are listed alphabetically. We thank Gretchen Spreitzer for her very helpful comments on an earlier draft.
2. The broaden-and-build model indicates that positive emotions—a likely concomitant of vitality—induce individuals to enlarge their awareness and engage in novel and exploratory behavior (Fredrickson, 2003), suggesting that vitality may predict learning. At the same time, a sense of learning—of progress—is likely to encourage and energize the newcomer, such that learning predicts vitality.
3. Even unsuccessful attempts may promote PsyCap if the individual derives important and actionable lessons from the failures.
4. Ironically, however, some research suggests that the very success of an extensive job search may heighten expectations of the work and organization to unrealistic levels, thus *undermining* adjustment (e.g., Takeuchi & Takeuchi, 2009).
5. Van Maanen and Schein (1979) argued that the fixed and investiture tactics actually inhibit a "custodial orientation" (p. 253), but research generally supports Jones' contention (see Ashforth, Sluss, & Harrison's, 2007, review).
6. The fact that newcomer proactivity has been consistently linked to positive outcomes bodes well for POS, as it suggests that organizations tend to be quite receptive to proactivity.

References

Anderson, C.M., Riddle, B.L., & Martin, M.M. (1999). Socialization processes in groups. In L.R. Frey, D.S. Gourin, & M.S. Poole (Eds.), *The handbook of group communication: Theory and research* (pp. 139–163). Thousand Oaks, CA: Sage.

Anderson, N., & Thomas, H.D.C. (1996). Work group socialization. In M.A. West (Ed.), *Handbook of work group psychology* (pp. 423–450). Chichester, UK: Wiley.

Ashford, S.J., & Black, J.S. (1996). Proactivity during organizational entry: The role of desire for control. *Journal of Applied Psychology, 81*, 199–214.

Ashford, S.J., Blatt, R., & VandeWalle, D. (2003). Reflections on the looking glass: A review of research on feedback-seeking behavior in organizations. *Journal of Management, 29*, 773–799.

Ashforth, B.E. (2001). *Role transitions in organizational life: An identity-based perspective*. Mahwah, NJ: Erlbaum.

Ashforth, B.E., & Saks, A.M. (1996). Socialization tactics: Longitudinal effects on newcomer adjustment. *Academy of Management Journal, 39*, 149–178.

Ashforth, B.E., Saks, A.M., & Lee, R.T. (1997). On the dimensionality of Jones' (1986) measures of organizational socialization tactics. *International Journal of Selection and Assessment, 5*, 200–214.

Ashforth, B.E., Sluss, D.M., & Harrison, S.H. (2007). Socialization in organizational contexts. In G.P. Hodginson, & J.K. Ford (Eds.), *International review of industrial and organizational psychology* Vol. 22 (pp. 1–70). Chichester, UK: Wiley.

Ashforth, B.E., Sluss, D.M., & Saks, A.M. (2007). Socialization tactics, proactive behavior, and newcomer learning: Integrating socialization models. *Journal of Vocational Behavior, 70*, 447–462.

Avey, J.B., Luthans, F., & Youssef, C.M. (2010). The additive value of positive psychological capital in predicting work attitudes and behaviors. *Journal of Management, 36*, 430–452.

Bandura, A. (1977). *Social learning theory*. Englewood Cliffs, NJ: Prentice-Hall.

Barley, S.R. (1989). Careers, identities, and institutions: The legacy of the Chicago School of Sociology. In M.B. Arthur, D.T. Hall, & B.S. Lawrence (Eds.), *Handbook of career theory* (pp. 41–65). Cambridge, UK: Cambridge University Press.

Bartlett, C.A. (2001). *Microsoft: Competing on talent* (Case 9–300-001). Boston: Harvard Business School Publishing.

Bauer, T.N., Bodner, T., Erdogan, B., Truxillo, D.M., & Tucker, J.S. (2007). Newcomer adjustment during organizational socialization: A meta-analytic review of antecedents, outcomes, and methods. *Journal of Applied Psychology, 92*, 707–721.

Bauer, T.N., Morrison, E.W., & Callister, R.R. (1998). Organizational socialization: A review and directions for future research. In G.R. Ferris (Ed.), *Research in personnel and human resources management* Vol. 16 (pp. 149–214). Greenwich, CT: JAI Press.

Bauer, T.N., & Taylor, M.S. (2002). Toward a globalized conceptualization of organizational socializations [sic]. In N. Anderson, D.S. Ones, H.K. Sinangil, & C. Viswesvaran (Eds.), *Handbook of industrial, work and organizational psychology* Vol. 1 (pp. 409–423). Thousand Oaks, CA: Sage.

Baumeister, R.F., & Leary, M.R. (1995). The need to belong: Desire for interpersonal attachments as a fundamental human motivation. *Psychological Bulletin, 117*, 497–529.

Boswell, W.R., Shipp, A.J., Payne, S.C., & Culbertson, S.S. (2009). Changes in newcomer job satisfaction over time: Examining the pattern of honeymoons and hangovers. *Journal of Applied Psychology, 94*, 844–858.

Bourassa, L., & Ashforth, B.E. (1998). You are about to party *Defiant* style: Socialization and identity onboard an Alaskan fishing boat. *Journal of Contemporary Ethnography, 27*, 171–196.

Bridges, W. (1995). *Jobshift: How to prosper in a workplace without jobs*. New York: Perseus/HarperCollins.

Carmeli, A., & Spreitzer, G.M. (2009). Trust, connectivity, and thriving: Implications for innovative behaviors at work. *Journal of Creative Behavior, 43*, 169–191.

Chan, D., & Schmitt, N. (2000). Interindividual differences in intraindividual changes in proactivity during organizational entry: A latent growth modeling approach to understanding newcomer adaptation. *Journal of Applied Psychology, 85*, 190–210.

Chao, G.T. (1997). Unstructured training and development: The role of organizational socialization. In J.K. Ford, S.W.J. Kozlowski, K. Kraiger, E. Salas, & M.S. Teachout (Eds.), *Improving training effectiveness in work organizations* (pp. 129–151). Mahwah, NJ: Erlbaum.

Chao, G.T., O'Leary-Kelly, A.M., Wolf, S., Klein, H.J., & Gardner, P.D. (1994). Organizational socialization: Its content and consequences. *Journal of Applied Psychology, 79,* 730–743.

Conti, N. (2009). A Visigoth system: Shame, honor, and police socialization. *Journal of Contemporary Ethnography, 39,* 409–432.

Cooper-Thomas, H., & Anderson, N. (2002). Newcomer adjustment: The relationship between organizational socialization tactics, information acquisition and attitudes. *Journal of Occupational and Organizational Psychology, 75,* 423–437.

Cooper-Thomas, H.D., & Anderson, N. (2005). Organizational socialization: A field study into socialization success and rate. *International Journal of Selection and Assessment, 13,* 116–128.

Cooper-Thomas, H.D., & Anderson, N. (2006). Organizational socialization: A new theoretical model and recommendations for future research and HRM practices in organizations. *Journal of Managerial Psychology, 21,* 492–516.

Crant, J.M. (2000). Proactive behavior in organizations. *Journal of Management, 26,* 435–462.

Dutton, J.E., & Heaphy, E.D. (2003). The power of high-quality connections at work. In K.S. Cameron, J.E. Dutton, & R.E. Quinn (Eds.), *Positive organizational scholarship: Foundations of a new discipline* (pp. 263–278). San Francisco: Berrett-Koehler.

Evans, W.R., & Davis, W.D. (2005). High-performance work systems and organizational performance: The mediating role of internal social structures. *Journal of Management, 31,* 758–775.

Feldman, D.C. (1981). The multiple socialization of organization members. *Academy of Management Review, 6,* 309–318.

Feldman, M.S., & Khademian, A.M. (2003). Empowerment and cascading vitality. In K.S. Cameron, J.E. Dutton, & R.E. Quinn (Eds.), *Positive organizational scholarship: Foundations of a new discipline* (pp. 343–358). San Francisco: Berrett-Koehler.

Finkelstein, L.M., Kulas, J.T., & Dages, K.D. (2003). Age differences in proactive newcomer socialization strategies in two populations. *Journal of Business and Psychology, 17,* 473–502.

Fisher, C.D. (1986). Organizational socialization: An integrative review. In K.M. Rowland, & G.R. Ferris (Eds.), *Research in personnel and human resources management* Vol. 4 (pp. 101–145). Greenwich, CT: JAI Press.

Folkman, S., & Moskowitz, J.T. (2004). Coping: Pitfalls and promise. In S.T. Fiske, D.L. Schacter, & C. Zahn-Waxler (Eds.), *Annual review of psychology* Vol. 55 (pp. 745–774). Palo Alto, CA: Annual Reviews.

Fredrickson, B.L. (2003). The value of positive emotions. *American Scientist, 91,* 330–335.

Frese, M., Garst, H., & Fay, D. (2007). Making things happen: Reciprocal relationships between work characteristics and personal initiative in a four-wave longitudinal structural equation model. *Journal of Applied Psychology, 92,* 1084–1102.

Gallagher, E.B., & Sias, P.M. (2009). The new employee as a source of uncertainty: Veteran employee information seeking about new hires. *Western Journal of Communication, 73*(1), 23–46.

Gould, S. (1979). Characteristics of career planners in upwardly mobile occupations. *Academy of Management Journal, 22,* 539–550.

Gruman, J.A., Saks, A.M., & Zweig, D.I. (2006). Organizational socialization tactics and newcomer proactive behaviors: An integrative study. *Journal of Vocational Behavior, 69,* 90–104.

Gundry, L.K., & Rousseau, D.M. (1994). Critical incidents in communicating culture to newcomers: The meaning is the message. *Human Relations, 47,* 1063–1088.

Hafferty, F.W. (1991). *Into the valley: Death and the socialization of medical students.* New Haven, CT: Yale University Press.

Hale, R. (2000). To match or mis-match? The dynamics of mentoring as a route to personal and organizational learning. *Career Development International, 5,* 223–234.

Hall, D.T. (2002). *Careers in and out of organizations.* Thousand Oaks, CA: Sage.

Hart, Z.P., & Miller, V.D. (2005). Context and message content during organizational socialization: A research note. *Human Communication Research, 31,* 295–309.

Haueter, J.A., Macan, T.H., & Winter, J. (2003). Measurement of newcomer socialization: Construct validation of a multidimensional scale. *Journal of Vocational Behavior, 63,* 20–39.

Hess, J.A. (1993). Assimilating newcomers into an organization: A cultural perspective. *Journal of Applied Communication Research, 21,* 189–210.

Holder, T. (1996). Women in nontraditional occupations: Information-seeking during organizational entry. *Journal of Business Communication, 33,* 9–26.

Holton, E.F., III, Bates, R.A., & Ruona, W.E.A. (2000). Development of a generalized learning transfer system inventory. *Human Resource Development Quarterly, 11,* 333–360.

Ibarra, H. (1999). Provisional selves: Experimenting with image and identity in professional adaptation. *Administrative Science Quarterly, 44,* 764–791.

Jablin, F.M. (1984). Assimilating new members into organizations. In R.N. Bostrom (Ed.), *Communication yearbook* Vol. 8 (pp. 594–626). Beverly Hills, CA: Sage.

Jablin, F.M. (2001). Organizational entry, assimilation, and disengagement/exit. In F.M. Jablin, & L.L. Putnam (Eds.), *The new handbook of organizational communication: Advances in theory, research, and method* (pp. 732–818). Thousand Oaks, CA: Sage.

Jones, G.R. (1986). Socialization tactics, self-efficacy, and newcomers' adjustments to organizations. *Academy of Management Journal, 29,* 262–279.

Kammeyer-Mueller, J.D., & Judge, T.A. (2008). A quantitative review of mentoring research: Test of a model. *Journal of Vocational Behavior, 72,* 269–283.

Kammeyer-Mueller, J.D., & Wanberg, C.R. (2003). Unwrapping the organizational entry process: Disentangling multiple antecedents and their pathways to adjustment. *Journal of Applied Psychology, 88,* 779–794.

Kanfer, R., Wanberg, C.R., & Kantrowitz, T.M. (2001). Job search and employment: A personality-motivational analysis and meta-analytic review. *Journal of Applied Psychology, 86,* 837–855.

Kark, R., & Carmeli, A. (2009). Alive and creating: The mediating role of vitality and aliveness in the relationship between psychological safety and creative work involvement. *Journal of Organizational Behavior, 30,* 785–804.

Katz, R. (1985). Organizational stress and early socialization experiences. In T.A. Beehr, & R.S. Bhagat (Eds.), *Human stress and cognition in organizations* (pp. 117–139). New York: Wiley.

Kim, T.-Y., Cable, D.M., & Kim, S.-P. (2005). Socialization tactics, employee proactivity, and person-organization fit. *Journal of Applied Psychology, 90*, 232–241.

Klein, H.J., Fan, J., & Preacher, K.J. (2006). The effects of early socialization experiences on content mastery and outcomes: A mediational approach. *Journal of Vocational Behavior, 68*, 96–115.

Klein, H.J., & Weaver, N.A. (2000). The effectiveness of an organizational-level orientation training program in the socialization of new hires. *Personnel Psychology, 53*, 47–66.

Korte, R.F. (2009). How newcomers learn the social norms of an organization: A case study of the socialization of newly hired engineers. *Human Resource Development Quarterly, 20*, 285–306.

Kozlowski, S.W.J., & Salas, E. (Eds.). (2009). *Learning, training, and development in organizations*. New York: Routledge/Taylor & Francis.

Kraimer, M.L. (1997). Organizational goals and values: A socialization model. *Human Resource Management Review, 7*, 425–447.

Kram, K.E. (1988). *Mentoring at work: Developmental relationships in organizational life*. Lanham, MD: University Press of America.

Kramer, M.W. (2004). *Managing uncertainty in organizational communication*. Mahwah, NJ: Erlbaum.

Lankau, M.J., & Scandura, T.A. (2002). An investigation of personal learning in mentoring relationships: Content, antecedents, and consequences. *Academy of Management Journal, 45*, 779–790.

Louis, M.R. (1980). Surprise and sense making: What newcomers experience in entering unfamiliar organizational settings. *Administrative Science Quarterly, 25*, 226–251.

Luthans, F., Avey, J.B., & Patera, J.L. (2008). Experimental analysis of a web-based training intervention to develop positive psychological capital. *Academy of Management Learning & Education, 7*, 209–221.

Luthans, F., Youssef, C.M., & Avolio, B.J. (2007). *Psychological capital: Developing the human competitive edge*. New York: Oxford University Press.

Macey, W.H., & Schneider, B. (2008). The meaning of employee engagement. *Industrial and Organizational Psychology, 1*, 3–30.

Manz, C.C. (1983). *The art of self-leadership: Strategies for personal effectiveness in your life and work*. Englewood Cliffs, NJ: Prentice-Hall.

Menguc, B., Han, S.L., & Auh, S. (2007). A test of a model of new salespeople's socialization and adjustment in a collectivist culture. *Journal of Personal Selling & Sales Management, 27*, 149–167.

Mignerey, J.T., Rubin, R.B., & Gorden, W.I. (1995). Organizational entry: An investigation of newcomer communication behavior and uncertainty. *Communication Research, 22*(1), 54–85.

Miller, V.D. (1996). An experimental study of newcomers' information seeking behaviors during organizational entry. *Communication Studies, 47*, 1–24.

Miller, V.D., & Jablin, F.M. (1991). Information seeking during organizational entry: Influences, tactics, and a model of the process. *Academy of Management Review, 16*, 92–120.

Moreland, R.L., & Levine, J.M. (2001). Socialization into organizations and work groups. In M.E. Turner (Ed.), *Groups at work: Theory and research* (pp. 69–112). Mahwah, NJ: Erlbaum.

Morrison, E.W. (1993). Longitudinal study of the effects of information seeking on newcomer assimilation. *Journal of Applied Psychology, 77*, 173–183.

Morrison, E.W. (1995). Information usefulness and acquisition during organizational encounter. *Management Communication Quarterly, 9*, 131–155.

Morrison, E.W. (2002). Newcomers' relationships: The role of social network ties during socialization. *Academy of Management Journal, 45*, 1149–1160.

Morse, B.J., & Popovich, P.M. (2009). Realistic recruitment practices in organizations: The potential benefits of generalized expectancy calibration. *Human Resource Management Review, 19*, 1–8.

Myers, K.K. (2005). A burning desire: Assimilation into a fire department. *Management Communication Quarterly, 18*, 344–384.

Myers, K.K., & McPhee, R.D. (2006). Influences on member assimilation in workgroups in high reliability organizations: A multilevel analysis. *Human Communication Research, 32*, 440–468.

Nelson, D.L., & Quick, J.C. (1991). Social support and newcomer adjustment in organizations: Attachment theory at work? *Journal of Organizational Behavior, 12*, 543–554.

Nicholson, N. (1987). The transition cycle: A conceptual framework for the analysis of change and human resources management. In K.M. Rowland, & G.R. Ferris (Eds.), *Research in personnel and human resources management* Vol. 5 (pp. 167–222). Greenwich, CT: JAI Press.

Ostroff, C., & Kozlowski, S.W.J. (1992). Organizational socialization as a learning process: The role of information acquisition. *Personnel Psychology, 45*, 849–874.

Pascale, R. (1985). The paradox of "corporate culture": Reconciling ourselves to socialization. *California Management Review, 27*(2), 26–41.

Phillips, J.M. (1998). Effects of realistic job previews on multiple organizational outcomes: A meta-analysis. *Academy of Management Journal, 41*, 673–690.

Porath, C.L., & Bateman, T.S. (2006). Self-regulation: From goal orientation to job performance. *Journal of Applied Psychology, 91*, 185–192.

Quinn, R.W. (2007). Energizing others in work connections. In J.E. Dutton, & B.R. Ragins (Eds.), *Exploring positive relationships at work: Building a theoretical and research foundation* (pp. 73–90). Mahwah, NJ: Erlbaum.

Ricks, T.E. (1997). *Making the Corps*. New York: Scribner.

Saks, A.M. (2005). Job search success: A review and integration of the predictors, behaviors, and outcomes. In S.D. Brown, & R.W. Lent (Eds.), *Career development and counseling: Putting theory and research to work* (pp. 155–179). Hoboken, NJ: Wiley.

Saks, A.M., & Ashforth, B.E. (1996). Proactive socialization and behavioral self-management. *Journal of Vocational Behavior, 48*, 301–323.

Saks, A.M., & Ashforth, B.E. (1997a). Organizational socialization: Making sense of the past and present as a prologue for the future. *Journal of Vocational Behavior, 51*, 234–279.

Saks, A.M., & Ashforth, B.E. (1997b). Socialization tactics and newcomer information acquisition. *International Journal of Selection and Assessment, 5*, 48–61.

Saks, A.M., & Gruman, J.A. (2011). Organizational socialization and positive organizational behaviour: Implications for theory, research, and practice. *Canadian Journal of Administrative Sciences, 28*, 14–26.

Saks, A.M., Uggerslev, K.L., & Fassina, N.E. (2007). Socialization tactics and newcomer adjustment: A meta-analytic review and test of a model. *Journal of Vocational Behavior, 70*, 413–446.

Salzinger, L. (1991). A maid by any other name: The transformation of "dirty work" by Central American immigrants. In M. Burawoy, A. Burton, A.A. Ferguson, K.J. Fox, J. Gamson, N. Gartell, et al. (Eds.), *Ethnography unbound: Power and resistance in the modern metropolis* (pp. 139–160). Berkeley: University of California Press.

Scott, C.W., & Myers, K.K. (2010). Toward an integrative theoretical perspective of membership negotiations: Socialization, assimilation, and the duality of structure. *Communication Theory, 20*, 79–105.

Sluss, D.M., & Ashforth, B.E. (2008). How relational and organizational identification converge: Processes and conditions. *Organization Science, 19*, 807–823.

Sluss, D.M., & Thompson, B.S. (2009). *Socialization and social exchange: Leader-member exchange as mediator between tactics and attachment.* Best Paper Proceedings of the 2009 Academy of Management conference, Chicago.

Sluss, D.M., van Dick, R., & Thompson, B.S. (2010). Role theory in organizations: A relational perspective. In S. Zedeck (Ed.), *Handbook of industrial and organizational psychology Vol. 1: Building and helping the organization* (pp. 505–534). Washington, DC: American Psychological Association.

Sonnentag, S., Niessen, C., & Ohly, S. (2004). Learning at work: Training and development. In C.L. Cooper, & I.T. Robertson (Eds.), *International review of industrial and organizational psychology* Vol. 19 (pp. 249–289). Chichester, UK: Wiley.

Spreitzer, G., Sutcliffe, K., Dutton, J., Sonenshein, S., & Grant, A.M. (2005). A socially embedded model of thriving at work. *Organization Science, 16*, 537–549.

Staw, B.M., & Boettger, R.D. (1990). Task revision: A neglected form of work performance. *Academy of Management Journal, 33*, 534–559.

Swap, W., Leonard, D., Shields, M., & Abrams, L. (2001). Using mentoring and storytelling to transfer knowledge in the workplace. *Journal of Management Information Systems, 18*(1), 95–114.

Takeuchi, N., & Takeuchi, T. (2009). A longitudinal investigation on the factors affecting newcomers' adjustment: Evidence from Japanese organizations. *International Journal of Human Resource Management, 20*, 928–952.

Teboul, J.C.B. (1994). Facing and coping with uncertainty during organizational encounter. *Management Communication Quarterly, 8*, 190–224.

Teboul, J.C.B. (1995). Determinants of new hire information-seeking during organizational encounter. *Western Journal of Communication, 59*, 305–325.

Turner, V. (1969). *The ritual process: Structure and anti-structure.* Chicago: Aldine.

Underhill, C.M. (2006). The effectiveness of mentoring programs in corporate settings: A meta-analytic review of the literature. *Journal of Vocational Behavior, 68*, 292–307.

Van Maanen, J. (1976). Breaking in: Socialization to work. In R. Dubin (Ed.), *Handbook of work organization, and society* (pp. 67–130). Chicago: Rand McNally.

Van Maanen, J., & Schein, E.H. (1979). Toward a theory of organizational socialization. In B.M. Staw (Ed.), *Research in organizational behavior* Vol. 1 (pp. 209–264). Greenwich, CT: JAI Press.

Vaught, C., & Smith, D.L. (1980). Incorporation and mechanical solidarity in an underground coal mine. *Sociology of Work and Occupations, 7*, 159–187.

Wanberg, C.R., & Kammeyer-Mueller, J.D. (2000). Predictors and outcomes of proactivity in the socialization process. *Journal of Applied Psychology, 85*, 373–385.

Wanberg, C.R., Welsh, E.T., & Hezlett, S.A. (2003). Mentoring research: A review and dynamic process model. In J.J. Martocchio, & G.R. Ferris (Eds.), *Research in personnel and human resources management* Vol. 22 (pp. 39–124). Amsterdam: Elsevier.

Wanous, J.P., & Colella, A. (1989). Organizational entry research: Current status and future directions. In G.R. Ferris, & K.M. Rowland (Eds.), *Research in personnel and human resources management* Vol. 7 (pp. 59–120). Greenwich, CT: JAI Press.

Wrzesniewski, A., & Dutton, J.E. (2001). Crafting a job: Revisioning employees as active crafters of their work. *Academy of Management Review, 26*, 179–201.

A Positive Approach to Studying Diversity in Organizations

Lakshmi Ramarajan *and* David Thomas

Abstract

In this chapter, we distinguish between positive findings in diversity research and a positive approach to studying diversity. We first review and integrate research on diversity from organizational behavior, social psychology, and sociology from 1998 to 2010, which has already documented positive findings in relation to diversity. We discuss this research using two broad categories: What is positively affected by diversity? (*Positive for what*)? This category consists of research that has shown instances of intergroup equality, positive intergroup relations, and the high performance of diverse groups. And, when is diversity positive (*Positive when*)? This category describes organizational and individual level conditions under which intergroup outcomes, relations, and group performance are positive. Second, we discuss a positive approach to studying diversity and describe some examples of organizational scholarship that have taken such an approach. We also discuss some of the limitations of taking a positive approach to diversity and propose some ways in which diversity scholars interested in taking a positive approach can overcome these limitations. By illuminating both positive findings in diversity research and a positive approach to studying diversity, we hope to spark more research that examines the beneficial and empowering aspects of difference for individuals and groups in organizations.

Keywords: Diversity, positive

In a recent edited volume on diversity in organizations, Chugh and Brief (2008) noted that research on diversity in organizations is sparse—only 5% of articles published in management journals from 2000 to 2008 included race or gender in their keywords. They further speculated that the low percentage of research on diversity reflected an assumption of whiteness and homogeneity in our workplaces. We had an additional concern: Could any of the scholarship on diversity be construed as positive?

We reflect on the term *positive* in relation to diversity scholarship in two ways: positive *findings* of diversity research and a positive *approach* to studying diversity. We consider positive findings of diversity research to be instances in which research on diverse teams, groups, and organizations indicate evidence of intergroup equality, positive intergroup relations, or positive group outcomes. These outcomes exemplify the kinds of phenomena in which diversity scholars are typically interested. For instance, do minority group members have access to opportunities? What is the relationship between majority and minority group members? How does diversity impact group performance? We consider a positive approach to studying diversity to be a lens that helps us define the questions we ask. Positive organizational scholars have argued that positive scholarship highlights those mechanisms that "push beyond optimal functioning" (Roberts, 2006). In the case of diversity research, this would be when scholars examine phenomena that exemplify a just, equal, and close society in which difference is empowering. Such a stance often transforms the questions we ask in diversity research and goes beyond establishing a positive finding in diverse contexts.

For example, a positive finding would be that the top ranks of corporations are slowly becoming more diverse, but a positive approach would entail asking "under what conditions do minority group members 'break through' and get to the top ranks of corporations?"

In this chapter, we first map the terrain of recent diversity research that has documented positive findings, specifically with regard to the three types of outcomes noted above: intergroup equality, positive intergroup relations, and positive group outcomes. We also describe the contingent nature of these positive findings by reviewing evidence of the organizational- and individual-level conditions under which diversity tends to be positive. Second, we describe a positive approach to studying diversity and how this has shaped our own research. We conclude by discussing some of the limitations of taking a positive approach to studying diversity and ways in which diversity scholars can overcome those limitations.

Highlighting both positive findings of diversity research and a positive approach to studying diversity is important for two reasons. First, for scholars who may not be studying diversity because of the idea that it is associated with prejudice, isolation, and intergroup conflict (Roberts, 2006), this chapter offers a review and integration of evidence that diversity can be beneficial. Second, staying open to the positive can present opportunities for novel research in diversity. We highlight four tenets of a positive approach to studying diversity. By illuminating both positive findings of diversity research and a positive approach to studying diversity, we hope to spark more research that examines the beneficial and empowering aspects of difference for individuals and groups in organizations.

Positive Findings in Diversity Research

We define diversity as a characteristic of a group (of two or more people) that refers to demographic differences among group members in race, ethnicity, gender, social class, religion, nationality, sexual identity, or other dimensions of social identity that are marked by a history of intergroup prejudice, stigma, discrimination, or oppression (Ely & Roberts, 2008; Ely & Thomas, 2001). This is one form of what Harrison and Klein (2007) call diversity as variety.

To gather evidence of positive findings in diversity research, we began by conducting a search for research articles on diversity[1] published between January 1998 and April 2010 in widely read management, psychology, and sociology journals.[2] This search yielded 135 articles.[3] We then examined and discussed whether the articles provided evidence of any one of our three types of positive outcomes: *intergroup equality, positive intergroup relations*, and *positive group outcomes.*

We defined *intergroup equality* as instances in which a stigmatized or disadvantaged group achieves a positive outcome. That is, evidence that members of a stigmatized or disadvantaged group are receiving more equal outcomes than stigmatized groups have received traditionally. We defined *positive intergroup relations* as instances in which the relationships between members of stigmatized or disadvantaged groups and members of unstigmatized or advantaged groups are experienced as positive. We defined *positive group outcomes* as instances in which the diversity of a group is positive for the performance of the group as a whole. That is, evidence that diversity positively influenced outcomes for the larger group as a whole (i.e., members of stigmatized/disadvantaged groups and unstigmatized/disadvantaged groups perform well together as a group).

Despite the fact that positive processes and outcomes are not just the opposite of negative processes and outcomes (Cacioppo & Berntson, 1994; Taylor, 1991; Watson, Clark & Tellegen, 1988), we deliberately included articles that showed a reduction or minimization of negative relationships and outcomes. For instance, if the outcome of a study was framed as reducing privilege or disadvantage instead of improving equality, it was still included in our sample. We felt that this was appropriate because the underlying enterprise of much diversity research is often to understand negative relationships, such as prejudice, stigma, and intergroup conflict, to transform them into positive relationships, even if the goal is not clearly stated as such (e.g., Allport, 1954). We found that only about 25% of the articles from our search fit our criteria. We then closely examined the articles we coded as indicating positive findings for the conditions under which intergroup equality, positive intergroup relations, and high performance were most likely to occur.

We describe select articles and findings in detail for illustrative purposes, but we do not provide an exhaustive account of all the articles we examined. We occasionally draw upon chapters in edited volumes, books, special issues on positive psychology, annual reviews, and working papers where relevant. Also, although we present work in sociology and psychology, where possible, we describe research findings focused on diversity in organizational contexts.

In the following sections, we discuss this research using two broad categories: What is positively affected by diversity? (*Positive for what*)? This category consists of research that has shown instances of intergroup equality, positive intergroup relations, and the high performance of diverse groups. And, when is diversity positive (*Positive when*)? This category describes organizational- and individual-level conditions under which intergroup outcomes, relations, and group performance are positive. The findings reviewed here have implications for creating positive conditions in organizations.

Positive for What?
INTERGROUP EQUALITY
Compared to the 1960s and 1970s, members of stigmatized and disadvantaged groups have made progress achieving more equal outcomes in organizations in several realms. The primary outcome of interest has been the increase in diversity itself. This has been measured largely through examining the proportion or representation of women and minorities, their advancement, and their retention at all levels of the organization. For instance, in a study of over 800 organizations, Kalev (2009) reports that the proportion of white women, black men, and black women has increased in the last 20 years as a result of the move in organizations to restructure jobs and do more team-based work. In an earlier study, Kalev and colleagues (2006) also showed that the proportion of white women, black men, and black women in firms increased the most due to programs that established organizational responsibility for diversity. In a study of women partners in law firms, Beckman and Phillips (2005) show that the percentage of female partners in law firms is growing and that this growth is related to the gender diversity of the firms' corporate clients.

Increased diversity in organizations is also the result of retaining and developing members of stigmatized or disadvantaged groups. Zatzick and colleagues (2003) documented that the turnover rates of members of a minority group decrease when there are greater numbers of representation at higher levels of the firm, and that for minority group members, working with others of one's own race (or even with members of other minority groups) improves minority retention and hence the diversity of the organization itself. These articles highlight the fact that diversity both within and outside the organization can have a positive impact on increasing the

representation of members of stigmatized and disadvantage groups in the workplace. However, measuring representation alone does not offer a complete picture of intergroup equality. One avenue for future work could be documenting additional dimensions, such as power or career trajectories. For instance, in a study of minority board members, Westphal and Milton (2000) showed that minority directors could exert even more influence than majority directors on corporate boards in direct proportion to their prior experience as a minority on majority boards and their social ties to majority board members through other boards.

POSITIVE INTERGROUP RELATIONS
Positive intergroup relations are likely to be antecedents to equality in the outcomes we described above. Furthermore, they are important in and of themselves as they capture the daily cognitive and emotional experiences of both the majority and minority members of a diverse group or organization. Creating positive relationships between members of stigmatized or disadvantaged groups and their more socially and materially well-situated counterparts has been a core part of social psychological research for many years.

Allport's (1954) seminal work on prejudice suggested that interaction and contact between members of majority and minority groups could lead to positive relations, but only under particular circumstances, such as equal status between groups and support from authorities for contact among others. Research on intergroup contact is still flourishing (Dovidio, Kawakami, & Gaertner, 2002; Pettigrew & Tropp, 2006; Pittinsky & Simon, 2007; Richeson & Shelton, 2003; Shelton & Richeson, 2005; Tropp & Pettigrew, 2005). For instance, Pettigrew and Troop's (2006) meta-analysis of the contact hypothesis conclusively showed that the basic contact hypothesis itself can be supported. Establishing the conditions that Allport suggested simply enhance the basic effect of intergroup contact, and this seems to be true for both experimental laboratory groups and real ethnopolitical conflict situations (Pettigrew & Tropp, 2006). Furthermore, recent work shows that these reductions in prejudice seem to extend beyond just the immediate contact situation; that is, individuals seem to generalize beyond the immediate person they are in contact with and exhibit positive attitudes toward that person's whole group after the contact situation (Pettigrew & Tropp, 2006).

Although actually making contact across group boundaries may be difficult, intergroup contact research has also shown that individuals of both majority and minority groups *desire* to have contact with members of other groups (Shelton & Richeson, 2005). This is a critical finding for positive intergroup relations, because contact is fundamentally inhibited when group members assume that members of other groups do not wish to interact with them (Shelton & Richeson, 2005; Turner, Voci, Hewstone, & Vonofakou, 2008). Thus, an Asian individual may desire to be friends with non-Asians, but may believe that non-Asians are not interested in close relationships with him. To the extent that these positive intentions toward interacting with members of other groups can be shared or communicated, they may spur reciprocity and eventually positive perceptions and relationships across group lines. For instance, research shows that an in-group member who is aware that other in-group members have friendships with members of an out-group is likely to perceive out-group members positively, and this effect is partially mediated by a positive perception that the out-group is interested in cross-group interactions (Turner et al., 2008). Thus, an Asian individual who is aware that other Asian people have friendships with African Americans may perceive African Americans positively because he may come to believe that African Americans are not opposed to forming friendships with Asians.

As might seem apparent from the studies above, positive intergroup relations in social psychology have largely been seen as a reduction in prejudice and negative attitudes toward out-groups. However, researchers have recently also introduced the construct of *allophilia*, or out-group liking (Pittinsky & Montoya, 2009; Pittinsky & Simon, 2007). Drawing on research that suggests positive and negative phenomena, such as emotions and motivations, are independent (Cacioppo & Berntson, 1994; Taylor, 1991; Watson, Clark & Tellegen, 1988), these researchers argue that decreasing negative attitudes toward out-group members is independent of increasing positive attitudes, and the two can act in distinctive ways. For example, they argue that allophilia, or positive intergroup attitudes, distinctively predicts proactive support for out-groups, whereas reduced prejudice or low levels of negative intergroup attitudes do not (Pittinsky, 2010). Furthermore, perceptions that out-group members desire to interact with one's own group are posited to be antecedents of allophilia (Pittinsky & Simon, 2007).

Organizational scholars of diversity have also used constructs and terms that distinctively denote the presence of positive aspects of relationships between members of different groups, as opposed to the absence or decrease of negative aspects. Terms used in research on positive relationships—such as resilience, respect, openness, and inclusion, among others (Carmeli & Gittell, 2009; Dutton & Heaphy, 2003; Dutton & Ragins, 2007)—have been transported to diversity research. For example, Ely and Roberts (2008) have argued that changing the emphasis of diversity research from differences to relationships focuses scholars on positive aspects of diversity, such as resilience and generativity. Similarly, Brickson (2000) argues that a relational identity orientation, an orientation toward meaningful interpersonal relationships in which minority members feel integrated in the organization and majority members see the minority member as a unique individual with social identity characteristics, is likely to be the most beneficial for intergroup relations.

POSITIVE GROUP PERFORMANCE

One major thrust of diversity research in organizations has been to support the *value-in-diversity* hypothesis (Williams & O'Reilly, 1998). That is, diversity brings value to the group as a whole—diverse groups perform better and have greater value than do homogenous groups. This has been documented in two ways. The first conceptualizes the value in diversity arising from the direct contributions of members, based on each members' unique attributes. Much research on the benefits of diversity refers to diversity as bringing multiple, diverse perspectives to the group, which allows the group to excel (Jehn, Northcraft, & Neale, 1999; Pelled, Eisenhardt, & Xin, 1999; Polzer, Milton, & Swann, 2002). Research by van Knippenberg and colleagues (2007, 2004; Homan, van Knippenberg, Van Kleef, & De Dreu, 2007) on diversity mindsets and the information-elaboration model has suggested that groups that value diversity pay more attention to the different perspectives of members; thus, the value in diversity comes from differences in information that each member uniquely holds and is exchanged under the right conditions.

Although this perspective has continued over the last 20 years, recent research has also exposed other relational and motivational processes that occur in diverse groups that lead to better group performance. For instance, Sommers (2006) conducted a study of group decision making in mock juries, in which he showed that diverse jury groups made better decisions than did homogenous groups due to better information, but the information was driven by motivated majority group members who paid more attention to information in the presence of a minority or out-group member than by the minority group member. This finding challenges the notion that, in diverse groups, it is minority members who bring unique information to the table that leads to improved performance. In this case, mere membership in a diverse group is sufficient to motivate enhanced information sharing and processing and thereby improve group performance (see also Phillips & Loyd, 2006). Recent research also suggests that, in diverse groups, sometimes having a small subgroup can be beneficial for outcomes such as team learning because the subgroup offers a supportive atmosphere in which team members can put forth individual opinions (Gibson & Vermeulen, 2003).

DISCUSSION

The three types of positive outcomes of diversity—intergroup equality, positive intergroup relations, and group performance—are independent of one another. They can be decoupled or interact with one another. For instance, one of the most consistent arguments made in diversity research since Williams and O'Reilly's (1998) review is that workgroup diversity may lead to positive group performance, but that it is often undermined by negative intergroup relationships and processes. However, some of the research discussed above shows that demographically heterogeneous groups may have positive intergroup relations, positive group processes, and positive performance under the right conditions, which we elaborate on more in the following section. In contrast, some research shows that, even when positive intergroup emotions are present, such as liking, there may not be respect for minority members' competence, for instance, in the case of housewives or the elderly and disabled (Cuddy, Fiske, & Glick, 2004; 2007), which can potentially result in unequal intergroup outcomes and low group performance.

The opposite is also true. Negative intergroup relations in the short term can improve unequal intergroup outcomes and help create long-term social change (Boen & Vanbeselaere, 2001). For instance, if a minority group member confronts a majority group member who displays bias, this can induce negative emotions for the majority group member, leading to negative intergroup relations in the short-term. However, in the long-term, this confrontation can influence more positive intergroup attitudes and less bias by the majority group member (Czopp, Monteith, & Mark, 2006). One need only think about the civil rights movement or the women's movement, which were based on short-term confrontation but influenced long-term social change, to understand the importance of looking at these three dimensions of positive findings independently.

One interesting pattern apparent from our review is that the attention to intergroup equality seems to be concentrated at the macro-organizational and institutional level of analysis, whereas many intergroup relations and group performance outcomes have been studied at the individual and group level. Research that crosses levels, for instance, bringing higher levels of analysis to understanding performance at the group level and examining intergroup equality at the more micro-level have received little attention. Research by Joshi and colleagues has taken such a direction, showing that demographic diversity at the occupation level moderates the effects of group diversity on group-level performance (Joshi & Roh, 2009) and that diversity at the group level influences intergroup equality in the form of reducing earnings inequalities for members of disadvantaged groups (Joshi, Hui, & Jackson, 2006).

Positive When?

Given the prevailing image of diversity as a problem to manage, our first objective was to review and integrate research that showed diversity could be positive for individuals and organizations. As the review above indicates, diversity research has documented instances of intergroup equality, positive intergroup relations, and positive group performance. However, we did not systematically focus our attention on the contingent nature of these findings, nor on the processes by which these outcomes arise. A careful examination of the research we reviewed above will indicate that many of these positive findings occur under particular conditions. Scholars have paid close attention to many moderators (see Jackson, Joshi, & Erhardt, 2003 for a review). In this section, we review organizational research that has closely examined the conditions under which organizations can positively influence intergroup equality, intergroup relations, and group performance. We organized the conditions covered by existing research into three broad themes: organizational or group-level conditions, individual-level conditions, and work or task-level conditions.

ORGANIZATIONAL OR GROUP-LEVEL MODERATORS

One thread in recent diversity research suggests that organizations and groups need to establish the right approach to diversity in order to realize positive intergroup outcomes, relations, and performance. For example, research at the firm level shows that diversity initiatives focused on organizational responsibilities for diversity are best able to exhibit increases in intergroup equality (i.e., see the greatest proportion of women and minorities in managerial positions) (Kalev, Dobbin, & Kelly, 2006). Organizational responsibilities for diversity include affirmative action plans, diversity committees, and diversity staff positions. Such approaches are distinguished from diversity training, education, and feedback, which have no noticeable effect on intergroup equality, and from approaches such as mentoring and networking programs that address the social connections of women and minorities as ways of managing diversity, which have a modest effect on intergroup equality (Kalev, Dobbin, & Kelly, 2006).

At the group level, Ely and Thomas (2001) describe three types of perspectives that groups may hold regarding diversity: discrimination-and-fairness, access-and-legitimacy, and integration-and-learning. In the discrimination-and-fairness perspective, groups operate under the belief that diversity is a moral imperative and, as a result, attempt to ensure justice and fair treatment for all. Groups with the access-and-legitimacy perspective believe that diversity is a means to gain access to and legitimacy for the organization among culturally diverse market segments. Groups with an integration-and-learning perspective recognize that diversity can be a resource for learning and adaptive change. Their study finds that the integration-and-learning perspective is most associated with sustainable, positive intergroup relations and group performance (Ely & Thomas, 2001).

Diversity research has also examined other group-level constructs closely related to an integration-and-learning perspective that capture the beliefs and attitudes regarding diversity and moderate the influence of diversity on group performance. For instance, van Knippenberg and colleagues investigated constructs such as a diversity mindset, and beliefs about the value in diversity (Homan et al., 2007; van Knippenerg, De Dreu, & Homan, 2004; van Knippenberg, Haslam, & Platow, 2007). They show that each of these constructs are important conditions under which diverse groups experience positive intergroup processes, such as sharing and elaborating on information, and hence achieve high performance.

Researchers have also examined moderators that broadly capture how groups vary in their acceptance of group members' differences. Some of these include climate for inclusion (Nishii, 2010; defined as environments in which members of all identity groups perceive they are fairly treated, valued for who they are, and included in core decision making), interpersonal congruence (the extent to which a group verifies each members' self-view; Polzer et al., 2002), and "openness to experience" (a Big-Five personality trait associated with openness to learning, novel experiences, and exploring difference; Homan et al., 2008). In such situations, diverse groups are more likely to experience positive intergroup relations that enhance group performance. For example, Nishii (2010) shows that organizational units that have high gender diversity experience lower conflict and greater satisfaction (more positive intergroup relations) and less turnover when they also have a climate for inclusion. In groups of MBA students, Polzer and colleagues (2002) find that when diverse groups also have high interpersonal congruence they show both positive intergroup relations and performance on creative tasks. Another approach to moderating the potentially damaging aspects of group diversity on intergroup relations and group performance is a common group identity (e.g., Gaertner & Dovidio, 2000; Jehn & Bezrukova, 2010) in which individuals share a sense of self as members of a common workgroup or organization and hence are less susceptible to negative intergroup processes.

Last, a qualitatively different type of condition under which diversity has been shown to result in intergroup equality and positive intergroup relations is the diversity of the larger context or environment in which groups and organizations are embedded. For example, in Phillips et al's (2009) study of promotion rates of female law partners, the demographic composition of the firm's clients was an important factor that contributed to intergroup equality; law firms with clients that had female executives were more likely to have female partners themselves. At the group level, recent work by Williams (2008) indicates that demographically diverse dyads develop more interpersonal trust than do demographically similar dyads when they are embedded in a larger group that is diverse rather than homogenous.

INDIVIDUAL-LEVEL MODERATORS

In addition to organizations and groups fostering the right set of conditions for diversity to be positive, individuals may also be able to positively influence the conditions under which they interact. Specifically, when in a diverse setting, one critical issue for members of stigmatized and disadvantaged groups is influencing how they are perceived by members of other groups. For example, both positive and negative stereotypes of women and minorities can limit the equality of their outcomes, the quality of their relationships, and their personal performance. Although these effects of diversity are measured at the individual level, it is likely that they also have implications for the ways in which intergroup dynamics play out in organizations (Alderfer & Smith, 1982).

Research suggests that the personality characteristics and identity management strategies of members of minority groups can be important moderators of these effects. For example, people form positive impressions of demographically distinct individuals in organizations when those individuals are high in the personality traits of extraversion (characterized by positive emotions, social interaction, and engagement with others) and self-monitoring (i.e., individuals who can observe their own and others reactions and regulate their behavior to adapt to the circumstance) (Flynn & Ames, 2006; Flynn & Chatman, 2001).

Along with personality, impression management strategies, targeted specifically around one's distinct social identity, can also positively moderate the influence of diversity on intergroup relations in organizations. For instance, although much research shows that concealing important aspects of oneself can have negative implications for minority group members' personal well-being (Clair, Beatty, & MacLean, 2005; Hewlin, 2003, 2009), Phillips and colleagues argue that this is not uniformly the case; for example, concealing negative information about one's distinct social identity may close status distance, bringing high- and low-status individuals together and leading to close relationships (Phillips, Rothbard, & Dumas, 2009). Disclosing positive information can also contribute to forming close relationships (Phillips et al., 2009); for instance, Roberts and colleagues (2009) note that for women and minorities who may be expected to conform or assimilate to the culture of dominant groups, displaying important aspects of oneself can lead to an experience of alignment or consistency between one's internal feelings and external expression that positively influences high-quality relationships (see also Roberts, 2005).

Despite these potentially positive consequences of managing one's image around a distinct social identity for positive intergroup relations (Phillips et al., 2009; Roberts, 2005; Roberts, Dutton, Spreitzer, Heaphy, & Quinn, 2005), Ely and Meyerson (2010) suggest that proving a particular image (whether highlighting positive aspects or concealing negative aspects) around one's distinct social identity can be detrimental for the work of the group as a whole. They argue that in traditionally masculine organizational cultures in which men are doing dangerous work and are oriented toward proving a gendered image of themselves as "tough," "macho," and "heroic," work suffers. In contrast, in their study of an offshore oil platform that created an organizational culture of safety and contribution to the organization, they argue that men were oriented away from maintaining a traditional masculine image. Instead, they were oriented toward one another and the organization as a whole, which enabled a safer and more efficient work environment.

In addition to managing impressions regarding their distinct social identity, minority group members also vary in how their social identities relate to other identities they hold. For instance, how does identifying with a gender role, or with one's cultural background, such as being African American or Asian, relate to one's work role or organizational identity? And how could this impact our interactions across group lines?

Recent research suggests that positive relationships between identities—when identities are experienced as compatible and/or enhancing one another (Benet-Martinez & Haritatos, 2005; Dutton, Roberts, & Bednar, 2010; Greenhaus & Powell, 2006; Rothbard & Ramarajan, 2009)—can lead to intergroup tolerance and openness (Ramarajan, 2009) and more diverse social networks (Dutton et al., 2010), and also influence a diverse team's innovative performance (Cheng, Sanchez-Burks, & Lee, 2008). Thus, individuals' management of multiple identities may also be an important aspect of understanding how individual-level identity factors may moderate the relationship between diversity and positive outcomes.

WORK AND TASK-LEVEL CONDITIONS

Last, in diverse groups, the work or task characteristics themselves can be important moderating conditions of the relationship between diversity and intergroup equality, as well as of intergroup relations and group performance. In terms of work characteristics, Kalev (2009) indicates that changes in the structure of work, with less job segregation and more teamwork, increase the visibility of women and minorities, and hence leads to a greater proportion of women and minorities in managerial positions. Group size is another element of the work environment that could moderate the effects of diversity on group performance. For example, Wegge and colleagues (2008) argue that gender diversity has a more positive influence on performance in larger groups than in smaller groups because the diversity of gender-based behaviors that contribute to positive performance is amplified in large groups. Characteristics of the group's task may also influence diverse group performance. In their study of MBA teams, Polzer et al. (2002) find that diversity has a positive impact on group performance under conditions of interpersonal congruence only for creative tasks, but not for computational tasks. However, for routine tasks, the impact of diversity on performance is inconsistent—sometimes negative (Wegge, Roth, Neubach, Schmidt, & Kanfer, 2008), and sometimes positive (Pelled et al., 1999). Last, time has been examined as a moderator, particularly in terms of decreasing the negative effects of demographic diversity on group processes (e.g., Chatman & Flynn, 2001; Pelled et al., 1999) and occasionally in showing the positive effects of demographic diversity over time (Earley & Mosakowski, 2000), but more longitudinal research is still needed. In general, research on the moderating effects of work and task characteristics is very limited (Joshi & Roh, 2009) and only a small fragment of this work emphasizes the positive aspects of diversity for intergroup outcomes, relations, or performance.

DISCUSSION

Recent research has examined a number of different moderators at the group and organizational levels, including the demography of units at different levels in the organization, as well as the context in which the organization or group is embedded, how organizations take responsibility for diversity, how groups may value differences, and the degree to which organizations embrace "the whole person." One potential avenue for future work could be investigating the antecedents of organizational conditions that are positive for diversity. Questions to explore include: What are the characteristics of organizations that strongly promote taking responsibility for diversity or an integration-and-learning perspective? And, how have successful diverse groups learned pro-diversity attitudes over time?

At the individual level, research suggests that members of stigmatized groups may enact complex identity and impression management processes to transform negative intergroup relations into positive ones. One could examine how minority group members' management of their distinct social identity or their multiple identities is perceived by majority group members. For instance, in the case of stigmatized group memberships, it could be that conflict among one's identities could have an important positive influence on creating social change or high-quality relationships.

Another avenue for research would be to examine how dominant group members enact identity processes that positively influence the link between demographic diversity and intergroup relations. Research that has examined dominant group members' identities and attitudes, such as white racial identity salience, has often linked it to intolerance (Ziegert & Hanges, 2005) and motivations to maintain privilege (Unzueta & Lowery, 2008; Unzueta, Lowery, & Knowles, 2008). In contrast, Flynn (2005) shows that, for whites, the personality trait of "openness to experience" is positively associated with attitudes of racial tolerance. In Sommers' (2006) study on jury decision making, better decision making outcomes of diverse juries were due to the white members, who were motivated to investigate the situation rather than from black participants bringing in a distinct point of view. Thus, research could examine how majority group members construct and enact identities that lead to more positive relations with minorities and better group performance; for example, how do people construct a "best white self"? This is crucial in understanding the potential for social change. For many minority groups, alliances with supportive members of the majority group are critical. What are the situational conditions, and identity and personality processes of majority group members that compel them to act in ways that promote positive intergroup outcomes and relations?

Some of the research we reviewed also shows that the magnitude of the positive findings varied by the actual minority group category (e.g., U.S./non-U.S.; black/Hispanic/Asian) (e.g., Zatzick, Elvira, & Cohen, 2003). For instance, Kalev and colleagues' work showed that intergroup equality differed by three different groups, white women (least unequal), black men, and black women (most unequal) (2009; Kalev, Dobbin, & Kelly, 2006). Castilla (2008) also shows that salary increases in a large U.S. organization differ by race, gender, and nationality, with women experiencing the least bias and non-U.S. citizens experiencing the most bias in rewards for their performance compared to white men. In a study on school friendship, research shows that cross-race friendships between whites and members other groups were more likely to occur when the other group members were Asian or Hispanic than when they were black (Quillian & Campbell, 2003). Despite research suggesting that there are important differences in identities, attitudes, and outcomes among different minority groups and interactions among multiple minority status categories (cf. Purdie-Vaughns & Eibach, 2008; Berdahl & Moore, 2006), very few diversity studies in organizations closely examine these differences. To fully understand the contingent nature of positive findings, future work should also try to take these distinctions into account.

A Positive Approach to Diversity Research

Our work in writing this chapter has been a process of review and reflection. We initially focused on reviewing the diversity research literature for the presence of positive findings. Although most of the studies in this literature are focused on examining the problematic nature of identity group dynamics in organizations, we did indeed find a number of studies whose findings highlight positive influences of diversity on individual and organizational outcomes and the conditions under which these positive results are likely to appear. We completed the review of this literature quite conscious of the fact that a positive approach to diversity research is distinct from positive findings that may arise from diversity research.

Taking a "positive approach to diversity" may seem ironic, idealistic, or perhaps even misguided to many organizational scholars on diversity. Here, we would like to acknowledge the concerns with such an approach and suggest some ways in which researchers can move forward while holding them in mind.

First, researchers may not believe that positivity and diversity can be studied together. Summarizing 40 years of diversity research in 1998, Williams and O'Reilly famously concluded that results for the value-in-diversity hypothesis were inconsistent—it was not clear that there were positive findings for diversity (at least with regard to group performance). Ten years later, diversity scholars acknowledged that their conclusion was still largely true (Chugh & Brief, 2008). In this chapter, we highlight the studies of diversity that have shown some positive

outcomes, and the conditions under which these happen, as a way to generate ideas and enthusiasm for paying attention to positive findings when studying diversity in organizations.

Second, given that scholars do not yet fully understand or include diversity in general in organizational studies, some may wonder if it is premature to take an approach that is explicitly positive. Just as improving representation of women and minorities in organizations is in and of itself an instance of positive intergroup outcomes, one suggestion is that creating more scholarship on diversity in and of itself could be a positive outcome for organizational scholarship. Perhaps rather than a call for more scholarship utilizing a positive approach to diversity, our field simply needs a call for more research on diversity?

Third, an emphasis on discussing the positives of diversity may seem too idealistic when societies and organizations still have much work to do to eliminate inequalities along the lines of race, gender, and other major categories (Chugh & Brief, 2008). We stated at the start of this chapter that one-quarter of the articles we coded showed a positive finding for diversity based on our admittedly broad categorization of research that showed instances of positive (and less negative) intergroup equality, intergroup relations, or group performance. One could ask at what level would diversity scholars consider diversity research to be "blinded" by documenting the positive (Roberts, 2006)? Perhaps as long as diversity research continues to take a mixed and contingent approach, examining the positive without ignoring or eliding the negatives, we can navigate this line.

What would a positive approach to diversity research entail? What would be the tenets or heuristics of such an approach? Is it possible to take a positive approach and not fall into an idealistic trap that distorts the reality of identity group dynamics in organizations? An observation by Roberts (2006) forced us to reflect on these questions in a more personal manner. In an article articulating the "value add" of taking a positive organizational studies approach, she noted the limited attention that diversity research has received in positive organizational studies literature. She also cited five diversity studies as noteworthy for their emphasis on and illumination of positive dynamics and organizational outcomes (Ely & Thomas, 2001; Polzer, Milton, & Swann, 2002; Richard, 2000; Thomas, 2004; Thomas & Gabarro, 1999). The Thomas noted in these citations is one of the authors of this chapter, David Thomas. The studies cited refer to his work on the influence of cultural diversity on individual and organizational performance (Ely & Thomas, 2001; Thomas & Ely, 1996; Thomas, 2004), the influence of race on developmental relationships (Thomas, 1990, 1993, 2001) and minority executive development and advancement (Thomas & Gabarro, 1999).

Upon reflection, we began to consider how consistent these studies were with the tenets of positive organizational scholarship (POS). According to Roberts (2006), the motivating idea of positive organizational studies is "to identify and understand the generative mechanisms that create positive deviance in people, groups and organizations." Against that criterion, we found that much of David's work could be seen as having a positive orientation.

His work with Robin Ely began with a focus on understanding the influence of racial diversity on organizations that transformed themselves from very homogeneous, predominantly white organizations, to being racially diverse across all levels of the hierarchy. The condition of racial diversity across all levels of the hierarchy was assumed to be positive and definitely was atypical or deviant for the industries in which these focal organizations existed. The theoretical contribution of this work was to identify that racial diversity alone did not lead to better organizational performance or individual outcomes. This occurred when diversity was accompanied by an integration-and-learning perspective about diversity and the relevance of diversity to the organization's work (Ely & Thomas, 2001).

Thomas (1993) examined the conditions under which cross-race developmental relationships evolve into intimate and positive mentor–protégé relationships that provide both significant instrumental career support (i.e., coaching, advocacy, exposure) and psychosocial support (i.e., trust, counseling, role modeling) rather than becoming only an instrumentally supportive but psychosocially distant sponsor–protégé relationship. A prior study in the same organization revealed that these cross-race mentor–protégé relationships were indeed rare (Thomas, 1990). The theoretical contribution of this work was identifying the complementarity between the perspectives of the mentor and the protégé regarding how to manage racial difference as the key mechanism that determined whether the cross-race dyad would evolve into a full-blown mentor–protégé relationship.

In a third stream of research, Thomas and Gabarro (1999) set out to identify the individual

and organizational factors that corresponded with racial minorities achieving C-suite level executive positions in large, predominantly white organizations. The study was comparative as it included minority executives (positive deviants), white executives, minorities who plateaued in middle management, and whites who plateaued in middle management. At the time, this was the first study to focus on the population of minorities in executive jobs with a comparative research design. A central contribution of the book was to isolate the unique pathway of mobility and the pattern of career experiences that differentiated minority executives from minorities who plateaued and from white executives who achieved comparable positions. During the design phase of the project, some scholars of race relations and inequality criticized it for focusing too much on an aberrant positive condition since race so overdetermined the fact that, on average, minorities will not reach executive-level positions regardless of their human and social capital assets in their early careers. The criticism is reminiscent of some of the reasons Roberts (2006) cited for why some scholars—and in particular diversity researchers—might be skeptical of a positive approach to studying diversity. The ultimate product of the research was an award-winning book, *Breaking Through: The Making of Minority Executives in Corporate America*, that in reviews did not receive criticism of this sort from the same scholars who were initially skeptical.

Discussion

Looking across these studies, we see threads consistent with POS. Some prominent elements of these studies also suggest four tenets or heuristics that might form the basis for a positive approach to diversity research that is consistent with positive organizational studies, and this approach would not negate the importance of examining the normative and problematic aspects of identity group dynamics in positive diversity research. First, a positive approach to diversity begins by examining a phenomenon in which identity group–based differences are thought to matter. The research must therefore be informed by the relevant diversity research, regardless of its emphasis on the positive or problematic. Although this may seem too obvious to state as the first tenet, it is important so that positive diversity scholarship does not become divorced from the literature on social identity group dynamics. For example, David Thomas's work on mentoring is very much informed by the literature on the tortured nature of cross-race relationships, stemming from the legacy of slavery in the United States (Thomas, 1989).

Second, the motivating question guiding the ultimate design of the study must focus on an established condition of positive deviance. For example, Thomas's work on mentoring (1990, 1993) evolved out of his statistical observation that cross-race developmental relationships did form, but that the mentor–protégé variety, characterized by high degrees of both instrumental career and psychosocial support, were rare. It was also clear that relationships that provided high degrees of both career and psychosocial support were longer lasting and seen as having a greater impact on positive career outcomes.

Third, a positive approach to diversity research requires that, where possible, empirical studies must include the nonpositive deviant or average condition for purposes of comparison. This ensures that unique identity group-related dynamics are not lost. The advantage of this was evident in Thomas's studies of both cross-mentoring relationships and minority career advancement (Thomas, 1993, 2001; Thomas & Gabarro, 1999). Without the presence of the more common cross-race sponsor–protégé condition in the mentoring study, the significance of complementarity in racial perspective would not have emerged because what was important was not the content of the perspective, but whether it was congruent with the dyad partner's perspective with regard to whether race was a positive issue to acknowledge and explore in the relationship or one deemed problematic and best left out of the relationship. Similarly, without the presence of white executives and plateaued minority managers in the study of minority executives, much of the race-related dynamics identified in the book would not have emerged.

Fourth, the researchers must treat the targeted positive deviance as a hypothesis rather than a fact. In other words, there must be openness to discovering the shadow side of positive deviance and modifying our understanding of the condition. The work by Ely and Thomas (1996, 2001) illustrates the importance of this tenet. The research originally began with the assumption that racial diversity across the organizational hierarchy was a condition of positive deviance. As the research progressed, it was discovered that, although deviant, the condition of racial diversity alone did not lead to the most positive outcomes or experience of being diverse. Those outcomes were dependent on a moderating condition, the integration-and-learning

diversity perspective. Thus, the researchers had to refine their initial understanding of what constituted the positive deviance.

Conclusion

Our narrative review and integration of positive findings on diversity, and our discussion on a positive approach to diversity scholarship, reveal some complementary directions for future diversity research in general and also research within POS. A positive approach to diversity research can yield theory that more powerfully facilitates individual and collective agency in making diversity a resource for positive outcomes in organizations, as well as in the mitigation of barriers. Even research designed to influence organizational policy could benefit. Today, most of the laws and policies governing issues related to areas such race, gender, and sexual orientation come out of studies of discrimination. Although these have helped open up institutions to broader participation, they also sometimes have unintended negative consequences. A prime example occurs when managers refrain from giving constructive and honest feedback to minorities in a timely manner for fear of lawsuits. We wonder whether policies developed from positive diversity research might be more helpful in shaping the kinds of relationships across difference that would have the potential to enhance people's ability to connect in more authentic ways.

The heuristics for a positive approach to diversity research that we articulate may also be relevant for the still-evolving general paradigm of positive organizational studies. Two dimensions are particularly obvious to us. First, just as we argue in tenet three of our positive diversity research approach, we believe that POS needs to be clearer about how studies should take into account the problematic or nonpositive conditions that motivate most research on diversity. Second, our positive approach to diversity research calls for an explicit openness to learning about and refining one's understanding of the presumed positive deviant condition and even acknowledging its shadow side. Such a learning stance would likely benefit all manner of positive organizational research.

Notes

1. Our own keyword search from 2008 to 2010 on diversity more generally (not only race and gender) yielded very similar percentages as did Chugh and Brief's (2008): 5% in management journals and 14% when we included psychology and sociology journals. We started our search in 1998, because this encompasses the years since William and

O'Reilly's (1998) review of the diversity literature in organizational scholarship.

2. We searched the following journals: *Administrative Science Quarterly, Organization Science, Academy of Management Journal, Academy of Management Review, Journal of Applied Psychology, Journal of Organizational Behavior, American Journal of Sociology, American Sociological Review, Journal of Personality and Social Psychology, Psychological Science,* and *Organizational Behavior and Human Decision Processes*

3. A list of these articles can be provided by the authors upon request.

References

Alderfer, C.P., & Smith, K.K. (1982). Studying intergroup relations embedded in organizations. *Administrative Science Quarterly, 27*(1), 35–65.

Allport, G.W. (1954). *The nature of prejudice.* Reading, MA: Addison-Wesley.

Benet-Martínez, V., & Haritatos, J. (2005). Bicultural Identity Integration (BII): Components and psychosocial antecedents. *Journal of Personality, 73*(4), 1015–1050.

Beckman, C.M., & Phillips, D.J. (2005). Interorganizational determinants of promotion: Client leadership and the attainment of women attorneys. *American Sociological Review, 70,* 678–701.

Berdahl, J., & Moore, C. (2006). Workplace harassment: Double jeopardy for minority women. *Journal of Applied Psychology, 91*(2), 426–436.

Boen, F., & Vanbeselaere, N. (2001). Individual versus collective responses to membership in a low-status group: The effects of stability and individual ability. *The Journal of Social Psychology, 141*(6), 765–783.

Brickson, S. (2000). The impact of identity orientation on individual and organizational outcomes in demographically diverse settings. *The Academy of Management Review, 25*(1), 82–101.

Carmeli, A., & Gittell, J.H. (2009). High-quality relationships, psychological safety, and learning from failures in work organizations. *Journal of Organizational Behavior, 30,* 709–729.

Castilla, E. (2008). Gender, race, and meritocracy in organizational careers. *American Journal of Sociology, 113*(6), 1479–1526.

Chatman, J., & Flynn, F.J. (2001). The influence of demographic heterogeneity on the emergence and consequences of cooperative norms in work teams. *Academy of Management Journal, 44,* 956–974.

Chugh, D., & Brief, A.P. (2008). Introduction: Where the sweet spot is: Studying diversity in organizations. In A.P. Brief (Ed.), *Diversity at work* (pp. 1–12). New York: Cambridge University Press.

Cacioppo, J.T., & Berntson, G.G. (1994). Relationship between attitudes and evaluative space: A critical review, with emphasis on the separability of positive and negative substrates. *Psychological Bulletin, 115,* 401–423.

Cheng, C., Sanchez-Burks, J., & Lee, F. (2008). Taking advantage of differences: Increasing team innovation through identity integration. In E. Mannix & M. Neale (Eds.), *Diversity and groups, research on managing groups and teams* Vol. 11 (pp. 55–73). Bingley, UK: JAI Press.

Clair, J., Beatty, J., & MacLean, T. (2005). Out of sight but not out of mind: Managing invisible social identities in the workplace. *Academy of Management Review, 30*(1), 78–95.

Cuddy, A., Fiske, S., & Glick, P. (2004). When professionals become mothers, warmth doesn't cut the ice. *Journal of Social Issues, 60*(4), 701–718.

Cuddy, A., Glick, P., & Fiske, S. (2007). The BIAS map: Behaviors from intergroup affect and stereotypes. *Journal of Personality & Social Psychology, 92*(4), 631–648.

Czopp, A.M., Monteith, M.J., & Mark, A.Y. (2006). Standing up for a change: Reducing bias through interpersonal communication. *Journal of Personality and Social Psychology, 90*(5), 784–803.

Dovidio, J.F., Kawakami, K., & Gaertner, S.L. (2002). Implicit and explicit prejudice and interracial interaction. *Journal of Personality and Social Psychology, 82*(1), 62–68.

Dutton, J.E., & Heaphy, E.D. (2003). The power of high quality connections. In K.S. Cameron, J.E. Dutton, & R.E. Quinn (Eds.), *Positive organizational scholarship* (pp. 263–278). San Francisco: Berrett-Koehler Publishers.

Dutton, J.E., & Ragins, B.R. (2007). *Exploring positive relationships at work: Building a theoretical and research foundation.* Mahwah, NJ: Lawrence Erlbaum.

Dutton, J.E., Roberts, L.M., & Bednar, J. (2010). Pathways for positive identity construction at work: Four types of positive identity and the building of social resources. *Academy of Management Review, 35*(2), 265–293.

Earley, P.C., & Mosakowski, E.M. (2000). Creating hybrid team cultures: An empirical test of international team functioning. *Academy of Management Journal, 43,* 26–49.

Ely, R., & Meyerson, D.E. (2010). *An organizational approach to undoing gender.* Working paper.

Ely, R.J., & Roberts, L.M. (2008). Shifting frames in team-diversity research: From difference to relationships. In A.P. Brief (Ed.), *Diversity at work* (pp. 175–201). New York: Cambridge University Press.

Ely, R.J., & Thomas, D.A. (2001). Cultural diversity at work: The effects of diversity perspectives on work group processes and outcomes. *Administrative Science Quarterly, 46,* 229–273.

Flynn, F.J. (2005). Having an open mind: The impact of openness to experience on interracial attitudes and impression formation. *Journal of Personality and Social Psychology, 88*(5), 816–826.

Flynn, F.J., & Ames, D. (2006). What's good for the goose may not be good for the gander: The benefits of self-monitoring for men and women. *Journal of Applied Psychology, 91,* 272–283.

Flynn, F.J., Chatman, J.A. (2001). Getting to know you: The influence of personality on impressions and performance of demographically different people in organizations. *Administrative Science Quarterly, 46,* 414–442.

Gaertner, S.L., & Dovidio, J.F. (2000). *Reducing intergroup bias: The common ingroup identity model.* Philadelphia: The Psychology Press.

Gibson, C., & Vermeulen, F. (2003). A healthy divide: Subgroups as a stimulus for team learning behavior. *Administrative Science Quarterly, 48,* 202–239.

Greenhaus, J.H., & Powell, G. (2006). When work and family are allies: A theory of work-family enrichment. *Academy of Management Review, 31,* 72–92.

Harrison, D.A., & Klein, K.J. (2007). What's the difference? Diversity constructs as separation, variety, or disparity in organizations. *Academy of Management Review, 32,* 1199–1228.

Hewlin, P. (2003). And the award for best actor goes to . . . facades of conformity in organizational settings. *Academy of Management Review, 28*(4), 633–642.

Hewlin, P. (2009). Wearing the cloak: Antecedents and consequences of creating facades of conformity. *Journal of Applied Psychology, 94*(3), 727–741.

Homan, A.C., van Knippenberg, D., Van Kleef, G.A., & De Dreu, C.K.W. (2007). Bridging faultlines by valuing diversity: Diversity beliefs, information elaboration, and performance in diverse work groups. *Journal of Applied Psychology, 92*(5), 1189–1199.

Homan, A., Hollenbeck, J., Humphrey, S., van Knippenberg, D., Ilgen, D., & Van Kleef, G. (2008). Facing differences with an open mind: Openness to experience, salience of intragroup differences, and performance of diverse work groups. *Academy of Management Journal, 51*(6), 1204–1222.

Jackson, S.E., Joshi, A., & Erhardt, N. (2003). Recent research on team and organizational diversity: SWOT analysis and implications. *Journal of Management, 29*(6), 801–830.

Jehn, K.A., Northcraft, G.B., & Neale, M.A. (1999). Why differences make a difference: A field study of diversity, conflict, and performance in workgroups. *Administrative Science Quarterly, 44*(4), 741–763.

Jehn, K.A., & Bezrukova, K. (2010). The faultline activation process and the effects of activated faultlines on coalition formation, conflict, and group outcomes. *Organizational Behavior and Human Decision Processes, 112*, 24–42.

Joshi, A., Hui, L., & Jackson, S.E. (2006). Cross-level effects of workplace diversity on sales performance and pay. *Academy of Management Journal, 49*(3), 459–481.

Joshi, A., & Roh, H. (2009). The role of context in work team diversity research: A meta-analytic review. *Academy of Management Journal, 52*(3), 599–627.

Kalev, A. (2009). Cracking the glass cages? Restructuring and ascriptive inequality at work. *American Journal of Sociology, 114*(6), 1591–1643.

Kalev, A., Dobbin, F., & Kelly, E. (2006). Best practices or best guesses? Assessing the efficacy of corporate affirmative action and diversity policies. *American Sociological Review, 71*(4), 589–617.

Nishii, L. (2010). *The benefits of climate for inclusion for diverse groups.* Working paper.

Pelled, L.H., Eisenhardt, K.M., & Xin, K.R. (1999). Exploring the black box: An analysis of work group diversity, conflict, and performance. *Administrative Science Quarterly, 44*, 1–28.

Pettigrew, T., & Tropp L.R. (2006). A meta-analytic test of intergroup contact theory. *Journal of Personality and Social Psychology, 90*(5), 751–783.

Phillips, K.W., & Loyd, D.L. (2006). When surface and deep-level diversity collide: The effects on dissenting group members. *Organizational Behavior and Human Decision Processes, 99*, 143–160.

Phillips, K.W., Rothbard, N.P., & Dumas, T.L. (2009). To disclose or not to disclose? Status distance and self-disclosure in diverse environments. *Academy of Management Review, 34*(4), 710–732.

Pittinsky, T.L., & Montoya, M.R. (2009). Is valuing equality enough? Equality values, allophilia, and social policy support for multiracial individuals. *Journal of Social Issues, 65*(1), 151–163.

Pittinsky, T.L., & Simon, S. (2007). Intergroup leadership. *The Leadership Quarterly, 18*, 586–605.

Pittinsky, T.L. (2010). A two-dimensional model of intergroup leadership. *American Psychologist, 65*(3), 194–200.

Polzer, J.T., Milton, L.P., & Swann, W.B. (2002). Capitalizing on diversity: Interpersonal congruence in small work groups. *Administrative Science Quarterly, 47*, 296–324.

Purdie-Vaughns, V., & Eibach, R. (2008). Intersectional invisibility: The distinctive advantages and disadvantages of multiple subordinate-group identities. *Sex Roles, 59*(5–6), 377–391.

Quillian, L., & Campbell, M.E. (2003). Beyond black and white: The present and future of multiracial friendship segregation. *American Sociological Review, 68*, 540–566.

Ramarajan, L. (2009). *Opening up or shutting down? The effects of multiple identities on problem solving.* Harvard Business School working paper, No. 10–041, Boston.

Richard, O.C. (2000). Racial diversity, business strategy, and firm performance: A resource-based review. *Academy of Management Journal, 43*, 164–177.

Richeson, J.A., & Shelton, J. (2003). When prejudice does not pay: Effects of interracial contact on executive function. *Psychological Science, 14*(3), 287–290.

Roberts, L.M. (2005). Changing faces: Professional image construction in diverse organizational settings. *Academy of Management Review, 30*(4), 685–711.

Roberts, L.M. (2006). Shifting the lens on organizational life: The added value of positive scholarship. *Academy of Management Review, 31*(2), 292–305.

Roberts, L.M., Cha, S.E., Hewlin, P.F., & Settles, I. (2009). Bringing the inside out: Enhancing authenticity and positive identity in organizations. In L.M. Roberts, & J.E. Dutton (Eds.), *Exploring positive identities and organizations: Building a theoretical and research foundation* (pp. 149–170). New York: Routledge.

Roberts, L.M., Dutton, J.E., Spreitzer, G.M., Heaphy, E.D., & Quinn, R.E. (2005). Composing the reflected best-self portrait: Building pathways for becoming extraordinary in work organizations. *Academy of Management Review, 30*(4), 712–736.

Rothbard, N., & Ramarajan, L. (2009). Checking your identities at the door? Positive relationships between nonwork and work identities. In L.M. Roberts, & J.E. Dutton (Eds.), *Exploring positive identities and organizations: Building a theoretical and research foundation* (pp. 125–148). New York: Routledge.

Shelton, N.J., & Richeson, J.A. (2005). Intergroup contact and pluralistic ignorance. *Journal of Personality and Social Psychology, 88*(1), 91–107.

Sommers, S.R. (2006). On racial diversity and group decision making: Identifying multiple effects of racial composition on jury deliberations. *Journal of Personality and Social Psychology, 90*(4), 597–612.

Taylor, S. (1991). Asymmetrical effects of positive and negative events: The mobilization-minimization hypothesis. *Psychological Bulletin, 10*, 67.

Thomas, D.A., & Alderfer, C.P. (1989). The influence of race on career dynamics. In M. Arthur, D.T. Hall, & B. Lawrence (Eds.), *Handbook of career theory.* Cambridge, UK: Cambridge University Press.

Thomas, D.A. (1990). The impact of race on managers' experiences of developmental relationships (mentoring and sponsorship): An intra-organizational study. *Journal of Organizational Behavior, 11*, 479–492.

Thomas, D.A. (1993). Racial dynamics of cross–race developmental relationships. *Administrative Science Quarterly, 38*, 169–194.

Thomas, D.A., & Ely, R.D. (1996). Making differences matter: A new paradigm for managing diversity. *Harvard Business Review, 74*(5), 79–90.

Thomas, D.A, & Gabarro, J.J. (1999). *Breaking through: The making of minority executives in corporate America.* Boston: Harvard Business School Press.

Thomas, D.A. (2001). The truth about mentoring minorities: Race matters. *Harvard Business Review, 79*(4), 98–112.

Thomas, D.A. (2004). Diversity as strategy. *Harvard Business Review, 82*(9), 98–108.

Tropp, L.R., & Pettigrew, T.F. (2005). Relationships between intergroup contact and prejudice among minority and majority status groups. *Psychological Science, 16*(12), 951–957.

Turner, R.N., Voci, A., Hewstone, M., & Vonofakou, C. (2008). A test of the extended intergroup contact hypothesis: The mediating role of intergroup anxiety, perceived ingroup and outgroup norms, and inclusion of the outgroup in the self. *Journal of Personality and Social Psychology, 94*(4), 843–860.

Unzueta, M., & Lowery, B. (2008). Defining racism safely: The role of self-image maintenance on white Americans' conceptions of racism. *Journal of Experimental Social Psychology, 44*(6), 1491–1497.

Unzueta, M., Lowery, B., & Knowles, E. (2008). How believing in affirmative action quotas protects White men's self-esteem. *Organizational Behavior & Human Decision Processes, 105*(1), 1–13.

van Knippenberg, D., De Dreu, C.K.W., & Homan, A.C. (2004). Work group diversity and group performance: An integrative model and research agenda. *Journal of Applied Psychology, 89*, 1008–1022.

van Knippenberg, D., Haslam, S., & Platow, M. (2007). Unity through diversity: Value-in-diversity beliefs, work group diversity, and group identification. *Group Dynamics: Theory, Research, and Practice, 11*(3), 207–222.

van Knippenberg, D., & Schippers, M.C. (2007). Work group diversity. *Annual Review of Psychology, 58*, 515–541.

Watson, D., Clark, L.A., & Tellegen, A. (1988). Development and validation of brief measures of positive and negative affect: The PANAS scales. *Journal of Personality and Social Psychology, 54*(6), 1063–1070.

Wegge, J., Roth, C., Neubach, B., Schmidt, K.H., & Kanfer, R. (2008). Age and gender diversity as determinants of performance and health in a public organization: The role of task complexity and group size. *Journal of Applied Psychology, 93*(6), 1301–1313.

Westphal, J., & Milton, L. (2000). How experience and network ties affect the influence of demographic minorities on corporate boards. *Administrative Science Quarterly, 45*(2), 366–398.

Williams, K.Y., & O'Reilly, C.A. (1998). Demography and diversity in organizations: A review of 40 years of research. In B. Staw, & R. Sutton (Eds.), *Research in organization behavior* Vol. 21 (pp. 77–140). Greenwich, CT: JAI Press.

Williams, M. (2008). *To be or not to be trusted: The influence of team demographic dissimilarity on dyadic trust across boundaries.* Paper presented at the annual Academy of Management Meetings, Anaheim, CA.

Zatzick, C.D., Elvira, M.M., & Cohen, L.E. (2003). When is more better? The effects of racial composition on voluntary turnover. *Organization Science, 14*(5), 483–496.

Ziegert, J.C., & Hanges, P.J. (2005). Employment discrimination: The role of implicit attitudes, motivation, and a climate for racial bias. *Journal of Applied Psychology, 90*(3), 553–562.

The Role of Communication in Positive Organizational Scholarship

Larry Browning, G. H. Morris, *and* Kerk F. Kee

Abstract

This chapter offers a position on organizational communication as a positive force by drawing together the literature on organizational communication, social interaction, and communication technology as they apply to organizations. We organize these ideas around two themes. First is integrative communication, which includes the subsets of inclusiveness, respectfulness, and supportiveness. Second is constructive interaction, which includes the subsets of solution focus, a future orientation, and collaborative interaction. These topics are elaborated as we offer orientations and practices that show evidence of their use. We conclude with an example of positive communication from the medical community and offer a glimmer of hope for the future based on current practice.

Keywords: Integration, dialogue, respectful interaction, information sharing

If part of the aim of positive organizational scholarship is to learn how to cultivate positive human processes and dynamics in organizations, then no concept is more ripe for examination than communication. Communication is a quintessential human good and, at least in popular views, the more of it, the better. Most people harbor very favorable assessments of communication because it can generate understanding, spread knowledge, overcome isolation, enable coordination, and improve problem solving. Communication technology, likewise, is well thought of because it can enable pooling of intelligence, conquer distances, speed activities, and expand networks. However, communication is playing with fire. It does not necessarily live up to its marvelous potential, and it can also be dangerous, disruptive, dull, disappointing, distracting, and even destructive. Just a few instances of destructive communication are enough to spoil a much larger number of successful communication experiences. Very commonly, a communication event that is positive for some purposes is simultaneously negative for others; events that uplift some may suppress others (Putnam, 2009). Because of its affirmative orientation, positive communication is susceptible to masking error and harm (Deetz, 2009). How is it possible to have directness, honesty, on the one hand, yet embrace communication acceptance at the same time? Because of these doubts, we feel an urgent need to better understand what counts as positive communication and to spark more consideration of the circumstances under which positive communication might contribute to other positive processes and dynamics in organizations.

In this chapter, we offer a model to organize images of positive communication. We begin with a brief historical overview of images of "good communication" from ancient Greece to the present. Next, we derive a definition of positive communication. The concepts of organizational integration and constructive interaction are key to our definition of positive communication, and we devote a section of the chapter to each. In each section, we mention particular orientations and practices that constitute positive communication (see Table 42.1 for a summary of concepts). After a brief conclusion, we close

Table 42.1 Characteristics and practices of positive communication

Integrative Communication		Constructive Interaction	
Characteristics	Practices	Characteristics	Practices
• Inclusiveness (coherence, cohesiveness, and relevance of diverse and unique voices) • Respectfulness (trust, honesty, self-respect, and being considerate facework) • Supportiveness (willingness to help, encouragement, comforting communication, and validating others' feelings)	• Dialogues (elaboration, connections beyond boundaries, social ties, etc) • Information sharing (being informed, forming group memory, speaking for interests of members, STICC formulation) • Creating public goods (knowledge management, e-mail copies, pass along effect) • Generating engagement (social capital, social network sites, city/community websites)	• Solution-focused (believe in becoming better, seeing possibilities, being optimistic) • Future-oriented (vision of the future, shadow of the future) • Collaborative (cogency, timeliness, nexting, aligning actions)	• Conversation (answer a question, accept a proposal, comply with a request, etc) • Therapeutic interaction (equitable, flexible, blaming-free, etc) • Future search conferences (discovering common ground, building cooperation, etc.) • Narrative vision (beyond belief, uncertainty absorption, argument centered, evidence centered)

this chapter with an example of positive communication in organizations.

Evolving Images of Good Communication

As a discipline, the communication field has drawn upon several images of good communication over the years. The field is heir to a centuries-long evolution in views of good communication, which can be seen by looking into the kinds of instruction offered to persons seeking to improve as communicators. The Greek and Roman ideals were persuasive oratory to be used by individuals defending their interests in court and the assembly. The European ideal, drawn from the conversation salon, was erudite, learned, sophisticated conversation. The Victorian ideal, also conversational in nature, was polite and nonconfrontive. More recently, the U.S. civic ideal was democratic discussion of the issues of the day by small groups of neighbors. Although they may be de-emphasized in the contemporary era, these models are remarkably durable. Today's views of good communication combine previous sensibilities while incorporating new interaction styles.

We discern four aspects of a contemporary idea of good communication by individuals. First, it is rhetorically effective. Communicators harness language use and nonverbal communication to meet the purposes at hand. Second, it stresses individuals' abilities to relate to others in face-to-face (FTF) interaction that features assertiveness, attentiveness, directness, openness, friendliness, and empathy in organizational relationships and groups (Cameron, 2000). Third, it is technologically sophisticated, calling for quick, responsive, efficient use of information and communication technologies (ICTs). Fourth, it is culturally and situationally appropriate and accountable. Increasingly, good communication involves working out ways to handle the rhetorical, relational, and technological aspects of the positive style, for the particular cultural and situational circumstance, at the same time, and under circumstances that may not be ideal.

Defining Positive Communication

A crucial purpose served by communication in all organizations is to enable people to arrive at sensible, workable, accurate, consensual, and contemporary understandings of the meaning of situations and events influencing them. Organization communication comprises an interpretation system, and one key purpose of positive communication is to improve that system. In other words, in a general sense, positive communication is that which enhances organizational intelligence (Johnson, 1977). More colloquially, positive communication improves how the organization understands the world in which it is operating. In the two following sections, we concentrate on two key standards of positive communication that make it suitable to help organizations better understand the world.

Integrative Communication

Integration is a master term across the social sciences including differentiation–integration (Lawrence & Lorsch, 1967) and integrative complexity in social psychology and public policy theory (Maruyama, 1992; Suedfeld & Leighton, 2002). To communicate integratively is to speak as one. In a way consistent with the idea of workplace democracy, positive communication integrates disparate parts, even through hard-fought discussions, and gives them a single voice. To have a voice is to become part of the whole, to join the discussion (Putnam, 2001). Recent research in communication suggests that ICTs may have a democratizing influence over organizations. For instance, "the Web tends to reduce the significance of offline hierarchies in accessing information—thereby 'democratizing' access to worldwide resources" (Caldas, Schroeder, Mesch, & Dutton, 2008, p. 679). Adoption of ICTs makes knowledge contribution and information more accessible to a wider audience.

Similarly, in a recent study of distributed teams, Yuan and Gay (2006) found that "homophily in gender and in race had no significant impact on the development of either instrumental or expressive ties. In instrumental networks, both homophily in group assignment and in location had significant impact on the development of network ties" (p. 1062). Thus, the use of ICTs can promote inclusiveness beyond the influence of demographic variables visible in most FTF interactions. This finding is encouraging because it suggests that organizational integration can be created based on group assignment and geographic location when the process is facilitated by ICTs.

Three characteristics that enable communication to be integrative, hence positive, are inclusiveness, respectfulness, and supportiveness.

INCLUSIVENESS
To be integrative, communication must add to the number and kind of voices that participate in sense-making while remaining coherent, cohesive, and relevant. Positive communication practices bring people together across distances, ideological divides, language barriers, and diverse cultural and individual experiences, enabling them to merge into single incorporated entities (Gibbs, 2009). Members each bring something unique, including experiences, strengths, and knowledge to the table, and they also appreciate what others bring (Browning & Shetler, 2000).

RESPECTFULNESS
Respectfulness is also a key to positive communication because disparate voices bring with them the possibility that others will ignore or discount what is said. According to Weick (2003), at least for high-reliability organizations, action in potentially problematic circumstances requires members to provide accurate reports on evolving situations. This is because mismanaging them could have catastrophic consequences. Weick's view of respectful interaction emphasizes the roles of trust, honesty, and self-respect as preconditions for respectful interaction. Being respectful necessitates willingness to trust others' accounts, reporting honestly oneself, and having respect for one's own interpretations of what is happening. The essence of respectful interaction, in this view, is to be able to trust each other's reports because they are presumed to be honest. Respectful interaction has been shown to have beneficial outcomes. A focus on respectful interactions allowed one group to maintain their motivation, as observed in their persistent behavior and objective job performance (Granta et al., 2007). In other instances, it has increased awareness of joint decision making in hospitals, on firefighting teams, and in promoting client care on physical therapy teams (Browning, 2007).

In an extension of Weick's (2003) approach, Morris (2008) argued that respectful interaction must also be considerate. Morris (2008) drew upon Goffman's work (1967, 1971) to suggest that people who are being respectful interact to save their own and others' faces and that "there is no time out" from this facework. Thus, besides being trusting, honest, and self-respecting, they are also considerate, not only in strategy sessions dealing with dynamic circumstances, but throughout their daily round of interactions with fellow organization members, leaders, and customers.

Whether or not communication is respectful shows in the small rituals of interaction, such as the making of introductions or in passing greetings. An individual can recognize and use another person's name or fail to remember it. One can choose whether to fill in a newcomer to a group meeting about what happened so far (offering a summary) or not consider his or her ability to follow what is going on. If a summary is offered, the individual can play it straight and not disparage anyone's contributions, or can deprecate them (e.g., "John was just telling us about his *brilliant* design"). Based on the literature on facework (i.e., Brown & Levinson, 1987; Goffman, 1971), part of what is respectful is the act of being considerate of others' goals and interests; what is negative is obstructing their desire to be free of interference.

ICTs may contribute to respectful communication in an unexpected way, because trust and honesty play out differently in computer-mediated communication (CMC). In a recent study,

Giordano, Stoner, Brouer, and George (2007) found that deception is lower and satisfaction is higher in CMC, such as in the use of instant messaging tools for negotiation, than in FTF interactions. In another study of lying behaviors in ICTs, Hancock and colleagues (2004) argue that the automatic recordability of ICTs is the condition that reduces participants' willingness to risk being caught lying; therefore, deception is less likely when people use instant messaging and e-mail communication compared to FTF communication; ICTs might increase the prevalence of trust and honesty by users and thereby facilitate organizational integration.

SUPPORTIVENESS

Supportiveness can be understood as "a desire and willingness to help others succeed . . . by encouraging someone whose confidence is wavering" (LaFasto & Larson, 2001, pp. 14–15). Such support is especially valuable under conditions of personal stress. A community of support of particular individuals will provide both emotional energy and strength. It will cause one to take good advice. Such declarations are sometimes the most memorable gifts a person can receive. One of the most studied examples of the role of communication in relationship maintenance is the research on social support, which shows that it can increase participants' well-being and happiness and act as a vanguard against depression. Social support also enhances peoples' ability to withstand stress. On the other side, the lack of a confidant is a major risk factor for developing depression. "Social support is enacted through interpersonal communication" (Segrin, 2003, p. 318).

Social support and comforting are the focus of emotional help-giving. Comforting communication consists of messages that bring about positive change in emotional states, including person-centered messages, through which a helper validates the feelings of the other and encourages talk about the troubling event. Comforting communication reflects interpersonal warmth (Jones & Wirtz, 2006). Although it may or may not include advice giving, when it does, advice is given in a way that does not threaten the target's face or undermine his or her competence (MacGeorge, Lichtman, & Pressey, 2002).

In sum, the three features of positive communication that support organizational integration are inclusiveness, respectfulness, and supportiveness. They may work in concert by enabling people who might not ordinarily be willing or able to work together successfully to lend their voices to organizational dialogue, have their voices be treated as valuable, and be buoyed up by others when they experience difficulties that the less fortunate would have to handle alone.

Orientations and Practices of Integrative Communication

In this section, we turn to a discussion of some of the orientations and practices that might facilitate organizational integration and lead to organizational intelligence. These key orientations/practices are dialogues, information sharing, building public goods, and engagement. We treat both FTF communication and the use of ICTs to generate CMC as a range of channels that members can employ. When communicators select among communication media, FTF is viewed as a technology with rules and protocols, just as electronic ICTs are (Browning, Sætre, Stephens, & Sørnes, 2008).

Dialogue

Dialogue can be construed as a process of elaborating on the information and perspectives others offer. van Knippenberg and colleagues (2004) define the process of elaboration as "the exchange of information and perspectives, individual-level processing of the information and perspectives, the process of feeding back into the group, and discussion and integration of its implications" (p. 1011). When members engage in elaboration, "diverse groups should outperform homogeneous groups. The idea is that diverse groups are more likely to possess a broader range of task-relevant knowledge" (van Knippenberg, De Dreu, & Homan, 2004, p. 1009). Discussion of a topic by a diverse group of people can both lead to creative solutions and produce ownership as a result of participation.

One of the premises of integrative communication is that the more of it that crosses barriers, whether cultural or academic, the greater the likelihood of people understanding each other. One of the greatest difficulties of cooperative scientific efforts is the natural chauvinism that goes with being a part of a scientific discipline. One of the downsides of commitment and professionalism is that other disciplines are flawed in some way; they are lesser and wanting. The positive communication value is that direct conversations lead to insights that would not have been possible for a brilliant, but isolated individual.

An example of cross-barrier communication is the National Academy of Science's call for increasing understanding among academic disciplines via the use of communication using a concept called the interdisciplinary research process (IDR). "At the heart of interdisciplinary understanding is communication—the conversations, connections, and combinations that bring new insights to virtually every kind of scientist and engineer" (Project Kaleidescope, 2006). Skill at communicating across disciplines has to do with overcoming language differences, building trust—both in the short and long term—and the ability to press forward with task and relational goals. Otherwise, a lack of communication creates a cultural divide (Rosenfeld, Richman, & May, 2004). Since "communication and language are the mechanisms through which social identity is created, maintained, and modified" (Riedlinger, Gallois, McKay, & Pittam, 2004, p. 61), integrative communication in the scientific arena holds promise for constructing interdisciplinary identities and, hence, cooperation.

At the interpersonal level, ICTs can promote the creation of social ties underlying dialogues. The development of social ties within structures is critical for organizational integration. In a study of the use of ICTs and social ties, Zhao (2006) found that "social users of the Internet have more social ties than nonusers do. Among social users, heavy e-mail users have more social ties than do light e-mail users. [Furthermore] . . . e-mail users communicate online with people whom they also contact offline" (p. 844). The use of ICTs, such as e-mails, generates social ties that enable the communication process. When multiple collaborations overlap among dispersed members, the formation of a virtual organization can further promote organizational integration. Based on complexity theory and a case of collaboration among 2,000 scientists, Bird, Jones, and Kee (2009) argue that the use of a range of technologies and remote instruments can create three paradoxical characteristics that promote the effective functioning of a virtual organization as dispersed but coordinated, diverse yet coherent, and flexible nonetheless secured. When an organization is too big to easily allow for FTF dialogues, ICTs expand dialogues beyond time and space.

Information Sharing/Being Informed

Having information to share and being informed by others go hand in hand as key practices for organizational integration. Communication tends to level information across groups because the asymmetrical knowledge becomes distributed when the knowing person communicates to the unknowing through the act of sharing. The result of sharing is to increase the amount of information held by a broad group of people, which creates an opportunity for group memory and a broadly felt sense of competence. Such shared knowledge that is recalled means that a group "re-members" by harkening back to what everyone knows when it is pooled into a single culture (Corbett, Faia-Correia, Patriotta, & Brigham, 1999). Interaction among groups serves to inform members about organizational wisdom, which is knowledge known by its members. "Groups recall more information than individuals" (Wittenbaum, 2003, p. 617). Since some members know more than others, communication allows for that information to be shared.

One version of membership in a network is being well enough informed to speak for the interests of members. For example, an association's board of directors may be affirmed and trusted because members believe that the board protects the interests of its members. Harter and Krone's (2001) study of the Nebraska Cooperative Council reported that members used the metaphor of voice to depict how they view the council as protecting the larger cooperative's interests. Voice serves as a kind of representation for stakeholders. Key to the voice metaphor is access (Harter & Krone, 2001). Part of the communication process is to become informed, so that information seeking is a kind of adaptation based on gaining a seat at the table. This allows a person to be involved in a learning process and subsequently to contribute to problem solving and decision making as an informed participant. One version of being informed and knowing what is going on is exemplified by African American women executives, who emphasize the importance of being open to information and paying attention to active listening (Parker, 2001).

An orientation for integrating diverse views under potentially catastrophic conditions is Weick's (2003) sequence of statements for respectful interaction about dynamic, potentially consequential events. In this STICC formulation, the leader sets up the interaction by saying:

1. *Situation*: Here's the situation we face.
2. *Task*: Here's what I think we should do.
3. *Intent*: Here's why we should do that.
4. *Concerns*: Here's what we should keep our eyes on because if that changes, we're in a new situation.
5. *Calibration*: Now talk to me.

Under conditions of trust, honesty, and self-respect, members are willing to offer their perspectives when called upon to do so, to disagree, and to work successfully through disagreements as they calibrate their determination of what is to be done. Indeed, willingness to disagree could sometimes display commitment to the collective's goal and work toward integrating the individual into the group.

Information and communication technologies can support the practice of information sharing/being informed, especially in the processes of organizational socialization, coordination, and collaboration. Flanagin and Waldeck (2004) proposed a theoretical orientation of ICT use, and they argue that accurate, appropriate, and sufficient information via ICTs can promote successful organizational socialization of newcomers. They suggest that group and organizational norms about the use of ICTs play an important role in a newcomer's socialization and organizational integration process. After members have been socialized into an organization, ICTs can facilitate coordination and collaboration. In a study by Walsh and Maloney (2007), the use of e-mail was found to be associated with fewer coordination problems in collaborations. Furthermore, communication research on the use of ICTs for collaboration has shown encouraging results. Sooryamoorthy and Shrum (2007, p. 733) found that "Internet use, as measured by time spent on e-mail, is positively associated with collaboration." Studies like this one lead us to believe that the use of ICTs can promote organizational integration. Additionally, a unique practice of ICTs for information sharing is the *pass-along effect*, which is similar to the practice of traditional word-of-mouth communication. Norman and Russell (2006) argue that the use of e-mails generated a pass-along effect in the spread of information because spreading information via e-mail is easy and low cost. Technology amplifies the opportunity to communicate to a great extent. As an example, we call it "viral" when large numbers of people e-mail interesting information to each other or pass along a YouTube videos to friends. Information and communication technology users prefer to send positive messages (Tierney, 2010). Because of the ease of communication and the lack of cost to send someone an electronic message, people who have access to ICTs simply send items—"whether websites that offer good bargains, or foods that are rich in antioxidants"—to others because they think it might be useful (Berger & Milkman, 2010, p. 6).

Public Goods

The practice of information sharing/being informed can produce shared knowledge in the form of public goods, which are "goods, such as parks, roads, libraries, neighborhood brush removal for fire prevention, beach cleanups, or other organized collective goals" (Fulk, Flanagin, Kalman, Monge, & Ryan, 1996). One of the values of positive communication is when it is directed toward a public good and information is meaningfully incorporated into the body of knowledge. Like an inoculation against a deadly disease, the knowledge can be available without regard to power and position in a hierarchy. In this way, positive communication is associated with a democratic process. "Traditional conceptions of deliberation emphasize quality, fairness, analysis, and a focus on the public good" (Gastil, Black, Deess, & Leighter, 2008, p. 139). Deliberation is a communication process that emphasizes weighing views and understanding each other's perspectives. People deliberate when they "carefully examine a problem and range of solutions through an open, inclusive discussion that respects diverse points of view" (Gastil, Black, Deess, & Leighter, 2008, p. 141).

When the practice of creating public goods is enabled by ICTs, we call the information repository *knowledge management* (KM). Knowledge management can be understood as "how distributed group members and their organizational colleagues locate, store and retrieve data, information and knowledge that they need for their individual and collective work" (Hollingshead, Fulk, & Monge, 2002, p. 335). When infused with technologies, organizations use KM systems to electronically create, transfer and apply knowledge to achieve their goals (Alavi & Leidner, 2001). The use of KM systems can lead to organizational viability (Palazzolo, Serb, She, Su, & Contractor, 2006) because knowledge is "information with assigned meaning that is stored and can be used in daily interactions to solve dilemmas or problems . . . [and] enables the individual to act" (Child & Shumate, 2007, p. 31).

Since the introduction of e-mails in the workplace in the 1990s (Rogers, 2003), the practice of e-mail copies is prevalent. Skovholt and Jan (2006) found that the practice of e-mail copies in a distributed work group serves to promote knowledge sharing, build a common information pool, and form alliance networks. Furthermore, in a study of 500 large companies, Lai (2001) found that organizations that implement an intranet system for employees to collaborate tend to have higher organizational and employee performance in general. Knowledge management systems have been studied as organizational platforms that would facilitate the development of a "group mind" to promote performance of organizational work teams (Yuan, Fulk, & Monge, 2007).

In order for successful implementation of KM systems, there needs to be a knowledge-oriented culture, stable organizational infrastructure, a high level of motivation, and support from senior management (Davenport, De Long, & Beers, 1999). In a study by Gold and colleagues (2010), they argue that "a knowledge infrastructure consisting of technology, structure, and culture along with a knowledge process architecture of acquisition, conversion, application, and protection are essential organizational capabilities or 'preconditions' for effective knowledge management" (p. 185). Last, in a study of organizational merger, Empson (2001) argues that an acquiring company can obtain useful information about the acquired company's policy and expertise through possessing their computerized KM databases, which can lead to more effective organizational integration despite an awkward transition. All these studies demonstrate how KM systems and the use of intranet systems promote organizational integration.

ENGAGEMENT

Much of the work on positive communication recognizes that the behavior that builds a reputation is the amount of sustained involvement of those in a network. Engagement that enables social capital can be seen in different settings, including structures held together by a groups' ability to communicate together effectively, and relationship building among nongovernmental organizations (NGOs) in a civil society effort. Rich communication channels allow groups to become central to information flow. Traditionally, engagement is enhanced when communication occurs in the presence of another, such that the feel of the person behind the discourse is visible, sensory, and directly experienced by those involved in the exchange. Such a position is structurational (Giddens, 1984) in that the communication itself signifies the centrality of and regard for individuals.

New social media platforms featuring increased interactivity and social presence seem to be just as effective as FTF interactions in generating social capital. Valenzuela, Park, and Kee (2009) found that higher-intensity Facebook users are also more likely to participate actively in civic engagement. High-intensity Facebook users also report a higher level of social trust and a greater degree of life satisfaction in general. In a subsequent analysis, Park,

Kee, and Valenzuela (2009) found that Facebook groups represent a social space in which online interactions often translate into offline activities. These studies suggest that social media can promote social capital that positively contributes to organizational integration. They argue in both studies that social capital exists in the use of social network sites such as Facebook.

When we extend the scope of engagement to a larger community, such as a city and metropolitan area, ICTs continue to show relevance. In a study of official websites of the core cities in the 50 largest U.S. metropolitan areas by population, Jeffres and Lin (2006) argue, "The Internet offers cities new opportunities to communicate with their constituents at a time when metropolitan areas struggle with their community identity and cohesion . . . [T]he vast majorities of all sample sites contained high frequencies of information links to reflect all major communication functions" (p. 975). We have identified four orientations and practices that constitute integrative communication. By engaging in dialogue with other members, sharing information, building public goods, and becoming engaged, individuals involve themselves substantively and symbolically in the sense-making activities of the organization and move closer together in the sense of a more common understanding and a greater sense of belonging to the organizational community.

Constructive Interaction

Integrative communication is positive, but it does not necessarily lead to improved ways of making sense of the world of the organization. We use the term *constructive interaction* to designate interpersonal and intergroup activities that involve participants "making things better." Although the focus of constructive interaction can be broadly conceived, at the heart of constructive interaction is an orientation that participants show as they speak or write, listen to or read others' contributions, and respond to them. This constructive orientation can be discerned when participants make their contributions solution focused, future oriented, and collaborative.

Solution Focus

This orientation is an insistence on talking about things being better, along with a persistent refusal to remain mired in talk about problems. Whereas communication that leads to disillusionment is negative, its positive counterpart is illusionment. It means building and holding on to the idea that those things that are not working well can be improved, things that impede progress can be overcome, current actions might work, and we have the resources we need. Zander and Zander (2000) call it "creating a framework of possibility" (p. 160). The solution focused nature of positive communication is well illustrated by a pilot project that says, "If we can do this here, you can do it anywhere." Such optimism also means keeping naysayers at bay. Whereas an orientation to problem solving includes both attention to the nature of the problem and attention to the characteristics of potential solutions, an orientation to the positive finds people imagining things being better, discounting evidence that things are staying the same or getting worse, recommending actions that can be tried, and encouraging quick trials and rapid abandonment of things that aren't working. It might be that the most basic idea of positive communication is that it keeps the flicker of hope alive for things to get better. Or, as Sematech CEO Bob Noyce said to encourage performance at the consortium he led, "Go out and do something wonderful!" instead of "That will never work!" (Browning & Shetler, 2000).

Future Orientation

One way that positive communication and ICTs can assist in improving organizational intelligence is to become bound up with a vision of the future. Organizations think hopefully about how technology will help them move into a future they want. People have a futuristic, sentimental attachment to technology. For people, communication technology is the great hope—especially when they do it because they imagine a brighter future. Communication technology is double-powered, in that it can both inspire hope and expand opportunities to accomplish desired futures.

In the language of the cooperation literature, participants are conscious of a "shadow of the future," which means that their day-to-day activities are conducted with an awareness that their long-term relationship makes a difference (Cohen, Riolo, & Axelrod, 2001; Kee & Browning, 2010). Logically, interacting constructively relies upon consciousness of a future together.

Collaborative Interaction

Part of being constructive is shown in the cogency and timeliness of participants' responses to what others say and do. Following Grice's (1975) model, participants in conversation provide what is needed at every given point according to the purpose and direction of the talk exchange. To respond cooperatively, they make contributions that are relevant, informative, truthful, and stylistically appropriate. So strong is the pressure to be cooperative that when participants fail to provide the appropriate contributions, it is presumed they are nevertheless attempting to be cooperative, but have chosen to say something by implication rather than directly. To enact conversation, then, it is necessary for people to apprehend the purpose of the conversation, to be able to project where it is going, and make contributions that advance the conversation. The ability to say what is needed at the point when it is needed has been termed "nexting" by Stewart (2009). Nexting means "doing something helpful next, responding fruitfully to what's just happened, taking an additional step in the communication process" (Stewart, 2009, p. 30). In conversation, it "takes two to tango," and every next move affords the opportunity for things to go in a better or worse direction or for things to stay the same. Every time we respond to what another person is doing, we are putting on display an orientation to abandon it or to build on it. They can't build on it without our cooperation.

However, any human action can be done well or poorly, so part of being constructive is to strive to do what would be appropriate, help to rectify errors, and continuously help fellow interactants make sense of what is going on. Conversation participants align their own conduct with others' expectations for it (Morris & Hopper, 1987) and, should their contributions be questioned, they utilize a large variety of aligning actions (Stokes & Hewitt, 1976) to normalize and make sense of their actions. The capacity to notice and to rectify errors is central to the ability to react to problems and keep organizational activities on track.

Orientations and Practices of Constructive Interaction
Conversation
We have already noted that every next contribution to any conversation can be or fail to be constructive. Conversation analysts have identified numerous interaction sequences, organized such that when a first conversational action is provided, a paired second action becomes relevant and usually follows immediately (Schegloff & Sacks, 1973). For example, when a participant asks another a question, the answer becomes relevant; when a participant makes a proposal, an acceptance or rejection of the proposal becomes relevant; and when a participant makes a request, either compliance with or refusal of the request is immediately relevant. Analysts have

also noted that the preferred next action usually follows without delay and that departures from what would be preferred include elements that mark them as unusual. In other words, there is structural evidence that to answer a question, accept a proposal, or comply with a request—each of which displays a constructive orientation to the interaction—is the preferred type of conversational contribution (Pomerantz, 1984). This orientation is also shown in how participants design their contributions specifically for those for whom they are intended (Nofsinger, 1991).

Therapeutic Interaction

Popular images of constructive interaction have usually been derived from other types of interaction than conversation, most especially therapy talk. For instance, client-centered therapy (Rogers, 1951) became the basis for instruction in how to listen actively. Strategic psychotherapy (Watzlawick, Beavin, & Jackson, 1967; Watzlawick, Weakland, & Fisch, 1974) is the origin of the contemporary idea of "thinking outside of the box." More recent forms of therapy are fertile ground for contemporary views of constructive interaction. Such approaches, which typically draw on a social constructionist standpoint (McNamee & Gergen, 1992), include collaborative therapy (Anderson & Goolishian, 1992), possibility therapy (Friedman, 1993), narrative therapy (Aronsson & Cederborg, 1994), constructive therapy (Hoyt, 1994) and solution-focused therapy (de Shazer & Berg, 1992; O'Connell, 1998). These approaches feature equitable and flexible dialogue between therapist and clients, in which they collaborate to understand what is going on and identify new possibilities.

Discourse analysis of these kinds of therapy has investigated how therapists and clients collaborate to arrive at understandings of their problems (Buttny, 2004), break through impasses (Couture & Strong, 2004), and define new possibilities for solutions (Couture, 2007). In solution-focused brief therapy (de Shazer & Berg, 1992; O'Connell, 1998) for example, the aim is to get couples to consider how things would be different if they weren't having the problem that brought them into therapy. Therapists inquire about "What would you be doing? What would you be saying to each other? How would other people notice? How would it affect them?" Such questions are about what people want and the possibilities they can discover (Zander & Zander, 2000). Couples are invited to imagine a world that is not so full of problems. When this world is revealed, the therapist and couple co-construct actions that can be taken to move in the desired direction. Since people in therapy often try to revert to a discussion of problems and blaming (Buttny, 2004), therapists strive to be "relentlessly positive" (de Shazer, 1985). To do so, they get clients to talk about the exceptions to their problems; they have clients estimate on a scale how much better they feel now than before and then ask clients to explain what they did to feel better. "How is the world better because of something you did?" This is a very concrete example of focusing on capabilities and building on strengths (Frederickson, 2003).

Future Search Conferences

Constructive interaction can also occur in much larger scale consultation. Building on years of work at the Tavistock Institute, Weisbord (1992) and his colleagues developed interaction formats that brought together several dozen, and often hundreds, of participants into future-oriented dialogue about their common interests and futures. In future search conferences, consultants guide participants from different parts of a large organization or different organizations in a community, over a period of two or more days, in an effort to discover and build on common ground. For example, a 2010 future search conference on youth violence in Santa Maria, California, brought together approximately 90–100 participants, including business owners, government officials, law enforcement personnel, probation officers, school officials, nonprofits, faith-based organizations, selected parents, and youth. Weisbord and his coauthors (1992) unveiled numerous designs for future search conferences they had facilitated, and they sought to account for their unusual success in uncovering common ground that enabled participants to work cooperatively toward solutions. The common sequence of topics discussed in future search conferences included, (1) describing the histories that led up to the present, (2) achieving consensus about the key aspects of the present situation, (3) shared ideas about mutually desired futures, and (4) commitments about actions to be taken. Despite the large numbers of participants, the complexity of the situations they faced, and the disparity in participants' perspectives, future search conferences usually resulted in more cooperative relationships and definitive action plans.

Narrative Vision

One positive communication practice, as it applies to leadership, is foreseeing a vision that gives direction to a company by the goal and projection of the future it provides. It is common for a leader to know more of a real and dire story than her or his subordinates know. This may be true for both hierarchical subordination and for information subordination. Both operate from the privileged premise: "You don't have the information that I have. You don't carry the burden I carry." One of the meanings of hierarchy is that the person at the top has greater access to scarcity, whether money or information. Being in the know justifies action. In organization theory, this is called *uncertainty absorption*. As a result, leaders are obligated to have a view of a positive future—a vision that is more controlled by her or him. Paradoxically, the compelling vision makes explicit, rational, data-driven arguments promoting a belief in the organization that is beyond what is rationally supported. The leader takes on the risk of being wrong, but her belief sees the organization over the uncertain chasm. This is akin to the promise a coach might see and build upon in a young athlete of modest accomplishments. Of course, seeing a direction and its invigorating possibilities that no one else sees is not automatically productive. The positive version of this kind of vision is Robert Noyce, inventor of the microchip, who led Intel to promote the chip as an innovative solution and later led the Sematech consortium at a time when the American chip manufacturing industry was in shambles. The negative example is Kenneth Lay, the CEO of Enron, who looked and sounded like a person with vision even while the company around him was disintegrating. The behavior of the two men looked the same, in that they promoted a future that was beyond contemporary belief, yet the results were different.

Conclusion

In summary, this chapter has focused on two streams of thought that enhance positive communication. First, we elaborated on the integrative power of communication. The more information is shared, the greater the use of overlapping groups for decision making, the less marginalized and fragmented the thinking—and thus the members—of an organization are likely to be. Second, we conceptualized constructive interaction, which accounts for both the emotions that arise as a part of communication and the way emotions and facts lead to solutions that seem to fit future circumstances. Constructive interaction takes into account the ability to exchange information and give it additional meaning that adds human value to it. With these ideas, we reaffirm

communication as a source model—what the speaker says is paramount, but it also includes the responsiveness of the listener, so that the pair of utterances is the basic unit for understanding interpersonal communication in organizations.

One advantage of the positive communication position is that communication operates at specific and theoretical spheres simultaneously (Hartelius & Browning, 2008). It is possible to talk about rhetorical and communication theory from the time of Plato and address the likelihood of communication being used for honorable or pitiful purposes and refer to a specific set of practices from which to make such an ethical assessment.

Example of Positive Communication

Let us end this essay on positive organizational communication with the same hope and sense of tradition with which we began, by offering an example drawn from one of the most important sites for positive communication performance—the medical community (Browning & Morris, in press). The story offered here, which we have excerpted from the *New Yorker,* is an analysis offered by Gawande (2009), for which he won the 2010 National Magazine Award category for Public Interest. In his *New Yorker* piece, he analyzes the delivery of medical care in the city of McAllen, Texas, which is in the Rio Grande Valley. In that area, the medical costs are nearly double the national average, yet medical care remains no better and in fact even poorer that most of the United States. Gawande's conclusion—affirmed by interviews in the Valley—is that, in the Valley, there is a culture of overtesting and of piling up costs by treating medicine as a profit center. Given the incentives for such a culture, Gawande wonders why more medical communities do not follow the same practice.

To counter the McAllen example, Gawande showcases two settings where medical care is driven by a different value, one enhanced by positive communication practices. First is the Mayo Clinic, which operates at half the costs of McAllen per patient, with drastically better results. They do so by emphasizing communication that seeks inputs from everyone in the medical system when making decisions about patients. As one doctor from Mayo says, "When doctors put their heads together in a room, when they share expertise, you get more thinking and less testing" (Gawande, 2009, from webpage). Gawande's second example of positive communication is the hospital system in Grand Junction, Colorado, where doctors decided on a program that paid them a similar fee whether from "Medicare, Medicaid, or private-insurance patients," which had the effect of reducing the incentive to select patients based on their ability to pay. Their practice of positive communication was to meet regularly "on small peer-review committees to go over their patient charts together. They focused on rooting out problems like poor prevention practices, unnecessary back operations, and unusual hospital-complication rates. Problems went down. Quality went up." These instances exemplify the precepts of positive communication as developed in this chapter in that these medical professionals (a) follow a design that values varied communication input, (b) seek information from expertise other than their own, and (c) consciously involve themselves in a give-and-take conversation that surfaces solutions that they would not have thought of operating as single individuals.

It is possible to use communication for useful purposes, to be productive and satisfied with the outcomes of speaking. It is also possible to misspeak and correct the errors it produces, and finally to gain strength from that same communicative repair work on those errors. Of all the features of communication, its capacity to help in adapting to new circumstances by reframing what is understood, and its ability to generate a force for change makes us hopeful about communication's contribution to the positive study of organizations.

References

Alavi, M., & Leidner, D.E. (2001). Review: Knowledge management and knowledge management systems: Conceptual foundations and research issues. *MIS Quarterly, 25*(1), 107–136.

Anderson, H., & Goolishian, H. (1992). The client is the expert: A not-knowing approach to therapy. In S. McNamee, & K. J. Gergen (Eds.), *Therapy as social construction* (pp. 25–39). Newbury Park, CA: Sage.

Aronsson. K., & Cederborg (1994). Conarration and voice in family therapy: Voicing, devoicing and orchestration. *Text, 14,* 345–370.

Berger, J., & Milkman, K.L. (2010). Social transmission and viral culture. Retrieved September 10, 2010, from http://opim.wharton.upenn.edu/~kmilkman/Virality_Feb_2010.pdf.

Bird, I., Jones, B., & Kee, K.F. (2009). The organization and management of grid infrastructures. *Computer, 42*(1), 36–46.

Brown, P., & Levinson, S. (1987). *Politeness: Some universals of language usage.* Cambridge: Cambridge University Press.

Browning, L.D. (2007). *Respectful interaction: A Weickian perspective.* Paper presented at the National Communication Association conference, Chicago.

Browning, L.D., Sætre, A.S. Stephens, K., & Sørnes, J.O. (2008). *Information and communication technologies in action: Linking theory and narratives of practice.* New York: Routledge.

Browning, L.D., & Shetler, J.C. (2000). *Sematech: Saving the U.S. semiconductor industry.* College Station, TX: Texas A & M University Press.

Browning, L.D., & Morris, G.H. (in press). *Narratives in the workplace.* New York. Taylor and Francis.

Buttny, R. (2004). *Talking problems: Studies of social construction.* Albany, NY: SUNY Press.

Caldas, A., Schroeder, R., Mesch, G.S., & Dutton, W.H. (2008). Patterns of information search and access on the World Wide Web: Democratizing expertise or creating new hierarchies? *Journal of Computer-Mediated Communication, 13*(4), 769–793.

Cameron, D. (2000). *Good to talk.* London: Sage.

Child, J.T., & Shumate, M. (2007). The impact of communal knowledge repositories and people-based knowledge management on perceptions of team effectiveness. *Management Communication Quarterly, 21*(1), 29–54.

Cohen, M.D., Riolo, R., & Axelrod, R. (2001). The role of social structure in the maintenance of cooperative regimes. *Rationality and Society, 13*(1), 5–32.

Corbett, J.M., Faia-Correia, M., Patriotta, G., & Brigham, M. (1999). *Back up the organisation: How employees and information systems re-member organizational practice.* Paper presented at the 32nd annual Hawaii International Conference on System Sciences (HICSS-32), Maui, Hawaii.

Couture, S.J., & Strong, T. (2004). Turning differences into possibilities: Using discourse analysis to investigate change in therapy with adolescents and their families. *Counselling and Psychotherapy Research, 4*(1), 90–101.

Couture, S.J. (2007). Multiparty talk in family therapy: Complexity breeds opportunity. Journal of Systemic Therapies, *26*(1), 63–80.

de Shazer, S. (1985). *Keys to solution in brief therapy.* New York: Norton.

de Shazer, S., & Berg, I.K. (1992). Doing therapy: A poststructural re-vision. *Journal of Marital and Family Therapy, 18,* 71–81.

Deetz, S. (2009). *Remarks on positive organizational communication scholarship.* Presented at the National Communication Association Convention, Chicago.

Davenport, T.H., De Long, D.W., & Beers, M.C. (1999). Successful knowledge management projects. *The Knowledge Management Yearbook 1999–2000,* 89–107.

Empson, L. (2001). Fear of exploitation and fear of contamination: Impediments to knowledge transfer in mergers between professional service firms. *Human Relations, 54,* 839–862.

Flanagin, A.J., & Waldeck, J.H. (2004). Technology use and organizational newcomer socialization. *Journal of Business Communication, 41*(2), 137–165.

Frederickson, B.L. (2003). Positive emotions and upward spirals in organizations. In K.S. Cameron, J.E. Dutton, & R.E. Quinn (Eds.), *Positive organizational scholarship* (pp. 163–175). San Francisco: Berrett-Koehler.

Friedman, S. (1993). Possibility therapy with couples: Constructing time-effective solutions. *Journal of Family Psychotherapy, 4,* 35–52.

Fulk, J., Flanagin, A.J., Kalman, A.J., Monge, P.R., & Ryan, T. (1996). Connective and communal public goods in interactive communication systems. *Communication Theory, 6* (1), 60–87.

Gastil, J., Black, L.W., Deess, E.P., & Leighter, J. (2008). From group member to democratic citizen: How deliberating with fellow jurors reshapes civic attitudes. *Human Communication Research, 34*(1), 137–169.

Gawande. (2009). The cost conundrum: What a Texas town can teach us about the cost of health care. Retrieved from http://www.newyorker.com/reporting/2009/06/01/090601fa_fact_gawande.

Gibbs, J. (2009). Dialectics in a global software team: Negotiating tensions across time, space, and culture. *Human Relations, 62*(6), 905–935.

Giddens, A. (1984). *The constitution of society: Outline of the theory of structuration.* Berkeley: University of California Press.

Giordano, G.A., Stoner, J.S., Brouer, R.L., & George, J.F. (2007). The influences of deception and computer-mediation on dyadic negotiations. *Journal of Computer-Mediated Communication, 12*(2), 362–383.

Goffman, E. (1967). *Interaction ritual.* Garden City, NY: Anchor.

Goffman, E. (1971). *Relations in public.* New York: Harper & Row.

Gold, A.H., Malhotra, A., & Segars, A.H. (2001). Knowledge management: An prganizational capabilities perspective. *Journal of Management Information Systems, 18*(1), 185–214.

Granta, A.M., Campbella, E.M., Chena, G., Cottonea, K., Lapedis, D., & Leea, K. (2007). Impact and the art of motivation maintenance: The effects of contact with beneficiaries on persistence behaviors. *Organizational Behavior and Human Decision Processes, 103,*(1), 53–67.

Grice, H.P. (1975). Logic and conversation. In P. Cole, & J.L. Morgan (Eds.), *Syntax and semantics* Vol. 3, *Speech acts.* New York: Academic Press.

Hancock, J.T., Thom-Santelli, J., & Ritchie, T. (2004). Deception and design: The impact of communication technology on lying behavior. In E. Dykstra-Erickson, & M. Tscheligi (Eds.), *Proceedings of the SIGCHI conference on Human Factors in Computing Systems* (pp. 129–134). New York: ACM.

Hartelius, E.J., & Browning, L.D. (2008). The application of rhetorical theory in managerial research: A literature review. *Management Communication Quarterly, 22*, 13–39.

Harter, L., & Krone, K. (2001). The boundary-spanning role of a cooperative support organization: Managing the paradox of stability and change in non-traditional organizations. *Journal of Applied Communication Research, 29*(3), 248–277.

Hollingshead, A.B., Fulk, J., & Monge, P. (2002). Fostering intranet knowledge-sharing: An integration of transactive memory and public goods approaches. In P.J. Hinds, & S. Keisler (Eds.), *Distributed work: New research on working across distance using technology* (pp. 335–355). Cambridge, MA: MIT Press.

Hoyt, M.F. (1994). *Constructive therapies.* New York: Guilford.

Jeffres, L.W., & Lin, C.A. (2006). Metropolitan websites as urban communication. *Journal of Computer-Mediated Communication, 11*(4), 957–980.

Johnson, B. (1977). *Communication: The process of organizing.* Boston: Allyn & Bacon.

Jones, S.M., & Wirtz, J.G. (2006). How does the comforting process work? An empirical test of an appraisal based model of comforting. *Human Communication Research, 32*(3), 217–243.

Kee, K.F., & Browning, L.D. (2010). The dialectical tensions in the funding infrastructure of cyberinfrastructure. *Computer Supported Cooperative Work, 19* (3–4), 283–308.

LaFasto, F., & Larson, C. (2001). *When teams work best: 6,000 team members and leaders tell what it takes to succeed.* Thousand Oaks, CA: Sage.

Lai, V.S. (2001). Intraorganizational communication with intranets. *Association for Computer Machinery, 44*, 95–100.

Lawrence, P.R., & Lorsch, J.W. (1967). Differentiation and integration in complex organizations. *Administrative Science Quarterly, 12*(1), 1–47.

MacGeorge, E.L., Lichtman, R.M., & Pressey, L.C. (2002). The evaluation of advice in supportive interactions: Facework and contextual factors. *Human Communication Research, 28*(3), 451–463.

Maruyama, M. (1992). *Context and complexity: Cultivating contextual understanding.* New York: Springer-Verlag.

McNamee, S., & Gergen, K.G. (1992). *Therapy as social construction.* Newbury Park, CA: Sage.

Morris, G.H. (2008). *Grafting Goffman's ideas to Weick's in a theory of respectful interaction.* Paper presented at the National Communication Association, San Diego.

Morris, G.H., & Hopper, R. (1987). Symbolic action as alignment: A synthesis of rules approaches. *Research on Language and Social Interaction, 21*, 1–30.

Nofsinger, R.E. (1991). *Everyday conversation.* Newbury Park, CA: Sage.

Norman, A.T., & Russell, C.A. (2006). The pass-along effect: Investigating word-of-mouth effects on online survey procedures. *Journal of Computer-Mediated Communication, 11*(4), 1085–1103.

O'Connell, B. (1998). *Solution-focused therapy.* Thousand Oaks, CA: Sage.

Palazzolo, E.T., Serb, D.A., She, Y., Su, C., & Contractor, N.S. (2006). Coevolution of communication and knowledge networks in transactive memory systems: Using computational models for theoretical development. *Communication Theory, 16*(2), 223–250.

Park, N., Kee, K.F., & Valenzuela, S. (2009). Being immersed in social networking environment: Facebook groups, uses and gratifications, and social outcomes. *CyberPsychology & Behavior, 12*, 729–733.

Parker, P.S. (2003). Control, resistance, and empowerment in raced, gendered, and classed work contexts: The case of African American women. *Communication Yearbook, 27*, 257–292.

Pomerantz, A. (1984). Agreeing and disagreeing with assessments: Some features of preferred/dispreferred turn shapes. In J.M. Atkinson, & J. Heritage (Eds.), *Structures of social action: Studies in conversation analysis* (pp. 57–101). Cambridge: Cambridge University Press.

Project Kaleidescope (2006). *Interdisciplinary research.* Retrieved September 10, 2010, from http://www.pkal.org/collections/Vol4InterdisciplinaryResearch.cfm.

Putnam, L. (2009). *Remarks on positive organizational communication scholarship.* Presented at the National Communication Association Convention, Chicago.

Putnam, L. (2001). Shifting voices, oppositional discourse, and new visions for communication. *Journal of Communication, 51*(1), 38–51.

Riedlinger, M.E., Gallois, C., McKay, S., & Pittam, J. (2004). Impact of social group processes and functional diversity on communication in networked organizations. *Journal of Applied Communication Research, 32*(1), 55–79.

Rogers, C. (1951). *Client-centered therapy: Its current practice, implications, and theory.* Boston: Houghton Mifflin.

Rogers, E.M. (2003). *Diffusion of innovations* (5th ed.). New York: Free Press.

Rosenfeld, L.B., Richman, J.M., & May, S.K. (2004). Information adequacy, job satisfaction and organizational culture in a dispersed-network organization. *Journal of Applied Communication Research, 32*(1), 28–54.

Segrin, C. (2003). Age moderates the relationship between social support and psychosocial problems. *Human Communication Research, 29*(3), 317–342.

Schegloff, E.A., & Sacks, H. (1973). Opening up closings. *Semiotica, 7,* 289–327.

Skovholt, K., & Jan, S. (2006). Email copies in workplace interaction. *Journal of Computer-Mediated Communication, 12*(1), 42–65.

Sooryamoorthy, R., & Shrum, W. (2007). Does the Internet promote collaboration and productivity? Evidence from the scientific community in South Africa. *Journal of Computer-Mediated Communication, 12*(2), 733–751.

Stewart, J. (2009). Communicating and interpersonal communication. In J. Stewart (Ed.), *Bridges not walls* (pp. 15–78). New York: McGraw Hill.

Stokes, R., & Hewitt, J.P. (1976). Aligning actions. *American Sociological Review, 41,* 838–849.

Suedfeld, P., & Leighton, D.C. (2002). Early communications in the war against terrorism: An integrative complexity analysis. *Political Psychology, 23*(3), 585–599.

Tierney, J. (2010, February 8). Will you be e-mailing this column? It's awesome. *New York Times.* Retrieved September 10, 2010, from http://www.nytimes.com/2010/02/09/science/09tier.html?pagewanted=all.

Valenzuela, S., Park, N., & Kee, K.F. (2009). Is there social capital in a social network site? Facebook use and college students' life satisfaction, trust, and participation. *Journal of Computer-Mediated Communication, 14*(4), 875–901.

van Knippenberg, D., De Dreu, C.K. W., & Homan, A.C. (2004). Work group diversity and group performance: An integrative model and research agenda. *Journal of Applied Psychology, 89*(6), 1008–1022.

Walsh, J., P., & Maloney, N., G. (2007). Collaboration structure, communication media, and problems in scientific work teams. *Journal of Computer-Mediated Communication, 12*(2), 712–732.

Watzlawick, P., Beavin, J.H., & Jackson, D.D. (1967). *Pragmatics of human communication.* New York: Norton.

Watzlawick, P., Weakland, C.E., & Fisch, R. (1974). *Change.* New York: Norton.

Weick, K.E. (2003). Positive organizing and organizational tragedy. In K.S. Cameron, J.E. Dutton, & R.E. Quinn (Eds.), *Positive organizational scholarship* (pp. 66–80). San Francisco: Berrett-Koehler.

Weisbord, M. (1992). *Discovering common ground.* San Francisco: Berrett-Kohler.

Wittenbaum, G.M. (2003). Putting communication into the study of group memory. *Human Communication Research, 29*(4), 616–623.

Yuan, Y.C., Fulk, J., & Monge, P.R. (2007). Access to information in connective and communal transactive memory systems. *Communication Research, 34*(2), 131–155.

Yuan, Y.C., & Gay, G. (2006). Homophily of network ties and bonding and bridging social capital in computer-mediated distributed teams. *Journal of Computer-Mediated Communication, 11*(4), 1062–1084.

Zander, R.S., & Zander, B. (2000). *The art of possibility.* New York: Penguin.

Zhao, S. (2006). Do Internet users have more social ties? A call for differentiated analyses of Internet use. *Journal of Computer-Mediated Communication, 11*(3), 844–862.

Parallel and Divergent Predictors of Objective and Subjective Value in Negotiation

Jared R. Curhan *and* Ashley D. Brown[1]

Abstract

The negotiation field has been dominated by a focus on *objective value* (or economic outcomes) with relatively less attention paid to *subjective value* (or social psychological outcomes). This chapter proposes a framework that highlights the duality of negotiation outcomes by identifying predictors of both objective and subjective value. Whereas some predictors tend to have parallel effects, benefiting objective and subjective value in tandem, other predictors tend to have divergent effects, benefiting objective value while simultaneously undermining subjective value, or vice versa. We further distinguish between predictors typically outside of the negotiator's control, such as personality traits and individual differences, versus predictors typically within the negotiator's control, such as behaviors and strategies. We offer 12 examples of predictors that illustrate this new framework, with the aim of advising individuals on how best to manage both objective and subjective value, thereby achieving peak performance in negotiations.

Keywords: Negotiation, subjective value, objective value, individual differences, negotiator behaviors, negotiator strategies

Conventional wisdom and decades of research in American behavioral science have tended to portray negotiation as a process of joint decision-making over the terms of exchange for scarce resources (Neale & Bazerman, 1985; Pruitt, 1983; Wall, 1985; Young, 1991). From this perspective, it is understandable that the vast majority of studies on negotiation have focused on how to achieve tangible, objective outcomes, whereas only a small fraction of studies have included subjective measures of performance, such as attitudes and perceptions (Bendersky & McGinn, 2010; Mestdagh & Buelens, 2003). Yet, in the spirit of positive organizational scholarship (POS) (e.g., Cameron, Dutton, & Quinn, 2003; Dutton & Glynn, 2008), we argue that this imbalance in the field may lead negotiators astray, because the same prescriptions that are intended to benefit objective outcomes sometimes have unintended negative consequences for social

psychological outcomes. In this chapter, we propose a new framework and use it to identify specific predictors of objective and subjective outcomes in negotiation.

Underlying our framework is a distinction between two kinds of outcomes in negotiation. *Economic outcomes* are the terms of the deal (or lack thereof), whereas *social psychological outcomes* are the attitudes and perceptions of the negotiators (Thompson, 1990). Economic outcomes refer to goods and services and can be said to have an *objective value* (OV), or worth defined by a market or by a negotiator's ex ante preferences. Social psychological outcomes, such as satisfaction or liking, can be said to have a *subjective value* (SV) as evaluated by a negotiator ex post (Curhan, Elfenbein, & Xu, 2006). The construct of SV emerged from a series of studies by Curhan et al. (2006), who defined SV as the "social, perceptual, and emotional consequences of a negotiation" (p. 494), comprising the negotiator's feelings about the instrumental outcome, feelings about him- or herself, feelings about the process, and feelings about the relationship.[2]

Given that SV is less tangible or concrete relative to OV, many behavioral scientists who study negotiation and professionals in business and law construe negotiation as being primarily about OV and tend to "write off" SV as amounting to a fleeting perception that is difficult to measure reliably and is subject to heuristics and biases. This emphasis on OV is also consistent with a broader tendency in traditional organization studies to attend to economic outcomes more so than positive states and processes (Cameron et al., 2003). For instance, Walsh, Margolis, and Weber (2003) coded all articles published by the Academy of Management from 1958 to 2001 and found a diminishing focus on social outcomes and a rising focus over time on economic outcomes. By contrast, the POS movement has been described as a potential corrective to this predominant concern with economic and financial considerations (Dutton & Glynn, 2008). Similarly, our framework is intended as a corrective to an overemphasis on OV—drawing upon a growing literature that has demonstrated a number of important benefits associated with fostering SV in negotiation.

Subjective value in negotiation is important for at least four reasons. First, negotiators frequently care more about subjective outcomes, such as feeling positive, being respected, or having a favorable relationship, than about the substance of an agreement (Blount & Larrick, 2000; Gelfand, Major, Raver, Nishii, & O'Brien, 2006; Tyler & Blader, 2003). In other words, SV may in some cases represent a good unto itself, or even the primary interest of a negotiating party (Lax & Sebenius, 1986).

Second, those who build solid relationships with their counterparts or who develop positive reputations are more likely to be sought after as a partner or a counterpart in future exchanges (Tenbrunsel, Wade-Benzoni, Moag, & Bazerman, 1999; Tinsley, O'Connor, & Sullivan, 2002). For example, in two longitudinal studies, individuals who reported high SV immediately following a negotiation subsequently reported greater intent to remain in professional contact, greater desire to work on the same team, and greater willingness to negotiate again with their counterpart, whereas OV from the initial negotiation showed none of these predictive effects (Curhan, Elfenbein, & Eisenkraft, 2010; Curhan et al., 2006). Having more parties with whom to negotiate increases one's bargaining power in any

single negotiation to the extent that it increases one's best alternative to a negotiated agreement.

Third, related to the previous point, SV resulting from one negotiation may "pay off" in terms of OV, particularly in the context of long-term interactions (Croson & Glick, 2001; Drolet & Morris, 2000; Fortgang, Lax, & Sebenius, 2003; Mannix, Tinsley, & Bazerman, 1995). In one of the few research studies in which negotiation performance has been examined longitudinally, individuals achieved greater individual and joint OV in a second negotiation if they experienced greater SV in an initial negotiation with the same counterpart, even after controlling for initial OV (Curhan et al., 2010).

Finally, SV is associated with commitment to upholding a deal. To the extent that negotiation outcomes are not self-enforcing, SV can serve as an "insurance policy," increasing the chances that the parties will follow through on their obligations set forth in the terms of the agreement. Counter to the conventional wisdom that SV is fleeting or labile, longitudinal research has demonstrated that SV can be remarkably robust over time—perhaps even more robust than OV. For example, Curhan, Elfenbein, and Kilduff (2009) examined OV and SV resulting from MBA students' job offer negotiations and demonstrated a remarkably strong correlation between these predictors and the students' subsequent job attitudes and turnover intentions an entire year later. Subjective value from these high-stakes, real-world employment negotiations predicted greater subsequent compensation satisfaction and job satisfaction, as well as lower subsequent turnover intention (i.e., intent to leave the job). In contrast, negotiators' OV had no apparent long-term effects on these important outcomes (see also Ferguson, Moye, & Friedman, 2008; Robinson & Morrison, 2000; Robinson & Rousseau, 1994).

Given the new wealth of evidence for the importance of SV as an outcome variable in negotiation, the question naturally arises, where does SV come from? In this chapter, we focus on specific predictors of SV, organized in a new theoretical framework, as depicted in Figure 43.1. By no means do we consider this to be a complete list of relevant predictors. Our purpose is illustrative rather than exhaustive, and several of our predictors were selected due to their close associations with the core mechanisms discussed in the POS literature. For example, we highlight self-efficacy and positive affect, which relate to the POS mechanisms of positive meaning making and positive emoting, respectively (Dutton & Glynn, 2008).

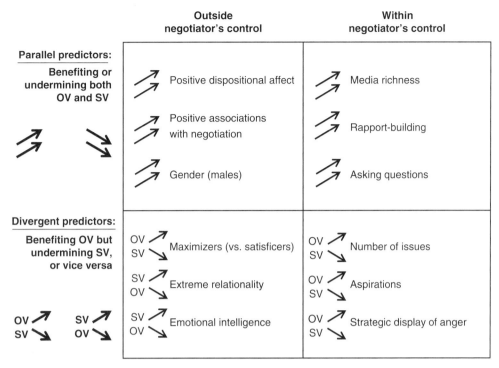

	Outside negotiator's control	Within negotiator's control
Parallel predictors: **Benefiting or undermining both OV and SV**	↗↗ Positive dispositional affect ↗↗ Positive associations with negotiation ↗↗ Gender (males)	↗↗ Media richness ↗↗ Rapport-building ↗↗ Asking questions
Divergent predictors: **Benefiting OV but undermining SV, or vice versa**	OV ↗ SV ↘ Maximizers (vs. satisficers) SV ↗ OV ↘ Extreme relationality SV ↗ OV ↘ Emotional intelligence	OV ↗ SV ↘ Number of issues OV ↗ SV ↘ Aspirations OV ↗ SV ↘ Strategic display of anger

Fig. 43.1 A theoretical framework populated with example predictors of objective and subjective value.

Our aim is to build a new framework for researchers and practitioners alike that highlights the duality of negotiation outcomes, incorporating not only OV, but also the frequently ignored elements of SV.

In addition to the aforementioned distinction between OV and SV, our framework draws two distinctions among potential predictors of those outcomes. The first distinction is between parallel and divergent predictors. We use the term *parallel predictors* to refer to predictors with uniform effects on both OV and SV. These predictors have relatively clear implications in that their effects tend to be either generally beneficial or generally detrimental for a negotiator. We use the term *divergent predictors* to refer to predictors with bidirectional effects, benefiting OV while undermining SV, or vice versa. By definition, divergent predictors are beneficial in some respects but detrimental in others, which may make them useful under certain circumstances, depending on the negotiator's relative prioritization of OV and SV. Judgments regarding the relative weightings of OV and SV may depend on features of the situation, such as the expectation of a future relationship.

We draw a further distinction in our framework between predictors that tend to be outside the control of an individual negotiator, such as personality or gender, versus predictors that could be under a negotiator's control and could, thereby, enter explicitly into a negotiator's tactical decision-making. In the final section of this paper, we include advice for negotiators on how to manage the tension between fostering OV and fostering SV, as well as ways in which one might deal with predictors that are within or beyond the negotiator's control.

Predictors Outside of the Negotiator's Control

Predictors outside of the negotiator's control tend to involve individual differences, such as personality or gender. In this respect, the findings discussed here contribute to an ongoing debate regarding the extent to which individual differences explain variance in negotiation outcomes (Barry & Friedman, 1998; Lewicki, Litterer, Minton, & Saunders, 1994; Terhune, 1970; Thompson, 1990). Although an individual negotiator may have limited or no ability to transform his or her stable characteristics (and even less ability to influence a counterpart's traits), an understanding of how particular individual differences are likely to influence one's negotiation performance is itself an advantage to the negotiator. Research on systematic individual differences helps one understand and even predict behavior.

More specifically, such knowledge can help negotiators diagnose their own negotiation style, predict the behaviors of their counterparts, or choose who to employ as negotiation advocates on their behalf. Therefore, we start with an overview of both parallel and divergent predictors of SV and OV that tend to be outside of the negotiator's control.

Parallel Predictors Outside of the Negotiator's Control

To begin, we consider predictors outside of the negotiator's control that have a parallel or uniform effect on OV and SV. For these predictors, the negotiator need not reconcile how to balance trade-offs between OV and SV.

DISPOSITIONAL AFFECT

Studies involving dispositional positive affect have emerged from a literature increasingly concerned with the effects of trait and state affect in negotiation (Barry, Fulmer, & Van Kleef, 2004; Carnevale & Isen, 1986; Forgas, 1998). With regard to SV, it is not surprising that dispositional positive affect—i.e., the extent to which people have extraverted personalities or a stable tendency to feel enthusiastic (Watson & Clark, 1984)—would tend to correlate with more positive feelings at the end of a negotiation. Less obvious is the fact that positive mood has been found to predict joint OV by reducing reliance on contentious or competitive tactics (Carnevale & Isen, 1986). Consistent with these findings, Elfenbein, Curhan, Eisenkraft, Shirako, and Baccaro (2008) demonstrated empirically that dispositional positive affect is a robust predictor of both one's own OV ($r = 0.17$, $p < 0.05$) and one's own SV ($r = 0.25$, $p < 0.01$). As such, dispositional positive affect tends to be a beneficial trait for individuals to have under most circumstances in a negotiation.

ASSOCIATIONS WITH NEGOTIATION

Even more promising than positive affect in general is the positivity of one's associations, attitudes, and beliefs about negotiation per se. For example, Sullivan, O'Connor, and Burris (2006) identified a form of self-efficacy specifically related to negotiation. Integrative self-efficacy refers to one's confidence in enlarging the pie and fostering rapport. Elfenbein et al. (2008) found that integrative self-efficacy results in a parallel effect, increasing one's own OV and SV.[3] Another parallel effect can be found among those who believe negotiation ability is a skill that can be learned, as opposed to a fixed

trait that is set at birth (Kray & Haselhuhn, 2007). Individuals who view negotiation skills as malleable in this respect achieve greater OV for themselves and tend to feel better about their relationships with their counterparts (Elfenbein et al., 2008). In sum, many empirical findings suggest that both OV and SV are benefited by positive attitudes concerning one's ability to enlarge the pie, one's ability to establish rapport, and one's ability to improve as a negotiator.[4]

GENDER

Gender is another individual difference measure related to negotiation that has been studied for many years. As Kray and Thompson (2005) describe, people have lay theories about what it takes to succeed in negotiations, and these perceptions generally place females at a disadvantage. Recent meta-analyses and literature reviews also have suggested that men tend to achieve higher individual OV in negotiations than do women, and this tendency emerges across a range of study designs, including archival analyses, collective bargaining tasks, and coalition games (Kray & Thompson, 2005; Stuhlmacher & Walters, 1999; Walters, Stuhlmacher, & Meyer, 1998). Although there has been less research on integrative than distributive negotiations, male–male dyads also tend to create more joint OV than female–female dyads (Kray & Thompson, 2005; Miles & LaSalle, 2004; Neu, Graham, & Gilly, 1988). One explanation for men achieving higher individual and joint OV is that men tend to set higher goals in their negotiations (Kray, Thompson, & Galinsky, 2001; Stevens, Bavetta, & Gist, 1993), and high goals have been associated with improved OV (Bazerman, Magliozzi, & Neale, 1985; Huber & Neale, 1987; Neale & Bazerman, 1985; Stevens et al., 1993). Men also tend to report lower apprehension prior to negotiating (Babcock, Gelfand, Small, & Stayn, 2006), greater confidence while negotiating (Watson, 1994), and higher SV post-negotiation (Watson, 1994; Watson & Hoffman, 1996). These parallel effects of gender on OV and SV may be explained by differential treatment of men and women. Bowles, Babcock, and Lai (2007) found that male evaluators penalized women more than men for attempting to negotiate for higher compensation. As such, the effects of gender on OV and SV may be reinforced by gender stereotypes. It should be noted, however, that particular situational characteristics can mitigate some of these gender differences.[5]

Divergent Predictors Outside of the Negotiator's Control

In contrast to the parallel predictors, the examples presented in this section tend to drive OV and SV in opposite directions. We offer one example of a trait that benefits OV yet undermines SV followed by two examples of traits that benefit SV yet undermine OV.

MAXIMIZING VERSUS SATISFICING

Building on a perspective first articulated by Herbert Simon (1955), Schwartz and colleagues (2002) proposed a distinction between two kinds of decision-makers in the face of choices involving many alternatives. Maximizers seek the "best outcome" and feel pressure to examine as many alternatives as possible, whereas "satisficers" seek an outcome that is "good enough" and then stop searching. Maximizing tendencies have been associated with improved objective outcomes at the expense of subjective outcomes. Specifically, Iyengar, Wells, and Schwartz (2006) found that students who scored high on a personality scale designed to measure maximizing tendencies secured 20% higher starting salaries compared to students with low maximizing tendencies. At the same time, these maximizers were less satisfied with the jobs that they secured and also experienced more negative feelings throughout the job search process, including stress, fatigue, anxiety, and worry. Iyengar et al. (2006) argue that, in seeking out an undefined "best" outcome, maximizers are more susceptible to experiencing regret associated with unrealistically high expectations.

EXTREME RELATIONAL ORIENTATION

An extreme concern or unhealthy anxiety over interpersonal relationships in negotiation can result in lower individual and joint OV. This phenomenon dates back to the classic negotiation study by Fry, Firestone, and Williams (1983) in which dating couples—particularly those couples who were defensive or possessive about their relationships (Rubin, 1970)—achieved lower joint OV compared to strangers. More recently, Gelfand et al. (2006) developed a theoretical model involving the broader concept of "relational self-construal," which refers to a cognitive representation of the self as fundamentally connected to other individuals. One prediction of this model is that dyads in which both parties have high relational self-construal accessibility[6] will experience a "relational satisficing" dynamic, resulting in higher SV but lower individual and joint OV (Gelfand et al., 2006). Consistent with this prediction, Curhan, Neale, Ross, and Rosencranz-Engelmann (2008) empirically demonstrated that dyads negotiating within highly relational contexts[7] had greater SV in that they trusted and liked their counterparts more and believed their counterparts liked them more. However, these same dyads reached outcomes of lower joint OV. Similarly, within a negotiation context, Amanatullah, Morris, and Curhan (2008) examined a construct called "unmitigated communion," or a dispositional orientation marked by anxiety about social relationships with others coupled with low concern for oneself (Fritz & Helgeson, 1998). They found that unmitigated communion led negotiators to make concessions in order to avoid straining relationships, which resulted in lower individual OV. Furthermore, high unmitigated communion on both sides of a negotiation resulted in greater SV in the form of relational satisfaction but lower joint OV (Amanatullah et al., 2008). In summary, the pattern across all of these studies is that individual and joint OV is forfeited in deference to relational concerns when both members of a dyad show extreme concern for the other.

EMOTIONAL INTELLIGENCE

The construct of emotional intelligence captures a range of abilities that includes perceiving emotion, facilitating thought with emotion, understanding emotion, and regulating emotion (Mayer, Salovey, & Caruso, 2000)—all factors that relate to the management of SV in negotiation (Fulmer & Barry, 2004). Indeed, those who are high on emotional intelligence tend to experience greater SV themselves and tend to induce greater SV in their counterparts (Der Foo, Elfenbein, Tan, & Aik, 2004; Mueller & Curhan, 2006). However, those who are high in emotional intelligence also tend to have lower individual OV (Der Foo et al., 2004) and counterparts with higher OV (Mueller & Curhan, 2006) than those who are low in emotional intelligence. Der Foo et al. (2004) argue that perhaps emotionally intelligent negotiators show too much sympathy and are more trusting relative to low emotional intelligence negotiators and thus may be more conciliatory.

In summary, this section has provided examples of predictors over which negotiators may not have extensive control, yet these predictors influence OV and SV. Dispositional positive affect, positive attitudes about negotiation, and gender serve as examples of a broad class of predictors that tend to have parallel or uniform influences on both OV and SV. Perhaps of greater concern to both researchers and practitioners, however, are those predictors that create a tension between OV and SV, such as maximizing tendencies, relational self-construal, and emotional intelligence. The divergent consequences of these predictors for OV and SV mean that the negotiator must attempt to weigh or calculate which outcomes are of greatest importance in any particular negotiation.

Predictors Within the Negotiator's Control

Although most negotiators have limited ability to alter the predictors discussed above, many situational characteristics or behavioral strategies tend to be within the control of the negotiator. Some of these strategies can enhance both OV and SV, whereas others result in a tension between the two kinds of outcomes.

Parallel Predictors Within the Negotiator's Control

Once again, we begin with a consideration of predictors within the negotiator's control that do not require a tradeoff between OV and SV. Specifically, choosing a rich medium of communication, building rapport, and asking questions are valuable strategies for enhancing OV and SV under a broad range of circumstances.

MEDIA RICHNESS

Media richness refers to the degree of information, such as rapid feedback or personal presence, that can be conveyed through a particular communication medium (Poole, Shannon, & DeSanctis, 1992). Although there has been a great deal of mixed evidence regarding how face-to-face negotiations compare to computer mediated, video-conferencing, or telephone negotiations, in general, media richness benefits both OV and SV—which is consistent with the notion so central to the POS literature that high-quality connections between individuals are vital for positive organizational dynamics (Dutton & Glynn, 2008).[8] Stuhlmacher and Citera (2005) conducted a meta-analysis reviewing studies that compared various mediums and concluded that face-to-face negotiations are less hostile and result in higher individual profit than other communication media. McGinn and Croson (2004) also argue that visual access increases social awareness and lends itself to more cooperation, coordination, truth

telling, and rapport building. Face-to-face negotiators tend to experience greater rapport, trust, and cooperation (Drolet & Morris, 2000) and complete negotiations in less time, with a greater desire for future interaction (Purdy, Nye, & Balakrishnan, 2000). By contrast, online negotiators have lower SV, are less confident in their outcomes, and express lower levels of trust both before and after the negotiation (Naquin & Paulson, 2003). Negotiators communicating via less rich media may also be less accurate in judging counterpart interests, resulting in lower individual and joint OV (Arunachalam & Dilla, 1995). Although there are some exceptions, including situations that are emotionally charged (Carnevale, Pruitt, & Seilheimer, 1981; Carnevale & Isen, 1986) or situations in which negotiators need time to reflect (Pesendorfer & Koeszegi, 2006), greater media richness generally benefits both OV and SV.

RAPPORT BUILDING

Using humor and developing rapport uniformly benefit both OV and SV and are also within the negotiator's control. Specifically, humor has been found to "ease" the pain when trying to influence or make final demands in a negotiation. Across three different final offer levels, O'Quin and Aronoff (1981) found that negotiators made larger concessions, evaluated the task more positively, and reported marginally less tension when the final offer was requested in a humorous way. A related strategy is to establish rapport either prior to or during the negotiation. Moore, Kurtzberg, Thompson, and Morris (1999) found that sharing personal information and in-group affiliation reduced the rate of impasse with electronically mediated negotiations. Similarly, Morris, Nadler, Kurtzberg, and Thompson (2002) found that a brief telephone conversation prior to a negotiation conducted over e-mail resulted in greater rapport and higher rates of agreement.[9] This finding is particularly astonishing, given that the phone call had such effects after a week of e-mail negotiating, suggesting that the benefits of rapport are by no means fleeting.

ASKING QUESTIONS

Tactics such as asking questions have also been found to be advantageous. Fairfield and Allred (2007) found that the more positive regard negotiators have for each other the more that they ask questions, which in turn, produces better understandings of the other side's interests and higher joint OV. This is consistent with Thompson's (1991) findings that negotiators achieved higher joint OV after asking more questions of the counterpart. In conflict situations, another advantage of asking questions is that it signals an interest in the other side's view, which enhances relationships and counterpart SV (Carnegie, 1963; Chen, Minson, & Tormala, 2010); furthermore, the person asking the questions becomes more open to the idea of having a conversation and tends to view the counterpart more positively (Chen et al., 2010). As such, asking questions can have benefits for both parties involved.

Divergent Predictors Within the Negotiator's Control

Despite being within the negotiator's control, other predictors are likely to represent a dilemma for the negotiator because they introduce a tradeoff between OV and SV. The use of these predictors requires more careful consideration, given that strategies aimed at achieving higher OV may undermine SV, and vice versa. In this section, we review three predictors that tend to enhance OV at the expense of SV.

NUMBER OF ISSUES

One of the main defining features of a negotiation is the number of issues under consideration (Raiffa, 1982). The prescriptive advice often provided is that negotiators should try to include as many issues as possible in any given deal-making process and strive to resolve those issues simultaneously rather than sequentially (Erickson, Holmes, Frey, Walker, & Thibaut, 1974; Froman & Cohen, 1970; Kelley, 1966; Pruitt, 1981; Yukl, Malone, Hayslip, & Pamin, 1976). More issues allow for more creative problem solving via *logrolling*—or trading off issues based on differences in relative priorities (Fisher, Ury, & Patton, 1991; Froman & Cohen, 1970; Lewicki, Saunders, & Minton, 1997; Pruitt, 1983; Raiffa, 1982; Thompson, 2001)—thereby resulting in higher joint OV. However, more recent research has found that the number of issues in any given negotiation is associated with lower levels of SV due to counterfactual thought processes (Naquin, 2003). Although Naquin (2003) found that the participants negotiating over more issues did indeed achieve higher joint OV, which is consistent with the prescriptive advice to include more issues, this tactic simultaneously undermined SV. The negotiator is caught between maximizing payoffs yet feeling worse about the outcome. This phenomenon is consistent with the findings discussed above regarding maximizers versus satisficers, in which maximizers had higher OV yet lower SV. Too many issues in

a negotiation may be analogous to facing too many decision alternatives and, therefore, may undermine the negotiator's SV, particularly if the negotiator is a maximizer. Thus, the negotiator is presented with a dilemma, in which she or he can either try to incorporate more issues in the negotiation, prioritizing OV, or incorporate fewer issues in the negotiation, prioritizing SV.

ASPIRATIONS

Another common negotiation strategy with a wealth of empirical support is to focus on aspiration values to achieve higher OV (Huber & Neale, 1986, 1987; Northcraft, Neale, & Earley, 1994; Thompson, 2001). However, Galinsky, Mussweiler, and Medvec (2002) found that negotiators who focus on their ideal outcomes or aspiration values cannot resolve the dissonance experienced at the end of the negotiation and, subsequently, have lower SV. The negotiators in their study who focused on their aspiration values (or goals) obtained higher individual OV compared to those who focused on their reservation prices (or backup plans), as expected, yet they had lower SV. Similarly, Thompson (1995) found that negotiators have lower SV when they have high aspirations relative to when they have low aspirations, even when reservation prices and individual OV are identical. As Loewenstein, Thompson, and Bazerman (1989) argue, satisfaction is often a function of perceived relative gain or comparison to others, rather than absolute gain (see also Novemsky & Schweitzer, 2004).

STRATEGIC DISPLAY OF ANGER

Finally, a burgeoning literature on emotion in negotiation, and the strategic display of anger, in particular, has received a great deal of attention. Intuition and initial evidence suggested that negative emotion, such as anger, would bring about suboptimal behaviors (Barry & Oliver, 1996) and would be associated with a range of negative consequences such that it should be avoided (Ury, 1991). Indeed, the strategic display of anger has negative repercussions for SV. Expression of anger may violate certain justice principles (Van Kleef & Côté, 2007); damage reputations (Clark, Pataki, & Carver, 1996); breed mutual anger, hostility, and aggression (Baron, Neuman, & Geddes, 1999; Kennedy, Homant, & Homant, 2004); and lead to a desire to get even (Bies & Tripp, 2001; Skarlicki & Folger, 1997). More broadly, negotiators with angry counterparts have been found to experience more anger themselves, have reduced SV, and express less willingness to engage in future negotiations (Friedman et al., 2004; Kopelman, Rosette, & Thompson, 2006; Van Kleef, De Dreu, & Manstead, 2004b). However, the expression of anger has also been found to benefit OV. The display of anger can convey the magnitude or significance of an issue and, subsequently, may influence or change behavior. Negotiators generally make lower demands and concede more when their counterparts display anger compared to happiness[10] (Sinaceur & Tiedens, 2006; Van Kleef, De Dreu, & Manstead, 2004a; Van Kleef et al., 2004b), and angry negotiators are able to claim more value when their counterparts have few alternatives (Sinaceur & Tiedens, 2006). Furthermore, the effects of anger may carry over across negotiations, in which negotiators may demand less when they encounter a counterpart who expressed anger in a previous negotiation (Van Kleef & De Dreu, 2008). As such, the strategic display of anger has a divergent effect on OV and SV, where the expression of anger is associated with benefits for OV but at the expense of SV.

In this section, we have reviewed predictors that are within the control of the negotiator, or examples of situational characteristics and behavioral strategies that negotiators can use to their advantage. Three of these examples benefit both OV and SV, whereas three other examples benefit OV yet tend to be detrimental for SV. With these latter examples, negotiators may need to prioritize either OV or SV or otherwise try to overcome the tension between the two. We discuss this at greater length below.

Conclusion

In this chapter, we have presented a new framework and 12 illustrative predictors of two kinds of outcomes in negotiation—OV and SV. Whereas some predictors have parallel effects on OV and SV, other predictors have divergent effects, driving the two kinds of outcomes in opposite directions.

One prescriptive implication of our proposed framework is that negotiators should account for the fact that some strategies will help both OV and SV, whereas others may help one while hindering the other. In the latter case, a negotiator needs to gauge which types of ends are most important. Moreover, some predictors tend to be outside of the negotiator's control while others tend to be within the negotiator's control. By managing the predictors within the negotiator's control and recognizing the predictors outside of one's control, one can maximize the chances of achieving peak performance.

Although we advise that negotiators deliberately consider which outcomes are most important in any particular negotiation, such decisions are unlikely to be straightforward. This mental accounting may be biased toward an overvaluation of short-term objective outcomes. However, a prioritization of SV might serve the negotiator better in the long-term. Research from the procedural justice domain suggests that people tend to emphasize instrumental concerns when they make choices, yet focus on procedural justice when asked about experiences already encountered. Tyler and Blader (2004) suggest that this tendency may have important implications and extensions to the negotiation context, where economic outcomes may be valued prior to and during the negotiation but subjective criteria may be valued more heavily retrospectively. As such, negotiators could be caught in a bind as preferences or the relative weighting of OV and SV shift over time. One of our goals in presenting our proposed framework is to emphasize the importance of SV, which may help negotiators in overcoming this bias if both OV and SV are considered in advance as important outcomes.

Notwithstanding these difficulties, consciously weighing the relative importance of OV and SV represents one method of handling divergent predictors (e.g., Savage, Blair, & Sorenson, 1999). Another method involves reappraising the situation so as to eliminate the bind altogether. For example, Galinsky et al. (2002) found that negotiators' whose satisfaction had been undermined by their own high aspiration values could increase their satisfaction after the negotiation by shifting their focus from their aspiration prices (or goals) to their reservation prices (or backup plans). Still another strategy may be to compensate for any harm done to SV. For example, Van Kleef and De Dreu (2008) found that offering an apology can offset some of the negative effects of displaying anger on SV.

Future Directions

As mentioned earlier, the examples offered here are intended to be illustrative of the kinds of predictors that might be researched in the future. Since less than 20% of negotiation studies focus on subjective outcomes (Mestdagh & Buelens, 2003), there is a great deal still to be learned. We hope that this chapter will provide a framework for future research on predictors of SV. For example, one area for future research is in the domain of self-enhancing biases, which may lead negotiators to overestimate their own performance (Kramer et al., 1993), contributing to greater SV, yet undermine their ability to reach agreements due to unrealistic expectations. Another domain for future research is the tenet of negotiation theory that prescribes the use of objective criteria, or principles of legitimacy to strengthen one's arguments in a negotiation (Fisher et al., 1991). This practice may potentially enhance OV, but the use of rights-based arguments may also undermine relationships because conflicting parties tend to disagree over what constitutes a fair settlement (Babcock & Loewenstein, 1997; Ury, Brett, & Goldberg, 1988).

It is our hope that the framework presented in this chapter will underscore the danger of measuring just one type of outcome in negotiation and help to motivate further research exploring the duality of negotiation outcomes. Additionally, negotiation serves as an illustrative context that highlights the broader POS perspective that positive dynamics and subjective outcomes are crucial for organizational scholars and practitioners to take into account above and beyond instrumental concerns.

Notes

1. Both authors contributed equally.
2. For the sake of parsimony, we conflate the subdimensions of SV throughout this chapter.
3. To the contrary, distributive self-efficacy, which refers to one's confidence in claiming a greater share of resources for oneself, results in a divergent effect—benefiting one's own OV at the expense of the counterpart's SV.
4. An exception to the benefits of self-efficacy in negotiation may be a negotiator who is overly positive or high in self-efficacy. These negotiators may be biased in their judgments or assessments of the negotiation. Kramer, Newton, and Pommerenke (1993) found that positive mood and motivation to maintain high self-esteem contribute to negotiator overconfidence and overly positive self-evaluations; to the extent that an impasse occurs, these negotiators may be high in SV but at the expense of not reaching an agreement.
5. Gender may have less of an effect, for example, when situations are low in ambiguity (i.e., economic structure is clear) or when women are negotiating on behalf of others (Bowles, Babcock, & McGinn, 2005). Similarly, although gender stereotypes are pervasive and powerful, how they are activated (implicitly or explicitly) and which gender-specific traits are connected to negotiator effectiveness may alter how the stereotypes influence negotiation performance (Kray, Galinsky, & Thompson, 2002; Kray et al., 2001); for instance, an explicit endorsement of stereotypes that are negative for women actually led women to outperform men as they behaved in a manner inconsistent with the stereotype (see also Curhan & Overbeck, 2008; Kray et al., 2001).
6. Many factors increase relational self-construal accessibility, including situational contexts, which contribute to temporary accessibility, and individual differences, which may foster chronic accessibility. As such, relational self-construal may be a predictor that is both within and outside the negotiator's control.
7. Situations in which individuals hold a representation of themselves as being fundamentally interdependent.
8. Some studies have found benefits to face-to-face negotiations (Arunachalam & Dilla, 1995), whereas other studies have found benefits to computer mediated negotiations (Croson, 1999). Still others have found few differences at all (Rangaswamy & Shell, 1997). Poole, Shannon, and DeSanctis (1992) argue that all mediums have their strengths and weaknesses (e.g., some mediums are better at surfacing conflict, while others are better at providing time for reflection, etc.), and the optimal choice depends on the specifics of the negotiation.
9. These two studies suggest that rapport building may also be a strategy to overcome some of the potential drawbacks associated with online negotiations.
10. Transitions between happy and angry states also impact negotiation outcomes, where negotiators who become angry yield higher concessions and reach agreements more than negotiators displaying steady-state anger (Filipowicz, Barsade, & Melwani, 2010).

References

Amanatullah, E.T., Morris, M.W., & Curhan, J.R. (2008). Negotiators who give too much: Unmitigated communion, relational anxieties, and economic costs in distributive and integrative bargaining. *Journal of Personality and Social Psychology, 95*(3), 723–738.

Arunachalam, V., & Dilla, W.N. (1995). Judgment accuracy and outcomes in negotiation: A causal modeling analysis of decision-aiding effects. *Organizational Behavior and Human Decision Processes, 61*, 289–304.

Babcock, L., Gelfand, M.J., Small, D., & Stayn, H. (2006). Gender differences in the propensity to initiate negotiations. In D.D. Cremer, M. Zeelenberg, & J.K. Murnighan (Eds.), *Social psychology and economics* (pp. 239–259). Mahwah, NJ: Lawrence Erlbaum.

Babcock, L., & Loewenstein, G. (1997). Explaining bargaining impasses: The role of self-serving biases. *Journal of Economic Perspectives, 11*, 109–126.

Baron, R.A., Neuman, J.H., & Geddes, D. (1999). Social and personal determinants of workplace aggression: Evidence for the impact of perceived injustice and the type A behavior pattern. *Aggressive Behavior, 25*, 281–296.

Barry, B., & Friedman, R.A. (1998). Bargainer characteristics in distributive and integrative negotiation. *Journal of Personality and Social Psychology, 74*, 345–359.

Barry, B., Fulmer, I.S., & Van Kleef, G. (2004). I laughed, I cried, I settled: The role of emotion in negotiation. In M.J. Gelfand, & J. Brett (Eds.), *The handbook of negotiation and culture* (pp. 71–94). Palo Alto, CA: Stanford University Press.

Barry, B., & Oliver, R.L. (1996). Affect in dyadic negotiation: A model and propositions. *Organizational Behavior and Human Decision Processes, 67*(2), 127–143.

Bazerman, M.H., Magliozzi, T., & Neale, M.A. (1985). Integrative bargaining in a competitive market. *Organizational Behavior and Human Decision Processes, 35*(3), 294–313.

Bendersky, C., & McGinn, K.L. (2010). Open to negotiation: Phenomenological assumptions and knowledge dissemination. *Organization Science, 21*(3), 781–797.

Bies, R.J., & Tripp, T.M. (2001). A passion for justice: The rationality and morality of revenge. In R. Cropanzano (Ed.), *Justice in the workplace: From theory to practice* Vol. 2 (pp. 197–208). Mahwah, NJ: Erlbaum.

Blount, S., & Larrick, R.P. (2000). Framing the game: Examining frame choice in bargaining. *Organizational Behavior and Human Decision Processes, 81*, 43–71.

Bowles, H.R., Babcock, L., & Lai, L. (2007). Social incentives for gender differences in the propensity to initiate negotiations: Sometimes it does hurt to ask. *Organizational Behavior and Human Decision Processes, 103*(1), 84–103.

Bowles, H.R., Babcock, L., & McGinn, K.L. (2005). Constraints and triggers: Situational mechanisms of gender in negotiation. *Journal of Personality and Social Psychology, 89*, 951–965.

Cameron, K.S., Dutton, J.E., & Quinn, R.E. (2003). Foundations of positive organizational scholarship. In K.S. Cameron, J.E. Dutton, & R.E. Quinn (Eds.), *Positive organizational scholarship: Foundations of a new discipline.* San Francisco: Berrett-Koehler Publishers, Inc.

Carnegie, D. (1963). *How to win friends and influence people.* New York: Simon & Schuster.

Carnevale, P., Pruitt, D.G., & Seilheimer, S. (1981). Looking and competing: Accountability and visual access in integrative bargaining. *Journal of Personality and Social Psychology, 40*, 111–120.

Carnevale, P.J., & Isen, A.M. (1986). The influence of positive affect and visual access on the discovery of integrative solutions in bilateral negotiation. *Organizational Behavior and Human Decision Processes, 37*(1), 1–13.

Chen, F.S., Minson, J.A., & Tormala, Z.L. (2010). Tell me more: The effects of expressed interest on receptiveness during dialogue. *Journal of Experimental Social Psychology, 46*(5), 850–853.

Clark, M.S., Pataki, S.P., & Carver, V.H. (1996). Some thoughts and findings on self presentation of emotions in relationships. In G.J.O. Fletcher, & J. Fitness (Eds.), *Knowledge structures in close relationships: A social psychological approach* (pp. 247–274). Mahwah, NJ: Erlbaum.

Croson, R., & Glick, S. (2001). Reputations in negotiations. In S. Hoch, & H. Kunreuther (Eds.), *Wharton on making decisions* (pp. 177–186). New York: Wiley.

Croson, R.T. (1999). Look at me when you say that: An electronic negotiation simulation. *Simulation & Gaming, 30*, 23–37.

Curhan, J.R., Elfenbein, H.A., & Eisenkraft, N. (2010). The objective value of subjective value: A multi-round negotiation study. *Journal of Applied Social Psychology, 40*(3), 690–709.

Curhan, J.R., Elfenbein, H.A., & Kilduff, G.J. (2009). Getting off on the right foot: Subjective value versus economic value in predicting longitudinal job outcomes from job offer negotiations. *Journal of Applied Psychology, 94*(2), 524–534.

Curhan, J.R., Elfenbein, H.A., & Xu, H. (2006). What do people value when they negotiate? Mapping the domain of subjective value in negotiation. *Journal of Personality and Social Psychology, 91*(3), 493–512.

Curhan, J.R., Neale, M.A., Ross, L., & Rosencranz-Engelmann, J. (2008). Relational accommodation in negotiation: Effects of egalitarianism and gender on economic efficiency and relational capital. *Organizational Behavior and Human Decision Processes, 107*, 192–205.

Curhan, J.R., & Overbeck, J.R. (2008). Making a positive impression in a negotiation: Gender differences in response to impression motivation. *Negotiation and Conflict Management Research, 1*, 179–193.

Der Foo, M., Elfenbein, H.A., Tan, H.H., & Aik, V.C. (2004). Emotional intelligence and negotiation: The tension between creating and claiming value. *International Journal of Conflict Management, 15*(4), 411–429.

Drolet, A.L., & Morris, M.W. (2000). Rapport in conflict resolution: Accounting for how face-to-face contact fosters mutual cooperation in mixed-motive conflicts. *Journal of Experimental Social Psychology, 36*, 25–50.

Dutton, J.E., & Glynn, M.A. (2008). Positive organizational scholarship. In J. Barling, & C.L. Cooper (Eds.), *The Sage handbook of organizational behavior* Vol. 1 *Micro Approaches.* London: Sage.

Elfenbein, H.A., Curhan, J.R., Eisenkraft, N., Shirako, A., & Baccaro, L. (2008). Are some negotiators better than others? Individual differences in bargaining outcomes. *Journal of Research in Personality, 42*, 1463–1475.

Erickson, B., Holmes, J.G., Frey, R., Walker, L., & Thibaut, J. (1974). Functions of a third party in the resolution of conflict: The role of a judge in pretrial conferences. *Journal of Personality and Social Psychology, 31*, 864–872.

Fairfield, K.D., & Allred, K.G. (2007). Skillful inquiry as a means to success in mixed-motive negotiation. *Journal of Applied Social Psychology, 37*(8), 1837–1855.

Ferguson, M., Moye, N., & Friedman, R. (2008). The lingering effects of the recruitment experience on the long-term employment relationship. *Negotiation and Conflict Management Research, 1*(3), 246–262.

Filipowicz, A., Barsade, S.G., & Melwani, S. (2010). *Emotional transitions in social interactions: The effects of changing emotions in a negotiation.* Manuscript submitted for publication.

Fisher, R., Ury, W., & Patton, B. (1991). *Getting to yes: Negotiating agreements without giving in* (2nd ed.). New York: Penguin Books.

Forgas, J. (1998). On feeling good and getting your way: Mood effects on negotiator cognition and bargaining strategies. *Journal of Personality and Social Psychology, 74*(3), 565–577.

Fortgang, R.S., Lax, D.A., & Sebenius, J.K. (2003). Negotiating the spirit of the deal. *Harvard Business Review, 81*(2), 66–76.

Friedman, R., Anderson, C., Brett, J., Olekalns, M., Goates, N., & Lisco, C.C. (2004). The positive and negative effects of anger on dispute resolution: Evidence from electronically mediated disputes. *Journal of Applied Psychology, 89*, 369–376.

Fritz, H.L., & Helgeson, V.S. (1998). Distinctions of unmitigated communion from communion: Self-neglect and overinvolvement with others. *Journal of Personality and Social Psychology, 75*, 121–140.

Froman, L.A., & Cohen, M.D. (1970). Compromise and logroll: Comparing the efficiency of two bargaining processes. *Behavioral Science, 15*, 180–183.

Fry, W.R., Firestone, I.J., & Williams, D.L. (1983). Negotiation process and outcome of stranger dyads and dating couples: Do lovers lose? *Basic and Applied Social Psychology, 4*, 1–16.

Fulmer, I.S., & Barry, B. (2004). The smart negotiator: Cognitive ability and emotional intelligence in negotiation. *International Journal of Conflict Management, 15*, 245–272.

Galinsky, A.D., Mussweiler, T., & Medvec, V.H. (2002). Disconnecting outcomes and evaluations: The role of negotiator focus. *Journal of Personality and Social Psychology, 83*(5), 1131–1140.

Gelfand, M.J., Major, V.S., Raver, J.L., Nishii, L.H., & O'Brien, K. (2006). Negotiating relationally: The dynamics of the relational self in negotiations. *Academy of Management Review, 31*, 427–451.

Huber, V.L., & Neale, M.A. (1986). Effects of cognitive heuristics and goals on negotiator performance and subsequent goal setting. *Organizational Behavior and Human Decision Processes, 38*(3), 342–365.

Huber, V.L., & Neale, M.A. (1987). Effects of self and competitor goals on performance in an interdependent bargaining task. *Journal of Applied Psychology, 72*(2), 197–203.

Iyengar, S.S., Wells, R.E., & Schwartz, B. (2006). Doing better but feeling worse: Looking for the "best" job undermines satisfaction. *Psychological Science, 17*, 143–150.

Kelley, H.H. (1966). A classroom study of dilemmas in interpersonal negotiations. In K. Archibald (Ed.), *Strategic intervention and conflict* (pp. 49–73). Berkeley, CA: University of California, Institute of International Studies.

Kennedy, D.B., Homant, R.J., & Homant, M.R. (2004). Perception of injustice as a predictor of support for workplace aggression. *Journal of Business and Psychology, 18*, 323–336.

Kopelman, S., Rosette, A.S., & Thompson, L. (2006). The three faces of Eve: Strategic displays of positive, negative, and neutral emotions in negotiations. *Organizational Behavior and Human Decision Processes, 99*(1), 81–101.

Kramer, R.M., Newton, E., & Pommerenke, P.L. (1993). Self-enhancement biases and negotiator judgment: Effects of self-esteem and mood. *Organizational Behavior and Human Decision Processes, 56*(1), 110–133.

Kray, L.J., Galinsky, A., & Thompson, L. (2002). Reversing the gender gap in negotiations: An exploration of stereotype regeneration. *Organizational Behavior and Human Decision Processes, 87*(2), 386–409.

Kray, L.J., & Haselhuhn, M.P. (2007). Implicit negotiation beliefs and performance: Experimental and longitudinal evidence. *Journal of Personality and Social Psychology, 93*, 49–64.

Kray, L.J., & Thompson, L. (2005). Gender stereotypes and negotiation performance: A review of theory and research. In B. Staw, & R.M. Kramer (Eds.), *Research in organizational behavior series* Vol. 26 (pp. 103–182). Greenwich, CT: JAI Press.

Kray, L.J., Thompson, L., & Galinsky, A. (2001). Battle of the sexes: Gender stereotype confirmation and reactance in negotiations. *Journal of Personality and Social Psychology, 80*, 942–958.

Lax, D.A., & Sebenius, J.K. (1986). Interests: The measure of negotiation. *Negotiation Journal, 2*, 73–92.

Lewicki, R.J., Litterer, J.A., Minton, J.W., & Saunders, D.M. (1994). *Negotiation* (2nd ed.). Burr Ridge, IL: Irwin.

Lewicki, R.J., Saunders, D.M., & Minton, J.W. (1997). *Essentials of negotiation*. Boston, MA: Irwin/McGraw-Hill.

Loewenstein, G.F., Thompson, L., & Bazerman, M.H. (1989). Social utility and decision making in interpersonal contexts. *Journal of Personality and Social Psychology, 57*, 426–441.

Mannix, E.A., Tinsley, C.H., & Bazerman, M. (1995). Negotiating over time: Impediments to integrative solutions. *Organizational Behavior and Human Decision Processes, 62*(3), 241–251.

Mayer, J.D., Salovey, P., & Caruso, D.R. (2000). Models of emotional intelligence. In R.J. Stemberg (Ed.), *Handbook of intelligence* (pp. 396–420). Cambridge, UK: Cambridge University Press.

McGinn, K.L., & Croson, R. (2004). What do communication media mean for negotiators? A question of social awareness. In M.J. Gelfand, & J. Brett (Eds.), *The handbook of negotiation and culture* (pp. 334–349). Palo Alto, CA: Stanford University Press.

Mestdagh, S., & Buelens, M. (2003). Thinking back on where we're going: A methodological assessment of five decades of research in negotiation behavior. Paper presented at the International Association of Conflict Management Conference, Melbourne, Australia.

Miles, E.W., & LaSalle, M.M. (2004). *Dyad gender composition and negotiation of joint gains: A comparison of three theoretical perspectives*. Unpublished manuscript, Georgia State University, Atlanta, GA.

Moore, D.A., Kurtzberg, T.R., Thompson, L., & Morris, M.W. (1999). Long and short routes to success in electronically mediated negotiations: Group affiliations and good vibrations. *Organizational Behavior and Human Decision Processes, 77*(1), 22–43.

Morris, M.W., Nadler, J., Kurtzberg, T.R., & Thompson, L. (2002). Schmooze or lose: Social friction and lubrication in e-mail negotiations. *Group dynamics: Theory, research, and practice, 6*(1), 89–100.

Mueller, J.S., & Curhan, J.R. (2006). Emotional intelligence and counterpart mood induction in a negotiation. *International Journal of Conflict Management, 17*(2), 110–128.

Naquin, C.E. (2003). The agony of opportunity in negotiation: Number of negotiable issues, counterfactual thinking, and feelings of satisfaction. *Organizational Behavior and Human Decision Processes, 91*, 97–107.

Naquin, C.E., & Paulson, G.D. (2003). Online bargaining and interpersonal trust. *Journal of Applied Psychology, 88*, 113–120.

Neale, M.A., & Bazerman, M.H. (1985). The effects of framing and negotiator overconfidence on bargaining behaviors and outcomes. *Academy of Management Journal, 28*(1), 34–49.

Neu, J., Graham, J.L., & Gilly, M.C. (1988). The influence of gender on behavior and outcomes in retail buyer-seller negotiation simulation. *Journal of Retailing, 64*, 427–451.

Northcraft, G.B., Neale, M.A., & Earley, C.P. (1994). The joint effects of goal-setting and expertise on negotiator performance. *Human Performance, 7*, 257–272.

Novemsky, N., & Schweitzer, M.E. (2004). What makes negotiators happy? The differential effects of internal and external social comparisons on negotiator satisfaction. *Organizational Behavior and Human Decision Processes, 95*(2), 186–197.

O'Quin, K., & Aronoff, J. (1981). Humor as a technique of social influence. *Social Psychology Quarterly, 44*(4), 349–357.

Pesendorfer, E.M., & Koeszegi, S.T. (2006). Hot versus cool behavioural styles in electronic negotiations: The impact of communication mode. *Group Decision and Negotiation, 15*, 141–155.

Poole, M.S., Shannon, D.L., & DeSanctis, G.L. (1992). Communication media and negotiation process. In L.L. Putnam, & M.E. Roloff (Eds.), *Communication and negotiation* (pp. 46–66). Newbury Park, CA: Sage.

Pruitt, D.G. (1981). *Negotiation behavior*. San Diego, CA: Academic Press.

Pruitt, D.G. (1983). Achieving integrative agreements. In M.H. Bazerman, & R.J. Lewicki (Eds.), *Negotiating in organizations* (pp. 35–49). Beverly Hills: Sage Publications.

Purdy, J.M., Nye, P., & Balakrishnan, P.V. (2000). The impact of communication media on negotiation outcomes. *International Journal of Conflict Management, 11*, 162–187.

Raiffa, H. (1982). *The art and science of negotiation*. Cambridge, MA: Belknap Press of Harvard University Press.

Rangaswamy, A., & Shell, G.R. (1997). Using computers to realize joint gains in negotiations: Towards an "electronic bargaining table." *Management Science, 8,* 1147–1163.

Robinson, S.L., & Morrison, E.W. (2000). The development of psychological contract breach and conflict: A longitudinal study. *Journal of Organizational Behavior, 21,* 525–546.

Robinson, S.L., & Rousseau, D.M. (1994). Violating the psychological contract: Not the exception but the norm. *Journal of Organizational Behavior, 15*(3), 245–259.

Rubin, Z. (1970). Measurement of romantic love. *Journal of Personality and Social Psychology, 16,* 265–273.

Savage, G.T., Blair, J.D., & Sorenson, R.L. (1999). Consider both relationships and substance when negotiating strategically. In R.J. Lewicki, D.M. Saunders, & J.W. Minton (Eds.), *Negotiation: Readings, exercises, and cases* (pp. 32–49). New York: Irwin McGraw-Hill.

Schwartz, B., Ward, A., Monterosso, J., Lyubomirsky, S., White, K., & Lehman, D.R. (2002). Maximizing versus satisficing: Happiness is a matter of choice. *Journal of Personality and Social Psychology, 83,* 1178–1197.

Simon, H.A. (1955). A behavioral model of rational choice. *Quarterly Journal of Economics, 59,* 99–118.

Sinaceur, M., & Tiedens, L.Z. (2006). Get mad and get more than even: When and why anger expression is effective in negotiations. *Journal of Experimental Social Psychology, 42*(3), 314–322.

Skarlicki, D.P., & Folger, R. (1997). Retaliation in the workplace: The roles of distributive, procedural, and interactional justice. *Journal of Applied Psychology, 82,* 434–443.

Stevens, C.K., Bavetta, A.G., & Gist, M.E. (1993). Gender differences in the acquisition of salary negotiation skills: The roles of goals, self-efficacy, and perceived control. *Journal of Applied Psychology, 78,* 723–735.

Stuhlmacher, A.F., & Citera, M. (2005). Hostile behavior and profit in virtual negotiation: A meta-analysis. *Journal of Business and Psychology, 20*(1), 69–93.

Stuhlmacher, A.F., & Walters, A.E. (1999). Gender differences in negotiation outcomes: A meta-analysis. *Personnel Psychology, 52,* 653–677.

Sullivan, B.A., O'Connor, K.M., & Burris, E.R. (2006). Negotiator confidence: The impact of self-efficacy on tactics and outcomes. *Journal of Experimental Social Psychology, 42*(5), 567–581.

Tenbrunsel, A.E., Wade-Benzoni, K.A., Moag, J., & Bazerman, M.H. (1999). The negotiation matching process: Relationships and partner selection. *Organizational Behavior and Human Decision Processes, 80,* 252–283.

Terhune, K. (1970). The effects of personality in cooperation and conflict. In P. Swingle (Ed.), *The structure of conflict* (pp. 193–234). Beverly Hills: Sage.

Thompson, L. (1990). Negotiation behavior and outcomes: Empirical evidence and theoretical issues. *Psychological Bulletin, 108,* 515–532.

Thompson, L. (1991). Information exchange in negotiation. *Journal of Experimental Social Psychology, 27,* 161–179.

Thompson, L. (1995). The impact of minimum goals and aspirations on judgments of success in negotiations. *Group Decision and Negotiation, 4*(6), 513–524.

Thompson, L. (2001). *The mind and heart of the negotiator* (2nd ed.). Upper Saddle River, NJ: Prentice Hall.

Tinsley, C.H., O'Connor, K.M., & Sullivan, B.A. (2002). Tough guys finish last: The perils of a distributive reputation. *Organizational Behavior and Human Decision Processes, 88,* 621–642.

Tyler, T.R., & Blader, S.L. (2003). The group engagement model: Procedural justice, social identity, and cooperative behavior. *Personality and Social Psychology Review, 7,* 349–361.

Tyler, T.R., & Blader, S.L. (2004). Justice and negotiation. In M.J. Gelfand, & J. Brett (Eds.), *The handbook of negotiation and culture* (pp. 295–312). Palo Alto, CA: Stanford University Press.

Ury, W. (1991). *Getting past no: Negotiating with difficult people.* London: Business Books.

Ury, W., Brett, J., & Goldberg, S. (1988). *Getting disputes resolved: Designing systems to cut the costs of conflict.* San Francisco: Jossey-Bass.

Van Kleef, G., & De Dreu, C.K.W. (2008). *Longer-term consequences of anger expression in negotiation: Retaliation or spill over?* Paper presented at the International Association of Conflict Management conference, Chicago, IL.

Van Kleef, G.A., & Côté, S. (2007). Expressing anger in conflict: When it helps and when it hurts. *Journal of Applied Psychology, 92,* 1557–1569.

Van Kleef, G.A., De Dreu, C.K.W., & Manstead, A.S. (2004a). The interpersonal effects of anger and happiness in negotiations. *Journal of Personality and Social Psychology, 86*(1), 57–76.

Van Kleef, G.A., De Dreu, C.K.W., & Manstead, A.S. (2004b). The interpersonal effects of emotion in negotiations: A motivated information processing approach. *Journal of Personality and Social Psychology, 87*(4), 510–528.

Wall, J.A. (1985). *Negotiation, theory and practice.* Glenview, IL: Pearson Scott Foresman.

Walsh, J.P., Margolis, J., & Weber, K. (2003). Social issues and management: Our lost cause found. *Journal of Management, 29*(6), 859–881.

Walters, A.E., Stuhlmacher, A.F., & Meyer, L.L. (1998). Gender and negotiator competitiveness: A meta-analysis. *Organizational Behavior and Human Decision Processes, 76,* 1–29.

Watson, C. (1994). Gender versus power as a predictor of negotiation behavior and outcomes. *Negotiation Journal, 10,* 117–127.

Watson, C., & Hoffman, R.L. (1996). Managers as negotiators: A test of power versus gender as predictors of feelings, behavior, and outcomes. *Leadership Quarterly, 7,* 63–85.

Watson, D., & Clark, L.A. (1984). Negative affectivity: The disposition to experience aversive emotional states. *Psychological Bulletin, 96*(3), 465–490.

Young, H.P. (1991). *Negotiation analysis.* Ann Arbor, MI: University of Michigan Press.

Yukl, G.A., Malone, M.P., Hayslip, B., & Pamin, T.A. (1976). The effects of time pressure and issue settlement order on integrative bargaining. *Sociometry, 39,* 277–281.

The Mindful Negotiator

Strategic Emotion Management and Well-being

Shirli Kopelman, Orli Avi-Yonah, *and* Akshaya K. Varghese

Abstract

This chapter adopts a positive organizational scholarship lens to examine negotiation theory. Whether focusing on cognitive or social processes, the basic assumptions of most negotiation research are drawn from social exchange theory (Blau, 1964; Emerson, 1976; Homans, 1958; Thibaut & Kelley, 1959), which conceptualizes relationships as economic transactions of material or nonmaterial goods. Building on humanistic psychology (Rogers, 1959, 1961), we suggest that engaging in mindful and strategic emotion management through a process of self-narration (Kopelman, Chen, & Shoshana, 2009) enables negotiators to develop positive regard for the self and others. Our framework suggests that negotiating mindfully will improve instrumental outcomes and well-being.

Keywords: Negotiation, positive organizational scholarship, mindfulness, holistic, emotion, emotion regulation, affect, strategic emotions, social exchange, humanistic psychology

This chapter adopts a positive organizational scholarship (POS) (Cameron, Dutton, & Quinn, 2003) lens to develop a mindful and strategic approach to negotiation theory. Individuals in and across organizations constantly engage in social interactions, which can be conceptualized as a *negotiation*. A negotiation is "an interpersonal decision-making process necessary whenever we cannot achieve our objectives single handedly" (Thompson, 2009, p. 2) in the context of deal making, decision making, or dispute resolution (Brett, 2001). Deal making may include negotiations between buyers and sellers at the product level, and also large-scale transactions, such as mergers and acquisitions. Decision making negotiations commonly take place in the context of project management in teams, for example, allocation of roles and tasks that will lead to increased productivity. Disputes are also prevalent in organizational life, whether among colleagues, across hierarchical roles, or interdepartmentally, as well as between firms. Negotiations play an essential role in the maintenance, adaptation, and management of

organizations (Barley & Tolbert, 1997; Follett, 1918; Pondy, 1967; Ranson, Hinings, & Greenwood, 1980; Scott, 1992). Although few domains in the field of organizational behavior have developed as rapidly as that of negotiations (Bazerman, Curhan, Moore, & Valley, 2000; Kramer & Messick, 1995), we suggest that, despite the breadth and depth of negotiation research, the literature has been bounded by social exchange theory. In the context of a social exchange approach, research focused mainly on instrumental process and outcome variables.

Early negotiation research was heavily influenced by mathematical modeling and by the field of economics. It focused on prescriptive and descriptive dimensions of deviations from rationality. Subsequently, social psychology began to have a large impact on empirical negotiation research, emphasizing the social and interpersonal context. However, both economic and social perspectives are grounded in a social exchange approach (Blau, 1964; Emerson, 1976; Homans, 1958; Thibaut & Kelley, 1959), which views relationships as economic transactions of material (e.g., money) or nonmaterial (e.g., status) goods. Rooted in a broader humanistic approach to personality and social relationships (Rogers, 1959, 1961), we introduce a framework of *negotiating mindfully*. We suggest that mindful and strategic emotion management through a process of self-narration (Kopelman et al., 2009) enables negotiators to develop positive regard for the self and other, which leads to better negotiation outcomes and also individual and organizational well-being.

A Social Exchange Approach to Negotiation

Beginning in the early 1960s and continuing through the 1990s, empirical research in negotiation was predominantly grounded in economic theory, behavioral decision making, and cognitive psychology traditions that either assumed people were rational or demonstrated how and why they departed from rationality (e.g., Bazerman et al., 2000; Dawes, 1998; Kahneman & Tversky, 1973; Simon, 1957; Thompson, Wang & Guinea 2010). Economic theory provided the benchmark for optimal negotiation performance assuming perfect rationality. Most research demonstrated that the "suboptimality that can be observed in negotiation is the result of deviations from rationality in the judgmental processes of negotiators" (Bazerman & Neale, 1992, p. 247). Behavioral decision research (BDR) offered a descriptive, rather than prescriptive perspective, by highlighting systematic decision making "errors" that resulted from simplifying strategies or cognitive heuristics employed by negotiators. Examples of such heuristics are the escalation of commitment, mythical fixed pie, anchoring and adjustment, framing, availability of information, and the winner's curse. Despite the important contributions of BDR to our understanding of negotiation behavior, a major criticism is that the meta-assumptions leave out the social aspect of negotiations that by definition take place in the context of a social interaction between two or more parties (Greenhalgh & Chapman, 1995; Greenhalgh & Gilkey, 1993; Kolb & Coolidge, 1991). The literature is characterized by an arelational bias—emphasizing autonomy, competition, and rationality over interdependence, cooperation, and relationality (Gray, 1994).

Grounded in social psychology, negotiation studies examining relational factors began to proliferate in the late 1980s. Broadening the theoretical lens to include the integral relational dimensions of negotiations introduced an array of independent variables that shed light on negotiation behavior. Some of the many factors studied include emotions (e.g., Barry & Oliver, 1996; Kopelman, Rosette, & Thompson, 2006; Van Kleef, De Dreu, & Manstead, 2010); ethics, fairness, and values (e.g., Lewicki & Litterer, 1985; O'Connor & Carnevale 1997); culture (e.g., Brett & Okumura, 1998; Carnevale & Pruitt, 1992); relationships (e.g., Gelfand, Major, Raver, Nishii, & O'Brien, 2006; McGinn, 2006); and personality (Elfenbein, Curhan, Eisenkraft, Shirako, & Baccaro, 2008). Rather than measuring negotiation success based on purely financial and objective benchmarks (e.g., material goods such as individual and/or joint financial profits), relational benchmarks are also emphasized (e.g., nonmaterial goods such as relative gains, reputation, and long-term relationships). However, whether assessing the objective or subjective value of financial or relational benchmarks (Curhan & Brown, 2010; Curhan, Elfenbein, & Xu, 2006) and whether grounded in open- or closed-system assumptions (Bendersky & McGinn, 2009), most empirical studies to date conceptualize negotiations as a social exchange and focus on financial and/or relational instrumental outcomes.

Social exchange theory (e.g., Blau, 1964; Emerson, 1976; Homans, 1958; Thibaut & Kelley, 1959) characterizes social relationships as interactions in which self-interested actors transact with other self-interested actors to accomplish individual goals they cannot achieve independently. Interdependence and self-interest are central assumptions. In contrast to economic theory, social exchange theory takes into consideration subjective utility models (e.g., Loewenstein, Thompson, & Bazerman, 1989; Messick & Sentis, 1979). That is, it includes assumptions of maximizing not only financial value, but also idiosyncratic personal preferences and relational value in an exchange process that includes subjective cost–benefit analyses and the comparison of alternatives. To maximize objective and/or subjective utility, individuals are not assumed to conform to strict rational choice or reinforcement principles; rather they are given the latitude of imperfect cognitive information processing and emotional processes (Lawler & Thye, 1999). Whether focusing on cognitive or social processes, construing the self as independent or interdependent, or taking into account emotional factors, the theoretical foundations of negotiation research have been grounded in social exchange theory. Although social exchange theory illuminates important dimensions of negotiation behavior, it reduces relationships (business or personal) to economic transactions of material or nonmaterial goods.

Beyond Social Exchange

A social exchange lens of negotiations illuminates how role-based economic transactions influence negotiation outcomes (Figure 44.1a). These negotiation outcomes include individual financial gains, maximizing the pie of joint resources (win–win), building rapport, and developing long-term business relationships that maximize the potential for future economic gains. However, the quality of an interpersonal process can have noninstrumental consequences beyond the negotiation task. For example, a positive negotiation process can improve the well-being of the parties (e.g., reduced stress or increased respect can lead to physiological and psychological health). The quality of the negotiation process can also impact organizational values and norms of behavior. On one hand, highly competitive internal negotiations can deteriorate the culture of trust in an organization. On the other, expertise in identifying interests and value creation can lead to a culture of abundance and thriving. These individual- and organizational-level noninstrumental consequences fall outside the scope of a social exchange approach to negotiations.

Rather than proposing a framework that replaces social exchange, we suggest a theoretical approach that complements it, and argue that both need to be espoused in order to understand the full range of negotiation processes and outcomes. A negotiation, by definition, has instrumental financial (resource distribution) and relational dimensions that social exchange theory illuminates. We build on humanistic psychology (i.e., Roger's [1959, 1961] person-centered

theory of personality and interpersonal relationships) to capture elements of the interaction that go beyond the role-based economic transaction. Humanistic psychology provides a positive conceptualization of social interactions that is aligned with POS. We suggest that it illuminates noninstrumental negotiation benefits to individual and organizational well-being. We propose that both a social exchange *and* a humanistic approach are necessary to fully understand negotiations in the context of social interactions in organizations (Figure 44.1b).

Humanistic psychology emerged in the 1950s in reaction to the bleak pessimism and despair presented by the psychoanalytic view of humans on the one hand, and the robotic-like conception of humans portrayed by behaviorism on the other. At its essence, humanistic psychology assumes that every person has the potential for healthy and creative growth. It is akin to existential psychology, placing a strong emphasis on the phenomenological experiences of the person, along with his or her feelings and values. Examples include Maslow's (1943) developmental theory, which emphasizes a hierarchy of needs and motivations, and Roger's person-centered therapy, which asserts that behavior cannot be "adequately accounted for by a knowledge of the individual's previous conditionings, but only if we [the therapist] grant the presence of a spontaneous force within the organism which has the capacity of integration and redirection" (Rogers, 1946, p. 422).

According to a person-centered theory of personality (Rogers, 1959, 1961), to promote positive

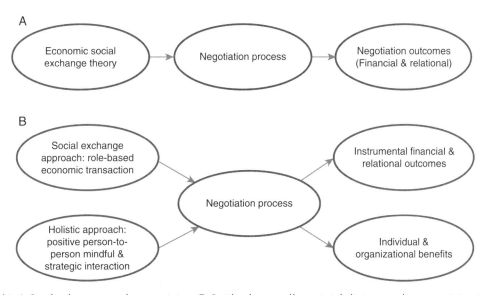

Fig. 44.1 A: Social exchange approach to negotiations. **B**: Social exchange *and* humanistic holistic approaches to negotiations in organizational contexts.

human interactions, negotiators would need to approach the other party, not only in a role-defined relationship, but as a *person* to a *person*. This requires a holistic engagement of one's own self and others, beyond the role of manager and employee, or buyer and seller (Rogers, 1959, 1961 discusses a holistic engagement beyond the role of therapist). Note that a holistic engagement is different from multirole relationship between negotiators (e.g., interacting both as a colleague and as a golf player). The basic assumption of humanistic psychology is that both the self and the other are primarily a person who deserves to be valued, no matter what his condition, role, or behavior. At the core, each person has unconditional self-worth. Furthermore, drawing on a person-centered theory of personality (Rogers, 1959, 1961), to promote positive human interactions, a negotiator must be genuine. Being genuine entails not hiding behind a defensive façade (e.g., cultural norms of behavior), but meeting the other with the full gamut of feelings one is experiencing (this does not necessitate displaying them). This facilitates letting go of one's situation-based role and meeting the other person without inner barriers that might keep one from fully sensing what it feels like to be the other party at each moment in the interaction. Such a humanistic approach is challenging because it requires a level of comfort in fully entering an interaction without knowing cognitively where it will lead. Relating in this manner would enable a negotiator to convey empathic understanding for oneself and to the internal frame of reference of the other party and lead a negotiator to experience unconditional positive regard toward the self and the other.

Building on these assumptions, we propose a framework for developing positive person-to-person interactions that lead to improved negotiation outcomes, as well as individual and organizational well-being (Figure 44.2). We suggest that a reflective process of self-narration (Kopelman et al., 2009) enables negotiators to develop positive regard for the self and others through mindful and strategic emotion management.

POSITIVE PERSON-TO-PERSON MINDFUL AND STRATEGIC INTERACTION

We suggest that a holistic person-to-person approach (Rogers, 1959, 1961) requires an ability to mindfully engage in social interactions. A psychological definition of mindfulness is bringing one's complete attention to the experiences occurring in the present moment, in a nonjudgmental or accepting manner (Baer, 2003; Brown & Ryan, 2003; Kabat-Zinn, 1982;

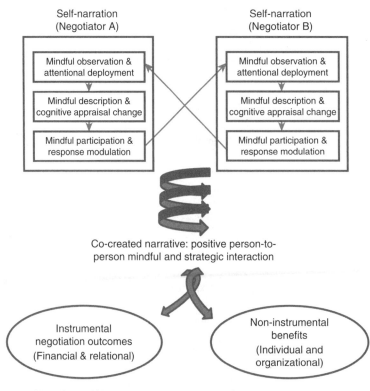

Fig. 44.2 The mindful negotiator: Narrative process of strategic emotion management.

Linehan, 1993a). This includes the individual's thoughts, feelings, and behaviors, as well as external stimuli such as the other party's verbal and nonverbal behavior. In psychology, mindfulness is conceptualized at the individual level and differs, for example, from collective mindfulness, which has been studied in the context of high-reliability organizations (e.g., Weick & Sutcliffe, 2007; Weick, Sutcliffe, & Obstfeld, 1999). Whereas collective mindfulness in high-reliability organizations is conceptualized as an enhanced quality of attention, the psychological concept of mindfulness differs in that it focuses on nonjudgmental and nonreactive integration of an individual's emotional and cognitive responses.

In dialectical behavioral psychology, Linehan (1993a, 1993b) suggests that mindfulness is the vehicle for integrating one's reasonable and emotional states into a holistic mind. A person in a state of reasonable mind approaches a situation intellectually, thinks rationally and logically, attends to facts, and plans responsive behavior with a purpose. However, a person in a *purely* reasonable state of mind may ignore or discount important emotional information. In contrast, when the emotional mind is dominant, thinking and behavior are controlled primarily by a person's current emotional state. The emotional mind suppresses cognitions, reasoning, and logical thinking; distorts perceptions to make them fit with current affect; and makes behaviors congruent with the current emotional state. The integration of the emotional state with the reasonable state represents the transformation of dialectical opposites (reasonable and emotional mind) into a more adaptive and holistic state of mind (*wise mind*; Linehan, 1993a, 1993b).

Mindfulness necessitates a reflective capacity. It is a state of mind that allows for objective observation and acceptance of a one's thoughts and feelings in the moment. A nonjudgmental and nonreactive attitude would require a negotiator to become aware of the constant stream of judging and reacting to inner and outer experiences, step back from it, and assume the stance of an impartial witness to one's own experience (Kabat-Zinn, 2009). Mindfulness can be contrasted with states of mind in which attention is focused elsewhere and behavior is automatic (Brown & Ryan, 2003); that is, one interacts socially without awareness of one's actions. "The habit of categorizing and judging our experience locks us into mechanical reactions that we are not aware of and that often have no objective [or current strategic] basis," (Kabat-Zinn, 2009, p. 33).

Paradoxically, being aware of the present moment and fully accepting it provides an opportunity for change. Nonjudgmental and nonreactive acceptance allows a negotiator to reflectively harness adaptive cognitive and emotional resources and behave in a strategic and effective manner.

Self-narration is a reflective process that enables a negotiator to rescript or replot the current moment. Self-narration is defined as a process of mindful and strategic emotion management (Kopelman et al., 2009). Self-narration integrates what Linehan (1993a, 1993b) conceptualizes as the "what" skills of mindfulness (observe, describe, and participate) with the modal model of emotion and emotion regulation (Gross & Thompson, 2007) and strategic emotion management in negotiations (Kopelman et al., 2006; Kopelman & Rosette, 2008; Kopelman, Gewurz, & Sacharin, 2008; Potworowski & Kopelman, 2008). The modal model of emotions defines emotions as sequential and iterative stages that include a situation (internal or external stimuli) that compels attention, has particular meaning represented by a cognitive appraisal, and results in a multisystem physiological manifestation. Emotion regulation can occur at the stage of perceptual attention (e.g., notice the time), cognitive appraisal (e.g., think that time is running out), and/or physiological manifestation (e.g., experience anxiety). A negotiator could renarrate the current moment by changing the cognitive appraisal and reframing the situation (e.g., thinking to oneself that "time is running out, but actually, it's almost time for lunch, which will energize us"). Rather than feeling anxiety, this cognitive appraisal change may lead to a feeling of relief about the upcoming well-earned break and excitement about the opportunities that may arise in the afternoon. The negotiator may then strategically display (Kopelman et al., 2006) the genuinely felt emotion of happiness and excitement.

Self-narration includes three possible stages of mindful and strategic emotion management (Figure 44.2). Mindful observation enables attentional deployment, for example, by perceiving and paying attention to other stimuli in the environment, not only the salient one that triggered a reaction (e.g., noticing not only the clock that indicates it's late, but the people around the table who seem worn out and tired). Mindful description enables cognitive appraisal change, or reinterpreting the meaning assigned to stimuli at the focus of one's attention (e.g., it's late, and we have had a productive morning). Finally, mindful participation enables response modulation, for example, by changing one's physiological response in the moment (e.g., although noticing it is late and appraising this as stressful, taking a deep breath to slow down one's heart rate and decrease the experienced anxiety). Modulation of any one level can impact other levels. For example, modulating the physiological response may enable paying attention to additional information. Thus, the process of self-narration can iteratively go back and forth between mindful observation and attentional deployment, mindful description and cognitive appraisal change, or mindful participation and response modulation. Thus, renarration of the present moment allows a negotiator to avoid a non-adaptive judgmental and reactive response; fully engage broader personal cognitive and emotional resources; and respond in an adaptive, effective, goal-oriented, and therefore a strategic manner.

Self-narration is conceptualized at the individual level of analysis. On the dyadic level, one negotiator's participation and displayed modulated response will serve as the stimuli that the other negotiator observes (Figure 44.2, self-narration of negotiator A and B). As the negotiation process proceeds, self-narration by both parties will generate a co-created shared narrative characterized by positive regard. This interface is conceptualized as a positive person-to-person mindful and strategic interaction. We suggest that this interaction improves instrumental negotiations outcomes—financial and/or relational. Moreover, it has broader individual and organizational benefits.

Consider, for example, the following negotiation scenario. At 47, Alicia spent her post-MBA career ascending to the top ranks of a venerable financial institution. The daughter of a banker father and a homemaker mother, she grew up excelling in math and science. A fine athlete, she was comfortable with men and assumed, despite several setbacks, that she would be rewarded according to her value to the firm. Although, in retrospect, that assumption was erroneous, it was not until she was suddenly widowed that she became aware of the apparent disparity in compensation between her male colleagues and herself. She requested a meeting with the managing partner of her firm. Uncharacteristically emotional and driven by hurt and fear, she blurted out "I have been treated unfairly here, and I resent having to work harder for less." This outburst was not well received by her superior, who responded by advising her to "calm down," a statement that further escalated the interaction. Alicia was flooded by emotions she had not

experienced since her early days with the firm, when after being subjected to the unwanted advances of a superior, she finally approached a supervisor but was advised to "grow up" and "enjoy the compliment." Alicia was completely unaware how deeply rooted and intense these emotional patterns were or how sensitive and potentially unprofessional she would be, and she was therefore unprepared for her meeting. Overwhelmed by her emotions, she fell into a completely reactive state in which she lost perspective, and left the meeting feeling ashamed and humiliated that she "fell apart and lost all hope of leading the firm one day."

Several months later, and upon careful reflection, which included mindfulness training and daily practice, Alicia developed an empathic view of her reaction and, equally important, an empathic and expansive view of her boss's position and the organizational needs he was managing. Eventually, she was prepared; she approached the meeting ready to negotiate for a new compensation contract, knowing and accepting (both cognitively and emotionally) she might not succeed. She also kept in mind the larger organizational context. She was aware of the recent downturn in the economy and the mounting pressure on the firm to justify generous annual bonuses. She wanted to stay with the firm, and at the meeting she let him know that she was eager to help him steer the firm into safety during these turbulent times. She made her case calmly, regulating her breathing, reminding herself that regardless of the outcome, she is and will be fine. She reminded herself that she loves her job and the people who work for her, and that she professionally and personally respects her managing partner. When he mentioned that he could not increase her bonus, she felt let down (physically she felt her stomach tighten). However, she did not immediately respond. She noted this (mindful observation) and thought, "Here I go again" and "This feeling will not serve me or the firm" (mindful description). To buy time, she breathed deeply and asked (mindful participation) why and whether this was true only for her, or also for others at her level (although she knew that at least one other person did recently get a raise).

Alicia decided not to challenge him, knowing that a confrontation would not help her achieve her goals and would be a conversation-ending action. She reminded herself that her goal was to stay with the firm. She then noticed (with an expanded view of positive regard beyond self) that the managing partner seemed uncomfortable (mindful observation and attentional deployment). She realized that he might be constrained by external factors and therefore not able to help her (mindful description and cognitive reappraisal). She was able to relax and feel more settled and connected to her boss and the company's mission (mindful participation and physiological response modulation). They continued to discuss the topic and then transitioned to more general company matters. He ended the meeting by thanking her for her dedicated contribution. Several days later, he informed her that, although he couldn't increase her bonus this year, he was able to raise her deferred compensation. He also commented on how pleasant the meeting with her was, and asked if she would be willing to assume a more senior position on the executive committee of the firm. Following this conversation, Alicia noticed that she had fewer headaches, slept better at night, and experienced higher levels of energy at work. Her group of direct reports also appeared more relaxed, creative, and effective.

This scenario contrasts an unexpected emotionally reactive response to an adaptive and positive process of self-narration in the moment. The two responses differ not only with respect to the strategic preparation, but in the negotiator's ability to nonjudgmentally observe, describe, and participate in the moment. Adopting this mindful approach enabled strategic management of emotions that emerged during the negotiation. Thus, the negotiator was able to *strategically display* her emotions (e.g., Kopelman et al., 2006; Kopelman & Rosette, 2008) and *strategically respond* to the other party's emotions (e.g., Kopelman, Gewurz, & Sacharin, 2008). Avoiding an emotionally reactive state helped Alicia evaluate the situation from multiple perspectives. No longer purely self-focused, the negotiator was able to experience positive regard toward herself and the managing partner. Her mindful approach also changed the power dynamics. It broadened the relationship from a narrow and hierarchical role-based salary negotiation to a broader person-to-person interaction between colleagues. Authentic presence emerged from the ability to psychologically let go of future outcomes and negotiate mindfully in the moment, while paradoxically staying true to task-related financial and relational goals (Kopelman et al., 2008). Alicia's approach was more holistic, as it integrated the full gamut of her feelings toward herself, the situation, and the managing partner, not simply the fear-based and angry part of herself.

Our framework suggests that a positive person-to-person mindful and strategic interaction can improve instrumental financial and relational negotiation outcomes. Engaging a purely reasonable mindset might lead a negotiator to become stuck in the domain of rights-based positional bargaining. For example, a purely reasonable mindset may lead a negotiator to argue that the facts as he perceives them is the only logical perspective, and he deserves full compensation while the other party receives nothing. Engaging in a purely emotional mindset also might lead to a purely rights-based perspective, if, for example, a negotiator is dominated by feelings of insult and therefore demands outrageous compensation. An exclusively reasonable or emotional mindset could thus lead to extreme positions that are difficult to resolve; similarly, either one might lead to a power-based escalation or derailing of the negotiation. In contrast to rights- and power-based approaches, integrative pie-expanding negotiations and dispute resolution require a consideration of interests and problem solving (Ury, Brett, & Goldberg, 1988). Whether the goal of a negotiator might be to maximize individual or joint economic gains, creating value (integrative negotiations) will lead to better financial outcomes. A mindful and nonreactive negotiator is more likely to comprehend the complexity of the situation, focus on the underlying needs and priorities of all parties, and integrate their interests into a mutually beneficial economic agreement. Mutually beneficial economic agreements are likely to lead to long-term business relationships. Likewise, a negotiator who engages in self-narration and develops positive regard for the self and other is likely to improve instrumental relational outcomes, such as the building of trust and development of rapport. Thus, self-narration can improve instrumental negotiation outcomes.

We also suggest that a positive person-to-person mindful and strategic interaction will lead to individual and organizational well-being. Research suggests that mindfulness leads to an array of positive psychological and physiological outcomes at the individual level and improves well-being (Baer, 2003; Baer, Smith, Hopkins, Krietemeyer, & Toney, 2006; Baer et al., 2008; Carmody & Baer, 2008). Although there are individual differences in the ability to be mindful, it is a skill that can be developed. A reliable and validated measure of mindfulness (Baer et al., 2006) includes five factors: observing, describing, acting with awareness, nonjudging of inner experience, and nonreactivity to inner experience. Long-term meditation practice appears to cultivate these mindfulness skills (Baer et al., 2008), and empirical studies have shown that increases in mindfulness resulting from meditation practice statistically explain the effect of meditation on improved well-being (Carmody & Baer, 2008). Interestingly, mindful meditation increases brain activation in areas associated with positive affect and immune functioning (Davidson et al., 2003). Mindfulness also improves task persistence (Evans, Baer, & Segerstrom, 2009). Therapeutic interventions that incorporate mindfulness training, such as mindfulness-based stress reduction (MBSR; Kabat-Zinn, 1982, 2009), mindfulness-based cognitive therapy (MBCT; Segal, Williams, & Teasdale, 2002), dialectical behavioral therapy (DBT; (Linehan, 1992b, 1993a), and acceptance and commitment therapy (ACT; Hayes, Strosahl, & Wilson, 1999), led to clinically significant improvements in psychological functioning related to chronic pain, eating disorders, anxiety, depressive relapse, emotion regulation in borderline personality disorders, and medical disorders such as fibromyalgia and psoriasis (for a review, see Baer, 2003). Reduced stress and the improved well-being of individuals in an organization has positive ripple effects at the dyadic and organizational level. For example, self-narration may lead to resilient positive relational identities (Kopelman et al., 2009). Positive social interactions at work build physiological resourcefulness and physical health, as well as increase engagement (Heaphy & Dutton, 2008). Thus, the process of mindful and strategic emotion management via self-narration in negotiations is likely to increase individual and organizational well-being.

Conclusion

Negotiations are interpersonal situations that, by definition, include a social exchange component (Blau, 1964; Emerson, 1976; Homans, 1958; Thibaut & Kelley, 1959), but can also be modeled as holistic person-to-person (Rogers, 1959, 1961) interactions. The POS perspective adopted in this chapter illuminates the positive negotiation processes and outcomes that social exchange theory does not capture. Drawing on humanistic psychology (Rogers, 1959, 1961), we suggest that mindful (Baer, 2003; Brown & Ryan, 2003; Kabat-Zinn, 1982; Linehan, 1993a) and strategic (Kopelman et al., 2006; Kopelman & Rosette, 2008; Kopelman et al., 2008; Potworowski & Kopelman, 2008) emotion management through a reflective process of self-narration (Kopelman et al., 2009) leads to the development of positive regard for the self and other. Such mindful and strategic person-to-person

interactions enable negotiators to recognize and integrate interests and priorities to achieve better financial and relational instrumental negotiation outcomes. In parallel, we propose that these positive social interactions lead to noninstrumental benefits to individual and organizational well-being.

Future Directions

We hope that this chapter will spur empirical research that will contribute to both the negotiation and POS literatures. Research in clinical psychology suggests that mindful emotion management improves individual well-being. Negotiation research demonstrates that strategic emotion management influences relational and financial outcomes; however, a direct link between mindfulness skills and instrumental negotiation processes and outcomes needs to be empirical established. That is, does mindfulness influence the ability of negotiators to identify interests and priorities to create more value; substantiate positions to claim more value; and build rapport that can lead to long-term business relationships? Furthermore, evidence in clinical psychology and POS suggests that mindful and strategic emotion management in negotiations will lead to individual and organizational well-being. Future research will need to test if this is the case; for example, do positive person-to-person mindful and strategic negotiation interactions energize individuals and lead to positive outcomes such as flourishing, growth, and fulfillment? Instrumental negotiation outcomes could be tested in a laboratory setting with negotiation simulation-based research; however, noninstrumental outcomes might be more conducive to field research and a collaborative project between a negotiation scholar and a positive organizational scholar.

A puzzling philosophically and empirical challenge is gauging whether an interaction between mindful and strategic negotiators lifts them (Quinn & Quinn, 2009) beyond an instrumental social exchange to become a positive force. Does a mindful negotiator need to be aware that the social interaction is broader than an instrumental social exchange? Or, is it sufficient that the researcher recognizes and measures different features of the social interaction to predict positive outcomes? Future research could also test whether and how a holistic relationship that engages the full person as defined by Rogers (1959, 1961) through mindful and strategic self-narration differs from instrumental business rapport and potentially complements the conceptualization of high-quality connections/relationships (Dutton, 2003; Stephens,

Heaphy, & Dutton (2011), Chapter 29, this volume). Finally, how do negotiators become genuinely "mindful and strategic"? Merely being aware of the complexity of negotiations (e.g., simultaneously accepting the status quo and striving for strategic change) may be sufficient to instigate a different quality of being and interacting that promotes positive growth and well-being.

Acknowledgments

We wish to thank Kim Cameron, Gretchen Spreitzer, Jane Dutton, Jeanne Brett, and Anne Lytle for comments on earlier versions of the chapter.

References

Barley, S., & Tolbert, P. (1997). Institutionalisation and structuration: Studying the links between action and institution. *Organization Studies, 18* (1), 93–117.

Baer, R.A. (2003). Mindfulness training as a clinical intervention: A conceptual and empirical review. *Clinical Psychology: Science and Practice, 10*, 125–143.

Baer, R.A., Smith, G.T., Hopkins, J., Krietemeyer, J., & Toney, L. (2006). Using self-report assessment methods to explore facets of mindfulness. *Assessment, 13*, 27–45.

Baer, R.A., Smith, S.T., Lykins, E., Button, D., Krietemeyer, J., Sauer, S., et al. (2008). Construct validity of the five facet mindfulness questionnaire in meditating and non-meditating samples. *Assessment, 15*, 329–342.

Barry, B., & Oliver R.L. (1996). Affect in dyadic negotiation: A model and propositions. *Organizational Behavior and Human Decision Processes, 67*(2), 127–143.

Bazerman, M.H., Curhan, J.R., Moore, D.A., & Valley, K.L. (2000). Negotiation. *Annual Review of Psychology, 51*(1), 279–314.

Bazerman, M.H., & Neale, M.A. (1992). *Negotiating rationally.* New York: Free Press.

Bendersky, C., & McGinn, K.L. (2009). Open to negotiation: Phenomenological assumptions and knowledge dissemination. *Organization Science, 21*(3), 781–797.

Blau, P.M. (1964). *Exchange and power in social life.* New York: Wiley.

Brett, J.M., & Okumura, T. (1998). Inter- and intracultural negotiation: U.S. and Japanese negotiators. *Academy of Management Journal, 41*(5), 495–510.

Brett, J.M. (2001). *Negotiating globally.* San Francisco: Jossey-Bass.

Brown, K.W., & Ryan, R.M. (2003). The benefits of being present: Mindfulness and its role in psychological well-being. *Journal of Personality and Social Psychology, 84*, 822–848.

Cameron, K., Dutton, J., & Quinn, R.E. (2003). *Positive organizational scholarship: Foundations of a new discipline.* San Francisco: Berrett-Koehler Publishers.

Carmody, J., & Baer, R.A. (2008). Relationships between mindfulness practice and levels of mindfulness, medical and psychological symptoms and well-being in a mindfulness-based stress reduction program. *Journal of Behavioral Medicine, 31*, 23–33.

Carnevale, P.J., & Pruitt, D.G. (1992). Negotiation and mediation. *Annual Review of Psychology, 43*, 531–582.

Curhan, J.R., & Brown, A.D. (2010). Parallel and divergent predictors of objective and subjective value in negotiation.

In K. Cameron, & G. Spreitzer (Eds.), *Handbook of positive organizational scholarship.* Oxford, UK: Oxford University Press.

Curhan, J.R., Elfenbein, H.A., & Xu, H. (2006). What do people value when they negotiate? Mapping the domain of subjective value in negotiation. *Journal of Personality and Social Psychology, 91*, 493–512.

Davidson, R.J., Kabat-Zinn, J., Schumacher, J., Rosenkranz, M., Muller, D., Santorelli, S.F., et al. (2003). Alterations in brain and immune function produced by mindfulness meditation. *Psychosomatic Medicine, 65*(4), 564–570.

Dawes, R.M. (1998). Behavioral decision making and judgment. In D.T. Gilbert, S.T. Fiske, & G. Lindzey (Eds.), *The handbook of social psychology* Vol. 1 (4th ed., pp. 497–548). New York: McGraw-Hill.

Dutton, J.E. (2003). *Energize your workplace: How to create and sustain high-quality connections at work.* San Francisco: Jossey Bass.

Elfenbein, H.A., Curhan, J.R., Eisenkraft, N., Shirako, A., & Baccaro, L. (2008). Are some negotiators better than others? Individual differences in bargaining outcomes. *Journal of Research in Personality, 42*, 1463–1475.

Emerson, R. (1976). Social exchange theory. *Annual Review of Sociology, 2*, 335–362.

Evans, D.R., Baer, R.A., & Segerstrom, S.C. (2009). The effects of mindfulness and self-consciousness on persistence. *Personality and Individual Differences, 47*, 379–382.

Follett, M.P. (1918). *The new state: Group organization, the solution of popular government.* London: Longman.

Gelfand, M.J., Major, V.S., Raver, J.L., Nishii, L.H., & O'Brien, K. (2006). Negotiating relationally: The dynamics of the relational self in negotiations. *Academy of Management Review, 31*(2), 427–451.

Gray, B. (1994). The gender-based foundations of negotiation theory. In R. Lewicki, B. Sheppard, & R. Bies (Eds.), *Research in conflict and negotiation* Vol. 3 (pp. 59–92). Greenwich, CT: JAI Press.

Greenhalgh, L., & Chapman, D.I. (1995). Joint decision making: The inseparability of relationships and negotiation. In R. Kramer, & D. Messick (Eds.), *Negotiation as a social process: New trends in theory and research* (pp. 166–185). Thousand Oaks, CA: Sage.

Greenhalgh, L., & Gilkey, R.W. (1993). Effects of relationship-orientation on negotiators' cognitions and tactics. *Group Decision and Negotiation, 2*, 167–183.

Gross, J.J., & Thompson, R.A. (2007). Emotion regulation: Conceptual foundations. In J.J. Gross (Ed.), *Handbook of emotion regulation* (pp. 3–24). New York: Guilford Press.

Hayes, S.C., Strosahl, K., & Wilson, K.G. (1999). *Acceptance and commitment therapy: An experiential approach to behavior change.* New York: Guilford.

Heaphy, E.D., & Dutton, J.E. (2008). Positive social interactions and the human body at work: Linking organizations and physiology. *Academy of Management Review, 33*(1), 137–162.

Homans, G.C. (1958). Social behavior as exchange. *American Journal of Sociology, 63*(6), 597–606.

Kabat-Zinn, J. (1982). An outpatient program in behavioral medicine for chronic pain patients based on the practice of mindfulness meditation: Theoretical considerations and preliminary results. *General Hospital Psychiatry, 4*, 33–47.

Kabat-Zinn, J. (2009). *Full catastrophe living: Using the wisdom of your mind and body to face stress, pain, and illness.* New York: Random House, Inc.

Kahneman, D., & Tversky, A. (1973). On the psychology of prediction. *Psychological Review, 80*, 237–251.

Kolb, D.M., & G.G. Coolidge. (1991). Her place at the table: A consideration of gender issues in negotiation. In J.W. Breslin, & J.Z. Rubin (Eds.), *Negotiation theory and practice*. Cambridge, MA: PON Books.

Kopelman, S., Chen, L., & Shoshana, J. (2009). Re-narrating positive relational identities in organizations: Self-narration as a mechanism for strategic emotion management in interpersonal interactions. In L.M. Roberts, & J. Dutton (Eds.), *Exploring positive identities and organizations: Building a theoretical and research foundation* (pp. 265–287). New York: Routledge.

Kopelman, S., Gewurz, I., & Sacharin, V. (2008). The power of presence: Strategic responses to displayed emotions in negotiation. In N.M. Ashkanasy, & C.L. Cooper (Eds.), *Research companion to emotions in organizations* (pp. 405–417). Northampton, MA: Edward Elgar.

Kopelman, S., & Rosette, A. (2008). Cultural variation in response to strategic display of emotions during negotiations. *Group Decision Making and Negotiations, 17*(1), 65–77.

Kopelman, S., Rosette, A.S., & Thompson, L. (2006). The three faces of Eve: Strategic displays of positive, negative and neutral emotions in negotiations. *Organizational Behavior and Human Decision Processes, 99*, 81–101.

Kramer, R.M., & Messick, D.M. (Eds.). (1995). *Negotiation as a social process*. Beverley Hills: Sage.

Lawler, E.J., & Thye, S.R. (1999). Bringing emotions into social exchange. *Annual Review of Sociology, 25*, 217–244.

Lewicki, R., & Litterer, J. (1985). *Negotiation*. Homewood, IL: Irwin.

Linehan, M.M. (1993a). *Cognitive-behavioral treatment of borderline personality disorder*. New York: Guilford Press.

Linehan, M.M. (1993b). *Skills training manual for treating borderline personality disorder*. New York: Guilford Press.

Loewenstein, G.F., Thompson, L., & Bazerman, M. (1989). Social utility and decision making in interpersonal contexts. *Journal of Personality and Social Psychology, 57*, 426–441.

Maslow, A.H. (1943). A theory of human motivation. *Psychological Review, 50*, 370–396.

McGinn, K. (2006). Relationships and negotiations in context. In L. Thompson (Ed.), *Negotiation theory and research* (pp. 129–144). Madison, CT: Psychosocial Press.

Messick, D.M., & Sentis, K.P. (1979). Fairness and preference. *Journal of Experimental Social Psychology, l5*, 418–434.

O'Connor, K.M., & Carnevale, P.J. (1997). A nasty but effective negotiation strategy: Misrepresentation of a common-value issue. *Personality and Social Psychology Bulletin, 23*, 504–515.

Pondy, L.R. (1967). Organizational conflict: Concepts and models. *Administrative Science Quarterly, 12*, 296–320.

Potworowski, G., & Kopelman, S. (2008). Developing evidence-based expertise in emotion management: Strategically displaying and responding to emotions in negotiations. *Negotiation and Conflict Management Research, 1*(4), 333–352.

Quinn, R.W., & Quinn, R.E. (2009). *Lift: Becoming a positive force in any situation*. San Francisco: Berrett-Koehler Publisher.

Ranson, S., Hinings, B., & Greenwood, R. (1980). The structuring of organizational structures. *Administrative Science Quarterly, 25*, 1–17.

Rogers, C. (1946). Significant aspects of client-centered therapy. *American Psychologist, 1*, 415–422.

Rogers, C. (1959). A theory of therapy, personality and interpersonal relationships as developed in the client-centered framework. In S. Koch (Ed.), *Psychology: A study of a science*. Vol. 3: *Formulations of the person and the social context*. New York: McGraw Hill.

Rogers, C. (1961). *On becoming a person: A therapist's view of psychotherapy*. London: Constable.

Scott, R.W. (1992). *Organizations: Rational, natural, and open systems*. New Jersey: Prentice Hall.

Segal, Z.V., Williams, J.M.G., & Teasdale, J.D. (2002). *Mindfulness based cognitive therapy for depression: A new approach to preventing relapse*. New York: Guilford.

Simon H.A. (1957). *Models of man*. New York: Wiley.

Stephens, J.P., Heaphy, E., & Dutton, J.E. (2011). High-quality connections. In K. Cameron, & G. Spreitzer (Eds.), *Handbook of positive organizational scholarship*. New York: Oxford University Press.

Thibaut, J.W., & Kelly, H.H. (1959). *The social psychology of groups*. New York: Wiley.

Thompson, L. (2009). *The mind and heart of the negotiator* (4th ed.). Upper Saddle River, NJ: Pearson.

Thompson, L., Wang, J., & Guinea, B. (2010). Negotiation. In S. Fiske (Ed.). *Annual Review of Psychology, 61*, 491–515.

Ury, W.L., Brett, J.M., & Goldberg, S.B. (1988). *Getting disputes resolved: Designing systems to cut the costs of conflict*. San Francisco: Jossey-Bass.

Van Kleef, G.A., De Dreu, C.K.W., & Manstead, A.S.R. (2010). An interpersonal approach to emotion in social decision making: The emotions as social information model. *Advances in Experimental Social Psychology, 42*, 45–96.

Weick, K.E., & Sutcliffe, K.M. (2007). *Managing the unexpected: Resilient performance in an age of uncertainty*. San Francisco: Jossey-Bass.

Weick, K.E., Sutcliffe, K.M., & Obstfeld, D. (1999). Organizing for high reliability: Processes of collective mindfulness. In R. Sutton, & B. Staw (Eds.), *Research in organizational behavior* (pp. 81–124). Greenwich, CT: JAI.

Positive Work–Family Dynamics

Jessica Keeney *and* Remus Ilies

Abstract

This chapter focuses on the positive interconnections between work and family. It provides a brief overview of historical perspectives that have been influential in this literature, followed by a delineation of the focal constructs (enhancement, spillover, enrichment, facilitation) and some subtle but important distinctions between them. The resources thought to enable work–family enrichment are reviewed, as well as the antecedents and consequences that have been studied in relation to self-reported work–family enrichment. Finally a large portion of the chapter is devoted to presenting a within-individual model of positive work–family spillover and crossover, focusing specifically on the transference of positive affective states across domains and across individuals. Interpersonal capitalization, or sharing positive work events with others, is proposed as one mechanism by which work experiences impact the well-being of employees and their families. In closing, unanswered questions in positive work–family dynamics are identified as potentially fruitful avenues for future research.

Keywords: Positive work–family spillover, work–family enrichment, work–family facilitation, interpersonal capitalization, crossover

As is true for many areas of psychology and organizational scholarship, an overwhelming emphasis has been placed on negative phenomena in the study of the work–family interface. Not only is work–family conflict a negative outcome, but it is also associated with a wide range of other deleterious states (e.g., depression, burnout, turnover intentions; Allen, Herst, Bruck, & Sutton, 2000). Although this focus is understandable given the potency that negative experiences hold (Baumeister et al., 2001), it undoubtedly ignores all the ways in which work and family benefit one another.

Fortunately, considerable progress has been made over the past decade in understanding the positive interdependencies of work and family. An exclusive focus on the positive side of the work–family interface can be useful, because research has shown that work–family conflict and work–family enrichment are relatively independent phenomena (Greenhaus

& Powell, 2006). Understanding work–family conflict and how to reduce it tells us very little about how to create the conditions for work–family enrichment. The purpose of this chapter is to review the literature on positive work–family dynamics and to highlight directions for future research.

We first provide a brief overview of historical perspectives that have been influential in the literature on positive work–family dynamics. In the section following, we delineate the focal constructs within this literature and some subtle but important distinctions between them. We review the nomological network of work–family enrichment. Finally, we devote a large portion of the chapter to presenting a within-individual model of positive work–family spillover and crossover, focusing specifically on the transference of positive affective states across domains and across individuals. In closing, we identify unanswered questions both in this model and in positive work–family dynamics more generally that should serve as fruitful areas for future investigations.

Early Roots of the Positive Work–Family Perspective

Although it would be quite some time before their ideas would be embraced by organizational scholars, over three decades ago, two sociologists challenged the dominant view of multiple roles as conflict-ridden. Sieber (1974) questioned why researchers frequently measured negative aspects of roles, such as strain and overload, but rarely measured the gratification and rewards provided by roles. Sieber argued that to adequately test the consequences of multiple role occupation, both the positive and negative features of roles need to be considered.

Similarly, Marks (1977) was skeptical of the idea that engagement in multiple roles always results in a sense of strained time and energy (i.e., reduced resources). Marks contrasted two perspectives: the scarcity and expansionist approaches. According to the scarcity approach, multiple role occupancy results in a net loss of energy. The expansionist approach, on the other hand, acknowledges that resources are renewable and, therefore, abundant. Interestingly, Marks highlighted the subjective nature of time and energy and suggested that the perceived depletion versus availability of these resources depends on an individual's degree of commitment to an activity. After some activities to which we are highly committed, we feel energized and ready to take on the world, whereas other activities seem to leave one feeling spent or drained.

Importantly, neither Marks (1977) nor Sieber (1974) denied the existence of role overload or conflict, but simply suggested that there are enough benefits of holding multiple roles that may just outweigh the costs. The data thus far lend some support to their perspective. On average, people perceive at least as much positive as negative effects of work and family on one another (e.g., Grzywacz & Marks, 2000; Hammer, Cullen, Neal, Sinclair, & Shafiro, 2005; Sumer & Knight, 2001). Furthermore, in support of the idea that conflict does not preclude enrichment, several studies provide evidence that enrichment and conflict are not simply two ends of the same continuum (Greenhaus & Powell, 2006; Tiedje et al., 1990; van Steenenbergen, Ellemers, & Mooijaart, 2007). These studies show that enrichment and conflict are not highly correlated, are differentially related to other variables,

and provide incremental prediction over one another for a variety of outcomes (e.g., work, home, life satisfaction).

Definition and Delineation of Positive Work–Family Constructs

A variety of terms have been used to describe the positive connections between work and family, including enhancement, enrichment, positive spillover, and facilitation. Although these terms have often been used interchangeably, some researchers have argued that they represent distinct constructs (Carlson, Kacmar, Wayne, & Grzywacz, 2006; Wayne, Grzywacz, Carlson, & Kacmar, 2007). Wayne (2009) provided one framework for distinguishing between these constructs, which we will draw upon here.

Enhancement refers to the acquisition of benefits, privileges, or other gains within a particular role (i.e., work or family). When a person experiences an increase in self-esteem after a successful presentation at work, for example, he or she has experienced a form of enhancement within the work role. Enhancement occurs at the individual level and is a prerequisite to any positive transfer between work and family. After enhancement occurs, positive spillover from one role to another can take place. *Positive spillover* occurs when experiences at work generate similar experiences at home, or vice versa (Edwards & Rothbard, 2000). For instance, if a person's positive affect at home carries over into the work environment and changes the way that he or she feels at work (e.g., Heller & Watson, 2005), spillover has occurred.

The next two processes are unique because they are contingent on a person perceiving or experiencing real improvements in their work or family role. They are distinguished from one another by their level of analysis (i.e., individual or system). *Work–family enrichment* (WFE) is "the extent to which experiences in one role improves the quality of life in the other role" (Greenhaus & Powell, 2006, p. 73) with quality of life defined at the individual level. An example of WFE is when self-esteem gained from work accomplishments makes a person a better role model to his or her child. Unsuccessful application of gains from work to family, or vice versa, would not be considered WFE. Thus, if work-derived self-esteem spills over into the home environment, but results in poor role modeling, then—according to Wayne (2009)—the conditions for WFE have not been met. In line with this conceptualization, all the items in the Carlson et al.

(2006) self-report scale of WFE ask respondents to consider whether a given resource helps them be "a better family member" or "a better worker" (depending on the direction of enrichment). *Work–family facilitation* (WFF) is similar to WFE but results in improved quality of life at the system level (i.e., workplace or family unit). System-level indicators of effective functioning in the workplace might include workgroup cooperation, whereas indicators in the family domain might include family cohesion. The next sections are constrained mostly to discussing WFE and its correlates because it has been the most heavily researched of these four constructs.

Subtle But Important Distinctions

One critical issue for the construct development of WFE is defining what is considered to be an improvement in quality of life. This issue is important because it determines what is contained within the definition of WFE and what constitutes valid measurement of WFE. Carlson et al. (2006) contend that performance improvement is the ultimate criterion for WFE. Greenhaus and Powell (2006) recognize positive affect as an additional component of quality of life, but ultimately their model specifies positive affect as a by-product of performance improvements. Thus, based on current theory, the direct influence of positive affective states experienced in one domain on positive affective states exhibited in another domain would be considered positive spillover but not WFE. In their review of work–family linking mechanisms, Edwards and Rothbard (2000, p. 180) argued quite effectively that "this version of spillover [experiences transferred intact] does not represent a linking mechanism, because, by itself, it does not entail a relationship between a work construct and a family construct."

Consistent with the above conceptualization of WFE, the majority of self-report scales measuring positive linkages between work and family contain items that reflect performance improvements, although some of the items reference performance in a loose sense (e.g., increased confidence in a domain). An exception is the Hanson, Hammer, and Colton (2006) work–family positive spillover scale, which contains many items within the instrumental spillover subscales that would be considered WFE (e.g., "I am better able to perform my family responsibilities as a result of skills acquired at work"), but also other items within the affective spillover subscale that would only qualify as spillover ("Being happy at work improves my spirits at home").

In the next section, we review findings regarding the nomological network of WFE, as reflected by correlations between self-report measures of WFE and other variables. To be clear, we use the term WFE to refer to both directions of enrichment and, otherwise, specifically note the direction of enrichment.

The Nomological Network of Work–Family Enrichment
Resources As Enablers of Work–Family Enrichment

Before WFE can occur, an individual must experience enhancement within a role. Enhancement has been operationalized as the acquisition of resources (Wayne, Grzywacz, Carlson, & Kacmar, 2007; Greenhaus & Powell, 2006). Work–family researchers have proposed a number of dimensions of positive spillover and WFE that correspond to the type of resource that is acquired and subsequently transferred across domains (see Table 45.1). Crouter (1984) first distinguished between the transfer of skills and perspectives ("educational spillover") and the transfer of affective states ("psychological spillover"). The more recent conceptualizations summarized in Table 45.1 encapsulate a more diverse array of resources that enable WFE (e.g., flexibility, values, interpersonal relationships). In line with Crouter's model, however, the most commonly examined resources are skills, perspectives, and positive affective states.

Antecedents of Work–Family Enrichment

What characteristics of work and families generate the resources that make positive spillover and WFE possible? Work characteristics that positively predict WFE include *job control/decision latitude/autonomy* (Butler, Grzywacz, Bass, & Linney, 2005; Carlson et al., 2006; Grzywacz & Butler, 2005; Grzywacz & Marks, 2000); *job variety, substantive complexity,* and *skill level* (only the relationship with work-to-family enrichment has been examined; Grzywacz & Butler, 2005; Butler et al., 2005); *social support at work* (Grzywacz & Marks, 2000); *developmental opportunities* and *supervisor relationship quality* (Carlson et al., 2006); and *job salience* (Carlson et al., 2006; Wayne, Randel, & Stevens, 2006). Family characteristics shown to positively predict WFE include *social support* (Grzywacz & Marks, 2000; Wayne et al., 2006) and *family salience* (Grzywacz & Marks, 2000).

A common proposition is that work resources should more strongly predict work-to-family

Table 45.1 Dimensions of positive spillover and work–family enrichment

Work or Family Resource	Description/Examples	Sample Item	Dimension of Spillover/WFE				
			Greenhaus & Powell (2006)	Kirchmeyer (1992)	Carlson et al. (2006)	Hanson, Hammer, & Colton (2006)	Van Steenbergen et al. (2007)
Affect	Mood, spirits	Being in a positive mood at home helps me to be in a positive mood at work.[a]			Affective gains	Affective	Energy-based
Positive emotions	Optimism, hope	Having a good day at work allows me to be optimistic with my family.[a]	Psychological and physical resources		Affective gains	Affective	Energy-based
Skills	Task-based or interpersonal skills/knowledge	Being a parent develops skills in me that are useful at work.[b]	Skills and perspectives	Personality enrichment	Developmental gains	Behavior-based	Behavioral
Positive sense of self	Self-esteem, security, personal fulfillment	My involvement in my work provides me with a sense of success, and this helps me be a better family member.[c]	Psychological and physical resources		Capital gains		
Perspectives/ Frame of Reference	Ways to perceive and handle situations	My involvement in my work helps me to understand different viewpoints, and this helps me be a better family member.[c]	Skills and perspectives	Personality enrichment	Developmental gains		Psychological

Interpersonal relationships	Connections, influence, information	*Being a parent provides me with contacts who are helpful for my work.*[b]	Social capital	
Material resources	Money, gifts	N/A	Material resources	
Flexibility	Discretion in where, how, and when role requirements are met	N/A	Flexibility	
Rights/Privileges	Liberties inherent in a role (e.g., being able to make suggestions)	*Being a parent earns me certain rights and privileges that otherwise I could not enjoy.*[b]	Privileges gained	Status enhancement
?	Using one domain to compensate for failure in the other domain	*Being a parent makes disappointments on the job seem easier to take.*[b]	Status security	Status enhancement
Values	Work ethic, obedience, self-direction	*Values developed at work make me a better family member.*[a]	Value-based	
?	Power of family life to motivate increased efficiency at work	*My involvement in my family requires me to avoid wasting time at work and this helps me be a better worker.*[c]	Efficiency gains	Behavioral

N/A = not available.
[a]Hanson, Hammer, and Colton (2006);
[b]Kirchmeyer (1992);
[c]Carlson et al. (2006).

enrichment, whereas family resources should more strongly predict family-to-work enrichment (Boyar & Mosley, 2007; Grzywacz & Butler, 2005; Wayne et al., 2007; Voydanoff, 2004). Although this pattern of results tends to hold true overall, this is not always the case. For example, job autonomy (or decision latitude) has been shown in two studies to predict enrichment in both directions (Carlson et al., 2006; Grzywacz & Marks, 2000). One explanation for this finding is that autonomy not only serves as a resource for work-to-family enrichment, but also serves as a facilitator for the occurrence of family-to-work enrichment. Autonomy gives employees the option of changing the way they work and thus enabling them to apply resources from another domain successfully (e.g., apply skills learned from the family role).

In addition to environmental antecedents, certain personality traits predispose individuals to experience WFE. Out of the Big Five traits, extraversion has the largest correlations (rs in the 0.20s) with both directions of WFE (Grzywacz & Marks, 2000; Wayne, Musisca, & Fleeson, 2004). Wayne et al. suggested that extraverts' high levels of positive affect, energy, and attentiveness to positive events makes it more likely that they will generate positive resources and transfer them across domains. The Wayne et al. study also found that extraversion did not predict conflict (which was better predicted by neuroticism), thus providing support for the independence of conflict and enrichment. Two other studies provide insight into the traits that relate to WFE. Sumer and Knight (2001) found that securely attached individuals have higher WFE. Boyar and Mosley (2007) found that individuals with high self-esteem and an internal locus of causality have higher WFE.

Finally, gender may relate to experienced levels of WFE. The few studies that have examined gender in the context of WFE suggest that, compared to men, women report higher WFE, as well as display stronger relationships between WFE and job satisfaction (McNall, Nicklin, & Masuda, 2010; van Steenenbergen, Ellemers, & Mooijaart, 2007). Wayne et al. (2007) proposed that gender may influence the types of resources that are sought and acquired in work and family, or the extent to which they are utilized. For example, women may be more likely to use family-friendly work resources (e.g., flextime) that contribute to WFE. Women may also be more likely to utilize their social relationships at work in a way that benefits family life (Friedman & Greenhaus, 2000).

Consequences of Work–Family Enrichment

Many of the same outcomes examined in the work–family conflict literature have also been studied in relation to WFE. The term "outcome" is used tenuously because the majority of studies have employed cross-sectional designs. A recent meta-analysis of 25 studies (McNall et al., 2010) found that WFE is positively related to *job satisfaction, job affective commitment, family satisfaction,* and *psychological and physical health.* The estimated relationships were small to moderate in magnitude, and in many cases, results suggested the presence of moderators, including the construct label used (e.g., spillover versus enrichment). Although WFE is related to many of the same outcomes as work–family conflict (in the opposite direction), an exception is that WFE appears to have little to no relationship with turnover intentions.

Contrary to findings in the work–family conflict literature, the McNall et al. meta-analysis showed that work-to-family enrichment is more strongly related with work-related outcomes, and family-to-work enrichment is more strongly related with non–work related outcomes. That is, more positive outcomes are seen within the domain from which enrichment originates. For example, family satisfaction correlated 0.34 with family-to-work enrichment and only 0.11 with work-to-family enrichment (McNall et al.). Wayne et al. (2004) found that both satisfaction and investment of effort are strongest in the domain from which enrichment originates. Wayne et al. suggested that individuals may be more satisfied and invest effort in roles they see as providing benefit; however, an alternative explanation worthy of consideration is that variables such as satisfaction and effort in a role actually precede enrichment. Longitudinal research is needed to help ascertain the direction of causality in these relationships.

Studies examining the relationship between WFE and performance are scarce, but the few that have been conducted show promising results. There is some evidence to suggest that skills, perspectives, and self-confidence gained in nonwork domains relate to higher job performance (as rated by supervisors; Weer, Greenhaus, & Linnehan, 2010). The Weer et al. study is unique because it considers not only family, but also a variety of other nonwork domains (e.g., religion, study, and leisure) as sources of enrichment. In a study of call center employees, van Steenbergen and Ellemiers (2009) examined the relationship between WFE and objective performance metrics. Enjoying time spent outside of work more as a result of one's job (a form of work-to-family enrichment) predicted whether sales targets were met 1 year later. Additionally, the study suggested possible health benefits of WFE. Individuals who felt more energized after coming home from work had lower cholesterol 1 year later. Also, feeling better able to focus on work as a result of recovery experiences at home (a form of family-to-work enrichment) was negatively correlated with an employee's number of sickness absences.

Overall, these studies demonstrate that WFE is relevant to employee well-being and performance. On the one hand, perhaps these results should not be surprising, given that most measures of WFE ask respondents to attribute positive effects of one domain on performance and affective states in the other domain. On the other hand, it is reassuring for the construct validity of WFE measures that those individuals who report enrichment actually are more satisfied and feel as though they can function better at work and at home.

Elucidating Process: Within-individual Spillover–Crossover Model of Affective States

Another stream of research does not rely upon individuals' self-report of positive work–family linkages, but instead infers their existence from an observed positive relationship between work constructs and family constructs. Like Greenhaus and Powell (2006), we believe that investigations of this nature have potential to shed light on the processes through which work and family enrich one another. In the next section of this chapter, we propose such a model of positive work–family spillover (i.e., a model that maps relationships of work and family constructs), focusing specifically on the spillover of affective states or well-being. In this model, we also introduce the concepts of crossover and interpersonal capitalization. *Crossover* refers to the transference of affective states between people (e.g., spouses), whereas interpersonal capitalization refers to sharing positive events with others and thereby reaping additional benefits beyond those of the events themselves. Together, these three bodies of research—spillover, crossover, and interpersonal capitalization—help explain the interrelatedness of affective states across roles (work and home) and across individuals within these roles (e.g., between family members). The model presented in Figure 45.1 is used both to describe relevant findings and to frame remaining issues for future research.

The proposed model (Figure 45.1) begins with the acquisition of resources in the work domain and reflects work-to-family spillover and crossover between family members. It should be noted that we could have just as easily begun with the acquisition

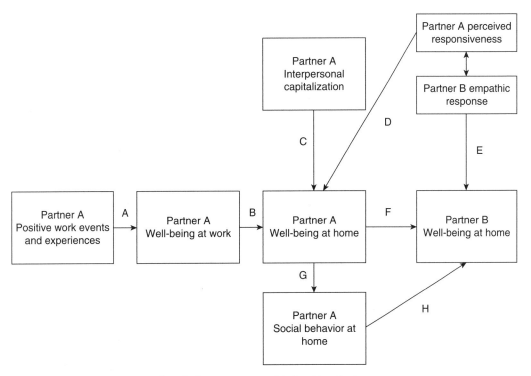

Fig. 45.1 Spillover–crossover model of positive affective states.

of resources in the family domain, capturing family-to-work spillover and crossover between coworkers. Additionally, we present the spillover of Partner A and the crossover from Partner A to B for sake of simplicity, but a parallel process should also operate in the opposite direction.

Importantly, the processes depicted in the model take place within individuals over time. Within-person studies of spillover and enrichment constitute a potentially fruitful area of inquiry. Several studies that have collected repeated measures of WFE suggest that a large percentage of the variance in WFE is within-person (69%, Butler et al., 2005; 72%, Sanz-Vergel, Demerouti, & Moreno-Jimenez, 2010). The crossover of positive states has only been studied at the between-person level and extending investigations of crossover to the within-person level will allow researchers to ask interesting questions, such as whether a person feels more engaged by his work on days when his spouse is more engaged by her work.

It is worth noting that the model presented within Figure 45.1 concerns the spillover and cross-over of positive affective states (e.g., mood, emotion, satisfaction, engagement), also referred to collectively as well-being. As such, the model does not explicitly address the process by which resources other than positive affective states gained in one role (e.g., skills, perspectives, social capital) benefit another role. We believe focusing on affective states is appropriate when examining variation within people that takes place over a relatively short time period (e.g., across days). Crouter (1984) suggested that the spillover of affective states is an episodic, dynamic phenomenon, whereas other forms of spillover (e.g., skill-based) take place more slowly over long time periods.

Antecedents of Positive Affective Spillover

As described earlier, stable work characteristics are antecedents of a person's general level of work-to-family enrichment. In contrast, positive work events and experiences are more theoretically relevant antecedents when studying daily fluctuations in work-to-family positive spillover and enrichment (Ilies, Schwind, & Heller, 2007). According to affective events theory (AET; Weiss & Cropanzano, 1996), positive occurrences at work (e.g., receiving recognition for a job well done) generate positive affect and other indicators of well-being, which represent individual enhancement (path A). The relationship between work events and subsequent well-being has been supported empirically

at the within-person level of analysis (e.g., Miner, Glomb, & Hulin, 2005). The spillover portion of the model stipulates that well-being at work, in turn, positively predicts well-being at home (path B). Affective states can persist throughout the day, traversing the work–home boundary. This path has been well-supported in experience sampling studies that correlate daily well-being measures obtained at work (i.e., affect and satisfaction) with measures of well-being at home later in the day (Heller & Watson, 2005; Ilies, Wilson, & Wagner, 2009; Judge & Ilies, 2004; Williams & Alliger, 1994). For example, Ilies and colleagues (2009) examined whether job satisfaction reported during the day by 101 university employees predicted their positive affect, as rated by their spouses, later the same night. Analyses showed that employees were more likely to arrive home in a positive, energized state on days when they felt highly satisfied by their job than on days when they had low job satisfaction.

Several studies have examined the link between work events or experiences and spillover (paths A and B combined). Ilies, Keeney, and Scott (2011) found that positive affect at work served as a mediator of the relationship between positive work events and well-being at home (i.e., job satisfaction assessed at nighttime). Studies using self-report measures of WFE also support the notion that work experiences are relevant antecedents of daily fluctuations in spillover. Sanz-Vergel et al. (2010) found that people report higher WFE on days when they experience recovery after breaks at work, and Butler et al. (2005) found that the opportunity to control one's work and utilize a high level of skill was a significant predictor of daily WFE.

Work–Family Interpersonal Capitalization

Although affective spillover is often conceptualized as a passive and unintentional process (Edwards & Rothbard, 2000; Greenhaus & Powell, 2006; Wayne, 2009), evidence suggests that individuals play an active role in regulating and maintaining their affective states (Bryant, 1989). As described above, people are likely to experience boosts in well-being after the occurrence of positive events at work, which do linger for some time and extend to the home environment. However, these effects can and will eventually dissipate (Suh, Diener, & Fujita, 1996), unless a person makes deliberate attempts to preserve or savor them. The construct of *savoring* has been introduced to capture how individuals mindfully attend to and appreciate positive events or experiences (Bryant, 1989; Bryant & Veroff, 2007).

This behavior has also been referred to as *capitalization* (Langston, 1994) as individuals are capitalizing on or taking advantage of the already positive effects of the events. In theory, savoring or capitalizing on positive events is thought to prolong or intensify their effects. We suggest that capitalization is an intentional, behavioral mechanism that partially accounts for the spillover of positive affective states between work and home.

One manner in which people frequently capitalize on positive events is by recounting them to close others (Bryant & Veroff, 2007; Langston, 1994; Gable et al., 2004). We have adopted the term *interpersonal capitalization* to refer to the process of disclosing positive events to others, and *work–family interpersonal capitalization* to reflect a situation where the domain in which an event occurs differs from the domain in which it is disclosed (Ilies, Keeney, & Scott, 2011). An example is when a person excitedly arrives home from work with good news (e.g., manuscript acceptance) to share with his or her spouse. Interpersonal capitalization on positive events has been shown to result in incremental prediction of positive affect and satisfaction, above and beyond the effects of positive events themselves (Gable et al., 2004; Hicks & Diamond, 2008; Ilies et al., 2010, Langston, 1994). Whereas the majority of research on interpersonal capitalization has focused on the sharing of events in general, Ilies et al. (2011) focused specifically on the sharing of positive work events with spouses. They found that—independent of how many positive work events had been experienced and the valence of the most positive work event that day—sharing the most positive work event with one's spouse was positively associated with job satisfaction reported at night. Thus, path C in the model, linking interpersonal capitalization on positive work events to well-being at home has some initial empirical support.

Research on interpersonal capitalization has stressed the importance of how one's partner responds to the sharing of a positive event (Gable et al., 2004, 2006; Maisel, Gable, & Strachman, 2008). People pay attention to others' reactions to their disclosures in order to gauge the appropriateness (e.g., too strong? too weak?) of their own affective response (Taylor, Buunk, & Aspinwall, 1990). Thus, one may calibrate one's own affective state based on the perceived responsiveness of one's partner, experiencing even greater positive affect if one's partner is especially enthused. Perceived responsiveness also has important implications for relationship satisfaction. Intimacy involves listening and understanding

(Prager, 2000). To the extent that a partner responds supportively, the person doing the sharing should experience greater psychological closeness and relationship satisfaction. In support of path D, several studies have found a positive relationship between the responsiveness of an individual's partner when disclosing a positive event and individual well-being (Gable et al., 2004, 2006; Ilies et al., 2011).

Crossover of Positive Affective States

All of the processes described thus far concern the well-being of Partner A. Whereas spillover captures an intraindividual phenomenon in which affective states are transferred across domains, crossover refers to an interindividual phenomenon in which affective states are transferred across people. An emerging area of research is represented by spillover–crossover models, which focus on the mechanisms by which one's work ultimately affects the well-being of one's intimate partner (e.g., Bakker, Demerouti, & Dollard, 2008). Crossover can be defined as "the process that occurs when the psychological well-being experienced by one person affects the level of well-being of another person" (Bakker & Demerouti, 2009, p. 220). Crossover is an important addition to the study of spillover, because it is one process-level explanation for how individuals' experiences in one domain (e.g., work or family) can not only enrich their experiences in a different domain, but can also enrich the experiences of close others in the recipient domain (e.g., coworkers or family members). This integrated perspective brings us closer to the concept of *facilitation*, in which not only an individual but also an entire system benefits from positive work–family dynamics (Wayne et al., 2007).

Crossover was first defined and studied as the process by which a person's strain leads to the strain of a closely related person (Bolger, DeLongis, Kessler, & Wethington, 1989; Westman, 2001). The majority of crossover research has thus focused on the transmission of negative states, most commonly between intimate partners. A variety of strain symptoms have been investigated including stress, dissatisfaction, negative emotions and mood, burnout, depression, poor physical health, and work–family conflict (Westman, Brough, & Kalliath, 2009). Several mechanisms are thought to be responsible for negative crossover (Bakker, Westman, & van Emmerik, 2009). First, negative states can be transmitted directly between partners due to empathy experienced in response to a partner's distress. *Empathy* refers to the process of interpreting the emotional state of another person and experiencing similar feelings (Barsade, 2002; Gruen & Mendelsohn, 1986). One partner expresses negative emotions (or other symptoms of his or her distress), and the listening partner identifies with these emotions and feels them as if they are his or her own. Second, negative states can be transmitted directly from one partner to another through a process of *emotional contagion*. Whereas empathy requires some level of consciousness, emotional contagion is considered to be relatively nonconscious and automatic. People tend to mimic their partners' fleeting emotional expressions (e.g., facial expression, voice, and posture) and begin to feel what their partners feel (Hatfield, Cacioppo, & Rapson, 1993). Third, negative states can be transmitted indirectly through interaction between partners. The strained spouse may be withdrawn, hostile, withhold social support, and engage in social undermining (i.e., criticism and behavior intended to thwart the partner's goals). Finally, it should be noted that an apparent crossover of negative states can be due to spurious effects—common stressors experienced by both partners.

Relevant to the focus of this chapter, Westman (2001) argued that the notion of crossover should be expanded to include positive states as well. At least three studies have examined positive crossover effects of work engagement between intimate partners. Bakker, Demerouti, and Schaufeli (2005) and Bakker and Demerouti (2009) found bidirectional effects of one partner's work engagement on the other partner's work engagement, controlling for both demands and resources on the job and at home. Westman, Etzion, and Chen (2009) found that business travelers' work vigor was positively related to their spouses' work vigor. Additionally, one study has examined the crossover of positive states between coworkers. Carlson, Ferguson, Kacmar, Grzywacz, and Whitten (2011) found that the work-to-family enrichment of supervisors crossed over onto the work-to-family enrichment of their subordinates.

The types of mechanisms postulated to account for the crossover of positive states (see Bakker et al., 2005) largely mirror those for negative crossover. The crossover of positive states between Partners A and B is captured by three distinct processes, depicted in Figure 45.1, that correspond to the major mechanisms for crossover, which are elaborated upon below.

First, on days when Partner A chooses to discuss a positive work event (i.e., interpersonal capitalization), a transference of positive states may occur as Partner B empathizes with his partner's experience. The happiness of one becomes "shared" when the listener is able to live vicariously, or is reminded of aspects of one's own job that generate similar, positive feelings. Partner B's empathic response should positively influence his or her own well-being (path E). One study provides direct support for this idea, showing that listening to one's partner recount his or her most positive event of the day was associated with higher positive affect at the end of the day for the listener (Hicks & Diamond, 2008). However, this study examined positive events in general (i.e., not specific to work), and partners mutually participated in some of the events that were included in the study. Other support comes from Bakker and Demerouti (2009), who found evidence that empathy plays a role in the crossover of work engagement; crossover from women to men was greater to the extent that the men were higher in trait perspective taking.

Second, Partner B may benefit from the positive affective state of Partner A through an automatic process of emotional contagion (i.e., the direct effect of Partner A's well-being on Partner B's well-being, shown by path F). This mechanism of crossover is differentiated from interpersonal capitalization because it does not rely on verbal communication about a positive event. Simply being around another person and observing his or her facial expression, mannerisms, and verbal intonation can be enough to trigger mimicry of these same behaviors. Once a person engages in mimicry, they begin to feel similarly, although at first they may not be aware of the affective transformation. There is evidence that people pick up on one another's positive affective states just as easily as they do negative states (e.g., Barsade, 2002). Larson and Almeida (1999, p. 5) suggest emotional contagion is best demonstrated when "events or emotions in one family member's immediate experience show a consistent, predictive relationship to subsequent emotions or behaviors in another family member." There is a small but growing literature in which a person's positive affective states are used to predict later positive affective states of his or her partner (e.g., Butner, Diamond, & Hicks, 2007). In one of the only studies to examine positive spillover and crossover, Song, Foo, and Uy (2008) found that positive mood spilled over from work to home, and then from one partner to another.

Third, positive states can be transmitted indirectly to Partner B through Partner A's social behaviors in the family domain (paths G and H).

Positive affective states at home may influence two primary categories of social behavior. When people are high in positive affective states, they are more likely to engage in positive interactions with their partners. Positive affect is associated with increased energy and activity (Watson, 2000). Partner A should engage in more frequent and positive interactions with Partner B on days when he or she arrives home after a satisfying day at work. In support of this idea, people have been found to engage in more social activities with their families on days when they have higher positive affective spillover from work (Ilies et al., 2007). Additionally, because positive affect is associated with increased prosocial behavior (Watson, 2000), positive work-to-home spillover may lead to the provision of more social support to partners. Aspinwall (1998) posited that a high level of pleasant affective states reduces one's self-focus and therefore frees resources for helping others. Bakker et al. (2005) explained, for example, that individuals experiencing high positive affect are more likely to help with household chores, putting their spouse in a better mood and freeing his or her own resources.

Conclusion

From the empirical evidence reviewed, it should be clear that rich resources are derived from work and family roles. What we suggest the field could most benefit from is a more dynamic consideration of the antecedents of WFE and how resources are transferred across domains. The model in Figure 45.1 was used to help organize a summary of findings relevant to the spillover and crossover of positive affective states. However, the model also brings to light some areas where researchers can make meaningful contributions.

Future Directions

To begin, although paths A and B have been tested in prior empirical research, one important question that remains is to determine what aspects of positive work events are most relevant for facilitating well-being and subsequent work-to-family spillover. Extant research and theory demonstrate that the frequency, intensity, and perceived importance of these events contribute independently to positive affective states (De Longis, Coyne, Dakof, Folkman, & Lazarus, 1982; Miner, Glomb, & Hulin, 2005; Weiss & Cropanzano, 1996). However, other features of events deserve attention, such as the extent to which they fulfill fundamental psychological needs (e.g., competency, relatedness, and autonomy;

Reis, Sheldon, Gable, Roscoe, & Ryan, 2000; Warner & Hausdorf, 2009). Some evidence suggests that events that meet basic psychological needs are particularly satisfying (Sheldon, Elliot, Kim, & Kasser, 2001). Consistent with the findings of Butler et al. (2005) described earlier, Zautra and Reich (1980) found that people had more intense and longer-lasting affective reactions to events that required their control and competence. Future work can focus on identifying the types of work experiences that generate the lasting positive affective states that employees ultimately bring home with them. Positive organizational scholars have already outlined some experiences that seem to be relevant in this regard (e.g., task focus, exploration, heedful relating; Spreitzer et al., 2005).

Research is needed in which positive spillover and crossover are examined within the same study. The within-individual spillover of positive states (i.e., from work to home, or vice versa) is a prerequisite for the between-individual crossover of these states (i.e., between spouses or coworkers) or, stated more succinctly, "first spillover, then crossover" (Bakker, Westman, & van Emmerik, 2009, p. 207). However, spillover and crossover have rarely been examined together. Research demonstrating crossover of work engagement from one spouse to another, for example, has not conclusively established that this state first originates in the workplace and then manifests itself at home (i.e., spillover). Studying the process from beginning to end should help validate the mediated relationships that are implied by spillover–crossover models.

Future studies should better elucidate the mechanisms responsible for the spillover and crossover of positive affective states. It has often been assumed that spillover occurs automatically, with no action on the part of individuals, an assumption that manifests itself in the lack of attention paid by researchers to more intentional processes. Furthermore, the negative crossover literature offers several theoretical explanations for crossover effects, but these have yet to withstand empirical testing for positive crossover. We described one process—interpersonal capitalization on positive events—that provides a behavioral explanation for both positive spillover and crossover. Telling one's spouse about positive events and experiences at work can have beneficial effects for oneself as well as for one's spouse. The well-being of the listening spouse is affected primarily by how he or she responds to the positive event disclosure or, more specifically, the degree of empathy he or she experiences. The perceived responsiveness of the listener, in turn, has implications for the well-being of the person doing the sharing. Although empathy has traditionally been associated with commiserating, research on interpersonal capitalization shows that empathy can also take the very different form of shared joy.

Whereas past studies have measured interpersonal capitalization in an all-or-none fashion (Gable et al., 2004, 2006; Ilies et al., 2010), future research would benefit from a richer assessment of this phenomenon. What characteristics of interpersonal capitalization impact its effectiveness? In other words, what are its boundary conditions? In addition to assessing whether a positive event is shared and how the listener responds, of potential interest is whether the event is mentioned in passing or discussed extensively (i.e., duration of interpersonal capitalization). It is possible that simply bringing up the event is sufficient to rekindle its associated positive feelings. Also of interest is the intensity of emotion with which it is shared and whether it is shared in person. Intensity of emotion can be conveyed even in today's world of technology-mediated communication; people who are happy or excited, for example, produce more words and exchange messages at a faster rate (Hancock, Gee, Ciaccio, & Lin, 2008).

To fully understand the spillover–crossover of positive affective states requires both well-developed theory and evidence regarding the mechanisms that underlie these processes. In addition to empathic response, the other two mechanisms that have been found to account for negative crossover (i.e., emotional contagion, social behavior) also provide solid starting points for researchers to begin their investigations of positive crossover. Although some research supports the idea that behavior in the home is a mediating mechanism between spillover and crossover (e.g., Ilies et al., 2007), this mechanism has yet to be formally tested.

Although the model presented in the latter half of this chapter focuses on work-to-family spillover and crossover between family members, we mentioned that a similar process may operate in reverse. We encourage researchers to more thoroughly consider the positive impact of family life on work life and whether the same mechanisms can explain the family-to-work direction of spillover and crossover of well-being between coworkers. It is quite possible that the extent to which workers discuss the positive aspects of their family lives has implications for their well-being at work.

Although the focus of this chapter is on the positive dynamics between work and family, we recognize that individuals are involved in a variety of nonwork domains including but not limited to family (e.g., friendships, leisure, health). There have been numerous calls to widen the focus of work–family research to be more inclusive in this regard (Bellavia & Frone, 2005; Carlson & Kacmar, 2000; Crooker, Smith, & Tabak, 2002; Sturges & Guest, 2004). These calls are well overdue, as Marks (1977) and Sieber (1974) described the benefits that come from occupying a myriad of roles several decades ago. One recent study suggests that participating in certain activities outside of work, such as hobbies and exercise, provide unique resources (e.g., skills, energy) that make one a better worker (Weer et al., 2010). Moving from WFE to work–life enrichment is a promising avenue for future research.

We began this chapter recognizing that the work–family conflict perspective could be supplemented by an appreciation of how the work and family roles benefit one another. The proliferation of constructs reflecting the positive interface between work and family provides some confirmation that a focus on the negative was truly providing an incomplete picture. Work in particular has been viewed mostly as a source of stress and has been underappreciated for the variety of psychological and material resources that it provides. Ironically, without the income provided by work, many individuals would not be able to afford the lifestyles and activities with which their work interferes. Putting things into perspective is a key strength of positive organizational scholarship. We hope that some of the ideas we have presented within this chapter stimulate research that helps to build a more well-balanced view of work–family dynamics.

References

Allen, T.D., Herst, D.E.L., Bruck, C.S., & Sutton, M. (2000). Consequences associated with work-to-family conflict: A review and agenda for future research. *Journal of Occupational Health Psychology, 5*, 278–308.

Aspinwall, L.G. (1998). Rethinking the role of positive affect in self-regulation. *Motivation and Emotion, 22*, 1–32.

Bakker, A.B., & Demerouti, E. (2009). The crossover of work engagement between working couples: A closer look at the role of empathy. *Journal of Managerial Psychology, 24*, 220–236.

Bakker, A.B., Demerouti, E., & Dollard, M.F. (2008). How job demands affect partners' experience of exhaustion: Integrating work-family conflict and crossover theory. *Journal of Applied Psychology, 93*, 901–911.

Bakker, A.B., Demerouti, E., & Schaufeli, W.B. (2005). The crossover of burnout and work engagement among working couples. *Human Relations, 58*, 661–689.

Bakker, A.B., Westman, M., & van Emmerik, I.J.H. (2009). Advancements in crossover theory. *Journal of Managerial Psychology, 24*, 206–219.

Barsade, S.G. (2002). The ripple effect: Emotional contagion and its influence on group behavior. *Administrative Science Quarterly, 47*, 644–675.

Bellavia, G.M., & Frone, M.R. (2005). Work-family conflict. In J. Barling, E.K. Kelloway, & M.R. Frone (Eds.), *Handbook of work stress*. Thousand Oaks, CA: Sage Publications.

Baumeister, R.F., Bratslavsky, E., Finkenauer, C., & Vohs, K.D. (2001). Bad is stronger than good. *Review of General Psychology, 5*, 323–370.

Bolger, N., DeLongis, A., Kessler, R., & Wethington, E. (1989). The contagion of stress across multiple roles. *Journal of Marriage and the Family, 51*, 175–183.

Boyar, S.L., & Mosley, D.C. (2007). The relationship between core self evaluations and work and family satisfaction: The mediating role of work-family conflict and facilitation. *Journal of Vocational Behavior, 71*, 265–281.

Bryant, F.B. (1989). A four-factor model of perceived control: Avoiding, coping, obtaining and savoring. *Journal of Personality, 57*, 773–797.

Bryant, F.B., & Veroff, J. (2007). *Savoring: A new model of positive experience*. Mahwah, NJ: Lawrence Erlbaum Associates.

Butler, A.B., Grzywacz, J.G., Bass, B.L., & Linney, K.D. (2005). Extending the demands-control model: A daily diary study of job characteristics, work-family conflict and work-family facilitation. *Journal of Occupational and Organizational Psychology, 78*, 155–169.

Butner, J., Diamond, L.M., & Hicks, A.M. (2007). Attachment style and two forms of affect coregulation between romantic partners. *Personal Relationships, 14*, 431–455.

Carlson, D.S., Ferguson, M., Kacmar, M.K., Grzywacz, J.G., & Whitten, D. (2011). Pay it forward: The positive crossover effects of supervisor work-family enrichment. *Journal of Management, 37*, 770–789.

Carlson, D.S., & Kacmar, K.M. (2000). Work-family conflict in the organization: Do life role values make a difference? *Journal of Management, 26*, 1031–1054.

Carlson, D.S., Kacmar, K.M., Wayne, J.H., & Grzywacz, J.G. (2006). Measuring the positive side of the work-family interface: Development and validation of a work-family enrichment scale. *Journal of Vocational Behavior, 68*, 131–164.

Crooker, K.J., Smith, F.L., & Tabak, F. (2002). Creating work-life balance: A model of pluralism across life domains. *Human Resource Development Review, 1*, 387–419.

Crouter, A.C. (1984). Spillover from family to work: The neglected side of the work-family interface. *Human Relations, 37*, 425–442.

DeLongis, A., Coyne, J.C., Dakof, G., Folkman, S., & Lazarus, R.S. (1982). Relationship of daily hassles, uplifts, and major life events to health status. *Health Psychology, 1*, 119–136.

Edwards, J.E., & Rothbard, N.P. (2000). Mechanisms linking work and family: Clarifying the relationship between work and family constructs. *Academy of Management Review, 25*, 178–199.

Friedman, S.D., & Greenhaus, J.H. (2000). *Work and family– Allies or enemies? What happens when business professionals confront life choices*. New York: Oxford Press.

Gable, S.L., Gonzaga, G.C., & Strachman, A. (2006). Will you be there for me when things go right? Supportive responses to positive event disclosures. *Journal of Personality and Social Psychology, 9*, 904–917.

Gable, S.L., Reis, H.T., Impett, E.A., & Asher, E.R. (2004). What do you do when things go right? The intrapersonal and interpersonal benefits of sharing positive events. *Journal of Personality and Social Psychology, 87*, 228–245.

Greenhaus, J.H., & Powell, G.N. (2006). When work and family are allies: A theory of work-family enrichment. *Academy of Management Review, 31*, 72–92.

Gruen, R.J., & Mendelsohn, G. (1986). Emotional responses to affective displays in others: The distinction between empathy and sympathy. *Journal of Personality and Social Psychology, 51*, 609–614.

Grzywacz, J.G., & Butler, A.G. (2005). The impact of job characteristics on work-to-family facilitation: Testing a theory and distinguishing a construct. *Journal of Occupational Health Psychology, 10*, 97–109.

Grzywacz, J.G., & Marks, N.F. (2000). Reconceptualizing the work-family interface: An ecological perspective on the correlates of positive and negative spillover between work and family. *Journal of Occupational Health Psychology, 5*, 111–126.

Hammer, L.B., Cullen, J.C., Neal, M.B., Sinclair, R.R., & Shafiro, M. (2005). The longitudinal effects of work-family conflict and positive spillover on depressive symptoms among dual-earner couples. *Journal of Occupational Health Psychology, 10*, 138–154.

Hancock, J.T., Gee, K., Ciaccio, K., & Lin, J.M. (2008). I'm sad you're sad: Emotional contagion in CMC. *Proceedings of the ACM Conference on Computer-Supported Cooperative Work*, 295–298.

Hanson, G.C., Hammer, L.B., & Colton, C.L. (2006). Development and validation of a multidimensional scale of perceived work-family positive spillover. *Journal of Occupational Health Psychology, 11*, 249–265.

Hatfield, E., Cacioppo, J.T., & Rapson (1993). Emotional contagion. *Current directions in psychological science, 2*, 96–99.

Heller, D., & Watson, D. (2005). The dynamic spillover of satisfaction between work and marriage: The role of time and mood. *Journal of Applied Psychology, 90*, 1273–1279.

Hicks, A.M., & Diamond, L.M. (2008). How was your day? Couples' affect when telling and hearing daily events. *Personal Relationships, 15*, 205–228.

Ilies, R., Keeney, J., & Scott, B. (2011). Work-family interpersonal capitalization: Sharing positive work events at home. *Organizational Behavior and Human Decision Processes, 114*, 115–126.

Ilies, R., Schwind, K.M., & Heller, D. (2007). Employee well-being: A multilevel model linking work and nonwork domains. *European Journal of Work and Organizational Psychology, 16*, 326–341.

Ilies, R., Wilson, K.S., & Wagner, D.T. (2009). The spillover of daily job satisfaction onto employees' family lives: The facilitating role of work-family integration. *Academy of Management Journal, 52*, 87–102.

Judge, T.A., & Ilies, R. (2004). Affect and job satisfaction: A study of their relationship at work and at home. *Journal of Applied Psychology, 89*, 661–673.

Kirchmeyer, C. (1992). Nonwork participation and work attitudes: A test of scarcity vs. expansion models of personal resources. *Human Relations, 45*, 775–792.

Langston, C.A. (1994). Capitalizing on and coping with daily-life events: Expressive responses to positive events. *Journal of Personality and Social Psychology, 67*, 1112–1125.

Larson, R.W., & Almeida, D.M. (1999). Emotional transmission in the daily lives of families: A new paradigm for studying family processes. *Journal of Marriage and the Family, 61*, 5–20.

Maisel, N.C., Gable, S.L., & Strachman, A. (2008). Responsive behaviors in good times and in bad. *Personal Relationships, 15*, 317–338.

Marks, S.R. (1977). Multiple roles and role strain: Some notes on human energy, time, and commitment. *American Sociological Review, 42*, 921–936.

McNall, L.A., Nicklin, J.M., & Masuda, A.D. (2010). A meta-analytic review of the consequences associated with work-family enrichment. *Journal of Business and Psychology, 25*(3), 381–396.

Miner, A.G., Glomb, T.M., & Hulin, C. (2005). Experience sampling mood and its correlates at work. *Journal of Occupational and Organizational Psychology, 78*, 171–193.

Prager, K.J. (2000). Intimacy in personal relationships. In C. Hendrick, & S.S. Hendrick (Eds.), *Close relationships: A sourcebook* (pp. 229–242). Thousand Oaks, CA: Sage.

Reis, H.T., Sheldon, K.M., Gable, S.L., Roscoe, J., & Ryan, R.M. (2000). Daily well-being: The role of autonomy, competence, and relatedness. *Personality and Social Psychology Bulletin, 26*, 419–435.

Sanz-Vergel, A.I., Demerouti, E., Moreno-Jimenez, B., & Mayo, M. (2010). Work-family balance and energy: A day-level study on recovery conditions. *Journal of Vocational Behavior, 76*, 118–130.

Sheldon, K.M., Elliot, A.J., Kim, Y., & Kasser, T. (2001). What is satisfying about satisfying events? Testing 10 candidate psychological needs. *Journal of Personality and Social Psychology, 80*, 325–339.

Sieber, S.D. (1974). Toward a theory of role accumulation. *American Sociological Review, 39*, 567–578.

Song, Z., Foo, M., & Uy, M.A. (2008). Mood spillover and crossover among dual-earner couples: A cell phone event sampling study. *Journal of Applied Psychology, 93*, 443–452.

Spreitzer, G., Sutcliffe, K., Dutton, J., Sonenshein, S., & Grant, A.M. (2005). A socially embedded model of thriving at work. *Organization Science, 16*, 537–549.

Sturges, J., & Guest, D. (2004). Working to live or living to work? Work/life balance early in the career. *Human Resource Management Journal, 14*, 5–20.

Suh, E., Diener, E., & Fujita, F. (1996). Events and subjective well-being: Only recent events matter. *Journal of Personality and Social Psychology, 70*, 1091–1102.

Sumer, H.C., & Knight, P.A. (2001). How do people with different attachment styles balance work and family? A personality perspective on work-family linkage. *Journal of Applied Psychology, 86*, 653–663.

Taylor, S.E., Buunk, B.P., & Aspinwall, L.G. (1990). Social comparison, stress, and coping. *Personality and Social Psychology Bulletin, 16*, 74–89.

Tiedje, L.B., Wortman, C.B., Downey, G., Emmons, C., Biernat, M., & Lang, E. (1990). Women with multiple roles: Role-compatibility perceptions, satisfaction, and mental health. *Journal of Marriage and the Family, 52*, 63–72.

van Steenenbergen, E.F., & Ellemers, N. (2009). Is managing the work-family interface worthwhile? Benefits for employee health and performance. *Journal of Organizational Behavior, 30*, 617–642.

van Steenenbergen, E.F., Ellemers, N., & Mooijaart, A. (2007). How work and family can facilitate each other: Distinct types of work-family facilitation and outcomes for women and men. *Journal of Occupational Health Psychology, 12*, 279–300.

Voydanoff, P. (2004). The effects of work demands and resources on work-to-family conflict and facilitation. *Journal of Marriage and Family, 66*, 398–412.

Warner, M.A., & Hausdorf, P.A. (2009). The positive interaction of work and family roles: Using need theory to further understand the work-family interface. *Journal of Managerial Psychology, 24*, 372–385.

Watson, D. (2000). *Mood and temperament*. New York: Guilford Press.

Wayne, J.H. (2009). Reducing conceptual confusion: Clarifying the positive side of work and family. In D.R. Crane, & E.J. Hill (Eds.), *Handbook of families and work: Interdisciplinary perspectives*. New York: University Press of America.

Wayne, J.H., Grzywacz, J.G., Carlson, D.S., & Kacmar, K.M. (2007). Work-family facilitation: A theoretical explanation and model of primary antecedents and consequences. *Human Resource Management Review, 17*, 63–76.

Wayne, J.H., Randel, A.E., & Stevens, J. (2006). The role of identity and work-family support in work-family enrichment and its work-related consequences. *Journal of Vocational Behavior, 69*, 445–461.

Wayne, J.H., Musisca, N., & Fleeson, W. (2004). Considering the role of personality in the work-family experience: Relationships of the big five to work-family conflict and facilitation. *Journal of Vocational Behavior, 64*, 108–130.

Weer, C.H., Greenhaus, J.H., & Linnehan, F. (2010). Commitment to nonwork roles and job performance: Enrichment and conflict perspectives. *Journal of Vocational Behavior, 76*, 306–316.

Weiss, H.M., & Cropanzano, R. (1996). Affective events theory: A theoretical discussion of the structure, causes, and consequences of affective experiences at work. *Research in Organizational Behavior, 18*, 1–74.

Westman, M. (2001). Stress and strain crossover. *Human Relations, 54*, 717–751.

Westman, M., Brough, P., & Kalliath, T. (2009). Expert commentary on work-life balance and crossover of emotions and experiences: Theoretical and practice advancements. *Journal of Organizational Behavior, 30*, 587–595.

Westman, M., Etzion, D., & Chen, S. (2009). Crossover of positive experiences from business travelers to their spouses. *Journal of Managerial Psychology, 24*, 269–284.

Williams, K.J., & Alliger, G.M. (1994). Role stressors, mood spillover, and perceptions of work-family conflict in employed parents. *Academy of Management Journal, 37*, 837–868.

Zautra, A., & Reich, J. (1980). Positive life events and reports of well-being: Some useful distinctions. *American Journal of Community Psychology, 8*, 657–670.

PART 6

Positive Organizational Practices

The Generative Potency of Cultural Symbols

Implications for Positive Organizational Scholarship

Mary Ann Glynn *and* Lee Watkiss

Abstract

In this chapter, we explore the affinities between cultural symbols and positive organizational scholarship at the collective level of analysis. Drawing on the extant literature, we advance a conceptual framework that outlines three mechanisms by which symbols can have generative potency (i.e., the capability to enrich collective strengths, virtues, and capabilities in organizations). These mechanisms are: cognitive (meaning-making), affective (experienced emotions), and relational (collective connectedness). We advance ideas for future research that might probe the complexities of this process, particularly the relationships among these mechanisms, the potency of different forms of cultural symbols, and the contextual contingencies that affect symbolic potency.

Keywords: Symbols, generativity, mechanisms

Five score years ago, a great American, in whose symbolic shadow we stand today, signed the Emancipation Proclamation. This momentous decree came as a great beacon light of hope to millions of Negro slaves who had been seared in the flames of withering injustice. It came as a joyous daybreak to end the long night of captivity. (King, 1963)

The time has come to reaffirm our enduring spirit; to choose our better history; to carry forward that precious gift, that noble idea passed on from generation to generation: the God-given promise that all are equal, all are free, and all deserve a chance to pursue their full measure of happiness. (Obama, 2009)

Reverend King and President Obama, in their speeches and in their persons, exemplify the generative potency of symbols—the capability to enrich collective strengths, virtues, and capabilities; in turn, such "life building, capability enhancing" processes (Dutton & Glynn, 2008, p. 694) can lead to positive outcomes such as vitality, thriving, or resilience (Cameron, Dutton, & Quinn, 2003). The generative potency of symbols is evident in the King and Obama speeches, particularly through the meaning-making and emotionality of their rhetoric and their exhortation to the American people to leave behind "the long night of captivity" and,

instead, "choose our better history" and "a chance to pursue happiness."

In many ways, these glimpses of rhetoric are suggestive of how symbolic vehicles like meanings, beliefs, language, stories, and leaders are carriers of cultural resources. Resources, generally speaking, are "forms of wealth" that have economic, social, or emotional value (Rousseau & Ling, 2007, p. 374); moreover, collective resources have the capability to bind together a community and enlarge possibilities for collective action (Swidler, 1986). The cultural symbols that carry these can encode the negative as well as the positive. This is evident, for instance, in

King's juxtaposition of "a great beacon light of hope" against the "flames of withering injustice," an antithesis that yields a vision of a more hopeful future. Here, we highlight the positive features of cultural symbols, focusing on their potential to affect desired, valued, or positive outcomes for a collective or organization. Such potential is evident in the confident rhetoric of Obama, urging that Americans "carry forward that precious gift." We seek to link the symbolic realm of organizational life to positive organizational scholarship (POS), a link that is suggested in this chapter's illustrative opening quotes.

In this chapter, we aim to understand the role of cultural symbols in enlarging collective capacities and in enabling positive outcomes in organizations. Our work is a response to the call that "organizational researchers should consider ways in which symbols enrich the organizational processes that contribute to collective organizing" (Dutton, Worline, Frost, & Lilius, 2006, p. 67). Among the primary "ways" through which symbols accomplish this, we propose, is by engaging a set of cognitive, relational, and affective mechanisms that enable forward "progress and momentum" and positive outcomes (Spreitzer, Sutcliffe, Dutton, Sonenshein, & Grant, 2005, p. 547).

A symbol can be "anything that represents a conscious or an unconscious association with some wider, usually more abstract, concept or meaning" (Hatch, 1993, p. 669). Symbols, generally speaking, convey meanings that go beyond their intrinsic or functional use to express the beliefs, emotions, or identity of the collective (e.g., Dandridge, Mitroff, & Joyce, 1980; Gioia, 1986; Morgan, Frost, & Pondy, 1983). In organizations, symbols can be viewed as "visible, physical manifestations of organizations and indicators of organizational life" that are experienced as real and as having significant organizational consequences (Rafaeli & Worline, 2000, p. 73). Symbols can take any number of forms, including physical, behavioral, or verbal, as well as events, images, and people (Pfeffer, 1977; Trice & Beyer, 1984, 1993). In this chapter, we use the term *symbol* to refer to any of these possible forms.

The generative potency of symbols has been implied by a number of researchers who have explored various facets of organizational or collective phenomena. For instance, Dutton, Worline, Frost, and Lilius (2006) find that symbols, such as leaders' actions and caring stories, are configural in compassion organizing because they focus the community's attention, evoke people's emotions, ease respondents' coordination, foster members' trust, and enable organizational legitimacy. Quinn and Worline (2008) demonstrate that symbols are critical in shaping and mobilizing courageous collective action under the darkest of circumstances: a counterattack against hijackers aboard Flight 93 on September 11, 2001 (9/11). They show how collective action is predicated upon a set of narratives about the individuals involved, their situation, and their shared call to action. Moreover, Quinn and Worline (2008) reveal how these symbols function as resources that enable courage by helping passengers to manage emotions, frame meanings, and define their relationships to each other as part of a collective. In short, symbols are central to the social construction and realities of organizations.

Organizational scholars working in fields as diverse as organizational identity, institutions, entrepreneurship, and social networks have shown that symbols can generate positive outcomes. For instance, in her study of the musician's strike at a symphony orchestra, Glynn (2000) shows how symbols of artistic excellence (e.g., complex musical pieces) and of fiscal solvency (e.g., endowment growth) are deployed as resources in making claims about the organization's identity.

Institutionalists alert us to how symbols (and symbolic systems) in the forms of cognitive templates, normative rules, and formal structures are inherent in organizational action (Meyer & Rowan, 1977); moreover, organizational alignment with such institutional symbols enhances legitimacy which, in turn, can expand favorable resource flows (e.g., Lounsbury & Glynn, 2001). Glynn and colleagues (Glynn & Abzug, 2002; Glynn & Marquis, 2005) demonstrate that the choice an organization makes for its name is intrinsically linked to the external audience's perceptions of, and preferences for, the institutional conformity that enhances legitimacy.

Entrepreneurship scholars show that symbols, and particularly the stories that entrepreneurs tell, are critical in the acquisition of organizational resources and wealth creation (Lounsbury & Glynn, 2001; Martens, Jennings, & Jennings, 2007; Navis & Glynn, 2010). Zott and Huy (2007), in their study of entrepreneurial ventures in the United Kingdom, demonstrate that different types of symbolic action—personal credibility, professional organizing, organizational achievement, and the quality of stakeholder relationships—conveyed by entrepreneurs shape different forms of legitimacy during the acquisition of these resources.

Ansell (1997) shows how even abstract ideas about a workers' "strike" function as "'condensation symbols'—symbols that condense meaning and thereby evoke an emotional response (p. 372)"— representing a potent meaning that integrated and connected a diverse set of workers. Furthermore, symbols have been shown to be powerful in linking together a loose set of actors around an issue to create community for a single event, such as the Olympic Games (Glynn, 2008), or for a 30-year project to improve the infrastructure of a large urban area (Hoffman, Krumholz, O'Brien, & Geyer, 2000). Across this diverse body of work, symbols have been shown to be a critical resource for organizations or collectives that can enable positive outcomes, even under conditions of adversity (e.g., Dutton et al., 2006; Glynn, 2000), uncertainty, or ambiguity (e.g., Lounsbury & Glynn, 2001; Martens et al., 2007; Zott & Huy, 2007). Taken together, these researchers offer preliminary evidence of the potency of symbols in collective engagement and organizing.

Building on these ideas, we focus on the underlying mechanisms that facilitate the generative potency of symbols. By using mechanism-based theorizing, we highlight explanations for *why* there is a relationship among symbols, generativity, and positive outcomes and *how* these processes work (Davis & Marquis, 2005). Two mechanisms broadly applicable to organizational phenomena, according to Davis and Marquis (2005, p. 336; drawing from McAdam, Tarrow, & Tilly, 2001, pp. 25–26) are: "*cognitive mechanisms* (which 'operate through alternations of individual and collective perception'), and *relational mechanisms* (which 'alter connections among people, groups, and interpersonal networks')." Given the prominence of emotions in accounts of symbolic processes and action (e.g., Dutton et al., 2006; Quinn & Worline, 2008), and drawing from Dutton and Glynn (2008), we also explore a third mechanism: *affective* or *emotional mechanisms* that evoke or elicit individual or collective feelings. Together, we propose that these three mechanisms—cognitive, relational, and affective— are the motors whereby symbols generate strengths and capabilities in organizations. In this chapter, we explicate this process.

Our contributions are twofold. First, we seek to contribute to the burgeoning POS literature by showing how symbols have generative potency in expanding collective capabilities and positive outcomes. Moreover, because we focus on the collective level, we complement more microperspectives that focus on individuals or psychological processes. Second, we seek to contribute to the literature on symbols by illuminating the mechanisms that underlie their functioning in organizations. Together, these contributions begin to expand the realm of the POS perspective and investigate a relatively unexplored aspect of symbols, their generative potency. We begin by reviewing the relevant literature on symbols in organizations and then theorize their link to the POS perspective. Next, we detail three focal mechanisms—cognitive, relational, and affective—whereby symbols have generative potency. Finally, we conclude with a discussion and directions for future research.

The Strength-building Capabilities of Organizational Symbols

Organizational symbolism refers to "those aspects of an organization that its members use to reveal or make comprehensible the unconscious feelings, images, and values that are inherent in that organization" (Dandridge et al., 1980, p. 77). Organizational symbols serve a variety of purposes that are both functional (Dandridge et al., 1980; Gioia, Thomas, Clark, & Chittipeddi, 1994; Heap & Roth, 1973; Murray, 1960; Pfeffer, 1981) and expressive (Ashforth, 1985; Cohen, 1985; Trice & Beyer, 1984). When organizational symbols are collectively shared, they create a common sense about what constitutes organizational reality and identity (Ashforth, 1985; Pfeffer, 1981). And, when this reality objectifies meaning in terms of everyday life (Verkuyten, 1995), while at the same time communicating the underlying emotions of the organization, the symbols become powerful influences (Ansell, 1997) that can persist over time.

Organizational symbols include a wide range of objects, events, speech–acts, and persons, as well as stories and myths, logos, ceremonies, and ritualized events, along with day-to-day affective and political life (Dandridge et al., 1980). The variety of symbols that can carry meaning is evident in our opening quotes; these include the event of the speech (e.g., presidential inauguration), rhetorical devices or language (e.g., imagery, antithesis, metaphors), cultural referents and resources (e.g., Lincoln's "symbolic shadow"), and the speakers themselves, who represent American ideology, aspiration, democracy, and the populace ("our enduring spirit").

By themselves, symbols have no inherent meaning, but rather, are understood, interpreted, and made sensible through figural actors, like King and Obama, as well as through the broader context in which they are embedded (Rafaeli & Worline, 2000), such as the public speeches on the Washington mall. Other researchers have highlighted the importance of interpretation in understanding the significance of symbols. For instance, Dutton and colleagues (2006) show that the mundane act of writing a check takes on greater significance when it is a spontaneous gesture by a leader—interrupting an annual speech he is delivering—to highlight the importance of "taking care of our own" when some in his community had, earlier in the day, lost all their belongings in a devastating fire. Glynn (2000) shows how a musician's cymbal becomes an assertive statement about professional ideology, while a concern for the bottom line becomes a utilitarian tool for administrators in the wake of an orchestral strike. Quinn and Worline (2008) demonstrate how a spouse's affirmation can symbolically define one's own identity under threat and provide the resources from which courageous action can be undertaken even in the midst of a terrorist attack. Like other resources, symbols are not static or scarce but "potentially varied, expansive, and emergent. Resources can be produced, unlocked, expanded or innovatively bricolaged via multiple organizing dynamics" (Dutton & Glynn, 2008, p. 695). Similarly, Pratt and Rafaeli (2001, p. 105) note the malleability of symbols: "Different communities may ascribe different meanings to physical symbols. Moreover, changes in a community can lead to changes in language."

The malleability of organizational symbols to construct and reconstruct organizational reality makes symbolic systems critical resources in organizations that can be used either to reinforce the status quo (Creed, DeJordy, & Lok, 2010) or animate organizational change (e.g., Gioia et al., 1994), with far-reaching consequences that include legitimacy (Cavanaugh & Prasad, 1994; Elsbach, 1994), resource infusions (e.g., Lounsbury & Glynn, 2001; Martens et al., 2007; Zott & Huy, 2007), and attention (Dutton et al., 2006). And, because symbols are resources themselves, they have the generative capacity to be assembled and reassembled creatively to enlarge the stock of resources and, in turn, enable organizational resourcefulness.

Resourcefulness is the use of any type of resource or series of resources that "can be activated by organizational structures, processes, systems, cultures or leaders to aid in the development of strengths and cultivation of flourishing" (Dutton & Glynn, 2008, p. 695). Fine (1996), in his studies of restaurant kitchens, demonstrates both the malleability and resourcefulness of symbols by showing that chefs use a variety of occupational rhetorics to define their work and their identities. Furthermore, Zott and Huy (2007) show that entrepreneurial symbolic action, such as those emphasizing a prestigious degree, the winning of awards, professional service, or the quality of relationships with key stakeholders, increases resource flows in new venture start-ups. More generally, entrepreneurial stories and storytelling can be an effective tool in securing and enlarging firm resources (Lounsbury & Glynn, 2001; Martens et al., 2007; Navis & Glynn, 2010). Taken together, this research, conducted across very different contexts, demonstrates the potent role of symbols (and symbolic action) in enabling organizational assets and enhancing the organizational capability for resourcefulness.

The generativity of symbols can also be triggered when actors have reason to reconsider their meaning. For instance, Christianson, Farkas, Sutcliffe, and Weick (2009) show how events, even disastrous ones like the collapse of the roof of the Baltimore & Ohio (B&O) Railroad Museum Roundhouse onto the world's most historic and comprehensive collection of American railroad equipment, can serve as symbols that trigger organizational learning, action, and recovery. Importantly, they demonstrate how it is the symbol of the past (and not simply the past) that serves as a resource that enables action in the present and the claiming of an identity that resonates symbolically with "who we were." Such legacy identities can persist over time, so as to energize collective identities and action (Walsh & Glynn, 2008). The links between the past and the future encoded in symbols attest to the role of resourcefulness in organizational resilience (Dutton et al., 2006).

This review of the relevant literature is indicative of the richness of the link between symbols and the POS perspective. Using theoretical and empirical analyses, in a diverse set of research settings, organizational scholars have demonstrated the critical role symbols can play in initiating, energizing, and enabling organizational resourcefulness and, in turn, positive outcomes for the organization as a whole. We now theorize three of the critical mechanisms that can explain *how* symbols have generative potency.

The Symbolic Mechanisms of Generative Potency

Drawing from theoretical accounts generally and POS specifically (e.g., Davis & Marquis, 2005; Dutton & Glynn, 2008), we focus on three mechanisms that explain symbols' generative potency: cognitive,

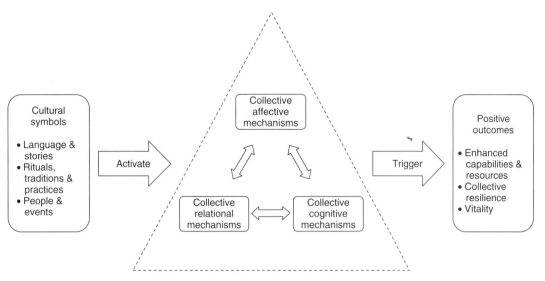

Fig. 46.1 Model of mechanisms underlying generative potency of cultural symbols.

relational, and affective. Cognitive mechanisms operate through changes in collective perceptions and understandings; relational mechanisms alter the social connections among members, groups, or networks in an organization; and affective mechanisms elicit, evoke, or shift collective feelings or emotions. We summarize these mechanisms in Figure 46.1 and discuss each in the following sections.

Symbols as Cognitive Mechanisms

Symbols function as cognitive mechanisms when they enable the construction of meaning, the articulation of understandings or causal beliefs, or the labeling and interpretation of events, actions, or persons. This occurs through perceptual processes of sense-making, interpretation, meaning-making, or other forms of cognition. Symbolic systems in organizations (e.g., rhetoric, artifacts, practices, labels, traditions, etc.) provide a structure by which people define the collective as well as themselves. To return to our earlier quotes, King's reference to the Emancipation Proclamation called forth a powerful symbol of America that reflected its core beliefs in freedom, the evils of slavery, and the rights of all citizens; similarly, Obama evoked collective understanding and acceptance of our "God-given promise that all men are equal." Thus, the choice of symbols, as well as the orator's highlighting of their positive meaning, activated cognitive understandings of the situation, the issues, and Americans' sense of national identity.

Symbols can encode positive meanings or "imbue stimuli with significance, implications, and consequences that imply something is good, desirable, or beneficial in some way" (Dutton & Glynn, 2008, p. 702). Although there has been extensive work by organizational scholars on symbols and meaning-making (e.g., Hatch, 1993; Meyer, 1984; Smith & Simmons, 1983; Trice & Beyer, 1984), only a few examples of scholarly attention relate symbols to positive meaning-making. Perry-Smith and Blum (2000), in their study of 527 firms across the United States, find that nonmandatory human resource policies can serve as positive symbols of organizational values for potential and current employees. Feldman and March's (1981) empirical study of information in organizations recognizes that symbols can represent organizational competence, have the power to affirm social virtue, and legitimize widely held values. Pratt and Rafaeli (1997) show how organizational members of a rehabilitation unit in a hospital used dress as a concrete and safe focus of communication to resolve a dispute pertaining to their unit's values and purpose, thereby reaffirming the role of symbolic acts in restoring harmony and shared values (Meyer, 1984). However, Bechky (2003) hints at the limits of such acts by showing how the diverse backgrounds and practices of engineers and assemblers at a Silicon Valley semiconductor company can reinforce differences among such subcommunities. In accordance with Fine's (1996) findings on the different use of occupational rhetorics among chefs, Bechky's work suggests that these differences are not inherently negative, and in many cases can be positive. Moreover, symbols at an even higher level of abstraction—condensation symbols (Ansell, 1997)—can bring together constituencies with different interests around a common meaning with which different types of actors can identify (e.g., Glynn, 2008).

Thus far, we have focused on a shared or a common meaning of symbols, perhaps implying that symbols are singular in their meaning. Clearly, this is not always the case. For instance, Turner (1967) reminds us that symbols can speak to different people in different ways, thereby having multiple layers of meaning. Such symbols, standing at the center of the relationship among actors, "are powerful precisely because of their multivocality and because of their metaphorical linkage between different levels of meaning" (Ansell, 1997, p. 373).

The positive meaning-making that can arise from symbols (and symbolic acts) is a resource that enables collective coping with traumatic events (e.g., Dutton et al., 2006; Quinn & Worline, 2008) and can decrease the ambiguity or uncertainty of organizational events (Dutton & Glynn, 2008); in turn, it can enable resilience. Goddard, LoGerfo, and Hoy's (2004) study of 96 high schools in a large Midwestern state suggests that when positive meanings are paired with perceived collective efficacy, improved organizational performance can result. More generally, positive meaning and interpretation are associated with increased capacities for action or resourcefulness (Dutton, 1993); one potential explanation for this is that positivity removes distractions, making it possible for people to see more clearly what the situation needs (Weick, personal communication, May 5, 2007).

Positive meanings may increase the appeal of an organization to diverse audiences and, in turn, strengthen members' identification and organizationally desirable behaviors (Elsbach & Glynn, 1996). For instance, Dutton, Dukerich, and Harquail (1994) show that the attractiveness of an organization's identity affects employee commitment and cooperation; greater cooperation can, in turn, cultivate collective capabilities that enable positive outcomes (Dutton & Glynn, 2008). For organizational newcomers, adjustment is harder in the absence of symbols that enable access to one's own past (Ibarra & Barbulescu, 2010) or, we speculate, to that of the organization's history.

To summarize, symbols can serve as cognitive mechanisms of generative potency because they offer wellsprings of positive meanings that function as resources to decrease uncertainty, increase attention, and bring together diverse (or potentially conflicting) interests. By drawing out members' commitment and cooperation, symbols can further strengthen the collective as a whole. Moreover, the positive meanings,

beliefs, aspirations, or values that symbols encode can define or affirm an organization's identity. Next, we turn to how symbols function as relational mechanisms.

Symbols as Relational Mechanisms

Symbols function as relational mechanisms when they enable structural, functional, or friendship connections among the members of a collective. To return to our opening excerpts from King and Obama, we observe a number of symbolic vehicles that foster relationships among the American people; these include symbolic language, particularly the use of the first person plural pronouns "we" and "our," as well as invoking the common values or ideology shared by Americans, such as "all are equal, all are free, and all deserve a chance to pursue their full measure of happiness." Such symbols create a sense of entitivity and identity for the collective, helping to define the bases of connectivity among members (Baker & Dutton, 2007), and forge common, positively valued ground among often disconnected people or groups. More generally, crafting a positive connection among people through symbolic vehicles "captures modes of interacting where the parties engaged experience their connection as mutual, trusting, respectful of other high quality attributes and they experience some form of mutual benefit" (Dutton & Ragins, 2006).

Physical symbols are particularly influential in shaping interrelationships among organizational members. Barley's (1983) study of funeral homes shows how funeral directors pose a corpse's features to imitate those of a sleeping person in order to put the deceased's family at ease and ensuring a smoothly flowing funeral. In turn, these relationships affect the meanings made (Trevino, Webster, & Stein, 2000) and the emotions felt.

In a study of people working in 212 organizations, across a wide variety of industries, with a wide range of experience and responsibility, Carmeli, Brueller, and Dutton (2009) find that, when these connections foster high quality relationships, they enlarge the emotional carrying capacity of a collective and enable it to withstand greater stress. Other studies have found that physical symbols are suited for enacting relationships within organizations (Pratt & Rafaeli, 2001). Elsbach (2004, p. 99) demonstrates that "individuals working in corporate office settings interpret office decor as indicators of their displayers' workplace identity" and that members' sense of belonging to their groups was affected by teams transitioning to nonterritorial work environments (Elsbach, 2003). Ashforth (1985) discovers that even something as seemingly innocuous as the seating arrangements in an office has effects on whether actors work cooperatively or competitively. These relationships are not necessarily based on shared self-interest but, rather, on the basis of shared symbols that encode priorities and structure relationships (Wolfe & Putler, 2002).

Symbols can function as mechanisms of community because artifacts enable communication and a shared sense of organizational reality, even when linguistic differences exist among communities; symbolic objects transform understandings to create common ground across occupational communities (Bechky, 2003). Physical symbols themselves constitute a language that can express and enact relationships among individuals and collectives (Pratt & Rafaeli, 2001).

In addition to enabling informational flows and communication, relationships can also carry emotions and energy that create patterns of connections among individuals and groups. Baker and Dutton (2007) show how relationships within organizations constitute a form of positive social capital that, in turn, increases access to, and combinatorial flexibility with, resources. Similarly, Glynn and Wrobel (2007) demonstrate how extraorganizational relationships, such as multigenerational family ties, can be used as symbols that suggest organizational expertise and legitimacy, often yielding positive social capital. Overall, positive relationships can build strengths and enable positive outcomes because they foster trust, legitimacy, and resource exchanges that build social, economic, and human capital (Aldrich & Fiol, 1994; Dutton & Glynn, 2008; Lounsbury & Glynn, 2001).

Relationships may be even more important under periods of social, cultural, or organizational transformation because they mark these eras, much as the content of the speeches of King and Obama signified. Swidler (1986, p. 279) proposes that symbols can be more causally powerful in contested cultural arenas because a symbolic vehicle like a ritual "reorganizes taken-for-granted habits and modes of experience. People . . . depend on cultural models to learn styles of self, relationship, cooperation, authority, and so forth." Such breaks from the habitual allow new combinations of resources that can expand collective strengths and capabilities.

In summary, symbols can function as relational mechanisms of generative potency when they enable communication, forge connections among intraorganizational persons and groups, and create a shared identity or a sense of "who we are as a collective." Symbolic vehicles such as language, artifacts, physical objects, and values can be effective relational mechanisms that increase resource capabilities and enable collective positive outcomes. Next, we turn to how symbols function as affective mechanisms.

Symbols as Affective Mechanisms

Symbols function as affective mechanisms when they elicit, excite, or evoke collective emotions or feelings. When these are positive, symbols express "short-term states of felt activation by individuals or collectives that are associated with a 'pleasantly subjective feel'" (Fredrickson, 1998, p. 300). Affective mechanisms are related to cognitive mechanisms in that both necessitate interpretation. For instance, in the weeks prior to 9/11, the American flag was flown as an everyday artifact whose emotional reach was often overlooked; however, the terrorist attacks on the World Trade Center towers that day reframed feelings about the U.S. flag to heighten emotionality and encourage pride of country by placing the symbol in storefronts, windows, and outside people's homes. Similarly, Dutton and colleagues (2006) demonstrate how a tragedy can elicit positive emotions in a collective. They found that a residential fire in which three members lost all their belongings evoked an outpouring of community caring, support, sympathy, and compassion; these resources, in turn, functioned to organize efforts by the collective to provide donations of money and household goods and to add an emotional dimension to the collective identity people shared.

To return to the speeches by King and Obama, we note how their language is often emotional, expressing hope, joy, and happiness. Moreover, when powerful leaders, like King and Obama, express positive emotion, those with less power typically experience positive emotion (Anderson, Keltner, & John, 2003); this tends to cultivate better performance by groups in tasks such as negotiation (Anderson & Thompson, 2004). Emotions, whether positive or negative, are propagated and diffused throughout a collective via processes of emotional contagion (e.g., Barsade, 2002), which in turn can lead to improved cooperation, decreased conflict, and increased perceived task performance. All of these tend to amplify mechanisms of positive organizing (Dutton et al., 2006).

Positive emotions also enlarge the resources available to the collective. Fredrickson (2003) formalized a broaden-and-build theory of positive emotions; she and Branigan (2005) theorize that positive emotions broaden the scope of attention and thought-action repertoires that expands the resources available. Moreover, the durable nature of these emotions provides a reserve of resources that can be drawn upon later (e.g., Fredrickson & Branigan, 2005; Rhee, 2006). Generally speaking, the expression of "collective joy," through symbolic rituals or celebrations tends to unify a group through strong affective ties forged by a "communal emotional connection" (Ehrenreich, 2007, p. 254).

To summarize, symbols can function as affective mechanisms of generative potency when they excite emotions that are positive; in turn, these tend to build emotional connections within a collective, and foster cooperation, creativity, and the expansion of collective resources and capabilities. We now discuss potential avenues for future research into the generative potency of cultural symbols.

Future Directions

In this chapter, we have tried to link the study of the symbolic realm with the POS perspective because we believe that there are mutual gains to be had. Positive organizational scholarship informs the study of symbols by highlighting symbols' generative potency to build strengths, enable resource flows and capacities, and facilitate positive outcomes. In turn, symbols enrich POS research because they provide a fulcrum for understanding the multilevel dynamics that connect cognitive, relational, and affective aspects of organizational life that can result in positive outcomes. Our articulation of three core mechanisms—cognitive, relational, and affective—provides a general framework for understanding these dynamics. However, we understand our work is but an initial foray into exploring these dynamics; more research is clearly warranted to understanding the nuances of such processes. Here, we offer some ideas for future research.

Relationships Among the Three Symbolic Mechanisms

For clarity, we have treated the three mechanisms as if they were somewhat independent. In reality, we suspect that this is not the case. Rather, symbols may function as complex mechanisms that simultaneously involve cognitive, relational, and affective elements. Cognition has long been linked to emotions, albeit with some argument (e.g., Folkman, Lazarus, Dunkel-Schetter, DeLongis, & Gruen, 1986; Zajonic, 1968). As well, relationships may have their basis in shared understandings or emotions and are

difficult to disentangle from either of these. In addition, we have looked at cases in which the three mechanisms generally act in concert. But this may not always hold; clearly, there is the potential for these mechanisms to conflict with, or contradict, each other. For instance, to many Americans, the symbol of the fallen World Trade Center towers elicits not only strong negative emotions of anger, fear, and injustice, but also strong positive emotions of resolve and resilience. How these different and potentially conflicting elements come together in a symbol and impact its potency is an interesting area for exploration. Therefore, understanding the interactivity among the different mechanisms of generative potency awaits future scholarship.

Alternatively, researchers might investigate whether some mechanisms have greater potency than others. Social movement theorists have shown how collective emotion can fuel collective action, meaning, and connections (e.g., Davis, McAdam, Scott, & Zald, 2005). Activists who experience strong negative emotions of social injustice or inequality (not unlike those expressed by King and Obama) can leverage powerful emotions in the service of the collective good, by envisioning alternative, more positive states and mobilizing actors to achieve them. Furthermore, our discussion of the generative potency of cultural symbols raises several research questions, including: Is positive interrelating sufficient to enlarge resource capabilities? Is a collectively held meaning sufficient to mobilize large numbers of actors? Can positive emotions be sustained to achieve desired outcomes? These questions can shape research investigations into the "necessary and sufficient" conditions of activating all three mechanisms synergistically to fully realize the generative potency of symbols.

In addition, these questions beg consideration of all three mechanisms. In our reading of the literature on symbols, we found that the cognitive (meaning-making) and relational (mobilization) aspects of symbols have gotten relatively more attention than emotional capacities or effects.

Symbolic Forms

For the sake of parsimony, we have treated all symbolic forms as fairly similar and interchangeable; however, it is likely that some symbolic forms may be more potent than others or that the aggregation of symbolic forms may have a multiplicative effect. In reading the relevant literature, we observe that scholars have focused on certain types of symbolic forms over others. For instance, there is far more work on physical or tangible symbols, in forms such as artifacts, objects, or material space, as well as language and rhetoric, than there is on the symbolic forms of persons or events. Our examples of the speech acts of King and Obama hopefully illustrate how much potency exists in these relatively neglected forms of symbols. For example, Obama's act of delivering his Inaugural Address is likely a more potent symbol than the act of reading the printed text. The symbol of the person, the collective event, the values, feelings, and relationships expressed in his voice can together increase its impact and potency. How multiple forms of symbols can converge to enable (or disable) positivity is a key agenda item for future research.

Finally, we examined the generativity of symbols with fairly broad strokes and did not discriminate among different kinds of positive outcomes, such as resourcefulness, thriving, or resilience. Different symbolic vehicles—or different types of mechanisms—may be more or less associated with each of these. For instance, because resilience may require a sustained effort over a long period of time, perhaps more enduring or permanent symbols, such as tangible objects, may have greater potency. Christianson and colleagues (2009) show how the symbol of past acts of resilience fueled the resolve to rebuild the B&O Railroad Museum; these acts are represented in various artifacts that can be referenced at will to sustain ongoing efforts over time. More ephemeral symbols, such as a leader's appearance or cheerleading, may be less potent in sustaining such resolve over time. Correspondingly, however, engendering the resourcefulness to find a creative solution to an immediate problem might benefit from symbols that interject high levels of meaning or energy, but are brief in their duration; in this case, a leader's appearance or cheerleading may be more effective than a physical artifact in rousing ideas and emotions.

Contextual Contingencies of Symbols

As we have discussed, symbols do not have inherent meaning, but rather derive meaning from the contexts in which they are embedded and through the actors who interpret them. Thus, there is an implication that the potency of symbols, and their associated mechanisms, may vary with the contexts in which they are present. As we have noted, the symbol of the American flag changed in its generativity from pre- to post-events of 9/11. Similarly, Apple Computer's ability to stir strength-building capabilities in consumers and suppliers changed

markedly following the introduction of the iPhone in 2007. The iPhone symbolized the revolution in smart phone technology and resonated with the public in general and Apple's consumers in particular. During the launch of the iPad in 2010, this symbol of the past seemed to enable the sale of twice the number of iPads as iPhones in their respective first month of sales. Without the symbolic power of the post-iPhone Apple Computer, such vigorous sales of iPad may not have been possible.

Noting how different periods of time may be "settled" or "unsettled," Swidler (1986) shows how symbols function as different kinds of resources under these different kinds of contingencies. In "unsettled" periods of social transformation, for instance, symbols tend to be resourced in creative efforts, through the bricolage of existing elements or the propagation for new ones, to enable adaptation under changing circumstances. Conversely, in more "settled" periods, symbols tend to be resourced in order to maintain institutionalized values and beliefs that reinforce an ongoing, steady state of activity. Swidler (1986) suggests the importance of understanding the functioning of symbols as resources in response to critical contingencies. As well, such a perspective raises questions about how different types of symbolic forms may be more or less evident or potent in different contexts. For instance, the relative permanence of physical symbols may have enduring potency during settled times; as well, they may function as an important anchor in changing circumstances, acting as legacy symbols for generating possibilities and change.

Symbols may also be used as boundary objects that differentiate work and occupational contexts within organizations or fields. Researchers have shown how symbolic systems can reinforce these boundaries (e.g., Bechky, 2003; Fine, 1996); however, symbols do not only divide, they also construct bridges across these divides. We see this in the King and Obama rhetorics, exhorting unity where there had been division. Moreover, other scholars have suggested how symbols can bridge across different temporal periods and events (Christianson et al., 2009; Walsh & Glynn, 2008). Examining such a bridging function would afford a window on generativity that can enlarge the scope of the collective.

Conclusion

In this chapter, we explored the affinity between organizational symbols and POS dynamics and outcomes. Drawing from the relevant literatures, we outlined a rudimentary conceptual framework that shows how symbols have the generative potency to enable positive outcomes, such as resourcefulness, resilience, and thriving in organizations. Underlying this generative potency are three mechanisms—cognitive, relational, and affective—that furnish symbolic gears which can motor the achievement of positive states. Moreover, understanding the complexities of this process, the potency of different forms of symbols, and the contextual contingencies that affect symbolic potency are key areas that await future inquiry. Our hope is that our ideas provoke future research in these arenas and others.

References

Aldrich, H., & Fiol, C. (1994). Fools rush in? The institutional context of industry creation. *Academy of Management Review, 19*(4), 645–670.

Anderson, C., Keltner, D., & John, O. (2003). Emotional convergence between people over time. *Journal of Personality and Social Psychology, 84*(5), 1054–1068.

Anderson, C., & Thompson, L. (2004). Affect from the top down: How powerful individuals' positive affect shapes negotiations. *Organizational Behavior and Human Decision Processes, 95*(2), 125–139.

Ansell, C.K. (1997). Symbolic networks: The realignment of the french working class, 1887–1894. *American Journal of Sociology, 103*(2), 359–390.

Ashforth, B. (1985). Climate formation: Issues and extensions. *Academy of Management Review, 10*(4), 837–847.

Baker, W., & Dutton, J. (2007). Enabling positive social capital in organizations. In J. Dutton, & B. Ragins (Eds.), *Exploring positive relationships at work: Building a theoretical and research foundation* (pp. 325–345). Mahwah, NJ: *Lawrence Erlbaum Associates.*

Barley, S. (1983). Semiotics and the study of occupational and organizational cultures. *Administrative Science Quarterly, 28*(3), 393–413.

Barsade, S.G. (2002). The ripple effect: Emotional contagion and its influence on group behavior. *Administrative Science Quarterly, 47*(4), 644–675.

Bechky, B. (2003). Sharing meaning across occupational communities: The transformation of understanding on a production floor. *Organization Science, 14*(3), 312–330.

Cameron, K., Dutton, J., & Quinn, R. (2003). *Positive organizational scholarship: Foundations of a new discipline.* San Francisco: Berrett-Koehler Publishers.

Carmeli, A., Brueller, D., & Dutton, J. (2009). Learning behaviours in the workplace: The role of high-quality interpersonal relationships and psychological safety. *Systems Research and Behavioral Science, 26*(1), 81–98.

Cavanaugh, J., & Prasad, P. (1994). Drug testing as symbolic managerial action: In response to "A case against workplace drug testing." *Organization Science, 5*(2), 267–271.

Christianson, M., Farkas, M., Sutcliffe, K., & Weick, K. (2009). Learning through rare events: Significant interruptions at the Baltimore & Ohio railroad museum. *Organization Science, 20*(5), 846–860.

Cohen, A. (1985). *The symbolic construction of community.* Chichester, UK: Ellis Horwood Publishers.

Creed, DeJordy, R., & Lok, J. (2010). Being the change: Resolving institutional contradiction through identity work. *Academy of Management Journal, 53*(6), 1336–1364.

Dandridge, T., Mitroff, I., & Joyce, W. (1980). Organizational symbolism: A topic to expand organizational analysis. *Academy of Management Review, 5*(1), 77–82.

Davis, G., & Marquis, C. (2005). Prospects for organization theory in the early twenty-first century: Institutional fields and mechanisms. *Organization Science, 16*(4), 332–343.

Davis, G., McAdam, D., Scott, W., & Zald, M. (Eds.). (2005). *Social movements and organization theory.* New York: Cambridge University Press.

Dutton, J. (1993). The making of organizational opportunities: An interpretive pathway to organizational change. *Research in Organizational Behavior, 15*, 195–195.

Dutton, J., Dukerich, J., & Harquail, C. (1994). Organizational images and member identification. *Administrative Science Quarterly, 39*(2), 239–263.

Dutton, J., & Glynn, M. (2008). Positive organizational scholarship. In C. Cooper, & J. Barling (Eds.), *The SAGE handbook of organizational behavior* (pp. 693–712). London: Sage Publications, Ltd.

Dutton, J., & Ragins, B. (2006). *Exploring positive relationships at work: Building a theoretical and research foundation.* Mahwah, NJ: Lawrence Erlbaum.

Dutton, J., Worline, M., Frost, P., & Lilius, J. (2006). Explaining compassion organizing. *Administrative Science Quarterly, 51*(1), 59–96.

Ehrenreich, B. (2007). *Dancing in the streets: A history of collective joy.* New York: Henry Holt.

Elsbach, K. (1994). Managing organizational legitimacy in the California cattle industry: The construction and effectiveness of verbal accounts. *Administrative Science Quarterly, 39*(1), 57–88.

Elsbach, K. (2003). Relating physical environment to self-categorizations: Identity threat and affirmation in a non-territorial office space. *Administrative Science Quarterly, 48*(4), 622–654.

Elsbach, K. (2004). Interpreting workplace identities: The role of office decor. *Journal of Organizational Behavior, 25*(1), 99–128.

Elsbach, K., & Glynn, M. (1996). Believing your own "PR": Embedding identification in strategic reputation. *Advances in Strategic Management, 13*, 65–90.

Feldman, M., & March, J. (1981). Information in organizations as signal and symbol. *Administrative Science Quarterly, 26*(2), 171–186.

Fine, G.A. (1996). Justifying work: Occupational rhetorics as resources in restaurant kitchens. *Administrative Science Quarterly, 41*(1), 90–115.

Folkman, S., Lazarus, R., Dunkel-Schetter, C., DeLongis, A., & Gruen, R. (1986). Dynamics of a stressful encounter: Cognitive appraisal, coping, and encounter outcomes. *Journal of Personality and Social Psychology, 50*(5), 992–1003.

Fredrickson, B. (1998). What good are positive emotions? *Review of General Psychology, 2*, 300–319.

Fredrickson, B. (2003). Positive emotions and upward spirals in organizations. In K. Cameron, J. Dutton, & R. Quinn (Eds.), *Positive organizational scholarship: Foundations of a new discipline* (pp. 163–175). San Francisco: Berrett-Koehler Publishers.

Fredrickson, B., & Branigan, C. (2005). Positive emotions broaden the scope of attention and thought-action repertoires. *Cognition & Emotion, 19*(3), 313–332.

Gioia, D. (1986). Symbols, scripts, and sensemaking: Creating meaning in the organizational experience. In H.P. Sims & D.A. Gioia, *The Thinking Organization: Dynamics of Organizational Social Cognition* (49–74). San Francisco: Jossey-Bass.

Gioia, D., Thomas, J., Clark, S., & Chittipeddi, K. (1994). Symbolism and strategic change in academia: The dynamics of sensemaking and influence. *Organization Science, 5*(3), 363–383.

Glynn, M.A. (2000). When cymbals become symbols: Conflict over organizational identity within a symphony orchestra. *Organization Science, 11*(3), 285–298.

Glynn, M.A. (2008). Configuring the field of play: How hosting the Olympic games impacts civic community. *Journal of Management Studies, 45*(6), 1117–1146.

Glynn, M.A., & Abzug, R. (2002). Institutionalizing identity: Symbolic isomorphism and organizational names. *Academy of Management Journal, 45*(1), 267–280.

Glynn, M.A., & Marquis, C. (2005). Fred's Bank: How institutional norms and individual preferences legitimate organizational names. In A. Rafaeli & M. Pratt (Eds.), *Artifacts and organizations: Beyond mere symbolism* (pp. 223–240). Mahwah, NJ: Lawrence Erlbaum Associates.

Glynn, M., & Wrobel, K. (2007). My family, my firm: How familial relationships function as endogenous organizational resources. In J. Dutton, & B. Ragins (Eds.), *Exploring positive relationships at work: Building a theoretical and research foundation* (pp. 307). Mahwah, NJ: Lawrence Erlbaum Associates.

Goddard, R., LoGerfo, L., & Hoy, W. (2004). High school accountability: The role of perceived collective efficacy. *Educational Policy, 18*(3), 403–425.

Hatch, M. (1993). The dynamics of organizational culture. *Academy of Management Review, 18*(4), 657–693.

Heap, J.L., & Roth, P.A. (1973). On phenomenological sociology. *American Sociological Review, 38*(3), 354–367.

Hoffman, S., Krumholz, N., O'Brien, K., & Geyer, B. (2000). How capital budgeting helped a sick city: Thirty years of capital improvement planning in Cleveland. *Public Budgeting & Finance, 20*(1), 24–37.

Ibarra, H., & Barbulescu, R. (2010). Identity as narrative: Prevalence, effectiveness, and consequences of narrative identity work in macro work role transitions. *Academy of Management Review, 35*(1), 135–154.

King, M.L. (1963). *I have a dream*. Retrieved August 21, 2010, from http://www.americanrhetoric.com/speeches/mlki haveadream.htm.

Lounsbury, M., & Glynn, M. (2001). Cultural entrepreneurship: Stories, legitimacy, and the acquisition of resources. *Strategic Management Journal, 22*(6/7), 545–564.

Martens, M.L., Jennings, J.E., & Jennings, P.D. (2007). Do the stories they tell get them the money they need? The role of entrepreneurial narratives in resource acquisition. *Academy of Management Journal, 50*(5), 1107–1132.

McAdam, D., Tarrow, S., & Tilly, C. (2001). *Dynamics of contention*: Cambridge, UK: Cambridge University Press.

Meyer, A. (1984). Mingling decision making metaphors. *Academy of Management Review, 9*(1), 6–17.

Meyer, J., & Rowan, B. (1977). Institutionalized organizations: Formal-structure as myth and ceremony. *American Journal of Sociology, 83*(2), 340–363.

Morgan, G., Frost, P., & Pondy, L. (1983). Organizational symbolism. In L.R. Pondy, P.J. Frost, G. Morgan, & T.C. Dandridge (Eds.), *Organizational symbolism* (pp. 3–35). Greenwich, CT: JAI Press.

Murray, H. (1960). Introduction. *Myth and mythmaking*. New York: George Braziller.

Navis, C., & Glynn, M. (2010). How new market categories emerge: Temporal dynamics of legitimacy, identity, and entrepreneurship in satellite radio, 1990–2005. *Administrative Science Quarterly, 55*(3), 439–471.

Obama, B. (2009). Presidential inaugural address. Retrieved August 21, 2010, from *http://www.america.gov/st/usg-english/2009/January/20090120130302abretnuh0.2991602.html*.

Perry-Smith, J., & Blum, T. (2000). Work-family human resource bundles and perceived organizational performance. *Academy of Management Journal, 43*(6), 1107–1117.

Pfeffer, J. (1977). The ambiguity of leadership. *Academy of Management Review, 2*(1), 104–112.

Pfeffer, J. (1981). Management as symbolic action: The creation and maintenance of organizational paradigms. *Research in Organizational Behavior, 3*(1), 1–52.

Pratt, M., & Rafaeli, A. (1997). Organizational dress as a symbol of multilayered social identities. *Academy of Management Journal, 40*(4), 862–898.

Pratt, M., & Rafaeli, A. (2001). Symbols as a language of organizational relationships. *Research in Organizational Behavior, 23*, 93–132.

Quinn, R., & Worline, M. (2008). Enabling courageous collective action: Conversations from United Airlines Flight 93. *Organization Science, 19*(4), 497.

Rafaeli, A., & Worline, M. (2000). Symbols in organizational culture. In N.M. Ashkanasy, C.P. M. Wilderom, & M.F. Peterson (Eds.), *Handbook of organizational culture and climate* (pp. 71–84). Los Angeles: Sage.

Rhee, S.-Y. (2006). *Shared emotions and group effectiveness: The role of broadening-and-building interactions*. Paper presented at the Academy of Management Proceedings.

Rousseau, D., & Ling, K. (2007). Commentary: Following the resources in positive organizational relationships. *In* J.E. Dutton, & B.R. Ragins (Eds.), *Exploring positive relations at work: Building a theoretical and research foundation* (pp. 373–384). Mahwah, NJ: Lawrence Erlbaum Associates.

Smith, K., & Simmons, V. (1983). A Rumpelstiltskin organization: Metaphors on metaphors in field research. *Administrative Science Quarterly, 28*(3), 377–392.

Spreitzer, G., Sutcliffe, K., Dutton, J., Sonenshein, S., & Grant, A.M. (2005). A socially embedded model of thriving at work. *Organization Science, 16*(5), 537–549.

Swidler, A. (1986). Culture in action: Symbols and strategies. *American Sociological Review, 51*(2), 273–286.

Trevino, L., Webster, J., & Stein, E. (2000). Making connections: Complementary influences on communication media choices attitudes, and use. *Organization Science, 11*(2), 163–182.

Trice, H., & Beyer, J. (1984). Studying organizational cultures through rites and ceremonials. *Academy of Management Review, 9*(4), 653–669.

Trice, H., & Beyer, J. (1993). *The cultures of work organizations*. Englewood Cliffs, NJ: Prentice Hall.

Turner, V. (1967). *The forest of symbols: Aspects of Ndembu ritual*. Ithaca, NY: Cornell University Press.

Verkuyten, M. (1995). Symbols and social representations. *Journal for the Theory of Social Behaviour, 25*(3), 263–284.

Walsh, I.J., & Glynn, M.A. (2008). The way we were: Legacy organizational identity and the role of leadership. *Corporate Reputation Review, 11*(3), 262–276.

Wolfe, R., & Putler, D. (2002). How tight are the ties that bind stakeholder groups? *Organization Science, 13*(1), 64–80.

Zajonic, R. (1968). Cognitive organization and processes. *International Encyclopedia of the Social Sciences, 15*, 615–622.

Zott, C., & Huy, Q.N. (2007). How entrepreneurs use symbolic management to acquire resources. *Administrative Science Quarterly, 52*(1), 70–105.

Resources, Resourcing, and Ampliative Cycles in Organizations

Martha S. Feldman *and* Monica Worline

Abstract

This chapter presents an overview of resourcing theory, comparing it with other perspectives such as resource dependence and the resource based view of the firm. After developing an understanding of the basic tenets of resourcing theory, the chapter goes on to explicate three mechanisms of resourcing in context that arise from recent empirical research and are likely to be of value to positive organizational scholars. The chapter concludes with an exploration of how the endogenous nature of resourcing and the potential for ampliative cycles can support positive spirals, a subject of vital interest to those studying positive organizational scholarship.

Keywords: Resources, practices, resourcing, organizational process, organizational change

Having resources is generally considered crucial for success in any context, and the study of resources has long had a central role in organizational scholarship. This focus on resources has given rise to several perspectives on organizations and organizing, such as resource dependence (Pfeffer, 1982; Pfeffer & Salancik, 1978), the resource-based view of the firm (Barney, 1991, 2001), dynamic capabilities realized through organizational processes (Eisenhardt & Martin, 2000; Teece, Pisano, & Shuen, 1997), and resourcing as an organizational process (Brickson & Lemmon, 2009; Feldman, 2004; Howard-Grenville, 2007; Quinn & Worline, 2008; Spreitzer, Sutcliffe, Dutton, Sonenshein, & Grant, 2005).

This chapter focuses primarily on resourcing as an organizational process because of its potential to contribute to positive organizational scholarship. Although it is in the nature of resources that they can be used for good or for evil (and often for both simultaneously), we argue that understanding the process of resourcing is a powerful tool for scholars and managers who want to promote positive spirals in organizations. Understanding the process of resourcing contributes to positive spirals in two ways. First, it enables managers and other organizational participants to understand how they can use the process endogenously to create ampliative cycles. *Ampliative* is a term that has been used primarily in logic and is based on the Latin verb meaning to enlarge. Webster's unabridged dictionary defines ampliative as: "Enlarging a conception by adding to that which is already known or received" (1998). Ampliative cycles enlarge the outcome of the process. Second, understanding the resourcing process can help managers and other organizational participants to separate the evaluation of the process from the evaluation of the outcome and thus promote attention not only to whether the process is ampliative but also to whether the outcome is desirable.

This chapter is organized around some central questions in the study of resources. The first section explores how resourcing theory influences our ideas about what constitutes a resource and how our actions create resources. The second section describes three mechanisms of resourcing that are commonly available in organizations and in everyday life. The third section explores ampliative cycles and positive outcomes. The chapter concludes with a discussion of some questions raised by resourcing theory that are important in the development of POS.

What Is Resourcing?

The most typical view of resources in organization theory, adopted in resource dependence theories (Pfeffer & Salancik, 1978) and in the resource-based view of the firm (Barney, 1991), imagines them as tangible or intangible assets that can be possessed or owned (Amit & Shoemaker, 1993; Barney, 1991; Penrose, 1959; Wang, 2009). This view suggests that resources are valuable because of some innate qualities contained within them. In keeping with this view, Eisenhardt and Martin (2000, p. 1107) define resources as "specific physical (e.g., specialized equipment, geographic location), human (e.g., expertise in chemistry), and organizational (e.g., superior sales force) assets that can be used to implement value creating strategies." The resource-based view of the firm argues that the innate qualities of resources are highly valuable: "competitive advantage derives from the resources and capabilities a firm controls that are valuable, rare, imperfectly imitable, and not substitutable" (Barney, Wright, & Ketchen, 2001, p. 625).

Resourcing theory defines resources differently. Feldman (2004) suggests that the typical view of resources hinders scholars' understanding of how resources are useful in organizations because it focuses on the innate features of assets, rather than how they are brought into use. Resourcing theory points to a definition of resources focusing on how organizational members take up and use assets as they pursue activities in line with what they wish to make happen in the world. This more expansive and less innate characterization leads to a new definition of a resource as anything that allows an actor to enact a schema (Feldman, 2004; Feldman & Orlikowski, forthcoming, Sewell, 1992).[1] This way of defining resources acknowledges that things have innate qualities (e.g., rocks are heavy) and that these qualities give them potential as resources (e.g., rocks can be used as building material). Resourcing theory emphasizes that, until action is taken to use these qualities, the thing does not fulfill its potential and become a resource, or what we refer to as a *resource in use* (e.g., rocks just sit there until people develop the ability to use rocks to build). Moreover, how the potential resource is used determines what kind of a resource it becomes or what is resourced (e.g., rocks can be used to build bridges and resource connections or to build fortresses and resource defense).[2]

Resourcing in "Real Life": Making Meatballs Without Meat

To illustrate the differences in these definitions of resources as possessing innate qualities versus resources as enacted through use, we invite you to engage in a thought experiment with us. Imagine you are a homemaker during World War II. You want to make meatballs for dinner, a favorite family meal. Because of the war, however, your family is working with ration points that allow you to purchase only a small amount of meat (see Cohen, 1991). Rationing ensures that there is not enough meat to make all the meatballs you need. What would you do next? Different theories of resources make different predictions about your behavior. Theories of resource dependence (Pfeffer & Salancik, 1978) might predict that the homemaker would skip making meatballs and make something else for the family meal, since meat is the key resource in meatballs and it is scarce.

In contrast with resource dependence, theories of dynamic capabilities (Eisenhardt & Martin, 2000; Teece et al., 1997) make a slightly different prediction. According to this body of theory, as a capable homemaker who is adapting to rationing, you might recognize that meatballs are a family favorite and therefore focus on accumulating rationing stamps in adaptable ways. Thus, you could serve meatballs, but less often, making them a rare and special treat for the family. This theory predicts that you can make meatballs during rationing, but only infrequently, after accumulating and leveraging resources in certain ways.

Theories of resourcing offer a third prediction, in part because this body of theory posits the relationship between resources and action as it is lived in practice. In this view, your cooking practices themselves provide an array of alternative actions for your use (de Certeau, 1984). Although it is true that you don't have meat, you do have bread. You do some experimenting with adding the bread to the meat. You toast it and crumble it and add bread crumbs to the meat in order to stretch it. You even add some new ingredients like tomato sauce to help preserve flavor. You make meatballs for the family meal— it just turns out that they don't contain much meat. But, in fact, your family likes these modified meatballs, maybe even more than they liked the originals.

Thus, theories of resourcing provide an explanation for how homemakers cooking under rationing were able to continue to serve meatballs regularly as a favorite family meal. Using everyday experience and experiments in cooking practices, they came up with new ways of making meatballs. Such experiments in practice are suggested in the historical record of the time, with governmental rationing boards offering ration-friendly recipes, *Good Housekeeping Magazine* printing a section on rationed foods in 1943, and a wartime edition of *The American Woman's Cook Book* offering recipes and advice for homemakers coping with rationing (Cohen, 1991). As theory focused on the relationship between asset and action, resourcing explains how different assets are taken up and put into use as new resources that enable homemakers to continue to enact the schema (or framework) of meatballs. The meatball story illustrates a number of ways in which redefining resources as related to practices affects our understanding of how resources are constituted.

THE ACTIVE TRANSFORMATION OF POTENTIAL RESOURCES INTO RESOURCES IN USE

Theories of resourcing posit that potential resources only become resources, or what we will term *resources in use*, when they are used to enact some schema or framework (Feldman, 2004). In the meatball story, bread was not initially related to the activity of making meatballs—it was not a resource in use to enact the meatball framework. By virtue of changes in their circumstances, however, and through practices of cooking that involved experimentation with different techniques, homemakers hit upon ways to incorporate bread into meatballs. In resourcing theory, it is these cooking practices that transformed bread from a potential resource to a resource in use. Emphasizing practices as central to resources is a unique and important aspect of theories of resourcing.

In the abstract, it may appear that by focusing on practices we may be creating an absurd situation in which anything can be defined as a resource. Although it is true that our approach may expand the range of potential resources, the connection to practice is in itself a boundary. Here again, our meatball example is useful. There are many things besides meat that can be used to create meatballs, but there are also many things that would not be potentially useful in making meatballs. Shards of glass, pellets of metal, or rat poison immediately jump to mind. We could put such things into meatballs, but it would stretch the limits of credibility to serve the result as a family meal. This suggests that the designation of resource is not just about the innate qualities of a material or nonmaterial asset, but about the nature of the relationship between the asset and what it helps to create. Rat poison does not help to create a family meal, and therefore is not a potential resource in the meatball framework.[3] In contrast to rat poison or shards of glass, however, we can think of many things (e.g., olives, hummus, tabouli) that could be put into meatballs and still help to create a family meal, even though they are not ordinarily associated with this food. These are what we refer to as *potential resources* because they could be taken up and put to use in creating meatballs. In other words, these potential resources could be turned into resources in use. The result would be a different kind of meatball that would nonetheless be a way of creating the family meal. In sum, then, resourcing theory suggests that potential resources become resources in use when they are taken up in enacting a framework. In this way, resourcing theory expands our focus from the innate qualities of things to include how those things are used (resourcing) and what they are used for (what is being resourced).

RESOURCING AS A DYNAMIC PROCESS

In showing meatballs as a metaphor for resourcing the family meal, we do not want to imply that frameworks exist independent of their enactment through resourcing. Indeed, our meatball story illustrates that the process is not one of matching two static objects (ingredients and meatballs), but of mutual adjustment between potential resources and emerging frameworks. In the meatball example, by incorporating bread into their meatballs, World War II-era homemakers did not just shift bread from a potential resource to a resource in use, they also changed the meatballs themselves. Families liked the "meatless" meatballs so much that homemakers turned the modified meatballs into a staple of family meals even after the war effort had ended. When the war ended and rationing was over, everyone had enough meat to go back to making meatballs without the bread, but few did. Stretching the meat during rationing has changed making meatballs, and meatballs themselves, for good.

RESOURCING CYCLES CAN BE ENDOGENOUS

Seeing the dynamic nature of resources as a key feature in the process of resource use leads to our final point about resourcing—that resourcing cycles can connect everyday actions to something larger, making them important in understanding complex organizing dynamics. In our meatballs example, what seems like a relatively simple action, adding bread to meat, and the resulting resource of a "meatless meatball" is actually tied to a much larger organizing effort of supporting the war effort. Figure 47.1 shows a collage of images from the World War II era that make an explicit link between daily home activities, such as cooking, and victory in the broader war effort. One war poster urged families to change their eating patterns to support the war effort by proclaiming: "Be patriotic, sign your country's pledge to save the food." In this way, cooking meatballs without meat becomes linked to something larger than the family meal. Meatless meatballs aren't simply an effort to feed the family, but also become part of the broader organizing to support the war effort. As shown in Figure 47.1, new ways of resourcing family life became an important part of government efforts to direct resources to the war effort.

Other ways of reducing the use of meat (not making meatballs or making them infrequently) would also serve the needs of the country. Being able to reduce the use of meat in a way that produced a popular food, however, contributes to a sense of being able to overcome obstacles, whether the obstacle is scarce meat or enemies of the state. Although making meatballs with little meat was only a small part of the war effort, that homemakers could use their practices on the home front was a significant enough contribution to prompt General MacArthur to write an encouraging preface to the *Victory Cookbook*.[4]

Comparing the Resourcing View with Other Approaches to Resources

We have used the description of homemakers making meatballs under rationing to accomplish two aims. Our first aim was to introduce the main concepts from theories of resourcing and demonstrate them in use. Our second aim was to set the stage for a comparison of the conceptualization of resources across different theoretical views. In this section, we draw those comparisons out more fully.

Figure 47.2 depicts the similarities, differences, and interconnections between three approaches to understanding resources: theories of resource dependence (e.g., Pfeffer, 1982; Pfeffer & Salancik, 1978), theories of dynamic capabilities that arise from a resource-based view of the firm (e.g., Barney, 2001; Eisenhardt & Martin, 2000; Teece, Pisano, & Shuen, 1997), and theories of resourcing (e.g., Feldman, 2004; Howard-Grenville, 2007; Quinn & Worline, 2008). The left column of Figure 47.2

Fig. 47.1 Rationing changes the relationship between resources, family cooking practices, and the broader war effort. Image Source: http://www.ameshistoricalsociety.org/exhibits/events/rationing.htm.

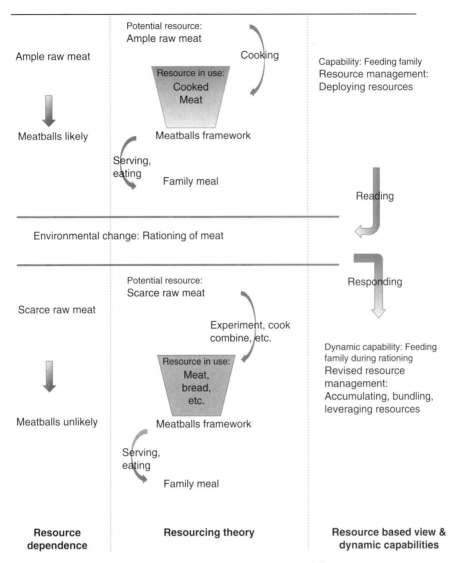

Ample raw meat

Potential resource:
Ample raw meat

Cooking

Capability: Feeding family
Resource management:
Deploying resources

Resource in use:
Cooked
Meat

Meatballs likely

Meatballs framework

Serving,
eating

Family meal

Reading

Environmental change: Rationing of meat

Responding

Scarce raw meat

Potential resource:
Scarce raw meat

Experiment, cook
combine, etc.

Resource in use:
Meat,
bread,
etc.

Dynamic capability: Feeding
family during rationing
Revised resource
management:
Accumulating, bundling,
leveraging resources

Meatballs unlikely

Meatballs framework

Serving,
eating

Family meal

**Resource
dependence**

Resourcing theory

**Resource based view &
dynamic capabilities**

Fig. 47.2 Three theoretical perspectives on meatball story.

conveys the main assumptions about resources that stem from theories of resource dependence. Particularly notable in this theory is the primary assumption that the ability to accomplish something (e.g., making meatballs) depends on the availability of particular resources (e.g., meat). Following this assumption, approaches to explanations that adopt the resource dependence view posit competition for scarce resources and the cessation of activity when those resources are absent. Thus, the prediction from a resource dependence view that, without meat, meatballs become scarce and unlikely as the family meal.

The right column of Figure 47.2 conveys the main ideas about resources that follow from resource-based views of the firm, and especially the

dynamic capabilities approach that emerges from the resource-based view. The resource-based view suggests that the organization, system, or firm (in this case the family) possesses resources as assets with innate qualities that make them valuable because they allow for certain kinds of capabilities (in this case, meat is a resource that allows homemakers to feed the family). In this theoretical view, when the environment changes, the resources available to the organization or firm (e.g., family) are also altered, and the organization must read the environment and understand it well enough to respond with appropriate resource management (Sirmon, Hitt, & Ireland, 2007). Organizations that successfully adapt to the changed resource environment exhibit a dynamic capability (Eisenhardt &

Martin, 2000); in this case, the dynamic capability is feeding the family during rationing. From this theoretical perspective, we might understand variation in the success of families eating under rationing by specifying that successful families engage in actions like accumulating, stabilizing, or mobilizing assets such as meat in order to structure, bundle, or leverage their resources (Sirmon, Hitt, & Ireland, 2007). Beyond these actions in relation to the environment, though, we would not necessarily be able to explain much about how the capability is created or enacted in the family.

The middle column of Figure 47.2 depicts resourcing theory. The figure helps make the distinctions between the theoretical perspectives clear by placing them in side-by-side comparison. Figure 47.2 conveys the uniqueness of resourcing theory in that it portrays the significance of specific actions that people (or sometimes machines) take in the organization or firm that enable a dynamic capability. In our example, people took actions to create potential resources and undertook experiments in practice that allowed them to move new assets from potential resources to resources in use to make meatballs. These microprocesses underlie the production of the capability and produce variations in outcomes; in this case, a family meal with meatballs with an Italian flavor (with tomato and onion) or our hypothetical Lebanese meatball with tabouli and hummus. By focusing on specific action and the transformation of potential resources into resources in use, resourcing theory not only reveals microprocesses that remain invisible in the other perspectives, but also turns attention to the changes in practice that lie behind innovations, changes that would be observed as outcomes from the resource-based view.

Although action is either implicit or explicit in all of the theories described in Figure 47.2, each of the theories reveals a different focus on the relationship between resources and action. Resource dependence theories (in the left column) see the taking of actions as dependent on the availability of resources with specific innate qualities. Resource-based views of the firm and dynamic capabilities in organizations (in the right column) posit actions at the level of the organization or firm that affect the availability of resources. Firms accumulate, bundle, and leverage resources to respond to environmental uncertainty (Sirmon, Hitt, & Ireland, 2007). Because the resource-based view emphasizes actions of the firm to respond to demands of the external environment, this theory tends to focus on the role of managers as agents who work on behalf of the firm. Thus, it is mostly managerial or executive action that is of consequence (e.g., Sirmon et al., 2007).

The focus of resourcing theory, by contrast, is on actions in organizations (specific, identifiable actions taken by specific people (or sometimes machines, such as computers) at specific times and places) rather than the actions of organizations in relation to their environments. This focus broadens the emphasis to actors throughout an organization by emphasizing practices as a way of understanding how a firm accomplishes outcomes. This broadens the explanatory power of resourcing theory in relation to practices and experiments in practice that emerge from the "bottom up" to generate change in organizations. Resourcing theory reveals that these practices have endogenous dynamics—they differ according to the ways in which people in organizations engage in them—that are consequential for the development of the practice and for understanding the microdynamics of production.

Mechanisms of Resourcing

Regardless of their view of the essence of resources, most organizational theories agree that it is hard to do much of anything without them—in other words, resources must be put to use. In the prior section, we established that theories of resourcing are likely to consider a broad range of actions as consequential in relation to resources. We also showed that these actions are likely to be oriented toward the microdynamics of productivity and relevant to internal organizational processes. In this section, we build on those assumptions to flesh out an important conceptual move in resourcing theory: the transition from potential resources to resources in use. The question of how potential resources become resources in use reveals action as key to the way in which resources are taken up and become valuable (Feldman, 2004; Goldsworthy, 2010; Howard-Grenville, 2007; Quinn & Worline, 2008; Feldman & Quick, 2009).

To illustrate the central role of action in generating the value of resources as they are taken up and used, we draw upon research related to three resourcing mechanisms in organizations. We find these three mechanisms important for POS scholars for two reasons: First, they emerge from the broad domain of recent POS research as empirically based examples of resourcing theory and how it explains the relationship of resources and action; second, they illustrate the potential of resourcing theory to expand organizational scholars' views of the relationship between resources and action. In this section, we review these three specific mechanisms and how they unfold in context, showing the relationship of action to potential resources and resources in use. These specific mechanisms help illustrate ways that resourcing contributes to the development of internal organizational capabilities (broadly defined) and constitutes process in relation to significant outcomes. These mechanisms are illustrative, but are not an exhaustive set. We feel confident that many other mechanisms are likely to emerge as scholars engage in research that combines resourcing theory and POS.

Mutual Adjusting As a Mechanism for Resourcing

A focus on the move from potential resource to resource in use makes clear that simply having something available doesn't mean it will be taken up and used. In addition, resourcing theory helps make clear that how something is taken up and used impacts the available frameworks for organizing. Thus, resourcing offers a view into a recursive relationship between a resource in use and the framework it energizes. Mutual adjusting as a resourcing mechanism helps illuminate the link between resources in use and frameworks for organizing by showing how potential resources and frameworks are adjusted to one another in the context of practice. This mechanism operates in contrast with matching—an activity in which one static concept is compared to another. In doing matching, we might think of a hammer and the need to build a house. We ask: "Does this tool match the job I need to do?" When the answer is affirmative, as, for instance, when we need to pound nails, we would use the tool. Otherwise it would sit idle. Contrast this with the notion of mutual adjusting, in which both the tool and the framework for its use are mutually adjusting to one another in ways that give rise to new potential resources.

The concept of mutual adjusting as a mechanism for resourcing is developed in an organizational context by Jaquith (2009), who describes the ways that teachers identify, take up, and use instructional resources in school contexts. Jaquith calls this process "fitting" instructional resources to their context for use, and makes clear that fitting resources to contexts involves an ongoing, recursive relationship between the resource in use and the framework that the resource is energizing. Jaquith suggests that teachers employ a combination of their sense of the

instructional purpose, the content of their lessons, the structure of their schools or classrooms, and the nature of their participants to fit or adjust instructional resources to the framework of student learning. Jaquith's study suggests that mutual adjusting as a mechanism for resourcing in organizations is likely to involve agentic actors who evaluate, compare, and fit potential resources with their unique purposes, knowledge, existing structures, and relationships to shape the resource in use and the frameworks that they want to energize.

As an example of mutual adjusting as a mechanism for resourcing, Jaquith (2009) describes how teachers take up and use tools for generating classroom participation to energize a community of learners in the classroom. "Equity sticks" are a tool created by instructional designers in which teachers write each student's name on a wooden stick, similar to a Popsicle stick, and draw sticks at random as a way of passing the floor. Equity sticks became useful for teachers to attempt to create fair distributions of turn-taking in their classrooms. Jaquith explores how equity sticks became a resource that was relatively easy for teachers to take up and use, showing that teachers adjust the use of the equity sticks to their particular classrooms in active and agentic ways that take into account their purposes, the content of their lessons, and characteristics of their students. For instance, teachers may begin using equity sticks with what they think of as "low-stakes" participation—questions that students find easy to answer from their own experience—as a way of energizing safety and support in the classroom community.

Jaquith's teachers hint that the example can be expanded. For instance, this low-stakes participation and the safety and support it generates becomes a potential resource. Teachers can take up and use the safety and support in a variety of ways, including using the equity sticks differently to facilitate different learning processes. The teacher might draw a stick and ask that student multiple questions to help engage critical thinking. Once this critical thinking becomes available as a potential resource in the classroom, along with safety and support, the students and teachers may then adjust their use of the equity sticks again, perhaps dividing the large bundle of sticks into small bundles as a way to form discussion groups that resource learning through conversation and peer-to-peer interaction. As peer relationships and peer-based conversation become potential resources in the classroom, the small groups may then again adjust the use equity sticks use. This process of mutual adjustment can continue indefinitely.

Although these different ways of promoting participation are familiar to people who have attempted to manage the floor in a classroom, the equity sticks example makes the mechanism of mutual adjusting between resource in use and framework for organizing tangible and visible. Equity sticks were designed as a tool with one use in mind. Through their practices, however, teachers and students adjust the tool to their purposes, similar to any technology in use (Orlikowski, 2000), and new frameworks become available. As they do so, the resource in use energizes the framework in ways that make new potential resources available and creates new possibilities for action.

Although Jaquith's (2009) study is situated in education, the mechanism of mutual adjusting in the recursive relationship between resources in use and frameworks is likely to generalize theoretically in many organizational contexts. People are likely to consider an amalgam of their purposes, content, structure, and relationships as they undertake actions that enable them to adjust resources in use to frameworks for organizing (Jaquith, 2009). In relation to any tool, members of organizations must agentically adjust the tool as potential resource to resource in use and then adjust the resource in use in relation to the frameworks that become available and that they want to energize. In the process of this mutual adjusting between resources in use and frameworks for organizing, a resource in use is altered at the same time that the resource in use continuously alters the nature of the framework it is used to energize. This process of mutual adjusting is likely to be of interest to POS scholars who want to understand how resources are taken up and used to energize positive frameworks such as community, safety and support, and learning.

Juxtaposing As a Mechanism for Resourcing

To juxtapose is "to place close together or side by side" (Random House Dictionary, 2010). Recent research on processes of cultural change in organizations (Howard-Grenville, Golden-Biddle, Irwin, & Mao, 2010) emphasizes the action of juxtaposing as an important means by which actors in organizations create resources and energize frameworks to facilitate change. Howard-Grenville and colleagues (2010) suggest that organizational actors who create cultural change use mundane or everyday settings to actively bring together different symbolic forms, juxtaposing the familiar with the unfamiliar in a way that creates liminality as a resource for change. In terms of resourcing theory, mundane or everyday events such as workshops are potential resources that are taken up and used by change agents within the framework of the organizational culture as a site for actively juxtaposing familiar and unfamiliar symbols in context. The use of these everyday organizational events as a resource for juxtaposing the old and the new gives rise to a new resource, liminality, defined as a sense of being between. This new sense of being between things in turn becomes available as a potential resource for changing the cultural repertoires in the organization.

Howard-Grenville and colleagues (2010) report a case of culture change in a health care context, in which one change agent used a strategy retreat to bring different principles for organizing into juxtaposition, using practices such as encouraging people from all levels to contribute, diminishing emphasis on formal boundaries, and inviting interaction focused on people's visions and hopes for the organization rather than their particular roles or status. The retreat became a site for the emergence of liminality—a sense of being between or at the threshold of things (Turner, 1967). By using the retreat to resource liminality, the leader helped to create an experience in which participants could safely try out new or different possibilities for being and doing in the organization. The authors also report on a case of culture change in an athletic wear firm, in which a central change agent who did not occupy a formal leadership or executive position organized workshops that tied branding and supply chain management issues to carbon scenarios and oil use, thus juxtaposing sustainability issues with everyday business concerns. The change agent actively made use of an everyday event, such as a business planning workshop, as a resource for juxtaposing familiar considerations with unfamiliar issues. The juxtaposition of business planning questions and sustainability issues created a sense of liminality for participants—being in between the issues in a new way that opened a threshold for seeing differently. Experiencing the liminal in the athletic wear company became a resource in use as people took up the opportunity to see the business differently and used it to interact in new ways, form new insights, and make new meanings of sustainability in relation to their business plan, ultimately contributing to change in the culture of the organization.

Although Howard-Grenville and colleagues (2010) propose juxtaposing as a mechanism for resourcing cultural change, we would suggest here that juxtaposing as a resourcing mechanism is likely to be theoretically generalizable, and thus put into specific types of use in different contexts in a variety of ways. As one example, consider that many organizations and managers seek to promote learning by bringing together cross-functional teams (Parker, 2003). Managers in essence create a context for resourcing knowing by juxtaposing people with different practices. Focusing on juxtaposition as the important mechanism sheds light on different ways that these teams may actually generate (or fail to generate) potential resources. Simply bringing people into proximity isn't likely to work well for energizing the knowledge creation framework, because proximity doesn't necessarily juxtapose ways of knowing. In the cross-functional teams example, bringing people together without practices that help them easily share their different knowledge domains can resource frustration and withdrawal rather than enthusiasm and engagement (Parker, 2003). Practices by which the context enables people to place their knowledge "side by side"—or juxtapose how they work—enable new ways of knowing and doing work. Practices that facilitate the juxtaposition of different repertoires for thinking, feeling, and acting are able to generate resources by enriching the available frameworks for knowing. For instance, work on boundary objects has shown that some kinds of objects and some uses of objects promote more fruitful juxtaposition than not using objects or using them in ways that are primarily based on confirming existing power relations or knowledge structures (Bechky, 2003; Carlile, 2002, 2004). This resourcing mechanism could be useful for scholars of POS who want to understand the processes underlying instances of positive organizational change.

Narrating As a Mechanism for Resourcing

Narratives are central to social life, in part because they provide a means of ordering events into a past, present, and future, and in so doing, enable people to know and make sense of the world around them (Ricoeur, 1984). In a study of the response of the passengers on United Flight 93 to the hijacking of the plane on September 11, 2001, Quinn and Worline (2008) suggest narrating as a central mechanism for resourcing. Narrating is action that transforms potential resources to resources in use by altering the framework or what is being resourced (Cooren, 2000; Quinn & Worline, 2008). The case evidence from Flight 93 suggests that passengers used everyday practices to create a narrative of the situation that made possible actions that were different from the actions they would have taken before creating this narrative. Specifically, using their communications with people outside the plane about the elapsed time and the fate of the other hijacked planes, the passengers were able to generate a narrative that they were in the midst of a hijacking that was likely to end disastrously. As earlier hijackings had ended in ransom demands rather than suicide attacks, creating this new narrative was an important move in this resourcing cycle.

The passengers were able to use this narrative to resource a sense of shared or collective identity, where before they had been separate individuals who happened to be in the same plane. The collective identity became a resource in use for generating collective action. The sense of "we" was critical to energizing a framework of resistance in which they acted together to launch a counterattack on the hijackers with all of the passengers sharing a common fate.

Collective identity is one key to showing how people aboard the plane began to narrate new possible actions as part of a framework of resistance, and how this framework enabled people to shift from victims of a hijacking to active participants in a counterattack. Quinn and Worline (2008) mark particular moments that reveal the process of collective identity moving from potential resource to resource in use aboard the plane, energizing a framework of resistance. For instance, one passenger was overheard by his wife saying "We have to do something!" This statement drew upon a shift that had already taken place as passengers began referring to themselves as a collective "we" rather than an individual "I" and energized the resistance framework through a call to action. The resourcing cycle aboard Flight 93 was generative enough to allow a group of strangers to become a collective capable of imagining and enacting previously unthinkable collective action within a narrow and highly stressful timeframe.

The powerful example of a generative resourcing cycle aboard Flight 93 suggests that narrative may be a resourcing mechanism of particular interest to POS scholars interested in generativity and change. Narrating is a powerful mechanism for resourcing in that it draws upon language, which is one of the most readily available potential resources in organizations (Weick, 1995). Because a large part of managing is talking, understanding how particular communication acts transform potential resources to resources in use, and how the resulting narratives energize certain frameworks, is central to research in POS. This mechanism is likely to be of particular interest to POS scholars who want to understand the processes by which managers, leaders, and organization members use language and positive stories to help shape new realities that resource different frameworks for organizing.

Endogenous Resourcing, Ampliative Cycles and Positive Outcomes

Scholars have noted that a framework or schema in one context can be a resource in another (Barney, 2001; Eisenhardt & Schoonhoven, 1996; Leblebici, 1991; Sewell, 1992). Resourcing theory helps us to see that action is an essential feature of this relationship. As we showed in the previous section, action is the driving force that creates, alters, and combines assets with frameworks. Here, we point out that action is also essential for the creation of ampliative cycles through endogenous resourcing, which involves using a resourced framework as a new resource.

The examples of resourcing mechanisms in organizational contexts provide illustrations of endogenous resourcing or the ways that resourced frameworks can become resources for other frameworks. They also illustrate a somewhat different point: that the endogenous resourcing can be ampliative. This feature of resourcing theory is particularly important for understanding the productivity of resourcing, and therefore for highlighting its relevance to POS. What makes endogenous resourcing ampliative is that the potential resources created in the recursive resourcing cycles are harnessed to move in a general direction, thereby keeping the resourcing cycles in motion and further enlarging the available potential resources. We use the term *ampliative* to refer to resourcing cycles that grow in a general direction, providing more energy for what one might refer to as a meta-framework or a larger framework that the resourcing cycles contribute to (Feldman & Quick, 2009).

Examples of Ampliative Cycles

The passengers aboard Flight 93 on September 11, 2001, engaged in resourcing cycles that energized individual identities and emotion in a bewildering situation (Quinn & Worline, 2008). They used these identities and emotions as potential resources in new resourcing cycles that helped them create a collective narrative of the duress they faced aboard the plane, and that narrative in turn became a potential resource that they took up to enact collective action in response to the hijacking (Quinn &

Worline, 2008). The agentic and improvisational actions of people aboard the plane kept the overlapping cycles of resourcing going and moved them in a general direction of constructive opposition to the situation (Quinn & Worline, 2008). Since the initial hijackings, we have seen several instances of passengers on airplanes intervening in actions that could have had disastrous outcomes. This observation raises the possibility that the narrative of Flight 93 has resourced a framework of dispersed courage and responsibility for flight safety in which passengers take action that would previously have been unthinkable or inappropriate.

In the example of the use of equity sticks in classrooms, we described how the simple tool of a participation routine could produce a different kind of classroom with more engaged learners, who then could be engaged in more critical thinking. In that case, the equity sticks were repurposed for use in the new framework (critical thinking) and combined with the more engaged learners that had been produced in the previous resourcing cycle. The equity sticks can be used in such a way that a new potential resource (engaged learners) emerges. These engaged learners can be considered an endpoint, but they can also be used in another resourcing cycle. Many readers of this chapter are likely to be teachers who can appreciate how much more you can teach when the students are engaged than when they are not. If teachers use the equity sticks routine simply to randomize participation, so that the people at the beginning or end of the alphabet are not always being called first (or last), then they have resourced the framework of more equitable participation, but they have not used the resource endogenously to create an ampliative cycle.[5] Indeed, such a use of the equity sticks may produce resources that make teaching and learning more difficult, if, for instance, students come to dread the randomness and uncertainty of the equity stick process. For the cycle to be ampliative, the framework energized (engaged learners) must be picked up (with or without the equity sticks) and used as a resource to extend a meta-framework, which in this case might be the kinds of learning or the extent of learning in the classroom.

Positive and Negative Outcomes

As the illustration of using equity sticks simply to randomize roll-calling indicates, endogenous resourcing is not always ampliative. Another illustration arose in the context of public engagement in a Midwestern city (Feldman & Quick, 2009). The city had developed a track record for inclusive engagement of residents in decision making over a period of several years, when the city managers decided to confront their budget problems by eliciting participation in a survey. The survey met the scientific standards for such data gathering, but fell short of the expectations of the community members for engagement in deliberative decision making. As a result, the community responded negatively to the survey process, as well as to the proposed budget based on the survey results. Angry members of the community began to organize a process that entailed opportunities for discussion and engagement. In this way, anger over the survey became a new resource that energized the community. From the perspective of the city managers, this endogenous resourcing was not an ampliative cycle, as the engagement of the community in the mode of us versus them is limiting in the long run if the goal is for the residents to work with government toward the solution of community problems. The result could have been years of antagonistic relations that would make it more difficult to develop and implement constructive ideas.

The next move by the city management shows the utility of understanding the resourcing cycle. They asked the most vocal critics of the unpopular survey process to advise them about how to organize a process that would engage the community in a more constructive manner; in this way, they used the energy associated with the anger that they had inadvertently generated as an unexpected resource. They worked with these critics, now advisors, providing them with information they requested and following suggestions they made. Through these actions, they showed both the critics/advisors and other community members their intent to be part of and work with the community rather than to manipulate or do an end-run around the community. Although one interpretation is that the managers simply bought off the most vocal critics, the resulting budget required the city managers to take action they did not want to take. It also, however, produced something they cared even about more—a return to constructive engagement. The move showed the ability to manage the resourcing flow to produce an ampliative cycle, in this case increasing the breadth of the engaged community and strengthening ties across the community.

Resourcing and Positive Organizational Scholarship

Resourcing theory is relevant to POS for several reasons. First, the awareness of resourcing dynamics on the part of organizational participants affects their ability to engage these dynamics constructively. Although endogenous and ampliative resourcing dynamics may occur as unintended consequences, the ability to recognize and direct resourcing enables people to make choices about what they would like to promote. We recognize that there is much legitimate debate about what outcomes are positive. The lack of awareness of resourcing dynamics, however, tends to support assumptions of inevitability about the direction of resourcing, which are unwarranted. Understanding the consequentiality of action creates opportunities not only to direct actions toward specific outcomes, but also to surface subjective valuations about what is positive and for whom.

In our examples, the outcomes that are amplified through endogenous resourcing are ones that many people would find positive—greater ability to stand up to terrorism, deeper learning, stronger and more engaged communities. The ability to produce ampliative cycles, however, does not necessarily produce positive outcomes. One of the strengths of focusing on the process is the ability to separate evaluation of the process from evaluation of the outcome. Indeed, an essential question raised by resourcing theory is "what is being resourced?" Because resourcing theory focuses on the relationship between potential resources, actions, and frameworks rather than the innate qualities of things, it shows that resources can only be judged as good or bad in the context of their use.

Future Directions

We see many future directions for research stemming from resourcing theory, some of which we have identified above. Here, we briefly discuss five promising ideas for developing resourcing theory in relation to POS.

1. *Develop and explore potential synergies between different theoretical views of resources, particularly between dynamic capabilities and resourcing theory.* Research on dynamic capabilities in organizations would benefit from a focus on the microdynamics of such capabilities, as would much of the research centered in the resource-based view of the firm, as articulated by Sirmon et al. (2007):

> Unfortunately, there is minimal theory explaining "how" managers/firms transform resources to create value (Priem & Butler, 2001). Therefore, the RBV [resource-based view] requires further elaboration to explain the link between the management of resources and the creation of value. (Sirmon, Hitt & Ireland, 2007, p. 273).

Resourcing theory offers a powerful view into the resource dynamics in organizations, representing a potential site of synergy between resourcing and the resource-based view of the firm. Resourcing theory also provides a way of theorizing how dynamic capabilities emerge and change, which is crucial for further development of the body of research (Eisenhardt & Martin, 2000). Many POS scholars are interested in understanding more about the emergence and processes involved in cultivating positive dynamic capabilities such as innovation or resilience.

2. *Develop the potential for resourcing theory to inform how innovation happens and how people and firms respond to change.* Many POS scholars are interested in practices that help sustain positive organizational change. Scholars interested in the microdynamics of innovation and change in organizations could benefit from taking up resourcing theory, because the resourcing view reveals the incremental nature of the experimentation involved in getting from "what do I have?" to "what actions can I take to create outcomes I care about?" As a result, resourcing theory provides a potentially valuable way of understanding how innovations happen and the role of everyday action in innovation and in other positive organizational change.

3. *Pursue more research on ampliative cycles and how they unfold in different contexts.* The concepts of endogenous resourcing and ampliative cycles have a great deal of potential for POS, especially for scholars interested in virtuous cycles, positive spirals, and broaden-and-build theories of positive emotion in organizations (e.g., Fredrickson, 2003). Finding out more about how these cycles can be used to perpetuate and enlarge the values we most want to promote in organizations might involve exploring questions about, for instance, the kinds of meta-frameworks that lend themselves to ampliative cycles. We have identified courage, learning, and community building possibilities, and we imagine further research could identify many more.

4. *Explore the agentic ability to alter the direction of resourcing cycles.* Recent research has shown that organizational participants can agentically direct the resourcing cycle such that energy can be diverted from negative cycles and directed to more positive cycles (Feldman & Quick, 2009). This agentic ability involves recognizing and engaging resourcing cycles that are often unpredictable and

generate surprising results (Howard-Grenville et al., 2010). Scholars interested in managing positive change could benefit from looking more closely into organizational members' abilities to direct resourcing cycles as a skill that could be understood, explained, and developed within organizations.

5. *Examine the availability of practices in specific contexts.* Resourcing theory makes clear that the ability to resource positive frameworks depends on the availability of practices or the ability to create practices that enable people to take up potential resources to energize these frameworks. Yet, we know little about how practices become available or whether practices available in specific contexts (e.g., health or education) are able to energize positive frameworks. The seeding of practices that can energize positive frameworks in and through organizations is an important potential area of new research.

Notes

1. Based on Sewell's 1992 definition of resource as "anything that can be used as a source of power in social interaction" (1992, p. 9).
2. This example was developed by Torsten Schmidt, University of St. Gallen. We are grateful to him for the use of the example.
3. We use the term *framework* (rather than schema as Feldman [2004] did) to refer to what a resource helps to create. We could also have used *schema*. Framework has the disadvantage of appearing to be static; schema's association with matters cognitive is also problematic.
4. We might also note that stretching food with various additives has become a standard feature of American processed foods since World War II and is one of the distinctions between American food and European food. This resourcing has benefited corporations but appears to have produced negative health outcomes.
5. Previous scholarship has used the term *cascade* to refer to these ampliative cycles or spirals (Feldman & Quick, 2009; Feldman & Khademian, 2003).

References

Amit, R., & Shoemaker, P. (1993). Strategic assets and organizational rents. *Strategic Management Journal, 14*, 33–46.

Barney, J.B. (1991). Firm resources and sustained competitive advantage. *Journal of Management, 17*, 99–120.

Barney, J.B. (2001). Is the resource-based "view" a useful perspective for strategic management research? Yes. *Academy of Management Review, 26*, 41–56.

Barney, J.B., Wright, M., & Ketchen, D. (2001). The resource-based view of the firm: Ten years after 1991. *Journal of Management, 27*(6), 625–641.

Bechky, B.A. (2003). Sharing meaning across occupational communities: The transformation of understanding on a production floor. *Organization Science, 14*(3), 312–330.

Brickson, S.L., & Lemmon, G. (2009). Organizational identity as a stakeholder resource. In L.M. Roberts, & J.E. Dutton (Eds.), *Exploring positive identities and organizations* (pp. 411–434). New York: Routledge.

Carlile, P.R. (2002). A pragmatic view of knowledge and boundaries: Boundary objects in new product development. *Organization Science, 13*(4), 442–455.

Carlile, P.R. (2004). Transferring, translating, and transforming: An integrative framework for managing knowledge across boundaries. *Organization Science, 15*(5), 555–568.

Cohen, S. (1991). V for victory: America's home front during World War II. Missoula, MT: Pictorial Histories Publishing Inc.

Cooren, F. (2000). *The organizing property of communication.* Philadelphia: John Benjamins.

De Certeau, M. (1984). *The practice of everyday life.* (P. Rendell, Trans.). Berkeley: University of California Press.

Eisenhardt, K.M., & Martin, J.A. (2000). Dynamic capabilities: What are they? *Strategic Management Journal, 21,* 1105–1121.

Eisenhardt, K.M., & Schoonhoven, C.B. (1996). Resource-based view of strategic alliance formation: Strategic and social effects of entrepreneurial firms. *Organization Science, 7,* 136–150.

Feldman, M.S. (2004). Resources in emerging structures and processes of change. *Organization Science, 15,* 295–309.

Feldman, M.S., & Khademian, A.M. (2003). Empowerment and cascading vitality. In K.S. Cameron, J.E. Dutton, & R.E. Quinn (Eds.), *Positive organizational scholarship* (pp. 343–358). San Francisco: Berrett-Koehler.

Feldman, M.S., & Quick, K.S. (2009). Generating resources and energizing frameworks through inclusive public management. *International Public Management Journal, 12*(2), 137–171.

Feldman, M.S., & Orlikowski, W.J. (2010). Theorizing practice and practicing theory. *Organization Science.* Forthcoming.

Fredrickson, B. (2003). Positive emotions and upward spirals in organizations. In Kim S. Cameron, Jane E. Dutton, and Robert E. Quinn (eds.) *Positive organizational scholarship* (pp. 163–175). San Francisco: Berrett-Koehler Publishers.

Goldsworthy, H. (2010). Compassionate capitalism: Institutionalization and legitimacy in microfinance. Ph.D. dissertation, University of California, School of Social Ecology, Irvine, CA.

Howard-Grenville, J.A. (2007). Developing issue-selling effectiveness over time: Issue selling as resourcing. *Organization Science, 18,* 560–577.

Howard-Grenville, J.A., Golden-Biddle, K., Irwin, J., & Mao, G. (2010). Liminality as cultural process for cultural change. *Organization Science.* (Manuscript under review.)

Jaquith, A.C. (2009). *The creation and use of instructional resources: The puzzle of professional development.* Ph.D. dissertation, Stanford University, School of Education, Stanford, CA.

Leblebici, H., Salancik, G.R., Copay, A., & King, T. (1991). Institutional change and the transformation of interorganizational fields: An organizational history of the U.S. radio broadcasting industry. *Administrative Science Quarterly, 36,* 333–363.

Orlikowski, W.J. (2000). Using technology and constituting structures: A practice lens for studying technology in organizations. *Organization Science, 11,* 404–428.

Parker, G.M. (2003). *Cross-functional teams: Working with allies, enemies, and other strangers.* San Francisco: Jossey-Bass.

Penrose, E. (1959). *The theory of the growth of the firm.* Oxford: Basil Blackwell.

Pfeffer, J. (1982). *Organizations and Organization Theory.* Boston: Pitman Publishing.

Pfeffer, J., & Salancik, G. (1978). *The External Control of Organizations: A resource dependence perspective.* New York: Harper and Row.

Priem, R.L., & Butler, J.E. (2001). Is the resource-based "view" a useful perspective for strategic management research? *The Academy of Management Review, 26,* 22–40.

Quinn, R., & Worline, M. (2008). Enabling courageous collective action: Conversations from United Airlines Flight 93. *Organization Science, 19*(4), 497–516.

Ricoeur, P. (1984). *Time and narrative.* Chicago: University of Chicago Press.

Sewell, W.H. (1992). A theory of structure: Duality, agency and transformation. *American Journal of Sociology, 98,* 1–29.

Sirmon, D.G., Hitt, M.A., & Ireland, R.D. (2007). Managing firm resources in dynamic environments to create value: Looking inside the black box. *Academy of Management Review, 32*(1), 273–292.

Spreitzer, G., Sutcliffe, K., Dutton, J., Sonenshein, S., & Grant, A. (1995). A socially embedded model of thriving at work. *Organization Science, 16*(5), 537–549.

Teece, D.J., Pisano, G., & Shuen, A. (1997). Dynamic capabilities and strategic management. *Strategic Management Journal, 18,* 509–533.

Turner, V.W. (1967). *The forest of symbols: Aspects of Ndembu ritual.* Ithaca, NY: Cornell University Press.

Wang, D. (2009). *Constructing the life cycle of resources: Resource artifacts and resources-in-use.* Working paper, Center for Work, Technology and Organization, School of Engineering, Stanford University, Stanford, CA.

Webster's revised unabridged dictionary. (1996, 1998). MICRA, Inc.

Weick, K. (1995). *Sensemaking in organizations.* Thousand Oaks, CA: Sage.

Collective Efficacy Beliefs, Organizational Excellence, and Leadership

Roger D. Goddard *and* Serena J. Salloum

Abstract

Those interested in positive organizational scholarship (POS) seek ways to understand how humans and organizations reach extraordinary levels of performance. This chapter explains the unique role of collective efficacy beliefs in fostering such positive deviance in organizations. A robust literature demonstrates that collective beliefs enable excellence in a variety of sectors. This analysis synthesizes existing research to discuss how collective efficacy is considered across various disciplines. Collective efficacy—a group's belief in its capabilities to organize and execute courses of action required to reach a specific goal—is understood to be an important organizational property because the strength of social institutions depends in part on communal ability and willingness to solve problems (Bandura, 1997). Understanding the choices that individuals and groups make in pursuit of organizational goals is a key need for POS. Our purpose is to advance awareness of collective efficacy as a facet of POS by examining the connections among collective efficacy, organizational excellence, and leadership.

Key words: Collective efficacy beliefs, leadership, organizational performance, self-efficacy, social cognitive theory

Organizations that achieve their best depend daily on the choices of individual members to creatively and resiliently pursue and reach challenging goals. At their core, decisions to tackle difficult work—whether they involve coaching a single worker to develop her capacity, transforming an unresponsive workgroup, or redesigning an organization's central mission in response to changing external environments—require individuals to exercise agency in ways that affirm self-assuredness and confidence. We argue that the degree to which group members work together effectively to accomplish such challenges depends heavily on their sense of collective efficacy. When organizational members are confident in the capabilities of their coworkers and leadership to reach given goals, it is likely that such expectations will positively influence the normative environment of the workgroup. Such expectations, in turn, tend to energize individuals and help them

manage their personal and interdependent capabilities to achieve organizational goals. Groups that thrive are thus likely to be characterized by normative expectations among team members that support excellence and goal attainment. In contrast, groups possessed by a debilitated sense of collective efficacy are likely to avoid challenges and at best accept or diminish the status quo. Importantly, in the case of organizations characterized by either high or low collective efficacy, human agency is a central concern. The exercise of control that flows from human agency can lead to self-actualization when collective efficacy beliefs are robust but can also spur downward spirals in organizational and personal performance when collective efficacy is weak.

Collective efficacy aligns well with positive organizational scholarship (POS) because it helps us understand the choices individuals and groups make in pursuit of organizational goals (Cameron, Dutton, & Quinn, 2003). A group possessed by a debilitated sense of collective efficacy easily succumbs to pressures that suggest that goals are unattainable. In contrast, groups characterized by a robust sense of collective efficacy interpret setbacks as challenges to be overcome. A workgroup with a strong sense of collective efficacy thus tends to exhibit the creativity, resiliency, and commitment required to reach performance goals. Collective efficacy beliefs can therefore have vitalizing or demoralizing effects on how well organizations function (Brophy & Good, 1986; Purkey & Smith, 1983).

Not surprisingly, research has demonstrated that collective beliefs enable excellence in a variety of sectors. For example, research suggests that collective efficacy is associated with positive outcomes as diverse as sports team effectiveness (Watson, Chemers, & Preiser, 2001), reduced neighborhood obesity (Cohen, Finch, Bower, & Sastry, 2006), decreased neighborhood crime (Sampson, Raudenbush, & Earls, 1997), and the academic learning of public school students (Bandura, 1997; Goddard 2001).

Given the importance of collective efficacy beliefs to effective organizational performance and human flourishing, we ask, across disciplines, what outcomes does collective efficacy predict? Likewise, across fields, what are the predictors of collective efficacy? To answer these questions, we first introduce the reader to the social cognitive theoretical underpinnings of collective efficacy. We do this not only because collective efficacy, as a construct, is so firmly rooted in social cognitive theory, but also to demonstrate one way in which a contemporary psychological theory can inform POS. Next, we discuss the extant social science evidence concerning the outcomes and predictors of collective efficacy. In particular, we synthesize existing theory and research to argue that leaders make a difference to collective efficacy beliefs in organizations. Finally, we discuss limitations of current research on collective efficacy and suggest new lines of inquiry that can further develop our understanding of positive psychology in organizations.

The Social Cognitive Underpinnings of Collective Efficacy

The study of efficacy beliefs is grounded in social cognitive theory, which espouses reciprocal causation among the self, the environment, and behavior (Bandura, 1977, 1986, 1997); it is concerned with agency, or the capacity for people to make and impress choices. Efficacy beliefs are a key element of social cognitive theory (Bandura, 1993, 1997). However, self-efficacy beliefs are just one component of this theory; self-efficacy operates in concert with other determinants to govern human thought, motivation, and action.

Collective efficacy is defined as a "group's shared belief in its conjoint capabilities to organize and execute courses of action required to produce given levels of attainment" (Bandura, 1997, p. 477). Because the strength of social institutions depends in part on communal ability and willingness to solve problems, collective efficacy beliefs are an important organizational feature. Individuals working within organizations both contribute to and are influenced by collective efficacy beliefs. Indeed, no matter how loosely coupled the technical work of an organization, persons acting individually do not do so without awareness of the beliefs, motivation, and performance of their coworkers. The interactive dynamics embedded in the social milieu of organized activity thus make collective efficacy beliefs an emergent group property that is more than the sum of its parts. As such, collective efficacy is a key characteristic of any organization's operative environment that conditions the degree to which individuals choose to enthusiastically embrace workgroup challenges. Indeed, it is difficult to imagine sustained effectiveness that is informed by a sense of inability to exercise control over immediate and long-term circumstances.

All efficacy beliefs are future orientated judgments about the capability to produce desired levels of performance (Bandura, 1997). It is also important to clarify that efficacy beliefs are judgments about capability, not necessarily accurate assessments of such skills. However, the self-assurance with which people approach and manage complicated problems dictates the degree to which they make better or worse use of their capabilities (Bandura, 1997). Therefore, the stronger individual or organizational efficacy beliefs, the more likely the sustained effort and persistence required to meet given goals. To ground our discussion of collective efficacy beliefs as a key concern for positive organizational functioning, we begin first with a discussion of the more longstanding concept of self-efficacy beliefs.

Self-efficacy Beliefs

Self-efficacy is the mechanism through which experience and thought lead to agency. A self-efficacy belief represents an individual's overall judgment of her capacity to successfully organize and execute the tasks required to reach a specific goal. For example, athletic success in any domain requires more than mastery of physical skills; athletic performance also depends on an individual's understanding of her own capability. Not surprisingly, a firm sense of efficacy positively influences athletic performance (Bandura, 1997).

According to social cognitive theory, people characterized by high levels of self-efficacy approach difficult tasks as challenges. They set ambitious goals for themselves and maintain a strong commitment to meeting these goals. When faced with a setback, they are resilient and therefore tend to recover quickly. Those with a strong sense of efficacy tend to attribute failure to insufficient effort, knowledge, or skill. In comparison, those with lower levels of efficacy are more likely to shy away from difficult tasks, viewing requisite performances as intimidating or impossible instead of challenging. Not surprisingly, people with a low sense of self-efficacy tend to have modest ambitions and weak commitment to the goals they set. When faced with a setback, these individuals often focus on their personal shortcomings and give up quickly. Because they view poor performance as a deficit in aptitude, they are unlikely to be sufficiently resilient and thus lose faith in their capability. *Therefore, people with similar skill levels but variant levels of self-efficacy may perform at different levels* (Bouffard-Bouchard, 1990; Bouffard-Bouchard, Parent, & Larivee, 1991; Gist & Mitchell, 1992).

One's self-efficacy evolves from a variety of sources, including past performance, previous history, and social influence. However, experience alone does not determine efficacy beliefs; rather it is the cognitive interpretations that individuals and groups make regarding those events that shape efficacy beliefs. According to Bandura (1986, 1997), four primary sources of experience inform cognitions that lead to self-efficacy beliefs. These include mastery experience, modeling and vicarious experience, verbal persuasion, and physiological arousal. *Mastery experience* is one of the most important sources of information influencing efficacy beliefs. Recurrent success tends to bolster self-efficacy beliefs, whereas consistent failure tends to produce thoughts of self-doubt and a lowered sense of efficacy. *Modeling and vicarious experience* impact self-perception because the social comparison involved in watching skilled others perform a task can build knowledge that positively informs one's own sense of self-efficacy. Watching an expert perform a task

can offer strategies to manage similar tasks in different contexts. In addition, seeing others in a similar position can alter self-efficacy beliefs. *Verbal persuasion* is a strategy employed to convince people that they can accomplish their goals. The persuasive skills of coaches, colleagues, and leaders all have the power to influence the ways in which individuals understand their self-capabilities and capacity to attain challenging goals. Finally, people rely on their *physiological and affective states* to judge their capability. Individuals make judgments about their anticipated performance based on positive arousal such as excitement and enthusiasm, or on negative factors such as fear and anxiety.

The assumptions of social cognitive theory were originally developed to explain the formation and effects of *self*-efficacy beliefs. More recently, however, these theoretical underpinnings have been extended to the organizational level to explain the formation and effect of *collective* efficacy beliefs in groups. We turn now to how the understanding of self-efficacy beliefs informs our understanding of collective efficacy.

Collective Efficacy

Although self-efficacy refers to an individual's belief in his or her own capabilities, the parallel organizational concept is *collective efficacy*. Central to the exercise of organizational agency is a group's collective belief in its ability to successfully execute the coordinated actions required to attain a given goal. Similar to self-efficacy, organizational agency operates through the actions of individual group members but is coordinated in ways that account for group interdependence in the pursuit of collective goals. The key question, put simply, is: "Can *we* orchestrate the thoughts and actions necessary to successfully perform the task?"

As with self-efficacy, a group's sense of collective efficacy is shaped by four sources of information: mastery experience, vicarious experience, verbal persuasion, and physiological and affective states (Bandura, 1986, 1997). Supporting the importance of mastery experience, researchers have documented that prior student achievement is positively related to the sense of collective efficacy found in schools (e.g., Bandura, 1993; Goddard, 2001). In addition, the accomplishments of other organizations facing similar pressures and external environments can provide vicarious learning experiences that inform group members' thoughts about their collective capabilities. Social persuasion also plays a role in group members' thinking about their sense of collective efficacy. For example, group members may be socially persuaded about their collective capabilities in response to highly effective continuing education opportunities or leaders who effectively persuade them of their capability to achieve difficult goals. Finally, organizations, like individuals, have affective states; they react to stress, pressure, success, and challenges. Organizations with effective coping skills effectively build on success in ways that enhance their affective states and react to stresses in ways that do not emphasize inadequacies. As we observe later, leaders may play a key role in influencing the ways in which organizational members interpret all of these experiences and hence their sense of collective efficacy for various organizational pursuits.

Having reviewed the ways in which the assumptions of social cognitive theory may hold at the group level, we turn next to a discussion of research on the outcomes and predictors of collective efficacy beliefs, with a special emphasis on the role of leadership. Although relatively unexplored in the literature, it is possible that strong leadership across the sources of efficacy belief-shaping information facilitates the development and maintenance of collective efficacy.

Outcomes and Predictors of Collective Efficacy Beliefs

In this section, we synthesize research on the outcomes and predictors of collective efficacy beliefs. In our discussion of the predictors of collective efficacy beliefs, we argue that emergent research evidence coalesces to suggest that organizational leadership is vital to the level of collective efficacy characterizing groups.

Outcomes of Collective Efficacy Beliefs

Collective efficacy beliefs may be conceived of as an organizational property at many different group levels and, because such beliefs are task specific, with respect to any number of specific group goals. Depending on the researcher, the groups for which collective efficacy beliefs have been examined have varied from small nursing teams with a few members, to sports teams, schools, neighborhoods, and even nations in studies of collective political efficacy (Bandura, 1997). Importantly, one of the most striking findings across studies of collective efficacy is that *regardless of the level of aggregation involved in the conceptualization of the group or the particular group goal examined, collective efficacy beliefs have consistently predicted group success on diverse measures*

of attainment. To illustrate the potential of collective efficacy beliefs to group success, we offer a summary of several prominent contexts in which collective efficacy beliefs and their effects have been studied.

COLLECTIVE EFFICACY AND NEIGHBORHOOD HEALTH

Several important studies have considered collective efficacy beliefs and their relationship to questions of medicine and public health in neighborhood settings. These studies have posited collective efficacy as a fundamental aspect of neighborhood context that may reduce vulnerability to disease. For example, Browning and Cagney (2002) found that, across neighborhoods, variation in levels of collective efficacy for intervening in ways that support health, such as intervening in the face of threats or providing help, were positively associated with reports of overall health. Similarly, Cohen, Finch, Bower, and Sastry (2006) found that neighborhood collective efficacy was negatively related to risk of being overweight and adolescent body mass index (BMI), net of levels of neighborhood disadvantage. Another study of neighborhood health found that neighborhood collective efficacy predicts lower levels of asthma and breathing problems (Cagney & Browning, 2004). Finally, Chung et al. (2009) discovered that neighborhood collective efficacy beliefs regarding the likelihood for access to care for clinical depression predicted community engagement in addressing depression. Collective efficacy beliefs may thus foster decisions to gather health-related resources, eliminate environmental hazards to health, and promote communication among neighbors, each of which in turn could facilitate dissemination of health information, prevent disease, and increase the likelihood of treatment. In sum, a positive sense of collective efficacy in neighborhoods regarding health care seems to promote pro-health outcomes for residents.

COLLECTIVE EFFICACY AND VIOLENCE

Neighborhood collective efficacy also has a negative relationship with violence and disorder. Sampson, Raudenbush, and Earls (1997) found that the stronger the sense of neighborhood collective efficacy for intervening to decrease violence, the less likely was the occurrence of neighborhood violence. Recent work supports this finding, as Browning (2009) found that collective efficacy was negatively associated with property crimes and social disorder in Chicago. In neighborhoods with a high sense of collective efficacy, residents seem more likely to intervene in the presence of violent activity and thus reduce crime rates. Related work suggests that observed physical disorder in schools may serve to increase fear and decrease collective efficacy to affect threatening or violent interactions among people, which in turn increase perceptions of social disorder in schools (Plank, Bradshaw, & Young, 2009). Together, these findings illustrate that collective efficacy is a key determinant of neighborhood safety.

COLLECTIVE EFFICACY IN ATHLETIC TEAMS

Another important area of inquiry has concerned the role of collective efficacy beliefs in successful performance for athletic teams. Among athletic teams, collective efficacy is positively related to group cohesion (Heuze, Raimbault, & Fontayne, 2006; Kozub & McDonnell, 2000), and both team cohesion and collective efficacy contribute to successful team performance (Watson, Chemers, & Preiser, 2001). Collective efficacy beliefs may also enhance a team's performance by strengthening its communication, cohesion, and utilization of skills. Furthermore, consistent with social cognitive theory, the more success or mastery experience a team has, the more robust the team's sense of collective efficacy (Feltz & Lirgg, 1998; Kozub & McDonnell, 2000).

COLLECTIVE EFFICACY IN EDUCATION

Because of their central role in developing human, social, and economic capital for society, schools have served as a key organizational context in which researchers have conducted research on the effects of collective efficacy. Indeed, several studies have shown collective efficacy to be a powerful predictor of student achievement, net of past academic success and sociodemographic context. For example, in Bandura's (1993) seminal study, collective efficacy was positively and significantly related to differences among schools in student achievement in both mathematics and reading. This study further indicated that collective efficacy was more strongly related to student achievement than socioeconomic status (SES). Building on Bandura's single-level study, Goddard, Hoy, and Woolfolk Hoy (2000) employed multilevel modeling to show that collective efficacy beliefs (an emergent organizational-level characteristic) were related to differences among urban elementary schools in student achievement in mathematics and reading (student-level attributes), even after controlling for the influence of prior achievement, race, SES, gender, and school context. Since then, researchers have confirmed that

the sense of collective efficacy found in schools is a critical predictor of academic achievement in elementary (Goddard, 2001; Goddard, Hoy, & Woolfolk Hoy, 2000), middle (Tschannen-Moran & Barr, 2004), and high school (Goddard, LoGerfo, & Hoy, 2004; Hoy, Sweetland, & Smith, 2002).

Although most research on collective efficacy in schools has examined student achievement as the dependent or outcome variable, a few researchers have considered the ways in which a strong sense of group capability may enhance job satisfaction and professional collaboration. For example, Caprar et al. (2003) employed multilevel structural equation modeling to show that schools' sense of collective efficacy for successfully achieving their educational missions was predictive of teachers' job satisfaction. In addition, Somech and Darch-Zahavy (2000) demonstrated that the greater the level of collective efficacy in schools, the more likely were teachers to help their colleagues improve their practice. Such decisions to exercise agency in ways that lead to individual and organizational learning are particularly important in light of more recent evidence that the degree to which teachers collaborate on instructional issues is positively related to student achievement in schools (Goddard, Goddard, & Tschannen-Moran, 2007).

Predictors of Collective Efficacy Beliefs

Given the importance of collective efficacy beliefs across performance domains and group types, it is vital to understand how groups can foster and sustain a robust sense of collective efficacy. Fortunately, several researchers have taken up questions related to the predictors of collective efficacy. In this section, we consider studies that have examined the sources and predictors of collective efficacy beliefs in organizations. Fundamental to our review is the suggestion that both social cognitive theory and emergent research evidence underscore the importance of leadership to the sense of collective efficacy characterizing groups.

PREDICTING COLLECTIVE EFFICACY BELIEFS IN SCHOOLS

Because social cognitive theory specifies that collective efficacy beliefs are influenced by prior levels of mastery experience, and because group members consider the nature of the task they face in concert with their collective competence when assessing their sense of collective efficacy (Goddard, Hoy, & Woolfolk Hoy, 2000), it is important to consider whether the collective efficacy beliefs a group possesses for a given pursuit are more than outcomes of prior experience and contextual factors. In other words, if past success predicts future success, do collective efficacy beliefs play an additive role in explaining group flourishing? Or, in contrast, are collective efficacy beliefs just artifacts of past experience and context?

Importantly, scholars have considered this question. For example, in a study of the predictors of collective efficacy beliefs for academic success in a large urban school district known for successfully decreasing student achievement gaps, Goddard and Skrla (2006) employed multilevel modeling to examine predictors of collective efficacy beliefs. Specifically, this study examined the degree to which levels of recent academic success and contextual features were predictive of variation in collective efficacy beliefs among schools. The researchers discovered that past academic achievement (i.e., mastery experience), the rate of student placement into gifted education programs, and faculty ethnic composition explained 46% of the variation among schools in collective efficacy beliefs (student SES and minority concentration were nonsignificant predictors). An important lesson from this study is that, although teachers' sense of collective efficacy varies by school membership, it is not simply an artifact of past success and social context. On the one hand, the relationship detected between prior experience and current levels of collective efficacy is consistent with the social cognitive assumption that pervious mastery experience is a powerful source of efficacy belief-shaping information for groups. On the other hand, the finding that prior experience and social context together explain less than half the variation among schools in collective efficacy beliefs is also consistent with the assumption that the social cognition of group members plays a key role in interpreting past events to determine levels of collective efficacy. This is an important theoretical finding because it suggests the need for more knowledge regarding those factors that influence the interpretation of past events and current context in the formation of collective efficacy beliefs. To shed light on this important question, we turn next to a discussion of the role of leadership in the formation of collective efficacy beliefs.

LEADERSHIP AND COLLECTIVE EFFICACY BELIEFS

As we have argued, a group's sense of collective efficacy is a key dimension of its work climate (Bandura, 1997). Yet, we also know that leaders make a difference to organizational climate (Cosner, 2009; Leithwood & Rheil, 2003). For example, in a study of school improvement in the Chicago Public Schools, Bryk and colleagues (2010) found that school leadership was a strong predictor of differences in the levels of relational trust across schools. Therefore, it is reasonable to conjecture that leaders may also influence the levels of collective efficacy that characterize their organizations. Even so, social cognitive theory does not specify a direct link between leadership and a group's sense of collective efficacy. Based on our review of the extant research, however, we argue that it is possible that leaders influence collective efficacy beliefs in several distinct ways. In this section, we synthesize the relatively scant extant research evidence relating group leadership to collective efficacy beliefs to sketch these possibilities.

One clear way in which leaders may influence collective efficacy beliefs is by directly sharing efficacy belief-shaping information. Indeed, Skrla and Goddard (2002) found that leaders influenced collective efficacy beliefs in urban schools by communicating socially persuasive expectations that positively affected group members' sense of conjoint capability to achieve their goals. Social persuasion provided by leaders also seems to have a unique opportunity to influence group members' interpretation of each of the four sources of efficacy belief-shaping information specified by social cognitive theory, regardless of the source of this information. Within athletics, for example, Watson, Chemers, and Preiser (2001) found that the more confident the leadership of National Collegiate Athletics Association (NCAA) basketball teams, the higher the levels of collective efficacy at the beginning of their season. Moreover, it is possible that a coach plays a key role in influencing whether an athletic team recovers from a major loss by renewing its sense of confidence in collective capability or by succumbing to a sense of diminished capability. These examples suggest that the interpretations group members make about their ability to make effective use of their skills are influenced by the degree of confidence espoused by their leaders.

Another important way in which leaders may influence collective efficacy beliefs in groups is by establishing organizational structures and designs that enable groups to make the most of their skills. For example, one factor that enhances a group's sense of collective efficacy is the degree to which group members are provided opportunities to exercise agency through collective decision-making.

Indeed, Bandura (1997) argued that "collective enablement programs take many different forms, but the shared assumption is that they work in part by enhancing people's sense of efficacy to bring about change in their lives" (p. 503). One test of this idea was conducted by Goddard (2003), who found that a one unit change in the extent to which teachers were enabled to influence instructionally relevant decisions in schools was positively associated with a 0.41 unit change in collective efficacy beliefs. All else equal, groups that have input over issues concerning their futures are more likely to have higher levels of collective efficacy than those that do not. Research in other sectors is consistent with the finding that group empowerment may foster collective efficacy beliefs. For example, Jung and Sosik (2002) discovered that across 47 Korean firms, transformational leadership was positively related to empowerment, which in turn positively predicted collective efficacy. Given that the exercise of agency for both individuals and groups is a fundamental assumption of social cognitive theory, it makes sense that empowerment is a key organizational condition required to maximize a group's sense of collective efficacy. For those interested in POS, such research provides both theoretical and empirical warrant for the importance of group empowerment and shared decision making alike.

Notably, the degree of influence over decisions that groups possess is only one of several structural features of organizations through which leaders might influence collective efficacy beliefs. For example, Adams and Forsyth (2006) examined the relationship between collective efficacy beliefs and organizational structure, which they conceptualized to range from enabling to hindering. Using hierarchal multiple regression, these researchers found that the more an organization's structure promotes policies, regulations, and procedures that are helpful and conducive to problem solving, the greater their sense of collective efficacy. In other words, the more leaders emphasize structures that are characterized as flexible and enabling, the greater the collective efficacy beliefs characterizing their workgroups.

Evidence outside the field of education also corroborates the importance of leadership to collective efficacy beliefs. For example, Chen and Bliese (2002) investigated the relationship between leadership climate and the sense of collective efficacy characterizing military combat units. Using random coefficient modeling on data collected from 2,585 soldiers in 86 combat units, leadership climate was found to be the strongest predictor of collective efficacy. In fact, leadership climate was more strongly related to collective efficacy than group members' self-efficacy beliefs. This suggests that leadership is more closely related to group motivation than individual motivation, at least in the combat units studied.

In sum, this section makes several important contributions. First, the research reviewed suggests that leaders may influence the degree of collective efficacy in their organizations by providing socially persuasive encouragement that serves both directly as a source of efficacy belief-shaping information and also indirectly by influencing the ways in which group members interpret the relationships among themselves, their environment, and their behaviors. Moreover, we have explained that, although important in ways that are consistent with social cognitive theory, research on the relationship between enactive experience and group contextual factors does not tend to explain the majority of variation in the levels of collective efficacy characterizing groups. Thus, other factors must be at work that influence the social cognitions of group members regarding their collective efficacy beliefs. Leaders may, for example, positively influence groups to action in much the same way as coaches help athletes make the best use of their skills in future performances. Evidence also suggests that leaders may also influence collective efficacy through the designs they put in place in organizations. For example, the more group members report being empowered to make important decisions regarding their work, the greater the sense of collective efficacy characterizing their work organization (Goddard, 2003). In sum, although the research to date has not been organized around the role of leaders in promoting collective efficacy, it seems that much of the evidence regarding the predictors of collective efficacy suggests that leaders play a unique role in shaping the experiences and cognitive interpretations of group members.

Conclusion

The purpose of this chapter was to provide an introduction to collective efficacy beliefs as a key concern for POS. The social cognitive theoretical underpinnings reviewed suggest that the exercise of agency, or the choices individuals and groups make in pursuit of goals, are heavily influenced by the strength of their efficacy beliefs. Indeed, a key finding across domains as diverse as neighborhood safety, athletic performance, and student academic outcomes is that collective efficacy beliefs are potent predictors of successful organizational performance.

According to social cognitive theory, beliefs influence group performance by strengthening the degree of creativity and tenacity with which group members approach prospective situations. The more robust a group's sense of collective efficacy, the more likely is it to overcome obstacles and setbacks that might persuade the less efficacious to give up.

Thus, it seems clear that collective efficacy is a vital aspect of an organization's operative culture. Yet, much more remains to be known. As we have discussed, although social cognitive theory describes social persuasion as one of four primary sources of efficacy belief-shaping information, it does not specify a direct role for leaders in the formation of collective efficacy beliefs. However, the evidence we have reviewed suggests it is likely that leaders strongly influence the cognitive interpretations and attributions of group members when they consider their conjoint capability to successfully manage prospective situations. Indeed, our review describes several pathways through which organizational leaders may positively influence collective efficacy beliefs. Chief among these involves providing primary workers with some control over decisions affecting their circumstances in pursuit of organizational goals. Indeed, in varied settings, shared and collaborative leadership positively predict collective efficacy beliefs after accounting for other contextual factors. This suggests that group members require the opportunity to exercise agency in order to make the best possible use of the skills they possess. We believe, therefore, that collective efficacy beliefs are key determinants of organizational flourishing and a serious concern for future POS. Indeed, scholars and practitioners alike need to know more about how to enhance collective efficacy. A primary area worthy of further investigation therefore regards the ways in which leaders make a difference to collective efficacy beliefs. Thus, there is ample room to advance POS related to the role of collective efficacy in new types of groups and performance domains and to map the role and social cognitive underpinnings of leadership in promoting collective efficacy beliefs.

References

Adams, C.M., & Forsyth, P.B. (2006). Proximate sources of collective teacher efficacy. *Journal of Educational Administration, 44*(6), 625–642.

Bandura, A. (1977). Self-efficacy: Toward a unifying theory of behavioral change. *Psychological Review, 84*(2), 191–215.

Bandura, A. (1986). *Social foundations of thought and action: A social cognitive theory.* Englewood Cliffs, NJ: Prentice-Hall.

Bandura, A. (1993). Perceived self-efficacy in cognitive development and functioning. *Educational Psychologist, 28*(2), 117–148.

Bandura, A. (1997). *Self-efficacy: The exercise of control.* New York: W.H. Freeman and Company.

Bouffard-Bouchard, T. (1990). Influence of self-efficacy on performance in a cognitive task. *Journal of Social Psychology, 130*(3), 353–363.

Bouffard-Bouchard, T., Parent, S., & Larivee, S. (1991). Influence on self-efficacy on self-regulation and performance among junior and senior high school age children. *International Journal of Behavioral Development, 14*(2), 153–164.

Brophy, J.J., & Good, T. (1986). Teacher behavior and student achievement. In M.C. Wittrock (Ed), *Handbook of research on teaching.* New York: Macmillan.

Browning, C.R., & Cagney, K.A. (2002). Neighborhood structural disadvantage, Collective efficacy and self-rated physical heath in an urban setting. *Journal of Health and Social Behavior, 43*(4), 383–399.

Browning, C.R. (2009). Illuminating the downside of social capital: Negotiated coexistence, property crime, and disorder in urban neighborhoods. *American Behavioral Scientist, 52*(11), 1556–1578.

Bryk, A.S. (2010). Organizing schools for improvement. *Phi Delta Kappan, 91*(7), 23–30.

Cagney, K.A., & Browning, C.R. (2004). Exploring neighborhood-level variation in asthma and other respiratory diseases: The contribution of neighborhood social context. *Journal General Internal Medicine, 19*, 229–236.

Cameron, K.S., Dutton, J.E., & Quinn, R.E. (2003). *Positive organizational scholarship: Foundations of a new discipline.* San Francisco: Berrett-Koehler Publishers, Inc.

Caprara, G.V., Barbaranelli, C., Borgogni, L., & Steca, P. (2003). Efficacy beliefs as determinants of teachers' job satisfaction. *Journal of Educational Psychology, 95*(4), 821–832.

Chen, G., & Bliese, P.D. (2002). The role of different levels of leadership in predicting self- and collective efficacy: Evidence for discontinuity. *Journal of Applied Psychology, 87*(2), 549–556.

Chung, B., Jones, L., Jones, A., Corbett, C.E., Booker, T., Wells, K.B., & Collins, B. (2009). Using community arts events to enhance collective efficacy and community engagement to address depression in an African American community. *American Journal of Public Health, 99*(2), 237–244.

Cohen, D.A., Finch, B.K., Bower, A., & Sastry, N. (2006). Collective efficacy and obesity: The potential influence of social factors on health. *Social Science & Medicine, 62*(3), 769–778.

Cosner, S. (2009). Building organizational capacity through trust. *Educational Administration Quarterly, 45*, 248–291.

Feltz, D.L., & Lirgg, C.D. (1998). Perceived team and player efficacy in hockey. *Journal of Applied Psychology, 83*(4), 557–564.

Gist, M.E., & Mitchell, T.R. (1992). Self-efficacy: A theoretical analysis of its determinants and malleability. *The Academy of Management Review, 17*(2), 183–211.

Goddard, R.D. (2001). Collective efficacy: A neglected construct in the study of schools and student achievement. *Journal of Educational Psychology, 93*(3), 467–476.

Goddard, R.D. (2003). The impact of schools on teacher beliefs, influence, and student achievement: The role of collective efficacy. In J. Raths, & A. McAninch (Eds.), *Advances in teacher education* Vol. 6 (pp. 183–204). Westport, CT: Information Age Publishing.

Goddard, Y.L., Goddard, R.G., & Tschannen-Moran (2007). A theoretical and empirical investigation of teacher collaboration for school improvement and student achievement in public elementary schools. *Teachers College Record, 109*(4), 877–96.

Goddard, R.D., Hoy, W.K., & Woolfolk Hoy, A. (2000). Collective teacher efficacy: Its meaning, measure, and effect on student achievement. *American Educational Research Journal, 37*(2), 479–507.

Goddard, R.D., LoGerfo, L., & Hoy, W.K. (2004). High school accountability: The role of collective efficacy. *Educational Policy, 18*(3), 403–425.

Goddard, R.D., & Skrla, L. (2006). The influence of school social composition on teachers' collective efficacy beliefs. *Educational Administration Quarterly, 42*(2), 216–235.

Goddard, Y.L., & Goddard, R.D. (2006). *Connecting teaching practice to school climate: An examination of the relationship between differentiated instructional practice and collective efficacy beliefs.* Paper presented at the American Education Research Association annual conference, San Francisco.

Heuze, J.P., Raimbault, N., & Fontayne, P. (2006). Relationships between cohesion, collective efficacy and performance in professional basketball teams: An examination of mediating effects. *Journal of Sports Sciences, 24*(1), 59–68.

Hoy, W.K., Sweetland, S.R., & Smith, P.A. (2002). Toward an organizational model of achievement in high schools: The significance of collective efficacy. *Educational Administration Quarterly, 38*(1), 77–93.

Jung, D.I., & Sosik, J.J. (2002). Transformational leadership in work groups: The role of empowerment, cohesiveness, and collective-efficacy on perceived group performance. *Small Group Research, 33*(3), 313–336.

Kozub, S.A., & McDonnell, J.F. (2000). Exploring the relationship between cohesion and collective efficacy in rugby teams. *Journal of Sports Behavior, 23*(2), 120–129.

Leithwood, K.A., & Riehl, C. (2003). What we know about successful school leadership. Philadelphia: Laboratory for Student Success, Temple University.

Plank, S.B., Bradshaw, C.P., & Young, H. (2009). An application of "broken-windows" and related theories to the study of disorder, fear, and collective efficacy in schools. *American Journal of Education, 115*, 227–247.

Purkey, S.C., & Smith, M.S. (1983). Effective schools: A review. *The Elementary School Journal, 83*(4), 426–452.

Sampson, R.J., Raudenbush, S.W., & Earls, F. (1997). Neighborhoods and violent crime: A multilevel study of collective efficacy. *Science, 277*, 918–924.

Skrla, L., & Goddard, R.D. (2002). *Accountability, equity, and collective efficacy in an urban school district: A mixed methods study.* Paper presented at the annual conference of the University Council for Educational Administration, Pittsburgh, PA.

Somech, A., & Drach-Zahavy, A. (2000). Understanding extra-role behavior in schools: The relationships between job satisfaction, sense of efficacy, and teachers' extra-role behavior. *Teaching and Teacher Education, 16*, 649–659.

Tschannen-Moran, M., & Barr, M. (2004). Fostering student learning: The relationship of collective teacher efficacy. *Leadership and Policy in Schools, 3*(3), 189–209.

Watson, C.B., Chemers, M.M., & Preiser, N. (2001). Collective efficacy: A multilevel analysis. *Personality and Social Psychology Bulletin, 27*(8), 1057–1068.

The Design of Jobs

A Strategy for Enhancing the Positive Outcomes of Individuals at Work

Greg R. Oldham

Abstract

This chapter examines the link between the design of employee jobs and five positive employee experiences and actions suggested by the positive organizational scholarship literature: satisfaction with the job, satisfaction with opportunities to grow and develop at work, internal work motivation, creativity, and altruism. The chapter first defines job design and then describes an approach to the design of jobs that has received the most empirical attention: *job characteristics theory* (JCT). I then review the literature that has focused on the effects of the core job characteristics included in JCT on the aforementioned positive outcomes. The implications of these findings for the design of individuals' jobs are then presented. I conclude with a discussion of several topics for future research, including the possible effects of the design of jobs on several positive employee outcomes (e.g., new learning and resilience) that have received little research attention.

Keywords: Job design, positive organizational scholarship, satisfaction, creativity, altruism, learning, resilience

During the past several years, a substantial amount of attention has focused on the emerging discipline of positive organizational scholarship (POS) (see Cameron, Dutton, & Quinn, 2003a; Fineman, 2006; Luthans & Youssef, 2007; Roberts, 2006). In contrast to disciplines that focus on negative outcomes and behaviors (e.g., errors, overcoming resistance, and unethical actions), POS emphasizes the importance of especially *positive* outcomes, processes, and attributes of organizations and their members (Cameron et al., 2003a). Thus, POS scholars encourage research and theory that attempt to explain such positive individual experiences and actions as psychological well-being, personal growth, and altruistic behavior (Cameron, Dutton, Quinn, & Wrzesniewski, 2003b; Spreitzer & Sonenshein, 2004). Moreover, many scholars connected to the POS discipline argue that the management of organizations should be concerned with developing those practices and strategies that

foster these positive outcomes among individual employees (Cameron et al., 2003a; Grant, 2008a). If organizations are successful in developing strategic approaches that promote positive experiences and actions, such as altruism and employee well-being, it is expected that both individual employees and the organizations that employ them will thrive and prosper over the long term.

It has long been established that one organizational strategy—the design of jobs—can make a significant contribution to an employee's positive experiences and positive actions at work (Grant, 2008a). The goal of the current chapter is to examine the job design literature and discuss the way that the design of jobs shapes employees' positive outcomes. To this end, I review the empirical research that has examined the effects of a job's structure and design on several positive employee outcomes and behaviors that have been the focus of earlier research attention. Three of the outcomes included in this review can be considered direct indicators of employee psychological well-being: satisfaction with the job, satisfaction with opportunities to grow and develop at work, and internal work motivation. I also discuss two other outcomes (creativity and altruism) that reflect positive actions on the part of the employee that have the potential to contribute to the well-being of that employee's coworkers and colleagues and to the growth and effectiveness of the organization itself.

I begin the chapter by defining job design and briefly summarizing some the most significant historical developments related to this topic. I then present one well-researched approach to the design of jobs, *job characteristics theory* (JCT; Hackman & Oldham, 1976, 1980), and discuss how the job properties associated with this theory might contribute to the positive outcomes and responses described above. Finally, I conclude with a discussion of the implications of these findings for enhancing positive outcomes at work and some possible future research directions concerning the design of jobs and positive employee experiences and actions.

Early Approaches to Job Design

For the past 50 years, few topics in the organizational sciences have received as much research attention as job design (Clegg & Spencer, 2007; Fried, Levi, & Laurence, 2008). At its most basic level, job design refers to the actual structure of jobs that employees perform. Thus, job design focuses squarely on the work itself—on the tasks or activities that individuals complete in their organizations on a daily basis. It is this focus on the work itself that is undoubtedly most responsible for the popularity of job design as a research topic. Individuals may be able to avoid contact with many aspects of the context in which they work, but it is very difficult for them to avoid contact with their jobs. Therefore, the way jobs are structured and designed should play a significant role in determining how people respond in their employing organizations.

Most of the early ideas concerned with the design of jobs have their origins in the philosophy set forth a century ago by Taylor (1911) and subsequently carried forward by industrial engineers who sought to bring greater control and efficiency to the workplace. Taylor's basic idea was to increase employee work efficiency by designing jobs that were simplified and standardized, so that any unnecessary work could be eliminated and employees could be just as interchangeable as standardized machine parts. The problem with this approach was that many employees

did not much like the routine, repetitive jobs they now were required to perform—so much so that they sometimes behaved in ways that negated the efficiencies engineers had built into the work. For example, employees often were late to work or restricted their productivity on such jobs, or they sabotaged their work or equipment, resulting in productivity losses (Walker & Guest, 1952). As a result, the gains in productive efficiency that were expected by early industrial engineers were often more than offset by the losses incurred when these engineering principles were implemented.

To address the problems that resulted from job simplification and standardization, behavioral scientists in the 1960s began considering ways to redesign jobs by expanding both their content and scope. Much of this early work was based on ideas developed by Herzberg (1966), who argued that, to enhance employee motivation and job satisfaction, jobs should be *enriched* rather than simplified. That is, work should be designed to foster responsibility, achievement, growth in competence, recognition, and advancement. Conditions extrinsic to the work itself, such as good supervisory practices and pleasant working conditions, were "hygiene factors" that could create dissatisfaction if poorly managed but never motivate employees to work hard or boost employees' satisfaction with the work itself.

Although empirical research did not provide much support for the conceptual model on which job enrichment was based (see King, 1970), Herzberg's approach did spawn a large number of job enrichment projects, many of them successful (see Herzberg, 1976). And, it provided a valuable point of departure for JCT (Hackman & Oldham, 1976, 1980), which has been the most widely researched and debated approach to the design of jobs from the 1970s until the present day (Fried et al., 2008).

Job Characteristics Theory

The primary objective of JCT was to identify the characteristics of jobs that contributed to employees' work effectiveness and several positive experiences, including internal work motivation (i.e., the extent to which individuals experienced personal satisfaction when they performed well), satisfaction with the job, and satisfaction with opportunities to grow and develop at work. Building upon work by Turner and Lawrence (1965) and Hackman and Lawler (1971), JCT identified five core job characteristics (Hackman & Oldham, 1976) that were expected to contribute to these outcomes: skill variety (i.e., the degree to which the job requires a variety of different activities in carrying out the work, involving the use of a number of different skills and talents of the person), task identity (i.e., the degree to which the job requires doing a whole and identifiable piece of work from beginning to end), task significance (i.e., the degree to which the job has a substantial impact on the lives of other people, whether those people are in the immediate organization or the world at large), autonomy (i.e., the degree to which the job provides substantial freedom, independence, and discretion to the individual in scheduling the work and in determining the procedures to be used in carrying it out), and job-based feedback (i.e., the degree to which carrying out the work activities required by the job provides the individual with direct and clear information about the effectiveness of his or her performance).

Each of the five core job characteristics was expected to contribute to the employee's outcomes and experiences via its effects on one of three psychological states. Specifically, the first three of these characteristics were expected to contribute to the *experienced meaningfulness* of the work (i.e., the degree to which the jobholder experiences the work as inherently meaningful, as something that "counts" in his or her own system of values). Skill variety was expected to boost meaningfulness because this characteristic required the employee to engage in activities that challenged or stretched his or her skills and abilities. Similarly, an employee was expected to experience the work as meaningful when the job had high task identity. In this circumstance, such as when an employee provides a complete unit of service or produces an entire product, the employee is likely to view the task as more meaningful than if he or she were responsible only for a small part of the job. Finally, the employee was expected to experience meaningfulness when the job had high task significance and he or she understood that the work being completed had a substantial impact on the physical or psychological well-being of others.

Autonomy was expected to contribute to employees' *experienced responsibility* for work outcomes (i.e., the degree to which the jobholder feels personally accountable and responsible for the results of the work he or she does). When the job provides the employee with substantial discretion, independence, and freedom, work outcomes should be viewed as depending on his or her own efforts. Thus, as autonomy increases, the employee should feel more personal responsibility for successes and failures that occur on the job and should be more willing to be personally accountable for the outcomes of the work.

Finally, job-based feedback was expected to provide direct *knowledge of the results* of the work (i.e., the degree to which the jobholder has confident knowledge about how well he or she is performing). When the job provides the employee with information about how well he or she is performing, such as when a physician treats a patient and sees the patient get healthy, the knowledge of results derives directly from the work activities themselves.

When a job contains high levels of the five core characteristics, all three psychological states should be simultaneously present. And when this occurs— that is, when the employee experienced the work to be meaningful, felt personally responsible for work outcomes, and had knowledge of the results of the work—JCT posited that individuals would be internally motivated to perform well because it felt good when they did, and it felt bad when they did not. Moreover, it was expected that individuals in these circumstances would be excited and enthusiastic about their work activities and fully engaged in their jobs (de Lange, De Witte, & Noelaers, 2008; Saavedra & Kwun, 2000), resulting in relatively high levels of satisfaction with the job itself and with opportunities for growth and development.

Job characteristics theory also proposed three conditions that were expected to moderate the effects of the core job characteristics on employee responses: growth need strength (GNS; i.e., the degree to which a jobholder values opportunities for personal growth and development at work), satisfaction with the work context (i.e., the degree to which the jobholder is satisfied with pay, supervision, coworkers, and security), and job-relevant knowledge and skill. Specifically, JCT posited that employees would respond positively to well-designed jobs that had high levels of the core job characteristics when they had high GNS and therefore valued the opportunities for accomplishment and self-direction provided by jobs with such characteristics, when they were satisfied with the context and could therefore focus their attentions and energies on the work itself, and when they had the competencies to complete a job high on the five core characteristics.

Results of Research on Job Characteristics Theory

This section reviews the research that has tested JCT, with an emphasis on those studies that have examined the three positive experiences included in the theory itself: internal motivation, job satisfaction, and satisfaction with opportunities for growth and development. Since extensive reviews of this literature are available elsewhere (e.g., Fried & Ferris, 1987; Fried et al., 2008; Humphrey, Nahrgang, & Morgeson, 2007; Oldham, 1996), I will not review the individual studies in detail here. Instead, I provide a brief overview of some of the major conclusions of these reviews.

Results of previous studies show that the five core job characteristics have substantial, positive effects on each of the three positive outcomes described above. Specifically, results indicate that employees generally experience high internal motivation, high satisfaction with their jobs, and high satisfaction with opportunities for growth and personal development when they work on complex, challenging jobs characterized by high levels of autonomy, skill variety, task identity, task significance, and job-based feedback (Fried & Ferris, 1987; Humphrey et al., 2007; Oldham, 1996). Moreover, although results of previous studies provide general support for the proposed mediating effects of the psychological states of experienced meaningfulness, experienced responsibility, and knowledge of results (Fried & Ferris, 1987; Oldham, 1996), a recent meta-analysis by Humphrey and colleagues (2007) also concluded that one of these psychological states—*experienced meaningfulness*—was quite effective in explaining the effects of *all* five core job characteristics on internal motivation and job satisfaction. That is, each of the five core properties was found to enhance the extent to which the employee experienced the work as meaningful and worthwhile, which then contributed to the internal motivation and job satisfaction outcomes included in JCT.

The results involving the three proposed moderators were not completely supportive of the arguments in JCT (Fried et al., 2008; Oldham, 1996). First, no studies directly tested the moderating effects of knowledge and skill, so it is unclear if individuals' competencies play a role in how they respond to the five core characteristics. The context satisfaction moderator did receive research attention, but the results of these studies were mixed and inconsistent and it is not clear that employees respond differently to the job characteristics if they are more or less satisfied with the work context (Oldham, 1996). Finally, the most recent meta-analysis of the literature concerning the GNS moderator (Fried & Ferris, 1987) concluded that GNS was generally ineffective in moderating the relationships between job characteristics and the

internal motivation, job satisfaction, and growth satisfaction outcomes. In total, then, differences among individual employees appear to play little role in determining how they respond to the core job characteristics.

In summary, research on JCT demonstrated that employees had generally positive experiences at work (i.e., high internal motivation and satisfaction) when their jobs were characterized by high levels of autonomy, skill variety, task identity, task significance, and job-based feedback. These effects appeared to flow to these positive outcomes through the three proposed psychological states, with experienced meaningfulness representing the most important and critical of these states. Thus, boosting a job's standing on the five core characteristics is likely to increase the jobholder's beliefs that the job counts and is worthwhile, which, in turn, should enhance his or her internal motivation and satisfaction. It should be noted that this latter finding provides support for arguments by Cameron et al. (2003b) that organizational conditions and practices often influence a variety of positive outcomes via their effects on an employee's sense of meaningfulness. Finally, empirical results described above involving moderators included in JCT were quite weak and suggest that they do not play a consistent role in shaping the effects of the job characteristics on the positive outcomes included in the theory.

The Design of Jobs, Employee Creativity, and Altruism

Thus far, I have discussed the effects of a job's design on three positive experiences included in JCT. In this section, I focus on two positive actions on the part of employees that are not included in the JCT model itself but have been shown to be affected by the structure and design of employees' jobs: employee creativity and altruistic behavior. In the paragraphs that follow, I define the creativity and altruism outcomes and discuss how the design of jobs might influence them. I then separately review the literature that has examined these proposed effects.

Creativity

This refers to the production of ideas concerning organizational products, practices, services, or procedures that are novel and potentially useful to the organization (Amabile, 1996; Shalley, Zhou, & Oldham, 2004). Ideas are considered *novel* if they are unique relative to other ideas currently available in the organization. Ideas are considered *useful* if they have the potential for value to the organization or its members, in either the short- or long-term. Scholars have long argued that when an employee generates creative ideas, he or she increases the likelihood that these ideas will be informally adopted by colleagues and coworkers and that the management of the organization will formally implement the ideas and introduce them in the organization as a whole or in the marketplace (Oldham & Baer, in press). Thus, the production of ideas by an employee has the potential to benefit the employee's coworkers by providing them with new ideas or perspectives that might facilitate the completion of their work activities. Moreover, the implementation of these creative ideas by management might benefit the organization by allowing it to adjust to shifting market conditions, respond to opportunities, and thereby, to adapt and grow (Lee, Rho, Kim, & Jun, 2007; Nonaka, 1991).

Based on earlier research and theory (e.g., Amabile, 1996; Kahn, 1990; Oldham & Baer, in press), I expect individual employees to generate creative ideas when they work on well-designed jobs characterized by high levels of the five core characteristics included in JCT. As noted earlier, when individuals work on jobs with these core characteristics, they should be excited by their work activities and fully engaged in their jobs. As a result of this engagement, individual employees are likely to step outside the bounds of their formally defined jobs and engage in acts that might benefit coworkers or the organization (Rich, LePine, & Crawford, 2010), such as generating ideas for improving the organization's products, processes, or service offerings (Oldham & Baer, in press). Moreover, previous research suggests that individuals who are fully engaged in their work are not only more curious but also more willing to take risks, such as engaging in exploratory behaviors and experimentation—all of which should facilitate creativity (Baer & Oldham, 2006; Zhou & Shalley, 2003).

A number of investigations have focused on the effects of a job's design on employee creativity and provide results that are generally consistent with these arguments. For example, studies have shown positive, significant correlations between objective, general indicators of a job's complexity and challenge derived from the *Dictionary of Occupational Titles* (DOT; Roos & Treiman, 1980) and supervisors' ratings of employee creativity (Tierney & Farmer, 2002, 2004) and employee self-reported creativity (Shalley, Gilson, & Blum, 2009). Other studies have obtained similar findings using employee descriptions of their jobs' complexity and challenge (e.g., Amabile Conti, Coon, Lazenby, & Herron, 1996; Farmer, Tierney, & Kung-McIntyre, 2003; Martin, Salanova, & Peiro, 2007). For example, Ohly, Sonnentag, and Pluntke (2006) found a positive association between employee descriptions of their job's overall complexity and self-reported creativity. Hatcher, Ross, and Collins (1989) found a significant correlation between a measure composed of three job characteristics (autonomy, variety, and feedback) and the number of new ideas employees submitted to an organization suggestion program. Oldham and Cummings (1996) found a significant correlation between an index composed of employee descriptions of the five core characteristics and a supervisory rating of employee creativity. And Zhang and Bartol (2010) found a positive relationship between a supervisor rating of employee creativity and an index composed of three core characteristics: variety, identity, and significance.

Only a few studies obtained results that were not consistent with the arguments concerning the expected positive effects of well-designed jobs on creativity. For example, across two samples, Jaskyte (2008) showed that an index composed of the five core characteristics had nonsignificant relationships to employee self-reports of creativity. Grant and Berry (2011) found a positive, significant association between supervisor-rated creativity and the job characteristic of autonomy, but a nonsignificant association involving skill variety.

In total, despite a few studies showing weak or negligible effects of a job's design, the large majority of studies that have examined the job design–creativity link indicate that when employees work on complex, challenging jobs they tend to exhibit relatively high levels of creativity at work. Unfortunately, most of the earlier research used measures of overall job complexity and challenge, and it is not yet clear which of the five core characteristics has the strongest impact on employees' creative idea generation. Research is needed to sort this out. It is also unclear *how* the job characteristics actually affect creativity. Although it may be that the characteristics affect creativity via the three psychological states included in JCT, it is also possible that they have their effects via experienced meaningfulness alone, via more general affective states (e.g., excitement and enthusiasm) that have been connected to the core job characteristics and creativity (Fisher, 2002; Madjar, Oldham, & Pratt, 2002; Saavedra & Kwun, 2000), or via other conditions such as creative self-efficacy (Tierney & Farmer, 2002).

Research is needed that compares and contrasts these possible mediating conditions. Finally, although a few studies have examined the possibility that individual differences (e.g., GNS, ability, personality) moderate the effects of job characteristics on creativity (Binnewies Ohly, & Niessen, 2008; Choi, Anderson, & Veillette, 2009; Oldham & Cummings, 1996; Shalley et al., 2009), there is insufficient evidence to suggest that specific individual difference characteristics consistently moderate the effects of a job's design on employee creative responses. More research is needed in this area as well.

Altruism

This refers to an employee voluntarily helping another individual with a problem or issue that emerges at work (Organ & Konovsky, 1989). This other individual could be located either inside or outside the boundaries of the organization. Thus, the beneficiary of altruistic behavior could be a colleague, coworker, manager, customer, or client. To the extent that a focal employee engages in any behavior that helps or assists an individual with a work-related or personal problem (e.g., providing information, support or resources), he or she is exhibiting altruism. Beyond the obvious benefits to the individual who is the recipient of the altruistic behavior, Katz (1964) has argued persuasively that such behavior is essential for a functioning organization.

I expect individual employees to engage in more altruistic behaviors when they work on jobs characterized by high levels of the five core characteristics. As argued above, employees holding jobs with the core characteristics are likely to be fully engaged in their jobs and to step outside the bounds of their formal job descriptions (Rich et al., 2010) by engaging in acts that might benefit others. Such acts might include providing help or assistance to others—even if such behavior is not a requirement of the individual's job and does not directly benefit him or her.

A number of studies have tested these general ideas and examined the effects of a job's design on employee altruistic behaviors (see Podsakoff, MacKenzie, Paine, & Bacharach, 2000). These early studies are of two general types: those that include separate and independent measures of employee helping and those that include items tapping altruism in more general measures of Organizational Citizenship Behavior (OCB; Organ & Konovsky, 1989). These latter measures also include items that tap such behaviors as sportsmanship, courtesy, and

conscientiousness. I review these studies separately below.

The results of studies that include independent measures of altruism provide substantial support for the argument that the design of an employee's job can impact his or her altruistic behavior. For example, Farh, Podsakoff, and Organ (1990) examined relationships between employee descriptions of the five core characteristics and supervisor reports of that employee's altruistic behavior in the workplace. Results showed that each of the characteristics was positively related to altruism, although only the relations involving three characteristics (skill variety, autonomy, and job-based feedback) were statistically significant. Bell and Menguc (2002) found a positive, significant relationship between employee reports of their job autonomy and manager reports of that employee's altruism. Todd and Kent (2006) found positive, significant correlations between employee self-reports of helping behavior and two core job characteristics: autonomy and task significance. Grant (2008b, study 2) examined the effects of changes in task significance on the helping behavior of lifeguards. Results showed that lifeguards who read a story about the impact of their work on the lives and well-being of others engaged in more helping behavior than did those who read stories about the benefits of their job to themselves. Only a study by Fisher (2002) failed to provide support for the proposed job complexity–altruism link. She found that a job complexity index composed of employee descriptions of the five core characteristics had a nonsignificant relationship to a self-report index of helping composed of five measures (provide extra help to customers/clients, help colleagues with heavy workloads, orient newcomers, do extra tasks, and volunteer to learn new tasks).

Studies that include altruism items in more general OCB measures also provide results generally consistent with my arguments. For example, Chen and Chiu (2009) examined relationships between each of the core characteristics and a supervisor rating of each employee's OCBs that included altruism items. Results showed that each of the five characteristics related positively to the OCB index. Chiu and Chen (2005) showed that employee self-reports of three of the five core characteristics (skill variety, task significance, and job feedback) were positively and significantly related to an overall OCB measure. Purvanova, Bono, and Dzieweczynski (2006) found positive, significant relationships between an overall measure of OCB and two measures of job complexity: a measure based on employee self-reports that taps the five core characteristics and an objective measure based on the DOT. Finally, Cappelli and Rogovsky (1998) demonstrated that three core characteristics (autonomy, skill variety, task significance) made positive and statistically significant contributions to an OCB index.

In summary, the large majority of previous studies suggest that employees engage in more altruistic activities in the workplace when they work on well-designed jobs that contain high levels of the five core characteristics included in JCT. However, a number of questions about the design of jobs and employee altruistic behavior remain unanswered. For example, it is not yet clear which job characteristic or characteristics explain most of the variance in altruistic behavior, or if different characteristics contribute to different types of altruism (e.g., providing emotional versus informational support). Research is needed that examines the independent effects of each of the five characteristics on different types of altruistic behaviors. In addition, research is needed that systematically examines the mediating conditions that might explain the effects of job design on altruism. For example, research might contrast the mediating effects of the individual psychological states included in JCT with more general affective states (e.g., positive mood). Finally, no study has examined the possibility individual differences moderate the effects of job design on altruism. Research is needed on this topic as well.

Implications for Practice

Considerable evidence indicates that the five core characteristics in JCT (autonomy, skill variety, task significance, task identity, and job-based feedback) have substantial effects on the five positive outcomes discussed in this chapter: internal motivation, job satisfaction, satisfaction with opportunities for growth and development, creativity, and altruism. Apparently, individuals feel good when they perform well on jobs that include the five core characteristics and are generally satisfied with their jobs and with their enriched opportunities to grow and develop when they work on such jobs. Moreover, individuals who work on well-designed jobs are likely to engage in creative and altruistic behaviors that may be of benefit to their clients, colleagues, and coworkers, as well as to their organization as a whole.

These results suggest that improving the standing of the core job characteristics by engaging in well-established job redesign practices (see Hackman & Oldham, 1980; Herzberg, 1976; Kopelman

1985) should result in significant improvements in the positive outcomes experienced and exhibited by employees. For example, providing each employee with a larger module of work should boost the skill variety and task identity characteristics. Putting the employee in direct contact with his or her clients and giving him or her continuing responsibility for managing those relationships should boost the characteristics of autonomy, skill variety, and feedback. And, changes in these job characteristics via the redesign practices just described should foster significant improvements in the five positive outcomes discussed in this chapter.

Future Directions

In this section, I discuss three areas related to the design of jobs and positive employee experiences and actions that warrant future research attention. I first focus on the possible effects of a job's social characteristics on positive outcomes. Next, I discuss the possibility that other positive outcomes that have received little research attention might be affected by both the core job characteristics and these social characteristics. I conclude with a discussion of the possibility that enhancing one employee's positive outcomes via job design might have spillover effects on the positive outcomes experienced by others.

Social Job Characteristics

As described earlier, JCT focused on five core job properties that were expected to shape employees' internal work motivation, job satisfaction, and satisfaction with growth opportunities. The model excluded job characteristics involving social aspects of the work since such characteristics were expected to have little motivational consequence (Oldham & Hackman, 2010). However, early research by Turner and Lawrence (1965) and Hackman and Oldham (1975) did identify and discuss several social job dimensions that were expected to supplement the effects of the core properties. These include *feedback from agents* (i.e., the degree to which managers and coworkers let the employee know how well he or she is doing on the job) and *dealing with others* (i.e., the degree to which the job requires an employee to work closely with other people inside or outside the organization). These social job dimensions have received less research attention than the five core characteristics (Oldham, 1996), and we know far less about their possible effects on the positive outcomes described in this chapter. Yet, as discussed below, I argue that such social dimensions have the potential to make substantial contributions to employees' positive actions and experiences at work.

A few studies have shown that the social dimensions of feedback from agents and dealing with others are related to the positive outcomes included in JCT (i.e., internal motivation, job satisfaction, and growth satisfaction), as well as to the three psychological states (Hackman & Oldham, 1975; Humphrey et al., 2007; Oldham, Hackman, & Stepina, 1979). Thus, individuals appear to be more internally motivated and satisfied with their jobs and with their opportunities to grow and develop when they work on jobs that require them to interact with others and when they receive feedback about their work performance from these others. However, it is not yet clear if these effects are transmitted through the three psychological states included in JCT or if only one state (e.g., experienced meaningfulness) may explain the effects. Research is now needed that examines these issues.

Research is also needed that links the social characteristics to the other positive outcomes considered in this chapter, creativity and altruism. For altruism, it may be that, when jobs are designed to encourage employee contact with others, those who perform them may empathize, identify with, and take the perspective of the others with whom they interact, resulting in more altruistic behavior (Grant, 2007). Research is needed to systematically test this possibility. With regard to employee creativity, it may be that increased interaction with others exposes the jobholder to new and different ideas and perspectives about work-related practices and policies (Oldham & Hackman, 2010). This enhanced exposure might contribute to an employee's creativity not only by directly triggering new ideas (Madjar, 2008; Perry-Smith, 2006) but also by energizing the combinatory processes that underlie the production of such ideas (Perry-Smith & Shalley, 2003). Thus, to the extent that social job characteristics facilitate access and exposure to new, unique information from other individuals to the focal employee, the creativity of that employee should be enhanced. Research is now needed that directly examines this possibility.

Finally, research is needed that examines the possibility that individual differences moderate the effects of the social job characteristics on employees' positive experiences and actions. A good start in addressing this issue has been provided by Mount, Barrick, and Stewart (1998). These authors conducted research on employees in jobs that required interpersonal interaction (i.e., teamwork or customer service) and demonstrated that these employees performed at higher levels when they scored high on three dimensions from the Big Five model of personality (Costa & McCrae, 1992): conscientiousness, agreeableness, and emotional stability. Research is needed to further specify the interactions between the social aspects of jobs and jobholder personality for positive outcomes (e.g., altruistic and creative behavior), as well as studies that explore the moderating effects of individual differences other than those specified in the Big Five model (e.g., GNS).

Job Design and Other Positive Outcomes

This chapter has focused on the connection between a job's design and five positive experiences and actions that might have received substantial attention in the literature. However, POS scholars have described numerous other positive outcomes (e.g., virtuousness, resilience, positive deviance) that address the best of the human condition (Cameron et al., 2003a; Spreitzer, Sutcliffe, Dutton, Sonenshein, & Grant, 2005). Unfortunately, little research has examined the connection between the design of jobs and such positive employee outcomes. In the paragraphs below, I discuss the possibility that the core and social characteristics of jobs described earlier might have an impact on four positive outcomes that have received little empirical research attention.

Employee *new learning* (Cameron et al., 2003b) is the first of these positive outcomes deserving of attention. I propose that both the core and social job characteristics described earlier have the potential to contribute to an employee's learning and acquisition of new knowledge at work (Clegg & Spencer, 2007; Oldham & Hackman, 2010). For example, it may be that high levels of skill variety offer the employee the chance to extend his or her skill set. And, high autonomy may permit the individual to hone his or her self-management capabilities. The social job characteristics described might also contribute to employee knowledge acquisition. For example, required interaction between the focal employee and clients or customers can provide new information to the employee that expands his or her knowledge, invite the cultivation of relationship management skills, and, if those with whom the jobholder interacts have background and demographic characteristics different from his or her own, expose the person to novel perspectives or behavioral styles (Baer, 2010; Oldham & Hackman, 2010; Perry-Smith, 2006).

Future research on the independent and combined effects of the core and social job characteristics on employee new learning and skill acquisition is clearly warranted. This research might attempt to sort out which characteristics are most powerful in shaping new learning and whether the acquisition of new knowledge has implications for other positive employee outcomes.

A second outcome that may warrant attention is employee *self-efficacy* (i.e., the extent to which an individual believes that he or she is capable of performing a particular job) (Bandura, 1986; Luthans & Youssef, 2007). Self-efficacy "is concerned not with the skills one has but with the judgments of what one can do with whatever skills one possesses" (Bandura, 1986). I propose that individuals who work on well-designed jobs characterized by high levels of the core characteristics should develop higher levels of self-efficacy than would those who work on simple, routinized jobs. The reason is that employees who work on such well-designed jobs often have considerable freedom and discretion at work and experience a good deal of personal control (Hackman & Oldham, 1980). Since personal control is considered a critical determinant of individuals' self-efficacy (Bandura, 1986), well-designed jobs that provide such control should boost jobholders' self-efficacy.

In addition to the possible effects of the freedom and discretion provided by a job, the social characteristics of a job also might make substantial contributions to employee self-efficacy. For example, if jobs that require social interaction expand an employee's knowledge and skill sets, as suggested earlier, these acquired skills may enhance the extent to which the employee feels capable of performing a given job.

A few studies provide indirect support for these arguments. For example, Buchanan and McCalman (1989) described how employees developed a stronger sense of self-efficacy at work after autonomous work groups were introduced in the organization. And Parker (1998) showed that a measure of task control (i.e., the extent to which the employee had control over work pace, scheduling, and how to carry out tasks) was positively associated with a measure of "role breadth self-efficacy" (i.e., the extent to which employees feel comfortable carrying out a broader and more proactive role at work). Research is now needed that directly examines the effects of core and social job characteristics on employee self-efficacy. This work might focus on identifying the job characteristic or characteristics that have the

strongest effects on self-efficacy and whether the effects of these job characteristics become stronger (or weaker) over time as individuals continue to work on jobs with these characteristics.

A third positive outcome that warrants attention is *resilience* (i.e., the extent to which the employee is capable of rebounding or adapting to threats, pressures or significant adversity) (Frederickson, Tugade, Waugh, & Larkin, 2003; Spreitzer et al., 2005). I suggest that when individuals work on well-designed jobs characterized by high levels the five core characteristics, they will become more resilient to external threats and adversity than if they work on jobs that are relatively simple and routine in nature. As argued earlier, well-designed jobs provide individuals with ample personal and psychological rewards for performing well. As a result of the availability of these personal rewards, individuals are likely to be fully absorbed and involved in their jobs and to experience positive affective states (Fisher, 2002; Saavedra & Kwun, 2000). It is the presence of these positive affective states in well-designed jobs that allows individuals to cope and thrive despite adversity or threat from external sources (Frederickson et al., 2003; Ong, Bergeman, Bisconti, & Wallace, 2006).

According to Frederickson et al. (2003), it is the cognitive broadening that accompanies the presence of positive affective states that allows individuals to develop enhanced resilience to adversity. That is, positive affective states broaden people's attention, thinking, and behavioral repertoires, thereby, boosting individuals' ability to cope and bounce back when threatened. In addition, Frederickson (2001) argues that, over time, the broadening triggered by positive affective states enables the individual to build a range of personal resources (e.g., physical, social, and intellectual) that allow individuals to become resilient to threat and pressures.

Although no studies have examined the possibility that positive affective states produced by a job's design enable employees to develop resilience to adversity in the workplace, numerous studies in nonwork settings have demonstrated that positive affective states have a restorative function enabling individuals to cope with adverse situations (see Frederickson et al., 2003, Ong et al., 2006; Tugade, Frederickson, & Barrett, 2004). Research is now needed that systematically examines the extent to which the work itself produces the specific affective states that allow individuals to bounce back from adversity. Research is also needed to determine if the presence of these positive states allows individuals to cope more effectively with threats from certain sources than from others (e.g., from supervisors vs. coworkers). Finally, research is needed that examines whether the redesign of jobs *after* adversity has been experienced by an employee is an effective strategy for restoring the effectiveness and well-being of individuals.

Finally, a fourth positive outcome that deserves research attention is the *quality of family and marital relationships* (Oldham, 1996). There are a number of possible ways that a job's design might impact family relationships. For example, if jobs are well-designed and contain the five core characteristics, individuals should be engaged and absorbed in their work, which could then compromise the time and energy they have for family-related activities. Alternatively, it may be that well-designed jobs allow the employee to participate in family activities by providing him or her with autonomy and discretion in work scheduling (Grzywacz & Butler, 2005). With regard to social job characteristics, it was noted earlier that jobs that require interaction between the focal employee and others enable the employee to develop new relationship management skills. And, it is possible that the acquisition of such new skills might affect the way an individual interacts with his or her spouse and family. Research is now needed that explores these possibilities and examines the long-term effects of an employee's job design on the quality of family and marital relations.

Positive Outcomes and Social Contagion

Thus far, I have focused on the possible effects of a job's structural properties on the positive actions and experiences of the employee who holds that job. This work suggests that boosting a job's standing on the core or social characteristics might have positive effects on the employee's positive outcomes such as satisfaction, creativity, and altruism. In this section, I discuss the possibility that an improvement in the positive outcomes for a single employee as a function of a job's design might have unintended spill-over effects on the related outcomes of individuals in that employee's network of contacts (e.g., coworkers, clients, and customers). That is, I discuss whether the enhanced satisfaction, creativity, and altruism that might result from changes in the design of one employee's job might have implications for improvements in the identical outcomes for others with whom that employee interacts.

A good deal of evidence that has focused on the topic of social contagion suggests that the enhancement of one individual's experiences might have

implications for the experiences of others (see Felps, Mitchell, Hekman, Lee, Holtom, & Harmon, 2009; Homburg & Stock, 2004; Olson, 2006). Totterdell, Kellett, Briner, and Teuchman (1998) offer two explanations for such effects. First, individuals might compare themselves with others by consciously processing information about how others are feeling, which sometimes leads them to feel the same way themselves. Second, it may be that people nonconsciously mimic people's expressive displays (face and voice) and consequently experience feedback from their own expressive displays that causes reactions to converge with those of the person they are mimicking. In support of these arguments, several studies have found a positive link between employee and customer satisfaction (see Bernhardt, Donthu, & Kennett, 2000; Schlesinger & Zornitsky, 1991) and suggest that this link might be strengthened when there is frequent contact between employee and customer (Homburg & Stock, 2004).

It is also possible that boosting one individual's creativity by improving the standing of that person's job on the core or social characteristics will result in improvements in creativity among the individuals with whom that employee interacts (Amabile, 1996). This prediction is based on two arguments. First, if an individual observes a colleague producing creative work, that colleague's motivation for engaging in creative work will spontaneously spread to him or her. Thus, if the creative colleague is engaged and excited about his or her work, that will result in increased engagement on the part of the other employee and higher subsequent creativity. Also, it may be that observing creative others allows individuals to acquire relevant strategies and approaches that enable them to exhibit higher creativity in their own work (Shalley & Perry-Smith, 2001).

A few studies have been conducted that support these arguments (see Amabile, 1996). For example, in two field studies, Zhou (2003) showed that the presence of creative coworkers had positive effects on an individual's creativity, as long as supervisors engaged in supportive behavior. Research is now needed that examines the effects of one employee's creativity on the creativity of others in the workplace and that attempts to sort out the ways that creativity spreads across individuals.

Finally, it may be that altruistic behavior is also contagious (Deckop, Circa, & Andersson, 2003). Based on the norm of reciprocity (Gouldner, 1960), individuals who receive help from a colleague are likely to feel indebted to that colleague and to engage in helping behavior toward him or her as a way to reduce this sense of indebtedness. It is also possible that individuals will model their motivational orientations after those of the individual who provided the help, thereby engaging in increased altruistic behavior toward others.

A few studies provide evidence that supports these arguments (Bateman & Organ, 1983; Tsai, Chen, & Liu, 2007). For example, Deckop and his colleagues (2003) showed that when employees perceived that they received a high level of assistance from their coworkers, they engaged in more helping behaviors toward their coworkers. And Tsai et al. (2007) showed that the more sales agents engaged in helping behaviors, the more help and support they received from their coworkers. More research is now needed that examines the effects of different forms of altruistic behavior exhibited by one employee on the altruism exhibited by the beneficiaries. For example, does an employee who receives help in the form of emotional support exhibit only this type of altruistic behavior toward others, or does he or she exhibit other forms of altruism (e.g., providing informational resources to others)?

In summary, this section discussed the possibility that changes in the design of one employee's job that resulted in improvements in that employee's satisfaction, creativity, and altruism might have widespread effects on the identical outcomes of others with whom that employee interacts. Thus, boosting the standing of one employee's job on the core or social characteristics might have effects on that employee's positive outcomes, but, perhaps more importantly, on the positive outcomes of many others in the workplace and beyond. More work is now needed to test these ideas with the regard to the positive outcomes discussed in this chapter as well as other positive outcomes identified by POS scholars (e.g., Cameron et al., 2003b; Luthans & Youssef, 2007).

References

Amabile, T.M. (1996). *Creativity in context*. Boulder, CO: Westview Press.

Amabile, T.M., Conti, R., Coon, H., Lazenby, J., & Herron, M. (1996). Assessing the work environment for creativity. *Academy of Management Journal, 39*, 1154–1184.

Baer, M. (2010). The strength-of-weak-ties perspective on creativity: A comprehensive examination and extension. *Journal of Applied Psychology, 95*, 592–601.

Baer, M., & Oldham, G.R. (2006). The curvilinear relation between experienced creative time pressure and creativity: Moderating effects of openness to experience and support for creativity. *Journal of Applied Psychology, 91*, 963–970.

Bandura, A. (1986). *Social foundations of thought and action: A social-cognitive view*. Englewood Cliffs, NJ: Prentice-Hall.

Bateman, T.S., & Organ, D.W. (1983). Job satisfaction and the good soldier: The relationship between affect and employee "citizenship." *Journal of Applied Psychology, 68*, 439–445.

Bell, S.J., & Menguc, B. (2002). The employee-organization relationship, organizational citizenship behaviors, and superior service quality. *Journal of Retailing, 78*, 131–146.

Bernhardt, K.L., Donthu, N., & Kennett, P.A. (2000). A longitudinal analysis of satisfaction and profitability. *Journal of Business Research, 47*, 161–171.

Binnewies, C., Ohly, S., & Niessen, C. (2008). Age and creativity at work: The interplay between job resources, age, and idea creativity. *Journal of Managerial Psychology, 23*, 438–457.

Buchanan, D.A., & McCalman, J. (1989). *High performance work systems: The digital experience*. Surrey, UK: Routledge.

Cameron, K.S., Dutton, J.E., & Quinn, R.E. (2003a). Foundations of positive organizational scholarship. In K. Cameron, J. Dutton, & R. Quinn (Eds.), *Positive organizational scholarship: Foundations of a new discipline* (pp. 5–27). San Francisco: Barrett-Koehler.

Cameron, K.S., Dutton, J.E., Quinn, R.E., & Wrzesiewski, A. (2003b). Developing a discipline of positive organizational scholarship. In K. Cameron, J. Dutton, & R. Quinn (Eds.), *Positive organizational scholarship: Foundations of a new discipline* (pp. 361–370). San Francisco: Barrett-Koehler.

Cappelli, P., & Rogovsky, N. (1998). Employee involvement and organizational citizenship: Implications for labor lab reform and "lean production." *Industrial and Labor Relations Review, 51*, 633–650.

Chen, C-C., & Chiu, S-F. (2009). The mediating role of job involvement in the relationship between job characteristics and organizational citizenship behavior. *The Journal of Social Psychology, 149*, 474–494.

Chiu, S-F., & Chen, H-L. (2005). Relationship between job characteristics and organizational citizenship behavior: The mediating role of job satisfaction. *Social Behavior and Personality, 33*, 523–540.

Choi, J.N., Anderson, T.A., & Veillette, A. (2009). Contextual inhibitors of employee creativity in organizations: The insulating role of creative ability. *Group & Organization Management, 34*, 330–357.

Clegg, C., & Spencer, C. (2007). A circular and dynamic model of the process of job design. *Journal of Occupational and Organizational Psychology, 80*, 321–339

Costa, P.T., & McCrae, R.R. (1992). *Revised NEO Personality Inventory (NEO-PI-R) and NEO Five-Factor Inventory (NEO-FFI) professional manual*. Odessa, FL: Psychological Assessment Resources.

de Lange, A.H., De Witte, H., & Notelaers, G. (2008). Should I stay or should I go? Examining longitudinal relations among job resources and work engagement for stayers versus movers. *Work & Stress, 22*, 201–223.

Deckop, J.R., Circa, C.C., & Andersson, L.M. (2003). Doing unto others: The reciprocity of helping behavior in organizations. *Journal of Business Ethics, 47*, 101–113.

Farh, J-L., Podsakoff, P.M., & Organ, D.W. (1990). Accounting for organizational citizenship behavior: Leader fairness and task scope versus satisfaction. *Journal of Management, 47*, 705–721.

Farmer, S.M., Tierney, P., & Kung-McIntyre, K. (2003). Employee creativity in Taiwan: An application of role identity theory. *Academy of Management Journal, 46*, 618–630.

Felps, W., Mitchell, T.R., Hekman, D.R., Lee, T.W., Holtom, B.C., & Harmon, W.S. (2009). Turnover contagion: How coworkers' job embeddedness and job search behaviors influence quitting. *Academy of Management Journal, 52*, 545–561.

Fisher, C.D. (2002). Antecedents and consequences of real-time affective reactions at work. *Motivation and Emotion, 26*, 3–30.

Fineman, S. (2006). On being positive: Concerns and counterpoints. *Academy of Management Review, 31*, 270–291.

Fredrickson, B.L. (2001). The role of positive emotions in positive psychology: The broaden-and-build theory of positive emotions. *American Psychologist, 56*, 218–226.

Frederickson, B.L., Tugade, M.M., Waugh, C.E., & Larkin, G.R. (2003). What good are positive emotions in crises? A prospective study of resilience and emotions following the terrorist attacks on the United States on September 11th, 2001. *Journal of Personality and Social Psychology, 84*, 365–376.

Fried, Y., & Ferris, G.R. (1987). The validity of the job characteristics model: A review and meta-analysis. *Personnel Psychology, 40*, 287–322.

Fried, Y., Levi, A.S., & Laurence, G. (2008). Motivation and job design in the new world of work. In C. Cooper & S. Cartwright (Eds.). *The Oxford handbook of personnel psychology* (pp. 586–611). Oxford, UK: Oxford University Press.

Gouldner, A.W. (1960). The norm of reciprocity: A preliminary statement. *American Sociological Review, 25*, 161–178.

Grant, A.M. (2007). Relational job design and the motivation to make a prosocial difference. *Academy of Management Review, 32*, 393–417.

Grant, A.M. (2008a). Designing jobs to do good: Dimensions and psychological consequences of prosocial job characteristics. *The Journal of Positive Psychology, 3*, 19–39.

Grant, A.M. (2008b). The significance of task significance: Job performance effects, relational mechanisms, and boundary conditions. *Journal of Applied Psychology, 93*, 108–124.

Grant, A.M., & Berry, J. (2011). The necessity of others is the mother of invention: Intrinsic and prosocial motivations, perspective-taking, and creativity. *Academy of Management Journal, 54*, 73–96.

Grzywacz, J.G., & Butler, A.B. (2005). The impact of job characteristics on work-to-family facilitation: Testing a theory and distinguishing a construct. *Journal of Occupational Health Psychology, 10*, 97–109.

Hackman, J.R., & Lawler, E.E. (1971). Employee reactions to job characteristics. *Journal of Applied Psychology Monograph, 55*, 259–286.

Hackman, J.R., & Oldham, G.R. (1975). Development of the job diagnostic survey. *Journal of Applied Psychology, 60*, 159–170.

Hackman, J.R., & Oldham, G.R. (1976). Motivation through the design of work: Test of a theory. *Organizational Behavior and Human Performance, 16*, 250–279.

Hackman, J.R., & Oldham, G.R. (1980). *Work redesign.* Reading, MA: Addison-Wesley.

Hatcher, L., Ross, T.L., & Collins, D. (1989). Prosocial behavior, job complexity, and suggestion contribution under gainsharing plans. *Journal of Applied Behavioral Science, 25*, 231–248.

Herzberg, F. (1966). *Work and the nature of man.* Cleveland: World.

Herzberg, F. (1976). *The managerial choice.* Homewood, IL: Dow Jones-Irwin.

Homburg, C., & Stock, R.M. (2004). The link between salespeople's job satisfaction and customer satisfaction in a business-to-business context: A dyadic analysis. *Journal of the Academy of Marketing Science, 32*, 144–158.

Humphrey, S.E., Nahrgang, J.D., & Morgeson, F.P. (2007). Integrating motivational, social, and contextual work design features: A meta-analytic summary and theoretical extension of the work design literature. *Journal of Applied Psychology, 92*, 1332–1356.

Jaskyte, K. (2008). Employee creativity in U. S. and Lithuanian nonprofit organizations. *Nonprofit Management & Leadership, 18*, 465–483.

Kahn, W.A. (1990). Psychological conditions of personal engagement and disengagement at work. *Academy of Management Journal, 33*, 692–724.

Katz, D. (1964). The motivational basis of organizational behavior. *Behavioral Science, 9*, 131–146.

King, N.A. (1970). A clarification and evaluation of the two-factor theory of job satisfaction. *Psychological Bulletin, 74*, 18–30.

Kopelman, R.E. (1985). Job redesign and productivity: A review of the evidence. *National Productivity Review, 4*, 237–255.

Lee, K., Rho, S., Kim, S., & Jun, G.J. (2007). Creativity-innovation cycle for organizational exploration and exploitation: Lessons from Neowiz-a Korean internet company. *Long Range Planning, 40*, 505–523.

Luthans, F., & Youssef, C.M. (2007). Emerging positive organizational behavior. *Journal of Management, 33*, 321–349.

Madjar, N. (2008). Emotional and informational support from different sources and employee creativity. *Journal of Occupational and Organizational Psychology, 81*, 83–100.

Madjar, N., Oldham, G.R., & Pratt, M.G. (2002). There's no place like home? The contributions of work and non-work creativity support to employee's creative performance. *Academy of Management Journal, 45*, 757–767.

Martin, P., Salanova, M., & Peiró, J.M. (2007). Job demands, job resources and individual innovation at work: Going beyond Karasek's model? *Psicothema, 19*, 621–626.

Mount, M.K., Barrick, M.R., & Stewart, G.L. (1998). Five-factor model of personality and performance in jobs involving interpersonal interactions. *Human Performance, 11*, 145–165.

Nonaka, I. (1991). The knowledge-creating company. *Harvard Business Review, 69*, 96–104.

Ohly, S., Sonnentag, S., & Pluntke, F. (2006). Routinization, work characteristics, and their relationships with creative and proactive behaviors. *Journal of Organizational Behavior, 27*, 257–279.

Oldham, G.R. (1996). Job design. In C. Cooper & I. Robertson (Eds.), *International review of industrial and organizational psychology* Vol. 11 (pp. 33–60). New York: Wiley.

Oldham, G.R., & Baer, M. (in press). Creativity and the work context. In M. Mumford (Ed.), *Handbook of organizational creativity.* Oxford, UK: Elsevier.

Oldham, G.R., & Cummings, A. (1996). Employee creativity: Personal and contextual factors at work. *Academy of Management Journal, 39*, 607–634.

Oldham, G.R., & Hackman, J.R. (2010). Not what it was and not what it will be: The future of job design research. *Journal of Organizational Behavior, 31*, 463–479.

Oldham, G.R., Hackman, J.R., & Stepina, L.P. (1979). Norms for the job diagnostic survey. *Psychological Documents, 9*, 14, Ms. No. 1819.

Olson, K.R. (2006). A literature review of social mood. *The Journal of Behavioral Finance, 7*, 193–203.

Ong, A.D., Bergeman, C.S., Bisconti, T.L., & Wallace, K.A. (2006). Psychological resilience, positive emotions, and successful adaptation to stress in later life. *Journal of Personality and Social Psychology, 91*, 30–749.

Organ, D.W., & Konovsky, M. (1989). Cognitive versus affective determinants of organizational citizenship behavior. *Journal of Applied Psychology, 74*, 157–164.

Parker, S.K. (1998). Enhancing role breadth self-efficacy: The roles of job enrichment and other organizational interventions. *Journal of Applied Psychology, 83*, 835–852.

Perry-Smith, J.E. (2006). Social yet creative: The role of social relationships in facilitating individual creativity. *Academy of Management Journal, 49*, 85–101.

Perry-Smith, J.E., & Shalley, C.E. (2003). The social side of creativity: A static and dynamic social network perspective. *Academy of Management Review, 28*, 89–106.

Podsakoff, P.M., MacKenzie, S.B., Paine, J.B., & Bacharach, D.G. (2000). Organizational citizenship behaviors: A critical review of the theoretical and empirical literature and suggestions for future research. *Journal of Management, 26*, 513–563.

Purvanova, R.K., Bono, J.E., & Dzieweczynski, J. (2006). Transformational leadership, job characteristics, and organizational citizenship performance. *Human Performance, 19*, 1–22.

Rich, B.L., LePine, J., & Crawford, E.R. (2010). Job engagement: Antecedents and effects on job performance. *Academy of Management Journal, 53*, 617–635.

Roberts, L.M. (2006). Response—shifting the lens on organizational life: The added value of positive scholarship. *Academy of Management Review, 31*, 292–305.

Roos, P.A., & Treiman, D.J. (1980). Worker functions and work traits for the 1970 U.S. census classification. In A. Miller et al. (Eds.), *Work, jobs and occupations* (pp. 336–389). Washington, DC: National Academy Press.

Saavedra, R., & Kwun, S.K. (2000). Affective states in job characteristics theory. *Journal of Organizational Behavior, 21*, 131–146.

Schlesinger, L.A., & Zornitsky, J. (1991). Job satisfaction, service capability, and customer satisfaction: An examination of linkages and management implications. *Human Resource Planning, 14*, 141–149.

Shalley, C.E., Gilson, L.L., & Blum, T.C. (2009). Interactive effects of growth need strength, work context, and job complexity on self-reported creative performance. *Academy of Management Journal, 52*, 489–505.

Shalley, C.E., & Perry-Smith, J.E. (2001). Effects of social-psychological factors on creative performance: The role of informational and controlling expected evaluation and modeling experience. *Organizational Behavior and Human Decision Processes, 84*, 1–22.

Shalley, C.E., Zhou, J., & Oldham, G.R. (2004). The effects of personal and contextual characteristics on creativity: Where should we go from here? *Journal of Management, 30*, 933–958.

Spreitzer, G.M., & Sonenshein, S. (2004). Toward the construction of positive deviance. *American Behavioral Scientist, 47*, 828–847.

Spreitzer, G., Sutcliffe, K., Dutton, J., Sonenshein, S., & Grant, A.M. (2005). A socially embedded model of thriving at work. *Organization Science, 16*, 537–549.

Taylor, F.W. (1911). *Principles of scientific management.* New York: Harper.

Tierney, P., & Farmer, S.M. (2002). Creative self-efficacy: Potential antecedents and relationship to creative performance. *Academy of Management Journal, 45*, 1137–1148.

Tierney, P., & Farmer, S.M. (2004). The Pygmalion process and employee creativity. *Journal of Management, 30*, 413–432.

Todd, S.Y., & Kent, A. (2006). Direct and indirect effects of task characteristics on organizational citizenship behavior. *North American Journal of Psychology, 8*, 253–268.

Totterdell, P., Kellett, S., Briner, R.B., & Teuchman, K. (1998). Evidence of mood linkage in work groups. *Journal of Personality and Social Psychology, 74*, 1504–1515.

Tsai, W-C., Chen, C-C., & Liu, H-L. (2007). Test of a model linking employee positive moods and task performance. *Journal of Applied Psychology, 92*, 1570–1583.

Tugade, M.M., Frederickson, B.L., & Barrett, L.F. (2004). Psychological resilience and positive emotional granularity: Examining the benefits of positive emotions on coping and health. *Journal of Personality, 72*, 1161–1190.

Turner, A.N., & Lawrence, P.R. (1965). *Industrial jobs and the worker.* Boston: Harvard Graduate School of Business Administration.

Walker, C.R., & Guest, R.H. (1952). *The man on the assembly line.* Cambridge, MA: Harvard University Press.

Zhang, X., & Bartol, K.M. (2010). Linking empowering leadership and employee creativity: The influence of psychological empowerment, intrinsic motivation, and creative process engagement. *Academy of Management Journal, 53*, 107–128.

Zhou, J. (2003). When the presence of creative coworkers is related to creativity: Role of supervisor close monitoring, developmental feedback, and creative personality. *Journal of Applied Psychology, 88*, 413–422.

Zhou, J., & Shalley, C.E. (2003). Research on employee creativity: A critical review and directions for future research. In J. Martocchio (Ed.), *Research in personnel and human resource management* (pp. 165–217). Oxford, UK: Elsevier.

Mindful Organizing

Establishing and Extending the Foundations of Highly Reliable Performance

Timothy J. Vogus

Abstract

Consistent with the positive organizational scholarship (POS) focus on positively deviant performance, mindful organizing represents a set of social processes that underlie the near-flawless performance of high-reliability organizations (HROs). This chapter details the foundations of mindful organizing, reviews recent empirical developments, and proposes five potential directions for further theoretical and empirical development, each of which deepens its contribution and connection to POS. The first proposed direction is to conceptually and empirically link both Eastern and Western conceptions of individual mindfulness and mindful organizing. The second is to establish the affective foundations of mindful organizing, namely how emotion affects the relationships between mindful organizing and error-free performance, the discrete emotions that constitute mindful organizing, and how emotional narratives sustain mindful organizing. Third is to examine a broader range of outcomes of mindful organizing, including its effects on employees. Fourth is to better link mindful organizing to leader attributes and leadership processes. Last, the impact of mindful organizing also requires further construct validation, including differentiating it from related constructs and establishing its responsiveness to interventions.

Keywords: Mindful organizing, mindfulness, high reliability, error, safety, safety culture

Positive organizational scholarship (POS) seeks to rethink organization studies through an affirmative bias (i.e., understanding excellence), a focus on endogenous resourcefulness (i.e., emergent organizational capabilities), and a careful rendering of the subjective experience of work (Cameron, Dutton, & Quinn, 2003). Over the past several years, it has made significant contributions to understanding positive deviance (Cameron & Lavine, 2006; Spreitzer & Sonenshein, 2003) and the organizational capabilities that make such outcomes possible (e.g., compassion organizing, Dutton, Worline, Frost, & Lilius, 2006). In that spirit, I look to the literature on high-reliability organizations (HROs), organizations that are positively deviant in their nearly error-free performance despite operating in complex, dynamic, interdependent, and time pressured settings in which errors should be plentiful

(Roberts, 1990; Schulman, 1993; Weick, Sutcliffe, & Obstfeld, 1999). In that literature, we find the capability that underlies the exceptional performance of HROs is mindful organizing—the collective capability to detect and correct errors and unexpected events (Weick, Sutcliffe, & Obstfeld, 1999; Weick & Sutcliffe, 2001; Weick & Sutcliffe, 2007; see also Sutcliffe & Christianson (2011), Chapter 64, this volume, for a broader discussion of managing the unexpected). More recently, mindful organizing has become a burgeoning, if still nascent, literature in its own right.

At first blush, the collective capability to detect and correct errors and unexpected events might seem to be a poor fit for POS. Error-free performance seems like it should be a jumping-off point for a POS approach rather than the destination. However, if we consider that organizational systems in dynamic environments tend toward disorder and entropy, then preserving order, reversing chaos, and containing errors and near misses becomes exceptional (Weick, 2003). In other words, an organization performing in a nearly flawless manner is an extraordinary organization. I review the foundations of such flawless organizing in this chapter and offer five areas for future development.

Mindful Organizing: Definition and Dimensions

Reliability is essential for survival, but difficult to achieve. Reliability is so challenging because many organizations operate in trying conditions rife with complexity, dynamism, interdependence, and time pressure. *Complexity* refers to the nature of the technical knowledge required. *Dynamism* refers to the fact that the knowledge base is ever-changing and growing, and that novel problems are regularly emerging. *Interdependence* means that reliability is a collective achievement rather than a sum of individual achievements. *Time pressure* means that action cannot be postponed. High-reliability organizations are those (e.g., aircraft carrier flight decks, air traffic control, nuclear power plants) that demonstrate an exceptional ability to navigate these conditions in a nearly error-free manner (Roberts, 1990; Schulman, 1993; Weick et al., 1999; Weick & Sutcliffe, 2007). They do so by solving the challenges of complexity, dynamism, interdependence, and time pressure through mindful organizing.

Mindful organizing is the collective capability for detecting and correcting errors and unexpected events (Weick et al., 1999). As a collective capability, it is a social process grounded in the actions and interactions of a workgroup. It becomes a shared property of a collective because the members of a given collective (e.g., a workgroup) encounter the same situational cues and, due to the interdependent nature of their work, often consult one another in the interpretation of those cues (Hofmann, Lei, & Grant, 2009; Klein, 2003), which results in interpretations and actions that converge (Salancik & Pfeffer, 1978; Weick & Roberts, 1993).

The capability of mindful organizing is a function of a collective's (e.g., workgroup) attention to context and capacity to act (Levinthal & Rerup, 2006). Attention to context is the sustained attention to operational challenges in the form of efforts to develop, deepen, and update a shared understanding of local context. Capacity to act is the collective's ability to marshal the necessary resources to

act on that understanding in a flexible manner that is tailored to the unexpected event.

Attention to context and capacity to act is produced on the front line through a set of interrelated organizational processes—preoccupation with failure, reluctance to simplify interpretations, sensitivity to operations, commitment to resilience, and deference to expertise (Weick et al., 1999; Weick & Sutcliffe, 2001; Weick & Sutcliffe, 2007). Preoccupation with failure directs attention and effort to complex threats to the system, through proactive and preemptive analysis of potential novel sources of error or conditions that can produce the unexpected (LaPorte & Consolini, 1991; Weick & Sutcliffe, 2007). Reluctance to simplify interpretations means that a collective does not take the past as an infallible guide to the future. Instead, its members actively question received wisdom and ensure that key variables are not overlooked by frequently discussing alternatives as to how to go about their everyday work (Fiol & O'Connor, 2003; Schulman, 1993; Weick & Sutcliffe, 2007). Sensitivity to operations means creating and maintaining an up-to-date understanding of the distribution expertise, so that it is appropriately utilized in the face of unexpected events (Weick et al., 1999; Weick & Sutcliffe, 2001, 2007). Together, these three processes richly represent the complexity of potential threats, dynamically deepen this understanding with new data, and manage interdependence through collective knowledge of relevant expertise. Commitment to resilience is discussing errors and deriving lessons learned, such that a collective is able to extract the most value from the error data they have (vanDyck, Frese, Baer, & Sonnentag, 2005; Weick et al., 1999; Weick & Sutcliffe, 2001, 2007; see also Barker Caza (2011), Chapter 68, this volume; Sutcliffe & Christianson (2011), Chapter 64, this volume). Last, deference to expertise occurs when, in the face of an unexpected event, a collective pools the necessary expertise and utilizes it by allowing the person or people with the greatest expertise in handling the problem at hand to make decisions, regardless of formal rank (Roberts, Stout, & Halpern, 1994). Commitment to resilience and deference to expertise jointly comprise the pool of expertise and the capacity to use it in a flexible manner tailored to the unexpected event. Taken as a whole, these processes constitute mindful organizing. That is, no one process or subset of processes is sufficient for mindful organizing.

The discussion of mindful organizing that follows refers to the construct as conceptualized and

Table 50.1 Correspondence theory and measurement of the processes of mindful organizing

Concept	Definition	Survey Item(s)
Preoccupation with failure	Operating with a chronic wariness of the possibility of unexpected events that may jeopardize safety by engaging in proactive and preemptive analysis and discussion.	When handing off an activity to another employee, we usually discuss what to look out for. We spend time identifying activities we do not want to go wrong.
Reluctance to simplify interpretations	Taking deliberate steps to question assumptions and received wisdom to create a more complete and nuanced picture of ongoing operations.	We discuss alternatives as to how to go about our normal work activities.
Sensitivity to operations	Creating and maintaining an up-to-date understanding of the distributed of tasks and expertise, so that these are appropriately utilized in the face of unexpected events.	We have a good "map" of each other's talents and skills. We discuss our unique skills with each other so we know who on the unit has relevant specialized skills and knowledge.
Commitment to resilience	Discussing errors and deriving lessons learned, such that a collective is able to extract the most value from the error data they have to prevent more serious harm.	We talk about mistakes and ways to learn from them. When errors happen, we discuss how we could have prevented them.
Deference to expertise	During high-tempo times (i.e., when attempting to resolve a problem or crisis), decision making authority migrates to the person or people with the most expertise with the problem at hand, regardless of their formal authority.	When attempting to resolve a problem, we take advantage of the unique skills of our colleagues. When a crisis occurs, we rapidly pool our collective expertise to attempt to resolve it.

Adapted from Vogus, T. J., & Sutcliffe, K. M. (2007a). The safety organizing scale: Development and validation of a behavioral measure of safety culture in hospital nursing units. *Medical Care, 45*(1), 46–54, with permission of Wolters Kluwer Health.

measured by Vogus and Sutcliffe (2007a).[1] Table 50.1 illustrates how each conceptual component of mindful organizing relates to specific survey items in Vogus and Sutcliffe's (2007a) measure. The table contains all nine survey items measured using a seven-point Likert scale (from "not at all" to "to a very great extent"). Mindful organizing is then constructed for a collective by averaging all nine items across all respondents. It is important to note that all items are behavioral (to capture the fact that mindful organizing is a social process) and that the referent of each item is "we" (to capture the fact that mindful organizing is a collective capability).

Relationship with Other Safety Constructs

Mindful organizing also differs from existing constructs that characterize a workgroup's orientation toward error (error management climate), safety (safety climate), and speaking up (psychological safety). Error management culture (van Dyck et al., 2005)—communicating about errors, analyzing and correcting errors quickly, sharing error knowledge, and helping in error situations—is most closely linked to mindful organizing in that it

captures processes that are highly similar to commitment to resilience and deference to expertise. In other words, error management culture is much like the components of mindful organizing that encapsulate a capacity to act. However, error management culture differs in that it does not simultaneously encompass the proactive elements of mindful organizing, including preoccupation with failure, reluctance to simplify interpretations, and sensitivity to operations (Weick & Sutcliffe, 2007). Safety climate is the shared perceptions regarding the safety policies, practices, and procedures that an organization expects, rewards, and supports (Zohar, 1980). Safety climate focuses on managerial commitment to safety (e.g., through investments in safety), priority placed on safety (i.e., the extent to which safety is subordinated to other goals), and the extent to which safety information is disseminated (Katz-Navon, Naveh, & Stern, 2005). As such, safety climate focuses on the initiating and enabling role of managers in promoting safety and compliance with safety procedures. In contrast, mindful organizing focuses on the interactions of workgroup members directed at anticipating and responding to the unexpected.

Similarly, psychological safety—a shared belief that it is safe to take interpersonal risks—is also a function of leader behaviors and discursive practice (Edmondson, 1999, 2004) that facilitate, but are distinct from, front-line action (Edmondson, 1996). As such, safety climate and psychological safety are potential antecedents of mindful organizing rather than analogues of it.

The Performance Effects of Mindful Organizing

Empirical examinations of the effect of mindful organizing on organizational reliability and other performance outcomes remains in its infancy. Despite this small number of studies, some clear findings have emerged. There is consistent qualitative and, more recently, quantitative evidence that higher levels mindful organizing improve safety and quality outcomes in health care contexts. In a multiyear qualitative study of a pediatric intensive care unit (PICU), Roberts and colleagues (2005; Madsen, Desai, Roberts, & Wong, 2006) found that diligent leaders trained in the principles of HROs enabled mindful organizing that corresponded with higher levels of performance. Frontline staff were constantly alert to the possibility that they had missed something (preoccupation with failure), regularly interpreted and questioned data that appeared relevant to their working hypotheses (reluctance to simplify interpretations), collaboratively constructed an up-to-date picture of potential threats to safety for each patient (sensitivity to operations), discussed errors and incidents to enlarge the repertoire of possible actions that caregivers could take to manage the unexpected (commitment to resilience), and migrated decisions to bedside caregivers who had more experience with a specific patient (deference to expertise). Together, these enactments of mindful organizing were associated with infrequent patient deterioration on the unit, a significant improvement from prior to the HRO intervention (Madsen et al., 2006; Roberts et al., 2005). In a study of perinatal units, Knox, Simpson, and Garite (1999) found that units that systematically enacted the processes of mindful organizing had better safety performance and fewer malpractice claims. In a first quantitative study of mindful organizing in 94 hospital nursing units, Vogus and Sutcliffe (2007a) found that higher levels of their measure of mindful organizing were associated with fewer medication errors and patient falls in the subsequent 6 months. In contrast, when the processes of mindful organizing are absent or underdeveloped,

different outcomes obtain. For example, the less mindful action characteristic of the cardiac unit of the Bristol Royal Infirmary was associated with shocking levels of excess deaths among infants, which forced a governmental inquiry (Weick & Sutcliffe, 2003).

There is more suggestive evidence that mindful organizing produces highly reliable performance in other contexts. Bigley and Roberts (2001) document a set of five "structural processes" analogous to mindful organizing that allows the fire-fighting Incident Command System (ICS) to function reliably in crisis conditions. For each structural process, the corresponding process or processes of mindful organizing are denoted. Role switching assigns and reassigns people based on situational demands. This builds a deeper attention to context and the likelihood that the system they create might fail to conform to the situation's needs (preoccupation with failure). Cognitive management and constrained improvisation further deepen the appreciation of context as they allow for refinement in the face of emerging data from the field that creates a more nuanced and holistic picture (reluctance to simplify interpretations). The ICS frequently refines its image of the big picture through "size ups" that construct and disseminate increasingly high-fidelity models of the evolving emergency. System resetting is the ability to disengage and reset the structure to confront a "nasty surprise" or an evolving problem (commitment to resilience). Last, authority migration allows for the necessary resources and skills to flow to emerging problems (deference to expertise). Taken together, these five interrelated processes lead to highly reliable management of emergencies. In a rigorous longitudinal case study of Novo Nordisk, Rerup (2009) found three attentional processes focused on attending to weak signals led to recovery from crisis and subsequent highly reliable performance. Each of the three attentional processes is akin to an equivalent process of mindful organizing (denoted in parentheses). Attentional stability is the deep consideration of issues that led to a more nuanced understanding and an awareness of potential pathways of failure (preoccupation with failure). Attentional vividness is the development of increasingly rich, detailed, and complex representation of issues (reluctance to simplify interpretations). Attentional coherence is the merging of vividness and stability into an integrated big picture (sensitivity to operations). In an intriguing qualitative study of habitual entrepreneurs, Rerup (2005) found that the processes of mindful organizing contribute to their success, but that the relationship may be curvilinear (i.e., mindful organizing is helpful only up to a point).

Emerging evidence also suggests that pairing mindful organizing with other supportive practices enhances the impact of mindful organizing on performance. Specifically, in a study of 73 hospital nursing units, Vogus and Sutcliffe (2007b) found that fewer medication errors occurred over the subsequent 6 months on units with high levels of mindful organizing and registered nurses reported high levels of trust in their nurse managers (i.e., these managers had created a sense of psychological safety). In addition, they found that mindful organizing paired with extensive use of standardized care protocols also resulted in fewer medication errors over time (Vogus & Sutcliffe, 2007b).

Antecedents of Mindful Organizing

The earliest studies of high reliability tended to focus on the organizational practices of HROs (e.g., Roberts, 1990). Studies of mindful organizing have built on this tradition and expanded it to include microprocesses (e.g., respectful interaction) and employee characteristics (e.g., professional tenure). I review this small, but growing body of work next.

Human resource (HR) and work design practices have been qualitatively and quantitatively examined as antecedents of mindful organizing. Vogus (2004) built on earlier descriptions of the importance of training and empowerment in HROs to examine the effect of a bundle of HR practices, including selective staffing, extensive training, developmental performance appraisal, and decentralized decision making on mindful organizing and reliability. He found that HR practices produced higher levels of mindful organizing through dyadic respectful interactions (i.e., interactions characterized by trust, honesty, and mutual respect; Vogus, 2004). In a sample of software firms, Vogus and Welbourne's (2003) results suggested that HR practices unleashed similar practices of mindful organizing that led to reliable innovation over time. In their study of the PICU, Roberts and colleagues (Madsen et al., 2006; Roberts et al., 2005) found that implementing practices derived from research on HROs, including regularly training (in-servicing) staff, team briefings (i.e., collaborative rounding), empowerment (decision migration to bedside caregiver), and frequent and inclusive post-event debriefings, generated and sustained more mindful organizing. At Novo Nordisk, the Novo Way of Management—a commitment to openness, continuous learning, and dialogue—was reinforced by organizational audits of the Novo Way and "facilitation" to coordinate weak signals across the organization to produce attentional processes analogous to mindful organizing (Rerup, 2009).

In focusing on structure (e.g., Roberts, 1990) and process (e.g., Weick et al., 1999), the characteristics of the personnel on the front line charged with organizing more or less mindfully have been minimized. This is a significant oversight because mindful organizing and reliable performance are a function of "reliability professionals" (Roe & Schulman, 2008). Reliability professionals

> [are] plural and deliberately so. Professionals work together in their domain of competence. They may see themselves as individual operators but they are networked into crews, teams, and support staff . . . the knowledge base [is] interconnected across their individual domains of competence. Change the network of professionals, say by changing one professional and his or her knowledge, and you affect the interconnected knowledge base. (Roe & Schulman, 2008, p. 121)

In other words, mindful organizing and reliable performance are a function of the cumulative knowledge base of front-line employees and their ability and willingness to effectively access the experience and expertise embedded in the knowledge base. In a sample of 122 hospital nursing units Vogus, Ramanujam, and Tangirala (2010) examined the effects of workgroup-level professional experience, the workgroup's variability in experience, and workgroup professional commitment on mindful organizing. They found that professional experience had a positive nonlinear relationship with mindful organizing. That is, the benefits of experience are positive, but they increase at a decreasing rate over time. They also found that this relationship was moderated by workgroup variability in professional experience (makes the diminishing returns to experience set in sooner) and workgroup professional commitment (delays diminishing returns to experience). Taken together, these studies provide an impressive and systematic, if incomplete, basis for future research.

Future Directions

Mindful organizing presents organizational researchers and practitioners with a largely untapped resource for understanding and unleashing positively deviant performance in very difficult circumstances. Furthermore, it is a construct that is conceptually well grounded in a set of rich case studies on HROs conducted over the past two decades (see Weick et al., 1999 for a review). More recently, quantitative work has shown that mindful organizing is also measurable and significantly predictive of safety outcomes in the workplace. However, at this early stage, there are numerous potential directions for future research on mindful organizing. I propose five necessary and promising directions for future research. In developing each future direction, I attempt to outline plausible study designs and potential hypotheses to test.

Eastern and Western Conceptions of Individual Mindfulness

Mindful organizing has been defined as a collective capability. As such, it is a social process that becomes collective through actions and interactions among individuals, rather than in the minds of individuals (e.g., Langer, 1989). However, distinguishing mindful organizing in order to achieve construct clarity is different from saying individual and collective mindfulness are unrelated. Mindful organizing was developed with Langer's (1989) work on individual mindfulness as a foundation. More recent writings on mindful organizing have begun to link it to Eastern mindfulness, with foundations in Buddhist thought (Weick & Putnam, 2006; Weick & Sutcliffe, 2006). I briefly review each of these perspectives, their linkages to mindful organizing, and offer some suggestions for future empirical investigation.

The Western perspective on mindfulness largely derives from Langer's (1989) work. A Western perspective means that this approach is a variant of an information processing approach (Weick & Sutcliffe, 2006). For Langer (1989), mindfulness is expressed through active differentiation and refinement of existing categories and distinctions (p. 138), creation of new discontinuous categories out of streams of events (p. 157), and a more nuanced appreciation of context and alternative ways to deal with it (p. 159). From this definition, it is evident how it deeply influences the processes of mindful organizing. Active differentiation and refinement, creating new categories to make sense experience, and more nuanced appreciation of context and ways to cope with it are all found in preoccupation with failure, reluctance to simplify interpretations, sensitivity to operations, and commitment to resilience. Deference to expertise is the way in which the work of mindfulness is put into practice to resolve a crisis.

In contrast, Eastern mindfulness is a state of consciousness in which attention is focused on present-moment phenomena occurring both externally and internally (Dane, forthcoming) or moment-to-moment, nonreactive, nonjudgmental awareness (Weick & Putnam, 2006). This also has workplace implications. For example, in a qualitative study of trial lawyers, Dane (2010) found that mindfulness permits lawyers to attend to a wide range of phenomena, such as reactions of the judge, jury members, and opposing counsel, and tailor their arguments to be most persuasive. Eastern mindfulness also has some speculative connections with mindful organizing. The processes of mindful organizing can be viewed in terms of their effects on concentration and strength of insight (Weick & Putnam, 2006). Weick and Putnam (2006, p. 282) provide interesting connections for each of the processes of mindful organizing. Preoccupation with failure, with its focus on emerging failures above all else, induces concentration and potentially vivid insights. Reluctance to simplify interpretations and sensitivity to operations increase the vividness of insight by replacing conceptual categories with awareness of current details, but possibly at the expense of concentration. Commitment to resilience is concentration complemented with vivid representation of errors as the means to achieve insights for future actions. Last, deference to expertise increases concentration by routing decisions to experts who are best able to focus on the present phenomenon without distraction.

The preceding discussion of individual mindfulness suggests interesting directions for future conceptual and empirical work. First, what factors moderate the relationship between individual mindfulness and mindful organizing? That is, does the value of individual mindfulness for mindful organizing depend on other traits (e.g., extraversion), skills (e.g., task expertise, Dane, forthcoming), work characteristics (e.g., task interdependence), or practices (e.g., protocols for interaction) that ensure that individual insights are socially shared? Second, if individual mindfulness is an antecedent of mindful organizing, how widespread must individual mindfulness be for mindful organizing to emerge? For example, Fiol and O'Connor (2003) suggest that an organization is less likely to adopt a management fad if it has more mindful senior managers that scan more broadly and question interpretations. Does the individual mindfulness of top managers have cascading effects for employees on the front line? That is, does leader individual mindfulness lead to mindful organizing on the front lines? Or, does it affect individual mindfulness on the front line? Similarly, what proportion of a workgroup needs to be mindful in order for mindful organizing to emerge? Which form of individual mindfulness (Western or Eastern) has greater impact on the emergence of mindful organizing? In addition to answering these questions, work that examines this question would also be beneficial for empirically differentiating Eastern mindfulness, Western mindfulness, and mindful organizing.

Moreover, is the individual mindfulness of senior managers sufficient to secure the operational benefits of mindful organizing? If so, what proportion of senior managers needs to be mindful? Under what conditions might individual mindfulness capture all the performance benefits of mindful organizing (e.g., task interdependence; individual mindfulness may capture performance benefits for work with low levels of interdependence). Examining these questions would provide important insight into whether hiring mindful managers or selecting mindful employees are viable substitutes for mindful organizing. Blending these three perspectives on mindfulness in organizations offers many exciting opportunities for further empirical and theoretical development.

Affective Foundations of Mindful Organizing

As is evident from the review of the emerging research on mindful organizing, prior work has emphasized its structural antecedents and cognitive processes. In doing so, this literature overlooks the degree to which effectively marshalling emotion may be necessary for mindful organizing to lead to nearly error-free performance, how emotion helps constitute the processes of mindful organizing, and how emotion, in the form of narratives, may sustain mindful organizing over time.

Mindful organizing, in part, is a capability to detect weak signals of danger and mobilize swifter interventions to avoid or curtail harm. Detecting weak signals and nearly error-free performance partly rely on effectively recognizing and interpreting one's own (Klein, 2003) or other's emotions (e.g., Benner, Tanner, & Chesla, 1996). Emotional information is especially important because it is often a leading indicator of deeper changes. Weak signals are often expressed emotionally through subtle changes in tone, facial expression, body language, or energy level; information might not be able to be expressed through another (nonemotional) channel (Madsen et al.,

2006). Klein offers numerous examples from high-reliability contexts (e.g., fire fighting, health care) of how individuals detect weak signals as a result of their own emotion in the form of gut instincts and intuition (Klein, 2003). Benner, Tanner, and Chesla (1996) describe how nurses work to construct an "intimate and particular understanding" of their patients and become "emotionally attuned" to them. Attuned nurses have the capacity to "read" the emotional tone of a patient situation to know when something is "off" when it looks okay on the surface, or to sense that something is actually all right despite appearances to the contrary. Thus, emotional attunement can help mobilize appropriate action in the face of deteriorating conditions and militate against a strong response to every weak signal that might otherwise overwhelm a workgroup (Rudolph & Repenning, 2002). As such, a collective's emotional attunement to their work (e.g., their patients) should enhance the benefits of mindful organizing on performance (i.e., moderate the relationship between mindful organizing and performance).

The traditional conception of emotion in studies of mindful organizing and high reliability is ostensibly in tension with the conception of emotion in POS. Positive organizational scholarship has emphasized the benefits of positive emotion for broadening and building cognitive and behavioral capabilities (Fredrickson, 1998). The literatures on mindful organizing and high reliability have emphasized that positive emotions associated with success (Miller, 1993) produce an unwarranted illusion of control and optimism that can create blind spots that leave important discrepancies unnoticed (Landau & Chisholm, 1995) or arrogance that creates a reluctance to adapt and change (Schulman, 1993). The two can be reconciled through a deeper consideration of how mindful organizing operates. The process of preoccupation with failure illustrates how emotion is potentially constitutive of mindful organizing and how it relies upon the benefits of both positive and negative emotion.

Preoccupation with failure has emotional underpinnings as a state of tension and alertness. As such, a preoccupation with failure runs the risk of deteriorating into a debilitating state of fear and paranoia. To prevent this descent into negative emotions that can debilitate an organization (e.g., Weick, 1993), mindful organizing couples in the inherent fallibility of a system with the efficacy of proactive and preemptive discussion. That is, although mindful organizing is not an optimistic process, it is not as pessimistic as it may seem to POS scholars, with its focus on failure. Mindful organizing may be best characterized as *hopeful*. Hope is an emotion grounded in a realistic appraisal of the challenges in one's environment and one's capabilities for navigating around them (Groopman, 2004). Hope combats the vagaries of unexpected events by making it more likely that threats will be labeled challenges, thus instilling a belief in an organization's ability to be resilient, and emphasizing the importance of updating and refining one's appraisal of the environment (Lazarus, 1999). As such, hopefulness is akin to a simultaneous focus on both success and failure that begets scanning for confirming and disconfirming data (Fiol & O'Connor, 2003).

Emotion may also play a crucial role in sustaining the fragile processes of mindful organizing (Weick & Sutcliffe, 2007) over time. Specifically, to maintain focus on error-free operations, members of HROs produce and widely share evocative accounts that preserve and communicate emotions (Weick et al., 1999). Weick and Roberts (1993) describe how personnel on aircraft carrier flight decks recount "war stories" that emphasize how "most positions on this deck were bought in blood." When these accounts are shared, they serve to socialize newcomers and resocialize insiders to the importance of executing tasks with care and attention to their impact on the overall safety of the system. Emotion-laden accounts can help create and sustain performance over time because they are durable, discursive resources that transcend the specific individuals participating and the circumstances surrounding a war story. That is, they possess an ongoing emotional resonance that shapes subsequent action, such that prior learning is not lost and vigilance and alertness remain high.

Employee Outcomes of Mindful Organizing

At this early stage in its development, little is known about the subjective experience of engaging in mindful organizing and its effects over time. Although it is rarely acknowledged, mindful organizing is effortful and costly (Levinthal & Rerup, 2006; Vogus & Welbourne, 2003). Mindful organizing is costly in the sustained commitment and effort it demands from employees on the front line (Roe & Schulman, 2008). High commitment and effort coupled with the potential hazards inherent in the work can result in employee exhaustion and turnover. However, it is possible that mindful organizing may reduce the likelihood of turnover because it provides a great deal of social support and resources that improve the experience of work and enhance

performance. These competing hypotheses merit further exploration.

The effects of turnover on mindful organizing also merit investigation. There is suggestive evidence that employee turnover, to the extent that it creates greater variability in experience, may negatively impact mindful organizing (Vogus et al., 2010). However, research in HROs seems to suggest that mindful organizing is maintained and possibly even enhanced by turnover (e.g., Weick & Roberts, 1993). There are two potential explanations for why HROs, like aircraft carrier flight operations, may seem to handle turnover well. First, the turnover facing these organizations may only be planned turnover and should therefore be less disruptive to ongoing organizational processes than more unexpected turnover events. Second, and related, there is some evidence that HROs have strong socialization practices in place that minimize the disruption caused by turnover on processes of mindful organizing (see Weick & Roberts, 1993). That said, exploring the effects of differing types of turnover (e.g., planned/unplanned, voluntary/involuntary) on mindful organizing, as well as the practices that might mitigate the deleterious effects of turnover on mindful organizing (e.g., practices that ease accessing experts, Hofmann, Lei, & Grant, 2009) deserve further empirical examination.

A similarly reciprocal process might also occur between affective commitment to one's profession and mindful organizing over time. For example, Vogus, Ramanujam, and Tangirala (2010) found that professional affective commitment has a direct and moderating effect on mindful organizing, but it is also plausible that, over time, mindful organizing can influence professional commitment. That is, engaging in mindful organizing and its intense focus on delivering error-free performance corresponds with the deeply held professional values that inspired professionals to enter their field (e.g., in nursing, Benner et al., 1996; Institute of Medicine, 2004).

It is equally possible that professional normative commitment (i.e., feeling one ought to remain in the profession, Meyer, Allen, & Smith, 1993) might also be an outgrowth of mindful organizing. As mindful organizing is consistent with ideals of professional practice, it is possible that it could generate normative commitment in the form of a moral duty rather than indebtedness (Meyer & Parfyonova, in press) and lead employees to fulfill their obligations to their profession (i.e., by using all of their skills, collaborating with coworkers, and staying up-to-date on new knowledge). Mindful organizing may also generate a commitment profile—for example, by simultaneously possessing high levels of affective and normative commitment—that in turn drives subsequent discretionary behaviors like mindful organizing (Gellatly, Meyer, & Luchakm 2006; Wasti, 2005). Therefore, the effects of mindful organizing on multiple forms of commitment to a profession might also further reinforce and deepen the processes of mindful organizing over time.

Relationship with Leader Attributes and Leadership Processes

Leaders can enable mindful organizing on the front line in at least two ways: first, by directing attention to safety, and second, by creating contexts in which practitioners feel safe to speak up and act in ways that improve safety. Directing attention to safety and ensuring that the front line speaks up enable greater attention to context and a richer capacity to act, and these constitute mindful organizing (Levinthal & Rerup, 2006). Both directing attention to safety and ensuring employees speak up are a function of leadership style and leader process. Leader style (e.g., empowering transformational leadership, Yun, Faraj, & Sims, 2005) and leader process (e.g., safety climate, psychological safety, and leader–member exchange [LMX]) can affect what employees attend to and how they carry out their work.

Transformational leadership is a leadership style that holds potential for influencing mindful organizing. Prior research has found that the commitment to employee welfare and empowerment characteristic of a transformational style are strongly associated with employee (e.g., satisfaction and commitment) and organizational (unit performance) outcomes in high-hazard industries (Gilmartin & D'Aunno, 2007). Such an empowering leadership style also allows employees to think, apply their knowledge (e.g., speak up), and learn by doing. For example, in a study of trauma units, Yun and colleagues found that applying an empowering approach during low- to moderate-severity trauma events resulted in greater learning by team members without compromising patient safety (Yun et al., 2005). As such, empowering transformational leadership may enable the processes of mindful organizing.

Leaders may be able to influence the processes of mindful organizing through employee perceptions of safety climate. As mentioned earlier, safety climate is a function of perceptions of a leader's commitment to safety, priority placed on safety, and dissemination of safety information (Katz-Navon

et al., 2005). For example, a supervisor who disregards safety procedures whenever production falls behind schedule or who punishes people for mistakes, signals a low commitment to safety and that a low priority is placed on safety (Carroll & Quijada, 2004; Zohar, 2000). Safety climate potentially influences mindful organizing by directing employees' attention to their context and the factors influencing its safety. Specifically, a strong safety climate means people more clearly understand threats to safer practice (Carroll & Quijada, 2004; Zohar, 2000) and attend more closely to errors and other incidents (Naveh, Katz-Navon, & Stern, 2006; Weingart, Farbstein, Davis, & Phillips, 2004), consistent with a preoccupation with failure. A safety climate also heightens safety motivation (i.e., willingness to exert effort) and participation in voluntary safety activities (e.g., helping coworkers with safety-related issues and attending safety meetings) (Neal & Griffin, 2006) necessary for reluctance to simplify interpretations and sensitivity to operations. Last, a safety climate produces more open and constructive problem solving in the face of errors (Hofmann & Mark, 2006; Singer, Lin, Falwell, Gaba, & Baker, 2009), commitment to resilience, and deference to expertise. Examining safety climate could also help illuminate the microfoundations of mindful organizing as leaders who are personally committed to safety and give it a high priority have employees who are more likely to make internal attributions for safety incidents (i.e., incidents are seen as being more correctable; Hofmann & Stetzer, 1998), which is consistent with a preoccupation with failure, a reluctance to simplify interpretations, and a commitment to resilience. Further study of the attribution process for errors, near misses, and other threats to safety would deepen our understanding of the microfoundations of mindful organizing.

Mindful organizing may also be enabled when leaders create a context in which employees are empowered to speak up and act to resolve threats to patient safety. Speaking up is more likely to occur in an organization when psychological safety is present (Edmondson, 1999). Leaders create psychological safety through subtle acts, such as changing the language used in an organization from threatening terms like "errors" and "investigations" to more psychologically neutral terms such as "accidents" and "analysis" (Edmondson, 2004). Leaders also create psychological safety through being more inclusive, by means of words and deeds that appreciate others' contributions (Nembhard & Edmondson, 2006) and by pardoning employees who disclose their unintentional mistakes (Edmondson, 1996). This leads to a greater disclosure of errors and close calls (Edmondson, 1996) that produces richer understanding of context and allows for the more detailed processing of a wider range of safety data, as in pre-occupation with failure. Psychological safety also produces higher levels of engagement in patient safety improvement projects (Nembhard & Edmondson, 2006; Tucker, 2007) that create the capacity to act in response to errors and unexpected events required of commitment to resilience and deference to expertise.

In high-quality LMX relationships, the leader and subordinate engage in collaborative sense-making that produces a richer and more elaborate set of role behaviors to enact (Hofmann, Morgeson, & Gerras, 2003). High-quality LMX relationships make it more likely that employees expand role definitions to include additional safety tasks (Hofmann et al., 2003) and foster open and constructive communication about safety and errors (Hofmann & Morgeson, 1999). However, prior work on LMX has tended to focus on individual processes and individual safety. It would be fruitful to see if high-quality LMX leads to improved higher levels of mindful organizing and organizational performance outcomes.

Additional Construct Validation

For mindful organizing to have maximum impact on research and practice, the construct needs further empirical validation and conceptual development. Prior work has established convergent validity (see Vogus & Sutcliffe, 2007a), criterion validity (mindful organizing has been shown to reduce medication errors and patient falls over time, Vogus & Sutcliffe, 2007a, b), and to a limited extent discriminant validity (i.e., empirical differentiation from related constructs, Vogus & Sutcliffe, 2007a). A starting point for further construct validation would be to move beyond the conceptual differentiation from related constructs presented in this chapter to empirical differentiation. Specifically, future research should use confirmatory factor analysis to test the discriminant validity of error management culture (van Dyck et al., 2005), psychological safety (Edmondson, 1999), safety climate (Zohar, 1980), and mindful organizing.

Another conceptual and empirical area ripe for development is the behavior of mindful organizing over time. Prior work paradoxically suggests that mindful organizing is fragile and needs to be

continuously reaccomplished, but at the same time suggests that mindful organizing is a stable characteristic of HROs (Weick et al., 1999; Weick & Sutcliffe, 2001; Weick & Sutcliffe, 2007). Rerup's (2009) excellent longitudinal study of Novo Nordisk seems to support the fragility of mindful organizing (see also Roberts et al., 2005 for a different example). He finds that mindful organization gradually erodes into more mindless organizing in the face of other (financial) pressures. At Novo, mindful organizing was only restored after instituting a bundle of practices designed to sustain vigilance to weak signals of threats to quality and safety—the Novo Way of Management (Rerup, 2009). This work offers a strong qualitative foundation for further examination of the processes of mindful organizing over time.

The generalizability of mindful organizing remains poorly understood because prior work has either been qualitative examinations of HROs in which mindful organizing was deeply ingrained (e.g., Schulman, 1993) or, more recently, how variation in mindful organizing relates to safety outcomes (e.g., Vogus & Sutcliffe, 2007a). We are lacking in intervention studies in which an organization moves from less mindful organizing to more mindful organizing and, in turn, from reliable performance to highly reliable performance. There are promising leads in the existing literature in the form of two longitudinal case studies. Roberts and colleagues' (Madsen et al., 2006; Roberts et al., 2005) study of a PICU suggests that a change in leadership—specifically leaders trained in high-reliability principles—can improve mindful organizing and move an organization from low reliability to high reliability. Similarly, Rerup's (2009) research at Novo Nordisk suggests that comprehensively implementing a new set of management practices (the Novo Way of Management) can restore mindful organizing after its collapse. Future research can build on these retrospective qualitative accounts to a more traditional assessment of change effectiveness. For example, one might assess baseline levels of mindful organizing and then implement leader training on high-reliability principles, front-line employee training in high-reliability principles, or a systematic implementation of a new set of management practices, and track the effects on mindful organizing and reliability over time. Another option might be assessing levels of mindful organizing prior to a new leader taking over an organization or organizational unit and tracking those effects over time. Yet another possibility would be to implement a more focused intervention shown to be effective in improving safety (e.g., Executive WalkRounds; Frankel, Grillo, Pittman, Thomas, Horowitz, Page, & Sexton, 2008) and see if it operated through enhancing processes of mindful organizing.

In sum, these future directions indicate that, even though mindful organizing is a promising construct for understanding positively deviant safety performance, there is a great need for further conceptual and empirical work.

Conclusion

This chapter has outlined the mindful organizing construct, detailed its contributions, and proposed five new directions for further theoretical development and empirical testing: exploring the relationship between individual mindfulness and mindful organizing, building affective foundations of mindful organizing, expanding outcomes of mindful organizing examined to include employee outcomes, investigating the roles leaders and leadership processes play in fostering mindful organizing, and finally, conducting further construct validation. This agenda also holds the potential to deepen mindful organizing's connection and contribution to POS.

Part of the strength of POS is its focus on richly capturing the subjective experience of organizational life. Mindful organizing offers a compelling lens for understanding the cognitive and social processes through which those on the front lines successfully navigate high-risk, high-hazard work. Further research on the affective foundations of mindful organizing will only enrich our understanding of the subjective experience of exceptional performance in trying circumstances. The research on high reliability and mindful organizing also provocatively prods POS to rethink positive emotions. Specifically, in high-hazard organizations, positive emotions like happiness may lead to deleterious outcomes (e.g., Landau & Chisholm, 1995). Therefore, in these organizations, positivity might need to strike the more balanced tone of hope or even emotional ambivalence (e.g., simultaneously holding positive and negative conceptions of a situation).

In POS, positivity is socially embedded. Mindful organizing embodies this embeddedness as a collective capability. Existing research on mindful organizing further shows how social practices enable it, and some of the suggested future directions will further reveal how it emerges. For example, studying the relationship between individual mindfulness and mindful organizing will demonstrate if and

when a group of mindful individuals mindfully organize. This has implications for other emergent capabilities that are hallmarks of POS (e.g., compassion, resilience).

In addition to being a powerful lens for understanding organizational life, POS is also a science (Cameron et al., 2003). Mindful organizing offers substantial contributions to the science of POS as a construct that has been rigorously developed, well validated, and strongly related to important outcomes across a number of organizations. As such, it provides one possible template for developing measures of positive organizational capabilities and building a systematic research program through which they are tested and refined. For all these reasons, POS and mindful organizing enrich each other in important ways. I hope this chapter plays a role in deepening and sustaining this fruitful relationship.

Note

1. In this chapter, I view Vogus and Sutcliffe's (2007a) measure of mindful organizing as "the" measure of mindful organizing because it is the best validated—its items emerge directly from theory and field observation (Vogus, 2004), it demonstrates strong psychometric properties (i.e., reliability and validity), it is a collective measure (i.e., the referent of the items is the collective, and it meets statistical criteria for aggregation to the group level), is linked to theoretically justified antecedents (professional experience, human resources practices), and is significantly related to performance over time (e.g., medication errors and patient falls). I know of two alternative measures of collective mindfulness. Knight's (2004) master's thesis measures collective mindfulness of lifeguards working at community swimming pools, but this measure demonstrated poor psychometric properties and failed to impact performance outcomes. Ray, Baker, and Plowman (forthcoming) developed a measure of "organizational mindfulness" and validated it using a sample of business schools. Their measure had strong psychometric properties and was well grounded in theory (Weick et al., 1999), but also has significant limitations. First, it treats each process of mindful organizing as independent. Prior theorizing views these processes as observable indicators of the underlying process of mindful organizing (e.g., Weick et al., 1999). Second, it did not link its measure to any performance indicators (i.e., no evidence of criterion validity) or antecedents. Third, they did not demonstrate that their measure was collective in a statistical sense. That is, they offered no evidence for aggregating perceptions of organizational mindfulness to a collective level.

References

Barker Caza, B., & Milton, L.P. (2011). Resilience at work: Building capability in the face of adversity. In K.S. Cameron & G.M. Spreitzer (Eds.), *The Oxford handbook of positive organizational scholarship*. New York: Oxford University Press.

Benner, P., Tanner, C.A., & Chesla, C.A. (1996). *Expertise in nursing practice: Caring, clinical judgment, and ethics.* New York: Springer Publishing Company.

Bigley, G.A., & Roberts, K.H. (2001). The incident command system: High-reliability organizing for complex and volatile environments. *Academy of Management Journal, 44*(6), 1281–1299.

Cameron, K.S., Dutton, J., & Quinn, R. (Eds.). (2003). *Positive organizational scholarship.* San Francisco: Berrett-Koehler.

Cameron, K.S., & Levine, M. (2006). *Making the impossible possible.* San Francisco: Berrett-Koehler.

Carroll, J.S., & Quijada, M.A. (2004). Redirecting traditional professional values to support safety: Changing organizational culture in health care. *Quality and Safety in Health Care, 13*(1), 16–21.

Dane, E. (in press). Paying attention to mindfulness and its effects on task performance in the workplace. *Journal of Management.*

Dane, E. (2010). *Developing mindfulness in a dynamic environment: Unpacking the role of job experience.* Working paper.

Dutton, J.E., Worline, M.C., Frost, P.J., & Lilius, J. (2006). Explaining compassion organizing. *Administrative Science Quarterly, 51*(1), 59–96.

Edmondson, A.C. (1996). Learning from mistakes is easier said than done: Group and organizational influences on the detection and correction of human error. *Journal of Applied Behavioral Science, 32*(1), 5–28.

Edmondson, A.C. (1999). Psychological safety and learning behavior in work teams. *Administrative Science Quarterly, 44,* 350–383.

Edmondson, A.C. (2004). Learning from failure in health care: Frequent opportunities, pervasive barriers. *Quality and Safety in Health Care, 13,* 3–9.

Fiol, M., & O'Connor, E.J. (2003). Waking up! Mindfulness in the face of bandwagons. *Academy of Management Review, 28*(1), 54–70.

Frankel, A., Grillo, S.P., Pittman, M., Thomas, E.J., Horowitz, L., Page, M., & Sexton, J.B. (2008). Revealing and resolving patient safety defects: The impact of leadership WalkRounds on frontline caregiver assessments of patient safety. *Health Services Research, 43*(6), 2050–2066.

Fredrickson, B.L. (1998). What good are positive emotions? *Review of General Psychology, 2,* 300–319.

Gellatly, I.R., Meyer, J.P., & Luchak, A.A. (2006). Combined effects of the three commitment components on focal and discretionary behaviors: A test of Meyer and Herscovitch's propositions. *Journal of Vocational Behavior, 69,* 331–345.

Gilmartin, M.J., & D'Aunno, T.A. (2007). Leadership research in health care: A review and roadmap. *Academy of Management Annals, 1,* 387–438.

Groopman, J.E. (2004). *The anatomy of hope.* New York: Random House.

Hofmann, D.A., Lei, Z., & Grant, A.M. (2009). Seeking help in the shadow of doubt: The sensemaking processes underlying how nurses decide who to ask for advice. *Journal of Applied Psychology, 94*(5), 1261–1274.

Hofmann, D.A., & Mark, B. (2006). An investigation of the relationship between safety climate and medication errors as well as other nurse and patient outcomes. *Personnel Psychology, 59,* 847–870.

Hofmann, D.A., & Morgeson, F.P. (1999). Safety-related behavior as a social exchange: The role of perceived organizational support and leader-member exchange. *Journal of Applied Psychology, 84*(2), 286–296.

Hofmann, D.A., Morgeson, F.P., & Gerras, S.J. (2003). Climate as a moderator of the relationship between leader-member exchange and content specific citizenship: Safety climate as an exemplar. *Journal of Applied Psychology, 88*(1), 170–178.

Hofmann, D.A., & Stetzer, A. (1998). The role of safety climate and communication in accident interpretation: Implications for learning from negative events. *Academy of Management Journal, 41*(6), 644–657.

Institute of Medicine. (2004). *Keeping patients safe: Transforming the work environment of nurses.* Washington, DC: National Academy Press.

Katz-Navon, T., Naveh, E., & Stern, Z. (2005). Safety climate in healthcare organizations: A multidimensional approach. *Academy of Management Journal, 48,* 1073–1087.

Klein, G. (2003). *Intuition at work: Why developing your gut instincts will make you better at what you do.* New York: Doubleday.

Knight, A. (2004). *Measuring collective mindfulness and exploring its nomological network.* Master's thesis, University of Maryland, College Park.

Knox, G.E., Simpson, K.R., & Garite, T.J. (1999). High reliability perinatal units: An approach to the prevention of patient injury and medical malpractice claims. *Journal of Healthcare Risk Management, 19*(2), 24–32.

Landau, M., & Chisholm, D. (1995). The arrogance of optimism: Notes on failure-avoidance management. *Journal of Contingencies and Crisis Management, 3,* 67–80.

Langer, E.J. (1989). *Mindfulness.* Reading, MA: Addison-Wesley.

LaPorte, T.R., & Concolini, P.M. (1991). Working in practice but not in theory: Theoretical challenges of "high reliability organizations." *Journal of Public Administration and Theory, 1*(1), 19–47.

Lazarus, R.S. (1999). Hope: An emotion and a vital coping resource against despair. *Social Research, 66,* 653–678.

Levinthal, D.A., & Rerup, C. (2006). Crossing an apparent chasm: Bridging mindful and less mindful perspectives on organizational learning. *Organization Science, 17*(4), 502–513.

Madsen, P.M., Desai, V.M., Roberts, K.H., & Wong, D. (2006). Mitigating hazards through continuing design: The birth and evolution of a pediatric intensive care unit. *Organization Science, 17*(2), 239–248.

Meyer, J.P., Allen, N.J., & Smith, C.A. (1993). Commitment to organizations and occupations: Extension and test of a three-component conceptualization. *Journal of Applied Psychology, 78*(4), 538–551.

Meyer, J.P., & Parfyonova, N.M. (in press). Normative commitment in the workplace: A theoretical analysis and reconceptualization. *Human Resource Management Review.*

Miller, D. (1993). The architecture of simplicity. *Academy of Management Review, 18,* 116–138.

Naveh, E., Katz-Navon, T., & Stern, Z. (2006). Readiness to report medical treatment errors: The effects of safety procedures, safety information, and priority of safety. *Medical Care, 44*(2), 117–123.

Neal, A., & Griffin, M.A. (2006). A study of the lagged relationships among safety climate, safety motivation, safety behavior, and accidents at the individual and group levels. *Journal of Applied Psychology, 91*(4), 946–953.

Nembhard, I.M., & Edmondson, A.C. (2006). Making it safe: The effects of leader inclusiveness and professional status on psychological safety and improvement efforts in health care teams. *Journal of Organizational Behavior, 27,* 941–966.

Ray, J.L., Baker, L.T., & Plowman, D.A. (in press). Organizing mindfulness in business schools. *Academy of Management Learning & Education*.

Rerup, C. (2009). Attentional triangulation: Learning from unexpected rare crises. *Organization Science, 20*(5), 876–893.

Rerup, C. (2005). Learning from past experience: Footnotes on mindfulness and habitual entrepreneurship. *Scandinavian Journal of Management, 21*, 451–472.

Roberts, K.H. (1990). Some characteristics of one type of high reliability organization. *Organization Science, 1*(2), 160–176.

Roberts, K.H., Madsen, P.M., Desai, V.M., & Van Stralen, D. (2005). A case of the birth and death of a high reliability healthcare organization. *Quality and Safety in Health Care, 14*, 216–220.

Roberts, K.H., Stout, S.K., & Halpern, J.J. (1994). Decision dynamics in two high reliability military organizations. *Management Science, 40*(5), 614–624.

Roe, E., & Schulman, P.R. (2008). *High reliability management: Operating on the edge*. Stanford, CA: Stanford Business Books.

Rudolph, J.W., & Repenning, N.P. (2002). Disaster dynamics: Understanding the role of quantity in organizational collapse. *Administrative Science Quarterly, 47*, 1–30.

Salancik, G.R., & Pfeffer, J. (1978). A social information processing approach to job attitudes and task design. *Administrative Science Quarterly, 23*(2), 224–253.

Schulman, P.R. (1993). The negotiated order of organizational reliability. *Administration & Society, 25*(3), 353–372.

Singer, S.J., Lin, S., Falwell, A., Gaba, D.M., & Baker, L. (2009). Relationship of safety climate and safety performance in hospitals. *Health Services Research, 44*(2), 399–421.

Spreitzer, G.M., & Sonenshein, S. (2003). Positive deviance and extraordinary organizing. In K.S. Cameron, J. Dutton, & R.E. Quinn (Eds.), *Positive organizational scholarship* (pp. 207–224). San Francisco: Berrett-Koehler.

Sutcliffe, K.M., & Christianson, M.K. (2011). Managing the unexpected. In K.S. Cameron & G.M. Spreitzer (Eds.), *The Oxford handbook of positive organizational scholarship*. New York: Oxford University Press.

Tucker, A.L. (2007). An empirical study of system improvement by frontline employees in hospital units. *Manufacturing & Service Operations Management, 9*(4), 492–505.

van Dyck, C., Frese, M., Baer, M., & Sonnentag, S. (2005). Organizational error management culture and its impact on performance. *Journal of Applied Psychology, 90*(6), 1228–1240.

Vogus, T.J. (2004). *In search of mechanisms: How do HR practices affect organizational performance?* Doctoral dissertation, University of Michigan, Ann Arbor, MI.

Vogus, T.J., Ramanujam, R., & Tangirala, S. (2010). *The nonlinear effects of professional tenure and commitment on mindful organizing: Evidence from health care*. Working paper.

Vogus, T.J., & Sutcliffe, K.M. (2007a). The safety organizing scale: Development and validation of a behavioral measure of safety culture in hospital nursing units. *Medical Care, 45*(1), 46–54.

Vogus, T.J., & Sutcliffe, K.M. (2007b). The impact of safety organizing, trusted leadership, and care pathways on reported medication errors in hospital nursing units. *Medical Care, 45*(10), 997–1002.

Vogus, T.J., & Welbourne, T.M. (2003). Structuring for high reliability: HR practices and mindful processes in reliability-seeking organizations. *Journal of Organizational Behavior, 24*, 877–903.

Wasti, S.A. (2005). Commitment profiles: Combinations of organizational commitment forms and job outcomes. *Journal of Vocational Behavior, 67*, 290–308.

Weick, K.E. (2003). Positive organizing and organizational tragedy. In K.S. Cameron, J.Dutton, & R.E. Quinn (Eds.), *Positive organizational scholarship* (pp. 66–80). San Francisco: Berrett-Koehler.

Weick, K.E. (1993). The collapse of sensemaking in organizations: The Mann Gulch disaster. *Administrative Science Quarterly, 38*, 628–652.

Weick, K.E., & Putnam, T. (2006). Organizing for mindfulness: Eastern wisdom and western knowledge. *Journal of Management Inquiry, 15*(3), 275–287

Weick, K.E., & Roberts, K.H. (1993). Collective mind in organizations: Heedful interrelating on flight decks. *Administrative Science Quarterly, 38*, 357–381.

Weick, K.E., & Sutcliffe, K.M. (2007). *Managing the unexpected: Resilient performance in an age of uncertainty* (2nd ed.). San Francisco: Jossey-Bass.

Weick, K.E., & Sutcliffe, K.M. (2001). *Managing the unexpected: Assuring high performance in an age of complexity* (1st ed.). San Francisco: Jossey-Bass.

Weick, K.E., & Sutcliffe, K.M. (2003). Hospitals as cultures of entrapment: A reanalysis of the Bristol Royal Infirmary. *California Management Review, 45*(2), 73–84

Weick, K.E., & Sutcliffe, K.M. (2006). Mindfulness and the quality of organizational attention. *Organization Science, 16*(4), 409–421.

Weick, K.E., Sutcliffe, K.M., & Obstfeld, D. (1999). Organizing for high reliability: Processes of collective mindfulness. In B.M. Staw, & L.L. Cummings (Eds.), *Research in organizational behavior* Vol. 21 (pp. 81–123). Greenwich, CT: JAI Press, Inc.

Weingart, S.N., Farbstein, K., Davis, R.B., & Phillips, R.S. (2004). Using a multihospital survey to examine the safety culture. *Joint Commission Journal on Quality and Safety, 30*(3), 125–132.

Yun, S., Faraj, S., & Sims, H.P. (2005). Contingent leadership and effectiveness of trauma resuscitation teams. *Journal of Applied Psychology, 90*(6), 1288–1296.

Zohar, D. (1980). Safety climate in industrial organizations: Theoretical and applied implications. *Journal of Applied Psychology, 65*(1), 96–102.

Zohar, D. (2000). A group-level model of safety climate: Testing the effect of group climate on microaccidents in manufacturing jobs. *Journal of Applied Psychology, 85*(4), 587–596.

The Defining Role of Organizational Identity for Facilitating Stakeholder Flourishing

A Map for Future Research

Celia V. Harquail *and* Shelley L. Brickson

Abstract

Organizations can aggregate, intensify, and radiate positive influence through their connections with many types of stakeholders. An organization's identity, the distinctive and meaningful characteristics that define it, can support and foster stakeholders' flourishing. This chapter explores organizational identity (OI) through the lens of positive organizational scholarship (POS), to sketch a provisional map of opportunities for research at their intersection. The chapter identifies ways in which OI content and dynamics may promote stakeholder flourishing by influencing stakeholder identity and broader stakeholder functioning. The first section describes how OI content might promote positive self-evaluations and valued identity content, and explores how OI content can help stakeholders create meaning, establish connections, and gain access to resources. The second section describes how OI dynamics might meet stakeholders' identity and sense-making needs, so that stakeholders derive benefits through their relationships with the organization. The final section identifies additional research opportunities at the intersection of OI and stakeholder flourishing.

Keywords: Organizational identity, identity change, stakeholders, flourishing

Organizations hold a privileged place in our world. They are granted social, legal, and economic status that makes them powerful actors. Their influence pulses outward to their environments, and their gravity coheres not only the organization's members but also the stakeholders who surround it. As centers of human relatedness (Cooperrider & Sekerka, 2003), organizations have the potential to aggregate, intensify, and radiate positive influence that can foster the flourishing of the organization's stakeholders. Organizations' influence can even reach beyond stakeholders to affect stakeholders' contexts. Of the many features of an organization that might contribute to stakeholders' flourishing, we look to what is central, distinctive, and enduring about the organization—its identity—as a source of positive influence.

Organizational identity (OI) has received much attention from organizational scholars, who have

come to understand a great deal about how OIs are created, how they attract stakeholders and resources, how they direct collective energy, and how they remain consistent yet transform over time. In this chapter, we turn our attention to how OI might serve as a positive support or even as a catalyst for stakeholder flourishing. The positive organizational scholarship (POS) perspective invites us to focus on ways that organizations might direct their energy and power toward benefiting their stakeholders and the larger system, to have the broadest, most positive net impact (Brickson & Lemmon, 2009). By exploring OI through the lens of POS, we can begin to chart the paths that connect what defines an organization to what fosters stakeholder flourishing.

Although little research explicitly resides at the intersection of OI and POS, embarking upon this chapter revealed to us a number of existing pathways in and around this intersection that offer some direction for such research. Our goal in this chapter is to offer an initial, provisional map of the relationships that span this terrain. With this map, we hope to tempt scholars interested in OI or POS to consider how their own work may deepen and extend existing pathways or forge new paths around this intersection. We guarantee that a great many opportunities await curious, creative, and passionate scholars.

We begin by defining the constructs we will explore, clarifying our approach and its limitations, and noting the work that already addresses OI through a POS lens. Then, we turn to our central question: How might OI foster stakeholder flourishing? We organize our initial response to that question by drawing from a heuristic distinction between OI content and OI dynamics. And, we fill out these two domains by applying a POS intent to what we already understand about OI. Specifically, we underscore how OI content and dynamics might contribute to stakeholder flourishing through their influence on stakeholder identity and through their broader influence on stakeholder functioning. The resulting map, sketchy as it may be, describes incipient links between OI and stakeholder flourishing. Each of these links serves as a suggestion for future research.

Definitions, Approach, and Limitations
Definitions
In our own quest to discern the rough contours of the terrain at the intersection of OI and POS, we found that the question, "How can OI enhance stakeholder flourishing in a net positive fashion?" helped to orient us. We therefore emphasize three constructs here—flourishing, stakeholders, and OI—recognizing that they present but one perspective on the intersection between OI and POS. We also engage in some level of definitional simplification for all three terms to help clarify our exposition and permit us to emphasize basic connections rather than intricate relationships between these constructs.

- *Flourishing*: We draw upon the construct of *flourishing* to capture in one simple term what is, in reality, a wide range of potentially positive influences and outcomes. By "flourishing" we mean the optimal experience and functioning of any particular stakeholder (Dutton & Sonenshein, 2008, p. 738).

- *Stakeholders*: By 'stakeholders' we mean entities that affect and can be affected by the organization (Freeman, 1984). Stakeholders include human as well as nonhuman entities (e.g., animals, the Earth) at any level of analysis, that are directly or indirectly "in relationship" with the organization. Stakeholders may be external or internal to the organization. Obviously, there are tremendous differences between stakeholders. The influences and processes that might support the flourishing of an individual, a strategic alliance partner, or the Earth are quite different. We elide these differences across stakeholders, so that it is easier to see just how far the influence of OI might reach. Further, for any particular type of stakeholder, relationships with an organization and processes engaging that stakeholder with OI will hold their own unique questions. We hope that colleagues will take what they know about the specifics of any given stakeholder and unfold the particular, more complex processes that apply to them.

- *Organizational identity*: Organizational identity is, in the most general way, the understanding of "who the organization is," an understanding of what qualities seem to define the organization and distinguish it from other organizations. Organizational identity is the aspect of culturally embedded sense-making that is focused on collective self-definition (Fiol, Hatch, & Golden-Biddle, 1998). Although different epistemological paradigms of OI are associated with somewhat discrepant distinctions about OI's source and ontological nature (Harquail & King, 2010) scholars generally agree that OI enables, influences, and legitimatizes organizational goals and actions (Ashforth & Mael, 1996; Brickson & Lemmon, 2009; Corley et al., 2006). And, OI is enacted, performed, or demonstrated though an organization's collective decisions and behaviors (Schultz, Hatch & Larsen, 2000).

Just as light is both particle and wave, OI is both content and process (Corley et al., 2006). When scholars consider the content of OI, they are usually referring to the attributes that express the defining values, goals, beliefs, stereotypic traits, knowledge, skills, and abilities of the organization. (Ashforth, Harrison, & Corley, 2008, p. 330). Focusing on the content of OI makes it possible to treat OI as a variable in a larger model explaining the experience and behavior of a focal organization's stakeholders. Meanwhile, when scholars consider the dynamic nature of OI, they investigate how it is construed, how it changes and endures, and how it is influenced by internal and external evaluations and responses. Focusing on the dynamics of the OI process makes it possible to look at the influence of OI over time, and at the role of stakeholders in negotiating that influence.

Approach and Limitations

In preparing to write this chapter, we sought to identify and review research that already addresses the role of OI from a POS perspective, as well as to identify potentially relevant emerging trends in the larger OI research stream. Our aim was to help craft an emergent picture of where OI and POS momentum might converge. A search through publication and conference proceedings databases over the past 20 years, as well as through various websites, revealed only seven articles explicitly about OI from a POS perspective. Six of these articles (Brickson & Lemmon, 2009; Corley & Harrison, 2009; Glynn & Walsh, 2009; Hamilton & Gioia, 2009; Marquis & Davis, 2009; Pratt & Kraatz, 2009) appeared in the same volume of research on positive identities (Roberts & Dutton, 2009). This set of articles explicitly addresses the OI–POS intersection, considering the nature and function of positive OIs. The seventh article addresses the inherent normative nature of OI, and considers the ethical implications of OI construction (Oliver, Statler, & Roos, 2010).

Although little work explicitly focuses on OI from a POS perspective, a wealth of research on OI dwells in and around this intersection. We have tried to include as much as possible in this chapter, while recognizing that we could not mention every OI-related study that might provide a springboard into POS. We also want to point out that our treatment of the terrain is more developed in some areas than in others. We believe this to be a function of the literature as well as our own biases. The literature has not been evenly distributed across levels of analysis or across types of stakeholders. For example, the influence of OI on individual members has received more attention than the influence of OI on external stakeholders. Further, most of the work within POS has drawn from social constructionist and psychological

perspectives. For our own part, we confess that our analysis reflects our own scholarly approaches, which draw from these same perspectives and a North American orientation. Although we will not attempt to mention all stakeholders at each level of analysis, research at the intersection of OI and POS can be anchored in stakeholder relationships at many levels of analysis. And, although our discussions emphasize a social constructionist paradigm, we are confident that the issues raised will be relevant to OI discussions within other paradigms.

How Can Organizational Identity Contribute to Stakeholder Flourishing?

We now turn to the challenge of organizing an overview of existing and possible pathways into the intersection of OI and POS. We divide our discussion into two sections, addressing possible links between OI and the flourishing of organizational stakeholders. The first section addresses the influence of OI content on positive outcomes, while the second section addresses the influence of OI dynamics on positive outcomes. In taking this approach, we collapse three previously identified domains for studying OI through a POS lens: positive content (i.e. attributes), dynamics (i.e. processes), and outcomes (Glynn & Walsh, 2009). We connect content and dynamics and processes to outcomes because we agree with others (Glynn & Walsh, 2009) that viewing these elements as interconnected may enhance the potency of the POS perspective. We recognize that OI content is dynamically created and that OI dynamics involve and are manifested in terms of content, but we found this distinction to be useful heuristically.

Our discussion of each of these domains has its own particular flavor. Research on OI content has focused on neutral and positive phenomena, such as Harquail's (2008) research demonstrating how elements of the Heartland Corporation's welcoming and Midwestern identity influenced the organization's product choices. Research on OI dynamics has often addressed more negative phenomena, such as strikes, over the definition of the organization and its future directions (e.g., Corley & Harrison, 2009; Glynn, 2000). Therefore, the first section outlines pathways that already exist between OI content and stakeholder flourishing and suggests ways to enrich and expand our understanding of these pathways. The second section sketches possible routes between OI dynamics and stakeholder flourishing by looking at findings about often-negative phenomena in a positive way.

Influence of Organizational Identity Content on Stakeholders' Flourishing

The content of an organization's identity may promote stakeholder flourishing through two broad means: by advancing positive identities among stakeholders and by advancing stakeholder functioning more generally. Although the bulk of existing work that addresses the influence of OI focuses on members and internal groups, OI can influence the identity and general functioning of stakeholders at any level of analysis, from individual to social movement. In the absence of research ranging evenly across levels of analysis, our strategy here is to extrapolate from research (usually on individuals and groups) to suggest some possible, parallel influences on stakeholders at other levels of analysis. We offer these extrapolated influences as preliminary propositions about mechanisms and relationships, and we hope readers will interpret these as invitations for future research.

The Positive Influence of Organizational Identity on Stakeholder Identity

One of the most central ways in which OI influences stakeholders is through shaping stakeholder identity itself. Shaping stakeholder identity is a particularly potent way that organizations can wield positive influence. Stakeholder identity itself has the potential to generate new cycles of positive dynamics and actions that affect other stakeholders, sending ripples of positive influence outward from the organization (Brickson & Lemmon, 2009) and promoting positive outcomes in a manner not predicted by linear models (Hamilton & Gioia, 2009). Existing literature underscores three routes through which OI can positively influence stakeholder identity: by directly promoting positive self-evaluations, by promoting identity content that is valued by the stakeholder or that ultimately generates net positive value to the stakeholder system as a whole, and by creating opportunities for stakeholders to enact and authenticate their identities, a positive experience. We address each of the three paths in turn.

The first route through which OI can positively influence stakeholder identity is by directly promoting positive self-evaluations among stakeholders (Dutton et al., 2010). This refers to the valance of one's identity generally speaking, rather than to specific content (Dutton et al., 2010). Favorable self-regard has long been considered positive and important (see Baumeister et al., 1998; Hogg & Terry, 2000). Attractive OIs allow stakeholders to "bask in their reflected glory" (Cialdini et al., 1976) by association and, as such, to enhance their own self-evaluations. This may be true for members (Dutton et al., 1994) as well as for a variety of external stakeholders, including customers (Bhattacharya & Sen, 2003), strategic alliance partners (Dacin, Oliver, & Roy, 2006), communities (Marquis & Davis, 2009), and social causes (Friedman & McAdam, 1992).

Research highlights two distinct ways that OIs secure attractiveness. First, certain OI content may lead organizations to be viewed as attractive, thus fostering positive self-evaluations among stakeholders, even without influencing the actual content of stakeholder identity itself. In social identity theory, OI attributes of "high status" and "distinctive" are considered to be attractive (Ashforth & Mael, 1989; Elsbach & Kramer, 1996). For example, business schools with elite identities may seem attractive to members who believe that this elite identity leads outsiders to think highly of the organization (Elsbach & Kramer, 1996). Other OI attributes may also be deemed generally attractive, such as virtues (Cameron, 2003; Wright & Goodstein, 2007) like 'just' (Rhee, Dutton, & Bagozzi, 2006; Tyler & Blader, 2000, 2003), 'ethical' (Belmer, Fukakawa, & Gray, 2007; Liedtka, 1996; Verbos et al., 2007), 'moral' (Matherne, 2009; Weaver, 2006), and 'sustainable' (Hamilton & Gioia, 2009). The second means by which OIs may garner attractiveness is through organizations meeting expectations. When organizations live up to the expectations held by insiders or outsiders, their identities are held in higher esteem (Brickson, 2010; Foreman & Whetten, 2002; Hsu & Hannan, 2005). From this perspective, the content of an organization's identity determines the particular standards by which an organization is evaluated as attractive such that, for example, acquiring high status may be attractive among organizations with individualistic identities, whereas being compassionate may be attractive among organizations with relational identities (Brickson, 2010).

Beyond directly promoting positive self-evaluations, the second route through which OI can positively influence stakeholder identity is by contributing identity content that stakeholders can use to define their own identities (see Dutton et al., 1994; Dutton et al., 2010). When contributed identity content is valued by stakeholders, or ultimately generates net positive value to the stakeholder system as a whole, these influences may be considered to foster stakeholder flourishing. Organizational identity shapes stakeholder identity content by enabling and constraining identity attributes available to stakeholders. Stakeholders, in their relationships with the organization, will be encouraged to define their identities in ways that incorporate, complement, fit with or are neutral with regard to the specific OI. Stakeholder identities related to intraorganizational roles (Birnholtz, Cohen, & Hoch, 2007; Golden-Biddle & Rao, 1997), occupations (Anteby, 2008), social identity groups (Hogg & Terry, 2000; Tretheway, 1997), and professions (Pratt, Rockmann, & Kaufmann, 2006) can all be shaped by OI because these other identities either fit within, overlap with, or envelope the organization's identity. Organizational identity has a cascading effect on internal stakeholder identities (Ashforth, Rogers, & Corley, 2010), in which identity content at one level is constrained by identity content at a higher level. For example, Anteby (2008) found that craftsmen in an aeronautical plant were able to define themselves as technically skilled experts, in contrast to assembly line workers, because the plant was known for its one-of-a-kind prototypes. For stakeholder groups in which the organization is a member, such as strategic groups (Peteraf & Shanley, 1997), industries (Czarniawska & Wolff, 1998), and communities (Marquis & Davis, 2009), OI has an upward influence by offering OI content as part of what might define these larger groups.

Organizational identity also constrains and enables stakeholder identity content by influencing OI-directed behavior. Stakeholder behavior is guided by OI through expressions of OI attributes, compliance with OI-based norms (Harquail, 2005), and enactment of organizational goals as outlined by the OI (Ashforth & Mael, 1996; Brickson & Lemmon, 2009). These behaviors then shape stakeholder identity. They directly elicit particular identity schemas among stakeholders (Brickson, 2007; Brickson & Lemmon, 2009). They also influence stakeholder self-definitions by serving as inputs into a sense-making process about "who" the stakeholders are (see Ashforth et al., 2010; Harquail, 1998, 2005); see also Ashforth et al., 2008; Ashforth & Mael, 1989; Dutton et al., 1994; Labianca et al., 2001; Pratt, 1998). Further, the organizational policies and practices that members enact in the service of organizational goals produce predictable intraorganizational and interorganizational relationship patterns and resources. These patterns and resources then help to entrench and broaden the effects of OI on stakeholder identities (Brickson & Lemmon, 2009). The content of the OI shapes emerging

stakeholder identities in ways that may potentially be positive.

Organizational identity shapes stakeholder identity content by generating new favorable attributes through positive social comparisons. As part of shaping the content of their own identity, entities engage in social comparison processes, choosing a target and comparing themselves to this target (Suls, Martin, & Wheeler, 2002). Stakeholders may use the organization as a target for social comparison, construing their positive similarity and positive distinctiveness relative to the organization's defining characteristics. Organizational identity is used as a social comparison target by individuals (Dutton et al., 1994; Harquail, 2005), groups (Sveningsson & Alvesson, 2003), organizations (Ashforth & Mael; Brickson, 2010), and within industries (Gnyawali & Madhavan, 2001; Staber, 2010). In some cases, these social comparisons suggest evaluatively positive attributes of the organization that stakeholders can adopt for characterizing their own identities in similar ways. In other cases, these comparisons are used by the stakeholder to make its own identity construal positively distinct from the organization's identity (Alvesson & Willmott, 2004; Elsbach & Bhattacharya, 2001; Greve & Rao, 2006).

The third route through which OI can positively influence stakeholder identity, in addition to promoting positive self-evaluations and advancing valued or valuable identity content, is by creating opportunities for stakeholders to enact their identities and thereby authenticate their sense of self (Harquail, 1998, 2005; Roberts et al., 2009). The organization's identity can provide a context in which members feel comfortable "being fully there" (Kahn, 1990), not only in terms of psychological presence and work engagement, but also in terms of experiencing personal authenticity (Harquail, 1998) or holism (Pratt & Ashforth, 2003). People value feeling internally consistent (Steele, 1988). In situations in which people can comfortably enact "who they are," they are able to align their external expressions and behaviors with their internal self-definition to experience pleasure (Harquail, 2005; Roberts et al., 2009).

Organizational identities can validate and mobilize stakeholders' identities in ways that invite stakeholders' identity expression. This may be due to OI–stakeholder identity alignment (Dutton et al., 1994; Dukerich, Golden, & Shortel, 2002) or to the ways in which the OI otherwise encompasses, resonates with, or facilitates the stakeholder's identity (Harquail, 2007). For example, OI enables the enactment of particular stakeholder roles (Birnholtz et al., 2007; Golden-Biddle & Rao, 1997) and social categories. With regard to internal stakeholders, OI shapes the nature of intraorganizational roles (Golden-Biddle & Rao, 1997) and enables the enactment of certain social identities, such as those related to sociocultural (Dougherty & Huyser, 2008), occupational (Anteby, 2008), and professional (Pratt et al., 2006) group memberships. For example, OIs associated with categories of organizational forms such as "orchestra" (Baron, 2004; Whetten & Mackey, 2002) enable members to enact cherished professional or occupational identities such as "musician" (see Anteby, 2008; Glynn, 2000). With regard to external stakeholders, OI can help to provide opportunities for others to enact positively valued societal roles, such as being "community oriented" (Brickson & Lemmon, 2009; Marquis & Davis, 2009), or to enact collectively shared and highly valued characteristics, such as being part of an elite "high-quality Scottish knitware" group (Porac, Thomas, & Baden-Fuller, 1989).

The Positive Influence of Organizational Identity on Stakeholder Functioning

Identity is a powerful determinant of an entity's well-being and its ability to engage effectively with others in its environment (Akerlof & Kranton, 2010; Kahn, 1990). Thus, to the extent that OI contributes positively toward stakeholder identity, it also contributes toward the functioning of those stakeholders. Yet, the power of OI goes beyond its influence on stakeholder identity. Organizational identity has a pervasive effect on much of the lived reality of internal and external stakeholders, because OI is central to all that organizations are and do, to the relationships that they forge and foster, and to the policies and practices enacted by their agents (Ashforth & Mael, 1996; Brickson, 2007). Although numerous other aspects of stakeholder functioning are surely relevant, we focus here on three: stakeholders' ability to create and act upon meaning, their sense of connection and belonging, and their ability to access resources. This list is not exhaustive, and the items are not mutually exclusive. For example, connection creates meaning, meaning enables connection, and both connection and meaning may be considered as resources.

One of the most fundamental things that OI contributes to stakeholders is meaning (Albert & Whetten, 1985; Ashforth & Mael, 1996; Hatch &

Schultz, 2002; Pratt & Ashforth, 2003). Organizational identity makes organizations ontologically possible by enabling entativity (Harquail, 2008) and allowing a sense of reflective and purposeful human-like selfhood (Sluss & Ashforth, 2008) to emerge out of a messy collective whose membership and boundaries are, in reality, challenging to discern (Bartel & Dutton, 2001; Wiesenfeld, 2007). As such, OI helps stakeholders construct a "we" or a "they" that is the organization. In addition, the content of OI gives the organization significant descriptive and normative character (Birnholtz et al., 2007; Wright & Goodstein, 2007). This character can include local attributes that are linked to and evoke larger, more global meaning systems, such as political perspectives, religions, social causes, and ideologies. Being in relationship with the organization that is embedded in these other meaning systems also connects stakeholders to a larger web of other meaning. Because people have a profound need to make sense of the world around them (Weick, 1995), such meaning is grounding and positive in its own right (Corley & Harrison, 2009; Harquail & King, 2010).

Further, the meaning associated with OI is functional because it makes action for the organization and stakeholders both possible and interpretable. In terms of making action possible, OI enables stakeholders to make sense of who the organization is, so that internal stakeholders know how to engage on behalf of the organization, and external stakeholders know how to interact with the organization (Albert & Whetten, 1985; Ashforth & Mael, 1996). For example, when employees at an extreme sports equipment company strategized about how to grow through acquisitions, the question "what does it mean to be who we are?" helped to guide them toward companies with similar values (Corley & Harrison, 2009). Perceptions of the organization's best interests (Livengood & Reger, 2010), normative declarations and esthetic imperatives (Harquail, 2008; Schultz, Hatch, & Larsen, 2000), and prioritization of goals (Brickson & Lemmon, 2009) that are driven by OI cohere and coordinate otherwise cumbersome stakeholder action. Shared goals focus the energy and attention of individuals and groups within the organization, enabling collective action (Albert, Ashforth, & Dutton, 2000). Further, when members (Dutton et al., 1994) or external stakeholders (Bhattacharya & Sen, 2003; Rowley & Moldoveanu, 2003) identify with the OI or the organization's goals, their energy and attention become supercharged to generate action even more productively (Tyler & Blader, 2000). In addition, as noted above, to the extent that OI includes inherently and normatively positive virtues, it focuses member effort on virtuous actions (Dutton & Dukerich, 1991; Hamilton & Gioia, 2009; Verbos, 2007). Organizational identities may also foster virtuous behavior on a grander scale by eliciting similarly virtuous identity schemas among other stakeholders through the kinds of relationships and resources engendered by the OI (Boyd et al., 2009; Brickson & Lemmon, 2009; Hardy & Carlo, 2005).

In addition to making action possible, OI also renders action interpretable. First, OI provides a lens through which stakeholders can understand organizational action. Organizational identities are associated with expectations on behalf of stakeholders about what kinds of roles and behaviors are appropriate (Brickson, 2007; Brickson & Lemmon, 2009; Harquail & King, 2010; Hsu & Hannan, 2005; Smith & King, 2009). These expectations make it possible to know what to expect from the organization, and serve as a basis of comparison for evaluating the organization (Brickson, 2010; see also Foreman & Whetten, 2002; Livengood & Reger, 2010). Importantly, when stakeholders decide to engage with an organization, they have both its identity and an associated set of expectations in mind. Based on the specific nature of the OI, stakeholders will expect the organization to behave toward themselves and toward other stakeholders in ways that reflect and express OI, treating OI as a commitment by the organization to "be" a specific way. An OI is a commitment not only to hold a certain set of values but also to behave in ways that reflect these values. An organization's stakeholder may see these values (and OI content as a whole) as part of what they "get" when they establish a relationship with the organization.

Second, in parallel fashion, OI also provides a lens through which stakeholders can understand their own behavior. Organizational identity offers a context for sense-making and sense-giving that helps to bring meaning to stakeholders' relationships with the organization and stakeholders' actions relative to the organization (Hamilton & Gioia, 2009). To the extent that stakeholders view their actions as based in virtuous and normative goals, these actions may be particularly pleasurable (Hamilton & Gioia, 2009). This is true for both internal stakeholders, who may view their work as virtue-based, and for outsiders, who may see their relationship with the organization as enabling virtuous behavior of

their own. For example, customers of virtuous organizations often view their purchases as virtuous behavior (Berger, Cunningham, & Drumwright, 2006).

Another way that OI fosters stakeholder functioning, beyond conferring meaning, is by enabling a sense of connection and belonging (Pratt, 1998) that helps to fulfill a deep-seated human need (Maslow, 1954). First, OI can provide opportunities for collective group membership by offering stakeholders a chance to affiliate themselves with the organization. Through this affiliation, stakeholders may experience membership and belonging to groups at higher levels of analysis, such as strategic groups (Czarniawska & Wolff, 1998; Peteraf & Shanley, 1997), communities (Marquis & Davis, 2009), and social movements (Berger et al., 2006; Meyer, 2004; Minkoff, 2002). Second, organizations are, themselves, relationship partners to stakeholders. Different types of OIs are likely to be associated with particular types of relationship ties with external and internal stakeholders, through which different types of content is apt to flow (Brickson, 2007; Brickson & Akinlade, 2010; Walsh, 2009; Walsh & Glynn, 2008). Further, these distinct relationship patterns between the organization and stakeholders are likely also to influence relationship ties and relationship content among stakeholders themselves (Brickson, 2007; Brickson & Akinlade, 2010; Walsh, 2009; Walsh & Glynn, 2008). For example, organizations with a relational identity orientation are apt to have strong socio-emotional bonds with employees, which are then manifested in strong bonds among employees (Brickson, 2007; Walsh, 2009).

A third way that OI can positively influence the functioning of stakeholders is by offering access to resources. An organization's core competencies are closely aligned with OI (Dutton & Dukerich, 1991; Fiol, 1991; Glynn, 2000; Livengood & Reger, 2010; Nag et al., 2007; Selznick, 1957), and these competencies influence which resources are made available to outsiders. For example, they may determine whether an orchestra offers the public exceptional-quality music or low-cost performances (Glynn, 2000). Further, since both the distinct features of the stakeholders' relationship ties and the currencies exchanged through these relationships are closely connected with OI content, organizations with different types of OIs provide internal and external stakeholders with unique types of resources (Brickson, 2007; Brickson & Lemmon, 2009; Brickson & Akinlade, 2010; Walsh, 2009; see also Dutton et al., 2010). For example, freedom, caring, and community were offered in a highly individualistic, relational, and collectivistic organization, respectively (Brickson & Akinlade, 2010).

Having established several preliminary ways that OI content can support stakeholder flourishing by positively influencing stakeholder identity and supporting stakeholders' functioning, we now shift from a focus on OI content to a focus on OI dynamics. When taking a dynamic view of OI, all the ways that OI content can lead to flourishing still apply, but have to be expanded to incorporate changes in OI content, as well as in the process of OI change itself.

Organizational Identity Dynamics and Stakeholder Flourishing

The concept of OI has a built-in illusion: OIs are composed of attributes that appear to be relatively enduring, even as some facets of OI change over time in concert with structural, material, and functional changes in the organization and the environment. Organizational identity dynamics are driven by the reexamination and adjustment of the reciprocal, dynamic relationships between beliefs about what defines the organization, perceptions of actions by the organization (and its members), and beliefs about how others see the organization (i.e., construed external image; Dutton et al., 1994) (Dutton & Dukerich, 1991; Gioia et al., 2000; Harquail & King, 2010; Hatch & Schultz, 1997). Organizational identity change can occur through dramatic episodes that punctuate what appears to be a steady and continuous collective construal, causing the organization to reconsider who it is, how it is seen, and how it should behave (Dutton & Dukerich, 1991; Fiol, 1991; Ravasi & Schultz, 2006). Organizational identity change can also occur in a more incremental, ongoing fashion, as stakeholders enact their beliefs about who the organization is, respond to others' perceptions of the organization's image, and interpret the organization's behaviors to understand "who it is" (Carlsen, 2006; Hatch & Schultz, 2002) and "what it means to be who we are" (Corley & Harrison, 2009). Through episodic and everyday dynamics of change, organizations and their identities are always in the process of "becoming" (e.g., Brown & Starkey, 2000; Corley & Harrison, 2009; Hatch & Schultz, 2002; Tsoukas & Chia, 2002) with OI always a work-in-progress.

Although much research on OI dynamics addresses the difficulties that OI change poses for stakeholders, OI dynamics also have much to offer from a POS perspective. Perceived OI continuity

and perceived OI change both meet distinct stakeholder needs, and the illusion of an enduring OI can help stakeholders bridge these needs. As above, we organize the discussion by first considering the possible benefits to stakeholder identity and then by considering the possible benefits to more general stakeholder functioning, on the way to stakeholder flourishing.

Effect of Organizational Identity Dynamics on Stakeholder Identity

The perception of OI continuity and the reality of OI change can benefit stakeholder identity because of the way that OI dynamics map onto an identity-specific paradox of stakeholders: Stakeholders are generally attached to their self-definitions, and thus anticipate potential change as a threat. At the same time, stakeholders also want to see themselves as growing and evolving (Eilam & Shamir, 2005; Kegan, 1982), and so they seek opportunities to renew their identities. The dynamics of OI, with their illusion of continuity gentling the disruption of change, offer stakeholders opportunities to bridge their own identity paradox. Organizational identity dynamics enable stakeholders both to be and to become.

On the "being" side of the equation, measures can be taken to help keep the OI feeling relatively coherent, consistent, and continuous (Dutton & Dukerich, 1991; Gioia et al., 2000; Pratt & Kraatz, 2009), thus allowing stakeholders to experience continuity in their self-definitions. Simple choices about how to describe OI change can enhance perceptions of continuity, such as using terms to describe OI that are more enduring than the evolving understanding of these terms. For example, the OI characteristic of "premier service provider" may mean "reliable" at one point in time and "first to market" at another (Corley & Gioia, 2004, p. 193). This tactic allows OI to look more stable than it may actually be (Gioia et al., 2000). And, when OI changes more dramatically, another tactic is to explicitly describe these changes as the outcome of intentional growth or natural evolution, making OI change sound more like continuity. The perception of OI continuity supports stakeholder flourishing because this perception allows stakeholders to expect continuity in the parts of their own identities that depend on the organization (Dutton et al., 1994; Eilam & Shamir, 2005).

Meanwhile, on the "becoming" side of the equation, changes in OI content provoke an accommodative response in stakeholder identities (Alvesson

& Robertson, 2006; Ashforth et al., 2010, Brickson & Lemmon, 2009; Carlsen, 2006). To the extent that OI content becomes more positive, this may inject additional positivity into stakeholders' own identities. For example, Eilam and Shamir (2005) found that a social service agency's image upgrade, through a move to modern and rather grand new offices, enabled members to reframe their self-concepts in ways that claimed their new place in the revised status hierarchy. Further, because stakeholder identities benefit from opportunities to develop, adjust, and grow (Dutton et al., 2010), changes in OI can make room for healthy stakeholder identity change and self-renewal.

Because organizations and stakeholders themselves can adjust their narratives about OI dynamics to incorporate claims of change and renewal alongside reassurances of continuity and stability (Chreim, 2005; Huy, 2002), stakeholders can craft their own interpretations of what is happening with OI in a way that meets their particular identity needs. Ultimately, when OI dynamics accomplish significant change (whether large or small) while being perceived as sufficiently consistent (Ravasi & Schultz, 2006), OI will support stakeholders' identity needs and promote the most flourishing.

Effects of Organizational Identity Dynamics on Stakeholder Functioning

In addition to their role in addressing stakeholder identity needs, OI dynamics can also advance stakeholder flourishing in other ways. Organizational identity dynamics help stakeholders continue to understand the organization even as it changes, to adjust their behavior with regard to the organization, and to determine the kinds of benefits they derive through their relationship with the organization. We address each in turn, acknowledging that other connections to stakeholder welfare surely exist.

Organizational identity dynamics can foster sense-making and action for both internal and external stakeholders (Ashforth & Mael, 1996; Albert & Whetten, 1985; Gioia & Thomas, 1996; Pratt & Kraatz, 2009). On the one hand, a sense of continuity allows stakeholders to feel confident in their knowledge of the organization (Albert & Whetten, 1985). This perception of OI continuity can also help stakeholders smooth over confusing and contradictory experiences of actual organizational change by guiding their focus and energy (Corley & Gioia, 2004). Because OI continuity facilitates making sense of who the organization is,

continuity is critical to helping stakeholders plot their own actions, whether in relation to, or on behalf of, the organization (Albert & Whetten, 1985; Ashforth & Mael, 1996). The perception of OI continuity also enables stakeholders to experience the organization as dependable and trustworthy. This makes it possible for stakeholders to derive a sense of comfort and safety through their relationship with the organization. Stakeholders can feel confident about depending on the organization both socially and materially, and this confidence can support stakeholder flourishing.

At the same time that perceived OI continuity facilitates some stakeholder needs, OI change facilitates other needs. Organizational identity change creates opportunities for stakeholders to revise their understanding of the organization, to reconsider their behaviors regarding the organization, and to renegotiate their relationship with the organization. Organizational change and changes in the organization's circumstances can trigger a sense of ambiguity about who the organization is, prompting stakeholders to revise their understanding of the organization's identity (Corley & Gioia, 2004; Gioia & Chittipeddi, 1991). The process of revising OI causes stakeholders to pay closer attention to identity-relevant information and to look closely at who the organization is becoming. Stakeholders can then draw on this new understanding to be more effective in their interactions with the organization (Scott & Lane, 2000). Organizational identity change also offers stakeholders the opportunity to reconsider how best to pursue the organization's goals. For example, if a commercial theater were to become a cooperative actors' workshop, with a corresponding shift from financial to educational goals, its employees, audiences, regulators, and other stakeholders would then reconsider how to respond to these changes and pursue these new goals.

Organizational identity changes can also prompt stakeholders to renegotiate the qualities and terms of their relationships with the organization, helping to establish new terms that will continue to support that stakeholder's flourishing (Glynn, 2000). Interestingly, stakeholders can continue to renegotiate their relationship to an organization even after the organization ceases to exist. Crafting a "legacy identity" (Walsh & Glynn, 2008) that defines "who we were" offers stakeholders opportunities to renegotiate their organizational relationship and enjoy some of the psychic, cognitive, and social benefits derived from this relationship, even if only through memory (Feldman & Feldman, 2006).

Stakeholders can also capitalize on OI change by actively renegotiating the OI itself (Scott & Lane, 2000). Stakeholders often have competing interests and will advocate for the view of OI that offers them the most advantage (Barbulescu & Weeks, 2007). For example, engineers may emphasize an organization's technical identity and focus on product performance, whereas sales managers may emphasize its commercial identity and focus on pleasing clients (Barbulescu & Weeks, 2007). In organizations with hybrid or multiple identities, such as church-sponsored schools that combine a religious identity and an academic identity (Albert & Whetten, 1985), the tensions between these identities and between the stakeholders' aligned with them are often delicately balanced in the OI structure. As OI is renegotiated, the balance between different identities and the concerns of competing stakeholders must be addressed. Periodic, constructive rebalancing efforts may sustain the organization's multiple identities (Price, Corley, & Gioia, 2008) while helping to resolve intergroup conflicts among stakeholders (Barbulescu & Weeks, 2007). When identity disagreements are resolved, and when leaders agree on an organization's identity, the organization's performance is improved (Giraud, Voss, & Cable, 2006). Moreover, when competing interests are successfully balanced or resolved, stakeholders can redirect their energy to other productive pursuits.

In sum, OI dynamics offer opportunities to benefit stakeholders by meeting identity and sensemaking needs and by providing benefits to stakeholders through their relationship with the organization. Perceptions of OI consistency allow stakeholders to remain confident in their understanding of the organization and their behavior regarding the organization. And, OI dynamics create timely, relevant opportunities for stakeholders to revise, reconsider and renegotiate their interdependence with the organization. In these ways, both perceived OI continuity and OI change can advance stakeholder flourishing.

Discussion

In this chapter, our goal was to sketch a rough map of the confluence of OI and POS by charting some paths that connect OI content and OI dynamics to stakeholder flourishing. We hope that this provisional map helps scholars recognize existing paths and identify where new paths may be forged. We encourage OI scholars to imagine where their own research might contribute, how POS might transform their research questions, and where they might establish inviting trailheads for new research linking OI to stakeholder flourishing.

We recognize that there are several potentially rich areas for future research that we were unable to include in this initial map. However, two particular topics of OI research deserve at least a brief mention because they seem especially ripe for inquiry guided by POS. These are research embracing the normative nature of OIs, and research supporting the rise of intentionally "positive" organizational structures.

Organizational identity research implicitly recognizes the normative nature of identity; the dynamic, processual, and temporal activities associated with OI always have an ethical dimension, whether "good" or "bad" (Matherne, 2009; Oliver et al., 2010; White, 1999). However, mainstream OI research has not directed much attention to OI's normative dimension (Kornberger & Brown, 2007). Where research has explored OI's normative dimension, it has tended to investigate how OI can be used to exert control over stakeholders, often in a negative way (see Alvesson & Willmott, 2004; Anteby, 2008; Gustavsson, 2005). Aside from initial forays in the positive identities book (Dutton & Roberts, 2009), we have yet to capitalize on how the normative dimension of OI can be used to support positive agency. Embracing the normative dimension of OI from a POS perspective might help scholars see how normative attributes and beliefs systems become significant to an organization as part of OI, enabling researchers to build links between norms, OI, and stakeholder flourishing.

Another area inviting attention from both OI and POS research is the study of social enterprises. Social enterprises are organizational forms such as B Corporations, triple bottom line companies (Norman & MacDonald, 2004), and low-profit limited liability companies (L3Cs) (Gottesman, 2007) that are intentionally designed to lead to stakeholder flourishing. By codifying hybrid OIs within the organization's legal identity, these forms intend to create inescapable, constructive, and dynamic tension within the organization's identity. Then, they aim to use this tension to impel the generative pursuit of goals that create net positive value across all stakeholders. Because these OIs are designed to be positive in their influence, they are likely to offer rich insights about stakeholder flourishing.

In the process of writing this chapter, we have become even more convinced that bringing POS to OI research has transformative and generative potential. Organizational identity is an enormously potent construct because it defines, organizes, and directs the energy and actions of the world's most powerful social actors toward their stakeholders, while also helping to define, orient, motivate, and generate outcomes for stakeholders themselves. Meanwhile, the POS perspective invites us to focus on ways that organizations might direct their energy and power toward benefiting their stakeholders and the larger system. We encourage scholars and practitioners to explore the transformative potential of the OI–POS intersection. Organizational identity, understood and employed through a positive perspective, can help organizations extend and inspire the positive flourishing of their stakeholders and the broader stakeholder system.

References

Ackerlof, G.A., & Kranton, R.E. (2010). *Identity Economics: How our identities shape our work, wages, and well-being.* Princeton, NJ: Princeton University Press.

Albert, S., Ashforth, B., & Dutton, J.E. (2000). Organizational identity and identification: Charting new waters and building new bridges. *Academy of Management Review, 25*(1), 13–17.

Albert, S., & Whetten, D. (1985). Organizational identity. In L.L. Cummings, & B.M. Staw (Eds.), *Research in organizational behavior* (pp. 263–295). Greenwich, CT: JAI Press.

Alvesson, M.H., & Willmott, H. (2004). Identity regulation as organizational control: Producing the appropriate individual. *Journal of Management Studies, 39*, 619–644.

Anteby, M. (2008). Identity incentives as an engaging form of control. *Organization Science, 19*(2), 202–220.

Ashforth, B.E., Harrison, S.H., & Corley, K.G. (2008). Identification in organizations: An examination of four fundamental questions. *Journal of Management, 34*, 325–374.

Ashforth, B., & Mael, F. (1989). Social identity theory and the organization. *Academy of Management Review, 14*(1), 20–39.

Ashforth, B.E., & Mael, F.A. (1996). Organizational identity and strategy as a context for the individual. In J.A. C. Baum, & J.E. Dutton (Eds.), *Advances in strategic management* Vol. 13 (pp. 19–64). Greenwich, CT: JAI.

Ashforth, B., Rogers, K., & Corley, K. (2010). Identity and organizations: Exploring cross-level dynamics. *Organization Science.* Manuscript submitted for publication.

Alvesson, M., & Robertson, M. (2006). The best and the brightest: The construction, significance and effects of elite identities in consulting firms. *Organization, 13*(2), 195–224.

Balmer, J.M.T., Fukukawa, K., & Gray, E.A. (2007). The nature and management of ethical corporate identity: A commentary on corporate identity, corporate social responsibility and ethics. *Journal of Business Ethics, 76*(1), 7–15.

Barbulescu, R., & Weeks, J. (2007). Why do managers talk about identity? In L. Lerpold, D. Ravasi, J. Van Rekom, & G. Soenen (Eds.), *Organizational identity in practice* (pp. 35–51). New York: Routledge Press.

Baron, J.N. (2004). Employing identities in organizational ecology. *Industrial and Corporate Change, 13*(1), 3–32.

Bartel, C. A., & Dutton, J.E. (2001). Ambiguous organizational memberships: Constructing organizational identities in interaction with others. In M.A. Hogg, & D. Terry (Eds.),

Social identity processes in organizational contexts (pp. 115–130). Philadelphia: Psychology Press.

Baumeister, R.F., Bratslavsky, E., Muraven, M., & Tice, D.M. (1998). Ego depletion: Is the active self a limited resource? *Journal of Personality and Social Psychology, 74*, 1252–1265.

Berger, E., Cunningham, P.H., & Drumwright, M.E. (2006). Identity, identification, and relationship through social alliances. *Journal of the Academy of Marketing Science, 34*, 128–137.

Bhattacharya, C.B., & Sen, S. (2003). Consumer-company identification: A framework for understanding consumers' relationships with companies. *Journal of Marketing, 67*, 76–88.

Birnholtz, J., Cohen, M., & Hoch, S. (2007). Organizational character: On the regeneration of Camp Poplar Grove. *Organization Studies, 18*(2), 1315–1332.

Boyd, B., Henning, N., Reyna, E., Wang, D.E., & Welch, M.D. (2009). *Hybrid organizations: New business models for environmental leadership.* Sheffield, UK: Greenleaf Publishing.

Brickson, S.L. (2007). Organizational identity orientation: The genesis of the role of the firm and distinct forms of social value. *Academy of Management Review, 32*, 864–888.

Brickson, S.L. (2010). *Athletes, best friends, and social activists: Modeling multiple paths to organizational identification.* Working paper, Department of Managerial Studies, University of Illinois, Chicago, IL.

Brickson, S.L., & Lemmon, G. (2009). Organizational identity as a stakeholder resource. In L.M. Roberts, & J.E. Dutton (Eds.), *Exploring positive identities and organizations: Building a theoretical and research foundation.* New York: Psychology Press.

Brickson, S.L., & Akinlade (2010). *The foundation, experience, and distribution of power in distinct organizational contexts: A resource-based perspective.* Working paper, Department of Managerial Studies, University of Illinois, Chicago, IL.

Brown, A., & Starkey, K. (2000). Organizational identity and learning: A psychodynamic perspective. *Academy of Management Review, 25*(1), 102–120.

Carlsen, A. (2006). Organizational becoming as dialogic imagination of practice: The case of the indomitable Gauls. *Organization Science, 17*, 132–149.

Cameron, K.S. (2003). Organizational virtuousness and performance. In K.S. Cameron, J.E. Dutton, & R.E. Quinn (Eds.), *Positive organizational scholarship: Foundations of a new discipline* (pp. 48–65). San Francisco, CA: Berrett-Koehler.

Chreim, S. (2005). The continuity-change duality in narrative texts of organizational identity. *Journal of Management Studies, 42*, 567–593.

Cialdini, R.B., Borden, R.J., Thorne, A., Walker, R.M., Freeman, S., & Sloan, L.R. (1976). Basking in reflected glory: Three (football) field studies. *Journal of Personality and Social Psychology. 34*(3), 366–375.

Cooperrider, D., & Sekerka, L.E. (2003). Elevation of inquiry into the appreciable world: Toward a theory of positive organizational change. In K. Cameron, J. Dutton, and R. Quinn (Eds.), *Positive organizational scholarship* (pp. 225–240). San Francisco: Berrett-Kohler.

Corley, K.G., & Gioia, D.A. (2004). Identity ambiguity and change in the wake of a corporate spin-off. *Administration Science Quarterly, 49*(2), 173–208.

Corley, K.G., Harquail, C.V., Pratt, M.G., Glynn, M.A., Fiol, C.M., & Hatch, M.J. (2006). Guiding organizational identity through aged adolescence. *Journal of Management Inquiry, 15*(2): 85–99.

Corley, K.G., & Harrison, S.H. (2009). Generative organizational identity change: Approaching organizational authenticity as a process. In L.M. Roberts, & J.E. Dutton (Eds.), *Exploring positive identities and organizations: Building a theoretical and research foundation.* New York: Psychology Press.

Czarniawska, B., & Wolff, R. (1998). Constructing new identities in established organization fields: Young universities in old Europe. *International Studies of Management & Organization, 28*(3), 32–56.

Dacin, M.T., Oliver, C., & Roy, J. (2006). The legitimacy of strategic alliances: An institutional perspective, *Strategic Management Journal, 28*(2), 169–187.

Dougherty, K.D., & Huyser, K.R. (2008). Racially diverse congregations: Organizational identity and the accommodation of differences. *Journal for the Scientific Study of Religion, 47*(1), 23–44.

Dukerich, J.M., Golden, B.R., & Shortell, S.M. (2002). Beauty is in the eye of the beholder: The impact of organizational identification, identity, and image on the cooperative behaviors of physicians. *Administrative Science Quarterly, 47,* 507–533.

Dutton, J.E., & Dukerich, J.M. (1991). Keeping an eye on the mirror: Image and identity in organizational adaptation. *Academy of Management Journal, 34*(3), 517–554.

Dutton, J., Dukerich, J., & Harquail, C.V. (1994). Organizational images and member identification. *Administrative Science Quarterly, 39*(2), 239–263.

Dutton, J.E., Roberts, L.M., & Bednar, J. (2010). Pathways for Positive Identity Construction at Work: Four Types of Positive Identity and the Building of Social Resources, *Academy of Management Review, 35* (2), 265–293.

Dutton, J.E., & Sonenshein, S. (2008). Positive Organizational Scholarship. In S. Lopez & A. Beauchamps (Eds.), *Encyclopedia of positive psychology.* London: Blackwell Publishing.

Eilam, G., & Shamir, B. (2005). Organizational change and self-concept threats: A theoretical perspective and a case study. *Journal of Applied Behavioral Science, 41,* 399.

Elsbach, K.D., & Bhattacharya, C.B. (2001). Defining who you are by what you are not: A study of organizational disidentification and the NRA. *Organization Science, 12,* 393–413.

Elsbach, K., & Kramer, R. (1996). Members' response to organizational identity threats: Encountering and countering the business week rankings. *Administrative Science Quarterly, 41*(3), 442–482.

Feldman, R.M., & Feldman, S.P. (2006). What links the chain: An essay on organizational remembering as practice. *Organization, 13*(6), 861–887.

Fiol, C.M. (1991). Managing culture as a competitive resource: An identity-based view of sustainable competitive advantage. *Journal of Management, 17*(1), 191–211.

Fiol, C.M., Hatch, M.J., & Golden-Biddle, K. (1998). Organizational culture and identity: What's the difference anyway? In D.A. Whetten, & P.C. Godfrey (Eds.), *Identity in organizations* (pp. 56–62). Thousand Oaks, CA: Sage Publications.

Foreman, P., & Whetten, D. (2002). Members' identification with multiple-identity organizations. *Organization Science, 13*(6), 618–635.

Freeman, R.E. (1984). *Strategic management: A stakeholder approach.* Boston, MA Pitman.

Friedman, D., & McAdam, D. (1992). Collective identity and activism: Networks, choices and the life of a social movement. In C. Mueller, & A. Morris (Eds.), *Frontiers in social movement theory* (pp. 156–173). New Haven, CT: Yale University Press.

Gioia, D., & Chittipeddi, K. (1991). Sensemaking and sensegiving in strategic change initiation. *Strategic Management Journal, 12,* 433–448.

Gioia, D., Schultz, M., & Corley, K. (2000). Organizational identity, image and adaptive instability. *Academy of Management Review, 25*(1), 63–81.

Gioia, D.A., & Thomas, J.B. (1996). Identity, image, and issue interpretation: Sensemaking during strategic change in academia. *Administrative Science Quarterly, 41*(3), 370–403.

Giraud, Z., Voss G.B., & Cable, D.M. (2006). Organizational identity and firm performance: What happens when leaders disagree about "who we are?" *Organization Science, 17*(6), 741–755.

Glynn, M.A. (2000). When cymbals become symbols: Conflict over organizational identity within a symphony orchestra. *Organization Science, 11*(3), 285–298.

Glynn M.A., & I.J. Walsh. (2009). Finding the positive in positive organizational identities. In L.M. Roberts, & J.E. Dutton (Eds.), *Exploring positive identities and organizations: Building a theoretical and research foundation* (pp. 471–486). New York: Psychology Press.

Greve, H.R., & Rao, H. (2006). A community ecology of ideology: Mutual insurance companies in norway, 1820–1905. *Proceedings of the annual meeting of the American Sociological Association.* Retrieved from http://www.allacademic.com/meta/p102942_index.html.

Gnyawali, D.R., & Madhavan, R. (2001). Cooperative networks and competitive dynamics: A structural embeddedness perspective. *Academy of Management Review, 26*(3), 431–445.

Golden-Biddle, K., & Rao, H. (1997). Breaches in the boardroom: Organizational identity and conflicts of commitment in a non-profit organization. *Organization Science, 8,* 593–611.

Gottesman, M.D. (2007). From Cobblestones to Pavement: The legal road forward for the creation of hybrid social organizations, *Yale Law & Policy Review, 26,* 345–350.

Hamilton, A., & Gioia, D.A. (2009). Fostering sustainability-focused organizational identities. In L.M. Roberts, & J.E. Dutton (Eds.), *Exploring positive identities and organizations: Building a theoretical and research foundation* (pp. 435–460). New York: Psychology Press.

Hardy, S.A., & Carlo, G. (2005). Identity as a Source of Moral Motivation. *Human Development, 48,* 232–256.

Harquail, C.V. (1998). Organizational identification and the "whole person": Integrating affect, behavior and cognition. In D.A. Whetten, & P.C. Godfrey (Eds.), *Identity in Organizations* (pp. 223–231). Thousand Oaks, CA: Sage Publications.

Harquail, C.V. (2005). Employees as animate artifacts: "Wearing the brand." In A. Rafaeli, & M.G. Pratt (Eds.), *Artifacts and organizations: Beyond mere symbolism* (pp. 161–180). Mahwah, NJ: Erlbaum Associates.

Harquail, C.V. (2007). *The power of the extra adjective: How and when organizations are marked with a social identity.* Paper presented at the Conference on Theorizing Culture: Culture Theory and International Management, Bjorkliden, Sweden. Sponsored by the Institute for International Business,

Stockholm School of Economics. March. Retrieved from http://authenticorganizations.com/articles/diversity-research/.

Harquail, C.V. (2008). Practice and identity: Using a brand symbol to construct organizational identity. In L. Lerpold, D. Ravasi, J. von Rekom, & G. Soenen (Eds.), *Organizational identity in practice* (pp. 135–150). London: Routledge Press.

Harquail, C.V., & King, A.W. (2010). Construing organizational identity: The role of embodied cognition. *Organization Studies.* Manuscript submitted for publication.

Hatch, M.J., & Schultz, M. (1997). Relations between organizational culture, identity and image. *European Journal of Marketing, 31*(5), 54.

Hatch, M.J., & Schultz, M. (2002). The dynamics of organizational identity. *Human Relations, 55*(8), 989–1018.

Hogg, M.A., & Terry, D.J. (2000). *Social identity and self-categorization processes in organizational contexts.* Philadelphia: Psychology Press.

Hsu, G., & Hannan, M.T. (2005). Identities, genres, and organizational forms. *Organization Science, 16,* 474–490.

Huy, Q.N. (2002). Emotional balancing of organizational continuity and radical change: The contribution of middle managers. *Administrative Science Quarterly, 47,* 31–69.

Kahn, W.A. (1990). Psychological conditions of personal engagement and disengagement at work. *Academy of Management Journal, 33*(4), 692–724.

Kegan, R. (1982). *The evolving self.* Cambridge, MA: Harvard University Press.

Kornberger, M.M., & Brown, A.D. (2007). 'Ethics' as a discursive resource for identity work. *Human Relations, 60*(3), 497–518.

Labianca, G., Fairbank, J.F., Thomas, J.B., Gioia, D.A., & Umphress, E.E. (2001). Emulation in academia: Balancing structure and identity. *Organization Science, 12*(3), 312–330.

Liedtka, J.J. (1996). Feminist morality and competitive reality: A role for an ethic of care. *Business Ethics Quarterly, 6*(2), 1679–1200.

Livengood, R., & Reger, R. (2010). That's our turf! Identity domains and competitive dynamics. *The Academy of Management Review, 35*(1), 48–66.

Matherne, C.F. (2009). *The relationship between moral identity congruence and extra-role behaviors in organizational settings.* Doctoral dissertation, ProQuest Dissertations & Theses database. (UMI No. 3352279).

Marquis, C., & Davis, G.F. (2009). Organization mechanisms underlying positive community identity and reputation. In L.M. Roberts, & J.E. Dutton (Eds.), *Exploring positive identities and organizations: Building a theoretical and research foundation.* New York: Psychology Press.

Maslow, A. (1954). *Motivation and personality.* New York: Harper & Row.

Meyer, M. (2004). Organizational identity, political contexts, and SMO action: Explaining the tactical choices made by peace organizations in Israel, Northern Ireland, and South Africa**.** *Social Movement Studies, 3*(2), 167–197.

Minkoff, D.C. (2002). The emergence of hybrid organizational forms: Combining identity based service provision and political action. *Nonprofit and Voluntary Sector Quarterly, 31*(3), 377–401.

Nag, R., Corley, K.G., & Gioia, D.A. (2007). The intersection of organizational identity, knowledge, and practice: Attempting strategic change via knowledge grafting. *Academy of Management Journal, 50*(4), 821–847.

Norman, W., & MacDonald, C. (2004). Getting to the Bottom of "Triple Bottom Line", *Business Ethics Quarterly, 14*(2), 243–262.

Oliver, D., Statler, M., & Roos, J. (2010). A meta-ethical perspective on organizational identity. *Journal of Business Ethics, 94*(3), 427–440.

Peteraf, M., & Shanley, M. (1997). Getting to know you: A theory of strategic group identity. *Strategic Management Journal, 18,* 165–186.

Porac, J.F., Thomas, H., & Baden-Fuller, C. (1989) Industries as cognitive communities: The case of Scottish knitwear manufacturers. *Journal of Management Studies, 26,* 397–416.

Pratt, M.G. (1998). To be or not to be: Central questions in organizational identification. In D.A. Whetten, & P.C. Godfrey (Eds.), *Identity in organizations: Building theory through conversation* (pp.171–207). Thousand Oaks, CA: Sage.

Pratt, M.G., & Ashforth, B.E. (2003). Fostering meaningfulness in working and at work. In K.S. Cameron, J.E. Dutton, & R.E. Quinn (Eds.), *Positive organizational scholarship: Foundations of a new discipline* (pp. 309–327). San Francisco: Berrett-Koehler.

Pratt, M.G., & Kraatz, M.S. (2009). E. Pluribus Unum: Multiple Identities and the Organizational Self. *In* L.M. Roberts & J.E. Dutton (Eds.), *Exploring positive identities and organizations: Building a theoretical and research foundation* (pp. 385–411). New York: Psychology Press.

Pratt, M.G., Rockmann, K.W., & Kaufmann, J.B. (2006). Constructing professional identity: The role of work and identity learning cycles in the customization of identity among medical residents. *Academy of Management Journal, 49*(2), 235–262.

Price, K.N., Gioia, D.A., & Corley, K.G. (2008). Reconciling scattered images: Managing disparate organizational expressions and impressions. *Journal of Management Inquiry, 17,* 173–185.

Ravasi, D., & Schultz, M. (2006). Responding to organizational identity threats: Exploring the role of organizational culture. *Academy of Management Journal, 49*(3), 433–458.

Rhee, S., Dutton, J.E., & Bagozzi, R.P. (2006). Making sense of organizational actions in response to tragedy: Virtue frames, organizational identification and organizational attachment. *Journal of Management, Spirituality and Religion, 3*(1 & 2) 34–59.

Roberts, L.M., Cha, S.E., Hewlin, P.F., & Settles, I.H. (2009). Bringing the inside out: Enhancing authenticity and positive identity in organizations. In L.M. Roberts, & J.E. Dutton (Eds.), *Exploring positive identities and organizations: Building a theoretical and research foundation.* New York: Psychology Press.

Roberts, L.M., & Dutton, J.E. (2009). *Exploring positive identities and organizations: Building a theoretical and research foundation.* New York: Psychology Press.

Rowley, T., & Moldoveanu, M.C. (2003). An interest and identity-based model of stakeholder mobilization. *Academy of Management Review, 28,* 204–219.

Scott, S., & Lane, V. (2000). A stakeholder approach to organizational identity. *Academy of Management Review, 25*(1), 43–62.

Schultz, M., Hatch, M.J., & Larsen, M.H. (2000). *The expressive organization: Linking identity, reputation and the corporate brand.* Oxford, UK: Oxford University Press.

Selznick, P. (1957). *Leadership in administration: A sociological interpretation.* New York: Harper & Row.

Sluss, D.M., & Ashforth, B.E. (2008). How relational and organizational identification converge: Processes and conditions. *Organizational Science, 19*, 807–823.

Smith, G.D., & King, B. (2009). Contracts as organizations. *Arizona Law Review, 51*(1), 1–46.

Steele, C.M. (1988). The psychology of self-affirmation: Sustaining the integrity of the self. *Advances in Experimental Psychology, 21*, 261–302.

Suls, J., Martin, R., & Wheeler, L. (2002). Social comparison: Why, with whom, and with what effect? *Current Directions in Psychological Science, 11*, 159–163.

Staber, U. (2010). Imitation without interaction: How firms identify with clusters. *Organization Studies, 31*(2), 153–174.

Sveningsson, S.F., & Alvesson, M. (2003). Managing managerial identities: Organizational fragmentation, discourse and identity struggle. *Human Relations, 56*(10), 1163–1193.

Tretheway, A. (1997). Resistance, identity, and empowerment: A postmodern feminist analysis of client service organization. *Communication Monographs, 64*, 281–301.

Tsoukas, H., & Chia, R. (2002). On organizational becoming: Rethinking organizational change. *Organization Science, 13*(5), 567–582.

Tyler, T.R., & Blader, S.L. (2000). *Cooperation in groups: Procedural justice, social identity, and behavioral engagement.* Philadelphia: Psychology Press.

Tyler, T.R., & Blader, S.L. (2003). The group engagement model: Procedural justice, social identity, and cooperative behavior. *Personality and Social Psychology Review, 7*, 349–361.

Verbos, A.K., Gerard, J.A., Forshey, P.A., Harding, C.S., & Miller, J.S. (2007). The positive ethical organization: Enacting a living code of ethics and ethical organizational identity. *Journal of Business Ethics, 76*, 17–33.

Walsh, I.J. (2009). Explaining post-death organizing: the role of organizational identification, working paper, Boston College, Boston, MA.

Walsh, I.J., & Glynn, M.A. (2008). The way we were: Legacy organizational identity and the role of leadership. *Corporate Reputation Review, 11*, 262–276.

Weaver, Gary R. (2006). Virtue in organizations: Moral identity as a foundation for moral agency. *Organization Studies, 27*(3), 341–368.

Weick, K.E. (1995). *Sensemaking in organizations.* Thousand Oaks, CA: Sage Publications.

Whetten, D.A., & Mackey, A. (2002). A Social Actor Conception of Organizational Identity and Its Implications for the Study of Organizational Reputation, *Business & Society, 41*(4), 393–414.

White, J. (1999). Ethical comportment in organizations: A synthesis of the feminist ethic of care and the Buddhist ethic of compassion. *International Journal of Value-Based Management, 12*(2), 109–128.

Wiesenfeld, B. (2007). The struggle to establish organizational membership and identification in remote work contexts. In C.A. Bartel, S. Blader, & A. Wrzesniewski (Eds.), *Identity and the modern organization* (pp. 119–135). Mahwah, NJ: Erlbaum Associates.

Wright T.A., & Goodstein, J. (2007). Character is not "dead" in management research: A review of individual character and organizational-level virtue. *Journal of Management, 33*(6), 928–958.

Organizational Energy

Bernd Vogel *and* Heike Bruch

Abstract

Research on organizational energy is an emerging field of inquiry. Organizational energy broadly refers to the force of a collective unit (an organization, department, or team) in pursuit of its goals. Studies investigate how and when collective units have mobilized their human potential. This chapter reviews conceptual and empirical studies focused on concepts such as momentum, energy in networks, or productive organizational energy. Research insights point to practices that managers might use to energize their organizations or work units. The chapter ends by identifying areas for future research in the field of organizational energy.

Keywords: Organizational energy, measurement of energy, productive energy, momentum, leadership

Organizational energy is a relatively new and emerging field of inquiry and refers to the force of a collective unit (an organization, department, or team) in pursuit of its goals (e.g., Bruch & Ghoshal, 2003, 2004; Bruch & Vogel, 2011). The majority of the research on organizational energy was published within the last 10 years (e.g., Bruch & Ghoshal, 2003 , 2004; Cole, Bruch, & Vogel, in press; Cross, Baker, & Parker, 2003; Dutton, 2003; Jansen, 2004; Kunze & Bruch, 2010; Walter & Bruch, forthcoming). A few early studies in sociology (Etzioni, 1968) and social psychology (Katz & Kahn, 1966) do elaborate on the concept of energy and its meaning for organizations. Nevertheless, most of the research on energy in organizations refers to the individual level of analysis: the energy of individuals in organizations (e.g., Atwater & Carmeli, 2009; Collins, 1990; Dutton, 2003; Quinn & Dutton, 2005). Less emphasis has been put on the collective level of analysis or organizational energy, which is the focus of this chapter.

Scholarly interest in investigating energy at the collective level of analysis (by referring to the organization, unit, or team) stems from various lines of thought. First, much of the work in today's organizations requires individuals to function as part of a collective entity such as a work unit, a team, or the organization as a whole (Mathieu, Maynard, Rapp, & Gilson, 2008). Recognizing this shift in emphasis (i.e., from individuals to higher-level entities), scholars have suggested that research and practice require a better understanding of when and how an organization or a team has mobilized its human forces collectively in pursuit of its goals. An emphasis on collective-level energy may provide us with a more complete understanding of energy in organizational settings (Bruch & Ghoshal, 2003; Cole et al., in press; Jansen, 2004, Walter & Bruch, forthcoming).

Second, various interventions in organizations, such as leadership and human resource practices, address not only the individual but also collective entities, or the entire organization. For instance, the effects of strategic leadership are likely to influence both individual employees within an organization and collective phenomena (Canella & Holcomb, 2005; Jansen et al., 2008; Shamir, 1995), of which organizational energy is one (Bruch, Vogel,

& Raes, 2009). This is in line with multilevel research that has repeatedly advocated investigating collective-level theories and constructs to explain collective outcomes such as organizational performance (Kozlowski & Klein, 2000; Morgeson & Hofmann, 1999; Ployhart & Moliterno, 2011). Correspondingly, recent research by Walter and Bruch (forthcoming) shows that a transformational leadership climate mobilizes productive organizational energy—that is, the human potential of entire organizations. Studies of the impact of high-performance work systems on performance show that this relationship is mediated by different organization-level mechanisms, including flexibility (Beltrán-Martín, Roca-Puig, Escrig-Tena, & Bou-Llusar, 2008), collective human capital (Takeuchi, Lepak, Wang, & Takeuchi 2007), and organizational energy (Bruch, Menges, Cole, & Vogel, 2009).

Third, recent research on energy has established links to various beneficial outcomes for organizations. At the individual level, research has shown that higher levels of energy are, for instance, related to enhanced well-being and performance (Dutton, 2003), personal development and health (Spreitzer, Sutcliffe, Dutton, Sonenshein, & Grant, 2005), and creative work involvement (Atwater & Carmeli, 2009; Kark & Carmeli, 2009). At the organizational or collective level, research has suggested or shown that energy is related to improved coordination (Quinn & Dutton, 2005), enhanced employee commitment (Cross et al., 2003), strategic change (Jansen, 2004; Levy & Merry, 1986), group collective goal commitment, and overall collective job satisfaction (Cole et al., in press).

Overall, research has acknowledged that it is worthwhile to conceptually and empirically investigate energy at the collective or organizational level of analysis (e.g., Bruch & Ghoshal, 2003; Spreitzer et al., 2005) to generate additional knowledge as necessary to understand organizations and develop practical insight.

The purpose of this chapter is threefold. First, it reviews the conceptual and empirical scope of the research on energy at the organizational level of analysis, including conceptual and empirical insights from research on the productive organizational energy concept. Second, this chapter presents the practical implications of organizational energy research; and third, it suggests potential avenues for future research. This chapter focuses exclusively on organizational energy, given that Chapter 12 of this volume, Spreitzer, Lam, and Quinn (2011) addresses human or individual energy.

Literature Review and Empirical Results
Early Work on Organizational Energy Constructs and Energy in Organizations

Organizational or collective energy identifies energy as a state of an organization or other collective such as a work unit or team. Despite its potential benefits, the domain of organizational or collective energy is a relatively new and developing area of inquiry that is in the process of defining its construct scope and conceptual space. Although it primarily refers to individual energy, the observation that energy has been "a construct that organizational scholars use but seldom define" (Quinn & Dutton, 2005, p. 36) also holds true for collective level energy. Similarly, Cross et al. (2003) note that "while the term energy is pervasive in much of organizational life, it is also a highly elusive concept in that context" (p. 51).

There is some early on research- and practitioner-oriented literature. In Katz and Kahn's (1966) seminal work on the social psychology of organizations, they refer to energy as a resource that is transformed within an organization. Von Cranach, Ochsenbein, and Valach (1986) suggested that energy exists at the individual and the collective level, although they offer little conceptual underpinning for the latter concept. Etzioni (1968) addresses the energy of societies and organizations. As with energy in physics, he distinguished between latent energy and energy in motion. *Latent* or *potential energy* (Etzioni, 1968) refers to the capacity or the human resources an organization possesses: that is, the energy that people can potentially exert and experience (see also Adams, 1984). Societies or organizations that demonstrate *energy in motion*, or kinetic energy (Etzioni, 1968) are using their organizational potential. That is, energy in motion implies the use of an organization's human potential (see also Levy & Merry, 1986).

Based on the distinction between latent energy and energy in motion, research investigates the shift from latent organizational energy to organizational energy in motion, which some authors call the mobilization of an organization's energy (Bruch & Ghoshal, 2003; Bruch & Vogel, 2011; Etzioni, 1968, Levy & Merry, 1986). In this regard, organizational energy may be influenced by interventions from individuals and organizations, such as leadership, that encourage energy in motion.

A second stream of research investigates energy *in* organizations rather than establishing energy as a collective-level construct. Dutton (2003), for instance, notes that "[p]ositive energy is experienced as a form of positive affect, making it a reinforcing experience that people enjoy and seek" (Dutton, 2003, p. 6). More importantly, she suggests that energy is a renewable resource and calls it the "fuel that makes great organizations run" (p. 7). Other scholars point to the effects of interaction and social processes that elevate the individual's experience of energy. Marks (1977) argues that people involved in social interaction become "far more enriched and vitalized than they are when left to their own 'resources'" (p. 925; see also Collins, 1990). Although these constructs are conceptualized at the individual level of analysis, these researchers point to the elevating effects of social interaction and related processes (e.g., contagion), which are also mechanisms for the emergence of collective energy.

In exploring the existing approaches, we distinguish between one-dimensional and multidimensional conceptualizations of collective energy.

One-dimensional Organizational Energy Concepts

Jansen (2004) works on the concept of changed-based momentum, which considers "the energy associated with movement along a new trajectory" (Jansen, 2004, p. 278). Jansen associates changed-based momentum with energy, great effort, and an organization's strong forces. Thus, energy is conceptualized as a facet of change-based momentum. Jansen also implicitly refers to the collective level of analysis by pointing to the critical mass of change supporters required to generate change-based momentum. Furthermore, change-based momentum refers to change-specific energy fluctuations and thus is not associated with work processes in general. The results of this mixed-method, qualitative, and quantitative study show that change-related commitment positively influences change-based momentum, whereas the gaps between momentum and new significant events have a negative influence. In addition, change-based momentum predicts goal attainment, which in turn influences subsequent momentum. The results thus support a spiraling relationship between momentum and goal attainment (see Table 52.1).

Although Jansen contributes significantly to our understanding of energy for change and particularly of energy over time, her conceptualization of energy as a facet of change-based momentum and as force or great effort remains somewhat ambiguous. Also, change-based momentum refers specifically to change-specific energy fluctuations, whereas others associate the energy construct and the need to

understand the energy construct also with other work processes.

Multidimensional Organizational Energy Concepts

GROUP DRIVE

Stogdill (1972) defines group drive as the "degree of group arousal, motivation, freedom, enthusiasm, or spirit" (p. 27). These facets represent different dimensions of group drive, including affective and cognitive dimensions. The author also states that drive can be analyzed according to its intensity. Group drive manifests itself in the individual group member, but the group context seems to have a decisive effect on the individual's level of drive because group drive "represents rather the intensity with which members invest expectation and energy on behalf of the group" (p. 27). Empirically, the study investigates the relationship between cohesion and productivity. The results show that group drive moderates the relationship between cohesion and productivity, so that it is positive under high group drive. However, given low group drive, or what Stogdill called "routine operating conditions" (p. 39), the relationship is negative.

Although the concept referred to is group drive, this study does not fully elaborate on the emergent processes by which group drive becomes a collective property of a group. Also, the definition of group drive blends potential core attributes of energy (e.g., enthusiasm) with factors such as freedom to act, which might impact the level of energy or arousal.

ENERGY IN NETWORKS

Studies by Baker, Cross, and Wooten (2003) and Cross et al. (2003) focus conceptually on multidyadic or network-based energizing relationships. This author group explores how energy (including that of organizations) might develop through these relationships at different levels: "we set out to assess how relationships with all of one's colleagues—in other words, within a social network—affect the energy of an individual, a group or an entire organization" (p. 52). Based on multiple dyadic relationships and social networks, organizations can create high or low levels of energy. Initially, Cross et al. (2003) follow the energy definitions developed by Collins (1990), Quinn and Dutton (2005), and Thayer (1989), considering energy as an experience of positive affective arousal. However, Baker et al. (2003) also observe that energy is "not merely affect or liking"; the interviewees reported experiences of

Table 52.1 Collective energy constructs: Main and indirect effects based on bootstrapping

Constructs	Definition
Early definitions of organizational energy	
Organizational energy (Levy & Merry, 1986)	Levy and Merry (1986) describe energy as "the level of spirit, morale, enthusiasm, motivation, pace, and volume of performance. It captures the vitality and stamina of organizational life" (p. 113).
Organizational energy (Adams, 1984)	Adams (1984) defines energy as the "potential for action or accomplishment of work" (p. 277).
One-dimensional collective energy constructs	
Momentum (Jansen, 2004)	Change-based momentum considers "the energy associated with movement along a new trajectory" (Jansen, 2004, p. 278).
Multidimensional collective energy constructs	
Group drive (Stogdill, 1972)	Group drive is described as the "degree of group arousal, motivation, freedom, enthusiasm, or spirit. . . . It represents rather the intensity with which members invest expectation and energy on behalf of the group" (p. 27).
Energy in networks (Baker, Cross, & Wooten, 2003; Cross, Baker, & Parker, 2003)	These authors apply the definition of energy by Quinn and Dutton (2005), which suggests that: "Energy is defined as 'a type of positive affective arousal, which people can experience as emotion—short responses to specific events—or mood—longer-lasting affective states that need not be a response to a specific event.'"
Organizational energy (Bruch & Ghoshal, 2003; 2004; Bruch & Vogel, 2011)	Organizational energy is defined as the force that an organization works with to purposefully put things like core initiatives, innovations, and changes into motion. The strength of organizational energy is the extent to which an organization has mobilized its emotional, cognitive, and behavioral potential in pursuit of its goals.
Productive organizational energy (Bruch, & Vogel, 2011; Cole, Bruch, & Vogel, 2005)	Productive organizational energy captures the joint experience of positive affect, cognitive activation, and agentic behavior in the shared pursuit of organizationally salient objectives (Cole et al., 2005).

cognitive vividness ("I am sure I literally think better and faster") and commented on behavioral ("willingly staying late to resolve important matters") aspects of energizing relationships (p. 340).

Empirically based on social network analysis and 63 interviews, the study by Cross et al. (2003) shows that energizers' ideas are more likely to be considered and implemented. Other high performers also seem to be more attached and committed to energizers. People associated with an energizer put more effort into their interactions with energizers. In sum, the authors find evidence that energizers and the people around them perform at a higher level.

Research on energy in networks constitutes an exceptional step in the work on collective energy. Less obvious are the conceptual underpinnings linking the core definition of energy as affect and the two additional dimensions, cognitive and behavioral factors. Also, although energy is proposed to exist at various levels in an organization (i.e., in relationships, dyads, teams, networks, and organizations), the theoretical foundation for the (different) emergence processes leading to collective energy remains unexplored. Finally, the focus on de-energizing relationships, measured as the lower end of the scale for energy in relationships, opens up a new topic: negative collective energy in organizations. Nonetheless, this idea may need to be more widely explored beyond the conceptual realm as the lower end of positive relationships.

Overall, we can identify the following three challenges associated with the recent research on energy in organizations: the need to more fully understand the underlying dimensionality of organizational energy, to specify the nature of the collectivity associated with the energy construct, and to consider that the scope of energy in organizations may also include negative energy, despite a general focus on the positive forces in organizations.

ORGANIZATIONAL ENERGY AND ENERGY STATES

The concept of organizational energy and, in particular, the construct of productive energy can be seen as a first attempt to address some of the challenges mentioned earlier. Organizational energy is defined as the force that an organization works with to purposefully put things into motion (Bruch & Ghoshal, 2003, 2004; Bruch & Vogel, 2011), for example core initiatives, innovation, and change. The strength of organizational energy is the extent to which an organization has mobilized its emotional, cognitive, and behavioral potential in pursuit of its goals. Adding to the concepts described earlier, Bruch and Ghoshal (2004) suggest that energy is not just inherently positive. Organizations may also experience negative or destructive forces, for example organizational burnout (Greenwood & Greenwood, 1979) or cynicism (Dean, Brandes, & Dharwadkar, 1998). Moreover, constructs such as inertia (Tushman & O'Reilly, 1996) or active inertia (Sull, 1999) point to less intense energy.

Bruch and Ghoshal (2004) suggest a framework for organizational energy that considers four different collective energy states based on two dimensions: *intensity* (high–low), which refers to the strength or level of organizational energy experienced in a collective unit—when it is active or alert—and the *quality* of organizational energy (positive–negative), that characterizes the extent to which a unit's energy is constructive or destructive regarding the company goals. Based on the different possible combinations of the two dimensions, organizations can face four energy states (Bruch & Ghoshal, 2004). In a slightly revised version of this concept, Bruch and Vogel (2011) suggest the following four organizational energy states (see Figure 52.1):

- *Productive energy* (high positive energy): Characterized by high employee emotion and mental alertness along with high activity levels, speed, and stamina.
- *Comfortable energy* (low positive energy): Characterized by high employee satisfaction and identification coupled with low activity levels and complacency.
- *Resigned inertia* (low negative energy): Characterized by high levels of employee frustration, mental withdrawal, cynicism, and low engagement.
- *Corrosive energy* (high negative energy): Characterized by aggression and destructive behavior—for example, through internal politics, resistance to change, and maximizing individual benefits.

Research on organization-level energy from this group of authors has thus far made the most progress in studying the intense and positive energy phenomenon termed *productive energy* or *productive organizational energy* (POE) which is therefore the focus of the following section.

Productive Organizational Energy
DEFINING PRODUCTIVE ORGANIZATIONAL ENERGY

Cole et al. (in press) suggest that being productively energized at work has far-reaching implications for employees and offers organizations competitive advantage; when collectively experienced among employees, higher levels of employee affect, cognitive alertness, and effort may lead to increased levels of organizational attachment and to better performance (e.g., Dutton, 2003). This may be particularly relevant in the growing number of work environments in which individuals must align with a workgroup, team, or organization (Mathieu et al., 2008). Nevertheless, advocates of the energy-at-work concept (Cameron, Dutton, & Quinn, 2003) note that research on energy remains scarce. Construct

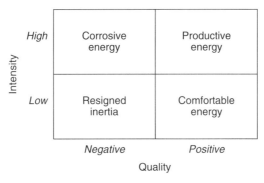

Fig. 52.1 The energy matrix.

definition in this field is at an early stage, and there are few valid and reliable measurement devices (Cameron, 2008; Cameron & Caza, 2004). Research on POE aims to address some of these deficiencies.

Productive organizational energy captures the joint experience of positive affect, cognitive activation, and agentic behavior in the shared pursuit of organizationally salient objectives (Cole et al., in press). The construct follows the view of energy in motion—productive energy captures the degree to which an organization or unit actually uses (has mobilized) its potential to perform work. The construct is thus labeled productive energy because it captures both the utilization of energy and the link to the goals of the unit. In terms of its three defining attributes, POE is a collective-level construct, it is multidimensional in nature, and it is an emergent state.

Productive Organizational Energy
As a Collective Construct
Productive energy is defined as capturing the shared affective, cognitive, and behavioral states of a collective. A growing body of research has suggested that individuals' energy may synergistically combine and thus materialize at the collective level. This emergence mechanism is referred to as a *bottom-up* process (see Kozlowski & Klein, 2000), suggesting that productive energy is isomorphic to individual energy. Thus, productive energy functions similarly to individual-level energy in its content and operation. However, individual-level energy and collective-level energy manifest themselves differently, in that the former most likely reflects individual differences among organization members, whereas the latter reflects the collective emotions, cognitions, and actions that are shared by or common to all members (see Chen & Kanfer, 2006), which in turn differ from one organization to another or between other collectives such as teams or divisions.

According to Cole et al. (in press), a defining characteristic of productive energy is that it is a shared phenomenon. Productive energy is jointly experienced by members of the same collective, for instance, via interaction processes. These processes amplify productive energy and establish it as a higher-level, collective construct (Morgeson & Hofmann, 1999). These positive interactions and exchanges may fuel positive and purposeful responses from others (Cole et al., in press). This pattern of mutual interaction (also known as a double interact; see, e.g., Morgeson & Hofmann, 1999) is the basic

building block upon which productive energy is constructed (Dutton & Heaphy, 2003). Cole et al. (in press) suggest additional emergence mechanisms, including common exposure to the same events (i.e., shared sense-making) (Kozlowski & Klein, 2000) and emotional and cognitive contagion processes (Barsade, 2002; Gibson, 2001; Levine, Resnick, & Higgins, 1993). In keeping with this logic, and consistent with multilevel theory of bottom-up processes (see, e.g., Kozlowski & Klein, 2000), productive energy is a shared or emergent phenomenon that is common to all members of a work unit. Thus, productive energy falls into the category of a collective construct that reflects the affective, cognitive, and behavioral properties of a collective unit as a whole.

Productive Organizational Energy As a
Multidimensional Construct
Cole et al. (in press; Bruch & Ghoshal, 2003; 2004) suggest that productive energy as a multidimensional concept consists of three dimensions: positive affect, cognitive arousal, and agentic purposeful behavior, as echoed in Baker and colleagues' (2003) conceptualization of energy. Working in the same vein, Thompson and Fine (1999) suggest that "social thought, affect, and behavior are explained not by studying people working alone but by studying groups of people engaged in social interaction" (p. 281), and others note that coordinated action is best accomplished when group members synchronize their feelings, thoughts, and behaviors (Hackman, 1992; see also Kahn, 1992).

Similarly, researchers have advocated studying multiple aspects of collective interaction instead of single variables because the former better capture the complex reality of how groups of people work together toward shared goals (e.g., Arrow, McGrath, & Berdahl, 2000).

Affective energy, as the emotional dimension of the POE construct, refers to the collective experience of positive feelings and emotional arousal due to members' enthusiastic assessments of the tasks and goals at hand. Unlike negative emotions, which limit one's actions to fight or flight responses, positive emotions encourage people to broaden their attention scope and their behavioral repertoires, thereby helping them be more effective at work (Fredrickson, 2001). Furthermore, it is widely acknowledged that the open expression of positive feelings is contagious, transferring the experience of positive emotion to other group members via emotional contagion (Barsade, 2002). Thus, positive goal-related shared affect not only produces individuals who function at higher levels but also does the same for organizational units (Fredrickson & Losada, 2005).

Cognitive energy, as the cognitive dimension of the POE construct, reflects the shared experience of being cognitively aroused and mentally alert in pursuit of shared goals. It represents the intellectual processes that propel group members to think constructively about work-related problems and to persist when searching for solutions. These include the ability to focus attention and shut out distractions and the desire to make "good things" happen (Lykken, 2005). Notably, the extant research has shown that the social and cognitive are intimately intertwined. Each member's capacity to function successfully thus depends on cognitive interactions with other group members, and consequently, the products emerging from these interactions cannot be attributed to single members (Levine et al., 1993). Given the extent to which cognitive energy is developed and spread through group interaction (Gibson, 2001), it seems reasonable to expect groups to perform tasks like learning, concept attainment, and problem solving better than individuals (e.g., Mathieu et al., 2008).

Behavioral energy, as the action-related dimension of the POE constructs, reflects group members' behavior as they collectively bring to bear extraordinary efforts to pursue shared goals (Spreitzer & Sonenshein, 2004). This facet of energy represents the pace, intensity, and volume with which members invest physical resources on behalf of the collective unit (e.g., Stogdill, 1972). The collective unit acts agentically to the degree that it engages in active, focused, and purposeful behaviors intended to help it realize its organizational objectives (Spreitzer et al., 2005). Through such agentic action and behavioral integration, members devise ways to transmit their behavioral routines to other members, thereby promoting patterns of productive behavior that enable collective units to fulfill desired outcomes (Bandura, 2001).

Productive Organizational Energy As a State
Third, the productive energy construct is believed to indicate a collective's positive, intense emergent state that can be mutable and fluid and may vary frequently, even during fairly short periods of time (Marks, Mathieu, & Zaccaro, 2001). Jansen (2004) notes that employees may experience fluctuations in organization energy during organiza-

tional change elicited by events, social information, or attentional processes. In contrast, group psychological traits (Cohen & Bailey, 1997) and collective personality (Hofmann & Jones, 2005) have the notion of permanency. Productive organizational energy is a collective property that is dynamic and thus can vary depending on the work context, inputs, processes, and outcomes of the collective (Marks et al., 2001). For example, each of the three productive energy dimensions (affect, cognition, and behavior) can be developed, changed, and managed by leaders or influential coworkers (see Kunze & Bruch, 2010; Walter & Bruch, forthcoming).

MEASURING PRODUCTIVE ORGANIZATIONAL ENERGY
Cole et al. (in press) present the Productive Energy Measurement (PEM) as a measurement of productive organizational energy. Walter and Bruch (forthcoming) recently used the measure at the organizational level of analysis, whereas Kunze and Bruch (2010) did the same at the team level of analysis. Developed from three studies, the measure is a 14-item scale. The three dimensions—emotional, cognitive, and behavioral energy—comprise a higher-order productive energy factor and are measured using three first-order factors. Example items include "people in my workgroup will go out of their way to ensure the company succeeds," "people in my workgroup really care about this company," and "people in my workgroup feel excited about their job" (Cole et al., in press). The measure has acceptable psychometric properties in terms of aggregation statistics and cross-cultural and cross-language measurement equivalence across five national cultures. A unit-level analysis also showed acceptable results for convergent and discriminant validity (with regard to cohesion, autonomy, efficacy, motivation, and exhaustion), as well as predictive validity (including a 6-month time lag with regard to group-level goal commitment, organizational commitment, and job satisfaction).

EMPIRICAL RESULTS FOR PRODUCTIVE ENERGY
The measure for POE has been used in another two published papers and in a series of working papers.

In the study by Walter and Bruch (forthcoming), POE functions as an outcome variable. With a sample of 125 organizations, the study empirically investigates organizational centralization, formalization, and size as antecedents of organizations' transformational leadership (TFL) climate and as moderators of the relationship between the TFL climate and productive organizational energy. The study results show that the TFL climate and POE are positively associated with one another but that centralization and formalization moderate this relationship. The TFL climate–POE linkage is diminished under conditions of high centralization and enhanced under conditions of high formalization. These findings point to the role of organizational structure as a boundary condition for both TFL occurrence and organizational effectiveness.

Kunze and Bruch's (2010) study addresses age-based fault lines in relation to work teams' perceived productive energy and considers transformational leadership as a potential moderator. Age-based fault lines in teams are defined as age subgroup formation reinforced by internal alignment with other demographic characteristics, such as tenure and gender. This paper argues that, based on social identity and social categorization theory, teams with strong age-based fault lines should display a lower level of perceived productive energy than would teams with weak fault lines. On teams with high levels of perceived transformational leadership, this effect should be reversed. The study's hypotheses were tested on a sample of 664 individuals on 72 teams from a multinational company. The results showed a marginally significant negative relationship between age-based fault lines and productive energy on teams. The moderating effect of transformational leadership was significant.

In summary, the study of organizational energy is an emerging field. Conceptually, and based on the first empirical results included in published and presented papers, there seems to be growing evidence not only that the construct of productive energy is conceptually legitimate but also that it makes a relevant contribution to the organizational phenomena of interest.

Practical Applications

The topic of energy has long attracted the interest of the company and the practitioner community, as proven by the range of practitioner-directed publications (e.g., Bruch & Ghoshal, 2003, 2004; Bruch & Vogel, 2011; Cross et al., 2003; Dutton, 2003; Schwartz, 2007). Although organizational energy research is an emerging area of interest, previous research insights into this domain have practical applications in four different areas.

Monitoring Organizational Energy

One practical application for organizations has to do with monitoring the development of and changes in organizational or productive energy. Existing research suggests and empirically shows that organizational energy can create a multitude of beneficial outcomes. Thus, productive energy may provide an early indicator for organizations of whether and to what extent proximal and distant performance criteria might change. Jansen (2004) recommends tracking momentum and the energy spent on a particular change. If the monitoring efforts are focused on "energy in use," organizations can also monitor whether people are actually collectively engaged, displaying high levels of enthusiasm, alertness, and effort or a lack thereof (for a version of the Organizational Energy Questionnaire OEQ and a process outline, see Bruch & Vogel, 2011). Rather than measuring the potential energy that people could collectively invest, monitoring actual energy in use provides organizations with a strong indication of the extent to which an organization has activated this energy and focused it on the right things. Tracking energy at different hierarchical levels or for different groupings within organizations will provide managers with valuable information about the state of energy—from the top team to particular unit line managers.

Identifying and Monitoring Energizers or De-energizers

The work by Cross et al. (2003) and their concept of social network–based energy indicate that individual energy levels should also be examined. Individuals' energizing or de-energizing behavior is a starting point for positive or negative energy contagion within organizations. This is even more important when organizations consider how energizing or de-energizing their leaders or managers might be (Bruch & Vogel, 2011). Managers are a focal point of attention because of their formal position and they play a natural role model function; whether they energized or de-energized may cause energy to increase or decrease in their environment. Hence, Cross et al. suggest that individuals themselves scrutinize their behavior using a battery of question and that organizations use social network techniques to identify energizers or de-energizers (e.g., individuals, leadership teams, projects), as this is crucial for the creation of negative or positive energy.

Energy and Change

The existing research on momentum and POE can be helpful because it provides organizations with insights and helps them to change and innovate. Jansen (2004) points out that there is a "limited amount of energy available that must be shared by multiple initiatives" (p. 292). Executives need to carefully choose the change initiatives on which the organization should focus; that is, which potential changes are worth mobilizing the collective emotional, cognitive, and behavioral forces of an organization.

If the aim is to lead change in organizations, it may also be beneficial that organizational energy is a collective state that seems to develop comparatively quickly in collectives. The POE pace of emergence differs from that indicated for previously outlined constructs such as organizational culture, which develop over a long period. Hence, organizations might concentrate on creating conditions including not only a sense of urgency (Kotter, 1995) but also energy organization directed toward change. In turn, this idea has implications for maintaining organizational momentum. If energy is conceptualized as a state, this also means that it could decrease more easily. Organizations therefore need to potentially reinforce the mobilization of their human potential. Consequently, Jansen (2004) suggests that "when trying to maintain momentum, the message may be 'the more news relevant to the focal change the better'" (p. 292).

Interventions and Organizational Energy

From the literature, we can draw a few first conclusions regarding interventions that organizations can employ to generate and maintain organizational energy. Leadership seems to play a role in generating positive forces (Cameron, 2008) and energizing organizations (e.g., Bruch & Ghoshal, 2004; Bruch & Vogel, 2011; Cross et al., 2003). The effects of leadership have been regarded as manifesting in the cognitive, affective, and behavioral dimensions (Kark & van Dijk, 2007). Bass (1985) suggests that transformational leadership exercises influence via cognitive, affective, and behavioral mechanisms that are typical facets of collective-level energy. Because transformational leadership and transformational leadership climate (Walter & Bruch, forthcoming) may influence organizational energy, an organization may wish to invest in developing leadership behavior across the hierarchy or scrutinize job candidates regarding their transformational leadership behavior. To facilitate a relevant underlying mechanism, organizations could encourage role model behavior among their leaders (Cameron, 2008; Cross et al., 2003) to energize the organization. Indeed, energized managers' sense of engagement might transfer to others.

In summary, if companies recognize the positive organizational benefits from organizational or productive energy, they may want to develop energy management as an explicit organizational ability.

Future Directions

As an emerging field, research on organizational energy has several areas for future research.

- *What are the core elements of the nomological networks for positive and negative organizational energy?* A growing stream of studies on positive or productive organizational energy examines its antecedents and outcomes. Future research should examine the cross-level effects of organizational energy. As Kozlowski and Klein (2000) explain, when tackling previously unexplored phenomena, researchers "may find it helpful to initially act as if the phenomena occur at only one level of theory and analysis" (p. 13). However, at a later stage, it might be fruitful to explore the cross-level linkages associated with organizational energy, considering factors like individuals' psychological capacities or health and well-being (Spreitzer et al., 2005).

- Future research might also pursue more research about negative energy states such as corrosive energy or resigned inertia (Bruch & Ghoshal, 2003; Bruch & Vogel, 2011). Although we believe that the focus on positive energy at the organizational level is valuable, it would be detrimental to knowledge progress and to practice to neglect the negative forces in organizations altogether (Bruch & Ghoshal, 2004; Bruch & Vogel, 2011; Fineman, 2006). Examining whether distinct leadership styles add to the level of corrosive energy or to collective detachment from an organization's overall goals may, for example, help to reduce negative leadership behavior. In turn, this could liberate potential emotional, cognitive, and behavioral energy for more productive use.

- *What is the nature of the relationship between organizational and individual energy?* Future work could conceptually and empirically explore the multilevel implications of organizational energy. A valid aim would be to examine the links between energy constructs at the individual-level energy constructs, such as thriving (Spreitzer et al., 2005), and organizational energy. Studies could explore the spiraling and recursive effects linking individual and organizational energy and ascertain which factors positively or potentially negatively influence spiraling. Furthermore, from a view of energy as building up in relationships (e.g., Quinn & Dutton, 2005), studies could investigate how energy emerges collectively in dyads from leaders' energy and that of their subordinates.

- *How does organizational energy behave over time?* Future research could use a longitudinal lens and further explore energy fluctuations and stability and the impact of organizational energy over time (Jansen, 2004). There might be a difference between mechanisms underlying the short-term mobilization of the collective emotional, cognitive, and behavioral forces in an organization—for instance, as necessary to start change initiatives—and mechanisms keeping organization's energy level stable and high. Studies could then examine the mechanisms that can be used to maintain organizational energy over time and how organization members seek out and promote conditions that reinforce and foster positive consequences, thereby sustaining productive energy levels over time. At the same time, from a practitioner point of view, Bruch and Menges (2010) point to the risk of losing energy through excessively high levels of activation or because there is no regeneration phase, calling the latter problem the "acceleration trap." Research could address the extent to which collectives can permanently work with fully mobilized forces and the conditions under which they need periods of less intense energy to revitalize.

- *Does organizational energy work as a generative force?* Some authors suggest that energy may become self-reinforcing and amplifying (Cameron, Dutton, & Quinn, 2003; Spreitzer et al., 2005). Experiencing energy as a group may, rather than just consuming resources, generate resources that fuel the systems in which they are embedded (Porath, Spreitzer, & Gibson, 2009). A preliminary indication in this

direction may be that team-level energy creates higher levels of leader empowerment, which in turn seems to be related to more transformational leadership behavior (Krummaker, Vogel, & Kunze, 2009). The latter has been linked to higher levels of organizational energy. Consequently, organizational energy may, to a certain extent, produce the resources required to maintain higher levels of energy over time.

Conclusion

Organizational energy is a relatively new field of inquiry and refers to the forces that an organization, work unit, or team work with in pursuit of its goals. In addition to research on individual energy, research also addresses how and when organizations or teams mobilize their human potential collectively. Much of today's work requires collective settings comprised of teams, units, or organizations that collaborate intensely and need to align and synchronize their emotions, cognitive processes, and behavior to create performance advantage. Research on organizational energy addresses this gap and has established itself as an emerging field, with an increasing number of studies and publications focused on research and practice. The conceptual foundation and empirical work that have been conducted so far hold implications for practice that include considerations such as monitoring organizational energy and leading organizational energy. However, this field of inquiry is only starting to build up evidence; it faces numerous open questions that invite scholars to pursue conceptual and empirical research in the domain of organizational energy.

References

Adams, J.D. (1984). *Transforming work: A collection of organizational transformation readings.* Alexandria, VA: Miles River Press.

Arrow, H., McGrath, J.E., & Berdahl, J.L. (2000). *Small groups as complex systems: Formation, coordination, development, and adaptation.* Thousand Oaks, California: Sage Publications, Inc.

Atwater, L., & Carmeli, A. (2009). Leader-member exchange, feelings of energy, and involvement in creative work. *The Leadership Quarterly, 20,* 264–275.

Baker, W., Cross, R., & Wooten, M. (2003). Positive organizational network analysis and energizing relationships. In K.S. Cameron, J.E. Dutton, & R.E. Quinn (Eds.), *Positive organizational scholarship. Foundations of a new discipline* (pp. 329–342). San Francisco: Berrett-Koehler.

Bandura, A. (2001). Social cognitive theory: An agentic perspective. *Annual Review of Psychology, 52,* 1–26.

Barsade, S.G. (2002). The ripple effect: Emotional contagion and its influence on group behavior. *Administrative Science Quarterly, 47,* 644–675.

Bass, B.M. (1985). *Leadership and performance beyond expectations*. New York: Free Press.

Beltrán-Martin, I., Roca-Puig, V., Escrig-Tena, A., & Bou-Llusar, J.C. (2008). Human resource flexibility as a mediating variable between high performance work systems and performance. *Journal of Management, 34*, 1009–1044.

Bruch, H., & Ghoshal, S. (2003). Unleashing organizational energy. *MIT Sloan Management Review, 45*, 45–51.

Bruch, H., & Ghoshal, S. (2004). *A bias for action. How effective managers harness their willpower, achieve results, and stop wasting time*. Boston: Harvard Business School Press.

Bruch, H., & Menges, J. (2010). The acceleration trap. *Harvard Business Review, 88*, 80–86.

Bruch, H., Menges, J., Cole, M.S., & Vogel, B. (2009). *High performance work systems and firm performance: The mediating role of organizational energy*. Working paper.

Bruch, H., & Vogel, B. (2011). *Fully charged: How great leaders boost their organization's energy and ignite high performance*. Boston: Harvard Business Review Press.

Bruch, H., Vogel, B., & Raes, A. (2009). *Productive organizational energy as a mediator between leadership and performance*. Working paper.

Cameron, K.S. (2008). *Positive leadership*. San Francisco: Berrett-Koehler.

Cameron, K.S., & Caza, A. (2004). Contributions to the discipline of positive organizational scholarship. *American Behavioral Scientist, 47*, 731–739.

Cameron, K.S., Dutton, J.E., & Quinn, R.E. (Eds.) (2003). *Positive organizational scholarship: Foundations of a new discipline*. San Francisco: Berrett-Koehler Publishers.

Cannella, A.A., Jr., & Holcomb, T.R. (2005). A multi-level analysis of the upper-echelons model. *Multi-Level Issues in Strategy and Methods, 4*, 197–237.

Chen, G., & Kanfer, R. (2006). Towards a systems theory of motivated behavior in work teams. *Research in Organizational Behavior, 27*, 223–267.

Cohen, S.G., & Bailey, D.E. (1997). What makes teams work: Group effectiveness research from the shop floor to the executive suite. *Journal of Management, 23*, 239–290.

Cole, M.S., Bruch, H., & Vogel, B. (in press). Energy at work: A measurement validation and linkage to unit effectiveness. *Journal of Organizational Behavior*.

Collins, R. (1990). Stratification, emotional energy, and the transient emotions. In T.D. Kemper (Ed.), *Research agendas in the sociology of emotions* (pp. 27–57). New York: State University of New York Press.

Cranach, M., Ochsenbein, G., &Valach, L. (1986). The group as a self-active system: Outline of a theory of group action. *European Journal of Social Psychology, 16*, 193–229.

Cross, R., Baker, W., & Parker, A. (2003). What creates energy in organizations? *Sloan Management Review, 44*, 51–56.

Dean, J.W., Brandes, P., & Dharwadkar, R. (1998). Organizational cynicism. *Academy of Management Review, 23*, 341–352.

Dutton, J.E. (2003). *Energize your workplace: How to create and sustain high-quality connections at work*. San Francisco: Jossey-Bass.

Dutton, J.E., & Heaphy, E.D. (2003). The power of high quality connections. In K.S. Cameron, J.E. Dutton, & R.E. Quinn (Eds.), *Positive organizational scholarship: Foundations of a new discipline* (pp. 263–278). San Francisco: Berrett-Koehler.

Etzioni, A. (1968). *The active society*. New York: Free Press.

Fineman, S. (2006). On being positive: Concerns and counterpoints. *Academy of Management Review, 31*, 270–291.

Fredrickson, B.L. (2001). The role of positive emotions in positive psychology: The broaden-and-build theory of positive emotions. *American Psychologist, 56*, 218–226.

Fredrickson, B.L., & Losada, M.F. (2005). Positive affect and the complex dynamics of human flourishing. *American Psychologist, 60*, 678–686.

Gibson, C.B. (2001). From accumulation to accommodation: The chemistry of collective cognition in work groups. *Journal of Organizational Behavior, 22*, 121–134.

Greenwood, J.W. III., & Greenwood, J.W., Jr. (1979). *Managing executive stress*. New York: Wiley.

Hackman, J.R. (1992). Group influences on individuals in organizations. In M.D. Dunnette, & L.M. Hough (Eds.), *Handbook of industrial and organizational psychology* (2nd ed., pp. 199–267). Palo Alto, CA: Consulting Psychologists Press.

Hofmann, D.A., & Jones, L.M. (2005). Leadership, collective personality, and performance. *Journal of Applied Psychology, 3*, 509–522.

Jansen, J.J.P., Vera, D., & Crossan, M. (2008). Strategic leadership for exploration and exploitation: The moderating role of environmental dynamism. *The Leadership Quarterly, 20*, 5–18.

Jansen, K. (2004). From persistence to pursuit: A longitudinal examination of momentum during the early stages of strategic change. *Organizational Science, 15*, 276–294.

Katz, D., & Kahn, R.L. (1966). *The social psychology of organizations*. New York: John Wiley.

Kahn, W.A. (1992). To be fully there: Psychological presence at work. *Human Relations, 45*, 321–349.

Kark, R., & Carmeli, A. (2009). Alive and creating: The mediating role of vitality and aliveness in the relationship between psychological safety and creative work involvement. *Journal of Organizational Behavior Journal, 30*, 785–804.

Kark, R., & Van Dijk, D. (2007). Motivation to lead, motivation to follow: The role of the self-regulatory focus in leadership processes. *Academy of Management Review, 32*, 500–528.

Kotter, J. (1995). Leading change: Why transformation efforts fail. *Harvard Business Review, 73*, 59–67.

Kozlowski, S.W.J., & Klein, K.J. (2000). A multilevel approach to theory and research in organizations: Contextual, temporal, and emergent processes. In K.J. Klein, & S.W.J. Kozlowski (Eds.), *Multilevel theory, research and methods in organizations: Foundations, extensions, and new directions* (pp. 3–90). San Francisco: Jossey-Bass.

Krummaker, S., Vogel, B., & Kunze, F. (2009). *Impact of team energy and leader empowerment on transformational leadership: A follower perspective*. Working paper.

Kunze, F., & Bruch, H. (2010). Age-based faultlines and perceived productive energy: The moderation of transformational leadership. *Small Group Research, 41(5)*, 593–620.

Levine, J.M., Resnick, L.B., & Higgins, E.T. (1993). Social foundations of cognition. *Annual Review of Psychology, 44*, 585–612.

Levy, A., & Merry, U. (1986). *Organizational transformation*. New York: Praeger.

Lykken, D.T. (2005). Mental energy. *Intelligence, 33*, 331–335.

Marks, S.R. (1977). Multiple roles and role strain: Some notes on human energy, time and commitment. *American Sociological Review, 42*, 921–936.

Marks, M.A., Mathieu, J.E., & Zaccaro, S.J. (2001). A temporally based framework and taxonomy of team processes. *Academy of Management Review, 26*, 356–376.

Mathieu, J.E., Maynard, M.T., Rapp, T., & Gilson, L. (2008). Team effectiveness 1997–2007: A review of recent advancements and a glimpse into the future. *Journal of Management, 34,* 410–476.

Morgeson, F.P., & Hofmann, D.A. (1999). The structure and function of collective constructs: Implications for multilevel research and theory development. *Academy of Management Review, 24,* 249–265.

Ployhart, R.E., & Moliterno, T.P. (2011). Emergence of the human capital resource: A multilevel model. *Academy of Management Review, 36,* 127–150.

Porath, C.L., Spreitzer, G., & Gibson, C.B. (2009). *Antecedents and consequences of thriving at work: A study of six organizations.* Working paper, University of Southern California, Los Angeles.

Quinn, R.W., & Dutton, J.E. (2005). Coordination as energy-in-conversation. *Academy of Management Review, 30,* 36–57.

Schwartz, T. (2007). Manage your energy, not your time. *Harvard Business Review, 85,* 63–73.

Shamir, B. (1995). Social distance and charisma: Theoretical notes and an exploratory study. *The Leadership Quarterly, 6,* 19–47.

Spreitzer, G.M., & Lam, C.F. (2011). Human energy in organizations: Implications for POS from six interdisciplinary streams. In K. Cameron, & G. Spreitzer (Eds.) *Oxford handbook of positive organizational scholarship.* New York: Oxford University Press.

Spreitzer, G.M., & Sonenshein, S. (2004). Toward a construct definition of positive deviance. *American Behavioral Scientist, 47,* 828–847.

Spreitzer, G., Sutcliffe, K., Dutton, J., Sonenshein, S., & Grant, A.M. (2005). A socially-embedded model of thriving at work. *Organization Science, 16,* 537–549.

Stogdill, R.M. (1972). Group productivity, drive, and cohesiveness. *Organizational Behavior and Human Performance, 8,* 26–43.

Sull, D. (1999). Why good companies go bad. *Harvard Business Review, 77,* 42–52.

Takeuchi, R., Lepak, D.P., Wang, H., & Takeuchi, K. (2007). An empirical examination of the mechanisms mediating between high-performance work systems and the performance of Japanese organizations. *Journal of Applied Psychology, 92,* 1069–1083.

Thayer, R.E. (1989). *The biopsychology of mood and arousal.* New York: Oxford University Press.

Thompson, L., & Fine, G.A. (1999). Socially shared cognition, affect, and behavior: A review and integration. *Personality & Social Psychology Review, 3,* 278–302.

Tushman, M.L., & O'Reilly, C.A., III. (1996). Ambidextrous organization: Managing evolutionary and revolutionary change. *California Management Review, 38,* 8–30.

Walter, F., & Bruch, H. (in press). Structural impacts on the occurrence and effectiveness of transformational leadership: An empirical study at the organizational level of analysis, *Leadership Quarterly.*

Innovativeness as Positive Deviance

Identifying and Operationalizing the Attributes, Functions, and Dynamics That Create Growth

Jeff DeGraff *and* Dan Nathan-Roberts

Abstract

This chapter situates organizational innovation within the field of positive organizational scholarship (POS) via the concept of positive deviance shared by both disciplines. It deconstructs the definition of innovation and its wide variance of use in research and suggests the concept of "innovativeness" as a more accurate and viable description of the activities and outcomes associated with organizational innovation. The interrelationship of levels of innovation is explored, and key dimensions of organizational innovation are summarized. The competing values framework is used to operationalize the specific attributes, functions, and dynamics of innovativeness within a POS context. Descriptions of generative activities such as moving from problem identification to appreciation and abundance, creating sustainability via the "heliotropic effect" of energy and momentum, and the importance of emotional connection in creating a sense of a destiny are all familiar themes in both fields. This chapter proposes that the field of organizational innovation may offer useful pathways for POS to translate some of its key insights and research findings into practices for organizational culture and capability development, and relate these to specific value propositions and other outcomes.

Keywords: Innovation, innovativeness, competing values framework, positive organizational scholarship, organization, clan, adhocracy, market, hierarchy, propositions, practices

Innovation in a business context is generally understood as one of the prime determinants of competitive advantage because of its productive role in driving both new market and revenue growth, as well as other value propositions (Schumpeter, 1939, 1942, 1947). Innovation is understandably one of the most widely researched topics across a vast range of disciplines and therefore susceptible to an array of interpretations and comparative discontinuities (Crossan & Apaydin, 2010). These gaps make translating innovation research into practice increasingly problematic for organizations attempting to transform, grow, and improve their value in multiple forms (Droge & Calantone, 1996). This chapter will attempt to integrate key theoretical and methodological concepts regarding innovation into an operational framework that will include the interactive role of the environment, organization, and individual. Finally, this operational framework will be related to the emerging field of positive organizational scholarship (POS).

The study of innovation is uniquely difficult because, at its core, it contains an epistemological problem regarding how we come to know and designate a thing, action, or expression as an innovation (Kimberly & Evanisko, 1981; Meyer & Goes, 1988). That is, an innovation is primarily distinguished by its unique qualities that allow us to recognize it as something better or new from that which currently exists. This means that what constitutes innovation emerges and changes over time. The higher the magnitude of the innovation, such as a breakthrough medicine, the more likely it is to be discontinuous from previous approaches and methodologies. Innovation therefore by description is a form of positive deviance. It is distinguished from non-innovations via its unique differences and perceived value.

Since we cannot fully see the future until it arrives, we are forced to study innovation as history and try to infer its basic principles of operation. In the words of philosopher Søren Kierkegaard "Life can only be understood backward, but it must be lived forward." So it is with the study of innovation, where its value is latent until it manifests itself sometime in the near or distant future. For researchers and leaders alike, innovation poses the challenge that the more revolutionary the speed and magnitude of an innovation, the more difficult it is to predict the ensuing outcomes with a high degree of accuracy or regularity (Damanpour & Wischnevsky, 2006). It is further complicated by the fact that we miss the interesting turn of events and confluence of factors that brings a company storming back from the brink of bankruptcy via a simple device that looks like a bar of soap (which eventually became the Apple iPod) but actually restructures the entire media industry. To move innovation from theory into practice, first the term itself must be defined and then integrated within a systematic framework in which it can be operationalized (Fagerberg, 2003b).

The Definition Problem

One of the key challenges of innovation research is defining the term itself. There is a wide range of accepted definitions for innovation. A case in point is the *Oxford English Dictionary,* which provides two distinctly different descriptions of the term:

1. The action or process of innovating
2. A new method, idea, product, etc.

The first describes the act of introducing something new, whereas the second identifies something newly introduced. So, innovation here is characterized as an activity in the case of the former and an outcome in the latter. In other words, it defines innovation as both a cause and effect. This dual definition is also true in the current literature (Crossan & Apaydin, 2010; Damanpour & Gopalakrishnan, 1998; Gopalakrishnan & Damanpour, 1997; Tushman & Nadler, 1986). Many researchers have characterized innovation as a process (Ettlie, 1980; Van de Ven, Angle, & Poole, 1989) or a product/outcome (Aiken & Hage, 1971; Damanpour & Evan, 1984; Kimberly & Evanisko, 1981; Meyer & Goes, 1988). Other common interpretations focus on the relationship between innovation and creativity. For instance, Amabile, Conti, Coon, Lazenby, and Herron (1996) posit that innovation is a stage at the end of a genealogical sequence of the creative process:

All innovation begins with creative ideas. . . . We define innovation as the successful implementation of creative ideas within an organization. In this view, creativity by individuals and teams is a starting point for innovation; the first is necessary but not sufficient condition for the second. (Amabile et al., 1996, pp. 1154–1155)

Other accepted definitions frame innovation from the sense-making vantage point of the interpreter or consumer of a particular innovation. Innovation is usually described in its usefulness, its ability to create something new or beneficial to an individual or groups of people:

An *innovation* is an idea, practice, or object that is perceived as new by an individual or other unit of adoption. It matters little, so far as human behavior is concerned, whether or not an idea is "objectively" new as measured by the lapse of time since its first use or discovery. The perceived newness of the idea for the individual determines his or her reaction to it. If an idea seems new to the individual, it is an innovation. (Rogers, 2003, p. 12, italics in original)

Differentiating innovation from invention by defining context and use is also a common theme in the literature:

An invention is the solution to a problem, often a technical one, whereas innovation is the commercially successful use of the solution. (Bacon & Butler, 1981, p. 12)

The challenge of defining innovation has become even more exacerbated in the current milieu, in which the act of creation and its outcomes are inextricably collapsed within an array of services, solutions, or designs. For example, a bookstore may sell commodity products like books and coffee but create a unique experience for the customer through the ambience of the space and service (Pine & Gilmore, 1999). This poses the question "What exactly is the innovation here, and how is it created?"

Several common definitions are (DeGraff & Quinn, 2007):

- The creation and customization of the product
- The combination of the two product categories
- The design and décor of the space
- The community that gathers in the space
- The business model that revitalizes a commodity market
- The marketing that describes the experience as desirable and unique
- The consumers who become innovative in the space

In this case, innovation is systemic (Fagerberg, 2003b). That is, it is produced not only by the activities that represent divergent definitions of the concept but also by their situation, combination, and interaction. Here then, innovation must be considered in a holistic light to be able to approach a definition.

Moving from Innovation to Innovativeness

The same diverse range of characteristics that make defining innovation problematic encompass a series of potentially oppositional attributes, functions, and dynamics associated with them:

- Innovation is created by both groups and individuals (see Anderson, Dreu, & Nijstad, 2004; Van de Ven, Polley, Garud, & Venkataraman, 2007).
- Innovation is a time-bound value proposition (Damanpour & Wischnevsky, 2006; Damanpour & Evan, 1984; Kimberly & Evanisko, 1981) and transitions into a commodity (non-innovation) or normative activities as it matures.
- Innovation is evolutionary and revolutionary in its speed (Gopalakrishnan & Damanpour, 1997).
- Innovation is incremental and radical in its levels of magnitude (Chandy & Tellis, 2000; Freeman & Soete, 1997).
- Innovation creates new opportunity and thus is anticipatory; moves first and responds as necessary when conditions dictate (Drucker, 1985).
- Innovation is both a discrete event and an ongoing process over time (Van de Ven et al., 2007).
- Innovation is a key strategic driver of value creation and an end unto itself (DeGraff & Quinn, 2007; Leifer, McDermott, O'Connor, Peters, Rice, & Veryzer, 2000).
- Innovation is diffusive and emerges at multiple places simultaneously (Grant, 2005; Rogers, 2003).
- Innovation is highly iterative and discontinuous (Anderson et al., 2004; Tushman & Nadler, 1986; Van de Ven et al., 2007).
- Innovation is highly influenced by both external environmental factors and internal organizational factors and hence, requires context specific organizational structures, practices, and processes (DeGraff & Quinn, 2007).

As a result of the variation in attributes, functions, and dynamics, innovation in practice tends toward a specific context that does not equally apply in all situations, or conversely to the nominal, which is typically too broad to distinguish it from the normative. So, in practice, what is innovation in one discipline may be a standard practice in another. For example, short message service or SMS as it is commonly called was used for years by network operators before social networking service providers caught on that this simple technology could be used to revolutionize communication between peer groups. Its relative uniqueness and value are predicated on its context and the subsequent forms of social and economic innovation built on the foundation of a technical one.

Although a wide range of definitions are scattered throughout the accepted literature and potentially make operationalizing innovation precarious, some common themes run through the widely held descriptions:

- Innovation has a generative power to transform inklings, ideas, and emotions into tangible outcomes (Anderson et al., 2004; West, 2002).
- Innovation creates or adds value to products, services, processes, or expressions (Anderson et al., 2004; Camison-Zornoza, Lapiedra-Alcami, Segarra-Cipres, & Boronat-Navarro, 2004; Lansisalmi, Kivimaki, Aalto, & Ruoranen, 2006; West, 2002).
- Innovation opens new opportunities and markets (Drucker, 1985).
- Innovation is compulsory to drive progress and organic growth in both a social and economic context (Fagerberg, 1994, 2003a; Fagerberg, Srholec, & Knell, 2007).
- Innovation displaces previous approaches and solutions (Chandy & Tellis, 1998, 2000; Clayton, Suárez, & Utterback, 1998; Ghemawat, 1991; Reinganum, 1983; Suárez & Utterback, 1995; Utterback & Suárez, 1993).
- Innovation is an amalgamation of several interrelated activities across disciplines and other boundaries (Tushman & Nadler, 1986).

So, although the varied attributes, functions, and one general description problematic, some common ground exists around the nature of innovation as a range of activities that create positive forms of deviance. This activity may be better described as "innovativeness," an attribute or distinguishing property of any number of actions and outcomes that create

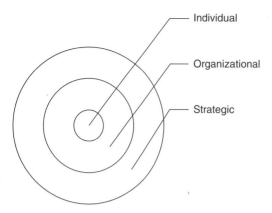

Individual

Organizational

Strategic

Fig. 53.1 Levels of innovativeness.

the useful novelty. By widening the net to accommodate many of the relevant definitions and variations of innovation within the context of POS, the attributes, functions, and dynamics of innovativeness on growth can more fully explored.

Levels and Dimensions of Innovativeness

Although there are multiple levels and dimensions of innovativeness, a few key classifications will be examined here.

Levels

Innovativeness has three levels, which can be characterized as starting with the most pervasive forces and working backward to appropriate organizational practices, and finally, personal leadership behaviors (Figure 53.1).

- *Strategic*: This level includes powerful and unseen drivers such as the market, the consumer, and the economy. These forces are real and quasi-perceptible, but typically the unruly environmental and situational factors that both produce opportunities for organizations to innovate and grow often confound those organizations' responses because of these forces' ambiguous structures and dynamics. This level might be characterized as the "macro" level of innovativeness.
- *Organizational*: This level may contain the entirety of a network that competes as an organization, the entity itself, or some division of that entity. This level is where the organization exhibits its agency through strategic planning, financial resource allocation, hiring, and staffing, as well as through research and new product development practices. This might be described as the collective "enterprise" level of innovativeness.

- *Individual*: This is the level of the leader, manager, and innovator. It is the most atomistic deconstruction of the entity but may exist as the entity in itself. There are some popular conceptualizations of innovators as "free agents" in a world connected in loose affiliations via seamless and ubiquitous technological platforms. At this level, individuals may participate in an organization because of their own self-interest. This can be depicted as the "personal" level of innovativeness.

It may be useful to think of this systemic view of innovativeness as a Russian nesting doll, in which each doll is contained inside another. Agency is achieved not at one level, but through the interplay of all levels. For example, a strategic change in the environment, such as a recession, may drive a business to change what it sells, how it sells, and the price it gets for its goods or services. The changes in the business may precipitate a change in behavior for leaders in that organization. Conversely, an individual may create a new design for a consumer electronics device that disrupts the new product development process within a firm. The company may incorporate this fresh design as a distinctive feature of its product, which in turn, may ignite a new market trend. What makes these levels significant is not so much what happens at each level, but rather the dynamics between them. It is between levels that innovativeness is amplified and produces cascading forms of deviance.

Dimensions

Innovativeness is the key pathway to achieving progress and growth and is typically seen as one of the distinguishing endeavors of humanity. So, it is no wonder that the process and act of innovating is studied across a wide array of fields and disciplines from various vantage points: Anthropology, business, economics, education, engineering, law, medicine, political science, psychology, and sociology have all made substantive contributions to the research on innovation. Although each discipline has particular areas of focus, the horizontal or cross-boundary functions of innovation typically create substantial overlap among these perspectives, which produces multifarious and countervailing explanations as to the how and why innovation happens.

For example, explanations of Thomas Edison's success with innovation range from development of

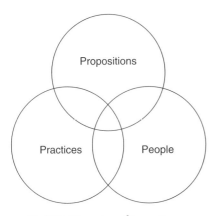

Fig. 53.2 Dimensions of innovativeness.

a sophisticated research and development process and community of practice to his singular creative genius. Although these views are not mutually exclusive, they are so wide ranging that they make functional replication extremely difficult if not improbable.

Although numerous dimensions inform organizational innovativeness, ranging from the diversity of the board of directors to indicators of manufacturability, much of the literature clusters around three main areas (Figure 53.2):

- *Propositions*: This dimension typically includes strategy, business models, financial measures, and commercialization.
- *Practices*: This dimension is characterized in widely different ways by different fields of study and may include organizational structure, product portfolio management, technological systems, standards and networks, research and development processes, and project management practices.
- *People*: This dimension has more continuity than the others due to its interrelatedness of the social sciences in research and publication. It often includes organizational development, knowledge management, leadership and management behavior, team building, decision making, personality attributes, and creativity initiation methods.

Although this list is not comprehensive, and considerable overlap exists among the dimensions, it is used here to help organize the dominant approaches in a useful pattern.

PROPOSITIONS

The focus here is the end game of innovativeness. That is, the value produced and harvested by the

organization is the central concern. In this view, innovativeness is characterized as starting with the result and working backward to the practices associated with producing it. Typically, in this view, the ends justify the means. These typologies of outcomes range from productivity, typically measured by factors such as rates of return or time to market, to the continuity and newness of the innovation. Implied in this view are factors of speed and magnitude. That is, how much innovativeness; how fast? For example, the more radical the innovativeness the more difficult it is to reliably predict its outcomes, given that the time to develop and commercialize an innovation and the returns produced by that innovation are more ambiguous than incremental innovations that have a greater degree of continuity. This partially explains why venture capitalists use different strategies and financial measures for managing innovation than the more conventional measures like net present value, which are typically used in corporations.

PRACTICES

Practices are often referred to as "processes" in the literature. However, what constitutes an innovation process varies greatly between the operations management and management and organizations literature, as well as that originating from other engineering and social science disciplines. So, the term *practices* is used here to subsume the work of multiple disciplines. Much of the theoretical basis for this dimension comes from practitioners and consulting firms specializing in increasing innovation efficacy and throughput. This dimension focuses on how to accelerate development processes, increase achievement of target goals, and select platforms; the innovation development processes; game changing business models; and resource allocation. The strong methodological bent of this dimension is aimed at articulating "how" innovation happens in an organizational context.

PEOPLE

This dimension is the oldest area of inquiry and is most closely associated with innovativeness, which is often taken as a collective form of creativity. Elements of the personal dimension of innovativeness are found in Plato, Freud, and Marx. This dimension commonly focuses on the creative initiation of the innovation process, the development of unique and resilient capabilities and culture, and the application of new and unique knowledge across the organization, as well as across wider networks. Issues such as the role of shared vision and values, the cohesiveness of governance, the ability to anticipate and respond to unexpected events, and risk taking are prominent.

As with levels, dimensions are intertwined and difficult to operationalize individually.

The Competing Values of Innovativeness

The competing values framework has been used extensively in both research and practice to categorize leadership, organizational culture, and competency (Cameron & Quinn, 1999; Quinn, 1988; Quinn & Cameron, 1983), and connect these to specific types of value propositions (Cameron, Quinn, DeGraff, & Thakor, 2006). Competing values has also been frequently used to organize the structures, dynamics, and practices associated with particular types of innovation (DeGraff & Quinn, 2007). The central tenet of the competing values framework is that oppositional factors can be productively engaged to create positive tensions that yield hybrid and novel solutions. This approach challenges conventional views that disagreements produce winners and losers and displace key types of innovation represented by weaker stakeholder groups. Like the POS precepts of abundance, appreciating, and valuing, the competing values framework view suggests that constructive conflict helps form a shared vision across diverse stakeholders and boundaries, and promotes a sense of destiny to pull the organization forward as opposed to reacting to problem sets. This holistic approach moves the tension from a dynamic to be avoided to the transformational power necessary to promote innovativeness.

Innovativeness, like positive deviance, is a context and culturally specific construct. Deviating from what norm? This section will explore the four general patterns or modalities (Figure 53.3) in which innovativeness occurs: *clan, adhocracy, compete,* and *hierarchy*:

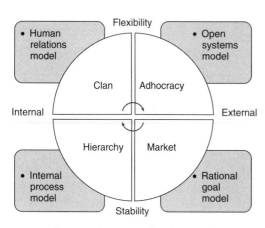

Fig. 53.3 Competing values framework.

- *Clan*: Human relations model, emphasizing flexibility and internal focus (Quinn, 1988):
  - *Primary cultural orientation*: Collaborate; social approaches to innovativeness
  - *Organizational focus*: High internal focus and integration; low external focus and differentiation
  - *Organizational preference for structure*: High flexibility and discretion; low stability and control
  - *Typical value propositions pursued*: Community development and relationship creation
  - *Typical innovativeness practices*: Knowledge management, mentoring and coaching, team building, collaborative communities of practice, search and reapply, culture and competency development, collaborating with customers and open source
  - *Leadership and organizational cohesiveness*: Shared values
  - *Role*: Idea and development sharing
- *Market*: Rational goal model, stressing control and external focus (Quinn, 1988):
  - *Primary cultural orientation*: Compete; commercial approaches innovativeness
  - *Organizational focus*: High external focus and differentiation; low internal focus and integration
  - *Organizational preference for structure*: High stability and control; low flexibility and discretion
  - *Typical value propositions pursued*: Speed and profits
  - *Typical innovativeness practices*: Mergers and acquisitions, portfolio management, rapid action problem solving teams, revenue insight processes, branding, market adjacencies, and business solutions
  - *Leadership and organizational cohesiveness*: Shared goals
  - *Role*: Competitive pressure
- *Adhocracy*: Open systems model, characterized by flexibility and external focus (Quinn, 1988):
  - *Primary cultural orientation*: Create; generative approaches innovativeness
  - *Organizational focus*: High external focus and differentiation; low internal focus and integration
  - *Organizational preference for structure*: High flexibility and discretion; low stability and control

- *Typical value propositions pursued*: Breakthrough innovation and discontinuous change
- *Typical innovativeness practices*: Futuring and scenario planning, new market speculation, innovation societies and fellows, diversified radical experiments, early technology adoption, corporate venturing and spinoffs, and greenhouse funding
- *Leadership and organizational cohesiveness*: Shared vision
- *Role*: Radical innovation
- *Hierarchy*: Internal process model, emphasizing control and internal focus (Quinn, 1988):
  - *Primary cultural orientation*: Control; technological approaches innovativeness
  - *Organizational focus*: High internal focus and integration; low external focus and differentiation
  - *Organizational preference for structure*: High stability and control; low flexibility and discretion
  - *Typical value propositions pursued*: Efficiency and quality
  - *Typical innovativeness practices*: Continuous process improvement, reverse engineering, benchmarking, lean manufacturing, total quality management, simulations, platform innovation, end-to-end IT systems, and supply chain innovation
  - *Leadership and organizational cohesiveness*: Shared processes
  - *Roles*: Process improvement and cost reduction

Clan

The clan modality represents the social approach to innovativeness through human connections. It emphasizes community, cooperation, and the development of relationships. Leaders build the organization by encouraging trust, commitment, and relationships, which results in empowered individuals. This unified behavior produces a cohesive organizational culture. The strong sense of identification with a shared set of values may even be discernible outside of the organization, as in the case of Singapore Air, which differentiates itself through its outstanding customer service. Clan-focused organizations are often ranked among the best places to work partly because of the premium they place on developing a harmonious workplace atmosphere and cultivating teamwork, as well as the development of personal and collective competencies. The POS precepts that

positive energizers tend to be high performers and enhance the work of others are easily recognizable here.

The ability to innovate across boundaries makes this approach particularly well suited for professional service providers that deliver complex solutions: Physicians, professors, consultants, and the like. Collaborative forms of innovation, such as open and crowd sourcing, is dependent on the trust and cooperation of groups with a shared set of values, as in the case of Linux, a not-for-profit organization that has patented its software so that anyone associated with its community can use it and add to it. The clan approach even extends the idea of community into the customer base, and customers often are seen as partners in the development of organization (see Pittaway, Robertson, Munir, Denyer, & Neely, 2004).

Typically the slowest form of innovativeness, the clan approach relies on the development of culture and competencies that are initially time intensive, but it is ultimately the most sustainable of all the approaches. This is because the ability to grow and develop innovativeness is contained within the talent base of the organization and community.

Market

The opposite of the communal or clan form of innovativeness is the market form, which represents a Darwinian approach that focuses on the rational pursuit of success, often at the expense of "weaker" participants. A game of winners and losers, aggressive competitors thrive in this course of action. The market approach is focused on performance and goals. These organizations are typically results-oriented environments in which overcoming challenges via highly focused problem solving abilities is necessary to "win." At first blush, the market modality may appear to be the antithesis of POS precepts, such as not focusing on troubleshooting barriers and gaps. However, upon closer examination, the market approach can be seen as having compatible tenets, such as rewarding high performers, transforming challenges into opportunities for abundance, and creating clear targets of success and encouraging their pursuit.

The market approach motivates leaders to move quickly on short- to mid-term opportunities for increasing profitability, market share, and brand equity through high-powered initiatives, mergers, and deals. Examples include valuable multinationals like General Electric in the United States and the Indian giant Tata Group, both with hundreds of companies working independently to crank out shareholder value year after year. Companies with the market approach invest in innovation acquisition instead of innovation generation within themselves and use it to enter new markets (Blonigen & Taylor, 2000; Roberts & Berry, 1985). This form of innovativeness is the fastest of all four, given its focus on short-term results. However, the generative abilities of the market modality often prove unsustainable because of a strong external focus that gives little concern to the development of the workforce. The predatory use of acquisitions to grow competencies and markets inorganically is one way that the market approach may overcome this potential deficiency.

Speed of Innovativeness as Clan–Market Positive Tension

There is a positive tension between the clan and market forms of innovativeness that shows up as everyday trade-offs regarding how fast an organization, team, or leader must move to act upon a perceived growth opportunity. The calibration of speed is the by-product of this constructive conflict. Does the organization pursue the development of competencies and culture, which take time to develop, or does it pursue a short-term opportunity, which must be acted upon quickly?

This temporal element of innovativeness may be used to determine which initiatives receive funding, who leads these efforts, and what strategic horizon the firm will focus on. The differences between these approaches are not so much personal preferences as they are competing forms of value. For example, training engineers in the aesthetics of new product design may provide a long-term competitive advantage for a company but require it to forego some of the short-term profits lost through the reduction of workflow. From the clan point of view, this is value enhancing because it is focused on a longer time horizon, although constituencies of the market view may see it as destroying shareholder value, which is typically calculated quarterly. Each sees the other as destroying its value proposition. This tension is constructive because it produces the hybrid, higher-level forms of innovativeness that are both sustainable and opportunistic. Productively managing and harnessing this opposition is one of the hallmarks of high-growth firms.

Adhocracy

The adhocracy approach pursues breakthrough innovativeness through open systems and a wide array of experiments to see what new opportunities emerge. Venture capitalists and high-tech firms alike embrace this high-risk, high-reward modality because it is often generative. That is, it produces new knowledge about products and markets, and, with a little luck, secondary solutions that may be even more valuable. Because radical approaches to innovativeness are more likely to succeed in high-risk and high-reward situations, both start-ups and failing corporations tend to gravitate to adhocracy (Greve, 2003; Kahneman & Tversky, 1979). Consider how Apple, only months out of near insolvency, developed the iPod, which became a huge success. However, it was the secondary solution, iTunes that created even greater opportunities for the firm and set the direction of pace of the entire industry segment.

Organizations with a strong tendency toward adhocracy are typically populated with entrepreneurs and artists, as well as with a very diverse range of individualists who enjoy launching a wide array of projects in pursuit of potentially unachievable aspirations. These organizations have an ability to easily shift directions to capitalize on opportunities as they become apparent. Because of its fluid, idea-generating nature, the adhocracy modality tends to lead to breakthrough products and services, which in turn can cause radical changes in the marketplace. Leaders employ the adhocracy practices to drive creative ideas that spur growth. They strive to develop unique products, services, and methods that will serve both existing and emerging customer groups in the future.

Like the clan modality, many POS principles can be readily observed in organizations that lean toward adhocracy, including a strong sense of destiny, an energetic and positively affirming culture, and the belief that the seemingly impossible can be achieved. To accomplish this, leaders often develop a compelling vision that emphasizes new ideas, technologies, flexibility, and adaptability. Adhocracy might be referred to as the "forward position" of innovativeness because it allows entrepreneurial concerns or radical experiments to provide some proof of concept that "it can be done." Companies like BMW and Genentech fit this description, as their basic approach to innovativeness involves providing very unique and proprietary products and solutions to the market. Although this approach provides the greatest magnitude of innovativeness, it also brings the greatest risk of failure.

Hierarchy

While adhocracy represents the forward position of innovativeness, exploring new ideas and markets first, hierarchy brings up the rear, focusing on internal process controls required to achieve scope and scale.

In its most accumulative form, innovativeness has a long tail that spans the entirety of the enterprise and supply chain, and cascades through the entire operation with continuous process improvements en masse. The hierarchy modality represents incremental innovativeness—taking something that exists and modifying it to make it better, cheaper, or faster. This approach has a built-in safety-net feature, and for this reason it is particularly useful in situations in which failure is not an option, as in the medical devices or aviation industries.

Like market, hierarchy has many aspects antithetical to espoused POS principles, such as a control-based orientation toward problem solving. But, here too, there are some oft-overlooked similarities. An ongoing commitment to excellence through constant review and revision is the driving principle of this modality. This emphasis on integrity and organizational learning is evident in multistep systematic technological and methodological improvement practices. In essence, it is the cumulative learning of an organization made manifest in tools, platforms, and techniques. This approach is highly sustainable because it builds on the learning of the organization and enhances these insights with each new cycle of review and revision.

Leaders using this approach also tend to focus on analytical, methodical, and practical solutions that allow large-scale and complex organization to operate efficiently. They engender a culture of planning, creating systems and processes, and ensuring compliance. The end result of these innovative practices is not so much an entirely new product or service, but instead an existing product with minor variations (see Chandy & Tellis, 1998; Chandy & Tellis, 2000). Firms like McDonalds and Dell, known for quality and value-based pricing, are good examples of the hierarchy approach. Although mitigating risk better than the other forms, this approach often brings unwanted bureaucracy.

Magnitude of Innovativeness as Adhocracy–Hierarchy Positive Tension

A second tension, involving the adhocracy and hierarchy approaches, is based on the magnitude and commensurate risk to be assumed in pursuit of innovativeness. The amount or measure of novelty of innovativeness is largely determined by this positive tension. Should the organization pursue revolutionary innovativeness, which brings great risk and expense, or pursue incremental and scalable innovativeness, which has less risk but often lacks sufficient inventiveness to develop new markets?

The level of ambition and corresponding risk often determines the course of action an organization will take.

For example, a biotech start-up will typically develop very novel therapies because it lacks the resources to compete on scope or scale, whereas an incumbent pharmaceutical company will develop relatively minor enhancements to an existing medication to extend the life of its patents and revenues. Again, these competing approaches also produce very different outcomes. The former pursues the relative radical result but assumes a higher level of risk, while the later pursues more incremental extensions of a medicine or therapy while mitigating as much risk as possible. When effectively balanced, these disparate forms of innovativeness work in concert to coordinate the cycle of the "new" as it transits into the "better."

Innovativeness As Integral and Context Specific

Of course, these modalities are meant to delineate the basic map to demonstrate countervailing approaches to innovativeness and provide a framework by which to explore possible intersections with POS. In reality, all environments, practices, and people express multiple approaches to innovativeness, but like people who are left- or right-handed, they tend to use one over the others. So, for example, investment banks tend to pursue market value propositions, such as short-term profits, and employ practices like portfolio management, while universities typically aspire to clan results and work across decades developing their community of scholars (see Table 53.1).

One size doesn't fit all. "Do this and you will succeed" lists may be useful but only in the context of a specific situation. As we have seen, many innovation practices are actually counterproductive if not applied in the right place at the right time; and, without proper coordination, they may actually displace other useful practices. Effective organizational innovativeness requires both alignment between intended outcomes and the practices that produce them, and also an appreciation of the diversity needed to develop innovativeness from ideation to scalable implementation. As with POS, a deep appreciation of the "other" is a common cause for the creation of abundance. The organization must aspire to and achieve a higher point of view, integrating the four approaches, to effectively grow in the face of complex demands and opportunities.

Table 53.1 Levels and dimensions of innovativeness and competing values

		Clan	Adhocracy	Market	Hierarchy
Levels of Innovativeness	*Strategic*	• Long-term development • Community-focused • Sustainable	• Small-scale • High variation • Accelerate failure	• Short time to market • Shareholder-focused • Competitive	• Large-scale • High complexity • Failure is not an option
	Organizational	• Collaborative workplace • Shared values and vision • Integrates personal goals • Informal	• Stimulating projects • New initiatives • Independent work streams • Diverse workforce	• High pressure and impact • Fast-moving • Quantifiable results • Winners and losers	• Clear roles and responsibilities • Replicable processes • Standards and regulations • Structured workflow
	Individual	• Sees potential • Builds commitment and trust • Encourages participation • Respects differences • Empowers people	• Visionary dreamers • Creative • Optimistic • Expressive • Big-picture thinkers	• Goal and action oriented • Assertive • Decisive • Challenging • Competitive	• Pragmatic • Organized and methodical • Scientific or technical • Problem solver • Objective
Dimensions of Innovativeness	*Proposition*	• Community • Knowledge	• Radical innovation • Growth	• Profits • Speed	• Efficiency • Quality
	Practices	• Values-centric • Culture and competency development • Team building • Training and coaching • Organizational learning	• Vision-centric • Creativity methods • Think tanks • Corporate venturing • Leading innovation and growth programs	• Goal-centric • Performance scorecards • Project portfolio management • Mergers and acquisitions • Branding programs	• Process-centric • Business process improvement • Benchmarking • Simulations • Supply chain management • Standards
	People	• Talent-focused • Community oriented • Patient • Empowering	• Visionary • Creative • Optimistic • Enthusiastic	• Goal-focused • Action oriented • Decisive • Competitive	• Pragmatic • Methodical • Objective • Persistent

Future Directions

The aim of this chapter is to demonstrate how the basic attributes, functions, and dynamics of innovativeness operate within an organizational context and help it achieve various forms of growth, a manifestation of abundance. The intent is to build upon the foundational concepts of POS and suggest where innovation practices and research may complement this work. Although some linkages are readily found, there is more work to be done to integrate the concept of innovativeness into POS theory and practice, particularly given the extensive number of domains that research innovation.

A few key areas of inquiry suggest a direction for future research:

- Although POS principles are easily reconciled with the clan and adhocracy modalities, in which the desired state of the organization is the principal concern, how do they function in the market and hierarchy modalities, in which the present state is the focus of the organization?
- Schumpeter's economic concept of "creative destruction," which pervades the theatrical basis for innovation strategy, suggests that it is through crisis, where risk and reward are reversed, that companies either perish or experience unprecedented growth. How can this financial concept of deficiency be directly addressed by POS principles of abundance?
- Given the trend that innovativeness, enabled by the web and the globalization of product development, is now occurring across organizations in federations, how do POS principles function in this virtual and collaborative environment?

References

Aiken, M., & Hage, J. (1971). The organic organization and innovation. *Sociology, 5*(1), 63–82.

Amabile, T.M., Conti, R., Coon, H., Lazenby, J., & Herron, M. (1996). Assessing the work environment for creativity. *The Academy of Management Journal, 39*(5), 1154–1184.

Anderson, N., Dreu, C.K. W.D., & Nijstad, B.A. (2004). The routinization of innovation research: A constructively critical review of the state-of-the-science. *Journal of Organizational Behavior, 25*(2), 147–173.

Bacon, F.R., & Butler, T.W. (1981). *Planned innovation*. Ann Arbor, MI: University of Michigan Press.

Blonigen, B.A., & Taylor, C.T. (2000). R&D intensity and acquisitions in high technology industries: Evidence from the US electronic and electrical equipment industries. *The Journal of Industrial Economics, 48*(1), 47–70.

Cameron, K.S., & Quinn, R.E. (1999). *Diagnosing and changing organizational culture based on the competing values framework.* Reading, MA: Addison-Wesley.

Cameron, K.S., Quinn, R.E., DeGraff, J., & Thakor, A.V. (2006). *Competing values leadership: Creating value in organizations.* Northampton, MA: Edward Elgar.

Camison-Zornoza, C., Lapiedra-Alcami, R., Segarra-Cipres, M., & Boronat-Navarro, M. (2004). A meta-analysis of innovation and organizational size. *Organization Studies, 25*(3), 331–361.

Chandy, R.K., & Tellis, G.J. (1998). Organizing for radical product innovation: The overlooked role of willingness to cannibalize. *Journal of Marketing Research, 35*(4), 474–487.

Chandy, R.K., & Tellis, G.J. (2000). The incumbent's curse? Incumbency, size, and radical product innovation. *The Journal of Marketing, 64*(3), 1–17.

Clayton, M.C., Suárez, F.F., & Utterback, J.M. (1998). Strategies for survival in fast-changing industries. *Management Science, 44*(12), S207–S220.

Crossan, M.M., & Apaydin, M. (2010). A multi-dimensional framework of organizational innovation: A systematic review of the literature. *Journal of Management Studies, 47*(6), 1154–1191.

Damanpour, F., & Wischnevsky, J.D. (2006). Research on innovation in organizations: Distinguishing innovation-generating from innovation-adopting organizations. *Journal of Engineering and Technology Management, 23*(4), 269–291.

Damanpour, F., & Evan, W.M. (1984). Organizational innovation and performance: The problem of "organizational lag." *Administrative Science Quarterly, 29*(3), 392–409.

Damanpour, F., & Gopalakrishnan, S. (1998). Theories of organizational structure and innovation adoption: The role of environmental change. *Journal of Engineering and Technology Management, 15*(1), 1–24.

DeGraff, J., & Quinn, S.E. (2007). *Leading innovation: How to jump start your organization's growth engine.* New York: McGraw-Hill.

Drucker, P.F. (1985). The discipline of innovation. *Harvard Business Review, 63*(3), 67–72.

Droge, C., & Calantone, R. (1996). New product strategy, structure, and performance in two environments. *Industrial Marketing Management, 25*(6), 555–566.

Ettlie, J.E. (1980). Adequacy of stage models for decisions on adoption of innovation. *Psychological Reports, 46*, 991–995.

Fagerberg, J. (1994). Technology and international differences in growth rates. *Journal of Economic Literature, 32*(3), 1147–1175.

Fagerberg, J. (2003a). [Review of the book The associational economy: Firms, regions and innovation, P. Cooke, & K. Morgan (Eds.)]. *Research Policy, 32*(6), 1146–1148.

Fagerberg, J. (2003b). *Innovation: A guide to the literature.* Oslo: Centre for Technology, Innovation and Culture, University of Oslo.

Fagerberg, J., Srholec, M., & Knell, M. (2007). The competitiveness of nations: Why some countries prosper while others fall behind. *World Development, 35*(10), 1595–1620.

Freeman, C., & Soete, L. (1997). *The economics of industrial innovation* (3rd ed.). London: Pinter.

Ghemawat, P. (1991). Market incumbency and technological inertia. *Marketing Science, 10*(2), 161–171.

Gopalakrishnan, S., & Damanpour, F. (1997). A review of innovation research in economics, sociology and technology management. *Omega, 25*(1), 15–28.

Grant, R.M. (2005). *Contemporary strategy analysis* (5th ed.). Cambridge, MA: Blackwell.

Greve, H.R. (2003). A behavioral theory of R&D Expenditures and Innovations: Evidence from shipbuilding. *The Academy of Management Journal, 46*(6), 685–702.

Kahneman, D., & Tversky, A. (1979). Prospect theory: An analysis of decision under risk. *Econometrica, 47*(2), 263–291.

Kimberly, J.R., & Evanisko, M.J. (1981). Organizational innovation: The influence of individual, organizational, and contextual factors on hospital adoption of technological and administrative innovations. *The Academy of Management Journal, 24*(4), 689–713.

Lansisalmi, H., Kivimaki, M., Aalto, P., & Ruoranen, R. (2006). Innovation in healthcare: A systematic review of recent research. *Nursing Science Quarterly,* 66–72.

Leifer, R., McDermott, C.M., O'Connor, D.C., Peters, L.S., Rice, M.P., & Veryzer, R.V. (2000). *Radical innovation: How mature companies can outsmart upstarts.* Boston: Harvard Business School Press.

Meyer, A.D., & Goes, J.B. (1988). Organizational Assimilation of Innovations: A Multilevel Contextual Analysis. *The Academy of Management Journal, 31*(4), 897–923.

Pine, B.J., & Gilmore, J.H. (1999). *The experience economy: Work is theatre & every business a stage.* Cambridge, MA: Harvard Business School Press.

Pittaway, L., Robertson, M., Munir, K., Denyer, D., & Neely, A. (2004). Networking and innovation: A systematic review of the evidence. *International Journal of Management Reviews, 5*(3–4), 137–168.

Quinn, R.E. (1988). *Beyond rational management: Mastering the paradoxes and competing demands of high performance.* San Francisco: Jossey-Bass.

Quinn, R.E., & Cameron, K.S. (1983). Organizational life cycles and shifting criteria of effectiveness; some preliminary evidence. *Management Science, 29,* 33–51.

Reinganum, J.F. (1983). Uncertain Innovation and the Persistence of Monopoly. *The American Economic Review, 73*(4), 741–748.

Roberts, E.B., & Berry, C.A. (1985). Entering new businesses: Selecting new strategies for success. *Sloan Management Review, 26,* 3–17.

Rogers, E.M. (2003). *Diffusion of innovations* (5th ed.). New York: Free Press.

Schumpeter, J.A. (1939). *Business cycles: A theoretical, historical, and statistical analysis of the capitalist process.* New York: McGraw-Hill.

Schumpeter, J.A. (1942). *Capitalism, socialism and democracy.* New York: Harper.

Schumpeter, J.A. (1947). The creative response in economic history. *Journal of Economic History, 7*(2), 149–159.

Suárez, F.F., & Utterback, J.M. (1995). Dominant designs and the survival of firms. *Strategic Management Journal, 16*(6), 415–430.

Tushman, M.L., & Nadler, D. (1986). Organizing for innovation. *California Management Review, 28*(3), 74–92.

Utterback, J.M., & Suárez, F.F. (1993). Innovation, competition, and industry structure. *Research Policy, 22*(1), 1–21.

Van de Ven, A., Angle, H.L., & Poole, M. (1989). *Research on the management of innovation.* New York: Harper and Row.

Van de Ven, A., Polley, D.E., Garud, R., & Venkataraman, S. (2007). *The innovation journey.* New York: Oxford University Press.

West, M.A. (2002). Sparkling fountains or stagnant ponds: An integrative model of creativity and innovation implementation in work groups. *Applied Psychology, 51*(3), 355–387.

Margins, Membership, and Mobility

Redefining Boundaries in Collaborative Endeavors

Rebekah Dibble *and* Cristina B. Gibson

Abstract

The focus of this chapter is on membership in team-based collaborative endeavors. Nearly a decade ago, Ancona and her colleagues introduced the concept of X-teams, highlighting membership by both core and peripheral participants in teams within an organization. Today, there is a growing prevalence of teams that are not embedded in any organizational context, which are even more temporary, more fluid, and operate in increasingly dynamic environments. Under these conditions, the margins around the team are permeable. Leaders of such organizationally independent collaborative endeavors may find themselves asking "Who is internal and who is external?" Boundaries may be in flux, and membership may vary over a short time. This variability may result in challenges for team management and effectiveness, but may also be liberating and productive. Here, we focus on the relationships between boundary mobility and identity, commitment, empowerment, and thriving, as well as the impact that boundary mobility has on collaboration effectiveness.

Keywords: Collaboration, positive organizational scholarship, boundaries, mobility, membership

Membership in Team-based Collaborative Endeavors

A critical problem facing organizational scholars of the 21st century is to address the abundance of "organizing" that takes place outside the realm of traditional organizations in more loosely structured formats, and to more fully understand the unique challenges and opportunities that participants in these collaborative endeavors experience. Variations of these collaborative entities may be found embedded within organizations in the form of committees (Lumsden, 2004), project teams (Jones, 1996; Shenhar, 2001), ad hoc teams (Hefke & Stojanovic, 2004), and X-teams (Ancona, Bresman, & Kaeufer, 2002); they may span organizations in the form of cross-organizational teams (Zuckerman & Higgins, 2002); or they may be independent of any overarching organization, in the case of team-based collaborations (Gibson & Dibble, 2008).

In this chapter, we focus on this last form: face-to-face team-based collaborations. We define team-based collaborations as temporary, multiparty, nonorganizationally embedded entities organized for the purpose of pooling expertise, resources, information, or social networks to create a specific product or service (Gibson & Dibble, 2008). Defining characteristics of such collaborative endeavors include dynamic sets of external constituents, emergent and shifting authority structures, and fluid membership. Hence, some of the most interesting and important questions associated with collaborative work relate to collaboration membership. As such, members of collaborative endeavors may find themselves asking who is "in" and who is "out," or wondering what marks the boundaries to their group. These questions, as will be noted below, have important implications at the individual and collaboration level of analysis. Although prior research has recognized blurred boundaries and migration across them as a critical dynamic in collaborative work, in team-based collaborations, these issues have even greater potential than previously recognized to create challenges for collaborative work—but they also have the potential to result in significant (potentially even liberating) opportunities for workers. In the spirit of the theme for this edited volume on positive organizational scholarship (POS), we focus on better understanding the opportunities created.

Consider the following example of a face-to-face team-based collaborative endeavor in the context of a humanitarian home building project. On a January morning in Central America, a group of people gathered together to participate in the construction of housing for needy families. It was the beginning of the second and final week of the project, and the group, consisting primarily of English-speaking Canadians, assembled to begin their day's work. Most of these people had met one another 1 week earlier, and had spent the previous week becoming acquainted, developing routines, and learning the tasks to be performed. During the course of the day, five new members were integrated into the group. Four women from the United States arrived, ranging in age from late teens to mid-30s, along with a middle-aged woman with a strong French accent who was originally from Switzerland. One participant who had been onsite during the previous week was ill and chose not to come to the site on this particular day. Maria, who was not the designated group leader, but one of the few bilingual participants, took the lead. She met briefly with Diego, a locally contracted construction foreman. Since Maria was one of the few people with whom Diego could communicate, instructions for the morning were given to Maria, who then called the group over and relayed the instructions to the group. Previous groups had come to work on this site under the direction of other construction leads, including Antonio, who had provided construction expertise for a similar group just weeks before. However, unlike Antonio, who merely oversaw work processes and provided instructions, Diego was clearly an integral part of this group. He made frequent attempts to interact with participants throughout the day and was proud of his affiliation with this group, to the extent that one newcomer had assumed that he must be an employee of the home building association and an integral leader on this work site.

This scenario illustrates some of the principal conundrums created by temporary collaborative endeavors with regard to membership, including a lack of shared history among members of the collaboration, an emergent and fluid leadership structure, a changing set of external constituents, difficulty that

may be experienced in identifying the boundaries between internal and external participants, and the question of whether some participants actually shift from "external" to "internal" status or vice versa. But it also illustrates the potential positive effects of shifting membership, in that new roles and identities may be created as a result of the changes that occur.

Margins, Membership, and Mobility

One intriguing aspect of collaboration membership is the concept of boundaries. Here, we examine three particularly important aspects of boundaries for temporary collaborative endeavors: the challenge of defining boundaries (i.e., where are the margins and how do these margins define membership?), the mobility of collaboration members across boundaries, and the relationship between boundary mobility and five critical outcomes at both the individual and collaboration level of analysis, including identity, commitment, empowerment, thriving, and collaboration effectiveness. In this chapter, we address each of these issues in turn, and in doing so, develop propositions along the way that contribute to an emerging theoretical framework for working in loosely structured team-based collaborative endeavors, and that highlight the positive organizational behaviors and outcomes that may be related to the unique contextual features of these collaborations.

Each of the relationships we propose has implications for boundary issues in collaborations and positive organizational themes. For example, we note that mobility across boundaries in collaborative entities often entails the development of multiple identities. As noted in Roberts and Creary (2010, p. 23), this resulting multiplicity and complexity of identities may result in positive organizational outcomes. They argue that, through the use of "identity expansion," a shared understanding may emerge "especially in situations where mistaken assumptions regarding the membership, significance, or valence of another person's multiple identities surface." Additionally, positive organizational attributes such as high quality connections may be one of the mechanisms through which boundary mobility has an impact on outcomes such as collaboration effectiveness. That is, the frequent movement across the boundaries of team-based collaborations may allow individuals to engage in short-term, high-quality connections. Stephens, Heaphy, and Dutton (2011, Chapter 29, this volume) have argued that the short-term nature of high-quality connections (in which individuals are interdependent but may not know one another well) may be associated with coordination and error detection that may result in enhanced performance of temporary work teams.

A key motivation for this research is to identify ways that participants in the current organizational environment, which is characterized more and more by short stints of engagement, temporary work, and brief contractual relationships, can find personal meaning, establish a professional identity, and enjoy commitment and success in each of their temporary collaborative endeavors. As illustrated in our arguments and propositions below, our point of view is that this is indeed possible!

Margins and Membership: Defining Boundaries

Group boundaries have been defined in a variety of ways in the literature. In traditional organizations, team boundaries are relatively clear. Hackman (2002) defined teams as groups of individuals working interdependently, with clear boundaries and membership stability. Similarly, Raven (2003, p. 294) noted that, in teams, "the distinction between members and nonmembers tends to be clear." However, with the emergence of more temporary, fluid, and dynamic forms of organizing, defining the boundaries of collaborative work has become more complex. New technologies, fast-changing markets, and global competition are revolutionizing business relationships; as companies blur their traditional boundaries to respond to this more fluid business environment, the roles that people play at work and the tasks they perform become correspondingly blurred and ambiguous (Hirschhorn & Gilmore, 1992, p. 5).

As a starting point, we begin with the definition of boundaries provided by Sundstrom, De Meuse, and Futrell (1990, p. 120), who described them as "features that (a) differentiate a work unit from others (Cherns, 1976); (b) pose real or symbolic barriers to access or transfer of information, goods, or people (Katz & Kahn, 1978); or (c) serve as points of external exchange with other teams, customers, peers, competitors, or other entities (Friedlander, 1987)." Continuing from the example above, participants who are volunteers or direct employees of the home building collaboration might be considered "internal," and those participants who are employed by an external entity and are contracted as a point of exchange to provide resources might be considered as "external." However, this distinction offered by Sundstrom et al. is not entirely clear in team-based collaborations such as this, because those who are contracted "externally" may in fact stay with the collaboration for as long (or longer) than those who were considered internal. Likewise, those who are "internal" may shift from collaboration to collaboration, or work on several simultaneously, and hence do not pose a point of differentiation for it, nor a symbolic barrier to it.

Ancona, Bresman, and Kaeufer (2002) provide a variation of this definition, defining the boundaries between the three tiers in their X-teams in the following way: *core members* are generally present at the start of the team, carry the team's history and identity, coordinate multiple parts of the team, create strategy, and make key decisions; *operational members* do the ongoing work, are often tightly connected to one another as well as to core members, and leave team oversight to the core; *outer-net members* often join the team to help with a particular task that is separable from the ongoing work, are generally loosely connected to one another but tightly connected to core members, bring specialized expertise, and may come and go as the nature of the team's task changes. Again, although some aspects of this conceptualization of boundaries apply in our home building example, it is difficult to determine whether any "core members" truly exist (given that the collaboration is so temporary and members lack any shared history); some of those individuals who are "external" may also be "operational"; and many of those who consider themselves "internal" may also be very short-term (and hence "outer-net")! Hence, we need to revisit these existing conceptualizations to better understand the nature of membership in loosely structured team-based collaborations.

Mobility

Other research has grappled with the challenge that boundaries present, not only because they are hard to define, but because they likely are permeable. Individuals may move across boundaries during the course of collaborating. For example, Sundstrom et al. (1990, p. 130) have argued that the group boundary "needs continual management to ensure that it becomes neither too sharply delineated nor too permeable, so that the team neither becomes isolated nor loses its identity." As noted above, collaboration boundaries might define participants who are directly affiliated with a collaborative entity to be internal, whereas those who are contracted from an external entity to provide resources for the collaboration may be considered external. However, this definition, as it applies to individual participants, may evolve as other criteria for internal status shift. For example, a change by an external participant in the percentage of time spent working for the focal entity, a change in the level of commitment to it, a shift in the primary purpose of working for the focal collaboration, or a change in the visibility of the external participant to recipients or key stakeholders may trigger a change in a participant's situation (i.e., internal vs. external).

Within the context of a team-based collaboration, it is likely that some external constituents will become so tightly connected to the collaborative endeavor that they may come to view themselves (and be viewed by others) as internal rather than external to the collaboration, effectively migrating across the boundary from one side to the other. An example of this might include a contract worker such as Diego (described in the opening example), who interacts on a regular basis with the internal members, has come to share similar goals and values with internal collaboration members, and works in close physical proximity to the end product. Such an example might also be found in the context of film making, in which a collaboration may commission the composition of a musical score to an independent, external musician. However, during the course of film production, the score writer may become such an integral part of the ability to fulfill the collaboration's central purpose that, despite the fact that this individual was afforded only a peripheral role as an independent contractor, she may begin to assume a role that is much more core to achieving the vision of the collaboration.

Ancona et al. (2002, p. 36) described mobility across boundaries in their theory of X-teams. They noted that "people may move in and out of the team during its life or move across layers." They provided an example of a product development team member who began as an external member (a member of the "outer-net" in their terminology) whose initial involvement entailed advising about components, then evolved to participation in product manufacturing, and concluded with his involvement as a leader and manager of the transition of other participants from one principal unit on the project to another. However, all members of X-teams exist within the context of an overarching organization (e.g., a company or firm), hence the "layers" of membership are more subtle. In team-based collaborative endeavors, in which all members may have different organizational affiliations (or no organizational affiliation), these distinctions are more difficult to migrate and may have even more pronounced results for identity, commitment, empowerment, thriving, and collaboration effectiveness.

Conversely, it is possible that some collaboration participants who may meet a collaboration's definition of an internal participant may become more peripheral and begin to be viewed as more external.

Individuals being integrated at later stages of the collaborative endeavor, individuals who do not share a similar passion for the collaborative vision, or participants who do not share a critical demographic dimension that is shared by all other collaboration members may have a harder time achieving full integration and internal participant status. Or, participants who begin as internal participants may migrate across the boundary to be classified as external as the needs of the project evolve.

Hence, one of the challenges associated with blurred boundaries is the difficulty that might be encountered in forming a professional identity. In the context of traditional teams, Sundstrom and colleagues (1990) argued that when boundaries become too loose, teams may become overwhelmed and may lose their identity. Further, Choi (2002, p. 182) noted that integration with external actors (e.g., boundary blurring) may "decrease the team's cohesiveness because 'external communication may signal an identification with outsiders' (Keller, 2001, p. 553)." Movement across boundaries (i.e., from external to internal status or vice versa) may also create challenges such as the need to redefine one's identity. This may be particularly problematic when such movement entails relinquishing internal status and moving to a more external role when one's skill set becomes less relevant or salient to the immediate needs of the collaboration.

However, these challenges notwithstanding, prior work has failed to address the many potential benefits of the blurring and migration across boundaries. Loosely structured, temporary team-based collaborations are becoming a fact of organizational life. If we take this as a given, what might be the upside of these organizational forms? The ability to move across boundaries may present opportunities at the individual and collaboration levels of analysis. For example, at the collaboration level, there may be less need for a large internal body of membership (and hence, an expensive payroll) if this type of mobility exists, allowing externally contracted participants to become more central (i.e., internal) as needed and returning to external status once their role is completed. From a participant's perspective, this type of arrangement may provide an opportunity that is simultaneously inclusive and enriching. That is, these participants may be able to enjoy many of the social benefits of working in teams without the limitations inherent in being tied to a single organization or position. Further, there may be underutilized benefits available to collaborative organizational forms with permeable boundaries, such as the ability to engage people who are both loosely affiliated and highly committed. We next examine the relationships between boundary mobility and identity, commitment, empowerment, and thriving, as well as the relationship between boundary mobility and collaboration effectiveness.

Identity

With regard to the relationship between individual identity and boundary mobility, we address the question of whether the ability to migrate across the boundaries of a collaboration (e.g., from internal collaborator to external collaborator or vice versa) will impact a participant's identification with the collaboration. Such a shift from external to internal status might entail a change by an external participant in the percentage of time he or she spends working for the collaboration, a change in his or her level of commitment to the collaboration, a shift in the primary purpose of working for the collaboration, working in closer proximity to a key deliverable, or becoming more visible to recipients or key stakeholders. A shift from internal to external status might entail a core volunteer returning to work in another organization or collaboration once her portion of the work is completed, a contractor taking on work for a different collaboration once his work for the collaboration has been accomplished, or a member of a supplier or customer organization returning to her primary organization or collaboration once the development phase of a collaboration's work is complete. We argue here that the ability to migrate across the boundaries of a collaboration will result in both internal and external participants having a stronger identification with the collaboration.

Drawing upon social identity theory (e.g., Tajfel, 1982; Tajfel & Turner, 1979), the identification with a collaboration by an internal or external participant may occur as a result of the collaborator feeling that association with the collaboration enhances "the positivity of their social identity and their self-esteem" (Sedikides, 1997, p. 126). Further, the opportunity for mobility across collaboration boundaries creates the possibility of developing and maintaining multiple collaborative or organizational identities. The literature on multiple identities (e.g., Turner, 1987) suggests that an individual has multiple self-concepts that form a cognitive system in which each part is different and can function independently of the others. Additionally, Fahr et al. (1998) have noted that individuals develop multiple identities, and that these various identities will have different degrees of salience depending on the social context. Hence, engaging simultaneously in multiple collaborative projects in both internal and external capacities, as well as shifting between internal and external membership in any given collaboration may allow for the development of such a multiplicity of professional identities. Further, we argue that the possibility of migrating across collaboration boundaries (i.e., being both internal and external to the collaboration at different points in time) may not only provide a multifaceted professional identity for participants in temporary entities, but may simultaneously be liberating and enriching, as this provides the opportunity to be engaged with multiple collaborative endeavors, each with varying and dynamic levels of intensity and engagement.

Beyond the idea that it is possible for an individual to identify with multiple collaborations, and that the ability to migrate across collaboration boundaries allows for this, we argue that the ability to migrate across collaboration boundaries will be associated with *greater* identification with a collaboration by both internal and external participants. This may be the case for a variety of reasons. Some literature has suggested that interaction with others outside of the group (which may be indicative of a blurred boundary) may serve to enhance group identity. For example, Choi (2002) has noted that group identity is the manifestation of a group's inherent propensity to differentiate itself from other groups in its environment by creating its own workspace, task structure, rules, and goals (Sundstrom et al., 1990). Choi (2002) has also argued that, through the process of social comparison, interactions with others may serve to sharpen these distinctions. Drawing upon this argument, we suggest that the more mobility across collaboration boundaries, the more frequently internal members will interact with external collaborators, and hence, have the opportunity to differentiate their work on the focal collaboration from other efforts. Stated another way, the ability to cross collaboration boundaries may allow for meaningful contact with a broader range of collaboration participants (both internal and external) than a collaborator might experience when participating on just one side of the collaboration boundary. A deeper connection with a greater proportion of collaboration participants may be associated with a stronger identification with a collaboration (Dutton, Dukerich, & Harquail, 1994). Hence, we propose that:

P1: The ability to migrate across collaboration boundaries (i.e., from internal to external and vice versa) will be associated with greater identification with a collaboration.

Commitment

Mowday et al. (1982) defined commitment as an individual's involvement in and identification with a particular organization, operationalized as motivation, identification, and intent to remain with an organization. Prior research has focused on the use of a core–periphery model (Atkinson, 1984; Nesbit, 2005) designed to allow organizations to achieve the dual objectives of maintaining employee commitment and also enhancing workforce flexibility. "Using this strategy, organizations seek to establish long-term employment relations with part of their workforce, a core of regular permanent workers with whom they seek commitment and motivation, while at the same time achieving labour cost effectiveness and varying degrees of numeric flexibility through the use of non-standard employment relations such as part-time, temporary, and contract workers" (Nesbit, 2005, p. 3). Further, Benson (1998) found empirical evidence that contract workers can have a dual commitment to their employer and the host firm for which they are working.

We extend this research by suggesting that it may be possible to achieve commitment among non-standard, peripheral workers (or "external collaboration participants" in the context of this research), as well as develop and maintain commitment from internal participants as a result of mobility across boundaries. That is, by making it possible for participants to migrate across the collaboration boundary (e.g., to go from internal to external status or vice versa), it may be possible to enhance the commitment of external collaborators as well as those who are more permanently situated near the core of the collaboration. This may be true because collaboration participants who begin as external participants and who are kept at arm's length may feel little sense of ownership in the work they do. Even if they share similar values and aspirations vís a vís the collaboration, without the option of fully engaging as a more central participant, external collaborators may have less incentive to fully commit. On the other hand, when external participants view the boundaries of the collaboration as permeable, and when external participants share a similar sense of values and vision with core collaboration members, it is likely that they will increase their commitment and engage more fully in the collaboration.

Further, collaborations with greater boundary mobility may provide greater freedom for internal collaborators who have the latitude to disengage for periods of time to pursue other endeavors and re-engage with the collaboration as needed. This type of freedom may prove to be richly rewarding and liberating, creating a greater affinity and appreciation for membership in a collaboration and, as a result, a greater sense of commitment. Pittinsky and Shih (2004, p. 794) examined "the possibility of organizational commitment *amid* worker mobility, instead of organizational commitment *at the expense of* worker mobility" and found empirical evidence of workers who are both strongly committed and highly mobile. They argued that "like nomadic people, Knowledge Nomads [similar to our concept of external collaborators] move frequently from place to place. But also, like nomadic people, they build homes and attachments to places when they stop. Knowledge Nomads are attached and committed to the organization while they are there, participating actively in the organizational community and working toward the organization's goals." They cite others (e.g., Kanter, 1995; Jones, 1996) who have either implicitly or explicitly suggested shifting the emphasis on organizationally bounded commitment to instead focusing on commitment to careers or projects. Although Pittinsky and Shih's (2004) research was conducted at the organizational level of analysis, we believe these arguments also have relevance for commitment and mobility in collaborative endeavors. That is, like the Knowledge Nomads, external collaborators will also likely find meaning, attachment, and fulfillment in their participation in temporary, collaborative endeavors. Hence, we propose the following:

> P2: The possibility of movement across collaboration boundaries (i.e., from external status to internal status or vice versa) will be associated with greater commitment from internal and external collaboration participants.

Boundary Mobility and Positive Organizational Behavior

One of the core missions of POS has been to identify the antecedents to and processes under which positively deviant outcomes occur, at both the individual and organizational levels of analysis. *Positive organizational behavior* is a subset of POS, focused specifically on positive individual-level states (Dutton, Glynn, & Spreitzer, 2006). Research in this domain has sought to discover the conditions under which individuals' careers flourish, individual functioning is optimized, episodes of career thriving take place, and where people view their jobs and careers as callings (Dutton et al., 2006). We contribute to this quest here by theoretically examining the impact of boundary mobility on empowerment and thriving. We develop two propositions with this goal in mind.

Empowerment

Empowerment has been defined as the act of distributing power (Druskat & Wheeler, 2003). We argue here that where extensive boundary mobility exists, collaborators will experience greater empowerment. The sheer complexity of managing these evolving roles and relationships may require anyone with formal power (i.e., a designated leader of the collaboration) to allow discretion, autonomy, and self-determination among those he or she leads (Gluesing & Gibson, 2004). In the opening example, as Diego became a more central member of the home building collaboration, Maria (who was not formally the leader of the group) was empowered to take on more leadership responsibility to facilitate the interaction between Diego and other core collaboration members. Further, as external collaborators are brought in to fill a particular need within the collaboration, they will likely at times (as Diego did in the opening example) take on leadership roles within the collaboration, thereby participating in the distribution of power as both recipients and distributors. Based on these ideas, we offer the following proposition.

> P3: Boundary mobility (the *possibility* of crossing the collaboration boundary from internal to external and vice versa) will enhance empowerment among both internal and external collaborators.

Thriving

When individuals thrive at work, their experience may be characterized by progress, momentum, increased understanding and knowledge, and a sense of vitality (Spreitzer et al., 2005). Thriving has been identified as "an adaptive function that helps individuals navigate and change their work contexts to promote their own development" (Spreitzer et al., 2005, p. 537). Further, Spreitzer et al. (2005, p. 539) have argued that thriving is socially embedded, and that learning (a critical element of thriving) "takes place through the social interactions that bind us together with others, both inside and outside the organizations in which we work." Hence, if thriving is contingent primarily upon a sense of vitality and opportunities for socially embedded learning, boundary mobility likely serves as a contextual feature that enhances participants' ability to thrive. That is, opportunities to move across collaboration boundaries and engage with individuals with a broad variety of skills, experiences, and organizational or collaborative affiliations will serve to add interest and variety to a collaborator's role, but also will serve to increase his or her chances for learning and development. Positive organizational scholarship suggests that there may be "many positively deviant workers who are energized by the opportunity to break out of old patterns and do something really different and meaningful" (Dutton et al., 2006, p. 8). Additionally, Spreitzer et al. (2005) noted that participation in a context that allows for broad information sharing (among other factors) will be associated with agentic behaviors that are likely to promote thriving. These ideas are reflected in the following proposition.

> P4: Boundary mobility (the possibility of crossing the collaboration boundary from internal to external and vice versa) will enhance individual thriving for both internal and external collaborators.

Collaboration Effectiveness

Outcomes such as empowerment and thriving are only a few of the many virtues and strengths to be found in collaborative settings that are important "not only as means to the desired end of strong economic performance, but also as ends worthy of explanation on their own" (Dutton et al., 2006, p. 6). Nevertheless, one critical issue to be addressed with respect to defining collaboration membership and the ramifications of boundary mobility is the impact that the ability to move across collaboration boundaries may have on collaboration effectiveness. Here, we propose that collaborations with more permeable boundaries will demonstrate more overall effectiveness than will collaborations with less permeable boundaries. This may be the case for several reasons. First, drawing upon the resource-based theory of the firm (e.g., Penrose, 1959), we argue that, if firms are to compete through the development of unique assets and knowledge, this suggests the need to outsource activities that are not central to a firm's resource base and to develop alliances with individuals, organizations, or other collaborations that have the potential to assist the collaboration to expand into novel areas (Rubery et al., 2002). Bringing on external collaborators serves these purposes—allowing a collaboration to outsource noncore functions and be introduced to novel practices and ideas.

Further, we argue that engaging external experts and allowing them to migrate from the periphery to the core of the firm will be associated with a collaboration's accumulation of new information, skills, and social networks that have been tried and proven to be essential to the collaboration. In this case, by incorporating new core collaboration membership through the periphery, a collaboration is able to examine external participants' fit with the collaboration with respect to shared values, commitment to the collaborative endeavor, and the fit of a particular skill set before engaging them in a more permanent collaboration–collaborator arrangement, which may involve the external participant assuming a more central position. In support of this, Rubery et al. (2002, p. 655) have argued that "permeable organizations may provide an effective means of learning and knowledge acquisition in situations where these are significant factors in competitiveness. . . ." Hence, we propose that:

> P5: Collaborations with permeable boundaries will be more effective than those with less permeable boundaries.

Membership at the Margins

Although some collaborations' boundaries are quite permeable, other collaborations are characterized by more rigid boundaries between internal and external members. However, even in such collaborative entities, it may be possible for external members to operate effectively at the margins and contribute to overall collaboration effectiveness. For example, a collaboration may contract with an external expert over the course of a long-term project. Consider the hypothetical example of a research consortium that has brought together a group of scholars to collaborate on the development of an emergent topic. Such a collaboration may have need of expertise in managing a large, complex data set. Rather than expend internal resources on database management, collaborators may opt to hire a database consultant who is a member of an external organization. During the course of this type of long-term research endeavor, the consultant may never be afforded formal membership in the consortium. However, due to her intimate familiarity with the subject matter, theory, and data under study, as well as frequent and meaningful interactions with consortium members, she may be able to comfortably span the boundary between her formal organizational affiliation and her external expert status with the research consortium. That is, although this expert may never actually become integrated into the core of the collaboration, she may continue to successfully fulfill a vital role. Based on collaborations that we have observed in action, some of the attributes of external collaborators who operate successfully at the margins of the collaboration include the ability to engage with a high

percentage of the collaboration's members on a frequent basis, the ability to adapt to changes in the collaboration's internal and external environment, the ability to span the boundary between core collaboration members and other external collaborators (e.g., people hired by the external collaborator), and the ability to identify with the collaborative endeavor despite other potentially conflicting identities.

Many of the critical characteristics needed by collaborators who reside at the boundaries are captured by the concept of *laterality*. Laterality is a skill that entails the individual ability to effectively relate and work with other individuals who may have different backgrounds, perspectives, and agendas, as well as the willingness to limit personal autonomy to achieve group goals that bring team or collaboration members together (Mankin, Cohen, & Bikson, 1996; Gibson & Dibble, 2008). Drawing upon these ideas, we argue that participants in collaborations with nonpermeable boundaries may not be devoid of the opportunities available to participants in collaborations with more boundary mobility. Rather, we argue that some of these same benefits achieved in collaborations with permeable boundaries can also be achieved in collaborations with nonpermeable boundaries when collaborators possess characteristics such as laterality. That is, collaborations that engage participants who are able to effectively relate to and communicate with individuals on both sides of the collaboration boundary may be able to avail themselves of the same benefits that accrue due to boundary mobility. These ideas are reflected in the following proposition.

> P6: Laterality may mitigate the negative effects of nonpermeable collaboration boundaries, such that when laterality exists, collaborations with nonpermeable boundaries achieve a similar level of effectiveness as do those collaborations with permeable boundaries (i.e., those in which participants have mobility across boundaries).

Discussion

In the current organizational climate, a deviation from traditional employer–employee relationships toward more complex organizational forms (including cross-organizational networking, partnerships, and the use of external agencies for both core and peripheral activities) (Rubery et al., 2002) has resulted in a need to rethink theories about identity, commitment, and collaboration effectiveness. Additionally, there has been a greater focus in recent years on the topic of positive organizational behavior, including an examination of ways in which organizations can foster empowerment, thriving, resilience, hope, confidence, optimism, and greater physical and mental well-being among organizational participants. We believe that research on boundaries in collaborative endeavors has particular relevance in this regard.

In this chapter, we proposed that boundary mobility (i.e., the ability for internal collaborators to move across collaboration boundaries to become external and vice versa) will be associated with greater identification with a collaboration among both internal and external collaborators. Hence, we argue that a permanent position in a traditional organization may not be the *only* way (or even the most *effective* way) for individuals to develop and sustain a sense of identity with the entity for which they work. Further, we argued that mobility across collaboration boundaries may be associated with greater collaboration commitment among both internal and external members. As commitment has been associated with positive outcomes such as decreased turnover intentions (Shore & Martin, 1989, cf. O'Reilly, 1991), decreased actual turnover (Farkas & Tetrick, 1989; O'Reilly & Chatman, 1986, cf. O'Reilly, 1991), and increased job performance (Meyer et al, 1989, cf. O'Reilly, 1991), understanding what drives commitment in collaborative endeavors is increasingly important. Additionally, there has been a growing interest in understanding features of organizing that contribute to enhanced physical and mental well-being among organizational participants. Here, we examined the impact of one prevalent characteristic of temporary collaborative endeavors—boundary mobility—on some of these features. Specifically, we proposed that boundary mobility will be positively associated with collaborator empowerment and participant thriving in the context of temporary collaborative endeavors.

Future Directions
We encourage empirical examination of the ideas presented above. Additionally, future research should examine ways in which collaborations establish a group identity in the midst of boundary mobility. Although contract and temporary workers often join an existing organization and may adapt their identities to fit into a preexisting organization, group formation in the context of a collaboration may present unique challenges. Given that many or all of the members of a collaboration may be unaffiliated with any organization, that membership may be very fluid, and that boundaries may be permeable, establishing a "group" identity may provide an interesting challenge, unique to team-based collaborative endeavors. Future research might examine how such group identities develop, as well as the potential for forming *strong* identities in short-lived, team-based collaborations, and the impact that group identity has on effectiveness in these contexts.

Additionally, future research should examine moderators of the relationships between boundary mobility and positive organizational outcomes. For example, it is possible that the relationship between boundary mobility and empowerment may be moderated by contextual conditions of the collaboration. In contexts in which collaborations work together virtually and formal leaders are well-connected to collaborators during critical decisions, this relationship may look different from face-to-face collaborations, in which the physical absence of a formal leader at critical junctures may necessitate greater empowerment. Additionally, the relationship between boundary mobility and thriving may be moderated by personality dimensions. For example, extraverted individuals may be more likely to seek out and experience social interactions that promote learning, high-quality connections, and other interactions related to frequent boundary crossing, which may be associated with thriving.

Conclusion
In conclusion, the inclusion of participants who function either at, or outside, the boundary surrounding core collaboration participants presents some important challenges and opportunities. In this chapter we have focused on the ways in which boundary mobility may be liberating. We suggested that defining margins and membership, as well as understanding the implications of mobility across the margins, have important implications for effectiveness and well-being at the individual and collaboration levels of analysis. For example, achieving both resource flexibility and participant commitment may not be mutually exclusive objectives, but may both be achieved by facilitating mobility across collaboration boundaries. We hope we have inspired scholars and practitioners to rethink current models describing team and organizational processes, as margins become blurred, defining membership becomes a subjective task, and mobility across the margins becomes the norm.

References
Ancona, D., Bresman, H., & Kaeufer, K. (2002). The comparative advantage of X-teams. *MIT Sloan Management Review, 43*(3), 33–39.

Atkinson, J. (1984). Manpower strategies for flexible firms. *Personnel Management, 16,* 28–31.

Benson, J. (1998). Dual commitment: Contract workers in Australian manufacturing enterprises. *Journal of Management Studies, 35*(3), 355–375.

Cherns, A. (1976). The principles of sociotechnical design. *Human Relations, 29,* 783–792.

Choi, J.N. (2002). External activities and team effectiveness: Review and theoretical development. *Small Group Research, 33,* 181–208.

Druskat, V.U., & Wheeler, J.V. (2003). Managing from the boundary: The effective leadership of self-managing work teams. *Academy of Management Journal, 46*(4), 435–457.

Dutton, J.E., Dukerich, J.M., & Harquail, C.V. (1994). Organizational images and member identification. *Administrative Science Quarterly, 39,* 239–263.

Dutton, J.E., Glynn, M.A., & Spreitzer, G. (2006). In J. Greenhaus & G. Callahan, (Eds.), *Encyclopedia of career development.* Thousand Oaks, CA: Sage.

Fahr, J., Tsui, A., Xin, K., & Cheng, B. (1998). The influence of relational demography and guanxi: The Chinese case, *Organization Science, 9*(4), 471–488.

Farkas, A.J., & Tetrick, L.E. (1989). A three-wave longitudinal analysis of the causal ordering of satisfaction and commitment on turnover decisions. *Journal of Applied Psychology, 74,* 855–868.

Friedlander, F. (1987). The ecology of work groups. In J. Lorsch (Ed.), *Handbook of organizational behavior* (pp. 301–314). Englewood Cliffs, NJ: Prentice-Hall.

Gibson, C.B., & Dibble, R. (2008). Culture inside and out: Developing the collective capability to externally adjust. In S. Ang, & L. Van Dyne (Eds.), *Advances in cultural intelligence* (pp. 221–240). New York: Sharpe.

Gluesing, J., & Gibson, C.B. (2004). Designing and forming global teams. In M. Maznevski, H. Lane, & M. Mendenhall (Eds.), *Handbook of cross–cultural management* (pp. 199–226). Oxford: Blackwell Publishing.

Hackman, J.R. (2002). *Leading teams: Setting the stage for great performances.* Boston: Harvard Business School Press.

Hefke, M., & Stojanovic, L. (2004). An ontology-based approach for competence bundling and composition of ad-hoc teams in an organization. *Proceedings of the 4th International Conference of Knowledge Management, Gratz, Austria,* 126–134.

Hirschhorn, L., & Gilmore, T. (1992). The new boundaries of the "boundaryless" company. *Harvard Business Review, May-June,* 4–16.

Jones, C. (1996). Careers in project networks: The case of the film industry. In M.B. Arthur, & D. Rousseau (Eds.), *The boundaryless career: A new employment principle for a new organizational era* (pp. 58–75). New York: Oxford University Press.

Kanter, R.M. (1995). Nice work if you can get it. *The American Prospect, 23,* 52–58.

Katz, D., & Kahn, R.L. (1978). *The social psychology of organizations* (2nd ed.). New York: Wiley.

Keller, R.T. (2001). Cross-functional project groups in research and new product development: Diversity, communications, job stress, and outcomes. *Academy of Management Journal, 44,* 547–555.

Lumsden, A.J. (2004). *The role and responsibilities of directors on board sub-committees.* Retrieved from SSRN: http://ssrn.com/abstract=990201.

Mankin, D., Cohen, S.G., & Bikson, T.K. (1996). Teams and technology: Tensions in participatory design. *CEO Publication, G,* 96–95 (299).

Meyer, J.P., Paunonen, S.V., Gellatly, I.R., Goffin, R.D., & Jackson, D.N. (1989). Organizational commitment and job performance: It's the nature of the commitment that counts. *Journal of Applied Psychology, 74,* 152–156.

Nesbit, P.L. (2005). HRM and the flexible firm: Do firms with "high performance" work cultures utilize peripheral work arrangements? *International Journal of Employment Studies, 13*(2), 1–17.

O'Reilly, C.A. III. (1991). Organizational behavior: Where we've been, where we're going. *Annual Review of Psychology, 42,* 427–458.

O'Reilly, C.A. III., & Chatman, J.A. (1986). Organizational commitment and psychological attachment: The effects of compliance, identification, and internalization on pro-social behavior. *Journal of Applied Psychology, 71,* 492–499.

Penrose, E. (1959). *The theory of the growth of the firm.* Oxford: Blackwell.

Pittinsky, T.L., & Shih, M.J. (2004). Knowledge nomads: Organizational commitment and worker mobility in positive perspective. *American Behavioral Scientist, 47,* 791–807.

Raven, A. (2003). Team or community of practice. In C.B. Gibson, & S.G. Cohen (Eds.), *Virtual teams that work: Creating conditions for virtual team effectiveness* (pp. 292–306). San Francisco: Jossey-Bass.

Roberts, L.M. & Creary, S.J. (2010). Positive individual identities: Insights from classical and contemporary theoretical perspectives. In K.S. Cameron & G. Spreitzer (Eds.), *Handbook of positive organizational scholarship.* Oxford, UK: Oxford University Press.

Rubery, J., Earnshaw, J., Marchington, M., Cooke, F.L., & Vincent, S. (2002). Changing organizational forms and the employment relationship. *Journal of Management Studies, 39*(5), 645–672.

Sedikides, C. (1997). Differential processing of ingroup and outgroup information: The role of relative group status in permeable boundary groups. *European Journal of Social Psychology, 27,* 121–144.

Shenhar, A.J. (2001). Contingent management in temporary, dynamic organizations: The comparative analysis of projects. *Journal of High Technology Management Research, 12,* 239–271.

Shore, L.M., & Martin, H.J. (1989). Job satisfaction and organizational commitment in relation to work performance and turnover intentions. *Human Relations, 42,* 625–638.

Spreitzer, G., Sutcliffe, K. Dutton, J., Sonenshein, S., & Grant, A.M. (2005). A socially embedded model of thriving at work. *Organization Science, 16*(5), 537–562.

Stephens, J.P., Heaphy, E., & Dutton, J.E. (2011). High-quality connections. In K.S. Cameron & G.M. Spreitzer (Eds.), The Oxford handbook of positive organizational scholarship. New York: Oxford University Press.

Sundstrom, E., De Meuse, K.P., & Futrell, D. (1990). Work teams: Applications and effectiveness. *The American Psychologist, 45*(2), 120–133.

Tajfel, H. (Ed.). (1982). *Social identity and intergroup relations.* Cambridge: Cambridge University Press.

Tajfel, H., & Turner, J.C. (1979). An integrative theory of intergroup conflict. In W.G. Austin, & S. Worchel (Eds.), *The social psychology of intergroup relations* (pp. 33–47). Monterey, CA: Brooks/Cole.

Zuckerman, D.S., & Higgins, M.B. (2002). Optimizing cross-organizational team performance and management. *Pharmaceutical Technology, 26*(6), 76–80.

PART 7

Positive Leadership and Change

The Spirits of Organization Development, or Why OD Lives Despite Its Pronounced Death

Jean M. Bartunek *and* Richard W. Woodman

Abstract

In Charles Dickens' book *A Christmas Carol*, Scrooge was visited by three Spirits, of the past, present, and future, who, by means of dire warnings, inspired him to reform his life. In this chapter, we describe four Spirits of organization development (OD) who, despite dire predictions of OD's demise over the past 30 years, suggest why OD still lives and why it is likely to continue to do so. These are the Spirits of organizing, practice, scholar–practitioner links, and paradox. We develop the positive contributions of these Spirits and suggest their importance for the vitality of OD's ongoing work.

Keywords: Organization development, organizing, practice, scholar practitioner, whole person

> Marley was dead, to begin with. There is no doubt whatever about that. The register of his burial was signed by the clergyman, the clerk, the undertaker, and the chief mourner. Scrooge signed it. And Scrooge's name was good upon 'Change, for anything he chose to put his hand to. Old Marley was as dead as a door-nail.
> —Charles Dickens, *A Christmas Carol*, 1843

No, it wasn't Marley who was dead. It was organization development (OD) that was dead, or very nearly so. There was no doubt whatever about that. Its demise, or at least its forthcoming replacement by something better, was signed by academics and practitioners alike, all people whose names were good upon 'change. It was signed by Burke (1976), who thought that the term OD might have run its course and perhaps would be replaced by quality of work interventions or quality of working life; by Jones and Pfeiffer (1977), who said that the term "organization development" was obsolete and should be replaced by more descriptive terms; and by Porras and Silvers (1991, p. 70) who suggested that organizational transformation was "second generation OD," an advancement over it. It was signed by Worren, Ruddle, and Moore (1999), who described how OD was being eclipsed by change

management; by Weidner (2004, p. 37), who saw OD as "a brand in dire straits" that is "at the margins of business, academe, and practice" with "no identifiable voice"; by Bunker, Alban, and Lewicki (2004), who described how OD's well of ideas had run dry; and by Greiner and Cummings (2004, p. 375) who questioned OD's future, given all the "troubling signs" that "suggest its possible demise." It was signed by Cox (2005), who feared that all the talk about OD's death would lead to a self-fulfilling prophecy; by Harvey (2005), who argued that someone "should take the tubes out of grandma," a phrase with contemporary currency, at least in the United States (no health care reform for OD!); by Argyris (2005), who said that its demise was due to the reasoning mindsets that OD practitioners typically use; and by Beitler (2007), who quite bluntly declared OD dead.

What is this thing called OD that has attracted so many predictions of its imminent demise? In the broadest sense, OD is both a "field of social action and an area of scientific inquiry" (Cummings & Worley, 2009, p. 1). Most professionals in the field would consider the following definition to have it about right: "Organization development is a systemwide application and transfer of behavioral science knowledge to the planned development, improvement, and reinforcement of the strategies, structures, and processes that lead to organization effectiveness; Cummings & Worley, 2009, pp. 1–2".

OD isn't a cat. It's not supposed to have nine lives. So, why in the *dickens* isn't it dead as a doornail? Or, to borrow a phrase from the vernacular, why does OD appear to be on its "second cat"? Why, despite the dire prognoses, does it still exhibit multiple signs of energy and life, even thriving (Spreitzer, Sutcliffe, Dutton, Sonenshein, & Grant, 2005)? Why is NTL (NTL Institute of Applied Behavioral Science, the source of much of the early development of OD) still active? Why are thousands of people actively involved in the OD Network and its regional affiliates? Why are large group interventions (Bunker & Alban, 1992, 2005; Manning & DelaCerda, 2003), and especially appreciative inquiry (Barrett & Fry, 2005; Cooperrider & Srivastava, 1987; Yeager, Sorensen, & Bengtsson, 2005) so popular around the world? Why are so many practitioner-oriented doctoral programs that emphasize OD springing up?

In *A Christmas Carol*, Marley sent three Spirits to warn Scrooge what would happen to him if he didn't change his ways. In this chapter, which, after all, is in a book that focuses on the positive, we ask four contemporary "Spirits"—of organizing, practice, scholar–practitioner links, and paradox—to suggest some reasons why OD is alive and well and might reasonably be expected to live and prosper for some time to come.

These Spirits aren't signs of OD simply being propped up, with death staved off for a little while. Rather, taking a positive approach to our subject, we want to examine how OD fully lives. Fittingly, we examine the field of OD through the lens of positive organizational scholarship (POS), which has been described, succinctly, as "the investigation of positive dynamics, positive attributes, and positive outcomes in organizations" (Cameron, 2008, p. 7). After all, OD has emphasized positive potentials in organizations throughout its history (e.g., Beckhard, 1969; French & Bell, 1995).

Toward this end, we advance four straightforward propositions for examination, one proposition for each Spirit:

- *Proposition 1:* The Spirit of Organizing: Organization development lives because it deals with a "core issue" of organizing.
- *Proposition 2:* The Spirit of Practice: Organization development lives because people keep using it. (We know this statement appears somewhat tautological, but bear with us.)
- *Proposition 3:* The Spirit of Scholar–Practitioner Links: Organization development lives because it effectively bridges the scholar–practitioner gap.
- *Proposition 4:* The Spirit of Paradox: Organization development lives because it engages paradox more effectively than most change approaches and philosophies.

The Spirit of Organizing

Organizations, particularly large ones, have a wonderful complexity. They may employ a rich diversity of human beings. They may operate in numerous economies and cultures around the world. They may possess a bewildering variety of processes, procedures, and goals both large and small. Their organizing structure—their "architecture"—may be almost a work of art. All of this real complexity may blind the student of organizations (read: organizational scientist) to a corresponding simplicity that also exists. There are fundamental tasks that all organizations, regardless of their purpose and complexity, must do reasonably well in order to exist. We call these fundamental tasks the "core issues" of organizing (Woodman, 1993, 2008).

As an example, consider that, no matter how elaborate and complex the design or architecture of an organization, all structure *must* do two fundamental, simple-to-understand things: divide up the work among the people doing it and coordinate their activities toward some common purpose (Thompson, 1967). Other examples of core issues include work process and system design, assessing individual and team performance, resource and reward allocation, employee participation and commitment—and managing change. Complex social systems are constantly changing. Thus, we regard the "management" of change as another core issue of organizing.

In addition to being so fundamental that all organizations must address them, another distinguishing characteristic of core issues is that they have the nasty habit of not remaining solved, but must be repeatedly addressed. The new performance appraisal and reward allocation system may work beautifully for a number of years, but the time will come when it will become suboptimal. The cutting-edge organizational architecture that so effectively allows the organization to adapt and change today will stifle it tomorrow. And so on.

So, the nature of the core issue of managing change could be regarded as the change agent's "full employment" act. Less tongue-in-cheek is the observation that organizations simply must do the things that OD was designed and created to do in order to remain (or become) effective. Organization development is not the only way to address organizational change, of course. Far from it. Nevertheless, considerable evidence with regard to OD's efficacy in changing organizations exists (e.g., Macy & Izumi, 1993; Robertson, Roberts, & Porras, 1993; Stebbins, Valenzuela, & Coget, 2009). Being able to deal effectively with "core issues" is crucial for organizational effectiveness and continued survival.

Organization development offers organizations ways of addressing the core issue of managing change that are robust across time and settings. Positive approaches to change, especially as embodied in large group interventions such as appreciative inquiry, have been very prominent in recent years. As Bushe and Marshak (2009) indicate, they have helped to lead OD away from a diagnostic focus on the negative that characterized early approaches to OD toward a more dialogical approach, based on social constructionist principles, that assumes that (p. 352) "social organization is open to infinite possibilities constrained only by the human imagination and collective will."

Listen! You can hear the "Spirit of organizing" speaking: "Organization development lives because it deals with a core issue of organizing."

The Spirit of Practice

The majority of the pronouncements of OD's death have come from academics or from practitioners who have an academic appointment. But what about working OD practitioners, both external consultants and OD professionals internal to their organization? It appears that, for many of them, OD is very much alive. We will develop two examples here, although there are many others as well.

Change Without Migraines

In late 2009, Jean had the opportunity to participate in a podcast with Rick Maurer, founder of the Change Management Open Source Project at http://introtochangewithoutmigraines.ning.com, an online community including about 400 members, primarily OD consultants, from about 20 different countries. Jean wondered whether OD was dead, and asked if other members of the online community had responses to the question. Several members responded at http://introtochangewithoutmigraines.ning.com/forum/topics/jean-bartunek-asks-is-od.

For example:

> I would suggest that OD is not dying; rather, the world as we've known it is about to end. But this is not a bad thing. In fact, this inevitable evolution creates a wonderful business opportunity for OD experts to help managers transition their organizations to succeed in the new and very different wiki world. . . . The new OD work will be more difficult because it involves changing the underlying social architecture that has remained constant for well over a century.

> I agree . . . that the domains for our work are in flux. I also agree that part of our work is to have familiarity with the new social architecture of the digital age. I am not sure that we need to be experts but we certainly need to bring something to this arena that adds value.

> For me, OD is not really dead but it languishes due in no small part to management having been directed by HR and senior managers to call on OD to be the 'fixer' of organizations. . . . viewing HR/OD as the 'fixer' results in management being forced (frequently colluding) to abdicate one of their primary organizational responsibilities—developing their organization.

Although these answers seem fairly clear about (some) OD practitioners' lack of agreement with the premise that OD is on its last legs, other discussions on this online forum about practitioner issues particularly contradict it. For example, Maurer asked forum members, "What are you looking for right now that's missing in all the books, etc.?" (http://introtochangewithoutmigraines.ning.com/forum/topics/ricks-big-question-about). This evoked a lively and thoughtful discussion about issues that academics typically do not address in ways that are helpful to practitioners, including "the tendency for change leaders to get pulled back into the daily operational demands too soon and too completely," "how to facilitate or lead or guide a team through major change, such that the team begins to learn from each other, from their customers and suppliers, from everywhere," and "as my company works only with social media for business . . . we have developed models that make change happen from both ends, so to speak. And the approach is absolutely not linear. It is an agile approach. We are testing it currently and it seems that this is working much better than other traditional change methodology(ies)." Many of the issues discussed here are absent from academic conversation.

The New Organization Development

In March 2010, Jean participated in a conference sponsored by NTL on "The new OD." The conference was fully subscribed (with a waiting list), primarily by practitioners, many of whom have received graduate degrees in practitioner-oriented doctoral and master-degree programs. Inspired by Bushe and Marshak's (2009) discussion of contemporary dialogic OD, they identified several opportunities and possible approaches for the development of OD. These include, among others, methods of organizing community leaders to transform their communities in the service of the larger society, developing ways that OD might be more directly involved in strategic change roles in their work organizations, working with discourse approaches to consulting, and making use of social media in consulting. Many of these were similar to the issues addressed in the online community.

Some of these topics are very congruent with POS directions. For example, Golden-Biddle and Dutton (in press) are editing a book on positive social change, and positive social change has already been addressed in some POS writings (e.g., Blatt & Camden, 2007; Cameron & Levine, 2006; McGinn, 2007). Further, the POS website (http://www.bus.umich.edu/Positive/) has available tools that OD practitioners are using, including reflected best self-feedback practices and job crafting.

Academics often wonder about the extent to which we should and can have impacts on practitioners (e.g., Rynes, Bartunek, & Daft, 2001). Rarely is the question reversed: How can and should practitioners have impacts on academics? For purposes of this chapter, the question can be reframed: How can the generativity embodied in OD practice impact academic thinking?

We suggest that OD practitioners who are dealing with serious day-to-day issues encountered by organizations have less luxury than academics do to obsess about questions within the more abstract academic realm, and that if academics pay attention to the issues practitioners are grappling with, they

may learn in ways that are pertinent to scholarly concerns (such as, for example, new developments in strategic change roles, relationships between social media and change). Certainly, it is an integral part of OD's legacy that learnings from practice inform scholarship (e.g., Lewin, 1951; Pasmore & Friedlander, 1982; Trist & Bamforth, 1951), and some of the newer work, such as large group interventions (e.g., Bunker & Alban, 2006; Holman, Devane, & Cady, 2007) can stimulate academic theorizing. What would be helpful now is devising contemporary means by which academics truly can learn practitioners' thinking patterns and rationales for their work.

The World of Practice Is Real

In any event, it is readily apparent that the world is full of people "doing" OD. It's not even that hard to find them (cf. McMahan & Woodman, 1992). They band together in networks of like-minded professionals (e.g., The OD Network). Some of them attend scholarly meetings and talk about what they are doing (for example, the Organization Development and Change Division of the Academy of Management currently has more than 500 practitioner members, many of whom are quite active). To an unbiased observer from another planet, it might seem like the academic/scholarly side of the field is constantly trying to "kill off" OD, but OD practitioners persist in keeping it alive through practicing it.

You can almost hear the "Spirit of practice" laughing at us: "Organization development lives because people keep using it."

The Spirit of Scholar–Practitioner Links

Despite frequent laments to the contrary, and despite the difficulties scholars may have understanding practitioners and practitioners understanding scholars (Pasmore, Woodman, & Simmons, 2008; Rynes et al., 2001; Van de Ven, 2007), OD is actually somewhat effective in bridging the scholar–practice gap. Tensions always exist between research and practice; these have been embodied in management schools for decades. Living with these tensions is not easy, as noted by the shifting stance of the founders of *Organization Science* (Daft & Lewin, 1990, 2008). But if they are handled appropriately, the tensions can be a sign of life, an index of activity, energy, and vitality (e.g., Lewis, 2000; Seo, Putnam, & Bartunek, 2004).

Organization development has been and continues to be at the forefront in linking scholarship and practice. This type of linkage is explicit in action research (Clark, 1972). It was a foundational principle for the *Journal of Applied Behavioral Science (JABS)* in 1965, and remains a central dimension of that journal's mission some 46 years later. For example, in 2005, the editor (Dick) stated that "The science of organizational change and the practice of OD, change management, and other applications of behavioral science knowledge sometimes exist in different worlds. We rededicate ourselves to the notion of bridging these worlds—of bringing together practical scholars and scholarly practitioners in meaningful dialogue" (Woodman, 2005, p. 8).

Academic–practitioner special issues are regularly published in *JABS* (e.g., Coghlan & Shani, 2009), and attempts are made to bridge academic–practitioner gaps, as in special issues on large group interventions and design science (Bunker & Alban, 1992, 2005; Bate, 2007). Organization development scholars' work has addressed academic–practice links for decades (e.g., Chris Argyris, Warner Burke, Ed Schein, Mike Beer, Barbara Bunker, Bill Pasmore). The Center for Effective Organizations at the University of Southern California (e.g., Lawler et al., 1985; Shani et al., 2008) is an explicit link, based on OD, to enable scholars and managers to collaborate. Further, it is from OD that the scholar–practitioner term has arisen and been developed (Wasserman & Kram, 2009). Most of the practitioner–scholar doctoral programs that have emerged in recent decades (e.g., at American University, Benedictine University, Cranfield University, George Washington University, Case Western Reserve University, FENIX, Saybrook University, and Fielding Graduate University) have links to OD.

Although balancing identities can be challenging, POS research suggests some potential benefits to individuals incorporating both scholar and practitioner identities. Scholar–practitioner is a type of complex identity, and Caza and Wilson (2009) suggest that such complexity might, in addition to tension, provide a buffer against adverse consequences of stress that come with one aspect of their identity.

For the organizational sciences to flourish, ongoing links must exist between scholarship and practice (Bartunek, 2007), and these are often embedded in individuals who take on both scholar and practitioner roles. Without OD, there would be much less institutionalized, long-term, enduring commitment to carrying out scholar–practitioner efforts. This bridging function, although far from perfect,

nevertheless brings constant renewal and energy to the field.

The "Spirit of scholar-practitioner links" smiles: "Organization development lives because it effectively bridges the scholar-practitioner gap."

The Spirit of Paradox

Allow us to anthropomorphize the organization for the moment. Society does this sort of thing all the time, of course. For example, in *Citizens United v. FEC,* the U.S. Supreme Court recently ruled—or "reaffirmed" depending on your politics—that the Constitutional right to free speech cannot be denied corporations. Academics anthropomorphize, too, when they write implications for practice that they expect "organizations" to carry out (Bartunek & Rynes, 2010).

Paradox of Whole People in Organizations

In the spirit of anthropomorphizing, we observe that organizations sometimes prefer to hire just a clever mind, or a skilled set of hands, or a strong back. But organizations cannot do that—they must employ the whole person. When the individual shows up for work, the organization gets the whole package, whether it wants it or not. The individual's personality, values, attitudes, cognitive map, information-processing capabilities, physical talents and limitations, all arrive at work. If the employee had a fight with her or his spouse last night—that comes along as well. If the person is a fantasy football or March Madness fanatic—that shows up too. There you have it, organization. That's the deal. Take it or leave it. It's with "whole people" that organizations must work to achieve their goals.

Now, one could argue that OD has always been about more than the "bottom line" in organizations. The earliest descriptions of OD stress the twin goals of changing organizations to make them more effective and improving the work experience of organizational members to make such work more fulfilling and satisfying. Formal definitions of OD typically stress the first of these objectives, whereas the underlying values of OD emphasize the second (cf. Cummings & Worley, 2009, pp. 1–14.) Needless to say, dialectical tensions can exist between these objectives. A primary and obvious concern is that it may be a challenge to attain a healthy balance in pursuit of these goals.

Beer and Nohria (2000) have offered a cogent and interesting argument for the importance of holding the tensions inherent in these goals. They suggest that organizations tend to approach change in essentially one of two dialectically opposed ways. "Theory E" approaches to organizational change emphasize the economic goals of the organization, manage change from the top, and tend to be highly structured in terms of process and procedures. "Theory O" approaches to organizational change emphasize the longer-term goal of developing organizational capabilities, are more participative and collaborative in change leadership, and are much less rigid in terms of process and procedures. Beer and Nohria provide numerous examples suggesting that an overemphasis on either the Theory E or Theory O change paradigm tends to produce a high probability of failure in the change or improvement effort. To survive and succeed, organizations must embrace this paradox by both creating value in the marketplace and developing the capabilities of their employees to function effectively, succeed, and, dare we say it, even be happy in their work. Their treatment of this complex duality mirrors the twin objectives of OD: to create effective organizations that are meaningful and rewarding for people–for whole people—to be a part of.

Paradox of Positive Organizational Change

Recent work on positive organizational change (Cameron, 2008) offers another paradox for OD. Considerable empirical evidence exists that there are natural tendencies toward the positive in human beings. As Cameron (2008, p. 11) states: "The inclination toward the positive . . . appears to characterize human beings in their thoughts, judgments, emotions, and language. A tendency toward the positive seems to be a natural human attribute, and empirical evidence suggests that positivity is the preferred and natural state of human beings, just as it is of biological systems." In a study of employees from a broad cross-section of jobs and organizations, Avey, Wernsing, and Luthans (2008) found that these employees' positive psychological capital (hope, optimism, resilience) and positive emotions were an important factor in reducing dysfunctional attitudes and behaviors during organizational change. Similarly, Gittell (2008), in a study in nine hospitals, found that positive relationships and "relational coordination" (operationalized as high levels of communication and strong task integration) led to higher degrees of organizational and work team resiliency in the face of work stressors stemming from external pressures.

All of this should bode well for OD, which, by most accounts, is a positive approach to organizational change with its emphasis on shared decision making, high levels of participation and collaboration, human growth and fulfillment through the work experience, and so on. But not so fast. The other side of the paradox that Cameron (2008) explores is the corresponding natural tendency of human beings to react more strongly to negative than to positive stimuli. As Cameron (2008, p. 13) observes: "Negative news sells more than positive news, people pay more attention to negative feedback than positive feedback, and traumatic events have greater impact on individuals than positive events." Cameron presents this as a paradox that must be held during organizational change. In a manner similar to the Beer and Nohria (2000) thesis, Cameron suggests that to overemphasize either the positive or the negative is dysfunctional.

At the same time, evidence clearly suggests that organizational change must emphasize (but not overemphasize) positive aspects of organizational change in order to succeed. We submit that, in the practice of OD, this notion is fairly well understood by experienced change agents and change leaders. For example, the OD professional knows that organizational diagnosis during change quite naturally tends to focus on the negative—the dysfunctions, disappointments, shortcomings, performance failings, and so on that have prompted the organization to undertake the change or improvement effort (Bushe & Marshak, 2009; Morgan Roberts, 2006). Such negative stimuli are common change drivers. Skilled change leaders know that overemphasizing the negative might well lower morale and expectations, such that people might despair: "It's hopeless; I didn't realize we were this bad; nothing can be done," and so on. Negative expectations can easily become a self-fulfilling prophecy. Among other things that might be done, skilled OD people often identify what individuals, teams, or departments are doing well; this is the explicit focus of appreciative inquiry (e.g., Cooperrider & Whitney, 2005). Even outside of appreciative inquiry, OD practitioners typically consider that it is as important to identify what the organization is doing well—and have the wisdom to leave it alone—as it is to identify what needs to be changed (Woodman, 1990). Thus, we would argue that OD has long been in the business of working with paradoxes surrounding positive organizational change. We would not argue, however, that we should be sanguine about the field's success, nor would we suggest that this is not a difficult challenge. Only that, as with the Theory E–Theory O paradox, OD's values and approaches embody the *potential* to live the paradox.

Paradox of Values

People tend to be passionate about OD. This passion arises, in part, from the values upon which OD is based, and in part from its engagement of the whole person. As managers and change agents, we can pretend that our actions (such as how we go about changing something) are value-free. But, of course, that is only pretense. There is no such thing as a "value-free" approach to organizational change, any more than there is an approach to change that is free of some template or model or theory of organization. That is, I must have some concept or theory of effective organizing—no matter how ill-formed or implicit—before I can even begin to improve the organization. Further, the organization is a collection of human beings who, as we noted above, each come with a complete set of attributes. We can design systems and manage them ignoring this reality and focusing only on the "technical" aspects of the system. Or, as sociotechnical systems theory suggested long ago (cf. Cherns, 1987; Pasmore & Sherwood, 1978; Trist & Bamforth, 1951), we can design change in these systems recognizing that every change in the technology, structure, etc. of the organization has an effect on the social fabric of that organization. At the end of the day, the values underlying OD, and the specific activities and behaviors utilized by OD for changing organizations, evoke both the cognitive and noncognitive parts of the mind and the social and technological aspects of the organization.

The "Spirit of the paradox" observes: "OD lives because it engages paradox more effectively than most other change approaches and philosophies."

Scrooge, Reprised

On Christmas morning the spirits left, and Scrooge awoke, flustered and glowing with good intentions. Yes! And the bedpost was his own. The bed was his own, the room was his own. Best and happiest of all, the Time before him was his own, to make amends in! "I will live in the Past, the Present, and the Future!" Scrooge repeated, as he scrambled out of bed. "The Spirits of all Three shall strive within me". . . . Scrooge was better than his word. He did it all, and infinitely more. (Charles Dickens, *A Christmas Carol*, 1843)

As did Scrooge going forward, OD lives (in part) in the past (Woodman, 2008). It functions (often reasonably effectively) in the present. And, if it continues to listen to and be true to its Spirits, it will exist long into the future. If you listen carefully, you might hear the "Spirit of organization development" speaking . . .

"I will honor the Spirits of organizing, of practice, of scholar-practitioner links, and of paradox," the Spirit of Organization Development repeated. "The Spirits of all four shall strive within me. . . ."

Future Directions

Like all good stories, *A Christmas Carol* has a beginning, middle, and an end. After finishing its final chapter, one can close the book with satisfaction. But, the book on OD continues to be written. With that recognition, here are our thoughts about the future of the "Spirit of Organization Development."

Positive Organizational Scholarship and Organization Development

A fundamental congruency exists between positive organizational change and OD (cf., Cameron & Powley, 2008). With its emphasis on developing human potential and fulfillment through the work experience as a crucial component of developing organizations, it could be argued that OD has always focused on the positive side of organizational life. How can the rapidly developing arena of POS further inform the field of OD? How can the intellectual energy in POS be harnessed to advance both the science of organizational change and the art of changing organizations? Further, what role might researchers and practitioners of OD play in the further development of POS? We see a positive direction as lying along a path where the fields of OD and POS further inform each other to their mutual benefit.

Bridging the Gap Between Scholars and Practitioners

Although we have argued, positively, that OD is a major "asset" for the organizational sciences in terms of its continued efforts to bridge gaps between scholars and practitioners, we acknowledge that this chapter of OD's book is far from finished. Indeed, using the same logic that we used to examine core issues of organizing, one could argue that gaps, both real and imagined, between practitioners and scholars are unlikely to ever be totally closed. Such is the nature, perhaps, of the "town and gown" relationship. However, an increasing emphasis seems to be placed on the importance of dealing with this gap (cf. Shani, et al., 2008). So, this challenge will require continuing attention.

Here the unanswered question is: What now? How can we capitalize on the current wave of interest?

What additional linkages, shared forums, and so on could be developed? How might we prevail upon POS and OD scholars to participate more in, for example, the OD Network or NTL? How might we encourage OD practitioners to take a more active role in POS events at Academy of Management meetings? Further, for the academics among us: There are already many ways to count academics' impacts (e.g., through citation counts), but few clear ways to assess practitioner impacts. How can we find ways to measure practitioner contributions to academic thought?

Creating Ethical Organizations

A great deal of pressure is placed on organizations to behave in an above-board, ethical manner. From managing diversity, to reducing discrimination and providing meaningful opportunities to all participants, to creating more sustainable organizations with reduced carbon footprints, to providing the engine of job creation during a recession, the expectations of society have moved far beyond notions of profit maximization as the only viable goal for the firm. We ignore the necessity for profits at our peril, of course. The long-term survival of the for-profit organization will always be a crucial goal. However, managers and organizations also ignore at considerable peril the expectations and demands of societies within which they must function. The news is constantly full of distressing stories of ethical lapses by managers and employees of our largest and most important organizations. People are not happy when they observe top management receiving millions of dollars in bonuses when the organization has performed so poorly that thousands of employees must be laid off. Men and women on Main Street are not terribly fond of reading that their government is bailing out some financial institution that has lost millions of dollars trading derivatives when they consider such trading to be little more than a form of legalized gambling. Not every lousy business decision or dumb mistake is an ethical lapse, of course. Nevertheless, there seem to be plenty of such ethical challenges around. We think that an important future direction for research and practice in OD will lie along the lines of developing a deeper understanding of ethical decision making and behavior (or the lack of same) in organizations.

How can OD help design and manage complex social systems such that they truly might be ethical in both spirit and operation? Ways of doing this are suggested by POS scholars, who discuss topics such as organizational virtuousness (Cameron, 2003)

and courageous action (Worline & Quinn, 2003). How can OD improve the ability to understand ethical dilemmas faced by managers and other employees—to more deeply appreciate the ethical consequences of actions taken by the organization, and to improve the probability that ethical decisions will be made? How do we balance the essential necessity for profits and success with the necessity to contribute to the greater good of society in terms of sustainability, equal opportunity, responsible corporate citizenship, and the like?

Certainly this line of inquiry is not new and considerable literature (and even some empirical evidence) already exists. However, organizations are failing currently in this arena and thus our argument that this might be (or should be) an explicit future direction for OD. Perhaps, for the sake of the future, it is crucial that OD continue to live, and, like Scrooge, to be "better than its word." And perhaps the Spirits visiting OD have not yet concluded their work.

References

Argyris, C. (2005). On the demise of organization development. In D.L. Bradford, & W.W. Burke (Eds.), *Reinventing organization development* (pp. 113–129). San Francisco: Pfeiffer.

Avey, J.B., Wernsing, T.A., & Luthans, F. (2008). Can positive employees help positive organizational change? Impact of psychological capital and emotions on relevant attitudes and behaviors. *Journal of Applied Behavioral Science, 44,* 48–70.

Barrett, F.J., & Fry, R.E. (2005). *Appreciative inquiry: A positive approach to building cooperative capacity.* Chagrin Falls, OH: Taos Institute.

Bartunek, J.M. (2007). Academic-practitioner collaboration need not require joint or relevant research: Towards a relational scholarship of integration. *Academy of Management Journal, 50,* 1323–1333.

Bartunek, J.M., & Rynes, S.L. (2010). The construction and contributions of "implications for practice": What's in them and what might they offer? *Academy of Management Learning and Education, 9,* 100–117.

Bate, P. (Ed.). (2007). Bringing the design sciences to organization development and change management. [Special issue]. *Journal of Applied Behavioral Science, 43*(1), 8–11.

Beckhard. R. (1969). *Organizational development: Strategies and models.* Reading, MA: Addison-Wesley.

Beer, M., & Nohria, N. (2000). Cracking the code of change. *Harvard Business Review, 78*(3), 133–141.

Beitler, M. (2007). The death of the OD practitioner. Retrieved from http://www.PopularArticles.com/article43135.html.

Blatt, R., & Camden, C.T. (2007). Positive relationships and cultivating community. In J.E. Dutton, & B.R. Ragins (Eds.), *Exploring positive relationships at work: Building a theoretical and research foundation* (pp. 243–264). Mahwah, NJ: Erlbaum.

Bunker B.B., & Alban, B.T. (Eds.). (1992). Large group interventions. [Special issue]. *Journal of Applied Behavioral Science, 28*(4).

Bunker, B.B., & Alban, B.A. (2006). *The handbook of large group methods: Creating systemic change in organizations and communities*. San Francisco: Jossey-Bass.

Bunker, B.B., & Alban, B.T. (Eds.). (2005). Large group interventions. [Special issue]. *Journal of Applied Behavioral Science, 41*(1).

Bunker, B.B., Alban, B.T., & Lewicki, R.J. (2004). Ideas in currency and OD practice. Has the well gone dry? *The Journal of Applied Behavioral Science, 40*, 403–422.

Burke, W.W. (1976). Organization development in transition. *Journal of Applied Behavioral Science, 12*, 22–43.

Bushe, G.R., & Marshak, R.J. (2009). Revisioning organization development: Diagnostic and dialogic premises and patterns of practice. *Journal of Applied Behavioral Science, 45*, 348–368.

Cameron, K.S. (2008). Paradox in positive organizational change. *Journal of Applied Behavioral Science, 44*, 7–24.

Cameron, K.S. (2003). Organizational virtuousness and performance. In K.S. Cameron, J.E. Dutton, & R.E. Quinn (Eds.), *Positive organizational scholarship: Foundations of a new discipline* (pp. 48–65). San Francisco: Berrett-Koehler.

Cameron, K.S., & Powley, E. (Eds.). (2008). Positive organizational change. [Special issue]. *Journal of Applied Behavioral Science, 44*(1).

Cameron, K., & Levine, M. (2006). *Making the impossible possible: Leading extraordinary performance, The Rocky Flats story*. San Francisco: Berrett-Koehler.

Caza, B.B., & Wilson, M.G. (2009). Me, myself, and I: The benefits of work-identity complexity. In L.M. Roberts, & J.E. Dutton (Eds.), *Exploring positive identities and organization: Building a theoretical and research foundation*. New York: Routledge, Taylor and Francis Group.

Cherns, A. (1987). Principles of sociotechnical design revisited. *Human Relations, 40*, 153–161.

Clark, P. (1972). *Action research and organizational change*. London: Harper & Row.

Coghlan, D., & Shani, R. (Eds.). (2009). The challenges of the scholar—practitioner. [Special issue]. *Journal of Applied Behavioral Science, 45*(1).

Cooperrider, D.L., & Srivastva, S. (1987). Appreciative inquiry in organizational life. In R.W. Woodman, & W.A. Pasmore (Eds.), *Research in organizational change and development* Vol. 1 (pp. 1–57). Greenwich, CT: JAI Press.

Cooperrider, D., & Whitney, D. (2005). *Appreciative inquiry: A positive revolution in change*. San Francisco: Berrett-Koehler Publishers.

Cox, C. (2005). The power of the question: Is OD dead? *Organization Development Journal, 23*(1), 73–80.

Cummings, T.G., & Worley, C.G. (2009). *Organization development & change* (9th ed.). Mason, OH: South-Western Cengage Learning.

Daft, R.L., & Lewin, A.Y. (2008). Rigor and relevance in organization studies: Idea migration and academic journal evolution. *Organization Science, 19*, 177–183.

Daft, R.L., & Lewin, A.Y. (1990). Can organization studies begin to break out of the normal science straitjacket? *Organization Science, 1*, 1–9.

Dickens, C. (1843). *A Christmas carol*. London: Chapman & Hall. Retrieved from http://www.stormfax.com/dickens.htm.

French, W.L., & Bell, C.H. (1995). *Organization development* (5th ed.). Englewood Cliffs, NJ: Prentice Hall.

Gittell, J.H. (2008). Relationships and resilience: Care provider responses to pressures from managed care. *Journal of Applied Behavioral Science, 44*, 25–47.

Golden-Biddle, K., & Dutton, J.E. (in press). *Exploring positive social change and organizations*. New York: Routledge, Taylor and Francis Group.

Greiner, L.E., & Cummings, T.G. (2004). Wanted: OD more alive than dead! *Journal of Applied Behavioral Science, 40*, 374–391.

Harvey, J.B. (2005). The future of OD: Or, why don't you take the tubes out of grandma? In D.L. Bradford, & W.W. Burke (Eds.), *Reinventing organization development* (pp. 15–18). San Francisco: Pfeiffer.

Holman, P., Devane, T., & Cady, S. (2007). *The change handbook: The definitive resource on today's best methods for engaging whole systems*. San Francisco: Berrett-Kohler.

Jones, J.E., & Pfeiffer, J.W. (1977). On the obsolescence of the term organization development. *Group & Organization Studies, 2*, 263–264.

Lawler, E., Mohrman, A., Mohrman, S., Cummings, T., & Ledford, G. (Eds.). (1985). *Doing research that is useful for theory and practice*. San Francisco: Jossey-Bass.

Lewin, K. (1951). *Field theory in social science*. New York: Harper.

Lewis, M.W. (2000). Exploring paradox: Toward a more comprehensive guide. *Academy of Management Review, 25*, 760–776.

Macy, B.A., & Izumi, H. (1993). Organizational change, design, and work innovation: A meta-analysis of 131 North American field studies—1961–1991. In R.W. Woodman, & W.A. Pasmore (Eds.), *Research in organizational change and development* Vol. 7 (pp. 235–313). Greenwich, CT: JAI Press.

Manning, M.R., & DelaCerda, J. (2003). Building organizational change in an emerging economy: Whole systems change using large group interventions in Mexico. In W.A. Pasmore, & R.W. Woodman (Eds.), *Research in organizational change and development* Vol. 14 (pp. 51–97). Oxford, UK: Elsevier Science.

McGinn, K. (2007). History, structure and practices: San Pedro longshoremen in the face of change. In J.E. Dutton, & B.R. Ragins (Eds.), *Exploring positive relationships at work: Building a theoretical and research foundation* (pp. 265–276). Mahwah, NJ: Erlbaum.

McMahan, G.C., & Woodman, R.W. (1992). The current practice of organization development within the firm: A survey of large industrial corporations. *Group & Organization Management, 17*, 117–134.

Morgan Roberts, L. (2006). Shifting the lens on organizational life: The added value of positive scholarship. *Academy of Management Review, 31*, 241–260.

Pasmore, W.A., & Friedlander, F. (1982). An action research program for increasing employee involvement in problem solving. *Administrative Science Quarterly, 27*, 343–362.

Pasmore, W.A., & Sherwood, J.J. (Eds.). (1978). *Sociotechnical systems: A sourcebook*. LaJolla, CA: University Associates.

Pasmore, W.A., Woodman, R.W., & Simmons, A.L. (2008). Toward a more rigorous, reflective and relevant science of collaborative management research. In A.B. Shani, N. Adler, S.A. Mohrman, W.A. Pasmore, & B. Stymne (Eds.), *Handbook of collaborative management research* (pp. 567–582). Thousand Oaks, CA: Sage.

Porras, J.I., & Silvers, R.C. (1991). Organization development and transformation. In M.R. Rosenzweig, & L.W. Porter (Eds.), *Annual review of psychology* Vol. 42 (pp. 51–78). Palo Alto, CA: Annual Reviews.

Robertson, P.J., Roberts, D.R., & Porras, J.I. (1993). An evaluation of a model of planned organizational change: Evidence from a meta-analysis. In R.W. Woodman, & W.A. Pasmore (Eds.), *Research in organizational change and development* Vol. 7 (pp. 1–39). Greenwich, CT: JAI Press.

Rynes, S., Bartunek, J., & Daft, R. (2001). Across the great divide: Knowledge creation and transfer between practitioners and academics. *Academy of Management Journal, 44,* 340–356.

Seo, M., Putnam, L., & Bartunek, J. (2004). Dualities and tensions of planned organizational change. In M.S. Poole & A.H. Van de Ven (Eds.), *Handbook of organizational change and innovation* (pp. 73–109). New York: Oxford.

Shani, A.B., Mohrman, S.A., Pasmore, W.A., Stymne, B., & Alder, N. (Eds.). (2008). *Handbook of collaborative management research.* Thousand Oaks: Sage Press.

Spreitzer, G.M., Sutcliffe, K., Dutton, J.E., Sonenshein, S., & Grant, A. (2005). A socially embedded model of thriving at work. *Organization Science, 16,* 537–549.

Stebbins, M.W., Valenzuela, J.L., & Coget, J. (2009). Long-term insider action research: Three decades of work at Kaiser Permanente. In R.W. Woodman, W.A. Pasmore, & A.B. Shani (Eds.), *Research in organizational change and development* Vol. 17 (pp. 37–75). Bingley, UK: Emerald Group Publishing.

Thompson, J.D. (1967). *Organizations in action.* New York: McGraw-Hill.

Trist, E., & Bamforth, W. (1951). Some social and psychological consequences of the long wall method of coal-getting. *Human Relations, 4,* 3–38.

Van de Ven, A.H. (2007). *Engaged scholarship: A guide for organizational and research knowledge.* New York: Oxford University press.

Wasserman, I.C., & Kram, K.E. (2009). Enacting the scholar-practitioner role: An exploration of narratives. *Journal of Applied Behavioral Science, 45,* 12–38.

Weidner, C.K. (2004). A brand in dire straits: Organization development at sixty. *Organization Development Journal, 22*(2), 37–47.

Woodman, R.W. (1990). Issues and concerns in organizational diagnosis. In C.N. Jackson, & M.R. Manning (Eds.), *Organization development annual* Vol. 3: *Diagnosing client organizations* (pp. 5–10). Alexandria, VA: American Society for Training and Development.

Woodman, R.W. (1993). Observations on the field of organizational change and development from the lunatic fringe. *Organization Development Journal, 11*(2), 71–75.

Woodman, R.W. (2005). Our legacy and the future. *Journal of Applied Behavioral Science, 41,* 7–8.

Woodman, R.W. (2008). Discourse, metaphor, and organizational change: The wine *is* new but the bottle is old. *British Journal of Management, 19,* S33–S37.

Worline, M.C., & Quinn, R.W. (2003). Courageous principled action. In K.S. Cameron, J.E. Dutton, & R.E. Quinn (Eds.), *Positive organizational scholarship: Foundations of a new discipline* (pp. 138–157). San Francisco: Berrett-Koehler.

Worren, N.A. M., Ruddle, K., & Moore, K. (1999). From organizational development to change management: The emergence of a new profession. *Journal of Applied Behavioral Science, 35,* 273–286.

Yaeger, T.F., Sorensen, P.F., & Bengtsson, U. (2005). Assessment of the state of appreciative inquiry: Past, present, and future. In R.W. Woodman, & W.A. Pasmore (Eds.), *Research in organizational change and development* Vol. 15 (pp. 297–319). Oxford, UK: Elsevier.

Positive Organization Development

Innovation-inspired Change in an Economy and Ecology of Strengths

David L. Cooperrider *and* Lindsey N. Godwin

Abstract

This chapter presents a framework for *innovation-inspired positive organization development* (IPOD); IPOD is presented as both a radical break from the problem solving approaches that have come to dominate the field, as well as a homecoming to OD's original affirmative spirit. The converging fields that inform the theory and practice of IPOD are detailed: appreciative inquiry, positive organizational scholarship, positive psychology, design theory, and the rise of sustainable enterprises. The theory of change underlying IPOD is articulated, including the three stages in creating strengths-based organizational innovation: the elevation-and-extension of strengths, the broadening-and-building of capacity, and the establishment of the new-and-eclipsing of the old. Recent work from the city of Cleveland, Ohio, illustrates how these stages unfold. The chapter concludes with an agenda for evolving the field of IPOD, calling for a focus on designing *positive institutions* that refract and magnify our highest human strengths outward into society.

Keywords: Innovation-inspired positive organization development, appreciative inquiry, managing as design, sustainability, positive institutions, strength-based management, innovation, theory of change

Fields change. And the field of organization development (OD) has been changing more than most (Cooperrider, Sorensen, Yaeger, & Whitney, 2005; Bushe & Marshak, 2009). Not only are the rules of the game changing for OD, but the very foundation of the field upon which it is played is transforming, thanks to the convergence of some exciting forces. There is currently a rewriting of many of the conventions of organization development and change thanks to breakthroughs in our theories of leadership—what has been called "the strengths revolution in management" (Buckingham & Clifton, 2001); the growing emergence of appreciative inquiry as a paradigm-altering form of action research that is permeating the fields of organization change and social innovation (Cooperrider & Srivastva, 1987); the mounting new database of human science research in fields of positive organizational scholarship (POS; Cameron, Dutton, & Quinn, 2003)

and positive psychology (Seligman, Steen, & Peterson, 2005); the growing permeation of design theory into management practice (Boland & Collopy, 2004); and the emergence of a social mandate to create sustainable enterprises that give back more (in all forms) to society than they consume. Increasingly, the call for OD *innovation* is eclipsing the call for OD *intervention,* and OD practitioners are needed to help build anew in organizations, not simply fix the old. Thus, the time has come to explore the foundations for a new, 21st-century field of organization development—what we refer to as *innovation-inspired positive organization development* (IPOD).

In this chapter, we present a framework for the nascent discipline of IPOD. To set the stage for this work, we first ascend into OD's history, highlighting the utopian spirit that set it apart and propelled its creativity. Names like McGregor, Lewin, Follett,

Shepherd, Schein, Boulding, Seashore, and Bennis stand out. Yet, the early days of OD were so much more than great personalities; there was a *positive ethos* that we want to underscore. In some ways, IPOD represents a radical break from some of the now-common OD assumptions; but, in another way, it is actually a homecoming to this original spirit. Next, we detail the forces noted above that are informing and shaping the development of IPOD and describe some of the innovative methodologies emerging around IPOD. We then outline the theory of change behind these methodologies, what we call *profusion*—the positive fusion of strengths—and the three stages in the process of creating strengths-based organizational innovation: the elevation-and-extension of strengths, the broaden-and-build approach to capacity, and the establish-and-eclipse stage of innovation. Using the bold steps currently being taken by the city of Cleveland to create a "Green City on a Blue Lake,"[1] we illustrate how these stages unfold in a live system. Last, we conclude the chapter with an agenda for evolving the field of IPOD, proposing that our future work will revolve around the design of positive institutions that not only elevate and connect human strengths, but also refract and magnify them outward into society.

Returning to Our Roots: Rethinking Our Approach to Organizational Change

In one of the first books on OD, Warren Bennis heralded what he saw as a signature theme in the field: the idea that OD was becoming an applied behavioral science built upon a "new attitude of 'optimism' or 'hope' or even conceit" (1969, p 3). Indeed, this "optimism" or "conceit" as Bennis so aptly amplified, had the feeling of a revolution. But what exactly was being overturned? In our view, it was nothing less than a rejection of the metaphysical pathos or bleak melancholy toward the idea of intentional change in human beings and their institutions that had dominated mindsets to that point.

Most change theories of the time had been erected on Weberian and Freudian foundations, resulting in a despairing zeitgeist in which the world was largely empty of choice. Bennis reflected on this proclivity, stating, "students of psychoanalysis and bureaucracy view their relevant units (people and organizations) as being mulishly resistant to most forms of alteration. Freud once said that he would be delighted if he could transform neurotic despair into normal unhappiness" (Bennis, 1963, p. 129). Weber pessimistically predicted that the march of bureaucracy, along with modernity's drive toward instrumental rationality, would advance like an automatic machine with a life of its own. He grimly forecast that bureaucracy would advance the more it was dehumanized, resulting in the routinization of every aspect of human life. In a word, Weber prophesied that we would see an ever-increasing "disenchantment"—with work in general, and in our institutions in particular (Weber, 2002).

The human sciences had their work cut out for them, as bureaucracy and neurosis were quickly becoming *the* macro forces of industry and modern society, with the issues associated with rigid hierarchies—authoritarianism, group conflict, stress, labor–management mistrust, etc.—being treated as givens to be managed. Imagine taking on Freud and Weber—and announcing, with confident fervor, that human beings and their institutions could be changed for the better. This is exactly what the OD pioneers did. They did it early on, with their interventions. For example, the invention of the T-group methodology was so powerful in terms of individual and group development that Carl Rogers called it "the most important social innovation of the 20th century" after using it in apartheid-riddled South Africa (Bradford, 1974). They did it in their writings, such as Maslow's visionary volume, *Euspsychian Management* (a title so audacious it was barely accepted for publication) (1998) and McGregor's *The Human Side of Enterprise* (1960), which became a classic resource for positive assumptions about people. They also did it in their institutes, such as the European Tavistock Institute[2] established in 1947, and MIT's Research Center for Group Dynamics,[3] established in 1945 around Lewin's new conception of action research. Likewise, they did it in the field. For example, University of Michigan's Survey Research Center demonstrated how systematic feedback of attitude survey data allowed for people to play a participative role in their organization's change process (Mann, 1961). In the late 1950s, Herb Shepherd, founder of the first doctoral program in organizational behavior at Case Western Reserve University, along with collaborators such as Robert Blake, helped coin the term "organization development" (French & Bell, 1973).

Soon, the field of OD took off, as Shepherd, Blake, and others demonstrated that the dehumanizing ills of bureaucracy could be countered through "planned change"—a daring notion at the time. In their classic on OD, French and Bell stated boldly, "this book is about an exciting and profound idea. The idea is this: it is possible for the people within and organization collaboratively to manage the culture of that organization in such a way that the goals and purposes of the organization are attained at the same time that *human values* of individuals within the organization are furthered" (1973, p. xiii). A new field was born, and OD became a champion for human values; organizational effectiveness and human development were now part and parcel of one another.

The Animating Spirit in Early Organization Development

The early work of OD was not only a call to repair and transform bureaucratic systems, it also protested the ivory tower, detached view of science and the hierarchical view of change that dominated organizational interventions at the time. Three overarching values gradually evolved to provide a foundation for the field. These included: a spirit of inquiry, an attitude of discovery embodied in a new willingness to expose ideas and beliefs to action, observation and reflection, and consensual conversation that countered the traditional advocacy-based approach of organizational change; *a collaborative design approach,* a belief that individuals' commitment to change is directly proportional to the degree to which they are engaged in designing the change and that everyone in the system—not just researchers and consultants—are potential "experts," with valuable insights for the change process; and *a positive view of humankind*, a belief in the fundamental potential of people that led to placing human development at the forefront of organizational work. These values secured OD's unique place in change management history. Change no longer needed to be something coercive or external. Organization development instead embraced Lewin's (1946) call for action research as a guide for organizational interventions, and sought to advance collaborative change approaches based on experiential learning and dialogical processes, and contextually conditioned through inquiry into the content *and* process of a human system.

IPOD: Completing Classical Organization Development's Incomplete Revolution

Somehow, the positive assumptions inherent in early OD, however, gave way to a storehouse of problem-focused interventions and diagnostic methods of analysis. Change became about diagnosing organizational ills and following up, albeit collaboratively, with carefully designed "interventions" to move from a problematic state to normalcy—a toss back

to the Freudian psychoanalytic model. Action research, the heart of OD, became formulated into a set of standardized steps: diagnosis, information gathering, feedback, and action planning, which were popularized by books such as Levinson's *Organizational Diagnosis* (1976). Bushe and Marshak (2009) trace the "problematizing" trajectory of classical OD, concluding that, like medicine, OD became a clinical science of what is wrong, focused on correcting the ills and excesses of bureaucracy. Whether intended or not, OD became almost exclusively a problem-solving science—what Bushe and Marshak labeled *Diagnostic OD* (2009, p. 3).

Unfortunately, the legacy of this diagnostic approach has become an approach and obsession that says, "Let's fix what's wrong and the strengths will take care of themselves." In fact, deficit-based management has itself become a self-perpetuating industry, with a mass-produced culture that revolves around sophisticated technologies for studying "what's wrong." Its error-focusing tendencies are woven tightly into everything from the global consulting industry, to Six-Sigma methodologies, to reengineering studies, variance analysis, and low-morale survey work. This type of consulting industry represents a $350 billion[4] market focused on problem analysis, error reduction, and repair. The deficit-based culture of consultancy has even led to tongue-in-cheek humor, reflected in a memo pad we saw recently that said, "Consulting: If you are not part of the solution, there is a lot of money to be made in prolonging the problem."

Since the days of Taylorism, organizations have regrettably become "problems to be solved." True to Maslow's observation, "It is tempting, if the only tool you have is a hammer, to treat everything as if it were a nail' (1966, p. 15), managers and consultants have become quite good at finding, analyzing, and solving organizational problems, armed with tools such as "gap analysis," "organizational diagnosis," "root causes of failure," "needs analysis," and "threat analysis." Deficit-based thinking has virtually become synonymous with the idea of any "helping profession." In management circles, it results in the 80/20 trap—where the pull of the problematic, the broken, and the deficient leaves us with an organization in which only a small minority of employees (only 20% globally) agree with the following statement: "At work, I have the opportunity to do what I do best every day" (Gallup, 2001). Sadly, the economic consequence of a severely underappreciated workforce is not just a demoralized "other 80%"; the disengagement that accrues as a result is estimated to cost the U.S. economy more than $300 billion annually (Gallup, 2001).

It is time for the organizational change revolution to surpass this deficit-based detour and come full circle, back to its positive roots. The emerging field of IPOD is cut from the same richly woven cloth of values as classical OD—except it does not have the same problematizing focus. As we will detail, IPOD embraces and advocates for the discovery-oriented spirit of inquiry and extends that spirit in its second-generation form of action research called appreciative inquiry (AI). It solidly preserves collaborative approaches and even expands those values in its large-group methodologies. The change theory underlying IPOD, however, illustrates a shift from collaborative *intervention* toward collaborative *innovation*. Furthermore, in IPOD, the idea of positivity becomes not just an end state to which we should aspire, but rather a catalytic resource for framing organizational change from the outset and a means for creating change. This new form of OD posits that change is not simply about moving from a "–7" to a neutral "0," but it also about a qualitatively different kind of change that moves us from a "+2" to a plus "+20" or "+200." That such a seemingly subtle shift can create seismic changes in the field is what the rest of this chapter is about.

Like classic OD, this new trajectory is emerging from exciting interdisciplinary connections and developments across the human sciences, including foundations in AI and strength-based management, positive psychology and POS, design theory, and the new sustainability domain of biomimicry. We now turn our attention briefly to each of these fields to detail how they form the foundation of this next generation of OD.

Appreciative Inquiry and Strengths-based Management

Contrasted with the dominant, deficit-based management culture, it is easy to see why the strengths-based movement is being called a revolution. The radical idea at the core of this movement is that, just as the Heisenberg principle holds true for the physical world (1949), so it is true for our social systems. In other words, the process of studying a phenomenon actually changes that phenomenon: We create new realities during the process of inquiry. The birth of AI extended this idea to the realm of organizational life by suggesting that the very act of asking a question has profound impact. Inquiry and change are not separate moments. Our questions focus our attention on what is "there" to be noticed. Reflecting its social constructionist roots (i.e., Gergen, 1982), AI refers to this as the *constructionist principle*, highlighting the relationship between inquiry and the simultaneous construction of reality (Cooperrider, Barrett, & Srivastva, 1995). An organization-wide survey on low morale, for example, produces ripple effects through the mere act of asking: "What are the causes of low morale?" This question concentrates attention on what or who is causing the low morale; it provides a more precise language for speaking about low morale, and provides a presumptive assurance that something can be done to help solve the problem. If we "figure out the problem," then we can apply the right intervention to help the system return to a more normal state. Most unfortunately, however, is the fact that one more expensive low-morale survey, even with all the good intentions, will not tell us one thing about how to create a supercharged, highly engaged workforce.

Appreciative inquiry offers a new change imperative by suggesting that we be aware of the negativity bias that pervades our investigations into organizational life. Appreciative inquiry posits that human systems move in the direction of the questions they most frequently and authentically ask; knowledge and organizational destiny are intimately interwoven; what we know and how we study it has a direct impact on where we end up (Cooperrider & Avital, 2003; Gergen, 1994). Given this new understanding of the power of questions, AI began to change the focus of what we typically study in organizational life, questioning the mindset that organizations are problems to be solved (Cooperrider & Srivastva, 1987). Inspired by their fieldwork at the Cleveland Clinic and Schweitzer's work on reverence for life (see Martin, 2007, for overview), Cooperrider and Srivastva engaged in a radical reversal of the traditional problem solving approach. They proposed that organizations are not machines incessantly in need of repair, but instead are mysteries and miracles of human relatedness; they are living systems, webs of infinite strength and limitless human imagination (1990). What emerged from this vantage point was an entirely different approach to organizational inquiry and change built fundamentally upon a new line of questions such as, "What gives life to the system when it is most alive?" The strengths-based philosophy that AI has helped inject into management practices is summarized in Table 56.1.

Because AI is so central to the emergence and practice of IPOD, we will return to discussing its

Table 56.1 Principles of strengths-based approaches to positive organization development and change

We live in worlds that our inquiries create; no change initiative outperforms its "return on attention," whether we are studying deficiencies or the best in life.
We excel only by amplifying strengths, never by simply fixing weaknesses; therefore, beware of the negativity bias of first framing because excellence is not the opposite of failure.
Small shifts make seismic differences; strengths-based change obeys a tipping point; instead of focusing 80% on what's not working and 20% on strengths, it is important to put this 80/20 rule in reverse to harness the transformative power of the "positivity ratio."
Strengths do more than perform, they transform—strengths are what make us feel stronger and therefore magnify "what is best" and imagine "what is next" in order to create upward spirals.
We live in a universe of strengths—the wider the lens, the better the view. The appreciable world is so much larger than our normal appreciative eye. What we appreciate (seeing value), appreciates (increases in value).

innovation-igniting methodologies, which are in direct contrast to diagnostic OD's focus on intervention or repair. We will explore how many of the exciting projects emerging in this realm are guided by the new action research phases of AI known as the *4-D cycle*—discovery, dream, design, and destiny (summarized in Figure 56.1).

For now, we will underscore one overarching point: We live in worlds that our inquiries create (Cooperrider, Barrett, & Srivastva, 1995). When we study excellence, there will be an impact. When we study low morale, there will be an impact. The questions we ask determine what we find, and what we find becomes a powerful resource for planning, imagining, and creating the future realities of organizations.

Positive Psychology and POS Create a Tectonic Shift

Failure and success are not opposites; they are merely different, and thus must be studied separately. Unfortunately, our research in the social sciences has not always reflected this truism. Until recently, the field of psychology—an important foundational discipline for organizational studies—had become consumed with a single topic: mental illness. Through decades of rigorous research, it built a rich understanding of the various psychological conditions that render the population below "normal." "This progress has come at a high cost," writes Seligman, "Relieving the states that make life miserable, it seems, has made building the states that make life worth living less of a priority . . . (if you were hoping for this) you have probably found the field of psychology to be a puzzling disappointment" (2002, p. ix). Indeed, when Seligman and Csikszentmihalyi (2000) and then Cameron, Dutton, and Quinn (2003) called for a new positive psychology and POS, respectively, another tectonic shift happened, opening a new frontier in our knowledge of human sciences.

In a mere decade since these initial calls for a science and scholarship of the positive, the impact has truly exploded. From the work on emotional

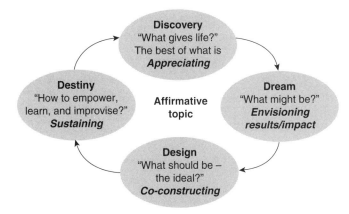

Fig. 56.1 The 4-D model of appreciative inquiry.

intelligence (Goleman, Boyatzis, & McKee, 2002), to better understanding of upward spirals of emotions in organizations (Fredrickson, 2003), to the continuing advances in AI (Cooperrider & Avital, 2003; Fry, Barrett, Seiling, & Whitney, 2001), to knowledge leaps on the science of happiness (Seligman, 2002), the implications for OD are vast. Even academic programs have begun to transform as a result. For example, in 2002, the University of Michigan established the Center for Positive Organizational Scholarship.[5] Then, in 2004, Case Western Reserve University, the birthplace of graduate education in OD, decided that the prolific research productivity of positive psychology was so profound that they changed the name of their top-ranked master's program from the masters in OD, to the masters in *positive* organization development (MPOD).[6] This simple change was a fork in the road, signaling that the knowledge base and scholarship of this generative form of study was so massive, an entire degree could be devoted to it. Similarly, Marty Seligman followed suit in 2005, with the establishment of the masters degree in applied positive psychology[7] at University of Pennsylvania.

Although other chapters serve to discuss positive psychology and POS in more detail, it is important to highlight three decisive components that make this whole arena one of the fresh foundations for the new discipline of IPOD. First, there has been a generation of a rich vocabulary of the positive. As Wittgenstein (1981) once reasoned, "the limits of language are the limits of our worlds," meaning that if we do not have nuanced vocabularies available, then not only will we not be able to converse about a phenomenon, but we also will be unlikely to act collaboratively in relation to the phenomenon. Thus, it is fitting that one of the very first pieces of scholarly work done in positive psychology was the production of an encyclopedia of human strengths, *Character Strengths and Virtues: A Handbook and Classification* (Peterson & Seligman, 2004), which offers a classification in contrast to the American Psychiatric Association's classic *Diagnostic and Statistical Manual of Mental Disorders (DSM)* (1994). All of a sudden, with a rich professional vocabulary of human courage, wisdom, love, vitality, emotional intelligence, gratitude, awe, open-mindedness, bravery, and many others, new forms of research proliferated.

The second significant component of the positive psychology–POS tandem came from an illuminating framework proposed by Cameron (2003). To help portray the idea of higher-order strengths (which had, to date, gone largely underdiscussed in the social sciences), Cameron created a continuum depicting a state of normality or healthy performance in the middle, with a condition of negatively deviant performance on the extreme left and extraordinary positive performance on the farthest right (2003). At the individual level, the left would be a focus on illness, in the middle the topic shifts to health, and on the right, topics shift to human flourishing. The same dynamic can be applied to organizations. Take, for instance, the notion of quality: on the left would be *error prone* organizations, the middle might be framed as *reliable*, and the positive deviance framing on the right is *flawless*.

Finally, it is in this search for positive deviancy that some of the most influential and exciting research of our times is taking place (i.e., Prahalad, 2004; Thachenkery, Cooperrider, & Avital 2010; Spreitzer & Sonenshein, 2003). As such, POS does not represent a single theory, but rather provides a compass to understanding dynamics described by words such as excellence, thriving, flourishing, life-giving, flawless, and extraordinary. Combined with positive psychology's inauguration of a science of human strengths, POS's razor-sharp clarifying framework truly sets the stage for a fundamental shift in our understanding of the human condition and its prospects.

The Design Thinking Movement

In the late sixties, Nobel Laureate Herb Simon outlined the three pillars of organization and management: intelligence, choice, and design (1969). Yet, somehow, over the years, the design pillar was conspicuously glossed over in favor of a decision-analytic stance. This is now changing as organizations everywhere discover the power and promise of design thinking. Increasingly, managers are turning to architects, creative artists, graphic specialists, and product designers as inspired models for innovation, improvisational leadership, and collaborative designing. Volumes such as *Managing as Designing* (Boland & Collopy, 2004); *Artful Making: What Managers Need to Know About How Artists Work* (Austin & Devin, 2003); *Discovering Design* (Buchanan & Margolis, 1995), and *The Design of Business* (Martin, 2009), are changing our conceptions of management. They portray the essence of management not as a science of rational decisions within a stable world, but rather as the art of generating artifacts and designs of a better future, rapid prototypes, feedback loops, and agile interactive pathways embedded within an increasingly uncertain and dynamic world.

Capitalizing on this new wave of innovation-inspired change in organizations, design firms, such as the acclaimed IDEO[8] in Silicon Valley, have expanded their mission from product design into organizational transformation. Their work is all about the art of creating, which is often quite different from solving. Extending this trend backward toward management schools that are responsible for preparing our future business leaders, many are beginning to ask what if our classes looked more like design studios, alive with hot interdisciplinary teams and innovation labs, bringing together the latest and best in applied creativity (Boland & Collopy, 2004). In line with this thinking, the head of *Harvard Business Review* recently wrote an article titled, "Magic by Design," in which he argued that the design field has much to teach managers, especially those with the explicit goal of succeeding at rapid, profuse innovation (Stewart, 2008).

The bridge between product designing and the spirit of design-thinking for the field of OD was outlined in a recent article in the *Journal of Applied Behavioral Sciences* (Coughlan, Suri, & Canales, 2008). Although the OD lexicon has traditionally included the word "design," and there are many epistemological ties between OD's roots in philosophical pragmatism and experiential learning (Kolb, 1984), a "rediscovered" pragmatism has emerged from the field of design thinking that argues for a new kind of logic beyond inductive or deductive reasoning. It is called *abductive reasoning* (a phrase coined by Peirce, 1938), which happens via "logical leaps of the mind" from even a single deviating data point that does not fit with the existing models (Martin, 2009). Ironically, many of the methods in the design field, for example group brainstorming on a flip chart, had their origins in the early days of OD (Marrow, 1967). Yet, it is design firms such as IDEO that are becoming the "go to" places for organization development. One reason, argues Avital, Boland, and Cooperrider (2008) is that design thinkers see the world through a positive lens, where even mistakes are valued as "material" for new possibilities. Similarly, Barrett (1998) describes how artists see everything as positive possibility; for example, jazz musicians who regularly say "yes to the mess." Indeed, an innovation-inspired positive OD discipline is rapidly emerging today, and it is being enriched by the question: What can we, as an OD field, learn bout nondeficit positive change from

architects, performing artists, musicians and product designers—especially the ways in which they create real-time change through the tools of visual representation, metaphor, and revolutionary innovation?

Biomimicry As Inquiry into Sustainable Value—and Life

Just as AI is the search for what gives life to human systems, biomimicry is a field of work dedicated to the conscious emulation of life's genius—it is all about innovation inspired by nature (Benyus, 1997). *Bios*, from the early Greeks, literally means "life," and unlike the Industrial Revolution, the biomimicry revolution is a call to relate to nature, not on what we can *extract* from it, but what we can *learn* from nature, with implications for organizations and industries. For example, biomimicry raises the question of how organizations, like true living organisms, can not only create less waste, but eliminate the very concept of waste (where every "waste" in transformed into a "food" for another part of the system), thus creating sustainable enterprises that help build a better world. Biomimicry invites OD to explore the fertile crests where ecology meets commerce, computing, human flourishing, energy, manufacturing, community, organizational design, and most importantly, the creation of *sustainable value*. What might it look like if we ran a business like a redwood forest, or compute like a cell, or gather energy like a leaf? The invitation is to appreciate the miracle of life and notice nature's strategies and strengths, sculpted over billions of years, then echo them in our own institutions.

Some of the most exciting and profoundly innovative work happening in OD today is at the intersection between AI, positive psychology and POS, design thinking, *and* biomimicry for the creation of sustainable value. With these forces taken together, we now see the earmarks of a breakthrough moment in the field of organization development and change. We see ideas coming together that can spread like an adaptive gene throughout our culture. The fresh approach to managing change is become clear: We need innovation inspired by the best in life.

From These Roots a New Branch Emerges: The Nature of IPOD

With the stage now set, we can now more fully consider the possibility of a theoretical and methodological transformation for the field of OD. Building on and extending the concepts of AI, positive human science, biomimicry's emulation of life, and the designer's mind, we now ask: What is the collective potential presented by merging these streams? To answer this question, we outline here the developing idea of IPOD—what it is, what it tries to accomplish, several illustrations, its new change theory, and directions for future research. Although our sketch remains high-level, we hope to demonstrate the enormous potential IPOD holds for the whole of OD. To begin, we situate these contributions by exploring what we call the *three-circles of the strengths revolution* (Cooperrider, 2008).

The Three Pillars of IPOD

Whether working with individuals, organizations, or broader social systems, there are three primary tasks in almost all positive organization development work: the *elevation* of strengths, the alignment or connected *magnification* of strengths, and the creation of strengths-based organizations to become positive institutions—vehicles for elevating, magnifying, and *refracting* our highest human strengths outward to the world. Figure 56.2 depicts these three interrelated spheres that form the framework for IPOD. At the center of the overlapping circles is

the individual capacity to see the world not as a problem-to-be-solved, but rather an invitation for inquiry into what gives life to a system when it is most alive. In this framework, strengths are defined as those things that make us feel stronger—the things that bring our institutions and ourselves to life. It is also important to highlight that AI provides the action research methodological architecture for this collaborative search into "what gives life." Although not exhaustive, this model begins to connect the many seemingly diverse streams of work that underpin the emerging discipline of IPOD.

With the aim to elevate strengths, the first circle highlights knowledge domains such as positive psychology and POS, the work on appreciative intelligence (i.e., Thachenkery & Metzker, 2006), and the leadership work on emotional intelligence and strengths-based management (i.e., Buckingham, 2006; Boyatzis & McKee, 2005). Exciting tools and resources for this domain include the VIA strengths-survey (Peterson & Seligman, 2004), best-self analysis (Roberts, Dutton, Spreitzer, Heaphy, & Quinn, 2005), resonant leadership tools (i.e., McKee, Boyatzis, & Johnston, 2008), strengths-finder surveys

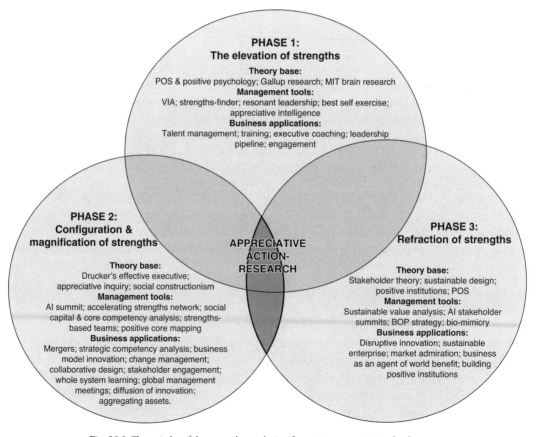

Fig. 56.2 Three circles of the strengths revolution for positive organization development.

(i.e., Rath, 2007), and appreciative coaching methodologies (i.e., Orem, Binket, & Clancy, 2007). The focus of this domain of work is largely at the individual and small group or team levels, and the applications range from corporate talent management, executive coaching, career and job crafting, to strengths-based leadership education and more.

The second circle goes beyond the lifting up of individual strengths and works with configurations and constellations of the whole. The primary work of this realm is to intensify and leverage existing positivity with an eye toward creating intentional *transformational uses* of a system's positive core. The guiding question here is: How do we take isolated strengths and help take them to a new octave? The social constructionist literature in anthropology, with its illustrations of the power of narrative and story (i.e., Miller, Potts, Fung, Hoogstra, & Mintz, 1990), the magic of intergenerational connections (i.e., Whitehouse, Bendezu, FallCreek, & Whitehouse, 2000), and the identity shaping power of symbols and ritual moments (i.e., Powley & Cameron, 2006), provides a rich array of approaches for amplifying individual strengths into a symphony of the whole. At this level, one also finds the management philosophy of Peter Drucker and others who wrote about the importance of the *alignments of strengths* (Drucker, 1966) and high-quality connections (Dutton & Heaphy, 2003). Methodologies include the macro-management method of the AI Summit, which brings together whole systems of 500 to 1,000 people, such as the recent business leaders summit at the United Nations (Cooperrider, 2010). Coupled with new web technologies, there are now AI Summits and similar "IBM Jam Sessions"[9] with 10,000 to 60,000 people combining their strengths and drawing from the positive core of the system. Other tools for this realm include the Strategic Core Competency work (Prahalad & Hamel, 1990), the World Café[10] model, Asset-Based Community Development (Kretzmann & McKnight, 1994), Future Search (Weisbord & Janoff, 1995), and an exciting new business planning and strategy approach called SOAR (versus SWOT). SOAR is an acronym for "strengths, opportunities, aspirations, and results" (Stavros & Hinrichs, 2009) and is further detailed in Chapter 63 (Stavros & Wooten, 2011). These methods are quickly demonstrating the effectiveness that ensues when everyone becomes an organizational designer.

The third circle represents the largest frontier for transforming OD. This level goes beyond the elevation of internal strengths; it involves the discovery and design of positive institutions—institutions that elevate, combine, magnify, and *refract* our highest human strengths into the world. In business, for example, it bespeaks of the stakeholder theory of the firm (Freedman, 1984), the call for sustainable value (Laszlo, 2008), and the search for business to act as an agent of world benefit (BAWB) (Piderit, Fry, & Cooperrider, 2007). Tools for accomplishing these lofty aims include the bottom of the pyramid protocol,[11] biomimicry (Benyus, 1997), cradle-to-cradle design (McDonough & Braungart, 2002), the next-generation AI Summit or "the sustainable design factory" (Cooperrider, 2008), and the BAWB world inquiry.[12] The work unfolding in this arena is increasingly informed and shaped by the lens of sustainable value creation. It is an innovation engine for management unlike anything we have ever seen, and it is becoming the driving business opportunity of the 21st century (Laszlo, 2003). In OD terms, it is the human dimensions of sustainability that we want to underscore. The myriad of terms surrounding the concept of sustainability—eco-efficiency, social entrepreneurship, social responsibility, triple bottom-line, sustainable development, green enterprise, and others—too often serve to mystify and cloud the underlying message of this concept. Today's pressing mandate for OD is to help create positive institutions—institutions that elevate, connect, and then help refract our higher human strengths, like a prism, into the world around us (Cooperrider & Dutton, 1999).

Taking these three circles as a coherent whole, we offer the following definition of IPOD: it is a strengths-based approach to organizational innovation and change that is *appreciative and inquiry-driven*, applying AI-based, action research methods for everything that gives strength and life to organizations and their surrounding ecosystems of stakeholders; *innovation inspired*, focused on amplifying widespread assets or constellations of strengths (systemic positivity) for transformational purposes—positioning an enterprise for distinctive breakthrough leadership in its domain; informed by the theory and technologies of the *positive human sciences*, especially social constructionist thought; an embodiment of the heart of *classic OD values,* including collaborative designing, the spirit of inquiry, and positive assumptions about human systems; seeking to *build positive institutions* that are increasingly exceptional at the connection and magnification of strengths and the extended refraction of our highest strengths into society; and applicable to *any* innovation or change agenda in organizational and societal life that can benefit from a strengths-based approach to innovation *as* change.

Establishing the New and Eclipsing the Old

The new model of OD is spreading rapidly around the world. With a blossoming array of initiatives informed by IPOD principles emerging across the globe—from Boeing to the United Nations (UN), to the U.S. Environmental Protection Agency (EPA), to World Vision, to women's empowerment projects in Nepal—it is easy to understand the popular spread of the strengths perspective. What is still missing in the scholarship of change, however, is a solid understanding of the term "positive change" versus "deficit change." What is needed now is a better articulation between ideas like OD *intervention* and OD *innovation*, between solving and creating. We need to understand the stages through which organizations progress as they move toward creating environments of *transformational positivity*—the intentional use of positive assets, strengths, positive emotions, and whole system network effects to initiate, inspire, and better manage change.

In diagnostic OD, the stages of change are commonly understood, such as the classic "unfreezing" "changing," and "freezing" model (Lewin, 1947). The negative assumption deeply ingrained in this and most OD change models is that people will instinctively resist change. Beckhard and Harris (1987), and later Jacobs (1994), codified the change model in the following formula: $D \times V \times F > R$, where D = Dissatisfaction with how things are now; V = Vision of what is possible; and F = First, or the concrete steps that have been taken toward the vision. If the product of these three factors is greater than R (Resistance), then change is possible. Because of the multiplication of D, V, and F, if any one element is absent or low, then the product will be low and therefore not capable of overcoming the resistance of restraining forces.

Guided by this formula, successful deficit-based change programs have worked to magnify urgency; the organization must recognize and accept the dissatisfaction that exists by communicating industry trends, customer dissatisfactions, and competitive analysis to build the necessity for change. Sometimes this is called "creating the burning platform" (Christensen & Shu, 1999). In his now classic HBR article, Kotter writes about how important deficit analysis is—even if it needs to be manufactured—to raising the state of dissatisfaction, stating that the most successful cases of change begin when "an individual or group facilitates a frank discussion of potentially unpleasant facts. . . . The purpose of all this activity . . . is to make the status quo seem more dangerous than launching into the unknown" (Kotter, 1995, p. 60). Bad business results, he concludes, are, in a way, a "blessing" for mobilizing the change agenda. Not pumping up the urgency, argues Kotter, is the "#1 error" in change management and the main reason why transformation efforts fail. With this framework guiding change initiatives, is it any wonder that our institutions are filled with cultures of fear and trembling? Positive OD proposes an alternative, perhaps more powerful, model of change. As William James championed over a century ago, "Emotional occasions, especially violent ones, are extremely potent in precipitating mental rearrangements. The sudden and explosive ways in which jealousy, guilt, fear, remorse, or anger can seize upon one are known to everybody. Hope, happiness, security, resolve—emotions characteristic of conversion, however, can be equally explosive. And emotions that come in this explosive way seldom leave things as they found them" (1902, pp. 163–164). Today, with the help of the latest in positive psychology research, we are able to more fully realize James' vision for more systematic attention to the kind of nondeficit positive change that happens when things are "hot and alive within us, and where everything has to re-crystallize about it" (James, 1902, p. 162).

Taking this thought from the ethereal to the organizationally pragmatic, we offer an alternative to the stages found in the formula of $D \times V \times F > R$, which places priority on the generation of dissatisfaction, fear, anxiety, anger, and the like. We propose that the most effective transformational change is really about *establishing the new and eclipsing the old*. In economics, this has been called "creative destruction" (Schumpeter, 1975), whereby something like the industrial age's oil problems will never be solved logically on their own terms (i.e., fixing one oil rig at a time), but will be eclipsed and made irrelevant through the invention of something new, like a bright, green solar economy. But how does this kind of change happen?

Building on the model proposed by Cooperrider and Sekerka (2003), we assert that the positive change embodied by IPOD moves through three phases: elevation-and-extension, broaden-and-build, and establish-and-eclipse. These stages are based on three assumptions: change is all about strengths and new creative configurations of strengths; we live in a universe of strengths, in which the appreciable world is profoundly larger than our normal appreciative

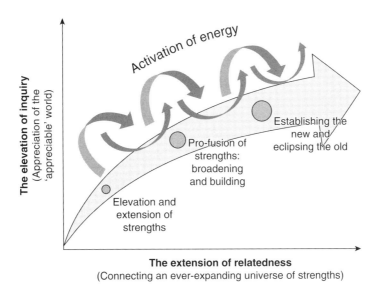

Fig. 56.3 The elevate-and-extend theory of positive change.

eye; and positive change is a powerful, self-renewing, and clean resource—much like an energy source that is abundant and renewable. As summarized in Figure 56.3, the DNA of positive change resembles a double helix—the *elevation* of inquiry, along one dimension, and *extension* of relatedness, which combines and connects strengths, along the other dimension. The process of positive change is initiated when one or both begin.

This dynamic change phenomenon is illustrated by the economic development work unfolding in Cleveland, Ohio. Determined to surmount their pollution-ridden industrial history as a city whose river infamously caught fire in the 1970s, Mayor Jackson called for an AI Summit in 2009, to bring 700 business leaders, entrepreneurs, scientists, and inventors together to envision a "Green City on a Blue Lake." The process included external companies such as IBM and its Smarter Planet technologies, as well as sustainable energy innovators from Sweden (Glavas, Senge, & Cooperrider, 2010). The AI process produced aspirations for green urban farming, fuel cell innovation, and visions of Lake Erie becoming a leading green energy provider for the nation.

Commenting on the surprising energy unleashed, the former editor of *The New Yorker* wrote, "summit-goers, exhausted but awakened to their new, collective power, gave the mayor a standing ovation. It was like uncorking a giant bottle of champagne left too long on the shelf and seeing the bubbles explode" (Michner, 2009, p. G-6). The AI Summit produced 21 prototype initiatives for Cleveland,

including a major partnership with General Electric for the city to become a premier freshwater wind energy location. New perspectives, new energy, and new vision were generated, and the traditional problem solving approach to OD was replaced by innovation-oriented IPOD. The city initiated a new positive trajectory.

Future Directions

We must still explore many questions within each of the three pillars of IPOD. First, as we seek to foster the elevation of strengths, we must improve our methods for identifying strengths within others and ourselves. Emerging work on appreciative intelligence (Thachenkery & Metzker, 2006) offers a beginning insight into why some individuals are better able to see hidden potential in situations and people. But, can this capacity be developed? If so, what methods are best at helping develop this type of strengths intelligence? Such queries have implications for affecting our management education pedagogies. Even as we seek to better recognize the strengths embedded in individuals and systems, we also need more rigorous tools to help measure and categorize strengths. Building on the strengths classification of Peterson and Seligman (2004) and the VIA strengths-survey (Peterson & Seligman, 2003), new instruments—even new language—are needed to help us catalogue all the strengths that exist in individuals and organizations.

Another needed area of research relates to AI Summits. Thus far, practice and application have outstripped research, so investigating what aspects of AI are most important, what processes are connected to what outcomes and why, what processes differentiate effective AI Summits from less-effective summits, and how the temporary positive energy associated with summits can be prolonged, all are areas in need of rigorous investigation.

Finally, investigations of the three pillars of IPOD will create an empirical foundation needed to lead planned, positive change efforts in organizations. Investigating not only how to *elevate* strengths but also how to *magnify* them and *refract* them, so that other individuals and organizations are affected—that is, to create upward-tending, virtuous cycles—is an important area of scholarly endeavor. The goal is to create the scholarly foundation that was missing in the early OD literature which, in its absence, produced a problem-centered, negative orientation in OD.

Notes

1. See www.gcbl.org
2. See www.tavinstitute.org
3. See www.rcgd.isr.umich.edu/history
4. See www.plunkettresearch.com
5. See www.bus.umich.edu/positive
6. See weatherhead.case.edu/mpod
7. See www.sas.upenn.edu/lps/graduate/mapp
8. See www.ideo.com
9. See www.collaborationjam.com
10. See www.theworldcafe.com
11. See www.bop-protocol.org
12. See worldbenefit.cwru.edu/inquiry

References

American Psychiatric Association. (1994). *Diagnostic and statistical manual of mental disorders.* Washington, DC: American Psychiatric Publishing.

Austin, R., & Devin, L. (2003). *Artful making: What managers need to know about how artists work.* Upper Saddle River, NJ: Prentice Hall.

Avital, M., Boland, R.J., & Cooperrider D.L. (Eds.). (2008). *Designing information and organizations with a positive lens: Advances in appreciative inquiry, volume 2.* Oxford, UK: Elsevier Science.

Barrett, F. (1998). Creativity and improvisation in jazz and organizations: Implications for organizational learning. *Organization Science, 9:* 605–622.

Beckhard, R., & Harris, R. (1987). *Organizational transitions: Managing complex change.* Reading, MA: Addison-Wesley.

Bennis, W. (1969). *Organization development: Its nature, origins, and prospects.* Reading, MA: Addison-Wesley.

Bennis, W. (1963). A New role for the behavioral sciences: Effecting organizational change. *Administrative Science Quarterly, 8*(2), 125–165.

Benyus, J. (1997). *Biomimicry: Innovation inspired by nature.* New York: Harper Collins.

Boland, R.J., & Collopy, F. (2004). Toward a design vocabulary for management. In R.J. Boland & F. Collopy (Eds.), *Managing as designing* (pp. 265–276). Stanford, CA: Stanford University Press.

Boyatzis, R.E., & McKee, A. (2005). *Resonant leadership: Renewing yourself and connecting with others through mindfulness, hope and compassion.* Boston, MA: Harvard Business School Press.

Bradford, L. (1974). *National training laboratories: Its history: 1947–1970.* Bethel, ME: Bradford.

Buchanan, R., & Margolin, V. (Eds.) (1995). *Discovering design: Explorations in design studies.* Chicago: University of Chicago Press.

Buckingham, M. (2006). *Go put your strengths to work.* New York: Free Press.

Buckingham, M., & Clifton, D. (2001). *Now, Discover your strengths.* New York: Free Press.

Bushe, G.R., & Marshak, R.J. (2009). Revisioning organization development: Diagnostic and dialogic premises and patterns of practice. *Journal of Applied Behavioral Science, 45*(3), 348–368.

Cameron, K.S., Dutton, J.E., & Quinn, R.E. (2003). Foundations of positive organizational scholarship. In K. Cameron, J.E. Dutton, & R.E. Quinn (Eds.) *Positive organizational scholarship: Foundations of a new discipline* (pp. 3–13). San Francisco, CA: Berrett-Koehler.

Cameron, K.S. (2003). Organizational virtuousness and performance. In K. Cameron, J.E. Dutton, & R.E. Quinn (Eds.) *Positive organizational scholarship: Foundations of a new discipline.* (pp. 48–65) San Francisco, CA: Berrett-Koehler.

Christensen, C., & Shu, K. (1999). What is an organization's culture? *Harvard Business School Note,* 399–104.

Cooperrider, D.L. (2010, in press). Foreword to advances in appreciative inquiry, Volume four. In T. Thachenkery, M. Avital, & D. Cooperrider (Eds.) *Positive design and appreciative construction: From sustainable development to sustainable value.* London: Emerald Group Publishing.

Cooperrider, D.L. (2008). Going green maximum velocity through AI's sustainable design factory. *Global HR News,* Mar 7.

Cooperrider, D.L. (2008). The 3-circles of the strengths revolution. *AI Practitioner,* November, 8–11.

Cooperrider, D.L., & Avital, M. (Eds.). (2003). *Constructive discourse and human organization (Volume 1).* San Diego, CA: Elsevier.

Cooperrider, D.L., Barrett, F., & Srivastva, S. (1995). Social construction and appreciative inquiry: A journey in organizational theory. In D. Hosking, P. Dachler, & K. Gergen (Eds.), *Management and organization: Relational alternatives to individualism* (pp. 157–200). Aldershot, UK: Avebury Press.

Cooperrider, D.L., & Dutton, J. (1999). *The organization dimensions of global change.* Thousand Oaks, CA: Sage.

Cooperrider, D.L., & Sekerka, L.E. (2003). Elevation of inquiry into the appreciable world: Toward a theory of positive organizational change. In K. Cameron, J. Dutton, and R. Quinn (Eds.), *Positive organizational scholarship* (pp. 225–240). San Francisco: Berrett-Kohler.

Cooperrider, D.L., Sorenson, P., Yaegar, T., & Whitney, D. (2005). *Appreciative inquiry: Foundations in positive organization development.* Chicago: Stipes Publishing.

Cooperrider, D.L., & Srivastva, S. (1987). Appreciative inquiry in organizational life. In Pasmore, W., Woodman, R. (Eds.), *Research in organization change and development* (Vol. 1). Greenwich, CT: JAI Press.

Cooperider, D.L., & Whitney, D. (2005). *Appreciative inquiry: A positive revolution in change.* San Francisco, CA: Berrett-Koehler.

Coughlan, P., Suri, J., & Canales, K. (2008). Prototypes as (design) tools for behavioral and organizational change: A design-based approach to help organizations change work behaviors. *The Journal of Applied Behavioral Science, 43*(1), 1–13.

Drucker, P. (1966). *The effective executive.* New York: Harper Collins.

Dutton, J., & Heaphy, E. (2003). The power of high-quality connections at work. In K. Cameron, J. Dutton, & R.E. Quinn (Eds.), *Positive organizational scholarship* (pp. 263–278) San Francisco, CA: Berrett-Koehler Publishers.

Fredrickson, B.L. (2003). The value of positive emotions. *American Scientist, 91,* 330–335.

Freeman, R.E. (1984). *Strategic Management: A stakeholder approach.* Boston: Pitman.

French, W., & Bell, C. (1973). *Organization development: Behavioral science interventions for organization improvement.* Englewood Cliffs, NJ: Prentice-Hall.

Fry, R., Barrett, F., Seiling, J., & D Whitney, J. (2001). *Appreciative inquiry and organizational transformation: Reports from the field.* Westport, CT: Quorum Books.

Gallup. (2001). What your disaffected workers cost. *Gallup Management Journal.* Retrieved from: http://gmj.gallup.com/content/439/What-Your-Disaffected-Workers-Cost.aspx.

Gergen, K. (1982). *Toward transformation in social knowledge.* New York: Springer-Verlag.

Gergen, K.J. (1994). *Realities and relationships: Soundings in social construction.* Boston, MA: Harvard University Press.

Glavas, A., Senge, P., & Cooperrider, D.L. (2010). Building a green city on a blue lake: A model for building a local sustainable economy. *People & Strategy,* March 1.

Goleman, D., Boyatzis, R., & McKee, A. (2002). *Primal leadership: Realizing the power of emotional intelligence.* Boston, MA: Harvard Business School Press.

Heisenberg, W. (1949), *The physical principles of quantum theory* (C. Eckart & F. C. Hoyt, Trans.) New York: Dover. (Original work published 1930).

Jacobs, R.W. (1994). *Real time strategic change: How to involve an entire organization in fast and far reaching change.* San Francisco, CA: Berrett-Koehler.

James, W. (1902). *The varieties of religious experience.* New York: Mentor Books.

Kolb, D.A. (1984). *Experiential learning.* Englewood Cliffs, NJ: Prentice Hall.

Kotter, J. (1995). Leading change: Why transformation efforts fail. *Harvard Business Review, 73*(2), 59–67.

Kretzmann, J.P., & McKnight, J.L. (1994). *Building communities from the inside out: A path toward finding and mobilizing a community's assets.* Evanston, IL: Institute for Policy Research.

Levinson, H. (1976) *Organizational Diagnosis.* Boston, MA: Harvard University Press.

Laszlo, C. (2008). *Sustainable value: How the world's leading companies are doing well by doing good.* Sheffield, UK: Greenleaf Publishing.

Laszlo, C. (2003). *The sustainable company: How to create lasting value through social and environmental performance.* Washington, DC: Island Press.

Lewin, K. (1946). Action research and minority problems. *Journal of Social Issues, 2*(4), 34–46.

Lewin, K. (1947). Frontiers in group dynamics. *Human Relations, 1*(1), 5–41.

Mann, F. (1961). Studying and creating change: A memo to understanding social organizations. In Bennis, W., Benne K., & Chin R. (Eds.), *The planning of change.* New York: Holt, Rinehart and Winston.

Marrow, A. (1967). Events leading to the establishment of the National Training Laboratories. *Journal of Applied Behavioral Science, 3,* 145–150.

Martin, M. (2007). *Albert Schweitzer's reverence for life: Ethical idealism and self realization.* Burlington, VT: Ashgate Gower.

Martin, R. (2009). *The design of business: Why design thinking is the next competitive advantage.* Boston, MA: Harvard Business School Press.

Maslow, A. (1998). *Maslow on management.* New York: Wiley. (Note: previously published as: *Eupsychian management: A journal.* Homewood, IL: Irwin-Dorsey, 1965.)

Maslow, A. (1966). *The psychology of science: A reconnaissance.* Chapel Hill, NC: Maurice Bassett Publishing.

McDonough, W., & Braungart, M. (2002). *Cradle to cradle: Remaking the way we make things.* New York, NY: North Point Press.

McGregor, D. (1960). *The human side of enterprise.* New York: McGraw-Hill.

McKee, A., Boyatzis, R.E., & Johnston, F. (2008). *Becoming a resonant leader: Develop your emotional intelligence, renew your relationships, sustain your effectiveness.* Boston, MA: Harvard Business School Press.

Michner, C. (2009). Mayor Jackson pulls off an amazing feat with an exhilarating idea-sparking summit. *Cleveland Plain Dealer,* August 23, p. G–6.

Miller, P.J., R. Potts, H. Fung, L. Hoogstra, J., & Mintz. (1990). Narrative practices and the social construction of self in childhood. *American Ethnologist, 17*(2), 292–311.

Orem, S. Binket, J., & Clancy, A. (2007). *Appreciative coaching: A positive process for change.* San Francisco, CA: Jossey-Bass.

Peirce, C.S. (1938). *Collected papers of Charles Sanders Peirce, Vols. 1–6, 1931–1935.* C. Hartshorne & P. Weiss (Eds.), Boston, MA: Harvard University Press.

Peterson, C., & Seligman, M. (2004). *Character strengths and virtues: A handbook and classification.* Washington, DC: APA Press and Oxford University Press.

Piderit, S.K., Fry, R.E., & Cooperrider, D.L. (Eds.) (2007). *Handbook of transformative cooperation.* Stanford, CA: Stanford University Press.

Powley, E., & Cameron, K. (2006). Organizational healing: Lived virtuousness amidst organizational crisis. *Journal of Management, Spirituality, & Religion, 3*(1), 13–33.

Prahalad, C.K. (2004). *The fortune at the bottom of the pyramid: Eradicating poverty through profit.* Upper Saddle River, NJ: Wharton School Publishing.

Prahalad, C.K., & Hamel, G. (1990). The core competence of the corporation. *Harvard Business Review, 68*(3), 79–87.

Rath, T. (2007). *Strengths Finder 2.0.* New York: Gallup Press.

Roberts, L., Dutton, J.E., Spreitzer, G.M., Heaphy, E.D., & Quinn, R.E. (2005). Composing the reflected best-self portrait: Building pathways for becoming extraordinary in work organizations. *Academy of Management Review, 30*(4), 712–736.

Seligman, M. (2002). *Authentic happiness: Using the new positive psychology to realize your potential for lasting fulfillment.* New York: Free Press.

Seligman, M., & Csikszentmihalyi, M. (2000). Positive psychology: An introduction. *American Psychologist, 55,* 5–14.

Seligman, M., Steen, T., Park, N., & Peterson, C. (2005). Positive psychology progress: Empirical validation of interventions. *American Psychologist, 60*(5), 410–421.

Schumpeter, J. (1975). Creative destruction. In *Capitalism, socialism and democracy* (pp. 82–85). New York: Harper.

Simon, H. (1969). *The Sciences of the artificial.* Cambridge, MA: MIT Press.

Spreitzer, G., & Sonenshein, S. (2003). Positive deviance and extraordinary organizing. In K. Cameron, J. Dutton & R. Quinn (Eds.), *Positive organizational scholarship* (pp. 207–224). San Francisco, CA: Berrett-Koehler Publishers.

Stavros, J., & Hinrich, G. (2009). *The thin book of SOAR: Building strengths-based strategy.* Bend, OR: Thin Book Publishing.

Stavros, J.M., & Wooten, L.P. (2011). Positive strategy: Creating and sustaining strengths-based strategy that SOARs and performs. In K.S. Cameron & G.M. Spreitzer (Eds.), *The Oxford handbook of positive organizational scholarship.* New York: Oxford University Press.

Stewart, T. (2008). Magic by design. *Harvard Business Review,* April.

Thatchenkery, T., Cooperrider, D.L., Avital, M., & Zandee, D. (Eds.). (2010). *Positive design and appreciative construction: From sustainable development to sustainable value.* Bingley, UK: Emerald Group Publishing.

Thatchenkery, T., & Metzker, C. (2006). *Appreciative intelligence: Seeing the mighty oak in the acorn.* San Francisco, CA: Berrett-Koehler.

Weber, M. (2002). *The Protestant ethic and "the spirit of capitalism"* (P. Baehr & G.C. Wells, Trans). New York: Penguin Books. (Original work published 1905).

Weisbord, M.R., & Janoff, S. (1995). *Future search.* San Francisco, CA: Berrett-Koehler.

Whitehouse P., Bendezu E., FallCreek S., & Whitehouse C. (2000). Intergenerational community schools: A new practice for a new time. *Education and Gerontology, 26,* 761–770.

Wittgenstein, L. (1999). *Tractatus Logico-Philosophicus,* German Text with an English Translation by C.K. Ogden, Introduction by B. Russell, London, UK, Routledge Press.

Seeing and Acting Differently

Positive Change in Organizations

Robert E. Quinn *and* Ned Wellman

Abstract

Positive organizational scholarship (POS) adopts an affirmative bias, seeking out and building upon the exceptional in organizational life. In this chapter, we contrast the POS perspective on organizational change with what we refer to as the "normal" or "traditional" perspective. We discuss 11 important individual- and organizational-level differences between the two approaches, and identify several promising new directions for change research.

Keywords: Change, positive organizational scholarship, leadership

Positive organizational scholarship (POS) is about seeing differently (Weick, 2003, p. 68). Although most organizational research focuses on problem solving, managing uncertainty, overcoming resistance, and competing against others, POS adopts an affirmative bias. Positive organizational scholarship researchers seek out individuals and organizations that are "exceptional, virtuous, life-giving and flourishing" (Cameron, Dutton, & Quinn, 2003, p. 5). This affirmative bias enables POS to complement traditional research by illuminating new, more positive patterns of organizing.

Most studies of change attempt to address the difficulties inherent in the change process by identifying the forces that impede change initiatives and seeking ways to overcome them. In this chapter, we refer to studies that adopt this approach as "traditional" or "normal" change research. The traditional approach has contributed much to what we know about change. However, it has also promoted a restrictive set of assumptions about organizational behavior. Normal change research depicts individuals who make utilitarian assumptions, comply with demands, endure constraints, minimize personal costs, prefer the status quo, and fail to grasp or even see all the opportunities in the work setting

(Bateman & Porath, 2003, p. 124). These individuals work in organizations that struggle to react to constraints imposed by their external environments (Thompson, 1967) and compete with each other for limited resources (Pfeffer & Salancik, 1978). Although the assumptions that typify the normal approach to studying organizational change are accurate in many cases, it is becoming clear they do not paint the full picture.

A smaller but rapidly growing body of POS research suggests that some individuals and organizations experience change very differently. This research reveals transcendent actors, people who "effect extraordinary change by exceeding demands, eliminating or overcoming constraints, and creating or seizing opportunities" (Bateman & Porath, 2003, p. 124–125). These are people who seek feedback, adapt to new environments, express voice, sell issues, take charge, expand their roles, craft jobs, break rules, implement ideas, and build social networks (Grant & Ashford, 2008). Studies of positive change also discover organizations that expand their resource pool by engaging in virtuous practices (Cameron, Bright, & Caza, 2004), facilitating the expression of positive emotions (Fredrickson, 2009) and responding with compassion to the pain and suffering of others (Dutton, Worline, Frost, & Lilius, 2006). Positive organizational scholarship reveals how change can unleash the positive forces inside organizations, a process that is characterized more by growth and transcendence than by rigidity and competition.

In reviewing the change literature, we found POS studies differ from traditional change research on 11 important dimensions, which are summarized in Table 57.1. The first five dimensions are relevant to the individual level of analysis; that is, they describe differences between the portrayal of individual change agents in traditional and POS research. The next six dimensions are organization-level differences. We should note at the outset that our comparison of the normal and POS approaches to change involves some degree of generalization. There are almost certainly examples of "normal" studies that adopt a perspective or assumption we have attributed to POS research, and vice versa. However, we believe that a comparison of the general trends in the two schools of thought is valuable and presents a more complete picture of the change process than either perspective provides on its own.

In the remainder of this chapter, we more fully articulate the differences between the traditional and POS perspectives on organizational change. After elaborating the contrasts, we offer our suggestions about how the two perspectives might be

reconciled and identify new possibilities for future change research to explore.

Individual-level Differences
Change Target: From Changing Others to Changing Self

We begin at the individual level, with the most important difference between the traditional and POS approaches to change. This difference involves the focus of the change agent. In the traditional perspective, change agents employ all the resources at their disposal to encourage others in the organization to change (Quinn & Sonenshein, 2008). Leaders campaign to acquire the necessary support for their predetermined objectives or agendas. They draw on their expertise to tell people how to change, and they draw on their hierarchical authority and political acumen to overcome resistance and leverage change (Ford & Ford, 1995). In both cases, they act "on" the human system just as they would act "on" any other object.

The POS literature, however, suggests change agents can access two additional strategies in addition to imposing change on others (Quinn & Sonenshein, 2008). The first is participation. The change agent can begin to act "with" others, co-creating trusting relationships and jointly constructed, attractive futures. This approach requires the surrender of control, the creation of trust, and the investment of time. Although the participating

Table 57.1 Comparing traditional and positive perspectives on organizational change

	Normal Change	Positive Change
Individual Level		
Change target	Others	Self
Orientation to purpose	Comfort-centered	Results-centered
Expectations	Externally directed	Internally directed
Relationships	Self-focused	Other-focused
Learning	Internally closed	Externally open
Organization Level		
Individual agency	Bounded	Limitless
Basic vision	Preserve the organization	Facilitate positive organizing
Knowledge	Expertise	Learning
Communication	Analyze the present	Symbolize the desired future
Search process	Find the problems	Find the possibilities
Ratio of positive to negative emotions	Low	High

strategy is often advocated in traditional discussions, it is less often practiced and sometimes used only to manipulate others. Positive change agents, however, trust participation and employ it with authenticity.

The next strategy is less recognized or employed. It is the strategy of self-change. It is based on the argument that the success of an intervention is most dependent upon the interior condition of the intervener (Scharmer, 2009). What a change agent knows and what a change agent does is less important than the inner state from which they are operating. Two people can engage in exactly the same behavior and get very different reactions. In this perspective, there is a shift from telling people what to do to showing people how to be. There is a focus on moral power (Weick & Quinn, 1999). As the change agent becomes more purposive, authentic, empathetic, and open, he or she models an elevated condition of positive influence (Quinn & Quinn, 2009). Moral power increases as the change agent becomes a living symbol, a "metaphor for metamorphosis" (Chatterjee, 1998). This elevated state repels some people, while it attracts others. As attracted people gather around the change agent, a new community forms and the way is open for new dialogs and new relationships.

Thus, self-regulating positive change agents launch others in their organizations on upward trajectories of increased virtue and goodness (Cameron, 2003; Peterson & Seligman, 2003). As these individuals engage in self-change, they become more vibrant and attractive, personifications of a vision that invites others into a new future. The notion of changing others by changing one's self can be difficult to comprehend, but represents a fundamental difference between the traditional and positive perspectives on change. Although the traditional perspective views change as forced *down* the organizational hierarchy through the exercise of formal authority, the POS perspective suggests change can also spiral *up* through organizations, driven by positive transformations in individual members who may or may not occupy positions of authority.

Focus: From Comfort Centered to Purpose Centered

Much of the traditional literature on organizational change views individuals as path dependent (Ford, Ford, & D'Amelio, 2008). They do what they have learned to do in the past. They therefore tend to be comfort-centered. Individuals who are comfort-centered feel tense and anxious when events force them outside of their normal routines (Weick, 1990). If they experience a gap between their expectations and reality, they label the gap as a problem (Smith, 1988). As a result, comfort-centered individuals view deviance, both positive and negative, as a threat, and go to great lengths to restore the status quo by removing the source of the disruption or by finding some other way to make events turn out the way they expect them to (Quinn & Quinn, 2009). They tend to use transactional leadership to influence others: rewarding those who meet their predetermined standards and expectations and punishing those who fail to do so (Burns, 1978; Podsakoff, Bommer, Podsakoff, & MacKenzie, 2006).

In contrast, a major theme in the positive literature is the notion of challenge and meaning (Garcea, Harrington, & Lindley, 2010). Positive organizational scholarship research reveals people who are purpose centered. They make a fundamental commitment to some aspect of their own highest potential (Fritz, 1989). When people choose to engage in challenging tasks that are at, or just beyond, their skill levels, they are more likely to experience task absorption and intrinsic motivation (Csikszentmihalyi, 1997). In the resulting state of flow, self-consciousness wanes, a sense of timelessness emerges, and personal energy expands. Attention becomes ordered and focused. People feel both aroused and in control. They feel more confident and are more open to learning and growth.

Positive change agents not only tolerate challenges and disruptions of the status quo, they encourage them by continually clarifying their higher purpose and helping others to do the same. Positive change agents tend to engage in transformational rather than transactional leadership behaviors. They recognize the existing routines and norms of the organization, but also appeal to the deeper motives and higher needs of others (Bass 1998; Burns, 1978). Transformational leaders display purpose and conviction, articulate compelling possibilities for a new and better future, and encourage others to think outside the box (Bass, 2008). By pursuing a higher moral purpose and transcending traditional norms, these individuals inspire creativity, innovation, and positive deviance (Van Dyne & Saavedra, 1996).

Expectations: From Externally Directed to Internally Directed

In normal change research, individuals are externally directed. They are microsystems residing in the larger macro-system of the organization. The prevailing assumption is that macro determines micro. Traditional research has confirmed that, in many situations, external pressures can indeed be a powerful determinant of individual behavior. For instance, participants in Stanley Milgram's (1974) iconic experiments delivered what they believed to be extremely painful or even deadly shocks to fellow participants simply because they were ordered to do so by an authority figure in a lab coat. In Milgram's study, the social pressure to obey authority overrode participant's internal standards governing ethical behavior (Quinn & Quinn, 2009). Social norms or stereotypes can also overwhelm individual intentions and values in determining behavior. For instance, when their gender was made salient, Asian women were found to perform worse than average on a math test, conforming to the stereotype that women struggle with math. When ethnicity rather than gender was made salient in the same group of women, they performed *better* than average, conforming to the stereotype that Asians excel at math (Shih, Pittinsky, & Ambady, 1999). Research in the traditional perspective reveals a number of external forces that can cause individuals to engage in behaviors that contradict their internal values and goals (Maio, Olson, Allen, & Bernard, 2001).

Studies that adopt a positive perspective, however, reveal change agents who are internally directed. They self-regulate as they move toward desired ends (Maddux, 2002) and choose behaviors that are consistent with their values (Maio, Olson, Allen, & Bernard, 2001). In so doing, they author a self with congruence between emotions, values, and actions (Rogers, 1961). When people exercise strengths such as wisdom and courage they become free from self-justification and experience an increased sense of dignity (Margolis, 2001). They also tend to perform more effectively (Sheldon & Elliot, 1999) and be happier (Sheldon et al., 2004). Indeed, internally directed behavior can produce an upward spiral in which self-concordant motivation increases the likelihood that individuals will achieve their personally valued goals, which in turn promotes satisfaction and further internally directed behavior (Sheldon & Houser-Marko, 2001). When people exercise the courage to be authentic, it inspires others to become more internally directed as well (Worline, Wrzesniewski, & Rafaeli, 2002). Positive change agents, who self-elevate through continuous value clarification, help others see their work as more important and more self-congruent (Bono & Judge, 2003).

Relationships: From Self-focused to Other Focused

Some of the foundational organization theories assume individual behavior is motivated by self-interest. For instance, transaction cost economics suggests organizational change results from self-interest seeking on the part of opportunistic individuals (Williamson, 1981). Agency theory argues managerial self-interest seeking is so pervasive that it must be curtailed by control mechanisms or it will disrupt the performance of the organization (Eisenhardt, 1989; Jensen & Meckling, 1976). Most psychological theories also view individuals as self-focused, adopting a perspective known as *social egoism,* that suggests people care for the well-being of others only to the degree that it affects their own welfare (Batson, 1990). The assumption that individuals are primarily self-interested may be accurate in many cases. Research suggests that 75% of all professionals hold a self-focused worldview (Quinn, Spreitzer, & Fletcher, 1995), and that powerful individuals tend to base important choices such as hiring decisions, intrapersonal judgments, and the selection of relationship partners on the other party's usefulness to their own personal goals (Gruenfeld, Inesi, Magee, & Galinsky, 2008).

Positive organizational scholarship research, however, reveals some individuals who are exceptional. These change agents transcend self-interest. They put the collective good ahead of their own personal good and are willing to sacrifice themselves to help the group accomplish its goals (Bass, 1998). Other-focused individuals, who make up approximately 18% of the total population, have, through self-change, adopted a more mature, more integrated perspective (Quinn, Spreitzer, & Fletcher, 1995). In addition to achieving objectives, they put an emphasis on teamwork, participation, and openness. They manage stress and conflict through mechanisms of consensus building. These people tend to be older, healthier, and more satisfied with coworkers and with life.

Positive organizational scholarship research also reveals that, under certain circumstances, people have a capacity for caring and helping that is driven by more than just self-interest. The best example of such research is the work of Batson (1990; Batson et al., 1988, 1989), who tested the social egoism perspective against the alternative hypothesis that experiencing empathy can lead individuals to behave altruistically—that is, to act with the ultimate goal of helping others. Batson identified the three most plausible egoistic explanations for helping: that people help to reduce the unpleasant feelings caused by witnessing others suffer, that people help to avoid social and self-punishments (e.g., shame and guilt), and that people help to obtain social rewards. In a series of controlled experiments, he then found that individuals who experienced empathy chose to assist others in distress even when they were presented with an easier alternative way of reaching the egotistic goals associated with helping (for example, leaving the room or justifying not helping). Batson's studies depict individuals who act with the greater good firmly in mind and who care about others as more than simply as a means to some personal end.

Learning: From Internally Closed to Externally Open

Change agents in normal research tend to be internally closed, that is, resistant to feedback and signals for change from their environments. This fear of feedback may stem from the belief that one's abilities are unchanging or unchangeable, or that one's success depends upon factors outside of one's control (Dweck, 2006). Or, it may stem from adopting goals that involve performing well or looking good rather than putting forth a sustained effort or learning new skills (Seijts, Latham, Taza, & Latham, 2004). Internally closed behavior on the part of managers causes others to withhold their opinions and concerns about potential problems, which contributes to the development of what has been termed a "climate of silence" in many organizations (Morrison & Milliken, 2000). Normal research has revealed that this type of climate is highly pervasive: One survey indicated that more than 70% of employees are afraid to speak up about issues or problems that they encounter at work (Ryan & Oestreich, 1991). Once formed, the climate of silence can further perpetuate internally closed behavior on the part of change agents by restricting the feedback available in their environment.

From a positive perspective, change agents are continuously engaged in the process of learning and development. People of influence are able to transcend their cultural programming and the tendency to repeatedly enact old scripts. They are able to recognize and respond to patterns that emerge in the present moment (Scharmer, 2009, p. 8; Avolio, Griffith, Wernsing, & Walumbwa, 2010). This requires adaptive self-reflection, the ability to examine one's own assumptions and behaviors in order to learn more about the self and thus increase understanding and capacity (Schön, 1983). Such self-reflection is often initiated in response to trigger events that provide unexpected feedback and stimulate episodes of self-reflection (Luthans & Avolio, 2003). Because externally open individuals believe growth is possible and desirable (Dweck, 2006), they embrace rather than defend against trigger events. Their external orientation endows them with a "capacity, sensitivity, and motivational orientation" to developmental aspects of their environment (Avolio, Griffith, Wernsing, & Walumbwa, 2010, p. 41). They are able to move forward, seeking out feedback and adapting in real time (Ashford, Blatt, & VandeWalle, 2003). This means they are more aware of the opportunities emerging in their environments and are more likely to see and engage them. By encouraging triggers and seeking feedback, externally open individuals also disrupt the climate of silence, encouraging others around them to voice their opinions and suggestions. These positive change agents model the process of moving with confidence into uncertainty while adapting effectively and attracting others into the learning process (Quinn, 2004).

Organization-level Differences
Individual Agency: From Bounded to Limitless

The traditional perspective holds that individual actors, particularly those who are not in top management positions, are limited in their ability to bring about organizational change. Theories of organizational culture, for example, suggest that once the culture of an organization is established it is rigid and little can be done to alter it (Schein, 2004). Similarly, contingency theories argue that the organization's external environment is the major driver of change and that the beliefs and actions of individual actors are largely unimportant (e.g., Thompson, 1967). Ecological theories take an even more extreme stance, suggesting that internal pressures toward inertia and rapid environmental fluctuations render meaningful organizational change impossible. Change, from an ecological perspective, occurs primarily at the organizational population level, as the result of births and deaths of individual organizations (Hannan & Freeman, 1984).

Recent studies adopting a POS perspective, however, suggest that individuals *can* initiate positive changes that spiral upward through organizations. For example, Dutton, Ashford, O'Neill, and Lawrence (2001) found that "issue selling," the process through which individuals bring events and agendas to the attention of top management, plays an important role in determining which change initiatives get activated and which actions ensue on the part of the organization. Similarly, Reay, Golden-Biddle, and GermAnn (2006) described how nurse practitioners were able to introduce a new work role into a well-established health care system in Alberta, Canada. By cultivating opportunities for change, fitting new practices into prevailing systems, proving the value of new policies, and recognizing and celebrating small wins, the practitioners legitimized their role, and it soon became incorporated into the existing institutions of the health care field. In another important study, Plowman and colleagues (2007) showed how individual actions sparked radical positive change at a southwestern church. The church decided to accept the suggestion of a few young members to begin offering breakfast to the homeless. This simple act of generosity became the catalyst for an emergent, radical change that fundamentally altered the church's mission and bolstered its declining membership.

Basic Vision: From Preserving the Organization to Facilitating Positive Organizing

Traditional studies of organizational change assume the hierarchy that dictates the process of organizing already exists (Biddle, 1986). It is a stable structure. It is reflected in a statement of predetermined roles and expectations. Human action is predictable because people respond to the predetermined roles and expectations. The goal of change is to preserve the organization in its current state by returning it to equilibrium while retaining as much of the prior structure as possible. Thus, the organization seeks to identify and repair the problems that alter its entropic trajectory.

In contrast, POS research acknowledges that preservation cannot happen without adaptation. Positive organizational scholarship studies reveal organizations that are receptive to progressive change agents, who in turn move the organizations to a more adaptive and effective state. The focus is on the creation of generative processes. The emphasis is not on organization but on organizing (Weick, 1979). The organization is not a thing, but a living system in the process of constant change. As such, an important part of its mission is to energize the process of positive organizing. According to Weick (2003, p. 69), positive organizing "occurs concurrent with wading into uncertain circumstances and dealing with whatever unexpected events occur using tools that themselves were unexpected recombinations of existing repertoires." He indicates that,

at the intergroup level, this process requires heedful interrelating, and at the organization level it requires mindfulness (Weick, 2003).

Heedful interrelating consists of contribution, representation, and subordination (Asch, 1952; Weick, 2003). Instead of seeing their work as a stand-alone effort, people see themselves as making a contribution to a system. Although the system may not exist, if people act like they are contributing to one, the system will materialize. Representation is about visualizing "meshed contributions." Each person in the emergent system has a cognitive representation that captures what others are doing and how those actions are related. Finally, individuals subordinate their self-interests, making the contributions necessary to keep the emergent systems functioning.

Mindful organizing involves an orientation to the present, focusing on the current moment and being fully aware of what is unfolding. It is the ability to engage in sense-making. Organizations that achieve mindful organizing are better able to examine failure, resist simple assumptions, observe operations, develop resilience, engage the unexpected, and locate and defer to local experts (Weick, 2003). Organizations engaged in positive change attract people to positive organizing. This means fostering relationships of trust – heedful relationships that give rise to synergy, to a state of mindfulness that connects with present reality and allows for facilitation of the emergent future. The objective is not to preserve the existing organization but to connect the existing organization with an emerging enhancement of itself.

Knowledge: From Expertise to Learning

Traditional research views change as incremental and linear (e.g., Gersick, 1994). Thus, it places a high value on expertise since experts are capable of making controlled alterations and adjustments to organizational processes. Because competent experts are promoted up the organizational hierarchy, organizations operate on a basis of knowledge and authority (Weber, 1968; Mintzberg, 1983).

In the process of positive organizing, change emerges from complex processes (Anderson, 1999). Rather than a stable hierarchy, the organization tends to move toward bounded instability (McKelvey, 1999). At the edge of chaos, structure exists but it is minimal. Relationships and processes tend to change. They become more dynamic. Traditional assumptions of linear analysis and control tend to fail (Higgs, 2010). The emphasis shifts from knowing to learning in real time.

The shift toward learning requires a change in leadership behaviors. Control gives way to the facilitation of the learning process. Organizations that successfully undertake complex change tend to engage in four types of behavior (Rowland & Higgs, 2008). First, they attract people to the big picture and future intent. Second, they challenge people by continually confronting reality and holding their attention. Third, they provide a "container" or supportive structure that provides confidence. Fourth, they create movement, thus enabling learning and change to happen. The leaders of these organizations do not assume expertise and control of a linear process. Rather, they bring about conditions that facilitate continual learning and the emergence of the new.

Communication: From the Literal Present to the Symbolized Future

The traditional approach to change research tends to view communication as factual. In the organizations depicted by normal studies, much effort and money goes into the generation and monitoring of control systems (e.g., Ouchi, 1977). From these systems come the data that give rise to many of the organizations' most important conversations. These conversations are assumed to be factual and objective.

In POS studies of change, the organization itself is seen as a conversation of conversations (Ford & Ford, 1995). The communication of the literal present is supplemented with the communication of the symbolized future. This symbolized future is most influential when it is drawn from the people in the organization. In the positive lens, we find that conversations of the symbolized future can become the most important conversations of all.

One of the most recognized methods for bringing forth such conversations is *appreciative inquiry* (Cooperrider & Srivastva, 1987; Cooperrider, 1986). The method is highly consistent with the notion of positive organizing. Appreciative inquiry assumes that organizations are living networks. The objective of appreciative inquiry is to call forth the positive core of organizational life by asking questions about what is most valued and what is most desired. The resulting image becomes the envisioned system around which people may begin to self-organize.

Appreciative inquiry involves four steps: discovery, dream, design and destiny. Based on the assumption that human systems are drawn to their deepest and most frequent explorations, the discovery phase is an inquiry into the positive capacities of the system. Members of the organization interview each other. As people throughout the organization become increasingly aware of the positive core, appreciation increases, hope expands, and community grows. In a state of increased positive emotions, the people are ready to engage in the dream phase. As they share the findings from the discovery phase, the conversations give rise to a shared vision. Because the dream is shared, there is less resistance to the process of designing new systems. In the final phase of appreciative inquiry, destiny, people experience a paradigm change, new routines emerge, and the organization transforms.

The lessons from appreciative inquiry may have long-term implications. Serkerka and Fredrickson (2010) suggest that the transformative cooperation that is seen in appreciative inquiry, and that emerges from positive emotions, and mutually beneficial, collective processes, can be stimulated as an ongoing process. Thus, organizations in POS research emphasize the symbolized future to attract people to continuous positive change.

Search Processes: From Problem Finding to Positive Deviance

In the normal change perspective, organizations place a high value on stability. Hierarchical efficiency calls for the elimination of variance (Hannan & Freeman, 1984). It is normal for authority figures to search for and identify problems. In this traditional perspective, the very purpose of management is to problem-solve.

In positive change research, organizations transcend the mindset of problem detection. Instead, there is recognition that excellence is, by definition, a form of deviance (Quinn, 1996). One way to stimulate excellence is to search for, observe, and spread the positive deviance that already exists in the system (Pascale, Sternin, & Sternin, 2010; Spreitzer & Sonenshein, 2003). Instead of searching for problems, organizational control systems seek out positive anomalies that have already emerged. Once identified, the positive patterns can be shared. By pointing to positive deviance, management can introduce new ideas that do not emanate come from a fantasy, but from an empirical reality that already exists in the organization. Organizational search processes can thus produce valid arguments for positive change by focusing on magnifying positive deviance rather than eliminating negative. This strategy can be extended beyond the organization by sending people to observe positive deviance in other organizations.

Ratio of Positive to Negative Emotions: From Low to High

Many organizations observed by normal researchers are characterized by low positivity ratios, that is, low ratios of positive to negative emotions (Fredrickson, 2009). Because these organizations are focused on identifying and correcting problems rather than on locating and rewarding excellence, they promote negative feelings such as anger and anxiety. Individuals in these organizations live in fear of making a mistake and feel hurt when they are reprimanded. These emotions cascade throughout the organization, causing it to become rigid and revert to narrow, prelearned behavioral patterns (Barsade, 2002; Fredrickson, 2001).

Organizations studied by POS scholars, however, tend to have higher positivity ratios. These organizations, which are characterized by an abundance of positive emotions, enable their members to play, explore, envision the future, savor experience, and integrate new views. Over time, this broadening process builds psychological and relational assets in the organization that can be called upon at later times (Fredrickson, 2001). Perhaps the best illustration of the benefit of high positivity ratios is found in the work of Losada and his colleagues (Fredrickson & Losada, 2005; Losada & Heaphy, 2004). Losada brought 60 management teams into a simulated board room where they could hold actual meetings. He divided the teams into three groups—high performance, mixed performance, and low performance—according to their performance on profitability, satisfaction, and 360-degree evaluations. Behind mirrors, researchers observed and coded every statement made by team members during the meetings. Losada used these observations to compare the internal processes and dynamics of thriving teams with those of teams that were less successful.

Losada found that the high-performance teams lived in flourishing relationships. They had positivity ratios as high as 6:1, they were very aware and responsive to one another (higher connectivity), and they were balanced on inquiry and on outward focus. These teams exhibited another remarkable characteristic: When their activities were graphed, the trajectory of their performance never retraced itself. The teams were always fresh and creative. Even if there was a big jolt of negativity, the teams would quickly recover and return to the creative edge. They had "infinite flexibility."

The performance trajectory of the middle teams started out the same as the high-performance teams but then dipped. The positivity ratio of these teams was much lower, and the range of inquiry and advocacy was narrow. Most importantly, the mixed teams were not resilient; they could not maintain the continual creative performance that was seen in the high-performing teams. Whenever a jolt of strong negativity occurred, the performance trajectory would collapse and the team would get stuck in a repetitive rut. Team members would get caught in negative, self-absorbed advocacy. The team would lose the ability to maintain positive emotions, to be flexible, and to question and explore. Participants tended to become critical of others while tightly maintaining their own position.

Low-performance teams started out where the middle teams ended up. From the outset, they were stuck in the rut of self-absorbed advocacy, criticism, and defensiveness. Their positivity ratios were low (1:1). There was no inclination to question and explore. They could only spiral downward to a completely static condition and lose all creative flexibility.

Discussion

We have suggested that POS research differs from normal or traditional research on a number of important dimensions relevant to change. Normal research views change agents as rigid and self-centered, focused on overcoming resistance and persuading others to adopt their preformulated agendas. Organizations depicted by normal research strive to preserve a preestablished hierarchical order by seeking out and correcting deviations to their typical patterns of organizing. In contrast, POS research suggests that individuals, through self-change, can move both themselves and their organizations to positive states that promote flexibility and enable flourishing. Organizations depicted by POS research encourage growth by embracing change as necessary and constant, and employ search processes, such as appreciative inquiry, to identify instances of positive deviance to create a vision of the improved future that serves as an attractor for other members.

Two important questions arise from our comparison of POS and traditional change research: Why is the POS perspective on change so different from the normal perspective when both perspectives ostensibly describe the same organizational reality? And, how do the two perspectives inform and complement each other? We address each of these questions in turn.

The key to understanding the differences between the findings of normal and POS research lies in understanding the affirmative bias adopted by

POS researchers. Assume organizational performance can be described by a normal curve. The middle of the curve, which contains the majority of organizations, represents those organizations that fall at or around the mean in terms of performance. At either end of the curve are a few exceptional organizations that exhibit either unusually poor or unusually strong performance. Normal research seeks to accurately describe the state of affairs in the majority of organizations. As such, it studies mostly organizations in the middle of the performance curve. These organizations experience extreme vulnerability as they struggle to meet the demands of turbulent environments. Therefore, questions involving sustainable performance, recovering from near disasters, and managing the unexpected become priorities for normal researchers (Weick, 2003). However, in addressing these questions, normal research tends to view organizations as "flawed and fragile," resistant to change and yet buffeted this way and that by the whimsical demands of their environments (Peterson & Seligman, 2003, p. 14).

In contrast, the objective of POS research is to explore how organizations function when they are at their very best. Positive organizational scholarship researchers start with different assumptions and ask different questions. They seek out organizations that are positive deviants, that are located at the far right of the normal performance curve. These organizations, and the individuals within them, are by definition unusual. They embrace opportunities for change as they move to ever more positive forms of organizing. The affirmative bias of POS shifts the focus of POS researchers away from problem solving and toward goodness and excellence. Although the POS approach can appear to contradict traditional change research, both POS and traditional studies offer accurate depictions of reality. The important difference is that normal research describes reality as it is for most organizations, whereas POS research focuses on the reality that is possible in organizations that are flourishing.

Both the POS and normal perspectives offer valuable contributions to what we know about change. The normal perspective has identified a number of important issues that arise in the "complex and fragile and entropic and unknowable" process of organizing people and technology (Weick, 2003, p. 67). Understanding these issues and how organizations attempt to overcome them is an important step in understanding why organizations behave the way they do with respect to change. However, simply overcoming the obstacles presented by the change process is not enough to ensure change initiatives that result in organizational flourishing. An understanding of the potential pitfalls of change must be supplemented by an appreciation for change's transformational potential, and an identification of the properties of individuals and organizations that facilitate flourishing through continual rebirth and renewal. The POS studies we have reviewed in this chapter provide this valuable supplement to traditional change research.

Normal change studies also contribute in important ways to POS research. Without understanding how ordinary organizations experience change, POS scholars would not be able to identify and appreciate organizations that change in ways that are extraordinary. Similarly, although the affirmative bias adopted by POS researchers enables valuable insights about positive change, it can also lead POS scholars to sample on the dependant variable. If only thriving organizations are studied, it is impossible to draw firm conclusions about which attributes of these organizations are causing the thriving. As such, it is important for POS change researchers to compare organizations that have extremely positive experiences with change with those that have normal or negative experiences. Only by comparing and contrasting their findings with those of normal research can POS researchers accurately understand the driving forces behind positive change.

Future Directions

Although POS research offers important insights concerning organizational change, because POS is a relatively new field many important questions related to positive change are yet to be answered. In the remainder of this chapter we highlight a few of these questions. First, in reviewing the extant change studies, we noticed a tremendous opportunity for additional research on organization-level positive change. Most studies adopting a POS perspective have focused on individual- or group-level phenomena. However, because organizations are bigger, more complex, and more hierarchical than groups, the complex dynamics that characterize the many positive phenomena might operate in new and different ways at the organizational level. For instance, organizations cannot rely as heavily on personal supervision and face-to-face communication as groups do. Therefore, positivity likely flows through organizations in different channels than it flows through groups or individuals. Further research investigating how aspects of organizations, such as formal (e.g., rewards programs) and informal (e.g., organizational culture) control systems, foster positive practices and enable positive change would be extremely valuable.

Second, the ideas in this chapter support a more agentic view of the organizational change process than is typically adopted. The predominant perspective seems to be that individual actors, particularly those who are not in top management positions, are incapable of stimulating organizational change. However, a positive lens suggests that the positive patterns produced by self-change can flow upward through groups and organizations. This argument is supported by recent empirical evidence suggesting that macro-level change can be initiated by the actions of individuals and groups (e.g., Hargadon & Douglass, 2001; Reay, Golden-Biddle, & GermAnn, 2006; Plowman et al., 2007). We believe these studies represent an important development in change research, and encourage others to continue to investigate the role of individual agency in organizational change.

Finally, although POS researchers have made tremendous contributions in identifying the benefits of positivity in the workplace, now that findings are accumulating there is a need to better integrate the research being conducted on the various POS topics. To date, POS research investigating topics such as virtuousness, compassion, positive emotions, and psychological capital has proceeded largely separately. However, it is likely that synergy exists between these topics and the potential for nonlinear dynamics in their interaction. Thus, future studies that integrate across the various POS research topics or explore the relationship of multiple positive phenomena in facilitating positive change efforts would constitute an important contribution.

Conclusion

If POS is about seeing differently, positive organizational change is about seeing and acting differently. We invite our readers to revisit their assumptions about organizations, about organizational change, and about themselves, so that they can see and act differently. We hope that this chapter will serve to attract change scholars to the employment of a new lens, a lens that puts the researcher into a new pattern of being, that changes the relationship of the observer to the observed, and opens both the observer and the observed to greater possibility.

References

Anderson, R. (1999). Complexity theory and organization science. *Organization Science, 10*, 216–232.

Asch, S. (1952). *Social Psychology*. Englewood Cliffs, NJ: Prentice-Hall.

Ashford, S.J., Blatt, R., & VandeWalle, D. (2003). Reflections on the looking glass: A review of research on feedback-seeking behavior in organizations. *Journal of Management, 29*, 773–799.

Avolio, B., Griffith, J., Wernsing, T.S., & Walumbwa, F.O. (2010). What is authentic leadership development. In P.A. Linley, S.H. Harrington, & N. Garcea (Eds.), *Oxford handbook of positive psychology and work* (pp. 39–52). New York: Oxford University Press.

Barsade, S.G. (2002). The ripple effect: Emotional contagion and its influence on group behavior. *Administrative Science Quarterly, 47*(4), 644–675.

Bass, B.M. (1998). *Transformational leadership: Industrial, military, and educational impact:* Lawrence Erlbaum Associates Mahwah, NJ.

Bass, B.M. (2008). *The Bass handbook of leadership* (4 ed.). New York: Free Press.

Bateman, T.S., & Porath, C. (2003). Transcendent behavior. In K.S. Cameron, J.E. Dutton, & R.E. Quinn (Eds.), *Positive organizational scholarship: foundations of a new discipline* (pp. 122–137). San Francisco: Berrett-Koehler.

Batson, C.D. (1990). How social an animal? The human capacity for caring. *American Psychologist, 45*(3), 336–346.

Batson, C.D., Dyck, J.L., Brandt, J.R., Batson, J.G., Powell, A.L., McMaster, M.R., et al. (1988). Five studies testing two new egoistic alternatives to the empathy-altruism hypothesis. *Journal of Personality and Social Psychology, 55*(1), 52–77.

Batson, C.D., Oleson, K.C., Weeks, J.L., Healy, S.P., Reeves, P.J., Jennings, P., et al. (1989). Religious prosocial motivation: Is it altruistic or egoistic? *Journal of Personality and Social Psychology, 57*(5), 873–884.

Biddle, B.J. (1986). Recent developments in role theory. *Annual Review of Sociology, 12*(1), 67–92.

Bono, J.E., & Judge, T.A. (2003). Self-concordance at work: Toward understanding the motivational effects of transformational leaders. *Academy of Management Journal, 46*, 554–571.

Burns, J.M.G. (1978). *Leadership*. New York: Harper & Row.

Cameron, K.S. (2003). Organizational virtuousness and performance. In *Positive Organizational Scholarship: Foundations of a new discipline* (pp. 48–65). San Francisco: Berrett-Koehler.

Cameron, K.S., Bright, D., & Caza, A. (2004). Exploring the relationships between organizational virtuousness and performance. *American Behavioral Scientist, 47*(6), 766.

Cameron, K.S., Dutton, J.E., & Quinn, R.E. (2003). Foundations of Positive Organizational Scholarship. In K.S. Cameron, J.E. Dutton, & R.E. Quinn (Eds.), *Positive Organizational Scholarship: Foundations of a new discipline* (pp. 3–13). San Francisco: Berrett-Koehler.

Chatterjee, D. (1998). *Leading consciously*. Boston: Butterworth-Heinemann.

Cooperrider, D.L. (1986). *Appreciative inquiry: Toward a methodology for understanding and enhancing organizational innovation*. Case Western Reserve University.

Cooperrider, D.L., & Srivastva, S. (1987). Appreciative inquiry in organizational life. *Research in organizational change and development, 1*, 129–169.

Csikszentmihalyi, M. (1997). *Creativity: Flow and the psychology of discovery and invention*. New York: Harper Perennial.

Dutton, J.E., Ashford, S.J., O'Neill, R.M., & Lawrence, K.A. (2001). Moves that matter: Issue selling and organizational change. *Academy of Management Journal, 44*(4), 716–736.

Dutton, J.E., Worline, M.C., Frost, P.J., & Lilius, J. (2006). Explaining compassion organizing. *Administrative Science Quarterly, 51*(1), 59–96.

Dweck, C.S. (2006). *Mindset: The new psychology of success.* New York: Random House.

Eisenhardt, K.M. (1989). Agency theory: An assessment and review. *Academy of Management Review, 14*(1), 57–74.

Ford, J.D., & Ford, L.W. (1995). The role of conversations in producing intentional change in organizations. *Academy of Management Review, 20*(3), 541–570.

Ford, J.D., Ford, L.W., & D'Amelio, A. (2008). Resistance to change: The rest of the story. *Academy of Management Review, 33*(2), 362–377.

Fredrickson, B. (2009). *Positivity: Groundbreaking research reveals how to embrace the hidden strength of positive emotions, overcome negativity, and thrive.* New York: Crown.

Fredrickson, B.L. (2001). The role of positive emotions in positive psychology: The broaden-and-build theory of positive emotions. *American Psychologist, 56*(3), 218–226.

Fredrickson, B.L., & Losada, M.F. (2005). Positive affect and the complex dynamics of human flourishing. *American Psychologist, 60*(7), 678–686.

Fritz, R. (1989). *The Path of Least Resistance: Learning to Become the Creative Force in Your Own Life.* New York: Fawcett.

Garcea, N., Harrington, S.H., & Linley, P.A. (2010). Building positive organizations. In P.A. Linley, S.H. Harrington, & N. Garcea (Eds.), *Oxford handbook of positive psychology and work* (pp. 323–334). New York: Oxford University Press.

Gersick, C.J.G. (1994). Pacing strategic change: The case of a new venture. *Academy of Management Journal, 37*(1), 9–45.

Grant, A., & Ashford, S.J. (2008). The dynamics of proactivity at work. *Research in organizational behavior, 28*, 3–34.

Gruenfeld, D.H., Inesi, M.E., Magee, J.C., & Galinsky, A.D. (2008). Power and the objectification of social targets. *Journal of Personality and Social Psychology, 95*(1), 111–127.

Hannan, M.T., & Freeman, J. (1984). Structural inertia and organizational change. *American Sociological Review, 49*(2), 149–164.

Hargadon, A.B., & Douglas, Y. (2001). When innovations meet institutions: Edison and the design of the electric light. *Administrative Science Quarterly, 46*(3), 476–501.

Higgs, M. (2010). Change and its leadership: The role of positive emotions. In P.A. Linley, S.H. Harrington, & N. Garcea (Eds.), *Oxford handbook of positive psychology and work* (pp. 67–80). New York: Oxford University Press.

Jensen, M.C., & Meckling, W.H. (1976). Theory of the firm: Managerial behavior, agency costs and ownership structure. *Journal of Financial Economics, 3*(4), 305–360.

Losada, M., & Heaphy, E. (2004). The role of positivity and connectivity in the performance of business teams: A nonlinear dynamics model. *American Behavioral Scientist, 47*(6), 740.

Luthans, F., & Avolio, B.J. (2003). Authentic leadership development. In K.S. Cameron, J.E. Dutton, & R.E. Quinn (Eds.), *Positive Organizational Scholarship: Foundations of a new discipline* (pp. 241–258). San Francisco: Berrett-Koehler.

Maddux, J.E. (2002). Self-efficacy: The power of believing you can. In C.R. Snyder & S.J. Lopez (Eds.), *Handbook of positive psychology* (pp. 277–287). New York: Oxford University Press.

Maio, G.R., Olson, J.M., Allen, L., & Bernard, M.M. (2001). Addressing discrepancies between values and behavior: The motivating effect of reasons. *Journal of Experimental Social Psychology, 37*(2), 104–117.

Margolis, J.D. (2001). Responsibility in an Organizational Context, Business Quarterly *11*(3), 431–455.

McKelvey, B. (1999). Avoiding complexity catastrophe in coevolutionary pockets: Strategies for rugged landscapes. *Organization Science, 10*, 294–321.

Milgram, S. (1974). *Obedience to authority.* New York: Harper.

Mintzberg, H. (1983). *Power in and around organizations.* Englewood Cliffs, NJ: Prentice-Hall.

Morrison, E.W., & Milliken, F.J. (2000). Organizational silence: A barrier to change and development in a pluralistic world. *Academy of Management Review, 25*, 706–725.

Ouchi, W.G. (1977). The relationship between organizational structure and organizational control. *Administrative Science Quarterly, 22*(1), 95–113.

Pascale, R., Sternin, J., & Sternin, M. (2010). *The Power of Positive Deviance: How Unlikely Innovators Solve the World's Toughest Problems.* Boston: Harvard Business Press.

Peterson, C.M., & Seligman, M.E.P. (2003). Positive organizational studies: Lessons from positive psychology. In K.S. Cameron, J.E. Dutton, & R.E. Quinn (Eds.), *Positive Organizational Scholarship: Foundations of a new discipline* (pp. 14–27). San Francisco: Berrett-Koehler.

Pfeffer, J., & Salancik, G.R. (1978). *The external control of organizations: A resource dependence perspective.* New York: Harper & Row.

Plowman, D.A., Baker, L.T., Beck, T.E., Kulkarni, M., Solansky, S.T., & Travis, D.V. (2007). Radical change accidentally: The emergence and amplification of small change. *Academy of Management Journal, 50*(3), 515–543.

Podsakoff, P.M., Bommer, W.H., Podsakoff, N.P., & MacKenzie, S.B. (2006). Relationships between leader reward and punishment behavior and subordinate attitudes, perceptions, and behaviors: A meta-analytic review of existing and new research. *Organizational Behavior and Human Decision Processes, 99*(2), 113–142.

Quinn, R.E. (1996). *Deep change.* San Francisco: Jossey-Bass.

Quinn, R.E. (2004). *Building the bridge as your walk on it: A guide for leading change.* San Francisco: Jossey-Bass.

Quinn, R.E., & Sonenshein, S. (2008). Four general strategies for changing human systems. In T.G. Cummings (Ed.), *Handbook of organization development* (pp. 69–78). Thousand Oaks, CA: Sage Publications, Inc.

Quinn, R.E., Spreitzer, G.M., & Fletcher, J. (1995). Excavating the Paths of Meaning, Renewal and Empowerment: A Typology of Managerial High Performance Myths. *Journal of Management Inquiry,* 4.1: (1995): 16–39

Quinn, R.W., & Quinn, R.E. (2009). *Lift: Becoming a positive force in any situation.* San Francisco: Berrett-Koehler.

Reay, T., Golden-Biddle, K., & Germann, K. (2006). Legitimizing a new role: Small wins and microprocesses of change. *Academy of Management Journal, 49*(5), 977–998.

Rogers, C.R. (1961). *On becoming a person: A therapist's view of psychotherapy.* London: Constable.

Rowland, D., & Higgs, M. (2008). *Sustaining change: Leadership that works.* San Francisco: Jossey-Bass.

Ryan, K., & Oestreich, D.K. (1991). *Driving fear out of the workplace: How to overcome the invisible barriers to quality, productivity, and innovation.* San Francisco: Jossey-Bass.

Scharmer, C.O. (2009). *Theory U: Learning from the future as it emerges.* San Francisco: Berrett-Koehler Publishers, Inc.

Schein, E.H. (2004). *Organizational culture and leadership*: Jossey-Bass.

Schön, D.A. (1983). *The reflective practitioner: How professionals think in action*: Basic Books.

Seijts, G.H., Latham, G.P., Tasa, K., & Latham, B.W. (2004). Goal setting and goal orientation: An integration of two different yet related literatures. *Academy of Management Journal, 47*(2), 227–239.

Serkerka, L.E., & Fredrickson, B. (2010). Working positively towards transformative cooperation. In P.A. Linley, S.H. Harrington, & N. Garcea (Eds.), *Oxford handbook of positive psychology and work* (pp. 81–94). New York: Oxford University Press.

Sheldon, K.M., & Elliot, A.J. (1999). Goal striving, need satisfaction, and longitudinal well-being: The self-concordance model. *Journal of Personality and Social Psychology, 76*(3), 482–497.

Sheldon, K.M., & Houser-Marko, L. (2001). Self-concordance, goal attainment, and the pursuit of happiness: Can there be an upward spiral? *Journal of Personality and Social Psychology, 80*(1), 152–165.

Sheldon, K.M., Elliot, A.J., Ryan, R.M., Chirkov, V., Kim, Y., Wu, C., et al. (2004). Self-concordance and subjective well-being in four cultures. *Journal of Cross-Cultural Psychology, 35*(2), 209.

Shih, M., Pittinsky, T.L., & Ambady, N. (1999). Stereotype susceptibility: Identity salience and shifts in quantitative performance. *Psychological Science, 10*, 80–83.

Smith, G.F. (1988). Towards a heuristic theory of problem structuring. *Management Science, 34*(12), 1489–1506.

Spreitzer, G.M., & Sonenshein, S. (2003). Positive deviance and extraordinary organizing. In K.S. Cameron, J.E. Dutton, & R.E. Quinn (Eds.), *Positive Organizational Scholarship: Foundations of a new discipline* (pp. 207–224). San Francisco: Berrett-Koehler.

Thompson, J.D. (1967). *Organizations in action*. New York: McGraw Hill.

Van Dyne, L., & Saavedra, R. (1996). A naturalistic minority influence experiment: Effects on divergent thinking, conflict and originality in work-groups. *British Journal of Social Psychology, 35*, 151–167.

Weber, M. (1968). *Economy and society.* New York: Bedminster.

Weick, K. (1990). The vulnerable system: An analysis of the Tenerife air disaster. *Journal of Management, 3*(16), 571–593.

Weick, K.E. (1979). *The social psychology of organizing*. New York: McGraw-Hill.

Weick, K.E. (2003). Positive organizing and organizational tragedy. In K.S. Cameron, J.E. Dutton, & R.E. Quinn (Eds.), *Positive organizational scholarship: Foundations of a new discipline* (pp. 66–80). San Francisco: Berrett-Koehler.

Weick, K.E., & Quinn, R.E. (1999). Organizational change and development. *Annual Review of Psychology, 50*, 361–386.

Williamson, O.E. (1981). The economics of organization: The transaction cost approach. *American Journal of Sociology, 87*(3), 548–577.

Worline, M.C., Wrzesniewski, A., & Rafaeli, A. (2002). Courage and work: Breaking routines to improve performance. In R.G. Lord, R.J. Klimoski, & R. Kanfer (Eds.), *Emotions in the workplace: Understanding the structure and role of emotions in organizational behavior* (pp. 295–330). San Francisco: Jossey-Bass.

What Makes an Organizational Change Process Positive?

Karen Golden-Biddle *and* Jina Mao

Abstract

In this chapter, we create a combined lens of positivity and process to explore what makes a change process positive. That is, what processes in changing strengthen and help people to build resilience, rather than deplete them? We examined field-based empirical studies that portrayed people's experiences of change in order to identify clusters of small acts in change that help people navigate even more difficult changes. From these, we culled out three to profile in this chapter: acting with compassion in change, fostering agency in change, and sustaining cultural continuity in change. We discuss each and conclude with possibilities for future research and the practice of implementing organizational change.

Keywords: Change process, compassion, agency, cultural continuity, positivity and process

And I can remember a conversation with my new boss . . . it was a conversation around goals— where we were headed. And I said that, as I look over my shoulder on the change that had occurred in the region, I see *all these human remains strewn in the ditches.* Moreover, I knew of an issue still brewing . . . and I knew that the lid was about to blow. But I was told it was just *street noise,* not to worry about it. And it was at that point that I said to myself ok, here is where we're never going to agree on how to deal with people in change; but I knew to trust my instincts since I had a lot more experience in knowing how *fragile communities* in change were—both in the local community and within the four walls of a facility.

—Gladys, former CEO and COO of health organizations

As the quote from Gladys expresses, people and communities in change can be fragile. Moreover, too easily are the different voices and issues that comprise human dynamics in change treated as "noise," and too readily are hunches to pay attention to them disregarded. Such dismissal not only renders change more difficult to implement but, more significantly, it closes down possibilities for creating generative change processes that respect people and their experiences of change.

Must change be so devastating and life depleting? Are we destined to leave "human remains strewn in the ditches" of change processes in organizations?

In articulating and pondering these questions, we do not deny the fear and anxiety, even pain, which can accompany individual and organizational change. Indeed, these emotions, along with ones such as joy and love, are vital aspects of all human experience. Yet, in spite of a large body of literature in our field that examines organizational change (Armenakis & Bedeian, 1999; Pettigrew, Woodman, & Cameron, 2001), people's actual experiences remain hidden. As a result, our literature has very little to say about whether change must be life depleting, and moreover, if not, how the alternative is achieved.

In this chapter, we create a combined lens of positivity and process to explore the question "What makes a change process positive?" That is, what change processes strengthen and help people to build resilience, rather than deplete them? Below, we describe the development of this combined lens and its use in identifying and selecting three clusters of small acts that make a change process more positive: acting with compassion in change, fostering agency in change, and sustaining cultural continuity in change. We then profile each cluster through the integration of relevant literature and excerpts from empirical studies of people's experience in change. Finally, we end by exploring further possibilities for research on change and for the practice of implementing change.

Developing a Combined Lens of Positivity and Process

Early on in this chapter's development, we read articles in the literatures on change and positive organizational studies to get an idea of what constituted "positive change processes." We came away with two insights for our work.

First, we noticed that what constituted "positive" was not a universal condition, at least not in the realm of organizational change. It was difficult to identify consistent characteristics or features of what made change processes "positive." Instead, what people perceived as positive in one situation (e.g., it bodes well that senior leadership is seeking our [employee] input), could be perceived as negative by people in another situation or at a different time (e.g., senior leadership is just trying to placate us by seeking our input). This fluidity complicated the notion of positivity. We found it useful, then, to conceive of positivity as a lens; a perspective-taking on our part as researchers in which, when reading studies, we pay attention to people's experiences in change that are or could be made more life enriching, and to how change processes enable (or not) the development of people and local capability. Thus, we use positivity to take note of and to better understand how organizational change can be implemented so as not to "leave human remains strewn" in its wake.

Second, we noticed that much of the change research adopted either variance- or stage-based analytic approaches. Although there is much to gain from this research, the downside is that it lowlights people's actual experiences during change. Here, we use a process lens (Langley, 1999, 2009) because analytically it incorporates the fluidity and open-endedness of changing. It illuminates what goes on during the change process—the realm of people's experience—between points or states along a trajectory of change (Tsoukas & Chia, 2002). The more familiar form of process theorizing conceives of phenomena over time (i.e., change evolves temporally). The less familiar process analysis concerns how processes—such as change processes—are themselves constituted. Here, we are interested both in how people's experiences of change unfold over time, and in the change processes themselves, specifically in how particular actions constitute a more positive change process.

We used this lens to inform our collection and analysis of empirical studies. In particular, we gathered those investigations that offered rich portraits of people's experiences during the implementation of organizational change. In our reading, we first took note of the experiences portrayed. Then, in rereading the studies, we sought to discern clusters of small acts in these experiences that could constitute a (more) positive change process. By "clusters of small acts" we mean groupings of small deeds or works representing a similar kind of effort. Anyone in an organization can and does enact these clusters; they are not the exclusive domain of officially designated leaders. We focused our attention on identifying those clusters oriented to strengthening people in change.

To select among the clusters for presentation in this chapter, we drew on a typology of positive mechanisms (Dutton & Glynn, 2008, p. 701) that represent "particularly relevant . . . dynamics central of flourishing: positive emoting, positive interrelating, and positive meaning-making." For each type of positive mechanism, we selected the most vivid and representative cluster of small acts distilled from the reading of people's experiences in change. We selected *acting with compassion in change* to represent the positive emoting mechanism. Similarly, *fostering agency in change* represents the positive interrelating mechanism and *sustaining cultural continuity in change* represents the positive meaning-making mechanism. Each cluster profiled helps people more readily, and potentially more adeptly, navigate experiences of change, however joyful or painful.

Clusters of Small Acts That Make Change (More) Positive
Cluster 1: Acting with Compassion in Organizational Change

> Compassion counts as a connection to the human spirit and to the human condition. In organizations

there is suffering and pain, as there is joy and fulfillment. There is a need for dignity and self-respect in these settings, and to the event that our theories, models, and practices ignore these dimensions, so do they distort our understanding of life in these enterprises. (Frost, 1999, p. 131)

As expressed in Peter Frost's comment, compassion "counts"; it matters deeply that we tap the human condition both in our practice and in our study of organizational life. The *Oxford English Dictionary* defines compassion as "the feeling or emotion, when a person is moved by the suffering or distress of another, and by the desire to relieve it." Compassion and suffering are inextricably linked. If we want to find out where more compassion is needed in organizations, we need simply to look for experiences of suffering. And if we want to explore compassion, we simply need to look for where people "notice, feel, and act in relation to suffering, both as individuals and as coordinated collectives" (Lilius, Kanov, Dutton, Worline, & Maitlis, 2011, Chapter 21, this volume).

Research (Lilius et al., 2008) has shown that attending to people's emotional needs shapes how they feel about themselves and about their organizations. It also conceives of relational systems, consisting of strong, weak, and nonexistent attachments in the system, as revealing how caregiving moves or fails to move within an organization (Kahn, 1998, p. 45). Organizational change brings emotions to the foreground as uncertainty, loss, and anxiety prevail. People's experiences may be painful and difficult for themselves, as well as for their families. Inevitably, whatever happens at work will also have a profound impact on their personal lives. As in Gladys's quote at the beginning of the chapter, organizational change brings forward human vulnerability and illuminates "fragile communities." Given the fact that people are emotionally vulnerable in times of change, this research helps to support people's efforts in tending to emotional needs and in paying attention to how and where such caregiving is facilitated or blocked. Indeed, there is evidence that experiencing compassion during difficult moments in change can help people better navigate the process (Huy, 2002).

It is in this context that acting with compassion in change represents a positive clustering of small acts that can make change more positive. Acting with compassion in change is oriented and dedicated to seeing suffering and acting to relieve suffering in change processes. In remaining mindful of painful or personally difficult experiences in organizational change, acting with compassion can inspire the creation of implementation processes that foreground the dignity and self-respect of each person. This cluster of small acts can also resource peoples' capabilities to navigate difficult experiences of change.

To illustrate the cluster of acting with compassion in change, we draw on two empirical field studies. Notably, neither study set out to examine compassion; indeed, they do not use the word "compassion." Nevertheless, they vividly depict how people in the midst of organizational change notice and act to relieve another's suffering.

HUY (2002): RADICAL CHANGE INITIATIVE

Compassion involves the proactive act of attending to and relieving others' suffering; it depicts a way of relating in response to people's sufferings. The three elements of compassion developed in Lilius et al. (2001; attention to or noticing of suffering, empathic concern or felt relation with the other, and action to lessen or relieve suffering), are readily disclosed in Huy's study (2002) of a radical change initiative that involved site closing, downsizing, and employee relocation. Huy found that middle managers played an important role in attending to change recipients' emotions to maintain continuity in operations in the midst of this change.

Attention to or Noticing of Suffering
Huy described a case in which middle managers failed to see the suffering caused by the change initially:

> We were affecting people's lives and it got extremely emotional . . . we found that we didn't allow the time to let their feelings out . . . people were still caught up in the emotions of leaving their [job or hometown] . . . and were bringing a lot of emotional baggage to the job . . . We didn't deal well with a lot of these soft issues. (p. 54)

Once the managers realized the importance of paying attention to the soft issues and started to attend to those emotions, they noticed a "night-and-day" difference. Other middle managers were more adept at noticing suffering in their subordinates. Huy described what he observed in one site:

> Managers mentioned that they watched for signs of burnout among their subordinates . . . Many managers shared with me their need to psyche themselves up, to blank out negative thoughts to deal

with employees in a more positive frame of mind in order not to exacerbate recipients' fear or hopelessness. (p. 41)

Attention to or noticing of suffering requires a form of relating that involves awareness and sensitivity to others' emotional state.

Empathic Concern: A Felt Relation with the Other
The middle managers also found ways to relate with the recipients to allow them to openly express their emotions. Huy observed that:

Middle managers set up focus groups in which front-line workers expressed the need to see their emotional hurt addressed. They wanted to see managers openly acknowledge the existence of problems. (p. 41)

Simply by acknowledging the existence of problems and talking about problems in an open setting help legitimate what the recipients are feeling. This builds a bond between the managers and their subordinates in a way that is empathic and sincere.

Acting to Lessen or Relieve Suffering
Middle managers also took actions to address people's hurt feelings in a practical way, by finding solutions to help the recipients in their everyday life. These actions extend beyond the realm of the workplace and, according to Huy, went a long way in helping to lessen or relieve suffering. As one middle manager describes:

I realized that one could not deal effectively with emotions when one was with a crowd. So, I began to set up smaller meetings in groups of seven or eight, and I told them I would be available for private meetings after the group discussion. . . . It was a winning formula. Every case was different: one service rep from a small town emotionally told me in a public meeting that she could not move to [Dallas] immediately. In private, she explained to me that she was going through a divorce. Another one was worried that her handicapped child could not find a specialized school, so I looked for a job that would suit her needs. Others have sick parents. Relocation is a very emotional thing. We addressed that by offering them paid visits to the new location a few months in advance. (p. 51)

Huy also found that middle managers offered paid psychological counseling and treatment, and provided company resources to people to take charge of employees' personal and family needs due to work relocation. The dedication of resources and the willingness to be flexible and to offer practical solutions to people in need is an act of compassion deemed to lessen the suffering caused by the change.

In summary, Huy portrayed compassion as a type of emotion-based organizational capability in which managers dedicated resources to alleviate recipients' suffering in radical change. The managers played an important role in noticing, discussing, and acting in relation to the negative emotions of the change recipients. They showed empathy toward the recipients, offering spaces to openly express their emotions, devoting resources and devising solutions to help relieve their suffering. Even though the word "compassion" was never used in the work, acts of compassion infused the portraits of what the middle managers did.

PLOWMAN, BAKER, BECK, KULKARNI, SOLANSKY, AND TRAVIS (2007): COMPASSION ORGANIZING

The study on radical change by Plowman et al. (2007) although not portrayed as such, can be conceived as an account of compassion organizing (Dutton, Worline, Frost, & Lilius, 2006). It is a portrait of how people collectively took action to relieve the suffering of homeless people in their church's community and how this action became institutionalized over time. Specifically, their decision to serve free hot breakfasts to homeless people sparked what turned out to be radical change in Mission Church.

The decision originated over dinner as "several young people from the church were discussing Sunday morning alternatives . . ." (Plowman et al., 2007, p. 515). A new member to the church first suggested the idea, and it generated interest among others present. In the study, the pastor describes this decision as a "novel gesture," in light of this church's history with the homeless. Up to this point, little attention was paid to the suffering of the homeless people. Indeed, discomfort was expressed when the homeless got too close to the church, as vividly described in the pastor's comment:

In the past, [the homeless] were invisible to us on Sunday mornings, intruding occasionally by asking for a handout. Our greeters were instructed to keep them away from our front doors because we knew they made people feel uncomfortable, especially visitors.

A small informal subgroup of those present at the dinner conversation started meeting to plan this initiative. The desire to relieve others' suffering infused not only their decision but also how they enacted it. For example, as noted by the authors (p. 526), they "named their idea Café Carazon in an effort to differentiate it from traditional soup kitchens, where, they believed, homeless people often were not treated with dignity." We learn that the initial small group of five or six church members who served 75 people at the first breakfast grew quickly into a group of more than 100 members who serve thousands of meals a year. Along the way, their efforts sparked other acts of compassion, including those of a physician who, during the course of serving breakfast, noticed that some people needed medical attention and began to offer medical services. Soon, he was joined by other medical professionals who offered vision and dental clinics. The breakfasts also fostered the "unintended establishment" of a day center providing shelter and services for homeless people throughout the week:

> A surprising challenge had developed when some of the homeless people who regularly attended breakfasts and worship services on Sunday mornings began to drop in to talk to church staff during the week and make requests of them. One person said: "We couldn't turn them away and . . . we (Mission Church staff) couldn't get any work done . . . Our decision to open up the Day Center was made before we knew 100% that we'd have funding for it, but we had to, you know . . . we either had to stop doing it and start stopping those people at the door saying we know you come to Church here on Sunday, but, you know, you look like you're from the streets and we can't let you in; or we had to open up the Day Center."

The breakfasts also created opportunities for people to act with compassion in ways barely visible to others. In a particularly poignant excerpt, the authors share the story of a staff member who, while serving breakfast on one particular Sunday, became the recipient of a compassionate act:

> The best experience I've had at that breakfast was . . . you know, I'm trying to help, I'm pouring syrup. I'm an emotional wreck because my mom just died and tears are coming down and this [homeless] man walks over and says "What's wrong?" and I said, "It's okay. My mom just died." And tears are coming down. He puts his hand on my shoulder and he says, "I'm sorry." And I've written [transformation] several times and okay, that was the moment I got it. You know, that was an awkward moment, and I realized

at that moment . . . I thought "your pain is the same as I have . . . I'm not feeling any worse than you are, you know, and maybe you've been through this. We're on an equal playing field." And from that, when people say "transformation," it's a little, okay, but have you really had a hard moment with it.

As profiled in the Plowman et al. study, serving breakfast to homeless people in the church's community was an act of compassion that generated radical change. It also inspired others to act with compassion in changing Mission Church.

This cluster of small acts highlights the realm of emotion, particularly in dealing with people's suffering in change. Although the studies do not incorporate compassion explicitly into their analytic frameworks, as we have shown, their data portray people acting with compassion in change. As such, these studies help us to notice and begin to theorize the relationship between compassion and change.

Cluster 2: Fostering Agency in Change

Unlike compassion, much scholarly attention has been accorded the topics of agency. In this chapter, we develop fostering agency in change as a positive clustering of small acts because it helps direct attention toward viable possibilities for people to act to create or shape the direction and impact of change, even in situations that might be considered beyond an individual's control.

One of the earliest conceptions of agentic action in organizations is that of empowerment, long an important topic in organizational behavior and other disciplines (Spreitzer & Bartunek, 2006). One example of agency as empowerment is found in the study by Feldman and Khademian (2003), who used the concept in examining how managerial action that encourages employee agency itself can catalyze other change. In particular, their model of cascading vitality shows how, by empowering public employees to reconsider how they do their everyday work, managers' efforts can lead to the generation of new, more inclusive processes to achieve government work. In turn, these new practices can also empower the public to become more involved in strengthening communities.

Their example is illustrative. In one city, a manager encouraged employees to stop the automatic processing of overdue and rarely paid bills (for mowing grass of houses with absentee landlords) and instead to "leave their desks" (Feldman & Khademian, 2003, p. 349) and talk with colleagues about alternate ways of dealing with the issue.

In their discussions, they realized they had lost sight of their original purpose in mowing the lawns: "to make a contribution to the aesthetics or . . . environmental quality of the neighborhood." In being empowered to work together, employees developed recommendations for working toward this purpose with community members. As Feldman and Khadamian suggest:

> Enabling employees to approach the task of the organization and to utilize and engage information and people in creative and alternative ways . . . is empowering, and nurtures individual vitality, which can expand and create organizational resources and enhance organizational vitality. . . . (p. 344)

In another study, by Dutton, Ashford, O'Neill, and Lawrence (2001, pp. 728–729), acting with agency is conveyed in the "behind-the scenes moves that in part compose the change process in organizations." Such moves are agentic and can also foster agentic action by others interested in the same issue. In this study, managers express agency in their issue-selling efforts. Analyses of more than 80 accounts of trying to sell issues disclose the type of moves managers take, such as packaging issues and deciding whom to involve in their efforts, and process moves such as timing of efforts. In addition, their analyses disclose three types of contextual knowledge critical to making the issue selling moves happen: relational, normative, and strategic.

In the study by Meyerson and Scully (1995), agency is represented in the strategies used by individuals whom they call "tempered radicals." These individuals identify with and are committed to their organization, while at the same time committed to an issue or cause that is at odds with their organization. In handling this tension, tempered radicals devise a number of strategies they use to try to create desired change in their organizations. These strategies can involve small wins or even small losses, from which they learn how to improve their efforts; direct expression of their beliefs with others; adeptness at using the language of those they are seeking to influence; and maintaining affiliations with others who represent aspects of both their commitment and identification with issues for change and their organization.

Reay, Golden-Biddle, and GermAnn (2006) examine the role of agency as deeply committed nurses sought to legitimize the role of nurse practitioner as an institutional change because they saw it as a core avenue for offering better care and advancing the nursing profession. Of special interest is their portrait of how these individuals, who are deeply embedded and context wise, are successful in their effort. And, they accomplished this in spite of many who dismissed their efforts as not being possible. In contrast to prior work showing embeddedness as constraint to change, the study by Reay et al. (2006, p. 978) shows evidence of a different relationship between agency and embeddedness, one in which "people use their embeddedness as a positive foundation for implementing desired change." Specifically, their analyses show how these individuals drew on their knowledge of their contexts to undertake change that was comprised of three microprocesses, as well as series of small wins.

Feldman (2000) analyzes the effect of agency on the enactment of routines. That is, when being performed by "people who think and feel and care" (p. 614), people can change routines. In this conception, routines are not static or fixed, but rather malleable and ongoing accomplishments as people participate in them. Her study of routines in a university housing organization depicts how, in people's performance of routines, some are altered. For example, changes in the hiring and training routines occurred when people thought they could do the work more efficiently with greater uniformity in their teams. Yet, this uniformity impeded the creation of teams less representative of the residence halls they were serving. But the change also produced new opportunities in the form of training a more uniformly qualified staff.

The article by Plowman et al. (2007) also provides examples of acting with agency in change in the form of amplifying action. In using "amplifying" the authors mean actions that broaden—amplify rather than counteract—deviations in the form of change. One example is that of the physician who began offering medical services on his own accord, "pushing the Sunday morning event in a new and unplanned direction" (Plowman et al., 2007, p. 530). His actions fostered the actions of others who began offering other kinds of medical services. After about a year, the church made a more formal commitment to both the breakfasts and expanded medical offerings.

Although agency is discussed in the organizational literature, as seen in the above examples of fostering of agency in change, adopting a combined positive-process lens highlights its variety. Although much of the literature has concentrated on a specific type of empowerment—that is, how managers can help employees become agentic— in these examples, agency is fostered by people at various levels in the organization. Such agentic action is perhaps less noticeable because it often occurs in fleeting, everyday micromoments of interaction that get overlooked in our investigations. Yet, blink, and we miss the important and positive acts of tempered radicals, the public manager, middle managers, nurses, church members, and others who make their own situations in change better, create desired change, and encourage others' agentic action. Moreover, and in contrast to an assumption in the change literature that people resist change because they are too embedded in the organization or too locked into prevailing ways of acting, the work above highlights how people not only foster agency in change, but also draw on this very embeddedness to foster agency for desired change.

Cluster 3: Sustaining Cultural Continuity in Change

A typical conception of change is that of breaking away from the past to create a new future. So, it may seem counterintuitive to suggest that continuity in change is desirable, let alone that it can make change processes more positive. Yet, in examining studies that form the basis of this cluster, we did not see experiences of people breaking away from the past. Rather, we saw portrayed managers and employees situating that which is existing or continuous from the past alongside what is new or the desired future. That is, they connected the past and future in the present (Golden, 1988; Shils, 1981) as they navigated change. These studies also show the meaningfulness for people experiencing change to carry forward some of what is familiar while embracing the unfamiliar that comprises change. Not all from the past is retained; continuity does not mean unwitting or even intentional adherence to a past or the old. But, neither is everything new adopted. Rather, this cluster highlights the continuous, even in fundamental change.

Sustaining *cultural* continuity in change suggests that certain meanings prevail, albeit often in altered form. The "cultural" descriptor of continuity in change brings forward a linguistic focus or cultural resource analyses of the studies profiled here. Each conceives continuity constituted in meaning: the connection between prior and emerging meanings and how people engage these meanings in creating a desired future. It is in this sense that "sustaining cultural continuity in change" represents a positive clustering of small acts because, in bringing together the past, present, and future, it seeks to draw on the best of the past while people build the future in the present.

In his study of narrating strategic change, Sonenshein (2010) finds that managers not only narrate how their organizations are changing (for example, by using discourse about innovation or new directions), but also and simultaneously narrate how these organizations are remaining the same. He calls this a "strategically ambiguous narrative" because it both reinforces as well as alters the status quo. Of particular interest is his finding that employees are not passive recipients of these narratives, but rather are quite active, "embellishing" them to interpret the change efforts and to imagine and articulate their reactions and responses. Although Sonenshein highlights some of the potential difficulties in change associated with strategic ambiguity, his study provides important evidence that managers do balance continuity with change in their narratives of how change is proceeding. And, rather than creating confusion, the narratives help employees consider the change and how they might variously welcome or dismiss the change efforts as they are living the change process.

A study by Thomas, Sargent, and Hardy (2011) highlights the active negotiation of meaning by organization members during a workshop that was part of a cultural change effort in a telecommunications company. What continues and what changes is a negotiated endeavor that emerges in people's interactions. Their analyses identified two different patterns, which they term *generative* and *degenerative*, occurring in two different discussions in the same workshop. One cultural change proposed involved the move to a common understanding of the company's "customer focus," with recognition that it was important for the company to have this focus. In what the authors call a "generative pattern," the workshop participants successfully negotiated discussion concerning who was the customer and whether they were currently customer-focused, and then revised the meaning of "customer focus" to the meaning "commercial focus." The generative pattern results from (Thomas et al., 2011, p. 12):

> The intersection of two sets of communicative practices: inviting, proposing, building, clarifying, and affirming by senior managers, and building, challenging, and reiterating by middle managers. The intersection of these practices produces what we refer to as relational engagement, by which we mean that both parties take active responsibility for the joint tasks in which they are involved and suspend 'irreducible social vulnerability and uncertainty as if they were favorably resolved.' (Mollering 2006, pp. 110–111)

In contrast, in the degenerative pattern, the group stalled, holding onto polarized meanings in their negotiations of the meaning of implementation. This pattern results from (Thomas et al., 2011, p. 12):

> Senior managers engage in dismissing, reiterating, deploying authority, invoking hierarchy, and reifying the culture toolkit, whereas middle managers rely primarily on challenging, reiterating, *holding* to account, and undermining. This leads to degenerative dialogue where . . . there is the polarized reproduction of two sharply contrasting existing meanings of implementation.

In these two patterns the meaning-making and interrelating mechanisms join; the generative (positive) interrelating mechanism leading to cultural change, whereas the degenerative pattern leads to polarization of meanings. In the generative interrelating mechanism (communicative practices), senior managers invite, propose, build, clarify, and affirm, and middle managers challenge and reiterate. This pattern of relating sustained cultural continuity in change as the resultant meaning of "commercial focus" incorporates the significance of customer and of being customer-focused while introducing a revised understanding of what customer meant.

The work by Howard-Grenville, Golden-Biddle, Irwin, and Mao (2011) offers a revised understanding of intentional cultural change that proceeds in a more gradual and diffuse way than the oft-depicted urgent and dramatic tempo of fundamental change. For example, it does not rely on "jolts" or an exogenously imposed sense of urgency that assumes organizational inertia and resistance to change. Their study shows how individuals adept at navigating the symbolic realm of organizations seed and energize longer-term change by opening up crevices (symbolically liminal or in-between regular, norm-governed relations) in everyday occurrences such as meetings. These "liminal" experiences provide opportunities for people to try out new meanings associated with a change (e.g., creating more sustainable production processes, or delivering health services based on a wellness model of caring, partnering, leadership, informed choice, and respect). In particular, juxtaposing new cultural resources alongside the organizations' existing repertoire generated cultural change by infusing new meaning into existing meanings. For example, the change toward more sustainable production processes infused the new idea of "sustainability as innovation" into existing meanings of "innovation" and "sustainability as risk."

This cluster of acts highlights the realm of meaning, in particular the relations between what is changing and what is staying the same, and the negotiation over what will become the new meanings. In all of these studies, people are active meaning makers, "embellishing" (Sonenshein, 2010), "juxtaposing" (Howard-Grenville et al., 2011), and "negotiating" (Thomas et al., 2011) meanings. Moreover, as the work from Thomas et al. (2011) conveys, the negotiation over how the new and old meanings will be ultimately combined can make a change process (more) positive when coupled with affirming relational systems.

Future Directions

In this chapter, we created a combined lens of positivity and process to explore the question: What makes a change process (more) positive? Using this lens to examine process studies that portray people's experiences of change enabled us to identify and develop three clusters of small acts that enabled the change process to become more positive: acting with compassion in change, fostering agency in change, and sustaining cultural continuity in change. These clusters show how the change process is made more positive in small, everyday acts rather than one large event. For example, in enacting these clusters, people express positivity in change—people care about others' and others' experiences of change when they act with compassion. As well, in enacting these clusters people cultivate positivity in change—people encourage others to act with compassion, foster agency, or sustain cultural continuity in the face of change.

We turn now to a consideration of further possibilities for future research and the practice of implementing organizational change.

For Research About Change

These cluster profiles highlight at least three possible avenues for future research. First, the combined positivity and process lens provides an analytic pathway for the study of implementing change that enables researchers to begin to take note of—to literally see—and then theorize generative clusters of small acts that constitute and cultivate a more positive change process. We were heartened to find these close-up process studies of change to examine and use in this chapter. And, we were struck with how much data about the positivity of these small clusters we found in the articles, but that was not systematically analyzed as such. The two exceptions were the study by Thomas et al. (2011), which discerned generative and degenerative patterns of negotiating meaning, and the study by Feldman and Khademian (2003), which examined cascading vitality. Even seeing how data could represent positive phenomena alongside more neutral and negative phenomena would begin to correct the prevailing tendency in studies of organizational change to investigate the negative (Cameron, 2008).

Second, the prevailing assumption in the literature on fundamental change, that exogenous "jolts" are needed to provoke people to make more fundamental change (see Weick & Quinn, 1999, for a contrast of episodic and continuous change models), may represent just one kind of fundamental change. The studies profiled in this chapter, which analyzed fundamental change, neither involved jolts nor did they bring into prominence a need to create a sense of urgency to motivate change. Consider the cases of serving breakfast to the homeless (Plowman et al., 2007) or creating a cultural change of wellness-based health delivery or sustainability as innovation (Howard-Grenville et al., 2011). These articles portray people working together to create a desired future in the present through fundamental change. They help us reconsider possibilities for creating and implementing major change, so that it is not so disruptive and life-depleting for people and the communities in which they live.

Third, although not profiled directly in the exploration of the clusters of small acts developed in this chapter, creating and implementing endogenously oriented change in a way that takes notice of and incorporates concern for peoples' experiences may require a different way of leading change. How do leaders lead transformational change processes that foreground acting with compassion, fostering others' agency, or not breaking from the past? How does the incorporation of these clusters change our notions and assumptions about leading change? More generally, how does consideration of these small acts help, provoke, prompt us to reconsider and to reconceive our models of change?

For the Practice of Change

The question of what makes a change process positive is a marked departure from the more traditional question of what makes a change effort so difficult to implement. In seeking to understand the question of how people better navigate change and also create desired change, this chapter connects with some practitioner-based books (Block, 2008; Westley, Zimmerman, & Patton, 2006; Zander & Zander, 2002), all of which deal with the complexity and ambiguity inherent in the experience of changing. As well, these sources are also based on the assumption that change efforts should bring out the best in people and communities who are collaborating to create desired futures. The present chapter adds to the spirit embodied in these books by portraying how individuals can make change processes more positive through clusters of small acts identified as acting with compassion, fostering agency in ourselves and others, and sustaining cultural continuity in change.

The cluster of acting with compassion asks us to remember and tend to emotions and human vulnerabilities in change. The cluster of fostering agency helps us see the multitude of ways people are agentic and actively consider how we might cultivate experiences or setting in which agency is mindfully cultivated. Finally, the cluster of sustaining cultural continuity helps us remember that instead of replacing the old with the new, change occurs through generative combination in dialogue and action of combining the old with the new.

A vivid consequence of overlooking compassion, agency, and cultural continuity is that employees are asked (sometimes demanded) in organizational change efforts to replace or shake up the past, in effect disrupting their lives through wholesale replacement of practices and values from one period in time to the next. In using a combined lens of positivity and process, we can accord due attention to considering and innovating in creating more possibilities for people's lived experience of change to be life-enriching and generative.

Conclusion

The clusters of small acts profiled here shines a light on the humanity and fragility of people and communities in change depicted in Gladys's opening quote, but all too often overlooked in our literature on change. We are enthusiastic to find exceptions in the field-based empirical studies profiled here that provided data disclosing the clusters of small acts. These studies represent efforts that can inform our theorizing of how these small acts help strengthen relational systems, relieve people's suffering, and generate alternative change patterns that enrich rather than deplete the human experience in change. In bringing forward the ideas of compassion, agency, and continuity in change in this chapter, we hope to inspire others to incorporate positivity and a more dynamic, process-based rendering of organizational change into our literature.

References

Armenakis, A.A., & Bedeian, A.G. (1999). Organizational change: A review of theory and research in the 1990s. *Journal of Management, 25,* 293–315.

Block, P. (2008). *Community: The structure of belonging*: Berrett-Koehler Publishers.

Cameron, K.S. (2008). Paradox in positive organizational change. *Journal of Applied Behavioral Science, 44*(7), 7–24.

Dutton, J.E., Ashford, S.J., O'Neill, R.M., & Lawrence, K.A. (2001). Moves that matter: Issue selling and organizational change. *Academy of Management Journal, 44*(4), 716–736.

Dutton, J.E., & Glynn, M.A. (2008). Positive organizational scholarship. In J. Barling & C.L. Cooper (Eds.), *The sage handbook of organizational behavior* (Vol. 1, pp. 693–712): Micro Approaches.

Dutton, J.E., Worline, M., Frost, P.J., & Lilius, J. (2006). Explaining compassion organizing. *Administrative Science Quarterly, 51*(1), 59–96.

Feldman, M.S., & Khademian, A.M. (2003). Empowerment and cascading vitality. In K.S. Cameron, J.E. Dutton, & R.E. Quinn (Eds.), *Positive organizational scholarship: Foundations in a new discipline* (pp. 343–358).

Feldman, M.S. (2000). Organizational routines as a source of continuous change. *Organization Science, 11*(6), 611–629.

Frost, P.J. (1999). Why compassion counts. *Journal of Management Inquiry, 8*(3), 127–133.

Golden, K.A. (1988). *Human resource management in a traditional organization.* Unpublished Doctoral Dissertation. Case Western Reserve University.

Howard-Grenville, J.A., Golden-Biddle, K., Irwin, J., & Mao, J. (2011). Crafting liminality as cultural process for cultural change. *Organization Science, 22*(2), 522–539.

Huy, Q.N. (2002). Emotional balancing of organizational continuity and radical change: The contribution of middle managers. *Administrative Science Quarterly, 47*(1), 31–69.

Kahn, W.A. (1998). Relational systems at work. *Research in Organizational Behavior, 20,* 39–76.

Langley, A. (1999). Strategies for theorizing from process data. *Academy of Management Review, 24*(4), 691–710.

Langley, A. (2009). Studying processes in and around organizations. In D.A. Buchanan & A. Bryman (Eds.), *Sage handbook of organizational research methods* (pp. 409–429). London, UK: SAGE Publications.

Lilius, J.M., Kanov, J., Dutton, J.E., Worline, M.C., & Maitlis, S. (2011). Compassion revealed: What we know about compassion at work (and where we need to know more). In K.S. Cameron & G.M. Spreitzer (Eds.), *The Oxford handbook of positive organizational scholarship.* New York: Oxford University Press.

Lilius, J., Worline, M., Maitlis, S., Kanov, J., Dutton, J.E., & Frost, P.J. (2008). The contours and consequences of compassion at work. *Journal of Organizational Behavior, 29*(2), 193–218.

Meyerson, D.E., & Scully, M.A. (1995). Tempered radicalism and the politics of ambivalence and change. *Organization Science, 6*(5), 585–600.

Pettigrew, A.M., Woodman, R.W., & Cameron, K.S. (2001). Studying organizational change and development: Challenges for future research. *Academy of Management Journal, 44*(4), 697–713.

Plowman, D.A., Baker, L.T., Beck, T.E., Kulkarni, M., Solansky, S.T., & Travis, D.V. (2007). Radical change accidentally: The emergence and amplification of small change. *Academy of Management Journal, 50*(3), 515–543.

Reay, T., Golden-Biddle, K., & Germann, K. (2006). Legitimizing a new role: Small wins and microprocesses of change. *Academy of Management Journal, 49*(5), 977–998.

Shils, E. (1981). *Tradition.* Chicago: University of Chicago Press.

Sonenshein, S. (2010). We're changing - or are we? Untangling the role of progressive, regressive and stability narratives during strategic change implementation. *Academy of Management Journal, 53*(3), 477–512.

Spreitzer, G.M., & Bartunek, J.M. (2006). The interdisciplinary career of a popular construct used in management: Empowerment in the late 20th century. *Journal of Management Inquiry, 15*(3), 255–273.

Thomas, R., Sargent, L.D., & Hardy, C. (2011). Managing organizational change: Negotiating meaning and power-resistance relations. *Organization Science, 22*(1), 22–41.

Tsoukas, H., & Chia, R. (2002). On organizational becoming: Rethinking organizational change. *Organization Science, 13*(5), 567–582.

Weick, K.E., & Quinn, R.E. (1999). Organizational change and development. *Annual Review of Psychology, 50*(1), 361–386.

Westley, F., Zimmerman, B., & Patton, M.Q. (2006). *Getting to maybe: How the world is changed*: Random House Publishers.

Zander, R.S., & Zander, B. (2002). *The art of possibility: Transforming professional and personal life*: Penguin Books.

Advances in Theory and Research on Authentic Leadership

Bruce J. Avolio *and* Ketan H. Mhatre

Abstract

This review tracks the evolution of the theory of authentic leadership from its theoretical conception to more recent empirical research. We begin this chapter by providing an overview of the construct of authenticity and various conceptualizations in the research literature. We follow that by an examination of the theoretical advances that have characterized the field of authentic leadership by outlining the competing models of authentic leadership proposed in prior research literature. Next, we summarize the empirical validation studies of the theory of authentic leadership in an effort to highlight the development that the field of authentic leadership has undergone over the past 6 years. And, finally, we synthesize research findings and use them as a platform for offering suggestions to facilitate future leadership research and practice.

Keywords: Authenticity, authentic leadership, research review

The concept of authenticity has been a prominent subject in philosophical writings for several centuries. Discussion on what constitutes authenticity and authentic leadership has recently begun to reemerge in the fields of psychology, organizational behavior, and leadership (among others), perhaps coinciding with the emergence of high-profile ethics violations in sports, industry, the military, and government. Its relevance seems especially ubiquitous given the moral inadequacies that have characterized the way organizations and their leaders have recently been vilified for their lack of concern for the consequences of their actions.

A 2007 national study by Harvard's Kennedy School examining the confidence the American public has in its leadership reported that 77% of participants responded as agreeing or strongly agreeing that there was a crisis of confidence regarding leaders in America (Rosenthal, Pittinsky, Purvin, & Montoya, 2007). Also revealed in this study was the fact that business and government leaders were in the lower third of all occupations, with respondents indicating they had moderate levels of trust or not much trust at all in leaders operating in these respective domains. These diminishing levels of trust will make it more difficult for both business and government to make the necessary changes to compete in a global economy to the extent the leaders are not trusted to be good stewards.

In the business sector, the mantra of satisfying shareholder wealth has resulted in a persistent and excessive focus on short-term profits, which has been described as one of the factors contributing to a lack of trust in business executives and, more importantly, as a potential causal factor driving unethical behavior (Ghoshal, 2005). Ghoshal (2005) specifically criticized business schools for contributing to this unconscious conspiracy of creating wealth at the expense of adhering to ethical standards, stating, "by propagating amoral theories business schools have actively freed their students from any sense of moral responsibility" (p. 76). Thus, it is not at all surprising that this apparent decline in the quality of the overall moral fabric of contemporary leadership would create an urgent need for new theories like authentic leadership and how it is developed that focus on promoting doing what's right versus just doing what's profitable in the short run.

The central focus of this chapter is to contribute to the expanding domain of positive organizational scholarship (POS; Cameron & Caza, 2004; Cameron, Dutton, & Quinn, 2003; Roberts, 2006), which involves a systematic study of positive outcomes, processes, and attributes of organizations and its members, by taking a closer look at the process of authentic leadership and reviewing and outlining the various theoretical and empirical advances that have characterized work in this area, with particular emphasis on the last 10 years. We start by shedding light on the conceptual origins of the work on authentic leadership that had its roots in research on POS and organizational behavior; next, we examine what has been discovered and what remains to be explored regarding the process of authentic leadership and followership, while also examining how current theory and research can inform leadership practice. Accordingly, the chapter is structured as follows. First, we examine some of the more recent discussions of authenticity with the goal of providing for the reader a solid foundation for what authors suggest constitutes authentic leadership. In this discussion, we present the different ways in which authenticity and its core components have been conceptualized, while also describing commonalities.

Second, we examine the theoretical advances that have characterized the field of authentic leadership over the last decade. In this section, our aim is to outline how models of authentic leadership have been conceptualized and integrated.

Third, we offer an overview of the emerging empirical research that has followed the initial conceptualizations of authentic leadership. Most of this research has focused on examining the nomological network of constructs associated with authentic leadership, as well as validating ways that it can be measured.

Fourth, we synthesize findings from recent empirical research and use the conclusions of this research to offer suggestions to facilitate leadership practice, followed by our ideas to direct future research and how that research may inform practice.

Authenticity and Authentic Leadership
Authenticity
Beyond early philosophical discussions of what constitutes an authentic person, authenticity has been defined and described in several different ways over the last 50 years. For example, Sartre (1966) defined authenticity as the absence of self-deception, which involves actually being true to who you are. According to Brumbaugh (1971), authenticity was characterized by the ability to make individual choices, take responsibility for one's errors, and recognize one's drawbacks, while working toward the fulfillment of one's potential.

More recent discussions of authenticity include those provided by Kernis (2003) and Avolio, Gardner, Walumbwa, Luthans, and May (2004). Kernis (2003) described authenticity as the "unobstructed operation of one's true, or core, self in one's daily enterprise" (p. 1), while Avolio and his colleagues defined it as knowing, accepting, and remaining true to one's self.

Kernis (2003) proposed that the construct of authenticity comprised four unique components. These components were awareness, unbiased processing, action, and relational orientation. Awareness refers to being aware of one's motives, feelings, desires, and other self-relevant cognitions. Such awareness involves a deeper understanding of one's strengths and weaknesses, traits, and the source and nature of one's emotions. Kernis (2003) proposed that because authentic individuals are more in tune with the different aspects of their selves, they are able to carry out more consistent, "genuine" social transactions with others within their environment.

The second component of authenticity, which is unbiased processing, involves the objective processing of self-relevant information. It complements the first component of awareness in the sense that it adds an element of objective accuracy to the self and other related knowledge derived from one's sense of self-awareness. Thus, individuals who are authentic are capable of processing self and other related information with greater accuracy that minimizes distortions, exaggerations, and biases.

The third component of authenticity is the actions one takes, and this constitutes the behavioral aspect of authenticity. It involves consistently behaving in a manner that is in accord with one's true self. Authentic individuals act in ways that are accurate representations of their beliefs and values. They stay true to their own selves and do not indulge in behaviors that involve pleasing others in pursuit of vested interests.

The fourth component of authenticity proposed by Kernis (2003) is relational orientation, which involves achieving openness and truthfulness in one's close relationships. Authentic individuals strive to achieve transparent relationships with others. They let others see them as they really are versus putting on a false front to pursue ulterior motives. This type of orientation results in the development of transparent relationships that are characterized by a high level of trust among the participating parties.

A noteworthy aspect of the way authenticity has been conceptualized lies in the fact that it is not an either–or condition (Erickson, 1995). Authenticity has been described as existing on a continuum ranging from highly inauthentic to highly authentic. This implies that individuals are not either completely authentic or completely inauthentic.

A Theoretical Evolution to Authentic Leadership

Building from prior conceptualizations of authenticity, Luthans and Avolio (2003) conceptualized and defined authentic leadership as "a process that draws from both positive psychological capacities and a highly developed organizational context, which results in both greater self-awareness and self-regulated positive behaviors on the part of leaders and associates, fostering positive self-development" (p. 243). This definition drew the concept of authenticity across levels of analysis, in that it incorporated a focus on the leader, follower, and the context in which they interacted. Furthermore, borrowing from Kernis' four components of authenticity, authentic leadership was theorized to be comprised of four core components including self-awareness, relational transparency, internalized moral perspective, and balanced processing. The authors described authentic leaders as striving to achieve authenticity through self-awareness, self-acceptance, authentic behavior, and open and transparent relationships. The same was applied to describing the authentic follower, who in interactions with the leader not only developed authenticity in him- or herself, but also in the leader.

This more recent conceptualization, along with the measurement tools that have been developed to assess authentic leadership, has paved the way for subsequent theoretical development of the construct and for empirically testing how authentic leadership predicts a variety of performance outcomes. These developments stand in contrast to prior discussions of authenticity and authentic leadership that were mainly philosophical or theoretical (Gardner, Avolio, & Walumbwa, 2006).

Avolio, Gardner, Walumbwa, Luthans, and May (2004) made an important contribution to the examination of authentic leadership by describing

authentic leadership as a "root" construct capable of grounding other leadership frameworks, such as transformational and ethical leadership. Building on the notion of a root construct, they proposed that authentic leaders could be directive, participative, or even authoritarian, and that these common leader behavioral styles in and of themselves do not differentiate whether a leader is authentic or inauthentic. According to Avolio and his colleagues, authentic leaders were leaders who acted in accordance with their core personal values and beliefs in order to build credibility and earn the respect and trust of their followers through the process of actively encouraging diverse viewpoints and building transparent and collaborative relationships with them. Such leaders could be described as charismatic, directive, participative, or transformational, in addition to being described as authentic.

Authentic leadership could also be viewed as being instrumental in orientation and/or goal-directed, without necessarily detracting from what represents the "authentic" aspect in authentic leadership. Most definitions of leadership include some sort of focus on achieving a particular aim or goal, which authentic leaders seek to attain by enlisting the support of their followers. However, the difference between authentic leadership and some other forms of leadership (e.g., transactional leadership) lies in the fact that authentic leaders strive to achieve their goals by offering followers a leader who will achieve those goals in a balanced and fair way, while being transparent, ethical, and self-aware. This is not to say that a transactional leader would not work in the same way with his or her followers. However, if that were the case, we would label such transactional leadership as being authentic. Such leaders are highly self-aware, so that acting in accordance with their core personal values and beliefs yields added benefits in terms of the transactional exchange by first building credibility with followers and then earning their trust and respect. Using authentic as the adjective for transactional leadership essentially adds in the four key components that will facilitate and sustain follower success in achieving the goals set.

Avolio et al. (2004) also proposed a theoretical framework linking authentic leadership to followers' attitudes and behaviors in their exploration of the authentic relationship that emerges between an authentic leader and follower. Avolio et al. (2004) went further in their proposed theoretical framework by also attempting to explain the potential mediating mechanisms that allow authentic leaders to exert their influence on followers' attitudes, behaviors, and performance. According to the authors, authentic leaders affect their followers' attitudes and behaviors by creating a sense of personal and social identification among their followers. They use positive role modeling and set high moral standards to connect with their follower's self-concepts, so that their followers' values and beliefs become more similar to those of their leader. Such leaders are identified with by their followers for "leading from the front," by transparently discussing their mutual vulnerabilities, and by having a constant focus on the growth and development of their followers, as well as themselves. Additionally, by creating an environment that is characterized by high levels of honesty and integrity, they create among followers a sense of pride in belonging to the group. This has been described as motivating followers to personally and socially identify with the authentic leaders and the leaders' group/organization. Again, such leaders can also be transactional or transformational and accomplish the same ends (Avolio & Luthans, 2006).

According to the proposed model of authentic leadership, such personal and social identification on the part of the followers leads to high levels of hope (Snyder, Irving, & Anderson, 1991) and trust (Dirks & Ferrin, 2002), as well as positive emotions (Seligman, 1998) and positive states (Luthans, Youseff, & Avolio, 2007). These mediating outcomes of trust and positive states/emotions, subsequently lead to higher levels of follower commitment, job satisfaction, meaningfulness, and engagement, which in turn would lead to increased extra effort, job performance, and a reduction in withdrawal behaviors by followers (Luthans et al., 2007). The theoretical framework proposed by Avolio and his colleagues offered a more comprehensive assessment of how the components of authentic leadership related to mediators and moderators, and how each related to the followers' authenticity and their performance.

Avolio and Gardner (2005) further extended the theoretical framework by outlining the various components associated with the process of authentic leadership. According to the authors, to fully examine core constructs comprising authentic leadership in action along with its subsequent impact involved an examination of nine major facets associated with the *authentic leadership process*. They were positive psychological capital, including the psychological states of efficacy, hope, optimism, and resiliency; positive moral perspective; leader

self-awareness; leader self-regulation; leadership processes/behaviors; follower self-awareness/regulation; follower development; organizational context; and veritable and sustainable performance beyond expectations.

This proposed framework has helped advance the research process on authentic leadership in three important ways. First, it presented a relatively comprehensive (although not all-inclusive) list of the elements associated with the emerging theory on authentic leadership, thus paving the way for more structured and organized efforts at subsequent theory development. Second, it offered a multilevel framework for examining authentic leadership that included the leader, follower, context, and performance. And third, it provided a broader platform for examining the discriminant validity of authentic leadership by comparing and contrasting it with other leading leadership frameworks, such as the transformational leadership theory, ethical leadership theory, the charismatic leadership theory, and theories of servant leadership and spiritual leadership.

It is important to distinguish the nine facets associated with the *authentic leadership process* theorized by Avolio and Gardner (2005) from the four core constructs comprising authentic leadership (i.e., self-awareness, relational transparency, internalized moral perspective, and balanced processing) in that the nine components encompass the entire process associated with authentic leadership and in part its development. Specifically, the process of authentic leadership minimally includes an authentic leader, his or her followers, the relationships between the two, the context and the outcomes that follow as a result. By contrast, the four constructs describe what constitutes the composition of an authentic leader.

Extending the work on authentic leadership further, Gardner, Avolio, Luthans, May, and Walumbwa (2005) focused on the follower component within a more dynamic authentic leadership framework, offering a multilevel self-based perspective of authentic leadership that also examined follower development. The authors introduced the concept of *authentic followership* as an integral component of authentic leadership development. They outlined the process through which authentic leaders use positive role modeling to create authentic followers who possess high levels of self-awareness and who practice self-regulatory behaviors that would mirror the values and beliefs of their authentic leaders. This mirroring of values and beliefs does not in any way discourage disagreements between authentic leaders and their followers because followers expect their authentic leaders to be transparent with them, to be fair when receiving criticism, to treat feedback with the highest moral standards, and to use that feedback to enhance their self-awareness. It is more a reflection of the fact that authentic leaders strive to develop authentic transparent relationships with their followers, in which followers are free to remain true to their own core values and beliefs while ultimately modeling their leader to display the same qualities with their peers and followers. It may also be the case that the follower becomes a role model for the leader, modeling aspects of authentic leadership that the leader then adopts.

Avolio and Luthans (2006) have also suggested that personal history and trigger events act as antecedents of both authentic leadership and authentic followership and the authentic relationship that results leads to outcomes of follower trust, engagement, workplace well-being, and sustainable and veritable performance. Including context in their discussion, they also examined the role played by an ethical and strengths-based organizational climate in fostering the development of authentic leaders and followers.

Extensions to the Base Theories of Authentic Leadership

Additional authors writing on what constitutes authentic leadership have offered several alternate theoretical frameworks and perspectives aimed at describing the multifaceted aspects constituting authentic leadership. For example, Ilies, Morgeson, and Nahrgang (2005) proposed a complementary multicomponent model of authentic leadership and follower development. Similar to other foundational work on authentic leadership, these authors described the four elements comprising authenticity (viz. self-awareness, unbiased processing, authentic behavior, and relational transparency), as well as the processes through which authentic leadership impacts the eudaemonic well-being of leaders and their followers. This model largely mirrored the theoretical frameworks proposed by Avolio and his colleagues, which in combination suggests that authentic leadership represents a normative view of leadership, albeit still early in its development.

Michie and Gooty (2005) examined the impact of values and emotions on leader authenticity. The authors suggested that self-transcendent values such as social justice, equality, and honesty, as well as positive other-directed emotions such as gratitude, goodwill, and appreciation, play a crucial role in the

emergence and development of authentic leadership. The authors proposed that "positive other-directed emotions, such as gratitude and appreciation, will motivate authentic leaders to behave in ways that reflect self-transcendent values, such as honesty, loyalty, and equality" (cited in Avolio & Gardner, 2005, p. 318).

One of the important aspects of determining whether a leader is authentic or ethical is how they make decisions. Turning to how authentic leaders make decisions, May, Hodges, Chan, and Avolio (2003) examined the factors that influence the ethical decision making processes and behaviors of authentic leaders and offered a glimpse into the inner workings of the authentic decision making process. They proposed that the process of authentic decision making involves "recognizing the level of intensity associated with each moral situation" (p. 247). They also suggested the crucial role played by the "transparent evaluation of all relevant alternatives and the development of intentions to act authentically" in the authentic decision making process. In a positive work climate in which transparency is the norm, authentic leaders should have greater situational awareness regarding what their followers think and feel. They should be balanced and fair in their approach toward considering the differing views of their followers. This balanced and fair processing of events and decisions should lead to authentic behaviors that involve doing the right thing, which in turn result in transparent leader–follower relationships.

According to their proposed model of authentic decision making, authentic leaders are capable of exhibiting a higher level of moral capacity to judge moral dilemmas from multiple angles and are able to take into account the different needs of the stakeholders involved. This leads to heightened intentions to act authentically, which is then subsequently translated into authentic moral actions. This represented an important contribution to research on authentic leadership because, not only did it extend the initial conceptualization of authentic leadership by Luthans and Avolio (2003), but it also bridged the gap between the cognitive and behavioral components of authentic decision making and taking action.

Eagly (2005) proposed some boundary conditions for authentic leadership theory. Specifically, she examined instances in which leaders failed to achieve relational authenticity with their followers by highlighting the significance of leader–follower value compatibility in the establishment of authentic relationships. Eagly also focused on the significance of follower-accorded legitimacy for the successful creation of authentic relationships and proposed that female leaders may find it more difficult to elicit personal and social identification from their followers as compared to male leaders. This does not, however, imply that the absence of personal and/or social identification on the part of the followers leads to the leader not being perceived as an authentic leader. It merely refers to the critical role played by personal and social identification with the leader's values and beliefs in the development of an authentic transparent leader–follower relationship. Often, followers come to identify with the leader as being self-aware, ethical, balanced, and transparent, even if they don't agree with the leader's vision or mission.

One of the more recent conceptualizations of authentic leadership includes an extensive focus on examining authentic leadership as a multilevel process. Yammarino, Dionne, Schriesheim, and Dansereau (2008) extended the conceptualization of authentic leadership to include multiple levels of analysis (i.e., individual, dyadic, group/team, and organizational) and suggested linkages between authentic leadership and performance that manifest at different levels of analysis. They offered a description of how the process of authentic leadership may operate within and between each level of analysis. More specifically, they theorized that, at the individual level, authentic leaders could display a leadership style "towards subordinates or followers in which they treat all followers or subordinates similarly" (p. 698). The authentic leadership style may differ across leaders, however, and it may display stable individual differences across time. Additionally, this view of leadership can apply to multiple levels of leaders across an organization, with increasing cognitive and task complexity for leaders at successively higher levels within an organization.

At a dyadic level of analysis, authentic leadership was theorized to "involve a leader and a follower or a superior and a subordinate having an interpersonal relationship" (p. 699). It constituted a one-to-one transparent relationship between a superior and a subordinate "involving the superior's investments in and returns from the subordinate and the subordinate's investments in and returns from the superior" (p. 699).

At the group or team level of analysis, authentic leadership was theorized with a focus on the entire group or a team and how they operate collectively. An "authentic team" was conceptualized as a collective whereby team members, including the authentic leader "view authentic leadership similarly and as a shared responsibility of all members" and involved a strong reliance on "shared mental models and shared knowledge and cognitions within a team" (p. 700). Last, at the organizational level, authentic leadership was theorized as "operating similarly to the strategic leadership approach regarding organizational values and managerial philosophy," resulting in an authentic organization and culture (p. 700). The authentic leadership philosophy and values may be an integral part of the entire organization, including all its subunits and subcultures.

Gardner, Fischer, and Hunt (2009) advanced a model of leader authenticity by examining how emotional labor played a role in producing authentic leadership. Specifically, they focused on the role of emotional labor in affecting perceptions of authenticity associated with a particular leader. According to their model, the extent of surface acting, deep acting, and genuine emotions on the part of a leader are indicative of followers' perceptions of a leader's authenticity. Moreover, this resulting perception of a leader's level of authenticity is subsequently related to the trust that followers experience with respect to their leader.

Ladkin and Taylor (2010) argued that followers' perceptions of leader authenticity are dependent upon the manner in which the leader's "true self" is enacted. Whether or not a leader succeeds in embodying his or her true self is indicative of the extent to which he or she is perceived as authentic. They proposed a theory of *embodied* authentic leadership in which they proposed that the creation of embodied authentic leadership involves three key aspects: self-exposure, relating, and leader-like decisions.

Several researchers have offered challenges regarding the way in which authentic leadership has been theorized. For instance, Cooper, Scandura, and Schriesheim (2005) pointed toward the lack of agreement associated with the way authentic leadership was theoretically defined and conceptualized in the early research literature. They suggested that, although most researchers agree on certain common components associated with authentic leadership, there still were discrepancies associated with the conceptualization that may need to be ironed out for research to progress in an organized manner. The authors suggested that the three most common components associated with the multiple conceptualizations of authentic leadership were the existence of a "true self" from which leaders tend to operate, the extent of self-awareness experienced by the leader, and the self-regulation or adherence to moral values associated with authentic actions.

Other researchers (e.g., Fields, 2007) have suggested that "it is not clear from authentic leadership theory how deeply self-referent aspects of a leader's self (authenticity) and the leader's underlying moral values (integrity) become apparent to followers" (p. 196). In a similar vein, Pittinsky and Tyson (2005) suggested that leaders' internal states may not be so easily apparent to followers and "on a practical level, followers' perceptions of the authenticity of a leader are as important to consider as are the actual thoughts and actions of the leader being perceived" (p. 254).

In sum, the theoretical and empirical literature focusing on authentic leadership has evolved considerably over the last 5 years, offering a more coherent and consistent view of what constitutes authentic leadership and the process of authentic leadership development. In the next section, we review some of the empirical support for the models just discussed.

Empirical Research on Authentic Leadership

Despite the multiple conceptualizations of what constitutes authentic leadership and the intermittent disagreements regarding how authentic leadership has been (and needs to be) defined in research literature, there has been a sizeable amount of empirical evidence supporting and validating the theory and constructs that have been proposed to constitute authentic leadership. Evidence of the growing interest in this area of research comes from the site where researchers can access the Authentic Leadership Questionnaire (www.mindgarden.com). This website has now received over 400 research project requests for use of the survey from around the globe.

Using the authentic leadership model as a guiding framework, Jensen and Luthans (2006) provided an exploratory examination of the link between employee perceptions of entrepreneurs as authentic leaders and employee attitudes and happiness. They found that employee perceptions of authentic leadership were the strongest single predictor of employee job satisfaction, organizational commitment, and work happiness. Focusing more on what comprised or even drove authentic leadership development, Shamir and Eilam (2005) proposed a life stories approach to examining authentic leadership development. Using this approach, the authors described how a leader's life story offers him useful insights into the meanings that he attaches to

life events to guide his followers, and to simultaneously develop himself through self-reflection. They suggested that life stories offer "authentic leaders with a self-concept that can be expressed through the leadership role" (p. 402). Walumbwa, Avolio, Gardner, Wernsing, and Peterson (2008) developed a theory-based measure of authentic leadership, the Authentic Leadership Questionnaire (ALQ), and tested it using five separate samples obtained from China, Kenya, and the United States. The authors found support for a higher-order, multidimensional model of the authentic leadership construct comprising leader self-awareness, relational transparency, internalized moral perspective, and balanced processing. They also found that the composite construct representing authentic leadership predicted work-related attitudes, behaviors, and supervisor-rated performance more significantly than each of its individual constructs. In addition, the authors found that authentic leadership predicted organizational citizenship behaviors (OCBs), organizational commitment, and follower satisfaction over and above ratings of ethical and transformational leadership using established measures in the literature for these two respective constructs.

In sum, this series of initial studies provided an important step in advancing the theory and research on authentic leadership because not only did it empirically verify some of the propositions associated with the authentic leadership framework, but it also offered a valid and reliable measure of authentic leadership in the form of the ALQ—a measure that can be obtained for research use at www.mindgarden.com. Moreover, this research established authentic leadership as a higher-order construct comprised of the four unique components described above (i.e., self-awareness, relational transparency, internalized moral perspective, and balanced processing).

Clapp-Smith, Vogelgesang, and Avey (2009) escalated the level of analysis to the group by exploring the relationship between ratings of authentic leadership and outcomes of trust and performance. They reported a positive relationship between ratings of authentic leadership and trust aggregated at the group level of analysis. Additionally, they found that trust partially mediated the relationship between ratings of authentic leadership and group performance. Using a longitudinal design, Tate (2008) investigated the role of authentic leadership in predicting initial perceptions of leadership, as well as changes in perceptions of leadership over time. Tate reported that individuals rated higher on authentic leadership were more likely to be perceived as leaders later in a group's tenure versus individuals rated lower. Additionally, Tate developed and utilized a 17-item measure for Authentic Leadership based on George's (2003) five dimensions of authentic leadership.

Walumbwa, Luthans, Avey, and Oke (2011) also raised the level of analysis by examining how authentic leadership affects group-level processes by exploring the mediating role of "collective" or group-level psychological capital (efficacy, hope, optimism, and resiliency) and trust in the relationship between authentic leadership and a workgroup's desired outcomes. Walumbwa et al. (2011) reported that collective psychological capital and trust mediated the relationship between ratings of authentic leadership and group citizenship behavior and group performance, after controlling for the effects of transformational leadership. Replicating the findings reported by Walumbwa et al. (2008), Walumbwa et al. (2011) provided further evidence to support the predictive validity of authentic leadership over and above other current leading leadership scales, such as transformational leadership.

Peterson, Walumbwa, Avolio, and Fredrickson (2010) examined the role of follower emotions in the relationship between authentic leadership and individual job performance. The authors reported a positive relationship between the frequency of authentic leadership exhibited by leaders and followers' job performance. Additionally, the authors found that followers' positive emotions mediated the relationship between authentic leadership behaviors and follower performance.

Walumbwa, Wang, Wang, Schaubroeck, and Avolio (2010) used hierarchical linear modeling to examine the direct and indirect effects of authentic leadership behavior on OCB and work engagement in followers. The authors reported that authentic leadership behavior was positively related to organizational citizenship behavior and work engagement in followers. Additionally, they found that the relationship between authentic leadership behavior and the outcomes of follower OCB and work engagement was mediated by followers' level of identification with the supervisor and follower's feelings of empowerment.

Hannah, Avolio, and Walumbwa (2010) examined whether ratings of authentic leadership predicted performance, while also examining several proposed mediators and moderators. In one of their three reported field studies, they assessed how the authenticity of military leaders predicted their followers' positivity and performance in a challenging military context 5 months after the collection of ratings of authentic leadership. Results from the 5-month field study demonstrated that, while controlling for the effects of a positive organizational climate, authentic leadership was positively related to follower performance, with that effect fully mediated through leaders' influence on followers' positivity. The predictive validity of ratings of authentic leadership was also replicated for leaders being rated by followers in a police organization and a separate military field study.

In sum, the accumulated research on authentic leadership has thus far provided the following outcomes:

- Authentic leadership can be reliably measured, and is comprised of four component factors (i.e., self-awareness, relational transparency, internalized moral perspective, and balanced processing) representing a higher-order construct of authentic leadership.
- Authentic leadership has been shown to be discriminantly valid in multiple field studies across multiple samples and settings when compared to measures of transformational and ethical leadership.
- Authentic leadership has been shown to predict a range of performance outcomes across time and organizational contexts.
- Authentic leadership relates to a number of mediators that have been hypothesized in the foundational models discussed at the outset of this chapter.
- Evidence for moderation of authentic leadership has also been provided.

Practical Implications

The growing research stream on authentic leadership has significant practical applications for organizational leaders across a wide range of varying organizational and cultural contexts. For example, one can use what is emerging as a well-validated measure and model of authentic leadership as a platform for developing authentic leadership and followership. To the extent that authentic leadership does represent a root construct underlying other positive forms of leadership, it would behoove organizations to build the four components of authentic leadership into every leadership intervention program, regardless of its focus, including team- and strategic-level leadership. Given below is a brief summary of some key practical implications derived from prior and current research on authentic leadership:

- Authentic leadership is measurable, and thus feedback can be provided to those leaders who aspire to be more authentically transactional, transformational, directive, or participative, or who aspire to other positive orientations toward leadership.
- Authentic leadership theory and practice, coupled with other well-validated leadership models, can enhance the impact of leadership interventions within organizations.
- Authentic leadership theory could be focused on both the leader and follower, such that future training interventions may want to include both in the development process.
- Research on escalating the effects of authentic leadership to the group level suggests that developing team authentic leadership and focusing on authentic strategic leadership development is something future intervention work needs to consider.

Future Directions

Although research on authentic leadership continues to grow, several important areas still remain untapped, the exploration of which could significantly add to our current understanding of what constitutes authentic.

Although authentic leadership has been theorized as a root construct that can be argued to lie at the heart of several different leadership theories (e.g., transformational leadership, ethical leadership, charismatic leadership, etc.), the exact nature of how it merges and interacts with those theoretical frameworks needs to be explored further. In this regard, it would be helpful to theorize the role of authentic leadership as a catalyst in augmenting the predictive power of other positive forms of leadership across differing contexts that vary from the extreme to the more normative (Hannah, Uhl-Bien, Avolio, & Cabarretti, 2009).

It would also be helpful for future research to explore a broader range of mediating and moderating mechanisms that help explain where authentic leadership may have a more positive impact on performance outcomes. These moderators might include such variables as the nature of the organization and work, national culture, level of experience the follower has with the leader, the level of experience of

the follower, organizational climate, and type of performance outcome. Mediators might include the learning or goal orientation of followers, openness to new experiences, perspective-taking capacity, cognitive complexity, self-concept clarity, and motivation to lead and learn.

Although prior research does support the added effects of authentic leadership over and above those of transformational and ethical leadership, we are currently unable to draw any definitive conclusions about cause and effect. This is because prior research has primarily used field survey research methods, and at best, we are able to determine temporal ordering, but not cause and effect. Thus, whether authentic leadership causes positive emotions in one's followers, or causes performance to increase remains for future research to explore.

Most conceptualizations of authentic leadership theorize authentic leadership as a higher-order construct comprised of four individual components—self-awareness, relational transparency, internalized moral perspective, and balanced processing—and view those components as being additive or even synergistic in nature. The primary validated measure of authentic leadership (i.e., the ALQ) also assumes an additive position, in which a mean score of authentic leadership is calculated after averaging the individual scores on all the items comprising the four individual components. Yet, we still don't know whether certain components are more or less important for perceptions of leader authenticity depending on the nature of the context in which followers are embedded or based on the followers' attributes themselves. For instance, future research could examine whether certain threshold levels of self-awareness (or transparency, internalized moral perspective, and balanced processing) need to be attained for some followers versus others to rate leaders as authentic. If yes, appropriate metrics need to be developed to estimate those threshold levels. Doing so would allow us to get a better understanding of the construct of authenticity and how it exists and functions within the specific domain of authentic leadership and more generally in terms of its relationship with other leadership constructs.

Much of the theorizing and empirical validation and testing of the authentic leadership framework has been performed in the context of Western cultures (with a few notable exceptions). Generalizing the current findings regarding authentic leadership to other cultural contexts would further consolidate the conceptual and empirical contribution of authentic leadership to the broader field of leadership studies.

Another avenue for extending research on authentic leadership is to theorize and assess the impact of gender, ethnicity, and race on authentic leadership. Given that the proportion of women assuming leadership positions is on the rise, it makes sense to examine if there are systematic differences in the way authenticity is enacted and perceived (authentic behaviors) across men and women in both leader and follower roles.

Additional studies need to be performed that examine the impact of authentic leadership across multiple levels of analysis. Some researchers have suggested examining how the effects of authentic leadership cascade across different levels and end up affecting cognitive, emotional, and performance outcomes of indirect followers of authentic leaders (Avolio & Luthans, 2006). Continuing along the same path, future research can be focused on determining the magnitude and the extent of the cascading effects across time, levels of analysis, and levels of organizations. For example, examining whether the effects of authentic leadership cascade two, three, or even more levels down an organization's hierarchy and studying the nature of the resulting impact would help to broaden the theoretical base underlying authentic leadership and to determine whether it is an emergent construct or not.

Additionally, researchers could also focus on assessing the time it takes for authentic leadership to generate an impact across lower and more distant levels of followers within certain organizational hierarchies and cultures. Not only would it enable future researchers to have a better understanding of how the cascading effect of authentic leadership works, but it would also allow future research to better design strategic leadership development interventions that view the entire organization as the leadership challenge.

Additionally, a greater focus on conducting longitudinal research could add to the current understanding of authentic leadership. Exploring the effects of authentic leadership across extended intervals of time and across a wide variety of contexts would help us get a firmer grasp on the developmental trajectory pertaining to the impact of authentic leadership on follower development and performance. Finally, some additional questions that could be addressed through future research include, how can damaged authenticity be repaired, and how long does it take? And, what are the boundary conditions for the effectiveness of authentic leadership across different contexts?

Conclusion

The field of authentic leadership theory has witnessed an increasing amount of activity over the last decade, and it continues to grow and integrate with other existing theories of leadership. Early empirical evidence suggests that the framework of authentic leadership holds a key place in the overall nomological network of leadership constructs and processes that adds value to what constitutes exemplary leadership and followership in organizations.

References

Avolio B.J., & Gardner W.L. (2005). Authentic leadership development: getting to the root of positive forms of leadership. *Leadership Quarterly, 16*, 315–338.

Avolio, B.J., Gardner, W.L., Walumbwa, F.O., Luthans, F., & May, D.R. (2004). Unlocking the mask: A look at the process by which authentic leaders impact follower attitudes and behaviors. *Leadership Quarterly, 15*, 801–823.

Avolio, B.J., & Luthans, F. (2006). High impact leader: Moments matter in authentic leadership development. NY: McGraw-Hill.

Brumbaugh, R.B. (1971). Authenticity and theories of administrative behavior. *Administrative Science Quarterly, 16*(1), 108–112.

Cameron, K.S., & Caza, A. (2004). Contributions to the discipline of positive organizational scholarship. American Behavioral Scientist, *47*, 731–739.

Cameron, K.S., Dutton, J.E., & Quinn, R.E. (Eds.). (2003). Positive organizational scholarship. San Francisco: Berrett-Koehler.

Clapp-Smith, R., Vogelgesang, G.R., & Avey, J.B. (2009). Authentic leadership and positive psychological capital: The mediating role of trust at the group level of analysis. *Journal of Leadership and Organizational Studies, 15*(3), 227–240.

Cooper, C., Scandura, T.A., & Schriesheim, C.A. (2005). Looking forward but learning from our past: Potential challenges to developing authentic leadership theory and authentic leaders. *The Leadership Quarterly, 16*, 475–493.

Dirks, K.T., & Ferrin, D.L. (2002). Trust in leadership: Meta-analytic findings and implications for research and practice. *Journal of Applied Psychology, 87*, 611–628.

Eagly, A.H. (2005). Achieving relational authenticity in leadership: Does gender matter? *The Leadership Quarterly, 16*, 459–474.

Erickson, R.J. (1995). The importance of authenticity for self and society. *Symbolic Interaction, 18*(2), 121–144.

Fields, D.L. (2007). Determinants of follower perceptions of a leader's authenticity and integrity. *European Management Journal, 25*(3), 195–206.

Gardner, W.L., Avolio, B.J., Luthans, F., May, D.R., & Walumbwa, F.O. (2005). "Can you see the real me?" A self-based model of authentic leader and follower development. *The Leadership Quarterly, 16*, 343–372.

Gardner, W.L., Avolio, B.J., & Walumbwa, F. (2006). *Authentic leadership theory and practice: Origins, effects and development.* Amsterdam: Elsevier JAI Press.

Gardner, W.L., Fischer, D., & Hunt, J.G. (2009). Emotional labor and leadership: A threat to authenticity? *The Leadership Quarterly, 20*, 466–482.

George, B. (2003). Leadership is authenticity, not style. In *Authentic leadership: Rediscovering the secrets to creating lasting value* (pp. 18–25). San Francisco: Jossey-Bass.

Ghoshal, S. (2005). Bad management theories are destroying good management practices. *Academy of Management Learning and Education, 4*, 75–91.

Hannah, S.T., Avolio, B.J., & Walumbwa, F. (2010). The influence of authentic leadership on follower behaviors: A three-study investigation. Unpublished manuscript.

Hannah, S.T., Uhl-Bien, M., Avolio, B.J., & Cabarretta, F. (2009). A framework for examining leadership in extreme contexts. *The Leadership Quarterly, 20*, 897–919.

Ilies, R., Morgeson, F.P., & Nahrgang, J.D. (2005). Authentic leadership and eudaemonic well-being: Understanding leader–follower outcomes. *The Leadership Quarterly, 16*, 373–394.

Jensen, S.M., & Luthans, F. (2006). Entrepreneurs as authentic leaders: Impact on employees' attitudes. *Leadership & Organization Development Journal, 27*(8), 646–666.

Kernis, M.H. (2003). Toward a conceptualization of optimal self-esteem. *Psychological Inquiry, 14*(1), 1–26.

Ladkin, D., & Taylor, S.S. (2010). Enacting the "true self": Towards a theory of embodied authentic leadership. *The Leadership Quarterly, 21*, 64–74.

Luthans, F., Youseff, C., & Avolio, B.J. (2007). *Psychological Capital: Developing the human Competitive edge.* Oxford, England: Oxford Press.

Luthans, F., & Avolio B.J. (2003). Authentic leadership: a positive developmental approach. In K.S. Cameron, J.E. Dutton, & R.E. Quinn (Eds.), *Positive organizational scholarship: foundations of a new discipline* (pp. 241–258). San Francisco, CA: Berrett-Koehler.

May, D.R., Chan, A.Y. L., Hodges, T.D., & Avolio, B.J. (2003). Developing the moral component of authentic leadership. *Organizational Dynamics, 32*, 247–260.

Michie, S., & Gooty, J. (2005). Values, emotions, and authenticity: Will the real leader please stand up? *The Leadership Quarterly, 16*, 441–457.

Peterson, S.J., Walumbwa, F.O., Avolio, B.J., & Fredrickson, B.L. (2010). The relationship between authentic leadership and job performance. The moderating role of follower emotions. Unpublished manuscript.

Pittinsky, T.L., & Tyson, C.J. (2005). Leader authenticity markers: Findings from a study of perceptions of African–American political leaders. In W.L. Gardner, B.J. Avolio, & F.O. Walumbwa (Eds.), *Authentic leadership theory and practice: Origins, effects and development* (pp. 253–280). London: Elsevier.

Roberts, L.M. (2006). Shifting the lens on organizational life: The added value of positive scholarship. *Academy of Management Review, 31*, 292–305.

Rosenthal, S.A., Pittinsky, T.L., Purvin, D.M., & Montoya, R.M. (2007). *National Leadership Index 2007: A National Study of Confidence in Leadership.* Center for Public Leadership, John F. Kennedy School of Government, Harvard University, Cambridge, Massachusetts.

Sartre, J.P. (1966). *The age of reason.* New York, NY: A.A. Knopf.

Seligman, M.E.P. (1998). Learned optimism. New York: Pocket Books.

Shamir, B., & Eilam, G. (2005). What's your story?: A life-stories approach to authentic leadership development. *The Leadership Quarterly, 16*, 395–417.

Snyder, C.R., Irving, L., & Anderson, J.R. (1991). Hope and health: Measuring the will and the ways. In C.R. Snyder, & D.R. Forsyth (Eds.), *Handbook of social and clinical psychology* (pp. 285–305). Elmsford, NY: Pergamon.

Tate, B. (2008). A longitudinal study of the relationships among self-monitoring, authentic leadership, and perceptions of leadership. *Journal of Leadership and Organizational Studies, 15*(1), 16–29.

Walumbwa, F.O., Avolio, B.J., Gardner, W.L., Wernsing, T.S., & Peterson, S.J. (2008). Authentic leadership: Development and validation of a theory-based measure. *Journal of Management, 34*(1), 89–126.

Walumbwa, F.O., Luthans, F., Avey, J.B., & Oke, A. (2011). Authentically leading groups: The mediating role of collective psychological capital and trust. *Journal of Organizational Behavior, 32*(1), 4–24.

Walumbwa, F.O., Wang, P., Wang, H., Schaubroeck, J., & Avolio, B. (2010). Psychological processes linking authentic leadership and follower behavior. *The Leadership Quarterly, 21*(5), 901–914.

Yammarino, F.J., Dionne, S.D., Schriesheim, C.A., & Dansereau, F. (2008). Authentic leadership and Positive Organizational Behavior: A meso, multi-level perspective. *The Leadership Quarterly, 19*, 693–707.

Toward a Positive and Dynamic Theory of Leadership Development

D. Scott DeRue *and* Kristina M. Workman

Abstract

In this chapter, we draw from the literature on positive organizational scholarship to inform and extend current theories and research on leadership development in organizational settings. Specifically, we highlight the value of a strengths-based approach to leadership development, draw attention to the emergence of positive cycles of leadership development, and emphasize the role of high-quality relationships and connections in facilitating leadership development. Our hope is that these theoretical insights provide the basis for new theory on cultivating extraordinary leadership capacity in organizations and stimulate future research on the positive and dynamic processes involved in leadership development.

Keywords: Leadership development, strengths, positive spirals, high-quality relationships

Leadership has long been recognized as an important source of competitive advantage for organizations (McCall, 1998; Tichy & Cohen, 1997; Vicere & Fulmer, 1998). Indeed, leadership is an important predictor of follower job performance and satisfaction, group effectiveness, and organizational performance (DeRue, Nahrgang, Wellman, & Humphrey, 2011; Waldman, Ramírez, House, & Puranam, 2001). Yet, leadership is not simply about meeting performance standards or individuals' being merely satisfied at work. Leadership is also about enabling individuals, groups, and organizations to thrive, be the best they can be, and dramatically exceed expectations. As Cameron states (2008, p. 13), "leaders focus on organizational flourishing, enabling the best of the human condition, and creating exceptionally positive outcomes, not merely on resolving problems, overcoming obstacles, increasing competitiveness, or even attaining profitability." People look to work for meaning in life (Wrzesniewski, 2002) and long to be part of something larger and more significant than themselves. Leadership can be a catalyst for enabling individuals to discover this meaning and realize their sense of purpose at work and beyond.

Recognizing the importance of leadership, organizations are spending approximately half of their organizational learning and development budgets on leadership development (O'Leonard, 2009). In fact, leadership development is often cited as one of the most important priorities for human resource and talent management in organizations and is becoming a strategic priority at all levels of the organization (O'Leonard, 2009; Hernez-Broome & Hughes, 2004). In parallel, organizational scholars are answering calls for more research on leadership development. Recent studies have examined the validity of experience-based leadership development (DeRue & Wellman, 2009; Dragoni, Tesluk, Russell, & Oh, 2009), explored how different people experience and go through the leadership development process (Day, Harrison, & Halpin, 2009; DeRue & Ashford, 2010a), and expanded the criterion domain to move beyond traditional leadership skills and consider the development of individuals' identities as leaders (DeRue & Ashford, 2010b; Day & Harrison, 2007; Van Knippenberg, Van Knippenberg, De Cremer, & Hogg, 2004), motivation to lead (Kark & Van Dijk, 2007), and ethical orientation (Lichtenstein, Smith, & Torbert, 1995; Schminke,

Ambrose, & Neubaum, 2005). Indeed, the interest in research on leadership development is evident across several special issues on the topic (McCall, 2010; Pearce, 2007; Yammarino, 2000).

Despite the attention that leadership development is receiving from scholars and practitioners alike, we contend that current theory and research on leadership development are limited in several important ways. Leadership has traditionally been equated with individuals in supervisory positions (Ancona & Backman, 2008; Bedian & Hunt, 2006), and as a result, most leadership development research focuses on addressing the skill or motivation deficiencies of individuals in these leadership positions. There are two fundamental problems with this approach to studying leadership development. First, by only focusing on individuals' deficiencies, it is possible that existing research does not capture the benefits associated with investing in and developing individuals' current strengths and talents (Spreitzer, 2006). Second, although there is value in developing individual-level leadership skills, leadership is often conceptualized as a social, mutual influence process that is embodied within a system of leader–follower relationships and patterns of influence that go beyond any single individual and evolve over time (Bedeian & Hunt, 2006; Collinson, 2005; Gemmill & Oakley, 1992; Gronn, 2002; Parry, 1998; Uhl-Bien, Marion, & McKelvey, 2007). In this sense, leadership development is not about simply building the capacity of an individual, but that of a collective to exhibit leadership through a relational network of mutual influence (Day, 2000). Unfortunately, current theory and research provide limited insight into the role of individuals' strengths and talents in the leadership development process, as well as the temporal and relational dynamics of the process.

In this chapter, we begin to address these limitations by examining the leadership development process through the lens of positive organizational scholarship (POS; Cameron, Dutton, & Quinn, 2003). Specifically, we explore the following question: How can POS enrich our understanding of leadership development in organizations? We organize the chapter around three specific objectives. First, we establish how and why adopting a POS perspective can inform and extend our understanding of leadership development in organizations. Second, we identify three areas in which POS can enrich leadership development theory and research. Within each of these, we identify specific insights that arise from examining leadership development

through a POS lens, develop the basis for new theory on leadership development, and highlight several propositions and research questions that can serve as the foundation for future research. Third, we offer a set of specific guidelines and recommendations for conducting research on the intersection of POS and leadership development.

What Is the Value in Adopting a Positive View of Leadership Development?

Positive organizational scholarship concerns the study of phenomena "associated with what individuals and organizations aspire to be when they are at their very best" (Cameron, Dutton, Quinn, & Wrzesniewski, 2003, p. 362). Leadership is one such phenomenon. Indeed, McCall (2010, p. 15) describes leadership as a process of "creating a context in which people can reach their full potential in serving the organization's mission." Likewise, Cameron (2008) suggests that leadership is most effective and most likely to enable extraordinary performance when individuals accentuate what is right, what is inspiring, and what is good in organizations. If we adopt this positive view of leadership, the fundamental question with respect to leadership development is as follows: How can organizations develop a capacity for leadership that enables people to reach their full potential and fosters extraordinary performance that exceeds expectations? We propose that adopting a POS perspective on leadership development begins to address this question in three important ways.

First, leadership development practices are most often grounded in a deficit approach to human development, whereby deficiencies in individuals' knowledge, skills, and abilities are identified and then targeted with specific developmental opportunities (Ohlott, 2004; Spreitzer, 2006). Likewise, most research on leadership development has focused on how organizations can assess, provide feedback on, and address individuals' deficiencies in leadership skills and abilities (Day, 2000). Although doing so is important, an alternative POS-based perspective suggests that building on people's strengths and not just focusing on their shortcomings is an important element of leadership development (Rath & Conchie, 2008; Spreitzer, 2006). Thus, one insight from POS is that we need theories and models for how best to build on individuals' strengths and talents during the leadership process, and POS offers a foundation for such research.

Second, a well-accepted tenet in current theories of leadership development is that the development process is dynamic and cyclical (Van Velsor, Moxley, & Bunker, 2004). At both individual and group levels of analysis, the capacity for leadership develops in different ways, at different times, and at different rates over time—ultimately taking on either positive or negative cycles of development (Day et al., 2009). For example, one idea often discussed in research on experience-based leadership development is that the developmental value of a job assignment is partially a function of an individual's prior job experiences, what lessons and skills were learned during his or her prior experiences, and how "ready" that individual is for the current experience (Avolio, 2005; Avolio & Hannah, 2008; Ohlott, 2004). When job assignments build on and extend the lessons learned from prior experiences, a positive developmental cycle can be created. When job assignments are disconnected or do not reinforce the lessons of past experiences, a negative cycle can be created. Similar negative development cycles have been documented in research on education and child development (Broidy et al., 2003; Nagin & Tremblay, 1999; Spreiker, Larson, Lewis, Keller, & Gilchrist, 1999). However, despite acknowledging that human development processes are cyclical, current theory and research on leadership development offer few insights into how positive and negative cycles of development are created in organizational settings. In contrast, POS is concerned with the study of generative, capability enhancing processes and structures, and thus provides insight into how positive, reinforcing cycles emerge in organizations (Dutton, Glynn, & Spreitzer, 2006). Thus, incorporating a POS perspective into theory and research on leadership development will help illuminate when and under what conditions positive developmental cycles occur.

The third reason for incorporating POS into our study of leadership development is because it addresses the relational aspects of leadership. Leadership is not an individual act but rather a social process of mutual influence that is enacted within a network of leader–follower relationships (Hollander, 1978; Parry, 1998). In this sense, leadership is very much a relational concept. However, with the exception of research on the development of leader–member exchange relationships (Graen & Uhl-Bien, 1995), most research on leadership development fails to account for the relational elements of leadership. Rather than consider the evolution of the content and quality of the interactions between leaders and followers, the literature on leadership development primarily focuses on the development of individuals' leadership skills and

behavioral competencies (e.g., McCall, 2004). As a result, current models of leadership development do not fully explain the process through which leader–follower relationships become a social reality in organizations and how those relationships evolve into high-quality, functioning leadership relationships over time. Positive organizational scholarship, on the other hand, emphasizes the importance of relational connections and helps explain the process of constructing high-quality connections between people (Dutton & Heaphy, 2003). By extending POS to the domain of leadership development, we hope to redirect existing theory toward a more relational-oriented approach to conceptualizing and studying the process of leadership development.

In sum, we contend that adopting a POS perspective establishes the foundation for at least three new insights related to the leadership development process: the value of a strengths-based approach, the cyclical nature of leadership development and need to understand the emergence of positive development cycles, and the role of high-quality relationships and connections in leadership development. We now examine each of these insights in turn, explaining how POS informs and extends current theories of leadership development.

Toward a Theory of Positive Leadership Development
Strengths-based Leadership Development
Positive organizational scholarship is grounded in an affirmative bias that results in a focus on enhancing strengths, affirming human potential, and maintaining a positive orientation toward what is right, as opposed to overcoming obstacles or deficiencies (Cameron et al., 2003a). The affirmative bias is grounded in an assumption that individuals, groups, and organizations have an innate desire and inherent latent ability not only to improve but also to prosper and excel above expectations. Some scholars have referred to this affirmative bias as an illustration of the *heliotropic effect*, whereby living systems are drawn toward positive energy and away from negative energy (Cooperrider & Srivastava, 1987). Applying an affirmative bias to leadership development implies that it might be more effective to frame individuals' positive qualities, existing strengths, and past successes as opportunities for building on what is already excellent, as opposed to focusing on individuals' existing liabilities and problems, such as negative or underdeveloped qualities, weaknesses, and performance gaps (Clifton & Harter, 2003).

The validity of a strengths-based approach to human development has been established in several different research domains. One of the first studies was an investigation of 10th-grade students' reading ability, in which Glock (1955) observed that high-ability students actually improved at faster rates over time than did low-ability students. As a result, the gap between high- and low-ability students actually increased over time, suggesting that building on one's current strengths and talents can be more effective than trying to develop talents that do not exist or are deficient in some way. These findings represent the beginning of a strengths-based movement in human development, and indeed, much of the current research on youth development has adopted a positive, strengths-based orientation (Larson, 2000; Lerner, Almerigi, Theokas, & Lerner, 2005; Smith, 2006). A similar focus on strengths can be found in recent theories of authentic leadership development (Avolio & Gardner, 2005), and in much of the research on leadership development emerging from the Gallup Organization (Clifton & Anderson, 2002; Clifton & Harter, 2003; Rath & Conchie, 2008). A consistent theme across all of this research is that some of the greatest gains in human development occur when training and development are targeted not at addressing people's deficiencies, but at improving what they already do well—what Seligman and Csikszentmihalyi (2000) refer to as people's positive traits.

A strengths-based approach stands in stark contrast to the existing literature on leadership development. For example, much of the research on learning from experience emphasizes the importance and developmental value of on-the-job experiences that are inherently stressful and unpleasant. Research as far back as McCall, Lombardo, and Morrison (1988), and as recent as DeRue and Wellman (2009), identifies job assignments that involve high pressure from outside constituencies, a lack of organizational support, or inherited problems as being particularly developmental. Likewise, Moxley and Pulley (2004) theorize that negative-valence experiences and hardships such as mistakes and failures, career setbacks, personal traumas, problem employees, and downsizing events develop individuals' capacity for leadership by addressing deficiencies in their self-awareness, resiliency, and consideration and compassion for others.

By looking beyond the hardships people face to also consider more positive developmental experiences, a POS perspective brings into focus questions about how leadership development processes can build on people's current leadership capacities and strengths in ways that foster the creation and growth of new leadership capacities. According to adult learning theories (Dewey, 1938; Kolb, 1984; Marsick & Watkins, 1990; Rogers, 1969), experience-based learning occurs when an individual's routines and thought patterns are disrupted by a novel experience, causing the individual to reassess and modify existing knowledge structures, approaches, and processes. Negative experiences, such as setbacks and hardships, can certainly disrupt existing routines and structures, but positive experiences can also provide a stimulus for learning from experience, and potentially without some of the negative consequences associated with hardship and trauma. To this point, Spreitzer (2006) advocates the idea of positive valence experiences ("positive jolts") that stimulate learning and development by energizing individuals and illuminating the possibilities for personal growth and development. Examples of positive developmental experiences might include receiving feedback about the positive contribution or impact that one has on another individual (Grant, 2008) or being granted the opportunity to shadow or be exposed to senior role models (Graen & Cashman, 1975). Not only can these positive experiences stimulate learning by breaking existing thought patterns and routines, but positive experiences also encourage individuals to create, consider, and work toward a more positive self-image. Moreover, because they are more likely to be perceived as supportive and validating, as opposed to threatening, positive experiences may foster psychological safety (Edmondson, 1999), a context that encourages risk taking and embraces personal growth (Dutton & Glynn, 2007; Spreitzer, Stephens, & Sweetman, 2009).

Based on these POS principles, we propose that positive developmental experiences will explain variation in leadership development above and beyond any effects associated with challenges and hardships. To establish support for this proposition, future research needs to expand the conceptualization of developmental experiences to encompass positive valence experiences, and then differentiate those experiences both conceptually and empirically from the predominantly negative valence experiences identified in prior research (e.g., McCall et al., 1988; McCauley, Ohlott, & Ruderman, 1999; McCauley, Ruderman, Ohlott, & Morrow, 1994). Similarly, scholars need to clarify the dimensionality of positive developmental experiences and identify the factors that explain why some positive experiences are more developmental than others. One way in which positive experiences may differ is whether the experience is self-focused (e.g., a celebration of one's extraordinary performance) or other-focused (e.g., being made aware of one's contribution to the success or well-being of others). It is possible that self-focused and other-focused experiences stimulate leadership development through different motivational pathways. On the one hand, self-focused experiences may create an awareness of what a person is truly capable of and motivate that person to strive for his or her full potential. On the other hand, other-focused experiences may stimulate learning and development by making salient how personal growth and development enable an individual to have a more positive impact on others, thereby creating a prosocial motivation for learning. Positive jolts, such as the Reflected Best Self-Exercise (RBSE; Spreitzer et al., 2009) that incorporate both self- and other-focused elements may be particularly developmental. Researchers should examine the utility of the RBSE as a leadership development intervention. By affording participants the chance to both identify their strengths and learn about the positive ways in which they affect others and the social system of which they are a part (Roberts, Dutton, Spreitzer, Heaphy, & Quinn, 2005), participants may experience synergistic motivations for self-improvement. By employing a POS lens to broaden the conceptualization of developmental experiences and examine alternative mechanisms to human development, we would construct a more comprehensive and holistic understanding of how positive and negative experiences influence leadership development processes.

Another area of study that will be important for establishing the validity of a strengths-based approach to leadership development is related to the impact that individuals' current strengths and talents have on future learning from experience. In contrast with the traditional deficit approach to leadership development, the prevailing wisdom among POS scholars is that learning and development are best achieved when people have an opportunity to leverage their talents in progressively more complex and significant tasks and situations. To establish the basis for our proposition, it will be important that future research address several issues. First, scholars need to establish the relative validity of a strengths-based approach above and beyond the deficit approach that pervades current theories of leadership development. Second, it will be particularly important to understand which strengths and talents are most important in predicting the developmental value of different types of experiences, how best to assess those strengths and talents, and how individuals can best leverage their strengths and talents in facilitating experience-based learning and development. One tool that should be explored is the Values in Action Inventory of Strengths (VIA-IS; Peterson, Park, & Seligman, 2005), which will enable researchers to identify individuals' character strengths such as hope, integrity, and perspective, and then explore how and to what extent building on these strengths promotes leadership development. Unfortunately, current theories of leadership development offer little insight into these questions. To advance a POS, strengths-based approach to leadership development, it is essential that future research explain how people's strengths and talents can be used to identify the optimal developmental experiences for an individual and how these experiences can be sequenced to facilitate learning and development.

Finally, we want to emphasize that adopting a POS perspective does not undermine or disregard the role of challenges, hardships, and setbacks in the leadership development process. Existing theory and research make very clear that people can learn from failures (Sitkin, 1992) and often emerge from hardships with key lessons learned about themselves and how to be more effective as leaders in organizations (Ohlott, 2004). Positive organizational scholarship does not deny the developmental value of such experiences. To the contrary, POS suggests that the developmental value of challenging hardships and setbacks can be enhanced by approaching, going through, and reflecting on negative valence experiences with a more positive orientation. Indeed, the literature on POS would suggest that individuals will experience extraordinary learning and development when negative valence experiences are framed and processed as opportunities to capitalize on existing strengths and talents, as opposed to challenges or tests of skills that might not exist or may be deficient in some way. When framed in more positive terms, we would expect individuals to enter into the experience with not only higher efficacy for the task (Bandura, 1997), but also a clearer sense of what strengths and talents they could build from and utilize to learn and grow as leaders. Additionally, negative valence experiences are necessary for positive leadership development because they serve as a foil against which people can cognitively process and interpret the meaning and value of positive developmental experiences (Cameron et al., 2003b). This foil may be particularly important for framing and interpreting positive feedback. Initial research on strengths-only feedback (Spreitzer et al., 2009) suggests that people receiving such feedback may "try to read between the lines" (p. 343), thereby interpreting strengths as weaknesses. Feedback that includes information about weakness as well as strengths may serve to help people process positive feedback as it is intended. Also, these negative valence experiences reduce the possibility of overconfidence, which can hinder learning processes (Chiu & Klassen, 2009), and enable the perspective and humility necessary to maintain a learning orientation (Spreitzer, 2006).

To establish the validity of these framing effects, future research needs to examine the effects of framing negative valence experiences around strengths and opportunities, and how different cognitive frames influence the leadership development outcomes of these experiences. Additionally, research should examine the relative and additive effects of developmental efforts targeted at addressing weaknesses and limitations and at building strengths and talents. It is likely that the former merely produces leaders of adequate ability, whereas the latter or some combination of the two enables leaders to excel (Spreitzer, 2006).

Positive Development Cycles in Leadership Development

Leadership development is, at its core, a process of human growth and change (McCauley, Moxley, & Van Velsor, 1998). Unfortunately, most of the existing literature on leadership development is concentrated on the efficacy of specific leadership development practices (e.g., action learning, feedback programs), and historically, very little scholarly attention has been directed at describing or explaining the dynamic change processes that take place during leadership development (Day, 2000; Day & Lance, 2004). Part of the problem is historical. Much of the research on leadership development has concentrated on rich descriptions of leadership behavior at different points in time (Conger & Kanungo, 1988), cross-sectional designs that connect individuals' current leadership behaviors to prior life experiences (Arvey, Zhang, Avolio, & Krueger, 2007; Zacharatos, Barling, & Kelloway, 2000), or pre–post designs that examine the efficacy of leadership development interventions (Collins, 2004; Tourangeau, Lemonde, Luba, Dakers, & Alksnis, 2003). Despite the value of such research, the result is essentially a gallery of studio portraits or

before and after snapshots of leaders at different developmental stages that offer little insight into the process of leadership development itself.

The leadership development process is complex and multifaceted, but one important aspect of the process that warrants scholarly attention is the trajectory or cycles of developmental change (Day & Lance, 2004; Halpern, 2004). Building on recent theory in developmental psychology that suggests the development process unfolds along different trajectories (Adolph, Robinson, Young, & Gill-Alvarez, 2008), the holy grail of leadership development is the construction of a positive cycle of development whereby prior learning sets the foundation for future learning, and future learning builds on and reinforces prior learning. DeRue, Ashford and Cotton (2009) offer one illustration of a positive development cycle in their theory of how individuals come to see "leader" as part of their personal identity. In the construction of a leader identity, a positive development cycle emerges when an individual behaves in ways that are consistent with a leader identity, and in turn, others within the social context respond to that person's behavior in ways that support and reinforce the individual's leader identity. In contrast, when an individual's claim of a leader identity is not supported and reinforced by others, for example by others openly challenging that person's right to leadership, then a positive development cycle is not created—and in fact, a negative development cycle can be created. What is unclear from the existing literature, however, is an understanding of what organizational structures and processes foster positive development cycles. The literature on POS helps inform current theories of leadership development by illuminating these organizational structures and processes.

Positive organizational scholarship seeks to understand how organizational structures and processes establish the foundation and conditions for the emergence of generative and capability-enhancing processes (Cameron et al., 2003a), and leadership development is one such process. Drawing from POS, we posit that three conditions are essential to creating a positive development cycle in leadership development. The first condition is that there must be a reinforcing nature to development experiences, such that current developmental experiences build on and reinforce the learning that took place in prior developmental experiences. Consistent with our earlier arguments about how developmental experiences need to leverage and build on individuals' strengths, in this case, we are proposing that experiences need to also leverage and build on individuals' prior experiences and the lessons from those experiences (not just their own individual strengths and talents). To fully internalize the lessons of experience and create a positive development cycle, it is important that the lessons of experience be reinforced through repetition over time and across experiences (Ericsson & Lehmann, 1996). In other words, it is when experiences are linked and reinforce each other that a positive development cycle will emerge. To this point, research that specifies how positive experiences can be sequenced with negative experiences to create a positive development cycle would be particularly noteworthy. Negative experiences are a fact of life in organizational settings and can often have harmful emotional and psychological consequences that impede the learning process. Yet, the presence of positive experiences or sequencing of positive experiences with negative experiences might offset those negative consequences and help facilitate the leadership development process. It is probable, therefore, that positive and negative valence experiences are both necessary for making people aware of their need to learn and for stimulating their motivation to learn, while also remaining hopeful and inspired by the possibilities for personal growth and development.

The second condition that is likely important for creating positive development cycles is related to the emotional experience of leadership development. Drawing from Fredrickson's (1998, 2001) broaden-and-build theory of emotions, we posit that the presence of positive emotions will be important for enabling positive development cycles to occur. The broaden-and-build theory suggests that positive emotions broaden people's momentary thought–action repertoires, thereby widening the array of thoughts and actions that come to mind and are considered in any given situation. For example, positive emotions such as joy create an urge to challenge existing routines, norms, and organizational boundaries, and can often lead to increased creativity (Isen, Daubman, & Nowicki, 1987). In the context of leadership development, these positive emotions should promote experimenting with new ways of leading or novel approaches to dealing with leadership challenges, and experimentation with new behavioral methods and approaches is central to learning and development (Kolb, 1984). Likewise, positive emotions such as interest create an urge to explore, take in new information and experiences, reassess current belief and knowledge structures, and increase people's preferences for variety and broaden their array of acceptable behavioral options (Estrada, Isen, & Young, 1997; Kahn & Isen, 1993)—all of which should promote learning and development. In this sense, positive emotions are resources that can be drawn on to facilitate positive cycles of development.

It is also possible that positive emotions can lead to positive cycles of development by regulating the negative emotions that can emerge from negative experiences such as hardships or dealing with adversity (Fredrickson & Levenson, 1998; Frederickson, Mancuso, Branigan, & Tugade, 2000). Given that many developmental experiences create discomfort and anxiety for the individuals involved (McCall et al., 1988; Ohlott, 2004), positive emotions can broaden the capacity for learning by building up resilience to any negative emotions that interfere with the learning process, and thereby help generate positive cycles of leadership development.

To explore the role of positive emotions in leadership development, it is important that future research investigate the extent to which positive emotions can shield people from the negatives associated with adversity and hardship, as well as the mechanisms through which this shielding occurs. Moreover, future research needs to illuminate the array of emotions that are created during developmental experiences, and the processes through which those emotions carry forward to affect learning and development. On the one hand, we do not want people to be overly positive and miss the stimulus for learning that is associated with negative emotions (e.g., discomfort), but at the same time, we do not want people feeling hopeless and lacking a motivation to learn. Thus, it might be that a complex balance of positive and negative emotions is needed to facilitate positive cycles of leadership development.

The third condition that we propose is essential to creating a positive cycle of leadership development is a climate of compassion in the organization. In the POS literature, a climate of compassion has been associated with a wide range of positive attitudes, behaviors, and feelings in organizations (Dutton, Frost, Worline, Lilius, & Kanov, 2002; Lilius, Worline, Dutton, Kanov, Frost, & Maitlis, 2008) and has been shown to foster stronger, more positive relationships between people (Frost, Dutton, Worline, & Wilson, 2000). Drawing from these findings, we contend that a climate of compassion will also have positive effects on learning processes and help sustain positive development cycles. In the service of learning and development, people will inevitably experience moments in which they stumble, mistakes are made, and failures occur. During these challenging times, people will experience a range of negative attitudes and feelings such as embarrassment and shame, and for many, levels of psychological stress will increase. Even though hardships, setbacks, and failures can be the source of much learning and growth (McCall et al., 1988), people have a tendency to focus on the negatives of difficult experiences and overlook the possible lessons that could be derived from these situations (Baumeister, Bratslavsky, Finkenauer, & Vohs, 2001). By constantly focusing on the negatives, people begin to define themselves according to their mistakes and failures, their efficacy for leadership decreases (Paglis & Green, 2002), their identity as a leader weakens (Day & Harrison, 2007; DeRue & Ashford, 2010b; DeRue et al., 2009), and a negative development cycle is created.

According to POS, however, a climate of compassion can help offset the negative effects of challenges at work. A compassionate climate is characterized by people who recognize that others are experiencing some sort of negative state, can empathize with their negative attitudes and feelings, and then respond in ways that help people not only overcome the negatives but also strengthen individuals' functional capacity (Dutton et al., 2002; Frost et al., 2000). In this sense, compassion is not simply about empathizing and showing concern for others. Compassion is also about enabling individuals to excel despite their hardships and engaging in actions that help develop a greater capacity for resilience and learning from challenging experiences (Dutton et al., 2006). Thus, when people encounter a developmental opportunity that is comprised of adversity and hardship, in a compassionate organization, these people are more likely to have colleagues who recognize their struggles and are ready to support and respond in ways that help facilitate learning and growth (e.g., through feedback, mentoring, coaching, training, provision of needed resources). In addition, people who receive compassion from others tend to experience more positive emotions (Dutton, 2003; Folkman & Moskowitz, 2000; Frost, 2003). These positive emotions can enhance resiliency and help foster the creation of positive development cycles. In this sense, a climate of compassion provides individuals with a resource that they can draw upon, in order to build upon and reinforce their developmental experiences, and in doing so, create a positive cycle of development.

Although the existing POS literature provides a solid theoretical basis for how a climate of compassion might help foster positive development cycles, there remain several important questions about the role of compassion in leadership development. For example, the concept of forgiveness (Bright, 2006) is often discussed in conjunction with compassion, and existing research shows that forgiveness can be instrumental in recovering from organizational hardships and setbacks (Cameron & Caza, 2002). Given that failures play such a meaningful role in leadership development (McCall et al., 1988), it would seem important that individuals be forgiven for their failures first, and only then will learning from mistakes occur and opportunities to demonstrate that learning be granted. Research that examines the role of forgiveness in relation to compassion and leadership development would be particularly noteworthy. In addition, we have conceptualized compassion in terms of an organization-level climate, but compassion is ultimately enacted within the context of dyadic relationships. Research that examines the process by which compassionate acts between people affect the learning process would go a long way toward advancing our understanding of how positive development cycles emerge and sustain over time.

High-quality Relationships and Connections

As stated in our introductory comments, leadership is not an individual act but rather an exchange relationship whereby social actors engage in a process of mutual influence (Hollander, 1978; Parry, 1998). Thus, to understand the development of leadership capacity in organizations, it would follow that we need to understand how leadership relationships emerge and develop in organizational settings. Yet, the leadership literature concentrates primarily on the influence tactics of the leaders to the exclusion of those enacted by followers. For instance, the relational dimension of transformational leadership (Bass, 1985; Burns, 1978) includes only leaders' behaviors toward followers (e.g., attending to follower needs, listening to their concerns), but it does not describe or explain follower behaviors or dynamic leader–follower interactions. Likewise, much of the leadership development literature focuses on individual-level development and does not fully explain the emergence or construction of leader–follower relationships.

In contrast, the literature on POS "examines the conditions, processes, and mechanisms in organizational relationships that increase the capacity for growth, learning, generativity, and resilience in individuals, groups and organizations" (Ragins & Dutton, 2007, p. 3). In particular, POS aims to understand how people construct relationships that are mutually beneficial, filled with positive emotions and regard for others, resilient to interpersonal strains and challenges, and open to new ideas and ways of interacting (i.e., high-quality connections; Dutton, 2003; Gittell, 2003). Not surprisingly, these attributes of interpersonal relationships are reflective of how Graen and colleagues (Graen & Uhl-Bien, 1995) describe high-quality relationships between leaders and followers. In this sense, high-quality leadership relationships are one form of high-quality connections discussed in the POS literature. Drawing from these ideas, we contend that adopting a POS perspective on leadership development can help illuminate how high-quality leadership relationships emerge and develop over time.

One mechanism through which positive relationships might facilitate leadership development is by establishing a context that enables people to learn about themselves, creates a safe environment for experimenting with new forms of the self, and provides a secure base for mutual learning and development (Roberts, 2007). A positive relationship is one in which there is a true sense of mutuality and relatedness, such that people experience mutual giving and receiving, caring, and safety in challenging times (Baumeister & Leary, 1995). This sense of mutuality and relatedness provides the psychosocial support and motivation for the construction and growth of positive relational identities that ultimately serve as a foundation in the construction of leadership relationships. Likewise, mutuality can reduce the likelihood that people in a leadership relationship experience identity threats or conflict over leader and follower identities. Rather, a sense of mutuality will enable people to co-create reinforcing identities as leader and follower, and through this identity construction process, generate a mutually reinforcing cycle of development that leads to high-quality leadership relationships.

Another way in which positive relationships can enable leadership development is through the provision of meaning and purpose. For many, leadership is the requisite source of meaning in organizational life (Podolny, Khurana, & Hill-Popper, 2005), but we contend that it is also the case that the purpose and meaning originating from positive relationships can also help enable and facilitate leadership development in organizations. A long history of research shows that individuals look to other people for validation in relation to the importance of the tasks they perform and the roles they assume (Aldefer, 1972). Such validation offers reinforcement that one's role in the organization is valued and that individuals are contributing to a meaningful and socially valued purpose (Kahn, 2007; Mitroff, 1993). In the context of leadership, positive relationships that provide such validation and reinforcement will link people to a larger purpose and motivate them to take on more leadership-like identities and roles in service of that purpose. To the extent organizations consist of a network of mutually reinforcing positive relationships that communicate purpose and meaning, we would expect to see the emergence of clear, well-defined leadership identities and relationships, which, in turn, will facilitate growth and development in the organization's leadership capacity.

Toward a Research Agenda on Positive Leadership Development

Table 60.1 provides a summary of the key propositions and research questions put forth in this chapter. In this section, we build on these propositions and research questions to offer several guidelines and suggestions for incorporating POS-based theories and models into the study of leadership development. First, our emphasis on strengths-based leadership development highlights how important it is that scholars explicitly consider where a person's current leadership knowledge, skills, abilities, and self-concept are when she begins the development process, and how these starting points shape the leadership development process going forward. Every individual will come to the development process with different levels and types of strengths and talents. Historically, leadership development research has used individuals' starting points simply as a baseline measure upon which to assess growth and change—that is, if the starting point is considered at all. In adopting a strengths-based approach, an individual's starting point in terms of leadership skills, for example, will affect the form and/or type of leadership development that occurs, as well as the role or trajectory of that development over time. Thus, an individual's starting point is a viable predictor of leadership development and not simply a baseline control measure. In addition, a strengths-based perspective on leadership development highlights how important the framing of developmental experiences might be to understanding why some people learn from hardships and others do not. In future research, scholars could design experimental

Table 60.1 Positive leadership development: Key propositions and research questions

	Propositions	Research Questions
Strengths-based Leadership Development	• Positive developmental experiences will explain variation in leadership development above and beyond any effects associated with challenges and hardships.	• What types of positive development experiences are most developmental? What types of positive development experiences are most developmental? • What are the mechanisms through which positive experiences facilitate leadership development?
	• Leveraging one's talents in progressively more complex and significant tasks will facilitate leadership development.	• What is the relative validity of a strengths-based approach, above and beyond a deficit-based approach of leadership development? • How can an individual's strengths and talents be used to identify appropriate developmental experiences?
	• Framing negative-valence experiences as positive opportunities to capitalize on existing strengths and abilities will facilitate leadership development.	• How do different positive and negative frames influence leadership development processes and outcomes?
Positive Cycles of Leadership Development	• Positive development cycles of leadership development occur when developmental experiences build on and reinforce the lessons of prior experiences.	• What characteristics of experiences determine how those experiences should be sequenced? • What is the optimum ratio and sequence of positive and negative valence experiences?
	• Positive emotions enable positive development cycles of leadership development to occur.	• To what extent and how do positive emotions shield people from the negatives associated with adversity and hardship? • What mix of positive and negative emotions best facilitates leadership development?
	• A climate of compassion leads to positive cycles of leadership development.	• How do compassionate acts between and among individuals affect the learning process? • When and how can forgiveness within the context of a compassionate organization facilitate leadership development?
High-quality Relationships and Connections	• Mutuality and relatedness among individuals provides a relational context for leadership development.	• Do mutuality and relatedness promote the development of more relational and shared forms of leadership?
	• Positive relationships facilitate leadership development through the provision of meaning and purpose.	• How does the structure of positive relationship networks influence the degree to which people seek out and take on leadership identities and roles in the organization?

or quasi-experimental studies in which the developmental experience is held constant but the cognitive framing of that experience for people is manipulated to focus on either the opportunity to build upon current strengths and talents, or in contrast, to address deficiencies in skills or knowledge. Studies such as these would go a long way toward building the empirical evidence necessary for establishing the validity of a strengths-based perspective on leadership development.

Adopting a POS perspective on leadership development also helps illuminate the need for multilevel theorizing and research designs. Developmental experiences are essentially events that occur and vary within people (DeRue & Wellman, 2009). Individuals' strengths and talents are at the individual-level and vary between people. The high-quality connections that we propose are important for facilitating the development of leadership relationships are dyad-level, relational connections between people (Ragins & Dutton, 2007). Finally, the context and climate for compassion that we discuss could operate at the group or organizational level (Cameron, 2008). Scholars have recently emphasized the need for more multilevel theory and research on leadership development (Avolio, 2005), and this chapter further illustrates that need. By identifying a set of POS-based factors that influence leadership development processes across multiple levels of analysis, we hope that this chapter continues to advance leadership research toward a more multilevel perspective in both our theorizing and empirical research.

Finally, we have presented leadership development as a relational and highly dynamic process that can take on different trajectories over time. With this in mind, it is essential that leadership development research adopt a more longitudinal and processual approach. For example, studies that measure leadership over multiple time periods, and then use latent-growth modeling to model the patterns and trajectories of leadership development, would go a long way toward providing insights into the leadership development process (Day & Lance, 2004). Likewise, research that employs observational and ethnographic methods would enable scholars to generate rich descriptions of individuals and groups learning leadership, and thus provide greater insight into the dynamic cycles of individual and relational development that comprise the leadership development process.

Conclusion

After Day argued that interest in leadership development had reached its "zenith" approximately 10 years ago (Day, 2000), we are observing a resurgence of people interested in the science of leadership development. Organizational scholars are now employing a variety of theoretical perspectives and research methods to study leadership development processes in organizations. In this chapter, we sought to build the case for a POS-based perspective on leadership development and identified several ways in which existing theories of leadership development could be enriched by incorporating POS theories and models. Specifically, we highlight the need to move from a deficit approach to also considering the importance of building on people's strengths in leadership development. We also emphasize how POS can inform our understanding of the dynamics in leadership development through the emergence and construction of positive development cycles. Finally, we underscore the importance of considering high-quality connections and relationships in the leadership development process. We ultimately hope that this chapter serves as the basis for new theory and research on how to cultivate extraordinary leadership capacity in organizations.

References

Adolph, K.E., Robinson, S.R., Young, J.W., & Gill-Alvarez, F. (2008). What is the shape of developmental change? *Psychological Review, 115,* 527–543.

Aldefer, C.P. (1972). *Existence, relatedness, and growth: human needs in organizational settings.* New York: Free Press.

Ancona, D., & Backman, E.V. (2008). *Distributed, shared or collective leadership: A new leadership model for the collaborative era?* Paper presented at the 68th Annual Meeting of the Academy of Management, Anaheim, CA.

Arvey, R.D., Zhang, Z., Avolio, B.J., & Krueger, R.F. (2007). Developmental and genetic determinants of leadership role occupancy among women. *Journal of Applied Psychology, 92*(3), 693–706.

Avolio, B.J. (2005). *Leadership in balance: Made/Born.* Mahwah, NJ: Erlbaum.

Avolio, B.J. (2005). Authentic leadership development: Getting to the root of positive forms of leadership. *Leadership Quarterly, 16,* 315–338.

Avolio, B.J., & Hannah, S.T. (2008). Developmental readiness: Accelerating leader development. *Consulting Psychology Journal: Practice and Research, 60,* 331–347.

Bandura, A. (1997). *Self-efficacy: The exercise of control.* New York: W.H. Freeman.

Bass, B.M. (1985). *Leadership and performance beyond expectations.* New York: Free Press.

Baumeister, R.F., Bratslavsky, E., Finkenauer, C., & Vohs, K.D. (2001). Bad is stronger than good. *Review of General Psychology, 5,* 323–370.

Baumeister, R.F., & Leary, M.R. (1995). The need to belong—desire for interpersonal attachments as a fundamental human-motivation. *Psychological Bulletin, 117*(3), 497–529.

Bedeian, A.G., & Hunt, J.G. (2006). Academic amnesia and vestigial assumptions of our forefathers. *Leadership Quarterly, 17*(2), 190–205.

Bright, D.S. (2006) Forgiveness as an attribute of leadership. In E.D. Hess & K.S. Cameron (Eds.), *Leading with values: Positivity, virtue, and high performance* (pp. 179–193). Cambridge, UK: Cambridge University Press.

Broidy, L.M., Tremblay, R.E., Brame, B., Fergusson, D., Horwood, J.L., Laird, R., et al. (2003). Developmental trajectories of childhood disruptive behaviors and adolescent delinquency: A six-site, cross-national study. *Developmental Psychology, 39,* 222–245.

Burns, J.M. (1978). *Leadership.* New York: Harper & Row.

Cameron, K.S. (2008). *Positive leadership: Strategies for extraordinary performance.* San Francisco: Berrett Koehler.

Cameron, K.S., & Caza, A. (2002). Organizational leadership virtues and the role of forgiveness. *Journal of Leadership and Organizational Studies, 9,* 33–48.

Cameron, K.S., Dutton, J.E., & Quinn, R.E. (Eds.) (2003a). *Positive organizational scholarship: Foundations of a new discipline.* San Francisco: Berrett-Koehler Publishers, Inc.

Cameron, K.S., Dutton, J.E., Quinn, R.E., & Wrzesniewski, A. (2003b). Developing a discipline of positive organizational scholarship. In K.S. Cameron, J.E. Dutton, & R.E. Quinn (Eds.), *Positive organizational scholarship: Foundations of a new discipline* (pp. 361–370). San Francisco: Berrett-Koehler Publishers, Inc.

Chiu, M.M., & Klassen, R.M. (2009). Calibration of reading self-concept and reading achievement among 15-year-olds: Cultural differences in 34 countries. *Learning and Individual Differences, 19,* 372–386.

Clifton, D.O., & Anderson, E. (2002). *StrengthsQuest: Discover and develop your strengths in academics, career, and beyond.* New York: Gallup Press.

Clifton, D.O., & Harter, J.K. (2003). Investing in strengths. In K.S. Cameron, J.E. Dutton, & R.E. Quinn (Eds.), *Positive organizational scholarship: Foundations of a new discipline* (pp. 361–370). San Francisco: Berrett-Koehler Publishers, Inc.

Collins, D.B., & Holton, E.F. (2004). The effectiveness of managerial leadership development programs: A meta-analysis of studies from 1982 to 2001. *Human Resource Development Quarterly, 15,* 217–248.

Collinson, D. (2005). Dialectics of leadership. *Human Relations, 58,* 1419–1442.

Conger, J.A., & Kanungo, R.N. (1988). The Empowerment Process—Integrating Theory and Practice. *Academy of Management Review, 13*(3), 471–482.

Cooperrider, D.L., & Srivastva, S. (1987). Appreciative inquiry in organizational life. *Research in Organizational Change and Development, 1,* 129–169.

Day, D.V. (2000). Leadership development: A review in context. *Leadership Quarterly, 11,* 581–613.

Day, D.V., & Harrison, M.M. (2007). A multilevel, identity-based approach to leadership development. *Human Resource Management Review, 17,* 360–373.

Day, D.V., Harrison, M.M., & Halpin, S.M. (2009). *An integrative approach to leader development: Connecting adult development, identity, and expertise.* New York: Routledge.

Day, D.V., & Lance, C.E. (2004). Understanding the development of leadership complexity through latent growth modeling. In D.V. Day, S.J. Zaccaro, & S.M. Halpin (Eds.), *Leader development for transforming organizations* (pp. 41–69). Mahwah, NJ: Lawrence Erlbaum.

DeRue, D.S., & Ashford, S.J. (2010a). Power to the people: Where has personal agency gone in leadership development? *Industrial and Organizational Psychology, 3,* 24–27.

DeRue, D.S., & Ashford, S.J. (2010b). Who Will Lead and Who Will Follow? A Social Process of Leadership Identity Construction in Organizations. *Academy of Management Review, 35,* 627–647.

DeRue, D.S., Ashford, S.J., & Cotton, N.C. (2009). Assuming the mantle: Unpacking the process by which individuals internalize a leader identity. In L.M. Roberts & J.E. Dutton (Eds.), *Exploring Positive Identities and Organizations: Building a Theoretical and Research Foundation* (pp. 217–236). New York: Routledge.

DeRue, D.S., Nahrgang, J.D., Wellman, N., & Humphrey, S.E. (2011). Trait and behavioral theories of leadership: A meta-analytic test of their relative validity. *Personnel Psychology, 64,* 7–52.

DeRue, D.S., & Wellman, N. (2009). Developing leaders via experience: The role of developmental challenge, learning orientation, and feedback availability. *Journal of Applied Psychology, 94,* 859–875.

Dewey, J. (1938). *Experience and education.* New York: Macmillan.

Dragoni, L., Tesluk, P.E., Russell, J.E.A., & Oh, I.S. (2009). Understanding managerial development: Integrating developmental assignments, learning orientation, and access to developmental opportunities in predicting managerial competencies. *Academy of Management Journal, 52,* 731–743.

Dutton, J.E. (2003). *Energize your workplace: How to create and sustain high-quality connections at work.* San Francisco: Jossey-Bass.

Dutton, J.E., Frost, P.J., Worline, M.C., Lilius, J.M., & Kanov, J.M. (2002). Leading in times of trauma. *Harvard Business Review, 80*(1), 54–61.

Dutton, J.E., & Glynn, M. (2007). Positive organizational scholarship. In C. Cooper, & J. Barling (Eds.), *Handbook of organizational behavior Vol. 1–Micro perspectives* (pp. 693–712). Thousand Oaks, CA: Sage.

Dutton, J.E., Glynn, M., & Spreitzer, G.M. (2006) Positive Organizational Scholarship. In J. Greehaus and G. Callanan (Eds.) *Encyclopedia of Career Development.* Thousand Oaks, CA: Sage Publishers.

Dutton, J.E., & Heaphy, E.D. (2003). The power of high-quality connections. In K.S. Cameron, J.E. Dutton, & R.E. Quinn (Eds.), *Positive organizational scholarship: Foundations of a new discipline* (pp. 361–370). San Francisco: Berrett-Koehler Publishers, Inc.

Edmonson, A. (1999). Psychological safety and learning behavior in work teams. *Administrative Science Quarterly, 44,* 350–383.

Ericsson, K.A., & Lehmann, A.C. (1996). Expert and exceptional performance: Evidence of maximal adaptation to task constraints. *Annual Review of Psychology, 47,* 273–305.

Estrada, C.A., Isen, A.M., & Young, M.J. (1997). Positive affect facilitates integration of information and decreases anchoring in reasoning among physicians. *Organizational Behavior and Human Decision Processes, 72,* 117–135.

Folkman, S., & Moskowitz, J.T. (2000). Positive affect and the other side of coping. *American Psychologist, 55,* 647–654.

Fredrickson, B.L. (1998). What good are positive emotions? *Review of General Psychology, 2,* 300–319.

Fredrickson, B.L. (2001). The role of positive emotions in positive psychology: The broaden-and-build theory of positive emotions. *American Psychologist, 56,* 218–226.

Fredrickson, B.L., & Levenson, R.W. (1998). Positive emotions speed recovery from the cardiovascular sequelae of negative emotions. *Cognition and Emotion, 12,* 191–220.

Fredrickson, B.L., Mancuso, R.A., Branigan, C., & Tugade, M. (2000). The undoing effect of positive emotions. *Motivation and Emotion, 24,* 237–258.

Frost, P.J. (2003). *Toxic emotions at work: How compassionate managers handle pain and conflict.* Boston: Harvard Business School Press.

Frost, P.J., Dutton, J.E., Worline, M.C., & Wilson, A. (2000). Narratives of compassion in organizations. In S. Fineman (Ed.), *Emotion in organizations* (pp. 25–45). Thousand Oaks, CA: Sage.

Gemmill, G., & Oakley, J. (1992). Leadership: An alienating social myth? *Human Relations, 45,* 113–129.

Gittell, J.H. (2003). A theory of relational coordination. In K.S. Cameron, J.E. Dutton, & R.E. Quinn (Eds.), *Positive organizational scholarship: Foundations of a new discipline* (pp. 279–295). San Francisco: Berrett-Koehler Publishers, Inc.

Glock, J.W. (1955). *The relative value of three methods of improving reading: Tachistoscope, films, and determined effort.* Unpublished PhD thesis, University of Nebraska-Lincoln.

Graen, G., & Cashman, J. (1975). A role-making model of leadership in formal organizations: A developmental approach. In J.G. Hunt & L.L. Larson (Eds.), *Leadership frontiers* (pp. 143–180). Kent, OH: Kent State University Press.

Graen, G.B., & Uhl-Bein, M. (1995). Development of leader-member exchange (LMX) theory of leadership over 25 years: Applying a multi-level multi-domain perspective. *Leadership Quarterly, 6,* 219–247.

Grant, A.M. (2008). Employees without a cause: The motivational effects of prosocial impact in public service. *International Public Management Journal, 11,* 48–66.

Gronn, P. (2002). Distributed leadership as a unit of analysis. *Leadership Quarterly, 13,* 423–451.

Halpern, D.F. (2004). The development of adult cognition: Understanding constancy and change in adult learning. In D.A. Day, S.J. Zaccaro, & S.M. Halpin (Eds.), *Leader development for transforming organizations.* Mahway, NJ: Lawrence Erlbaum Associates.

Hernez-Broome, G., & Hughes, R.L. (2004). Leadership development: Past, present, and future. *Human Resource Planning, 27,* 24–32.

Hollander, E.P. (1978). *Leadership dynamics: A practical guide to effective relations.* New York: Free Press.

Isen, A.M., Daubman, K.A., & Nowicki, G.P. (1987). Positive affect facilitates creative problem solving. *Journal of Personality and Social Psychology, 52,* 1122–1131.

Kahn, B.E., & Isen, A.M. (1993). The influence of positive affect on variety-seeking among safe, enjoyable products. *Journal of Consumer Research, 20,* 257–270.

Kahn, W.A. (2007). Meaningful connections: Positive relationships and attachments at work. In J.E. Dutton & R.B. Ragins (Eds.), *Exploring Positive Relationships at Work* (pp. 189–206). New York: Lawrence Erlbaum Associates.

Kark, R., & Van Dijk, D. (2007). Motivation to lead, motivation to follow: The role of the self-regulatory focus in leadership processes. *Academy of Management Review, 32,* 500–528.

Kolb, D.A. (1984). *Experiential learning: Experience as the source of learning and development.* Englewood Cliffs, NJ: Prentice-Hall.

Larson, R.W. (2000). Toward a psychology of positive youth development. *American Psychologist, 55,* 170–183.

Lerner, R.M., Almerigi, J.B., Theokas, C., & Lerner, J.V. (2005). Positive youth development: A view of the issues. *Journal of Early Adolescence, 25,* 10–16.

Lichtenstein, B.M., Smith, B.A., & Torbert, W.R. (1995). Leadership and ethical development: Balancing light and shadow. *Business Ethics Quarterly, 5:* 97–116.

Lilius, J.M., Worline, M.C., Dutton, J.E., Kanov, J.M., Frost, P.J., & Maitlis, S. (2008). The Contours and consequences of compassion at work. *Journal of Organizational Behavior, 29,* 193–218.

Marsick, V.J., & Watkins, K. (1990). *Informal and incidental learning in the workplace.* New York: Routledge.

McCall, M.W. (1998). *High flyers: Developing the next generation of leaders.* Boston: Harvard Business School Press.

McCall, M.W. (2004). Leadership development through experience. *Academy of Management Executive, 18,* 127–130.

McCall, M.W. (2010). Recasting leadership development. *Industrial and Organizational Psychology, 3,* 3–19.

McCall, M.W., Lombardo, M.M., & Morrison, A.M. (1988). *The lessons of experience: How successful executives develop on the job.* Lexington, MA: Lexington Books.

McCauley, C.D., Moxley, R.S., & Van Velsor, E. (Eds.). (1998). *The Center for Creative Leadership handbook of leadership development.* San Francisco: Jossey-Bass.

McCauley, C.D., Ohlott, P.J., & Ruderman, M.N. (1999). *Job challenge profile: Facilitator's guide.* San Francisco: Jossey-Bass.

McCauley, C.D., Ruderman, M.N., Ohlott, P.J., & Morrow, J.E. (1994). Assessing the developmental components of managerial jobs. *Journal of Applied Psychology, 79,* 544–560.

Mitroff, I. (1993). *Crisis Leadership.* New York: Wiley.

Moxley, R.S., & Pulley, M.L. (2004). Hardships. In C. McCauley & E.V. Velsor (Eds.), *The Center for Creative Leadership handbook of leadership development* (2nd ed., pp. 183–203). San Francisco: Jossey-Bass.

Nagin, D., & Tremblay, R.E. (1999). Trajectories of boys' physical aggression, opposition, and hyperactivity on the path to physically violent and nonviolent juvenile delinquency. *Child Development, 70,* 1181–1196.

Ohlott, P.J. (2004). Job assignments. In C. McCauley & E.V. Velsor (Eds.), *The Center for Creative Leadership handbook of leadership development* (2nd ed., pp. 151–182). San Francisco: Jossey-Bass.

O'Leonard, K. (2009). *The corporate learning factbook 2009: Benchmarks, Trends and Analysis of the U.S. Corporate Training Market.* Oakland, CA: Bersin & Associates.

Paglis, L.L., & Green, S.G. (2002). Leadership self-efficacy and managers' motivation for leading change. *Journal of Organizational Behavior, 23*(2), 215–235.

Parry, K.W. (1998). Grounded theory and social process: A new direction for leadership research. *Leadership Quarterly, 9,* 85–105.

Pearce, C.L. (2007). The future of leadership development: The importance of identity, multi-level approaches, self-leadership, physical fitness, shared leadership, networking, creativity, emotions, spirituality and on-boarding processes. *Human Resource Management Review, 17,* 355–359.

Peterson, C., Park, N., & Seligman, M.E.P. (2005). Assessment of character strengths. In G.P. Koocher, J.C. Norcross, & S.S. Hill, III (Eds.), *Psychologists' desk reference* (2nd ed., pp. 93–98). New York: Oxford University Press.

Podolny, J.M. Khurana, R., & Hill-Popper, M. (2005). Revisiting the meaning of leadership. *Research in Organizational Behavior: An Annual Series of Analytical Essays and Critical Reviews, Vol 26,* 1–36.

Ragins, R.B., & Dutton, J.E. (2007). Positive relationships at work: An introduction and invitation. In J.E. Dutton & R.B. Ragins (Eds.), *Exploring Positive Relationships at Work* (pp. 3–25). New York: Lawrence Erlbaum Associates.

Rath, T., & Conchie, B. (2008). *Strengths-based leadership.* New York: Gallup Press.

Roberts, L.M. (2007). From proving to becoming: How positive relationships create a context for self-discovery and self-actualization. In J.E. Dutton & R.B. Ragins (Eds.), *Exploring Positive Relationships at Work* (pp. 29–45). New York: Lawrence Erlbaum Associates.

Roberts, L.M., Dutton, J.E., Spreitzer, G.M., Heaphy, E.D., & Quinn, R.E. (2005). Composing the reflected best-self portrait: Building pathways for becoming extraordinary in work organizations. *Academy of Management Review, 30,* 712–736.

Rogers, C.R. (1969). *Freedom to learn.* Columbus, OH: Merrill.

Schminke, M., Ambrose, M.L., & Neubaum, D.O. (2005). The effect of leader moral development on ethical climate and employee attitudes. *Organizational Behavior and Human Decision Processes, 97,* 135–151.

Seligman, M.E.P., & Csikszentmihalyi, M. (2000). Positive psychology: An introduction. *American Psychologist, 55,* 5–14.

Sitkin, S.B. (1992). Learning through Failure—the Strategy of Small Losses. *Research in Organizational Behavior, 14,* 231–266.

Smith, E.J. (2006). The strength-based counseling model. *The Counseling Psychologist, 34*(1), 13.

Spieker, S.J., Larson, N.C., Lewis, S.M., Keller, T.E., & Gilchrist, L. (1999). Developmental trajectories of disruptive behavior problems in preschool children of adolescent mothers. *Child Development, 70,* 443–458.

Spreitzer, G.M. (2006). Leading to grow and growing to lead: Leadership development lessons from positive organizational studies. *Organizational Dynamics, 35,* 305–315.

Spreitzer, G.M., Stephens, J., & Sweetman, D. (2009). The Reflected Best Self field experiment with adolescent leaders: Exploring the psychological resources associated with feedback source and valence. *Journal of Positive Psychology, 4,* 331–348.

Tichy, N.M., & Cohen, E.B. (1997). *The leadership engine: How winning companies build leaders at every level.* New York: HarperCollins.

Tourangeau, A.E., Lemonde, Luba, M., Dakers, D., & Alksnis, C. (2003). Evaluation of a leadership development intervention. *Nursing Leadership, 16,* 91–104.

Uhl-Bien, M., Marion, R., McKelvey, B. (2007). Complexity leadership theory: Shifting leadership from the industrial age to the knowledge era. *Leadership Quarterly, 18,* 298–318.

Van Knippenberg, D., Van Knippenberg, B., De Cremer, D., & Hogg, M.A. (2004). Leadership, self, and identity. *The Leadership Quarterly, 15,* 825–856.

Van Velsor, E., Moxley, R.S., & Bunker, K.A. (2004). The Leadership Development Process. In C. McCauley & E. Van Velsor (Eds.), *The Center for Creative Leadership Handbook of Leadership Development* (2 ed., pp. 204–233). San Francisco, CA: Jossey-Bass.

Vincere, A.A., & Fulmer, R.M. (1998). *Leadership by design.* Boston: Harvard Business School Press.

Waldman, D.A., Ramírez, G.G., House, R.J., & Puranam, P. (2001). Does leadership matter? CEO leadership attributes and profitability under conditions of perceived environmental uncertainty. *Academy of Management Journal, 44,* 134–143.

Wrzesniewski, A. (2002). It's not just a job": Shifting meanings of work in the wake of 9/11. *Journal of Management Inquiry, 11,* 230–234.

Yammarino, F.J. (2000). Leadership skills: Introduction and overview. *Leadership Quarterly, 11,* 5–9.

Zacharatos, A., Barling, J., Kelloway, E.K. (2000). Development and effects of transformational leadership in adolescents. *Leadership Quarterly, 11,* 211–226.

Organizational Sustainability

Organization Design and Senior Leadership to Enable Strategic Paradox

Wendy K. Smith, Marianne W. Lewis, *and* Michael L. Tushman

Abstract

Positively deviant organizations are sustainable, achieving organizational peak performance today while creating the conditions to thrive tomorrow. We argue that organizational sustainability depends on attending to strategic paradox, simultaneously engaging contradictory yet interrelated strategies. Drawing on our research and the work of others, we explore the paradoxical nature of organizational sustainability and identify organization design and leadership characteristics of differentiating and integrating that can more effectively support seemingly contradictory strategies.

Keywords: Organizational sustainability, peak performance, strategic paradox, organizational design, senior teams

Southwest Airlines, Royal Dutch Shell, and IDEO have achieved sustained performance in industries defined by competition, consolidation, and turbulence. Financially, they have outperformed their rivals. Southwest posted profits for 37 consistent years, despite extensive bankruptcies and acquisition within the airline industry. Royal Dutch Shell holds the largest retail fuel network, and is the second largest oil and gas company. IDEO, a privately owned design firm, has been thriving and growing its number of offices and employees since 1991. In addition, these firms remain generative and creative places in which employees thrive and new ideas emerge. Southwest remained on *Fortune's* "Top Places to Work in America" for 10 consecutive years from 1995 to 2005. IDEO has been considered one of *Fortune's* "Most Favored Employers by MBA Students." In 2009, Royal Dutch Shell and IDEO were listed among *Business Week's* "50 Most Innovative Companies," with IDEO, an industrial design firm, winning more IDEA design awards than any of its competitors. What enables these organizations to thrive in the present, while flourishing for the future?

Traditional organizational research argues that the exemplary success that these firms demonstrate depends on focus and alignment. According to this perspective, success involves visionary leaders assessing the environment, aligning their strategies with that environment, and designing their organizations to execute those strategies (Beer, 1980; Lawrence & Lorsch, 1967). Changing environments demand that leaders shift their strategic focus and, in turn, alter their organizations in order to succeed (Tushman & Romanelli, 1985). Following this argument, focus facilitates consistent interactions among the many components of a complex organizational system, resulting in greater efficiency and effectiveness.

Yet, although focus and alignment enable short-term and local optimums, research suggests that these same efforts also thwart long-term, peak performance. First, such focus does not accommodate competing goals across multiple time horizons. The consistency that enables success today inhibits organizational adaptation and hosts the seeds of failure for tomorrow (Audia et al., 2000). Successful efforts blind leaders, preventing them from responding to threatening external shifts. Core competencies often become core rigidities (Leonard-Barton, 1992; Tripsas, 1997). Once creative decisions become cognitive commitments, as leaders get locked into successful strategies of their past (Tripsas & Gavetti, 2000). Great innovators, such as Polaroid, IBM, and Goodyear Tires, have fallen prey to such traps, failing or faltering when shifts in the market challenge their established means of success (Tushman & O'Reilly, 2002). Second, the pursuit of focused goals and aligned organization does not accommodate complex, competing demands across multiple stakeholders (Donaldson & Preston, 1995). Becoming entrenched in a singular pursuit to meet the demands of one stakeholder group often leads to long-term demise. Scandals at Enron, WorldCom, and Tyco highlight the dangers of pursuing shareholder profits at the expense of employee, customer, or community needs.

An alternative approach argues that organizational success depends not on building consistency and alignment, but on supporting inconsistency, tensions, and contradiction. According to this perspective, organizations inherently host paradoxical tensions, "contradictory yet interrelated" demands on the organization (Cameron & Quinn, 1988; Lewis, 2000). *Strategic paradox* refers to competing organizational agendas, including expectations to explore new opportunities while exploiting existing capabilities, achieve profits while engaging people and the planet, connect globally while responding to local demands, manage competition while enabling cooperation, and prioritize employee engagement while ensuring customer satisfaction. A paradoxical approach argues that long-term success depends on supporting these competing strategies *simultaneously*. Southwest Airlines, Royal Dutch Shell, and IDEO all adopt such a paradoxical approach. Southwest Airlines considers as its highest priority both employee and customer satisfaction, even when these priorities come in direct conflict with one another (Gittell, 2002). Royal Dutch Shell emphasizes learning and experimentation as vigorously as performance and discipline, despite the inconsistent design and cultures demanded for these activities (Senge, 1990). IDEO seeks to exploit its design process and products while exploring new processes and products, even as these activities compete for resources internally in the organization and externally in the market (Hargadon & Sutton, 1997).

Our central thesis in this chapter is that organizational sustainability—achieving peak performance today while creating conditions to thrive tomorrow—depends on leveraging strategic paradox. Although firms may achieve short-term optimums with alignment and focus, positive organizational deviants simultaneously accept and attend to contradictory strategic tensions. To that end, we review mounting research locating strategic paradox at the core of organizational sustainability. We argue that managing strategic paradox is challenging, and we describe organizational designs and leadership characteristics that attend to these challenges and unleash the power of paradoxes.

Organizational Sustainability: A Core POS Agenda

Positive organizational scholarship (POS) investigates positive deviance—intentional, extraordinary action that departs from the norm (Spreitzer & Sonenshein, 2003). At the firm level, positive deviants are flourishing, thriving, resilient, generative, and growing institutions (Dutton & Glynn, 2008; Dutton & Sonenshein, 2008). Organizational sustainability reflects positive deviance. Sustainable organizations achieve peak performance in the present, while also building resources and competencies that position them to excel in the future. Although "sustainability" can refer to a firms' capacity to effectively manage natural and environmental resources, we use the term more broadly to encompass the organization's capabilities to also cultivate human, financial, and organizational resources. From this perspective, sustainable organizations achieve employee satisfaction, motivation, and trust, while pushing employees for increased productivity and commitment. These organizations attend to divergent, and often competing, stakeholder needs while managing success across multiple time horizons. For example, Southwest Airlines addresses multiple stakeholder needs simultaneously, improving employee satisfaction by engaging employees' families and communities. Well cared for employees, in turn, provide excellent customer service, and are then recognized for doing so. IDEO has redesigned itself from a traditional industrial design firm into a firm that uses design principles to address challenges in education, government, and environmental impact, even as their new service often threatens their core processes and products.

What enables organizations to successfully support strategic paradoxes and achieve peak performance? Others have described conditions to achieve this peak performance at the individual level (i.e., Csikszentmihalyi, 1990; Keyes, 2002; Privette, 1983), or proposed systems to improve individual success for high-performing organizations (Harrell-Cook & Mahoney, 2001; Li-Yun et al., 2007). Optimum experiences are associated with challenge and confidence, expending energy and recovering (Loehrand & Schwartz, 2001), and with calm and intensity (Anshel, 1994). We shift this perspective, exploring conditions to achieve sustainability at the organizational level.

Sustainability is defined by plurality and temporality. Plurality determines success according to the varied demands from internal (Cyert & March, 1963) and external stakeholders (Donaldson & Preston, 1995). Beyond profits, sustainable organizations also attend to outcomes associated with employee needs (Gittell, 2004), social missions (Margolis & Walsh, 2003), and environmental impacts (Hoffman & Woody, 2008). Temporality reflects success across multiple time horizons. Sustainable organizations do not choose between today and tomorrow, but create conditions to enable both past and present, ends and means, stability and flexibility, exploration and exploitation (March, 1991; O'Reilly & Tushman, 2008). Like high-reliability organizations (i.e., Weick et al., 1999), sustainable organizations respond quickly to threats, even as they are also capable of learning and adapting in the absence of crises.

As sustainable organizations attend to multiple stakeholders and time horizons, they reflect positive dynamics. Leaders make dynamic decisions between supporting one strategy or another, or finding synergies between them (Smith et al., 2010). As a result, outcomes are not represented by a static endpoint, but a shifting, growing, and virtuous cycle, in which results from one action trigger spiraling, positive reactions (Sundaramurthy & Lewis, 2003). Rather than creating vicious cycles that foster strategic persistence (Audia et al., 2000) and organizational decline (Hambrick & D'Aveni, 1992), peak performance depends on fueling strategic flexibility, adaptability, and synergy. As a result, sustainability does not reflect a fixed outcome, but a positive and dynamic cycle. At Southwest Airlines, expanding employee engagement benefits, rather than deters from, attending to customer needs. At IDEO, new exploratory technologies and processes help reinvent, rather than render obsolete, existing capabilities that they exploit. Figure 61.1 depicts sustainability as a positive, virtuous, and dynamic cycle. We now examine these optimum states in more depth, proposing that organizational sustainability depends on attending to strategic paradoxes and creating the conditions for paradoxes to unleash virtuous cycles.

Strategic Paradox to Enable Sustainability

To achieve organizational sustainability, leaders must embrace strategic paradoxes (Lewis, 2000; Smith & Lewis, 2011). Conventionally, however,

Peak performing involves virtuous cycles between strategy A, strategy B and a synergy of A & B

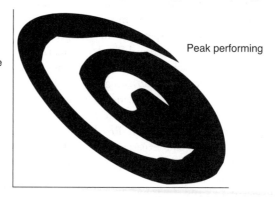

Strategy A
e.g.
• Exploit
• Financial performance
• Global needs
· Competition
• Customers

Peak performing

Strategy B
e.g.
• Explore
• Social performance
• Local needs
· Cooperation
• Employees

Fig. 61.1 Organizational sustainability as a positive, virtuous, dynamic spiral.

divergent goals are associated with inconsistent organizational designs and compete for scarce resources. Engaging a paradoxical approach, in contrast, seeks to engage opposing agendas simultaneously, encouraging their coexistence and seeking powerful synergies (Farjoun, 2010; Lewis, 2000). For example, exploiting existing capabilities is supported by stable structures and cultures that reward efficiency, whereas exploring new possibilities is associated with flexible structures and cultures that reward experimentation (Smith et al., 2005). Andriopoulos and Lewis (2009) found that in leading product design firms, exploration and exploitation foster tensions of strategic intent (profit vs. breakthrough emphasis), customer orientation (tight vs. loose coupling), and personal drivers (discipline vs. passion). Rather than view such tensions as dilemmas, requiring an either/or tradeoff, these exceptionally ambidextrous firms applied both/and approaches. In turn, simultaneously exploring and exploiting results in long-term organizational performance (Tushman et al., 2010). Similarly, even as social missions and financial outcomes attract contrary demographics (Battilana & Dorado, 2009), foster divergent logics (Sonenshein, 2006), and are associated with inconsistent outcomes and rewards (Jensen, 2002), research increasingly stresses that, if managed effectively, social and financial agendas benefit one another (Margolis & Walsh, 2003).

Yet, even as engaging strategic paradox enables organizational sustainability, attending to competing demands is cognitively and emotionally challenging. Competing demands raise uncertainty, ambiguity and conflict, fostering anxiety for senior leaders tasked with making and communicating strategic direction (Jarzabkowski & Sillince, 2007), as well as for middle managers tasked with implementing complex strategic initiatives (Balogun & Johnson, 2004; Luscher & Lewis, 2008). As early psychology research found, individuals often avoid inconsistency, often changing their beliefs or espoused attitudes to enable alignment (Cialdini et al., 1995; Festinger, 1957; Heider, 1958). In organizations, power and politics foster consistent behaviors as leaders competition fosters entrenched positions (Kaplan, 2008), or as leaders commit to historical realities. As a result, achieving organizational sustainability is unusual and reflective of positive deviants.

Although attending to paradox is complex and challenging, doing so surfaces opportunities. Supporting contradictory demands has been associated with individual career success (O'Mahony & Bechky, 2006), exceptional leadership capabilities (Denison et al., 1995), high-performing groups (Murnighan & Conlon, 1991), and organizational performance (Cameron & Lavine, 2006; Tushman et al., in press). We build from such studies, suggesting that leveraging strategic paradox unleashes positive cycles to foster sustainability. More specifically, we propose that engaging strategic paradox enables sustainability through three mechanisms: enabling learning and creativity, fostering flexibility and resilience, and unleashing human potential.

Embracing paradox fosters individual and team learning and creativity. In a study of 54 highly creative individuals, Rothenberg (1979) found that their genius stemmed from the capacity to juxtapose opposing ideas. Einstein's theory of relativity emerged from thinking about the same object simultaneously in motion and at rest. Mozart's music is a function of engaging harmony with discord, and Picasso's paintings reflect both calm and chaos. Similarly, Seudfeld and colleagues (1992) noted that world leaders addressing some of the most complex problems juxtapose contradictory elements to understand their differences and to explore points of synergy. Eisenhardt and Westcott (1988) found that linking conflicting strategies spurs organizational learning. Opposing forces may create the context for leaders to engage in creative problem solving, identify now solutions, and foster organizational change.

Attending to paradoxical tensions also helps individuals and organizations remain flexible and resilient, fostering more dynamic decision making (Smith, et al., 2010). Attending to competing demands simultaneously involves a consistent and mindful shifting of cognition, restructuring resources, altering structures, and rethinking goals (Weick et al., 1999). Such constant movement fosters adaptability, as leaders become less stuck in their existing paradigms (Farjoun, 2002; Weick & Quinn, 1999).

Finally, attending to strategic paradox unleashes human potential. Purposefully engaging contradictions offers opportunities for individuals to experience positive energy through the ongoing interplay of challenges and success. Positive energy creates the conditions for individuals to be more engaged in high-quality connections (Dutton & Heaphy, 2003), more resilient in the face of future challenges (Seligman & Csikszentmihalyi, 2000), and more dedicated to reaching their goals (Kirschenbaum, 1984). In turn, this energy helps raise team effectiveness (Losada & Heaphy, 2004), as well as organizational performance (Cameron & Lavine, 2006). In sum, attending to paradox reinforces commitment to multiple, competing agendas, enabling the organizing process to become fluid, reflective, and sustainable. The challenge for leaders therefore is to effectively harness these tensions and associated anxieties. In the next section, we identify features of organizational design that can help leaders to fuel virtuous cycles and unleash the power of strategic paradoxes.

Organizational Design to Engage Strategic Paradoxes

Paradoxical strategies challenge dominant tenets of organizational design. By organizational design, we refer to a set of choices that leaders make to enable their firms to execute their strategies. These features can include formal elements, such as roles, reporting relationships, and responsibilities, as well as more informal processes, social networks, organizational culture, and leadership characteristics (Nadler & Tushman, 1997). In the early 1960s, Burns and Stalker (1961) suggested that effective design types, specifically organic and mechanistic forms, fit an organization's strategy and environment. Building from this idea, a number of researchers in the late 1960s and early 1970s advocated for organizational fit as a core principle of design. Advocates viewed complex organizations as facing varied environmental challenges, with success determined by aligning their strategy with their organizational design (Beer, 1980; Tushman & Nadler, 1978) and with the external setting (Lawrence & Lorsch, 1967). Achieving fit continues to enable organizations to achieve short-term, local optimums, and it remains a focal objective in organizational theory and a critical principle taught to MBA students and to managers (Beer, 2009).

Despite the benefits, these design principles fail to support competing strategies. First, alignment is static, and does not account for the vicissitudes of the market. Environmental and technological shifts demand new strategies and major internal reorganizations to achieve realignment (Tushman & Romanelli, 1985). Yet, most organizations fail to adapt in the face of shifting environmental conditions. These limitations become amplified over time, as factors such as increased globalization and hypercompetition demand faster-paced innovation and shortened product life cycles (D'Aveni, 1994; Iansiti, 1995). Second, the principle of fit is most effective within a consistent and focused strategy, and does not account for the intricate and often divergent demands of multiple stakeholders. Yet conflicting voices within and outside organizations are not problematic or ancillary (Cyert & March, 1963), but normal and potential sources of competitive advantage (Gittell, 2002; Margolis & Walsh, 2003).How then can we design organizations that can attend to strategic paradoxes?

Drawing from an increasingly robust literature, we seek design principles that can enable consistent inconsistency—the capacity for organizations to consistently support competing demands (Smith et al., 2010). We propose that implementing strategic paradox entails designing organizations and senior leadership teams that have the capability of both differentiating and integrating. Figure 61.2 depicts the nature of these features, and Figure 61.3 creates a model that argues for the impact of these features on organizational sustainability.

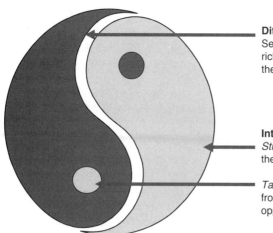

Differentiating
Seeking novel distinctions and taking into account rich, unique contexts and conditions; represented by the boundary between each sliver.

Integrating
Strategic integrating – points of synergies that benefit the overall system; represented by the unified circle.

Tactical integrating – tasks, knowledge and capabilities from one agenda benefit the other; represented by opposite colored circles inside each sliver.

Fig. 61.2 Features of a paradox.

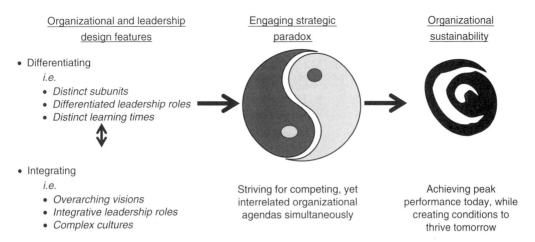

Organizational and leadership
design features

- Differentiating
  i.e.
  - *Distinct subunits*
  - *Differentiated leadership roles*
  - *Distinct learning times*

- Integrating
  i.e.
  - *Overarching visions*
  - *Integrative leadership roles*
  - *Complex cultures*

Engaging strategic
paradox

Striving for competing, yet
interrelated organizational
agendas simultaneously

Organizational
sustainability

Achieving peak
performance today, while
creating conditions to
thrive tomorrow

Fig. 61.3 Achieving organizational sustainability.

Differentiating

Differentiating involves formal and informal organizational features that build boundaries and make distinctions between competing agendas (Andriopoulos & Lewis, 2009; Langer, 1989; Smith, et al. 2010). Differentiation takes into account the unique context and conditions of a given agenda (Lawrence & Lorsch, 1967; Weick et al., 1999). Such differentiating is illustrated in the yin–yang symbol by the boundary between the distinct slivers (see Figure 61.2). Why seek design mechanisms to reinforce differentiating, especially as competitive contexts already dichotomize alternatives, framing them as inconsistent and irreconcilable (Fiol et al., 2009; Langer, 1989; Suedfeld et al., 1992)? Initial differences may be oversimplified and limited. In contrast, encouraging leaders to consistently "seek novel distinctions" results in mindfully approaching problems with greater focus, nuance, and specificity to understand the value of disparate strategies, while also identifying more specific leverage points (Langer, 1989).

Both formal and informal design features foster distinctions that enable more effective attention to strategic paradoxes. These features allow leaders to build boundaries between their paradoxical agendas (Raisch & Tushman, 2010). Structural ambidexterity advocates for creating *distinct subunits*, in which each subunit can host its own strategic agenda (O'Reilly & Tushman, 2008). Distinct subunits allow each agenda to be cultivated independently. Leaders of each subunit maintain focus, even while the overall organization attends to competing demands. Senior leaders can also engage strategic paradox in the context of decision making by explicitly *differentiating leadership roles*, identifying distinct

actors to attend to each strategic agenda (Brown & Eisenhardt, 1997; Smith et al., 2010). Finally, securing *distinct learning times* to discuss the competing agendas ensures that leaders focus on each, independently of the other. Leaders who create time to learn about and focus on competing agendas distinct from one another are most successful in managing tensions between exploration and exploitation (Andriopoulos & Lewis, 2009; Smith et al., 2010).

For example, IBM manages to explore and exploit simultaneously by creating *emerging business opportunity* (EBO) structures to incubate new ideas and products without pressures from existing subunits (see, e.g., Harreld et al., 2007). Leaders of these EBOs advocate for their emerging business among corporate senior leaders. Such focus helps ensure that senior leaders attend to their innovations, thus overcoming the structural inertia and short-term demands that otherwise draw leaders' attention to exploitative efforts. IBM also hosts forums, such as the Strategic Leadership Forum, to provide distinct time for business units to independently discuss their exploratory and exploitative agendas in depth.

Raising divergent perspectives is anxiety producing. Paradoxical agendas heighten conflict as they compete for scarce resources and demand inconsistent organizational structures and cultures. As a result, effectively differentiating demands design principles and senior team behaviors that permit these teams to attend to and deal with this conflict (Eisenhardt et al., 1997). Edmondson (1999), for example, found that teams raise and attend to more diverse perspectives and overall concerns when there is a culture of psychological safety. Similarly, Gilbert (2006) found that teams that framed strategic contradictions as opportunities systematically out-performed those teams that coded the same stimulus as a threat. These leaders are not only able to create individual cognitive frames to more effectively differentiate, but also effectively articulate these distinctions to one another.

Integrating

Strategic paradoxes accommodate conflicting approaches that, when taken together, enable a more effective organization. The benefit of bringing together contradictory agendas is that their integration unleashes synergies that trigger benefits greater than either would independently. Integration involves strategic as well as tactical synergies. Strategic synergies refer to the overall, long-term organizational benefits accrued from engaging paradoxical strategies. Royal Dutch Shell's attention to both exploring and exploiting results in a firm that is overall more strategically agile, as well as more exciting and engaging for its employees. Southwest's ability to prioritize both employees and customers results in positive virtuous spirals among these stakeholder groups. Organizations also gain benefits from tactical synergies, the sharing of tasks, knowledge, and capabilities from one agenda to the other. Exploring new opportunities can introduce new ideas, technology, and motivation that improve existing products. For example, IDEO creates new products and services, and uses the tacit knowledge from this exploration to improve upon its exploitation of existing capabilities and processes

The Taoist symbol of yin and yang depicts these different levels of integration (see Figure 61.2). As with strategic integration, two distinct slivers comprise the overall circle. The yin–yang is not complete without either one of these parts. Tactical integration is represented by the small black and white circles found inside the sliver of the opposing shade, suggesting that each side of the yin–yang benefits from the contributions of its opposite.

Faced with conflicting agendas, individuals tend to pull opposing forces apart and overemphasize their distinctions (Ford & Ford, 1994; Lewis, 2000; Smith & Berg, 1987). To balance this tendency, organizational design features can reinforce strategic and tactical integration. Even as differentiating design features seek to build boundaries, integrating features seek boundary spanning (Raisch & Tushman, 2010). First, an *overarching strategic aspiration* provides a platform for attending to strategic integration. Overarching aspirations are engaging, emotionally charged visions that demand the contributions of

both goals in order to succeed (Andriopoulos & Lewis, 2009; Tushman et al., 2010). By accommodating differences and interconnections, an overarching aspiration ties together competing agendas within a common understanding (Smith et al., 2010). Ciba Vision's goal to achieve "Healthy Eyes for Life" supported its cash cow, an existing hard contact lens and solution business, as well as its innovative and potentially cannibalizing disposable contact lens innovations. Other missions explicitly integrate social and financial goals. Timberland seeks to "Equip People to Make a Difference in the World," an aspiration to sell leading-brand rugged outdoor gear while attending to the ethics and responsibility of their products, processes, and people.

Overarching aspirations not only accommodate contradictory agendas, but also create the potential to find synergies between them. Juxtaposing contradictions within a single setting creates uncertainty and ambiguity, which demands creative solutions (Rothenberg, 1979). The Toyota Production System identifies ultimate goals that demand integration across conflicting agendas (Eisenhardt & Westcott, 1988; Osono et al., 2008). Toyota's leaders want zero cars on their lot, while always having cars to deliver to customers. They respond to these seemingly impossible demands by challenging themselves to create new solutions, and this results in continuous innovative process and product learning. Their just-in-time process resulted from seeking new ways to have access to parts without carrying unnecessary inventory.

Finally, overarching goals diminish the potentially detrimental conflicts that ensue between contradictory agendas. Sherif's (1958) historic Robber's Cave experiments demonstrated how a superordinate goal could diminish the detrimental friction between competing groups of boys. Similarly, reframing organizational goals to focus on the overarching vision, rather than on competing individual goals, enables synergies and minimizes detrimental conflict (Bartlett, 1989; Bartunek, 1988). Smith et al. (2010) found that senior leaders used overarching visions to increase cooperation and decrease competition.

Second, organizations can assign *integrative roles* for leaders. Organizations are more successful when senior leadership explicitly assumes an integrative role (Tushman et al., 2010). Integrative success can be managed by either the CEO alone, or by the entire senior leadership team. However, allocating this responsibility to middle managers, without the senior leaders' integrative support, results in detrimental conflict and ineffective designs (Smith et al., 2010). For example, Ray Stata, at Analog Devices, consistently recreated the organization by separating exploratory products from the core exploitative products. Each differentiated unit had its own leadership team. Stata managed the integration between these competing products, while the subunit leaders rarely spoke with one another. In contrast, although Glen Bradley, CEO of Ciba Vision also created distinct subunits and leaders for their exploratory contact lenses, these leaders worked in a highly integrative team alongside existing product leaders. Both this leader-centric and team-centric model prove successful for managing integration between exploratory and exploitative products (Smith & Tushman, 2005).

Finally, organizations can use informal structures to foster integration, particularly highlighting tactical synergies between competing goals. Research on contextual ambidexterity points to the role of a *complex culture* to enable integration. Gibson and Birkenshaw (2004) observed that organizations inspire individuals to attend to both stability and change by creating cultures that provide support and trust in service of learning and experimentation, while also integrating discipline and stretch to ensure performance. Andriopoulos and Lewis (2009) noted how product design teams integrate exploratory and exploitative tensions via cultures that embrace synergies between emerging possibilities and predetermined project constraints.

Suedfeld and colleagues (1992) stressed that individuals differ in their tendency to engage in integrative thinking. Doing so, they find, is associated with more creativity, diplomacy, and problem solving. Keller and Lowenstein (2010) noted that one of the factors influencing such a distinction is the extent to which the broader culture is predisposed to thinking about "lay dialectisms" or synergies between contradictory forces.

Engaging Both Integration and Differentiation

A key insight of our proposal is that processes of integrating and differentiating work together, reinforcing one another to support strategic paradox (Andriopoulos & Lewis, 2009; Smith & Tushman, 2005). First, greater clarity about the distinct needs of each agenda enables leaders to break seemingly intractable disputes over resource distribution and articulate more effective points of leverage (Bazerman, 1998; Langer, 1989; Lax & Sebenius, 2002). In addition, differentiating can minimize or

avoid "false synergies," in which leaders overzealously and ineffectively link one agenda with another, resulting in inertial behaviors (Smith et al., 2010). For example, without accentuating the distinct value of exploration versus exploitation, organizations can become too focused on one or the other approach to innovation. Firms facing short-term performance pressures often overextend their existing structures, strategies, and processes, leading to devastating consequences (Taylor & Helfat, 2009). Tripsas and Gavetti (2000) depicted how the demise of Polaroid stemmed from the senior team's unsuccessful search for synergies between their historical analog "razor and blade" strategy and their emerging digital strategy. So too, overly enthusiastic adoption of exploratory practices deters optimization and efficiency (Volberda & Lewin, 2003).

Finally, an integrative vision provides a context for exploring distinctions and differences without creating threatening and divisive conflict. Ely and Thomas' (2001) research on managing diversity at work suggests that organizations achieve greater benefit from diversity when they foster an overarching perspective rooted in "integration and learning." Such an overarching context encourages people to bring their distinctions together to improve the firm. Creating a context for diversity invites distinct identities, skills, experiences, and cultural norms without resulting in devastating conflict and competition.

Organizations can attend to differentiating and integrating simultaneously. Andriopoulos and Lewis (2009) found that exploring and exploiting in product design firms depends on attending to multiple, nested tensions. These firms built in processes that enabled differentiation and integration. Tushman and colleagues (2010) found that attending to exploration and exploitation at the strategic business unit level involves creating ambidextrous structures, in which differentiating and integrating are imbedded. Distinct subunits and leaders reinforce differentiating between existing products and novel innovations, while senior leadership is responsible for both overarching and tactical integration. Smith and Tushman (2010) further noted differentiation and integration efforts of senior leadership teams; these teams created distinct times to do "deep dives" and learn about each product, while also identifying overarching visions to support cooperation and synergy.

Others have pointed to a sequential pattern of differentiating and integrating. For example, Gilbert (2006) found that effectively exploring and exploiting involves organizational leaders attending to strategic opportunities and threats. *Opportunity frames* enable integrative thinking, whereas *threat frames* resulted in more differentiated thinking. Although Gilbert (2006) argued that organizations may be most successful when they attend to both at the same time, he noted a sequenced pattern that begins with attending to differentiation through threat frames, then seeking integration through opportunity frames, and only after attending to both of these, engaging these competing frames simultaneously. Organizations may first attend to distinctions and use these differences to seek integration, or firms may seek integration first and then use the overall context of trust to enable conversations about distinctions.

Future Directions
Organizational Sustainability and Strategic Paradox

Our assertion that sustainability is inherently paradoxical and that organizational design features can effectively attend to paradoxical strategies, suggests implications for the POS community as well as a future research agenda. A key objective of POS is to identify mechanisms by which individuals and organizations achieve positive deviance. The results of our work joins those of others (e.g., Cameron, 1986; Cameron & Lavine, 2006) in suggesting that a critical mechanism for positive, virtuous spirals involves attending to and engaging paradoxical demands. Indeed, we suggest that attending to paradox, specifically strategic paradox, is necessary to achieve sustainability, and that organizations can more effectively do so by building in designs that foster both differentiation and integration. Yet, we fully recognize that doing so is challenging. Organizational sustainability, as a positive deviant is, by definition, unusual and unique. To encourage future inquiry, we map out additional questions to explore the nature, implications, and management of strategic paradoxes.

What organization and senior team design characteristics most effectively enable firms to engage strategic paradoxes? A growing body of research investigates managing paradox in general, highlighting features of differentiating and integrating (for a review, see Smith & Lewis, 2011). The ability of senior teams to differentiate and integrate permits their to act paradoxically. An organization focused on a single agenda often remains static, whereas attending to paradox creates dynamic capabilities for organizations (Smith & Lewis, 2011). Attending to contradictory

demands provokes managers and leaders to dynamically shift their time, attention, financial resources, human resources, and organizational designs between competing agendas (Smith et al., 2010). Dynamic shifting unleashes virtuous cycles, in which firms build upon an ongoing, beneficial shift between opposing poles. Future research can link this research on paradoxical strategies with the research on dynamic capabilities (Helfat et al., 2007).

What individual leadership characteristics are necessary to support strategic paradoxes? Attending to strategic paradoxes is challenging for leaders and their teams. Paradoxes raise increased uncertainty, and ambiguity, and doing so requires complex emotional and cognitive capabilities. For example, Seudfeld and colleagues (1992) found that effectively attending to complex problem solving across competing stakeholders is associated with leaders who demonstrate higher levels of integrative complexity. Similarly, effectively managing strategic paradox requires paradoxical cognition—frames that welcome inconsistency and contradiction (Smith & Tushman, 2005). Others have pointed to the emotional capabilities necessary for mindfulness and the avoidance of defensive behaviors (Smith & Berg, 1987; Vince & Broussine, 1996). Whereas this research highlights features of leaders and their teams, others stress elements of the organizational system that can support these skills. For example, Keller and colleagues (2010) find that national cultures in China and the United States are associated with different levels of acceptances of contradictions and paradox. An important extension of this hypothesis therefore is to explore the leadership capabilities that support strategic paradoxes, and the conditions under which individuals can learn, develop, or adopt these capabilities.

Do organizations always benefit from attending to strategic paradox? What are the boundary conditions? We assert that attending to strategic paradoxes is imperative for organizational sustainability. We assume that engaging paradoxical strategies benefits organizations in the long run by enabling resilience for today, while renewing individual and organizational resources for tomorrow. Yet, there may be cases in which organizations may not be seeking such long-run success. Some situations may be created to achieve only a short-term goal, and not benefit from the costs of attending to paradoxical demands across time. For example, leaders may be actively managing organizational demise (Sutton, 1987), or short-term, bounded projects (Lewis et al., 2002).

How generalizable is this model across different strategic paradoxes? Organizations face a number of strategic paradoxes: exploring for today while exploiting for tomorrow, performing financially while attending to social and environmental needs, engaging globally while addressing local demands. These strategic paradoxes are all similar to one another in that they represent "contradictory yet interrelated elements" of the organization (Lewis, 2000). Such strategic dualities compete for organizational resources and are associated with inconsistent designs, and yet the organization benefits from attending to both simultaneously. Yet, do organizations attend to social and financial tensions, for example, in the same way that they attend to exploration and exploitation?

The level of interdependence between paradoxical agendas, as evident in shared tasks, knowledge, and capabilities, may be an important contingency in attending to strategic paradox (Tushman & O'Reilly, 1996). Some paradoxical agendas can be more easily split into distinct subunits than others. For example, high levels of tactical interdependence between some exploratory and exploitative initiatives may render distinct subunits implausible or too costly (Siggelkow & Levinthal, 2003). Similarly, social initiatives may require increased levels of structural integration to enable managers to effectively attend to both simultaneously (Weaver et al., 1999). For example, Nike's social initiative to reduce the environmental impact of their processes and products involves tasks with a high level of integration within the organization and requires greater structural integration across divisions. However, their initiative to build more public play spaces in impoverished communities may be only loosely integrated with tasks, knowledge, and capabilities throughout the organization, thus allowing more differentiated structures.

Finally, we have focused on the implication of attending to paradoxical strategies and argued that doing so impacts organizational sustainability. Yet, organizations face paradoxical demands at multiple levels of analysis (Smith & Lewis, 2011). Although we have focused on strategic paradoxes, organizations also face paradoxical demands in their processes, operations (Luscher & Lewis, 2008), organizational identities (i.e., Fiol et al., 2009; Pratt & Foreman, 2000), group interactions (Smith & Berg, 1987), and individual motivations (Rothbard, 2001). What is the impact of (not) attending to such organizational paradoxes? We encourage research at these multiple levels of analysis.

Implications for Research and Practice

Engaging strategic paradoxes to enable organizational sustainability has implications for what we teach managers and MBA students, and how we learn from organizations in our research. Traditionally, we teach managers to identify a strategy and align their organization with this strategy. As authors, we have taught and developed fit and alignment models. Our assertions suggest that we need to expand our teaching to help managers identify and unleash paradoxical tensions. Ambidextrous organizational models allow managers to explore structures (Harreld et al., 2007) and cultures (Gibson & Birkinshaw, 2004) that support competing strategies simultaneously. Cameron and Quinn's (2006) competing values framework helps managers understand how to embed paradoxical values and cultures into their organizations. In addition, the dynamic equilibrium model of organizing highlights the characteristics and management strategies to attend to paradoxes (Smith & Lewis, 2011). Engaging strategic paradox may encourage us to rethink the models and frameworks that we teach in areas such as innovation and change, social responsibility, globalization, and entrepreneurship.

Managing strategic paradoxes may also require us to consider the skills we help develop in leaders. If attending to paradox is cognitively and emotionally challenging, managers may need a varied toolset of cognitive, behavioral, and emotional capabilities to effectively attend to complexity, ambiguity, and uncertainty. Helping students develop and engage skills such as cognitive complexity, paradoxical thinking, emotional intelligence, and conflict management becomes even more critical to managers today.

The focus on strategic paradoxes also has implications for how we do research, and for how and what we learn from organizations. Our traditional research assumptions and methods build upon the underlying assumption that focused goals, alignment, and consistency breed success. Traditional research epistemologically adopts contingency assumptions, parsing out specific conditions under which alternative explanations best occur. Typical research methods to answer these questions include statistical analyses that identify central tendencies or single points of success. These methods obscure paradoxical dynamics. In contrast, adopting a paradoxical epistemology guides research to identify multiple competing goals. Rather than ask the conditions under which A or B should occur, paradox research asks how A and B can occur simultaneously.

Therefore, methods to explore this question must be able to identify multiple, competing goals, engage complex contexts, and highlight inconsistencies. Researchers exploring paradox typically resort to qualitative methods such as comparative case analysis (Andriopoulos & Lewis, 2009; Smith et al., 2010), ethnography (Huy, 2002), or action research (Luscher & Lewis, 2008). Going forward, we believe there is ripe opportunity to explore new methodological approaches that can integrate both qualitative and quantitative approaches in search of understanding paradox.

Conclusion

Engaging strategic paradoxes simultaneously is complex and challenging, and requires significant individual, team, and organizational energy to resist forces for simplicity, consistency, and status quo. Yet, doing unleashes organizational energy, fueling virtuous cycles that enable sustainability. In this chapter, we mapped out design principles for engaging strategic paradox. Continuing to investigate the opportunities and obstacles for engaging paradox provides a fruitful and critical set of questions for POS and for creating more sustainable organizations.

References

Andriopoulos, C., & Lewis, M.W. (2009). Exploitation-Exploration Tensions and Organizational Ambidexterity: Managing Paradoxes of Innovation. *Organization Science*, 20, 696–717.

Anshel, M.H. (1994). *Sport psychology: From theory to practice*. Scottsdale, AZ: Gorsuch Scarisbrick.

Audia, P.G., Locke, E.A., & Smith, K.G. (2000). The paradox of success: An archival and a laboratory study of strategic persistence following radical environmental change. *Academy of Management Journal*, 43, 837–853.

Balogun, J., & Johnson, G. (2004). Organizational restructuring and middle manager sensemaking. *Academy of Management Journal*, 47, 523–549.

Bartlett, C.A., & Ghoshal, S. (1989). *Managing across borders: The transnational solution*. Boston: Harvard Business School Press.

Bartunek, J. (1988). The dynamics of personal and organizational reframing. In R. Quinn & K. Cameron (Eds.), *Paradox and transformation: Toward a theory of change in organization and management* (pp. 137–162). Cambridge, MA: Ballinger Publishing Company.

Battilana, J., & Dorado, S. (2009). Building sustainable hybrid organizations: The case of commercial microfinance organizations. *Harvard Business School Working Paper*.

Bazerman, M. (1998). *Judgment in managerial decision making* (4th ed.). New York: Wiley.

Beer, M. (1980). *Organization change and development: A systems view*. Santa Monica: Goodyear Publishing Company.

Beer, M. (2009). *High commitment high performance: How to build a resilient organization for sustained competitive advantage*. Hoboken, NJ: Jossey-Bass.

Brown, S.L., & Eisenhardt, K.M. (1997). The art of continuous change: Linking complexity theory and time-paced evolution in relentlessly shifting organizations. *Administrative Science Quarterly*, 42, 1–34.

Burns, T., & Stalker, G.M. (1961). *The management of innovation*. London: Tavistock Publications.

Cameron, K. (1986). Effectiveness as paradox: Consensus and conflict in conceptions of organizational effectiveness. *Management Science*, 32, 539–553.

Cameron, K., & Quinn, R. (1988). Organizational paradox and transformation. In R. Quinn & K. Cameron (Eds.), *Paradox and transformation: Toward a theory of change in organization and management* (pp. 1–18). Cambridge, MA: Ballinger Publishing Company.

Cameron, K., & Lavine, M. (2006). *Making the impossible possible: Leading extraordinary performance*. San Francisco: Berrett-Koehler Publishers, Inc.

Cameron, K., & Quinn, R. (2006). *Diagnosing and changing culture: Based on the competing values framework* (2nd ed.). San Francisco: Jossey-Bass.

Cialdini, R., Trost, M., & Newsom, J. (1995). Preference for consistency: The development of a valid measure and the discovery of surprising behavioral implications. *Journal of Personality and Social Psychology*, 69, 318–328.

Csikszentmihalyi, M. (1990). *Flow: The psychology of optimal experience*. New York: Harper Collins.

Cyert, R.M., & March, J.G. (1963). *A behavioral theory of the firm*. Englewood Cliffs: Prentice-Hall, Inc.

D'Aveni, W. (1994). *Hypercompetition: Managing the dynamics of strategic maneuvering*. New York: Free Press.

Denison, D., Hooijberg, R., & Quinn, R. (1995). Paradox and performance: Toward a theory of behavioral complexity in managerial leadership. *Organization Science*, 6, 524–540.

Donaldson, T., & Preston, L.E. (1995). The stakeholder theory of the corporation: Concepts, evidence, and implications. *Academy of Management Review*, 20, 65–91.

Dutton, J., & Heaphy, E. (2003). The power of high quality connections. In K. Cameron, J. Dutton, & R.E. Quinn (Eds.), *Positive organizational scholarship: Foundations for a new discipline* (pp. 263–278). San Francisco: Berrett-Koehler.

Dutton, J.E., & Glynn, M.A. (2008). Positive organizational scholarship. In J. Barling & C.L. Cooper (Eds.), *The SAGE handbook of organizational behavior* (pp. 693–712). Los Angeles: SAGE Publisher.

Dutton, J.E., & Sonenshein, S. (2008). Positive organizational scholarship. In S. Lopez & A. Beauchamps (Eds.), *Encyclopedia of positive psychology*. Boston: Blackwell Publishing.

Edmondson, A. (1999). Psychological safety and learning behavior in work teams. *Administrative Science Quarterly*, 44, 350–383.

Eisenhardt, K.M., & Westcott, B. (1988). Paradoxical demands and the creation of excellence: The case of just in time manufacturing. In R. Quinn & K. Cameron (Eds.), *Paradox and transformation: Toward a theory of change in organization and management* (pp. 19–54). Cambridge, MA: Ballinger Publishing Company.

Eisenhardt, K.M., Kahwajy, J.L., & Bourgeois, L.J.I. (1997). Conflict and strategic choice: How top management teams disagree. *California Management Review*, 39, 42–62.

Ely, R.J., & Thomas, D.A. (2001). Cultural diversity at work: The moderating effects of work group perspectives on diversity. *Administrative Science Quarterly*, 46, 229–273.

Farjoun, M. (2002). The dialectics of institutional development in emergent and turbulent fields: The history of pricing conventions in the on-line database industry. *Academy of Management Journal, 45,* 848–874.

Farjoun, M. (2010). Beyond dualism: Stability and change as duality. *Academy of Management Review, 35,* 202–225.

Festinger, L. (1957). *A theory of cognitive dissonance.* Evanston, IL: Row Peterson.

Fiol, C.M., Pratt, M.G., & O'Connor, E.J. (2009). Managing intractable identity conflict. *Academy of Management Review, 34,* 32–55.

Ford, J.D., & Ford, L.W. (1994). Logics of dualities, contradiction and attraction in change. *Academy of Management Review, 19,* 756–795.

Gibson, C.B., & Birkinshaw, J. (2004). The antecedents, consequences and mediating role of organizational ambidexterity. *Academy of Management Journal, 47,* 209–226.

Gilbert, C. (2006). Change in the presence of residual fit: Can competing frames co-exist? *Organization Science, 17,* 150–167.

Gittell, J.H. (2002). *The Southwest Airlines way: Using the power of relationships to achieve high performance.* New York: McGraw-Hill.

Gittell, J.H. (2004). Paradox of coordination and control. *California Management Review:* 101–117.

Hambrick & D'Aveni. (1992). Top team deterioration as part of the downward spiral of large corporate bankruptcies. *Management Science, 38,* 1445–1466.

Hargadon, A., & Sutton, R.I. (1997). Technology brokering and innovation in a product development firm. *Administrative Science Quarterly, 42,* 716.

Harreld, J.B., O'Reilly, C., & Tushman, M. (2007). Dynamic capabilities at IBM: Driving strategy into action. *California Management Review, 49,* 21–43.

Harrell-Cook, G., & Mahoney, J.T. (2001). Manufacturing advantage: Why high-performance work systems pay off. *Academy of Management Review, 26,* 459–462.

Heider, F. (1958). *The psychology of interpersonal relations.* New York: Wiley.

Helfat, C., Finkelstein, S., Mitchell, W., Peteraf, M.A., Singh, H., Teece, D., & Winter, S. (2007). *Dynamic capabilities: Understanding strategic change in organizations.* Malden, MA: Blackwell Publishing.

Hoffman, A., & Woody, J.G. (2008). *Memo to the CEO: Climate change, what's your business strategy?* Cambridge, MA: Harvard Business School Press.

Huy, Q.N. (2002). The emotional balancing of organizational continuity and radical change: The contribution of middle managers. *Administrative Science Quarterly, 47,* 31–69.

Iansiti, M. (1995). Shooting the rapids: Managing new product development in turbulent environments. *California Management Journal, 38,* 1–22.

Jarzabkowski, P., & Sillince, J. (2007). A rhetoric-in-context approach to building commitment to multiple strategic goals. *Organizational Studies, 28,* 1639–1665.

Jensen, M.C. (2002). Value maximization, stakeholder theory and the corporate objective function. *Business Ethics Quarterly, 12,* 235–256.

Kaplan, S. (2008). Framing contests: Strategy making under uncertainty. *Organization Science, 19,* 729–752.

Keller, J., & Loewenstein, J. (2010). The cultural category of cooperation: A consensus model analysis of the United States and China. *Organization Science,* Epub before print Jun 21, 2010, DOI: 10.1287/orsc.1100.0530.

Keyes, C. (2002). The mental health continuum: From languishing to flourishing in life. *Journal of Health and Social Behavior, 43.*

Kirschenbaum, D. (1984). Self regulation and sport psychology: Nurturing and emerging symbiosis. *Journal of Sport Psychology, 8,* 26–34.

Langer, E. (1989). *Mindfulness.* Boston: Addison-Wesley.

Lawrence, P., & Lorsch, J. (1967). *Organizations and environment: Managing differentiation and integration.* Homewood, IL: Richard D. Irwin.

Lax, D.A., & Sebenius, J.K. (2002). Dealcrafting: The substance of three-dimensional negotiations. *Negotiation Journal, 18,* 5–28.

Leonard-Barton, D.A. (1992). Core capabilities and core rigidities: A paradox in managing new product development. *Strategic Management Journal, 13,* 111–125.

Lewis, M. (2000). Exploring paradox: Toward a more comprehensive guide. *Academy of Management Review, 25,* 760–776.

Lewis, M., Welsh, M.A., Dehler, G.E., & Green, S.G. (2002). Product development tensions: Exploring contrasting styles of product management. *Academy of Management Journal, 45,* 546–564.

Li-Yun, S.U.N., Aryee, S., & Law, K.S. (2007). High performance human resource practices, citizenship behavior, and organizational performance: A relational perspective. *Academy of Management Journal, 50,* 558–577.

Loehrand, J., & Schwartz, T. (2001). The making of a corporate athlete. *Harvard Business Review, 79,* 120–128.

Losada, M.F., & Heaphy, E. (2004). The role of positivity and connectivity in the performance of business teams. *Journal of Applied Behavioral Science, 47,* 740–765.

Luscher, L., & Lewis, M. (2008). Organizational change and managerial sensemaking: Working through paradox. *Academy of Management Journal, 51,* 221–240.

March, J. (1991). Exploration and exploitation in organizational learning. *Organization Science, 2,* 71–87.

Margolis, J.D., & Walsh, J. (2003). Misery loves company: Rethinking social initiatives by business. *Administrative Science Quarterly, 48,* 268–305.

Murnighan, J.K., & Conlon, D. (1991). The dynamics of intense work groups: A study of british string quartets. *Administrative Science Quarterly, 36,* 165–186.

Nadler, D., & Tushman, M. (1997). *Competing by design: The power of organizational architectures.* New York: Oxford University Press.

O'Mahony, S., & Bechky, B.A. (2006). Stretchwork: Managing the career progression paradox in external labor markets. *Academy of Management Journal, 49,* 918–941.

O'Reilly, C., & Tushman, M. (2008). Ambidexterity as a dynamic capability: Resolving the innovator's dilemma. In A.P. Brief & B.M. Staw (Eds.), *Research in organizational behavior* (Vol. 28, pp. 185–206). New York: Elsevier.

Osono, E., Shimizu, N., & Takeuchi, H. (2008). *Extreme Toyota: Radical contradictions that drive success at the world's best manufacturer.* Hoboken, NJ: John Wiley and Son.

Pratt, M.G., & Foreman, P.O. (2000). Classifying managerial responses to multiple organizational identities. *Academy of Management Review, 25,* 18–42.

Privette, G. (1983). Peak experience, peak performance and flow: A comparative analysis of positive human experiences. *Journal of Personality and Social Psychology, 45.*

Raisch, S., & Tushman, M. (2010). A dynamic perspective on organizational ambidexterity: Structural differentiation and boundary activities. *Harvard Business School Working Paper.*

Rothbard, N.P. (2001). Enriching or depleting? The dynamics of engagement in work and family roles. *Administrative Science Quarterly, 46,* 655–684.

Rothenberg, A. (1979). *The emerging goddess.* Chicago: University of Chicago Press.

Seligman, M., & Csikszentmihalyi, M. (2000). Positive psychology: An introduction. *American Psychologist, 55,* 5–14.

Senge, P. (1990). *The fifth discipline.* New York: Currency Doubleday.

Sherif, M. (1958). Superordinate goals in the reduction of intergroup conflict. *The American Journal of Sociology, 63,* 349–356.

Siggelkow, N., & Levinthal, D. (2003). Temporarily divide to conquer: Centralization, decentralization and reintegrated organizational approaches to exploration and adaptation. *Organization Science, 14,* 650–669.

Smith, K., & Berg, D. (1987). *Paradoxes of group life.* San Francisco: Josey-Bass Publishers.

Smith, W.K., & Tushman, M.L. (2005). Managing strategic contradictions: A top management model for managing innovation streams. *Organization Science, 16,* 522–536.

Smith, W.K., Binns, A., & Tushman, M. (2010). Complex business models: Managing strategic paradox simultaneously. *Long Range Planning, 43,* 448–461.

Smith, W.K., & Lewis, M.W. (2011). Toward a Theory of Paradox: A Dynamic Equilibrium Model of Organizing. *Academy of Management Review, 36,* 381–403.

Sonenshein, S. (2006). Crafting social issues at work. *Academy of Management Journal, 49,* 1158–1172.

Spreitzer, G., & Sonenshein, S. (2003). Positive deviance and extraordinary organizing. In K. Cameron, J. Dutton, & R. Quinn (Eds.), *Positive organizational scholarship: Foundations of a new discipline.* (pp. 207–224). San Francisco: Berrett-Koehler Publishers.

Suedfeld, P., Tetlock, P., & Streufert, S. (1992). Conceptual/integrative complexity. In C. Smith, J. Atkinson, D. McClelland, & J. Verof (Eds.), *Motivation and personality: Handbook of thematic content analysis* (pp. 393–400). Cambridge: Cambridge University Press.

Sundaramurthy, C., & Lewis, M. (2003). Control and collaboration: Paradoxes of governance. *Academy of Management Review, 28,* 397–415.

Sutton, R.I. (1987). The process of organizational death: Disbanding and reconnecting. *Administrative Science Quarterly, 32,* 542–569.

Taylor, A., & Helfat, C.E. (2009). Organizational linkages for surviving technological change: Complementary assets, middle management, and ambidexterity. *Organization Science, 20,* 718–739.

Tripsas, M. (1997). Unraveling the process of creative destruction: Complementary assets and incumbent survival in the typesetter industry. *Strategic Management Journal, 18,* 119–142.

Tripsas, M., & Gavetti, G. (2000). Capabilities, cognition and inertia: Evidence from digital imaging. *Strategic Management Journal, 18,* 119–142.

Tushman, M., & Nadler, D. (1978). Information processing as an integrating concept in organizational design. *Academy of Management Review, 3.*

Tushman, M., & Romanelli, E. (1985). Organizational evolution: A metamorphosis model of convergence and reorientation. In B.M. Staw & L. Cummings (Eds.), *Research in organizational behavior* (pp. 171–222). Greenwich, CT: JAI Press.

Tushman, M., & O'Reilly, C.A. (2002). *Winning through innovation: A practical guide to leading organizational change and renewal.* Boston, MA: Harvard Business School Press.

Tushman, M., Smith, W.K., Wood, R., Westerman, G., & O'Reilly, C. (2010). Organizational design and innovation streams. *Industrial and Corporate Change, 19,* 1331–1366.

Tushman, M.L., & O'Reilly, C.A.I. (1996). Ambidextrous organizations: Managing evolutionary and revolutionary change. *California Management Review, 38,* 8–30.

Vince, R., & Broussine, M. (1996). Paradox, defense and attachment: Accessing and working with emotions and relations underlying organizational change. *Organization Studies, 17,* 1–21.

Volberda, H.W., & Lewin, A. (2003). Co-evolutionary dynamics within and between firms: From evolution to co-evolution. *Journal of Management Studies, 40,* 2111–2136.

Weaver, G.R., Trevino, L.K., & Cochran, P.L. (1999). Integrated and decoupled corporate social performance: Management commitments, external pressures, and corporate ethics practices. *Academy of Management Journal, 42,* 539–552.

Weick, K., & Quinn, R. (1999). Organizational change and development. *Annual Review of Psychology, 50,* 361–386.

Weick, K., Sutcliffe, K.M., & Obstfeld, D. (1999). Organizing for high reliability: Processes of collective mindfulness. In R.I. Sutton & B.M. Staw (Eds.), *Research in organizational behavior* (pp. 81–123). Stamford: JAI Press.

Emotions and Strategic Change

Quy Nguyen Huy

Abstract

Strategic change represents a special form of organizational change that is particularly large-scale, disruptive, and elicits a wide range of strong emotions among employees. This chapter discusses how organizations can develop routines that deal constructively with employees' emotions, as well as the challenges that organization leaders face in perceiving and managing employees' collective emotions. The chapter ends by suggesting a number of important research questions in this vastly underexplored area.

Keywords: Leadership; emotions, strategic change, emotional intelligence, collective emotions, emotional contagion, culture

One of the many important questions facing positive organizational scholarship (POS) is its link to business strategy, which focuses on organizational performance. During relatively stable times, in which managers have more bountiful psychological and organizational resources to build stable, quality relationships, many dimensions of POS, such as thriving at work (Spreitzer, Sutcliffe, Dutton, Sonenshein, & Grant, 2005), relational quality (Dutton & Heaphy, 2003), and experiencing positive energy (R. W. Quinn & Dutton, 2005) seem relevant to increasing business performance, although more research is needed to explore the associated boundary conditions. But when organizations need to deal with the pressure of strategic change, which is often associated with low or declining organizational resources and time pressure, how can a POS perspective help us think about what organizations can do to create an enabling and constructive social-psychological context for beneficial change in business strategy?

This chapter explores this question and is organized as follows. First, strategic change will be defined as a distinct form of organizational change.

We then review the role of emotions in organizations experiencing strategic change. The chapter then elaborates the key constructs in this literature, namely individual versus collective emotions, and perceiving and managing emotions at work. Next, it highlights several psychological and contextual enablers and impediments to dealing with emotions at work. Finally, it suggests avenues for future research.

Strategic Change as a Distinct Form of Organizational Change

Strategic change refers to a qualitative change in the firm's philosophy or core perspective/identity (Bartunek, 1984; Johnson, 1987). Core identity is defined as the central, enduring, and distinctive characteristics of the organization that all members feel proud of and have personally identified with (Dutton & Dukerich, 1991). This deep change in core identity often requires concurrent shifts in all other organizational dimensions, such as structure, systems, and personnel, to preserve alignment. Thus, a strategic change is often deep and large-scale and not only causes a major and pervasive redistribution of resources and power, which is already highly upsetting in itself, but by definition demands a paradigm shift that challenges members' most basic assumptions about the nature of the organization (Reger & Gustafson, 1994). These assumptions define the domain of socially constructed reality and provide a patterned way of dealing with ambiguous, uncontrollable events (Schein, 1992). Organization members have "emotionally invested" in these non-negotiable assumptions that shape their cognitive structures for sense-making and sense-giving. Challenging this source of cognitive and emotional stability is tantamount to an attack on core identity and could trigger strong defense mechanisms, such as anxiety and defensiveness (Schein, 1992).

To the extent that strategic change is perceived as being in opposition to esteemed core values, the negative emotions can be more intense than the affect aroused by lack of cognitive understanding of the proposed change (Festinger, 1957). Opposing concepts are likely to trigger anger, threat, or fear (Reger et al., 1994). Disagreement on important issues provokes intense emotions (Jehn, 1997), and negative emotions tend to spread more rapidly than positive ones (Staw, Sutton, & Pelled, 1994).

Change leaders' tasks include recognizing cues that signal the need for strategic change and helping employees implement a new strategic direction (Huff, Huff, & Thomas, 1992). As this process unfolds, top and mid-level managers can face many challenges in their attempts to facilitate learning among their employees (Chakravarthy, 1982), and as they strive to empower, motivate, and inspire them (Quinn, 1980). To accomplish strategic change, leaders often have to manage the tension between deploying existing competencies and fostering the development and implementation of new ones (Crossan, Lane, & White, 1999). These conflicting goals can generate role conflict and emotional discord among employees who are already worried about time pressure and resources to carry out their tasks effectively (Floyd & Lane, 2000). The emotional reactions of individual employees, as well as of upper and middle managers, to alternative strategic direction can be particularly intense (Kanter, 1983) as these are amplified in a context of new, contested, and shifting ideas. To facilitate strategic change, organization leaders need to perceive employees' emotions accurately, then manage them in a constructive manner. We explore each dimension in turn.

Perceiving and Managing Emotions in Strategic Change

One important dimension of positive psychology involves how employees feel at work and how their emotions influence personal well-being and task performance (Spreitzer et al., 2005). Emotions refer to psychobiological responses elicited by an appraisal of a particular target or situation and often include subjective experiences and specific action tendencies (Frijda, 1986; Lazarus, 1991). Emotion and strategic change are linked insofar as emotions are not necessarily aroused by favorable or unfavorable conditions; sometimes they are aroused by actual or expected changes in these conditions (Frijda, 1988). People can express emotions verbally and through nonverbal behavior. Emotional cues, such as vocal intonations, facial displays, and other nonverbal gestures, indicate how others construe their role in changing events and social structures (Rafaeli & Sutton, 1987). Emotions help direct attention, prompt and inhibit particular behavioral tendencies, and allow employees to coordinate their efforts (Keltner & Haidt, 1999). Paying attention to emotional cues therefore provides useful information about opinions, preferences, and potential behaviors—even when people are unaware of their emotions or consciously try to control their expression (Ashkanasy, Härtel, & Zerbe, 2000).

Emotions in organizations, however, have implications that extend beyond those related to specific individuals. Personal emotions can play a significant role in the effectiveness of collective efforts (George, 1990; George & Brief, 1992). Collective reactions and informal coalitions can form in response to change proposals and their perceived implications for various groups that have different roles and interests in an organization (Cyert & March, 1992). Collective emotions can influence the ways in which various groups think and behave in relation to both the organization and other groups within it (Mackie, Devos, & Smith, 2000). These emotional responses arise and evolve throughout the process of strategic change, and they highlight the need for leaders to accurately perceive collective emotions then to manage them.

Perceiving Emotions in Strategic Change

Perceiving emotions accurately, both at an individual and collective level, has been theorized to be important in the context of strategic change (Sanchez-Burks & Huy, 2009).

PERCEIVING EMOTIONS IN INDIVIDUALS

The ability to recognize emotions in other people is a key component of social emotional intelligence

(Salovey & Grewal, 2005). Scholars have shown empirically that accuracy in respect to individuals' emotional displays is related to effectiveness in managing interpersonal relationships in many occupations and organizational roles (Côté & Miners, 2006; Elfenbein, Beaupré, Lévesque, & Hess, 2007; Elfenbein, 2007); For example, studies have shown that high emotion recognition ability among managers correlates positively with perceptions of transformational leadership among their subordinates (Bass, 1999; Rubin, Munz, & Bommer, 2005), and in negotiation, accuracy correlates with value for both parties (Elfenbein et al., 2007).

PERCEIVING COLLECTIVE EMOTIONS

Collective emotions refer to the composition of various shared emotions of the group's members (Barsade & Gibson, 1998). Collective emotions are important to study because they can influence a variety of group outcomes (van Zomeren, Spears, & Fischer, 2004). Collective emotions can reflect an emotionally homogenous group: All members of the group experience the same emotion. But the composition of a collective emotion can also consist of sizable proportions of different shared emotions. A sales unit reacting to a new change initiative, for example, could have 80% of members experiencing negative emotions and 20% experiencing positive emotions. Since strategic change is unlikely to affect all work units or groups in the same way, the composition of collective emotions might be diverse in large organizations inhabited by groups with distinctive roles, values, and interests (Cyert & March, 1992). For instance, some clusters of group members might feel proud because they perceive that managers are heeding their calls for a new strategic direction. On the other hand, other clusters of group members might feel contemptuous, because they believe their own ideas about new strategic directions are better than those their managers have proposed. In turn, these collective emotions can prompt either action or inaction among subgroups within the collective, motivating mobilization for or against strategic change.

Several mechanisms contribute to the emergence of collective emotions. These include similar interpretations, experiences, identities, and organizational culture (Mackie, Devos, & Smith, 2000). Faced with an important event (e.g., announcement of a new strategic direction), employees can experience emotions similar to one another if they have similar interpretations about the impetus for strategic change, or if they have had similar experiences

with regard to the ensuing costs and benefits for their work units (Gump & Kulik, 1997). For example, employees who strongly identify themselves with their companies are likely to experience emotions similar to one another when faced with events that enhance or threaten the organization's identity through a major shift in strategic focus (Dutton & Dukerich, 1991). Organizational culture represents another subtle yet powerful form of control that informs and guides the emotions of employees and contributes to shared emotional experiences (Van Maanen & Kunda, 1989).

Emotional contagion is another mechanism through which emotions spread from group member to group member, often occurring automatically without conscious knowledge (although it can be consciously induced), to produce shared emotions (Barsade, 2002). This mechanism reflects an innate human propensity to adopt the emotional experiences of those around us (Neumann & Strack, 2000). The mere perception of a person showing anguish, for example, can lead to a sad expression on the perceiver's face (Ekman, 2004). In turn, these unintentional changes in facial and other muscles can lead to similar emotional states in perceivers. Studies have found that these nonconscious but contagious effects produce clusters of shared emotional experiences in a variety of organizational settings (Barsade, 2002; Bartel & Saavedra, 2000).

Sanchez-Burks and Huy (2009) theorized that leaders' *emotional aperture* is distinct from their ability to perceive individual emotions, which represented the focus of the emotional intelligence literature (Mayer & Salovey, 1999). Emotional aperture refers to a person's ability to recognize dynamically the substantive yet shifting proportions of diverse shared emotions that are experienced by various subgroups in a given community. Upon the announcement of a pending change in a company's strategic direction, for example, nearly three-quarters of the marketing group may react with hope, whereas the other quarter reacts with fear. Four months later, the proportion of group members experiencing hope may decline, while the proportion of people feeling fear may increase significantly. The effective use of emotional aperture would involve distinguishing more than a single dominant group emotion and an ongoing perceptiveness to recognize such changes in the emotional composition of the collective. Emotional aperture requires taking a holistic orientation to emotion perception (Nisbett, Peng, Choi, & Norenzayan, 2001), wherein managers derive a relatively accurate portrait of an organization's emotional landscape from a brief but deeper focus on emotional distributions. Perceiving collective emotions and its effects on various strategic change processes and outcomes remains to be empirically investigated both in laboratory and field settings.

Managing Emotions in Strategic Change

Beyond accurately perceiving emotions at the individual and collective level, leaders need to deal with these when necessary in order to foster positive outcomes, such as employees' psychological well-being and optimum business performance during prolonged periods of disruption caused by strategic change. Anxious, fearful employees cannot devote their full attention to their current tasks and have little inclination or capacity to gain new knowledge and skills. Resentful and angry employees may engage in covert sabotage. Depressed and sick employees increase the burden of work on peers who are already overwhelmed (Noer, 1993). All of these emotion-related conditions slow and even thwart organizational learning and beneficial strategic change. Unfortunately, thoughtful management of employees' emotions during strategic change is little understood and even less systematically practiced in organizations.

Skillful emotion management seems necessary to create organizational contexts that foster innovation and beneficial change. This requires emotion-aware managers who systematically allocate organizational resources to develop procedures related to emotion management. Skillful enactment of these procedures constitutes the organization's emotional capability (Huy, 1999, 2005). Such a collective capability mobilizes aggregate emotion management efforts from many people and allows the organization to transcend the need for a large number of individuals with superior emotional intelligence.

Empirical research on emotion management in strategic change has introduced the importance of emotional balancing (Huy, 2002), whereas theoretical research has developed the concept of emotional capability (Huy, 1999, 2005). *Emotional balancing* involves the emotion management behavior of two distinct organizational groups: change agents and change recipients. Practicing emotional balancing could bring about positive organizational adaptation and help avoid the extremes of organizational chaos and inertia. *Emotional capability* then focuses on change recipients and elaborates how to enable those recipients to facilitate major change and innovation. Each concept—representing distinct but complementary forms of emotion management during strategic change—is described in turn.

EMOTIONAL BALANCING AS DISTINCT EMOTION MANAGEMENT FOR STRATEGIC CHANGE

Emotional balancing refers to a group-level process juxtaposing emotion-related organizational actions intended to drive change while fostering a sense of continuity among a group of employees (Huy, 2002). Huy's field research found that such balancing is necessary because too many and too rapid change could generate chaos in employee groups, whereas too little and too slow change could create inertia. Emotional balancing entails, at the organizational level, (a) the change agents' emotional commitment to champion and pursue change projects and (b) middle managers attending to the emotions of their employees to maintain their emotional well-being and necessary operational continuity. Different managers can play different roles, however. Some managers may choose to play the role of change agents who propose radically new ways of doing things, whereas others may focus on attending to organizational continuity and employees' emotions. Enacting emotional balancing at work thus does not require all influential organization members to display a high level of emotion management skills. The aggregation of various emotion management actions performed by different groups of managers and facilitated by the organization's procedures, resources, and training could help develop an enabling emotional climate that facilitates beneficial strategic change. Emotional balancing involves the management of emotions of both change agents and change recipients.

With regard to change agents, to create the emotional energy that helps them consider ambitious strategic change and persist in adversity, change agents manage their emotions by eliciting/increasing pleasant high-activation emotions (e.g., enthusiasm) and reducing unpleasant low-activation emotions (e.g., dejection). Positive emotions, in particular, can help increase people's resilience to hardship, increase their flexible thinking, and improve their interpersonal skills, all of which can increase change agents' effectiveness (Sekerka, Vacharkulksemsuk, & Fredrickson, 2011, Chapter 13, this volume). Emotional commitment to change provides agents with stamina and hope to persevere in sustained change efforts and reduces premature despair and early abandonment due to initial disappointing outcomes.

Meanwhile, employees as recipients of strategic change may feel powerless and fatigued when confronting change and, as a result, neglect to perform the mundane but critical organizational routines that serve the needs of key constituencies, such as delivering good customer service and ensuring safety and quality in production. Organizations need to mitigate the extreme effects of too much change and chaos by focusing managers' attention on the importance of maintaining operational continuity in their own workgroups (Huy, 2002).

The organization needs to display emotional sensitivity behaviors that distinguish, repair, and manage the emotions of change recipients. This requires managers to attend to their subordinates' emotional responses to achieve some emotional equanimity in their employees' work and private lives. Attendance to employees' private lives is crucial to enhancing their receptivity to strategic change, because during such disruptive change, employees tend to be less concerned about the organization's new strategy than about its potential effects on their personal and family welfare.

Huy (2002) found that managers' aggregate emotional balancing actions facilitated two important organizational outcomes: development of new skills and operational continuity. Through "learning by doing," certain organization members developed a more refined embodied understanding of the necessary skills involved in major, rapid change. With regard to operational continuity, middle managers' attention to work details and subordinates' emotions contributed to, for example, smooth downsizings in various work units. Managers' emotion management actions dampened in part employees' anger and fear, which could spread and amplify through emotional contagion. Some continuity in providing products and services allowed the organization to maintain some of its revenue-generating capability, thus providing part of the needed cash to fund various change projects. Inadequate attention to recipients' emotions was found to cause underperformance in organizational outcomes even when change agents' commitment to realizing operational efficiency and manpower savings are strong. Similarly, weak commitment to change in a high-pressure strategic change context or when emotions are not attended to can lead to workgroup inertia or chaos, thus resulting in deteriorating workgroup performance. This suggests that emotional balancing is particularly important for strategic change that requires both strong commitment to pursue ambitious change and, minimally, some moderate

acceptance from recipients to integrate the change while maintaining some of their traditional and still important tasks (e.g., serving customers).

In summary, emotional balancing involves broad categories of emotion management actions related to change agents (e.g., emotional commitment to the proposed changes) and recipients (e.g., the need to attend to their emotions). Huy (1999, 2005) further elaborates the theory of emotional capability, which specifically describes the links between specific emotion management actions that elicit recipients' various emotions in strategic change.

EMOTIONAL CAPABILITY

Emotional capability refers to the organizational ability to recognize, monitor, discriminate, and attend to emotions of employees at both the individual and the collective levels (Huy, 1999). This ability is built into the organization's routine procedures for action, which reflect the collective knowledge and skills demonstrated in local contexts to manage emotions related to strategic change. Organizations that develop procedures related to emotion management and that provide systematic training on this subject to various managers likely reduce the need to rely on the innate competence of individuals' emotional intelligence and their variable individual dispositions. In this respect, an organization's emotional capability can be far greater than the sum of the emotional intelligence of its individual members (Huy, 1999).

Huy (1999, 2005) elaborates the various emotion management action routines that constitute an organization's repertoire of emotional capabilities: the experiencing, reconciliation, identification, encouragement, display freedom, and playfulness that express or elicit specific positive emotions during strategic change. These actions are called *emotional dynamics*. These emotional dynamics are posited to influence three critical processes of strategic change—receptivity, collective mobilization, and organizational learning—as feedback mechanisms linking receptivity to mobilization. Each is summarized below.

Empathy and the Dynamic of Heedfulness

Empathy refers to a person's ability to understand someone else's feelings and to re-experience them. Empathy represents a core attribute of emotional intelligence and a prime motivator for altruistic behavior (Salovey & Mayer, 1990). Empathy is demonstrated in part through heedful behaviors related to others' feelings. At the organizational level, heedfulness refers to the quality of an organization's active efforts in recognizing the importance of emotion and in enacting emotion-focused activities during strategic change. These actions can involve organized activities, such as training and coaching all organization members, and especially change agents, to experience the same or other appropriate emotions in response to others' feelings and to communicate or act on this internal experience. Organization members can be trained in the ability to accurately recognize the subtle social cues and signals given by others in order to determine what emotions are being expressed and to understand the perspective of the other party (Huy, 1999).

The organization can establish anxiety reduction mechanisms, for example, informal communication structures that foster dialogue and sense-making during this disruptive period. Emotional support structures, such as psychological counseling services, self-help groups, and single- and double-loop learning interventions, may help employees come to grips with the new reality. The more these programs are made widely available in the organization and the more varied they are, the more likely the intensity of emotional pain will be attenuated. Heedfulness also means sensitivity to the impact of the timing, pacing, and sequencing of the various change actions, so that adequate emotional equanimity is maintained among those affected. In sum, the emotional dynamic of experiencing is posited to increase employees' receptivity to the proposed strategic change and their ability to react constructively to it (Huy, 1999, 2005).

Sympathy and the Dynamic of Reconciliation
At the individual level, sympathy is a less demanding emotional process than empathy, as it refers to the ability to feel for the general suffering of another with no direct sharing of that person's experience (Davis, 1983). Sympathy is a precursor to the development of empathy. Sympathy is partly demonstrated by conciliatory behaviors. At the organizational level, Albert (1984) conceptualizes most change as a juxtaposition of additions and deletions. To the extent that the proposed change can be framed and accepted by the recipients as an addition or an expansion of existing values, the easier it is to accept the proposed change. The more continuity is perceived to exist between the past and the future, the less the change is perceived as radical. On the other hand, the portion of the valued elements of the past

that must be "deleted" should be mourned to facilitate transition.

A process of reconciliation that bridges feelings about new and old values, therefore, has to be conducted. Emotional conversations between change agents and their targets to co-construct a new meaning are helpful. To the extent that strategic change requires abandonment of certain cherished values, mourning of these past, abandoned values has to be organized (Albert, 1984). Thus, one of the first steps toward achieving full emotional reconciliation is adequate grieving. Mourning is more likely to be effective if adequate time and resources are allocated for affected members to work through their emotional grief. The effectiveness of various reconciliation processes thus hinges on their aggregate ability to address various addition and deletion components that can co-exist in strategic change. This requires an artful combination of various activities, such as allocating appropriate time and resources, ensuring the quality and frequency of conversations to develop a new and meaningful synthesis, and involving influential stakeholders. The emotional dynamic of reconciliation is posited to increase employees' receptivity to strategic change (Huy, 1999, 2005).

Hope and the Dynamic of Encouragement
Hope is an emotional state that is elicited by appraisal of future positive prospects for self (Ortony, Clore, & Collins, 1988). Hope buffers people against apathy and depression and strengthens their capacity to persist under adversity; it bolsters people's beliefs that they have both the will and the means to accomplish goals (Snyder et al., 1991). Recently, scholars such as Carlsen, Hagen, and Mortensen (2011, Chapter 22, this volume) have argued for an understanding of hope that should not focus simply on the individual and her goals, but include the relational quality of hope that is experienced in social relationships. Hope grows when one places oneself in service to others, and it binds together members of a community. Hope can be elicited by a future that is open-ended and becoming, in which people toy with generative possibilities, improvise, and co-create a coherent image of the future.

At the organizational level, the emotional dynamic of encouragement refers to the organization's ability to instill hope among all its members during strategic change. Huy's (2002) research found that certain change agents aroused hope and collective action by promoting wide participation of, and active consultation with, employees right from the beginning of strategic change. They developed some enthusiastic supporters in recipient groups who, in turn, championed their cause inside their respective units in the "language" that their local peers could relate to. People who feel that they can influence the direction of change are also likely to feel more confident about their own future (Beer, Eisenstat, & Spector, 1990). Perceptions of personal control are related positively to maintaining the effort devoted to challenging tasks, such as the pursuit of ambitious change projects (Aspinwall & Taylor, 1997).

Examples of organizational actions that arouse hope among employees include establishing meaningful change goals; creating small wins to rekindle self-confidence; frequent and cheerful interaction between change agents and employees; uplifting rituals, such as rousing speeches and award ceremonies; and a compelling strategic vision (Ashkanasy & Tse, 2000; House, 1977). The higher the degree of encouragement to elicit hope among all employees, the higher the posited degree of collective mobilization for strategic change (Huy, 1999, 2005).

Authenticity and the Dynamic of Display Freedom
At the individual level, emotional authenticity refers to a person's ability to acknowledge, express, and be sincere about his or her feelings. Individuals who lose this ability bury their real self and a false self emerges (Hochschild, 1983). At the organizational level, the emotional dynamic of display freedom refers to the organization's ability to facilitate the variety of authentic emotions that can be legitimately displayed (and felt) in the organization during strategic change. The converse is an *alexithymic* organization that controls the types or intensity of emotions that can be expressed and felt through the oppressive use of culture and power (Lukes, 1974). Values and preferences are shaped so that individuals cannot visualize any better alternative than the status quo. Order is maintained partly through emotional underpinnings such as fear, guilt, or embarrassment. A failure to engage play-acting skills and to display representative emotions is read as an act of insubordination or a sign of incompetence in strong cultures (Flam, 1993). As a result, employees may privately feel trapped and fearful. In front of powerful persons, individuals are likely to restrict the range of displayed emotions to mainly positive expressions (Morris & Feldman, 1996). Negative displays could be interpreted as cynicism or detachment during strategic change.

Duck (1993) suggests that the content of emotions (negative vs. positive) is not as important as how leaders of change deal with them. Leaders who deny emotionality in the workplace will also block the emergence of new ideas from the base of the organization at a time when creativity and contextual knowledge are most needed to realize strategic change. Organization members should be encouraged to express their full range of emotions without fear of reprisal. Controlling the variety of emotions expressed in the organization during discontinuous transition periods may well lead to emotional acting, risk aversion, cynicism, and covert resistance to the proposed change. This further reduces the self-reflection time that is necessary for deep learning. This frustrating state could be interpreted as a failure in change that depresses further efforts at collective learning. The dynamic of display freedom is posited to facilitate organizational learning during strategic change (Huy, 1999, 2005).

Fun and the Dynamic of Playfulness
At the individual level, fun as an emotional state and process relates to the motivated search for pleasant experiences and aesthetic appreciation. From a neurophysiological perspective, a feeling of elation permits the rapid generation of multiple images, so that the associative process is richer. A happy person indulges more often in creative and exploratory behavior; in contrast, sadness slows image evocation (Damasio, 1994). In a related vein, research on creativity suggests that people who experience flow or timelessness are likely to be more creative. Cskszentmihalyi (1975, p. 43) defines flow as the experience of a series of actions in which one feels in control and in harmony with them and the feeling after which one nostalgically says, "That was fun." Mountain climbers, motivated artists, and researchers are likely to experience a high level of flow when they are totally immersed in their tasks, lose their self-consciousness and sense of time, and thus experience "timelessness" (Mainemelis, 2001). Fun replenishes people's energy as they undertake long and arduous work to reach a distant vision with uncertain outcomes, and enjoying the process of doing one's work helps people to persevere in the face of difficulties and disappointments (Csikszentmihalyi, 1997).

It is thus critical that leaders of strategic change allocate special attention to rekindling employees' creative energy by enacting a set of actions that display playfulness (Huy, 2005). Playfulness refers to the organizational ability to arouse "serious" fun in employees, to create a context that encourages the generation of creative ideas leading to organizational innovation (Amabile, 1996; Amabile, Conti, Coon, Lazenby, & Herron, 1996; Huy, 1999). "Serious" or "deep fun" here should be distinguished from the superficial fun elicited by traditional social activities such as telling jokes, organizing office parties, or attending sports events, all of which can elicit fleeting pleasure, provide temporary release, and strengthens social bonding but that exert little long-term effect on work creativity and innovation (Csikszenmihalyi, 1997). "Deep fun" is reflected in feelings of timelessness and flow, when one engages in personally motivating and challenging activities. This state, however, should be distinguished from more holistic and transcendent spiritual experiences (see Sandelands, Chapter 76, this volume).

The literature on organizational creativity has suggested a number of organizational actions that create a playful climate fostering "deep fun." These involve emotional states of interest and task enjoyment. These actions are at three different levels—task, organization, and workgroup—and are discussed in Huy (2005).

Love and the Dynamic of Identification

At the individual level, the ability to love refers to the attunement process, whereby emotions are accepted and reciprocated, which begins early between parents and children (Goleman, 1995). At the organizational level, the emotional dynamic of identification refers to the collective behavior whereby organization members express their deep attachment to salient organization characteristics (Dutton, Dukerich, & Harquail, 1994). Identifying is analogous to "falling in love"; that is, to the extent that one's expectations are fulfilled and reciprocated, the initial attraction ripens into a deep and abiding attachment (Ashforth, 1998). Members in a collective group stay together because there are mutual benefits, and among the most important of these are the emotional bonds that develop over time in relation to self-identified and shared organization characteristics. Proposed major changes to identity can arouse intense anxiety, especially when a meaningful new identity is not present or not yet proven. People tend to dismiss or deny warnings that increase anxiety by practicing selective attention and various forms of information distortion: This is known as *defensive avoidance* (Janis & Mann, 1977).

Thus, strategic change requires a certain level of psychological safety (Edmondson, 1999). Emotional identification often translates into resilient loyalty to the organization experiencing disruptive change. Organizations with a high turnover rate have difficulty in learning since their experience base is being continually eroded: Much of the organization's know-how and know-why is tacit and involves understanding and operationalization of the subtle interconnections between routines that have been developed among various members (Kim, 1993). This collective yet distributed memory enables revisions to existing routines and the addition of new ones, thereby enabling organizational learning. To the extent that strategic change does not require a complete destruction of the past involving organizational memory and distinctive competence, veteran employees who remain loyal to the organization can help operationalize new knowledge more quickly. Thus, emotional attachment to the organization is posited to foster organizational learning during strategic change (Huy, 1999, 2005).

Thus far, discussion has focused on how leaders in organizations can enact practices related to the perception and management of employees' emotions to facilitate strategic change. This is by no means an easy task. The next section discusses why perceiving and managing emotions in strategic change can be difficult in organizations.

Barriers to Perceiving and Managing Emotions

Theoretical research has identified a number of challenges for organizations perceiving emotions in strategic change (Sanchez-Burks & Huy, 2009). These include attending to emotional information at work, adjusting emotional aperture from the individual to the collective, asymmetry in perceiving accurately negative emotions versus positive emotions, and challenges posed by culturally diverse organizations. Each is elaborated below.

Attending to Emotional Information At Work

Recent research indicates a widespread perceptual habit among Westerners to filter out much of what unfolds in the social and emotional domains (Sanchez-Burks, 2005). Although it is neither uncommon nor inappropriate to focus on emotional cues (such as someone's tone of voice, facial expression, or nonverbal gestures) beyond the workplace, it is often considered inappropriate to do so in the workplace. The cultural norms of professionalism, therefore, create emotional blind spots.

Scholars have explained this reduced sensitivity to emotions as a pervasive work ethos: the *Protestant relational ideology* (PRI) (Sanchez-Burks, 2002), a concept closely associated with beliefs about the moral importance of work that underpins the Protestant work ethic. One result of these deep-seated beliefs is the assumption that social and emotional matters will interfere with business effectiveness. To be professional, therefore, is to focus attention exclusively on tasks instead of on social emotional concerns. This denial is largely independent of high individual emotional intelligence: The same people who show impoverished attention to emotional cues at work might be highly alert to similar emotional cues away from work (Sanchez-Burks, 2002). The implication of PRI for organizations and managers during strategic change is that they must learn about the deep-seated habit of filtering out precisely the type of information they need in responding to emotional behaviors.

Thus, the first step in increasing emotional aperture is to overcome culturally grounded cognitive habits that restrict attention to emotional cues at work. A focus that includes emotion perception is especially important for leaders who manage the role conflicts and emotional tensions that arise during strategic change. Attention to collective emotions may provide leaders with the information they need, for example, during times of particular crisis, to deal sensitively and promptly with their employees' most acute emotional needs (Fox & Amichai-Hamburger, 2001; Huy, 2002; Liu & Perrewe, 2005).

Adjusting Emotional Aperture: From the Individual to the Collective

Recall that emotional aperture departs from other ability constructs of emotion perception by switching from a research focus on sensitivity to the emotion-laden cues of an individual to cues that are embedded in a collective. This focus on collective emotions does not downplay the importance of paying attention to individual-level emotional cues. Accurate perception of a specific individual's emotional cues has been shown to improve the quality of interpersonal interactions, negotiations, and perceived leadership (Rubin et al., 2005). But a managerial focus on that alone, perhaps on the emotions of very close or very outspoken employees, could be misleading about the prevalence and distribution of that specific emotion, as well as other shared emotions, across the organization. Therefore, adjusting one's perception so as to read collective emotions is complementary to—rather than a substitute for—perceiving another individual's emotions.

The dynamic nature of strategic change suggests that, beyond simply perceiving the proportion of any specific emotion (e.g., contempt, fear, hope) that emerges upon the initial announcement of a strategic change, it is also necessary to perceive the extent to which this emotion spreads or fluctuates over time. Such dynamic perception of collective emotions could provide timely clues about whether the change initiative is being accepted or not.

Recent research on analytic versus holistic perception explains why it could be challenging for managers to perceive a collective's emotional composition (Nisbett et al., 2001). People vary widely in their ability to process social information holistically—seeing patterns in an entire field ("forest") as opposed to focusing on specific individuals ("trees"). Masuda and his colleagues (2006) showed that, when perceiving a group, it is not uncommon to narrow one's attention to a few individuals. Achieving this collective-level focus of attention seems more challenging for Westerners, who are more likely to focus on individuating information at the expense of social and contextual information (Nisbett et al., 2001).

Asymmetry in Accurately Perceiving Negative Versus Positive Emotions

During emotionally turbulent times, accurately recognizing clusters of shared positive emotions (e.g., the proportion of group members experiencing happiness or hope) and negative emotions (e.g., those exhibiting contempt or fear) is necessary for understanding a collective's emotional composition. Empirical evidence indicates a reliable asymmetry in emotion recognition, showing less accuracy for negative emotions than for positive ones (Hillary Anger Elfenbein & Ambady, 2002).

Misreading the proportion of negative emotions within either the organization as a whole or its departments in particular is posited to impede strategic change (Sanchez-Burks & Huy, 2009). The ability to detect shifting proportions of distinct negative emotions (e.g., contempt, fear, anger) during strategic change provides leaders with early valuable information about the effectiveness of past actions and the likely success of new ones. Unlike differentiating between global negative and positive emotions, differentiating between specific ones provides fine-grained cues about potential behavior, for example, emotions associated with a relational orientation to engage with or disengage from others (Kitayama, Markus, & Kurokawa, 2000). Consider, for example, two specific negative emotions, contempt and anger.

Whereas anger is amenable to resolution since it motivates engagement (Folger, 1987), the more disengaged emotion of contempt most often is not (Fischer & Roseman, 2007). Thus, misreading one negative emotion (anger) for another (contempt) can lead to adverse unintended consequences.

Despite the utility of recognizing specific negative emotions, because they typically signal a problematic state of affairs, many people are unable to detect negative emotions as accurately as they do positive emotions (Elfenbein & Ambady, 2002). The explanation for this handicap might have to do with the lower frequency with which people encounter displays of negative emotions. Another explanation is that, given their potentially destructive consequences in social interactions, most people might try to hide their own negative emotions—especially in front of their more powerful superiors (Argyris, 1993), thus inhibiting the latter's ability to decode their subordinates' negative emotions. This adversely affects change leaders' collective emotion recognition by increasing the odds of underestimating the proportion of negative emotions.

Challenges in Culturally Diverse Organizations

Although there is some degree of universality in nonverbal displays of emotions, enough variation remains to produce culturally unique nuances in emotional displays that create a handicap at decoding the emotions expressed by people with cultural backgrounds different from those of the perceivers (Elfenbein & Ambady, 2002). In increasingly culturally diverse companies that undergo various forms of strategic change (including global mergers acquisitions and international alliances), cultural differences in emotional display can present yet another challenge to accurately reading the composition of diverse collective emotions in a group. Scholars have suggested that this disadvantage is due to people's common greater exposure to people from similar backgrounds than to those from different ones (Beaupré & Hess, 2006; Elfenbein & Ambady, 2003). For example, Chinese people living in China are less accurate than Chinese people living in the United States at decoding Anglo-American faces. However, training in recognizing emotional facial expression produces greater improvement for recognizing emotions expressed by out-groups than by in-groups, thus supporting the argument that exposure increases accuracy (Elfenbein & Ambady, 2003). Although this disadvantage at decoding out-group emotions has been demonstrated only at the individual level, this finding suggests that, at the level of collective emotions, people's inferences about various shared emotions of the out-group will be less accurate than those related to the in-group. This bias presents another challenge to accurate emotion perception.

Although research to date has conceptualized only some of the barriers to perceiving accurately collective emotions in organizations, one can hypothesize that similar, if not more difficult and diverse barriers exist at managing and modifying others' emotions at work during strategic change. This represents an area for potentially rich research, which is discussed next.

Future Directions

This chapter suggests that much work remains to be done, notably empirical research. Huy's work (2002) is one of the very few empirical studies that link perception and management of emotions in a context of strategic change, whereas other works have been conceptual (e.g., Huy, 1999, 2005; Sanchez-Burks & Huy, 2009). Much research, therefore, can be done with respect to perceiving and managing emotions in strategic change.

Perceiving Emotions

It remains an empirical question as to whether individuals who are skilled at recognizing emotions in others at the individual level will be similarly competent in doing so at the collective level. Sanchez-Burks and Huy (2009) posited that this might not always be the case. Using emotional aperture to bring into focus the composition of collective emotions could represent a distinct ability complementary to existing notions of social emotional intelligence. Empirical tests of this and the other proposed relationships are needed in future research to validate and deepen our understanding of perceiving collective emotions.

For example, one could empirically explore, using qualitative or quantitative research in a longitudinal cross-panel research of diverse employee groups inhabiting one organization in flux, whether the importance of emotional aperture for leader success in realizing strategic change likely increases with the level of emotional turbulence and with the level of cultural diversity in that organization. Researchers could also investigate the degree to which emotional aperture is an ability that people can be trained to improve. The ability measures of emotional aperture required to assess the effectiveness of such training also would provide a metric that organizations could use to evaluate their success in building this managerial capability. Importantly, such a metric should avoid exclusive reliance on self-reported measures of accuracy and include, instead, various multichannel stimuli with ecological validity (e.g., audio, pictures, or movies of people in context). People are generally overconfident about their accuracy when making judgments about others (Todorov, Pkrashi, & Engell, 2007), yet the most confident judgments are not the most accurate. Studying emotional aperture in more naturalistic settings also may further our understanding about moderating factors. For example, although research show a disadvantage in recognizing negative emotions compared to positive ones, this effect may not exist when the perceiver has access to both vocal and visual cues (e.g., Wallbott & Scherer, 1986).

Managing Emotions

Huy's (2002) field research on emotional balancing involves management of four groups of emotions in the quadrants of low–high activation and pleasant–unpleasant hedonic valence. Within each of these four groups, discrete emotions can be quite different in terms of what people experience (e.g., anger is distinct from fear, disappointment is different from depression). This suggests that the antecedents and consequences of discrete emotions can also differ in strategic change. Future research should go beyond the effects of these broad emotion categories to tackle the effects of discrete emotions. Emotional capability, with its focus on certain discrete emotions (Huy, 1999, 2005), represents only a first step toward greater specificity. Future research on emotional balancing (Huy, 2002) can also explore individual differences that led some managers to emphasize emotions related to change and others to focus on managing employees' emotions. Scholars can distinguish the effects of organizational conditions from individual competences in managing employees' emotions versus emotional commitment to realizing strategic change.

The challenge of realizing beneficial strategic change raises another issue. Would developing emotional balancing and capability in organizations vary according to organizational age and employee turnover? In large and established organizations with a long history, people (including middle managers) who perceive and manage employees' emotions generally had a long tenure and knew many of their subordinates well, and this might explain in part their good-will efforts to attend to their subordinates' emotions. In young companies, such as entrepreneurial start-ups, in which many employees expect short tenure or share few, if any, core organizational values, people may be less likely to expend prolonged, extraordinary personal efforts to deal with their colleagues' emotions when faced with adversity. Future research could validate whether and how emotional balancing emerges in young organizations undergoing stressful change, and whether emotional capability can be developed in such transient contexts.

It is also unclear what kinds of emotional balancing and capability might be developed during strategic change in flatter or networked organizations, and who might be willing and able to do it. The majority of the employees in these organizations will be front-line workers or professionals rather than experienced personnel managers. It is possible that emotional balancing and capability, and thus beneficial strategic change, in these organizations might depend mainly on individuals' skills and predispositions. This raises the hypothesis that organizations that tend not to value emotional awareness, such as certain engineering or financial trading companies, may have less emotional resilience and adaptive capacity under strategic change than would organizations that value it more, such as The Body Shop (Martin, Knopoff, & Beckman, 1998).

Finally, much research has theorized on the positive effects of positive emotions. Little research has systematically examined the adaptive, beneficial effects of negative emotions in the context of strategic change. Huy (2008) represents only a preliminary step in this regard. The combination of contrasting emotions—both positive and negative—is theorized to influence various processes of strategic change. Much empirical research remains to be done to validate the various hypotheses and delineate boundary conditions.

Conclusion

In sum, the field of positive psychology can be enriched by exploring the rich diversity of specific positive and negative emotions, how these interact with each other, as well as various organizations' emotional capabilities to perceive and manage individual and collective emotions to achieve both employees' well-being and high organizational performance and adaptation.

References

Albert, S. (1984). A delete model for successful transition. In J.K.R. Quinn (Ed.), *Managing organizational transitions* (pp. 149–191). Homewood, IL: Richard Irwin.

Amabile, T.M. (1996). *Creativity in context*. Boulder, CO: West View.

Amabile, T.M., Conti, R., Coon, H., Lazenby, J., & Herron, M. (1996). Assessing the work environment for creativity. *Academy of Management Journal, 39*(5), 1154–1184.

Argyris, C. (1993). *Knowledge for action: A guide to overcoming barriers to organizational change*. San Francisco, CA: Jossey-Bass.

Ashforth, B.E. (1998). Becoming: How does the process of identification unfold? In D.A. Whetten & P.C. Godfrey (Eds.), *Identity in organizations: Developing theory through conversations*. Thousand Oaks, CA: Sage.

Ashkanasy, N., & Tse, B. (2000). Transformational leadership as management of emotion: A conceptual review. In N. Ashkanasy, C. Härtel, & W. Zerbe (Eds.), *Emotions in the workplace: Research, theory and practice* (pp. 221–235). Westport, CT: Quorum Books.

Aspinwall, L.G., & Taylor, S.E. (1997). A stitch in time: Self-regulation and proactive coping. *Psychological Bulletin, 121*(3), 417.

Barsade, S.G. (2002). The ripple effect: emotional contagion and its influence on group behavior. *Administrative Science Quarterly, 47*(4), 644–675.

Barsade, S.G., & Gibson, D.E. (1998). Group emotion: A view from top and bottom. In M.A. Neale & E.A. Mannix (Eds.), *Research on managing groups and teams* (Vol. 1, pp. 81–102). Stamford, CT: JAI Press.

Bartel, C.A., & Saavedra, R. (2000). The collective construction of workgroup moods. *Administrative Science Quarterly, 45*(2), 197–231.

Bartunek, J.M. (1984). Changing interpretive schemes and organizational restructuring: The example of a religious order. *Administrative Science Quarterly, 29*(3), 355–387.

Bass, B.M. (1999). Two Decades of Research and Development in Transformational Leadership. *European Journal of Work & Organizational Psychology, 8*(1), 9.

Beaupré, M.G., & Hess, U. (2006). An in-group advantage for confidence in emotion recognition judgments: The moderating effect of familiarity with the expressions of out-group members. *Personality and Social Psychology Bulletin, 32*(1), 16–26.

Beer, M., Eisenstat, R.A., & Spector, B. (1990). Why change programs don't produce change. *Harvard Business Review, 68*(6), 158.

Carlsen, A., Landsverk Hagen, A., & Mortensen, T.F. (2011). Imagining hope in organizations: From individual goal attainment to horizons of relational possibility. In K.S. Cameron & G.M. Spreitzer (Eds.), *The Oxford handbook of positive organizational scholarship*. New York: Oxford University Press.

Chakravarthy, B.S. (1982). Adaptation: A promising metaphor for strategic management. *Academy of Management Review, 7*(1), 35.

Carlsen, A., Hagen, A.L., & Mortensen, T.F. (2011). Imagining hope in organizations: From individual goal-attainment to horizons of relational possibility. In K. Cameron & G. Spreitzer (Eds.) *The Oxford handbook of positive organizational scholarship*. New York: Oxford University Press.

Côté, S., & Miners, C.T.H. (2006). Emotional intelligence, cognitive intelligence, and job performance. *Administrative Science Quarterly, 51*(1), 1–28.

Crossan, M.M., Lane, H.W., & White, R.E. (1999). An organizational learning framework: from intuition yo institution. *Academy of Management Review, 24*(3), 522–537.

Csikszentmihalyi, M. (1997). *Finding flow: The psychology of engagement with everyday life*. New York: Basic Books.

Cskszentmihalyi, M. (1975). Play and intrinsic rewards. *Journal of Humanistic Psychology*(15), 41–63.

Cyert, R.M., & March, J.G. (1992). *A behavioral theory of the firm* (First published in 1963 ed.). Cambridge, MA: Blackwell Publishers.

Damasio, A.R. (1994). *Descartes' error emotion, reason, and the human brain*. New York: Putnam's Sons.

Davis, M.H. (1983). Measuring individual differences in empathy: Evidence for a multidimensional approach. *Journal of Personality and Social Psychology, 44*, 113–126.

Duck, J.D. (1993). Managing change: The art of balancing. *Harvard Business Review, 71*(6), 109–118.

Dutton, J.E., & Dukerich, J.M. (1991). Keeping an eye on the mirror: Image and identity in organizational adaptation. *Academy of Management Journal, 34*(3), 517–554.

Dutton, J.E., Dukerich, J.M., & Harquail, C.V. (1994). Organizational images and member identification. *Administrative Science Quarterly, 39*(2), 239–263.

Dutton, J.E., & Heaphy, E. (2003). The power of high-quality connections. In K.S. Cameron, J.E. Dutton & R.E. Quinn (Eds.), *Positive organizational scholarship: Foundations of a new discipline* (Vol. 17, pp. 263–268). San Francisco: Berrett-Koehler Publishers.

Edmondson, A.C. (1999). Psychological safety and learning behavior in work teams. *Administrative Science Quarterly, 44*, 350–383.

Ekman, P. (2004). Emotions revealed. New York: Henry Holt and Company.

Elfenbein, H.A. (2007). Emotion in Organizations. *Academy of Management Annals, 7*.

Elfenbein, H.A., & Ambady, N. (2002). On the universality and cultural specificity of emotion recognition: A meta-analysis. *Psychological Bulletin, 128*(2), 203–235.

Elfenbein, H.A., & Ambady, N. (2003). Cultural similarity's consequences: A relational perspective on cross-cultural differences in emotion recognition. Journal of Cross Cultural Psychology, 85(2), 276–290.

Elfenbein, H., Beaupré, M., Lévesque, M., & Hess, U. (2007). Toward a dialect theory: Cultural differences in the expression and recognition of posed facial expressions. *Emotion, 7*(1), 131–146.

Festinger, L. (1957). *A theory of cognitive dissonance*. Stanford, CA: Stanford University Press.

Fischer, A.H., & Roseman, I.J. (2007). Beat them or ban them: The characteristics and social functions of anger and contempt. *Journal of Personality and Social Psychology, 93*(1), 103–115.

Flam, H. (1993). *Fear, loyalty and greedy organizations*. London: Sage.

Floyd, S.W., & Lane, P.J. (2000). Strategizing throughout the organization: Managing role conflict in strategic renewal. *Academy of Management Review, 25*(1), 154.

Folger, J.C. (1987). Low prices: A strategy for the foolhardy? *Hospitals, 61*(4), 112.

Fox, S., & Amichai-Hamburger, Y. (2001). The power of emotional appeals in promoting organizational change programs. *Academy of Management Executive, 15*(4), 84–94.

Frijda, N.H. (1986). *The emotions*. Cambridge/Paris: Cambridge University Press; Editions de la Maison des sciences de l'homme.

Frijda, N.H. (1988). The laws of emotion. *American Psychologist, 43*, 349–358.

George, J.M. (1990). Personality, affect, and behavior in groups. *Journal of Applied Psychology*, 75, 107–116.

George, J.M., & Brief, A.P. (1992). Feeling good-doing good: A conceptual analysis of the mood at work-organizational spontaneity. *Psychological Bulletin, 112*(2), 310.

Goleman, D. (1995). *Emotional intelligence*. New York: Bantam.

Gump, B.B., & Kulik, J.A. (1997). Stress, affiliation, and emotional contagion. *Journal of Personality & Social Psychology, 72*(2), 305–319.

Hochschild, A.R. (1983). *The managed heart: Commercialization of human feeling*. Berkeley, CA: University of California Press.

House, R.J. (1977). A theory of charismatic leadership. In J.G. Hunt & L.L. Larson (Eds.), *Leadership: The cutting edge*. Carbondale: Southern Illinois University Press.

Huff, J.O., Huff, A.S., & Thomas, H. (1992). Strategic renewal and the interaction of cumulative stress and inertia. *Strategic Management Journal, 13*(5), 55–75.

Huy, N.Q. (1999). Emotional capability, emotional intelligence, and radical change. *Academy of Management Review, 24*(2), 325–345.

Huy, N.Q. (2005). An emotion-based view of strategic renewal. In G. Szulanski, J. Porac, & Y. Doz (Eds.), *Strategy process* (pp. 3–37): Elsevier.

Huy, Q. (2002). Emotional balancing of organizational continuity and radical change: The contribution of middle managers. *Administrative Science Quarterly, 47*(1), 31–69.

Huy, Q. (2008). How contrasting emotions can enhance strategic agility. In N.M. Ashkanasy & C.L. Cooper (Eds.), *Research companion to emotion in organizations*. Cheltenham, UK; Northampton, MA: Edward Elgar.

Janis, I.L., & Mann, L. (1977). Emergency decision-making—Theoretical analysis of responses to disaster warnings *Journal of Human Stress, 3*(2), 35–45.

Jehn, K.A. (1997). A qualitative analysis of conflict types and dimensions in organizational groups. *Administrative Science Quarterly, 42*(3), 530–557.

Johnson, G. (1987). *Strategic change and the management process*. New York: Basic Blackwell.

Kanter, R.M. (1983). Change masters and the intricate architecture of corporate culture change. *Management Review, 72*(10), 18.

Keltner, D., & Haidt, J. (1999). Social functions of emotions at four levels of analysis. *Cognition & Emotion, 13*(5), 505–521.

Kim, D.H. (1993). The link between individual and organizational learning. *Sloan Management Review, 35*(1), 379–500.

Kitayama, S., Markus, H.R., & Kurokawa, M. (2000). Culture, emotion, and well-being: Good feelings in Japan and the United States. *Cognition & Emotion, 14*(1), 93–124.

Lazarus, R.S. (1991). *Emotion and adaptation*. New York: Oxford University Press.

Liu, Y., & Perrewe, P.L. (2005). Another look at the role of emotion in the organizational change: A process model. *Human Resource Management Review, 15*(4), 263.

Lukes, S. (1974). *Power: A radical view*. New York: Macmillan, Basingstoke.

Mackie, D.M., Devos, T., & Smith, E.R. (2000). Intergroup emotions: Explaining offensive action tendencies in an intergroup context. *Journal of Personality & Social Psychology, 79*(4), 602.

Mainemelis, C. (2001). When the muse takes it all: A model for the experience of timelessness in organizations. *Academy of Management Review, 26*(4), 548–565.

Martin, J., Knopoff, K., & Beckman, C. (1998). An alternative to bureaucratic impersonality and emotional labor: Bounded emotionality at the body shop. *Administrative Science Quarterly, 43*(2), 429–469.

Masuda, T., Ellsworth, P.C., Mesquita, B., Leu, J., Tanida, S., & Veerdonk, E. (2006). Placing the face in context: Cultural differences in the perception of facial emotion. Unpublished Manuscript under review. University of Michigan.

Mayer, D., & Salovey, P. (1999). Emotional intelligence meets traditional standards for an intelligence. *Intelligence, 27*(4), 267–298.

Morris, J.A., & Feldman, D.C. (1996). The dimensions, antecedents, and consequences of emotional labor. *Academy of Management Review, 21*(4), 986–1010.

Neumann, R., & Strack, F. (2000). Mood contagion: The automatic transfer of mood between person. *Journal of Personality and Social Psychology, 79*, 211–223.

Nisbett, R.E., Peng, K., Choi, I., & Norenzayan, A. (2001). Culture and systems of thought: Holistic versus analytic cognition. *Psychological Review, 108*(2), 291–310.

Noer, D.M. (1993). Leadership in an age of layoffs. *Issues & Observations, 13*(3), 1–6.

Ortony, A., Clore, G.L., & Collins, A. (1988). *The cognitive structure of emotions*. Cambridge, UK: Cambridge University Press.

Quinn, J.B. (1980). Managing strategic change. *Sloan Management Review, 21*(4), 3–20.

Quinn, R.W., & Dutton, J.E. (2005). Coordination as energy-in-conversation. *Academy of Management Review, 30*(1), 36.

Rafaeli, A., & Sutton, R.I. (1987). Expression of emotion as part of the work role. *Academy of Management Review, 12*(1), 23–37.

Reger, R.K., & Gustafson, L.T. (1994). Reframing the organization: Why implementing total quality is easier said than done. *Academy of Management Review, 19*(3), 565–584.

Rubin, R.S., Munz, D.C., & Bommer, W.H. (2005). Leading from within: The effects of emotion recognition and personality on transformational leadership behavior. *Academy of Management Journal, 48*(5), 845–858.

Salovey, P., & Grewal, D. (2005). The science of emotional intelligence. *Current Directions in Psychological Science, 14*(6), 281–285.

Salovey, P., & Mayer, J.D. (1990). Emotional intelligence. *Imagination, Cognition and Personality, 9*, 185–211.

Sanchez-Burks, J. (2002). Protestant relational ideology and (in)attention to relational cues in work settings. *Journal of Personality & Social Psychology, 83*(4), 919–929.

Sanchez-Burks, J. (2005). Protestant relational ideology: The cognitive underpinnings and organizational implications of an American anomaly. *Research in Organizational Behavior, 26*, 265–305.

Sanchez-Burks, J., & Huy, Q.N. (Writers). (2009). Emotional aperture and strategic change: The accurate recognition of collective emotions [Article], Organization Science.

Sandelands, L. (2011). In God we trust: A comparison of spiritualities at work. In K. Cameron & G. Spreitzer (Eds.), *The Oxford handbook of positive organizational scholarship*. New York: Oxford University Press.

Schein, E.H. (1992). *Organizational culture and leadership* (2nd ed.). San Francisco: Jossey-Bass.

Sekerka, L.E., Vacharkulksemsuk, T., & Fredrickson, B.L. (2011). Positive emotions: Broadening and building upward spirals of sustainable development. In K. Cameron & G. Spreitzer (Eds.), *The Oxford handbook of positive organizational scholarship*. New York: Oxford University Press.

Snyder, C.R., Harris, C., Anderson, J.R., Holleran, S.A., Irving, L.M., Sigmon, S., et al. (1991). The will and the ways: Development and validation of an individual-differences measure of hope. *Journal of Personality & Social Psychology, 60*(4), 570.

Spreitzer, G., Sutcliffe, K., Dutton, J.E., Sonenshein, S., & Grant, A.M. (2005). A socially embedded model of thriving at work. *Organization Science, 16*(5), 537–549.

Staw, B.M., Sutton, R.I., & Pelled, L.H. (1994). Employee positive emotion and favorable outcomes at the workplace. *Organization Science, 5*(1), 51–71.

Todorov, A.M., Pkrashi, A., & Engell, A. (2007). *Judging trustworthiness from faces.* Paper presented at the Annual meeting of the Society for Personality and Social Psychology.

Van Maanen, J., & Kunda, G. (1989). Real feelings: Emotional expression and organizational culture. In L.L. Cummings & B.M. Staw (Eds.), *Research in organizational behavior* (Vol. 11, pp. 43–104). Greenwich, CT: JAI Press.

van Zomeren, M., Spears, R., & Fischer, A.H. (2004). Put your money where your mouth is! Explaining collective action tendencies through group-based anger and group efficacy. *Journal of Personality and Social Psychology 87*(5), 649–664.

Wallbott, H.G., & Scherer, K.R. (1986). Cues and channels in emotion recognition. *Journal of Personality and Social Psychology, 51*(4), 690–699.

Positive Strategy

Creating and Sustaining Strengths-based Strategy that SOARs and Performs

Jacqueline M. Stavros *and* Lynn Wooten

Abstract

SOAR is an approach for framing strategy through a positive organizational scholarship (POS) lens. SOAR stands for *strengths, opportunities, aspirations, and results*. As a framework, SOAR focuses on formulating and executing a positive strategy by identifying and building strengths, feeding creativity in the form of opportunities, encouraging individuals and groups to share aspirations, and determining results. To explore SOAR as an approach for framing strategy through a POS perspective, this chapter examines the SOAR framework through several concepts in the strategy literature. In addition, this chapter presents recent empirical studies on SOAR to demonstrate why and how the SOAR framework supports positive strategy and future research questions. The chapter concludes with directions for future research.

Keywords: Positive strategy, strategy processes, SOAR, strengths-based, strategy formation, strategic learning

Today's challenging business climate makes it necessary to create and execute strategy that delivers results and makes stakeholders believe in the future. A growing number of strategy researchers are suggesting that we need to rethink our strategy concepts, frameworks, and models for competing in the 21st century (Hamel & Prahalad, 1996; Hitt, Keats, & DeMarie, 1998; Lowendahl & Revang, 1998; Kim & Mauborgne, 2005). Strategy must be generated in real time to create and anticipate opportunities proactively. Historical ways of thinking about strategy may limit its ability to effectively address and adapt to the ever-changing conditions and turbulent environment in which organizations exist today (Selsky, Goes, & Baburoglu, 2007). A recent study of organizations in *McKinsey Quarterly* echoes this sentiment. This research found that organizations with the highest performance had a clear purpose, an understanding of *strengths*, shared *aspirations*, and leaders who know how to unleash ideas (*opportunities*) with a *result*-driven process (Isern & Pung, 2007).

In essence, these organizations have found an alternative way for creating strategy that moves beyond a problem solving mentality by purposely focusing on strengths to create a shared image of potential (Barrett, Cooperrider, & Fry, 2005). This is a perspective of strategy that seeks out and transforms glimpses of future possibilities into actionable images that provide direction for goal setting and a pathway for achieving the desired results (Hamel & Prahalad, 1994). It allows for organizational flexibility through a continuous process of improvising and learning as strategy evolves through discovery, dialoging, and deliberating (Mintzberg, 1994).

Developing mental models from a POS perspective of strategy entails a different way of framing how the organization perceives and enacts its strategy. Frames are lenses that bring the world into focus by drawing on theories and knowledge of a given concept (Bolman & Deal, 2008). Frames help organizational members by providing mental models for analyzing situation cues (Senge, 1990;

Dane & Pratt, 2007). Through the use of frames, organizational members can organize information to think strategically and plan actions because frames provide a lens for understanding, identifying, responding, and adapting to the opportunities and challenges confronting them (Pisapia et al., 2009). In a world of complexity and equivocality, organizational members use frames as maps to focus their attention, make sense of their world, and direct their strategic actions (Bolman & Deal, 1991; Weick, 1979).

In this chapter, we propose that SOAR is an approach for framing strategy through a positive organizational scholarship (POS) lens. SOAR stands for *strengths, opportunities, aspirations, and results*. SOAR focuses on the formulation and implementation of strategy through a POS lens by identifying and building strengths, feeding creativity in the form of opportunities, encouraging individuals and groups to share aspirations, and determining results. The result is the capacity to see, acknowledge, and use the contributions of each member in an organization. Thus, SOAR can best be understood as a strengths-based framework with a participatory approach to strategic thinking that allows an organization's stakeholders to co-construct and execute its future through collaboration, shared understanding, and a commitment to action. As a framework, SOAR provides a foundation for the creation of strategy. SOAR has proved to be a useful method for exploring strategy and identifying strategic courses of action. It should be noted that SOAR provides the underpinnings to the discussion of strategy formulation, strategic plans, and execution, but it is not intended to provide a roadmap or set of specific instructions.

To explore SOAR as an approach for framing strategy through a POS lens, we begin this chapter by presenting the emergent concept of *positive strategy*. Then, the SOAR framework is examined through the lens of several concepts in the strategy literature that relate to or are consistent with SOAR. Next illustrated are several recent empirical studies on SOAR to demonstrate why and how the SOAR framework supports positive strategy and future research questions.

Positive Strategy: An Emergent Concept

The traditional view of strategy describes it as a central, integrated plan for achieving objectives that define approaches for managing resources, customers, competition, and growth (Hambrick & Fredrickson, 2005; Thompson, Strickland, &

Gamble, 2007). An ideal strategy is internally focused, but also takes into account external opportunities and threats as it defines criteria of effectiveness (Hofer & Schendel, 1978). Furthermore, in most cases, a traditional approach to strategy is a separation of the planners from the implementers, in which the experts at the top of the organization pass down the decisions to those responsible for the execution.

Positive strategy differs by focusing on positive processes that enable collective resourcefulness and generative dynamics that lead to positive states or outcomes (Barney, 1986; Glynn & Dutton, 2007; Wooten & Cameron, 2008). Collective resourcefulness refers to the manner in which all organizational members work together to develop and implement strategy (Barney & Hansen, 1994; Grant, 2002), which enhances the organization's likelihood of positive outcomes. Generative dynamics refers to an organization's activities that create, develop, transform, multiply, and leverage its resources and capabilities (Collis & Montgomery, 1997; Glynn & Dutton, 2007). The creation and development of new capabilities make it possible for organizations to respond to changing environments with value-enhancing strategies (Eisenhardt & Martin, 2000; Zollo & Winters, 2002).

At the heart of a POS approach to strategizing is the ability of organizational members to frame strategy by inquiring into its positive core—the sum total of the organization's unique strengths, assets, networks, resources, and capabilities—to create a future (Cooperrider, Whitney, & Stavros, 2003). Inquiry into the organization's positive core requires organizational members to engage in strategic conversations that are multidirectional communication mechanisms for framing the strategic intent of the organization (Miles, Munilla, & Darroch, 2006). A strategic conversation is generative when it facilitates the process of organizational members coming together to develop a mental map of the complete system for value creation and the strengths that support this system (Barrett, Cooperrider, & Fry, 2005). This helps organizational members unpack the assumptions and behaviors that produce success (Pisapia, 2009). By using the strategic conversation as an open forum for dialogue and the exchange of diverse perspectives, it fosters participation and commitment to the organization's strategic initiatives (Barrett, 1995).

Strategic conversations stimulate and sustain positive strategy by enabling organizational members to collectively see the potential in a situation and their role as participants (Liedtka & Rosenblum, 1996). The process of formulating and implementing a positive strategy evolves as the organization draws on its human capacity to appreciate and leverage its strengths, successes, and potentials (Barrett, 1995). Organizational members learn how to challenge conventional practices by provoking each other to experiment and stretch in new directions (Cameron, Quinn, DeGraff, & Thakor, 2006; Lee, Caza, Edmondson, & Thomke, 2003;). Furthermore, they learn to formulate and implement a strategy while understanding how to construct systems that keep track of results and provide feedback (Kaplan & Norton, 2000).

Why SOAR Framework Supports Positive Strategy

There is a growing demand for strategy to be more innovative and implemented more rapidly (Isern & Pung, 2007). An organization must create and communicate a strategy and plan that invigorates and engages its stakeholders with a shared set of values (ways to operate together), a vision (future direction), a mission (present purpose and organization offering), and set of strategic initiatives (foundations for goal and objective setting). According to Peter Drucker:

> Strategy is not a goal; it is a direction, a blueprint for putting the pieces together and building. It must have continuous feedback to translate real-time results into refinements and changes as appropriate. (Edersheim, 2007, p. 40)

Need for a New Assumption

The pressures for strategy to be innovative, invigorating, and inclusive call for a new approach to framing it. Traditional SWOT (strengths, weaknesses, opportunities, and threats) analysis frames strategy from the assumption that there is an objective environment in which the organization competes. When the SWOT analysis is complete, organizational members have defined the "as-is" state of the organization's environment. Then what? SWOT was designed in the 1960s and does not take into account the fluid design that requires stakeholder connections to adjust to new information (Valentin, 2001). Also, in most cases, SWOT analysis does not take into account how organizational members should "ideally" think to develop value producing strategies, because it is not intended to create a compelling mental model that provokes people to take action (Bushe & Kassam, 2005;

Mintzberg, 1994). As a result, the output produced from SWOT analysis can lack relevancy, adequate insights, or commitment, and this is in part because organizational members do not have a meaningful way to conceptualize the strategy and how they contribute to it (Hill & Westbrook, 1997).

Somewhat different from SWOT, the SOAR framework focuses on the process, formulation, planning, and implementation of strategy rather than on simply the analysis of internal strengths and weaknesses and external opportunities and threats to them. By using SOAR, stakeholders can have a shared understanding of the ultimate vision, mission, and goals, so that they are able to respond dynamically through creating the strategy and iterating the implementation. For example, a task force leader needed to formulate a strategy and create a plan to obtain funding for a youth leadership development program. This leader convened a 5-hour strategy meeting to build into the proposal the shared vision and mission, goals, and strategies for program. Within 3 months, the funding was received for the program. Four months later, one of the goals was achieved—to send a core group of youth leaders to the president of the United States inauguration in Washington, D.C. (Stavros & Hinrichs, 2009). This is because SOAR nurtures a culture of strategic learning by building a widespread *appreciative intelligence*. Appreciative intelligence is "the ability to perceive the positive inherent generative potential within the present. Put in a simple way, Appreciative Intelligence is the ability to see the mighty oak in the acorn" (Thatchenkery & Metzker, 2006, p. 4). Thatchenkery and Metzker explain that appreciative intelligence creates a powerful construct for high performance, creativity, and innovation in people and organizations by reframing the present view, appreciating the positive possibilities in any situation, and envisioning how the future unfolds. Once these strategic factors are identified, they need to be shared with other stakeholders. Likewise, SOAR provides a framework with an upward spiral, as illustrated in Figure 63.1.

In an Esperanza school system strategic planning meeting, many participants commented that the most powerful part of the meeting was the team's reading of the *Inspiration to SOAR* (Stavros, Cooperrider, & Kelly, 2003). After using the SOAR framework, the "energy and optimism in the room during and after this meeting was incredible" (Daly, Millhollen, & DiGuilio, 2007, p. 39). "Grounded in the SOAR framework, participants were provided with time to engage in powerful discourse that led

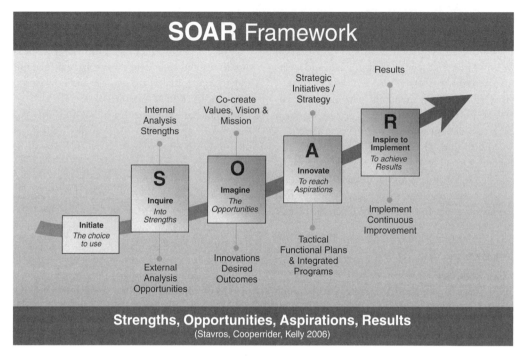

SOAR Framework

Results

Strategic
Initiatives /
Strategy

R

Co-create
Values, Vision &
Mission

Internal
Analysis
Strengths

A

**Inspire to
Implement**
*To achieve
Results*

S

O

Innovate
*To reach
Aspirations*

Inquire
*Into
Strengths*

Imagine
*The
Opportunities*

Implement
Continuous
Improvement

Initiate
*The choice
to use*

Tactical
Functional Plans
& Integrated
Programs

External
Analysis
Opportunities

Innovations
Desired
Outcomes

Strengths, Opportunities, Aspirations, Results
(Stavros, Cooperrider, Kelly 2006)

Fig. 63.1

to substantive change and lifted their spirits. Through the conversation, I could feel a shift in my own thinking and paradigm," explained one school principal (p. 41).

Positive Lens of Strategy: Connecting the Positive Framework of SOAR in Strategy

A close connection exists between SOAR and positive strategy. This was made possible through appreciative inquiry (AI). Appreciative inquiry is a positive concept with a 4-D approach (discovery, dream, design, and destiny) that has been used successfully throughout the world in recent decades to address issues by looking at what is going right in a system. SOAR builds on AI and creates a strategic framework that makes it possible to discover the strengths, opportunities, aspirations, and results of the organization through the eyes of stakeholders, as illustrated in Figure 63.1. The 5-I approach (initiate, inquiry, imagine, innovation, and implementation) is an earlier version of the 4-D approach (Watkins & Kelley, 2011). Appreciative inquiry is a philosophy and change approach that builds on an organization's strengths and on the life-giving forces of the organization. Its assumption is:

> Every organization has something that gives it life when it is most alive, effective, successful, and connected in healthy ways to its stakeholders and communities. AI begins by identifying what is

positive and connecting to it in ways that heighten energy, vision, and action for change. (Cooperrider, Whitney, & Stavros, 2008, p. xv)

Originally developed by David Cooperrider (1986), AI rests on five core principles: constructionist, simultaneity, poetic, anticipatory, and positive (additional information at http://appreciativeinquiry.case.edu/). This chapter recognizes their role in developing the elements of the SOAR framework.

- "S" (strengths) offers the foundation for discovering and aligning an organization's best capabilities to a process of focusing on a stronger competitive advantage and more sustainable future.
- "O" (opportunities) moves into the realm of location and positive enhancement of potentially unexplored endeavors and innovations.
- "A" (aspirations) expands and gives voice to the desires of those focusing on the future of the organization.
- "R" (results) reinforces and activates the motivation, resources, and commitment of those involved to attain the desired outcomes.

Although the term *positive strategy* may appear new to the organizational world, the closely related term *strengths-based* is well known, according to Cameron, Dutton, and Quinn (2003). Gallup researchers have collected data related to strengths development in hundreds of studies over the last 30 years. The focus was often on excellence, high performance, successful managers, employees, successful teams, and the like across a wide range of industries. The question remains: Can SOAR be utilized as an effective framework to impact an organization's performance?

Before we provide the empirical evidence to support SOAR, this next section offers further understanding of SOAR as a strengths-based framework, highlights several strategic concepts and theories whose underlying assumptions support the SOAR framework, and develops a perspective of the value and nature of SOAR as a framework for strategic thinking and strategy formulation and implementation. These concepts are highlighted in Table 63.1.

In Table 63.1, capacity building supports all the elements of SOAR by reconceptualizing strategy that allows an organization to "build the internal relational components of the organization so it can better use its resources (i.e., people, time, and money) to achieve its mission, attain its vision and goals/objectives, and sustain these over time" (Stavros, 1998, p. 43). *Capacity building* is a social process that uses interdependent relationships to sustain the collective existence of organizations committed to a common cause (Stavros, 1998). Thus, capacity building moves from strategic thinking and conversations to strategy formulation and implementation based on core dialogues, knowledge creation, and engagement of stakeholders (Ganz, 2000). An organization must be able to bring together all its relevant stakeholders to create meaningful strategies to achieve its goals.

SOAR embraces capacity building through the stakeholder view and the importance of relationships in building positive strategy. To gain a perspective and take appropriate action, the whole system must be more fully understood. This can be achieved by using an approach that allows for stakeholder involvement, buy-in, and commitment both inside and outside the organization's environment. The SOAR framework provides an application of new language, metaphors, and perspectives to create positive strategy. SOAR continues to emerge as an effective and flexible strategic framework that fosters an organization's energy, creativity, and engagement through the stakeholder relationships (Stavros & Hinrichs, 2009).

Strengths (S)

Foundational to the SOAR framework is the research on strengths. Research has shown that "identifying and building on people's strengths can produce greater benefit than finding and correcting their weaknesses" (Clifton & Harter, 2003; Seligman, 2002, as cited in Cameron, 2008, p. 46). Focusing on strengths means that the SOAR framework invites conversations on "what an organization is doing right, what skills could be enhanced, and what is compelling to those who have a 'stake' in the organization's success" (Stavros & Hinrichs, 2009, p. 6).

STRENGTH(S) THEORY

Over 40 years ago, Clifton and Nelson (1992), with their colleagues, began studying *strengths theory*. This research has led to three major conclusions (pp. 21–22):

- The study of strengths creates a new theory of what people are like.
- Maximum productivity can be gained by focusing on strengths and managing weaknesses.
- The study of strengths leads to an understanding of the difference between good and great.

Over a decade later, Clifton and Harter (2003) reported that, in organizations where workers focus on building and elevating strengths, productivity is one and a half times greater than in organizations

Table 63.1 Strategic concepts in support of SOAR framework

S	O	A	R
Capacity Building			
Strengths Theory	Innovation	Visioning	Balanced Scorecard
Resource-based View	Abundance	Strategic Intent	Triple Bottom Line
Dynamic Capabilities	Complex Adaptive Systems (CAS)	Strategic Storytelling	Constructive Accountability Theory

that focus on weaknesses. Their findings show that focusing on improving weaknesses zaps the strength needed for focusing on producing a heightened future strategy for expansive effectiveness. According to Peter Drucker (2004), "Effective leadership is the aligning of strengths that makes the weaknesses irrelevant."

As a strengths-based approach, SOAR builds on the work of these authors by asking "what are our greatest assets?" as the starting point for the strategic conversation. A key distinction of SOAR is to identify strengths and expand on existing strengths, rather than drill down on problems, weaknesses, deficiencies, and threats.

RESOURCE-BASED VIEW

The current, developing field of strategy is located in the resource-based view (RBV) that focuses attention on an organization's distinctive core competencies that are superior to that of the competition (Collis & Montgomery, 1997; Grant, 1991; Prahalad & Hamel, 1990). A methodological and theoretical approach that examines RBV is called *resource-based analysis*, which requires that "each resource or capability be examined for its potential to provide the business with a sustainable competitive advantage" (Bamford & West, 2010, p. 179). The location of these unique resources or distinctive competencies creates opportunities for leveraging organizational strengths. According to RBV, locating the strengths and opportunities of organizational members and then acting on those discoveries expands the organization's competitive advantage.

The RBV focuses on explaining competitive advantage as an outcome of the development and deployment of valuable organizational resources (Colbert, 2004). It is, according to Porter (1998), about being different and successfully exploiting that difference. Sustaining competitive advantage is increasingly being explained as occurring through human- or knowledge-based assets (Coff & Rousseau, 2000) and management of those assets (Simon, Hitt, & Ireland, 2007).

By starting with a discovery of the organization's strengths or distinctive core competencies, SOAR supports the strategy of identifying, protecting, and expanding organizational resources to sustain a competitive advantage. These resources, and the ability to create new resources, are reinforced in the minds, experiences, and strengths of the participants and located through the collaborative and conversational process of exchange applied in the SOAR framework.

DYNAMIC CAPABILITIES

Although RBV discusses the importance of an organization's core competencies, it does not explain how to identify or build new distinctive competencies. *Dynamic capabilities* provide a perspective on how organizational members can begin to reconfigure or build new core competencies. Dynamic capabilities are "the firm's ability to integrate, build, and reconfigure internal and external competencies to address rapidly changing environments" (Teece, 1997, p. 516).

Ten years later, Helfat, Finkelstein, Mitchell, Peteraf, Singh, Teece, and Winter (2007) further defined *dynamic capabilities* as "the capacity of an organization to purposefully create, extend, or modify its resource base" (p. 4). Their research supports that dynamic capabilities are developed through organizational members' willingness to contribute and learn. Dynamic capabilities are best determined through dialogue between organizational members (Teece, 2009).

The SOAR framework builds on the evolving study of dynamic capabilities and supports its approach to creating distinctive core competencies through the use of dialogue. Further, SOAR acknowledges the importance of member interaction as a primary mechanism for generating willingness to become actively engaged in the process. This is important, because it is through focused and directed strengths-based dialog that SOAR captures and refines the organization's competencies into capabilities, while simultaneously encouraging member participation by giving them a say in the organization's direction and outcome.

Opportunities (O)

Focusing on an organization's strengths and opportunities will offer a better chance for success (deKluyver & Pearce, 2009; Thompson, Strickland, & Gamble, 2007). Opportunities move into the realm of locating possibilities (or combinations of possibilities) that can enhance the search for unexplored endeavors that may lead to innovations of products and services. The strategic conversations build on the strengths to identify opportunities for growth.

INNOVATION THEORY

In Sundbo's (1998) book *The Theory of Innovation: Entrepreneurs, Technology, and Strategy*, he defines the theory of innovation as something that is *new*, such as a new product or service, process, strategy or structure, type of marketing, opportunity, etc. In further discussing innovation theory, we open with a statement from Mayer (1996): "In *reproductive thinking*, problem solvers apply solution procedures they have been used to solve identical or similar problems in the past. In *productive thinking*, problem solvers must invent a new way of solving a problem—that is, they must produce a novel solution" (p. 3). Providing the opportunity to be innovative and adventurous is important to hearing new ideas, gaining energy within the process, and having participants engage in productive conversations within an innovative and adventurous activity of exchange. SOAR addresses these criteria.

The emergence of scholarly writing around "combination capability" (Nahapiet & Ghoshal, 1998) and "absorptive capacity" (Zahra, 2002) has brought to the forefront the organizational tactics essential to influencing the occurrence of innovation and exploitation of innovative ideas for benefit. The essence of innovation is either to *absorb* new information and *combine* it with already known information or to take already known information and combine it in new generative ways. SOAR asks positive questions in its inquiry and imagine phase to engage the organizational stakeholders in a dialogue to discover possible innovations, as shown in Figure 63.1.

ABUNDANCE APPROACH

In their case study, Cameron and Lavine (2006) explored the extraordinary success achieved in the clean-up and closure of the Rocky Flats nuclear weapon production facility, which was termed by the media as the most dangerous building in the United States. Four basic enablers were found for this success, which Cameron and Lavine called "an abundance approach to change" (Table 63.2) as described below:

> An *abundance approach* to change refers to the striving for positive deviance, pursuing the best of the

human condition, and working to fulfill the highest potential of organizations and individuals. *An abundance approach* focuses on resilience, flourishing, and vitality rather than mere goal achievement . . . *An abundance approach* stands in contrast to a problem-solving or a deficit-based approach to change. Rather than being consumed by difficulties and obstacles, an abundance approach is consumed by strengths and human flourishing. Rather than an exclusive focus on problem solving, an abundance approach pursues possibility finding. Rather than addressing change that is motivated by challenges, crises, or threats . . . *the abundance approach* addresses affirmative possibilities, potentialities, and elevating processes and outcomes. (p. 6)

The five themes identified in the right column of Table 63.2 by Cameron and Lavine (2006) are embedded in the SOAR framework (left column in Table 63.2). They represent the dualities of fostering innovation versus seeking stability and developing relationships/human capital versus managing power/politics. Although this research represents just one case study and therefore cannot be generalized, the Rocky Flats case study offers some interesting propositions that align with positive strategy and SOAR. The abundance approach has recurrent themes of inclusiveness–whole system approach (inviting relevant stakeholders into the strategic dialogue), relationships, collaboration, leveraging strengths, identifying enablers/opportunities, collective learning, and utilizing an appreciative paradigm to explore and achieve an organization's highest potential.

Applying abundance approach to strategy helps an organization tap into its strengths and identify opportunities that create strategies to leverage these strengths, leading to more generative ways of strategizing. Cameron et al. (2003) contend that "POS seeks to be a generative lens for linking theories in

Table 63.2 SOAR framework and abundance approach

SOAR Framework	Abundance Approach
• Describe peak organizational experiences. • Identify strengths and opportunities. • Identify stakeholders' aspirations. • Design 5-I Summits and Quick SOARs to create strategic plans and positive strategy to produce results. • Basic assumption: Our job is to identify the best strategies and plans to enable the organization to perform to meet desired results.	• Describe peak experiences. • Identify enablers of the highest past performance. • Identify what could be continued and replicated in the future. • Design interventions that create an ideal future with extraordinary performance. • Basic assumption: Our job is to embrace and enable our highest potential.

Adapted from Cameron, K., & Lavine, M. (2006). *Making the impossible possible. Leading extraordinary performance. The Rocky Flats story.* San Francisco; Berrett-Koehler. Reprinted with permission of the publishers. All rights reserved. www.bkconnection.com.

organizational studies" (p. 10). As such, the application of abundance theory can offer a generative approach for helping organizations identify strategies that bridge the gap between their current performance and their potentiality.

Like the abundance approach, SOAR focuses on an organization's strengths and opportunities. Weaknesses and threats are not ignored. Instead, they are reframed and given the appropriate focus within the opportunities and results conversation. Ultimately, it becomes a question of balance. SOAR seeks to focus an organization's dialogue around what they do well and how to do more of that. What gives the organization more energy to take action? What gives them the confidence to set a stretch goal?

COMPLEX ADAPTIVE SYSTEMS

At all levels of the organization, research by Liedtka and Rosenblum (1996) advocates for widespread strategic thinking and dialogue around strengths and opportunities that, combined with a culture of empowerment and engagement, lead to strategies that *promote continuous adaptation*. This requires a set of "metacapabilities" (p. 149) of learning, collaboration, and the ability to redesign strategy, structure, and processes. A metacapability is defined as "the skills and knowledge that underline the process of capacity building itself. Metacapabilities enable the continuous recreation of specific business-related capabilities over time" (Liedtka, 1996, p. 21). These metacapabilities depend upon the strategic conversations at all levels of the organization aimed at implementing existing strategies but also at identifying new opportunities for emergent strategies.

Recently, the theories of complexity and chaos have been applied from the organization development field to strategy. Complexity theory compares the nature of organizations to living organisms, considering an organization to be a complex adaptive system (CAS) (Stacey, 1996). Complex adaptive systems consist of agents interacting with each other according to a set of simple rules that require them to examine and respond to each other's behavior in a way that improves the behavior of the individual agent and the system as a whole (Eoyang, 2010).

SOAR is a framing mechanism that produces positive strategy by identifying and building strengths, feeding creativity in the form of opportunities, encouraging individuals and groups to share aspirations, and determining results, which provides the capacity to see, acknowledge, and use the contributions of every agent in the complex system. This aligns with the most recent research in CAS, which requires a "focus on positive patterns to build strengths, reinforce effectiveness, feed creativity, and encourage energy for individuals and groups" (Eoyang, 2010, p. 469). SOAR framework proposes a dialogue for continuous strategic engagement and adaptation at all levels.

Aspirations (A)

An organization's aspirations play a significant role in a positive view of strategy, because aspirations describe the organization's strategic intent by taking into account its strengths and opportunities, then explicitly stating what the organization wants to become (Stavros & Hinrichs, 2009). Aspirations represent how an organization's strategy conveys its envisioned future and the roadmap for creating this future. The supporting pillar of an organization's aspirations is its core ideology that defines its character through a consistent identity that transcends changes in leadership, market life cycles, and technological breakthroughs (Collins & Porras, 1996).

VISIONING

Frequently, strategic management research discussions of aspirations are embedded in the discourse of visioning in organizations. This aspect of strategy making is described as symbolic and viewed as interpretive; it is expressed as metaphors and frames of reference that enable the organization and its environment to be understood by stakeholders (Chaffee, 1985; Hart, 1992). In some instances, visioning clarifies aspirations by helping organizational members confront uncertainty and resolve confusion through visual images and verbal expressions (Bolman & Deal, 2008). Research has validated the positive impact of visioning on both employee productivity and organizational-level performance, as measured by sales growth and profitability (Baum, Locke, & Kirkpatrick, 1998).

The visioning mode of strategy making entails cognitively constructing conceptual representation of the aspirations that will guide future actions (Mumford & Strange, 2005). This requires perspective taking and reframing, so that the organization can envision new ways to approach its strategic opportunities (Hughes & Beatty, 2005). Reframing is an important aspect of visioning because it challenges organizational members to reflect upon what they can do differently for a competitive advantage and to follow up these reflections with system thinking that maps out the interrelationships of variables that produce extraordinary results (Collins, 2001; Senge, 1990).

SOAR acknowledges the value of visioning as a tool to inspire and guide action. The framework invites participants to visualize the organization's future by asking questions designed to elicit a vision of its desired future and outcomes through a discussion of individuals' aspirations. One of the core questions that SOAR asks illustrates this by asking stakeholders to describe the preferred future of the organization, in an ideal situation, and where they see the organization 5 years from now. Table 63.3 provides a list of standard SOAR questions.

STRATEGIC INTENT

In some instances, aspirations are discussed as an organization's strategic intent. Strategic intent has been described as an organization's ambitious and compelling dream, that which energizes stakeholders and provides the emotional and intellectual energy for the journey into the future (Prahalad & Hamel, 1994). Strategic intent challenges the organization to create an extreme misfit between resources and its aspirations (Hamel & Prahalad, 2005). Therefore, the emphasis on strategic intent is to formulate stretch aspirations and then leverage current resources and acquire new resources to accomplish aspirations.

STRATEGIC STORYTELLING

Similar to strategic conversations, strategic storytelling is another vehicle for communicating aspirations and engaging organizational members. A strategic story is an imagined future that serves as a planning platform for an organization's aspirations by using narratives to set the stage to define the current situation, present a dramatic conflict that challenges members to identify opportunities, and develop an approach for winning (Shaw, Brown, & Bromiley, 1998). Strategic storytelling exemplifies the ethos of SOAR by presenting the art of what is possible through inviting listeners to co-create a course of action, envisioning its effects on others, and deciding how to contribute. This helps organizational members find their role in a strategic story through sense-making and sense-giving within the given situation (Boje, 1995). When strategic stories can be used for visualizing or as a metaphorical representation of aspirations, organizational members can more easily see the big picture and think in terms of holistic systems (Hauden, 2008).

Results (R)

Aspirations motivate and energize organizational members to act in ways that are consistent with producing results for the organization (Hart, 1992). However, how does an organization know when it is succeeding at producing these results? From a positive strategy perspective, conscientious identification and the use of meaningful measures indicate if the organization is on track to achieve its goals, considering its strengths, opportunities, and aspirations (Stavros & Hinrichs, 2009). From a POS perspective, a results-oriented strategy embraces a broaden-and-build perspective by framing the attainment of performance objectives as opportunities for learning, growth, and expanded awareness (Cravens, Oliver, & Stewart, 2009).

BALANCED SCORECARD

The balanced scorecard (BSC) provides a lens to explore how results can be enacted in a SOAR framework of positive strategy. Based on research and practice, BSC was designed as a management and measurement system for specifying organizational strategies and the translation of strategic vision into action (Kaplan & Norton, 1996). The design of the BSC assumes that strategy is a set of hypotheses about cause and effect that can be expressed by a sequence of if–then statements.

The BSC tells the story of an organization's strategy through a measurement system that makes the explicit relationships (hypotheses) among objectives (measures) for four perspectives: financial, customer satisfaction, learning and growth, and internal processes. The four perspectives of the BSC are integrative components that reinforce each other in indicating the present and future prospects of an

Table 63.3 Standard SOAR questions

Strengths	Opportunities
What are we most proud of as an organization?	What are the best possible opportunities?
What are our greatest assets?	How might we best partner with others?
Aspirations	Results
What do we care deeply about?	How do we know we are succeeding?
What is our preferred future?	What are our measurable results?

organization (Nguyen, 2007). Conceptualizing the results dimension of the SOAR framework from a BSC view illustrates the importance of linking strategic vision to performance metrics by providing a map for how organizations can convert resources and capabilities into strategic initiatives and desired outcomes (Kaplan & Norton, 2000). A key point regarding the measurement system is the focus on more meaningful results than solely profit.

TRIPLE BOTTOM LINE

Recently, the balanced scorecard has been extended to include social and environmental issues (Hubbard, 2006). In some instances, these additional components are integrated from a triple bottom line (TBL) perspective (Jamali, 2006), which offers another lens for organizations to incorporate the "results" aspects of SOAR. The TBL emphasizes that when an organization is measuring results, it should consider that there are multiple impacts on society with associated bottom lines. The TBL is a value-based aspiration that requires the organization to acknowledge the relationship between its economic performance and its performance in social and environmental terms (Colbert & Kurucz, 2007). This entails managing and balancing responsibilities that are often depicted as the three Ps—profits, planet, and people—to create sustainability strategies (Wirtenberg, Russell, & Lipsky, 2009).

The TBL now is being used to capture the values, vision (aspirations), opportunities, and practices that organizations use to maximize positive impact and generate sustainable value for the economy, society, and environment (Elkington, 1997; Jamali, 2006; Laszlo, 2008). Consequently, the focus on TBL results are reinforced when an organization adopts a whole-system approach to learning that is conceived as attunement with the environment and permeates boundaries to create feedback cycles with various stakeholders (Jamali, 2006; Luthans, Rubach, & Marsnik, 1995).

ACCOUNTABILITY THEORY

By formulating and enacting strategy through SOAR, it holds organizational members accountable for achieving results. Managers have been attempting to move accountability inside the activity of working for decades, instead of locating it after something or someone has gone wrong and asking the involved party to explain and rationalize. To continue this traditional accountability process jeopardizes the desire of organization members to participate in making decisions.

Constructive accountability recognizes and emphasizes that the performance of one organization's member impacts the performance of others. Thus, accountability is experienced and understood as constructive and contributing to mutual accomplishment during the performance of the work (Seiling, 2005). It occurs spontaneously and purposely during the exchange of conversations that include suggestions, acknowledgements, answers, challenges of right or wrong, and opportunities to contribute to the success of others. Inside these activities, there occurs a constructive exchange of accountability—people purposely join together to be responsible and accomplish the work.

SOAR activates constructive accountability, exponentially expanding energy and interest in contributing to the welfare within the organization. For example, John Deere has been using SOAR at multiple levels for 7 years, and the leading indicators for success were "confidence, energy, alignment, commitment, accountability, and relationships" (Hinrichs, 2010, p. 34). There were also lagging indicators including: "a 50% reduction in project completion cycle time; a 25% increase in stretch projects and goals; and accomplishments of SBU and functional department goals" (p. 34). People pull themselves and others into the process to create a future that is mutually beneficial. Commitment and dedication to the future spreads across the group and extends outward to other groups. They become constructively accountable for deciding and performing what must be done to reach results.

SOAR: Empirical Evidence

The *International Journal of Appreciative Inquiry* features many case studies on the benefits resulting from employing the SOAR framework (2003, 2007, 2008). There are more recent case studies in other books (Stavros & Sprangel, 2008; Wankel & Stoner, 2009; Watkins & Kelley, 2011). The following three examples provide insights from one organization that has been using the SOAR framework for over 4 years. Two other examples are based on two dissertations, one that demonstrates SOAR's effectiveness for building trust and impacting customer/supplier relationships and performance in a global chemical supplier organization, and the second on building strategic capacity by a variety of users of SOAR.

Professional Global Service Provider

In a 3-year case study, a senior management team and its divisional employees decided to use the SOAR framework to build on the practice's financial and

Table 63.4 Change in client and financial position

Results	Initial	Year 1	Year 2	Year 3
Client Satisfaction	8th	8th	6th	1st
Revenue	8th	5th	4th	1st
Income	12th	6th	2nd	1st

Adapted from Stavros & Saint (2010). Reprinted with permission of John Wiley and Sons.

operational successes. Based on 30 offices, this office was ranked eighth in client satisfaction and revenue and 12th in income (see results in Table 63.4). The managing director wanted to take a good office and make it great. He wanted to be ranked number one in client satisfaction and profits.

The leadership team moved from a top-down approach to a strengths-based whole-system strategic planning approach that developed a learning network focusing on the search and strategic dialogues for strengths, innovations, opportunities, and results between employees and clients. At this office, quarterly meetings and monthly strategy meetings were designed around the SOAR framework to inquire into the past year's most powerful innovations and service deliveries. These meetings demonstrated the effectiveness of SOAR in action. SOAR was foundational in creating the strategic marketing operating plans. Some of the results are shown in Table 63.4.

As the results suggest, this form of strengths-based whole-system learning and development builds momentum and magnifies the reason for clients to place confidence and trust in this financial management practice's people. This work resulted in this management practice office being awarded Office of the Year, the firm's highest award, in Year 2 and 3.

Global Chemical Management Service Provider

Sprangel's study (2009) examined the interrelationship among SOAR framework, trust, environmental management system (EMS)/chemcial management system (CMS), and supplier performance with 71 program managers and customers at a global chemical management services provider. Sprangel's study proposed how the elements of the SOAR framework can build trust and increase supplier performance to answer the research question (p. 39): How can a CMS program better manage implementation activities to achieve high levels of CMS supplier performance as measured by perceptions of program manager and customer supplier performance?

The results support a combined framework in which utilization of the elements of SOAR built trust and pro-environmental behaviors to train suppliers to develop collaborative relationships with customers. There were two major findings. First, the results suggested that supplier performance can improve through the use of the SOAR framework. Second, the effect of SOAR on supplier performance was mediated by the dimensions of trust and EMS/CMS. This study validated the role of the SOAR framework, trust, and EMS/CMS on the desired outcome of improved supplier performance for a CMS program.

SOAR Exemplars Build Strategic Capacity

More findings include Malone's (2010) research. Her qualitative dissertation explores a generative approach to strategy through the application of capacity building that views strategy as a "fluid, deeply embedded capability for thinking and functioning strategically" (p. 4). Through 39 in-depth interviews with strategy and SOAR exemplars, along with supporting case study material, Malone concluded that the metacapabilities (i.e., SOAR) that support strategic capacity lead to an increased capacity for strategic change that allows for combining and generating new capabilities to positively impact performance. Strategic capacity was conceptualized as:

> [T]he ability of an organization to obtain its vision, mission, and goals, ultimately leading to its sustainability. Strategic capacity involves every individual in the organization acting in relationship with others and the organization in collectively making strategic choices (Grant, 2005) and dynamically building competencies and deploying critical resources (Hamel & Prahalad, 2005) necessary to successfully deliver the organization's contribution to its shareholders, employees, customers, and communities. In short, strategic capacity is a deeply embedded ability that enables an organization to bridge the gap between its current performance and its potential. (Malone, 2010, p. 8)

This concept of strategic capacity represents an opportunity to reframe strategy, creating new perspectives and frames and leading to the generation of new opportunities for "creating and doing strategy." In this study, the SOAR framework was found to be "a versatile, simple, and powerful framework that can be utilized in a multitude of ways for applications such as strategic planning, leadership development, coaching, conflict resolution, and continuous improvement, among others" (Malone, 2010, p. 261). In summary, from her data, Malone summarizes SOAR as a framework that:

> [E]ngages the entire system (including all stakeholders) to build upon strengths, engage in possibility thinking, and expand participation in the development of goals and objectives for strategy implementation. SOAR creates energy that informs action. SOAR also fosters learning and engagement and can be utilized as a shared learning system in many different applications. SOAR can also function as a sense-managing tool that enables individuals across the organization and multiorganizations to better understand the mission, vision, and strategies of the organization and relate them back to individual actions. (pp. 262–263)

Future Directions

This chapter focuses on the conceptual development and application of SOAR to create *positive strategy*. As such, there are many areas for future research.

Malone's concept on strategic capacity is a construct that has been barely studied to date. Ganz (2000, 2009) first defined this construct in his seminal work on California unionization. Then, Malone's study expanded his theory and created a framework in which SOAR was foundational to building strategic capacity. The theoretical frameworks and propositions developed through her study, which focuses on the efficacy and application of SOAR, can be a springboard from which future research can be built. An area that would benefit from future research may be how strategic capacity leads to positive strategy through the application of the SOAR framework.

Another major area for future research would be quantitative or mixed-methods studies that allow for the linkage of SOAR to organizational performance or transformation. For example, how much does the combination of all the SOAR elements contribute to building a positive strategy that ultimately impacts performance or transformation? Are some SOAR elements stronger contributors to

building positive strategy than others? This could be accomplished through mixed methods of surveys, interviews, and case studies from those who have used SOAR over a period of time.

In addition, there is a need to understand how positive strategy develops over time and can be measured and sustained. Only one longitudinal study exists to date of positive strategy development with an organization (Stavros & Saint, 2010). Similarly, another area for future research would be to better understand the specific capabilities that support the continuous development of positive strategy through the application of the SOAR framework.

Conclusion
Creating a Positive Strategy

Strategies should be living and generative actions. Furthermore, strategy should be part of everyone's job. The SOAR framework provides a fresh and innovative approach to traditional strategy conversations and strategic planning efforts that encourages positive strategy. This chapter begins to identify the current strategic concepts and theories in the strategy field that support the SOAR framework.

The SOAR framework focuses on how to complete a strategic inquiry with an appreciative intent into what works best, the best possible market or product/service opportunities to be considered, the collective aspirations and dreams of stakeholders, the measurable and meaningful results, and how all stakeholders get involved in the strategic planning process. What are the resources and rewards required to successfully implement the strategy? SOAR accelerates the strategic planning efforts that give life and energy to the organization's members and their future.

References

AI Practitioner: The International Journal of AI Best Practices (ISSN: 1741–8224), London, England: November 2003, Appreciative strategy, co-editors: J. Stavros, M. Schiller, & J. Sutherland. August 2007; SOARing to high and engaging performance: An appreciative approach to strategy, co-editors: J. Stavros & G. Hinrichs. August 2008; The sustainability journey and appreciative inquiry: How a whole system, positive change approach can accelerate the adoption and integration of a new business paradigm, co-editors: Mona Amodeo, C.K. Cox, D.K. Saint, & J.M. Stavros.

Bamford, C.E., & West, G. (2010). *Strategic management: Value creation, sustainability, and performance.* Mason, OH: South-Western Cengage Learning.

Barney, J.B. (1986). Organizational Culture: Can it be a source of sustained competitive advantage? *Academy of Management Review, 11(3)*: 656–665.

Barney, J.B., & Hansen, M.H. (1994). Trustworthiness as a source of competitive advantage. *Strategic Management Journal, 15*, 175–190.

Barret, F. (1995). Creaing appreciative learning cultures. *Organizational Dyamics 24*(2), 36–49.

Barrett, F.J., Cooperrider, D.L., & Fry R.E. (2005). Bringing every mind into the game to realize the positive revolution in strategy. The Appreciative Inquiry summit. In William J., Rothwell, R.S., & Gary N. (Eds.*), Practicing organization development: A guide for consultants* (pp. 501–549). San Francisco: John Wiley & Sons Inc.

Baum, J.R., Locke, E.A., & Kirkpatrick, S.A. (1998). A longitudinal study of vision and vision communication to venture growth in entrepreneurial firms. *Journal of Applied Psychology, 83*(1), 43–54.

Boje, D.M. (1995). Stories of the storytelling organization: A postmodern analysis of Disney as "tamara-land." *Academy of Management Journal. 38*(4), 997–1035.

Bolman, L., & Deal, T. (2008). *Reframing organizations: Artistry, choice and leadership.* San Francisco, CA: John Wiley & Sons.

Bolman, L., & Deal, T. (1991). Leadership and management effectiveness: A multi-frame, multi-sector analysis. *Human Resource Management 30*(4), 509–534.

Bushe, G., & Kassam, A. (2005). When is appreciative inquiry transformational? A meta-case analysis. *Journal of Applied Behavioral Science, 41*, 161–181.

Cameron, K. (2008). *Positive leadership: Strategies for extraordinary performance.* San Francisco, CA: Berrett-Koehler.

Cameron, K.S., Dutton, J.E., & Quinn, R.E. (2003). Foundations of positive organizational scholarship. In *Positive organizational scholarship: Foundations of a new discipline* (pp. 3–13). San Francisco, CA: Berrett-Koehler.

Cameron, K., & Lavine, M. (2006). *Making the impossible possible. Leading extraordinary performance: The Rocky Flats story.* San Francisco, CA: Berrett-Koehler Publishers.

Cameron, K.S., Quinn, R.E., DeGraff, J., & Thakor, A.V. (2006). *Competing values leadership: Creating value in organizations.* Northampton, MA: Edward Elgar.

Chaffee, E. (1985). Three models of strategy. *Academy of Management Review, 10*(1), 89–98.

Clifton, D., & Nelson, P. (1992). *Soar with your strengths.* New York, NY: Dell Publishing.

Clifton, H., & Harter, J. (2003). Investing in strengths. In K. Cameron, J. Dutton, & R. Quinn (Eds.), *Positive organizational scholarship: Foundations of a new discipline* (pp. 111–121). San Francisco, CA: Berrett-Koehler Publishers.

Coff, R.W., & Rosseau, D.M. (2000). Sustainable competitive advantage from relational wealth. In C.R. Leana & D.M. Rousseau (Eds.), *Relational wealth: The advantages of stability in a changing economy* (pp. 27–48*).* New York, NY: Oxford University Press.

Colbert, B.A. (2004). The complex resource-based view: Implications for theory and practice in strategic human resource management. *Academy of Management Review, 29*, 341–358.

Colbert, B.A., & Kurucz, E.C. (2007). Three conceptions of triple bottom line: Business sustainability and the role of HRM. *Human Resource Planning, 30*(1), 21–29.

Collins, J. (2001). *Good to great.* New York, NY: Harper Collins Publishers, Inc.

Collins, J., & Porras, J. (1996). *Built to last.* New York, NY: Harper Collins Publishers, Inc.

Collis, D.J., & Montgomery, C.A. (1997). *Corporate strategy: Resources and scope of the firm.* Irwin, IL: Homewood.

Cooperrider, D. (1986). *Appreciative inquiry: Toward a methodology for understanding and enhancing organizational innovation.* Unpublished Dissertation. Case Western Reserve University.

Cooperrider, D.L., Whitney, D., & Stavros, J. (2003). *The appreciative inquiry handbook* (1st ed.). San Francisco, CA: Berrett-Koehler.

Cooperrider, D.L., Whitney, D., & Stavros, J. (2008). *The appreciative inquiry handbook* (2nd ed.). San Francisco, CA: Berrett-Koehler.

Cravens, K.S., Oliver, E.G., & Stewart, J.S. (2009)., Can a positive approach to performance evaluation help accomplish your goals?, *Business Horizons, 53*(3), 269–279.

Dane, E., & Pratt, M.G. (2007). Exploring intuition and its role in managerial decision making. *Academy of Management Review, 32*(1), 33–54.

Daly, A., Millhollen, B., & DiGuilio, L. (2007). SOARing toward excellence in an age of accountability: The case of Esperanza school district. *International Journal of Appreciative Inquiry, 37*, 43.

deKluyver, C., & Pearce, J. (2009). *Strategy: A view from the top.* Englewood Cliffs, NJ: Pearson Prentice Hall.

Drucker, P. (2004). David Cooperrider interview with Peter Drucker in Summer 2004.

Edersheim, E. (2007). *The definitive Drucker.* New York, NY: McGraw-Hill.

Eisenhardt, K.M., & Martin, J.A. (2000). Dynamic capabilities: What are they? *Strategic Management Journal, 21*(10/11), 1105–1121.

Elkington J. (1997). *Cannibals with forks: The triple bottom line of 21st century business.* Oxford: Capstone Publishing.

Eoyang, G. (2010). Human systems dynamics: Competencies for a new organizational practice. In W.J. Rothwell, J.M. Stavros, R. Sullivan, & A. Sullivan (Eds.), *Practicing organization development: A guide for leading change* (3rd ed., pp. 446–456). San Francisco, CA: Jossey-Bass Publishers.

Hambrick, D.C., & Fredrickson, J.W. (2005). Are you sure you have a strategy? *Academy of Management Executive, 19*(4), 51–62.

Ganz, M. (2000). Resources and resourcefulness: Strategic capacity in the unionization of California agriculture, 1959–1966. *The American Journal of Sociology, 105*(4), 1003–1062.

Ganz, M. (2009). *Why David sometimes wins: Leadership, organization, and strategy in the California farm worker movement.* Oxford, NY: Oxford University Press.

Glynn, M.A., & Dutton, J. (2007). The Generative Dynamics of Positive Organizing. Working Paper. Ross School of Business, University of Michigan.

Grant, R.M. (1991). The resource-based theory of competitive advantage: Implications for strategy formulation. *California Management Review, 33*. 114–135.

Grant, R. (2002). *Contemporary strategic analysis: Concepts, techniques and applications.* New York, NY: Wiley.

Grant, R. (2005). The resource-based theory of competitive advantage: Implications for strategy formulation. In S. Segal-Horn (Ed.), *The strategy reader* (pp. 177–194). Malden, MA: Blackwell Publishing Ltd.

Hamel, G., & Prahalad, C.K. (1994). Strategy as a field of study: Why search for a new paradigm? *Strategic Management Journal, 15*, 5–16.

Hamel, G., & Prahalad, C. (1996). Competing in the new economy: Managing out of bounds. *Strategic Management Journal, 17*, 237–242.

Hamel, G., & Prahalad, C.K (2005). Strategy as stretch and leverage. In S. Segal-Horn (Ed.), *The Strategy Reader* (pp. 29–40). Malden, MA: Blackwell Publishing Ltd.

Hart. S. (1992). An integrative framework for strategy making processes. *Academy of Management Review, 17*(2), 327–351.

Hauden, J. (2008). *The art of engagement: Bridging the gap between people and possibilities*. New York, NY: McGraw-Hill.

Helfat, C., Finkelstein, S., Mitchell, W., Peteraf, M., Singh, H., Teece, D., & Winter, S. (2007). *Dynamic capabilities: Understanding strategic change in organizations*. Malden, MA: Blackwell Publishing.

Hill, T., & Westbrook, R. (1997). SWOT analysis: It's time for a product recall. *Long Range Planning, 30*(1), 46–52.

Hinrichs, G. (2010). SOARing for sustainability: Longitudinal organizational efforts applying appreciative inquiry. *International Journal of Appreciative Inquiry, 12*(3), 31–36.

Hitt, M., Keats, B., & DeMarie, S. (1998). Navigating in the new competitive landscape: Building strategic flexibility and competitive advantage in the 21st century. *Academy of Management Executive, 12*(4), 22–42.

Hofer, C.W., & Schendel, D. (1978). *Strategy formulation: Analytical concepts*. St. Paul, MN: West Publishing.

Hubbard, G. (2006). Measuring organizational performance. *Business Strategy and the Environment, 18*, 1–17.

Hughes, R.L., & Beatty, K.C. (2005). *Becoming a strategic leader: Your role in your organization's enduring success*. San Francisco, CA: Jossey-Bass.

Isern, J., & Pung, C. (2007). Driving radical change. *The McKinsey Quarterly, 4*, 1–12.

Jamali, D. (2006). Insights into triple bottom line integration from a learning organization perspective, *Business Process Management Journal, 12*, 809–821.

Kaplan R.S., & Norton D.P. (2000). *The strategy focused organization*. Boston, MA: Harvard Business School Press.

Kaplan, R., & Norton, D. (1996). *The Balanced Scorecard: Translating strategy into action*. Boston, MA: Harvard Business Press.

Kim, C., & Mauborgne, R. (2005). *Blue ocean strategy*. Boston, MA: Harvard Business School Press.S

Laszlo, C. (2008). *Sustainable value: How the world's companies are doing well by doing good*. Stanford, CA: Stanford University Press.

Lee, F., Caza, A., Edmondson, A., & Thomke, S. (2003). New knowledge creation in organizations. In K.S. Cameron, J.E. Dutton, & Quinn, R.E. (Eds.), *Positive organizational scholarship* (pp. 194–206). San Francisco, CA: Berrett-Koehler.

Liedtka, J. (1996). Collaborating across lines of business for collaborative advantage. *Academy of Management Executive, 10*(2): 20–34.

Liedtka, J., & Rosenblum, J. (1996). Shaping conversations: Making strategy, managing change. *California Review, 39*(1), 141–157.

Lowendahl, B., & Revang, O. (1998). Challenges to existing strategy theory in a postindustrial society. *Strategic Management Journal, 19*, 755–733.

Luthans, F., Rubach, M.J., & Marsnik, P. (1995). Going beyond total quality: The characteristics, techniques and measures of learning organizations. *International Journal of Organizational Analysis, 3*(1), 24–28.

Malone, P. (2010). *An appreciative exploration of strategic capacity and the impact of the SOAR framework in building strategy capacity*. Unpublished dissertation, College of Management, Lawrence Technological University, Southfield, MI.

Mayer, R.E. (1996). The search for insight: Grappling with Gestalt Psychology's unanswered questions. In R.J. Sternberg & J.E. Davidson (Eds.), *The nature of insight* (pp. 3–32). Cambridge, MA: MIT Press.

Miles, M., Munilla, L., & Darroch, J. (2006). The role of strategic conversations with stakeholders in the formation of corporate social responsibility strategy. *Journal of Business Ethics, 69*, 195–205.

Mintzberg, H. (1994). *The rise and fall of strategic planning*. Englewood Cliffs, NJ: Prentice Hall.

Mumford, M.D., & Strange, J.M. (2005). The origins of vision: Effects of reflection, models, and analysis. *Leadership Quarterly, 16*, 121–148.

Nahapiet, J., & Ghoshal, S. (1998). Social capital, intellectual capital, and the organizational advantage. *Academy of Management Review, 23*, 242–266.

Nguyen, C. (2007). *Resource allocation with the use of the Balanced Scorecard and the Triple Bottom Line in education*. Accessed April 2010 from Educational Resource Information Center. Retrieved from http://eric.ed.gov/ERICWebPortal/custom/portlets/recordDetails/detailmini.jsp?_nfpb=true&_&ERICExtSearch_SearchValue_0=ED496206&ERICExtSearch_SearchType_0=no&accno=ED496206.

Pisapia, J, Pang, N., Hee, T., Lin, Y., & Morris, L. (2009). A comparison of the use of strategic thinking skills of aspiring leaders in Hong Kong, Malaysia, Shanghai, and the United States: An exploratory study. *International Education Studies, 2*(2), 46–58.

Porter, M. (1998). What is strategy? In S. Segal-Horn (Ed.), *The strategy reader* (pp. 73–99). Malden, MA: Blackwell Business.

Prahalad, C.K., & Hamel, G. (1990). The core competence of the corporation, *Harvard Business Review, 68*(3), 79–91.

Prahalad, C.K., & Hamel, G. (1994). *Competing for the future*. Boston, MA: Harvard Business School Press.

Seiling, J.G. (2005). *Moving from individual to constructive accountability*. Published dissertation. Taos Institute/University of Tilburg, Netherlands.

Seligman, M.E.P. (2002). *Authentic happiness*. New York, NY: Free Press

Selsky, J., Goes, J., & Baburoglu, O. (2007). Contrasting perspectives of strategy making: Applications in hyper environments. *Organization Studies, 28*(1), 71–94.

Senge, P. (1990). *The fifth discipline: The art and practice of the learning organization*. New York, NY: Doubleday.

Shaw, G.B.R., & Bromiley, P. (1998). Strategic stories: How 3M is rewriting business planning. *76*(3), 41–50.

Simon, D.G., Hitt, M.A., & Ireland, R.D. (2007). Managing firm resources in dynamic environments to create value: Looking inside the black box. *Academy of Management Review, 32*, 273–292.

Sprangel, J. (2009). *A study of the direct and meditational effects of the SOAR framework, trust, and environmental management systems on chemical management services supplier performance at the Haas TCM Group*. Unpublished dissertation, College of Management, Lawrence Technological University, Southfield, MI.

Stacey, R. (1996). *Complexity and creativity in organizations*. San Francisco, CA: Berrett-Koehler Publishers.

Stavros, J. (1998). *Capacity building using a positive approach to accelerate change*. Unpublished dissertation, Case Western Reserve University.

Stavros, J., Cooperrider, D., & Kelley, D. (2003). Strategic Inquiry - Appreciative intent: Inspiration to SOAR. *AI Practitioner*, November, 2–19.

Stavros, J., & Hinrichs, G. (2009). *Thin book of SOAR: Building strengths-based strategy*. Bend, OR: Thin Book Publishers.

Stavros, J., & Saint, D. (2010). SOAR: Linking strategy and OD to sustainable performance. In W.J. Rothwell, J.M. Stavros, R. Sullivan, & A. Sullivan (Eds.), *Practicing Organization Development: A guide for leading change* (pp. 377–394). San Francisco, CA: Jossey-Bass.

Stavros, J., & Sprangel, J. (2008). Applying appreciative inquiry to deliver strategic change: Orbseal technology center. In J. Passmore, S. Lewis, & S. Castore (Eds.), *Appreciative inquiry for change management* (pp. 210–224). Philadelphia: Kogan Page Publishers.

Sundbo, G. (1998). *The theory of innovation: entrepreneurship, technology, and strategy*. Oxford, UK: Edward Elgar Publishers.

Teece, D., Pisano, G., & Shuen, A. (1997). Dynamic capabilities and strategic management. *Strategic Management Journal, 18*(7), 509–533.

Teece, D. (2009). *Dynamic capabilities and strategic management*. Oxford, UK: Oxford University Press.

Thatchenkery, T., & Metzker, C. (2006). *Appreciative intelligence*. San Francisco, CA: Berrett Koehler Publishers.

Thompson, A., Strickland. A., & Gamble, J. (2007). *Crafting and executing strategy: The quest for competitive advantage: Concepts and cases* (14th ed.). New York: McGraw-Hill.

Valentin, E. (2001). SWOT analysis from a resource-based view. *Journal of Marketing Theory and Practice, 9*, 54–68.

Wankel, C. & Stoner, J. (2009). *Management education for global sustainability*. Charlotte, NC: Information Age Publishing.

Watkins, J., & Kelley, R. (2011). *Change at the imagination of speed* (2nd ed.). San Francisco, CA: Jossey-Bass Publishers.

Weick, K. (1979). *The social psychology of organizations*. Reading, MA: Addison-Wesley.

Wirtenberg, J., Russell, W., & Lipsky, D. (2009). *The sustainable enterprise fieldbook: When it all comes together*. New York: AMACOM.

Zahra, S.A. (2002). Absorptive capacity: A review, re-conceptualization, and extension. *Academy of Management Review, 27*:185–203.

Zollo, M., & Winter, S.G. (2002). Deliberate learning and the evolution of dynamic capabilities. *Organization Science, 13*, 339–351.

PART 8

A Positive Lens on Problems and Challenges

Kathleen M. Sutcliffe *and* Marlys K. Christianson

Abstract

Positive organizational scholarship is concerned with dynamics that enable organizational strength and flourishing. In this chapter, we argue that organizations that manage unexpected events and prevent small problems from becoming large crises are engaged in important acts of positive organizing. We assume that adverse events, crises, and accidents are not inevitable; rather, they result from small problems, surprises, and lapses that shift, grow, and escalate until they are too big to handle. This chapter focuses on a set of capabilities that allows organizations to contain and repair vulnerability. Specifically, we identify a set of critical capabilities that involve attention, awareness, and action: these include capabilities for attending to, making sense of, and not explaining away discrepancies; capabilities for updating and coordinating understanding as problems unfold; and capabilities for actively managing problems through containment and resilience. We end with avenues for future research and practice.

Keywords: Managing unexpected events, perturbations, weak signals, problem finding, coping with surprise, resilience, high reliability organizing,

On the evening of April 20, 2010, a sudden blow-out explosion on the Deepwater Horizon offshore oil drilling platform, located 40 miles southeast of the Louisiana coast, killed 11 platform workers and injured 17 others (CNN.com, 2010; Robertson, 2010). It also initiated a massive ongoing oil spill in the Gulf of Mexico that gushed for 4 months beneath the ocean, at an estimated rate of between 35,000 and 65,000 barrels of crude oil per day (Finard, 2010), until early August when the runaway well was finally capped. Estimates of the short- and long-term ecological and economic damage from one of the largest spills in the world and perhaps the largest spill in U.S. history suggested costs would be massive (Weisman, Chazan, & Power, 2010). Cleanup costs, damages, and fines for British Petroleum (the well's owner) alone were estimated to be in the range of $50 billion (Sandler, 2010).

The day after the accident, executives of the platform's owner, Transocean Ltd., stated that, before

the blast occurred, workers had been performing their standard routines and *had no indications* of impending problems (CNN.com, 2010). Yet, as investigators sifted through internal documents from BP, Transocean, and other involved companies and interviewed those involved, a different story began to emerge (Casselman & Gold, 2010). Warning signs of problems—such as possible contamination of the cement used to seal off the well from volatile natural gas, failure to monitor the well closely for signs that gas was leaking in, and a decision to continue work after a test that checks for leaks in the well suggested that something was wrong—were prominent; not only in the hour before the explosion, but also in the days, weeks, and months before. In fact, there were many ways in which workers, leaders, and others either knew or should have known that something was amiss. For example, prompted by a December 2009 near-disaster on one of its North Sea drilling rigs, Transocean Ltd., on April 5, in a 10-page operations advisory warned the Deepwater crew "Do not be complacent . . . Remain focused on well control" (Casselman, 2010).

The preceding story highlights the central issue of concern in this chapter, which is summed up in the following compact sentence: Managing the unexpected is about curbing the temptation to treat small perturbations and discrepancies as normal, and then dealing with the consequences when curbing that temptation fails.

Unexpected, by definition, means to come without warning; something unforeseen. Yet, even though it may seem like an apparent contradiction, several decades of research on the underpinnings of crises/accidents and more recent work on predictable surprises (e.g., Bazerman & Watkins, 2004) reveal that unexpected events rarely develop instantaneously or occur without warning (see, for examples, Reason, 1997; Starbuck & Farjoun, 2005; Turner, 1978). Their seeds are sown long before turmoil arrives in small problems, mistakes, or failures that are unnoticed, ignored, misunderstood, or discounted, and subsequently concatenate and escalate into crises or catastrophes (Reason, 1997). To manage the unexpected requires problem insight— becoming alert and aware of small disturbances and vulnerabilities as they emerge, making sense of their possible problematic consequences, and making adjustments to ongoing action before they can turn into a tragic flaw (Perin, 2006). The earlier organizations try to catch problems, the more options are available to deal with them. At the same time, the earlier organizations try to catch problems, the harder they are to spot (Weick & Sutcliffe, 2007).

A chapter focused on "problems" in a book devoted to scholarship that aims to explore "especially positive outcomes, processes, and attributes of organizations and their members" (Cameron, Dutton, & Quinn, 2003, p. 4) may seem ironic. Yet, if we take seriously the idea that small perturbations underlie unexpected events and are a key to their evasion, and that "to go through a day filled with a million accidents waiting to happen, and to find at the end of the day that they are still waiting to happen, *is amazing*" (Weick, 2003, p. 79, emphasis added), then the study of the mechanisms through which organizations can discern and manage small disturbances before they grow bigger is a "nonobvious outcropping" (Weick, 2003, p. 79) of *positive organizing*, and an important area of inquiry.

Positive organizational scholarship (POS) emphasizes how supportive and "virtuous" organizations can be characterized by climates that enable strength and flourishing. But through what mechanisms does strengthening—the capability to resist attack—come about? In this chapter, we propose that strengthening comes about by organizing in ways to become aware of problems earlier, so that they can be remedied before they become large and unwieldy. In this way, impermanent organizations that tend toward disorder, chaos, and entropy enact structures that facilitate positive adjustment no matter what the conditions (Sutcliffe & Vogus, 2003). We begin with the assumption that the "presumed solidity of organizations is not so obvious" (Weick, 2009, p. 7) and that coordination and interdependence are impermanent and need to be continually reaccomplished (Weick, 2009). Moreover, we assume that organizations tend toward mistakes, errors, and failures. Consistent with Paget (1988), we assume that actions become mistaken but don't start out that way. Given the tendencies toward entropy in interdependent systems, it is clear that episodes of positive organizing occur when the invisible or less visible initial stages of potential organizational failures turn positive rather than negative (Weick, 2003).

The virtuousness and criticality of exploring how systems can be strengthened, so that their operations remain neutral or at least not negative, is heightened by research demonstrating the pervasiveness of *positive asymmetry* (Cerulo, 2006). Positive asymmetry is the cultural tendency of people (especially Americans) to focus on and exaggerate the best-case characteristics, the most optimistic outlook or outcomes. This tendency "to see only the best characteristics and potential of people, places, objects, and events" until it is too late, often leads to situations that "we never saw coming" (Cerulo, 2006, p. 6). In other words, small problems, mistakes, mishaps, or lapses are a natural part of organizational life, but strong tendencies to pay careful attention to best cases and careless attention to worst cases often means that small details don't get attention until too late. We argue that this doesn't have to be the case.

In the remainder of this chapter, we enlarge these introductory ideas in three ways. First, we explore issues of organizational attention and recognition. Second, we explore issues of containment and resilience once the unexpected has broken through. Third, we conclude with a set of ideas for future research that follow from our analysis.

Toward a Capability Model for Managing the Unexpected

We propose that issues of alertness, awareness, and action underpin an organization's ability to manage the unexpected. Specifically, we argue that processes that enable competent action to deal with these issues in various domains (e.g., Dutton, Worline, Frost, & Lilius, 2006; Eisenhardt & Martin, 2000; Orlikowski, 2002) are critical capabilities that underpin organizational strength. Specifically, we explore seven key capabilities: first, the capability to allocate attention, either proactively or reactively; second, the capability to discern and make sense of weak signals/small problems as they emerge; third, the capability to avoid normalizing anomalies away; fourth, the capability to stay flexible and update understandings as situations evolve over time; fifth, the capability to coordinate understanding through intraorganizational communication and interaction; sixth, the capability to contain the unexpected as it manifests; and, seventh, the capability to be resilient in the face of adversity.

Allocating Attention

Managing the unexpected naturally requires attention. To attend to something means "to direct the mind or observant faculties, to listen, apply oneself; to watch over, minister to, wait upon, follow, frequent; to wait for, await, expect" (*Oxford English Dictionary*). By definition, attending is a deliberate act, in which cognitive effort is being actively expended, and the moment of attending can be seen as a type of "switching of cognitive gears," in which automatic thinking changes to active thinking (Louis & Sutton, 1991). Attention can be allocated proactively or reactively. Proactively, attention can be allocated to scan the environment, looking for potential problems, often those that fit a particular set of criteria (i.e., certain cues to watch for, issues that trigger alerts etc). Reactively, attention can be allocated in response to some sort of stimulus.

Research on organizational attention has been conducted mostly at the level of the organization and its top management team (Ocasio, 1997; Ocasio & Joseph, 2005; Sonpar & Golden-Biddle, 2008; Starbuck & Milliken, 1988; Sutcliffe, 1994), primarily on the topic of proactive attention allocation (which has become synonymous with scanning). For instance, *scanning*—an organizational "process of monitoring the environment and providing environmental data to managers"—is a first step in Daft and Weick's (1984) model of organizations as interpretation systems. Scanning can be either the simple observation of stimuli or a stimulus-driven search carried out through formal data collection systems or the personal contacts of managers (p. 286). Scanning systems have been characterized as irregular, periodic,

or continuous, reflecting the increasing formalization, intensity, and complexity of the system (Fahey & King, 1977), and can vary "from high vigilance, active scanning, to the routine scanning or mere maintenance of a state of alertness for nonroutine (but relevant) information" (Huber, 1991, p. 97).

A key idea in these perspectives is that the more attention that is directed to active scanning, the better the recognition of problems, threats, or changes. However, there are at least two problems with the idea that top management team attention leads to better problem finding. First, we know that scanning by top leaders is often flawed. Actors who are scanning on behalf of the organization (i.e., executives) are themselves prone to biases and may notice certain cues instead of other cues (Starbuck & Milliken, 1988) or have the accuracy of their perceptions shaped by structural factors within the organization (Sutcliffe, 1994). Second, we know that organizational leaders are often unaware of problems that others in the organization have noticed, either because others are not willing to speak up (Morrison & Milliken, 2000) or because they believe that—as experts—they would be aware of problems if they existed (Westrum, 1982).

Unfortunately, few studies have investigated how front-line workers attend to emerging problems or how attention is collectively distributed within teams and organizations (for an exception, see Rerup, 2009). This is a particularly critical issue in complex interdependent work, when both the recognition and resolution of unfolding problems depend on the combined knowledge and action of multiple individuals: For instance, one person may notice that there is a problem, but if they are not able to focus the attention of the team on the problem, they won't be able to resolve the issue (Christianson, 2009).

Research on the reactive allocation of attention suggests that the individual who perceives the cue is important; that one executive may notice something that another executive has filtered out (Kiesler & Sproull, 1982) or an expert may notice something that a novice might not (Benner, Hooper-Kyriakidis, & Stannard, 1999; Dreyfus & Dreyfus, 1986; Klein, Pliske, Crandall, & Woods, 2005). Other studies suggest that the nature of the stimulus is important, that attention is reactively triggered when there is a gap or discrepancy (Cowan, 1986; Klein et al., 2005). A gap or discrepancy can be triggered in several ways: something expected doesn't happen, something unexpected happens, or something completely inconceivable happens (i.e., "bolt from the blue") (Weick & Sutcliffe, 2007). The amount of attention directed toward a problem depends on the magnitude of the problem: Larger problems or crises demand more attention (Christianson, Farkas, Sutcliffe, & Weick, 2009; Meyer, 1982), and smaller problems often escape notice. Ultimately, managing the unexpected is about managing the flow of attention of both top management and front-line workers, so that they are able to proactively and reactively notice small problems before they become big problems and to manage and coordinate the flow of attention within teams of front-line workers, achieving a balance so team members can both attend to their individual tasks and to the collective work of the team.

Sensemaking

Managing the unexpected not only requires attention, becoming aware of details, but also requires discernment, understanding what those details might mean. Scholars grounded in the computational information processing perspective assume that discernment results from a linear latency period of gestation in which conditions are changing and building and discrepancies accumulate until some kind of threshold is reached and the problem or situation is understood (Cowan, 1986).

In contrast, scholars grounded in the interpretive aspects of information processing (Klein et al., 2005; Weick, 1995) privilege the idea that part of organizational information processing necessitates the creation of "meaning around information in a social system" (Lant, 2002, p. 345). In other words, discernment isn't simply an information processing problem of perceiving cues that add up until a threshold is reached. Rather, because cues and discrepancies unfold in the context of other information and multiple projects are under way at the same time that reflection takes place (Weick, 1995, p. 27), there is equivocality and confusion rather than uncertainty and ignorance. Thus signals are subtle and context dependent (Klein et al., 2005), which means that discernment is an issue of sensemaking. Moreover, we often recognize problems concurrently or after discrepancies signaling their development have already occurred, thus we are always playing catch-up in trying to make sense of their implications.

The point is that discernment is an issue of appreciating the "significance of data elements in the first place" (Klein et al., 2005, p. 20). To call something a cue or discrepancy, one has to already appreciate its meaning. "The same datum can change meaning as context changes, which means that it is fruitless to mount a search for the 'important stuff'" (Sutcliffe & Weick, 2008, p. 66). In other words, meaning is sensitive to some details of the current situation, what is, has, and could be, going on, and what "the observer expects or intends to happen" (Woods, Patterson, & Roth, 2002). Expectancies (expectations) are critical to sensemaking, as cues and anomalies are not given by the situation. They are constructed and inferred. And, expectancies form the basis for what counts as a cue and is singled out—in sum, they are sensegiving structures for sensemaking. In fact, they form the basis for virtually all deliberate actions because expectancies about how the world operates serve as implicit assumptions that guide behavioral choices (Olson, Roese, & Zanna, 1996, p. 220). But they also create blind spots because they direct attention to certain features of events. Thus, they act like an invisible hand, affecting what people notice, take for granted, ignore, overlook, and discount. Coupled with cognitive biases and heuristics that increase the propensity to search for evidence that confirms the accuracy of our original expectations, these blind spots get larger, often concealing small problems that are getting bigger and harder to solve. Still, expectancies "are critical for detecting 'negative' cues—events that did not happen, but were supposed to occur" (Klein et al., 2005, p. 21–22), and because they are sticky, there is a need to generate alternative expectancies. This means that problem discernment "requires people to reframe the way they understand the situation" (Klein et al., 2005, p. 23). This is harder than it might seem.

Research suggests that cultivating expertise (often through deliberate practice; Ericsson & Charness, 1994) strengthens the ability to generate expectancies critical for noticing cues, as well as for discerning their meaning (Klein et al., 2005). Experts can more quickly recognize patterns, spot things that violate expected patterns, or, conversely, piece together into patterns seemingly unrelated cues (Benner, 1984; Dreyfus & Dreyfus, 1986). Moreover, expertise may influence the capability to judge urgency, and "the need to respond quickly rather than waiting to see how things will develop" (Klein et al., 2005, p. 22).

Anomalizing

Managing the unexpected requires capabilities to avoid treating small perturbations (e.g., unexpected cues, events or discrepancies) as normal. In other words, to manage the unexpected well requires capabilities to enhance the stability and vividness of attention. Stable, vivid attention means that people can hang onto discrepant details long enough to weaken the tendency to normalize—to treat small unexpected events or weak signals of deviation as no big deal (Weick & Sutcliffe, 2006).

Vaughan's (1996) reanalysis of the 1986 *Challenger* space shuttle disaster revealed evidence of the tendency to normalize anomalies and uncertainties into acceptable deviations or risks or to simply ignore them (Starbuck & Farjoun, 2005, p. 46–47). A variant on this pattern was found in the *Columbia* space shuttle accident, when NASA staff interpreted the burst of debris at the root of the left wing of the shuttle as an "almost in-family event" (Starbuck & Farjoun, 2005, p. 146). This interpretation meant that the event was not a serious "problem," and may have been normal (or expected) because "in-family" events referred to problems that had been previously experienced, analyzed, and understood.

If we assume that anomalies foreshadow potential problems, but that the tendency exists to sweep the details into everyday experience, particularly when people and organizations face performance and production pressures, the obvious question is: What decreases the tendency to normalize? According to Weick and colleagues (Weick & Sutcliffe, 2001, 2007; Weick, Sutcliffe, & Obstfeld, 1999), mindful organizing decreases tendencies to normalize and increases tendencies to *anomalize* (Weick & Sutcliffe, 2006, p. 518)—to become more alert to discrepant details, more able to hold on to those details, less likely to simplify those details into familiar events, and overall to become more aware of their significance. The more people hold on to differences, nuances, discrepancies, and outliers, the more slowly they normalize the details. In other words, the longer that people are able to appreciate the distinctiveness of a cue (e.g., delaying stereotyping), either by avoiding lumping it into a broader category or by developing more varied categories, the more nuanced and fine-grained an understanding they can create. This means that the nuances of anomalies can be more deeply examined and acted on more quickly, so that they don't build up until events become unmanageable.

Patterns of mindful organizing are especially visible in so-called high reliability organizations (HROs), which face special problems of learning and acting because of risky technologies that are not fully comprehended and continuous exposure to dynamic contingencies. The best HROs institutionalize processes and practices that "induce a rich awareness of discriminatory detail and a capacity for action" (Weick et al., 1999, p. 88) by spending more time examining failures to assess the health of the system, resisting the urge to simplify assumptions, observing operations and their effects, developing resilience, and locating local expertise and creating a climate of deference to those experts (Weick & Sutcliffe, 2006, p. 516). A mindful infrastructure guards against misspecifying, misestimating, and misunderstanding things (Schulman, 2004; Vogus & Sutcliffe, 2007b) and increases the organization-wide sense of vulnerability that can mitigate the competing performance and production pressures that can exacerbate normalizing. Consequently, organizations can continuously manage fluctuations and more quickly discover and correct minor perturbations that can build and cause major disruptions. Research on mindful organizing in health care appears to confirm these ideas. Vogus (2004; Vogus & Sutcliffe, 2007a, 2007b), for example, found strong negative associations between mindful organizing practices and errors and falls, and concluded that the ongoing actions and interactions embedded in safety organizing practices contributed to greater alertness and discernment of unsafe conditions.

Updating

Managing the unexpected requires updating—that is, the ability to modify understanding of a situation (and the corresponding response to that situation) either because the situation has changed or evolved over time, or the initial assessment of the situation was flawed. This ability to update goes to the heart of adapting and remaining resilient in the face of adversity. However, we know that it is extremely difficult—if not impossible—for people to engage in updating, particularly if they have already started down a particular trajectory/pathway of cognition and action (e.g., Klayman, 1995; Nisbett & Ross, 1980; Rudolph, Morrison, & Carroll, 2009; Staw & Ross, 1987). Updating is made even more complicated by the fact that unexpected discrepancies are often perceived as threats and, under threat, people tend to restrict information processing (i.e., attend only to dominant cues) and constrict control (i.e., revert to first learned responses) (Staw, Sandelands, & Dutton, 1981; Weick, 1990)

Much of the research on why effective updating is so difficult (Nisbett & Ross, 1980; Rudolph, 2003; Staw & Ross, 1987) centers on cognitive biases, and how they act as barriers to updating. *Confirmation bias* is one example (Klayman, 1995; Nickerson, 1998). Confirmation bias pertains to a class of biases in which individuals privilege information that supports their hypotheses and dismiss information that challenges them, interfering with both noticing and interpreting, which are essential for updating. To update understanding, one must notice that something has changed and also must interpret that change as a cue worth paying attention to. Furthermore, one must convert that change into a new understanding. In addition to interfering with updating, cognitive biases can also interfere with activities discussed earlier in this chapter: the allocation of attention, sensemaking, and anomalizing.

If people are able to revisit their understanding—which requires breaking the inertia (or momentum) of the current trajectory—and to reconsider whether they are on the right path, the next question is: How effectively are they updating? Effective updating is characterized by arriving at a more plausible or closer correspondence between the actor's interpretation of the situation and the situation itself, which can be characterized as "more comprehensive, incorporates more of the observed data, and is more resilient in the face of criticism" (Weick, Sutcliffe, & Obstfeld, 2005, p. 415). Yet, studies show that high variance exists, both in terms of frequency and accuracy, in the extent to which effective updating is accomplished. Rudolph's (2003) study of the diagnostic strategies used by anesthesiology residents showed that only 23% of the sample engaged in effective updating (28% of the sample got stuck on their initial diagnosis, 5% considered only a few alternate diagnoses but did not test them sufficiently, and 44% considered multiple diagnoses but did not spend time to determine if they were correct). Even more strikingly, Christianson (2009) found a 32-fold difference in terms of the speed with which interdisciplinary teams of health care providers were able to detect and correct an equipment malfunction.

Updating requires doubt. Doubt—that "state of uncertainty with regard to the truth or reality of anything; undecidedness of belief or opinion" (*Oxford English Dictionary*)—is necessary for overcoming the many forces that make it difficult to question a trajectory of cognition and action once under way (Weick, 1979). As people make sense of unfolding events, doubt either can be a prompt to consider other courses of action, or it can be the outcome of the chosen course of action. Doubt can be generative, resulting in new ideas (Locke, Golden-Biddle, & Feldman, 2008)

Although questions remain about how to facilitate updating, one promising finding suggests that updating is more likely when people work in groups. Individuals are able to effectively update about 25% of the time (Rudolph, 2003), whereas groups are able to effectively update about 50% of the time (Christianson, 2009; LePine, 1998). It may be easier for groups to make sense of problems because partners make social constructions easier: "A partner is a second source of ideas. A partner strengthens independent judgment in the face of a majority. And a partner enlarges the pool of data that are considered" (Weick, 1993, p. 642). Consequently, as we argue in the next section, interactions are critical for managing the unexpected.

Interacting and Communicating
Managing the unexpected is about interacting and communicating. Attending, sensemaking, anomalizing, and updating occur in the context of complex organizations that are loosely connected. Interconnecting is critical to "finding" emerging problems (as well as putting them right). As Taylor and Van Every (2000, p. 207) argue, *re*-cognition occurs when "groups composed of individuals with distributed—segmented, partial—images of a complex environment. . .through interaction, synthetically construct a representation. . .that works; one which in its interactive complexity, outstrips the capacity of any single individual in the network to represent and discriminate events." A pool of knowledge may result from the summation of people's ideas, "but, a representation of the world that none of those involved individually possessed or could possess" (Taylor & Van Every, 2000, p. 207) emerges out of dense interconnections. This is consistent with Hutchins's (1995, p. 176) view that "the cognitive properties of human groups may depend on the social organization of individual cognitive capabilities."

The basic point is that the organization's design (task and workflow interdependence [Thompson, 1967] and patterns of interaction and communication) and the culture that results from it can help or hinder how individuals become alert and aware of perturbations as it influences patterns of cognition, and also the extent to which individuals link their cognitions. More controlled cognition, which, as we argued earlier, will affect patterns of attention, results from reciprocal interdependence and mutual adjustment (Weick, 2009, p. 54). After all, problems in complex organizations rarely emerge full-blown; they are constructed and created through various bits of information that must be assembled and consolidated before understanding can emerge. But, it isn't simply a matter of assembling information parts. The meaning of one part may relate "to some other part whose meaning, in turn, is dependent on the meaning of the initial part" (Weick, 2009, p. 54). Moreover, organizations are filled with ambiguous and messy details, so that people can draw different yet equally plausible conclusions from observing the same "objective" data. Ambiguity cannot be resolved through collecting more information; rather it requires debate, discussion, and active listening (Weick et al., 1999). The important insight for our purposes is that detecting and making sense of anomalies is an iterative process of making sense of divergent information and perceptions that requires dense interaction and communication.

Still, reciprocal interaction does not guarantee that that a clear view of the problem will be generated. Challenges to creating a common representation among diverse individuals are many. First, individuals may be embedded in organizations in which silence about emerging problems is more the norm than the exception (Morrison & Milliken, 2000). Moreover, people refrain from speaking up because they fear negative social consequences (Edmondson, 1999), think their input will be dismissed or disregarded (Blatt, Christianson, Sutcliffe, & Rosenthal, 2006), or defer to the expertise of others (Barton & Sutcliffe, 2009; Van Dyne, Ang, & Botero, 2003).

Second, research shows that people tend to surface and discuss commonly held information much more so than unique information (Stasser & Titus, 1985), possibly because of status dynamics or because the bearer of unique news incurs social costs (Stasser & Titus, 2003). Third, even if people do surface details and come together to discuss them, groups with different types of expertise may have difficulty exploiting their diverse perspectives, in part because of cross-functional communication and coordination problems that complicate sense-making (see Bunderson & Sutcliffe, 2002). Finally, making sense of cues and disparate details and creating a coherent representation of an emerging problem is made difficult because people's understandings are changing at different rates. This issue, labeled *variable disjunction* (Turner, 1976, 1978), refers "to a complex situation in which a number of parties handling a problem are unable to obtain precisely the same information about it so that many differing interpretations of the problem exist" (Turner, 1978, p. 50). It is a situation of high complexity and continuous change. People may be continuously exchanging information, but because the content of the disjoined sets of information is always varying, it is almost impossible to reach consensus about what exists. In part, it is difficult because one has to convince others of the status (legitimacy) of one's own set of information, and also has to convince others of the validity of one's own analysis.

Containing the Unexpected

Managing the unexpected is about containing. We deliberately chose the word "contain" to signify two relevant dimensions of its meaning: contain means both to "hold or encompass" and to "restrain or control" (*Oxford English Dictionary*). These subtly different meanings draw attention to the point that the capability of containing the unexpected requires two types of skills: *encompassing* relates to the ability to delineate the boundaries of a specific problem and encapsulate it, and *controlling* relates to the ability to work within the problem space to begin to resolve the problem.

Containing, in the sense of encompassing a problem, requires that the problem be fully comprehended. People make sense of the nature and scope of a problem by categorizing and labeling the problem (Weick et al., 2005). Once the problem is labeled, the next step in containing is to determine the scope or boundaries of the problem. Underestimating the size or consequences of a problem can occur for several reasons. First, just as weak signals (small problems) or vague concerns (ill-defined problems) are difficult to notice and attend to, they are also difficult to contain, because it's hard to know how far the problem extends and hard to forecast what potential consequences may be. This is particularly an issue in tightly coupled systems, in which taking any action to encompass and contain a problem can have potentially unintended consequences (Perrow, 1986). Second, and more generally, as people take steps to address the problem, they enact changes in the environment that can then change the scope and nature of the problem (Weick, 1979, 1988). Because understanding always lags actions (i.e., actions always are a little ahead of understanding), individuals can unwittingly negatively intensify situations before they know what they are doing. To avoid this, people need to make sense more quickly and fully. Last, problems can evolve over time and may not be immediately apparent. Marianne Paget (1990, p. 142), who studied medical errors, argued that errors are not always detectable in real time: "The journey of error, the dynamic experience of going wrong, is crucial in understanding medical mistakes. They are rarely simple events like errors in addition. Rather they are complex activities and cognitions that unfold in time."

Containing, in the sense of controlling a problem, is often what people have in mind when they talk about "managing the unexpected." There are different elements of controlling a problem. First, and most obviously, it's important to keep the problem from getting bigger. Second, once the problem is no longer enlarging or escalating, it is important to attempt to minimize or mitigate the damage caused by the problem. But those dealing with the problem must also, themselves, exhibit control—they must avoid panic or overload, keep their emotional responses in check, and avoid returning to first learned responses.

Naturally, organizations do not address problems in a vacuum. Problems emerge amid—or even sometimes from—the organization's regular ongoing activity. The unexpected interrupts organizational routines. By routines, we mean "repetitive, recognizable patterns of interdependent actions, carried out by multiple actors" (Feldman & Pentland, 2003, p. 95). Routines rarely come to mind in the context of managing the unexpected, but understanding them is critical for understanding containing capabilities.

When the unexpected breaks through, organizations can respond in at least three ways: first, by enacting a preexisting routine (i.e., contingency plan, standard operating procedure) intended to manage unexpected (yet not inconceivable) events; second, by modifying an existing routine to fit the unexpected event; or, third, by innovating a completely new routine—either de novo (i.e., like the creation of the "escape fire" made famous in the Mann Gulch disaster) or as a bricolage of other existing routines. One challenge is to identify, more or less correctly, what routine to engage in—modifying an existing routine when the problem calls for an entirely novel response is a problem in and of itself. Many organizations, particularly those in dynamic and high-risk settings, try to defend against the unexpected through conventional "prevention" mechanisms such as contingency plans, standard operating procedures, and professional protocols. In these settings, the particular manifestation of the event may be unexpected, but this does not mean the event is unimaginable, just that it is out of the ordinary. In fact, in some organizations, the work consists of managing unexpected events (Okhuysen, 2005). For example, it might be unexpected that a particular patient within a hospital will go into cardiac arrest, but hospitals have protocols for handling cardiac arrests.

Sometimes, organizations don't have a routine that will exactly work, but they can modify their existing routines so that they are able to address this problem. Put another way, they are able to restructure their routines. For example, a study of the collapse of the Baltimore and Ohio Railroad Museum recounted how curators taught steelworkers how to identify artifacts so that—as the steelworkers were clearing the rubble—they could hold up the artifacts and curators could look at them through binoculars (as they weren't allowed to be on the construction site) and indicate whether the item should be saved or discarded (Christianson et al., 2009).

Sometimes, an event is so completely unexpected that there are no available routines with which to respond. These "cosmology episodes" generate a sense of "vuja de" (I've never been here before) and are so shocking that people "suddenly and deeply feel that the universe is no longer a rational, orderly system" (Weick, 1993, p. 633). In this situation, people must either invent a completely new routine/response to match the new problem or cobble together something (i.e., bricolage) from existing routines. Completely novel solutions are quite rare; more common is a solution that is comprised from the materials on hand, in this case the preexisting routines in an organization. Creative and resourceful use of preexisting routines is consistent with the idea of bricolage, in which people, based on deep knowledge of resources, are able to recombine often seemingly disparate elements into a useful solution (Weick, 2001).

Skill is associated with enacting routines that are most useful for containing the unexpected. At the same time, staying flexible and modifying understanding of how well routines are working is critical—in other words, updating around the course of action is critical. It may be that a problem starts off looking familiar but then spirals out of control, requiring the use of other routines. It may be that something that seems completely new is actually similar to something the organization has encountered before.

Resilience and the Unexpected

Finally, managing the unexpected is about resilience, bouncing back from or coping with dangers that have become manifest (Wildavsky, 1991, p. 77). To become aware of the unexpected earlier, so that actions can be taken to contain problems before they grow bigger and unmanageable, is desirable. Yet, because unexpected events often unfold before they are noticed, and actions in response to weak signals are rare, unexpected problems that do show up are often more severe. This means a well-developed capability to withstand and bounce back from unanticipated surprises is critical (Wildavsky, 1991, p. 120).

Resilience requires "improvement in overall capability, i.e., a generalized capacity to investigate, to learn, and to act, without knowing in advance what one will be called to act upon" (Wildavsky, 1991, p. 70). In this way, resilience relies upon past learning and fosters future learning, but exists independently of learning activities, in that resilience represents a store of capabilities and the presence of latent resources that can be activated, combined, and recombined in new situations as challenges arise (Sutcliffe & Vogus, 2003). As such, resilience implies more than a specific adaptation.

Operating resiliently means "learning through fast negative feedback, which dampens oscillations" (Wildavsky, 1991, p. 120), and highlights the importance of general knowledge, technical facility, and command over resources, so that knowledge can be combined in unexpected ways to address emerging threats. In fact, resilience is enhanced by capacity (i.e., ability) and response repertoires, which paradoxically affect alertness and awareness of emerging problems. As Westrum (1994, pp. 336 and 340) concluded after analyzing the battered child syndrome, "a system's willingness to become aware of problems is associated with its ability to act on them," meaning that systems cannot see that over which they have no control.

Resilience results from processes and dynamics that create or retain resources (cognitive, emotional, relational, or structural) in a form sufficiently flexible, storable, convertible, and malleable to enable organizations to successfully cope with and learn from the unexpected (Sutcliffe & Vogus, 2003). For example, processes, structures, and practices that promote competence, encourage growth, and enhance efficacy (e.g., expanding people's general response repertoires by improving their knowledge, their technical capabilities, and their understanding of how to recombine the resources they have at hand) improve organizational capabilities to mediate perturbations and strain. These capabilities and their associated salutary responses work in part by

contributing to a different way of sensemaking. In particular, they counteract tendencies toward threat rigidity (Staw et al., 1981) by increasing capabilities to better sense, process, interpret, and manage small discrepancies as they emerge. This increases the likelihood that disruptive events will be treated as opportunities rather than threats. Rebounding from challenges initiates a positive feedback loop to an organization's capabilities, such that they are strengthened and further resilience is promoted in the face of unexpected events.

Future Directions

Managing the unexpected is often portrayed as a reactive activity directed at problems or surprises that catch organizations unawares. We have tried to show the flaws in that portrayal; we have argued that managing the unexpected is less about reacting to surprises and more about proactively paying attention to the small perturbations and discrepancies that can escalate into large problems. The unexpected is not a given, nor is it an inherent part of complex organizations and organizational life. Rather, it is often set in motion by the (mis)perceptions, (mis)conceptions, and (in)actions of organizational actors. We have argued that a constellation of capabilities—*attending, sensemaking, anomalizing, updating, interconnecting, containing,* and *resiling*—undergird organizational abilities to find problems and put them right before they explode into crises and adverse consequences. These instances of positive organizing build a system's strength and are important sites for POS research. Here, we discuss a few of these opportunities for future research and enhancing practice.

By identifying a set of capabilities for managing unexpected events, we provide a more nuanced vocabulary for thinking about how organizations approach small perturbations and weak signals. These capabilities are, of course, interrelated, but it may be that organizations can demonstrate mastery of some capabilities but still have significant difficulty enacting others. Future research may wish to further disentangle how these capabilities relate to each other and determine whether certain capabilities are more difficult to master than others. As well, research can identify whether there are recurrent organizational "blind spots," in which particular capabilities are neglected. Fundamentally, our model extends previous work on high reliability organizing and is premised on the idea that organizations can intentionally develop capabilities and become more expert in handling all aspects of managing unexpected events (Christianson et al, 2009). We hypothesize that those organizations that are more adept at more of the capabilities will be more likely to sustain high performance, which links back to our argument that the absence of catastrophes in high-risk settings is, in itself, an important form of positive organizing.

Specific antecedents to managing the unexpected also influence the capabilities we have identified: expertise, the design of work, and the role of interruptions. The primary presumption of this chapter is that many crises and accidents develop from *failures of insight.* This understanding is based on a stream of studies suggesting that disaster results from a failure to notice critical cues (e.g., Turner, 1976, 1978). The failure to become aware of small perturbations and discrepancies is not only an issue of failing to detect them, but also an issue of failing to make sense of them in context. Expertise is one potential factor that may play a role in influencing detection as well as sensemaking. For example, Klein et al. (2005) propose that experts are more able to perceive (detect) and conceive (make sense of) subtle signs in part because they have a deeper experience base that "provides a sense of typicality" (p. 21), which would serve to affect the ability to detect anomalies and to understand when expectations are violated. Experts also have more sophisticated mental models, so they are more able to generate explanations for events and tie them into a story. Yet, expertise also has a downside: Experts may fixate on initial explanations and explain anomalies away (De Keyser & Woods, 1993; Klein et al., 2005). This interesting juxtaposition of the possible positive and negative effects of expertise suggests a rich area for research.

In addition to examining the role that individuals may play, it is also important to examine the effects of an organization's (and unit's) design on both attention and containment. Weick and colleagues (Weick & Sutcliffe, 2006; Weick et al., 1999) argue that mindful organizing increases the quality of organizational attention (its stability and vividness) and, at the same time, the ability to act on what is "seen." Yet, they go on to say that, under some conditions, particular practices may inadvertently serve to make attention more scattered (less stable) (Weick & Sutcliffe, 2006, p. 519). Empirical studies examining the effects of mindful organizing on the stability and vividness of attention, as well as how these practices affect the capability to contain the unexpected after it is manifest, are needed.

We have focused on failures of insight and the idea that unexpected events occur because cues are missed, ignored, or dismissed. However, recent work by Barton and Sutcliffe (2009) suggests an important alternative. Noticing small cues may be important for managing unexpected events; however, it may not be sufficient to interrupt ongoing patterns of action that are under way. Rather, psychological and contextual factors create strong "dysfunctional" momentum that is not easily slowed or stopped. Continuing action without interruptions in the face of emerging problems threatens "organizations' abilities to adapt and adjust flexibly" (Barton & Sutcliffe, 2009, p. 1331). Thus, researchers need to better understand the role interruptions play in both sensing and managing the unexpected.

Conclusion

Several implications for managing the unexpected in practice follow from our work. The practice-related literature on managing the unexpected often focuses on controlling or solving the problem (i.e., keeping the problem from enlarging, minimizing the damage from the problem). Finding the problem in the first place is often thought to be the easy part. The present chapter should help to highlight the weakness in that view. As we have argued, capabilities for noticing and making sense of problems, being resistant to explaining them away, and updating and reconsidering whether the course of action is really the right one—capabilities that all precede problem solving or containment—are vital components of managing for unexpected events. Second, until recently, much of the literature related to managing unexpected events presumed that people and organizations were able to adaptively and resiliently negotiate through unexpected events, incorporating new information and modifying the plan as the situation evolved (Christianson, 2009). However, there is considerable evidence that this adaptation and change is extraordinarily difficult. Put simply, it's easy for people to get stuck (or entrained) in a certain trajectory of cognition and action, even if there are many cues that they are on the wrong path. This chapter acknowledges the difficulties involved and draws attention to key capabilities that organizations can develop in order to become more skilled at managing unexpected events.

References

Barton, M.A., & Sutcliffe, K.M. (2009). Overcoming dysfunctional momentum: Organizational safety as a social achievement. *Human Relations, 62*(9), 1327–1356.

Bazerman, M.H., & Watkins, M.D. (2004). *Predictable surprises: The disasters you should have seen coming, and how to prevent them.* Boston, MA: Harvard Business School Press.

Benner, P. (1984). *From novice to expert: Excellence and power in clinical nursing practice.* Menlo Park, CA: Addison-Wesley Publishing Company.

Benner, P., Hooper-Kyriakidis, P., & Stannard, D. (1999). *Clinical wisdom and interventions in critical care: A thinking-in-action approach.* Philadelphia, PA: W.B. Saunders Company.

Blatt, R., Christianson, M.K., Sutcliffe, K.M., & Rosenthal, M.M. (2006). A sensemaking lens on reliability. *Journal of Organizational Behavior, 27,* 897–917.

Cameron, K.S., Dutton, J.E., & Quinn, R.E. (2003). *Positive organizational scholarship: Foundations of a new discipline.* San Francisco, CA: Berrett-Koehler Publishers, Inc.

Casselman, B. (2010, Aug 17). Warning preceded blast, *Wall Street Journal,* p. A5.

Casselman, B., & Gold, R. (2010, May 27). Unusual decisions set stage for BP disaster, *Wall Street Journal,* p. A1.

Cerulo, K.A. (2006). *Never saw it coming: Cultural challenges to envisioning the worst.* Chicago: University of Chicago Press.

Christianson, M.K. (2009). *Updating as part of everyday work: An interactional perspective.* Dissertation, University of Michigan, Ann Arbor, MI.

Christianson, M.K., Farkas, M.T., Sutcliffe, K.M., & Weick, K.E. (2009). Learning through rare events: Significant interruptions at the Baltimore & Ohio Railroad Museum. *Organization Science, 20*(5), 846–860.

CNN.com. (2010). At least 11 missing after blast on oil rig in Gulf Retrieved May 28, 2010, from http://www.cnn.com/2010/US/04/21/oil.rig.explosion/index.html.

Cowan, D.A. (1986). Developing a process model of problem recognition. *Academy of Management Review, 11*(4), 763–776.

Daft, R.L., & Weick, K.E. (1984). Toward a model of organizations as interpretation systems. *Academy of Management Review, 9*(2), 284–295.

De Keyser, V., & Woods, D.D. (1990). Fixation errors: Failures to revise situation assessment in dynamic and risky systems. In A.G. Colombo & A. Saiz de Bastamente (Eds.), *Advanced systems in reliability modeling.* (pp. 231–252). Dordrechts, The Netherlands: Kluwer Academic Publishers.

Dreyfus, H.L., & Dreyfus, S.E. (1986). *Mind over machine: The power of human intuition and expertise in the era of the computer.* New York: Free Press.

Dutton, J.E., Worline, M.C., Frost, P.J., & Lilius, J. (2006). Explaining compassion organizing. *Administrative Science Quarterly, 51*(1), 59–96.

Edmondson, A. (1999). Psychological safety and learning behavior in work teams. *Administrative Science Quarterly, 44*(2), 350–383.

Eisenhardt, K.M., & Martin, J.A. (2000). Dynamic capabilities: What are they? *Strategic Management Journal, 21*(10/11), 1105–1121.

Ericsson, K.A., & Charness, N. (1994). Expert performance. *American Psychologist, 49*(8), 725–747.

Fahey, L., & King, W.R. (1977). Environmental scanning for corporate planning. *Business Horizons*(August), 61–71.

Feldman, M.S., & Pentland, B.T. (2003). Reconceptualizing organizational routines as a source of flexibility and change. *Administrative Science Quarterly, 48*(1), 94–118.

Finard, A. (2010). BP oil spill live feed. Retrieved August 16, 2010, from http://www.zimonet.com/bp-oil-spill-live-feed-record-loss-expected/229/.

Huber, G.P. (1991). Organizational learning: The contributing processes and literature. *Organization Science, 2*(1), 88–115.

Hutchins, E. (1995). *Cognition in the wild.* Cambridge, MA: MIT Press.

Kiesler, S., & Sproull, L. (1982). Managerial response to changing environments: Perspectives on problem sensing from social cognition. *Administrative Science Quarterly, 27*(4), 548–570.

Klayman, J. (1995). Varieties of confirmation bias. *Psychology of Learning and Motivation, 32,* 385–418.

Klein, G., Pliske, R., Crandall, B., & Woods, D.D. (2005). Problem detection. *Cognition, Technology and Work, 7*(1), 14–28.

Lant, T.K. (2002). Organizational cognition and interpretation. In Baum, J.A. C. (Ed.), *The Blackwell companion to organizations* (pp. 344–362). Oxford, UK: Blackwell.

LePine, J.A. (1998). *An integrative model of team adaptation.* Doctoral dissertation, Michigan State University.

Locke, K., Golden-Biddle, K., & Feldman, M.S. (2008). Making doubt generative: Rethinking the role of doubt in the research process. *Organization Science, 19*(6), 907–918.

Louis, M.R., & Sutton, R.I. (1991). Switching cognitive gears: From habits of mind to active thinking. *Human Relations, 44*(1), 55–76.

Meyer, A.D. (1982). Adapting to environmental jolts. *Administrative Science Quarterly, 27*(4), 515–537.

Morrison, E.W., & Milliken, F.J. (2000). Organizational silence: A barrier to change and development in a pluralistic world. *Academy of Management Review, 25*(4), 706–725.

Nickerson, R.S. (1998). Confirmation bias: A ubiquitous phenomenon in many guises. *Review of General Psychology, 2*(2), 175–220.

Nisbett, R., & Ross, L. (1980). *Human inference: Strategies and shortcomings of social judgment.* Englewood Cliffs, NJ: Prentice-Hall, Inc.

Ocasio, W. (1997). Towards an attention-based view of the firm. *Strategic Management Journal, 18*(6), 187–206.

Ocasio, W., & Joseph, J. (2005). An attention-based theory of strategy formulation: Linking micro- and macroperspectives in strategy processes. *Strategy Process, 22,* 39–61.

Okhuysen, G. (2005). Understanding group behavior: How a police SWAT team creates, changes, and manages group routines. In K.D. Elsbach (Ed.), *Qualitative organizational research* (pp. 139–168). Greenwich, CT: Information Age Publishing.

Olson, J., Roese, N., & Zanna, M.P. (1996). Expectancies. In E.T. Higgins & A.W. Kruglanski (Eds.), *Social psychology: Handbook of basic principles* (pp. 211–238). New York: Guilford Press.

Orlikowski, W.J. (2002). Knowing in practice: Enacting a collective capability in distributed organizing. *Organization Science, 13*(3), 249–273.

Oxford English Dictionary. 2010. http://www.oed.com/ (last accessed May 24, 2010).

Paget, M.A. (1990). Life mirrors work mirrors text mirrors life. *Social Problems, 37*(2), 137–148.

Perin, C. (2006). *Shouldering risks: The culture of control in the nuclear power industry.* Princeton, NJ: Princeton University Press.

Perrow, C. (1986). *Complex organizations: A critical essay* (3rd ed.). New York: McGraw-Hill.

Reason, J. (1997). *Managing the risks of organizational accidents.* Aldershot, UK: Ashgate.

Rerup, C. (2009). Attentional triangulation: Learning from unexpected rare crises. *Organization Science, 20*(5), 876–893.

Robertson, C. (2010, April 22). 11 remain missing after oil rig explodes off Louisiana; 17 are hurt, *The New York Times,* p. A13.

Rudolph, J.W. (2003). *Into the big muddy and out again: Error persistence and crisis management in the operating room.* Doctoral dissertation, Boston College.

Rudolph, J.W., Morrison, J.B., & Carroll, J.S. (2009). The dynamics of action-oriented problem solving: Linking interpretation and choice. *Academy of Management Review, 34*(4), 733–756.

Sandler, L. (2010). *Bloomberg Businessweek, August 16–29,* 45–46.

Schulman, P.R. (2004). General attributes of safe organizations. *Quality & Safety in Health Care, 13*(Supplement 2), ii39–ii44.

Sonpar, K., & Golden-Biddle, K. (2008). Using content analysis to elaborate adolescent theories of organization. *Organizational Research Methods, 11*(4), 795–814.

Starbuck, W.H., & Farjoun, M. (2005). *Organization at the limit.* New York: Blackwell Publishing.

Starbuck, W.H., & Milliken, F.J. (1988). Executives' perceptual filters: What they notice and how they make sense. In D.C. Hambrick (Ed.), *The executive effect: Concepts and methods for studying top managers* (pp. 35–65). Greenwich, CT: JAI Press.

Stasser, G., & Titus, W. (1985). Pooling of unshared information in group decision making: Biased information sampling during discussion. *Journal of Personality and Social Psychology, 48*(6), 1467–1478.

Stasser, G., & Titus, W. (2003). Hidden profiles: A brief history. *Psychological Inquiry, 14*(3/4), 304–313.

Staw, B.M., & Ross, J. (1987). Behavior in escalation situations: Antecedents, prototypes, solutions. In L.L. Cummings & B.M. Staw (Eds.), *Research in organizational behavior* (Vol. 9, pp. 39–78). Greenwich, CT: JAI Press.

Staw, B.M., Sandelands, L.E., & Dutton, J.E. (1981). Threat-rigidity effects in organizational behavior: A multilevel analysis. *Administrative Science Quarterly, 26*(4), 501–524.

Sutcliffe, K.M. (1994). What executives notice: Accurate perceptions by top management teams. *Academy of Management Journal, 37*(5), 1360–1379.

Sutcliffe, K.M., & Vogus, T.J. (2003). Organizing for resilience. In K.S. Cameron, J.E. Dutton & R.E. Quinn (Eds.), *Positive organizational scholarship: Foundations of a new discipline* (pp. 94–110). San Francisco, CA: Berrett-Koehler Publishers, Inc.

Taylor, J.R., & Van Every, E.J. (2000). *The emergent organization: Communication as its site and surface.* Mahwah, NJ: Erlbaum.

Thompson, J.D. (1967). *Organizations in action.* New York: McGraw Hill.

Turner, B. (1976). The organizational and interorganizational development of disasters. *Administrative Science Quarterly, 21*(3), 378–397.

Turner, B. (1978). *Man-made disasters.* London: Wykeham Publications.

Van Dyne, L., Ang, S., & Botero, I.C. (2003). Conceptualizing employee silence and employee voice as multidimensional constructs. *Journal of Management Studies, 40*(6), 1359–1392.

Vaughan, D. (1996). *The Challenger launch decision: Risky technology, culture, and deviance at NASA.* Chicago: The University of Chicago Press.

Vogus, T.J. (2004). *In search of mechanisms: How do HR practices affect organizational performance?* Doctoral dissertation, University of Michigan, Ann Arbor.

Vogus, T.J., & Sutcliffe, K.M. (2007a). The impact of safety organizing, trusted leadership, and care pathways on reported medication errors in hospital nursing units. *Medical Care, 45*(10), 997–1002.

Vogus, T.J., & Sutcliffe, K.M. (2007b). The Safety Organizing Scale: Development and validation of a behavioral measure of safety culture in hospital nursing units. *Medical Care 45*(1), 46–54.

Weick, K.E. (1979). *The social psychology of organizing* (2nd ed.). New York: McGraw-Hill.

Weick, K.E. (1988). Enacted sensemaking in crisis situations. *Journal of Management Studies, 25*(4), 305–317.

Weick, K.E. (1990). The vulnerable system: An analysis of the Tenerife air disaster. *Journal of Management, 16*(3), 571–593.

Weick, K.E. (1993). The collapse of sensemaking in organizations: The Mann Gulch disaster. *Administrative Science Quarterly, 38*(4), 628–652.

Weick, K.E. (1995). *Sensemaking in organizations.* Thousand Oaks, CA: Sage Publications.

Weick, K.E. (2001). *Making sense of the organization.* Oxford: Blackwell Business.

Weick, K.E. (2003). Positive organizing and organizational tragedy. In K.S. Cameron, J.E. Dutton, & R.E. Quinn (Eds.), *Positive Organizational Scholarship: Foundations of a New Discipline*: 66–80. San Francisco: Berrett Koehler.

Weick, K.E. (2009). *Making sense of the organization: The impermanent organization.* Southgate Chichester, UK: John Wiley & Sons.

Weick, K.E., & Sutcliffe, K.M. (2001). *Managing the unexpected: Assuring high performance in an age of complexity.* San Francisco, CA: Jossey-Bass.

Weick, K.E., & Sutcliffe, K.M. (2006). Mindfulness and the quality of organizational attention. *Organization Science, 17*(4), 514–524.

Weick, K.E., & Sutcliffe, K.M. (2007). *Managing the unexpected: Resilient performance in an age of uncertainty* (2nd ed.). San Francisco, CA: Jossey-Bass.

Weick, K.E., Sutcliffe, K.M., & Obstfeld, D. (1999). Organizing for high reliability: Processes of collective mindfulness. In B.M. Staw & L.L. Cummings (Eds.), *Research in organizational behavior* (Vol. 21, pp. 81–123). Greenwich, CT: JAI Press.

Weick, K.E., Sutcliffe, K.M., & Obstfeld, D. (2005). Organizing and the process of sensemaking. *Organization Science, 16*(4), 409–421.

Weisman, J., Chazan, G., & Power, S. (2010, May 28). Spill tops Valdez disaster, *Wall Street Journal,* p. A1.

Westrum, R. (1982). Social intelligence about hidden events. *Knowledge, 3*(3), 381–400.

Westrum, R. (1994). Thinking by groups, organizations, and networks: A sociologist's views of the social psychology of science and technology. In W.R. Shadish & S. Fuller (Eds.), *The social psychology of science* (pp. 329–342). New York: Guilford Press.

Wildavsky, A. (1991). *Searching for safety* (4th ed.). New Brunswick, NJ: Transaction.

Woods, D.D., Patterson, E.S., & Roth, E.M. (2002). Can we ever escape data overload? A cognitive systems diagnosis. *Cognition, Technology, & Work, 4*(1), 22–36.

Organizational Healing

A Relational Process to Handle Major Disruption

Edward H. Powley

Abstract

Disruptions to operational and organizational processes represent an important area of study for organizational scholars. Although scholars and practitioners have written much about prevention and post-crisis communication and management, this chapter focuses on how organizations heal. Organizational healing is a process that focuses on compassionate interpersonal relationships that enable action and which cumulatively restructure an organization after major harm and disruption. Both endogenous and exogenous factors facilitate organizational healing. Endogenous resources act as antibodies to strengthen organizational bonds, enable new connections, and promote protective measures against future threat; external resources include community support and institutional support from parent organizations that provide resources for organizations on the path of recovery. A key aspect for healing is an organization's capacity for discovering, developing, and cultivating positive connections. The chapter concludes with questions for future research.

Keywords: Organizational healing, interpersonal connection, compassion, structuration theory, disruption

Stark examples of disruption and crisis are reminders that, at times, organizational life is painful and rife with difficulty and distress (Frost, 2003). This is especially true because crises interrupt work, create ambiguity, and threaten important relationships at work. Disruptive events in organizations can take place anywhere and at any time. For example, Hurricane Katrina interrupted community services, university programs, the tourism industry, and other vital services in New Orleans. In war-torn areas, military units face a multitude of risks in security operations. Roadside and suicide bombings, resulting in post-traumatic stress and often death, cause distress in integrated military units (Powley & Taylor, 2010). To illustrate the challenges and difficulties of disruption from crises, consider two extreme examples: a suicide bombing and a shooting in an industrial plant in the United States.

What began as an orderly process to allow local civilians to pass through a crowded entry control point ended when a lone man detonated explosives strapped to his body. The blast killed several Marines and severely wounded nearly a dozen others. Military personnel had been processing civilians as usual that afternoon when the suicide bomber entered the checkpoint. Standing between the barriers, he raised his arms in preparation for a search when he triggered the explosive device. The blast radiated in front of him causing harm to those in close range. The senior enlisted leader, working alongside with his men that afternoon, noticed the nervous and agitated behavior of the apparent suicide bomber, and immediately positioned himself in front of one of his men to shield him from the blast. Although his act preserved the lives of several Marines, he lost his life. This particular unit's mission was to secure a small but significant city, but frustrations among unit members flared due to an overextended timetable, which meant they would return home several months after their scheduled departure. Now, with the death of one of their most important leaders, the unit risked losing its focus, leadership, and togetherness. Less experienced junior officers leading the various companies faced the challenge of maintaining a high-paced operational tempo to minimize any decrease in momentum as they completed their deployment. Moreover, the senior enlisted leader's loss threatened the organizational culture and the sense of stability and continuity he helped establish.

In 2003, one industrial plant experienced similar trauma:

> An assembly-line worker who had talked openly about shooting people walked out of an ethics and sensitivity training session at his factory [one] morning, returned [from the parking lot] moments later with a semiautomatic rifle and a shotgun, and opened fire, killing five coworkers before fatally shooting himself. . . . Dozens of workers at the Lockheed Martin aircraft parts plant ran screaming from the cavernous hilltop building . . . as the gunman, dressed in his usual black T-shirt and camouflage pants, but now wearing bandoliers full of extra shotgun shells slung across his chest, suddenly started blasting away at about 9:40 A.M. . . . When the police arrived minutes later, nine people had been wounded, one critically, in what was [one of] the nation's deadliest plant shooting[s]. (Halbfinger & Hart, 2003)

Among other traumatic incidents, difficult circumstances due to the economy, ethical problems of organizational leadership, and violence causing operational disruption significantly affect organizations. Although extreme, crisis in war is not unlike the trauma experienced in work organizations when rupture from normal operations occurs. Regardless of their intensity or severity, these types of incidents raise the following questions: How do organizational units not only manage crises but also heal from disruption? And, what does it mean to heal from such situations? When faced with crises, the kind that involve threat to human life and organizational functioning, mechanisms evolve to enable individuals and groups to weather the difficulty (Powley, 2009; Powley & Piderit, 2008). Recent high-profile disasters and crises (e.g., the September 11, 2001 terrorist attacks in the United States, earthquakes and tsunamis in Southeast Asia and Japan, Hurricane Katrina, the Haitian and Chilean earthquakes, and the like) generated interest for practitioners and scholars studying crisis communication and crisis management. The process of organizational healing complements crisis management

scholarship and practice by bringing together organizational scholarship, positive psychology, and social support processes that describe how social interactions mend an organization's social structure and repair operational routines (Powley & Cameron, 2006). Organizational healing represents an important contribution to positive organizational scholarship because it pays particular attention to the positive social dynamics inherent among individual organization members who face seemingly insurmountable challenges.

The purpose of this chapter is to describe the process of organizational healing and its outcomes for organizations, groups, or communities during and after major disruption, like the examples described above. Following a discussion of healing in the context of the organizational sciences, I articulate the endogenous and exogenous resources that enable healing and promote long-term recovery. The chapter continues with a discussion of the relationship between healing and an organization's capacity for connections, and concludes with a discussion of key questions for future research.

Literature Review
A Definition of Organizational Healing
Organizational healing is a kind of restoration after loss—with loss defined as any event that disrupts routines, structures, relationships between individuals, and an individual's life experience (Fazio & Fazio, 2005). I define organizational healing as a process of positive, enabling social interactions to restore and renew organization members' interpersonal connections and allow the organization to resume routines, practices, or operations. In one sense, healing is an organizing mechanism because it involves human action patterns (Weick, 1979) that create positive social interactions among organizational members; healing is about organizing those relationships to resume organizational functioning. The theoretical emphasis is on process, to show how structures and actions interrelate to create positive outcomes (Dutton et al., 2006). Social interaction at the group or organizational level intimates the collective nature of healing, which is consistent with war trauma studies (Ayalon, 1998; Jareg, 1995; Lumsden, 1997; Terr, 1991). Organizational healing, situated in the domain of relationship sciences (Dutton & Ragins, 2007; Kelley et al., 1983), refers to the actual work of repairing relationships and continuity in support of recovery of vital practices, routines, structures, and organizational functions (Powley & Cameron, 2006).

Organizational healing is associated somewhat with resilience (bouncing back) (Sutcliffe & Vogus, 2003), adaptation (adjusting to changes) (Cyert & March, 1963), hardiness (being tough, durable) (Maddi & Khoshaba, 2005), or recovery (movement from acute crisis to normalcy) (Petterson, 1999). Maddi and Khoshaba (2005) define hardiness as the capacity for toughness and durability. Hardiness refers to individual endurance, an individual characteristic, describing how well an individual might handle setbacks with poise and manage difficult conditions. Toxin handlers (Frost, 2003), as examples of hardiness, facilitate endurance when they help people endure experiences of negative emotions in the workplace. In short, they possess the capacity to help people cope with difficulty. Healing is also related to resilience. Resilience is a latent capacity of both individuals and organizations; it exists before any trauma occurs and translates into the capacity to bounce back from untoward events and the ability to withstand setbacks (Sutcliffe & Vogus, 2003). In contrast though, healing is an active process involving social interaction that unfolds after crises to enable the restoration of critical relationships.

Healing is closely associated with recovery, but is also conceptually distinct. Recovery is a long-term process measured in months, years, or decades (Mitchell, 1996), and it may involve dealing with a number of setbacks, whereas healing occurs early and in fairly short order and focuses specifically on an acute incident. Healing leads to restoration of routines and functions immediately following setbacks, whereas recovery is about systems functioning (Mitchell, 1996) *after* healing occurs. Healing is a short-term process that begins immediately following crisis, in the critical period after crisis, and is measured in hours, days, or weeks (Powley, 2009; Stein, 2004). Moreover, whereas recovery deals with functional operability, systemic concerns, and organizational processes, healing is about repairing social dynamics and processes, and attending to the immediate needs of affected groups and individuals. As such, the process of healing repairs an organization's social fabric and affords subsequent strengthening as the organization moves from a wounded state toward a condition of strength, thus enabling longer-term recovery.

Healing occurs during and immediately following the critical period of crisis (Stein, 2004), during a liminal state, or a space between past and future, and between organizational states (Powley, 2009; Powley & Cameron, 2006; Turner, 1967). During this time, existing social structures such as roles, positions, status, and responsibility temporarily suspend established interactions, practices, and relationships. Immediate safety concerns and attention toward others as human beings receive higher priority over operational processes. An organization's response and actions taken by key organizational stakeholders influence the healing process. For example, dysfunctional, destructive, and potentially vengeful actions inhibit healing, yet actions encouraging connection, opportunities to help those affected, and organizational efforts to restore organizational processes engender healing.

Using disciplined imagination as a framework (Weick, 1989), wound healing in medicine (Schilling, 1968) serves as a metaphor for the process of organizational healing, which takes places in three stages (see Powley & Piderit, 2008). First, we recognize *inflammation*. After an acute moment or drawn-out crisis, healing begins with intense focus and attention on the crisis at hand (swelling), heightened emotions related to role ambiguity and the unknown (tenderness), and concern for others and the well-being of the organization (sensitivity). Just as blood and coagulants rush to the site of a wound to protect it and provide necessary resources, individuals and groups show a high degree of interest in the crisis location. This is demonstrated when organization members prioritize individuals in need of urgent care and minimize recriminations—the organizations attends to those most needing help.

Next, we observe *proliferation*. After the initial reaction at the crisis site, interpersonal connections, like connective tissue, begin to proliferate to reestablish lost or damaged relationships. This is demonstrated when organization members foster positive connections and improvise organizational routines. The final stage is *remodeling*. Organization members look forward to strengthening relationship ties, thus remodeling and reshaping the relationships in the organization, in the same way a wound closes up and, despite potential scar tissue, is ready for basic functioning. This is demonstrated when organization members strengthen family-like bonds and initiate ceremonies and rituals that create a sense of closure.

The process of healing is not limited to social dynamics among organization members; rather, the pattern of healing permits the organization to resume routines and practices that further promote longer-term recovery. This may include coordinating mechanisms, such as meetings and strategy sessions to deal with questions and concerns about an incident, or engaging with internal and external stakeholders to share information or seek help to restore operations. Embedded in the process of healing are the deployment of and access to internal organizational resources and external support and help.

Disruption and Crisis

Healing occurs in the context of disruption and crisis. It departs somewhat from the normative management processes of emergency crisis to enable recovery from crisis. Healing is about what occurs *after* individuals are safe and secure, and the crisis is being managed. That is, healing begins after police, fire, and emergency medical teams leave the scene, have secured the situation, and the initial moment of crisis has passed. Metaphorically, crisis management might be summarized as getting to the hospital in an ambulance, whereas healing refers to processes beginning in the emergency room that initiate focused patient care.

Workplace disruption comes in multiple and unique forms, each requiring expertise, although discernible patterns cut across crises and offer a potentially rich way to understand how organizations heal. Definitions for crisis and disaster vary widely in the scholarly literature (Britton, 1986; Creamer, Buckingham, & Burgess, 1991; Norris, Friedmans, Watson, Bryne, Diaz, & Kaniasty, 2002b; Rosenthal, Charles, & t'Hart, 1989). Britton (1986) reviewed a broad range of definitions and called for a more rigorous differentiation of various kinds of disaster situations. Disasters represent "widespread and near-complete disruption of ALL social processes, social structures, and primary/secondary interactions," whereas emergencies are "disruptions interfering with ongoing activities of specific people involved," and accidents are disruptions affecting a specific interest group of victims (Britton, 1986, p. 267). Despite Britton's call for more rigor, other researchers have defined disaster more broadly as "overwhelming events that test the adaptational responses of communities or individuals beyond their capability, and result in massive disruption to normal functioning" (Creamer et al., 1991, p. 99; see also Rapheal, 1986). Definitions such as these do not provide a nuanced view of disaster and crisis situations, but they do provide a general framework in which to situate disruptive action.

The crisis management literature tends to examine prevention and management of crisis (LaLonde, 2007). Psychologists place emphasis on the traumatic impact of victims (Katz et al., 2002; McNally, et al.,

2003) and focus on immediate responses. For example, crisis management is about mobilization: ensuring that severely affected individuals receive emergency care, securing buildings from physical threat, removing others in proximity to safety, and providing materials (fire trucks, ambulances, and the like). Historically, scholars highlight causal factors and systemic interrelationships inherent in disasters (Meyer, 1982; Vaughan, 1996, 1999; Snook, 2000); anticipation, prevention, management of, and processes to mitigate potential crises are common themes in high-reliability organization research (Weick & Sutcliffe, 2001; Weick, Sutcliffe, & Obstfeld, 1999). Research and practice in this field concentrates on normative processes of organizational design and structure, policies, and communication strategies (Pauchant & Mitroff, 1990; Rosenthal et al., 1989; Shrivastva, 1987).

Frameworks for Organizational Healing

Organizational healing incorporates research on positive relationships in groups and organizations (Cameron, Dutton, & Quinn, 2003; Dutton & Ragins, 2007). Extant research on workplace recovery (Marks, 1995) explores specific themes and offers new insight on how social relationships among organization members enable recovery in times of crisis. This is particularly important since the majority of research on disaster scenarios and tragedy deals primarily with recovery of critical systems and functions, and less on the social connections that make up affected organizations (Weick, 2003). Organizational healing draws from three theoretical domains: compassion organizing, relationship sciences, and structuration theory. These scholarly domains represent guideposts to study healing after disruption. They inform theoretical analysis of organizational healing and raising potential research questions.

COMPASSION ORGANIZING

Compassion organizing (Dutton et al., 2006) explains the spontaneity of a compassionate response to crises. Compassion, which is more than empathy and sympathy, involves the three active processes of feeling, noticing, and responding (Kanov et al., 2004). That is, more than seeing and feeling another's pain, compassion is action-oriented (von Dietze & Orb, 2000), and is an inborn desire to reach out to others needing social support (Weingarten, 2003). When work colleagues face crises in organizational life, difficult emotions emerge and must be dealt with for healing to occur (Boyatzis et al., 2004;

Frost, 2003). Positive emotions in compassionate responses activate positive emotions that enable positive individual, group level, and organizational outcomes.

INTERPERSONAL CONNECTIONS

Organizational healing involves interpersonal connections that restore important relationships in organizations. Connections are the basis of relationships in organizational life (Dutton & Ragins, 2007) and therefore the restoration of connections has the potential to enable healing of social units. When dealing with hurt or pain, individuals tend to turn toward each other in a supportive and caring manner indicative of high degrees of social support (Fazio & Fazio, 2005). Research on communities and social groups in difficult experiences suggest that positive relationships in communities are necessary to ensure their viability (Ayalon, 1998; Blatt & Camden, 2007; McGinn, 2007). Scholars studying effects of war on families and communities agree that healing is not a solitary or individual task; rather, healing, as relationship-based activity, always requires social intervention and collective support, either from those within the community or external agencies (see Ayalon, 1998; Jareg, 1995; Lumsden, 1997; Terr, 1991). Blatt and Camden (2007) studied temporary workers and found that their workplace affiliation derived primarily from positive relationships with other temporaries. Through swift "positive in-the-moment connections," they created a sense of community. Likewise, McGinn's (2007) analysis of San Pedro dock workers suggests that positive communities, based on networks of supportive relationships, serve as one indicator of membership and belonging.

STRUCTURATION THEORY

Finally, structuration theory, a third framework to understand how healing is accomplished in disruption, emphasizes the dual nature of human agency and structure, in which organization members reproduce their social structure as they share and legitimize the meaning of everyday experiences and interactions (Giddens, 1982)—actions and interactions being "both a reflection and revision of the social order" (Meyerson, 1994). In this way, organizations are remade (Barley & Tolbert, 1997) as social structures resume through the actions and interactions of individual agents. Central to this perspective is the role of social relations among individual actors: how they interact, the types of relationships they form, and the extent to which the quality of

their relations affects the process of structuration and the quality of healing that follows. Structure, action, and agency enable the process of healing in the social architecture by restoring basic organizing routines and relationships within an organization.

Endogenous and Exogenous Resources

Workplace relationships, operations, routines, and practices have a high probability of severing due to crisis or major transition because they significantly alter established relationship patterns. In these situations, various sources of support are critical to enable the organization and its members to heal from crisis. In the examples above, military units or for-profit organizations face similar challenges and opportunities. They draw upon established relationships or reach outward for support to meet critical needs. Embedded military units must draw on the social support provided by their immediate group of soldiers, but they also rely on staff support back home to support their operational needs.

What these examples suggest is that healing requires both endogenous and exogenous resources. Endogenous resources, or enablers, internal to the organization promote healing and growth from within; exogenous resources, or external interventions, aid healing from beyond an organization's boundaries. Endogenous resources include elements internal to the organization that activate the rebuilding of social connections in disrupted organizations. These include social processes, actions by leaders, or interactions emerging from individuals and groups working together to support and help one another. Entities outside the organization provide exogenous resources to support organizational processes, as well as individuals and groups needing special help.

Exogenous resources may include networked stakeholders who come to an organization's aid, community support mechanisms offered to the organizations (e.g., Red Cross, and the like), and interventions that recognize and empathize with affected organizational units (e.g., counseling services). Exogenous and endogenous resources work in a coordinated and combinatory fashion. The type of resources and connections, however, are qualitatively different, thus adding to the available set of possible resources. External agents and service providers may be important in the inflammation phase—synonymous with medication, bandages, or health care provider actions. The availability of resources to deploy may be important in the proliferation phase—synonymous with ambulances, hospital availability, or colleague support after an injury.

Three sources of endogenous and exogenous resources include the coordination of safety, providing compassion, and establishing connections. These resources enable interpersonal connections and compassionate support for affected parties, and provide the structures necessary to maintain continuity and restore essential routines and processes. Individuals connect with colleagues, multiply connections with others, and strengthen existing relationships both inside and outside the organization; those interpersonal relationships begin to mend (Dutton, 2003). Underlying each of these sources of help is an organization's capacity for positive social connections.

COORDINATE SAFETY

A prominent feature of the inflammation stage of healing, individual employees and organizational leaders quickly recognize the immediate effects of crisis and then refocus energy and attention to deal with primary concerns, simultaneously providing support and supplying needed resources. Specifically, they coordinate action related to the physical security and safety of organization members. Within crises, finding safety is achieved most likely first from those also experiencing the incident, then from those outside the organization who are called upon to help. The expediency for resolution prompts organizational leaders and those close to the incident to demonstrate concern for colleagues and others in need, increase the speed of decision-making on critical issues (Haas, 1977), and therefore secure the safety of organization members. The goal is to secure exposed individuals or groups and know work colleagues' whereabouts relative to the incident. Coordinated efforts enable fellow victims to strengthen bonds through the shared experience and achieve a sense of safety.

In the example of the suicide bombing, the first reaction was to secure others in the unit. This occurred as individuals checked in with senior leaders and ensured their people's safety. In a university shooting incident (Powley, 2009), personnel accounted for each other through phone trees or other established mechanisms. A counselor activated a network of resident hall assistants and thereby mobilized them to respond to specific questions and issues. These initial connections internally served as a primary way to ensure and retain a sense of stability amid crisis. Simply knowing where people were assured others that the organization was intact.

From an external position, those providing help send a secure message to victims: We are here to help, and we have the needed physical resources to make that happen. Exogenous resources may include parent organization support, community partnerships, police, and emergency medical personnel who offer and provide needed support (sometimes unexpectedly). These organizational bodies provide initial help to secure individuals' safety. Critical to their ability to succeed are the coordinating mechanisms that often exist between internal leaders and external service providers. These mechanisms might include joint planning, pre-crisis drills, or the development of integrated crisis management and communication plans. Coordinating mechanisms then are deployed during an incident (as in the examples above), although often the plans resemble actionable templates for an emergent process dictated by particular nuances of the unique crisis situation. From a structuration theory perspective, safety and security action develops as agents respond to situational needs. In summary, coordinating mechanisms connecting endogenous and exogenous sources of help structure action that enables safety and security of organization members in the midst of crisis.

PROVIDE COMPASSION

Crisis events create fear and anxiety for individuals, and therefore an empathetic and compassionate response is critical to dealing with the potentially high degree of negative affect (Dutton et al., 2006). Crisis research in psychology has tended to emphasize post-traumatic stress disorder triggered by seeing or experiencing disturbing acts, feeling pain and anxiety, and dealing with loss (Norris, Friedmans, & Watson, 2002; Norris et al., 2002). Crisis induces undesirable psychological effects, and chances for frustration and recrimination increase. In response, work colleagues from within may work together to counteract negative effects that require time and positive relationships. For example, organization members share their anxiety, discuss fears, or express feelings and emotions about safety and security. It is critical that multiple, optional opportunities are provided for individuals to share pain, demonstrate compassion, and thereby decrease anxiety (Herman, 1997; Kahn, 2001; Pennebaker & Harber, 1993; Swatton & O'Callaghan, 1999). Moreover, sharing fosters attachments because of the highly affective quality coupled with the significant common experience.

Exogenous sources of care and compassion serve as an additional resource to respond to fear and anxiety. In cases in which exposure to trauma is significant, offers of support from external agencies for counseling provide forums for individuals and groups to work through the pain and distress of the incident. For example, after the September 11, 2001 terrorist attacks, offers of support flooded New York to help affected workplaces, families, and neighborhoods. The Red Cross and other providers offered opportunities to share their experiences collectively. An employee assistance program may serve this function as well. Opportunities for debriefing and access to counseling and professional help have the power to alleviate stress. The aim of outside resources is to mitigate the effects of post-traumatic stress, relieve stress of physical harm, and ensure that the most affected receive proper and adequate care.

Three active elements of compassion (feeling, noticing, and responding; Kanov et al., 2004) represent endogenous and exogenous resources. Care and compassion by those witnessing the events potentially diminish the ill effects produced by the crisis. For example, the organization may offer alternative work schedules or adjust deadlines. In environments in which operational tempo is expected to remain constant, adjusting work schedules and shifts or temporary reassignments could alleviate possible stress. These compassionate responses are action-oriented (von Dietze & Orb, 2000) and provide a way to extend social support and reduce fear and anxiety (Weingarten, 2003) for organization members. To accomplish healing at the organizational unit level requires specific actions, social interactions, and compassionate responses on the part of individuals, leaders, and groups of individuals to coordinate their activity to restore routines, structures, social continuity, roles, responsibilities, and relationships.

ESTABLISH CONNECTIONS

Crises and disruptions temporarily suspend an organization's work and social interaction patterns and give way to new structures (Turner, 1967, 1969). Basic relationship norms shift to allow for a new kind of equality at a human level (Turner, 1967). Several scholars highlight how triggering events shift perceptions of relationships and norms (Perrow, 1999; Shrivastva, 1987; Weick, 1990). Weick suggests that the newly enacted situation often intensifies crisis (Weick, 1988), but this structural shift is more nuanced, in that within the new situation are seeds for new relationships. Instead of intensifying the crisis, new relational forms open pathways for creating bonds to reduce fear and anxiety as individuals turn toward each other and thus fulfill basic social and affiliation needs (de Waal, 1996).

Fulfillment of such needs is an endogenous factor that involves finding others, making contact with them, and clinging to any relationship that provides a sense of stability and belonging (Ashmos & Duchon, 2000). New and emerging connections provide initial structure for organizations that then build longer-lasting routines. Connecting in this way with others during and after major disruption is a social support mechanism (Fazio & Fazio, 2005) that enables attachment and closeness (Kahn, 2001). Moreover, attachments across boundaries support ongoing organizational tasks even amid disruption.

Additionally, connections made with external individuals or organizations serves a similar purpose. Exogenous resources include critical information for survival and future functioning unknown to those embedded in the crisis. Even beyond connections made in the immediate perimeter of the crisis event, additional parties (city officials, supporting government offices, humanitarian and first-responder organizations) may provide support to the organization indirectly. Those indirect channels of support make important resources available, including social, psychological, and material aid (i.e., financial and physical). Organizations draw on these resources to deal with immediate concerns, such as helping with counseling and responding to questions about security, and to rebuild organizational infrastructures, such as repairing damaged property. Therefore, new situational structures enable new patterns of interpersonal connection that begin to reassemble a sense of order and continuity. Making connections with others (internal or external to the incident), and thus sharing information across spatial and functional boundaries, reduces fear, anxiety, and ambiguity.

Connective Capacity

Coordination, compassion, and connection reflect an organizational capacity embedded in a system of social interactions. Healing, as an organizing process, rests on the ability to foster positive social connections and to encourage the needed support internally and externally. Organizational capacity for connections that enable healing involves three characteristics: cohesion, flexibility, and interrelatedness. *Cohesion* is the degree to which organization members' relations come together, form bonds, and connect emotionally (Mooney, 2009). In the language of Gittell and her colleagues (2006), cohesion is the essence of "positive social relationships." *Flexibility* involves individualized, human agency (rather than institutionalized processes) to support and help those affected by adverse events; it is inherent in a compassionate response to trauma and distress. In this sense, to adapt flexibly amid disruption means to extend options. Sutcliffe and Vogus (2003) refer to this as positive adaptive capacities (a central theme of psychological resilience). *Interrelatedness* between external and internal parties reflects the interdependent interactions among individuals, groups, and larger units within organizational or ecological systems.

Structuration theory provides one explanation for how connective capacity aids organizational healing. Foremost is the role of human agency to reshape and restore an organization and its basic functions. In so doing, the internal structure of relationships takes shape, and through agents' action, organization members are able to remake the social connections necessary for coordinating and organizing new routines and practices. Both the structure and dynamics of interpersonal relationships are important (Dutton & Ragins, 2007; Giddens, 1982): Individuals join, draw strength from one another, reestablish and create new connections, and allow the emergence of redundant communication patterns in the informal and formal social interaction networks. These actions prompt a loosening of previously constricted information and relationship ties, especially as people communicate across functional and organizational boundaries (Sutcliffe & Vogus, 2003). Moreover, the heightened emotional tone in the organization subsides as individuals resume their work and daily routines, help close communication gaps, and complete work tasks unfinished because of the crisis. The "undoing" of an organization that is caused by the crisis is now tempered with calls for action to maintain order as agents act together to reproduce necessary structures and routines through the emergent social structure that a crisis precipitates. The crisis ultimately resolves through structural transformation, either as healthy, new structures and relationships (the topic of this chapter) or as severe, irreparable damage.

Healing restores social functions even though organizational processes and structures are modified. Relational structures foster cohesion between organization members, which enables close communal ties, filial bonds, or high quality connections (Dutton & Heaphy, 2003). Individualized responses (through alternatives and options) demonstrate flexibility. Connections across boundaries (internal to external) that link unlikely pairs or groups facilitate interrelatedness among organizational units and relationships throughout the system.

Contribution

This chapter provides a nuanced perception that there are "positive implications buried somewhere in the tragedies" (Weick, 2003, p. 68). Healing adds to what we know about compassion organizing: The focus in compassion organizing is the confluence of resources necessary to organize a compassionate response. Healing is about a process of rejoining social connections, and additionally explains how compassion organizing can take place in disruption. The social element of compassion organizing is about the role that interpersonal connection plays to enable an empathetic response.

In the domain of relationship science (Berscheid, 1999) and high quality connections (Dutton, 2003; Dutton & Heaphy, 2003), organizational healing emphasizes the study of interpersonal connections. It unites anthropological conceptions of time and space (liminality) with empathic responses to trauma (compassion). This work also draws out the nonrational and emotional aspects of networks and connection (Mooney, 2009), which have followed primarily a rational, instrumental paradigm (Burt, 1997, 1992; Granovetter, 1973). Like recent work on compassion in organizational life (Dutton et al. 2006; Frost, 2003), organizational healing acknowledges the presence of painful realities amid emergency crises and thus helps to "fill a gap in the organizational literature that often fails to portray organizations as human institutions" (Kanov et al., 2004, p. 810). This research domain addresses the positive side of trauma in discussions of appreciation, care, and comfort as facilitators for dealing with difficulty (Janoff-Bulman, 1992; Janoff-Bulman & Berger, 2000; Tennen & Affleck, 1999; Tedeschi & Calhoun, 1995, 1996).

Organizational healing also affords additional contributions and outcomes consistent with the endogenous and exogenous resources needed to replenish organizational routines and operational processes.

Little Inclination to Blame

When healing goes well, individuals find fewer instances of recrimination. Healing supports and enables other organization members rather than negatively targeting those responsible. This does not mean that perpetrators are absolved from due process and personal responsibility, but that victims (intended or not) are less inclined to seek adverse, mean-spirited retribution. When organization members focus attention on work processes and routines, they are less likely to be consumed with matters associated with blame and frustration. Blame and retribution are counterintuitive in warfare though, but these may be attenuated somewhat with respect to organizational relationships (within the unit and command, as well as at higher levels of a military organization).

Predominant Focus on Others over Self
Whereas self-absorption tends to isolate affected individuals, urgent care is aimed toward the most affected. Focusing on others is associated with the inflammation stage of healing. Selfless acts replace self-protection—a reflection of the priority placed on individual needs—and organizational units ensure that their members are accounted for, so that the integrity of the whole is not compromised. When individuals focus on others, they are more inclined to provide compassion and offer support to affected individuals. This element of the healing process ensures the safety and security of individuals.

Development of High Quality Connections
Along with a predominant focus on others—a key element of the proliferation stage of healing—organization members have greater potential to establish deeper ties with each other and external to the organization. Characterized as positive regard and a sense of mutuality, high quality connections have the potential to strengthen existing and emergent relationships among organization members (Dutton & Heaphy, 2003). As they feel supported, they desire to be with each other and share personal experiences, both individually and in groups. Opportunities to share experiences and show empathy enable organizational units to mend ties between department members and beyond. In some cases, relationships across functional boundaries and outside of the organization emerge.

Adaptive Organizational Routines and Practices
At the organizational level, leaders may modify employment practices to adapt to specific employee needs as healing unfolds. Adaptation is a key aspect of the remodeling phase of healing. Such adaptation makes it possible to alter work routines and offer flexibility for how work is accomplished during and immediately after a disruptive incident. When organizations adjust policies and procedures, they enable social relations to mend rather than create potential friction between the organization and its people.

Emphasis on Building a Positive Organizational Culture
Aspects of organizational culture, often hidden but brought to the surface in crisis, may signal opportunities to engage organization members, bring them together, and identify themselves with their common purpose and a common set of assumptions, values, and rituals. Social gatherings, so vital for high quality connections, foster and reinforce a positive organizational culture that acts as a binding agent—another element of the remodeling phase. Culture itself structures current and future action to encourage and foster improved routines and organizational processes as the crisis event subsides.

Power of Ritual and Ceremony
Rituals and ceremonies reinforce a sense of community and encourage individual members to be optimistic and oriented toward the future. Ceremonies celebrate moments in human life and death, often carrying with them sensitivity for others' positive and negative emotions (Beyer & Trice, 1987; Turner, 1967). Engaging in ritual, rites, and ceremonies throughout the healing process attenuates tension, fears, negative emotions, and ambiguities in order to provide a sense of continuity amid disruption. They help reestablish a sense of peace, stability, and order; moreover, rituals serve as a holding space for organization members to grieve, to regroup, and to reorient themselves toward the future (Kahn, 2001).

Future Directions
Healing as an organizational construct and as an approach to post-crisis relief promises to be an important field of research. Opportunities for empirical research in organizational systems that have faced intense challenges are many. Examining and differentiating the role and dynamics of both endogenous and exogenous resources in the different phases of healing is a first step: What do social networks of internal and external organizational systems look like during disruption? What matters most for healing? Do internal or external resources predict organization success through crisis? These questions and others offered here suggest a potential research agenda in this field.

Organizational healing depends on several dimensions. The magnitude and severity of crises—whether one examines a special forces unit in wartime or a company faced with deadlines due to inclement weather, natural disasters (e.g., volcanoes, floods, or hurricanes), or human error or terrorist activity (e.g., car bombs, suicide attacks, or failure to pay attention to critical systems issues)—will determine the outcomes of crisis. Timing, duration, and scale of individual and organizational actions also need consideration. More severe "injuries" causing major disruption will, of course, require immediate and more direct action to enable healing to occur. The time it takes for an organization to emerge from the liminal period can vary dramatically depending on the extent to which the healing process begins right away or is delayed.

A number of organizations experience major change and trauma but may not fully recover. The key question here is: What is strengthened after crisis? Moreover, what outcomes are important to examine with respect to healing? That is, how does one know whether an organization has "healed?" Organizations or their subunits may hobble along, with compromised health, optimizing their situation the best they can and thereby place stress on other parts of the organization. Healing may not always imply strength, but may result in deformed structures and organizational forms. Therefore, does a "fully" recovered organization relieve stress or pressure from other units? In addition, is it able to improve the quality of life for organization members and its stakeholders? Effects of the crisis may be ever present despite resultant changes, and healing may not be not automatic. Perhaps the important part of healing and future recovery takes place after all the attention is gone and the organization is left to address lingering issues.

Finally, the practical implications of healing offer additional opportunities to examine how to handle disruption in organizations when it occurs. Emergency crises allow organizations to activate their capacity for a wide range of social connections, the possibility to see novel distinctions (Langer & Moldoveanu, 2000), and to understand the capacity for organizations to adapt and flex under pressure. Wildavsky (1988) suggests that organizations ought to develop ways to test their adaptational capacity. Organizational scholars might ask how leaders should manage the aftermath of serious disruptive events: To what degree do organizations cohere in crisis? To what degree do individuals and groups within the system adapt and flex in such incidents? To what degree do groups and departments collectively interrelate across boundaries? Responses to these questions form the basis of a potentially interesting and insightful body of research.

Conclusion

Healing is a coordinated effort by individuals working together to restore harmony, security, and integrity to others, as well as to routines and structures. Therefore, a healed organization is one that has become whole, such that the underlying social tissue or the vital organizational relationships are renewed and restored, and the organization is enabled to resume its operations. This chapter presents a framework for understanding organizational healing and opens the potential for future opportunities to study healing in organizations.

References

Ashmos, D.P., & Duchon, D. (2000). Spirituality at work: A conceptualization and measure. *Journal of Management Inquiry, 9*(2), 134–145.

Ayalon, O. (1998). Community healing for children traumatized by war. *International Review of Psychiatry, 10*, 224–233.

Barley, S.R., & Tolbert, P.S. (1997). Institutionalization and structuration: Studying the links between action and institution. *Organization Studies, 18*(1), 93–117.

Berscheid, E. (1999). The greening of the relationship science. *American Psychologist, 54*(4), 260–266.

Beyer, J.M., & Trice, H.M. (1987). How an organization's rites reveal its culture. *Organizational Dynamics, 15*: 5–24.

Blatt, R., & Camden, C.T. (2007). Positive relationships and cultivating community. In J.E. Dutton & B.R. Ragins (Eds.), *Exploring positive relationships at work: Building a theoretical and research foundation* (pp. 243–264). New Jersey: Lawrence Erlbaum Associates.

Boyatzis, R.E., Bilimoria, D., Godwin, L., Hopkins, M., & Lingham, T. (2004). Effective leadership in extreme crisis. In Y. Neria, R. Gross, R. Marshall, & E. Susser (Eds.), *9/11: Public health in the wake of terrorist attacks.* New York: Cambridge University Press.

Britton, N.R. (1986). Developing an understanding of disaster. *Australian and New Zealand Journal of Sociology, 22*(2), 254–271.

Burt, R.S. (1992). *Structural holes: The social structure of competition.* Cambridge, MA: Harvard University Press.

Burt, R.S. (1997). The contingent value of social capital. *Administrative Science Quarterly, 42*(2), 339–366.

Cameron, K.S., Dutton, J.E., & Quinn, R.E. (Eds.). (2003). *Positive organizational scholarship: Foundations of a new discipline.* San Francisco, CA: Berrett-Koehler.

Creamer, M., Buckingham, W.J., & Burgess, P.M. (1991). A community based mental health response to a multiple shooting. *Australian Psychologist, 26*(2), 99–102.

Cyert, R.M., & March, J.G. (1963). *A behavioral theory of the firm.* Englewood Cliffs, NJ: Prentice Hall.

de Waal, F. (1996). *Good natured: The origins of right and wrong in humans and other animals.* Cambridge, MA: Harvard University Press.

Dutton, J.E. (2003). *Energize your workplace: How to create and sustain high quality connections at work.* San Francisco, CA: Jossey-Bass.

Dutton, J.E., & Heaphy, E.D. (2003). The power of high quality connections. In K.S. Cameron, J.E. Dutton, & R.E. Quinn (Eds.), *Positive organizational scholarship: Foundations of a new discipline* (pp. 263–278). San Francisco, CA: Berrett-Koehler.

Dutton, J.E., & Ragins, B.R. (Eds.). (2007). *Exploring positive relationships at work: Building a theoretical and research foundation.* New Jersey: Lawrence Erlbaum Associates.

Dutton, J.E., Worline, M.C., Frost, P.J., & Lilius, J.M. (2006). Explaining compassion organizing. *Administrative Science Quarterly, 51*, 59–96.

Fazio, R.J., & Fazio, L.M. (2005). Growth through loss: Promoting healing and growth in the face of trauma, crisis, and loss. *Journal of Loss and Trauma, 10*, 221–252.

Frost, P.J. (2003). *Toxic emotions at work: How compassionate managers handle pain and conflict.* Boston: Harvard University Press.

Giddens, A. (1982). *Profiles and critiques in social theory.* Berkeley, CA: University of California Press.

Gittell, J.H., Cameron, K.S., Lim, S., & Rivas, V. (2006). Relationships, layoffs, and organizational resilience: Airline industry responses to September 11th. *Journal of Applied Behavioral Science, 42*(3), 300–329.

Granovetter, M. (1973). The strength of weak ties. *American Journal of Sociology, 78*, 1360–1380.

Haas, J.E., Kates, R.W., & Bowden, M.J. (Eds.). (1977). *Reconstruction following disaster.* Cambridge, MA: MIT Press.

Halbfinger, D.M., & Hart, A. (2003, July 8). Man kills 5 co-workers at plant and himself. *The New York Times*, p. A1.

Herman, J. (1997). *Trauma and recovery: The aftermath of violence—from domestic abuse to political terror.* New York: Basic Books.

Janoff-Bulman, R. (1992). *Shattered assumptions: Towards a new psychology of trauma.* New York: Free Press.

Janoff-Bulman, R., & Berger, A.R. (2000). The other side of trauma: Towards a psychology of appreciation. In J.H. Harvey & E.D. Miller (Eds.), *Loss and trauma: General and close relationship perspectives.* (pp. 29–44). Philadelphia: Brunner-Routledge.

Jareg, E. (1995, May 18–19). *Main guiding principles for the development of psychological interventions for children affected by war.* Paper presented at the ISCA Workshop, Stockholm, Sweden.

Kahn, W.A. (2001). Holding environments at work. *Journal of Applied Behavioral Science, 37*(3), 260–279.

Kanov, J.M., Maitlis, S., Worline, M.C., Dutton, J.E., Frost, P.J., & Lilius, J.M. (2004). Compassion in organizational life. *American Behavioral Scientist, 47*(6), 808–827.

Katz, C.L., Pellegrino, L., Pandya, A., Ng, A., & DeLisi, L.E. (2002). Research on psychiatric outcomes and interventions subsequent to disasters: A review of the literature. *Psychiatry Research, 110*(3), 201–217.

Kelley, H.H., Berscheid, E., Christensen, A., Harvey, J.H., Huston, T.L., Levinger, G. et al. (Eds.). (1983). *Close relationships.* New York: W.H. Freeman and Company.

LaLonde, C. (2007). The potential contribution of the field of organizational development to crisis management. *Journal of Contingencies and Crisis Management, 15*(2), 95–104.

Langer, E., & Moldoveanu, M. (2000). The construct of mindfulness. *Journal of Social Issues, 56*(1), 1–9.

Lumsden, M. (1997). Breaking the cycle of violence: Are "communal therapies" a means of healing shattered selves. *Journal of Peace Research, 34*(4), 377–383.

Maddi, S.R., & Khoshaba, D.M. (2005). *Resilience at work.* New York: American Management Association.

Marks, M.L. (1995). Sustaining change: Creating the resilient organization. In D.A. Nadler, R.B. Shaw, A.E. Walton, & Associates (Eds.), *Discontinuous change: Leading organizational transformation* (pp. 97–117). San Francisco: Jossey-Bass.

McGinn, K.L. (2007). History, structure, and practices: San Pedro longshoremen in the face of change. In J.E. Dutton & B.R. Ragins (Eds.), *Exploring positive relationships at work: Building a theoretical and research foundation* (pp. 265–276). New Jersey: Lawrence Erlbaum Associates.

McNally, R.J., Bryant, R.A., & Ehlers, A. (2003). Does early psychological intervention promote recovery from posttraumatic stress? *Psychological Science in the Public Interest, 4*(2), 45–79.

Meyer, A.D. (1982). Adapting to environmental jolts. *Administrative Science Quarterly, 27*(4), 515–537.

Meyerson, D.E. (1994). Interpretations of stress in institutions: The cultural production of ambiguity and burnout. *Administrative Science Quarterly, 39*, 628–653.

Mitchell, J.K. (Ed.). (1996). *The long road to recovery: Community responses to industrial disaster.* Tokyo: United Nations University Press.

Mooney, C.G. (2009). *Theories of attachment: An introduction to Bowlby, Ainsworth, Gerber, Brazelton, Kennell, and Klaus.* St. Paul, MN: Redleaf Press.

Norris, F.H., Friedmans, M.J., & Watson, P., J. (2002). 60,000 disaster victims speak: Part II. Summary and implications of the disaster mental health research. *Psychiatry, 65*(3), 240–260.

Norris, F.H., Friedmans, M.J., Watson, P., J., Bryne, C.M., Diaz, E., & Kaniasty, K. (2002). 60,000 disaster victims speak: Part I. An empirical review of the empirical literature, 1981–2001. *Psychiatry, 65*(3), 207–239.

Pauchant, T.C., & Mitroff, I.I. (1990). Crisis management: Managing paradox in a chaotic world—The case of Bhopal. *Technological Forecasting and Social Change, 38*(2), 117–134.

Pennebaker, J.W., & Harber, K.D. (1993). A social stage model of collective coping: The Loma Prieta earthquake and the Persian Gulf War. *Journal of Social Issues, 49*(4), 125–145.

Perrow, C. (1999). *Normal accidents: Living with high-risk technologies.* Princeton, NJ: Princeton University Press.

Petterson, J. (1999). *A review of the literature and programs on local recovery from disaster.* Working Paper 102, Natural Hazards Research and Applications Information Center, Institute of Behavioral Science. Boulder, CO: University of Colorado.

Powley, E.H. (2009). Reclaiming resilience and safety: Resilience activation in the critical period of crisis. Human Relations, 62(9), 1289–1326.

Powley, E.H., & Cameron, K.S. (2006). Organizational healing: Lived virtuousness amidst organizational crisis. *Journal of Management, Spirituality, and Religion, 3*(1 & 2), 13–33.

Powley, E.H., & Piderit, S.K. (2008). Tending wounds: Elements of the organizational healing process. *Journal of Applied Behavioral Sciences, 44*(1), 134–149.

Powley, E.H., & Taylor, S.N. (2010). *Leading healing in a broken unit.* Washington, DC: NDU Center for Complex Operations.

Rapheal, B. (1986). *When disaster strikes.* London: Century Hutchinson.

Rosenthal, U., Charles, M.T., & t'Hart, P. (Eds.). (1989). *Coping with crisis: The management of disasters, riots, and terrorism.* Springfield, IL: Charles C.Thomas Publisher.

Schilling, J.A. (1968). Wound healing. *Physiological Reviews, 48*(2), 374–423.

Shrivastva, P. (1987). *Bhopal: Anatomy of a crisis.* Cambridge, MA: Ballinger.

Snook, S. (2000). *Friendly fire: The accidental shoot down of U.S. Black Hawks over Northern Iraq.* Princeton: Princeton University Press.

Stein, M. (2004). The critical period of disasters: Insights from sensemaking and psychoanalytic theory. *Human Relations, 57*(10), 1243–1261.

Sutcliffe, K.M., & Vogus, T.J. (2003). Organizing for resilience. In K.S. Cameron, J.E. Dutton, & R.E. Quinn (Eds.), *Positive organizational scholarship: Foundations of a new discipline* (pp. 94–110). San Francisco, CA: Berrett-Koehler.

Swatton, S., & O'Callaghan, J. (1999). The experience of "healing stories" in the life narrative: A grounded theory. *Counseling Psychology Quarterly, 12*(4), 413–429.

Tedeschi, R.G., & Calhoun, L.G. (1995). *Trauma and transformation: Growing in the aftermath of suffering.* Newbury Park, CA: Sage.

Tedeschi, R.G., & Calhoun, L.G. (1996). The posttraumatic growth inventory: Measuring the positive legacy of trauma. *Journal of Traumatic Stress, 9*(3), 455–472.

Tennen, H., & Affleck, G. (1999). Finding benefits in adversity. In C.R. Synder (Ed.), *Coping: The psychology of what works* (pp. 279–304). New York: Oxford University Press.

Terr, L.C. (1991). Childhood traumas: An outline and overview. *American Journal of Psychiatry, 148*(1), 10–20.

Turner, V.W. (1967). *The forest of symbols: Aspects of Ndembu ritual.* Ithaca NY: Cornell University Press.

Turner, V.W. (1969). *The ritual process: Structure and anti-structure.* Ithaca, NY: Cornell University Press.

Vaughan, D. (1996). *The challenger launch decision: Risky technology, culture, and deviance at NASA.* Chicago: University of Chicago Press.

Vaughan, D. (1999). The dark side of organizations: Mistake, misconduct, and disaster. *Annual Review of Sociology, 25*, 271–305.

von Dietze, E., & Orb, A. (2000). Compassionate care: A moral dimension of nursing. *Nursing Inquiry, 7*(3), 166–174.

Weick, K.E. (1979). *The social psychology of organizing.* New York: McGraw Hill.

Weick, K.E. (1988). Enacted sensemaking in crisis situations. *Journal of Management Studies, 25*(4), 305–317.

Weick, K.E. (1989). Theory construction as disciplined imagination. *Academy of Management Review, 14*(4), 516–531.

Weick, K.E. (1990). The vulnerable system: An analysis of the Tenerife air disaster. *Journal of Management, 16*(3), 571–593.

Weick, K.E. (2003). Positive organizing and organizational tragedy. In K.S. Cameron, J.E. Dutton, & R.E. Quinn (Eds.), *Positive organizational scholarship: Foundations of a new discipline* (pp. 66–80). San Francisco, CA: Berrett-Koehler.

Weick, K.E., & Sutcliffe, K.M. (2001). *Managing the unexpected: Assuring high performance in an age of complexity.* San Francisco: Jossey-Bass.

Weick, K.E., Sutcliffe, K.M., & Obstfeld, D. (1999). Organizing for high reliability: Processes of collective mindfulness. In R.I. Sutton & B.M. Staw (Eds.), *Research in organizational behavior* (Vol. 21, pp. 81–123). Stamford, CT: JAI Press.

Weingarten, K. (2003). *Common shock: Witnessing violence every day: How we are harmed, how we can heal.* New York: Penguin Group.

Wildavsky, A.B. (1988). *Searching for safety.* New Brunswick, NJ: Transaction Books.

Recovery

Nonwork Experiences That Promote Positive States

Sabine Sonnentag, Cornelia Niessen, *and* Angela Neff

Abstract

This chapter gives an overview of research on work-related recovery processes. Recovery can be conceptualized as a process that reverses the strain process and that restores well-being. The chapter focuses on the question of how recovery processes improve positive affective states, work engagement, and job performance. The chapter stresses that it may not only be important to gain distance from negative work experiences, but also to capitalize on positive work events and experiences.

Keywords: Recovery, restoration, positive affect, work engagement, job performance, proactive behavior, psychological detachment

From the perspective of positive organizational scholarship (POS), it is highly desirable that employees feel energetic and have enriching social relationships with others at work in order to achieve positive outcomes for themselves and for the organizations in which they work (Dutton & Heaphy, 2003; Quinn & Dutton, 2005). Of course, leadership processes and specific job design efforts play a crucial role in fostering energy and positive relationships in organizational contexts (Grant, 2008; Spreitzer, 2006). However, how employees feel and how they interact with others at work is not only influenced by processes happening during working time. Experiences and events during nonwork time play also an important role in employee affect and in social interactions within organizations. For example, affect experienced at home may have an impact on affect experienced at work (Rothbard, 2001). In this chapter, we focus on one specific aspect of the interface between nonwork and work; namely, recovery processes (i.e., processes related to affective and energetic restoration) occurring during nonwork time. We argue that such recovery processes play a crucial role for positive states and performance at work.

In the first two sections, we introduce the recovery concept and briefly summarize theoretical models that are relevant for recovery research. In the third section, we introduce recovery activities, recovery experiences, and sleep as the core processes relevant for recovery. The fourth section is the core part of this chapter and summarizes empirical findings on the association between recovery processes and positive outcomes, including positive affective states, motivational states, and job performance. In the final section, we highlight a number of questions that future research should address.

Recovery Concept

Generally, recovery is a concept that refers to the process of regaining something that has been lost and of returning to a former state. In the field of psychology and organizational behavior, recovery refers to restoration or regeneration processes by which negative states (e.g., fatigue) are reduced and positive states (e.g., vigor) are enhanced (Craig & Cooper, 1992; Meijman & Mulder, 1998). The basic idea is that high levels of these negative states and low levels of positive states originate from job-related events and processes, particularly from job stressors and effort expenditure associated with these stressors. For example, an employee who faces many hassles at work will need to spend a lot of effort to overcome these hassles and to uphold a high performance level despite these hassles (Hockey, 1997). As a consequence, this employee will experience negative affect (e.g., anger) and other strain symptoms (e.g., fatigue). During a work break or while home at night, when this employee is no longer facing these hassles, it is most likely that he or she recovers from his or her negative affect and the other strain symptoms. However, physical distance from the hassles might not be sufficient for recovery to occur. For example, continued rumination or worry about work-related hassles while at home might impede recovery, even when the hassles are no longer present in a physical sense (Brosschot, Gerin, & Thayer, 2006).

It is important to note that recovery does not only imply that negative states, such as anger or fatigue, are reduced. Recovery also implies that positive states, such as positive affect and vitality, increase (Sonnentag & Niessen, 2008). From the perspective of POS, these changes in positive states are particularly important because positive affect and vitality are related to well-being (Shirom, Toker, Berliner, Shapira, & Melamed, 2008), job performance (Carmeli, Ben-Hador, Waldman, & Rupp, 2009), and organizational citizenship behavior (OCB) Ilies, Scott, & Judge, 2006), and because they stimulate creativity and innovation behavior at work (Amabile, Barsade, Mueller, & Staw, 2005; Carmeli & Spreitzer, 2009).

Recovery can occur during various occasions, such as work breaks (Trougakos, Beal, Green, & Weiss, 2008), free evenings (Sonnentag, Binnewies, & Mojza, 2008), weekends (Fritz & Sonnentag, 2005), vacations (Westman & Eden, 1997), and sabbaticals (Davidson et al., 2010). It may even occur during short, informal microbreaks; for example, after finishing one task and before addressing the next (cf. Elsbach & Hargadon, 2006).

Theoretical Approaches
Several theoretical approaches refer to recovery process: the effort-recovery model (ERM; Meijman & Mulder, 1998), conservation of resources theory (COR; Hobfoll, 1989, 1998), and a more recent approach focusing on psychological resources (Trougakos & Hideg, 2009). These approaches have substantial overlap and should therefore be seen as complementary rather than opposing views on recovery.

The ERM departs from the core assumption of stress research that working, per se, requires that the working individual invests effort. This effort investment has to be particularly high when job stressors are present. Effort investment leads to strain reactions in the individual (e.g., fatigue). The ERM postulates that recovery (for example, during breaks and other periods of nonwork time) has to occur to reduce these strain reactions and to prevent long-term negative consequences for the individual's health and well-being. If no (or insufficient) recovery occurs, strain reactions may accumulate and result in negative long-term consequences, such as burnout and physical illnesses: When returning to work without being sufficiently recovered, even greater effort investment is necessary to meet work demands, and as a consequence, strain levels will further increase (Hockey, 1997).

The COR regards resources as crucial factors in human lives. Within COR, resources are defined as "objects, personal characteristics, conditions, or energies that are valued by the individual or that serve as a means for attainment of these objects, personal characteristics, conditions, or energies" (Hobfoll, 1989, p. 516). It is assumed that humans strive to gain and protect their resources; according to COR, stress occurs when resources are lost, when resources are threatened, and when resource investment does not lead to the gain of new resources. With respect to recovery processes, affective and energetic resources are particularly important. Similar to the assumptions of the ERM, COR predicts that working per se and particularly working under stressful conditions depletes affective and energetic resources, and that recovery is necessary to replenish these resources. Resource replenishment can occur by temporarily reducing stressors. In addition to what ERM predicts, COR states that resources can be (re-)gained not only by reducing stressors, but also by investing additional resources. Thus, whereas ERM focuses on the absence of negative factors (i.e., stressors) as the core prerequisite for recovery, COR includes also the presence of positive factors (i.e., resources) as an additional mechanism by which recovery can occur. For example, affective and energetic resources might be regained through positive social interactions.

By drawing on the ego depletion model (Muraven & Baumeister, 2000), Trougakos and Hideg (2009) argue that self-regulation (i.e., regulatory efforts when engaging in a task that one does not want to engage in, or when actively inhibiting a preferred or dominant behavior) depletes resources.

Importantly, because the ego depletion model postulates that all acts of self-regulation utilize one common resource, replenishment of resources can only occur by reducing the degree of self-regulation, irrespective of the specific task or target of self-regulation. According to Trougakos and Hideg, resource replenishment can occur by stopping working on tasks that deplete resources or by engaging in preferred behaviors that do not require the investment of self-regulatory resources. Thus, recovery occurs when one refrains from engaging in behaviors that drain resources or when one takes part in activities that one finds enjoyable and desirable and that therefore do not ask for any regulatory effort. Similar to the COR model, Trougakos and Hideg also argue that recovery may not only occur if stressors (and the associated need to self-regulate) are reduced, but also when regulatory resources are preserved by engaging in preferred and enjoyable activities.

In both the COR model and in Trougakos and Hideg's (2009) approach, resources play a core role: resources are important as they facilitate recovery processes, and an increase in resources indicates that recovery has occurred. This high relevance of resources resembles other models that emphasize the role of resources for individuals (e.g., job demands resources model; Bakker & Demerouti, 2007). Particularly, when focusing on personal resources (as opposed to job resources; Xanthopoulou, Bakker, Demerouti, & Schaufeli, 2007), an integration of the recovery models described above with the job demands resources model would be a logical next step in theory development on recovery.

Recovery Activities and Recovery Experiences

When examining in more detail the processes that help employees to recover from work, Sonnentag and Fritz (2007) suggested distinguishing between recovery activities and recovery experiences. Recovery activities refer to what a person is doing; recovery experiences refer to how a person is perceiving what he or she is doing.

Activities

Recovery activities are leisure time activities that have the potential to promote recovery. To examine which activities contribute to recovery, Sonnentag (2001) differentiated between activities with a high duty profile (i.e., obligatory activities) and activities with a potential for recovery. High-duty profile activities comprise activities such as job-related activities at home or household and childcare activities.

Activities with a potential for recovery are low-effort activities (e.g., reading a novel, relaxing at home), social activities (e.g., meeting friends), and sport and physical exercise. Similarly, in their study on the benefits of work break activities, Trougakos et al. (2008) differentiated between chores and more freely chosen respite activities. Chores included activities such as working with customers, running errands, practicing material, and preparing for an upcoming work period. Respite activities included napping, relaxing, and socializing.

Although the categories suggested by Sonnentag (2001) and Trougakos et al. (2008) make sense intuitively, the distinction between the various categories are less clear-cut. For example, although childcare is an obligatory category, specific childcare activities, such as playing with one's children, might contribute substantially to recovery. Moreover, voluntary work would be a typical activity with a high duty profile. Despite its obligatory nature, voluntary work activities have been shown to be related to recovery processes and other positive outcomes (Hecht & Boies, 2009; Mojza, Lorenz, Sonnentag, & Binnewies, 2010; Ruderman, Ohlott, Panzer, & King, 2002).

Sport and exercise belong to the most effective nonobligatory recovery activities. When employees spent time on sports and exercise after work, they generally felt better, more vigorous, and less depressed afterward, compared to evenings when they did not engage in sports or exercise (Rook & Zijlstra, 2006; Sonnentag, 2001; Sonnentag & Natter, 2004). These findings are in line with the broader research evidence on sports and exercise: People pursue sports and exercise activities to regulate their mood (Hsiao & Thayer, 1998; Thayer, Newman, & McClain, 1994) and in fact experience an increase in positive affect after having spent time on sports and exercise activities (Reed & Ones, 2006).

Experiences

Based on mood regulation research (Parkinson & Totterdell, 1999), Sonnentag and Fritz (2007) suggested four core recovery experiences: psychological detachment from work, relaxation, mastery experiences, and control. Psychological detachment from work during off-job time refers to a person's experience to be mentally disconnected from work. It means not only to refrain from job-related activities (e.g., finishing tasks, making job-related phone calls), but also to refrain from job-related thoughts. Relaxation refers to a psychological and physical state of low activation. Relaxation can be achieved by deliberate relaxation exercises, such as meditation or yoga, but also through other leisure time activities that calm the body and mind. For example, many people can relax when they listen to classical music. *Mastery experiences* refer to off-job experiences that provide challenges and opportunities for learning. Thus, recovery does not necessarily imply being passive or engaging in activities that calm down the activated systems. Recovery can also occur by getting fully immersed in an experience that stretches one's boundaries and broadens one's horizon. Finally, control refers to self-determination during off-job time. As many jobs are characterized by a low level of control, gaining control during off-job time is an important experience that helps to restore impaired mood.

Construct validation studies show that these four recovery experiences can be differentiated empirically (Sanz-Vergel et al., 2010; Sonnentag & Fritz, 2007). Nevertheless, as one might expect, the four experiences show positive correlations among each other. For example, being in a state of relaxation is positively associated with psychological detachment from work. Relaxation and mastery experiences might be incompatible in any given moment; however, within a larger time frame, they are positively associated: Persons who tend to relax during their off-job time also tend to enjoy mastery experiences (Siltaloppi, Kinnunen, & Feldt, 2009; Sonnentag & Fritz, 2007).

The four recovery experiences proposed by Sonnentag and Fritz (2007) might not be the only experiences that matter for recovery. For example, satisfaction of basic needs—as spelled out in self-determination theory (Ryan & Deci, 2000)—might matter as well (Mojza, Sonnentag, & Bornemann, 2011). Also, interaction with nature may constitute an important recovery experience. Research showed that interactions with nature (e.g., walking through nature) affect attention, memory, and cognitive control in a positive way (e.g., Berman, Jonides, & Kaplan, 2008; Berto, 2005; Hartig, Evans, Jamner, Davis, & Gärling, 2003). According to attention restoration theory (ART; Kaplan, 1995; 2001), nature helps directed attention, an attentional mechanism largely under intentional control (Kaplan, 2001); it replenishes by providing stimulation (e.g., flowers, sunset) that invoke involuntary attention. Although attention is distracted by environmental stimuli, mechanisms underlying voluntary attentional control can be restored. Thus, even after a short interaction with nature, cognitive functioning improves (Berman, et al., 2008). Kaplan (1995) proposed that stimuli of natural environments are superior to stimuli of urban environments in providing restoration because they are more modest. In urban environments, individuals are required to overcome strong stimulation, such as traffic noise, which hinders replenishment of voluntary attention.

Sleep

Sleep is a very specific "activity" to be mentioned in the context of recovery. Sleep can be characterized as a reversible condition of altered and decreased awareness (Carskadon & Dement, 2000). Sleep is highly relevant for recovery, but its restorative function is not a necessary constituent of the sleep concept because sleep might not always be restorative (Akerstedt, Nilsson, & Kecklund, 2009).

Outcomes of Recovery Processes

Recovery that occurs during off-job time is an important factor that contributes to positive individual outcomes within organizations. In this section, we describe empirical research that has shown that recovery is related to positive affective states, favorable motivational states, and performance-related outcomes. Studies that have addressed the benefits of recovery have looked at the state of being recovered (e.g., the subjective experience of feeling recovered; Binnewies, Sonnentag, & Mojza, 2009a; Sonnentag, 2003), specific recovery activities (e.g., sports and physical exercise; e.g., Sonnentag & Natter, 2004), specific recovery experiences (e.g., psychological detachment from work; Sonnentag & Bayer, 2005), and sleep (e.g., Scott & Judge, 2006).

In terms of the specific conceptual and methodological approaches used, researchers have conducted between-person and within-person studies. Between-person studies look at interindividual differences in recovery and its assumed outcomes. For example, studies following this approach test if persons who are more able to mentally detach from work during nonwork time enjoy a better well-being than other persons (e.g., Sonnentag & Fritz, 2007). Within-person studies look at intraindividual variation of recovery and associated outcomes. For example, such studies test if, on evenings when a person succeeds in detaching from work during nonwork time, this person feels better than on evenings when he or she still ruminates about work-related issues (e.g., Sonnentag & Bayer, 2005).

Positive Affective States

Recovery processes have the potential to increase positive affective states such as positive affect, vigor, or serenity. According to the circumplex model of affect, positive affective states can occur both at a high- and low-activation level (Russell & Carroll, 1999). Positive affect at a high-activation level comprises states such as excitement, elation, and enthusiasm; positive affect at a low-activation level comprises states such as contentment, serenity, satisfaction, and calmness (cf. also Watson, Wiese, Vaidya, & Tellegen, 1999). These positive affective states are highly important at work as they are related to positive work-related outcomes. For example, positive activated states predict creativity at work (Amabile et al., 2005; Binnewies & Wörnlein, 2011) and helping behavior (Ilies et al., 2006).

BETWEEN-PERSON STUDIES

Studies have provided empirical evidence that recovery experiences are related to life satisfaction. For example, after surveying a sample of 128 emergency professionals from Spain, Moreno-Jiménez and his coworkers (2009) found that psychological detachment was positively related to life satisfaction. Moreover, psychological detachment was a moderator in the negative relation between family–work conflict (i.e., the experience that one's family life interferes with meeting job demands) and life satisfaction. Family–work conflict was negatively related to life satisfaction when employees were unable to mentally detach from work while at home. However, work–family conflict was unrelated to life satisfaction when employees succeeded in detaching from work while at home. Poor psychological detachment from work during nonwork time may make it difficult to enjoy one's family life. When in a family–work conflict situation (i.e., in a situation when family interferes with work) one does not enjoy one's family life, because it becomes impossible to detach from work, and life satisfaction suffer. In a family–work conflict situation, however, when work-related thoughts do not intrude into one's family life, life satisfaction is less likely to be affected.

A recent study with administrative employees from U.S. colleges and universities also showed that psychological detachment from work during nonwork time predicted life satisfaction (Fritz, Yankelevich, Zarubin, & Barger, 2010), even after controlling for a range of background variables (including negative affectivity) and after taking measures to avoid same-source bias (cf. Podsakoff, MacKenzie, Lee, & Podsakoff, 2003).

Some studies examined if recovery experiences during specific respite occasions (e.g., weekends, sabbaticals) are related to favorable affective outcomes

after the respite. In a study with 229 German preschool teachers, Fritz, Sonnentag, Spector, and McInroe (2010) addressed the question of how recovery experiences during a free weekend are related to affective states at the end of the weekend and 1 week later on Friday night. To rule out that previous affect influenced both weekend experiences and post-weekend affect, the researchers controlled for affective states before the weekend. Analyses revealed that psychological detachment from work during nonwork time, mastery experiences, and relaxation during the weekend predicted joviality and serenity at the end of the weekend. Self-assurance at the end of the weekend was predicted by mastery experiences and relaxation, but not by psychological detachment from work during the weekend. When it comes to positive affective states 1 week later, relaxation during the weekend predicted joviality, serenity, and self-assurance. Moreover, psychological detachment from work during the weekend also predicted serenity one week later.

Davidson et al. (2010) conducted a unique study on the role of sabbaticals by comparing a multinational sample of 129 faculty members who were on sabbatical with a matched control group of 129 faculty members who continued to work in their regular setting. Overall, in the sabbatee group—but not in the control group—positive affect and life satisfaction increased during the sabbatical. Importantly, sabbatees with high respite self-efficacy, high levels of perceived control, high psychological detachment, and high respite quality experienced a greater increase in positive affect, and partly also in life satisfaction. This study demonstrates that a long respite is related to substantial affective gains and that specific features of the respite (e.g., psychological detachment) intensify these gains. Importantly, this study suggests that it is not the absence of work per se that is responsible for affective gains, but rather the distance from the regular work environment and work demands (cf. also Etzion, Eden, & Lapidot, 1998).

Taken together, these studies on between-person differences demonstrate that recovery experiences such as psychological detachment and relaxation are positively associated with positive affective experiences. Individuals who detach from their work and relax during their free time in general and during specific respites (e.g., weekends) are more satisfied with their lives and experience more positive emotions. One might argue that these associations are due to stable individual differences. However, some of the studies ruled out this interpretation by using a control group design and by controlling for pre-respite affect (Davidson et al., 2010; Fritz, Sonnentag et al., 2010).

WITHIN-PERSON STUDIES

Several studies conducted by Sonnentag and her team focused on recovery during evenings at home. Using a within-person approach, these studies tested if recovery activities and experiences during the evening predict affective states late in the evening (Sonnentag & Bayer, 2005; Sonnentag & Natter, 2004), in the next morning (Sonnentag, Binnewies et al., 2008), and after the subsequent working day (Sonnentag & Niessen, 2008).

In a first study of 47 flight attendants, Sonnentag and Natter (2004) aimed at predicting employee vigor at bedtime. Analyses showed that spending time on sports and physical exercise and experiencing leisure activities as recovering predicted vigor at bedtime, even when controlling for vigor at the end of the working day. In other words, exercising and experiencing one's activities as refreshing increased flight attendants' energy level throughout the evening. Sonnentag and Niessen (2008) went a step further and examined if recovery-related variables matter also for vigor at the end of the subsequent working day. In a daily survey study, 77 employees from various occupational backgrounds reported their degree of recovery in the evening and their level of vigor at the end of the next working day. Analyses showed that a measure of accumulated recovery (i.e., degree of recovery accumulated during the preceding evenings) predicted vigor at the end of the next working day. This effect was particularly pronounced for employees with a high trait vigor level. Interestingly, recovery of the immediately preceding evening did not predict next-day vigor. This finding might imply that the benefits of recovery do not become immediately evident; it might be that, for sustaining high levels of vigor, practicing recovery on a daily basis is important.

In another daily survey study with 87 professionals, Sonnentag and Bayer (2005) included psychological detachment from work during evening hours in the analyses. As hypothesized, psychological detachment turned out to be a significant predictor of positive mood at bedtime. In addition, and similar to the findings from the Sonnentag and Natter (2004) study, time spent on sports and physical exercise predicted positive mood at bedtime.

Sonnentag, Binnewies, et al. (2008) tested if specific recovery experiences (psychological detachment from work, mastery experience, relaxation) were related to affective states the next morning. Results from this study with 166 public service employees showed that mastery experiences during the evening predicted positive activation the next morning and that relaxation experiences predicted serenity. Psychological detachment from work during the evening predicted low levels of negative activation and low fatigue, but not positive affective states.

Employees' recovery experiences may not only differ from day to day, but also from week to week (Sonnentag, Mojza, Binnewies, & Scholl, 2008). In a study using a week-level perspective, Sonnentag et al. tested if psychological detachment from work on free evenings during the week is associated with higher levels of positive affect at the end of the week. Data from a sample of 159 employees showed that in weeks when employees succeeded in mentally detaching from their jobs during their free time, they had higher levels of positive activation on Friday afternoon than they did in weeks when they failed to detach, even when controlling for affect on Monday, time pressure during the week, and anticipation of a nice weekend. Interestingly, these researchers found that the association between psychological detachment during nonwork time and Friday positive activation was particularly strong for highly engaged employees (i.e., employees who get absorbed in their work and who are very dedicated to their jobs). This finding suggests that specifically employees who are engaged at work need psychological detachment from their jobs during nonwork time in order to protect a positive affective state.

An increasing number of studies addressed recovery processes during work breaks. In an experience sampling study using a unique sample of 64 cheerleader instructors, Trougakos and his coworkers (2008) examined activities during work breaks and their association with affective states. Their analyses showed that engaging in respite activities during the breaks (i.e., napping, relaxing, socializing), as opposed to chore activities (i.e., working with customers, running errands, practicing material, preparing for upcoming sessions), were associated with the positive affective states of happiness and love. Respite activities were also associated with a higher level of positive affective display during the session after the break.

A study by Sanz-Vergel, Demerouti, Moreno-Jiménez, and Mayo (2010) suggests that recovery during work breaks may spill over into employees' nonwork life. Over a period of 5 working days, 49 Spanish professionals reported the degree to which they felt recovered after their work at a first measurement occasion and their level of vigor at a second measurement occasion late at night. Analyses showed that feeling recovered and re-energized after the work break predicted employees' vigor level at the end of the day, even when controlling for a range of other variables, including hours worked and morning affect.

Sleep as a very specific recovery activity also is related to subsequent positive affective states. For example, Scott and Judge (2006) surveyed 45 administrative employees over a period of 3 weeks. Analyses showed that after nights when respondents experienced insomnia symptoms (e.g., problems falling asleep, waking up several times during the night), they reported low levels of joviality and attentiveness. Thus, the better the sleep quality during the night, the higher the level of positive affective states. Positive affective states, in turn, predicted job satisfaction. Interestingly, the negative association between insomnia symptoms and positive affective states was stronger for women than for men, implying that, in this study, women in particular benefited from good sleep. The daily survey study by Sonnentag et al. (2008) provides additional evidence that sleep matters for positive affective states. After nights when respondents enjoyed good sleep quality and slept longer than they did on average, they reported higher levels of positive activation and serenity. Overall, these within-person studies clearly demonstrate that day-specific and week-specific recovery activities and experiences matter for employees' positive affective states. Here, recovery activities (particularly sports and physical exercise) and recovery experiences (particularly psychological detachment from work, but also relaxation and mastery experiences), as well as sleep play a role. These affective benefits of recovery are highly relevant for organizational life because recovery is not only related to immediate affective responses, but seems to be also experienced during the subsequent working day.

Motivational States

Recovery does not only matter with respect to affect, but also with respect to motivational states. The general idea is that being recovered is beneficial for positive motivational states. Being recovered implies that energetic and regulatory resources are available (Trougakos & Hideg, 2009). When individuals experience that they have these resources available, they will be more inclined to invest these resources back into work, to spend effort on the tasks at hand,

and may even create new tasks by recrafting their jobs (Wrzesniewski & Dutton, 2001). When, on the other side, individuals do not feel well recovered and lack energetic and regulatory resources, they will be less able to exert deliberate effort on their work tasks. Moreover, based on COR theory one can assume that they will be reluctant to spend remaining resources on their work, but will try to protect these resources.

Work engagement is the motivational state that has received most empirical attention in recovery research. Work engagement is a broad concept comprising high involvement, affective energy, and self-presence at work (Britt, Dickinson, Greene-Shortridge, & McKibben, 2007; Macey & Schneider, 2008). Researchers have proposed different specific conceptualizations of work engagement (Kahn, 1990; Maslach & Leiter, 2008; May, Gilson, & Harter, 2004; Rothbard, 2001). Within recovery research, researchers concentrated on the work engagement concept as suggested by Schaufeli and Bakker (2004). These authors' engagement concept comprises three aspects: vigor (i.e., high levels of energy and mental resilience at work), dedication (i.e., work involvement and the experience of significance, inspiration, pride, and challenge), and absorption (i.e., full immersion in and concentration on one's work).

BETWEEN-PERSON STUDIES

A study of 527 Finnish employees from several occupational sectors examined whether the four recovery experiences suggested by Sonnentag and Fritz (2007) predict work engagement (Siltaloppi et al., 2009). Hierarchical regression analysis showed that psychological detachment from work during nonwork time, as well as mastery experiences, predicted work engagement. Importantly, psychological detachment and mastery explained variance in work engagement above demographic variables, working hours per week, job control, and justice of the supervisor. Thus, this study suggests that employees who tend to disconnect from their jobs while not at work are more engaged while at work. Moreover, spending an active leisure (characterized by mastery experiences such as learning and addressing challenges) goes hand in hand with work engagement. Of course, because of the cross-sectional nature of this study, we cannot rule out that third variables (e.g., personality) contribute to the empirical association between mastery experiences off the job and engagement on the job. In the study of Siltaloppi et al., the recovery experiences of relaxation and control were not associated with work engagement. It may be that relaxation lacks the energizing component that is important for work engagement; moreover, job control—rather then control during nonwork time— might be more important for work engagement (Bakker & Demerouti, 2007).

In a recent longitudinal study with 309 human service employees, Sonnentag, Binnewies, and Mojza (2010) examined if psychological detachment from work during nonwork time can predict work engagement over a period of 1 year. The initial level of work engagement and a broad range of other variables were controlled. Analyses showed an interaction effect between psychological detachment and job demands on work engagement. More specifically, when psychological detachment from work during nonwork time was low, high job demands predicted a decrease in work engagement over 1 year. However, when psychological detachment from work during nonwork time was high, work engagement remained stable, even when job demands were high. This study suggests that psychological detachment from work during nonwork time is an important protector of work engagement, particularly in contexts in which employees face a high level of job demands.

Kühnel und Sonnentag (2011) examined how work engagement develops after a vacation. In a longitudinal study of 131 teachers, they assessed work engagement before a 2-week vacation, immediately after the vacation, as well as for 2 and 4 weeks after the vacation. Consistent with earlier studies on the benefits of vacations (De Bloom, Kompier, Geurts, De Weerth, & Sonnentag, 2008; Westman & Eden, 1997), this study found that, after the vacation, work engagement increased significantly. However, 2 weeks after the vacation, work engagement showed a significant decline and nearly reached the pre-vacation level 4 weeks after the vacation. Thus, although causality could not be established in a strict sense, the study suggests that recovery during vacation increases work engagement and that the process of facing daily demands at work lets work engagement erode over time. Interestingly, relaxation during leisure time after the vacation period attenuated the decline in work engagement, at least for the first 2 weeks after vacation. In other words, teachers who experienced relaxation after the vacation weeks enjoyed a higher level of work engagement than did teachers who were less successful in relaxing after the vacation weeks. It seems that relaxation during free time has the potential to postpone vacation fadeout.

WITHIN-PERSON STUDY

Whereas the work engagement studies presented so far addressed differences between persons who enjoy good versus not so good recovery processes, other research addressed the question of whether recovery matters also within persons. Framed differently, this research tested if fluctuations in work engagement from day to day can be explained by an individual's day-specific state of recovery. In a day-level study of 147 employees working in public service organizations, Sonnentag (2003) examined how an individual's subjective experience of being recovered (assessed in the morning) predicted work engagement during the day. Hierarchical linear modeling showed that, on days when individuals felt well recovered in the morning, they reported higher levels of work engagement during the day, compared to days when they felt less recovered.

Taken together, these studies on work engagement suggest that recovery is important for motivational states. However, not all aspects of recovery seem to matter in all situations. The subjective experience of being recovered, psychological detachment, and mastery experiences are probably most important, particularly when job demands are high. In teaching jobs with high social demands, relaxation also seems to be important (for the prominent role of relaxation, cf. also Fritz, Sonnentag et al., 2010). It may be that in these jobs, in which high levels of activation are needed during the working day, the experience of "calming down" during the relaxation process is particularly important.

Performance-related Outcomes

Recovery is not only relevant for affective and motivational states. Empirical research suggests that recovery is also important for performance and other job-relevant behaviors, such as learning activities. Studies that looked at performance outcomes addressed both in-role and extra-role components of performance and examined performance implications of recovery, again both from a between-person and a within-person perspective.

BETWEEN-PERSON STUDIES

Using a longitudinal design, Binnewies, Sonnentag, and Mojza (2009b) examined the longer-term performance benefits of recovery. Specifically, they tested if the feeling of being recovered during leisure time predicts performance over the course of 6 months. Analyses showed that employees who felt well recovered during leisure time showed an increase in task performance, but not in other performance components including personal initiative, OCB, and creativity.

Research further suggests that detaching from work during nonwork time might play a role for performance-related variables. For example, in a study of 477 self-employed workers, Taris and his coworkers (2008) showed that persons who were unable to detach from work during nonwork time reported lower levels of professional efficacy and achievement. However, psychological detachment from work during nonwork time might not always be beneficial for performance. A recent study by Fritz and her coworkers (2010) found not a linear, but a curvilinear relation between psychological detachment from work during nonwork time and performance outcomes (task performance, personal initiative): At low levels and at high levels of psychological detachment, task performance and personal initiative were low, but at medium levels of psychological detachment, task performance and personal initiative were high. This finding suggests that lack of detachment might impair performance because lack of detachment depletes energy resources (Sonnentag et al., 2010), but at high levels of detachment during leisure time it might become very difficult to commit oneself to one's work and to concentrate on it while back at work.

Other studies examined if performance increases after a respite period, such as a weekend or a vacation. In a study using a sample of 87 emergency service workers, Fritz and Sonnentag (2005) found no change in self-rated performance from before to after a free weekend. It might be that, overall, no change in performance becomes evident because a weekend might have a positive effect on one group of employees and a negative on another group, depending on the specific weekend experiences. The data of this study partly support this assumption. Emergency service workers who engaged in social activities during the weekend reported an increase in task performance over the weekend. Moreover, the absence of hassles during the weekend was associated with an increase in task performance, personal initiative, and learning.

A similar picture emerged in another study by Fritz and Sonnentag (2006) that examined the potential benefits of vacations on task performance. In a sample of 222 university employees, no change in overall task performance became evident, although health complaints and emotional exhaustion decreased during the vacation. These findings suggest that respite periods, such as weekends and vacations, seem to impact affect-related outcomes,

but not performance. It might be that potential performance benefits of weekends and vacations are counteracted by some detrimental effects. For example, it might take some time to become again fully immersed in one's work when returning to work on Monday—and after a vacation. Moreover, it might be that, after a weekend or vacation, performance does not increase per se. Rather, specific experiences—as demonstrated in the weekend study (Fritz & Sonnentag, 2005)—and the degree to which one really recovered during the weekend or vacation might be more important.

WITHIN-PERSON STUDIES

In the study described above, Sonnentag (2003) tested if an employee's subjective experience of being recovered (assessed in the morning) predicts proactive behavior throughout the working day. Analyses revealed that on days when employees felt well recovered in the morning, they showed higher levels of personal initiative and higher levels of learning behavior throughout the working day. An additional mediation analysis suggested that work engagement mediated the association between the experience of being recovered and proactive behavior at work. Binnewies et al. (2009a) continued this line of research and included additional performance-related concepts in their study. This study, based on 99 public service employees who completed daily surveys over 1 working week, demonstrated that the subjective state of being recovered (assessed in the morning) was related to task performance, OCB, and personal initiative (measured at the end of the working day). However, this association between recovery and the performance-related outcomes was not uniform for all employees. Particularly, employees working in jobs with high levels of autonomy showed the positive association between state of being recovered and performance, whereas for employees working in low-autonomy jobs, the association was not significant. This pattern of findings suggests that a high level of job autonomy enables an employee to adjust his or her performance level to his or her current psychological state, whereas a low-autonomy job does not provide such an option.

In another study, Binnewies, Sonnentag, and Mojza (2010) tested a similar model at the week level (data overlapping with Sonnentag, Mojza, et al., 2008). Analyses showed that feeling well recovered on Monday predicted various performance outcomes throughout the week, specifically task performance, OCB, and personal initiative.

For personal initiative as outcome variable, Binnewies et al. could identify psychological detachment from work and relaxation during the weekend as the underlying recovery experiences that—via the state of being recovered—predicted this performance aspect.

In sum, empirical evidence suggests that recovery matters for job performance and related constructs. The subjective experience of being recovered is particularly important. The association between psychological detachment from work during nonwork and performance at work shows a more complex pattern. Whereas lack of detachment seems to have clear drawbacks, too much detachment might be detrimental as well. Probably, the mechanisms underlying the association between low versus high levels of detachment differ. Whereas at low levels of detachment, energy depletion might impede job performance, at high levels of detachment, a decrease in commitment to one's job might be detrimental for performance. It has to be noted that most studies on the association between recovery and performance relied on self-report data. However, the study by Fritz, Yankelevich, et al. (2010) also included performance ratings by others, and therefore suggests that the association between psychological detachment and performance cannot be solely attributed to common method bias. Nevertheless, more studies are needed that use more objective performance measures.

Beyond Recovery: Capitalizing on Positive Work Experiences

A substantial portion of the recovery research conceptualized recovery in the context of job stress (Geurts & Sonnentag, 2006). This job stress perspective implies that work is seen as something that is (potentially) stressful, and that gaining physical and mental distance from this stressful work while at home is needed so that recovery can occur. Recovery will manifest itself in the reduction of negative symptoms and in an increase in positive states.

However, viewing off-job time solely from the job stress perspective is rather limited. Research in the field of POS has demonstrated that work can also have positive sides and that it has the potential to contribute to individual well-being and growth (Dutton & Heaphy, 2003; Spreitzer, Sutcliffe, Dutton, Sonenshein, & Grant, 2005). Therefore, the benefits of positively spent off-job time should be addressed not only from the job stress perspective that focuses on the reduction of *negative* effects of work.

Rather, the benefit of off-job time can also be examined from a savoring (Bryant, 1989, 2003) or capitalizing (Langston, 1994) perspective. *Savoring* refers to cognitive or behavioral strategies for amplifying or prolonging enjoyment of positive events, to recalls of past positive events in ways that promote present well-being, and to the anticipation of future positive outcomes (Bryant, 1989). *Capitalizing*, a term used by Langston (1994), refers to the "process of beneficially interpreting positive events" (p. 1112). Such a perspective on savoring and capitalizing implies the assumption that work has positive features, and that mentally and behaviorally addressing these positive features improves positive states. Empirically, research on savoring and capitalizing has mainly addressed positive events and experiences outside work. For example, Langston (1994) has shown that expressive responses to positive events increased positive affect, in addition to the positive valence of the positive event. Findings from Gable and his coworker stress the importance of sharing positive experiences with others. Sharing a positive experience with others increased positive affect and other well-being indicators, again above and beyond the positive impact of the event itself (Gable, Reis, Impett, & Asher, 2004). Experimental research points in a similar direction: Expressing gratitude (as a specific positive reaction to positive experiences) was found to increase well-being indicators (Emmons & McCullough, 2003). Further studies have shown that reminiscing (i.e., deliberately remembering) about positive events is positively related to happiness indicators (Bryant, 2003, 2005); importantly, a field experiment demonstrated that reminiscence increased the percent of time persons felt happy during the week (Bryant, 2005).

A few studies started to examine savoring processes in relation to on-the-job experiences. These studies focused on positive work reflection (i.e., positively thinking about one's job and being aware of what one likes in one's job). For example, in the study of 87 emergency workers summarized above, Fritz and Sonnentag (2005) found that employees who reflected in a positive way about their job during the weekend experienced less emotional exhaustion and more engagement when returning back to work, even when pre-weekend levels of exhaustion and engagement were taken into account. Moreover, employees who reflected positively about their work engaged more in learning activities when back at work. A second study addressed positive work reflection with a longitudinal design (Binnewies et al., 2009b). Positively reflecting about one's work during leisure time predicted an increase in proactive work behavior, creativity, and OCB over the course of 6 months. Importantly, these associations remained significant when controlling for a range of variables, including the initial level of the outcome variables and negative affectivity.

Another recent study suggests that telling another person about a positive event is particularly important (Hicks & Diamond, 2008). A diary study of 48 couples demonstrated that disclosing the experience of a positive event to one's partner predicted end-of-day positive affect, after controlling for many other variables. Although this study was not limited to work-related positive events, it might indicate that talking about a positive work-related event while at home increases positive affective states (cf. also Ilies, Keeney, & Scott, 2011).

Conclusion
Future Directions
Empirical research summarized in this chapter clearly demonstrates that recovery is related to positive affective as well as motivational states, and that it is associated with performance outcomes. It seems that it is not only important for employees to have respite periods between intense working days or weeks, but the way employees spend and experience their free time is crucial. Psychological detachment from work and relaxation have been found to be beneficial in most of the respite settings. However, not only mental distance from work might help to foster positive affective and motivational states. Focusing on positive features and events of one's work should also help in increasing positive affect and positive job-related behaviors.

Despite the growing empirical evidence on the relevance of recovery processes, many questions in this research field still remain unanswered. In this last section of the chapter, we will highlight some of the most important and promising avenues for future research. In terms of theory, recovery research is still underdeveloped. Although several approaches clearly cover processes that are relevant for recovery (Hobfoll, 1998; Meijman & Mulder, 1998), an overall theoretical model that specifies in more detail the relevant mechanisms is still missing. A first framework focusing on the role of psychological detachment has been proposed (Sonnentag, 2010), but a much deeper elaboration is needed. In our view, the approach presented by Trougakos and Hideg (2009), focusing on regulatory resources, is an excellent starting point.

Empirical research has indicated that psychological detachment from work during nonwork is associated with positive affective and motivational outcomes, particularly when demands are high (Siltaloppi, et al., 2009). What is more, empirical studies have suggested that psychological detachment from work is particularly difficult when demands and other job stressors are high (Sonnentag & Bayer, 2005). Thus, a core question to be addressed in future recovery research is to determine what helps employees detach from their jobs during nonwork time. Here, one might think of nonwork activities that require full concentration and engagement, and that therefore leave no cognitive capacity for job-related thoughts. But also deliberate rituals that help employees to enact the separation between their work and nonwork lives might be highly relevant for the experience of detachment (Kreiner, Hollensbe, & Sheep, 2009).

Despite the positive association between psychological detachment from work during nonwork time and positive affective as well as motivational outcomes, very high levels of detachment from work are not necessarily beneficial for performance-related outcomes (Fritz, Yankelevich et al., 2010). Employees probably face difficulties in finding their way back into their job after having been fully detached from work. A particularly difficult time for attaching oneself to work might be Monday mornings or the first days after a vacation. Thus, research may also want to find answers to the question of how employees can attach themselves to work again.

In this chapter, we have argued that not only processes related to recovery from unfavorable work events and experiences are important to restore positive affective and motivational states. Capitalizing on positive features of one's job also may have benefits. In addition to the general need to study work-related capitalizing processes in a broader range of settings, researchers may also want to explicitly contrast recovery and capitalizing processes. In other words, it would be important to find out when capitalizing processes are sufficient for protecting employee well-being, and when deliberate recovery processes (including a mental distance to one's work) are needed.

The idea that work and nonwork are two areas of life that can be clearly separated is more and more challenged by the increased availability and use of technical devices (e.g., smartphones) and working arrangements that blend work and nonwork life (Boswell & Olson-Buchanon, 2007; Golden &

Geisler, 2007). Therefore, the notion that, at home, one recovers from one's job by gaining mental distance might no longer be realistic for many employees. Thus, future studies may want to address the question of how employees can gain sufficient recovery from the negative aspects of their work when they actually do work at home.

Empirical studies have shown that not only specific recovery experiences, such as psychological detachment, but also specific types of activities matter for recovery, with sports and exercise being particularly important activities (e.g., Sonnentag & Natter, 2004). Therefore, one might ask if future research should focus on experiences or on activities. In our view, we do not think that the experience perspective is superior to the activity perspective or vice versa. Rather, we would like to suggest that experiences could be conceptualized as the mediating mechanism between activities and positive outcomes. For example, one of several reasons why sports and exercise are so beneficial for recovery is that these activities help the individual to detach from work (Feuerhahn, Sonnentag, & Woll, 2010). Thus, when interested in the underlying processes that potentially facilitate recovery, researchers may want to focus on experiences. However, when looking for temporal processes, the assessment of activities might be more appropriate. For example, it is probably very difficult for respondents (and observers alike) to give an accurate estimation about how long they have detached from work; to provide time estimates of activities might be more feasible here.

In addition, the notion that recovery takes place outside the workplace has to be challenged. Recovery occurs also at the workplace, with formal work breaks being a prominent recovery occasion. Recovery, however, may not only happen during formal work breaks, but also during the course of the working day, for example during short episodes after having finished one task, but before switching to the next one (Beal, Weiss, Barros, & MacDermid, 2005). One might speculate that these microbreaks have an enormous potential for protecting and restoring positive states.

One largely neglected field within recovery research concerns the role of personality in the recovery process. For example, Grant and Langan-Fox (2007) examined the relation between personality traits and peoples' job-related psychological and physical strain reactions. This study showed that people especially high in neuroticism are prone to develop psychological and physical strain symptoms, whereas extraversion showed direct salutary effects on psychological and physical strain. These findings suggest that people with specific personality traits such as neuroticism and low extraversion might need to recover more to protect their well-being and positive states. Furthermore, Trougakos and Hideg (2009) also discussed the moderating role of personality in the recovery process. According to these authors, extraversion and neuroticism might moderate the recovery process, for example, by influencing how a person experiences and arranges his or her own work breaks. Definitively, more studies are needed to investigate the role of personality in the recovery process.

One of the core assumptions in recovery research is that recovery processes restore personal resources (Hobfoll, 1998; Trougakos & Hideg, 2009). However, researchers have just begun to include explicit measures of resources in empirical studies on recovery (Davidson et al., 2010). The next generation of recovery studies should not only demonstrate that recovery processes are related to positive outcomes, but should also shed more light on resource gain as the underlying mechanism.

Until now, recovery research has focused on individual-level outcomes. Team- and organization-level outcomes remain largely unexplored. However, one might expect that when several people within a workgroup lack sufficient recovery, team climate might deteriorate. Consequences of poor recovery processes, such as burnout and low work engagement, might crossover to other team members (Bakker & Xanthopoulou, 2009; Westman, 2001). In addition, one can assume that the benefits of recovery go further than influencing immediate affect, motivational states, and performance outcomes. For example, is it reasonable to assume that well-recovered employees and supervisors have a positive influence on social interaction processes at work and thereby influence also others.

In terms of methodology, stronger study designs are needed. Most of the existing recovery studies rely on correlational methods, often using cross-sectional designs. Without doubt, the inclusion of daily survey and experience sampling methods (Trougakos et al., 2008), longitudinal (Sonnentag et al., 2010) as well as quasi-experimental designs (Davidson et al., 2010) indicate substantial progress. In the future, we also need experimental and intervention studies to bring more light into the causal processes underlying recovery. Still, recovery research largely relies on self-report measures. Notable exceptions include the studies by Trougakos et al. (2008) and Fritz, Yankelevich et al. (2010)

that included observational data and reports from others, respectively. Scholars conducting future studies should continue to walk this path. Moreover, physiological measures might be included (Heaphy & Dutton, 2008). Without doubt, it would be also very interesting and fruitful to integrate qualitative research methods into recovery research.

Taken together, we believe that these suggestions point to exciting avenues for future studies on recovery. Ultimately, we hope that addressing these new questions and methodological challenges will help to develop a better understanding of the processes that help employees to protect and enhance positive affective and motivational states at work as well as job performance. We expect that well-recovered employees will contribute to better and more fulfilling organizational lives.

References

Akerstedt, T., Nilsson, P.M., & Kecklund, G. (2009). Sleep and recovery. In S. Sonnentag, P.L. Perrewé, & D.C. Ganster (Eds.), *Current perspectives on job-stress recovery* (pp. 205–247). Bingley, UK: Emerald.

Amabile, T.M., Barsade, S.G., Mueller, J.S., & Staw, B.M. (2005). Affect and creativity at work. *Administrative Science Quarterly, 50*, 367–403.

Bakker, A.B., & Demerouti, E. (2007). The job demands-resources model: State of the art. *Journal of Managerial Psychology, 22*, 309–328.

Bakker, A.B., & Xanthopoulou, D. (2009). The crossover of daily work engagement: Test of an actor-partner interdependence model. *Journal of Applied Psychology, 94*, 1562–1571.

Beal, D.J., Weiss, H.M., Barros, E., & MacDermid, S.M. (2005). An episodic process model of affective influences on performance. *Journal of Applied Psychology, 90*, 1054–1068.

Berman, M.G., Jonides, J., & Kaplan, S. (2008). The cognitive benefits of interacting with nature. *Psychological Science, 19*, 1207–1212.

Berto, R. (2005). Exposure to restorative environments helps restore attentional capacity. *Journal of Environmental Psychology, 25*, 249–259.

Binnewies, C., Sonnentag, S., & Mojza, E.J. (2009a). Daily performance at work: Feeling recovered in the morning as a predictor of day-level job performance. *Journal of Organizational Behavior, 30*, 67–93.

Binnewies, C., Sonnentag, S., & Mojza, E.J. (2009b). Feeling recovered and thinking about the good sides of one's work: A longitudinal study on the benefits of non-work experiences for job performance. *Journal of Occupational Health Psychology, 14*, 243–256.

Binnewies, C., Sonnentag, S., & Mojza, E.J. (2010). Recovery during the weekend and fluctuations in weekly job performance: A four-week longitudinal study examining intra-individual relationships. *Journal of Occupational and Organizational Psychology, 83*, 419–441.

Binnewies, C., & Wörnlein, S. (2011). What makes a creative day? A diary study on the interplay between affect, stressors, and job control. *Journal of Organizational Behavior, 32*, 589–607.

Boswell, W.R., & Olson-Buchanon, J.B. (2007). The use of communications technologies after hours: The role of work

attitudes and work-life conflict. *Journal of Management, 33*, 592–610.

Britt, T.W., Dickinson, J.M., Greene-Shortridge, T.M., & McKibben, E. (2007). Self engagement at work. In C.L. Cooper, & D. Nelson (Eds.), *Positive organizational behavior* (pp. 143–158). Thousand Oaks, CA: Sage.

Brosschot, J.F., Gerin, W., & Thayer, J.F. (2006). The perseverative cognition hypothesis: A review of worry, prolonged stress-related activation, and health. *Journal of Psychosomatic Research, 60*, 113–124.

Bryant, F.B. (1989). A four-factor model of perceived control: Avoiding, coping, obtaining, and savoring. *Journal of Personality, 57*, 773–797.

Bryant, F.B. (2003). Savoring Beliefs Inventory (SBI): A scale fore measuring beliefs about savoring. *Journal of Mental Health, 12*, 175–196.

Bryant, F.B. (2005). Using the past to enhance the present: Boosting happiness through positive reminiscence. *Journal of Happiness Studies, 6*, 227–260.

Carmeli, A., Ben-Hador, B., Waldman, D.A., & Rupp, D.E. (2009). How leaders cultivate social capital and nurture employee vigor: Implications for job performance. *Journal of Applied Psychology, 94*, 1553–1561.

Carmeli, A., & Spreitzer, G.M. (2009). Trust, connectivity, and thriving: Implications for innovative behaviors at work. *Journal of Creative Behavior, 43*(169–191).

Carskadon, M.A., & Dement, W.C. (2000). Normal human sleep: An overview. In M.H. Kryger, T. Roth, & W.C. Dement (Eds.), *Principles and practice of sleep medicine* (pp. 15–25). Philadelphia: W.B. Saunders Company.

Craig, A., & Cooper, R.E. (1992). Symptoms of acute and chronic fatigue. In A.P. Smith, & D.M. Jones (Eds.), *Handbook of human performance* Vol. 3 (pp. 289–339). London: Academic Press.

Davidson, O.B., Eden, D., Westman, M., Cohen-Charash, Y., Hammer, L.B., Kluger, A.N., et al. (2010). Sabbatical leave: Who gains and how much? *Journal of Applied Psychology, 95*, 953–964.

De Bloom, J., Kompier, M.A.J., Geurts, S.A.E., De Weerth, C., & Sonnentag, S. (2008). Do we recover from vacation? Meta-analysis of vacation effects on health and well-being. *Journal of Occupational Health, 51*, 13–25.

Dutton, J.E., & Heaphy, E.D. (2003). The power of high quality connections. In K.S. Cameron, J.E. Dutton, & R.E. Quinn (Eds.), *Positive organizational scholarship: Foundations of a new discipline* (pp. 263–278). San Francisco: Berrett-Koehler.

Elsbach, K.D., & Hargadon, A.B. (2006). Enhancing creativity through "mindless" work: A framework of workday design. *Organizational Science, 17*, 470–483.

Emmons, R.A., & McCullough, M.E. (2003). Counting blessings versus burdens: An experimental investigation of gratitude and subjective well-being in daily life. *Journal of Personality and Social Psychology, 84*, 377–389.

Etzion, D., Eden, D., & Lapidot, Y. (1998). Relief from job stressors and burnout: Reserve service as a respite. *Journal of Applied Psychology, 83*, 577–585.

Feuerhahn, N., Sonnentag, S., & Woll, A. (2010). *Physical exercise as a daily recovery activity: A closer look on how it works.* Working paper, Jacobs University, Bremen and University of Konstanz.

Fritz, C., & Sonnentag, S. (2005). Recovery, health, and job performance: Effects of weekend experiences. *Journal of Occupational Health Psychology, 10*, 187–199.

Fritz, C., & Sonnentag, S. (2006). Recovery, well-being, and performance-related outcomes: The role of work load and vacation experiences. *Journal of Applied Psychology, 91,* 936–945.

Fritz, C., Sonnentag, S., Spector, P.E., & McInroe, J. (2010). The weekend matters: Relationships between stress recovery and affective experiences. *Journal of Organizational Behavior, 31,* 1137–1162.

Fritz, C., Yankelevich, M., Zarubin, A., & Barger, P. (2010). Happy, healthy and productive: The role of detachment from work during nonwork time. *Journal of Applied Psychology, 95,* 977–983.

Gable, S.L., Reis, H.T., Impett, E.A., & Asher, E.R. (2004). What do you do when things go right? The intrapersonal and interpersonal benefits of sharing positive events. *Journal of Personality and Social Psychology, 87,* 228–245.

Geurts, S.A.E., & Sonnentag, S. (2006). Recovery as an explanatory mechanism in the relation between acute stress reactions and chronic health impairment. *Scandinavian Journal of Work, Environment and Health, 32,* 482–492.

Golden, A.G., & Geisler, C. (2007). Work-life boundary management and the personal digital assistant. *Human Relations, 60,* 519–551.

Grant, A.M. (2008). The significance of task significance: Job performance effects, relational mechanisms, and boundary conditions. *Journal of Applied Psychology, 93,* 108–124.

Grant, S., & Langan-Fox, J. (2007). Personality and the occupational stressor-strain relationship: The role of the big five. *Journal of Occupational Health Psychology, 12,* 20–33.

Hartig, T., Evans, G.W., Jamner, L.D., Davis, D.S., & Gärling, T. (2003). Tracking restoration in natural and urban field settings. *Journal of Environmental Psychology, 23,* 109–123.

Heaphy, E.D., & Dutton, J.E. (2008). Positive social interactions and the human body at work: Linking organizations and physiology. *Academy of Management Review, 33,* 137–162.

Hecht, T.D., & Boies, K. (2009). Structure and correlates of spillover from nonwork to work: An examination of nonwork activities, well-being and work outcomes. *Journal of Occupational Health Psychology, 14,* 414–426.

Hicks, A.M., & Diamond, L.M. (2008). How was your day? Couples' affect when telling and hearing daily events. *Personal Relationships, 15,* 205–228.

Hobfoll, S.E. (1989). Conservation of resources: A new attempt at conceptualizing stress. *American Psychologist, 44,* 513–524.

Hobfoll, S.E. (1998). *Stress, culture, and community: The psychology and physiology of stress.* New York: Plenum.

Hockey, G.R.J. (1997). Compensatory control in the regulation of human performance under stress and high workload: A cognitive-energetical framework. *Biological Psychology, 45,* 73–93.

Hsiao, E.T., & Thayer, R.E. (1998). Exercising for mood regulation: The importance of experience. *Personality and Individual Differences, 24,* 829–836.

Ilies, R., Keeney, J., & Scott, B. (2011). Work-family interpersonal capitalization: Sharing positive events at home. *Organizational Behavior and Human Decision Processes, 114,* 115–126.

Ilies, R., Scott, B.A., & Judge, T.A. (2006). The interactive effects of personal traits and experienced states on intraindividual patterns of citizenship behavior. *Academy of Management Journal, 49,* 561–575.

Kahn, W.A. (1990). Psychological conditions of personal engagement and disengagement at work. *Academy of Management Journal, 33,* 692–724.

Kaplan, S. (1995). The restorative benefits of nature: Toward an integrative framework. *Journal of Environmental Psychology, 15,* 169–182.

Kaplan, S. (2001). Meditation, restoration, and the management of mental fatigue. *Environment and Behavior, 33,* 480–506.

Kreiner, G., Hollensbe, E., & Sheep, M.L. (2009). Balancing borders and bridges: Negotiating the work-home interface via boundary work tactics. *Academy of Management Journal, 52,* 704–730.

Kühnel, J., & Sonnentag, S. (2011). How long do you benefit from vacation? A closer look at the fade-out of vacation effects. *Journal of Organizational Behavior, 32,* 125–143.

Langston, C.A. (1994). Capitalizing on and coping with daily-life events: Expressive responses to positive events. *Journal of Personality and Social Psychology, 67,* 1112–1125.

Macey, W.H., & Schneider, B. (2008). The meaning of employee engagement. *Industrial and Organizational Psychology: Perspectives on Science and Practice, 1,* 3–30.

Maslach, C., & Leiter, M.P. (2008). Early predictors of job burnout and engagement. *Journal of Applied Psychology, 93,* 498–512.

May, D.R., Gilson, R.L., & Harter, L. (2004). The psychological conditions of meaningfulness, safety, and availability and the engagement of the human spirit at work. *Journal of Occupational and Organizational Psychology, 77,* 11–37.

Meijman, T.F., & Mulder, G. (1998). Psychological aspects of workload. In P.J.D. Drenth, & H. Thierry (Eds.), *Handbook of work and organizational psychology* Vol. 2: *Work psychology* (pp. 5–33). Hove, UK: Psychology Press.

Mojza, E.J., Lorenz, C., Sonnentag, S., & Binnewies, C. (2010). Daily recovery experiences: The role of volunteer work during leisure time. *Journal of Occupational Health Psychology, 15,* 60–74.

Mojza, E.J., Sonnentag, S., & Bornemann, C. (2011). Volunteer work as a valuable leisure time activity: A day-level study on volunteer work, non-work experiences, and well-being at work. *Journal of Occupational and Organizational Psychology, 84,* 123–152.

Moreno-Jiménez, B., Mayo, M., Sanz-Vergel, A.I., Geurts, S.A.E., Rodríguez-Munoz, A., & Garrosa, E. (2009). Effects of work-family conflict on employee's well-being: The moderating role of recovery experiences. *Journal of Occupational Health Psychology, 14,* 427–440.

Muraven, M., & Baumeister, R.F. (2000). Self-regulation and depletion of limited resources: Does self-control resemble a muscle? *Psychological Bulletin, 126,* 247–259.

Parkinson, B., & Totterdell, P. (1999). Classifying affect-regulation strategies. *Cognition and Emotion, 13,* 277–303.

Podsakoff, P.M., MacKenzie, S.B., Lee, J.Y., & Podsakoff, N.P. (2003). Common method biases in behavioral research: A critical review of the literature and recommended remedies. *Journal of Applied Psychology, 88,* 879–903.

Quinn, R.W., & Dutton, J.E. (2005). Coordination as energy-in-conversation. *Academy of Management Review, 30,* 36–57.

Reed, J., & Ones, D.S. (2006). The affect of acute aerobic exercise on positive activated affect: A meta-analysis. *Psychology of Sport and Exercise, 7,* 477–514.

Rook, J.W., & Zijlstra, F.R.H. (2006). The contribution of various types of activities to recovery. *European Journal of Work and Organizational Psychology, 15,* 218–240.

Rothbard, N.P. (2001). Enriching or depleting? The dynamics of engagement in work and family roles. *Administrative Science Quarterly, 46*, 655–684.

Ruderman, M.N., Ohlott, P.J., Panzer, K., & King, S.N. (2002). Benefit of multiple roles for managerial women. *Academy of Management Journal, 45*, 369–386.

Russell, J.A., & Carroll, J.M. (1999). On the bipolarity of positive and negative affect. *Psychological Bulletin, 125*, 3–30.

Ryan, R.M., & Deci, E.L. (2000). Self-determination theory and the facilitation of intrinsic motivation, social development, and well-being. *American Psychologist, 55*, 68–78.

Sanz-Vergel, A.I., Demerouti, E., Moreno-Jiménez, B., & Mayo, M. (2010). Work-family balance and energy: A day-level study on recovery conditions. *Journal of Vocational Behavior, 76*, 118–130.

Sanz-Vergel, A.I., Sebastián, J., Rodrígez-Munoz, A., Garrosa, E., Moreno-Jiménez, B., & Sonnentag, S. (2010). Adaptaciòn der "Cuestionario de Experiencias de Recuperación" a una muestra espanola. *Psicothema, 22*, 990–996.

Schaufeli, W.B., & Bakker, A.B. (2004). Job demands, job resources, and their relationship with burnout and engagement: A multi-sample study. *Journal of Organizational Behavior, 25*, 293–315.

Scott, B.A., & Judge, T.A. (2006). Insomnia, emotions, and job satisfaction: A multilevel study. *Journal of Management, 32*, 622–645.

Shirom, A., Toker, S., Berliner, S., Shapira, I., & Melamed, S. (2008). The effects of physical fitness and feeling vigorous on self-rated health. *Health Psychology, 27*, 567–575.

Siltaloppi, M., Kinnunen, U., & Feldt, T. (2009). Recovery experiences as moderators between psychological work characteristics and occupational well-being. *Work & Stress, 23*, 330–348.

Sonnentag, S. (2001). Work, recovery activities, and individual well-being: A diary study. *Journal of Occupational Health Psychology, 6*, 196–210.

Sonnentag, S. (2003). Recovery, work engagement, and proactive behavior: A new look at the interface between non-work and work. *Journal of Applied Psychology, 88*, 518–528.

Sonnentag, S. (2010). Recovery from fatigue: The role of psychological detachment. In P.L. Ackerman (Ed.), *Cognitive fatigue: The current status and future for research and application.* Washington, DC: American Psychological Association.

Sonnentag, S., & Bayer, U.V. (2005). Switching off mentally: Predictors and consequences of psychological detachment from work during off-job time. *Journal of Occupational Health Psychology, 10*, 393–414.

Sonnentag, S., Binnewies, C., & Mojza, E.J. (2008). "Did you have a nice evening?" A day-level study on recovery experiences, sleep, and affect. *Journal of Applied Psychology, 93*, 674–684.

Sonnentag, S., Binnewies, C., & Mojza, E.J. (2010). Staying well and engaged when demands are high: The role of psychological detachment. *Journal of Applied Psychology, 95*, 965–976.

Sonnentag, S., & Fritz, C. (2007). The recovery experience questionnaire: Development and validation of a measure assessing recuperation and unwinding from work. *Journal of Occupational Health Psychology, 12*, 204–221.

Sonnentag, S., Mojza, E.J., Binnewies, C., & Scholl, A. (2008). Being engaged at work and detached at home: A week-level study on work engagement, psychological detachment, and affect. *Work & Stress, 22*, 257–276.

Sonnentag, S., & Natter, E. (2004). Flight attendants' daily recovery from work: Is there no place like home? *International Journal of Stress Management, 11*, 366–391.

Sonnentag, S., & Niessen, C. (2008). Staying vigorous until work is over: The role of trait vigor, day-specific work experiences and recovery. *Journal of Occupational and Organizational Psychology, 81*, 435–458.

Spreitzer, G., Sutcliffe, K., Dutton, J., Sonenshein, S., & Grant, A.M. (2005). A socially embedded model of thriving at work. *Organization Science, 16*, 537–549.

Spreitzer, G.M. (2006). Leading to grow and growing to lead: leadership development lessons from positive organizational studies. *Organizational Dynamics, 232*, 1–12.

Taris, T.W., Geurts, S.A.E., Schaufeli, W.B., Blonk, R.W.B., & Lagerveld, S.E. (2008). All day and all of the night: The relative contribution of two dimensions of workaholism to well-being in self-employed workers. *Work & Stress, 22*, 153–165.

Thayer, R.E., Newman, J.R., & McClain, T.M. (1994). Self-regulation of mood: Strategies for changing a bad mood, raising energy, and reducing tension. *Journal of Personality and Social Psychology, 67*, 910–925.

Trougakos, J.P., Beal, D.J., Green, S.G., & Weiss, H.M. (2008). Making the break count: An episodic examination of recovery activities, emotional experiences, and positive affective displays. *Academy of Management Journal, 51*, 131–146.

Trougakos, J.P., & Hideg, I. (2009). Momentary work recovery: The role of within-day work breaks. In S. Sonnentag, P.L. Perrewé & D.C. Ganster (Eds.), *Current perspectives on job-stress recovery* (pp. 37–84). Bingley, UK: Emerald.

Watson, D., Wiese, D., Vaidya, J., & Tellegen, A. (1999). The two general activation systems of affect: Structural findings, evolutionary considerations, and psychobiological evidence. *Journal of Personality and Social Psychology, 76*, 820–838.

Westman, M. (2001). Stress and strain crossover. *Human Relations, 54*, 717–751.

Westman, M., & Eden, D. (1997). Effects of a respite from work on burnout: Vacation relief and fade-out. *Journal of Applied Psychology, 82*, 516–527.

Wrzesniewski, A., & Dutton, J.E. (2001). Crafting a job: Revisioning employees as active crafters of their work. *Academy of Management Review, 26*, 179–201.

Xanthopoulou, D., Bakker, A.B., Demerouti, E., & Schaufeli, W.B. (2007). The role of personal resources in the job demands-resources model. *International Journal of Stress Management, 14*, 121–141.

Orientations of Positive Leadership in Times of Crisis

Erika Hayes James *and* Lynn Perry Wooten

Abstract

This chapter identifies three crisis leadership orientations that research suggests are necessary for leaders and their organizations to manifest positivity in crisis. We argue that leaders who have a mindset for learning and adapting to rapidly changing circumstances, seeing possibilities amid the tragic circumstances of a crisis, and expecting trust and trustworthiness will be more inclined to identify positive outcomes in crisis situations. This chapter also offers a set of corresponding behaviors that characterize the three crisis leadership orientations. The chapter begins with a brief introduction to crises and crisis phases. We then introduce the leadership orientations and their respective behaviors, followed by a discussion of the types of positive outcomes that can be manifested from the leadership orientations. These outcomes include benefits for the individual crisis leader, the organization, and its stakeholders. As we discuss in the section on future directions, the manifestation of these outcomes may be contingent upon both organizational factors and the nature and source of the crisis.

Keywords: Crisis, leadership, positive organizational scholarship, crisis leadership, crisis management, learning, trust

Undeniably, the past decade has been fraught with crises on both a domestic and international scale. At the outset of the decade, people all over the world scrambled to address the potential technological disruption of the Y2K bug. Then, in 2001, the United States (although ramifications have been felt worldwide) was traumatized by the terrorist attacks on September 11. A few years later, areas along the U.S. Gulf Coast region were severely compromised by Hurricane Katrina, the response to which left indelible images of a community in suffering and a government struggling to respond. We closed out the decade with the near collapse of the financial markets, the H1N1 pandemic, and the Deepwater Horizon oil rig explosion, which resulted in 11 deaths and became potentially one of the world's biggest environmental disasters. Given such devastation, it seems almost ludicrous and insensitive to suggest any link between positivity and crisis.

And yet, that is precisely what this chapter attempts to do.

Here, we highlight three crisis leadership orientations that allow for positive organizing in response to crisis events. We further suggest a set of behaviors associated with these leadership orientations that can yield positive outcomes for the organization in crisis. Thus, a fundamental assumption underlying the ideas presented in this chapter is that crises have the potential to be a catalyst for positive organizational change (Brockner & James, 2008). Further, it is incumbent upon organizational leaders to manifest positivity in times of crisis.

As a result of this assumption, this chapter is entrenched in the positive organizational scholarship (POS) domain that is based on the premise that "understanding how to enable human excellence in organizations will unlock potential, reveal possibilities, and facilitate a more positive course of human and organizational welfare" (Cameron, Dutton, Quinn, & Spreitzer, 2006a), even in times of crisis. Doing so, however, requires that leaders have a perspective that orients them to see the potential for positivity amid crisis and necessitates that they enact a concomitant set of behaviors. Although both the crisis leadership orientations and the behaviors may be observed in leaders operating in noncrisis contexts, we argue that they are essential to realize positive results during and following a crisis.

In recent years, the study of the positive has been applied to areas such as organizational scholarship (Cameron, Dutton, & Quinn, 2003), leadership (Cameron, 2008), psychology (e.g. Seligman & Csikszentmihalyi, 2000), and change (Brockner & James, 2008), all of which are grounded in three fundamental connotations: a focus on abnormally positive deviant performance; a bias toward the affirmative rather than the negative, strengths rather than weaknesses, and optimism over pessimism; and a focus on virtuousness or the best of the human condition (Cameron, 2008). In light of this burgeoning literature, POS offers a conceptually and theoretically rich domain for examining positivity in crisis. We argue, for example, that in times of crisis an overarching positive orientation can help leaders and their organizations achieve resilience or the ability to bounce back following a threatening event (Sutcliffe & Vogus, 2003). Likewise, positivity is implied in the ability for crisis handlers to see opportunities in crisis. In the remainder of this chapter, we highlight specific crisis leadership orientations that are grounded in the concept of positivity.

Defining Crisis

Organizations have always been and will likely continue to be vulnerable to crises in some form or another. Although each type of crisis poses a unique threat, it helps to understand what differentiates a crisis situation from an unfortunate or unpleasant business challenge. Dutton (1986) described a business crisis as a type of strategic issue that, in the absence of corrective action, can lead to a negative outcome. She further argued that crises reflect situations that are critically important to an organization and that they can be distinguished from noncrisis strategic issues because they are accompanied by time pressure and ambiguity. The more important, immediate, and uncertain the issue, the more likely it is to be characterized as a threat or a crisis. Similar to Dutton, Pearson and Clair (1998)

defined a crisis as a low-probability, high-impact event that threatens the security and well-being of the public, and is characterized by ambiguity of cause, effect, and means of resolution. Consequently, such situations require decisions to be made swiftly. These and other definitions of crisis include three key elements: ambiguity, high stakes, and urgency—all of which distinguish business crises from other problems or challenges an organization and its leadership may face. In addition to these features, we believe that crises are unique in the infrequency of their occurrence, their reach and magnitude of effect on stakeholders, and the likelihood and impact of publicity. To more fully appreciate a business crisis, we define it as:

> A rare and significant situation that has the potential to become public and bring about highly undesirable outcomes for the firm and its stakeholders, therefore requiring immediate corrective action by firm leaders (James & Wooten, 2010).

Crises are clearly complicated events. Although many crises seem to happen instantaneously, in truth, they generally unfold over a period of time. Researchers have established a minimum of five phases through which business crises pass (Pearson & Clair, 1998).

Crisis Phases

- *Phase 1: Signal Detection.* Although these are less evident in many crises that occur suddenly and without warning (e.g., a natural disaster), most other types of crisis have several early warning signs that lead an enlightened manager to know that something is wrong. A slowly building increase in customer complaints or defect rates, for example, can be a sign of trouble in product quality.
- *Phase 2: Preparation/Prevention.* The preparation and prevention phase is one in which managers engage in activities to plan for or avert a crisis. These activities may include developing crisis policies and procedures, identifying a crisis response team, and performing crisis drills. As Pearson and Mitroff (1993) cautioned, the preparation and prevention stage of crisis management should not imply that the goal for managers is to prevent all crises, but rather to engage in realistic planning to better position the organization to prevent

some crises and manage those that are unavoidable.

- *Phase 3: Containment/Damage Control.* The goal of the containment/damage control phase is to limit the reputational, financial, and other threats to firm survival in light of the crisis. This is achieved through activities that limit the encroachment of a localized crisis into otherwise unaffected parts of the business or the environment (Pearson & Clair, 1998). Containment and damage control tend to preoccupy management time and attention when crises occur. Indeed, it is these activities that people associate with crisis management, and they represent an important step toward the next phase: business recovery.

- *Phase 4: Business Recovery.* One of the ultimate goals of any crisis situation is to return the organization to its pre-crisis condition. In earlier research of firms involved in class action discrimination lawsuits, we found that executives try to constantly reassure stakeholders that, despite the disruption, business affairs are operating smoothly or will be returning to normal soon (James & Wooten, 2006). In the business recovery stage, crisis handlers should have a set of short- and long-term initiatives designed to return the business to normal operations.

- *Phase 5: Learning.* Organizational learning is the process of acquiring, interpreting, acting upon, and disseminating new information throughout the firm. When managing crisis situations, firm leadership runs the risk of adopting a reactive and defensive posture that prevents learning. Firms taking a learning stance, however, are still subject to the earlier crisis phases *and* their efforts are enhanced by an explicit attempt to understand the underlying organizational factors contributing to the crisis. Leaders can then leverage this insight to facilitate fundamental change in firm systems and procedures (Wooten & James, 2004).

Crisis Leadership Orientations

A crisis leadership orientation is a frame of mind accompanied by a key set of behaviors. The frame of mind determines the perspective from which leaders view the crisis and the criteria for selecting a course of action (Klann, 2003). It is characterized by openness to new experiences, willingness to learn and take risks, the ability to perceive possibilities for resolving the crisis, and a belief that, even in times of a crisis, people and organizations can emerge better off after the crisis than before (James & Wooten, 2010). The mindset associated with crisis leadership orientations represents repertoires of cognitive capabilities that develop before, during, and after a crisis as a result of information gathering, experiences, preparation, and feedback from external sources (Schoenberg, 2004; Weick, 2003). Developing this mindset is a continuous process of finding ways to integrate previously acquired knowledge, while building new mental models to prevent or resolve the crisis situation (Roberts, Madsen, & Desai, 2007). This requires analysis and reflection to gain insight, accompanied by decision making and actions to produce positive change (Edmondson, 2002; Hooijberg, Hunt, & Dodge, 1997).

The behaviors associated with crisis leadership orientations are complex and demand the ability to perform multiple roles and behaviors that adapt to the organizational and environmental context. The complexity of crisis leadership orientations manifest as the capacity to exhibit contradictory or opposing behaviors (as appropriate or necessary), while still maintaining integrity, credibility, and direction (Denison, Hooijberg, & Quinn, 1995). Similar to the dimensions of the competing values framework (CVF), crisis leadership orientations encompass behaviors that balance flexibility versus control and an internal versus external focus (Cameron, Quinn, DeGraff, & Thakor, 2006b). The control versus flexibility of a crisis leadership orientation entails actions focused on planning, goal clarity, and efficiency, but also on improvising and innovating as the crisis unfolds (Rego & Garau, 2007). These behaviors are a combination of short-term responses to urgent events associated with containing or resolving the crisis and long-term planning for resilience—the ability to absorb the strain of the crisis, recover from the crisis, and improve the functioning of the organization (Sutcliffe & Vogus, 2003). The internal versus external focus of crisis leadership orientations involve creating an organizational culture of compassion, optimism, hope, trust, and collaboration, while working with and responding to the demands of external stakeholders (Cameron & Lavine, 2006).

We propose that crisis leadership orientations enable positive organizing in crisis situations when it produces generative dynamics at the collective level. This, in turn, results in organizational resourcefulness that can lead to positive states such as resilience, enhanced organizational capabilities, or expanded organizational action repertoires (Glynn & Dutton, 2007). In the next sections, we present three crisis leadership orientations that allow for positive organizing in response to crisis events. In addition, we discuss the set of behaviors associated with these leadership orientations that can yield positive outcomes for the organization in crisis.

Crisis Leadership Orientation #1: Propensity to Reflect, Learn, and Adapt

Organizational learning is an adaptive process, in which firms use prior experience to develop new routines or behaviors that create opportunities for enhanced performance (Levitt & March, 1988). In keeping with this idea, researchers have referred to organizational learning as a change in routines (e.g., rules, procedures, strategies, and codes) and beliefs as a result of failure or an identified need to improve action through better knowledge and understanding (Fiol & Lyles, 1985). This assertion is based on three central tenets: firm behavior is based on routines; behavior in an organization is history-dependent and therefore focused on activities and interpretations of the past, rather than on expectations of the future; and firms are target-oriented and measure their success according to the achievement of goals.

Organizational learning can be planned and reflective or an urgent reaction to problem (Argyris & Schon, 1978). Somewhat similar to individual learning, organizational learning manifests as a change in thoughts and actions through trial-and-error experimentation of assimilating new knowledge and using what has already been learned (Bandura, 1977; Vera & Crossan, 2004). Through the learning process, therefore, an organization's dysfunctional routines will cease when they are associated with failure (e.g., inability to meet targets) and the organization's functional routines will continue or increase when they are associated with success (Cyert & March, 1963).

Crises are high-impact situations that require immediate and decisive action by organizational leaders. Given the speed with which decisions must be made and actions taken, there is presumably little time to think retrospectively (e.g., how or why did this happen?), or futuristically (e.g., what is the long-term impact?). This thereby potentially limits the opportunities for learning to occur. The result is that the vast majority of crisis management activity is focused on damage control and crisis containment (how do we solve this problem?).

Clearly, in the midst of a crisis, solving the problem should take precedence because the affected stakeholders need relief. Yet, if the opportunity exists for an organization to come through a crisis better than it was beforehand, then leaders must engage in reflection and learning in order to adapt positively to their new circumstances (Sitkin, 1992). Crises offer tremendous learning opportunities throughout the crisis life cycle, and yet too often firm leaders fail to take advantage of the learning that crises can provide.

Bazerman and Watkins (2004) argued that there are four ways in which organizations fail to learn how to anticipate a crisis:

- *Scanning failures*: As a result of arrogance, a lack of resources, or simple inattention, leadership fails to pay attention to internal or external warning signs that a potential problem is imminent.
- *Integration failures*: Failure to understand how seemingly disparate pieces of information (e.g., data, evidence) fit together to provide lessons for avoiding crisis.
- *Incentive failures*: Failure to provide adequate rewards or reinforcement for people who bring potential problems to the attention of others. Likewise, punishing people for surfacing such information is also a form of incentive failure.
- *Learning failures*: Failure to draw the appropriate lessons from prior crises and to preserve those lessons in the organization's memory.

In addition to Bazerman and Watkins' (2004) four ways organizations fail to learn how to anticipate a crisis, we suggest that framing crises as threats also contributes to an organization's inability to learn. By their nature, crises are threats to an organization, and leaders respond to threats in fairly consistent ways. Emotionally, threats elicit negative responses in people such as anger, anxiety, guilt, hopelessness, and depression (Smith & Ellsworth, 1985), as they contemplate the enormity of the threat. Staw, Sandelands, and Dutton (1981) theorized how organizational decision makers react to the stress and anxiety of strategic issues perceived as threatening. Their research suggested that threats can restrict the amount of information and how it is processed, as well as the extent to which information is shared. The 2010 Deepwater Horizon oil rig explosion and subsequent oil spill along the U.S. Gulf Coast is a perfect example. Given the magnitude, impact, and long-term consequences of the spill, the crisis facing the British Petroleum (BP) executives and others seemed overwhelming at times. Although BP did not have the "luxury" of being paralyzed by indecision and inaction, the emotional toll likely contributed to them making numerous errors in judgment in communicating with the media (Goodman, 2010).

In light of the emotional and behavioral tendencies in response to crisis, it is unlikely that many leaders are positioned to see opportunity or positivity from them. In fact, the general tendencies in responding to crisis are antithetical to those needed for learning and creativity to emerge (Amabile, 1996). Stated more affirmatively, crises are more apt to be seen as sources of opportunity when organizational leaders have a learning orientation.

Dweck (1990) distinguished between people who are motivated by the learning process and by opportunities for growth and development (learning oriented) from those who are motivated primarily by performance and achievement (achievement oriented). She and others demonstrated that people with a learning orientation elicit more adaptive responses to adverse conditions (Dweck, 1990; Cron, Slocum, VandeWalle, & Fu, 2005). This is not to say that leaders with an inherent orientation to learn, reflect, and adapt are no less susceptible to the negative emotional and behavioral responses to threats described above; rather, they have an added perspective that allows them to see crises not only as threats, but *also* as opportunities (Brockner & James, 2008). A learning orientation enables adaptive responses to adverse situations because the focus is on cognitive experimentation, divergent thinking, and feedback loops that inform, direct action, and create dialogue between the leader, stakeholders, and the environment (Hadley, Pittinsky, Sommer, & Zhu, 2009; Palus & Horth, 2002).

Crisis Leadership Orientation #1: Behaviors

Leaders who possess the crisis leadership orientation toward reflecting, learning, and adapting demonstrate a set of behaviors that we believe distinguishes them in their ability to lead through times of crisis, and positions them to ultimately identify and manifest positivity. These behaviors are: seek diverse learning sources, accept all forms of data, and search for the root causes of problems.

SEEKS DIVERSE LEARNING SOURCES

Organizational audiences, or stakeholders, are an important constituency during a crisis (Ginzel,

Kramer, & Sutton, 1993). Too often, crisis handlers and decision-makers are sensitive to stakeholders who are the most influential or have the most power in the organization (James & Wooten, 2006). This may or may not include stakeholders most affected by the crisis, or others who may have relevant information and perspectives that would be helpful to the decision making and crisis response process. Unfortunately, by limiting the sources from which a leader gathers information, he or she also potentially limits his or her understanding of the root causes of the crisis, possible means for addressing the crisis, and possible outcomes beyond damage control and containment. Leaders who seek diverse learning sources are not only open to external expertise from nonobvious sources, but proactively test ideas, logic, and strategy with these experts as well (Hargadon & Bechky, 2006.

Kim's (1998) research on crisis construction and organizational learning at Hyundai Motor illustrates how leaders sought and applied knowledge acquired from diverse sources as a proactive strategy for the global shakeout of the automotive industry in the 1990s. Hyundai's leaders sought information from international alliance partners, suppliers, literature searches, and design experts, and by observing technologies in other industries. In addition to the acquisition of information, Hyundai used the knowledge by engaging in a cycle of studying the information, experimenting, and improving on its application. This created a "can-do" organizational culture and closed performance gaps amid a crisis.

AN OPEN MIND FOR FILTERING DATA

The euphemism "don't shoot the messenger" suggests that communicating bad or undesirable information, particularly to those in more senior positions, can be threatening. Consequently, unless explicitly instructed to serve as a devil's advocate, many employees are unwilling to communicate bad news. Information that could be helpful in decision making is often never shared with those making the decisions. This was a critique of the decision making and communication process in the 1986 launch of the fateful space shuttle *Challenger* (Vaughn, 1996), and continues to play out in organizational settings. When leaders have an open mind for different forms of data, they both affirm and disconfirm information, regardless of how uncomfortable or undesirable it may be. Furthermore, these leaders have the capacity to not only accept data from various sources, but actively solicit the data, recognizing that there is as much to be learned from mistakes and failures as there is from success (Cannon & Edmonson, 2001; Sitkin, 1992). This approach creates a psychologically safe climate in which organizational members will seek help, discuss errors, and speak up. Empirical evidence from stressful work environments such as hospital operating rooms suggests this promotes a learning orientation throughout an organization's hierarchy (Edmondson, Bohmer, & Pisano 2001).

SEARCHES FOR ROOT CAUSES

Not all crises are human-made, but all responses to crises are. As we have stated (James & Wooten, 2010), it is often the responses to the crisis that can have the most deleterious reverberations and long-standing organizational consequences. The most effective responses are those that include adequate investigation into the underlying root causes of the crisis. Such an investigation is critical regardless of whether the crisis was human-made or an act of nature, because leaders have a responsibility to prepare adequately for or prevent threats regardless of their source, especially if the organization's systems, practices, or norms contributed to the crisis or prevented effective responses to it.

Searching for root causes means that leaders engage in information searches that provide a solid understanding of why the crisis occurred or why they may have mishandled it. Argyris and colleagues (1977, 1978) refer to this as *double-loop learning* and propose that organizations engaged in double-loop learning reexamine and reflect upon fundamental organizational norms, policies, or objectives to discern the underlying reason for a problem. To the contrary, firms engaged in single-loop learning take corrective actions for a problem without questioning or changing fundamental aspects of the organization that may have contributed to it. In responding to a crisis, firms that focus primarily on single-loop learning are unlikely to reap the same lessons and therefore the same opportunities for positive change as are firms that engage in double-loop learning (Wooten & James, 2005). Finally, fully enacting the searching for root causes behavior requires that leaders seek information from multiple, even nonobvious, sources, such a competitors and experts from different industries (Brockner & James, 2008).

In a longitudinal study of 20 business crises, several leaders of organizations that received positive feedback for their management of crisis situations conducted root cause analysis by investigating what happened and using this knowledge to learn how to not only contain the crisis, but also to prevent future crises (Wooten & James, 2008). One example discussed in this research was the Tyco case's leadership team. After a financial scandal, Tyco's leadership team inquired into what happen in the past that caused the crisis and probed deeply to identify systematic accounting fraud and audit the company's internal operations (Pilmore, 2003). The ability to ask difficult questions and learn from the answers helped Tyco understand its mistakes and reevaluate its processes, so that problematic issues would not surface in the future.

Crisis Leadership Orientation #2: Propensity for Seeing Possibilities

To lead positivity before, during, and following a crisis requires a leadership orientation toward seeing possibilities. In other words, organizations must have leaders with a proclivity to take in a vast amount of information, frame it from multiple perspectives, and see not only the potential for threat, but also the potential for opportunity. Generally, however, people are limited in their cognitive capacity to process and use all the information to which they are exposed. This is especially true in contexts marked by uncertainty (Tversksy & Kahneman, 1974). Consequently, seemingly innate tendencies manifest in ways that influence how leaders deal with environmental cues and ambiguous data. As stated, leaders tend to interpret data negatively and respond defensively by, in part, limiting what they choose to pay attention to and how they use the information they have (Staw et al., 1981).

Inherent to the crisis leadership orientation for seeing possibilities is Weick's notion of sense-making (1988, 1993, 1995). *Sense-making* refers to the process by which people give meaning to various experiences or stimuli. It is the act of turning circumstances into a situation that can be comprehended explicitly in words and that serves as a springboard into action. A particularly noteworthy and relevant property of sense-making is that it is influenced by context (Brown, Stacey, & Nandhakumar, 2007; Salancick & Pfeffer, 1978). Leaders, for example, read contextual information into whatever situation they are confronting; indeed, how they interpret that context influences how they make order—or make sense—of what they are facing. When leaders are confronted by something new, unusual, or something they do not understand, or for which they have no reference, the tendency is to seize data that will force the anomaly into something they can comprehend or upon which they can make decisions or take actions (Weick, 1988). In responding to a crisis, then, leaders may be inclined to make sense of the situation as if it can be resolved with only previously tested policies or procedures or other previously used behavioral responses and communication patterns. Crises, by their nature, however, require innovation and improvisation. To see the possibilities for resolving a crisis entails learning how to "drop tools" that are irrelevant, so that the organization can be flexible and adaptable in its response to the situation (Weick, 1993).

The orientation for seeing possibilities invites crisis leaders to make sense of crisis situations not as a typical problem, but rather as a new set of circumstances for which a new awareness and a new set of responses is required. Further, leaders who possess this orientation may be primed to act in ways that may counteract the natural tendency toward rigidity in response to a crisis. As a result, they will be more receptive to seeing previously untapped means for dealing with crises and personal or organizational opportunities that are unlikely to be recognized at all, much less seriously considered, for those without this orientation (Brockner & James, 2008; James & Wooten, 2010). We further propose that leaders who are oriented to see possibilities will be more inclined to see new possibilities for crisis handling, as well as read the context in ways that makes them more attuned to seeing the warning signs of a pending crisis, thereby leading to the possibility for crisis prevention. The following behaviors exemplify the crisis leadership orientation for seeing possibilities in crisis: perspective taking, using technology to manage complexity, and forecasting and assessing risk.

Crisis Leadership Orientation #2: Behaviors
PERSPECTIVE TAKING
Perspective taking refers to the ability to consider another person's or group's point of view (Galinsky & Moskowitz, 2000), which can lead to a connection between one's self and someone else in such a way that greater understanding is engendered. Perspective taking has been linked positively to one's social competence and self-esteem (Davis, 1983), cognitive functioning (Piaget, 1932), and moral reasoning (Kohlberg, 1976), and negatively to social aggression (Richardson, Hammock, Smith, Gardner, & Signo, 1994) and stereotyped thinking (Galinsky & Moskowitz, 2000). Perhaps most germane for manifesting positivity in crisis, though, is that the act of considering how someone is affected by his or her situation is more likely to yield an empathic

response than not taking such a perspective. Crises offer important and meaningful opportunities for leaders to connect and empathize with their employees and other critical stakeholders. In fact, during a crisis, one of the core responsibilities of a leader is ensuring the well-being of those affected by the crisis. Perspective taking allows leaders to better understand and empathize with others, and, in turn, act in the best interest of stakeholders.

For example, during the 2008 financial crisis, the CEO and senior leadership team of the Genworth Financial Corporation made communicating with stakeholders a key priority (Goldberg & James, 2008). The communication, however, was two-way: Information was both sent out and taken in from affected stakeholder. In the process of truly listening and caring about what employees, creditors, and others were saying about their fears and concerns during this troubling time, Genworth leadership identified a set of actions in the course of handling the crisis that addressed these issues. In this case, the company's willingness to engage in perspective taking allowed them to emerge from the crisis successfully. Indeed, they retained—and in some cases gained—the trust of important stakeholders.

USING TECHNOLOGY TO MANAGE COMPLEX INFORMATION
To lead an organization effectively and resolutely throughout the crisis life cycle requires coordinating people and other resources, synthesizing and interpreting information, and communicating with multiple stakeholders (Dantas & Seville, 2006). The broader the crisis, the more coordinating and collaborative mechanisms will be required, and the more technology will play a role in effective crisis resolution. In the book *Good to Great*, Jim Collins (2001) devotes a chapter to technology accelerators and offers data indicating that great companies think about and use technology differently than do average companies. It is not that technology itself propels a company past its competition, but rather that technology aids an existing innovative business idea or solution.

To extend this logic, we suggest that using technology effectively, coupled with a solid crisis response strategy, will lead to the proliferation of creative thinking with respect to crisis handling, a faster crisis response, and the recognition of various possibilities for generating positive organizational adaptation post-crisis. Leidner and her colleagues' (2009) research on the Singaporean government's effective management of the severe acute respiratory syndrome (SARS) and Asian tsunami disasters highlights the role of technology as a resource for recognizing signals and seeing the big picture. In both crisis situations, the Singaporean government was able to enact a crisis response plan efficiently because its information technology infrastructure was coupled with the interaction of collaborative network stakeholders. The information technology infrastructure enabled communication across organizational boundaries, the search for and distribution of information, and the agile mobilization of people. Thus, technology served as a mechanism to identify the possibilities for transforming and coordinating resources into crisis resolution actions.

FORECASTING SCENARIOS AND ASSESSING RISK

Crisis leadership requires that leaders recognize all phases of the crisis, from the prodromal (early or pre-crisis) stages, through the acute (immediate action is required) stage, to the recovery and resolution stage (Kash & Darling, 1998; Pearson & Mitroff, 1993). An important set of activities during the prodromal stage is to forecast and assess risk. Moreover, effective crisis leaders will identify organizational vulnerabilities and assess risk not only for obvious crisis triggers, but for potential situations that are not readily apparent. This is particularly difficult for many leaders because ego needs and psychological defense mechanisms can often impede their ability to take the threat of a crisis seriously (James & Wooten, 2005).

Forecasting techniques involve predictions. The predictions are based on a fundamental assumption that the organization is in fact capable of responding to, and more importantly, adapting to the changing circumstances that crises impose. Leaders oriented to focus on the prodromal stage, and in turn engage in forecasting and risk assessment, will position their firms better to prevent crises or, at the very least, limit the impact and severity of a crisis should it occur. Leaders without this orientation are unlikely to hold this assumption and will therefore make decisions and take action in ways that emphasize damage control rather than considering or recognizing possibilities for positive adaptation.

Scenario planning, a process of visualizing probable future events, their consequences, and responses, is one technique that can be used to enhance a leader's propensity to forecast and assess risks. By engaging in scenario planning, crisis leaders learn how to expand their view of what is possible and create a script for actions (Moats, Chermack,

& Dooley, 2008). Although the specific scenario may differ when the crisis occurs, that act of scenario planning develops the ability of leaders to discover opportunities for resolving and learning from the crisis because they have analyzed various alternatives (Penrose, 2000).

Crisis Leadership Orientation #3: Expectation of Trust

On the surface, the notion of trust seems a simple construct. It is one of the first lessons in childhood, and it factors into every stage and phase of life. In reality, though, the feelings, emotions, and experiences of trust suggest that it is a complex phenomenon, one that has implications for emotional, interpersonal, and organizational well-being. Despite the tendency to talk about trust in one-dimensional ways, scholars have begun to recognize and explore trust as a multidimensional construct (Butler, 1991; Swan, Trawick, Rink, & Roberts; 1988). According to Mishra's (1996) review of the trust literature, four distinct dimensions of trust lead to the following definition: "*Trust* is one party's willingness to be vulnerable to another party based on the belief that the latter party is: 1) competent, 2) open, 3) concerned, and 4) reliable". Fundamental to this definition is the notion of vulnerability; in this case *vulnerability* refers to the willingness to take action when the potential for loss exceeds the potential for gain (Luhmann, 1979). Vulnerability, in turn, implies risk. It is one thing, for example, for a manager to say she trusts her employees. It is quite another to leave employees in complete charge of a work product for a client. The rhetoric of trust does not require risk, whereas the behavioral component does. In our example, when the risk is enacted, the manager becomes vulnerable to the employee.

The implications for trust in organizational settings have been well documented (see for example Kramer & Tyler's 1996 seminal book on trust in organizations). Moreover, scholars have examined the role of trust in the specific context of organizational crises (Mishra, 1996). As James and Wooten (2010) discussed, crises invoke vulnerability for all stakeholders affected by a crisis event. Leaders in crises, for example, are vulnerable in that the consequences of their decisions and actions have the power to affect, positively or negatively, themselves and their organizations. Similarly, victims, or potential victims, are vulnerable in that they may find themselves lacking control over their own circumstances, with the actions of another party potentially determining their fate. Thus, crisis leaders are faced with an awesome responsibility to manage vulnerability—which is shared across multiple parties—carefully.

Leaders oriented to expect trust in times of crisis are likely to act in ways that demonstrate trust by clearly working to serve in the best interest of the stakeholders. Over time, stakeholders begin to recognize the leader as someone who can be trusted, and the expectation of trust is eventually reciprocated. Consider, for example, the quick response and outpouring of support by firm leaders following the 1982 Johnson & Johnson (J&J) product tampering crisis (Barton, 2008). In this case, someone maliciously introduced cyanide poison into bottles of Tylenol, killing seven people and introducing fear into the minds of tens of thousands of consumers. Up to that point, J&J had built a solid reputation of being one of the most trusted brands in the world, and they were distinguished from their competitors in the extent to which they were guided by their company credo to put people first (Pauly & Hutchinson, 2005. In order of priority were customers, employees, communities in which they operated, and stockholders. Although the J&J credo does not specifically mention trust, the sense that trust is at the core of their operating philosophy is evident by the way it refers to the company's responsibilities to people and its commitment to ideals such as fairness, dignity, openness, and citizenship.

In response to the Tylenol crisis, firm leaders were guided by the firm's credo in their decision making, which included pulling the product from store shelves across the country despite the incidences of poisoning being localized to the Chicago region (Paine, 1994). This action clearly made J&J vulnerable to potentially severe financial ramifications, and yet it was precisely their willingness to put the company in this position of vulnerability (i.e., to take the risk on behalf of their consumers) that allowed them to sustain their reputation of trust. In turn, customers remained loyal to the firm. Almost 30 years later, J&J continues to be lauded for its actions and has preserved its trustworthy reputation—both of which are two positive outcomes of effective crisis handling. Three behaviors uniquely exemplify the crisis leadership orientation around the expectation of trust: communicating effectively, demonstrating concern, and acting reliably.

Crisis Leadership Orientation #3: Behaviors
COMMUNICATING EFFECTIVELY
Communication is the primary mechanism through which firm leaders influence the perceptions that

organizational stakeholders hold of the organization. Communicating in a way so that the firm's values can be recognized and understood clearly is an important part of not only reputation building, but also of creating a relationship between the firm and its various audiences. When the Baltimore & Ohio Railroad Museum's Roundhouse roof collapsed after a blizzard, the staff communicated via telephone, Internet, and the media the status of the crisis and its plans for managing the crisis (Christianson, Farkas, Sutcliffe, & Weick, 2009). The response was deep concern and support, revealing the significant role the museum played in the community and energizing support for rebuilding the museum.

DEMONSTRATING CONCERN
Thomas and Kilmann (1974) identified a model of conflict resolution (based largely on the managerial grid created by Blake & Mouton, 1964) grounded along two axes: assertiveness and cooperation. Underlying these axes is the extent to which a focal individual is primarily concerned with self or other. The more one is motivated by self concerns, the more likely one is believed to resolve conflict in assertive ways. Conversely, being motivated largely by concerns for other should yield cooperative approaches to conflict resolution. These approaches are not necessarily mutually exclusive, but rather are captured along a continuum, suggesting that people can have varying degrees of concern for self and other. The same is true for trust. Where one falls along the self versus other continuum has implications for the possibility of trust developing in the relationship (Kanter, 1983, 1989; Nanus, 1989). A leader's demonstration of concern for others in times of crisis should reap an expectation of trust by stakeholders.

Flight Director Eugene Krantz's behavior when leading Apollo 13 after an explosion that aborted the space vehicle's planned moon landing exemplifies demonstrating concern for others in a crisis situation (Glynn & Dutton, 2007; Useem, 1998) During the astronaut's return to earth, Krantz demonstrated concern for his team members that worked to safely direct the space shuttle by emphasizing their psychological well-being. Krantz created a team climate of optimism and hope using both words and actions. This produced a work environment centered on trust, in which members learned the difference between the "I" and the "we" component of the team and how they could contribute (Foust, 2005).

ACTING RELIABLY

At the root of almost every definition of trust is the notion of reliability or consistency (see for example Gabarro, 1987; McGregor, 1967; Ouchi, 1981). Without the expectation of being able to count on a person or a particular behavior, trust is simply not feasible. Moreover, reliability is important regardless of whether the relied upon behavior is desirable or undesirable. Research in the area of leadership and trust has also suggested that acting reliably is central to the manifestation of perceived trustworthiness by and for leaders (Kilpatrick & Locke, 1991). In times of organizational crisis, we believe it is important that leaders provide some semblance of normalcy in contexts marked by ambiguity and change. Consistent and redundant behavior is one way to generate a sense of normalcy and reliability. For example, when leaders put reliable communication systems or messaging in place to convey important information to key stakeholders about the crisis, organizational audiences will likely feel more informed and more trusting of their leadership.

Crisis leaders who act reliably build trust through their values, how they communicate these values, and their associated behaviors that validate these values. Seeger and Ulmer's (2001, 2002) research on crisis leadership highlights the significance of acting reliably and with sensitivity to the human aspects of a crisis. In their research, they found that leaders who demonstrated this behavior had a reservoir of support and goodwill with stakeholders. In addition, the trust that was a by-product of reliable actions committed stakeholders to rebuilding the organization and opened the possibility of exploring opportunities for renewal rather than issues of blame or culpability.

Future Directions

Just as there are positive outcomes to be reaped from effective crisis leadership, there are also opportunities for scholars of crisis research. The opportunities are both methodological and theoretical in nature. Methodologically, crisis research has been hampered by the sheer nature of crises. Crises often take us by surprise and yet generally require an immediate response. Moreover, because of the intense focus required in crisis management, as well as the negativity and potential legal ramifications that surround organizations in crisis, there is generally little desire for firm leaders to talk openly (or provide survey or other forms of data) about their experiences. Consequently, the ability to prepare an empirically sound and pretested research protocol is limited.

Crisis scholars, therefore, have the opportunity to develop innovative research methods to capture data from organizations and their leaders experiencing a crisis. For future research, the methodologies may want to consider using simulations to study the effectiveness of crisis leadership orientations or conducting event histories to understand how specific crisis leadership behaviors unfold before, during, and after a crisis manifests. Likewise, to circumvent the challenges associated with the unwillingness or inability of organizational leaders to communicate about their experiences leading in times of crisis, insider–outsider teams may be a solution (Bartunek & Louis,1996). This could entail external researchers collaborating with key stakeholders associated with the crisis to gain a greater understanding of how specific leadership orientations are enacted in crisis situations. In comparison to traditional research partnerships, this type of research team may be in a better position to capture real-time data at the evolution of an organization in crisis.

Moreover, future research should explore what types of empirical data would be most beneficial for enhancing our understanding about the positive outcomes that are experienced from crises. This may require developing and validating measures for organizational learning during and after a crisis, and exploring what leaders do with knowledge acquired in crisis situations. Also, creating and testing measures for organizational resilience would contribute to our understanding of how organizations recover after a crisis. Measures for resilience may help us understand what leadership behaviors enable organizations to implement positive organizing practices that not only result in recovery, but also improve the organization's effectiveness.

Theoretically, there continue to be numerous questions to address regarding the relationship between leadership and the ability to bring about positive outcomes in times of crisis. We address this topic in some of our earlier work (e.g., Brockner & James, 2008; James & Wooten, 2010). For example, beyond the learning orientation, are there other stable individual traits that differentiate leaders who are able to realize and manifest positivity in crisis from those who do not? It would also be interesting to draw on various leadership theories to study how leaders develop these traits overt time by considering factors such as life experiences, educational background, and different career assignments.

Another research topic for the future would be to explore the extent that organizational culture influences the likelihood that positive outcomes will manifest. Examining the culture of organizations managing a crisis would allow for the studying of those values and practices that enable some organizations to thrive while other organizations struggle. Connecting various theoretical perspectives of organizational culture with specific leadership orientations that emphasize behavioral norms, such as trust, collaboration, innovation, would help in understanding how organizations balance the competing demands of adapting while preserving the positive core.

Conclusion

We conclude this chapter by explicitly joining with the POS community to find ways to introduce positivity into organizational scholarship. On the surface, organizational crises may seem like an unlikely place to explore for positivity, but we believe our ideas with respect to the crisis leadership orientations and their concomitant behaviors illustrate one such opportunity. We believe that leadership orientations consistent with learning and adaptation, a penchant for seeing possibilities, and expectations of trust are more inclined to bring about positive individual and organizational outcomes post-crisis than are orientations that are more neutral or that embrace negative leadership perspectives. Such orientations are pillars of crisis leadership (James & Wooten, 2010).

Throughout this chapter, we have attempted to provide insights to help scholars better understand leadership amid crisis, demonstrating that a central component of crisis leadership is the ability to seize and manifest opportunity from the crisis, while realizing that positivity in crisis is no easy task. To do so often requires the ability to counter human defense tendencies. Yet, there are examples of people and organizations that have adopted a positive frame of mind in response to threat and that have demonstrated positive organizing during a crisis. Consequently, what these individuals and organizations do in response to crises is worth examining. There are potential benefits for both theory and practice if we can better understand the factors that contribute to leaders enacting positive organizing in crisis situations. Thus, it is our hope that this chapter stimulates future research and enables organizations to develop leadership capabilities in this vitally important area.

References

Amabile, T.M. (1996). *Creativity in context*. Boulder, CO: Westview Press.

Argyris, C. (1977). Double-loop learning in organizations. *Harvard Business Review, 55*(5), 115–125.

Argyris, C., & Schon, D.A. (1978). *Organizational learning: A theory of action perspective*. Reading, MA: Addison-Wesley.

Bandura, A. (1977). *Social learning theory*. Englewood Cliffs, NJ: Prentice-Hall.

Barton, L. (2008). *Crisis leadership now: A real-world guide to preparing for threats, disaster, sabotage and scandal*. New York: McGraw Hill.

Bartunetk, J., & Louis, M. (1996). *Insider/outsider team research. Qualitative research methods series (40)*. Thousand Oaks, CA: Sage.

Bazerman, M.H., & Watkins, M.D. (2004). *Predictable surprises: The disasters you should have seen coming and how to prevent them*. Boston: Harvard Business School Press.

Blake, R., & Mouton, J. (1964). *The managerial grid: The key to leadership excellence*. Houston, TX: Gulf Publishing Co.

Brockner, J.B., & James, E.H. (2008). Toward an understanding of when executives see opportunity in crisis. *Journal of Applied Behavioral Science, 44*(7), 94–115.

Brown, A.D., Stacey, P., & Nandhakumar, J. (2007). Making sense of sensemaking narratives. *Human Relations, 61*(8), 1035–1062.

Butler, J. (1991). Toward understanding and measuring conditions of trust: Evolution of conditions of trust inventory. *Journal of Management, 17*(3), 643–663.

Cameron, K.S. (2008). *Positive leadership: Strategies for extraordinary performance*. San Francisco: Berrett-Koehler.

Cameron, K.S., & Lavine, M. (2006). *Making the impossible possible: Leading extraordinary performance: The Rocky Flats story*. San Francisco: Berrett-Koehler.

Cameron, K.S., Dutton, J.E., & Quinn, R.E. (2003). *Positive organizational scholarship: Foundations of a new discipline*. San Francisco: Berrett-Koehler.

Cameron, K.S., Dutton, J.E., Quinn, R.E., & Spreitzer, G.M. (2006a). What is positive organizational scholarship? Retrieved November 23, 2006 from http://www.bus.umich.edu/Positive/WhatisPOS/.

Cameron, K.S., Quinn, R.E., DeGraff, J., & Thakor, A. (2006b). *Competing values leadership: Creating value in organizations*. Northampton, MA: Edward Elgar.

Cannon, M., & Edmonson, A. (2001). Confronting failure: Antecedents and consequences of shared beliefs about failure in organizational work groups. *Journal of Organizational Behavior, 22*(2), 161–177.

Christianson, M.K., Farkas, M.T., Sutcliffe, K.M., & Weick, K.E. (2009). Learning through rare events: Significant interruptions at the Baltimore & Ohio Railroad Museum. *Organization Science, 20(5)*, 846–860.

Collins, J. (2001). *Good to great*. New York: HarperCollins.

Cron, W.L., Slocum, J.W., Jr., VandeWalle, D., & Fu, Q.F. (2005). The role of goal orientation on negative emotions and goal setting when initial performance falls short of one's performance goal. *Human Performance, 18*(1), 55–80.

Cyert, R.M., & March, J.G. (1963). *A behavioral theory of the firm*. Englewood Cliffs, NJ. Prentice-Hall.

Dantas, A., & Seville, E. (2006). Organizational issues in implementing an information sharing framework: Lessons from the Matata flooding events in New Zealand. *Journal of Contingencies and Crisis Management, 14*(1), 38–52.

Davis, M.H. (1983). Measuring individual differences in empathy: Evidence for a multidimensional approach. *Journal of Personality and Social Psychology, 44(1)*, 113–126.

Denison, D.R., Hooijberg, R., & Quinn, R.E. (1995). Paradox and performance: Toward a theory of behavioral complexity in managerial leadership. *Organization Science, 6*(5), 524–540.

Dutton, J.E. (1986). The processing of crisis and non-crisis strategic issues: A situationalist perspective. *Journal of Management Studies, 23*(5), 501–517.

Glynn. M.A., & Dutton, J.E. (2007). *Generative dynamics of positive organizing.* Unpublished manuscript.

Dweck, C. (1990). Motivation. In R. Glaser, & A. Lesgold (Eds.), *Foundations for a cognitive psychology of education.* Hillsdale, NJ: Lawrence Erlbaum.

Edmondson, A. (2002). The local and variegated nature of learning in organizations: A group-level perspective. *Organization Science, 13*(2), 128–146.

Edmondson, A., Bohmer, R.M.J., & Pisano, G. (2001). Disrupted routines: Team learning and new technology adaptation. *Administrative Science Quarterly, 46*(4), 698–716.

Fiol, C.M., & Lyles, M.A. (1985). Organizational learning. *Academy of Management Review, 10*(4), 803–813.

Foust, J. (2005, April 18). We must never fail. Gene Kranz, Apollo 13, and the future. *The Space Review.* Retrieved from http://www.thespacereview.com/article/357/1.

Gabarro, J. (1987). *The dynamics of taking charge.* Boston: Harvard Business School Press.

Galinsky, A.D., & Moskowitz, G.B. (2000). Perspective-taking: Decreasing stereotype expression, stereotype accessibility, and in-group favoritism. *Journal of Personality and Social Psychology, 78*(4), 708–724.

Ginzel, L.E., Kramer, R.M., & Sutton, R.I. (1993). Organizational impression management as a reciprocal influence process: The neglected role of the organizational audience. In B.M. Staw, & L.L. Cummings (Eds.), *Research in organizational behavior* Vol. 15 (pp. 227–266). Stamford, CT: JAI Press.

Goldberg, R., & James, E.H. (2008). *Building stakeholder trust during crisis: Genworth Financial.* Case Study, Charlottesville, Virginia: Darden Publishing, University of Virginia.

Goodman, P. (2010, August 21). In case of an emergency: What not to do. *New York Times.* Retrieved August 25, 2010 from http://www.nytimes.com/2010/08/22/business/22crisis.html?_r=1&sq=Peter%20S.%20Goodman&st=cse&scp=2&pagewanted=print.

Hadley, C., Pittinsky, T., Sommer, S., & Zhu, W. (2009). *Measuring the efficacy of leaders to access information and make decision in a crisis: The C-LEAD scale.* Working paper series RWP09–021, John F. Kennedy School of Government, Harvard University, Cambridge, MA.

Hargadon, A., & Bechky, B. (2006). When collections of creatives become creative collectives: A field study of problem solving at work. *Organization Science, 17*(4), 484–500.

Hooijberg, R., Hunt J., & Dodge. G. (1997). Leadership complexity and development of the leaderplex model. *Journal of Management, 23*(3), 375–408.

James, E.H., & Wooten, L.P. (2005). Leadership as (un)usual: How to display competence in times of crisis. *Organizational Dynamics, 34*(2), 141–152.

James, E.H., & Wooten, L.P. (2006). Diversity crises: How firms manage discrimination lawsuits. *Academy of Management Journal, 49*(6), 1103–1118.

James, E.H., & Wooten, L.P. (2010). *Leading under pressure: From surviving to thriving before, during, and after a crisis.* New York: Routlege Press.

Kanter, R.M. (1983). *The change masters: Innovation and entrepreneurship in the American corporation.* New York: Simon & Schuster.

Kanter, R.M. (1989). *When giants learn to dance.* New York: Simon & Schuster.

Kash, T.J., & Darling, J.R. (1998). Crisis management: Prevention, diagnosis and intervention. *Leadership and Organization Development Journal, 19*(4), 179–186.

Kilpatrick, S.A., & Locke, E.A. (1991). Leadership: Do traits matter? *The Executive, 5*(1), 48–60.

Kim, L. (1998). Crisis construction and organizational learning: Capability building in catching up at Hyundai Motor. *Organization Science, 9*(4), 506–521.

Klann, G. (2003). *Crisis leadership: Using military lessons, organizational experiences, and the power of influence to lessen the impact of chaos on the people you lead.* Greensboro, NC: Center for Creative Leadership.

Kohlberg, L. (1976). Moral stages and moralization: The cognitive-developmental approach. In T. Lickona (Ed.), *Moral development and behavior* (pp. 31–53). New York: Holt, Rinehart, & Winston.

Kramer, R.M., & Tyler, T. (1996). *Trust in organizations.* Newbury Park, CA: Sage.

Leidner, D., Pan, G., & Pan, S. (2009). The role of IT in crisis response: Lessons from SARS and Asian Tsunami disasters. *Journal of Strategic Information Systems, 18*(2), 80–99.

Levitt, B., & March, J.G. (1988). Organizational learning. *Annual Review of Sociology, 14*, 319–338.

Luhmann, N. (1979). *Trust and power.* Hoboken, NJ: John Wiley & Sons.

Moats, J., Chermack, T., & Dooley, L. (2008). Using scenarios to develop crisis managers: Applications of scenario planning and scenario-based training. *Advances in Developing Human Resources, 10*(3), 397–324.

McGregor, D. (1967). *The professional manager.* New York: McGraw-Hill.

Mishra, A. (1996). Organizational responses to crisis: The centrality of trust. In R. Kramer, & T. Tyler (Eds.), *Trust in organizations* (pp. 261–287). Newbury Park, CA: Sage.

Nanus, B. (1989). *The leader's edge: The seven keys to leadership in a turbulent world.* Chicago: Contemporary Books.

Ouchi, W.G. (1981). *Theory Z: How American business can meet the Japanese challenge.* Reading, MA: Addison-Wesley.

Paine, L. (1994). Managing for organizational integrity. *Harvard Business Review, 72*(2), 106–117.

Palus, C., & Horth, D. (2002). *The leader's edge.* San Francisco: Jossey-Bass.

Pauly, J.J., Hutchison, L.L. (2005). Moral fables of public relations practice: The Tylenol and Exxon Valdez cases. *Journal of Mass Media Ethics, 20*(4), 231–249.

Pearson, C., & Clair, J. (1998). Reframing crisis management. *Academy of Management Review, 23*(1), 59–76.

Pearson, C., & Mitroff, I. (1993). From crisis prone to crisis prepared: A framework for crisis management. *Academy of Management Executive, 7*(1), 48–59.

Penrose, J. (2000). The role of perception in crisis planning. *Public Relations Review, 26*(2), 155–171.

Piaget, J. (1932). *The moral judgment of the child.* London: Kegan, Paul, Trench, & Trubner.

Pilmore, M. (2003). How we're fixing up Tyco. *Harvard Business Review, 81*(12), 96–103.

Richardson, D.R., Hammock, G.S., Smith, S.M., Gardner, W., & Signo, M. (1994). Empathy as a cognitive inhibitor of interpersonal aggression. *Aggressive Behavior, 20*(4), 275–289.

Rego, L., & Garau, R. (2007). *Stepping into the void: Reflections and insights from a forum on crisis leadership convened at the Center for Creative Leadership*. Greensboro, NC: Center for Crisis Leadership.

Roberts, K.H., Madsen, P., & Desai, V. (2007). Organizational sense-making during crisis. In C. Pearson, C. Roux-Dufort, & J. Clair (Eds.), *The international handbook of organizational crisis management* (pp. 107–122). London: Sage.

Salancik, G.R., & Pfeffer, J. (1978). A social information processing approach to job attitudes and task design. *Administrative Science Quarterly, 23*, 224–253.

Schoenberg, A. (2004). *What it means to lead during a crisis*. Unpublished doctoral thesis, Syracuse University, Syracuse, New York.

Seeger, M.W., & Ulmer, R.R. (2001). Virtuous responses to organizational crisis: Aaron Feuerstein and Milt Cole. *Journal of Business Ethics, 31*, 369–376.

Seeger, M.W., & Ulmer, R.R. (2002). A post-crisis discourse of renewal: the cases of Malden. *Journal of Applied Communication Research, 30*: 126–142.

Seligman, M.E.P., & Csikszentmihalyi, M. (2000). Positive psychology: An introduction. *American Psychologist, 55*(1), 5–14.

Sitkin, S.B. (1992). Learning through failure: The strategy of small losses. In B.M. Staw, & L.L. Cummings (Eds.), *Research in organizational behavior* Vol. 14 (pp. 231–266). Greenwich, CT: JAI Press.

Smith, C.A., & Ellsworth, P.C. (1985). Patterns of cognitive appraisal in emotion. *Journal of Personality & Social Psychology, 48(4)*, 813–838.

Staw, B.M., Sandelands, L.E., & Dutton, J.E. (1981). Threat-rigidity effects on organizational behavior. *Administrative Science Quarterly, 26*(4), 501–524.

Sutcliffe, K.M., & Vogus, T. (2003). Organizing for resilience. In K.S. Cameron, J.E. Dutton, & R.E. Quinn (Eds.), *Positive organizational scholarship: Foundations of a new discipline* (pp. 94–110). San Francisco: Berrett-Koehler.

Swan, J., Trawick, I., Rink, D., & Roberts, L. (1988). Measuring dimensions of purchaser trust of industrials salespeople. *Journal of Personal Selling & Sales Management, 8*, 1–9.

Thomas, K.W., & Kilmann, R.H. (1974). *Thomas-Kilmann conflict mode instrument*. Mountain View, CA: Xicom.

Tversky, A., & Kahneman, D. (1974). Judgment under uncertainty: Heuristics and biases. *Science,* 185(4157), 1124–1131.

Useem (1998). *The leadership moment: Nine true stories of triumph and disaster and their lessons for us all*. New York: Three Rivers Press.

Vaughn, D. (1996). *The Challenger launch decision: Risky technology, culture, and deviance at NASA*. Chicago: University of Chicago Press.

Vera, D., & Crossan, M. (2004). Strategic leadership and organizational learning. *The Academy of Management Review, 29*(2), 222–240.

Weick, K.E. (1988). Enacted sensemaking in crisis situations. *Journal of Management Studies, 25*(4), 305–317.

Weick, K.E. (1993). The collapse of sensemaking in organizations: The Mann Gulch disaster. *Administrative Science Quarterly, 38*, 628–652.

Weick, K.E. (1995). *Sensemaking in organizations*. London: Sage.

Weick, K.E. (2003). Positive organizing foreshadowed in organizational tragedies. In K.S. Cameron, J.E. Dutton, & R.E. Quinn (Eds.), *Positive organizational scholarship: Foundations of a new discipline* (pp. 66–80). San Francisco: Berrett-Koehler.

Wooten, L.P., & James, E.H. (2008). Linking crisis management and leadership competencies: The role of human resource development. *Advances in Human Resource Management Development, 10*(3), 352–379.

Wooten, L.P., & James, E.H. (2004). When firms fail to learn: The perpetuation of discrimination in the workplace. *Journal of Management Inquiry, 13*(1), 23–33.

Wooten, L.P., & James, E.H. (2005). Challenges of organizational learning: Perpetuation of discrimination against employees with disabilities. *Behavioral Sciences and the Law, 23(1)*, 123–141.

Resilience at Work

Building Capability in the Face of Adversity

Brianna Barker Caza *and* Laurie P. Milton

Abstract

Building on and extending beyond current definitions, we define resilience at work as a positive developmental trajectory characterized by demonstrated competence in the face of, and professional growth after, experiences of adversity in the workplace. In this chapter, we review, consider, and comment on the research history, nature, and consequences of resilience at work; share our perspective on resilience at work and situate this in current debate; and identify promising directions for future research. Our primary objective is to stimulate a productive conversation about resilience at work in ways that enable our research community to advance this important area of inquiry.

Keywords: Resilience, stress, coping, identity

Turbulent, ambiguous, complex—sound familiar? Uncertain, exhausted, afraid—this too? Every era has its challenges. The fact is that bad things happen. They happen to individuals, to groups, to organizations, and to industries. A large literature on coping has taught us, however, that difficult events do not themselves determine the trajectories of individuals, groups, or organizations. How each responds differentiates those that succeed in the present and into the future. Experiencing negative events and stressors in the workplace can lead to poor personal and professional outcomes such as burnout (e.g., Buunk & Schaufeli, 1993; Lee, 1993; Malach, 1982; Maslach, 2001; Pines, Aronson, & Kafry, 1981), but does not always do so. Many individuals recover and are able to cope with adversity (e.g., Pines et al., 1981). Some even thrive as they experience difficult circumstances (Bonanno, 2004, 2005, 2010; Bonanno et al., 2002). In fact, many individuals actually emerge from adversity with competency, efficacy, and growth (Sutcliffe & Vogus, 2003). These "resilient" individuals, groups, and organizations adapt positively during and following

adversity or risk. In this chapter, we focus on such exemplars, those who demonstrate excellence in adverse situations—situations that often undermine others. In a field in which research on adversity has focused largely on negative coping trajectories, our approach, which focuses on a positive resilience trajectory, contributes to a more complete understanding of how individuals react to adversity at work.

Our primary objectives are to provide an overview of what we know about individual resilience at work, and to pave the way for future research in this important area of inquiry. First, we define resilience at work and situate our definition within the perspectives of other researchers. To this end, we examine how others define resilience in various contexts, explain choices we made in crafting our definition, and distinguish it from similar concepts. Second, we review bodies of literature that illuminate resilience at work. Third, we consider how individuals, groups, and organizations may cultivate individual resilience at work. In so doing, we pay particular attention to connections between identity and the process of resilience. To conclude, we offer suggestions for future research and briefly discuss the theoretical and practical importance of studying resilience at work

Defining Resilience at Work

Resilience had been defined in multiple ways over time and across disciplines. Bridges (1995, p.57) defines resiliency simply, as "the ability to bend and not break." This definition is consistent with the way in which resilience has been used in the physical sciences to refer to a property of a material that enables it to resume its original shape or position after being bent, stretched, or compressed. In contrast, the social sciences use the term *resilience* in a number of ways to describe a general state of being that allows living organisms to positively adapt to adversity. Some have thus defined resilience as a relatively stable personality trait characterized by the ability to bounce back from negative experience and by flexible adaptation to the ever-changing demands of life (Block & Block, 1980; Block & Kremen, 1996). Others have defined resilience as the ability to maintain psychological stability and experience fewer mental health problems when presented with a threat (Bonanno et al., 2005; Bonanno, Wortman, & Nesse, 2004; Fredrickson, Tugade, Waugh, & Larkin, 2003). Yet another group has taken a more dynamic view, defining resilience as a process encompassing positive adaptation within the context of adversity (Luthar & Chicchetti 2000; Luthar, Cicchetti, & Becker, 2000; Masten,1994; 2001; Masten, Best, & Germanzy, 2001).

Two consistent aspects of resilience emerge from these definitions (Luthar et al., 2000). The first is that resilience requires a precondition of some negative stressor, or exposure to a significant threat. The second is the individual's achievement of positive adaptation in the face of this stress or threat (Garmezy, 1990; 1993; Luthar et al., 2000; Masten & Reed, 2002). Positive adaptation is defined in terms of behaviorally manifested social competence (Luthar & Cicchetti, 2000). In other words, resilience involves the ability of an individual to meet developmental tasks (Masten, Best, & Garmezy, 1990; Masten & Coatsworth, 1998). For example, research on resilience in children has demonstrated that a child of schizophrenic parents positively adapts when that child consistently meets social and cognitive developmental standards as he or she grows. Resilience in the context of work also benefits from a developmental perspective. Just as children are prone to rapid growth and development, so too are adults who are progressing in their careers.

An adult's resilience in the process of career growth often depends on his ability to meet developmental standards in his profession even when he is exposed to adversity. As Sutcliffe and Vogus (2003, p. 97) explain: "An entity not only survives/thrives by positively adjusting to current adversity, but also in the process of responding strengthens its capabilities to make future adjustments." A developmental approach to resilience thus requires that an individual follow a positive developmental trajectory.

Following from this logic, we define *resilience at work* as a developmental trajectory characterized by demonstrated competence in the face of, and professional growth after, experiences of adversity in the workplace. Each enables an individual to handle future challenges. From our perspective, resilience at work encompasses behavioral, affective, and psychological manifestations of positive adaptation and professional growth within the context of significant adversity at work.

Although most researchers generally agree that resilience entails both adversity and positive adaptation, there is controversy over more specific aspects of the concept of resilience (e.g., Luthar et al., 2000; Masten, 1990; Masten & Reed, 2002). The most important debates encompass three issues (e.g., Bonanno, 2004; Roisman, 2005) that our definition of resilience at work takes a firm position on: whether resilience is conceptualized as a fixed trait (outcome), a developmental process, or a phenomenon; what counts as adversity; and what counts as a positive adjustment.

Is Resilience a Trait, Process, or Phenomenon?

The distinction between resilience as a trait and resilience a process is one of the most heated debates in the psychological study of resilience. Much of the psychological research on resilience has described it as an individual trait (e.g., Fredrickson et al., 2003; Tugade & Fredrickson, 2004; Tugade, Fredrickson, & Barrett, 2004). Psychological researchers often label a person as "resilient" or "invulnerable" and thereby imply that resilience is a fixed state (Luthar et al., 2000). In fact, psychological resilience is defined in many sources as a relatively stable personality trait characterized by the ability to bounce back from negative experience and by flexible adaptation to the ever-changing demands of life (Block & Block, 1980; Block & Kremen, 1996; Fredrickson et al., 2003). Individuals who are able to bounce back from stressful experiences quickly and efficiently are considered resilient.

Yet, studies demonstrating the role of contextual factors suggest that resilience may not be merely a personality attribute. For instance, Luthar and colleagues (2000) argue that resilience is a dynamic process, which changes over time and by situation, and is separate from those who subscribe to Block and Block's (1980) influential conceptualization of the ego resilience. Ego resilience does not require exposure to substantial adversity, whereas by definition resilience presupposes prior substantial adversity (Luthar, 1991).

More recently, researchers have extended the process-based view of resilience further, defining resilience as "a phenomenon defined by the success (positive developmental outcomes) of the (coping) processes involved" (Leipold & Greve, 2009, p. 41). This conceptualization suggests that resilience is a developmental trajectory that should itself be explained rather than a resource that explains a developmental outcome. This definitional shift focuses attention on the underlying mechanisms and processes that lead to a developmental trajectory. Greve and Staudinger (2006) conceptualize resilience as a constellation that encompasses the fit among individual resources (capacities, competencies, and attributes), social conditions (e.g., social support), and developmental challenges or problems (e.g., obstacles, deficits, and losses). In the study of organizational resilience, Sutcliffe and Vogus (2003) recognize that for resilience to occur, resources need to be activated as challenges at work arise (Sutcliffe & Vogus, 2003). Our definition of resilience at work is consistent with that of Greve and colleagues' and Sutcliffe and Vogus's (2003) conceptualization of organizational resilience, as a developmental trajectory characterized by competence, efficacy, and professional growth in the face of work-related adversity. We thus capture the idea that resilient individuals are developing in their careers, even when obstacles are in the way. We also suggest that resilience results from an interaction of the individual, the adversity, and the individual's social environment.

What Is Adversity At Work?

Resilience researchers vary in their views about what qualifies as adversity (Luthar et al., 2000). Although studies of childhood resilience have examined both single stressful experiences and an aggregate of multiple risk factors, studies of adult resilience have mainly focused on single critical incidents (e.g., death of a spouse or experience of an extreme event such as September 11, 2001; e.g., Bonanno, 2004,

2005; Mancini & Bonanno, 2009). In contrast, we take a broad, subjective approach to defining adverse events, considering adversity to encompass any events that the person perceives to be disruptive to his or her working environment. We expect adverse events to vary in magnitude, impact, and duration. However, our subjective approach does not place boundaries around what can be experienced as an adverse event. This approach is consistent with field research that found much variability in what nurse-midwife informants considered to be a critical event (Caza, 2010). For some, the death of a patient or being named in a lawsuit was an adverse event. For others, the event was a single negative interaction with a physician. Thus, it is difficult to objectively define an adverse event. Adversity is a subjective experience; an event itself only becomes a stressor if it is perceived as such.

The Role of Adversity

Beyond definitions, the exact role of adversity in a resilience trajectory is debated. Some researchers talk about resilience "in the face of" adversity (e.g., Bonanno, 2004, p. 602), or "despite" adversity (Luthar et al., 2000, p. 554), or "in the context of" adversity (Masten & Reed, 2002, p. 75). Others conceptually assign a more active role to adversity. Roosa (2000), for example, argues that individuals emerge with new knowledge, skills, and increased competence not *despite* but *because* of their experience with an adversity. Experiencing adversity is thus seen as helping to promote growth in individuals in some way. This latter perspective is consistent with the developmental perspective of resilience that Sutcliffe and Vogus (2003) take by positioning resilience as the capacity to rebound from adversity strengthened and more resourceful. They thereby imply that an adversity has a role in promoting growth by serving as a platform for learning.

What Is Positive Adjustment?

Just as the conditions associated with resilience vary, so too do the ways that resilience has been operationally defined. These latter definitions have ranged from viewing resilience as the absence of psychopathology in a child of a mentally ill parent, to the recovery of function in a brain-injured patient (Cicchetti & Garmezy, 1993), to the ability to gain capacity during a crisis (Sutcliffe & Vogus, 2003). Definitions thus vary on three dimensions. First, whereas some researchers focus exclusively on the maintenance of functioning, others require evidence of developmental growth. As noted earlier, the definition of "positive adjustment" that we include in our conceptualization of resilience at work requires that the latter show evidence of developmental growth. As individuals proceed through their careers, they are expected to become more professionally competent with time and experience. A resilient individual should be able to continue to achieve developmental milestones in the face of adversity, thereby demonstrating professional growth. Further, the process of responding to the adversity will enable the person to increase his or her ability to handle future adversities (Sutcliffe & Vogus, 2003). Substantial, career-altering growth is not required. Simply cultivating a new practice that works efficiently in a crisis or developing a better understanding of the nature of one's work would signal growth.

A second distinction between definitions of positive adjustment is that, although some researchers claim that resilient individuals must excel in only one domain, others argue that they must achieve above-normal functioning in multiple domains (Masten & Reed, 2002). The latter is a more global definition of resilience (e.g., Tolan, 1996). Each recognizes, however, that individuals may be resilient in one life domain or sphere, but not in others. Tusaie and Dyer (2004, p. 3) illustrate the domain-specificity of resilience by noting that: "an individual from an abusive, impoverished childhood may demonstrate education and work resilience by obtaining a doctoral degree and a high-paying job, but be unable to maintain intimate relationships, and demonstrate impairment in the psychosocial domain." Similarly, a police officer may cope well with the death of a spouse, but fail to cope or fall into a negative spiral of coping when faced with adversity at work—or, vice versa.

Mounting research supports the notion that resilience is not one dimensional and monolithic, but encompasses multiple domains (e.g., Hunter, 2001; Luthar et al., 1993; Werner & Johnson, 1999). Werner and Johnson (1999) argue that, in research and in practice, it is more useful to recognize domain-specificity than to focus on global resilience since behaviors across domains are not often highly correlated. In fact, as Luthar and colleagues (1993) demonstrated, an individual's level of resilience may vary across domains. Individuals can show signs of substandard functioning in some domains but positive development in others. We concur; the way individuals react to adversity is domain-specific. We thus accept that individuals can excel in their personal lives, but succumb to adversity in their work lives and vice versa. Our focus is primarily on how individuals respond to negative stressors in the workplace. Although some contagion effects in resilience across life domains may be likely, it is not necessarily present (e.g., Luthar & Cushing, 1999). We thus treat *resilience at work* and *personal resilience* as separate constructs. An individual may be able to demonstrate growth in the face of adversity at work but not during a general life crisis or vice versa.

Distinguishing Resilience from Similar Concepts

Resilience is distinct from other positive trajectories such as recovery, thriving, and post-traumatic growth (see Table 68.1 for a summary). First, resilience is conceptually and empirically distinct from recovery because of its developmental component (Bonanno, 2004; Luthar et al., 2000; Masten & Reed, 2002). An individual who has recovered will have returned to his or her prior level of competence (Sonnentag & Neff, 2011, Chapter 66, this volume), whereas an individual who demonstrates resilience will have emerged from the adversity with growth and strengthened capabilities for dealing with future challenges (Sutcliffe & Vogus, 2003).

Second, resilience is also distinct from thriving, defined as the psychological state in which individuals experience both a sense of vitality and a sense of learning at work (Spreitzer, Sutcliffe, Dutton, Sonenshein, & Grant, 2005), because resilience presupposes an element of significant adversity (Cicchetti, 1996; Luthar et al., 2000) before individuals experience vitality and learning, whereas thriving does not. In this way, resilience is also different from positive adjustment, which examines how individuals adjust to varying situations, again not requiring the element of significant adversity (Cicchetti, 1996; Luthar et al., 2000). Highlighting the importance of development with and without adversity, research has demonstrated that these two trajectories have different antecedents (Cicchetti & Rogosch, 1997) and correlates (Luthar et al., 2000).

The emphasis on the role of adversity in promoting growth aligns the concept of resilience at work most closely with the psychological construct labeled *post-traumatic growth* (PTG; as reviewed by Maitlis (2011, Chapter 69, this volume). Post-traumatic growth is defined as a positive psychological change experienced as a result of the struggle with highly challenging life circumstances (Calhoun & Tedeschi, 1999). Both resilience as we define it and PTG thus

Table 68.1 Comparison of resilience to similar concepts (in the context of work)

Term	Definition	Role of Adversity	Reaction to Adversity	Functioning After the Event
Recovery	The process of regaining something that has been lost and of returning to a former state (Sonnentag & Neff, Chapter 66, this volume).	Negative events are considered a necessary precondition.	Negative states are reduced, but positive states are also increased.	Return to an earlier state of functioning.
Resilience	A developmental trajectory characterized by demonstrated competence in the face of, and professional growth after, experiences of adversity in the workplace.	Essential precondition that causes a trajectory of positive adaption.	Demonstrated competence during the adversity, and some degree of professional growth post-adversity.	The individual continues on a positive developmental trajectory and is better prepared for future challenges.
Posttraumatic Growth	The experience of positive change that occurs as a result of the struggle with highly challenging life crises (Maitlis, Chapter 69)	Large adversity that shatters previously held schemas is essential.	The individual endures a period of distress after the event that leads to a significant positive transformation.	Transformational growth after the event.
Thriving	A psychological state in which individuals experience both a sense of vitality and a sense of learning at work (Spreitzer, Sutcliffe, Dutton, Sonenshein, & Grant, 2005).	Thriving does not require adversity as a precondition	This state is not in reaction to an external event.	Individuals demonstrate vitality and learning.

involve improvement rather than simply returning to baseline functioning. Yet, these concepts are distinguishable in two important ways: the magnitude of change/growth and the source of the change/growth. Post-traumatic growth is most often described as a transformational process, as a complete change in an established set of schemas (Tedeschi & Calhoun, 2004). Post-traumatic growth would be evident, for example, in individuals who completely change their profession in order to find their true calling after experiencing an adverse event at work. In contrast, we conceptualize resilience at work in terms of professional growth that individuals exhibit after experiences of adversity. Although this growth may in fact well be a significant qualitative change in functioning, it may also be more subtle. For example, in response to adversity, a resilient individual may demonstrate growth and learning by deepening his or her knowledge of some aspect of his or her profession, such as a medical procedure or flight protocol, or by coming to a better understanding of his or her own capacity to perform under pressure. Another important distinction between resilience and PTG is the source of change/growth. In the PTG literature, growth is

achieved primarily through cognitive processing and disclosure that takes place post-adversity (Tedeschi & Calhoun, 2004). In contrast, resilience focuses on growth and development gained through the process of doing one's work during adversity rather than via a mental crisis endured after the experience of adversity.

Learning About Resilience at Work

One of the challenges in studying resilience is the requirement for both vulnerability and adaptability to an adverse event. As noted, operationalizing these terms can be difficult. And, even if definitions are agreed, it may be difficult to create or find situations to study that involve both. Much knowledge of resilience in adults is based on a rich literature on resilience in vulnerable children (Sutcliffe & Vogus, 2003). The psychological study of resilience emerged from studies of individuals' (primarily children's) positive adaptation despite extremely difficult circumstances, such as familial mental illness or poverty (Garmezy, 1971; Luthar, 1999; Luthar et al., 2000; Masten & Reed, 2002; Werner & Smith, 1982). Early research on resilience was thus largely dominated by a focus on childhood resilience, and definitions were based upon development-based that would be expected in a child.

Only in the past decade have researchers focused their attention on understanding resilience in adult populations (Bonnano, 2004; Sutcliffe & Vogus, 2003). It has thus become necessary to recalibrate the construct of resilience at work to anchor it to developmental outcomes expected in an adult. Bonnano's (2004) research on adults' psychological and physical functioning after exposure to an isolated and potentially highly disruptive event, such as the death of a close relation or a violent or life-threatening situation, has confirmed that the process of resilience in adults is qualitatively different from resilience in children. Although the childhood resilience literature may provide a starting point for understanding the process of resilience in adults, there are likely key differences in protective factors and process in the two populations (Bonanno, 2004).

To date, most empirical research studies on adult populations have focused primarily on acute, critical life events such as individuals facing illness, disability, or the loss of a loved one (Bonanno & Manacini, 2008). These studies have sought to understand how some individuals overcome and even thrive in the face of negative events while others are unable to do so. Much research has studied resilience in individuals with chronic illness and disabilities (Davidson et al., 2005; Farber, Schwartz, Schaper, Moonen, & McDaniel, 2000), chronic pain (Karoly & Ruehlman, 2006; Zautra, Johnson, & Davis, 2005), mental health disorders (e.g.; Tugade & Fredrickson, 2004), and even learning disorders (Sorensen et al., 2003; Werner, 1993). A second stream of research has focused on understanding how individuals cope with disasters, such as the loss of a loved one or national tragedies like 9/11 (e.g., Bonanno, 2004, 2005).

Three different, yet complementary, streams of research are aimed specifically at building an understanding of resilience in the context of work. First, in the field of positive organizational scholarship, a literature on organizational resilience (Sutcliffe & Vogus, 2003), examines ways that individuals, groups, and organizations are collectively resilient in the face of adversity at work. A second stream of research has focused on career resilience, defined as "the ability to adapt to changing circumstances" (London, 1993, p. 55) in individuals who are faced with the sudden loss of a job (Waterman, Waterman, & Collard, 1994). The third, practitioner-focused stream aims to understand and promote individual correlates of resilience at work (e.g., Maddi &

Khoshaba, 2005). Although these three literatures appear to overlap minimally, and to approach resilience from different angles, they all focus on ways in which resilience at work can be cultivated. They thus seek to understand the trajectory that illuminates ways in which individuals, social groups, and organizations can cultivate resilience at work. Toward this end, in the next section, we summarize the findings and propose a framework for understanding how to promote resilience at work.

Cultivating Resilience at Work

One could easily infer from the literature that, to develop resilience in their workforces, organizations should select and hire people who are resilient and release (fire) those who do not maintain and develop their competence in adverse circumstances. The underlying view would be that resilience is an individual difference; some have it and others do not, some can develop it and others cannot, so selecting those who do is good for business. This would be an impoverished viewpoint. As we have pointed out, resilience at work should be viewed as a developmental process rather than a fixed trait (Sutcliffe & Vogus, 2003). It is therefore essential to understand the dynamics that help to cultivate resilience at work.

Psychological resilience scholars use the terms *risk factors* and *protective factors* to describe an individual's potential for resilience (e.g., Werner & Smith, 1982). A risk factor is an aspect of the individual (or environment) that makes him or her more likely than other individuals to develop a specific negative outcome after experiencing adversity (Luthar et al., 1993; Rutter, 1993). In contrast, a protective factor is an aspect of the individual (or environment) that lessens or eliminates the effects of risk factors, thus protecting individuals from the effects of risk factors (Tusaie & Dyer, 2004). The defining feature of a protective factor is that its presence modifies an individual's response to a risk situation (Luthar et al., 2000). Debate continues about whether protectors must only work under adversity (e.g., akin to an airbag on an automobile), or may also operate under normal conditions, but become stronger in adverse times (Masten & Reed, 2002).

Reviews of the psychological resilience literature indicate that three broad sets of protective factors promote resilience: aspects of the individuals, characteristics of their family, and components of the wider social context (e.g., Garmezy, 1985; Luthar et al., 2000; Masten, Morrison, Pellegrini, &

Tellegen, 1990; Rutter, 1987, 1993; Werner & Smith, 1982). This work suggests that, to cultivate resilience at work, individual, social, and organizational factors must be considered. Resilience emerges through an interaction of these three factors, which we now explore. We first consider how individuals can develop and maintain their resilience, and how others at work can help them do so. Our premise is that individual and social factors work in tandem to create, maintain, and develop resilient individuals, work groups, units, and organizations. We focus on individual resilience and thus consider how individuals themselves, the organizational members with whom they interact, and organizations can develop and maintain a resilient workforce.

After considering how individuals can cultivate their own resilience, we consider the pivotal role of social support and, in our concluding sections, bridge to the role of organization culture and structure. We argue that colleagues and organizations themselves may support and develop or, alternatively, undermine the resilience of organization members however resilient these members are when they are recruited. Research suggests that shared identity bonds, high-quality relationships, and identity validation and confirmation are social processes that facilitate individual resilience. At the system level, organizations that value and normalize resilience and that affirm and otherwise support the value and practice of resilience via organization culture and structure will similarly do so.

Individual Protective Factors

Scholars have emphasized the importance of individual variables, or resources, in fostering resilience (e.g., Sutcliffe & Vogus, 2003; Wildavsky, 1991). For instance, Wildavsky (1991) discussed three essential elements of resilience resources: storability, malleability, and the ability for useful conversion when challenge arises. In organizational resilience literature, Sutcliffe and Vogus (2003) focus on knowledge and adaptability as important capacity building resources for resilience. Maddi and Khoshaba (2005) insist that the key to resilience is the development of psychological hardiness, which is composed of three attitudes: commitment, control, and challenge (Kobasa, 1979). Other work on career resilience proposes that those who are resilient in the face of sudden job loss are high in self-efficacy and risk taking, but low in dependency (London, 1993). Outside the workplace, personality researchers have found evidence suggesting that individual differences (e.g., self-enhancing biases,

attachment style, repressive coping and positive emotions) promote resilience to life's stressors (Fraley & Bonanno, 2004; Fredrickson et al., 2003; Tugade & Fredrickson, 2004; Mancini & Bonanno, 2009).

Individual differences such as these are important correlates of resilience at work. However, to cultivate resilience, individuals need to also know how to create and mobilize these resources. Molinsky and Stoltz (2010) suggest that individuals can build their capacity for resilience by viewing adversity from four different lenses: controlling the factors causing the crisis, the impact of management's actions, the breadth of the crisis, and duration of the situation. Similarly, Mancini and Bonanno (2009) posit that the appraisal process is a key mechanism to the resilience process. We agree that how individuals understand a situation affects their resilience base. We complement this perspective by proposing that an individual's view of him or herself, identity, constitutes another key mechanism through which individuals can cultivate, mobilize, and maintain resources that support resilience.

Identity As a Key Factor in the Resilience Process

Research suggests and we argue that one's identity encompasses a cognitive schema that includes the individual's goals, values, and practices at work (Schein, 1978), and can be a key source of resources that enable individuals to be resilient at work. For instance, research on resilience to loss has indicated that identity plays a key role in shaping how individuals respond (Mancini & Bonanno, 2006). Experiencing adversity at work often increases the salience of one's professional identity (Caza, 2010). A literature on meaning-focused coping posits that individuals react to adverse events by trying to understand the experience and integrate it with their self-views (Park & Folkman, 2004). As a result, identity processes and mechanisms become important resources that shape individuals' responses to adversity. We posit that identity plays three key roles in the resilience process: as a resource that affects resilience potential, as a mechanism for behavioral elasticity, and as a key sense-making framework.

First, a valued professional identity may provide an individual with a sense of efficacy, control, positive emotion, and a strong sense of self, each of which affects his or her resistance. In a study of mental health crisis clinicians, Edwards (2005) found that sense of self was a primary factor of resilience. Other researchers have found that individuals who display resilience to loss are more likely to feel continuity within their selves and identities; they are thus more able respond effectively to external demands (Mancini & Bonanno, 2006).

Second, an individual's identity may be useful as a resource that helps guide behavior in times of crisis and thereby fosters capability and effectiveness. Recently, Mancini and Bonanno (2009) proposed flexible adaptation or behavioral elasticity as a key to individual resilience. Flexible adaptation entails the ability to match behavior to the demands of a stressor. We believe that complex identity structures enable individuals to engage in flexible adaptation. An individual's identity is an important source of practice schemas and resources that individuals can rely on and combine creatively to react appropriately in adverse situations (Callero, 1986; 1994; Caza & Bagozzi, 2010). These findings suggest that not only is it important to have a valued identity, but that the structure of one's identity may influence resilience. Specifically, having a complex identity may provide individuals with more practice-based schemas or resources for flexible adaptation. Indeed, Mancini and Bonanno (2009) posit that identity complexity serves as an important coping factor that is operative at high distress levels.

Third, an individual's identity serves as an important meaning-making framework that will help individuals to understand and to grow from the adversity (Caza, 2010). Research has shown that identity construction is critical for sense-making behavior in organizations (Pratt, Rockmann, & Kaufmann, 2006; Weick, Sutcliffe, & Obstfeld, 2005). Making sense of adversity is pivotal to helping individuals follow a positive developmental trajectory and emerge with increased learning and competence.

In addition to these three functions of identity during the resilience process, identity change can also be an important indicator of the resilience process. Through the process of experiencing and responding to adversity at work, individuals may learn more about themselves, including their capabilities and professional strengths. As a result, their identities may broaden and become more complex, thus enabling them to more capably handle future adversities via the three mechanisms noted above.

Social Protective Factors

Individuals undoubtedly play an important role in shaping resilience, but it is indeed true that no person is an island. Individuals are social creatures embedded in social systems (Granovetter, 1985), and therefore the process of resilience at work is often shaped by supportive relationships with other people (Peterson, 2006) and social structure. Research on organizational resilience has underlined the critical role of relationships in fostering resilience at the collective level (Gittell, 2008; Gittell, Cameron, & Lim, 2006; Sutcliffe & Vogus, 2003). Specifically, the way in which individuals relate to one another before, during, and after an adverse event has been shown to impact resilience. Building on this work, we focus on how others in the organization can help to foster individual resilience at work. Our premise is that colleagues and organizations themselves may support and develop or, alternatively, undermine the resilience of organization members.

Social relationships play a pivotal role in buffering individuals from the negative effects of adversity (Cohen & Willis, 1985) and in allowing individuals to function at a higher level in the face of adversity (Mancini & Bonanno, 2009; Shih, 2004). Studies have found that children are more likely to be resilient if they have close relationships with caregiving adults (Luthar, Cicchetti, & Becker, 2000; Masten & Reed, 2002; Rutter, 1990). Social support has also been found to reduce the harmful effects of stress during times of adversity (Aspinwall & Taylor, 1997; Cohen & Willis, 1985) and to prevent workplace burnout (for a review see Lee & Ashforth, 1996). We posit that three sets of social forces affect the relationship between perceived social support and resilience: shared social identities, high-quality relationships, and confirming identities.

Individuals who share social identities with others at work are more likely to perceive themselves as having strong social support. Haslam and Reicher (2006) demonstrated that having a strong identification with a social group increases an individual's ability to respond to stressors through its impact on social support. Individuals who are strongly identified with a group are more likely to feel empowered when facing adversity, even when the group they receive social support from is stigmatized (Shih, 2004).

Individuals who share common identities or who have complementary identities may be particularly able to help one another become and remain resilient. Such individuals relate particularly effectively in adverse circumstances inasmuch as sharing similar outlooks and behaviors facilitates their interdependent work. Individuals who share identities may spend more time together, become more familiar with one another (Shah & Jehn, 1993), and develop other bonds (e.g., work friends, social friends, mentor and mentee). Over time, as they acquire a history of relating successfully to one another, they may develop protocols for dealing with adversity and providing one another with support in so doing. For example, they may develop debriefing routines within which they help one another learn from adverse circumstances or share material, social, or other forms of help.

Relationships do not have to stem from a shared-identity in order to facilitate individual resilience at work. Researchers have shown that relationships can be critical during adversity experiences by influencing core collective processes such as coordination (Gittell, 2008) and error detection (Weick & Roberts, 2003). High-quality relationships in particular are likely to have a potent and positive impact on how individuals respond to stressors (Dutton & Heaphy, 2003). More specifically, these high-quality relationships help individuals to feel valued and connected. We propose that high-quality relationships foster individual resilience, in part, because these confirm the identities of others. As discussed earlier, individuals tend to behave in ways that are consistent with their identities (Bem, 1972). Those who work in occupations or who engage in work that is consistent with their identities will tend to enact their roles competently, and go that extra mile to contribute (Milton, 2003). Those who work in organizations whose image is consistent with their personal professional identities cooperate more therein than do others (Dukerich, Golden, & Shortell, 2002). Even in emergency response teams, to the extent that a workmate validates and values and in multiple ways thus confirms a person's identity, this person tends to cooperate more with the workmate (Milton & Westphal, 2005), which often leads to resilience (Gittell, 2008). Individuals who work with others who confirm their identities will tend to be more psychologically centered and behaviorally predictable and hence reliable and able to perform at their best. Their social situation is consistent with and supportive of who they are; they are valued and can be authentic. In interviews, members of these groups attributed positive performance to being able to rely on others to help them stay centered in difficult circumstances and to debrief experiences and lessons learned thereafter.

The social support (by way of cooperation and helping) that emanates from identity confirmation ties may be the bedrock that supports (behavioral and emotional) resilience in diverse group members operating in demanding contexts. Polzer, Milton, and Swann (2002) found that diverse groups characterized by high levels of interpersonal congruence—one form of confirmation—tended to outperform other groups on innovative tasks. These may be groups within which strong mutual identity confirmation-based networks and the cooperation and support associated with these are embedded (Milton & Westphal, 2005). High-quality relationships, characterized by identity confirmation, may also help individuals to grow and learn from the adverse situations they encounter together. High-quality connections are more likely to be associated with learning behaviors in the workplace (Carmeli, Brueller, & Dutton, 2009), which is critical to a resilience trajectory (Sutcliffe & Vogus, 2003).

Summary

Research on coping with loss, childhood resilience, career resilience, and organizational resilience has all contributed to our understanding of individual resilience at work. In this section, we have explored the individual and relational factors that help to cultivate individual resilience at work. Specifically, we found that identity is an important mechanism of resilience at work, and that relational practices that support and enrich an individual's identity will influence his or her ability to follow a resilient trajectory.

Future Directions

Research on resilience at work has several important directions to pursue and many questions to answer. In this section, we propose three research pathways that we believe will enrich our understanding of resilience at work. The first is an examination of resilience in individuals working in high-risk professions. The second is research investigating the role of organizational protective factors in developing individual resilience at work. The third is the development of measurement tools for resilience at work.

Resilience At Work in High-risk Professions

Although the formal study of resilience at work is still in its infancy, resilience trajectories have been captured for decades in studies of individuals in high-risk professions. Those who work in these professions either endure chronic stressors or are frequently exposed to critical acute adversity, or both. The burnout literature suggests that individuals in some professions are constantly faced with stress and adversity at work. Most often, these professions either entail large amounts of emotional labor (e.g., nursing, teaching) (Halbesleben & Buckley, 2004; Maslach, 1982; Maslach Schaufeli, Leiter, P., 2001), or constant role stress (e.g., nursing managers, pharmacists) (Bakker, Schaufeli, Sixma, Bosveld, & van Dierendonck, 2000; Lee & Ashforth, 1996; Sitkin & Sutcliffe, 1991 Zellars, Perrewe, Hochwarter, 2006). Other professions are at risk for severe, acute forms of adversity. For example, due to the nature of their work, emergency care workers, doctors, social workers, and police often face tragedies at work (e.g., the unexpected death of a patient or client). Dealing with such events takes a psychological and emotional toll on individuals and thereby increases the likelihood that they will experience burnout (e.g., Razavi, Delvaux, Farvacques, & Robaye, 1988).

Examining individuals in these professions indicates that, despite the focus on burnout in these professionals, a large number of these individuals refuse to burn out in the context of chronic or acute stressors. Many display resilience, although the label "resilience" may not have been applied. Noting this reality, there has been a recent surge of interest in resilience within these populations. For example, Edward (2005) examined resilience in mental health care crisis clinicians who were constantly at risk of burnout. Gillespie, Chaboyer, Wallis, and Grimbeek (2007) built and tested a model of resilience in operating rooms. We believe that organizational scholars can learn a great deal by examining resilience that takes place constantly in many high-risk professions, and we suggest that additional research in this domain would be valuable.

Organizational Protective Factors

Organizations play an important role in shaping individual resilience at work. Although organizations may do so in many ways, we suggest that research on whether and how organization culture and structure affect resilience shows particular promise. Organizations whose cultures and structures support individual resilience may benefit considerably. Organizational culture forms the social context and provides structure for organization members and for relations among them. To fully develop the resilience of their members, research suggests that organizations themselves adopt an ideology that espouses beliefs, values, and norms that are consistent with and advance resilience. To the extent that their symbols, language, narratives, and practices are aligned with this ideology, the culture would be said to support resilience (cf. Trice & Beyer, 1993, for a related argument).

From a cultural perspective, just as cooperative group norms mediate the effect of demographic heterogeneity on work processes and outcomes such as satisfaction, individual performance, team efficiency, and effectiveness in groups (Chatman & Flynn, 2001), so too may organizational norms that support resilience in organizations (e.g., recognize that effective professionals learn to cope over time and benefit from social support) foster resilience within the organization. Just as organization practices, such as addressing conflict constructively, helped members of SEMATECH (a consortium of competitors such as Intel and Motorola) cooperate to revitalize the U.S. semiconductor industry in the 1990s (Browning, Beyer, & Shetler, 1995), so too may practices such as debriefing tough situations as they unfold and providing support to those experiencing adversity help organization members to resile. Symbols that recognize individual learning and excellence in the face of adversity may similarly do so. In organizations whose culture validates and values and in other ways confirms the identities of organization members and thereby embeds cooperation (Milton & Westphal, 2005), social and structural systems that advance individual resilience may be prevalent. Differences between the cultures of organizations within which individuals do and do not resile warrant research scrutiny, as do mechanisms through which organization culture affects resilience.

Organizations seem to have recognized the impact of structure on resilience (e.g., by creating staff wellness centers, structures to control workload and workflow and to reconcile competing demands). However, we believe that research evaluating the effectiveness of different structures and illuminating mechanisms through which structures affect individual resilience, prevent the erosion of resilience, and resolve fractures in resilience warrants attention. We similarly call for additional research investigating the impact of organization culture on resilience. Formalized support practices and critical incident debriefing practices that are embedded in the organizational culture are likely to impact the ways in which organizational members play a key role in each other's resilience process.

Measuring Resilience At Work

A third high-priority direction for future research is to develop and validate a reliable measure of resilience at work. To do so, it is imperative to develop a concrete understanding of the concept of resilience at work that can be operationalized. Critics have noted that, depending upon how resilience is defined and measured, the prevalence of resilience in any given population ranges from 15% to 50% (Rutter, 1987; Werner, 1993). Confusion regarding the antecedents, processes, and outcomes of resilience has similarly hindered research progress. In multiple ways, the lack of conceptual clarity has and continues to create theoretical confusion.

Whereas some measures of resilience focus on traits associated with resilience (e.g., ER89, Block & Block, 1980; Bernard et al., 1991), others concentrate on psychological resources included in the construct of psychological capital (Luthans, Avolio, Avey, & Norman, 2007). Each aims to distinguish individuals who have the capacity for resilience from others who do not. Although they abstractly measure capacity for resilience, they do not assess whether a resilience trajectory has been activated or followed by individuals.

Mancini and Bonanno (2009) insist that resilience can only be measured by operationalizing it as an outcome that follows a highly stressful event. By doing so, one can assess the extent to which individuals function after adversity. In contrast, we adopt a developmental approach that requires individuals to emerge from adversity demonstrating professional growth. Thus, we argue that it is important for measures of resilience to capture more than the absence of pathogenic symptoms (Luthar et al., 2000), but also the presence of development and growth. Doing so requires that one's level of functioning before the event is captured and compared to functioning after the event, so that a level of growth or development can be assessed. Ideally, levels of functioning would be assessed periodically during an adverse event so that resilience trajectories could be examined.

Doing so would also allow for a better understanding of the trajectory of resilience over time. To date, we and other researchers have posited that one of the distinguishing factors of a resilience trajectory is that the individual is able to display competence during the adversity. This suggests that individual performance and well-being is relatively stable during and right after the adversity. In this way, resilience is different from recovery and post-traumatic growth, which both entail lower levels of functioning during and after an adversity. It also would be interesting to better understand whether the developmental growth observed in resilient individuals is constant or whether it proceeds in fits and starts—via, for example, periods of growth in resilience punctuated by periods of consolidation or trauma or both.

Conclusion

Resilience is much needed in today's business environment. In fact, organizational resilience is often pinned as a critical strategic advantage in businesses today (Hamel & Välikangas, 2003), and an increasing number of articles and cases have been aimed at teaching individuals how to build resilience at work (e.g., Coutu, 2002; Margolis & Stoltz, 2010). Yet, despite this energy around the importance of resilience, research on resilience in adults has taken off only recently (Bonanno, 2004; Sutcliffe & Vogus, 2003). Most of this research has focused on resilience to critical life stressors, such as the death of a spouse or a traumatic life event. And, although disciplines such as psychology and education have been studying resilience for almost half a century (Masten, Cutuli, Herbers, & Reed, 2009), organization scientists have only recently joined the conversation. The fact that our understanding of the nature, antecedents, and consequences resilience at work is still evolving bespeaks this broader history. In this chapter, we have reviewed the literature on individual resilience at work, providing an overview of what we currently know and suggesting what we have yet to learn. We hope that our perspective motivates and excites other organizational researchers to help illuminate resilience at work.

References

Bakker, A.B., Demerouti, E., & Schaufeli, W.B. (2003). The socially induced burnout model. In S.P. Shokov (Ed.), *Advances in psychological research* Vol. 25 (pp. 13–30). New York: Nova Science Publishers.

Bakker, A.B., Schaufeli, W.B., Sixma, H.J., Bosveld, W., & van Dierendonck, D. (2000). Patient demands lack of reciprocity, and burnout: A five-year longitudinal study among general practitioners. *Journal of Organizational Behavior*, *21*, 425–441.

Bem, D.J. (1972). Self-Perception Theory1. *Advances in experimental social psychology*, 6, 1–62.

Block, J.H., & Block, J. (1980). The role of ego-control and ego-resiliency in the organization of behavior. In W.A. Collins (Ed.). Development of cognition, affect, and social relations: The Minnesota symposia on child psychology (Vol. 13). Hillsdale, NJ: Erlbaum.

Block, J., & Kremen, A.M. (1996). IQ and ego-resiliency: Conceptual and empirical connections and separateness. *Journal of Personality and Social Psychology*, 70, 349–361.

Bonanno, G.A., Wortman, C.B., Lehman, D.R., Tweed, R.G., Haring, M., Sonnega, J., et al. (2002). Resilience to loss and chronic grief: A prospective study from pre-loss to 18 months post-loss. *Journal of Personality and Social Psychology*, *83*, 1150–1164.

Bonanno, G.A. (2004). Loss, trauma, and human resilience: Have we underestimated the human capacity to thrive after extremely aversive events? *American Psychologist*, *59*, 20–28.

Bonanno, G.A. (2005). Clarifying and extending the concept of adult resilience. *American Psychologist, 60*(3), 63–64.

Bonnano, G.A., Rennicke, C., & Dekel, S. (2005). Self-enhancement among high exposure survivors of the September 11th terrorist attack: Resilience or social maladjustment? *Journal of Personality and Social Psychology, 88*(6), 984–998.

Browning, L.D., Beyer, J.M., & Shetler, J.C. (1995). Building cooperation in a competiotive industry: Sematech and the semiconductor industry. *Academy of Management Journal, 38*(1), 113–151.

Bridges, W. (1995). *Jobshift: How To Prosper In A Workplace Without Jobs* (1st ed.). Da Capo Press.

Buunk, B.P., & Schaufeli, W.B. (1993). Professional burnout: A perspective from social comparison theory. In W.B. Schaufeli, C. Maslach, & T. Marek (Eds.), *Professional burnout: Recent developments in theory and research* (pp. 53–69). New York: Taylor & Francis.

Calhoun, L.G., & Tedeschi, R.G. (1999). Posttraumatic growth: Future directions. In R.G. Tedeschi, C.L. Park, & L.G. Calhoun (Eds.), *Posttraumatic growth: Positive change in the aftermath of crisis* (pp. 215–238). Mahwah, NJ: Lawrence Erlbaum Associates.

Callero, P.L. (1986). Toward a median conceptualization of role. *Sociological Quarterly, 27*, 343–358.

Callero, P.L. (1994). From role-playing to role-using: Understanding role as a resource. *Social Psychology Quarterly, 57* (Special Issue on Conceptualizing Structure), 228–243.

Carmeli, A., Brueller, D., & Dutton, J. (2009). Learning behaviors in the workplace: The role of high-quality interpersonal relationships and psychological safety. *Systems Research and Behavioral Science, 26*, 81–98.

Caza, B. (2010). *Telling tales of adversity.* Working paper.

Caza, B, & Bagozzi, R. (2010). *A model of resilience at work.* Working paper.

Chatman, J.A., & Flynn, F.J. (2001). The influence of demographic heterogeneity on the emergence and consequences of cooperative norms in work teams. *Academy of Management Journal, 44*, 956–974.

Cicchetti, D. (1996). Regulatory processes in development and psychopathology. *Development and Psychopathology, 8*, 1–2.

Cicchetti, D., & Rogosch, F.A. (1997). The role of self-organization in the promotion of resilience in maltreated children. *Development and Psychopathology, 9*, 799–817.

Cohen, S., & Wills, T.A. (1985). Stress, social support, and the buffering hypothesis. *Psychological Bulletin, 98*, 310–357.

Coutu, D. (2002). How resilience works. *Harvard Business Review, 80*(5), 46–51.

Dukerich, J.M., Golden, B.R., & Shortell, S. (2002). Beauty is in the eye of the beholder: The impact of organizational identification, identity, and image on the cooperative behaviors of physicians. *Administrative Science Quarterly, 47*, 507–533.

Dutton, J.E., & Heaphy, E.D. (2003). The power of high quality connections. In J.E. Dutton, R.E. Quinn, & K.A. Cameron (Eds.), *Positive organizational scholarship.* San Francisco: Berrett-Koehler Publishers.

Edward, K. (2005). The phenomenon of resilience in crisis care mental health clinicians. *International Journal of Mental Health Nursing, 14*(2), 142–148.

Fredrickson, B.L. (2004). The broaden-and-build theory of positive emotions. *Philosophical Transactions of the Royal Society B: Biological Sciences, 359,* 1367.

Fredrickson & Losada, M.F. (2005). Positive affect and the complex dynamics of human flourishing. *American Psychologist, 60*(7), 678–688.

Fredrickson, B.L., Tugade, M.M., Waugh, C.E., & Larkin, G. (2003). What good are positive emotions in crises?: A prospective study of resilience and emotions following the terrorist attacks on the United States on September 11th, 2001. *Journal of Personality and Social Psychology, 84,* 365–376.

Garmezy, N. (1971). Vulnerability research and the issue of primary prevention. *American Journal of Orthopsychiatry, 41,* 101–116.

Garmezy, N. (1985). Stress resistant children: The search for protective factors. In J. Stevenson (Ed.), *Recent research in developmental psychopathology* (pp. 213–233). Oxford, UK: Pergamon.

Garmezy, N. (1991). Resiliency and vulnerability to adverse developmental outcomes associated with poverty. *American Behavioral Scientist, 34,* 417–430.

Garmezy, N. (1993). Children in poverty: Resilience despite risk. *Psychiatry, 56,* 127–136.

Garmezy, N., & Masten, A. (1990). The adaptation of children to a stressful world: Mastery of fear. In A.L. Eugene (Ed.), *Childhood stress* (pp. 460–473). New York: Wiley.

Gillespie, B.M., Chaboyer, W., Wallis, M., & Grimbeek, P. (2007). Resilience in the operating room: Developing and testing of a resilience model. *Journal of Advanced Nursing, 59*(4), 427–438.

Gittell, J.H. (2008). Relationships and resilience: Care provider responses to pressures from managed care. *Applied Behavioral Science, 44*(1), 25–47.

Gittell, J.H., Cameron, K., Lim, S., & Rivas, R. (2006). Relationships, layoffs, and organizational resilience. *Journal of Applied Behavioral Science, 42*(3), 300–329.

Granovetter, Mark (1985). Economic Action and Social Structure: The Problem of Embeddedness", *American Journal of Sociology 91*(3), 481–510.

Greve, W., & Staudinger, U.M. (2006). Resilience in later adulthood and old age: Resources and potentials for successful aging. In D. Cicchetti and D.J. Cohen (Eds.), *Developmental psychopathology, Vol. 3: Risk, disorder, and adaptation* (2nd ed.), pp. 796–840. Hoboken, NJ: Wiley.

Hamel, G., & Välikangas, L. (2003). The quest for resilience. *Harvard Business Review, 81*(9), 52–63.

Halbesleben, J.R.B., & Buckley, R.M. (2004). *Burnout in organizational life, 30,* 859–879.

Haslam, S.A., & Richer, S. (2006). Stressing the group: Social identity and the unfolding dynamics of response to stress. *Journal of Applied Psychology, 91*(5), 1037–1052.

Kobasa, S. (1979). Stressful life events, personality, and health: An inquiry into hardiness. *Journal of Personality and Social Psychology, 37*(1), 1–11.

Lee, R.T., & Ashforth., B.E. (1993). A longitudinal study of burnout among supervisors and managers: Comparisons between the Leiter and Maslach (1988) and Golembiewski et al. (1986) models. *Organizational Behavior and Human Decision Processes, 54,* 369–398.

Lee, R.T., & Ashforth, B.E. (1996). A meta-analytic examination of the correlates of the three dimensions of job burnout. *Journal of Applied Psychology, 81,* 123–133.

Leipold, B., & Greve, W. (2009). Resilience: A conceptual bridge between coping and development. *European Psychologist. 14*(1), 40–50.

London, M. (1993). Career motivation of full- and part-time workers in mid and late career. *International Journal of Career Management, 5*(1), 21–29.

Luthans, F., Avolio, B.J., Avey, J.B, & Norman, S.M. (2007). Psychological capital: Measurement and relationship with performance and satisfaction. *Personnel Psychology, 60*, 541–572.

Luthar, S.S., & Cichetti., D. (2000). The construct of resilience: Implications for interventions and social policies. *Developmental Psychology, 12*, 857–885.

Luthar, S.S., Cicchetti, D., & Becker, B. (2000). The construct of resilience: A critical evaluation and guidelines for future work. *Child Development, 71*(3), 543–562.

Luthar, S.S., & Cushing, G. (1999). Measurement issues in the empirical study of resilience: An overview. In M. Glanz & J.L. Johnson (Eds.), *Resilience and development: Positive life adaptations* (pp. 129–160). New York, NY: Plenum.

Luthar, S.S., Doernberger, C.H., & Zigler, E. (1993). Resilience is not a unidimensional construct: Insights from a prospective study of inner-city adolescents. Development and Psychopathology. *Special Issue: Milestones in the development of resilience, 5*, 703–717.

Maddi, S.R. (2005). On hardiness and other pathways to resilience. *American Psychologist, 60*, 261–262.

Maddi, S.R., & Khoshaba, D.M. (2005). *Resilience at work: How to succeed no matter what life throws at you.* New York: Amacom.

Maitlis, S. (2011). Post-traumatic growth: A missed opportunity for positive organizational scholarship. In K.S. Cameron & G.M. Spreitzer (Eds.), *The Oxford handbook of positive organizational scholarship*. New York: Oxford University Press.

Mancini, A.D., & Bonanno, G.A. (2006) Resilience in the face of potential trauma: Clinical practices and illustrations, *Journal of Clinical Psychology, 62*(8), 971–985.

Maslach, C. (1982). *Burnout: The cost of caring.* Englewood Cliffs, NJ: Prentice Hall.

Maslach C. (2001). What have we learned about burnout and health? *Psychology and Health, 16*, 607–11.

Maslach, C., Schaufeli, WB., Leiter, MP. (2001). Job burnout. In: Fiske ST, Schacter DL, Zahn-Waxler C, (Eds). *Annual Review of Psychology, 52*, 397–422.

Masten, A.S., Best, K.M., & Garmezy, N. (1990). Resilience in development: Contributions from the study of children who overcame adversity. *Development and Psychopathology, 2*, 425–444.

Masten, A.S. (1994). Resilience in individual development: Successful adaptation despite risk and adversity. In M.C. Wang, & G.W. Gordon (Eds*.), Educational resilience in inner-city America*. Hillsdale, NJ: Lawrence Erlbaum Associates.

Masten, A.S. (1999). Resilience comes of age: Reflections on the past and outlook for the next generation of research. In M.D. Glantz, & J.L. Johnson (Eds.), *Resilience and development: Positive life adaptations* (pp. 291–296). New York: Kluwer Academic/Plenum Publishers.

Masten, A.S., Cutuli, J.J., Herbers, J.E., & Gabrielle-Reed, M.J. (2009). Resilience in development. In C.R. Snyder, & S.J. Lopez (Eds.), *The handbook of positive psychology* (2nd ed., pp. 117–131). New York: Oxford University Press.

Masten, A.S. (2001). Ordinary magic: Resilience processes in development. *American Psychologist, 53*(3), 227–238.

Masten, A.S., & Coatsworth, J.D. (1998). The development of competence in favorable and unfavorable environments: Lessons from successful children. *American Psychologist, 53*, 205–220.

Masten, A.S., & Reed, M.J. (2002). Resilience in development. In C.R. Snyder, & S.J. Lopex (Eds.), *The handbook of positive psychology (*pp. 74–88). Oxford, UK: Oxford University Press.

Margolis, J., & Stoltz, P. (2010). How to bounce back from adversity. (cover story). *Harvard Business Review, 88*(1), 86–92.

Mancini, A.D., & Bonanno, G.A. (2009). Predictors and parameters of resilience to loss: Toward an individual differences model. *Journal of Personality, 77*, 1–27.

Milton, L.P. (2003). An identity perspective on the propensity of high-tech talent to unionize. *Journal of Labor Research, 24*, 31–53.

Milton, L.P., & Westphal, J.D. (2005). Identity confirmation networks and cooperation in workgroups. *Academy of Management Journal, 48*, 191–212.

Peterson, C. (2006). *A primer in positive psychology.* Oxford, UK: Oxford University Press.

Pines, A.M., Aronson, E., & Kafry, D. (1981). *Burnout: From tedium to personal growth.* New York: The Free Press.

Pratt, M.G., Rockmann, K.W., & Kaufmann, J.B. (2006). Constructing professional identity: The role of work and identity learning cycles in the customization of identity among medical residents. *Academy of Management Journal, 49*(2), 235–262.

Polzer, J.T., Milton, L.P., & Swann, W.B., Jr. (2002). Capitalizing on diversity: Interpersonal congruence in small work groups. *Administrative Science Quarterly, 47*, 296–324.

Razavi, D., Delvaux, N., Farvacques. C., Robaye, E. (1988). Immediate effectiveness of brief psychological training for health professionals during terminially ill cancer patients: a controlled study. *Social Science and Medicine, 77*(4), 369–375.

Roosa, M.W. (2000). Some thoughts about resilience versus positive development, main effects versus interactions, and the value of resilience. Child Development, *71*(3), 567–569.

Roisman, G.I. (2005). Conceptual clarifications in the study of resilience. *American Psychologist, 60*(3), 264–265.

Rutter, M. (1987). Psychosocial resilience and protective mechanisms. *American Journal of Orthopsychiatry, 57,* 316–331.

Rutter, M. (1990). Psychosocial resilience and protective mechanisms. In J. Rolf, A.S. Masten, D. Cocchetti, K.H. Nuechterlein & Weintraub (Eds.) *Risk and protective factors in developing psychopathology* (pp 181–214). Cambridge, UK: Cambridge University Press.

Rutter, M. (1993). Resilience: Some conceptual considerations. *Journal of Adolescent Health, 14*(8), 622–628.

Schein, E.H. (1978). *Career Dynamics: Matching Individual and Organizational Needs.* Reading, MA.: Addison-Wesley.

Shah, P., & Jehn, K. (1993). Do friends perform better than acquaintances? *The interaction of friendship, conflict and task. Group Decision and Negotiation, 2*, 149–166.

Shih, M. (2004). Positive stigma: Resilience and empowerment in overcoming stigma. *The Annals of the American Academy, 571*, 175–185.

Sonnentag, S., & Neff, A. (2011). Recovery: Nonwork experiences that promote positive states. In K.S. Cameron & G.M. Spreitzer (Eds.), *The Oxford handbook of positive organizational scholarship*. New York: Oxford University Press.

Spreitzer, G., Sutcliffe, K., Dutton, J., Sonenshein S., & Grant A. (2005). A Socially Embedded Model of Thriving at Work, *Organization Science, 16*(5), 537–49.

Sutcliffe, K.M., & Vogus, T.J. (2003). Organizing for resilience. In J.E.D.K.S. Cameron, & R.E. Quinn (Ed.), *Positive Organizational Scholarship: Foundations of a New Discipline*. San Francisco, CA: Berret-Kohler Publishers, Inc.

Tedeschi, R.G., & Calhoun, L.G. (2004). Posttraumatic growth: Conceptual foundations and emperical evidence. *Psychological Inquiry, 15*(1), 1–18.

Tolan, P.T. (1996). How resilient is the concept of resilience? *The Community Psychologist, 29*, 12–15.

Trice, H.M., & Beyer, J.M. (1993). *The cultures of work organizations.* Englewood Cliffs, NJ: Prentice-Hall.

Tugade, M.M., & Fredrickson, B.L. (2004). Resilient individuals use positive emotions to bounce back from negative emotional experiences. *Journal of Personality and Social Psychology, 86*(2), 320–333.

Tugade, M.M., Fredrickson, B.L., & Barrett, L.F. (2004). Psychological resilience and positive emotional granularity: Examining the benefits of positive emotions on coping and health. *Journal of Personality, 72*(6), 1162–1190.

Tusaie, K., & Dyer, J. (2004). Resilience: A historical review of the construct. *Holistic Nursing Practice, 18*(1), 3.

Waterman, R.H., Waterman, J.D., & Collard, B.A. (1994). Toward a career resilient workforce. *Harvard Business Review, 72*(4), 87–95.

Weick, K.E., Roberts, K.H. (1993). Collective mind in organization: Heedful interrelating on flight decks. *Administrative Science Quarterly, 38,* 357–381.

Weick, K., Sutcliffe, K.M., & Obstfeld, D. (2005). Organizing and the process of sensemaking. *Organization Science, 16*(4), 409–421.

Werner, E. (1993) Risk, resilience and recovery. Perspectives from the Kauai Longitudinal Study. *Development and Psychopathology, 5,* 503–515.

Werner, E., & Johnson, J. (1999) Can we apply resilience? In *Resilience and Development: Positive Life Adaptations* (eds M. Glantz & J. Johnson), pp. 259–268. Academic Press/Plenum Publishers.

Werner, E.E., & Smith, R.S. (1982). *Vulnerable but invincible: A study of resilient children.* New York: McGraw-Hill.

Wildavsky A. (1991). *Searching for Safety.* New Brunswick (USA) and London: Transaction Books.

Zellars, K.L., Perrewe, P.L., Hochwarter, W.A. (2006). Burnout in health care: The role of five factors of personality. *Journal of Applied Social Psychology, 30*(8), 1570–1598.

Posttraumatic Growth

A Missed Opportunity for Positive Organizational Scholarship

Sally Maitlis

Abstract

This chapter introduces the concept of posttraumatic growth (PTG), considering its prevalence among trauma survivors, the contexts in which it has typically been studied, and the critical role of meaning making in the growth process. Examining key findings from empirical studies of PTG reveals the dearth of research in occupational and organizational contexts, and highlights the potential contribution of a PTG lens to positive organizational scholarship. The chapter closes with a discussion of key challenges for our understanding of PTG and an agenda for future research in this important area.

Keywords: Trauma, growth, meaning making, emotion, narrative

Posttraumatic growth (PTG) is the "the experience of positive change that occurs as a result of the struggle with highly challenging life crises" (Tedeschi & Calhoun, 2004, p. 1). Underlying the concept of PTG is the notion that, although trauma causes a variety of intense and distressing emotions, such as anxiety, sadness, guilt, and anger (Herman, 1997), it can also act as a catalyst for transformational positive change. This change, or growth, is manifest in a stronger sense of self, richer relationships with others, and changes in life philosophy that often include radically altered priorities (Calhoun & Tedeschi, 2001, 2006; Joseph & Linley, 2008). Posttraumatic growth does not occur in place of pain, and those experiencing growth are unlikely to view a trauma as a desirable or positive event. They do, however, believe that good has come from having to deal with it. Thus, as a concept rooted in affirmative qualities such as growth, strength, and appreciation, PTG has a clear place in positive organizational scholarship (POS), but, in contrast to most other POS constructs, it is inherently connected to experiences of pain and loss.

In this chapter, I first explore different ways in which the concept of PTG has been used in the rapidly developing literature, and I consider its relationship to other concepts, such as resilience and thriving. I then discuss the prevalence of PTG and examine the contexts in which it has been studied, followed by an overview of themes from prominent models from the literature. Next, I consider the role of meaning making in PTG, reviewing research from psychological and narrative perspectives. This is followed by a summary of key findings from empirical studies, exploring individual characteristics associated with PTG and its health-related outcomes. I then examine the limited literature on PTG in the context of work, highlighting the dearth of research and showing the potential contribution that a PTG lens can make to POS. The chapter ends with a discussion of key challenges for our understanding of PTG, and concludes with an agenda for future research in this important area.

Introducing Posttraumatic Growth
Early Origins

The term *posttraumatic growth* has appeared in the literature only in the last 15 or so years, but the idea that positive change can emerge from pain and suffering is not new. This theme runs through the writings of major world religions, in which the power of trauma to transform can be found in the writings of Buddhism, Christianity, Hinduism, Islam, and Judaism (O'Rourke, Tallman, & Altmaier, 2008; Tedeschi & Calhoun, 1995). It is a central motif within literature, music, and other cultural forms (Campbell, Brunell, & Foster, 2004; Siltala, 1998), and it underpins existential and other psychological perspectives on human suffering (Frankl, 1963; May, 1981; Yalom, 1980). In the psychological literature, an interest in the nature of PTG, the contexts in which it can occur, and its concomitants has grown rapidly in the last decade (Park, 2010). It has received much less attention in management writings, and only a very small number of studies have considered PTG in the context of work and work organizations (e.g., Britt, Adler, & Bartone, 2001; Linley & Joseph, 2006; Paton, 2006a).

Conceptualizing Posttraumatic Growth

Posttraumatic growth, as the transformative positive change that can follow an adverse life event, has been described through a variety of terms, including stress-related growth, perceived benefits, positive adaptation, and adversarial growth (Linley & Joseph, 2004). All are used to capture broadly similar kinds of changes, although different studies and measures emphasize different facets of growth. For example, Tedeschi and Calhoun (1995), two of the most prominent writers in this field, initially identified three broad categories of change: perceptions of self, relationships with others, and philosophy of life. Thus, those who have survived a trauma may begin to see themselves as stronger and better able to deal with difficult events in the future (self-perception). They may also change how they see and feel around others, experiencing a greater sense of intimacy and belonging, and feeling more compassion for those who are suffering (relationships with others). In addition, these individuals often gain a greater sense of purpose and appreciation for life, and experience changed beliefs about what is most important (life philosophy). Three domains expanded to five factors in the Posttraumatic Growth Inventory (PTGI; Tedeschi & Calhoun, 1996): personal strength, new possibilities, relating to others, appreciation of life, and spiritual change. Other scales assessing positive change post-trauma have identified growth in areas such as community closeness, empathy, and appreciation of life, but research has also suggested that PTG may best be regarded as a single construct with three second-order components (Joseph & Linley, 2008).

The PTG construct is further complicated by the fact that it is at times treated as an outcome and at other times as a process. Thus, although scholars often see growth as an outcome of a meaning making process (e.g., Calhoun & Tedeschi, 2006; Janoff-Bulman, 2006), others regard it as the coping process through which growth is pursued (Affleck & Tennen, 1996; Nolen-Hoeksema & Davis, 2004). This distinction is well-captured by Park (2010; Park, Edmondson, Fenster, & Blank, 2008) in her discussion of "meaning made" versus "meaning making," and seen throughout the literature. For example, Neimeyer (2006, p. 69) describes PTG as "a form of meaning reconstruction in the wake of crisis and loss" (the process of meaning making), whereas Janoff-Bulman (2006, p. 82) characterizes it as "expansions and developments in survivors' cognitive-emotional understandings of themselves and their world" (the expanded meanings made). Similarly, cognitive strategies such as "benefit finding" (process) and "perceived benefits" (outcome) are often used interchangeably with "posttraumatic growth" (e.g., Helgeson, Reynolds, & Tomich, 2006; Stanton, Bower, & Low, 2006), a problem intensified by the use of participants' reports of cognitive strategies in which they have engaged as a way of measuring growth (e.g., Davis & Morgan, 2008; Helgeson et al., 2006; Thompson, 1985).

Although recognizing that "growth" is not some stable endpoint achieved by individuals at the conclusion of a clearly defined meaning making process, in this chapter, I consider PTG as a kind of meaning made, manifest in individuals' changed understandings of themselves, their relationships with others, and their life philosophies, and generated through meaning making processes that take place following a traumatic event.

Posttraumatic Growth and Related Concepts

Given the blurred conceptual boundaries of the PTG construct, it is perhaps unsurprising that there is much discussion and at times confusion in the literature about the relationship between PTG and certain other concepts, such as resilience, thriving, and flourishing. Resilience has been defined in a variety of ways (Barker Caza & Milton, 2011, Chapter 68, this volume), but is commonly understood as the ability to maintain relatively stable, healthy levels of functioning after a highly disruptive event (Bonanno 2004, 2005) or the maintenance of positive adjustment under challenging conditions (Sutcliffe & Vogus, 2003). Resilience can thus be seen to differ from PTG in that it emphasizes stability in the context of trauma, rather than a trajectory of increased positive functioning. Yet, overlaps in the PTG literature are quite common, with certain kinds of growth seen as enabling increased resilience (Calhoun & Tedeschi, 2006), or as being a form resilience (Lepore & Revenson, 2006).

Posttraumatic growth can be still more clearly differentiated from other related concepts such as thriving and flourishing. Thriving has been defined as "the psychological state in which individuals experience both a sense of vitality and a sense of learning" (Spreitzer, Sutcliffe, Dutton, Sonenshein, & Grant, 2005, p. 538), and flourishing individuals are defined as those who are "filled with emotional vitality . . . functioning positively in the private and social realms of their lives" (Keyes & Haidt, 2003, p. 6). Although thriving, flourishing, and PTG all involve individuals' positive functioning at a level beyond normal expectations, in PTG this occurs only in the context of significant adversity, whereas in thriving and flourishing it may or may not occur after a negative event. Further, PTG entails transformation, in a way that is less prominent in thriving or flourishing, and this transformation is focused on quite specific realms—the self, relationships with others, and life priorities.

Prevalence of Posttraumatic Growth and Contexts of Study
Prevalence of Growth

Posttraumatic growth is not a rare phenomenon. Its prevalence, however, is much debated, with studies reporting figures ranging from 3% to 98% in individuals who have experienced a traumatic event (Linley & Joseph, 2004). The very high prevalence reported in some studies can be partly explained by the lack of random sampling in research on PTG (e.g., McMillen, Smith, & Fisher, 1997; Weiss, 2002), but this does not fully account for the range of 30% to 80% that is found across the majority of studies (Linley & Joseph, 2004). Other questions are raised, however, by scholars who note that reports of growth are sometimes accompanied by a raft of depressive and depleting outcomes (Wortman, 2004). From this perspective, growth prevalence should be assessed by the proportion of individuals who show positive changes that are not overshadowed by negative changes also experienced.

Contexts of Study
Studies of PTG have been carried out in the context of a very great variety of traumas, but few consider trauma in work or organizations. Typical contexts of study include bereavement (e.g., Davis, Nolen-Hoeksema, & Larson, 1998), cancer (e.g., Cordova, Cunningham, Carlson, & Andrykowski, 2001), heart attacks (e.g., Affleck, Tennen, Croog, & Levine, 1987), HIV/AIDS (Milam, 2006), other medical conditions (e.g., Evers et al., 2001), sexual assault and abuse (e.g., Frazier, Conlon, & Glaser, 2001), terrorism (Updegraff, Silver, & Holman, 2008), plane crashes, and natural disasters (e.g., McMillen et al., 1997). Very few attempts have been made to compare PTG across different types of traumas, in part because it is thought that differences in growth levels are most likely a function of characteristics of the subjective experience of an event, such as helplessness, uncontrollability, and threat, rather than of the kind of event itself (Linley & Joseph, 2004). More generally, it is argued that, to trigger growth, an event must challenge an individual's assumptive world, activating the cognitive processing that leads to growth (Tedeschi & Calhoun, 2004). Although some research suggests that growth is more likely to occur following more rather than less intensely traumatic experiences (McMillen, Smith, & Fisher, 1997), other studies report a curvilinear relationship, with growth levels highest for intermediate levels of trauma exposure (Fontana & Rosenheck, 1998; Linley & Joseph, 2004).

Research has explored many aspects of the phenomenon and in a great variety of situations, but it is notable, especially in the context of this handbook, that PTG has received almost no attention in organizational contexts. Important exceptions include studies of the military and peacekeeping forces (e.g., Britt et al., 2001; Dohrenwend et al., 2004; Elder & Clipp, 1989) and of those engaged in law enforcement and emergency services (e.g., Paton, 2006a, b). Research on trauma and PTG occurring in the service of "ordinary" work, however, is extremely rare. This is surprising, given the likelihood that people in a range of occupations have traumatic experiences in the course of their work. Indeed, although increasing attention in organization studies has been paid to painful experiences such as abusive bosses, sexual harassment, unfair treatment, and job loss (e.g., Latack, Kinicki, & Prussia, 1995; Schneider, Swan, & Fitzgerald, 1997; Tepper, 2007), the field has been slow to consider positive changes that may follow for some individuals. This is not to minimize the intense distress experienced by people dealing with these situations, or to imply that these—or any other—traumatic events should be seen as positive. Rather, I suggest that, by not considering the possibility of growth from these experiences, we risk a significant oversight in organizational research and the loss of a particularly valuable opportunity for POS.

Theorizing Posttraumatic Growth

Central to theories of PTG is the shattering by a traumatic event of an individual's assumptive world and the subsequent rebuilding of that world through meaning making. Prominent models theorize the emotional and cognitive processes through which growth is achieved and the key factors that enable passage through these processes.

A common theme of process models of PTG is the notion of "accommodation." Joseph and Linley's (2005) organismic valuing model suggests that growth comes as survivors revise their schemas to *accommodate* the trauma (e.g., "Bad things can happen to good people because the world is not a just place") rather than *assimilating* the trauma into their existing models of the world (e.g., "Bad things happen to bad people, so I must deserve what happened"). Similarly, Tedecschi and Calhoun's (1995, 2004) functional descriptive model emphasizes accommodation of trauma that involves survivors moving from trying to grasp what has happened to them to establishing whether and how they can deal with it, and ultimately making sense of the trauma in ways that highlight its positive meaning and future possibilities.

Janoff-Bulman (2004, 2006) provides a more complex process model that allows three different paths through which changes in the content and structure of a trauma survivor's "assumptive world" can lead to different elements of growth. In the "strength through suffering" pathway, growth comes through an individual's struggle to cope and the discovery of previously unrealized strengths. The "existential reevaluation" path describes how growth occurs as the trauma survivor acknowledges the randomness and uncontrollability of life events and searches for two kinds of meaning "meaning as comprehensibility" ("Why has this happened to me?") and "meaning as significance" ("What point or value can this have?") (Janoff-Bulman & Frantz, 1997). The third path is "psychological preparedness," which occurs through an immunity, or resilience, that is established as a result of the more complex and differentiated schema developed through meaning making following the shattering of core assumptions.

The factors that have been theorized as supporting PTG primarily involve social support and various forms of disclosure. Joseph and Linley (2005) argue that positive accommodation of trauma is facilitated by a supportive social context that endorses survivors changing the meaning they accord to their lives and relationships (e.g., "Bad things can happen any time, so it is important to live fully and appreciate what I have right now"). In contrast, social environments that do not support such a worldview can lead survivors to make a negative accommodation (e.g., "Bad things can happen at any time so it is impossible to live fully"), leading to helplessness and depression. Tedeschi and Calhoun (1995, 2004) emphasize the importance of disclosing thoughts and feelings in writing or talk, as well as in interactions with others who respond with understanding, and especially those who model PTG.

In sum, PTG is seen as coming through the meaning making processes triggered by the loss of a person's assumptive world. These processes, which occur alongside the management of great emotional distress, can be enabled by a supportive social context, writing, and other means that enable the development of new schemas or narratives. Counter to this portrayal, some have questioned whether one's assumptive world must "shatter" to precipitate PTG. Park (2010), for example, suggests that many traumatic events may cause only modest shifts in individuals' meaning systems, and Wortman (2004) suggests that trauma-induced threats to mortality may be more important for growth than shattered worldviews. Although we do not yet know how much people's assumptive worlds are affected by trauma, it is widely held that they *are* affected by these intensely negative and unexpected events (Janoff-Bulman, 1992; Linley & Joseph, 2004; Tedeschi & Calhoun, 2004), and that growth is more likely to occur when individuals' assumptions about the world have been severely challenged (Davis & Nolen-Hoeksema, 2009; Davis, Wohl, & Verberg, 2007).

Studying Meaning Making in Posttraumatic Growth

Consistent across models of PTG is the central role given to how individuals think about what has happened to them and its impact on their future lives. Such cognitive processing is important because it enables individuals to make acceptable meaning out of this traumatic turning point (Bulman & Wortman, 1977; Gillies & Neimeyer, 2006). Not surprisingly, therefore, there has been much research on meaning making in PTG, represented by two different but overlapping literatures: psychological studies that use survey measures to gather individuals' reports on their cognitive processing, and narrative research that explores meaning making in the stories people tell or write about their experiences.

Psychological Research

Most typically, psychological studies ask individuals whether they have engaged in a meaning making activity, for example, if they have talked about the event with others (e.g., Cordova et al., 2001), if they have searched for meaning in the event (e.g., Downey, Silver, & Wortman, 1990), or more specifically, if they have looked for something good in what happened to them (e.g., Park et al., 2008). Meaning making is thus assessed by participants' reports of whether they have tried to make meaning. Other studies have assessed meaning *making* by asking participants whether they have *made* meaning of what happened (e.g., Eton, Lepore, & Helgeson, 2005), rather than their efforts to do so. Very little research has thus explored meaning making *as a process,* and therefore how it may lead to growth. Some insight has been gained through studies that inquire into specific cognitive processing strategies, finding positive relationships between growth and the strategies of positive cognitive restructuring (e.g., "There is ultimately more good than bad in this situation"), downward comparison ("Other people have had worse experiences than mine"), and acceptance ("I have come to terms with this experience") (Gangstad, Norman, & Barton, 2009; Park, Cohen, & Murch, 1996; Phelps, Williams, Raichle, Turner, & Ehde, 2008; Williams, Davis, & Millsap, 2002). Yet, this work still relies on individuals' reports of their cognitive strategies, rather than exploring meaning making directly and as a process.

Narrative Research

Scholars who take a narrative perspective see a person's narrative, or life story, as constructed from related events or cohesive themes through which that individual understands and shares who she is (Bruner, 1987; Gergen, 1994; McAdams, 1991). This story is extremely powerful, influencing how a person acts in the world and how the world reacts to her, as captured in Howard's (1991) observation, "We are lived by the stories we tell" (cited in Meichenbaum, 2006, p. 358).

Narrative scholars propose that PTG can be understood as the "process of constructing a narrative understanding of how the self has been positively transformed by the traumatic event" (Pals & McAdams, 2004). Neimeyer (2000, 2004, 2006), who has written extensively on bereavement as a "narrative disrupting event," examines how different forms of narrative disruption trigger meaning making processes that enlarge and deepen the survivor's identity to enable growth. Some kinds of narrative disruption lead to evolutionary changes to identity, achieved through an elaboration of a pre-loss narrative, similar to the idea of assimilation discussed earlier (Joseph & Linley, 2005). Other forms of narrative disruption produce more radical identity change, as individuals construct new capacities that allow them to live in ways richer than before. It is this latter kind of narrative disruption and reconstruction that is most closely associated with PTG (Neimeyer, 2006).

Although a narrative perspective on PTG is associated with a relatively small amount of empirical work, research in this tradition shows how growth naturally emerges in survivors' stories of trauma and themselves post-trauma. It highlights the kinds of meaning making embedded in growth narratives, including acknowledging the trauma's emotional impact, analyzing its effect on and meaning for the self, and constructing a positive ending that explains the self-transformation (King, Scollon, Ramsey, & Williams, 2000; Pals & McAdams, 2004; Pals, 2006a, b). For example, writing about the "springboard effect" in life narratives, Pals (2006b) describes how meaning making about the emotional impact of trauma can act as a narrative springboard for positive self-transformation and growth. Consistent with writings in emotion-focused psychotherapy (e.g., Greenberg, 2004; Greenberg & Pavio, 1997), Pals' (2000) research suggests that individuals who use their emotion as a resource for thinking about themselves differently open up the possibility for growth. In narrative terms, the individual brings the negative experience into his narrative by identifying causal connections between what happened previously and subsequent events that have shaped the person he is today. The narrative is resolved by transforming negative into positive, making meaning of the traumatic event in a way that connects the negative experience to positive changes in the self. Thus, the trauma becomes "the opening act in a transformative and redemptive sequence" (Pals & McAdams, 2004, p. 66) that concludes by affirming and explaining the positive transformation.

Such findings are in keeping with research that examines the use of different "micronarratives" within stories of traumatic loss (Neimeyer & Anderson, 2002; Neimeyer, 2006). This work explores different perspectives taken within a narrative, such as an external voice that reports on what happens, an internal voice that focuses on personal reactions to the event, and a reflexive voice that focuses on meaning making. Research suggests that trauma is better integrated when the narrator shifts between voices, constructing a coherent external account, then exploring her emotional response, and going on to search for the meaning it contains for her (Neimeyer & Anderson, 2002). Another significant body of work explores individuals' reactions to trauma through "illness narratives" (e.g., Becker, 1997; Frank, 1995; Kleinman, 1988), the stories of those whose lives have been significantly disrupted by illness. Here, we see the importance of metaphor, especially when linked to normalizing cultural ideologies, in integrating extraordinary life experiences into identity (Becker, 1997).

One area of narrative-based research that has generated a large stream of work focuses on the healing qualities of writing about painful live events (see Pennebaker & Chung, 2007, for a review). This work shows that participants in experiments who write narratives of their thoughts and feelings about a highly stressful event tend to show better psychological and physical well-being than do a control group (Pennebaker & Chung, 2007), and that the effect is strengthened by engaging in meaning making over multiple sessions (Pennebaker, Mayne, & Francis, 1997; Rivkin, Gustafson, Weingarten, & Chin, 2006). Studies have found increased PTG for participants writing about their trauma-related thoughts and feelings relative to participants in other conditions (Ullrich & Lutgendorf, 2002; Smyth, Hockemeyer, & Tulloch, 2008), and a positive relationship between growth and depth of processing in the narratives (Weinrib, Rothrock, Johnsen, & Lutgendorf, 2006).

Looking across the emergent body of narrative research on PTG, we see that this work adds considerably to psychological studies of meaning making and growth by providing valuable insights into *how* meaning making enables growth.

Predictors and Outcomes of Posttraumatic Growth
Individual Characteristics
Research on predictors of PTG has typically been cross-sectional, exploring how various individual characteristics covary with growth, and generally showing mixed results. No clear sociodemographic indicators exist, with positive, negative, and statistically insignificant findings for age, gender, socioeconomic status, and ethnicity (see Linley & Joseph, 2004; Stanton et al., 2006, for reviews). Across a smaller number of studies, certain personality characteristics seem to be related to PTG, most consistently optimism (Davis et al., 1998; Evers et al., 2001; Tennen, Affleck, Urrows, Higgins, & Mendola, 1992; Updegraff, Taylor, Kemeny, & Wyatt, 2002). Positive relationships have also been found with extraversion and openness to experience (Tedeschi & Calhoun, 1996), whereas the relationship with neuroticism is less clear, with some research showing a negative association and other finding no significant relationship (Evers et al., 2001; Helgeson et al., 2006; Stanton et al., 2006; Tedeschi & Calhoun, 1996).

A number of studies have found a positive relationship between positive affect and PTG (Linley & Joseph, 2004; Stanton et al., 2006), both when measured concurrently and when growth is assessed months or years after measures of positive affect were obtained (Abraido-Lanza, Guier, & Colon, 1998; Evers et al., 2001; Park et al., 1996; Tennen et al., 1992; Tomich & Helgeson, 2002; Sears, Stanton, & Danoff-Burg, 2003; Weinrib et al., 2006). The studies are fewer and findings less consistent for negative affect. Although some research suggests a negative relationship between negative affect and growth, it may be wholly mediated by neuroticism (Evers et al., 2001; Linley & Joseph, 2004). Other studies find no relationship between negative affect and growth (Weinrib et al., 2006). Longitudinal studies of PTG are still few in number, and their findings in this regard are inconsistent (e.g., Abraido-Lanza et al., 1998; Davis et al., 1998; King et al., 2000; McMillen et al., 1997; Park et al., 1996).

Health-related Outcomes
From the perspectives of POS and positive psychology, growth is a critically important outcome for individuals. Many psychological theories see growth as a universal human tendency and propose that people will take opportunities for growth when available (Maslow, 1968; Perls, 1969; Rogers, 1964). This is even the case when growth does not offer the easy path, as is the case post-trauma, when growth is often infused with sorrow and existential wisdom (Janoff-Bulman, 2006; Calhoun & Tedeschi, 2004). However, despite the inherent value of PTG, there has also been considerable interest in its outcomes, or the relationship between growth and various

measures of psychological and physiological adjustment, both positive and negative. Key findings from this body of research are summarized briefly below. Because of the dearth of longitudinal studies, however, we currently know more about concomitants of growth than its outcomes.

As with the research on predictors of growth, findings on the relationship between growth and adjustment are mixed. In a recent meta-analysis of 87 cross-sectional studies relating PTG to health outcomes (Helgeson et al., 2006), growth was found to be positively related to measures of well-being, including self-esteem and life satisfaction, negatively related to depression, and unrelated to anxiety, global distress, quality of life, and subjective physical health. Findings on the relationship between growth and distress are also mixed. Some cross-sectional research shows a negative relationship between growth and distress (e.g., Davis et al., 1998; Frazier et al., 2001), whereas several other studies find no relationship (e.g., Cordova et al., 2001; Sears et al., 2003). These varied findings are mirrored in longitudinal studies of the growth–distress relationship (see Stanton et al., 2006). Helgeson and colleagues considered the possible moderating effect of time since the trauma, and found that the relationships between growth and well-being, and growth and depression are stronger with the greater elapse of time since the event, and that growth was related to distress only when the event is quite recent. These findings suggest that the adaptive value of PTG may only come into effect over time, a proposition supported by some longitudinal studies of growth and adjustment (see Park & Helgeson, 2006; Zoellner & Maercker, 2006).

A small but intriguing set of studies has explored the relationship between PTG and various physiological health outcomes. In their review of PTG after cancer, Stanton et al. (2006) report on studies that find growth linked to reductions in serum cortisol, a hormone normally released in response to stress and that suppresses the immune system (Cruess et al., 2000), and to increases in lymphocyte proliferation, an immune function associated with breast cancer progression and recurrence (McGregor et al., 2004). Similarly, in a study of PTG and HIV disease prevention, a relationship was found between growth and CD4 T-cell counts, a measure of immune system functioning (Milam, 2006). These studies do not permit causal claims, but they do show that PTG is associated with changes in immune functioning over time, with implications for the progression of potentially terminal diseases. In addition, Affleck et al. (1987) found that patients who reported growth after a heart attack were less likely to suffer a subsequent attack and more likely to have better general health. Posttraumatic growth has also been linked to decreases in pain (Katz, Flasher, Cacciapaglia, & Nelson, 2001). Although research in this area is still in its infancy, it clearly indicates important relationships between PTG and physiological outcomes.

Posttraumatic Growth at Work

Despite the burgeoning literature on PTG, only a very small number of studies examine it in the context of work. To some extent, this is understandable, given the association of trauma with events in individual's personal lives, such as bereavement, illness, and sexual assault. However, it is surprising when we consider how much time people spend at work and the emotional challenges of contemporary working life (Fineman, 2000). Bullying, sexual harassment, unfair dismissal, and redundancy are just a few of the experiences that regularly occur in the workplace (Frost, 2003; Lilius, Kanov, Dutton, Worline, & Maitlis, 2011, Chapter 21, this volume; Martin, 2000; Schneider et al., 1997), and which, despite their prevalence, are deeply distressing to the individuals who experience them. In addition, recent research on "necessary evils"—work tasks that involve an act causing emotional or physical harm to another in the service of a greater good (Molinsky & Margolis, 2005)—highlights the potential for work-related trauma on the part of the deliverer, as well as recipient, of intensely painful experiences. Given PTG's basis in meaning making, and since work is a primary source of meaning for many individuals (Baumeister, 1991; Wrzesniewski, 2002; Wrzesniewski, McCauley, Rozin, & Schwartz, 1997), the dearth of research in a work context is especially striking.

The small body of research on PTG at work emerges out of a larger literature that has examined conditions such as posttraumatic stress disorder (PTSD) in job contexts that are especially likely to engender trauma and distress, such as disaster work, emergency services, and police work (Carlier, Voerman, & Gersons, 2000; Clohessy & Ehlers, 1999; Gersons, Carlier, Lamberts, & van der Kolk, 2000; Paton, 2006a). A few of these studies have explored the possibility of positive outcomes of trauma, and show that soldiers and disaster workers can derive benefits from work that is stressful and potentially traumatic (Britt et al., 2001; Dyregrov, Kristofferson, & Gjestad, 1996; Linley & Joseph, 2006; Raphael, Singh, Bradbury, & Lambert, 1984).

For example, in Britt et al.'s (2001) longitudinal examination of peacekeepers, "perceived benefits" assessed 4–5 months after soldiers' deployment on a peacekeeping mission were found to be positively associated with the extent to which they regarded their deployment as meaningful work, as well as with the personality construct of hardiness. Linley and Joseph (2006) explored PTG in disaster workers, whose jobs are considered traumatic due to the routine exposure to death. Although unable to link growth to any specific traumatic event, the authors found a positive association with workers' feelings of fear, horror, and helplessness during their work experiences. Earlier studies of disaster workers have also found that, alongside the distress these employees feel in doing their jobs, many of them are more positive about their lives (Raphael et al., 1984) and have a greater sense of their own strengths (Dyregrov et al., 1996).

Another body of research explores "vicarious" or "secondary" trauma and growth in professionals whose work is inherently traumatic because of its focus on others' suffering. These include studies of psychotherapists (Linley & Joseph, 2007), the clergy (Profitt, Calhoun, Tedeschi, & Cann, 2002), psychologists (Radeke & Mahoney, 2000), and funeral directors (Linley & Joseph, 2005). This work reveals that individuals in such roles may experience more emotional exhaustion than those in parallel professions (e.g., professional vs. research psychologists), but are also more likely to experience growth.

Thus, we know that growth can occur in people doing jobs that are inherently traumatic, although our understanding of the conditions under which PTG at work is most likely to occur, or the processes through which it happens, is still limited. In addition, and despite the insights provided by this research, we continue to know very little about the possibility for PTG in more ordinary work contexts. A small set of literature exists that examines the experience of trauma for workers in "normal" jobs who experience a highly distressing event, such as armed robbery or an office shooting, while at work (Creamer, Burgess, & Pattison, 1992; Harrison & Kinner, 1998; Kamphuis & Emmelkamp, 1998; MacDonald, Colotla, Flamer, & Karlinsky, 2003), and there is also increasing interest in highly distressing but less sensational workplace traumas, such as bullying or mobbing (Leyman & Gustaffson, 1996; Matthiesen & Einarsen, 2004; Mikkelson & Einarsen, 2002). This work is important in highlighting the presence of trauma in a variety of work contexts, but the focus has been on trauma, PTSD, and other negative symptoms, rather than on exploring the possibility of any positive aftermath. Overall, then, our knowledge about PTG in the context of work is very limited, and the potential for research to shed insight into growth following traumatic experiences in ordinary jobs extremely high.

One of the few studies of PTG at work is Maitlis' (2009) exploration of professional musicians who, because of an injury, have been forced to give up their life's work. Through the analysis of their life stories, Maitlis shows how these individuals re-narrate themselves after an occupational trauma that significantly and distressingly challenges their core sense of self. Over time, and as they come to terms with what has happened to them, the injured musicians engage in identity work that allows them to separate from their former selves and construct new, expanded identities that are agentic, resourceful, and robust in ways previously unknown to them. Here, we see PTG in a work setting not normally associated with ongoing trauma, offering an example of "ordinary" occupational trauma. The possibilities for trauma at work are, however, sadly endless. At the same time, this means that the opportunity to explore possible positive outcomes that follow or accompany the distress for employees experiencing harassment, abuse, and other forms of injustice—and perhaps even for those who witness the events—is enormous, and one that the field of POS would do well to seize.

Challenging Questions in Posttraumatic Growth

As the field of PTG develops, so too do questions about its meaning and significance. Here, I consider some of the issues arising with greatest frequency and urgency in the literature.

Is Growth "Real"?

The question that dominates many recent writings in the field is whether individuals' reports of growth reflect actual, or *veridical* change (Nolen-Hoeksema & Davis, 2004; Park & Helgeson, 2006; Wortman, 2004). This issue is important because most of the studies of PTG use self-reported measures of growth, gathered through a variety of inventories (see Joseph & Linley, 2006; Park & Lechner, 2006 for reviews). As Park and Helegson (2006, p. 793) inquire of study participants, "are they reporting changes in their lives that have actually occurred because of the trauma or are they manufacturing positive changes as an attempt to cope with the trauma and reduce their feelings of psychological distress?".

Frazier and Kaler (2006) identify several reasons that self-reported growth may not represent actual life changes. Perhaps the most powerful one rests on research on "positive illusions" (Taylor & Brown, 1988), which shows that most people view themselves in unrealistically positive terms, have unrealistically optimistic views of the future, and exaggerated perceptions of control over events. It could therefore reasonably follow that reports of PTG represent illusory perceptions that survivors unwittingly generate to alleviate their distress, perhaps by derogating their earlier selves and lives (McFarland & Alvaro, 2000; Wilson & Ross, 2001). More generally, research on self-reports in other areas has shown that people are not very accurate in assessing how they have changed over time or how they were at some prior time point, for example, with regard to their personality (Robins, Notfle, Wrzesniewski, & Roberts, 2005), emotional state (Parkinson, Briner, Reynolds, & Totterdell, 1995), and other psychosocial variables (Henry, Moffitt, Caspi, Langley, & Silva, 1994). The same could be true for respondents answering questions about changes in feelings of self-reliance, closeness with others, and so on, since a trauma. In particular, survivors influenced by certain cultural scripts may feel they have grown because they believe that they are meant to grow as a result of crisis (Frazier & Kaler, 2006; Linley & Joseph, 2004). It addition to these unintended self-delusions, inflated reports of growth may also come from survivors concerned to present themselves well to others so as to be seen as coping effectively (Frazier & Kaler, 2006).

Clearly, there are strong arguments against the validity of self-reported measures of PTG. Empirically, some research is consistent with these concerns, whereas other studies suggest that perceived growth reflects more tangible changes in an individual. For example, two studies of trauma survivors and their intimates found significant positive correlations between survivors' reports of growth and assessments of their growth made by close friends and family, suggesting that the survivors had grown in ways evident to those close to them (Park et al., 1996; Weiss, 2002). Other studies, however, provide evidence that self-reported, retrospective measures of growth do not capture veridical growth (Frazier & Kaler, 2006; Lehman, Wortman, & Williams, 1987; Wortman, 2004). In a rare prospective study, Frazier and colleagues (2009) explored whether self-reported growth was associated with actual change in domains of growth that were measured before and after the traumatic event.

They found little relationship between perceived growth and actual growth. They also found that perceived growth was associated with increased distress over time, whereas actual growth was associated with decreased distress, and they hypothesize that this may reflect different underlying processes. Indeed, some have argued for a "two-component model" of PTG (Maercker & Zollner, 2004; Zoellner & Maercker, 2006), which incorporates both constructive and illusory forms of growth. *Illusory growth* is triggered by the perception of threat and operates as an acute coping mechanism that decreases over time, whereas *constructive growth* emerges from the struggle for meaning, increases over time, and is linked to psychological adjustment. Evidence for this model is still, however, quite preliminary.

Other research suggests that survivors' perceptions of growth may provide more insight into their post-trauma experiences than can measures of veridical growth gathered across time points. For example, the social support literature has found that perceptions of support matter more to individual well-being than does actual received support (Cohen & Wills, 1985), and recalled experience may better predict behavior than actual experience (Kahneman, Fredrickson, Schreiber, & Redelmeier, 1993). Perhaps, as Park and Helgeson (2006) suggest, it depends on the question one seeks to answer. If we are interested in learning about how survivors enhance their psychological and social resources to cope with possible future crises, it may be more valuable to investigate their veridical growth. If we want to understand survivors' experience following a trauma, we may do better exploring their accounts of growth.

How Important Is Meaning Making to Growth?

As outlined earlier, meaning making plays a central role in prominent models of PTG (Janoff-Bulman, 1998, 2004, 2006; Joseph & Linley, 2005; Tedeschi & Calhoun, 1995, 2004). It is through this process, both carried out privately and in discussion with others, that individuals are said to come to terms with what has happened to them, and what it means for how they understand themselves and their future lives. Despite its dominance in writings on growth, the importance of meaning making has been challenged. Some consider that, although this kind of cognitive processing is important, it has been overemphasized in models of growth while the significance of emotional processing (Kennedy-Moore &

Watson, 2001; Rachman, 2001) and the role of supportive others (McMillen, 2004) have been underplayed. Others have suggested that meaning making may not help, and may even hinder people's recovery from trauma (Wortman, 2004). This may be especially likely when individuals try but fail to find meaning in what has happened to them (Bower, Kemeny, Taylor, & Fahey, 1998). Rather than show that meaning making *per se* is unhelpful, therefore, such research highlights the importance of facilitating meaning making that enables the development of narratives that explain what has happened.

A stronger challenge to the role of meaning making in PTG comes from Hobfoll et al. (2007), who argue that meaning making alone does not enable growth and that it must be translated into action in order to restore the basic psychological needs challenged by trauma. Drawing on Deci and Ryan's self-determination theory (Deci & Ryan, 1985, 2000), and Hofoll's conservation of resources theory (Hobfoll, 1989, 2002), Hobfoll and colleagues explain how feelings of autonomy, competence, and relatedness—which are significantly undermined by trauma—can rarely be regained through meaning making alone. Examining studies of growth in terrorism and war, they show the importance of *action growth*—daily actions in restoring resources (not simply meaning) lost through trauma (Hobfoll et al., 2007). This work does not show that action is necessary for PTG, but it provides valuable evidence for the importance of action in connecting PTG narratives to positive adjustment, in the form of fewer depressive and PTSD symptoms. These ideas are consistent with goal-oriented models of growth that propose that making meaning may be less important to growth than is disengaging from goals that are no longer attainable and the construction of new, more realistic life goals (O'Leary, Alday, & Ickovics, 1998; Ransom, Sheldon, & Jacobsen, 2008).

Must One Grow?

Finally, scholars have noted the danger of PTG becoming a "must have" outcome, blighted by the "tyranny of the positive attitude" (Held, 2002) that is increasingly prevalent in North American culture (Lechner, Stoelb, & Antoni, 2008; Lepore & Revenson, 2006; Meichenbaum, 2006). Lechner and colleagues (2006) note that individuals diagnosed with cancer are often beseeched to "stay positive" and "look on the bright side," even suggesting that maintaining such a positive outlook may itself be critical in preventing the cancer's spread or return.

Although this can feel empowering to some, to others, striving to be cheerful and upbeat in the context of a life-threatening trauma may only add to their burden (Holland & Lewis, 2000). Indeed, a recent study of patient adaptation to disability found that hoping for a reversal (for those with a potentially short-term condition) was associated with poorer life satisfaction and quality of life than was acceptance of the condition (Smith, Loewenstein, Jankovic, & Ubel, 2009). Here, hope seemed to prevent individuals from getting on with life, and potentially from growth. In addition, as an awareness of the possibility of PTG grows in the wider population, individuals may feel under pressure to experience it, or claim to be experiencing it. Such expectations expressed by others, or implicit in survivors' understandings of their own healing process, will likely amplify survivors' feelings that they are not functioning as they ought and are therefore failing in some way to feel and act appropriately post-trauma. Again, this compounds their painful experience and is unlikely to assist them in recovery and adjustment to their new situations.

Future Directions

Research on PTG has blossomed in the last decade, offering richer conceptualizations and increasingly sophisticated studies of the phenomenon. With this have come many questions, both theoretical and empirical. Although these are all important, the most compelling and urgent contribution for POS is doubtless the study of PTG in more occupational and organizational contexts. The possibilities here are numerous, including further investigation of PTG in organizations where members have witnessed a deeply troubling event, such a shooting or armed robbery (e.g., Harrison & Kinner, 1998; Powley, 2009) and in trauma-prone professions, such as peacekeeping forces, disaster work, and emergency department nursing (e.g., Britt et al., 2001; Dyregrov et al., 1996; Laposa, Alden, & Fullerton, 2003; Paton, 2006a). However, perhaps the richest opportunities lie in studies of growth in work settings not normally associated with trauma. This is where we may discover the possibility for growth alongside very painful experiences that are all too common in normal organizational life, such as workplace aggression, coercive bosses, and excruciating moral dilemmas, to name but a few (e.g., Schat & Kelloway, 2003; Sonenshein, 2007). Of course, these situations cannot be in any way regarded as positive, and organizations should never encourage them to enable the chance of employee growth.

However, given the sad inevitability of such experiences at work, POS can make a major contribution to the field of organizational behavior by increasing our understanding of how and when growth can emerge out of such traumas.

A second powerful opportunity for future research lies in narrative approaches to PTG, a suggestion consistent with Neimeyer's (2004, p. 53) observation that the "literature concerned with the construction, deconstruction, and reconstruction of narratives may be among the richest, but also least utilized" in the study of PTG. Indeed, this field has traditionally relied heavily on survey methods, which, as discussed earlier, has led to certain problems. In addition to debate about the veracity of self-reported growth, we have seen questions about the validity of the many existing measures of growth, and different opinions about its underlying factor structure. Further, conceptual difficulties in separating out processes leading to growth from measures of growth itself have been compounded by measures that do not distinguish between them, as well as meaning making processes assessed through single item responses, or individuals' reports of the cognitive strategies that they believe they used to make meaning. Clearly, there is value in continuing to refine growth inventories and tease apart the operationalization of different growth-related constructs. There is also, however, an overlooked opportunity for research that allows the exploration of growth in alternative ways. Specifically, narrative studies provide a powerful means for the examination of individuals' experience of PTG, and especially for the in-depth study of the meaning making process that is so important to growth. Moreover, narrative research enables not only the careful investigation of individuals' stories, but also the analysis of both the proximal and broader cultural narratives that are so influential in shaping individuals' movement toward growth (Ibarra & Barbulescu, 2010; McAdams, 2006).

These are just two suggestions for future research in a field that holds immense promise for POS, and indeed for organizational studies more generally.

Conclusion

As this chapter has shown, although the study of PTG is flourishing in psychology and related disciplines, it is almost absent from organizational behavior. This is not because people rarely experience trauma in the course of their work, or because organizational members' ability to work goes unaffected by trauma in their personal lives. On the contrary, individuals' working lives can be profoundly affected by painful experiences that occur within the organization and beyond, and this is likely to continue (Frost, 2003). As scholars and colleagues, we must do all that we can to prevent trauma at work. At the same time, we should recognize the possibility for growth in its aftermath, and work to increase knowledge of how, when, and where this can happen.

References

Abraido-Lanza, A.F., Guier, C., & Colon, R.M. (1998). Psychological thriving among Latinas with chronic illness. *Journal of Social Issues, 54,* 405–424.

Affleck, G., & Tennen, H. (1996). Construing benefits from adversity: Adaptational significance and dispositional underpinnings. *Journal of Personality, 64*(4), 899–922.

Affleck, G., Tennen, H., Croog, S., & Levine, S. (1987). Causal attribution, perceived benefits, and morbidity following a heart attack: An eight-year study. *Journal of Consulting and Clinical Psychology, 55,* 29–35.

Barker Caza, B., & Milton, L.P. (2011). Resilience at work: Building capability in the face of adversity. In K.S. Cameron & G.M. Spreitzer (Eds.), *The Oxford handbook of positive organizational scholarship.* New York: Oxford University Press.

Baumeister, R.F. (1991). *Meanings in life.* New York: Guilford.

Becker, G. (1997). *Disrupted lives: How people create meaning in a chaotic world.* Berkeley & Los Angeles: University of California Press.

Bonanno, G.A. (2004). Loss, trauma and human resilience: Have we underestimated the human capacity to thrive after extremely aversive events? *American Psychologist, 59*(1), 20–28.

Bonanno, G.A. (2005). Resilience in the face of potential trauma. *Current Directions in Psychological Science, 14*(3), 135–138.

Bower, J.E., Kemeny, M.E., Taylor, S.E., & Fahey, J.L. (1998). Cognitive processing, discovery of meaning, CD4 decline, and AIDS related mortality among bereaved HIV-seropositive men. *Journal of Consulting and Clinical Psychology, 66,* 979–986.

Britt, T.W., Adler, A.B., & Bartone, P.T. (2001). Deriving benefits from stressful events: The role of engagement in meaningful work and hardiness. *Journal of Occupational Health Psychology, 6*(1), 53–63.

Bruner, J. (1987). Life as narrative. *Social Research, 54*(1), 11–32.

Bulman, R.J., & Wortman, C.B. (1977). Attributions of blame and coping in the "real world": Severe accident victims react to their lot. *Journal of Personality and Social Psychology, 35*(May), 351–363.

Calhoun, L.G., & Tedeschi, R.G. (2001). Posttraumatic growth: The positive lessons of loss. In R.A. Neimeyer (Ed.), *Meaning reconstruction and the meaning of loss* (pp. 157–172). Washington, DC: American Psychological Association.

Calhoun, L.G., & Tedeschi, R.G. (2004). The foundations of posttraumatic growth: New considerations. *Psychological Inquiry, 15*(1), 93–102.

Calhoun, L.G., & Tedeschi, R.G. (2006). The foundations of posttraumatic growth: An expanded framework. In L.G. Calhoun, & R.G. Tedeschi (Eds.), *Handbook of posttraumatic growth: Research and practice* (pp. 1–23). Mahwah, NJ: Erlbaum.

Campbell, W.K., Brunell, A.B., & Foster, J.D. (2004). Sitting in limbo: Ego shock and posttraumatic growth. *Psychological Inquiry, 15*(1), 22–26.

Carlier, I.V.E., Voerman, A.E., & Gersons, B.P.R. (2000). The influence of occupational debriefing on post-traumatic stress symptomatology in traumatized police officers. *British Journal of Medical Psychology, 73*(1), 87–98.

Caza, B. (2003). Resilience in organizations. In K. Cameron, & G. Spreitzer (Eds.), *Handbook of positive organizational scholarship*. New York: Oxford University Press.

Clohessy, S., & Ehlers, A. (1999). PTSD symptoms, response to intrusive memories and coping in ambulance service workers. *British Journal of Clinical Psychology, 38*(3), 251–265.

Cohen, S., & Wills, T.A. (1985). Stress, social support and the buffering hypothesis. *Psychological Bulletin, 98*(2), 310–357.

Cordova, M.J., Cunningham, L.L., Carlson, C.R., & Andrykowski, M.A. (2001). Posttraumatic growth following breast cancer: A controlled comparison study. *Health Psychology, 20*(3), 176–185.

Creamer, M., Burgess, P., & Pattison, P. (1992). Reaction to trauma: A cognitive processing model. *Journal of Abnormal Psychology, 101*(3), 452–459.

Cruess, D.G., Antoni, M.H., McGregor, B.A., Kilbourn, K.M., Boyers, A.E., Alferi, S.M., & Kumar, M. (2000). Cognitive behavioral stress management reduces serum cortisol by enhancing benefit finding among women being treated for early-stage breast cancer. *Psychosomatic Medicine, 62*, 304–308.

Davis, C.G., & Morgan, M.S. (2008). Finding meaning, perceiving growth, and acceptance of tinnitus. *Rehabilitation Psychology, 53*(2), 128–138.

Davis, C.G., & Nolen-Hoeksema, S. (2009). Making sense of loss, perceiving benefits, and posttraumatic growth. In C.R. Snyder, & S.J. Lopez (Eds.), *Oxford handbook of positive psychology* (pp. 641–649). New York: Oxford University Press.

Davis, C.G., Nolen-Hoeksema, S., & Larson, J. (1998). Making sense of loss and benefiting from the experience: Two construals of meaning. *Journal of Personality and Social Psychology, 75*, 561–574.

Davis, C.G., Wohl, M.J.A., & Verberg, N. (2007). Profiles of posttraumatic growth following an unjust loss. *Death Studies, 31*(8), 693–712.

Deci, E.L., & Ryan, R.M. (1985). *Intrinsic motivation and self-determination in human behavior*. New York: Plenum.

Deci, E.L., & Ryan, R.M. (2000). The "what" and "why" of goal pursuits: Human needs and the self-determination of behavior. *Psychological Inquiry, 4*, 227–268.

Dohrenwend, B.P., Neria, Y., Turner, J.B., Turse, N., Marshall, R., Lewis-Fernandez, R., & Koenen, K.C. (2004). Positive tertiary appraisals and posttraumatic stress disorder in US male veterans of the war in Vietnam: The roles of positive affirmation, positive reformulation, and defensive denial. *Journal of Consulting and Clinical Psychology, 72*, 417–433.

Downey, G., Silver, R.C., & Wortman, C.B. (1990). Reconsidering the attribution-adjustment relation following a major negative event: Coping with the loss of a child. *Journal of Personality and Social Psychology, 59*(5), 925–940.

Dyregrov, A., Kristofferson, J.I., & Gjestad, R. (1996). Voluntary and professional disaster-workers: Similarities and differences in reactions. *Journal of Traumatic Stress, 9*, 541–555.

Elder, G.H., Jr., & Clipp, E.C. (1989). Combat experience and emotional health: Impairment and resilience in later life. *Journal of Personality, 57*(2), 311–341.

Eton, D.T., Lepore, S.J., & Helgeson, V.S. (2005). Psychological distress in spouses of men treated for early-stage prostate carcinoma. *Cancer, 92*, 2412–2418.

Evers, A.W., Kraaimaat, F.W., van Lankveld, W., Jongen, P.J., Jacobs, J.W., & Bijlsma, J.W. (2001). Beyond unfavorable thinking: The illness cognition questionnaire for chronic diseases. *Journal of Consulting and Clinical Psychology, 69*(6), 1026–1036.

Fineman, S. (2000). *Emotion in organizations*. Thousand Oaks, CA: Sage Publications Ltd.

Fontana, A., & Rosenheck, R. (1998). Psychological benefits and liabilities of traumatic exposure in the war zone. *Journal of Traumatic Stress, 3*, 485–503.

Frank, A.W. (1995). *The wounded storyteller: Body, illness and ethics*. Chicago: The University of Chicago Press.

Frankl, V. (1963). *Man's search for meaning: An introduction to logotherapy*. New York: Pocket Books.

Frazier, P.A., Conlon, A., & Glaser, T. (2001). Positive and negative life changes following sexual assault. *Journal of Consulting and Clinical Psychology, 69*(6), 1048–1055.

Frazier, P.A., & Kaler, M.E. (2006). Assessing the validity of self-reported stress-related growth. *Journal of Consulting and Clinical Psychology, 74*(5), 859.

Frazier, P., Tennen, H., Gavian, M., Park, C., Tomich, P., & Tashiro, T. (2009). Does self-reported posttraumatic growth reflect genuine positive change? *Psychological Science, 20*(7), 912–919.

Frost, P. (2003). *Toxic emotions at work: How compassionate managers handle pain and conflict*. Boston: Harvard Business School Press.

Gangstad, B., Norman, P., & Barton, J. (2009). Cognitive processing and posttraumatic growth after stroke. *Rehabilitation Psychology, 54*(1), 69–75.

Gergen, K. (1994). *Realities and relationships: Soundings in social construction*. Cambridge, MA: Harvard University Press.

Gersons, B.P., Carlier, I.V., Lamberts, R.D., & van der Kolk, B.A. (2000). Randomized clinical trial of brief eclectic psychotherapy for police officers with posttraumatic stress disorder. *Journal of Traumatic Stress, 13*(2), 333–347.

Gillies, J., & Neimeyer, R.A. (2006). Loss, grief and the search for significance: Towards a model of meaning reconstruction in bereavement. *Journal of Constructive Psychology, 19*(1), 31–65.

Greenberg, L.S. (2004). Emotion-focused therapy. *Clinical Psychology & Psychotherapy, 11*(1), 3–16.

Greenberg, L.S., & Pavio, S.C. (1997). *Working with emotions in psychotherapy*. New York: Guilford Press.

Harrison, C.A., & Kinner, S.A. (1998). Correlates of psychological distress following armed robbery. *Journal of Traumatic Stress, 11*(4), 787–798.

Held, B.S. (2002). The tyranny of the positive attitude in America: Observation and speculation. *Journal of Clinical Psychology, 58*(9), 965–991.

Helgeson, V.S., Reynolds, K.A., & Tomich, P.L. (2006). A meta-analytic review of benefit finding and growth. *Journal of Consulting and Clinical Psychology, 74*(5), 797–816.

Henry, B., Moffitt, T.E., Caspi, A., Langley, J., & Silva, P.A. (1994). On the "remembrance of things past": A longitudinal evaluation of the retrospective method. *Psychological Assessment, 6*(2), 92–101.

Herman, J. (1997). *Trauma and recovery* (2nd ed.). New York: Basic Books.

Hobfoll, S.E. (1989). Conservation of resources: A new attempt at conceptualizing stress. *American Psychologist, 44*, 513–524.

Hobfoll, S.E. (2002). Social and psychological resources and adaptation. *Review of General Psychology, 6*(4), 307–324.

Hobfoll, S.E., Hall, B.J., Canetti-Nisim, D., Galea, S., Johnson, R.J., & Palmieri, P.A. (2007). Refining our understanding of traumatic growth in the face of terrorism: Moving from meaning cognitions to doing what is meaningful. *Applied Psychology, 56*(3), 345–366.

Holland, J.C., & Lewis, S. (2000). *The human side of cancer: Living with hope, coping with uncertainty*. New York: Harper Collins.

Howard, G.S. (1991). Cultural tales: A narrative approach to thinking, cross-cultural psychology, and psychotherapy. *American Psychologist, 46*, 187–197.

Ibarra, H., & Barbulescu, R. (2010). Identity as narrative: Prevalence, effectiveness, and consequences of narrative identity work in macro work role transitions. *Academy of Management Review, 35*(1), 135–154.

Janoff-Bulman, R. (1992). *Shattered assumptions: Towards a new psychology of trauma*. New York: Free Press.

Janoff-Bulman, R. (1998). From terror to appreciation: Confronting chance after extreme misfortune. *Psychological Inquiry, 9*(2), 99–101.

Janoff-Bulman, R. (2004). Posttraumatic growth: Three explanatory models. *Psychological Inquiry, 15*(1), 30–34.

Janoff-Bulman, R. (2006). Schema-change perspectives on posttraumatic growth. In L.G. Calhoun, & R.G. Tedeschi (Eds.), *Handbook of posttraumatic growth: Research and practice* (pp. 81–99). Mahwah, NJ: Erlbaum.

Janoff-Bulman, R., & Frantz, C.M. (1997). The impact of trauma on meaning: From meaningless world to meaningful life. In M.J. Power, & C.R. Brewin (Eds.), *The transformation of meaning in psychological therapies: Integrating theory and practice* (pp. 91–106). Hoboken, NJ: Wiley.

Joseph, S., & Linley, P.A. (2005). Positive adjustment to threatening events: An organismic valuing theory of growth through adversity. *Review of General Psychology, 9*(3), 262–280.

Joseph, S., & Linley, P.A. (2006). Growth following adversity: Theoretical perspectives and implications for clinical practice. *Clinical Psychology Review, 26*(8), 1041–1053.

Joseph, S., & Linley, P.A. (Eds.). (2008). *Trauma, recovery and growth: Positive psychological perspectives on posttraumatic stress*. Hoboken, NJ: John Wiley & Sons.

Kahneman, D., Fredrickson, B.L., Schreiber, C.A., & Redelmeier, D.A. (1993). When more pain is preferred to less: Adding a better end. *Psychological Science, 4*(6), 401–405.

Kamphuis, J.H., & Emmelkamp, P.M. G. (1998). Crime-related trauma: Psychological distress in victims of bank robbery. *Journal of Anxiety Disorders, 12*(3), 199–208.

Katz, R.C., Flasher, L., Cacciapaglia, H., & Nelson, S. (2001). The psychosocial impact of cancer and lupus: A cross-validational study that extends the generality of "benefit-finding" in patients with chronic disease. *Journal of Behavioral Medicine, 24*, 561–571.

Kennedy-Moore, E., & Watson, J. (2001). How and when does emotional expression help? *Review of General Psychology, 5*, 187–212.

Keyes, C.L.M., & Haidt, J. (Eds.). (2003). *Flourishing: Positive psychology and the life well lived*. Washington, DC: American Psychological Association.

King, L.A., Scollon, C.K., Ramsey, C., & Williams, T. (2000). Stories of life transition: Subjective well-being and ego development in parents of children with Down Syndrome. *Journal of Research in Personality, 34*, 509–536.

Kleinman, A. (1988). *The illness narratives: Suffering, healing and the human condition*. New York: Basic Books.

Laposa, J.M., Alden, L.E., & Fullerton, L.M. (2003). Work stress and posttraumatic stress disorder in ED nurses/personnel (CE). *Journal of Emergency Nursing, 29*(1), 23–28.

Latack, J.C., Kinicki, A.J., & Prussia, G.E. (1995). An integrative process model of coping with job loss. *Academy of Management Review, 20*(2), 311–342.

Lechner, S.C., Stoelb, B.L., & Antoni, M.H. (2008). Group based therapies for benefit finding in cancer. In S. Joseph, & P.A. Linley (Eds.), *Trauma, recovery and growth* (pp. 207–231). Hoboken, NJ: John Wiley & Sons.

Lehman, D.R., Wortman, C.B., & Williams, A.F. (1987). Long-term effects of losing a spouse or child in a motor vehicle crash. *Journal of Personality and Social Psychology, 52*, 218–231.

Lepore, S., & Revenson, T. (2006). Relationships between posttraumatic growth and resilience: Recovery, resistance, and reconfiguration. In L.G. Calhoun, & R.G. Tedeschi (Eds.), *Handbook of posttraumatic growth: Research and practice* (pp. 24–46). Mahwah, NJ: Erlbaum.

Leymann, H., & Gustaffson, A. (1996). Mobbing at work and the development of post-traumatic stress disorders. *European Journal of Work and Organizational Psychology, 5*(2), 251–275.

Lilius, J.M., Kanov, J., Dutton, J.E., Worline, M.C., & Maitlis, S. (2011). Compassion revealed: What we know about compassion at work (and where we need to know more). In K.S. Cameron & G.M. Spreitzer (Eds.), *The Oxford handbook of positive organizational scholarship*. New York: Oxford University Press.

Linley, P.A., & Joseph, S. (2004). Positive change following trauma and adversity: A review. *Journal of Traumatic Stress, 17*(1), 11–21.

Linley, P.A., & Joseph, S. (2005). Positive and negative changes following occupational death exposure. *Journal of Traumatic Stress, 18*(6), 751–758.

Linley, P.A., & Joseph, S. (2006). Positive and negative aspects of disaster work. *Journal of Loss and Trauma, 11*, 229–245.

Linley, P.A., & Joseph, S. (2007). Therapy work and therapists' positive and negative well-being. *Journal of Social and Clinical Psychology, 26*(3), 385–403.

MacDonald, H.A., Colotla, V., Flamer, S., & Karlinsky, H. (2003). Posttraumatic stress disorder (PTSD) in the workplace: A descriptive study of workers experiencing PTSD resulting from work injury. *Journal of Occupational Rehabilitation, 13*(2), 63–77.

Maercker, A., & Zollner, T. (2004). The Janus face of self-perceived growth: Toward a two-component model of posttraumatic growth. *Psychological Inquiry, 15*(1), 41–48.

Maitlis, S. (2009). Who am I now? Sensemaking and identity in posttraumatic growth. In L.M. Roberts, & J.E. Dutton (Eds.), *Positive identities in organizations* (pp. 47–76). New York: Psychology Press.

Martin, B. (2000). Mobbing: Emotional abuse in the workplace. *Journal of Organizational Change Management, 13*(4), 401–406.

Matthiesen, S.B., & Einarsen, S. (2004). Psychiatric distress and symptoms of PTSD among victims of bullying at work. *British Journal of Guidance and Counselling, 32*(3), 335–356.

Maslow, A.H. (1968). *Toward a psychology of being* (2nd ed.). New York: Van Nostrand.

May, R. (1981). *Freedom and destiny*. New York: Norton.

McAdams, D.P. (1991). The psychology of life stories. *Review of General Psychology, 5,* 100–122.

McAdams, D.P. (2006). The redemptive self: Generativity and the stories Americans live by. *Research in Human Development, 3*(2&3), 81–100.

McFarland, C., & Alvaro, C. (2000). The impact of motivation on temporal comparisons: Coping with traumatic events by perceiving personal growth. *Journal of Personality and Social Psychology, 79*(3), 327–343.

McGregor, B.A., Antoni, M.H., Boyers, A., Alferi, S.M., Blomberg, B.B., & Carver, C.S. (2004). Cognitive-behavioral stress management increases benefit finding and immune function among women with early-stage breast cancer. *Journal of Psychosomatic Research, 56,* 1–8.

McMillen, J.C. (2004). Posttraumatic growth: What's it all about? *Psychological Inquiry, 15*(1), 48–52.

McMillen, J.C., Smith, E.M., & Fisher, R.H. (1997). Perceived benefit and mental health after three types of disaster. *Journal of Consulting and Clinical Psychology, 65*(5), 733–739.

Meichenbaum, D. (2006). Resilience and posttraumatic growth: A constructive narrative perspective. In L.G. Calhoun, & R.G. Tedeschi (Eds.), *Handbook of posttraumatic growth: Research and practice* (pp. 355–368). Mahwah, NJ: Erlbaum.

Mikkelsen, E.G., & Einarsen, S. (2002). Basic assumptions and symptoms of post-traumatic stress among victims of bullying at work. *European Journal of Work and Organizational Psychology, 11*(1), 87–111.

Milam, J. (2006). Posttraumatic growth and HIV disease progression. *Journal of Consulting and Clinical Psychology, 74*(5), 817–827.

Molinsky, A., & Margolis, J. (2005). Necessary evils and interpersonal sensitivity in organizations. *Academy of Management Review, 30*(2), 245–268.

Neimeyer, R.A. (2000). Searching for the meaning of meaning: Grief therapy and the process of reconstruction. *Death Studies, 24,* 541–557.

Neimeyer, R.A. (2004). Fostering posttraumatic growth: A narrative contribution. *Psychological Inquiry, 15*(1), 53–59.

Neimeyer, R.A. (2006). Re-storying loss: Fostering growth in the posttraumatic narrative. In L.G. Calhoun, & R.G. Tedeschi (Eds.), *Handbook of posttraumatic growth: Research and practice* (pp. 68–80). Mahwah, NJ: Erlbaum.

Neimeyer, R.A., & Anderson, A. (2002). Meaning reconstruction theory. In N. Thompson (Ed.), *Loss and grief: A guide for human service practitioners* (pp. 45–64). New York: Palgrave.

Nolen-Hoeksema, S., & Davis, C. 2004. Theoretical and methodological issues in the assessment and interpretation of posttraumatic growth. *Psychological Inquiry, 15*(1), 60–64.

O'Leary, V.E., Alday, C.S., & Ickovics, J.R. (1998). Life changes and posttraumatic growth. In R.G. Tedeschi, C.R. Park, & L.G. Calhoun (Eds.), *Posttraumatic growth: Positive changes in the aftermath of crisis* (pp. 127–151). Mahwah, NJ: Lawrence Erlbaum Associates, Inc.

O'Rourke, J.J.F., Tallman, B.A., & Altmaier, E.M. (2008). Measuring post-traumatic changes in spirituality/religiosity. *Mental Health, Religion & Culture, 11*(7), 719.

Pals, J.L. (2000). *Self-narrative of difficult life experiences in adulthood*. Unpublished doctoral dissertation, University of California, Berkeley.

Pals, J.L. (2006a). Authoring a second chance in life: Emotion and transformational processing within narrative identity. *Research in Human Development, 3*(2), 101–120.

Pals, J.L. (2006b). Constructing the "springboard effect": Causal connections, self-making, and growth within the life story. In D.P. McAdams, R. Josselson, & A. Lieblich (Eds.), *Identity and story: Creating self in narrative* (pp. 175–199). Washington, DC: American Psychological Association.

Pals, J.L., & McAdams, D.P. (2004). The transformed self: A narrative understanding of posttraumatic growth. *Psychological Inquiry, 15*(1), 65–69.

Park, C.L. (2010). Making sense of the meaning literature: An integrative review of meaning making and its effects on adjustment to stressful life events. *Psychological Bulletin, 136*(2), 257–301.

Park, C.L., Cohen, L.H., & Murch, R. (1996). Assessment and prediction of stress-related growth. *Journal of Personality, 64,* 71–105.

Park, C.L., Edmondson, D., Fenster, J.R., & Blank, T.O. (2008). Meaning making and psychological adjustment following cancer: The mediating roles of growth, life meaning, and restored just-world beliefs. *Journal of Consulting and Clinical Psychology, 76*(5), 863–875.

Park, C.L., & Helgeson, V.S. (2006). Introduction to the special section: Growth following highly stressful life events–Current status and future directions. *Journal of Consulting and Clinical Psychology, 74*(5), 791–796.

Park, C.L., & Lechner, S. (2006). Measurement issues in assessing growth following stressful life experiences. In L.G. Calhoun, & R.G. Tedeschi (Eds.), *Handbook of posttraumatic growth: Research and practice* (pp. 47–67). Mahwah, NJ: Erlbaum.

Parkinson, B., Briner, R.B., Reynolds, S., & Totterdell, P. (1995). Time frames for emotion: Relations between momentary and generalized ratings of affect. *Personality and Social Psychology Bulletin, 21,* 331–339.

Paton, D. (2006a). Posttraumatic growth in disaster and emergency work. In L.G. Calhoun, & R.G. Tedeschi (Eds.), *Handbook of posttraumatic growth: Research and practice* (pp. 225–247). Mahwah, NJ: Erlbaum.

Paton, D. (2006b). Critical incident stress risk in police officers: Managing resilience and vulnerability. *Traumatology, 12*(3), 198–206.

Pennebaker, J.W., & Chung, C.K. (2007). Expressive writing, emotional upheavals, and health. In H.S. Friedman, & R.C. Silver (Eds.), *Foundations of health psychology* (pp. 263–284). New York: Oxford University Press.

Pennebaker, J.W., Mayne, T.J., & Francis, M.E. (1997). Linguistic predictors of adaptive bereavement. *Journal of Personality and Social Psychology, 72,* 863–871.

Perls, F.S. (1969). *Ego, hunger and aggression*. New York: Random House.

Phelps, L.F., Williams, R.M., Raichle, K.A., Turner, A.P., & Ehde, D.M. (2008). The importance of cognitive processing to adjustment in the 1st year following amputation. *Rehabilitation Psychology, 53*(1), 28–38.

Powley, E.H. (2009). Reclaiming resilience and safety: Resilience activation in the critical period of crisis. *Human Relations, 62*(9), 1289–1326.

Profitt, D.H., Calhoun, L.G., Tedeschi, R.G., & Cann, A. (2002). *Clergy and crisis: Correlates of posttraumatic growth and well-being*. Poster presented at the annual meeting of the American Psychological Association, Chicago.

Rachman, S. (2001). Emotional processing, with special reference to post-traumatic stress disorder. *International Review of Psychiatry, 13,* 164–171.

Radeke, J.T., & Mahoney, M.J. (2000). Comparing the personal lives of psychotherapists and research psychologists. *Professional Psychology: Research and Practice, 31*(1), 82–84.

Ransom, S., Sheldon, K.S., & Jacobsen, P.B. (2008). Actual change and inaccurate recall contribute to posttraumatic growth following radiotherapy. *Journal of Consulting and Clinical Psychology, 76*(5), 811–819.

Raphael, B., Singh, B., Bradbury, L., & Lambert, F. (1984). Who helps the helpers? The effects of a disaster on the rescue workers. *Omega, 14*, 9–20.

Rivkin, I.D., Gustafson, J., Weingarten, I., & Chin, D. (2006). The effects of expressive writing on adjustment to HIV. *AIDS and Behavior, 10*, 13–26.

Robins, R.W., Noftle, E.E., Wrzesniewski, K.H., & Roberts, B.W. (2005). Do people know how their personality has changed? Correlates of perceived and actual personality change in young adulthood. *Journal of Personality, 73*(2), 489–522.

Rogers, C.R. (1964). Toward a modern approach to values: The valuing process in the mature person. *Journal of Abnormal and Social Psychology, 68,* 160–167.

Schat, A.C.H., & Kelloway, E.K. (2003). Reducing the adverse consequences of workplace aggression and violence: The buffering effects of organizational support. *Journal of Occupational Health Psychology, 8*(2), 110–122.

Schneider, K.T., Swan, S., & Fitzgerald, L.F. (1997). Job-related and psychological effects of sexual harassment in the workplace: Empirical evidence from two organizations. *Journal of Applied Psychology, 82*(3), 401–415.

Sears, S.R., Stanton, A.L., & Danoff-Burg, S. (2003). The yellow brick road and the Emerald city: Benefit finding, positive reappraisal coping, and posttraumatic growth in women with early-stage breast cancer. *Health Psychology, 22*(5), 487–497.

Siltala, P. (1998). I made a picture of my life—a life from the picture: The life of the body in the pictures and writings of Frida Kahlo. *International Forum of Psychoanalysis, 7,* 133–155.

Smith, D.M., Loewenstein, G., Jankovich, A., & Ubel, P.A. (2009). Happily hopeless: Adaptation to a permanent, but not to a temporary, disability. *Health Psychology, 28*(6), 787–791.

Smyth, J.M., Hockemeyer, J.R., & Tulloch, H. (2008). Expressive writing and post-traumatic stress disorder: Effects on trauma symptoms, mood states, and cortisol reactivity. *British Journal of Health Psychology, 13*, 85–93.

Sonenshein, S. (2007). The role of construction, intuition, and justification in responding to ethical issues at work: The sensemaking-intuition model. *Academy of Management Review, 32*(4), 1022–1040.

Spreitzer, G., Sutcliffe, K., Dutton, J., Sonenshein, S., & Grant, A.M. (2005). An embedded model of thriving at work. *Organization Science, 16*(5), 537–549.

Stanton, A.L., Bower, J.E., & Low, C.A. (2006). Posttraumatic growth after cancer. In L.G. Calhoun, & R.G. Tedeschi (Eds.), *Handbook of posttraumatic growth: Research and practice* (pp. 138–175). Mahwah, NJ: Erlbaum.

Sutcliffe, K.M., & Vogus, T. (2003). Organizing for resilience. In K.S. Cameron, J.E. Dutton, & R.E. Quinn (Eds.), *Positive organizational scholarship* (pp.94–110). San Francisco: Berrett-Koehler.

Taylor, S.E., & Brown, J.D. (1988). Illusion and well-being: A social psychological perspective on mental health. *Psychological Bulletin, 103*(2), 193–210.

Tedeschi, R.G., & Calhoun, L.G. (1995). *Trauma and transformation: Growing in the aftermath of suffering.* Thousand Oaks, CA: Sage Publications.

Tedeschi, R.G., & Calhoun, L.G. (1996). The posttraumatic growth inventory: Measuring the positive legacy of trauma. *Journal of Traumatic Stress, 9*, 455–471.

Tedeschi, R.G., & Calhoun, L.G. (2004). Posttraumatic growth: Conceptual foundations and empirical evidence. *Psychological Inquiry, 15*(1), 1–18.

Tennen, H., Affleck, G., Urrows, S., Higgins, P., & Mendola, R. (1992). Perceiving control, construing benefits, and daily processes in rheumatoid arthritis. *Canadian Journal of Behavioural Science/Revue Canadienne des Sciences du Comportement, 24*(2), 186–203.

Tepper, B.J. (2007). Abusive supervision in work organizations: Review, synthesis, and research agenda. *Journal of Management, 33*(3), 261–289.

Thompson, S.C. (1985). Finding positive meaning in a stressful event and coping. *Basic and Applied Social Psychology, 6*, 279–295.

Tomich, P.L., & Helgeson, V.S. (2002). Five years later: A cross-sectional comparison of breast cancer survivors with healthy women. *Psycho-Oncology, 11*, 154–169.

Ullrich, P.M., & Lutgendorf, S.K. (2002). Journaling about stressful events: Effects of cognitive processing and emotional expression. *Annals of Behavioral Medicine, 24*, 244–250.

Updegraff, J.A., Silver, R.C., & Holman, E.A. (2008). Searching for and finding meaning in collective trauma: Results from a national longitudinal study of the 9/11 terrorist attacks. *Journal of Personality and Social Psychology, 95*(3), 709–722.

Updegraff, J.A., Taylor, S.E., Kemeny, M.E., & Wyatt, G.E. (2002). Positive and negative effects of HIV infection in women with low socioeconomic resources. *Personality and Social Psychology Bulletin, 28*, 382–394.

Weinrib, A.Z., Rothrock, N.E., Johnsen, E.L., & Lutgendorf, S.K. (2006). The assessment and validity of stress-related growth in a community-based sample. *Journal of Consulting and Clinical Psychology, 74*(5), 851.

Weiss, T. (2002). Posttraumatic growth in women with breast cancer and their husbands: An intersubjective validation study. *Journal of Psychosocial Oncology, 20*, 65–80.

Williams, R.M., Davis, M.C., & Millsap, R.E. (2002). Development of the cognitive processing of trauma scale. *Clinical Psychology & Psychotherapy, 9*(5), 349–360.

Wilson, A.E., & Ross, M. (2001). From chump to champ: People's appraisals of their earlier and present selves. *Journal of Personality and Social Psychology, 80*(4), 572–584.

Wortman, C.B. (2004). Posttraumatic growth: Progress and problems. *Psychological Inquiry, 15*(1), 81–90.

Wrzesniewski, A. (2002). "It's not just a job": Shifting meanings of work in the wake of 9/11. *Journal of Management Inquiry, 11*(3), 230–234.

Wrzesniewski, A., McCauley, C.R., Rozin, P., & Schwartz, B. (1997). Jobs, careers, and callings: People's relations to their work. *Journal of Research in Personality, 31*, 21–33.

Yalom, I.D. (1980). *Existential psychotherapy.* New York: Basic Books.

Zoellner, T., & Maercker, A. (2006). Posttraumatic growth in clinical psychology–A critical review and introduction of a two component model. *Clinical Psychology Review, 26*(5), 626–653.

Just a Good Place to Visit?

Exploring Positive Responses to Psychological Ambivalence

Michael G. Pratt *and* Camille Pradies

Abstract

Although historically ambivalence has been treated as something to be avoided or resolved, we argue that research increasingly suggests the benefits of being ambivalent. Specifically, we show how *traditional* responses to ambivalence, which largely view ambivalence negatively—paralysis, moving against, moving away, moving toward, and vacillation—can sometimes have positive benefits. We also discuss the positive nature of *emerging* responses to ambivalence: commitment, trust, creativity, openness to change, as well as wisdom and adaptation. We map both the emerging and traditional responses to ambivalence to reveal the various dimensions that underlie them. We also show how emerging responses appear to cluster around two different targets of ambivalence (e.g., relationships vs. knowledge) and discuss the properties of these targets (e.g., hotter vs. colder cognitions). Finally, we discuss the relationship between positivity and ambivalence, and we posit avenues for future research.

Keywords: Positive responses to ambivalence, wisdom and adaptation, stability–flexibility, trust and commitment, openness to change, creativity

Ambivalence is a reasonable place to visit, but you wouldn't want to live there.
—Miller & Rollnick, 2002, p. 14

Even though it might be most appropriate to have mixed feelings about it, both its origin and much subsequent use of psychological ambivalence have tended to emphasize its negative aspects and our need to escape it. The epigraph captures the sentiment well. First, although scholars suggest that everyone encounters ambivalence—some even equating ambivalence to being central to the human condition (e.g., Boehm, 1989; Smelser, 1998)—the preponderance of research appears to agree that it is not something you either want to have lot of or want to experience over long periods of time. However, in the past 40 years, there has been a growing consensus that how we respond to ambivalence can have salutary effects (e.g., Brickman, 1987; Fong, 2006; Plambeck & Weber, 2009;

Weick, 2004). While we do not deny that ambivalence and our responses to it may have negative effects—and indeed, we review some of them here—the purpose of this chapter is to bring attention to the more positive responses to ambivalence. Specifically, our focus is on positive responses to salient psychological ambivalence, and to a lesser degree, on the conditions that enable these positive responses for individuals and the collectives to which they belong (Cameron, Dutton, & Quinn, 2003, p. 5).

We begin by briefly reviewing what ambivalence is and identifying some boundary conditions of our chapter. We then summarize both traditional and emerging research that discuss how we respond to ambivalence, and emphasize the positive elements of these various responses. Building on this work, we propose an organizing framework for these various types of responses to ambivalence. Finally, we conclude our chapter with some implications of our research, and ideas for where future scholarship on positivity and ambivalence might go.

Ambivalence: A Brief Review

Even if definitions of ambivalence have varied somewhat, there is consensus around the notion of ambivalence as the simultaneous experience of contradictory emotions and cognitions (see Ashforth, Rogers, & Pratt, 2011, for review). Drawing from Lüscher (2002, p. 566), we view ambivalence as "competing perspectives oriented to one and the same object . . . that cannot be fully reconciled within a limited or even an unlimited time span." This definition highlights the unique features of ambivalence, including its essentially irreconcilable nature. According to Meyerson and Scully (1995), ambivalence comes from the Latin *ambo* ("both") and *valere* ("to be strong"), and refers to powerful and competing forces.

Although a full review of the literature on psychological ambivalence is beyond the scope of this chapter, we follow Wang and Pratt (2008) and divide this field into two main approaches. The first approach addresses what has been the historical focus of ambivalence research: discussing how ambivalence characterizes interpersonal relationships (Freud, 1950/1920; Horney, 1945), such as the love–hate relationship one might have with family members. As noted by Lüscher (2002), the focus on ambivalence in relationships can be traced at least back to Greek mythology, such as in the story between Oedipus and his father. The parent–child relationship as a source of ambivalence is also evident in developmental psychology. Bowlby (1982), for example, saw ambivalence as characterizing one of the main attachment types between infants and caregivers. Research in this tradition has continued and has been extended to include relationships among adults (Hazan & Shaver, 1994). More generally, ambivalence has moved from defining primarily pathological relationships to defining a wider range of human relationships (e.g., cross-generational; Lüscher, 2002), as well as relationships with nonhuman "others," such as artifacts or symbols (Smelser, 1998). In the organizational literature, this relationship perspective continues in a variety of ways (Pratt & Doucet, 2000). For example, research on ambivalent identification (Kreiner & Ashforth, 2003; Pratt, 2000) discusses individual

bonds with groups and organizations that are characterized by both approach (identification) and avoidance (disidentification) elements. Moreover, as described below, research on relational commitment and on some forms of trust would also be relevant here.

The second psychological approach studies ambivalence as an attitude (King & Emmons, 1990; Thompson & Zanna, 1995). Conner and Armitage (2008) identified two broad categories, top-down and bottom-up, which refer to the antecedents of attitudinal ambivalence. Top-down approaches refer to chronic psychological tendencies, such as individual differences or conflicts over internalized values. To illustrate, Thompson and Zanna (1995) have studied how different personality traits can influence how individuals process and accept duality. Bottom-up approaches refer to how conflicting stimuli associated with the object of ambivalence itself may influence ambivalence. Specifically, the research shows how some objects (e.g., condoms) can evoke ambivalent attitudes in some individuals but not others (e.g., Dahl, Darke, Gorn, & Weinberg, 2005). Although an attitudinal approach is less common in the organizational literature, it can be found most directly in discussions of ambivalence and wisdom (Weick, 1998).

While we are inclusive and draw upon both approaches, our chapter does have some important boundary conditions. First, by focusing on psychological ambivalence, we do not emphasize sociological approaches that stress the social and structural (e.g., norms, roles) roots of ambivalence (e.g., Coser, 1979; Merton & Barber, 1976). Rather, we see norms, roles, and the like as potential antecedents for ambivalence (Pratt & Doucet, 2000; Wang & Pratt, 2008). Following its earliest uses (Sincoff, 1990), we also focus on the affective-cognitive aspects of ambivalence (e.g., Lavine, Thomsen, Zanna, & Borgida, 1998) rather than on its behavioral manifestations. Finally, we focus on ambivalence that is salient or strong enough so that people are aware of it and are motivated to respond to it (Ashforth et al., 2011).

Our approach to ambivalence is decidedly positive as well. Similar to Baggozi (2003), who discussed the positive effects of negative emotions, we draw upon emerging work in organizational scholarship that emphasizes various positive responses to ambivalence. By *positive responses to ambivalence*, we refer to individual-level reactions to ambivalence that foster enhanced personal functioning or flourishing. In this way, we break away from and enrich extant conceptualizations of ambivalence, a concept that, when coined by Bleuler, was viewed as negative at best, and a sign of pathology at worst (Lüscher, 2002). Moreover, given our focus on positive *responses* to ambivalence, we do not focus much on the antecedents of ambivalence (see Ashforth et al., 2011; Wang & Pratt, 2008, for recent reviews).

Traditional Responses to Ambivalence

As noted, ambivalence and its consequences have traditionally been perceived as largely negative; ambivalence is an anxiety-producing state that individuals often want to avoid (Ashforth et al., 2011; Smelser, 1998) or escape. We may even be predisposed to not hold onto ambivalence. In their study linking recollection and emotion, Aaker, Drolet, and Griffin (2008) demonstrated that experiences of ambivalence are not only more difficult to recall accurately than those of univalent emotions, but that, over time, the experience of mixed emotions is simplified such that individuals recall it as univalent. This effect, they argue, is due to the fact that ambivalence creates feelings of conflict within individuals, who escape the accompanying discomfort by altering their experiences a posteriori. Even though "forgetting" problems may be viewed as a negative or ultimately ineffective response, it may allow individuals to cope in inhospitable environments. The mixed blessing of responses such as these represents a fundamental tension that continues through our discussion of all ambivalence responses, especially the traditional ones.

Pratt and Doucet (2000) have identified five traditional or classic responses to ambivalence. First, they note that *paralysis*—understood as the incapacity to act—can result from ambivalence. Indeed, ambivalent individuals might suffer from strong indecision (Sincoff, 1990) and may lose the capacity to take action or to form an opinion. Paralysis is most likely when the opposing elements comprising ambivalence are of relatively equal strength. Although they did not find evidence of this response in their data, Pratt and Doucet (2000) argue that paralysis, if it occurs, may be an initial response to ambivalence, and that other responses may follow. If we take seriously the notion that ambivalence can be uncomfortable, then one would expect that, over time, an individual will likely come to take some action to resolve his or her ambivalence (Weigert & Franks, 1989). Examples of such action include the other four responses to ambivalence that they posit. Three of these responses follow from Horney's (1945) typology of "acting out" ambivalence: moving toward,

moving away, and moving against the target of one's ambivalence. This typology also mirrors Hirschman's (1970) notions of exit (moving away), voice (moving against), and loyalty (moving toward).

A "*moving against*" or "negative/approach" response to ambivalence occurs when individuals want to retain some attachment to the target of their ambivalence, but enact this attachment by attempting to bring harm to this target. Psychoanalytic literature, for example, shows that individuals might be aggressive and attack the target of their ambivalence (Horney, 1945). A similar reaction can be found in work on prejudice toward stigmatized minorities. Katz and Glass (1979) argue that individuals in a majority group are often initially ambivalent toward those in the minority. To resolve this ambivalence, majority in-group members will seek out additional information about the minority out-group. If they observe an out-group member doing something bad or incorrectly, their attitudes will become decidedly negative toward the entire minority group. These negative sentiments, in turn, can be translated into action. For instance, MacDonald and Zanna (1998) found that negative response amplification among those ambivalent toward feminists led to less liking and lower intentions to hire a feminist.

Other moving against approaches responses have been suggested as well. To illustrate, Piderit (2000) notes that when ambivalence involves emotions, it may lead to resistance to change. Coser (1979) suggests a less extreme form of moving against by showing how ambivalent psychiatric residents manage their mixed thoughts and emotions toward their patients by referring to them as "sick." Similarly, Pratt and Dutton (2000) describe how some librarians deal with their ambivalence surrounding homeless patrons of the library by calling them "bums."

A third classic response to ambivalence is to escape or to *move away*. This negative avoidance response involves ambivalent people physically or psychologically distancing themselves from the targets of their ambivalence. Pratt and Doucet (2000) identified escapist behaviors—such as nail filing or lunch ordering rather than taking care of customers—as common moving away responses in call centers.

A fourth response is *moving toward* someone. Building on the works of Merton (1957) and Weigert and Franks (1989), Pratt and Doucet (2000) argue that individuals may engage in positive/approach responses, whereby an individual comes to feel positive regard toward his or her target of ambivalence. Positive response amplification is the mirror image of negative response amplification described above, and it occurs when individuals are strongly ambivalent toward members of an out-group. Here, however, rather than receiving negative information about the out-group and making one's attitudes toward them more negative, the individual receives positive information (e.g., "That minority group member did a great job!"). The consequence is that ambivalence is resolved in such a way that the majority member is highly positive about the minority member—possibly even more positive than he or she is of fellow in-group majority members (Katz & Glass, 1979). Pratt and Doucet (2000) illustrate this positive response ambivalence with a rural doctor who was ambivalent about joining a managed care operation, but in resolving his ambivalence came to view his new arrangement very positively—so much so that all negatives were pushed aside. He stated, "I don't see any down side at all, I have no complaints about what is going on" (Pratt & Doucet, 2000, p. 215). Although this approach is positive, in that it leads to favorable assessment of the target of one's ambivalence, it may also lead to biased and simplistic views of this target. Pushing out all negative assessments is likely, at minimum, to lead to disappointment when undesirable aspects of the new relationship invariably appear.

A fifth and final classic response to ambivalence is a mix of moving toward and moving away. *Vacillation* involves alternating between attraction toward the target of ambivalence and revulsion. Vacillation often results from the splitting defense mechanism whereby the target of ambivalence is divided into good and bad elements (Sincoff, 1990). For example, Gutierrez, Howard-Grenville, and Scully's (2010) work on "Voice of the Faithful" discusses how active and engaged Roman Catholics responded to the sex-abuse scandal in their Church by separating the Church as an institution (which they continued to follow) from the Church as an organization/clerical hierarchy (which they moved away from).

Emphasizing the Positive in Traditional Ambivalence Responses

Research has tended to frame these classic responses to ambivalence in a negative light. We agree to some extent: It is doubtful that any of the above will lead to healthy and generative outcomes in the long run. However, we do argue that these responses may not be as negative in certain situations, and that they may have some positive benefits in the short run.

We have, for example, argued that ambivalence can lead to paralysis (Wang & Pratt, 2008; Weigert & Franks, 1989). Although inaction may appear negative, it may be masking more positive responses. To illustrate, some researchers link paralysis with increased information processing (Rothman & Wiesenfeld, 2007). Indeed, when an individual is paralyzed by his or her experience of ambivalence, he or she stops taking action and instead analyzes the conflicting thoughts and emotions at hand. Such a behavior provides time to reflect and make better decisions. For instance, when doctors are performing diagnoses, initial ambivalence and paralysis may be useful. By not acting immediately, it may help them avoid fixating exclusively on one potential disease. Of course, in the long term, an adaptive reasoning process combining action and reflection is needed for successful diagnosis (Rudolph, Morrison, & Carroll, 2009).

Similarly, vacillation can be potentially good in the short term as it delays taking committing actions. This may be especially helpful when the decision someone is making is important and more information is needed. Thus, an individual may feel ambivalent about leaving one's current organization to start another job (Ibarra, 2003). Given the magnitude of the decision, it might be good to go back-and-forth for a while: one day feeling convinced to stay, and then moving toward being convinced of leaving. This, in turn, may motivate gathering information about both alternatives. As more information comes in, or as one processes existing information more deeply, it may be that the decision one needs to make becomes clearer.

Vacillation may also help if someone is trying to appease multiple stakeholders. In the above example, expressing confidence about staying with an organization to one's current peers and confidence about moving to potential peers may have some short-term benefits by keeping options open and appearing to be thorough. As Rothman and Wiesenfeld (2007, p. 286) suggest:

> The mixed and inconsistent emotional cues given off by the ambivalent expresser are likely to suggest to others that the expresser has not yet arrived at a conclusion, and that he/she is experiencing and possibly exploring multiple sides of a situation . . . [and] are likely to be perceived as more cognitively complex than more consistently happy and angry expressers.

However, in the long term, such "waffling" may be a threat to one's perceived authenticity.

Moving away responses may be positive when they allow the individual to escape, even momentarily, the discomfort that may accompany ambivalence. This may be especially critical when an individual has little control over the sources of ambivalence—such as when the sources of ambivalence are embedded in social roles or structures. It may also be functional when the source of ambivalence is not important to an individual. As Ashforth and colleagues (2011, p. 16) argue, "Generally, avoidance is most effective and therefore most likely if the issue prompting the ambivalence is relatively unimportant or insoluble."

Finally, moving against and moving toward (negative/approach and positive/approach) responses may have their appropriate times as well. For example, actively resisting change may be good when the proposed change will be harmful to an individual or organization. Hence, in her discussion of ambivalence and resistance to change, Piderit (2000, p. 785) notes:

> [W]hat some may perceive as disrespectful or unfounded opposition might also be motivated by individuals' ethical principles or by their desire to protect the organization's best interests. It is worth entertaining efforts to take those good intentions more seriously by downplaying the invalidating aspect of labeling responses to change "resistant."

It is also possible that resistance may take on a more positive form, such as *voice*, whereby an individual confronts the target of his or her ambivalence, but in such a way that the person is "actively and constructively trying to improve conditions" (Rusbult, Farrell, Rogers, & Mainous, 1988, p. 601). Positive outcomes may also come from moving toward responses, too. To illustrate, having positive appraisals of an out-group member with whom one was ambivalent about may decrease in-group–out-group tensions and facilitate cooperation and interaction—at least in the short term.

Emerging "Positive" Responses to Ambivalence

Traditional approaches toward ambivalence focus on how one responds to the target of ambivalence (e.g., to approach or avoid it). However, emerging perspectives broaden this focus to include the ambivalence itself that one experiences. Moreover, these emerging approaches also emphasize how ambivalence can be used to create conditions or states that are beneficial to the ambivalence holder.

In this chapter, we highlight five responses that we believe are integral to individuals in organizations: (1) commitment, (2) trust, (3) creativity, (4) openness to change, and (5) wisdom and adaptation.

Commitment

For Brickman (1987, p. 15), "commitments are about ambivalence." Specifically, he argues that commitments involve the binding together of positive and negative "elements" though choice. He uses the example of marriage to illustrate his point. On the one hand, marriage allows you to be with one, special individual. On the other hand, a marriage commitment also involves foregoing opportunities to be with other people. Commitments transform this ambivalent state when individuals willingly take on both these positive and negative aspects. Thus, even in commitment, ambivalence remains. Consequently, sometimes commitments are experienced enthusiastically and with joy, while at other times commitments are perceived as burdens that must be endured. No matter whether the positive or negative "face" of commitment is experienced, individuals remain attached to the choices they make.[1]

Pratt and Rosa (2003) build on Brickman's foundational work, but move the focus of commitment from choices to relationships, referring to Brickmanian commitment as "relationship-based" commitment. In particular, they discuss how leaders in network marketing organizations, such as Mary Kay and Amway, foster commitments by either highlighting existing sources of ambivalence in people's relationships (e.g., between work and family obligations) or creating new ones (e.g., pointing out that your [non-Amway/non-Mary Kay] "boss" pays you, but never what you are worth). These leaders then provide tools, such as scripts or sayings, which help individuals to accept these oppositional forces in their relationships with both members and nonmembers. Consistent with Brickman's thesis, both positive and negative elements remain salient in the commitments made by those who work in network marketing organizations. For example "building the business" involves many lonely nights away from home, but with the promise that someday one will have the resources to be with their family full time. Hence, commitments among distributors are experienced with a mixture of both sadness and hope.

Trust

In a similar vein, Pratt and Dirks (2006) build from Brickman's core logic to explain the resilient nature of trust. Trust is often conceptualized as "a psychological state comprising the intention to accept vulnerability based upon positive expectations of the intentions or behavior of another" (Rousseau, Sitkin, Burt, & Camerer, 1998, p. 395). Pratt and Dirks argue that trust, by its very nature, is fraught with ambivalence. For trust to occur, one must be vulnerable to another party (a negative element) for the promise of achieving some future rewards (a positive element). This tension is evident in a phrase made popular by President Ronald Reagan: "Trust, but verify."

When trust is conceptualized from a social-exchange perspective, it does little to explain the hardiness of trust. In particular, if it was just a matter of social exchange, one would expect trust to be broken every time one party did not deliver on its promised "intentions or behaviors" toward the other party. But people do not easily break off trust, and at least some forms of trust are highly robust (McKnight, Cummings, & Chervany, 1998). As with commitment, trust transforms ambivalence through choice—when people enter into relationships and accept both the inherent costs and rewards, it allows them to form a strong bond. This bond, in turn, enables both parties to remain engaged with each other, even when the different faces of trust are evident (e.g., feeling vulnerable or feeling rewarded in the relationship).

Creativity

Creativity has been defined as the production of useful and novel ideas by individuals (Amabile, Barsade, Mueller, & Staw, 2005). It is often viewed as part of a larger creativity-innovation process, with the latter involving the implementation of new ideas (Driver, 2008). Whether stated implicitly or explicitly, ambivalence has long been thought to be central to the creative process. To illustrate, Rothenberg (1990) reported that experiencing simultaneous opposite thoughts increases the probability that these conflicting thoughts will be integrated into a new creation. Similarly, Amabile and her colleagues (2005) have offered a possible explanation as to why ambivalence leads to creativity. Drawing on arguments from mood congruence theory (Blaney, 1986), they note that specific mood states are often associated with specific memories. Therefore, individuals who experience positive and negative emotions might activate more memories that would not have been connected to each other otherwise, and the net result is increased creative thinking (Amabile et al., 2005). Empirical support for this linkage was found by Fong (2006) whose experimental research has shown a positive effect of emotional ambivalence on creativity. However, Fong explains the relationship between ambivalence and creativity slightly differently than do Amabile and colleagues. Fong views emotions as information about the type of environments individuals are in; ambivalence signals an unusual environment that calls for creative thinking. Taken together, this research suggests that ambivalence may encourage divergent or complex thinking, which may result in creative responses.

Openness to Change

Another positive response to ambivalence—or perhaps better said, a *set* of responses to ambivalence—refers to the notion that ambivalence allows an individual to be more open to change. More specifically, being ambivalent has been linked to unlearning, enhanced information seeking and processing, and openness to new learning. Taking these together, these responses mirror Lewin's (1958) classic model of change. The logic of Lewin's model is that change begins with a destabilization of a system (unfreezing), which creates readiness for change (Burke, 2008). The second phase of the model is the "movement" part, whereby perspectives are altered and individuals engage in behaviors to enact their new understandings. The final phase of the model is the refreezing stage that aims at stabilizing the new ways of behaving that have been adopted during the change process. Although only some authors who discuss the benefits of ambivalence directly link their work to Lewin's, we find it a useful organizing framework for this set of responses, which we refer to as openness to change.

Unlearning corresponds with "unfreezing." Specifically, Pratt and Barnett (1997) link ambivalence and unfreezing at the individual level through their discussion of ambivalence and unlearning. They showed how Amway distributors strategically used ambivalence with their new recruits to facilitate their recruits' letting go of preexisting assumptions about the world and their place in it (e.g., that their non-Amway bosses do care about them). Thus, ambivalence was raised to make individuals more receptive to the Amway message.

Enhanced information seeking and processing, a key component in movement, has also been strongly linked with ambivalence. With regard to greater information seeking, Plambeck and Weber (2009) have shown that CEO's ambivalence was aligned with a greater search for possible action and broader input in the decision making process. Zhao and Cai

(2008) similarly find that ambivalent college smokers are the most likely to search for antismoking information.

Ambivalent individuals may not only seek out more information; research suggests that they also process it more systematically and more thoughtfully (Petty, Tormala, Brinol, & Jarvis, 2006; Rothman & Wiesenfeld, 2007). This systematic processing may facilitate one's ability to change by making alternatives clearer. This may explain Zhao and Cai's (2008) argument that the increased information processing associated with ambivalence is also linked with an overall greater acceptance of new antismoking information.

This emphasis on ambivalence and acceptance of new information echoes linkages made by other researchers between ambivalence and new learning, which corresponds with "refreezing." With regard to this link, March and Olsen (1976) have emphasized the need to hold competing evaluations as a source of learning within organizations. Similarly, educational scholars have acknowledged the fact that ambivalence resulting from the experience of dilemmas that occurred in the classroom sparks the push for new resolutions and increases learning opportunities for teachers (Smith, 2000; Wood, 1995; Wood, Cobb, & Yackel, 1991).

Taken together, this research suggests that ambivalence is associated with openness to change. In closing, we want to note that the strongest link between ambivalence and Lewin's model is most likely in the first portion of the model. Given that incompatibility and instability are at the core of what ambivalence is, its connection to unfreezing seems apparent. Although we have reviewed research that links ambivalence to each of Lewin's later stages, it may be that those who find linkages between ambivalence and (a) information seeking, (b) information processing, and (c) the internalization of new information (i.e., learning) are capturing more distal effects of ambivalence. Moreover, as we discuss at the end of this chapter, the nature of the relationship between ambivalence and change may be even more complex than what we have argued to this point, which is why ambivalence may sometimes lead to resistance to change, and at other times, openness to change (e.g., Piderit, 2000).

Wisdom and Adaptation

Related to the idea of openness to change is the connection between ambivalence and wisdom and adaptation. However, whereas the goal of the former is to return to a new steady state ("refreezing"), the goal of wisdom and adaption is to remain "unfrozen." According to Weick (1998, 2004), wisdom involves the successfully retaining and navigating oppositional forces, such as between overconfidence and overcautiousness and between doubt and knowing (Weick, 1998). Building from Campbell (1965), he further notes that the functional value of ambivalence or ambivalence-based wisdom is in its ability to foster successful adaptation:

> In multiple-contingency environments, the joint presence of opposing tendencies has a functional survival value. Where each of two opposing tendencies has survival relevance, the biological solution seems to be an ambivalent alternation of expressions of each rather than the consistent expression of an intermediate motivational state. Ambivalence rather than averaging, seems the "optimal compromise." (Campbell, 1965, as quoted in Weick, 1998, p. 61)

Even if "wisdom" is not evoked, similar arguments have been made linking ambivalence and adaptation. For example, Larsen, McGraw, and Cacioppo (2001) have shown that accepting and even maintaining ambivalence enables individuals to accept a higher degree of complexity. This capacity to accept complexity, in turn, can be understood as a prerequisite to engaging in highly adaptive behaviors. As Cavazza and Butera (2008, p. 2) put it:

> [T]he positive and the negative components allows people to express their position by putting forward the component that best fit the specific normative context . . . with no need to change or to feel inappropriate. For example, Monica—who holds ambivalent attitudes toward traffic restrictions—is perfectly able to contend that the level of pollution is now too high and traffic restrictions should be implemented, when talking about the children's health at kindergarten, but also to contend that living in cities is absolutely impossible without a car when discussing with a group of commuters. Ambivalence allows her to participate in both discussions without changing her general attitude. In other words, the structural flexibility of ambivalent attitudes would be a strength rather than a weakness.

Similarly, Larsen and his colleagues (Larsen, Hemenover, Norris, & Cacioppo, 2003) emphasize that the ability to experience both positive and negative emotions at the same time (e.g., simultaneously venting negative emotions and cultivating more positive ones) enhances the capacity to successfully adapt to key life stressors.

Mapping Emerging Responses to Ambivalence

Although we can advance the field by naming and describing the five aforementioned emerging positive responses to ambivalence, we feel that to further push our understanding of positive responses to ambivalence, we need to explore their similarities and differences. In doing so, we identified at least two key dimensions underlying these emerging responses—as well as traditional responses: response flexibility versus stability, and the degree of ambivalence resolution. These responses are mapped in Figure 70.1, and the emerging responses are circled.

Dimension 1: Flexibility Versus Stability in Response Potentials

One of the key differences among the emerging ambivalence responses is that some tend to motivate individuals to behave more consistently and narrowly (e.g., trust and commitment), whereas others seem to leave the individual open to a broad range of acting (e.g., creativity, wisdom, and openness to change). We refer to this dimension in terms of "response potentials" rather than "response outcomes" because there may be some slippage between how one thinks and feels and how one acts (Piderit, 2000; Weigert & Franks, 1989). That is, we do not predict a one-to-one correspondence between certain responses to ambivalence and specific behaviors; rather, some responses to ambivalence have a higher probability of narrowing one's behavioral set,

whereas others have a higher probability of expanding one's behavioral set.

To illustrate, trust allows individuals the opportunity to engage in consistent and considerate actions despite feelings of vulnerability and the potential for harm by the other party (Pratt & Dirks, 2006). Similarly, one reason for forming a commitment is to provide an individual a rudder when navigating the positive and negative valences surrounding a relationship (Brickman, 1987). In short, the emerging responses in the third quadrant of Figure 70.1 have a greater potential to lead to more stable behaviors than do those in Quadrant II.

By contrast, the emerging ambivalence responses in Quadrant II have greater potential for behavioral instability or flexibility. Thus, adopting an "attitude of wisdom" allows one to keep options for action open (Weick, 1998). Similarly, the entire purpose of "unfreezing" is to make people more open to change and thereby break them out of routine and habitual ways of acting. In the same way, creativity involves breaking out of established patterns. By spurring divergent thinking, ambivalence may lead to the creation of a wide variety of new ideas. As more ideas are formed, the potential response set that a person can enact increases as well.

Dimension 2: Degree of Resolution

Whereas the first dimension dealt with potential outcomes of ambivalence responses, the second dimension is more closely associated with the antecedents

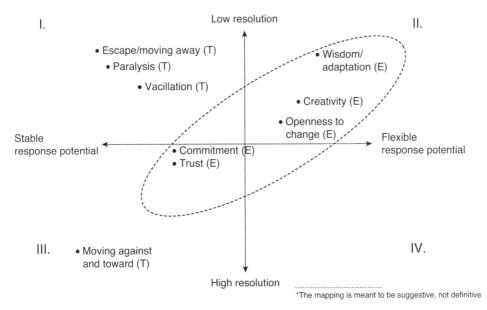

Fig. 70.1 Mapping emerging (E) and traditional (T) ambivalence responses.

of these responses. This second dimension is the degree to which ambivalence is "resolved"—that is, the degree to which the person still actively experiences the ambivalence while committing, trusting, being open to change, creating, etc. Although it is important to note that each of the emerging responses keeps ambivalence unresolved to some degree, there is some variance in responses. This variance is evident as we move diagonally from the top right to the bottom left of Figure 70.1.

For wisdom to occur, for example, it is vital that the opposing thoughts and emotions be cultivated and maintained. Thus, we see it as involving the least amount of resolution. Unfreezing (key to openness to change) and creativity, by contrast, both involve the maintenance of ambivalence; however, unlike wisdom, which is often seen as a desirable end in itself, both unfreezing and creativity are traditionally part of broader processes that do not maintain ambivalence over time. As noted, in Lewin's (1958) classic model, the main purpose of unfreezing is to allow for the acceptance of change and then eventual refreezing. Thus, as the epigraph states, you might want to "visit" ambivalence, but it is not a desired long-term state. In more recent depictions of change, messages about stability and change co-occur (Sonenshein, 2010); however, even here one would expect that ambivalence is eventually resolved.

Similarly, creativity is often part of a larger creativity-innovation process (Van de Ven, 1986; West, 2002). Innovation often involves putting what comes from the creative process into practice. Critical to this process is "selling" a narrower set of creative ideas to a group or organization via an idea champion; this idea champion, however, is often depicted as decidedly unambivalent about the creative ideas he or she is advocating. Thus, although we see wisdom, openness to change, and creativity as each involving low resolution of ambivalence in the short run, we would expect that the latter two would tend toward less ambivalence over time.

Commitment and trust may appear, at least on the face of it, as involving a fair amount of resolution. However, it is more accurate to say that they involve more resolution than some other responses, like wisdom, but ambivalence is maintained. To illustrate, even though commitment is sometimes experienced as a burden, and at other times as a source of enthusiasm, both "faces" are always present to some degree. As Brickman (1987, p. 10) argues, people "should experience commitment as having two faces, but two faces that co-occur, more

complementary than contradictory. This is quite different from the idea that one face of commitment will show itself only when the other face is hidden." Consequently, sometimes one face will dominate, sometimes the other, and sometimes both will be more equally evident; but even though there is certainly some processing and resolution—or, perhaps better said, there is a "transformation"—of ambivalence, the ambivalence does not "go away." Similarly, the interplay of vulnerability and benefit are always in play, to some degree, in trust.

What Mapping Reveals

When mapping the emerging ambivalence responses, it appears that they cluster along the diagonal of our two dimensions (see Figure 70.1). That is, responses with more flexible potentials appear to also involve less resolution of ambivalence. By contrast, responses that are more likely to lead to stability are also those with more resolution of ambivalence. It should be noted, however, that these dimensions need not coincide in this way. For example, paralysis and vacillation are both relatively stable responses, but here ambivalence remains unresolved.

The clustering into different quadrants (II & III) also suggests two very different perspectives on ambivalence: relationships and knowledge—a distinction that roughly parallels the relationship and attitude divide in ambivalence research in psychology. The responses in Quadrant III are often embedded in interpersonal relationships (commitment and trust). Although Brickman (1987) focuses broadly on choices, a prime illustration of ambivalence for Brickman was marriage. Moreover, refinements of Brickman's work by Pratt and colleagues (Pratt & Dirks, 2006; Pratt & Rosa, 2003) have focused primarily on how ambivalence is transformed in the context of relationships, be they internal or external to one's organization. What is also common here is the presence of strong emotions: The cognitions in this quadrant are relatively "hot."

The responses in Quadrant II are, broadly speaking, linked with a more knowledge-based perspective. This linkage is clearest in the creativity, as well as in the wisdom and adaptation responses. For both, the purpose is to keep conflicting notions in one's head so that new ideas, new linkages, and new pathways are more readily apparent. For example, Plambeck and Weber's (2009) CEOs used their ambivalence to broaden their thinking and create novel ideas. Another contrast between these two responses and those in Quadrant III is that the cognitions are often cooler.

This is not to say that they are without emotion, but research in this area to date has tended to have a more cognitive focus. That said, as we move toward openness to change (and closer to Quadrant III), the cognitions may heat up a bit.

Differentiating hotter cognition/relationship-based from cooler cognition/knowledge-based ambivalence in particular—and mapping responses to ambivalence more generally—also helps us advance in several ways what it means to respond positively to ambivalence. First, mapping allows us to better understand why emergent, positive responses to ambivalence are so different from their traditional counterparts. On the face of it, ambivalence has traditionally been posited to lead to a wide range of outcomes from inaction to vacillation to strongly committed action (Pratt & Doucet, 2000). But as we map them onto Figure 70.1, they all fall on left half of the model, emphasizing stability. Emergent responses tend to fall to the right of these traditional ones. Thus, they emphasize more flexibility in response potentials. Such flexibility may allow individuals more paths for action, resilience, and thriving.

Although flexibility is important, it is also essential to note that the responses most associated with relationships (and hotter cognitions) are associated with the most stability—especially among the emerging responses. This may be, at least in part, because predictability is very helpful in forming meaningful bonds with other human beings. A partner's predictability has been linked to the formation of intimacy, and the predictability of a stranger's attitudes mediates the oft-found relationship between similarity and attraction (see Worthen, Coats, McGlynn, & Rossano, 2007). Predictability has also been linked to one's willingness to cooperate with another (Mayer, Davis, & Schoorman, 1995). Consequently, responding to ambivalence in relationships in such a way that predictability is increased—as would be expected when ambivalence has been somewhat resolved and behavioral responses are more stable—would be critical. That said, one must not take this notion of predictability too far. To begin, predictability itself is not enough, as hating someone may lead to predictable but conflict-ridden relationships. In addition, it is important to note that, in any healthy relationship, flexibility is also critical—which is why commitment and trust are toward the midpoint of the stability–flexibility axis.

The relatively cooler knowledge-based responses to ambivalence, by contrast, are particularly useful when individuals are faced with a complex environment, similar to those faced by the "adaptive" CEOs noted by Plambeck and Weber (2009) and the "wise" wild-land firefighters noted by Weick (1998). Again, this is not surprising if you believe that responsiveness and openness are critical for successfully operating in complex environments (Dane, in press; Rudolph et al., 2009). Responding to ambivalence in this manner is valued as it helps create the potential to attain the necessary requisite variety in matching responses with the environment, and allows individuals and their organizations to nimbly navigate difficult and ever-changing situations. Taken together, our mapping indicates the importance of answering the question, "Ambivalent about what?" when discussing how to positively respond to ambivalence. Is it about who we relate to, or about some idea or notion?

Second and similarly, our mapping gives us an opportunity to think about the dimensions along which ambivalence responses may vary more generally (see also Ashforth et al., 2011), and to point out areas in which positive responses have yet to be uncovered. As illustrated in Figure 70.1, we could not find a response to ambivalence whereby the ambivalence was largely resolved, but still led to a highly flexible response. It may be that such responses are impossible to achieve: that if you totally resolve the ambivalence, you lose your source of flexibility (e.g., conflicting thoughts). However, less extreme responses may exist (largely resolved but still flexible). But if so, what would they look like? What positive function might they serve? As research continues, it will be interesting to continue to explore, map, and uncover the positive aspects of a wider range of ambivalence responses.

Third, mapping helps us better understand when "negative" versus "positive" responses to ambivalence are likely to occur. To illustrate, Piderit (2000) notes that when emotions are implicated, ambivalence is likely to lead to neglect responses: a type of resistance to change (Quadrant III response). However, when ambivalence is more cognitive, people are more likely to be open to change (Quadrant II response). Hence, Piderit's work would be consistent with our theorizing about the types of responses that follow from hot versus cold cognitions. However, juxtaposing her work and ours raises a broader issue: What might cause some ambivalence to be experienced as hotter versus cooler, and potentially more positive or more negative? We speculate that relationships and emotions may be related to a third variable: identity. Research in social identity and relational identity suggest that who one relates to influences one's identity and vice versa; moreover, when identity is involved, ambivalence may be more emotion-laden (Wang & Pratt, 2008). If true, then we *predict that changes associated with relationship-based ambivalence may be more likely to be resisted than those associated with knowledge-based ambivalence* because the former threatens identity and may be more emotional.

Fourth, mapping positive ambivalence responses also opens up dialogue for what "positive" means. We started our chapter by linking positivity with an individual outcome: enhanced individual functioning. However, we discovered that, like ambivalence itself, "positive" can mean many things when it comes to ambivalence. A quick glance at Figure 70.1 shows that positivity can be both personal and social. Although responding to ambivalence may make you feel better, more confident about how to act in an ambivalent relationship, or more wise, it can also help dyads (e.g., commitment and trust) or even larger systems (e.g., as creativity leads to innovation or openness to change). Positivity can even be thought of in terms of process and outcomes. Thus, we can think of the positivity of committing and of being committed, of trusting and of having trust, of creating and of having created something, etc. More generally, we even note how positivity can be contextual and temporal. Thus, even if paralysis is often viewed as a negative response to ambivalence, it can lead to a positive outcome for an individual in the long run, especially if it is associated with more and better information processing.

Finally, mapping reveals that emerging responses do not fully resolve ambivalence. Perhaps the power of ambivalence is not in how you get rid of it, but in how you keep it. This casts doubt on our epigraph—perhaps ambivalence *is* a place where you might want to live.

Future Directions

We are excited to draw attention to positive ambivalence responses. Although we hope we have advanced research in this area, we also realize that there is much more work to be done. Thus, others may wish to look at positive ambivalence responses more broadly than we have here. For example, we have focused on largely conscious responses to ambivalence. However, true to its psychodynamic roots, many responses might be less conscious, such as denial, splitting, and the like (see Ashforth et al., 2011, for review). Future research may wish to explore how positivity and ambivalence relate when examining nonconscious responses.

In addition, prospective research may also explore in more depth a dimension underlying ambivalence responses that we have only touched upon: the temporal dimension. We have argued that some traditional responses to ambivalence may be positive in the short run. Conversely, do emerging responses to ambivalence also have a range of time when they are positive? For example, on the face of it, it appears that most of the benefits that accrue to emerging responses are somewhat long term. Trust, commitment, openness to change, and creativity, for example, may only bear fruit as relationships mature and as ideas get implemented. Similarly, just as there are benefits to traditionally negatively responses to ambivalence, there may also be a "dark side" to the more positive responses, such as remaining committed to someone or something that is not healthy for you, being open to a change that is harmful, focusing on being wise when swift action is needed. Thus, important contingencies and contextual conditions need to be identified.

In a similar vein, much more work needs to be done on the conditions that predict when individuals will respond with a Quadrant I, II, III, or even IV response. We have suggested that relationships may require more stability and that complex environments may require more flexibility, but do these requirements evoke specific types of ambivalence responses? We have also speculated that the implication of personal identity may differentiate the degree of emotionality associated with ambivalence. However, we remain tentative.

In this chapter, we have addressed to some degree what role organizations might play in managing ambivalence for positive responses. For example, we explicitly noted that leaders in direct selling organizations foster commitment by highlighting sources of ambivalence in salespeople's relationships, such as the tension between work and family, and then offering these salespeople ways to transform that ambivalence (Pratt & Rosa, 2003). However, more implicitly, we have suggested that hotter relationship-based ambivalence may need to be managed differently than cooler knowledge-based ambivalence. For the former, you may want to provide stories, scripts, or techniques for at least partially resolving ambivalence (Pratt & Rosa, 2003), whereas for the latter, you may want to emphasize techniques (e.g., devil's advocate) that help individuals surface and retain (i.e., not resolve) opposing thoughts and emotions. But might there be other means of managing these types of ambivalence? Moreover, might there be unique benefits of managing for Quadrant II and III responses simultaneously? To illustrate, it would appear that organizations would greatly benefit from individuals who both trust their leaders, but are at the same time open to organizational change. In this situation, fostering trust may help provide the psychological safety necessary to allow ambivalence about organizational change to be maintained (e.g., Pratt & Barnett, 1997). And, if there are benefits of managing for different responses to ambivalence simultaneously, we might further ask how this can be best accomplished.

Finally, we have focused our arguments primarily at the individual level of analysis. Although we believe there is much work to be done here, we also think there is potential in moving beyond this level. For example, it may be interesting to view ambivalence as a logic for organizing. As Farjoun (2010, p. 202) notes, "the dual search for stability and change pervades all forms of organizing." Like the amphitheater that shares the root "amphi" with ambivalence, groups (Pradies & Pratt, 2010; Smith & Berg, 1987), organizations (Farjoun, 2010) and institutions (Lounsbury, 2007) are often places where contradicting forces meet (Lüscher, 2002). Can we organize organizations to productively retain these oppositional forces without simply vacillating between them (e.g., exploring then exploiting)? Can we organize to create a "wise organization"? Similarly, can we harness positive ambivalence among individuals to facilitate healthier functioning at higher levels of analysis, such as groups, organizations, or even institutions? If so, our responses to ambivalence would undoubtedly be more positive.

Notes

1. This is not to say that commitment triggered by ambivalence will always remain and never dissolve. As Pratt and Rosa (2003, p. 411) argue, ambivalence is "fuel" for commitment, and when "the fuel is absent or not the right mix, commitment suffers." For example, individuals can lose the capacity for transforming ambivalence into commitment when the positive elements of the relationship consistently and repeatedly fail to materialize.
2. Although extant research on trust and commitment has often involved relationships, it may be possible that these responses may also occur in relation to ideas or objects. Due to space constraints, we cannot tackle this issue here. However, to the degree that such nonhuman relationships are relevant in Quadrant III, we suggest that they would likely involve hot cognitions—likely due to a connection between these beliefs and objects and one's identity (Pratt, 2000).

References

Aaker, J., Drolet, A., & Griffin, D. (2008). Recalling mixed emotions. *Journal of Consumer Research, 35*(2), 268–278.

Amabile, T.M., Barsade, S.G., Mueller, J.S., & Staw, B.M. (2005). Affect and creativity at work. *Administrative Science Quarterly, 50*(3), 367–403.

Ashforth, B.E., Rogers, K.M., & Pratt, M.G. (2011). *Ambivalence in organizations.* Working paper.

Bagozzi, R.P. (2003). Positive and negative emotions in organizations. In K.S. Cameron, J.E. Dutton, & R.E. Quinn (Eds.), *Positive organizational scholarship: Foundations of a new discipline* (pp. 176–193). San Francisco: Berrett-Koehler Publishers.

Blaney, P.H. (1986). Affect and memory: A review. *Psychological Bulletin, 99*(2), 229–246.

Boehm, C. (1989). Ambivalence and compromise in human nature. *American Anthropologist, 91,* 921–939.

Bowlby, J. (1982). *Attachment and loss.* New York: Basic Books.

Brickman, P. (1987). Commitment. In C.B. Wortman, & R. Sorrentino (Eds.), *Commitment, conflict, and caring* (pp. 1–18). Englewood Cliffs, NJ: Prentice Hall.

Burke, W.W. (2008). *Organization change: Theory and practice.* Los Angeles, London, New Dehli, Singapore: Sage Publications, Inc.

Cameron, K.S., Dutton, J.E., & Quinn, R.E. (Eds.). (2003). *Positive organizational scholarship: Foundations of a new discipline.* San Francisco: Berrett-Koehler Publishers.

Campbell, O.T. (1965). Ethnocentric and other altruistic motives. In D. Levine (Ed.), *Nebraska symposium on motivation.* Lincoln, NE: University of Nebraska Press.

Cavazza, N., & Butera, F. (2008). Bending without breaking: Examining the role of attitudinal ambivalence in resisting persuasive communication. *European Journal of Social Psychology, 38*(1), 1–15.

Conner, M., & Armitage, C.J. (2008). Attitudinal ambivalence. In W.D. Crano, & R. Prislin (Eds.), *Attitudes and attitude change: Frontiers of social psychology* (pp. 261–286). New York: Psychology Press.

Coser, R.L. (1979). *Training in ambiguity: Learning through doing in a mental hospital.* New York: Free Press.

Dahl, D.W., Darke, P.R., Gorn, G.J., & Weinberg, C.B. (2005). Promiscuous or confident? Attitudinal ambivalence toward condom purchase. *Journal of Applied Social Psychology, 35*(4), 869–887.

Dane, E. (in press). Paying attention to mindfulness and its effects on task performance in the workplace. *Journal of Management.* Forthcoming.

Driver, M. (2008). New and useless. A psychoanalytic perspective on organizational creativity. *Journal of Management Inquiry, 17*(3), 187–197.

Farjoun, M. (2010). Beyond dualism: Stability and change as a duality. *Academy of Management Review, 35*(2), 202–225.

Fong, C.T. (2006). The effects of emotional ambivalence on creativity. *Academy of Management Journal, 49,* 1016–1030.

Freud, S. (1950/1920). *Beyond the pleasure principle.* London: Norton.

Gutierrez, B., Howard-Grenville, J., & Scully, M.A. (2010). The faithful rise up: Split identification and an unlikely change effort. *Academy of Management Journal, 53*(4), 673–699.

Hazan, C., & Shaver, P.R. (1994). Attachment as an organizational framework for research on close relationships. *Psychological Inquiry, 5*(1), 1–22.

Hirschman, A.O. (1970). *Exit, voice, and loyalty: Responses to decline in firms, organizations, and states.* Cambridge, MA: Harvard University Press.

Horney, K. (1945). *Our inner conflicts: A constructive theory of neurosis*. New York: W.W. Norton & Co. Inc.

Ibarra, H. (2003). *Working identity: Unconventional strategies for reinventing your career*. Cambridge, MA: Harvard Business School Press.

Katz, I., & Glass, D.C. (1979). An ambivalence-amplification theory of behavior toward the stigmatized. In W. Austin, & S. Worchel (Eds.), *The social psychology of intergroup relations* (pp. 55–70). Monterrey, CA: Brooks/Cole.

King, L.A., & Emmons, R.A. (1990). Conflict over emotional expression: Psychological and physical correlates. *Journal of Personality and Social Psychology, 58*(5), 864–877.

Kreiner, G.E., & Ashforth, B.E. (2003). Evidence toward an expanded model of organizational identification. *Journal of Organizational Behavior, 25*(1), 1–27.

Larsen, J.T., Hemenover, S.H., Norris, C.J., & Cacioppo, J.T. (2003). Turning adversity to advantage: On the virtues of the coactivation of positive and negative emotions. In L.G. Aspinwall, & U.M. Staudinger (Eds.), *A psychology of human strengths: Fundamental questions and future directions for a positive psychology* (pp. 211–225). Washington, DC: American Psychological Association.

Larsen, J.T., McGraw, A.P., & Cacioppo, J.T. (2001). Can people feel happy and sad at the same time? *Journal of Personality and Social Psychology, 81*(4), 684–696.

Lavine, H., Thomsen, C.J., Zanna, M.P., & Borgida, E. (1998). On the primacy of affect in the determination of attitudes and behavior: The moderating role of affective-cognitive ambivalence. *Journal of Experimental Social Psychology, 34*, 398–421.

Lewin, K. (1958). Group decision and social change. In E.E. Maccoby, T.M. Newcomb, & E.L. Hartley (Eds.), *Readings in social psychology* (pp. 197–211). New York: Holt, Rinehart & Winston.

Lounsbury, M. (2007). A tale of two cities: Competing logics and practice variation in the professionalizing of mutual funds. *Academy of Management Journal, 50*(2), 289–307.

Lüscher, K. (2002). Intergenerational ambivalence: Further steps in theory and research. *Journal of Marriage and Family, 64*, 585–592.

MacDonald, T.K., & Zanna, M.P. (1998). Cross-dimension ambivalence toward social groups: Can ambivalence affect intentions to hire feminists? *Personality and Social Psychology Bulletin, 24*(4), 427–441.

March, J.G., & Olsen, J.P. (1976). *Ambiguity and choice in organizations*. Bergen: Universitetsforlaget.

Mayer, R.C., Davis, J.H., & Schoorman, F.D. (1995). An integrative model of organizational trust. *Academy of Management Review, 20*(3), 709–734.

McKnight, D.H., Cummings, L.L., & Chervany, N.L. (1998). Initial trust formation in new organizational relationships. *Academy of Management Review, 23*(3), 473–490.

Merton, R.K. (1957). *Social theory and social structure*. New York: The Free Press.

Merton, R.K., & Barber, E. (1976). Sociological ambivalence. In R.K. Merton (Ed.), *Sociological ambivalence and other essays* (pp. 3–31). New York: Free Press.

Meyerson, D.E., & Scully, M.A. (1995). Tempered radicalism and the politics of ambivalence and change. *Organization Science, 6*, 585–600.

Miller, W.R., & Rollnick, S. (2002). *Motivational interviewing: Preparing people for change* (2nd ed.). New York: Guilford Press.

Petty, R.E., Tormala, Z.L., Brinol, P., & Jarvis, W.B. (2006). Implicit ambivalence from attitude change: An exploration of the past model. *Journal of Applied Psychology, 90*(1), 21–41.

Piderit (2000). Rethinking resistance and recognizing ambivalence: A multidimensional view of attitudes toward an organizational change. *Academy of Management Review, 25*(4), 783–794.

Plambeck, N., & Weber, K. (2009). CEO ambivalence and responses to strategic issues. *Organization Science, 20*(6), 993–1010.

Pradies, C., & Pratt, M.G. (2010). Ex uno plures: Toward a conceptualization of group ambivalence. In L.A. Toombs (Ed.), *Proceedings of the seventieth annual meeting of the Academy of Management*. Montreal.

Pratt, M.G. (2000). The good, the bad, and the ambivalent: Managing identification among Amway distributors. *Administrative Science Quarterly, 45*, 456–493.

Pratt, M.G., & Barnett, C.K. (1997). Emotions and unlearning in Amway recruiting techniques: Promoting change through safe ambivalence. *Management Learning, 28*(1), 65–88.

Pratt, M.G., & Dirks, K.T. (2006). Rebuilding trust and restoring positive relationships: A commitment-based view of trust. In J. Dutton, & B. Ragins (Eds.), *exploring positive relationships at work: Building a theoretical and research foundation* (pp. 117–136). Mahwah, NJ: Lawrence Earlbaum Associates.

Pratt, M.G., & Doucet, L. (2000). Ambivalent feelings in organizational relationships. In S. Fineman (Ed.), *Emotions in organizations* (pp. 204–226). London: Sage.

Pratt, M.G., & Dutton, J.E. (2000). Owning up or opting out: The role of emotions and identities in issue ownership. In N.M. Ashkanasy, C.E.J. Haertel, & W.J. Zerbe (Eds.), *Emotions in the workplace: Research, theory, and practice* (pp. 103–129). New York: Quorum Books.

Pratt, M.G., & Rosa, J.A. (2003). Transforming work-family conflict into commitment in network marketing organizations. *Academy of Management Journal, 46*, 395–418.

Rothenberg, A. (1990). *Creativity and madness: New findings and old stereotypes*. Baltimore, MD: Johns Hopkins University Press.

Rothman, N.B., & Wiesenfeld, B.M. (2007). Social consequences of expression emotional ambivalence. In E.A. Mannix, M.A. Neale, & C.P. Anderson (Eds.), *Affect and groups* (pp. 275–308). Oxford, Amsterdam, San Diego: Elsevier/JAI Press.

Rousseau, D.M., Sitkin, S.B., Burt, R.S., & Camerer, C. (1998). Not so different after all: A cross-discipline view of trust. *Academy of Management Review, 23*(3), 393–404.

Rudolph, J.W., Morrison, J.B., & Carroll, J.S. (2009). The dynamics of action-oriented problem solving: Linking interpretation and choice. *Academy of Management Review, 34*(4), 733–756.

Rusbult, C., Farrell, D., Rogers, G., & Mainous, A. (1988). Impact of exchange variables on exit, voice, loyalty & neglect: An integrative model of responses to declining satisfaction. *Academy of Management Journal, 31*(3), 599–627.

Sincoff, J.B. (1990). The psychological characteristics of ambivalent people. *Clinical Psychology Review, 10*(1), 43–68.

Smelser, N.J. (1998). The rational and the ambivalent in the social sciences. *American Sociological Review, 63*, 1–16.

Smith (2000). Balancing old and new: An experienced middle school teacher's learning in the context of mathematics instructional reform. *The Elementary School Journal*, 351–375.

Smith, K.K., & Berg, D.N. (1987). *Paradoxes of group life*. San Francisco, London: Jossey Bass Inc.

Sonenshein, S. (2010). We're changing or are we? Untangling the role of progressive, regressive and stability narratives during strategic change implementation. *Academy of Management Journal, 53*(3), 477–512.

Thompson, M.M., & Zanna, M.P. (1995). The conflicted individual: Personality-based and domain-specific antecedents of ambivalent social attitudes. *Journal of Personality and Social Psychology, 63*(2), 259–288.

Van de Ven, A.H. (1986). Central problems in the management of innovation. *Management Science, 32*(5), 590–607.

Wang, L., & Pratt, M.G. (2008). An identity-based view of emotional ambivalence and its management in organizations. In N. Ashkanasy, & C. Cooper (Eds.), *Research companion to emotion in organizations* (pp. 589–604). London: Edward Elgar.

Weick, K.E. (1998). The attitude of wisdom: Ambivalence as the optimal compromise. In S. Srivastva, & D.L. Cooperrider (Eds.), *Organizational wisdom and executive courage* (pp. 40–64). San Francisco: The New Lexington Press.

Weick, K.E. (2004). Mundane poetics: Searching for wisdom in organization studies. *Organization Studies, 25*(4), 653–668.

Weigert, A., & Franks, D. (1989). Ambivalence: A touchstone of the modern temper. In D.M. Franks, & E. McCarthy (Eds.), *The sociology of emotions: Original essays and research papers* (pp. 205–227). Greenwich, CT: JAI Press.

West, M.A. (2002). Sparkling fountains or stagnant ponds: An integrative model of creativity and innovation implementation in work groups. *Applied Psychology, 51*(3), 355–387.

Wood, T. (1995). An emerging practice of teaching. In P. Cobb, & H. Bauersfeld (Eds.), *The emergence of mathematical meaning: Interaction in classroom cultures* (pp. 203–227). Hillsdale, NJ: Erlbaum.

Wood, T., Cobb, P., & Yackel, E. (1991). Change in teaching mathematics: A case study. *American Educational Research Journal, 28*(3), 587–616.

Worthen, J.B., Coats, S., McGlynn, R.P., & Rossano, M.J. (2007). Cognitive factors in the prediction of liking of social groups: Prototypes, predictability and familiarity. In J.A. Zebowski (Ed.), *New research on social perception* (pp. 161–179). New York: Nova Science Publishers.

Zhao, X., & Cai, X. (2008). The role of ambivalence in college nonsmokers' information seeking and information processing. *Communication Research, 35*(3), 298–318.

Stress Interventions Versus Positive Interventions

Apples and Oranges?

Caroline Biron, Cary L. Cooper, *and* Philip Gibbs

Abstract

The term *stress* is one that has received much attention over the past 30 years, particularly within occupational settings. At an individual level, stress represents a real risk to an employee's quality of life, and at an organizational level, there are heavy financial costs due to absenteeism and presenteeism. In recent years, this field of research has received criticism that too much emphasis has been placed on negative issues, while largely ignoring any positive ones. With the growing influence of the positive movement, this chapter attempts to revisit the implications of the intervention it entails. Given the adverse health effects of occupational stress, preventing it by alleviating or eliminating psychosocial risks should be one of the priorities of researchers in occupational health psychology. From a positive perspective, there is also a need to understand the characteristics of healthy, thriving, and flourishing people and organizations. This chapter aims to explore the implications of using a positive approach as opposed to a stress management one. Although we acknowledge that the traditional occupational stress models and the more recent positive trends are distinct conceptually, both approaches ultimately aim to bring about changes to improve in the workplace. However, these changes are not conceptually distinct when arising from the positive (promoting health) and the negative (preventing stress) perspectives.

Keywords: Positive stress, organizational stress interventions, risk management, psychosocial characteristics, health promotion

In the past three decades, the literature on stress at work has been dominated by studies attempting to demonstrate the causal relationship between exposure to stressors in the workplace, workers' health and well-being, and organizational performance. Although many debates still exist, many would agree that psychosocial risks, such as the lack of job control, social support, recognition for ones' efforts, and work overload are, in the long term, strong predictors of poor of physical and psychological health (Semmer, 2006) and other effects of strain on workers (psychological distress, exhaustion, psychosomatic complaints, health problems) and on organizations (increased absenteeism, presenteeism, productivity losses). Theoretically, interventions aiming to modify aspects of the work (work-oriented) or of the organization (organization-oriented) should reduce exposure to or eliminate the source of stress. We use work- and organization-level interchangeably to refer to changes brought to bear on aspects of the workplace, in contrast to the individual. These changes should, at least theoretically, be associated with decreased strain reactions, which in turn should be linked with decreased adverse consequences for individuals and organization.

Recently, a call has been made for a less disease-oriented approach to psychology and to organizational behavior. This is particularly evident in the establishment of several new scholarly movements within the past 10 years that emphasize the study of more positively oriented phenomena. In this chapter, we wish to enquire how interventions emerging from more positively oriented approaches differ and resemble those implemented from within the stress management framework. We delve into the nature of positive and stress interventions, to verify to what extent they are conceptually distinct. We then look at the pros and cons of each approach. We conclude by arguing for a more integrated approach, encompassing a comprehensive approach to both preventing stress and promoting health and well-being.

Conceptualization of Interventions
Stress Interventions
Ample evidence demonstrates that stress at work can have detrimental effects on workers' psychological and physical health (see for example Belkic, Landbergis, Schnall, & Baker, 2004; Bourbonnais, Brisson, Vézina, & Moisan, 1996; Bourbonnais & Mondor, 2001; de Lange, Taris, Kompier, Houtman, & Bongers, 2003; Ylipaavalniemi et al., 2005). Employees chronically exposed to high pressure, conflicting demands, or lack of resources (such as job control, social support, recognition or other rewards) show higher risks of various strain symptoms compared to employees exposed to lower levels of constraints.

Since job stress is a major health risk to employees' health and well-being, much research has addressed the effectiveness of interventions to reduce it. According to preventive stress management theory (Quick, Quick, & Nelson, 2000), several approaches exist to manage occupational stress. Cooper and Cartwright (1997) suggest a three-prong intervention strategy, based on public health and preventive medicine concepts that are transposed and applied onto an organizational stress process framework. Primary prevention is generally used to refer to elimination or control of the sources of stress, such as psychosocial risk factors, which exist in the working environment. Reducing and preventing psychosocial risks in the workplace implies an action on the causes of stress rather than on its consequences. As far as secondary prevention programs are concerned, these aim to help individuals manage stress by improving or modifying their strategies for adapting to the sources of stress (i.e., time management, cognitive restructuring), or by relieving the symptoms associated with stress (i.e., relaxation, physical exercise, therapy, etc.). As for tertiary-level actions, these are concerned with treatment, rehabilitation, procedures for returning to work, and monitoring of individuals who are suffering or have suffered from mental health problems in the workplace. Murphy (1988) and Quick et al. (2000) also use the terms from preventive medicine and public health models, and classify interventions according to their level, namely the primary level (i.e., reducing sources of stress), the secondary level (i.e., improving stress management by the individual), and the tertiary level (i.e., rehabilitation and treatment).

DeFrank and Cooper (1987) suggest a different prevention model based on the targets of interventions. Interventions to reduce stress in the workplace may target the individual, the organization, or the interface between the individual and the organization. Individual actions seek to increase the physical and psychological capacity of the individual to enable him or her to adapt to the stressful situation. In turn, organizational interventions aim to reduce stress on a macro level; for example, by modifying certain aspects of the organizational structure or revising personnel selection processes and policies, so that they adapt the working environment to employees' needs. Finally, actions that are taken on a more local level (i.e., within a team or a department) tend to put the emphasis on the interface between the individual and the organization; for example, by clarifying roles or by increasing staff involvement and autonomy.

As pointed out by Jordan et al. (2003), the preventive stress management theory proposed by Cooper and Cartwright (1997) and Quick et al. (2000) is not directly transposable to the approach by DeFrank and Cooper (1987); that is, primary level does not necessarily entail a modification of the work and the organization, whereas secondary and tertiary levels are not always directed at individuals. For example, coaching for managers could potentially help them develop better management practices, which in return are likely to have a positive effect on employees' well-being (Dellve, Skagert, & Vilhelmsson, 2007). If such a coaching initiative was integrated within a corporate policy, and groups of managers would be coached, it would be considered an organizational intervention. However, if this coaching initiative was intended for one or a few specific managers whose management practices were considered problematic, it could be considered an individual intervention. Because it aims to prevent employees becoming ill due to inappropriate management practices, the coaching initiative (individual or organizational) would also be considered a primary-level intervention.

Positive Interventions

One of the criticisms about the positive movement concerns its emphasis, at least so far, on individual-level phenomena. For instance, Hackman (2009) argues that: "Positive organizational scholars appear to have jumped on Seligman's bandwagon without pausing to reflect on where the gaps really are in organizational research. And they have done so in a way that subtly moves the focus of their research from organizational dynamics to intrapersonal phenomena" (p. 310). Although Luthans and Avolio (2009a) reply to this criticism by pointing out that both positive organizational behavior (POB) and positive organizational scholarship (POS) research has shown examples of organizational, group, and multilevel research, it does appears as though the bulk of intervention research in the field is so far concerned with individual-level constructs, and with defining, validating, and relating these constructs to each other and to more traditional constructs (Hackman, 2009; Luthans & Avolio, 2009a). As described later in this chapter, organizational-level stress interventions share common aims with the positive discipline. Indeed, organizational interventions aim to reduce or eliminate sources of stress, but by doing so, they also aim to provide healthy work organization and individual health and well-being. In this sense, positive and stress interventions share some common grounds in terms of their ultimate goals.

Another criticism about the positive discipline is whether it is conceptually different the from traditional, negative perspective. According to the POS discipline, the experience of positive and negative emotions is conceptually different. For example, Roberts (2006) argues that, at the individual level, the experience of positive and negative emotions elicits different action tendencies. In the same line, Nelson and Simmons (2004) describe how individuals' physiological responses to events interpreted positively and negatively are different. This emphasis is methodologically important, assuming that positive states are not merely the opposite of negative states. Roberts (2006) argues that positive dynamics will not emerge by simply reversing negative dynamics, although the two are closely connected. Although we acknowledge that, in terms of physiological responses and experiences, positive and negative states are different, we agree with Fineman (2006a) that the two should not be separated. Indeed, they can be seen as two opposing sides of the same continuum and thus are mutually informative. To make positive appraisals, people must experience negative emotions and vice versa, and it is this interaction that helps derive meaningful experiences and emotions. For example, Fineman (2006a) explains that "hope can give strength, but also shut one's receptiveness to different possibilities (blind hope)" (p. 275). Consequently, there is an argument to be made that negative and positive emotions and experiences cannot be easily separated, and thus both need to be considered when attempting to understand important outcomes.

In line with this, Nelson and Simmons (2004) contrast positive and negative stress. Following Selye (1976), they define *eustress*: "A positive psychological response to a stressor, as indicated by the presence of positive psychological states." Distress is defined as: "A negative psychological response to a stressor, as indicated by the presence of negative psychological states." (p. 292). They specify that both negative and positive responses can be experienced simultaneously after exposure to any given stressor. For example, a tight deadline can produce distress, yet workers can respond to this demand with vigor and engage with the challenge it presents. Simmons, Nelson, and Neal (2001) found that nurses with high exposure to death and dying patients were more engaged in their work than were their counterparts who worked in other departments, thus experiencing both negative and positive responses after exposure to this particular stressor. They underline the need to identify work conditions that are the antecedents of eustress at work by identifying what makes a healthy workplace, or in other words, those jobs and organizational characteristics that produce positive responses.

Having clarified our view of the inseparability of positive and negative responses, we now consider how interventions emerging from each movement compare with each other. The chapter does not aim to describe exhaustively the constructs used in each field, but simply to draw on a few of them to contrast positive and stress interventions. This is exploratory and thus not aimed to be clear-cut, as some interventions could very well be coherent within both the positive and the stress frameworks. Table 71.1 illustrates examples of each type of interventions. It should be noted that we do not use the three-prong model with primary, secondary, and tertiary levels, not because it is conceptually incoherent, but because it is simpler to highlight the positive versus stress differences and similarities. It appears to us that the public health model could, however, be used to conceptualize positive interventions. The public health model is originally based on

Table 71.1 Typical classification of interventions

Approach	Intervention level	
	Organizational	Individual
Stress	Establish fair reward system and employment policies Improve physical and environmental constraints Staff selection Work–family conciliation policy Encourage a participatory management style Promote/support healthy work organization Enhance job design (autonomy, task significance, task feedback, skill variety, etc.) Promote social support and collaboration Flexible work schedules Encourage participation Establish clear roles and objectives Build cohesive teams Train managers on UK Health & Safety Executive's stress management competencies (Yarker, Donaldson-Feilder, Lewis, & Flaxman, 2008) Develop psychosocial safety climate (Dollard & Bakker, 2009) Return-to-work programs (to improve working environment and prevent worker from becoming ill again; St-Arnaud, 2007) Employee assistance programs	Psychological flexibility (ability to focus on the present moment and, depending upon what the situation affords, persist with or change one's (even inflexible, stereotypical) behavior in the pursuit of goals and values; Bond, Flaxman, & Bunce, 2008) Relaxation session, biofeedback, meditation Training in strategies to adapt to stress Training in time management Chair massage Working hours adapted to particular cases Resolution of interpersonal conflicts Promote health and a healthy lifestyle (fitness club, wellness programs)
Positive	Train managers to adopt practices creating positive stress (Quick, Mack, Gavin, Cooper, & Quick, 2004) Transformational leadership training (Barling, Moutino, & Kelloway, 1996) Appreciative inquiry and organizational development (Cooperrider & Whitney, 2005) Design jobs to promote flow (Csikszentmihalyi, 1990; Nielsen & Cleal, 2010) Psychologically Healthy Workplace Program (Grawitch, Gottschalk, & Munz, 2006) "Fit-note" policy to maintain the employment relationship (fit notes describe what a worker can do at work instead of a sick note, which describes what he cannot do; Black 2008)	Psychological capital (Luthans, Avey, Avolio, Norman, & Combs, 2006; Luthans, Avey, & Patera, 2008) "Fun at work" policies Engineering humor (Collinson, 2002) Implementing emotional intelligence programs (Cherniss & Caplan, 2001)

Note: Several interventions could be seen from both the positive and the stress perspectives, as they share similar goals.

a deficit approach, with an aim to prevent people from getting ill either by eliminating the source of illness, by strengthening their capacities to face that source, or by preventing further damages in those who are already ill. However, one could also argue that primary-level interventions can be positively framed to promote organizational health, vigorousness, and flourishing, whereas secondary-level interventions can focus on enhancing individuals' core strengths, and tertiary-level ones could involve using a positive approach in the context of a therapy to treat people who are (or not) necessarily ill, but who

want to feel better and develop certain strengths. With a view to explore the nature of interventions emerging from each perspective, we categorize interventions based on whether they target individuals versus work and organizational aspects. In the following section, we use a few examples from each type of intervention described in Table 71.1.

The examples of interventions given in Table 71.1 are classified on the basis of their aim, namely the organization or the individual. The classification is meant to underline the similarities between both approaches. Several interventions have traditionally been considered as aiming to prevent stress or to promote positive outcomes. However, as illustrated in the following section, a lot of common ground exists between the two perspectives, and several interventions could be considered within both perspectives, given the similarities of their aims.

Organizational-level Stress Interventions

Empirical evidence supporting the relevance of organizational interventions in the workplace to improve stress outcomes is surprisingly scarce. Systematic reviews and meta-analyses of quasi-experiments and randomized control trials generally conclude that there is insufficient or limited evidence to concur about their effectiveness (Graveling, Crawford, Cowie, Amati, & Vohra, 2008; Marine, Ruotsalainen, Serra, & Verbeek, 2006; Parkes & Sparkes, 1998; Richardson & Rothstein, 2008; Van Der Klink, Blonk, Schene, & Van Dijk, 2001). However, reviews including other types of research designs tend to support their relevance to improve organizational outcomes, as well as individual's health and well-being (Giga, Noblet, Faragher, & Cooper, 2003; Kompier, Cooper, & Geurts, 2000; Semmer, 2003, 2006). In his review of the organizational stress intervention literature, Semmer (2003) characterizes organizational interventions as being focused on one or more of the following targets: clarifying roles and improving relations, improving working conditions (e.g., ergonomics, workload, schedules), or changing tasks and technical characteristics (e.g., improving job design). Some interventions target one particular aspect, whereas many studies have several simultaneous targets. His review suggests that "overall, results imply that social interventions do have the potential for positive effects. These effects are by no means certain, and again, it is difficult to predict which outcome will be influenced by which interventions" (p. 337). Semmer (2003) concludes by arguing that the question is not so much whether organizational interventions are effective in reducing job stress, but rather what can be expected under particular circumstances.

Interventions aiming to develop stress management competencies also appear promising. Research conducted by Yarker and colleagues (2008) for the Health and Safety Executive (HSE) in Great Britain highlights the importance of line managers in preventing stress. They developed a model based on several interviews with managers and employees, which allowed identifying key managerial competencies for stress. These competencies refer to specific manager behaviors (positive and negative) that are linked with stressors. This approach integrates both positive and negative aspects in the training of managers. In line with this, Quick et al. (2004) provide several examples of how managers can generate positive states at work by, for example, crafting challenging goals, encouraging learning culture, communicating openly, or creating trusting relationships. Managerial leadership is important for positive outcomes such as well-being, but is also linked with negative ones such as absenteeism, stress, and cardiovascular diseases, as the leadership literature acknowledges (Dellve et al., 2007; Kelloway & Barling, 2010; Nyberg, Westerlund, Hanson, & Theorell, 2008).

In the same vein, Dollard and Bakker (2009) have developed a psychosocial safety climate concept, which is a construct referring to the policies, practices, and procedures for the protection of workers' psychological health and safety (Dollard, 2007). Their results show that the psychosocial safety climate is a precursor to psychosocial work conditions. Senior managers who failed to value worker well-being were associated with employees having higher job demands. Psychosocial climate is an upstream construct, which is causally prior to working conditions. Their research showed a top-down effect of the psychosocial safety climate on longitudinal changes in skill discretion, work pressure, and emotional demands. They suggest that top managers' beliefs and support for employees' well-being is a concept having an effect on work conditions and on workers' health through their working conditions. Workers perceiving a high psychosocial climate have better work conditions in terms of demands and resources, perhaps because managers pay more attention to ensuring balanced workloads and flexible adjustments of schedules. The concept of psychosocial safety climate appears to have resonance with the aims of the positive approach, in that it thrives to find a balance and compatibility between the ideals of productivity and health. As the next section illustrates, this is highly similar to the logic of positively oriented organizational interventions.

It should be noted that organizational-level stress interventions not only aim to reduce stress but also to promote health and well-being. For example, redesigning jobs to promote higher job control, participation in decisions, and more social support are likely to reduce stress symptoms but also to promote positive outcomes. This highlights the notion that positive and stress interventions share common grounds and should be seen as complementary approaches, instead of as two separate streams.

Positive Organizational-level Interventions

An example of a positive approach to encourage healthy work is the American Psychological Association's Psychologically Healthy Workplace Program. The program presents awards to organizations that foster employee health and well-being while also enhancing organizational productivity and performance. The practices that distinguish psychologically healthy workplaces include employee involvement, work–life balance, employee growth and development, health and safety, and employee recognition.

As the review by Grawitch, Gottschalk, and Munz (2006) highlights, these practices are associated with both improvements in employee well-being, as well as in organizational outcomes such as absenteeism reduction. The definition of organizational health implies a continuum ranging form the promotion of positive health outcomes to prevention of the negative outcomes of poor health (Adkins, Quick, & Moe, 2000). As Grawitch et al. (2006) indicate, organizational health is a continuous process, not an obtainable state. It requires attention and action to be maintained or, in other words, it requires a climate of psychosocial safety in which the policies, practices, and procedures are geared toward the protection of worker psychological health and safety (Dollard & Bakker, 2009).

Studies evaluating flow in organizations can also be considered with the positive approach and can be linked with modifications of the workplace. Although flow is a state and not an intervention, it is tightly linked with job design and management practices. Bakker (2005) and Demerouti (2006) define flow as a state in which the worker is highly absorbed in the activity, with a high level of concentration and involvement; enjoying the activity; and intrinsically motivated, which is characterized by a fascination with the activity. Nielsen and Cleal (2010) measured flow as a transient state associated with specific activities on the job, such as brainstorming, planning, problem solving, and evaluation, as well as in relation to more stable job characteristics (role clarity, influence, and cognitive demands). Their study examined the predictors of flow in managers. Their results showed that managers experienced higher levels of flow when they were engaging in cognitively challenging activities such as planning, problem solving, and evaluation. Their results also suggests that these activities are of greater significance to flow than are more stable job characteristics, although other studies have found otherwise using a different operationalization of the flow construct. In a study including ten organizations, Demerouti (2006) found that skill variety, autonomy, job feedback, and task identity were significantly related to flow. Similarly, social support, support for innovative practices at work, and clear rules and goals were all found to be related to flow in school teachers (Salanova, Bakker, & Llorens, 2006). These studies have implications in terms of those job design and management practices that are associated with healthy organizations. The concept of flow is inherently coherent with the focus of the positive approach. Yet, in terms of management practices and interventions, it is still coherent with concepts traditionally included in stress studies, such as the demand-control model (Karasek & Theorell, 1990) or the job characteristics model (Hackman & Oldham, 1980).

The *appreciative inquiry* method is another example of interventions aiming to change aspects of the workplace using a positive approach (Cooperrider & Whitney, 2005). Appreciative inquiry is an organizational development approach that aims to produce changes by enhancing the positive aspects of the workplace, instead of focusing on identifying problems and devising ways to solve them. Contrary to the risk management approach to prevent stress (Cox et al., 2000), it does not start with a diagnosis; rather, the inquiry process implies phases, during which members of an organization are asked to analyze successes and peak performances (a phase called discovery), envision what might be in the future in an unrestricted manner (dream), design plans for the future (design), then plan what will need to happen to fully realize the propositions (delivery). The delivery phase involves thinking about specific activities and who will commit which task (Cooperrider & Sekerka, 2003). The process of building an action plan based on successes and positive aspects is considered a source of learning and growth. As highlighted by Caza and Cameron (2009), formal research on the effects of this approach is still limited, although it is widely used by organizational development practitioners.

Individual-level Stress Interventions

As indicated by Biron, Cooper, and Bond (2009), reviews of the scientific literature on stress prevention programs in the workplace still reveal the dominance of secondary- and tertiary-level interventions (DeFrank & Cooper, 1987; Giga, Noblet et al., 2003; Marine et al., 2006; Murphy & Sauter, 2003; Richardson & Rothstein, 2008; Van Der Hek &

Plomp, 1997; Van Der Klink et al., 2001). Even though interventions of this type are popular within organizations and studies tend to show that they are associated with a reduction in psychological and physiological stress symptoms, these positive effects are likely to be of relatively short duration and limited extent (Murphy & Sauter, 2003). In addition, programs focusing on individuals generally don't have any impact on organizational measures, such as job satisfaction or productivity, whereas organizational measures are linked to improvements in the health of individuals and the performance of the organization (Giga, Noblet et al., 2003). However, a meta-analytic study by Parks and Steelman (2008) showed that participation in organizational wellness programs (providing on- or off-site membership to health clubs and other wellness approaches) was associated with decreased absenteeism and increased performance. Nevertheless, even though preventive methods focused on individuals can be both useful and necessary, they do not change the work organization since they tend to target the consequences rather than the sources of the problem. Individual-level interventions can be usefully combined and integrated within a more comprehensive approach. For instance, a review by Lamontagne, Keegel, Louie, Ostry, and Landbergis (2007) showed that intervention programs encompassing more than one level of prevention were more likely to yield positive results.

An example of this combination of individual and work-related intervention is given by Bond, Flaxman, and Bunce (2008) in describing *psychological flexibility*, which refers to "an ability to focus on the present moment and, depending upon what the situation affords, persist with or change one's (even inflexible, stereotypical) behavior in the pursuit of goals and values." (p. 645). In a study with customer service centers in the financial sector, Bond et al. (2008) found that people who had higher levels of psychological flexibility benefited more from a participative action research that aimed to increase job control. People with higher levels of psychological flexibility showed larger improvements in mental health and absenteeism. Future research should investigate the most efficient balance between approaches encompassing several types and levels of interventions.

Positive Individual-level Interventions
Psychological capital (PsyCap) is one construct that has been studied in an interventional context at the individual level. Hope, resilience, optimism, and self-efficacy are four constructs that make up what

Luthans, Youssef, and Avolio (2007) calls PsyCap. This composite construct has been found to be malleable through interventions. Luthans et al. (2007) explicitly argue that PsyCap is founded on recognized theoretical frameworks, namely social cognitive theory (Bandura, 1986) and hope theory (Snyder, 2000). Consequently, they argue that this should not be confused with management fads that promote unsubstantiated claims of happiness, health, and well-being from self-proclaimed management gurus and self-help guidelines from popular literature. It is state-like, and therefore open to development, contrary to other dispositional models. Luthans and Avolio (2009b) distinguish PsyCap, which is inherently part of the POB movement, with the broader POS movement. They indicate that POB is concerned with micro and meso levels of interventions, and that it focuses on state-like and performance criteria. POS is different, in that is it more concerned with interpersonal and organizational levels in addition to individual- level phenomena. Avey, Wernsing, and Luthans (2008) investigated the impact of PsyCap in relation to organizational change. Their study suggests that employees who had more positive levels of PsyCap and positive emotions were more likely to view organizational change favorably and less likely to have negative reactions. Studies investigating the effects of training (Luthans et al., 2008) have found PsyCap to be a malleable construct that can be enhanced through training, an individual-level intervention that could potentially influence the organizational climate or the way in which organizational transitions are experienced.

Also at the individual level, Seligman, Steen, Park, and Peterson (2000) describe psychological interventions to increase happiness. Their results showed that some very simple exercises increased happiness and decreased depressive symptoms for up to 6 months. As the authors pointed out, the participants were well educated, white, financially comfortable, and motivated to become happier.

A word of caution should be said about individual-level strategies. Warren (2005) takes an ironic perspective to analyze "fun at work" policies, which she describes as a "quick fix" for flagging staff morale, in which employees are encouraged to have fun when they work. She points out the ironical assumptions behind these programs. For example, it assumes that employees don't know how to enjoy themselves if left to their own device, and it highlights that structured fun is probably unlikely to be much fun for those involved.

Table 71.2   Pros and cons of positive versus stress interventions

	Positive interventions	Stress interventions
Advantages	**1** Managers' and other stakeholders' buy-in Aiming for more than mere elimination of stressful aspects of work Potential to generate strong ownership and commitment from managers and employees	**2** Based on a risk assessment that highlights the need for change Discrepancy between actual and desired situation increases readiness to change Several existing tools measuring constructs known to have effects on health
Disadvantages	**3** Risk of being perceived as tyrannical Stigmatizing distressed employees Possibility that employees prioritize stressor-elimination instead of building strengths Healthy organization/manager effect: Possibility that only already well-functioning organizations/skilled managers will participate, leaving out those who most need help	**4** Legal motive: Extrinsic motivation might impede stakeholders' ownership and commitment to implement the intervention program Can be perceived as "opening a can of worms" Can be difficult to manage if several/profound changes need to be made

Positive Versus Stress Interventions: Pros and Cons

Now that we have described interventions arising from both positive and stress research, and their similarities and differences, we point out a few advantages and limits of each approach. These are summarized in Table 71.2.

Readiness to Change

As indicated by the advantages of using the stress approach to design interventions (Table 71.2, Quadrant 2), and as highlighted by Beer, Eisenstat, and Spector (1990), the first step for any type of organizational change is to mobilize commitment to change through joint diagnosis of business problems. The starting point of any effective change effort is a clearly defined business problem. One criticism put forward by adherents to the more positive approach is that defining problems and attempting to correct them is based on the deficit model, which implies that too much emphasis is placed on negative issues while ignoring positive ones. However, based on the stress intervention literature, it is crucial to establish whether there is even a need to change and whether specific groups should be targeted (Comcare, 2005; Cox et al., 2000; Giga, Cooper, & Faragher, 2003; Jordan et al., 2003; Semmer, 2006). If they are not under strain, as Semmer (2006) puts it, then we might be delivering smoking cessation programs to nonsmokers. This need for change can trigger a more proactive reaction. For instance, a study of 81 organizations in the Dutch domiciliary care sector, with a sample size exceeding 26,000 employees,

was conducted by Taris et al. (2003). It showed that organizations with suboptimal scores with regards to job demands, social support, decision latitude, and skill discretion took more steps to reduce job stress, as compared to organizations with better scores on these work characteristics.

At the individual level, it would also be useful to understand more how readiness to change influences the effects of positive and traditional stress interventions. Holt, Armenakis, Field, and Harris (2007) reviewed of existing measures of readiness to change and also validated a new scale that could usefully be integrated into intervention measures. The findings from such a scale would allow researchers to determine if interventions have a differential impact on people according to expectation levels and their readiness for change. Combined with measures of positive constructs, it would also enable us to determine whether people who experience more positive states, or who present more positive traits, benefit differently from interventions.

As described in Quadrant 1 of Table 71.2, there are also advantages to using a positive approach to interventions, for example by integrating or combining individual-level positive interventions within a comprehensive approach involving modification of stressful aspects workplace. Such a comprehensive approach could generate a stronger commitment to the intervention program and to improving the workplace. However, if the organizational context is cynical and highly stressful, it is likely that positively oriented interventions on their own will not be a popular option, as employees might prioritize stressor-reduction strategies instead. In a context in which participants have a negative and cynical view of their organization, positive interventions might not only be a hard sell—indeed, as shown by Atwater, Waldman, Atwater, and Cartier (2000), it is likely that the benefits of positive interventions will be diminished.

Obtaining Commitment and Buy-in

As far as employee involvement is concerned, the stress literature on this subject is very clear: Employee involvement is essential if the prevention actions are to succeed (Elden, 1983; Jordan et al., 2003; Kompier, Geurts, Grundemann, Vink, & Smulders, 1998; Mikkelsen & Gundersen, 2003; Mikkelsen, Saksvik, & Landsbergis, 2000). However, Brun, Biron, and Ivers (2008) highlight that obtaining employees' buy-in in a stress intervention project is not always an easy task. Employees have expressed doubts as to management's good faith, the proposed projects, and the anticipated repercussions on a systematic basis. As described in Table 71.2 (Quadrant 4), stress interventions can be difficult to manage and may be perceived as "opening a can of worms." Providing support for managers (i.e., by means of an external consultant, an HR representative, a line manager) to enable them to deal with these attitudes was a crucial stage in Brun et al.'s study. This comment made by an employee during a group discussion to identify problems and solutions illustrates this point:

> I found it really difficult to persuade my team to come along [to a focus group on identifying sources of stress in the unit]. If this process doesn't lead to anything, you can forget about us, because we won't be coming again; time and time again people LISTEN to us, but don't DO anything about it. We are not frightened of coming here; we're just not under any illusions. (Brun et al. 2008., p. 24).

It is possible that a more positive approach would help managers and employees to accept the change project. As Peterson and Seligman (2004, p. 17) note, "positive social science is an easy sell to the general public and a hard sell to the academic community." Luthans and Avolio (2009b) indicate that this reflects their own experience, as they have had enthusiastic responses from their work with various populations in different cultural contexts.

Carrot or Stick?

As described in Quadrant 4 of Table 71.2, using legislation to ensure a certain level of commitment to reducing stress can be seen as an advantage.

For example, according to legislation in the United Kingdom, employers have a duty to "assess the risk of stress-related ill health arising from work activities under the Management of Health and Safety at Work Regulations, 1999 and under the Health and Safety at Work etc Act 1974, and to take measures to control that risk" (Health and Safety Executive, 2009). The HSE offers ample guidance on risk assessments and undertakes enforcement action when employers fail to carry out the legally required suitable and sufficient risk assessment. Although inspectors can issue improvement notices, and action may be taken when the law is breached, the approach is not enforcement-led. Given the strong business case for stress (see Bond, Flaxman, & Loivette, 2006), not to mention the costs of a successful lawsuit, it is hoped that employers will take action following the risk assessment. However, as highlighted by Biron, Gatrell, and Cooper (2010), the idea that the legal requirements will be sufficient to enforce the implementation of corrective solutions is not necessarily realistic. Even when organizations do have specific measures in place to conduct risk assessments, it does not means that shop floor managers are actually using them appropriately and implementing corrective solutions. Theoretically, when conducting stress risk assessments, managers would see the benefits and make it a priority if needed. Motivation theories show that external regulation (e.g., legal requirement) is not the most effective way to engage people in their actions with a full sense of choice (Ryan & Deci, 2000). As shown by Biron et al. (2010), to build managers' intrinsic motivation to use stress risk assessment tools and implement corrective solutions, different and more theoretically sound strategies need to be instituted to create ownership and commitment (Dawson, Willman, Clinton, & Bamford, 1988; Fullan, 2003). It is likely that more positively framed interventions carry the potential to generate this type of ownership and commitment from managers and employees.

In summary, and as shown in Quadrant 3 of Table 71.2, although positively framed interventions have the potential to go beyond eliminating the effects and sources of stress, as well as to increase manager and employee buy-in and ownership, they also bear the risk of stigmatizing distressed employees and targeting already well-functioning teams. Stress interventions, on the other hand, bear the risk of being seen as a Pandora's box or slippery slope if too many problems are targeted all at once (Parkes & Sparkes, 1998). Yet, when based on a sound risk assessment and a systematic approach (several tools and approaches have already been suggested and tested), interventions emerging from the stress perspective can highlight the need for change and thus trigger change initiatives. From an interventionist perspective, one can question whether organizations are more willing to intervene proactively on the elimination and reduction of sources of stress, or on developing strengths, virtues, and building on what they are doing right. Although a positive approach might make the theory of change more appealing for all, the discrepancy has to be perceived to generate the motivation to change something.

Future Directions
A Call for an Integrative Approach

A few points must be made regarding positive and stress interventions. One argument is that, by focusing solely on desirable positive states and emotions, the positive approach could isolate and exploit some employees who do not fit this positive mold (Fineman, 2006a). For instance, not all employees necessarily feel the need to be happy and positive at work in order to be productive and good at their job. Fineman (2006b) also goes on to suggest that, although a positive lens may have good intentions, it could be misused by senior managers as a form of control and exploitation. Consequently, organizations have to be careful that by promoting positive workplaces they do not exclude or stigmatize employees who do not fit within this positively oriented framework.

Some scholars have alos asked if more recent movements, which accentuate the positive, are actually that different from movements that have accentuated the negative (Held, 2004). For instance, are such efforts simply relabeling or rebranding negative oriented phenomena to give the impression they are more positive? Indeed, Luthans and Avolio (2009b) stated that there is a "need to inquire whether positive organizational behavior is simply old wine in a new bottle?" (p. 292). Taking everything into account, however, it is our opinion that, at the organizational level, both positive and stress perspectives share the ultimate aim of helping organizations to manage and develop employee's psychological states to facilitate a positive organizational climate.

Along the same line, Fineman (2006a) argues that focussing exclusively on positive aspects represents a reductionist, one-eyed view of the social world that excludes sufferings and frustrations. For example, he criticizes appreciative inquiry (a positive organizational-level intervention; Cooperrider & Whitney, 2005) in the following way:

> But in exclusively favoring positive narratives, appreciative inquiry fails to value the opportunities for positive change that are possible from negative experiences, such as embarrassing events, periods of anger, anxiety, fear, or shame (Barge & Oliver, 2003; Fineman, 2004). For Argyris (1994), such a positive skew is anti-learning. He sees it as closing access to crucial data for double-loop learning, thus undermining the capacity for individuals and groups to engage in anything more than superficial changes. (p. 275)

In line with these arguments, future research should consider the possibilities offered by a more integrated approach, as opposed to a dichotomized one. Stress research and work psychology in general have been characterized by paradigmatic wars. These wars have kept researchers from using methodologies and theoretical perspectives that they perceive as irreconcilable with their own. It is likely that the limits of one approach can be compensated by the strengths of another. However, as argued by Cox, Karanika, Griffiths, and Houdmont (2007), "a more broadly conceived and eclectic framework" is needed for evaluating interventions with methods and study designs that are "fit for purpose" and adapted to the organizational reality (p. 349). As Griffiths (1999) argues, there is no need to abandon our efforts to accumulate evidence on the effectiveness of stress programs, but rather a need to adapt our methods, so that they are fit for the purpose of querying this subject area. Evaluating the context in which the intervention is going to take place, for example by assessing the stakeholders' readiness to change could help determine which approach is most fit for the purpose. In line with Lamontagne et al. (2007), who showed that comprehensive programs encompassing primary, secondary, and tertiary levels of prevention are more likely to have positive effects, future research should investigate whether integrating both positive and stress interventions produces differential or stronger effects on various outcomes from both perspectives.

Conclusion

This chapter aimed to contrast the positive approach to interventions with more traditional stress management interventions. We attempted to illustrate that, although positive well-being and stress might be distinct constructs from a theoretical perspective, from an interventional perspective, they are highly similar in their aims. Indeed, it highlights that, in terms of preventative measures, the two approaches are complementary to each other. However, each approach has advantages and disadvantages that need to be taken into account.

From the employer's perspective, it is much easier and often cheaper to put in place measures that address an individual's capability to cope with stressful aspects of his or her work, instead of attempting to reduce or eliminate these aspects. As shown in this chapter, several organizational interventions modifying work-related aspects exist, both within the positive and the stress management frameworks. Albeit more demanding and difficult, intervening on work-related and organizational aspects instead of (or in addition to) aiming to reduce their adverse effects on individuals is thought to be a much more effective, viable, and sustainable preventive strategy (Lamontagne et al., 2007; Semmer, 2006). This point is best summarized by Hackman:

> The findings and tools of positive organizational scholarship clearly can help guide adaptation by individual human beings as they deal with the inevitable stresses and challenges of life and work. But that is only half the story. We hope that research within the POB paradigm one day soon will give at least as much attention to identifying and creating those organizational conditions that promote learning and growth as they do to strategies for helping people adapt and adjust to their work circumstances. Doing that, however, will require that positive organizational scholars move beyond their present focus on individual persons and explicitly explore ways to develop and exploit the positive structural features of the social systems within which people live and work. (Hackman, 2009, p. 316)

Refereces

Adkins, J.A., Quick, J.C., & Moe, K.O. (2000). Building world-class performance in changing times. In L.R. Murphy, & C.C.L. (Eds.), *Healthy and productive work: An international perspective* (pp. 107–132). London: Taylor & Francis.

Argyris, C. (1994). Good communication that blocks learning. *Harvard Business Review, 72*(4), 77–86.

Atwater, L.E., Waldman, D., Atwater, D., & Cartier, J. (2000). Supervisors' cynicism, follow-up, and commitment to subordinates. *Personnel Psychology, 53*, 275–297.

Avey, J.B., Wernsing, T.S., & Luthans, F. (2008). Can positive employees help positive organizational change? *The Journal of Applied Behavioral Science, 44*, 48–70.

Bakker, A.B. (2005). Flow among music teachers and their students: The crossover of peak experiences. *Journal of Vocational Behavior, 66*, 26–44.

Bandura, A. (1986). *Social foundations of thought and action.* Englewood Cliffs, NJ: Prentice-Hall.

Barge, J.K., & Oliver, C. (2003). Working with appreciation in managerial practice. *Academy of Management Review, 28*, 124–142.

Barling, J., Moutino, K., & Kelloway, E.K. (1996). Effects of transformational leadership training on attitudinal and financial outcomes. *Journal of Applied Psychology, 81*, 827–832.

Beer, M., Eisenstat, R.A., & Spector, B. (1990). Why change programs don't produce change. *Harvard Business Review, 68*(6), 158.

Belkic, J.L., Landbergis, P.A., Schnall, P.L., & Baker, D. (2004). Is job strain a major source of cardiovascular disease risk? *Scandinavian Journal of Work and Environmental Health, 30*(2), 85–128.

Biron, C., Cooper, C.L., & Bond, F.W. (2009). Mediators and moderators of organizational interventions to prevent occupational stress. In S. Cartwright, & C.L. Cooper (Eds.), *Oxford handbook of organizational well-being* (pp. 441–465). Oxford, UK: Oxford University Press.

Biron, C., Gatrell, C., & Cooper, C.L. (2010). Autopsy of a failure: Evaluating process and contextual issues in an organizational-level work stress intervention. *International Journal of Stress Management, 17*(2), 135–158.

Black, C. (2008). *Working for a healthier tomorrow.* London: TSO Publications.

Bond, F.W., Flaxman, P.E., & Bunce, D. (2008). The influence of psychological flexibility on work redesign: Mediated moderation of a work reorganization intervention. *Journal of Applied Psychology, 93*(3), 645–654.

Bond, F.W., Flaxman, P.E., & Loivette, S. (2006). *A business case for the management standards for stress* (No. RR 431). Norwich, UK: Health & Safety Executive.

Bourbonnais, R., Brisson, C., Vézina, M., & Moisan, J. (1996). Job strain and psychological distress in white collar workers. *Scandinavian Journal of Work, Environment and Health, 22*(2), 139–145.

Bourbonnais, R., & Mondor, M. (2001). Job strain and sickness absence among nurses in the province of Quebec. *American Journal of Industrial Medicine, 39*, 194–202.

Brun, J.P., Biron, C., & Ivers, H. (2008). *Strategic approach to preventing occupational stress* (Studies/Research No. R-577). Québec, Canada: Institut de recherche Robert-Sauvé en santé et en sécurité du travail.

Caza, A., & Cameron, K.S. (2009). Positive organizational scholarship: What does it achieve? In S.R. Clegg, & C.L. Cooper (Eds.), *The Sage handbook of organizational behavior* Vol. 2: *Macro approaches* (pp. 99–116). London: Sage Publications.

Cherniss, C., & Caplan, R.D. (2001). Implementing emotional intelligence programs in organizations. In C. Cherniss, & D. Goleman (Eds.), *The emotionally intelligent workplace* (pp. 286–304). San Francisco: Jossey-Bass.

Collinson, D. (2002). Managing humour. *Journal of Management Studies, 39*(3), 269–288.

Comcare. (2005). *An organisational approach to preventing psychological injury—a guide for corporate, HR and OHS managers.* Retrieved from www.comcare.gov.au.

Cooper, C.L., & Cartwright, S. (1997). An intervention strategy for workplace stress. *Journal of Psychosomatic Research, 43*(1), 7–16.

Cooperrider, D.L., & Sekerka, L.E. (2003). Toward a theory of positive organizational change. In K. Cameron, J.E. Dutton, & R.E. Quinn (Eds.), *Positive organizational* scholarship: Foundations of a new discipline (pp. 225–240). San Francisco: Berrett-Koehler.

Cooperrider, D.L., & Whitney, D. (2005). *Appreciative inquiry: A positive revolution in change*. San Francisco: Berrett-Koehler.

Cox, T., Griffiths, A.J., Barlowe, C.A., Randall, R.J., Thomson, L.E., & Rial-Gonzalez, E. (2000). *Organisational interventions for work stress: A risk management approach*. Sudbury: HSE Books.

Cox, T., Karanika, M., Griffiths, A., & Houdmont, J. (2007). Evaluating organizational-level work stress interventions: Beyond traditional methods. *Work & Stress, 21*(4), 348–362.

Csikszentmihalyi, M. (1990). *Flow: The psychology of optimal experience*. New York: Harper & Row.

Dawson, S., Willman, P., Clinton, P., & Bamford, M. (Eds.). (1988). Conclusion: The future of self regulation. In *Safety at work: The limits of self-regulation*. Cambridge, UK: Cambridge University Press.

de Lange, A.H., Taris, T.W., Kompier, M., Houtman, I.L.D., & Bongers, P.M. (2003). The very best of the millennium: Longitudinal research and the demand-control- (support) model. *Journal of Occupational Health Psychology, 8*(4), 282–305.

DeFrank, R.S., & Cooper, C.L. (1987). Worksite stress management interventions: Their effectiveness and conceptualisation. *Journal of Managerial Psychology, 2*(1), 4–10.

Dellve, L., Skagert, K., & Vilhelmsson, R. (2007). Leadership in workplace health promotion projects: 1- and 2-year effects on long-term work attendance. *European Journal of Public Health, 17*(5), 471–476.

Demerouti, E. (2006). Job characteristics, flow, and performance: The moderating role of conscientiousness. *Journal of Occupational Health Psychology, 11*, 266–280.

Dollard, M.F. (2007). *Psychosocial safety culture and climate; Definition of a new construct*. Adelaide, AU: University of South Australia.

Dollard, M.F., & Bakker, A.B. (2009). Psychosocial safety climate as a precursor to conducive work environments, psychological health problems, and employee engagement. *Journal of Occupational and Organizational Psychology, 83*(3), 579–599.

Elden, M. (1983). Democratization and participative research in developing local theory. *Journal of Occupational Behavior, 4*(1), 21.

Fineman, S. (2004). Getting the measure of emotion—and the cautionary tale of emotional intelligence. *Human Relations, 57*, 719–740.

Fineman, S. (2006a). On being positive: Concerns and counterpoints. *Academy of Management Review, 31*(2), 270–291.

Fineman, S. (2006b). Reply: Accentuating the positive. *Academy of Management Review, 31*(2), 306–308.

Fullan, M. (2003). *Change forces with a vengeance*. London, New York: Routledge.

Giga, S.I., Cooper, C.L., & Faragher, B. (2003). The development of a framework for a comprehensive approach to stress management interventions at work. *International Journal of Stress Management, 10*(4), 280–296.

Giga, S.I., Noblet, A.J., Faragher, B., & Cooper, C.L. (2003). The UK perspective: A review of research on organisational stress management interventions. *Australian Psychologist, 38*(2), 158–164.

Graveling, R., Crawford, J.O., Cowie, H., Amati, C., & Vohra, S. (2008). *Workplace interventions that are effective for promoting mental well-being: Synopsis of the evidence of effectiveness and cost-effectiveness*. Edinburgh: National Institute for Health and Clinical Excellence (NICE).

Griffiths, A. (1999). Organizational interventions: Facing the limits of the natural science paradigm. *Scandinavian Journal of Work and Environment Health, 25*(6), 589–596.

Grawitch, M.J., Gottschalk, M., & Munz, D. (2006). The path to a healthy workplace: Critical review linking healthy workplace practices, employee well-being, and organizational improvements. *Consulting Psychology Journal: Practice and Research, 58*(3), 129–147.

Hackman, J.R. (2009). The perils of positivity. *Journal of Organizational Behavior, 30*, 309–319.

Hackman, J.R., & Oldham, G.R. (1980). *Work redesign*. Reading, MA: Addison-Wesley.

Health and Safety Executive. (2009, October 30). *What does the HSE require employers to do?* Retrieved from http://www.hse.gov.uk/stress/faqs.htmleg.

Held, B.S. (2004). The negative side of positive psychology. *Journal of Applied Humanistics, 44*, 9–46.

Holt, D.T., Armenakis, A.A., Feild, H.S., & Harris, S.G. (2007). Readiness for organizational change: The systematic development of a scale. *Journal of Applied Behavioral Science, 43*(2), 232–255.

Jordan, J., Gurr, E., Tinline, G., Giga, S., Faragher, B., & Cooper, C. (2003). *Beacons of excellence in stress prevention* (No. RR-133). Manchester, UK: Health and Safety Executive.

Kelloway, K.E., & Barling, J. (2010). Leadership development as an intervention in occupational health psychology. *Work & Stress, 24*(3), 260–279.

Karasek, R., & Theorell, T. (1990). *Healthy work: Stress, productivity and the reconstruction of working life*. New York: Basic Books.

Kompier, M.A.J., Cooper, C.L., & Geurts, S.A.E. (2000). A multiple case study approach to work stress prevention in Europe. *European Journal of Work & Organizational Psychology, 9*(3), 371.

Kompier, M.A.J., Geurts, S.A.E., Grundemann, R.W.M., Vink, P., & Smulders, P.G.W. (1998). Cases in stress prevention: The success of a participative and stepwise approach. *Stress Medicine, 14*, 155–168.

LaMontagne, A.D., Keegel, T., Louie, A.M., Ostry, A., & Landbergis, P.A. (2007). A systematic review of the job-stress intervention evaluation literature, 1990–2005. *International Journal of Occupational and Environmental Health, 13*, 268–280.

Luthans, F., Avey, J.B., Avolio, B.J., Norman, S.M., & Combs, G.M. (2006). Psychological capital development: Toward a micro-intervention. *Journal of organizational behavior, 27*, 387–393.

Luthans, F., Avey, J.B., & Patera, J.L. (2008). Experimental analysis of a web-based training intervention to develop positive psychological capital. *Academy of Management Learning and Education, 7*(2), 209–221.

Luthans, F., & Avolio, B.J. (2009a). Inquiry unplugged: Building on Hackman's potential perils of POB. *Journal of Organizational Behavior, 30*(323–328).

Luthans, F., & Avolio, B.J. (2009b). The "'point'" of positive organizational behavior. *Journal of Organizational Behavior, 30*, 291–307.

Luthans F., Youssef, C.M., Avolio, B.J. (2007). *Psychological capital*. New York: Oxford University Press.

Marine, A., Ruotsalainen, J., Serra, C., & Verbeek, J. (2006). Preventing occupational stress in healthcare workers. *Cochrane Database of Systematic Reviews* (4).

Mikkelsen, A., & Gundersen, M. (2003). The effect of a participatory organizational intervention on work environment, job stress, and subjective health complaints. *International Journal of Stress Management, 10*(2), 91–110.

Mikkelsen, A., Saksvik, P.Ø., & Landsbergis, P. (2000). The impact of a participatory organizational intervention on job stress in community health care institutions. *Work & Stress, 14*(2), 156–170.

Murphy, L.R. (1988). Workplace interventions for stress reduction and prevention. In C.L. Cooper & R. Payne (Eds.), *Causes, coping and consequences of stress at work*. New York: Wiley.

Murphy, L.R., & Sauter, S.L. (2003). The USA perspective: Current issues and trends in the management of work stress. *Australian Psychologist, 38*(2), 151–157.

Nelson, D.L., & Simmons, B.L. (2004). Eustress: An elusive construct, an engaging pursuit. In P.M. Perrewé, & D. Ganster (Eds.), *Emotional and physiological processes and positive intervention strategies. Research in occupational stress and well being* Vol. 3 (pp. 265–322). Oxford: Elsevier.

Nielsen, K., & Cleal, B. (2010). Predicting flow at work: Investigating the activities and job characteristics that predict flow states at work. *Journal of Occupational Health Psychology, 15*(2), 180–190.

Nyberg, A., Westerlund, H., Hanson, L.L.M., & Theorell, T. (2008). Managerial leadership is associated with self-reported sickness absence and sickness presenteeism among Swedish men and women. *Scandinavian Journal of Public Health, 36*(8), 803.

Parkes, K.L., & Sparkes, T.J. (1998). *Organizational interventions to reduce work stress: Are they effective? A review of the literature* (No. RR-193). Sudbury, UK: Health and Safety Executive.

Parks, K.M., & Steelman, L.A. (2008). Organizational wellness programs: A meta-analysis. *Journal of Occupational Health Psychology, 13*(1), 58–68.

Quick, J.C., Mack, D., Gavin, J.H., Cooper, C.L., & Quick, J.D. (2004). Executives: Engines for positive stress. In P.M. Perrewé, & D. Ganster (Eds.), *Emotional and physiological processes and positive intervention strategies. Research in occupational stress and well being* Vol. 3 (pp. 359–405). Oxford, UK: Elsevier.

Quick, J.D., Quick, J.C., & Nelson, D.L. (2000). The theory of preventive stress management in organizations. In C.L. Cooper (Ed.), *Theories of organizational stress*. New York: Oxford University Press.

Richardson, K.M., & Rothstein, H.R. (2008). Effects of occupational stress management intervention programs: A meta-analysis. *Journal of Occupational Health Psychology, 13*(1), 69–93.

Roberts, L.M. (2006). Shifting the lens on organizational life: The added value of positive scholarship. *Academy of Management Review, 31*(2), 292–305.

Ryan, R.M., & Deci, E.L. (2000). Self-determination theory and the facilitation of intrinsic motivation, social development, and well-being. *American Psychologist, 55*(1), 68–78.

Salanova, M., Bakker, A., & Llorens, S. (2006). Flow at work: Evidence for an upward spiral of personal and organizational resources. *Journal of Happiness Studies, 7*, 1–22.

Seligman, M.E.P., & Csikszentmihalyi, M. (2000). Positive psychology: An introduction. *American Psychologist, 55*, 5–14.

Selye, H. (1976). *Stress in health and disease*. Boston: Butterworths.

Semmer, N.K. (2003). Job stress interventions and organization of work. In J.C. Quick, & L.E. Tetris (Eds.), *Handbook of occupational health psychology*. Washington, DC: American Psychological Association.

Semmer, N.K. (2006). Job stress interventions and the organization of work. *Scandinavian Journal of Work and Environmental Health, 32*(6, special issue), 515–527.

Simmons, B.L., Nelson, D.L., & Neal, L.J. (2001). A comparison of the positive and negative work attitudes of home health care and hospital nurses. *Health Care Management Review, 26*, 63–74.

Snyder, C.R. (2000). *Handbook of hope*. San Diego: Academic Press.

St-Arnaud, L. (2007). Determinants of return-to-work among employees absent due to mental health problems. *Relations Industrielles (Industrial Relations), 62*(4), 690.

Taris, T.W., Kompier, M.A.J., Geurts, S.A.E., Schreurs, P.J.G., Schaufeli, W.B., de Boer, E., et al. (2003). Stress management interventions in the Dutch domiciliary care sector: Findings from 81 organizations. *International Journal of Stress Management, 10*(4), 297–325.

Van Der Hek, H., & Plomp, H.N. (1997). Occupational stress management programmes: A practical overview of published effect studies. *Occupational Medicine, 47*(3), 133–141.

Van Der Klink, J.J.L., Blonk, W.W.B., Schene, A.H., & Van Dijk, F.J.H. (2001). The benefits of interventions for work-related stress. *American Journal of Public Health, 91*(2), 270–276.

Warren, S. (2005) Humour as a Management Tool? The irony of structuring fun in organizations. In U. Johannson & J. Woodilla (Eds.) *Irony & Organization: Epistemological claims and supporting field stories*, pp.174–199. Copenhagen: Copenhagen Business School Press.

Yarker, J., Donaldson-Feilder, E., Lewis, R., & Flaxman, P.E. (2008). *Management competencies for preventing and reducing stress at work: Identifying and developing the management behaviours necessary to implement the HSE management standards: Phase 2*. London: HSE Books.

Ylipaavalniemi, J., Kivimaki, M., Elovainio, M., Virtanen, M., Keltikangas-Jarvinen, L., & Vahtera, J. (2005). Psychosocial work characteristics and incidence of newly diagnosed depression: A prospective cohort study of three different models. *Social Science & Medicine, 61*(1), 111.

PART 9

Expanding Positive Organizational Scholarship

Positive Deviance for a Sustainable World

Linking Sustainability and Positive Organizational Scholarship

Andrew J. Hoffman *and* Nardia Haigh

Abstract

This chapter examines the linkages between the positive organizational scholarship (POS) and sustainability research domains; examining ways in which each domain can enrich the other, their mutual research agendas, and practical contributions. Positive organizational scholarship can help sustainability make a shift from addressing "deficit gaps" to instead addressing "abundance gaps." Sustainability can help expand the scope of the POS research domain from explaining how people and organizations can flourish, to also considering ways in which human and organizational flourishing is embedded within the state of the natural environment. To do this, the chapter first outlines the issues and domain of sustainability scholarship, then discusses the linkages in more detail, and explores the scholarly implications for each domain. It concludes by suggesting potentially fruitful research questions posed by these sustainability–POS linkages, and discusses the implications of these linkages for business education.

Keywords: Sustainability, sustainable development, natural environment, positive organizational scholarship, cultural creatives, LOHAS, hybrid organizations

This chapter explores the fit between the research domains of sustainability and positive organizational scholarship (POS), both of which are grounded in the core concept of flourishing. Positive organizational scholarship is concerned with "conditions that foster flourishing at the individual, work group, and organizational levels" (Dutton & Glynn, 2008). Sustainability holds "the possibility that human and other life will flourish on the planet forever" (Ehrenfeld, 2008, p. 6). As a vision, POS research seeks to explore organizational and institutional contexts that help to realize the fullest human potential. Sustainability research explores economic development that will "meet the needs of present generations without compromising the ability of future generations to meet their own needs" (World Commission on Environment and Development, 1987). With these as foundational starting points, we explore two fundamental ways in which these domains are interconnected; each emerging from the other.

On the one hand, scholars and practitioners in the sustainability literature have long sought to explain and prescribe how individuals and organizations can live and organize *less unsustainably*. More recent scholars have begun to push the literature into focusing instead on living *more sustainably* (Ehrenfeld, 2008; McDonough & Braungart, 2002). This distinction represents a shift from addressing "deficit gaps" to instead addressing "abundance gaps" (Cameron, 2007). However, this shift has not been adequately explained within the sustainability literature. Positive organizational scholarship can help sustainability scholars explain and make this transition by offering a conceptual basis by which to understand it. Further, contributions from POS can make sustainability issues more actionable and sustainability more achievable by suggesting tangible skills and actions that individuals can use to transform their lives and organizations. For sustainability scholars, this means focusing beyond the managed destruction or regeneration of the natural world, to instead understanding and working with nature's bias toward abundance without waste.

On the other hand, POS scholars focus on the study of especially positive (or "positively deviant") contexts, systems, practices, and outcomes that foster and enable individuals and collectives to flourish (Cameron, 2007; Dutton & Glynn, 2008; Dutton & Sonenshein, 2008). By introducing sustainability issues more directly into POS scholarship, researchers can expand the scope of the research domain, from explaining how people and organizations can flourish to also considering ways in which human and organizational flourishing is embedded within the flourishing of the natural environment.

By highlighting these linkages, we hope that sustainability and POS scholars will see how their domains can enrich each other, their mutual research agendas, and practical contributions. We invite readers to examine these linkages, and to identify other ways in which the two domains are complementary. To more fully explore these possibilities, this chapter first outlines the issues and the domain of sustainability scholarship. We then discuss the linkages in more detail, examining the scholarly implications for each domain. We conclude by suggesting potentially fruitful research questions posed by these sustainability–POS linkages, and we discuss the implications of the linkages for business education.

Issues of Sustainability

The past century has witnessed unprecedented economic growth and human prosperity. World population increased by a factor of four, the world economy increased by a factor of 14 (Thomas, 2002), global per capita income tripled (World Business Council on Sustainable Development, 1997), and average life expectancy increased by almost two-thirds (World Resources Institute, 1994). In the United States alone, life expectancy rose from 47.3 to 77.3 years between 1900 and 2002 (National Center for Health Statistics, 2004).

But, although these and other advances are notable, widening income disparities mean that not all people share in the material and economic progress of the past century. According to the United Nations (UN), the richest 20% of the world's population consume 86% of all goods and services while the poorest 20% consume just 1.3%. In fact, the richest three people in the world have assets that exceed the combined gross domestic product of the 48 least developed countries. Of the 4.4 billion people in the developing world, almost 60% lack access to safe sewers, 33% do not have access to clean water, 25% lack adequate housing, and 30% have no modern health services (Crossette, 1998).

At the same time, the past century has witnessed unprecedented human impacts on the natural environment. The Millennium Ecosystem Assessment (Reid et al., 2005) commissioned by the UN (involving more than 1,360 experts worldwide) concluded that, of the 24 global ecosystem services analyzed, 60% were degraded or used unsustainably, and that humans have changed Earth's ecosystems over the past 50 years more quickly and more extensively than comparable historical periods. Humans have increased the species extinction rate by as much as 1,000 times over background rates typical of the planet's history. In the last 100 years, 816 species have become extinct, and 11,046 more are threatened with extinction (United Nations, 2001). Nearly 25% of the world's most important marine fish stocks are depleted, overharvested, or just beginning to recover from overharvesting. Another 44% are being fished at their biological limit and are, therefore, vulnerable to depletion (World Resources Institute, 2000).

In short, the exploitative relationship between the economy and the natural and social environments, which took shape in the Industrial Revolution of the 19th century and that continues to grow with globalized industrial production in this century, cannot be sustained. We are today in the throes of a commons tragedy of global proportions, and this has caused a great deal of concern among many within society (Sandelands & Hoffman, 2008). This concern produced the modern sustainable development movement.

The Sustainable Development Movement and Sustainability Scholarship

The sustainable development movement and the interdisciplinary domain of sustainability scholarship emerged in the mid-1980s. The United Nations' World Commission on Environment and Development (1987) Brundtland Commission report, *Our Common Future*, promoted sustainable development by calling for economic growth to be pursued in a manner that assures the protection of both social and environmental systems. The report followed an environmental conservation movement that can be traced back to the late 1800s, which led to the protection of large tracts of American land for national parks. The movement gained momentum throughout the 1900s, with events such as the publication of Rachel Carson's (1962) *Silent Spring*, the first Earth Day in 1970, and the 1972 United Nations Conference on Human Environment in Stockholm (the first UN conference to attend to global environmental issues).

The Brundtland Commission report advanced the sustainability issue by using the term "sustainable development" to highlight ways in which economic development was causing environmental degradation and social inequities. Nongovernmental organizations (NGOs), policy makers, scholars, and members of the general public have taken inspiration from the Brundtland report and advocated for organizations to address environmental and social issues in communities and the economy, while sustainability scholars investigated the interconnections between business strategy and issues such as ecosystem protection, species extinction, pollution, community development, and human health and well-being.

Sustainability scholarship is an interdisciplinary domain that encompasses a holistic view of firms and their relationships with the natural environment and societies in which they operate, and includes topics such as corporate social responsibility and environmental management. Work has progressed over the past 15 years to identify how organizations can reduce their impact on both society and the natural environment. For instance, pollution prevention, product stewardship, and sustainable development have been identified as strategic organizational capabilities (Hart, 1995), as have the ability to integrate matters concerning the natural environment into strategic planning processes (Judge & Douglas, 1998), process innovation (Christmann, 2000), stakeholder integration, higher-order learning, and continuous innovation (Sharma & Vredenburg, 1998) to reduce environmental impact. In many cases, the strategic importance of these capabilities has been measured through correlations with company profitability or cost advantages (Christmann, 2000; Judge & Douglas, 1998; Menguc & Ozanne, 2005; Russo & Fouts, 1997). One of the most widely used concepts for measuring sustainability action has been the notion of the triple bottom line (TBL) (Elkington, 1997), which advocates for companies to maximize three bottom lines: the three e's (equity, environment, and economy) or the three p's (people, planet, and profit).

But, with its focus on operating *less unsustainably* rather than *more sustainably*, or on addressing the deficit gaps rather than identifying and addressing abundance gaps (Cameron, 2007), sustainability has drawn criticism both from the left and right, and both from advocates and opponents. The harshest criticisms come from those who believe that pursuing sustainability misappropriates the purpose of the corporation and is contrary to the true intentions of capitalism. For example, *The Economist* magazine published a cover story in January 2005 that derided sustainability and corporate social responsibility as misguided concepts driven by people with little knowledge or a downright fear of capitalism. Similarly, when the U.S. Climate Action Partnership, a consortium of ten blue-chip corporations (including DuPont, Alcoa, BP America, GE, Lehman Brothers, PG&E, and two environmental NGOs) called for federal standards on greenhouse gas emissions in early 2007, a *Wall Street Journal* editorial ridiculed them as the "10 jolly green giants" and challenged their motives as being economically opportunistic rather than environmentally altruistic (Strassel, 2007). In 2005, when GE announced plans to publish its first "Citizenship Report," the *Wall Street Journal* wrote that environmentalists had made their "biggest catch yet" and pondered whether "capitalists are abandoning capitalism" (Murray, 2005, p. A2). Such critics believe that economic growth remains the primary goal of development planning, whereas sustainability is a social and political constraint (Colby, 1991). Rather than harmonizing economic, environmental, and social considerations into a synergistic whole, such critics believe the prevailing regimen remains one of making trade-offs while holding to economic growth as the paramount objective.

At the opposite extreme, some advocates of sustainability argue that the TBL does not go far enough. They argue alongside opponents that sustainability is nothing but a label for actions or strategies that are actually driven by the standard social, economic, and institutional mechanisms (e.g., Jacobs, 1993; Schnaiberg, 1980). They further argue that simple metrics, such as internal rate of return or net present value, contribute significantly to present-day sustainability problems by obscuring broader responsibilities that cannot be measured easily, if at all. Thus, it seems beyond optimistic to suppose that metrics for sustainability, such as the TBL, could resolve these problems. And, if they could, it seems beyond hopeful to suppose they would be embraced when opposition to intertwining environmental, social, and economic development remains (and many still assume they are mutually exclusive). In short, the sustainability movement could be seen as having become as intractable as the problems it aims to solve, because it has been defined and enacted using the same logics that created the problem in the first place—a focus on the deficit gaps—and attempts to explore abundance gaps and operate more sustainably remain outweighed by challenges and underexplored opportunities.

Positive Deviance in Practice

Today, at the onset of the 21st century, a growing number of individuals and organizations have begun to alter their lifestyles and business models to enact their vision of sustainability toward "intentional behaviors that depart from the norms . . . in honorable ways" (Spreitzer & Sonenshein, 2004, p. 828). They act as positive deviants seeking to change the organizations, industries, and socioeconomic systems of which they are a part. There are several proposed explanations as to why this shift is happening at this point in time (Hoffman, 2003). First, society has advanced in terms of leisure time, such that people are searching for more meaning in the work realm of their lives (Neck & Milliman, 1994). Many people are reaching a stage in their development in which they feel secure in their basic needs, such that they are striving for the highest stage of human development, self-actualization (Maslow, 1954). These individuals derive a sense of self-actualization through their actions, and a sense of sacredness and purpose through their work that allows them to feel more genuine and authentic (Ray & Anderson, 2000). They tend not to spend their whole career within a single company. Instead, their career path represents a more personal journey of self-discovery (Hall & Mirvis, 1996). For this demographic, leading a sustainable lifestyle may be explained as a calling or vocation (Wrzesniewski, McCauley, Rozin, & Schwartz, 1997) on that journey. People now strive to develop and express their entire selves at work (Mitroff & Denton, 1999) and therefore bring their personal values into the workplace (Hoffman, 2003; McDonald, 1999).

Second, many in the current workforce are Baby Boomers, who grew up in the idealistic 1960s and 1970s and are trying to maintain their idealistic roots (Cash, Gray, & Rood, 2000; Hall & Richter, 1990). These people may be among the many who search for ways to leave a legacy and the satisfaction of knowing their lives made the world a better place (Covey, 1995). Third, as educational experience, social values,

and religious doctrine increasingly support sustainability, it becomes more tightly tied to individual identity and becomes an important motivator of personal action (Wade-Benzoni et al., 2002).

By observing the actions of proactive individuals and organizations through a POS lens, we can begin to explain why and how sustainability can be achieved through discrete shifts in values, beliefs, skills, capabilities, and strategies. In the next sections, we will discuss key examples of individual and organizational positive deviance within the sustainability domain, and explore how using a POS lens can help to explain them.

Positive Sustainability Deviance At the Individual Level

To address sustainability issues and their frustration with policy solutions, many people are taking direct action that reflects their personal beliefs and values about their proper role within the natural environment and among fellow human beings. These positive deviants have been recognized as a growing demographic segment within America, with labels such as Cultural Creatives (Ray & Anderson, 2000) or Lifestyles of Health and Sustainability (LOHAS) consumers (LOHAS, 2009; The Natural Marketing Institute, 2008). These are people who value design, health, environmental and social justice, and ecological sustainability in the products they purchase, the careers they pursue, and the lifestyles they lead.

Rather than acquiesce to societal values, these positive deviants act and seek meaning according to their beliefs, and growth in the segment suggests that, in doing so, they are affecting those same societal values. This segment values authenticity, nature, and community (Ray & Anderson, 2000). They actively pursue a life they feel is environmentally and socially fulfilling by expressing themselves and making a practical difference (Neal, 2000). They are careful consumers who reject products that are imitations, of poor quality, disposable, or cliché in style, and they want to know where products originate, how they are manufactured, by whom, and what becomes of them in disposal (Ray & Anderson, 2000). In 2001, the LOHAS demographic was estimated at 50 million people, approximately 25% of American adults. By 2003, that figure had grown to 68 million Americans, or about 33% of the adult population (Cortese, 2003). In 2008, LOHAS consumers represented an estimated $209 billion U.S. industry for goods and services focused on health, green building, eco-tourism, alternative energy and transport, and natural lifestyles (LOHAS, 2009).

Not content to project their values and beliefs only in the safety of their homes, these individuals often take them into the workplace. Many choose to pursue careers in companies with values that match their own. Or, if the values of the organization clash with their own, they seek to change the organization's culture in ways that fit their personal beliefs, rather than succumb to organizational pressures (Hall & Richter, 1990).

For example, Interface Inc. CEO Ray Anderson describes having a personal epiphany after reading *The Ecology of Commerce* by Paul Hawken (1993), which changed how he thought about the legacy of his company, its products, and manufacturing processes. With an increasing awareness of the environmental destructiveness of the carpets and fabrics it manufactured, Anderson came to believe the company could no longer pursue profits in the way it had. He not only changed the materials and processes it used to manufacture carpet to be less environmentally impactful and to recycle all materials, but went further and introduced a service business model to the carpet industry by leasing rather than selling carpet to consumers (therefore retaining responsibility for refurbishing worn carpet) without forgoing profitability (Anderson, 2007; Fishman, 1998).

Sustainability scholars and practitioners have celebrated Anderson's work and the change he continues to orchestrate in and through Interface, Inc., and have held him up as an example of what is possible. However, the field has done less to explain the shift he initiated. Through a POS lens, several explanations become available. First, the combination of reducing environmental impact *and* developing new markets in sustainable goods can be explained as organizing in a way that not only addresses deficit gaps, but also addresses abundance gaps (Cameron, 2007). Second, we can investigate the change that Anderson implemented in Interface as a result of switching to positive meaning making (Dutton & Sonenshein, 2008). Anderson realized that Interface's ways of operating were not sustainable, but rather than seeing this only as a threat (and considering ways to reduce environmental impact to avoid consequences), he also saw opportunities. Anderson identified how a service business model could work in a manufacturing industry and identified ways of operating that were both significantly more sustainable and full of profit potential and market leadership.

Third, there are significant leadership components to Anderson's actions. By combining sustainability and profitability through innovative business models, Anderson's style embodies positive leadership through his demonstration of virtuousness and focus on creating positive outcomes from negative situations, and his determination to drive his organization to exceptional achievement (Cameron & Lavine, 2006; Cameron, 2008; Flynn, 2008). Interface embodies Flynn's (2008, p. 359) argument that "[t]he coalescence of virtue and profit is possible only when daring, creative, and insightful business leadership is practiced in society."

But not all change emerges from positive deviants at the top of the corporate hierarchy, like Anderson. Often, sustainability-driven individuals are rank-and-file members who find themselves in the middle, mediating between conflicting value sets—their personal beliefs and those of the organizations in which they work. To resolve this tension, they seek to "fit" within both cultures. Known to both sustainability and POS scholars, these "tempered radicals" succeed according to the rules, protocols, and reward systems of the organization, but act in ways that concur with their personal beliefs (Meyerson & Scully, 1995). They continue to look like what the organization determines to be valid and appropriate, but are ambivalent to these norms. Through discrete, visible, positively biased actions that reflect individualized motivations, their programs of positive deviance become infectious and help to sculpt new beliefs and behaviors in the workplace that align with their own.

Peter Grant, an African American who had worked his way up to an executive-level banking position, is an example of a tempered radical identified by Meyerson (2001). Grant had a long-term aim of hiring highly qualified minorities and helping them to be successful in the bank. He did this at every opportunity, "chipping away at the organization's demographic base," one person at a time over a 30-year career (Meyerson, 2001, p. 95).

Tempered radicalism is a powerful concept for exploring the challenges that individuals face as they reconcile the competing demands and expectations of different value systems (Meyerson & Scully, 1995). For instance, they may be perceived (or perceive themselves) as hypocritical (Goffman, 1969), and feel isolated from both value systems. They must also withstand pressures for co-optation, to forfeit one side or the other. These perceptions and pressures may lead to emotional burdens of guilt or self-doubt about their effectiveness and importance (Kolb & Williams, 1993). Tempered radicals overcome these challenges by programmatically "chipping away" at them with initiatives that act as "small wins" on a path toward lasting organizational change (Hammonds, 2000). These individuals bring energy, creativity, and vitality to the organization and spiritual satisfaction for themselves. By thinking differently than the organizational norm, these positive deviants can also be critics of the status quo; identifying opportunities for change that may be overlooked by others.

Cultural creatives, LOHAS consumers, positive leaders, and tempered radicals use their positive deviance to pursue sustainability in their personal lives, organizations, and society. These change agents remind us (in the spirit of Gandhi) that individuals can be the change they want to see in the world. Drawing upon concepts and models from POS, sustainability scholars can gain greater insights into the ways that individuals play these key roles in the pursuit of sustainability. The next section will consider ways in which positive deviance manifests at the organizational level of analysis.

Positive Sustainability Deviance at the Organizational Level

Moving beyond the level of the individual, we can also observe organizations that are playing instrumental roles in changing industrial norms by addressing social and environmental issues, and competing on the basis of sustainability to yield positive social, environmental, and economic benefits. The most evocative examples of positive organizational deviance can be found among companies with business models that blur the boundary between the for-profit and nonprofit worlds. These companies have been described as *fourth sector, blended value, for-benefit, values driven* or *mission driven organizations,* or *B-corporations*—or, what we use in this chapter: *hybrid organizations* (Alter, 2004; Boyd, Henning, Reyna, Wang, & Welch, 2009; Hoffman, Badiene and Haigh, forthcoming). These new organizational forms adopt social missions like a nonprofit but generate income to accomplish that mission like a for-profit entity. They operate on the notion that traditional nonprofit operating models are no longer adequate to address the environmental and social problems of our day (Boyd, et al., 2009) and that a new emphasis on social enterprise models provides promise for achieving sustainability goals. Their business models do not seek to comply with prevailing environmental regulation or community expectations, or address the ills of the past. Rather, they seek to build profitable organizations and markets in the service of addressing their causes while creating broad-scale institutional change. In effect, sustainability is simply a core aspect of their organizational identity (Hamilton & Gioia, 2009) that enhances their ability to innovate and generate revenues in ways that enrich the social and environmental systems in which they operate.

One such example is Guayakí, a for-profit company that sells organic, fair trade, rainforest-grown Yerba maté (a type of tisane, or herbal tea) to deliver products that are beneficial to well-being and health while using business models that drive and facilitate reforestation and provide employees with living wages that benefit farmers and indigenous communities (Boyd et al., 2009). Guayakí pays its farmers above-market wages and devotes significant time and resources to training them in sustainable farming techniques. There are easier and cheaper ways to obtain their raw materials and resources, and CEO Chris Mann acknowledges that his company could expand faster if it were willing to compromise its mission and source the ingredients in ways that do not promote the protection of Atlantic rainforests. But the social mission of the company holds equal prominence with the profit mandate. For instance, Mann noted that the company had struggled with the decision to bring on partner financing, because venture capitalists want high percentages of control, which would make it more difficult to maintain Guayakí's mission (Boyd et al., 2009).

Hybrid organizations like Guayakí are becoming a force for social change by resetting the norms of business practice—one of their stated goals. Their mission is about driving change in the norms, values, and beliefs of organizational and market systems. Sustainability scholars have studied their business models, strategies, structures, missions, market tactics, and measures of success. However, by examining hybrid organizations through a POS lens, we can begin to explore the ways in which they pursue profit to support sustainability-oriented missions through positive deviance.

Another example of positive sustainable deviance is Green Mountain Coffee Roasters (GMCR). GMCR competes on the basis of its ethical and environmental principles, and has been rated by *Forbes* magazine as the leading ethical company in the United States, while growing to $180 million in sales revenue (Neville, 2008). GMCR takes the view that "knowledgeable and dedicated farmers and distributors are just as important to GMCR as employees within the corporate headquarters," and that they all contribute to an exceptional coffee experience for consumers (Neville, 2008, p. 565). Employees retell stories of how they travel to where the coffee is grown to help them appreciate the natural environment, and of how an executive personally extended a $3,000 interest-free loan to a new employee whose partner was diagnosed with cancer. Such stories reflect a culture embedded in values of compassion, integrity, optimism, and corporate success. They represent a shift to an "abundance approach" to management (Cameron & Lavine, 2006) and demonstrate that organizational virtuousness can be correlated with high performance (Cameron, Bright, & Caza, 2004).

Neville (2008, p. 569) termed the philosophy of GMCR as "conscience capitalism," which recognizes the interconnectedness between people, organizations, and society; sees wealth as stretching far beyond financial status; and operates on organizational time horizons that span multiple generations. A key mechanism underpinning GMCR's ability to flourish was its use of appreciative inquiry methods. In this case, the use of Whitney and Cooperrider's (2000) 4-D discovery, dream, design, and destiny process helped to facilitate strategy development within the company and enabled it to affirm an image infused with positive meaning. This, in turn, yielded action that had positive implications for how stakeholders interrelated and related to the natural environment.

These examples, and the use of the POS lens to understand them, are in counterpoint to the predominant sustainability research that investigates ways in which individuals and organizations address their negative deviance—focusing on how they become less unsustainable. They represent a redirection toward understanding how and why companies become more sustainable and positively deviate. This shift is vastly open to future research (Neville, 2008). The holistic and interconnected thinking found at hybrid organizations like GMCR and Guayakí leads to a critical linkage between sustainability and POS perspectives; the relationship between human/organizational flourishing and natural environmental flourishing.

Environmental and Human/Organizational Flourishing

Positive organizational scholars recognize that human flourishing is contextually embedded (Dutton & Glynn, 2008), whereas sustainability scholars recognize that the ability for people and organizations to flourish is embedded within a stable and balanced natural and social environment (Stead & Stead, 2009). As Harper (2001, p. 37) explains:

> [H]umans and human systems are unarguably embedded in the broader webs of life in the

biosphere. We are one species among many, both in terms of our biological makeup and our ultimate dependence for food and energy provided by the earth.

At the most rudimentary level, the natural environment provides people and organizations with raw materials, water, air, energy, and the bare physical context in which life and business is conducted (Haigh & Griffiths, 2009; Starik, 1995; Stead & Stead, 2004). Services provided by the natural environment, such as air and water purification provided by forests, waste assimilation, and air and water currents provided by oceans and wind, makes many of these resources renewable (therefore making our relationship with them more sustainable).

But, at a deeper level, the connection between the natural environment and flourishing extends and enhances POS principles and demonstrates the embeddedness of human flourishing in the natural environment. If humans can learn to work with natural systems rather than exploit them, both humans and nature will flourish. The difficulty is in avoiding the temptation to think of ways to "fix" nature (beyond restoring ecosystems that have been severely affected by humans), since nature is not broken. If sustainability is to be achieved, the need is for humans to understand, work with, and flourish within the bounds and dynamics presented by biophysical systems. Below, we offer to two examples to explain this connection.

Individual Flourishing and the Natural Environment

Richard Louv (2005) studied the reasons and implications for people (children specifically) losing their connection to the natural environment through modern Western lifestyles. Similar to what Wilson describes as "biophilia," the "the innate tendency [in human beings] to focus on life and lifelike processes" (Wilson, 1984), and Kaplan and Kaplan's (1989, p. 119) work showing that time spent in natural settings "restores depleted mental energies," Louv argued that the loss of connection to the natural environment could be a factor in the rise in emotional, mental, and physical maladies, such as attention-deficit hyperactivity disorder, childhood heart and circulatory problems, and diminished use of the senses. Louv (2005) cited a host of reasons for children spending less time in nature, including stranger danger fears, liability concerns, a reduced appreciation by parents of unstructured playtime, computer games, increased homework, and the simple fact of there being less nature available. He argued that all these factors have contributed to the growing divide between children and nature, or "nature-deficit disorder," and advocated for the restorative power of nature and the importance that time spent in nature has for the emotional and mental development of children. As an example of nature's positive influences, Louv highlighted that children who attend schools sited within natural settings "are more physically active, more aware of nutrition, more civil to one another, and more creative" (Louv, 2005, p. 220).

Teachers of these students also benefit, expressing "renewed enthusiasm for teaching" and a realization of their passion for teaching when doing so outdoors and at schools with more green space (Louv, 2005, p. 220). Thus, natural settings appear to have strong implications for the ability of these teachers to thrive at work. Extending Spreitzer et al.'s (2005) work on the social aspects of the work unit and resources produced in doing work, there appears an opportunity to explore how nature (or natural settings) is an equally important element of the work context. Human thriving at work can be seen as both socially and environmentally embedded by complementing POS and sustainability perspectives. For example, exposure to natural settings could moderate the ability of work contexts to facilitate the agentic work behaviors that Spreitzer et al. (2005) argue contribute to thriving.

The processual aspects of Louv's (2005) work are also worth highlighting, as natural settings appear to enhance key processes that the POS literature advocates as being central to flourishing: positive meaning making, positive emoting, and positive interrelating (Dutton & Glynn, 2008; Dutton & Sonenshein, 2008). Specifically, this work shows positive meaning making and positive emoting among teachers through statements about "renewed enthusiasm" and "passion" for their chosen profession, and positive interrelating among students as they treat each other with more civility if they have experienced schools with green spaces.

Organizational Flourishing and the Natural Environment

Organizations also have a very close relationship with the natural environment, although this is often overlooked outside the sustainability literature. For instance, it has been shown that the reintroduction of previously lost species (e.g., salmon into Lake Erie and the Thames; Harper, 2001) can play a significant role in rejuvenating heavily degraded ecosystems.

The rejuvenation improves the health of surrounding communities and industry by improving the ability to utilize resources from the ecosystem (in the salmon example, these resources may be fresher water, the salmon themselves, predators of salmon, etc.). Sustainability is not about helping to "save the planet," since Earth has survived significant previous stresses to its systems (e.g., the comet or meteor credited with dinosaur extinction). Rather, sustainability is about reestablishing and sustaining a "human-friendly habitat" on the planet (Stead & Stead, 2009, p. 3).

To exemplify this key point, we turn to companies that seek not only to understand their relationship with the natural environment, but also to actively use an understanding of natural dynamics to enhance their business models. For example, PAX Scientific is an engineering research and development company that uses *biomimicry* (Benyus, 2002) to design improved air- and fluid-handling equipment (Boyd et al., 2009). Biomimicry is the practice of learning from and imitating nature's designs and/ or processes in man-made systems. Well-known products that are the result of biomimicry include hypodermic needles and Velcro® (Environment, 2002; Post, 2007). The founder of PAX Scientific calls nature the "supreme designer" (Boyd et al., 2009, p. 129), and the company leveraged the design and efficient function of nature's vortices and spirals (e.g., hurricanes) to develop technologies such as water mixers, air fans, propellers, and turbines, which they patent and license. In addition to using nature's design principles, these products also have positive environmental and health outcomes. For instance, one potable water mixer designed by PAX Scientific provided higher-quality water that averted bacterial growth, thus enhancing health not only through bacteria control, but also by enabling an 85% reduction in the use of chemical disinfectant.

Just as Louv (2005) argued that nature nurtures creativity among children, PAX Scientific demonstrates that nature also provides design templates for creativity and innovation (Boyd et al., 2009) for organizations, topics of great interest within the POS literature (Dutton & Glynn, 2008). Such considerations potentially extend to studies of the role of nature in innovation. For instance, in their study of the relationship between trust, connectivity, thriving, and employees' innovative behaviors at work, Carmeli and Spreitzer (2009) found that connectivity mediated the relationship between trust and thriving, and thriving mediated the relationship between connectivity and innovative behaviors. Louv's (2005) observations and PAX Scientific's (Boyd et al., 2009) practices prompt us to ask questions about the role that human connectivity with the natural environment might play in innovation. More broadly, the PAX Scientific case study and Louv's (2005) work lead us to consider the possibility that connectivity encompasses not only that between humans (Dutton & Heaphy, 2003; Losada & Heaphy, 2004), but also that between humans and the natural environment.

Human flourishing is embedded in the natural environment. People and organizations draw value from and generate new ideas through connections with the natural environment, as well as better connections with each other. The two comprise a complete system managing the complexity, diversity, and irreducibility of sustainability issues and the relationship of organizations to them (Cooperrider, Sorenson, Whitney, & Yeager, 2000; Shrivastava & Cooperrider, 1999). This encompassing system generates an ecological perspective in which "all the pieces of the puzzle come together in one place and everyone can gain an appreciation for the whole" and "environmental and social performance [becomes] an opportunity for innovation, profit, and growth" (Laszlo & Cooperrider, 2008, p. 18).

These examples show how the sustainability domain can provide ground for POS scholars to not only explain human and organizational flourishing in a social sense, but to extend this expertise to exploring ways in which human and organizational flourishing is embedded within the condition of the natural world. In this sense, we see that POS capabilities, such as generativity, resilience, thriving, and endogenous resourcing, may enable a fuller appreciation of how humanity and our economic activity relates to the natural environment, and we see potential value in both fostering them on a practical level within organizations and communities, and studying them to track their sustainability.

Future Directions

The objective of this chapter is to invite POS and sustainability scholars to further examine the linkages between their domains, and to identify and pursue ways in which the two may complement and improve each other. These linkages highlight ways in which complementing POS and sustainability research domains can help scholars to revisit existing research questions in their own domain and generate new questions.

Revisiting Existing Research Questions and Developing New Ones

This chapter motivates us to revisit existing research questions and develop new questions in three ways. First, it prompts us to consider ways in which a POS perspective can help to shift sustainability from a focus on people and organizations being less unsustainable, to becoming more sustainable, from explaining deficit gaps to instead addressing abundance gaps (Cameron, 2007). Questions in this track include: What is the form of the shift from addressing less unsustainable ways of organizing to more sustainable ways? What contexts, processes, and mechanisms can explain the dynamics that lead to this shift? What are the antecedents and implications of this shift for organizations? What measures track the move? What can firms that were established under the traditional (rational) premises of organizing learn from organizations (such as hybrids) that were established under sustainability premises? What are the tactics and strategies that can be used by positive deviants to facilitate this shift? What are the underlying cognitive and cultural beliefs that may impede this shift in consciousness, and how can they be overcome?

The second track in which existing research questions are revisited involves an expansion of the POS perspective beyond a focus on human flourishing to include an appreciation for its embeddedness within the natural environment. This linkage raises questions such as: What underpins individual and organizational learning about and from nature's systems, communities, designs, and dynamics? What can organizations borrow from nature's ecosystems and communities? How do natural contexts and dynamics explain human flourishing? How does an integration of human flourishing within the natural environment change basic conceptions of what it means to be human?

Third, this chapter raises new research questions and opens a new stream of research that challenges POS and sustainability scholars to identify new variables, explanatory mechanisms, processes, and measures. In this area, key new questions are: Does working toward environmental sustainability simultaneously enhance human flourishing? What aspects of social and environmental sustainability sustain positive deviance? Does concern for the natural environment alter conceptions or tactics of positive deviance? How do we measure human flourishing in conjunction with natural environment flourishing?

Before closing, we consider one final issue in our examination of the POS–sustainability linkages.

Since academic scholars live not only in the world of research, but also in the world of business education, the linkages between these domains offer critical opportunities for addressing pressing issues in management education.

Future Directions in Business Education

At the time of writing this chapter, confidence in the business world is very low and resentment is directed toward MBA education programs that do not promote critical thinking and moral reasoning skills development among their students, that take a fragmented approach to management, and that have trained graduates who played central roles in scandals such as Enron and Worldcom, and in the financial crisis (Podolny, 2009). Calling attention to these issues means asking questions about what and who managers are and asking about the purpose of leadership (Khurana, 2007). Today, within modern business schools, little sustained attention is paid to critical sustainability issues like poverty, climate change, species extinction, social unrest, equity, and fairness in a rapidly globalized world. These social and environmental ills present challenges to the dominant organizing models of business education (such as agency theory and investor capitalism) that POS and sustainability can begin to address.

Although scholars can begin to push this shift in emphasis, change may also be promoted from within. New MBA applicants are increasingly drawn from the cultural creatives, tempered radicals and LOHAS consumers demographic sectors noted earlier. Students are driving business school administrators to address environmental and social awareness in curricula, operations, and development. The rise of alternative business school and university rankings, such as The Aspen Institute's *Beyond Grey Pinstripes* and the Sierra Club's *Cool Schools* list, and the introduction of sustainability into Association to Advance Collegiate Schools of Business (AACSB) requirements are testament to this.

Linked, sustainability and POS scholars can help to address the growing issues facing business schools today by bringing a more holistic and humanistic approach to business education. Positive organizational scholarship and sustainability curricula and research have the scope to help students and managers understand the complexity of businesses and issues facing them without becoming overwhelmed by them, to learn ways to develop and meet short- and long-term business goals that extend beyond earning money, and to learn ways in which organizations can be naturally generative, competitive, and innovative. A broader educational approach that addresses sustainability and is guided by POS works toward developing managers who have the ability to question dominant mindsets and play the role of social or institutional entrepreneur to develop innovative solutions to intractable global issues (in which firms have historically only played a negative role).

Conclusion

Perspectives from the POS research domain provide sustainability scholars with an avenue to investigate the role that individuals and organizations play in shifting society toward becoming *more sustainable* rather than *less unsustainable*. Correspondingly, perspectives from the sustainability research domain push POS scholars beyond an appreciation of human flourishing, to recognizing its embeddedness within the natural world. In this sense, POS traits such as generativity, resilience, and endogenous resourcing can enable a fuller appreciation of how humanity relates to the natural environment, and may be viewed as measures of our ability to pursue and achieve sustainability.

The empirical platform that grounds sustainability scholars—the natural environment—is the essence of generativity and abundance without waste. This platform also provides POS scholars with great destructive and regenerative polar contexts and a full range of states from birth/generation through to growth, maturity, decay, death, and rebirth/regeneration to study topics such as resilience, vitality, endogenous resourcing, meaningfulness and flourishing. Sustainability challenges us to develop a vision, mission, purpose, calling, or vocation through work that will sustain a positively deviant balance between social, environmental, and competitive realms. Positive organizational scholarship challenges us to ensure that we, our colleagues, and our organizations develop or retain high levels of compassion, virtue, resourcefulness, and care, with the understanding that the vision is not achievable or sustainable without them. Together, the two domains can enrich each other, their mutual research agendas, and practical contributions toward achieving a sustainable world.

Acknowledgments

The authors would like to acknowledge the financial support of the Frederick A. and Barbara M. Erb Institute for Global Sustainable Enterprise at the University of Michigan.

References

Alter, K. (2004). *Social enterprise typology*. Seattle: Virtue Ventures LLC.

Anderson, R.C. (2007). Refining the vision. *Environmental Design & Construction, 10*(2), 28–30.

Benyus, J.M. (2002). *Biomimicry: Innovation inspired by nature*. New York: Harper Collins Publishers.

Boyd, B., Henning, N., Reyna, E., Wang, D.E., & Welch, M.D. (2009). *Hybrid organizations: New business models for environmental leadership*. Sheffield, UK: Greenleaf Publishing.

Cameron, K., Bright, D., & Caza, A. (2004). Exploring the relationships between organizational virtuousness and performance. *American Behavioral Scientist, 47*(6), 1–24.

Cameron, K., & Lavine, M. (2006). *Making the impossible possible: Leading extraordinary performance: The Rocky Flats story*. San Francisco: Berrett-Koehler Publishers.

Cameron, K.S. (2007). Positive organizational scholarship. In S. Clegg, & J. Bailey (Eds.), *International encyclopedia of organizational studies*. Beverly Hills: Sage.

Cameron, K.S. (2008). *Positive leadership: Strategies for extraordinary performance*. San Francisco: Berrett-Koehler.

Carmeli, A., & Spreitzer, G. (2009). Trust, connectivity, and thriving: Implications for innovative work behavior. *Journal of Creative Behavior, 43*(3), 169–191.

Carson, R. (1962). *Silent spring*. Boston: Houghton Mifflin.

Cash, K., Gray, G., & Rood, S. (2000). A framework for accommodating religion and spirituality in the workplace. *Academy of Management Executive, 14*, 124–134.

Christmann, P. (2000). Effects of "best practices" of environmental management on cost advantage: The role of complementary assets. *Academy of Management Journal, 43*(4), 663–680.

Colby, M. (1991). Environmental management in development: The evolution of paradigms. *Ecological Economics, 3*, 193–213.

Cooperrider, D.L., Sorenson, P.E., Whitney, D., & Yeager, T.E. (Eds.). (2000). *Appreciative inquiry*. Champaign, IL: Jossey Bass.

Cortese, A. (2003, July 20). Business: They care about the world (and they shop, too). *New York Times*.

Covey, S. (1995). *First things first*. New York: Simon & Schuster.

Crossette, B. (1998, September 27). Kofi Annan's astonishing facts. *New York Times*, 4–16.

Dutton, J.E., & Glynn, M.A. (2008). Positive organizational scholarship. In J. Barling, & C.L. Cooper (Eds.), *The SAGE handbook of organizational behavior* (pp. 693–712). Los Angeles: Sage.

Dutton, J.E., & Heaphy, E.D. (2003). The power of high-quality connections. In K.S. Cameron, J.E. Dutton, & R.E. Quinn (Eds.), *Positive organizational scholarship: Foundations of a new discipline*. San Francisco: Berret-Koehler.

Dutton, J.E., & Sonenshein, S. (2008). Positive organizational scholarship. In S. Lopez, & A. Beauchamps (Eds.), *Encyclopedia of positive psychology*. Oxford, UK: Blackwell Publishing.

Ehrenfeld, J.R. (2008). *Sustainability by design*. New Haven, CT: Yale University Press.

Elkington, J. (1997). *Cannibals with forks: The triple bottom line of 21st century business*. Oxford, UK: Capstone.

Environment. (2002). Natural designs. *Environment, 44*(2), 4.

Fishman, C. (1998). Sustainable growth - Interface, Inc. *Fast Company*. Retrieved from http://www.fastcompany.com/magazine/14/sustaing.html.

Flynn, G. (2008). The virtuous manager: A vision for leadership in business. *Journal of Business Ethics, 78*(3), 359–372.

Goffman, E. (1969). *The presentation of self in everyday life*. New York: Doubleday.

Haigh, N.L., & Griffiths, A. (2009). The natural environment as primary stakeholder: The case of climate change. *Business Strategy and the Environment, 18*(6), 347–359.

Hall, D.T., & Mirvis, P. (1996). The new protean career: Psychological success and the path with a heart. In D.T. Hall (Ed.), *The career is dead, long live the career: A relational approach to careers* (pp. 15–45). San Francisco: Jossey-Bass.

Hall, D.T., & Richter, J. (1990). Career gridlock: Baby boomers hit the wall. *Academy of Management Executive, 4*, 7–22.

Hamilton, A., & Gioia, D.A. (2009). Fostering sustainability-focussed organizational identities. In L.M. Roberts, & J.E. Dutton (Eds.), *Exploring positive identities and organizations: Building a theoretical and research foundation* (pp. 162–174). New York: Routledge.

Hammonds, K. (2000). Practical radicals: You say you want a business revolution? Not so fast. *Fast Company*, September, 162–174.

Harper, C.L. (2001). *Environment and society: Human perspectives on environmental issues*. Upper Saddle River, NJ: Prentice Hall.

Hart, S.L. (1995). A natural-resource-based view of the firm. *Academy of Management Review, 20*(4), 986–1014.

Hawken, P. (1993). *The ecology of commerce: A declaration of sustainability*. New York: HarperCollins.

Hoffman, A. (2003). Reconciling professional and personal value systems: The spiritually motivated manager as organizational entrepreneur. In R. Giacalone, & C. Jurkiewicz (Eds.), *The handbook of workplace spirituality and organizational performance* (1st ed., pp. 193–208). New York: M.E. Sharpe.

Hoffman, A., Badiene, K., & Haigh, K. (*forthcoming*). Hybrid organizations as agents of positive social change: Bridging the for-profit & non-profit divide. In K. Golden-& J. Dutton (Eds) *Exploring positive social change and organizations: Building and theoretical and research foundation* New York: Routledge, Taylor and Francis Group.

Jacobs, M. (1993). *The green economy: Environment, sustainable development and the politics of the future*. Vancouver, BC: UBC Press.

Judge, W.Q., & Douglas, T.J. (1998). Performance implications of incorporating natural environmental issues into the strategic planning process: An empirical assessment. *Journal of Management Studies, 35*(2), 241–262.

Kaplan, R., & Kaplan, S. (1989). *The experience of nature: A psychological perspective*. Cambridge, UK: Cambridge University Press.

Khurana, R. (2007). *From higher aims to hired hands: The social transformation of American business schools and the unfulfilled promise of management as a profession*. Princeton, NJ: Princeton University Press.

Kolb, D., & Williams, S. (1993). Professional women in conversation: Where have we been and where are we going? *Journal of Management Inquiry, 2*, 14–26.

Laszlo, C., & Cooperrider, D. (2007). Design for sustainable value: A whole system approach, In M. Avital, R. Boland, & D. Cooperrider (Eds.) *Designing information and organizations with a positive lens (Advances in Appreciative Inquiry, Volume 2)*, (pp. 15–29). Bingley, UK: Emerald Group Publishing Limited.

LOHAS. (2009). *Lifestyles of health and sustainability*. Retrieved from http://www.lohas.com/.

Losada, M., & Heaphy, E. (2004). The role of positivity and connectivity in the performance of business teams: A nonlinear dynamics model. *American Behavioral Scientist, 47*(6), 740–765.

Louv, R. (2005). *Last child in the woods: Saving our children from nature-deficit disorder*. Chapel Hill, NC: Algonquian Books of Chapel Hill.

Maslow, A. (1954). *Motivation and personality*. New York: HarperCollins.

McDonald, M. (1999). Shush. The guy in the next cubicle is meditating. *U.S. News & World Report, 126*(7), 46.

McDonough, W., & Braungart, M. (2002). *Cradle to cradle: Remaking the way we make things*. New York: North Point Press.

Menguc, B., & Ozanne, L.K. (2005). Challenges of the "green imperative": A natural resource-based approach to the environmental orientation—business performance relationship. *Journal of Business Research, 58*(4), 430–438.

Meyerson, D.E. (2001). Radical change the quiet way. *Harvard Business Review, 79*(9), 92–100.

Meyerson, D.E., & Scully, M.A. (1995). Tempered radicalism and the politics of ambivalence and change. *Organization Science, 6*(5), 585–600.

Mitroff, I., & Denton, E. (1999). A study of spirituality in the workplace. *Sloan Management Review, 40*(Summer), 83–92.

Murray, A. (2005, May 18). Will "social responsibility" harm business? *Wall Street Journal,* A2.

National Center for Health Statistics. (2004). *Health, United States, 2004*. Washington, DC: Department of Health and Human Services.

Neal, J. (2000). Work as service to the divine. *American Behavioral Scientist, 43,* 1316–1334.

Neck, C., & Milliman, J. (1994). Thought self-leadership: Finding spiritual fulfillment in organizational life. *Journal of Managerial Psychology, 9,* 9–16.

Neville, M.G. (2008). Positive deviance on the ethical continuum: Green Mountain Coffee as a case study in conscientious capitalism. *Business & Society Review, 113*(4), 555–576.

Podolny, J.M. (2009). The buck stops (and starts) at business school. *Harvard Business Review, 87*(6), 62–67.

Post, N.M. (2007). Designers begin to look to nature to render buildings in harmony with the planet. *ENR: Engineering News-Record, 258*(6), 23.

Ray, P.H., & Anderson, S.R. (2000). *The cultural creatives: How 50 million people are changing the world*. New York: Harmony Books.

Reid, W.V., Mooney, H.A., Cropper, A., Capistrano, D., Carpenter, S.R., Chopra, K., et al. (2005). *Millennium ecosystem assessment synthesis report*. London: World Resources Institute. Retrieved from www.millenniumassessment.org.

Russo, M.V., & Fouts, P.A. (1997). A resource-based perspective on corporate environmental performance and profitability. *Academy of Management Journal, 40*(3), 534–559.

Sandelands, L., & Hoffman, A.J. (2008). Sustainability, faith and the market. *Worldviews: Global Religions, Culture and Ecology, 12,* 129–145.

Schnaiberg, A. (1980). *The environment: From surplus to scarcity*. New York: Oxford University Press.

Sharma, S., & Vredenburg, H. (1998). Proactive corporate environmental strategy and the development of competitively valuable organizational capabilities. *Strategic Management Journal, 19,* 729–753.

Shrivastava, S., & Cooperrider, D.L. (1999). *Appreciative management and leadership: The power of positive thought and action in organization*. San Francisco: Jossey Bass.

Spreitzer, G., Sutcliffe, K., Dutton, J., Sonenshein, S., & Grant, A.M. (2005). A socially embedded model of thriving at work. *Organization Science, 16*(5), 537–549.

Spreitzer, G.M., & Sonenshein, S. (2004). Toward the construct definition of positive deviance. *The American Behavioral Scientist, 47*(6), 828–847.

Starik, M. (1995). Should trees have managerial standing? Toward stakeholder status for non-human nature. *Journal of Business Ethics, 14*(3), 207–217.

Stead, J.G., & Stead, W.E. (2004). *Sustainable strategic management*. Armonk, NY: M.E. Sharpe.

Stead, J.G., & Stead, W.E. (2009). *Management for a small planet*. Armonk, NY: M.E.Sharp.

Strassel, K. (2007, January 26). If the cap fits. *Wall Street Journal,* A10.

The Natural Marketing Institute. (2008). Excerpts from the 2006 understanding the LOHAS market report. In M.V. Russo (Ed.), *Environmental management: Readings and cases*. Thousand Oaks, CA: Sage Publications.

Thomas, W. (2002, June). Business and the journey towards sustainable development: Reflections on progress since Rio. *Environmental Law Reporter.*

United Nations. (2001). *Global status of biological diversity*. New York: United Nations Commission on Sustainable Development.

Wade-Benzoni, K., Hoffman, A., Thompson, L., Moore, D., Gillespie, J., & Bazerman, M. (2002). Barriers to resolution in ideologically based negotiations: The role of values and institutions. *Academy of Management Review, 27*(1), 41–57.

Whitney, D., & Cooperrider, D.L. (2000). The appreciative inquiry summit: An emerging methodology for whole system positive change. *Journal of the Organization Development Network, 32,* 13–26.

Wilson, E.O. (1984). *Biophilia*. Cambridge, MA: Harvard University Press.

World Business Council on Sustainable Development. (1997). *Exploring sustainable development: WBCSD global scenarios*. London: World Business Council on Sustainable Development.

World Commission on Environment and Development. (1987). *Our common future*. Oxford, UK: Oxford University Press.

World Resources Institute. (1994). *World resources*. Oxford, UK: Oxford University Press.

World Resources Institute. (2000). *World resources, 2000–2001: People and ecosystems*. Washington, DC: World Resources Institute.

Wrzesniewski, A., McCauley, C., Rozin, P., & Schwartz, B. (1997). Jobs, careers, and callings: People's relations to their work. *Journal of Research in Personality, 31,* 21–33.

Critical Theory and Positive Organizational Scholarship

Arran Caza *and* Brigid Carroll

Abstract

This chapter uses a critical theory perspective to consider previous work in positive organizational scholarship (POS). Questions raised by the critical management studies (CMS) concepts of performativity, denaturalization, and reflexivity highlight areas in which POS could benefit from a more critical approach. Specifically, this chapter calls on POS to be more explicit about its intended aims, to be careful of universalizing notions of positivity, and to consider the implications of some its seemingly innocent choices. Specific examples of how POS has done well and poorly in these areas are offered, as a first step toward an informative dialogue between POS and CMS. Such a dialogue is important, both for the likelihood of POS achieving its stated aim of creating beneficial change and for the continuing relevance of POS in the larger field of organizational studies.

Keywords: Critical management studies, performativity, reflexivity, denaturalization

To introduce this chapter, we invite the reader to imagine that they are preparing a presentation about their latest research. You will be speaking to a cross-section of military personnel. It will be a large group of late-career, senior officers, and almost entirely men. Imagine that you prepare your presentation for this audience, but then arrive to find that, instead, you will be speaking to a small group, almost entirely women, all of whom are new officers who have been identified as future leaders. Would you have prepared differently if you had known? Would you be thinking about how to adjust your talk even as you approached the podium? We suspect so. As a result of mistaken assumptions, your efforts to create a useful talk may go awry. At a minimum, your talk will not be as effective as it might have been, and it could be a failure.

In this example, we would have liked to correct your misunderstanding before you finalized the talk, to give you the chance to help your audience as much as possible. This chapter has the same intent. Our reading suggests that some prevalent assumptions

may be stopping positive organizational scholarship (POS) from achieving what its participants intend, and our aim is to highlight those assumptions. Specifically, we challenge the POS community to consider the possibility of managers and nonmanagers working together in new, strikingly different ways to create futures that are more dynamic and ambiguous than those envisioned by mainstream organizational studies, but which are also more empowering and more humane. We hope that this chapter will help to prevent the enthusiasm and good intentions of POS from going astray. As stated repeatedly in descriptions of POS, the goal is to improve the lives of those in organizations, to encourage flourishing and thriving. This is a laudable goal, and one we would like to support.

However, as we tried to suggest with the opening example, good intentions and good research do not guarantee good outcomes. Assumptions determine what actions are taken, and the consequences they produce. Highlighting this powerful influence from assumptions is an important part of critical management studies (CMS), and is at the heart of our chapter. We adopt a critical perspective here, because we worry that without it, POS may not be as effective as it could be in contributing to beneficial change. We hope to provoke insights and new thinking by using a critical perspective to highlight aspects of POS that may not have been explicitly examined before, but which nonetheless have significant consequences. By examining some of the assumptions and language used in POS, we intend to highlight potential contradictions and to create space for different interpretations and perspectives.

In some ways, this chapter is an example of how a POS–CMS dialogue might begin, because it is a product of addressing contradictions. One of the authors self-describes as a critical management researcher similar to Alvesson (2008, p. 17) in having "a moderate version of constructionism, some interest in 'reality out there,' some in ideologies/discourses and subjectivity, plus some interest in the specifics and details of language . . . radical humanism with a clear postmodernist (poststructuralist) bent." In contrast, the other author has pronounced positivist and modernist leanings, and despite being sensitive to the critiques of those positions, agrees with Parker (1995) in believing in the utility of "truth" as a concept. Writing together led to negotiation between our differing views about knowledge, the role of the researcher, and the aim of the argument. These differences are not resolved, nor should they be. The goal here is dialogue, not conclusion. We hope to provoke similar dialogue and rethinking between CMS and POS.

In keeping with this goal, we have made an effort to engage POS in its own terms when possible. Our reading of POS suggests that it is based in a modernist, science-oriented ontology. The majority of POS research that we examined makes assumptions about the "true" nature of people and aims to use the scientific method to uncover enduring, universal knowledge in the service of progress. This contrasts with most of CMS, in which the prevalent position is constructionism, in which any "truth" is a product of complex relational, situational, and contextual dimensions (Alvesson, 2008). In this view, knowledge can never be treated as "facts," in the sense of being value neutral; any claim of truth is an exercise of power that favors some at the expense of others. Because of this ontological difference between POS and CMS, our comments sometimes take two forms. The first tries to express our concerns within the ontology adopted by POS. The second adopts a more consciously CMS paradigm,

one that is often essential for the critique to be meaningful. We hope that this two-part format provokes new considerations for readers.

The chapter is organized in five sections. The first describes what we mean by CMS, and the second explains how we understand POS. These are followed by two sections in which we bring these understandings into contact. We first consider issues in how the aims of POS are formally stated, and then we do the same with some examples of how POS research has been reported. We conclude with possibilities for continuing the dialogue.

Critical Theory in Management Studies

We begin by describing the specific critical perspective that we use in this chapter. This is important, because there is no normative agreement on the aims and content of critical theory. In the most traditional and historical sense, critical theory refers to the work of the Frankfurt school and associated scholars such as Adorno, Marcuse, Habermas, and Anderson. However, in practice, "critical theory," and the even narrower "critical management studies," involves a range of perspectives, which have been characterized as different branches (Alvesson, 2008) or competing arguments (D. Grant, Iedema, & Oswick, 2010). As a general approach, CMS is probably most widely known for its critique of management and life inside organizations, and is often characterized as displaying a negative attitude toward organizations. In fact, it is the "experience of unhappiness which is the wedge critical theory uses to justify" its observations and critique (Alvesson & Willmot, 1992, p. 439). Implicit in this is an oppositional stance toward management, which suggests that "to be engaged in critical management studies means, at the most basic level, to say there is something wrong with management as a practice and as a body of knowledge" (Fournier & Grey, 2000, p. 16). This view argues that organizations should not be "presented as a self-evident force for good" (Alvesson, Bridgeman, & Willmot, 2010, p. 6) and that there is always a dark side in management practice (Alvesson, 2008).

Described this way, CMS would seem to be the opposite of POS. Where POS seeks to highlight the positive aspects of organizational life, CMS is often seen as most concerned with the negative. However, we do not agree. For one, as we discuss below, "positive" and "negative" are descriptors that require significant qualification. They are only meaningful if one answers fundamental questions such as "positive for whom?" and "to what effect?" Moreover, although

CMS may be most visible in its antimanagement position, the intent of critical theory is not inherently antimanagement (Alvesson & Willmot, 1992). In our view, being critical means paying attention to that which is absent, marginalized, or silenced in the business of organizing (Alvesson, 2008). Critical management studies recognize that people are shaped by the interdependence of organizing, and that this shaping inevitably favors some parties at the expense of others. It is therefore important to recognize these asymmetries in an effort to make organizations "less irrational and socially divisive" (Fournier & Grey, 2000, p. 23). In particular, Horkheimer (1976, p. 220) described critical theory as being "motivated by the effort to transcend the tension and to abolish the opposition between the individual's purposefulness, spontaneity, and rationality, and those work-process relationships on which society is built."

Our approach in this chapter builds on Fournier and Grey's (2000) three elements of performativity, denaturalization, and reflexivity, supplemented by Spicer, Alvesson, and Karreman's (2009) critique of the performativity component. Fournier and Grey (2000) offered their three elements as a minimal set that could be used to characterize CMS as a whole. Their formulation has attracted many supporters, but also many detractors. For example, Thompson (2004) noted that some work that is not part of CMS involves aspects of the three elements, and that some work that all would agree is part of CMS does not consider the three elements particularly significant. Even allowing these concerns, we believe that Fournier and Grey's (2000) three elements offer a promising place to begin our pursuit of a CMS–POS dialogue. Therefore, we discuss each of the three elements below, then use them as a framework to highlight how a critical perspective might influence the development of POS.

Following Fournier and Grey (2000), we use *performativity* to refer to the issue of automatically making traditional business-related outcomes (e.g., efficiency, profit) the top priority in organizations. Adopting a critical perspective helps to highlight the default and unquestioned dominance of economic performance in mainstream organizational studies; financial results are typically treated as the most important of all outcomes. Admittedly, profit may be a valid and important goal in many situations, but its validity and importance should be assessed, not treated as automatic or exclusive of other concerns. The logic of maximizing output from minimum input is only one way to assess

organizational life, and its preeminence should be challenged. There may be many other outcomes of equal or greater value (e.g., health, peace, development).

However, as Spicer and colleagues (2009) note, simply challenging the dominance of economic performance is not sufficient. A purely antiperformance stance commits to negativism by failing to offer a solution for change. As such, an alternative performance standard must be provided. Spicer and colleagues (2009) propose a critical performativity comprised of five elements: affirmative stance, normative orientation, working with potential, pragmatism, and ethic of care. Their argument is that judgments of organizational success must include these criteria, not simply financial results. Outcomes other than business performance can be valuable in themselves, not just as means to economic ends. Autonomy, democracy, equality, ecological balance, and other outcomes may be desirable for their own sake, independent of, and potentially even in conflict with, organizations' economic performance (Alvesson, 2008).

Denaturalization concerns revealing the constructedness of organizations and organizing processes. That is, it makes visible the "'un-naturalness' or irrationality" of current practice (Fournier & Grey, 2000, p. 18). In the absence of denaturalization, existing social processes can be reified or experienced as "natural," and this assumption of naturalness prevents the consideration of alternatives (Weick, 2006). Activities and relationships established for the sake of organizing become legitimized and inviolable when they are viewed as inevitable, objective states. For example, if all business organizations are arranged in part around power-based hierarchies, one may come to believe that hierarchy is inherently part of organizing, rather than merely an aspect of how organizing is currently practiced. Denaturalization calls for examination of the historical, cultural, and social construction of current practices, so that they cannot be assumed to be inevitable or inherent.

Reflexivity calls for an awareness of one's personal practice and its implications. This applies both to philosophical and methodological concerns. In the absence of reflexivity, one imposes one's own assumptions on what is treated as relevant, and even possible (Fournier & Grey, 2000). Reflexivity asks that researchers consider the influence that arises from what they pay attention to and what they create through their actions. For example, reflexivity highlights that "objectivity, neutrality, and universality" are working ideologies, rather than existential realities (Alvesson, Bridgeman, & Willmott, 2010, p. 9). As such, positivism is an approach to be argued for, not an assumption from which to begin. Epistemologies and ideologies are always part of research, but they should be handled with an awareness of their presence and their consequences.

These three elements are closely interrelated, and serve not so much as a template, but as a guide to inquiry. Each element suggests questions with which one may consider the work of a discipline such as POS (see Table 73.1). In this chapter, we begin to ask these questions of POS. In doing so, we hope to prevent POS from falling into the traps its predecessors have, so that it does not become a "false and stunted humanism . . . wanting change without really changing anything" (Aktouf, 1992, p. 412).

Our Interpretation of Positive Organizational Scholarship

To say anything about POS requires first clarifying what constitutes POS. Doing so involves defining boundaries, which is of particular significance to those advocating a critical perspective. Critical management studies are concerned with the marginalized and the excluded, with the exercise of power inherent in allocating status. Assigning membership is necessarily an act of exclusion: Some will be given status and recognition while others are excluded.

Since POS is still comparatively new, and is intended to be encompassing of diverse work

(Cameron, Dutton, & Robert E. Quinn, 2003b), the specifics of what is and is not POS are ambiguous. In recognition of this, we adopted a conservative approach, with the intent of choosing an interpretation of POS that we believe would be recognized and accepted by most insiders. This influenced several of our decisions about what we would treat as constituting POS. For one, we chose to follow stated POS practice and restrict our consideration to studies of organizational phenomena (Cameron et al., 2003a; Dutton & Sonenshein, 2009). Positive organizational scholarship has been described as the contextualized cousin of positive psychology, as it pursues the same humanistic aims, but does so with particular attention paid to the role of organizational processes and environments (Dutton & Glynn, 2008; Dutton, Glynn, & Spreitzer, 2006). In keeping with this, we limited ourselves to organizational studies. As well, consistent with prior POS claims (Dutton et al., 2006; Roberts, 2006), we considered research identifying itself as part of the positive organizational behavior (POB) tradition to be part of the larger POS whole.

The second decision we made was to restrict our consideration to peer-reviewed journal articles. In doing so, we do not intend to denigrate the importance of nonreviewed scholarship, but we believe that this decision is consistent with the stated aims of POS, which stress the importance of "empirical

Table 73.1 Three elements of critical inquiry

Element	Description	Questions Raised
Critical performativity	Challenge the automatic dominance of financial and economic performance; consider other outcomes that may be of equal or greater importance in organizations.	What goals and values does POS explicitly pursue? What goals and values are implicitly supported, because they are not challenged? What, if any, outcomes are just as important as profit? What, if any, outcomes are worth pursuing, even at the expense of profit?
Denaturalization	Recognize the constructed nature of judgments and labels.	What is being taken for granted about: Individuals? Groups? Relations among people? The nature of organizing? What possibilities do these assumptions preclude?
Reflexivity	Consider the implications of one's choices and the possibilities that those choices preclude.	Who and what are (implicitly) made negative by not receiving the label "positive"? What does POS make most important in organizations? Who and what is studied? In what ways? How do these choices influence what POS can say, and how it can say it?

credibility and theoretical explanations [based on] rigorous, systematic, and theory-based foundations [that show] consistency with scientific procedures in drawing conclusions" (Cameron et al., 2003a, p. 6; also see Cameron, 2007; Dutton et al., 2006). The only exception we made to the reviewed article decision was the inclusion of eight book chapters that are formal statements of the nature of POS (discussed below).

However, even restricting attention to peer-reviewed articles addressing organizational phenomena still leaves considerable uncertainty about what constitutes POS. For example, since POS has repeatedly been described as "not new," in the sense that it makes no claim to have invented a focus on positive phenomena, but rather aims to unite relevant previous work (Cameron, 2007; Cameron et al., 2003a; Dutton & Glynn, 2008; Dutton & Sonenshein, 2009), there are many scholars who could be understood to have been "doing" POS before POS existed. This raises the question of whether their recent work should be considered part of POS. As well, in addition to the work that explicitly draws on statements of POS, an even larger body of research appears to be studying phenomena claimed as part of POS. For example, using the Social Science Citation Index to conduct forward citation searches on the 11 formal statements of the domain of POS, as well as on Luthans' (2002) description of POB, we found more than 100 articles (based on a search conducted March 20, 2010). If one expands this to an ABI-INFORM database search of the years 2002–2010 using POS keywords such as "thriving" and "flourishing," the potential literature of POS increases by more than 200 articles (again, as of March 20, 2010). We suspect that POS insiders would assign these more than 300 articles varying degrees of inclusion, and that some would be excluded.

Therefore, to be confident that what we are critiquing is only what "truly is" POS, we adopted a more restrictive list. Using the website of the Center for Positive Organizational Scholarship (http://www.bus.umich.edu/Positive) and the publication records of the three POS founders (i.e., Cameron, Dutton, and Quinn; see Bernstein, 2003), we were able to identify three articles and eight chapters that appear to be official statements about the nature of POS. We used these to form our interpretation of what POS is formally espoused to be. We then developed a list of 35 peer-reviewed articles that appear to be unequivocally POS research, as they are officially endorsed by the Center for POS.[1] We used the Center's own list of recent publications (http://www.bus.umich.edu/Positive/CPOS/Publications/recentworkingpapers.html, accessed March 18, 2010), historical report (Center for Positive Organizational Scholarship, 2007), report of research impact (Center for Positive Organizational Scholarship, n.d.), and current activity highlight report (Center for Positive Organizational Scholarship, 2010) to identify the 35 articles that we used in our analysis of enacted POS.

Positive Organizational Scholarship As Espoused

In this section, we ask questions that are raised by a critical examination of the 11 formal statements of the domain of POS. These statements often summarize the nature of POS by contrasting it with what POS is not. For example, "theories of problem solving, reciprocity and justice, managing uncertainty, overcoming resistance, achieving profitability, and competing successfully against others" are used as examples of organizational phenomena that are of relatively little concern to POS (Cameron et al., 2003a, p. 3). Although not denying the importance of these issues, POS is positioned as a call to emphasize other phenomena, including "excellence, transcendence, positive deviance, extraordinary performance, and positive spirals of flourishing" (Cameron et al., 2003a, p. 3). Positive organizational scholarship describes itself as being concerned with every aspect of positive organizational phenomena, including their causes, consequences, and mechanisms (Dutton et al., 2006; Roberts, 2006; Spreitzer, 2008). It is argued that studying positive phenomena may provide new ways to understand familiar outcomes (e.g., authenticity's role in leadership, Avolio & Gardner, 2005; the role of virtue in organizational performance, Cameron, Bright, & Caza, 2004), and it may reveal important outcomes that have previously been neglected (e.g., compassion organizing, Dutton, Worline, Frost, & Lilius, 2006; flow states, Ryan W. Quinn, 2005).

However, the specifics of positivity remain unclear (Caza & Cameron, 2008; Fineman, 2006; George, 2004). The formal statements of POS have consistently stated that the discipline is concerned with understanding positive phenomena, but offered little guidance for distinguishing positive from negative. The most common device used to describe what constitutes positivity is reference to positive deviance: to "especially positive deviance from anticipated patterns . . . that which is unexpectedly positive" (Cameron, 2007) or to "above normal, extraordinary states that are good, honorable, or virtuous" (Dutton et al., 2006, p. 642). However, these descriptions only defer the question, rather than answer it. One must then ask: Positively deviant relative to what? Who judges the honor or virtue of the result?

In this matter of emphasizing the positive, we are encouraged that POS explicitly recognizes its "positive bias" (Cameron, 2007, 2008b; Roberts, 2006), avowing a consciously normative perspective (Cameron et al., 2003a; Dutton & Glynn, 2008). It is helpful that POS openly positions itself as committed to advancing a value-based agenda and to creating change in service of that agenda (Caza & Cameron, 2008; Dutton & Glynn, 2008): "The focus is on the creation, diffusion, and legitimation of POS practices in business units and organizations" (Dutton et al., 2006, p. 642). This forthright admission of intent is an important change from more traditional work that hides behind the facade of value neutral science.

Nonetheless, more is required. It is not enough to admit bias and espouse a value-based agenda. The values in question must be made explicit, and their implications considered. Which specific values are being advanced? By implication, which other values are being denied? Why these values? Who chose? Who should choose? And what effect will advancing the preferred values have, particularly on those who may not share them? The benefit of admitting bias can only be realized if these sorts of questions are addressed, so that the likely effects of the bias may be examined. The POS failure to clarify the meaning of "positive" is subject to critique in at least two ways, each reflecting our (the authors') differing perspectives.

If one allows the positivist, modernist assumptions of POS, it might be argued that comprehensive definitions of complex empirical phenomena are difficult to achieve. Biology, for example, does not have a final definition of "life" (McKay, 2004), and in fact some scientists claim that trying to define life is not useful. They argue that definitions involve semantics, while the proper concern of biology is understanding organisms (Cleland & Chyba, 2002). In keeping with this orientation, biology does not have a comprehensive definition of what life is, but it does have specific criteria for recognizing whether something is alive (e.g., homeostasis, metabolism, etc.). In this perspective, if POS cannot provide a final definition of what is positive, it should at least offer concrete criteria for its recognition. Examples of this include biology's characteristics of life and

psychology's criteria for healthy mental functioning (American Psychiatric Association, 1994).

In contrast, a postmodern view would argue that positivity, like all phenomena, is open to multiple, partial, and often contradictory definitions, so that any attempt to delineate or define it is an act of power. This view would argue that a definition must be advanced, and that in doing so, POS must engage with the issues that arise from the act of defining. In particular, POS should consider how any definition of positivity includes some phenomena while excluding others. All uses of the label positive are consequential choices, not natural or neutral observations of fact. Defining positivity and recognizing that definition's constructedness would allow for contestation. It would reveal which parties and perspectives are legitimized (or not) by the stated nature of positivity. It would also create the possibility of alternative definitions, potentially allowing otherwise marginalized voices to be heard.

We believe that both critiques reveal the need for POS to clearly state its goals and desired outcomes, in the way that Spicer and colleagues (2009) advocated their five-part framework. Positive organizational scholarship should specify what it is trying to achieve in the name of positivity. For example, an important part of many CMS views is the emancipatory project, which is an aim to move individuals and groups toward greater freedom and autonomy (Alvesson & Willmott, 1992). Critical management studies scholars who explicitly seek this aim must consider the meaning of emancipation, and how their actions and language facilitate its progress. Positive organizational scholarship would benefit from doing likewise concerning its own aims. Being clear about what is intended and whether a given action supports those aims will be crucial for POS to achieve its goal of improving organizational life.

Moreover, we would argue that the need for clarity is especially important for POS because it involves the study of organizations, in which the traditional, economic performance standards have de facto dominance. If POS is not explicit about what constitutes positivity, then POS risks defaulting to the status quo of serving business outcomes. For example, one could read the claim that "by focusing on the generative dynamics of human organizing, POS provides an expanded view of how organizations can create sustained competitive advantage" (Cameron et al., 2003a, p. 10), as an effort to use positivity solely for profit. Even when a stronger position is taken, advocating for the inherent value of positive outcomes in themselves, an apologetic tone is often taken, with the promise that these positive outcomes will not interfere with the pursuit of profit. For example, "POS represents a perspective that includes instrumental concerns but puts an increased emphasis on ideas of 'goodness'" (Cameron, 2007) and " . . . not only as a means to the desired end of strong economic performance, but also as ends worthy of explanation on their own" (Dutton et al., 2006, p. 642). In contrast to this tepid position, we agree with those who have observed that the greatest potential from POS may be in the establishment of new "dependent variables," in defining new criteria that replace profit as the best standard of organizational success (Caza & Cameron, 2008; Dutton & Glynn, 2008). But if POS is going to do this and be the force for change that it aspires to be, it needs to be explicit about the nature of positivity.

Similarly, our reading suggests that POS would benefit from engaging in denaturalization. At present, most formal statements of POS assert universal agreement on, and desire for, positive states (Cameron, 2008b; e.g., Cameron & Caza, 2004; Dutton et al., 2006). Positive organizational scholarship "advocates the position that the desire to improve the human condition is universal and that the capacity to do so is latent in most systems" (Cameron et al., 2003a, p. 10). The use of terms such as "instinct," "latent potential," and "universal" make the authors' views of what is positive automatic, even teleological. This is problematic for its implicit denigration of any state that the author does not endorse. Except for some brief and undeveloped mention of potential cultural differences (Caza & Cameron, 2008; Dutton & Glynn, 2008), the assumption of some universally positive state dominates POS. We commend POS authors for openly asserting their desire to move toward what they consider to be positive outcomes, but urge that those same authors be careful not to implicitly position their own desired states as a "natural" part of being human.

As an extension of this claim of universal positives, statements of POS also have a disturbing tendency to treat positivity as an unequivocal characteristic. In this view, anything either is or is not positive, in its entirety. References are made to positive states, positive processes, and positive outcomes, with relatively little discussion of the possibility that the same state might have both positive and negative aspects, or be perceived simultaneously as positive and negative by different parties (but see Dutton & Sonenshein, 2009). In response, we

would ask whether Wal-Mart, one of the world's largest and most influential organizations, is positive or negative. Evidence suggests that Wal-Mart creates economic success at the expense of locally owned, small firms offering similar goods and services (Irwin & Clark, 2006). Moreover, although Wal-Mart clearly contributes to a reduced cost of living (Basker, 2005a), it also seems to increase local poverty (Goetz & Swaminathan, 2006). The presence of a Wal-Mart raises local employment levels, but does so by shifting jobs away from some sectors toward others (Basker, 2005b), and Wal-Mart's presence may simultaneously contribute to reduced social capital (Goetz & Rupasingha, 2006) and increased entrepreneurial success (Goetz & Shrestha, 2009). Given all of this, it is hard to imagine that Wal-Mart is solely positive or negative, thus demonstrating the problems of assuming that anything can be entirely positive or not.

An important implication of this observation is the value of greater reflexivity when advocating POS. Although every statement of POS includes the caveat that the authors do not deny the importance of negative phenomena, there are nonetheless powerful implications in the use of positive–negative labeling. Even if the negative phenomena are not explicitly denigrated, they are cast in opposition to phenomena described as creating "goodness, generativity, growth" (Dutton & Sonenshein, 2009), and which foster "excellence, thriving, flourishing, abundance, resilience, or virtuousness" (Cameron, 2007). Moreover, it is not only organizational phenomena, but, by implication, the people who participate in them and who research them, that are cast as being contrary to these evocative, powerful states. Even if POS authors do not intend harm, we urge consideration of the unintended consequences of the powerful language used by POS.

In addition, POS authors should consider the criteria that they are implicitly advancing when judging one state positive and another not. As we noted earlier, no explicit standard of positivity has been offered, but every use of the label "positive" nonetheless implies one. Since positivity involves "desirable deviance" relative to some standard, any act of labeling something positive implicates a specific set of desires and reference standards. To the extent that these desires and standards remain unstated, they are protected from scrutiny. This has the effect of implying their unquestionable rightness, which brings us back to the point that began this section: We laud the fact that POS is open about its advocacy, but suggest that unless the intent of that advocacy is to perpetuate the status quo, it is crucial to specify the change that is desired.

Positive organizational scholarship As Enacted

In this section, we consider several themes that we see running through the 35 peer-reviewed articles that are officially part of POS. These themes concern the nature of positivity, the problem of performance standards, the relative importance of managers versus employees, and a disturbing historical trend. In each case, we summarize the theme, and then raise questions suggested by the critical perspective we have adopted. We also offer examples of POS research that does not fit the theme, and which seems to be moving in a direction that we consider more promising.

Problematic Positivity

In addressing the issue of what is positive, POS articles tend to adopt one of three approaches (Cameron, 2008b). The first is to assert the natural or obvious character of positivity. In this approach, it is claimed that everyone has an instinctive drive toward the same ideals; that in our true hearts, we all know and agree on what is positive (e.g., Caza, Barker, & Cameron, 2004). These claims are usually based in some historical tradition, such as ancient Greek philosophy (Cameron et al., 2004) or world religious practice (Kanov et al., 2004). In all cases, it is problematic for reasons we have already addressed. Giving one's belief about what is good the label "instinctive" or "natural" makes other beliefs wrong and unnatural, even inhuman.

The second approach is related, in that it also presumes the obviousness of positivity, but does so by not addressing the matter at all (e.g., Carmeli & Spreitzer, 2009; Dutton et al., 2006; Ryan W. Quinn, 2005). These articles may mention POS or the importance of studying positive phenomena, but little effort is made to define what constitutes positivity. These articles typically argue for the important consequences associated with their focal construct, but offer no explanation for why those consequences are positive or to be preferred over any others. This approach takes the risk of having the positive label seem arbitrary. As a concrete example, we found six of the 35 articles particularly mysterious (Berg, Wrzesniewski, & Dutton, 2010; James & Wooten, 2005; Lawrence, Lenk, & Robert E. Quinn, 2009; Ryan W. Quinn & Dutton, 2005; Wooten et al., 2005). These articles make no explicit mention of positivity, and it is not obvious to us

why they have been designated as POS research while any number of other articles has not.

In contrast to these two, the third approach tries to define positivity explicitly by focusing on its exceptional nature. In this approach, POS concerns phenomena "exceeding normal happiness and excellence . . . an affirmative exception to typical organizational behavior" (Cameron & Caza, 2002, pp. 33–34). This "positive deviance" approach is concerned with "intentional behaviors that depart from the norms of a referent group in honorable ways" (Spreitzer & Sonenshein, 2004, p. 834). In other words, if it is good and rare or unlikely, it is positive. Although this does not constitute a satisfactory definition, it has at least recognized the subjective nature of judgments about goodness. In particular, Spreitzer and Sonenshein (2004) proposed that POS be concerned with four reference groups for judging positive deviance: the unit or organization, the industry, professional practitioners, and what they refer to as "general principles." In each case, it is suggested that knowledgeable insiders should determine how honorable a given deviation is. These authors also recognize that two groups may judge the same act in different ways, but do not develop the matter.

From a critical perspective, it is useful to have defined the reference groups and to have proposed judges because doing so allows for discussion of whether these choices are desirable ones. We encourage POS researchers to have this discussion, to consider whether these four groups are the best referents and whether expert insiders are the preferred judges. They may not be. For example, if POS is concerned with creating change, then using insider judges may be counterproductive. A deviance that is beneficial to a group disempowered by the existing social structure may seem threatening and dishonorable to the insiders favored by current practice. As a result, the use of insider judges could restrict the status of "positive" to that which perpetuates the status quo. This will work against change, rather than for it. A better approach would be to recognize the contentious nature of defining positive, and to examine the implications of competing interpretations. A POS example of this appears to be developing in discussions of identity. Dutton and colleagues have recognized that it is problematic to simply label an identity as positive or not; they consider four different bases for assigning such a label, and the differing implications of each (Dutton, Roberts, & Bednar, 2010). We believe that this sort of reflexive, multiperspective approach is a more fruitful direction as POS grapples with the meaning of "positive."

Economic Performance

Earlier, we noted that if POS did not clearly define its own positive performance criteria, then it was at risk of adopting the economic criteria that have priority in mainstream organizational studies. The large majority of POS articles published so far confirm this fear. Most of the 35 articles treat organizations' economic performance or related business goals as the ultimate end of positive states and practices.

In many cases, the use of POS to serve economic ends was framed as incidental. That is, the positive phenomenon was described as inherently valuable, but also having the happy side effect of enhancing profits. For example, one article on the virtue of organizational forgiveness noted that instrumental motives are antithetical to virtue, that "if forgiveness produced no personal or organizational advantage, it would still be desirable because of its intrinsic goodness. Nonetheless, . . . there is some reason to believe that virtues in general, and forgiveness in particular, may lead to personal and social benefits" (Cameron & Caza, 2002, p. 40). Similarly, although compassion was argued to be important because it was a natural human response to the suffering of others, it was also noted that such compassion "may be particularly important for sustained organizational survival and effectiveness. . . . Pain and suffering have serious implications for organizational performance and productivity," (Kanov et al., 2004, pp. 810–811), because "compassion shown by work colleagues can strengthen emotional connections at work and boost people's ability to function as productive employees" (Lilius et al., 2008, p. 194). Other POS articles made similar observations about phenomena such as humanistic organizational practices (Wooten & Crane, 2004), employee self-actualization (Wooten & Crane, 2002), and energizing communication (Ryan W. Quinn & Dutton, 2005).

In other cases, the preeminence of economic gain was more explicit: POS was required to serve monetary aims. One article observed that "an irony associated with organizational virtuousness is that without demonstrated benefits, virtuousness is unlikely to capture much interest in organizational research . . . without pragmatic outcomes" (Cameron et al., 2004, p. 770). In another, organizational resilience was promoted as a promising management strategy for preserving shareholder profit (Gittell, Cameron, Lim, & Rivas, 2006). Some articles went even further, with alarming undertones that seem to offer POS constructs as a way to further management control of employees. For example,

one article described how most people have altruistic inclinations, and how organizations can use these inclinations as a tool for increasing employees' organizational commitment (A. M. Grant, Dutton, & Rosso, 2008). Another article observed that the knowledge-based nature of modern work is undermining managers' ability to monitor and evaluate subordinate employees and proposed the use of POS constructs as new performance metrics for managers' control (Ryan W. Quinn, 2005). In the most disturbing case, promoting employee thriving was explicitly suggested as a less expensive way to get more from employees:

> Today's work environment requires more ingenuity and fresh ideas from employees. . . . Organizations can no longer survive by doing more of the same. Although we often hear about the impressive benefits and perks that companies like Google or SAS offer their employees to motivate creative and innovative behaviors, this research suggests that there may be cheaper and more sustainable ways to enable employee innovative behaviors. Generative relationships that enable human thriving at work (i.e., learning and vitality) are less expensive alternatives than high priced gourmet meals, workplace concierges, or in-house masseuses (Carmeli & Spreitzer, 2009, p. 196).

Admittedly, only this last article was so explicit as to say that POS offers a way for management to squeeze more from employees, but most were implicitly compatible with this view. In advancing the observation that positivity is also good for the bottom line, POS does nothing to challenge the dominance of financial measures as the ultimate performance standards. As a result, the priorities of mainstream organizational studies may co-opt the humanistic mission of POS.

However, there were also exceptions, articles that challenged the dominance of profit by at least proposing other outcomes that were equally important (e.g., Wooten et al., 2005). For example, in defining the construct of thriving, the authors focused on it as a source of health, individual achievement, and growth in all aspects of life (Spreitzer, Sutcliffe, Dutton, Sonenshein, & A. M. Grant, 2005). It was noted that thriving could also contribute to work performance, but this was clearly secondary; it was presented as an incidental consequence of the fact that the thriving individual had a job. Similarly, the POS call for more participatory leadership and empowerment in organizations was not grounded in any potential benefit for business, but rather in the ability to contribute to world peace (Spreitzer, 2007). Going further still, one article presented a case study in which organizational resources and routines were subverted to care for members whose lives outside the organization were in turmoil (Dutton et al., 2006). This article celebrated the act of compassion for its own sake, making no effort to justify compassion in terms of economic or financial gain.

It is our belief that POS will make its most important and transformative contributions only if these exceptions become the rule. In this, we will restate our claim from the previous section. Positive organizational scholarship must be conscious and explicit about the nature of the positive change it wishes to promote. Stating a goal of greater physical health, increased world peace, more compassionate organizations, or something else of this sort will provide direction and the possibility of resisting the dominant economic metrics. Without such a goal, as suggested by the majority of POS research already published, financial concerns will take control.

Privileging Management

If a dominant narrative runs through the POS articles, it is of formal organizational leaders who are well-intentioned and innocent victims that prevail despite challenging environments. Bad things happen to these good people, but their essential heroism allows them to take actions that engender positive states in their employees and produce unexpected organizational performance. Consistent with this narrative, most of the positivity in POS articles is described as originating in authority figures. Thus, the articles emphasized how leaders and managers provide role models for employees (Cameron & Caza, 2002; Heaphy & Dutton, 2008), create policies that lead employees to do good deeds (A. M. Grant et al., 2008; Wooten & Crane, 2002), and generally shepherd employees from crisis to success (James & Wooten, 2005; Spreitzer, 2006; Wooten & James, 2008). The prevalent assumption that employees need their positive inclinations to be legitimized or institutionalized by leaders (e.g., Bright, Cameron, & Caza, 2006; Cameron, 2008a; Kanov et al., 2004), means that educators must teach tomorrow's managers how to put virtue into their organizations (Cameron, 2006). In this view, except for participating in the processes created by leaders, there is relatively little role for employees in contributing to positive states or outcomes.

This view is problematic for at least two reasons. The first is that it is untenable given what others have learned about leading. One hundred years ago, the study of leadership focused on "great men" who made things happen by exerting their will on effectively inert followers, but leadership scholars have since come to a consensus that this not a useful way to understand leaders (Avolio, Walumbwa, & Weber, 2009). Leading is a negotiated outcome, in which the leader's social environment plays a fundamental role (Brass, 2001; Hunt & Dodge, 2001; Salancik, Calder, Rowland, Leblebici, & Conway, 1975). Followers are the most important and influential force in that social environment. They are contributors in leadership; leadership does not happen to them (Cogliser & Schriesheim, 2000; Dirks & Ferrin, 2002; Uhl-Bien, 2006). As such, we have trouble believing that there is no role for employees in fostering organizational positivity.

Moreover, the view that positivity arises primarily from formal leaders is fundamentally disempowering for employees. If employees have no role, except perhaps as transmitters in a process created by management, they are little more than automatons. Adopting and promoting such a narrative implies that employees cannot contribute to positivity, and therefore should not try; they should simply accept what is given or done to them by management. This view is incompatible with the emancipatory aims of CMS, and does not seem especially appropriate for the POS goal of fostering flourishing and generative states.

However, within the POS articles, there were exceptions to this leader-centric narrative. These articles challenged the assumption that managers were the key players in positivity. Some made individuals the most important determinants of their own outcomes (e.g., Roberts et al., 2005; Spreitzer et al., 2005). Others adopted more interactive views, with employees and management jointly creating positivity (e.g., Dutton et al., 2006; Spreitzer, 2007). Some went even further, and began to challenge mainstream assumptions about management control, questioning whether traditional bureaucratic structures were conducive to positivity (Wooten & Crane, 2004) or calling for participation from those outside the organization, including communities, families, and individuals (Wooten et al., 2005). As before, we believe that these exceptions offer a better direction for POS. It is not clear to us how promoting management dominance and employee passivity will contribute to the stated aims of POS.

Declining Relevance

Spreitzer (2008) made the provocative admission that she wants POS to be a temporary phenomenon. She stated her hope that POS would reach its aims of creating positive change, and in doing so, make itself obsolete. In this hope, POS would no longer matter as a research perspective, because positive phenomena would be institutionalized and accepted to the extent that researchers and practitioners alike would give them the attention they deserve. Positive organizational scholarship would no longer need to champion positivity. Our reading of the POS articles leaves us suspecting that Spreitzer may have been correct about the coming obsolescence of POS, but we see a more dire cause: POS may be losing its impetus for change.

In the previous parts of this section, we have discussed our worries about POS being subordinated to economic goals and its potential role in disempowering employees. We have also noted that there are promising exceptions to these patterns. However, a striking feature of these exception articles is that they were all published between 2004 and 2007. None of the earliest or latest POS articles give much evidence of challenging the dominance of managers and economic performance. We find this troubling.

We suspect that the early articles may have been based on a strategic decision to avoid challenging traditional assumptions. Since POS was apparently intended to create change from within mainstream organizational studies (Bernstein, 2003), it may have been judged necessary to launch POS in terms that were familiar to the mainstream. Once those first, tame articles had established POS (i.e., 2002–2004), the subsequent articles could then begin to push against the boundaries, to challenge assumptions. Early POS work may have been intended as a bridge from the mainstream.

However, this logic does not explain why POS articles published in the last 3 years seem to have stopped challenging mainstream assumptions. If anything, we might have expected and hoped that the most recent work would have extended the trend, that it would be even more radical. Instead, the most recent articles either explicitly serve economic and management dominance, or do so complicitly by failing to offer any challenge and by carefully couching the value of positivity in terms consistent with mainstream priorities. This suggests that our fears about POS being co-opted by mainstream priorities are well-founded. If this apparent trend in POS research continues, then POS may indeed become obsolete, but not for the optimistic reasons that Spreitzer (2008) hoped. Rather, it will be because POS has nothing new to say.

Conclusion

It may seem ironic to bring a critical view to a movement explicitly founded to overcome negative scholarship (Cameron, Dutton, & Robert E. Quinn, 2003a), but we believe there is a surprising potential for synergy between POS and CMS. At present, POS is in danger of failing to achieve its goal of creating beneficial change, because unquestioned assumptions are subverting positivity to financial gain and management dominance. However, as highlighted in this chapter, there are exceptions that show how POS has the potential to avoid this failure and do remarkable things. In service of that, we have tried to show how the questions raised by a critical perspective could benefit POS. If POS can offer an alternative performance criterion, one that is reflexively conscious of its implications, we believe it could contribute greatly to thriving in organizations.

However, doing so will require different ways of working. For example, returning to the military talk that opened the chapter, the traditional response to

Table 73.2 Future directions

What constitutes "positive"? What specific aims is POS trying to achieve? What is the agenda?
If positivity lies in honorable deviance, who should judge the honor of the act? Which interests and groups are favored by that choice of judges? Which ones are hurt?
Can anything be entirely positive (or negative)? If not, what implications does that have for the meaning of positivity?
What is implicitly being labeled negative by not being included in positive? What effect will that have?
What new outcomes and dependent variables represent the greatest potential value of the POS perspective?
In defining positivity, which groups might have differing views? How many of those groups are included in the conversation? How could the excluded parties be involved?

the mistaken assumption about the audience might be to give the talk as planned or to revise as you go. But what if you worked with your audience instead? You have your expertise, but they also have theirs. Perhaps you admit to them your assumptions and how they influenced you. In addition to discussing your findings, you might discuss what other findings could be useful, and the assumptions you made, with their implications for yourself and also for the military. This would create a very different conversation. To spark such conversations within POS, we end with some questions for consideration (see Table 73.2). Combined with the issues discussed here, we hope that these questions can help to direct POS toward reaching its laudable aims.

Acknowledgments

We appreciate the assistance of Jane Dutton, Gail Fairhurst, Eric Guthey, and Jim Walsh in helping us with the development of this chapter.

Note

1. The Center for POS sources actually suggested 36 articles, but we excluded the article by Spreitzer, Stephens, and Sweetman (2009), because its report on the effect of the Reflected Best Self Exercise (RBSE) did not seem to fit the "organizational" criterion of POS. Although the RBSE was developed by POS researchers, this particular study examined its effects on a group of high school students at a three-day conference, rather than in an organizational or work context.

References

Alvesson, M. (2008). The future of critical management studies. In D. Barry, & H. Hansen (Eds.), *Sage handbook of new approaches in management and organization* (pp. 13–26). Thousand Oaks, CA: Sage Publications. Aktouf, O. (1992). Management and theories of organizations in the 1990s: Toward a critical radical humanism? *Academy of Management Review, 17*(3), 407–431.

Alvesson, M., Bridgeman, T., & Willmot, H. (2010). Introduction. In M. Alvesson, T. Bridgeman, & H. Willmot (Eds.), *Oxford handbook of critical management studies* (pp. 1–23). Oxford, UK: Oxford University Press.

Alvesson, M., & Willmot, H. (1992). On the idea of emancipation in management and organization studies. *Academy of Management Review, 17*(3), 432–484.

American Psychiatric Association. (1994). *Diagnostic and statistical manual of mental disorders.* Washington, DC: American Psychiatric Association.

Avolio, B.J., & Gardner, W.L. (2005). Authentic leadership development: Getting to the root of positive forms of leadership. *Leadership Quarterly, 16*(3), 315–338.

Avolio, B.J., Walumbwa, F.O., & Weber, T.J. (2009). Leadership: Current theories, research, and future directions. *Annual Review of Psychology, 60*, 421–449.

Basker, E. (2005a). Selling a cheaper mousetrap: Wal-Mart's effect on retail prices. *Journal of Urban Economics, 58*(2), 203–229.

Basker, E. (2005b). Job creation or destruction? Labor-market effects of Wal-mart expansion. *Review of Economics and Statistics, 87*(1), 174–183.

Berg, J.M., Wrzesniewski, A., & Dutton, J.E. (2010). Perceiving and responding to challenges in job crafting at different ranks: When proactivity requires adaptivity. *Journal of Organizational Behavior, 31*(2–3), 158–186.

Bernstein, S.D. (2003). Positive organizational scholarship: Meet the movement: An interview with Kim Cameron, Jane Dutton, and Robert Quinn. *Journal of Management Inquiry, 12*(3), 266–271.

Brass, D.J. (2001). Social capital and organizational leadership. In S.J. Zaccaro, & R.J. Klimoski (Eds.), *The nature of organizational leadership.* San Francisco: Jossey-Bass.

Bright, D., Cameron, K.S., & Caza, A. (2006). The amplifying and buffering effects of virtuousness in downsized organizations. *Journal of Business Ethics, 64*(3), 249–269.

Cameron, K. (2006). Good or not bad: Standards and ethics in managing change. *Academy of Management Learning & Education, 5*(3), 317–323.

Cameron, K.S. (2007). Positive organizational scholarship. In S.R. Clegg, & J.R. Bailey (Eds.), *International encyclopedia of organizational studies.* Beverly Hills: Sage Publications.

Cameron, K.S. (2008a). Positively deviant organizational performance and the role of leadership values. *Journal of Values Based Leadership, 1*, 67–83.

Cameron, K.S. (2008b). Paradox in positive organizational change. *Journal of Applied Behavioral Science, 44*(1), 7–24.

Cameron, K.S., Bright, D., & Caza, A. (2004). Exploring the relationships between organizational virtuousness and performance. *American Behavioral Scientist, 47*(6), 766–790.

Cameron, K.S., & Caza, A. (2002). Organizational and leadership virtues and the role of forgiveness. *Journal of Leadership & Organizational Studies, 9*(1), 33–48.

Cameron, K.S., & Caza, A. (2004). Contributions to the discipline of positive organizational scholarship. *American Behavioral Scientist, 47*(6), 731–739.

Cameron, K.S., Dutton, J.E., & Quinn, R.E. (2003a). Foundations of positive organizational scholarship. In K.S. Cameron, J.E. Dutton, & R.E. Quinn (Eds.), *Positive organizational scholarship: Foundations of a new discipline* (pp. 3–13). San Francisco: Berrett-Koehler Publishers Inc.

Cameron, K.S., Dutton, J.E., & Quinn, R.E. (2003b). *Positive organizational scholarship: Foundations of a new discipline.* San Francisco, CA: Berrett-Koehler Publishers Inc.

Cameron, K.S., Dutton, J.E., Quinn, R.E., & Wrzesniewski, A. (2003). Developing a discipline of positive organization scholarship. In K.S. Cameron, J.E. Dutton, & R.E. Quinn (Eds.), *Positive organizational scholarship: Foundations of a new discipline* (pp. 361–370). San Francisco: Berrett-Koehler Publishers Inc.

Carmeli, A., & Spreitzer, G.M. (2009). Trust, connectivity, and thriving: Implications for innovative behaviors at work. *Journal of Creative Behavior, 43*(3), 161–191.

Caza, A., Barker, B.A., & Cameron, K.S. (2004). Ethics and ethos: The buffering and amplifying effects of ethical behavior and virtuousness. *Journal of Business Ethics, 52*(2), 169–178.

Caza, A., & Cameron, K.S. (2008). Positive organizational scholarship: What does it achieve? In S. Clegg, & C.L. Cooper (Eds.), *SAGE handbook of organizational behaviour* (pp. 99–116). Thousand Oaks, CA: Sage.

Center for Positive Organizational Scholarship. (n.d.). *Positive organizational scholarship: Measuring impact*. University of Michigan, Ann Arbor, MI. Retrieved March 18, 2007 from http://www.bus.umich.edu/Positive/PDF/POS-Measuring_Impact.pdf

Center for Positive Organizational Scholarship. (2007). *The first five years: July 2002-June 2007*. University of Michigan, Ann Arbor, MI. Retrieved March 18, 2007 from http://www.bus.umich.edu/Positive/CPOS/About%20the%20Center/reports.html.

Center for Positive Organizational Scholarship. (2010). *CPOS: 2008–2009 highlights of activities*. University of Michigan, Ann Arbor, MI.

Cleland, C.E., & Chyba, C.F. (2002). Defining 'life.' *Origins of Life and Evolution of the Biosphere, 32*, 387–393.

Cogliser, C.C., & Schriesheim, C.A. (2000). Exploring work unit context and leader-member exchange: A multi-level perspective. *Journal of Organizational Behavior, 21*, 487–511.

Dirks, K.T., & Ferrin, D.L. (2002). Trust in leadership: Meta-analytic findings and implications for research and practice. *Journal of Applied Psychology, 87*(4), 611–628.

Dutton, J.E., & Glynn, M. (2008). Positive organizational scholarship. In J. Barling & C.L. Cooper (Eds.), *Sage Handbook of Organizational Behavior* Vol. 1 (pp. 693–712). London: Sage Publications.

Dutton, J.E., Glynn, M., & Spreitzer, G.M. (2006). Positive organizational scholarship. In J.H. Greenhaus & G.A. Callanan (Eds.), *Encyclopedia of Career Development* (pp. 641–644). Thousand Oaks, CA: Sage Publications.

Dutton, J.E., Roberts, L.M., & Bednar, J. (2010). Pathways for positive identity construction at work: Four types of positive identity and the building of social resources. *Academy of Management Review, 35*(2), 265–293.

Dutton, J.E., & Sonenshein, S. (2009). Positive organizational scholarship. In S.J. Lopez (Ed.), *Encyclopedia of positive psychology* (pp. 737–742). Malden, MA: Blackwell Publishing.

Dutton, J.E., Worline, M.C., Frost, P.J., & Lilius, J. (2006). Explaining compassion organizing. *Administrative Science Quarterly, 51*(1), 59–96.

Fineman, S. (2006). On being positive: Concerns and counterpoints. *Academy of Management Review, 31*(2), 270–291.

Fournier, V., & Grey, C. (2000). At the critical moment: Conditions and prospects for critical management studies. *Human Relations, 53*(1), 7–32.

George, J.M. (2004). [Review of the book *Positive organizational scholarship: Foundations of a new discipline,* by K.S. Cameron, J.E. Dutton, & R.E. Quinn (Eds.)]. *Administrative Science Quarterly, 49*(2), 325–330.

Gittell, J.H., Cameron, K., Lim, S., & Rivas, V. (2006). Relationships, layoffs, and organizational resilience: Airline industry responses to September 11. *Journal of Applied Behavioral Science, 42*(3), 300–329.

Goetz, S.J., & Rupasingha, A. (2006). Wal-Mart and social capital. *American Journal of Agricultural Economics, 88*(5), 1304–1310.

Goetz, S.J., & Shrestha, S.S. (2009). Explaining self-employment success and failure: Wal-Mart versus Starbucks, or Schumpeter versus Putnam. *Social Science Quarterly, 91*(1), 22–38.

Goetz, S.J., & Swaminathan, H. (2006). Wal-Mart and county-wide poverty. *Social Science Quarterly, 87*(2), 211–226.

Grant, A.M., Dutton, J.E., & Rosso, B.D. (2008). Giving commitment: Employee support programs and the prosocial sensemaking process. *Academy of Management Journal, 51*(5), 898–918.

Grant, D., Iedema, R., & Oswick, C. (2010). Discourse and critical management studies. In M. Alvesson, T. Bridgeman, & H. Willmot (Eds.), *Oxford handbook of critical management studies* (pp. 213–231). Oxford, UK: Oxford University Press.

Heaphy, E.D., & Dutton, J.E. (2008). Positive social interactions and the human body at work: Linking organizations and physiology. *Academy of Management Review, 33*(1), 137–162.

Horkheimer, M. (1976). Traditional and critical theory. In P. Connerton (Ed.), *Critical sociology: Selected readings* (pp. 206–224). Harmondsworth, UK: Penguin.

Hunt, J.G., & Dodge, G.E. (2001). Leadership déjà vu all over again. *Leadership Quarterly, 11*, 435–458.

Irwin, E.G., & Clark, J. (2006). Wall street vs. Main street: What are the benefits and costs of Wal-Mart to local communities? *Choices, 21*(2).

James, E.H., & Wooten, L.P. (2005). Leadership as (Un)usual: How to display competence in times of crisis. *Organizational Dynamics, 34*(2), 141.

Kanov, J., Maitlis, S., Worline, M.C., Dutton, J.E., Frost, P.J., & Lilius, J.M. (2004). Compassion in organizational life. *American Behavioral Scientist, 47*(6), 808–827.

Lawrence, K.A., Lenk, P., & Quinn, R.E. (2009). Behavioral complexity in leadership: The psychometric properties of a new instrument to measure behavioral repertoire. *The Leadership Quarterly, 20*(2), 87–102.

Lilius, J.M., Worline, M.C., Maitlis, S., Kanov, J., Dutton, J.E., & Frost, P. (2008). The contours and consequences of compassion at work. *Journal of Organizational Behavior, 29*(2), 193–218.

Luthans, F. (2002). The need for and meaning of positive organizational behavior. *Journal of Organizational Behavior, 23*(6), 695–706.

McKay, C.P. (2004). What is life—and how do we search for it in other worlds? *Public Library of Science Biology, 2*(9), e302.

Parker, M. (1995). Critique in the name of what? Postmodernism and critical approaches to organization. *Organization Studies, 16*(4), 553–564.

Quinn, R.W. (2005). Flow in knowledge work: High performance experience in the design of national security technology. *Administrative Science Quarterly, 50*(4), 610–641.

Quinn, R.W., & Dutton, J.E. (2005). Coordination as energy-in-conversation. *Academy of Management Review, 30*(1), 36–57.

Roberts, L.M. (2006). Shifting the lens on organizational life: The added value of positive scholarship - Response. *Academy of Management Review, 31*(2), 292–305.

Roberts, L.M., Dutton, J.E., Spreitzer, G.M., Heaphy, E.D., & Quinn, R.E. (2005). Composing the reflected best-self portrait: Building pathways for becoming extraordinary in work organizations. *Academy of Management Review, 30*(4), 712–736.

Salancik, G.R., Calder, B.J., Rowland, K.M., Leblebici, H., & Conway, M. (1975). Leadership as an outcome of social structure and process: A multidimensional analysis. In J.G. Hunt, & L.L. Larson (Eds.), *Leadership frontiers* (pp. 81–101). Kent, OH: Kent State University.

Spicer, A., Alvesson, M., & Karreman, D. (2009). Critical performativity: The unfinished business of critical management studies. *Human Relations, 62*(4), 537–560.

Spreitzer, G., Stephens, J.P., & Sweetman, D. (2009). The reflected best self field experiment with adolescent leaders: Exploring the psychological resources associated with feedback source and valence. *Journal of Positive Psychology, 4*(5), 331–348.

Spreitzer, G., Sutcliffe, K., Dutton, J., Sonenshein, S., & Grant, A.M. (2005). A socially embedded model of thriving at work. *Organization Science, 16*(5), 537.

Spreitzer, G.M. (2006). Leading to grow and growing to lead: Leadership development lessons from positive organizational studies. *Organizational Dynamics, 35*(4), 305.

Spreitzer, G.M. (2007). Giving peace a chance: Organizational leadership, empowerment, and peace. *Journal of Organizational Behavior, 28*, 1077–1095.

Spreitzer, G.M. (2008). A note on the future of positive organizational scholarship. In D. Barry & H. Hansen (Eds.), *Sage handbook of new approaches in management and organization* (pp. 501–503). Thousand Oaks, CA: Sage Publications.

Spreitzer, G.M., & Sonenshein, S. (2004). Toward the construct definition of positive deviance. *American Behavioral Scientist, 47*(6), 828–847.

Thompson, P. (2004). Brands, boundaries and bandwagons: A critical reflection on critical management studies. In S. Fleetwood, & S. Ackroyd (Eds.), *Critical realism in action and organization studies* (pp. 54–70). London: Routledge.

Uhl-Bien, M. (2006). Relational leadership theory: Exploring the social processes of leadership and organizing. *Leadership Quarterly, 17*, 654–676.

Weick, K.E. (2006). Faith, guesses, and action: Better guesses in an unknowable world. *Organization Studies, 27*, 1723–1736.

Wooten, L.P., & Crane, P. (2002). Nurses as implementers of organizational culture. *Nursing Economics, 21*(6), 275–279.

Wooten, L.P., & Crane, P. (2004). Generating dynamic capabilities through a humanistic work ideology: The case of a certified-nurse midwife practice in a professional bureaucracy. *American Behavioral Scientist, 47*(6), 848–866.

Wooten, L.P., & James, E.H. (2008). Linking crisis management and leadership competencies: The role of human resource development. *Advances in Developing Human Resources, 10*(3), 352–379.

Wooten, L.P., Schultz, C., Ford, B., Anderson, L., Waller, A., & Ransom, S. (2005). Leadership and prenatal health disparities: It takes a village. *African American Research Perspectives, 11*(1), 17–30.

Strange Bedfellows

Homo economicus and Positive Organization Scholarship

Paul C. Godfrey

Abstract

The assumptions about the human actors at the base of positive organizational scholarship (POS) seem diametrically opposed to the view of human actors found in current economic theory. In this chapter, I review the received view of economic man, *Homo economicus*. I then look back at economic history and show that the narrow view of *H. economicus* currently in vogue is of recent origin; economists such as Adam Smith, Alfred Marshall, and John Maynard Keynes held much more expansive views of human motivations, actions, and outcomes. I also investigate the findings of a new field, behavioral economics, to show that *H. economicus*, although a recent construction, appears more as a cognitive simplification than an accurate description of human behavior. I conclude that the assumptions of economic man are in fact not inconsistent with ones needed to generate the positive behaviors studied in POS and pose a set of questions for further study to advance the field.

Keywords: Economics, economic history, morality, human behavior

How can positive organizational scholarship (POS) benefit from a study of the fundamental assumptions about economic actors? The common, descriptively positive conception of *Homo economicus* appears antithetical to the tenets of POS's normatively positive theory of organizations and the actors who populate them. Peterson and Seligman (2003) counsel POS leaders to focus on horses, not unicorns, as they build the field; in other words, to focus on the obvious areas for theory development first, then go for the unique and different. A water cooler conversation with economics-trained colleagues leads to the somewhat obvious conclusion that the conceptions of individuals studied by POS and standard behavioral assumptions of economics taught today seem quite opposite. *Homo economicus* and *H. positivus* appear to be, at best, strange bedfellows, but what can each discipline learn from the other? Can their relationship be complementary rather than antagonistic? This is the fundamental question I take up in this chapter.

I begin by outlining the loosely held behavioral assumptions of POS. In their seminal book, Cameron, Dutton, and Quinn (2003, p. 4) provide a domain statement:

> POS is concerned with the study of especially positive outcomes, processes, and attributes of organizations and their members . . . it focuses on dynamics that are typically described by words such as *excellence, thriving, flourishing, abundance, resilience,* or *virtuousness.* . . . It encompasses attention to *the enablers* (e.g., processes, capabilities, structures, methods), *the motivations* (e.g., unselfishness, altruism, contribution without regard to self), and *the outcomes or effects* (e.g., vitality, meaningfulness, exhilaration, high-quality relationships) associated with positive phenomena [emphasis in original].

It follows logically that for the list of organizational dynamics listed above to come to fruition, organizations must be composed of actors capable of acting excellently, with an abundance orientation, resiliently, from deeper meaning, and be capable of developing high-quality relationships.

The old saw that "politics makes strange bedfellows" implies that, in the course of getting beneficial work done, parties may work together who would typically be antagonistic; they may hold divergent views on most issues but share a common concern on one, hence their working relationship becomes one of "strange bedfellows." A cursory look at a set of word pairs exposes the apparent contradictions between POS and *H. economicus*:

- POS's concern with *abundance* versus economics focus on *scarcity*
- Actors motivated by *altruism* as opposed to those driven by *self-interest*
- A vibrant outcome such as *vitality* compared with a clearly second-best condition known as *Pareto optimality*
- *Meaningfulness* and *flourishing* juxtaposed with *profit* or *utility* maximization
- High-quality *relationships* standing against arms length *transactions*

As if these differences are not stark enough, POS uses "positive" in a distinctly normative sense—if people would engage in certain virtuous behaviors, then the world would be a richer and better place—whereas economics describes itself as a positive science in both an opposite and similar sense: It posits how people behave and argues that, when people behave according to its dictates, the outcomes are positive for individuals and society (Freidman, 1953). Resolving the apparent tensions between *H. economicus* and the *H. positivus* of POS would appear to be one of Seligman's horses for the development of POS as a sustainable field of inquiry.

My chapter proceeds as follows. I first outline the standard view of *H. economicus* prevalent in economics, business, and finance teaching and research today. I then look back at three luminaries of economic theorizing, Adam Smith, Alfred Marshall, and John Maynard Keynes to examine their views on the behavioral undergirding of economics. I then look forward to current work in behavioral economics that sheds additional light on the robustness, veracity, and ultimate usefulness of *H. economicus* as a construct. In each section, I hope to outline key implications for *H. positivus*. I intend to use extensive quotations from historical and current sources to provide readers with a real sense of the context of many oft-heard quotations, context that helps refine and polish the views of different thinkers on the nature of economic man.

Homo economicus: The standard view

The received view represented in most current economics textbooks can be summed up as a view of human beings as rational, self-interested, utility maximizers. Rationality encompasses the ability to gather information about the world, understand our own preferences, and calculate the expected costs and payoffs of different courses of action (Nicholson, 1995); self-interest focuses the decision criteria on the ultimate beneficiary of action—the self—while utility broadly defines the end goal of action. Utility can be broadly construed as the desirability of actions or goods (Nicholson, 1995) or more narrowly as the pursuit of pleasure and the avoidance of pain (Mill, 1863/1987).

The rational actor view of *H. economicus* has existed in some form or another since the advent of economics as a separate study; indeed, modern economists cite with vigor the writings of Adam Smith: "It is not from the benevolence of the butcher, the brewer, or the baker, that we expect our dinner, but from their regard to *their own interest*. We address ourselves, not to their humanity but to their *self-love*, and never talk to them of our own necessities but of their *advantages*" (Smith, 1776/1965, p. 14, emphasis added).

The belief, however, that "self-love" motivates human behavior, economic or not, is of more recent origin. Economic historian Stephen Medema (2009, p. 193) traces the origin of an expansive rational actor view to Gary Becker:

> Becker (1976, p. 4), whose work in this vein is without parallel, made this clear when he described the method that motivated his own work: "the combined assumptions of maximizing behavior, market equilibrium, and stable preferences, used relentlessly and unflinchingly, form the heart of the economic approach as I see it." The logic of this extension is a simple one: economics is the study of choice, and all of life involves making choices; should not economics, then, apply to all manner of human decisions and thus all areas of human life?

Becker's extension of economic man into other domains includes economic analyses of crime and punishment (1968), the allocation of time (1965), marriage (1976), and voting behavior (1976). Oliver Williamson's (1985) focus on opportunism—the tendency of actors to pursue their own self-interest though deception, obfuscation, or other forms of guile—amplifies the extent to which individuals will go to secure their own interests. The received view of *H. economicus* can be summed up as follows: Wherever choice is involved, people can safely be viewed as rational, self-interested utility maximizers, with some willing to abandon social or moral convention to get what they want.

It appears clear that the Becker-Williamson view of economic man runs counter to the existence and persistence of *H. positivus.* Such an actor would be considered irrational unless his or her actions could be subsumed within the paradigmatic assumption of self-interest. Such a subsumption occurs as economists, or their disciples, argue that all behavior is guided by self-interest: Other-regarding behaviors or actions are merely crafty moves by *H. economicus* to maximize his or her own welfare. If we accept such an explanation, we are left with an overly expansive economics that explains the whole of human behavior.

The recency of such an expansive view of *H. economicus,* coupled with powerful voices in economics and its business school sister discipline—finance—supporting such a view, often create the illusion that this view of human nature carries the day. As I now outline, however, the long history of economics adopts a much more circumspect view of *H. economicus.*

Adam Smith: *Homo economicus* Within *Homo moralis*

I return to Adam Smith, the universally acknowledged founding father of modern economics. Smith's *Inquiry into the Nature and Causes of the Wealth of Nations* (1776) outlines classical economic theory, including powerful concepts of the division of labor, the power of market mechanisms to generate individual and national wealth, a critique on the fallacies of mercantilism, and many insightful comments about government policies and the creation of new business ventures and models. As a scholarly aside, the tome deserves its rank as a classic; Smith considers issues both timely, in terms of current economic problems, and timeless, with keen insight and wisdom we would do well to follow. Central to our purposes is Smith's notion of the role of self-love, self-interest, and greed, which can be found early in the book. Smith offers a more tempered version of self-love further into the book, in the famed "invisible hand" passage:

> [By acting in his own interest] He generally, indeed, neither intends to promote the public interest, nor knows how much he is promoting it. By preferring the support of domestic to that of foreign industry, he intends only his own security; and by directing

that industry in such a manner as its produce may be of the greatest value, he intends only his own gain, and he is in this, as in many other cases, led by an invisible hand to promote an end which was no part of his intention. Nor is it always the worse for the society that it was not part of it. By pursuing his own interest he frequently promotes that of the society more effectually than when he really intends to promote it. I have never known much good done by those who affected to trade for the public good. It is an affectation, indeed, not very common among merchants, and very few words need be employed in dissuading them from it. (1776/1965, p. 423)

Smith outlines here the doctrine that Becker and his contemporaries seem to rely upon two centuries later. However, for Smith, what would constitute "pursuing his own interest" turns out to be somewhat different than the standard Becker-Williamson interpretation. The *Wealth of Nations* was Smith's masterpiece on economics and trade, but not on human nature. His earlier work, *The Theory of Moral Sentiments* (1759) provides a longer and more thorough exposition of his views on human nature. In the *Theory,* Smith outlines several virtues; a critical and perhaps paramount virtue in humans is *prudence.* Smith describes and defines prudence and its relationship to other virtues:

> Wise and judicious conduct, when directed to greater and nobler purposes than the care of the health, the fortune, the rank and reputation of the individual, is frequently and very properly called prudence. . . . Prudence is, in all these cases, combined with many greater and more splendid virtues, with valour, with extensive and strong benevolence, with a sacred regard to the rules of justice, and all these supported by a proper degree of self-command. This superior prudence, when carried to the highest degree of perfection, necessarily supposes the art, the talent, and the habit or disposition of acting with the most perfect propriety in every possible circumstance and situation. It necessarily presupposes the utmost perfection of all the intellectual and of all the moral virtues. It is the best head joined with the best heart. It is the most perfect wisdom combined with the most perfect virtue. It constitutes very nearly the character of the Academical or Peripatetic sage, as the inferior prudence does that of the Epicurean. (1759/1984, p. 216)

Note in this passage three things: First, there are ends of human action nobler than the mere pursuit of self-interest, described as health, fortune, rank, and reputation; second, the importance of the virtues of self-command—regard for rules, justice, and valor; and third, the purpose of life as the creation of a character, as opposed to the maximization of utility. Smith's *H. economicus* could focus on his or her self-interest precisely because, in his or her best incarnation, *H. economicus* was transcended by a *H. moralis*, an individual primarily concerned with the development of a virtuous character and endowed with a strong sense of propriety and self-control. Self-interest, the Epicurean, could pursue its ends because those ends were tightly bounded within the larger objective of obtaining a moral character.

Smith's view of the social nature of man reflects this preference for virtue.

> It is thus that man, who can subsist only in society, was fitted by nature to that situation for which he was made. All the members of human society stand in need of each other's assistance, and are likewise exposed to mutual injuries. Where the necessary assistance is reciprocally afforded from love, from gratitude, from friendship, and esteem, the society flourishes and is happy. All the different members of it are bound together by the agreeable bands of love and affection, and are, as it were, drawn to one common centre of mutual good offices.

> But though the necessary assistance should not be afforded from such generous and disinterested motives, though among the different members of the society there should be no mutual love, affection, the society, though less happy and agreeable, will not necessarily be dissolved. Society may subsist among different men, as among different merchants, from a sense of its utility, without any mutual love or affection; and though no man in it should owe any obligation, or be bound in gratitude to any other, it may still be upheld by a mercenary exchange of good offices according to an agreed valuation. (1759/1984, p. 85–86)

Here, we see two social orders juxtaposed: one built on prudence, benevolence, and virtue; the other built on self-interest. To use a modern economic phrase, Smith clearly viewed a society built on self-interest to be "second-best," inferior in happiness *and* prosperity from one built on virtue. Smith's classical economics teaches POS that a concern for virtue and virtuous action may lead to better organizational societies. The logic of classical theory suggests that POS may not only lead to happier but also more prosperous organizations because the actions of *H. moralis* may lead to both happiness and prosperity.

Alfred Marshall: *Homo economicus* and *Homo marginalus*

The story continues as we fast-forward a century to the dawn of the neo-classical, or marginalist, economic model and the impressive writings of Sir Alfred Marshall. The marginalist paradigm differed from Smith's classical conception in many ways: a theory of value based on consumer utility rather than supplier inputs, the role of price as a market clearing signal and mechanism, and the importance of decision making "at the margin" in determining both individual choice and economy-wide equilibrium. Marshall's thinking and writing on these and other topics are clear and concise enough that his fundamental text, *Principles of Economics* (1890), could still be used in most economics classes today.

The marginalists parted company with Smith's classical system on many elements. Did they also move away from the *H. moralis* postulated by Smith? Marshall notes some wandering in this direction by his contemporaries: "Attempts have indeed been made to construct an abstract science with regard to the actions of an 'economic man,' who is under no ethical influences and who pursues pecuniary gain warily and energetically, but mechanically and selfishly" (1890, p. xii). It seems the proponents of rational choice theory were already at work. Marshall, however, builds his theory upon

> [M]an as he is: not with an abstract or "economic" man; but a man of flesh and blood. They [economists] deal with a man who is largely influenced by egoistic motives in his business life to a great extent with reference to them; but who is also neither above vanity and recklessness, nor below delight in doing his work for its own sake, or in sacrificing himself for the good of his family, his neighbors, or his country; a man who is not below the love of a virtuous life for its own sake. (1890/2006, p. 27)

For Marshall, as for Smith, *H. economicus* exists as a bounded individual, bounded in this passage less by absolute moral constraint than by a mixture of ethical and social considerations, an early form of the *H. socialus* posited by later Granovetter (1985) and others, in whom extreme self-interest is limited by the embedded character of the actor and the social relationships in which he or she lives.

In light of this, Marshall notes that "the problems, which are grouped as economic, [sic] relate specially to man's conduct under the influence of motives that are measurable by a money price, are found to make *a fairly homogeneous group*"

(1890/2006, p. 27, emphasis added). *Homo economicus* makes decisions in a limited sphere about a set of problems that have uniform characteristics, namely that they can be solved by the rational, calculating tools available through marginal analysis. However, for Marshall, as for Smith, the Becker-Williamson notion of a hegemonic *H. economicus* operative in all aspects of life would be inconsistent with their pragmatism and moral leanings.

Marshall's analysis suggests to POS that organizational actions motivated by social concerns, as opposed to those purely made on price considerations, may operate on a different logic—a logic of forgiveness, compassion, altruism. To the extent that the behaviors central to POS become more ingrained in organizational life, those organizations will become centers of deep meaning as well as economic gain (John Paul II, 1991). The phenomena considered by POS exist in a world in which organizational life, and its outcomes, has meaning beyond products, profits, or projects; organizational membership bestows identity, builds community, and spawns relationships not "measureable by a money price." One potential consequence of being in an organization operating according the transcendent logic of POS would be positive behaviors that exhibit a deviation-amplifying pattern: an organization in which compassion breeds compassion, for example (Weick, 1979).

John Maynard Keynes: *Homo economicus* trumped by *Homo animalus*—The Irrationality of Animal Spirits

Discussions of human nature in economics have not been limited to the sphere of microeconomics, the study of households and firms. The nature of economic man plays a prominent role in economics *writ large* as well, or the study of macroeconomics. The most prominent macroeconomist of our time is John Maynard Keynes, for as economists often quip, comparing Keynes to Freud: "We're all Keynesians now." Although Keynesianism suffered a fall from grace during the Reagan revolution and the rise of neo-conservatism, Keynesian principles form the foundation of most macroeconomics courses and neo-Keynesians such as George Ackerloff and Robert Schiller (2009) see a renaissance of Keynesian supremacy in policy making realms.

Economic historian Robert Heilbroner (1999) sets Keynes' views on human nature in its historical and theoretical context. Economists always assumed that business cycles (aka recessions or depressions) would be a self-correcting phenomenon. As business

conditions deteriorated, unemployment would rise, inventories would fall, and the economy would contract. As the process went on, however, a bottom would be reached. Eventually inventories would need to be restocked, which would lead to hiring and expansion of economic activity, which would eventually lead to growth and a rebound from recession. Economic downturns would end as if by an automatic mechanism (perhaps the macro version of an invisible hand) that would restore growth and prosperity.

The great depression of the 1930s seemed to defy this "invisible hand" logic; economic activity continued to wane, even in the face of low inventory stocks and other traditional triggers for growth. Keynes' masterwork, *The General Theory of Employment, Interest, and Money* (1936) considers how such an economic outcome might exist and what could be done to solve the problem. Heilbroner notes that

> *The General Theory* has a startling conclusion. There was no automatic safety mechanism after all! Rather than a seesaw that would always right itself, the economy resembled an elevator: it could be going up or down, but it could also be standing perfectly still. And it was just as capable of standing still on the ground floor as at the top of the shaft. A depression, in other words, might not cure itself at all; the economy could lie stagnant indefinitely, like a ship becalmed. (1999, p. 270)

What would cause such a halt in the self-correcting cycle of repair? For Keynes, the culprit here was human nature, as he explains:

> There is the instability due to the characteristic of human nature that a large proportion of our positive activities depend on spontaneous optimism rather than on a mathematical expectation, whether moral or hedonistic or economic. Most, probably, of our decisions to do something positive, the full consequences of which will be drawn out over many days to come, can only be taken as a results of *animal spirits*—of a spontaneous urge to action rather than inaction, and not as the outcome of a weighted average of quantitative benefits multiplied by quantitative probabilities . . . this means, unfortunately, not only that slumps and depressions are exaggerated in degree, but that economic prosperity is excessively dependent on a political and social atmosphere which is congenial to the average business man. (1936/2009, p. 174, emphasis added)

For Keynes, people are not rational thinkers, they don't engage in precise calculations, either in the short term or especially in considering the long run. They make decisions to invest or act based on things like "spontaneous optimism" (emotion) or "congenial" political and social conditions (temporary states of social nature). Decisions to hoard or to withhold action can just as easily be made based on "spontaneous pessimism" or "unfriendly" external conditions. In short, *H. economicus* may not be transcended by but rather supplanted by *H. animalus*: economic actors driven by "animal spirits" rather than rational, logical utility maximizing calculations. Unlike Smith and Marshall, Keynes had no particular belief that *H. economicus* existed but was constrained by either moral or social constraints; Keynes worried about the economic effects of human behavior that could just as easily be irrational as rational, and may exhibit a fundamental tendency toward irrationality.

Nobel laureate George Ackerloff and his colleague Robert Schiller (2009) recently revisited Keynes' notion of animal spirits. They note four particular manifestations of *H. animalus* that confound economic reasoning: the nature of confidence, or optimism, as a self-fulfilling prophecy; the propensity of humans to prefer interpersonally fair outcomes to maximizing ones; the presence of corruption and bad faith (as opposed to the ethical egoism posited by *H. economicus*); the inability of people to rationally calculate things such as real versus nominal income (i.e., the money illusion); and a strong preference for stories as heuristics for dealing with uncertainty. Each element represents a unique way in which economic actors systematically vary from the dictates of *H. economicus*.

Consider the fun example of fairness and how it plays out in the ultimatum game. Two individuals play: Player One is given a sum of money (say $5.00 if done with undergraduates, $20 in the MBA classroom, $100 in an executive setting). The money must be shared between the two, and Player One proposes a split. Player Two can either accept the split, leading to a distribution of funds, or she can refuse, leading to a forfeiture of funds for both players. Given a $5.00 fund, what is the "rational" payoff for *H. economicus*? A $4.99 and $0.01 split, which leaves both players better off than before. Player One maximizes her revenue (utility), and Player Two also sees a gain that would be foregone by refusing.

I've done this experiment in class and the most common result is that Player One offers to split the money with Player Two, with each taking home $2.50. Although pleasing, these results run counter

to the dictates of *H. economicus*, both for the proposer and the responder. Empirical results on large samples find not only a similar outcome, but also find that "responders [Player Two] reject even substantial offers a in the range $0 < \alpha < p/2$, which they apparently regard as unfair, and proposers [Player One] shy away from excessively low offers; the most frequent (modal) offer is usually the equal split $p/2$" (Guth & Ortmann, 2006, p. 407).

Rational choice theorists explain away these "nonrational" results in terms of reputation effects; actors see long-term utility in being perceived as fair. Although this sounds plausible, the explanation suffers from two problems. First, MBA players often see greater reputational gains by playing the role of ruthless economic actors, meaning that reputation may work in the opposite direction than theorized. Second, Francois (2002) notes that markets for reputation presume a set of ex ante meaningful relationships—social capital—that predate the beginning of economic transacting. In other words, markets for economic reputations build on relational-social, not economic-rational, foundations.

Confidence stands as another of Keynes' "animal spirits." Ackerloff and Shiller explain:

> But if we look up *confidence* in the dictionary, we see that it is more than a prediction. The dictionary says that it means "trust" or "full belief." The word comes from the Latin *fido*, meaning "I trust." The confidence crisis that we are in at the time of this writing is also called a *credit crisis*. The word *credit* derives from the Latin word *credo*, meaning "I believe."
>
> Given these additional shades of meaning, economists' point of view, based on dual equilibria or rosy versus bleak predictions, seems to miss something. Economists have only partly captured what is meant by *trust* or *belief*. Their view suggests that confidence is rational: people make use of the information at hand to make rational predictions; they then make a rational decision based on those rational predictions. Certainly people often do make decisions, confidently, in this way. But there is more to the notion of *confidence*. The very meaning of trust is that we go beyond the rational. Indeed the truly trusting person often discards or discounts certain information. She may not even process the information that is available to her rationally; even if she has *processed* it rationally, she still may not *act* on it rationally. She acts according to what she *trusts* to be true. (2009, p. 12; emphasis in original)

How do policy makers deal with this animal spirit? Ackerloff and Shiller (2009), standard macroeconomics texts (Mankow, 2006), and popular writers (Schmick, 2008) all call for expectations management as a key determinant of economic policy. Thus, the Federal Reserve plays a substantive economic role in determining discount rates and the money supply, but a larger symbolic economic role of managing the expectations (i.e., confidence) of a jittery public about coming economic conditions. Shcmick (2008) notes that the jittery, often irrational, public includes professional investors as well as the nonprofessional public. At the policy level, those who may espouse a belief in *H. economicus* must play roles that make sense only if he is a fiction.

The existence of *H. animalus* suggests another role for the positive behaviors of interest to POS: To the extent that these behaviors create a set of "optimistic" or "congenial" expectations about the future, they are likely to lead to investment and action on the part of organizational participants. Put simply, under conditions of environmental uncertainty, a presumption of trust encourages action rather than inaction; the positive outcomes of POS behaviors may be economic as well as social and/or moral.

Behavioral Economics: *Homo economicus* as *Homo sapiens*

Smith, Marshall, and Keynes all preceded the introduction of the narrow *H. economicus* of Becker and Williamson. Just as Marshall's analysis corrected errors in Smith's reasoning, and Keynes considered an economy far different from the one confronting Marshall, does the Becker-Williamson view of *H. economicus* represent an evolutionary advance over previous theorizing? Is *H. economicus* the last and best word on human nature?

A look at recent work in behavioral economics indicates no. *Homo economicus* looks more like a theoretical simplification than an advanced description of human behavior. Economists and other social scientists working in the broad, multidisciplinary field known as behavioral economics have been working to modify the Becker-Williamson received conception of economic man since the initial work of Simon (1957). Simon noted that economic actors aren't rational in any complete sense; they don't have access to all relevant economic information and would be unable to process it even if they could get it.

Altman (2006) describes the assumption behind the growing body of work known as behavioral economics: "behavioral economists find that individuals, firms, particular markets, and economies all often behave differently than is predicted by conventional wisdom. The manner in which individuals actually do behave critically depends on psychological, institutional, cultural, and even biological considerations that affect and constrain the choices individuals can and do make" (Altman, 2006, p. xvii). Put simply, behavioral economists study why people behave in ways inconsistent with the prescriptions of *H. economicus*, but rather act like *H. animalus, H. moralis,* or *H. socialus,* or more generally *H. sapiens.*

I cite two brief examples here. Behavioral economics has recently drawn on the emerging science of evolutionary neurobiology to better understand the human hard-wiring that underlies behavior. Cory (2006) explains that the current view in neurobiology models the human brain as "interconnected, modular [and] tri-level: a set of features referred to as the 'reptilian complex,' another known as the 'paleomammalian complex,' and a 'neocortex/neomammalian complex'" (Cory, 2006, p. 25). The reptilian complex houses the set of emotions, cognitions, and wiring that controls the ego, or self-interested, response. The paleomammalian complex produces our empathic, other-interested responses, and evolved as a result of our need to live in families and larger social groups to enhance survival prospects. The neocortex serves as a type of executive program, working to create a dynamic balance between the two competing urges and is the most recent evolutionary development.

Homo economicus, by definition, works only on self-interest; he is power seeking, assertive, competitive, and values his own needs above all. *Homo economicus* fits the prescriptions and behaviors of the reptilian brain. However, behavior dominated by the ego suppresses the human empathic, mammalian, response and the hard-wired desire for self-sacrifice, supportiveness, and other-interested behaviors. This suppression results in biological stress that inexorably moves behavior toward the other-interested pole (Cory, 2006). Since human behavior is driven by both centers of the brain, the best the neocortex can hope to do is maintain a dynamic balance between the two, characterized by behaviors such as compromise and concerns for fairness and justice.

The work in neurobiology implies that *H. economicus* may not be a fiction. There exists a part of our natures that wants to behave according to its dictates. *Homo economicus* is naturally and inevitably in conflict with *H. empathicus,* our other-interested self. As Cory (2006, p. 27) notes, this may not be such a bad thing:

> The evolutionary process by which the two opposite promptings of self-preservation and affection were combined in us helped us survive by binding us in social interaction and social exchange, thereby providing us with the widest range of behavioral responses to our environment. Our inborn conflicting programs are a curse, then, only to the degree that we fail to recognize them as a blessing. Our self-preservation and affection programs allow us a highly advanced sensitivity to our environment, keeping our interactive social exchange behaviors homeostatically within survival limits as well as enabling us to perceive and appreciate the survival requirements of others. Ironically, the accompanying behavioral tension—even the stress—is an integral part of this useful function.

In sum, neurobiology implies that *H. economicus* represents at best part of our nature—but only a part—and the assumption of behavior exclusively or primarily driven by self-interest may not only be impoverished, it may be patently false. The findings from behavioral economics suggest that the behaviors of interest to POS may not be merely praiseworthy—they appear fundamentally critical to the long run effective functioning of organizations and institutions. They seem as hardwired into our consciousness as rationality or self-interest.

If the findings from neurobiology question the value of the assumption of self-interest seeking behavior, psychological findings around the topic of intuition raise doubts as to whether it is, in fact, irrational not to engage in the type of rational analysis and calculation that exemplify *H. economicus*. Frantz (2006, p. 51) lays out the case for the efficiency of intuition, or "a form of thinking, but not a conscious analytical (logical, sequential, step-by-step, and reasoned) process of thinking":

> The difficulty with rational decision making is that calculating costs and benefits so as to maximize subjective expected utility will take too much time and is subject to too much error. Two reasons are offered: the human attention span is too short, and the capacity of our working memory is too small. Second, the strategy of eliminating emotion from decision making "has far more to do with the patients with pre-frontal damage [i.e., brain damage] than with how normals usually operate. (Frantz, 2006, p. 57).

To respond to these difficulties, healthy humans use intuition. We engage in numerous shortcuts, including relying on our unconscious perceptions of situations (Gladwell, 2005), rules of thumb, or heuristics (Girgerenzer, 2007; Rieskamp, Hertwig, & Todd, 2006), or on our emotions and values—for example, Pascal's famous phrase "the heart has reasons that reason does not know at all" (in Cory, 2006). Rieskamp et al. (2006, p. 230) note that "there are two main reasons why simple heuristics often perform so well in comparison with more complex strategies. First, many problems have 'flat maxima,' meaning that the best solution does not differ substantially from other (e.g., heuristic) solutions. Second, heuristics can outperform other strategies in terms of generalization, that is, when applied to new situations."

The work around intuition suggests, similar to Simon's (1957) original formulation of satisficing, that cognitive processing limits often preclude the type of reasoning familiar to *H. economicus*, and if that is not enough, the complexities and novelties of living in a rapidly changing environment mean that gut feelings (Girgerenzer, 2007), emotion-driven reasoning (Stewart, 2004), or values-based decision making may prove superior to calculative reasoning. This finding further supports the view of humanity central to POS—a complete human being often willing to forego calculative reasoning so that he can work and play well with colleagues.

The important findings from behavioral economics suggest that the Becker-Williamson version of *H. economicus*, a rational, self-interested, amoral utility maximizer does not seem to be a descriptive or predictive advance over more classical conceptions, but rather a cognitive simplification and iconic representation that yields insights (consider the importance of Williamsonian analysis in strategic management) but may obscure as much about human behavior and motivation as it reveals.

Conclusion

I have argued here that the view of economic, and most likely organizational, man described in the *H. economicus* heuristic is at odds with a more normatively positive set of behavioral assumptions. Indeed, modern economics and POS appear to be strange bedfellows. The historical weight of economic thinking, however, reveals a different conception—an economic and organizational actor not only consonant with POS but likely to engage in the behaviors of self-sacrifice, altruism, concern for relationships, meaning, and excellence as often as not.

There seems to be no inconsistency between economic man and the *H. positivus* postulated by POS. The inconsistency arises when economic man is conceived of narrowly in the Becker-Williamson model.

The view of individuals posited classically by Adam Smith and most recently by behavioral economists implies something far deeper than merely that actors are more than calculating, narrow, rational, utility maximizers. Positive organizational scholarship behaviors may prove remarkably efficient as they help resolve fundamental challenges to information processing and cooperative action. Returning to the goals of POS outlined at the beginning—a study of excellent, meaningful, high-quality organizational outcomes—such outcomes may exist in multiple manifestations: economic, social, and moral. Before finishing with such a rosy prediction, however, I note three areas where further work is needed, or where Peterson and Seligman's (2003) proverbial horses need to be tamed.

First, if not *H. economicus*, then who?: *Homo moralis, H. socialis, H. animalus,* or *H. sapiens*? Although pleasing to note that *H. positivus* is not a strange bedfellow with an expansive *H. economicus* found in economic theorizing, the solid and detailed work to outline the behavior basis of *H. positivus* remains to be done. *Homo economicus* may be undersocialized and -moralized and overrationalized. The extreme notions of *H. moralis, H. socialis,* or *H. animalus* would likewise suffer the same malady: focusing on one aspect of human nature at the exclusion of others. My suggestion here would be a focus on humans as *H. sapiens* to capture the entire range of behavioral drivers that influence human action in individual and organizational settings. Whatever the ultimate resolution, one horse POS needs to harness is a clear and cogent set of behavioral priors that motivate action.

Second, whither Organization? How does the act of organizing to gain cooperation change individuals? If organizations are filled with complex people acting on multiple motivations, how do the simplifying features of organizational life, such as the division of labor and articulated roles, constrain, but also enable, different actions, particularly those considered positive? What types of cultures exacerbate/mitigate the different aspects of *H. sapiens*? How do different structures, compensations systems, and information processing systems influence the balance between *H. economicus* and *H. empathicus*? And, what about the managerially relevant question

of how does one create organizational alignment to support the balance between these two hard-wired facets of human nature?

Finally, do POS behaviors lead to economically, as well as socially or morally, superior outcomes? This is the strategy question: Do organizations that engage in POS behaviors actually create greater happiness and prosperity as Adam Smith stipulated? If the first two questions are clearly theoretical then this last one invites serious empirical research. For example, do organizations with high-quality interpersonal relationships, or those rich in meaning, win in the marketplace, and for labor and/or products? Such a question forces research beyond network models of relationships because there is no guarantee that network centrality correlates to anything like quality of human interaction. Similarly, how does one define meaning and create some type of empirical scale that differentiates organizations rich in meaning with those less rich? Finally, what is the appropriate time frame for measuring "superior outcomes?" Do POS-driven organizations win in the short run, long run, before, during, or after a crisis? Answering questions such as these will force POS scholars to confront and tame many of Peterson and Seligman's (2003) horses, but they will also expose many unicorns, the unique and different features of POS organizations.

As POS enters its second decade as an area of organizational scholarship, there is much to be grateful for. Research and theorizing are moving forward, and the impressive list of authors and the wide range of topics found in this volume testify to the fundamental utility and interest in the notions of positive organizations. The conclusion of this chapter is that such work need not disparage, and may in fact draw support from, the assumptions underlying economic behavior.

References

Ackerlof, G.A., & Shiller, R.J. (2009). *Animal spirits: How human psychology drives the economy, and why it matters for global capitalism.* Princeton, NJ: Princeton University Press.

Altman, M. (2006). Introduction. In M. Altman (Ed.), *Handbook of contemporary behavioral economics: Foundations and developments* (pp. xv–xxii). Armonk, NY: M.E. Sharpe.

Becker, G. (1976). *The economic approach to human behavior.* Chicago: The University of Chicago Press.

Becker, G.S. (1965). A theory of the allocation of time. *The Economic Journal, 75,* 493–517.

Becker, G.S. (1968). Crime and punishment: An economic approach. *Journal of Political Economy, 76,* 169–217.

Cameron, K.S., Dutton, J.E., & Quinn, R.E. (2003). Foundations of positive organizational scholarship. In K.S. Cameron, J.E. Dutton, & R.E. Quinn (Eds.), *Positive organizational scholarship* (pp. 3–14). San Francisco: Berrett-Koehler.

Cory, G.A. (2006). Physiology and behavioral economics: The new findings from evolutionary neuroscience. In M. Altman (Ed.), *Handbook of contemporary behavioral economics: Foundations and developments* (pp. 24–49). Armonk, NY: M.E. Sharpe.

Francois, P. (2002). *Social capital and economic development.* London: Routledge.

Frantz, R. (2006). Intuition in behavioral economics. In M. Altman (Ed.), *Handbook of contemporary behavioral economics: Foundations and developments* (pp. 50–65). Armonk, NY: M.E. Sharpe.

Friedman, M. (1953). *Essays in positive economics.* Chicago: University of Chicago Press.

Girgerenzer, G. (2007). *Gut feelings: The intelligence of the unconscious.* London: Penguin Books.

Gladwell, M. (2005). *Blink: The power of thinking without thinking.* New York: Back Bay Books.

Guth, W., & Ortmann, A. (2006). A behavioral approach to distribution and bargaining. In M. Altman (Ed.), *Handbook of contemporary behavioral economics: Foundations and developments* (pp. 405–422). Armonk, NY: M.E. Sharpe.

Heilbroner, R.L. (1999). *The worldly philosophers: The lives, times, and ideas of the great economic thinkers.* New York: Touchstone Books.

John Paul II. (1991). *Centessimus annus.* Rome.

Keynes, J.M. (2009). *The general theory of employment, interest, and money.* Hamburg, Germany: Management Laboratory Press. (Original work published 1936).

Mankiw, N.G. (2006). *Macroeconomics* (6th ed.). New York: Worth Publishers.

Marshall, A. (2006). *Principles of economics, abridged edition.* New York: Cosimo Classics. (Original work published 1890).

Medema, S.G. (2009). *The hesitant hand: Taming self-interest in the history of economic ideas.* Princeton, NJ: Princeton University Press.

Mill, J.S. (1863/1987). *Utilitarianism.* Buffalo, NY: Prometheus Books.

Nicholson, W. (1995). *Microeconomic theory: Basic principles and extensions.* Fort Worth, TX: The Dryden Press.

Peterson, C.M., & Seligman, M.E.P. (2003). Positive organizational studies: Lessons from positive psychology. In K.S. Cameron, J.E. Dutton, & R.E. Quinn (Eds.), *Positive organizational scholarship* (pp. 14–28). San Francisco: Berrett-Koehler.

Risekamp, J., Hertwig, R., & Todd, P.M. (2006). Bounded rationality: Two interpretations from psychology. In M. Altman (Ed.), *Handbook of contemporary behavioral economics: Foundations and developments* (pp. 218–236). Armonk, NY: M.E. Sharpe.

Schmick, D.M. (2008). *The world is curved: Hidden dangers to the global economy.* New York: Penguin Books.

Simon, H.A. (1957). *Models of man: Social and rational.* New York: Wiley.

Smith, A. (1984). *The theory of moral sentiments.* Indianapolis: Liberty Fund. (Original work published 1759).

Smith, A. (1965). *An inquiry into the nature and causes of the wealth of nations.* New York: The Modern Library. (Original work published 1776).

Stewart, T.A. (2004). The highway of the mind. *Harvard Business Review,* January, 116.

Weick, K.E. (1979). *The social psychology of organizing* (2nd ed.). New York: McGraw-Hill.

Williamson, O.E. (1985). *The economic institutions of capitalism.* New York: Free Press.

Social Movements in Organizations

Debra Guckenheimer

Abstract

This chapter examines the linkages between positive organizational scholarship (POS) and social movements scholarship. Positive organizational scholarship is interested in prosocial and citizen behavior as well as corporate responsibility. Social movements can influence those within formal organizations to engage in prosocial and citizen behavior and can be an important force in driving corporate social responsibility. Activists bring social movement agendas into the formal organizations they engage in during their everyday lives, including their workplace. This chapter is based upon a review of the social movement literature and the author's multimethod empirical research on faculty efforts to increase institutional diversity as a case study of insider activism.

Keywords: Social movements, organizations, social change, diversity, collective behavior

Scholarship on social movements has much to offer positive organizational scholars. Social movements contribute to two components of positive organizational scholarship (POS) noted by Cameron, Dutton, and Quinn (2003): prosocial and citizen behavior, and corporate social responsibility. These may be driven by activists located either inside or outside an organization. External activists shape organizations directly through boycotts, publicity campaigns, and lawsuits, or indirectly by shaping laws and codes that govern organizations. Internal activists can directly lobby for change within organizations. Although social movement scholarship has long recognized the activism of unions, which have a long history of targeting corporations as well as the state, social movements also form their own organizations, which create important social change on their own. Unions and social movement organizations, however, are not the focus of this chapter. Instead, this chapter focuses on how progressive social movement activists become insiders within mainstream organizations and bring movement goals with them. I demonstrate how prosocial and

citizen behavior, as well as corporate responsibility, are sometimes driven by social movements.

Social movement activists organize to advance collective goals that they view as positive, although the values of social movement activists may not be positive from the view of others in society and may even lead to counter-movements and resistance. Individuals participating in social movement activity do so out of shared values; however, others outside that movement might find those values abhorrent and respond by participating in counter-movements.[1] For example, those within the pro-choice movement see themselves as working for positive social change, but those within the pro-life movement organize against the shared beliefs within the pro-choice movement. Some organizations are more able to handle opposing values than are others, and this chapter is of value to those who wish to be inclusive by allowing for disagreements about values. Although other types of values-driven change efforts can be analyzed by some of the concepts and tools offered by this chapter, I focus on change efforts that are influenced by social movements. Therefore, this chapter will be of particular interest to POS scholars interested in organizational change.

This chapter is based on both the existing literature on social movements and organizations and my own empirical research. The empirical research is a case study of activism within organizations, exploring the influence of social movements on faculty diversity work or efforts to increase institutional diversity in higher education. This research occurred under two phases with a team of scholars[2] from 2004 to 2008. The first phase involved interviewing 35 faculty members identified as change agents on issues of diversity at the University of California, Santa Barbara. The second phase of research was an online survey of the faculty at nine colleges and universities across the United States. Quotes provided in this chapter are from the first phase of research. The case of faculty diversity work provides an example of individuals organizing together within a formal organization to make what they consider to be positive changes. Not all diversity work is social movement organizing; however, I focus on efforts that are connected to or influenced by civil rights, black power, Chicano, and feminist movements.

Although organizational change may occur because of a multitude of factors, I focus this chapter on change making efforts within formal organizations by social movements. This chapter begins with a definition of social movements. Next, I explain how social movements drive organizations to change, and how organizational change may be an outcome of social movement activism. I outline the multitude of ways in which movements enter organizations. Last, I discuss the role of insider activists within organizations. I conclude by providing three categories of change created by social movements inside organizations and offer suggestions for future research. Because of the nature of my data, my analysis focuses on progressive social movements of the Left.

What Are Social Movements?

Positive change can occur only after people become aware of and identify problems or grievances. Social movements arise after groups identify a grievance and then decide to collectively challenge that grievance. Grievances tend to arise from societal strains, conflicts, and injustices (Gurr, 1970; Taylor, 2000; Turner & Killian, 1972). But a grievance is not enough to bring about a social movement. Social movement scholars disagree about what exactly movements are and why they form, and it is

important to distinguish between individuals working to create change and social movements. In this section, I provide a definition of social movements within the context of this debate about movements.

Definitions of social movements are highly variable and contested within social movement scholarship, but having a framework for understanding social movements in organizations is important. Therefore, I have identified the essential elements of the social movements for the purpose of understanding their operation within organizations. The first element is drawn from Taylor's (2000) assertion that social movements are composed of "forms of collective action where solidarity is employed with some temporal continuity to transgress, challenge, or defend the values, institutions, and structures of society" (p. 220). A social movement can thus be viewed as a group of people who share a common identity based on experiencing collective injustice and are working to change society in some way. People may participate in a social movement who do not share an identity, such as feminist men, and some of those who provide social movements with financial resources, labor, and facilities may have ideological connection to them (McCarthy & Zald, 1977). Still, solidarity is important in the mobilization of activists—movements do not organize around personal problems, only around those seen as shared problems; collective identity is important to the maintenance of movements over time (Taylor, 2010). The second key element of a social movement framework is described by Zald and Berger (1978, p. 828) who say that a social movement is an "expression of a preference for change among members of a society." Activists express this preference for change by organizing, utilizing a limited array of possible tactics and other actions, and these have been called "collective action repertoires" (Tarrow, 1997). A social movement requires groups of people who share solidarity and collective action repertoires engaged in contentious politics to create change on a particular issue. Actions that are not collective and that fail to challenge systems of inequality are excluded from this framework (Armstrong & Bernstein, 2008).

Social movement scholars are just beginning to look at how movements can bring about change in organizations. Traditionally activism directed at the state was recognized by movement scholars. Social movement theory has often assumed that activists are disenfranchised (Taylor, 2000), but social movement actors have varying levels of power within the multiple institutions they struggle to change. Some social movement actors are located inside organizations and institutions and wield considerable power. For example, although sexism negatively impacts all women, some individual women do have power within their organizations. Increasingly, social movement theorists understand that movements broadly target society including the state, organizations, power, and culture (Armstrong & Bernstein, 2008; Taylor, 2010). Figure 75.1 shows outlining how social movements operate within organizations. I will explain the figure throughout this chapter.

Organization scholars do not need to identify a social movement within an organization in order to benefit from social movement scholarship. People within organizations may try to create change without forming a new movement or participating in an established one. For example, people may be influenced by social movements even if they do not directly participate in them. It is helpful, however, to identify the effect of social movements on organizational change when apparent.

Driving Organizations to Change

In this section, I argue that social movements can cause important organizational change. The marriage between social movement and organizational scholarships was largely developed by Mayer Zald

(Morrill, Zald, & Rao, 2003; Zald, 2005; Zald & Berger, 1978; Zald, Morrill, & Rao 2005). Morrill, Zald, and Rao (2003, p. 392) examine what they term *covert political conflict* in organizations, as they argue that many movement scholars overlook organized efforts to create change within organizations. Although they recognize that these challenges are often embedded in broader social conflicts and that covert political conflict is a way for subordinated groups to express grievances against superiors within an organization, challenges by subordinated groups are not seen as connected to broader social movements. Covert political activity offers a framework for subordinated groups to make sense of how social forces contribute to their otherwise seemingly personal problems (Morril, Zald, & Rao, 2003).

Indeed, many types of organizational change can be understood through social movement concepts. Strang and Jung (2005, p. 280) claim that, "Many efforts at organizational change are better understood as social movements." Claims such as this have led social movement scholars to analyze organizational change with social movement concepts. Zald and Berger (1978) looked at coup d'etat, insurgency, and mass movements inside organizations that they termed "corporate hierarchical forms" (as opposed to voluntary organizations), noting how organized groups of people inside organizations can cause organizational change.

Fig. 75.1 Social movements inside organizations.

Traditional social movement scholars who look at the impact of social movement actors inside the government can help us understand how social movement insiders bring about change in organizations. Moore (1999) used the term *mediators* to describe activists who are also members of an institution. She describes mediators as those occupying a middle ground who can argue the positions of activists to those inside institutions. However, even this term implies that those acting in institutions are somehow separate from those actually engaging in the activism. Santoro and McGuire (1997) term social movement actors inside the government *institutional activists*. This framework can be extended to analyzing activists inside other types of bureaucratic organizations. Santoro and McGuire (1997) state that institutional activists can impact change by influencing policy outcomes by being a part of the decision making process, countering opposition to their movement, and monitoring policy implementation.

Organizations are one arena for social movements to engage in change making efforts. Social movement efforts inside organizations are influenced by factors internal and external to the organizations themselves. In a study of activism of lesbian, gay, and bisexuals for workplace rights, Raeburn (2004) presents an "institutional opportunity framework" of factors that facilitate social movement success on the macro and meso institutional levels. On the macro level, there are three types of processes: sociopolitical (e.g., boycotts and lawsuits), organizational field (e.g., career mobility and structure of the field), and professional and cultural (e.g., outsider activists and culture of the organization). On the meso level, there are structural templates (i.e., preexisting supports for the movement), organizational realignments (e.g., change in elite office holders), allies (i.e., coalition partners or support from management), and cultural supports (i.e., corporate culture). As employees engage in activism, they improve the organizational field for their movement. Improvements in one field can affect another, even in the absence of visible insider activists as the improvements become institutionalized (Raeburn, 2004). By operating from within organizations, social movement activists create durable changes, although sometimes vis-à-vis compromise and co-optation of their ideas, as I will explain later in this chapter.

Movements Shift Organizational Contexts

The accomplishments of social movements *outside* organizations can cause pressure for organizations to shift or at least create opportunities for change *inside* organizations. Clemens (2005) notes how conflict within organizations is sometimes the result of outside tensions (caused by social movements) and how actors aligned with social movements may heighten said conflict. Social movements in organizations may be more successful when movement activism is also taking place outside organizations. Katzenstein (1998) argues that activists inside organizations may rely on activist work outside organizations, especially when they are more accountable to authority within the institution. If activism is risky and may result in retribution from supervisors, including job loss, activists inside organizations are more likely to be dependent upon activism outside the organization. In part, this process is about how cultural and political shifts caused by social movements create space for those inside organizations to make political challenges. In turn, cultural and political shifts also can stimulate activism (Taylor, 1996).

Social movements can change the organizational context and create legitimacy for their claims. For example, Rojas (2007) notes how the civil rights and black nationalist movements' successes in shifting race relations led to a legitimacy for African American students' claims and subsequent protests. Without the achievements of the broader movement, the organizational context at colleges and universities in the United States would have been less receptive to the organizing efforts of black students. Subsequently, the success of creating and institutionalizing black studies changed the organizational context of higher education further. In this case, the achievements of the civil rights and black nationalist movements created space for black students' demands aimed at universities, which were themselves located within a larger context of activism on university campuses.

Whether organizations will change according to movement pressure depends on multiple factors, including type of tactics used, organizational context, and length of protest. Moore (1999) argues that disruptive tactics may support success in change making efforts.

Disruptive challenges do not necessarily need to take place from outside the organization. Insiders can also bring challenges, and the disruption might be subtle. The level of disruption needed to influence change may depend on the power of those causing the disruption. Moore (1999) also argues that protest over longer periods of time is more likely to be effective than shorter-term actions.

Organizations have multiple options for responding to demands from social movements. Goldner (2005) describes six options: avoiding the pressure from activists, providing resources to movements, preexisting members of the organization coming to participate in the movement, allowing activists from the movement to join the organization, co-opting the movement by allowing it insider status but restricting its work to a limited set of reforms, and constraining a movement by creating a counter-movement. Goldner (2005) argues that institutional theories demonstrate that organizations can avoid the pressure to change by hiding their resistance. For example, in terms of efforts to increase institutional diversity, college and university administrators may talk about diversity and hire someone to work on diversity issues but not give them power or authority.

Zald, Morrill, and Rao (2005) suggest viewing organizations and social movements in interaction. No matter how organizations respond, social movements change the costs and benefits of pursuing particular policies and practices (Zald, Morrill, & Rao, 2005). Still, Zald, Morrill, and Rao (2005, p. 257) assume that organizations are "more or less unified actors whose responses to differential pressures vary according to organizational commitments (or resistance) to the intents or goals of the movement and organizational capacity." But, organizations are not necessarily unified actors, and some organizational actors are also social movement actors.

To really see organizations and movements in interaction, attention must be paid to how they are intertwined and interconnected. For example, Feminist, Black Power, and Chicano movements led to the establishment of Women's Studies, Black Studies, and Chicano Studies programs and departments within colleges and universities across the United States. In turn, these departments hire scholar-activists who often have ties to social movements, and those faculty members recruit colleagues and students to become involved in diversity work.

Organizational Leadership

Organizational leaders or elites can greatly affect the success of social movement activism. Although Cress and Myers (2004) note that sociopolitical elites can either facilitate or constrain movement success, the importance of elites is more complicated than just considering if elites are supportive or opposed to a particular movement. Organizational elites create organizational cultures that shape social

movements' ability to create change. For example, Rojas' (2007) study noted the importance of the administrators to social movement activism at universities. In his study of black student activism at San Francisco State from 1968 to 1969, Rojas notes how social movement activity shifted with a changing of college presidents, both of whom were resistant to student demands, but who had different approaches and skill sets in countering those demands.

Culture

Culture (both on a broad societal and localized organizational levels) can operate either to facilitate or constrain movements. Culture provides institutional schemas, shared meanings, or the rules of the game, which are self-sustaining and can reproduce institutions and/or be the impetus for social movement activity (Polletta, 2004). Since changes to culture within an organization will thus change practices (Polletta, 2004), culture is an important factor for movement activity in organizations. Polletta, therefore, argues that practices around less prestigious cultural objects will be easier to change than cultural objects endowed with higher prestige (such as a school mascot).

Tactics

Social movements raise grievances and pressure organizations to change through a variety of tactics. They bring attention to grievances, lobbying organizational authorities to change policies and practices, and working through government influence over organizations (Zald, Morrill, & Rao, 2005). Movements can exploit rifts among people inside organizations, as well as organizational weaknesses, to encourage support, or at least reduce resistance, from organizational insiders (Binder, 2002; Rojas 2007). Movements will likely choose tactics based on their target, and organizations will respond differently, depending upon the tactics used. Although traditionally social movement scholars focused on protest and contentious politics, those inside organizations often utilize tactics that take advantage of their insider status.

Performing particular roles inside a formal organization can be a tactic to create change, as insiders recognize the power of their organizations. My empirical data about faculty diversity work provide an example of this. Although operating within an office is not traditionally thought of as activism, some see a measure of what they do in their office as a part of achieving social movement goals. In an interview, a Chicano studies professor said, "Activism can sometimes be defined even functioning in an office. Believe it or not, sometimes even in certain moments even pushing paper the right way [is an act of activism]. Activism is something you do when you get the opportunity to make the case and promote that type of agenda." Faculty members have varying levels of power within institutions of higher education, and when they engage in diversity work, they wield that power to achieve social movement goals.

How Do Movements Enter Organizations?

People inside organizations may have ties to outside social movements, and their activism may come to "spill over" into their place of work, worship, etc. For example, Raeburn (2004) looks at how the gay rights movement led to activists creating changes in their places of employment. Raeburn calls these activists operating from within organizations *internal activists* (2004, p. 241). Diversity activism in the workplace is one mechanism by which social movements move into organizations (Clemens & Minkoff, 2004). Ideas, tactics, style, organizational structures, frames, and participants spread from one movement to another; this is *spillover* (Meyer & Whittier, 1997). When activists in a movement raise their issues to the institutions they deal with in their daily life (such as their places of work), their movement spills over into this new institution. Entrenchment in organizations occurs as social movement actors create connections with their targets of change (e.g., repeatedly meeting with a member of Congress) and bring their activism to their places of employment, religious institutions, and community groups (see Figure 75.1).

As social movements successfully make claims to organizations, organizations may be pressured to consider these claims when hiring. Some employees may be hired specifically because of their ties to social movements (Davis et al. 2005, p. 249). A Chicano studies professor described his faculty position as an extension of his participation in the Chicano movement: "When I came to [this campus] in '78 to be in this position, this position was really an extension of my previous studies and previous participation in a social movement, the Chicano movement." Social movements also pressure organizations to be cognizant of racial, gender, and sexual identity orientation inequalities when hiring.

Movements also enter organizations as those inside organizations become sympathetic to social movement claims. In the case of feminist activism inside labor unions, Fonow (2003) describes how the broader feminist movement created legitimacy for women in unions to bring feminist challenges forward, even when activists were not necessarily directly connected with the broader feminist movement. Similarly, Katzenstein (1998) argues that the majority of feminist social changes occur within institutions through people who may not at all be connected with the feminist movement. For example, many academic men who do not identify with or connect to the feminist movement participate in committees and workgroups to reduce barriers for women in academic science because they are sympathetic to feminist claims of inequality relating to women in science. Even though social change may be created by those not connected to a social movement, they still may be affected by the movement in a positive way.

HIGH-RISK ACTIVISM THROUGH MICROEVENTS

One way that individuals can function as a site of political activity is through *microevents* that reframe issues of inequality. Microevents are interactions between individuals that challenge taken-for-granted arrangements that support discrimination (Creed & Scully, 2000). Creed and Scully (2000) look at lesbian, gay, and bisexual (LGB) employees that challenge homophobia and heterosexism in their workplace. They describe "encounters" as one type of microevent involving an interaction with a focus of displaying one's identity. Encounters involve LGB employees displaying their sexual identity with a coworker. By coming out, employees challenge homophobia in the workplace. The work of Creed and Scully (2000) demonstrates that bringing "invisible, marginalized, or even stigmatized aspects" (p. 391) of identity into encounters with coworkers can be social activism. Taylor and Raeburn (1995) call this "high-risk activism" since the individual is the site of political activity that could lead to bias, discrimination, and even job loss. Coming out is an act of activism since it tends to decrease homophobia: It is harder to hate those you know than those you do not (Herek & Glunt, 1993). Microevents can be important in creating change, especially in organizations.

Activists Inside Organizations

Just who are these activists inside organizations? Some are activists before entering organizations, and they bring their activism to their places of work either on their own or through the encouragement of the organization. Others only become activists once inside the organization, either motivated by other activists inside the organization or swayed by social movement activity from outside the organization.

Participation in social movements is likely to impact activists and can cause them to be involved in other forms of movement or political activity, including inside mainstream organizations. According to McAdam (1989) and Whalen and Flacks (1989), 1960s activists are likely to continue to hold leftist attitudes and remain active in movements or politics. Therefore, social movement participation affects activists, and once driven to participate in movements, they are likely to become active in other ways. If activists become involved in movements outside organizations, they will be likely to bring that activism to the other organizations in which they are involved, including their places of work.

For movements to succeed, activists must balance their activism with assimilation within their organizational environment. For some activists in the workplace, balancing work expectations with activism is a difficult task. Meyerson's (2001) book *Tempered Radicals* describes how people committed to social justice agendas find ways to make change inside their places of work while still finding ways of fitting in. These activists "want to rock the boat, and they want to stay in it" (p. xi). To do so successfully, workplace activists need to find a balance between pushing for small changes, choosing their battles, and educating their coworkers.

Organizations tend to change through small, incremental steps, which can be especially frustrating for activists. Those who fail to find a balance between pushing for change and fitting in with their organization will eventually give up, conform to the organization, or leave. Those who stay must be able to adapt and make the most of opportunities for change. One of the ways in which change agents adapt is by recognizing that they cannot achieve their goals on their own and by working with others who are not activists (Meyerson, 2001).

Change in organizations is slow, and, therefore, change making efforts from inside organizations may be less radical. Meyerson (2001) argues that radicals become tempered when they value the platform offered by their position within a mainstream organization. Although insider social movements may appear conservative, they can bring about radical changes through long-term, slow, incremental steps. However, in the case of the insider activists' achievements described by Rojas (2007), although activists achieved the creation of the first black studies department, the department became depoliticized as it worked to achieve institutional survival and legitimacy. Still, earlier forms of black studies, according to Rojas, were not institutionalized at colleges and universities before social movement organizing pushed for it. Institutional context plays a role in determining how much radical voices must compromise to succeed. Within universities, particularly within departments that themselves support radicalism, faculty may not have to compromise their radicalism at all to maintain their employment, especially after receiving tenure.

Activists will be faced with both challenges and supports for their activism. In her study of tempered radicals, Meyerson (2001) found that the challenges include feelings of loneliness, frustration, burnout, lures of co-option, and potential damage to their reputation within their organization. Although activist work inside one's place of employment is tough, Meyerson also found supports to include company appreciation of differences and progressives, a diverse composition of peers, cultural legitimacy for activists' issues or identity group, and positive relationships between activists and others inside the organization. A supportive environment can be nurtured by activists, between one's boss or one's employees, and in mentoring other activists (Meyerson, 2001).

What propels people to become involved in insider activism? From my study, I found that some become involved because of commitments to broader social movements. They in turn recruit their colleagues to become involved. Once activists' achievements are institutionalized, others become involved as a part of their job instead of for ideological reasons (see Figure 75.1). Many of those who are most committed to faculty diversity work identify with feminist, civil rights, black power, ethnic, and gay rights movements. They bring movement goals of challenging sexism, racism, and homophobia to the academy. One faculty member interviewee said: "In the '60s and '70s, I was something of an activist. . . . I was someone who was in the streets a lot even when I was in high school. But, then I devoted my political passions to teaching. . . . I felt that I could make more headway in my professional work." For her, diversity work as a faculty member is a way to accomplish the same political goals of the civil rights and feminist movements in which she participated in earlier periods in her life. Although many may see teaching as a way to create positive change, for this faculty member, it is also a way to achieve social movement goals. Campuses and departments vary in their support of diversity work, and this frames the type, sustainability, and success of diversity work.

Activist Networks

Another way that workplace activism is important is through the creation of social networks. Networks are an important path for the spread of norms and practices and can lead to social movement mobilization (McAdam, 1982; Vogus & Davis, 2005). Networks allow movements to flourish in periods of movement latency or abeyance (Crossley, 2002; Taylor, 1997). Social networks of activists can change an opportunity structure and expand tactical repertoires (Raeburn, 2004). Activism in organizations relating to issues of identity can take the form of mentoring, mutual support of group members, and the development of caucuses (Zald, Morrill, & Rao, 2005). On a very basic level, social networks allow activists to interact with one another and support each other's work (Meyerson, 2001).

How are activist networks created? Development of social movement activity within organizations is facilitated by separate spaces for activists to meet, connect, and strategize (Fonow, 2003; Katzenstein, 1998). Having space allows for social networks to be created, and social networks are necessary for social movements. For example, Taylor (1996) describes how sex-segregated spaces encourage feminist activism. Social networks can transform to become activist networks, and indeed movements are most likely to form through preexisting social ties between those with shared values and practices (Taylor, 1996, 2000). Not all activist networks will be formalized, as friendship networks and larger social movement communities support participants in engaging in activist work (Meyer & Whittier, 1997). Conferences, national organizations, and indirect means of communicating (such as the Internet) are all important means of forming social networks (Raeburn, 2004; Schussman & Earl, 2004; Taylor, 1996, 2000). Within universities, faculty engaged in diversity efforts create committees, councils, and workgroups to foster the achievement of movement goals, and these build and support networks of faculty engagement with diversity.

Organizational Change As a Social Movement Outcome

Organizations are constantly changing and evolving, often to preserve what is believed to be the organization's interests. Sometimes organizations change because of external and/or internal pressures. When these pressures come from social movements, they may not be seen, especially if they come from social movement insiders. However, social movements create important changes within organizations, and organizations that desire organizational change that reflect social movement interests, such to increase diversity and inclusion, should consider utilizing social movement activists and organizations, such as those from the civil rights and Chicano movements.

Although it is relatively easy to track the goals and targets of social movements, tracking the outcomes of movements is much more difficult (McAdam, McCarthy, & Zald, 1988; Raeburn, 2004; Tarrow, 1999). Movement outcomes include mobilization, new laws and subcultures, changes in policies and culture, effects on other movements and activists, and the creation of identities and communities (Earl, 2004; Raeburn, 2004; Staggenborg, 1995; Whittier, 2004). Movements also make systems of power more visible (Melucci, 1985), for example the feminist movement created awareness about systems of gender inequality. The actual outcomes of social movements may be different from the goals set out by activists (Giugni, 1999; Goldner, 2005). Plus, not all social movement actors will agree on the goals or how to define success (Giugni, 1999; Goldner 2005).

It is difficult to isolate the impact of a specific social movement. A social movement success in one arena will have impacts in other arenas (Rochon, 1998; Tarrow, 1997). Social movements operate within larger and overlapping systems of power, so identifying the impact of a single movement becomes especially problematic because of the effects of nonmovement events and actions (Tilly, 1999). Even if changes are observed, it can be difficult to prove causality (Earl, 2004; Giugni, 1999).

The impact of social movements on organizations is difficult to track because it is often outside the public view. In an interview, a woman faculty member in science described her efforts to increase the representation of women in the applicant pool in her department while serving on hiring committees: "Inevitably, the first list of candidates will never include a woman. I can never remember a time when that happened. And then maybe someone like me will say, 'Wait a minute! How come there aren't any women on this list?' And they'll go, 'Well, who could it be?' And then they'll look and go, 'Oh, she's really good; put her on the list.'" Without her efforts, women would not be seriously considered for faculty positions within this science department. With her efforts, the number of women in her department has increased. This will have a positive ripple effect as students have more women role models of successful academic scientists.

The quantity of outcomes a movement achieves is important, but so is the durability of these achievements. According to Rojas (2007), achievement is important, but also important is how long an impact can be sustained. Faculty diversity work increases the pipeline of students from underrepresented backgrounds; recruits underrepresented students, faculty, and staff; makes institutional climates more welcoming; and changes campus policies regarding diversity. The durability of outcomes of diversity work depends upon institutional and political environments, which are constantly shifting. Several interviewees mentioned the importance of their sustained efforts over time because of opposing forces, such as a lack of institutional support and budget constraints. For example, one said, "One of the biggest lessons is that you can't assume that things have been accomplished and that they will stay in place unless you keep trying to make sure that they stay in place." Individuals engaged in diversity work may become frustrated at the slow pace of change and numerous roadblocks, but the collectivity of their efforts does create important changes.

Institutionalization Transformation

Sometimes movements in organizations are about more than changing just the organization. Institutionalization is the product of struggle and conflict evoked by social movements that challenge taken-for-granted arrangements (Goldner, 2005; Schneiberg & Soule, 2005). Some movements can change institutions. For example, Moore (1999) described that anti-Vietnam War activists changed the relationship between science and the American public and thus led to the formation of university departments in science and technology studies. As movements challenge institutions, they do so on multiple and interacting levels.

The National Science Foundation created a set of grants specifically geared at institutional transformation related to women in science, technology, engineering, and math (STEM). Large grants are given out to organizations desiring to reduce barriers for women in STEM fields, with special attention paid to barriers for women of color. Some of those connected to these grants are feminist faculty, whereas others are not but are influenced by feminist and other social movements that called for reducing inequality for women.

Although some see the transformation of movements from street protests to inside institutions as co-optation, movements forge important changes when they become embedded in institutions. Movements can also co-opt "tools of authority control" (Cress & Myers, 2004, p. 288). Lounsbury (2001) notes the complexity of movements embedded in organizations, stating that they are not necessarily co-opted as they enter organizations, but that social movements are embedded within multiple institutions that overlap. For example, Lounsbury saw that when recycling advocacy groups became effective at policy negotiation as well as grassroots activism, they became more successful. Also, Fonow (2003) argued that since the women were already members of the union, they were uniquely positioned to be able to bring about change relating to increasing women's representation and participation in the union.

Conclusion and Future Directions

Social movements inside organizations create important changes, but documenting the activism itself is difficult since it often takes place outside of the public view, and movements have multiple targets. Nevertheless, there are three categories of outcomes to consider. The first category is direct outcomes. This includes achievements outlined by insider activists as the goal of their efforts. In the case of diversity work, a direct outcome is the hiring of a professor of color within an individual department.

The second category is the institutionalization of movements. Recognized social movement activists are hired in a mainstream organization, such as hiring an anti-rape activist as an organizational sexual harassment representative. Diversity work is institutionalized as it becomes recognized as a part of the expected role of faculty members. A strong case of institutionalization took place when social movements drove the establishment of departments (Feminist movement led to Women's Studies, the Black Power movement led to Black Studies). Social movements and institutions operate in interaction, even though insider social movement efforts may not be visible.

The third category is cultural change. Sometimes this change occurs through institutionalization, but even with a lack of institutionalization, social movement efforts may change culture and taken-for-granted social arrangements. For example, through diversity work, campus climates for underrepresented groups are improved and diversity itself given a higher value. These changes affect not only the institution within which the activism takes place, but also may influence similar organizations to follow suit. Plus, as individuals themselves change, they bring their new beliefs to every field with within which they interact. In this way, changes to localized cultures may influence broader cultures.

Social movements operate within organizations in four ways, as shown in Figure 75.1. First, movements target organizations with traditional tactics, such as protest (Fonow, 2003; Rojas, 2007). Second, activists become entrenched in organizations and bring movement goals to their work within those organizations (Katzenstein, 1998; Kurtz, 2002; Meyerson, 2001; Raeburn, 2004; Taylor, 2002; Taylor & Raeburn, 1995). Third, those activists recruit others within their social network to contribute to achieving movement goals within the organization (Katzenstein, 1998; Meyerson, 2001; Raeburn, 2004).[3] Finally, movement achievements become institutionalized, and this encourages others to participate as a part of their job or other regular participation in their organization.

Social movements create important changes inside organizations. In this chapter, I presented a framework for understanding the operation of social movements in organizations. In particular, I demonstrated how social movements enter, operate, and achieve successful outcomes within formal organizations. Social movements are relevant for positive organizational scholars since corporate social responsibility often stems from the efforts of social movements by activists external and internal to formal organizations. Positive organizational scholarship is relevant for social movement scholars since it acknowledges value-driven, change making efforts inside organizations, which are difficult to track. Future scholarship is needed to address the following questions:

- How is prosocial and citizen behavior within formal organizations influenced by social movements? In this chapter, I argued for a bridging of social movement scholarship and positive organizational scholarship and the need for research to address the influence of social movements on prosocial and citizen behaviors.
- How does organizational context shape the type of activism? What organizational features encourage or discourage activism? How can social movements adjust to increase their success depending upon the type of

organization they target? Although much research tends to make broad arguments from individual cases, more research is needed on the impact of organizational context for those who wish to create institutional transformation, in order to know how to best shift their organizations to create friendly climates.

- How do social movements influence nonactivists to work for social movement goals within mainstream organizations? As movements are institutionalized, nonactivists will begin to work for social movement goals within mainstream organizations. The downside to this phenomenon is deradicalization; however, it does lead to sustainable change. More work is needed to know how to institutionalize movements in ways which lead to real, sustainable change that allows for continued connections to the original social movements that drove these changes.
- Do social movements of the political Right operate inside organizations in the same way as movements of the Left? Although this chapter and my research focus on movements of the Left, work is needed to explore if conservative movements fit the framework presented here. What dynamics occur when organizations have insider activists from the Left and from the Right? How can organizational elites reduce conflict between those with conflicting goals?

Notes

1. See Zald (1999) for a discussion of how social movements create common culture and social change but also conflict.
2. The other team members involved in this research are Drs. Sarah Fenstermaker, John Mohr, and Joseph Castro.
3. Taylor (2002) argued that activist bureaucrats operating within a public secondary school were more likely to form ties with those outside the organization. Those she studied were unlikely to mentor younger replacements. Those within other organizations are likely to form social networks with colleagues. Faculty members, in particular, often form social networks with colleagues and, at least to some degree, mentor junior faculty members.

References

Armstrong, E., & Bernstein, M. (2008). Culture, power, and institutions: A multi-institutional politics approach to social movements. *Sociological Theory, 26*, 74–99.

Binder, A. (2002). *Contentious curriculua: Afrocentrism and creationism in American public schools.* Princeton, NJ: Princeton University Press.

Cameron, K., Dutton, J., & Quinn, R. (2003). Foundations of positive organizational scholarship. In K. Cameron, J. Dutton, & R. Quinn (Eds.), *Positive organizational scholarship* (pp. 3–13). San Francisco: Berrett-Koehler.

Clemens, E. (2005). Two kinds of stuff: The current encounter of social movements and organizations. In D. McAdam, G. Davis, W. Scott, & M. Zald (Eds.), *Social movements and organizational theory* (pp. 351–365). New York: Cambridge University Press.

Clemens, E., & Minkoff, D. (2004). Beyond the iron law: Rethinking the place of organizations in social movement research. In D. Snow, S. Soule, & H. Kriesi, *The Blackwell companion to social movements* (pp. 155–170). Malden, MA: Blackwell Publishing.

Creed, D., & Scully, M. (2000). Songs of ourselves: Employees' deployment of social identity in workplace encounters. *Journal of Management Inquiry, 9,* 391–412.

Cress, D., & Myers, D. (2004). Authorities in contention. In D. Meyers, & D. Cress (Eds.), *Authorities in contention, research in social movements, conflicts and change* (pp. 279–293). San Diego: Elsevier.

Crossley, N. (2002). *Making sense of social movements.* Philadelphia: Open University Press.

Davis, G., McAdam, D., Scott, W.R., & Zald, M. (2005). *Social movements and organizational theory.* New York: Cambridge University Press.

Earl, J. (2004). The cultural consequences of social movements. In D. Snow, S. Soule, & H. Kriesi (Eds.), *The Blackwell companion to social movements* (pp. 508–530). Malden, MA: Blackwell Publishing.

Fonow, M. (2003). *Union women: Forging feminism in the united steelworkers of America.* Minneapolis: University of Minnesota Press.

Goldner, M. (2005). The dynamic interplay between Western medicine and the complementary and alternative medicine movement: How activists perceive a range of responses from physicians and hospitals. In P. Brown, & S. Zavestoski (Eds.), *Social Movements in Health* (pp. 17–56). Malden, MA: Blackwell Publishing.

Giugni, M. (1999). Introduction: How social movements matter: Past research, present problems, future developments. In M. Giugni, D. McAdam, & C. Tilly (Eds.), *How social movements matter* (pp. xiii–xxxiii). Minneapolis: University of Minnesota Press.

Gurr, T. (1970). *Why men rebel.* Princeton, NJ: Princeton University Press.

Herek, G.M., & Glunt, E.K. (1993). Interpersonal contact and heterosexuals' attitudes toward gay men: Results from a national survey. *The Journal of Sex Research, 30,* 239–244.

Katzenstein, M. (1998). *Faithful and fearless: Moving feminist protest inside church and military.* Princeton: Princeton University Press.

Kurtz, S. (2002). *Workplace justice: Organizing multi-identity movements.* Minneapolis: University of Minnesota Press.

Lounsbury, M. (2001). Institutional sources of practice variation: Staffing college and university recycling programs. *Administrative Science Quarterly, 46,* 29–56.

McAdam, D. (1982). *Political process and the development of black insurgency, 1930–1970.* Chicago: University of Chicago Press.

McAdam, D. (1989). The biographical impact of activism. *American Sociological Review, 54,* 744–760.

McAdam, D., McCarthy, J., & Zald, M. (1988). Social movements. In N. Smelser (Ed.), *Handbook of sociology* (pp. 695–737). Beverly Hills: Sage.

McCarthy, J., & Zald, M. (1977). Resource mobilization and social movements: A partial theory. *American Journal of Sociology, 82,* 1212–1241.

Melucci, A. (1985). The symbolic challenge of contemporary movements. *Social Research, 52,* 789–816.

Meyer, D., & Whittier, N. (1997). Social movement spillover. In D. McAdam, & D. Snow (Eds.), *Social movements: Readings on their emergence, mobilization, and dynamics* (pp. 480–493). Los Angeles: Roxbury Publishing Company.

Meyerson, D. (2001). *Tempered radicals.* Boston: Harvard Business School Press.

Moore, K. (1999). Political protest and institutional change: The Anti-Vietnam war movement and American science. In M. Giugni, D. McAdam, & C. Tilly (Eds.), *How social movements matter* (pp. 97–118). Minneapolis: University of Minnesota Press.

Morrill, Zald, C.M., & Rao, H. (2003). Covert political conflict in organizations: Challenges from below. *Annual Review of Sociology, 29,* 391–415.

Polletta, F. (2004). Culture in and outside institutions. In D. Meyers, & D. Cress (Eds.), *Authorities in contention, research in social movements, conflicts and change* (pp. 161–183). San Diego: Elsevier.

Raeburn, N. (2004). *Changing corporate America from the inside out: Lesbian and gay workplace rights.* Minneapolis: University of Minnesota Press.

Rochon, T. (1998). *Culture matters: Ideas, activism, and changing values.* Princeton, NJ: Princeton University Press.

Rojas, F. (2007). *From black power to black studies: How a radical social movement became an academic discipline.* Baltimore: John Hopkins University Press.

Santoro, W., & McGuire, G. (1997). Social movement insiders: The impact of institutional activists on affirmative action and comparable worth policies. *Social Problems, 44,* 503–519.

Schneiberg, M., & Soule, S. (2005). Institutionalization as a contested, multilevel process: The case of rate regulation in American fire insurance. In G. Davis, D. McAdam, W. Scott, & M. Zald (Eds.), *Social movements and organizational theory* (pp. 122–160). New York: Cambridge University Press.

Schussman, A., & Earl, J. (2004). From barricades to firewalls? Strategic voting and social movement leadership in the internet age. *Sociological Inquiry, 74,* 439–463.

Staggenborg, S. (1995). Can feminist organizations be effective. In M.M. Ferree, & P. Martin (Eds.), *Feminist organizations: Harvest of the new women's movement* (pp. 339–355). Philadelphia: Temple University Press.

Strang, D., & Jung, D. (2005). Organizational change as an orchestrated social movement. In G. Davis, D. McAdam, W. Scott, & M. Zald (Eds.), *Social movements and organizational theory* (pp. 280–309). New York: Cambridge University Press.

Tarrow, S. (1997). Cycles of collective action: Between madness and the repertoire of contention. In D. McAdam, & D. Snow (Eds.), *Social movements* (pp. 328–339). Los Angeles: Roxbury Publishing Company.

Tarrow, S. (1999). Forward. In M. Giugni, D. McAdam, & C. Tilly (Eds.), *How social movements matter* Vol. 10, *Social movements, protest, and contention* (pp. vii–ix). Minneapolis: University of Minnesota Press.

Taylor, J. (2002). *Activist bureaucrats: A study of people who turn movement ideals into institutional logics*. Ph. D. dissertation, University of California, Santa Barbara.

Taylor, V. (1996). *Rock-a-by baby: Feminism, self-help, and postpartum depression*. New York: Routledge.

Taylor, V. (1997). Social movement continuity: The women's movement in abeyance. In D. McAdam, & D. Snow (Eds.) *Social movements* (pp. 409–420). Los Angeles: Roxbury Publishing Company

Taylor, V. (2000). Mobilizing for change in a social movement society. *Contemporary Sociology, 29*, 219–230.

Taylor, V. (2010). Culture, identity, and emotions: Studying social movements as if people really matter. *Mobilization*. Forthcoming.

Taylor, V., & Raeburn, N. (1995). Identity politics as high-risk activism: Career consequences for lesbian, gay, and bisexual sociologists. *Social Problems, 42*, 252–273.

Tilly, C. (1999). Conclusion: From interactions to outcomes in social movements. In M. Giugni, D. McAdam, & C. Tilly (Eds.), *How social movements matter* (pp. 253–270). Minneapolis: University of Minnesota Press.

Turner, R., & Killian, L. (1972). *Collective behavior*. Englewood Cliffs, NJ: Prentice-Hall.

Vogus, T., & Davis, G. (2005). Elite mobilizations for antitakeover legislation, 1982–1990. In G. Davis, D. McAdam, W. Scott., & M. Zald (Eds.), *Social movements and organizational theory* (pp. 96–121). New York: Cambridge University Press.

Whalen, J., & Flacks, R. (1989). *Beyond the barricades: The sixties generation grows up*. Philadelphia: Temple University Press.

Whittier, N. (2004). The consequences of social movements for each other. In D. Snow, S. Soule, & H. Kriesi (Eds.), *The Blackwell companion to social movements* (pp. 531–551). Malden, MA: Blackwell Publishing.

Zald, M. (1999). Transnational and international social movements in a globalizing world: Creating culture, creating conflict. In D. Cooperrider, & J. Dutton (Eds.), *Organizational dimensions of global change: No limits to cooperation* (pp. 168–184). Thousand Oaks, CA: Sage Publications.

Zald, M. (2005). The strange career of an idea and its resurrection: Social movements in organizations. *Journal of Management Inquiry, 14*, 157–166.

Zald, M., Morrill, C., & Rao, H. (2005). The impact of social movements on organizations. In G. Davis, D. McAdam, W. Scott., & M. Zald (Eds.), *Social movements and organizational theory* (pp. 253–279). New York: Cambridge University Press.

Zald, M., & Berger, M. (1978). Social movements in organizations: Coup d'Etat, insurgency, and mass movements. *The American Journal of Sociology, 83*, 823–861.

In God We Trust

A Comparison of Spiritualities at Work

Lloyd E. Sandelands

Abstract

Lacking an idea of "human spirit," business science cannot account for the trust that makes business possible. This chapter reviews recent writings about spirituality in management to see whether and how they illuminate this still dark territory of business life. The aim of the chapter is not bibliographic, but critical: to compare rival ideas of spirituality so that a choice can be made among them. Distinguishing between and among immanent and transcendent types of spiritualities, the chapter concludes that only those centered upon a transcendent personal God (as for example the God of Abraham identified in the world's three great religions) are adequate to fulfill our understanding of business life. The chapter concludes by noting that if business science is to produce a true humanism—a humanism adequate for building positive forms of business life—it must be informed by the knowledge of God that comes by religious faith.

Keywords: God, immanence, markets, meaning, organization, science, transcendence, trust

Editors' Note: This chapter's examination of the meaning of spirituality in organizations draws a particular conclusion, namely that fully understanding organizations depends on acknowledging a personal God. Some readers may judge this to be inappropriately theological, but the author intends to compare and contrast approaches to spirituality and to stimulate thoughtful scrutiny and investigation of this concept, even though different conclusions may be drawn.

> Without God man neither knows which way to go, nor even understands who he is. . . . . Paul VI recalled in *Populorum Progressio* that man cannot bring about his own progress unaided, because by himself he cannot establish an authentic humanism. Only if we are aware of our calling, as individuals and as a community, to be part of God's family as his sons and daughters, will we be able to generate a new vision and muster new energy in the service of a truly integral humanism. . . . *A humanism which excludes God is an inhuman humanism*. Only a humanism open to the Absolute can guide us in the promotion and building of forms of social and civic life. . . .
> —Pope Benedict XVI, 2009, #78, p. 41

It seems that our scientific understanding of business is built on sand. There are indications large and small—gaping fissures and ominous hairline cracks— that its theoretical foundations cannot stand up to the stresses of an increasingly technocratic, global, and consumerist economy. In particular, there are indications that its central pillar—its idea of the human person—cannot bear the weight placed upon it.

In the large of business we see the faults in theories of economics and management. Oversimplifying only a little, the first think it foundation enough for a well-functioning market that persons (or economic entities regarded as persons) act in self-interest.[1] Yet, in diffuse markets, in which business costs can be "externalized," self-interest can turn ugly and destructive. Thus, manufacturers outsource pollution to Third World countries, retailers squeeze costs at the expense of decent wages, financiers foist flagrantly overrated securities upon unsuspecting investors, and we ourselves enjoy these exploitations in checkout lines at big-lot discount stores. However, even while in self-interest all of us are capable of indifference or worse to others, the market is not a Hobbesian war of "all against all" but an arena in which compassion and kindness take a place. There is something more to the person than economic theories say. And again, oversimplifying only a little, theories of management think it foundation enough for a well-functioning organization that persons (or units of organization regarded as persons) obey authority.[2] To be sure, as Milgram (1974) showed, our susceptibility to authority can be exploited even to the pitch of holocaust. But, as Milgram also showed, we can also maintain moral integrity, in spite of authority. There is something more to the person than management theories say.

And, likewise, in the small of personal experience we see the faults in social and behavioral science theories of work. These think it foundation enough to explain the human experience of work causally by taking account of the worker's internal states (instincts, needs, values, abilities, beliefs, skills) and his or her personal, social, and cultural circumstances (opportunities, constraints, affiliations, roles, responsibilities, norms) (cf. Rosso, Dekas, & Wreszniewski, 2010). But such a scientific vocabulary of cause and effect can say nothing of the meanings people find in their work and for which they live. Meaning is not effect to any cause, but a uniquely human invention of language, a genuine act of creation beyond the physical world. In the talk of mechanism, the human person disappears. There is something more to the person than theories of work say.

This chapter is about the "something more" missing in our understanding of the human person in business. It is in answer to the questions posed above, of what makes a market or an organization if not economic self-interest or obedience to authority, and of what makes work meaningful if not its causes and effects. At base, these are questions about

trust; about the trust by which persons set aside self-interest and obedience for the good of all and about the trust by which persons believe their work is meaningful. Although such questions are not new, they have been given new currency by growing interest in what has come to be called *positive organizational studies* (Cameron, Dutton, & Quinn, 2003). In this chapter, I hope to add to this interest with a look at the growing literature on spirituality in business. I do so with the hope of every humane inquiry; to learn what is true about the human person. Finally, in introduction, I wish to express my thanks—first to Professors Cameron and Spreitzer for inviting me to write about this topic and second to Pope Benedict XVI for his "just-in-time" instruction on how to do so in his encyclical letter on charity in truth, *Caritas in Veritate*. It is my good fortune to have both my editors and Pope pulling me in the same direction, calling me to a renewed idea of the human person in business and reminding me of God's presence in the world.

Spiritualities At Work

If today's literature on spirituality in business is united about anything, it is in the claim that there *is* "something more" to the human person; namely, his or her human essence or spirit. Many see this claim as a brief for change—as a challenge to values of scientific materialism and selfish individualism and as a shift in thinking "from modernity's exaltation of reason to an appreciation of feeling, emotion and experience" and "from a dominance of masculinity and patriarchy to a celebration of femininity, in individuals and in society."[3] Perhaps uniquely, this literature evinces its subject, finding "inspiration" in its study of "spirit."

Unfortunately, this literature often leaves the "something more" of spirit unsaid. This occurs perhaps for several reasons. One is a modesty that thinks spirit is intensely personal, as a beauty known only to the eye of the beholder. Thus, for Hill, Pargament, Hood, McCullough, Swyers, Larson, and Zinnbauer (2000) spirituality is "subjective feelings, thoughts, and behaviors that arise from a search for the sacred," where the sacred refers broadly to "a divine being, divine object, ultimate reality, or Ultimate Truth as perceived by the individual" (p. 68). A second is a scientific focus on the function of spirit apart from its details. Thus, in their *Handbook of Workplace Spirituality and Organizational Performance*, Giacalone and Jurkiewicz (2003) define spirituality as "a framework of organizational values evidenced in the culture that promotes employees' experience of transcendence through the work process, facilitating their sense of being connected to others in a way that provides feelings of completeness and joy" (p. 13). And a third is a reluctance to preempt or offend anyone's idea of that which they hold dear.

Moreover, for going unsaid, spirit is allowed to be whatever one wants it to be. In their widely cited *Spiritual Audit of Corporate America* (1999), Mitroff and Denton asked business executives to describe their spirituality. Most distinguished it from religious beliefs and identified it at work with the ability to realize my full potential as a person, being associated with a good organization, having interesting work, making money, having good colleagues and serving humankind, service to future generations, and service to my immediate community. In their comprehensive survey of academic writing on the subject, Dent, Higgins, and Wharff (2005) found more definitions of spirituality than writers to define it. Spirit, they discovered, was identified with beauty, creativity, insight, quiet, openness, extraordinary performance, wonder, play, spontaneity, joy, imagination, discernment, grace, celebration, magic, and miracle (p. 632). Impressed by such variety, other writers wonder if the "something more" of spirit is so subjective, fluid, and idiosyncratic to be nearly "anything" (Ashforth & Pratt, 2003) or perhaps "everything" (Sperry, 1997).

With so many "spiritualities" at hand, how are we to choose among them? Useful as it is to know what business people and academics say about spirituality, it is more useful to know what their different ideas mean for business and for the lives of persons in them. In the sections that follow, I survey conceptions of spirit in business to delineate two basic types—immanent and transcendent—and within each of these types two subtypes. My interest in taking this comprehensive view is not primarily bibliographic but critical. I compare spiritualities so that we might choose between them. I do so with an eye upon the questions about business with which we began.

Immanent Spiritualities

The immanent business spiritualities begin with the idea that spirit lies within and is discovered by the illuminations of meditation or contemplation. Thus, according to Conger (1994) spirituality "gives expression to the being that is in us; it has to do with feelings, with the power that comes from within, with knowing our deepest selves and what is sacred to us" (p. 9). Immanent spirituality is distinguished from transcendent spirituality, which begins with an idea of a superior power or force that is often supposed to be divine. There is no such superior power or force in immanent spirituality. If there is a divine at all, it is just that of inner being. According to Ashmos and Duchon (2000) "whether the spirit deals with the divine is not the crucial issue. What is crucial [is that] there are dispiriting forces that will eat away at the inner spirit if people are not fully aware of the condition of their inner life" (p. 136).

Immanent spirituality is of two types—individual and whole. Individual immanence is the idea that spirit lies within the self, that it is indivisible, and that it is realized in the growth and development of consciousness. In Western culture, this spirituality traces to the esoteric-theosophical tradition widely accepted by European intellectuals in the 18th and 19th centuries. To this tradition, a key element was added by the largely American philosophy of pragmatism, which saw spirituality, not as religious doctrine about God, but as personal experience. This nondoctrinal spirituality of experience, which was largely a rejection of Judeo-Christianity, is seen particularly in James' (1902) *Varieties of Religious Experience,* which became a touchstone for much American thinking about spirituality that followed. This emphasis on personal experience opened the way to a "spiritualization" of experience generally, whereby spirit is found in all kinds of experiences, from peak performance (Privette, 1981), flow (Csikszentmihalyi, 1990), play (Koch, 1956), and today, increasingly, business (Kinjerski & Skrypnek, 2004; King & Nicol, 1999; Milliman, Ferguson, Trickett & Condemi, 1999; Milliman, Czaplewski & Ferguson, 2003; Waddock, 1999).

In business writing, the leading exponent of individual immanence is Maslow, who found answer to man's existential dilemma of identity and value in "self-actualization"; in his words, "There's no place else to turn but inward, to the self, as the locus of values" (1968, p. 10). This, he supposed, is a spiritual quest, as the perfect or godlike in man is found in the farthest reaches of his own being:

> Human beings strive perpetually toward ultimate humanness. . . . It's as if we were doomed forever to try to arrive at a state to which we could never attain. Fortunately, we now know this not to be true, or at least it is not the only truth. There is another truth which integrates with it. We are again and again rewarded for good Becoming by transient states of absolute

Being, by peak-experiences. Achieving basic-need gratifications gives us many peak-experiences, each of which are absolute delights, perfect in themselves, and needing no more than themselves to validate life. (1968, p. 154)

Following Maslow, Burak (1999) confirms that spirituality comes from within. "In the last analysis, it is the person who takes on the expression of spirituality, albeit, the organization culture or environment is conducive to this process" (p. 283). Spirituality, suggests Burak, is identified with mental growth and development. And this, according to Dehler and Welsh (2003, p. 114) is not only or mainly a cognitive state, but fundamentally one of feeling:

> [W]hen spirit is described as a search for meaning, aspirations beyond instrumentality, deeper self-knowledge, or transcendence to a higher level, writers are in actuality defining spirit in terms of emotion—internalized and personal feelings of meaning, purpose, knowing, and being. Such felt emotion serves to energize action; thus spirit is a form of energy. Feelings and emotions themselves can't be observed until they are expressed as behaviors; thus spirituality is the expression of spirit; behaviorally or cognitively . . . Csikszentmihalyi's (1990) notion of a 'flow state' is perhaps the closest analogy to inspirited behavior.

Writing about business practice, Sheep (2006) summarized a decade of scientific study of spirituality by finding agreement on four dimensions of self-actualization: self–workplace integration, meaning in work, transcendence of self, and growth and development of one's inner self at work. Likewise, Pfeffer (2003, p. 32) described four desires that people have in seeking immanence at work: "(1) interesting work that permits them to learn, develop, and have a sense of competence and mastery, (2) meaningful work that provides some feeling of purpose, (3) a sense of connection and positive social relations with their coworkers, and (4) the ability to live an integrated life, so that one's work role and other roles are not inherently in conflict and so that a person's work role does not conflict with his or her essential nature. . . ."

Whole immanence, on the other hand, is the idea that spirit lies in the entirety of the cosmos, including all humankind. Everything in the universe is interrelated, such that every part is an image of the totality; the whole is in everything and everything is in the whole. There is no opposition between God and the world; the universe itself is divine and undergoes a progression from inert matter in the Big Bang through geologic transformations through terrestrial and human biological evolution, culminating in the highest and most perfect forms of consciousness. Accordingly, enlightenment comes to the self as it becomes of one mind with the divinity of the cosmos. This is the truth behind all appearances. Often, in inspiration and practice, such spirituality draws upon Eastern traditions of Zen, Buddhism, Hinduism, and Confucianism, either directly or as these have been interpreted in the West by such scholars as Emerson, Jung, Brown, Watts, and Remen. For example, as described by Brown (1966) in *Love's Body*, this spirituality is that of unconscious mind, of an integral awareness before words or categories:

> The unconscious is that immortal sea which brought us hither; intimations of which are given in moments of "oceanic feeling"; one sea of energy or instinct; embracing all mankind, without distinction of race, language, or culture; and embracing all the generations of Adam, past present, and future, in one phylogenetic heritage; in one mystical or symbolical body. (pp. 88–89)

In business writing, there are particular influences of holism in the transpersonal spiritualities of Wilber (1985) and Peck (1988), which offer concepts of Universal Mind, Higher Self, collective and personal holons, and the individual ego and which suggest that the Higher Self is our real identity and bridge between God as divine Mind and humanity. Accordingly, spiritual development is achieved as consciousness overcomes all forms of dualism, such as between subject and object, mind and body, life and death, and finally God and Man. Thus, nodding to Wilber, Steingard (2005) develops a spiritually informed management theory upon a holism that finds spirit in all things. Also nodding to Wilber, Mitroff (2003) idealizes spirituality as feeling "totally integrated and connected with the entire universe such that there are no boundaries between where one starts and where one leaves off" (p. 378). And nodding to Mitroff, Parboteeah, and Cullen (2003) describe spirituality as a feeling of wholeness, connectedness, and deeper values. For his part, Mirvis (1997) looks to Peck for guidance in speaking about the spiritual unity of the organization, about the "company as community." He finds examples of such in People Express Airlines (now defunct), Ben & Jerry's Ice Cream, The Body Shop, and Mary Kay Cosmetics. Holism is the focus as well for Ashar and

Lane-Maher (2004), who quote Rachel Remen in noting that "the spiritual is inclusive" and that "we all participate in the spiritual all the time, whether we know it or not"; for Fornaciari and Dean, who write of the new "whole-person thinking" and "new science of wholeness" in business; for Korac-Kakabadse et al. (2002), who write of the "wider spiritualities" needed in the practice of leadership; for Butts (1999), who writes of "sacred/ultimate/whole-system values which enable the human spirit to grow and flourish" (p. 329); and for Eisler and Moutuori (2003), who write of a "partnership spirituality" with four keys: listening to inner wisdom; being fully conscious of others; learning moral standards of empathy, caring, and responsibility; and putting partnership into practice.

Finally, although individual and whole spiritualities think of immanence differently—one beginning with self, the other with community—they agree in thinking of spirit as an impersonal divine.[4] They join in regarding the personal God of monotheistic religion as an unfortunate fiction that diverts people from the divinity intrinsic to self and the world. Whereas a personal God divides Man from God, profane from sacred, finite from infinite, male from female, relative from absolute, and present from past and future, the immanent spiritualities unite these through fusion of Man and God, profane and sacred, finite and infinite, male and female, relative and absolute, and past, present, and future.

Transcendent Spiritualities

The transcendent spiritualities begin with the idea that spirit lies neither in the self alone nor in the totality of the cosmos, but in a personal and/or communal relation to a superior force or power. These spiritualities are also of two types, which differ as to whether this relation is impersonal or personal.

Within the impersonal type are two subtypes; one "uncommitted," which refers to unspecified powers (gods unnamed); the other "neo-pagan," which refers to worldly powers (gods with a small "g"). The first is ably described by Berger (1970) who, in *A Rumor of Angels*, shows how ordinary human experiences of order, play, hope, damnation, and humor imply an extraordinary transcendence. In business writing, Paloutzian, Emmons, and Keortge (2003) identify this spirituality with "the tendency to guide thoughts, feelings, and behavior by the gist or idea of whatever is beyond and seen as ultimately important, which can be expressed religiously and nonreligiously" (p. 124). Likewise,

McCormick (1994, by way of Clark, 1958) characterizes this spirituality as "the inner experience of the individual when he senses a Beyond, especially as evidenced by the effect of this experience on his behavior when he actively attempts to harmonize his life with the Beyond" (p. 22). If there is a virtue in such uncommitted expressions of transcendent spirituality, it may be that they make room for the reader's preferred transcendent (Bene el, 2003; Brown, 2003; Konz & Ryan, 1999).

The second neo-pagan type of impersonal transcendent spirituality recalls the pagan spiritualities of Greek and Roman antiquity, as well as those of pre- and post-Christian agrarian cultures in Europe. These are spiritualities of small gods (gods with a small "g") with circumscribed ambits and powers (in the Greek pantheon, for example, there were the Olympian gods of sky, marriage, sea, the dead, love and beauty, music and healing, war, hunt, wisdom, fire, hearth, and harvest). Business examples of this second type of impersonal transcendent spirituality abound in the myriad idols and cults of business life. Aside from the obvious cult of Mammon (in worship of the "almighty dollar"), there are innumerable particular idolatries of business organizations. Not least is worship of the CEO which, as Khurana (2004) describes, pervades American business thinking and has resulted in a labor market for CEO talent distorted by charisma. When a CEO is regarded as a sort of worldly god, the organization and its shareholders become a sort of cult. Such are seen in the business press, in stories of Sam Walton and Wal-Mart, Jack Welsh and General Electric, and Herb Kelleher and Southwest Airlines. Writing in a more general and theoretical vein, Ashforth and Vaidyanath (2002) describe how business organizations can become "secular religions" by presenting employees "cosmologies tied to something transcendent" in the world. Such organizations, they argue, offer "a system of beliefs and practices that address fundamental questions about the meaning of life and one's role in the world . . . without necessarily invoking a supernatural being or power" (p. 361). This parallel, they maintain, is no mere metaphor. Organizational persons or practices become religious by a "process of sacralization," in which a generic "hunger for transcendence" and a diffuse "susceptibility to edifying cosmologies" are recruited to the organization.[5]

It is perhaps more than a parenthesis to note that in speaking of spirituality as they do—that is, objectively as a process of sacralization—Ashforth and Vaidyanath (2002) take part (along with Ashmos &

Duchon, 2000; Bell & Taylor, 2003; Giacalone & Jurkiewicz, 2003; and others) in perhaps the greatest neo-Pagan spirituality of our age; namely, that of science itself. Taking cue from pioneers such as Comte and Durkheim in sociology; Mauss, Levi-Strauss, and Levy-Bruhl in anthropology; and Canetti and Freud in psychology, this spirituality lords over all particular others, seeing them not as human verities but as social, cultural, and psychic functions met in interchangeable ways. Here, the transcendent power is not a named or unnamed god, but an impersonal method whose powers of observation and conscientious inference define objective truth.[6] This is the actual spirituality of many scientific accounts of spirit in business; this is the spirituality of which Vitz (1994) writes in describing modern psychology as religion, and this is the spirituality that Percy (1983, p. 115) identifies as the chief means of self-transcendence available in our post-religious age:

> The scientist is the prince and sovereign of the age. His transcendence of the world is genuine. That is to say, he stands in a posture of objectivity over against the world, a world which he sees as a series of specimens or exemplars, and interactions, energy exchanges, secondary causes—in a word: dyadic events.

At last and not least, there are the transcendent spiritualities of a personal God (God with capital "G") propounded by the great monotheistic religions of the world: Judaism, Christianity, and Islam. In these religions, spirituality takes the definite form of a relation with a supernatural God that illuminates and deepens one's relations with self, others, and with the cosmos. About the fact of this relation, the monotheistic religions agree. They differ in how they construe the relation and how they suggest it be pursued. For Jews, the relation is revealed in the Torah and especially by the prophet Moses and is cultivated in careful adherence to God's law (as for example the Decalogue). For Muslims, the relation is articulated by the Qur'an and especially by the prophet Muhammad and is set forth in the Five Pillars of Islam that unite Muslims into a community. And for Christians, the relation is given by God's redemption of man by the sacrifice of his only son, Jesus Christ—the so-called "lamb of God"[7]—and is fulfilled by turning back to the Father, through the Son, in docility to the power of the Holy Spirit. In view of the prominence of these three great world religions, it is surprising that business examples of this personal God-centered transcendent spirituality are few (e.g., Ali, Camp & Gibbs, 2000; Cavanagh, 1999; Delbecq, 1999; Sandelands, 2003, 2008, 2009, Zaman, 2008). In writing about business, it seems there is a bias against spirituality of a specifically religious bent.

Among the transcendent spiritualities, those that invoke a personal God differ most dramatically from the immanent spiritualities. Whereas these last find salvation in self-realization and self-redemption, the former find salvation in obedience to the one and only God of creation. And whereas these last see no right or wrong (no good or bad) in the spirit, and see spiritual growth as an ever-increasing perfection of consciousness, the former locate the spirit in a moral order of right and wrong (in an economy of sin) and insist that spiritual growth comes by faithful obedience to God's law.[8] According to the former, we are responsible to God and need His help to be faithful.

Spiritualities Compared

Certainly, the generosity that welcomes the myriad spiritualities of business does not make them equally true or good. Spiritualities differ in how they conceive of the person and in what they make of his or her life. Each is an anthropology—an account of the human that can be fruitfully compared to the others. Although this much might be obvious (for it is the reason for having a literature about spirituality in the first place) this is just what most writing on the subject denies. To the contrary, there is a sort of political correctness that denies priority to *any* understanding of human spirit.[9] "Who are you," goes the admonishing question, "to claim superior understanding of something so personal and so bound up with the divine?" Thus, Freshman (1999) argues for a business spirituality that is whatever people make it out to be (see also Krishnamakumar & Neck, 2002). Reviewing academic treatments of the subject, she finds "there is no 'one answer' to the question, 'What is spirituality in the workplace?'" and that "the definitions and applications of 'spirituality in the workplace' are unique to individuals." For this reason, she warns that one "must be careful not to presuppose otherwise." The problem with this sort of political correctness, of course, is that it is not interested in the truth.[10]

Assuming that spiritualities are not equal in truth or good, I reclaim the idea that we can be right or wrong about them. I submit that the "something more" of human spirit in business is not a subjectivity that affords to each his or her own, and is not a referendum for popular vote, but is a discoverable truth written into our being. Following Pope Benedict XVI (2009), I suppose that this spiritual truth is for us to discern:

> [W]hile it may be true that development needs the religions and cultures of different peoples, it is equally true that adequate discernment is needed. Religious freedom does not mean religious indifferentism, nor does it imply that all religions are equal. Discernment is needed regarding the contribution of cultures and relations, especially on the part of those who wield political power, if the social community is to be built up in a spirit of respect for the common good. Such discernment has to be based on the criterion of charity and truth. (p. 31)

Thus we do well to compare business spiritualities to see if they speak in charity and truth about the human person in business, especially in answer to our touchstone questions of trust in markets and organizations and trust in the meaning of work.

Immanent Spiritualities

The immanent spiritualities speak truth about the divine in human being—about the tragedy of egoism and about the totality of a cosmos in which we are one human family before all category and distinction. But it is truth in falsehood; truth that fails the human spirit, truth that fails our touchstone questions of trust in business.

The immanence of the individual is a great realization of human being. Maslow (1968) spoke in truth of self-actualization. His voice in the "human potential movement" was an encouragement to "the God within"—he saw that to realize one's potential one had to go beyond ego to the authentic self deep down. This is an answer to the question of meaning at work. If one could realize his or her inner divinity through "peak experiences" at work—if one could thereby "self-actualize"—then one could be fulfilled in the joy of a higher and more perfect consciousness. The meaning of work is the consciousness it affords—a consciousness that Hackman and Oldham (1976) suggest reaches its height in "feeling personally responsible for performing well on a meaningful task."

The danger in this truth of self-actualization is that it is false when taken as the whole truth, when it is supposed that a person can bring about the "God within" on his or her own, in a process of self-discovery. This is false both in what it asserts and in what it denies. What it asserts is that the human good consists in realizing one's inner being. This is the error in what Pope Benedict XVI (2009) described as

religious and cultural attitudes that "do not oblige men and women to live in communion but rather cut them off from one another in a search for individual well-being, limited to the gratification of psychological desires" (#55, p. 31). The human good is greater than this—it also involves relations to others. What it denies is that the person needs help in the good. This is the error of self-transcendence. The quest to find one's self is quixotic, a tilting at windmills. As Percy (1983, pp. 106–107) explains, its futility is a logical feature of meaning itself:

> The fateful flaw of human semiotics is this: that of all the objects in the entire Cosmos which the sign-user can apprehend through the conjoining of signifier and signified (word uttered and thing beheld), there is one which forever escapes his comprehension— that is the sign-user himself. Semiotically, the self is literally unspeakable to itself. . . . The self of the sign-user can never be grasped, because, once the self locates itself at the dead center of its world, there is no signified to which a signifier can be joined to make a sign. The self has no sign of itself. No signifier applies. All signifiers apply equally.

This flaw of human semiotics is fateful, Percy elaborates, because "As soon as the self becomes self-conscious—that is, aware of its own unique unformulability in its world of signs—from that moment forward, it cannot escape the predicament of its placement in the world" (p. 109). For this "catastrophe of the self," the human person is condemned to a lifetime of futile search—both heroic and absurd— for his or her meaning.

It is worth noting in this connection that Maslow himself was aware of this dilemma of individual immanence and saw that meaning could not be gained by the self alone but only by reaching to something beyond self. And it is doubly worth noting what he imagined that "something beyond" to be. In terms that he describes as recalling Christian teaching, he speaks of the need to see self and others in sacred rather than secular terms. In particular, he speaks of the need to "resacralize":

> Resacralizing means being willing, once again, to see a person "under the aspect of eternity," as Spinoza says, or to see him in the medieval Christian unitive perception, that is, being able to see the sacred, the eternal, the symbolic. It is to see Woman with a capital "W" and everything which that implies, even when one looks at a particular woman. (1971, p. 48)

Suffice it here to note that such unitive perception—that is, perception open to the sacred and eternal—is possible only by making reference to something greater than the self and greater than the human.

In the same way, the immanence of the whole is a great realization of human being—we *are* united in one being, one consciousness. And experiencing this harmony—this "oceanic feeling" as Brown says—does restore the soul; upon its discovery, people can set upon a path of healing both their own lives and their relations to others. But this spiritual truth about the whole is not the whole truth of the human spirit. In overlooking human division or distinction, this truth overlooks the human person (and indeed every human division of race, nation, tribe, community, organization, and family). The human person is sui generis; a unique self, a personality apart from every other. This is his or her essence, his or her dignity, his or her spirit. Overlooking this essence, dignity, and spirit, the immanent spirituality of holism offers no ground for trust of one person for another and thereby no ground for a market or an organization. This is the cardinal flaw of holism. When no quarter is given to individual uniqueness and to personal freedom, the "oneness" of the community or cosmos becomes a "noneness" of persons. Such is the flaw in the "partnership spirituality" described by Eisler and Montuori (2003). This spirituality is loud and clear about the need for collaboration based on empathy, caring, and collegiality, but is mute about the divisions and spaces required for persons to be persons. As the authors reckon it, this feminine spirituality is to be set against the masculine spirituality of hierarchy and domination. But for its tilt to the feminine, it denies the masculine and the needful balance of the two. Partnership, like love, requires persons able to unite in and through their differences. To be partners, persons must first be persons.

Finally, one might hope that the partialities of individualistic and holistic immanent spiritualities could be allayed by combining them to gain the benefits of both and the liabilities of neither. But such hope is betrayed in the attempt. To wit, after identifying spirituality with desires to "realize full potential," "work for ethical organizations," "do interesting work," and "make money" (p. 376), Mitroff (2003) observes that in higher forms of spirituality "all distinctions, all dichotomies, all boundaries, all dualities and either–ors, vanish entirely" (p. 378). One is led to ask if by distinctions, boundaries, dualities, and either–ors Mitroff excludes those required to define full potential, eth-

ical organization, interesting work, and money. In another example, Buchholz and Rosenthal (2003) propose that the good "emerges" in interaction of the individual and the whole by means of "bipolar dynamics of adjustment." However, while offering enthusiastic detail about the ends of spirit—including "responsibility in directing the course of growth in the most workable ways," "imaginative grasp of authentic possibilities," and "attunement to the sense of concrete human existence in its richness diversity, and multiple types of relatedness" (p. 161)—the authors are unspecific about its means. One is led to ask how or even if it is possible to get there from here.

At the end of the day, one sees the immanent spiritualities as aspirations for the spirit rather than descriptions of the spirit. We long to be at peace with ourselves and not turned inside-out and bogged down by the pettiness of ego. And, we long to be one with others undivided by conflicts or group animosities. These worthwhile aspirations are true human hopes, but they are sentiments not spiritualities, statements of seeking not statements of being. From them we learn about how persons would like to be, not about how they are. In them, we seek the "something more" of trust that makes markets, organizations, and meaningful work possible, but we do not learn what this something more is.

Transcendent Spiritualities

In contrast to the oneness of immanent spiritualities, the transcendent spiritualities speak a different truth about the human person in business. This is the truth of love—of division in unity—potentiated and nurtured by the relation of persons to a transcendent power or force. The human spirit subsists in personal relations as a quality of the love and trust intrinsic to them. This spirit both defines who a person is and how he or she is related to others. Thus, whereas the immanent spiritualities take the person out of place and time and out of relations to others, the transcendent spiritualities locate the person in place and time and in relations to others. In a word, the transcendent spiritualities give the person a "home," a secure grounding in the physical, temporal, and social world.

In the case of uncommitted transcendent spirituality, this "home" has no particular address. Although it offers a prospect of unity and cooperation in something larger, it is a prospect only. Until we know what the transcendent "Beyond" is, and until we know what it demands, we cannot fix ourselves in place or time, and we cannot collect and coordinate ourselves in its service. To trust others in markets and organizations, and to trust that our work has meaning, we must have our bearings—we must know who God is, what He wants, and that He is the god of all. But this is just what an uncommitted transcendent spirituality, such as proposed by McCormick (1994), shies from saying. Such is not a true spirituality, but an idea of spirituality. Such is not the stuff of which trust and meaning are made.

In the case of neo-pagan transcendent spirituality, the issue is not that of not knowing where "home" is, but of living in an impoverished and sometimes rough neighborhood. This spirituality establishes relations to various masters whose worldly multiplicity leave us in question and doubt. As we strive to answer the often conflicting local deities of home, community, organization, CEO, society, Mammon, and self, we are hard put to trust others in markets or organizations who may answer such deities differently. And, as we strive to answer more than one god, we are hard put to trust in the meaning of work that differs from god to god. Such is the dilemma of worldly multiplicity in neo-pagan business spiritualities, such as proposed by Ashforth and Vaidyanath (2002), which put faith in diverse business elements such as leaders, rituals, creeds, stories, and material artifacts. The danger, as Mary Follett (1942) saw long ago, is that to serve more than one master is to serve none. Writing of business, she noted that effective coordination of the whole can come only when there is "functional unity" of parts; that is, when parts are united in a single transcending value. This led to her emphasize the significance of spiritual values that transcend the organization itself.[11]

Of the transcendent business spiritualities, only those that predicate a personal God (such as described in the great monotheistic religions of Judaism, Islam, and Christianity) meet the need identified by Follett and furnish the "home" in which we can trust others in markets and organizations and in which we can find the meaning in work. The personal God who is literally Father to every human spirit establishes by his paternity both the ultimate dignity and sibling relation of all persons.[12] The trust that enables business is just that which begins in the transcendent personal God who created us in his image. We are able to trust one another in markets to exchange goods fairly and for mutual benefit because we can trust in the God in whom we are brother and sister. We are able to trust one another in organizations to obey authority within moral bounds because we can trust in the God whose paternity is model for our relations of authority.[13] And we are able to trust that our work has meaning because we can trust in the God whose love gives meaning to all creation. To these ends, we recognize that God is the source and perfect example of the trust and love that we, his human children, have an inherent although imperfect tendency to emulate. When we approach or achieve these ends, we are most God-like and thereby most spiritual.

It is therefore crucial that God be both *transcendent* and related to us as a *person*. Only a transcendent God can provide the unitary and absolute commonality in which persons of every stripe and background can abandon their differences to join productively with others in markets and organizations. This necessary commonality is denied by immanent spiritualities in which there are no fixed points and is limited by impersonal transcendent spiritualities in which there is no specific or universal god. And only a personal God can supply a sufficient model for the human person and for human relations. To be a person is to be in his image, a creative being of infinite dignity and free to act for the good. And to be related to other persons is again to be in his image, in a spirit of love, in a spirit of charity and truth.[14] This necessary model is missing in immanent spiritualities, in which persons and relations are dissolved in the one ultimate consciousness and incompletely sketched in impersonal transcendent spiritualities in which persons and relations have no specific or single god as model.

And, finally, we can note that a transcendent spirituality centered upon a personal God is more needful than ever in today's increasingly global economy, in which persons are less able to rely on local cultures to discipline markets (Scruton, 2009) and organizations (Jackall, 1988). What is needed is the universality that the world's great monotheistic religions provide—one God in which all persons can find a basis to trust one another. Thus, according to Islamic law (Shari'ah) economic activity is to be directed not only toward self-interested competition, but more importantly toward cooperation and generosity as well (Zaman, 2008). And, according to Christian teaching, where a strictly commercial logic of contracts cannot sustain the fraternity necessary for economy what is needed is a divine principle of gratuitousness and logic of the gift.

> Economic life undoubtedly requires contracts, in order to regulate relations of exchange between goods of equivalent value. But it also needs just laws and forms of redistribution governed by politics, and

what is more, it needs works redolent of the spirit of gift. The economy in the global era seems to privilege the former logic, that of contractual exchange, but directly or indirectly it also demonstrates its need for the other two: political logic, and the logic of the unconditional gift. (#37, p. 20)[15]

Conclusion

This comparison of business spiritualities reminds us of the danger in mistaking a part-truth for the whole truth. Each of the spiritualities described above conveys a truth. It is true that we are each an authentic individual beyond our tragically compromised ego. It is true that we are one humanity and united in one "cosmic" consciousness. And it is true that we can ally ourselves with many kinds of transcendent powers, including unnamed gods of the "great beyond" and neo-pagan gods of the secular world. But the whole truth of spirituality, the inclusive and emancipating truth, the truth that incorporates the others and puts them in their place, is the personal God of Abraham observed and respected by the monotheistic religions of the world. The spirituality of a transcendent personal God includes those of individual and whole immanence. In Christian doctrine, this is the meaning of the Holy Trinity, in which these immanent spiritualities are realized together in its divine model for the human.[16] And the spirituality of a transcendent personal God incorporates the spiritualities of impersonal transcendence by specifying who God is and by establishing that He is before all lesser pagan "gods."

God is the truth missing in theories of business. We are able to act together with others, in business and everywhere else, only because we are made and long to be in God's image. By this natural law (so-called because it is written into our hearts) we seek, however imperfectly, to love and trust one another as we are loved and trusted by God. This law of our being—this law of our spirit—remains true whether or not we believe in God (for His love, which He has written into our creation, does not require our assent). Thus, it is by virtue of our relationship to God that we are able to enter together into markets and organizations and that we are able to find the meaning in work. This truth of the human spirit, known to faith, underscores the partiality and error in theories of economics, which assume that rational self-interest is grounding enough for markets, and the partiality and error in theories of management, which assume that simple obedience is grounding enough for organization. Markets and organizations stand firm only when built upon the concrete foundation of personal trust and benevolence toward others. When philosopher-economists such as Ayn Rand or Milton Friedman enthuse about individual freedom in markets, or when sociologist-economists such as Richard Scott or Oliver Williamson praise obedience to authority, they do so without acknowledging the dependence of these upon our unshakable relationship to God. In this, they too speak a partial truth unfaithful to the whole truth. By not taking account of God, and thereby not taking account of our spiritual being, their theories of business are built on shifting sands of self-interest, obedience, and the logic of cause and effect. God is the cement needed to turn these shifting sands into concrete foundations for markets, organizations, and meaningful work.

Finally, if there is a lesson for positive organization studies in today's literature on business spirituality it is just this—that our understanding of business must begin with the personal God who makes all things possible and who answers our most basic questions about the human person. This is a large lesson for it means that we cannot rely only upon science to teach us what we need to know about business but must turn to religion as well. If our business science is to lead to a true humanism, to a humanism mindful of our spiritual essence that can guide us in building positive forms of business life, it must be informed by the knowledge of God that comes by religious faith.

Acknowledgments

I thank Kim Cameron, Jane Dutton, Gretchen Spreitzer, and Jim Walsh for their helpful comments on earlier drafts of this chapter.

Notes

1. The "little" in this oversimplification is that economics is broader than the neo-classical models that dominate its discourse. There are today strands of evolutionary and behavioral theory that recognize the limitations of the assumption that economic actors maximize self-interest and that argue, to the contrary, that economic actors sometimes sacrifice self-interests for social justice (cf. Boehm, 1999; Dawes, Fowler, Johnson, McElreath, & Smirnov, 2007). Calling attention to altruistic or pro-social economic motives, this new work reinforces the claim that the human person has not been adequately described by economic theories. Offering instead an evolutionary explanation for altruistic or pro-social motives, this new work ventures a speculation that may or may not rival the claims of spirituality discussed in this paper.

2. The "little" in this oversimplification is that organization studies is broader than its models of power and authority.

There have been and continue to be strands of work on pro-social behavior and organizational citizenship (e.g., Brief & Motowidlo, 1986; Smith, Organ & Near, 1983) to suggest that organization requires more than obedience from workers, that it requires workers to not simply work to rule but to go beyond the call of duty. Calling attention to such pro-social or civic motives for cooperation, this work reinforces the claim that the human person has not been fully described by theories of organization focused on power and authority.

3. Pontifical Council for Culture, "Jesus Christ the Bearer of the Water of Life: A Christian Reflection on the 'New Age,'" #2.1, p. 9–10. www.vatican.va/roman_curia/pontifical_councils/interelg/documents.

4. As noted by the Catholic Church's *Pontifical Councils for Culture and Interreligious Dialogue* (2003):

> There is talk of a God, but it is . . . neither personal nor transcendent. Nor is it the Creator and sustainer of the universe, but an "impersonal energy" immanent in the world, with which it forms a "cosmic unity." "All is one." This unity is monistic, pantheistic or, more precisely, panentheistic. God is the "life-principle," the "spirit or soul of the world," the sum total of consciousness existing in the world. In a sense, everything is God. God's presence is clearest in the spiritual aspects of reality, so every mind/spirit is, in some sense, God. (# 2.3.4.2, pp. 17–18).

5. According to Ashforth & Vaidyanath (2002, p. 365):

> In time, then, the substantive and symbolic practices that once merely imparted the organization may come to define the organization. . . . Ultimately, the founder may become a larger-than-life figure, a deity of sorts. Executives and key insiders and experts may assume the mantle of clergy. Institutionalized processes, such as strategic planning and cost–benefit analyses, may be consecrated as sacred rights even where they do not serve "rational" purposes. There may even be sacred "texts," such as creation stories from the early days and great sayings of the founder. Individual exemplars of the organizational identity may be beatified, nonconformists may be demonized and excommunicated, precedents may be recast as commandments and failings as sins, job may be sanctified as callings, and incidents may be expanded into sacred legends.

6. Such is the ironic power in the godlike pronouncements by certain of today's critics of religion—among them Dawkins, Wilson, and Hitchens—who argue that if spirituality is a variously met function whose parameters and effects can be objectively described, then there is no need for a hidden and mysteriously powerful God. These critics have not defeated spirituality, as they suppose, but have elevated their own spirituality over that of religion and God.

7. As described by the Catholic Church, through its Pontifical Councils for Culture and Interreligious Dialogue (2003), for Christians, Christ is:

> [T]he one who is present actively in the various members of his body, which is the Church. They do not look to impersonal cosmic powers, but to the loving care of a *personal* God; for them cosmic bio-centrism has to be transposed into a set of *social* relationships (in the Church); and they are not locked into a cyclical pattern of cosmic events, but focus on the *historical* Jesus, in particular on his crucifixion and resurrection. . . . . The Christian conception of God is one of a Trinity of Persons who has created the human race out of a desire to share the communion of Trinitarian life with creaturely persons. Properly understood, this means that authentic spirituality is not so much *our* search for God but *God's* search for us. (#3.3, 24–25)

8. For Christians in particular salvation depends on:

> [P]articipation in the passion, death, and resurrection of Christ, and on a direct personal relationship with God rather than on any technique. The human situation, affected as it is by original sin and by personal sin, can only be rectified by God's action: sin is an offense against God, and only God can reconcile us to himself. In the divine plan of salvation, human beings have been saved by Jesus Christ who, as God and man, is the one mediator of redemption. In Christianity salvation is not an experience of the self, a meditative and intuitive dwelling within oneself, but much more the forgiveness of sin, being lifted out of profound ambivalences in oneself and the calming of nature by the gift of communion with a loving God. (Pontifical Councils for Culture and Interreligious Dialogue, 2003, #4, p. 29)

9. Lamentably, this academic failing need not have happened. It was not so long ago when theology reigned as "queen of the sciences" on the university campus (Newman, 1996) and when needful questions of the wholeness and completeness of spiritual truth were engaged as a matter of course.

10. Complicit in this political correctness, Wilber, Peck, Senge, Mitroff, and Giacalone and Jurkiewicz, among many others, insist upon a distinction between "spirituality" and "religion," in which the latter is at best a divisive specialization and at worst an absurd practice of the former. Mitroff (2003), in barely disguised agreement with his informants, finds religion to be a crabbed and intolerant spirituality:

> Religion is seen as dividing people through dogma and its emphasis on formal structure. It is viewed as intolerant, closed-minded, and excluding all those who do not believe in a particular point of view. Spirituality, on the other hand, is viewed as both personal and universal. It is perceived as tolerant, open-minded, and potentially including everyone. (p. 377)

And Giacalone and Jurkiewicz deride religion as a scientifically absurd spirituality:

> Workplace spirituality based on religion is ill-defined and untestable and therefore cannot contribute to a scientific body of knowledge. Application of religious principles to the workplace is tantamount to physicians practicing medicine based upon idiosyncratic religious beliefs rather than scientifically proven protocols. While one can certainly take a religious approach, the absurdity of doing so is no less apparent for organizational science than it is for medical practice. (2003, p. 6)

It is hard to imagine a distinction more harmful to understanding than this one between spirituality and religion. The whole point and glory of religion is to bring spirit into the light of reason so that we may know its fullness. In its dogma, if not always in its imperfect and all-too-human institutions, religion issues claims that are comprehensive (encompass the whole person—body, mind, and soul) and universal (include all persons). Thus, religion is not as its detractors would have it, a category of spirituality; to the contrary it is the working out and realization of spirituality. To cast religion aside in a literature on spirituality is not a benign openness, but a malignant intolerance for the contest of ideas and pursuit of truth. At the least, it is a cowardly gerrymandering that shrinks before the challenge religion poses to thought.

11. As Follett describes:

> The leader releases energy, unites energies, and all with the object not only of carrying out a purpose, but of creating further and larger purposes. And I do not mean here by larger purposes mergers or more branches; I speak of larger in the qualitative rather than the quantitative sense. I mean purposes which will

include more of those fundamental values for which most of us agree we are really living. (Follett, 1942, p. 168)

12. According to Christian teaching, this spirituality attains its apotheosis in Christ who is more than an idea or image of God, but is literally God made Man. In Christ, human being is perfected. In Christ we come to the Word and Way of human being.

13. "Authority" is thus a theological idea. As I describe in Sandelands (2008, p. 139), the word derives from the Latin *auctoritas* meaning authorship and *augere* meaning augmentation. In antiquity, human authority was invested in those able to interpret and/or augment the will of the gods. In the Judeo–Christian West, the will in question was the God of revelation to whom moral truth is uniquely known.

14. Here the Christian Holy Trinity is a powerful image. In its perfection of love in the three-in-one union of Father, Son, and Holy Spirit, each divine element is at once an autonomous indivisible person and a member of the one indivisible God.

15. This last is the demand for charity in truth for which the Church stands:

> Charity in truth, in this case, requires that shape and structure be given to those types of economic initiative which, without rejecting profit, aim at a higher goal than the mere logic of the exchange of equivalents, of profit as an end in itself. (Benedict XVI, #38, p. 20)

16. Again from Benedict XVI (2009):

> In this regard reason finds inspiration in Christian revelation, according to which the human community does not absorb the individual, annihilating his autonomy, as happens in the various forms of totalitarianism, but rather values him all the more because the relation between individual and community is a relation between one totality and another. . . . This perspective is illuminated in a striking way by the relationship between the Persons of the Trinity within the one divine Substance. The Trinity is absolute unity insofar as the three divine Persons are pure relationality. The reciprocal transparency among the divine Persons is total and the bond between each of them complete, since they constitute a unique and absolute unity. God desires to incorporate us into this reality of communion as well: "that they may be one even as we are one" (Jn 17:22). The Church is a sign and instrument of this unity. Relationships between human beings throughout history cannot but be enriched by reference to this divine model. (#53, p. 30)

References

Ali, A.J., Camp, R.C., & Gibbs, M. (2000). The Ten Commandments perspective on power and authority in organizations. *Journal of Business Ethics, 26*, 351–361.

Ashar, H., & Lane-Maher, M. (2004). Success and spirituality in the new business paradigm. *Journal of Management Inquiry, 13(3)*, 249–260.

Ashforth, B.E., & Pratt, M.G. (2003). Institutionalized spirituality: An oxymoron? In R.A. Giacalone & C.L. Jurkiewicz (Eds.), *Handbook of workplace spirituality and organizational performance* (pp. 93–107). New York: M.E. Sharpe.

Ashforth, B.E., & Vaidyanath, D. (2002). Work organizations as secular religions. *Journal of Management Inquiry, 11*(4), 359–370.

Ashmos, D.P., & Duchon, D. (2000). Spirituality at work: A conceptualization and measure. *Journal of Management Inquiry, 9*(2), 134–145.

Bell, E., & Taylor, S. (2003). The elevation of work: Pastoral power and the new age work ethic. *Organization, 10*(2), 329–349.

Bene el, M. (2003). Irreconcilable foes: The discourse of spirituality and the discourse of organization science. *Organization, 10*(2), 383–391.

Benedict XVI. (2009, July 18). *Encyclical letter caritas in veritate.* Retrieved from www.vatican.va/holy_father/benedict_xvi/encyclicals/documents/.

Berger, P.L. (1970). *A rumor of angels.* Garden City, NY: Anchor Books.

Boehm, C. (1999). *Hierarchy in the forest: The evolution of egalitarian behavior.* Cambridge, MA: Harvard University Press.

Brief, A.P., & Motowidlo, S.J. (1986). Prosocial organizational behaviors. *Academy of Management Review, 11*(4), 710–725.

Brown, N. (1966). *Love's body.* New York: Norton.

Brown, R.B. (2003). Organizational spirituality: The skeptic's version. *Organization, 10*(2), 393–400.

Buchholz, R.A., & Rosenthal, S.B. (2003), Spirituality, consumption, and business. In R.A. Giacalone & C.L. Jurkiewicz (Eds.), *Handbook of workplace spirituality and organizational performance* (pp. 152–180). New York: M.E. Sharpe.

Burack, E.H. (1999). Spirituality in the workplace. *Journal of Organizational Change Management, 12*(4), 280–292.

Butts, D. (1999), Spirituality at work: An overview, *Journal of Organizational Change Management, 12*(4): 328-332.

Cameron, K., Dutton, J.E., & Quinn, R.E. (Eds.) (2003). *Positive organizational scholarship: Foundations of a new discipline.* San Francisco: Barrett Kohler.

Cavanagh, G.F. (1999). Spirituality for managers: Context and critique. *Journal of Organizational Change Management, 12*(3), 186–199.

Clark, W.H. (1958). *The psychology of religion.* New York: Macmillan.

Conger, J.A. (1994). *Spirit at work.* San Francisco: Jossey-Bass.

Csikszentmihalyi, M. (1990). *Flow: The psychology of optimal experience.* New York: Harper-Collins.

Dawes, C.T., Fowler, J.H., Johnson, T., McElreath, R., & Smirnov, O. (2007). Egalitarian motives in humans. *Nature, 446* (April 12), 794–796.

Dehler, G.E., & Welsh, M.A. (2003), The experience of work: Spirituality and the new workplace. In R.A. Giacalone & C.L. Jurkiewicz (Eds.), *Handbook of workplace spirituality and organizational performance* (pp. 108–122). New York: M.E. Sharpe.

Delbecq, A. (1999). Christian spirituality and contemporary business leadership. *Journal of Organizational Change Management, 12*(4), 345–354.

Dent, E.B., Higgins, M.E., & Wharff, D.M. (2005). Spirituality and leadership: An empirical review of definitions, distinctions, and embedded assumptions. *Leadership Quarterly, 16*, 625–653.

Eisler, R., & Montouri, A. (2003), The human side of spirituality. In R.A. Giacalone & C.L. Jurkiewicz (Eds.), *Handbook of workplace spirituality and organizational performance* (pp. 46–56). New York: M.E. Sharpe.

Freshman, B. (1999). An exploratory analysis of definitions and applications of spirituality in the workplace. *Journal of Change Management, 12*(4), 318–327.

Follett, M.P. (1942). *Dynamic administration: The collected papers of Mary Parker Follett.* H.C. Metcalf, & L. Urwick (Eds.). New York: Harper Brothers.

Giacalone, R.A., & Jurkiewicz, C.L. (2003). *Handbook of workplace spirituality and organizational performance.* Armonk, NY: M.E. Sharpe.

Hackman, J.R., & Oldham, G.R. (1976). Motivation through the design of work: Test of a theory. *Organizational Behavior and Human Performance, 16*(2), 250–279.

Hill, P.C., Pargament, K.I., Hood, R.W., McCullough, M.E., Swyers, J.P., Larson, D.B., & Zinnbauer, B.J. (2000). Conceptualizing relation and spirituality: Points of commonality, points of departure. *Journal of the Theory of Social Behaviour, 30*(1), 51–77.

Jackall, R. (1988). *Moral mazes*. New York: Oxford University Press.

James, W. (1902). *Varieties of religious experience*. New York: Random House.

Khurana, R. (2004). *Searching for a corporate savior: The irrational quest for charismatic CEOs*. Princeton, NJ: Princeton University Press.

King, S., & Nicol, D.M. (1999). Organizational enhancement through recognition of individual spirituality. *Journal of Organizational Change Management, 12*(3), 234–243.

Kinjerski, V., & Skrypnek, B.J. (2004). Defining spirit at work: Finding common ground. *Journal of Organizational Change Management, 17*(1), 26–42.

Koch, S. (1956). Behavior as intrinsically regulated: Work notes toward a pre-theory of a phenomena called 'motivational'. In M.R. Jones (Ed.), *Nebraska symposium on motivation*. Lincoln, NE: University of Nebraska.

Konz, G.N.P., & Ryan, F.X. (1999). Maintaining an organizational spirituality: No easy task. *Journal of Organizational Change Management, 12*(3), 200–210.

Korac-Kakabadse, N, Kouzmin, A., & Kakabadse, A. (2002). Spirituality and leadership praxis. *Journal of Managerial Psychology, 17*(3), 165–182.

Krishnakumar, S., & Neck, C.P. (2002). The 'what,' 'why' and 'how' of spirituality in the workplace. *Journal of Managerial Psychology, 17*(3), 153–164.

Maslow, A. (1968). *Toward a psychology of being* (2nd ed.). New York: Van Nostrand Reinhold.

McCormick, D.W. (1994). Spirituality and management. *Journal of Managerial Psychology, 9*(6), 5–8.

Milgram, S. (1974). *Obedience to authority*. New York: Harper & Row.

Milliman, J., Czaplewski, A.J., & Ferguson, J. (2003). Workplace spirituality and employee work attitudes. *Journal of Organizational Change Management, 16*(4), 426–447.

Milliman, J., Ferguson, J., Trickett, D., & Condemi, B. (1999). Spirit and community at Southwest Airlines. *Journal of Organizational Change Management, 12*(3), 221–233.

Mirvis, P.H. (1997). 'Soul work' in organizations. *Organization Science, 8*, 193–206.

Mitroff, I.I. (2003). Do not promote religion under the guise of spirituality. *Organization, 10*(2), 375–382.

Mitroff, I.I., & Denton, E.A. (1999). *A spiritual audit of corporate America*. San Francisco: Jossey-Bass.

Newman, J.H. (1996). *The meaning of the university*. New Haven, CT: Yale University.

Paloutzian, R.F., Emmons, R.A., & Keortge, S.G. (2003). Spiritual well-being, spiritual intelligence, and healthy workplace policy. In R.A. Giacalone & C.L. Jurkiewicz (Eds.), *Handbook of workplace spirituality and organizational performance* (pp. 73–92). New York: M.E.Sharpe.

Peck, M.S. (1988). *The road less traveled: A new psychology of love, traditional values and spiritual growth*. New York: Touchstone.

Percy, W. (1983). *Lost in the cosmos*. New York: Farrar, Straus & Giroux.

Pfeffer, J. (2003). Business and the spirit: Management practices that sustain values. In R.A. Giacalone & C.L. Jurkiewicz (Eds.), *Handbook of workplace spirituality and organizational performance*. Amonk, NY: M.E. Sharpe.

Privette, G. (1981). Dynamics of peak performance. *Journal of Humanistic Psychology, 21*(1), 57–67.

Rosso, B.D., Dekas, K.H., & Wrzesniewski, A. (2010). On the meaning of work: A review. In B.M. Staw & A.P. Brief (Eds.), *Research in organizational behavior*. Forthcoming.

Sandelands, L.E. (2003). The argument for God from organization studies. *Journal of Management Inquiry, 12*(2), 168–177.

Sandelands, L.E. (2008). Thy will be done? *Journal of Management Inquiry, 17*, 137–142.

Sandelands, L.E. (2009). The business of business is the human person: Lessons from the Catholic social tradition. *Journal of Business Ethics, 85*, 93–101.

Scruton, R. (2009). The journey home. *Intercollegiate Review, 44*(1), 31–39.

Sheep, M.L. (2006). Nurturing the whole person: The ethics of workplace spirituality in a society of organizations. *Journal of Business Ethics, 66*, 357–375.

Smith, C.A., Organ, D.A., & Near, J.P. (1983). Organizational citizenship behavior: Its nature and antecedents. *Journal of Applied Psychology, 68*, 653–663.

Sperry, L. (1997). Leadership dynamics: Character and character structure in executives. *Consulting Psychology Journal: Practice and Research, 49*(4), 268–280.

Steingard, D.S. (2005). Spiritually-informed management theory: Two profound possibilities for inquiry and transformation. *Journal of Management Inquiry, 14*(3), 227–241.

Vitz, P. (1994). *Psychology as religion: The cult of self-worship*. Grand Rapids, MI: Eerdman's.

Waddock, S.A. (1999). Linking community and spirit: A commentary and some propositions. *Journal of Organizational Change Management, 12*(4), 332–345.

Wilber, K. (1985). *No boundary: Eastern and western approaches to personal growth*. Boston, MA: Shambhala.

Zaman, A. (2008). *Islamic economics: A survey of the literature*. Working paper No. 22, University of Birmingham, Religions and Development Research Programme, Birmingham, AL. Retrieved from SSRN: http//ssrn.com/abstract=128786.

Positive Deviance

A Metaphor and Method for Learning from the Uncommon

Marc Lavine

Abstract

The term *positive deviance* (PD) has primarily been used to describe uncommon behavior that is norm-defying yet socially desirable, as well as a formal method for learning from this behavior. Organization scholars have largely used this concept metaphorically, whereas those in the health and nutrition sciences have developed PD into a robust learning and social change method. This chapter is an attempt to merge insights from these diverse disciplines and provide an overview of work to date on the subject, as well as to offer a revised construct definition and comparison to related topics such as pro-social rule breaking, tempered radicalism, and appreciative inquiry. The chapter also includes a consideration of key contextual variables that influence the diffusion of PD and proposed directions for future research at varied levels of analysis. This potent concept can serve as a key building block for positive scholarship and positive organizing.

Keywords: Positive deviance, positive, deviance, organizational change, social change

Positive psychology and positive organizational scholarship (POS) embrace the notion that there is as much to be learned about favorable individual and organizational outcomes as failed or pathological ones. Positive deviance (PD) focuses our attention on the extreme end of the positive spectrum, to the uncommon cases that represent unusually successful behaviors amid unlikely odds. In settings where child malnutrition is pervasive, why do children from certain households, that possess no greater resources than others, remain adequately nourished while the majority of others do not? In hospitals where antibiotic-resistant infection rates are endemic, how do some facilities, with no greater resources, radically minimize this threat?

Positive deviance involves people behaving in ways that notably depart from expected norms, albeit in a direction that some group of others (i.e., a referent group) finds positive. The family that staves off malnutrition among its children may defy dietary norms and supplement the children's diet with readily available plants and indigenous protein sources. Although some might grouse about their "uncivilized" neighbors eating foods that have largely become the domain of livestock—meaning that agreement about positive behaviors is often not universal—those who care about healthy children would see this local foraging as a wonderfully clever tactic. In fact, solutions along these lines contributed to a 65%–85% reduction in childhood malnutrition in locations in the developing world where 60%–70% of the population was affected by malnutrition (Goldstein, Hazy, & Lichtenstein, 2010). Positive deviance is also widely used in organizations. For example, a hospital staffer developed a nontraditional method of removing his gloves and gown that more effectively traps germs. This method can easily be taught to others. The Centers for Disease Control estimate that antibiotic-resistant hospital-acquired infections affect more than 90,000 Americans annually and kill an estimated 19,000 each year (Klevans et al., 2007), but a PD approach has resulted in reductions of 85%–95% where it has been used (Lindberg, Norstrand, Munger, DeMarisco, & Buscell, 2009). In ways that are often modest but fundamentally powerful, positive deviants (i.e., those who engage in acts of PD) act in ways that others find more effective, successful, or desirable.

For most of its history, deviance has been understood as aberration from expected, or socially desirable, norms. The concept of deviance has been widely considered by criminologists, psychologists, and sociologists throughout the 20th century. Studies of deviance are widespread enough to warrant a scholarly journal devoted to the topic (see *Deviant Behavior*). The sociological literature treats normalcy as the opposite of deviance. Yet, just as positive psychology and POS have highlighted positive states beyond baseline normalcy—states of thriving and flourishing, rather than a simple lack of illness, or of extraordinary performance, rather than standard operating procedures—researchers in a series of fields (including nutrition, public health, psychology, and organization studies) have begun to posit that there is a "positive correlate" to deviance comprised of highly desirable, resilient, or virtuous behavior.

Organization scholars have used the frame of PD somewhat loosely or metaphorically to describe outlier organizational success (Cameron & Lavine, 2006; Hartman, Wilson, Arnold, 2005) or to encourage others to learn from uncommon excellence (Dutton, 2003). Elsewhere in this book, for example, authors use PD as a evocative frame or metaphor, rather than a precise concept or practice. The title of chapter 53 begins with the words "Innovativeness as Positive Deviance" and Chapter 72 is entitled "Positive Deviance for a Sustainable World." In other instances management scholars have attempted to carefully elaborate the PD concept, including Warren (2003), Spreitzer and Sonenshein (2003, 2004), and Morrison (2006). This work helped establish the legitimacy of positive forms of deviance and make the case that PD must be construed in normative terms, meaning that some party or referent group deems behaviors positive according to their values rather than by some universal standard. Spreitzer and Sonenshein are responsible for the greatest development of the PD concept among management scholars to date. Surprisingly, the authors' work (2003, 2004), which provides considerable added clarity by providing a carefully reasoned construct definition that positions PD in relation to its sociological antecedents and

describes how PD could be empirically validated and incorporated in future research agendas, has gone largely undeveloped. Little subsequent work has deepened our understanding of this important topic.

Yet, in fields outside of the management realm, PD has flourished. Most notably, it has grown into an increasingly important topic in the health and nutrition sciences. In these fields, scholars and practitioners have developed a methodology based on learning from the strategies of positive deviants. This approach differs from a best practices orientation in ways I delineate in this chapter. A PD approach (what I will call the action learning/social change method based on PD) has primarily been used to address deeply entrenched social problems, such as child malnutrition, endemic poverty, and the spread of infectious disease in hospital settings. In addition to substantial scholarly literature in public health and nutrition journals (Buscell, 2008; Friedman, Mateu-Gelabert, Sandoval, Hagan, & Des Jarlais, 2008; Guastelli et al., 2010; Lindberg, et al., 2009; Vossenaar et al., 2009; Singhal, McCandless, Buscell, & Lindberg, 2009; Walker, Sterling, Hoke, & Dearding, 2007, see also the Food and Nutrition Bulletin special issue on PD Vol.: 23, 4, 2002), a PD approach has garnered substantial public attention with coverage in places such as the *New York Times* (Sack, 2009), *Harvard Business Review* (Pascale & Sternin, 2005; Sternin & Choo, 2000), and the CBS *Evening News* (Miller, 2009). The Rockefeller Foundation considers a PD approach a breakthrough social innovation, and supports the Tufts University-based Positive Deviance Initiative in its aims to reach 15 million people through its work by 2015. The organization's website contains voluminous literature on the topic, and the newly released book *The Power of Positive Deviance: How Unlikely Innovators Solve the World's Toughest Problems* (Pascale, Sternin, & Sternin, 2010), is the most comprehensive treatment of an applied PD approach to date.

In this chapter, I propose that organization and management scholars follow the lead of the health and nutrition sciences and make greater use of PD as a learning method or applied technology. In part, this exhortation is a practical one. Those of us in organization studies or psychology can learn from the comparatively greater development of PD and capitalize on the level of attention that the topic is receiving in these other disciplines. Because PD is still something of a metaphor in the organization sciences, but a real-world practice in the worlds of health and nutrition, we have the opportunity for deep experience to inform our theorizing. Staying closer to a practice orientation as we theorize about PD should help us develop it as a learning method and improve our theorizing by considering "existence proofs" of this phenomenon and avoiding theoretical claims that can easily be disproved in practice. Monique Sternin, one of the founders of the Positive Deviance Initiative and a primary developer of a PD approach, notes "any new application has to be evidence based. It must be observable" (personal communication, March 5, 2010).

Yet, beyond opportunistic or instrumental motivations, there are more compelling normative reasons for following the lead of these other disciplines. Connecting research on PD from the health and nutrition sciences to those of management and organization studies is an opportunity to forge interdisciplinary connections and connect theory to practice. All too often in the behavioral and social sciences, we bemoan silos between and within fields that result in scholars speaking primarily to small groups of others who share our precise interests. Furthermore, those who use PD in the health and nutrition sciences do so to help address some of the most pressing social problems facing humanity. Adopting this orientation as our starting point can help us consider how we might employ insights from the behavioral and management sciences to address the great social issues of the day. In other words, it can help us ensure the social importance of our research.

Based on these goals, in this chapter, I first briefly characterize foundational work to date on PD. I present key developments from multiple disciplines. I then propose an updated and revised construct definition for PD. Finally, I address further directions for PD research and provide a vision of how PD could enliven and organize a broad range of research.

Origins and Development of Positive Deviance
Early Roots in Sociology
Positive deviance grew out of more prevalent conceptualizations of deviance as a negative state. Social deviance has been a robust topic in the sociological literature over the past century. Although often understood as behavior that defies prevailing social norms, common definitions include "conditions, persons, or acts that a society disvalues" (Saragin, 1975), and can include voluntary and involuntary behaviors. Different schools of thought about deviance have prevailed at different times among

sociologists: functionalist views (e.g., considering its social function, demarcating that which is taboo); absolutist views (judging deviance against absolute or seemingly universal social standards); reactivist definitions, including labeling theories that contended that deviance was not an intrinsic state but required an audience to react against or deem (e.g., label) something, or someone, deviant; normative views (deviance is based on defying social norms of a specific referent group); and statistical views (deviance determined by that which is in the statistical minority) (Clinard & Meier, 2007).

Even though the sociological literature, including literature on workplace deviance, adopts an overwhelmingly negative conception of deviance, literature on social deviance provides some basis on which to establish a positive vision of deviance. Functionalist views acknowledge that some acts of social deviance were enacted as forms of social resistance. This suggests that some deviant behaviors are based on principled actions (and likely ones that some subset of actors construe as virtuous). Reactivist theories, such as labeling theory, have illustrated that the same behavior could be seen as positive or negative deviance depending on the viewpoint of the actors or the historical perspective of the society. One study illustrates that French Impressionists were seen as negatively defying norms in their day but are seen as convention-defying masters today (Heckert, 1989). Normative views show the subjective and malleable nature of deviance assessments and the degree to which they are rooted in time, place, and context. Noted sociologists and social deviance scholars Clinard and Meier write: "To understand deviance, one must first understand this contradiction: no consensus reliably identifies people, behavior, or conditions that are deviant although most people would say they know deviance when they see it" (2007, p. 22). Statistical views of deviance provide an easy pathway to PD. If deviance is construed as that which departs from the statistical norm, then outlier behavior—including atypically positive acts—would exist on either side of a standard curve.

Prevailing sociological views of deviance continue to treat it as an almost purely negative phenomenon, and some leading scholars have deemed PD an oxymoron or as theoretically nonviable (Goode, 1991; Saragin, 1985). Sociological views of deviance gave rise to the study of workplace deviance, which similarly treats deviance as purely negative behavior (Bennett & Robinson, 2000). Yet, there are limited signs that some sociologists are beginning to acknowledge that deviance may indeed have a positive aspect. In *Sociology of Social Deviance*, a widely used teaching text in its 13th edition, Clinard and Meier acknowledge at the outset that "society may encounter positive and negative deviance" (2001, p. 4) and work by Heckert (1989), Jensen (2001), and Heckert and Heckert (2002) also acknowledges this possibility.

Positive Deviance in Management and Organizational Research

Among organization and management scholars, a precursor to PD was Bill Starbuck's work making the case for the importance and generativity of studying "extreme cases" because they can "expose overlooked causal factors" and "discourage overgeneralization" (Starbuck, 2006). Starbuck reminds us that, in extreme cases, organizational dynamics may be comparatively exaggerated relative to less extreme situations. As a result, important actions and routines may be more visible than in more conventional settings. Other fields echo this sentiment. Education researchers note the value of "extreme, deviant (in a statistical sense) or unique case sampling" (Ary, Jacobs, Razavieh, & Sorenson, 2009, p. 430) and suggest: "You might choose to study a high poverty inner-city elementary school that has achieved exemplary reading and mathematics scores. Such a study might identify practices, teaching methods and student characteristics that may be relevant to their superior performance" (Ary et al., 2009, p. 430).

Some of the first and most visible examples of management scholars adopting a specific frame of PD begin to appear early in the 21st century. Warren (2003), drawing on normative and labeling theories, identified a series of destructive *and* constructive organizational or workplace behaviors that imply deviation from expected norms. Warren notes that, whereas behaviors such as aggression, lying, and theft have been addressed by management scholars as deviance, pro-social behaviors, tempered radicalism, and whistle blowing have all been characterized as examples of constructive deviation from organizational norms.

The most substantial scholarship on this topic among management scholars has been seen in efforts by Spreitzer and Sonenshein, who first explored the topic at length (2003) and further refined their work by creating a construct definition and proposing methods of validating the concept and using it in further research (2004). In their 2003 chapter, the authors theorize that PD may be facilitated by psychological conditions of meaning, a pro-social (other-centered) orientation, self-determination, personal efficacy, and courage. They also identify contextual factors, such as transformational leadership and situations of crisis, as conditions more likely to bring forth PD. The authors note that PD is likely to enhance a sense of greater subjective well-being for the positive deviant, create higher-quality relationships between the deviant and those helped by the deviants' actions, and increase the effectiveness of individuals and organizations. Importantly, the authors acknowledge that PD can gradually shift organizational norms. Citing examples of companies that exhibited PD by embracing unusually strong environmental practices, the authors note that many of these behaviors have now become mainstream (therefore positive, but not deviant), and previously acceptable operating practices are now considered negatively deviant as PD has gradually helped shift norms of acceptability.

Spreitzer and Sonenshein also call for more rigorous theoretical development of the PD construct. They begin to explore definitional issues when they address the importance of clarifying the referent group whose norms an actor may defy, noting that unit-, organizational-, or field-level norms are all possible considerations. The authors heed the call for more construct development in a 2004 piece, wherein they offer the following construct definition for PD: *intentional behaviors that significantly depart from norms of a referent group in honorable ways.* The authors provide a detailed explanation of the sociology of deviance as an inductive means to make the case for their choice of a decidedly normative definition of PD. They differentiate PD from related constructs, showing that PD is likely to be related to, but theoretically distinct from, organizational citizenship behaviors, whistle-blowing, corporate social responsibility, and behaviors of creativity and innovation.

Spreitzer and Sonenshein provide a clear pathway forward for empirical validation of PD and an agenda for future research. Yet, other organizational and management researchers have not significantly built on the strong foundation provided by these authors. Of the 18 times their 2004 article was cited in the remainder of the decade (using the ISI Social Science Index), a rough assessment (based on informal review of article titles and abstracts for the citations) shows that two-thirds of the citations were made to explore topics of negative deviance. Of the six citations devoted to positive topics, none is devoted to advancing PD as an overall construct.

Because Spreitzer and Sonenshein describe how PD may be related to but is distinct from organizational citizenship behaviors, whistle-blowing, corporate social responsibility, and behaviors of creativity and innovation (2004), I will not repeat this effort here. Instead, I address the possible relationship between PD, pro-social rule breaking, and tempered radicalism. Later in this chapter, I also address the differences between a PD approach and appreciative inquiry.

Early conceptualizations of rule breaking have been based on the assumption that it inherently had selfish or organizationally damaging intent. Morrison (2006) shows that rule breaking is also utilized to benefit the organization or key stakeholders of the organization, such as instances when an employee exercises discretion and defies a rule to better accommodate a customer. Morrison notes that pro-social rule breaking is a form of PD but only one manifestation, in that it pertains to defying formal organizational rules, whereas PD may involve departing from social norms rather than formal rules. Pro-social rule breaking can be one form of PD. The important conceptual differences are that pro-social rule breaking can be commonplace, or a de facto norm in a given setting, whereas PD is by definition rare or uncommon. Just as anachronistic laws often remain "on the books" well beyond the time of their routine enforcement, some rules may be defied by a majority of an organization's members for pro-social reasons. Furthermore, PD may involve rule breaking though it need not, by definition, do so. It may instead involve defying norms while not breaking formal rules.

Tempered radicalism (Meyerson & Scully, 1995; Meyerson, 2001; Creed, 2003) describes people who act in counter-normative ways in an effort to balance their commitment to their workplace and their own social values and identity. Many examples of tempered radicals seem akin to positive deviants, such as an employee who works with the company as it is, but quietly acts to improve the organization's commitment to diversity, or its policy on volunteerism. Yet, tempered radicalism is an explanation of identity rather than change, and narratives of tempered radicalism are often used to explain an actor's decision to refrain from action, or to act with ambivalence, because of conflicting commitment to one's workplace and personal values. Positive deviance typically describes action. It is possible for PD to describe the rare actor who refrains from activity for positive effect though the focus of PD is

nonetheless on behavioral acts, not on identity considerations that may inform the action.

Positive Deviance in Health and Nutrition Research

Positive deviance that began through field observation, such as the work of Jerry and Monique Sternin, was inspired by the work of nutritionist Marian Zeitlin and colleagues (1990), who approached PD in a manner akin to studies of resilience or hardiness. Zeitlin and colleagues asked why some people in difficult circumstances seem to emerge relatively healthy, whereas the same conditions are so deleterious for the majority (Hegsted, 1967; Wray, 1972; Greaves, 1979). These scholars questioned whether differing behaviors, or tangible actions by some subset of actors, might explain differences in outcomes (Alvarez, Wurgaft, & Wilder, 1982; Mata, 1980). Zeitlin, who has written extensively on PD and studied it in the field, is often seen as an originator of PD, although she credits comments made decades earlier by colleague Mark Hegsted that "we should pay more attention to the reasons for nutritional success than nutritional failure" (Hegsted, 1967) as the first use of the PD concept. Jerry and Monique Sternin are considered pioneers of the PD approach, having extensively used positive methods throughout the world and having established the clearinghouse and think tank, the Positive Deviance Initiative.

Insights from PD in the health and nutrition sciences make three important contributions to our understanding of PD. First, they demonstrate that the question of what is positive is always a relative one. In instances in which a reasonable expectation is for tragedy, an outcome of only limited harm can be exceptionally positive. This is consonant with sociological labeling theory and supports Weick's (2003) reminder that positivity need not be shining success, but a better outcome than can reasonably be expected. When absolute calamity seems likely, mere difficulty can represent an astonishing and hard-fought success. Second, a PD approach, in the tradition of Zeitlin, is firmly rooted in the study of especially entrenched social problems such as child malnutrition; serious child protection situations, such as child trafficking; rehabilitation of child soldiers; combating methicillin-resistant *Staphylococcus aureus* (MRSA) virus in hospitals; other health care issues, such as cancer and HIV/AIDS reduction; and female genital mutilation. It can also include broad social issues such as poverty reduction, agricultural development, and country-level corruption reform efforts. Finally, PD rooted in the health and nutrition tradition differentiates the actions of "positive deviants" (e.g., those engaging in acts of PD in a given situation) from a PD approach, which is a strategy to learn from the behaviors of positive deviants by enabling others to emulate their actions. This allows the power of PD to multiply far beyond the impact of the original actor.

Learning from Positive Deviance as a Method

In considering how the flames of PD could be fanned such that others could learn from the success strategies of positive deviants, the Sternins, and others who experimented with a PD approach, developed a series of supportive practices that aid the dissemination of PD behaviors. One key mechanism is an inquiry-based *discovery process* whereby people hoping to make use of PD strategies search for the solutions that might produce more favorable results. Structured dialogue is used to identify whether anyone is aware of people who have found solutions or better results (i.e., PD) for a problem that is broadly confounding. In many cases, even if a solution is identified, those who need to implement the new solution observe and discover for themselves the better outcome.

One example of this discovery process comes from the use of a PD approach to battle the deadly MRSA bacteria that kills an estimated 19,000 Americans annually (Klevans et al., 2007). MRSA is an infection largely spread in hospitals, and simple practices, such as increased hand washing, significantly reduce its transmission. Among one group of collectively managed hospitals, the infection rates at a few of the hospitals were far lower than at the vast majority of locations. Methods to ensure more routine hand washing among medical personnel and an innovative method developed by a hospital orderly for removing surgical scrubs and gloves (Miller, 2009) were key methods responsible for the better results. Yet, rather than simply presenting these data to the assembled staff from all the hospitals, the facilitators of the PD intervention gave everyone data that showed the infection rates for each hospital, with the identifying data of each locale removed. After the entire assembled group had time to review the data, some of the gathered members noticed the pattern of much lower infection rates in a couple of locations and said something to the effect of, "Gosh, I don't know what's going on at those locations, but if these data are accurate, they're sure doing something that no one else is." The next step was visiting those locales and observing practices. Such a process might seem slow and labor intensive, yet it resulted in a much higher uptake for the rest of the facilities emulating the successful practices because they felt a sense of ownership in having "discovered" the practices.

This discovery phase can seem challenging for many organizations that, once they find a more workable solution, simply want to change rules through fiat or edict to make the better approach the new official policy. This is a key way in which PD differs from a best-practices approach. It also differs in that it is always organic or indigenous to the system and has, therefore, proven that it can take root in the context that is relevant to the organization, unlike many best practices that are imported from foreign contexts. Those who regularly employ a PD approach contend that a discovery-based process is necessary to overcome skepticism, ego-defense, or a sense of being criticized for the failures of the prior approach. In some cases, this discovery process is necessary simply to find or assess whether positive deviants exist who have found a better way. In other cases, even when data are in hand that point to pockets of unusual success, a discovery process is still necessary to overcome resistance among those who would need to change to amplify the strategies of the positive deviants.

A PD approach aims to identify actors who have developed more successful solutions using readily available resources that don't substantially differ from those available to others. As those who are familiar with "model projects" have all too often seen, some shining examples gain their luster from far greater resources than what aspiring projects have available. Yet, it is always the case that "separate is never equal." There will almost always be some variation in the resources available among actors. A PD approach relies, therefore, on having those who seek to replicate the PD strategies pass each success factor through a *conceptual sieve* or filter to methodically separate those resources that may not be available in another situation from those that are widely available. Positive deviance facilitators refer to this conceptual filter as "TBU" for "True but Useless" to identify features of a successful strategy that may not be available to all. Thus, rather than wholesale benchmarking, PD replication is considered an adaptive customization process more akin to a well-executed design process (Brown & Wyatt, 2010).

Those involved in the Positive Deviance Initiative note that PD has some *baseline success requirements.*

First, there needs to be a problem in which behavioral change is part of what is required for a solution. Positive deviance also requires that people enacting better solutions can indeed be identified. A PD approach functions on the basis of social proof, not hypothetical solutions. Those well-versed in the PD approach also note important contextual factors. A PD approach works best for addressing particularly intractable problems, when other approaches have not worked. Because PD represents a departure from accepted norms, this approach can be threatening and tends to be engaged in as a method of last resort. Additionally, sufficient leadership buy-in is crucial to uncover and support positive deviance solutions. Although this may seem uncontroversial, or obvious, because PD involves defying norms, it is seen as a threat to organizational control and often quelled or not supported even if it yields superior outcomes.

Successful PD interventions in social systems often build capacity for actors to respond to future challenges because they develop the ability of people to come together around a common problem and recognize that expertise to solve problems can often be found within a social system, rather than requiring outside expertise. These sorts of claims are often made about other so-called strengths- or asset-based organizational intervention approaches. A PD approach starts with a recognized challenge and assumes that solutions exist within the system or organization. Notwithstanding that the PD approach often involves outsiders as facilitators, it operates on the assumption that the insiders are the experts and that the community or organization itself will need to establish success criteria and identify its own PD solutions.

Given the asset-based intervention orientation of a PD approach, it is useful to address how PD differs from other asset-based organizational development methods such as appreciative inquiry. *Appreciative inquiry* (AI) can loosely be described as posing affirming questions designed to provoke and guide change. Although both approaches rely on identifying and cultivating latent strength within a system (whether organizational or societal) AI and PD differ in important ways. Whereas PD employs strengths to solve problems, the starting point for PD is a dilemma, often a seemingly intractable one. Appreciative inquiry may not take a problem as its starting point and is often credited for not starting with the assumption that things are necessarily wrong and broken. Appreciative inquiry can be applied to take something that is going well and seek to make it better; it can work whether or not alternative solutions are identified (Cooperrider, Sorensen, Whitney, Yaeger, 2000). Positive deviance requires success examples and is largely used to address intractable problems, rather than to make incremental improvements. Positive deviance focuses specifically on concrete behavioral change and "acting your way into new ways of thinking," whereas AI may directly attempt to address and alter mental models. Appreciative inquiry generates questions about what might be possible and allows for what people can imagine or envision as the basis for goal setting, not simply what people can directly observe. Positive deviance requires observable behavior. Appreciative inquiry is often used for large-scale change efforts, bringing thousands of people together to engage in shared questions about change, whereas PD is more carefully adapted to the varied resources and contexts of specific communities and organizations.

Although both approaches embrace a positive core they differ in the range of problems they are suited to address, and their philosophy of change differs in crucial ways. Yet, because of their shared strengths-based approach, practitioners using a PD approach see AI as a complementary approach. Ochieng (2006) suggests that, a PD approach may be more concrete and targeted, whereas AI methods can help strengthen a PD learning process. Marian Zeitlin frames this as a "basket approach" to organizational change, in which a series of intervention methods, including PD and AI, can be adapted or used in beneficial conjunction with one another (e-mail communication, September 5, 2009).

Expanding Positive Deviance Research and Theory: A Revised Construct Definition

Building on the strong foundation of Spreitzer and Sonenshein, let us revisit their construct definition of PD as a starting point: *intentional behaviors that depart from the norms of a referent group in honorable ways* (2004). Before delving into conceptual matters, it is worth noting two structural differences between this definition and the one I offer at the end of this section. This previous definition makes the departure from norms the centrally honorable act. I contend that the primary concern is whether a referent group deems the behavior honorable. I also treat behavior as a singular act (behavior) rather than a plural (behaviors) one. Although PD may describe repeated or plural behaviors, even one behavior could be considered PD, and a singular behavior can be strung together from a subrepertoire of microbehaviors.

Spreitzer and Sonenshein are careful to note that their definition takes a normative stance, as departure from norms and evaluation of honorable intent must be determined by some referent group. I agree with their assessment. As with any normative claim, we must acknowledge that there will never be universal agreement about the positive or honorable nature of a PD claim. One referent group may deem something positive, and another might just as vigorously disagree. Terrorists, in the eyes of one referent group, are freedom fighters to another. Recalling the sociological insights derived from labeling theory, it is also important to remember that factors such as historical context and accompanying shifts in social norms may alter the normative sentiments among members of a referent group over time.

Despite the fact that certain virtues are broadly regarded as positive, behavior is inherently subject to varied interpretations even if it is propelled by virtue. The applied PD tradition (what I refer to as a PD approach) often deals with social challenges that intersect with cultural taboos. There may be deep-seated normative sentiments about the appropriateness, meaning, and value of behaviors. A PD approach has been used, for example, by human rights activists and health care workers to combat female genital mutilation. Other referent groups see the practice as a time-honored ritual and would insist that the correct term for the practice is female circumcision. They see those who hope to change this practice as negative deviants and meddling outsiders. Thus, the positive in PD may be hotly contested.

Spreitzer and Sonenshein cite Dodge (1985) to note that a normative definition differs from a statistical appraisal of PD, which would construe any outlier behavior as deviance (whether positive or negative). A purely statistical perspective does not allow for normative claims about the nature of the outlier behavior. The authors offer the example of someone who has the ability to spit a particularly long distance. Despite their atypical prowess, this unusual talent is unlikely to be seen as normatively honorable or socially desirable by any referent group.

Although a statistical perspective is inadequate to define PD, it is important to note that norm-defying behavior must be uncommon. Positive deviance need not describe actions that are the exclusive domain of true statistical outliers, but it is inherently a minority behavior. Of course, if a behavior becomes common, it may be laudable but often signals that norms have shifted to accept the behavior.

Spreitzer and Sonenshein note as much when they show that PD can shift organizational norms, where a behavior such as environmental stewardship becomes mainstream. Once that happens, the behavior is no longer deviant, even if it is still honorable or positive. Conversely, some behavior can become fairly widespread, even while a norm against it persists. I contend, therefore, that the word "uncommon" provides important clarity and qualification to the construct definition.

Drawing on the extensive body of PD practice from the work of the Positive Deviance Initiative, it does not appear that PD behavior needs to be intentional, nor that the intentions necessarily need to be honorable in the mind of the positive deviant (even if the behavior is deemed honorable by referent others). Monique Sternin notes that some positive deviants do not even realize that what they are doing is norm-defying (personal communication, March 5, 2010). It is possible that, due to social isolation, accident, improvisation, or lack of formal training, an individual might act in a way that others would deem honorable and positive when the original intent may have been practical or arbitrary. Imagine that a mother who is an agricultural worker has a mildly crippling injury. As a result of the injury, she pauses more often between working and, when pausing, feeds her child. Feeding a child smaller portions more often can support healthy body weight, but the mother's act of feeding her child more often may be an adaptation to circumstance, not an act with deliberately honorable intent. The hospital worker who devises a method for removing and disposing of his hospital gown and gloves that diminishes the potential to spread infection from those garments may have simply devised a routine he found efficient, not realizing that another benefit was limiting the spread of infection. Spreitzer and Sonenshein state (p. 833) that:

> It is also important to point out that the definition of positive deviance focuses on behaviors with honorable *intentions*, independent of *outcomes*. Positive intentions do not always lead to positive outcomes. We consider intentions the important criterion for positive deviance, and not outcomes. There is a long intellectual tradition of understanding noteworthy behaviors independent of outcomes (e.g., Kant, 1993).

Those who work with a PD approach note that its success relies on identifying observable behaviors. In that sense, a behavior *is* an observable outcome. Intention without behavior is merely internal thought. An idea may represent PD (imagining freedom where repression is the norm for example), yet it is only when a thought is enacted that it becomes replicable. For the purposes of refining a construct definition that has utility for organizational theory, where coordination among actors is basic to organizations and organizing, some sort of action or behavior must be part of our definition. Of course, outcomes deemed more visibly successful by a referent group would be more likely to be identified and emulated.

In fact, very subtle or undetected action could be considered PD. As Monique Sternin acknowledges, "Many positive deviants don't want to be found" (personal communication, March 5, 2010). This may be true because, in some cases, detection brings attention that makes the positive deviant less able to engage in PD. John Taylor Gatto, the former New York City and New York State Teacher of the Year, noted that once he won awards, he felt compelled to stop teaching because his success ran the risk of recrimination from other programs that felt they were made to look bad in light of his greater success with fewer resources (Gatto, 1992).

Although stealth might provide cover for PD, another explanation is that some PD behavior is neither intentional nor motivated by pro-social (i.e., focused on helping others) aims. Some secret acts of PD may be accidental or motivated by survival instinct, not a desire to remain quiet in order to continue helping others. If a sex worker devises a way to persuade clients to follow safer sex guidelines, such actions may be motivated out of self-protection or survival. What is important is that a referent group finds the action normatively/subjectively honorable or positive, regardless of the actor's intent. Of course, the process of helping others to learn from and adopt the behavior (i.e., a PD approach, not just PD) is inherently pro-social, as is any learning process.

Thus far, the two issues I have raised would simply result in a substitution of words within Spreitzer and Sonenshein's definition: removing *intentional* and adding *uncommon*. Another semantic, but also symbolically and practically important question, is whether to use the word *honorable* rather than *positive* in any construct definition of PD. Although others have labored to characterize the meaning of the word "positive" within POS (Cameron, Dutton, & Quinn, 2003; Cameron, 2008), given the varied connotations of the term, it merits clarification in the context of PD.

The most fitting definitions of the word "positive" describe it as "an affirmative element or characteristic"

and "a constructive nature." A common synonym is "favorable" (American Heritage Dictionary, 1978). Given a normative definition of PD, a referent group would deem behavior positive because they judge the behavior constructive and/or favorable.

Spreitzer and Sonenshein's construct definition made use of the term "honorable" rather than positive. Certainly "honorable" is close in meaning to "positive." A common definition is "deserving and winning of honor and respect, credible" (American Heritage Dictionary, 1978). I maintain that it is pragmatically preferable to use the word positive rather than to introduce a synonymous variant such as "honorable." The meaning of the word "positive" needs to be defined regardless, simply because it is part of the term *positive deviance*. Therefore, using the word "honorable" adds complexity because it necessitates the introduction of two additional definitions (of the word itself as well as its root "honor"). Using "honorable" instead of "positive" does not add clarity but creates added potential for confusion. In addition to these practical considerations, there are more conceptual reasons for favoring the word positive. Although both terms (positive and honorable) can be used normatively, honor adheres more closely to the language of virtue and therefore carries a greater possible risk of misinterpretation, as it may more readily imply that a given behavior is inherently honorable. Positivity may be more universally understood as an abstract category that requires normative interpretation.

Some view the use of the same word in a definition and the term it defines as inherently circular, if not tautological. Yet, tautology connotes "needless repetition of the same sense *in different words*" (American Heritage Dictionary, 1978). Thus, If the first sin of tautology is redundancy then the second is synonymous substitution. This makes the use of terms closely similar in concept to positive, such as honorable, more tautologically problematic. The use of the word "positive" in the term PD and its definition is indeed somewhat circular although this is no more the case than defining honorable as "acting with honor" (which is typically the first definition of the word). Using the word "positive" also has the benefit of greater consonance with POS. The same affirmative stance that broadly characterizes POS: "toward an emphasis on strengths, capabilities, and possibilities"(Cameron, 2008, p. 8) holds true for PD. Members of a referent group may well find acts of PD "exceptional, virtuous, or life-giving" (Cameron et al., 2003, p. 5).

In summation, PD describes behavior that has three essential qualities that distinguish it from other laudable forms of action. First, because this definition is normative, it requires that some referent group must deem the behavior positive. Yet, because this is not a reactivist definition, it is not imperative that a group actually deem the behavior positive, simply that a referent group would do so were it aware of the behavior. For this reason, I use the conditional phrasing "would deem" in my proposed construct definition. Second, the behavior must depart from the norms of the referent group and/or the norms that the referent group expects from the behavior of the actor (whether an individual, group, organization, or society) in question. In other words, it could be that you and I work together, and you do not adhere to some organizational norm; yet, other coworkers and I would deem your behavior positive nonetheless. In that case, you departed from a norm held by the same referent group that would deem the behavior positive. Alternately, in the case of women who defy the norm of female circumcision in societies where this is a traditional practice, this behavior is deemed positive by "Westerners." Yet, the behavior of these women does not depart from a norm held by Westerners. The behavior departs from the norms the Westerners would expect from members of a society in which the practice of female circumcision was the norm. This is an example of PD as a departure from the norms the referent group expects from the actors in question. Finally, as I describe earlier in this section, PD behavior must be relatively rare or uncommon.

Based on the points I have addressed in this section, an updated definition of PD is: *uncommon behavior that does not conform to expected norms but would be deemed positive by a referent group.* I shift from the language of "norm departure" to that of "nonconformity" because the phrasing makes it unambiguous that it is the behavior, rather than the departure from norms, that is of central importance to the referent group. Furthermore, in the sociological literature, nonconformity often implies a link to social change (Marshall, 1998; Merton, 1971). The phrase "expected norms" allows that the norms may be those of the referent group or those that the group expects of the actor in question. A definition of a PD approach could be: *a process whereby members of a referent group learn from PD.*

Notably absent from this definition is anything about the resources that positive deviants have at their disposal. Those who use a PD approach as a

learning method are quick to emphasize that the material resources that the positive deviant uses to support his or her PD must be roughly similar to, or no greater than those available to others. If a parent keeps her child well-nourished while others go hungry because hers is the only family in the community who has the money to purchase more food, the outcome for the child is clearly positive but that is not an approach that is easily replicable or scalable. It is also possible that a referent group would be inherently less likely to consider the behavior positive because they would not think of the behavior as norm-defying relative to that of people with similar resources, only to themselves with fewer. Although this caveat is critical to assess the suitability of the positive deviant's actions for emulation by others— a key moderator when considering a PD approach—it need not prevent, by definition, classification of an act as PD. At the time of this writing, for example, David DeRothschild is sailing a catamaran made entirely of recycled plastic bottles from California to Australia to raise awareness of environmental issues. Environmentalists may well consider this an act of PD. That the sailor happens to be the heir to the Rothschild banking fortune explains his ability to have spent 4 years creating the boat and 100 days sailing it. These facts explain why others may consider it PD, but not consider it feasible to follow suit.

Further Directions

The study of PD has the potential to energize and enlighten our research (Dutton, 2003). Individuals, groups, and organizations acting in nonconforming ways for positive ends can be both insight-granting and inspiring and we, as social researchers, comprise a legitimate group to deem such behavior positive. Spreitzer and Sonenshein are quite right to note that more work can and should be done to validate PD as a construct. The updated construct definition I provide in this chapter should aid in that goal. In what follows, I pose questions and propose directions for development of PD as a construct, theory of action, and resource for social change.

Positive Deviance at Different Level of Analysis

Individuals, groups, and organizations all seem to engage in PD. Our theorizing must contend with this complexity. We must also consider PD as an act—or set of actions and behaviors— as well as a PD approach: an action learning and social change methodology based on PD. In that spirit, I suggest future directions for research organized around these matters.

- *Positive deviants*: This designation is a bit of a misnomer (though the longer but more accurate designation "individuals who perform acts of PD" is a bit cumbersome), there is far more to be understood about the antecedents of PD. What makes positive deviants deviate? What internal factors should be considered, and what contextual factors are important? Others have described this as a consideration of both subjective states as well as externally observable traits (Roberts, 2006). It is understandable that we think of admirable features as precursors to PD, such as greater hardiness, resilience, resourcefulness, and self-efficacy. Yet, it is entirely possible that qualities we do not wish upon people influence PD—considerations such as social isolation (it's easier to break norms if you don't realize what they are or are socially less bound by them to begin with) and sheer desperation. Necessity may indeed be the mother of invention. We don't break norms easily or naturally, and counter-normative behavior is often born out of deep desperation.

- *Positive deviance in groups*: Much of what we consider individual-level PD may, in fact, be group-level phenomena. Often, an act that an individual engages in requires cooperation and coordination with others to be successful. Efforts to combat female genital mutilation, for example, typically require the support of a broad circle of family members. In other instances, what may appear to be individual behavior, such as women enriching the diet of their young children, may be a group-level phenomenon if a counter-normative "pocket" of behavior takes root in which information exchange and influence between a subgroup enables PD. What social factors support or constrain group-level PD? How might this differ when some social actors play "accomplice" roles than when all actors are engaged in PD? This suggests a role for network and relational considerations about the nature and features of relationships among actors.

- *Positive deviance in organizations*: Key questions here revolve around contextual forces that enable or constrain PD. Scholars suggest that transformational leadership is necessary to see organizational level PD (Foster & Torbert, 2005), whereas others simply note the general importance of leadership in the equation (Cameron & Lavine, 2006; Spreitzer & Sonenshein, 2003). Although pockets of PD sometimes emerge in organizations, often there is a "return to the median," whereby the desire for managerial control exceeds an organizational willingness to prioritize positive results from well-intentioned but norm-defying or rule breaking actors. What kind of leadership can encourage increased norms of PD? How can leaders foster organizations that routinely welcome innovative and unconventional methods for favorable results?

- *A positive deviance approach*: Moving from PD itself to the process of its replication, or its role in inspiring learning, change, and innovation, opens up new levels of complexity. Many other research streams can inform such an approach. Scholars of organizational change and innovation could explore local or situational factors that enable or constrain PD adoption. We must also examine contextual adaptation of PD solutions. Harkening back to the distinction that some factors contribute to PD are "true but useless" when it comes to PD's diffusion, because they exist in one context but not another, forces us to ask: What must be true, and what can be useless? Additionally, not enough is known about key criteria for skillful PD facilitation. Many who have long used a PD approach suggest that it may be strengthened when used in conjunction with complementary methodologies. This too suggests further avenues for research.

Beyond the transmission of PD from positive deviants to others, a PD approach also raises questions about the nature of positive behaviors themselves. For fairly basic tasks, simply learning a new behavior may be an adequate approach. What about more complex tasks? This raises questions about the emulation process between positive deviants and those who seek to learn from their behaviors. What pedagogies best support effective PD diffusion?

All of these questions focus on how we might better understand and improve a PD approach.

Yet another extension of PD research could be to "look from the inside out" and examine the organizational consequences of PD organizing. At its best, there is the suggestion that a PD approach not only supports great strides in combating seemingly intractable problems but also paves the way for organizations to experience enduring improvement in intraorganizational relations and collaboration thereafter (Buscell, 2008). Understanding the consequences and variation in outcomes of a PD approach is another important area for study.

KEY CONTEXTUAL VARIABLES

In addition to the various contextual factors that may support or inhibit PD, the moment we think about how others might learn from PD behaviors and actions, we must consider similarity or difference in resources available to the positive deviants and others. We must also conduct a more thorough appraisal of the success, or lack thereof, of the positive deviants' behavioral approach to decide whether their approach merits emulation. We must make sure this sentiment is shared by referent others who would adopt the behavior. This is not to suggest that resources must be identical among actors, or that there exist complete consensus about the success of the behaviors or actions, but these two forces will significantly influence the feasibility and desirability of implementing strategies based on PD. We must treat these contextual considerations as important moderating variables in our theorizing about PD.

Conclusion

A continued exploration of PD, especially through deeper dialogue among an academically and professionally diverse range of actors who consider and practice PD in varied settings, has the potential to ensure that PD is ever more theoretically robust and practically useful. Further inquiry about PD also has the potential to invigorate our own research (Dutton, 2003) by deepening our understanding about the circumstances of atypical success. Positive deviance can indeed be one of the "generative mechanisms" (2006, p. 292) that can contribute to better theoretical and empirical understanding of optimal individual and organizational functioning. Positive deviance research also has the potential to ensure that some of the possible risks of a "positive perspective" are unlikely to take hold. As Roberts rightly notes (2006), a positive perspective carries a risk of naiveté, of under-perceiving negative conditions, or failing to address injustice. Because the applied PD tradition has so steadfastly addressed pervasive tragedy, endemic difficulty, and deep injustice, our continued refinement of this frame reminds us to cultivate knowledge and practice that is cognizant of suffering and aimed toward social betterment.

References

Alvarez, M., Wurgaft, F., & Wilder, H. (1982). Non verbal language in mothers with malnourished infants, a pilot study. *Social Science & Medicine, 16*(14), 1365–1369.

American heritage dictionary (New College Ed.). (1978). Boston: Houghton-Mifflin.

Ary, D., Jacobs, L., Sorenson, C., & Razavieh, A. (2009). *Introduction to research in education.* Belmont, CA.: Wadsworth Publishing.

Bennett, R.J., & Robinson, S.L. (2000). Development of a measure of workplace deviance. *Journal of Applied Psychology, 85*(3), 349–360.

Brown, T., & Wyatt, J. (2010). Design thinking for social innovation. *Stanford Social Innovation Review, Winter.*

Buscell, P. (2008). More me than we: How the fight against MRSA led to a new way of collaborating at Albert Einstein Medical Center. *Deeper Learning, 1*(5), 1–15.

Cameron, K. (2008). Paradox in positive organizational change. *Journal of Applied Behavioral Science, 44*(1), 7–24.

Cameron, K., Dutton, J., & Quinn, R. (2003). Foundations of positive organizational scholarship. In K. Cameron, J. Dutton, & R. Quinn (Eds.), *Positive organizational scholarship* (pp. 3–13). San Francisco: Berrett-Koehler.

Cameron, K., & Lavine, M. (2006). *Making the impossible possible: Leading extraordinary performance.* San Francisco: Berrett-Koehler.

Clinard, M.B., & Meier, R.F. (2007). *Sociology of deviant behavior* (13th ed.). Fort Worth, TX.: Harcourt.

Cooperrider, D., Sorensen, P., Whitney, D., & Yaeger, T. (2000). *Appreciative inquiry: Rethinking human organization toward a positive theory of change.* Champaign, IL: Stipes Publishing.

Creed, W.E.D. (2003). Voice lessons: Tempered radicals and the use of voice and silence. *Journal of Management Studies, 40*(6), 1353–1358.

Dodge, D. (1985). The over-negativized conceptualization of deviance: A programmatic exploration. *Deviant Behavior, 6*(1), 17–37.

Dutton, J. (2003). Breathing life into organizational studies. *Journal of Management Inquiry, 12,* 5–19.

Foster, P., & Torbert, W. (2005). *Leading through PD: A developmental action learning perspective on institutional change.* In R. Giacolone (Ed.), *Positive psychology in business ethics and corporate responsibility* (pp. 123–142). Charlotte, NC: Information Age Publishing.

Friedman, S., Mateu-Gelabert, P., Sandoval, M., Hagan, H., & Des Jarlais, D. (2008). PD control-case life history: A method to develop grounded hypotheses about successful long-term avoidance of infection. *BMC PublicHealth, 8*(94). doi:10.1186/1471-2458-8-94.

Gatto, J. (1992). *Dumbing us down: The hidden curriculum of public schooling.* Gabriola Island, BC, Canada: New Society Publishers.

Goldstein, J., Hazy, J., & Lichtenstein, B. (2010). The innovative power of PD. *Complexity and the nexus of leadership. Leveraging nonlinear science to create ecologies of innovation.* Englewood Cliffs, NJ: Palgrave-MacMillan Press.

Goode, E. (1991). PD: A viable concept. *Deviant Behavior, 12*(3), 289–309.

Greaves, J.P. (1979). Nutrition delivery system. *Journal of Nutrition and Diet, 16*, 75–82.

Guastelli, M., Pereira de Arau, L., Saraiva dos Santos, C.M., Lamblet, J., Silva, L., de Lima, G., et al. (2010). PD: A new strategy for improving hand hygiene compliance. *Infection Control and Hospital Epidemiology, 31*(1), 12–20.

Hartman, L., Wilson, F., & Arnold, D. (2005). Positive ethical deviance inspired by moral imagination: The entrepreneur as deviant. *Zfwu, 6/3*, 343–358.

Heckert, D.M. (1989). The relativity of PD: The case of the French impressionists. *Deviant Behavior, 10*(2), 131–144.

Heckert, A., & Heckert, D. (2002). A new typology of deviance: Integrating normative and reactivist definitions of deviance. *Deviant Behavior, 23*, 449–479.

Hegsted, D.M. (1967). *Comment on agricultural development and economic growth.* In H.M. Southworth, & B.F. Johnston (Eds.), *Agricultural development and economic growth* (p. 361). Ithaca, NY: Cornell University Press.

Jensen, G. (2001). *"Definition of Deviance."* In: C.D. Bryant, (Ed.), *Encyclopedia of Criminology and Deviant Behavior* (pp. 88–92). NewYork, N.Y.: Taylor and Francis.

Kant, I. (1993). *Grounding for the metaphysics of morals.* Indianapolis, IN: Hackett.

Klevens, R., Morrison, M., Nadle, J., Petit, S., Gershman, K., Ray, S., et al. (2007). Invasive methicillin-resistant staphylococcus aureus infections in the United States. *Journal of the American Medical Association, 298*, 1763–1771.

Lindberg, C., Norstrand, P., Munger, M., DeMarsico., & Buscell, P. (2009). Letting go, gaining control: PD and MRSA prevention. *Clinical Leader, 2*(2), 60–67.

Marshall, G. (1998). *A dictionary of sociology.* Cambridge, UK: Oxford University Press.

Mata, L.J. (1980). Child malnutrition and deprivation: Observations in Guatemala and Costa Rica. *Food Nutrition, 6*(2), 7–14.

Merton, R. (1971). *Social problems and sociological theory.* In R. Merton, & R. Nisbet (Eds.), Contemporary social problems (pp. 697–738). New York: Harcourt Brace Jovanovich.

Meyerson, D. (2001). *Tempered radicals: How people use change to inspire difference at work.* Cambridge, MA.: Harvard Business School Press.

Meyerson, D., & Scully, M. (1995). Tempered radicalism and the politics of ambivalence and change. *Organization Science, 6*(5), 585–600.

Miller, M. (Producer). (2009, March 22). Health care workers battle superbugs: Hospital workers taking innovative steps to curb the spread of deadly infections. *CBS Evening News.* (Television Broadcast). New York: Central Broadcasting Service.

Morrison, E. (2006). Doing the job well: An investigation of pro-social rule breaking. *Journal of Management, 32*(5), 5–28.

Ochieng, C. (2006). Development through PD and its implications for economic policy making and public administration in Africa: The case of Kenyan agricultural development, 1930–2005. *World Development, 35*(3), 454–479.

Pascale, R., & Sternin, J. (2005). Your company's secret change agents. *Harvard Business Review, 83*(5), 72–81.

Pascale, R., Sternin, J., & Sternin, M. (2010). *The power of PD. How unlikely innovators solve the world's toughest problems.* Cambridge, MA: Harvard Business Press.

Roberts, L.M. (2006). Shifting the lens on organizational life: The value of positive organizational scholarship. *Academy of Management Review, 31*(2), 292–305.

Sack, K. (Reporter). (2009, March 26). Hospitals reap benefits of PD. *New York Times.*

Sagarin, E. (1975). *Deviants and deviance: An introduction to the study of disvalued people.* New York: Praegar.

Sagarin, E. (1985). PD: An oxymoron. *Deviant Behavior, 6*(1), 169–181.

Singhal, A., McCandless, K. Buscell, P., & Lindberg, C. (2009). Spanning silos and spurring conversations: PD for reducing infection levels in hospitals. *Performance, 2*(3), 78–83.

Spreitzer, G., & Sonenshein, S. (2004). Toward a construct definition of PD. *American Behavioral Scientist, 47*(6), 828–847.

Spreitzer, G.M., & Sonenshein, S. (2003). PD and extraordinary organizing. In K. Cameron, J. Dutton, & R. Quinn (Eds.), *Positive organizational scholarship* (pp. 207–224). San Francisco: Berrett-Koehler.

Starbuck, W. (2006). The production of knowledge: The challenge of social science research. Oxford, UK.: Oxford University Press.

Sternin, J., & Choo, R. (2000). The power of positive deviancy. *Harvard Business Review, 78*, 14–15.

Vossenaar, M., Mayorga, E., Soto-Mendez, M.J., Medina-Monchez, S., Campos, R., Anderson, A., & Solomons, N. (2009). The PD approach can be used to create culturally appropriate eating guides compatible with reduced cancer risk. *The Journal of Nutrition: Nutritional Epidemiology.* doi:10.3945/jn.108.100362.

Walker, L., Sterling, B.S., Hoke, M., & Dearden, K. (2007). Applying the concept of PD to public health data: A tool for reducing health disparities. *Public Health Nursing, 24*(6), 571–576.

Warren, D. (2003). Constructive and destructive deviance in organizations. *Academy of Management Review, 28*, 622–632.

Weick, K. (2003). Positive organizing and organizational tragedy. In K. Cameron, J. Dutton, & R. Quinn (Eds.), *Positive organizational scholarship* (pp. 207–224). San Francisco: Berrett-Koehler.

Wray, J.D. (1972). Can we learn from successful mothers? *Journal of Tropical Pediatric Environmental Child Health, 18*(3), 279–283.

Zeitlin, M., Ghassemi, H., & Mansour, M. (1990). *PD in child nutrition -with emphasis on psychosocial and behavioural aspects and implications for development.* Tokyo: United Nations University Press.

Five Steps Toward Peacemaking

*Using Positive Organizational Scholarship to Build
a Better World*

J.B. Ritchie *and* Scott C. Hammond

Abstract

This chapter uses journal recollections from the lead author, as he worked with Palestinians leading up to the 1992 Oslo Peace Accords, to propose five steps toward peace, as supported by positive organizational scholarship (POS). The authors propose that POS is informed by and informs successful peace processes by noting the shift in identity from a victim or victimizer to a peacemaker; a change from a view of power as coercive power to a view of power as holistic; a shift in the view that relationships are historically fixed and immovable to a sense that relationships are complex and fluid; a dialectic view of the peace process, in which compromise is the best possible outcome to a dialogic model, and in which new and creative solutions can be envisioned; and the change from goal-oriented outcomes, in which objectives must be achieved, to a commitment to a process that is ongoing and honored. The conclusion offers general and specific research questions related to peace processes that could guide future research.

Keywords: Peacemaking, sustainable peace, Middle East Peace, Oslo Accords

The path to peace between Israel and Palestine has never been smooth. The history of U.S. involvement goes back to before the American Revolution, long before the State of Israel was established in 1948. Americans have played a role in escalating conflict, mediating peace, and as direct victims of violent acts. Many Americans hold both a deep desire for peace and a profound puzzlement as to why all the conflict, negotiations, and diplomacy have failed to make a significant difference (Oren, 2007).

In recent years, several U.S. presidents with good intentions have offered weak and ill-timed initiatives that failed (Tessler, 1995). On August 18, 2010, Secretary of State Hillary Clinton announced yet another initiative, launching talks that offer some hope for progress. Clinton and other international diplomats have underlined success, while also trying to suppress expectations (http://www.haaretz.com/news/diplomacy-defense/un-chief-direct-peace-talks-must-not-be-wasted-1.309391).

A similar peace initiative, the Oslo Accords, was started in 1992, and made some significant progress toward peace. Signed in 1993, in a public ceremony in Washington D.C., the Oslo Accords represented an important agreement between Israel and Palestine that was hammered out in a series of 14 secret meetings and three other meetings held in different locations. The Accords recognized the Palestinian Authority as a legitimate democratic government in exchange for the withdrawal of Israeli defense forces from the West Bank and Gaza. Permanent issues such as Israeli settlements, refugees, the status of Jerusalem, security, and borders were postponed for 5 years.

We acknowledge that the Oslo Accords did not bear the promised fruit of peace. But their failure to live up to expectations should not overshadow the shift in thinking that made progress possible. In this chapter, we use some of the elements of positive organizational scholarship (POS) to explain how progress toward peace was made. The new ways of thinking or paradigm shifts that led to the Nobel Peace Prize for Palestinian Liberation Organization Chairman Yasser Arafat, former Israel Prime Minister Yitzhak Rabin, and Foreign Minister Shimon Peres were refined in an old French Villa in Tunis, as witnessed by lead author Bonner Ritchie.

> Ritchie: In the fall of 1992, I found myself and my colleague, Omar Kader, in a hotel in Tunis waiting for a call from Yasser Arafat, the Chairman of the Palestinian Liberation Organization (PLO). Arafat had been labeled as a terrorist, a freedom fighter, a villain, and a liberator, depending on whether the press was Western, Israeli, or Arab. Tunis seemed an appropriate place to meet. It was the temporary headquarters for the PLO and had a history as one of the most important cities in the Roman Empire, Carthage, which sits on the outskirts of Tunis. The stories of the Punic wars, Hannibal, the destruction of and rebuilding of Carthage, and the questionable story of the Romans sowing salt in the soil, all added intrigue to the upcoming rendezvous. The PLO had been invited to go to Oslo, Norway, to negotiate with Israel, but they were still uncertain about the venture. During that time, I observed significant changes in the PLO's approach to negotiation, including a shift in identity, a change in their view and application of power, a rethinking of long traditions of how relationships should be conducted, and a new practice of dialogue rather than dialectic communication that contributed to a greater commitment toward peace.

This chapter will show how advances in POS and positive psychology can facilitate and smooth the path to peace. We will use the Oslo Accords as an illustration in hopes that future peace efforts can be informed of the positive lessons from Oslo, acknowledging negative and unfulfilled aspects as well. In this chapter, we will show the five shifts toward peace that Ritchie described above, supported by the new theory and research on POS. The five steps we describe are the shift in identity from a victim or victimizer to a peacemaker; a change from a view of power as coercive power to a view of power as holistic; a shift in the view that relationships are historically fixed and immovable to a sense that relationships are complex and fluid; a dialectic view of the peace process, in which compromise is the best possible outcome to a dialogic model, and in which new and creative solutions can be envisioned; and the change from goal-oriented outcomes, in which objectives must be achieved, to a commitment to a process that is ongoing and honored.

> Richie: When we landed in Tunis, we were met by two impressive men clothed in black. They ushered us from the plane to a black Mercedes, where we began a winding trip through the city to a hotel. When I developed enough courage, I asked the individual in the right front seat why he was caring an Uzi machine gun (I had spent enough time in Israel, the West Bank, and Gaza to know the difference between an Uzi and Kalashnikov, a Soviet weapon used by many in the Arab world). His answer was fun and provocative. He said, "It was to keep us alive." I told him I liked the motive, but why an Israeli weapon? Again, a "learning opportunity" response: "Why wouldn't we have the best weapons?" I didn't push the issue as to how the weapons were acquired.

Step 1: Changing Identity to Being a Peacemaker

> Ritchie: That evening at dinner (about 1 A.M.), I was intrigued by Arafat's dietary habits. He liked honey on a variety of foods (we took Utah honey as a gift) and was a sort of health food connoisseur. Using his hands, he literally took a handful of green salad and put it on my plate. I don't usually eat fresh salads when traveling in order to stay reasonably healthy, but I ate that one and I didn't get sick.
>
> At dinner, I presented the PLO leader with *Tom and Jerry* cartoons as a gift. My wife had read (Hart) that he liked *Tom and Jerry* cartoons because the "little guy" wins or at least he holds his own. The videos were received with enthusiasm. In fact, Suha Arafat, recently married to Yasser, said that most visitors bring things like swords to Arafat, but how symbolic that we brought cartoons.

Kenneth Burke (1939) said humans create their identity by narrating themselves into being. The concept of symbolic creation of self is extended by McAdams (1993) who says the oft-cited notion of identity construction is the "story a person constructs and internalizes to organize and make sense of his or her new life as a whole." Carlsen (2009) suggests that positive dramas in the work environment contribute to positive identity formation. They influence peak performance and give people a sense of empowerment and control.

It is not hard to see how these positive work and life experiences were very limited for the Palestinians in 1992, and are substantially limited today. Although the literature on POS shows the process by which a positive identity construction emerges, we can also imagine how a negative identity can develop from deep and ongoing conflict that, in the case of the Palestinians, has lasted for generations.

For the Palestinians, the long history of displacement that began in 1949, inter-tribal conflict, and dismal economies have led to a largely negative identity. In this environment, the narratively constructed identity of the Palestinians was often seen as that of victims, unable to bring a positive outcome to their situations. In a peace process, the first change was a change toward a new positive identity as a peacemaker. The 1992 peace process was the first step toward a new and more positive identity that required transcendence toward a new and more positive view of the self and the collective.

The identity of the Palestinians was symbolized in the *Tom and Jerry* cartoon, in which the little and powerful mouse is more clever than the bigger and more powerful cat. The mouse is highly mobile, stunningly violent, although never quite able to shake the persistent cat—but in the end, the mouse is clearly the ultimate survivor and symbolic winner. In a less metaphorical way, the Palestinian leaders saw themselves as freedom fighters, pushed to a violent solution by continued occupation and oppression. They felt that the confiscation of lands followed by the immigration of hundreds of thousands of Jews justified actions to protect an ancestral homeland.

In 1992, Palestinian leaders seemed ready to accept the kind of identity transcendence described by Nobel Peace Prize winner, Vaclav Havel. Havel, who was the first president of the Czech Republic following its peaceful separation of Slovakia, said in a July 4, 1994 speech in Boston, that transcendence comes as people begin to see themselves differently. Havel, himself a revolutionary turned peacemaker, said most eloquently that peace begins with change or self-transcendence:

> Transcendence as a hand reached out to those close to us, to foreigners, to the human community, to all living creatures, to nature, to the universe.
> Transcendence as a deeply and joyously experienced need to be in harmony even with what we ourselves are not, what we do not understand, what seems distant from us in time and space, but with which we are *nevertheless* mysteriously linked because, together with us, all this constitutes a single world.
> Transcendence as the only real alternative to extinction.

If current and future efforts are to succeed, both Israelis and Palestinians will need to shed their roles as victim or victimizer. They will need to transcend to different roles in which they begin to see themselves first as peacemakers. Those willing to commit violent acts have always known that they can derail any peace process by simply making one side or the other accept or compete for the role of victim. Only when that role shifts to a shared role, where all sides see themselves more fully responsible for peace, will progress be made.

Step 2: Seeing the Powers of the Weak

> Ritchie: It was at dinner that Suha Arafat (Yasser's new wife) told me that, since 1964, Yasser has been married to the PLO. His every waking hour had been dedicated to working to bring food, shelter, honor, and peace to his people, though many Palestinians and certainly Israelis and Americans were often troubled by his method. Suha said, "Now he is married to me, and we are going to have children (I didn't realize she was pregnant at that time), and those children must grow up in peace in a Palestinian state. It is time to negotiate peace with Israel."

Although the traditional view of power reflects a Newtonian physics view of the world, the POS approaches to power more closely resemble field theory. *Field theory* attempts to explain how complex multidimensional interactive systems behave over time. It stands in contrast to linear systems in which only "significant" variables are considered in relationship to other "significant" variables. Hayles (1990) says that in a field, symbols become self-referent, connected by means of the mediating field. For Hayles (1990), Turner (1995), and others, language is the field of meaning through which social interaction is connected.

A simpler way to look at this is to suggest that the dominant metaphor for traditional views of power is a linear contest, such as a tug-o-war between two teams. In our example, the teams might be the PLO and the Israeli Defense Force (IDF), who square off in a Tom and Jerry-like mismatch in which the "terrorist" or freedom fighter can only strike in the place of the other. Although this view of power may be useful in describing the behavior of participants in a single contest, a field theory view of power helps explain the behavior of a league of teams. A single contest or a single player is placed in the context of a family of teams over time.

In Ritchie's journal cited above, Arafat's recent marriage had clearly moved his thinking away from winning (or stale mating) the contest between his organization and the IDF toward a more family view that included multiple players in a field over time.

Especially important was the introduction of the metaphor of children. The reality of the pending birth of Arafat's own child and the metaphor of children, "insignificant" variables in the traditional view, became powerful fields and the reason for making the future better.

Step 3: Sustainable Individual Relationships

The view of power is less temporal and clearly more aligned with POS because it takes a holistic view of power, in which the goal is to build long-term sustainable relationships. Returning to the game metaphor, a traditional view of power looks at an outcome at the end of the game, when time for the game has expired. A field theory view of power is less concerned about the outcome of a single game but more concerned that the league is sustained over time, with sufficient compliance to rules, recruiting procedures and reputations.

For Arafat, a new and more sustainable view of relationships emerged when he had a near-death experience in the desert of Tunisia.

> Ritchie: His plane was caught in a sandstorm and was forced to make a crash landing. Arafat was a sort of mystic, and he often changed seats (and had others change seats). In this instance, he moved from one seat to another prior to a crash landing. The seat he moved to resulted in a safe landing, while if he had stayed seated in the other seat it could have been fatal. He said that God didn't preserve his life to keep on fighting—it was time to make peace; to turn your enemies into friends.

As the leader of a state without a place, Arafat had spoken at the United Nations and met with many world leaders. He was viewed by some with sympathy, by others as a freedom fighter, and yet by others as the original terrorist. Like many at war, his strategy was to identify his enemies and destroy them. But after his near death experience, his strategy changed and he began to try to convert his enemies into advocates.

Step 4: On a Dialogic Approach to Peace

> Ritchie: The *relationship* between the Palestinians and Israelis facilitated by key Norwegian government officials and academics prior to the formal Oslo negotiations pointed toward productive dialogue. Mahmoud Abbas, serving since 2006, as President of the Palestinian Authority, told me that after decades of destructive conflict, "There is now no substitution for dialogue." He and Yossi Beilin, a member of the

Israeli Knesset, developed a framework for ongoing discussions in secret meetings in Norway. Other key Israeli and Palestinian representatives were involved in direct exchanges with the blessing of top officials in Israel and the PLO. He said it was critically important to not have the ongoing pressure, speculation, and distortions that public meetings would generate. The press and the reactions of the Israeli and Palestinian public would make it difficult to engage in honest and creative exploration of new alternatives to the peace. And, out of these meetings came the Declaration of Principles, which stated that it was time to "put an end to decades of confrontation and conflict, recognize their mutual legitimate and political rights, and strive to live in peaceful coexistence and mutual dignity and security to achieve a just, lasting and comprehensive peace settlement and historic reconciliation."

Recent scholars have focused on dialogue as a generative means of moving toward nonviolent complex problem resolution. In Europe during the last 30 years, Bakhtin (1981), Delueze (1995) and others, have examined the difference between the conflict-with-words dialectic approach and a discovering-common-ground dialogic approach to conflict resolution.

In the United States, popular books by Senge (1992), Tannen (1998), Isaacs (1999), and scholarly works by Hawes (1999), Anderson, Baxter and Cissna (1994), and others have emphasized the need for empirical research in the study of dialogue. Courses in the academy have emerged and are being taught on college campuses (Hyde & Bineham, 2000) in corporate training, and some scholars have argued that dialogue skills should be a part of modern education in developing countries such as China (Hammond & Gao, 2001). Even the popular press has argued for offering dialogue as an essential skill for the citizen of the 21st century (Weisbord, 1992; Wheatley, 1992).

The dialogic method seemed to be what the PLO wanted to be used to approach peace in these early stages of preparation for the Oslo Accords, although there were often reversions to the old and familiar dialectic rhetoric of victimhood. Central to the dialogic approach over the dialectic approach is the idea of construction over compromise. In a constructive approach, peacemakers take time to listen and articulate needs rather than declare positions. When negotiations are based on positions, then a dialectic compromise is the best hope for the outcome. But when dialogue is used, new, previously unconsidered approaches emerge in a co-construction of the outcome by stakeholders.

Dialogue can be used to discover new roles and to reframe conflict toward more workable solutions (De Mare, 1989). For example, a new peacemaking framework consistent with the values of POS comes from the work of John Paul Lederach at the U.S. Institute of Peace. His books, Sampson and Lederach's (2000) *From the Ground Up: Mennonite Contributions to International Peacebuilding*, describes how a positive organizational-spiritual commitment can be translated into a proactive, early intervention strategy, instead of one that simply tries to put out fires after the damage is done. Lederach helps to move the paradigm from conflict resolution (eliminating the problem) to conflict management (living with conflict) to peacemaking (developing love and understanding) that only comes through a dialogic form of communication.

Step 5: Commitment

> Ritchie: The fundamental change in paradigms was illustrated by a comment of Mahmoud Abbas, as we were discussing possible strategies with a new prime minister in Israel (Yitzhak Rabin) and a new administration in Washington (Bill Clinton).
> We talked about the fact that since the announcement of the Partition Plan of the United Nations creating the state of Israel and the state of Palestine, the Palestinians had an all-or-nothing strategy. They felt that no outside power had the authority to create another state on their land of Palestine. For decades afterward, the Palestinians and most of the Arab world did not recognize the right of Israel to exist at all. They felt it was all their land. The Jews, on the other hand, had an incremental strategy. They might not get all they wanted in the determination of the boundaries of Israel, but they would take the increment available at the time and work out details later. I pointed out that now, almost 50 years later, the Israelis had all, and the Palestinians had nothing. Maybe it was time for a new paradigm. In elaborating, he stated that, "in the past it was unacceptable to advocate peace negotiations with Israel, now it is unacceptable not to."

When there is a shift in identity from a victim or victimizer to a peacemaker, a reconceptualization of power to a view of power as holistic, a new sense that relationships are complex and fluid, and a new dialogue related to peace, then it is not surprising that there is a change from a goal-oriented outcome, in which objectives must be achieved, to a commitment to a process that is sustainable and ongoing.

A helpful model of this process started with Anatel Rapoport's, *Fights, Games and Debates* (1960). In proposing ways of transcending the Cold War arms race, he suggests that we should not be in a fight with a goal of destruction, or a game with a criterion of winning, but rather in a debate in which we try to understand and change perceptions. We would add two other variables to this list. Each of Rapoport's dimensions is focused on the protagonist's frame of reference.

We add love and children as metaphors for peacemaking. With love, you are more concerned with the well-being of another. With children, you are committed to creating a better future for those who will inhabit the organizations of tomorrow.

Future Directions

The Oslo Accords are at the edge of memory for many following the current peace process in Palestine and Israel. The prerequisite events to the Clinton/Obama initiative, such as the blockade-running of ships trying to get into Gaza, are a return to the "them against us" roles of the past. It's *Tom and Jerry* all over again, with Israel and Hamas both claiming to be victims of the other's aggressive strategy.

Positive organizational scholarship does much to enlighten and enable the illusive peace that most hope for. Although our five steps are based on the observations of a single process, they do lean toward research questions that could be more generalizable and instrumental in facilitating peace processes.

Before suggesting additional research questions, we need to acknowledge the problematics of understanding the peacemaking processes using positive organizational scholarship. The first and most obvious problematic is that every conflict has unique characteristics, making us question whether techniques and practices gained in one process are portable to another. If practitioners of peacemaking want to mine positive organizational research for real techniques, then scholars need to find ways to ensure that these techniques are truly portable between conflicts.

A second and related problematic is related to the rareness of global conflict. Because family, organizational, and community conflict is more common, we often assume that techniques used in resolving those conflicts can be scaled to larger global conflicts. Although this is certainly true in some cases, there are indeed aspects of global conflict that are unique to that scale of conflict, and thus warrant additional exploration. The complexity, historical persistence, number of stakeholders, and long-term implications of global conflict are just a few of the many variables that make it different.

Still, all conflicts are rooted in basic human relations. A careful analysis of informed observers' descriptions of global conflict may be a good starting point for further study. Many books, such as George Mitchell's (1999) reflective work on his role as a peacemaker in Ireland, or Dennis Ross's (2004) and Mahmoud Abbas's (1995) reflections on their role in Middle East peace can be seen as informed participants with reflective observations. Although they often lack the theory building of more academic work, they begin to help sort out what is generalizable and what is idiosyncratic in each process.

More specific questions for future researchers come out of the five steps to peace offered above. Our first step is related to a change in identity. Although we note that the move from victim or victimizer to peacemaker can facilitate peace, we also note historically that Egyptian President Anwar Sadat and Israeli Prime Minister Yitzhak Rabin were both assassinated as a result of their public shift in identity to peacemaker. In both cases, they were killed by people on their side who were vested in the continuation of conflict. Research that further nuances identity shifts within conflict could help avoid future retaliatory violence.

Our discussion of the reconceptualization of power, as defined in second step, could be further investigated with research that shows how marginalized groups once seen as powerless are empowered through the peace process. But more importantly, further study needs to reveal how groups with the new powers that peace brings can cope with their new powers. Nelson Mandela's now famous Truth and Reconciliation Commission in South Africa has done much to reduce violence in situations in which the once empowered are now sharing power with the powerless (Mandela, 1995). Positive organizational studies could do much to tell us more about how humans can productively share power where conflict once poisoned their relationships.

Our third step clearly has power implications as well and is also related to sustainability. Clearly, peace processes are both personal and global for those who are directly involved as negotiators or facilitators (Mitchell, 1999). Participants in peace processes cannot go home to their nation with a treaty in hand and no new friendships (Hart, 1994). This problem of scale, previously mentioned in this section, is a ripe area for exploration for researchers who want to rediscover what medieval monarchs knew: that personal relationships, such as a marriage between a prince and a princess, can indeed bind countries together. Positive organizational studies researchers can tell us how to manage these personal relationships, so that their implications can be writ large and turned into peace levers.

Our fourth step deals with dialogue. As dialectic practices require controlled conflict to determine right action, dialogic communication is more creative (Tannen, 1998). It offers a transformational and transcendent opportunity for parties to address conflict while suspending certainties, and while facing the future (Hammond, Cissna, & Anderson, 2003). Researchers in both positive organizational studies and communication can explore the prerequisite peace dialogues, processes for progress, and rhetorical patterns that are productive.

Our final step was related to a more sustainable commitment to peace. High-profile peace processes are marked by manufactured events that signal a beginning, progress, and an end. The end often includes a bright-light media event in which a treaty is signed and peace is declared. Treaty or agreement violations often occur as conflict returns. Positive organizational studies can help us understand how to sustain peace in proactive ways. Additional research can show how forgiveness, hope, and well-being can be sustained until the embers of conflict are fully extinguished. Conflict often takes generations to end. Positive organizational studies can help us see how to fill in the gap between the generations of conflict and the generations of peacemakers.

Conclusion

The most recent peace process in the Middle East will offer researchers yet another opportunity to solve one of history's most puzzling problems. Positive organizational studies informs and is informed by this opportunity to reduce conflict and herald peace, but the claims are high and the stakes are perilous. But what will actually happen? Former Israeli Prime Minster and Nobel Peace Prize winner Shimon Peres is quoted as saying, "History is like a horse that gallops past our window, and the true test of statesmanship is to jump from the window onto the horse" (www.nytimes.com/2010/08/27/opinion/27indyk.html). Leap or no leap, scholars are sure to learn something about the process that will make the next leap less perilous.

References

Abbas, M. (1995). *Through secret channels*. Reading, UK: Garnet.

Anderson, R., Baxter, L.A., & Cissna, K.N. (1994). *Dialogue: Theorizing difference in communication studies*. Thousand Oaks, CA: Sage.

Bakhtin, M.M. (1981). Discourse in the novel. In M.M. Bakhtin, C. Emerson, & M. Holquist (Eds.), *The dialogic imagination* (pp. 259–422). Austin, TX: University of Texas Press.

Burke, K. (1939). *Attitudes towards history*. Berkeley: University of California Press.

Carlsen, A. (2009). After James on identity. In P.S. Adler (Ed.), *Oxford handbook of sociology and organizational studies: Classical foundations* (pp. 431–443). New York: Oxford University Press.

Deleuze, G. (1995). *Negotiations*. New York: Columbia University Press.

Hart, A. (1984). *Arafat: A political biography*. Bloomington, IN: Indiana University Press.

Hayles, K.N. (1990). *Chaos bound: Orderly disorder in contemporary literature and science*. Ithaca, NY: Cornell University Press.

Hammond, S.C., Cissna, K., & Anderson, R. (2003). The problematics of dialogue as empowerment. *Communication Yearbook 27*.

Hammond, S.C., & Gao, H. (2001). *Dialogic method and Chinese education policy*. Unpublished paper.

Hawes, L.C. (1999). The dialogs of conversation: Power, control, vulnerability. *Communication Theory, 9*, 229–264.

Hyde, B., & Bineham, J.L. (2000). From debate to dialogue: Toward a pedagogy of non-polarized public discourse. *Southern Communication Journal, 65*, 208–223.

Isaacs, W. (1999). *Dialogue and the art of thinking together*. New York: Doubleday.

Lederach, P. (1997). *Building peace: Sustainable reconciliation in divided societies*. Washington, DC: United States Institute of Peace.

Mandela, N. (1995). *The long walk to freedom*. Boston: Little, Brown and Company.

Mitchell, G. (1999). *Making peace*. San Francisco: University of California Press.

Oren, M. (2007). *Power, faith and fantasy: America in the Middle East 1776 to the present*. New York: W.W. Norton.

Rapoport, A. (1960). *Fights, Games and Debates*. Ann Arbor, MI: University of Michigan Press.

Ross, D. (2004). *Missing the peace: The inside story of the fight for Middle East peace*. New York: Farrar, Straus and Giroux.

Sampson, C., & Lederach, J.P. (2000). *From the ground up: Mennonite contribution to international peacebuilding*. New York: Oxford University Press.

Senge, P. (1992). *The fifth discipline: The art and practice of learning organizations*. New York: Doubleday.

Tannen, D. (1998). *The argument of culture*. New York: Random House.

Tessler, M. (1994). *A history of the Israeli-Palestinian conflict*. Bloomington, IN: Indiana University Press.

Turner, F. (1995). *The culture of hope: A new birth of the classical spirit*. New York: Free Press.

Weisbord, M. (1992). *Discovering common ground*. San Francisco: Berrett-Koehler.

Wheatley, M. (1992). Future search conferences and the new science: What process should we trust? In M. Weisbord (Ed.), *Discovering common ground* (pp. 105–110). San Francisco: Berrett-Koehler.

A Path Forward

Assessing Progress and Exploring Core Questions for the
Future of Positive Organizational Scholarship

Gretchen M. Spreitzer *and* Kim C. Cameron

Abstract

In this concluding chapter, we survey this handbook's abundant content to synthesize the many findings and highlight what has been learned from positive organizational scholarship research since its infancy. These findings are grouped into six key categories: complicating the meaning of positive; specifying mechanisms undergirding generative dynamics; noting key outcomes; identifying positive human resource and organizational practices; and advancing construct development. As we discuss various authors' work, we include associated chapter number for your reference. We conclude this chapter by identifying core questions that can help shape an agenda for future research and help increase the impact and insights of a POS lens.

Keywords: positive, mechanisms, generative

Less than a decade ago, Cameron, Dutton, and Quinn (2003) published the edited volume titled *Positive Organizational Scholarship.* The volume helped introduce positive organizational scholarship (POS) as a new lens for understanding the conditions and processes that explain flourishing in organizational contexts. A POS lens enriches organizational studies by expanding the range of topics and constructs seen as valuable within organizational behavior and organizational theory (Dutton & Sonenshein, 2009). Positive organizational scholarship helps us see new possibilities for organizational studies—it helps move constructs and ideas to the foreground that are often in the background or are even invisible. Progress over the last decade indicates a coming of age, in which core questions are being raised and answered. Yet, there is still much to be learned and more maturing is warranted. In this concluding chapter, we highlight what has been learned from POS research since its infancy as we look across the preceding chapters. We also highlight core questions that can help shape an agenda for future research and help increase the impact and insights of a POS lens.

What We've Learned from the Handbook Chapters

In the sections that follow, we highlight some of this Handbook's most important insights, which we have grouped into six categories: complicating the meaning of positive; specifying mechanisms undergirding generative dynamics; noting key outcomes; identifying positive human resource and organizational practices; and advancing construct development.

Complicating What We Mean by Positive

As we look across the preceding chapters, we see several different perspectives on *positive*. Most of the chapters do not explicitly provide a definition of positive, but many of the approaches to positive can be aligned with the four domains of positive offered in the introductory chapter. In other chapters, we see subtleties that enrich our understanding of the term positive. Thus, here we come full circle to look at how the chapters address the four domains of positive and discuss some nuances that have emerged.

A Positive Lens

A positive lens is an orientation toward, for example, strengths rather than weaknesses, optimism rather than pessimism, and supportive rather than critical communication (Cameron, 2008b). A POS lens foregrounds strengths, capabilities, and possibilities, and backgrounds weaknesses, problems, and threats. Indeed, Baumeister, Bratslavsky, Finkenauer, and Vohs (2001) provided compelling evidence that human beings overattend to negative events and dynamics. Counteracting this tendency, POS theory and research focuses more directly on strengths, capabilities, and possibilities. Adopting a positive lens regarding traditionally nonpositive phenomena is particularly explicit in the following chapters:

- Stansbury and Sonenshein (2011, Chapter 26) suggest that much research on ethics focuses on unethical behaviors and the decision processes that lead to them. They counter such research by developing the notion of good works.
- Mayer (2011, Chapter 24) notes how much of the justice literature focuses on one's own reactions to injustice. He counters by looking at third-party reactions, particularly in terms of constructive and prosocial responses.
- Hoffman and Haigh (2011, Chapter 72) make the case that sustainability is more than the absence of unsustainable practices – something more is important for environmental flourishing.
- Godfrey (2011, Chapter 74) takes a historical look at economic theory to uncover clues to a positive perspective to economics.
- Ramarajan and Thomas (2011, Chapter 41) articulate how the literature tends to foreground the problematic nature of identity group dynamics in organizations. These groups create a more positive approach to diversity research that foregrounds the positive influences of diversity on individual and organizational outcomes, including intergroup equality, positive intergroup relations, and group performance.
- Kopelman, Avi-Yonah, and Varghese (2011, Chapter 44) propose moving beyond an instrumental, social-exchange lens on negotiation to a mindfulness lens that focuses on developing the self and other parties.
- Biron, Cooper, and Gibbs (2011, Chapter 71) evaluate the potency of interventions that promote health and well-being, rather than simply reduce or prevent stress.
- Baker (2011, Chapter 31) makes the case that more altruistic moral sentiments explain generalized reciprocity just as much as traditional models of self-interested reputation do.

An Affirmative Bias that Fosters Resourcefulness

Adopting an affirmative bias is associated with resourcefulness, or with creating, unlocking, and multiplying latent resources in individuals and organizations. *Resourcefulness* means that an amplifying effect occurs when individuals and organizations are exposed to positivity (Feldman & Worline, 2011, Chapter 47, this volume). Some chapters, for example, discuss POS as life-giving or life-enhancing (Lilius et al., 2011, Chapter 21, this volume; Sandelands, 2011, Chapter 76, this volume; Spreitzer, Lam, & Quinn, 2011, Chapter 12, this volume). The focus is on elevating life, whether physiological or psychological, and on life-giving resources such as positive energy. Similarly, Keeney and Illies (2011, Chapter 45, this volume) articulate how positive work–family interconnections enhance well-being in both contexts and how positivity spills over, enriches, and facilitates resourcefulness in work and family life.

Virtuousness

Virtuousness is defined as the best of the human condition and that which human beings consider to be inherently good (Cameron, 2008a). This definition captures the focus in POS on what is virtuous (Cameron & Winn, 2011, Chapter 18, this volume), morally praiseworthy (Stansbury & Sonenshein, 2011, Chapter 26, this volume), honorable (Spreitzer & Sonenshein, 2004; Lavine, 2011, Chapter 77, this volume), and away from maximizing utility (Godfrey, 2011, Chapter 74, this volume). Positive organizational scholarship research indicates that an array of human virtues or character strengths are deemed to reflect the highest aspirations of humankind (Cameron & Winn, 2011, Chapter 18); Rego, Clegg, & e Cunha, 2011, Chapter 28, this volume; Owens, Rowatt, & Wilkins, 2011, Chapter 20, this volume; Bright & Exline, 2011, Chapter 19, this volume).

Extraordinarily Positive Outcomes or Positive Deviance

Positive deviance can be defined as successful performance that dramatically exceeds the norm in a positive direction. Positive deviance departs from the norms of a referent group in positive ways (Lavine, 2011, Chapter 77, this volume). This definition of positive is explicit in POS research that focuses on identifying and explaining spectacular results, surprising outcomes, and extraordinary achievements (Cameron & Lavine, 2006), including those in the context of change (Golden-Biddle & Mao, 2011, Chapter 58, this volume). This use of the term positive captures the optimal functioning of individuals, groups, or organizations (Dutton & Sonenshein, 2009) and is adopted by several chapter authors, including Pratt and Pradies (2011, Chapter 70) (on the unexpected positive outcomes that come from ambivalence), Asplund and Blacksmith (2011, Chapter 27) (engagement and productivity), and Stavros and Wooten (2011, Chapter 63) (organizational performance).

Fineman (2006) noted a lack of clarity on what is meant by the term positive, and the plurality in defining positive may be perplexing to those looking for focus and clarity (Kilduff & Brands, 2010). Although many of the chapters clearly illustrate one or more of the four domains of positive noted above, we do find a more complicated understanding of what positive means.

For example, Pratt and Pradies' (2011, Chapter 70, this volume) perspective on positive is particularly insightful with regard to the value of plurality in definitions:

> . . . [M]apping positive ambivalence responses also opens up dialogue for what "positive" means. We started our chapter by linking positivity with an individual outcome: enhanced individual functioning. However, we discovered that like ambivalence itself, positive can mean many things when it comes to ambivalence. . . . positivity can be both personal and social. While responding to ambivalence may make you feel better, more confident about how to act in an ambivalent relationship, or more wise; it can also help dyads (e.g., commitment and trust), or even larger systems (e.g., as creativity leads to innovation or openness to change). Positivity can even be thought of in terms of process and outcomes. Thus, we can think of the positivity of committing and of being committed, of trusting and of having trust, of creating and of having created something, etc. More generally, we even note how positivity can be contextual and temporal. Thus, while paralysis is often viewed as a negative response to ambivalence, it can lead to a positive outcome for an individual in the long run, especially if it is associated with more and better information processing (p. 934).

Similarly, Golden-Biddle and Mao (2011, Chapter 58) notice in their work on positivity in change processes that what constituted positive was not a universal condition. What some people perceived as positive in one situation (senior leadership being perceived as caring when asking for input), could be perceived as negative in another (senior leadership trying to placate employees by asking for input). They found it useful to

> [C]onceive of positivity as a lens; a perspective-taking on our part as researchers, in which we pay attention when reading studies to people's experiences in change that are or could be made more life enriching, and to how change processes enable (or not) the development of people and local capability (p. 764).

The chapters also offer insights on the subtlety and nuance in the meaning of positive—whether as a lens, an outcome, a value, or a process. They indicate that sometimes what is positive is in the eye of the beholder or is influenced by the culture or context.

Understanding the Core Outcomes of Positive Organizing

Several clusters of outcomes have been a primary focus of POS research. One cluster of outcomes has focused on *individual flourishing and well-being*. These kinds of outcomes capture a "pleasant life"—a life that successfully pursues positive emotions (Sekerka, Vacharkulksemsuk, & Fredrickson, 2011, Chapter 13) about the present, past, and future. People experience positive emotions, beyond just being satisfied with their work life, to be happy and joyful (Fredrickson, 2003), to thrive (Spreitzer, Sutcliffe, Dutton, Sonenshein, & Grant, 2005), to develop higher traits of extraversion and core self-evaluations (Bono, Davies, & Rasch, 2011, Chapter 10, this volume), to be fully engaged (Bakker & Oerlemans, 2011, Chapter 14, this volume), and to be healthy (Pressman & Cohen, 2005). Many of the chapters set their sights on understanding the individual and organizational factors that enable human well-being.

A second cluster of outcomes relates to a "meaningful life"—*personal fulfillment* through a life worth living. This includes theory and research on one's calling/meaning (Wrzesniewski, 2011, Chapter 4, this volume), the fundamental state of leadership (Quinn & Wellman, 2011, Chapter 57, this volume), prosocial motivation (Grant & Berg, 2011, Chapter 3, this volume), identity (Morgan Roberts & Creary, 2011, Chapter 6, this volume), and spirituality (Sandelands, 2011, Chapter 76, this volume). In these chapters, the authors point to actions that individuals can take to "craft" more meaning into their work life and how organizations can provide opportunities for individuals to find their purpose and best contribute.

A third cluster of outcomes has to do with *exemplary performance*, sometimes individual performance (Asplund & Blacksmith, 2011, Chapter 27, this volume; Kopelman, Avi-Yonah, & Varghese, 2011, Chapter 44, this volume), but more typically team (Dibble & Gibson, 2011, Chapter 54, this volume; Rhee & Yoon, 2011, Chapter 17, this volume) or organizational (Cameron, Bright, & Caza, 2004; Smith, Lewis, & Tushman, 2011, Chapter 61, this volume; Stavros & Wooten, 2011, Chapter 63, this volume) performance. In fact, Luthans and Avolio (2009) insist that to fall within the domain of positive organizational behavior, research must have a performance impact.

A fourth cluster of outcomes deals with *adaptation and learning*. Here, researchers are interested in how organizations build their agility/flexibility for innovation (DeGraff & Nathan-Roberts, 2011, Chapter 53, this volume) and creativity (Zhou & Ren, 2011, Chapter 8, this volume). Inherent in this theme of adaptation and learning is understanding how to build individual resilience (Barker Caza & Milton, 2011, Chapter 68, this volume), psychological capital (Youssef & Luthans, 2011, Chapter 2, this volume), personal growth (Asplund & Blacksmith, 2011, Chapter 27, this volume), and growth through trauma (Maitlis, 2011, Chapter 69, this volume). At the collective level, this set of outcomes also includes research on healing (Powley, 2011, Chapter 65, this volume), forgiveness (Bright & Exline, 2011, Chapter 19, this volume), and responding to crises (James & Wooten, 2011, Chapter 67, this volume). Through the dynamics generated by a POS lens, we see more transformation (Quinn & Wellman, 2011, Chapter 57, this volume), transcendence (Ritchie & Hammond, 2011, Chapter 78, this volume), and collective imagination (Carlsen, Landsverk Hagen, & Mortensen, 2011, Chapter 22, this volume) because the possibility for something dramatically new and better is revealed.

A fifth cluster of outcomes addresses the long-term *sustainability of people, organizations, society, and the environment* (Hoffman & Haigh, 2011, Chapter 72, this volume). Sustainability can be defined as ensuring our ecosystem supports life over time; it includes efforts to preserve, conserve, renew,

and generate resources to support life (Pfeffer, 2010). The focus shifts from short-term performance results to longer-term outcomes that can be sustained over time. Here, the focus is on how to build in recovery (Sonnentag & Neff, 2011, Chapter 66, this volume), so that the organization and individuals do not get bogged down with resistance, stagnation, or burnout.

Articulating Generative Mechanisms More Clearly

Perhaps the most substantial progress revealed in these chapters is that the explanatory mechanisms that enable flourishing within organizations are richly articulated. Mechanisms explain the how and why of something (Hedstrom & Swedberg, 1998). They describe "a set of interacting parts—an assembly of elements producing an effect not inherent in any one of them. A mechanism is not so much about 'nuts and bolts' as about 'cogs and wheels'—the wheelwork or agency by which an effect is produced" (Hernes, 1998, p. 74). By generative, we mean life-building, capability-enhancing, and capacity-creating (Dutton & Glynn, 2007). In their chapter on symbols, Glynn and Watkiss (2011, Chapter 46, this volume) note three key mechanisms that enable flourishing within organizations: cognitive, affective, and relational. These are similar to Dutton and Glynn's (2007) tripartite typology of positive meaning-making, positive emoting, and positive interrelating. Other chapters add agentic and structural mechanisms to the mix of explanatory mechanisms; we discuss each in the next section. In many of the chapters, these mechanisms operate within a single level of analysis, but are sometimes elaborated by crossing levels.

Cognitive Mechanisms

Cognitive mechanisms operate through changes in how people become aware, know, think, learn, and judge. Several chapters illustrate a variety of cognitive mechanisms that produce flourishing in organizations. One cognitive mechanism is *meaning*. For example, Wrzesniewski (2011, Chapter 4, this volume) describes how callings create meaning related to how people construct why they work, which this leads to positive outcomes. Taking another perspective on meaning, Carlsen et al. (2011, Chapter 22, this volume) describe how hope is rooted in creating meaning in ongoing experience by weaving stories of possibilities in new experience.

Identity is another cognitive mechanism. Again, Carlsen et al. (2011, Chapter 22, this volume) describe the importance of hope in constructing identity, as captured in the favorable progression in life stories of individual and organizations. Morgan Roberts and Creary (2011, Chapter 6, this volume) describe a range of mechanisms for constructing a positive identity that draw on four different theoretical traditions of identity scholarship (i.e., social identity, identity theory, narrative as identity, and identity work). Likewise, Barker Caza, and Milton (2011, Chapter 68, this volume) describe how identity is a key resource that enables individuals to be resilient at work. At an organization level, Harquail and Brickson (2011, Chapter 51, this volume) make a case for how organizational identities facilitate stakeholder flourishing.

Learning is a third kind of cognitive mechanism. For example, Hall and Las Heras (2011, Chapter 38, this volume) describe the self-discovery process in terms of the importance of aspirations, hopes, and dreams for positive career development. And Maitlis (2011, Chapter 69, this volume) describes how post-traumatic growth occurs through learning to create meaning from the loss of a person's assumptive world.

Sense-making or interpreting is another kind of cognitive mechanism. For example, Bono et al. (2011, Chapter 10, this volume) describe how extraverts flourish more at work because they tend to interpret or evaluate situations more positively. Glynn and Watkiss (2011, Chapter 46, this volume) describe how symbols encode positive meanings, beliefs, and interpretations to enrich strengths, virtues, and capacities in organizations.

Affective Mechanisms

Affective mechanisms operate through changes that evoke or elicit individual or collective feelings. Fredrickson's (2003) broaden-and-build theory of positive emotions is the key affective mechanism in POS research (Sekerka, et al., 2011, Chapter 13, this volume). Unlike negative emotions, which tend to create tendencies to "fight or flight," positive emotions such as joy, interest, or appreciation "function in the short term to broaden one's attention and quell heightened bodily reactivity to build one's cognitive, social, psychological, and physical resources over the long term" (Sekerka et al., 2011, Chapter 13, p. 169, this volume). To illustrate this mechanism, Porath (2011, Chapter 33, this volume) articulates how civility (even witnessing civility) facilitates negotiations, promotes teamwork, and spreads goodwill because it generates positive emotions toward the self and others. In another example,

Baker (2011, Chapter 31, this volume) explains how the act of generalized reciprocity generates positive emotions, what is sometimes termed a "warm glow" that fuels future acts of giving.

The broaden-and-build mechanism is not only applicable at an individual level of analysis, but also at the organizational level through shared emotions and emotional contagion. For example, Rhee and Yoon (2011, Chapter 17, this volume) review various mechanisms (i.e., mimicry, shared experiences, and emotional comparisons) through which individuals share their emotions and moods with others within their workgroups. Golden-Biddle and Mao (2011, Chapter 58, this volume) also suggest a positive emoting mechanism of "acting with compassion" to buffer the uncertainty, loss, and anxiety inherent in change.

Relational Mechanisms

Relational mechanisms operate through changes in connections among people and groups. Although positive relationships can be one dimension of flourishing (an end in itself), many of the chapters describe how relationships act as the generative mechanisms to achieve flourishing within organizations. For example, chapters on high-quality connections (Stephens, Heaphy, & Dutton, 2011, Chapter 29, this volume), relational coordination (Hoffer Gittell, 2011, Chapter 30, this volume), trust (Mishra & Mishra, 2011, Chapter 34, this volume), and civility (Porath, 2011, Chapter 33, this volume) describe how connections with others can unlock resources endogenous to the system. For example, Keeney and Illies (2011, Chapter 45, this volume) describe how interpersonal capitalization (sharing positive work events with others) is a relational mechanism by which work experience impacts the well-being of employees and their families. Williams (2011, Chapter 35, this volume) describes how the relational act of perspective taking facilitates high-quality connections and trustworthy actions in organizations. James and Wooten (2011, Chapter 67, this volume) build on the relational mechanism of perspective taking to show how it can enable opportunity in the context of crisis. Bono et al. (2011, Chapter 10, this volume) describe how extraverts are more likely to flourish given their tendency to develop and maintain rich social relationships and receive more social support from others.

Other chapters highlight social mechanisms that have been largely ignored in prior organizational studies. In particular, Vogus (2011, Chapter 50, this volume) describes mindful organizing as a social process grounded in interactions with coworkers for detecting and correcting errors and unexpected events. Powley (2011, Chapter 65, this volume) describes healing as a process involving social interactions that mend the organization's social structure and repair operational routines. Baker (2011, Chapter 31, this volume) demonstrates how reciprocity, particularly generalized reciprocity, generates moral sentiments and reputational effects that unlock latent resources in organizational systems and beyond. Finally, Dibble and Gibson (2011, Chapter 54, this volume) describe how the process of laterality (i.e., the ability to work effectively with others who are different), as well as a willingness to limit personal autonomy to achieve group goals, facilitates collaboration in teams.

Agentic Mechanisms

Agentic mechanisms operate through changes in how people interpret their relationship with their environment in terms of what they can do. When people take action, they co-create their world, rather than just being influenced by it. This includes not only bold, heroic actions, but also the fleeting, everyday micromoments of small acts in organizations (Golden-Biddle & Mao, 2011, Chapter 58, this volume). For example, proactive behaviors are a key agentic mechanism within POS. Proactivity is a goal-driven process of "self-initiated efforts to bring about change in the work environment and/or oneself in order to achieve a different future" (Wu & Parker, 2011, Chapter 7, p. 84, this volume). Proactive behaviors unlock capabilities by allowing individuals to transform the status quo. Through proactive behaviors, such as job crafting (Wrzesniewski & Dutton, 2001), individuals grow, develop, and learn to leverage strengths and capabilities in order to play out their passions at work (Perttula & Cardon, 2011, Chapter 15, this volume).

Endogenous resourcefulness (Dutton & Glynn, 2007) is another key agentic mechanism. *Endogenous* refers to coming from within the system rather than from outside of it. Feldman and Worline's (2011, Chapter 47, this volume) resourcing perspective describes how resources are not merely innate qualities, but are things that may be assembled and reassembled creatively to enlarge the supply of resources. The endogeneity reflects that resources are created in the process of doing work in organizations (Vogel & Bruch, 2011, Chapter 52, this volume), not just supplied from outside the system (Spreitzer et al., 2005). The process highlights the mutability of resources through actions such as mutual adjusting,

juxtaposing, and narrating that create amplifying cycles and positive spirals (Sekerka et al., 2011, Chapter 13, this volume). This endogenous resourcefulness demonstrates the accumulating generativity over time as small acts/outcomes build on one another. This is precisely the opposite of the dynamics that lead to failure in high-reliability work—where small events accumulate and build on each other to create trouble (Sutcliffe & Christianson, 2011, Chapter 64, this volume).

Another agentic mechanism inherent in POS research is the voice or participation that enables positive deviance (Lavine, 2011, Chapter 77, this volume). Positive deviance involves departing from the norms of a reference group (Spreitzer & Sonenshein, 2004). These departures require self-empowerment (Spreitzer, 1995) and courage (Worline, 2011, Chapter 23, this volume) to step beyond normal patterns of behavior. The experience of psychological safety at work facilitates organizational learning, better performance, and more satisfying work by enabling employees to speak up or find a voice (Nembhard & Edmondson, 2011, Chapter 37, this volume). Likewise, more trust among leaders and followers creates more capacity for followers to be empowered (Mishra & Mishra, 2011, Chapter 34, this volume).

Structural Mechanisms

Structural mechanisms operate through routines and leadership. Structural mechanisms involve institutionalized practices, systems, and structures that enable positive outcomes. For example, Harrison (2011, Chapter 9, this volume) describes how routines such as brainstorming or problem solving can stimulate curiosity that in turn create unexpected creativity. He further articulates how leaders can stimulate curiosity by deliberately problematizing followers' view of the world. Likewise, Stavros and Wooten (2011, Chapter 63, this volume) identify several strategic processes that shape organizational reactions to their competitive environment which, in turn, enables organizational performance. Oldham (2011, Chapter 49, this volume) highlights how work design enhances positive outcomes and how relying on positive practices in work structure improves individual and organizational performance. Smith, Lewis, and Tushman (2011, Chapter 61, this volume) highlight the role of structural paradoxes and leadership in accounting for organizational performance.

These are just some of the ways the research that adopts a POS lens has helped uncover enriched cognitive, affective, relational, agentic, and structural mechanisms that explain desired outcomes.

Understanding the "O" in Positive Organizational Scholarship Better

Although a substantial number of the chapters focus at the micro level of analysis, we have seen progress on the macro front as well. There are several ways that the handbook's authors offer new insights on theory and research relevant to the "O" in POS. The first is through increasing focus on organizational functions and practices; what Heath and Sitkin (2001) refer to as "Big O" in their commentary about making organizational behavior (OB) more organizational. The handbook chapters offer theory and research on organization practices such as socialization (Ashforth, Meyers, & Sluss, 2011, Chapter 40, this volume), mentoring (Ragins, 2011, Chapter 39, this volume), communications (Browning, Morris, & Kee, 2011, Chapter 42, this volume), career development (Hall & Las Heras, 2011, Chapter 38, this volume), leadership development (DeRue & Workman, 2011, Chapter 60, this volume), organizational development (Cooperrider & Godwin, 2011, Chapter 56, this volume; Bartunek & Woodman, 2011, Chapter 55, this volume), and diversity (Ramarajan & Thomas, 2011, Chapter 41, this volume).

These chapters look at how POS sheds new light on a traditional organizational function or practice. For example, Stavros and Wooten (2011, Chapter 63, this volume) review the role of POS in strategic management. They examine several strategy concepts (including the resource-based view, dynamic capabilities, and the balanced scorecard) through a positive lens to provide new insights into strategy. Baker (2011, Chapter 31, this volume) also uses POS in his research on networks. Typically, network research focuses on how power and information are distributed throughout the network. Baker brings a POS lens to network theory by adding positive energy as a key variable in network dynamics. Browning, Morris, and Kee (2011, Chapter 42, this volume) describe the integrative, constructive, and even therapeutic dynamics that can result from positive organizational communications.

Although these and other chapters advance our understanding of the field, we still have much to learn about the "O" in POS (Hackman, 2009). For example, to date, we know little about how POS might offer new insights to HR functions such performance management, compensation, hiring, staffing, training, labor/management relationships, and

workplace safety. One interesting example of a promising approach is open-book finance—in which employees are educated and involved in the workings of an organization's finances (Baker & Gunderson, 2005). Future research could look specifically at what new insights a POS lens might bring to core macro organizational theories such as institutional theory or transaction cost economics.

A second way that the chapters in the handbook offer insight on the "O" in POS is by transcending constructs that have been studied originally at the individual level of analysis to an organizational or collective level. For example, Goddard and Salloum (2011, Chapter 48, this volume) build on the work of others (e.g., Bandura, 1977) to understand the social cognitive underpinnings of collective efficacy—a construct most often studied at an individual level of analysis. Powley (2011, Chapter 65, this volume) moves the notion of healing to the collective level by focusing on healing as an organizing mechanism in which human action patterns help restore organizational functioning. Similarly, Lilius et al. (2011, Chapter 21, this volume) examine compassion from an organizational lens to understand processes of compassion organizing and how compassionate practices can be institutionalized.

Another point regarding the "O" in POS involves the need to understand how organizational context affects phenomena that have been studied largely without focus on the role of context or embeddedness (Maitlis, 2011, Chapter 69, this volume). Colloquially, this has been called "contextualized B" in the provocative commentary by Heath and Sitkin (2001), which discusses what is "organizational" about organizational behavior. For example, whereas courage has been studied from a psychological perspective (especially the courage of the hero), Worline (2011, Chapter 23, this volume) makes the case that everyday courage in a work context is a relevant and important area of investigation. Rather than studying the image of the "mythic hero," we need to find courage in "every corner of every cubicle (Worline, 2011)." Courage goes beyond individual personality qualities and has implications for the organizational context and how it enables or impedes performance at work. Similarly Ybarra, Rees, Kross, & Sanchez-Burks (2011, Chapter 16, this volume) propose a model of emotional intelligence that "carefully, deliberately, and explicitly" considers the social world that people navigate. This focus on social context helps inform the "when" and "why" of emotional intelligence. As another example, Perttula and Cardon (2011, Chapter 15, this volume) drill down to understand passion in the specific context of entrepreneurial activity. In doing so, they examine a specific contextual embeddedness of passion at work.

Juxtaposing to Negative Events

As several chapters suggest, good things can emanate from negative events or circumstances, such as compassion (Lilius et al., 2011, Chapter 21, this volume), resilience (Barker Caza & Milton, 2011, Chapter 68, this volume), healing (Powley, 2011, Chapter 65, this volume), post-traumatic growth (Maitlis, 2011, Chapter 69, this volume), and crisis response (James & Wooten, 2011, Chapter 67, this volume). These handbook authors embrace, rather than ignore, the limits, setbacks, and problems that occur in organizations by looking at the good that result from them. Positive organizational scholarship treats positive phenomena as figure rather ground (Dutton & Sonenshein, 2007). Rather than viewing negative events as failures and threats, POS researchers often theorize they are catalysts or opportunities that can facilitate adaptation, resilience, and growth.

In addition, several chapter authors demonstrate how positive phenomena are not merely the opposite, or even the absence, of negative phenomena. For example, peace is not merely the absence of war. It requires something more in terms of the relationship between two parties or nations (Spreitzer, 2007). Indeed, positive and negative phenomenon may have different mechanisms that drive different outcomes (Biron, Cooper & Gibbs, 2011, Chapter 71, this volume). Yet, positive emotions may buffer and even undo the untoward effects of negative phenomenon, as has been shown in research on individual resilience after the U.S. terrorist attacks of September 11, 2001 (Fredrickson, 2003).

Advances in Developing Positive Organizational Scholarship Constructs and Measures

For POS to mature as a discipline, clear definitions and validated measures of core constructs are required. Hackman (2009, p. 312) asserted that "construct validity is the sine qua non of theory development." In the first POS volume (2003), several constructs were newly developed or transplanted from other disciplines into organizational studies. These included empowerment, compassion, virtuousness, relational coordination, transcendent behavior, high-quality connections, positive energy, meaning, resilience, positive deviance, relational

coordination, and authentic leadership. Almost a decade later, we have made substantial progress in defining, grounding in the literature, differentiating from conceptually similar constructs, and measuring these and other constructs of interest. Numerous chapters in this handbook highlight the explicit progress made to date in more clearly understanding definitions and inherent dimensions. Examples include:

- Articulating the three subjective experiences (vitality, positive regard, and felt mutuality) and three structural features (emotional carrying capacity, tensility, and connectivity) of high-quality connections (Stephens, Heaphy, & Dutton, 2011, Chapter 29, this volume)
- Defining humility as "a deeply held belief of shared human limits and worth that shapes how individuals view themselves (objectively), others (appreciatively), and new information (openly)" (Owens, Rowatt, & Wilkins, 2011, Chapter 20, p. 262, this volume)
- Conceptualizing organizational healing as a process and an outcome that results from effectively managing liminality (Powley, 2011, Chapter 65, this volume)
- Articulating the different roles for appraisal-related, affective, and cognitive perspective taking (Williams, 2011, Chapter 35, this volume)
- Uncovering the four dimensions of trustworthiness: reliability, openness, competence, and compassion (Mishra & Mishra, 2011, Chapter 34, this volume)
- Conceptualizing compassion as a three-part process consisting of noticing suffering, demonstrating empathy, and acting to reduce the observed suffering (Lilius et al., 2011, Chapter 21, this volume)
- Describing resilience at work as a developmental trajectory characterized by competence in the face of, and professional growth after, experiences of adversity (Barker Caza & Milton, 2011, Chapter 68, this volume)
- Conceptualizing calling as a source of intrinsic fulfillment and a way to contribute in the wider world (Wrzeniewski, 2011, Chapter 4, this volume)
- Defining positive deviance as "uncommon behavior that does not conform to expected norms but would be deemed positive by a

referent group" (Lavine, 2011, Chapter 77, p. 1023, this volume).

We have also made progress on measuring and validating several POS-related constructs including psychological capital (Youssef & Luthans, 2011, Chapter 2, this volume), mindful organizing (Vogus, 2011, Chapter 50, this volume), and thriving at work (Porath, Spreitzer, Gibson & Stevens, 2010). Validated measures are crucial for research studies to build upon one another to compile a coherent body of evidence. Many of these constructs have been operationalized at an individual level of analysis, but several are specifically organizational in their focus, including relational coordination (Gittell, 2011, Chapter 30, this volume), virtuousness (Cameron & Winn, 2011, Chapter 18, this volume), civility (Porath, 2011, Chapter 33, this volume), and resourcefulness (Feldman & Worline, 2011, Chapter 47, this volume). Given the importance of the "O" in POS, however, our hope is that future research will escalate the conceptual and empirical development of POS-related constructs at the group, unit, or organizational levels.

Puzzles and Core Questions: Articulating a Path Forward
Are Virtues and Character Strengths Culturally Determined?
Much debate has ensued on whether virtues and character strengths are universal or culturally dependent (Rego, Clegg, & e Cunha, 2011, Chapter 28, this volume). Indeed, Fineman (2006) argued that even the term positivity may have a "moncultural tint." As such, we need to understand the cultural distinctions that may be at play across a globe based on varying traditions, rituals, values, and religions. We need a clearer understanding of how positive dynamics may be universal or culturally dependent. In this handbook, we sought a global set of contributors, with the hope of generating a better cultural understanding of a POS lens in a global context. Clearly though, more cross-cultural comparative theorizing and research is warranted.

Can There Be Too Much Positivity?
Grant and Schwartz (2011) suggested the possibility of positive state, traits, and experiences having an inverted-U relationship with key outcomes. They suggest that positive phenomenon can reach inflection points at which their effects may turn negative. For example, too much persistence can lead to escalated commitment. Or, too much choice can lead to decision paralysis (Iyengar & Lepper, 2000). Indeed, this non-monotonicity may be true for many things in life; humans can, indeed, experience too much of a good thing. In their chapter on virtuousness, Cameron and Winn (2011, Chapter 18, this volume) provided a possible answer to this question. They suggested a distinction between strengths and virtues. Focusing too much on a particular strength, they suggested, can create negative dynamics. Yet, they argued that virtues are different. One should not put an upper limit on compassion or forgiveness when others may be suffering. These virtues enable an upward spiral of positive dynamics that can lengthen the distance to the point of inflection. Future research could examine how much of a given positive trait, state, or experience may be too much, including if and when a tipping point might occur.

It may also be the case that fine-tuning our theories can help us see important nuances that explain why we might see unexpected negative dynamics from what appear to be positive states. For example, Perttula and Cardon (2011, Chapter 15, this volume) review Vallerand et al.'s (2003) research, which demonstrated that there are two different manifestations of passion: harmonious and obsessive. Although harmonious passion is related to positive outcomes such as performance and health, obsessive passion is related to negative outcomes such as shame and interference with social relationships. These important theoretical distinctions can help clarify the ambiguity and disagreements associated with the question whether there "can there be too much positivity?"

Targets for Positive Organizational Scholarship
To whom does POS research apply? Primarily to managers and executives as opposed to front line workers or even people who are not even at the line? Positive organizational scholarship research and, indeed, organizational scholarship more broadly, has been accused of neglecting nonmanagerial and nonelite populations and perspectives. Positive organizational scholarship research can do more work to benefit our understanding of how to create more a more positive work context for those in the lower rungs of society—for example, low-wage workers, older employees, workers without a home, employees with salaries that put them below the poverty line, noncore/temporary workers, invisible and marginalized workers (e.g., those with mental health problems), or stigmatized populations (e.g., felons)

(Caza & Carroll, 2011, Chapter 73, this volume). This concern aligns with a recent editorial by Bamberger and Pratt (2010), which called for enhanced understanding in organizational studies of critical organization phenomena by focusing on lower-echelon employees or contexts outside for-profit business organizations, such as health care, schools, nonprofits, and social movements.

Researchers in this handbook offer theorizing that may be helpful to people with little power and material resources in organizations. For example, research on compassion (Lilius et al., 2011, Chapter 21, this volume) offers insights regarding how sympathy can move people to action that makes a difference in the lives of others who may be suffering. Research on psychological safety (Nembhard & Edmondson, 2011, Chapter 37, this volume) articulates how leaders can create a context whereby those with low formal power can have voice. Additionally, Ramarajan and Thomas (2011, Chapter 41, this volume) discuss how practices that retain and develop members of stigmatized and disadvantaged groups can increase intergroup equality that in turn improves the performance of the group as a whole.

What about the Full Range of Virtues?

Although the chapters in this volume suggest progress on understanding the role of several virtues in organizational contexts, other virtues have received considerably less attention in organizational studies (although some have received more attention in positive psychology). We use Peterson and Seligman's (2004) typology of virtues and character strengths to inventory the current state of research in this domain. They developed a classification to organize 24 character strengths into six categories of virtues: courage, justice, humanity, wisdom, temperance, and transcendence. Although other typologies of virtues exist, the Peterson and Seligman typology is best known. Note, too, that Asplund and Blacksmith (2011, Chapter 27, this volume) also use the term strengths, but they are referring to building human competence and capacity rather than virtues or character strengths per se.

Several of the Peterson and Seligman virtues have received attention in this handbook: courage, justice, and humanity.

- Courage deals with accomplishing goals in the face of opposition. This handbook includes chapters on courage (Worline, 2011, Chapter 23, this volume), behavioral integrity (Simons, Tomlinson, & Leroy, 2011, Chapter 25, this volume), passion (Perttula & Cardon, 2011, Chapter 15 this volume), and energy (Spreitzer, Lam, & Quinn, 2011, Chapter 12, this volume). Although there is no chapter on persistence (an additional component of courage), we know quite a bit about this topic thanks to the extensive research on motivation.

- Justice deals with building a healthy community. The handbook includes chapters on justice (Mayer, 2011, Chapter 24, this volume), trust (Mishra & Mishra, 2011, Chapter 34, this volume), leadership (DeRue & Workman, 2011, Chapter 60, this volume; Quinn & Wellman, 2011, Chapter 57, this volume), prosocial motivation (Grant & Berg, 2011, Chapter 3, this volume), and ethics (Stansbury & Sonenshein, 2011, Chapter 26, this volume).

- Humanity deals with befriending and tending to others. This handbook includes chapters on social-emotional intelligence (Ybarra et al., 2011, Chapter 16, this volume), high-quality connections (Stephens, Heaphy, & Dutton, 2011, Chapter 29, this volume), compassion (Lilius et al., 2011, Chapter 21, this volume), civility (Porath, 2011, Chapter 33, this volume), generalized reciprocity (Baker, 2011, Chapter 31, this volume), prosocial motivation (Grant & Berg, 2011, Chapter 3, this volume), and intimacy (Kark, 2011, Chapter 32, this volume). We note, however, that we know less about love, generosity, or charity.

The remaining virtue categories in Peterson and Seligman's framework have more obvious gaps: wisdom, temperance, and transcendence:

- Wisdom deals with acquiring and using knowledge. Several of our chapters fit this bill: curiosity (Harrison, 2011, Chapter 9, this volume), innovation (DeGraff & Nathan-Roberts, 2011, Chapter 53, this volume), creativity (Zhou & Ren, 2011, Chapter 8, this volume), ambivalence (Pratt & Pradies, 2011, Chapter 70, this volume), and perspective-taking (Williams, 2011, Chapter 35, this volume). Still missing is research on open-mindedness and love of learning.

- A second underresearched virtue category is *temperance*, which protects against excess. The handbook includes chapters on forgiveness (Bright & Exline, 2011, Chapter 19, this volume) and humility (Owens, Rowatt, & Wilkins, 2011, Chapter 20, this volume). We know little, however, about other components of temperance such as prudence, patience, honor, moderation, tolerance, sacrifice, and wisdom.
- The final virtue category with significant research gaps is transcendence, which focuses on meaning and seeking connections to the larger universe. Chapters in this handbook focus on spirituality (Sandelands, 2011, Chapter 76, this volume), calling (Wrzeniewski, 2011, Chapter 4, this volume), transcendence through hope (Carlsen et al., 2011, Chapter 22, this volume), humor (Cooper & Sosik, 2011, Chapter 36, this volume), mindful organizing (Vogus, 2011, Chapter 50, this volume), peace (Ritchie & Hammond, 2011, Chapter 78, this volume), and virtuousness (Cameron & Winn, 2011, Chapter 18, this volume). We know less about calmness, harmony, consciousness, faith, gratitude, appreciating beauty, and gentleness.

In addition to filling these gaps on specific virtues and strengths, future research could conceptualize the key distinctions between virtues and strengths better and can focus more precisely on the "O" level of analysis.

Methodological Issues

Are certain methodological issues of interest for the discipline of POS? We conclude this section articulating a path forward by offering some insights on methods for future POS research. Much quantitative research on POS topics is still cross-sectional in nature (although frequently research employs other outcome assessments to avoid common method bias). Research that is nonlongitudinal by design limits our ability to study fluidity and dynamics over time. We need more longitudinal research that looks at trajectories, delays, and accelerations. More longitudinal or field experiments with interventions can also enable us to examine the direction of causal influence among constructs.

A more qualitative process focus could also help us understand people's actual lived experiences

(Golden-Biddle & Mao, 2011, Chapter 58, this volume). For example, Worline (2011, Chapter 23, this volume) discusses courage as an emergent pattern of activity in context. It can also help POS researchers think about studying verbs rather than nouns (e.g., resiling rather than resilience; forgiving rather than forgiveness). For example, Carlsen et al. (2011, Chapter 22, this volume) recommend a phenomenological approach to studying "acts of hoping" (a verb) rather than the state of hope (a noun). By following people in their work settings over time, we can understand the process of hoping or even "hope organizing."

Much of POS research operates at a single level of analysis, be it individual, team, unit, or organization. Organizational dynamics, however, do not operate within a single level of analysis. Positive organizational scholarship research needs to address the cross-level interactions among individuals, their work relationship, and the broader organization, cultural, and societal context in which they are embedded more effectively. As Hackman (2009, p. 313) suggested, "robust explanations more often than not require simultaneous attention to factors that operate at both higher and lower levels than the level of the focal phenomenon itself . . . the most satisfying explanations for the dynamics of positive organization phenomena will require cross-level analyses." One particularly good example of a chapter that takes a cross-level approach is Carlsen et al. (2011, Chapter 22, this volume). They look at three paths of hope research, each at a different level of analysis: hope as an individual attaining goals, hope as a relational possibility, and hope as an organizational process. In this way, they open up a more positive vocabulary of hope across levels for organizational studies.

Finally, although progress has been made on defining constructs, we still need better instrumentation. We need validated measures of core POS constructs inasmuch as this is a crucial requirement for building a cumulative body of research knowledge.

Conclusion

In summary, in this concluding chapter, we hope to convey the progress achieved over the last decade, but also convey the energy and excitement about what questions have been raised as we move beyond the first decade of POS. Positive organizational scholarship provides an enriching lens for organizational studies. It encourages organizational scholars to expand their horizons in theorizing about and empirically investigating OB and OT topics. It expands the range of topics seen as valuable and legitimate in organizational science.

The plethora of emerging research questions highlighted in these chapters primes us to invite other scholars to look for the POS-related issues in their own research programs. We hope this can build a "deluge" (Wright & Quick, 2009, p. 147) that can dramatically escalate a promising trajectory of POS research. We invite you to join us as we continue the POS journey in organizational studies.

Acknowledgments

Thank you to the participants in the POS incubator session who offered helpful feedback on an earlier version of this concluding chapter. A special thanks to Jane Dutton who offered constructive feedback as well.

References

Ashforth, B.E., Myers, K.K., & Sluss, D.M. (2011). Socialization perspectives and positive organizational scholarship. In K.S. Cameron & G.M. Spreitzer (Eds.), *The Oxford handbook of positive organizational scholarship*. New York: Oxford University Press.

Asplund, J., & Blacksmith, N. (2011). Productivity through strength. In K.S. Cameron & G.M. Spreitzer (Eds.), *The Oxford handbook of positive organizational scholarship*. New York: Oxford University Press.

Baker, W. (2011). A dual model of reciprocity in organizations: Moral sentiments and reputation. In K.S. Cameron & G.M. Spreitzer (Eds.), *The Oxford handbook of positive organizational scholarship*. New York: Oxford University Press.

Baker, W.B., & Gunderson, R. (2005). Zingerman's community of businesses. Case. Centre for Positive Organizational Scholarship, University of Michigan.

Bakker, A.B., & Oerlemans, W.G.M. (2011). Subjective well-being in organizations. In K.S. Cameron & G.M. Spreitzer (Eds.), *The Oxford handbook of positive organizational scholarship*. New York: Oxford University Press.

Bamberger, P., & Pratt, M. (2010). Moving forward and looking back: Reclaiming unconventional research contexts and samples in organizational research. *Academy of Management Journal, 53*, 665–671.

Bandura, A. (1977). Self-efficacy: Toward a unifying theory of behavioral change. *Psychological Review, 84*(2), 191–215.

Barker Caza, B., & Milton, L.P. (2011). Resilience at work: Building capability in the face of adversity. In K.S. Cameron & G.M. Spreitzer (Eds.), *The Oxford handbook of positive organizational scholarship*. New York: Oxford University Press.

Bartunek, J.M., & Woodman, R.W. (2011). The spirits of organization development or why OD lives despite its pronounced death. In K.S. Cameron & G.M. Spreitzer (Eds.), *The Oxford handbook of positive organizational scholarship*. New York: Oxford University Press.

Baumeister, R.F., Bratslavsky, E., Finkenauer, C., & Vohs, K.D. (2001). Bad is stronger than good. *Review of General Psychology, 5*(4), 323–370.

Biron, C., Cooper, C.L., & Gibbs, P. (2011). Stress interventions versus positive interventions: apples and oranges? In K.S. Cameron & G.M. Spreitzer (Eds.), *The Oxford handbook of positive organizational scholarship*. New York: Oxford University Press.

Bono, J.E., Davies, S.E., & Rasch, R.L. (2011). Some traits associated with flourishing at work. In K.S. Cameron & G.M. Spreitzer (Eds.), *The Oxford handbook of positive organizational scholarship*. New York: Oxford University Press.

Bright, D.S., & Exline, J.J. (2011). Forgiveness at four levels: Intrapersonal, relational, organizational, and collective-group. In K.S. Cameron & G.M. Spreitzer (Eds.), *The Oxford handbook of positive organizational scholarship*. New York: Oxford University Press.

Browning, L.D., Morris, G.H., & Kee, K.F. (2011). The role of communication in positive organizational scholarship. In K.S. Cameron & G.M. Spreitzer (Eds.), *The Oxford handbook of positive organizational scholarship*. New York: Oxford University Press.

Cameron, K.S. (2003). Organizational virtuousness and performance. In Cameron, K., Dutton, J., & Quinn, R. (Eds.). *Positive organizational scholarship*: Foundations of a new discipline. San Francisco: Berrett-Koehler.

Cameron, K. (2008a). *Positive leadership: Strategies for Extraordinary performance*. San Francisco: Berrett-Koehler.

Cameron, K.S. (2008b). Paradox in positive organizational change. *Journal of Applied Behavioral Science, 44*, 7–24.

Cameron, K., Bright, D., & Caza, A. (2004). Exploring the relationships between organizational virtuousness and performance. *American Behavioral Scientist, 47*, 731–739.

Cameron, K., & Lavine, M. (2006). *Making the impossible possible: Leading extraordinary performance: The Rocky Flats Story*. San Francisco: Berrett-Koehler.

Cameron, K.S., Dutton, J.E., & Quinn, R.E. (2003). *Positive organizational scholarship: foundations of a new discipline*. San Francisco, CA: Berrett-Koehler.

Cameron, K.S., & Winn, B. (2011). Virtuousness in organizations. In K.S. Cameron & G.M. Spreitzer (Eds.), *The Oxford handbook of positive organizational scholarship*. New York: Oxford University Press.

Carlsen, A., Landsverk Hagen, A., & Mortensen, T.F. (2011). Imagining hope in organizations: From individual goal-attainment to horizons of relational possibility. In K.S. Cameron & G.M. Spreitzer (Eds.), *The Oxford handbook of positive organizational scholarship*. New York: Oxford University Press.

Caza, A., & Carroll, B. (2011). Critical studies and POS. In K.S. Cameron & G.M. Spreitzer (Eds.), *The Oxford handbook of positive organizational scholarship*. New York: Oxford University Press.

Cooper, C.D., & Sosik, J. (2011). The laughter advantage: Cultivating high-quality connections and workplace outcomes through humor. In K.S. Cameron & G.M. Spreitzer (Eds.), *The Oxford handbook of positive organizational scholarship*. New York: Oxford University Press.

Cooperrider, D.L., & Godwin, L.N. (2011). Positive organizational development: Innovation-inspired change in an economy and ecology of strengths. In K.S. Cameron & G.M. Spreitzer (Eds.), *The Oxford handbook of positive organizational scholarship*. New York: Oxford University Press.

DeGraff, J., & Nathan-Roberts, D. (2011). Innovativeness as positive deviance: Identifying and operationalizing the attributes, functions and dynamics that create growth. In

K.S. Cameron & G.M. Spreitzer (Eds.), *The Oxford handbook of positive organizational scholarship*. New York: Oxford University Press.

DeRue, D.S., & Workman, K.M. (2011). Toward a positive and dynamic theory of leadership development. In K.S. Cameron & G.M. Spreitzer (Eds.), *The Oxford handbook of positive organizational scholarship*. New York: Oxford University Press.

Dibble, R., & Gibson, C.B. (2011). Margins, membership, and mobility: Redefining boundaries in collaborative endeavors. In K.S. Cameron & G.M. Spreitzer (Eds.), *The Oxford handbook of positive organizational scholarship*. New York: Oxford University Press.

Dutton, J.E., & Glynn, M. (2007). Positive organizational scholarship. In C. Cooper & J. Barling (Eds.), *Handbook of organizational behavior*. Thousand Oaks, CA: Sage.

Dutton, J.E., & Sonenshein, S. (2009). Positive organizational scholarship. In Lopez, S. (Ed.). *Encyclopedia of positive psychology* (pp. 737–742) Oxford: Wiley-Blackwell.

Feldman, M., & Worline, M. (2011). Resources, resourcing, and ampliative cycles in organizations. In K.S. Cameron & G.M. Spreitzer (Eds.), *The Oxford handbook of positive organizational scholarship*. New York: Oxford University Press.

Fineman, S. (2006). On being positive: Concerns and counterpoints. *Academy of Management Review, 31*(2), 270–291.

Fredrickson, B. (2003). The value of positive emotions. *American Scientist, 91*, 339–335.

Glynn, M.A., & Watkiss, L. (2011). The generative potency of organizational symbols: Implications for positive organizational scholarship. In K.S. Cameron & G.M. Spreitzer (Eds.), *The Oxford handbook of positive organizational scholarship*. New York: Oxford University Press.

Goddard, R.D., & Salloum, S.J. (2011). Collective efficacy beliefs, organizational excellence, and leadership. In K.S. Cameron & G.M. Spreitzer (Eds.), *The Oxford handbook of positive organizational scholarship*. New York: Oxford University Press.

Godfrey, P.C. (2011). Strange bedfellows: Homo economicus and positive organization scholarship. In K.S. Cameron & G.M. Spreitzer (Eds.), *The Oxford handbook of positive organizational scholarship*. New York: Oxford University Press.

Golden-Biddle, K., & Mao, J. (2011). What makes an organizational change process positive? In K.S. Cameron & G.M. Spreitzer (Eds.), *The Oxford handbook of positive organizational scholarship*. New York: Oxford University Press.

Grant, A.M., & Berg, J.M. (2011). Prosocial motivation at work: When, when, why, and how making a difference makes a difference? In K.S. Cameron & G.M. Spreitzer (Eds.), *The Oxford handbook of positive organizational scholarship*. New York: Oxford University Press.

Grant, A., & Schwartz, B. (2011). Too much of a good thing: The challenge and opportunity of the inverted-U. *Perspectives in Psychological Science, 6*, 61–76.

Hackman, J. (2009). The perils of positivity. *Journal of Organizational Behavior, 30*, 309–319.

Hall, D.T., & Las Heras, M. (2011). Personal growth through career work: A positive approach to careers. In K.S. Cameron & G.M. Spreitzer (Eds.), *The Oxford handbook of positive organizational scholarship*. New York: Oxford University Press.

Harquail, C.V., & Brickson, S.L. (2011). The defining role of organizational identity for facilitating stakeholder flourishing: A map for future research. In K.S. Cameron & G.M. Spreitzer (Eds.), *The Oxford handbook of positive organizational scholarship*. New York: Oxford University Press.

Harrison, S. (2011). Organizing the cat? Generative aspects of curiosity in organizational life. In K.S. Cameron & G.M. Spreitzer (Eds.), *The Oxford handbook of positive organizational scholarship*. New York: Oxford University Press.

Heath, C., & Sitkin, S. (2001). Big-B versus Big-O: What is organizational about organizational behavior? *Journal of Organizational Behavior 22*, 43–58.

Hedstrom, P., & Swedberg, R. (1998). *Social mechanisms: An analytical approach to social theory*. New York: Cambridge University Press.

Hernes, G. (1998). Real virtuality. In P. Hedstrom & R. Swedberg (Eds.), *Social mechanisms: An analytical approach to social theory* (pp. 74–101). New York: Cambridge University Press.

Hoffer Gittell, J. (2011). New directions for relational coordination theory. In K.S. Cameron & G.M. Spreitzer (Eds.), *The Oxford handbook of positive organizational scholarship*. New York: Oxford University Press.

Hoffman, A.J., & Haigh, N. (2011). Positive deviance for a sustainable world: Linking sustainability and positive organizational scholarship. In K.S. Cameron & G.M. Spreitzer (Eds.), *The Oxford handbook of positive organizational scholarship*. New York: Oxford University Press.

Iyengar, S., & Lepper, M. (2000). When choice is demotivating: Can one desire too much of a good thing? *Journal of Personality and Social Psychology, 79*, 994–1006.

James, E.H., & Wooten, L.P. (2011). Orientations of positive leadership in times of crisis. In K.S. Cameron & G.M. Spreitzer (Eds.), *The Oxford handbook of positive organizational scholarship*. New York: Oxford University Press.

Kark, R. (2011). Workplace intimacy in leader-follower relationships. In K.S. Cameron & G.M. Spreitzer (Eds.), *The Oxford handbook of positive organizational scholarship*. New York: Oxford University Press.

Keeney, J., & Illies, R. (2011). Positive work–family dynamics. In K.S. Cameron & G.M. Spreitzer (Eds.), *The Oxford handbook of positive organizational scholarship*. New York: Oxford University Press.

Kilduff, M., & Brands, R. (2010). Book Review: Exploring positive identities and organizations. *Administrative Science Quarterly, June*, 347–349.

Kopelman, S., Avi-Yonah, O., & Varghese, A.K. (2011). The mindful negotiator: Strategic emotion management and well-being. In K.S. Cameron & G.M. Spreitzer (Eds.), *The Oxford handbook of positive organizational scholarship*. New York: Oxford University Press.

Lavine, M. (2011). Positive deviance: A metaphor and method for learning from the uncommon. In K.S. Cameron & G.M. Spreitzer (Eds.), *The Oxford handbook of positive organizational scholarship*. New York: Oxford University Press.

Lilius, J.M., Kanov, J., Dutton, J.E., Worline, M.C., & Maitlis, S. (2011). Compassion revealed: What we know about compassion at work (and where we need to know more). In K.S. Cameron & G.M. Spreitzer (Eds.), *The Oxford handbook of positive organizational scholarship*. New York: Oxford University Press.

Luthans, F., & Avolio, B.J. (2009). The point of positive organizational behavior. *Journal of Organizational Behavior, 30*, 291–307.

Maitlis, S. (2011). Post-traumatic growth: A missed opportunity for positive organizational scholarship. In K.S. Cameron & G.M. Spreitzer (Eds.), *The Oxford handbook of positive organizational scholarship*. New York: Oxford University Press.

Mayer, D.M. (2011). A positive lens on organizational justice: Toward a moral, constructive, and balanced approach to reactions to third-party (in)justice. In K.S. Cameron & G.M. Spreitzer (Eds.), *The Oxford handbook of positive organizational scholarship*. New York: Oxford University Press.

Meyerson, D. (2001). *Tempered radicals: How people use change to inspire difference at work*. Cambridge, MA: Harvard Business School Press.

Mishra, A.K., & Mishra, K.E. (2011). POS and trust in leaders. In K.S. Cameron & G.M. Spreitzer (Eds.), *The Oxford handbook of positive organizational scholarship*. New York: Oxford University Press.

Morgan Roberts, L., & Creary, S.J. (2011). Positive identity construction: Insights from classical and contemporary theoretical perspectives. In K.S. Cameron & G.M. Spreitzer (Eds.), *The Oxford handbook of positive organizational scholarship*. New York: Oxford University Press.

Nembhard, I.M., & Edmondson, A.C. (2011). Psychological safety: A foundation for speaking up, collaboration, and experimentation in organizations. In K.S. Cameron & G.M. Spreitzer (Eds.), *The Oxford handbook of positive organizational scholarship*. New York: Oxford University Press.

Oldham, G.R. (2011). The design of jobs: A strategy for enhancing the positive outcomes of individuals at work. In K.S. Cameron & G.M. Spreitzer (Eds.), *The Oxford handbook of positive organizational scholarship*. New York: Oxford University Press.

Owens, B.P., Rowatt, W.C., & Wilkins, A.L. (2011). Exploring the relevant and implications of humility in organizations. In K.S. Cameron & G.M. Spreitzer (Eds.), *The Oxford handbook of positive organizational scholarship*. New York: Oxford University Press.

Peterson, C., & Seligman, M.E. P. (2004). *Character strengths and virtues: A handbook and classification*. Oxford: Oxford University Press.

Perttula, K.H., & Cardon, M.S. (2011). Passion. In K.S. Cameron & G.M. Spreitzer (Eds.), *The Oxford handbook of positive organizational scholarship*. New York: Oxford University Press.

Pfeffer, J. (2010). Building sustainable organizations: The human factor. *Academy of Management Perspectives, 8*, 34–45.

Porath, C.L. (2011). Civility. In K.S. Cameron & G.M. Spreitzer (Eds.), *The Oxford handbook of positive organizational scholarship*. New York: Oxford University Press.

Porath, C., Spreitzer, G., Gibson, C., & Stevens, F. (2010). *Construct validation of a measure of thriving at work*. Working paper.

Powley, E.H. (2011). Organizational healing: A relational process to handle major disruption. In K.S. Cameron & G.M. Spreitzer (Eds.), *The Oxford handbook of positive organizational scholarship*. New York: Oxford University Press.

Pratt, M.G., & Pradies, C. (2011). Just a good place to visit? Exploring positive responses to psychological ambivalence. In K.S. Cameron & G.M. Spreitzer (Eds.), *The Oxford handbook of positive organizational scholarship*. New York: Oxford University Press.

Pressman, S.D., & Cohen, S. (2005). Does positive affect influence health? *Psychological Bulletin, 131*, 925–971.

Quinn, R.E., & Wellman, N. (2011). Seeing and acting differently: Positive change in organizations. In K.S. Cameron & G.M. Spreitzer (Eds.), *The Oxford handbook of positive organizational scholarship*. New York: Oxford University Press.

Ragins, B.R. (2011). Relational mentoring: A positive approach to mentoring at work. In K.S. Cameron & G.M.

Spreitzer (Eds.), *The Oxford handbook of positive organizational scholarship*. New York: Oxford University Press.

Ramarajan, L., & Thomas, D. (2011). A positive approach to studying diversity in organizations. In K.S. Cameron & G.M. Spreitzer (Eds.), *The Oxford handbook of positive organizational scholarship*. New York: Oxford University Press.

Rego, A., Clegg, S., & e Cunha, M. (2011). The positive power of character strengths and virtues for global leaders. In K.S. Cameron & G.M. Spreitzer (Eds.), *The Oxford handbook of positive organizational scholarship*. New York: Oxford University Press.

Rhee, S.Y., & Yoon, H.J. (2011). Shared positive affect in workgroups. In K.S. Cameron & G.M. Spreitzer (Eds.), *The Oxford handbook of positive organizational scholarship*. New York: Oxford University Press.

Ritchie, J.B., & Hammond, S.C. (2011). Five steps toward peacemaking: Using positive organizational scholarship to build a better world. In K.S. Cameron & G.M. Spreitzer (Eds.), *The Oxford handbook of positive organizational scholarship*. New York: Oxford University Press.

Sandelands, L.E. (2011). In God we trust: A comparison of spiritualities at work. In K.S. Cameron & G.M. Spreitzer (Eds.), *The Oxford handbook of positive organizational scholarship*. New York: Oxford University Press.

Sekerka, L.E., Vacharkulksemsuk, T., & Fredrickson, B.L. (2011). Positive emotions: Broadening and building upward spirals of sustainable enterprises. In K.S. Cameron & G.M. Spreitzer (Eds.), *The Oxford handbook of positive organizational scholarship*. New York: Oxford University Press.

Simons, T., Tomlinson, E.D., & Leroy, H. (2011). Research on behavioral integrity: A promising construct for positive organizational scholarship. In K.S. Cameron & G.M. Spreitzer (Eds.), *The Oxford handbook of positive organizational scholarship*. New York: Oxford University Press.

Smith, W.K., Lewis, M.W., & Tushman, M.L. (2011). Organizational sustainability: Organization design and senior leadership to enable strategic paradox. In K.S. Cameron & G.M. Spreitzer (Eds.), *The Oxford handbook of positive organizational scholarship*. New York: Oxford University Press.

Sonnentag, S., & Neff, A. (2011). Recovery: Nonwork experiences that promote positive states. In K.S. Cameron & G.M. Spreitzer (Eds.), *The Oxford handbook of positive organizational scholarship*. New York: Oxford University Press.

Spreitzer, G. (2007). Participative organizational leadership, empowerment, and sustainable peace. *Journal of Organizational Behavior, 28*(8), 1077–1096.

Spreitzer, G., Sutcliffe, K., Dutton, J., Sonenshein, S., & Grant, A. (2005). A socially embedded model of thriving at work. *Organization Science, 16*(5), 537–549.

Spreitzer, G., & Sonenshein, S. (2004). Toward a construct definition of positive deviance. *American Behavioral Scientist, 74*(6), 828–847.

Spreitzer, G.M. (1995). Psychological empowerment in the workplace: Dimensions, measurement, and validation. *Academy of Management Journal, 38*(5), 1442–1465.

Spreitzer, G.M., Lam, C.F., & Quinn, R.W. (2011). Human energy in organizations: Implications for POS from six interdisciplinary streams. In K.S. Cameron & G.M. Spreitzer (Eds.), *The Oxford handbook of positive organizational scholarship*. New York: Oxford University Press.

Stansbury, J.M., & Sonenshein, S. (2011). Positive business ethics: Grounding and elaborating a theory of good works. In K.S. Cameron & G.M. Spreitzer (Eds.), *The Oxford hand-*

book of positive organizational scholarship. New York: Oxford University Press.

Stavros, J.M., & Wooten, L.P. (2011). Positive strategy: Creating and sustaining strengths-based strategy that SOARs and performs. In K.S. Cameron & G.M. Spreitzer (Eds.), *The Oxford handbook of positive organizational scholarship*. New York: Oxford University Press.

Stephens, J.P., Heaphy, E., & Dutton, J.E. (2011). High-quality connections. In K.S. Cameron & G.M. Spreitzer (Eds.), *The Oxford handbook of positive organizational scholarship*. New York: Oxford University Press.

Sutcliffe, K.M., & Christianson, M.K. (2011). Managing the unexpected. In K.S. Cameron & G.M. Spreitzer (Eds.), *The Oxford handbook of positive organizational scholarship*. New York: Oxford University Press.

Vallerand, R., et al. (2003). Les passion de l'ame: On obsessive and harmonious passion. *Journal of Personality and Social Psychology, 85*, 756–767.

Vogel, B., & Bruch, H. (2011). Organizational energy. In K.S. Cameron & G.M. Spreitzer (Eds.), *The Oxford handbook of positive organizational scholarship*. New York: Oxford University Press.

Vogus, T.J. (2011). Mindful organizing: Establishing and extending the foundations of highly reliable performance. In K.S. Cameron & G.M. Spreitzer (Eds.), *The Oxford handbook of positive organizational scholarship*. New York: Oxford University Press.

Williams, M. (2011). Perspective taking: Building positive interpersonal connections and trustworthiness one interaction at a time. In K.S. Cameron & G.M. Spreitzer (Eds.), *The Oxford handbook of positive organizational scholarship*. New York: Oxford University Press.

Worline, M.C. (2011). Courage in organizations: An integrative review of the "difficult virtue." In K.S. Cameron & G.M. Spreitzer (Eds.), *The Oxford handbook of positive organizational scholarship*. New York: Oxford University Press.

Wright, T.A., & Quick, J.C. (2009). The emerging positive agenda in organizations: Greater than a trickle, but not yet a deluge. *Journal of Organizational Behavior, 30*, 147–159.

Wrzesniewski, A. (2011). Callings. In K.S. Cameron & G.M. Spreitzer (Eds.), *The Oxford handbook of positive organizational scholarship*. New York: Oxford University Press.

Wrzesniewski, A., & Dutton, J.E. (2001). Crafting a job: Employees as active crafters of their work. *Academy of Management Review, 26*, 179–201.

Wu, C., & Parker, S.K. (2011). Proactivity in the workplace: Looking back and looking forward. In K.S. Cameron & G.M. Spreitzer (Eds.), *The Oxford handbook of positive organizational scholarship*. New York: Oxford University Press.

Ybarra, O., Rees, L. Kross, E., & Sanchez-Burks, J. (2011). Social context and the psychology of emotional intelligence: A key to creating positive organizations. In K.S. Cameron & G.M. Spreitzer (Eds.), *The Oxford handbook of positive organizational scholarship*. New York: Oxford University Press.

Youssef, C.M., & Luthans, F. (2011). Psychological capital: Meaning, findings, and future directions. In K.S. Cameron & G.M. Spreitzer (Eds.), *The Oxford handbook of positive organizational scholarship*. New York: Oxford University Press.

Zhou, J., & Ren, R. (2011). Striving for creativity: Building positive contexts in the workplace. In K.S. Cameron & G.M. Spreitzer (Eds.), *The Oxford handbook of positive organizational scholarship*. New York: Oxford University Press.

INDEX

Page numbers followed by "*f*", "*t*", or "*n*" denote figures, tables, or notes, respectively.

C

cache cycle, in relational mentoring, 524–25
callings, 2, 45–54
    ability calibration and, 52
    as action-oriented, 47
    antecedents of, 49–51
    capitalism and, development of, 46
    careers as, 509
    centrality of work and, 48–49
    in Christian theology, 46
    definition of, 46
    development of, 50
    economic stability and, 53
    evolution of, 49–50
    future research on, 52–54
    idealism and, 45
    identity theory and, 50
    individualism and, 46
    influences on, 50
    intrinsic prosocial motivation and, 51
    introspection as part of, 49
    job involvement and, 49, 51
    measurement of, 52–53
    as mission, 47
    as moral imperative, 53
    in moral psychology research, 53
    neoclassical, 52
    in object relations theory, 50
    origins of, 50
    outcomes of, 51–52
    parameters of, 48–49
    passions and, 47
    POS and, 45
    positivity and, 45
    as prosocial, 47
    during Protestant Reformation, 46–47
    qualitative studies on, 52
    religion and, 46–47
    sampling issues and, 52
    as secular entity, 48
    self-definition and, 48
    self-fulfillment and, 48
    self-reflection and, 49
    social class as influence on, 50
    in social learning theory, 50
    in social reproduction theory, 50–51
    sources of, 49–51
    in theories of social representations of reality and, 50
    as work orientation, 47–48
Calvin, John, 46
Cameron, Kim, 4
Campbell, David, 511
capability models
    in emotional management, 814–18
    for unexpected event management, 844–51
capacity building, 829
capital. *See* human capital; psychological capital; social capital
capitalism, callings and, 46
careers, 507–17
    adaptability in, 514–15
    as calling, 509
    choices of, stages for, 511–12
    content theories for, 510–11
    Cross-Cultural Study of Contemporary Careers researchers, 516
    definition of, 507
    development models for, 511–12
    as dream, 511–12
    extrinsic dimensions of, 512
    extrinsic success, 512
    as fulfillment of potential, 508
    future research applications for, 516–17
    growth of, challenges to, 514–15
    human development growth and, 508
    identity from, 508
    individual control of, 508
    intrinsic dimensions of, 512
    job satisfaction and, 509*f*
    literature overview, 508–12
    locus of appraisal for, 513*t*
    mentoring in, 514, 520
    metacompetencies and, 514
    objective, 507
    orientations toward, 509–10
    passion for, 510
    personal interpretation of, 508
    personality types and, 511
    positive meaning of, 507–8
    as possibility, 515
    process theories for, 511–12
    prosocial outcomes from, 508
    psychological success, 512–14
    retirement and, 516–17
    smart jobs and, 514
    studies of, approaches to, 510–12
    subjective, 507
    synthesizing process for, 511
    vocational choice and, 511
career development
    in high-quality mentoring, 526
    models for, 511–12
caring, 238
causality
    relational coordination theory and, 405
    virtuousness and, in organizations, 237–38
ceremony, in organizational healing, 863
CFA. *See* confirmatory factor analysis
chain-generalized reciprocity, 415, 420n1
change. *See* openness to change; positive change, in organizations; strategic change; veridical change
change management, 729–30
Chappell, Tom, 514
character strengths, 235–36, 240n2. *See also* strengths-based development, for employees
    classification for, 235
    for global leaders, 366–79
    humanity as, 372, 376

    humility as, 261–62
    humor as, 374, 376, 475
    immersion as, 370
    learning orientation for, 235–36
    temperance as, 372–73, 376
    transcendence as, 373–74
    virtues and, 368*t*, 1042
Character Strengths and Virtues: A Handbook and Classification (Peterson/Seligman), 742
charismatic leadership, humility and, 267
charismatic relationships, 35
charity, 236
cheerfulness, 235
Chouinard, Melinda, 514
Chouinard, Yvon, 514
Christian theology, 46
A Christmas Carol (Dickens), 727–28
circumplex model of affect, 179
citizenship behaviors, 36
civility, 439–46. *See also* incivility
    biological foundations for, 445
    broaden-and-build theory and, 443
    communication and, 443
    continuum of, 439
    courtesy and, 440
    CREW process for, 445
    for customers as witnesses, 443–44
    definition of, 439–40
    emotional contagion and, 443
    between employees, 444
    future research for, 445–46
    individual outcomes and, 440–44
    interventions for, 444–45
    in management literature, 439–40
    manners and, 440
    negative deviance for, 439
    organizations influenced by, 443
    politeness and, 440
    positive deviance for, 439
    positive emotions and, 440
    practical applications of, 444–45
    social development of, 440
    teams and, effect on, 442–43
    witnesses and, effect on, 442
Civility, Respect, and Engagement at work (CREW) process, 445
claiming, identity development through, 77
clan modality, for innovativeness, 708–9
Clifton StrengthsFinder (CSF), 356–57
Clinton, Bill, 205
Clinton, Hillary, 1027
closed ideas, 98
closeness, humor as result of, 478
CMC. *See* computer-mediated communication
CMS. *See* critical management studies
cognition
    as context for creativity, 99
    forgiveness and, 249
    hotter/cooler, psychological ambivalence and, 933

value-in-diversity hypotheses, 555
work-level conditions for, 558–59
diversive curiosity, 112–13
divestiture, in socialization, 544
DOT. *See Dictionary of Occupational Titles*
double-loop learning, 887
downsizing. *See* corporate downsizing
dream careers, 511–12
DRM. *See* day reconstruction method
Drucker, Peter, 745
DSM. See Diagnostic and Statistical Manual of Mental Disorders
dual identification, 78
Dutton, Jane, 4
dynamics. *See* generative dynamics
dynamic change phenomenon, 746–47
dynamism
EI and, 210
mindful organizing and, 665

E

EAP. *See* employee assistance program
EBO. *See* emerging business opportunity
The Ecology of Commerce (Hawken), 957
economic models, 979–87
behavioral, 20, 985–86
domains and, 979
human nature as influence on, 983
prudence in, 981
rational choice theory for, 980–82, 984
Edelman Global Trust Barometer, 449
Edison, Thomas, 706–7
education, collective efficacy in, 646–47
education hypothesis, 254–55
Edwards, John, 205
efficacy. *See also* collective efficacy, as belief system; self-efficacy
as future-oriented, 643
as psychological capital, 18
in social cognitive theory, 643
work engagement and, 57, 64
effort-recovery model (ERM), 868
ego depletion models, 868–69
ego-depletion theory, 156–57
biological foundations in, 156–57
POS, 163–64
egoism
prosocial motivation and, 30
reciprocity and, 416–17
EI. *See* emotional intelligence
elevation, 2
from organizational justice, 320
in psychological safety, 498
Ely, Robin, 561
embodied authentic leadership, 778
emerging business opportunity (EBO), 803
Emerson, Ralph Waldo, 293
emotions. *See also* collective emotions; emotional management, strategic change and; positive emotions
authentic leadership influenced by, 777

collective, 813–14
courage and, 311
definition of, 224n1
forgiveness and, 248–49
in individuals, 812–13
information theories of, 112. *See also* moods
in leadership development, 790
management of, strategic change and, 812–21
in mindful organizing, 670
perception of, strategic change and, 812–21
perspective-taking influenced by, 464
positive, 168–75
symbolism and, 623–24
emotional aperture, 813–14, 819
emotional balancing, 814–15, 821
emotional capability, 814
emotional contagion
as character strength, for global leaders, 372
civility and, 443
in collective emotions, 813
crossover and, in work-family dynamics, 610
energetic arousal and, 160
HQCs and, 390
incivility and, 443
job design and, 660–61
shared positive affect and, in workgroups, 218
emotional control, 207–8
social, 208
emotional engagement, 58
emotional exhaustion, 182
emotional intelligence (EI), 201–11
ability models of, 203
assessment of, 202–4
assumptions about, 204–5
biases and, 206–7
communication and, 207
conceptualization of, 202–4
as deliberate, 207
deliberate processing in, 209
development history of, 205
dynamism and, 210
emotional control and, 207–8
emotional displays, 206–7
emotional recognition and, 207–9
EQ-i and, 203
flexibility of, 210
future research on, 210–11
general abilities of, 207–10
incivility and, 446
integrative models of, 203
as intuitive, 207–10
MEIA and, 203
mental processes with, 207
mixed models for, 203
in mixed-motive environments, 206–7
in negotiations, 583–84
nonsocial implications of, 205

organizational outcomes, 202
processing types of, 207–10
psychology of, 203–4
salary increases influenced by, 202
social, 201, 208t
social cognition, 204, 206
social context of, 203–5
social outcomes, 204–6
social skills and, 202
SREIT and, 203
transformational leadership and, 202
emotional labor, 282
emotional management, strategic change and, 812–21
in alexithymic organizations, 817
for anger, 820
antecedents of, 821
asymmetry in, 819–20
authenticity in, 817
balancing as part of, 814–15, 821
barriers to, 818–20
capability in, 814–18
commitment in, 814
cultural diversity as influence on, 820
defensive avoidance and, 818
emotional information in, 818–19
empathy in, 815–16
encouragement in, 816–17
future research for, 820–21
heedfulness in, 815–16
hope in, 816–17
innovation and, 812–15
love and, as influence on, 818
playfulness in, 817–18
positive emotions and, 814
PRI and, 818–19
psychological safety and, 818
reconciliation in, 816
sympathy and, 816
Emotional Quotient Inventory (EQ-i), 203
emotional recognition, 207–9
cultural contexts for, 209
social, 208
emotional stability, 130
emotional well-being, WFE and, 606
empathetic sharing, 221
empathy
bottom-up emotional response to, 145–46
compassion and, 275, 280
crossover and, in work-family dynamics, 609–10
dispositional, 321
emotional aspects of, 148
in emotional management, 815–16
in HQCs, 389–90
imitative aspects of, 148
monitoring mechanism in, 145
organizational justice and, 320
perspective-taking and, 463
positive change and, 766
as positive emotion, 170

impulsivity and, 127
leadership and, 129
learning and, 129
mechanisms for, 128*f*
positive evaluations of, 128–29
social relationships and, 129
extreme relational orientation, 583
extrinsic career success, 512
extrinsic prosocial motivation, 36
rewards for creativity and, 105
eye-tracking, positive emotions and, 169
Eysenck, H.J., 128

F

face-to-face communication, 567, 587n7
failure, preoccupation with, 665, 670–971
fairness, reciprocity and, 417
faith, 236
hope and, 293
false synergies, 805
fatigue, 155
feedback. *See also* negative feedback
creativity and, 104
proactive behaviors and, 93
in relational job design, 33
field theory, 1029
Fights, Games and Debates (Rapoport), 1031
Fiorina, Carly, 373
flexibility
ambivalence and, 931
cognitive, in shared positive affect, 216
of EI, 210
from organizational healing, 861–62
in positive strategies, 825–26
psychological, 944
work engagement and, 56
flourishing, 125–35, 1036. *See also*
extraversion, flourishing and;
stakeholders, in OI
autonomy and, 127
broaden-and-build theory and, 134
conscientiousness and, 135
conservation of resources theory
and, 132
CSE for, 126, 130–31, 131*f*
definition of, 125–26
extraversion and, 126–30
future research for, 133–34
goals and, 132
intrinsic prosocial motivation, 127
job characteristics and, 131–32
job satisfaction and, 126
literature of, 126
mean level changes and, 125
mentoring as influence on, 133
meta-analytic work for, 127
motivation influenced by, 131
natural environment and, 959–61
in OI, 679
organizational sustainability and,
959–61
personality as trait for, 126
in POS, 1, 3, 126

positive emotions and, 134
PTG and, 911
relational mentoring and, 522
self-consistency theory and, 131
self-determination and, 126–27
sociability and, 127
of stakeholders, in OI, 678–87
use of resources and, 132–33
work as determinant for, 126
flow, 155
fMRI. *See* functional magnetic resonance
imaging
Folkes, Valerie, 443
Follett, Mary Parker, 401
followers. *See also* leader-follower
relationships
authentic followership, 776–77
behavioral integrity for, 333–36
humor for, between leaders, 479–80
forecasting scenarios, in crisis
management, 889
forgiveness, 238, 244–56
anger and, 248–49
appreciative inquiry and, 252
cognition and, 249
at collective-group level, 248, 252–54
communication of, 251
contact hypothesis for, 254–55
counseling and, 249
as culture, 251–52
definition of, 244
education hypothesis for, 254–55
emotions and, 248–49
empathy and, 253–54
employee error, 251
forgivers and, 245, 255
forms of, 245, 246*t*
future research on, 254–55
general properties of, 244–45, 248
illocutionary force and, 251
individual-to-individual configurations
of, 245–46
as intentional response, 245
intergroup, 248, 253
at interpersonal level, 248–50, 255
intervention models and, 249
intrapersonal, 255
mental health benefits and, 250–51
as multilevel concept, 245
offenders and, effect on, 250–51
at organizational level, 251–52
organization-initiated offenses, 245
organization-to-individual
configurations of, 248
personality and, 249
positive outcomes and, 3
pragmatic mode of, 252
as process, 249
at relational level, 249–51
restorative justice and, 250
rumination and, 249
sociopolitical, 253
transcendent mode of, 252

truth-and-reconciliation process,
253–54
as unconditional, 248
as virtue, 244
forgivers, 245, 255
formal mentoring, 520
Foucault, Michel, 343
frame innovation, 704
Frankfurt school, 966
free-rider problem, 216
Friedman, Milton, 1010
*From the Ground Up: Mennonite
Contributions to International
Peacebuilding* (Lederach/
Sampson), 1031
Frost, Peter, 765
fulfillment, personal, 1036
callings as, 53
career as, 508
as self-fulfillment, 48
functional magnetic resonance imaging
(fMRI), 138

G

Gadiesh, Orit, 117
Galarraga, Amando, 231
Gatto, John Taylor, 1022
gender
authentic leadership influenced
by, 782
negotiations and, as influence on, 582,
587n4
proactive behaviors and, 90
relational coordination theory
and, 405
salaries influenced by, 559–60
in work-family dynamics, 606
workplace intimacy as influence
on, 434
generalized exchange, 412
generalized reciprocity, 412–13, 413*f*
in chains, 415, 420n1
in groups, 414–15
in networks, 414–15
*The General Theory of Employment, Interest,
and Money* (Keynes), 983
generative dynamics, 3–4, 1037
in mentoring, 522
generosity, 235
George, Bill, 372
Gerstner, Lou, 373
Ghosn, Carlos, 370
Giacalone, R.A., 1002
Gillies, James, 111
global chemical management service
provider, 835
global leaders, character strengths for,
366–79
aesthetic appreciation as, 374
antecedents of, 375*f*
competencies of, 366–67
as core virtues, 377*t*
courage as, 370–71, 376